Abrams' Angiography

Interventional Radiology

Abrams' Angiography

Interventional Radiology

EDITED BY

Stanley Baum, MD

Eugene P. Pendergrass Professor of Radiology
and Chairman, Department of Radiology
University of Pennsylvania School of Medicine
Chairman, Department of Radiology
Hospital of the University of Pennsylvania
Philadelphia

Michael J. Pentecost, MD

Associate Professor and Vice-Chairman
Department of Radiology
University of Pennsylvania School of Medicine
Chief of Interventional Radiology
Hospital of the University of Pennsylvania
Philadelphia

VOLUME III

Little, Brown and Company

BOSTON   NEW YORK   TORONTO   LONDON

Copyright © 1997 by Stanley Baum, M.D.

Library of Congress Cataloging-in-Publication Data

Abrams' angiography : interventional radiology. / Stanley Baum, Michael J. Pentecost, editors.
    p.   cm.
    Includes bibliographical references and index.
    ISBN 0-316-08432-8
    1. Angiography. 2. Interventional radiology. I. Baum, Stanley. II. Pentecost, Michael J.
    [DNLM: 1. Angiography. WG 500 A157a 1997]
  RC691.6.A53A27 1997
  616.1'307572—dc20
  DNLM/DLC
  for Library of Congress   96-24525
                                     CIP

Vol. III ISBN 0-316-08432-8

Printed in the United States of America

EB-M

Editorial: Nancy E. Chorpenning, Deeth K. Ellis
Production Services: Julie Sullivan
Indexer: AlphaByte, Inc.
Production Supervisor: Michael A. Granger
Designer: Marty Tenney
Cover Designer: Louis C. Bruno, Jr.

To **Jeanne**
and **Judy**

Contents

II. Revascularization of the Aorta and Its Branches

V. Interventional Radiology of the Central Nervous System

VI. Interventional Radiology of the Thorax

Contributing Authors

J. FRITZ ANGLE, M.D.
Assistant Professor, Division of Angiography, Interventional Radiology, and Special Procedures, University of Virginia Health Sciences Center, Charlottesville, Virginia

KLEMENS H. BARTH, M.D.
Professor of Radiology and Medicine, Georgetown University, Washington, D.C.; Associate Professor of Radiology, Johns Hopkins University, Baltimore; Director, Vascular and Interventional Radiology, Georgetown University Hospital, Washington, D.C.

RICHARD A. BAUM, M.D.
Assistant Professor, Department of Radiology, and Assistant Professor of Radiology in Surgery, University of Pennsylvania; Staff Interventional Radiologist, Department of Radiology, Hospital of the University of Pennsylvania, Philadelphia

STANLEY BAUM, M.D.
Eugene P. Pendergrass Professor of Radiology and Chairman, Department of Radiology, University of Pennsylvania; Chairman, Department of Radiology, Hospital of the University of Pennsylvania, Philadelphia

GARY J. BECKER, M.D.
Clinical Professor of Radiology, University of Miami School of Medicine; Medical Director, Interventional Radiology, Miami Vascular Institute, Miami

YORAM BEN-MENACHEM, M.D.
Professor of Radiology, UMDNJ-New Jersey Medical School; Chief, Trauma Radiology, Department of Radiology, UMDNJ-University Hospital, Newark, New Jersey

ALEJANDRO BERENSTEIN, M.D.
Professor, Department of Radiology and Neurosurgery, New York University School of Medicine; Attending Physician, Department of Radiology and Neurosurgery, New York University Medical Center, New York City

GILES W. BOLAND, M.D.
Instructor in Radiology, Department of Radiology, Harvard Medical School; Clinical Assistant, Department of Radiology, Massachusetts General Hospital, Boston

JOSEPH BONN, M.D.
Assistant Professor, Department of Radiology, Jefferson Medical College; Cardiovascular/ Interventional Division, Department of Radiology, Thomas Jefferson University Hospital, Philadelphia

JOSEPH J. BOOKSTEIN, M.D.
Professor Emeritus, Department of Radiology, University of California, San Diego; Research Professor, Department of Radiology, University of California Medical Center, San Diego

FLAVIO CASTAÑEDA, M.D.
Clinical Associate Professor of Radiology and Radiology Research Director, University of Illinois College of Medicine at Peoria; Staff, Cardiovascular and Interventional Radiology, Saint Francis Medical Center, Peoria, Illinois

CONSTANTIN COPE, M.D.
Professor of Radiology and Staff, Angiography and Interventional Radiology, University of Pennsylvania School of Medicine, Philadelphia

J. A. GORDON CULHAM, M.D.
Professor of Radiology, University of British Columbia; Head, Cardiovascular and Interventional Radiology, British Columbia's Children's Hospital, Vancouver, British Columbia, Canada

MICHAEL D. DAKE, M.D.
Assistant Professor of Radiology and Pulmonary Medicine, Stanford University School of Medicine; Chief of Cardiovascular and Interventional Radiology, Stanford University Hospital, Stanford, California

MICHAEL D. DARCY, M.D.
Associate Professor, Mallinckrodt Institute of Radiology, Washington University Medical Center, St. Louis

STEVEN L. DAWSON, M.D.
Assistant Professor, Department of Radiology, Harvard Medical School; Head of GI/GU Interventional Radiology, Department of Radiology, Massachusetts General Hospital, Boston

GARY S. DORFMAN, M.D.
Professor, Department of Diagnostic Imaging, Brown University School of Medicine; Medical Director, Office of Clinical Management, and Co-Director, Vascular and Interventional Radiology, Rhode Island Hospital, Providence

PETER J. EISENBERG, M.D.
Radiologist, Florida Medical Center, Fort Lauderdale, Florida

RICHARD G. FISHER, M.D.
Associate Professor, Department of Radiology, Baylor College of Medicine; Director, Vascular/Interventional Radiology, Ben Taub General Hospital, Houston

GEORGE I. GETRAJDMAN
Assistant Professor, Department of Radiology, New York Hospital/Cornell Medical College; Assistant Attending Radiologist, Department of Radiology, Memorial Hospital, New York City

ROY L. GORDON, M.D.
Professor of Radiology, University of California; Chief of Interventional Radiology, Moffit/Long Hospital, University of California, San Francisco

SUE E. HANKS, M.D.
Assistant Professor of Radiology, University of Southern California; Interventional Radiology Staff, USC Affiliated Hospitals, Los Angeles

ZIV J. HASKAL, M.D.
Assistant Professor of Radiology, University of Pennsylvania School of Medicine; Assistant Professor of Radiology, Hospital of the University of Pennsylvania, Philadelphia

JOSÉ M. HERNANDEZ-GRAULAU, M.D., F.A.C.S.
Clinical Associate Professor of Surgery, Department of Surgery (Urology), University of Illinois School of Medicine; Staff, Department of Surgery (Urology), St. Francis Medical Center, University of Illinois School of Medicine, Peoria

HOWARD C. HERRMANN, M.D.
Associate Professor, Department of Medicine, University of Pennsylvania School of Medicine; Director, Interventional Cardiology, University of Pennsylvania Medical Center, Philadelphia

RANDALL T. HIGASHIDA, M.D.
Clinical Professor, Department of Radiology and Neurological Surgery, University of California, San Francisco; Associate Chief, Department of Interventional Neuroradiology, University of California, San Francisco

JOHN W. HIRSHFELD, JR., M.D.
Professor of Medicine, Department of Medicine, University of Pennsylvania School of Medicine; Director, Cardiac Catheterization Laboratory, University of Pennsylvania Medical Center, Philadelphia

ROBERT W. HURST, M.D.
Associate Professor and Director of Interventional Neuroradiology, Department of Radiology, Neurosurgery, and Neurology, University of Pennsylvania, Philadelphia

MARCY B. JAGUST, M.D.
Assistant Professor of Radiology, Cornell University Medical College; Assistant Attending, Department of Interventional Radiology, The New York Hospital, New York City

PAUL F. JAQUES, M.D.
Professor, Department of Radiology and Surgery, University of North Carolina; Chief of Vascular and Interventional Radiology, Department of Radiology, University of North Carolina Hospitals, Chapel Hill, North Carolina

ALLEN M. JOHNSON, M.D.
Chief, Section of Special Procedures, Department of Radiology, Brooke Army Medical Center, San Antonio, Texas

JOHN A. KAUFMAN, M.D.
Assistant Professor of Radiology, Department of Radiology, Harvard Medical School; Staff Angiographer/Interventionalist, Department of Radiology, Massachusetts General Hospital, Boston

MICHAEL D. KATZ, M.D.
Assistant Professor, Department of Radiology, University of Southern California; Director, Interventional Radiology, USC Affiliated Hospitals, Los Angeles

FREDERICK S. KELLER, M.D.
Cook Professor and Director, Dotter Interventional Institute, and Chairman, Department of Diagnostic Radiology, Oregon Health Sciences University; Director of Interventional Radiology, Dotter Interventional Institute, Oregon Health Sciences University, Portland

PAUL C. LAKIN, M.D.
Associate Professor, Dotter Interventional Institute, Oregon Health Sciences University; Attending Physician, Vascular/Interventional Radiology, University Hospital and Clinics, Portland, Oregon

ROBERT E. LAMBIASE, M.D.
Clinical Assistant Professor of Radiation Biology, Brown University Program in Medicine; Staff Radiologist, Department of Diagnostic Imaging, Rhode Island Hospital, Providence

STEVEN V. LOSSEF, M.D.
Associate Professor of Radiology, Department of Radiology, Georgetown University Hospital, Washington, D.C.

ERIC S. MALDEN, M.D.
Fellow, Vascular and Interventional Radiology, Mallinckrodt Institute of Radiology, Washington University School of Medicine, St. Louis, Missouri

ERIC C. MARTIN, M.D.
Professor of Radiology, College of Physicians and Surgeons of Columbia University; Director of Cardiovascular and Interventional Radiology, Columbia-Presbyterian Medical Center, New York

ALAN H. MATSUMOTO, M.D.
Associate Professor of Radiology, and Director, Fellowship Program in Angiography, Interventional Radiology, and Special Procedures, University of Virginia Health Sciences Center, Charlottesville, Virginia

MATTHEW A. MAURO, M.D.
Professor of Radiology and Surgery, and Vice-Chairman of Radiology, University of North Carolina School of Medicine, Chapel Hill, North Carolina

JEFFREY S. MOULTON, M.D.
Clinical Assistant Professor, Department of Radiology, University of Colorado School of Medicine; Staff Radiologist and Co-Director of Vascular and Interventional Radiology, Department of Radiology, St. Anthony Hospital, Denver

TIMOTHY P. MURPHY, M.D.
Assistant Professor, Brown University School of Medicine; Director, Division of Vascular and Interventional Radiology, Department of Diagnostic Imaging, Brown University School of Medicine, Providence, Rhode Island

PETER KIM NELSON, M.D.
Assistant Professor of Radiology, New York University Medical School; Staff Radiologist, Department of Radiology and Neuroradiology, New York University Medical Center, New York City

PHILIP D. ORONS, D.O.
Assistant Professor of Radiology and Surgery, Department of Radiology, University of Pittsburgh; Attending Radiologist, Section of Vascular/Interventional Radiology, Department of Radiology, University of Pittsburgh, Pittsburgh

FLOYD A. OSTERMAN, JR., M.D.
Associate Professor, and Director, Department of Radiology, Johns Hopkins University School of Medicine, Baltimore

STEVE H. PARKER, M.D.
Director, Breast Diagnostic and Counseling Centers, Englewood, Colorado

MICHAEL J. PENTECOST, M.D.
Associate Professor and Vice-Chairman, Department of Radiology, University of Pennsylvania; Chief of Interventional Radiology, Hospital of the University of Pennsylvania, Philadelphia

DANIEL PICUS, M.D.
Professor of Radiology and Surgery and Chief, Vascular and Interventional Radiology, Mallinckrodt Institute of Radiology, Washington University School of Medicine, St. Louis

JEFFREY S. POLLAK, M.D.
Chief, Section of Vascular and Interventional Radiology, Department of Diagnostic Radiology, Yale University School of Medicine, New Haven, Connecticut

PARVATI RAMCHANDANI, M.D.
Associate Professor, Department of Radiology, Section of Genito-urinary Radiology, University of Pennsylvania Medical Center, Philadelphia

KENNETH S. RHOLL, M.D.
Associate Clinical Professor, Department of Radiology, George Washington University, Washington, D.C.; Director, Noninvasive Vascular Lab, Department of Radiology, Alexandria Hospital, Alexandria, Virginia

ANNE C. ROBERTS, M.D.
Associate Professor, Department of Radiology, University of California, San Diego; Director, Vascular and Interventional Radiology, Department of Radiology, USCD Medical Center/Thornton Hospital, La Jolla, California

JOSEF RÖSCH, M.D.
Director and Professor, Research Laboratory, Dotter Interventional Institute, Oregon Health Sciences University, Portland, Oregon

ROBERT J. ROSEN, M.D.
Associate Professor, Department of Radiology, New York University School of Medicine; Director, Vascular and Interventional Radiology, New York University Medical Center, New York City

DONALD E. SCHWARTEN, M.D.
Director, Vascular and Interventional Radiology, St. Vincent Hospital and Health Care Center, Indianapolis, Indiana

SALVATORE J. A. SCLAFANI, M.D.
Professor of Radiology, Emergency Medicine and Surgery, State University of New York Health Science Center at Brooklyn; Director, Department of Radiology, Kings County Hospital Center, Brooklyn, New York

AVI SETTON, M.D.
Assistant Professor of Radiology, Department of Radiology and Neurosurgery, New York University School of Medicine; Attending Physician, Department of Radiology and Neurosurgery, New York University Medical Center, New York City

RICHARD D. SHLANSKY-GOLDBERG, M.D.
Assistant Professor of Radiology and Surgery, University of Pennsylvania Medical School; Staff Interventional Radiologist, University of Pennsylvania Medical School, Philadelphia

JOSEPH L. SKEENS, M.D.
Clinical Faculty, Department of Diagnostic Radiology, West Virginia University; Interventional Radiologist, Department of Radiology, West Virginia University, Charlestown, West Virginia

GREGORY J. SLATER, M.B.B.S., F.R.A.C.
Clinical Senior Lecturer, Department of Radiology, University of Queensland Medical School, Brisbane; Radiologist, Mater Private Radiology, Brisbane, Australia

TONY P. SMITH, M.D.
Professor of Radiology and Chief, Vascular/Interventional Radiology, Duke University Medical Center, Durham, North Carolina

THOMAS A. SOS, M.D.
Professor of Radiology, Cornell University Medical College; Director, Interventional Radiology, The New York Hospital, New York City

MICHAEL C. SOULEN, M.D.
Associate Professor of Radiology, Department of Radiology, and Associate Professor of Radiology in Surgery, University of Pennsylvania School of Medicine; Staff Interventional Radiologist, Department of Radiology, University of Pennsylvania Medical Center, Philadelphia

CHARLES J. TEGTMEYER, M.D.
Professor of Radiology and Anatomy, Director of Angiography, Interventional, and Special Procedures, University of Virginia Health Sciences Center, Charlottesville, Virginia
Deceased

AMY S. THURMOND, M.D.
Associate Professor of Obstetrics and Gynecology, Oregon Health Sciences University, Portland; Radiologist, Department of Radiology, Legacy Meridian Park Hospital, Tualatin, Oregon

KARIM VALJI, M.D.
Associate Professor, Department of Radiology, University of California, San Diego; Head, Division of Vascular and Interventional Radiology, University of California San Diego Medical Center, San Diego

ANTHONY C. VENBRUX, M.D.
Associate Professor and Associate Director of Cardiovascular and Interventional Radiology, Department of Radiology, Johns Hopkins University School of Medicine, Baltimore

BRUCE F. WALLER, M.D.
Clinical Professor of Pathology and Medicine, Indiana University School of Medicine; Director, Cardiovascular Pathology Registry, St. Vincent's Hospital; Cardiologist, Nasser, Smith, and Pinkerton, Inc., Indianapolis, Indiana

ARTHUR C. WALTMAN, M.D.
Associate Professor of Radiology, Harvard Medical School; Director, Division of Vascular and Interventional Radiology, Massachusetts General Hospital, Boston

ROBERT I. WHITE, JR., M.D.
Professor and Past Chairman, Diagnostic Radiology, Yale University School of Medicine; Interventional Radiologist, Yale–New Haven Hospital, New Haven, Connecticut

ALBERT B. ZAJKO, M.D.
Professor of Radiology and Surgery, University of Pittsburgh Medical School; Chief, Vascular and Interventional Radiology, Department of Radiology, University of Pittsburgh Medical Center, Pittsburgh

Preface

The third volume of the fourth edition of *Abrams' Angiography* is new—a stand-alone text devoted to interventional radiology rather than scattered chapters as in the previous editions. This separate volume was chosen after considerable deliberation and, in many ways, it symbolizes another stage in the growth and evolution of interventional radiology practice.

Increasingly, alternative imaging methods permit accurate and less invasive diagnosis of many conditions. With advances in ultrasound, magnetic resonance imaging, and helical CT, the number of diagnostic angiograms is declining in most practices; to some extent, this decrease has been offset by the growth in interventional procedures. In fact, in most practices interventional procedures are more common than diagnostic examinations.

Whatever the numbers, the rise of interventional radiology has certainly changed the tenor of practice. While some of the tools may be the same, interventional radiology is different than angiography. When attempting to change the course of disease rather than simply study its appearance, a radiologist assumes a whole different level of responsibility—from outpatient clinics to rounds to admitting services. And all of these changes have been good for radiology.

Creating a new field of medicine such as interventional radiology took intelligence, self-confidence, and vision—all traits that characterized our pioneers, many of whom contributed to the first, second, and third editions of *Abrams' Angiography*. The ensuing wave of radiologists are similar to those who fall in the ranks behind forerunners in other disciplines—perhaps less individualistic than their forebears, greater in number, a little narrower in scope, more engineers than pioneers. Their work—filling in the clinical and scientific gaps, quantifying the risks and benefits, developing and codifying training programs, haranguing insurers—is no less important. Whatever their contributions, these two groups gave birth to a new branch of medicine. This volume, to which many of them contributed, is a tribute to them all.

A physician can hope for two great professional pleasures. First, and always foremost, is the satisfaction of caring for an individual patient. The other is a contribution to society—the expansion of scientific knowledge, a public policy initiative, an organizational change that optimizes and improves health care. Those involved in the inception of this field over the past two decades have been fortunate to sample both pleasures.

Of course, interventional radiology is only one facet of the much larger field of minimally invasive therapy. These powerful trends—to less violative surgery, to a smaller incision, a shorter hospitalization, a quicker return to the normal function—are fueled by ever more knowledgeable patients. Fittingly, patients are the prime beneficiaries of interventional techniques as well as advances in allied fields of cardiology, gastroenterology, urology, and laparoscopic and arthroscopic surgery.

A labor of this size requires many hands. A great debt is owed to our administrative assistants, Flora Cauley and Jennifer Waechter, who handled the organization of this project in Philadelphia. The editorial assistance of Mary Frawley and Julie Sullivan was enlightening, understanding and, frankly, indispensable. A task of this magnitude would have been impossible without the steadfast encouragement of Nancy Chorpenning and Deeth Ellis at Little, Brown in Boston. In concert with Little, Brown and Dr. Abrams, we selected a satin enamel finish over more "traditional" enamel gloss papers, as we determined that it provides superior definition and gray-scale reproduction. We hope you find it easier on your eyes!

The counsel and aid of the interventional radiology attendings at the University of Pennsylvania, Drs. Constantin Cope, Ken Fellows, Parvi Ramchandani, Robert Hurst, Richard Shlansky-Goldberg, Michael Soulen, Ziv Haskal, Richard Baum, and Doug Redd, were critical to this effort. Finally, we appreciate the faith and confidence of Dr. Herb Abrams in entrusting us with this important duty.

Stanley Baum
Michael J. Pentecost

Notice

The indications and dosages of all drugs in this book have been recommended in the medical literature and conform to the practices of the general medical community. The medications described do not necessarily have specific approval by the Food and Drug Administration for use in the diseases and dosages for which they are recommended. The package insert for each drug should be consulted for use and dosage as approved by the FDA. Because standards for usage change, it is advisable to keep abreast of revised recommendations, particularly those concerning new drugs.

I

General Considerations

1

Mechanisms of Balloon Angioplasty and Restenosis

GARY J. BECKER
BRUCE F. WALLER

The introduction of percutaneous transluminal angioplasty (PTA) in 1964 did not immediately clarify the important pathophysiologic mechanisms responsible for enlargement of the lumen and improvement in flow beyond the lesion. Rather, our current understanding of this process and the body's response to the injury of PTA have evolved over time. Although the earliest in vitro experiments and animal studies focused primarily on mechanisms of PTA, the past decade has brought enormous interest in the topic of postangioplasty healing and restenosis. Initially, scientific and medical curiosity and intellectual pursuit were sufficient to generate this level of interest. Currently, the major driving forces are medical/scientific and medical/economic. From the medical/scientific side, there has been a veritable explosion in information about the biology of the endothelium and the vessel wall in the past 10 years. From the medical/economic side, interventionalists are developing processes to determine the clinical outcomes of angioplasty, and industry is deeply involved in the development of devices, drugs, and bioengineered substances to inhibit or prevent restenosis.

The scope of the following discussion of pathophysiologic mechanisms is confined to PTA of atherosclerotic plaque. It is highly likely that the important mechanisms of PTA in fibromuscular dysplasia, postsurgical anastomotic stenoses, and other arteriopathies are quite different. However, because of the relative importance of atherosclerosis and its treatment and the much higher level of our current understanding of the topic, this chapter will only discuss atherosclerosis.

Pathophysiologic Mechanisms of Angioplasty

Historical Background

It seemed clear to Dotter and Judkins that their "transluminal treatment of arteriosclerotic obstructions" was a technique that worked, since it produced clinical results. But they believed that the success of PTA using the coaxial dilator method ("Dotter method") was due to compression of atherosclerotic plaque.[1] Since they did not commonly see emboli downstream from the PTA site on post-PTA angiography and there was no clinical evidence of plaque fragmentation and embolization, this was a logical conclusion to draw. Where else could the plaque have gone? One analogy that they used was the footprint in the snow caused by the force of one's foot against the relatively compressible snow. Another was the displacement of wood that occurs when a nail is driven into it. The flaw in this reasoning is that both the snow and the wood have significant gaseous components that the atherosclerotic plaque does not have. The gas can be easily displaced from the snow by the force of one's foot and the wood by the force of the nail. The angioplasty catheter, however, cannot displace plaque components in this way.

Even 14 years later, after the introduction to clinical use of polyvinyl chloride (PVC) balloon angioplasty catheters, Gruentzig still believed the compression theory.[2] Zeitler had adhered to it as well.[3] Because follow-up angiography in PTA patients typically showed that the lumen was smooth in the site of previous PTA, these pioneers believed that in the healing process the compressed material was eventually covered by new endothelium. None of the aspects of this entire theory have ever been substantiated.

Investigative Approach Disproves Compression Hypothesis

The closest concept to compression that could be demonstrated to some small extent in the laboratory was that of redistributive remodeling. In a rather simple but elegant set of experiments aimed at revealing all potentially important mechanisms of PTA, Wolf and coworkers discovered that although a plaque could not be compressed in the sense described above, its mass and shape could be redistributed along a longer length of the vessel wall, as it is literally flattened or molded by an angioplasty catheter (redistributive remodeling).[4] However, this phenomenon probably occurs to a significant degree only with the coaxial dilator method of PTA and not with balloon PTA. There is evidence that with balloon PTA redistributive remodeling can account for only a very small portion of the increase in lumen size, because the vast majority of the increase is accounted for on the basis of other mechanisms.

Studies Document Important Pathophysiologic Mechanisms of PTA

From 1980 to 1987, a number of investigators studied and reported on the mechanical and histologic effects of PTA.[4-19] A review of these works verifies that neither

compression nor remodeling is an important pathophysiologic mechanism of successful balloon PTA. As would be expected from our knowledge of the clinical success of PTA, neither is embolization of plaque fragments or constituents an important mechanism.

Numerous studies have identified plaque fracture (Fig. 1-1) with or without localized dissection into the underlying media to be the principal mechanism of successful balloon PTA in humans.[5,6,8–10,13–20] In a necropsy study of coronary arteries from patients who underwent percutaneous transluminal coronary angioplasty (PTCA), Waller and colleagues reported that deep intimal fractures and underlying dissection of the media subjacent to the plaque (Fig. 1-2) are requisite pathologic changes to produce immediate and long-term improvement in luminal cross-sectional area.[19]

Several studies have combined to strongly suggest that stretching of the media is an important mechanism of PTA.[4,7,9–11,13–16,18,20] This is especially likely to be true with respect to angioplasty's effect on the disease-free arc of the vessel wall in cases of eccentric (rather than concentric) atherosclerotic plaque. In the coronary arteries in particular, approximately 70 percent of atherosclerotic plaques are eccentric.[21] There is much about the effects of PTA on the arterial media that still needs to be elucidated, particularly in regard to the long-term effects, the role of the smooth muscle cell (SMC) in the development of intimal hyperplasia and so on. However, some of the more acute pathologic effects have been determined. Castaneda-Zuniga and colleagues showed that irreversible overstretching results in disruption of some of the intercellular junctions between medial SMCs.[20] Pyknosis of nuclei was identified on canine studies of PTA. Disruption of the

Figure 1-1. Diagram showing intimal-medial plaque fracture after balloon angioplasty. Medial involvement (localized dissection) is an important component of the dilation process.

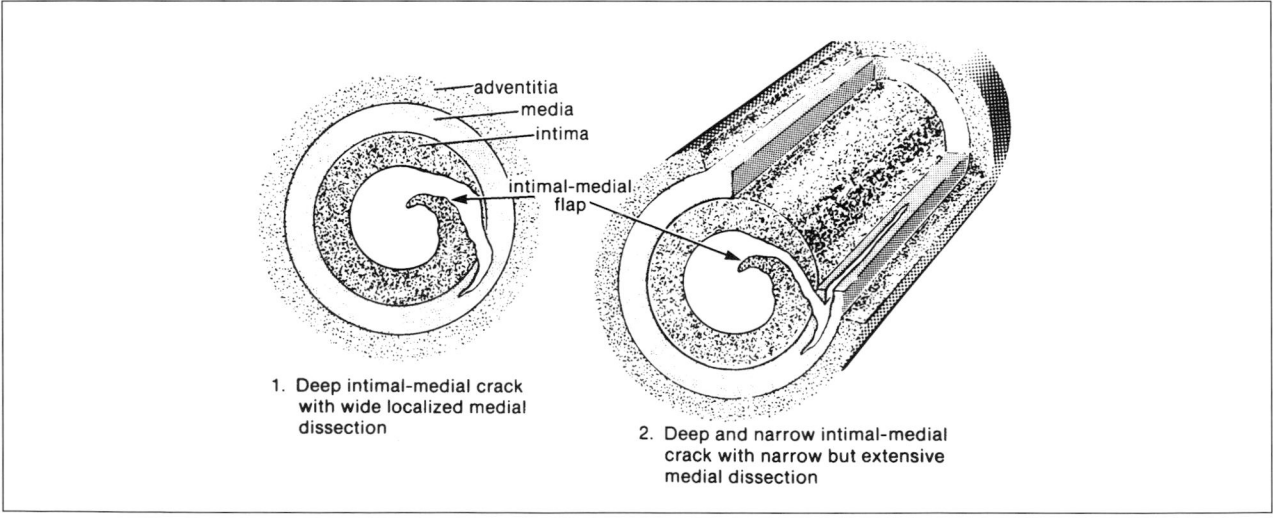

1. Deep intimal-medial crack with wide localized medial dissection

2. Deep and narrow intimal-medial crack with narrow but extensive medial dissection

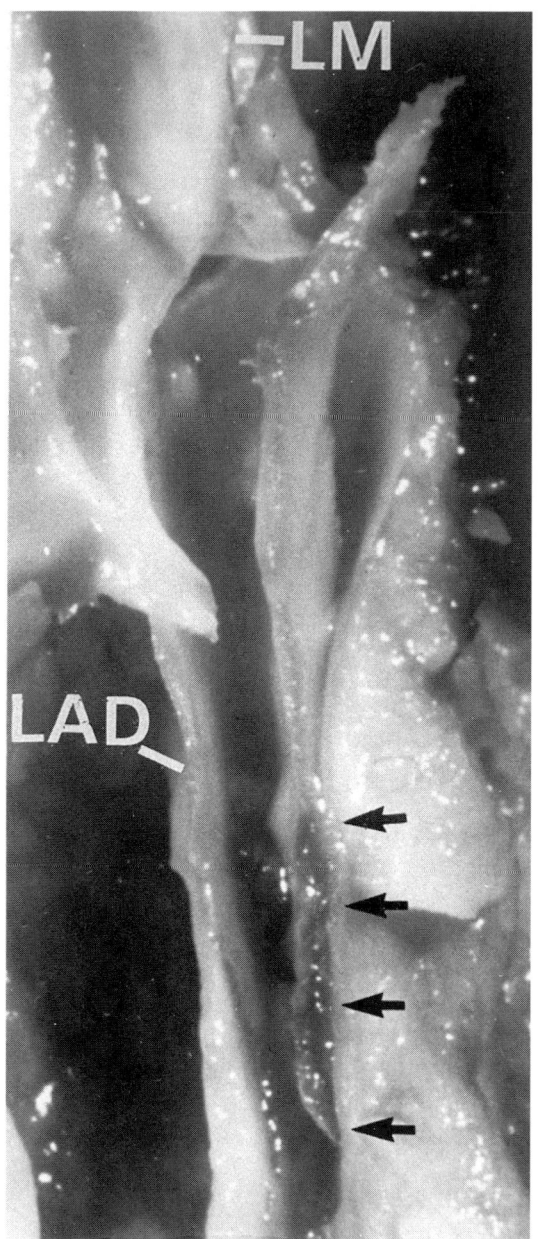

Figure 1-2. Gross pathologic specimen showing intimal-medial dissection (*arrows*) after successful balloon angioplasty of the left anterior descending coronary artery (LAD). *LM,* left main coronary artery.

internal elastic lamina was consistent in additional morphologic studies on necropsy specimens with atherosclerotic disease.[22] (Note: Disruption of the external elastic lamina is much less common and implies that the "localized" dissection of PTA has extended into the adventitia. It does not necessarily mean that a patient will manifest a rupture clinically, though the patient is much more likely to be symptomatic with pain.) In chronic studies of vascular wall histopathol-ogy several weeks after PTA, macrophages were found to be present, presumably removing the necrotic debris that remained. We can conclude that although, intuitively, overstretching to the point of adventitial rupture is an undesirable outcome of PTA, lesser degrees of stretching constitute an important component of the so-called controlled injury we associate with PTA.

An important feature of the vessel wall that determines the degree of injury with PTA is the extent of calcification. Calcification is directly related to the risk of rupture and to the extent of vessel wall dissection that occurs with angioplasty. Waller and colleagues conducted a study of 100 necropsy coronary arteries, in which arteries were graded for calcification on a 0 to 4+ scale (0 calcification, $n = 30$; 1–2+ calcification, $n = 35$; and 3–4+ calcification, $n = 35$). The investigators showed a direct correlation between the amount of vessel calcification and the likelihood of "overinjury" with balloon angioplasty.[23] Of 24 extensive dissections and 8 ruptures occurring in this necropsy study, all were in the 3–4+ or 4+ calcification group. Figure 1-3 depicts the relationship between degree of calcification and extent of injury with angioplasty.

Finally, with respect to morphologic changes after PTA, a number of investigators have concentrated on the vasa vasorum.[24–27] They have demonstrated transient hyperemia, an increase in the number and/or size of the vasa vasorum, or both. The significance of these changes is not well understood.

Pathophysiologic Mechanisms of Restenosis

Clinical features or recurrence of symptoms and signs late after balloon angioplasty (weeks to 1 year) may be due to (1) restenosis or occlusion at the original PTA site, (2) progression of disease proximal or distal to the original treatment site, or (3) unrelated causes. Discussions of progressive atherosclerosis remote from the treatment site and other causes are beyond the scope of this chapter. The current focus, therefore, will be on restenosis at the site of previous balloon PTA.

To those working in the field, at times it seems as if no progress has been made in the prevention or control of restenosis. However, as Eric Topol pointed out in his introduction to the 1994 Restenosis Summit at the Cleveland Clinic and as discussed below, 1994 will be remembered as the year in which both a device and a drug proved effective in reducing restenosis in clinical trials.

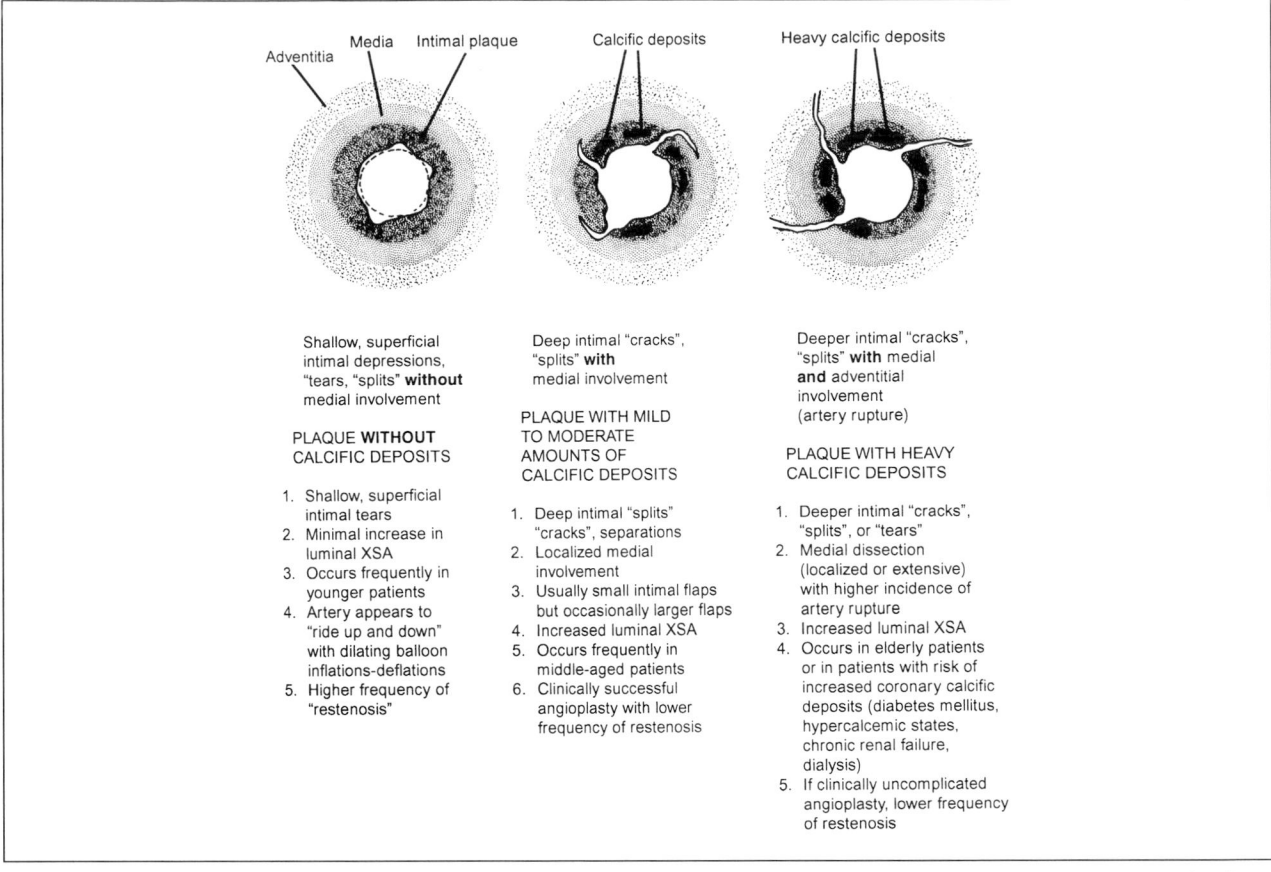

Figure 1-3. Diagram showing the effect of varying degrees of plaque calcific deposits on the morphologic results of balloon PTA. Plaques with moderate amounts of calcification appear to have the best results of angioplasty.

Angiographic, Clinical, and Histopathologic Restenosis

Kuntz and Baim have underscored the complexity of the concept of restenosis by citing the differences and interrelationships between *angiographic restenosis, clinical restenosis,* and *histopathologic restenosis.*[28] They further explored the view of restenosis as a dichotomous outcome (present or absent) versus restenosis as a continuous outcome (such as height). In the latter view, restenosis would occur to some extent in all individuals with vessels injured by PTA or other intervention. To view restenosis dichotomously, a threshold by which to diagnose restenosis must be identified. Since recurrent angina after PTCA necessitates a binary decision (to revascularize or not), late failure after PTCA certainly can be quantified as a dichotomous event. Since the vast majority of post-PTCA restenosis occurs between 2 and 6 months, the 6-month angiogram emerged as the gold standard to diagnose restenosis. The angiogram is also capable of distinguishing between true restenosis and progression of disease at other sites.

Angiographic Restenosis

Several reasonable but distinctly different angiographic definitions of restenosis exist in the coronary literature. The first is a stenosis of greater than 50 percent at the site of previous PTA (the Emory definition). This was not universally adopted because it failed to take into account whether the initial result was better than a 50 percent stenosis. The second is a loss of 50 percent or more of the previous gain in lumen diameter at the site of previous PTA (NHLBI-IV definition). Even this definition fails to correlate well with recurrent clinical symptoms. There are also several others. Reiber and colleagues have proposed that any change in minimal lumen diameter of 0.72 mm or more represents a significant reduction that can be termed restenosis.[29] This figure represents twice the standard deviation of the difference of duplicate measurements made at disparate times under similar conditions. Obviously, since this figure results in part from the blurred appearance of vessel edges on cineangiography, and in turn the effect on inter- and intraobserver variability in measurements, it is not directly applicable to peripheral vessels. Perhaps another value would be more applicable in the peripheral circulation. All in all, there are at least a dozen definitions of restenosis in the coronary angiography literature.

The fundamental problem remaining was that the view of restenosis as a binary event seemed always clouded by angiographic measurement error. Furthermore, incomplete angiographic follow-up (<80 percent of patients) had been clearly associated with significant selection bias.[30] Several studies with careful angiographic follow-up went on to document that late luminal renarrowing actually occurs as a continuous process, whereas initially the observation was thought to be due to inherent measurement errors in quantitative coronary angiography. Beatt and colleagues were the first to suggest that restenosis takes place to some extent in virtually all lesions after PTCA.[31] Kuntz and colleagues studied late angiographic results after Palmaz-Schatz stenting, atherectomy, or laser balloon angioplasty.[32,33] They considered the ultimate lumen gain as the difference between early gain and late loss. They found the results to be in a nearly normal continuous distribution not suggestive of a bimodal pattern of "restenosers" and "nonrestenosers." The continuous view supported previously published pathologic observations.[34,35] Modern quantitative coronary angiography is associated with a 0.2-mm standard deviation in measurements, rather than the 0.36-mm standard deviation mentioned above, and measurement errors tell more about the measurement methods than they do about the biologic process of restenosis.

Since restenosis turned out to be a continuous process, parametric statistical tests rather than weak categorical tests (such as chi square) can be used, and use of sophisticated regression techniques became possible. Many analyses have gone on to show that the most important aspect of device performance is its ability to initially provide a large lumen.[36] Balloon angioplasty (PTCA) results in 17 to 50 percent loss of inflated balloon diameter due to recoil.[37-40] However, Kuntz and colleagues determined that laser balloon PTA, Palmaz-Schatz stenting, and directional coronary atherectomy all provide a larger initial lumen diameter than PTCA.[33] The long-term outcome (lumen diameter) is actually better with these devices, despite the fact that the late loss due to restenosis is more than twice that with PTCA. The reason is that the initial gain is so much greater that the resulting late lumen diameter is larger. This extremely important concept is depicted diagrammatically in Figure 1-4. Linear regression models that relate either absolute acute gain to absolute late loss or relative acute gain to relative late loss reveal an amazingly stable slope of these relationships (0.45–0.50) for PTCA, directional atherectomy, stenting, and excimer laser PTA followed by adjunctive balloon dilatation. Kuntz and colleagues go on to point out that although the absolute amount of late loss may be important, particularly in pharmacologic trials, they find it difficult to feel too badly about a group of stent patients whose mean lumen diameter is 2.18 mm, whose mean late diameter stenosis is 33 percent, and whose binary stenosis rate is 26 percent,

Figure 1-4. Diagram depicting the importance of early gain in lumen diameter with intervention. Ultimate lumen gain is extremely dependent on the immediate postintervention lumen diameter. Lumen gain is much greater for stents than for PTCA. Therefore, although intimal hyperplasia causes more neointimal volume after stenting than after PTCA, the ultimate lumen gain (ULG = early gain minus late loss) is greater for stenting.

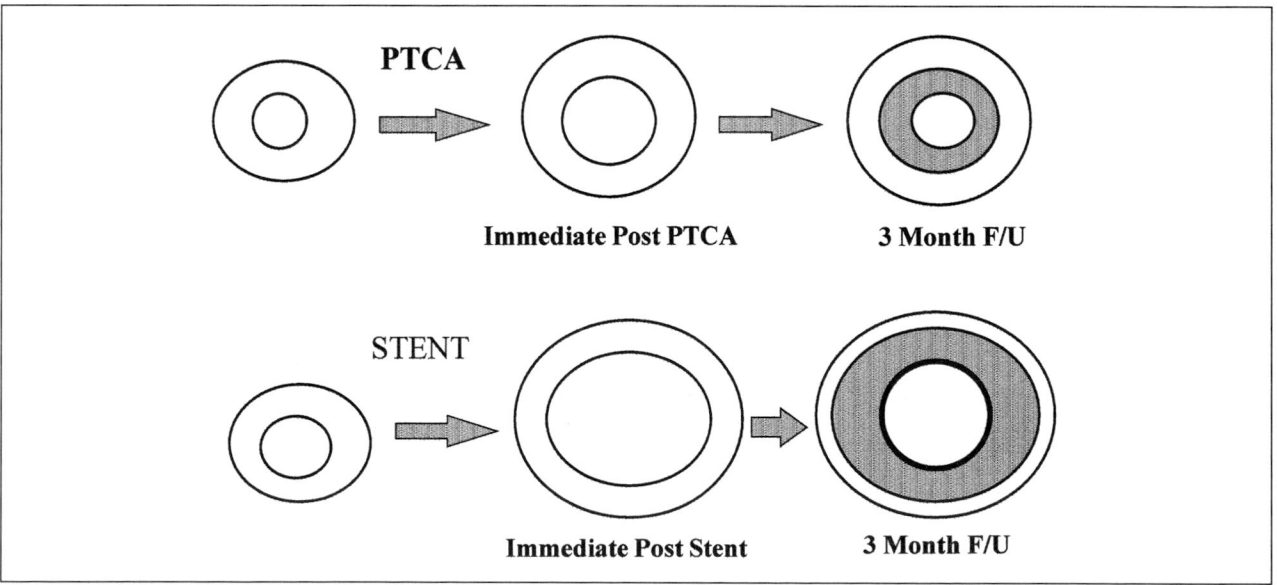

simply because 85 percent of them had an absolute late loss of over 0.72 mm.

The most important point is that it is clinically more relevant to measure restenosis by the late percent stenosis (by the hole, not the doughnut). It is also important to realize the virtues of attempting to achieve the greatest possible acute lumen within the limits of safety. It is possible to be too aggressive with directional atherectomy, and not all devices work well simply because they provide a large initial lumen. The Wallstent had an 18 percent reclosure rate within 2 weeks of treatment.[41] In general, however, as long as a slope of 0.5 or lower is achieved in the *loss index* (measured absolute late loss divided by the absolute initial gain in lumen diameter), the late result in lumen diameter will be acceptable. If the loss index reaches 0.75, then the result will not be better than that for PTCA. There is still a good deal of variation in late loss at follow-up angiography, and mechanical factors explain only 10 to 20 percent of the disparity. Biologic factors come into play in explaining these differences. Two factors that have been shown to portend a high rate of restenosis are a left anterior descending coronary artery location of the treated lesion (loss index of 0.52 versus loss index of 0.35 for right coronary artery lesions following stenting and atherectomy)[42] and diabetes mellitus (0.68 for diabetics versus 0.48 for non-diabetics after stenting).[43] Figures 1-5 and 1-6 depict lower extremity arterial and renal arterial cases of restenosis, respectively.

Clinical Restenosis

Because of the limitations and expense of the 6-month follow-up angiogram and clinical definitions of restenosis, Kuntz and Baim[28] have suggested *target vessel revascularization* as an improved clinical restenosis end point. The virtues of this concept include the following: it is concentrated in the same time period in which maximum luminal renarrowing is known to occur, it correlates well with dichotomous angiographic restenosis defined as over 50 percent diameter stenosis, and it is statistically sensitive to the strongest determinant of angiographic restenosis (acute lumen diameter). This end point misses asymptomatic restenosis, but such patients do not have worse clinical courses than those without restenosis.[44–47]

Finally, since almost all coronary revascularizations after PTCA occur within 240 days of the initial intervention (15:1 ratio of before 240 days and after),[48] target vessel revascularization before 240 days may be considered a dichotomous time-limited end point. Under these terms, it is inappropriate and unnecessary to analyze results of PTCA with Kaplan-Meier life-table analysis or other time-dependent methods. The

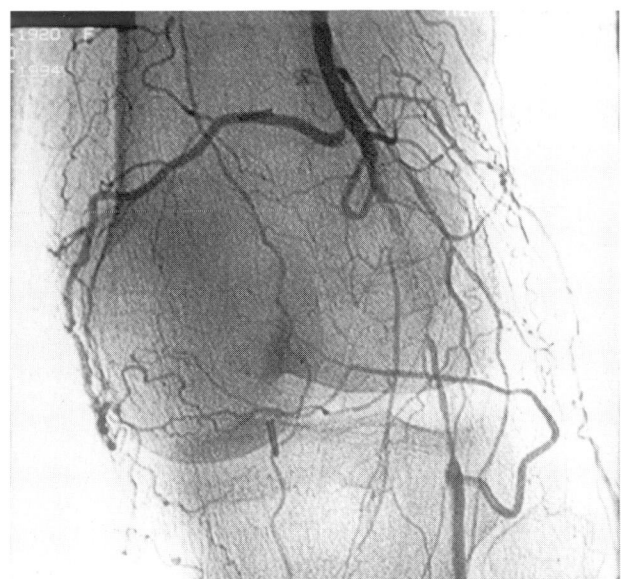

A

Figure 1-5. An elderly woman with severe claudication and flat pulse volume recordings below the knee. (A) Arteriogram demonstrating short-segment popliteal artery occlusion. (B and C) Recanalization and PTA are performed under road-mapping guidance. D. Immediate post-PTA arteriogram shows numerous dissection clefts but a widely patent lumen. The dorsalis pedis and posterior tibialis pulses were normal. The patient was asymptomatic for 9 months, but then returned with recurrence of calf claudication. (E) Arterial digital subtraction angiography showing severe popliteal restenosis.

challenge for interventionalists is to reduce restenosis as defined by target vessel revascularization in the first 8 months; progression of coronary artery disease remains the domain of controlling risk factors or reversing atherosclerosis that is already present.

Histopathologic Restenosis

In a necropsy study of coronary arteries proven to have restenosis angiographically, Waller and colleagues demonstrated that 60 percent of the lesions exhibited histologic findings of a response to PTA, including intimal fibrous proliferation (IFP), also known as myointimal hyperplasia; 40 percent exhibited absolutely no evidence that a PTA had previously occurred.[49] Prior to this, Waller[50] and other investigators[34,35,51,52] had proved that IFP identical to that associated with post-carotid-endarterectomy restenosis[53] occurs after PTA, but the percentages were not known. The 40 percent lacking findings specifically showed the presence of plaque, but no IFP, no evidence of previous plaque fracture, and no evidence of new immature plaque formation. The lack of immature plaque formation in both these and the other 60 percent with IFP provides

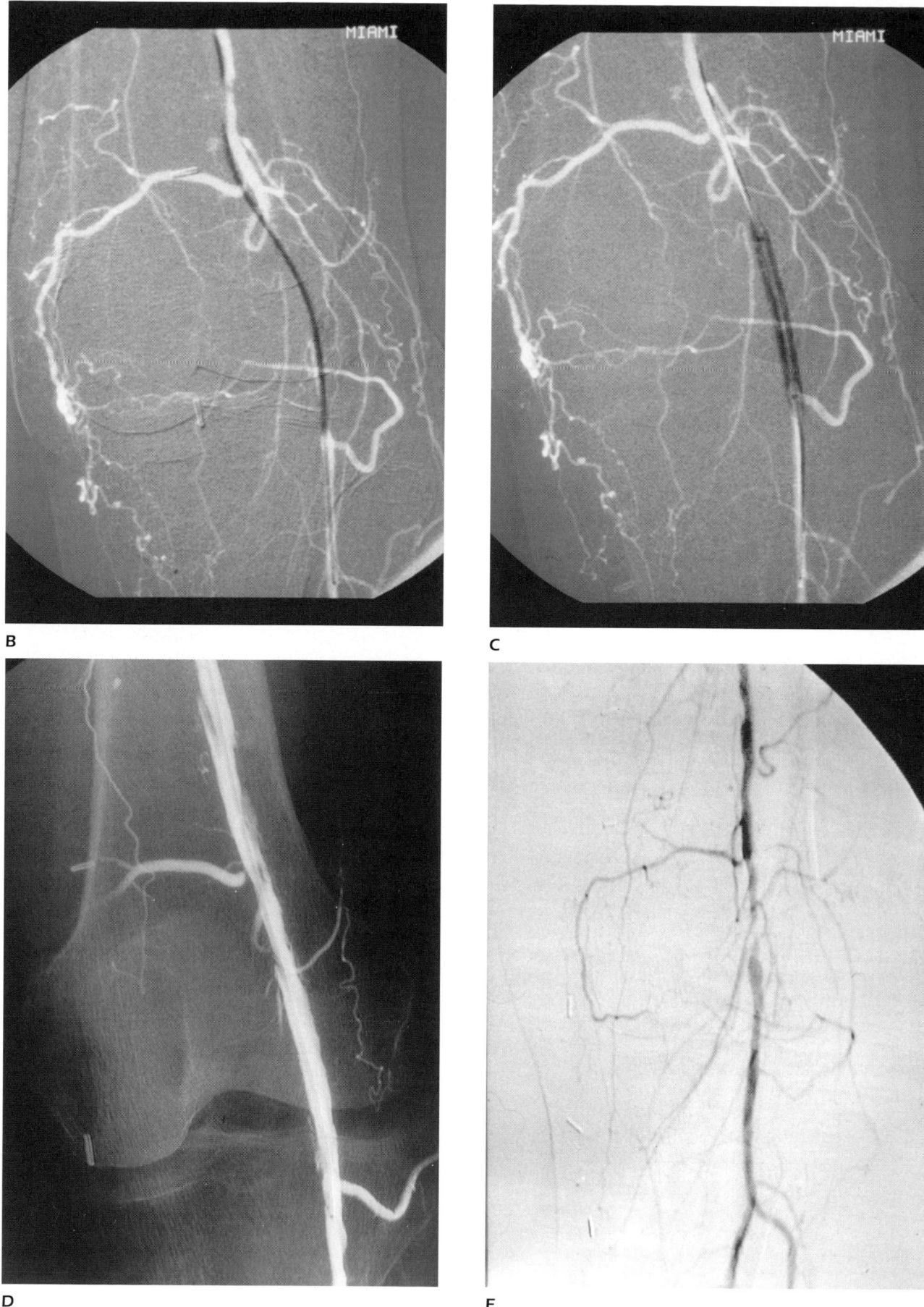

B

C

D

E

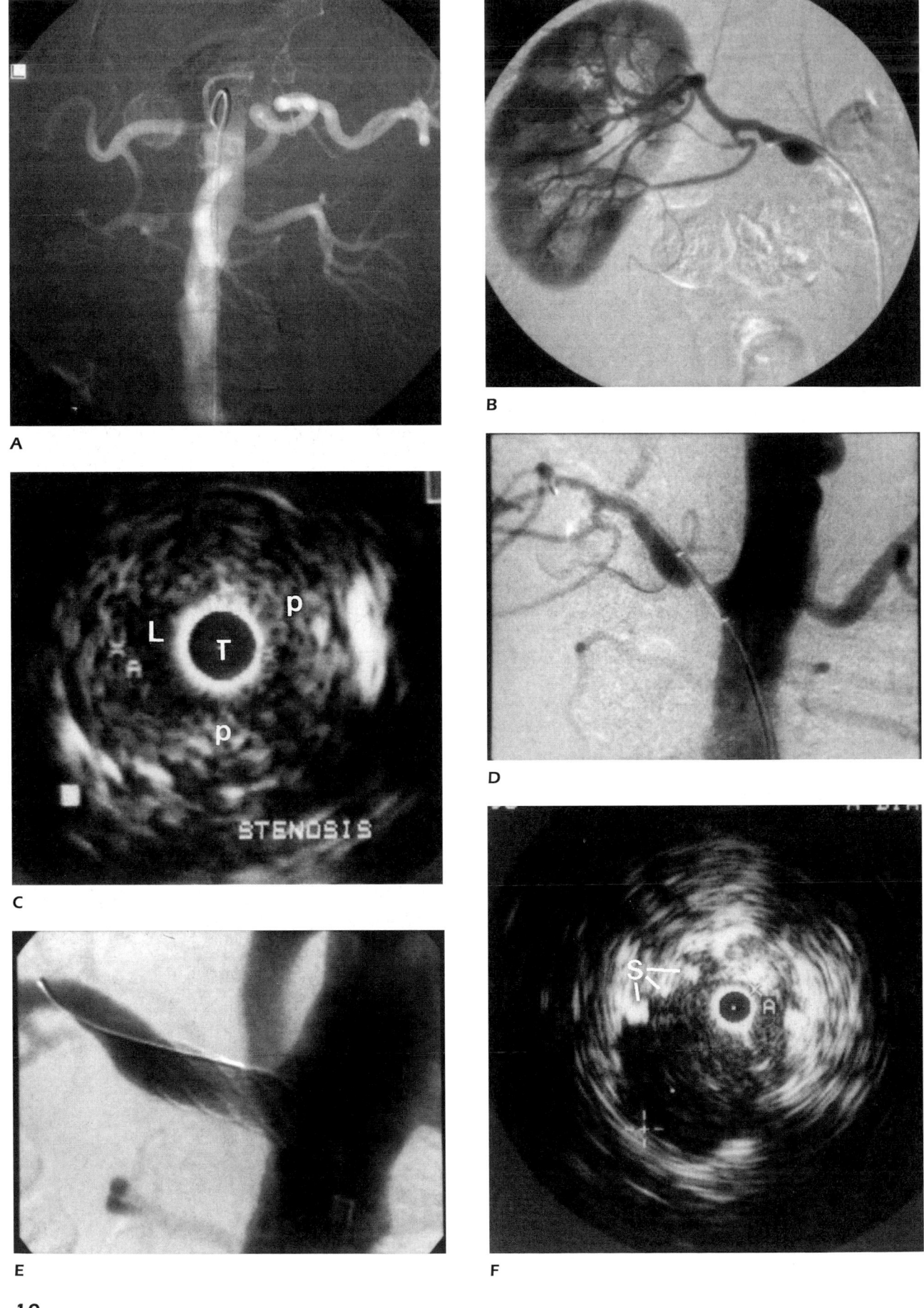

A

B

C

D

E

F

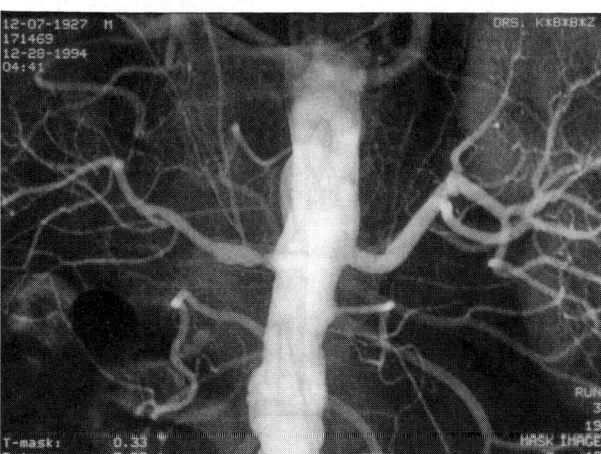

G

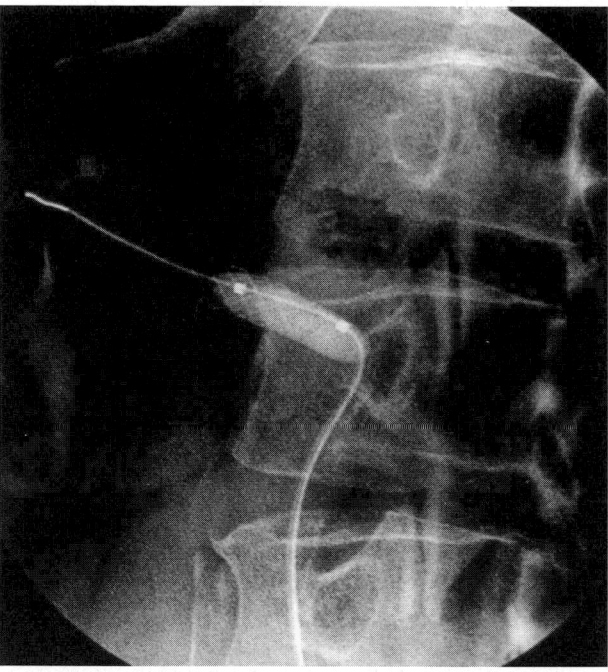

H

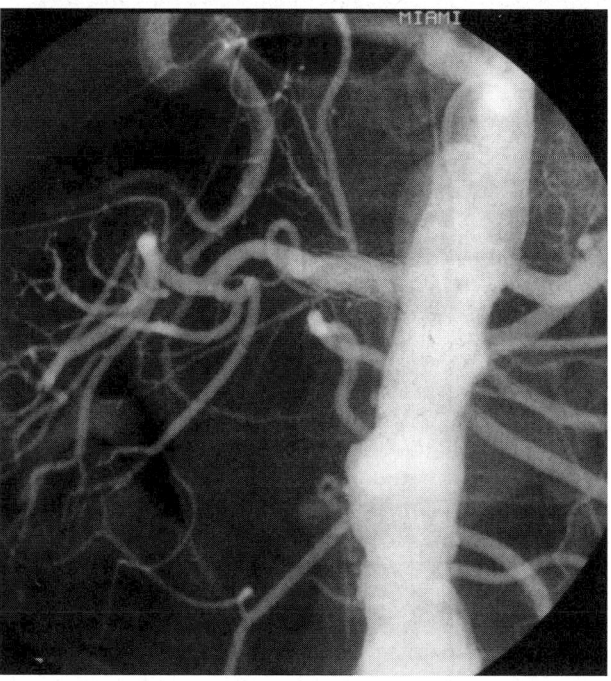

I

Figure 1-6. A 51-year-old man with severe new-onset hypertension. (A) Digital aortogram reveals severe proximal right renal artery stenosis. (B) Selective right renal arteriogram with catheter tip beyond stenosis. (C) Intravascular ultrasound study (IVUS) immediately after PTA. *T,* transducer; *p,* plaque, which appears homogeneously echogenic in this image; *L,* lumen. Only a small crescent of lumen is identifiable between the transducer and the adjacent plaque. Therefore, PTA had failed to alleviate the stenosis due to this eccentric atherosclerotic plaque. The most likely cause of failure here is elastic recoil. (D) Palmaz-Schatz stent in position before deployment. (E) Aortogram immediately after stenting reveals an excellent anatomic result. (F) IVUS after stent deployment reveals a widely patent stented lumen. The transducer is eccentrically positioned. *S,* stent struts. The patient was well until hypertension suddenly recurred 15 months after stenting. (G) Aortogram revealed intimal hyperplasia throughout the stented lumen of the right renal artery, plus a focal stenosis (restenosis) due to intimal hyperplasia. (H) Digital spot film of balloon angioplasty for this restenosis. (I) Post-PTA aortogram revealing an excellent anatomic result. The patient once again became normotensive.

evidence against theories that PTA can accelerate atherosclerosis. Moreover, the lack of findings in the 40 percent group suggests (1) that mechanisms other than plaque fracture may be important in a high percentage of technically successful PTAs, and (2) that elastic recoil, recovery of myocyte function, and perhaps other processes yet to be delineated are important in a high percentage of restenosis cases detected clinically and angiographically. The finding that not all restenosis is due to IFP suggests that stents, thermal molding of the vessel wall, and other efforts to optimize lumen geometry may offer promise of both improved technical success and longer-term patency. The clinical studies cited above provide further evidence that this is true.

Pathogenesis of Restenosis: Conventional View and Results of Treatment Strategies

Pathogenesis

Restenosis due to IFP is considered by some to be the "Achilles' heel" of PTA. Liu and colleagues summarized much of the important research in this area in their excellent review article.[54] Much of our present

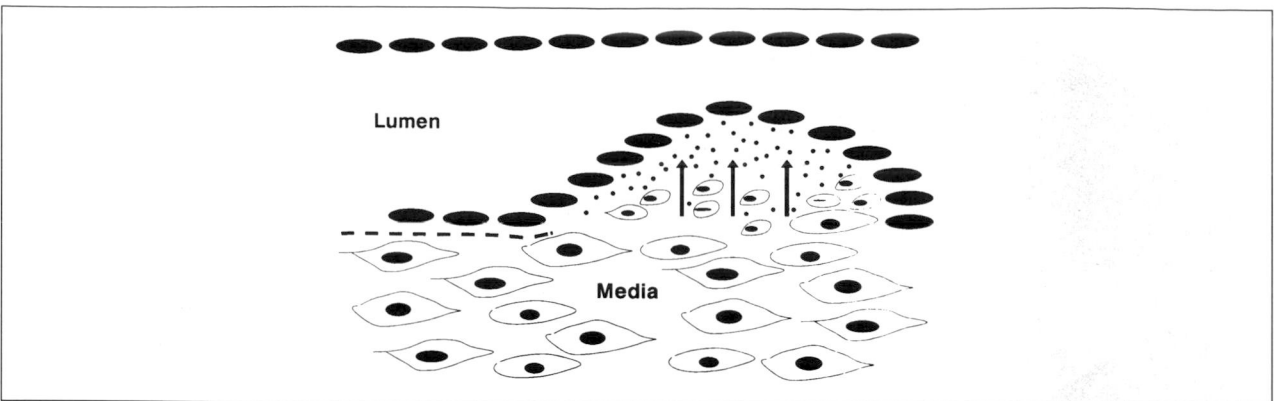

Figure 1-7. Diagrammatic representation of the process of restenosis due to neointimal hyperplasia (intimal fibrous proliferation). Smooth muscle cells from the media adopt a synthetic, noncontractile phenotype and migrate into the intima and proliferate. They produce a matrix that constitutes 90 percent of neointimal volume. (From Schwartz RS, Holmes DR, Topol EJ. The restenosis paradigm revisited: an alternative proposal for cellular mechanisms. J Am Coll Cardiol 1992;20:1284–1293. Used with permission.)

knowledge about IFP derives from necropsy studies of human coronary arteries, angiographic studies, studies of atherosclerotic vessels in animals, and studies of normal vessels in animals following injury. In clinical PTA, IFP is nearly impossible to predict, nearly impossible to prevent, and difficult to treat. It detracts significantly from the economic advantage of PTA over surgical bypass grafting, and has become the focus of intense investigation worldwide.

IFP tissue is made of SMCs and extracellular matrix.[55] There are two major distinct phenotypes of SMC: contractile and synthetic. The synthetic ones lack the contractile mechanism responsible for SMC contraction, but contain, as demonstrated on transmission electron microscopy, the subcellular organelles associated with protein synthesis (e.g., rough endoplasmic reticulum). IFP tissue contains predominantly synthetic SMCs that have populated the intima by migrating from the media through the internal elastic membrane and then dividing.[56] Most SMCs begin their mitotic activity within 2 to 3 days after injury of the arterial wall.[57] By approximately 1 week after the injury, the number of SMCs peaks; then it plateaus. IFP thickness (including increases in cell size and elaboration of matrix) peaks at about 8 weeks in animals, and probably at about 8 to 12 weeks in humans.[58] Figure 1-7 reviews the process diagrammatically; Figure 1-8 is a histologic depiction of intimal hyperplasia in a patient without angiographic or clinical restenosis; Figure 1-9 is a histologic depiction of a fatal coronary restenosis.

To mount an effective attack on IFP requires that we understand the factors contributing to its development. To date, we have a small amount of knowledge in this area. Platelets, growth factors, the extent and nature of injury, endothelial cells, SMCs, lumen geometry and hemodynamics, and various risk factors all have important roles in modulating the IFP response to balloon PTA.

In animal models, platelets adhering at the site of arterial injury within 10 minutes of arterial injury[59] are known to degranulate within 30 minutes of the injury. Alpha granule contents can be detected in the subjacent vessel wall.[60] It is thought that platelet-derived growth factor (PDGF) and other factors may enter the wall in this way. Although only 3 percent of alpha granules are retained in the adherent platelets by 40 minutes after the injury, the aggregating platelets are quite different.[61] They lose only a small percentage of their granule contents, and of those that are released, the vast majority are inactivated in the circulation.[62] Since the adhering platelet layer would seem much more important than aggregating layers in the pathogenesis of IFP, a shadow of doubt is cast upon studies examining the association between indium-platelet scintigraphic results on the one hand and the likelihood and/or severity of restenosis on the other. A scintigraphic study specific for activated platelets would seem to have great potential value. Recently, an agent for this purpose has been proposed and tested.[63] As important as adhering platelets may be in the early pathogenesis of IFP, they are not a necessary condition for its development. After arterial injury, IFP occurs even in the circumstance of extreme thrombocytopenia.[64]

PDGF is the most potent SMC mitogen known.[64] Although it is capable of causing SMCs to advance from interphase to prophase in the mitotic cycle, other factors are required to advance SMCs to and through the DNA synthetic phase.[65] Some factors that may be

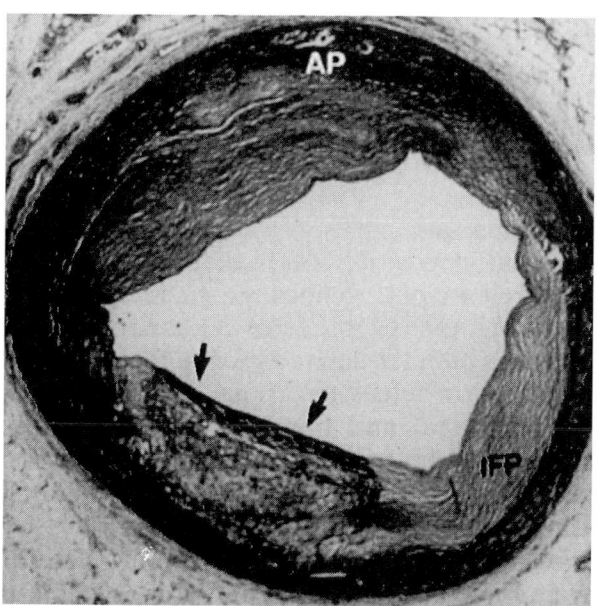

Figure 1-8. Cross section of a coronary artery 24 months after successful percutaneous transluminal coronary angioplasty. *Arrows* point to atherosclerotic plaque (*AP*). *IFP*, intimal fibrous proliferation or intimal hyperplasia.

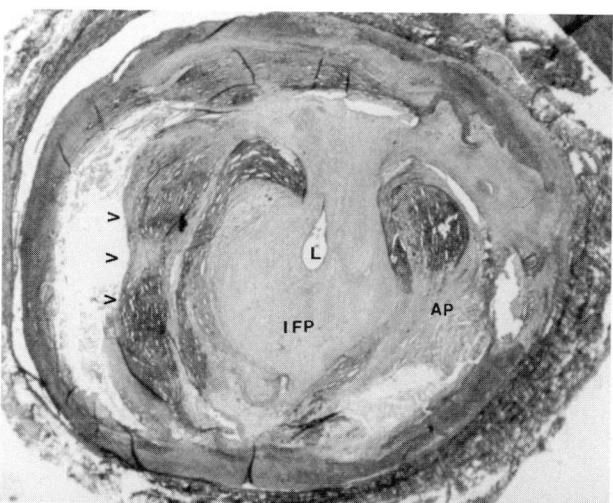

Figure 1-9. Fatal coronary restenosis due to intimal hyperplasia (intimal fibrous proliferation, *IFP*). *Arrowheads* indicate separation of plaque from vessel wall, which occurred at the time of balloon angioplasty and plaque fracture. *AP*, atherosclerotic plaque; *L*, the very narrow, teardrop-shaped lumen.

important in the modulation of IFP include PDGF, transforming growth factor-beta, and epidermal growth factor from platelets; basic fibroblast growth factor and interleukin-1 from macrophages; and somatomedin-C from serum. Insulinlike growth factor is another that acts together with PDGF to stimulate SMC proliferation. PDGF and others may also derive from dead or dying SMCs. In addition, endothelial cells are a source of growth factors.

Endothelial cells produce not only growth factors, but heparin. The latter has antiproliferative effects on SMCs.[54] In fact, certain low-molecular-weight heparin fragments now in clinical trials have been shown to inhibit SMC proliferation, but to have little anticoagulant effect.[66] Loss of endothelial surface due to injury (e.g., balloon PTA) has interesting implications with respect to SMC response according to extent of injury.

The extent and nature of injury seem to play important roles in modulation of the SMC response to injury. Mechanical and inflammatory processes can both cause IFP. However, examination of mechanical injuries provides insights into the relationship between the type and extent of injury on the one hand and the SMC response on the other. In animal studies, a wide area of endothelial denudation without injury to the internal elastic lamina (IEL) results in slow endothelial coverage of the site of injury and marked SMC hyperplasia.[67] But since migration of SMCs into the intima does not occur, there is no IFP. On the other hand,

a tiny area of endothelial denudation (for example, by a very sharp instrument) with penetration through the IEL results in IFP, despite rapid endothelial coverage.[68] Obviously, it matters whether the extent of injury is defined according to depth or width. Interestingly, recent studies of directional atherectomy suggest that when elements of the media are contained in the initial atherectomy specimens in de novo atherosclerotic lesions, the likelihood of restenosis is higher than if no medial elements are present.[69] This finding provides clinical supporting evidence for the contention that extent of injury is related to IFP, and that injury to the media is an important determinant.

SMC injury is integral to the development of IFP, and disruption of the IEL is not a necessary precondition. In animal models, it has proved possible to place a constricting band on arteries, inducing a pressure injury of SMCs. Following such an injury and in the absence of significant injury to the luminal surface of the arteries, IFP occurs.[70,71] Thus, despite the presence of an intact IEL, injury to the SMCs results in migration of SMCs into the intima, proliferation of SMCs, and elaboration of matrix.

A wealth of information from angiographic studies in the coronary circulation has provided us with valuable insights and theories regarding the importance of lumen geometry, hemodynamics, and restenosis. Restenosis after coronary angioplasty occurs with increased frequency in arteries with relatively low flow,[72,73] in arteries with 35 percent or more stenosis remaining after angioplasty, at PTA sites with a residual gradient of 15 mmHg (systolic) or greater, in vessels with marked tortuosity, and in still other specific morphologic circumstances, such as extensive disease and eccentric lesions.[74] Investigators have also postulated that there is a relationship between shear stress and restenosis. Shear stress is greatest when flow velocity is high. Fluctuation in shear stress is great in poststenotic areas with turbulent flow and reversal of flow (areas of flow separation), such as that beyond a residual stenosis following PTA. The theory is that when lumen geometry and flow are optimal, shear stress is high and fluctuation in shear stress is low. In such circumstances there is little or no restenosis; when lumen geometry and/or flow is suboptimal, shear stress is low and fluctuation in shear stress is great. Under these circumstances, there is a high likelihood of restenosis.[74] In any case, the concept lends credence to the strategy of optimizing both lumen geometry and the hemodynamic result of PTA.

In addition to the above, there are certain clinical risk factors known to predispose to a higher likelihood of restenosis (following coronary angioplasty). These include diabetes mellitus (particularly if current PTA is for treatment of restenosis), continued cigarette smoking, absence of a previous myocardial infarction, and unstable angina.[75] A high total-cholesterol–HDL-cholesterol ratio has been reported to be an important predictor of restenosis,[76] but some investigators have disagreed.[77,78]

Despite our lack of knowledge, several different strategies are being and have been tried in efforts to prevent IFP. Each strategy fits into one of the following categories: technical, pharmacologic, molecular biologic, or a combination of these.

Strategies for the Prevention of Restenosis

Technical Strategies. First are the technical approaches. These include all of the new devices. Simple laser heat probe thermal angioplasty has been tried. In part, the rationale was that debulking the vessel wall of much of its plaque burden by vaporization would accomplish two objectives toward reducing clinical restenosis. The first was that debulking would rid the vessel lumen of plaque burden; thus, when IFP did occur, it would occur on a background of less atheromatous material. Therefore, it would take relatively longer for IFP to produce a clinical restenosis. The second was that laser vaporization of plaque would smooth out the treated surface and thereby reduce the amount of post-PTA platelet activation; the ultimate result would be less IFP. In addition to these proposed benefits, it was hoped that heating of the media would result in destruction of some of the medial SMCs responsible for IFP. Unfortunately, laser heat probe an-

gioplasty does not reduce IFP or clinical restenosis,[79] and in fact may worsen them.

Thermal balloon angioplasty with attempts to control the thermal injury producing SMC injury and necrosis, and thereby to reduce recoil, spasm, and intimal hyperplasia, is being tried. Simple thermal balloon angioplasty (TBA),[80] radiofrequency balloon angioplasty (RFBA),[81,82] and laser balloon angioplasty (LBA)[83,84] are some approaches. They have also been used in attempts to mold the vessel wall,[85] a concept that is only just beginning clinical testing. So far, although these balloons have proved capable of molding vessels and even sealing dissection clefts, there is no direct evidence that they reduce the IFP response to PTA, either in frequency or severity. In fact, the IFP that occurs is greater than that observed for PTCA.[33] However, as noted above, they do provide a larger acute lumen diameter increase in coronary interventions than does PTCA alone.

Atherectomy has been used in attempts to debulk the lesion and thereby set back the starting point of IFP and the onset of clinical restenosis. One of the other proposed benefits of atherectomy was the supposedly smoother resultant surface, which would be less likely to activate platelets and therefore more likely to reduce platelet-mediated SMC hyperplasia. None of these concepts have yet been shown to reduce intimal hyperplasia. However, directional atherectomy in the coronary studies has resulted in a larger acute lumen diameter than that achievable with PTCA.[33] Since it does cause approximately three times the absolute late loss in lumen diameter that PTCA causes, it would seem that incomplete atherectomy could lead to an increased frequency of clinical and angiographic restenosis. There is also some evidence that atherectomy cuts into the media (presumably associated with more SMC injury) are associated with a greater frequency of restenosis.[79] In clinical application, the Coronary Angioplasty Versus Excisional Atherectomy Trial (CAVEAT) did not document a therapeutic advantage of directional coronary atherectomy (DCA) over PTCA.[86] Instead, the most important determinant of lumen diameter at 6 months was the lumen diameter achieved at the time of the procedure, regardless of whether that lumen was achieved with PTCA or DCA.

Finally, stents have been used to help prevent or manage this problem. As mentioned above, stents have proved valuable in the management of eccentric lesions, elastic recoil, and PTA-induced dissection. Early data also suggest that stents may have a role in ostial renal artery lesions.[87] Although intimal hyperplasia sufficient to result in clinical restenosis can and does occur within stented vessel segments, the early gain is great and the loss index is approximately 0.5.[28] Therefore, at least in coronary studies, the benefits of early lumen diameter increase seem to outweigh the late loss. That clinically apparent restenosis is less with Palmaz-Schatz stents than with PTCA, at least in 6-month follow-up, has been shown in the prospective randomized BENESTENT[88] and STRESS[89] studies.

Pharmacologic Strategies. Many pharmacologic maneuvers have been tried in attempts to reduce restenosis, and only one has proved efficacious (see glycoprotein IIb/IIIa platelet antagonists and the EPIC trial below). Conventional antiplatelet therapy, for instance, seems reasonable, since PDGF is known to stimulate SMC hyperplasia. However, antiplatelet drugs have their greatest impact in preventing accretion of new platelet layers once platelet adhesion to the exposed connective tissue has already occurred. As detailed above, there is evidence that growth factors from these additional platelet layers have little if any effect on SMCs in the media. A metaanalysis of several studies employing aspirin after coronary angioplasty has failed to reveal a significant reduction in restenosis.[90] Growth factors from the adherent platelet layer probably enter the vessel wall extremely rapidly after PTA. Inhibition of platelet adhesion would seem an important avenue to explore. This, in fact, is being explored with such investigational compounds as hirudin, a leech enzyme that has antithrombin effects and, unlike heparin, is capable of preventing the growth of an acute thrombus.[91] Local delivery of a synthetic hirudinlike compound, D-Phe-Pro-Arg chloromethyl ketone (PPACK), effectively inhibits thrombosis in doses more than 100 times less than those required with intravenous PPACK administration.[92] Heparin does decrease platelet deposition and thrombus growth after arterial injury in a dose-dependent fashion.[93] It is now clear from multiple studies that, after arterial injury deep to the endothelial surface, thrombosis is mediated predominantly by thrombin activation of platelets.[94,95] In trials of warfarin, therapy was not preceded by consistently adequate anticoagulant doses of heparin during the periangioplasty period. Therefore, warfarin has been inadequately studied to date.[96] Prostacyclin (PGI$_2$) is a naturally occurring prostaglandin produced by endothelial cells that is known to be a potent vasodilator, a potent inhibitor of platelet aggregation, and a potent disaggregator of platelet clumps.

A synthetic PGI$_2$ analogue known as ciprostene has been used in extensive laboratory studies and more recently in clinical trials in attempts to reduce clinical restenosis.[97] Thus far only a trend toward lower frequency of angiographic restenosis has been identified (without statistical significance). Even if it were to prove somewhat effective, there are numerous practical problems with the development of suitable regimens for the administration of ciprostene. Thromboxane-A$_2$ receptor inhibitors, including ticlopidine, GR 32191B, and sulotroban, have failed to demonstrate a therapeutic effect.[98–100] Other compounds known to have antiproliferative effects on SMCs, such as the calcium channel antagonists, have proved clinically ineffective in the prevention of restenosis.[101–102] The low-molecular-weight heparin compounds have antiproliferative properties and little or no anticoagulant properties. They have demonstrated limited efficacy in reducing restenosis in animal studies[66] and have undergone limited study in randomized clinical trials without demonstration of efficacy.[103] Colchicine, which causes metaphase arrest in mitosis, has proved capable of inhibiting DNA synthesis in vascular smooth muscle cells and in reducing restenosis in laboratory studies.[104,105] However, it has so far failed to reduce restenosis in clinical trials.[106–107]

Antineoplastic drugs have also been tried in animal studies of arterial injury. In low doses, they have proven effective in decreasing the early SMC proliferative response.[108] Whether the results will have longer-term benefit or eventual clinical application is not known. In laboratory studies, corticosteroids have been shown to inhibit SMC proliferation, growth, and chemotaxis, and possibly even PDGF production.[109–112] Also, in vitro the antiproliferative SMC effects of corticosteroids and low-molecular-weight heparin are additive.[112] However, thus far clinical trials of corticosteroids have not shown a significant reduction in restenosis.[113] Other potential pharmacologic agents include antagonists to platelet membrane glycoprotein IIb/IIIa receptor complex that could effectively prevent platelet adhesion to exposed collagen.[114] The potential benefit of such an agent has already been demonstrated in a large coronary clinical trial (EPIC trial).[115] Angiopeptin, a somatostatin analogue that inhibits SMC hyperplasia in response-to-injury animal models,[116] has not proved to be of benefit in clinical trials. Cilazapril, an angiotensin-converting enzyme inhibitor that inhibits SMC hyperplasia in animals,[117] has also been assessed in clinical trials.[118] So far, clinical trials of angiotensin-converting enzyme inhibitors have been disappointing.[118–120] Interest in fish oils was prompted by their antiaggregatory effects on platelets, antimitogenic qualities, and lipid effects. However, clinical trials (five studies in all) have failed to demonstrate a clear reduction in restenosis.[90] One final pharmacologic strategy is that of cholesterol-lowering agents to reduce total cholesterol and to reduce the total-cholesterol–HDL-cholesterol ratio. The angiographic results of the two best studies are at odds with one another. One claims a marked reduction in restenosis after cholesterol control on diet and cholesterol-lowering agents after coronary angioplasty,[121] and the other shows no advantage at all.[122]

Combined Technical and Pharmacologic Strategies. The combined technical and pharmacologic approach is not in common use, nor has it been tried in any large-scale trial. The idea is that an interventional device is used to deliver drugs or bioengineered growth factor inhibitors to the vessel wall in the PTA microenvironment in an effort to prevent IFP. One example of such devices is a local infusion angioplasty balloon catheter that achieves pressures adequate for PTA, yet has microholes in the balloon surface drug delivery.[123–125] Another is so-called endoluminal paving with hydrogel polymers, a technique that has recently been shown in animal models to reduce both early thrombus formation after vascular injury and long-term intimal hyperplasia.[126] Such polymers may have potential to serve not only as a barrier to blood-borne growth factors, but also as a delivery system for timed release of antirestenosis drugs. Ideally, the drug(s) should be effective against one or more steps in the development of the IFP response. Limited feasibility studies of both local infusion balloons and biodegradable and bioresorbable stents have been performed.

Molecular Genetic Strategies. The newest and perhaps most exciting avenues of attack on IFP—gene transfer and other molecular genetic approaches—are being investigated in genetics laboratories today. One idea is to identify and isolate genes known to encode for the synthesis of compounds that may be used to prevent IFP, then transfer the gene(s) or gene products directly to the vessel wall. Two methods of gene transfer—liposomal transfection and retroviral and adenoviral infection—are in experimental use today. Nabel and colleagues have shown that the process is feasible.[127] They isolated the *Escherichia coli* gene that encodes for the synthesis of beta-galactosidase and successfully transferred it to the iliac arteries of swine by perfusing the experimental iliac segments (in vivo), using a double balloon catheter. The perfusion fluid carried the genes within replication-defective retroviral vectors directly into the intima, media, and adventitia of the vessel wall. Weeks to months after perfusion the gene was proven to be in the vessel wall and functioning. The beta-galactosidase produced by the experimental vessels gave a positive blue histochemical stain, while the control vessels did not. Subsequently, the investigators were also successful in transferring the gene to porcine iliac arteries in vivo using liposomal transfection (no viruses). In another laboratory, investigators have succeeded in transferring the gene that encodes for firefly luciferase to canine coronary and carotid arteries.[128] Using an assay for luminescence, the investigators have been able to determine that the gene is present and expressing (producing luciferase) in the vessel wall. The implications are obvious. Transfer of desirable genes, such as those producing growth factor inhibitors or gene products (various proteins), is a real possibility. Delivery of such genes or products to the target site at the time of PTA would be the next generation in intravascular therapy. In a more recent experiment designed to determine whether genes can be transferred to human vessels, luciferase expression has been documented after successful transfer of the gene to normal human internal mammary arterial endothelial cells and to endothelial cells from atherectomy-derived atherosclerotic plaque.[129] In atherosclerotic rabbits, PTA has been shown not to interfere with transfection efficiency.[130]

Regarding identification of potentially useful molecular strategies, in humans, a gene known as c-*myc* protooncogene is activated in the process of SMC proliferation. The region of this gene that is responsible for translation initiation could potentially be blocked if a complementary strand of DNA could be used to block the corresponding mRNA synthesis (antisense approach). Recently, a 15-mer oligonucleotide complementary to the translation initiation region (antisense oligomer) has been used in this way to successfully inhibit SMC proliferation in a dose-dependent fashion.[131] Addition of excess sense oligomers succeeded in reversing this effect. In a recent opinion paper on the subject, Epstein and colleagues from the NIH were critical of current antisense strategies.[132] They cited the lack of specificity of the antisense oligonucleotides for their intended target genes, the tendency of investigators to publish positive results (showing inhibitory effects of antisense oligomers) but not to publish negative results or results showing inhibitory effects of other oligomers (such as those with only partial homology or those that are scrambled), nonantisense mechanisms of action of some antisense oligonucleotides, difficulties with cellular uptake of the oligonucleotides, and other problems. The authors, however, remained cautiously optimistic, predicting that antisense approaches to restenosis will become more logical as we understand more of the basic mechanisms of antisense.

Another unique strategy invokes the concept of targeted delivery of SMC toxins. Pickering and colleagues showed that they could produce a fusion protein, $DAB_{389}EGF$, which is expressed by a gene in which the sequences for the receptor-binding domain of diphtheria toxin have been replaced by those encoding human epidermal growth factor (EGF).[133] The protein was therefore designed to take the diphtheria toxin directly to the cellular targets bearing receptors for EGF (including SMCs). They showed (in culture) that $DAB_{389}EGF$ was extremely toxic to rapidly proliferating SMCs. Complete inhibition occurred at a concentration of 10^{-8} pM. The toxic effect was inhibited by adding excess EGF and by adding antibody to human EGF receptors.

Combined Technical, Pharmacologic, and Molecular Biologic Strategy. At the Howard Hughes Medical Institute of the University of Michigan Medical Center in Ann Arbor, Ohno and colleagues reported striking reduction of post-PTA intimal hyperplasia in porcine iliofemoral arteries following an experimental treatment protocol employing a combination of local delivery, gene transfer, and pharmacotherapeutics.[134] In experimental animals, injured vessel walls were transfected with adenoviral vectors encoding herpesvirus thymidine kinase (tk). Subsequently, ganciclovir administered intravenously was phosphorylated by tk and then incorporated into DNA, where it induced chain termination and cell death (in replicating cells). When compared with controls, the intima-media area ratio, as determined by quantitative histomorphometry in experimental animals, was markedly reduced ($p<.05$). Controls (none of which had ratios as low as those of experimental animals) included animals that received saline instead of ganciclovir, those that received adenoviral vector without the tk gene, and finally those that received neither the tk gene nor ganciclovir.

Pathogenesis of Restenosis: Newer Concepts and Potential Therapeutic Implications

An Infectious Basis for Restenosis?

New molecular concepts have emerged in the study of restenosis, but perhaps none so ingenious as the one recently published by Speir and colleagues. They began a series of studies based on the hypothesis that the formation of intimal hyperplasia may be controlled by events and alterations that confer a selective growth advantage to SMCs.[135] They investigated two possible molecular processes: (1) p53 tumor suppressor protein (which normally inhibits cell cycle progression and which is functionally inactivated in some human cancers) might be aberrantly expressed in restenosis lesions; and (2) latent human cytomegalovirus (HCMV, a herpesvirus) may be activated. HCMV has already been associated with the development of atherosclerosis.[136] Conceivably, an HCMV protein could impair the tumor suppressor action of p53. This mechanism has been established in the case of other DNA tumor viruses.[137-138] For their series of experiments, atherectomy specimens were obtained from 60 patients at

sites of angiographically proven coronary restenosis; the control specimens obtained were 20 primary atherectomy specimens from human coronary arteries. The investigators were able to show that 38 percent of restenosis lesions were immunopositive for p53 (a condition which prevails when it is stable enough to measure, such as when it has lost its inhibitory function in certain tumors), but none of the control lesions were immunopositive. Only wild-type (nonmutated) p53 was found in the restenosis lesions. Using polymerase chain reaction (PCR) analysis, they found HCMV sequences in 11 of the 13 (85 percent) human restenosis lesions that were immunopositive for p53, but in only 3 of 11 (27 percent) that were immunonegative for p53. They then immunostained SMC cultures with antibody to HCMV protein IE84 and found that not only was the protein present, but that there was significant concordance between p53 accumulation and IE84 expression. The authors then took SMCs that were negative for p53 and IE84 at baseline and infected them with HCMV. Two days after infection, they were immunopositive for both proteins. Subsequent studies documented a protein-protein interaction between p53 and IE84. The authors postulated that PTA-induced vessel wall injury may reactivate latent HCMV. They further postulated in their concluding remarks that IE84 may block p53's inhibition of cell cycle progression in restenosis lesions.

Thrombus Replacement Theory

In a unique editorial and review paper, Schwartz and colleagues posit that almost all therapies aimed at clinical restenosis have failed because we have failed to recognize the fundamental processes involved.[139] Their alternative theory (Fig. 1-10), based on their own work in a porcine model, includes three stages. In stage I, thrombus occurs at the injury site. In stage II, the thrombus is covered by endothelium. A mononuclear leukocytic infiltrate then begins to develop on the lumen side of the vessel. Finally, in the proliferative stage (III), a cap of actin-positive cells accumulates on the luminal surface. The cap thickens as additional cells are recruited and additional matrix is deposited. The cells do not arise from the vascular media. The authors assign major importance to thrombus, which is viewed as providing the matrix for SMC proliferation.

Vascular Remodeling Theory

Recently, observations in humans with atherosclerosis have shown that untreated arteries undergo compensatory enlargement and preserve luminal cross-sectional area for long periods of time.[140-143] Expanding on this concept, investigators have studied whether some of the late lumen loss after PTA might

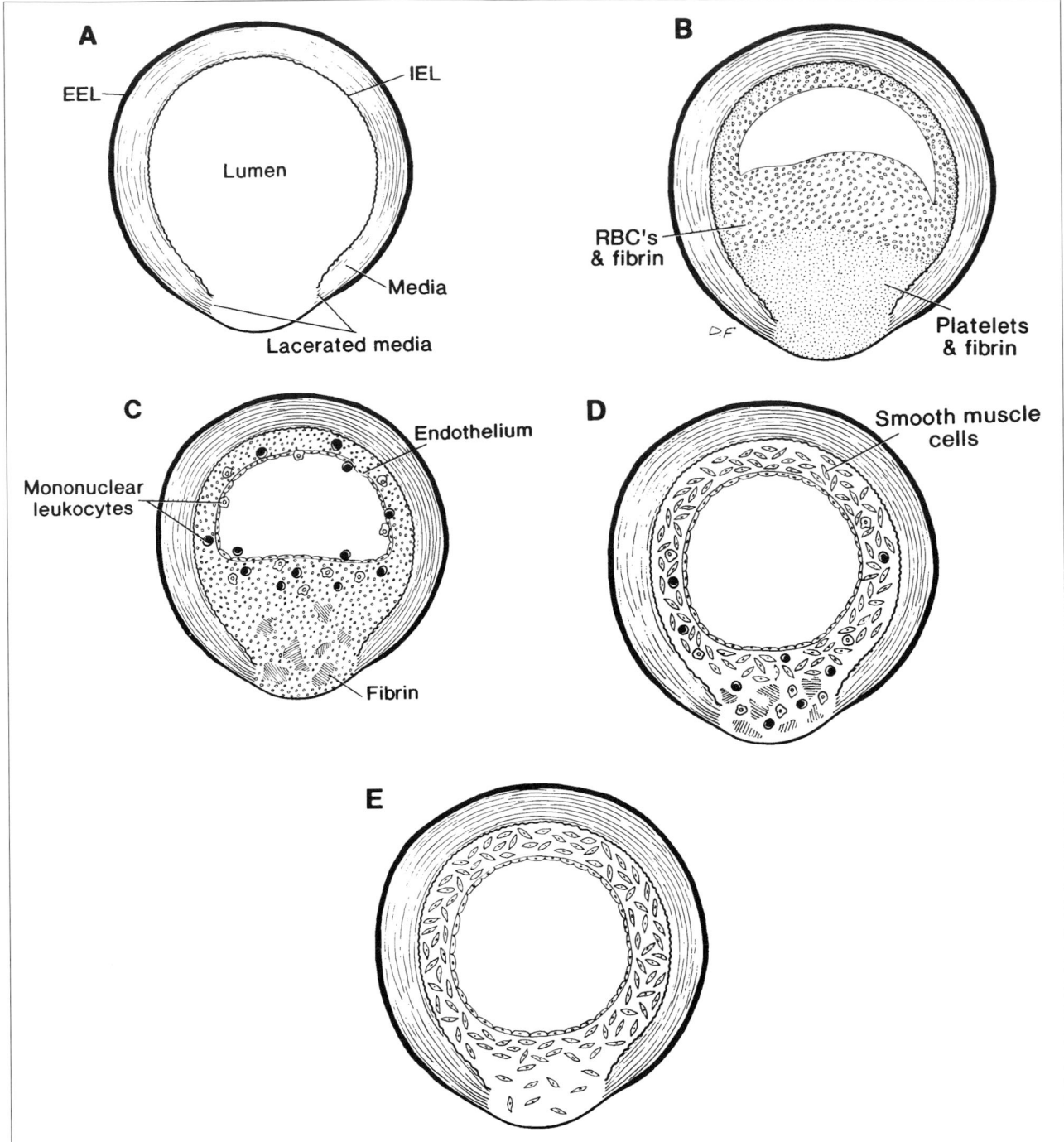

Figure 1-10. Alternative hypothesis for restenosis. (A) Angioplasty produces vessel injury, including break in the internal elastic lamina (*IEL*). The external elastic lamina (*EEL*) is intact. (B) Stage I: Thrombus formation. Platelets adhere to injured surface and platelets and fibrin form a plug. Additional fibrin–red blood cell accumulates. (C) Stage II: An endothelial lining develops. Monocytes adhere to the surface, then migrate into the subendothelium. Monocytes or monocyte-derived cells release fibrinolytic enzymes that lyse the surrounding fibrin. (D) Stage III: Lysis of fibrin continues, but a cap of actin-positive cells develops on the luminal surface. (E) As these cells proliferate, thrombus is completely replaced by actin-positive cells (smooth muscle cells) and matrix. The cap thickens toward rather than away from the injury site. (From Schwartz RS, Holmes DR, Topol EJ. The restenosis paradigm revisited: an alternative proposal for cellular mechanisms. J Am Coll Cardiol 1992;20:1284–1293. Used with permission.)

be due to a remodeling phenomenon rather than to intimal hyperplasia alone. Post and colleagues used quantitative angiography and quantitative histomorphometry on conventional and thermal balloon PTA-treated vessels in normal rabbits and conventional balloon PTA-treated vessels in Yucatan micropigs on normal or atherogenic diet.[144] They observed a consistent discrepancy between the angiographic late loss in lumen diameter by angiography and the diameter reduction that could be explained histomorphometrically by intimal hyperplasia. The discrepancy was due to a reduction in the area circumscribed by the internal elastic lamina (IEL) (arterial remodeling). They concluded that in these animal models restenosis after PTA is due to both intimal hyperplasia and arterial remodeling. Kakuta and colleagues used an atherosclerotic rabbit model to study the same question.[145] In the late follow-up group, animals were divided into restenosis and nonrestenosis groups. The intimal areas turned out to be virtually identical in the two groups ($p=$NS); however, the IEL area was greater in the nonrestenosis group ($p<.05$). The authors concluded that in their model the iliac artery compensates for intimal hyperplasia by vessel enlargement, and that the degree of enlargement is more important than intimal area in determining late lumen diameter and area. Isner was openly critical of the methods in these studies,[146] most notably the lack of intravascular ultrasound for the in vivo portion. However, he conceded that vascular remodeling in some form probably has heretofore unrecognized significance in untold numbers of restenosis cases. The important conclusion is that since numerous processes seem to be involved, no single therapeutic or preventive strategy is likely to succeed in managing all cases.

Summary

Our understanding of the pathophysiologic mechanisms of PTA has evolved since 1980. The basic mechanisms of plaque and intimal fracture with localized dissection into the arterial media and overstretching of the disease-free wall are the most important. Disruption of the internal elastic lamina occurs in most cases, but disruption of the external elastic lamina is synonymous with extension of the "controlled injury" of PTA into the adventitia. The usual response of the vessel wall following PTA involves proliferation of medial SMCs, migration of SMCs into the intima, and elaboration of matrix. The result is a neointima that, in some patients, produces a clinically and/or angiographically evident restenosis.

Restenosis is a complex problem that follows PTA, atherectomy, intravascular stenting, and other endoluminal interventions. Intimal hyperplasia (IH), a pathologic substrate of restenosis, is one common denominator in the majority of lesions. An overwhelming body of evidence suggests that medial SMCs are the cells of origin of IH; however, one newer theory proposes that circulating monocytes are involved in the process, which is characterized by thrombus replacement by a cellular, proliferative lesion that grows toward the site of arterial injury. Vascular remodeling, manifested as an increase in arterial size to compensate for intimal hyperplasia, may be an important mechanism of lumen preservation late after PTA, just as it is an important mechanism for lumen preservation in situations of untreated atherosclerotic plaque in humans. One recent study from NIH has shown that human CMV may be reactivated after PTA and that one of its protein products, IE86, may inactivate p53's cell cycle suppressive activity, conferring a selective growth advantage to medial SMCs and resulting in restenosis in human coronary arteries.

With the exception of the results of the EPIC trial, which attempted to prevent coronary restenosis by administration of a glycoprotein IIb/IIIa antagonist, pharmacologic treatments and preventive strategies for restenosis have been miserable failures. Drug delivery catheters, such as porous balloons and biodegradable stents, are still being investigated today, in hopes that newer pharmacologic or biotechnologic agents will become available for targeted delivery to the treatment site in the vessel wall.

Biotechnologic strategies including direct gene therapy to the vessel wall, targeted infusion of antisense oligomers into the vessel wall, local delivery of fusion proteins, and other approaches will continue to develop in an effort to control the process of intimal hyperplasia.

One of the most important and promising recent discoveries is the concept of loss index. Using this concept, we have learned that the new devices—namely, stents, directional atherectomy catheters, and laser balloons (used in the coronary circulation)—provide a greater initial gain in lumen diameter than balloon PTA. Since the loss index for each intervention is approximately 0.45 (0.45 mm lost for each initial 1.0 mm of gain), the larger the initial lumen, the larger the late lumen diameter (and the lower the clinical appearance of restenosis). In other words, when it comes to early gain in lumen diameter, bigger is clearly better. Thankfully, we have in our armamentarium various devices with which to produce a large initial lumen diameter.

Acknowledgments

We wish to thank Carol A. Mascioli and Tony Chirinos for their kind and skillful assistance with the illustrations in this chapter.

References

1. Dotter CT, Judkins MP. Transluminal treatment of arteriosclerotic obstructions: description of a new technic and a preliminary report of its application. Circulation 1964;30:654–670.
2. Gruentzig AR. Transluminal dilatation of coronary artery stenosis. Lancet 1978;1:263.
3. Zeitler E, Schoop W, Zahnow W. The treatment of occlusive arterial disease by transluminal catheter angioplasty. Radiology 1971;99:19.
4. Wolf GL, LeVeen RF, Ring EJ. Potential mechanisms of angioplasty. Cardiovasc Intervent Radiol 1984;7:11–17.
5. Block PC, Fallon JT, Elmer D. Experimental angioplasty: lessons from the laboratory. AJR 1980;135:907–912.
6. Hoffman MA, Fallon JT, Greenfield AJ, Waltman AC, Athanasoulis CA, Block PC. Arterial pathology after percutaneous transluminal angioplasty. AJR 1981;137:147–149.
7. Waller BF. Pathology of transluminal balloon angioplasty used in the treatment of coronary heart disease. Hum Pathol 1987;18:476–484.
8. Kinney TB, Chin AK, Rurik GW, et al. Transluminal angioplasty: a mechanical-pathophysiological correlation of its physical mechanisms. Radiology 1984;153:85–89.
9. Castaneda-Zuniga WR, Laerum F, Rysavy J, Rusnak B, Amplatz K. Paralysis of arteries by intraluminal balloon dilatation: an experimental study. Radiology 1982;144:75–76.
10. Saffitz JE, Totty WG, McClennan BL, Gilula LA. Percutaneous transluminal angioplasty: radiological-pathological correlation. Radiology 1981;141:651–654.
11. Castaneda-Zuniga WR, Formanek A, Tadavarthy M, et al. The mechanism of balloon angioplasty. Radiology 1980;135:565–571.
12. Faxon DP, Weber VJ, Haudenschild C, Gottsman SB, McGovern WA, Ryan TJ. Acute effects of transluminal angioplasty in three experimental models of atherosclerosis. Arteriosclerosis 1982;2:125–133.
13. Block PC, Myler RK, Stertzer S, Fallon JT. Morphology after transluminal angioplasty in human beings. N Engl J Med 1981;305:382–385.
14. Sanborn TA, Faxon DP, Haudenschild C, Gottsman SB, Ryan TJ. The mechanism of transluminal angioplasty: evidence for formation of aneurysms in experimental atherosclerosis. Circulation 1983;68:1136–1140.
15. Block PC, Baughman KL, Pasternak RC, Fallon JT. Transluminal angioplasty: correlation of morphologic and angiographic findings in an experimental model. Circulation 1980;61:778–785.
16. Zollikofer CL, Redha FH, Bruhlmann WF, et al. Acute and long-term effects of massive balloon dilation on the aortic wall and vasa vasorum. Radiology 1987;164:145–149.
17. Cragg AH, Einzig S, Rysavy JA, Castaneda-Zuniga WR, Borgwardt B, Amplatz K. The vasa vasorum and angioplasty. Radiology 1983;148:75–80.
18. Lyon RT, Zarins CK, Lu C-T, Yang C-F, Glagov S. Vessel, plaque, and lumen morphology after transluminal balloon angioplasty: quantitative study in distended human arteries. Arteriosclerosis 1987;7:306–314.
19. Waller BF, Dillon JC, Cowley MH. Plaque hematoma and coronary dissection with percutaneous transluminal angioplasty (PTCA) of severely stenotic lesions: morphologic coronary observations in 5 men within 30 days of PTCA. Circulation 1983;68(Suppl III):111–144.
20. Castaneda-Zuniga WR, Amplatz K, Laerum F, et al. Mechanics of angioplasty: an experimental approach. Radiographics 1981;1(3):1–14.
21. Vlodaver Z, Edwards JE. Pathology of coronary atherosclerosis. Prog Cardiovasc Dis 1971;14:256.
22. Zollikofer CL, Cragg AH, Hunter DW, Yedlicka JW Jr, Castaneda-Zuniga WR, Amplatz K. Mechanism of transluminal angioplasty. In: Castaneda-Zuniga WR, Tadavarthy SM, eds. Interventional radiology. 2nd ed. Baltimore: Williams & Wilkins, 1992:249–297.
23. Waller BF, Miller J, Morgan R, Tejada E. Atherosclerotic plaque calcific deposits: an important factor in success or failure of transluminal coronary angioplasty (TCA). Circulation 1988;78(Suppl II):376.
24. Cragg AH, Einzig S, Rysavy JA, Castaneda-Zuniga WR, Borgwardt B, Amplatz K. The vasa vasorum and angioplasty. Radiology 1983;148:75.
25. Cragg A, Einzig S, Rysavy J, Borgwardt B, Castaneda W, Amplatz K. Effect of aspirin on angioplasty-induced vessel wall hyperemia. Am J Roentgenol 1983;140(6):1233–1238.
26. Train JS, Mitty HA, Efremidis SC, Rabinowitz JG. Visualization of a fine periluminal vascular network following transluminal angioplasty: possible demonstration of the vasa vasorum. Radiology 1982;143:399.
27. Pisco JM, Correia M, Esperanca-Pina JA, de Sousa LA. Changes in the vasa vasorum following percutaneous transluminal angioplasty in a canine model of aortic stenosis. J Vasc Intervent Radiol 1994;5:561–566.
28. Kuntz RE, Baim DS. Defining coronary restenosis: new clinical and angiographic paradigms. Circulation 1993;88(3):1310–1323.
29. Reiber JHC, Serruys PW, Kooijman CJ, et al. Assessment of short-, medium-, and long-term variations in arterial dimensions from computer-assisted quantitation of coronary cineangiograms. Circulation 1985;71:280–288.
30. Kuntz RE, Keaney KM, Senerchia C, Baim DS. Estimating the late results of coronary intervention from incomplete angiographic follow-up. Circulation 1993;87:815–830.
31. Beatt KJ, Luijten HE, deFeyter PJ, van den Brand M, Reiber JHC, Serruys PW. Change in diameter of coronary segments adjacent to stenosis after percutaneous transluminal coronary angioplasty: failure of percent diameter stenosis measurement to reflect morphologic changes induced by balloon dilation. J Am Coll Cardiol 1988;12:315–323.
32. Kuntz RE, Schmidt DA, Levine MJ, Reis GJ, Safian RD, Baim DS. Importance of post-procedure luminal diameter on restenosis following new coronary interventions. Circulation 1990;82(Suppl III):1245.
33. Kuntz RE, Safian RD, Levine MJ, Reis GJ, Diver DJ, Baim DS. Novel approach to the analysis of restenosis following three new coronary interventions. J Am Coll Cardiol 1992;19:1493–1499.
34. Nobuyoshi M, Kmura T, Ohishi H, et al. Restenosis after percutaneous coronary angioplasty: pathologic observations in 20 patients. J Am Coll Cardiol 1991;17:433–439.
35. Ueda M, Becker AE, Tsukada T, Numano F, Fujimoto T. Fibrocellular tissue response after percutaneous transluminal coronary angioplasty. Circulation 1991;83:1327–1332.
36. Kuntz RE, Gibson CM, Nobuyoshi M, Baim DS. A generalized model of restenosis following conventional balloon angioplasty, stenting, and directional atherectomy. J Am Coll Cardiol 1993;21:15–25.
37. Hanet C, Wijns W, Xavier M, Schroderer E. Influence of balloon size and stenosis morphology on immediate and delayed elastic recoil after percutaneous transluminal coronary angioplasty. J Am Coll Cardiol 1991;18:506–511.
38. Hjemdahl-Monsen CE, Ambrose JA, Borrico S, et al. Angiographic patterns of balloon inflation during percutaneous transluminal coronary angioplasty: role of pressure-diameter curves in studying distensibility and elasticity of the stenotic lesion and the mechanism of dilatation. J Am Coll Cardiol 1990;16:569–575.

39. Rensing BJ, Hermans WRM, Beatt KJ, et al. Quantitative angiographic assessment of elastic recoil after percutaneous transluminal coronary angioplasty. Am J Cardiol 1990;66:1039–1044.

40. Ardissino D, Di Somma S, Kubica J, et al. Influence of elastic recoil on restenosis after successful coronary angioplasty in unstable angina pectoris. Am J Cardiol 1993;71:659–663.

41. Serruys PW, Strauss BH, Beatt KJ, et al. Angiographic follow-up after placement of a self-expanding coronary artery stent. N Engl J Med 1991;324:13–17.

42. Kuntz RE, Hinohara T, Robertson GC, Safian RD, Simpson JB, Baim DS. The influence of vessel selection on the observed restenosis rate following endoluminal stenting or directional atherectomy. Am J Cardiol 1992;70:1101–1108.

43. Carrozza JP, Kuntz RE, Fishman RF, Baim DS. Restenosis following arterial injury in diabetics: an analysis of intimal hyperplasia following coronary stenting. Ann Intern Med 1993;118:344–349.

44. Wijns W, Serruys PW, Reiber JHC, de Feyter PJ, van den Brand M, Simoons ML, Hugenholtz PG. Early detection of restenosis after successful percutaneous transluminal coronary angioplasty by exercise-redistribution thallium scintigraphy. Am J Cardiol 1985;55:357–361.

45. Hernandez RA, Macaya C, Iniguez A, Alfonso F, Goicolea J, Fernandez-Ortiz A, Zarco P. Midterm outcome of patients with asymptomatic restenosis after coronary balloon angioplasty. J Am Coll Cardiol 1992;19:1402–1409.

46. Popma JJ, van den Berg EK, Dehmer GJ. Long-term outcome of patients with asymptomatic restenosis after percutaneous transluminal coronary angioplasty. Am J Cardiol 1988;62:1298–1299.

47. Rosen DR, Cannon RO, Watson RM, et al. Three year anatomic, functional and clinical follow-up after successful percutaneous transluminal coronary angioplasty. J Am Coll Cardiol 1987;9:1–7.

48. Freidrich SP, Gordon PC, Leidig GA, et al. Clinical events following new interventional devices are determined by time-dependent hazards. Circulation 1992;86(Suppl I):785.

49. Waller BF, Pinkerton CA, Orr CM, Slack JD, VanTassel JW, Peters T. Restenosis 1 to 24 months after clinically successful coronary balloon angioplasty: a necropsy study of 20 patients. J Am Coll Cardiol 1991;17(Suppl B):58–70.

50. Waller BF, McManus BM, Garfinkel HJ, et al. Status of the major epicardial coronary arteries 80 to 150 days after percutaneous transluminal coronary angioplasty: analysis of 3 necropsy patients. Am J Cardiol 1983;51:81–84.

51. Essed CE, van den Brand M, Becker AE. Transluminal coronary angioplasty and early restenosis: fibrocellular occlusion after wall laceration. Br Heart J 1983;49:393–396.

52. Giraldo A, Esposo OM, Meis JM. Intimal hyperplasia as a cause of restenosis after percutaneous transluminal coronary angioplasty. Arch Pathol Lab Med 1985;109:173–175.

53. Stoney RJ, String ST. Recurrent carotid stenosis. Surgery 1976;80:705–710.

54. Liu MW, Roubin GS, King SB III. Restenosis after coronary angioplasty: potential biologic determinants and role of intimal hyperplasia. Circulation 1989;79:1374–1387.

55. Clowes AW, Reidy MA, Clowes MM. Mechanism of stenosis after arterial injury. Lab Invest 1983;49:208–215.

56. Ohara T, Nanto S, Asada S, Komamura K, Wang D. Ultrastructural study of proliferating and migrating smooth muscle cells at the site of PTCA as an explanation for restenosis. Circulation 1988;78(Suppl II):290.

57. Clowes AW, Schwartz SM. Significance of quiescent smooth muscle migration in the injured rat carotid artery. Circ Res 1985;56:139–145.

58. Serruys PW, Luijten HE, Beutt KJ, et al. Incidence of restenosis after successful coronary angioplasty: a time-related phenomenon: a quantitative angiographic follow-up study in 342 patients at 1, 2, 3, and 4 months. Circulation 1988;77:361–371.

59. Stemerman MB. Thrombogenesis of the rabbit arterial plaque. Am J Pathol 1973;73:7–18.

60. Goldberg ID, Stemerman MB. Vascular permeation of platelet factor 4 after endothelial injury. Science 1980;209:611–612.

61. Baumgartner HR, Muggli R. Adhesion and aggregation: morphological demonstration and quantitation in vivo and in vitro. In: Gordon JL, ed. Platelets in biology and pathology. Amsterdam: Elsevier, 1976:23–60.

62. Ross R, Raines EW, Bowen-Pope DF. The biology of platelet-derived growth factor. Cell 1986;46:155–169.

63. Rivera FJ, Miller DD, Garcia OJ, Palmaz JC, Weisman HF, Berger HJ. Noninvasive detection of platelet activation at human postangioplasty sites with S-12 monoclonal antibody imaging. J Vasc Intervent Radiol 1991;2(1):31.

64. Liu MW, Roubin GS, King SB III. Restenosis after coronary angioplasty. Potential biologic determinants and role of intimal hyperplasia. Circulation 1989;79:1374–1387.

65. Stiles CD, Pledger WJ, Tucker RW, Martin RG, Scher CD. Regulation of the Balb/C 3T3 cell cycle effects of growth factors. J Supramol Struct 1980;13:489–499.

66. Currier JW, Pow TK, Haudenschild CC, Minihan AC, Faxon DP. Low molecular weight heparin (Enoxaparin) reduces restenosis after iliac angioplasty in the hypercholesterolemic rabbit. J Am Coll Cardiol 1991;17:118B–125B.

67. Tada T, Reidy MA. Endothelial regeneration IX: arterial injury followed by rapid endothelial repair induces smooth-muscle-cell proliferation but not intimal thickening. Am J Pathol 1987;129:429–433.

68. Walker LN, Ramsay MM, Bowyer DE. Endothelial healing following defined injury to rabbit aorta: depth of injury and mode of repair. Atherosclerosis 1983;47:123–130.

69. Johnson DE, Hinohara T, Selmon MR, Braden LJ, Simpson JB. Primary peripheral arterial stenoses and restenoses excised by transluminal atherectomy: a histopathologic study. J Am Coll Cardiol 1990;15:419–425.

70. Gebrane J, Roland J, Orcel L. Experimental diffuse intimal thickening of the femoral arteries in the rabbit. Virchows Arch [A] 1982;396:41–59.

71. Cole CW, Hagen P-O, Lucas JF, et al. Association of polymorphonuclear leukocytes with sites of aortic catheter-induced injury in rabbits. Atherosclerosis 1987;67:229–236.

72. Faulkner SL, Fisher RD, Conkle DM, Page DL, Bender HW Jr. Effect of blood flow rate on subendothelial proliferation in venous autografts used as arterial substitutes. Circulation 1975;51, 52(Suppl I):163–172.

73. Zarins CK, Bomberger RA, Glagov S. Local effects of stenoses: increased flow velocity inhibits atherogenesis. Circulation 1981;64(Suppl II):221–227.

74. Ku DN, Giddens DP, Zarins CK, Glagov S. Pulsatile flow and atherosclerosis in human carotid bifurcation: positive correlation between plaque location and low and oscillating shear stress. Arteriosclerosis 1985;5:292–302.

75. Califf RM, Ohman EM, Frid DJ, et al. Restenosis: the clinical issues. In: Topol EJ, ed. Interventional cardiology. Philadelphia: Saunders, 1989:363–394.

76. Bergelson BA, Jacobs AK, Small DM. Lipoproteins predict restenosis after PTCA. Circulation 1989;80(Suppl II):65.

77. Hearn JA, Donohue BC, King SB, et al. Does serum lipoprotein-a predict restenosis after PTCA? J Am Coll Cardiol 1990;15(Suppl A):205.

78. Austin GE, Hollman J, Lynn MJ, Meier B. Serum lipoprotein levels fail to predict postangioplasty recurrent coronary artery stenosis. Clevel Clin J Med 1989;56:509–514.

79. Sanborn T, Cumberland D, Greenfield A, Welsh C, Guben J. Percutaneous laser thermal angioplasty: initial results and 1-year follow-up in 129 femoropopliteal lesions. Radiology 1988;168:121–125.

80. Gleason T, Cragg AH, Smith TP, Landas SK, De Jong SC. Thermal balloon angioplasty in a canine model: preliminary results. J Vasc Intervent Radiol 1990;1:121–126.

81. Becker GJ, Lee BI, Waller BF, et al. Radiofrequency balloon angioplasty: rationale and proof of principle. Invest Radiol 1988;23:810–817.

82. Becker GJ, Lee BI, Waller BF, et al. Potential of radiofrequency balloon angioplasty: weld strengths, dose response relationships, and correlative histology. Radiology 1990;174: 1003–1008.

83. Spears JR, Reyes VP, James LM, Sinofsky EL. Laser balloon angioplasty: initial clinical experience. Circulation 1988;78 (Suppl II):296.

84. Ferguson JJ, Dear WE, Leatherman LL, et al. A multi-center trial of laser balloon angioplasty for abrupt closure following PTCA. J Am Coll Cardiol 1990;15(Suppl A):25.

85. Lee BI, Becker GJ, Waller BF, et al. Thermal compression and molding of atherosclerotic vascular tissue with use of radiofrequency energy: implications for radiofrequency balloon angioplasty. J Am Coll Cardiol 1989;13:1167–1175.

86. Topol EJ, Leya F, Pinkerton CA, et al. A comparison of directional atherectomy with coronary angioplasty in patients with coronary artery disease. N Engl J Med 1993;329:221–227.

87. Rees CR, Palmaz JC, Becker GJ, et al. Preliminary report of a multi-center study of the Palmaz stent in atherosclerotic stenoses involving the ostia of the renal arteries. Radiology 1991; 181:507–514.

88. Serruys PW, de Jaegere P, Kiemeneij F, et al. for the BENESTENT Study Group. A comparison of balloon-expandable-stent implantation with balloon angioplasty in patients with coronary artery disease. N Engl J Med 1994;331:489–495.

89. Fischman DL, Leon MB, Baim DS, et al. for the STRESS investigators. A randomized comparison of coronary-stent placement and balloon angioplasty in the treatment of coronary artery disease. N Engl J Med 1994;331:496–501.

90. Ohman EM, Califf RM, Lee KL, Fortin DF, Frid DJ, Bengtson JR. Restenosis after angioplasty: overview of clinical trials using aspirin and omega-3-fatty acids. J Am Coll Cardiol 1990;15(Suppl A):88.

91. Badimon L, Badimon J, Lassila R, Heras M, Chesebro JH, Fuster V. Thrombin inhibition by hirudin decreases platelet thrombus growth on areas of severe vessel wall injury. J Am Coll Cardiol 1989;13(Suppl A):145.

92. Nunes GL, King SB, Hanson SR, Sahatjian RA, Scott NA. Hydrogel-coated PTCA balloon catheter delivery of an antithrombin inhibits platelet-dependent thrombosis. Circulation 1992;86(4):I-380.

93. Heras M, Chesebro JH, Webster MWI, et al. Hirudin, heparin, and placebo during deep arterial injury in the pig: the in vivo role of thrombin in platelet-mediated thrombosis. Circulation 1990;82:1476–1484.

94. Mruk JS, Chesebro JH, Webster MWI. Platelet aggregation and interaction with the coagulation system: implications for antithrombotic therapy in arterial thrombosis. J Coronary Artery Dis 1990;1:149–158.

95. Chesebro JH, Badimon L, Fuster V. Importance of antithrombin therapy during coronary angioplasty. J Am Coll Cardiol 1991;17(Suppl B):96–100.

96. Thronton MA, Gruentzig AR, Hollman J, et al. Coumadin and aspirin in prevention of recurrence after transluminal coronary angioplasty: a randomized study. Circulation 1984;69: 721–727.

97. Knudtson ML, Flintoft VA, Roth DL, Hansen JL, Duff HJ. Effect of short-term prostacyclin administration on restenosis after percutaneous transluminal coronary angioplasty. J Am Coll Cardiol 1990;15:691–697.

98. White CW, Knudson M, Schmidt D. Neither ticlopidine nor aspirin-dipyridamole prevents restenosis post PTCA: results from a randomized placebo-controlled multicenter trial. Circulation 1987;76(Suppl IV):213.

99. Serruys PW, Rutsch W, Heyndricks GR, et al. Prevention of restenosis after percutaneous transluminal coronary angioplasty with thromboxane A2 receptor blockade: a randomized, double-blind, placebo-controlled trial. Circulation 1991;84:1568–1580.

100. Pepine C, MacDonald R, Bass T, et al. for the M-Heart Group. Effect of selective and non-selective TxA2 blockade on events after PTCA: M-Heart II. J Am Coll Cardiol 1992; 19(Suppl A):209.

101. Corcos T, David PR, Val PG, et al. Failure of diltiazem to prevent restenosis after percutaneous transluminal coronary angioplasty. Am Heart J 1985;109:926–931.

102. Whitworth HB, Roubin GS, Hollman J, et al. Effect of nifedipine on recurrent stenosis after percutaneous transluminal coronary angioplasty. J Am Coll Cardiol 1986;8:1271–1276.

103. Faxon D, Spiro T, Minor S, et al. Enoxaparin, a low molecular weight heparin, in the prevention of restenosis after angioplasty: result of a double blind randomized trial. J Am Coll Cardiol 1992;19(Suppl A):258.

104. Currier JW, Pow TK, Minihan AC, Haudenschild CC, Faxon DP, Ryan TJ. Colchicine inhibits restenosis after iliac angioplasty in the atherosclerotic rabbit. Circulation 1989;80 (Suppl II):66.

105. March K, Mohanraj S, Ho P, Wilensky R, Hathaway D. Biodegradable microspheres containing a colchicine analog inhibit DNA synthesis in vascular smooth muscle cells. Circulation 1992;86(4):I-381.

106. O'Keefe JH, McCallister BD, Bateman TM, Kuhnlein D, Ligon RW, Hartzler GO. Colchicine for the prevention of restenosis after coronary angioplasty. J Am Coll Cardiol 1991; 17(Suppl A):181.

107. Muller DWM, Ellis SG, Topol EJ. Colchicine and antineoplastic therapy for the prevention of restenosis after percutaneous coronary interventions. J Am Coll Cardiol 1991;17 (Suppl B):126–131.

108. Barath P, Arakawa K, Cao J, et al. Low dose of antitumor agents prevents smooth muscle cell proliferation after endothelial injury. J Am Coll Cardiol 1989;13(Suppl A):252.

109. Berk BC, Vallega G, Griendling KK, et al. Effect of glucocorticoids on Na/H exchange and growth in cultured vascular smooth muscle cells. J Cell Physiol 1988;137:391–401.

110. Longnecker JP, Kilty LA, Johnston LK. Glucocorticoid influence on growth of vascular wall cells in culture. J Cell Physiol 1982;113:197–202.

111. Berk BC, Raines EW. Vascular smooth muscle growth inhibition by hydrocortisone is associated with decreased PDGF A chain expression. FASEB J 1989;3:A611.

112. Gordon JB, Berk BC, Bettmann MA, Selwyn AP, Renke H, Alexander RW. Vascular smooth muscle cell proliferation following balloon injury is synergistically inhibited by low molecular weight heparin and hydrocortisone. Circulation 1987; 76(Suppl IV):213.

113. Pepine CJ, Hirshfeld JW, Macdonald RG, et al. A controlled trial of corticosteroids to prevent restenosis after coronary angioplasty. Circulation 1990;81:1753–1761.

114. Ellis SG, Bates ER, Schaible T, Weisman HF, Pitt B, Topol EJ. Prospects for the use of antagonists to the platelet glycoprotein IIb/IIIa receptor to prevent postangioplasty restenosis and thrombosis. J Am Coll Cardiol 1991;17(Suppl B):89–95.

115. Topol EJ, Califf RM, Weisman HF, Anderson K, Want A, Willerson JT, for the EPIC investigators. Six-month follow-up after acute phase platelet IIb/IIIa integrin blockade in the EPIC trial: reduction in need for revascularization procedures. J Am Coll Cardiol 1994;23(Suppl A):60.

116. Lundergan CF, Foegh ML, Ramwell PW. Peptide inhibition of myointimal proliferation by angiopeptin, a somatostatin analogue. J Am Coll Cardiol 1991;17(Suppl B):132–136.

117. Powell JS, Muller RKM, Baumgartner HR. Suppression of the vascular response to injury: the role of angiotensin-converting enzyme inhibitors. J Am Coll Cardiol 1991; 17(Suppl B):137–142.

118. The Multicenter European Research Trial with Cilazapril After Angioplasty to Prevent Transluminal Coronary Obstruction and Restenosis (MERCATOR) Study Group. Does the new angiotensin converting enzyme inhibitor cilazapril prevent restenosis after percutaneous transluminal coronary angioplasty? Results of the MERCATOR study: a multicenter, randomized, double-blind placebo-controlled trial. Circulation 1992;86:100–110.

119. Faxon DP. Angiotensin converting enzyme inhibition and restenosis: the final results of the MERCATOR trial. Circulation 1992;86(Suppl I):53.
120. Desmet W, Vrolix M, De Scheerder I, van Lierde J, Piessens J. Fosinopril sodium in restenosis prevention after coronary angioplasty. Circulation 1992;86(Suppl I):54.
121. Sahni R, Maniet AR, Voci G, Banka VS. Prevention of restenosis by lovastatin. Circulation 1989;80(Suppl II):65.
122. Hollman J, Konrad K, Raymond R, Whitlow P, Michalak M, Van Lente F. Lipid lowering for the prevention of recurrent stenosis following coronary angioplasty. Circulation 1989; 80(Suppl II):65.
123. Wolinsky H, Lin C-S. Use of the perforated balloon catheter to infuse marker substances into diseased coronary artery walls after experimental postmortem angioplasty. J Am Coll Cardiol 1991;17(Suppl B):174–178.
124. Lambert CR, Leone J, Rowland S. The microporous balloon: a minimal-trauma local drug delivery catheter. Circulation 1992;86(4):I-381.
125. Hong MK, Farb A, Unger EF, Wang JC, Jasinski LJ, Mehlman MD. A new PTCA balloon catheter with intramural channels for local delivery of drugs at low pressure. Circulation 1992;86(4):I-380.
126. Hill-West JL, Chowdhury SM, Slepian MJ, Hubbell JA. Inhibition of thrombosis and intimal thickening by in situ photopolymerization of thin hydrogel barriers. Proc Natl Acad Sci 1994;91:5967–5971.
127. Nabel EG, Plautz G, Nabel GJ. Gene transfer into vascular cells. J Am Coll Cardiol 1991;17(Suppl B):189–194.
128. Lim CS, Chapman GD, Gammon RS, et al. Direct in vivo gene transfer into the coronary and peripheral vasculatures of the intact dog. Circulation 1991;83:2007–2011.
129. Pickering JG, Jekanowski J, Weir L. Demonstration that gene transfer may be successfully accomplished in human vascular smooth muscle cells obtained from atherosclerotic lesions by directional atherectomy. Circulation 1992;86(4):I-798.
130. Takeshita S, Leclerc G, Gal D, Weir L. In vivo arterial gene transfer: effect of angioplasty on transfection efficiency in atherosclerotic arteries. Circulation 1992;86(4):I-799.
131. Shi Y, Hutchinson HG, Hall DJ, and Zalewski A. Downregulation of c-*myc* expression by antisense oligonucleotides inhibits proliferation of human smooth muscle cells. Circulation 1993;88(3):1190–1195.
132. Epstein SE, Speir E, Finkel T. Do antisense approaches to the problem of restenosis make sense? Circulation 1993;88(3): 1351–1353.
133. Pickering JG, Bacha P, Jekanowski J, Weir L, Nichols JC, Isner JM. Prevention of smooth muscle cell proliferation and

134. outgrowth from human atherosclerotic plaque by a recombinant fusion protein. Circulation 1992;86(4):I-226.
134. Ohno T, Gordon D, San H, Pompili VJ, Imperiale MJ, Nabel GJ, Nabel EG. Gene therapy for vascular smooth muscle cell proliferation after arterial injury. Science 1994;265:781–784.
135. Speir E, Modali R, Huang E-S, Leon MB, Shawl F, Finkel T, Epstein SE. Potential role of human cytomegalovirus and p53 interaction in coronary restenosis. Science 1994;265:391–394.
136. Melnick JL, Hu C, Burek J, Adam E, DeBakey ME. Cytelomegalovirus DNA in arterial walls of patients with atherosclerosis. J Med Virol 1994;42(2):170–174.
137. Werness BA, Levine AJ, Howley PM. Association of human papillomavirus types 16 and 18 E6 proteins with p53. Science 1990;248:76–79.
138. Zhang Q, Gutsch O, Kenney S. Functional and physical interaction between p53 and BZLF1: implications for Epstein-Barr virus latency. Mol Cell Biol 1994;14:1929.
139. Schwartz RS, Holmes DR, Topol EJ. The restenosis paradigm revisited: an alternative proposal for cellular mechanisms. J Am Coll Cardiol 1992;20:1284–1293.
140. Steinke W, Els T, Hennerici M. Compensatory carotid artery dilatation in early atherosclerosis. Circulation 1994;89(6): 2578–2581.
141. Glagov S, Weisenberg E, Zarins CK, Stankunavicius R, Kolettis GJ. Compensatory enlargement of human atherosclerotic coronary arteries. N Engl J Med 1987;316:1371–1375.
142. Zarins CK, Weisenberg E, Kolettis G, Stankunavicius R, Glagov S. Differential enlargement of artery segments in response to enlarging atherosclerotic plaques. J Vasc Surg 1988;7: 386–394.
143. Stiel GM, Stiel LSG, Schofer J, Dnath K, Mathey DG. Impact of compensatory enlargement of atherosclerotic coronary arteries on angiographic assessment of coronary artery disease. Circulation 1989;80:1603–1609.
144. Post MJ, Borst C, Kuntz RE. The relative importance of arterial remodeling compared with intimal hyperplasia in lumen renarrowing after balloon angioplasty: a study in the normal rabbit and the hypercholesterolemic micropig. Circulation 1994;89(6):2816–2821.
145. Kakuta T, Currier JW, Haudenschild CC, Ryan TJ, Faxon DP. Differences in compensatory vessel enlargement, not intimal formation, account for restenosis after angioplasty in the hypercholesterolemic rabbit model. Circulation 1994;89(6): 2809–2815.
146. Isner JM. Vascular remodeling. Honey, I think I shrunk the artery. Circulation 1994;89(6):2937–2941.

2

Balloon Angioplasty Catheters

GARY J. BECKER

Historical Background

Coaxial Dilating Catheter Method

For nearly a decade after the introduction by Dotter and Judkins of percutaneous transluminal angioplasty (PTA),[1] at a time when little significance was ascribed to therapeutic catheter techniques in the United States and throughout the world, Zeitler and colleagues kept the method alive in Europe.[2,3] Despite their enthusiasm, Dotter, Judkins, Zeitler, and a few other pioneers in this field recognized that the technique, which employed tapered Teflon coaxial dilating catheters (Fig. 2-1), imposed a very real limitation on the size of vessel that could be treated. The larger the vessel to be treated, the larger the catheter shaft required. This meant that the puncture site had to be dilated to very large sizes in order to treat large arteries, and the result was a greater risk of puncture site complications, particularly hematoma and pseudoaneurysm. Dotter and Judkins recognized this limitation quite early in their experience. They described it and predicted the future development of radially expanding catheters to treat arterial stenoses.[1]

In addition to size limitations, the relative inflexibility of the coaxial catheters imposed a limitation on the specific anatomic areas that could be catheterized and treated. To reach a coronary artery lesion with one of these catheters would have been unthinkable. But in the mid-1960s, the design of the coaxial dilating catheters was only one of many limitations, each of which would have made coronary angioplasty unthinkable. Among these limitations were the lack of soft-tipped, steerable, highly radiopaque guidewires, the lack of torque control catheters and guiding catheters, the relatively early point in time of the development of sophisticated cardiac catheterization laboratories, and the relative lack of adjunctive pharmacotherapeutics. Confronted with these very real limitations, Dotter and Judkins still predicted applications of angioplasty in the coronary, renal, and carotid arteries.[1]

Finally, it was known that the coaxial dilator method applied not only a radial force to the diseased vessel wall at the site of the lesion, but also a shearing force that was undesirable. Therefore, efforts were undertaken to develop a catheter that would, after delivery to the site of the atherosclerotic lesion, radially expand and thereby deform or mold the plaque and enlarge the vessel lumen.

Early Balloon PTA Catheters

Porstmann's "korsett balloon catheter"[4] and Dotter's reinforced balloon dilating catheter (Fig. 2-2)[5,6] and caged balloon catheter (Fig. 2-3)[5,7] were early products of these efforts. The last-mentioned device was a Teflon catheter with short parallel slits in its long axis near the leading end that were arranged about the circumference of the catheter shaft. Inside this Teflon catheter, a coaxial latex balloon on a 22-gauge metal cannula positioned at the site of the slits (cage) was expanded at the time of angioplasty. The result of this design was a radial force applied to the stenosis during angioplasty. The cage restricted the size the balloon could reach and thereby provided a safeguard against bursting. The catheter was dilated up to 9.3 mm from a minimum diameter of 3.0 mm. Dotter and colleagues reported their success with the caged balloon catheter in more than 90 percent of 48 consecutive cases of atherosclerotic iliac artery obstruction.[7] Follow-up in the series was up to 6 years. Despite these results, the use of Dotter's caged balloon catheter was associated with very real limitations, such as inflexibility and occasional thromboembolic complications. These detracted from its clinical utility and encouraged investigators to develop better angioplasty catheters.

The Beginnings of Modern Balloon PTA

The first major advance leading to balloon catheters as we know them today was the development of polyvinyl chloride (PVC) balloon PTA catheters by Gruentzig and Hopff. Encouraged by Dotter's work and armed

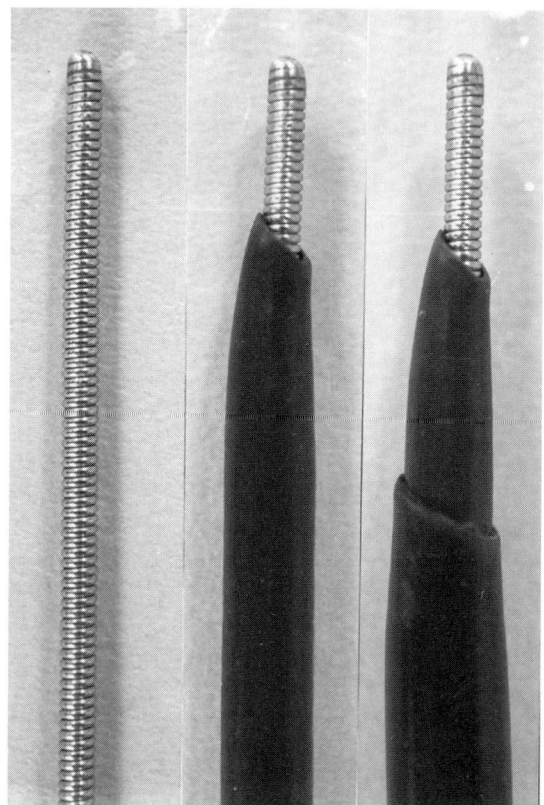

Figure 2-1. Dotter coaxial dilating catheters.

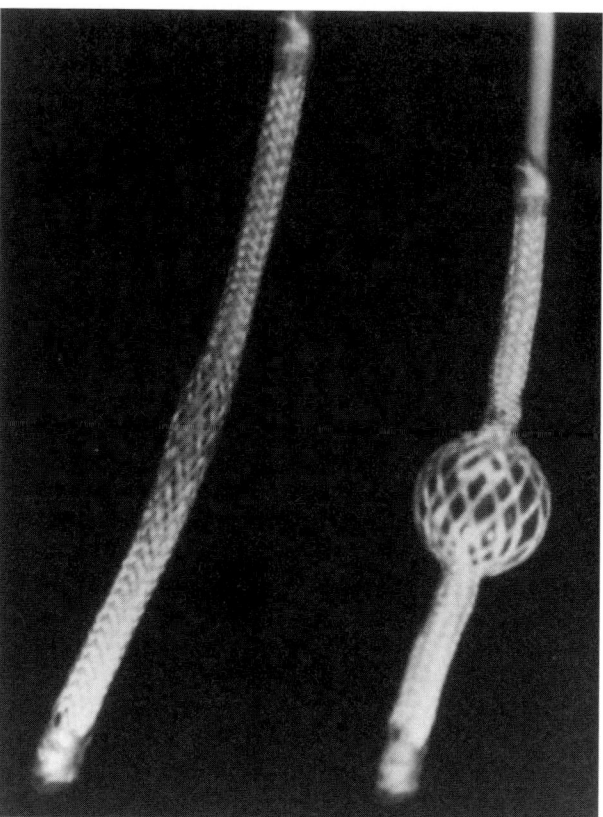

Figure 2-2. Dotter's reinforced balloon dilating catheter.

with his own cardiology background, training under Zeitler, and experience with peripheral PTA, Gruentzig had been continuing the search for a more suitable material with which to build a balloon catheter specifically for coronary angioplasty. He teamed up with a professor emeritus of organic chemistry from the Eidgenossischen Technischen Hochschule of Zurich by the name of Hopff, and PVC was selected.[8] Walter Schlumpf, husband of Maria Schlumpf, Gruentzig's assistant, actually built the first PVC balloon catheters that Gruentzig used on patients for peripheral PTA. The first case series of PTA with use of the new PVC catheters (1974) comprised a group of patients with atherosclerotic obstructions in the lower extremities.[9] In 1976 and 1977, the new catheters were used intraoperatively to dilate human coronary artery stenoses,[10] and on September 16, 1977, Gruentzig performed the first percutaneous transluminal coronary angioplasty (PTCA). He reported his first five patients in a letter to the editor of *Lancet,* which was published in February of 1978.[11] His clinical report of a series of patients followed in 1979.[12] By 1980, angioplasty's flame had been reignited in the United States, preparing the way for all of the ensuing developments we have witnessed.

Basic Properties and Functions of Balloon PTA Catheters

Since the earliest beginnings of balloon PTA, experience has helped to determine the problems with and limitations of existing technologies in various applications. The understanding thus derived has helped manufacturers focus on the most important balloon catheter characteristics and to develop better products.

Balloon compliance and dilating force, hoop strength, profile, trackability, kink resistance, pushability, and balloon inflation and deflation times are the most important attributes of angioplasty balloon catheters. For a modern treatment of balloons, we might add a discussion of stent compatibility. Although stents will be mentioned below, no formal guidelines or standards have been established.

Balloon Compliance and Dilating Force

In the strictest sense, compliance is the change in volume per unit change in pressure. For most PTA balloon catheters, the changes in length that occur in

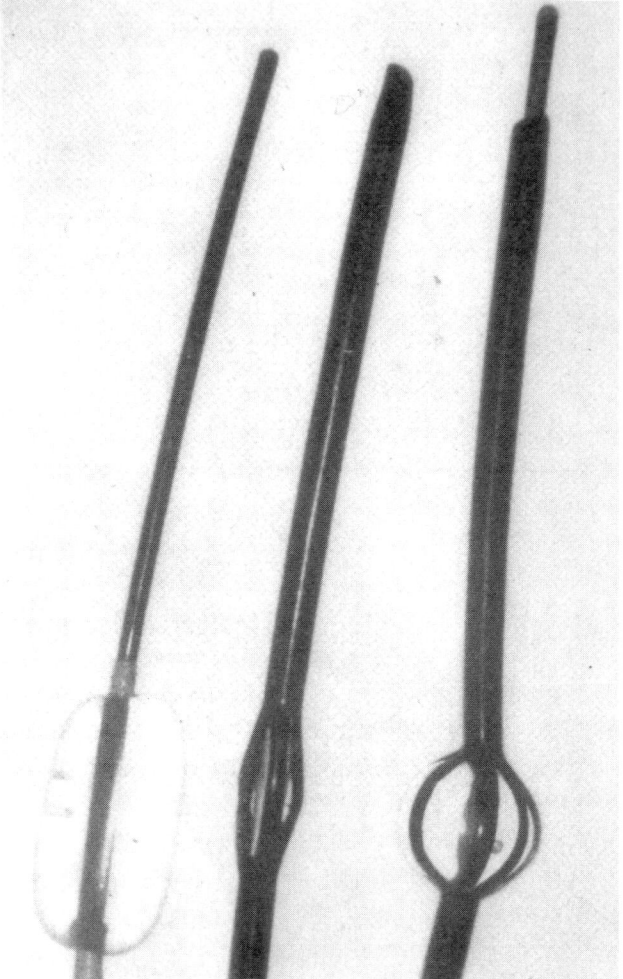

Figure 2-3. The caged balloon catheter.

balloons can result in (1) unpredictable balloon diameters, (2) overstretching of the balloon material not abutting the lesion (i.e., that portion contacting the normal vessel wall), (3) overstretching and possible rupture of adjacent normal vessel segments, (4) a poor tactile sense of the lesion, and (5) decreased dilating force at the lesion site.[13,14]

Since the introduction of PTA balloons, developments in polymer science and technology have led to thin-walled balloons made of less compliant materials, including polyethylene (PE), polyethylene teraphthalate (PET), nylon, and polyurethane. These materials are less compliant than PVC, and are therefore generally better suited for PTA, although PE is the most compliant among them. Noncompliant balloons increase very little in diameter before reaching burst. Therefore, the selection of the correct balloon size to match the vessel size all but guarantees that a vessel rupture (transmural tear) will not occur during angioplasty. The balloon itself may rupture if the limits of tensile strength are exceeded, but the vessel should remain intact. Figure 2-4, a graph of compliance of various balloon materials, illustrates the differences between some of these materials. Other than the specific balloon material, variables related to compliance and burst include temperature, number of inflations,[15] and balloon diameter. PVC balloons tend to stretch before burst, not only in response to increasing pressure, but also in response to repeated inflations.[16] Such balloon overstretching has led to vessel rupture in clinical angioplasty.[17,18]

response to increased pressure are negligible. Therefore, volume changes occur primarily because of changes in balloon diameter, and balloon compliance is best represented by the expression

$$C \cong \frac{\Delta D}{\Delta P}$$

where C is balloon compliance, D is balloon diameter, and P is pressure inside of the PTA balloon. Gruentzig's original balloons and all of the early PTA balloons were made of PVC, a relatively compliant balloon material by today's standards. These balloons tended to yield under pressure and increase their diameter significantly before reaching the limits of tensile strength (burst). The result during PTA was often a balloon diameter significantly larger than that stated by the manufacturer. Abele has provided an excellent discussion of how, with increasing force applied to such materials in a severe stenosis, expansion of compliant

Hoop Strength

The nonradial force applied to the surface of the balloon circumferentially during balloon expansion is known as *hoop stress*. Since pressure is force per unit area, for a given pressure, a large balloon surface experiences greater hoop stress than does a smaller balloon. The hoop stress, T, is the product of pressure, P, and balloon diameter, D.

$$T = P \times D$$

For a given balloon material and inflation pressure, a balloon of larger diameter has greater hoop stress applied to its surface. Therefore, large balloons burst at lower pressures than small balloons of the same material. Stated another way, in a selection of various balloon sizes of the identical material, each balloon bursts at the same level of hoop stress. However, because of the above relationship, for a given level of hoop stress, the pressure and balloon diameter are inversely related. Therefore, for large balloons, relatively low pressures

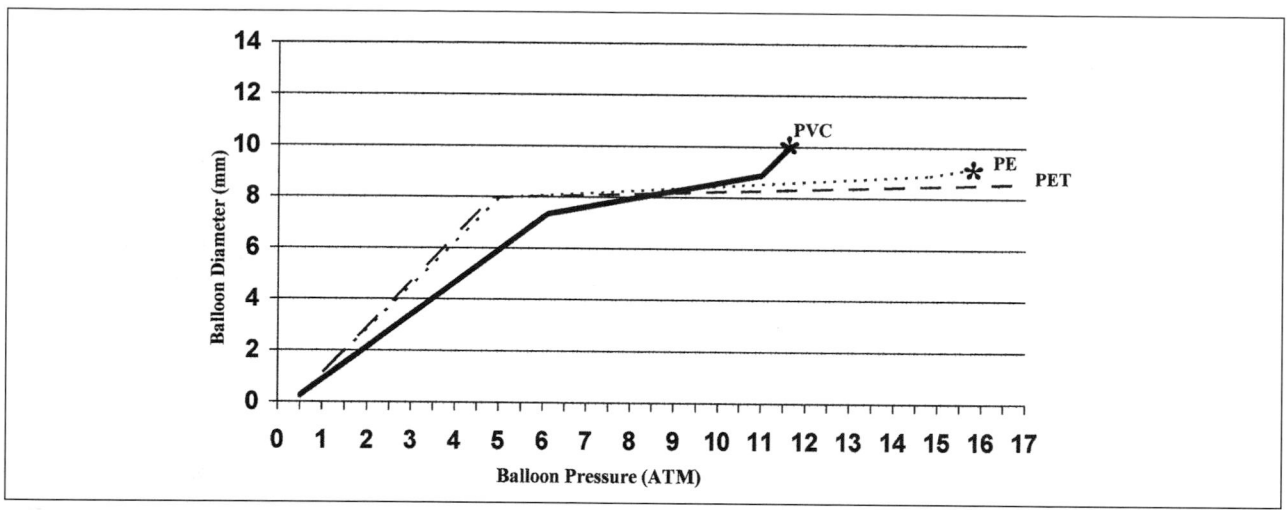

Figure 2-4. Compliance curves for various balloon catheters of 8 mm nominal diameter. Since length is assumed to be constant, compliance is represented by change in balloon diameter as a function of pressure. From most compliant to least compliant: *PVC*, polyvinyl chloride; *PE*, polyethylene; *PET*, polyethylene teraphthalate. *Asterisks* represent burst point.

are required to reach the hoop stress at which burst will occur. Consequently, the largest balloons have the lowest burst pressure ratings. "High-pressure balloons" that withstand up to 20 atm of pressure (but whose advertised maximum inflation pressures are 10–16 atm) are available and in use in clinical PTA.

The most important underlying cause of vessel rupture angioplasty is overdistention of the vessel. The simplest way to ensure that overdistention will not occur and that the maximum dilating force will be applied to the lesion site is to select a noncompliant balloon with the appropriate diameter. Since one uses a noncompliant balloon to perform PTA, dilating force increases linearly with the inflation pressure.[14] Finally, one alternative to the ideal noncompliant PTA catheter is a controlled compliance catheter. This concept, which is used by the manufacturers of some of the nylon balloons, entails using a PTA balloon catheter in conjunction with an inflation device. For any inflation pressure chosen, the balloon has a known diameter, because its compliance curves are accurate and reproducible. Using such a system, it is possible, for example, to expand an 8.0-mm balloon to 7.5 or 8.5 mm (or whatever diameter between these two extremes is needed) by choosing the correct pressure to reach the corresponding predicted balloon diameter.

Balloon Profile

Profile may be thought of as the maximum cross-sectional area or diameter of the PTA catheter. It is usually expressed in French size. Thus a 5 French PTA catheter whose balloon increases the profile slightly

may be a true 5.7 French. Most modern PTA is performed through an angiographic sheath with hemostatic valve and side port. A 5.7 French profile would necessitate use of a 6 French sheath. Balloon catheters with significantly larger profiles at the balloon site than throughout the remainder of the shaft length have a propensity for causing blood leakage at the catheter insertion site when used without an angiographic sheath.

Low profile confers two tangible benefits: a smaller arterial access sheath (and the potential of fewer local entry site complications) and lesion crossability. The latter property refers to the ability of the balloon to cross the target lesion so that PTA can be performed. Aside from profile, another factor related to crossability is the frictional force between the lesion surface and the balloon surface. To decrease this frictional force, some manufacturers have added hydrophilic coatings to the balloon surfaces.

The early PTA catheters had 9 French shafts. Adding the balloon wrap to the catheter shaft often produced a true profile in the 10 to 11 French range. Such prohibitively large catheters could never have been used to track over a wire through tortuous vessels for visceral or coronary angioplasty. To actually decrease the profile of most PTA catheters, manufacturers have used better catheter materials and modern extrusion technology to reduce the overall catheter shaft size, decreased the diameter of the portion of the catheter shaft beneath the balloon, used very thin but noncompliant balloon materials, and perfected the balloon wrap. The specific balloon catheter design (coaxial, double-lumen, balloon-on-a-wire) is another determi-

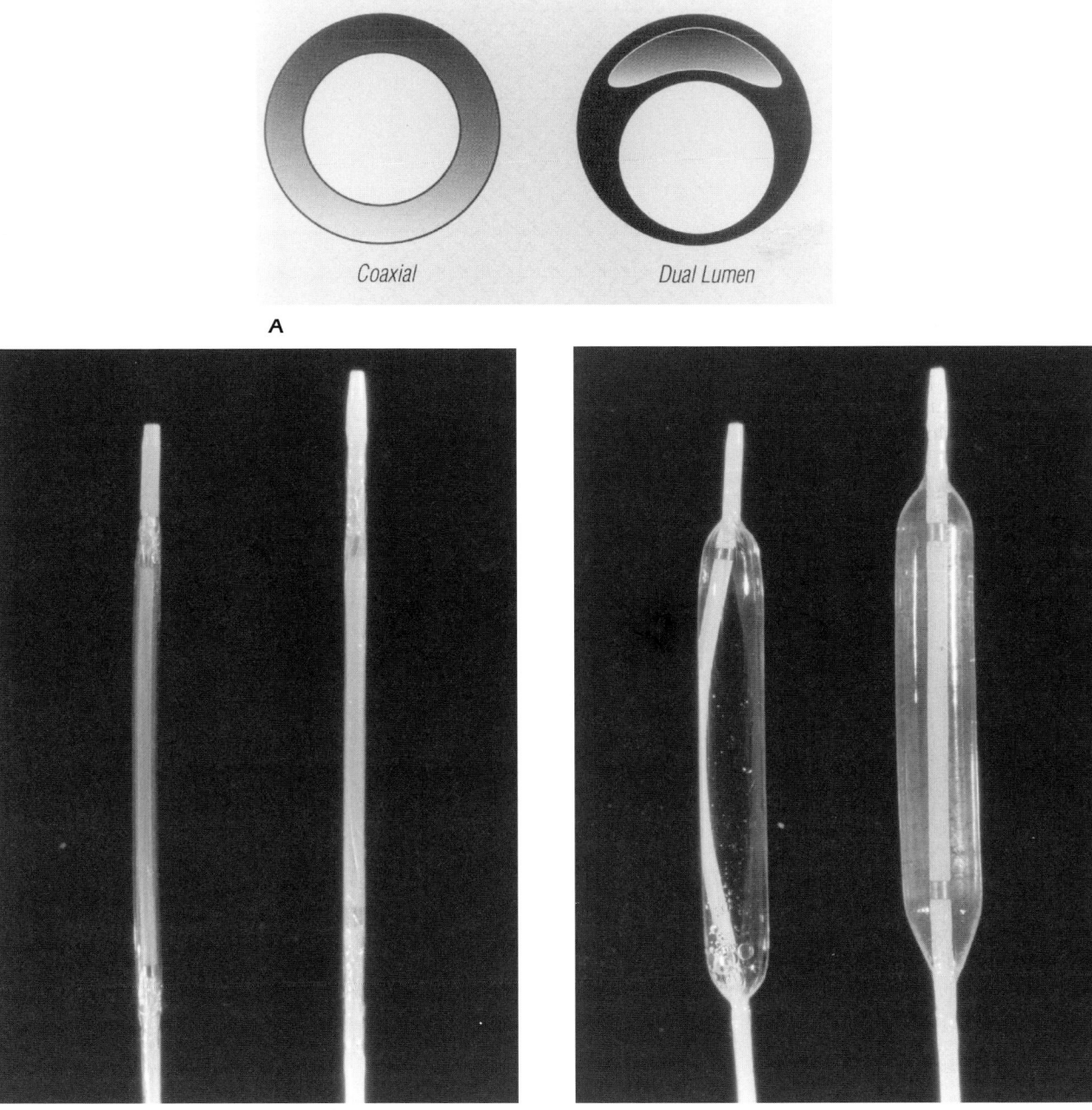

Figure 2-5. Peripheral PTA balloons are available in a variety of designs and sizes on 5 French catheter shafts. (A) Cross sections of coaxial and double-lumen balloon catheters. (B and C) Double-lumen (*left*) and coaxial (*right*) 5 French balloon catheters before (B) and after (C) inflation.

nant of profile. All commonly used PTA balloon sizes are available on 5 French catheter shafts. At least two of the manufacturers have balloons up to 12 mm in diameter on a 5 French shaft (Fig. 2-5), and two have high-pressure balloons on 5 French shafts. The profile, including the balloon wrap, on these 12-mm balloon catheters is approximately 7 French. Therefore, a 7 French sheath is required to use them.

Some vessels are so small that the most important catheter characteristic is profile. Small-vessel balloon catheters used for tibial PTA, pediatric renal PTA, and renal branch PTA are available on shafts ranging from 3.1 to 5.0 French (Fig. 2-6). These balloon diameters range from 2 to 6 mm, and the balloons are rated at 6 to 16 atm, depending on balloon material, diameter, and manufacturer. Problems related to profile exist in interventional cardiology, too. In PTCA, some severe stenoses in mid- to distal coronary arterial segments are not crossable without extremely low profile balloon catheters. The manufacturers have responded to this challenge, however, and a wide array of low-profile PTCA balloons is now available.

The angiographer also has some control over profile. For almost all balloon catheters, including those that "wing" significantly upon deflation, counterclockwise torque decreases balloon profile to the lowest possible level. Occasionally, when faced with a situation in which the balloon catheter cannot be advanced over a wire through the area of stenosis, minimizing profile with counterclockwise rotation on the catheter enables passage of the balloon through the lesion. Profile must even be kept in mind when a balloon has been deflated and is about to be removed from the angiographic sheath. Often a balloon catheter that resists withdrawal through the sheath may be successfully retrieved once counterclockwise torque is applied. If there is any question about which direction

of rotation produces the lowest profile of the balloon catheter, the balloon should be rotated with one hand of the angiographer while the index and forefinger of the other hand are used to grip the balloon. Winging should not occur when the proper direction has been selected. In addition, some of the high-pressure balloons wing markedly when negative pressure is forcefully applied to the balloon inflation syringe (Fig. 2-7). For the safest, least traumatic removal of these balloons, it may be necessary to deflate forcefully and patiently, and then open the balloon port to ambient pressures prior to withdrawal.

Trackability

Trackability is the tendency of a PTA catheter to follow a guidewire through a tortuous path to the lesion site without loss of wire position. In any given case, the specific anatomy, the skill and experience of the operator, and the guidewire-catheter combination all contribute to the likelihood that the catheter will track

Figure 2-6. (A and B) Small-vessel angioplasty balloons for tibial and branch renal angioplasty: 4-mm × 2-cm balloon on a 4 French shaft (*left*) and 2-mm × 4-cm balloon on a 3.7 French shaft (*right*) before (A) and after (B) inflation.

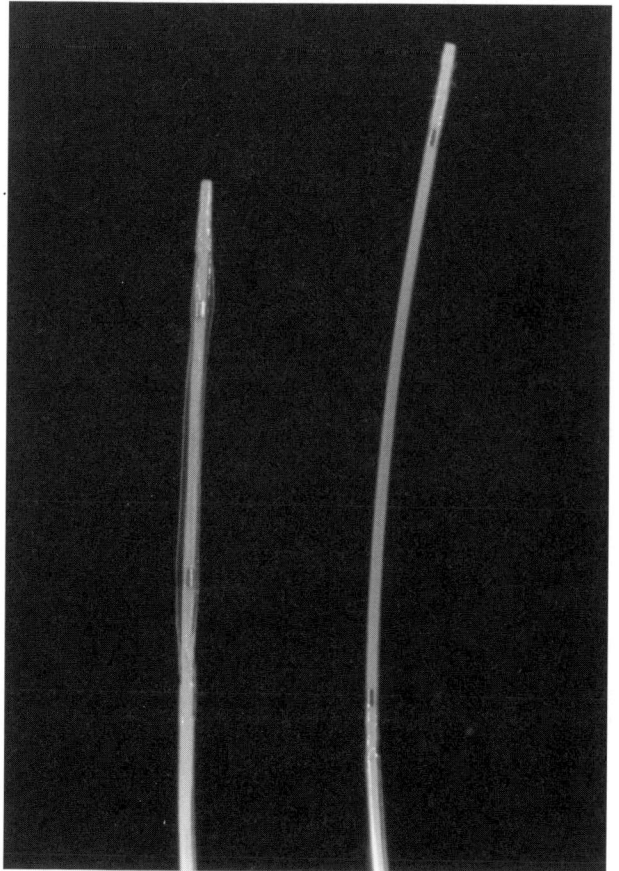

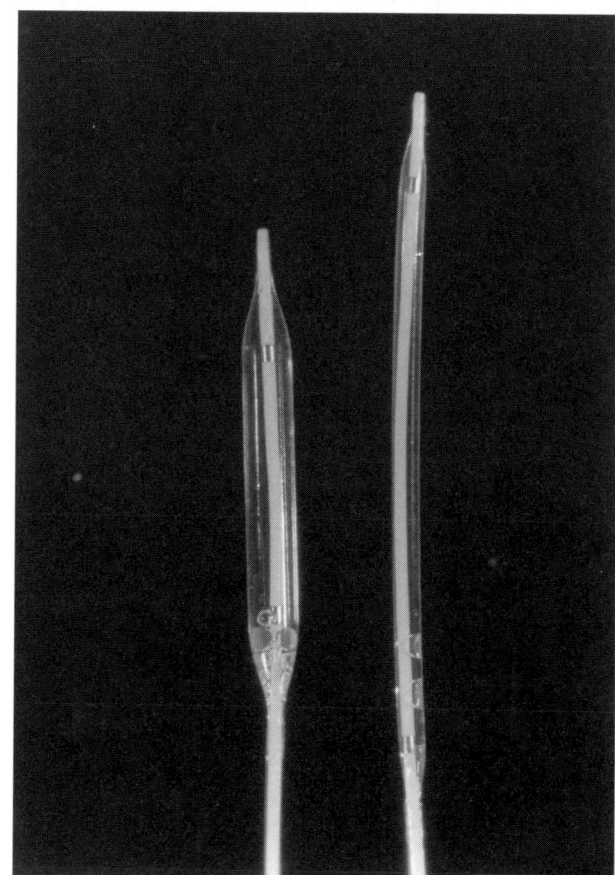

A

B

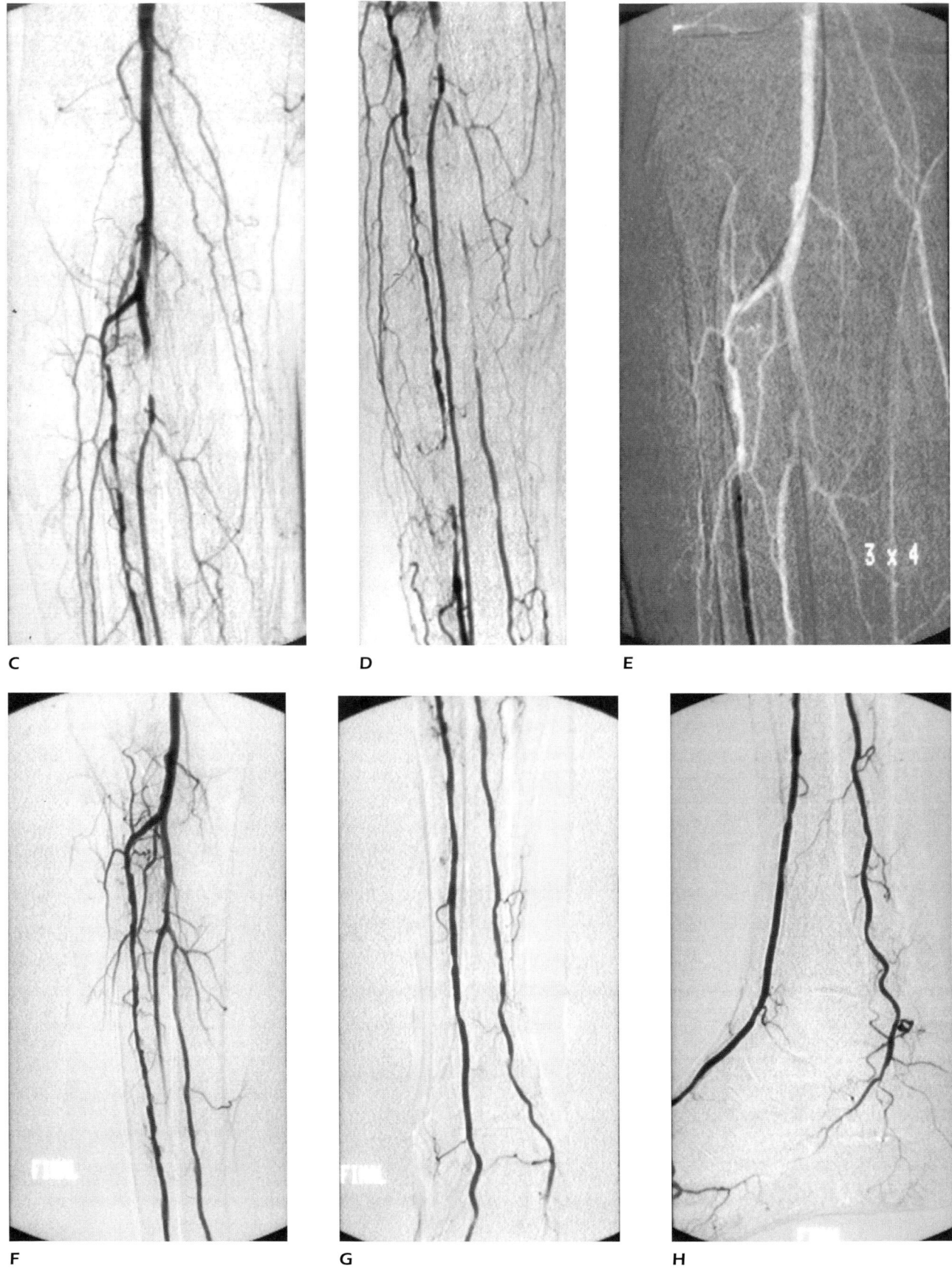

to the desired location. In the early days of superficial femoral and retrograde iliac angioplasty, trackability was never a necessary feature. Therefore, the relatively large, stiff PTA catheters seemed quite acceptable. Because their stiffness made them pushable, most lesions could be traversed and dilated. But the need to do over-the-bifurcation iliac and femoral PTA, renal PTA, and visceral PTA placed new demands on the manufacturers (Fig. 2-8). Sufficient flexibility had to be incorporated into catheter design to enable angiographers to do these procedures. To a great degree, this flexibility came about with the reduction in profile that the manufacturers achieved. Much of this reduction has been achieved by manufacturing thin-walled catheters. Two prices that are paid for the thinner walls are an increased tendency for the catheter to kink and a decrease in pushability (see below). In addition to thinner catheter walls, another factor that has enhanced the trackability of modern PTA catheters is the wide variety of guidewires currently in use. A veritable array of exchange wires and steerable wires in 0.035-inch size are now available. The ideal wire enables the operator to steer across the site, has a flexible, soft, radiopaque tip, and has a relatively stiff body over which the catheter can track. In practice, however, it is often necessary to use more than one wire to complete a procedure. For instance, in renal PTA (Fig. 2-9), crossing a stenosis with a sidewinder catheter led by a Bentson wire may provide the ideal combination of catheter shape and soft wire tip. Once the catheter has crossed the lesion and the correct intraluminal position is confirmed by injection of contrast material, the Bentson wire may be exchanged for a Rosen wire, a TAD (torsional attenuating diameter) wire, or other relatively stiff wire with a safe tip, over which the PTA catheter will track through the stenosis. A balloon catheter that tracks poorly will erase the previous selective catheterization efforts by pulling the exchange wire out of the target vessel into the aorta or parent vessel as it is being advanced (Fig. 2-10).

Kink Resistance

Ideally, a catheter used to negotiate tortuous paths and severe stenoses should also be able to resist kinking when the shaft is being advanced through a curve with a narrow radius. In PTA, this problem is perhaps most frequently encountered when the operator needs the PTA to also double as a diagnostic angiographic cathe-

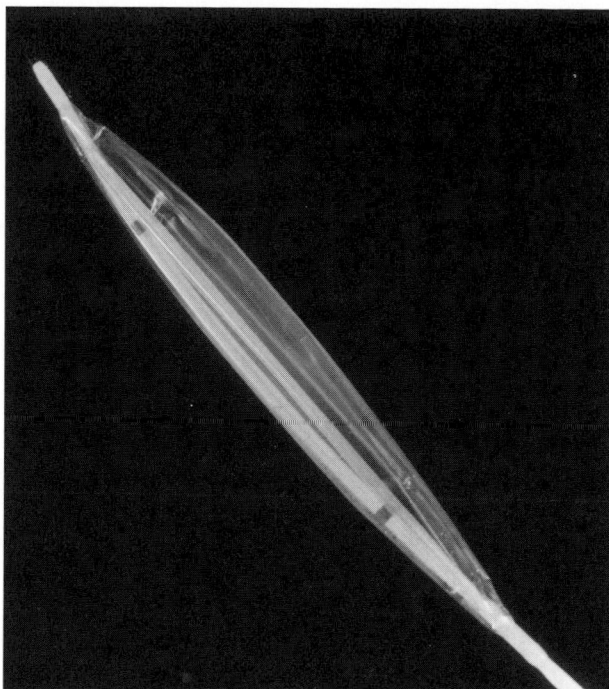

Figure 2-7. "Winging" of a high-pressure balloon during aspiration on the balloon port. This balloon will not rewrap to its original low profile upon deflation and removal. However, the profile can be minimized and the effects of "winging" diminished by aspirating the balloon and then opening the balloon port to ambient pressure prior to removal.

ter. For instance, in over-the-bifurcation PTA of the superficial femoral artery (SFA), the operator may wish to withdraw the guidewire temporarily so that the guidewire lumen may be used to inject contrast material for the post-PTA arteriogram. When the guidewire is being withdrawn, the catheter shaft (along with its balloon lumen and guidewire lumen) is most susceptible to kinking. In PTCA, kinking is not as much of a problem because of the use of guiding catheters and because the PTCA balloon catheters are never used for injecting contrast material.

Most if not all of the 5 French PTA balloon catheters have demonstrated this kinking problem in over-the-bifurcation PTA and other applications. Once kinking occurs, it can sometimes be overcome by withdrawing the catheter in small increments while advancing a tapered-tip guidewire. Usually, however, the catheter must be withdrawn and the vessel must be recatheterized. To avoid this problem, there are a few

◄ **Figure 2-6** (continued). (C and D) A patient with a non-healing ulcer of the right foot. Angiogram before PTA depicts numerous stenoses and segmental occlusions in the anterior tibial and tibioperoneal vessels of the right lower leg. (E) Road-map image during PTA of the anterior tibial artery with a 3-mm × 4-cm small-vessel balloon catheter. (F through H) Images from the angiogram after PTA of all trifurcation vessels reveal an excellent morphologic result.

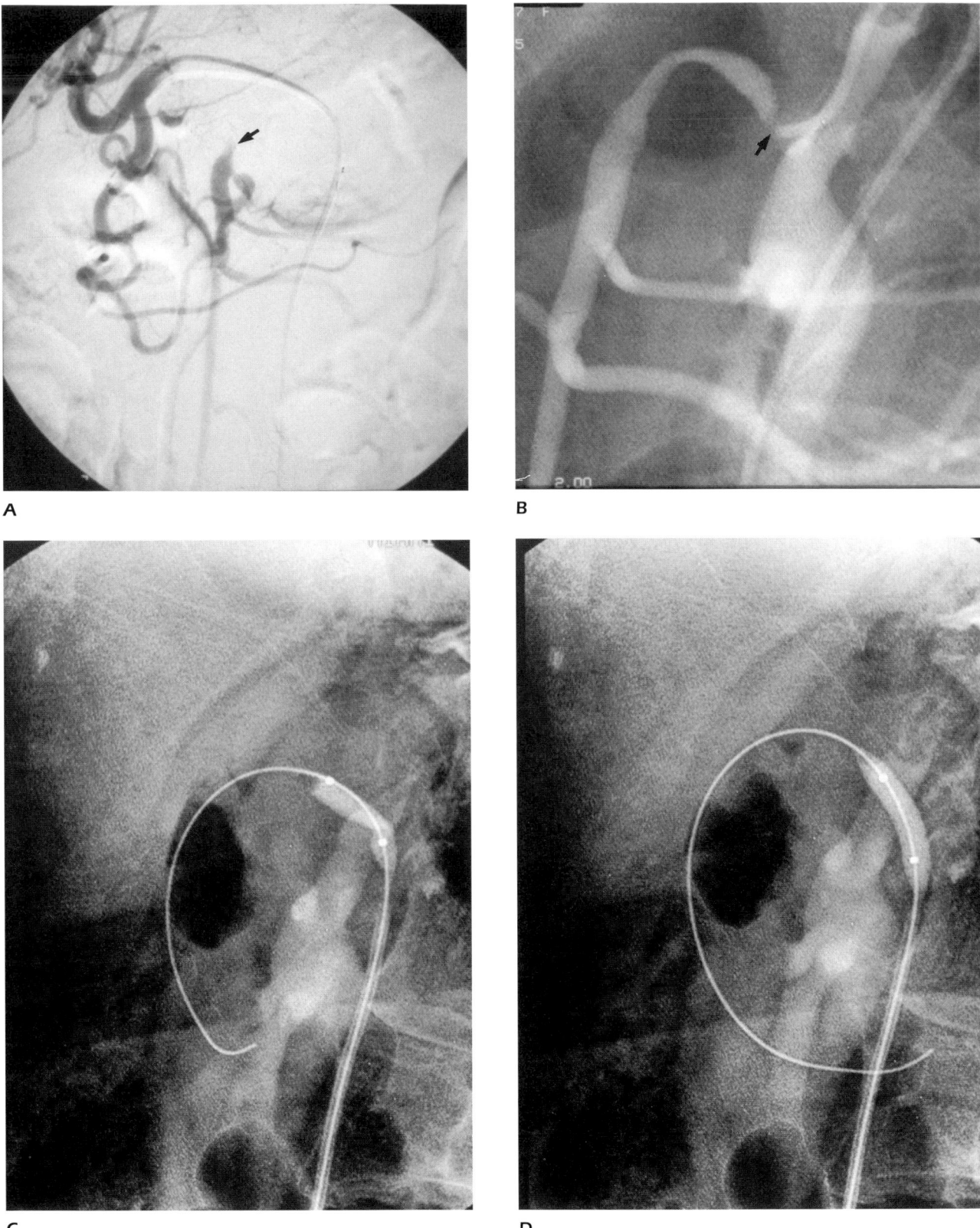

A

B

C

D

Figure 2-8. Trackability and low profile are two important characteristics that enable peripheral PTA balloon catheters to function in stenoses located along difficult curves, particularly in renal and visceral PTA. (A and B) Even with these properties, sometimes a guiding catheter is required to successfully negotiate a difficult stenosis. Posteroanterior proper hepatic (A) and lateral selective superior mesenteric artery

(B) injections in a patient with abdominal angina attributable to inferior mesenteric artery occlusion (not shown), severe superior mesenteric artery (SMA) stenosis (*arrows*), and moderate celiac stenosis (not shown). (C and D) PTA with a 6-mm × 2-cm balloon catheter positioned within the SMA stenosis through a guiding catheter.

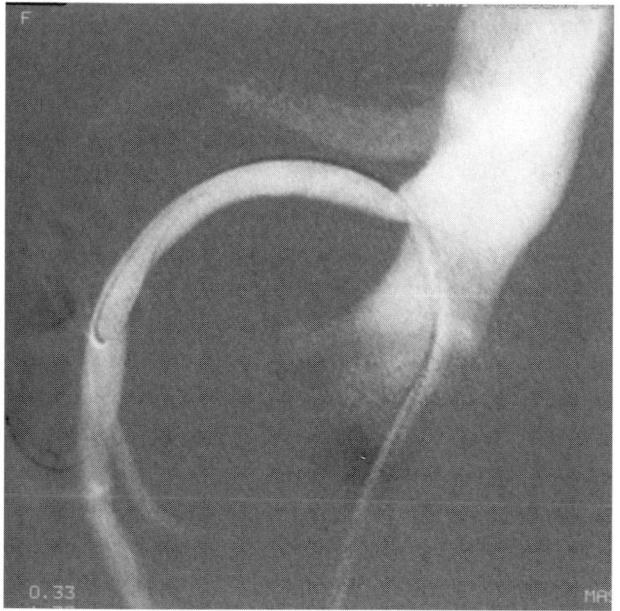

E

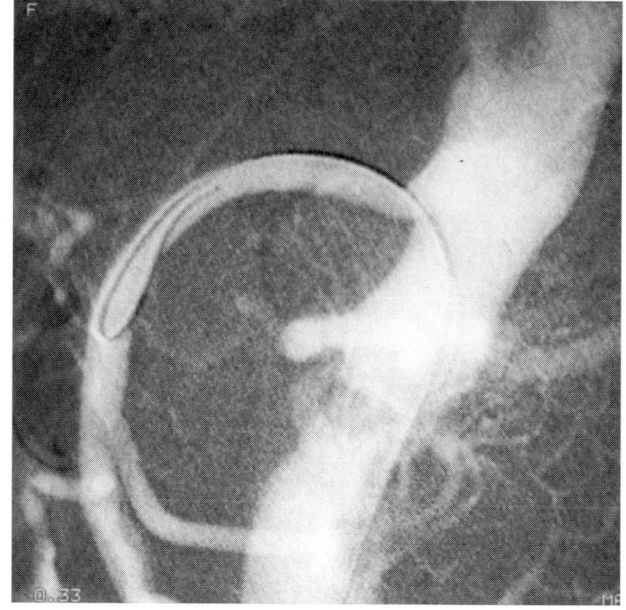

F

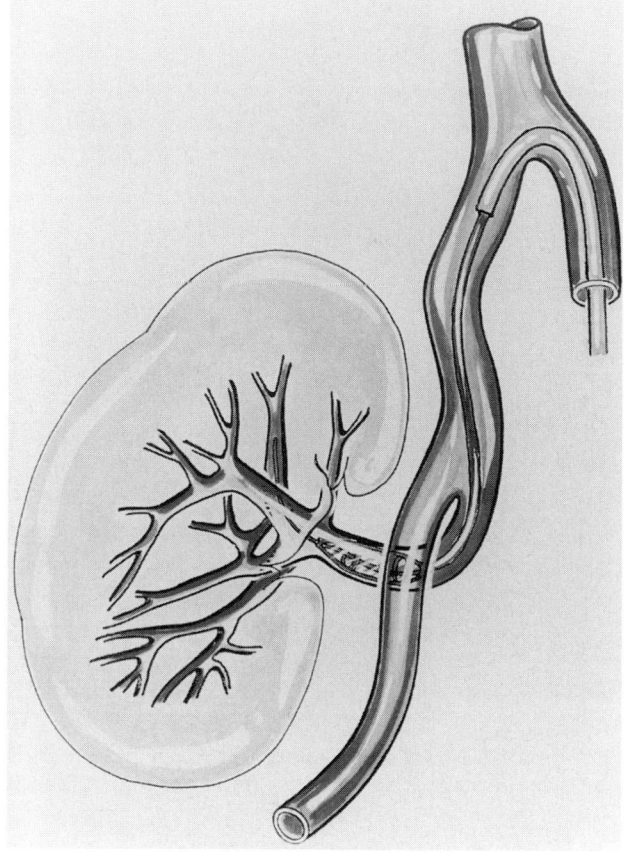

G

H

Figure 2-8. (continued). (E and F) Post-PTA angiograms showing marked angiographic improvement. (G) Artist's rendering of an over-the-bifurcation PTA of a contralateral renal transplant arterial stenosis. *Arrows* at the bifurcation indicate that the angiographer "shimmies" the catheter shaft over the aortic bifurcation to avoid pulling the wire out of position or pushing it up into the aorta. In so doing, the operator is taking advantage of the fact that the coefficient of dynamic friction is lower than that of static friction. (H) The over-the-bifurcation iliac guide catheter is a very reasonable alternative that results in a larger arterial puncture site.

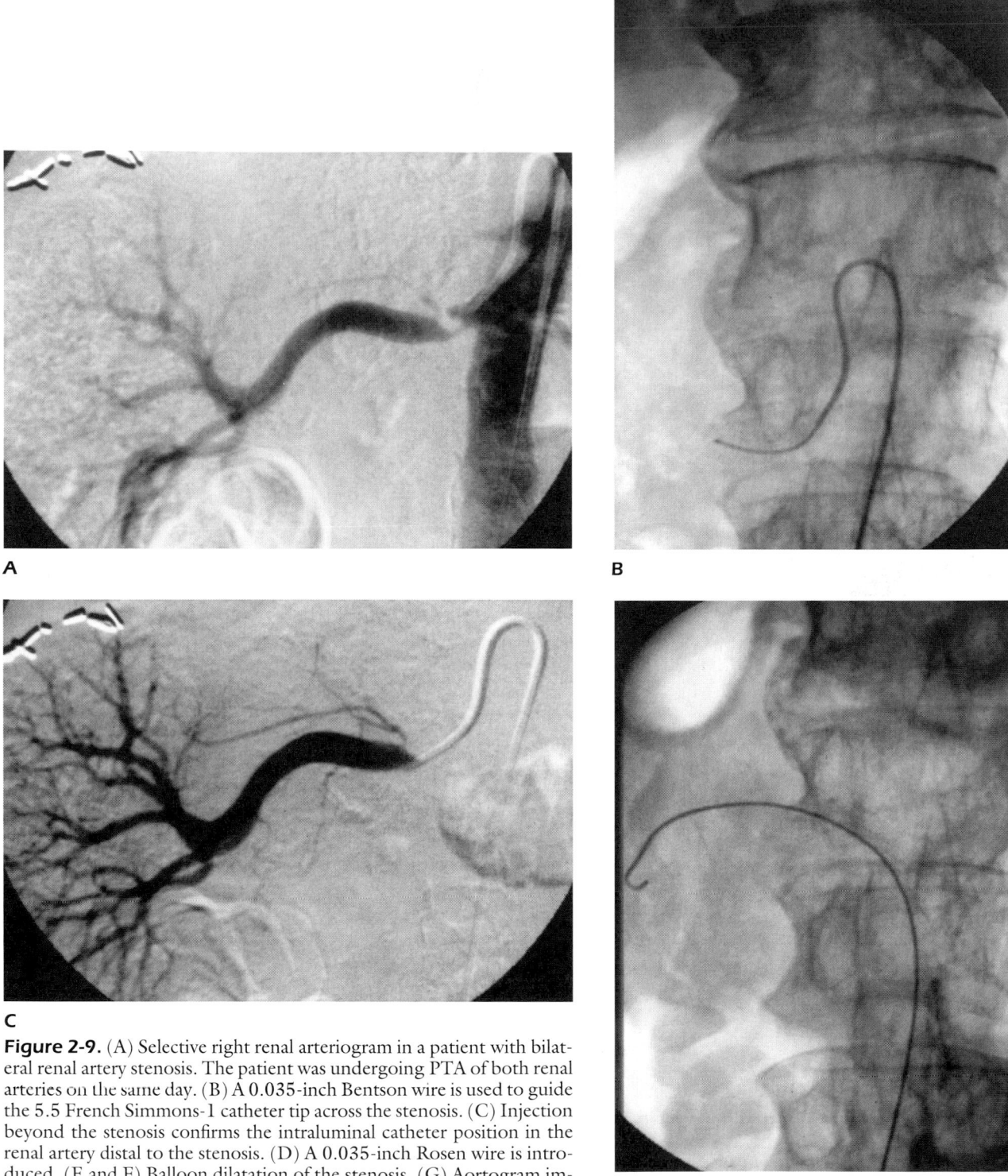

A

B

C

D

Figure 2-9. (A) Selective right renal arteriogram in a patient with bilateral renal artery stenosis. The patient was undergoing PTA of both renal arteries on the same day. (B) A 0.035-inch Bentson wire is used to guide the 5.5 French Simmons-1 catheter tip across the stenosis. (C) Injection beyond the stenosis confirms the intraluminal catheter position in the renal artery distal to the stenosis. (D) A 0.035-inch Rosen wire is introduced. (E and F) Balloon dilatation of the stenosis. (G) Aortogram immediately after right renal PTA demonstrates marked improvement.

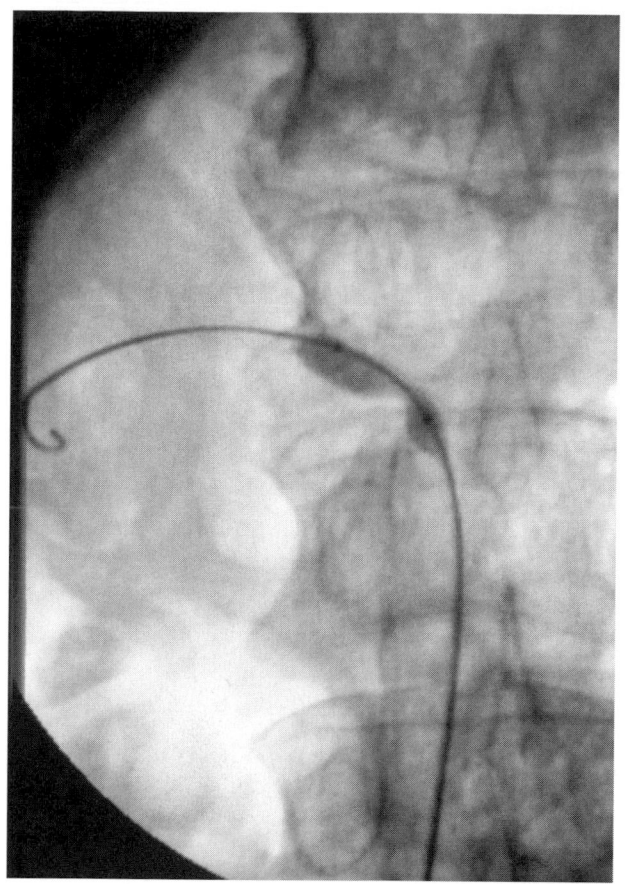

E

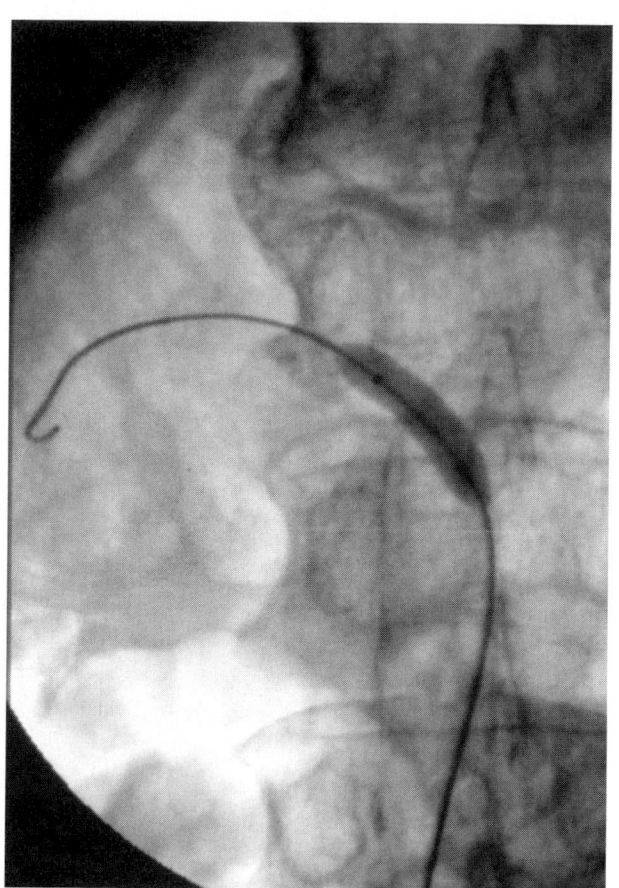

F

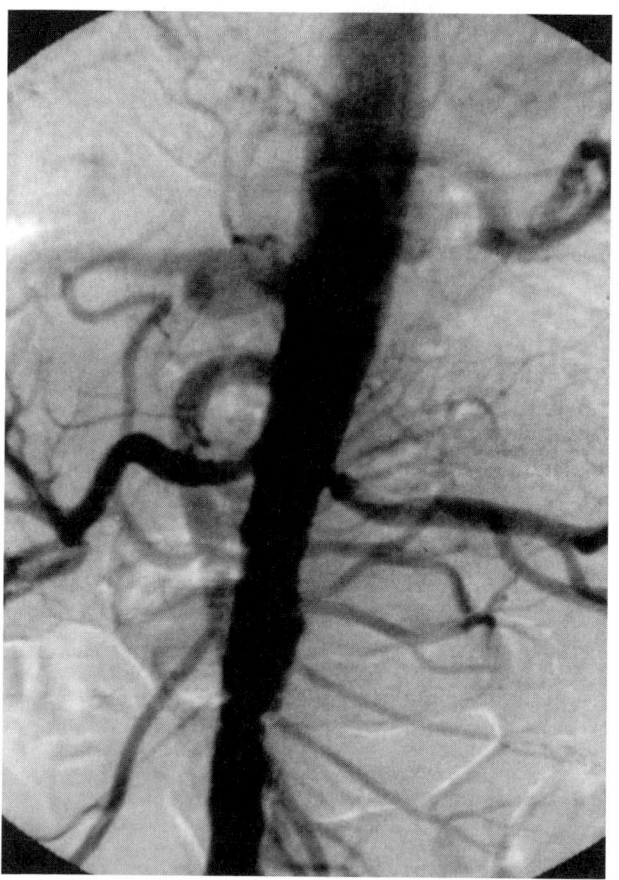

G

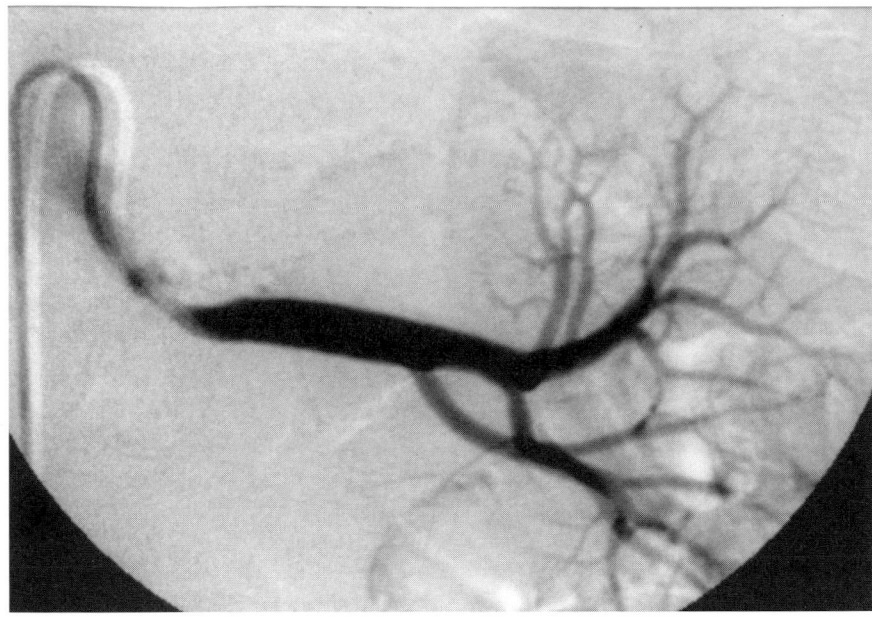

A

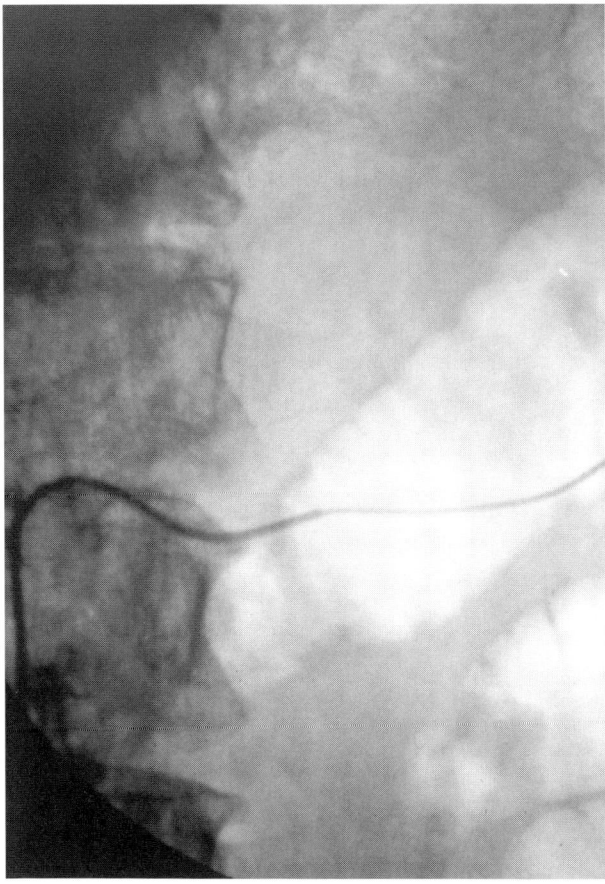

B

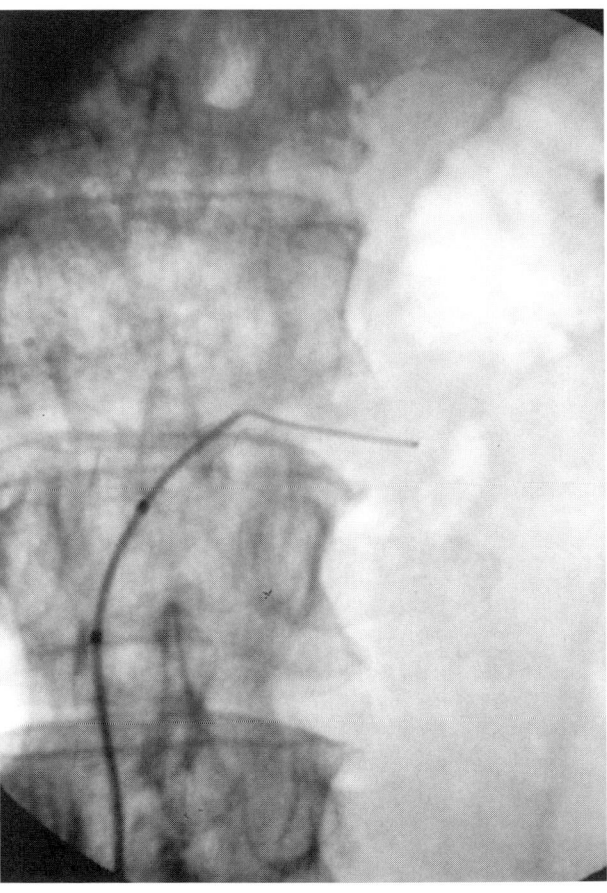

C

Figure 2-10. Attempted angioplasty of a left renal artery stenosis. (A) Selective left renal arteriogram demonstrates severe stenosis. (B) A 5.5 French Simmons-1 catheter is introduced safely through the stenosis over a wire. (C) The bal- loon will not track over the straight, fixed-core exchange wire through the stenosis; instead it continues up the aorta and in the process pulls the wire out of the renal artery.

maneuvers that can be done. The first is to position a relatively stiff 0.018-inch wire with a soft tip beyond the stenosis and to affix a Y adapter with a hemostatic valve to the injection port of the balloon PTA catheter. A sufficiently trackable balloon PTA catheter may then be brought into position over the wire, and the side port of the Y adapter may be used to inject contrast material, nitroglycerin, saline flush, or other substances (Fig. 2-11). The second is to use an over-the-bifurcation iliac guide or sheath that broadens the curve (increases the radius of curve) required of the 5 French catheter during contralateral work. Kinking may thus be avoided; however, the advantage of low profile at the catheter entry site is lost.

Virtually all materials have a high susceptibility to kinking when the catheter wall is too thin. However, for a given thickness of catheter wall, different materials have different kink resistances. Braided catheters may have the best kink resistance, but there are prices to be paid in profile and in trackability. A 5 French braided catheter with a balloon lumen added for PTA would increase profile significantly above 5 French and would be less trackable than a nonbraided catheter. Therefore, although some sheaths and guide catheters and many selective catheters are braided, balloon PTA catheter shafts generally are not.

To summarize, low-profile balloon catheters manufactured from very thin materials are susceptible to kinking, particularly when advanced through a curve with a narrow radius, and when the guidewire is removed. No manufacturer has a completely kink resistant low-profile PTA catheter. The best way to deal with kinking is to avoid it with one of the maneuvers described above.

Pushability

It is perhaps easiest to conceptualize the problem of pushability by considering PTCA rather than PTA, although the principle comes into play in over-the-bifurcation femoropopliteal PTA, in tibial PTA, in renal and visceral PTA, and now in intracranial PTA. The very-low-profile PTCA catheters may have no problem reaching a severe stenosis; however, if the catheter lacks pushability, it may not be able to cross the stenosis. To overcome this problem, manufacturers have now come up with very floppy catheters at the balloon end (leading end) that also have a relatively stiffer shaft for pushing at the trailing end. The longer and smoother the transition between stiff portion and floppy portion, the more resistance to kinking the catheter has. The pushability property of PTA catheters takes on a different meaning in over-the-wire ap-

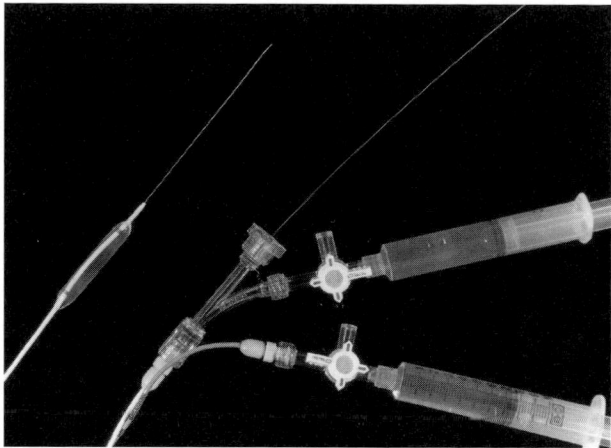

Figure 2-11. Catheter setup for over-the-bifurcation work that enables contrast material injection without losing wire position and without allowing kinking of the balloon port or central lumen at the aortic bifurcation. The procedure for contralateral superficial femoral PTA would be (1) catheterize the contralateral superficial femoral artery with a cobra or other curved catheter, (2) replace the 0.035-inch guidewire with a 200-cm, 0.018-inch guidewire, (3) place the PTA balloon (5 French) over 0.018-inch wire to the site of lesion, (4) dilate, (5) deflate and withdraw the balloon catheter but leave wire in position across the treated area, and (6) perform angiogram through Y adapter.

plications (i.e., most circumstances encountered in peripheral PTA). Here the angiographer is able to use the stiffness of the guidewire to support the catheter as it is being pushed through the lesion. Even under such circumstances, it is helpful to use an angioplasty balloon catheter with a well-tapered tip and a low profile. Perhaps the epitome of reliance on the guidewire for support as the catheter is pushed through a lesion is the pull-through technique for recanalization PTA and stenting of chronic iliac occlusions (Fig. 2-12).

Balloon Catheter Tip

Balloon catheter tips should taper well to fit the guidewire and to aid in crossing stenoses. An excessively bulky or poorly tapered tip design can result in a catheter that will not cross severe stenoses, even over a stiff guidewire. A poorly tapered tip and poor pushability of the shaft make an especially undesirable combination. The only other major property of balloon catheter tips is length. In many applications, such as retrograde balloon PTA of the common iliac artery, tip length may not be an issue. However, wherever branch vessels beyond the catheter tip are susceptible to tip trauma (as in renal artery and tibial applications), a short tip length is required.

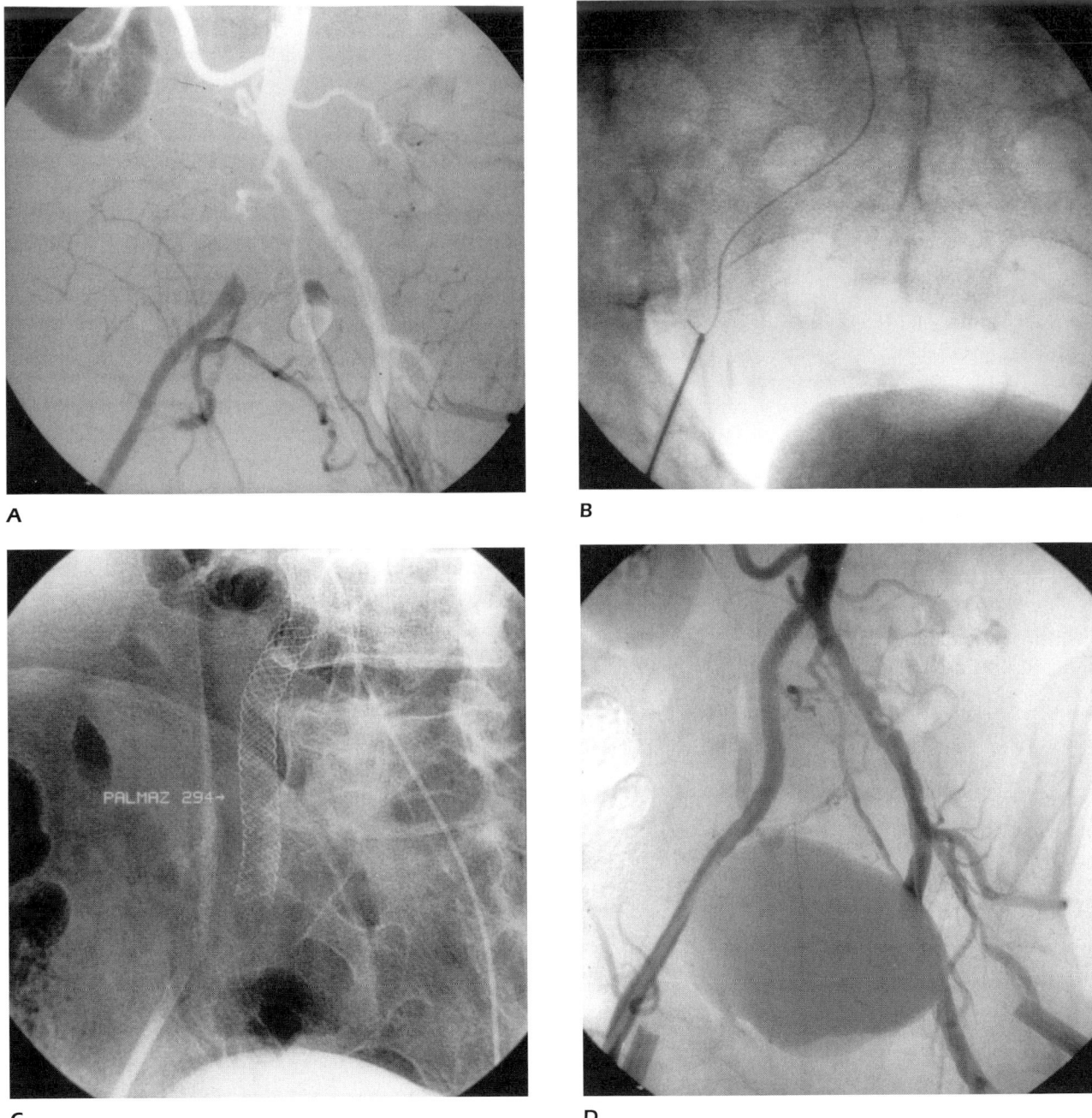

A

B

C

D

Figure 2-12. Pull-through method for recanalization, PTA, and stenting of chronic iliac artery occlusions. (A) Arteriogram of right common iliac artery occlusion in a patient with claudication. Early arterial phase film is used for subtraction mask; the result is black and white arteries due to late filling of the right external iliac artery by collaterals. (B) After a sidewinder catheter has been used to successfully pass a wire through the occlusion from a contralateral approach, the wire is snared from the right with a snare through a sheath that has been placed in the right groin. (C) Stents are placed using a right retrograde approach. (D) Completion angiogram shows an excellent anatomic result.

Balloon Inflation and Deflation Times

Even though the "flow" of dilute contrast material through the balloon port of a PTA catheter during inflation and deflation is not laminar, it is useful to think of it as such to understand the factors contributing to observed inflation and deflation times. Modern PTA catheters have a low profile and a proportionately small diameter balloon port or channel. "Flow" of liquid through this channel is proportional to the fourth power of the radius. It is also inversely related to the length of the catheter. Therefore, if we compare two 12-mm-diameter PTA balloon catheters that have the same-diameter balloon ports but different lengths, one 40 cm and the other 80 cm, we find that the 80-cm catheter takes approximately twice as long to deflate as the 40-cm one.

Stent Compatibility

Stent compatibility may be thought of as that property or collection of properties of a balloon catheter that determine its suitability as a delivery device for balloon-expandable stents. As of this writing, only one balloon-expandable stent, the Palmaz balloon-expandable intraluminal stent (Johnson and Johnson Interventional Systems) is available for human use in the United States, although others are in development. Therefore, at present, a stent-compatible balloon catheter is appropriately considered to be one that is suitable for deploying a Palmaz stent. Desirable properties such balloons should possess for peripheral vascular work include a sufficiently low profile with the stent mounted to pass through a 7 French sheath with hemostatic valve, resistance to slippage of the stent on the balloon surface during passage through the sheath and deployment, and scratch resistance. Most of the 5 French PTA balloon catheters fulfill the profile criterion, and virtually all of these balloons allow manual crimping of the stent sufficient to avoid slippage during passage through the sheath to the target site. However, once balloon inflation begins, two serious problems can still occur. The first, slippage off the balloon surface, occurs with balloons that have coatings to reduce friction and enhance lesion crossability. Therefore, it is unwise to choose these balloons as a first choice for stent deployment. The second problem that can occur is balloon rupture. This tends to happen with scratch-sensitive balloons. These balloons lose their structural integrity when scratched by a stent or even by a sharp, calcified plaque. Both balloon rupture during stent deployment and stent slippage off the balloon surface during deployment may lead to loss of the stent in the vessel or in a nontarget vessel. Figure 2-13 depicts a situation in which a balloon catheter exchange was required to salvage a stenting procedure after a partial deployment. Although no carefully controlled trials are available to compare the utility and safety of the various balloon types in stent deployment, many experienced interventionalists have concluded that Duralyn (nylon) balloons are the most scratch-resistant (least likely to develop holes and fail during stent deployment). The next most scratch-resistant balloons are PE. Of the balloon materials in common usage in peripheral PTA, PET is the most scratch-sensitive. The experience in the author's institution is that approximately 30 to 40 percent of attempted stent deployments with PET balloons result in rupture and a need to exchange balloon catheters. With Duralyn, balloon ruptures still occur but much less frequently (5–10 percent of attempted deployments). Because of these differences, Duralyn is an excellent choice of balloon material for stent deployment. The author has deployed up to five iliac stents in a procedure using a single 5 French Duralyn balloon.

Other Functions of Balloon PTA Catheters

In recent years, the high frequency of postangioplasty restenosis, the economic impact of restenosis, and the added risk to patients of subsequent revascularization procedures have generated widespread interest in basic and clinical research aimed at reducing or eliminating the problem. Approaches have been mechanical (stents, atherectomy), pharmacologic, and even genetic. Current theory holds that once PTA occurs, growth factors cause a fundamental change in medial smooth muscle cells (SMCs) that results in a synthetic rather than a contractile phenotype. These transformed SMCs migrate into the intima and elaborate an organic matrix that constitutes 90 percent of the volume of neointimal hyperplastic tissue. The latter is responsible for most cases of restenosis.

Many of the drugs, cytotoxic agents, and other potentially antiproliferative substances that have been investigated for their ability to control restenosis will never be delivered intravenously because their effects in high doses would be too toxic to patients. Others, including oligopeptides, oligonucleotides, and various drugs cannot be given orally because of their susceptibility to digestive enzymes and the various pH conditions of the stomach and intestine. Therefore, an interest has developed in delivering control substances directly into the target site at the time of PTA. Naturally, the PTA balloon has been considered a potential delivery device for such strategies. Hydrogel-coated angioplasty balloons with the capability of using the hydrogel as a drug delivery vehicle have been used in

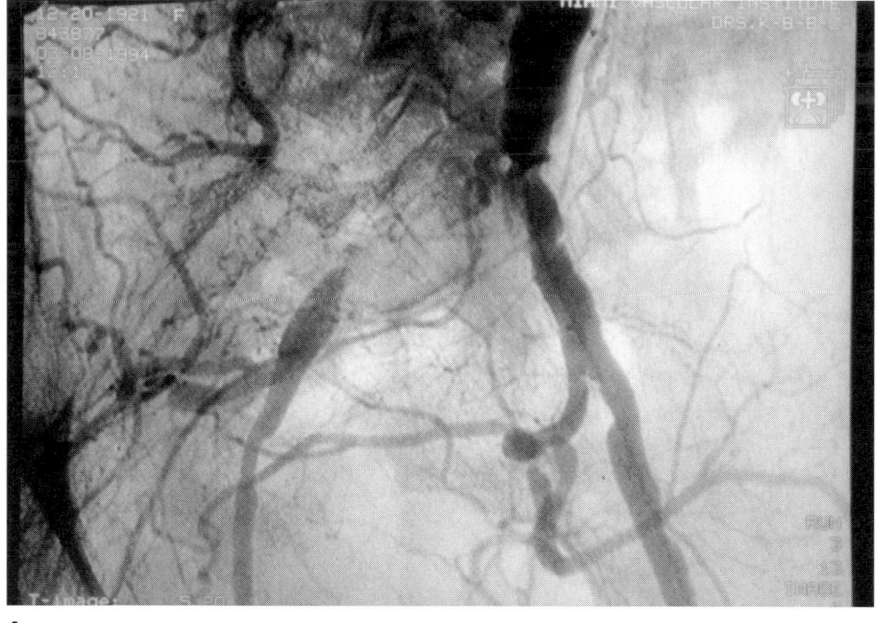

A

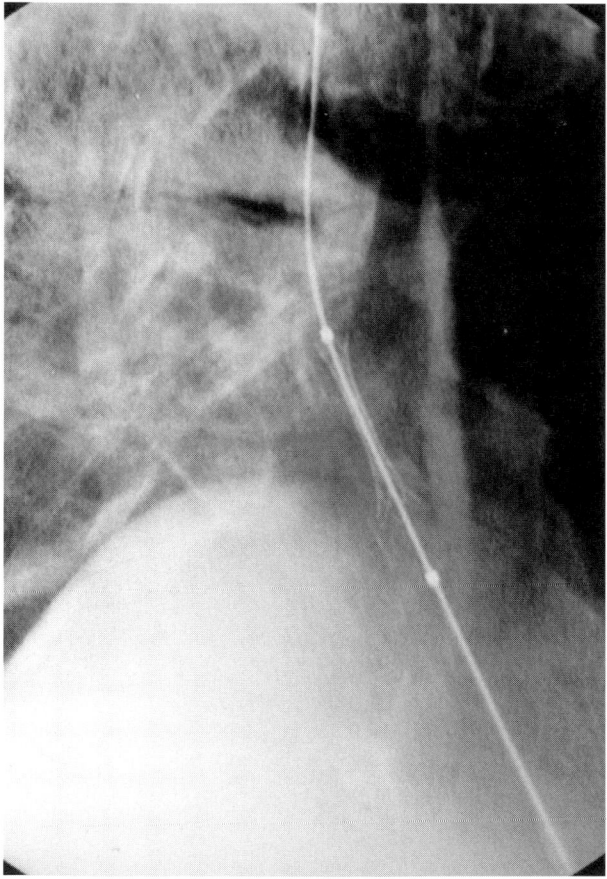

B

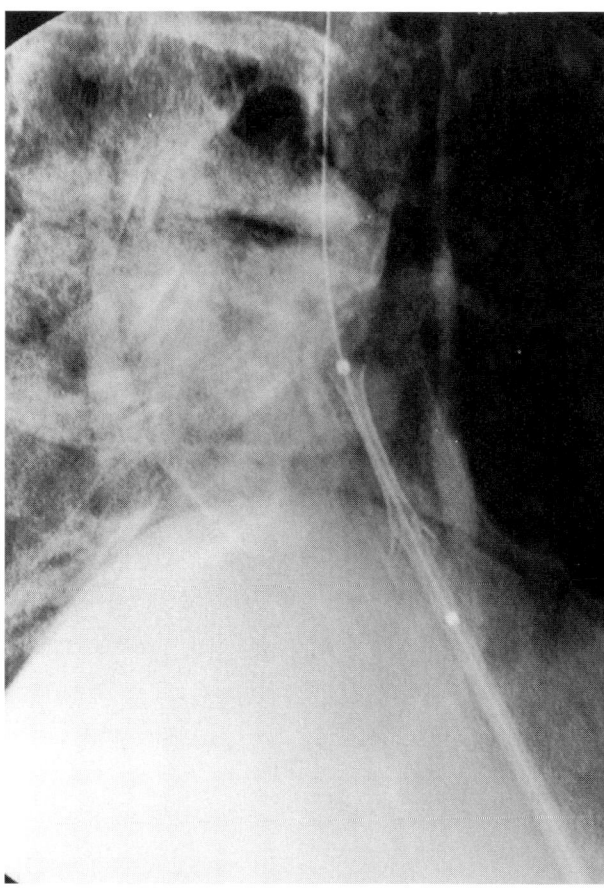

C

Figure 2-13. Patient with bilateral claudication. (A) Preliminary angiogram reveals right iliac occlusion and left iliac stenoses. (B) Attempted stent deployment results in balloon rupture and only partial expansion of the stent (minimal flaring on leading and trailing edges). Attempted rapid expansion of the balloon, first with a 10-ml and then a 5-ml syringe, in an effort to complete stent deployment failed because of a large rent in the balloon. (C) The sheath was advanced to the trailing edge of the stent to prevent stent migration during subsequent manipulations. A decision was made to exchange balloon catheters; however, a 5 French catheter would have been too large to traverse the stent lumen, so a low-profile balloon was used. In preparation for using a low-profile balloon, the 0.035-inch wire was exchanged for an 0.018-inch guidewire. The balloon was withdrawn as the partially flared stent edge was held against the leading edge of the sheath.

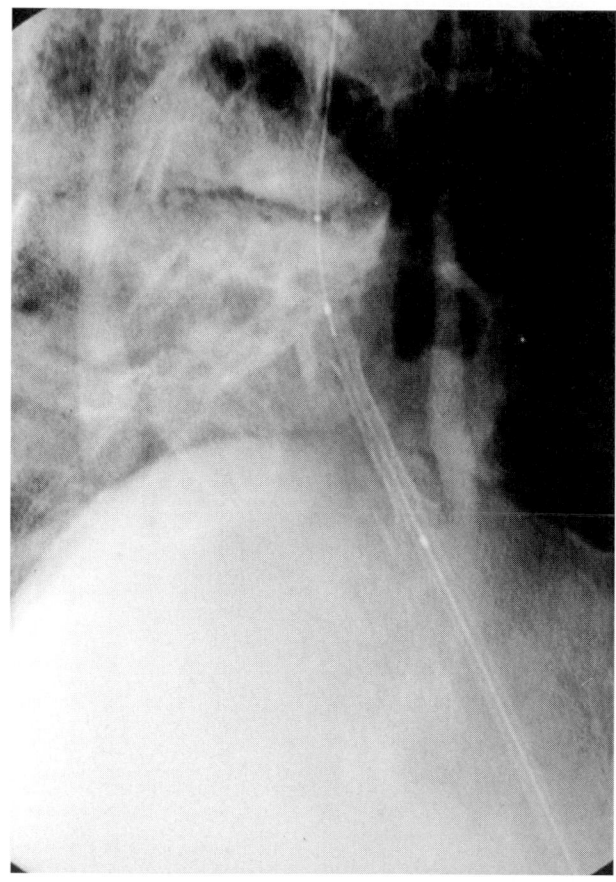

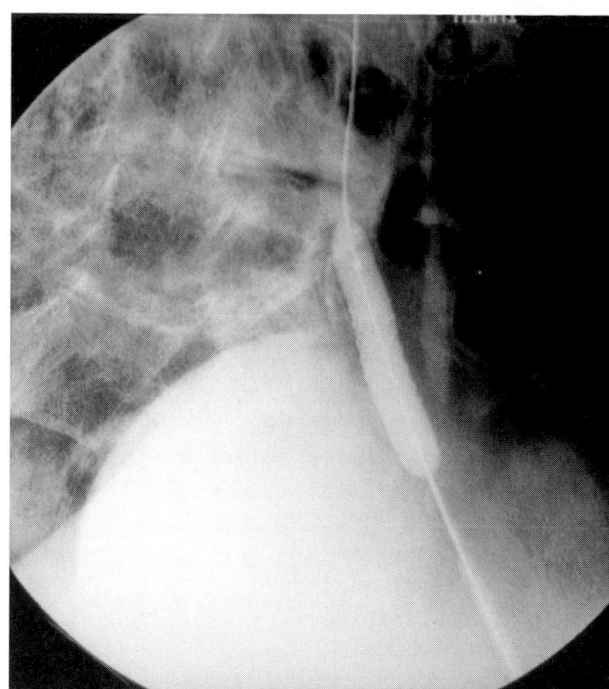

E

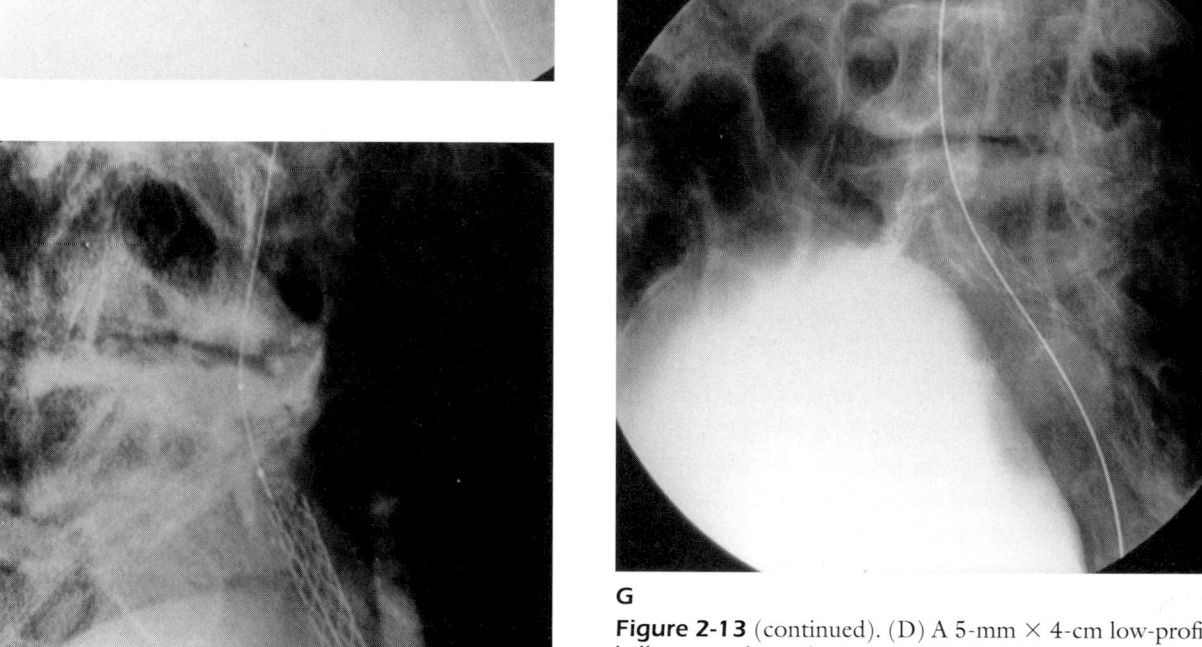

G

Figure 2-13 (continued). (D) A 5-mm × 4-cm low-profile balloon was brought into position inside the stent. (E and F) Preliminary deployment was accomplished with the 5-mm balloon. (G) Deployment was completed with an 8-mm balloon. (H) Completion angiogram after stenting on left and recanalization and stenting on right.

D

F

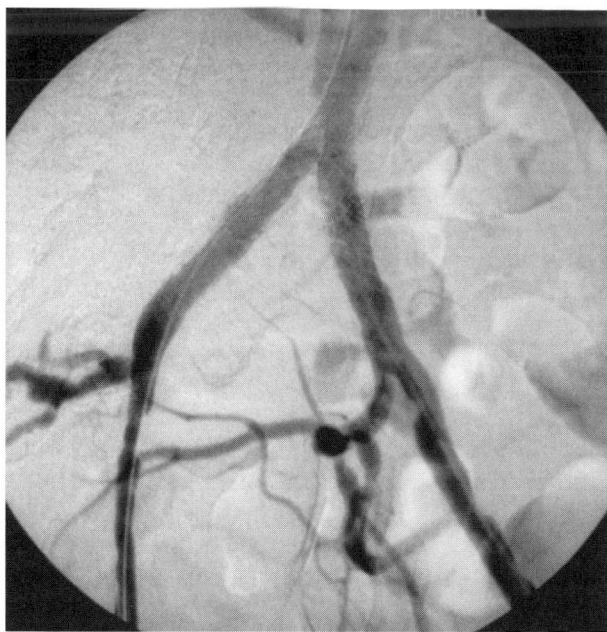

H   **Figure 2-13** (continued).

experiments aimed at this goal.[19] Others have used microporous balloon angioplasty catheters of various types in their own experiments to deliver drugs to the vessel wall.[20-22]

It is also possible that angioplasty balloons could be used to deliver energy to the vessel wall and thus prevent or inhibit restenosis. Radiofrequency energy delivery via a specially modified angioplasty balloon has been proposed as a means of sealing PTA-induced dissections and of molding the vessel wall with PTA without producing a dissection.[23-25] Laser energy has also been delivered via optical fibers in attempts to reduce restenosis.[26,27]

Finally, others have proposed using balloons as a delivery device for liquid polymers that would solidify upon endovascular delivery and "pave" the vessel wall injured by PTA, thereby protecting it from growth factors in the circulation and other substances that may induce restenosis.[28] At the same time, the paved vessel would be protected against closure due to PTA-induced dissection. Some of the polymers proposed include polylactic acids and other substances degradable by the body. Although the mechanical properties of these substances pose problems for the concept of stenting, they offer the possibility of temporary stenting without having to remove a device.

Nomenclature

All interventionalists confront the need to describe the various portions of the balloon catheter in clinical dictation, in writing a scientific report, and in verbal com-

munication with a colleague or assistant during a procedure, or in oral presentations. Inevitably, the terms *proximal* and *distal* spring up as the interventionalist attempts to describe the balloon catheter at a critical point of the procedure. Also inevitably, the interventionalist feels uneasy as he or she realizes his or her uncertainty about which end of the balloon is which. For example, in a PTA of the cavoatrial junction for Budd-Chiari syndrome, if the balloon is placed from a transfemoral approach so that it is partially across the cavoatrial junction, partially in the right atrium, and partially in the inferior vena cava, which end of the balloon is "proximal"? If one said the end in the inferior vena cava, one has probably been consistent with one's own common practice of referring to the end of the balloon closest to the operator as "proximal." However, the truth is that the term *proximal* has no meaning without anatomic reference points. When anatomic references are chosen, it is always the centralmost position that is proximal; therefore, the right atrial end would be the correct answer. The problem is that since the catheter itself is nonanatomic, it cannot have a proximal or distal end.

In a previous publication, the author made a plea with the interventional community to avoid this confusion by abandoning attempts to use the terms *proximal* and *distal* with respect to devices, and to replace them with terms that would be consistently understood in the context of the action that is taking place.[29] The terms are *leading* and *trailing*. Whenever there is a need to describe the catheter in use or a portion thereof, it is simple to refer to the leading end and the trailing end. For example, in the case described above, a rather precise description can derive from applying these terms to the radiopaque markers on the balloon catheter: "with the wire tip in the superior vena cava, the trailing marker of the balloon catheter was positioned 2 cm below the stenotic cavoatrial junction, while the leading marker was midatrial." The terminology works for guidewires and diagnostic catheters as well.

Stents and other devices for deployment are unique. The terminology works for stents, as long as they are on the catheter up to and including the time of deployment. As long as a stent is on its delivery catheter, it has a leading and trailing end, to which one can refer until it is delivered. Once it is deployed, it is free of the operator and of any ongoing action. It therefore assumes the anatomic reference points of the body tube or cavity it inhabits. If a stent were being deployed in the above example, during the deployment the end of the stent nearest the leading tip of the catheter would be the leading end of the stent, and that nearest the trailing end of the catheter would be the trailing end of the stent. Once it was deployed, *leading* and *trailing* would no longer have meaning. The atrial end of it would be proximal and the inferior vena caval end would be distal. The same principles apply to inferior vena cava filters and other devices that are deployed in the body.

Widespread adoption of these simple rules about nomenclature would improve our spoken and written communications about devices and procedures immeasurably.

Summary

In less than 2 decades since the beginning of balloon angioplasty, balloon catheter and guidewire technology has advanced in response to clinical need and a competitive marketplace. *High-pressure, low-compliance, controlled-compliance, low-profile, trackable, pushable,* and (for some balloons) *scratch-resistant* are a few of the terms that can be used to accurately describe the modern peripheral PTA balloon catheters now available. Specialty guidewires that are steerable, radiopaque, stiff, floppy, and variable in stiffness are all available. Commonly used wire sizes include 0.014 to 0.018 inch for small-vessel balloon catheters and 0.035 to 0.038 inch for low-profile 5 French balloon catheters. Future development should focus on kink resistance, scratch resistance, stent compatibility, and balloons for delivery of pharmacotherapeutic agents, genes, and biodegradable or bioresorbable stents. Research should also focus on miniaturization of all balloon functions for application in intracranial interventions.

Acknowledgments

I wish to thank Carol A. Mascioli and Tony Chirinos for their kind and skillful assistance with the illustrations in this chapter, and Barry Uchida for providing photographs from the Dotter Museum at the Dotter Institute.

References

1. Dotter CT, Judkins MP. Transluminal treatment of arteriosclerotic obstructions: description of a new technic and a preliminary report of its application. Circulation 1964;30:654–670.
2. Zeitler E, Schoop W, Zahnow W. The treatment of occlusive arterial disease by transluminal catheter angioplasty. Radiology 1971;99:19.
3. Zietler E, Schmidtke J, Schoop W. Die perkutane Behandlung von arteriellen Durchblutungsstorungen der Extremitaten mit Katheter. Vasa 1973;2:401.
4. Porstmann W. Ein neuer Korsett-Ballonkatheter zur transluminalen Rekanalisation nach Dotter unter besonderer Berucksichtigung von Obliterationen an der Beckenarterien. Radiol Diagn (Berlin) 1973;14:239–244.
5. Geddes LA, Geddes LE, eds. The catheter introducers. Chicago: Mobium, 1993:60–61.
6. Dotter CT, Judkins MP, Frische LH. The nonsurgical treatment of iliofemoral arteriosclerotic obstruction. Radiology 1966;86:871–875.
7. Dotter CT, Rosch J, Anderson JM, Antonovic R, Robinson M. Transluminal iliac artery dilation. JAMA 1974;230:117–124.
8. Geddes LA, Geddes LE, eds. The catheter introducers. Chicago: Mobium, 1993:71–77.
9. Gruentzig A, Hopff M. Perkutane Rekanalisation chronischer arterieller Verschlusse mit einem neuen Dilatationskatheter: Modifikation der Dotter-Technik. Dtsch Med Wochenschr 1974;99:2502–2510.
10. Gruentzig AR, Myler RK, Hanna ES, Turina MI. Coronary transluminal angioplasty. Circulation 1977;56(Suppl III):84.
11. Gruentzig A. Transluminal dilation of coronary-artery stenosis. Lancet 1978;1(8058):263.
12. Gruentzig AR, Senning A, Siegenthaler WE. Nonoperative dilatation of coronary-artery stenosis. N Engl J Med 1979;301:61.
13. Abele JE. Balloon catheter technology. In: Castaneda WR, Tadavarthy SM, eds. Interventional radiology. 2nd ed. Baltimore: Williams & Wilkins, 1992:345–350.
14. Abele JE. Balloon catheters and transluminal dilatation: technical considerations. AJR 1980;135:901–906.
15. Gerlock AJ, Regen DM, Shaff MI. An examination of the physical characteristics leading to angioplasty balloon rupture. Radiology 1982;144:421–422.
16. Simonetti G, Rossi P, Pasariello R, et al. Iliac artery rupture: a complication of transluminal angioplasty. AJR 1983;140:989–990.
17. Zollikofer CL, Salomonowitz E, Castaneda-Zuniga WR, Bruhlmann WF, Amplatz K. The relation between arterial and balloon rupture in experimental angioplasty. AJR 1985;144:777–779.
18. Zollikofer CL, Cragg AH, Hunter DW, Castaneda-Zuniga WR, Amplatz K. Mechanism of transluminal angioplasty. In: Castaneda-Zuniga WR, Tadavarthy SM, eds. Interventional radiology. 2nd cd. Baltimore: Williams & Wilkins, 1992:249–297.
19. Consigny PM, Barry JJ, Vitali NJ. Local delivery of an antiproliferative drug with use of hydrogel-coated angioplasty balloons. J Vasc Intervent Radiol 1994;5(1):9–10.
20. Lambert CR, Leone J, Rowland S. The microporous balloon: a minimal-trauma local drug delivery catheter. Circulation 1992;86(4):I-381.
21. Hong MK, Farb A, Unger EF, et al. A new PTCA balloon catheter with intramural channels for local delivery of drugs at low pressure. Circulation 1992;86(4):I-380.
22. Wolinsky H, Lin C-S. Use of the perforated balloon catheter to infuse marker substances into diseased coronary artery walls after experimental postmortem angioplasty. J Am Coll Cardiol 1991;17(Suppl B):174.
23. Becker GJ, Lee BI, Waller BF, et al. Radiofrequency balloon angioplasty: rationale and proof of principle. Invest Radiol 1988;23:810–817.
24. Becker GJ, Lee BI, Waller BF, et al. Potential of radiofrequency balloon angioplasty: weld strengths, dose response relationships, and correlative histology. Radiology 1990;174:1003–1008.
25. Lee BI, Becker GJ, Waller BJ, et al. Thermal compression and molding of atherosclerotic vascular tissue with use of radiofrequency energy: implications for radiofrequency balloon angioplasty. J Am Coll Cardiol 1989;13:1167–1175.
26. Spears JR, Reyes VP, James LM, Sinofsky EL. Laser balloon angioplasty: initial clinical experience. Circulation 1988;78(Suppl II):296.
27. Ferguson JJ, Dear WE, Leatherman LL, et al. A multi-center trial of laser balloon angioplasty for abrupt closure following PTCA. J Am Coll Cardiol 1990;15(Suppl A):25.
28. Slepian MJ, Schindler A. Polymeric endoluminal paving/sealing: a biodegradable alternative to intracoronary stenting. Circulation 1988;78(Suppl II):409.
29. Becker GJ. Suggested standard terms for interventional procedures. J Vasc Intervent Radiol 1993;4:616.

3

Atherectomy Catheters

JOSEPH L. SKEENS
MICHAEL D. DAKE

*A*ll atherectomy catheters are designed to remove atheroma from the wall of stenotic vascular structures. Over the past 5 to 7 years, the clinical evaluation of several catheter designs has led to a clearer understanding of how atherectomy can be used in the primary treatment of atherosclerotic lesions as well as in combination with other techniques, including angioplasty. Atherectomy has also found an unanticipated utility in treating several clinical situations other than routine peripheral occlusive disease.

Atherectomy catheters can be classified by their mechanism of action and method of plaque elimination (Table 3-1). The major mechanisms of action for treating atheroma are extirpative, using cutting and resection, and ablative, using pulverizing or grinding. Methods of plaque elimination include directional, with a cutting window of less than 360 degrees, and circumferential.

The theoretical advantages of atherectomy compared to angioplasty relate to its ability to remove a portion of the atheromatous plaque with relatively little trauma to the remainder of the arterial wall. This material is then retrieved or small particles are allowed to pass antegrade. The common drawback to all atherectomy designs is their inability to reliably assess the position of the device within the lumen and the expected depth of tissue removal relative to normal wall elements.

Atherectomy rather than angioplasty may be indicated whenever there are short, eccentric, or calcified stenoses or atherosclerotic plaques associated with "blue toe syndrome." It may also be used in the treatment of intimal flaps after percutaneous transluminal angioplasty, particularly in the superficial femoral artery. Several niche applications of atherectomy have been explored, including treatment of dialysis access fistulas, both native and transplant renal artery stenosis, and intimal hyperplasia within intravascular stents. Atherectomy may be used as a biopsy tool in the biliary and vascular systems.

The following paragraphs briefly describe the four atherectomy catheters approved by the U.S. Food and Drug Administration (FDA) (Fig. 3-1) as well as the Pullback Atherectomy Catheter, which is investigational. The description includes application, restenosis rate, and complication rate in selected references. For a more detailed understanding of the use of an individual catheter, the reader should contact the manufacturer.

Simpson AtheroCath

Probably the best-evaluated atherectomy catheter is the Simpson peripheral atherectomy catheter (Devices for Vascular Intervention Inc.), which uses either a 0.018- or 0.035-inch fixed-tip guidewire design or an over-the-wire (0.018-inch) configuration. This device uses an eccentric balloon to oppose the resection window of the cylindrical housing against the vessel wall. After the catheter is positioned across the stenosis, the resection window is directed precisely at the lesion. The positioning balloon is then inflated and the atheroma is forced into the cutting chamber. This process is facilitated by imaging in multiple projections and by using real-time fluoroscopic guidance to control the position of the resection window. A hand-held, battery-powered motor drive unit attached to the base of the catheter is activated and rotates the cutter at speeds of approximately 2000 rpm. The rotating blade is manually advanced through the cutting chamber to collect atheromatous debris in the distal collection chamber. When, under fluoroscopic observation, the collecting chamber is full, the catheter can be removed and the atheromatous material can be sent for histopathologic evaluation if desired.

The most suitable application for the Simpson catheter is to treat a short eccentric stenosis (Fig. 3-2), because the 90-degree cutting window allows for directed removal of a focal plaque involving less than 360 degrees of the circumference of the vessel wall. The disadvantage of the design relates to its inability to efficiently treat concentric lesions.

Results of treatment of peripheral vascular disease

Table 3-1. Classification of Atherectomy Catheters

Catheter	Mechanism of Action	Method of Plaque Elimination
Simpson AtheroCath	Directional	Cut and resect
Trac-Wright	Circumferential	Pulverize
Auth Rotoblator	Circumferential	Pulverize
Transluminal Extraction Catheter	Circumferential	Cut with suction removal
Pullback Atherectomy Catheter	Circumferential	Cut and resect

with the Simpson catheter, including both stenoses and occlusions, are varied. A large series of 131 patients with 139 stenoses and 56 occlusions[1] reported initial success in 98 percent of stenoses, with a lesion recurrence rate of 17 percent using angiographic follow-up at a mean time of 17 weeks after atherectomy. Occlusions were successfully recanalized in 100 percent of cases (56 cases, mean length 10.5 cm). Angiographic follow-up was available in 14 cases of treated occlusion, with a 50 percent recurrence rate (5 stenoses, 2 occlusions) at a mean follow-up interval of 17 weeks. Another series[2] reported treatment results for 195 lesions. Initial angiographic results were successful in 90 percent of stenoses treated from the level of the aorta to the tibial arteries; there were no clinical or angiographic follow-up results. These high primary success rates were later confirmed but were found to be associated with a 53 percent lesion recurrence rate at a mean angiographic follow-up time of 5.4 months in 74 patients from a series of 126 patients.[3] In this

series, the lesion recurrence rate was influenced by the site of atherectomy, with a 54 percent restenosis rate in the superficial femoral and popliteal arteries compared to 80 percent in the tibial vessels. These authors also found that the length of the stenosis treated was associated with restenosis. A 100 percent recurrence rate was noted for superficial femoral lesions greater than 10 cm, compared to only 59 percent for those less than 10 cm in length. A series of 77 patients[4] reported initial success in 92 percent of cases with a mean follow-up of 13.5 months. Noninvasive studies demonstrated a 3-year patency rate of 84 percent. These authors found a higher restenosis rate among diabetic patients with no significant difference in restenosis rates based on lesion location, calcification, or eccentricity. Although these series differed greatly in experimental design, they represent larger numbers of patients than the earlier clinical trials.[5,6]

The complications involved in these trials were relatively few in number. One atherectomy series in 100 patients[2] documented 2 cases of distal embolization and 1 case each of delayed occlusion, transient thrombosis, and groin hematoma requiring blood transfusion. Two out of 134 procedures required surgical intervention. In contrast, a series of 77 patients[4] included a 21 percent complication rate, mostly due to groin hematomas; however, 3 puncture site pseudoaneurysms required surgical repair, and 1 case of retroperitoneal bleeding required transfusion. A series of 131 patients[1] described a 6 percent incidence of arterial tear and a 4 percent incidence of distal embolization.

Figure 3-1. Atherectomy catheters. *Top to bottom:* Auth Rotoblator, Transluminal Extraction Catheter (TEC), Trac-Wright, and Simpson AtheroCath.

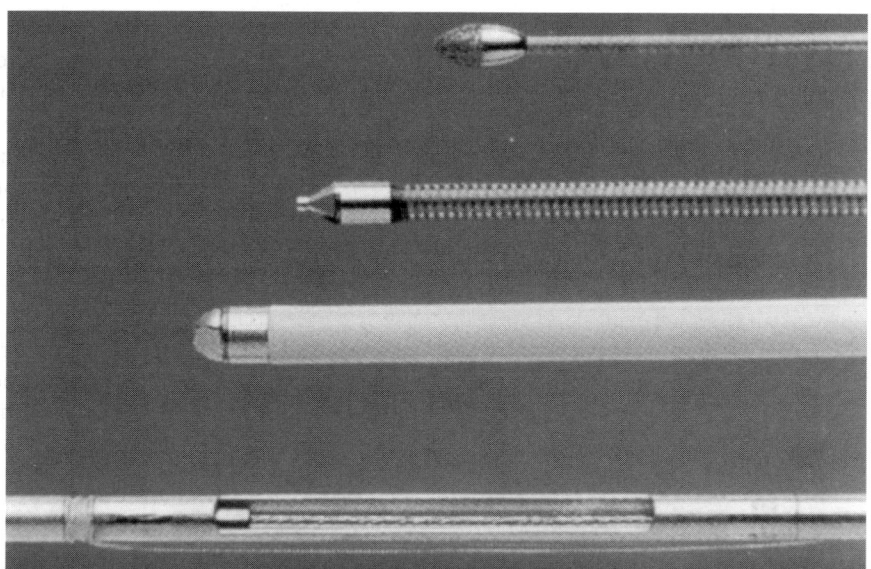

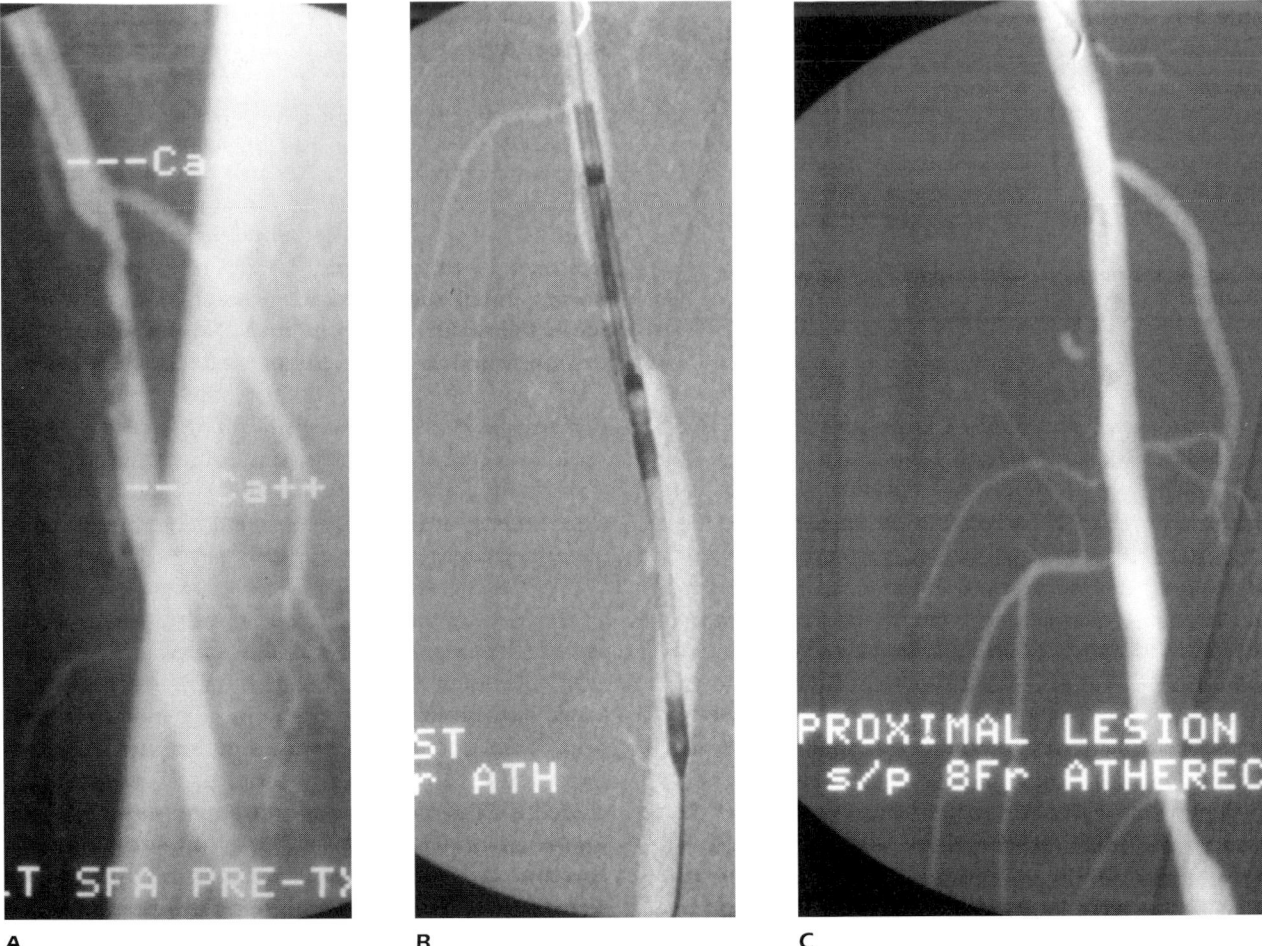

Figure 3-2. (A) Arteriogram demonstrating short segment eccentric superficial femoral artery stenosis. (B) Percutaneous therapy using an 8 F Simpson atherectomy catheter from an antegrade femoral approach. (C) Postatherectomy arteriogram shows no residual stenosis.

Trac-Wright

The Trac-Wright atherectomy catheter (formerly known as the Kensey catheter, Dow Corning Wright) uses an internal torsion-driven wire to drive a rotating cam tip with rotational speed of up to 100,000 rpm. The catheter is advanced to the proximal margin of the stenosis or occlusion with or without the aid of a guidewire, depending on the exact catheter model. Atherectomy is performed with variable rotational speeds from 30,000 to 100,000 rpm, with simultaneous irrigation using an integrated high-pressure system.

Early results in a series of 20 patients with 23 treated extremities[7] demonstrated initial improvement in lumen caliber in 10 of 13 stenoses and in 4 of 10 occlusions of the superficial femoral artery. Follow-up consisted of noninvasive evaluation, with a mean follow-up period of 5.4 months. Stable ankle-arm indices were recorded in all 14 initial successes. A series of 44 patients with 46 femoropopliteal occlusions[8] demonstrated 87 percent immediate success in recanalizing occlusions ranging from 2 to 24 cm in length. In this series, follow-up of 20 of these patients for 12 months resulted in a patency rate of 70 percent. Another series[9] of 12 patients described a 75 percent rate of successful initial recanalization. One group[7] encountered 9 cases of unsuccessful catheter passage with vascular perforation in 8 cases out of 23 treated limbs. Another series[8] encountered 4 cases of vascular perforation in 46 treated lesions. In addition to vascular perforation, distal embolization was encountered in 3 of 46 treated occlusions in one series,[8] in 1 of 23 treated vascular occlusions in another series,[7] and in 1 of 12 cases ultimately requiring above knee amputation in another series.[9]

Overall, the Trac-Wright catheter is perhaps best suited for use in long occlusive lesions; however, the possibility of vascular perforation, particularly in densely calcified lesions, represents a significant drawback of the device.[8] Further, the various reports of distal embolization would support the contention that distal particle microemboli are capable of producing clinically significant vascular occlusions.

Auth Rotoblator

The Auth Rotoblator (Heart Technology) uses a rotating metal burr tip fitted with multiple small (22- to 45-μ) diamond chips driven by an air turbine at rotational speeds of more than 150,000 rpm. The catheter is advanced under fluoroscopic observation with gentle manual pressure over a 0.005-inch central guidewire with a 0.014-inch flexible tip. The Rotoblator is best suited for recanalization of hard, calcified atheromatous lesions, but it initially requires successful passage of a guidewire through occlusive lesions without dissection or perforation.

A series of 20 patients with 25 atherectomy procedures[10] was reviewed, with initial success in 92 percent of cases. Follow-up consisting of noninvasive evaluations showed a cumulative patency rate of 66 percent at 6 months and 17 percent at 2 years. Complications in this series consisted of 5 cases of thrombosis, 4 cases of emboli, 1 case of intimal dissection, and 1 case of limb loss, but no cases of vascular perforation. These authors concluded that the long-term patency rates were poor, with large numbers of thromboembolic complications and restenosis due to late intimal hyperplasia.

Transluminal Extraction Catheter

The Transluminal Extraction Catheter (TEC) (Interventional Technologies) uses rotating cutting blades on a pyramidal distal tip tapered to a 0.014-inch guidewire. A hand-held, battery-powered motor drive unit rotates the blades at speeds of approximately 900 rpm. An externally attached vacuum device removes atheromatous debris through the catheter proximal to the cutter.

In a series of 95 patients with 126 lesions,[9] initial success was achieved in 92 percent of the cases. Six-month angiographic follow-up was available in 16 cases in this series. Four occlusions were noted, all in patients whose original lesion was an occlusion greater than 8 cm in length. The remaining 12 patients with angiographic follow-up had a satisfactory angiographic appearance at the site of atherectomy. Two patients in the series experienced temporary thrombotic occlu-sions that responded to thrombolytic therapy. No cases of vascular perforation or significant distal microembolization were reported in this series.

The TEC catheter may be more advantageous in treating long lesions. Although not specifically addressed in this large series, another author[11] describes significant blood loss, possibly requiring a transfusion, to be a possible limitation because of the suction required to aspirate the atheromatous debris.

Pullback Atherectomy Catheter

Although not yet FDA-approved, the Pullback Atherectomy Catheter (PAC) (Arrow/Med Innovations) consists of a coaxial system with a distal outer cannula with a cutting edge attached to an inner rotating catheter driven by an external motor drive at speeds of approximately 2000 rpm. The catheter is advanced over a 0.018-inch guidewire. This system differs from other atherectomy catheters in its use of simultaneous external compression of the diseased arterial segment around the catheter by a blood pressure cuff and retraction of the rotating cutter through the lesion. The prolapsed atheroma is circumferentially resected and deposited in the collection chamber of the cutter housing. This catheter has the theoretical advantage of being able to remove larger amounts of plaque.

Preliminary results in a series of 8 patients[12] with femoropopliteal stenoses demonstrated a decrease in mean stenosis from 95 to 28 percent with clinical improvement in 75 percent of patients. A series of 12 cases found successful removal of atheroma in all cases with a decrease in mean stenosis from 90 to 30 percent.[13] No significant complications were encountered. Further clinical trials are under way with this new atherectomy device to establish long-term patency rates.

Niche Applications

Although atherectomy catheters were designed and tested with a goal of revascularizing atherosclerotic occlusive disease, several niche applications have been explored in both the vascular and biliary systems. Treatment of stenotic dialysis access fistulas with the Simpson atherectomy device (Fig. 3-3) was reported[14] in 13 patients, with initial success in 10 patients. After a mean follow-up period of 6 months, 7 dialysis fistulas remained patent. Another series of 24 patients with 12 intragraft stenoses and 14 venous outflow stenoses[15] were treated with the Simpson atherectomy catheter. Initial success was achieved in 81 percent of cases with

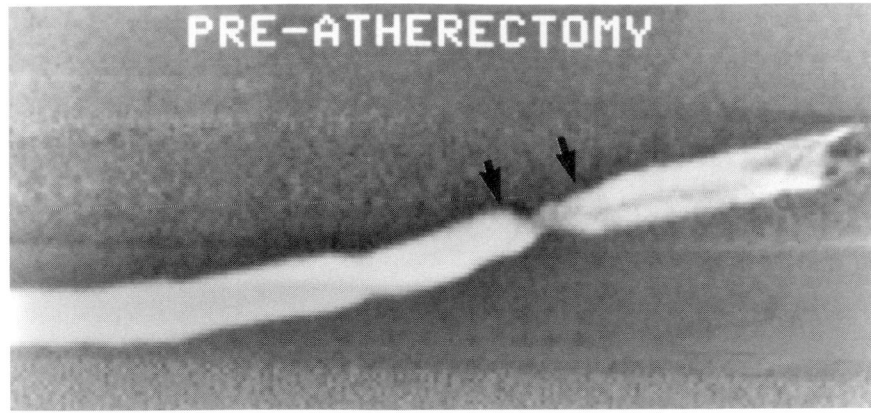

Figure 3-3. (A) Arteriovenous fistulagram demonstrating focal high-grade venous outflow stenosis. (B) Simpson atherectomy catheter in area of stenosis. (C) Postatherectomy fistulagram with no residual luminal stenosis.

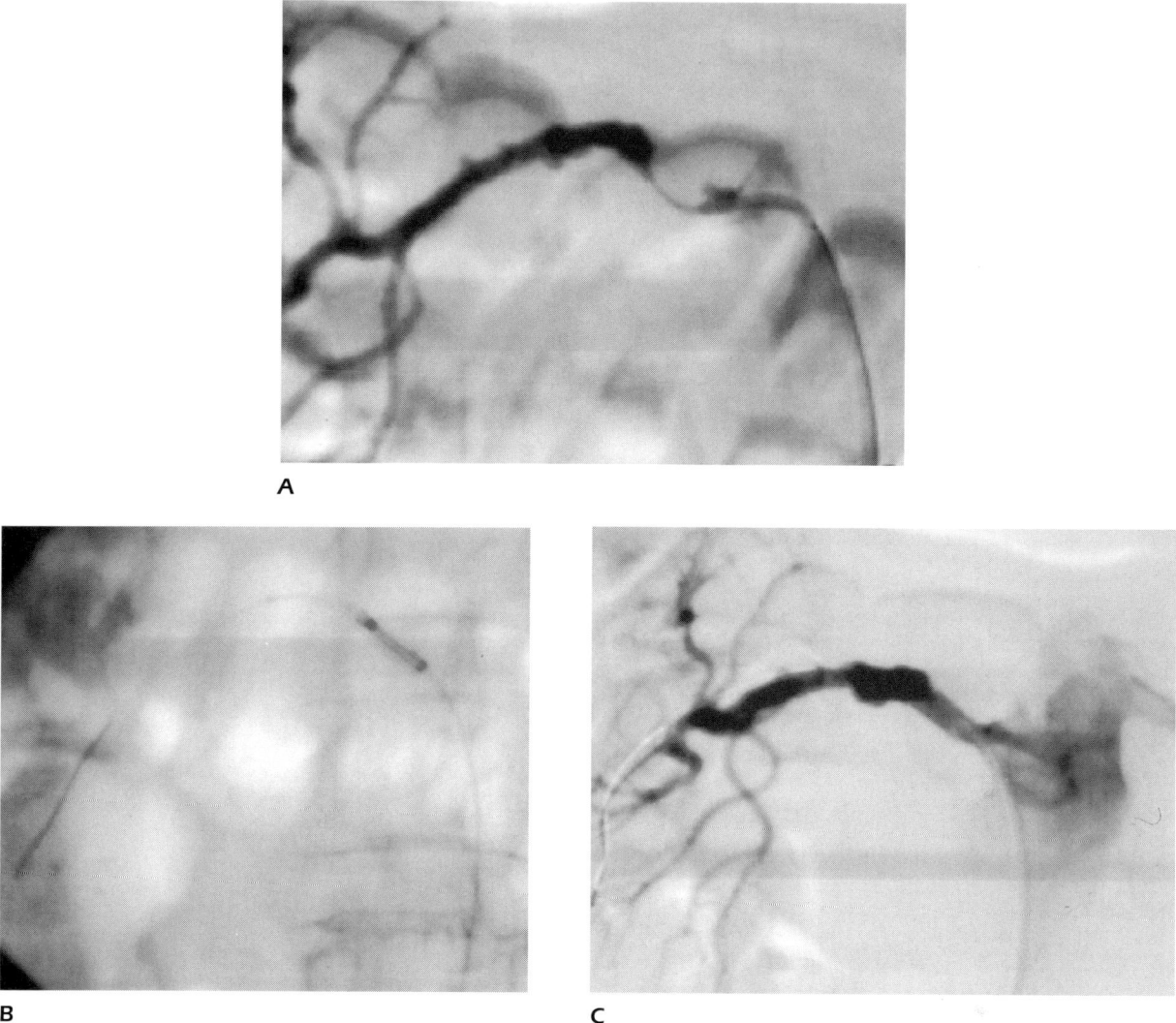

Figure 3-4. (A) Renal arteriogram 6 months after percutaneous transluminal angioplasty demonstrates eccentric, nonostial renal artery stenosis. (B) Simpson atherectomy catheter across area of stenosis. (C) Postatherectomy arteriogram demonstrates less than 20 percent residual diameter stenosis.

venographic follow-up demonstrating 50 percent patency of intragraft stenoses at 6 months and 67 percent patency of subclavian vein stenoses at 6 months. These results would indicate that the patency rates for atherectomy treatment of dialysis access fistulas are similar to and potentially better than those reported for percutaneous transluminal angioplasty. Other intravascular niche applications for directional atherectomy treatment include atherectomy of the aorta[16] and femoral arteries[17] for treatment of "blue toe syndrome,"

atherectomy of vein bypass grafts of the lower extremities, and treatment of renal artery stenosis (Fig. 3-4),[18,19] renal transplant artery stenosis,[20] vascular endoprosthesis restenosis caused by intimal hyperplasia,[21] and postangioplasty obstructive intimal flaps.[22]

The use of the atherectomy catheter as a biopsy device has also been studied in a small number of cases of superior vena cava syndrome[23,24] and common bile duct strictures (Fig. 3-5).[25]

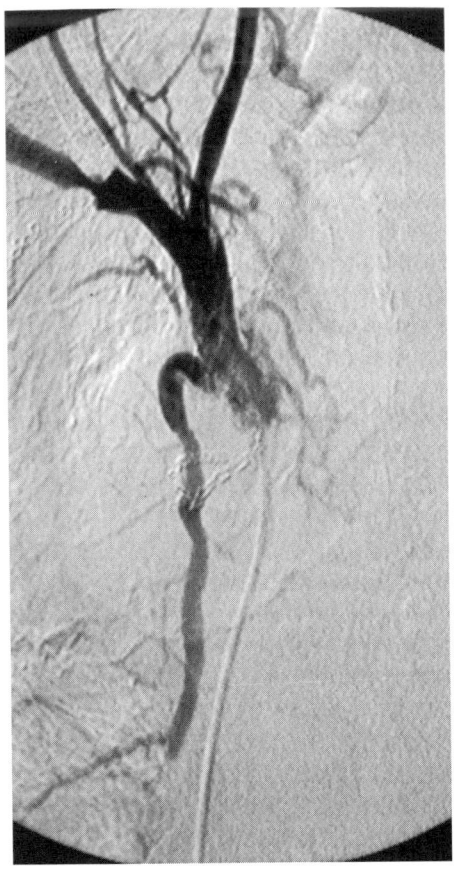

A

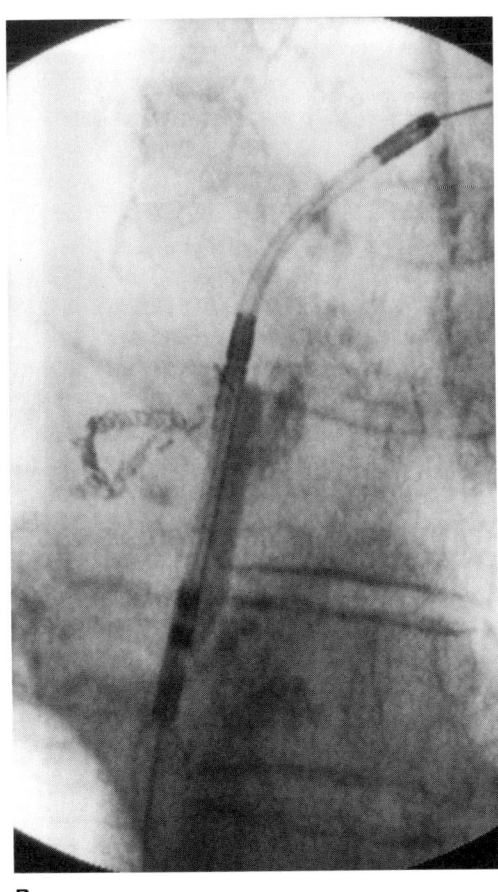

B

Figure 3-5. (A) Superior vena cavogram identifies occlusion of unknown etiology. (B) Percutaneous biopsy using Simpson atherectomy catheter yields soft tissue fragments leading to histologic diagnosis of malignant tumor.

References

1. Dorros G, Lewin RF, Sachdev N, et al. Percutaneous atherectomy of occlusive peripheral vascular disease: stenoses and/or occlusions. Cathet Cardiovasc Diagn 1989;18:1–6.
2. Hinohara T, Selmon MR, Robertson GC, et al. Directional atherectomy: new approaches for treatment of obstructive coronary and peripheral vascular disease. Circulation 1990;81 (Suppl IV):79–90.
3. Dorros G, Iyer S, Lewin R, et al. Angiographic follow-up and clinical outcome of 126 patients after percutaneous directional atherectomy (Simpson AtheroCath) for occlusive peripheral vascular disease. Cathet Cardiovasc Diagn 1991;22:79–84.
4. Kim D, Gianturco LE, Porter DH, et al. Peripheral directional atherectomy: 4-year experience. Radiology 1992;183:773–778.
5. Langes K, Schofer J, Bleifeld W, et al. Catheter atherectomy: functional results in peripheral arterial disease. Angiology 1989; 18:830–834.
6. Wilms G, Pauwels P, Peene P, et al. Percutaneous transluminal atherectomy: preliminary results. Cardiovasc Intervent Radiol 1990;13:18–21.
7. Snyder SO, Wheeler JR, Gregory RT, et al. The Kensey catheter: preliminary results with a transluminal atherectomy tool. J Vasc Surg 1988;8:541–543.
8. Desbrosses D, Petit H, Torres E, et al. Percutaneous atherectomy with the Kensey catheter: early and midterm results in femoropopliteal occlusions unsuitable for conventional angioplasty. Ann Vasc Surg 1990;4:550–552.
9. Wholey MH, Jarmolowski CR. New reperfusion devices: the Kensey catheter, the atherolytic reperfusion wire device, and the transluminal extraction catheter. Radiology 1989;172: 947–952.
10. Ahn SS, Eton D, Yeatman LR, et al. Intraoperative peripheral rotary atherectomy: early and late clinical results. Ann Vasc Surg 1992;6:172–280.
11. Ahn SS. Status of peripheral atherectomy. Surg Clin North Am 1992;72:869–878.
12. Pollack JS, Denny DF, White RI, Fischell RE, Fischell TA, Wilkenson LA. Phase I results of Pullback Atherectomy: potential value of external compression. Radiology 1991;181(Suppl): 295.
13. Benenati JF, Becker GJ, Zemel G, Katzen BT, Brown JA, Semba CP. Initial results with the Pullback Atherectomy Catheter. Radiology 1992;185(Suppl):278.
14. Zemel G, Katzen BT, Dake MD, et al. Directional atherectomy in the treatment of stenotic dialysis access fistula. J Vasc Intervent Radiol 1990;1:35–38.
15. Gray RJ, Dolmatch BL, Buick MK. Directional atherectomy treatment for hemodialysis access: early results. J Vasc Intervent Radiol 1992;3:497–503.
16. Clugston RA, Eisenhauer AC, Matthews RV. Atherectomy of the distal aorta using a "kissing-balloon" technique for the treatment of blue toe syndrome. AJR 1992;159:125–127.
17. Dolmatch BL, Rholl KS, Moskowitz LB, et al. Blue toe syn-

drome: treatment with percutaneous atherectomy. Radiology 1989;172:799–804.

18. Zaitoun R, Dorros F, Lyer SS, et al. Percutaneous high-speed rotational atherectomy (Rotoblator) of a restenosed ostial renal artery: a case report. Catheter Cardiovasc Diagn 1990;20:254–256.

19. Dake MD, Oesterle SN, Robertson GC, Eisenhauer AE, Wexler L, Wittich GW. Percutaneous directional atherectomy for treatment of renal artery stenosis. Radiology 1991;181(Suppl): 295.

20. Polnitz A, Hofling B. Percutaneous atherectomy of a recurrent renal transplant artery stenosis. Transplantation 1989;4:880–883.

21. Vorwerk D, Guenther RW. Removal of intimal hyperplasia in vascular endoprostheses by atherectomy and balloon dilatation. AJR 1990;154:617–619.

22. Maynar M, Reyes R, Cabrera V, et al. Percutaneous atherectomy as an alternative treatment for postangioplasty obstructive intimal flaps. Radiology 1989;170:1029–1031.

23. Castaneda F, Moradian G, Hunter D, et al. Percutaneous intravascular biopsy using a Simpson atherectomy catheter: technical note. Cardiovasc Intervent Radiol 1990;12:342–343.

24. Dake MD, Zemel G, Dolmatch BL, et al. The cause of superior vena cava syndrome: diagnosis with percutaneous atherectomy. Radiology 1990;174:957–959.

25. Kim D, Porter DH, Siegel JB, et al. Common bile duct biopsy with the Simpson atherectomy catheter. AJR 1990;154:1213–1215.

4

Agents for Small-Vessel and Tissue Embolization

MICHAEL C. SOULEN

Since the first crude efforts at embolization of vascular territories in the beginning of the century,[1] highly sophisticated catheterization tools and numerous embolic materials have been developed that permit interventional radiologists to perform vascular occlusion with greater precision than is possible in surgery. Control of hemorrhage and ablation of tumors, organs, and vascular malformations can be accomplished with minimum hazard to nontarget tissues. The proper use of embolization techniques requires an understanding of the vascular anatomy and pathology being treated, the tools used to deliver embolic agent(s), and the embolic agents themselves. This chapter focuses on the embolic agents used in these procedures.

The choice of embolic agent depends on the size of the vessel to be occluded and the duration of occlusion desired. Large-vessel occlusion requires mechanical devices such as coils or balloons, which are discussed in another chapter. Occlusion of higher-order branches on down to the capillary level can be performed with particulate or liquid agents. The most commonly used materials are listed in Table 4-1.

An ideal embolic agent would be precisely sized, nonclumping, highly radiopaque, nontoxic, nonallergenic, and inexpensive. It would allow easily controlled delivery through conventional or microcatheter systems to a specific vascular territory, and would provide reliable occlusion for the desired length of time. None of the agents listed in Table 4-1 meet all these qualifications; rather, each has its particular niche among the varied clinical indications for embolization, with its own nuances in preparation and delivery. It is the task of the interventional radiologist to find the appropriate embolic agent to match the clinical setting and to deliver that agent effectively and safely.

Gelfoam

Gelfoam is an inexpensive gelatin sponge that comes in sterile sheets or in powder form. It causes vascular occlusion by mechanical obstruction, induction of thrombosis, and inflammation of the vessel wall. The gelatin dissolves and permits recanalization of the artery within days to weeks.[2] Since it does not cause permanent occlusion, Gelfoam is useful in treating benign sources of bleeding such as trauma or peptic disease where healing of the underlying lesion is expected, or for temporary devascularization of masses or organs immediately before resection to minimize blood loss.

Arteries 2 to 4 mm in diameter are best embolized with torpedoes of Gelfoam formed by cutting 2- to 3-mm-wide by 5- to 10-mm-long strips with a scissors or scalpel and rolling them between two fingers or against a sterile drape into a tight cigar shape. The torpedo is then loaded into the tip of a 1-ml syringe filled with dilute contrast and injected slowly under fluoroscopic guidance into the target vessel. The catheter should be well seated in the artery to avoid reflux into a nontarget vessel. When smaller branches need to be embolized, such as ramifications of the left gastric artery or pancreaticoduodenal branches off the gastroduodenal artery feeding a peptic bleed, Gelfoam can be cut into 1- to 2-mm pieces and loaded into a 3-ml syringe. This is connected to another 3-ml syringe filled with dilute contrast via a three-way stopcock, and the contrast and Gelfoam are pumped rapidly back and forth to create a slurry. The slurry is carefully injected until near stasis is observed in the distal branch vessels. Torpedoes can be added to embolize the larger parent artery. Care should be taken not to create complete stasis, since injection at that point will cause reflux of

Table 4-1. Commonly Used Embolization Materials

Material	Size	Duration
Biodegradable particles		
Gelatin sponge (Gelfoam)	40 μ–4 mm	2 days–6 weeks
Microfibrillar collagen (Avitene, Angiostat)	5 × 70 μ	1–8 weeks
Starch microspheres (Spherex)	20–70 μ	30–60 min
Permanent particles		
Polyvinyl alcohol sponge	100–1000 μ	
Plastic, glass, and metal microspheres (± encapsulated drugs or radioactivity)	40–500 μ	
Liquids		
Ethanol		
Iodized oil (Ethiodol, Lipiodol)		
Glue		
Sodium tetradecyl sulfate (Sotradecol)		
Boiling contrast		
Hypertonic glucose		

Gelfoam out of the target artery. The slurry is fine enough to pass through a microcatheter. Since it will float upward in the contrast-filled syringe, the syringe should be pointed up during injection to avoid clumping of the Gelfoam in the back of the syringe. When slurry is used in the gastroduodenal artery to treat duodenal hemorrhage, coil blockade of the proximal right gastroepiploic artery can be performed to protect the greater curve of the stomach and direct the slurry into the pancreaticoduodenal branches.

Gelfoam powder measures 40 to 60 μ and, because of clumping, causes occlusion of vessels 100 to 200 μ in diameter. This distal level of embolization is beyond most collaterals and so causes more severe ischemia than slurry or torpedoes. Gelfoam powder is good for preoperative embolization of tumors or organs but should not be used in the gut because of the risk of tissue necrosis.

Microfibrillar Collagen

Avitene and Angiostat are preparations of collagen fibers derived from cowhide. The fibers are 5 μ in diameter by 70 to 200 μ in length, and they cause vascular occlusion at the 25- to 250-μ level. Avitene causes a granulomatous reaction, whereas Angiostat is inert and works primarily by mechanical obstruction of the lumen.[3,4] Recanalization of the vessels begins at about a week and continues over 1 to 2 months. The collagen itself is broken down and resorbed after 3 months. As with Gelfoam powder, the small size of the collagen fibers makes them unsuitable for embolization of the gut because of the risk of infarction. Collagen is useful for tumor embolization, either preoperatively or palliatively, and has been used for chemoembolization in the liver. The small fibers when suspended in contrast are easily administered through microcatheters.

Starch Microspheres

These biodegradable particles are manufactured from potato starch. They are spherical, precisely sized, and deformable to allow easy passage through microcatheters. The starch is rapidly metabolized by amylase, with a half-life of 25 minutes, so the ischemia is short-lived but intense because of the peripheral level of occlusion. The primary application is for chemoembolization, to allow a high level of drug extraction with only transient ischemia.[5]

Polyvinyl Alcohol

Polyvinyl alcohol (PVA) is an inert plasic sponge that comes in blocks or sheets or that is ground into coarsely shaped particles of graded dimensions from 100 to 1000 μ. It causes permanent mechanical occlusion of the vessel lumen with subsequent ingrowth of thrombus and fibrin.[6] The irregular, cratered surface of the particles makes them prone to clump into aggregates, so that occlusion occurs at the level of vessels larger than the nominal size of the particles used. Occlusion of the catheter lumen is an occasional problem as well, particularly if the suspension of particles is too thick. Suspensions of PVA can be created by pouring a 1-ml vial into 25 ml of contrast in a sterile metal bowl and then placing the tip of a 3- to 5-ml syringe below the surface of the contrast and pumping the plunger to agitate. Care should be taken not to cause air bubbles, which trap the particles. A lower ratio of particles to contrast can be used for smaller or less vascular territories, such as spinal malformations. An alternative method is to pack 0.1 to 0.2 ml of PVA into a 5-ml syringe and then connect this via a three-way stopcock to another 5-ml syringe filled with dilute contrast and pump back and forth, described above for making Gelfoam slurry. Only particles less than 250 μ should be injected through microcatheters to avoid clogging the catheter. Like Gelfoam, PVA particles tend to float in contrast, so the syringe must be pointed upward during injection to avoid clumping at the back of the barrel.

The permanence and distal level of occlusion caused by PVA make it well suited for treatment of arteriovenous malformations and tumors.

Other Permanent Particles

A variety of microspheres made from organic compounds, glass, or metal exist or are under development, particularly outside the United States. Features of these particles include smooth, spherical geometry; precise sizing; coatings or materials that expand on contact with blood to occlude vessels larger than the delivery catheter; and incorporation of radioactive or chemotherapeutic agents. Reported applications include treatment of neurovascular lesions, peripheral vascular malformations, and tumors.

Liquid Embolization Agents

Unlike particles, which by virtue of their size are arrested at a precapillary level, liquid sclerosants can pass to the capillary level and through to the venous circulation. This feature makes them desirable agents when tissue destruction is warranted, such as for ablation of tumors, organs, veins, or vascular malformations. Vascular occlusion occurs from a combination of thrombosis and destruction of the vessel endothelium, which is usually permanent.

Liquid sclerosants are more challenging to use than particulates. Their lack of radiopacity and their deeper penetration into tissue make their distribution harder to control and increase the risk of nontarget embolization. A typical example would be the use of alcohol to ablate a renal tumor. Alcohol washing through the tumor is harmless because of rapid dilution in the high-flow renal venous system; however, perfusion of angiographically occult retroperitoneal branches communicating with perineural vasculature can cause paralysis, and undetected reflux into the aorta can lead to visceral infarction. The use of an occlusion balloon to deliver liquid sclerosants is therefore recommended whenever possible. The usual technique is to inflate the occlusion balloon in the renal artery and inject enough contrast to determine the volume of contrast needed to fill the tumor. The balloon is then deflated, the alcohol drawn up, the balloon reinflated, and the alcohol injected. The balloon is left up for a few minutes to allow for thrombosis to occur, and the catheter is aspirated before the balloon is deflated to remove any alcohol remaining in the artery and in order to prevent reflux into the aorta. If an occlusion balloon cannot be used, then the alcohol can be made partially radiopaque by shaking it with Ethiodol in a 8:2 or 7:3 ratio.[7] The suspended oil droplets make it possible to observe the flow of the alcohol fluoroscopically. The oil also improves the distribution and embolic effect of the alcohol.[8]

When liquid agents are used to sclerose the gonadal vein in the treatment of a varicocele, the inguinal ring must be compressed to prevent reflux into the scrotum and testicular infarction.[9]

References

1. Dawbarn G. The starvation operation for malignancy in the external carotid area. JAMA 1904;43:792–795.
2. Barth KH, Strandberg JD, White RI Jr. Long-term follow-up of transcatheter embolization with autologous clot, Oxycel, and Gelfoam in domestic swine. Invest Radiol 1977;12:273–280.
3. Kaufman SL, Strandberg JD, Barth KL, White RI Jr. Transcatheter embolization with microfibrillar collagen in swine. Invest Radiol 1978;13:200–204.
4. Daniels JR, Kerlan RK, Dodds L, et al. Peripheral hepatic arterial embolization with crosslinked collagen fibers. Invest Radiol 1987;22:126–131.
5. Civalleri D, Esposito M, Fulco RA, et al. Liver and tumor uptake and plasma pharmacokinetics of arterial cisplatin administered with and without starch microspheres in patients with liver metastases. Cancer 1991;68:988–994.
6. Castañeda-Zuñiga WR, Sanchez R, Amplatz K. Experimental observations on short- and long-term effects of arterial occlusion with Ivalon. Radiology 1978;126:783–785.
7. Soulen MC, Faykus MH, Shlansky-Goldberg RD, et al. Elective embolization for prevention of hemorrhage from renal angiomyolipomas. J Vasc Intervent Radiol 1994;5:587–591.
8. Wright KC, Loh G, Wallace S, et al. Experimental evaluation of ethanol-Ethiodol for transcatheter renal embolization. Cardiovasc Intervent Radiol 1990;13:309–313.
9. Hunter DW, Castañeda-Zuñiga WR, Coleman CC, et al. Spermatic vein embolization with hot contrast medium or detachable balloons. Semin Intervent Radiol 1984;1:163–166.

5

Mechanical Embolic Agents

JEFFREY S. POLLAK
ROBERT I. WHITE, JR.

The last two decades have seen tremendous growth in the availability and refinement of methods for transcatheter occlusive therapy. Advances in agents for embolization and in catheter and guidewire technology have increased the reach of the interventional radiologist in treating a variety of pathologic conditions, from traumatic hemorrhage to congenital arteriovenous malformations. Although this chapter centers on mechanical embolization agents, it is important to remember that these agents often need to be used in conjunction with other methods. Furthermore, as the size of available mechanical devices continues to shrink, the distinction between these and particulate embolization agents has started to blur.

General Concepts

The ideal vascular occlusive agent should have the ability to do the following:

1. Permit simple and easy delivery to the desired location
2. Test-occlude, reversing the occlusion if it is improper in location
3. Reliably occlude for the desired time
4. Spare other vascular structures
5. Be stable over time
6. Be biologically inert other than for producing vascular occlusion
7. Be inexpensive

Methods for embolization can be categorized by the duration of effect and the type of agent. Resorbable agents such as Gelfoam generally give temporary occlusion, although permanent occlusion may result, especially when there is poor collateral flow and necrosis occurs. Nonresorbable agents usually give permanent occlusion. The types of agents include liquids, particulates, mechanical devices, and coagulants. Liquid and particulate agents tend to give distal occlusion, whereas mechanical agents are generally larger

and tend to give proximal vessel occlusion. Large embolic agents give selective occlusion at the site of the agent with variable thrombosis of vessels distally and proximally, depending on the adequacy of collateral flow. In effect, they simulate surgical ligation.

Early descriptions of percutaneously introduced mechanical occlusive agents appeared in the mid-1970s with several reports of detachable balloons[1-4] and the development of the wool coil.[5] Extensive experience with these agents since then has resulted in a better understanding of their roles and clinical indications. Mechanical agents are most useful when they can be placed directly within or across the origin of the vascular structure to be occluded (such as the origin of an arteriovenous fistula). In addition to being able to occlude large fistulas or shunts, they are useful for treating aneurysms or pseudoaneurysms, large-vessel hemorrhage, and in redistributing blood flow away from nontarget organs before transvascular therapy of the target organ. These devices have more limited roles in treating small-vessel hemorrhage, arteriovenous malformations, and in causing tumor or organ infarction. They also have a variety of nonvascular uses.

Mechanical embolization agents can be considered in the following categories:

1. Metal-based agents
   a. Wires with threads (coil emboli)
   b. Bare wires
   c. Wires that induce electroocclusion
   d. Metal devices with attached occlusive plugs (e.g., polyvinyl alcohol foam)
2. Balloons
   a. Nondetachable (occlusion balloon)
   b. Detachable
3. Other devices
   a. Devices for closing defects and shunts associated with congenital heart disease
   b. Endovascular grafts
   c. Plain threads
   d. Bristle brushes
   e. Lasers that induce occlusion

55

Metal-Based Emboli

Reports on the insertion of wire to produce thrombosis of aortic aneurysms appeared as early as 1864.[6] Although results were suboptimal,[7] this technique continued to be popular in this century, with and without the addition of an electrical current to produce electrothermic coagulation.[8] In 1975, Gianturco et al.[5] described two novel occlusive devices designed for percutaneous transcatheter delivery, both consisting of a combination of metal and threads.

Wires with Threads (Coil Emboli)

The first of the devices described by Gianturco was a 3-mm-long 19-gauge piece of steel tubing with cotton threads attached to it, and the second was the original steel coil embolus (Fig. 5-1). This consisted of a 5-cm-long coiled piece of 0.038-inch-gauge steel guidewire with its central mandrel core removed and four 3-cm-long woolen strands attached to its tip. This was introduced into a 7 French nontapered Teflon catheter by a thin mandrel extending from a 19-gauge steel tubing. The mandrel fit inside the core of the wire embolus, straightening it for placement within the catheter. A 0.045- or 0.052-inch guidewire was then used to advance the device through the catheter.

Early experience demonstrated that complete vascular occlusion rapidly developed in the local segment containing these devices,[9–11] although several coils were needed in larger vessels. Whereas the metal and fabric created physical obstruction of the vessel lumen,

more complete occlusion was due to the formation of thrombus. Both animal and clinical studies showed long-term occlusion on follow-up. Late recanalization appeared to be a rare phenomenon.[12] Histologic studies depicted intraluminal thrombus and a dense, granulomatous inflammatory reaction extending to the perivascular tissue, with destruction of the vessel wall.[10,11,13] This intense reaction appeared related to the wool, and in at least one instance appeared to result in the development of an aneurysm 4 months after embolization.[14] Plain steel coils were less likely to cause vessel occlusion because of inadequate wire coiling and insufficient thrombus formation.[10,13] Indeed, multiple bare wires are needed to produce complete obstruction.

Over the next few years, refinements[15,16] resulted in thinner embolization coils, permitting their use through conventionally tapered 5 French catheters, and, more recently, the development of coil emboli for use through 3 French or smaller catheter systems.[17–19] In addition, wool has been replaced by polyester (Dacron), which creates a less severe inflammatory reaction in the vessel wall.

Material

A host of coil or spring emboli are available in varying wire sizes, lengths, coiled diameters, and shapes. The conventional steel coil embolus (Cook, Inc.) consists of a short length of guidewire with multiple polyester strands attached transversely along most of its length between the turns of the wire (Fig. 5-2). These devices come prepackaged and stretched out in metal cartridges, eliminating the need for a special mandrel in-

Figure 5-1. Original steel spring coil embolus with woolen strands attached to its tip. (Courtesy of James H. Anderson, Ph.D.)

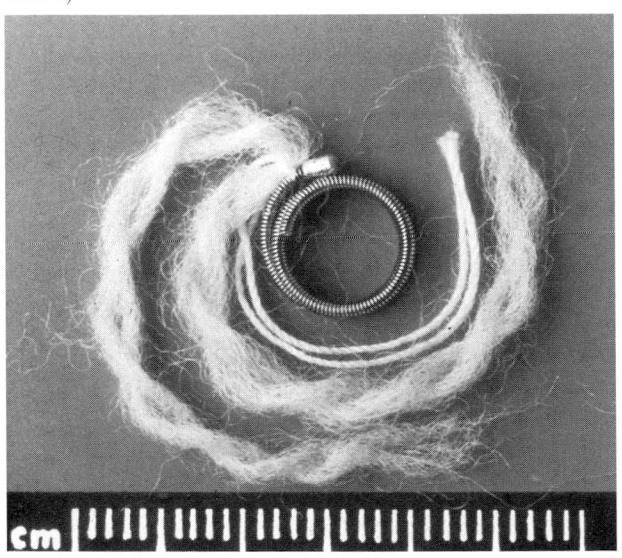

Figure 5-2. An 8-mm-diameter, 5-cm-long conventional 0.038-inch-gauge coil embolus (Cook, Inc.). Resting coiled shape at bottom, stretched out appearance in center, and cartridge at top. The polyester threads are well demonstrated on the elongated coil.

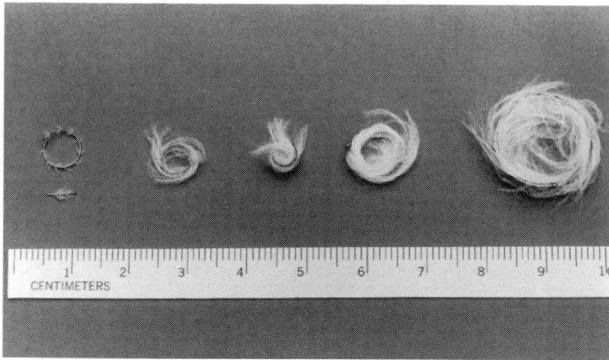

Figure 5-3. Coils available from Cook, Inc. *Left to right:* coiled and straight 0.018-inch Hilal Microcoils, 0.025-inch coil, and three varying-diameter 0.038-inch coils. (Courtesy of Cook, Inc.)

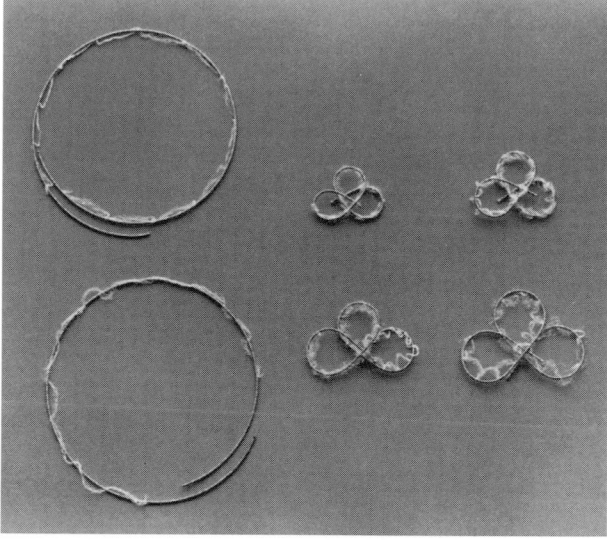

Figure 5-4. Several 0.018-inch-gauge fibered occlusive devices made by Target Therapeutics. *Left:* 20- and 30-mm-diameter "vein of Galen" coils; *right:* various-diameter complex helical coils.

Figure 5-5. Conventional coil exiting a catheter. (Courtesy of Cook, Inc.)

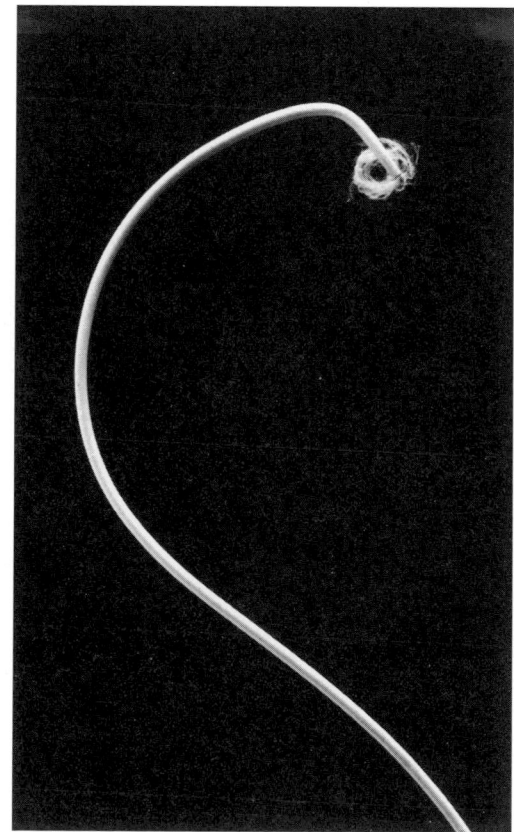

troducer and permitting their delivery through conventional 5 French, 0.035- and 0.038-inch tapered catheters using conventional, floppy guidewires. Helical diameters of 3, 5, and 8 mm are stocked, but diameters of 4, 10, 12, and 15 mm can be ordered as well (Fig. 5-3). In addition, 0.052-inch wires are available in coiled diameters up to 20 mm.

Spring emboli for use through microcatheter systems are also available. The 0.025-inch coils (see Fig. 5-3) come in diameters between 2 and 5 mm and can be delivered through the T3.0S (Cook) or the Cragg infusion wire (Medi-Tech). The 0.018-inch platinum wire emboli, with and without threads, are made by Cook (Hilal Embolization Microcoils) (see Fig. 5-3) and Target Therapeutics (Fig. 5-4). These are recommended for use with 0.018-inch inner lumen catheters, such as the Tracker 18 (Target Therapeutics), although the authors have had no difficulty delivering them through the T3.0S or Cragg wire as well. Target supplies complex helical shapes that provide greater cross-sectional coverage of the vessel lumen as well as "vein of Galen" coils that reach diameters of 30 mm. The 0.025- and 0.018-inch emboli have extended the use of coil occlusion to small and peripherally located vascular lesions.

Technique

Coil embolization depends on selective catheterization of the vessel to be occluded. Because of the potential need for a variety of catheter shapes and the possibility that a catheter still containing a coil may need to be removed prematurely, the authors recommend using a sheath. The coil is usually deposited just distal to the tip of the catheter (Fig. 5-5); however, when the coil's diameter is smaller than the vessel's, it will migrate, potentially to an improper position. For this

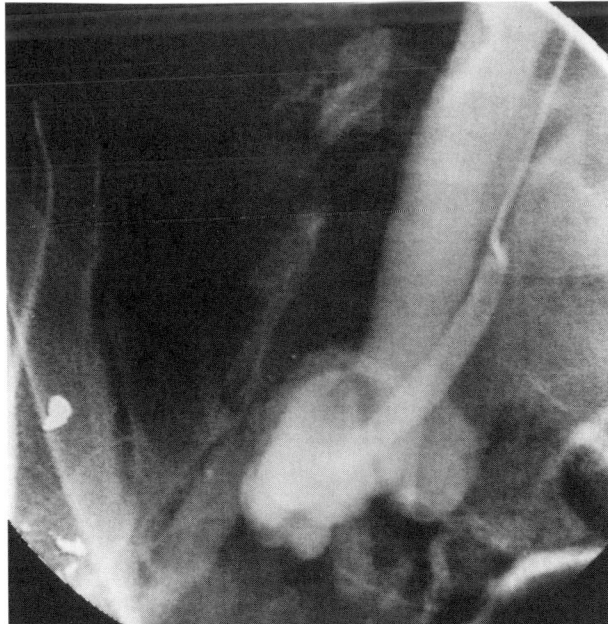

A

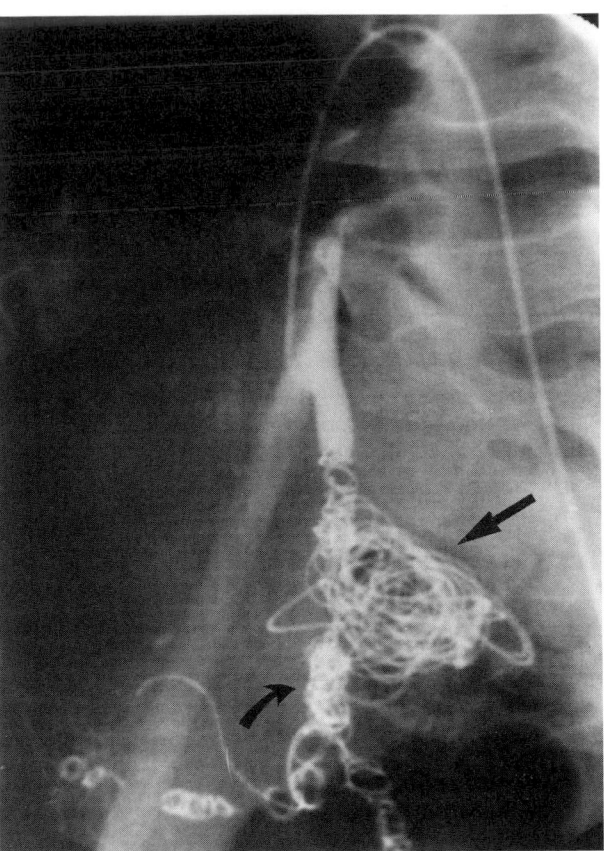

B

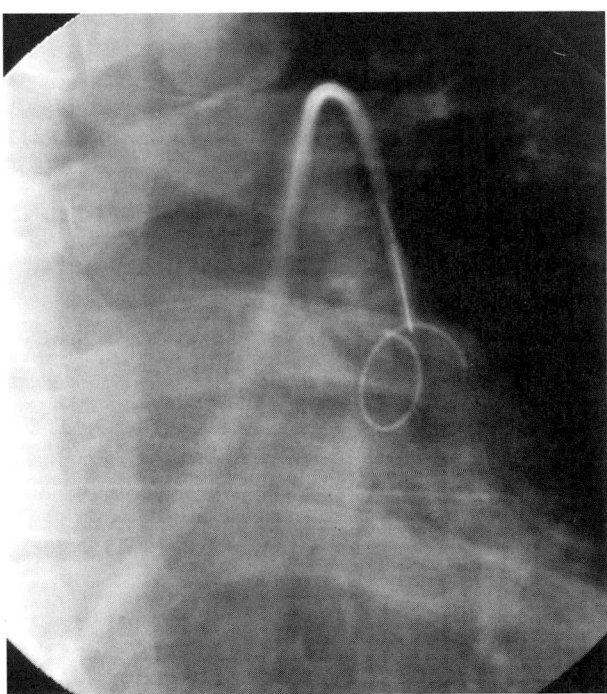

C

Figure 5-6. (A) Large pseudoaneurysm and arteriovenous fistula from the right internal iliac artery (selectively injected) to the internal iliac vein. The condition was caused by a gunshot wound 8 days earlier and was felt to be responsible for a more recent sudden drop in hematocrit. (B) The branches distal to the aneurysm were embolized with conventional coils. A nest of coils is well demonstrated in the internal iliac trunk distal to the pseudoaneurysm (*curved arrow*). The aneurysm and connection to the vein were later embolized using a curled removable core wire (*straight arrow*) to create a baffle for the deposition of conventional coils. An occlusion balloon was used during the procedure to reduce flow and permit better visualization of the pathology. The final angiogram after further coil deposition within the baffle and artery proximal to the aneurysm showed complete occlusion. (C) The initial 15-mm-diameter coil released in the pseudoaneurysm (before placement of the baffle) migrated through the fistula to the left pulmonary artery. A 10-mm nitinol gooseneck snare (Microvena) was used to retrieve this after the fistula was occluded.

reason, the first coil placed should have a slightly larger diameter than the channel where it is expected to lodge. After the catheter tip is in position, the coil is introduced by placing the tip of the metal cartridge containing the elongated coil into the hub of the catheter and advancing a floppy-tipped wire through the metal tubing, pushing the coil ahead of it. The authors prefer to use a 0.035-inch Newton straight wire for

this. The wire is then used to advance the coil to the tip of the catheter while the stability of the catheter in the vessel is ascertained fluoroscopically. If there is any concern that the catheter might shift position during the embolization, depositing the coil too proximally, advancing the pusher wire alone can test the system. The coil is released by further advancement of the delivery wire, although retraction of the catheter is occasionally necessary. This latter maneuver is only done if the system is sufficiently far within a vessel that back-positioning into the parent vessel will not occur. Complete release is confirmed by careful fluoroscopy, observation of the tip of the pusher wire exiting the catheter, and careful removal of the catheter at the end of the embolization. A gentle contrast injection is performed after depositing a spring embolus to assess for occlusion. If blood flow is sluggish, waiting several minutes for further thrombosis is generally sufficient.

Vessels larger than 3 to 5 mm frequently require several coils for occlusion. Progressively smaller diameter coils "nested" within larger ones are effective (Fig. 5-6A and B). Very large vessels may require ancillary devices to form a framework or baffle for the coils (see Fig. 5-6B). Small vessels are generally best approached with coaxial microcatheter systems. In addition to permitting superselective, distal catheterization, these systems, used in conjunction with soft, steerable wires, appear to induce less spasm. The smaller coils can be delivered through them with special coil pushers (Target Therapeutics), 0.025- or 0.018-inch Glidewires (Medi-Tech) that resist kinking, or a forceful saline flush.

In addition to the smaller coils, conventional-size coils can also be delivered by using a flush technique.[20] A forceful preliminary injection of saline or contrast with a 10-ml or smaller syringe is made to assess the stability of the catheter, after which the coil is loaded into the proximal part of the catheter and the saline-filled syringe is used to eject the coil. Although the authors do not use this method primarily, it is sometimes useful for ejecting emboli that are difficult to advance with a wire.

Pitfalls

A thorough knowledge of the equipment is important for correct use. The spring coil, catheter, and guide-wire must be properly matched to avoid wedging in the catheter. Several factors govern the ease of coil passage through a catheter[16,21]: (1) the material of the catheter, which determines the degree of resistance, with Teflon, polyethylene, and polyamide having less friction than polyurethane; (2) the amount and manner in which the fibers are attached; (3) the relative diameters of the coil and that of the inside of the catheter—whereas clearly too small an inner diameter will create difficulty, too large a diameter will permit partial coiling and also prevent easy passage; (4) the size of the delivery wire—too thin a wire may wedge alongside the coil; (5) the diameter of the curled coil, which affects the degree of tension against the catheter; (6) the shape of the catheter; (7) kinking of the catheter; and (8) the size of the tapered tip of the catheter. In

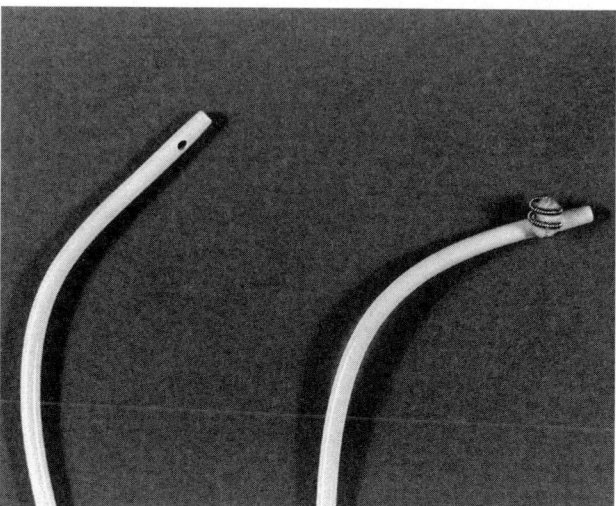

Figure 5-7. *Left:* catheter with a side hole. *Right:* partially extruded 5-mm-diameter coil inadvertently advanced through a side hole.

addition, end-hole-only catheters should be used because the tip of the coil may catch in a side hole and become jammed (Fig. 5-7). Lastly, contrast in the catheter increases the resistance to coil passage and can cause the embolus to stick in the lumen; therefore, the catheter should be flushed with saline before the coil is advanced. This is especially important with the 0.025- and 0.018-inch systems. If there is any question of the ability of a coil to safely pass through a particular catheter, an in vitro test before using it is helpful.

With careful fluoroscopic monitoring of the coil, incomplete release is rarely undetected. With the original coil, occasionally release of the wire with incomplete release of the long wool or polyester tails would occur.[21] This is infrequently seen with the new design in which multiple short threads are placed transversely along the wire but sparing the proximal segment. Detecting complete release of the 0.025-inch emboli is occasionally a problem because of their small size and poor radiopacity. Nevertheless, careful fluoroscopy to see the pusher wire exit the catheter and observation of the coil during the initial removal of the catheter should detect this problem and permit complete extrusion.

Selection of the proper coil diameter for the size of the vessel being occluded will determine its stability and position once released.[21,22] The optimal diameter to enhance stability is probably about 20 percent larger than that of the vessel. Too small a coil can migrate distally or proximally back into the parent vessel (such as the aorta) with subsequent embolization elsewhere. Proper sizing to prevent migration may be especially difficult in large vessels; arteriovenous fistulas (see Fig. 5-6), especially those with short connections or no tapering of the feeding artery; and veins, which are compliant and change their diameters with changes in respiration and blood volume. Furthermore, not only do veins not taper in the direction of blood flow, but they enlarge as blood returns to the heart. The authors have seen even properly sized coils migrate through high-flow arteriovenous fistulas, perhaps because hemodynamic forces cause deformity of the spring embolus as it pushes through the communication. Baffles[23] and barbed systems[24–26] that engage the vessel wall have been devised to deal with these challenges (see below). Too large a coil will remain elongated, resulting in less cross-sectional coverage of the vessel and therefore less occlusive ability. In addition, too large a coil can cause the catheter to back out of the vessel, with the coil then projecting into the parent vessel. Although it is unlikely to be dislodged completely by blood flow in the parent vessel, it can act as the nidus for thromboemboli.[10,21] Lastly, the edge of an elongated coil may traumatize a nonoccluded vessel, leading to intimal damage and possibly pseudoaneurysm.

When one is occluding a vessel preoperatively, care should be taken to leave a sufficient stump of proximal, noncoiled vessel for the surgeon to safely ligate.[21,27,28] This is done to reduce the risk of operatively induced reflux of coils. After resection, the specimen should be examined to be sure it contains the appropriate number of coils; if any are missing, intraoperative radiography is necessary to search for them. Depending on their location, they may need to be retrieved.

Placing excessive numbers of coils runs the risk of the proximal one extending into the parent vessel[21] (Fig. 5-8). This can be avoided by placing the catheter in a more distal location before starting the embolization, by waiting several minutes before placing tenuous, proximal coils to see if the channel will thrombose with time, or by using the Amplatz coil positioner[29] (see below) to nest coils within each other over a short distance.

Following coil placement, the contrast injection to assess the adequacy of occlusion should be gentle to avoid creating turbulence about the proximal coils, which could result in reflux, especially if the proximal coils are not firmly embedded in the vessel. Malpositioned or migrated coils can be retrieved with a loop snare (see Fig. 5-6) or basket (see Fig. 5-8).[30]

Rarely, coil embolization may be accompanied by vessel rupture, perhaps because of an unusually weak wall, excessive trauma from the coil, or hemodynamic alterations in which the pressure rises with the occlusion. Generally, the anatomy will permit treatment of this with further embolization.

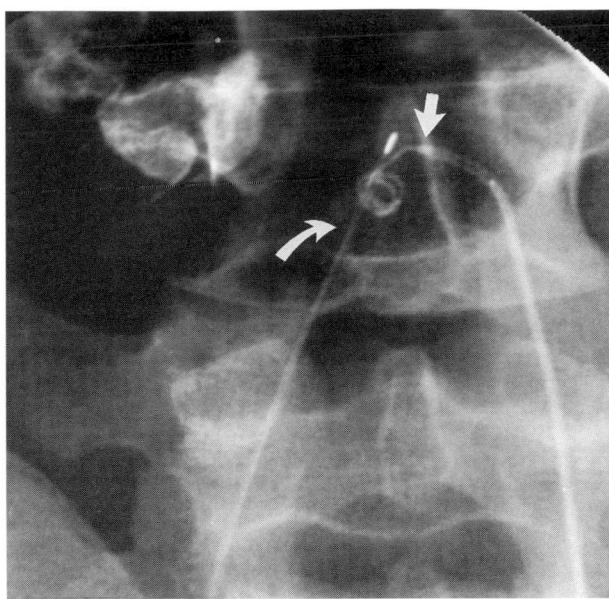

Figure 5-8. The last coil placed during an embolization backed out of the vessel while still partly within the catheter (*straight arrow*). A basket (*curved arrow*) from the opposite femoral artery was used to retrieve it.

Since coil emboli rely in large measure on inducing thrombosis to occlude a vessel, difficulties may be encountered in patients with severe hemostatic disorders, large vessels, and high-flow lesions. Furthermore, recanalization of the thrombus can occur. A cross-sectional occluding agent such as a detachable balloon may be effective in these situations.

Modifications

More precise delivery of coils is possible with the Amplatz coil positioner[29] (Cook, Inc.) (Fig. 5-9). This device is an open-ended guidewire with a retractable, thin, inner mandrel. The mandrel fits inside the core of the coil, straightening it out for delivery beyond the tip of the catheter. Once the coil is at the desired location, one releases it by retracting the mandrel. The coil can be positioned as far in the vessel as the wire assembly will go; however, once it exits the catheter, the coil cannot be pulled back into it because it will preferentially slip off the mandrel due to traction against the vessel wall or against the tip of the catheter. This device has also been used to precisely nest coils[31]—the "coil-in-coil" technique—and to thereby contain the emboli within a short length of vessel. This technique is most useful for occluding short channels.

When there is a short length of vessel, it may be difficult to stabilize the catheter for coil delivery. Delivering the coils through an occlusion balloon, with

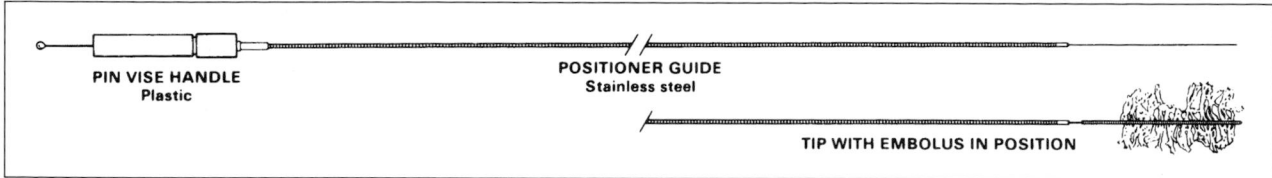

Figure 5-9. Amplatz coil positioner, with thin, retractable inner mandrel extending distally that fits inside the wire of the coil.

the balloon inflated, can prevent undesirable catheter movement. Abnormalities difficult to reach with transluminal catheterization or with feeding vessels that are preferentially not occluded have also been approached through direct percutaneous or intraoperative puncture.[32–34]

Soaking coils in thrombin may promote thrombus formation when the coil embolus may be inadequate in itself,[35] particularly in patients with coagulopathies (e.g., acquired after massive transfusions for bleeding) and high-flow arteriovenous abnormalities. The cartridge containing the coil is placed vertically (to let air escape) into a container containing a solution of 200 to 2000 units of thrombin/ml (Parke-Davis).[36,37] For 8-mm-diameter by 5-cm-long 0.038-inch Gianturco coils, the absorption of thrombin appears to plateau at 1 minute, with 40 to 80 units of thrombin per coil at higher concentrations. These doses are sufficiently low to avoid a systemic effect; only a local effect would be expected unless numerous coils are required.

The use of barbed coils have been described as a method to enhance stability of the embolus. The first of two types described by Castaneda-Zuniga[24] consists of a coil with several steel barbs attached to its leading end, forming an "umbrella" that opens and embeds into the vessel wall. These coils have been used for closing large arteriovenous fistulas. The second consists of a conventional coil that is modified by straightening the proximal 3 to 4 mm of the wire and cutting the tip to form a sharp point.[38] This is then delivered on a coil positioner. This modification has been recommended for use in veins where correct vessel sizing is difficult because of their compliance and their increase in diameter in the direction of flow, two factors predisposing to migration.

Several concepts for detachable spring emboli have been suggested. The first[10,39] consists of a screw-on device in which the tip of the delivery wire screws into the back of the coil. The second[40] employs a coaxial delivery cannula with a monofilament running longitudinally through the inner cannula, exiting a distal side hole, and attaching to the back of the spring embolus. Retraction of the monofilament permits retrieval while advancement and twisting of the outer cannula of the delivery system brings its cutting edge

against the monofilament, releasing the coil. More recently, Cook has released a detachable coil in which the pusher wire is a 2.6 French "coil positioning catheter" that has a moveable, thin, inner wire with a bulbous tip. This tip lies in a groove in the proximal end of the coil, firmly holding it in the lumen of the 2.6 French catheter, and permitting removal of the entire device. The coil is released by advancing the inner wire; once out of the lumen of the positioning catheter, the wire and coil separate from each other.

Plugs of polyvinyl alcohol (PVA) sponge have been compressed about the straightened end of a spring embolus ("coilon")[41] to provide more rapid crosssectional vessel occlusion as the PVA expands.

Ancillary Devices

Occluding large vascular channels may require special devices to form a framework for later placement of coil emboli. The risk of migration is especially great in arteriovenous shunts and large veins. The use of inappropriately small agents can lead to paradoxical embolization to the lungs from systemic shunts and to systemic arteries from pulmonary shunts. Although 0.038-inch coil emboli can be obtained in diameters up to 15 mm, these flexible wires may still deform and migrate.

Spider. To enhance stability and form a framework for coil emboli, Castaneda-Zuniga and others described the stainless steel spider (Cook, Inc.) (Fig. 5-10).[25,26] This device consists of a short central metal

Figure 5-10. Amplatz stainless steel spiders.

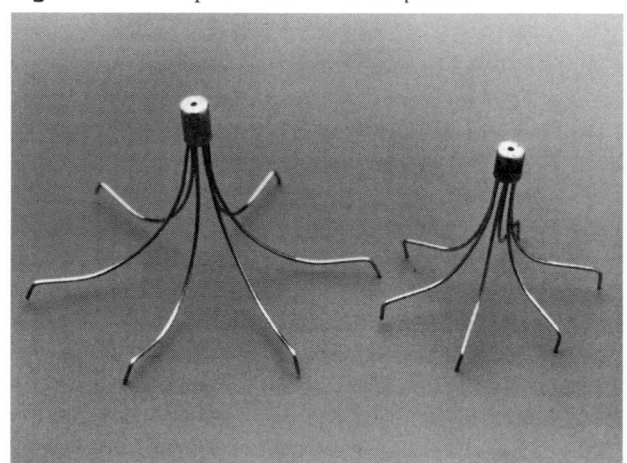

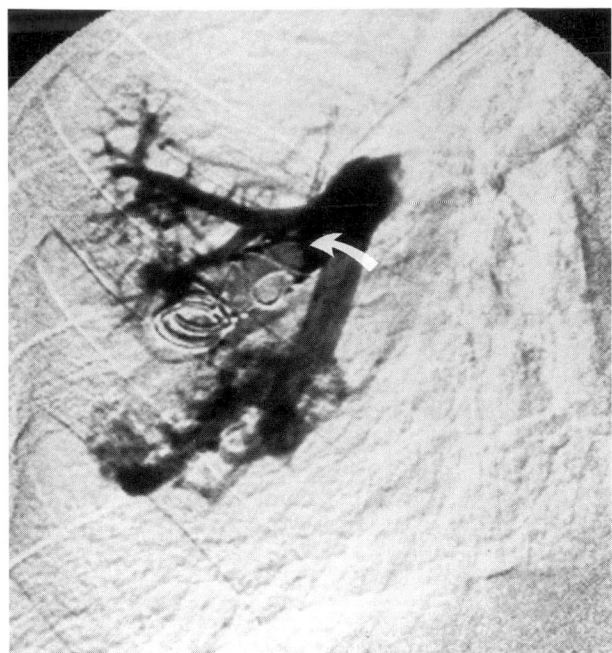

Figure 5-11. Complex, large right lower lung pulmonary arteriovenous malformation with many feeding arteries, the first of which has been embolized using a detachable balloon (*arrow*) placed within a framework of coils.

tube with six curved metal prongs that pierce the vessel wall. It comes in four sizes, indicated for vessels of diameters up to 9, 13, 15, and 20 mm. Coil emboli and other agents can be deposited behind the devices.

Wire Baffles. Another adjunct for occluding large channels is the coil baffle described by Chuang and Szwarc.[23] This consists of a 15- to 20-cm length of guidewire, with or without transverse bundles of Dacron fibers every 3 cm, that can be coiled into varying diameters to match the structure to be embolized. To create a similar device, the authors have modified movable core wire (see Fig. 5-6), by removing most of the core, curling it to the desired diameter, replacing the core to introduce and advance the wire in the catheter, and then depositing it using a pusher wire after the core has been removed. Large coil emboli can then be placed within this framework to cause complete occlusion.

Detachable Balloons. Coils can be used with detachable balloons that provide cross-sectional occlusion (Fig. 5-11).

Imaging of Wire Emboli

Wire emboli are generally obvious on plain radiographs; however, there has been a report of an unnecessary operation done because coils were confused for the radiopaque stripe of a surgical swab.[42] The compatibility of coils with magnetic resonance imaging (MRI) depends on the potential of interaction with the magnetic field, which is significant for highly ferromagnetic steel coils but minimal for nonferromagnetic platinum coils. Compatibility is assessed in terms of safety and picture quality. Safety is principally a function of the risk from any motion of the device caused by the magnetic field. Since coils become firmly incorporated in the occluded vessel, they all appear to be safe,[43,44] although it is probably best to wait a sufficient time for a firm occlusion to occur when steel coils are used in an area with adjacent critical structures. Severe "black-hole" artifacts and image distortion occur with steel coils,[45] limiting magnetic resonance imaging. This problem is minimal with platinum coils.

Other Metal-Based Embolic Agents

Bare Wires

Bare wires appear to be less effective at causing vessel occlusion than wires with fibers, apparently because of decreased thrombogenicity. Consequently, a denser matrix of wire is required. Plain steel coils were of limited value experimentally.[10,13] Plain platinum wires, 0.018 inch and thinner, have been used successfully,[17-19] but the fibered ones are preferred. Thin copper wires have also been reported for endovascular occlusion.[46]

Wire-Induced Electroocclusion

The ability of an electric current passed through a vessel to produce vascular occlusion has been known since the 19th century.[6] Theories for the development of thrombosis with the application of direct current include the precipitation of negatively charged blood elements (red cells, white cells, platelets, and fibrinogen) about a positively charged electrode (anode),[47] injury to the intima,[48] and the release of clotting factors. The advantages of the first direct current devices were precise control of the site of occlusion by the position of the anode, effectiveness in the face of heparinization and thrombocytopenia, and long-term occlusion. However, the drawbacks included difficulty in placing the anode in superselective positions, the long time needed to produce occlusion, especially in vessels larger than 5 mm (frequently 30 to 60 minutes), skin burns from the metal ground plate before an intervening lubricating sponge was used, and corrosion of the steel anode due to electrolysis, with the tip occasionally breaking off.[48] Using platinum anodes instead of steel gives the advantages of greater radiopacity, of no corrosion, since platinum does not undergo electroly-

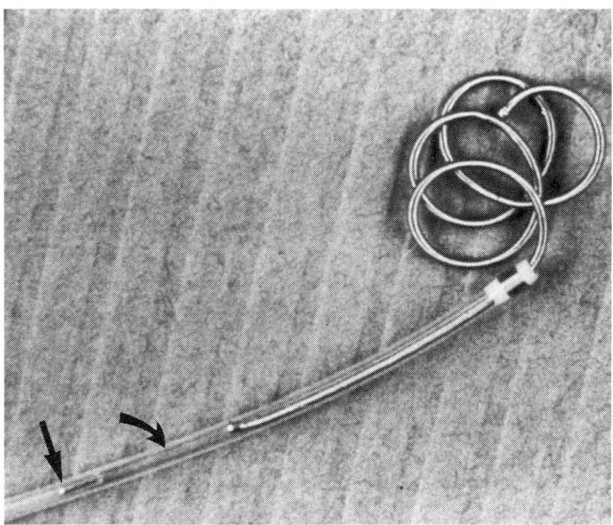

Figure 5-12. Guglielmi detachable embolization coil, partly in catheter. Note the curled platinum wire tip, the soft stainless connecting section (*curved arrow*), which lyses, and the stainless steel delivery section (*straight arrow*). (Courtesy of John Chaloupka, M.D.)

sis, and of producing larger clots.[49] Recently, Guglielmi reported a detachable embolization coil[49-51] (Target Therapeutics) that uses both the electrothrombotic and electrolytic effects of a direct current to occlude aneurysms. The device consists of a 0.010- to 0.015-inch curled platinum wire attached to the distal end of a 3-cm length of soft stainless steel, which in turn is attached to a 175-cm-long stainless steel wire (Fig. 5-12). The platinum component can be designed in various lengths and coiled diameters. After the platinum is coiled in proper position, a low-voltage direct current results in thrombosis and dissolution of the connecting soft steel segment through electrolysis. This process takes 4 to 12 minutes.

Vessel occlusion has also been produced by an alternating current electrode (endovascular diathermy)[52] and a radiofrequency probe,[53] although neither device is commercially available. These techniques create a thermal response that is greatest about the intravascular electrode, resulting in coagulation of the surrounding tissue, including the vessel wall. *Diathermy* is the term for a thermal response in biologic tissue to an alternating electrical current.

Spiderlon

The spiderlon consists of a cylindrical plug of PVA foam compressed about a wire attached to a spider.[54] This device can occlude vessels 3 to 8 mm in diameter. Although the spider is designed to form a stable baffle for the deposition of other embolic agents, the spiderlon can be used alone: the plug of PVA will expand to occlude the vessel in several minutes.

Balloon Devices

Nondetachable Occlusion Balloons

Early balloons used to occlude vessels consisted of nondetachable devices for the temporary cessation of blood flow.[55-59] Interest was principally directed toward preoperative occlusion of the abdominal aorta for ruptured aneurysms, but the potential for controlling hemorrhage elsewhere and other conditions was soon realized.[60-62] Both single- and double-lumen catheters have been developed, the former requiring placement through an introducer and the latter permitting advancement over a guidewire (Fig. 5-13) and injections of contrast. The balloon material is generally latex, although silicone is acceptable, and the balloon can be inflated with dilute contrast or air.

Early experience with the use of temporary occlusion balloons for the nonoperative control of hemorrhage was discouraging. Even when the procedure was successful, prolonged inflation times were required, up

Figure 5-13. Medi-Tech 5 French dual-lumen occlusion balloons, uninflated (*left*) and inflated (*right*), with guidewire exiting end hole.

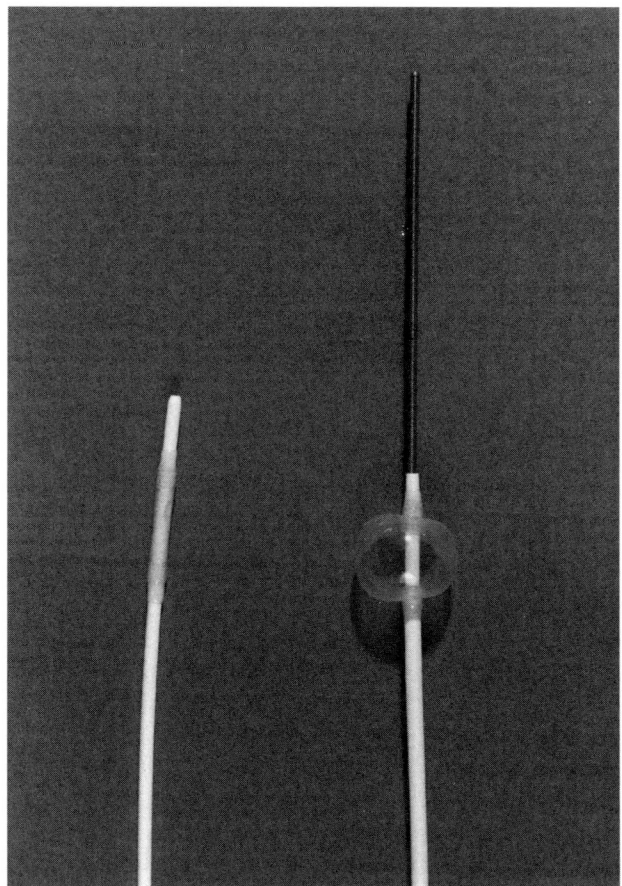

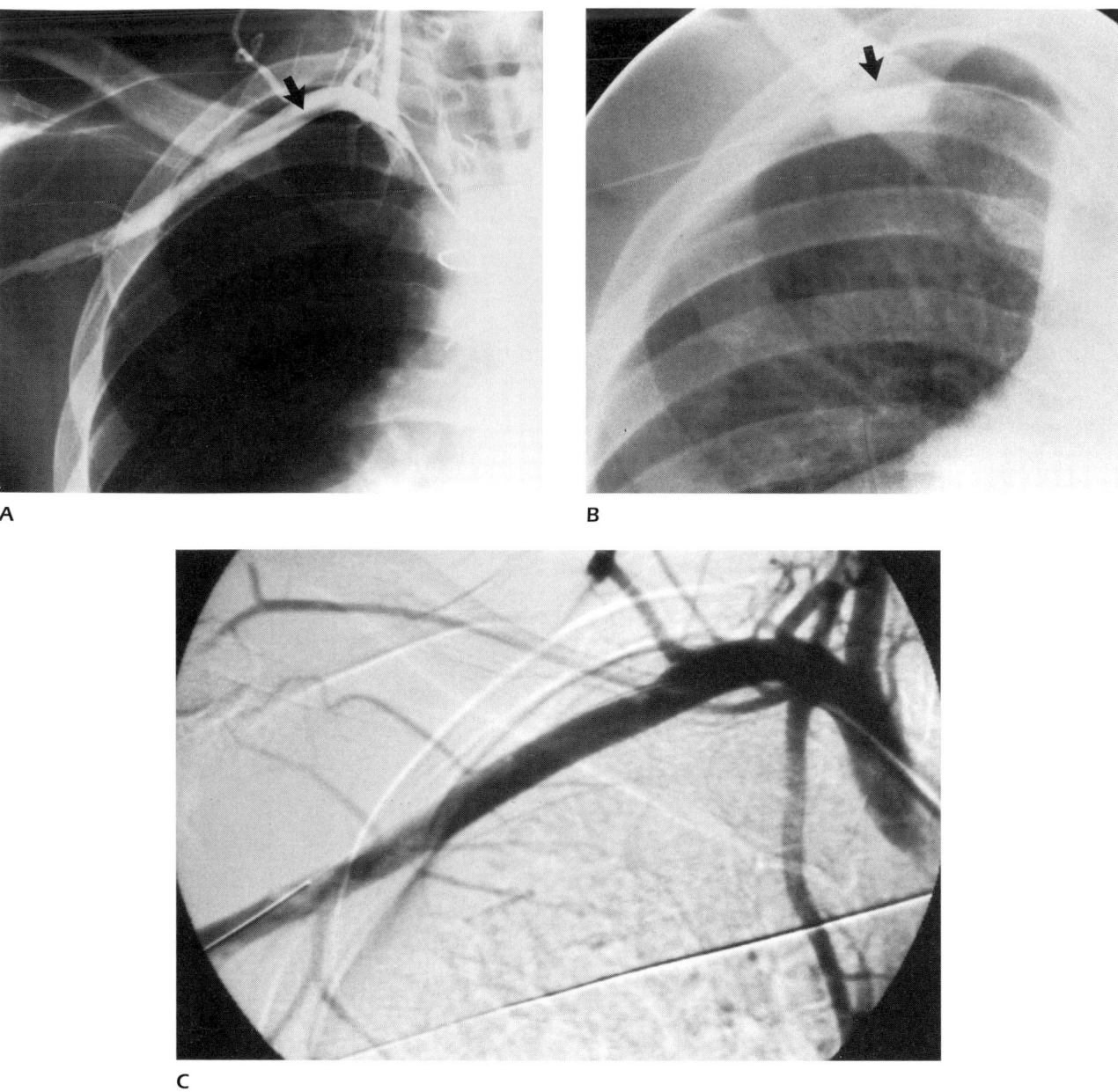

Figure 5-14. (A) Right subclavian artery inadvertently catheterized with a 7 French sheath (*arrow*) in a patient with cyanotic congenital heart disease. (B) Because of brisk hemorrhage after removal of the sheath, an occlusion balloon previously placed across the prior entry site of the sheath was inflated (*arrow*). Although recurrent bleeding occurred with deflation of the balloon after an initial 10-minute occlusion, no further bleeding was noted after the second 10-minute inflation or during a 30-minute subsequent observation period. (C) Final angiogram shows no extravasation or other pathology.

to 48 hours. The authors use these types of balloon catheters to occlude vessels in a limited number of situations, such as for preoperative control of the renal or splenic artery and for temporary or definitive control of bleeding from a vessel that cannot be sacrificed (Fig. 5-14).

Occlusion balloons also have a role in controlling blood flow when embolizing with another agent and in preventing reflux of another agent.[63] Limiting the inflow of nonopacified blood may be the optimal method for visualizing a high-flow abnormality. These balloons are also useful for test occlusion of the carotid artery before embolization or surgery.[64]

Potential complications with occlusion balloons are rupture of the balloon, balloon-catheter separation, and vascular injury.

Calibrated Leak Balloons

In addition to the dual-lumen catheters, another solution to permit intravascular fluid injections was the single-lumen calibrated leak balloon.[65–68] This balloon consists of a catheter with a balloon at its tip that has a small hole. This hole only begins to leak fluid after the balloon has been inflated to a certain degree; before that, the hole is constricted by the balloon shell. These devices can be made small in caliber and very flexible, permitting superselective catheterization and flow directionality. They are most useful for occluding flow during diagnostic angiography and during the administration of liquid glues (e.g., isobutyl-2-cyanoacrylate) into arteriovenous malformations. Inflation of the balloon limits flow in the vessel while the tissue adhesive is injected, thereby limiting dilution, escape into the venous system, and maximizing deposition in the nidus. A detachable type of calibrated leak balloon permits release of the balloon if it becomes embedded in the glue.

Detachable Balloons

The desire to produce a permanent occlusion eventually led to the development of detachable systems.[1–4] The major interest has been in using these in the neurovascular circulation because of the desirable characteristics of exact placement and reversibility.

Material and Techniques

All detachable balloon systems consist of the balloon, a delivery-inflation catheter, and an introducer catheter (Fig. 5-15). A variety of sizes are made, as well as various different expanded shapes: cylindrical, oval, and spherical[67] (Fig. 5-16). The balloons may be made of latex or silicone. Silicone is stable and is not subject to degradation as is latex.[69] In addition, silicone has a more gradual inflation profile than latex, which tends to build up pressure and then suddenly expand. Because silicone acts as a semipermeable membrane, when a silicone balloon is filled with a hypertonic solution it can enlarge, potentially to the point of rupture and balloon deflation.[70] Consequently, the preferred filling fluid should have an osmolarity close to that of blood. The authors use slightly hypotonic iohexol 140 (Omnipaque 140, Winthrop Pharmaceuticals, 273 mOsm. Late deflation of silicone balloons may also be due to fatigue of the balloon shell or leaking from its valve.[71] Latex does not appear to be osmotically active to any significant degree, and therefore has no osmotic requirement for its filling agent[72,73]; however, deflation over time has been seen, probably due to physical degradation or leaking from its base.

In certain situations, it is desirable to keep the bal-

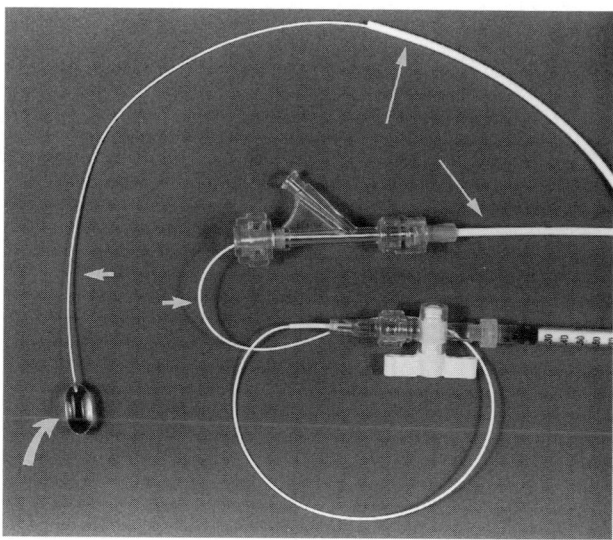

Figure 5-15. Interventional Therapeutics Corporation Detachable Silicone Balloon (*curved arrow*) on Hieshima Taper Select Delivery Catheter (*short straight arrows*) through an 8 French introducer catheter (*long straight arrows*). Y adapter at hub of introducer permits injections around the delivery catheter.

loon inflated indefinitely at a particular size and shape. This is especially important when there is a significant potential of incomplete occlusion or of recanalization if the balloon undergoes late deflation, as in aneurysms. To produce a permanently inflated embolic agent, the balloon can be filled with a solidifying liquid such as silicone[67] or various mixtures of 2-hydroxyethyl methylacrylate (HEMA)[71,74] instead of contrast medium. These can be made radiopaque by adding a small amount of bismuth oxide or tantalum dust to liquid silicone or powdered or liquid conventional contrast agents to HEMA, depending on the type of mixture. The hardening time for silicone is generally

Figure 5-16. Debrun tie-on latex balloons. After a latex ligature is used to firmly attach the balloon to the delivery catheter, the sleeve is cut away.

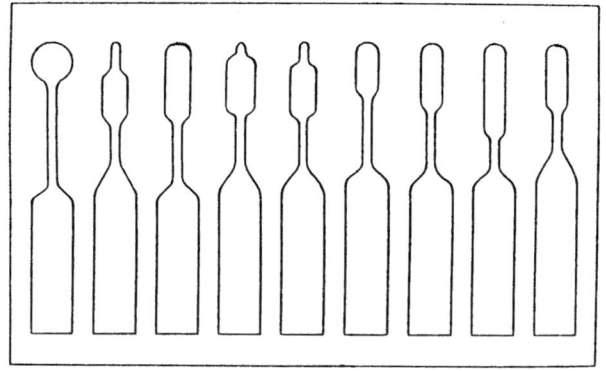

10 to 15 minutes, whereas for HEMA it is about 40 to 60 minutes, although this can be modified by altering the amount of catalyst. The lower viscosity and longer hardening time of HEMA are advantageous because it can be injected more easily through the catheter still in its liquid form. Introduction of these agents is limited by the volume of contrast contained within the delivery-inflation catheter. If this volume represents a significant percentage of the volume needed to inflate the balloon, little or none of the polymer will reach the balloon. This problem can be solved by using a dual-lumen inflation catheter, but it is then larger and more rigid, making balloon delivery to tortuous, small destinations difficult. A vent tube can be used within the inflation catheter to permit more complete exchange for the solidifying solution, but again this generally results in a more rigid delivery system. Detachable calibrated leak balloons[65,67] permit intravascular leaking of the unwanted contrast but also run the risk of leaking the polymer. Although this may be acceptable with superselective catheter positioning within an arteriovenous malformation, this would be dangerous when embolizing an aneurysm. Care must be taken when choosing a solidifying agent; commercially available latex balloons and filling agents need to be compatible, since there have been reports of latex degradation.[75,76] HEMA may cause chemical degradation by bonding to components of latex, depending on the materials used to cure the latex, possibly leading to deterioration of the balloon shell and leakage during the polymerization stage.[69] No reports of silicone balloon degradation from polymerizing filling agents have appeared.

Long-term vascular occlusion of systemic vessels appears to reliably occur if the balloon remains inflated for at least 3 weeks.[77] The histology of vessels occluded with silicone balloons shows organizing thrombus surrounding the balloons and intimal fibrosis in the vessel wall.[77] One experiment[78] suggested that silicone Debrun balloons may produce delayed thrombogenesis, organization, and endothelial covering of aneurysms as compared to latex ones. The reduced thrombogenicity of silicone was hypothesized to be related to its smoother surface; latex had a rough surface on scanning electron microscopy.

The size of the vessel that can be occluded and of the required delivery catheter system for a detachable balloon depends on its elasticity. The maximum recommended expansion ratios of silicone and latex balloons are about four to six times their uninflated diameters. Recent reports of reactions to latex products,[79,80] including barium enema balloons and gloves, have raised concern over the potential for allergic reactions to detachable intravascular latex devices; however, this has yet to be reported. Silicones are well known to be biologically inert. Lastly, latex balloons are generally less expensive.

Delivery-inflation catheters have been made from polyethylene, polyurethane, and Teflon. They must be attached to the balloon firmly yet permit reliable detachment. Types of attachment mechanisms include the elastic grip of the balloon material, elastic ligatures, and self-sealing valves (Fig. 5-17). Clearly, relying on the elastic grip of the balloon material is the least reliable, being prone to premature release and immediate deflation of the balloon.[67] Ligatures have the advantage of the firmest attachment with little risk of premature or inadvertent release, but are more cumbersome to prepare. Furthermore, this design requires a hub to the balloon, which may project back from the oc-

Figure 5-17. Methods for attaching detachable balloon to delivery-inflation catheters.

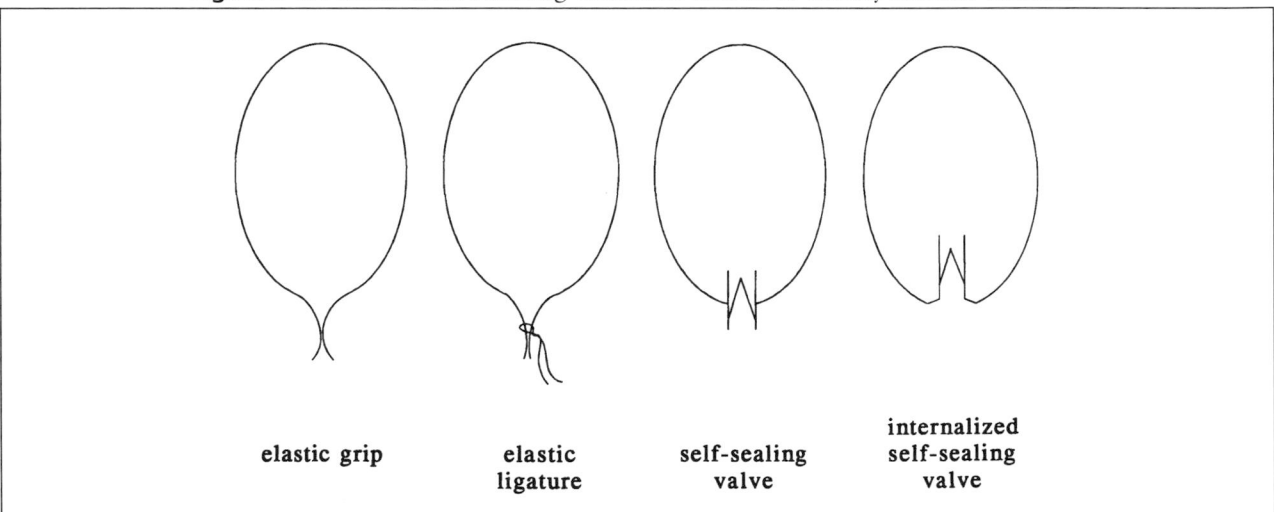

elastic grip   elastic ligature   self-sealing valve   internalized self-sealing valve

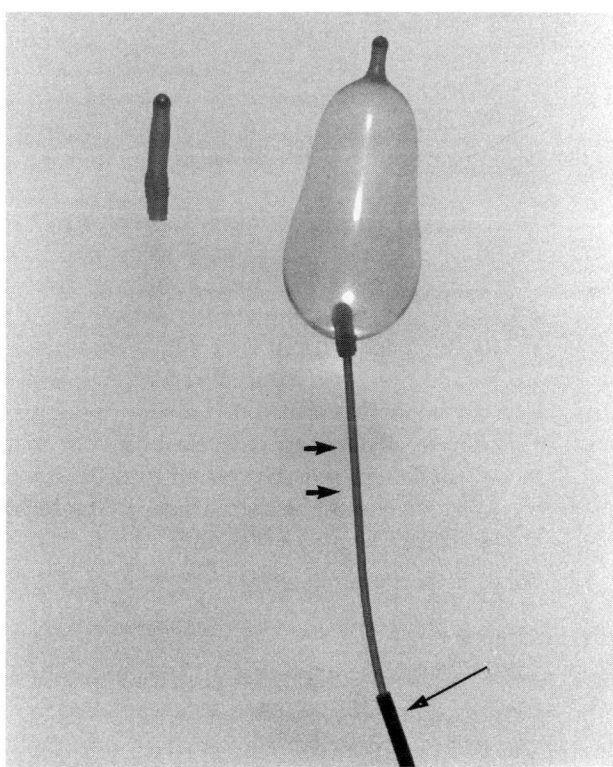

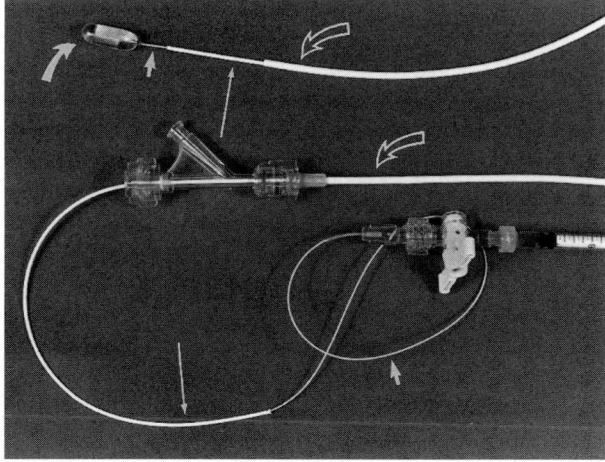

Figure 5-19. Interventional Therapeutics Corporation Detachable Silicone Balloon (*curved closed arrow*) on 2 French delivery catheter (*short straight arrows*) with outer, coaxial, 4.2 French detachment catheter (*long straight arrows*) and 8 French introducer catheter (*curved open arrows*).

Figure 5-18. Goldvalve balloons, uninflated on *left* and inflated on *right*. The gold bead is at the tip. The inflated balloon is mounted on a 2 French delivery catheter (*short arrows*) with a coaxial 3 French detachment catheter (*long arrow*).

cluded lesion into a nonoccluded segment (e.g., project back from an embolized aneurysm into the nonoccluded vessel of origin). This hub, or the tails of a ligature, could potentially act as sources of thromboemboli. Valve mechanisms have been designed that are incorporated into the geometry of an inflated balloon.

The delivery catheter may be a single catheter (see Fig. 5-15), in which case detachment relies on balloon traction against the vessel wall as the catheter is pulled out, or a coaxial catheter system (Figs. 5-18 and 5-19), in which the outer catheter can be used to stabilize the balloon as the inner one is retracted. A balloon attached by a valve may use either system; one attached by a ligature generally requires the coaxial one to release it. Relying on traction may carry a higher risk of rupture when one is embolizing a structure with a fragile wall, such as an aneurysm[67]; however, the inherently greater flexibility of a single catheter facilitates negotiation of tortuous vessels.

After the vessel to be embolized has been catheterized, exchange for the introducer catheter is performed. This is generally a nontapered, thin-walled polyethylene catheter that is placed through a sheath. Large introducers are frequently most easily advanced in conjunction with an inner, coaxial guiding catheter. The required introducer size will of course depend on the diameters of the uninflated balloon and catheter delivery system. Balloons may be passed through the introducer by manual advancement of the delivery catheter or carried along with an injection of saline (hydraulic propulsion). Silicone spray can facilitate passage of the balloon. With flexible delivery catheters, balloons have a tendency to be carried along with the flow. This can be enhanced by slight inflation of the balloon. A Y adapter at the back of the introducer permits injections of contrast to assess balloon position and occlusion.

Pitfalls

Premature release of a balloon may occur because of inadvertent stripping against the coaxial detachment catheter or the introducer catheter, events of special concern when trying to remove a balloon. Caution is especially needed when attempting to remove valved systems because there is a step-off between the rim of the valve or balloon and the catheter. It is safest to remove the introducer at the same time, although this does involve losing selective catheterization.

When a balloon is partially inflated, it creates a stenosis in the vessel with resultant high flow velocities and drag forces. In large, high-flow channels, this force could overcome the force of attachment to the delivery catheter, resulting in premature release and distal embolization of the incompletely inflated balloon, possibly to an undesirable location. Occasionally, a "teardrop" deformity of the balloon will act as a warning, permitting deflation and removal. If this situation is anticipated, balloons with firm attachments to their catheters should be used. In addition, an occlusion balloon introduced into the more proximal vessel from another puncture can be used to reduce flow.

A balloon may migrate if it is improperly sized to the vessel. Anatomic and physiologic characteristics may also predispose toward balloon instability. A sharply tapered vessel may have a tendency to expel the balloon. Compliant vessels may enlarge in diameter with deep respiratory excursions or in response to the occlusion because greater hemodynamic forces are transmitted to the wall. Furthermore, drag forces with partial inflation in high-flow vessels or arteriovenous fistulas can cause elongation of these deformable detachable balloons. With poor traction against the wall, the balloon may embolize distally (e.g., across an arteriovenous shunt) or even reflux into the parent vessel and embolize elsewhere. In the appropriate setting, an alternative to trying to retrieve the balloon is to percutaneously puncture it, permitting its smaller, deflated fragments to travel distally and occlude a smaller territory.

Difficulty in detaching a balloon may be due to geometric, anatomic, or physical factors. Sharp retrograde angulation of the balloon on its delivery catheter, the most extreme example being a balloon that has folded back on itself, makes it difficult to detach because the direction of force needed for release will not be the same as the direction in which the catheter moves when pulled back. Furthermore, the catheter can kink, making it difficult to deflate the balloon. Percutaneous puncture of the balloon may be necessary in this situation.

The small size and limited tensile strength of delivery catheters, the firmness of their attachment to the balloon, and the limited transmission of retraction force when working through tortuous vessels can also result in difficult detachment and even rupture of delivery catheters. If this occurs, the balloon should be allowed to deflate, after which the catheter should be firmly grasped and removed. If the rupture occurs internally, it can be retrieved using a number of methods, such as a snare or basket, or immobilized against the introducer catheter using a small balloon dilatation catheter.

Thromboembolic events have been described,[81] presumably due to clot forming on the catheter system. If possible, systemic anticoagulation should be administered during balloon embolotherapy in critical circulations. The authors use between 45 and 100 units of heparin per kilogram, depending on the region being treated.

Rupture of a vessel by the balloon appears to be a rare phenomenon. If this occurs, rapid occlusion with additional embolic agents may be effective. Immediate rupture of a balloon may occur if it has been overinflated, if inflation forces it against a bony spur, or if it is defective.

Early deflation, especially before 3 weeks, may result in nonocclusion and migration. This may occur if the balloon has a defective or injured shell or valve, if it is inflated beyond its recommended volume, or if a silicone balloon is not inflated with a near isoosmotic solution. In addition, the authors' recent experience has raised the possibility that too vigorous manipulation of a balloon adjacent to embolization coils may result in early deflation, possibly related to shell injury. Therefore, caution should be used when placing these two types of agents next to each other.

Late deflation is generally only of concern in abnormalities that have a propensity to recanalize or that were incompletely occluded to begin with. In this situation, a liquid polymer can be used to keep the balloon inflated indefinitely. The isolated occlusion of aneurysms represents such a situation, since they are difficult to completely fill with balloons and may recanalize if their neck does not become endothelialized.

Ancillary Techniques

The flexible delivery catheter of a detachable balloon that normally permits flow guidance may be stiffened for better manual-guided delivery by inserting an appropriately thin guidewire.[82] The wire can also have a distal bend to give this type of system steerability.

Occlusion of large vascular channels may be difficult with the isolated use of balloons because of the need for a prohibitively large introducer for the uninflated device. In this situation, the preliminary use of large coils (see Fig. 5-11),[83] a spider,[84] or a wire baffle can reduce the size of the balloon needed to complete the occlusion.

Specific Detachable Balloons

Although a variety of detachable balloons have been described, we will concentrate on three in detail.

Mini-balloon. Although the Bard-Parker (division of Becton-Dickinson and Company) Mini-balloon (MB) is no longer in production, it is historically important for the role it played as the major nonneurological detachable balloon and for its delivery through hydraulic propulsion, a concept described by Dotter et al. in 1972.[85]

The MB (Fig. 5-20) was a silicone balloon preattached by a silicone tie onto a 2 French polyurethane delivery catheter. One- and 2-mm uninflated-diameter balloons were designed for occlusion of vessels up to 4

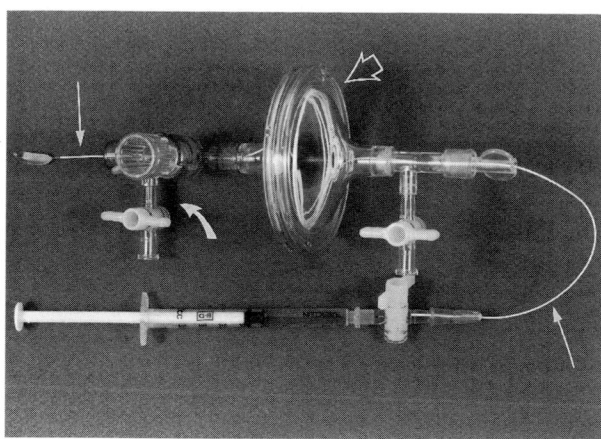

Figure 5-20. Inflated Mini-balloon on 2 French delivery catheter (*straight arrows*), most of which is in the coiling chamber (*open arrow*). Tuohy-Borst (*curved arrow*) through which forceful saline injection is given to carry the balloon forward.

and 8 mm. The introducer catheters were thin-walled, nontapered polyethylene catheters of 4.9 French (0.044-inch-diameter lumen) and 8.8 French (0.088-inch lumen).

The MB was delivered by a forceful saline flush given through a Tuohy-Borst located at the front of the delivery assembly. This would hydraulically carry the balloon forward, out of its coiling chamber. If the introducer was in a nonselective position, the balloon would still have a tendency to find its way into high-flow abnormalities. If not, gentle manipulation of the delivery catheter with the balloon slightly inflated would frequently succeed. Once in proper position, the MB was detached by pulling the delivery catheter away from the inflated balloon, which was held in place against the vessel wall. If the position was not acceptable, the balloon could be deflated and moved.

The MB was contraindicated in large vessels with high flow because of the risk of premature detachment related to large drag forces. The MB also had a relatively long tail.[86]

Debrun and Goldvalve Balloons. The Debrun latex balloon[4,67,87] (Nycomed-Ingenor) (see Fig. 5-16) is made from latex sleeves with narrow proximal portions to grip the catheter. Different shapes (e.g., cylindrical, spherical) and inflated sizes from less than 4 mm to 30 mm are made. After the balloon is mounted on the delivery catheter, it is test-inflated and then firmly attached by being tied at the base with a latex thread (12 one-half turns followed by three to four knots). The base and ligature can project over 2 mm from the inflated balloon. A small radiopaque metal marker can be placed within the balloon for visibility. Coaxial

Teflon or polyethylene delivery and detachment catheters are 1.5 to 2.0 French and 3.0 French in size. The hub of the outer 3 French catheter has a valve that can be tightened down on the inner catheter to keep it relatively immobile. A Y adapter should also be placed about the catheter before mounting the balloon, to be used for injections of saline or contrast after the adapter is connected to the hub of an appropriate introducer (generally an 8 or 9 French thin-walled, nontapered polyethylene catheter). The balloon is delivered by advancing the coaxial catheters. After the tip of the introducer is reached, only the inner catheter is advanced to precisely place the balloon. Detachment is accomplished by sliding the outer catheter over the inner one until it reaches the balloon and then pulling the inner catheter while holding the balloon steady with the outer one. These balloons are recommended for large, relatively proximal occlusions (e.g., traumatic carotid-cavernous sinus fistulas, vertebral fistulas, and cavernous aneurysms) because the coaxial system limits the distal extent to which they can be advanced.

The two other Debrun balloons are the Goldvalve balloon and the leaking detachable balloon, a detachable calibrated leak balloon (Nycomed-Ingenor). The Goldvalve balloon (see Fig. 5-18) is a variant of the classic Debrun latex balloon with a manufactured valve at its base that replaces the need for an operator-tied latex ligature. The valve may project back from the balloon as a collar or may be incorporated into the inflated balloon (integrated valve). It also has a gold marker bead at its tip. The 2 French polyethylene delivery catheter is inserted through the valve mechanism at the base and has a 3 French coaxial detachment catheter. After the balloon is advanced, it can be detached by pulling the inner catheter alone; it is not necessary to advance the outer catheter. The Debrun and Goldvalve balloons are not approved by the U.S. Food and Drug Administration.

Detachable Silicone Balloon. The Interventional Therapeutics Corporation system consists of a silicone balloon with a self-sealing silicone valve inside that has a radiopaque base[69] (Fig. 5-21). A variety of sizes are available in uninflated diameters of 0.85 to 2.20 mm, maximally inflating to diameters of 4 to 13 mm. The Detachable Silicone Balloons (DSB) come with valves that release within three predetermined ranges of force: low (blue) for 20 to 30 g, medium (red) for 30 to 40 g, and high (white) for 40 to 55 g. Although the DSB has a hub that projects back from the balloon, there is also a collarless variant. Depending on the uninflated diameter, the delivery and coaxial detachment catheters are either 1.5 and 3.6 French (for 0.85-mm uninflated balloons) or 2.0 and 4.2 French (for 1.5-

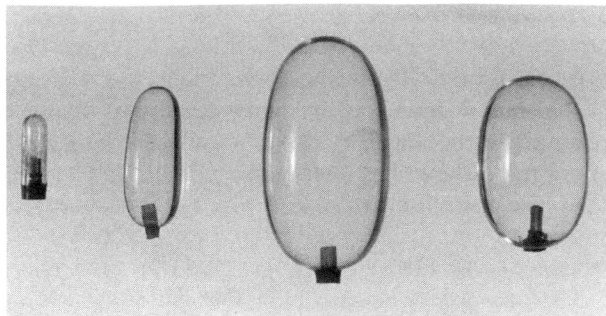

Figure 5-21. Several detachable silicone balloons made by Interventional Therapeutics Corporation. *Left to right:* uninflated 1.8-mm-diameter balloon, 0.85-mm balloon inflated to diameter of 4 mm, 1.5-mm balloon inflated to 8.5 mm, 2.2-mm collarless balloon inflated to 8.5 mm. The first three have hubs projecting back from the balloon, the fourth has the valve incorporated into the balloon shell.

mm and larger balloons) polyethylene catheters (see Fig. 5-19). The larger balloons can also use a tapered single delivery catheter (Hieshima Taper Select Delivery Catheter) (see Fig. 5-15). The delivery catheter is inserted through the balloon valve by the physician at the time of the procedure after a Y adapter is placed over the coaxial catheter.

The introducer catheters are 6.3 to 9.0 French. Once the introducer catheter is in position, the DSB is advanced to its tip and placed or flow-guided to the proper location. Angiography of a test occlusion can be performed through the Y adapter, followed by coaxial detachment or traction detachment. These balloons are being used under an investigational device protocol in the United States.

Other Detachable Balloons

A balloon with two valves, one at either end, has also been described[88,89] that permits advancement and test inflation over a guidewire. The wire traverses both valves, whereas the delivery catheter only extends through the proximal valve.

Rand has described a thrombogenic balloon[90] that is coated with a thrombogenic ferromagnetic substance. This substance permits more limited inflation of the balloon and therefore reduces the chance of traumatic rupture of fragile aneurysms or other structures, with subsequent thrombosis causing obliteration of the aneurysm.

Imaging of Balloons

Although balloons are radiolucent, when filled with contrast they are generally readily visible. Balloons are essentially free of artifacts on MRI.[91]

Other Mechanical Embolization Agents

Devices for Occluding Defects and Shunts in Congenital Heart Disease

Since Porstmann et al.'s description of transluminal closure of patent ductus arteriosus (PDA) in 1971[92] using a plug of PVA foam, a variety of devices and techniques have been described for closing this lesion, as well as atrial septal defects (ASDs) and small ventricular septal defects.[93,94] The Rashkind double-disk occluder device (USCI) (Fig. 5-22) is a double umbrella device that comes in 12- and 17-mm-diameter sizes. Each umbrella consists of three or four steel wire arms covered by polyurethane that spring open when released from a delivery catheter. Although principally designed for PDAs, this device has been used to close other lesions, including small ASDs and valvular and paravalvular leaks.[95] Variations of the double umbrella concept that have been tried for larger ASDs[96,97] include the Rashkind ASD Occluder (USCI Angiographics), which has had problems with improper placement and partial dislodgement; the Lock Clamshell Occluder (USCI Angiographics); and the buttoned double-disk device (Sideris). Another device described for occluding PDA is the Botallooccluder (NTK SovECs), which consists of a conically shaped plug of compressible polyurethane foam mounted on a stainless steel frame with fixing hooks that extend out of the polyurethane cone.[98] These devices may have applications in occluding large, abnormal vascular shunts elsewhere in the body.

Figure 5-22. Rashkind double-disk occluder device with two opposing umbrella-shaped disks that spring open when released from the delivery catheter. (Courtesy of William E. Hellenbrand, M.D.)

Percutaneous Stents and Endovascular Grafts

Stents and endovascular grafts (e.g., covered stents) offer the advantage of thrombosing vascular pathology by excluding it from the circulation while preserving flow in the feeding channel. These devices hold potential for treating lesions when the parent vessel must be preserved.

Miscellaneous Agents

Plain Threads

Silk sutures[24,99] and polylene threads[100] have been used for occluding fistulas and cerebral arteriovenous malformations. Silk threads require a baffle to hold them in large channels. Polylene threads have been shown to have less of an inflammatory effect on the vessel wall than isobutyl-2-cyanoacrylate.

Bristle Brushes

Bristle brushes consist of numerous nylon bristles attached to a stainless steel core. In the experimental setting, 4- and 8-mm-diameter brushes[101] appeared to produce vessel occlusion through a combination of mechanical obstruction and thrombus formation, with little injury to the vessel wall. They have not received much attention since the original report.

Laser-Induced Occlusion

Experimental occlusion of aneurysms by laser-induced thermal energy has been described with a device in which the metal thermal diffusing cap of the laser fiber detaches.[102]

Comparison of Embolization Coils and Detachable Balloons

Among the mechanical embolic agents, the most widely used are embolization coils and detachable balloons. Although either may be adequate for many situations, there are clear differences between these two devices that can affect the decision over which may be preferred.

Detachable balloons have the advantages of flow directionality, reversibility, and rapid mechanical cross-sectional occlusion of a channel, without relying on acute thrombus formation. Flow directionality permits selective embolization of vessels that have not been catheterized. This is generally readily achieved in the setting of high-flow fistulas; however, selection of other lesions may be more difficult. When a competing branch is preferentially entered, introducing a second balloon to temporarily occlude that route may be helpful.[2] Reversibility imparts a high degree of safety. If a test occlusion demonstrates an inappropriately positioned balloon, it can be deflated and repositioned or removed. In addition, detachable balloons do not degrade magnetic resonance images as steel coils do.

The disadvantages of detachable balloons are that they require larger, special introducer catheters (making them more cumbersome) as well as greater preparation time, are more complex, and are generally more expensive. Because they cannot be introduced through conventional catheters, an exchange is frequently necessary for each vessel to be embolized. To avoid this difficulty, it may be possible to leave the introducer catheter in a proximal location and use selective catheters through it. In addition, the size considerations may be prohibitive in small vessels if flow direction has failed. Although these devices are generally more expensive than coils, the cost differential is mitigated in large lesions, where a single balloon may suffice as compared to multiple nested coils.

Coils require no preparation time and can be delivered through conventional diagnostic catheters. Furthermore, although they are more expensive than steel coils, 0.018-inch platinum coils have made possible coil embolization of more distal vessels. Still, coils rely on inducing thrombus to produce vessel occlusion and are not easily retrieved.

Although most situations are well served by coils, in several situations detachable balloons are preferred. Principal among these is when precise positioning and reversibility of the embolic agent are needed and when the risk of inadvertent embolization of other vessels is high. This is true for large arteriovenous fistulas, especially in the pulmonary circulation (Fig. 5-23), where paradoxical embolization can result in stroke or other serious systemic sequelae. Embolization of large neurovascular structures is also benefited by these advantages. In addition, patients with hemostatic dysfunction or a lesion in which the risk of recanalization of thrombus is greater than usual may require the cross-sectional occlusion of a detachable balloon. Lastly, the flow directionality of a detachable balloon may be helpful when a specific location cannot otherwise be catheterized.

Clinical Indications

An extensive review of the clinical experience of embolization with mechanical agents is better left to the individual chapters dealing with specific disease entities; however, a general discussion of the value of these agents in different types of conditions follows. As a

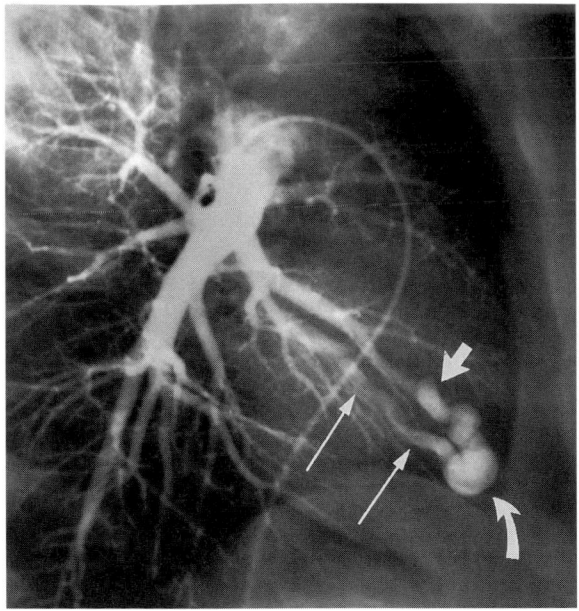

A

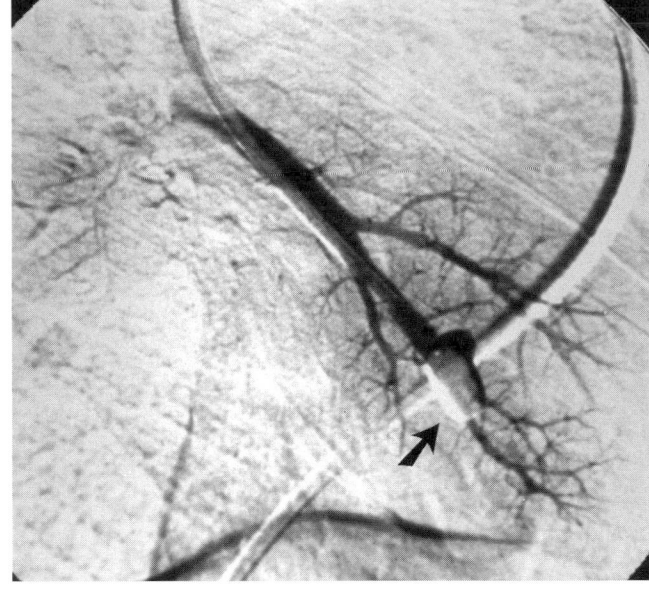

B

Figure 5-23. (A) Lateral right pulmonary angiogram depicting a right middle lobe simple pulmonary arteriovenous malformation, with feeding artery (*short straight arrow*), draining vein (*long straight arrows*), and aneurysmal commu nication (*curved arrow*). (B) Selective angiogram during test occlusion of the feeding artery with a detachable balloon (*arrow*). The balloon was later released.

rule of thumb, mechanical agents are most suitable for discrete, macroscopic vascular lesions where they can be placed precisely across the desired site of occlusion.

Aneurysms and Pseudoaneurysms

The major indications for treating aneurysms are to prevent hemorrhagic or thromboembolic complications. Less frequently, they may create difficulties due to mass effect on adjacent structures (of greater concern intracranially) and rupture into an adjacent vein with arteriovenous shunting. Percutaneous occlusion is most effective when the origin of the aneurysm is securely closed. Methods include the following[103]:

1. Occlusion of the afferent, feeding channel. This is especially effective in end arteries where there is no potential for retrograde filling of the aneurysm by reconstituted distal vessels.
2. Occlusion of the efferent channel, with the expectation of thrombosis of the aneurysm in a retrograde fashion.

3. Occlusion of the afferent and efferent channels, generally including the origin of the aneurysm.
4. Obliteration of the aneurysmal sac directly, with or without extension into feeding vessels (Fig. 5-24).

Mechanical agents can provide occlusion for all of these methods. Although isolated aneurysmal thrombosis is ideal because it will maintain patency of the feeding channel, it is limited by the risk of recanalization if there is subtotal occlusion and the origin of the aneurysm does not develop an endothelial or mature fibrous cover. Occlusion extending into the afferent and efferent vessels is the most definitive method but cannot be done if it will result in infarction of a critical organ.

Placing a stent or endovascular graft so that it crosses the orifice of an aneurysm holds promise as an alternative method of occlusion while preserving the vessel. A noncovered stent has been reported in the treatment of an iliac aneurysm,[104] and covered stents are being investigated as a method to exclude fusiform aneurysms such as of the abdominal aorta.[105–107] Long-

Figure 5-24. (A) Lateral angiogram of selective right posterior tibial artery injection in a patient with traumatic fractures of the tibia and fibula. The proximal posterior tibial artery ended in a pseudoaneurysm (*arrow*). (B) Three-millimeter-diameter 0.025-inch coils were placed into the aneurysm (*curved arrow*) and the feeding artery (*straight arrow*) through a Cragg infusion wire (Medi-Tech). (C) Postembolization frontal angiogram confirms occlusion of the proximal right posterior tibial artery and the pseudoaneurysm. The distal posterior tibial artery reconstituted (*arrow*). The anterior tibial and peroneal arteries showed spasm and displacement but were continuous.

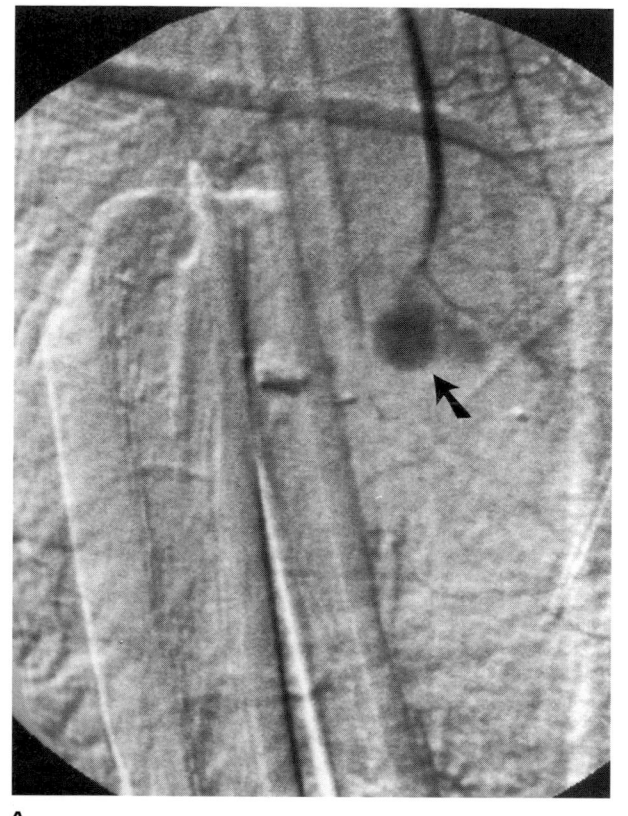

A

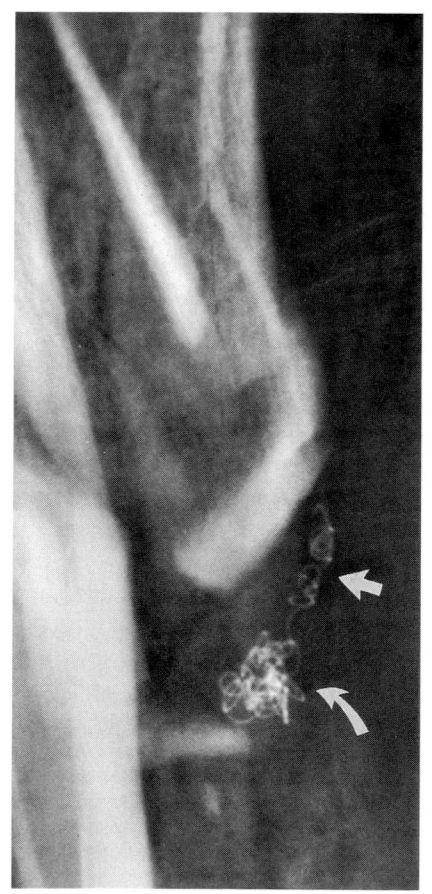

B

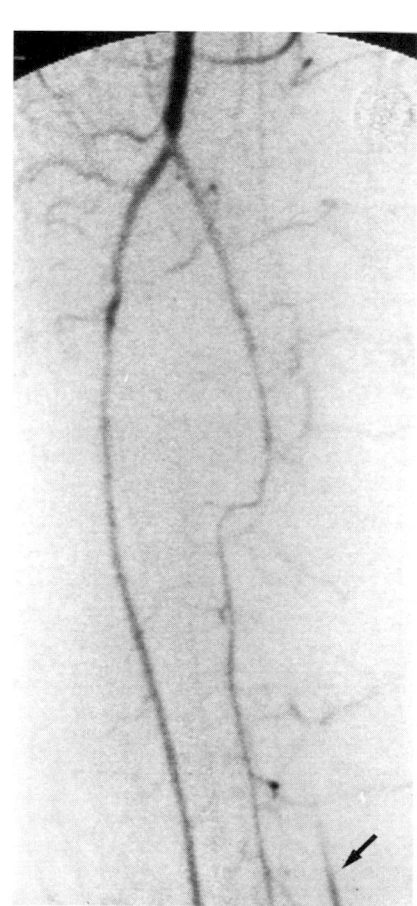

C

term theoretical concerns over the use of these devices, especially for fusiform lesions, are whether thrombosis of the aneurysm will prevent recanalization, enlargement, and rupture.

Although the most common approach to embolization of aneurysms has been transvascular, reports of direct percutaneous and intraoperative puncture of the aneurysm with the introduction of embolic agents have also appeared.[32–34,103] In addition to coils, thrombin and Gelfoam have been used. The tract is frequently embolized as well, as the catheter or needle is removed.

Arteriovenous Fistulas

Arteriovenous fistulas are direct arteriovenous connections that bypass the capillary bed. Acquired lesions are most commonly due to trauma, including iatrogenic sources. Other acquired causes are surgical shunts (e.g., persistent Blalock-Taussig shunt after more definitive corrective surgery), aneurysms that rupture into adjacent veins, erosive inflammatory or malignant processes, and persistent venous communicators after in situ saphenous vein bypass.[108] Examples of congenital lesions include a simple form of arteriovenous malformation, simple pulmonary arteriovenous malformations, and persistent primitive vascular connections, such as patent ductus arteriosus and congenital systemic-to-pulmonary artery collaterals seen in disorders with pulmonary outflow obstruction (e.g., tetralogy of Fallot).

Although the term *arteriovenous fistula* generally refers to simple, macroscopic connections, easily distinguished from complex arteriovenous malformations, long-standing lesions can develop a rich source of inflow, making the distinction difficult. The major sequelae of these lesions include rupture and hemorrhage, high-output heart failure, paradoxical embolization, local mass effect, and ischemia due to vascular steal phenomena. Pulmonary arteriovenous fistula, generally seen in patients with hereditary hemorrhagic telangiectasia (Osler-Weber-Rendu syndrome), carries the additional risk of hypoxemia. Furthermore, paradoxical embolization from these will travel to the systemic arterial circulation, potentially causing stroke or brain abscess.

Therapy of these lesions depends on occluding all potential routes into the shunt. Congenital lesions frequently have a well-defined single feeding channel that can be embolized (see Fig. 5-23). Acquired, traumatic lesions (see Fig. 5-6) have a false channel connecting the artery and vein. These are best treated by occluding the origin of this false channel. Embolization of only the artery proximal to this runs the risk of persistent retrograde filling of the lesion from a reconstituted more distal artery (the "back door" to the lesion). Acquired lesions may be embolized by creating a continuous occlusion of the vessel distal to, at the origin of, and proximal to the false channel, or by a continuous occlusion of the false channel back to the feeding vessel. Isolated occlusion of an acquired false channel runs the risk of recanalization. Care must be taken to properly size the embolic agent to avoid paradoxical embolization, giving mechanical agents an advantage over other types.

Devices designed to close shunts related to congenital heart disease hold potential for closing arteriovenous fistulas while maintaining patency of the feeding channel. Endovascular grafts may also achieve this goal.

Arteriovenous Malformations

Complex arteriovenous malformations may cause complications due to hemorrhage, mass effect, high-output heart failure, or local ischemia due to vascular steal. Depending on the size of the arteriovenous connections, paradoxical embolization may also be significant. These lesions are best treated by eradicating the nidus; the isolated occlusion of feeding vessels afforded by mechanical devices frequently only results in at best temporary benefit as collateral vessels enlarge to supply the malformation. Furthermore, the most direct routes for future embolization will be eliminated. The smaller mechanical agents, such as 0.018-inch wire emboli, do have a role because they can be placed closer to the nidus. Also, there is a role for preoperative large-vessel embolization and occlusion balloon placement to help in the control of these vessels. Malformations that are simple arteriovenous fistulas or in which eradication of the nidus is not essential, such as pulmonary arteriovenous malformations, are well treated by mechanical embolization devices.

Hemorrhage

The choice of the proper embolization agent for hemorrhage depends on the source, location, and etiology of bleeding. The goal is to stop the hemorrhage yet preserve normal tissue.

Large-Vessel Hemorrhage

Bleeding from large vessels may be due to laceration with free extravasation, aneurysm, pseudoaneurysm,

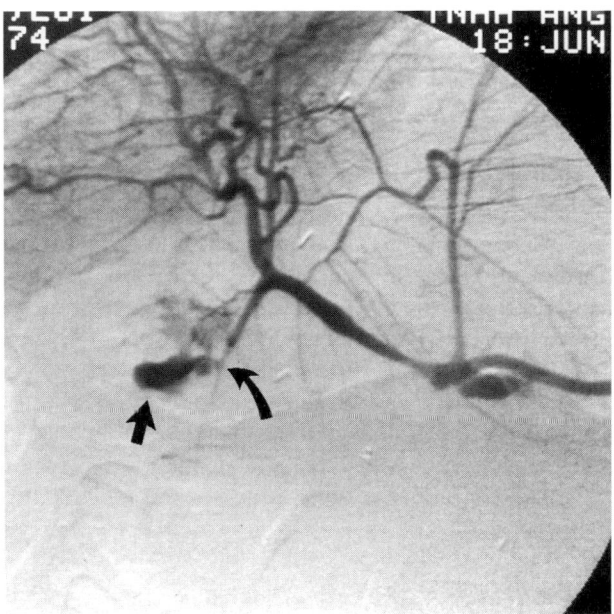

A

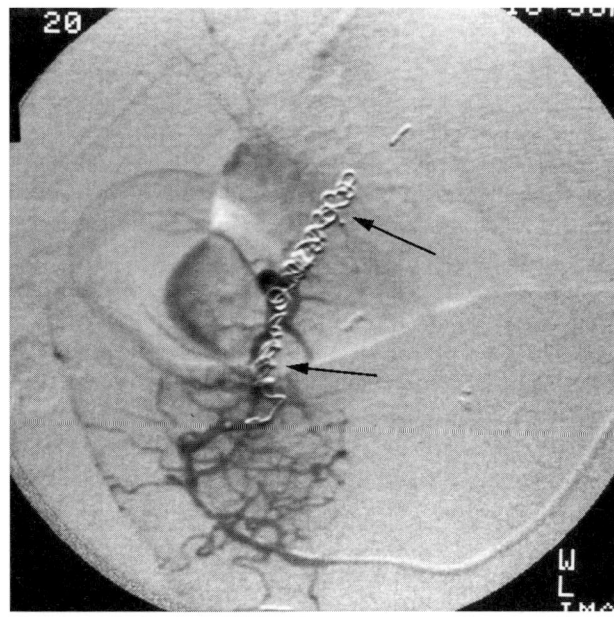

B

Figure 5-25. (A) A 46-year-old man with gastrointestinal lymphoma and massive hemorrhage localized to the duodenum on endoscopy. Celiac angiography demonstrated gross extravasation (*arrow*) directly from the gastroduodenal artery (*curved arrow*). (B) Because of difficulty catheterizing from the celiac route, the gastroduodenal artery was successfully entered with a microcatheter from the inferior pancreaticoduodenal artery and embolized with 0.018-inch-gauge complex helical coils (Target Therapeutics) (*arrows*). The patient stopped bleeding.

arteriovenous fistula, or occasionally spontaneous rupture due to intrinsic or extrinsic related mural disease (e.g., arteritis or erosion from a peptic ulcer or a malignancy). Mechanical agents may be preferred if the site of extravasation can be covered with them (Fig. 5-25). When the vessel cannot be sacrificed, an occlusion balloon may offer preoperative control[109] or even definitive therapy (see Fig. 5-14). If angiography after a trial of balloon occlusion shows no extravasation, surgery may be avoided; however, the patient must be carefully monitored to assess for recurrent bleeding. Also, hemorrhage from a subclavian artery inadvertently catheterized with a large-bore tunneled venous line has been controlled with a covered stent.[110]

Small-Vessel Hemorrhage

It is recommended that proximally occluding agents be avoided when treating small-vessel bleeding if the device cannot be placed across the origin of the hemorrhage. The isolated use of agents traveling distally, such as small particulates, is preferred. In benign conditions, the ideal particle size is that which will create a sufficient diminution in perfusion to permit cessation of hemorrhage yet not cause infarction. Generally, the concern over infarction is less when bleeding is due to a tumor.

Proximal occlusion for small-vessel hemorrhage may not only fail to control the problem but may also restrict the ability to do so in the future by eliminating the direct, most easily catheterizable route for repeat embolization. A good example of this concept is systemic embolotherapy for the control of hemoptysis. Repeat bleeding is known to occur in a significant number of patients, both acutely and on long-term follow-up.[111] If only small particulate agents are used to occlude the bronchial arteries and other systemic vessels, repeat embolization is more easily accomplished through these channels because they will become the primary feeders to the recanalized or newly developed small vessels, as opposed to numerous collateral pathways, which are frequently smaller (having had less time to hypertrophy), more tortuous, and more difficult to catheterize.

Exceptions to this rule include situations in which the rapid occlusion of a vessel is needed in a life-threatening situation and when the risk of undesirable infarction from distal, particulate embolization is high and a nonselective drop in perfusion pressure has a reasonable chance of stopping the bleed. In addition, it may be possible to place the newer, smaller agents directly into submillimeter vessels, potentially across the site of extravasation.

Organ or Tumor Ablation

Embolization of a variety of organs and tumors has been performed for the treatment of benign and malignant disorders, both preoperatively and as isolated therapy. Examples of benign conditions include splenic embolization for thrombocytopenia or gastric variceal bleeding due to splenic vein occlusion and renal embolization for hypertension due to renin-producing end-stage kidneys. Embolization of tumors is done for preoperative vascular control and to palliate unresectable lesions. In addition to bland embolization, occlusion with chemotherapeutic and radioactive agents can be done for selective, high-dose cancer therapy.

In general, the isolated use of mechanical agents to occlude proximal vessels has a limited role, especially if the organ is to remain in the patient, since collateral flow will quickly result in reperfusion; reembolization, if necessary, will then be difficult. Even in organs with end-arteries, such as the kidney, agents traveling to the distal, small-vessel level give a more definitive occlusion. This is less critical in the preoperative situation, where control of the major vessels may be the primary goal.

As an alternative to using releasable agents, perioperative placement of a temporary occlusion balloon may be sufficient. The authors frequently do this for large renal tumors. An occlusion balloon is placed in the operating room after the patient is under general anesthesia, using a prior aortogram to identify the location and number of renal arteries. This approach avoids the complications of postembolization syndrome.

Broad-spectrum antibiotics are recommended if the organ or tumor is not immediately resected. In addition, consultation with anesthesia for postembolization pain control is beneficial.

Redistribution of Blood Flow

Mechanical agents are ideal for protecting a nontarget organ prior to other transvascular therapy. The proximal occlusion they provide permits collateral supply from other routes to maintain perfusion while eliminating significant perfusion from the embolized path. This is most commonly encountered before embolization when avoidance of the nontarget organ is difficult. Placing a coil embolus or detachable balloon in the gastroduodenal artery before hepatic embolization or in the distal inferior gluteal artery before pelvic embolization can prevent occlusion of the pancreaticoduodenal region or gluteal musculature. In addition, occlusion of a small left inferior vena cava has been described as a means of redirecting flow toward the larger right vena cava, which had a filter.[112]

Disorders Related to Venous Insufficiency

Varicocele

Dilatation of the pampiniform plexus is believed to be due to elevated hydrostatic pressure secondary to incompetent valves in the internal spermatic vein or compression of the left renal vein by the superior mesenteric artery.[113] Treatment is indicated when it results in patient discomfort or infertility.

A variety of materials have been used for transcatheter occlusion of the internal spermatic vein, including tissue adhesives, sclerosants, detachable balloons, coils, and hot contrast. The advantage of mechanical agents is greater control over their placement with less risk of proximal or distal migration. The authors use either a series of coils or a combination of detachable balloons with dextrose 70 as a sclerosant between them, with the occasional addition of coils as needed.

Penile Venous Leakage

Impotence related to incompetence of the corpora cavernosal sinusoids has been treated with a variety of embolic agents placed in the draining veins, including coils and detachable balloons.[114]

Nonvascular Indications

Ureter

Patients with intractable urinary fistulas may benefit from occlusion of the ureter and chronic urinary diversion. Among the mechanical agents, coils in conjunction with gelatin sponge (Gelfoam) and glue have been used with success,[115-117] as have detachable balloons.[118] The authors' experience with detachable balloons has been less favorable. They tend to migrate because of ureteral peristalsis, frequently back into the renal pelvis. If these methods fail, renal embolization can be considered.

Biopsy Tracks

Steel coils and Gelfoam have been used to embolize the tracks of percutaneously performed biopsies[119-122] in an effort to enhance the safety of the procedure, especially in patients with bleeding disorders.

Bronchopleural Fistulas

Various methods have been described to occlude bronchi supplying a persistent air leak. In addition to tissue adhesives, fibrin glue, and other agents, both balloons and spring coils have been used.[123-125]

Adverse Events

Major determinants for the occurrence of a complication from embolotherapy appear to be the nature of the underlying lesion,[126] the overall clinical status of the patient, and the level of the occlusion. Other factors that play a role are the vascular anatomy, the experience of the interventionalist, the catheters and contrast used, the embolic material, and the adequacy of follow-up care. The adverse events may result from the diagnostic angiographic procedure, a technical mishap, hemodynamic alterations induced by the occlusion, or the consequences of infarction.

Occlusive or hemorrhagic vascular injuries and contrast reactions may occur from the diagnostic or therapeutic procedure. Nontarget embolization can result from inadvertent embolization or early or late migration. The postembolization syndrome is a benign, self-limiting condition consisting of malaise, fever, nausea, vomiting, pain, and occasionally leukocytosis and adynamic ileus. It is more commonly seen in the setting of extensive tissue infarction or vascular thrombosis and therefore is unlikely with the isolated use of proximally occluding mechanical agents. It generally lasts 3 to 5 days and should be distinguished from a more ominous complication such as infection. Other consequences of infarction (intended or unintended) are abscess, sepsis, and organ-specific events such as perforation of a hollow viscus, stricture formation, neurologic injury, hyperuricemia, and skin sloughing. An understanding of the principles of embolization, the material, the vascular anatomy, and the clinical condition of the patient is important before attempting this form of treatment.

References

1. Prolo DJ, Hambery JW. Intraluminal occlusion of a carotid cavernous sinus fistula with a balloon catheter. Technical note. J Neurosurg 1971;35:237–242.
2. Serbinenko FA. Balloon catheterization and occlusion of major cerebral vessels. J Neurosurg 1974;41:125–145.
3. Picard L, Lepoire J, Montaut J, et al. Endarterial occlusion of carotid-cavernous sinus fistulas using a balloon tipped catheter. Neuroradiology 1974;8:5–10.
4. Debrun G, Lacour P, Caron JP, et al. Experimental approach to the treatment of carotid cavernous fistulas with an inflatable and isolated balloon. Neuroradiology 1975;9:9–12.
5. Gianturco C, Anderson JH, Wallace S. Mechanical devices for arterial occlusion. AJR 1975;124:428–435.
6. Linton RR. Intrasaccular wiring of abdominal arteriosclerotic aortic aneurysms by the "pack" method. Angiology 1951;2:485–498.
7. Inahara T, Geary GL, Mukherjee D, et al. The contrary position to the nonresective treatment for abdominal aortic aneurysm. J Vasc Surg 1985;2:42–48.
8. Blakemore AH, King BG. Electrothermic coagulation of aortic aneurysms. JAMA 1938;111:1821–1827.
9. Wallace S, Gianturco C, Anderson JH, et al. Therapeutic vascular occlusion using steel coil technique: clinical applications. AJR 1976;127:381–387.
10. Anderson JH, Wallace S, Gianturco C. Transcatheter intravascular coil occlusion of experimental arteriovenous fistulas. AJR 1977;129:795–798.
11. White RI Jr, Strandberg JV, Gross GS, et al. Therapeutic embolization with long-term occluding agents and their effects on embolized tissues. Radiology 1977;125:677–687.
12. Jhaveri HS, Gerlock AJ Jr, Ekelund L. Failure of steel coil occlusion in a case of hypernephroma. AJR 1978;130:556.
13. Barth KH, Strandberg JD, Kaufman SL, et al. Chronic vascular reactions to steel coil occlusion devices. AJR 1978;131:455–458.
14. Struthers NW, Samu P, Chalvardjian A. Renal artery aneurysm: a complication of Gianturco coil embolization of renal adenocarcinoma. J Urol 1980;123:105–106.
15. Anderson JH, Wallace S, Gianturco C. "Mini" Gianturco stainless steel coils for transcatheter vascular occlusion. Radiology 1979;132:301–303.
16. Chuang VP, Wallace S, Gianturco C. A new improved coil for tapered-tip catheter for arterial occlusion. Radiology 1980;135:507–509.
17. Yang P, Hallbach VV, Higashida RT, et al. Platinum wire: a new transvascular embolic agent. AJNR 1988;9:547–550.
18. Morse SS, Clark RA, Puffenbarger A. Platinum microcoils for therapeutic embolization: nonneuroradiologic applications. AJR 1990;155:401–403.
19. Teitelbaum GP, Reed RA, Larsen D, et al. Microcatheter embolization of non-neurologic traumatic vascular lesions. J Vasc Intervent Radiol 1993;4:149–154.
20. Makita K, Furui S, Irie T, et al. Embolization with steel coils using a saline flush technique. Br J Radiol 1991;64:708–710.
21. Mazer MJ, Baltaxe HA, Wolf GL. Therapeutic embolization of the renal artery with Gianturco coils: limitations and technical pitfalls. Radiology 1981;138:37–46.
22. Nancarrow PA, Fellows KE, Lock JE. Stability of coil emboli: an in vitro study. Cardiovasc Intervent Radiol 1987;10:226–229.
23. Chuang VP, Szwarc I. The coil baffle in the experimental occlusion of large vascular structures. Radiology 1982;143:25–28.
24. Castaneda-Zuniga WR, Tadavarthy SM, Murphy W, et al. Nonsurgical closure of large arteriovenous fistulas. JAMA 1976;236:2649–2650.
25. Castaneda-Zuniga W, Tadavathy SM, Galliani CA, et al. Experimental venous occlusion with stainless-steel spiders. Radiology 1981;141:238–242.
26. Lund G, Cragg AH, Rysavy JA, et al. Detachable stainless-steel spider. Radiology 1983;148:567–568.
27. Tisnado J, Beachley MC, Shao-Ru C, et al. Peripheral embolization of a stainless steel coil. AJR 1979;133:324–326.
28. Klein FA, Texter JH Jr, Mendez-Picon G. Complications of the Gianturco coil in preoperative infarction of renal cell carcinoma. J Urol 1981;125:105–107.
29. Castaneda-Zuniga W, Zollikofer C, Barnets A, et al. A new device for the safe delivery of stainless steel coils. Radiology 1980;136:230–231.
30. Chang VP. Nonoperative retrieval of Gianturco coils from the abdominal aorta. AJR 1979;132:996–997.
31. Butto F, Hunter DW, Castaneda-Zuniga W, et al. Coil-in-coil technique for vascular embolization. Radiology 1986;161:554–555.
32. Rosen RJ, Rothberg G. Transhepatic embolization of hepatic artery pseudoaneurysm following biliary drainage. Radiology 1982;145:532–533.
33. Rothbarth LJ, Redmond PL, Kumpe DA. Percutaneous transhepatic treatment of a large intrahepatic aneurysm. AJR 1989;153:1077–1078.

34. Capek P, Rocco M, McGahan J, et al. Direct aneurysm puncture and coil occlusion: a new approach to peripancreatic arterial pseudoaneurysms. J Vasc Intervent Radiol 1992;3:653–656.

35. McLean G, Stein EJ, Burke DR, et al. Steel occlusion coils: pretreatment with thrombin. Radiology 1986;158:549–550.

36. Harman JT, Becker GJ. Thrombin-soaked coils: estimation of thrombin dose. J Vasc Intervent Radiol 1991;2:166–168.

37. Nicholson DA, Cockburn JF, Bradshaw AE, et al. Thrombin-soaked embolization coils: the effect of whole blood clotting time. Clin Radiol 1992;46:108–110.

38. Castaneda-Zuniga WR, Tadavarthy SM, Gonzalez R, et al. Single barbed stainless steel coils for venous occlusion: a simple but useful modification. Invest Radiol 1992;17:186–188.

39. Lund G, Rysavy J, Kotula F, et al. Detachable steel spring coils for vessel occlusion. Radiology 1985;155:530.

40. Hawkins J, Quisling RG, Mickle JP, et al. Retrievable Gianturco-coil introducer. Radiology 1986;158:262–264.

41. Zollikofer C, Castaneda-Zuniga WR, Galliani C, et al. A combination of stainless steel coil and compressed Ivalon: a new technique for embolization of large arteries and arteriovenous fistulas. Radiology 1981;138:229–231.

42. Van Lanschot JJB, Meijssen MAC, de Witte MT, et al. Intra-arterial embolisation coils mimicking retained swab in the peritoneal cavity. Eur J Surg 1993;159:57–58.

43. Marshall M, Teitelbaum GP, Kim HS, et al. MR imaging safety and artifacts of platinum embolization microcoils. Cardiovasc Intervent Radiol 1991;14:163–166.

44. Shellock FG, Curtis JS. MR imaging and biomedical implants, materials, and devices: an updated review. Radiology 1991; 180:541–550.

45. Teitelbaum GP, Bradley WG Jr, Klein BD. MR imaging artifacts, ferromagnetism, and magnetic torque of intravascular filters, stents, and coils. Radiology 1988;166:657–664.

46. Takahashi A, Yoshimoto T, Kawakami K, et al. Transvenous copper wire insertion for dural arteriovenous malformations of the cavernous sinus. J Neurosurg 1989;70:751–754.

47. Sawyer PN, Pate JW. Bioelectric phenomena as an etiologic factor in intravascular thrombosis. Am J Physiol 1953;175:103–107.

48. Thompson WM, Johnsrude IS. Vessel occlusion with transcatheter electrocoagulation. Cardiovasc Intervent Radiol 1980;3:244–255.

49. Guglielmi G, Vinuela F, Sepetka I, et al. Electrothrombosis of saccular aneurysms via endovascular approach: Part 1. Electrochemical basis, technique, and experimental results. J Neurosurg 1991;75:1–7.

50. Guglielmi G, Vinuela F, Dion J, et al. Electrothrombosis of saccular aneurysms via endovascular approach: Part 2. Preliminary clinical experience. J Neurosurg 1991;75:8–14.

51. Guglielmi G, Vinuela F, Duckwiler G, et al. Endovascular treatment of posterior circulation aneurysms by electrothrombosis using electrically detachable coils. J Neurosurg 1992;77:515–524.

52. Cragg AH, Galliani CA, Rysavy JA, et al. Endovascular diathermic vessel occlusion. Radiology 1982;144:303–308.

53. Yamanashi WS, Saksanen SJ, Valentine JL, et al. Intervascular occlusion of canine renal, splenic, and vertebral arteries using electromagnetic field focusing (EEF) probe. Angiology 1991; 42:195–201.

54. Castaneda-Zuniga WR, Galliani CA, Rysavy J, et al. "Spiderlon": new device for simple, fast arterial and venous occlusion. AJR 1981;136:627–628.

55. Dotter CT, Lukas DS. Acute cor pulmonale: an experimental study utilizing a special cardiac catheter. Am J Physiol 1951; 164:254–262.

56. Edwards WS, Salter PP, Carnaggio VA. Intraluminal aortic occlusion as a possible mechanism for controlling massive intra-abdominal hemorrhage. Surg Forum 1953;4:496–499.

57. Hesse FG, Kletschka HD. Rupture of abdominal aortic aneurysm: control of hemorrhage by intraluminal balloon tamponade. Ann Surg 1962;155:320–322.

58. Heimbecker RO. An aortic tampon for emergency control of ruptured abdominal aneurysm. Can Med Assoc J 1964;91:1024–1025.

59. Rubenstein RB, Wolvek S. Percutaneous aortic balloon occlusion. Surg Gynecol Obstet 1987;164:561–563.

60. Wholey MH, Stockdale R, Hung TK. A percutaneous balloon catheter for the immediate control of hemorrhage. Radiology 1970;95:65–71.

61. Paster SB, Van Houten FX, Adams DF. Percutaneous balloon catheterization: a technique for the control of arterial hemorrhage caused by pelvic trauma. JAMA 1974;230:573–575.

62. Wholey MH. The technology of balloon catheters in interventional angiography. Radiology 1977;125:671–676.

63. Greenfield AJ, Athanasoulis CA, Waltman AC, et al. Transcatheter embolization: prevention of embolic reflux using balloon catheters. AJR 1978;131:651–655.

64. Eckard DA, Purdy PD, Bonte FJ. Temporary balloon occlusion of the carotid artery combined with brain blood flow imaging as a test to predict tolerance prior to permanent carotid sacrifice. AJNR 1992;13:1565–1569.

65. Kerber C. Balloon catheter with a calibrated leak: a new system for superselective angiography and occlusive catheter therapy. Radiology 1976;124:547–550.

66. Pevsner PH. Micro-balloon catheter for superselective angiography and therapeutic occlusion. AJR 1977;128:225–230.

67. Debrun G, Lacour P, Caron J-P, et al. Detachable balloons and calibrated-leak balloon techniques in the treatment of cerebral vascular lesions. J Neurosurg 1978;49:635–649.

68. Kerber CW, Bank WO, Cromwell LD. Calibrated leak balloon microcatheter: a device for arterial exploration and occlusive therapy. AJR 1979;132:207–212.

69. Higashida RT, Halback VV, Dormandy B, et al. Endovascular treatment of intracranial aneurysms with a new silicone microballoon device: technical considerations and indications for therapy. Radiology 1990;174:687–691.

70. White RI Jr, Urasic TA, Kaufman SL, et al. Therapeutic embolization with detachable balloons: physical factors influencing permanent occlusion. Radiology 1978;126:521–523.

71. Goto K, Halbach VV, Hardin CW, et al. Permanent inflation of detachable balloons with a low viscosity hydrophilic polymerizing system. Radiology 1988;169:787–790.

72. Tomsick TA. Osmotic effects upon long term inflation of latex detachable balloons. Neurosurgery 1985;17:952–954.

73. Hawkins TD, Szaz KF. The permeability of detachable latex rubber balloons: an in vitro study. Invest Radiol 1987;22:969–972.

74. Taki W, Handa H, Yamagata S, et al. Radiopaque solidifying liquids for releasable balloon technique: a technical note. Surg Neurol 1980;13:140–142.

75. Monsein LH, Debrun GM, Chazaly JR. Hydroxyethyl methacrylate and latex balloons. AJNR 1990;11:663–664.

76. Forsting M, Sartor K. Hema and latex: a dangerous combination? Neuroradiology 1991;33:338–340.

77. Kaufman SL, Strandberg JD, Barth KH. Therapeutic embolization with detachable silicone balloons: long-term effects in swine. Invest Radiol 1979:14:156–161.

78. Miyachi S, Negoro M, Handa T, et al. Histopathological study of balloon embolization: silicone versus latex. Neurosurgery 1992;30:483–489.

79. Ownby DR, Tomlanovich M, Sammons N, et al. Anaphylaxis associated with latex allergy during barium enema examinations. AJR 1991;156:903–908.

80. Warpinski JR, Folgert J, Cohen M, et al. Allergic reaction to latex: a risk factor for unsuspected anaphylaxis. Allerg Proc 1991;12:95–102.

81. Barrow DL, Fleischer AS, Hoffman JC. Complications of detachable balloon catheter technique in the treatment of traumatic intracranial arteriovenous fistulas. J Neurosurg 1982; 56:396–403.

82. Nelson M. A versatile, steerable, flow-guided catheter for the delivery of detachable balloons. AJNR 1990;11:657–658.

83. Lammert GK, Merine D, White RI Jr, et al. Embolotherapy

of a high-flow false aneurysm by using an occlusion balloon, thrombin, steel coils, and a detachable balloon. AJR 1989; 152:382–384.

84. Grinnell VS, Flanagan KG, Mehringer CM, et al. Occlusion of large fistulas with detachable valved balloons and the spider. AJR 1983;140:1259–1261.

85. Dotter CT, Rösch J, Lakin PC, et al. Injectable flow-guided coaxial catheters for selective angiography and controlled vascular occlusion. Radiology 1972;104:421–423.

86. Pollak JS, Lee GK, White RI Jr, et al. Comparison of the mechanical properties of detachable balloons for embolotherapy. J Vasc Intervent Radiol 1993;4:91–95.

87. Debrun GM: Embolotherapy with detachable balloons: the Debrun balloons. In: Kadir S, ed. Current practice of interventional radiology. Philadelphia: Decker, 1991:100–104.

88. Makita K, Furui S, Machida T, et al. Wire-directed detachable balloon: work in progress. Radiology 1991;180:139–140.

89. Makita K, Kazuhiro T, Furui S, et al. Nondissecting vertebral fusiform aneurysm: embolization using wire-directed detachable balloons. AJNR 1993;14:340–342.

90. Rand RW. Thrombogenic microballoon for cerebral aneurysms, arteriovenous malformations, and carotid cavernous fistula occlusion: preliminary technical note. Surg Neurol 1991;35:403–407.

91. Tsuruda JS, Sevick RJ, Halbach VV. Three-dimensional time-of-flight MR angiography in the evaluation of intracranial aneurysms treated by endovascular balloon occlusion. AJNR 1992;13:1129–1136.

92. Portstmann W, Wierny L, Warnke H, et al. Catheter closure of patent ductus arteriosus: 62 cases treated without thoracotomy. Radiol Clin North Am 1971;9:203–218.

93. Hellenbrand WE, Mullins CE. Catheter closure of congenital cardiac defects. Cardiol Clin 1989;7:351–368.

94. Transcatheter occlusion of persistent arterial duct: report of the European registry. Lancet 1992;340:1062–1066.

95. Hourihan M, Perry SB, Mandell VS, et al. Transcatheter umbrella closure of valvular and paravalvular leaks. J Am Coll Cardiol 1992;20:1371–1377.

96. Rome JJ, Keane JF, Perry SB, et al. Double-umbrella closure of atrial septal defects: initial clinical applications. Circulation 1990;82:751–758.

97. Schlesinger AE, Folz SJ, Beekman RH. Transcatheter atrial septal defect occlusion devices: normal radiographic appearances and complications. J Vasc Intervent Radiol 1992;3:527–533.

98. Saveliev VS, Prokubovski VI, Kolody SM. Patent ductus arteriosus: transcatheter closure with a transvenous technique. Radiology 1992;184:341–344.

99. Halbach VV, Higashida RT, Hieshima GB, et al. Transarterial occlusion of solitary intracerebral arteriovenous fistulas. AJNR 1989;10:747–752.

100. Benati A, Beltramello A, Colombari R, et al. Preoperative embolization of arteriovenous malformations with polylene threads: techniques with wing microcatheter and pathologic results. AJNR 1989;10:579–586.

101. Gomes AS, Rysavy JA, Spadaccini CA, et al. The use of the bristle brush for transcatheter embolization. Radiology 1978; 129:345–350.

102. O'Reilly GV, Forrest MD, Schoene WC, et al. Laser-induced thermal occlusion of berry aneurysms: initial experimental results. Radiology 1989;171:471-474.

103. Cope C, Zeit R. Coagulation of aneurysms by direct percutaneous thrombin injection. AJR 1986;147:383–387.

104. Lugmayr H, Hartl P, Schwarz C, et al. Stent implantation in solitary aneurysm of the common iliac artery. Dtsch Med Wochenschr 1993;118:499–502.

105. Mirich D, Wright KC, Wallace S, et al. Percutaneously placed endovascular grafts for aortic aneurysms: feasibility study. Radiology 1989;170:1033–1037.

106. Laborde JC, Parodi JC, Clem MF, et al. Intraluminal bypass of abdominal aortic aneurysm: feasibility study. Radiology 1992;184:185–190.

107. Lazarus HM. Endovascular grafting for the treatment of abdominal aortic aneurysms. Surg Clin North Am 1992;72:959–968.

108. Schwarz W, Nozick J, Richmand D, et al. The in situ saphenous vein bypass graft: radiologic aspects. AJR 1986;146:605–608.

109. Scalea TM, Sclafani SJ. Angiographically placed balloons for arterial control: a description of a technique. J Trauma 1991;31:1671–1677.

110. Becker GJ, Benenatl JF, Zemel G, et al. Percutaneous placement of a balloon-expandable intraluminal graft for life-threatening subclavian artery hemorrhage. J Vasc Intervent Radiol 1991;2:225–229.

111. Stoll JF, Bettmann MA. Bronchial artery embolization to control hemoptysis: a review. Cardiovasc Intervent Radiol 1988;11:263–269.

112. Smith D, Kohne RE, Taylor FC. Steel coil embolization supplementing filter placement in a patient with a duplicated inferior vena cava. J Vasc Intervent Radiol 1992;3:577–580.

113. Thomas AJ Jr, Geisinger MA. Current management of varicoceles. Urol Clin North Am 1990;17:893–907.

114. Schwartz AN, Lowe M, Harley JD, et al. Preliminary report: penile vein occlusion therapy: selection criteria and methods used for the transcatheter treatment of impotence caused by venous-sinusoidal incompetence. J Urol 1992;148:815–820.

115. Gaylord GM, Johnsrude IS. Transrenal ureteral occlusion with Gianturco coils and gelatin sponge. Radiology 1989;172:1047–1048.

116. Bing KT, Hicks ME, Figenshau RS, et al. Percutaneous ureteral occlusion with use of Gianturco coils and gelatin sponge: Part I. Swine model. J Vasc Intervent Radiol 1992;3:313–317.

117. Bing KT, Hicks ME, Picus D, et al. Percutaneous ureteral occlusion with use of Gianturco coils and gelatin sponge: Part II. Clinical experience. J Vasc Intervent Radiol 1992;3:319–321.

118. Gunther R, Klose KJ, Alken P, et al. Transrenal ureteral occlusion with a detachable balloon. Radiology 1982;142:521–523.

119. Chuang VP, Alspaugh JP. Sheath needle for liver biopsy in high-risk patients. Radiology 1988;166:261–262.

120. Allison DJ, Adams A. Percutaneous liver biopsy and track embolization with steel coils. Radiology 1988;169:261–263.

121. Crummy AB, McDermott JC, Wojtowycz M. A technique for embolization of biopsy tracts. AJR 1989;153:67–68.

122. Dawson P, Adam A, Edwards R. Technique for steel coil embolization of biopsy track for use with the "Biopty" needle. Br J Radiol 1992;65:538–540.

123. Ellis JH, Sequeira FW, Weber TR, et al. Balloon catheter occlusion of bronchopleural fistula. AJR 1982;138:157–159.

124. Pace R, Rankin RN, Finley RJ. Detachable balloon occlusion of bronchopleural fistulae in dogs. Invest Radiol 1983;18:504–506.

125. Salmon CJ, Ponn RB, Westcott JL. Endobronchial vascular occlusion coils for control of a large parenchymal bronchopleural fistula. Chest 1990;98:233–234.

126. Hemingway AP, Allison DJ. Complications of embolization: analysis of 410 procedures. Radiology 1988;166:669–672.

6

Principles of Regional Chemotherapy

MICHAEL J. PENTECOST

The regional infusion of a chemotherapeutic agent is a means of increasing the drug exposure of a tumor. By injecting the agent directly into the arterial supply, one can increase the concentration of the drug substantially and, correspondingly, decrease the systemic exposure.

Several principles underlie such treatments.[1] First, the tumor should be confined to the area of infusion. Regional therapies of any kind, whether involving drugs, surgery, or radiation, make little sense if widespread disease is present. Second, a window of tumor sensitivity should be present. If a tumor is very sensitive, systemic levels should be adequate; if insensitive, increased levels of antineoplastic agent will have no effect. Third, a practical catheter system should be available that infuses the entire area of tumor on a repeated and chronic basis.

The pharmacokinetics of regional arterial infusion have been well described.[2,3] The advantages are determined by the clearance of agent by the body, the extraction of agent by the tumor, and the arterial flow to the neoplasm, according to the following formula:

$$\text{Advantage} = 1 + \frac{C}{F(1 - E)}$$

where

- C = total body clearance from the rest of the body except the tumor
- F = blood flow through artery infused
- E = extraction of the drug in the affected area

As clearance of an agent increases, so does the advantage of regional infusion. If the clearance of an agent were minimal, the drug would constantly recirculate through the tumor bed and no advantage would be conferred by direct injection. The rate of flow varies inversely to the advantage because a slower tide prolongs exposure time. Advantage varies directly with the extraction of agent by the target; the greater the extraction, the greater the advantage.

However, this formula does make certain assumptions that may not be accurate.[4] The perfusion of normal and neoplastic tissue may vary throughout an area and change over time. Since advantage varies inversely to flow, any factor that alters the ratio of flow between normal and tumor tissue (e.g., clot formation, catheter migration, neovascularity, etc.) could decrease the benefit of regional infusion. Although the concentration of drug in the systemic, afferent arterial and effluent venous circulation is relatively easy to measure, tissue and compartment levels are more difficult to obtain, particularly over time. Another important yet unproved assumption is that there is no streaming of drug in the bloodstream. Although this may be the case, experimental studies have suggested otherwise.[5]

Drug Classes and Mechanisms of Action

Chemotherapeutic agents can be divided into five broad categories: antimetabolites, antitumor antibiotics, platinum analogues, alkylating agents, and vinca alkaloids (Table 6-1). For some, such as methotrexate, the mechanism of action is relatively well understood; in others, there are large gaps in the fundamental understanding of their action. All of the following agents are FDA-approved, the subject of considerable study in the clinic, and used either in regional infusions or in alternative therapies.

Antimetabolites

Antimetabolites interfere with DNA synthesis during the S phase of cell division. The antifolate compound methotrexate is one of the most commonly used and best-understood antimetabolites. Methotrexate inhibits and depletes the intracellular concentration of dihydrofolate reductase, thus interfering with purine and pyrimidine synthesis. It is used in treating leukemia, lymphoma, breast cancer, and head and neck cancer.

The fluoropyrimidine 5-fluorouracil (5-FU) is well tolerated, relatively nonmyelosuppressive, and syner-

Table 6-1. Classification of Chemotherapeutic Agents by Method of Action

Antimetabolites
    Methotrexate
    5-fluorouracil
Antibiotics
    Bleomycin
    Doxorubicin
    Mitomycin
Platinum analogues
    Cisplatin
Alkylating agents
    Cyclophosphamide
    Melphalan
    Chlorambucil
    Busulfan
    Ifosfamide
Vinca alkaloids
    Vincristine

Table 6-2. Exposure with Hepatic Artery Infusion

Agent	Increase in Hepatic Exposure
Fluorouracil (5-FU)	50–100 fold
Floxuridine (FUDR)	100–400 fold
Mitomycin	3–5 fold
Cisplatin	2–4 fold

Adapted from Ensminger WD, Syves JW. Regional cancer chemotherapy. Cancer Treat Rep 1984;68:101–115.

gistic with other cytostatic agents and radiation. It is a commonly used agent in treating breast, gastrointestinal, and head and neck tumors. Since cell division and DNA synthesis are minimal in these solid tumors, few cells are in the S phase. To increase the probability of catching cells during division, these agents are used in prolonged or infusion therapy rather than in bolus injections. The intracellular derivative of 5-FU, fluorodeoxyuridine (floxuridine or FUDR), inhibits thymidine synthetase activity, leading to the depletion of deoxythymidine triphosphate, which is essential for DNA synthesis. FUDR is commonly used for regional hepatic infusions because there is a 95 percent extraction or first-pass clearance, compared to 50 percent for 5-FU (Table 6-2).[6]

Antibiotics

Bleomycin, an antibiotic with anticancer and antimicrobial activity, is commonly used in treating lymphoma and germ-cell tumors, particularly testicular cancer. Bleomycin works by creating breaks in DNA strands and is most active in the premitotic or G2 phase. It has well-known pulmonary toxicity but little myelosuppressive activity.

The anthracycline doxorubicin is used to treat leukemia and solid tumors such as soft tissue sarcomas and breast and lung cancer. It has two methods of activity—DNA fragmentation and free radical formation. It causes DNA fragmentation by triggering activity of topoisomerase II, an enzyme responsible for strand passing and coiling during replication. The cellular generation of superoxide, hydrogen peroxide, and hydroxyl radical by doxorubicin results in destruction of DNA and cell membrane lipids. Doxorubicin causes myelosuppression, but its most characteristic side effect is cardiac toxicity.

Mitomycin is used in the therapy of gastrointestinal and small-cell lung tumors. The antibiotic, after alkylating, cross-links with adenine and guanine, causing inhibition of DNA synthesis. Mitomycin is most active in a hypoxic environment and is therefore used in solid tumors and chemoembolization. Toxic effects include myelosuppression and renal failure.

Platinum Analogues

The platinum analogue cisplatin is effective in treating bladder, lung, germ-cell, and head and neck tumors. The mechanism of action is unclear but seems to be related to DNA binding to guanine and adenine. Since the predominant toxicity is renal insufficiency, careful screening and monitoring of kidney function are necessary. Other side effects include peripheral neuropathy, ototoxicity, nausea, and vomiting.

Alkylating Agents

Alkylating agents used in oncology practice include cyclophosphamide, melphalan, chlorambucil, busulfan, and ifosfamide. All share a positively charged, electrophilic alkyl group that combines with DNA and interferes with replication and transcription.

Most recently, interest has centered on cyclophosphamide, which is used in the treatment of lymphoma, myeloma, and breast cancer. A potent immunosuppressant, cyclophosphamide is also used to treat rheumatoid arthritis, vasculitis, and graft versus host reactions. In addition to immunosuppression, adverse effects include hemorrhagic cystitis and myocardial damage.

Vinca Alkaloids

Vincristine, the most commonly used vinca alkaloid, is employed in the treatment of leukemia, lymphoma, sarcomas, and breast and lung tumors. Vincristine works by binding with and preventing polymerization of tubulin; this disrupts the formation of intracellular microtubules, which are essential for intracellular transport and preservation of cell shape. It is most active in the G1 or S phase of the cell cycle. Vincristine is metabolized by the liver, and its use must be modified in the face of hepatic dysfunction. Side effects include neurotoxicity, myelosuppression, and gastrointestinal dysfunction.

Clinical Applications

Intraarterial infusion chemotherapy has been used for a number of malignancies, most commonly liver (Chapter 27) and musculoskeletal neoplasms (Chapter 61). Limited experience has been reported with breast, pelvic, and head and neck tumors.

Because of better screening, presentation with stage III (or locally advanced) breast cancer is uncommon, occurring in only 5 percent of patients in the United States. Surgery, radiation, and/or chemotherapy (particularly doxorubicin) allows for local control in most patients, with a 10-year survival in 15 to 40 percent. The success of this combination treatment has restrained the use of intraarterial chemotherapy infusion, despite encouraging early results.[7] The patient with previously treated, locally recurrent disease presents a more difficult problem because repeat surgery, radiation therapy, or systemic chemotherapy may not be possible. A recent study described experience with the intraarterial infusion of mitoxantrone, an antitumor antibiotic, in such a setting.[8] With the infusion into the lateral thoracic, thoracodorsal, and internal mammary branches of the subclavian artery, a beneficial effect was observed in 77 percent of patients. The appropriate branch of the subclavian artery was selected by using CT angiography. The unavoidable infusion of surrounding normal tissues was well tolerated.

Up to 15 percent of patients with bladder cancer present with or progress to muscle invasion. With primary, or neoadjuvant, chemotherapy and/or radiation, the 5-year survival with radical cystectomy in such patients is 50 percent, with less than 5 percent operative mortality. Sumiyoshi et al. describe similar survival after bladder-sparing surgery preceded by radiation and intraarterial infusion of doxorubicin.[9] The agent was infused into the common iliac artery during compression of the common femoral artery; this approach was chosen to include potential nutrient vessels from the internal and external iliac distribution.

The incidence of cervical carcinoma has greatly declined with cytologic screening. Early-stage macroscopic cancer (stages I and II) can be treated with either radiation or surgery. Stage III and IV diseases are typically treated with radiation. Promising results with intraarterial chemotherapy in 16 patients with advanced cervical carcinoma have recently been reported by Morris et al.[10] Using surgically implanted catheters, the anterior divisions of the internal iliac arteries were infused with FUDR and cisplatin over 4 weeks during concurrent radiation therapy. Eight patients had a complete response, and 6 had partial responses.

The conventional therapy for stage I and stage II (cervix involvement) carcinoma of the endometrium is total hysterectomy and oophorectomy with or without radiation therapy. Preoperative pharmacologic manipulation with intraarterial angiotensin, doxorubicin, and cisplatin has been tested in such patients by Hata et al.[11] The rationale for this combination is to selectively increase blood flow to tumor tissue during chemotherapy infusion, angiotensin being the hypertensive and hyperperfusion agent. Using Doppler ultrasound and magnetic resonance imaging, Hata and colleagues documented the increased flow to malignant tissue and the subsequent tumor response with this technique.

Unlike most tumors, head and neck cancers are fatal because of locoregional rather than metastatic disease. Thus emphasis is placed on staging and controlling local disease. Radiation, limited or radical neck dissection, and systemic chemotherapy in various combinations are used in various combinations; no compelling advantage has been demonstrated with any particular treatment or combination. Robbins et al. recently reported an ingenious method of delivering very high doses of cisplatin to patients with stage III and IV head and neck tumors.[12] Using techniques first conceived for intraperitoneal administration,[13] they administered doses up to 200 mg/m^2/week via microcatheters selectively placed into branches of the carotid artery (Fig. 6-1). Thiosulfate, which neutralizes cisplatin, was simultaneously infused intravenously. Nontarget perfusion occurred in 2 patients. Of 22 patients with untreated disease, 86 percent responded to the therapy.

Complications

The indwelling catheters necessary for long-term infusion of antitumor agents pose unique problems that differ from problems due to the embolization therapy for cancer (see Chapter 27). These include pericatheter thrombus formation, local toxic effect of chemotherapy, and catheter migration. At first these complications limited acceptance for percutaneously placed catheters and regional cancer therapies.[14] More recently, complications from surgically placed catheters have also limited acceptance of this mode of ther-

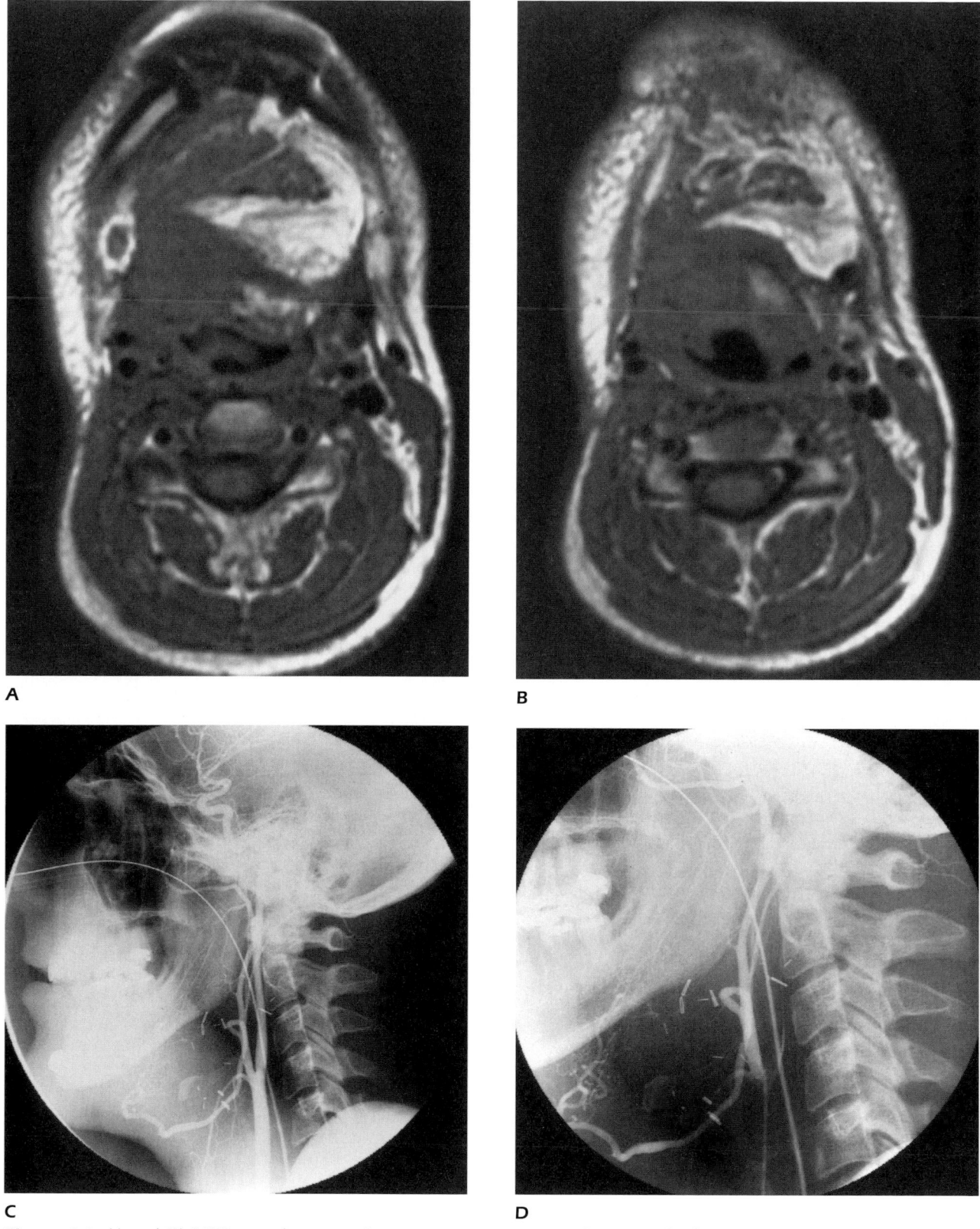

Figure 6-1. (A and B) MRI scan demonstrating recurrent squamous-cell carcinoma at the base of the tongue extending into the preepiglottic space. The carcinoma is adja

cent to the pectoralis flap. The patient had had a previous mandibular resection. (C and D) External carotid angiography prior to cisplatin infusion.

apy.[15-18] Techniques have now been developed to place infusion port catheters percutaneously[19]; whether such techniques permit one to avoid earlier-reported complications remains unclear.

Iatrogenic arterial injuries at the point of infusion (unrelated to the puncture site) are particularly common in vessels of the extremity.[20] This is probably due to their small size, their proclivity for developing spasm, and the frequent use of such therapies in patients with extremity sarcoma and melanoma.

Conclusion

With appropriately selected agents, regional infusion therapy for cancer is physiologically well founded. Changes in flow, which inevitably result when an indwelling catheter infuses a vasoactive agent, have to date been an intractable problem. Most clinicians have turned their interests to therapies with very short catheter swell time or to chemoembolization. In these treatments, flow dynamics can be monitored continuously.

References

1. Ensminger WD, Gyves JW. Regional chemotherapy of neoplastic diseases. Pharmcol Ther 1983;21:277–293.
2. Eckman WW, Patlak CS, Fenstermacher JD. A critical evaluation of principles governing the advantages of intraarterial infusions. J Pharmacokinet Biopharmacol 1974;2:257–285.
3. Chen HSG, Gross JF. Intra-arterial infusion of anti-cancer agents: theoretic aspects of drug delivery and review of responses. Cancer Treat Rep 1980;64:31–40.
4. Dedrick RL. Arterial drug infusion: pharmacokinetic problems and pitfalls. J Natl Cancer Inst 1988;80:84–89.
5. Lutz RJ, Dedrick RL, Boretos JW, et al. Mixing during intra-carotid artery infusions in an in vitro model. J Neurosurg 1986; 64:277–283.
6. Ensminger WD, Gyves JW. Regional cancer chemotherapy. Cancer Treat Rep 1984;68:101–115.
7. Koyama H, Nishizawa Y, Wada T, et al. Intra-arterial infusion chemotherapy as an induction therapy in multidisciplinary treatment of locally advanced breast cancer. Cancer 1985;56: 725–729.
8. Gorich J, Hasan I, Majdali R, et al. Previously treated, locally recurrent breast cancer: treatment with superselective intra-arterial chemotherapy. Radiology 1995;197:199–203.
9. Sumiyoshi Y, Yokota K, Akiyama M, et al. Neoadjuvant intra-arterial doxorubicin chemotherapy in combination with low dose radiotherapy for the treatment of locally advanced transitional cell carcinoma of the bladder. J Urol 1994;152:362–366.
10. Morris M, Eifel PJ, Burke TW, et al. Treatment of locally advanced cervical cancer with concurrent radiation and intra-arterial chemotherapy. Gynecol Oncol 1995;57:72–78.
11. Hata K, Hata T, Fujiwaki R, et al. Hypertensive intra-arterial chemotherapy for endometrial carcinoma assessed by transvaginal Doppler ultrasound and magnetic resonance imaging. J Clin Ultrasound 1995;23:407–411.
12. Robbins KT, Storniolo AM, Kerber C, et al. Phase I study of highly selective supradose cisplatin infusions for advanced head and neck cancer. J Clin Oncol 1994;12:2113–2020.
13. Howell SB, Pfeifle CE, Wung WE, et al. Intraperitoneal cisplatin with systemic thiosulfate protection. Ann Intern Med 1982;97:845–851.
14. Clouse ME, Ahmed R, Ryan RB, et al. Complications of long term transbrachial hepatic arterial infusion chemotherapy. Am J Roentgenol 1977;129:799–803.
15. Kemeny N, Daly J, Reichman B, et al. Intrahepatic or systemic infusion of fluorodeoxyuridine in patients with liver metastases from colorectal carcinoma. Ann Intern Med 1987;107:459–465.
16. Hohn DC, Stagg RJ, Friedman MA. A randomized trial of continuous intravenous versus hepatic intraarterial floxuridine in patients with colorectal cancer metastatic to the liver. The Northern California Oncology Group Trial. J Clin Oncol 1989; 7:1646–1654.
17. Chang AE, Schneider PD, Sugarbaker PH, et al. A prospective randomized trial of regional versus systemic continuous 5-fluorodeoxyuridine chemotherapy in the treatment of colorectal liver metastases. Ann Surg 1987;206:685–693.
18. Martin JK, O'Connell MJ, Wieand HS, et al. Intra-arterial floxuridine vs. systemic fluorouracil for hepatic metastases from colorectal cancer. Arch Surg 1990;125:1022–1027.
19. Yoshikawa M, Ebara M, Nakano T, et al. Percutaneous transaxillary catheter insertion for hepatic artery infusion chemotherapy. AJR 1992;158:885–886.
20. Myers SI, Harward TRS, Putnam JB, et al. Vascular trauma as a result of therapeutic procedures for the treatment of malignancy. J Vasc Surg 1991;14:314–319.

7

Vascular Stents

GARY J. BECKER

This chapter focuses exclusively on the principles of metallic vascular stents and the applications of stents in lower extremity and renal arteries. The reasons are threefold: (1) plastic biliary and ureteral stents and metallic stents used in other organ systems are dealt with elsewhere in this text, (2) metallic stents used elsewhere (e.g., biliary ductal system, tracheobronchial tree, esophagus, etc.) are, for the most part, of the very same design and manufacture as those discussed here, and (3) a thorough discussion of stent properties and principles of arterial stenting embodies the important principles of all intraluminal stenting.

Historical Background

The potential benefits of endovascular "splinting" were first described by Dotter and Judkins in the original article on angioplasty in 1964.[1] They correctly predicted that endovascular "splints" would "reintimalize." In 1969, Dotter reported his laboratory experience with a spring-coil endoprosthesis in canine popliteal arteries.[2] This was the first report of transluminal endovascular metallic stent placement under fluoroscopic guidance, although metallic endovascular prostheses had been placed surgically for other purposes in the past. In the United States, further interest was not demonstrated until 1983, at which time Dotter and colleagues[3] and Cragg and colleagues[4] each published experimental findings with the use of nitinol self-expanding spring-coil endoprostheses in animals. However, since that time, many stents have been designed and evaluated in laboratory and clinical studies.

Current Experience in the United States and Abroad

Clinical experience with stenting for peripheral vascular disease (PVD) in the United States has been largely limited to the Palmaz stent (Johnson & Johnson Interventional Systems, JJIS) and the Wallstent (Schneider Stent Division, Pfizer), and as of this writing, only the Palmaz stent has been approved for peripheral vascular use by the U.S. Food and Drug Administration (FDA) for suboptimal iliac percutaneous transluminal angioplasty (PTA) results. The Palmaz-Schatz stent (JJIS) and the Gianturco-Roubin FlexStent (Cook, Inc.) have been approved for use in the coronary arteries. FDA approval of the Wallstent for use in failed iliac and femoral PTA and in transjugular intrahepatic portosystemic shunts (TIPS) is pending.

The Strecker woven tantalum balloon-expandable mesh stent (Strecker Stent), the Cragg nitinol stent, and the Memotherm stent have been implanted extensively for peripheral vascular disease in Europe and other international locations. The Gianturco Z stent has been used extensively in the treatment of benign and malignant vena cava syndromes. More recently, it has been used as metallic skeletal framework for the construction of endografts used investigationally in the treatment of aneurysms, pseudoaneurysms, and arteriovenous fistulas.

General Principles of Vascular Stents

The immediate success and long-term benefits of percutaneous transluminal angioplasty (PTA) are significantly diminished by the problems of acute closure and postangioplasty restenosis. Acute closures occur in 1 to 5 percent of peripheral PTAs[5-7] and in a similar number of coronary angioplasties (PTCAs).[8] Most of the former and approximately one-half of the latter are due to extensive, flow-limiting dissection. Restenosis occurs from weeks to months after balloon PTA. The most important causes are intimal hyperplasia (about 60 percent of cases)[9] and elastic recoil (most of the remaining cases). The process of restenosis and its relationship to the recurrence of clinical symptoms are more complex than this, but a discussion is beyond the present scope of this chapter.[10-19]

Intravascular stenting in all of its forms embodies

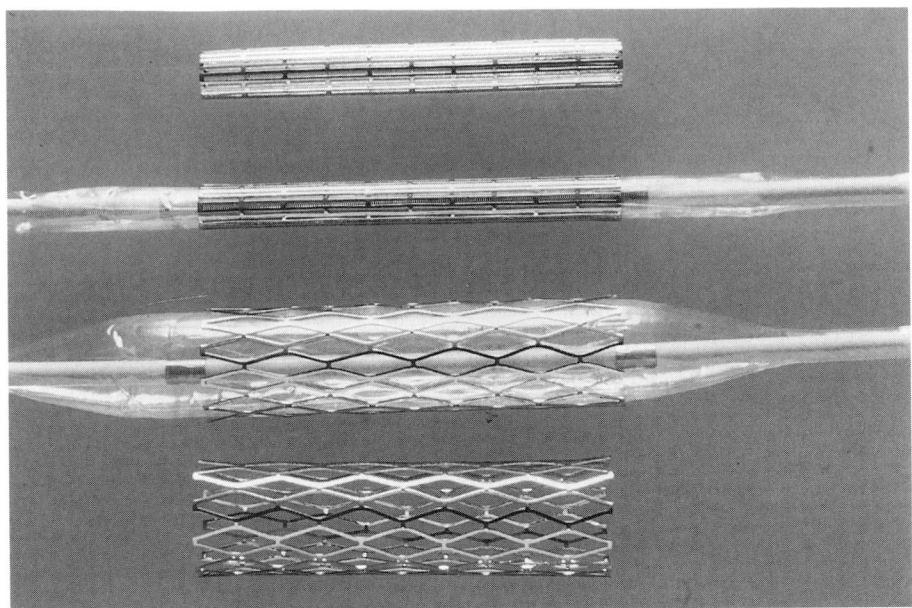

Figure 7-1. Palmaz balloon-expandable intraluminal stent. *Top to bottom:* unmounted stent; stent mounted and crimped on balloon; stent expanded by balloon inflation; stent deployed, balloon catheter removed.

one major strategy for dealing with the shortcomings of PTA. The essential function of all stents is to oppose the elastic recoil of the vessel wall and provide internal support and preservation of luminal patency and dimensions. Although all stents share this common function, there are many differences in design. Stents are best categorized by methods of deployment: the two major types are balloon-expandable and self-expanding. There is no ideal stent. There are important functional characteristics, in which stents differ in very significant ways. Table 7-1 lists the properties of the ideal metallic intravascular stent. Careful examination of this list enables one to evaluate the strengths and weaknesses of the various devices.

Types of Stents

Balloon-Expandable Stents

Palmaz Balloon-Expandable Intraluminal Stent

The Palmaz balloon-expandable intraluminal stent (Fig. 7-1) is the only stent thus far approved for peripheral arterial use in the United States,[20] although at the time of this writing, approval of the Wallstent is imminent, and the Wallstent has been approved for use in transjugular intrahepatic portosystemic shunt (TIPS) procedures. The Palmaz P308 stent has been approved by the FDA for deployment in iliac angioplasty cases with suboptimal results. Each stent is a single tube of 316L stainless steel with etched rectangular slots that are oriented in the long axis of the stent and

arranged in staggered rows around the entire circumference of the tube.

For delivery (Fig. 7-2), the stent-balloon assembly is introduced to the target site over a guidewire and within a protective outer sheath. When the target site is reached, the sheath is withdrawn and the stent is deployed by balloon inflation. This action produces balloon-mediated expansion, which results in plastic deformation of the metallic endoprosthesis beyond its elastic limit. Plastic deformation of the metal is the prin-

Table 7-1. Ideal Metallic Stent Characteristics

Deployed with familiar PTA techniques
Delivered on a very-low-profile catheter
Very high in expansion ratio
Available in a range of lengths and diameters
Highly radiopaque
Delivered precisely to the target site
Retrievable in the event of errant placement
High in hoop strength to resist recoil
Resistant to plastic deformation once deployed
Flexible for use in tortuous vessels
Stable in position, so as not to embolize or migrate
Thromboresistant
Incorporated into the vessel wall with thin neointima and
    functional endothelial coat
Isocompliant with adjacent vessel segments
Biologically inert or protective against restenosis
Patent in long-term follow-up
Structurally intact after billions of cardiocirculatory cycles
Amenable to noninvasive imaging follow-up, including MRI
Inexpensive

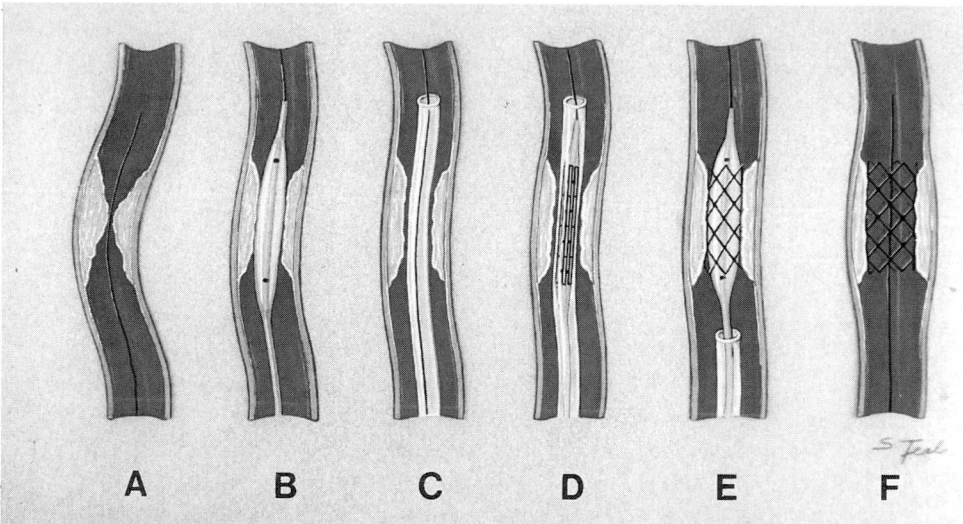

Figure 7-2. Artist's depiction of Palmaz stent placement for failed PTA. (A) Stenosis due to atherosclerotic plaque. (B) Balloon angioplasty. (C) Angioplasty has resulted in recoil and residual stenosis. A sheath has been introduced across the lesion and the dilator has been removed. (D) Stent-balloon assembly has been introduced to target site within sheath. (E) The sheath has been withdrawn to a trailing position behind the stent balloon assembly, and the stent has been expanded by balloon inflation. (F) Deployed stent remains in target site. The balloon catheter has been removed.

cipal mechanism by which the Palmaz stent provides endovascular support. The balloon is then deflated, the catheter is rotated to be certain that the balloon is free from the stent, and the catheter is removed. In the deployed condition, the openings in the stent appear as diamond-shaped rather than rectangular.

The major positive attributes of the Palmaz stent are its high hoop strength and high expansion ratio. It is intermediate in radiopacity and it lacks longitudinal flexibility; therefore, it cannot be readily delivered contralaterally over the aortic bifurcation. The stent is also susceptible to permanent plastic deformation by two-point compression. Renal stents and coronary stents have undergone clinical testing in the United States, and the coronary stents have received market approval from the FDA.

As suggested by its many applications, the Palmaz stent is available in many sizes and designs (Table 7-2), most of which have received FDA approval for use in the biliary tree. The only approved design for peripheral vascular use is the P308 stent, which is approximately 30 mm long and has an expansion range of 8 to 12 mm. It is approved only for suboptimal PTA results in the iliac arteries. As discussed below, experience has not been limited to this specific design or application.

Strecker Stent

The Strecker stent (Medi-Tech) is a highly radiopaque, balloon-expandable tantalum stent (Fig. 7-3).[21] It is a cylindrical, interwoven-wire mesh stent with a wire di-

ameter that may be varied to change such properties as hoop strength, but with an impact on profile. The method of deployment is slightly different from that of the Palmaz stent. In the unexpanded state, the stent is secured on the balloon surface by leading and trailing edge retainer sleeves made of silicone. As the balloon is inflated at the target site, the stent expands and shortens slightly as it is freed from the retainer sleeves.

The major strengths of this stent are its high radiopacity and its intermediate flexibility. It has a lower hoop strength than the Palmaz stent. Although there has now been considerable experience with this device in Europe, including long-term follow-up,[22] this stent has undergone only preliminary evaluation for the treatment of PVD in U.S. clinical trials.

Table 7-2. Palmaz Stent Sizes

Code #	Thickness (inches)	Length (mm)	Expansion Range (mm)
PS1530	0.0025	15	3–4
P104	0.0055	10	4–9
P154	0.0055	15	4–9
P204	0.0055	20	4–9
P294	0.0055	30	4–9
P394	0.0055	39	4–9
PS204	0.004	20 (articulated)	4–7
P128	0.005	12	8–12
P188	0.005	18	8–12
P308	0.005	30	8–12

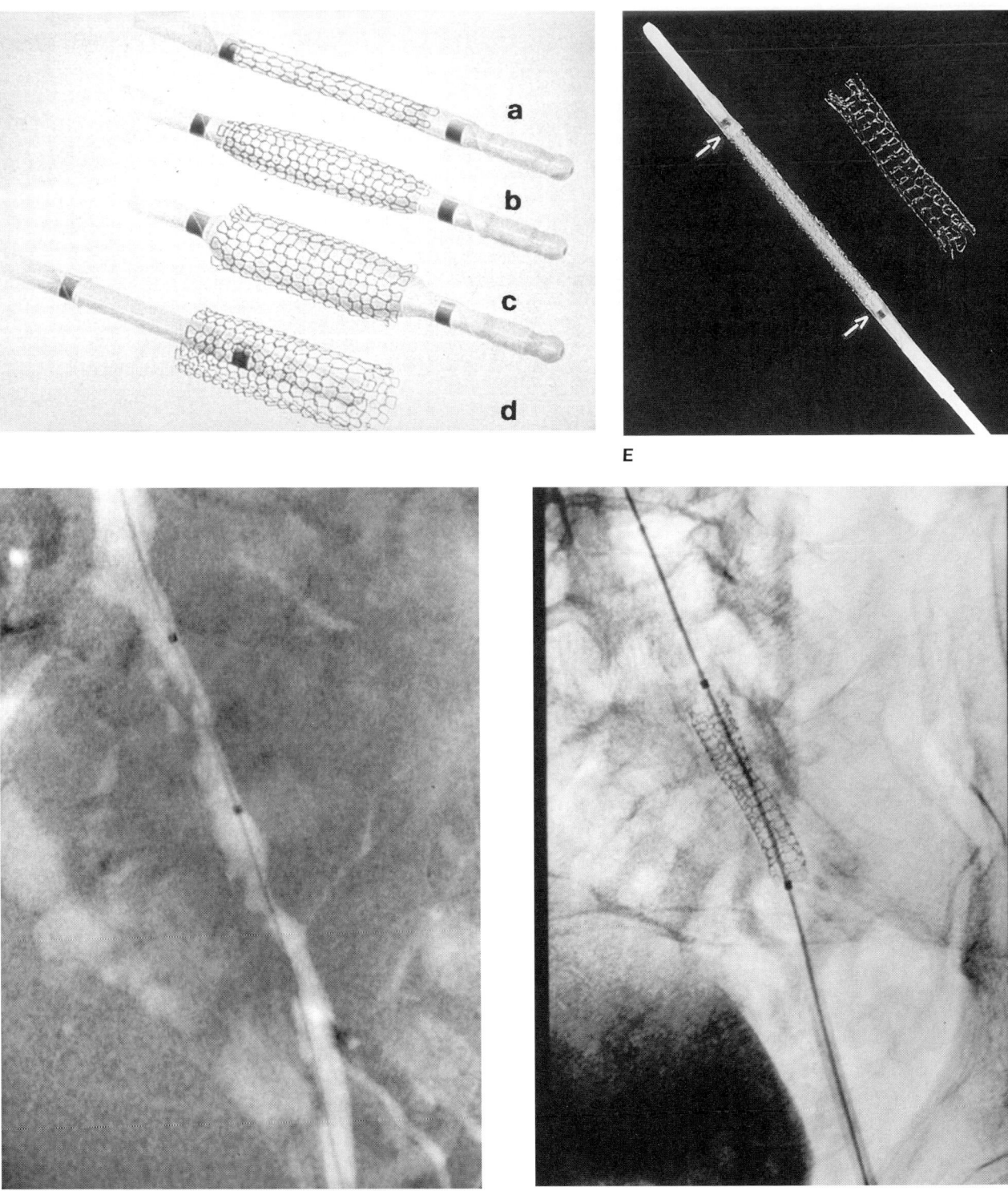

Figure 7-3. Strecker woven tantalum balloon-expandable stent. (A to D) Artist's rendering of deployment mechanism. Balloon expansion frees ends of stent from silicone retainer sleeves. After full expansion, the balloon is deflated and removed, leaving the stent deployed. (E) Photograph shows Strecker stent mounted and after deployment. *White arrows* point to silicone retainer sleeves that hold stent on catheter prior to balloon expansion and deployment. (F) Road map of an iliac artery stenosis during Strecker stent deployment. (G) Radiograph of deployed stent with balloon deflated shows the high radiopacity of the Strecker stent, due to tantalum.

Cordis Stent

Cordis Corporation has developed a stent (Fig. 7-4) that is flexible in the undeployed state, yet rigid once deployed.[23] It is a balloon-expandable, tantalum stent manufactured from a single 0.0075-inch-diameter tantalum wire formed into a single-plane sinusoidal wave pattern. The resulting planar "ribbon" is wrapped in a helical or spiral fashion around a mandrel to form a tube, whose shape is maintained by welded joints that connect tangential intersections of adjacent sine wave apices. Consecutive weld joints provide the stent with longitudinal stability. At each end, the stent has an end weld termination. Deployed diameters range from 4 to 12 mm and deployed lengths from 15 to 70 mm. The stents are very radiopaque, low in profile, and flexible in the undeployed state.

Upon deployment, the stent undergoes plastic deformation and assumes the new expanded shape. Once the stent is deployed, its hoop strength is intermediate between that of the Palmaz stent and the Wallstent (discussed below), but closer to that of the Palmaz stent. Preclinical testing[24] is complete, and human trials are about to begin.

Wiktor and Fontaine-Dake Stents

Other investigational balloon-expandable stents with similar characteristics to the Cordis stent are the Wiktor stent (Medtronics Corp.) (Fig. 7-5) and the Fontaine-Dake stent (Cook, Inc.).[25–27] They also have single tantalum wire zigzag and sinusoidal designs, respectively. The Fontaine-Dake stent employs welds, but the Wiktor stent does not. Neither has undergone clinical trials for PVD.

Gianturco-Roubin ("Bookbinder") FlexStent

One final balloon-expandable stent is the Gianturco-Roubin or "Bookbinder" stent, so named because it resembles the binding of a spiral notebook.[28] Its tradename is the FlexStent (Cook, Inc.). It is a flexible, stainless steel, small-vessel stent made of surgical suture wire (0.0006 inch or 0.15 mm in diameter). The wire is wrapped cylindrically with bends adopting alternating U and inverted U configurations every 360 degrees. The major strengths of this stent are its simplicity and its flexibility. It is minimally radiopaque. Of all the stents mentioned thus far, this one has the least potential for peripheral vascular applications because of its low expansion ratio. Because of the low ratio, stenting an iliac or femoral artery would require a large-bore catheter, and therefore a prohibitively large arterial sheath. Therefore, although this stent may ultimately find applications in the tibial arteries, its principal intended use is in the coronary circulation. It has

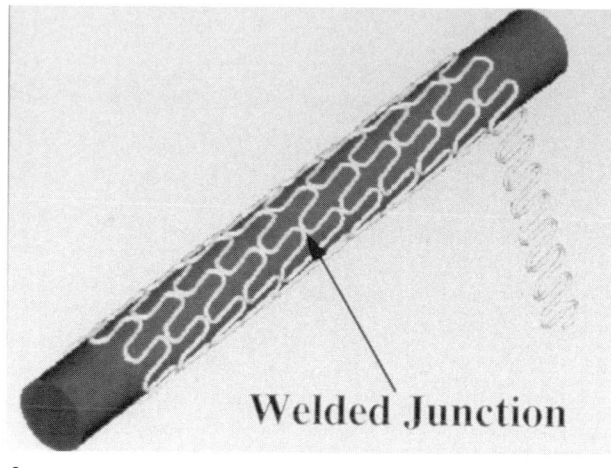

A

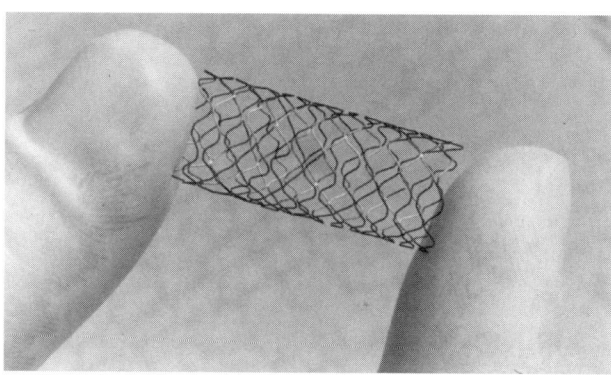

B

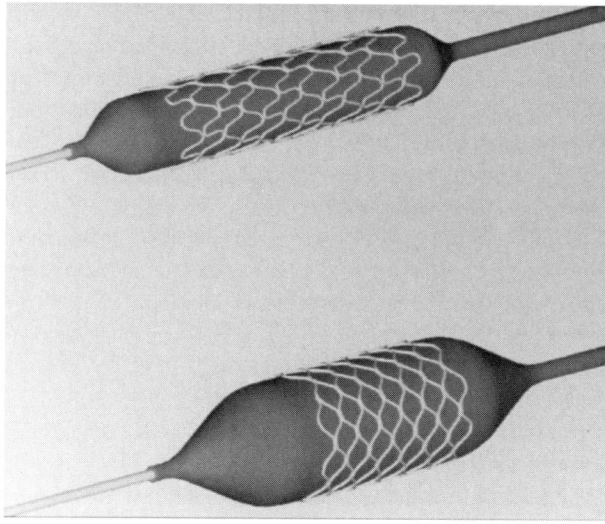

C

Figure 7-4. Cordis tantalum balloon-expandable stent. (A) The stent is made of tantalum wire shaped into a planar ribbon of alternating sine waves, the apices of which touch when the wire is wrapped in a tubular helix. Some of the apices are then welded. (B) Photograph of expanded stent. (C) Two different stent designs yield expansion ranges of 4 to 7 mm and 8 to 12 mm in diameter.

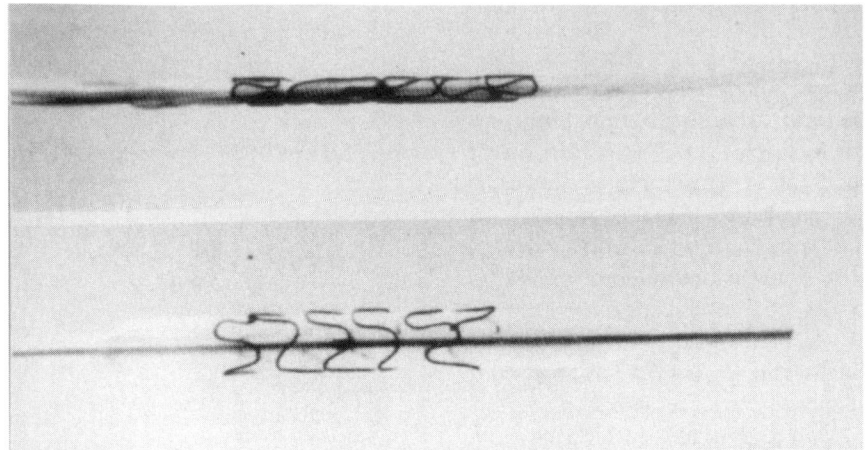

Figure 7-5. Wiktor stent before (*above*) and after (*below*) expansion.

received market approval from the FDA for use in the coronary arteries.

Self-Expanding Stents

Each self-expanding stent works by one of the following mechanisms: (1) a spring action triggered by unloading the device from a constraining delivery catheter, or (2) thermal shape memory that causes the stent to assume the proper configuration when warmed to body temperature.

It should be mentioned that although the basic mechanism of each of these devices is self-expanding, in most cases involving peripheral vascular disease, full expansion is achieved by balloon inflation inside the stented lumen after the initial deployment. Whereas balloon assistance may not be required in nonvascular applications, it is an important step in vascular applications, aimed at preventing acute thrombosis (i.e., thrombosis may be considered a likely outcome when a metallic foreign body is placed within a persistent stenosis). Figure 7-6 depicts an example of complete stent expansion that was accomplished only with the assistance of a balloon. This is routinely necessary when self-expanding stents are used in vascular stenoses.

Nitinol Spring-Coil Stents

Thermal memory stents are composed of nitinol, a nickel-titanium alloy with thermally triggered shape memory. Because of this property, they may be loaded into or onto a catheter in a relatively elongated state for delivery, yet they regain their useful configuration, such as a spring coil, upon deployment at body temperature. The interchangeable shapes correspond to distinct crystalline structures that the alloy assumes at different temperatures. The actual thermal trigger point for shape change can be controlled metallurgically by varying the proportions of nickel and titanium and by varying the annealing temperature. Although these stents have been used extensively for vascular applications in Russia,[29] and although they have undergone animal testing in the United States,[30] they have not been used in FDA-controlled clinical trials in the United States. There is a small amount of experience in Europe using a nitinol spring-coil stent (InStent, Inc.) (Fig. 7-7) to treat femoropopliteal disease.[31]

Schneider Wallstent

The most widely used self-expanding stent, the Wallstent (Schneider Stent Division, Pfizer) (Fig. 7-8),[32] is a stainless steel spring-loaded stent. It is manufactured in a range of sizes from 5 mm (expanded diameter) to 24 mm. Each stent comprises 16 to 20 spring-steel filaments (surgical grade of stainless steel alloy) woven into a tubular, flexible, self-expanding braid configuration. Hoop strength varies with the number and gauge of the wires. Filaments of the smallest stents are 0.075 to 0.100 mm in diameter; those of the larger stents are 0.12 to 0.17 mm in diameter. At the crossing points, the filaments are free to pivot. This allows for excellent longitudinal flexibility, the most out-

Figure 7-6. Incomplete Wallstent expansion rendered complete with balloon assistance. (A) Arteriogram showing superficial femoral artery occlusion. (B) Road map arteriogram during stent deployment shows incomplete expansion. (C) Further expansion of stent with a PTA balloon catheter. ▶ (D) Final arteriogram. (E) Color flow Doppler study of superficial femoral artery depicting the stent and a widely patent lumen.

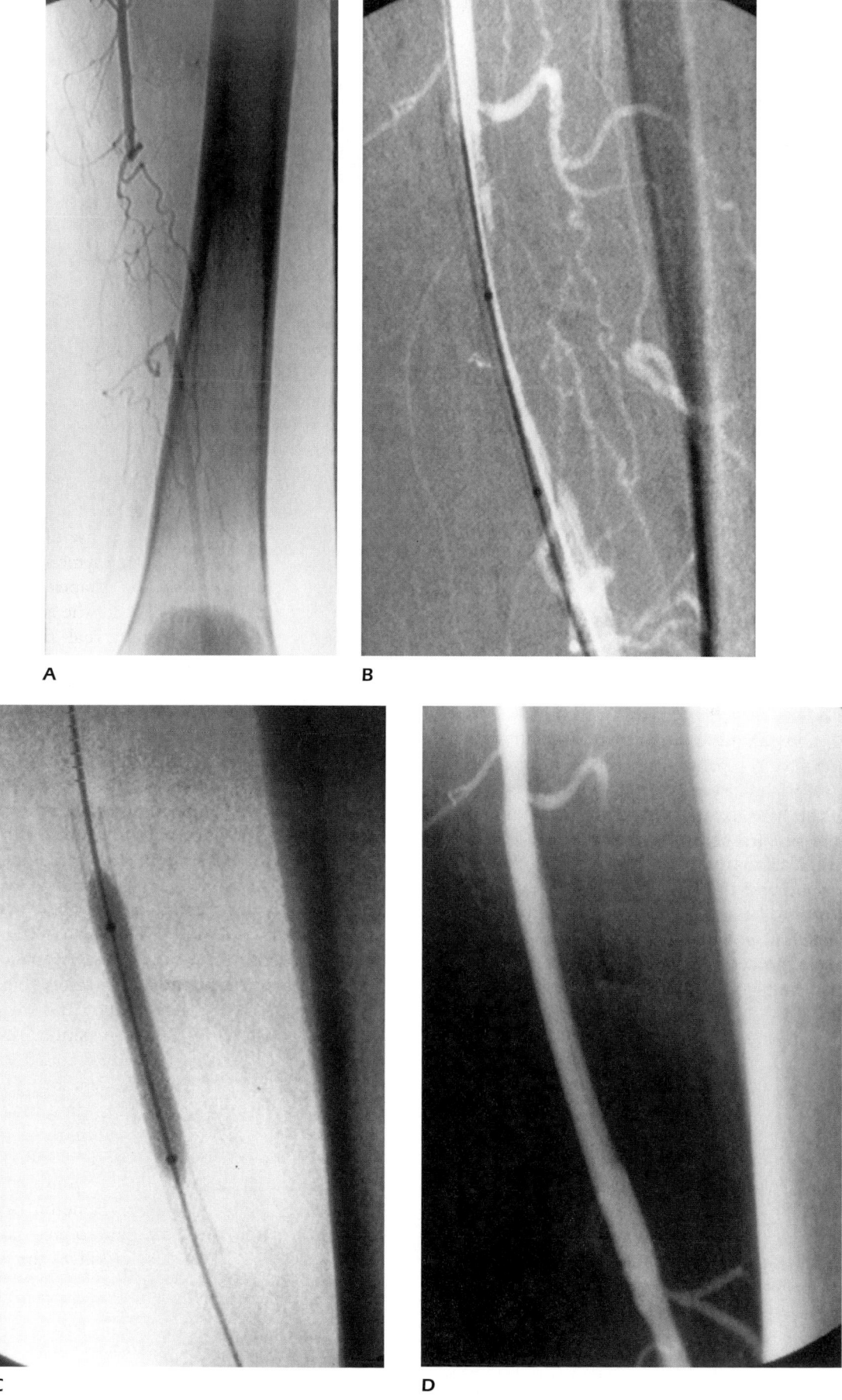

A

B

C

D

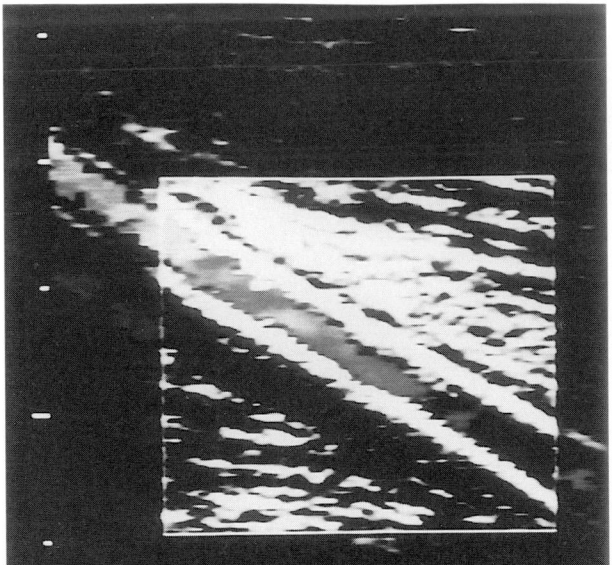

E   **Figure 7-6** (continued).

standing characteristic of this stent. The larger stents for peripheral applications are delivered on 7 French catheters over 0.035-inch guidewires. With the original design, the stent was mounted on the delivery catheter in such a way that it was stretched to a very low profile under a constraining rolling membrane. To deploy the stent, the operator first positioned it within the target site. A separate port that connected to the rolling membrane was injected with a 30 percent weight/volume mixture of contrast material under 3 atm of pressure. As the catheter was pulled back steadily against a stable pushing rod, the rolling membrane was retracted and the stent was thereby deployed by self-expansion. In an updated design (known as Unistep), there is no rolling membrane to pressurize in the deployment process. Instead, the outer constraining catheter is simply withdrawn to expose the stent.

The Wallstent has high hoop strength (though not as high as that of a Palmaz stent), excellent flexibility, and marginal radiopacity. Because it shortens substantially as it is deployed, it is often difficult to position the ends of the stent precisely. However, until the stent is approximately 75 to 80 percent deployed, it can still be withdrawn (but not advanced) slightly for repositioning. The Wallstent has undergone clinical trials in the iliac and superficial femoral arteries in the United States,[33] but is still awaiting market approval for vascular use from the FDA. It is also the most frequently used device for transjugular intrahepatic portosystemic shunt (TIPS) procedures,[34] and is currently awaiting FDA approval for that indication.

The Wallstents are available in a variety of diameters and lengths for nonvascular applications (Table 7-3). Various ones have been used to manage venous stenoses in upper extremity veins, subclavian veins, and brachiocephalic veins in patients with hemodialysis access–related stenoses.

Gianturco **Z** Stent

Another type of self-expanding stainless steel stent is the Gianturco zigzag (**Z** stent) (Cook, Inc.) (Fig. 7-9).[35] In this design, a wire is bent into a zigzag pattern and its ends are connected to form a cylinder. The stent is compressed radially and loaded into a nontapered delivery catheter. At the target site, the outer catheter is withdrawn against an inner pusher catheter without altering the position of the pusher or of the stent. This deploys the stent in its unconstrained configuration. In an experimental study of **Z** stent properties, Fallone and colleagues used a "tire-wrap" device and a simple spring gauge to describe a coefficient of stiffness for each **Z** stent.[36] The value of the coefficient is independent of the original fully expanded radius, linearly dependent on the caliber of the stent wire, and

Figure 7-7. InStent nitinol self-expanding helical coil stent.

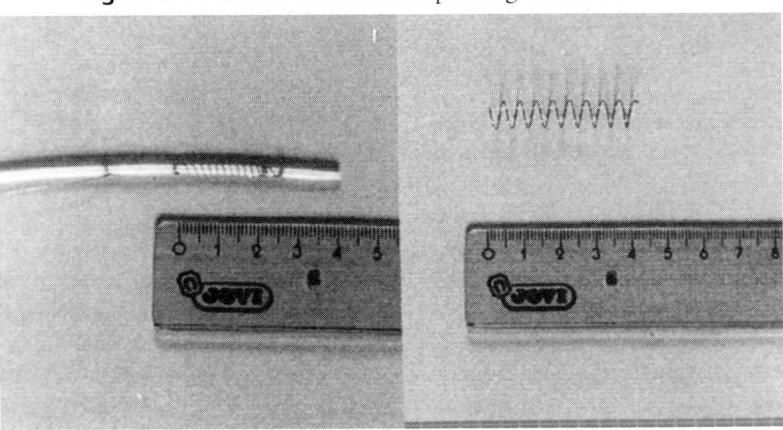

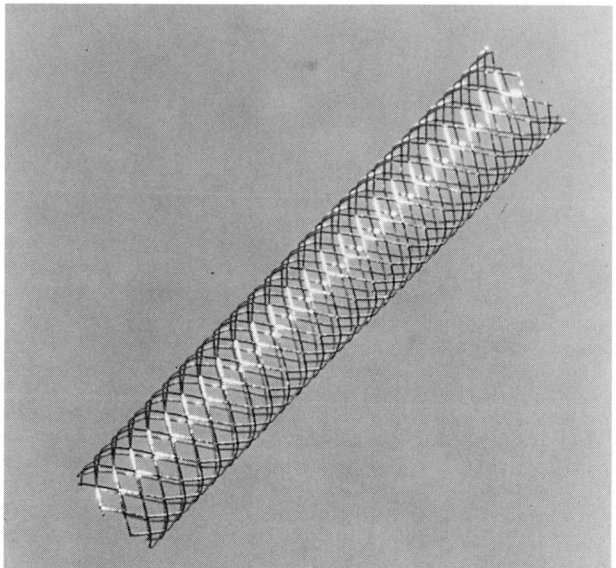

Figure 7-8. Wallstent.

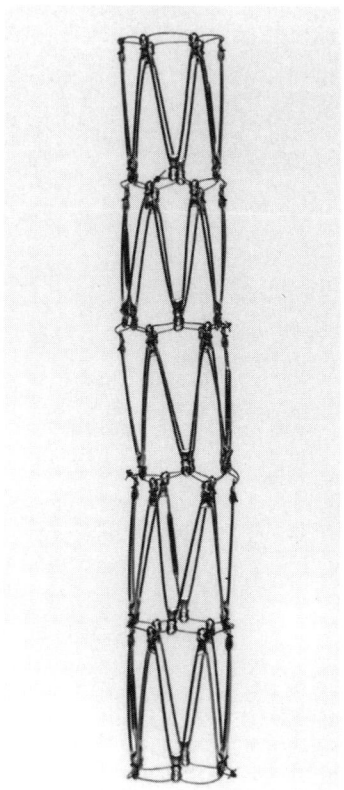

Figure 7-9. Multisegment Z stent.

inversely related to stent length. Small radial displacements are linearly related to the force required to compress the stent, and the coefficient of stiffness is the proportionality constant. Vascular applications of this device have been limited primarily to the treatment of vena cava syndromes,[35,37] although there is some experience in iliac atherosclerosis in Japan. Covered Z stents are now being used for transluminal treatment of thoracic aortic aneurysms (Fig. 7-10).[38] Various modifications of the original design have been made,[39] including multisegmented stents, stents with skirts to prevent embolization and migration, and barbs for anchoring. Monofilament lines made of nylon suture (Ethicon, Inc.) may be placed through "eyes" at each of the bends to prevent overexpansion of the stent and overdistention of the stented vessel.

Table 7-3. Wallstent Sizes

Diameter (mm)	Available Lengths (mm)
5	20, 40, 55, 80
6	20, 45, 60, 90
7	20, 40, 60, 90
8	20, 40, 60, 80
10	20, 42, 68, 94
12	40, 60, 90
14	40, 55, 80
16	40, 60, 90
18	40, 60, 90
20	40, 55, 80
22	35, 45, 70
24	35, 45, 70

Biological Response to Stent Implantation

Almost all metallic stents that have been studied in animal models and in humans have been shown (histologically and histochemically in animal studies) to develop a neointima with a functional overlying endothelium (Fig. 7-11). The neointimal layer thickens increasingly for approximately 6 months, and then recedes until it is measurably thinner. However, until approximately 2 years ago, the events leading up to this final result had never been described in adequate detail.

Palmaz has done an exquisite job of reviewing the physical characteristics of stents that affect their thrombogenicity and ultimate incorporation into the vessel wall.[40] In his review, he explains that the smoothness of the metallic surface (determined by the manufacturing process) is important, because rougher surfaces are more thrombogenic. Almost all metallic surfaces used in human implantations have an electropositive surface charge that attracts fibrinogen, a thin (<20-nm) layer of which forms within a few seconds of stent implantation. The fibrinogen layer lowers the critical surface tension (a measure of surface wettability) of the metal surface, thereby rendering it less

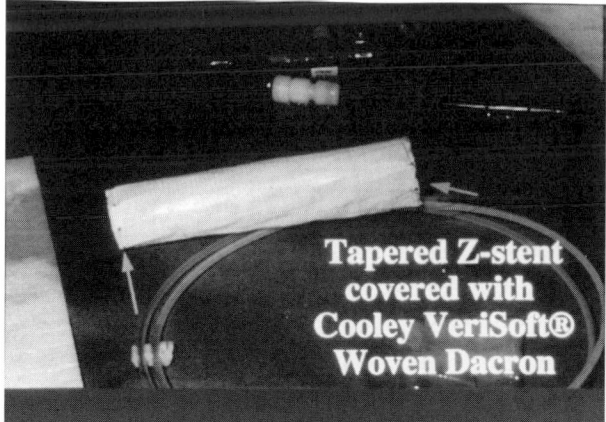

A

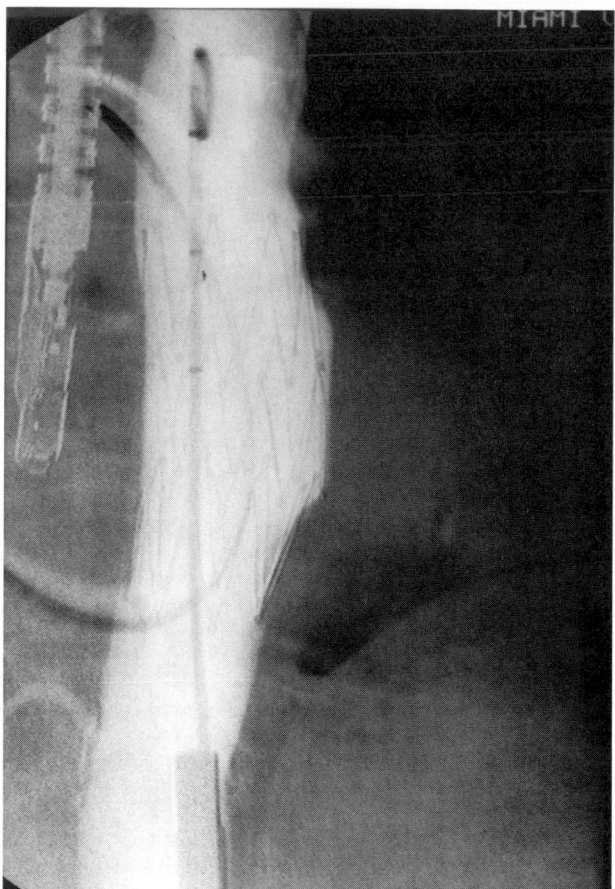

C

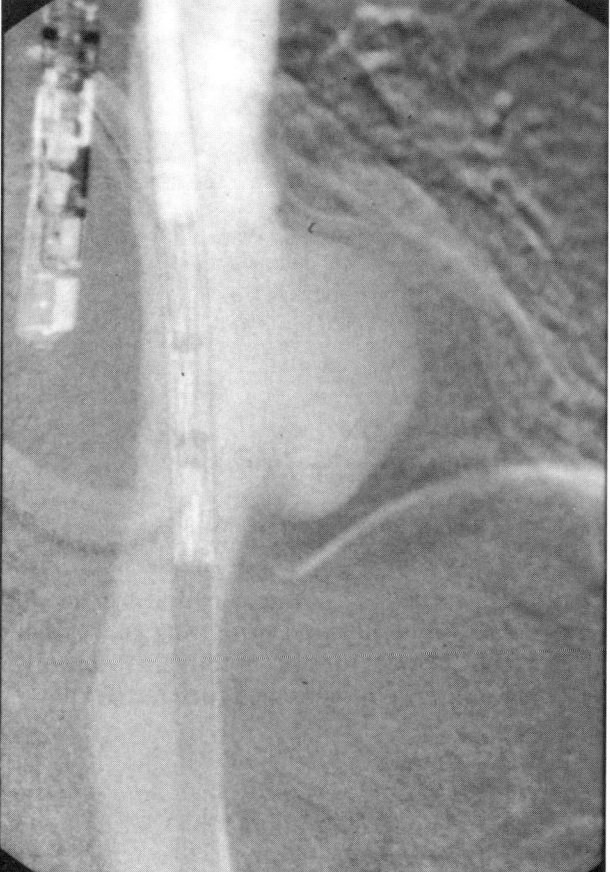

B

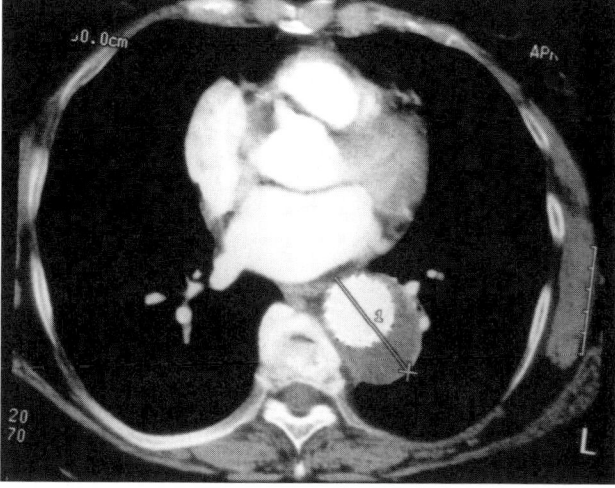

D

Figure 7-10. Covered Z stents for thoracic aortic aneurysm (TAA). (A) Tapered Z stent covered with Cooley Verisoft Dacron graft material with the crimps ironed out to achieve the lowest possible profile. This graft was used in a descending thoracic aortic aneurysm. (B) Arteriographic road map image of a descending TAA during endovascular treatment. Note the multisegment Z stent. The graft itself is radiolucent. (C) The same TAA after endograft deployment. The TAA has been excluded. (D) Follow-up axial CT scan with contrast demonstrating exclusion of the TAA. (E) Shaded surface display reconstruction from a follow-up spiral CT scan in another patient treated with an endograft for a descending TAA. The portion of the aorta with the endograft is clearly discernible.

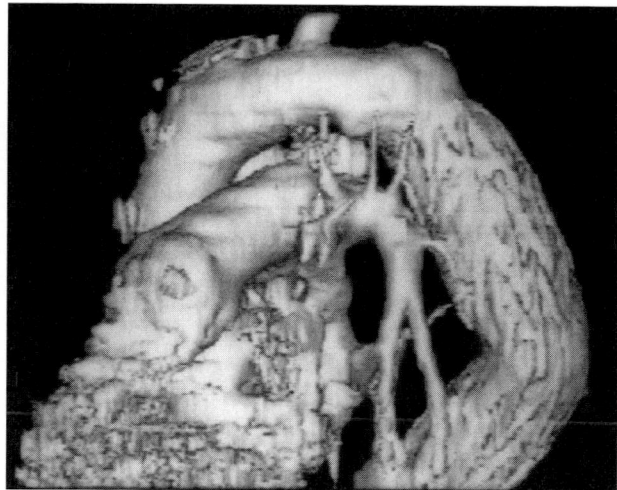

E   **Figure 7-10** (continued).

thrombogenic. In a previous work, Palmaz and colleagues showed that by 24 hours there is a complete layer of fibrin on the stent surface, with strands oriented in the direction of blood flow.[41] The authors postulated that the fibrin strands may serve as a framework for the ingrowth of endothelial cells.

Palmaz goes on to make the point that adequate stent expansion (generally to a diameter 10 to 15 percent larger than that of the vessel) is required to ensure embedding of the stent struts into the wall. He posits that such embedding is required to limit thrombus for-

mation to the mural troughs around the struts. Under these conditions, endothelium may grow from tissue mounds projecting up between the struts, provided the endothelial cells haven't been completely denuded. Stents incompletely applied to the vessel wall remain relatively thrombogenic.

Over the first few days to weeks after stent placement, the thrombus surrounding the struts is gradually replaced by neointimal hyperplasia, and the number of new vessels in each such area is related to the number of neointimal cells. In a series of elegant animal experi-

Figure 7-11. Histologic demonstration of the neointima forming after stent deployment. (A) Neointima 24 weeks after Palmaz stent deployment in an atherosclerotic rabbit.

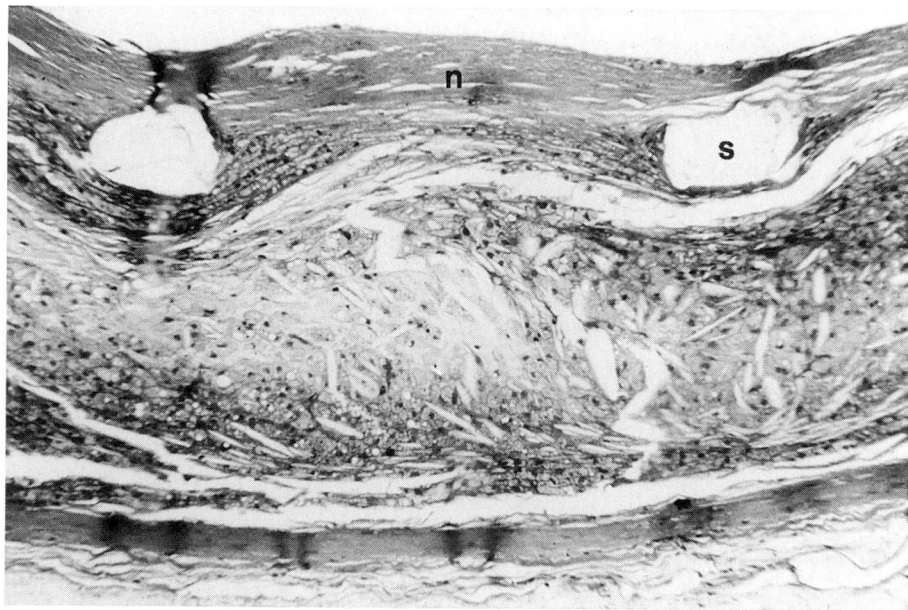

A

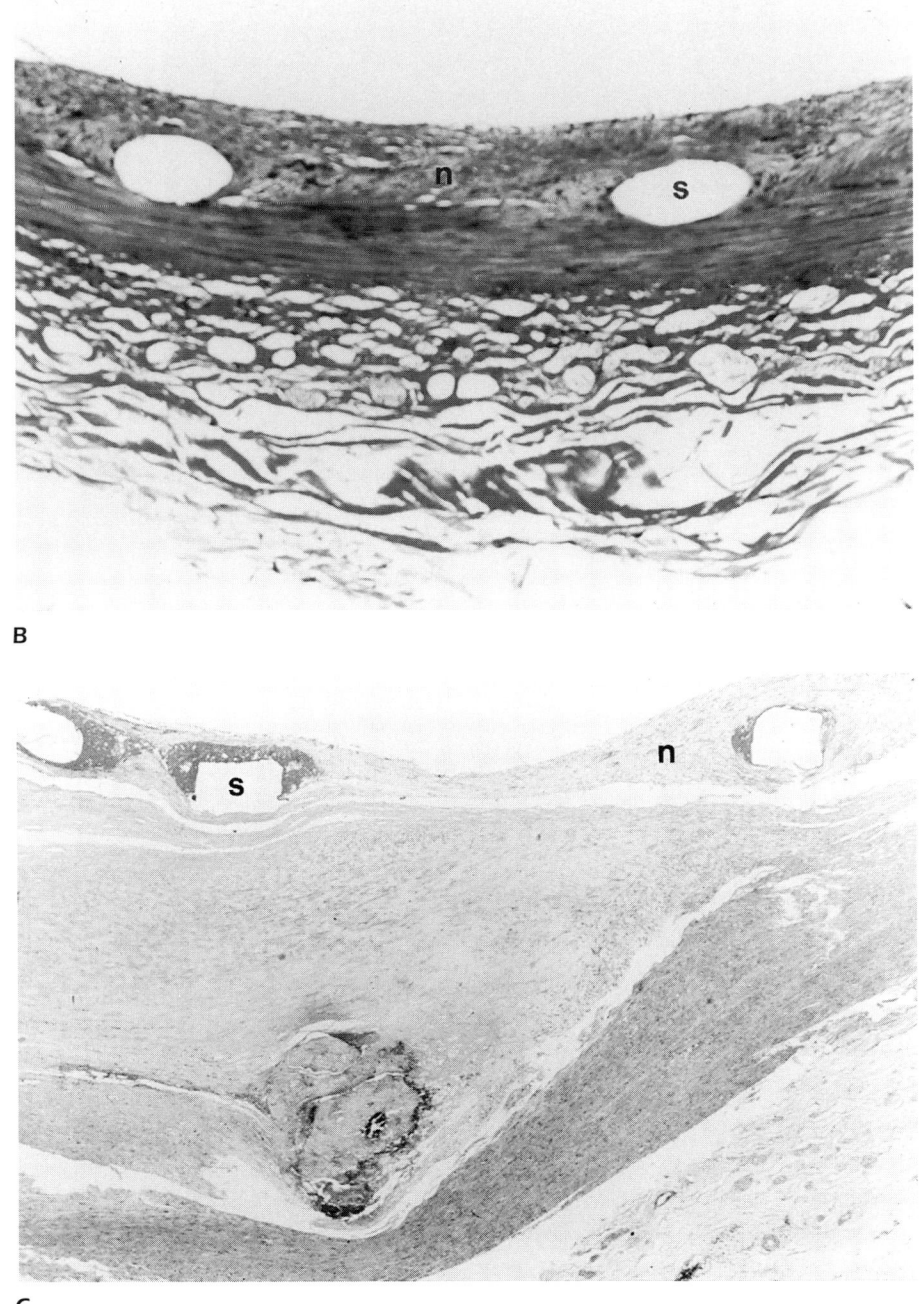

B

C

Figure 7-11 (continued). (B) Neointima after Wallstent deployment in a dog. (C) Neointima in a necropsy specimen of an atherosclerotic iliac artery from a human (*s, stent wire or strut; n,* neointima onthe above histologic sections). (D) Gross photograph of specimen shown in (C) depicts the stent struts and the neointima.

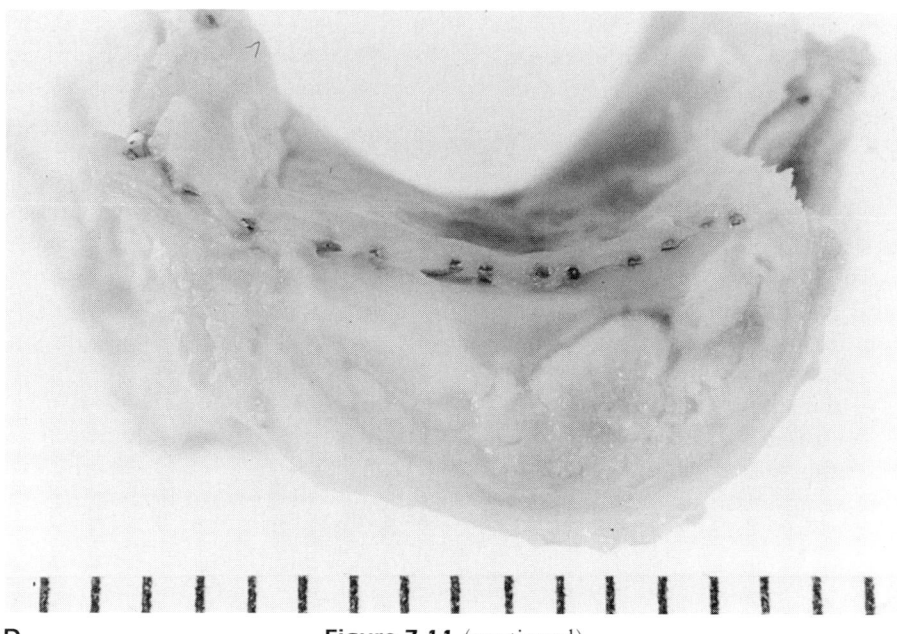

D   **Figure 7-11** (continued).

ments by Pisco and colleagues involving stenting of the abdominal aortas of canines, it was shown that the neovessels most likely derive from the vasa vasorum.[42] The cellular neointima of the canine model peaks at approximately 2 months after stent placement. Thereafter, it becomes thinner, much less cellular, and is ultimately nearly completely replaced by collagen.[43] Although it would seem that the decrease in neointimal thickness ought to be accompanied by an increase in lumen diameter, this concept has never been firmly established angiographically or by noninvasive means in humans.

Current and Potential Role of Stents in Peripheral Vascular Disease (PVD) of the Lower Extremities

Stents have been developed to deal with the major limitations of PTA, including (1) the unsuitability of some lesions for percutaneous therapy, (2) acute failures due to dissection and recoil, and (3) late failures due to restenosis. None of these problems have been completely ameliorated by stents. However, some have been significantly reduced. Increasing experience and clinical studies continue to shape our understanding of the role of stents in the management of PVD.

Before one can understand the current role of stents in peripheral vascular disease, it is necessary to know the results of PTA above and below the inguinal ligament and to appreciate the problems and limitations. Anticipated short- and long-term results are the major determinants of the role of PTA in the management of clinical problems due to disease in specific vascular distributions. To clearly delineate the role of PTA in PVD, guidelines for its appropriate application in specific clinical and morphologic circumstances have been developed.[44] These "Guidelines for Peripheral Percutaneous Transluminal Angioplasty of the Abdominal Aorta and Lower Extremity Vessels" were formulated by a joint committee of several councils of the American Heart Association. The committee used the available literature and consensus of experts to categorize lesions according to the applicability of PTA:

Category 1: Balloon angioplasty is the procedure of choice, and treatment by PTA results in a high rate of technical success and complete obliteration of pressure gradients with complete relief of symptoms generally expected.

Category 2: Generally well suited for PTA, and complete relief or improvement can be expected. This category includes patients whose PTA is to be followed by bypass to treat multilevel disease.

Category 3: Amenable to PTA, but in general because of location, disease extent, or severity, surgery offers a better chance of technical success and lasting patency.

Category 4: Surgical options are superior to PTA. PTA plays a minor role in selected cases.

In general, PTA is more successful when lesions are (1) short instead of long, (2) single instead of multiple, (3) concentric instead of markedly eccentric, (4) non-ostial, and (5) stenoses rather than occlusions (given equal lesion length).

It is understood that the guidelines require updating. In fact, the above-referenced guidelines represent an updated version of the original ones.[45] As technology advances and our scientific database increases, changes in recommendations are likely to evolve. Moreover, the committee realized that no two health care facilities are completely alike. In some hospitals, the operating skills of the surgeons may provide the most experience with a disease process and the operating suites may offer the most advanced technology and safest procedural environment. In such cases, no matter what the suitability of a lesion for PTA, surgery may be the safest approach. Conversely, even a category 3 lesion should be approached by the skilled and knowledgeable interventionalist if in his or her hospital the angiography suite and his or her level of experience offer the patient the best and safest alternative.

Aortoiliac PTA

Aortic PTA

The procedure of choice for diffuse atherosclerotic occlusive disease of the infrarenal abdominal aorta and iliac arteries is aortobifemoral bypass grafting. It is the most durable procedure, and in properly selected elective cases has a very low morbidity and mortality.

Percutaneous transluminal angioplasty (PTA) has been applied to more focal disease of the distal abdominal aorta, common iliac arteries, and external iliac arteries for the past 17 years or more. However, series involving strictly focal abdominal aortic lesions have been few and relatively small in number of patients. Hallisey and colleagues reported 15 lesions in 14 patients treated over a 10-year period and followed for a mean of 4.3 years.[46] Their initial clinical success was 93 percent, as compared to the angiographic success of 100 percent. At a mean follow-up of 4.8 years in the successfully treated group, the mean ankle-brachial index (ABI) was 0.95 and there were no clinical symptoms. There was no morbidity or mortality in this small series. Because of the small number of patients involved, these studies do not lend themselves to a detailed analysis. Focal aortic disease per se is not nearly as common as aortic atherosclerosis also involving the common iliac artery origins. In the series of aortic PTA reported by Yakes and colleagues, half of the aortic PTA patients had involvement of the iliac arteries.[47] A separate discussion of aortic stents is not warranted here. Stents have been used in the abdominal aorta,[48]

particularly in cases of polypoid or markedly irregular focal plaque in the abdominal aorta, when the fear of embolic complications may be quite high (Fig. 7-12).

Iliac PTA

The published "Guidelines for Peripheral Percutaneous Transluminal Angioplasty of the Abdominal Aorta and Lower Extremity Vessels"[44] have categorized iliac lesions as follows:

Category 1: Noncalcified, concentric stenoses less than 3 cm in length
Category 2: Stenoses 3 to 5 cm in length or calcified or eccentric stenoses less than 3 cm in length
Category 3: Stenoses 5 to 10 cm in length or chronic occlusions less than 5 cm in length after thrombolytic therapy
Category 4: (a) Stenoses over 10 cm in length, (b) chronic occlusions over 5 cm in length after thrombolytic therapy, (c) extensive aortoiliac disease, (d) iliac stenoses in a patient with abdominal aortic aneurysm or other lesion requiring aortic or iliac surgery

The technical and initial clinical success of iliac PTA in all series exceeds 90 percent, and for focal iliac stenosis approaches 100 percent. Reported long-term patencies have ranged from 50 percent to more than 90 percent. Only a few studies have carefully documented clinical results over a long period of follow-up using standard life-table methods. A 1991 report by Tegtmeyer and colleagues of 340 aortoiliac lesions treated in 200 patients used standard life-table methods.[49] The mean follow-up was approximately 29 months, and cumulative patency (clinical success) at 7.5 years was found to be 85 percent when only initially successful procedures were included and 79 percent overall (standard error [SE] = 3 percent). Complications occurred in 10.5 percent of patients. In a reanalysis of 662 balloon angioplasties of the iliac arteries from the University of Toronto series, Johnston examined variables associated with success or failure by Kaplan-Meier, Cox regression, and logistic regression analysis.[50] Cumulative clinical success was measured rather than cumulative patency by angiography. Of 82 iliac occlusions, there were 15 technical failures and 1 complication. For initially successful cases, cumulative clinical success ± SE was 91.0 ± 3.5 percent at 1 year and 58.8 ± 7.1 percent at 3 years. Of 580 iliac stenoses, there were only 8 technical failures. For 313 common iliac PTAs, the cumulative clinical success was 97.1 ± 0.9 percent at 1 month, 81.1 ± 2.3 percent at 1 year, 70.6 ± 2.9 percent at 2 years, 67.8 ± 3.0 percent at 3 years, 64.9 ± 3.3 percent at 4 years, 60.2 ± 4.0 percent at 5 years,

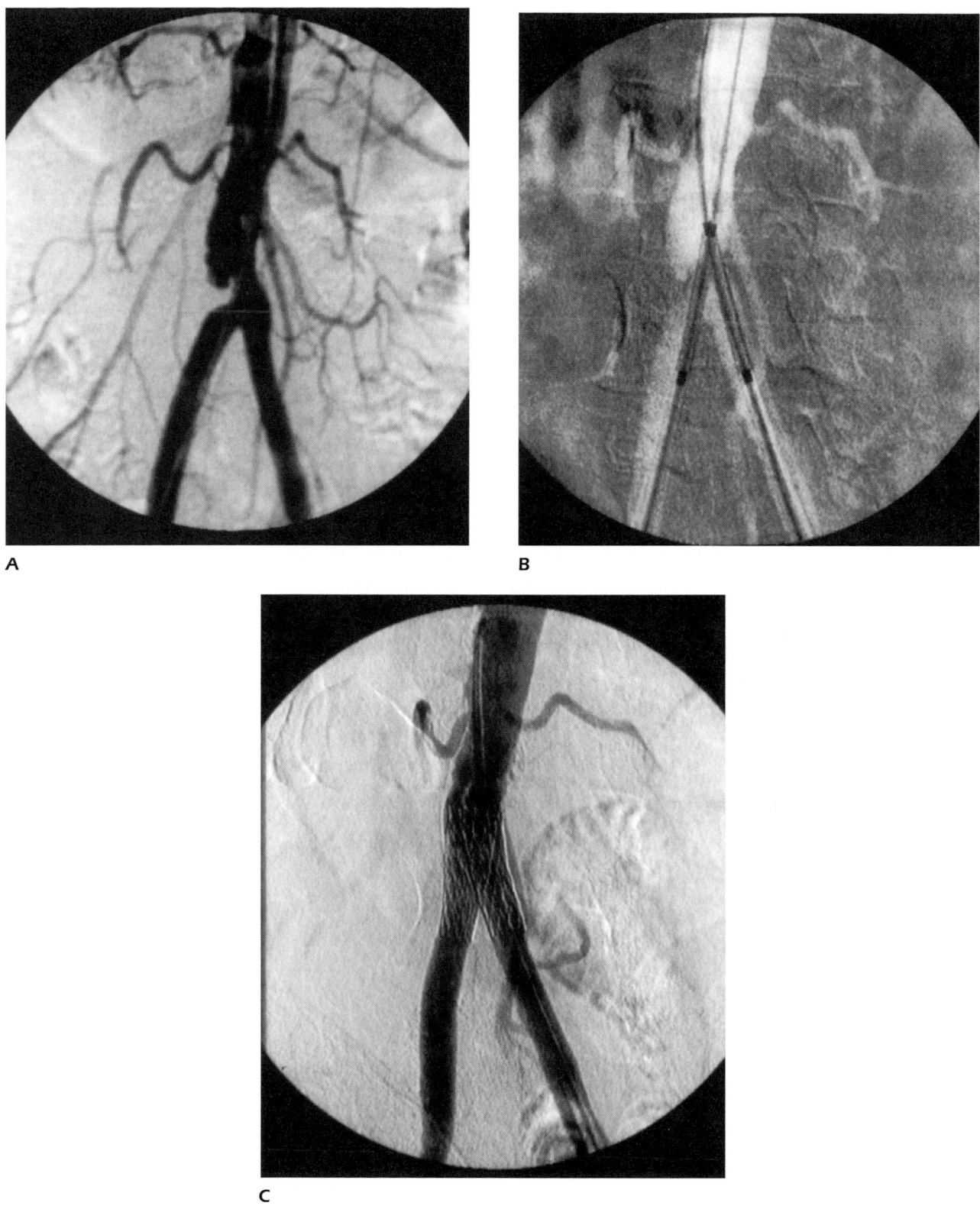

A

B

C

Figure 7-12. Focal distal abdominal aortic plaque. (A) Preliminary arteriogram demonstrates the lesion on the right lateral wall of the aorta above the bifurcation. (B) Arteriographic road map image during bilateral common iliac artery stent placement. (C) Poststenting completion arteriogram demonstrates an excellent morphologic result.

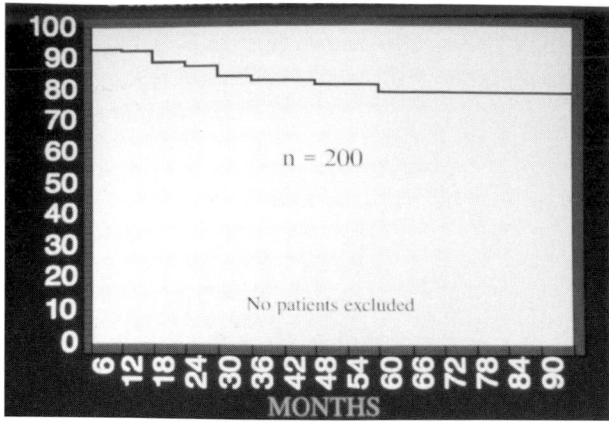

Figure 7-13. Cumulative clinical success of iliac angioplasty (Tegtmeyer). (Modified from Tegtmeyer CJ, et al. Results and complications of angioplasty in aortoiliac disease. Circulation 1991;83(Suppl I):53–60.)

tables for both the Tegtmeyer and the Johnston reports (Figs. 7-13 and 7-14, respectively).

Aortoiliac Stents

The availability of stents for use in aortoiliac PTA has modified our definition of a good or acceptable PTA result. Stents have improved the immediate hemodynamic results of iliac PTA and effectively managed recoil and PTA-related flow-limiting dissections. In addition, stents probably provide long-term patencies substantially higher than those of PTA alone.

Regarding the hemodynamic superiority of stenting over PTA alone, in a limited study by Bonn and colleagues at Thomas Jefferson University in Philadelphia, patients undergoing PTA followed by immediate intraluminal stenting with the Palmaz expandable intraluminal stent were studied as follows.[51] The translesional pressure gradient was found to average 52 mmHg (peak systolic) and 66 mmHg after vasodilation and before PTA. After PTA, the gradients were found to have decreased to a mean of 11 mmHg (personal communication). After intraluminal stenting, the gradients were found to have decreased to a mean of 2 mmHg. These differences in pressure gradient have been consistent across several studies since that time.

Another way in which intraluminal stenting provides immediate results superior to those of PTA alone

and 52.0 ± 5.7 percent at 6 years. For the 209 external iliac PTAs, the predicted 3-year cumulative clinical success was 57 percent for men and 34 percent for women. For 58 PTAs of common and external iliac arteries combined, the predicted 3-year cumulative clinical success was 73 percent for patients with good runoff and 30 percent for those with poor runoff. Adverse events included death in 0.3 percent of patients, complications requiring surgery in 1.0 percent, and delayed hospital discharge in 2.6 percent.

See the accompanying cumulative clinical success

Figure 7-14. Cumulative clinical success of iliac angioplasty (Johnston). (A) Kaplan-Meier life-table analysis for 667 iliac PTAs. The cumulative percentage success (mean $\pm$ 1 SE) is plotted versus time of follow-up. Five of the original 667 cases were excluded because the success or failure could not be determined. (B) Results of PTA of 82 iliac artery occlu-

sions (including 15 PTAs that failed for technical reasons). The cumulative percentage success (mean $\pm$ 1 SE) is plotted versus time of follow-up to 3 years, as calculated with the Kaplan-Meier method. (Modified from Johnston KW. Iliac arteries: reanalysis of results of balloon angioplasty. Radiology 1993;186:207–212. Used with permission.)

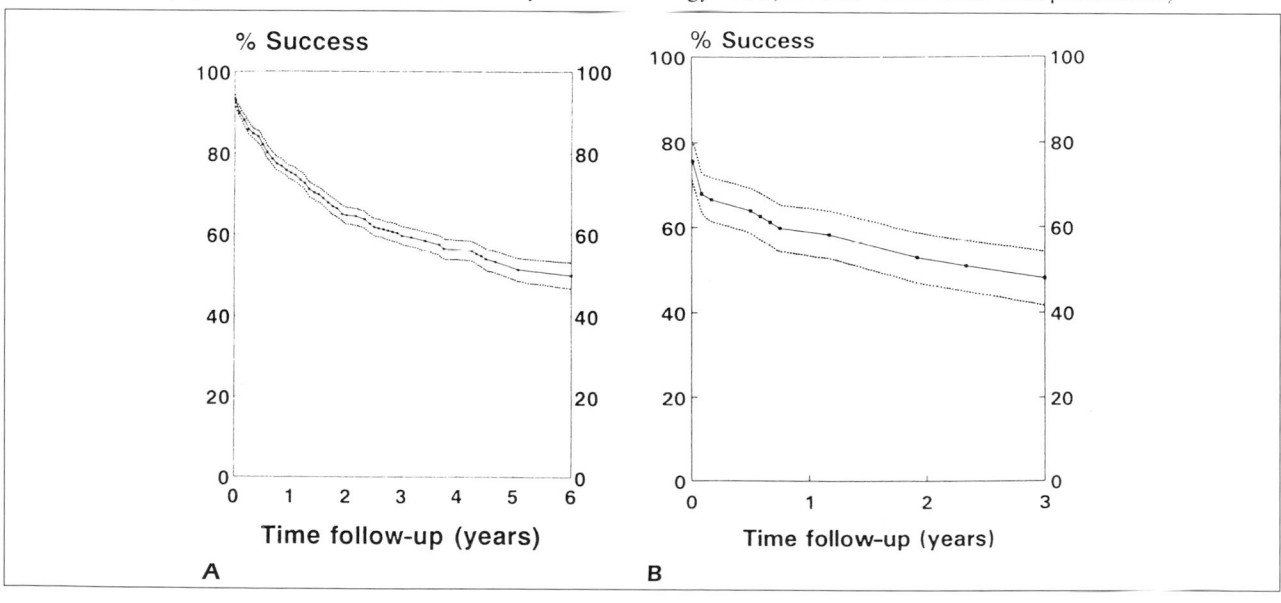

is in the management of PTA-induced iliac artery dissection (Fig. 7-15).[52] In the first clinical series on this topic, the frequency of flow-limiting PTA-related dissection in the iliac arteries was probably not less than 4.8 percent, and possibly significantly higher.[52] It was noted that extensively calcified iliac artery lesions seemed prone to PTA-induced dissection, but that these lesions were readily managed by intraluminal stent placement. Long-term patency was documented in that series. Since that report, intraluminal stenting has been applied widely and has become the standard treatment for PTA-induced, flow-limiting iliac artery dissection.

Another application of iliac stenting is for the treatment of chronic iliac artery occlusions (Fig. 7-16). Before 1988, the available literature (what limited amount there was) was overwhelmingly negative on the use of PTA for iliac artery occlusions. Then Rees and colleagues reported the use of recanalization techniques and PTA followed by intraluminal stenting as an improved way to manage iliac artery occlusions percutaneously.[53] In that series, 12 patients with complete

iliac occlusion underwent percutaneous treatment. Five of those were judged to be chronic iliac occlusion. More recently, Palmaz and colleagues reported the long-term follow-up results on 587 stent procedures in 486 patients.[54] In that series, ongoing clinical success was 87.8 percent at 40 months in the group originally treated for iliac occlusion and only 66.6 percent for those with iliac stenosis. Long and colleagues reported long-term follow-up in 49 consecutive patients treated with iliac artery stents.[55] Twenty-eight percent of 53 lesions in that series were iliac occlusions. Both Strecker stents and Wallstents were included in the series. Primary patencies were 85.3 percent at 12 months and 80.9 percent at 18 months. Secondary patencies were 96.1 percent at 12 and 18 months. Vorwerk and Gunther reported a 3-year experience with the use of Wallstents for iliac artery disease.[56] Eighty-five of their initial 147 patients presented with iliac artery occlusions, and 62 had stenoses. Failure to recanalize occurred in 22 percent of occlusions; therefore, only 63 patients underwent stenting for iliac artery occlusion. Complications occurred in 4 percent of the entire

Figure 7-15. Iliac stents for angioplasty-induced dissection. (A) Preliminary arteriogram in this claudicant shows a proximal left external iliac artery stenosis. (B) On arteriogram following PTA, a flow-limiting dissection is demonstrated.

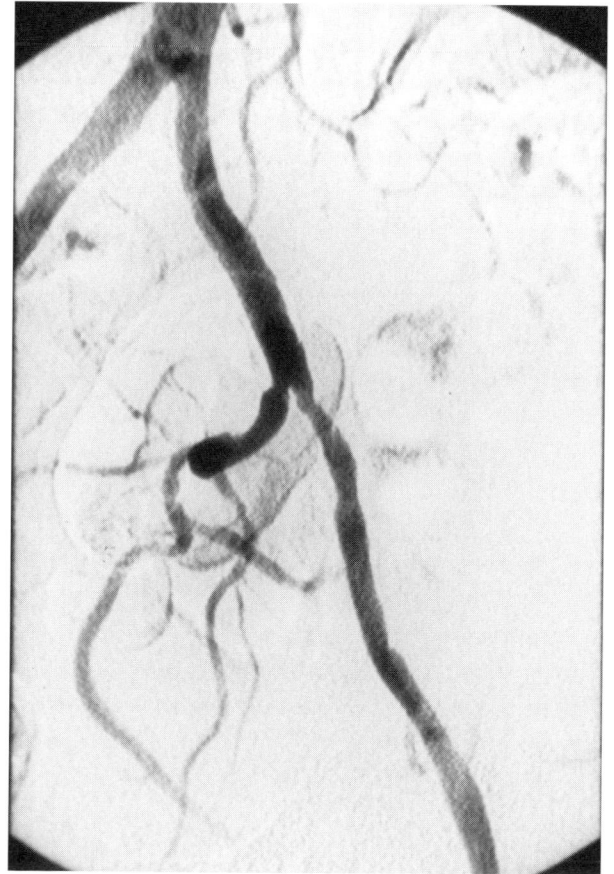

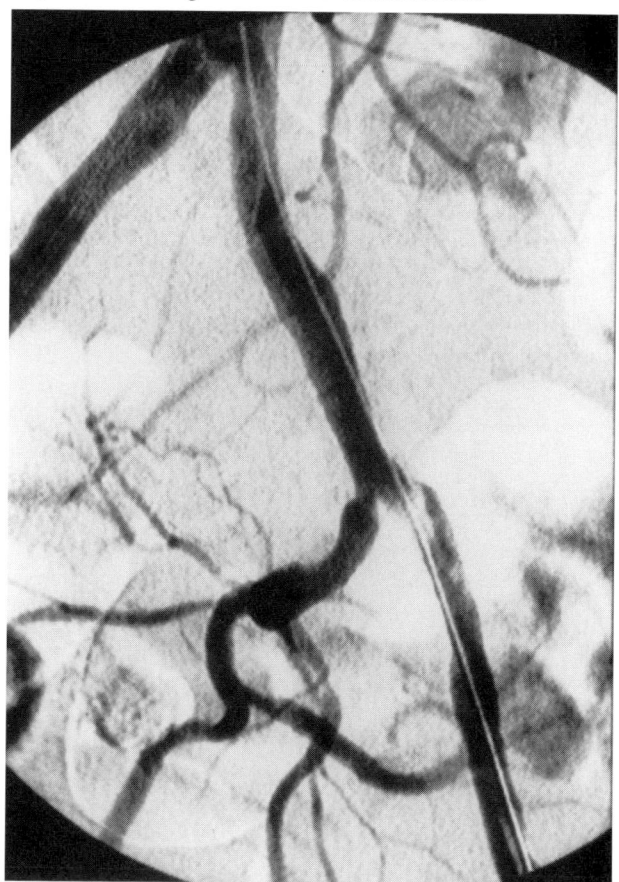

A

B

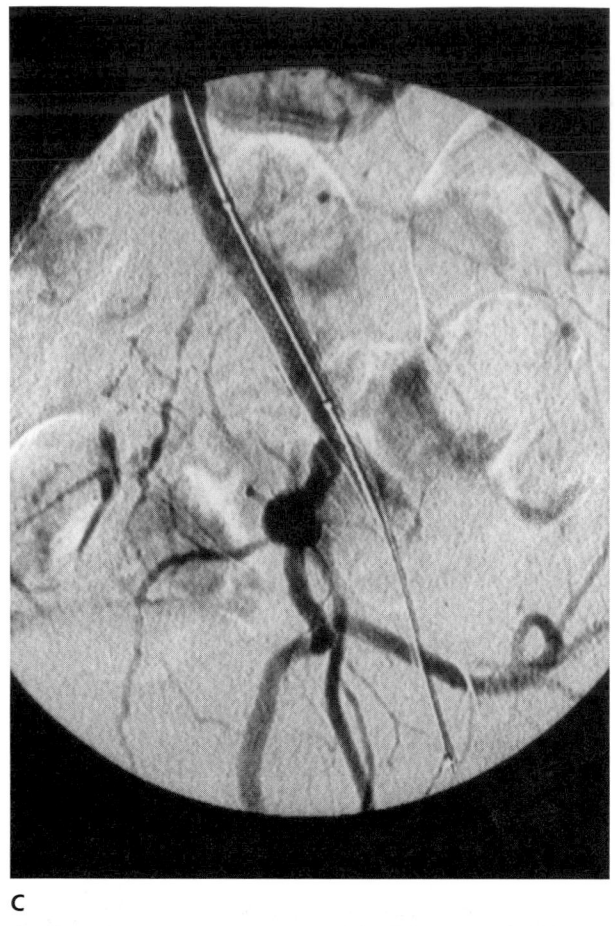

C

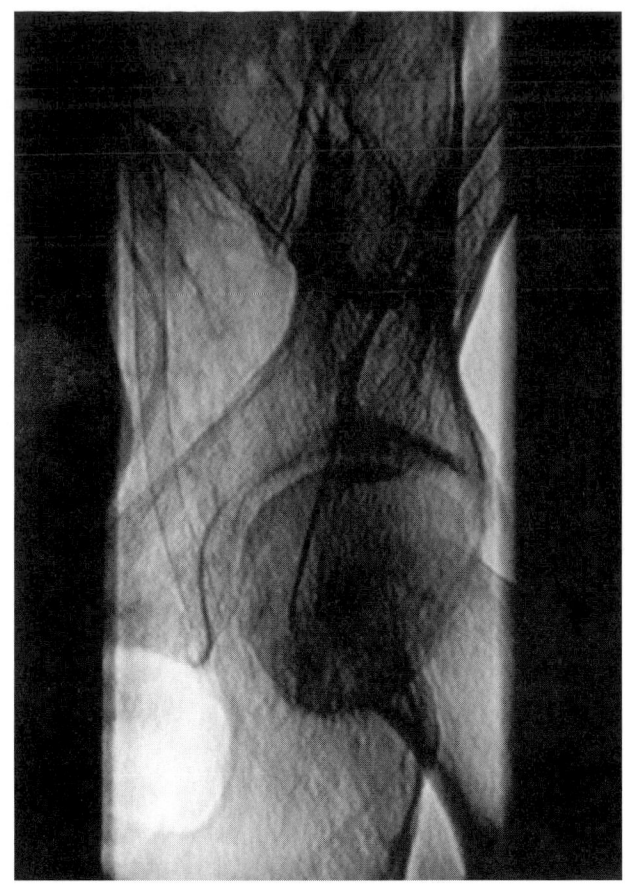

D

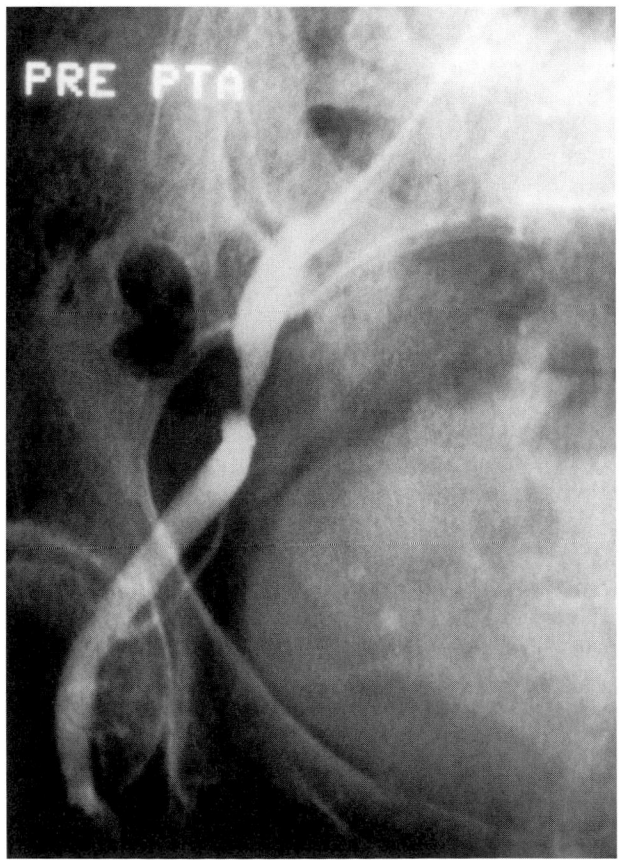

E

F

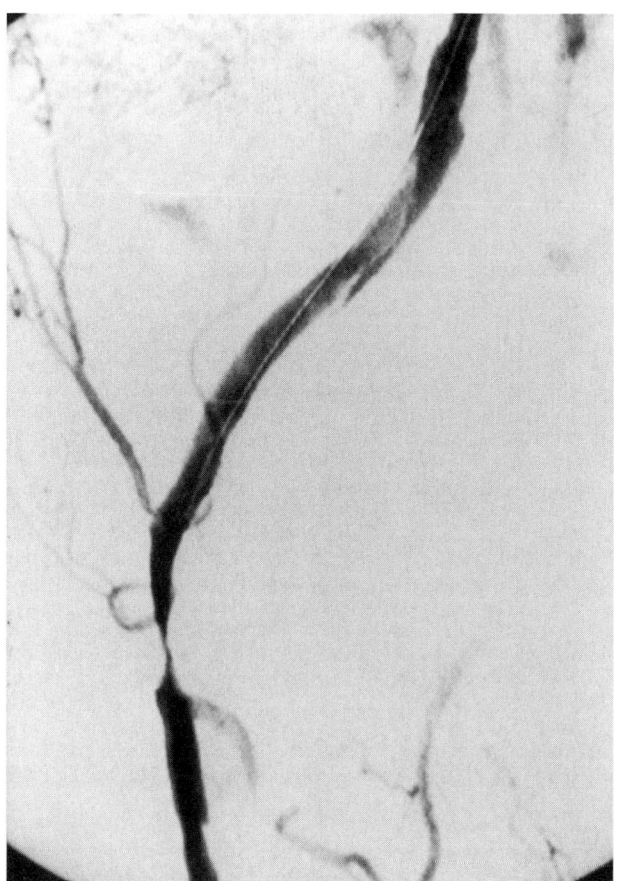

G

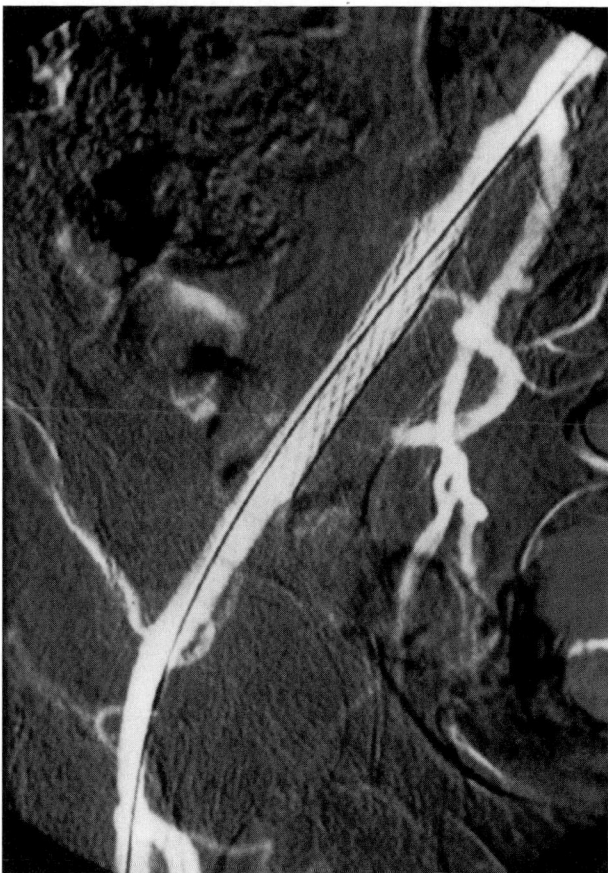

H

Figure 7-15 (continued). (C) Moments later, the dissection occludes the artery, and stenting with overlapping Wallstents is undertaken. (D) Digital spot film after deployment of two overlapping Wallstents. (E) Completion arteriogram shows an excellent result with a widely patent lumen. (F) Focal external iliac artery stenosis in a different patient immediately prior to PTA from a contralateral approach. (G) Arteriogram immediately after PTA reveals a severe spiral dissection of the external iliac artery extending into and nearly occluding the common femoral artery. (H) Completion arteriogram demonstrates that placement of two overlapping Palmaz stents in the external iliac artery has completely resolved the problem.

group, but all of the complications occurred in patients with iliac artery occlusion rather than stenosis. Importantly, 3 of the complications were embolic (1 ipsilateral and 2 contralateral). Only 2 complications required surgical or percutaneous intervention. Cumulative patency at 2 years in this series was 89.4 percent. In the author's own (unpublished) experience at the Miami Vascular Institute, using angiography, intraluminal pressure measurements, and intravascular ultrasound, the author identified at least two major reasons that PTA alone often fails in cases of iliac occlusion: dissection with residual gradient and marked elastic recoil with residual gradient. Using stents, the data for the first 45 patients were as follows. Technical success was 80 percent. At a mean follow-up of 15 months, the primary patency in the initially successful group was 82 percent and for all patients undergoing

attempted treatment was 64 percent; assisted primary patencies were 86 and 69 percent, respectively; secondary patencies were 89 and 72 percent, respectively.

Iliac stenting probably provides a more durable result than PTA alone, although published randomized controlled trials are lacking. One obvious reason is that stenting provides an excellent early result in many cases that would otherwise be PTA failures or suboptimal results. These include the chronic iliac artery occlusions plus the more severe cases of PTA-induced dissection and the cases of elastic recoil. The resulting increase in technical success raises the starting point of the life-table curve.

In the review of the nonrandomized multicenter trial of the Palmaz stent in iliac arteries[54] by Palmaz and colleagues of 587 procedures in 486 patients, the 30-day mortality was 1.9 percent. Ongoing clinical

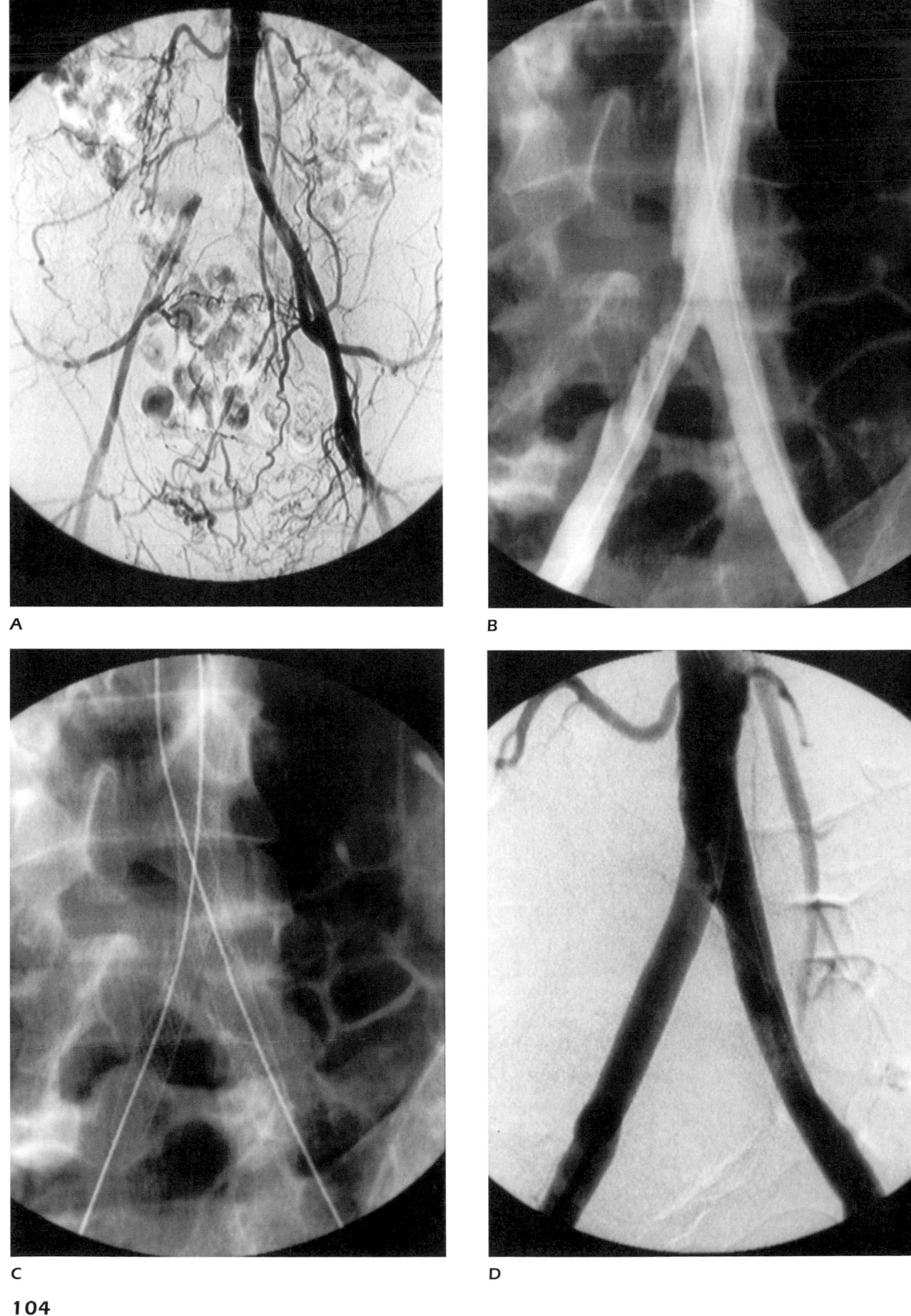

A

B

C

D

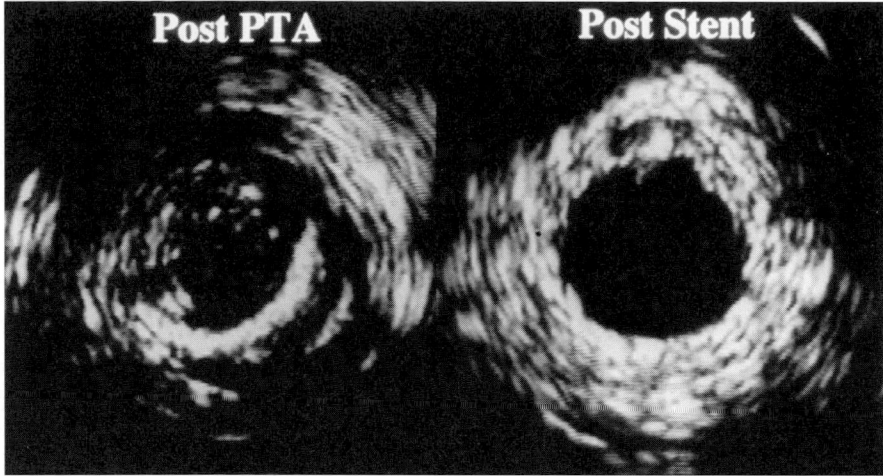

E

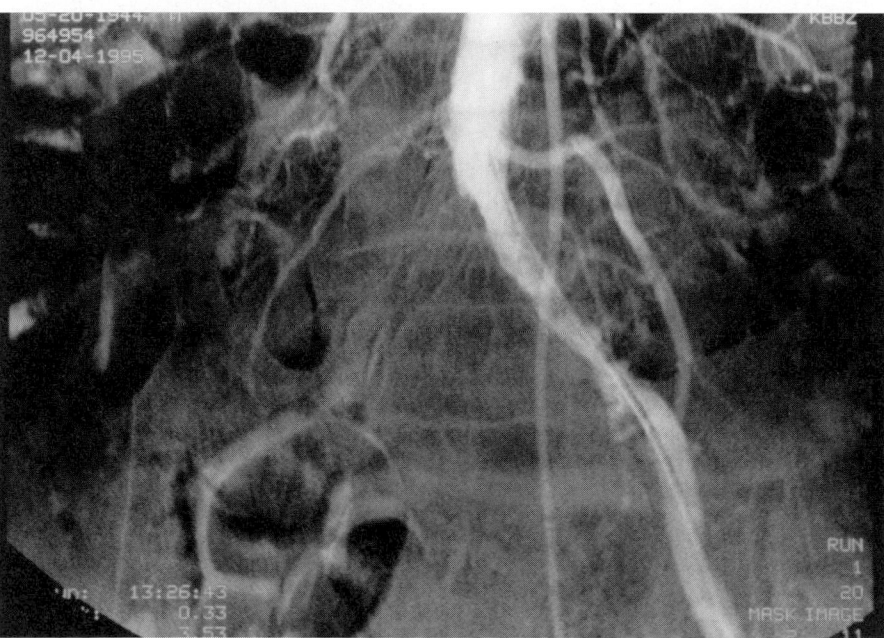

F

Figure 7-16. (A) Arteriogram in another patient with claudication shows complete right common iliac occlusion with reconstitution at the bifurcation into external and internal iliac arteries. (B) Arteriogram following recanalization and stenting demonstrates considerable recoil (compare diameters of right and left common iliac arteries) and dissection of the right common iliac artery. (C) Digital spot-film radiograph after placement of bilateral Wallstents. (D) Completion arteriogram. (E) Intravascular ultrasound in another patient depicts two of the reasons PTA alone (without stents) frequently fails in cases of chronic iliac artery occlusion. The image on the *left* shows dissection and marked recoil after PTA. The image on the *right* depicts an excellent morpho-logic result following stent placement in the same patient. (F and G) Long-segment right iliac artery occlusion and left external iliac artery stenosis in another patient. Arteriogram demonstrates the above findings and reconstitution of the distal right external iliac artery. (H) Attempted recanalization of right iliac artery with a Simmons-1 curve and an LLT wire. (I) Wire shown passing into right external iliac artery. After this image, the wire was snared from the right, and then used for the remainder of the case. (J) A stent has been deployed and expanded in the right common and external iliac arteries. (K) Completion arteriogram taken immediately after placement of bilateral iliac stents.

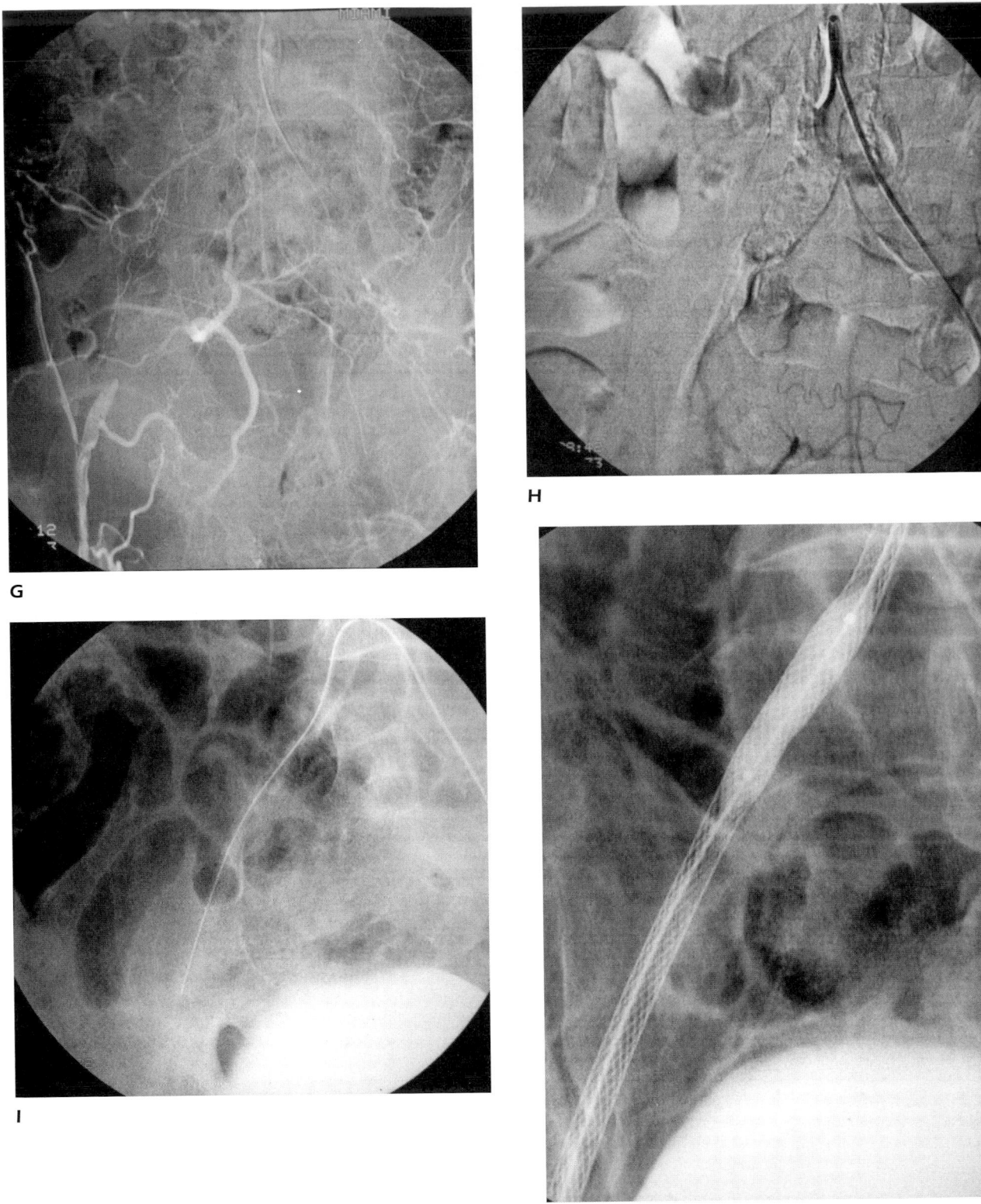

G

H

I

J

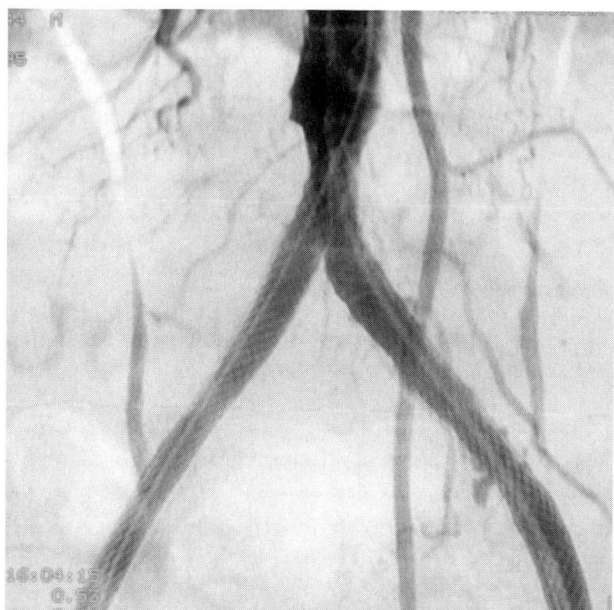

K   **Figure 7-16** (continued).

and in 68.6 percent at 43 months. Angiographic follow-up ($n = 201$ at a mean follow-up of 8.7 months) yielded a cumulative patency rate of 91.9 percent. The mean loss of lumen diameter was 15 percent, including the few who had developed total occlusions. The Wilcoxon test revealed significantly better long-term clinical success in nondiabetics than in diabetics ($p < 0.00001$) and in patients with good runoff versus those with poor runoff ($p = 0.0013$).

In a recent reanalysis of the Palmaz multicenter iliac data, Laborde and colleagues determined the influence of anatomic distribution of atherosclerosis (i.e., disease severity) on the outcome of revascularization by stenting.[57] They divided the 455 patients of the study population into three groups according to the Brewster classification of disease patterns (Fig. 7-17)[58] and then used a statistical analysis to determine differences in outcome between groups. Pattern type I includes only those patients with focal aortoiliac disease and/or common iliac disease (39.6 percent of the study group); pattern type II includes external iliac artery lesions (12.8 percent of the study group); pattern type III, or multilevel disease involving the infrainguinal vessels, was seen in 47.7 percent of study patients. Complete relief of symptoms occurred in 88.3 and 85.4 percent of pattern type I and II patients, respectively, whereas only 60.1 percent of those with pattern type III experienced complete relief ($p < 0.05$).

success was considered to be the retention of at least one stage of improvement in the ischemic ranking system. Using this definition, ongoing clinical success was present in 99.2 percent immediately after treatment, in 90.9 percent at 1 year, in 84.1 percent at 2 years,

Figure 7-17. Brewster classification of iliac artery disease. *Type I:* Focal aortoiliac disease or common iliac artery disease (39.6% of cases). *Type II:* Disease involving the external iliac artery (12.8% of cases). *Type III:* Multisegment disease, including the infrainguinal vasculature (47.7% of patients).

(From Brewster DC. Clinical and anatomical considerations for surgery in aortoiliac disease and results of surgical treatment. Circulation 1991;83(Suppl):42–52. Copyright 1991 American Heart Association. Used with permission.)

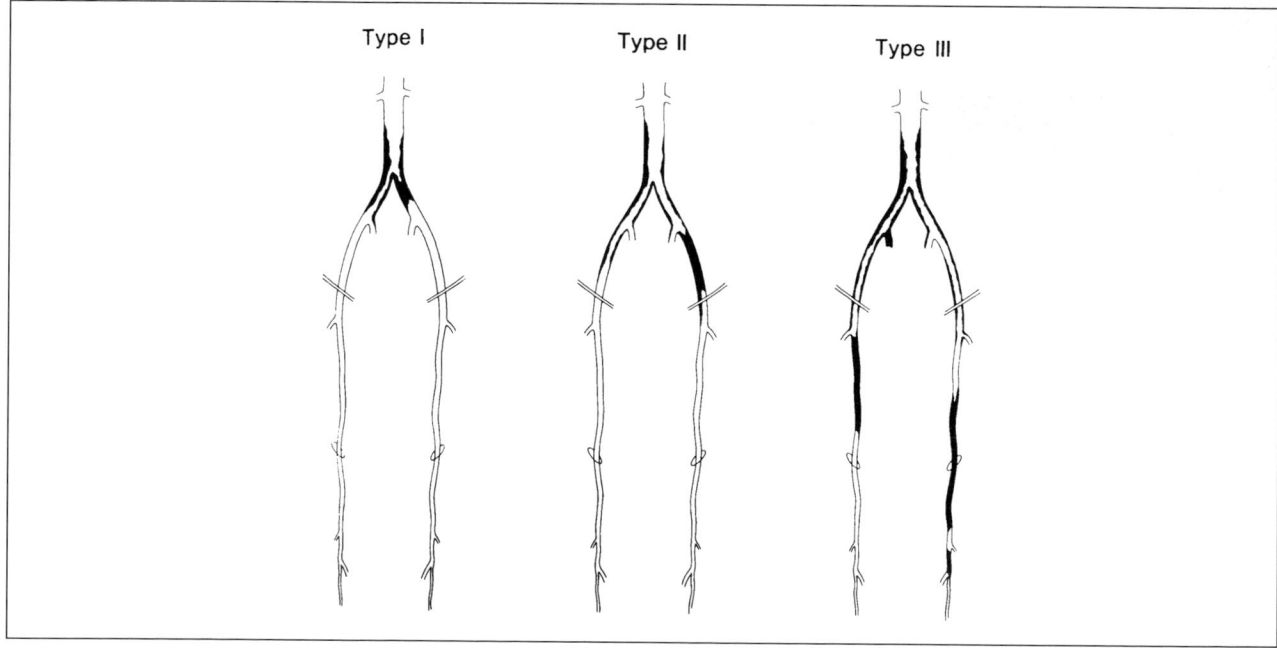

Type I   Type II   Type III

Persistent clinical benefit at 36 months was seen in 91.6 and 97.9 percent of patients with pattern type I and type II disease, respectively, as compared with 60.8 percent in type III ($p = 0.006$ for type II versus type III and $p = 0.001$ for type I versus type III, Wilcoxon test). No 30-day mortalities occurred in pattern type I or II patients; however, the 30-day mortality in type III was 2.9 percent ($p = 0.05$, Fisher's exact test). One-year mortalities were 3.0, 5.7, and 9.7 percent with pattern types I, II, and III, respectively (Fisher's exact test). Multivariate logistic regression showed that pattern type III was the most powerful indicator of unsatisfactory early outcome in iliac stenting ($p < 0.001$). Female gender also predicted unsatisfactory clinical outcome ($p < 0.01$) and higher periprocedural complications ($p < 0.001$).

Long-term follow-up for stents not available in the United States for intraarterial use (i.e., all stents other than the Palmaz stent) is more scant. Liermann and colleagues have reported their experience with placement of more than 100 Strecker stents in the iliac and femoral arteries.[59] Follow-up, which ranged from 8 to 48 months with a mean of 20 months, included noninvasive testing and intravenous digital subtraction angiography (DSA). Thirty iliac stenoses and 22 iliac occlusions were included in the report, and at a mean follow-up of 20 months, only 1 vessel had developed a restenosis. The long-term follow-up after treatment of iliac stenoses and occlusions with the Wallstent, as reported by Vorwerk and Gunther,[56] is indicated above.

In the U.S. clinical trial of the Wallstent in PVD,[33] 164 iliac lesions were stented for suboptimal PTA result in 137 patients. The 30-day mortality was 1.3 percent. ABIs before and after the procedure were 0.64 ± 0.18 and 0.86 ± 0.20, respectively. The relatively low postprocedure average ABI indicates that concomitant infrainguinal disease was common in the series, a fact that can profoundly influence the cumulative clinical success. For example, the 6-month cumulative clinical success in the study was 89 percent, and the angiographic patency (in 63 percent of patients) was 93 percent. The 1-year cumulative clinical success rate was 79 percent (SE = 3.6 percent). These numbers seem more impressive when one considers that all patients were entered after some form of PTA failure (occlusion, dissection longer than original lesion, residual stenosis ≥ 30 percent, or residual gradient > 5 mmHg).

The above discussion has attempted to show how profoundly stents have influenced modern aortoiliac PTA by providing a means to oppose elastic recoil, treat PTA-related dissections, and possibly improve the long-term clinical results. In addition to these benefits, stents have also provided a method to effectively treat category 3 and category 4 aortoiliac bifurcation disease in selected patients. For an area of vascular practice as seemingly established as aortoiliac surgery and iliac angioplasty for occlusive disease, developments are still occurring rapidly. A more complete understanding of the various roles of stents awaits further investigation and longer-term follow-up.

Femoropopliteal PTA

The American Heart Association categories for femoropopliteal lesions are as follows:

Category 1: Single stenoses up to 3 cm in length not at the origin of the superficial femoral artery (SFA) or the distal popliteal artery

Category 2: (a) Single stenoses 3 to 10 cm in length, not involving the distal popliteal; (b) heavily calcified stenoses up to 3 cm in length; (c) multiple lesions, each less than 3 cm (stenoses or occlusions); or (d) single or multiple lesions in the absence of continuous tibial runoff to improve inflow for distal surgical bypass

Category 3: (a) Single, 3 to 10 cm in length, involving distal popliteal; (b) multiple, each 3 to 5 cm, with or without heavy calcification; or (c) single stenoses or occlusions over 10 cm

Category 4: Complete common femoral artery (CFA) and/or SFA occlusions or complete popliteal and proximal trifurcation occlusion.

Five very important studies of femoropopliteal PTA have appeared in the literature in recent years. The first was a report by Morgenstern and colleagues from Columbia Presbyterian in New York that documents a 95 percent success rate at crossing femoropopliteal occlusions 1 to 4 cm in length and an 86 percent success rate in occlusions 5 to 10 cm in length using modern imaging and catheters together with a variety of steerable and specialty function guidewires.[60] Overall, technical success at balloon PTA for these occlusions was achieved in 64 out of 70 patients (91 percent). These figures update the authors' experience to a total of 160 femoropopliteal recanalizations. Importantly, this 91 percent initial success, which was achieved with standard guidewires and catheters, represents an expected frequency of success in clinical practice today. Considering the costs involved in using any of the new recanalization devices, Morgenstern and colleagues have made it clear that substantial advantages in safety, technical success, or long-term benefit will be required to justify the expenditures.

A second important paper by Murray and colleagues provides data on recanalization and PTA for very-long-segment femoropopliteal occlusions using modern angiographic technique and steerable guide-wires.[61] Lesions ranged from 10 to 40 cm in length, with an average of 24.3 cm. Success was defined as less than 30 percent residual diameter stenosis *and* an increase of 0.2 or more in the ABI. Patency at follow-up was defined as less than 50 percent diameter stenosis by color flow imaging. Initial success was achieved in 41 out of 44 attempts (93 percent). There was no mortality. At 18-month follow-up, the mean ABI had increased from 0.53 (preprocedure) to 0.80. The cumulative primary patency at 18 months was 69 percent, but clinical symptoms had improved in 83 percent.

In the third important study, Capek and colleagues reported the long-term results of 217 PTA procedures in the superficial femoral and popliteal arteries over an 8-year period.[62] Patients were followed with serial noninvasive studies and in 71 cases with angiography. Follow-up ranged from 2 to 11 years, with a mean of 7 years. In this study, life-table analysis was used to assess factors that had a potential impact on the long-term outcome of PTA. Most of the cases in this series were enrolled in 1979 and 1980, before the advent of DSA, road-mapping, steerable soft-tipped guidewires, calcium channel blockers, low-profile catheters, and several other important advances. Still, the technical success rate was 93 percent for stenoses and 82 percent for occlusions. Excluding initial failures in 10 percent, the patencies at 1, 3, and 5 years were 81, 61, and 58 percent, respectively. Inclusion of the initial failures according to the new standards (i.e., accounting for *all* patients subjected to this form of therapy) results in overall patencies at 1, 3, and 5 years of 73, 55, and 52 percent, respectively. Complications occurred in 10 percent of cases, but one-quarter of these were technical "complications" without clinical consequence. Clinical factors that were found to negatively influence long-term patency included diabetes mellitus ($p = 0.04$), diffuse atherosclerotic cardiovascular disease ($p = 0.05$), and threatened limb loss at the time of initial presentation for treatment ($p = 0.01$). Morphologic factors found to negatively influence long-term outcome included long lesion length (overall $p = 0.004$; for 0–2 cm versus >2 cm, $p = 0.001$; for 0–2 cm versus >10 cm, $p = 0.007$; for 2–5 cm versus >10 cm, $p = 0.015$); moderate eccentricity ($p = 0.04$); and residual stenosis on post-PTA angiogram ($p = 0.02$).

The fourth important study was Johnston's reanalysis of data from the femoropopliteal angioplasty subgroup in the Toronto series.[63] The author analyzed data from 254 femoropopliteal PTAs that were performed for all severities of chronic ischemia. Cumulative clinical success was measured by standard objective criteria, and the Kaplan-Meier method was used

to recalculate the data. Cox multiple regression analysis was used to determine variables predictive of late results. For stenoses with good runoff, the 5-year cumulative clinical success was 53 percent; with poor runoff it was 31 percent. For occlusions, cumulative clinical success was 36 percent at 5 years for patients with good runoff and 16 percent for those with poor runoff. Occlusion may have been a confounding variable in this study, just as it was in the study of Capek and colleagues. In other words, in the Capek study, patients with femoropopliteal occlusion who underwent successful recanalization and PTA were just as likely to have lasting patency as those who began with stenoses. The differences in cumulative clinical success were almost all due to the differences in technical success from the very beginning. The data in Johnston's reanalysis suggest a similar phenomenon. In the overall study group (failures included), the cumulative clinical success ± SE was 88.8 ± 2.0 percent at 1 month, 62.5 ± 3.2 percent at 1 year, 52.6 ± 3.5 percent at 2 years, 50.7 ± 3.5 percent at 3 years, 44.1 ± 4.0 percent at 4 years, and 38.1 ± 4.4 percent at 5 years. When only initially successful cases were included, the cumulative clinical successes were 70.4 ± 3.3 percent at 1 year, 59.4 ± 3.7 percent at 2 years, 57.1 ± 3.8 percent at 3 years, 49.7 ± 4.3 percent at 4 years, 42.9 ± 4.9 percent at 5 years, and 40.2 ± 5.3 percent at 6 years. It seems from these data that initial success portends a high likelihood of long-term clinical benefit. Importantly, initial success occurred in 88.8 percent of cases in the study.

See Figures 7-18 and 7-19 and Table 7-4 for life-table data from the Capek and Johnston studies, respectively.

The fifth and final important femoropopliteal study is a decision and cost-effectiveness analysis of revascularization procedures for femoropopliteal disease by Hunink and colleagues.[64] The authors used a literature review of mortality, morbidity, patency, and cost data as a source. They included only procedures performed after 1985. There were 4800 PTAs and 4511 bypass operations. They developed a decision analytic model to examine the choice between bypass surgery and PTA for lesions amenable to either procedure. Outcomes measured included 5-year patency, quality-adjusted life expectancy (QALE), lifetime costs, and incremental cost-effectiveness ratios. Six treatment strategies were analyzed: (1) no treatment, (2) initial PTA, no further revascularization, (3) initial PTA, subsequent PTA, (4) initial PTA, subsequent bypass surgery, (5) bypass surgery followed by no further therapy, and (6) bypass surgery followed by graft revision. The results showed that for a 65-year-old man with disabling claudication and a femoropopliteal stenosis or occlusion, the initial PTA strategy increased QALE

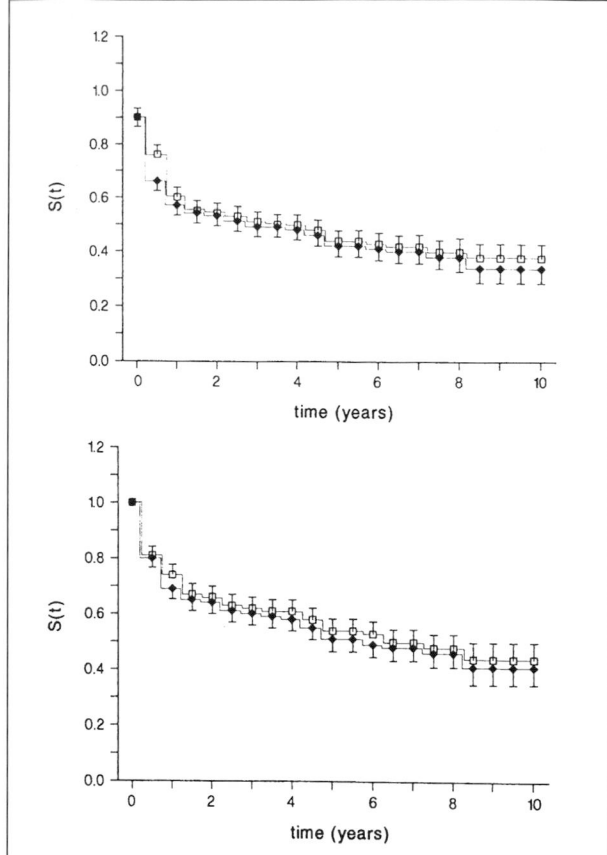

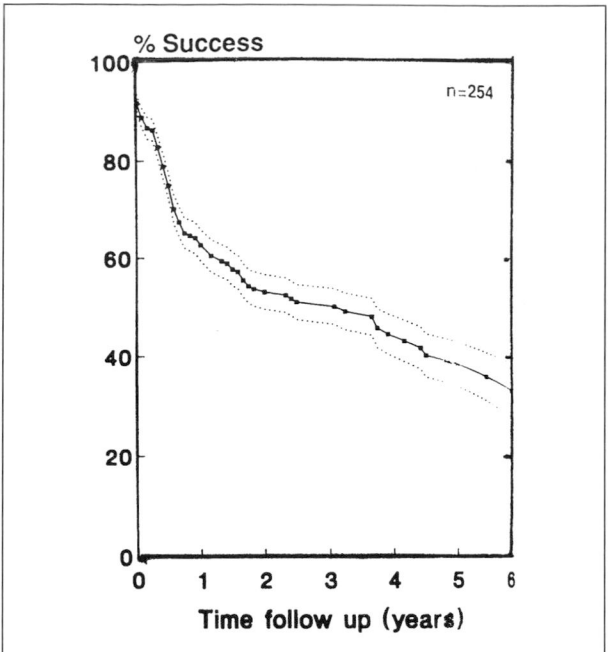

Figure 7-19. Cumulative clinical success of femoropopliteal angioplasty. Results for all 254 femoral and popliteal PTAs calculated with the Kaplan-Meier method. The mean, +1 standard error, and −1 standard error are shown. (From Johnston KW. Femoral and popliteal arteries: reanalysis of results of balloon angioplasty. Radiology 1992;183:767–771. Used with permission.)

Figure 7-18. Cumulative clinical success of femoropopliteal angioplasty. Overall survival curve showing primary (◆) and secondary (□) patencies, including (A) and excluding (B) primary technical failures. The similarity between the two curves reflects the fact that most patients presenting with recurrent symptoms were treated surgically and consequently terminated from the analysis. Error bars show the standard error of the cumulative proportion of survivors. (From Capek P, McLean GK, Berkowitz HD. Femoropopliteal angioplasty: factors influencing long-term success. Circulation 1991;83(Suppl I):74. Copyright 1991 American Heart Association. Used with permission.)

by 2 to 13 months and resulted in decreased lifetime expenditures as compared to bypass surgery. The same was true for chronic critical ischemia and a femoropopliteal stenosis. For femoropopliteal occlusion and critical ischemia, an initial strategy of bypass surgery increased QALE by 1 to 4 months and decreased lifetime expenditures compared to PTA. Sensitivity analysis showed that when the 5-year patency of PTA exceeds 30 percent, PTA is always the preferred initial strategy. The authors concluded that PTA is the preferred initial strategy in patients with disabling claudication and femoropopliteal stenosis or occlusion and in those with chronic critical ischemia and a stenosis. In patients with chronic critical ischemia and an occlusion, bypass surgery is the preferred initial strategy.

Femoropopliteal Stents

The most troublesome lesions for percutaneous intervention include eccentric stenoses, long-segment occlusions, long-segment stenoses, obstructing intimal flaps after PTA, and stenoses due to intimal hyperplasia at graft anastomoses. All of these morphologic problems occur commonly in the femoropopliteal distribution, and not surprisingly, stents have been applied as a potential solution. In general, the immediate and early results have been excellent, and many cases of angioplasty failure have been converted to early successes

Table 7-4. Cumulative Clinical Success of Femoropopliteal Angioplasty

Years	Percent
1	70.4 ± 3.3
2	59.4 ± 3.7
3	57.1 ± 3.8
4	49.7 ± 4.3
5	42.9 ± 4.9
6	40.2 ± 5.3

Reanalysis of 254 PTAs. Figures are after exclusion of initial (30-day) failures. Data from Johnston KW. Femoral and popliteal arteries: reanalysis of results of balloon angioplasty. Radiology 1992;183:767–771. Used with permission.

due to the impact of stents. However, intimal hyperplasia has resulted in a very high frequency of restenosis.

Preliminary studies using a variety of stents show less than promising results because of intimal hyperplasia and occlusion. In a study of 22 femoropopliteal lesions in 21 patients, Sapoval et al. used the Wallstent and found a primary patency of 49 percent at 1 year.[65] In a study of 26 patients, Do-dai-Do and colleagues reported a secondary patency rate of 69 percent at 1 year using the same device.[66] Zollikofer used Wallstents in 15 patients with an inadequate response to recanalization and angioplasty for femoropopliteal occlusion.[67] At a mean follow-up of 20 months in 11 patients available for follow-up, only six arteries were patent. Using the Strecker stent, Liermann and colleagues found a patency rate of 70.8 percent at a mean follow-up of 19 months.[59] A few centers have accumulated an experience with the Palmaz stent in femoropopliteal disease (Fig. 7-20). These studies have been done in Europe, and to date, no randomized clinical trials have been concluded. The U.S. multicenter trial of the Palmaz stent in femoropopliteal arteries, which was a prospective randomized trial against PTA, has been terminated by the manufacturer.

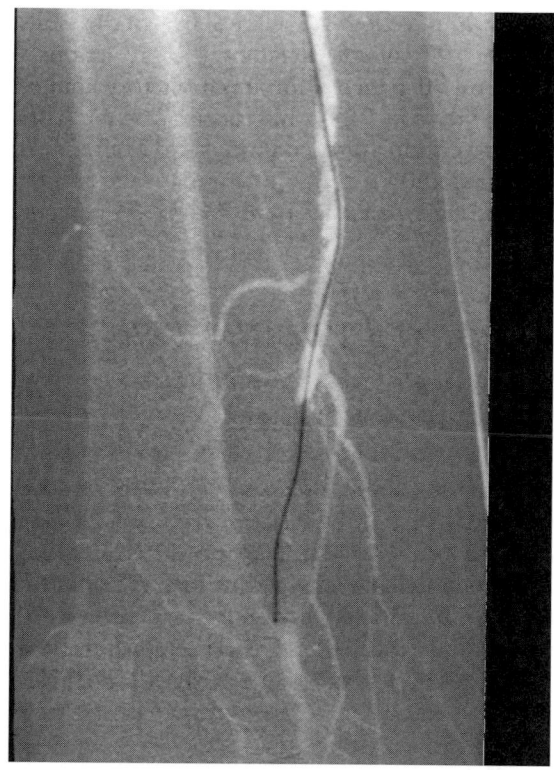

A

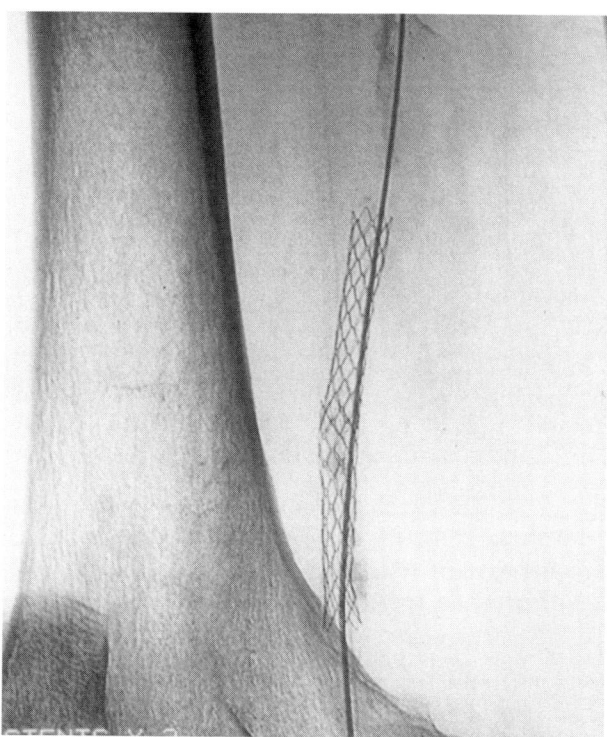

B

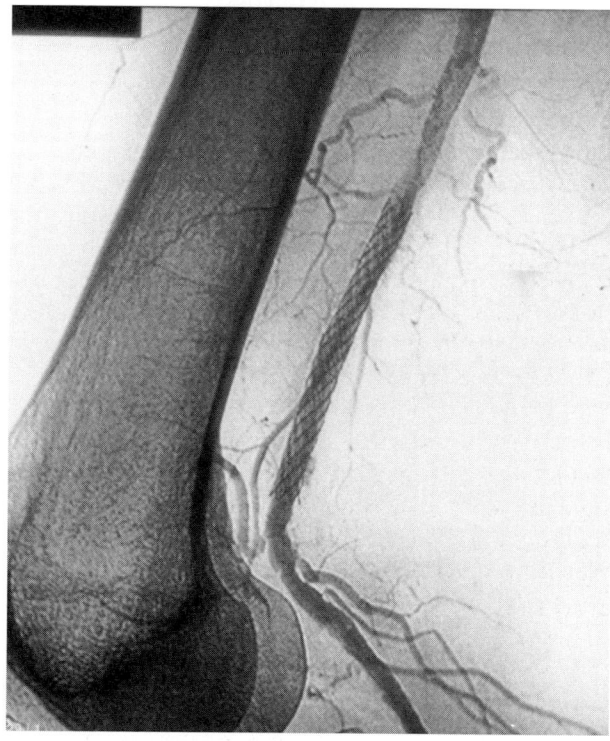

C

Figure 7-20. Femoropopliteal Palmaz stents. (A) Short-segment chronic above-knee popliteal occlusion is successfully traversed with a guidewire. (B) Two stents are placed in tandem with slight overlap. (C) Arteriogram with flexion demonstrates a widely patent lumen that is not disturbed by this positioning. Stents in the femoropopliteal segment have not proved unequivocally superior to PTA. They do, however, make manageable some cases of failure due to dissection or recoil.

In the multicenter U.S. clinical trial of the Wallstent in PVD,[33] 97 superficial femoral artery lesions were stented in 90 patients for unsatisfactory immediate PTA results ($n = 91$) or restenosis ($n = 6$). ABIs before intervention averaged 0.65 ± 0.19; after stenting they averaged 0.96 ± 0.27. Cumulative 6-month and 1-year primary patencies were 73 and 54 percent, respectively.

Current and Potential Role of Stents in Atherosclerotic Renal Artery Disease

Although only about 5 percent of all hypertensive patients have true renovascular hypertension (RVHTN), certain historical features increase the likelihood of a renovascular cause. Patients with such histories should undergo diagnostic evaluation for renal artery stenosis and RVHTN with an eye toward therapy if the workup is positive. Any of the features listed in Table 7-5 should initiate a search for renovascular hypertension (RVHTN).

Diagnostic Tests for RVHTN

Scintigraphy

Technetium 99m–DTPA renal flow scanning and mercapto-acetyl-triglycine (MAG-3) scanning are useful in the detection of unilateral renal artery stenosis. The diagnostic sensitivity is enhanced by captopril challenge. Whereas these tests are quite sensitive for unilateral renal artery stenosis, their diagnostic utility is lower in the presence of bilateral renal artery disease. Importantly, bilateral disease is common, particularly in patients with athcrosclerosis of the aorta and renal artery stenosis. It has been claimed that split-function scintigraphy (combined ^{99m}Tc-DMSA and ^{99m}Tc-DTPA scanning, or "D & D scanning") is useful in predicting which patients will benefit (blood pressure and/or renal function benefit) from renal revascularization (angioplasty or surgery). The general rule has been that if a kidney contributes less than 10 to 20 percent of the total function as measured by scintigra-

Table 7-5. Clues to the Diagnosis of Renovascular Hypertension

1. Sudden-onset (especially in women), accelerated, or difficult-to-control HTN
2. HTN without a family history
3. Poor compliance on medical therapy
4. HTN and a bruit suggestive of renal artery stenosis
5. Onset of renal insufficiency during captopril therapy

phy, then it is not worth revascularizing, because the risks outweigh the potential benefits. This has not been uniformly true in the author's experience. The author has seen patients derive both blood pressure and renal function benefits of revascularization by angioplasty, starting with as little as 6 percent function in the affected kidney and achieving up to 30 percent after revascularization.

Hypertensive Intravenous Pyelogram (IVP)

Although popular in the past, hypertensive IVP as a stand-alone method of screening for renovascular HTN is more of a historical curiosity than a useful test.

Renal Vein Renins

A positive or lateralizing renal vein renin ratio is equal to or greater than $1.5:1.0$. Unfortunately, although lateralizing renal vein renins predict a beneficial outcome of revascularization with an accuracy of 90 percent, the ratio turns out to be an insensitive detector of patients who can benefit from revascularization. Approximately 60 percent of patients with a nonlateralizing ratio benefit from surgical revascularization, and similar results have been shown with percutaneous transluminal renal angioplasty (PTRA). Therefore, many nephrologists and hypertensologists have adopted an aggressive approach to diagnosis and management.

Arteriography

Since current arteriographic methods are quite safe and accurate, angiography for RVHTN can be done on an outpatient basis with the use of a 4 or 5 French catheter. Intraarterial DSA is commonly employed as a substitute for standard cut-film arteriography in the workup of RVHTN. Although there is a very slight compromise in spatial resolution when this approach is used, the benefits are substantial. The lower concentrations of contrast material used in DSA maximize patient comfort and minimize the total iodine dose and risk to the kidneys.

Treatment of RVHTN: Relationship to Renal Function

There are several major questions to answer with respect to the management of the patient with HTN and renal artery stenosis. First, is the stenosis related to the HTN? Second, are there likely to be other causes of HTN in the same patient? Should we treat? If so, should the patient get angioplasty or surgery? Is medical therapy reasonable? What results should we expect?

These are complex questions, and their answers are intertwined. One major problem is that even in essential hypertensives with renal artery stenosis, blood pressure and renal function are not independent. In many instances, medical control of blood pressure in the presence of renal artery stenosis leads to a decline in renal function. In a study comparing medical and surgical therapy for atherosclerotic renal vascular disease, 46 percent of patients treated medically for 1 to 9 years showed a decline in renal function while those treated surgically did not.[68]

One concept that continues to surface is that of "preocclusive" (destined to occlude) renal artery stenosis. How severe of a stenosis is "preocclusive"? Which ones should we dilate and when? The problem is that our knowledge of the natural history of renal artery stenosis is limited. To some extent, the answer to the question depends on the disease entity causing the renal artery stenosis, as determined by angiography. In at least one series, atherosclerotic disease progressed in severity in 39 percent of cases over a follow-up period of 6 months to 7 years in 39 patients.[69] Fibromuscular disease (FMD) progressed in only 16 percent. In a retrospective study of 85 patients with atherosclerotic renal artery stenosis who underwent renal angiography more than once, 37 (44 percent) progressed. This small study also demonstrated a 39 percent likelihood of progression to complete occlusion (mean angiographic follow-up of 13 months) when the stenosis on the original angiogram was in the 75 to 99 percent category.[70] In a more recent study by Tollefson and Ernst,[71] 194 aortograms done primarily for evaluation of aneurysm or occlusive disease in 48 patients were studied to define variables predictive of the development of progressive renal artery stenosis or occlusion. Each patient had a minimum of two aortograms at least a year apart. Disease progressed in 53 percent of renal arteries, and occlusion occurred in seven arteries. The seven had a mean stenosis rate of 80 percent (range 61–94 percent) on the aortogram immediately preceding the one showing occlusion. None of the patients without progression to occlusion had renal artery stenoses of 60 percent or more on their aortograms. The authors concluded that aggressive revascularization may be warranted in patients with the most severe stenoses.

Percutaneous Transluminal Renal Angioplasty (PTRA) for HTN

For morphologically true renal artery lesions, whether fibromuscular or atherosclerotic, the technical success rate of PTRA exceeds 90 percent,[72,73] and PTRA is the procedure of choice. The success rate for ostial stenoses due to atherosclerosis of the aortic wall is considerably lower because plaque in the aortic wall is not responsive to PTA of a branch vessel perpendicular to

Table 7-6. Guidelines for Reporting Results of Interventional or Surgical Therapy for Hypertension

Cured: DP is less than or equal to 90 mmHg with at least a 10-mmHg decrease from pre-PTA.

Improved: 15% decrease in DP and DP is less than 110 but greater than 90 mmHg.

Failed: Less than 15% decrease in DP with DP greater than 90 mmHg, or a DP greater than 110 mmHg.

Benefited: Cured + Improved. About 90% of patients experience BP benefit from PTRA, and nearly 70% demonstrate long-term benefit as determined by clinical follow-up. Cures are not common, and long-lasting benefit is more likely to occur in patients with fibromuscular dysplasia than in patients with atherosclerosis.

DP = diastolic pressure

the offending plaque. In general, surgical bypass grafting is the procedure of choice in such patients, since the main renal arteries are often free of disease, and bypass grafts can be expected to work quite well. Nonetheless, currently, percutaneous renal artery stenting is beginning to prove efficacious in ostial renal artery stenosis.

Results of PTRA for RVHTN have traditionally been reported according to the guidelines in Table 7-6. Table 7-7 shows results.

Percutaneous Transluminal Angioplasty for Preservation of Renal Function

A major cause of renal insufficiency in the elderly is atheromatous renal artery stenosis. In one study, 48 percent of patients over the age of 50 years presenting with advanced renal failure had renal artery obstructions as the underlying cause.[74] Usually, untreated atheromatous renal artery stenoses are progressive. Timely revascularization by percutaneous transluminal renal angioplasty (PTRA) may prevent further functional deterioration of the kidneys and/or postpone initiation of dialysis. In fact, PTRA can provide dramatic improvement in renal function in cases of azotemia due, at least in part, to renal artery stenosis.

Martin and colleagues employed PTRA in the treatment of 79 patients with a serum creatinine (CR) level greater than or equal to 1.8 mg/dl.[73,74] In 43 percent of the study group, the serum CR decreased from an average of 2.7 mg/dl to 1.7 mg/dl in a mean follow-up period of 16 months. Significant decreases were found in 61 percent of patients with bilateral stenoses, in 38 percent of patients with unilateral stenoses and absence of flow to the contralateral kidney, and in 38 percent of patients with unilateral stenosis and normal flow to the contralateral kidney. The least benefit was encountered in patients with serum creatinine levels greater than 4.0 mg/dl. Sos has reported a similar experience with up to 2 years of follow-up.[75]

Table 7-7. Results of Renal PTA for Hypertension due to Nonostial Atherosclerotic Renal Artery Stenosis

	Number of Patients	Successfully Dilated		Cured		Improved		Follow-up (mo)	
Author		*n*	%	*n*	%	*n*	%	Mean	Range
Tegtmeyer et al. Radiology 1984;153:77–84.*†	65	61	94	15	25	129	55	NA	1–60
Schwarten et al. Radiology 1980;135:601.	54	49	91	23	47	25	51	NA	1–18
Geyskes et al. Br Med J 1983;287:333.*	44	44	100	4	9	19	43	NA	12–48
Martin and Cork. SCVIR Intervent Radiol 1990;F-57:174.†	38	?38	?100	10	25	19	47	19	3–36
Sos et al. N Engl J Med 1983;309:274–279.	20	15	75	4	27	9	60	16	4–40
Martin et al. Am J Radiol 1981;128:951.	15	13	87	2	15	4	31	13	NA
Grim et al. Ann Intern Med 1981;95:439.	16	16	100	1	7	8	50	10	3–24
Total	252	236	94	59	25	130	55		

*Includes some patients with bilateral disease.
†Includes some patients with ostial stenoses.
NA = not available.
Source: From Sos TA. Angioplasty for the treatment of azotemia and renovascular hypertension in atherosclerotic renal artery disease. Circulation 1991;83(Suppl II):I–164. Copyright 1991 American Heart Association. Used with permission.

In a retrospective study at the Miami Vascular Institute, the author and colleagues assessed the effect of PTRA on renal function in 40 azotemic patients (all with serum creatinine levels over 1.5 mg/dl) with atherosclerotic renal artery stenosis.[76] The study group included 29 men and 11 women. The patients had hypertension ($n = 35$), diabetes mellitus ($n = 19$), and a history of smoking ($n = 14$). During the preprocedural year, the mean serum creatinine level rose from 1.9 ± 0.15 mg/dl to 2.4 ± 0.17. The slope of the regression line of serum creatinine against time in individual patients before PTRA had a positive value of 0.6 ± 0.22 mg/dl per year, indicating a statistically significant rise ($p < 0.05$). After PTRA, the renal function curve reached a plateau with a mean serum creatinine level of 2.5 ± 0.57 mg/dl at 1 year. The slope of the regression line after PTRA (0.2 ± 1.24 mg/dl per year) was not statistically significantly different from 0. This indicated on the average that renal function did not deteriorate further, but rather tended to stabilize after intervention. It should be remembered that patients with chronic renal insufficiency and atherosclerotic renal artery stenosis show a steady decline in renal function (as did this study group in the year before intervention). Successful revascularization at one point along the curve may therefore not manifest as a decrease in creatinine, but rather as a plateau or interruption in the upward rise of creatinine. Some patients may be saved from dialysis by revascularization.

In the author's study, clinical success was not related to the initial level of serum creatinine or the rate of deterioration of renal function prior to PTRA. Clinical failure was, however, related to residual stenosis after PTRA and to claudication.

Results of several series are summarized in Table 7-8.[73–78]

Table 7-8. Comparison of Renal Function of Stented Versus Nonstented Renal Angioplasty

	Renal Function After PTRA: Atheromatous Renal Artery Stenosis		
	Series	No. Pts.	% Improved or Stabilized
Nonstented	Pickering et al. Nephron 1986; 44(Suppl 1): 8–11.	55	47
	Bell et al. Q J Med 1987; 63(241):393–403.	22	85
	Martin[74]	72	43
	Pattison et al. Q J Med 1993; 86(3):215–216.	60	80
	Pattynama et al.[76]	40	60
Total		249	55
Stented	Rees[78]	124 (U.S. multicenter Palmaz trial stent)	73

*Ten of 13 were able to cease dialysis.

Complications of renal angioplasty include death (0.2 percent); injury to the renal artery (0.5–2.0 percent); loss of a kidney (0.2 percent); renal failure, either transient or permanent, due to contrast material (1 percent); and arterial puncture site problems, most commonly hematoma (1–5 percent, the majority of which are minor and do not require intervention). Approximately 2.5 percent of patients require surgery because of or in association with some problem of PTA. However, most of these are not urgent operations.

Surgical Approach to Renal Artery Disease

Aortorenal bypass grafting can have an excellent initial success rate of 97 percent and an operative mortality rate of 0.5 percent in a highly selected population. However, these figures are not the norm for surgical management of RVHTN, particularly in centers where a preponderance of patients have diffuse atherosclerosis and coronary or cerebrovascular comorbidity. Nor should these figures be used to select patients for surgical management in centers where the surgeons are less experienced. The figures for surgical cure of RVHTN and surgical improvement are similar to those of PTRA, and PTRA remains less invasive. Post-PTRA restenosis can be managed with repeat PTRA.

Importantly, splenorenal and hepatorenal grafting are important new renal bypass procedures that may exhibit relatively less morbidity and mortality than those of aortorenal bypass grafting. Still, aortorenal bypass is performed more commonly. Aortorenal endarterectomy is another option in patients with severe aortic atherosclerosis and proximal renal artery stenosis.

Surgery is an excellent option for preservation of renal function, particularly in patients with bilateral renal ostial disease refractory to PTA. However, stents have begun to assume an important role in these patients.

Renal Artery Stents

To address the limitations of PTRA, intraarterial stent investigations have been undertaken throughout the world. The major ones in use are the Palmaz-Schatz stent (Johnson & Johnson Interventional Systems), the Wallstent (Sneider Stent Division, Pfizer), and the Strecker stent (Medi-Tech). The overwhelming majority of experience has been gleaned with the Palmaz-Schatz stent.

Thousands of patients have now undergone placement of Palmaz-Schatz stents for suboptimal renal angioplasty results. Figure 7-21 depicts one illustrative case. In the most recent analysis of the results of a U.S. multicenter trial of the Palmaz-Schatz stent in the renal arteries, Rees and colleagues analyzed 263 patients

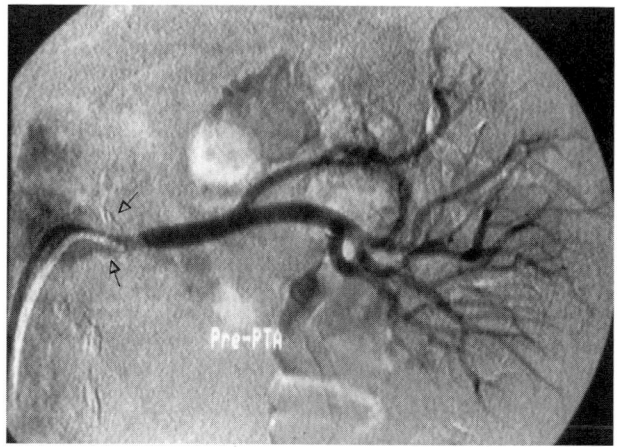

A

B

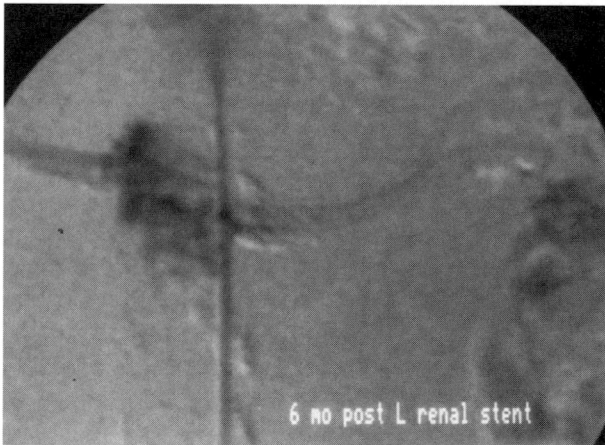

C

Figure 7-21. Palmaz stent for ostial renal artery stenosis in a patient with new onset of hypertension. (A) Selective left renal arteriogram shows aortorenal ostial plaque. The catheter is in the stenosis. *Arrows* indicate the calcified plaque extending from the aorta into the origin of the renal artery. The patient was treated with a renal artery stent. (B) Film from 6-month follow-up renal arteriogram shows criss-cross pattern of stent, a smooth renal artery lumen, and a definite neointimal lining without stenosis. (C) Later frame from same sequence shows trailing edge of well-expanded stent buttressing the ostial renal artery plaque.

who underwent this procedure for suboptimal PTRA result, restenosis, dissection, or ostial atheroma (high risk of poor outcome).[78] The mean patient age was 66 years $\pm$ 10.1; 98 percent of the lesions were atherosclerotic, and 80 percent were ostial. Forty-seven percent of patients had renal insufficiency (CR > 1.5 mg/dl). Follow-up included blood pressure measurements, laboratory studies, and 6-month angiography.

Technical success was achieved in 95 percent, and the poststent residual stenosis rate was 4.2 percent $\pm$ 8.6 percent. Cumulative cure or improvement in HTN using Kaplan-Meier analysis was 91 percent at 1 month, 84 percent at 3 months, 70 percent at 6 months, and 61 percent at 12 months. In patients with renal insufficiency, benefit was realized in 73 percent (improvement in 34 percent, stabilization in 39 percent). Deterioration had occurred in 27 percent at longest follow-up (mean follow-up 7.9 months). Angiography in 150 patients revealed restenosis (diameter at treated site < 50 percent of normal adjacent vessel) in 32.7 percent. Restenosis was lower in males (23 percent, $p < 0.05$) and for stents dilated to 6 mm or more (26 percent, $p < 0.05$). It was lowest of all for patients in both groups (10.5 percent, $p < 0.05$).

Summary

Metallic stents have added significantly to the armamentarium of interventionalists. They come in two varieties: balloon-expandable and self-expanding. The balloon-expandable devices work by plastic deformation of the metal beyond its elastic limit. The result is a relatively rigid device with high hoop strength. The self-expanding devices work by a simple spring-coil mechanism or by thermal shape memory. There are many properties of the ideal metallic stent; however, no single stent is ideal.

The Palmaz stent is approved by the FDA for use in the iliac arteries and in the coronary arteries. The other balloon-expandable stents are under evaluation. The Wallstent is the self-expanding stent with the most use in the vascular system in the United States. It is currently awaiting approval from the FDA for failed iliac and superficial femoral artery PTAs, and for transjugular intrahepatic portosystemic shunts (TIPs).

Stents for PVD have had their greatest impact in the aortoiliac segment, where they have proved effective in managing PTA-induced dissection, elastic recoil, and residual hemodynamic gradients after PTA. They have also provided the means by which chronic iliac artery occlusions can be managed percutaneously. In other words, stents have rendered successful many PTA cases that would otherwise have been deemed failures or un-

satisfactory results. Most of the available clinical data are for the Palmaz stent and the Wallstent. Stents probably provide long-term patency superior to that of PTA alone, although this has not been established by peer-reviewed publication of clinical trials.

There is a significant but smaller experience with infrainguinal stents for PVD. In most of the reported experience, the Wallstent has been used. Stents have proved invaluable in the management of acute PTA failures and suboptimal results. Intimal hyperplasia continues to result in restenosis; however, the 6-month and 1-year results are comparable to those of PTA alone. These results are significant, since most of the cases included in the stent studies have been done for an indication of PTA failure or suboptimal result.

Percutaneous transluminal renal angioplasty (PTRA) is a safe and effective method of renal revascularization in cases of main renal artery atherosclerosis and fibromuscular dysplasia. Major shortcomings of PTRA include restenosis and the poor short- and long-term response of ostial atheromatous lesions. Transluminal arterial stenting in cases of suboptimal PTRA, restenosis, and ostial disease has a 95 percent technical success rate, provides the mechanical support necessary to resist elastic recoil, and is associated with benefit in both blood pressure and renal function. Therefore, stents have already established their clinical utility in enhancing short- and midterm PTRA results. Metallic stents do not prevent restenosis in the stented segment of the renal artery; the most durable results have been seen in men and in arteries dilated to at least 6-mm diameter.

Acknowledgments

I wish to thank Tony Chirinos for his kind and skillful assistance with the illustrations in this chapter.

References

1. Dotter CT, Judkins MP. Transluminal treatment of arteriosclerotic obstructions: description of a new technic and a preliminary report of its application. Circulation 1964;30:654–670.
2. Dotter CT. Transluminally-placed coilspring endarterial tube grafts: long-term patency in canine popliteal artery. Invest Radiol 1969;4:327–332.
3. Dotter CT, Buschmann RW, McKinney MK, Rösch J. Transluminally expandable nitinol coil stent grafting: preliminary report. Radiology 1983;147:259–260.
4. Cragg A, Lund G, Rysavy J, Castaneda F, Castaneda-Zuniga W, Amplatz K. Nonsurgical placement of arterial endoprosthesis: a new technique using nitinol wire. Radiology 1983;147:261–263.
5. Gardiner GA Jr, Meyerovitz MF, Stokes KR, Clouse ME, Harrington DP, Bettmann MA. Complications of transluminal angioplasty. Radiology 1986;159:201–208.
6. Martin LG, Casarella WJ, Alspaugh JP, Chuang VP. Renal ar-

tery angioplasty: increased technical success and decreased complications in the second 100 patients. Radiology 1986;159: 631–634.

7. Becker GJ, Palmaz JC, Rees CR, et al. Angioplasty-induced dissections in human iliac arteries: management with Palmaz balloon-expandable intraluminal stents. Radiology 1990;176: 31–38.

8. Cowley MJ, Dorros G, Kelsey SF, Van Raden M, Detre KM. Acute coronary events associated with percutaneous transluminal angioplasty. Am J Cardiol 1984;53(12):12c–16c.

9. Waller BF, Pinkerton CA, Orr CM, Slack JD, VanTassel JW, Peters T. Restenosis 1 to 24 months after clinically successful coronary balloon angioplasty: a necropsy study of 20 patients. J Am Coll Cardiol 1991;17(6 Suppl B):58B–70B.

10. Kuntz RE, Baim DS. Defining coronary restenosis: new clinical and angiographic paradigms. Circulation 1993;88(3):1310–1323.

11. Reiber JHC, Serruys PW, Kooijman CJ, et al. Assessment of short-, medium-, and long-term variations in arterial dimensions from computer-assisted quantitation of coronary cineangiograms. Circulation 1985;71:280–288.

12. Kuntz RE, Keaney KM, Senerchia C, Baim DS. Estimating the late results of coronary intervention from incomplete angiographic follow-up. Circulation 1993;87:815–830.

13. Beatt KJ, Luijten HE, deFeyter PJ, van den Brand M, Reiber JHC, Serruys PW. Change in diameter of coronary segments adjacent to stenosis after percutaneous transluminal coronary angioplasty: failure of percent diameter stenosis measurement to reflect morphologic changes induced by balloon dilation. J Am Coll Cardiol 1988;12:315–323.

14. Kuntz RE, Schmidt DA, Levine MJ, Reis GJ, Safian RD, Baim DS. Importance of post-procedure luminal diameter on restenosis following new coronary interventions. Circulation 1990; 82(Suppl III):1245.

15. Kuntz RE, Safian RD, Levine MJ, Reis GJ, Diver DJ, Baim DS. Novel approach to the analysis of restenosis following three new coronary interventions. J Am Coll Cardiol 1992;19:1493–1499.

16. Nobuyoshi M, Kmura T, Ohishi H, et al. Restenosis after percutaneous coronary angioplasty: pathologic observations in 20 patients. J Am Coll Cardiol 1991;17:433–439.

17. Ueda M, Becker AE, Tsukada T, Numano F, Fujimoto T. Fibrocellular tissue response after percutaneous transluminal coronary angioplasty. Circulation 1991;83:1327–1332.

18. Kuntz RE, Gibson CM, Nobuyoshi M, Baim DS. A generalized model of restenosis following conventional balloon angioplasty, stenting, and directional atherectomy. J Am Coll Cardiol 1993;21:15–25.

19. Hanet C, Wijns W, Xavier M, Schroderer E. Influence of balloon size and stenosis morphology on immediate and delayed elastic recoil after percutaneous transluminal coronary angioplasty. J Am Coll Cardiol 1991;18:506–511.

20. Palmaz JC, Richter GM, Noeldge G, et al. Intraluminal stents in atherosclerotic iliac artery stenosis: preliminary report of a multicenter study. Radiology 1988;168:727–731.

21. Strecker EP. Flexible, balloon expandable percutaneously insertable vascular prosthesis: experimental and clinical results. Radiology 1988;169:388.

22. Strecker EP, Hagen B. Iliac artery stenting: long-term patency rate and complications. Cardiovasc Intervent Radiol 1995; 18(Suppl I):S73.

23. Becker GJ, Cottone RJ Jr, Nguyen A. The new Cordis tantalum balloon-expandable peripheral vascular stent: design features and properties. J Vasc Intervent Radiol 1995;6(1):2–3.

24. Becker GJ, Cottone RJ Jr, Scagnelli T, et al. Evaluation of the new Cordis tantalum balloon-expandable peripheral vascular stent in canine arteries. J Vasc Intervent Radiol 1995; 6(1):3.

25. Fontaine AB, Dake MD, Tschang TP, Guertin S, Stabbe MT, Dos Passos S. Tantalum balloon-expandable stent: in vivo swine studies. J Vasc Intervent Radiol 1993;4:749–752.

26. Fontaine AB, Koelling K, Clay J, Spigos DG, et al. Decreased platelet adherence of polymer-coated tantalum stents. J Vasc Intervent Radiol 1994;5:567–572.

27. Fontaine AB, Spigos DG, Eaton G, Dos Passos S, Christoforidis G, Khabiri H, Jung S. Stent-induced intimal hyperplasia: are there fundamental differences between flexible and rigid stent designs? J Vasc Intervent Radiol 1994;5:739–744.

28. Duprat G Jr, Wright KC, Charnsangavej C, Wallace S, Gianturco C. Flexible balloon-expanded stent for small vessels. Radiology 1987;162:276–278.

29. Rabkin JE, Matevosov AL, Gothman LN. Roentgenovascular surgery. Moscow: "Medicine" Publisher, 1987:176–198.

30. Cragg AH, DeJong S, Barnhart W, Landas S, Smith TP. Preclinical evaluation of the Cragg stent. Radiology 1992; 185(Suppl):162.

31. Henry M, Amor M, Henry I, Ethevenot G, Le Borgne EL, Beyar R. Initial clinical experience with the Instent nitinol permanent and temporary stents. Program syllabus of the Sixth International Symposium on Vascular Diagnosis and Intervention. Sponsored by Miami Vascular Institute, Miami Beach, Florida, January 10–13, 1994:205.

32. Rousseau H, Puel J, Joffre F, et al. Self-expanding endovascular prosthesis: an experimental study. Radiology 1987;164:709–714.

33. Martin EC, Katzen BT, Deitrich EB, et al. A multicenter trial of the Wallstent in the iliac and femoral arteries. J Vasc Intervent Radiol 1995;6(6):843–849.

34. Ring EJ, Lake JR, Roberts JP, Gordon RL, LaBerge JM, Read A. Percutaneous intrahepatic portosystemic shunts to control variceal bleeding prior to liver transplantation. Ann Intern Med 1992;166:304–309.

35. Charnsangavej C, Carrasco CH, Wallace S, Wright KC, Ogawa K, Richli W, Gianturco C. Stenosis of the vena cava: preliminary assessment of treatment with expandable metallic stents. Radiology 1986;161:295–298.

36. Fallone BG, Wallace S, Gianturco C. Elastic characteristics of the self-expanding metallic stents. Invest Radiol 1988;23:370–376.

37. Lakin PC, Petersen BD, Barton RE, Uchida B, Rösch J, Saxon RR. Expandable stents in the treatment of central obstruction in the venous system. J Vasc Intervent Radiol 1994;5(1):1.

38. Dake MD, Miller DC, Semba CP, et al. Transluminal placement of endovascular stent-grafts for the treatment of descending thoracic aortic aneurysms. N Engl J Med 1994;331(26): 1729–1734.

39. Uchida BT, Putnam JS, Rösch J. Modifications of Gianturco expandable wire stents. Am J Roentgenol 1988;150:1185–1187.

40. Palmaz JC. Intravascular stents: tissue-stent interactions and design considerations. AJR 1993;160:613–618.

41. Palmaz JC, Tio FO, Schatz RA, Alvarado R, Rees C, Garcia FS. Early endothelialization of balloon-expandable stents: experimental observations. J Intervent Radiol 1988;3:119–124.

42. Pisco JM, Correia M, Esperanca-Pina JA, de Sousa LA. Vasa vasorum changes following stent placement in experimental arterial stenoses. J Vasc Intervent Radiol 1993;4:269–273.

43. Schatz RA, Palmaz JC, Tio FO, Garcia FJ, Reuter SR. Balloon-expandable intracoronary stents in the adult dog. Circulation 1987;76:450–457.

44. Pentecost MJ, Criqui MH, Dorros G, et al. Guidelines for peripheral percutaneous transluminal angioplasty of the abdominal aorta and lower extremity vessels. Circulation 1994;89(1): 511–531.

45. Spies JB, LeQuire MH, Brantley SD, Williams JE, Beckett WC, Mills JL. Comparison of balloon angioplasty and laser thermal angioplasty in the treatment of femoropopliteal atherosclerotic disease: initial results of a prospective randomized trial. Work in progress. J Vasc Intervent Radiol 1990;1:39–42.

46. Hallisey MJ, Meranze SG, Parker BC, et al. Percutaneous transluminal angioplasty of the abdominal aorta. J Vasc Intervent Radiol 1994;5:679–687.

47. Yakes WF, Kumpe DA, Brown SB, et al. Percutaneous translu-

minal aortic angioplasty: techniques and results. Radiology 1989;172:965–970.

48. Long AL, Gaux JC, Raynaud AC, et al. Infrarenal aortic stents: initial clinical experience and angiographic follow-up. Cardiovasc Intervent Radiol 1993;16:203–208.

49. Tegtmeyer CJ, Harwell GD, Selby JB, Roberston R Jr, Kron IL, Tribble CG. Results and complications of angioplasty in aortoiliac disease. Circulation 1991;83(Suppl I):53–60.

50. Johnston KW. Iliac arteries: reanalysis of results of balloon angioplasty. Radiology 1993;186:207–212.

51. Bonn J, Gardiner GA Jr, Shapiro MJ, Sullivan KL, Levin DC. Palmaz vascular stent: initial clinical experience. Radiology 1990;174:741–745.

52. Becker GJ, Palmaz JC, Rees CR, et al. Angioplasty-induced dissections in human iliac arteries: management with Palmaz balloon-expandable intraluminal stents. Radiology 1990;176:31–38.

53. Rees CR, Palmaz JC, Garcia O, et al. Angioplasty and stenting of completely occluded iliac arteries. Radiology 1989;172:953–959.

54. Palmaz JC, Laborde JC, Rivera FJ, Encarnacion CE, Lutz JD, Moss JG. Stenting of the iliac arteries with the Palmaz stent: experience from a multicenter trial. Cardiovasc Intervent Radiol 1992;15:291–297.

55. Long AL, Page PE, Raynaud AC, et al. Percutaneous iliac artery stent: angiographic long-term follow-up. Radiology 1991;180:771–778.

56. Vorwerk D, Gunther RW. Stent placement in iliac arterial lesions: three years of clinical experience with the Wallstent. Cardiovasc Intervent Radiol 1992;15:285–290.

57. Laborde JC, Palmaz JC, Rivera FJ, Encarnacion CE, Picot MC, Dougherty SP. Influence of anatomic distribution of atherosclerosis on the outcome of revascularization with iliac stent placement. J Vasc Intervent Radiol 1995;6:513–521.

58. Brewster DC. Clinical and anatomical considerations for surgery in aortoiliac disease and results of surgical treatment. Circulation 1991;83(Suppl):42–52.

59. Liermann D, Strecker EP, Peters J. The Strecker stent: indications and results in iliac and femoropopliteal arteries. Cardiovasc Intervent Radiol 1992;15:298–305.

60. Morgenstern BR, Getrajdman GI, Laffey KJ, Bixon R, Martin EC. Total occlusions of the femoropopliteal artery: high technical success rate of conventional balloon angioplasty. Radiology 1989;172:937–940.

61. Murray JG, Apthorp LA, Wilkins RA. Long-segment (≥10 cm) femoropopliteal angioplasty: improved technical success and long-term patency. Radiology 1995;195:158–162.

62. Capek P, McLean GK, Berkowitz HD. Femoropopliteal angioplasty: factors influencing long-term success. Circulation 1991;83(Suppl I):70–80.

63. Johnston KW. Femoral and popliteal arteries: reanalysis of results of balloon angioplasty. Radiology 1992;183:767–771.

64. Hunink MGM, Wong JB, Donaldson MC, Meyerovitz MF, de Vries J, Harrington DP. Revascularization for femoropopliteal disease: a decision and cost-effectiveness analysis. JAMA 1995;274:165–171.

65. Sapoval MR, Long AL, Raynaud AC, Beyssen BM, Fiessinger J-N, Gaux JC. Femoropopliteal stent placement: long-term results. Radiology 1992;184:833–839.

66. Do-dai-Do, Triller J, Walpoth BH, Stirnemann P, Mahler F. A comparison study of self-expandable stents vs. balloon angioplasty alone in femoropopliteal artery occlusions. Cardiovasc Intervent Radiol 1992;15:306–312.

67. Zollikofer CL, Antonucci F, Pfyffer M, et al. Arterial stent placement with use of the Wallstent: midterm results of clinical experience. Radiology 1991;179:449–456.

67a. Liermann D, Strecker EP, Peters J. The Strecker stent: indications and results in iliac and femoropopliteal arteries. Cardiovasc Intervent Radiol 1992;15(5):298–305.

68. Dean RH, Kieffer RW, Smith BM, et al. Renovascular hypertension: anatomic and renal function changes during drug therapy. Arch Surg 1981;116:1408–1415.

69. Meaney TF, Dustan HP, McCormack LJ. Natural history of renal artery disease. Radiology 1968;91:881–887.

70. Schreiber MJ, Pohl MA, Novick AC. The natural history of atherosclerotic and fibrous renal artery disease. Urol Clin North Am 1984;11:383–392.

71. Tollefson DFJ, Ernst CB. Natural history of atherosclerotic renal artery stenosis associated with aortic disease. J Vasc Surg 1991;14:327–331.

72. Becker GJ, Katzen BT, Dake MD. Noncoronary angioplasty: state of the art. Radiology 1989;170(3):921–940.

73. Martin LG, Price RB, Casarella WJ, et al. Percutaneous angioplasty in clinical management of renovascular hypertension: initial and long-term results. Radiology 1985;155:629–633.

74. Martin LG, Casarella WJ, Gaylord GM. Azotemia caused by renal artery stenosis: treatment by percutaneous angioplasty. AJR 1988;150:839–844.

75. Sos TA. Angioplasty for the treatment of azotemia and renovascular hypertension in atherosclerotic renal artery disease. Circulation 1991;83(Suppl I):I–164.

76. Pattynama PMT, Becker GJ, Brown JM, Zemel G, Benenati JF, Katzen BT. Percutaneous angioplasty for atherosclerotic renal artery disease: effect on renal function in azotemic patients. Cardiovasc Intervent Radiol 1994;17:143–146.

77. Bell GM, Reid J, Buist TAS. Percutaneous transluminal angioplasty improves blood pressure and renal function in renovascular hypertension. Q J Med 1987;63:393–403.

78. Rees CR, Snead DB, Niblett RL. Multicenter study of Palmaz-Schatz stents in the renal arteries. J Vasc Intervent Radiol 1995;6(1):60.

8

Principles of Selective Thrombolysis

JOSEPH J. BOOKSTEIN
KARIM VALJI

With advancing methodology, thrombolysis has become an effective therapeutic adjunct in the clinical management of a wide variety of thromboembolic disorders. The advances in clinical methodology are largely derived from advances in relevant basic science. This chapter considers selected scientific concepts and advances that underlie current clinical methodology, particularly the authors' own method, *pulse-spray pharmacomechanical thrombolysis*. In addition, this chapter considers major residual problems of thrombolysis (such as lysis resistance) and research directions that may be useful in overcoming these problems.

To exploit current and approaching methodology, the vascular interventionalist should be familiar with a range of disciplines well beyond the usual radiologic curriculum. These disciplines incorporate (1) thrombology and the coagulation system, (2) the physiology of endogenous fibrinolytics, (3) the pharmacodynamics of exogenous fibrinolytics, (4) platelet-fibrinolytic relationships, (5) pharmacologic adjuncts of fibrinolysis such as antiplatelet and antithrombic agents, (6) the methodology of fibrinolytic delivery, (7) methods of mechanical thrombolysis, and (8) results of clinical thrombolysis. A comprehensive consideration of all these subjects is beyond the scope of a single chapter; an overview is provided here instead. In Chapter 9 details of clinical implementation will be emphasized, along with results and complications.

Inasmuch as fibrin constitutes the basic structural component of thrombi, thrombolysis is largely synonymous with fibrinolysis, a proteolytic process through which fibrin is converted into soluble fibrin degradation products (FDPs). To supplement the endogenous fibrinolytic system, exogenous fibrinolytic agents can be administered for therapeutic purposes. Thrombi can also be treated by physical modalities, a process for which the term *mechanical thrombolysis* is gaining recognition.

Although systemic administration of fibrinolytics is common, particularly for treatment of acute myocardial infarction, selective administration is generally used in treating peripheral thromboemboli. Selective methods provide intrathrombic concentrations of fibrinolytic agent several thousandfold higher than those achievable by intravenous administration, and also allow specific targeting of the offending thrombus with relative sparing of thrombi elsewhere, and of circulating fibrinogen.

Components of the Fibrinolytic System

The endogenous fibrinolytic system involves a large number of blood and endothelial elements, including fibrin, plasminogen, plasmin, plasminogen activators, plasminogen activator inhibitors, and antiplasmins. Recent progress in protein chemistry has made possible complete amino acid sequencing, cloning of human cDNA, and identification of the responsible gene for most of these proteins.[1]

Fibrinogen and Fibrin

Fibrinogen is a large symmetrical protein with three long polypeptide chains, designated alpha, beta, and gamma,[2] in each half of the molecule (Fig. 8-1). Two short central branches, termed *fibrinopeptides A and B*, are attached to the alpha or beta chains, respectively, connecting the two halves of the molecule with disulfide bridges. Fibrinogen is present in blood plasma in concentrations of 200 to 400 mg/dl, and is also released from platelet alpha granules after platelet activation.[3]

Molecules of fibrin are formed from fibrinogen after cleavage of fibrinopeptides A and B by thrombin. The fibrin molecules form a three-dimensional lattice via self-polymerization of the alpha, beta, and gamma chains. A few minutes after fibrin formation, stabilizing cross-linkages begin to form between gamma chains and later between alpha chains (but not

119

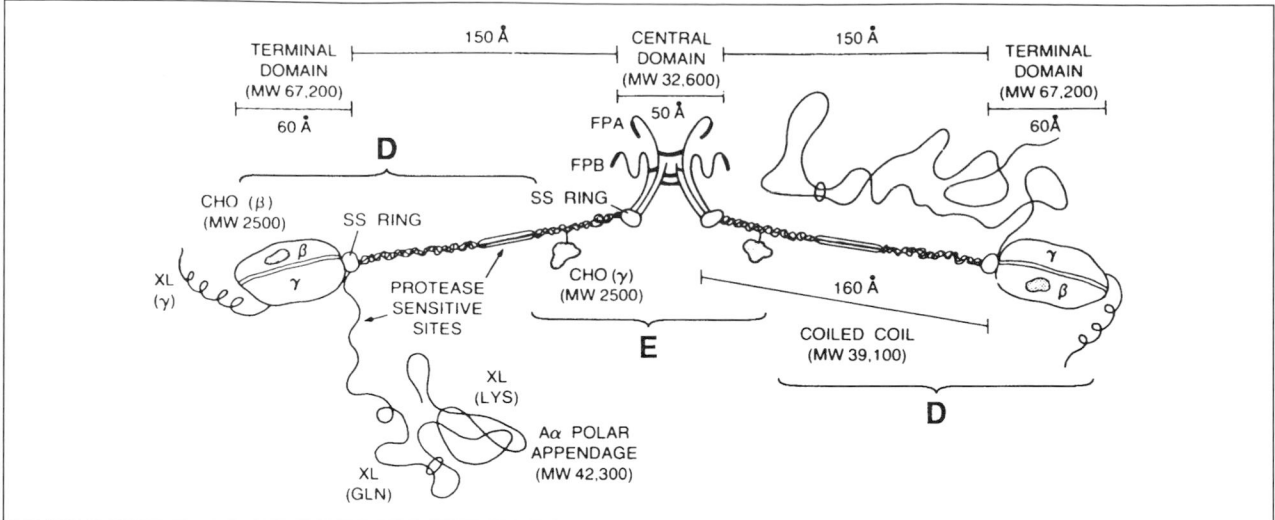

Figure 8-1. Fibrinogen molecule, schematic diagram. Molecular weight is about 340,000 daltons. The symmetrical structure of the molecule is evident, with three separate chains, alpha, beta, and gamma, one each side, connected by three disulfide bonds centrally. The molecule is shown with four major protein regions: the *central domain,* which contains the amino-terminal ends of all six chains; the thin connecting alpha-helical *coiled coils* of three chains each, the two carboxy-*terminal domains,* and the alpha-chain *polar appendages.* Fibrinopeptides A and B (*FPA* and *FPB*) are noted as slightly thickened parts of the amino-terminal ends of the alpha and beta chains. Factor XIII$_a$–related sites of cross linking (*XLs*) are situated near the carboxy terminus of the gamma and alpha chains. The multiple sites of lysine throughout the molecule are not illustrated. SS = disulfide; CHO = carbohydrate cluster. (Courtesy of R. Doolittle.) During conversion of fibrinogen to fibrin by thrombin, the four A and B fibrinopeptides are cleaved. After proteolysis by plasmin, the molecule is divided into various fibrinogen degradation products, indicated as *D* and *E.* Fragment *D* plus *E* constitute a fragment known as Y. Both *Ds* and an *E* constitute a fragment known as X. Fibrin degradation products consist of these same fragments, but cross-linked.

between beta chains)[4] under the influence of factor XIII$_a$.[4–6] Cross-linking is essentially complete within 24 hours.[7] Cross-linkages moderately inhibit, but do not prevent, fibrinolysis.[8–10]

Practical Implications: The fact that cross-linking is complete within 24 hours excludes progressive cross-linking as an explanation for the relative lysis resistance of clots older than 2 to 3 weeks. Release of fibrinopeptides A and B during conversion of fibrinogen to fibrin provides a convenient biochemical marker of ongoing rethrombosis during thrombolysis.

Plasminogen

Plasminogen is a single-chain glycoprotein[11] that is synthesized in the liver,[12] and that normally circulates in the plasma at concentrations of 20 to 30 mg/dl.[13] Variable amounts of plasminogen also exist within thrombus,[14–16] at least partially bound to fibrin. The amount of plasminogen bound to thrombus is sufficient for thrombolysis, regardless of clot age.[17]

Plasminogen exists in two forms, the Lys-plasminogen form with lysine at the amino-terminal end, and Glu-plasminogen, with glutamic acid at the amino-terminal end. The two forms of plasminogen differ some-

what functionally, with the lysine form predominant in fibrin- or endothelial-bound plasminogen, and the glutamic acid form more prevalent in plasma.[18] The estimated biologic half-lives of Glu- and Lys-plasminogen are 2.2 and 0.8 days, respectively.[16] Under the influence of plasmin, Glu-plasminogen undergoes partial degradation to the lysine form.[19]

Practical Implications: The fact that sufficient plasminogen is already bound to fibrin within thrombus obviates inflow of circulating plasminogen as a prerequisite for lysis, and helps explain the efficacy of intrathrombic administration of fibrinolytic agents.

Plasmin

Under the influence of plasminogen activators, plasminogen is converted into plasmin, its active form, through hydrolysis of the arginine$_{560}$-lysine$_{561}$ peptide bond. Simultaneously, the single-chain plasminogen becomes two-chain plasmin. The heavier of the two chains contains five loops (kringles) and retains fibrin-binding capacity, and the light chain contains the protease activity. Under physiologic intravascular conditions, the conversion of plasminogen to plasmin is catalyzed primarily by tissue-type plasminogen activator (tPA).[1,16] Fibrin-bound plasminogen is converted into fibrin-bound plasmin, which can be neutralized by fibrin-bound alpha$_2$-antiplasmin.[1]

The major substrate of plasmin is fibrin, which is cleaved into various soluble FDPs termed *X,Y,D,* or *E.* The X fragment can participate in fibrin polymerization, whereas incorporation of Y, D, or E fragments terminates the polymerization process (Doolittle, personal communication). Plasmin is a nonspecific proteolytic agent and also digests other coagulation factors, particularly fibrinogen and factors V and VIII.[20] It, as well as thrombin, is also an extremely potent platelet activator.[21] The half-life of intrathrombic plasmin, when plasmin is partially fibrin-bound and protected from circulating inhibitors, is approximately 10 seconds.[16] On the other hand, plasmin in plasma is rapidly neutralized by alpha$_2$-antiplasmin, so that the estimated half-life of circulating plasmin is only 100 milliseconds.[16]

Practical Implications: The abundance of plasmin inhibitors in plasma and thrombus and the lack of fibrin specificity of plasmin largely explain the inapplicability of plasmin itself as a direct therapeutic agent.

Tissue Plasminogen Activator (tPA)

Under physiologic conditions, plasminogen is predominantly activated by tPA, a serine protease released from endothelial cells and other tissues. tPA is synthesized by endothelial cells as a single-chain (sc) protein of molecular weight 60,000 to 72,000 daltons (d).[22] Release from endothelial cells is augmented by thrombin,[23] heparin, dDAVP, and other substances.[24] sctPA binds to fibrin and then develops an affinity to form a trimolecular complex with plasminogen.[25] In the absence of fibrin, tPA is an inefficient activator of plasminogen, but when bound to fibrin, its efficacy in converting plasminogen to plasmin is augmented 1000-fold.[26] Plasmin in turn performs a limited hydrolysis on sctPA and converts it into a two-chain molecule (tctPA) of identical molecular weight.[27] The single- and double-chain forms of tPA have essentially equivalent fibrinolytic and plasminogen-activating properties.[28] The half-life of sctPA is 5 minutes, and for tctPA 8 minutes[29] because of neutralization by plasminogen activator inhibitor 1 or 2,[30] or hepatic clearance.[31]

Although it was anticipated that the fibrin specificity of tPA would decrease the incidence of hemorrhage relative to other fibrinolytics, the clinical incidence of hemorrhagic complications after the use of tPA is considerable, approximately equivalent to that of streptokinase (SK)[32] and probably greater than that of urokinase (UK). In one study of thrombolysis in myocardial infarction, there was a 2.1 percent incidence of intracranial hemorrhage after the use of large doses (150 mg) of tPA.[33] One possible reason for the less-than-expected safety of tPA is that FDPs reduce the fibrin specificity of tPA, thus promoting fibrinogenolysis.[34] tPA shows a greater tendency to bind to endothelial cells than SK or UK, another possible factor related to hemorrhagic complications of tPA.[35]

tPA is manufactured commercially by recombinant DNA technology, with most tPA used in the United States manufactured by Genentech, brand name *Activase,* generic name *alteplase.* The specific activity of alteplase is 550,000 to 667,000 IU/mg.[36] Typical therapeutic doses of alteplase range from 35 mg (about 21,000,000 units) for selective therapy of peripheral thrombi[37] to 80 to 100 mg (about 48,000,000 to 60,000,000 units) for systemic therapy of myocardial infarction.[38] This dose can be compared to the usual 500,000 to 2,000,000 units of UK used for peripheral vascular thrombolysis. The much greater usual dose of tPA than of UK partially reflects the fact that UK units are 3.5 to 5.3 times more potent than tPA units,[39] as well as the fact that the biological half-life of tPA is approximately one-half that of UK. Nevertheless, the usual dose of tPA still seems considerably greater than that of UK, possibly partially explaining the considerable incidence of hemorrhage associated with tPA.[37]

Practical Implications: Fibrin selectivity is of much less importance when agents are administered by the selective intrathrombic route than when administered systemically. The high molecular weight of tPA (and the other plasminogen activators) contributes to slow diffusion within thrombus, one factor limiting the rate of thrombolysis. Table 8-1 compares various properties of commonly used fibrinolytic agents.

Streptokinase

Streptokinase (SK) is a single-chain polypeptide derived from beta-hemolytic streptococci,[40] with a molecular weight of about 53,000. It is an indirect activator of plasminogen that first forms irreversible activator complexes with plasminogen (or plasmin).[41,42] The activator complex may then activate any plasminogen remaining. The biologic half-life of SK is approximately 23 minutes.[1] The plasminogen-SK complex shows slight fibrin selectivity, much less than that of tPA.[43] Because of the prevalence of prior streptococcal infections, antibodies against SK that inhibit formation of SK-activator complexes are present in many populations. This inhibitory effect can be overcome by a loading dose of SK, typically about 250,000 units in North Americans. For 6 months after SK

Table 8-1. Comparison of Common Plasminogen Activators

Agent	SK	APSAC	scuPA	tcuPA (UK)	r-sctPA[a]	r-tctPA[b]
Activation	Indirect	Indirect	Direct	Direct	Direct	Direct
Half-life (min)	23	60–105	7	16	5	8
Fibrin selectivity	+	++	++++	++	+++	+++
Antigenicity	++	++	–	–	–	–

[a]r-sctPA = recombinant single-chain tissue plasminogen activator.
[b]r-tctPA = recombinant two-chain tissue plasminogen activator.

therapy, antibody titers can be sufficiently elevated to block the fibrinolytic effect of further SK administration.[44]

Practical Implications: At present, it is our impression that SK has been largely superceded by UK for peripheral vascular therapy in the United States. Disadvantages of SK include its antigenicity (precluding frequently repeated therapy) and its increased consumption of plasminogen associated with the two-step process of activation. The increased consumption of intrathrombic plasminogen by SK obviates the usefulness of highly concentrated SK for pulse-spray thrombolysis.

Anisoylated Plasminogen Streptokinase Complex (APSAC)

Acylation increases the half-life of the SK-plasminogen complex from 23 to 90 minutes, enabling relatively prolonged lysis from a single intravenous injection.[45,46] Another form of acylated SK has a functional half-life of 7 hours.[1] Acylation appears to significantly increase fibrin specificity[45,46] but is not thought to alter antigenicity.[47]

Practical Implications: The relatively prolonged fibrinolytic effects of a single intravenous dose of APSAC seem to offer most promise for initial management of coronary thrombi in patients with acute myocardial infarction, perhaps during ambulance transport.

Urokinase

Urokinase (UK) is a two-chain polypeptide that activates plasminogen in a one-step process. Originally derived from human urine, UK has also been isolated from fetal kidney cells and will soon be commercially available via recombinant DNA techniques (personal communication, Abbott Laboratories). The molecular weight is approximately 55,000, and the biologic half-life about 16 minutes.[48] UK is synthesized by the endothelial cells as a relatively inactive single-chain mole-

cule (scuPA), which is activated by plasmin through conversion to a two-chain enzyme (i.e., high-molecular-weight UK).[23] A low-molecular-weight (33,000 d) form of UK exists after further plasmin hydrolysis.[49] Urokinase probably plays little physiologic role in fibrinolysis. Few or no natural antibodies exist against UK, and UK seems not to be antigenic.[47]

Single-Chain Urokinase Plasminogen Activator (scuPA or pro-uPA)

scuPA may be obtained from endothelial cell tissue-culture media, urine, plasma, or transformed bacteria.[50] Molecular weights vary from about 54,000 to 68,000 d.[41] scuPA is only about 1 percent as effective a plasminogen activator as is UK, the two-chain variety.[51] scuPA, however, has fibrin selectivity comparable to tPA, and after binding to fibrin may be activated to produce relatively selective *fibrin*olysis. Fibrin also enhances the catalytic efficacy of scuPA from 10- to 2000-fold.[52] The half-life of scuPA in blood is about 7 minutes.[53]

Practical Implications: Despite very limited fibrin specificity, UK is gaining acceptance, at least in the United States, as the agent of choice for selective peripheral thrombolysis. It has a number of desirable features, including lack of antigenicity, high efficacy, and a very low incidence of serious hemorrhage. Along with tPA, its short biologic half-life allows surgical intervention relatively soon after thrombolysis, should that prove necessary.

In in vitro investigations,[54] tPA, UK, SK, and plasmin at 10^{-6} molar concentration produced approximately equivalent rates of lysis of thrombi aged 2 hours. (These concentrations were clinically relevant, and corresponded to approximately 13,200 units/ml tPA, 11,000 units/ml UK, and 5000 units/ml SK.) Increasing concentrations of tPA accelerated lysis with a slope of 1.37 as molarity increased from 10^{-7} to 10^{-5}. The comparable slope for UK was 1.17. The slope for SK became steeply negative as molarity was increased from 10^{-6} to 10^{-5}, reflecting disproportionate consumption of intrathrombic plasminogen in forming activator complex (see above). By increasing the surface area of clot via clot maceration, lysis was significantly accelerated for each of the above agents.

Plasminogen Activator Inhibitors (PAI)

Two types of plasminogen activator inhibitors (PAI-1 and -2)[55] are synthesized and secreted by the endothelium.[23] PAI is also released from activated platelets.[9]

Practical Implications: The amount of PAI released from endothelium and platelets is relatively small[1,56] and probably insufficient to significantly interfere with the large concentrated doses of plasminogen activator used for selective intrathrombic thrombolysis.

Alpha$_2$-antiplasmin

Alpha$_2$-antiplasmin is the primary inhibitor of plasmin, and is found in plasma and thrombus.[1,57,58] It is an irreversible inhibitor, and during thrombus formation alpha$_2$-antiplasmin, along with plasminogen, binds to fibrin.[57] On a molar basis, plasma contains about twice the amount of plasminogen as alpha$_2$-antiplasmin, so that unneutralized plasmin can circulate following large exogenous doses of plasminogen activators,[58] producing a so-called fibrinolytic state.

Alpha$_2$-macroglobulin

Alpha$_2$-macroglobulin is a general proteinase inhibitor, and slowly inactivates many components of the fibrinolytic system, including plasmin, tcuPA, tPA, and the streptokinase-plasmin(ogen) complex. Once alpha$_2$-antiplasmin has been consumed, alpha$_2$-macroglobulin is the major residual antiplasmin.

Practical Implications: The presence of powerful circulating antiplasmins provides some of the rationale for intrathrombic deposition of fibrinolytic agents, in sufficient concentration to overwhelm intrathrombic plasmin inhibitors. The amount of inhibitory agent within thrombus is currently unknown.

Composition of the Thrombus

Major advances have been made recently in understanding the formation of thrombus, particularly with regard to the role of platelets, and the assembly of fibrin fibrils and their susceptibility of fibrinolysis.

Although much emphasis has been placed on the fibrin network of thrombus, it must be emphasized that thrombi contain other ingredients—red cells, white cells, and platelets. The influence of red cells and white cells on thrombolysis is beyond the scope of this chapter. Platelets, however, play critical, primarily (but not exclusively) prothrombotic and antifibrinolytic roles in hemostatic balance,[59] and an understanding of thrombolysis requires consideration of the role of platelets.

Platelets

Platelets contribute to normal hemostasis by adhering to subendothelial surfaces of injured vessels via receptors for von Willebrand factor, collagen, and possibly fibronectin. Adhesion activates the platelet, which, among other effects, exposes the GP IIb/IIIa surface receptor. GP IIb/IIIa binds to several proteins, including fibrinogen, the protein primarily responsible for platelet aggregation. Activated platelets release a cofactor to plasma prothrombinase that markedly accelerates the conversion of prothrombin to thrombin. Other procoagulants released by activated platelets include fibrinogen; ADP, which further activates platelets; platelet factor 4 (a heparin inhibitor); factor XIII, which stimulates fibrin x-linking; and plasminogen activator inhibitor-1. Platelets also promote late clot retraction, which impairs tPA thrombolysis, perhaps by sheltering tPA binding sites.[9] Platelets also contain fibronectin,[3] a structural protein critical in providing a network along which fibroblasts can migrate into clot to subsequently form collagen.[60]

Platelet-rich thrombi have been shown experimentally to be much more resistant to lysis than thrombi rich in red cells.[10] Platelets release a number of factors, in general the same prothrombotic factors listed above, that contribute to lysis resistance: PAI-1[61]; alpha$_2$-antiplasmin[62]; TGF-beta (a potent stimulus for endothelial release of PAI-1)[63]; platelet factor 4, which inactivates heparin[64]; and platelet-activating factor.[65] Furthermore, platelets provide cofactors that increase prothrombinase activity as much as 300,000-fold.[66] Platelets also contain nearly 50 percent of factor XIII, which has three antifibrinolytic properties: (1) it strongly promotes fibrin cross-linkages that in turn decrease the rate of fibrinolysis by 32 to 55 percent from non-cross-linked fibrin,[8] (2) it accelerates cross-linking of alpha$_2$-antiplasmin to fibrin,[67] and (3) it promotes cross-linkage of fibronectin to fibrin,[68] in turn facilitating intrathrombic migration of fibroblasts.[69] The amount of cross-linked alpha-chains, as well as the final molecular weight of the fibrin polymer, increases progressively with platelet counts from 30,000 to 900,000/ml.[7] The *rate* of alpha-chain cross-linking also depends on platelet count, but even with counts as low as 30,000/ml, alpha-chain cross-linking is complete by 24 hours.[7]

The platelet concentration and activity in clot vary

considerably, and the factors influencing platelet concentration are poorly understood. In addition to a tendency for increased platelet concentration at the leading edge of thrombi, foci and columns of concentrated platelets associated with dense fibrin (lines of Zahn) can be found throughout thrombus.[70] Intrathrombic platelets are often incompletely degranulated, suggesting that further activation and secretion may occur during thrombolysis, thus emphasizing the need for concomitant antiplatelet and antithrombic measures during thrombolysis.

Clot Retraction

Activation of platelets during fibrin formation results in platelet filopodia that attach to fibrin fibers,[71] mediated at least partially by the GP IIb/IIIa complex. Subsequent contraction by activated contractile proteins[72] produces clot retraction, with as much as 90 percent reduction in clot volume.[9] Under experimental conditions, clot retraction is 90 to 100 percent complete in 1 hour.[73] As stated above, clot retraction has been associated with moderately increased lysis resistance, perhaps secondary to shielding of tPA binding sites on fibrin.[9]

Practical Implications: We believe that high platelet foci contribute significantly to the clinical problem of lysis resistance. Thrombi that form in the arterial system often harbor foci of high platelet concentration, particularly at their leading edges or at sites of rupture of atherosclerosis.[74] On gross examination these foci are pale, and hence are called *white thrombus.*[70,72,75] Clinically the authors have observed that a lysis-resistant portion often is situated at the proximal end of an arterial or graft thrombus. In a limited number of transluminal biopsies, this resistant material has revealed dense collections of fibrin and relatively few red cells, features typical of white thrombus. The high-platelet region of thrombus can become very firm within hours of formation and resistant to passage of a guidewire, as judged by the authors' experience in a few acutely rethrombosed dialysis grafts. Rethrombosis after experimental thrombolysis has also been frequently found to consist of white thrombus.[76]

Surface Characteristics of Clot

A single personal (JJB) case provided strong angiographic evidence that the surface of a thrombus may have greater structural integrity than its depth. In this case, contrast medium was inadvertently injected into a large thrombus of the inferior vena cava (IVC) (Fig. 8-2). A thin radiolucent surface membrane of the clot became apparent, indicating that the contrast had pref-

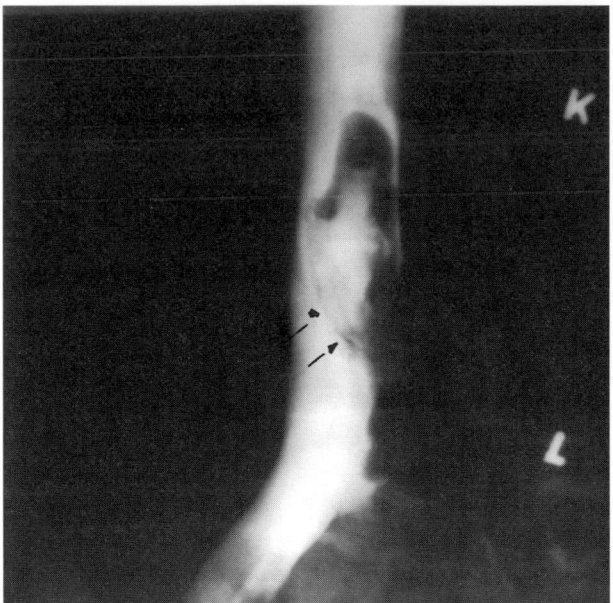

Figure 8-2. Inadvertent injection into IVC thrombus. Note the clear demonstration of the clot surface membrane about 1 mm thick (*arrows*), indicating accumulation of contrast medium beneath the membrane, as well as in the adjacent IVC. Preservation of the membrane indicates greater structural integrity than the subjacent thrombus. The structure and explanation for this membrane are not known with certainty, but albumen binding to fibrin, or progressive platelet accumulation leading to dense fibrin deposition, are postulated causes. A second nearly parallel line is seen to the patient's left of the first, probably representing an intrathrombic line of Zahn, of the same composition. Catheter penetration of these lysis-resistant membranes may partially explain the increased efficacy of intrathrombic over parathrombic infusions.

erentially dissected beneath the clot surface before perforating into the IVC. This behavior indicated greater structural integrity of the thrombic surface than its subsurface. This observation nicely confirms textbook descriptions of relatively dense fibrin layers at or near the surface of thrombus,[70] which seem to be in relation to dense accumulations of degranulated (i.e., fully activated) platelets.

There is also experimental evidence that the surface of a clot differs in composition from its deeper structure. Galanakis[77] has observed that the peripheral fibrin fibrils (termed *leptofibrils*) are finer and more tightly woven than the deeper ones (termed *pachyfibrils*), and postulates that the decreased surface porosity retains intrathrombic thrombin or prevents ingress of plasminogen and/or plasminogen activators, thus inhibiting thrombolysis. He has also shown binding of albumin fragments to surface fibrin, which he postulates blocks plasmin-accessible sites, further explaining surface lysis resistance. Collagen also interacts with fibrin, conferring marked resistance to lysis, and this interaction seems to occur more easily at the thrombus surface.[69] Platelets demonstrate moderate adherence to fibrin surfaces, although less so than to collagen surfaces.[78] Adherent platelet layers have been demonstrated to block diffusion of molecules as small as 8 Kd,[78a] molecules far smaller than plasminogen or tPA.

Practical Implications: The relative lysis resistance of the thrombic surface may partially explain the much greater efficacy of intrathrombic over parathrombic infusion of lytic agents. By breaking through a resistant membrane with the catheter, the lytic agent is deposited within less resistant thrombus. Thrombic emboli incident to thrombolysis may be expected to lack a complete surface membrane and to lyse relatively rapidly with further lytic infusion, as we have observed clinically. Dense strands of fibrin can be found throughout thrombus, also in relation to dense columnar accumulation of platelets, and these fibrin strands probably also interfere with intrathrombic diffusion of fibrinolytic agents. By moving the catheter within thrombus or by using principles of pulse-spray thrombolysis (see below), relatively homogeneous deposition of material throughout clot is achieved, partially circumventing these diffusion barriers. The fact that intrathrombic platelets often appear only partially degranulated[70] suggests that continued release of platelet contents can occur during thrombolysis, consistent with experimental evidence of the profibrinolytic effects of concomitant administration of antiplatelet agents by intrathrombic or other means (see below).[79]

Age of Thrombus

It is generally assumed that older clots (> 2 weeks) lyse much more slowly than younger ones, and that they may become clinically unlysable. Various explanations have been offered, but none seem entirely convincing. Gottlob[15] found diminished plasminogen concentration with age in some experimental clots, but more recent evidence indicates that the plasminogen concentration is adequate for lysis in both young and old human thrombi.[17] Lysis resistance has been ascribed to increased cross-linkage of fibrin, but experimental evidence demonstrates only about 35 to 50 percent slower lysis of cross-linked as compared to non-cross-linked fibrin.[8] Likewise, retracted clots are less lysable than nonretracted ones.[9] Retraction and cross-linking, however, are essentially complete within 1 or 24 hours, respectively, and would not explain postulated differences in the behavior of clots 3 days versus 3 weeks of age.[8] The markedly increased lysis resistance of platelet-rich clots has already been commented on, and it is possible that sequential layers of

platelets bind to thrombus over time. However, no correlation between clot age and platelet content has been shown. Certainly fibrous organization of clots will reduce or eliminate the possibility of lysis, but organized clots are not considered here. Current postulates explaining relative lysis resistance of older thrombi include progressive binding of albumin to fibrin[77,78] or early collagen deposition by fibroblasts migrating along fibronectin pathways.[69]

Regardless of the cause of increased lysis resistance of older thrombi, we believe that the degree of resistance has been considerably exaggerated. In our own experience with the pulse-spray method, mean lysis times of clots 1 to 3 days of age (mean 56 ± 51 minutes) differed statistically but hardly clinically from mean lysis times of clots aged 4 to 1000 days (mean 94 ± 53 minutes).[80] The minimal effect of clot age on lysis times when using intrathrombic pulse-spray techniques suggests that much of the observed differences may be attributable to the relatively resistant surface membrane.

The Dynamic Nature of Thrombolysis (Concurrent Rethrombosis)

There is abundant evidence of prothrombotic sequelae of thrombolysis that lead to a dynamic equilibrium between thrombolysis and concurrent rethrombosis. During thrombolysis, thrombin bound to fibrin is released as thrombin-bound FDP. This thrombin is thought to retain the capacity to convert fibrinogen to fibrin, as well as to activate platelets.[2,81–84] Elevated levels of thrombin-antithrombin III complex were associated with failure of thrombolysis in one series,[84] suggesting that concurrent rethrombosis rather than primary failure of lysis was the cause. Both thrombin and plasmin are powerful platelet activators,[21] so that platelet activation and all the sequelae described above are brought into play.[66,85] Shear activation of platelets[86,87] almost certainly occurs during pulse-spray methods of thrombolysis, along with destruction of red cells and presumed release of (platelet-activating) ADP and other procoagulants.[88]

In addition to prothrombotic sequelae of thrombolysis, preexisting systemic or local conditions also contribute to rethrombosis. Stressful clinical situations, such as myocardial infarction[89] or perhaps severe ischemic leg pain, increase epinephrine levels. Even the mental stress of arithmetic problems can produce detectable increases in platelet aggregation in coronary patients.[90] Epinephrine in turn is an activator of platelets,[91,92] and epinephrine levels may be related to the shortened bleeding times and aspirin resistance of patients with myocardial infarction.[93] Finally, the underlying vascular conditions that initially predisposed to thrombosis, usually stenosis and/or exposed mural elements, persist during and immediately following lysis.[94]

Lysis-Resistant Thrombi: Summary

Table 8-2 summarizes the factors associated with lysis resistance.

As a result of clinical observations of concurrent and immediate postthrombolytic rethrombosis, as well as theoretical reasons for a local hypercoagulant state at the site of thrombolysis, antithrombin and antiplatelet measures during thrombolysis have been investigated extensively and are now being incorporated into thrombolytic regimens. Heparin has been shown to accelerate thrombolysis in vitro.[95–97] Aspirin has been long used in conjunction with thrombolysis, despite the fact that the benefit is probably only moderate.[98–101] Newer antiplatelet agents such as prostaglandin E_1 (PGE_1)[102] or monoclonal antibody against the platelet GP IIb/IIIa receptor[101,103–105] have significantly augmented the rate of experimental thrombolysis. Newer thrombin inhibitors such as hirudin[81,101,106] or argatroban[107] seem to be more effective than heparin. In experimental evaluation of the pulse-spray methodology with tPA, admixture of heparin, PGE_1, or argatroban demonstrated significant advantage over intravenous or nonuse of these agents in accelerating thrombolysis.[108–110]

Practical Implications: On the basis of these experimental observations, as well as clinical observations, we have for several years[80] advocated rigorous anticoagulant and antiplatelet therapy during pulse-spray thrombolysis. Heparin is used liberally: 5000 units admixed with the first 250,000-unit ampule of UK plus several thousand units systemically. (This large and highly concentrated dose of intrathrombic heparin is highly empiric, and probably at least an order of magnitude beyond that necessary to fully activate estimated amounts of intrathrombic antithrombin-III. The excess heparin presumably contributes to systemic anticoagulation.) Systemic activated clotting times (ACTs) are checked during the procedure by an automated device (Hemotec, Englewood, CO), particularly if thrombolysis is progressing slowly or rethrombosis becomes evident. With the Hemotec device, we prefer to work with the ACT at near 300 seconds. The patients also receive aspirin shortly before the procedure. Furthermore, if concurrent rethrombosis be-

Table 8-2. Recognized Factors Contributing to Lysis Resistance

Factor	Comment
Cross-linking of alpha and beta fibrin chains	Complete by 24 hr
Clot retraction	Complete by 24 hr
Platelet-rich thrombus	Especially leading edge of clot
Hypercoagulable states	Concurrent rethrombosis
Clot membrane	Composition uncertain
Older clots	Several possible reasons
Persistent underlying obstruction	Stagnation promotes thrombosis
Persistent underlying stenosis	Shear activation of platelets
Exposure of subendothelial components	Collagen binds and activates platelets

comes evident, dextran (low molecular weight in 10 percent solution, 40-ml bolus plus 40 ml/hr during lysis) has, in several cases, appeared to abruptly terminate the rethrombosis process. Dextran has a number of poorly understood antithrombotic, antiplatelet, and profibrinolytic effects.[111–113]

Delayed Rethrombosis

In addition to concurrent rethrombosis, discussed above, delayed rethrombosis may occur within hours or days of technically successful thrombolysis. In the coronary circulation, for example, rethrombosis has been observed after hours or days in 10 to 20 percent of initially reperfused arteries.[114] The factors leading to delayed rethrombosis are probably similar to those leading to concurrent rethrombosis: (1) the continued presence of the initiating vascular lesion, (2) incompletely lysed thrombus yielding partial obstruction and enhanced platelet adhesion,[94] (3) residual activation of platelets and clotting factors secondary to thrombolysis, (4) gradual waning of anticoagulant effects of heparin or fibrin(ogen) degradation products, and (5) discontinuance of anticoagulant or antiplatelet therapy. Rethrombosis occurs in inverse frequency to the plasma half-life of the fibrinolytic, with the lowest incidence associated with APSAC and urokinase (about 10 percent), intermediate frequency with SK (about 15 percent), and highest incidence with tPA (20 percent).[47,115–117] The incidence would probably be considerably higher were it not for various regimens directed against rethrombosis, including continuing thrombolysis via a low-dose regimen, use of anticoagulants or antiplatelet agents, or early angioplasty. Several investigators have reported a significantly reduced incidence of rethrombosis with combined use of tPA and UK.[115,116,118]

Clinical Application of Selective Thrombolysis

The preceding reflects some of the basic science upon which present clinical practices of thrombolysis are based. Clinical application of this information has evolved through various stages, to which many have contributed, including ourselves, over the past two decades. This evolution will be considered in detail in Chapter 9.

Selective transcatheter parathrombic infusion of thrombolytic agent was suggested by Dotter et al. in 1974.[119] The method purportedly enabled lower doses of SK than systemic administration, with presumably augmented safety and efficacy. Our initial experience with the Dotter method reflected typical results for that time: a 75 percent success rate, a 33 percent rate of hemorrhagic complications, and mean lysis times of 38 hours.[120]

As would be anticipated from the above discussion, selective administration of thrombolytic agents proved much more effective than systemic administration in the management of peripheral vascular thromboembolism. For example, early reports after *systemic* administration of SK revealed restoration of patency in only 9 to 24 percent of arterial occlusions and required infusions of 1 to 3 days' duration.[121] These rates are inferior to those achieved by the Dotter method, and far below the 85 to 95 percent technical success rates currently obtained by selective infusion methods.[122-126] Systemic administration of thrombolytics for peripheral vascular thromboembolism is largely obsolete.

In 1985, McNamara described a modified method for selective thrombolysis using *intrathrombic* infusion of UK and intermittent catheter advance as thrombolysis progressed.[126] Lysis times were reduced to 18 $\pm$ 20 hours, the failure rate to 17 percent, and hemorrhagic complications to 4 percent. Also in 1985, our group began investigating manipulable variables for maximizing the speed, efficacy, and safety of selective thrombolysis.[54] The initial series of in vitro experiments evaluated the rate and extent of lysis and demonstrated (1) no relative advantage of SK, UK, tPA, or plasmin if used in equimolar concentrations, (2) a significant advantage of high concentrations of UK or tPA but not SK, and (3) a significant advantage of clot maceration. These laboratory observations led to the development of pulse-spray pharmacomechanical thrombolysis (PSPMT), a method first evaluated in a subacute canine venous thrombosis model[127] and then applied clinically.[128]

PSPMT consists of brief high-pressure pulsed injec-

tions of concentrated fibrinolytic agent throughout clot via a multi-side-hole catheter. In our experience, this method has markedly augmented the speed, efficacy, and safety of clinical thrombolysis. Indeed, PSPMT accelerates thrombolysis sufficiently to allow the entire procedure to be performed in a few hours while the patient is under observation in the angiography suite. Frequent angiographic observations during thrombolysis demonstrated a significant incidence of concurrent rethrombosis, as was anticipated from the known prothrombotic effects of thrombolysis discussed above. Further laboratory experiments were therefore conducted to determine the value of incorporating heparin or other antithrombic or antiplatelet agents into the PSPMT regimen. These results have been presented above, and in summary demonstrated significant advantage of the concomitant use of thrombin inhibitors or antiplatelet agents.[108-110] Because of these results, the current PSPMT method involves the admixture of heparin with UK and systemic administration of heparin and aspirin. If thrombolysis is slow or concurrent rethrombosis becomes evident, low-molecular-weight dextran is given systemically, as described above.

The principles of PSPMT are as follows:

1. Penetrating intrathrombic injections of fibrinolytic spray to macerate clot and augment the interactive surface area, as well as to penetrate the lysis-resistant surface membranes of the thrombus, and the intrathrombic, presumably lysis-resistant, lines of Zahn
2. Circulatory isolation of thrombolytic agents to minimize dilution, minimize inhibition of fibrinolysis by plasmin inhibitors in plasma, and minimize systemic effects
3. Simultaneous treatment of the entire thrombus to increase the rate of lysis
4. Concentrated agent, usually UK (25,000 IU/ml), to increase the rate of lysis and to overwhelm intrathrombic inhibitors
5. Intrathrombic heparin and systemic aspirin to significantly inhibit concurrent rethombosis
6. Small pulse volumes (0.2 ml) and briefly delayed treatment of a small distal plug of thrombus (15 minutes) to minimize embolization
7. Transluminal angioplasty to eliminate residual luminal compromise, including possible residual thrombus, after lytic stagnation[129] (see Chapter 9)
8. Transluminal angioplasty or atherectomy upon completion, as indicated

Chapter 9 elaborates further on the clinical aspects of

thrombolysis, emphasizing details of methodology, results, and complications.

Acknowledgments

The authors are grateful to Dr. Russell Doolittle for his review of this chapter and his numerous suggestions, which contributed to clarity and scientific accuracy.

References

1. Margaglione M, Grandone E, Di Minno G. Mechanisms of fibrinolysis and clinical use of thrombolytic agents. Prog Drug Res 1992;39:197–217.
2. Doolittle RF, Watt HWK, Cottrell BA. Fibrinogen: a highly evolved regulatory agent for maintaining the integrity of the vertebrate circulatory system. In: Li CH, ed. Versatility of proteins. New York: Academic, 1978:393–411.
3. Stenberg PE, Bainton DF. Storage organelles in platelets and megakaryocytes. In: Phillips DR, Shuman MA, eds. Biochemistry of platelets. Orlando, FL: Academic, 1986:257–295.
4. Mosesson MW. The assembly and structure of the fibrin clot. Nouv Rev Fr Hematol 1992;34:11–16.
5. Doolittle R. Fibrinogen and fibrin. Ann Rev Biochem 1984;53:195–229.
6. Hermans J, McDonagh J. Fibrin: structure and interactions. Semin Thromb Haemostasis 1982;8:11–24.
7. Francis CW, Marder VJ. Rapid formation of large molecular weight α-polymers in cross-linked fibrin induced by high factor XIII concentrations. J Clin Invest 1987;80:1459–1465.
8. Francis CW, Marder VJ. Increased resistance to plasmic degradation of fibrin with highly crosslinked α-polymer chains formed at high factor XIII concentration. Blood 1988;71:1361–1365.
9. Kunitada S, FitzGerald GA, Fitzgerald DJ. Inhibition of clot lysis and decreased binding of tissue-type plasminogen activator as a consequence of clot retraction. Blood 1992;79:1420–1427.
10. Jang I-K, Gold HK, Ziskind AA, et al. Differential sensitivity of erythrocyte-rich and platelet-rich arterial thrombi to lysis with recombinant tissue-type plasminogen activator. Circulation 1989;79:920–928.
11. Collen D, Verstraete M. Molecular biology of human plasminogen: metabolism in physiological and some pathological conditions in man. Thromb Diath Haemorrh 1975;34:403–408.
12. Bohmfalk J, Fuller G. Plasminogen is synthesized by primary cultures of rat hepatocytes. Science 1980;209:408–410.
13. Akikazu T, Ymilo T. Activation pathway of Glu-plasminogen to Lys-plasminogen by urokinase. Thromb Res 1982;27:671–677.
14. Alkjearsig N, Fletcher A, Sherry S. The mechanism of clot dissolution by plasmin. J Clin Invest 1959;38:1086–1095.
15. Gottlob R. Mechanisms of intravascular thrombus dissolution as induced by streptokinase. In: Martin M, Schoop W, Hirsch J, eds. Concepts in streptokinase dosimetry. Bern: Hans-Huber, 1978.
16. Collen D. On the regulation and control of fibrinolysis. Thromb Haemostasis 1980;43:77–89.
17. Brommer EJ, van Bockel JH. Composition and susceptibility to thrombolysis of human arterial thrombi and the influence of their age. Blood, Coagulation and Fibrinolysis 1992;3:717–725.
18. Hajjar K, Nachman R. Endothelial cell–mediated conversion of Glu-plasminogen to Lys-plasminogen: further evidence for assembly of the fibrinolytic system on the endothelial cell surface. J Clin Invest 1988;82:1769–1778.
19. Claeys H, Molla A, Verstraete M. Conversion of NH_2-terminal glutamic acid to NH_2-terminal lysine human plasminogen by plasmin. Thromb Res 1973;3:515–523.
20. Marder V, Shulman N. High molecular weight derivatives of human fibrinogen produced by plasmin. J Biol Chem 1969;244:2120–2124.
21. Penny WE, Ware JA. Platelet activation and subsequent inhibition by plasmin and recombinant tissue-type plasminogen activator. Blood 1992;79:91–98.
22. Pennica D, et al. Cloning and expression of human tissue-type plasminogen activator cDNA in *E. coli*. Nature 1983;301:214–221.
23. van Hinsbergh V. Regulation of the synthesis and secretion of plasminogen activators by endothelial cells. Haemostasis 1988;18:307–327.
24. Agnelli G, Levi M, Cosmi B, et al. Additive effect of dDAVP and standard heparin in increasing plasma t-PA. Thromb Haemostasis 1989;61:507–510.
25. Hoylaerts M, Rijken D, Lijnen H, Collen D. Kinetics of the activation of plasminogen by human tissue plasminogen activator: role of fibrin. J Biol Chem 1992;257:2912.
26. Zamarron C, Lijnen H, Collen D. Kinetics of the activation of plasminogen by natural and recombinant tissue-type plasminogen activator. J Biol Chem 1984;259:2080–2083.
27. Rijken D, Collen D. Purification and characterization of the plasminogen activator secreted by human melanoma cells in culture. J Biol Chem 1981;256:7035–7041.
28. Rijken D, Hoylaerts M, Collen D. Fibrinolytic properties of one-chain and two-chain human extrinsic (tissue-type) plasminogen activator. J Biol Chem 1982;257:2920–2925.
29. Garabedian HD, Gold HK, Leinbach RC, et al. Comparative properties of two clinical preparations of recombinant human tissue-type plasminogen activator in patients with acute myocardial infarction. J Am Coll Cardiol 1987;9:599–607.
30. Collen D. Report of the meeting of the subcommittee on fibrinolysis, Jerusalem, Israel, June 2, 1986. Thromb Haemostasis 1986;56:415–416.
31. Tanswell P, Seifried E, Su PC, Feuerer W, Rijken DC. Pharmacokinetics and systemic effects of tissue-type plasminogen activator in normal subjects. Clin Pharmacol Ther 1989;46:155–162.
32. Rao AK, Pratt C, Berke A, et al. Thrombolysis in Myocardial Infarction (TIMI) Trial: Phase 1. Hemorrhagic manifestations and changes in plasma fibrinogen and the fibrinolytic system in patients treated with recombinant tissue plasminogen activator and streptokinase. J Am Coll Cardiol 1988;11:1–11.
33. Bovill EG, Terrin ML, Stump DC, et al. Hemorrhagic events during therapy with recombinant tissue-type plasminogen activator, heparin, and aspirin for acute myocardial infarction: results of the thrombolysis in myocardial infarction (TIMI), phase II trial. Ann Intern Med 1991;115:256–265.
34. Weitz JI, Leslie B, Ginsberg J. Soluble fibrin degradation products potentiate tissue plasminogen activator–induced fibrinogen proteolysis. J Clin Invest 1991;87:1082–1090.
35. Hajar KA, Hamel NM, Harpel PL, Nachman RL. Binding of tissue plasminogen activator to cultured human endothelial cells. J Clin Invest 1987;80:1712–1719.
36. Loscalzo J, Braunwald E. Tissue plasminogen activator. N Engl J Med 1988;319:925–931.
37. Meyerovitz MF, Goldhaber SZ, Reagan K, et al. Recombinant tissue-type plasminogen activator versus urokinase in peripheral arterial and graft occlusions: a randomized trial. Radiology 1990;175:75–78.
38. Topol ER, George BS, Keriakes DJ, et al. Comparison of two dose regimens of intravenous tissue plasminogen activator for acute myocardial infarction. Am J Cardiol 1988;61:723–728.
39. Creighton-Kempsford LJ, Pring JB, Gaffney PJ. A comparison of the plasminogen activator activity units of urinary-type plasminogen activator (u-PA) and tissue-type plasminogen activator (t-PA). Blood, Coagulation and Fibrinolysis 1992;3:481–483.

40. Tillett W, Garner R. The fibrinolytic activity of hemolytic streptococci. J Exp Med 1933;58:485–502.
41. Robbins KC, Markus G. The interaction of human plasminogen with streptokinase. In: Gaffney PJ, Balkuv-Ulitin S, eds. Fibrinolysis: current fundamentals and clinical concepts. London: Academic Press, 1978:61–75.
42. Reddy KNN. Streptokinase: biochemistry and clinical applications. Enzyme 1988;40:79–89.
43. Robbins KC. Fibrinolytic therapy: biochemical mechanisms. Semin Thromb Hemostasis 1991;17:1–6.
44. Fletcher AP, Alkjaersig N, Sherry S. The maintenance of a sustained thrombolytic state in man: I. Induction and effects. J Clin Invest 1959;38:1096–1110.
45. Monk J, Heel R. Anisoylated plasminogen streptokinase activator complex (APSAC): a review of its mechanism of action, clinical pharmacology and therapeutic use in acute myocardial infarction. Drugs 1987;34:25–49.
46. Runge M, Quertermous T, Haber E. Plasminogen activators; the old and the new. Circulation 1989;79:217–224.
47. Marder VJ, Sherry S. Thrombolytic therapy: current status. New Engl J Med 1988;318:1512–1520, 1585–1595.
48. Fletcher A, Alkaersig N, Sherry S, Genton E, Hirsch J, Bachmann F. The development of urokinase as a thrombolytic agent: maintenance of a sustained thrombolytic state in man by its intravenous infusion. J Lab Clin Med 1965;65:713–731.
49. Gunzler W, Steffens G, Otting F, et al. Structural relationship between human high and low molecular mass urokinase. Hoppe-Seyler's Z Physiol Chem 1982;363:133–141.
50. Holden RW. Plasminogen activators: pharmacology and therapy. Radiology 1990;174:993–1001.
51. Lijnen H, Van Hoef B, De Cock F, Collen D. The mechanism of plasminogen activation and fibrin dissolution by single chain urokinase-type plasminogen activator in a plasma milieu in vitro. Blood 1989;73:1864–1872.
52. Lee P, Wohl RC, Boreisha IG, Robbins KC. Kinetic analysis of covalent hybrid plasminogen activators; effect of CNBr-degraded fibrinogen on kinetic parameters of Glu_1-plasminogen activation. Biochemistry 1988;27:7506–7513.
53. Collen D, Stassen J, Blaber M, Winkler M, Verstraete M. Biological and thrombolytic properties of proenzyme and active forms of human urokinase: III. Thrombolytic properties of natural and recombinant urokinase in rabbits with experimental jugular vein thrombosis. Thromb Haemostasis 1984;52:27–30.
54. Bookstein JJ, Saldinger E. Accelerated thrombolysis: in vitro evaluation of agents and methods of administration. Invest Radiol 1985;20:731–735.
55. Schleef R, Loskutoff D. Fibrinolytic system of vascular endothelial cells: role of plasminogen activator inhibitors. Haemostasis 1988;18:328–341.
56. Kruithof EKO, Tran-Thang C, Bachmann F. The fast-acting inhibitor of tissue-type plasminogen activator in plasma is also the primary plasma inhibitor of urokinase. Thromb Haemostasis 1986;55:201–205.
57. Tamaki T, Aoki N. Cross-linking of α_2-antiplasmin inhibitor and fibronectin to fibrin by fibrin stabilizing factor. Biochim Biophys Acta 1981;661:280–286.
58. Verstraete M, Vermylen J, Schetz J. Biochemical changes noted during intermittent administration of streptokinase. Thromb Haemostasis 1978;39:61–68.
59. Shuman MA, Greenberg CS. Platelet regulation of thrombus formation. In: Phillips DR, Shuman MA, eds. Biochemistry of platelets. Orlando, FL: Academic, 1986:319–347.
60. Mirshahi M, Azzarone B, Soria J, Mirshahi F, Soria C. The role of fibroblasts in organization and degradation of a fibrin clot. J Lab Clin Med 1991;117:274–281.
61. Erickson LA, Ginsburg MH, Loskutoff DJ. Detection and partial characterization of an inhibitor of plasminogen activator in human platelets. J Clin Invest 1984;74:1465–1472.
62. Plow EF, Collen D. The presence and release of alpha$_2$-antiplasmin from human platelets. Blood 1981;58:1069–1074.
63. Loskutoff DJ. Type 1 plasminogen activator inhibitor and its potential influence on thrombolytic therapy. Semin Thromb Hemostasis 1988;14:100–109.
64. Bock PE, Luscombe M, Marshall SE, Pepper D, Holbrook J. The multiple complexes formed by the interaction of platelet factor 4 with heparin. Biochem J 1980;191:769–776.
65. Golino P, Ambrosio G, Ragni M, et al. Short-term and long-term role of platelet activating factor as a mediator of in vivo platelet aggregation. Circulation 1993;88:1205–1214.
66. Miletich JP, Jackson CM, Majerus PW. Interactions of coagulation factor Xa with human platelets. Proc Natl Acad Sci USA 1977;74:4033–4036.
67. Reed GL, Matseuda GR, Haber E. Fibrin-fibrin and alpha$_2$-antiplasmin-fibrin cross linking by platelet factor XIII increase the resistance of platelet clots to fibrinolysis. Thromb Haemostasis 1991;68:881–887.
68. Mosher DF. Cross-linking of cold-insoluble globulin by fibrin-stabilizing factor. J Biol Chem 1975;250.6614–6621.
69. Knox P, Crooks S, Rimmer CS. Role of fibronectin in the migration of fibroblasts into plasma clots. J Cell Biol 1986;102:2318–2323.
70. Freiman DG. The structure of thrombi. In: Colman RW, Hirsh J, Marder VJ, Salzman EW, eds. Hemostasis and thrombosis: basic principles and clinical practice. Philadelphia: Lippincott, 1982.
71. Cohen I, Burk DL, White JG. The effects of peptides and monoclonal antibodies that bind glycoprotein IIb-IIIa complex on the development of clot tension. Blood 1989;73:1880–1887.
72. Fox JEB, Phillips DR. Polymerization and organization of actin filaments within platelets. Semin Hematol 1983;20:243–260.
73. Widmer K, Moake JL. Clot retraction: evaluation in dilute suspensions of platelet-rich plasma and gel-separated platelets. J Lab Clin Med 1976;87:49–57.
74. Friedman M, van den Bovenkamp GJ. The pathogenesis of a coronary thrombus. Am J Pathol 1966;48:19–44.
75. Chandler AB. The anatomy of a thrombus. In: Sherry S, Brinkhous K, Genton E, Stengle JM, eds. Thrombosis. Washington, DC: National Academy of Science, 1969:279–299.
76. Yasuda T, Gold HK, Fallon JT, et al. Monoclonal antibody against the platelet glycoprotein (GP) IIb/IIIa receptor prevents coronary artery reocclusion following reperfusion with recombinant tissue-type plasminogen activator in dogs. J Clin Invest 1988;81:1284–1291.
77. Galanakis DK. Anticoagulant albumin fragments that bind to fibrinogen/fibrin: possible implications. Semin Thromb Hemostasis 1992;18:44–52.
78. Jen CJ, Lin JS. Direct observation of platelet adhesion to fibrinogen- and fibrin-coated surfaces. Am J Physiol 1991;261:H1457–H1463.
78a. Loike JD, Silverstein R, Cao L, et al. Activated platelets form protected zones of adhesion on fibrinogen and fibronectin-coated surfaces. J Cell Biol 1993;121:945–955.
79. Coller BS. Platelets and thrombolytic therapy. N Engl J Med 1990;322:33–42.
80. Bookstein JJ, Valji K. How I do it: pulse-spray pharmacomechanical thrombolysis. Cardiovasc Intervent Radiol 1992;15:228–233.
81. Mirshahi M, et al. Evaluation of the inhibition by heparin and hirudin of coagulation activation during r-tPA-induced thrombolysis. Blood 1989;74:1025–1030.
82. Francis CW, Markham RE, Barlow GH, Florack TM, Dobrzynski DM, Marder VJ. Thrombin activity of fibrin thrombi and soluble plasmic derivatives. J Lab Clin Med 1983;102:220–230.
83. Bloom AL. The release of thrombin from fibrin by fibrinolysis. Br J Haematol 1962;8:129–133.
84. Gulba DC, Barthels M, Westhoff-Bleck M, et al. Increased thrombin levels during thrombolytic therapy in acute myocardial infarction: relevance for the success of therapy. Circulation 1991;83:937–944.

85. Fitzgerald DJ, FitzGerald GA. Antiplatelet and anticoagulant therapy during coronary thrombolysis. Trends Cardiovasc Med 1991;1:29–35.

86. Bernstein EF, Marzec U, Johnston GG. Structural correlates of platelet functional damage by physical forces. Trans Am Soc Artif Intern Organs 1977;23:617–625.

87. Colantuoni G, Hellums JD, Mbake JL, Alfrey CP. The response of human platelets to shear stress at short exposure times. Trans Am Soc Artif Intern Organs 1977;23:626–631.

88. Bookstein JJ, Valji K. Pulse-spray pharmacomechanical thrombolysis: updated clinical and laboratory observations. Semin Intervent Radiol 1992;9:174–181.

89. Karlsberg RP, Cryer PE, Roberts R. Serial plasma catecholamine response early in the course of clinical acute myocardial infarction: relationship to infarct extent and mortality. Am Heart J 1981;102:872–874.

90. Grignani G, Soffiantino F, Zucchella M, et al. Platelet activation by emotional stress in patients with coronary artery disease. Circulation 1991;83(Suppl II):128–136.

91. Grant JA, Scrutton MC. Novel alpha$_2$-adrenoreceptors primarily responsible for inducing human platelet aggregation. Nature 1979;277:659–661.

92. Becker RC. Seminars in thrombosis, thrombolysis and vascular biology: 3. Platelet activity in cardiovascular disease. Cardiology 1991;79:49–63.

93. Kristensen SD, Bath PMW, Martin JF. Differences in bleeding time, aspirin sensitivity and adrenaline between acute myocardial infarction and unstable angina. Cardiovasc Res 1990;24:19–23.

94. Badimon L, Badimon JJ. Mechanisms of arterial thrombosis in nonparallel streamlines: platelet thrombi grow on the apex of stenotic severely injured vessel wall. An experimental study in the pig model. J Clin Invest 1989;84:1134–1144.

95. Andrade-Gordon P, Strickland S. Interaction of heparin with plasminogen activators and plasminogen: effects on the activation of plasminogen. Biochemistry 1986;25:4033–4040.

96. Fears R. Kinetic studies on the effect of heparin and fibrin on plasminogen activators. Biochem J 1988;249:77–81.

97. Susawa T, Yui Y, Hattori R, et al. Heparin requirements in tissue-type plasminogen activator–induced experimental coronary thrombolysis: comparison with urokinase-induced coronary thrombolysis. Jpn Circ J 1987;51:431–435.

98. Curl GR, Jakubowski JA, Deykin D, Bush HL. Beneficial effect of aspirin in maintaining the patency of small-caliber prosthetic grafts after thrombolysis with urokinase or tissue-type plasminogen activator. Circulation 1986;74(Suppl I):21–24.

99. Ratnatunga CP, Rees GM, Kovacs IB. High-dose aspirin inhibits shear-induced platelet reaction involving thrombin generation. Circulation 1992;85:1077–1082.

100. Third International Study of Infant Survival Collaborative Group. ISIS-3: a randomized comparison of streptokinase vs tissue plasminogen activator vs anistreplase and of aspirin plus heparin vs aspirin alone among 41,299 cases of suspected acute myocardial infarction. Lancet 1992;339:753–770.

101. Haskel EJ, Prager NA, Sobel BE, Abenschein DR. Relative efficacy of antithrombin compared with antiplatelet agents in accelerating coronary thrombolysis and preventing early reocclusion. Circulation 1991;83:1048–1056.

102. Vaughan DE, Plavin SR, Schafer AI, Loscalzo J. PGE$_1$ accelerates thrombolysis by tissue plasminogen activator. Blood 1989;73:1213–1217.

103. Haskel TJ, Adams SP, Feigen LP, Saffitz JE, Gorczynski RJ, Sobel BE, Abendschein DR. Prevention of reoccluding platelet-rich thrombi in canine femoral arteries with a novel peptide antagonist of platelet glycoprotein IIb/IIIa receptors. Circulation 1989;80:1775–1782.

104. Yasuda T, et al. Lysis of plasminogen activator–resistant platelet-rich coronary artery thrombus with combined bolus injection of recombinant tissue-type plasminogen activator and antiplatelet GPIIb/IIIa antibody. J Am Coll Cardiol 1990;16:1728–1735.

105. Yasuda T, Gold HK, Yaoita H, et al. Comparative effects of aspirin, as synthetic thrombin inhibitor and a monoclonal antiplatelet glycoprotein IIb/IIIa antibody on coronary artery reperfusion, reocclusion and bleeding with recombinant tissue-type plasminogen activator in a canine preparation. J Am Coll Cardiol 1990;16:714–722.

106. Heras M, et al. Hirudin, heparin, and placebo during deep arterial injury in the pig. Circulation 1990;82:1476–1484.

107. Jang I-K, Gold HK, Leinbach RC, Fallon JT, Collen D. In vivo thrombin inhibition enhances and sustains arterial recanalization with recombinant tissue-type plasminogen activator. Circ Res 1990;67:1552–1561.

108. Valji K, Bookstein JJ. Efficacy of adjunctive intrathrombic heparin with pulse spray thrombolysis in rabbit inferior vena cava thrombosis. Invest Radiol 1992;27:912–917.

109. Valji K, Bookstein JJ. Effects of intrathrombic administration of prostaglandin E$_1$ during pulse-spray thrombolysis with tissue-type plasminogen activator in experimental thrombosis. Radiology 1993;186:873–876.

110. Valji K, Bookstein JJ. The effect of intrathrombic deposition of a specific thrombin inhibitor (Argatroban) on pulse-spray thrombolysis in an experimental clot model. Presented, Society of Cardiovascular and Intervention Radiology, March 1994, San Diego, CA.

111. Carlin G, Saldeen T. On the interaction between dextran and the primary fibrinolysis inhibitor α$_2$-macroglobulin. Thromb Res 1980;19:103–110.

112. Ljungstrom K-G. The antithrombotic efficacy of dextran. Acta Chir Scand 1988;543(Suppl):26–30.

113. Pasternak RC, Baughman KL, Fallon JT, Block PC. Scanning electron microscopy after coronary transluminal angioplasty of normal canine coronary arteries. Am J Cardiol 1980;45:591–598.

114. Sherry S. Appraisal of various thrombolytic agents in the treatment of acute myocardial infarction. Am J Med 1987;83(2A):31–46.

115. Morris JA, Muller DWM, Topol EJ. Combination thrombolytic therapy: a comparison of simultaneous and sequential regimens of tissue plasminogen and urokinase. Am Heart J 11;122:375–380.

116. Califf RM, Topol EJ, Stack RX, et al for the TAMI Study Group. Evaluation of combination thrombolytic therapy and timing of cardiac catheterization in acute myocardial infarction: results of Thrombolysis and Angioplasty in Myocardial Infarction: Phase 5 randomized trial. Circulation 1991;83:1543–1556.

117. Neuhaus K-I, Tebber U, Gottwik M, et al for the GAUS Group. Intravenous recombinant tissue plasminogen activator (rt-PA) and urokinase in acute myocardial infarction: results of the German Activator Urokinase Study (GAUS). J Am Coll Cardiol 1988;12:581–587.

118. Grines CL, Nissen SE, Booth DC, et al. A prospective, randomized trial comparing combination half-dose tissue-type plasminogen activator and streptokinase with full-dose tissue-type plasminogen activator. Circulation 1991;84:540–549.

119. Dotter CT, Rösch J, Seaman AJ. Selective clot lysis with low-dose streptokinase. Radiology 1974;111:31–37.

120. Mori K, Bookstein JJ, Hoagie C. Selective streptokinase infusion: clinical and laboratory correlates. Radiology 1983;148:677–682.

121. Martin M. Thrombolytic therapy in arterial thromboembolism. Prog Cardiovasc Dis 1979;21:351–374.

122. Sullivan KL, Gardiner GA, Kandarpa K, Bonn J, Shapiro M, Carabasi RA, Smullens S, Levin DC. Efficacy of thrombolysis in infrainguinal bypass grafts. Circulation 1991;83(Suppl I):99–105.

123. McNamara TO, Bomberger RA, Merchant RF. Intra-arterial urokinase as the initial therapy for acutely ischemic lower limbs. Circulation 1991;83(Suppl I):106–119.

124. Bookstein JJ, Valji K, Roberts AC. Pulse-spray pharmacomechanical thrombolysis in the peripheral vasculature. In:

Comerato AJ, ed. Thrombolytic therapy for peripheral vascular disease. Philadelphia: JB Lippincott, 1995.

125. LeBlang SD, Becker GJ, Benenati JF, Zemel G, Katzen BT, Sallee SS. Low-dose urokinase regimen for the treatment of lower extremity arterial and graft occlusions: experience in 132 cases. J Vasc Intervent Radiol 1992;3:475–483.

126. McNamara T, Fischer J. Thrombolysis of peripheral arterial and graft occlusions: improved results using high dose urokinase. AJR 1985;144:755–769.

127. Valji K, Bookstein JJ. Fibrinolysis with intrathrombic injection of urokinase and tissue-type plasminogen activator: results in a new model of subacute venous thrombosis. Invest Radiol 1987;22:23–27.

128. Bookstein JJ, Fellmeth B, Roberts A, Valji K, Davis G, Machado T. Pulsed-spray pharmacomechanical thrombolysis: preliminary clinical results. AJR 1989;152:1097–1100.

129. Valji K, Bookstein JJ. Lytic stagnation: an endpoint for pulse-spray pharmacomechanical thrombolysis of occluded peripheral arteries and bypass grafts.

9

Thrombolysis:
Clinical Applications

KARIM VALJI
JOSEPH J. BOOKSTEIN

*T*he pharmacologic dissolution of thrombus has become a widely practiced and accepted method for treating vascular occlusions over the last two decades. The clinical practice of thrombolysis is the byproduct of a better understanding of the fibrinolytic process in humans and of the effect of exogenous plasminogen activators on clot, and of the development of catheter and guidewire systems that have allowed for direct application of these agents. The important milestones in the evolution of thrombolytic therapy in noncoronary vessels are outlined in Table 9-1.[1-11]

Refined methods for thrombolytic therapy have led to greater reliability in clot lysis, shortened treatment times, and reduction in bleeding complications. These modifications have largely occurred in three areas: the use of more predictable and clot-specific fibrinolytic agents; increasingly selective deposition of agents at the site of occlusion; and the combination of mechanical dissolution with enzymatic degradation of clot. The scientific principles and pharmacology of thrombolysis are discussed in Chapter 8. This chapter considers clinical applications of transcatheter thrombolysis in all vascular beds except the coronary and cerebral circulations.

Indications

Thrombolytic therapy, often in conjunction with supplementary operative or transcatheter procedures, is an acceptable alternative to primary surgical revascularization in the following conditions:

- Thrombosed hemodialysis access grafts
- Iliac artery occlusions of any length or age in patients with severe claudication, ischemic rest pain, or tissue loss (Rutherford class I-3, II, or III)[12]
- Short (2–20 cm) infrainguinal arterial occlusions of

any age in patients with Rutherford class I-3, II, or III symptoms
- Acute peripheral arterial or bypass graft occlusions of any length in the presence of demonstrable runoff vessels
- Upper extremity arterial thromboses of any length or age
- Acute thromboses that occur during diagnostic angiography or transcatheter therapy
- Symptomatic upper extremity venous occlusions not responsive to anticoagulation
- Iliac and lower extremity venous thrombosis in selected cases
- Pulmonary artery embolism in patients with impending cardiorespiratory collapse

Thrombolytic therapy is occasionally performed in other vascular beds (e.g., aorta, renal arteries and veins, mesenteric arteries), but the published experience has been limited and the relative benefits and risks in these settings have not been established.

The decision to attempt thrombolysis is based on several factors, including the patient's symptoms, findings at angiography, and an assessment of the relative benefit and risk of the procedure compared with alternative therapies. As a rule, transcatheter therapy is considered when surgical intervention is indicated. However, because of the lower morbidity and mortality associated with thrombolysis, indications for percutaneous treatment may be liberalized in selected cases (e.g., treatment of peripheral arterial occlusions in patients with mild to moderate claudication, symptomatic upper extremity venous occlusions).

Thrombolysis may be preferable to surgical intervention in patients at high operative risk, in peripheral bypass graft candidates without a suitable autologous vein, and in patients with infection at the proposed operative site without infection in the vicinity of the occluded vessel.

Table 9-1. Milestones in Noncoronary Vascular
Thrombolytic Therapy

1933: Tillett and Garner discover fibrinolytic substance in streptococci.[1]

1946: MacFarlane and Pilling isolate human urokinase (UK).[2]

1952: Johnson and Tillett report lysis of rabbit thrombi with IV
streptokinase (SK).[3]

1954: Sherry describes the interaction between SK and the fibrinolytic system.[4]

1959: Johnson and McCarty use intravenous SK to lyse clot in humans.[5]

1960s: Streptokinase used widely in the treatment of thrombotic
disorders.

1970s: Intravenous SK and UK used in therapy of pulmonary embolism and deep venous thrombosis.[6]

1974: Dotter et al. describe intraarterial clot lysis with low-dose SK.[7]

1981–83: Katzen and van Breda[8] and Becker et al.[9] popularize local
thrombolytic therapy.

1985: McNamara and Fischer describe technique of selective local
infusion of high-dose UK.[10]

1989: Bookstein et al. define method for accelerating thrombolysis
using the pulse-spray pharmacomechanical technique (PSPMT).[11]

Contraindications

Thrombolysis should be avoided in patients at increased risk for bleeding from the use of anticoagulant
or fibrinolytic agents:

- Recent intracranial, thoracic, or abdominal surgery
- Recent major trauma
- Recent gastrointestinal hemorrhage
- Recent stroke or presence of intracranial neoplasm
- Pregnancy
- Severe hypertension
- Bleeding diathesis

Patients with suspected infection at the site of
thrombosis should not be treated with thrombolytic
agents. The sites most likely to harbor infected thrombus include hemodialysis access grafts, the anastomoses of peripheral bypass grafts, and upper extremity and
thoracic veins containing vascular access catheters. Infected clot appears to be relatively resistant to exogenous fibrinolytic agents. More importantly, lysis of infected clot may cause systemic sepsis.[13]

Patients with profound ischemia from acute arterial
or bypass graft occlusions are at high risk for limb loss.
Signs of irreversible ischemia include severe pain, gross
sensorimotor deficits, lack of arterial or venous Doppler signal, and laboratory evidence of muscle necrosis
(e.g., myoglobinuria). Because rapid treatment is critical to limit the amputation level and decrease mortality, infusion thrombolysis is generally not indicated.
Pulse-spray thrombolysis may be considered in se-

lected cases because blood flow can be restored quickly
to the ischemic limb. Even with accelerated thrombolysis, a reperfusion syndrome may occur, manifested by
acidosis, hemodynamic instability, myoglobinuria,
hyperkalemia, and compartment syndrome.[14]

In situ thrombosis in the absence of underlying obstructive disease is often due to the presence of a hypercoagulable state.[15] Such occlusions may not benefit
from thrombolytic therapy unless the coagulation defect can be temporarily corrected or alleviated.

Choice of Fibrinolytic Agent

Streptokinase (SK) was the first fibrinolytic drug to be
widely used in clinical practice. Streptokinase is derived
from group C streptococci and is a single-chain polypeptide of 47,000 daltons.[16] The agent forms a complex with plasminogen, and the SK-plasminogen complex catalyzes the conversion of plasminogen to
plasmin. Streptokinase is a moderately effective thrombolytic agent. In the treatment of peripheral arterial
thromboses, complete clot lysis is achieved in 40 to
80 percent of cases.[17-21] However, lysis of peripheral
occlusions requires large doses of the agent and long
infusion times (24–48 hours) to effect complete lysis.
Streptokinase use is associated with several important
side effects. Because the protein is derived from a bacterial source, it is antigenic. Fever or allergic reactions
are seen in up to 42 percent of cases.[22] More importantly, SK infusion causes a fall in plasma levels of
fibrinogen, alpha$_2$-antiplasmin, and factors V and
VII, leading to a systemic lytic state. Minor or major
bleeding complications occur in about 25 percent of
cases.[17-21]

Urokinase (UK) is safer and more effective than
streptokinase. UK is obtained from human fetal kidney
tissue culture and more recently by recombinant DNA
techniques. It is a double-chain polypeptide of 54,000
daltons.[16] Unlike streptokinase, UK is not antigenic
and therefore will not be neutralized by circulating antibodies. In addition, UK is a direct plasminogen activator; because SK requires complexing with plasminogen before activation, fibrin-bound plasminogen may
be depleted before complete lysis occurs. Urokinase
has been shown to be a more effective thrombolytic
agent than streptokinase. In a study of occluded infrainguinal bypass grafts comparing the two agents directly, lysis was achieved in 48 percent of grafts treated
with SK and in 84 percent of grafts treated with UK.[23]
Finally, hemorrhagic complications are less frequent
with UK than with SK.[24]

Tissue-type plasminogen activator (tPA) is a serine
protease originally isolated from cultured melanoma

cell lines and now produced commercially by recombinant DNA techniques. The activity of tPA is markedly enhanced by fibrin-bound plasminogen. Although tPA is theoretically less likely than SK or UK to produce a systemic lytic state, this advantage has not been realized clinically.[25,26] Numerous experimental and clinical studies have shown that the clot specificity of tPA is dose-dependent, and intravenous doses necessary for effective clot dissolution produce systemic fibrinolysis.

Tissue plasminogen activator has been shown to be an effective agent for treating peripheral arterial and bypass graft occlusions. Technical success is achieved in 75 to 95 percent of cases, and infusion times range from 3 to 22 hours.[27–30] Intraarterial tPA is favored over intravenous administration for reasons of efficacy and overall safety.[31] In a small series of patients, Krupski and associates found tPA to be an effective agent in lower extremity vascular occlusions, but mild systemic fibrinolysis developed in most patients and minor hemorrhagic complications occurred in half of the cases.[32] In a randomized study comparing UK and tPA in native arteries and bypass grafts, Meyerovitz et al. found a slight acceleration in lysis but equivalent rates of complete lysis and slightly increased bleeding complications with tPA.[33] Circulating fibrinogen levels were lower in patients treated with tPA than in those with comparable doses of UK. Similarly, experience in the treatment of coronary thromboses has shown no decline in bleeding complications from the use of tPA compared with SK.[34] In fact, the frequency of minor or major bleeding complications may be as high as 25 percent with tPA.[35] Although some studies have shown a slight advantage of tPA over UK in efficacy of lysis, the increased frequency of minor bleeding complications and significantly higher cost make this agent less attractive than UK in clinical practice.

Several new natural and synthetic fibrinolytic agents are currently being tested for use in the coronary circulation. However, none of these agents has undergone extensive evaluation in the treatment of peripheral vascular disease.

Methods of Thrombolysis

Thrombolytic therapy is performed only after diagnostic angiography. For peripheral vascular occlusions, access is usually gained by ipsilateral femoral artery puncture. Sometimes occlusions can be treated from the contralateral side using the initial access site from the diagnostic arteriogram. This approach avoids a second arterial puncture, but it may be more difficult to cross the occlusion. In peripheral bypass grafts, direct puncture may be considered if the graft is superficial.[36] A popliteal artery approach may be advantageous in certain cases, including markedly obese patients, graft occlusions without a nipple at the proximal anastomosis to allow entry into the graft, or grafts in which the proximal anastomosis is near the top of the common femoral artery.[37]

The occlusion is initially crossed with a guidewire. Soft-tipped wires are less likely to produce a subintimal passage and are usually tried first. Hydrophilic guidewires are particularly useful in negotiating difficult occlusions. If other methods fail, the combination of a Rosen wire and straight catheter may be successful. There is some controversy regarding the value of thrombolytic therapy when the occlusion cannot be traversed with a guidewire. McNamara and others believe that inability to cross an arterial obstruction predicts a poor response to thrombolysis.[10] On the other hand, Smith and coworkers found that the inability to cross an occlusion with a guidewire had no significant bearing on the success of clot lysis.[38] Most authorities will attempt thrombolytic therapy if at least some portion of the occlusion can be penetrated.

Infusion Thrombolysis

The current techniques for infusion thrombolysis are modified versions of the method originally described by McNamara and Fischer.[10] Once the occlusion has been crossed with a guidewire, a therapeutic catheter is placed for infusion. Thrombolysis may be performed with an end-hole catheter positioned at the top of the obstruction, a multi-side-hole catheter with tip-occluding wire for intrathrombic infusion, or a coaxial system for split infusion at the proximal and midportions of the occlusion.[39,40] Most practitioners favor intrathrombic infusions to optimize the delivery of fibrinolytic agent into the clot. Before infusion, thrombolysis may be initiated by lacing the thrombus with UK or injecting small pulses of UK solution through a side-hole catheter. Sullivan and coworkers demonstrated more rapid lysis with a lower overall UK requirement after initial lacing of thrombi with large doses of UK (120,000–250,000 IU) before infusion.[41]

Both high-dose (60,000–240,000 IU/hr) and low-dose (up to 50,000 IU/hr) urokinase infusion techniques have been used. Proponents of the high-dose technique point to an increase in speed and efficacy from more rapid infusions. Advocates of the low-dose method suggest that hemorrhagic complications are lower. Cragg and coworkers have performed the only large study to date comparing low-dose (50,000 IU/hr) and high-dose (125,000–250,000 IU/hr)

UK infusions in both native arteries and bypass grafts.[42] The rates of recanalization and bleeding complications were similar in both groups. The very limited effect of modest increases in dose is consistent with experimental studies that showed that very marked differences in UK concentration are associated with only modest acceleration of thrombolysis.[43]

When practical, angiograms are obtained every 2 to 6 hours to monitor lysis and allow for adjustments in dose and catheter position. After several hours of high-dose therapy, the infusion rate is often decreased to permit slow delivery of large doses of UK overnight.

The catheter is secured in place, and the patient is transferred to an intermediate or intensive care unit for monitoring. The patient is observed for hemorrhagic complications by evaluation of the puncture sites and serial hematocrits. If thrombolysis was begun early in the morning, the patient may be returned to the angiography suite in the afternoon to assess the extent of clot lysis. Otherwise, infusion is continued overnight and angiography is repeated the following day. If clot lysis is judged complete, underlying stenoses are usually treated at that time with balloon angioplasty, atherectomy, or intravascular stents. If the angiogram suggests the presence of residual clot, the infusion may be continued. However, infusions are usually stopped after 36 to 48 hours of therapy or when more than 2.5 million units of urokinase have been given.

Pulse-Spray Pharmacomechanical Thrombolysis

Acceleration of thrombolysis by forceful pulsed injection of fibrinolytic agents directly into clot has been observed in vitro[43] and in animal models.[44,45] The technique of pulse-spray pharmacomechanical thrombolysis (PSPMT) is the other currently accepted method for noncoronary thrombolysis. Once the occlusion is traversed with a guidewire, a pulse-spray catheter is placed within the thrombus (Fig. 9-1). Several infusion systems are available for use. The essential element of a pulse-spray system is a noncompliant catheter with very small side slits or side holes. The active catheter length (length of distal catheter with side slits) is chosen on the basis of the length of the occlusion. The catheter is initially placed with the tip about 1 to 2 cm above the bottom of the occlusion to leave a small untreated segment of clot. This plug may prevent embolization of large clot fragments in the early stages of thrombolysis. The catheter is later advanced to treat this distal segment. The end hole is obstructed with a tip-occluding wire, and the catheter is fitted with a hemostatic valve. The system is purged of air using heparinized saline.

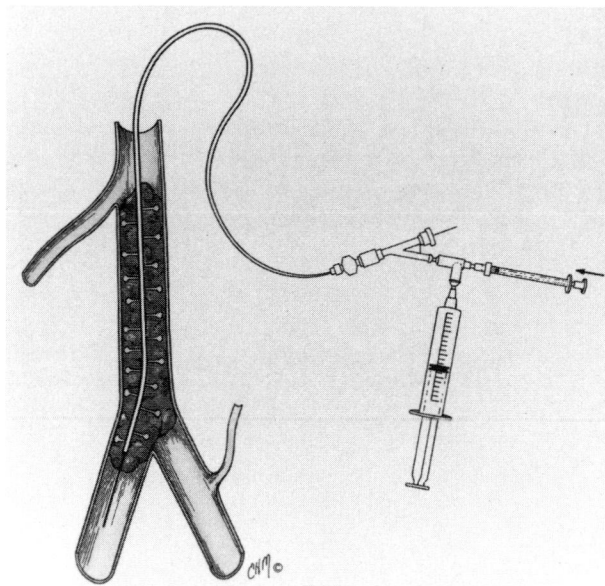

Figure 9-1. Line drawing of pulse-spray catheter and tip-occluding wire within arterial occlusion. The catheter is fitted with a hemostatic adapter and three-way stopcock. Injections are made with a tuberculin syringe. The 12-ml syringe serves as a reservoir for the urokinase/heparin mixture. (From Valji K, Bookstein JJ. Pulsed-spray thrombolysis accelerates clot dissolution. Diagn Imaging 1991;13:58–63. Used with permission.)

The injectate is prepared from one vial of UK (Abbokinase, Abbott Laboratories; 250,000 IU) in 9 ml of sterile water and 1 ml of heparin (5000 U/ml). If the patient is already anticoagulated, 2000 to 3000 units of heparin is added to the UK. No heparin is added if additional vials of UK are required. Drugs are injected into the obstruction by forceful manual thrusts of a tuberculin syringe in 0.2- to 0.3-ml increments every 30 seconds. Care is taken to keep gas bubbles out of the system. Angiograms are obtained every 20 to 30 minutes to monitor the progress of lysis. A suitable end point for thrombolytic therapy can be defined when serial angiograms show no change in the appearance of residual disease after treatment with additional doses of fibrinolytic agent. This condition has been termed *lytic stagnation* (Fig. 9-2).[46] Underlying disease may be treated safely at this point with a balloon catheter provided that large intraluminal filling defects are not present.

Residual disease found after thrombolysis may represent organized clot, lysis-resistant clot, atherosclerotic plaque, intimal hyperplasia, or embolus composed of one or more of these materials. Mural disease can be treated with balloon angioplasty with little risk of distal embolization. Large residual intraluminal material can also be treated by angioplasty, but with a

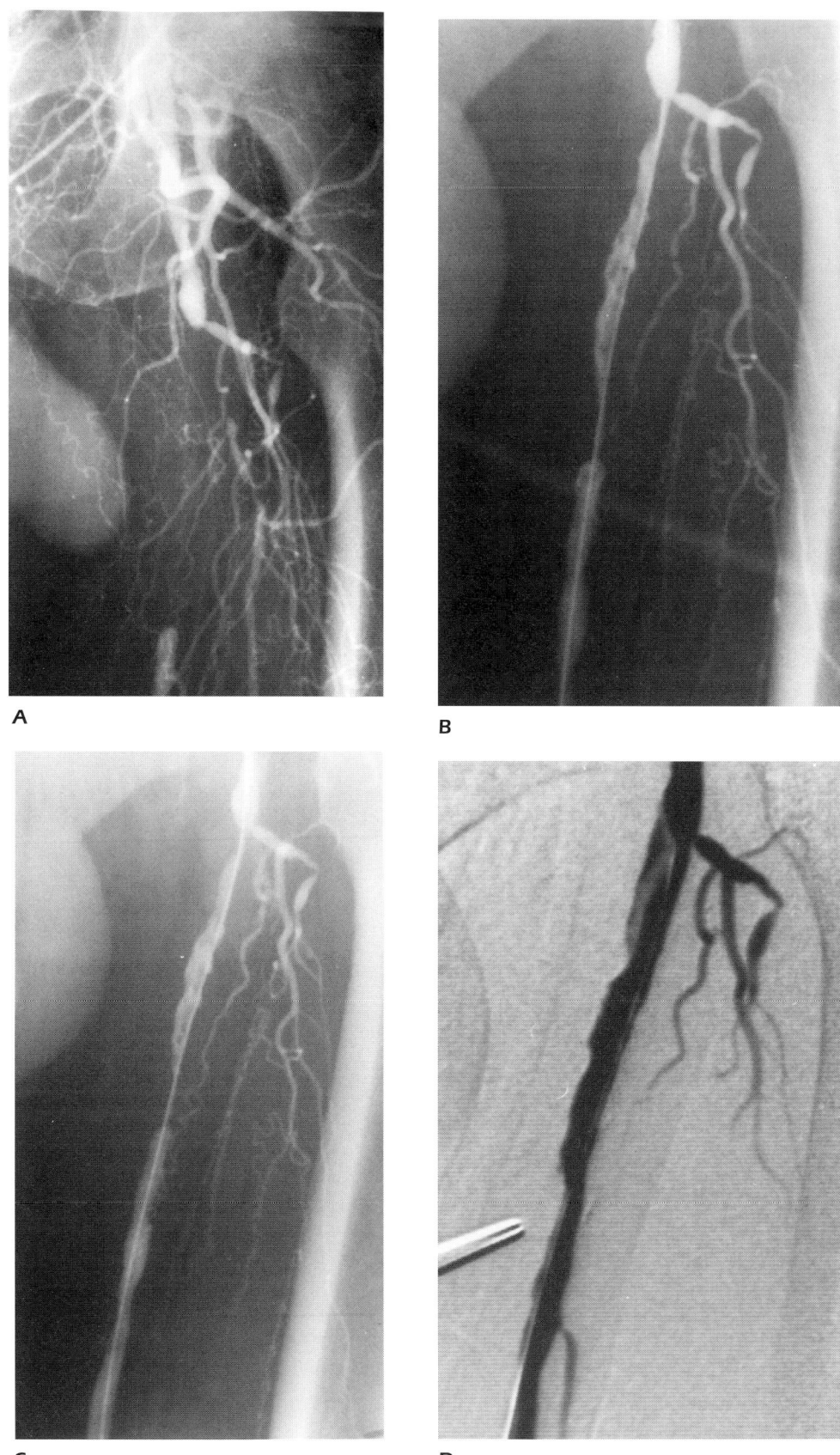

A

B

C

D

substantial risk of distal embolization. Surgical thrombectomy may be warranted in such cases, particularly when the distals vessels are severely compromised.

Although the efficacy and safety of PSPMT have been proven by several investigators, a direct comparison of PSPMT and infusion thrombolysis has not been made. Most studies have only evaluated one modality. Those studies that have directly compared the two methods are limited by comingling of techniques and by important variations in the pulse-spray methodology.[47] Favorable results with the pulse-spray method depend on careful adherence to technique, including the use of appropriate catheters, the inhibition of concurrent rethrombosis with aspirin and intrathrombic heparin, and the use of lytic stagnation as an end point for thrombolysis.[48]

Use of Antithrombin and Antiplatelet Agents

When a thrombus forms in a vessel, a dynamic balance between endogenous fibrinolysis and ongoing thrombosis takes place. When exogenous fibrinolytic agents are infused around or within a clot, concurrent rethrombosis may occur during thrombolysis.[49,50] Studies in animal models of thrombosis have shown that adjunctive antithrombin and antiplatelet agents used during pulse-spray thrombolysis, including heparin,[51] prostaglandin E_1,[52] and the direct thrombin inhibitor argatroban,[53] enhance clot lysis. Clinical studies using a variety of antiplatelet and antithrombin agents during coronary artery thrombolysis are under way.[54]

The use of anticoagulants during thrombolytic therapy is still controversial. Because thrombolysis is followed by balloon angioplasty in most cases, and aspirin is considered essential to inhibit postangioplasty thrombosis, most practitioners give aspirin before beginning thrombolysis. Heparin therapy during thrombolysis became routine after thrombus formation around the infusion catheter was reported in a substantial number of patients by early investigators in the field.[19] However, frequent bleeding complications were reported with the use of heparin during thrombolysis with SK. Although the majority of practitioners routinely use adjunctive heparin during thrombolysis, some experienced investigators do not.[55] The reported technical success of thrombolysis without the use of

heparin[56] or with the use of low-dose heparin (100 U/hr) to prevent pericatheter thrombosis[57] is similar to results when heparin is given.

Rapid and effective clot lysis during PSPMT is critically dependent on inhibition of concurrent rethrombosis with aspirin and heparin. Patients who are not already anticoagulated at the time of therapy are empirically given 2000 to 3000 units of intravenous heparin and 5000 units of intrathrombic heparin admixed with UK. Maintenance doses of heparin (500–1500 U/hr) are given during the procedure. However, heparin metabolism varies widely among patients, largely because of its nonspecific binding with plasma proteins.[58] Thus the anticoagulative response may be unpredictable. When heparin is given during overnight UK infusion, the activated partial thromboplastin time (aPTT) can be used to guide therapy, with the heparin dose adjusted to maintain the aPTT about 1.5 to 2.0 times control. When heparin is given during pulse-spray thrombolysis, a more rapid method of monitoring anticoagulation is necessary. The activated clotting time (ACT, Hemotec, Englewood, CO) is an indicator of whole blood clotting and is useful in guiding anticoagulant therapy.[59] The ACT is normally about 120 to 140 seconds. The ACT should be prolonged to at least 250 to 300 seconds during thrombolytic therapy.

Low-molecular-weight dextran may be a useful adjunct during thrombolysis, particularly in patients with hypercoagulable states and when rethrombosis is observed during thrombolysis. Dextran 40 is a polysaccharide that inhibits platelet activity by coating of the platelet membrane surface and by reducing von Willebrand factor.[60] Dextran has been used as a plasma expander, in the prevention of deep venous thrombosis, and during vascular surgical procedures. In conjunction with thrombolysis, dextran 40 may be given as a single intravenous bolus injection of 40 to 50 ml, followed by continuous infusion of 20 to 40 ml per hour during treatment.

Use of Vasodilators

Prophylactic use of vasodilators is recommended in arteries that are prone to vasospasm, including renal, upper extremity, tibial, and pedal arteries. Oral or

◄ **Figure 9-2.** Lytic stagnation as an end point for pulse-spray thrombolysis in a 72-year-old man with a 10-week history of left leg rest pain. (A) Arteriogram shows short occlusion of left superficial femoral artery. (B) Following treatment by pulse-spray thrombolysis with 250,000 IU of urokinase over 30 minutes, significant lysis has occurred with residual disease present. (C) Treatment with an additional 150,000 IU of urokinase over 30 minutes produces no change in the appearance of residual disease. (D) The artery is widely patent following balloon angioplasty. (From Valji K, Bookstein JJ, Roberts AC, Sanchez RB. Occluded peripheral arteries and bypass grafts: lytic stagnation as an endpoint for pulse-spray pharmacomechanical thrombolysis. Radiology 1993;188: 389–394. Used with permission.)

sublingual nifedipine (10 mg) may be given before therapy. In addition, intraarterial nitroglycerin may be given in 150- to 200-μg aliquots immediately before thrombolysis or angioplasty. Intraarterial verapamil 1 to 2 mg is also an effective agent, but its use may be risky in patients with cardiac disease or conduction disturbances.

Technical Modifications for Treatment of Hemodialysis Grafts

Infusion thrombolysis has proven ineffective in treating thrombosed hemodialysis access grafts. On the other hand, the pulse-spray method has been found to be a safe, rapid, and reliable method for recanalizing clotted grafts. Several modifications of the standard pulse-spray technique are necessary. Direct punctures are made at two sites in the midportion of the graft, and dilators are placed in a criss-crossed fashion to allow access to the entire clot and to allow graft inflow and outflow for treatment of underlying stenoses (Fig. 9-3). The catheter directed toward the venous anastomosis should be inserted first. If the venous anastomosis cannot be crossed, thrombolysis should not be performed. The dilators are replaced with pulse-spray catheters. The active catheter length is chosen to allow exposure of the entire clot to fibrinolytic agents while keeping the side slits within the graft.

The thrombolytic mixture (UK 250,000 IU and heparin 5000 U) is divided between the two catheters and injected over about 15 minutes. Additional UK (without additional intrathrombic heparin) is only given if large amounts of clot are still present after the first dose has been given. Otherwise, residual clot is macerated with a dilatation balloon.

The composition of clot within a thrombosed dialysis graft is not homogeneous. The body of the graft is largely filled with red cell–rich thrombus that is quite sensitive to fibrinolytic agents. However, clot at the most proximal end of the graft is relatively insensitive to these agents. Surgeons frequently retrieve a small white plug from the arterial anastomosis of clotted grafts during operative thrombectomy. This residual filling defect is also noted in most cases after thrombolytic therapy (Fig. 9-4). In keeping with limited histologic examinations, this plug is thought to consist of dense concentrations of fibrin and few red cells, characteristics of "white" or platelet-rich clot (JJ Bookstein, unpublished data). The plug may be removed by several means. Maceration with a dilatation balloon is usually effective. If the clot is directly opposite the arterial anastomosis, dilation may produce downstream emboli. In such cases, an 8.5-mm occlusion balloon (Medi-Tech) can be inserted beyond the clot into the adjacent artery. When the balloon is gently inflated and then rapidly withdrawn, the plug will be pulled into the graft. Residual material can then be safely macerated with a dilatation balloon. If these methods fail, directional atherectomy may be considered.

Following clot lysis, an underlying cause for graft thrombosis should be sought. Venous anastomotic stenosis is the usual reason for graft failure. Other causes for thrombosis include venous outflow obstruction, arterial anastomotic or inflow stenosis, and intragraft stenosis.

Figure 9-3. Line drawing of criss-cross pulse-spray catheter technique for treatment of occluded hemodialysis grafts.

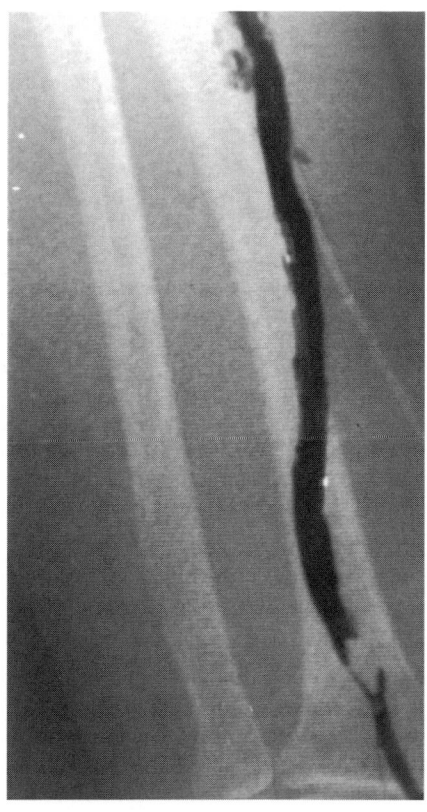

A

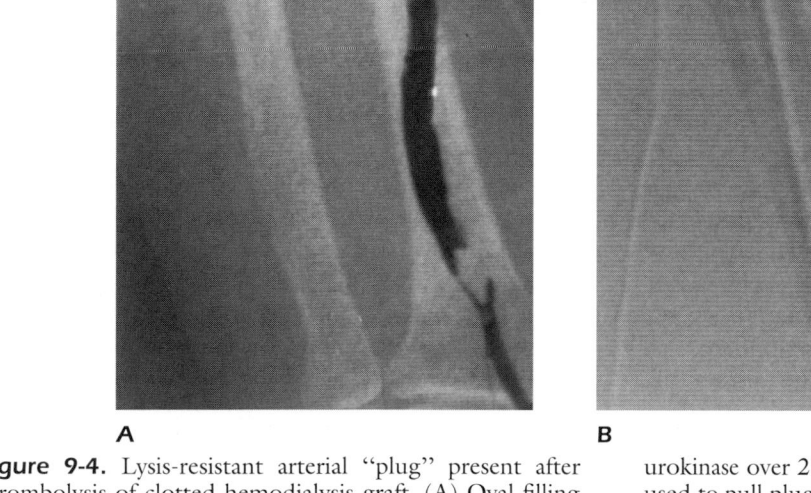

B

Figure 9-4. Lysis-resistant arterial "plug" present after thrombolysis of clotted hemodialysis graft. (A) Oval filling defect in proximal portion of the graft with otherwise complete clot lysis after pulse-spray therapy with 250,000 IU of urokinase over 20 minutes. (B) Occlusion balloon has been used to pull plug into midportion of graft; residual material was then macerated with a 6-mm dilatation balloon.

Specific Applications of Thrombolytic Therapy

Pelvic and Lower Extremity Arteries

By far the largest experience with noncoronary thrombolysis has been gained in the treatment of peripheral arterial occlusions. Table 9-2 summarizes the recent major clinical series in which UK was used to treat lower extremity occlusive disease.[61-67] The most frequently treated sites are the iliac and femoropopliteal arteries. Aortic thrombosis has also been successfully managed with thrombolytic techniques.[68] There is limited experience to date with treatment of occluded tibial and pedal vessels, although the same general principles are applicable.[24]

Technical success, defined as recanalization of the artery and clearing of about 90 to 95 percent of the occlusion with restoration of antegrade flow, is achieved in about 60 to 80 percent of cases using UK infusion therapy. With infusion methods, lysis times usually range from 18 to 24 hours. High-dose infusion therapy has not been consistently shown to improve technical efficacy over low-dose regimens, although many practitioners prefer the former. Similar technical results have been achieved with tPA but with a higher frequency of bleeding complications (20 percent).[29,35] Technical success can be achieved in greater than 95 percent of cases using PSPMT.[69,70] Pulse-spray therapy significantly accelerates clot dissolution, reducing lysis time to about 1 to 3 hours (Figs. 9-2 and 9-5).

Thrombolysis is more likely to be successful with short occlusions and with the presence of at least one runoff vessel below the occlusion. Clot age should not be considered a major factor in selecting patients for thrombolysis as long as the thrombus has not organized sufficiently to prevent passage of a guidewire and catheter. However, although clot age may not be an important determinant for success in occlusions less than 6 months old,[67,71] several studies have shown a significant reduction in technical success and long-term patency for occlusions older than 6 months.[35,72]

A poor outcome from transcatheter therapy may be anticipated with inability to traverse the occlusion with

Table 9-2. Thrombolytic Therapy with Urokinase for Peripheral Arterial Occlusions

Source (year)	Cases	Method	Dose (× 1000 IU)	Technical Success (%)	Lysis Time (hr)
McNamara, 1985[10]	61	Infusion	120–240/hr	81	18.0
Pilger, 1986[61]	30	Infusion	48/hr	80	2.1
Pernes, 1987[62]	46	Infusion	50–80/hr	75	11.0
van Breda, 1987[63]	24	Infusion	40–60/hr	80	22.0
Koltun, 1987[21]	35	Infusion	60/hr	71	36.0
Katzen, 1988[64]	125	Infusion	40–100/hr	85	20.0
Motarjeme, 1989[65]	276	Infusion	60/hr	80	24.0
Eisenbud, 1990[66]	27	Infusion	40 bolus 60–240/hr	56	23.0
Cragg, 1991[42]	17	Infusion	50/hr	65	26.0
	17	Infusion	125–250/hr	70	21.0
LeBlang, 1992[57]	72	Infusion	50–150/hr	94	20.0
Bookstein, 1992[67]	37	Pulse-spray	5–10/min	97	1.9

a guidewire, subintimal dissection during therapy, the presence of organized thrombus, rethrombosis occurring during lysis (Fig. 9-6), lack of adequate inflow to or outflow from the treated segment, the presence of a hypercoagulable state (Fig. 9-7), or significant residual disease after thrombolysis and angioplasty.

Patients with severe acute limb ischemia pose a difficult challenge. Thrombolysis has been found effective in such patients, with a 70 to 85 percent technical success rate and an amputation rate below 10 percent.[66,73] A recent review of the published experience indicated a 1.9 percent cumulative mortality rate after infusion thrombolysis in this patient population.[73] However, the time required for successful infusion thrombolysis may be prohibitive in some of these patients. Many have widespread thrombotic disease with occlusion of several or all tibial arteries and extensive disease in pedal vessels. Blood flow must be reestablished without delay to avoid or limit amputation. In particular, patients with sensorimotor deficits are at particular risk for limb loss if circulation is not restored rapidly. Accelerated thrombolysis with PSPMT has been found particularly useful in this subgroup of patients.[74]

Peripheral embolism represents a special category of peripheral vascular obstruction. Although it may be difficult to distinguish embolic occlusions from thrombotic ones, suggestive features include multiple separate branch occlusions, the absence of large collateral vessels, a convex margin at the proximal extent of oc-

clusion, a history of atrial fibrillation, known left atrial or ventricular thrombus, and acute onset of symptoms. Embolic occlusions may respond to thrombolytic therapy more readily than thrombotic occlusions because much of the occlusion is composed of fresh clot.[73] However, the treatment of embolic occlusions is somewhat controversial. Prolonged intraarterial UK infusions have the potential to cause further lysis of the original embolic source (usually within the heart), which may lead to repeated embolization. Although this complication has been described in case reports,[75] the vast majority of patients with embolic occlusions treated by thrombolytic infusion have not developed further emboli during therapy. The use of pulse-spray methods minimizes the systemic effects of fibrinolytics and may be especially advantageous in such cases.

Several studies have shown significantly higher rates of technical success with embolic occlusions.[35] On the other hand, emboli may consist of material that is not amenable to balloon angioplasty (e.g., organized clot or atherosclerotic plaque). Balloon angioplasty poses a significant risk of distal embolization if unlysable intraluminal material is dilated. If large intraluminal residua are present, directional atherectomy may be useful in removing residual disease. Otherwise, surgical embolectomy is usually required.

The long-term success of thrombolysis of peripheral lower extremity occlusions has not been thoroughly evaluated. Reports from large series of treated peripheral arterial occlusions have noted a 6-month patency

Figure 9-5. Pulse-spray thrombolysis of acute popliteal artery occlusion in a 47-year-old man. (A) Arteriogram shows complete occlusion of left popliteal artery. (B) Following PSPMT with 250,000 IU of urokinase, partial lysis is noted. (C) Treatment with a total of 400,000 IU of urokinase over 50 minutes demonstrates minimal additional lysis with residual mural disease present. (D) Widely patent popliteal artery following balloon angioplasty. No distal emboli were identified on runoff study. ▶

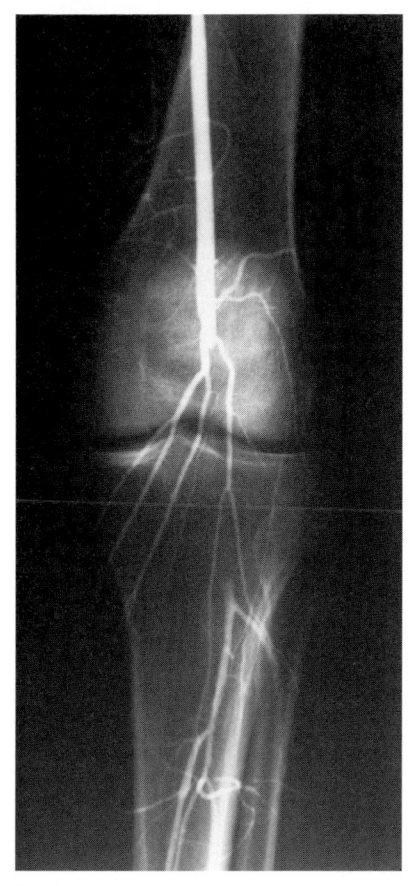

A

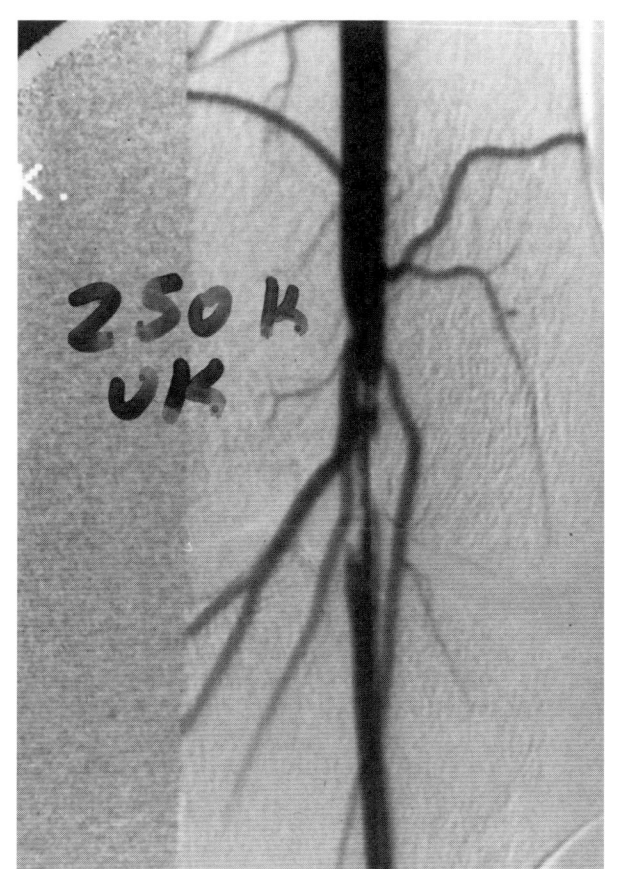

B

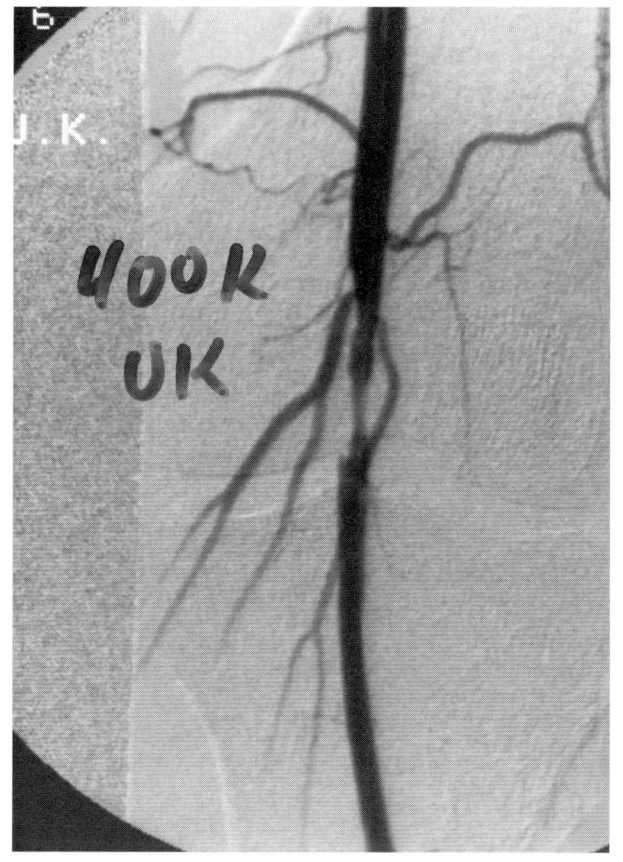

C

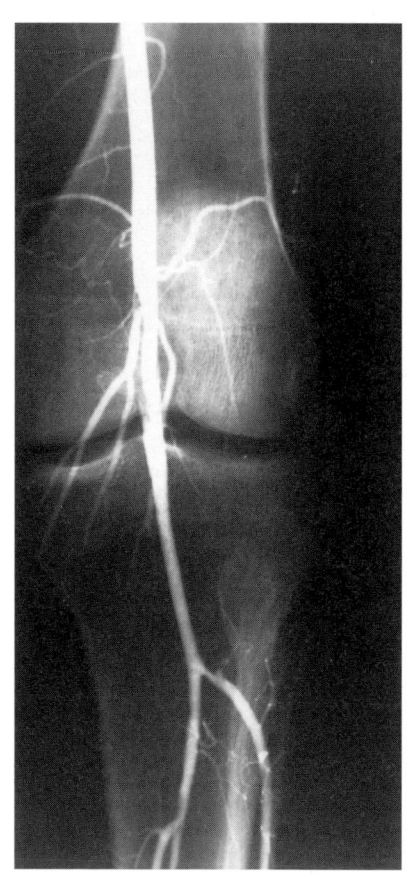

D

141

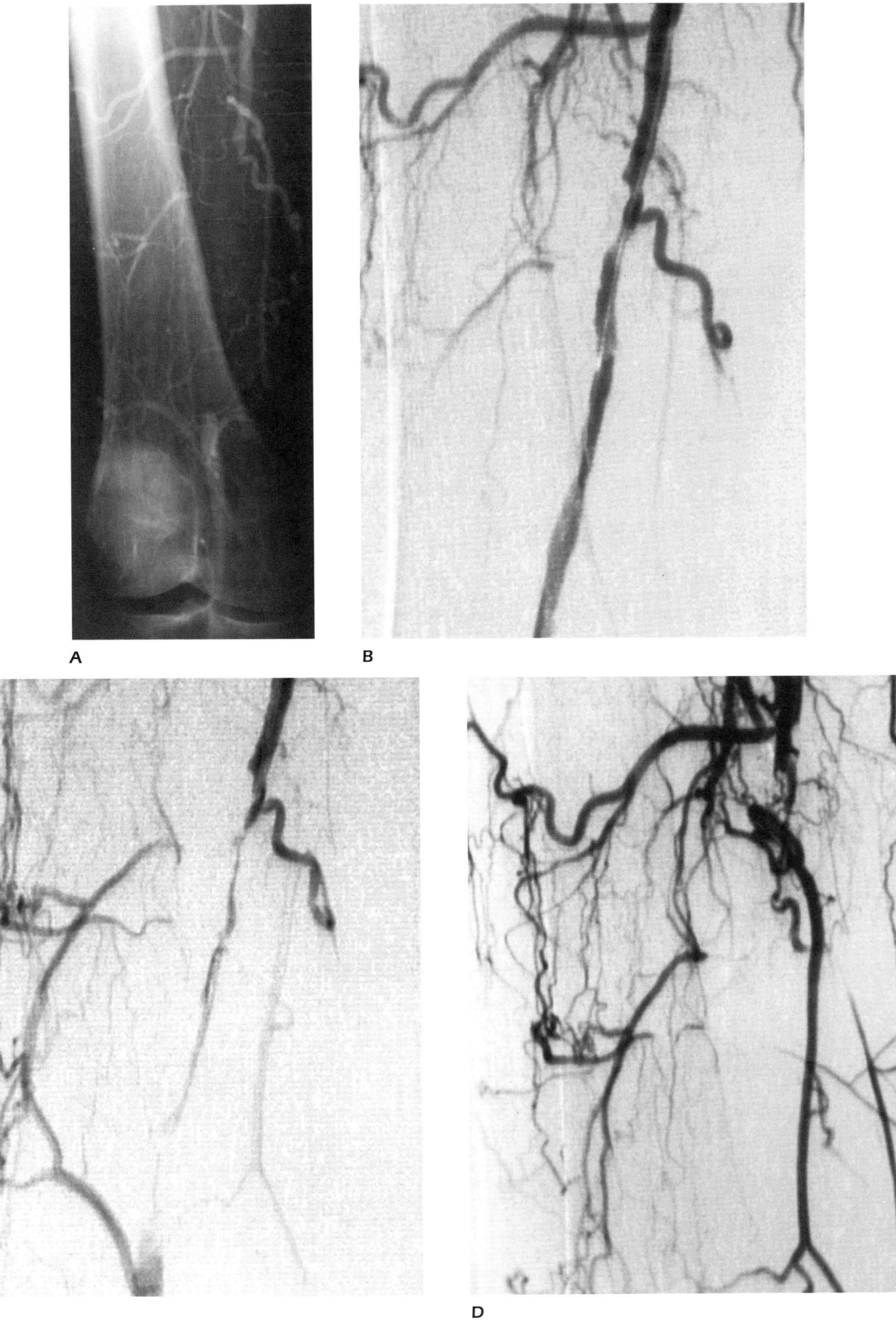

A

B

C

D

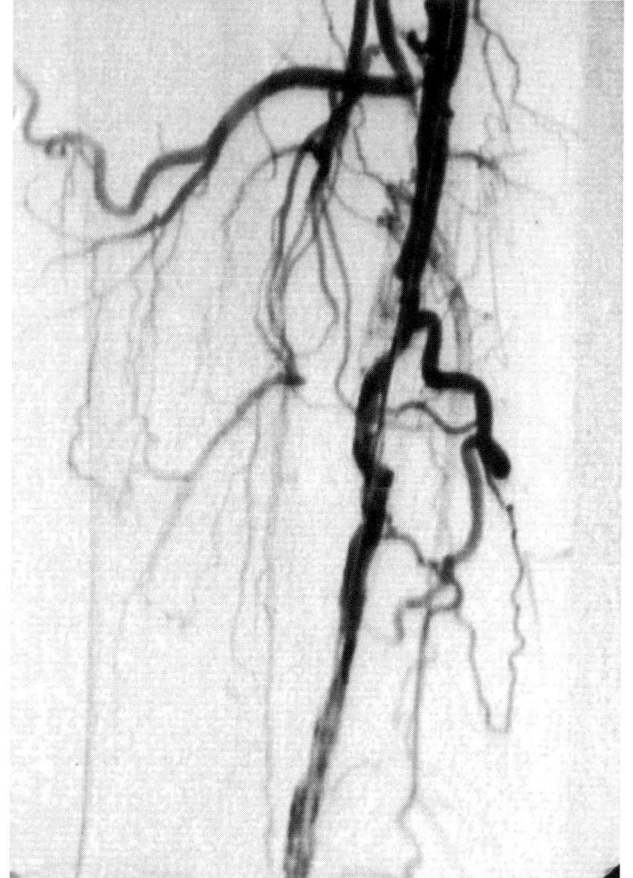

E

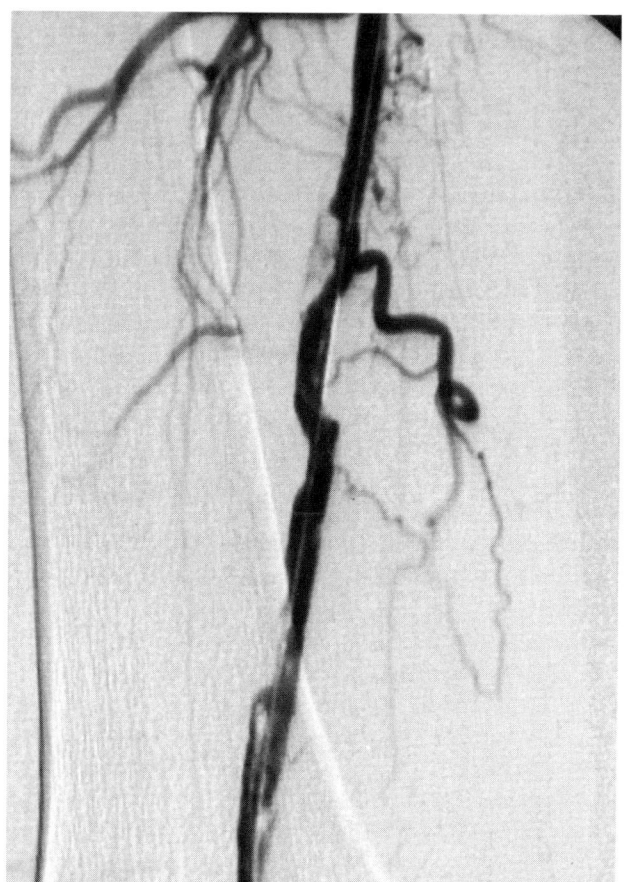

F

Figure 9-6. Rethrombosis during pulse-spray thrombolysis due to inadequate anticoagulation. (A) Arteriogram shows short distal right superficial femoral artery occlusion. (B) Pulse-spray thrombolysis with urokinase produced substantial lysis with minimal residual disease. (C) Arteriogram obtained immediately after (B) shows rethrombosis of treated segment. Patient had not received aspirin or adequate heparin therapy. (D) Arteriogram after overnight infusion of urokinase shows persistent occlusion. (E) Partial recanalization of artery after repeated pulse-spray therapy, full anticoagulation with heparin, and low-molecular-weight dextran infusion. (F) Additional treatment with urokinase shows minimal further lysis of clot. (G) Final arteriogram after balloon angioplasty shows a widely patent superficial femoral artery.

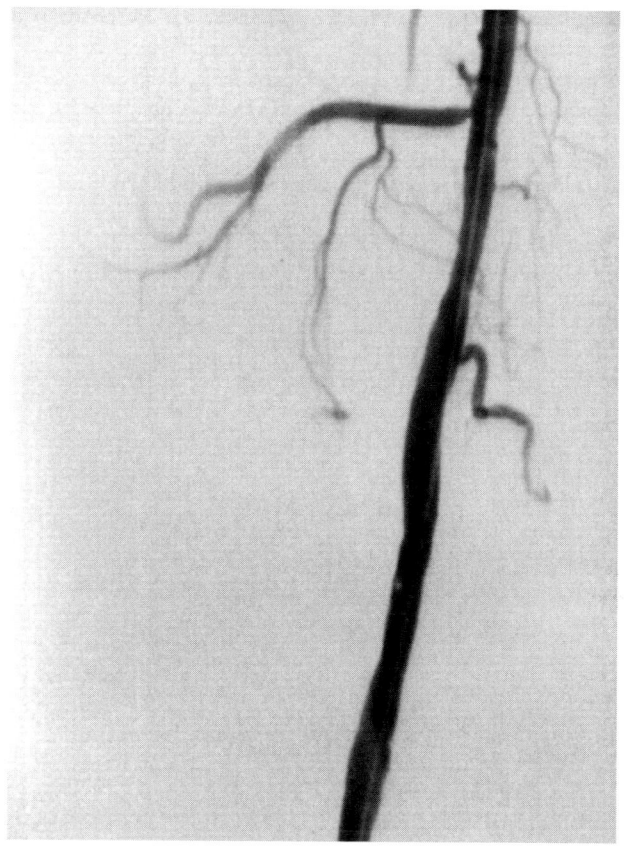

G

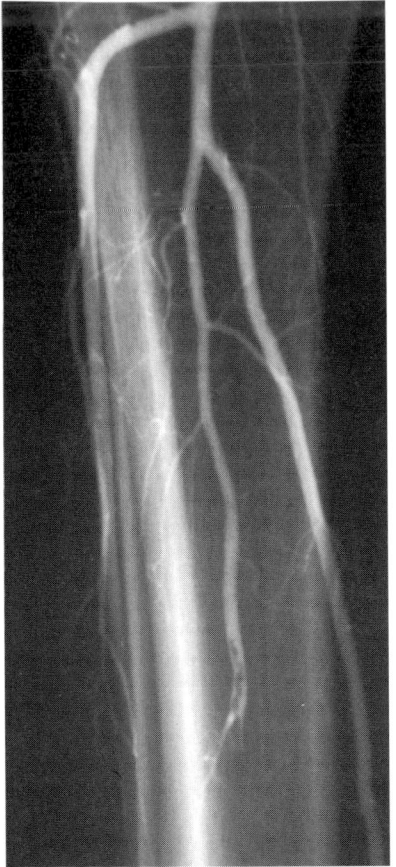

A

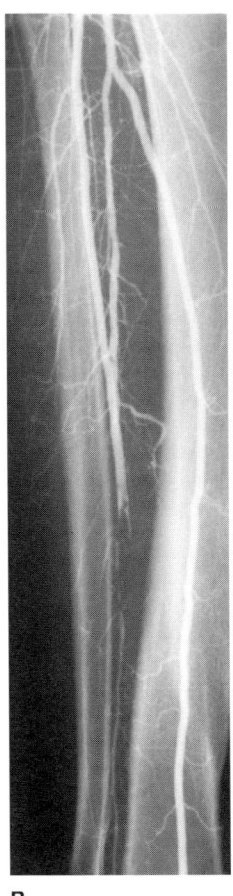

B

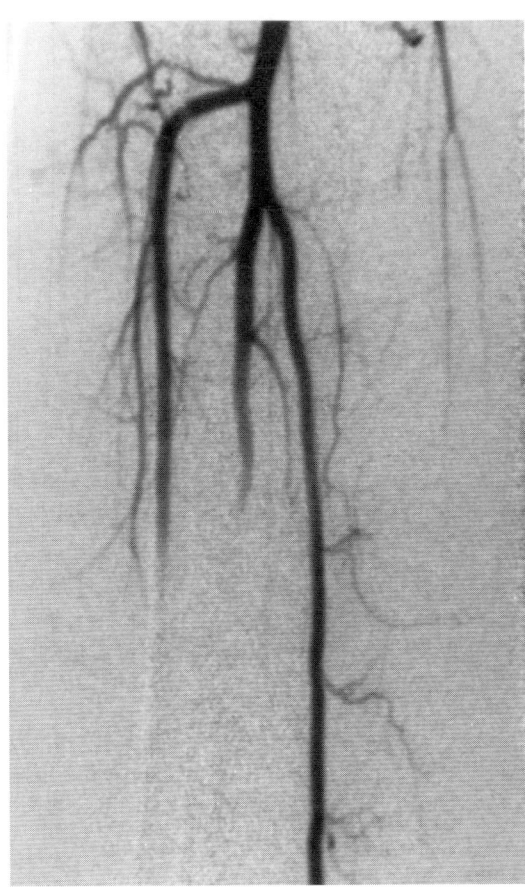

C

Figure 9-7. Poor response to thrombolysis due to hypercoagulable state in a 38-year-old woman with metastatic melanoma and thrombocytosis. (A) Right lower extremity arteriogram reveals emboli or in situ thrombosis in peroneal and anterior tibial arteries. (B) Almost no response to thrombolysis is noted after pulse-spray injections with 720,000 IU of urokinase. The patient was being treated with heparin, aspirin, and low-molecular-weight dextran. (C) After overnight infusion of 1.4 million IU of urokinase into the popliteal artery, no significant lysis is noted.

rate of 45 percent,[76] a 1-year patency rate of 50[77] and 83 percent,[78] and a 2-year patency rate of 18[72] and 72 percent.[79] These inconsistent results reflect varying definitions of long-term patency, the exclusion of initial treatment failures or lack of objective evidence for vessel patency in some series, and a combination of results from different arterial sites.

Several factors may affect the durability of treated arteries after thrombolysis. Browse et al. found that the 1-year patency rate was significantly greater for occlusions less than 1 week old (71 percent) than for older occlusions (36 percent).[77] McNamara and Bomberger noted that 6-month patency rates were higher for iliac arteries (92 percent) than for femoral arteries (50 percent).[76] Decrinis and coworkers observed that treated embolic occlusions had better long-term patency than thrombotic occlusions.[35]

Peripheral Bypass Grafts

Recent advances in the practice of vascular surgery have improved the long-term patency of peripheral bypass grafts. The 3-year patency rate of infrainguinal in situ saphenous vein grafts is greater than 80 percent.[80,81] Vein bypass grafts to small vessels in the foot are becoming routine. Periodic surveillance of grafts, using such techniques as color Doppler sonography, can significantly increase their longevity. Similarly, Cohen and coworkers noted an 82 percent cumulative 5-year patency rate for failing grafts that were revised before thrombosis occurred, compared with a 28 percent 5-year patency rate for occluded grafts that required surgical thrombectomy and revision.[82]

However, despite efforts to maintain graft patency, graft thrombosis remains a vexing problem. About 3 to 5 percent of in situ saphenous vein grafts fail within

Table 9-3. Thrombolytic Therapy of Peripheral Bypass Grafts

Source (year)	Cases	Method	Agent	Dose (× 1000 IU for UK)	Technical Success (%)	Lysis Time (hr)
Graor, 1988[84]	22	Infusion	tPA	0.05–0.10 mg/kg/hr	86	4–5
Durham, 1989[56]	71	Infusion	UK	100/hr	75	20
Motarjeme, 1989[65]	35	Infusion	UK	60/hr	83	—
Eisenbud, 1990[66]	40	Infusion	UK	40 bolus 60–240/hr	66	23
Sullivan, 1991[85]	43	Infusion	UK	30–250 bolus 60–240/hr	88	22
Seabrook, 1991[86]	30	Infusion	UK	30–240/hr	100	3–40
Bookstein, 1992[67]	25	Pulse-spray	UK	5–10/min	97	1.9
Guest, 1992[87]	29	Infusion	tPA	5mg q10 min	69	2.5
Miller, 1992[15]	23	Infusion	UK	125–250/hr 0.05 mg/kg/hr	91	—
LeBlang, 1992[57]	60	Infusion	UK	50–150/hr	97	20

1 month of operation, usually because of inadequate outflow, technical error, or abnormalities of the venous conduit.[82,83] Late graft occlusion is noted in about 4 percent of cases despite aggressive surveillance; the most common causes for failure are thromboembolism and low flow states.

Thrombolysis has been found to be an effective means of recanalizing occluded peripheral bypass grafts. The results of recently reported large series are given in Table 9-3. Technical success is achieved in about 70 to 90 percent of cases. Therapy with UK usually requires 20 to 24 hours of infusion. In several series, local tPA infusion has been found to produce more rapid lysis (2–5 hours).[84,87] Thrombolysis is most effective with PSPMT, which enables graft recanalization in more than 95 percent of cases with a mean lysis time just under 2 hours (Fig. 9-8).[67]

There are several advantages of thrombolytic therapy over surgical thrombectomy and revision. Complete clot lysis can be achieved with thrombolytic techniques. Damage to the endothelium of vein grafts is minimized by avoiding Fogarty embolectomy. Fibrinolytic agents may lyse clot in vessels distal to the graft in areas that are inaccessible to embolectomy. In some cases, balloon angioplasty of underlying stenoses will provide definitive therapy. When transcatheter techniques are inadequate, a limited operation may be performed guided by angiographic findings following lysis (Fig. 9-9).[88]

After thrombolysis, an underlying anatomic cause for occlusion can be found in 50 to 90 percent of patients.[56,85,86,88] The most common reasons for graft failure are intragraft stenoses, distal or proximal anastomotic stenoses, diffuse graft disease, native proximal or distal arterial stenoses, and poor distal runoff. Addi-

tional causes of graft failure include emboli, technical errors, and persistent fistulas.

Although most grafts can be reopened with thrombolysis, the 1-year primary patency rate after thrombolysis of occluded bypass grafts is about 20 to 60 percent.[15,84,85,89] Hye and coworkers noted a 28 percent primary patency rate at 30 months for 33 occluded grafts treated with PSPMT.[90] On the other hand, long-term results after surgical thrombectomy and revision are also poor. Cohen et al. noted a 28 percent 5-year patency rate after reoperation of occluded vein grafts.[82] Ascer and coworkers noted a 3-year patency rate of 16 percent for reoperated infrainguinal polytetrafluoroethylene (PTFE) grafts.[91] Graor et al. found that for synthetic infrainguinal bypass grafts the long-term results of thrombolytic therapy and directed surgery were similar to those from surgical thrombectomy and revision.[84] These poor results after operative repair are probably due to a combination of factors, including permanent vessel wall injury from ischemia, endothelial injury from Fogarty embolectomy,[92] and incomplete clot extraction.

Because only modest long-term results can be expected with transcatheter therapy, proper selection of patients is important. Some studies have shown that technical success is more likely with prosthetic graft occlusions,[90] suprainguinal grafts,[65] and recent occlusions.[56] On the other hand, Sullivan et al. found that graft age, location, and clot age had little effect on immediate outcome.[85] Failure of therapy is usually due to rethrombosis, graft infection, organized clot, diffuse graft disease, inability to correct an underlying lesion, or intraprocedural complications that prevent complete therapy (bleeding or graft dissection).[85] Long-term patency is greater for vein grafts,[85] grafts

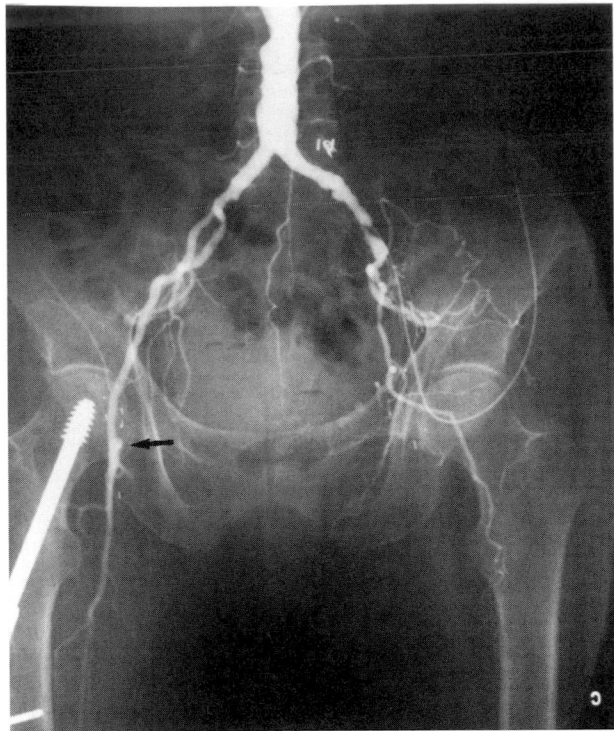

A

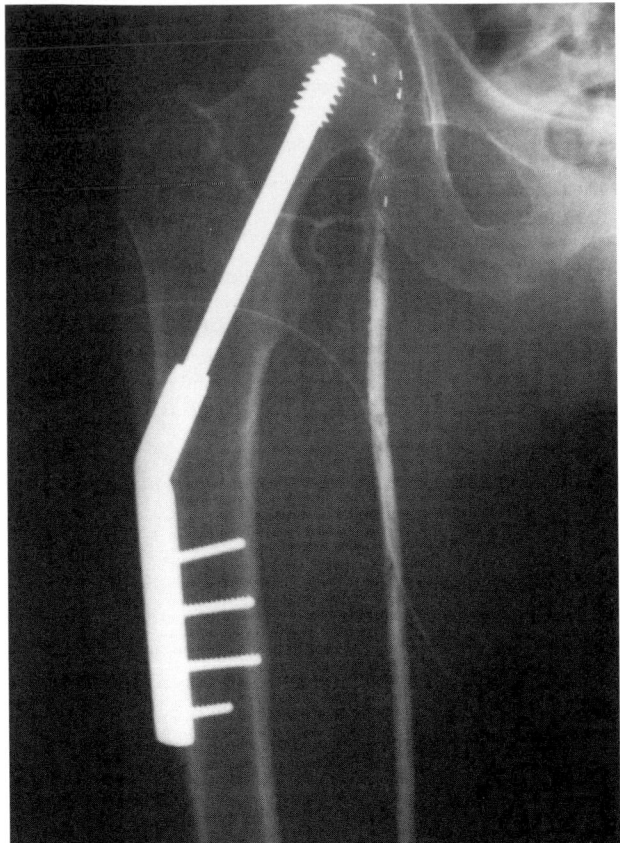

B

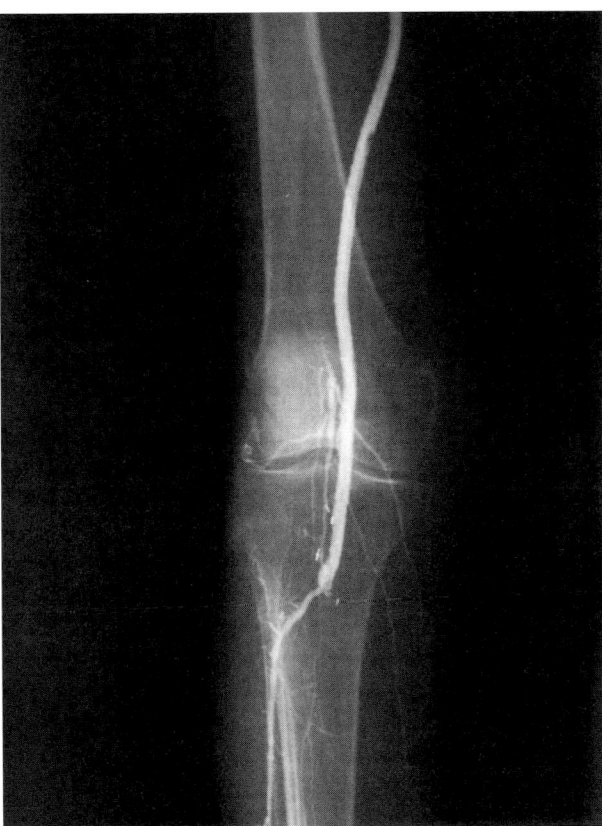

C

Figure 9-8. Pulse-spray thrombolysis of occluded right femoropopliteal synthetic graft in a 79-year-old woman. (A) Diagnostic arteriogram shows graft occlusion (*arrow*). (B) Pulse-spray therapy performed by direct graft puncture and criss-cross catheter technique. Nearly complete lysis is noted after 60 minutes of treatment with urokinase. (C) Graft and distal anastomosis are widely patent after thrombolysis and balloon angioplasty.

with underlying correctable lesions,[23] and grafts that have been functional for a long period.[90] Other studies have shown that long-term patency cannot be predicted by the presence of diabetes, hypertension, smoking, graft age, or graft type.[84] Durham et al. found no independent variable that predicted significantly better long-term patency.[56] Miller et al. was able to achieve a 70 percent 1-year secondary patency rate for successfully lysed grafts by careful graft surveillance using frequent color Doppler sonography.[15]

Hemodialysis Grafts

Thrombosis of vascular access grafts is a major problem for patients on chronic hemodialysis. Access grafts have a high rate of failure, with a 60 to 70 percent patency of synthetic grafts at 1 year.[93] As patients are being maintained on hemodialysis for longer periods of time, the need for preserving access sites has become more critical.

Thrombolysis of clotted hemodialysis access devices was attempted as early as the 1960s. Early methods of treatment by infusion of SK or UK were often unsuccessful because the underlying disease was not treated.[94,95] Local infusion therapy followed by balloon angioplasty of stenoses led to better results.[96–99] However, these techniques failed to compete with surgical thrombectomy and revision because prolonged infusions were required and bleeding complications were frequent.

Dialysis graft thrombolysis became practical with the development of PSPMT by Bookstein and Valji.[100–102] The efficacy of the technique has been confirmed by other investigators.[93,103] The cardinal features of the method include the following:

- Cross-catheter technique to allow access to the entire clot and graft inflow and outflow
- Rapid intrathrombic injection of a single dose of UK (250,000 IU) and heparin (5000 U) over 10 to 15 minutes
- Mobilization of lysis-resistant clot at the arterial anastomosis by withdrawal of an inflated occlusion balloon from the artery into the graft
- Maceration of residual clot with a dilatation balloon
- Identification and treatment of underlying stenoses from the arterial inflow to central venous outflow
- Long-term aspirin therapy to prevent restenosis and/or rethrombosis[104]

All thrombosed hemodialysis grafts are considered for PSPMT unless there are contraindications to therapy (see above). Surgical revision is preferred if operative revision has been performed within 2 weeks or if frequent, repeated trials of PSPMT have been required to maintain graft function.

Of 284 occluded grafts referred for treatment over a 6-year period, 10 failed to undergo complete therapy because of inability to cross the venous anastomosis (8 cases), extravasation during initial thrombolysis (1 case), and development of a large perigraft hematoma (1 case). Urokinase therapy was terminated in 2 cases because of perigraft bleeding. Of 274 cases that underwent complete therapy, lysis was achieved in 272 instances with 96 percent of all treated grafts patent at 24 hours. The mean lytic infusion time has been reduced to 23 minutes in the last several years, and the mean total procedure time is about 90 minutes (Fig. 9-10).

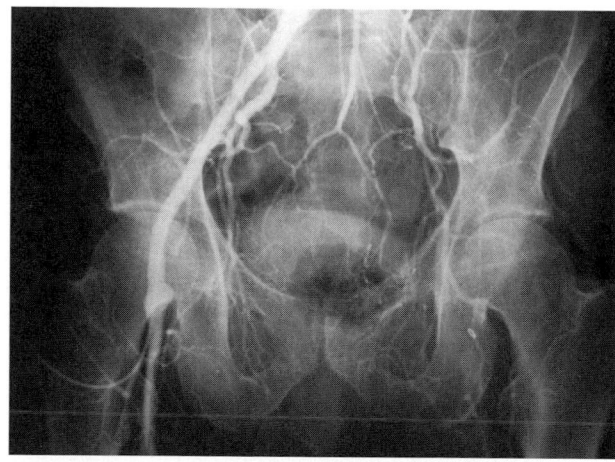

A

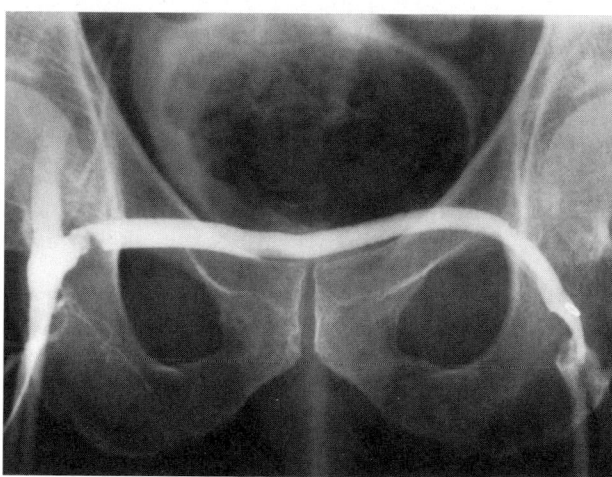

B

Figure 9-9. Treatment of occluded right-to-left femoro-femoral crossover graft in a 45-year-old man. (A) Initial arteriogram shows graft occlusion with prominent nipple at the right common femoral artery. (B) After graft access through the femoral artery and pulse-spray thrombolysis, complete clot dissolution is noted. Residual stenoses at both anastomoses were not responsive to balloon angioplasty. Elective graft revision was performed at a later date.

Underlying obstructions warranting angioplasty were found at the venous anastomosis (79 percent), at the arterial anastomosis or inflow (13 percent), at the venous outflow (20 percent), and within the graft (6 percent) (Figs. 9-11 and 9-12).

Long-term results with PSPMT for dialysis grafts have been favorable. Of 117 grafts treated by pharmacomechanical thrombolysis and angioplasty, the primary and secondary patency rates at 1 year were 26 and 51 percent, respectively.[101] These results are comparable to the 60 to 70 percent patency rate reported for surgical revision at 1 year.[105,106]

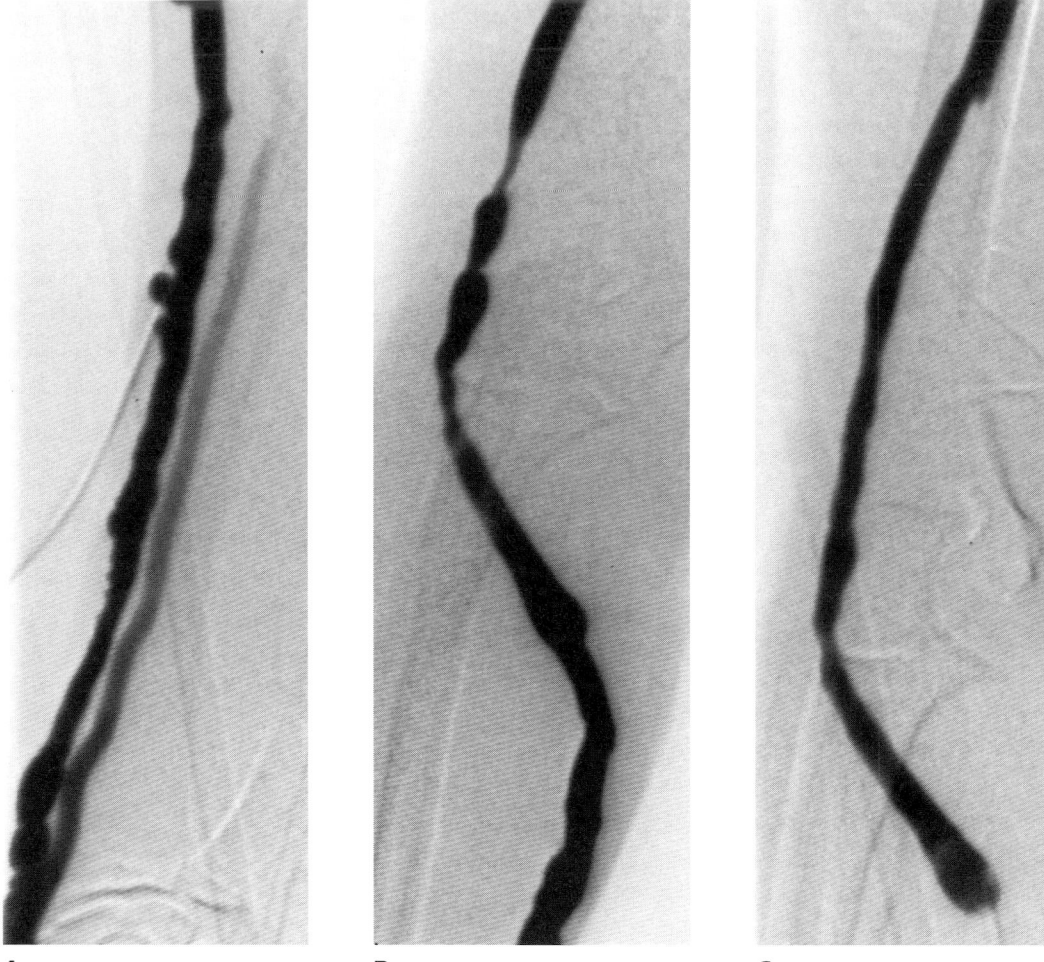

A　　　　　　　　**B**　　　　　　　　**C**

Figure 9-10. Pulse-spray thrombolysis of clotted hemodialysis graft. (A) Complete clot lysis is noted after treatment with 250,000 IU of urokinase over 30 minutes. Small pseudoaneurysms at dialysis puncture sites are seen throughout the graft. (B) Two significant stenoses are noted at and just beyond the venous anastomosis. (C) A good result from balloon angioplasty of the stenoses is achieved. (From Valji K, Roberts AC, Bookstein JJ. Thrombosed hemodialysis access grafts: management with pulse-spray thrombolysis and balloon angioplasty. In: Strandness ER, van Breda A, eds. Vascular diseases: surgical and interventional therapy. New York: Churchill-Livingstone, 1993:1087–1096. Used with permission.)

Upper Extremity Arteries

Although arterial thrombosis is a far less common problem in the arm than in the leg, the management of upper extremity occlusions is often more complex. Operative approaches to occlusive upper extremity disease include embolectomy, proximal bypass surgery, and microvascular reconstruction for distal thromboses. However, surgical therapy is often not feasible, and amputation may be required in a substantial number of cases.[107,108]

Early attempts at thrombolytic therapy of upper extremity occlusions using streptokinase often required 2 to 4 days of infusion (Fig. 9-13) and were often un-successful.[109] Results of local infusion of urokinase have been more encouraging.[110-112] Thrombolysis has been used successfully in the treatment of atherosclerotic and embolic occlusions, occluded upper extremity grafts, thoracic outlet syndrome, arteritis, thrombosis of brachial catheterization sites, posttraumatic thrombosis,[113] and thrombosis resulting from self-administration of illicit drugs.[109]

Successful therapy depends significantly on the duration of occlusion, with occlusions less than 2 days old responding most favorably.[109,110,112] Accelerated thrombolysis with PSPMT offers the same advantages in the upper extremity as in the leg (Fig. 9-14).[114]

Unlike disease in the leg, thrombosis is often exten-

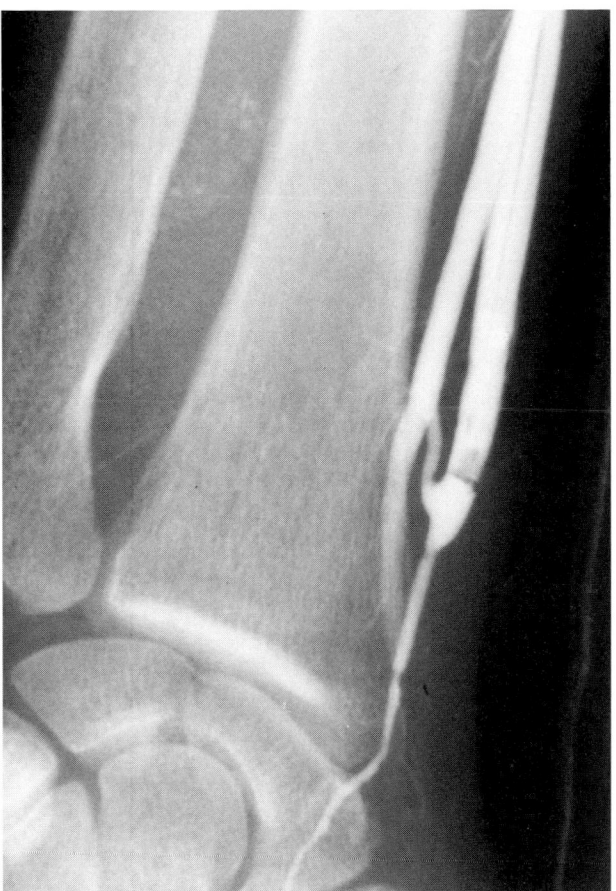

Figure 9-11. After treatment of an occluded dialysis graft with pulse-spray pharmacomechanical thrombolysis, an anastomosis between the graft and a small branch of the radial artery is found.

sive, with involvement of several forearm vessels, the palmar arch, and digital vessels, making operative therapy impractical. Therefore, UK infusion may be the preferred method of treatment. Clinically successful thrombolysis often requires 2 to 3 days of local infusion. Results of thrombolysis with pulse-spray or infusion methods are often incomplete. Nonetheless, most patients improve and have long-lasting benefit even when extensive disease is present, probably because collateral vessels are opened by the fibrinolytic agent.[109–112] Long-term anticoagulation is often required after successful lytic therapy.

One risk of thrombolysis of upper extremity occlusions not encountered with lower extremity disease is embolic stroke from pericatheter clot. Full anticoagulation with heparin may not prevent this severe complication. Therefore, an antegrade brachial approach should be considered when distal disease is present.[111]

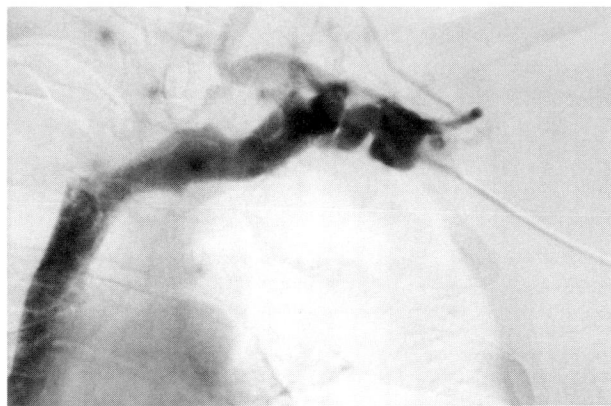

A

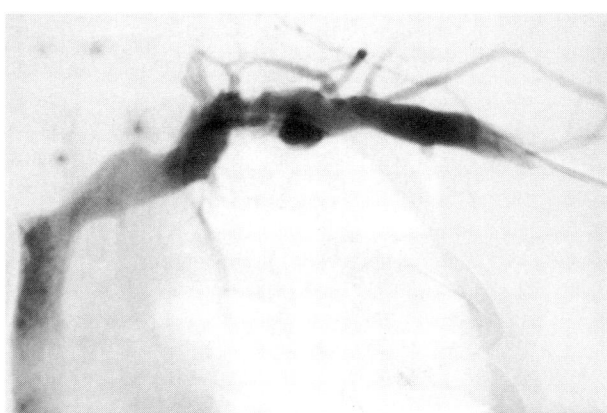

B

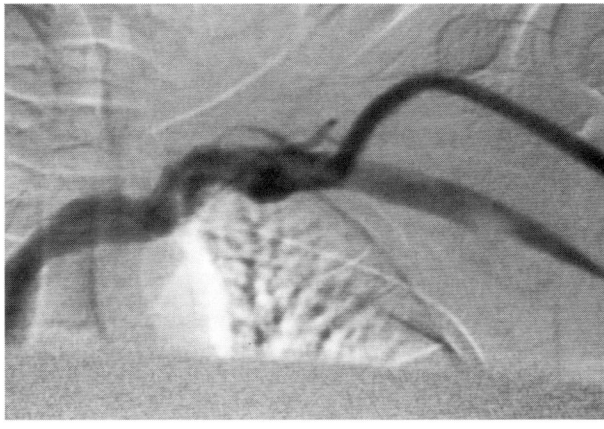

C

Figure 9-12. Central venous outflow stenosis in a 16-year-old girl identified after pulse-spray therapy of clotted hemodialysis graft. (A) Subclavian venogram demonstrates irregular stenosis of the midsubclavian vein with a 4-mmHg gradient. (B) Following angioplasty with a 12-mm balloon, the stenosis was largely resolved and the gradient fell to 1 mmHg. (C) Follow-up venogram 14 months after treatment shows wide patency of treated vessel. (Adapted from Bookstein JJ, Valji K, Roberts A, et al. Percutaneous recanalization of failing dialysis grafts: progress in thrombolytic and mechanical methods. In: Cope C, ed. Current techniques in interventional radiology. Philadelphia: Current Medicine, 1994:13.1–13.4. Used with permission.)

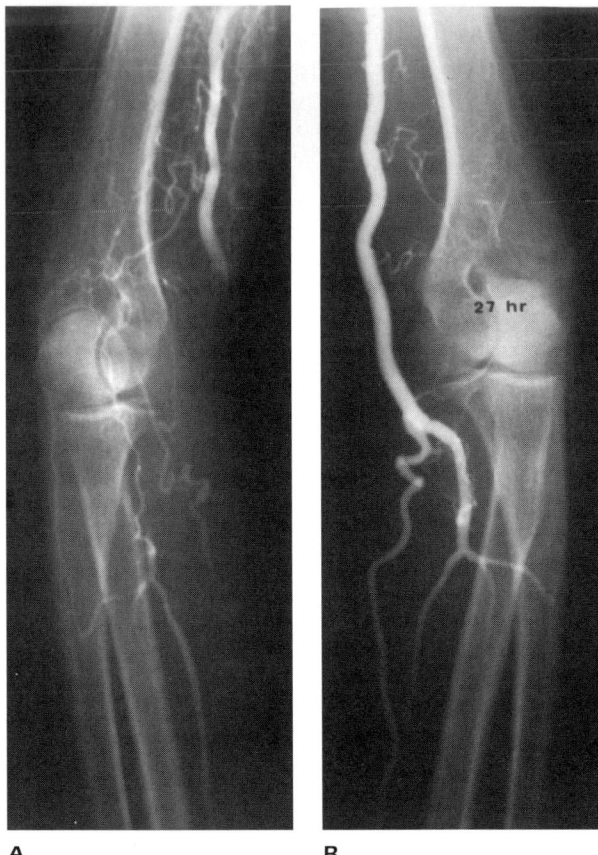

A   **B**

Figure 9-13. Local infusion thrombolysis for upper extremity arterial occlusion. (A) Arteriogram shows abrupt occlusion of the distal brachial artery with reconstitution below the elbow. (B) Following 27 hours of streptokinase infusion, complete clot lysis is observed.

Axillary and Subclavian Veins

There are several causes of central venous thrombosis.[115] Thrombosis may result from systemic disease or hypercoagulable states (e.g., local malignancy or radiation therapy). Central venous access devices are an increasingly frequent cause of subclavian or axillary vein thrombosis. Finally, primary or "effort" thrombosis accounts for 1 to 2 percent of cases and is due to extrinsic compression on the axillary or subclavian veins by muscles, tendons, or bony structures in the costoclavicular or subcoracoid spaces.[116] In most cases, repeated venous trauma or compression by these structures causes damage to the vein wall with subsequent thrombosis. Many of these patients will not respond to anticoagulation alone.

The diagnosis of subclavian or axillary vein thrombosis can be established by color Doppler sonography with a high degree of accuracy.[117] However, contrast upper arm venography is often necessary before treatment to establish the extent of disease. Many of these patients can be treated effectively with long-term anticoagulation and supportive therapy. Patients not responsive to conservative measures, those with underlying disease that predisposes to repeated thrombosis, and those with severe symptoms may benefit from clot dissolution or removal. Persistent symptoms of occlusion, including arm edema, exertional pain, or pulmonary embolism, may be present in 70 to 90 percent of patients with primary subclavian or axillary vein thrombosis.[118] Conventional treatment of subclavian or axillary vein thrombosis includes thrombectomy and correction of the underlying anatomic abnormality (e.g., first rib resection, division of the anterior scalene muscle, excision of the subclavius muscle) or autologous venovenous bypass.[119]

Thrombolytic therapy has recently become an accepted alternative to surgery in such patients.[120–122] After upper arm venography, local infusion or pulse-spray thrombolysis is performed through a sheath placed in an antecubital vein. Occasionally, access from the femoral vein may be necessary. Results of thrombolytic therapy have been encouraging.[123,124] Lysis is successful in most cases (Fig. 9-15). However, prolonged infusions over several days and large doses of UK (> 2 million units) are often required to achieve complete clot dissolution. Thrombolysis alone rarely provides long-term venous patency, but it allows time for the development of adequate collaterals to prevent recurrent symptoms. Most patients also require long-term anticoagulation to prevent repeated thrombosis.

Transluminal angioplasty is performed after thrombolysis to treat underlying stenoses. However, the long-term results of angioplasty of central venous stenoses are mixed.[125] Therefore, many patients require definitive surgical treatment of the underlying anatomic abnormality at some time after clot dissolution. Thrombolysis combined with delayed surgical decompression permits long-term benefit in over 75 percent of cases.[126]

Lower Extremity Veins

Anticoagulation with heparin is the treatment of choice for most patients with deep venous thrombosis of the lower extremity. Potential advantages of thrombolytic therapy in such patients include prompt symptomatic relief through rapid clot lysis, prevention of pulmonary embolism, and reduced vein wall and valve damage that predispose to the postphlebitic syndrome. Intravenous thrombolytic therapy with SK has been found to reduce the incidence of postphlebitic symptoms in patients with lower extremity deep venous thrombosis compared with heparin therapy alone.[127–129]

UK has also been found to be efficacious and has a lower frequency of hemorrhagic complications.[130] Although tPA has been shown to accelerate clot lysis compared with heparin therapy alone,[131] several trials using intravenous tPA at low and high doses have shown limited efficacy and bleeding complications in up to 30 percent of cases.[132,133] For these reasons, there has been little enthusiasm for the routine use of tPA

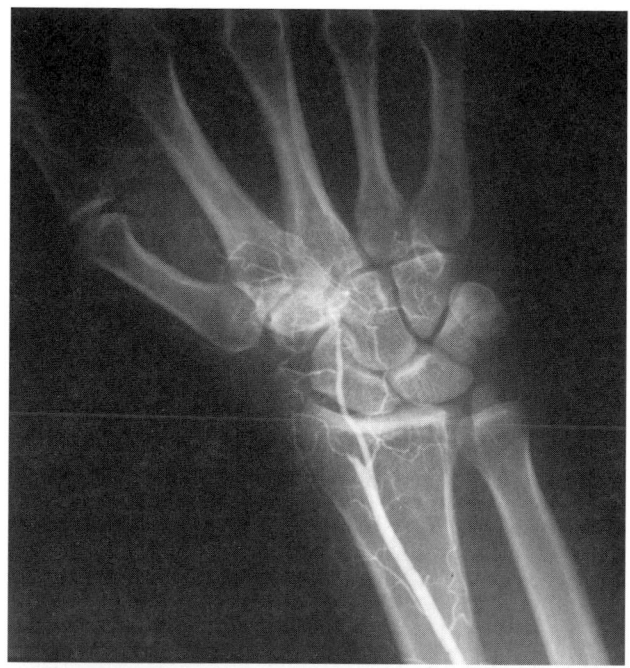

A

Figure 9-14. Pulse-spray thrombolysis of distal forearm arterial occlusion in a patient with Buerger disease. (A) Diagnostic study shows complete occlusion of the distal radial artery and palmar arch with collateral flow into the hand. (B) Pulse-spray thrombolysis with 200,000 IU of urokinase over 40 minutes reveals two segments of stenosis in the palmar arch. (C) Following balloon angioplasty, stenoses are resolved. Residual spasm is noted in the deep palmar arch, which otherwise fills normally. (From Lang EV, Bookstein JJ. Accelerated thrombolysis and angioplasty for hand ischemia in Buerger's disease. Cardiovasc Intervent Radiol 1989; 12:95–97. Used with permission.)

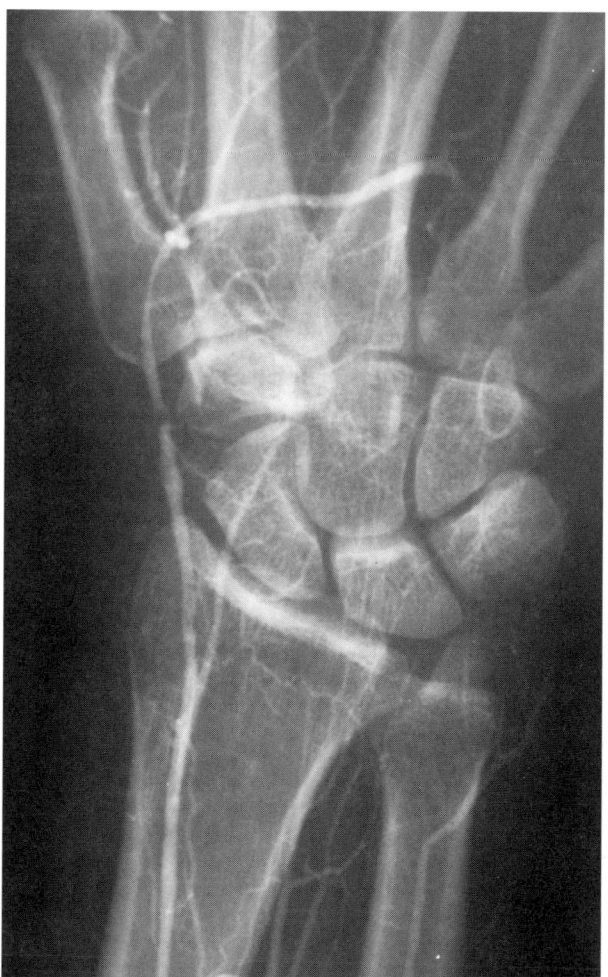

B

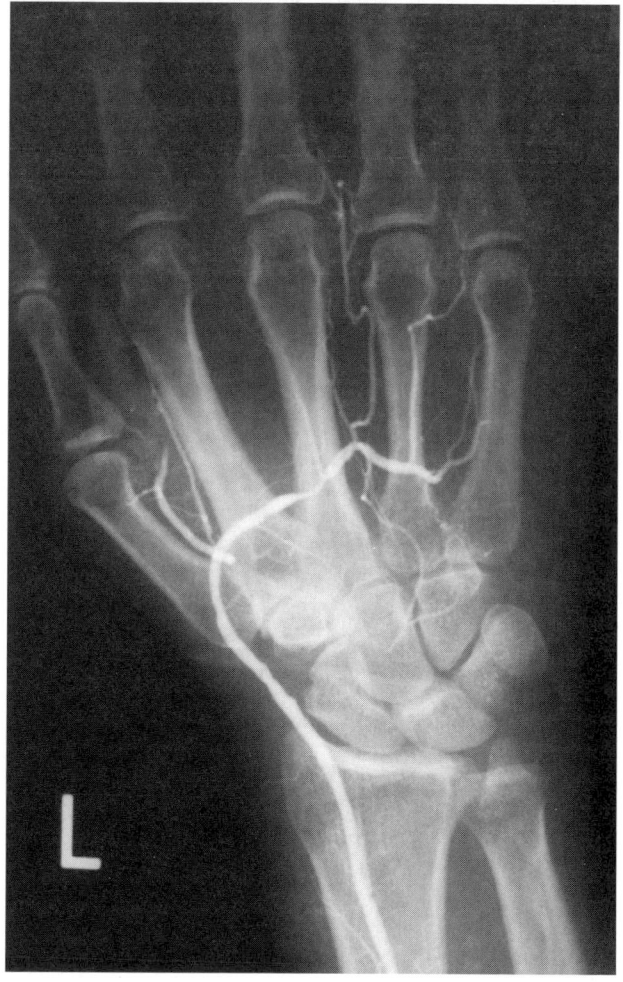

C

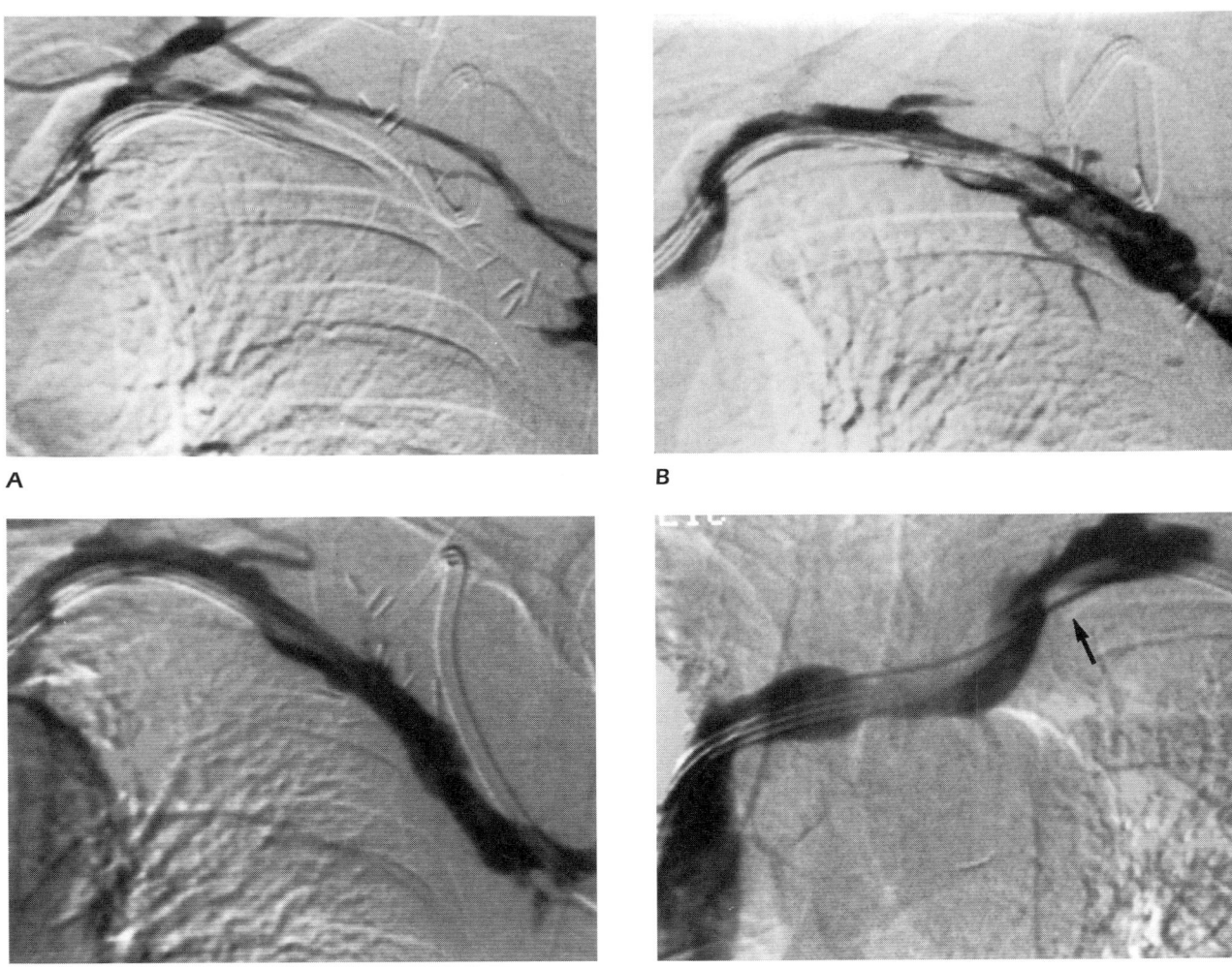

A

B

C

D

Figure 9-15. Pulse-spray and infusion thrombolysis of occluded subclavian vein in a 51-year-old woman with indwelling central venous catheter and hypercoagulable state from metastatic breast carcinoma. (A) Digital subtraction venogram shows complete left subclavian vein occlusion. (B) Following pulse-spray thrombolysis with 500,000 IU of urokinase, significant residual clot remains. (C) Overnight infusion of urokinase (total dose 1.7 million IU), low-molecular-weight dextran, and heparin enabled complete clot dissolution. (D) Underlying stenosis of subclavian vein at junction with jugular vein (*arrow*) following treatment with balloon angioplasty. The patient's arm swelling resolved and chronic anticoagulation was instituted.

in the treatment of lower extremity deep venous thrombosis.

Thrombolytic therapy may play an important role in patients with phlegmasia cerulea dolens. This syndrome is marked by complete thrombosis of one or both lower extremity venous systems, leading to pain, edema, cyanosis, and arterial insufficiency. Phlegmasia cerulea dolens is often associated with malignancy or with the presence of an inferior vena cava filter. Amputation is required in a significant number of cases, and the mortality from this disease has been estimated at 25 to 40 percent.[134] Thrombectomy or thrombolysis is usually indicated when symptoms fail to improve after 6 to 12 hours of anticoagulant therapy. Throm-

bolysis is particularly useful in patients presenting with venous gangrene, who virtually never respond to anticoagulation and supportive measures alone.[134] Several reports have described successful treatment of such patients with UK by local infusion[135] or pulse-spray therapy.[136]

Pulmonary Arteries

Most patients with pulmonary embolism only require treatment to prevent further embolization. Dissolution or direct removal of pulmonary emboli is rarely necessary. However, a small fraction of patients sustain acute massive pulmonary embolism that causes profound cardiovascular compromise and is associated with high mortality. Pulmonary embolectomy should be considered in these cases, particularly when there is a contraindication to fibrinolytic therapy or when the patient is too unstable to withstand a trial of thrombolysis. However, the overall mortality for surgical embolectomy when performed with cardiopulmonary bypass is about 30 to 40 percent.[137,138]

Results from phase I and phase II studies of the multicenter Urokinase Pulmonary Embolism Trial established that intravenous fibrinolytic agents were more effective than anticoagulation alone in the dissolution of pulmonary emboli, especially when clots were massive.[139,140] In those studies, significant improvement in angiographic abnormalities was observed in 9 percent of patients treated with heparin alone and in 53 percent of patients treated with UK. However, bleeding complications were frequent in both groups (27 and 45 percent, respectively). In addition, no significant difference in the final degree of resolution by radionuclide scanning, recurrence of pulmonary embolism, or mortality was found between the two treatment regimens.

The introduction of tPA has rekindled interest in thrombolytic therapy for pulmonary embolism. It has been shown to be a useful agent and more effective than UK[141] in the treatment of pulmonary embolic disease.[142] One popular protocol for the management of pulmonary emboli employs short-duration, high-dose intravenous tPA infusion.[143,144]

The optimal route for treating massive pulmonary emboli is subject to debate. Verstraete et al. found no added value to intrapulmonary tPA over intravenous administration.[142] However, several studies have shown significant benefit from intraarterial infusion of UK or SK with rapid improvement in cardiorespiratory function.[145–147] A bolus injection of tPA has been found to improve pulmonary perfusion compared with the standard 2-hour infusion.[148]

Renal Artery and Vein

Renal artery thrombosis usually results from underlying atherosclerotic disease, embolism, blunt abdominal trauma, dissection from catheterization or renal artery angioplasty, or complications of transplantation. Thrombolytic therapy with SK and UK has been applied in scattered cases of acute renal artery thrombosis[149–154] (Fig. 9-16) and to occluded renal artery grafts.[155] Muegge and coworkers recently reviewed the published experience with SK infusion in the treatment of renal artery occlusions.[156] Although lysis is successful in the majority of cases, full recovery of renal

function is unusual, and segmental renal infarctions are common.

Although results are most successful with fresh occlusions, lysis has been achieved in renal artery thromboses up to 7 days old. Although the warm ischemia time of explanted kidneys is about 3 hours, renal arteries have been successfully revascularized up to 6 weeks after occlusion.[157] Preservation of function largely depends on the extent of preexisting collateral blood flow through periureteric, capsular, lumbar, and inferior adrenal branches. In particular, late reconstitution of the distal renal artery by collateral vessels and the presence of a distinct nephrogram may predicate successful return of at least partial renal function after treatment. Flow may be insufficient for adequate renal function but sufficient to maintain organ viability. Therefore, thrombolysis is probably warranted even weeks after occlusion in a patient with suspected chronic renal artery disease. However, thrombolysis should not be delayed more than several hours in patients with probable acute occlusion (e.g., embolism or trauma).[158]

There has been limited experience with thrombolytic infusions for native renal vein thrombosis. Recanalization has been attempted in native kidneys using selective injection of SK or UK.[159] Although successful results have been achieved with preservation of renal function, prolonged infusions are often required.

Thrombosis of the vein in a transplanted kidney is a rare, potentially catastrophic event usually related to kinking of the vein, extension of lower extremity thrombophlebitis into the pelvic veins, or extrinsic compression by hematoma or lymphocele. To salvage the transplant and prevent spontaneous rupture, surgical thrombectomy or thrombolysis may be necessary. Thrombolysis for graft salvage by direct venous infusion has been successful in scattered cases.[160,161] Alternatively, renal vein thrombosis may be treated by infusion of fibrinolytic agents into the renal artery.[162]

Pediatric Applications

Vascular thromboses are rare in children, and therefore the experience with thrombolytic therapy in the pediatric population is limited. Ryan and Andrews[163] and Giacoia[164] recently published reports of thrombolysis in children. The majority of cases have involved neonates and infants with thrombosis of the aorta,[165–167] right atrium,[168,169] iliofemoral arteries,[170] or central veins.[171] In most cases, thrombosis resulted from indwelling vascular catheters, including umbilical artery, central venous, and extracorporeal membrane oxygenation devices. Surgical thrombectomy has been the

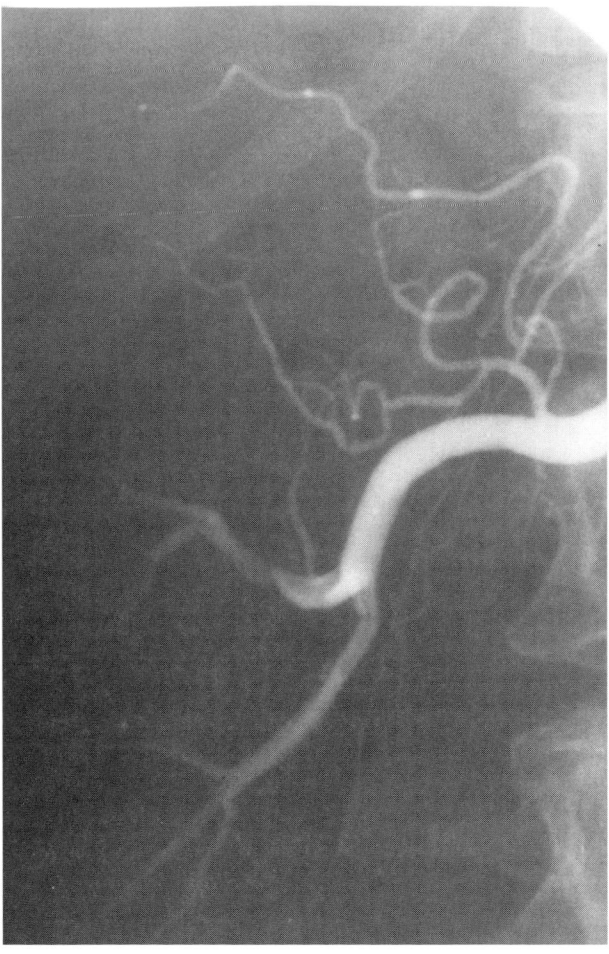

A

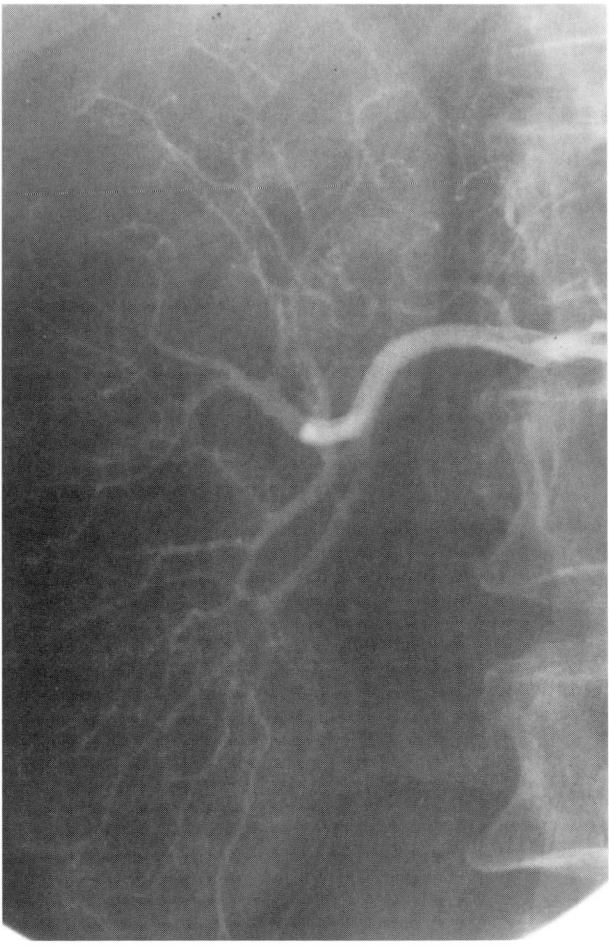

B

Figure 9-16. Infusion thrombolysis of renal artery embolus in patient with prosthetic mitral valve and history of cardiac arrhythmias. (A) Magnification renal arteriogram shows intraarterial thrombus extending into intraparenchymal branches. (B) After 24 hours of intraarterial streptokinase infusion at 5000 units per hour, repeat arteriography shows resolution of clot.

traditional treatment in these cases, particularly for aortoiliac thrombosis.[172]

Thrombolytic therapy using SK, UK, or tPA has been successful in most cases. The dose of plasminogen activator is usually extrapolated from adult regimens on a per kilogram basis. However, newborns may require larger doses of agents because of lower plasma concentrations of plasminogen and tPA and higher concentrations of plasminogen activator inhibitors compared with adults.[173,174]

Complications

The major complications resulting from thrombolytic therapy are bleeding, distal embolizations, allergic or idiosyncratic drug reactions, postreperfusion syn-drome, pericatheter thrombosis, and graft extravasation. Although current methods of thrombolysis rarely produce a systemic lytic state, fibrinolysis may occur at sites remote from the occluded vessel. The risk of hemorrhage with fibrinolytic therapy is compounded by the use of anticoagulants and aspirin. Minor bleeding at the puncture site is by far the most common complication of thrombolytic therapy for peripheral vascular occlusions and is reported in about 5 to 25 percent of cases.[42,56,57,66,85] Bleeding is usually self-limited and requires no further therapy. Hemorrhage requiring blood transfusion or surgical evacuation occurs in about 3 to 7 percent of cases.[42,56,57,85] The frequency of major bleeding complications is primarily related to the duration of infusion rather than the total dose of fibrinolytic agent. Bleeding may occur at sites with altered vascular integrity, including recent arterial punctures for catheterization, through surgical anastomoses, or through prosthetic graft material. Transgraft extravasation leading to significant hematoma formation has been reported with various types of graft material but is more common with Dacron grafts.[85,175] Hemorrhage at remote sites can largely be avoided by withholding treatment from patients with risk factors for bleeding (see above). Nonetheless, spontaneous intracranial, gastrointestinal, and retroperitoneal bleeding have been reported.

The risk of hemorrhage during PSPMT may be lower than for infusion thrombolysis. Reasons for this diminished risk include direct intrathrombic injection of fibrinolytic agents, reduced overall UK dose and time for infusion, and direct observation of patients during the entire course of therapy. In the treatment of peripheral arteries and bypass grafts using UK and PSPMT, Bookstein and Valji reported a 3 percent minor and 0.5 percent major bleeding rate, with no episodes of retroperitoneal or intracranial hemorrhage.[67] Minor perigraft bleeding is occasionally noted with treatment of dialysis fistulas, but major hemorrhagic complications are exceedingly unusual.

Distal embolization is the other major complication from thrombolytic therapy. Embolization is reported in 2 to 15 percent of patients treated for peripheral arterial occlusions.[42,56,57,73,85] However, angiographic assessment of distal vessels after the procedure was not routinely performed in all reported series. In many cases, the embolus consists of lysable material that can be treated successfully by local UK infusion. In a minority of cases, nonlysable material is embolized and surgical removal may be necessary.

There is a theoretical risk that distal embolization will occur more frequently with pharmacomechanical methods of thrombolysis because of the rapidity of lysis and early fragmentation of clot by the high-pressure spray. The incidence of distal embolization during PSPMT for occluded arteries and bypass grafts is 11 percent, a figure comparable to that after infusion thrombolysis.[67] Embolization can be minimized by avoiding angioplasty when large, clearly intraluminal filling defects are present after thrombolysis.[46]

The current method of PSPMT for clotted hemodialysis grafts involves rapid delivery of UK and early maceration of residual clot with a balloon catheter. Embolization of small clot fragments to the lung probably occurs in the majority of cases. However, symptomatic pulmonary embolism has not been definitely observed in any of the authors' cases. On the other hand, embolization of clot from the proximal portion of the graft into the efferent artery has been reported with PSPMT in several cases.[102] Embolization can be avoided by carefully manipulating guidewires and catheters within the proximal portion of the graft and by delaying angioplasty of residual clot near the arterial anastomosis until the plug is withdrawn into the body of the graft with an occlusion balloon.

Recently, idiosyncratic reactions to UK have been noted by many users.[176,177] The reaction has been reported in 10 to 30 percent of treatments and occurs more frequently with high-dose or bolus techniques. Symptoms usually develop 30 to 60 minutes after starting therapy and involve moderate to severe rigors, agitation, tachycardia, and occasionally nausea or vomiting. Several cases of severe hypotension and respiratory distress requiring intubation have also been reported. The nature of these reactions has not been established. Rigors respond promptly to 25 mg of intravenous meperidine. Anecdotal reports suggest that pretreatment with acetaminophen and antihistamines may prevent the reaction.

Revascularization complications that may occur after thrombolysis include compartment syndrome and the postrevascularization syndrome. Compartment syndrome is a rare complication after infusion thrombolysis and was seen in 4 percent of patients treated by McNamara et al. for acute lower extremity ischemia.[73]

Pericatheter thrombosis was a frequent problem in the early years of thrombolytic therapy. The routine use of systemic heparin has virtually eliminated this problem, but ongoing rethrombosis may occur in a small fraction of patients, particularly when a hypercoagulable state is present.

References

1. Tillett WS, Garner RI. The fibrinolytic activity of hemolytic streptococci. J Exp Med 1933;58:485–502.
2. MacFarlane RG, Pilling J. Observations of fibrinolysis: plasminogen, plasmin, and antiplasmin content of human blood. Lancet 1946;2:562–565.
3. Johnson AJ, Tillett WS. Lysis of intravascular blood clots by the streptococcal fibrinolytic system (streptokinase). J Exp Med 1952;95:449–464.
4. Sherry S. The fibrinolytic activity of streptokinase activated human plasmin. J Clin Invest 1954;33:1054–1063.
5. Johnson AJ, McCarty WR. The lysis of artificially induced intravascular clots in man by intravenous infusions of streptokinase. J Clin Invest 1959;38:1627–1643.
6. Thrombolytic therapy in thrombosis: a National Institutes of Health Consensus Development Conference. Ann Intern Med 1980;93:141–144.
7. Dotter CT, Rösch J, Seaman AJ. Selective clot lysis with low-dose streptokinase. Radiology 1974;111:31–37.
8. Katzen BT, van Breda A. Low dose streptokinase in the treatment of arterial occlusions. AJR 1981;136:1171–1178.
9. Becker GJ, Rabe FE, Richmond BD, et al. Low-dose fibrinolytic therapy: results and new concepts. Radiology 1983;148:663–670.
10. McNamara TO, Fischer JR. Thrombolysis of peripheral arteries

and bypass grafts: improved results using high dose urokinase. AJR 1985;144:769–775.

11. Bookstein JJ, Fellmeth B, Roberts A, et al. Pulsed-spray pharmacomechanical thrombolysis: preliminary clinical results. AJR 1989;152:1097–1100.

12. Rutherford RB, Flanigan DP, Gupta SK, et al. Suggested standards for reports dealing with lower extremity ischemia. J Vasc Surg 1986;4:80–94.

13. Davis GB, Dowd CF, Bookstein JJ. Thrombosed dialysis grafts: efficacy of intrathrombic deposition of concentrated urokinase, clot maceration, and angioplasty. AJR 1987;149:177–181.

14. Belkin M. Pathophysiology of acute extremity ischemia. In: Strandness DE, van Breda A, eds. Vascular diseases: surgical and interventional therapy. New York: Churchill-Livingstone, 1993:305–309.

15. Miller BV, Sharp WJ, Hoballah JJ, et al. Management of infrainguinal occluded vein bypasses with a combined approach of thrombolysis and surveillance. Arch Surg 1992;127:986–989.

16. Holden RW. Plasminogen activators: pharmacology and therapy. Radiology 1990;174:993–1001.

17. Hess H, Ingrisch H, Mietaschk A, et al. Local low-dose thrombolytic therapy of peripheral arterial occlusions. N Engl J Med 1982;307:1627–1630.

18. Mori KW, Bookstein JJ, Heeney DJ, et al. Selective streptokinase infusion: clinical and laboratory correlates. Radiology 1983;148:676–682.

19. Katzen BT, Edwards KC, Albert AS, van Breda A. Low dose direct fibrinolysis in peripheral vascular disease. J Vasc Surg 1984;1:718–722.

20. Graor RA, Risius JB, Deny K. Local thrombolysis in the treatment of thrombosed arteries, bypass grafts, and arteriovenous fistulae. J Vasc Surg 1985;2:406–414.

21. Koltun WA, Gardiner GA, Harrington DP, et al. Thrombolysis in the treatment of peripheral arterial vascular occlusions. Arch Surg 1987;122:901–905.

22. van Breda JA, Ribison JC, Feldman L. Local thrombolysis in the treatment of arterial occlusions. J Vasc Surg 1984;1:103–112.

23. Gardiner GA, Harrington DP, Koltun W, et al. Salvage of occluded arterial bypass grafts by means of thrombolysis. J Vasc Surg 1989;9:426–431.

24. Traughber PD, Cook PS, Micklos TJ, et al. Intraarterial fibrinolytic therapy for popliteal and tibial artery obstruction: comparison of streptokinase and urokinase. AJR 1987;149:453–456.

25. Vaughan DE, Goldhaber SZ, Kim J, et al. Recombinant tissue plasminogen activator in patients with pulmonary embolism: correlation of fibrinolytic specificity and efficacy. Circulation 1987;75:1200–1203.

26. Bovill EG, Terrin ML, Stump DC, et al. Hemorrhagic events during therapy with recombinant tissue-type plasminogen activator, heparin, and aspirin for acute myocardial infarction: results of the thrombolysis in myocardial infarction (TIMI) phase II trial. Ann Intern Med 1991;115:256–265.

27. Risius B, Graor RA, Geisinger MA, et al. Thrombolytic therapy with recombinant tissue-type plasminogen activator: a comparison of two doses. Radiology 1987;164:465–468.

28. Graor RA, Risius B, Lucas FV, Young JR, et al. Thrombolysis with recombinant human tissue-type plasminogen activator in patients with peripheral arterial and bypass graft occlusions. Circulation 1986;74:115–120.

29. Verstraete M, Hess H, Mahler F, et al. Femoro-popliteal artery thrombolysis with intra-arterial infusion of recombinant tissue-type plasminogen activator: report of a pilot trial. Eur J Vasc Surg 1988;2:155–159.

30. Earnshaw JJ, Westby JC, Gregson RHS, et al. Local thrombolytic therapy of acute peripheral arterial ischemia with tissue plasminogen activator: a dose-ranging study. Br J Surg 1988;75:1196–1200.

31. Berridge DC, Gregson RHS, Hopkinson BR, et al. Randomized trial of intra-arterial recombinant tissue plasminogen activator, intravenous recombinant tissue plasminogen activator, and intra-arterial streptokinase in peripheral arterial thrombolysis. Br J Surg 1991;78:988–995.

32. Krupski WC, Feldman RK, Rapp JH. Recombinant human tissue-type plasminogen activator is an effective agent for thrombolysis of peripheral arteries and bypass grafts: preliminary report. J Vasc Surg 1989;10:491–500.

33. Meyerovitz MF, Goldhaber SZ, Reagan K, et al. Recombinant tissue-type plasminogen activator versus urokinase in peripheral arterial and graft occlusions: a randomized trial. Radiology 1990;175:75–78.

34. Rao AK, Pratt C, Berke A, et al. Thrombolysis in myocardial infarction (TIMI) trial: Phase I. Hemorrhagic manifestations and changes in plasma fibrinogen and the fibrinolytic system in patients treated with recombinant tissue plasminogen activator and streptokinase. J Am Coll Cardiol 1988;11:1–11.

35. Decrinis M, Pilger E, Stark G, et al. A simplified procedure for intra-arterial thrombolysis with tissue-type plasminogen activator in peripheral arterial occlusive disease: primary and long-term results. Eur Heart J 1993;14:297–305.

36. Page JE, Buckenham TM, Taylor RS. Accelerated thrombolysis facilitated by direct puncture of occluded prosthetic femoral grafts. Australas Radiol 1992;36:230–233.

37. Dorros G, Hall P, Iyer SS. Urokinase infusion of chronically occluded femoropopliteal Gortex bypass grafts via the popliteal approach. Cathet Cardiovasc Diagn 1991;24:197–203.

38. Smith DC, McCormick MJ, Jensen DA, et al. Guide wire traversal test: retrospective study of results with fibrinolytic therapy. J Vasc Intervent Radiol 1991;2:339–342.

39. Hicks ME, Picus D, Darcy MD, et al. Multilevel infusion catheter for use with thrombolytic agents. J Vasc Intervent Radiol 1991;2:73–75.

40. Kaufman SL, Martin LG, Gilarsky BP, et al. Urokinase thrombolysis using a multiple side hole multilumen infusion catheter. Cardiovasc Intervent Radiol 1991;14:334–337.

41. Sullivan KL, Gardiner GA, Shapiro MJ, et al. Acceleration of thrombolysis with a high-dose transthrombus bolus technique. Radiology 1989;173:805–808.

42. Cragg AH, Smith TP, Corson JD, et al. Two urokinase dose regimens in native arterial and graft occlusions: initial results of a prospective, randomized clinical trial. Radiology 1991;178:681–686.

43. Bookstein JJ, Saldinger E. Accelerated thrombolysis: in vitro evaluation of agents and methods of administration. Invest Radiol 1985;20:731–735.

44. Valji K, Bookstein JJ. Fibrinolysis with intrathrombic injection of urokinase and tissue-type plasminogen activator: results in a new model of subacute venous thrombosis. Invest Radiol 1987;22:23–27.

45. Kandarpa K, Drinker PA, Singer SJ, et al. Forceful pulsatile local infusion of enzyme accelerates thrombolysis: in vivo evaluation of a new delivery system. Radiology 1988;168:739–744.

46. Valji K, Bookstein JJ, Roberts AC, Sanchez RB. Occluded peripheral arteries and bypass grafts: lytic stagnation as an endpoint for pulse-spray pharamacomechanical thrombolysis. Radiology 1993;188:389–394.

47. Kandarpa K, Chopra PS, Aruny JE, et al. Intraarterial thrombolysis of lower extremity occlusions: prospective, randomized comparison of forced periodic infusion and conventional slow continuous infusion. Radiology 1993;188:861–867.

48. Bookstein JJ, Valji K, Roberts AC. Pulsed versus conventional thrombolytic infusion techniques. Radiology 1994;193:318–324.

49. Coller BS. Platelets and thrombolytic therapy. N Engl J Med 1990;322:33–42.

50. Fitzgerald DJ, FitzGerald GA. Antiplatelet and anticoagulant therapy during coronary thrombolysis. Trends Cardiovasc Med 1991;1:29–35.

51. Valji K, Bookstein JJ. Efficacy of adjunctive intrathrombic heparin with pulse spray thrombolysis in rabbit inferior vena cava thrombosis. Invest Radiol 1992;27:912–917.
52. Valji K, Bookstein JJ. Effects of intrathrombic administration of prostaglandin E_1 during pulse-spray thrombolysis with tissue-type plasminogen activator in experimental thrombosis. Radiology 1993;186:873–876.
53. Valji K, Bookstein JJ. Use of a direct thrombin inhibitor (Argatroban) during pulse-spray thrombolysis in experimental thrombosis. J Vasc Intervent Radiol 1995;6:91–95.
54. Sharma B, Wyeth RP, Gimenez HJ, et al. Intracoronary prostaglandin E_1 plus streptokinase in acute myocardial infarction. Am J Cardiol 1986;58:1161–1166.
55. van Breda A, Katzen BT. Thrombolytic therapy of peripheral vascular disease. Semin Intervent Radiol 1985;2:354–366.
56. Durham JD, Geller SC, Abbott WM, et al. Regional infusion of urokinase into occluded lower-extremity bypass grafts: long-term clinical results. Radiology 1989;172:83–87.
57. LeBlang SD, Becker GJ, Benenati JF, et al. Low-dose urokinase regimen for the treatment of lower extremity arterial and graft occlusions: experience in 132 cases. J Vasc Intervent Radiol 1992;3:475–483.
58. DeSwart CAM, Nijmeyer B, Roelofs JMM, et al. Kinetics of intravenously administered heparin in humans. Blood 1982;60:1251.
59. Ogilby JD, Kopelman HA, Klein LW, et al. Adequate heparinization during PTCA: assessment using activated clotting times. Cathet Cardiovasc Diagn 1989;18:206–209.
60. Bergqvist D. Dextran and haemostasis. Acta Chir Scand 1982;148:633–640.
61. Pilger E, Lammer J, Bertuch H, et al. Intraarterial fibrinolysis: in vitro and prospective clinical evaluation of three thrombolytic agents. Radiology 1986;161:597–599.
62. Pernes JM, de Almeida Augusto M, Vitoux JF, et al. Local thrombolysis in peripheral arteries and bypass grafts. J Vasc Surg 1987;6:372–378.
63. van Breda A, Katzen BT, Deutsch AS. Urokinase versus streptokinase in local thrombolysis. Radiology 1987;165:109–111.
64. Katzen BT. Technique and results of "low-dose" infusion. Cardiovasc Intervent Radiol 1988;11:S41–S47.
65. Motarjeme A. Thrombolytic therapy in arterial occlusion and graft thrombosis. Semin Vasc Surg 1989;2:155–178.
66. Eisenbud DE, Brener BJ, Shoenfeld R, et al. Treatment of acute vascular occlusions with intra-arterial urokinase. Am J Surg 1990;160:160–165.
67. Bookstein JJ, Valji K. Pulse spray pharmacomechanical thrombolysis: updated clinical and laboratory observations. Semin Intervent Radiol 1992;9:174–182.
68. Bean W, Rodan B, Thebaut A. Leriche syndrome: treatment with streptokinase and angioplasty. AJR 1985;144:1285–1286.
69. Valji K, Roberts AC, Davis GB, Bookstein JJ. Pulse spray thrombolysis of arterial and bypass graft occlusions. AJR 1991;156:617–621.
70. Mewissen MW, Minor PL, Beyer GA, et al. Symptomatic native arterial occlusions: early experience with "over-the-wire" thrombolysis. J Vasc Intervent Radiol 1990;1:43–47.
71. Hallett JW, Greenwood LH, Yrizarry JM, et al. Statistical determinants of success and complications of thrombolytic therapy for arterial occlusion of lower extremity. Surg Gynecol Obstet 1985;161:431–437.
72. Hess H, Mietaschk A, Brueckl R. Peripheral arterial occlusions: a 6-year experience with local low-dose thrombolytic therapy. Radiology 1987;163:753–758.
73. McNamara TO, Bomberger RA, Merchant RF. Intra-arterial urokinase as the initial therapy for acutely ischemic lower limbs. Circulation 1991;83(Suppl I):106–119.
74. Lang EV, Stevick CA. Transcatheter therapy of severe acute lower extremity ischemia. J Vasc Intervent Radiol 1993;4:481–488.
75. Paulson EK, Miller FJ. Embolization of cardiac mural throm-
76. bus: complication of intraarterial fibrinolysis. Radiology 1988;168:95–96.
76. McNamara TO, Bomberger RA. Factors affecting initial and 6 month patency after intraarterial thrombolysis with high dose urokinase. Am J Surg 1986;152:709–712.
77. Browse DJ, Torrie EPH, Galland RB. Early results and one year follow-up after intra-arterial thrombolysis. Br J Surg 1993;80:194–197.
78. Lammer J, Pilger E, Neumayer K, et al. Intraarterial fibrinolysis: long-term results. Radiology 1986;161:159–163.
79. Lonsdale RJ, Whitaker SC, Berridge DC, et al. Peripheral arterial thrombosis: intermediate-term results. Br J Surg 1993;80:592–595.
80. Fogle MA, Whittemore AD, Couch NP, et al. A comparison of in situ and reversed saphenous vein grafts for infrainguinal reconstructions. J Vasc Surg 1987;5:46–52.
81. Leather RP, Shah DM, Chang B. Resurrection of the in situ saphenous vein bypass. Ann Surg 1988;208:435–441.
82. Cohen JR, Mannick JA, Couch NP, et al. Recognition and management of impending vein-graft failure. Arch Surg 1986;121:758–759.
83. Bandyk DF, Towne JB, Schmitt DD, et al. Therapeutic options for acute thrombosed in situ saphenous vein arterial bypass grafts. J Vasc Surg 1990;11:680–687.
84. Graor RA, Risius B, Young JR, et al. Thrombolysis of peripheral arterial bypass grafts: surgical thrombectomy compared with thrombolysis. J Vasc Surg 1988;7:347–355.
85. Sullivan KL, Gardiner GA, Kandarpa K, et al. Efficacy of thrombolysis in infrainguinal bypass grafts. Circulation 1991;83(Suppl I):99–105.
86. Seabrook GR, Mewissen MW, Schmitt DD, et al. Percutaneous intraarterial thrombolysis in the treatment of thrombosis of lower extremity arterial reconstructions. J Vasc Surg 1991;13:646–651.
87. Guest P, Buckenham T. Thrombolysis of the occluded prosthetic graft with tissue-type plasminogen activator—technique, results and problems in 23 patients. Clin Radiol 1992;46:381–386.
88. Turner C, Valji K, Wolf Y, et al. Value of pulse spray thrombolysis with adjunctive angioplasty or surgical revision for infrainguinal bypass graft occlusion. Radiology 1993;189(P):333.
89. Belkin M, Donaldson MC, Whittemore AD, et al. Observations on the use of thrombolytic agents for thrombotic occlusion of infrainguinal vein grafts. J Vasc Surg 1990;11:289–296.
90. Hye RJ, Turner C, Valji K, et al. Is thrombolysis of occluded popliteal and tibial bypass grafts worthwhile? J Vasc Surg 1994;20:588–597.
91. Ascer E, Collier P, Gupta SK, et al. Reoperation for polytetrafluoroethylene bypass failure: the importance of distal outflow site and operative technique in determining outcome. J Vasc Surg 1987;5:298–310.
92. Chidi C, DePalma R. Atherogenic potential of the embolectomy catheter. Surgery 1978;83:549–557.
93. Kumpe DA, Cohen MAH. Angioplasty/thrombolytic treatment of failing and failed hemodialysis access sites: comparison with surgical treatment. Prog Cardiovasc Dis 1992;34:263–278.
94. Mangiarotti G, Canavese C, Thea A, et al. Urokinase treatment for arteriovenous fistulae declotting in dialyzed patients. Nephron 1984;36:60–64.
95. Klimas VA, Denny KM, Paganini EP, et al. Low dose streptokinase therapy for thrombosed arteriovenous fistulas. Trans Am Soc Artif Intern Organs 1984;30:511–513.
96. Zeit RM, Cope C. Failed hemodialysis shunts: one year of experience with aggressive therapy. Radiology 1985;154:353–356.
97. Rodkin RS, Bookstein JJ, Heeney DJ, et al. Streptokinase and transluminal angioplasty in the treatment of acutely thrombosed hemodialysis access fistulae. Radiology 1983;149:425–428.

98. Young AT, Hunter DW, Castaneda-Zuniga WR, et al. Thrombosed synthetic hemodialysis access fistulas: failure of fibrinolytic therapy. Radiology 1985;154:639–642.

99. Poulain F, Raynaud A, Bourquelot P, et al. Local thrombolysis and thromboaspiration in the treatment of acutely thrombosed arteriovenous hemodialysis fistulas. Cardiovasc Intervent Radiol 1991;14:98–101.

100. Valji K, Bookstein JJ, Roberts AC, et al. Pulse spray pharmacomechanical thrombolysis of thrombosed hemodialysis access grafts: long-term experience and comparison of original and current techniques. AJR 1995;164:1495–1500.

101. Valji K, Bookstein JJ, Roberts AC, et al. Pharmacomechanical thrombolysis and angioplasty in the management of clotted hemodialysis grafts: early and late clinical results. Radiology 1991;178:243–247.

102. Valji K, Roberts AC, Bookstein JJ. Thrombosed hemodialysis access grafts: management with pulse-spray thrombolysis and balloon angioplasty. In: Strandness ER, van Breda A, eds. Vascular diseases: surgical and interventional therapy. New York: Churchill-Livingstone, 1993:1087–1096.

103. Summers S, Drazan K, Gomes A, et al. Urokinase therapy for thrombosed hemodialysis access grafts. Surg Gynecol Obstet 1993;176:534–538.

104. Abedon SI, Le H, Valji K, et al. Effect of aspirin on hemodialysis graft patency. Radiology 1993;189(P):175.

105. Palder SB, Kirkman RL, Whittemore AD, et al. Vascular access for hemodialysis: patency rates and results of revision. Ann Surg 1985;202:235–239.

106. Etheredge EE, Haid SD, Maeser MN, et al. Salvage operations for malfunctioning polytetrafluoroethylene hemodialysis access grafts. Surgery 1983;94:464–470.

107. Silcott GR, Polich VL. Palmar arch reconstruction for the salvage of ischemic fingers. Am J Surg 1981;142:219–225.

108. Schmidt FE, Hewitt RL. Severe upper limb ischemia. Arch Surg 1980;115:1188–1191.

109. Tisnado J, Bartol DT, Cho S-R, et al. Low-dose fibrinolytic therapy in hand ischemia. Radiology 1984;150:375–382.

110. Widlus DM, Venbrux AC, Benenati JF, et al. Fibrinolytic therapy for upper-extremity arterial occlusions. Radiology 1990;175:393–399.

111. Lambiase RE, Paolella LP, Haas RA, et al. Extensive thromboembolic disease of the hand and forearm: treatment with thrombolytic therapy. J Vasc Intervent Radiol 1991;2:201–208.

112. Pfyffer M, Schneider E, Jaeger K, et al. Lokale thrombolyse von akuten und subakuten Unterarm-, hand- und fingerarterien-verschluessen: Frueh- und spaetergebnisse. Vasa 1989;18:128–135.

113. Capek P, Holcroft J. Traumatic ischemia of the hand in a tennis player: successful treatment with urokinase. J Vasc Intervent Radiol 1993;4:279–281.

114. Lang EV, Bookstein JJ. Accelerated thrombolysis and angioplasty for hand ischemia in Buerger's disease. Cardiovasc Intervent Radiol 1989;12:95–97.

115. Machleder HI. Venous disorders. In: Machleder HI, ed. Vascular disorders of the upper extremity. Mount Kisco, NY: Futura, 1989:269–296.

116. Martin ED, Koser M, Gordon DH. Venography in axillary-subclavian vein thrombosis. Cardiovasc Radiol 1979;2:261–266.

117. Longley DG, Yedlicka JW, Molina EJ, et al. Thoracic outlet syndrome: evaluation of the subclavian vessels by color Doppler sonography. AJR 1992;158:623–630.

118. Swinton NW, Edgett JW, Hall RJ. Primary subclavian-axillary vein thrombosis. Circulation 1968;38:737–745.

119. Jacobson JH, Haimon M. Venous revascularization for the arm: report of three cases. Surgery 1977;81:599–604.

120. Fankuchen EI, Neff RA, Collins RA, et al. Urokinase perfusion for axillary-subclavian vein thrombosis. Cardiovasc Intervent Radiol 1984;7:90–93.

121. Taylor LM, McAllister WR, Dennis DL, et al. Thrombolytic therapy followed by first rib resection for spontaneous (effort) subclavian vein thrombosis. Am J Surg 1985;149:644–647.

122. Grassi CJ, Bettman MA. Effort thrombosis: role of interventional therapy. Cardiovasc Intervent Radiol 1990;13:317–322.

123. Becker GJ, Holden RW, Rabe FE, et al. Local thrombolytic therapy for subclavian and axillary vein thrombosis. Radiology 1983;149:419–423.

124. Druy EM, Trout HH, Giordano JM, et al. Lytic therapy in the treatment of axillary and subclavian vein thrombosis. J Vasc Surg 1985;2:821–827.

125. Glanz S, Gordon DH, Lipkowitz GS, et al. Axillary and subclavian vein stenosis: percutaneous angioplasty. Radiology 1988;168:321–323.

126. Malcynski J, O'Donnell TF, Mackey WC, et al. Long-term results of treatment for axillary-subclavian vein thrombosis. Can J Surg 1993;36:365–371.

127. Arneson H, Hoiseth A, Ly B. Streptokinase or heparin in the treatment of deep vein thrombosis: follow-up results of a prospective study. Acta Med Scand 1982;211:65–68.

128. Elliot MS, Immelman EJ, Jeffrey P, et al. A comparative randomized trial of heparin versus streptokinase in the treatment of acute proximal venous thrombosis: an interim report of a prospective trial. Br J Surg 1979;66:838–843.

129. Persson AV, Persson CA. Thrombolytic therapy for deep vein thrombosis. Am J Surg 1985;150:50–53.

130. Van de Loo JCW, Kriessman A, Truebenstein G, et al. Controlled multicenter pilot study of urokinase, heparin and streptokinase in deep vein thrombosis. Thromb Haemostasis 1983;50:660–663.

131. Goldhaber SZ, Meyerowitz MF, Green D, et al. Randomized, controlled trial of tissue plasminogen activator in proximal deep venous thrombosis. Am J Med 1990;88:235–240.

132. Verhaeghe R, Besse P, Bounameaux H, et al. Multicenter pilot study of the efficacy and safety of systemic rt-PA administration in the treatment of deep vein thrombosis of the lower extremities and/or pelvis. Thromb Res 1989;55:5–11.

133. Bounameaux H, Banga JD, Bluhmki E, et al. Double blind, randomized comparison of systemic continuous infusion of 0.25 versus 0.50 mg/kg/24h of alteplase over 3 to 7 days for treatment of deep venous thrombosis in heparinized patients: results of the European thrombolysis with rt-PA in venous thrombosis (ETTT) trial. Thromb Haemostasis 1992;67:306–309.

134. Weaver FA, Meacham PW, Adkins RB, et al. Phlegmasia cerulea dolens: therapeutic considerations. South Med J 1988;81:306–312.

135. Hood DB, Weaver FA, Modrall JG, et al. Advances in the treatment of phlegmasia cerulea dolens. Am J Surg 1993;166:206–210.

136. Robinson DL, Teitelbaum GP. Phlegmasia cerulea dolens: treatment by pulse spray and infusion thrombolysis. AJR 1993;160:1288–1290.

137. Del Campo C. Pulmonary embolectomy: a review. Can J Surg 1985;28:111–113.

138. Gray HH, Morgan JM, Paneth M, et al. Pulmonary embolectomy for acute massive pulmonary embolism: an analysis of 71 cases. Br Heart J 1988;60:196–200.

139. The Urokinase Pulmonary Embolism Trial: a national cooperative study. Circulation 1973;47(Suppl II):1–108.

140. Urokinase Pulmonary Embolism Trial Study Group. Urokinase-streptokinase embolism trial: phase II results. JAMA 1974;229:1606–1613.

141. Goldhaber SZ, Kessler CM, Heit J, et al. Randomized controlled trial of recombinant tissue plasminogen activator versus urokinase in the treatment of acute pulmonary embolism. Lancet 1988;2:293–298.

142. Verstraete M, Miller GAH, Bounameaux H, et al. Intravenous and intrapulmonary recombinant tissue-type plasminogen activator in the treatment of acute massive pulmonary embolism. Circulation 1988;77:353–360.

143. Heit JA. An analysis of current pulmonary embolism therapy. Int Angiol 1992;11:57–63.

144. Goldhaber SZ. Evolving concepts in thrombolytic therapy for pulmonary embolism. Chest 1992;4(Suppl):183S–185S.

145. Rosenthal D, Evans RD, Borrero E, et al. Massive pulmonary embolism: triple-armed therapy. J Vasc Surg 1989;9:261–270.

146. Schwarz F, Zimmerman K, Stelert M, et al. Local thrombolysis with urokinase in acute massive pulmonary embolism. Deutsch Med Wochensch 1984;109:55–58.

147. Arnesen LH, Eie H, Hol R. A controlled clinical trial of streptokinase and heparin in the treatment of major pulmonary embolism. Acta Med Scand 1987;203:465–470.

148. Levine M, Hirsh J, Weitz J, et al. A randomized trial of a single bolus dosage regimen of recombinant tissue plasminogen activator in patients with acute pulmonary embolism. Chest 1990;98:1473–1479.

149. Steckel A, Johnston J, Fraley DS, et al. The use of streptokinase to treat renal artery thromboembolism. Am J Kidney Dis 1984;4:166–170.

150. Pineo GF, Thorndyke WC, Steed BL. Spontaneous renal artery thrombosis: successful lysis with streptokinase. J Urol 1987;138:1223–1225.

151. Fischer CP, Konnak JW, Cho KJ, et al. Renal artery embolism: therapy with intraarterial streptokinase. J Urol 1981;125:402–404.

152. Cronan JJ, Dorfman GS. Low dose thrombolysis: a nonoperative approach to renal artery occlusion. J Urol 1983;130:757–759.

153. Zuckerman AM, Martin LG, Silverstein MI. Emergent renal artery revascularization for acute anuria. J Vasc Intervent Radiol 1993;4:489–492.

154. Cole PE, Bohner H, Sos TA. Role of thrombolysis in renal artery disease. J Vasc Intervent Radiol 1992;3:37.

155. Olin JW, Graor RA, Young JR. Thrombolytic therapy for renal artery occlusions: a preliminary report. Clevel Clinic J Med 1989;56:432–438.

156. Muegge A, Gulba DC, Frei U, et al. Renal artery embolism: thrombolysis with recombinant tissue-type plasminogen activator. J Int Med 1990;228:279–286.

157. De La Rocha G, Zorn M, Downs AR. Acute renal failure as a consequence of sudden renal artery occlusion. Can J Surg 1981;24:218–222.

158. Blum V, Billmann P, Krause T. Effect of local low-dose thrombolysis on clinical outcome in acute embolic renal artery occlusion. Radiology 1993;189:549–554.

159. Rowe JM, Rasmussen RL, Mader SL, et al. Successful thrombolytic therapy in two patients with renal vein thrombosis. Am J Med 1984;77:1111–1114.

160. Robinson JM, Cockrell CH, Tisnado J, et al. Selective low-dose streptokinase infusion in the treatment of acute transplant renal vein thrombosis. Cardiovasc Intervent Radiol 1986;9:86–89.

161. Schwieger J, Reiss R, Cohen JL, et al. Acute renal allograft dysfunction in the setting of deep venous thrombosis: a case of successful urokinase thrombolysis and a review of the literature. Am J Kidney Dis 1993;22:345–350.

162. Chiu AS, Landsberg DN. Successful treatment of acute transplant renal vein thrombosis with selective streptokinase infusion. Transplant Proc 1991;23:2297–2300.

163. Ryan CA, Andrews M. Failure of thrombolytic therapy in four children with extensive thromboses. Am J Dis Child 1992;146:187–193.

164. Giacoia GP. High dose urokinase therapy in newborn infants with major vessel thrombosis. Clin Ped 1993;32:231–237.

165. LeBlanc JG, Culham JAG, Chan K, et al. Treatment of grafts and major vessel thromboses with low dose streptokinase in children. Ann Thorac Surg 1986;41:630–635.

166. Strife JL, Ball WS, Towbin R, et al. Arterial occlusions in neonates: use of fibrinolytic therapy. Radiology 1988;166:395–400.

167. Vailas GN, Brouillette RT, Scott JP, et al. Neonatal aortic thrombosis: recent experience. J Pediatr 1986;109:101–108.

168. Marsh D, Wilkerson S, Cook L, et al. Right atrial thrombosis in neonates receiving central venous lines after extracorporeal membrane oxygenation. Crit Care Med 1988;16:202–203.

169. Pongiglione G, Marasini M, Ribaldone D, et al. Right atrial thrombosis in two premature infants: successful treatment with urokinase and heparin. Eur Heart J 1986;7:1086–1089.

170. Levy M, Benson LN, Burrows PE, et al. Tissue plasminogen activator for the treatment of thromboembolism in infants and children. J Pediatr 1991;118:467–472.

171. Curnow A, Idowu J, Behrens E, et al. Urokinase therapy for Silastic catheter induced intravascular thrombi in infants and children. Arch Surg 1985;120:1237–1240.

172. O'Neill JA, Neblett WW, Born ML. Management of major thromboembolic complications of umbilical artery catheters. J Pediatr Surg 1981;16:972–978.

173. Ekelund J, Hedner U, Nilsson IM. Fibrinolysis in newborns. Acta Pediatr Scand 1970;59:33–43.

174. Corrigan JJ, Sleeth, JJ, Jeter M, et al. Newborn's fibrinolytic mechanism: components and plasmin generation. J Hematol 1989;32:273–278.

175. Becker GJ, Holden RW, Rabe FE. Contrast extravasation from a Gore-tex graft: a complication of thrombolytic therapy. AJR 1984;142:573–574.

176. Matsumoto AH, Selby JB, Farr B, et al. Shaking rigors during regional infusion of urokinase: a recent development. J Vasc Intervent Radiol 1993;4(Abs):24.

177. Rholl KS, Parker BC, van Breda A. Increased reactions to urokinase: experience at a community hospital and results of SCVIR survey. J Vasc Intervent Radiol 1993;4(Abs):24.

10

Percutaneous Suction Thromboembolectomy

ROBERT E. LAMBIASE
GARY S. DORFMAN
TIMOTHY P. MURPHY

The percutaneous removal of embolized thrombus, in situ thrombus, or atheroma by means of suction applied to endovascular catheters is not a widespread procedure at this time. Its precise role in the setting of existing critical arterial thromboembolic disease or as treatment for embolized atheromatous debris is uncertain when compared to other well-accepted and well-documented interventions, such as thrombolysis and Fogarty thromboembolectomy. Few published series have specifically addressed this procedure. For these reasons, a brief historical overview of interventional treatment options in critical arterial thromboembolic disease is presented to clarify the potential role of percutaneous suction thromboembolectomy.

Background

The first reported arteriotomy for removal of an embolus was attempted (unsuccessfully) by Suabanejew in 1895.[1] The site was the common femoral artery. The first successful embolectomy was performed by Labey via common femoral arteriotomy in 1911.[1] Subsequent modifications of simple arteriotomy and clot removal involved retrograde "milking" of the extremity using Esmarch bandages to expel thrombus at the arteriotomy site, as well as retrograde flushing of the artery with saline solution for the same purpose. Various devices, including vein strippers and endarterectomy devices, were employed for mechanical retrieval of thrombus proximal or distal to the arteriotomy site. A corkscrew device was designed by Shaw for the removal of distal thrombi, and gained some popularity.[2,3]

Dale[4] in 1961 reported the use of endovascular suction catheters, which were soft, flexible, 30-cm long synthetic tubing of various diameters attached to 50-ml syringes used to create negative pressure. The catheters were threaded via a common femoral arteriotomy to the site of thrombotic occlusion. The catheters were removed and flushed when they became blocked with thrombus, and the procedure was repeated until there was restoration of inflow or back-bleeding.

In 1963 Fogarty and colleagues[3] revolutionized the treatment of acute thromboembolic disease with the introduction of a low-pressure, inflatable balloon embolectomy catheter that allowed for efficient thrombus removal at a site distal to the arterial cutdown. The procedure could be performed under local anesthesia, if necessary. In subsequent large published series, cumulative limb salvage rates following Fogarty thromboembolectomy ranged from approximately 60 to 95 percent, with most recent series in the 85 to 95 percent range.[5-10] The cumulative 30-day mortality rate ranged from 10 to 35 percent. Mortality remains high and is essentially unchanged compared to that associated with earlier methods of surgical thromboembolectomy. This reflects the severe generalized atherosclerotic condition of these patients, who commonly suffered cardiac-related deaths in the follow-up period.

Although Fogarty thromboembolectomy has been proved to be a safe and effective procedure in experienced hands, many potential mechanisms of arterial injury have been elaborated secondary to this technique.[11-21] The most common complications of this procedure are vessel perforation or rupture, intimal dissection or dislodgment of atheromatous plaque with luminal compromise, balloon rupture with embolization of balloon fragments, embolization of the catheter tip, and intima or media injury with subsequent myointimal hyperplasia or accelerated atherosclerosis. Overall, complications are seen in approximately 1 percent of Fogarty thromboembolectomy procedures.[20] However, true complication rates may be higher because completion angiograms are often not obtained, and some complications of Fogarty thromboembolectomy may occur on a delayed basis. This is particularly true of intimal or medial injury, which is stated to represent approximately 12 percent of complications[18]; in these cases accelerated atherosclerosis or myointimal hyperplasia may not be noted for months to years. This type of vessel injury is not localized to the obstructed segment but to the entire length of the vessel over which the balloon has been retracted while inflated.

The Fogarty catheter is not steerable, and thus there is no direct mechanism for selective catheterization of arterial branches, in particular the calf vessels. There is a risk that the initial passage of the catheter will advance the thrombus distally into a site where it is not easily dislodged. A further criticism of the Fogarty technique is that much residual thrombus remains after the procedure. This remaining thrombus may then act as a nidus for further clot propagation. That significant residual thrombus remains after Fogarty thromboembolectomy has been verified by postprocedural angioscopy of the treated vessel.[22] In light of the shortcomings of the Fogarty balloon for complete thrombus removal, endovascular brushes have been developed for this purpose.[23] It is also fairly routine at present for the vascular surgeon to infuse urokinase into the affected arterial tree after the Fogarty procedure in an attempt to lyse residual thrombus.[24] However, the dose used and the means of administration of urokinase or other thrombolytic agent vary widely from surgeon to surgeon. Thus the efficacy of this route of administration is uncertain at present. Again, this uncertainty is compounded by the lack of routine postprocedure angiography.

Despite its shortcomings, Fogarty thromboembolectomy remains a safe and effective means of rapidly reestablishing arterial blood flow to an ischemic limb.

In 1968, Greenfield et al.[25] reported on the experimental use of an endovascular, steerable transvenous vacuum cup catheter for removal of acute, life-threatening pulmonary emboli. Several small clinical series followed over the next several decades, not only documenting the usefulness of this technique in the appropriate clinical setting but also emphasizing the rarity of its usage.[26,27] The design of the device makes it unsuitable for intraarterial use. A device to mechanically fragment pulmonary emboli has recently been described.[28]

The most useful therapeutic innovation for acute thromboembolic disease since the advent of the Fogarty embolectomy catheter has been percutaneous transcatheter intraarterial thrombolytic therapy. This procedure is discussed in Chapter 9 and will not be discussed here. Suffice it to say that thrombolytic therapy remains the treatment of choice in many settings of acute thromboembolic disease when Fogarty thromboembolectomy is not indicated or is not elected as primary therapy.

Indications

The authors have employed percutaneous suction thromboembolectomy at their institution over a 7-year period. It is used when there is an absolute contra-indication to thrombolytic therapy, when "debulking" of clot is needed before thrombolytic therapy to accelerate the restoration of blood flow to the ischemic limb, when residual thrombus must be removed after thrombolytic therapy, or when the amount of urokinase must be limited because of a relative contraindication to lytic therapy. A major indication is the treatment of postangioplasty distal embolization. In the authors' experience, the embolized material in this setting is often atheromatous or mixed atheroma-thrombus rather than purely thrombotic in nature, and is well-treated by suction thromboembolectomy. Thrombolytic therapy in this setting would be expected to be entirely or partially unsuccessful.

Method

The equipment needed is simple and inexpensive: a 5 or 8 French vascular sheath, either a 5 or 8 French nontapered angiographic catheter, and a 50-ml syringe to apply negative pressure. After diagnostic angiography (which includes inflow to investigate a possible source of embolization), an antegrade puncture of the affected limb is made with placement of a 5 or 8 French vascular sheath. Fluoroscopic or digital "road map" guidance is used to negotiate the nontapered catheter to the level of obstruction. A "guidewire test" (relative ease in traversing the obstruction with a guidewire) of the obstruction gives information regarding the nature of the obstruction but, in the authors' experience, does not predict with accuracy the likelihood of success or failure for percutaneous suction removal. Once the catheter tip is embedded in thrombus (or embolized atheroma), suction is applied to the syringe (Fig. 10-1). If there is persistent blood entering through the catheter, it is repositioned until blood return stops, indicating occlusion of the catheter lumen, presumably secondary to aspirated embolic material. The catheter is then removed, and the contents are flushed out over a gauze. Often the aspirated specimen, when flushed out of the catheter, is significantly larger in diameter than the catheter lumen (Fig. 10-2). It is thus compressed as it is aspirated, which allows for more rapid removal than would be otherwise anticipated. Specimens are sent to the pathology department to determine embolus age or atheroma versus embolus. The procedure is repeated until patency of the vessel is restored. The underlying arterial morphology is assessed to determine the need for further therapy, such as short-term urokinase, further attempts at suction, or transluminal angioplasty. In the case of adherent, organized thrombus, the authors will often use balloon angioplasty as a mechanism to rapidly fragment the clot, which can then be removed by

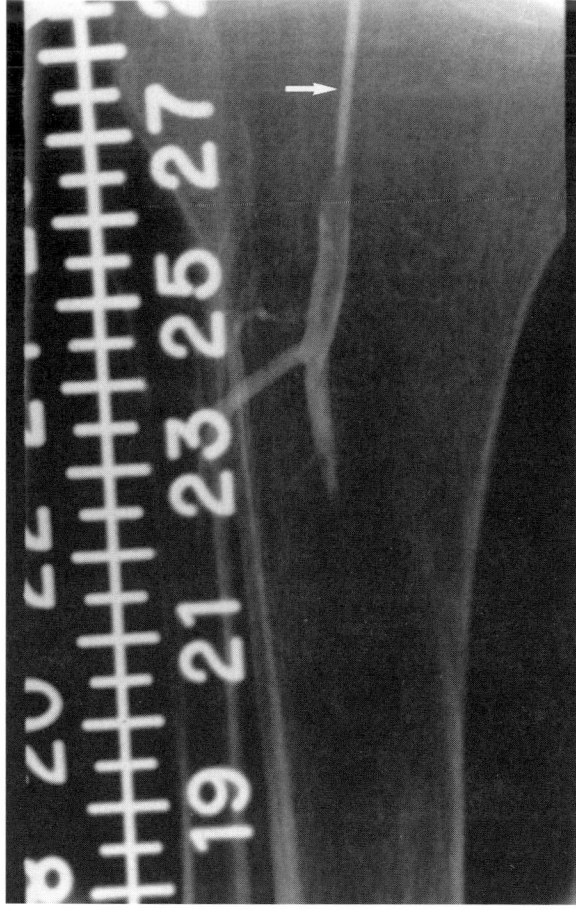

A

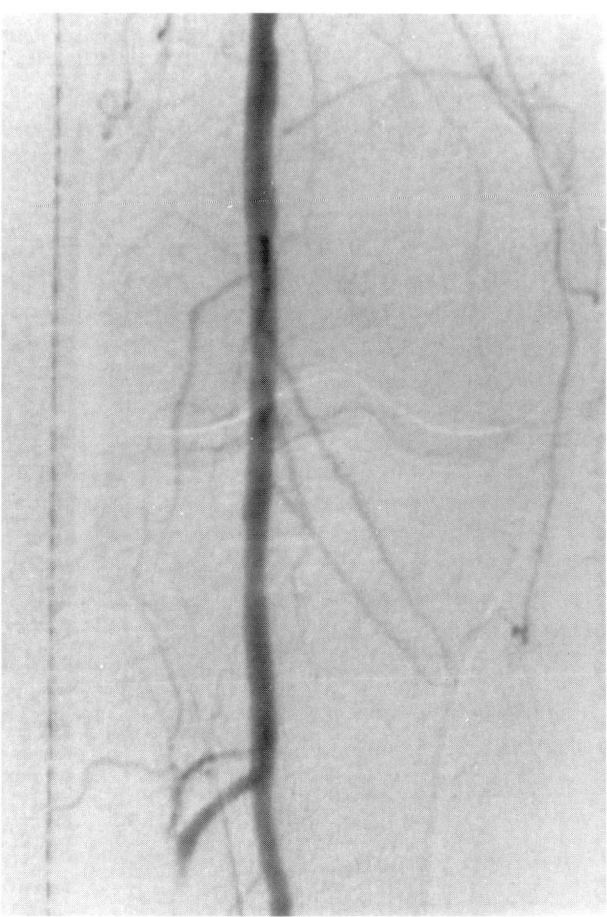

B

Figure 10-1. (A) The catheter (*arrow*) has been advanced to the site of thrombotic occlusion in the popliteal artery, and the tip is embedded in clot (thromboembolus). (B) After treatment with suction thromboembolectomy alone, the popliteal artery is patent without underlying stenosis. There is continuous runoff to the foot via the anterior and posterior tibialis arteries.

aspiration. Distal embolization, which occurs in approximately 10 to 15 percent of cases in our experience, is dealt with in a similar manner, with subselection of distal vessels as required. However, very distal embolizations into the foot are usually treated with thrombolytic therapy.

If upon removal of the catheter the aspirated material is dislodged into the vascular sheath, the sheath is removed over a guidewire while suction is applied, and the sheath is then flushed and replaced. A second guidewire is occasionally placed initially to act as a safety guidewire.

Wagner and Starck[29] describe several equipment modifications that seem useful. One is a removable hemostatic valve for the vascular sheath to reduce the need for sheath removal to clean out trapped thrombus. The second modification is an 8 French catheter with a double lumen, one of which accommodates a 0.018-inch guidewire. This allows for multiple passes of the catheter over a guidewire, without the need for renegotiating the vessel with each pass. This would be particularly useful if angioplasty were performed upstream, where each pass of the catheter would require renegotiation of the angioplasty site.

As mentioned, the aspirated specimens are routinely sent for pathologic examination, and many are found to be atheromatous in nature or mixed thrombus-atheroma. Many specimens that contained atheromatous material were not post-angioplasty embolization but most likely represented the treatment results of in situ thrombosis or thromboembolization to a site of atheromatous stenosis. The suction technique is thus capable of aspirating in situ atheroma as well as embolized material. The long-term clinical effects of in situ atheroma aspiration are unknown but may include accelerated atherosclerosis or myointimal hyperplasia. In the authors' experience, the site of denudation is not prone to rethrombosis; however, all patients were routinely anticoagulated during and after the procedure.

Drawbacks of the suction thromboembolectomy

procedure include the need to renegotiate the arterial tree to the site of occlusion every time the catheter is removed for flushing. The catheter often becomes occluded and is removed to be cleaned, but only a very small amount of embolic material is retrieved. Every pass of the catheter runs the risk of vessel injury in these often severely diseased vessels, particularly if angioplasty has been performed proximally. The need to avoid subintimal dissection at the angioplasty site is obvious. In addition, the procedure can be time-consuming, often requiring significant fluoroscopic time. The authors' approximately 20 percent failure rate was due primarily to the inability to "grasp" the embolic material to allow for its successful retrieval.

Results

Sniderman et al.[30] reported on a series of six patients in 1984 in whom percutaneous suction thromboembolectomy was performed. This was the first published clinical series based on this technique. The authors reported an 83 percent success rate. In all cases, treatment followed embolization secondary to upstream angioplasty, with embolization of occlusive thrombotic or atheromatous debris. Aspiration was performed using an 8 French nontapered catheter through an 8 French vascular sheath. The stated reason for employing this new technique, credited to a suggestion by Horvath et al. (and truly a percutaneous reworking of Dale's arteriotomy-based suction technique as well as Greenfield's suction device for pulmonary emboli), was to avoid the not uncommon "severe hemorrhagic complications" of thrombolytic therapy.[30]

In 1985, Starck et al.[31] reported a series of 41 patients in whom percutaneous suction thromboembolectomy had been performed urgently. They used a custom-designed catheter-sheath system with a minimally tapered catheter within a long (up to 80 cm) sheath, usually 8 French in diameter (although varying sizes were available). A removable hemostatic sheath valve was a custom addition that allowed for easier removal of clot impacted within the sheath. In this series, 40 percent of the patients were treated following embolization from transluminal angioplasty: 20 percent for postthrombolysis residual thrombus, and 20 percent for cardiogenic emboli. The remainder were treated for a variety of embolic events. In the 40 patients, 80 percent of the treated vascular beds improved from 51 to 100 percent in luminal patency or blood flow, and in 17 percent of patients from 30 to 50 percent. There were 3 percent failures. Seventy-eight percent of patients improved greater than or equal to 1 Fontaine stage, and 13 percent improved

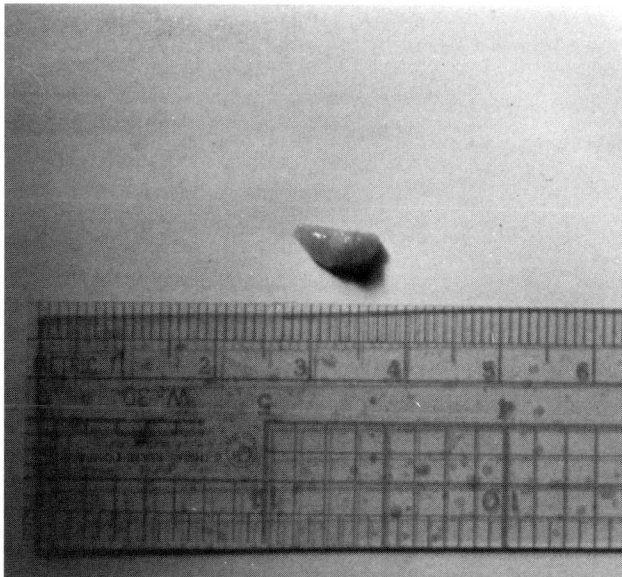

Figure 10-2. This specimen was aspirated from the popliteal artery after superficial femoral artery angioplasty with embolization. It was retrieved with an 8 French nontapered catheter. Pathologic evaluation revealed it to be atheromatous material.

within the same stage. No patients were made worse. However, the results were based on a combination of percutaneous transluminal angioplasty, thrombolysis, and suction thromboembolectomy. Of the series, approximately 20 percent of patients had aspiration alone, 27 percent had a combination of thrombolysis and aspiration, 20 percent had angioplasty and aspiration, and 22 percent had a combination of all three procedures. Thus it is difficult to separate out in a statistically meaningful manner the efficacy of suction thromboembolectomy in isolation from the other techniques.

Poulain et al.[32] reported in 1991 on the use of suction thromboembolectomy in the treatment of acutely thrombosed arteriovenous hemodialysis fistulas (both synthetic graft and direct arteriovenous anastomoses). This was performed using 65 procedures in 55 patients. In this study, suction thromboembolectomy was used only after lytic therapy had been employed (either because of failure of thrombolysis or to remove residual resistant clot). Of 26 failed procedures, in all cases surgery salvaged the fistula using thrombectomy alone or coupled with revision. However, results in arteriovenous fistulas are not analogous or comparable to results in the native arterial tree.

The largest series documenting clinical results of percutaneous suction thromboembolectomy was reported in 1992 by Wagner and Starck, who reported on treatment results in 102 patients.[29] This series only dealt with acute arterial thromboembolic occlusion distal to the inguinal ligament. None of the reported cases was due to postangioplasty embolization. In this series, approximately 21 percent of the occlusions were in the superficial femoral artery, 42 percent were in the popliteal artery, and 37 percent were in the tibial arteries. The majority of occlusions were from 3 to 10 cm in length.

The technique involved antegrade puncture of the involved extremity and placement of an 8 French vascular sheath. A catheter was passed through the obstruction, and the distal runoff was studied. The nature of the obstruction (i.e., fresh or organized thrombus) was gleaned from the "feel" of the catheter passing through the obstruction. Suction was then applied to the catheter with a 50-ml syringe. If the embolic material was partially organized, a specially manufactured spiral guidewire or rotating basket was placed through the catheter to detach adherent material and to fragment large particles to allow for aspiration. The spiral guidewire could be hand- or motor-driven. The authors claim that vessel injury was limited to the intima. Of 102 patients, 87 percent had aspiration therapy alone, and 13 percent had combined aspiration and dislodgment-fragmentation using the spiral guidewire or basket.

The authors defined angiographic success as reperfusion of the previously completely occluded vascular segment with a residual stenosis of less than 50 percent. Primary clinical success was defined as improvement of at least one stage on the Fontaine scale at the time of release from the hospital. Angiographic success was achieved in 93 percent, and clinical success in 87 percent of patients. No patients required surgical embolectomy after percutaneous suction thromboembolectomy. There was a 9 percent complication rate, primarily groin hematomas, with one patient requiring postprocedure fasciotomy. Limb salvage in this series was 94 percent, and the 30-day mortality was 3.9 percent. Both these indicators compare favorably with the cumulative results of Fogarty thromboembolectomy series. The authors concluded that percutaneous suction thromboembolectomy is the treatment of choice for embolic arterial occlusion distal to the inguinal ligament.

The authors' overall success rate for percutaneous suction thromboembolectomy is approximately 80 percent for both primary angiographic and clinical results. Several failures had subsequent successful Fogarty procedures. Complications have included several large groin hematomas and two cases of distal embolization resistant to all subsequent therapy. Although these latter complications did not result in limb loss, there was a reduction in the runoff bed after the procedure. We anticipate that the results of using this technique will vary significantly from institution to institu-

tion based on patient selection as well as on the persistence of the interventionalist.

Investigational Devices

A variety of mechanical thrombolysis catheters have undergone successful in vitro investigation; however, clinical experience in all of these devices is limited or nonexistent.[33–40] The principal strategy is the use of a propeller-blade system for mechanical maceration of clot. This may be used in conjunction with transcatheter suction to remove the fragmented debris (Hawkins, Beck, Guenther, Amplatz, and various propeller and loop designs). Alternatively, the design of the blade and the speed of rotation may be such that a vortex is created that continually pulverizes the fragments until they "disintegrate" and are then allowed to embolize distally (Bildsoe, Kensey). Although clinical results are generally lacking, conceptual criticisms arise a priori to all these devices. All at least risk significant arterial wall injury because of the inclusion of rotating parts. Acute injury may involve intima or media dissection or direct vessel perforation. As is well documented, intima or media injury of sufficient magnitude may predispose to myointimal hyperplasia or accelerated atherosclerosis.[14] Further, the mechanisms would be expected to be fairly expensive. The flexibility and steerability of such devices to allow for selective branch catheterization need to be evaluated, as does the role of such devices in small-caliber arteries. In addition, all rotating mechanical thrombolytic catheters have been shown to cause distal embolization to varying degrees.[38] All rotating catheters have been shown in vitro to be impaired by the aggregation of fibrin on the drive shafts.[38] Finally, the devices must prove to have an advantage over presently available flexible, steerable, inexpensive suction catheter systems.

Several in vitro studies of thrombolysis using ultrasonic probes have been published.[41–44] The mechanism of thrombolysis is felt to be mechanical. Cavitation effects may play a small role as well. No in vivo studies have been published, to the authors' knowledge, using ultrasonic thrombolysis. The technology is limited by expense as well as by the inflexibility of the ultrasonic probe in its present configuration. Schmitz-Rode et al.[44] claim that the principal advantage of ultrasound-assisted percutaneous thrombectomy is the rapid oscillation of the probe, which prevents the catheter from becoming clogged with fragments of clot and fibrin. The fragmentation and removal of the clot are mostly due to the applied transcatheter suction and are independent of the ultrasound probe.

Conclusions

The authors do not view percutaneous suction thromboembolectomy as a panacea for all thrombotic or embolic processes or complications, and we do not believe it will replace Fogarty thromboembolectomy or thrombolytic therapy. However, it is an effective primary or adjunctive procedure that is simple in theory and technique, that is quick and inexpensive to perform, that has minimal complications, and that can be performed at the time of diagnostic angiography. The procedure can result in rapid reestablishment of blood flow to the ischemic limb.

References

1. Key E. Embolectomy in the treatment of circulatory disturbances in the extremities. Surg Gynecol Obstet 1923;36:309–312.
2. Green RM, DeWeese JA, Rob CG. Arterial embolectomy before and after the Fogarty catheter. Surgery 1975;77:24–33.
3. Fogarty TJ, Cranley JJ, Krause RJ, et al. A method for extraction of arterial emboli and thrombi. Surg Gynecol Obstet 1963;116:241–246.
4. Dale WA. Endovascular suction catheters for thrombectomy and embolectomy. J Thorac Cardiovasc Surg 1962;44:557–558.
5. Levy J, Butcher H. Arterial emboli: an analysis of 125 patients. Surgery 1970;68:968–973.
6. MacGowan W, Mooneerian R. A review of 174 patients with arterial embolism. Br J Surg 1973;60:894–898.
7. Baxter-Smith D, Ashton F, Slaney G. Peripheral arterial embolism: a 20-year review. J Cardiovasc Surg 1988;29:453–457.
8. Satiani B, Gross W, Evans W. Improved limb salvage after arterial embolectomy. Ann Surg 1978;188:153–157.
9. Balas P, Bonatsos G, Xeromeritis N, et al. Early surgical results in acute arterial occlusion of the extremities. J Cardiovasc Surg 1983;26:262–269.
10. Abbott WM, Maloney RD, McCabe CC, et al. Arterial embolism: a 44-year perspective. Am J Surg 1982;143:460–464.
11. Dobrin PB. Mechanisms and prevention of arterial injuries caused by balloon embolectomy. Surgery 1989;106:457–466.
12. Foster JH, Carter JW, Graham CP Jr, et al. Arterial injury secondary to the use of the Fogarty catheter. Ann Surg 1970;171:971–978.
13. Byrnes G, MacGowan WA. The injury potential of Fogarty balloon catheters. J Cardiovasc Surg 1975;16:590–593.
14. Schwartz TH, Dobrin PB, Mikvicka R, et al. Early myointimal hyperplasia after balloon catheter embolectomy: effect of shear forces and multiple withdrawals. J Vasc Surg 1988;7:495–499.
15. Jorgensen RA, Dobrin PB. Balloon embolectomy catheters in small arteries: IV. Correlation of shear forces with histologic injury. Surgery 1983;93:798–808.
16. Dujovny M, Laha RK, Barrionuevo P. Endothelial changes secondary to the use of a Fogarty catheter. Surg Neurol 1977;7:39–41.
17. Dobrin PB, Jorgensen RA. Balloon embolectomy catheters in small arteries: a technique to prevent excessive shear forces. J Vasc Surg 1985;2:692–696.
18. Schweitzer DL, Aguam AS, Wilder JR. Complications encountered during arterial embolectomy with the Fogarty balloon catheter. Vasc Surg 1976;10:144–156.
19. Chidi CG, DePalma RG. Atherogenic potential of the embolectomy catheter. Surgery 1978;83:549–557.
20. Albrechtsson U, Einarsson E, Tylen U. Complications secondary to thrombectomy with the Fogarty balloon catheter. Cardiovasc Intervent Radiol 1981;4:15–16.
21. Greenwood LH, Hallett JW Jr, Yrizarry JM, et al. Diffuse arterial narrowing after thromboembolectomy with the Fogarty balloon catheter. AJR 1984;142:141–142.
22. White GH, White RA, Kopchok GE, et al. Angioscopic thromboembolectomy: preliminary observations with a recent technique. J Vasc Surg 1988;7:318–325.
23. Crispin HA. Experience with the vascular brush. J Cardiovasc Surg 1987;28:45–49.
24. Garcia R, Saroyan RM, Senkowsky J, et al. Intraoperative intraarterial urokinase infusion as an adjunct to Fogarty catheter embolectomy in acute arterial occlusion. Surg Gynecol Obstet 1990;171:201–205.
25. Greenfield LJ, Garman O, Kimmell MSE, et al. Transvenous removal of pulmonary emboli by vacuum-cup catheter technique. J Surg Res 1969;9:347–352.
26. Moore JH Jr, Koolpe AJ, Carabasi A, et al. Transvenous catheter pulmonary embolectomy. Arch Surg 1985;120:1372–1375.
27. Stewart JR, Greenfield LJ. Transvenous vena caval filtration and pulmonary embolectomy. Surg Clin North Am 1982;62:411–430.
28. Schmitz-Rode T, Günther RW. New device for percutaneous fragmentation of pulmonary emboli. Radiology 1991;180:135–137.
29. Wagner HJ, Starck EE. Acute embolic occlusions of the infrainguinal arteries: percutaneous aspiration embolectomy in 102 patients. Radiology 1992;182:403–407.
30. Sniderman KW, Bodner L, Saddekni S, et al. Percutaneous embolectomy by transcatheter aspiration. Radiology 1984;150:357–361.
31. Starck EE, McDermott JC, Crummy AB, et al. Percutaneous aspiration thromboembolectomy. Radiology 1985;156:61–66.
32. Poulain F, Raynaud A, Bourquelot P, et al. Local thrombolysis and thromboaspiration in the treatment of acutely thrombosed arteriovenous hemodialysis fistulas. Cardiovasc Intervent Radiol 1991;14:98–101.
33. Bildsoe MC, Moradian GP, Hunter DW, et al. Mechanical clot dissolution: new concept. Radiology 1989;171:231–233.
34. Hawkins IF, Helms R, Spencer C, et al. Mechanical spiral embolectomy catheter. Semin Intervent Radiol 1985;2:414–418.
35. Kensey RK, Nash JE, Abrahams C, et al. Recanalization of obstructed arteries with flexible rotating tip catheter. Radiology 1987;165:387–389.
36. Guenther RW, Vorwerk D. Aspiration catheter for percutaneous thrombectomy: clinical results. Radiology 1990;175:271–273.
37. Schmitz-Rode T, Günther RW. Functional properties of the Kensey arterial recanalization catheter: in vitro investigations. Invest Radiol 1990;25:631–637.
38. Schmitz-Rode T, Günther RW. Percutaneous mechanical thrombolysis: a comparative study of various rotational catheter systems. Invest Radiol 1991;26:557–563.
39. Günther RW, Vorwerk D. A new aspiration thromboembolectomy catheter with propeller-tipped rotating wire. J Intervent Radiol 1990;5:17–20.
40. Yasui K, Quian Z, Nazarian GK, et al. Recirculation-type Amplatz clot macerator: determination of particle size and distribution. J Vasc Intervent Radiol 1993;4:275–278.
41. Trübestein G, Engel C, Etzel F, et al. Thrombolysis by ultrasound. Clin Sci Mol Med 1976;51:697S–698S.
42. Siegel RJ, Cumberlan DC, Meler RK, et al. Percutaneous ultrasonic angioplasty: initial clinical experience. Lancet 1989;2:772–774.
43. Schmitz-Rode T, Günther RW. Oscillating probe aspiration thrombectomy: comparative in vitro evaluation of two concepts. Cardiovasc Intervent Radiol 1992;15:151–153.
44. Schmitz-Rode T, Günther RW, Müller-Leisse C. U.S.-assisted aspiration thrombectomy: in vitro investigations. Radiology 1991;178:677–679.

11

Percutaneous Image-Guided Biopsy

JEFFREY S. MOULTON

The first percutaneous needle biopsy procedure was performed in Germany in 1883. While the theoretical foundation for modern techniques was laid at that time, the pioneers would scarcely recognize the procedure given its current sophistication. Increasing acceptance by both practitioners and referring physicians has made it the most frequently performed interventional radiological procedure. This continued growth is attributable to three major factors. First, the development and evolution of cytologic techniques have allowed pathologic diagnoses to be made on the basis of the examination of individual cells. Second, recent advances in radiologic guidance techniques permit accurate and minimally invasive access to almost any site in the body. Third, the procedure has proved to be extremely safe when small-caliber aspiration needles are used.

Martin and Ellis from Memorial Hospital in New York are generally acknowledged as the founders of the needle aspiration technique. Martin, a head and neck surgeon, was reluctant to treat cancer patients without a preoperative pathologic diagnosis. He felt that surgery performed only for diagnosis carried an unacceptable risk of tumor dissemination in resectable disease and exposed patients to undue cost and morbidity in unresectable disease. Needle aspiration biopsy emerged as an alternative. The technique, which involved a simple handheld syringe and 18-gauge needle, was refined in the 1920s with initial results published in 1930.[1] The procedure did not initially gain widespread acceptance in the United States, in part because the cytologic specimens from 18-gauge needles were thick and poorly prepared, thus requiring unequivocal evidence of malignancy for diagnosis. At that time the use of larger cutting needles to obtain histologic cores carried an unacceptably high complication rate.

Ultimately, needle biopsy for the preoperative diagnosis of tumors was replaced by intraoperative frozen section techniques. In the 1950s percutaneous biopsy techniques were reborn in Europe with the development of small-caliber aspiration needles, which could obtain excellent cytologic specimens with minimal risk. Advancements in specimen preparation, largely refined in Sweden in the 1960s, improved the ability to interpret such specimens. The potential scope of percutaneous biopsy expanded dramatically with the development of cross-sectional guidance modalities, primarily ultrasound and computed tomography (CT). However, it was not until the 1970s that the procedure began to gain more widespread acceptance in the United States.

Over the last 20 years there has been further evolution of pathologic techniques, biopsy needle technology, and guidance modalities. Numerous investigators have advanced the technique with continued improvements in accuracy and safety. In the current cost-conscious medical environment, percutaneous biopsy will assume an even greater role as an inexpensive, safe, and effective diagnostic tool. This chapter summarizes the current status of percutaneous biopsy and the theoretical basis of modern techniques.

Pathologic Considerations

The accuracy of cytologic diagnosis is one of the major reasons for the widespread acceptance of percutaneous biopsy. The primary indication for biopsy is the nonsurgical diagnosis of cancer, and this task is well served. Malignant sensitivity is reported to range from 56 to 93 percent, with some of the variation depending on the biopsy site and the types of tumors included in different studies.[2-12] Most series report a diagnostic accuracy greater than 85 percent. However, as the practice of percutaneous biopsy has spread and expectations have grown, both the strengths and limitations of the cytologic technique have become apparent. It is important that the limitations are recognized and addressed if the procedure is to continue to evolve.

It cannot be overemphasized that the results of fine-needle aspiration biopsy to a significant degree depend on the cytologist. However, like all of medicine, cytology is an art as well as a science. Most pathologists are well schooled in classical surgical histology, but fewer are true experts in cytology. Practitioners should carefully review the results of percutaneous biopsy at their institution to determine whether accuracy and complication rates are acceptable. If so, then no significant changes in their biopsy technique should be undertaken. However, if results are suboptimal, it is important to understand why and to take steps to correct any deficiencies. It is not possible for a radiologist to control the available level of expertise in the pathology department, but it is possible to minimize its impact on biopsy results if necessary.

To better understand the capabilities of cytology and histology, it is helpful to more closely examine the pathologic nature of tumors and the techniques used to define them. There is a spectrum of pathologic change within all tissue from normal to frankly malignant. On a cellular basis certain benign neoplastic and reactive conditions resemble their tissue of origin to a remarkable degree. The spectrum continues into conditions in which cellular features and architectural organization are deemed atypical or dysplastic. There is a fine line between these pathologic conditions and well-differentiated malignant tumors. Poorly differentiated tumors represent the far end of the spectrum and bear only slight resemblance to the parent tissue. To differentiate benign from malignant conditions, pathologists rely on both cellular and architectural features. Cellular changes include alterations in the appearance of the cytoplasm, nuclei, nucleoli, and chromatin. Architectural changes include the loss of normal tissue organization, associated supporting stromal features, and capsular and vascular invasion. Cytologic interpretation involves the evaluation of a cellular monolayer and is therefore best suited to demonstrate individual cellular morphologic changes. Histologic interpretation involves evaluation of not only the cellular morphology but also the overall architectural organization of a tumor, including the intercellular matrix and supporting stromal components. These basic differences between cytologic and histologic examination help to explain some of the strengths and limitations of each.

The reported false-negative rates for percutaneous biopsy range from 7 to 44 percent.[2–12] False-negative diagnoses result from either sampling error or pathologic interpretive error and can occur with either cytologic or histologic specimens. Sampling error may occur simply because the target lesion was missed. This is somewhat unusual given modern guidance techniques but can still occur in small deep lesions, poorly visualized lesions, and uncooperative patients. More commonly, sampling error is due to retrieval of nonrepresentative tissue from the target lesion. Some large

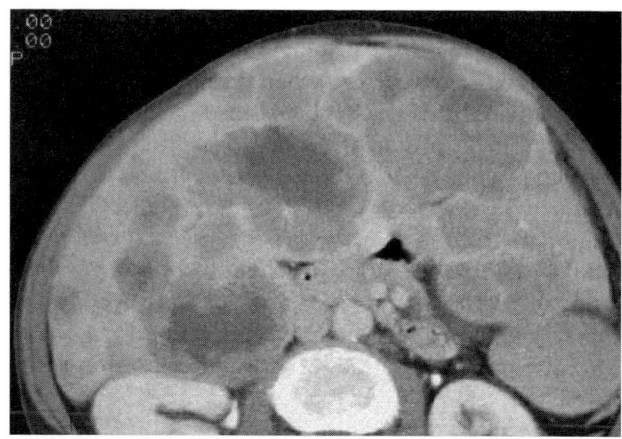

A

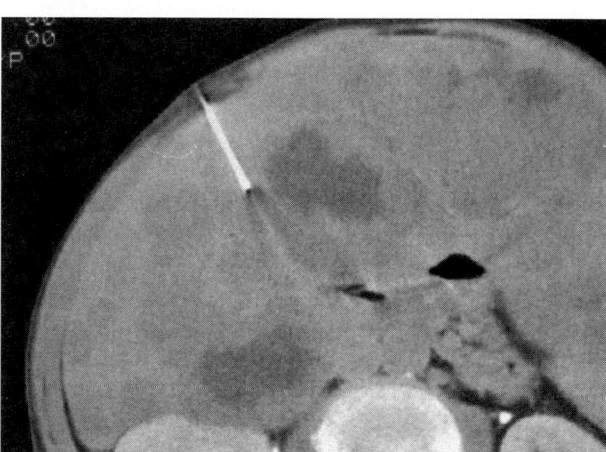

B

Figure 11-1. Metastatic adenocarcinoma of the colon. (A) Contrast-enhanced CT section shows multiple hypodense lesions, at least two of which show central necrosis. (B) A 19-gauge guiding needle is placed through a rim of normal liver parenchyma to the partially enhancing rim of a tumor nodule to avoid sampling error due to the central necrosis.

tumors have extensive areas of central necrosis that will not yield recognizable malignant cells if sampled (Fig. 11-1). Certain tumors elicit a dense, fibrous, desmoplastic reaction (e.g., breast and pancreatic carcinoma) or a surrounding inflammatory response (e.g., lung carcinoma or lymphoma). Sampling of these areas may yield nonspecific benign reactive tissue without diagnostic malignant cells. Extremely vascular tumors may yield only blood.

Pathologic interpretive error is less common but does occur.[13,14] In a retrospective review of cytologic specimens from lung cancer, Taft et al.[15] found a 6 to 16 percent intraobserver variability as to whether the specimens were deemed benign or malignant. Because cytology depends on morphologic changes in individual cells, the more closely the tumor cells resemble normal cells the more difficult is the cytologic diagnosis. For this reason, pathologic interpretive error is a more significant problem when dealing with very well differentiated malignant neoplasms. Such tumors may defy cytologic diagnosis because the determination of malignant potential requires histologic architectural changes such as vascular or capsular invasion.[14,16] The majority of tumors, however, are less well differentiated and have such striking cellular morphologic alterations that the diagnosis of malignancy is readily and reliably made by cytologic examination.

False-positive diagnoses are reported to occur in 1 to 2 percent of cases and contribute to the false-negative rate in an indirect way.[10-12] Certain benign neoplasms and reactive or inflammatory conditions have enough cellular atypia and pleomorphism to mimic a well-differentiated malignancy.[14,16] Because of the clinical and medicolegal implications of a false-positive diagnosis, pathologists are more likely to err on the conservative side when faced with a borderline specimen. Thus they may be more willing to accept a slightly higher false-negative rate rather than risk a false-positive diagnosis.

Accuracy in the cytologic diagnosis of benign conditions is lower than that for malignant tumors. Literature series report that a specific diagnosis can be made in up to 65 percent of benign lesions by cytologic examination alone.[4-8] This is not surprising if we remember that many benign lesions are defined histologically with little cytologic differentiation from the parent tissue. Histologic architecture is lost in aspiration specimens, and diagnoses that are based on histology are not possible.[14] A specific diagnosis can be made in conditions with characteristic cellular morphology such as a pulmonary hamartoma or hepatic steatosis, as well as in some infectious lesions and benign simple cysts; but most benign neoplasms, reactive changes, and inflammatory conditions present a greater problem for cytologic diagnosis (Fig. 11-2). The significance of this fact depends somewhat on the patient population seen in any given practice. If benign lesions represent only a small percentage of the cases seen, then the ability to make a specific benign diagnosis becomes less important.

A significant limitation of aspiration cytology is a variable negative predictive value that ranges from 17 to 69 percent.[1,5-8,11,12] The negative predictive value depends on both the false-negative rate and the prevalence of malignancy in a given series. Both a high false-negative rate and a high prevalence of malignancy will lead to a lower negative predictive value. A nonspecific true-negative specimen will appear, by cytologic examination, very similar to a false-negative specimen in which peritumoral inflammation or fibrosis is re-

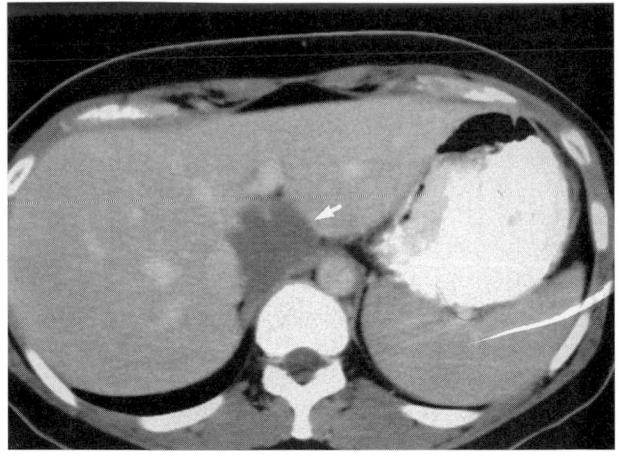

A

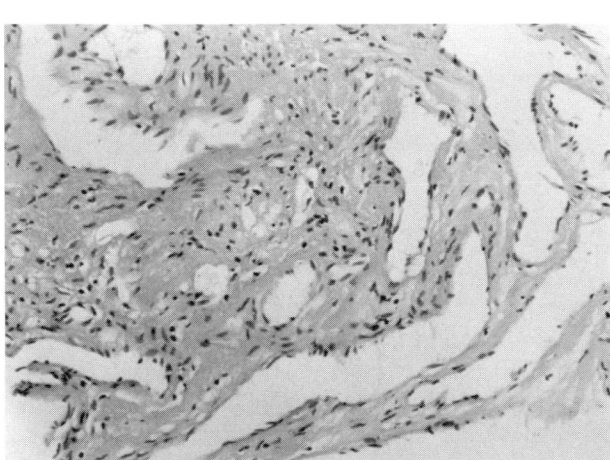

B

Figure 11-2. (A) Contrast-enhanced CT section shows an irregular nonenhancing mass (*arrow*) between the liver and the right crus of the diaphragm. (B) Histologic section reveals irregular dilated lymphatic spaces lined by flattened endothelial cells representing a retroperitoneal lymphangioma. The aspiration cytology specimen revealed only normal lymphocytes.

trieved. The result is that most nonspecific cancer negative diagnoses must undergo further diagnostic evaluation, either repeat biopsy or surgical excision. If a specific benign diagnosis is made, the negative predictive value improves considerably and no further evaluation is usually necessary.[17]

Both cytologic and histologic examination perform well in the diagnosis of malignancy, but the determination of the cellular subtype and origin of a tumor may be more difficult. It is usually possible to differentiate major classes of tumor such as epithelial versus mesenchymal malignancy. Certain tumors (e.g., melanoma and myeloma) have distinctive enough cytologic features to allow a specific diagnosis.[16,18] When there is

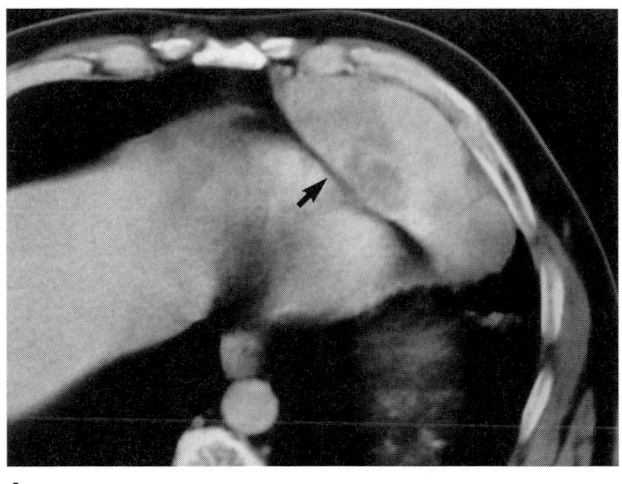

A

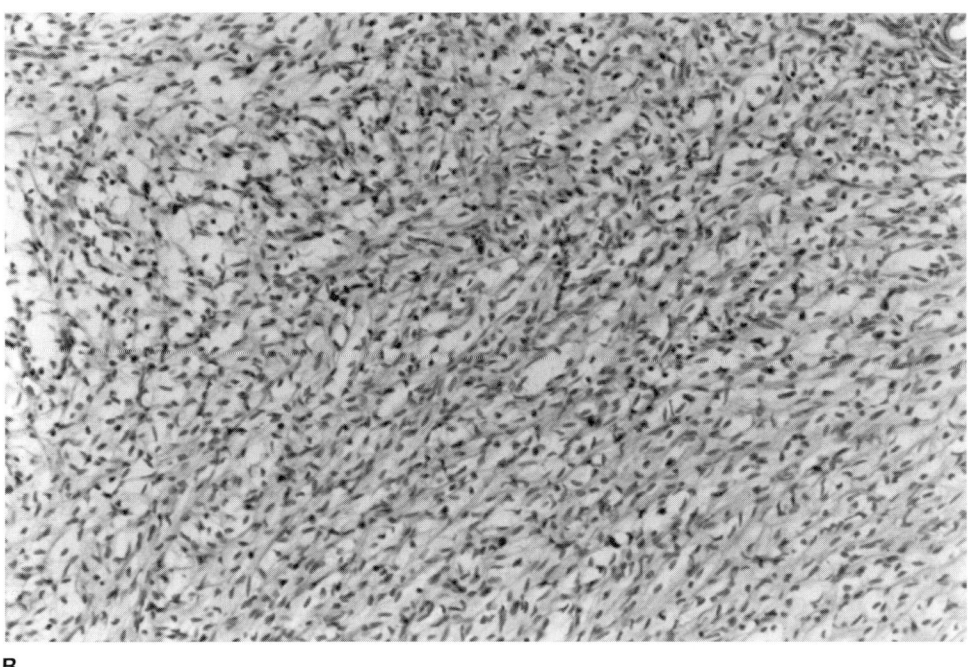

B

Figure 11-3. (A) CT section shows an enhancing mass (*arrow*) arising near the anterolateral pericardium and diaphragm. Coaxial biopsy was performed via an angled subxiphoid approach using both an 18-gauge automated gun and a 22-gauge Chiba needle. (B) Histologic section demonstrates a low-grade malignant spindle-cell neoplasm representing a primary pericardial fibrosarcoma. The aspiration cytology specimen was nondiagnostic.

glandular or squamous differentiation of an epithelial malignancy, the potential sources can be narrowed. Diagnosis and subtyping of mesenchymal malignancies (sarcomas and lymphomas) are more difficult by cytology alone (Fig. 11-3).[14,16,18] Such subclassification often depends on the histologic architecture and the relationship between supporting stromal components and the malignant cellular components. Because the stromal component is absent in cytologic specimens, further classification may be hampered.

There is some concern regarding the reliability of tumor subtyping by needle biopsy in relation to the ultimate surgical pathologic classification. Most studies on cytologic-histologic correlation have involved examination of resected thoracic malignancies. Cytologic-histologic correlation in regard to tumor subtyping is better for well-differentiated tumors and less reliable for poorly differentiated tumors.[10,11,15,19] It is known that there may be significant pleomorphism within a given tumor mass in terms of both differentiation and cell type.[14,15] The specific area of the tumor sampled may not reflect the dominant pathology of the tumor as a whole. This is a problem shared by both cytologic and histologic needle biopsy specimens.

There is also controversy surrounding the accuracy of surgical pathologic classification of resected specimens. For well-differentiated tumors a 2 to 5 percent interobserver variability in cell type designation has been reported; this increases to 20 to 42 percent for poorly differentiated tumors.[15,20] An intraobserver variability of 2 to 20 percent is reported in cell type determination. Given these data, it is clear that even histologic examination of resected specimens is a flawed gold standard. This places the reported subtyping inaccuracies of percutaneous biopsy in a more favorable light. Of primary importance is the impact of subtype determinations on clinical management. Determining a specific subtype is important only if there are significantly different effective therapeutic regimens for different tumors. The best example of this is small-cell undifferentiated carcinoma of the lung, which for the most part is treated chemotherapeutically rather than surgically, as in most other lung tumors. Studies have shown that cytology can adequately differentiate small-cell carcinoma from non-small-cell malignancies in over 90 percent of cases.[16,19] Cytologic-histologic correlation is probably also adequate for most nonpulmonary epithelial malignancies, although less information is available on this subject. On the other hand, adequate subclassification of lymphoma is achieved in only 40 to 80 percent of cases by cytology alone.[3,17,21] Overall it would seem that the accuracy of tumor subtyping by cytologic means is clinically adequate for epithelial malignancies but suboptimal for mesenchymal malignancies.

In 1930 Martin and Ellis[1] wrote that

> the chief disadvantage of biopsy by aspiration is that . . . the specimen is very small. In such a small specimen the characteristic cell arrangement is usually lost entirely. While the lack of definite cell arrangement in smears . . . often prevents accurate classification of the lesion, one is still able to determine whether such tissue is malignant or benign. The aspiration of [nonmalignant] tissue may not be considered alone as conclusive evidence of a benign process. The pathologist . . . must be capable of intelligently utilizing what may be called his pathological imagination.

It is remarkable that several of the limitations in cytologic diagnosis we face today were recognized in the first formal study of the technique. In the following years there has been continuous evolution and refinement of fine-needle aspiration biopsy techniques in an attempt to address these limitations. In general, the approaches may be summarized as obtaining more tissue for examination, obtaining better tissue specimens, and improving the techniques of pathologic examination of the specimens.

Obtaining more tissue for cytologic examination will decrease both sampling and interpretive errors. If a greater number of cells are retrieved, there is a greater likelihood that diagnostic cells will be present. The simplest way to do this is to make a greater number of biopsy passes, often using a tandem, coaxial, or modified coaxial system for ease of localization. Attempts should be made to sample several different areas within a given lesion to account for fibrous and inflammatory stromal reactions, necrosis, and intratumoral cellular pleomorphism. It has also been reported that the use of larger aspiration needles and aspiration needles with modified tip configurations allows one to retrieve more tissue and improve the diagnostic results.[22-24]

The "quick-stain" technique involves immediate staining and microscopic examination of cytologic specimens while the biopsy is still in progress. In theory this should decrease false-negative results due to sampling error, but the only controlled study of this method did not show a significant improvement in results.[25] Cytologic tissue preparation is not ideal with this technique, and in practice it primarily serves to determine whether an adequately cellular specimen has been retrieved rather than to render a definitive diagnosis. In addition, the equipment and properly trained personnel necessary for an accurate on-site specimen evaluation are not always available in community hospitals. If these are available, however, the technique can be useful in particularly difficult cases or in cases in which a repeat biopsy may expose the patient to undue risk. Although best suited for cytologic aspirates, touch preparations of histologic specimens may also be examined in this fashion.

Different methods of pathologic examination of specimens have improved both sensitivity and specificity. Special stains to identify subcellular architecture and cellular biochemical products have helped in determining tumor subtypes.[14,18] Electron microscopy for ultrastructural analysis can also help in this regard but is expensive, cumbersome, and not routinely available.[16] Immunocytochemical studies are helpful, particularly in the subclassification of lymphomas.[16,18,21] Special stains and cultures are useful in improving the specificity of diagnosis in benign infectious processes.[11]

The most effective method of improving biopsy accuracy is to obtain specimens for histologic as well as cytologic examination. Initial attempts to obtain histologic specimens focused on obtaining microhistologic fragments using modified 20- to 22-gauge aspiration needles.[2,11,12,23,26,27] These studies showed that, when evaluated separately, the results of cytologic examination were better than the results of microhistologic examination. When the results were combined, however, overall biopsy accuracy improved. Although the reports from different institutions varied, several conclusions could be made. In institutions with very high cytologic accuracy there was less additional benefit from microhistology.[11,17] A greater improvement in accuracy could be obtained if adequate microhistologic cores could be obtained in a high percentage of cases.[12,27,28] The improvement in results was generally better in terms of tumor subtype designation than in terms of malignant sensitivity.[2,11,12,27] Pathologists were also subjectively more comfortable in rendering a definitive diagnosis when both types of specimens were available for examination. Most importantly, each series reported cases in which the histology was diagnostic while the cytology was not and vice versa. This difference suggests that improvements in sampling error played a significant role in improved results. The conclusion was that cytologic and histologic examination were complementary. This conclusion is logical in that cytologic specimens are best suited to evaluate cellular and nuclear morphologic changes whereas histologic specimens are best suited to evaluate architectural changes. It is unreasonable to expect either technique to optimally evaluate both types of pathologic change.

Microhistologic fragments are quite small by pathologic standards and seem to be in an intermediate category between optimal cytologic specimens and optimal histologic specimens. Weisbrod et al.[23] referred to such fragments as "glorified cytologic specimens that had the disadvantage of being processed by a technique that is inferior for cytologic purposes." Recent studies have focused on using different needles to improve both the histologic recovery rate and the quality of histologic specimens. Obtaining true histologic cores with cutting needles has been shown to improve all aspects of biopsy accuracy.[17,29] Malignant sensitivity of greater than 90 percent can be routinely obtained.[6,8,9,17,29-33] Accuracy in diagnosing lymphoma and other mesenchymal malignancies can be improved from 20 to 70 percent by cytology alone to 80 to 90 percent by histology (Fig. 11-4).[8,17,34] There is also a dramatic improvement in the ability to obtain a specific pathologic diagnosis in benign disease.[6,8,17,33] The importance of a specific benign diagnosis is probably the single greatest contribution of histology because in such cases the negative predictive value approaches 100 percent (Fig. 11-5).[6,17,33] This has the potential to eliminate one of the key weaknesses of aspiration biopsy: the need for surgery or repeat biopsy in cancer-negative cases. Accurate subtyping of malignancies,

particularly those of mesenchymal origin, is also improved significantly when tumor architecture can be evaluated.[6,11,12,17,28] This will have a greater impact on tumors for which specific effective chemotherapeutic regimens are available.

Close cooperation between the radiology and pathology departments is critical in maximizing biopsy accuracy. Cases should be discussed in depth with the pathologist before the biopsy so that proper specimens can be obtained, depending on the needs of the pathologist. While decisions regarding specimen handling and preparation should be left to the pathologists, they are much better able to make these decisions if they know the clinical and radiographic differential diagnosis. With this knowledge they can choose which pathologic examination techniques are most appropriate to answer the clinicoradiologic questions. The pathologist can also advise the radiologist regarding specimen needs. This includes the need for histologic specimens, the transport medium in which specimens will be delivered, and the amount of tissue needed, which may be greater if additional studies such as special stains, immunohistochemical studies, or electron microscopy will be necessary.

Some uncertainty in diagnosis is inherent in the need for biopsy in the first place. Nevertheless, it is frequently possible to predict the pathologic nature of a lesion by clinical history and imaging characteristics prior to biopsy. The majority of biopsy cases encountered represent metastatic disease from known primary epithelial tumors. It can be argued that the accuracy of cytologic diagnosis is so high in this situation that histologic cores are not necessary. Larger needle core biopsies may then be reserved for more difficult pathologic questions or for repeat biopsies in those cases where the initial results were inconclusive. However, in a significant number of cases there are definite advantages to the addition of histology. If histologic specimens can safely be obtained, then there is no advantage to aspiration biopsy alone. We are now at a point where such specimens can be routinely and safely obtained by percutaneous methods. If high-quality specimens for both cytology and histology are obtained, there will be fewer pathologic interpretive errors and less dependence on an expert cytopathologist. Further improvements in biopsy accuracy will depend on reducing sampling error, which is primarily under the control of the radiologist.

Technical Considerations

Biopsy devices and techniques have been modified and refined in attempts to increase accuracy, decrease

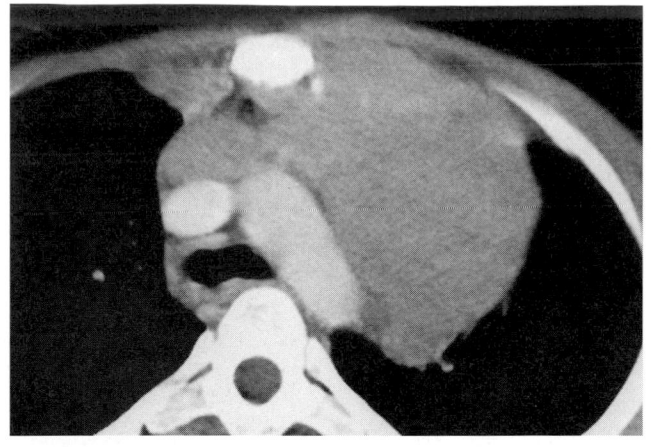

A

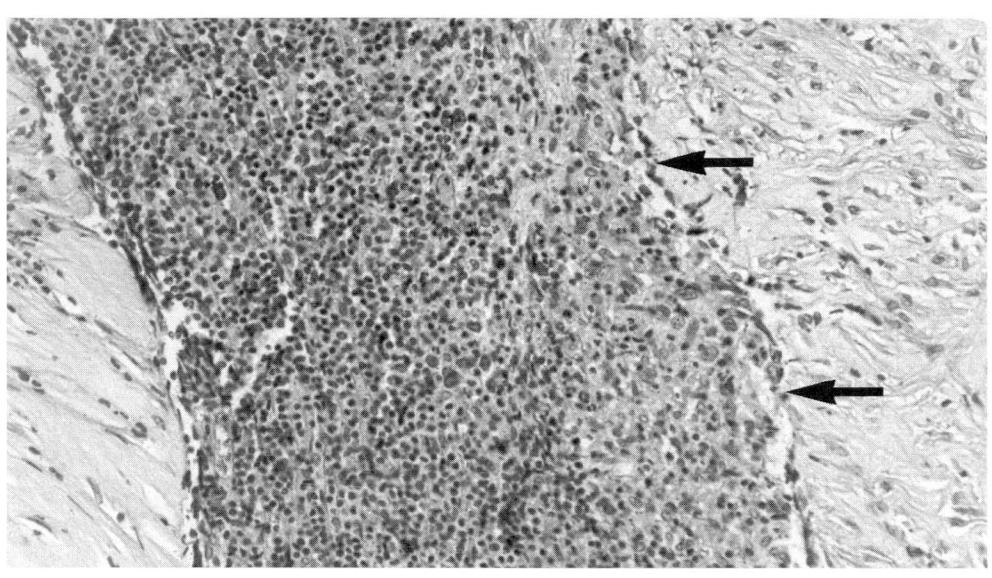

B

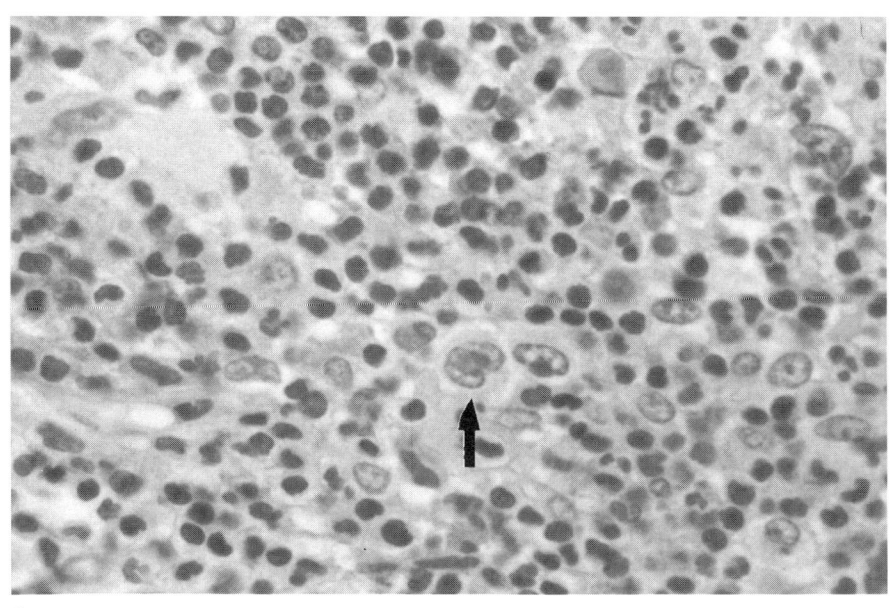

C

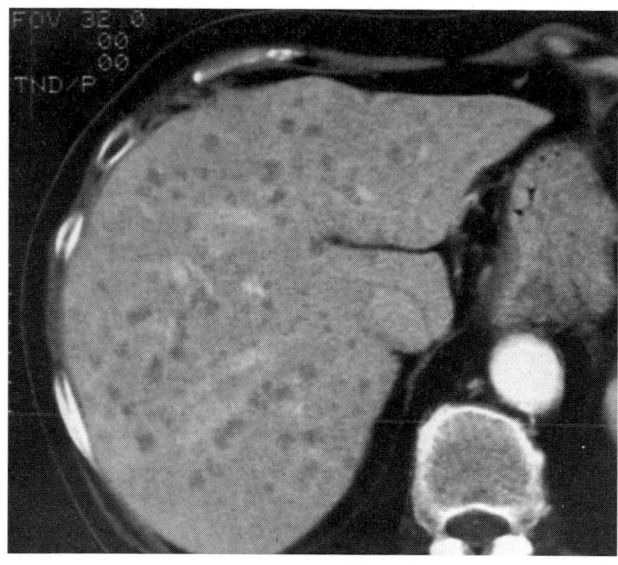

A

B

Figure 11-5. (A) Contrast-enhanced CT section shows multiple low-density liver lesions in a patient with rheumatoid arthritis and elevated liver enzymes. (B) Histologic section demonstrates pallisading epithelial macrophages (*curved arrow*) and a portion of a necrobiotic rheumatoid nodule (*straight arrows*). The aspiration cytology specimen revealed only nonspecific inflammatory cells. The liver lesions resolved after steroid therapy.

◄ **Figure 11-4.** Nodular sclerosing Hodgkin disease. (A) CT section demonstrates a large anterior mediastinal mass. Biopsy was performed using both an 18-gauge automated biopsy gun and a 22-gauge aspiration needle. The cytology specimen revealed only nonspecific inflammatory cells. (B) Low-power view of the histologic section shows a lymphoid tumor nodule (*arrows*) surrounded by bands of dense sclerosis. (C) Higher-power view of the histologic section shows several Reed-Sternberg cells (*arrow*) with a pleomorphic background of inflammatory cells and small lymphocytes.

complications, or both, with variable success. Although technique is determined largely by user preference, certain developments have emerged as being more significant in optimizing results.

Biopsy Devices

Biopsy needles may be classified by tip configuration and size. The three major needle tip configurations are aspiration needles, modified aspiration needles, and cutting needles. Aspiration needles are thin-walled cannulas with a varying degree of bevel angulation at the tip. The most widely used examples are the spinal and Chiba needles. Modified aspiration needles have sharpened cutting edges and differing tip shapes designed to enhance recovery of both cytologic and microhistologic specimens. Examples include the Greene, Turner, Franseen, and Westcott needles. Cutting needles are designed to obtain histologic cores rather than cytologic specimens. The two major mechanisms of action of cutting needles are the Menghini and tru-cut mechanisms. The Menghini-type needles are hollow cannulas with a sharpened beveled tip that cuts a cylindrical core of tissue during advancement while suction is maintained in the lumen. This is simply a larger version of a modified aspiration needle. The tru-cut type needles have a notched central stylet and outer cylindrical cannula. After the stylet is advanced, tissue enters the notch. A semicylindrical tissue core is then cut off by advancement of the outer cutting cannula. In theory the Menghini-type needles would retrieve a larger core for the same gauge as the tru-cut type needles. In practice, however, tru-cut type needles are more reliable in obtaining a satisfactory specimen.[35,36]

The latest biopsy devices are the automated guns that use a Menghini or tru-cut type needle attached to a spring-loaded handle that mechanically performs the steps of tissue retrieval. Tru-cut type needles are used much more commonly and, as with manual cutting needles, are more reliable in obtaining high-quality histologic cores.[35] Both "long-throw" and "short-throw" models are available, which vary the distance by which the stylet and cannula extend between the cocked and fired positions. The long-throw models have been shown to be more reliable than the short-throw models.[35,36] These devices greatly simplify the biopsy procedure and require less operator experience for optimal use than modified aspiration needles or manual cutting needles. A wide variety of automated devices are available, including disposable needles attached to a reusable gun, disposable gun-needle combinations (either one piece or detachable), and guns with variable throw lengths. Data are incomplete regarding the advantages and disadvantages of each.

There are three general categories of needle size. Small-caliber needles are 21 to 25 gauge, middle-caliber needles are 18 to 20 gauge, and large-caliber needles are 16 gauge or larger. In general, more tissue is retrieved by larger needles.[22] This does not mean, however, that larger needles are always better than smaller needles. If the intention is to obtain a specimen for cytologic evaluation, it is best to obtain a large number of individual cells separate from the supporting stroma so that a uniform monolayer of cells may be examined. Small-caliber aspiration and modified aspiration needles are best suited for this purpose. A common property of some cancer cells is poor intercellular cohesiveness, a feature that facilitates retrieval of a large number of malignant cells free of the surrounding stromal elements. The microhistologic fragments obtained using middle-caliber modified aspiration needles are not ideal for evaluation by cytologic techniques.[18,23]

If the intention is to obtain a specimen for histologic evaluation, cutting needles are clearly superior to modified aspiration needles.[22,36] Tissue fragments adequate for histologic evaluation are obtained in 38 to 92 percent of biopsies using modified aspiration needles.[2,11,12,23,26,27] In comparison, histologic recovery rates of 97 to 100 percent are achieved using automated tru-cut type biopsy devices.[17,29-31] Although larger cutting needles obtain larger cores, excellent specimens may be reliably retrieved with middle-caliber automated devices.[17,29,35] The choice depends on the estimated amount of tissue needed for adequate diagnosis and classification of a pathologic lesion and the risk factors attendant in biopsy in any given case.

Biopsy Technique

Optimal technique based on experience is probably more important than needle tip design or size when using aspiration or modified aspiration needles.[22,36] Manual Menghini- and tru-cut type needles also require some experience for proper use. Automated devices, on the other hand, have a more rapid and precise biopsy action that is less dependent on operator technique.

Several techniques have been developed to increase the amount of tissue retrieved, the simplest of which is to make multiple biopsy passes. If sequential separate biopsy passes are made, the needle tip must be localized with every pass. This is a more significant drawback when using CT guidance than when using ultrasound or fluoroscopic guidance. The tandem technique involves initial localization of a small-caliber needle followed by nonguided parallel placement of one or more biopsy needles to the same depth. The disadvantages of this method are that separate organ punctures are required for each biopsy pass and that tip localization is not precisely controlled. The coaxial technique involves placement of a thin-walled guiding needle, which is then used as a conduit for the biopsy needle. In the "short" coaxial method the guide is placed through the skin only and organ puncture is made by the biopsy needle. This may require localization of both the guide and the biopsy needle. In the "long" coaxial method the guide needle tip is placed in or at the margin of the lesion and requires localization of only the guiding needle. In the modified long coaxial method the initial localization is performed with a small-caliber needle. The hub of the small-caliber needle is removable so that a larger-caliber needle can be placed over it to the lesion and serve as the subsequent biopsy-guiding cannula. In this method the localization is performed with a small needle, which may be safer if multiple needle passes are necessary for adequate tip positioning.

There are several advantages to a coaxial system. Needle tip localization is performed only once, and multiple biopsy passes may be made with only one puncture of the target organ. It is relatively simple to use both small-caliber needles to obtain cytologic specimens and middle-caliber needles to obtain histologic cores via the same guiding needle. The most significant advantage is that virtually any needle may be placed through a coaxial guide, including automated devices. This negates all of the difficulties in localizing the cumbersome biopsy guns, particularly if CT guidance is used. The guide and biopsy needle may be manually angled for subsequent biopsy passes to sample different areas of a lesion. The guide may also be used for track embolization if necessary. The only disadvantage of the coaxial method is that the guide must have a larger caliber than the actual biopsy device, but this is not a significant drawback.

The purpose of percutaneous biopsy is to obtain diagnostic tissue samples with minimal risk to the patient. Even given the above advantages and disadvantages, the choice of needles and biopsy technique remains largely one of personal preference and experience. Practitioners should adopt a technique with which they are comfortable and should develop expertise in that technique. Nevertheless, results are the only true measure of technique, and physicians should remain open-minded regarding other methods that may improve both the accuracy and safety of biopsies in their particular institution.

Guidance Modalities

The evolution of guidance modalities has been a major factor in the increased acceptance of percutaneous biopsy. Initially percutaneous biopsies were either blind or guided only by palpation. Fluoroscopy was the first imaging tool used to guide biopsy needle placement, followed by ultrasound and CT. Each of these modalities has continued to evolve, becoming both more accurate and easier to use. Guidance by magnetic resonance imaging (MRI) is now being explored as well. More than any other aspect of technique, the choice of guidance modality is one of personal preference and experience. The basic tenet of guidance, regardless of which modality is chosen, is that it should allow safe and accurate placement of the biopsy needle with absolute documentation that the biopsy specimen was obtained from the target lesion. The best modality is usually that which best demonstrates the lesion and the adjacent vital structures.

Fluoroscopic guidance is now primarily used for lung biopsy. The major advantages are that needle advancement can be continuously monitored and that the length of time during which the needle is through the pleura is relatively short. Disadvantages are radiation exposure to the operator and difficulty in localizing small lesions and lesions in the hilum or mediastinum. Even with multiplanar fluoroscopy, it can be difficult to avoid crossing aerated lung during biopsy of pleural-based lesions.[37] Nonthoracic uses of fluoroscopic guidance are less common but very valuable in selected cases. Lesions of the appendicular skeleton may be biopsied under fluoroscopy, whereas lesions of the axial skeleton are best approached under CT guidance in order to avoid adjacent structures. Some lesions, such as mucosal tumors of the bile duct, are not visible on ultrasound or CT but are amenable to fluoroscopic-guided biopsy after ductal opacification. Endoluminal biliary histologic biopsy via a transhepatic track can be performed using devices designed for vascular atherectomy (Fig. 11-6).[38] This appears to be more accurate than endoluminal brush biopsy or percutaneous biopsy with small-caliber aspiration needles.

Ultrasound guidance has advanced tremendously in recent years with the advent of high-resolution scanners and small real-time phased array transducers. Ultrasound probably requires more operator expertise than other modalities but is also extremely flexible. Experienced practitioners favor a "free-hand" approach, controlling the biopsy needle with one hand and the transducer with the other. Mechanical needle guides attached to the transducer are also available if necessary. Advantages of ultrasound guidance include real-time visualization of the needle throughout placement, multiplanar approach capabilities, lack of ionizing radiation, speed, and cost (Fig. 11-7). The major disadvantage is that even with modern scanners it is occasionally difficult to precisely localize the needle tip in relation to the lesion. This drawback is evidenced

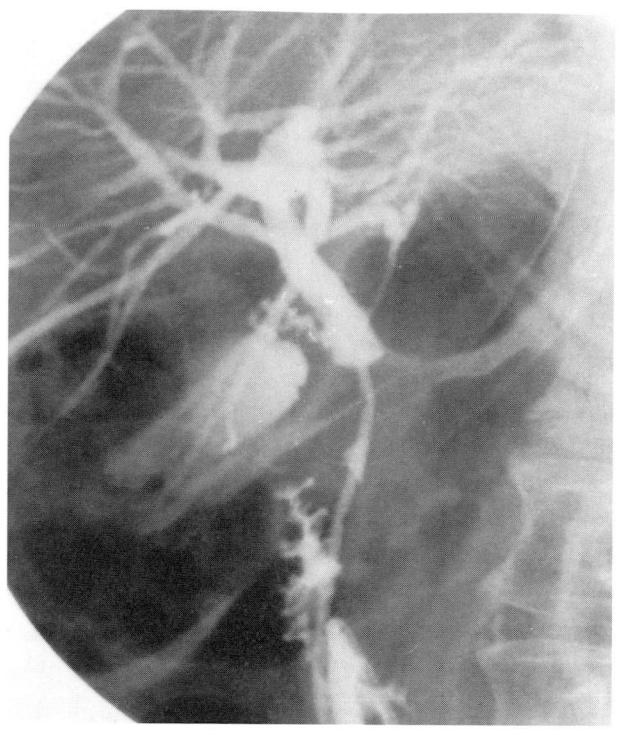

A

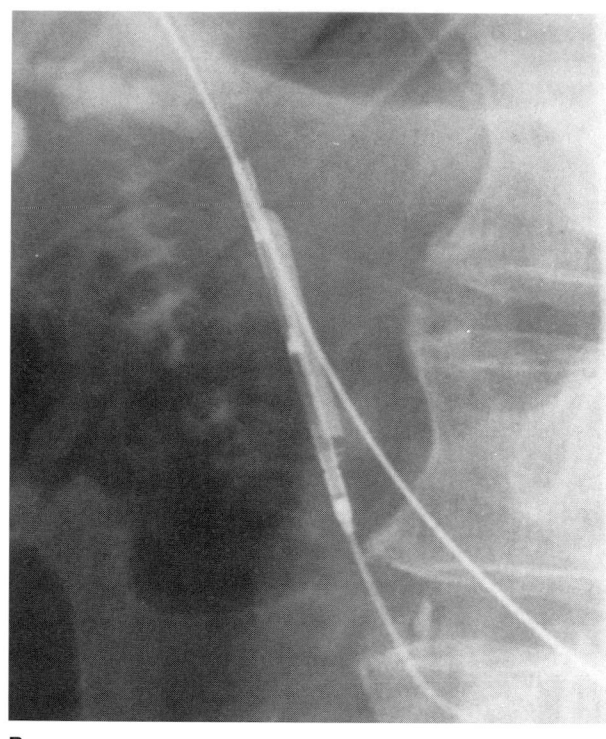

B

Figure 11-6. Extrahepatic cholangiocarcinoma. (A) Spot film from a transhepatic cholangiogram demonstrates an annular constricting lesion of the common bile duct. (B) An 8 French side-cutting atherectomy device is shown bridging

the common duct lesion with a safety guidewire in place. Histologic examination of the resected specimens revealed a cholangiocarcinoma.

Figure 11-7. Cavernous hemangioma of the liver. Imaging features were considered atypical by computed tomography. (A) Longutidinal ultrasound scan through the right lobe of the liver shows a well-defined hyperechoic mass (*arrows*).

(B) Scan during biopsy shows the distal needle shaft of an 18-gauge automated biopsy gun (*arrows*) within the mass. An oblique path was chosen to avoid puncturing the capsular surface of the mass. (Courtesy of Dr. Steve Parker.)

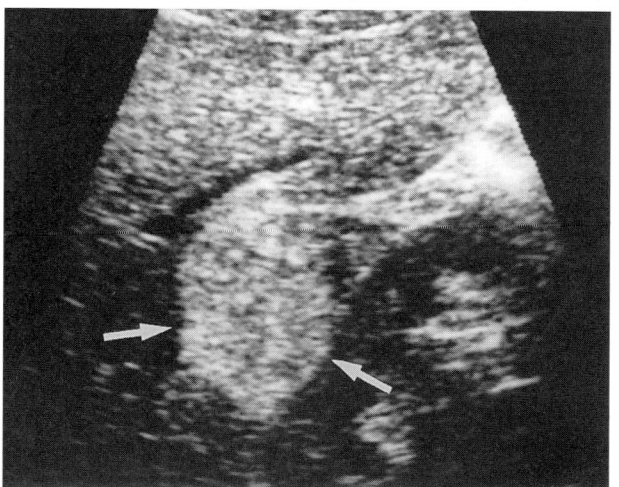

A

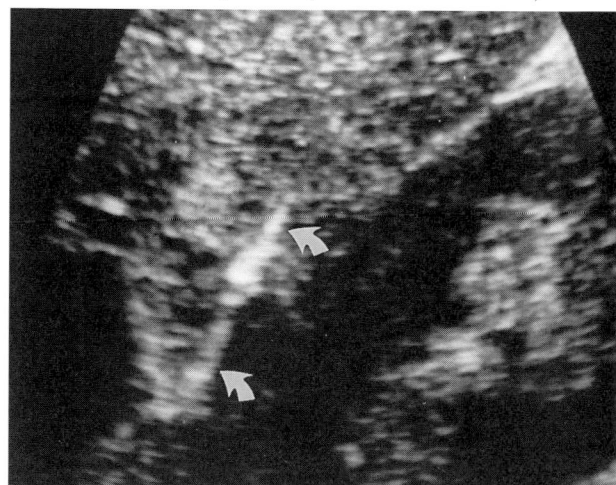

B

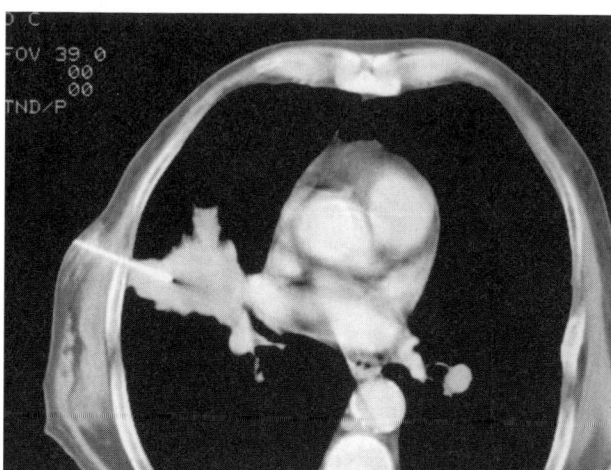

Figure 11-8. Small-cell anaplastic carcinoma of the right hilum with peripheral postobstructive atelectasis reaching the pleural surface. CT guidance allows precise placement of the guiding needle through the pleural attachment and into the central mass.

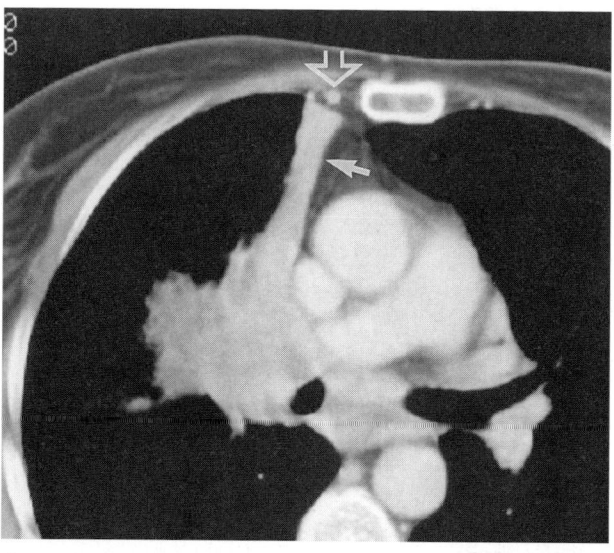

A

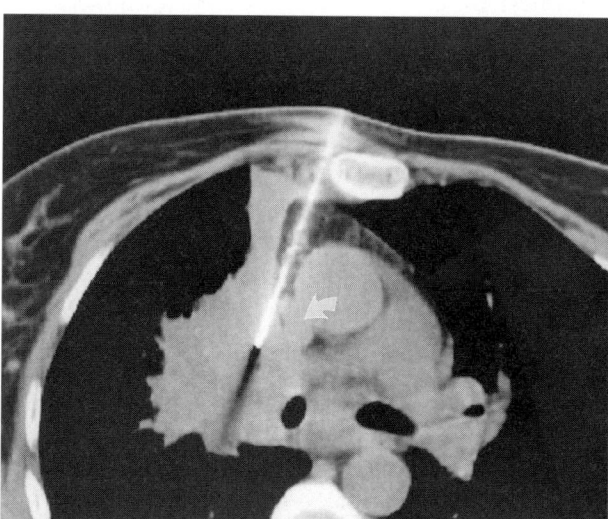

B

Figure 11-9. Small-cell anaplastic carcinoma of the right hilum. Bronchoscopic examination was nondiagnostic. (A) Contrast-enhanced CT section shows a 5-cm right hilar and mediastinal mass with a small linear wedge of collapsed upper lobe (*solid arrow*) extending to the anterior chest wall. *Open arrow*, internal mammary vein. (B) A 19-gauge guiding needle has been placed medial to the internal mammary vein and through the collapsed upper lobe into the central portion of the mass. The distal aspect of the guiding needle is immediately adjacent to the aorta and superior vena cava (*arrow*).

by attempts to design needles with greater visibility, including electronically enhanced passive transponders placed at the needle tip.[39] Overlying bone, bowel, or lung will obscure the underlying lesion, and deep or small lesions may be inadequately visualized for adequate localization.

CT guidance is the most accurate modality in terms of precise needle tip localization and can be applied to virtually any lesion in the body. It provides the best visualization of intervening and adjacent vital structures so that the safest biopsy path may be chosen. It is quite common to encounter lesions that cannot be safely approached by any other modality. Mediastinal and pleural-based lung lesions can be approached without crossing aerated lung in almost every case (Fig. 11-8). Biopsies may be safely performed immediately adjacent to major vascular structures in the mediastinum and retroperitoneum (Fig. 11-9). The optimal portion of a given lesion may be sampled to avoid regions of tumor necrosis. Mechanical needle-guiding devices are also available for CT, including devices designed specifically for use with automated biopsy guns. The use of such devices is largely one of personal preference.

In the past the most significant drawback of CT guidance has been the longer procedure time and the inability to visualize the needle in real time during placement. The latter has become less of a problem with greater experience. The recent development of high-speed scanners with much faster image reconstruction times has essentially eliminated the time constraints of CT guidance. Helical scanning also has the potential to greatly facilitate needle tip localization by minimizing respiratory misregistration.

Complications

The use of cutting needles to obtain tissue cores for histologic evaluation has been shown to have a significant impact on biopsy accuracy. It is equally important, however, that this be accomplished without an increase in complications. The demonstrated safety of 21- to 22-gauge aspiration needles is another major reason behind the growth of percutaneous biopsy techniques. Much of the reason that cytologic techniques evolved at all was the concern regarding the high complication rates associated with larger needles. This concern arose largely from early studies of lung biopsies using 14- to 16-gauge needles and has persisted despite a paucity of data regarding the risk of using such needles in biopsy of other organs.[40]

Martin and Ellis[1] again succinctly stated the problem in 1930, observing that "larger specimens uniformly fixed and stained offer more satisfactory material upon which to reach a definite opinion, but such a preparation can too often be obtained only at considerable disadvantage to the patient. A postmortem diagnosis never benefits the one most concerned, the donor of the specimen." All biopsies involve both risk and benefit. The benefits of core histology are clear, providing proper indications for the procedure are met. To completely justify their use, the risk associated with larger-caliber cutting needles must also compare favorably with that of small-caliber aspiration biopsy. Contraindications, although usually relative, must be considered.

Two complications, pneumothorax and bleeding, are of dominant concern and will be discussed separately. A third potential complication, needle track seeding, also crosses site-specific considerations and deserves special mention. Other less common complications are site-specific and will be discussed with regional biopsy considerations.

Indications and Contraindications

It is difficult to succinctly summarize the various indications that may apply in any given biopsy. The imaging characteristics of a lesion must present a differential diagnosis. If the imaging features are sufficiently characteristic of any given pathologic entity that would be treated by surgical resection, then a preoperative diagnosis is usually not necessary. An example would be a typical renal cell carcinoma in a patient with no contraindications to surgery. Second, entities in the differential diagnosis must be distinguishable by the biopsy method chosen, either cytologic or core histologic examination. An example would be a small nonfunctioning adrenal mass in a patient with no other

evidence of malignancy. One should expect considerable difficulty in distinguishing the two main diagnostic considerations, adenoma and nonfunctioning primary adrenal carcinoma, by examination of a needle biopsy specimen. Third, there must be significantly different treatment regimens for the entities in the differential diagnosis, and the patient should understand these considerations and have agreed to undergo the therapy dictated by the biopsy results. If the results of the biopsy will have no significant bearing on subsequent treatment, then the risk-benefit ratio becomes unacceptable. Finally, percutaneous biopsy should not be performed in lieu of other potential diagnostic modalities that would provide a safer means of securing the diagnosis.

The majority of contraindications to percutaneous biopsy are relative. In an uncooperative patient it will be much more difficult to secure a diagnosis and the risks of doing so will be higher. The combination of a false-negative diagnosis and a complication is the most frustrating situation we face. It is also important that a safe access route be available, although with modern guidance techniques this is almost always possible. There are well-defined conditions that would predispose a patient to a higher risk of pneumothorax or bleeding, and these are discussed in the following sections.

Pneumothorax

Pneumothorax is reported to occur in 10 to 40 percent of transthoracic biopsies.[7,11,41–47] Although unusual, it can also complicate biopsy of upper abdominal organs if the pleural space is crossed.[48] Several risk factors have been identified that increase the risk of pneumothorax. Obviously, the most significant factor is whether or not aerated lung is crossed by the needle.[30,41,42] Theoretically there should be no risk of pneumothorax if aerated lung is not crossed. In practice this can occur if a coaxial system is used and the guide needle is placed in the pleural space adjacent to a lesion that abuts but does not invade the pleura (Fig. 11-10).

The presence of chronic obstructive pulmonary disease (COPD) may be a factor in increasing the risk of pneumothorax.[43,46,47,49,50] Patients with COPD who develop a pneumothorax are more likely to require a tube thoracostomy for treatment.[49] An uncooperative patient is at higher risk, and the inability to suspend respiration during the biopsy should be considered a relative contraindication to biopsy. There is probably an increased risk of pneumothorax if multiple pleural punctures are made or if fissures are crossed. This potential risk is the rationale for using a coaxial technique so that multiple biopsies can be performed with fewer

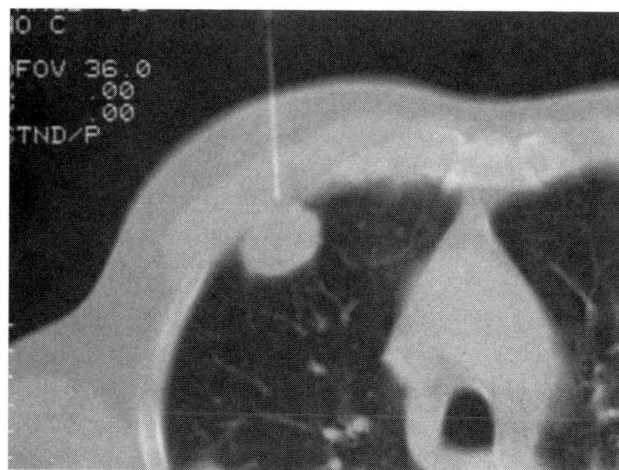

A

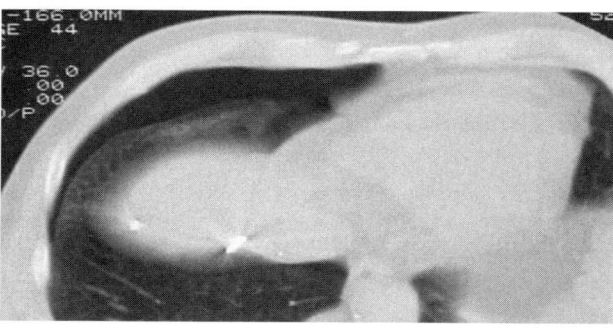

B

Figure 11-10. Pneumothorax complicating coaxial biopsy of a pleural-based lung mass (metastatic hepatocellular carcinoma). (A) The tip of the 19-gauge guiding needle is shown at the edge of the lesion where it abuts the pleural surface. (B) Postbiopsy scan demonstrates a small pneumothorax. This occurred because the lesion abutted but did not invade the pleura, thus allowing air ingress via the guiding needle during the coaxial biopsy.

pleural punctures. Increasing depth and decreasing size of a lesion have been implicated in increasing the risk as well, but these are most likely related to the greater number of biopsy passes needed.[37,49,50] The use of 16-gauge or larger cutting needles will result in a higher pneumothorax rate, but no significant difference has been demonstrated between needles ranging from 18- to 22-gauge.[17,30,43,50]

Although several modifications in technique have been proposed to decrease the risk of pneumothorax, few have been successful. The quick-stain technique should theoretically decrease the number of needle passes made but has not been shown to be beneficial in controlled studies.[25,43] The blood patch technique involves injection of autologous clot into the biopsy track during removal of a coaxial guide in an attempt to seal the pleural puncture site. The only controlled studies of this technique have failed to demonstrate

any benefit.[46,47] A more recent pilot study has shown some potential benefit in plugging the pleural tract with Gelfoam.[51] Positioning the patient with the biopsy side down immediately after the procedure is theoretically beneficial by creating dependent atelectasis and allowing tamponade of the pleural puncture site against the chest wall. Although the only controlled study has not shown this to be effective in decreasing the incidence of pneumothorax, it does appear to decrease the need for tube thoracostomy.[44] A similar effect is seen with the administration of 100 percent oxygen after the biopsy.[50]

Early reports have suggested that the use of CT guidance was associated with a higher incidence of pneumothorax.[4,5] These studies used both a coaxial system and the quick-stain technique, which resulted in pneumothorax rates of 43 to 61 percent. With this combination the guide needle is left in place across the pleura for an extended period of time, increasing the likelihood of an air leak or pleural laceration. Other potential explanations for the higher pneumothorax rate include the increased sensitivity of CT for small pneumothoraces and the difficult nature of the lesions selected for CT-guided biopsy in these series. In contrast, other studies of CT-guided thoracic biopsy have reported pneumothorax rates of 11 to 19 percent.[17,41] The quick-stain technique and coaxial system were not used in combination in these series. Fluoroscopic guidance has traditionally allowed quicker completion of the biopsy given the time delay in localization of the needle in CT. The advent of high-speed scanners with short reconstruction times has significantly narrowed the difference. This, in combination with the improved ability to avoid crossing aerated lung, has made CT a more attractive guidance modality without increasing the risk of pneumothorax.

Tube thoracostomy is necessary after 2 to 21 percent of transthoracic biopsies (7–60 percent of pneumothoraces).[17,44-47] The decision to place a chest tube is often subjective and is more frequently necessary if the size of the pneumothorax rather than the symptoms is used as the criterion for tube placement. Observation is certainly an option but often requires serial films over several days to be sure the pneumothorax is not enlarging. There is an understandable reluctance to observe pneumothoraces on an outpatient basis, and one can argue that placement of a small-caliber chest tube with a Heimlich valve results in much faster and safer resolution of the situation. A frequently successful alternative is simple aspiration of the pneumothorax without placement of a chest tube.[30] The choice is personal, but all radiologists performing transthoracic biopsies must be familiar with the technique of tube thoracostomy should it be urgently needed.

Bleeding Complications

Bleeding is the second most common complication of percutaneous biopsy. It occurs in up to 12 percent of cases, although most series report bleeding rates of 0 to 6 percent.[24,29,48,52–55] Most cases are minor and require no treatment. Significant bleeding complications requiring transfusion or surgical or radiologic intervention are reported in approximately 0 to 3 percent of cases.[29,48,55] The mortality rate is estimated at 0.01 to 0.10 percent.[56,57] It can be difficult to compare the incidence of bleeding complications in various series because of differences in patient populations, biopsy sites and technique, and methods used to detect complications. Most recent studies have the advantage (or disadvantage) of employing high-resolution imaging modalities, which are able to detect much more subtle bleeding. Ralls et al.[58] were able to detect some degree of hemorrhage in 91 percent of renal biopsy patients using CT. The great majority of these were asymptomatic and would probably not have been reported in other series. With this in mind, certain conclusions can be made regarding factors that may place a given patient at a higher risk for significant bleeding.

Coagulation Disorders

Some controversy exists regarding the risk imparted by coagulation defects and the value of prebiopsy coagulation screening. The most commonly used measures of coagulation are the prothrombin time, partial thromboplastin time, platelet count, and less commonly the skin bleeding time.[59] There are conflicting data as to the value of these tests for preintervention screening. Several laboratory and uncontrolled clinical studies have shown that defects in hemostasis do impart an increased risk of bleeding complications.[52,60–63] There is some evidence to suggest that defects in cellular hemostasis are more significant than defects in thrombin-mediated clot formation.[63] A conflicting viewpoint is presented in studies that found no correlation between peripheral blood coagulation measurements and the risk of bleeding from surgical or interventional procedures.[56,59,64,65] Because of this lack of correlation, several authors have questioned the value of performing preprocedure coagulation screening. Despite such recommendations, almost all clinical investigators list coagulation defects as a relative contraindication to biopsy, and most continue to perform prebiopsy screening.

Although it seems to defy common sense to assume that a defect in coagulation does not impart an increased risk of bleeding, at the same time currently available measurements of coagulation status do not allow us to quantify that risk in any given patient. Part of the problem is one of degree, in that the incidence of bleeding complications is so low that it is difficult to demonstrate a statistically significant difference without a very large number of patients, particularly if the coagulation defects are not severe. Controlled clinical studies of this issue would be unacceptable on ethical grounds. Laboratory studies suffer from the uncertainty as to whether controlled in vitro conditions accurately reflect in vivo conditions.

Several conclusions can be made from the data available. Currently available measures of hemostasis cannot be used to quantify the risk of bleeding in a given patient. It is clear that our understanding of hemostasis has limitations and that our methods of measuring it are imperfect. Defects in hemostasis do impart an increased risk in general, but the increase is relatively small and certain local tissue factors are more important in individual cases. This is not to imply that we should ignore the available measures. Preprocedure screening is still valuable in most cases, depending on the type of intervention and the site and nature of the pathologic lesion. Severe defects in hemostasis can be detected and steps can be taken to correct or counteract them if necessary.

Local Tissue Factors

Cellular and mechanical tissue factors may be the most important determinant of the risk of bleeding. The fact that skin bleeding time does not correlate well with liver bleeding time raises the possibility that local cellular and biochemical mediators of hemostasis exist and that these factors cannot be measured peripherally.[64,65] Mechanical factors are also extremely important. Normal liver tissue is soft, and the track left by a biopsy needle will collapse and aid in local hemostasis by promoting tamponade. Tumors, on the other hand, often have a very firm fibrous stroma that prevents collapse of the track. Benign processes such as severe cirrhosis also lead to a more fibrous and less pliable liver in which local tamponade may be less effective. This hypothesis is supported by studies demonstrating an increased risk of bleeding in biopsy of malignant nodules or cirrhotic livers independent of coagulation status.[52,56,61] The ability of normal liver to tamponade the biopsy track is also evidenced by an increased risk of bleeding from liver biopsy if the lesion is on the peritoneal surface of the liver (Fig. 11-11).[56,57] Biopsy of vascular lesions of the liver such as a cavernous hemangioma has been shown to be safe if a rim of normal liver tissue is interposed between the puncture site in the capsule and the edge of the lesion.[66] The lack of local mechanical tamponade is also a factor in the risk of bleeding from other nonhepatic lesions that abut ei-

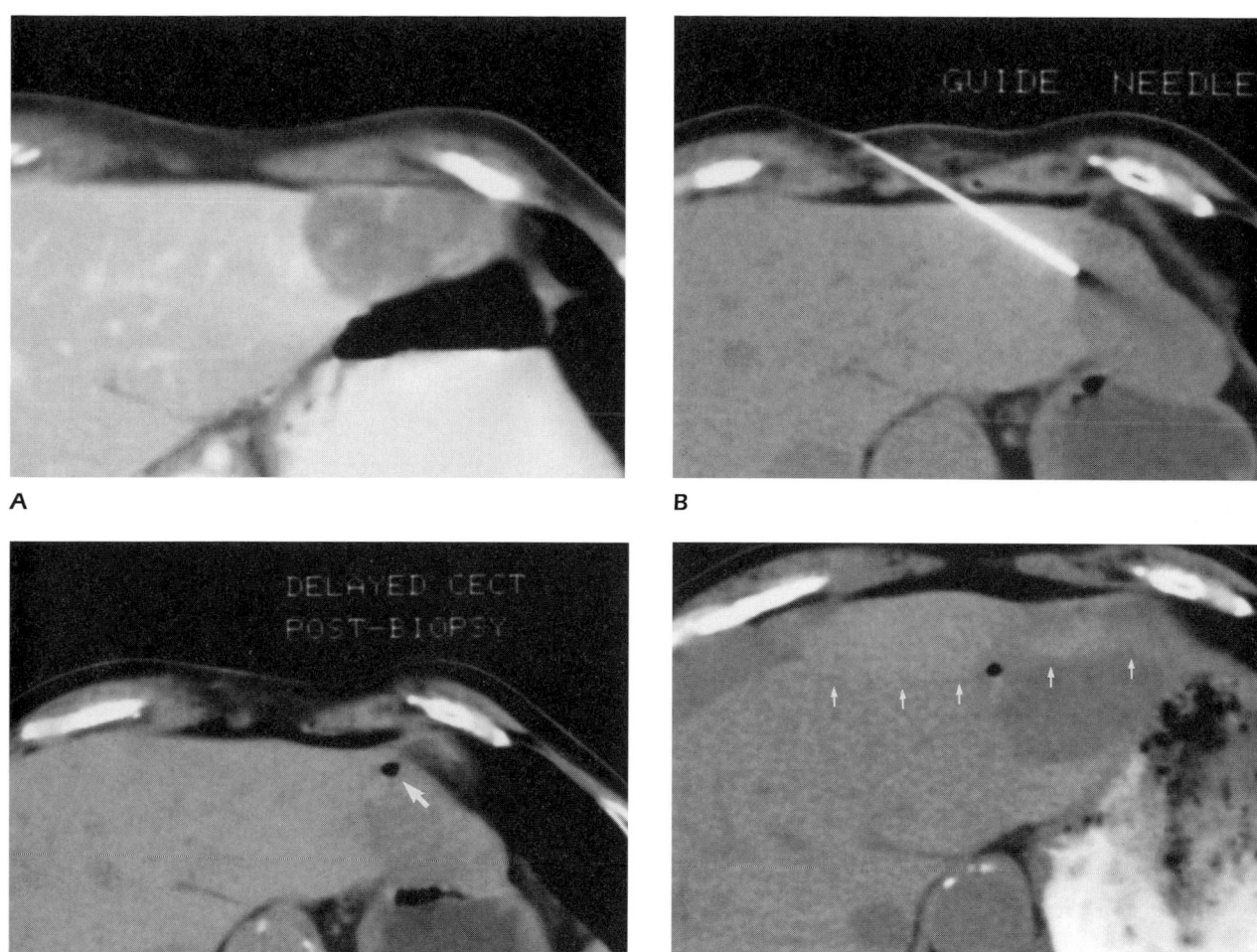

A

B

C

D

Figure 11-11. Atypical cavernous hemangioma of the liver. (A) Contrast-enhanced CT section shows a hypodense mass in the lateral segment of the left lobe. (B) An oblique guide needle approach was used to place a thin rim of normal liver tissue between the capsular puncture site and the proximal margin of the lesion. (C) Scan obtained immediately after the coaxial biopsy shows a small air bubble (*arrow*) between the lesion and the adjacent normal liver. The air bubble is 1.5 cm anterior to the point where the needle entered the lesion, suggesting that a potential space exists between the lesion and the liver. (D) Scan obtained 24 hours after the biopsy shows a large perihepatic hematoma (*arrows*). Continued bleeding necessitated a lateral hepatic segmentectomy. Examination of the resected specimen revealed an accessory fissure between the lesion and the adjacent liver. Because of this accessory fissure, the biopsy needle passed through the medial capsular surface of the lesion. The presence of a potential fissural space allowed continued bleeding without benefit of local tamponade within a track of normal liver.

ther the peritoneal surface or a potential space in which a significant amount of blood could collect.

Lesion Vascularity

Several studies have reported puncture of major vascular structures such as the aorta, superior vena cava, and pulmonary artery with 21- to 22-gauge needles without sequelae, although this has been advisedly avoided with larger cutting needles.[26,33,45] Local tamponade seems to play a role in this phenomenon. Puncture of retroperitoneal or extrapericardial mediastinal vessels is relatively safe, as evidenced by the low complication rate in translumbar aortography. However, if vessels are punctured in locations where local tamponade is limited, more serious sequelae can result. Both hemorrhagic pericarditis and pericardial tamponade have been reported after puncture of intrapericardial mediastinal vessels.[4,7] Given the accuracy of modern guidance modalities, it would seem prudent to avoid puncture of most vascular structures if possible.

Both malignant and benign tumors may demonstrate arterial hypervascularity. An increased incidence of bleeding and a higher mortality rate have been reported after biopsy of such lesions.[57,59,62] The importance of vascularity is also evidenced by the increased incidence of bleeding following renal biopsy as compared to liver biopsy. Liver tissue is soft and is supplied primarily by low-pressure veins, whereas renal tissue is more firm and has a much more extensive high-pressure arterial blood supply. Another important factor is the inherent pathologic difference between normal arteries and tumor vessels. Normal arteries develop smooth muscle contraction in the vessel wall after trauma, thus limiting blood loss. Neoplastic vessels do not have a smooth muscle media and cannot contract. Once severed, the vessel will freely bleed until external tamponade occurs. Increased vascularity of a lesion should not be considered a contraindication to biopsy, although the needle path should be carefully chosen so that local mechanical factors can be exploited to assist in tamponade of the tract.

Biopsy Technique

Although the use of large-caliber cutting needles in many sites has been reported, these are carefully selected series that limited biopsy to only the safest lesions. The data that are available indicate that there is a small but real increased risk of bleeding complications with 14- to 16-gauge needles as compared to 18- to 22-gauge needles.[6,24,48,53–55] The same studies have demonstrated no significant increase in risk with the use of 18- to 20-gauge needles as compared to 21- to 22-gauge needles. The stiffness of larger needles may also play a role in that there is a theoretical increase in the risk of organ capsular laceration with respiratory motion. Middle-caliber needles may offer enough flexibility to be safe while not suffering from the problem of tip deviation during placement that is seen with 21- to 22-gauge needles.

Some data suggest that there is an increased incidence of bleeding if multiple biopsy passes are made with larger cutting needles.[56] The effect appears to be minimal, and no similar data have been presented regarding middle- or small-caliber needles. There is also some evidence that the use of cutting needles carries a slightly higher risk as compared to aspiration needles of the same gauge, but the difference is small and probably not significant.[6,62] The literature to date supports the contention that middle-caliber cutting needles can reliably obtain histologic cores with no significant increase in complications.

Protective Measures

None of the above-described risk factors for bleeding are considered an absolute contraindication to biopsy. The relative potential significance of those risk factors that are present may be assessed in a subjective, if not a quantitative, fashion. Given this understanding,

there are certain steps that may be taken to prevent bleeding complications if a higher risk is foreseen. It is advisable to defer biopsy in patients with a severe coagulopathy if this can be corrected. Cessation of medications affecting either cellular or thrombin-mediated hemostasis is the most obvious example. Transfusion of platelets or cryoprecipitate has been used but carries the additional risks of viral agent contamination and transfusion reaction. In addition, such transfusions are marginally effective at best in correcting a significant coagulopathy. The single most important step is to carefully determine the biopsy needle path in order to avoid vascular structures and take advantage of the effects of local tamponade. The use of 14- to 16-gauge cutting needles should probably be avoided except when local mechanical tamponade is ensured.

Transjugular biopsy of the liver has been advocated in cases of severe coagulopathy. This technique has some strong advocates but has not been widely accepted because of the somewhat cumbersome technical difficulties in achieving an optimal performance. The transjugular modified aspiration needles used are not as reliable in obtaining adequate histologic specimens as are percutaneous cutting needles. Inadequate or nondiagnostic specimens are obtained in up to 30 percent of biopsies.[67,68] Complication rates are relatively low given the patient population but are still significant. Inadvertent carotid artery puncture and cardiac arrhythmias may occur in up to 2 percent of cases.[67] Capsular perforation is seen in 2 to 6 percent of cases, although bleeding from such sites can be minimized by embolization of the biopsy track before sheath withdrawal.[67,68]

Embolization of percutaneous biopsy tracks is an alternative when a higher risk of bleeding is anticipated.[60,69,70] This technique requires some form of coaxial system through which the biopsy is performed. After biopsy the guiding needle or cannula is used as a conduit for placing embolic material into the biopsy track (Fig. 11-12). Several different devices have been used as coaxial cannulas, including thin-walled guiding needles, back-loaded Teflon sheaths, and the outer cannula of the tru-cut type of biopsy needle. The last-mentioned has the advantage of not requiring a larger-gauge sheath or needle than the biopsy device but is more cumbersome to use. The embolic materials used have included Gelfoam plugs, autologous clot, steel coils, and thrombin. Each has its advocates, advantages, and disadvantages, and the choice may be one of personal preference. The use of autologous clot or Gelfoam plugs via a coaxial guiding needle is probably the simplest technique. The use of steel coils is reserved for cases in which communication with a large vascular channel is demonstrated. In such cases the smaller embolic agents may enter the vascular channel and embolize distally. Another innovative approach to track embolization is the use of a protein-polymer cylinder, which acts as both the sheath and the embolic agent.[63] This system is not commercially available and suffers from the disadvantage of not being able to make more than one biopsy pass through the sheath.

Biopsy and embolization may be performed with any guidance modality. Real-time control of the embolization is possible under fluoroscopic guidance, whereas embolization is essentially blind when using either CT or ultrasound guidance. When the need for track embolization is expected in the biopsy of focal lesions, the use of both ultrasound and fluoroscopic guidance offers the combination of both biopsy accuracy and embolic precision.[60,70] The majority of cases of track embolization reported in the literature have been performed under CT or ultrasound guidance. Despite the lack of real-time guidance, there have been no apparent technical difficulties.

To date there have been no controlled randomized trials demonstrating the efficacy of the track embolization technique, and indeed such trials may not be possible because of ethical concerns. The technique has been used in a large number of patients with coagulation defects in a noncontrolled fashion with very low complication rates.[60,69] No adverse effects related specifically to the embolization have been reported. Because standard large-caliber cutting needles can be used, the histologic recovery rate and diagnostic accuracy are considerably higher than with transjugular biopsy. This approach is also simpler to perform and can be used in the biopsy of any organ or location, not just hepatic biopsies. Although the main indication for embolization is coagulation disorders, it can be used for other indications, such as biopsy of hypervascular lesions or biopsies in which no tissue rim is present to aid in local tamponade.

Needle Track Seeding

Metastatic seeding of malignant cells into the needle track has been a concern since the earliest reports on percutaneous biopsy.[1] A major tenet of cancer surgery is that the tumor should not be disrupted prior to removal for fear of local spread of tumor cells.[1,71] The vascular supply is isolated and controlled before removal to prevent vascular embolization of cells. Similar spread of tumor cells during percutaneous biopsy was therefore also a theoretical consideration, but it has received relatively less attention because of its apparent rarity, with a reported incidence of less than 0.01 percent.[57,72] Although acknowledged, the risk of seeding

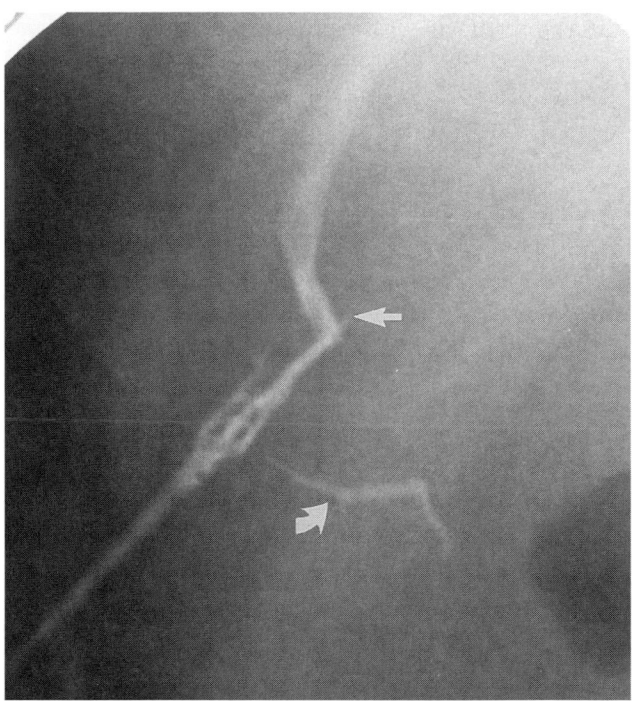

A

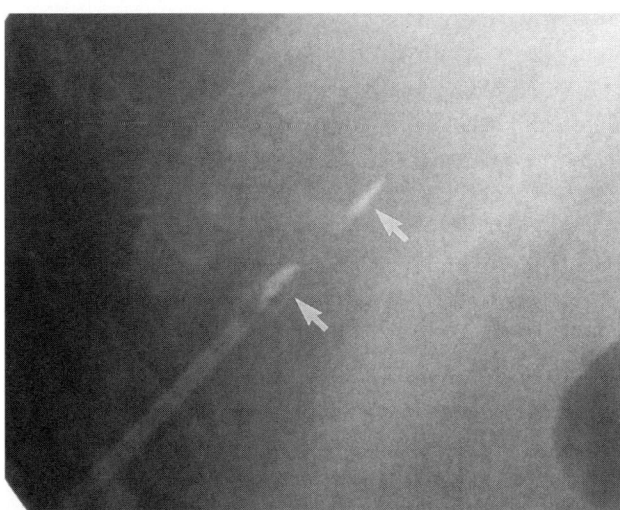

B

Figure 11-12. Fluoroscopic-guided liver biopsy with track embolization in a patient with suspected hemachromatosis and a moderate coagulopathy. These biopsy passes were performed coaxially with a 15-gauge automated cutting device through a 6 French hemostatic sheath. (A) Postbiopsy spot film during contrast injection into the sheath shows the trident shape of the three adjacent biopsy tracks. The inferior track communicates with a small portal vein branch (*curved arrow*) and the middle track communicates with a larger hepatic vein branch (*straight arrow*). (B) Spot film obtained after track embolization shows two contrast-opacified Gelfoam plugs (*arrows*) in the distal and mid portions of the biopsy track. A third Gelfoam plug was later placed just below the liver capsule.

has not generally been a strong consideration for most radiologists when evaluating the indications and contraindications to biopsy in a given case.

Recent studies have raised new concerns regarding this issue. Lundstedt et al.[73] in 1991 reported a 0.1 percent incidence of track seeding in 5000 biopsies. In a study of peritoneal fluid cytology in patients with pancreatic carcinoma, Warshaw[71] found positive cytology in 75 percent of patients who had undergone percutaneous biopsy, as compared to 19 percent in those who had not. In an older laboratory study of lymph node biopsy in rabbits, Engzell et al.[74] found tumor cells outside the node capsule at the puncture site in 80 percent of biopsies, although no vascular embolization of tumor cells was demonstrated. Clinically apparent seeding has been reported following biopsy of the liver, pancreas, thyroid, prostate, lung, breast, lymph nodes, and bowel.[57,72,73]

In contrast to these findings is the low overall incidence of clinically apparent seeding and the fact that no studies have demonstrated decreased survival in patients who have undergone biopsy as compared to those who have not.[72,74] There are several potential explanations for this discrepancy between laboratory and clinical results. Most important is the fact that the majority of patients undergoing percutaneous biopsy already have metastatic cancer at the time of the procedure. These patients often die of distant metastatic disease before track seeding can become apparent. It is also probable that in most studies no diligent search for track metastases was made and only those anecdotal cases brought to the attention of the radiologist were reported. Furthermore, it is known that a significant inoculum of cells is necessary for metastatic implantation.[72–74] Aspiration biopsies probably would seed only a small number of cells with no intact tumor stroma. In the majority of cases these small inocula are probably destroyed by host defense mechanisms prior to implantation. Larger cutting needles may deposit a greater number of cells with some intact stroma, and indeed a higher frequency of clinical seeding has been demonstrated with the use of these needles.[72–74]

The main concern in this issue is the possibility that a resectable tumor will be rendered incurable by the very test used to establish its presence. Despite the above theoretical concerns, the available data indicate that this is an extremely rare occurrence and the indications for biopsy should not change. However, this issue should be considered before biopsy of a suspected primary malignancy for which the treatment would be a potentially curative resection. Some surgeons may still feel that it is helpful to know the diagnosis before surgery so that the procedure may be appropriately planned and so that frozen-section diagnosis, with its attendant time delay and potential inaccuracy, can be avoided. There is also the concern that without a presurgical diagnosis certain patients may undergo resection of benign lesions or lesions for which surgery is not the procedure of choice. This issue is not clearcut, but it remains prudent to be aware of all possibilities when considering biopsy in any given case.

Regional Biopsy Considerations

Thoracic Biopsy

There is some controversy surrounding the role of percutaneous transthoracic needle biopsy versus competing endoscopic and surgical diagnostic modalities. Thoracic lesions may be approached by bronchoscopy, thoracoscopy, mediastinoscopy, parasternal mediastinotomy, or thoracotomy, with each modality having vocal proponents. Bronchoscopy is accurate and safe in the diagnosis of central lesions with an endobronchial component but is less accurate for peripheral lung lesions or mediastinal disease.[30,75,76] Thoracoscopy is limited to lesions near the pleural surface. Mediastinoscopy and mediastinotomy are accurate but can reach only specific limited nodal chains. The surgical modalities also carry significantly higher morbidity and mortality rates than either percutaneous or endoscopic techniques.[30,76] It is difficult to justify this increased risk when one considers the significant percentage of surgical procedures performed for the diagnosis of benign or nonresectable malignant disease. Surgery is more accurate, bronchoscopy is slightly safer, and needle biopsy is the most versatile and combines both accuracy and safety in the diagnosis of most thoracic lesions.

Because of the relative predominance of noncarcinomatous masses in the mediastinum, the accuracy of needle biopsy is significantly improved if cutting needles are used to obtain histologic specimens in addition to routine cytologic sampling. The best example of this is in the diagnosis of lymphoma. The reported sensitivity of cytology alone in the diagnosis of lymphoma ranges from 54 to 83 percent.[3,7,8,21] Better results are obtained in recurrent lymphoma because prior tissue samples are available for comparison.[17,21] Diagnosis and adequate subtyping are more difficult in primary lymphoma. With the addition of histology, both the diagnosis and subtype can be established in over 90 percent of cases.[17,30,34] Neither cytology nor histology can reliably differentiate nodular from diffuse forms of lymphoma, but this feature has little clinical significance. Results in general are better for non-Hodgkin lymphoma than for Hodgkin disease because the latter diagnosis rests in the demonstration of relatively sparse Reed-Sternberg cells. Histologic specimens are also superior in the diagnosis of thymoma, although it can be difficult to differentiate benign and malignant forms.[3,7] In general, cytology fares well in the diagnosis of carcinomatous mediastinal metastases. The addition of histology will be of benefit in accurate subtyping, particularly if prior tissue samples are not available for comparison.[3,8,11,17]

For lung lesions cytology alone fares well, with a reported malignant sensitivity of 65 to 93 percent.[4,5,8,10,11] When adequate histologic specimens are also obtained, the combined malignant sensitivity is 85 to 97 percent.[11,17,23,26,45] Accurate subtype determination is slightly better with histology, although cytology appears adequate in differentiating small-cell from non-small-cell carcinomas.[11,30] The most significant advantage of histology is the ability to obtain a specific diagnosis in benign nodules.[5,8,11,17] If a specific benign diagnosis is obtained, the negative predictive value approaches 100 percent.[17] The negative predictive value is much lower for non-specific cancer-negative diagnoses, and in this setting further diagnostic evaluation is usually necessary, either repeat biopsy or surgery.

Needle biopsy may also be performed for the diagnosis of diffuse parenchymal lung disease, although it is more difficult to obtain an adequate specimen because of the soft, elastic nature of lung tissue.[30,40,77] Fine-needle aspiration cytology alone can demonstrate an etiologic agent in approximately 75 percent of diffuse infections but does not fare well in the diagnosis of noninfectious interstitial disease.[40,77,78] The use of larger cutting needles improves accuracy in noninfectious disease but carries an unacceptably high complication rate. Not only are pneumothoraces more frequent, but significant hemoptysis is seen in up to 21 percent of cases and mortality rates approaching 1 percent have been reported.[77,78] In selected cases fine-needle aspiration biopsy seems an acceptable alternative in the diagnosis of infectious disease as long as the patient is not on mechanical positive pressure ventilation. In most cases, however, bronchoscopy and thoracoscopy are both more accurate and safer and should therefore be the primary diagnostic modalities.[75]

Complications specific to thoracic biopsy, in addition to pneumothorax, include hemoptysis and air embolism. Hemoptysis is reported to occur in 2 to 12 percent of cases.[4,5,11,37,45] Although usually minor and self-limited, hemoptysis can be severe and has been a significant contributing factor in several of the deaths reported after lung biopsy.[37] Hemoptysis is more frequent and more severe if larger airways or vessels are traversed; this fact explains the increased incidence in biopsy of hilar lesions and diffuse parenchymal lung disease.[30,37,77] Bleeding disorders and pulmonary arterial hypertension are considered relative contraindications to biopsy because of the potential for more severe hemoptysis. A suspected arteriovenous malformation should be considered an absolute contraindication to biopsy.

Air embolism may occur if a bronchovascular communication is created in the face of increased intrathoracic pressure (e.g., coughing or positive pressure ventilation) or if a needle is left open to air with the tip in a pulmonary vein in the face of decreased intrathoracic pressure (i.e., during inspiration). This is an extremely rare complication but can be fatal.[79] To minimize the risk of air embolism it is important to keep the needle tip within the lesion, particularly if a coaxial guide needle is used. The needle should be in the chest for as short a period of time as possible and not left open to air. These precautions assume greater importance in patients who are unable to suspend respiration during the biopsy. Patients on positive pressure mechanical ventilation should not undergo percutaneous thoracic biopsy unless absolutely necessary.

Although fluoroscopy is the time-honored standard guidance modality for thoracic biopsy, CT guidance is rapidly gaining favor. Fluoroscopy is faster and simpler but is limited to lesions well seen in two planes and is therefore suboptimal in demonstrating small nodules or abnormalities in or adjacent to the mediastinum.[4,37] After biopsy, perilesional parenchymal hemorrhage is seen in up to 25 percent of cases, often obscuring the lesion under fluoroscopy and precluding additional biopsy passes. It can also be difficult to avoid crossing aerated lung during fluoroscopically guided biopsy of pleural-based lung lesions if the pleural attachment is small.[37] Postobstructive lobar collapse may also obscure a central lesion, predisposing to sampling error.

CT is more accurate in determining the optimal needle path to avoid traversing aerated lung and bronchovascular structures. In the mediastinum it is almost always possible to traverse an extrapleural path to the lesion (Fig. 11-13). This is significant, because when both parenchymal and mediastinal abnormalities are present it is preferable to biopsy the mediastinal lesion to provide both diagnosis and staging with a single biopsy. Even if an extrapleural access route is not obvious, an artificial extrapleural window may be created by injecting saline outside the parietal pleura to displace the adjacent aerated lung away from the intended needle path (Fig. 11-14).[30,80] In pleural masses and peripheral pleural-based lung masses the pleural attachment can usually be traversed, although this occasionally requires a complex approach (Fig. 11-15). Regions of postobstructive collapse may also be used as a nonaerated path to central masses. Although some authors have suggested that ultrasound guidance has

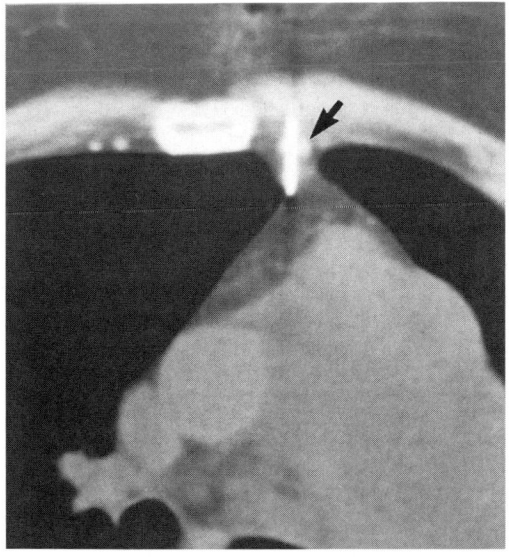
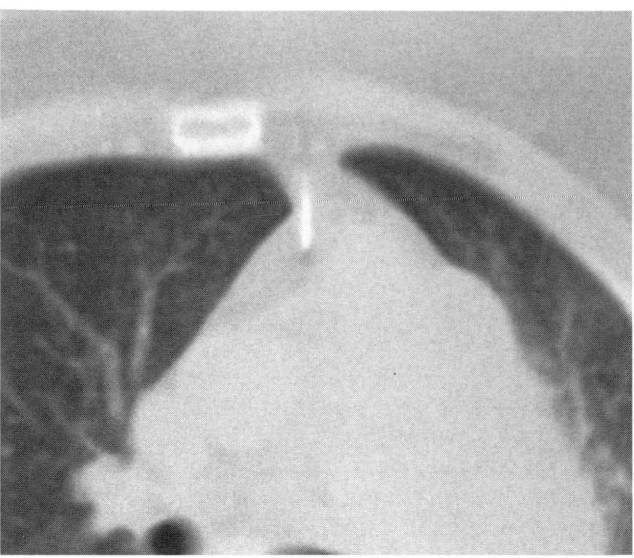

A   B

Figure 11-13. Metastatic small-cell anaplastic carcinoma in the left superior mediastinum. (A) A 19-gauge guiding needle has been placed between the internal mammary vein and the internal mammary artery (*arrow*). (B) Scan obtained after further advancement of the guiding needle shows the needle path to be within mediastinal fat medial to both the right and left mediastinal pleural reflections, thus avoiding traversal of aerated lung.

similar advantages to CT, it is limited to masses with a natural sonic window abutting the chest wall and is much less versatile.[81] CT-guided needle tip placement is more precise in both small and large masses and thus allows one to avoid necrotic portions of a tumor. If a coaxial system is used, it is easier to be certain the tip of the guiding needle is within the mass rather than in adjacent aerated lung.

The comparatively longer time during which the biopsy needle is in place during CT localization remains a drawback, although newer high-speed scanners have minimized this problem. More than in any other organ system, the experience of the physician in lung biopsy techniques correlates with lower complication rates. Physicians with greater experience are able to exploit the advantages of CT guidance to improve accuracy even for more complex lesions without an increase in complications.

Liver Biopsy

The two primary indications for liver biopsy are the diagnosis of suspected primary or secondary malignancy and the investigation of diffuse hepatocellular disease. Fine-needle aspiration cytology has a malignant sensitivity of 70 to 90 percent in the diagnosis of metastatic disease from epithelial malignancies.[2,6,9] However, cytology is not as accurate in the diagnosis of well-differentiated hepatocellular carcinoma or of metastases from nonepithelial malignancies such as

sarcomas or lymphoma.[2,16] With the addition of histologic specimens malignant sensitivities of 90 to 98 percent have been reported.[2,6,9–17,24]

Cytology alone plays no role in the diagnosis of diffuse hepatocellular disease because these entities are defined by histologic architecture rather than by cellular morphologic changes. Cirrhosis presents a very heterogeneous histologic pattern that requires excellent nonfragmented cores for accurate diagnosis.[52] Because of this microscopic heterogeneity, it has been common practice to use 14- to 16-gauge cutting needles when investigating suspected diffuse hepatocellular disease such as cirrhosis. Several recent studies, however, have reported excellent results in biopsy of both native hepatocellular disease and liver allografts using 18-gauge automated biopsy devices.[31,52] It would seem prudent for physicians performing liver biopsies to review the specimens with the pathology staff to determine which needle size is adequate in their institution.

Although the advantages of obtaining both histologic and cytologic specimens are well documented, it is equally important that this be accomplished with no increase in complications. Adequate histologic cores can be obtained in almost all cases using 18- to 20-gauge automated biopsy devices, with reported complication rates of 1 to 3 percent.[17,31,52] This is comparable to the complication rates reported for both small-caliber aspiration needles and middle-caliber manual cutting needles.[2,6,9,24] The use of 14- to 16-gauge cutting needles for diffuse hepatocellular disease is associ-

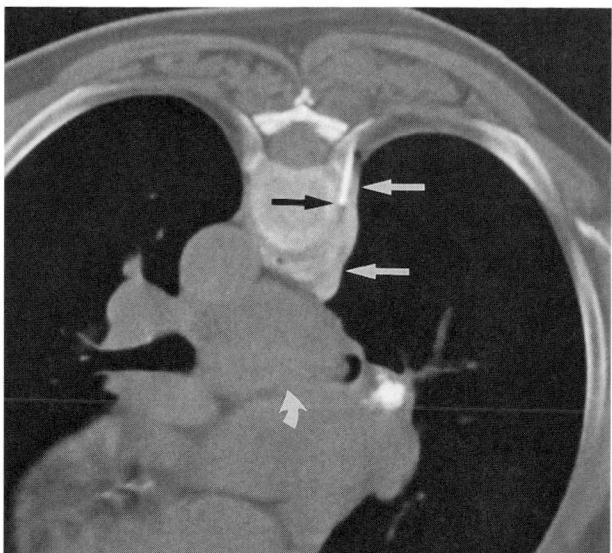

A

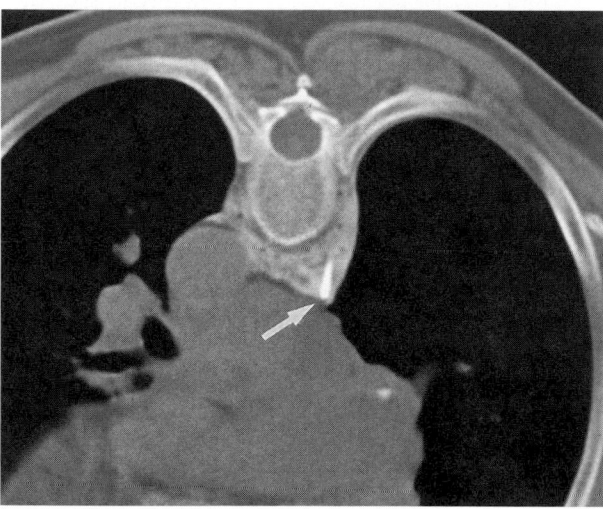

B

Figure 11-14. Use of an artificial extrapleural window for mediastinal biopsy. (A) Prone CT section shows a subcarinal mass (*curved white arrow*) and the tip of a 19-gauge guiding needle (*straight black arrow*) in a paraspinous position. Diluted contrast has been injected via the guiding needle to displace the right mediastinal pleura (*straight white arrows*) laterally away from the vertebral body. (B) Scan obtained after further guide needle advancement shows the needle tip (*arrow*) at the lesion margin. Additional saline was injected before the needle was advanced into the mass so that the needle path was entirely extrapleural. The biopsy revealed metastatic adenocarcinoma.

ated with a slight increase in bleeding complications.[2,24] If large-caliber needles are used, particularly in the face of abnormal coagulation studies, it is helpful to employ precautionary techniques such as postbiopsy track embolization.[60,69,70]

The best guidance modality is that which best dem-

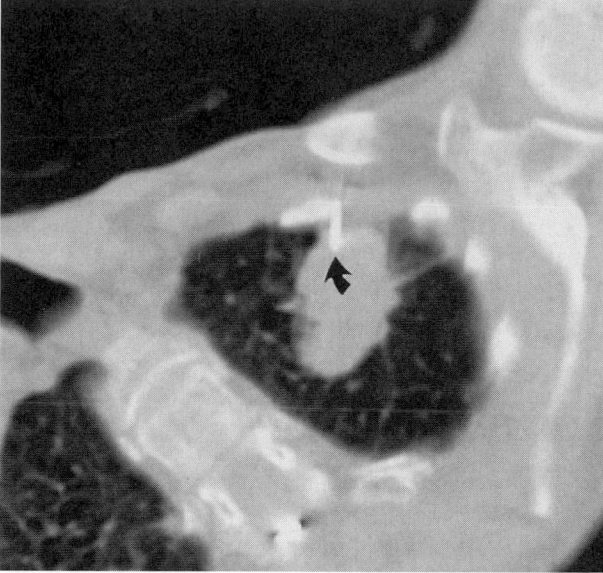

Figure 11-15. Primary left apical adenocarcinoma in a patient with chronic obstructive pulmonary disease. The guiding needle tip (*arrow*) is seen just within the anterior margin of the mass. An oblique supraclavicular approach with caudal needle angulation allowed placement of the guiding needle through the pleural-based portion of the mass.

onstrates the pathology and adjacent structures. CT and ultrasound are the most commonly used modalities, with the decision between the two being largely based on personal experience and preference. Fluoroscopic guidance may be used for diffuse hepatocellular disease when the need for track embolization is anticipated. Precise guidance not only increases accuracy but also decreases complications. Bleeding complications can be minimized, even with hypervascular lesions, by ensuring that a rim of normal liver tissue is interposed between the capsular puncture site and the margin of the lesion. Portal structures, dilated bile ducts, large vessels, lung, and adjacent organs are relatively easy to avoid with either CT or ultrasound. As a result, nonhemorrhagic complications such as colon or gallbladder perforation, pneumothorax, bile leak, and arteriovenous fistula or pseudoaneurysm formation have dramatically decreased in incidence when compared to blind biopsies.

Biopsy of the Pancreas

Most pancreatic biopsies are performed for suspected ductal adenocarcinoma. Occasionally masses of indeterminate nature are encountered, with the differential diagnosis primarily being adenocarcinoma versus chronic pancreatitis. Cystic neoplasms, rare solid epithelial neoplasms, and neuroendocrine tumors are

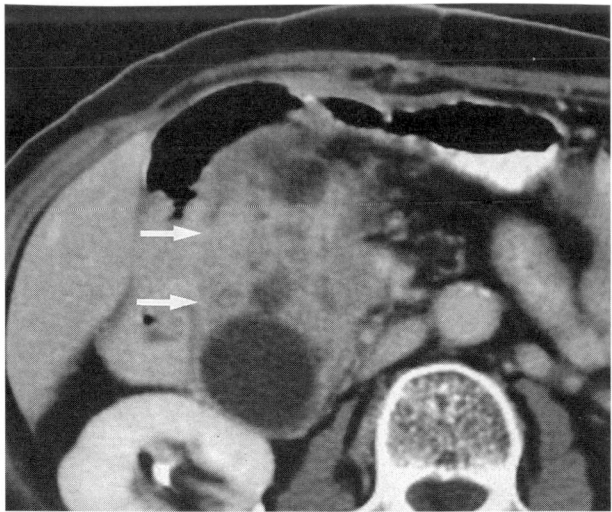

A

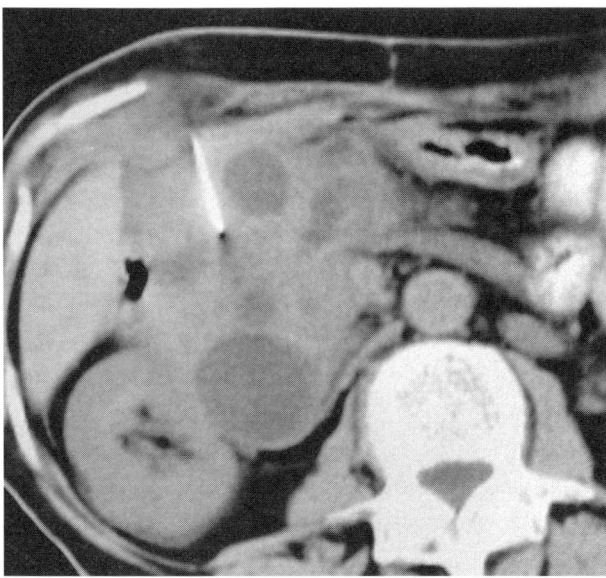

B

Figure 11-16. Ductal adenocarcinoma of the pancreas. (A) Contrast-enhanced CT section shows a large mass (*arrows*) in the head of the pancreas with several low-density areas of either necrosis or cystic degeneration. (B) Scan obtained for guiding needle localization documents specimen retrieval from the noncystic enhancing portion of the mass. Examination of the biopsy specimen revealed chronic pancreatitis and fibrosis. Subsequent open surgical biopsy revealed ductal adenocarcinoma.

much less common. Clinical and imaging characteristics are often highly suggestive of either a benign or malignant process, but overlap is sufficient such that a definitive diagnosis cannot be made without pathology. Because pancreatic carcinoma is usually unresectable at presentation, needle biopsy assumes a prominent role in establishing the diagnosis.

Pancreatic biopsy has a reported malignant sensitivity of 67 to 93 percent.[2,13,33,82,83] In these series better results were obtained with 18- to 20-gauge needles than with 22-gauge needles. Cytology fares well in biopsy of the pancreas because the primary diagnostic features of malignancy are cellular morphologic changes rather than histologic architectural changes.[14-18] Diagnostic difficulties arise because pancreatic carcinoma often incites an intense desmoplastic fibrotic response as well as a surrounding inflammatory reaction indistinguishable pathologically from chronic pancreatitis.[13,82] For this reason sampling error is the most common cause of false negatives and can occur with either cytologic or histologic specimens. A biopsy diagnosis of chronic inflammation and fibrosis cannot therefore be considered diagnostic of chronic pancreatitis (Fig. 11-16). Accurate guidance plays an important role in limiting sampling error. If ultrasound guidance is used, the hypoechoic central portion of the mass should be targeted.[82] Under CT guidance it is important to use contrast enhancement so that the lower-density central tumor may be sampled rather than the higher-density surrounding inflammatory mass, although this technique is not infallible.

The primary complications of pancreatic biopsy are bleeding and pancreatitis, which occur in 0 to 7 percent of cases.[2,13,24,33,82-84] In these series slightly lower complication rates were noted using 20-gauge or smaller needles. Despite its rarity, pancreatitis following biopsy can be fatal.[84] Most reported cases of pancreatitis have occurred after biopsy of small tumors, normal glands, or chronic pancreatitis.[82-84] It has been postulated that puncture of ducts or intact pancreatic tissue rather than tumor predisposes to peripancreatic leak of enzymes, leading to pancreatitis. Although this is difficult to prove given the small number of cases, it would still seem wise to avoid puncture of major ducts. The use of needles 16 gauge or larger is neither advisable nor necessary. Bowel loops frequently overlie the pancreas and can be traversed safely, although most authors have avoided puncture of the colon with 18-gauge or larger needles.[33,82] CT guidance may be necessary in such cases if bowel gas obscures the lesion to ultrasound.

Renal Biopsy

The imaging characteristics of large primary renal tumors are usually sufficiently specific to obviate preoperative biopsy. Biopsy is then reserved for small solid masses, for cases in which the imaging features suggest an atypical or noncarcinomatous tumor, for suspected metastatic disease to the kidney, and for the diagnosis of focal infection. Biopsy for the diagnosis of a focal renal mass has results and complications similar to those of other abdominal and retroperitoneal biopsies.

Biopsy for the diagnosis of diffuse parenchymal renal disease is quite different in that histologic cores of renal cortex with 5 to 10 glomeruli per core are required for adequate diagnosis. Until recently renal biopsies were performed either blind or under fluoroscopic guidance using 14-gauge or larger cutting needles, with diagnostic tissue obtained in 75 to 95 percent of cases.[55,85] In the majority of inadequate biopsies no renal tissue was obtained, either because the renal cortex was missed or because the needle did not penetrate the capsule. Complications occurred in 6 to 12 percent of biopsies, primarily hematuria, perinephric hemorrhage, and arteriovenous fistula formation. More recently results and complication rates have improved because of advancements in both guidance and needle technology.

Ultrasound is the most commonly used guidance modality for biopsy of diffuse parenchymal renal disease, although it may occasionally be suboptimal in obese patients, for whom CT guidance is preferable.[54,85] The use of cross-sectional guidance allows much more accurate targeting of the kidney. Within the kidney the operator may also selectively biopsy the lower pole cortex and avoid biopsy of the central sinus or medulla.

Automated tru-cut type biopsy devices are now the preferred needle for renal biopsy. More glomeruli are obtained per core with the larger devices, and for a given size more glomeruli are obtained with automated devices than with manual needles.[53,54] Adequate specimens can be obtained in 91 to 95 percent of cases with 18-gauge devices, with complication rates of 1 to 6 percent.[53–55] The use of 14- to 15-gauge devices is recommended by some investigators, who report an accuracy approaching 99 percent and no increase in complications.[85,86] Practitioners should review their own results to determine whether the smaller devices are satisfactory at a given institution.

Although the use of cross-sectional guidance certainly contributes to lower complication rates, the automated devices play a role as well. The rapid, reproducible firing action allows easier penetration of the capsule with less risk of capsular or vascular laceration. The needle is also within the kidney for a much shorter period of time. An additional advantage is that these devices allow one operator to perform the entire procedure using real-time ultrasound guidance, whereas manual cutting needles require a two-handed operation with the technologist providing guidance.

Biopsy of the Adrenal Glands

Adrenal masses are detected in 2 to 5 percent of all abdominal CT scans and thus present a common diagnostic dilemma.[87] The great majority of these are nonfunctioning benign adenomas and require neither a pathologic diagnosis nor treatment. Metastases are the second most common entity, and primary adrenal malignancy is quite rare. Benign neoplasms, granulomatous infection, cysts, and hemorrhage constitute the remainder. Although certain tumors such as myelolipomas often have diagnostic imaging features, most lesions are nonspecific in appearance. There has been considerable interest in attempting to predict the malignant or benign nature of adrenal masses by contrast-enhanced CT, ultrasound, and magnetic resonance imaging, but results to date show sufficient overlap that a definitive diagnosis is rarely possible.

In developing a diagnostic approach to adrenal masses, it is helpful to divide patients into oncologic and nononcologic groups. Oncologic patients are those who have either had a prior malignancy or who currently have clinical or radiologic evidence of cancer. Nononcologic patients are those who have no such prior history or current clinical or radiographic suspicions. In the presence of a unilateral adrenal mass, the diagnostic approach differs significantly in the two groups.

In nononcologic patients the clinically important differential diagnosis includes nonfunctioning adenoma, functioning adenoma, and primary malignancy. Biochemical screening for hormonal activity will detect the functioning adenomas and 85 percent of the primary adrenocortical carcinomas, which are then treated primarily by surgical excision. In nonfunctioning masses the approach is largely dictated by size. A unilateral adrenal mass smaller than 5 cm will essentially never be a metastatic lesion, and primary carcinoma of this size is exceedingly rare.[48,87,88] Masses of this size are almost always adenomas and may be followed with serial scans. Masses larger than 5 cm have a slightly greater likelihood of being malignant and require a pathologic diagnosis. Although biopsy may be performed in such cases, it can occasionally be difficult to differentiate a well-differentiated adrenocortical carcinoma from an andenoma, particularly by cytology alone.[14,16] Histology may be helpful in demonstrating capsular or vascular invasion, but false negatives still occur.

In oncologic patients the likelihood of an adrenal mass being a metastatic lesion varies with the primary cell type and stage. In patients with carcinoma of the lung, 40 to 50 percent of unilateral adrenal masses are

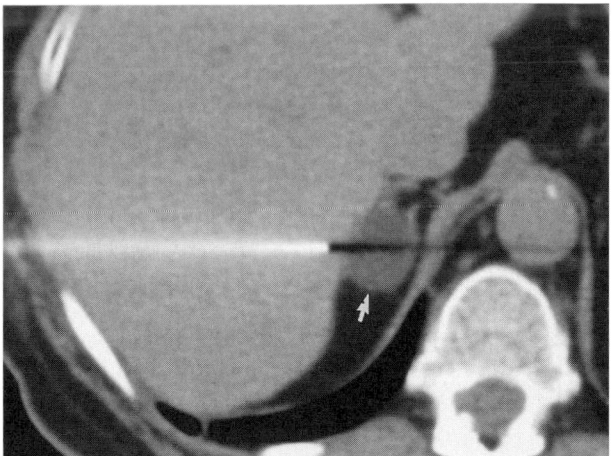

Figure 11-17. Nonfunctioning right adrenal adenoma (*arrow*) in a patient with adenocarcinoma of the lung. A lateral transhepatic approach in the supine position was used to avoid crossing aerated lung with the coaxial guiding needle.

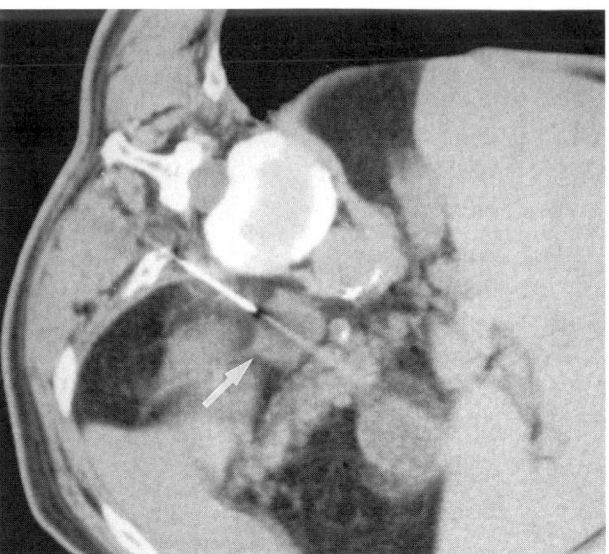

Figure 11-18. Left adrenal metastasis (*arrow*) in a patient with large-cell undifferentiated carcinoma of the lung. A posterior approach in the left lateral decubitus position was used to collapse the posterior costophrenic sulcus and thus avoid crossing aerated lung with the coaxial guiding needle.

metastases and the remainder benign adenomas (Fig. 11-17). The percentage representing metastatic disease will be much lower for other primary malignancies. Percutaneous biopsy is the primary diagnostic procedure in this situation, with a reported sensitivity of over 90 percent for epithelial metastases.[16,48,88] Retrieval of normal adrenal tissue is highly predictive of benignity.[88] Even in this setting, adrenal biopsy is not a common procedure because other more accessible metastatic lesions are often present.

Adrenal biopsy is technically more difficult than other abdominal biopsies because of the deep subphrenic location of the glands. As a result, complication rates are slightly higher, approaching 10 percent.[24,48,88] Minor hemorrhage and pneumothorax are the most common complications. The risk of pneumothorax can be minimized by using an angled subcostal approach, decubitus posterior approach, right transhepatic approach, or left anterior approach. The last-mentioned may necessitate traversing the pancreas, a problem not encountered with the posterior approach (Fig. 11-18). A rare but significant complication is hypertensive crisis after biopsy of a pheochromocytoma.[89] Although most pheochromocytomas are detected by hormonal screening, up to 14 percent are occult and may undergo biopsy. Such cases usually proceed without incident, but the need for treatment of a hypertensive crisis should be anticipated.[89]

Biopsy of the Peritoneum and Retroperitoneum

Epithelial metastases, lymphoma, and other rare primary mesenchymal tumors constitute the majority of

peritoneal and retroperitoneal masses referred for biopsy. In AIDS patients, infection with unusual organisms such as atypical mycobacterium is also a consideration. Aspiration cytology has a high sensitivity in the diagnosis of epithelial metastatic disease, whereas histologic specimens are often necessary for accurate diagnosis of mesenchymal tumors, just as in the mediastinum.[12,34] The major difference between mediastinal and retroperitoneal masses is that the latter are usually much easier to reach. Local mechanical tamponade in the retroperitoneum allows the use of 18-gauge or even larger cutting needles with minimal bleeding complications. Lesions in the peritoneum or mesentery, however, behave more like lesions on the capsular surface of the liver, with minimal effective local tamponade. Needles up to 18 gauge in size may be used safely if the access route is chosen carefully to avoid the colon and adjacent solid viscera. The bladder may be safely traversed with such needles if necessary. Track embolization may also be helpful if larger needles are used and it is expected that local tamponade may be ineffective. Because of overlying bowel and the deep location of most retroperitoneal masses, CT guidance is technically easier than ultrasound.

Biopsy of the Musculoskeletal System

Musculoskeletal lesions in almost any location are amenable to percutaneous biopsy. The technique var-

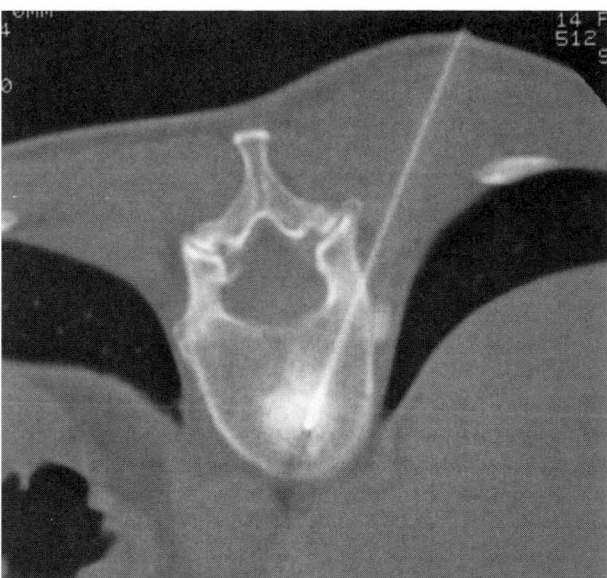

Figure 11-19. Sclerotic metastasis in the T11 vertebral body from carcinoma of the breast. Scan shows a 17-gauge trephine bone-coring needle in place via a transpedicular approach.

ies depending on whether the lesion is in bone or soft tissue, and if in bone on whether it is blastic or lytic. Blastic bone lesions require the use of 10- to 16-gauge trephine biopsy needles (Fig. 11-19).[90–92] Soft tissue masses or lytic bone lesions without an intact cortex may be biopsied with standard needles (Fig. 11-20). For lytic lesions with an intact cortex, a trephine needle may be placed through the cortex and used as a coaxial guide for standard needles.[92]

Lesions of the appendicular skeleton may be biopsied under either CT or fluoroscopic guidance, whereas CT is preferred for biopsy of the axial skeleton. CT more accurately depicts the lesion, the planned needle path, associated soft tissue abnormalities, and vital intervening structures. Complex approaches to vertebral body lesions may be necessary, including transforaminal, translaminal, transpedicular, and transcostovertebral paths.[93]

For optimal results it is important to obtain specimens for both cytologic and histologic evaluation.[91,92] Accuracy depends not only on technique but also on the nature of the lesion. Biopsy for the diagnosis of infection is accurate, but false negatives may occur if antibiotics have been administered before the biopsy. Cytologic or histologic features may be diagnostic in such cases even if cultures are negative. Accuracy is also high in cases of metastatic disease. Malignant sensitivity of 80 to 90 percent may be expected, with lytic lesions being easier to diagnose than blastic lesions.[90–93]

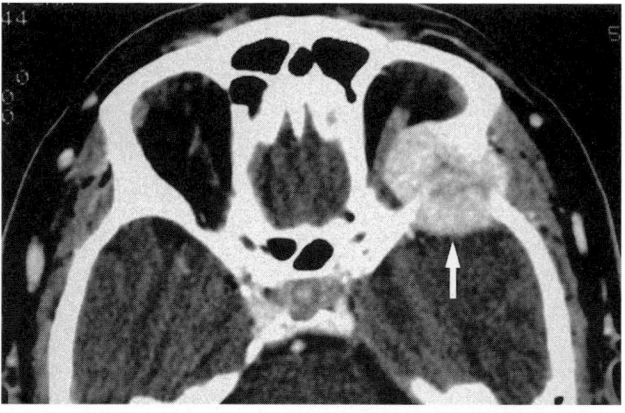

A

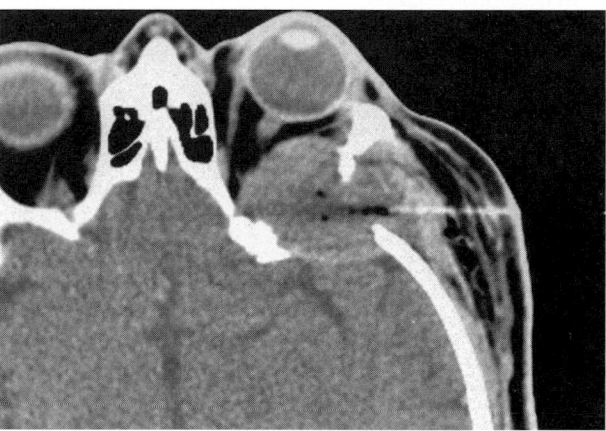

B

Figure 11-20. Metastatic thyroid carcinoma. (A) Hypervascular soft tissue mass (*arrow*) with lytic destruction of the sphenoid bone, intraorbital extension, and displacement of the optic nerve. (B) Postbiopsy scan with the 19-gauge guiding needle in place. The biopsy was performed coaxially using a 20-gauge automated gun. The two air bubbles in the center of the mass indicate the location from which the cutting needle biopsy specimen was taken.

Biopsy of suspected primary bone tumors is less commonly performed, for several reasons. Because most primary bone tumors are treated by surgical resection, there may be little benefit from the results of a preoperative biopsy. Whether to perform a preoperative biopsy is largely a matter of personal preference on the part of the surgeon, but biopsy can be helpful if preoperative radiation therapy or chemotherapy is anticipated. Diagnosis of bone lesions is more difficult with needle biopsy specimens than with resected specimens, and diagnosis in this area—more than any other area—requires an extremely skilled pathologist. Certain lesions, such as cartilaginous tumors and soft tissue sarcomas, are extremely difficult to classify by needle biopsy alone.[16,94] There is also tremendous pleomorphism in both malignant and benign bone tumors, and the distinction between the two may not be clear by the study of cellular morphologic changes.[14] In centers with a high volume, considerable experience, and expert pathologists, an accuracy of 70 to 90 percent may be obtained,[90,92,94] but it is doubtful that such results can be obtained at smaller institutions with less experience. Close cooperation between the radiologist and the orthopedic surgeon is mandatory, not only in selecting patients for biopsy but also in determining the biopsy needle path so that it may be resected along with the tumor at the time of surgery.[90]

Summary

The accuracy of cytologic diagnosis, the safety of fine-needle aspiration, and advances in guidance are responsible for the growth of percutaneous biopsy techniques. Cytology is very accurate in the diagnosis of epithelial malignancies, which are the most common lesions encountered in any given biopsy practice. However, the cytologic technique is suboptimal for the diagnosis of noncarcinomatous tumors and benign lesions. These limitations are best addressed by obtaining histologic core specimens in addition to cytologic aspirates. The improvement in biopsy accuracy realized by the addition of histology depends on the type of lesions encountered and the cytopathologic expertise available in any given practice. It it important that the proper needle is used to obtain each type of specimen. Small-caliber aspiration or modified aspiration needles are best suited to retrieve cytologic specimens. The advent of middle-caliber automated cutting needles allows for the reliable retrieval of high-quality histologic core specimens. Certain modifications in technique are necessary for the optimal use of these devices.

The roles of histologic and cytologic analysis remain complementary. Obtaining excellent-quality specimens for each makes pathologic interpretation easier and more accurate and lessens the dependence on highly experienced cytopathologists. With both techniques it is possible to safely obtain diagnostic tissue in over 95 percent of cases referred for biopsy. Sampling error is then the most significant obstacle to even greater biopsy accuracy, thus placing control of accuracy largely in the hands of the radiologist. Future efforts should be directed at minimizing complications and at developing methods to safely sample tissue from multiple areas of a lesion to minimize sampling error.

References

1. Martin HE, Ellis EB. Biopsy by needle puncture and aspiration. Ann Surg 1930;92:169–181.
2. Schwerk WB, Durr HK, Schmitz-Moormann P. Ultrasound guided fine-needle biopsies in pancreatic and hepatic neoplasms. Gastrointest Radiol 1983;8:219–225.
3. Herman SJ, Holub RB, Weisbrod GL, et al. Anterior mediastinal masses: utility of transthoracic needle biopsy. Radiology 1991;180:167–170.
4. van Sonnenberg E, Casola G, Ho M, et al. Difficult thoracic lesions: CT-guided biopsy experience in 150 cases. Radiology 1988;167:457–461.
5. Fink I, Gamsu G, Harter LP. CT-guided aspiration biopsy of the thorax. J Comput Assist Tomogr 1982;6:958–962.
6. Martino CR, Haaga JR, Bryan PJ, et al. CT-guided liver biopsies: eight years' experience. Radiology 1984;152:755–757.
7. Weisbrod GL, Lyons DJ, Tao LC, et al. Percutaneous fine-needle aspiration of mediastinal lesions. AJR 1984;143:525–529.
8. Goralnik CH, O'Connell PM, El Yousef, et al. CT-guided cutting needle biopsies of selected chest lesions. AJR 1988;151:903–907.
9. Pagani JJ. Biopsy of focal hepatic lesions: comparison of 18- and 22-gauge needles. Radiology 1983;144:673–675.
10. Todd TRJ, Weisbrod G, Tao LC, et al. Aspiration needle biopsy of thoracic lesions. Ann Thorac Surg 1981;32:154–161.
11. Greene R, Szyfelbein WM, Isler RJ, et al. Supplementary tissue-core histology from fine-needle transthoracic aspiration biopsy. AJR 1985;144:787–792.
12. Lieberman RP, Hafez GR, Crummy AB. Histology from aspiration biopsy: Turner needle experience. AJR 1982;138:561–564.
13. Hall-Craggs MA, Lees WR. Fine-needle aspiration biopsy: pancreatic and biliary tumors. AJR 1986;147:399–403.
14. Hajdu SI, Melamed MR. Limitations of aspiration cytology in the diagnosis of primary neoplasms. Acta Cytol 1984;28:337–345.
15. Taft PD, Szyfelbein WM, Greene R. A study of the variability in cytologic diagnoses based on pulmonary aspiration specimens. Am J Clin Pathol 1980;73:36–40.
16. Katz RL. The scope of fine-needle aspiration biopsy: cytologic diagnosis and techniques. Semin Intervent Radiol 1985;2:207–219.
17. Moulton JS, Moore PT. Coaxial percutaneous biopsy technique with automated biopsy devices: value in improving accuracy and negative predictive value. Radiology 1993;186:515–522.
18. Bocking A. Cytological vs. histological evaluation of percutaneous biopsies. Cardiovasc Intervent Radiol 1991;14:5–12.
19. Thornbury JR, Burke DP, Naylor B. Transthoracic needle aspiration biopsy: accuracy of cytologic typing of malignant neoplasms. AJR 1981;136:719–724.
20. Feinstein CR, Gelfman NA, Yesner R. Observer variability in the histopathologic diagnosis of lung cancer. Am Rev Respir Dis 1970;101:671–684.
21. Wittich GR, Nowels KW, Korn RL, et al. Coaxial transthoracic fine-needle biopsy in patients with a history of malignant lymphoma. Radiology 1992;183:175–178.
22. Andriole JG, Haaga JR, Adams RB, et al. Biopsy needle characteristics assessed in the laboratory. Radiology 1983;148:659–662.
23. Weisbrod GL, Herman SJ, Tao LC. Preliminary experience with a dual cutting edge needle in thoracic percutaneous fine-needle aspiration biopsy. Radiology 1987;163:75–78.
24. Welch TJ, Sheedy PF, Johnson CD, et al. CT-guided biopsy: prospective analysis of 1000 procedures. Radiology 1989;171:493–496.
25. Miller DA, Carrasco CH, Katz RL, et al. Fine needle aspiration biopsy: the role of immediate cytologic assessment. AJR 1986;147:155–158.

26. Westcott JL. Direct percutaneous needle aspiration of localized pulmonary lesions: results in 422 patients. Radiology 1980; 137:31–35.

27. Wittenberg J, Mueller PR, Ferrucci JT, et al. Percutaneous core biopsy of abdominal tumors using 22-gauge needles: further observations. AJR 1982;139:75–80.

28. Haaga JR, LiPuma JP, Bryan PJ, et al. Clinical comparison of small- and large-caliber cutting needles for biopsy. Radiology 1983;146:665–667.

29. Parker SH, Hopper KD, Yakes WF, et al. Image directed percutaneous biopsies with a biopsy gun. Radiology 1989;171:663–669.

30. Gunther RW. Percutaneous interventions in the thorax. J Vasc Intervent Radiol 1992;3:379–390.

31. Chezmar JL, Keith LL, Nelson RC, et al. Liver transplant biopsies with a biopsy gun. Radiology 1991;179:447–448.

32. Jaeger HJ, MacFie J, Mitchell CJ, et al. Diagnosis of abdominal masses with percutaneous biopsy guided by ultrasound. Br Med J 1990;301:1188–1191.

33. Elvin A, Andersson T, Scheibenpflug L, et al. Biopsy of the pancreas with a biopsy gun. Radiology 1990;176:677–679.

34. Erwin BC, Brynes RK, Chan WC, et al. Percutaneous needle biopsy in the diagnosis and classification of lymphoma. Cancer 1986;57:1074–1078.

35. Hopper KD, Abendroth CS, Sturtz KW, et al. Automated biopsy devices: a blinded evaluation. Radiology 1993;187:653–660.

36. Hopper KD, Baird DE, Reddy VV, et al. Efficacy of automated biopsy guns vs conventional biopsy needles in the pygmy pig. Radiology 1990;176:671–676.

37. Berquist TH, Bailey PB, Cortese DA, et al. Transthoracic needle biopsy: accuracy and complications in relation to location and type of lesion. Mayo Clin Proc 1980;55:475–481.

38. Kim D, Porter DH, Siegel JB, et al. Common bile duct biopsy with the Simpson atherectomy catheter. AJR 1990;154:1213–1215.

39. Perrella RR, Kimme-Smith C, Tessler FN, et al. New electronically enhanced biopsy system: value in improving needle-tip visibility during sonographically guided interventional procedures. AJR 1992;158:195–198.

40. Zavala DC, Bedell GN. Percutaneous lung biopsy with a cutting needle: an analysis of 40 cases and comparison with other biopsy techniques. Am Rev Respir Dis 1972;106:186–193.

41. Gobien RP, Stanley JH, Vujic I, et al. Thoracic biopsy: CT guidance of thin-needle aspiration. AJR 1984;142:827–830.

42. Haramati LB, Austin JHM. Complications after CT-guided needle biopsy through aerated vs. nonaerated lung. Radiology 1991;181:778.

43. Johnsrude IS, Silverman JF, Weaver MD, et al. Rapid cytology to decrease pneumothorax incidence after percutaneous biopsy. AJR 1985;144:793–794.

44. Moore EH, LeBlanc J, Montesi SA, et al. Effect of patient positioning after needle aspiration lung biopsy. Radiology 1991; 181:385–387.

45. Westcott JL. Percutaneous needle aspiration of hilar and mediastinal masses. Radiology 1981;141:323–329.

46. Bourgouin PM, Shepard JO, McLoud TC, et al. Transthoracic needle aspiration biopsy: evaluation of the blood patch technique. Radiology 1988;166:93–95.

47. Herman SJ, Weisbrod GL. Usefulness of the blood patch technique after transthoracic needle aspiration biopsy. Radiology 1990;176:395–397.

48. Bernardino ME, Walther MM, Phillips VM, et al. CT-guided adrenal biopsy: accuracy, safety and indications. AJR 1985;144: 67–69.

49. Fish GD, Stanley JH, Miller KS, et al. Postbiopsy pneumothorax: estimating the risk by chest radiography and pulmonary function tests. AJR 1988;150:71–74.

50. Poe RH, Kallay MC, Wicks CM, et al. Predicting risk of pneumothorax in needle biopsy of the lung. Chest 1984;85:232–235.

51. Engeler CE, Hunter DW, Castaneda-Zuniga W, et al. Pneumo-thorax after lung biopsy: prevention with transpleural placement of compressed collagen foam plugs. Radiology 1992;184: 787–789.

52. Sheets PW, Brumbaugh CJ, Kopecky KK, et al. Safety and efficacy of a spring-propelled 18-gauge needle for US-guided liver biopsy. J Vasc Intervent Radiol 1991;2:147–149.

53. Bogan ML, Kopecky KK, Kraft JL, et al. Needle biopsy of renal allografts: comparison of two techniques. Radiology 1990;174: 273–275.

54. Cozens NJA, Murchison JT, Allan PL, et al. Conventional 15-G needle technique for renal biopsy compared with ultrasound-guided spring-loaded 18-G needle biopsy. Br J Radiol 1992; 65:594–597.

55. Mostbeck GH, Wittich GR, Derflur K, et al. Optimal needle size for renal biopsy: in vitro and in vivo evaluation. Radiology 1989;173:819–822.

56. McGill DB, Rakela J, Zinsmeister AR, et al. A 21-year experience with major hemorrhage after percutaneous liver biopsy. Gastroenterology 1990;99:1396–1400.

57. Smith EH. Complications of percutaneous abdominal fine-needle biopsy. Radiology 1991;178:253–258.

58. Ralls PW, Barakos JA, Kaptein EM, et al. Renal biopsy-related hemorrhage: frequency and comparison of CT and sonography. J Comput Assist Tomogr 1987;11:1031–1034.

59. Silverman SG, Coughlin BF, Seltzer SE, et al. Current use of screening laboratory tests before abdominal interventions: a survey of 603 radiologists. Radiology 1991;181:669–673.

60. Zins M, Vilgrain V, Gayno S, et al. US-guided percutaneous liver biopsy with plugging of the needle track: a prospective study in 72 high-risk patients. Radiology 1992;184:841–843.

61. Mahal AS, Knauer CM, Gregory PB. Bleeding after liver biopsy. West J Med 1981;134:11–14.

62. Gazelle GS, Haaga JR, Rowland DY. Effect of needle gauge, level of anticoagulation, and target organ on bleeding associated with aspiration biopsy: work in progress. Radiology 1992; 183:509–513.

63. Gazelle GS, Haaga JR, Halpern EF. Hemostatic protein polymer sheath: improvement in hemostasis at percutaneous biopsy in the setting of platelet dysfunction. Radiology 1993;187:269–272.

64. Ewe K. Bleeding after liver biopsy does not correlate with the indices of peripheral coagulation. Dig Dis Sci 1981;26:388–393.

65. Rodgers RPC, Levin J. A critical reappraisal of the bleeding time. Semin Thromb Hemostasis 1990;16:1–20.

66. Cronan JJ, Esparza AR, Dorfman GS, et al. Cavernous hemangioma of the liver: role of percutaneous biopsy. Radiology 1988;166:135–138.

67. Corr P, Beningfield SJ, Davey N. Transjugular liver biopsy: a review of 200 biopsies. Clin Radiol 1992;45:238–239.

68. Gamble P, Colopinto RF, Stronell RD, et al. Transjugular liver biopsy: a review of 461 biopsies. Radiology 1985;157:589–593.

69. Tobin MV, Gilmore IT. Plugged liver biopsy in patients with impaired coagulation. Dig Dis Sci 1989;34:13–15.

70. Dawson P, Adam A, Edwards R. Technique for steel coil embolization of biopsy track for use with the "Biopty" needle. Br J Radiol 1992;65:538–540.

71. Warshaw AL. Implications of peritoneal cytology for staging of early pancreatic cancer. Am J Surg 1991;161:26–30.

72. Sinner WN, Zajicek J. Implantation metastasis after percutaneous needle aspiration biopsy. Acta Radiol 1976;17:473–480.

73. Lundstedt C, Stridbeck H, Andersson R, et al. Tumor seeding occurring after fine-needle biopsy of abdominal malignancies. Acta Radiol 1991;32:518–520.

74. Engzell U, Esposti PL, Rubio C, et al. Investigation on tumour spread in connection with aspiration biopsy. Acta Radiol Ther Phys Biol 1971;10:385–398.

75. Herman PG, Hessel SJ. The diagnostic accuracy and complications of closed lung biopsies. Radiology 1977;125:11–14.

76. Schenk DA, Bower JH, Bryan CL, et al. Transbronchial needle aspiration staging of bronchogenic carcinoma. Am Rev Respir Dis 1986;134:146–148.

77. Youmans CR, DeGroot WJ, Marshall R, et al. Needle biopsy of the lung in diffuse parenchymal disease: an analysis of 150 cases. Am J Surg 1970;120:637–643.

78. Palmer DL, Davidson M, Lusk R. Needle aspiration of the lungs in complex pneumonias. Chest 1980;78:16–21.

79. Tolly TL, Feldmeier JE, Czarnecki D. Air embolism complicating percutaneous lung biopsy. AJR 1988;150:555–556.

80. Moulton JS. Artificial extrapleural window for mediastinal biopsy. J Vasc Intervent Radiol 1993;4:825–829.

81. Yang PC, Chang DB, Yu CJ, et al. Ultrasound-guided core biopsy of thoracic tumors. Am Rev Respir Dis 1992;146:763–767.

82. Brandt KR, Charboneau JW, Stephens DH, et al. CT- and US-guided biopsy of the pancreas. Radiology 1993;187:99–104.

83. Phillips VM, Hersh T, Erwin BC, et al. Percutaneous biopsy of pancreatic masses. J Clin Gastroenterol 1985;7:506–510.

84. Mueller PR, Miketic LM, Simeone JF, et al. Severe acute pancreatitis after percutaneous biopsy of the pancreas. AJR 1988; 151:493–494.

85. Sateriale M, Cronan JJ, Savadier LD. A 5-year experience with 307 CT-guided renal biopsies: results and complications. J Vasc Intervent Radiol 1991;2:401–407.

86. Tung KT, Downes MO, O'Donnell PJ. Renal biopsy in diffuse renal disease: experience with a 14-gauge automated biopsy gun. Clin Radiol 1992;46:111–113.

87. Moulton JS, Moulton JS. CT of the adrenal glands. Semin Roentgenol 1988;23:288–303.

88. Silverman SG, Mueller PR, Pinkney LP, et al. Predictive value of image-guided adrenal biopsy: analysis of results of 101 biopsies. Radiology 1993;187:715–718.

89. Casola G, Nicolet V, van Sonnenberg E, et al. Unsuspected pheochromocytoma: risk of blood pressure alterations during percutaneous adrenal biopsy. Radiology 1986;159:733–735.

90. Kattapuram SV, Rosenthal DI. Percutaneous biopsy of skeletal lesions. AJR 1991;157:935–942.

91. Tikkakoski T, Lahde S, Puranen J, et al. Combined CT-guided biopsy and cytology in diagnosis of bony lesions. Acta Radiol 1992;33:225–229.

92. DeSantos LA, Lukeman JM, Wallace S, et al. Percutaneous needle biopsy of bone in the cancer patient. AJR 1978;130:641–649.

93. Brugieres P, Revel MP, Dumas JL, et al. CT-guided vertebral biopsy: a report of 89 cases. J Neuroradiol 1991;18:351–359.

94. Dollahite HA, Tatum L, Moinuddin SM. Aspiration biopsy of primary neoplasms of bone. J Bone Joint Surg 1989;71:1166–1169.

12

Intravascular Biopsy

JOSEPH BONN

*A*s with many interventional radiology procedures conceived over the past several decades, intravascular biopsy was orginally developed as an extension of conventional diagnostic angiography, eventually becoming a percutaneous alternative to traditional open surgical techniques. In its current form, it encompasses a range of techniques and tools, providing important vascular anatomic information to clinicians and accurate and reliable tissue specimens to pathologists, while subjecting patients to less risk and a more rapid, easier recovery, all at a lower cost.

The concept of intravascular biopsy was first described by Charles Dotter in a 1964 report on his early dog experiments using a new catheter and a new approach for transvenous liver biopsy.[1] As was his tendency, he speculated on the other possible uses for this technique, including the biopsy of tumor invading the superior vena cava, the sampling of a lung tumor accessible via the pulmonary artery, obtaining tissue from a renal tumor via an arterial approach during a diagnostic renal arteriogram, and the biopsy of a meningioma via the superior sagittal sinus. Although not all of his speculations came to pass, his foresight is clearly visible in the following passage:

> Blood vessels offer ready, nontraumatic access to nearly all large organs and regions of the body. They not only provide routes for observation but avenues of accomplishment that in many instances can replace the mutilating medical expediency we call surgical exposure.[1]

Overall, the topic of intravascular biopsy can be divided into two general categories: those techniques used to biopsy benign and malignant tumor masses or tissue protruding into the lumen of a vessel, and those techniques designed to use vessels as less invasive pathways through which to biopsy organs such as the liver or kidney, most commonly to obtain nonspecific parenchymal tissue, but occasionally directed at tissue from a specific intraparenchymal mass. The differences between these techniques make it worthwhile to examine each separately.

Biopsy of Intravascular Material

The first published case report of an intravascular biopsy was by Robins and Bookstein in 1972 describing the use of gastric biopsy forceps introduced through a common femoral vein access to successfully biopsy a mass occluding the inferior vena cava and causing Budd-Chiari syndrome.[2]

The 3-mm specimen they obtained under fluoroscopic guidance was found to be a renal cell carcinoma invading the venous system and growing into the inferior vena cava to the level of the hepatic vein inflow. Subsequently, three other case reports appeared in the scientific literature: (1) a report on suction applied through an 8.3 French catheter introduced through the brachial vein to biopsy another renal cell carcinoma invading and occluding the inferior vena cava to cause phlegmasia cerulea dolens,[3] (2) a report on an endomyocardial biopsy forceps introduced through a 7 French sheath in the common femoral vein to biopsy an oat cell lung tumor invading the medial wall of the superior vena cava and causing superior vena cava syndrome,[4] and (3) a report on a transcatheter suction biopsy from a common femoral vein approach to obtain cytology from a renal mass invading the inferior vena cava.[5]

In 1978 Mills et al.[6] published the first series of patients who had undergone intravascular biopsy. In their six patients with abdominal neoplasms, brush biopsies were performed using an endobronchial brush through tapered 6 or 7 French or untapered 8 French catheters to obtain cytologic samples to distinguish tumor thrombus from bland thrombus in the inferior vena cava of five patients with known primary malignancies and in one patient without a malignant diagnosis. The authors were successful in obtaining malignant cells in four of the six biopsies. Several important observations emerged from their experience: they advocated approaching the obstructing vena cava mass from a peripheral venous access so as not to embolize material centrally during the biopsy, and they noted that a host of malignancies may appear in the vena cava

195

as tumor thrombus, including renal, adrenal, liver, and testicular carcinomas, retroperitoneal sarcomas, pheochromocytoma, melanoma, and glomus tumors.

After this last paper from 1978, four separate case reports were published describing the successful intravascular biopsy of four different malignant tumors extending into venous lumina: a lymphoma obstructing the left innominate vein,[7] a poorly differentiated liver carcinoma extending into the inferior vena cava,[8] a leiomyosarcoma invading the inferior vena cava,[9] and a renal cell carcinoma tumor thombus in the inferior vena cava.[10] Whereas the first report mentions inadvertent retrieval of tissue from the tumor thrombus by an endomyocardial bioptome during a right ventricular biopsy to assess Adriamycin cardiotoxicity, the other reports were intentional biopsies using endobronchial brushes through a 7 French sheath and an endomyocardial biopsy forceps through an 8 French sheath. Only the authors of the last paper specify choosing femoral vein access to minimize the risk of embolizing fragments of the target mass into the pulmonary circulation.

It was not until Withers et al. in 1988 that another series of intravascular biopsies was published.[11] These authors were successful in obtaining diagnostic specimens in all four cases using pediatric endoscopic biopsy forceps via a 9 French sheath, favoring a transfemoral access to minimize central embolization. They observed that it was helpful to have a pathologist present in the angiography suite to confirm the adequacy of their specimen and that, although a peripheral approach (in this case femoral) to an intravascular tumor may lessen the risk of embolization, one was more likely to encounter bland thrombus on this side of the obstructing mass where flow was stagnant, and one needed to bury the biopsy tool into the mass, but not pass through it, to maximize one's chances of obtaining a diagnostic tissue sample.

On a different but related front, the advent of new technology to improve on balloon angioplasty of atherosclerotic occlusive vascular disease led to the introduction in the mid-1980s of the Simpson atherectomy catheter, whose laterally directed aperture, rotational cutting blade, and collecting chamber allowed one to slice away and remove material protruding eccentrically into a vessel lumen. In a variation on Simpson's theme, Bauriedel et al. in 1989 used this catheter not only to treat benign occlusive arterial disease but also to obtain samples of the material they observed that were narrowing previously angioplastied sites.[12] They applied cell culture techniques to this material, isolating smooth muscle cells and endothelial cells to study the composition of restenosis lesions. One year later, Dake et al.[13] and Castaneda et al.[14] published their ex-

periences using the Simpson directional atherectomy catheter to biopsy the occlusive material causing superior vena cava syndrome in three patients. Dake et al. distinguished recurrent lung tumor from fibrosis in two patients, and Castaneda et al. revealed chronic inflammation and fibrosis rather than malignancy in a single patient.

A summary of these 18 years of intravascular biopsy (excluding the sampling of material in arterial occlusive disease) reveals that the venae cavae, both inferior and superior, are the most likely sites for biopsy of intraluminal material. Patients most commonly present with vena cava syndromes, with cross-sectional imaging demonstrating extrinsic compression, encasement, or tumor growth into the vena cava lumen. The differential diagnosis in most of these patients is between extension or recurrence of a known malignancy, first presentation of a new malignancy, or benign inflammation or fibrosis, especially at the previous site of radiotherapy or surgery. Didier et al., in an analysis of cross-sectioning imaging modalities for inferior vena cava tumor thrombus, noted that transabdominal ultrasound was best in defining the cephalad extent of the tumor, and that computed tomography (CT) was better than ultrasound in describing the full cephalo-caudad extent and extraluminal extent of the tumor, as well as invasion of the vena cava wall.[15] Neither modality could adequately distinguish tumor from bland thrombus, especially because both can enlarge the vena cava (and tumor can be present without enlargement), and both can cause vein wall inflammation and the appearance of invasion. Although magnetic resonance imaging (MRI) has added the advantage of vascular imaging without contrast material and the possibility of greater specificity in distinguishing tumor from thrombus, clinical experience is still somewhat limited.

The technique of sampling intravascular material has not reached a point of standardization, and even the most experienced investigators have not randomized enough between the many available techniques to allow completely objective comparisons of biopsy approaches and devices. But the limited experiences described in the published reports above provide some perspective on the pros and cons of the many technical alternatives.

Most biopsies begin with a contrast venogram to outline the location, extent, and severity of the intraluminal mass and to provide a road map for the best pathway to the biopsy site, as well as the most accurate picture of collateral veins. Common femoral vein access is the route most familiar to angiographers, and when used to approach a mass in an occluded *inferior* vena cava, it allows one to obtain a biopsy with a minimal risk of embolizing material from the biopsy site centrally into the pulmonary circulation because the occlusive mass is interposed. On the contrary, the pressure in the venous system on the femoral vein side of the occluding mass, especially in a patient with inferior vena cava syndrome, may be elevated and the flow more stagnant, exposing the patient to a greater risk of puncture site complications or pericatheter thrombosis. In addition, femoral percutaneous access and access to the vena cava mass may be thrombosed in patients with particularly severe inferior vena cava syndrome. In patients with a patent vena cava, the portion of the mass presenting peripherally is more likely to be coated with bland thrombus in the presence of relatively stagnant flow. In comparison, biopsy of the centrally presenting portion of an inferior vena cava mass from a jugular or brachial approach, although less familiar to angiographers, may be more productive of an adequate tumor specimen but may increase the risk of embolizing material to the pulmonary circulation.

Similar considerations must be applied to *superior* vena cava intraluminal lesions: the more familiar femoral approach may be more likely to yield an adequate specimen from the central portion of the mass but may increase the risk of embolization. The jugular or brachial approach, however, may be precluded by interposed thrombosis or, if the route is patent, may increase the risk of puncture site bleeding because of high pressure or of a false-negative biopsy of bland thrombus on the stagnant, peripheral side of the mass. One unique advantage of the jugular approach is the opportunity it provides to limit postprocedure puncture site bleeding by elevating the patient's head, thereby lowering the pressure in the jugular vein.

Biopsy brushes designed for endobronchial or endourologic use tend to require the smallest introductory system and produce the least disruption of the mass and the least risk of embolization; however, they provide samples adequate only for cytopathology, which may be suboptimal in the evaluation of lymphoma or when acquired from the superficial surface of some tumors. Embedding the brush in the mass may improve the adequacy of the sample, but this maneuver increases the risk of vessel perforation or embolization from the mass.

Aspiration biopsy through a nontapered catheter or sheath requires less demanding catheter manipulation; however, it depends on the target material being friable enough to be suctioned into the catheter lumen. In addition, the sample becomes disrupted during the aspiration, which may make pathologic identification more difficult.

Cutting biopsy tools such as endomyocardial or endobronchial biopsy forceps or pediatric endoscopic forceps require a larger introductory system, between 8 and 10 French, but they produce samples large enough for full histologic evaluation. In general, they require greater catheter manipulation expertise than do brushes of aspiration catheters, they are more expensive, and they run a greater risk of vessel wall damage or embolization from the mass. In certain cases where the intraluminal pattern of tumor growth may not favor the relatively straight-ahead approach of these biopsy forceps, the directional Simpson atherectomy catheter may be more advantageous for cutting a sample through its laterally directed window. The disadvantages of the Simpson catheter, however, are its greater cost and the risk of vessel perforation; it is critical to choose from the cross-sectional imaging a thick-walled segment of the involved vena cava for biopsy.

Transvenous Liver and Kidney Biopsy

In contrast to the intravascular biopsy of abnormal tissue protruding into a vessel lumen, transvenous liver and kidney biopsy represents simply the use of the venous system as an alternative pathway to a target organ in a patient who might be at high risk for conventional percutaneous organ biopsy techniques. It is based on the principle that access into the venous system through a femoral or jugular vein approach, and biopsy of the organ parenchyma through its own vein wall, is easier for the interventionalist to control and for some patients to tolerate than passing a biopsy needle through the abdominal wall and the outer surface of the organ.

It was not until 9 years after Dotter first proposed the technique and tools of transjugular liver biopsy,[1] 6 years after Hanafee and Weiner described the first transjugular hepatic vein catheterization in humans,[16] and 1 year after Wallace et al.'s report on the spectrum of complications associated with percutaneous liver biopsy[17] that Rösch et al. published the first report on transjugular liver biopsy in humans.[18] Rösch was also the first to define patient selection criteria, prescribing the technique for those patients with contraindications to percutaneous biopsy due to coagulopathy or ascites. He also described the feasibility of either right or left jugular venous approaches, the importance of skills in fluoroscopy and catheter manipulation, and the opportunity in the procedure not only to obtain tissue with less risk to the patient but also to obtain venous pressures and to perform diagnostic venography in the liver, right kidney, and inferior vena cava.

Since this seminal publication, at least 16 other reports have presented series of transjugular liver biopsies in humans.[19-34] These series incorporate the full spectrum of ages and liver diseases, including more recently those in transplanted livers[30] and the hepatic complications of bone marrow transplantation.[31] On the basis of this growing experience, the indications for a transjugular approach have expanded to include not only patients with coagulopathies and ascites but also those with thrombocytopenia or massive obesity, those who are unable to maintain the respiratory control needed for percutaneous biopsy, those who require pressures and venography or multiple hepatic specimens, those who have had a previously unsuccessful percutaneous biopsy, and those who prefer the transjugular approach.

In most centers the technique of transvenous liver biopsy has remained a transjugular procedure because this access permits a more direct linear approach into most hepatic veins, the inferior venae cavae, and the renal veins and also gives one the opportunity to easily wedge a catheter into a distal hepatic vein to calculate corrected sinusoidal pressures with which to assess the portal venous system. This approach also is favored for the introduction of the stiff Colapinto needle, a commonly chosen biopsy tool. The straight line from the right internal jugular vein into the inferior vena cava is favored, but Rösch et al. note that approaching from the left internal jugular vein produced only mild upper chest pressure symptoms and no technical compromise in five patients.[18]

After a large-bore sheath is introduced into the right atrium, a selective catheter is used to cannulate preferably a right hepatic vein for free and wedged hepatic vein pressures, followed by inferior vena cava and left renal pressures in patients being considered for surgical splenorenal portosystemic shunt creation. After the catheter is repositioned in the right hepatic vein, it is exchanged over a guidewire for the needle cannula, through which the Colapinto needle is passed. The needle is directed out of the cannula at a segment midway in the hepatic vein to reduce the risk of liver capsule perforation, more prevalent during biopsy from a wedged or distal vein position. The needle is passed inferiorly, and usually anteriorly, also to minimize the risk of capsular perforation. If there is uncertainty as to whether a posterior or anterior direction is safer, a lateral-view hepatic venogram should reveal which direction would biopsy the larger segment of liver.

The aspiration technique during the passage of the needle through the vein wall into the parenchyma varies among investigators, but the principles are the same: to secure in the needle the largest specimen with the least fragmentation and with as little blood con-

taminating the sample. Colapinto and Blendis's modification of adding a perforated stylet to the needle during aspiration significantly reduces fragmentation of the sample, and their recommendation of maintaining suction on the stylet until it is out of the cannula helps maximize the size of the specimen and keeps it from dislodging during removal.[27] The published experience with this technique describes success in obtaining adequate pathologic specimens in more than 80 percent of patients (percutaneous biopsy is successful approximately 95 percent of the time),[23] but this varies with the type of liver. Lebrec et al. found in a very large series that their 99 percent success rate in nonfibrotic livers declined to a 64 percent success rate in fibrotic livers.[25] A series of over 2000 patients by Colapinto found success in 82 percent of biopsies.[35]

Other biopsy tools have been proposed, including a Vim-Silverman (TruCut) tip bonded to a flexible endoscopy forceps. The tip is forced into the parenchyma, and a metal sleeve is advanced over it to cut off the sample. Bull et al. in a large series with this system obtained adequate samples in 97 percent of patients, although they do not specify the quality of liver parenchyma they biopsied.[26] A caution is raised that, because this is a flexible system, the delivery cannula must be wedged in the hepatic vein to support the needle's passage into the parenchyma, theoretically increasing the risk of capsular perforation.[35]

Just as TruCut-like percutaneous biopsy needles have evolved from a manual, multistep device into spring-loaded, semiautomated systems, a similar device has recently been developed for transjugular liver biopsy, incorporating the rapid-fire biopsy mechanism onto the end of a long, flexible 18-, 19-, or 20-gauge thin-walled metal shaft, which is passed through a stiff guiding cannula into the hepatic vein (Quick-Core, Cook, Inc.). Little et al.[32] have described their initial use of this needle in 43 patients, and in the 42 hepatic biopsies obtained, 100 percent were adequate for diagnosis. This flexible system has the potential advantage of tracking into more acutely angled hepatic veins than can be reached by the stiff Colapinto core biopsy needle, as is often found in shrunken livers with end-stage disease. The authors' early experience also suggests that the TruCut mechanism yields more tissue with fewer needle passes and less sample fragmentation than the coring Colapinto needle.

In contrast to these reports, other investigators have reported their early experience with a *noncoring* technique using a femoral vein approach and a guiding catheter through which to pass a flexible-shaft cup biopsy forceps, as is more commonly used in endomyocardial biopsy. In two reports from the same institution using this device, technical success was achieved in 85 percent of biopsies.[31,36] Other authors have achieved similar success in large series: Bilbao et al. obtained pathologically adequate samples in 84 percent of 31 biopsies without complication;[33] and Teare et al. obtained adequate samples in 80 percent of 104 biopsies with four complications.[34] Although specimens typically are smaller than those obtained from the coring needles described above, they are large enough for all standard histologic examinations and may be less likely to fragment; the flexible shaft and biting action of the cup forceps make this device less likely to perforate the liver capsule. In contrast to the transjugular approach, the transfemoral approach may be more familiar to most angiographers. It avoids the risk of cardiac arrhythmia induced by catheters working across the right atrium from a transjugular approach, and it allows for easier entry into the sharply angled hepatic vein–inferior vena cava junction often seen in small, fibrotic, cirrhotic livers. The transfemoral approach still permits pressures to be measured and diagnostic venography to be performed.[31,33,34,36] However, it lacks the benefit of jugular vein puncture in the coagulopathic patients who often are candidates for transvenous liver biopsy, which is to reduce puncture site pressure and achieve more reliable hemostasis by elevating the patient's head.

After any biopsy device is used to obtain a parenchymal specimen, the delivery cannula should be left wedged into the biopsy site so that contrast can be injected to immediately determine whether the capsule has been perforated. If a perforation is seen by the extravasation of contrast outside the organ, the biopsy tract should be embolized with Gelfoam through the same cannula until repeat contrast injections no longer demonstrate extravasation. The incidence of capsular perforation probably varies directly by the degree of compulsion used to find it. Lebrec had 5 in 1033 biopsies, 4 of which were asymptomatic and 1 of which was fatal.[25] Colapinto's summary of all data available in publications on transvenous liver biopsy revealed significant bleeding from a capsular perforation in 8 of 2271 biopsies, for an incidence of 0.35 percent.[35] In a report published after Colapinto's, Hadengue et al.[30] revealed that they had no significant peritoneal bleeding in over 5000 transvenous liver biopsies, without describing whether they followed their biopsies immediately with a contrast injection and tract embolization.

Additional complications associated with a transjugular liver biopsy include jugular puncture site hematoma, pneumothorax, hepatic artery–portal vein fistula, hepatic artery pseudoaneurysm, and cardiac arrhythmia. In the large series described above, the fistula and the pseudoaneurysm were asymptomatic and discovered incidentally.[22,25]

A variation on transjugular liver biopsy has been developed by Mal et al.,[37] who performed transjugular kidney biopsies in 50 patients who had contraindications to conventional percutaneous biopsy. Using the same rigid Colapinto needle and favoring the right kidney because of its less acute angle with the inferior vena cava, they were able to obtain adequate samples in 88 percent of cases. Complications included three small perirenal hematomas seen on routine postbiopsy ultrasound and four briefly transient cases of microscopic hematuria.

In summary, transvenous techniques for obtaining specimens from the liver and the kidney are a safe and effective alternative to conventional percutaneous biopsy in patients who either have a contraindication to a percutaneous approach or who would be better managed by its alternative. Although the greatest experience and the largest number of published reports concern the transjugular approach using a coring needle through a cannula, newer series are being published demonstrating that the transfemoral approach with a flexible noncoring biopsy forceps may be equally safe and effective while offering several advantages. With either approach into the liver, venous access can also be used for measuring systemic and indirect portal pressures and for performing systemic diagnostic venography to provide additional diagnostic information, especially in the patient whose liver disease may have led to or may be associated with portal hypertension.

Conclusion

Both transvenous liver and kidney biopsy and the biopsy of intravascular material highlight some of the best features of interventional radiology; these procedures take advantage of advances in imaging guidance and catheter-based devices to provide critical diagnostic information in a safe, effective manner, with a cost and morbidity considerably lower than traditional surgical approaches. Each technique has found its niche in the diagnostic armamentarium of the interventional radiologist, and, as advances in biopsy device design and experience in new approaches develop, each technique will continue to mature and evolve over time.

References

1. Dotter CT. Experimental technic for transvenous liver biopsy. Catheter Biopsy 1964;82:312–314.
2. Robins JM, Bookstein JJ. Percutaneous transcaval biopsy technique in the evaluation of inferior vena cava occlusion. Radiology 1972;105:451–452.

3. Coel MN, Chalmers J. Percutaneous catheter transcaval tumor biopsy. Radiology 1975;116:222.
4. Armstrong P, Hayes DF, Richardson PJ. Transvenous biopsy of carcinoma of bronchus causing superior vena caval obstruction. Br Med J 1975;1:662–663.
5. Wendth AR, Garlick WB, Pantoja E, et al. Transcatheter biopsy of renal carcinoma invading the inferior vena cava. J Urol 1976; 115:331–332.
6. Mills SR, Doppman JL, Head GL, et al. Transcatheter brush biopsy of intravenous tumor thrombi. Radiology 1978;127: 667–670.
7. Meltzer RS, Stebbins R, Hunt SA, et al. Transvenous biopsy of mediastinal lymphoma invading the superior vena cava. Cathet Cardiovasc Diagn 1980;6:305–308.
8. Ellis JH, Becker GJ, Jackson VP, et al. Transcatheter brush biopsy of a liver mass with CT-proven intracaval extension. Comput Radiol 1985;9(3):173–176.
9. Pollanen M, Butany J, Chiasson D. Leiomyosarcoma of the inferior vena cava. Arch Pathol Lab Med 1987;111:1085–1087.
10. O'Donnell C, Adam A. Percutaneous transcaval tumour biopsy using bioptome forceps. J Intervent Radiol 1988;3:19–21.
11. Withers CE, Casola G, Herba MJ, et al. Intravascular tumors: transvenous biopsy. Radiology 1988;167:713–715.
12. Bauriedel G, Dartsch PC, Voisard R, et al. Selective percutaneous "biopsy" of atheromatous plaque tissue for cell culture. Basic Res Cardiol 1989;84:326–331.
13. Dake MD, Zemel G, Dolmatch BL, et al. The cause of superior vena cava syndrome: diagnosis with percutaneous atherectomy. Radiology 1990;174:957–959.
14. Castaneda F, Moradian G, Hunter D, et al. Percutaneous intravascular biopsy using a Simpson atherectomy catheter: technical note. Cardiovasc Intervent Radiol 1990;12:342–343.
15. Didier D, Racle A, Etievent JP, et al. Tumor thrombus of the inferior vena cava secondary to malignant abdominal neoplasms: US and CT evaluation. Radiology 1987;162:83–89.
16. Hanafee W, Weiner M. Transjugular percutaneous cholangiography. Radiology 1967;88:35–39.
17. Wallace S, Medellin H, Nelson RS. Angiographic changes due to needle biopsy of the liver. Radiology 1972;105:13–18.
18. Rösch J, Lakin PC, Antonovic R, et al. Transjugular approach to liver biopsy and transhepatic cholangiography. N Engl J Med 1973;289(5):227–231.
19. Rösch J, Lakin PC, Antonovic R, et al. Transjugular approach to the liver, biliary system, and portal circulation. Am J Roentgenol 1975;125(3):602–608.
20. Gilmore IT, Bradley RD, Thompson RPH. Transjugular liver biopsy. Br Med J 1977;2:100–101.
21. Gilmore IT, Bradley RD, Thompson RPH. Improved method of transvenous liver biopsy. Br Med J 1978;249.
22. Goldman ML, Gonzalez AC, Galambos JT, et al. The transjugular technique of hepatic venography and biopsy, cholangiography, and obliteration of esophageal varices. Radiology 1978; 128:325–331.
23. Choy OG, Shimkin PM, Link RJ, et al. The transjugular route as an alternative to direct percutaneous needle biopsy of the liver. Am J Gastroenterol 1978;70:653–656.
24. Henriksen JH, Matzen P, Christoffersen P, et al. Improved transvenous liver biopsy needle. Scand J Gastroenterol 1979; 14:593–598.
25. Lebrec D, Goldfarb G, Degott C, et al. Transvenous liver biopsy: an experience based on 1000 hepatic tissue samplings with this procedure. Gastroenterology 1982;83:338–340.
26. Bull HJM, Gilmore IT, Bradley RD, et al. Experience with transjugular liver biopsy. Gut 1983;24:1057–1060.
27. Colapinto RF, Blendis LM. Liver biopsy through the transjugular approach. Radiology 1983;148:306.
28. Velt PM, Choy OG, Shimkin PM, et al. Transjugular liver biopsy in high-risk patients with hepatic disease. Radiology 1984; 153:91–93.
29. Gamble P, Colapinto RF, Stronell RD, et al. Transjugular liver biopsy: a review of 461 biopsies. Radiology 1985;157:589–593.
30. Hadengue A, Lebrec D, Gaudin C, et al. Transvenous biopsy of orthotopic liver grafts—feasible and effective. Transplantation 1991;51:915–917.
31. Lipchik EO, Cohen EB, Mewissen MW. Transvenous liver biopsy in critically ill patients: adequacy of tissue samples. Radiology 1991;181:497–499.
32. Little AF, Zajko AB, Oruns PD. Transjugular liver biopsy: a prospective study in 43 patients with the Quick-Core biopsy needle. J Vasc Intervent Radiol 1996;7:127–131.
33. Bilbao JI, Sola J, Iglesias A, et al. Transvenous liver biopsy in patients with cirrhosis with use of the femoral venous approach and a flexible forceps. J Vasc Intervent Radiol 1994;5:460–462.
34. Teare JP, Watkinson AF, Siegfried RE, et al. Transfemoral liver biopsy by forceps: a review of 104 consecutive procedures. Cardiovasc Intervent Radiol 1994;17:252–257.
35. Colapinto RF. Transjugular biopsy of the liver. Clin Gastroenterol 1985;14(2):451–467.
36. Mewissen MW, Lipchik EO, Schreiber ER, et al. Liver biopsy through the femoral vein. Radiology 1988;169:842–843.
37. Mal F, Meyrier A, Callard P, et al. Transjugular renal biopsy. Lancet 1990;335:1512–1513.

13

Interventional Radiology and the Cancer Patient

MICHAEL J. PENTECOST

Developments such as percutaneous biopsy, biliary and genitourinary drainage, chemoinfusion, and embolization have brought many patients with cancer into the world of interventional radiology. Their numbers are expected to grow; by the year 2010, the National Cancer Institute estimates that cancer will replace cardiovascular disease as the leading cause of death in the United States. The care of the oncology patient—the psychological needs, the control of their pain, the unique therapeutic complications, the intensity and chronicity of care, and the evaluation of alternative treatments—presents a host of new challenges to the interventional radiologist.

Pain Control

The control of pain in the cancer patient has been the subject of increased attention, including a major guideline from the Agency for Health Care Policy and Research (AHCPR).[1,2] Estimates are that 30 to 90 percent of patients with cancer experience severe pain during the course of their illness. This is particularly common in patients with pancreatic, prostate, breast, and bone cancer. In patients with advanced disease, up to one-fourth die without adequate pain control.[3] The control of pain in two settings—acute intraprocedural analgesia and the relief of chronic distress—is pertinent to the interventional radiologist.

Acute Pain

The fear of pain is a major concern of patients undergoing diagnostic or interventional radiologic procedures. Intraprocedural management, including analgesia, is addressed in Chapter 15. Nonetheless, several treatments unique to the oncology patient pose especially difficult problems. Embolization and chemoembolization are increasingly being used to treat tumors of the liver unresponsive to systemic chemotherapy. Patient acceptance of these palliative treatments was initially hindered by intolerable levels of pain during liver embolization.

The etiology of the severe pain experienced by patients during hepatic embolization or chemoembolization is poorly understood. Hypotheses include stretching of the liver capsule due to hepatic parenchymal swelling, nontarget embolization of the gallbladder, and the presence of pain fibers in the hepatic arteries. Molgaard and colleagues used intraarterial lidocaine for analgesia during chemoembolization and observed a marked decline in the amount of morphine and midazolam needed for satisfactory pain control.[4] Their technique involved the periodic infusion of 30-mg aliquots of lidocaine during embolization. The total dose needed (about 100 mg) and the systemic levels of lidocaine were well within range of tolerance, and no untoward effects were encountered.

Coldwell and Lopez described the use of celiac plexus block as analgesia for hepatic embolization.[5] The preprocedural injection of bupivacaine into the celiac plexus was performed expeditiously with fluoroscopic guidance. The use of narcotic analgesia was substantially reduced in this group of patients compared to a cohort control group.

Chronic Pain

Severe pain is a common feature of upper abdominal malignancy, particularly pancreatic and gastric carcinoma. Permanent celiac ganglion block, using phenol or alcohol, has been proposed as an effective analgesic in such patients.[6,7] Lee et al., using CT guidance from the anterior approach, advanced needles into the tissues around the celiac axis and superior mesenteric artery origins.[7] After confirmatory contrast injection and repeat CT imaging, a neurolytic agent was instilled. Relief of pain was observed in 73 percent of patients with malignant disease.

The pain associated with skeletal metastases can usually be controlled with oral analgesics and radiation therapy. The use of percutaneous alcohol injection has been described in patients in whom such treatments are unsuccessful.[8] Using CT guidance, alcohol was injected into the bone metastases of patients with primary malignancies of the lung and breast. Most metastatic lesions were in the ribs, hip, vertebra, and scapula. Nearly three-fourths of the patients experienced lasting pain relief, and one-fourth demonstrated tumor regression.

The Postembolization Syndrome

Nearly every patient undergoing embolization therapy for cancer experiences the postembolization syndrome of nausea, vomiting, anorexia, lassitude, fever, and pain. The syndrome can hinder proper hydration and nutrition, prolong hospitalization, limit acceptance of further treatments, and mimic serious conditions such as abdominal abscess.

Postchemotherapy emesis has two peaks of occurrence—1 to 2 hours and 12 to 18 hours after treatment. The latter is more frequent with chemoembolization; in such patients, nausea and vomiting can be quite prolonged because of the longer dwell time of the chemotherapeutic agent. Emesis can jeopardize hemostasis at the arterial puncture site and prolong hospitalization by preventing oral hydration.

Cisplatin, a commonly used agent in chemoembolization, is by far the most emetic chemotherapeutic drug. Nonetheless, the use of recently developed serotonin receptor antagonists such as ondansetron allows for control of emesis in 65 to 80 percent of patients undergoing chemotherapy even with cisplatin. Ondansetron has become the single most important treatment of the postembolization syndrome.

Postembolization pain and fever can cause diagnostic dilemmas by raising the possibility of coexistent infection. Distinguishing necrotic tumor from abscess can be especially difficult. This diagnostic uncertainty can give rise to superfluous radiologic workup and occasionally even unnecessary intervention or surgery. Response to the nonsteroidal anti-inflammatory agents can help differentiate infection from the postembolization syndrome.

Clinical Trials

The growing acceptance of regional interventional cancer therapies raises new issues for the interventional radiologist. Their feasibility, safety, efficacy, and effectiveness must be evaluated and compared to alternative cancer treatments. The benchmarks of such comparisons are quite different from those of other well-known interventional therapies such as revascularization or drainage procedures.

The first stage in evaluating an interventional therapy is determining its feasibility. Can the procedure be accomplished? Is it possible to cannulate the hepatic, brachial, or external carotid artery? Can the antitumor agent be infused or injected through currently available catheters? Only when it is determined that the interventional treatment can be applied in a timely and rational manner can evaluation proceed to the next step.

Practically speaking, the safety of most chemotherapeutic agents used in regional treatments has already been established in systemic therapy trials. Safety concerns therefore usually center around the embolic agent or catheter delivery system. Does the procedure or embolic agent cause end-organ infarction? Do the higher local levels obtained during regional infusion of cytotoxic agent cause tissue damage? Can the vital surrounding tissues, such as the brain during external carotid artery infusion or the intestine during hepatic artery embolization, be spared?

Once the feasibility and safety are established, the treatment may be compared to currently accepted alternatives. The benchmarks used for comparison in oncology are the quality of life, response rate, and duration of survival. The use of quality-of-life end points in interventional radiology is in the formative stage. Response rates are well accepted and can be further classified into durable responses (how long until recurrences develop, the status of the patient between these times, etc.), complete responses (no detectable disease), partial responses (a certain amount of tumor shrinkage, usually 50 percent reduction in the product of the greatest two diameters), stable disease, and no response. In patients with advanced cancer, complete responses are few in number. The investigator is usually left to judge new treatments based on partial response rates. There are many flaws in such determinations. Partial responses are frequently fleeting and their benefit to patient health uncertain. Most interventional treatments are directed toward solid tumors; therefore, the responses are usually judged by tumor reduction on cross-sectional imaging. There is considerable controversy, particularly in the liver, as to whether such parameters are insensitive (i.e., a responding tumor may liquefy but not decrease in size).[9]

Survival benefit must be judged against a similar cohort of patients—patients with the same age, tumor histology, cancer stage, time from diagnosis, time from initiation of therapy, number of previous treatments, and other factors.

The randomized trial comparing a new therapy to

the existing standard is the pinnacle of clinical investigation. The randomized trial removes bias, standardizes selection criteria, provides for concurrent data collection, and systematizes treatment protocols. Before initiation of such a trial, one more step is critical: investigators must arrive at some consensus about what constitutes optimal therapy. For example, in the case of hepatic chemoembolization, there must be at least broad agreement about the selection of suitable patients, the proper chemotherapeutic agents and their dosages, the best embolic agent, the appropriate timing of treatments, the methods of supportive care such as antibiotics, the end points of therapy, and so on. Achieving such a consensus may take years, even decades. For example, 25 years elapsed between the initial description of regional infusion therapy for unresectable liver tumors and the first reports of the randomized trials.[10-12] If agreement about the best therapy is not achieved first, a credible randomized trial is impossible.

Finally, the treatments must have proven effectiveness in different settings. The skill necessary to perform interventional therapies of any type must be transferable from the research centers where they are developed to the community where they are practiced.

References

1. Jacox AK, Carr DB, Payne R. New clinical-practice guidelines for the management of pain in patients with cancer. N Engl J Med 1994;330:651–655.
2. Jacox AK, Carr DB, Payne R, et al. New clinical-practice guidelines for the management of pain in patients with cancer. N Engl J Med 1994;330(9):651–655.
3. World Health Organization. Cancer pain relief. Geneva, Switzerland, 1986.
4. Molgaard CP, Teitelbaum GP, Pentecost MJ, et al. Intraarterial administration of lidocaine for analgesia in hepatic chemoembolization. J Vasc Intervent Radiol 1990;1:81–85.
5. Coldwell DM, Lopez KA. Regional anesthesia for hepatic arterial embolization. Radiology 1989;172:1039–1040.
6. Lieberman RP, Lieberman SL, Cuka DJ, et al. Celiac plexus and splanchnic nerve block: a review. Semin Intervent Radiol 1988;5:213–222.
7. Lee MJ, Mueller PR, van Sonnenberg E, et al. CT-guided celiac ganglion block with alcohol. AJR 1993;161:633–636.
8. Gangi A, Kastler B, Klinkert A, et al. Injection of alcohol into bone metastases under CT guidance. J Comput Assist Tomogr 1994;18:932–935.
9. Venook AP, Stagg RJ, Lewis BJ, et al. Chemoembolization for hepatocellular carcinoma. J Clin Oncol 1990;8:1108–1114.
10. Clarkson B, Young C, Dierick W. Effects of continuous hepatic artery infusion of metabolites on primary and metastatic cancer of the liver. Cancer 1962;15:472–488.
11. Chang AE, Schneider PD, Sugarbaker PH, et al. A prospective randomized trial of regional versus systemic continuous 5-fluorodeoxyuridine chemotherapy in the treatment of colorectal liver metastases. Ann Surg 1987;206:685–693.
12. Kemeny N, Daly J, Reichman B, et al. Intrahepatic or systemic infusion of fluorodeoxyuridine in patients with liver metastases from colorectal carcinoma. Ann Intern Med 1987;107:459–465.

14

Preintervention Assessment

KLEMENS H. BARTH

Interventional radiology (IR) procedures are minimally invasive surgical procedures that inflict less pain and procedure-related morbidity and mortality than conventional open surgery. Most IR procedures do not require more than 24 hours of hospitalization; some are outpatient procedures. They do not pose significant cardiovascular risks and do not produce the circulatory and metabolic changes caused by open surgical procedures, particularly those of the major arteries. Since IR procedures are rarely performed under general anesthesia, they avoid the anesthetic impact on respiratory, cardiac, and hepatorenal function.

The Scope of Clinical Responsibilities

Interventional radiology is still evolving. Few techniques are definitively established, in contrast to the many surgical techniques that have been passed on for many generations of physicians. IR is largely represented by the first and second generation of practitioners who dedicated most of their professional efforts to develop IR procedures. A third generation of trainees is emerging from programs with a variety of practice styles. This lack of tradition and a limited database on IR procedures have certainly had an impact on risk and benefit assessments, which influence their acceptance by referring physicians and patients. Transjugular intrahepatic portosystemic shunting (TIPS) is a particularly prominent example of a procedure receiving intense scrutiny for its indications, complications, and longevity by gastroenterologists, surgeons, and public health organizations.[1]

For many interventional radiologists the idea that an IR procedure poses a much lower risk than surgery, and does not preclude its subsequent successful performance, provides a powerful rationale for applying it, even though failure or limited success may be encountered. Good examples are transluminal angioplasty thrombolysis and tumor embolization.[2] It is also clear that interventional radiologists strive to perform these procedures as true alternatives to more invasive therapy and not merely as temporizing or strictly preoperative measures.

In view of the potential benefits gained for the patient through state-of-the-art IR therapy, the radiologist's clinical responsibility becomes obvious.[3] Unlike in diagnostic radiology, where recognition of pathology constitutes the sole consultation to the referring physician, who in turn has full responsibility to convert the radiologic findings into clinical care, the interventional radiologist is a clinical consultant, like a surgeon, who converts diagnostic findings directly into clinical care and remains involved from the time a consultation is requested until such time when the consequences of the IR procedure are no longer of importance to the patient's care. This includes preprocedure workup, patient preparation, performance of the procedure, sedation and pain control, monitoring during the procedure, and postprocedure follow-up, which may extend over days or years.[4] Since most IR procedures do not require an anesthesiologist, the radiologist also prescribes and supervises sedation, pain control, and, if necessary, emergency measures to treat complications during the procedure (see Chapter 15). As a member of a clinical treatment team, the radiologist may delegate some of the workup and follow-up to other team members, such as a vascular surgeon, cardiologist, gastroenterologist, or nephrologist. However, only within that framework and in close communication with other team members, and with the patient's understanding that he or she is treated by a team of physicians, is delegation of responsibility appropriate. In any other situation, the radiologist needs to personally prepare and follow the patient. This statement is made expressly with respect to therapeutic procedures. For diagnostic procedures, the interventional radiologist's role as consultant is generally limited to the immediate procedure-related preparation, the procedure, and follow-up of less than 12 hours.

In the environment of managed and probably rationed care, the interventional radiologist will also become more and more a gatekeeper who prevents overuse of IR procedures. Perceived overuse of inferior vena cava filter placement and overuse of transluminal angioplasty have already become prominent examples.[5,6] Presentations to hospital staff, weekly specialty conferences, and grand rounds are important forums in which interventional radiologists can inform clinical colleagues about the proper indications for IR procedures.[4]

For most diagnostic radiologists, it is unusual to question the appropriateness of an ordered examination. This posture may be understandable because transmission of information about the patient is usually limited and research on the complete clinical background may be impossible within the context of a busy practice. However, this does not apply to therapeutic IR procedures. Interventional radiologists, therefore, must understand the different role they play in that part of their practice.[4]

These postulates appear straightforward, yet the priorities of radiologic practice do not necessarily favor them. If IR procedures are performed within the daily routine of diagnostic radiology, most of which are diagnostic image interpretations, it may be very difficult or impossible to personally review every requested procedure, pay an inpatient visit or conduct an office visit, discuss the procedure, and finally perform the procedure in an appropriate time. This situation goes to the heart of the way radiologists practice outside most university hospitals, and has no easy solution. It is often a question of personnel, sharing of responsibility among the members of a group, distribution of specialty skills, maintenance of those skills, sharing of on-call responsibilities, and so forth.[7] With the introduction of subspecialty boards for interventional radiology, there will be better standardization of training and the realization that clinical responsibilities are to be taken more seriously or IR procedures may be lost to other clinical specialties. Interventional radiologists will have to practice more or less full time or devote enough time to procedures and clinical obligations to receive full recognition as clinical specialists.[8,9] In turn, opposition will lessen to interventional radiologists seeking clinical privileges or maintaining privileges for those procedures of interest to physicians of other specialties.[10–12]

Auxiliary Personnel

To conduct patient care efficiently, the radiologist should have competent assistance.[8] A receptionist or secretary with good people-handling skills can take care of scheduling, including the preprocedure outpatient visits, inpatient consultations, and patient follow-ups; distribute patient information materials and maintain regular contact with the referring physician's office staff to arrange patient information transfer; schedule admissions; and deal with insurance preauthorization and notify the radiologist when input in the insurance process is required. Some of these functions may be performed by a nurse who is more familiar with the clinical situation, particularly regarding insurance companies, who frequently employ nurses for such tasks. A nurse could also obtain via telephone a patient history and workup; assess physical disabilities, transportation needs, and other matters; and discuss with the patient medication adjustment, dietary changes, and so forth. A direct nurse-to-patient contact the day before the procedure is considered an essential part of outpatient preparation. The nurse's function is equally important during the procedure for sedation and monitoring, as discussed in Chapter 15. A nurse practitioner or physician assistant may assist the radiologist in some expanded capacity, particularly with inpatient preparation and follow-up, including catheter exchange procedures.[13] In teaching institutions, fellows and residents complement the interventional radiology team by becoming directly involved in procedures under the supervision of the senior interventional radiologists. At present, the customary length of fellowship training is 1 year. During that time the fellow needs to quickly move from the stage of a closely supervised apprentice to a self-supportive and self-deciding interventional radiologist.

Inpatient Consultation

The clinical consultation is initiated for each patient by direct contact with the referring physician unless practice routine has been established between a referring physician or group of such physicians with the interventional radiologist so that typical diagnostic findings prompt a prearranged therapeutic intervention. For instance, after angiographic identification of a significant iliac artery stenosis, angioplasty follows immediately, because a decision was made with the referring physician to proceed in such fashion. This is communicated with the patient in advance and consent is obtained.

The initial physician contact gives the radiologist opportunity to review the reason for referral, the essential parts of the patient's history, physical findings, and pertinent diagnostic workup. Here the radiologist can clarify the approach and treatment planning. For example, if placement of an inferior vena cava filter is requested, questions to be settled are documented pulmonary emboli, relative or absolute contraindication to anticoagulation, and availability of venous access. During the conversation with the referring physician, the radiologist can also make an initial decision about the appropriateness of the procedure or suggest a modification thereof, request further workup, or determine whether the intervention should be performed emergently to realize its full benefit. The outcome of such conversation, particularly if disagreement as to the proper indication exists, will be heavily influenced by the radiologist's professional stature, clinical competence, and reasoning skills. It is important to ascertain that the referring physician has told the patient about the referral to an interventional radiologist; otherwise, the patient may refuse treatment for not having been able to discuss the matter with the physician.

When a problem-focused history is taken, specific questions are asked about such issues as onset of claudication on either side, bilateral symptoms, and which side may be preferable for angioplasty. Other specific questions will pertain to allergies of particular interest to radiologists, such as an allergy against contrast agents or against penicillins or cephalosporins if a drainage procedure is intended and those antibiotics are routinely used for prophylaxis. A procedure-oriented physical examination includes the entire pulse status for all vascular interventions and auscultation for possible bruits over the groin and the neck.[14] Finding a loud bruit over the carotid artery, for example, would prompt further workup for carotid stenosis before renal angioplasty to assess the risk of stroke following sudden decrease in blood pressure. All patients undergoing peripheral angioplasty have ankle or arm indices obtained and documented in the chart.

Additional patient information is obtained from the patient's chart, the nurses, and the house staff. If a change of plans results, the referring physician is immediately notified. For example, a patient scheduled to have a chronic catheter placed for hepatic artery chemotherapy infusion via the left transbrachial access may refuse to have any catheter placed through that arm because she was told by the surgeon "not to have any needles in the arm" because of a previous axillary node dissection.

Imaging studies pertinent to procedure planning include outside angiograms, computed tomography (CT) studies, and ultrasound studies, the latter particularly for hepatobiliary interventions, nephrostomies, and other deep-seated fluid drainages. Magnetic resonance imaging and angiography are particularly relevant for neurointerventions and peripheral arteriovenous malformation embolizations. Procedure-specific laboratory tests include tests for clotting functions,

creatinine levels, complete blood count, and so on. After the radiologist has established the "game plan," he or she obtains the patient's written consent. This consent needs to be secured in some temporary relationship to the procedure, most often within 24 hours. Many patients are comfortable with having the conversation lead to written consent conducted in the presence of a next of kin or caretaker, and the radiologist should encourage the patient to do this if feasible.

The main elements in the consent conversation are the nature of the procedure, the main risks and complications, and the alternatives.[15,16] In some jurisdictions, it is a requirement to put these three elements down in writing and hand a copy to the patient. What constitutes a significant complication is determined by its expected frequency and severity, which may vary depending on the clinical circumstances. For example, small peripheral emboli during peripheral angioplasty are usually of minimal significance if the trifurcation artery runoff is intact. However, if a patient has only a single trifurcation artery, even a small peripheral embolus could have serious consequences. Conversely, a patient with a history of asthma, a condition suggesting allergic diathesis, may not have significant exposure to a contrast-related allergy if the procedure involves nonvascular injection or if carbon dioxide can be used in place of iodinated contrast. Informed written consent documents the existence of a contract between physician and patient.

After the consent conversation, the radiologist completes the consultation report with a treatment recommendation and enters specific preparation orders into the patient's chart, which include the type of food to be withheld, the type of hydration, the antibiotic prophylaxis, and additional laboratory tests if needed. For most IR procedures there is no need for an extended fast. Solid food should be avoided for at least 8 hours before the procedure, whereas clear liquids can be maintained up to 2 hours before the procedure. If standby anesthesia is requested, anesthesiologists generally require a more extended fasting period.

The intramuscular administration of sedatives or narcotic analgesics on the patient's floor before transfer to the interventional laboratory should be discouraged because the patient is not likely to be monitored adequately (exceptions are given below under "Allergy Preparation"). Instead it is better practice to have the patient connected to monitoring devices in the angiographic laboratory before sedation is administered and after baseline vital signs have been recorded. Comforting behavior by the physician, technical staff, and nursing staff during such preparation will go a long way to alleviate patient anxiety.[17]

Outpatient Consultation

As in the inpatient setting, most outpatient referrals are initiated by direct physician-to-physician contact. For therapeutic interventions, the most desirable next step is a patient visit to the interventional radiologist's office, where all the necessary preparatory workup can be performed. If time has allowed, pertinent medical and imaging studies have been sent to the interventional radiologist before that visit or are brought along by the patient. The interventional radiologist may request further workup. For example, if a patient is referred for renal angioplasty, the radiologist may want to obtain a duplex ultrasound study to document and grade the renal artery stenosis by noninvasive means as a basis for postprocedure follow-up. A patient scheduled for hepatic chemoembolization may need an immediate preprocedure contrast-enhanced CT scan as a baseline for matching Lipiodol concentration with individual tumor nodules and for planning additional embolization procedures.

If overnight admission is required, admission arrangements will be made to the service of the radiologist, to the referring physician, or to another consultant, depending on the nature and circumstances of the procedure.

Immediate Preprocedure Preparation

The night before or the day of the IR procedure, certain medication adjustments, fasting periods, assessment of vital signs, and a review of the patient's laboratory tests, such as a renal function test, clotting status test, white blood cell count, hematocrit, and so on, are instituted. Also reviewed are changes in pulse status or venous patency for potential access. Outpatients may have the necessary laboratory tests performed immediately before the procedure, such as a creatinine level test for renal tolerance of vascular contrast, or a full clotting status test for fluid drainages and large-caliber needle biopsies. If not yet done, the definitive written consent is then finalized with the patient having already been informed verbally about the procedure. This is not the time for the initial patient-to-physician contact. The patient should be prepared to undergo the procedure after having had reasonable time for decision making, and finalization by written consent means just that.

Hydration and Medication Adjustment

Patients undergoing procedures with vascular contrast should not be dehydrated, and oral intake of clear fluids is generally allowed to within 2 to 3 hours of the IR procedures. Diuretics are withheld, which in most instances are prescribed for control of hypertension. Diabetic patients and those with borderline renal function who have creatinine levels greater than 1.5 mg/dl are prepared with oral hydration for at least 12 hours before the procedure and if necessary with intravenous hydration during overnight admission.[18] Diuresis may be induced during or immediately after the procedure with mannitol (12.5–25.0 g IV over 1 hr) together with additional intravenous fluids.[19,20] The only caveat regarding hydration is in patients with limited cardiac function. In these instances cardiology consultation is advised. Low-osmolality contrast agents are preferred over high-osmolality agents, and in any event the total amount should be minimized.[20,21]

The insulin dose in diabetic patients is reduced during procedure-related fasting. For morning procedures the author reduces the morning dose by one-half. Blood sugar levels can be monitored during the procedure, and 50 percent glucose injection should be available in case of hypoglycemia.

Testing and Adjustment of Spontaneous or Induced Coagulation Deficits

Screening for hemostatic function usually includes tests for coagulation function (Table 14-1). The partial thromboplastin time (PTT) test represents the *intrinsic pathway,* and the prothrombin time (PT) the *extrinsic pathway.* The platelet count completes the assessment. If a platelet deficiency is assumed (platelet aggregation inhibitors, renal failure), the bleeding time (BT) can be checked to assess the *primary hemostatic function.*

Patients already receiving heparin anticoagulation have the dose reduced to a PTT level around 45 seconds or less for procedures requiring arterial entry. Heparin can be restarted about 2 hours following hemostasis after catheter pullout. For venous procedures, higher PTT levels can be tolerated, but consideration must be given to limit catheter calibers (7 French), and the platelet count should be adequate (>100,000). This is particularly relevant for placement of inferior vena cava filters, which routinely require introducer catheters of 10 French or larger. Patients who need procedures via cutdowns, deep fluid drainages, or large-caliber needle biopsies should have normal clotting function.

Table 14-1. Testing and Management of Common Coagulation Deficiencies

Test	Normal Value	Cause of Abnormal Tests	Treatment
Prothrombin time (PT)—"extrinsic coagulation system"	Within 3 sec of control value	1. Warfarin treatment	1. Vitamin K 10–15mg IM or SQ q8h for 3 doses or FFP[a]
		2. Parenchymal liver disease	2. FFP[a] 3–4 units or 10–20 ml/kg
		3. Vitamin K absorption deficiency: parenteral nutrition, biliary obstruction, malabsorption, antibiotics	3. Vitamin K 10–15mg IM or SQ q8h for 3 doses or FFP[a] 3–4 units
		4. Consumption of factors: disseminated intravascular coagulation, thrombolytic therapy	4. Treat initiating cause
		5. Congenital: hemophilia	5. Consult hematologist
Partial thromboplastin time (PTT)—"intrinsic coagulation system"	Within 6 sec of control value	1. Warfarin treatment	1. As above
		2. Heparin treatment	2. Wait 3–4 hr after stopping heparin, check PTT, or give protamine (1mg/100 U heparin) IV very slowly (cave anaphylaxis)
		3. Lupus anticoagulant	3. No treatment necessary
Bleeding time (BT; indicates platelet function if PT and PTT are normal)	Less than 8 min	Platelet deficiency 1. Quantitative platelet count less than 50,000/μl	1. Platelet transfusion (10 U), hemodialysis, cryoprecipitate (0.1–0.2 bags/kg), and/or DDAVP[c] (0.4 mcg/kg over 30 min)
		2. Qualitative: a. uremia; b. ASA, dipyridamole, NSAID[b]	2. Stop medication (requires days to weeks to reverse effect)
		3. Spontaneous	3. Consult hematologist

[a]FFP = fresh-frozen plasma.
[b]ASA (aspirin), dipyridamole, and NSAID (nonsteroidal anti-inflammatory drugs) generally do not influence the indication for percutaneous vascular procedures, but may do so for deep-seated drainages, percutaneous stone extractions, and so forth.
[c]DDAVP = 1-deamino-(18-D-arginine)-vasopressin.

Patients receiving Coumadin generally require several days of treatment-free interval before the clotting function returns to normal or nearly normal levels. If continuation of anticoagulation is critical, as for patients with atrial fibrillation and artificial heart valves, switching to intravenous heparin is the preferred procedure. The above policy is then followed; otherwise treatment with vitamin K is necessary.

Patients with severe coagulation deficits require adjustment of the clotting function for vascular and nonvascular procedures. Patients likely to present these deficiencies have received chemotherapy, bone marrow transplantation, or high-volume blood transfusions,[22] or have severe liver disease, hypersplenism, renal failure, or disseminated intravascular coagulation after severe trauma or sepsis.[23] Much rarer in the general hospital environment are congenital hemophilias, spontaneous thrombocytopenias, and von Willebrand disease. Although the referring physician or the clinical service is generally aware of the patient's problem, the interventional radiologist needs to be equally aware and at least familiar with basic steps to correct the coagulation status. Specific tests are available for most clotting deficiencies. For platelet function, other than the overall count, determination of the bleeding time is usually the best test. In many instances the underlying process cannot readily be corrected; therefore, specific clotting factors, fresh-frozen plasma, or single-donor platelets are transfused in close temporal relationship to the IR procedure.

Although many patients receive platelet aggregation inhibitors such as aspirin and/or dipyridamole for prophylaxis of stroke or myocardial infarction or after percutaneous transluminal angioplasty or vascular surgery, correction of this platelet deficiency is not required for percutaneous vascular procedures performed through compressible arterial access. However, deep-seated drainages with larger-caliber catheters or access sheath placement for renal stone extraction may well encounter unusual bleeding in those patients. Correction of the platelet defect requires medication suspension for 7 to 10 days before the IR procedure.

Prophylactic Antibiotics

Prophylactic antibiotics (Table 14-2) are not routinely required for sterile vascular procedures except for embolizations that intend to infarct tissue, such as tumor embolization or end-stage kidney ablation.[24] Those patients are covered with antibiotics to avoid or reduce the bacterial seeding of necrosing tissue during or shortly after the procedure.[25,26] Several such procedural protocols have been established.[27–30] It is best to set up

Table 14-2. Antibiotic Prophylaxis for Interventional Radiology Procedures

Vascular Procedures and Biopsies

Patients undergoing sterile vascular procedures do not require prophylactic antibiotics, including those with a history of bacterial endocarditis and prosthetic implants. Strictly adhere to sterile procedure rules.

Exception: Chronic venous catheter implants, catheter introduction through area within 48 hours prior to surgery. Prophylaxis: cefotetan, 2 g IV; start 1 hour before the procedure. (For organ ablation by embolization and chemoembolization, specific procedure protocols apply.)

Biliary and Urinary Drainage Procedures

Antibiotics are administered within the hour before percutaneous biliary, urinary, and other fluid drainages not previously identified as infected (otherwise therapeutic antibiotics should already have been administered). Routine catheter checks during unimpaired drainage and routine catheter exchanges through established tracts do not require such prophylaxis unless the patient is immunocompromised.

Prophylaxis for biliary procedures: Inpatients receive cefoperazone sodium, 2 g IV, or ampicillin, 2 g IV, and gentamicin, 1.5 mg/kg IV. Outpatients receive a single dose of ceftriaxone sodium, 2 g IV. A bile specimen for culture and sensitivity is obtained as soon as the bile ducts are entered.

Prophylaxis for urinary tract procedures: Ampicillin, 2 g IV, and gentamicin, 1.5 mg/kg IV. Patients with limited renal function may receive cefoperazone, 2 g IV. Preferably, urinalysis and urine culture have been performed before the procedure; if not, a urine culture is performed from the first aspirated urine specimen.

Alternative Antibiotic Prophylaxis

Patients allergic to penicillins and cephalosporins receive vancomycin, 1 g IV, and gentamicin, 1.5 mg/kg IV.

---

a routine together with the infectious disease service of a particular hospital environment. Prophylaxis starts within the hour of the procedure and is usually carried on over 24 to 48 hours. For a few vascular procedures in which percutaneous entry is carried out in the area of synthetic bypass grafting, prophylactic antibiotics effective against skin pathogens reduce the possibility of synthetic graft infection.[29]

Adjustment of Cardiac Rhythm Abnormalities in High-Risk Cardiac Patients

Patients with cardiac arrhythmias, particularly those scheduled to undergo pulmonary arteriography or intrapulmonary thrombolysis by catheter, thrombus aspiration, embolization, and so on, should be adequately prepared by cardiology. If a left bundle branch block is present, a temporary transvenous pacemaker is inserted to treat a potential complete heart block.

Patients with severe ischemic[31] heart disease (unstable angina, ejection fraction less than 30 percent) belong to the high-risk group for any intervention and should be so identified in the preparatory process.

Allergy Preparation

For patients allergic to contrast agents, appropriate regimens have been designed over the years and consist of steroids or steroids with H_1 or H_2 receptor antagonists.[17,32,33]

It is generally recognized that the incidence of serious allergic reactions to nonionic contrast is rare and roughly equal to that in patients receiving high-osmolality contrast agents after preparatory medication.[34] It is also recognized that arterial contrast injections are less likely to evoke allergic reactions than intravenous contrast injections.

Preprocedure preparation with benzodiazepines is recommended for patients with recent seizures.[35]

Infected Fluid Drainages

Obstructed biliary or urinary tracts may become infected with or without clinical evidence of such infection. In the latter case the fluids are considered colonized. This concept also applies to internal fluid collections in proximity to the respiratory, gastrointestinal, and urogenital tracts. Percutaneous drainage of such obstructed fluids by IR procedures is most frequently the preferred technique. Prophylactic antibiotics should be administered (see Table 14-2). The procedures are considered "contaminated" or at least "clean-contaminated."[25] Even with antimicrobial protection, patients are still at risk for procedure-induced bacteremia and septic shock. The shock syndrome may be triggered by endotoxin release and not necessarily by overwhelming infection, and is therefore unrelated to the immediate effect of bacteriocidal antibiotics.[36] If patients develop rigor, 25 to 50 mg of meperidine IV provides an effective countermeasure and can be dosed repeatedly. The interventional radiologist can minimize the risk of seeding endotoxin or bacteria-laden fluid into the bloodstream by inducing the minimal trauma necessary for effective external drainage, by avoiding pressure during contrast opacification, and by postponing a more definitive entry, crossing of the obstruction, introduction of a larger-caliber drain, internal drainage, or other procedure to a later time.

References

1. National Digestive Diseases Advisory Board. Role of transjugular intrahepatic portal systemic shunt (TIPS) in therapy of portal hypertension. Workshop, Feb. 28–March 1, 1994, Bethesda, MD.
2. Creasy TS, McMillan PJ, Fletcher EWL, Collin J, Morris PJ. Is percutaneous transluminal angioplasty better than exercise for claudication? Preliminary results from a prospective randomized trial. Eur J Vasc Surg 1990;4:135–140.
3. Ring EJ, Kerlan RK. Inpatient management: a new role for interventional radiologists. Radiology 1985;154:543.
4. Katzen BT, Kaplan JO, Dake MD. Developing an interventional radiology practice in a community hospital: the interventional radiologist as an equal partner in patient care. Radiology 1989;170:955–958.
5. Arnold TE, Karabinis VD, Mehta V, et al. Potential of overuse of the inferior vena cava filter. Gynecol Obstet 1993;177:463–467.
6. Tunis SR, Bass EB, Steinberg EP. The use of angioplasty, bypass surgery, and amputation in the management of peripheral vascular disease. N Engl J Med 1991;325:556–562.
7. Levin DC. A new challenge to radiologists. Radiology 1988;169:855–856.
8. White RI, Denny DF, Osterman FA, Greenwood LH, Wilkinson LA. Logistics of a university interventional radiology practice. Radiology 1989;170:951–954.
9. Kinnison ML, White RI, Auster M, et al. Inpatient admissions for interventional radiology: philosophy of patient management. Radiology 1985;154:349–351.
10. Williams GM. Who should blow up balloons in arteries? Radiology 1988;169:857.
11. Hollier LH. Influence of nonsurgical intervention on vascular surgical practice. J Vasc Surg 1989;9:627–629.
12. Thrall JH, Wittenberg J. Specialization in radiology—trends, implications, and recommendations. AJR 1991;156:1276.
13. White RI Jr, et al. Streamlining operation of an admitting service for interventional radiology. Radiology 1988;168:127–130.
14. DeWeese JA, Leather R, Porter J. Practice guidelines: lower extremity revascularization. J Vasc Surg 1993;18:280–294.
15. Reuter SR. An overview of informed consent for radiologists. AJR 1987;148:219–227.
16. Morris KJ, Tarico VS, Smith WL, Altmaier EM, Franken EA. Critical analysis of radiologist-patient interaction. Radiology 1987;163:565–567.
17. Lasser EC, Berry CC, Talner LB, Santilini C, Lang EK. Pretreatment with corticosteroids to alleviate reactions to intravenous contrast material. N Engl J Med 1987;317:845–849.
18. Barth KH, Matsumoto AH. Patient care in interventional radiology: a perspective. Radiology 1991;178:11–17.
19. Anto HR, Chou S-Y, Porush JG, Shapiro WB. Infusion intravenous pyelography and renal function: effects of hypertonic mannitol in patients with chronic renal insufficiency. Arch Intern Med 1981;141:1652–1656.
20. Porter GA. Contrast medium–associated nephropathy recognition and management. Invest Radiol 1993;28(Suppl IV):11–18.
21. Polosky S. Management of diabetes in the surgical patient. Med Clin 1982;66:1361–1372.
22. Colman RW, Hirsh J, Marder VJ, Salzman EW, eds. Hemostasis and thrombosis: basic principles and clinical practice. 2nd ed. Philadelphia: Lippincott, 1987:920–925.
23. Levi M, ten Cate H, van der Poll T, van Deventer S. Pathogenesis of disseminated intravascular coagulation in sepsis. JAMA 1993;270:975–979.
24. Sternlicht M, Daniels JR, Sales SF, Daniels AM. Effect of antimicrobial protection on tolerance to hepatic chemoembolization with a fibrous collagen carrier. Radiology 1989;170:1067–1071.
25. Spies JB, Rosen RJ, Lebowitz AS. Antibiotic prophylaxis in vascular and interventional radiology: a rational approach. Radiology 1988;166:381–387.
26. Stone HH. Basic principles in the use of prophylactic antibiotics. J Antimicrob Chemother 1984;14(Suppl B):33–37.
27. Platt R, Zaleznik DF, Hopkins EP, et al. Perioperative antibiotic prophylaxis for herniorrhaphy and breast surgery. N Engl J Med 1990;322:153–156.
28. Bergquist EJ, Murphey SA. Prophylactic antibiotics for surgery. Med Clin North Am 1987;71:357–368.
29. DiPiro JT, Cheung RPF, Bowden TA, Mansberger JA. Single dose systemic antibiotic prophylaxis of surgical wound infections. Am J Surg 1986;152:552–559.
30. vanSonnenberg E, Varney RR, Casola G. Antibiotic commentary. Radiology 1988;166:901–902.
31. Grossmann W, Baim DS. Cardiac catheterization, angiography and intervention. 4th ed. Philadelphia: Lea & Febiger, 1991.
32. Greenberg PA, Patterson R. The prevention of immediate generalized reactions to radiocontrast media in high-risk patients. J Allergy Clin Immunol 87:867–872.
33. King J, Rothenberger KH, Clauss W. Prevention of anaphylactoid reactions after radiographic contrast media infusion by combined histamine H_1 and H_2 receptor antagonists: results in a prospective, controlled trial. Int Arch Allergy Appl Immunol 1985;78:9–14.
34. Bettman MA. Guidelines for use of low osmolality contrast agents. Radiology 1989;17:901–903.
35. Kelly JF, Patterson R, Lieberman P, Mathison DA, Svenson DD. Radiographic contrast media studies in high-risk patients. J Allergy Clin Immunol 1978;62:181–184.
36. Cronan JJ, Horn DL, Marchello A, et al. Antibiotics and nephrostomy tube care: preliminary observations: II. Bacteremia. Radiology 1989;172:1043–1045.

15

Intraprocedure Management

KLEMENS H. BARTH
ALAN H. MATSUMOTO
STEVEN V. LOSSEF

*I*n most interventional radiology (IR) procedure rooms, as in operating rooms, endoscopy rooms, and invasive cardiology rooms, a team of physicians, nurses, and technologists works together. Such team efforts, to which every team member contributes specific skills, require coordination by the team leader. In this instance, the interventional radiologist retains the overall responsibility for the care of each patient. Although coordination may be based on mutual understanding and work experience, most hospitals through their accreditation procedures require some written policy on standards of care, credentialing, continued education, conscious sedation, emergency procedures, and quality assurance.[1,2] Beyond that it is prudent to compile a 'laboratory manual' that contains current procedure protocol, basic equipment needs, a step-by-step description of infrequently performed procedures, specific precautions and management of complications, and standard dilutions for frequently infused medications such as vasopressin, urokinase, nitroglycerin, and so on. Periodic in-service meetings are held to address problems, update protocols, and discuss new ideas and developments in the field, such as those gathered from national meetings.

Coordination among nursing, radiologic technology, and medical staff on quality assurance issues will provide for the most efficient use of personnel. Data gathering on radiation exposure parameters, duration of procedures, room turnover time, in-out catheter time, total volume of contrast used, blood loss, hematoma formation, allergic reactions, and other complications is done most efficiently in computerized format using dedicated software such as that developed by the Society for Cardiovascular and Interventional Radiology.[3]

Immediate Preprocedure Assessment

Before entering the procedure room, the patient is reassessed with regard to change in clinical status and medications taken before arriving in the laboratory, particularly antihypertensive medications, antibiotics, oral hypoglycemic agents, or insulin (see Chapter 14). An allergy history is confirmed and compliance with the prescribed allergy preparation is verified. Results of pertinent blood tests are reviewed.

Once the patient enters the IR laboratory, the nurse is usually the first member of the team to assist. His or her posture should be initially geared to lessen the patient's anxiety by providing comfort and compassion. The nurse obtains and records the patient's vital signs. (Periodic monitoring data are added to the written record as well as the final nursing assessment at the conclusion of the procedure.) The nurse then connects the patient to the monitoring equipment, which includes a pulse oximeter, ECG, and blood pressure recorder (Table 15-1). Monitoring devices should be capable of producing a continuously updated digital as well as an analogue display and should allow hard copy printout, with the device's display unit clearly visible to the nurse and the physician operator during the procedure. The same unit should allow dual-channel pressure recording with hard copy printout for invasive pressure measurements, and should have variable scales for systemic arterial, pulmonary arterial, systemic venous, portal venous, biliary, and urinary tract pressures.

After the patient's baseline vital signs are recorded, an intravenous catheter of preferably 20-gauge caliber is placed into a forearm or antecubital vein to allow rapid intravenous fluid infusion if necessary. This line is kept open by continous infusion of either normal saline, 5 percent glucose, or 5 percent glucose with one-half normal saline solution. An existing venous catheter should only be used if it is of sufficient caliber.

Once intravenous access is established, it is appropriate to start intravenous sedation before further patient preparation is performed. With the radiologist's consent, the nurse may give a standard dose of a sedative (see below). The initial dose should take into account the patient's height and weight, age (advanced

Table 15-1. Automated Patient Monitoring During Interventional Radiology Procedures

1. Pulse oximetry (with adjustable alarm, e.g., <92%).
2. ECG (with alarm for bradycardia, tachycardia, arrhythmias).
3. Blood pressure (by cuff, with automatic inflation/deflation cycle and alarm).
4. Have oxygen supply and suction available.

Table 15-2. Oxygen Therapy (approximate percentage of oxygen in inspiratory air)

By Nasal Cannula		By Mask	
1 liter	24%	5–6 liters	40%
2 liters	28%	6–7 liters	50%
3 liters	32%	7–8 liters	60%
4 liters	36%		
5 liters	40%		
6 liters	44%		

age reduces medication tolerance), respiratory status, cardiac status (arrhythmias, limited cardiac output), blood pressure, level of consciousness, narcotic tolerance (patients on chronic narcotic medications or those with current or previous drug abuse may require unusually high doses), and hepatic function (reduced benzodiazepine and narcotics metabolism in patients with decreased liver function). After the initial sedation, the patient is prepared and draped for the procedure, and the radiologist administers local anesthesia by skin infiltration.

Sedation and Pain Control

Although minimally invasive compared to open surgery, IR procedures require percutaneous tracts and cause pain. The extent of manipulation rarely requires general anesthesia in adults; however, some procedures, such as biliary drainage with sizable transhepatic tracts, percutaneous kidney stone extraction, and dilation of biliary and urinary tract strictures, are known to elicit more pain than most patients are able to tolerate under the combination of local anesthesia and neuroleptic sedation and analgesia. Nerve blocks can be employed by those experienced in their technique; otherwise epidural or general endotracheal anesthesia, administered by anesthesiology, is advisable.[4] Intraductal lidocaine (1 percent solution) has been found to reduce pain during biliary duct dilation.[5]

IR procedures are typically performed under conscious sedation, with the exceptions noted above. This type of sedation maintains a comfortable state so that the patient can tolerate minor invasion and the discomfort often related to the extended motionless position. The patient remains easily arousable to allow cooperation during the procedure.

Blood oxygenation is the key parameter to monitor during conscious sedation.[6] A decrease in oxygen saturation due to respiratory depression may trigger carbon dioxide retention, deeper anesthesia, myocardial ischemia, cardiac arrhythmias, and cardiorespiratory arrest. Supplemental oxygen should be immediately available if oxygen saturation drops to the low 90 percent levels (Table 15-2). Encouraging the patient to take deeper breaths may be all that is needed in many situations. Oxygen saturation levels in patients with chronic lung disease may read below 90 percent at baseline. Nasal oxygen should be withheld unless the saturation drops further.

Sedation in most instances employs *benzodiazepines* or *morphine derivatives* or a combination of both, since it is desirable to both relax the patient and control pain (Table 15-3). Both medications together have a potentiating effect that also increases the risk of respiratory depression. Benzodiazepines and morphine derivatives are given in increments until a reasonable level of sedation and pain control is achieved. The end point of sedation may best be characterized by the patient's becoming somnolent (slurred speech) but easily arousable. If little pain is expected during the procedure, a benzodiazepine alone may be sufficient; otherwise a narcotic analgesic is added. As a group, benzodiazepines have an excellent sedative effect but differ in potency, duration of action, and amnestic and cardiovascular effects. A potent, short-acting, amnestic sedative with little cardiovascular suppressive effect is midazolam.[7] Agitated patients may benefit from the initial administration of 25 to 50 mg of diphenhydramine (Benadryl) IV, which has both antihistaminic and mild sedative effects and is generally well tolerated even by severely debilitated patients. Its administration may reduce the dose of subsequent benzodiazepines and narcotic analgesics. As a matter of general policy, the choice of drugs used should be limited so that the team becomes familiar with the wide variation of response among patients to one or two agents. Although the emphasis in this chapter is on adult conscious sedation, a suggested approach to sedation of children is given in Table 15-4.

With adequate monitoring and incremental dosing of medications, unexpected respiratory depression and cardiovascular effects should be minimal. Once an adequate level of sedation and pain control is achieved, supplemental doses may be given every 15 minutes after the patient's level of consciousness has been assessed. Timing of drug dosing becomes critical toward the end of the procedure because the lack of pain stim-

Table 15-3. Sedatives and Analgesics for Interventional Radiology Procedures in Adults

Agents	Initial Intravenous Dose	Total Dose*	Onset	Duration	Comments
Benzodiazepines					
Midazolam	0.5–2.0 mg	0.035–0.150 mg/kg	2 min	1–2 hr	Good amnestic agent, potent, short-acting.
Diazepam	1–5 mg	10–25 mg	2–3 min	6–24 hr	Delayed sedation from metabolites; do not give intramuscularly.
Lorazepam	0.5–2.0 mg	2–4 mg	10–20 min	6–16 hr	Best amnestic agent.
Flumazenil (antagonist)	0.2 mg over 15 sec	3 mg	15–60 sec	20–60 min	Resedation may occur due to short half-life. Repeat dose; monitor closely. If patient is a chronic benzodiazepine user, seizures may occur. Titrate dose.
Narcotic analgesics					
Fentanyl	25–100 µg	1–3 µg/kg	2 min	30–60 min	Minimal cardiovascular effects, chest wall rigidity, if given rapidly.
Morphine	1–5 mg	0.05–0.20 mg/kg	5–10 min	3–4 hr	May cause histamine release and/or a rise in common bile duct pressure.
Meperidine	12.5–50.0 mg	0.5–1.0 mg/kg	3–5 min	2–4 hr	Less effect on common bile duct pressure.
Naloxone (antagonist)	0.1–0.4 mg	Repeat dose in 1–2 min if no response	1–2 min	20–30 min	May need to repeat effective dose every 20 minutes; can precipitate pulmonary edema in higher doses.

*Dose may need to be reduced in elderly or frail patients and in patients with renal or hepatic insufficiency.

ulus may lead to deeper than anticipated sedation. Postprocedure monitoring is therefore important until the patient's level of consciousness has improved. In addition to monitoring the patient's vital signs, the nurse establishes verbal contact with the patient at least every 10 minutes. The nurse also routinely communicates with the physician during the procedure about the patient's clinical status. The need for continuation or termination of sedation and analgesia is determined. In addition, the interventional radiologist needs to keep the nurse informed about the need for additional pain control if he or she anticipates a period of increased pain such as for transhepatic tract dilation, catheter manipulation inside the peritoneal cavity, or renal or hepatic embolizations.

It is important to account for the time required for postpullout vascular compression and skin suture application. Femoral artery compression can be a particularly painful experience for an exhausted patient. It is also important to realize that a full bladder can make femoral compression even more painful and is also a potent hypertensive stimulus that should always be considered if the patient's blood pressure keeps rising. If the patient is unable to void spontaneously in the recumbent position, catheter drainage should be provided. This can be done expeditiously with a straight in-and-out catheter.

Nausea may complicate sedation and analgesia, particularly in nonfasted patients. Nausea may also be triggered by contrast injection, chemoembolization, or pain. Suction equipment should be readily available.[8] Potent antiemetics can be administered intrave-

nously, but all of them enhance sedation (Table 15-5). For other side effects, see also Table 15-5.

In addition to intravenous sedation and analgesia, local anesthesia is provided at the intended needle and catheter entry site. For vascular procedures, it is desirable to place anesthesia on both sides of the entry vessel to reduce vasospasm. If the catheter is to traverse the parietal peritoneum or the pleura, local anesthesia of that surface should be attempted with a small-caliber needle. Frequently, patients experience an initial burning sensation when the local anesthetic is infiltrated into the skin. This burning can be reduced by neutralizing the acidic anesthesia compound by mixing 10 ml of 1 percent lidocaine with 1 ml of 8.4 percent sodium bicarbonate.[9] The amount of the diluted agent has to be increased proportionally. Occasionally

Table 15-4. Sedation of Euvolemic Children Without Cardiopulmonary Disease

Sedative	Route	Initial Dose
Chloral hydrate with diphenhydramine	PO	50–75 mg/kg with 1 mg/kg
Benzodiazepines		
Midazolam	IV (IM)	0.01–0.03 mg/kg
Diazepam	IV only	0.1–0.2 mg/kg
Narcotic analgesics		
Fentanyl	IV	2–5 µg/kg
Morphine	IV (IM)	0.05–0.10 mg/kg

Barbiturates, ketamine, and propofol reserved for application and monitoring by anesthesiology.[21]

Table 15-5. Antiemetics for Interventional Radiology Procedures

Agent*	Single Intravenous Dose	Total Dose	Onset (min)	Duration (hr)	Comments
Metoclopramide	10 mg	0.5–1.0 mg/kg	1–3	1–2	Stimulates upper GI tract motility.
Prochlorperazine	2.5–10.0 mg	10 mg	10–20	4–6	Use a lower dose for elderly patients.
Promethazine	12.5–25.0 mg	25 mg	10–20	4–6	Enhances central nervous system depressant effect of narcotics and benzodiazepines; extravasation can cause tissue necrosis.
Droperidol	0.625–1.250 mg	Higher doses for sedative effect	10–15	4–6	Higher doses may cause dysphoria; potent antiemetic at low doses.
Ondansetron	10 mg over 15 min	0.15 mg/kg	<30	4–6	Very effective; use for chemoembolization; may be combined with dexamethasone (20 mg IV) once.

*All can cause extrapyramidal side effects.

a patient is allergic to a local anesthetic. If the allergenic agent belongs to the chemical group of esters, it can be substituted by one from the amide group or vice versa (Table 15-6). In addition, the rare allergy to solution preservatives (e.g., methylparaben) may occur, in which instance preservative-free preparations should be substituted. It is also worthwhile to note that local anesthetics have different potencies and thresholds for central nervous system toxicity (see Table 15-6). Similarly, agents with lower toxicity thresholds increase the risk of hypoxia during sedation.[10]

Supplemental injections of a local anesthetic should be considered if the catheterization time exceeds 60 minutes, particularly if catheter exchanges are undertaken without protection by an introducer sheath. At times, biliary or nephrostomy tube tracts remain very painful after the procedure. Relief can be provided by local infiltration with a long-acting local anesthetic such as bupivacaine (see Table 15-6).

In the special circumstance of chemoembolization, the use of intraarterial lidocaine (30 mg) immediately before the embolization can significantly reduce the pain associated with the postinfarction syndrome.[11]

Table 15-6. Local Anesthetics

Drug	Chemical Group	Relative Potency	CNS Toxicity Threshold (mg/kg)
Procaine	Ester	1	19.2
Chloroprocaine	Ester	1	12.8
Lidocaine	Amide	2	6.4
Mepivacaine	Amide	2	9.8
Etidocaine	Amide	6	3.4
Bupivacaine	Amide	8	1.6
Tetracaine	Ester	8	2.5

Note: When substituting amides for esters or vice versa in allergic patients, also consider preservative-free preparations, since an allergy may exist to the preservative of the individual preparation.

Fluid Balance

While the patient is under sedation, fluid requirements are assessed. Patients undergoing procedures early in the morning often have a low fluid balance from overnight fasting. Crystalloid infusion of 200 to 300 ml in the first hour may be required to maintain adequate renal tubular function during contrast injection. A hypotensive reaction with tachycardia early after routine sedation can be corrected by rapid saline infusion in many instances. For patients with reduced renal tubular function, hydration becomes even more critical. In addition to a preprocedure fluid load, the patient should be given mannitol (12.5 g IV) toward the end of the procedure to induce an osmotic diuresis and help eliminate the contrast agent (see also below on protection of renal function). Patients undergoing visceral arteriography; visceral artery, bronchial artery, and neuroembolization procedures; and pulmonary arteriography are likely to receive large amounts of intravascular contrast that challenge renal tolerance.

Adjustment of Blood Pressure, Heart Rate, Renal Function, and Blood Sugar Levels

Hypertensive Reactions

Many patients undergoing IR procedures have hypertension, and they should be advised to take their usual dose of antihypertensive medication before most IR procedures. Since preprocedure anxiety often increases the blood pressure further[12] and sedation helps suppress that stimulus,[13] the administration of additional antihypertensive medication should be delayed until the effect of sedation is established. Antihypertensive medication taken by the patient before the procedure

Table 15-7. Treatment of Hypertensive Crisis (not secondary to pheochromocytoma)

1. Reduce pain, anxiety.
2. Empty bladder.
3. Nifedipine 10 mg PO q30 min; adjust to effect (pierce capsule, have patient swallow it) in older patients; give 5 mg PO and repeat q15 min, if necessary.
4. Nitropaste 1–2 inches on shoulder or chest.
5. Labetalol 0.2 mg/kg IV over 2 min, 40–80 mg repeat injection every 10 min up to desired effect, maximum dose 300 mg. Maximum effect 5 min after injection (can worsen congestive heart failure, possible hepatotoxicity).
6. Hydralazine 10–20 mg IV (can cause hypotension and reflex tachycardia).
7. Nitroprusside IV, 5–10 mg/min initially, titrate (monitor blood pressure via arterial line).

may not have reached its peak effect; this, compounded by anxiety, may make the patient's blood pressure appear out of control. If needed, nifedipine (Table 15-7) is the antihypertensive agent of first choice. The nifedipine capsule should be punctured and the patient asked to swallow it with some liquid. Sublingual resorption is less efficient.[14] The dose can be repeated after about 20 minutes. As an alternative treatment for hypertension, or if the patient has a history of or develops angina, a nitroglycerin patch (Nitropaste) can be applied (1–2 inches to the chest or shoulder). Intravenous antihypertensive medication should be administered by the radiologist only if he or she has experience in its use, since blood pressure changes may be precipitous unless the doses are carefully titrated.[4,13] Otherwise emergency consultation with cardiology or critical care medicine should be undertaken.

A hypertensive crisis triggered by selective arteriography for the localization of a pheochromocytoma is probably no longer encountered because of the availability of other diagnostic tests. Those arteriograms were always performed with phentolamine available as an adrenergic blocker.[4]

Hypotensive Reactions

Hypotensive reactions during IR procedures are most likely the result of oversedation, vasovagal reaction, or blood loss. Hypotension on the basis of septic shock is rarely encountered during or immediately after an IR procedure; however, the prodromes of chills and fever are. These prodromes should be regarded as an indication for treatment with intravenous antibiotics (see Table 14-2) and fluids. Meperidine (25–50 mg IV) can be administered to suppress chills and rigor temporarily.

Hypotension on the basis of oversedation is usually the result of cardiorespiratory depression. Nasal oxygen, intravenous fluids, and a narcotic or sedative antagonist (see Table 15-3) should be given.

Bradycardic hypotension in connection with a vasovagal reaction should be readily recognizable; nausea may be a precursor. Atropine and fluids are the established countermeasures. The atropine dose should be at least 0.6 mg, since lower doses may aggravate bradycardia. If hypotension remains unresponsive to atropine and a fluid challenge, dopamine (2–5 mg/kg/min via large peripheral veins or preferably a central venous catheter) is started. The dopamine dose is titrated to the desired pressor effect. Above 10 mg/kg/min significant renal, peripheral, and mesenteric vasoconstriction occurs. Peripheral venous infusion of dopamine entails the risk of skin necrosis on extravasation.

Hypotension secondary to volume loss is usually secondary to bleeding from the vascular entry site or from deep-seated organs such as the kidneys during nephrostomies or the liver during biliary drainage procedures. Frequently, these bleeding sources can be tamponaded by the insertion of a larger-caliber sheath or catheter after pullout of the arterial catheter, by appropriate manual compression. Rapid crystalloid infusion is indicated, and the patient should be typed and crossed for blood transfusion.[13]

If the patient is anticoagulated with heparin, the effect can be reversed promptly with protamine sulfate (1 mg for each 90 units of heparin). Protamine should be given slowly at a rate of 2 mg/min IV to avoid a hypotensive reaction. Since excess protamine acts as an anticoagulant, the dose should be carefully titrated. The half-life of heparin depends on the dose administered and should average 30 to 60 minutes for doses customarily administered (3000–5000 units as bolus) during IR procedures.[15] Protamine can also cause anaphylactoid reactions, particularly in insulin-dependent diabetics.[16] Patients undergoing IR procedures with a high potential for bleeding (e.g., transluminal angioplasty with large introducer sheaths, large-bore nephrostomy, and stone retrieval procedures) should be typed and cross-matched for two units of packed red blood cells before the procedure.

Table 15-8. Drug Treatment of Cardiac Arrythmias

Symptoms	Medication	Dose	Dose Frequency	Maximum Dosage	Comments
Symptomatic sinus brady-cardia	Atropine	0.6–1.0 mg IV	5-min intervals	2 mg IV	Doses smaller than 0.5 mg may cause a paradoxical bradycardia and lead to ventricular fibrillation; demand pacemaker for refractory bradycardia.
Supraventricular tachycardia[a]	Adenosine	6-mg rapid IV bolus; if no response, repeat	1–2 min	12-mg IV bolus	
	Verapamil	0.1 mg/kg IV slowly (maximum of 10 mg)	0.15 mg/kg IV slowly 30 min after first dose	20 mg IV	Use is contraindicated in patients on beta blockers; can be used with patients receiving digitalis.
Ventricular tachyarrythmia[a]	Lidocaine	1-mg/kg bolus IV	Repeat 0.5 mg/kg IV every 8–10 min	3-mg/kg total bolus dose	Once arrhythmia is controlled, continuous infusion of lidocaine at 2–4 mg/min; if circulatory arrest occurs, call code team and defibrillate.
Ventricular fibrillation	Defibrillate: start with 200 joules, then follow ACLS[b] protocol (this treatment should only be administered by ACLS-certified interventional radiologists).				

[a]Consider cardioversion.
[b]ACLS = advanced cardiac life support.

Arrhythmias

Sustained ventricular ectopy, new-onset supraventricular tachycardia, symptomatic sinus bradycardia, heart block, and ventricular tachycardia require immediate management (Table 15-8). A detailed description of treating cardiac emergencies is beyond the scope of this chapter. If a situation arises that is not generally dealt with in the IR laboratory, help should be called as soon as possible. Cardiac lifesaving measures are well established.[17] Each hospital has a resuscitation team ("code team"). This team should be called as soon as tachyarrhythmias are observed that are unrelieved by initial therapy (see Table 15-8). While the interventional radiologist and his or her team are waiting for the code team, they should be ready to start chest compressions and maintain an airway.[18] It is desirable that the interventional radiologist and nurse are certified in advanced cardiac life support. The importance of a large venous access line becomes obvious in the resuscitation situation. Emergency supplies (Table 15-9) as well as defibrillation equipment should be readily available. Since early initiation of treatment to correct a dysrrhythmia is crucial, the radiologist may start to defibrillate as soon as ventricular fibrillation is seen on the monitor. The initial energy for defibrillation is 200 joules (see Table 15-8).

An adequate supply of emergency medication in the IR laboratory is essential and should be kept up to date by the IR nurse (see Table 15-9). Since virtually all emergency drugs are administered intravenously, the importance of a large-caliber venous access needs to be stressed again. The arterial catheter for emergency fluid administration or for continuous arterial pressure monitoring should not be forgotten.

Hypoglycemic Reactions

Oral hypoglycemic agents and insulin may induce hypoglycemia in diabetic patients. Oral agents of the sulfonylurea group (e.g., tolbutamide) are subject to po-

Table 15-9. Suggested Emergency Drugs and Equipment for Adults (individual needs may vary)

Drugs	Equipment
Adenosine	Intravenous access and infusion sets, including 22-, 20-, 18-, and 16-gauge IV catheters
Albuterol (by inhalation)	
Aminophylline	
Ammonia spirits	Intravenous fluids: lactated Ringer's solution, normal saline
Atropine	
Diazepam	Defibrillator
Digitalis	Face masks (small, medium, large), breathing bag and valve set
Diphenhydramine	
Dopamine	
Epinephrine (1:1000, 1:10,000)	Nasal airways (small, medium, large)
Flumazenil	
Glucose (50% bolus, 10% infusion)	Laryngoscope handles
Hydrocortisone	Laryngoscope blades (straight, curved)
Labetalol	
Lidocaine (cardiac)	Endotracheal tubes and stylets (cuffed and uncuffed)
Naloxone	
Nifedipine	Suction catheters
Nitroglycerin (sublingual spray)	Nasogastric tubes
Oxygen	Nebulizer with medication kits
Phentolamine	Wall suction
Sodium bicarbonate	Nasal cannulas
Verapamil	

tentiating effects by aspirin, certain other nonsteroidal anti-inflammatory drugs, Coumadin, and sulfonamide, which deepen and prolong hypoglycemia. This potential problem should be apparent from the patient's medication record. Dose reduction for insulin in preparation for an IR procedure is discussed in Chapter 14. A prudent measure is to determine any diabetic patient's blood glucose levels before and at regular intervals during the procedure. If the blood sugar level falls below normal ($\leq$80–100 mg percent) while the patient remains alert, oral glucose or sugar-containing liquids (orange juice) should be given, with continued close monitoring of glucose levels. If the patient's mental function is impaired (confusion, stupor or tremors, seizures), 50 ml of 50 percent dextrose is injected intravenously followed by infusion of 5 to 10 percent dextrose; blood glucose levels are adjusted to over 150 mg percent. The administration of high-osmolarity glucose can easily damage a small-caliber vein, a problem that again can be reduced by a larger-caliber venous access. Since mental impairment in the early stages of hypoglycemia is masked by intravenous sedation, infusion of 10 percent dextrose may be instituted even at normal to low-normal blood glucose levels.

Protection of Renal Function

Patients with normal renal function should be able to tolerate intravascular contrast volumes as needed for virtually all IR procedures. The authors limit the contrast dose for a single procedure to 5 mg/kg with a maximum of 300 ml of a 60 percent contrast solution. Patients with impaired renal function (creatinine $\geq$1.5 mg/dl) are at increased risk for contrast-induced nephrotoxicity. Older age is an additional independent risk factor, but diabetes mellitus without existing renal insufficiency is not.[19] Nonionic contrast reduces the risk of nephrotoxicity in patients with impaired renal function.[20] Although carbon dioxide can be substituted for ionic contrast in certain diagnostic arteriograms, this does not appear practical for many IR procedures. Protection of renal function includes adequate hydration, maintenance of blood pressure, and osmotic diuresis by mannitol (see also Chapter 14). Hydration needs to be accomplished before the contrast load. Patients on dialysis should receive contrast soon after or immediately before hemodialysis. In the first instance, they are best able to tolerate the contrast-induced increased intravascular volume; in the latter instance, the volume overload is immediately corrected. There is no need, however, to provide dialysis specifically to remove contrast.

Management of Anaphylactoid Reactions

Allergic or anaphylactoid reactions are encountered most frequently after intravascular contrast administration and are not unique to IR procedures. Such reactions are more likely to occur in patients who have an allergic diathesis (bronchial asthma), and are typically unpredictable in their severity. What starts out as hives may progress to laryngeal edema and cardiopulmonary arrest. However, most allergic reactions are limited to urticaria and are typically treated with 50 mg of diphenhydramine IV as soon as itching or the first urticaria is noted, typically in the face and neck area. Various guidelines have been issued for treating allergic reactions, and any of these can be posted in the laboratory or contained in the laboratory manual. A sample regimen is given in Table 15-10.

Table 15-10. Treatment of Anaphylactic Reactions

Symptom	Drug	Initial Dose	Dose Frequency	Comments
Urticaria	Diphenhydramine	25–50 mg IV	May repeat once	Treat if symptomatic or progressive.
Angioneurotic edema	Diphenhydramine or hydroxyzine	25–50 mg IM	May repeat once	For symptomatic subcutaneous angioedema.
	Epinephrine	0.3 mg SC or IM	Repeat every 10 min as needed	For mucocutaneous swelling or airway compromise.
Bronchospasm	Albuterol	2.5 mg inhaled over 5–15 min		
	Aminophylline	6 mg/kg IV over 20 min	Maintenance, 0.6 mg/kg/hr IV	For suboptimal response or recurrent symptoms after epinephrine. Reduce maintenance dose by $\frac{1}{2}$ in cardiac-risk and debilitated patients.
	Epinephrine	0.3 mg SC or IM	As above	May induce angina in patients with coronary artery disease.
Laryngospasm	Epinephrine	0.3 mg SC or IM	As above	For severe reaction, give 0.5 ml of 1:1000 diluted in 10 ml of normal saline IV slowly; call code team.

References

1. Spies JB, Bakal CW, Burke DR, et al. Practice Committee of the Society of Cardiovascular and Interventional Radiology. Standards for interventional radiology. J Vasc Intervent Radiol 1991;2:59–65.
2. Accreditation manual for hospitals. Chicago: Joint Commission on Accreditation of Healthcare Organizations, 1990.
3. Rholl K (chairman), Electronic Data Base Committee. HI-IQ 20 health information and inventory for quality control. Fairfax: Society of Cardiovascular and Interventional Radiology, 1995.
4. Barth KH, Matsumoto AH. Patient care in interventional radiology: a perspective. Radiology 1991;178:11–17.
5. Cheng YF, Chen TY, Ko SF, et al. Treatment of postoperative residual hepatolithiasis after progressive stenting of associated bile duct strictures through the T-tube tract. Cardiovasc Intervent Radiol 1995;18:77–81.
6. Alexander CM, Teller LE, Gross JB. Principles of pulse oximetry: theoretical and practical considerations. Anesth Analg 1989;68:368–376.
7. Lauven PM, Hörnchen U. Techniques used for conscious sedation. Curr Opin Anesthesiol 1991;4:530–533.
8. Grunberg SM, Hesketh PJ. Control of chemotherapy induced emesis. N Engl J Med 1993;329:1790–1796.
9. Matsumoto AH, Reifsnyder AC, Hartwell GD, et al. Reducing the discomfort of lidocaine administration through pH buffering. J Vasc Intervent Radiol 1994;5:171–175.
10. Bernards CM, Carpenter RC, Rupp SM, et al. Effect of midazolam and diazepam premedication on central nervous system and cardiovascular toxicity of bupivacaine in pigs. Anesthesiology 1989;70:318–323.
11. Molgaard CP, Teitelbaum GP, Pentecost MJ, et al. Intraarterial administration of lidocaine for analgesia in hepatic chemoembolization. J Vasc Intervent Radiol 1990;1:81–85.
12. Barth KH. Patient care aspects of vascular and nonvascular interventional radiology procedures. Semin Intervent Radiol 1994;11:83–88.
13. Kiowski W. Treatment of disturbances in blood-pressure regulation, volume homeostasis, and microcirculation during interventional radiology procedures. In: Steinbrich W, Gross-Fengels W, eds. Interventional radiology, adjunctive medication and monitoring. Berlin: Springer, 1993:49–58.
14. vanHarten J, Burggraaf K, Danhof M. Negligible sublingual absorption of nifedipine. Lancet 1987;2:1363–1365.
15. Olsson P, Lagergren H, Stig EK. The elimination from plasma of intravenous heparin: an experimental study on dogs and humans. Acta Med Scand 1963;173:619–630.
16. Cobb CA, Fung DL. Shock due to protamine hypersensitivity. Surg Neurol 1982;17:245–246.
17. Standards and guidelines for cardiopulmonary resuscitation (CPR) and emergency cardiac care (ECC). JAMA 1986;255:2905–2989.
18. Tortolani AJ, Risucci DA, Rosati RJ, et al. In-hospital cardiopulmonary resuscitation: patient arrest and resuscitation factors associated with survival. Resuscitation 1990;20:115–128.
19. D'Elia JA, Gleason RE, Alday M, et al. Nephrotoxicity from angiographic contrast material: a prospective study. Am J Med 1982;72:719.
20. Porter GA. Contrast medium–associated nephropathy: recognition and management. Invest Radiol 1993;28(Suppl IV):511–518.

16

Postintervention Care

KLEMENS H. BARTH

Postprocedure Routine for Inpatients and Outpatients

After the interventional radiology (IR) procedure is completed, the patient's monitoring records and the timed and dated medication orders are signed by the interventional radiologist. An entry into the patient's record briefly describes the type and results of the procedure, the amount of contrast used, the medications administered, the body fluids removed, blood loss, complications, and any recommendations for observation and treatment. Verbal instructions may be given to the patient depending on his or her level of alertness. Verbal instructions are always in addition to, not in lieu of, written postprocedure instructions. For outpatients, the written instructions include a plan for postprocedure care, emergency phone numbers, and a follow-up appointment, if applicable (Fig. 16-1). Follow-up by the interventional radiologist is particularly important for angioplasties, transjugular intrahepatic portosystemic shunting (TIPS), control venous access catheters, and long-term drainage catheter placements. Besides being good medical practice, follow-up provides essential information for any outcome assessment.[1]

The IR nurse communicates with his or her counterpart on the inpatient service or the nurse taking care of the outpatient recovery unless the IR laboratory is equipped and staffed with its own postprocedure outpatient recovery unit.[2] In that area, monitoring continues until the patient is able to ambulate and is ready to be discharged. It is wise to leave the intravenous access line in place until the patient ambulates, because postural hypotension is not unusual after intravenous sedation and hours of recumbency. Rapid fluid infusion will help to correct this condition. Evaluation of the vascular entry site for hematoma formation is always included in the postangiogram follow-up, as are frequent peripheral pulse checks. The patient is given a written sheet of postprocedure instructions (see Fig. 16-1). The nurse should review that information with the patient before discharge.

Intermediate and Long-Term Follow-up

Depending on the type of IR procedure, the follow-up may involve days to years. IR procedures with a short follow-up period of 1 day to 1 week are typically needle biopsies, needle aspiration of fluid, collections, inferior vena cava filter placements, foreign-body removals, embolization for acute bleeding, vasopressin infusion, and all procedures in which another clinical service typically provides most of the procedure-related follow-up as an integral part of its routine (e.g., urinary tract stone removal, central venous access catheters and ports). Some referring physicians insist on providing routine follow-up themselves and refer to the interventional radiologist only if problems arise.

Procedures requiring extended follow-up are transluminal angioplasties, TIPS, internal and external biliary drainages, nephrostomies, abscess drainages, and tumor embolizations. Biliary, urinary, and abscess drainage must be monitored, and the drainage catheters should be flushed periodically. Unless a team approach exists between interventional radiologist and clinical staff, the radiologist should perform his or her own follow-up on these patients and communicate directly with the referring physician on the results verbally and in writing.[3]

Some controversies exist about the need to provide antibiotic prophylaxis each time manipulation and exchanges of chronic catheters such as a biliary or urinary tract drainage catheter are performed. Once a tract is mature, the manipulation per se is not an indication for antibiotic prophylaxis. However, each time drainage is impaired, the fluid is considered infected and the pressure exerted by contrast injection alone can lead to bacteremia. Therefore, appropriate antibiotics are administered intravenously before the procedure (see Table 14-2).

The main aim of routine follow-up for patients with chronic drainage catheters is to avoid obstructive complications and sepsis. Since the interval for which a patient may maintain adequate patency of a drainage

To perform your . . . . procedure, it was necessary to puncture a major artery/vein. To prevent complications, the following precautions are recommended:

- Do not drive for at least 12 hours. If walking is necessary, walk slowly.

- Return home and relax on the bed or couch for the rest of the day.

- If possible, arrange for someone to stay with you.

- Avoid any strenuous activity such as bending over, long walks, stair climbing, housework, or lifting heavy objects.

- You may return to work the day after your procedure, if your job is sedentary. Do not perform rigorous or heavy physical activity for 3 days.

- The bandage covering the vessel entry site may be removed in one day. To keep the puncture site dry, wait until the bandage is removed to shower or bathe. If the bandage becomes wet or soiled, it should be changed.

- You may eat and take your medications as usual. Fluid intake is encouraged unless you have been advised otherwise.

- The puncture site may be sore, but if pain develops at the puncture site, observe the site for bleeding or swelling. Should bleeding develop, lie flat and apply *firm pressure* to the area for 10 to 15 minutes without interruption. Have someone contact us at the number below if bleeding occurs.

- If pain develops in the extremity of the vessel entered, inspect the extremity for change in color, coolness, or decreased sensation. Should these symptoms be present, contact us immediately at the number below.

- Contact us or your doctor if you develop fever, chills, or vomiting within 48 hours, or if you have any questions.

If you have problems or questions call: _____
　　　　　　　　　　　　　　　　　　　　Person or Institution

at _____ between _____
　　Tel　　　　　　　　hours Mon-Friday, Sat/Sun or after _____ call _____
　　　　　　　　　　　　　　　　　　　　　　　　　　hour

_____　　　　　_____
　　　PATIENT SIGNATURE　　　　　　　　　　　　　　RADIOLOGY STAFF SIGNATURE

　　　　　　　　　　　　　_____
　　　　　　　　　　　　　　　　DATE

Figure 16-1. Discharge Instructions for Outpatient Vascular Procedures

Clean the tube (catheter) insertion site with soap and water every 24 to 48 hours or whenever the dressing becomes wet or soiled. (Wash hands before and after handling the tube.) Dry the insertion site carefully. You may leave the insertion site open to air or apply a light dressing. Do not use a tight, occlusive dressing because moisture will accumulate and increase the risk of infection.

Avoid baths, but you may shower.

If you experience discomfort at the insertion site, you may take Tylenol, 1 to 2 tablets every 4 to 6 hours.

If you develop any of the following symptoms, notify your physician or present to an emergency department immediately.
1. Drainage emerging around the tube.
2. Pain and/or swelling at the insertion site, bleeding from the tube or at the insertion site, dizziness, fainting, weakness, or a rapid pulse (greater than 100 beats per minute).
3. Fever or chills.
4. Lack of drainage from the tube.

Drainage catheters require periodic exchange by the interventional radiologist who placed the tube. Your next catheter exchange needs to be done before _____. Please call our number below about 10 days before that date for an appointment. After the drainage tube exchange, you should resume caring for the tube as previously instructed, unless redirected by the radiologist.

If you require sedation for the tube change, you may not drive or operate heavy machinery for at least 12 hours after the procedure. You will need to arrange for transportation home.

If you have problems or questions call: _____
                                                Person or Institution

at _____ between _____
        Tel   hours Mon-Friday, Sat/Sun or after _____ call _____
                                                                              hour

_____   _____
        PATIENT SIGNATURE   RADIOLOGY STAFF SIGNATURE

                        _____
                              DATE

Figure 16-2. Ambulatory Care and Precautions for Patients with Percutaneous Drainage Catheters

catheter varies considerably, initial follow-ups are made at relatively short intervals (3 to 4 weeks) until a patient's individual tolerance is established. Although some patients with nephrostomy tubes may go unobstructed for 6 months, most nephrostomy and biliary drainage catheters require exchange at least every 3 months. The patient should receive written instructions about catheter care, precautions, warning signs of complications (Fig. 16-2), and a phone number to call if a problem arises.

After transluminal angioplasty and TIPS procedures, patients are followed at 3-month intervals up to a year, and thereafter semiannually or annually. The frequent initial follow-up is maintained to cover the critical time of the reaction of the vascular or stent wall to the transluminal procedure and potential restenosis or shunt stenosis. Ankle-to-brachial blood pressure comparison and duplex ultrasound are often valuable for qualitative and quantitative assessment of functional impairment before symptoms reappear.

References

1. Geigle R, Jones SB. Outcomes measurement: a report from the front. Inquiry 1990;27:7–13.
2. Barth KH, Matsumoto AH. Patient care in interventional radiology: a perspective. Radiology 1991;178:11–17.
3. Katzen BT, Kaplan JO, Dake MD. Developing an interventional radiology practise in a community hospital: the interventional radiologist as an equal partner in patient care. Radiology 1989; 170:955–958.

II

Revascularization of the Aorta and Its Branches

17

Percutaneous Aortoiliac Intervention in Vascular Disease

KENNETH S. RHOLL

Percutaneous transluminal angioplasty (PTA) of the iliac arteries is one of the most commonly performed and widely accepted interventional procedures, with multiple specialties claiming its "turf." Yet its acceptance was gradual and hard fought, and there was significant resistance from the surgical community. "Visualize, but do not try to fix!" was printed on an early requisition for angiographic evaluation, recalled Dotter in one of his early manuscripts.[1] Despite the initial lack of enthusiasm from the medical and surgical communities, Dotter correctly predicted the rapid application of percutaneous revascularization techniques to multiple organ systems.

After inadvertently crossing an occluded iliac segment, Dotter first wrote of possible percutaneous treatment of atheromatous occlusive disease in 1963.[2] In 1964, Dotter used a series of coaxial polyethylene catheters to restore perfusion in the leg of an elderly woman who had refused amputation.[3] Early gangrenous changes were reversed and the leg was saved. Ten years later, Gruntzig introduced the double-lumen balloon catheter for vessel dilation, which allowed one to dilate lesions to a larger diameter while using a smaller arteriotomy.[4] The next 10 to 15 years saw rapid advances in balloon technology, with development of balloon systems for vessels anywhere from less than 2 mm to well over a centimeter. With these advances, PTA of iliac lesions became routine and is now accepted as the procedure of choice for isolated, short-segment stenoses of the iliac arteries. Many studies have documented the high technical and clinical success of iliac PTA as well as its long-term efficacy.[5-68] Thrombolytic therapy, converting longer-segment occlusive disease, expanded the role of PTA[69-81] in treating iliac disease, as did the introduction of percutaneously placed intravascular stents.[82-96] The future of iliac recanalization may also include a role for percutaneously placed covered stents or "stent grafts." Although this technology is still in its infancy, there is great excitement and anxiousness in both the radiolog-ical and surgical communities. Assuredly, further technological refinements will follow, but we should recall the historical importance of iliac artery angioplasty as well as anticipate its future. At the time of its initial description, iliac angioplasty was a portent of the revolutionary potential of nonsurgical treatment of "surgical disease," a promise that is still being fulfilled with the evolution of other interventional, minimally invasive therapies. Its current clinical utility and applications are considered within this chapter.

Clinical Evaluation

Before any consideration of intervention, a complete evaluation of the patient should be undertaken, including a directed history and physical examination (H&P). A noninvasive vascular examination confirms the presence of disease, allows quantification and localization of the level of disease, and relates the patient's symptoms to the disease. All of this information helps the interventionalist decide whether intervention is indeed appropriate.

History and Physical Examination

Patients with aortoiliac disease may present with a variety of symptoms because of the proximal nature of the obstruction. Intermittent claudication is by far the most common presentation, with the dominant site being the calves. However, the claudication may involve the thighs, hips, and buttocks in varying combinations. The presence of more proximal symptoms should point the clinician toward aortoiliac disease, although these symptoms must be differentiated from those originating from musculoskeletal and neurologic disorders. Young women (ages 40–50) with a history of tobacco use have a unique pattern of atherosclerotic vascular disease consisting of diffuse disease of the distal abdominal aorta, or the "small aorta syndrome."[97] The young age and female predilection, and

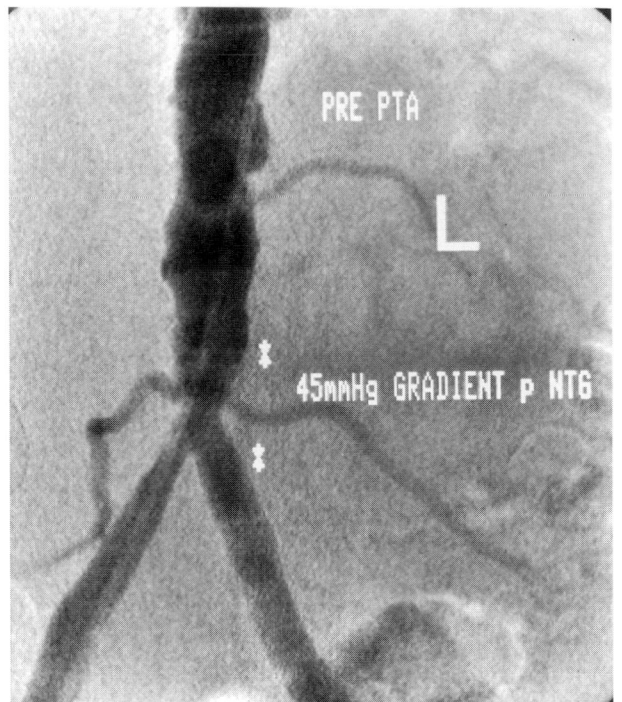

A

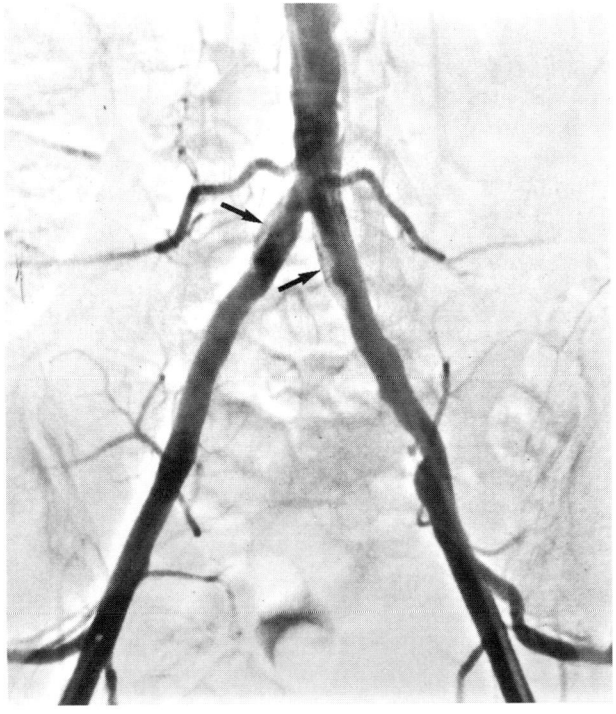

C

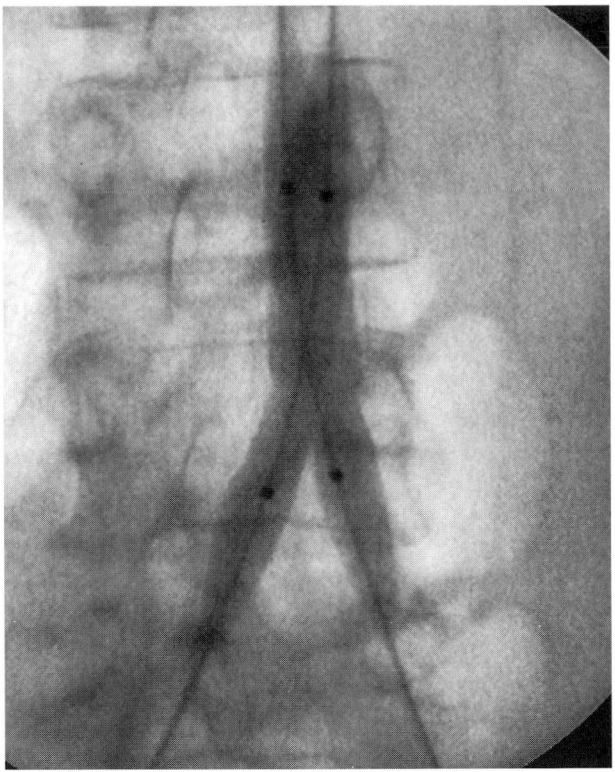

B

Figure 17-1. A 47-year-old woman th hip and thigh claudication. (A) Diagnostic aortography demonstrated atherosclerotic disease involving the distal abdominal aorta (*arrows*). A 25-mmHg transstenotic resting gradient was demonstrated, increasing to 40 mmHg after intraarterial nitroglycerin administration. (B) PTA of the distal abdominal aorta was performed using a bilateral retrograde "kissing balloon" approach. (C) After PTA, no residual gradients were present and the patient's symptoms resolved completely. Small intimal cracks are present in both common iliac arteries (*arrows*). (From Rholl, KS. Percutaneous intervention for aortoiliac disease. In: Strandness E, van Breda A, eds. Vascular diseases: surgical and interventional therapy. New York: Churchill-Livingstone, 1994. Used with permission.)

the difference from the classic clinical profile of atherosclerotic vascular disease, may lead to a delay in diagnosis (Fig. 17-1). Impotence may also be a presenting symptom, either in concert with intermittent claudication or as an isolated complaint. The Leriche syndrome includes symptoms of lower extremity ischemia and impotence secondary to a distal aortic occlusion. It should also be clear that presenting symptoms are extremely dependent on the activity level of the patient, a determination that should be made at the time of the initial interview. Quantification of distance, time to symptoms, degree of activity, and the time course of the evolution of symptoms are all important factors in assessing the patient's disease.

Embolic events may also be associated with aortoiliac disease, either as the primary occlusive event in these segments or as a distal event from a preexisting aortoiliac lesion. The sudden onset of ischemic symptoms in one or both lower extremities without preexisting claudication suggests a primary embolic event, whereas a sudden worsening of symptoms in a patient with preexisting symptoms may indicate occlusion of a previously stenotic segment. Distal emboli may also occur secondary to aortoiliac disease, with symptoms of ischemia presenting anywhere distal to the iliac vessels. Microemboli occluding the digital arteries results in focal severe ischemia of the digits, the "blue toe syndrome."[98] Bilateral simultaneous "blue toe syndrome" suggests an aortic or cardiac source of emboli. Alternatively, unilateral findings may occur with any lesion distal to the aortic bifurcation (Fig. 17-2). Although many "blue toe" patients may have claudication secondary to a stenosis with ulceration and embolization, patients may also present with embolization alone if the offending lesion is not significantly stenotic. Normal peripheral pulses and a normal noninvasive vascular study do not obviate angiography in this setting.

In addition to the history directed at the current symptom complex, an evaluation of risk factors should be undertaken. A smoking history is foremost in this evaluation, since this is the only truly reversible risk factor. In the absence of limb-threatening ischemia in a patient who continues to smoke, revascularization should be delayed until the patient has discontinued tobacco use. Most patients will improve without intervention when use of tobacco products is discontinued and a regular graded exercise program is undertaken. Risk factor delineation also includes evaluation of other sites of vascular disease, such as coronary and cerebrovascular disease and the presence of diabetes mellitus, hyperlipidemia, and a family history of vascular disorders. The last-mentioned may be particularly useful in patients with hitherto undiagnosed hypercoagulable syndromes, many of which are familial.

Physical examination of the patient with aortoiliac disease often reveals diffusely decreased or absent pulses of the femoral, popliteal, and pedal arteries. However, femoral pulses may be present and "normal" at rest and may significantly delay the diagnosis. Though present at rest, pulses will frequently disappear or decrease with exercise, pointing out the value of noninvasive testing with an exercise protocol. Auscultation may reveal a bruit over the aortoiliac segment. Auscultation should also be performed to evaluate other common sites of vascular disease, such as the renal and carotid arteries. Gentle palpation of the abdomen for the presence of an abdominal aortic aneurysm is also an important part of the routine evaluation of peripheral vascular disease. Finally, evaluation of the distal extremities should be undertaken for evidence of ischemia, both acute and chronic. Chronic ischemia leads to trophic changes in the nail beds and loss of hair over the foot and calf. As the ischemia progresses,

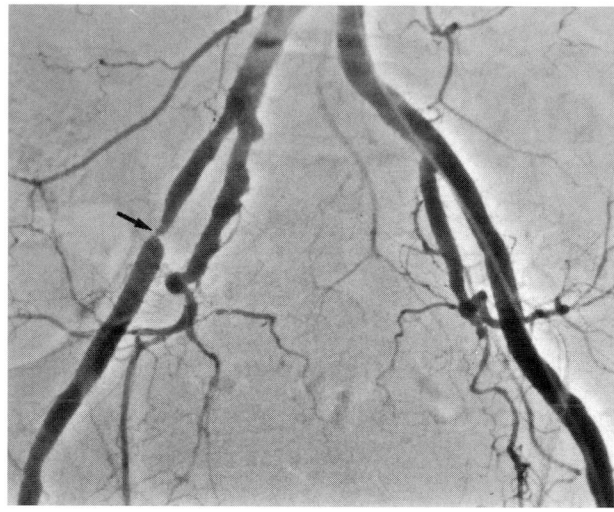

A

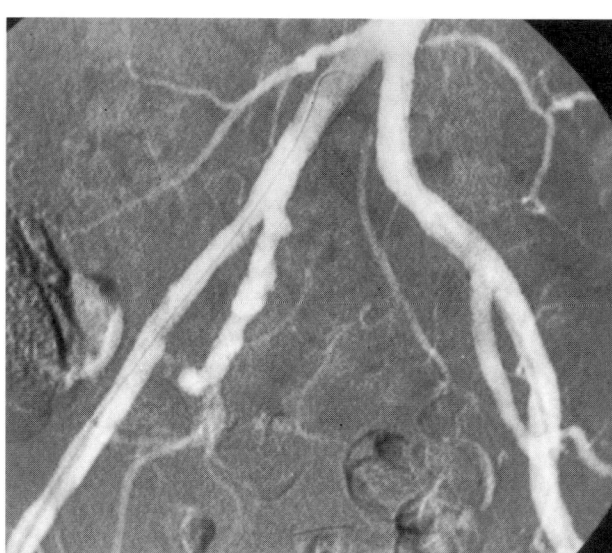

B

Figure 17-2. A 53-year-old man with digital embolization in the right foot, the "blue toe syndrome." The patient had a preceding history of right thigh and calf claudication. (A) Diagnostic arteriography revealed a high-grade right external iliac artery stenosis as the source of emboli (*arrow*). (B) After PTA of the lesion, there was no significant residual stenosis. At 4 years, there had been no further embolic events and the ischemic toes had healed.

the affected limb may demonstrate dependent rubor with pallor upon elevation of the extremity. The patient may have pain in the extremity at rest, which often is relieved by placing the extremity in the dependent position. Capillary refill time may be noticeably slowed. With more severe ischemia, tissue breakdown may occur with formation of ischemic ulceration. When advanced, gangrenous changes occur as tissue breakdown becomes irreversible. With acute severe ischemia, the viability of the extremity should be determined by evaluating capillary refill and sensory and motor function; this assessment is critical in determining the course of subsequent therapy. Both acute and chronic ischemia of the lower extremities should be classified by the criteria of the Society of Vascular Surgery, which was modified by Rutherford and accepted by both the surgical and interventional communities, providing a common definition of the clinical status.[99,100]

Noninvasive Vascular Testing

Although a directed history and physical examination is extremely useful in the evaluation of patients with suspected peripheral vascular disease, both false-positive and false-negative diagnoses may result from sole reliance on the H&P.[101] Noninvasive vascular testing (NVT) can be extremely useful, not only in detecting but also in quantifying and localizing the disease. Furthermore, NVT can help relate the patient's presenting constellation of symptoms to the vascular

disease present. Neurogenic claudication can present with symptoms very similar to those of vascular disease. Exercise testing can help differentiate vascular from nonvascular symptoms, and thus prevent unindicated intervention. It is imperative to remember that the mere presence of disease is not an indication for intervention.

Although a complete description of NVT is beyond the scope of this chapter, a brief description of the modalities available is in order. NVT modalities can be generally categorized by the information they provide as physiologic and anatomic tests. Common physiologic tests include segmental limb pressures, Doppler waveform analysis, volume plethysmographic tracings (PVRs), and photoplethysmographic tracings (PPGs). Anatomic tests include duplex ultrasound, with or without color, and magnetic resonance angiography (MRA). The choice of testing modality should depend on the information sought, with some consideration given to the cost of the examination. Physiologic testing is intended to provide information on the overall perfusion status of the extremity and affords localization and quantification, which are the basis for classi-

Table 17-1. Clinical Categories of Limb Ischemia

		Acute Limb Ischemia				
Category	Description	Capillary Refill	Motor Impairment	Sensory Impairment	Arterial Doppler	Venous Doppler
Viable	Not immediately threatened	Intact	None	None	Audible, ankle pressure >30 mmHg	Audible
Threatened	Salvageable if promptly treated	Intact, slow	Mild	Mild	Inaudible	Audible
Irreversible	Major tissue loss, amputation required regardless of treatment	Absent (marbling)	Profound, paralysis (rigor)	Profound, anesthetic	Inaudible	Inaudible

		Chronic Limb Ischemia	
Grade	Category	Clinical Description	Objective Criteria
I	0	Asymptomatic, no hemodynamically significant lesion	Normal results of treadmill[a]/stress test
	1	Mild claudication	Treadmill completed, postexercise AP[b] >50 mmHg but >25 mmHg below normal
	2	Moderate claudication	Symptoms between categories 1 and 3
	3	Severe claudication	Treadmill test cannot be completed, postexercise AP <50 mmHg
II	4	Ischemic rest pain	Resting AP ≤40 mmHg, flat or barely pulsatile metatarsal plethysmography, toe pressure <30 mmHg
III	5	Minor tissue loss, nonhealing ulcer, focal gangrene with diffuse pedal edema	Resting AP ≤60 mmHg, ankle or metatarsal plethysmography flat or barely pulsatile, toe pressure <40 mmHg
	6	Major tissue loss, extending above transmetatarsal level, functional foot not salvageable	Same as for category 5

[a]Treadmill at 2 mph with a 12 percent grade for 5 minutes.
[b]AP = ankle pressure.
Adapted from Rutherford RB, Becker GJ. Standards for evaluating and reporting the results of surgical and percutaneous therapy for peripheral arterial disease. J Vasc Intervent Radiol 1991;2:169–174; and Marinelli MR, Beach KW, Glass MJ, et al. Noninvasive testing vs. clinical evaluation of arterial disease: a prospective study. JAMA 1979;241:2031. Used with permission.

fication of disease (Table 17-1).[99,100] Exercise testing, an important part of physiologic testing in patients with exertional symptoms, helps relate the physiologic changes occurring with exercise to the patient's symptomatology. Anatomic testing confers greater localization and anatomic information but provides little physiologic information. It is important to remember that many patients with stenotic or occlusive disease in the extremities have "leg pain" that is not vascular in etiology, and therefore undue reliance on anatomic testing may lead to inappropriate treatment. No exercise equivalent is present in anatomic testing. In addition, the cost of anatomic testing is generally significantly higher than the physiologic alternatives. Finally, if one is considering percutaneous intervention, patients with positive anatomic tests will generally not be spared the need for the angiographic procedure, and therefore the costs of angiography will not be avoided. Thus the choice of NVT modality will depend on the information being sought and the equipment available. Physiologic testing is particularly suited to determining the presence of vascular disease and relating the disease to the patient's symptomatology. As such, it is the author's preferred test in the initial evaluation of a patient with suspected peripheral vascular disease. Anatomic testing is more suited to characterizing the disease and therefore may play a significant role in differentiating those patients who have lesions amenable to percutaneous therapy. Frequently, a modified combination of the two modalities may be useful, such as a limited duplex examination to differentiate arterial occlusion from stenosis after physiologic testing. The author reserves anatomic testing as a complement to physiologic testing in a select group of patients.

Percutaneous Revascularization Techniques

Patient Preparation

After a complete clinical evaluation, those patients who are felt to be candidates for aortoiliac intervention should undergo a thorough diagnostic arteriographic examination. A complete diagnostic arteriogram should include a study of the abdominal aorta and iliac arteries, not only for stenotic disease but also for aneurysmal disease, a relative contraindication to intervention in those segments. Loss of lumbar arteries even in the face of an apparently normal-caliber aorta should raise suspicion of an underlying aneurysm. Oblique imaging of the aorta to facilitate renal artery evaluation may be useful in the face of systemic hypertension. Similarly, oblique imaging of the pelvis is mandatory for thorough elucidation of the common

iliac and common femoral arterial bifurcations. In general, the contralateral oblique projection opens the iliac artery bifurcations, whereas the ipsilateral oblique projection is most useful for the femoral artery bifurcations. Finally, complete imaging of the infrainguinal runoff is a requisite prior to intervention. If imaging of the runoff is performed only after intervention is undertaken, the etiology of distal occlusion may be in doubt, possibly representing emboli rather than preexisting disease. This is particularly important when, despite a successful aortoiliac intervention, there is little improvement or perhaps worsening of the patient's vascular status. Because of advances in digital vascular imaging, extensive imaging of the runoff vessels is possible with lower contrast loads. Using carbon dioxide as a contrast agent may nearly eliminate the need for iodinated contrast in those patients who have compromised renal function or a history of significant contrast allergy.

The prior noninvasive evaluation will help the interventionalist in planning an approach to the patient, in terms of both the diagnostic angiogram and the subsequent intervention. Although some prefer to perform the diagnostic angiogram from the side of suspected disease, thereby possibly obviating a second arteriotomy, this approach has two significant drawbacks. First, if an occlusion is encountered at the outset of the study, the diagnostic examination cannot be completed without prior intervention or a second, contralateral arteriotomy. A complete diagnostic study prior to intervention allows for careful planning of the intervention, including anticipation of possible complications secondary to the intervention. The status of the distal runoff should be evaluated before the intervention, or it may be difficult to ascertain whether distal occlusions were preexisting or secondary to complicating emboli. Second, a contralateral approach helps avoid inadvertent occlusion of an iliac artery with a preexisting stenosis secondary to passage of the diagnostic catheter through the stenosis. When this occurs unexpectedly and an occlusion is found, the site of stenosis may be difficult to determine, possibly occurring anywhere from the arteriotomy site to the proximal end of the occlusion (Fig. 17-3). Distal external iliac and common femoral stenoses can be quite problematic in this regard. In instances of severe bilateral disease, alternative approaches may be considered, including brachial, axillary, translumbar, and venous digital subtraction angiography.

Hemodynamic assessment of the aortoiliac segment should be performed as part of any arteriographic study done for peripheral vascular disease. Just as anatomic NVT provides little physiologic information, so the hemodynamic significance of a lesion may not be

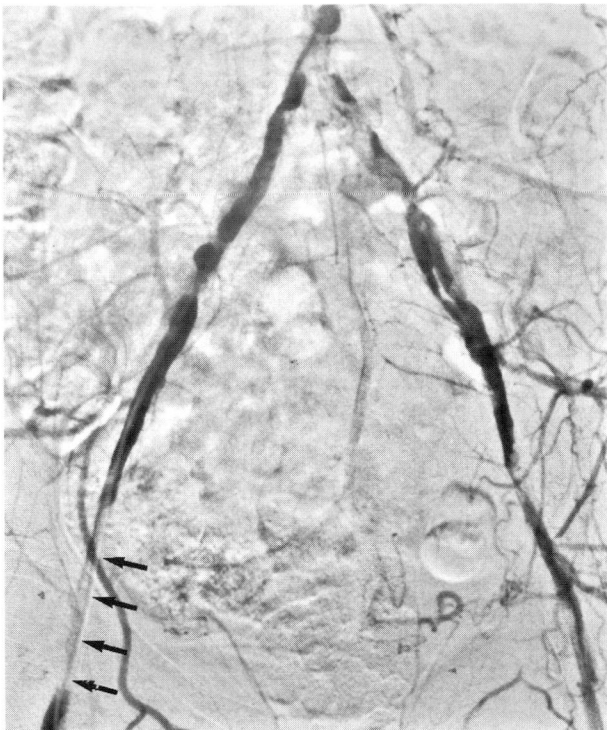

Figure 17-3. Diagnostic pelvic arteriogram in a patient with extensive severe disease. Without prior diagnostic arteriography from an alternate approach, it was difficult to assess whether the occlusion at the right iliofemoral junction (*arrows*) was preexistent or caused by catheter placement.

evident even with the most thorough arteriographic evaluation. Intraarterial pressure measurements through the aortoiliac segment can quantify the hemodynamic effect of a lesion. Occasionally, intraarterial pressure monitoring may uncover a lesion where none was suspected (Fig. 17-4). A resting peak systolic gradient of 10 to 15 mmHg across a lesion is considered hemodynamically significant. In the absence of a resting gradient, tolazoline, 25 mg, or nitroglycerin, 100 to 200 mcg, administered intraarterially distal to the runoff of the extremity in question may reveal the significance of a lesion. The vasodilation produced in the distal vascular beds simulates the increased arterial demand of exercise. A produced gradient of 15 to 20 mmHg or 15 percent of peak systolic pressure is considered hemodynamically significant. Repeat measurements after interventions such as PTA help to judge the technical success of the procedure, or conversely, to identify those areas where a significant flow-limiting lesion persists that may require further intervention. A diagnostic arteriogram should not be considered complete without this information.

Although extremely useful in the evaluation of stenotic disease, gradients must be evaluated with the entire angiographic and clinical picture in mind. Production of a gradient requires outflow beneath a lesion, and in the absence of outflow, no gradient may be measured despite the presence of a severe inflow stenosis. This fact becomes extremely important in multilevel disease in which correction of outflow obstruction is being considered. If one relies solely on hemodynamic data and fails to correct obvious inflow disease before treating the outflow disease, a distal graft may be compromised because these grafts are extremely dependent on adequate inflow.

Certain pharmacologic agents may also aid the interventionalist in performing revascularization procedures. Antiplatelet agents such as aspirin administered before the procedure and intraprocedural use of heparin are considered routine at many institutions. The use of anticoagulation during a procedure depends on the complexity of the procedure, including the general blood flow through the vessel during the procedure, the length of time a vessel is expected to be occluded, and the thrombogenicity of the device to be used. Atherectomy devices and stents are especially thrombogenic. For routine iliac balloon angioplasty, heparinization is frequently omitted. Many authors have also proposed the routine intraprocedural use of vasodilators such as nitrates and calcium channel blockers to minimize the likelihood of vasospasm complicating the procedure.[5,14,20,30,37,102-104] Finally, it is imperative that patients refrain from tobacco use before the procedure. Transdermal nicotine may have the same adverse vasoconstricting effect as tobacco, and its use should also be avoided in the periprocedural period.

Aortoiliac Angioplasty

Although the technique of balloon angioplasty has been thoroughly described in the literature, aspects of particular importance in aortoiliac disease are addressed here. It cannot be overstressed that adequate patient preparation, including informed consent, is mandatory before embarking on any form of intervention.

Historically, an ipsilateral retrograde approach has been preferred for iliac angioplasty. Its greatest advantage is that of excellent catheter and guidewire control during the procedure. Additionally, the treated region can be imaged either through the angioplasty catheter without excessive manipulation or withdrawal of the catheter across the lesion, or through a contralateral diagnostic catheter (Fig. 17-5). PTA has been performed from a contralateral approach without a significant increase in complications.[105,106] If this approach is considered, it is desirable to select those patients with less acute angulation of the aortic bifurcation and

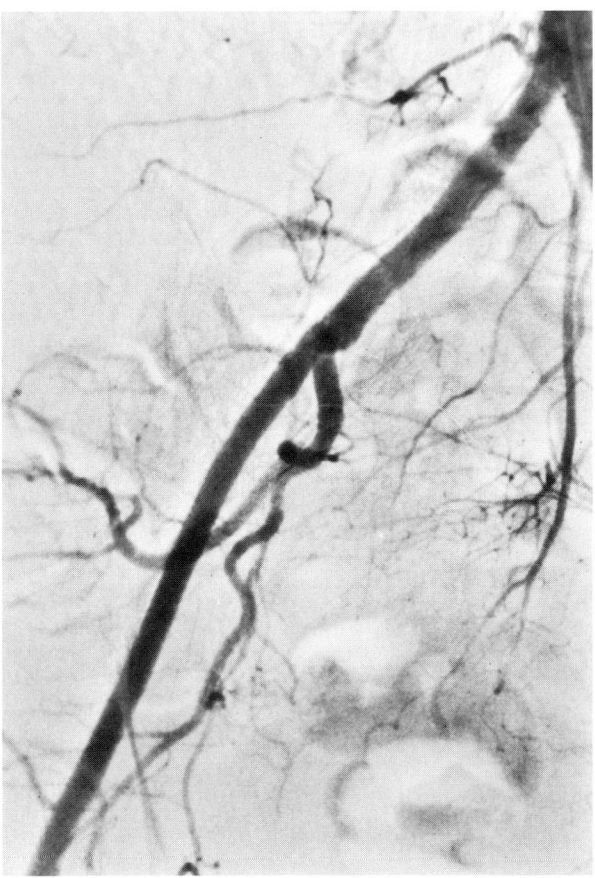

A

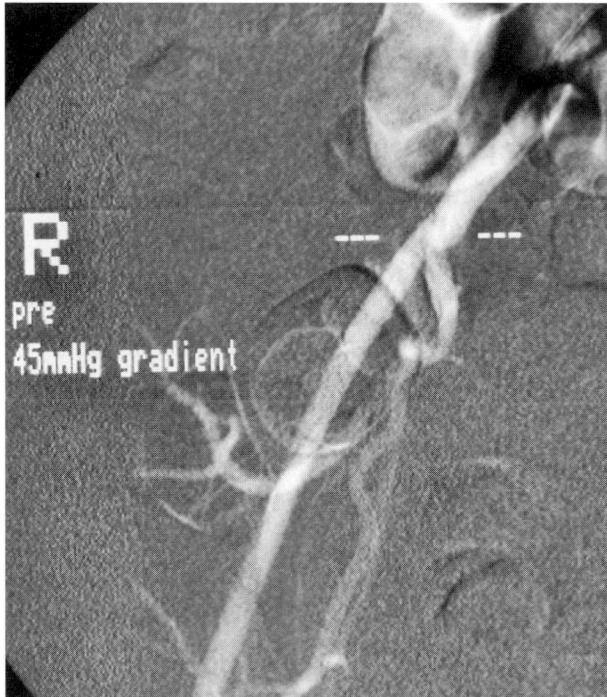

B

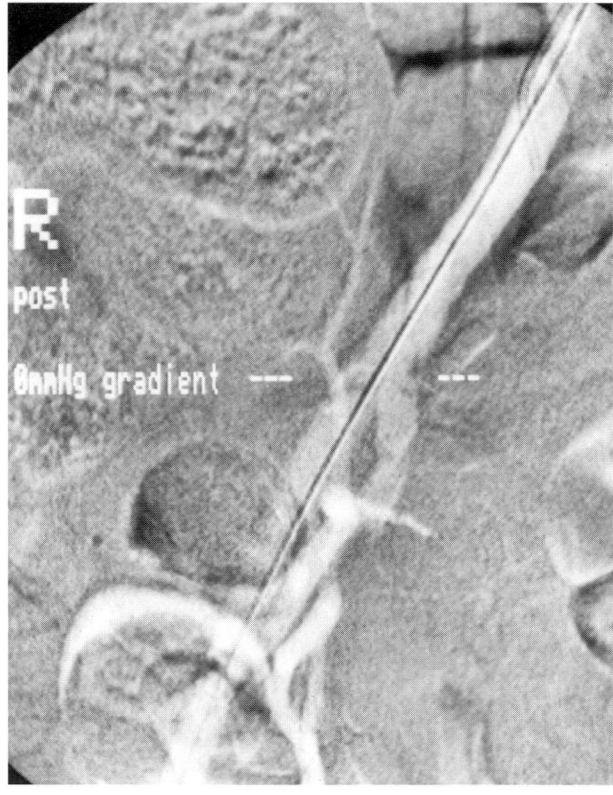

C

Figure 17-4. A 52-year-old woman with right calf and thigh claudication. (A) Diagnostic arteriography revealed no obvious high-grade stenosis. (B) Intraarterial pressure measurements, however, revealed a 45-mmHg gradient across the origin of the right external iliac artery. (C) After PTA, repeat intraarterial pressure measurements revealed no residual gradient and the patient was subsequently asymptomatic. (From Rholl, KS. Percutaneous intervention for aortoiliac disease. In: Strandness E, van Breda A, eds. Vascular diseases: surgical and interventional therapy. New York: Churchill-Livingstone, 1994. Used with permission.)

less tortuosity of the iliac vessels. A brachial or axillary approach is rarely necessary and should be avoided because of the greater risk of puncture site complications. This approach places the arm and the cerebral vasculature at risk for complications, including arterial occlusions, emboli, and hemorrhage. In addition, because of the necessary course, there is less control over catheters and guidewires.

The choice of angioplasty balloon diameter is important if one is to obtain an optimal result and yet avoid arterial rupture, which can be catastrophic. Most authors consider slight overdilation of the vessel necessary. This is provided by direct measurement of the

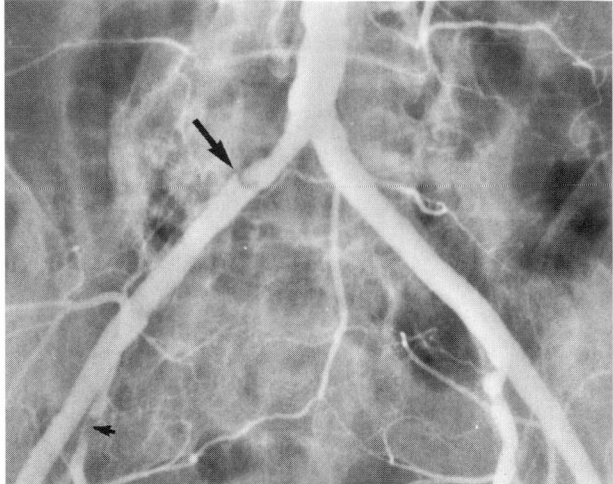

A

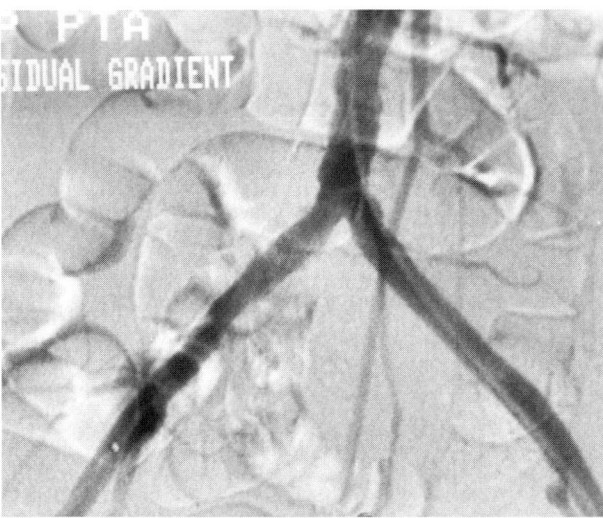

C

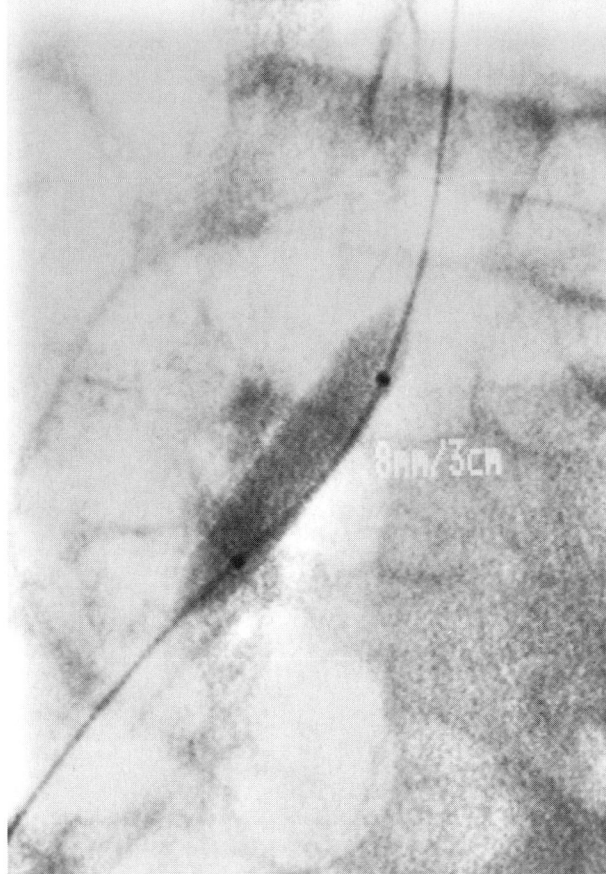

B

Figure 17-5. A 63-year-old man with right thigh and buttock claudication. (A) Diagnostic arteriography revealed an eccentric focal lesion (*large arrow*) in the right common iliac artery. Severe hypogastric artery disease (*small arrow*) was also present. (B and C) Angioplasty was performed from an ipsilateral retrograde approach; angiographic monitoring of the procedure could be performed using the contralateral diagnostic catheter. In this case, there was a good angiographic result with no significant residual stenosis or gradient.

"normal" segment of vessel from a film-screen angiogram, which confers a degree of magnification (usually 10–20 percent). Significant overdilation of an artery usually results in significant discomfort to the patient. The patient should therefore be monitored for discomfort related to the balloon inflation; if excessive, the balloon size should be decreased. Documentation of the results of PTA should include both angiographic study and intraarterial hemodynamic evalua-

tion as outlined above. Fluoroscopic "impressions" or intraoperative comments such as "the flow looked better" are inadequate and do not meet the standard of care for PTA.

Lesions involving the aortic bifurcation and origins of the common iliac arteries may require the use of bilateral retrograde PTA catheters extending across the aortic bifurcation with simultaneous inflation, referred to as the "kissing balloon" technique (Fig. 17-6).[45,46,48–50,53–58,107] Not only does this provide a larger dilation process in the distal aorta, but the simultaneous balloons may help avoid shifting of bifurcation plaque from one side to the other. Initially, aortic lesions often required more than one balloon to achieve an adequate lumen size. Indeed, the use of three balloons has been described. Larger balloon diameters are now available, and this multiple balloon technique is rarely necessary for aortic dilation.

Thrombolysis

Catheter-directed thrombolysis has been widely used for the treatment of occluded arteries and grafts.[69–80] In addition to acute occlusive disease, chronic arterial

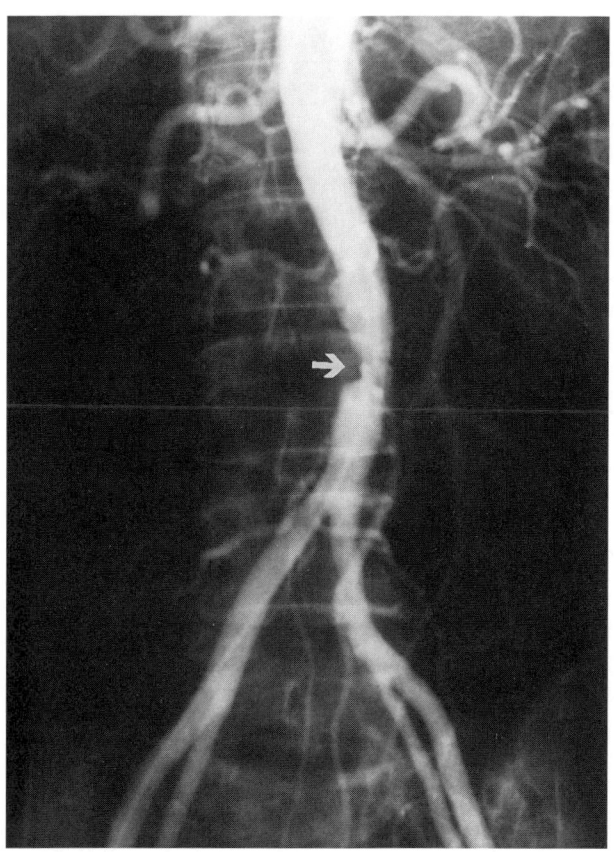

A

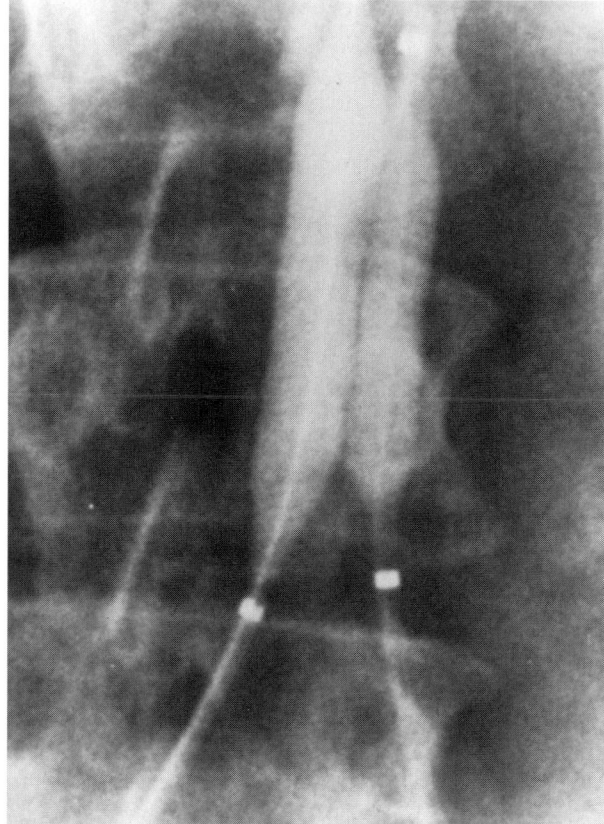

B

Figure 17-6. (A) An eccentric stenosis of the infrarenal abdominal aorta (*arrow*) was identified in this patient with symptoms of bilateral lower extremity claudication. (B) The "kissing balloon" technique was used to dilate the aorta to sufficient diameter. (C) After dilation, the transstenotic gradient resolved. An intimal cleft (*arrows*) is seen along the left lateral aspect of the dilation site.

occlusions have been successfully treated with this technique. The occluded segment is first traversed with a catheter and guidewire. This process has been greatly facilitated by the introduction of "steerable" guidewires with hydrophilic coatings. After successful negotiation of the occluded segment, an infusion system for thrombolysis is positioned in the occluded segment to bathe the segment during the infusion of a thrombolytic agent. Urokinase (UK; Abbott Laboratories) has become the most frequently used agent for catheter-directed thrombolysis because it has a high incidence of lysis with fewer complications than its predecessor, streptokinase (SK; Pharmicia Adria).[75] Another agent, recombinant tissue plasminogen activator (rtPA; Genetech) may be effective; however, there are inadequate data and a paucity of experience to recommend its routine use.

The choice of dose of UK is controversial and prob-

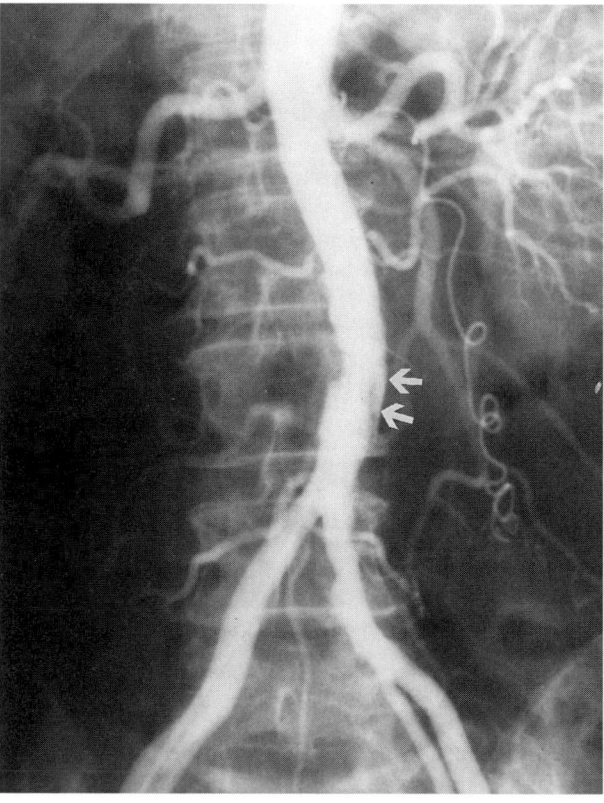

C

ably depends on the acuteness and severity of the ischemia. McNamara and his colleagues use an initial rate of 4000 IU per minute for the first 2 hours, followed as needed by a lower dose of 1000 to 2000 IU per minute until all thrombus has been cleared.[73,77] This may be particularly useful in the face of severe acute ischemia, where rapid restoration of flow is imperative. With chronic occlusions, however, many authors begin with the lower dose (60,000–120,000 IU/hr), which is continuously administered until the thrombus resolves.[70,72,75,81] Cragg et al., in a prospective randomized trial including native arteries and grafts, could demonstrate no significant difference between the two regimens.[108]

Also controversial is the use of concomitant anticoagulation in the form of heparin during the infusion. Although providing protection against pericatheter thrombus formation, the use of heparin does increase the incidence of bleeding complications. With catheter-directed thrombolysis, the systemic effects (and complications) seen with systemic therapy such as in the treatment of acute myocardial infarction can largely be avoided. After removal of the thrombus from an occluded vessel, the underlying offending atherosclerotic lesion can be evaluated and treated appropriately (Fig. 17-7). Occasionally, as with an embolus, no underlying lesion is identified and a widely patent vessel is restored.

Intravascular Stents

Balloon-expandable intravascular stents have greatly enhanced the arsenal of the interventionalist in aortoiliac disease.[82–96] The Palmaz stent (Johnson & Johnson) has been approved for use in the United States for treating lesions in the iliac arteries in which standard PTA techniques have resulted in a suboptimal outcome or in which there is a reasonable chance of failure of standard PTA techniques. In general, these lesions include eccentric calcified stenoses, stenoses in which there is significant elastic recoil, and intimal dissections in which there is obstruction to flow. The stent, which is mounted on a balloon angioplasty catheter, is positioned in the region of an offending lesion and deployed by balloon inflation (Fig. 17-8). The stent approved for use in the iliac arteries requires a larger entry sheath than is necessary for routine PTA (9–10 French), and its rigid nature generally requires a retrograde ipsilateral approach. Smaller Palmaz stents (at present approved only for use in the biliary system) have anecdotally been used successfully for the treatment of aortoiliac disease. Flexible, self-expanding stents (Wallstent, Schneider Inc.) have also been used in the treatment of aortoiliac disease. These

stents have the advantage of flexibility, which allows their deployment from a contralateral approach and in tortuous vessels (Fig. 17-9). In addition, they are available in various lengths that may be more suitable to longer lesions.

Intravascular stents have expanded the indications for percutaneous treatment of aortoiliac disease. Treatment of longer stenoses and occlusions is possible where PTA has a low likelihood of long-term success. Virtual reconstruction of occluded iliac systems has been accomplished with excellent results (Fig. 17-10).[90–92,109] The long-term success of these procedures is only now being evaluated. The role of stents in more advanced disease, although highly promising, remains as yet poorly undefined.

Atherectomy

Directional atherectomy, by removing the atheromatous material causing obstruction and eliminating the possibility of elastic recoil, in theory should produce a longer-lasting result than PTA (Fig. 17-11). Also, the smooth lumen produced by atherectomy might be less prone to thrombus formation, turbulence, and therefore restenosis. But although the use of directional atherectomy has been described in the iliac arteries, these theoretical advantages have not been proven in clinical applications.[30,110–112] Significant disadvantages of the currently approved Simpson Atherectomy Device (Mallinckrodt Medical) include size, rigidity, and relatively small working diameter. The largest available Simpson Atherocath device requires an 11 French introducer sheath yet affords a working diameter of less

Text continues on page 240

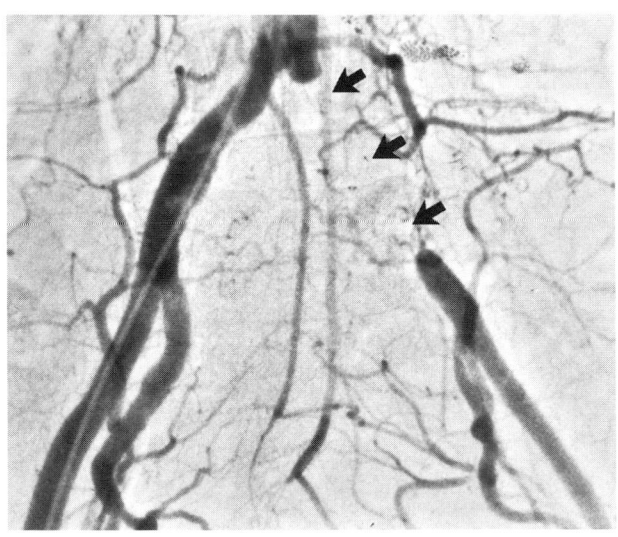

A

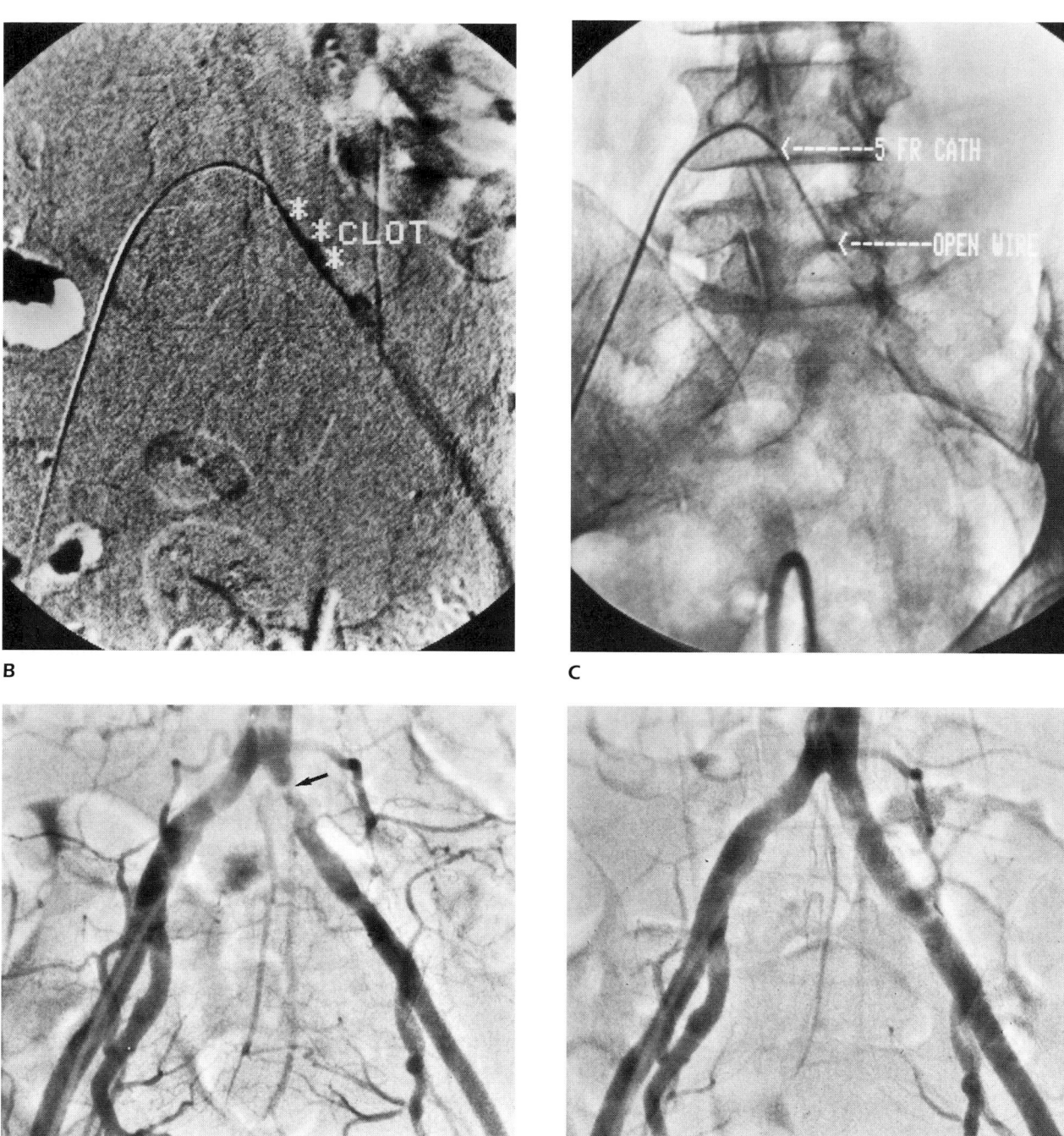

Figure 17-7. (A) A 6-cm occlusion of the left common iliac artery (*arrows*) was demonstrated in this patient with severe left thigh and calf claudication. (B) The occluded segment was traversed from a contralateral approach with a hydrophilic wire. Injection of the diagnostic catheter revealed thrombus within the occluded segment. (C) Thrombolytic infusion was performed through a coaxial catheter and infusion wire system at 100,000 units of urokinase per hour.

(D) After a 12-hour infusion, there was complete lysis of the thrombus, revealing an underlying focal concentric stenosis (*arrow*). (E) After PTA, a normal-caliber lumen was restored with no residual transstenotic gradient. (From Rholl, KS. Percutaneous intervention for aortoiliac disease. In: Strandness E, van Breda A, eds. Vascular diseases: surgical and interventional therapy. New York: Churchill-Livingstone, 1994. Used with permission.)

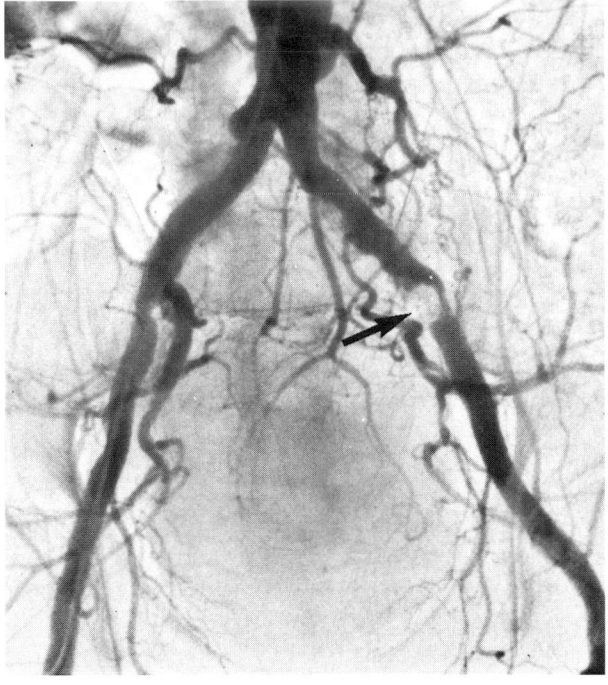

A

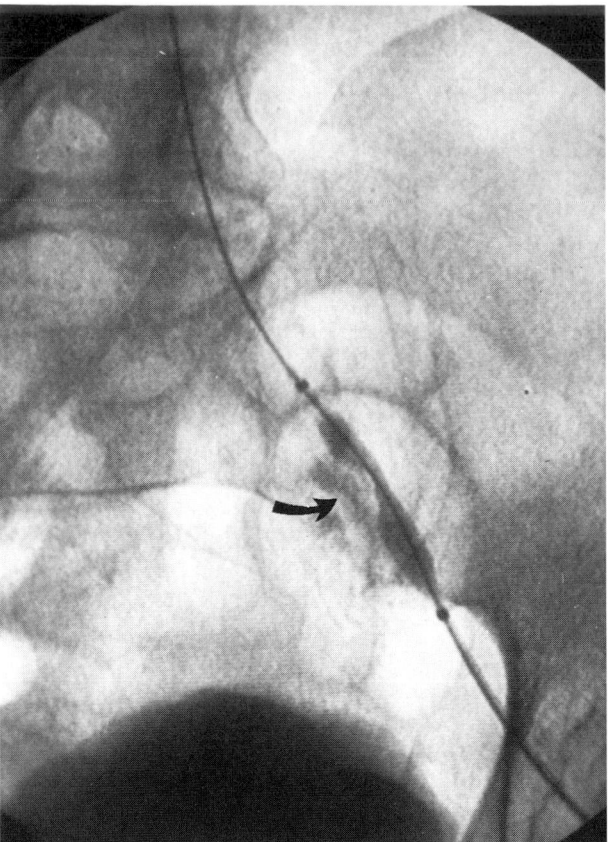

B

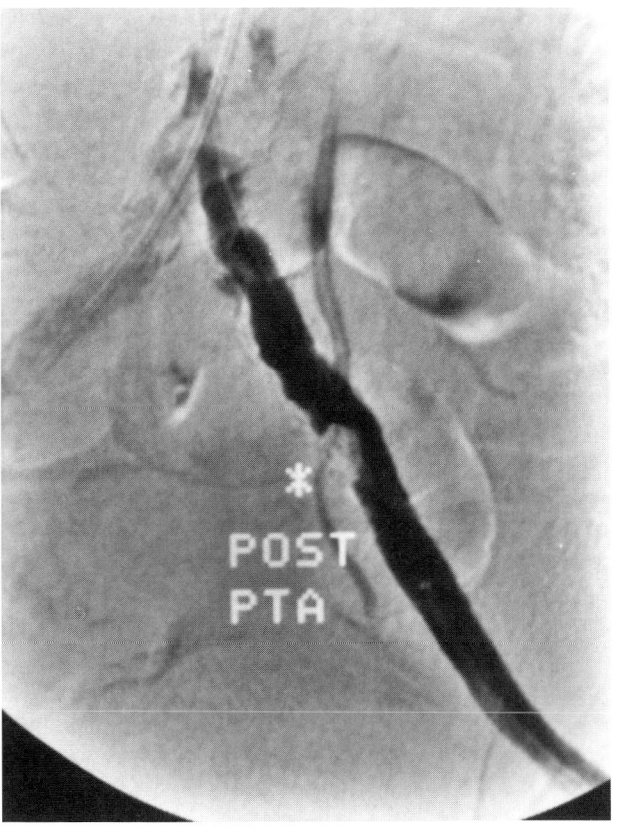

C

Figure 17-8. A 59-year-old man with one-block left calf claudication. (A) Diagnostic arteriography revealed an eccentric, densely calcified lesion (*arrow*) near the left common iliac bifurcation. The left hypogastric artery origin was occluded, filling from collateral pathways. (B) PTA was performed under fluoroscopy from a retrograde approach, possibly displacing the calcified lesion medially (*arrow*). However, with balloon deflation the calcified lesion returned to its initial position. (C) Although there was some improvement in the lesion after PTA, there was still significant elastic recoil and residual stenosis. (D) A Palmaz intravascular stent (*arrow*) was deployed to overcome lesion recoil. The calcified lesion is seen medial to the stent. (E) After stent deployment, there was no significant residual stenosis (*arrow*) or gradient. The patient remained asymptomatic for over 5 years. (From Rholl, KS. Percutaneous intervention for aortoiliac disease. In: Strandness E, van Breda A, eds. Vascular diseases: surgical and interventional therapy. New York: Churchill-Livingstone, 1994. Used with permission.)

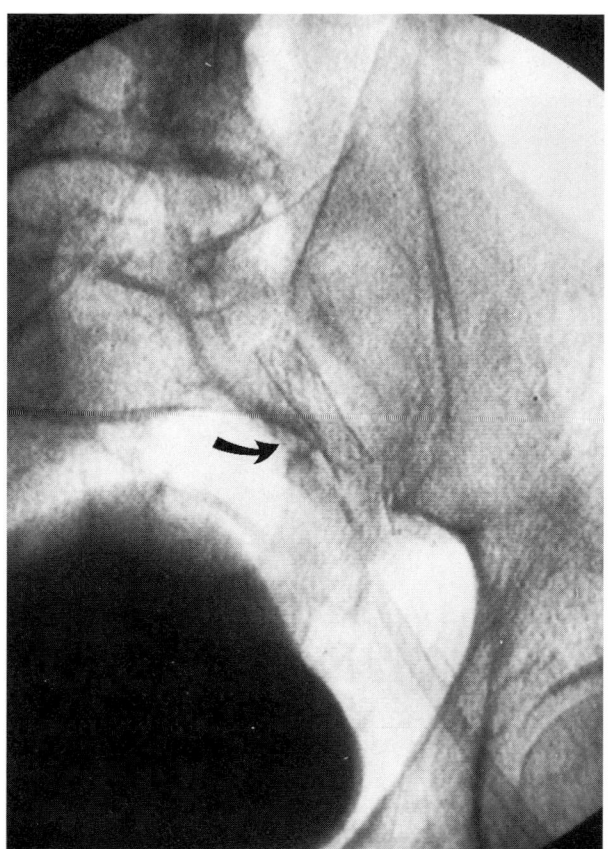

D

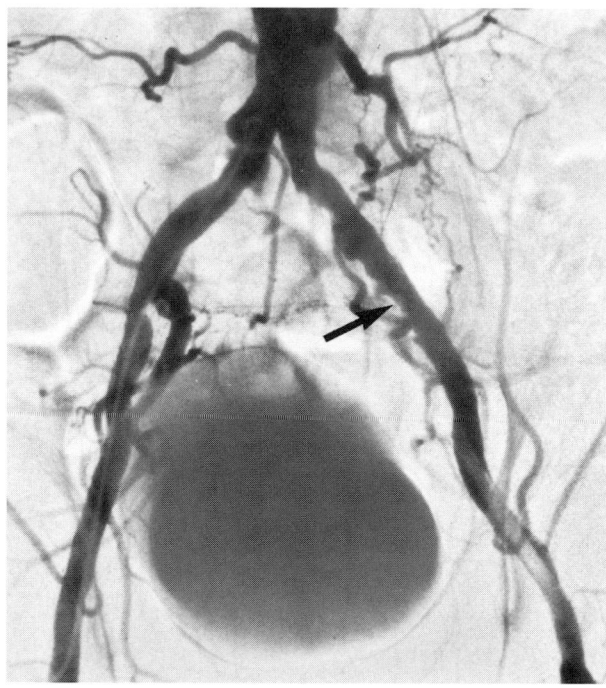

E

Figure 17-8 (continued).

Figure 17-9. (A) An extensive dissection of the external iliac artery was present after PTA in this patient who presented with nonhealing ulcers of several toes. A residual 40-mmHg gradient was measured across the dissected vessel. (B) A Wallstent was deployed from a contralateral approach. The flexibility of the Wallstent allowed deployment through a very tortuous vessel, completely eliminating the residual gradient.

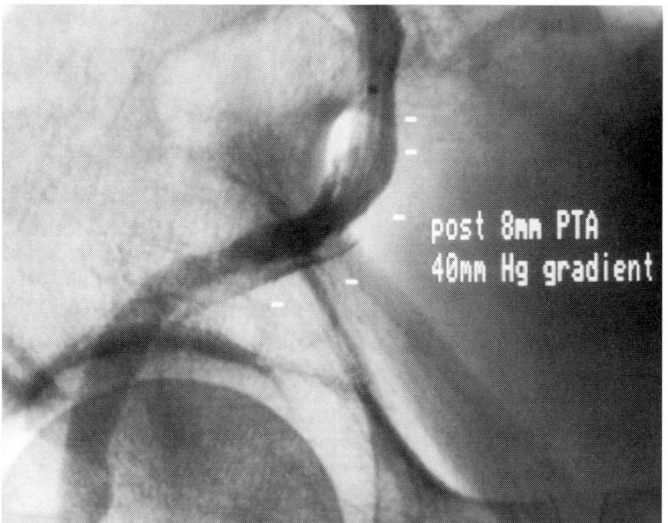

A

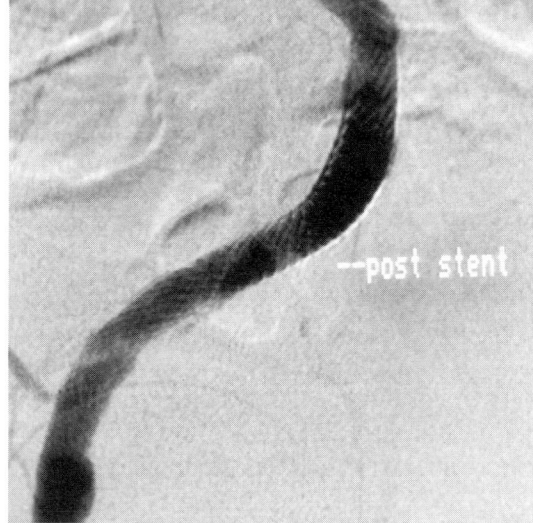

B

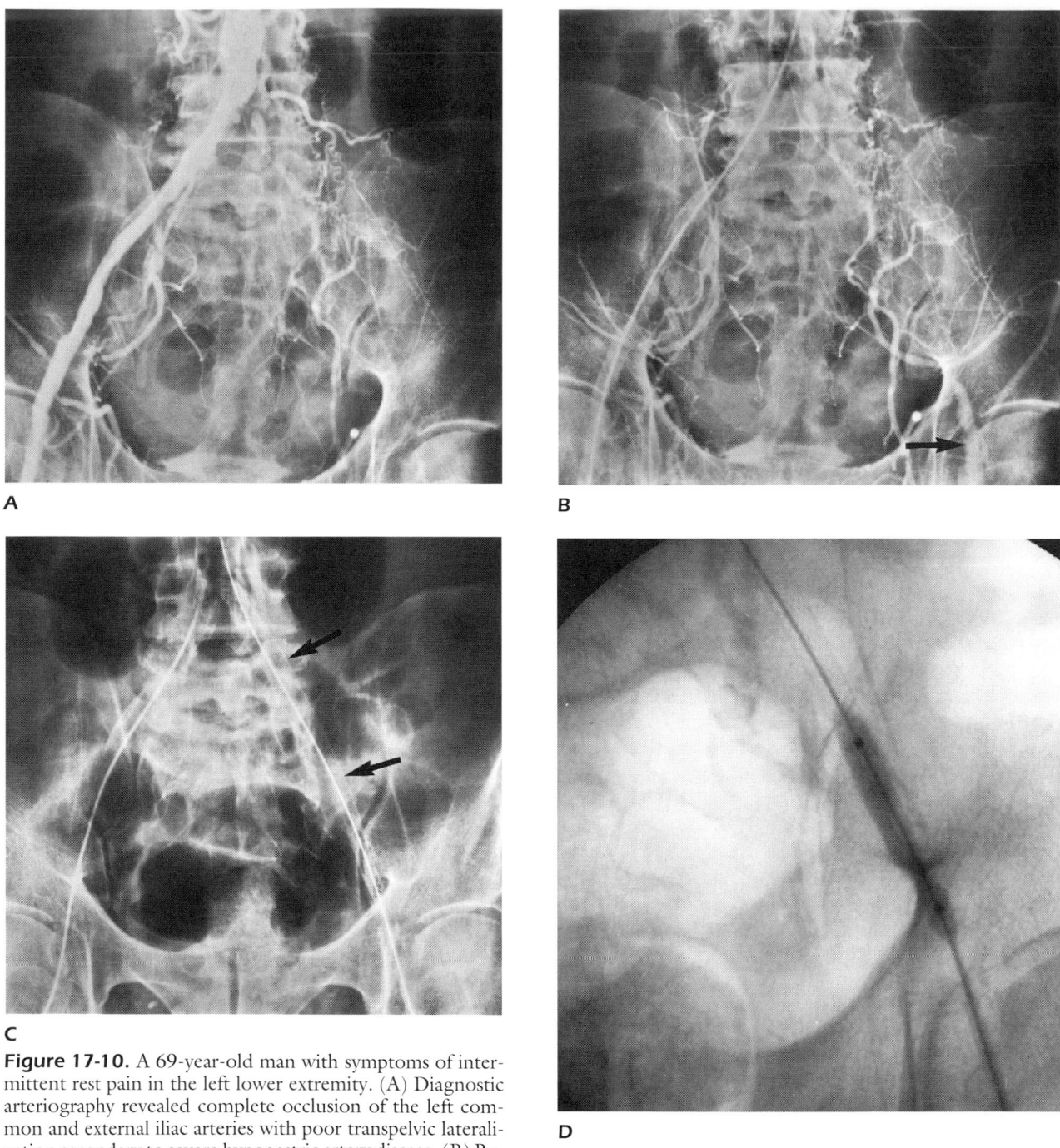

A

B

C

D

Figure 17-10. A 69-year-old man with symptoms of intermittent rest pain in the left lower extremity. (A) Diagnostic arteriography revealed complete occlusion of the left common and external iliac arteries with poor transpelvic lateralization secondary to severe hypogastric artery disease. (B) Reconstitution of the left common femoral artery (*arrow*) is seen on a delayed image. (C and D) After recanalization of the left iliac artery, two overlapping Wallstents (*arrows,*

C) were deployed and dilated to 8 mm with a PTA balloon. (E) Final completion arteriography revealed restoration of a widely patent left iliac system.

Figure 17-11. A 41-year-old woman with severe right lower extremity claudication. (A) Diagnostic arteriography revealed a long fusiform stenosis of the right external iliac artery (*arrows*). A moderate right common iliac artery stenosis (*curved arrow*) was also identified. (B) Since the external iliac artery lesion was suboptimal for PTA, atherectomy was performed with the Simpson atherectomy device. (C) After atherectomy, there was marked improvement in the lumen caliber. A nonobstructing intimal crack dissection (*arrows*) ▶ was noted. Although the patient initially did well, the lesion eventually recurred and the patient underwent subsequent bypass procedure. (From Rholl, KS. Percutaneous intervention for aortoiliac disease. In: Strandness E, van Breda A, eds. Vascular diseases: surgical and interventional therapy. New York: Churchill-Livingstone, 1994. Used with permission.)

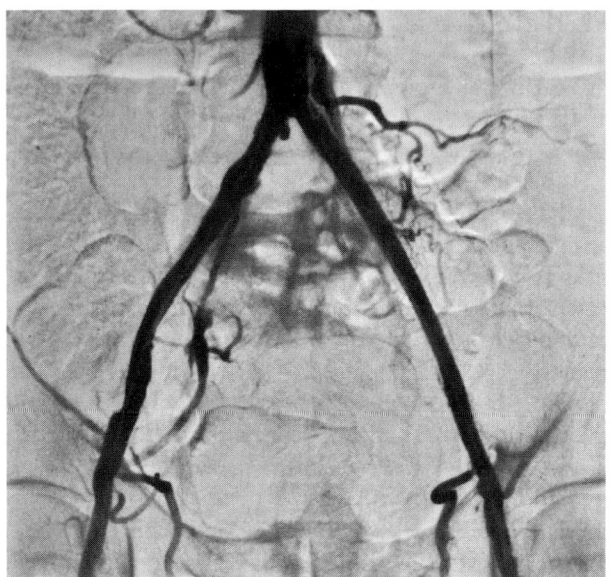

E

Figure 17-10 (continued).

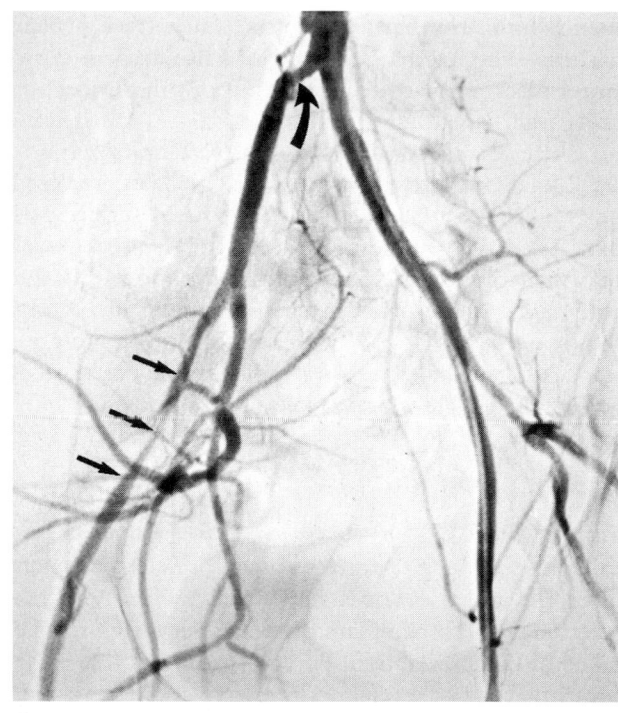

A

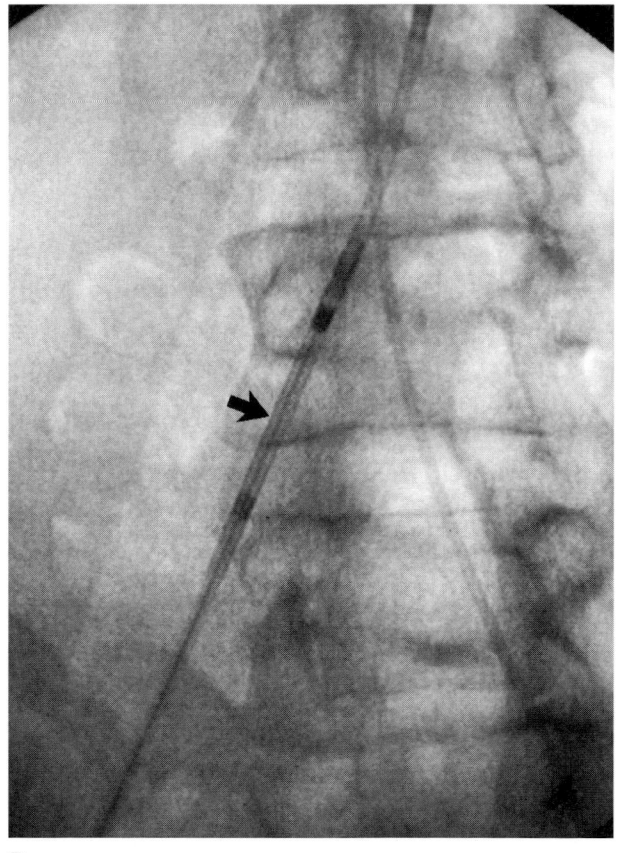

B

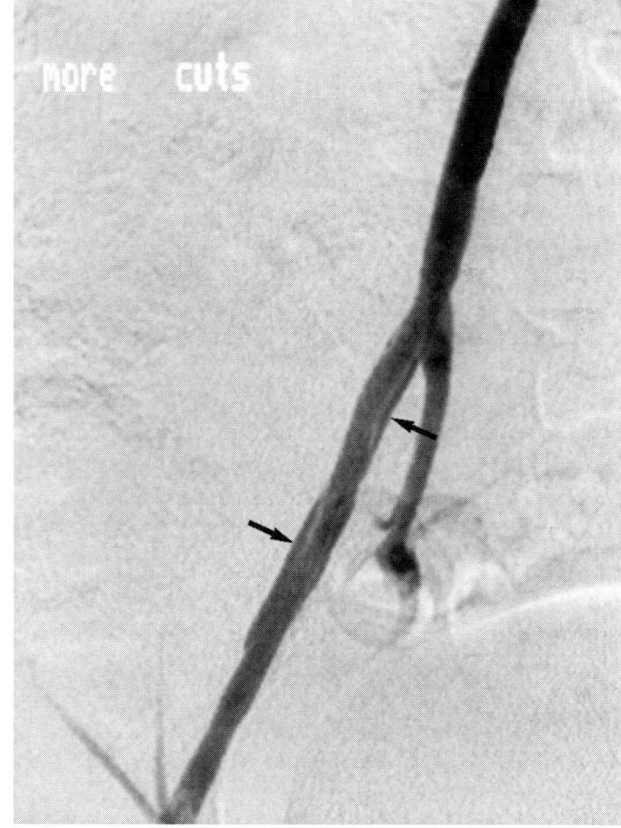

C

than 8 mm. The newer Simpson Atherotrack, which has the ability to track over a guidewire, has a slightly larger working diameter of 9.7 mm. Both devices are quite rigid, creating difficulty in tortuous, atherosclerotic arteries and making a contralateral approach unfeasible. Furthermore, densely calcified atheroma is not well removed by these devices. One described potential use of atherectomy devices involves the removal of obstructing intimal flaps after intervention.[113] In the aortoiliac system, however, the use of stents in treating these dissections has obviated atherectomy in most instances.[87] Thus there appears to be little role for atherectomy in iliac revascularization procedures.

Indications and Patient Selection

Options available for the treatment of aortoiliac disease include surgical revascularization, percutaneous intervention, and conservative management. When treatment is contemplated, several factors must be taken into consideration. Foremost among these is the severity of the ischemia and its effect upon the patient. Mild symptoms of claudication that do not limit the patient's lifestyle do not require aggressive intervention, but rather should be conservatively managed with appropriate follow-up.[114,115] All too often, the last option is forgotten even though most patients will improve with a graded exercise program and abstinence from tobacco use. Accordingly, every patient presenting with intermittent claudication deserves a trial of "conservative management" before consideration of more invasive therapies. This must be an appropriately monitored and reviewed trial of no less than 3 months. For more severe ischemic presentations such as rest pain or tissue breakdown, or in patients with rapidly progressive symptoms, this may not be an option. Those patients who are limited in their lifestyle and have failed an adequate trial of conservative management may be candidates for percutaneous intervention. Traditionally, these patients have not been candidates for surgical intervention until the limitation has become severe (lifestyle-limiting) or there is threatened limb loss. In conjunction with the severity of ischemia, the overall health of the patient should be assessed. The risks of any intervention must be weighed against possible benefits to be gained from the procedure. Percutaneous procedures, in general, have a lower rate of morbidity and mortality than do the corresponding surgical interventions. As the morbidity and mortality of procedures increases, so should the severity of the disease that would justify treatment. Therefore it may be appropriate to perform an iliac PTA on a patient who may not be a candidate for a surgical bypass. However, it should be kept in mind

that the rare complication of a percutaneous procedure may necessitate surgical intervention and thus place the patient at increased risk.[15,67,103] No procedure, no matter how "routine," should be taken lightly with respect to its possible consequences.

When one is considering percutaneous intervention, the anticipated immediate technical and long-term clinical success should be weighed against the risks as well as the anticipated results with surgical revascularization. The morphology of the patient's disease plays a major role in determining these outcomes.[11,15,29,34–36,39,67] A list of factors influencing the outcome of PTA is given in Table 17-2. Two common themes should be noted from this list. Those with more extensive disease, involving either the vessel treated or the runoff vessels, do worse than those with focal, less severe disease. Second, larger vessels do better than smaller vessels. Many additional factors have been studied, but most are interrelated with the two above. Patients referred for limb salvage generally have more diffuse disease than those with intermittent claudication. Although patients with diabetes as a group did worse than those without diabetes, Spence et al.[11] and Stokes et al.[35] did not find a significant difference when the pattern of disease was accounted for and only iliac lesions were studied. Despite this, information regarding the diabetic population as a whole can help predict outcomes prior to evaluation and treatment, and is therefore useful in the decision-making process. It is of great interest that, despite the widely held belief that patients who continue to smoke have a poorer long-term patency as a group than those who abstain from tobacco use, there is little supporting evidence for this in the literature.

Using the available data in the literature, the Society of Cardiovascular and Interventional Radiology (SCVIR) has published criteria for the performance of arterial PTA based on morphologic characteristics, including the length, severity, and the presence of calcified atheroma, as well as on coexisting disease such

Table 17-2. Factors Influencing the Outcome of Aortoiliac Angioplasty

Predictive Factor	Worse Outcome	Improved Outcome
Indication	Limb salvage	Claudication
Site	Distal (external iliac artery)	Proximal (common iliac artery)
No. of lesions	Multiple	Single
Runoff	Diseased	Intact
Severity of disease	Long occlusion, eccentric, calcified	Short stenosis, concentric, non-calcified
Diabetes	Present	Absent

Data from references 11, 15, 29, 34–36, and 39.

Table 17-3. SCVIR Guidelines for Iliac Angioplasty

Category	Description	Guidelines
1	Stenoses less than 3 cm, concentric, non-calcified.	PTA is treatment of choice.
2	Stenoses 3–5 cm, concentric, noncalcified. Stenoses less than 3 cm, eccentric, calcified.	Well suited for PTA. Includes lesions followed by distal bypass.
3	Stenoses 5–10 cm. Chronic occlusions less than 5 cm.	Amenable to PTA. Moderate chance of success vs. surgery. PTA may be performed in patients with high surgical risk or lack of surgical material.
4	Stenoses greater than 10 cm. Chronic occlusions greater than 5 cm, after thrombolysis. Extensive bilateral disease. Stenoses associated with aneurysms or other lesions requiring surgery.	PTA has a limited role. Low technical success. Poor long-term benefit. PTA only when no surgical options or in very-high-risk patients.

Adapted from Guidelines for percutaneous transluminal angioplasty: standards of Practice Committee of the Society of Cardiovascular and Interventional Radiology. Radiology 1990;177:619–626. Used with permission.

as aneurysm formation and concurrent emboli (Table 17-3).[116] Guidelines for treatment are then proposed for each category based on the clinical situation and expected results. PTA is the treatment of choice for short focal stenoses (Fig. 17-12). Conversely, in patients with diffuse disease including long chronic occlusions, PTA has a very limited role with a low likelihood of long-term patency (Fig. 17-13). However, the recommendations for each category are meant to serve only as guidelines when intervention is considered. In each case the entire clinical picture must be assessed by weighing the risks and expected benefits of the alternatives. Although the treating vascular specialist, interventionalist, or surgeon should be able to present these options to the patient, at times a multispecialty approach to complex cases with early involvement of the patient and family in the decision-making process is desirable to allow full consideration of all options and to ensure truly informed consent.

Lifestyle-limiting claudication is the most common clinical indication for aortoiliac PTA, including grade I, categories 1 to 3 of chronic limb ischemia (see Table 17-1). These categories include patients in whom there is no immediate threat to the affected limb but symptoms are severe enough to preclude them from their desired daily activities. Clearly this is an individual assessment. A very active person wishing to play tennis or golf will be limited with much milder disease than will a sedentary person needing to ambulate only one to two blocks to accomplish his or her routine. If after a trial of conservative management including regular exercise and reduction of risk factors there is significant limitation, either patient may be a candidate for percutaneous revascularization.

Grades II and III of chronic limb ischemia (categories 4–6) indicate severe ischemia with resting symptoms and tissue loss, and there is generally little place for a prolonged trial of conservative management if a suitable alternative intervention exists. These patients often have more extensive disease and thus are less than optimal candidates for PTA. Unfortunately, anatomy and coexisting risk factors frequently make them poor candidates for surgical revascularization as well. The lower morbidity and mortality of percutaneous revascularization may then warrant an attempt, especially since a failed percutaneous procedure generally does not preclude the surgical alternative, whereas a failed surgical procedure generally makes any further intervention extremely difficult.

These patients often have multilevel disease with both inflow and outflow obstruction. Depending on the anatomy, a combined surgical and percutaneous approach may be beneficial, such as PTA of an iliac stenosis prior to a femoropopliteal bypass.[117–131] PTA of an iliac stenosis in a patient with a contralateral iliac occlusion may also be used in conjunction with a femorofemoral bypass in patients who are not candidates for aortobifemoral or aortoiliac bypass (Fig. 17-14). Distal (femoropopliteal) PTA may be used to improve outflow from a proximal bypass graft.

Initial experience with PTA was limited to stenotic disease with occlusions deemed appropriate for surgical intervention.[132–136] Early trials of PTA of an occluded iliac artery noted both a higher failure rate and a higher incidence of complications.[62–64] However, more recent approaches have shown PTA to be effective in treating longer, chronic iliac occlusions.[65,66,68,70–72,75,76,80,81,88,90–92,109,121,137,138] Since most occluded arterial segments have consisted of a thrombosed vessel with a more focal occluding atheroma, thrombolysis has been used to convert these occluded segments into shorter regions of stenosis. At least in theory, these shorter-segment stenoses may convey the advantages of stenotic disease in terms of long-term efficacy and may therefore be good candidates for PTA after lysis (see Fig. 17-7). More recently there has been a movement toward direct recanalization and stenting of these chronically occluded segments (see Fig. 17-10). This has the advantage of decreasing procedural time and eliminating the possible bleeding complications associated with thrombolysis. Several studies have demonstrated a high initial success rate

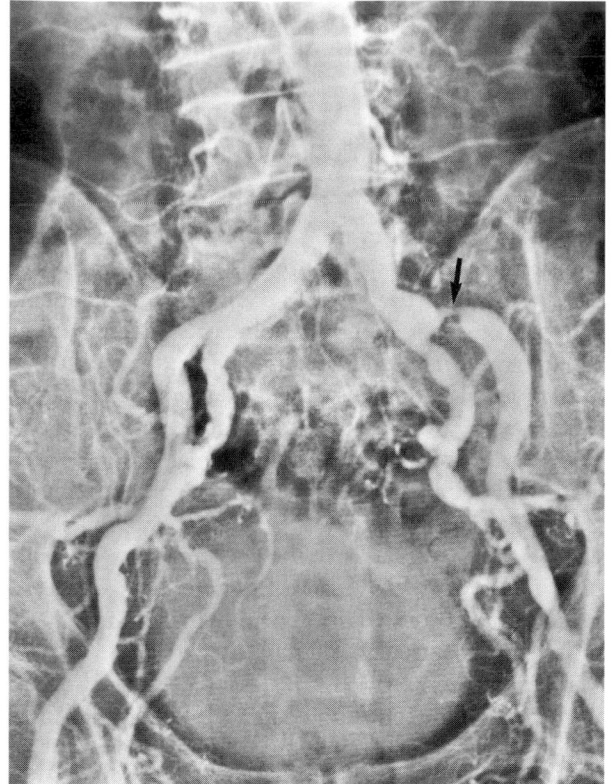

A

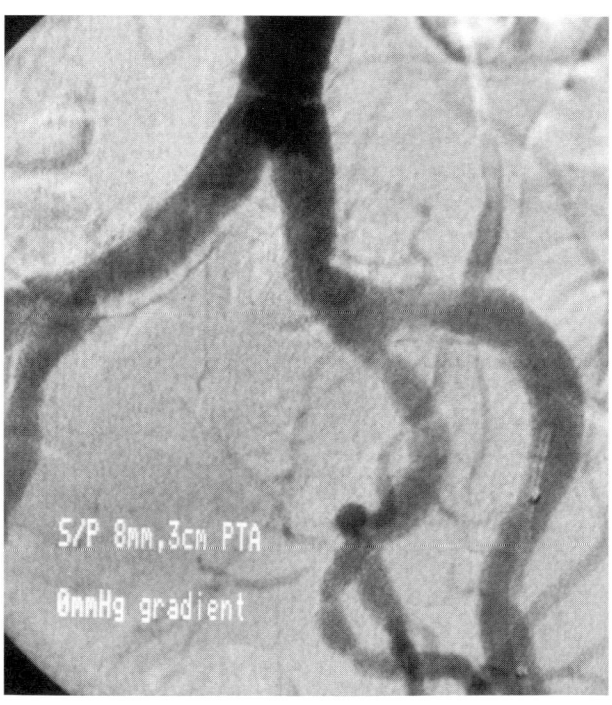

C

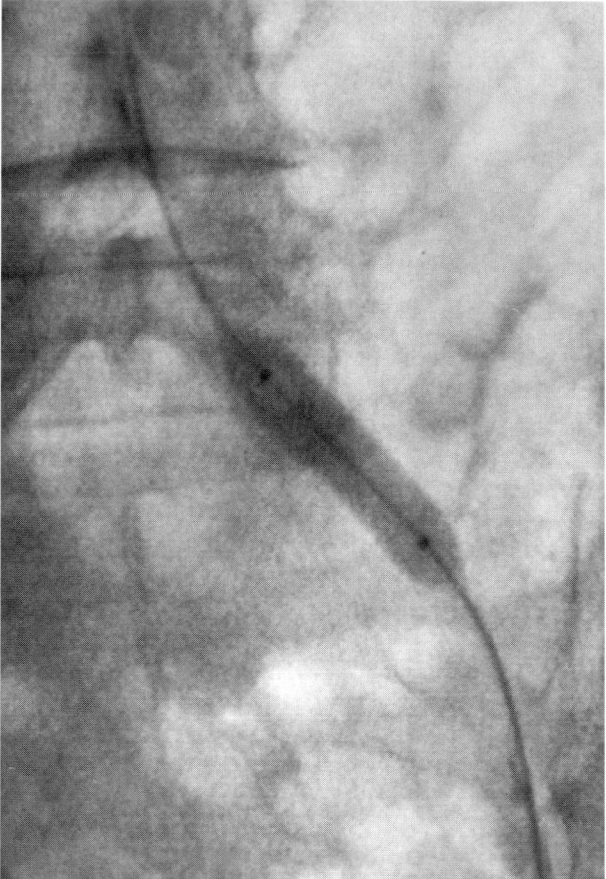

B

Figure 17-12. An 82-year-old man with ischemic ulcerations involving the left foot. (A) A focal concentric left external iliac artery (*arrow*) demonstrated by arteriography was ideally suited to PTA (SCVIR category 1). (B and C) PTA of the lesion was performed with good result, allowing healing of the left foot.

with this technique. Long-term follow-up is just now becoming available but looks quite promising. Thus the respective roles of thrombolysis and primary stenting, and the corresponding surgical alternatives, are continually evolving.

Aortoiliac lesions presenting with distal emboli such as those seen in "blue toe syndrome" were initially thought to represent relative contraindications to peripheral intervention such as angioplasty.[98] However, these lesions have been successfully treated with PTA and other percutaneous interventional techniques without a significant incidence of intraprocedural embolization.[139–141] Lesions resulting in distal embolization in general are either ulcerated or severely stenotic with thrombi forming in or below the stenosis (see Fig. 17-2). Angioplasty generally results in cessation of embolic events from the lesion, presumably secondary to some remodeling of the ulcerated lesion and/or

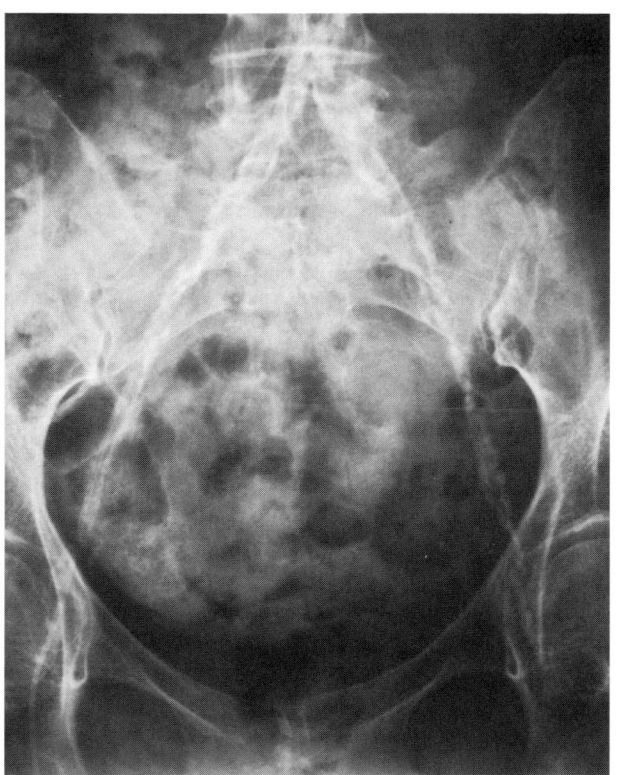

A

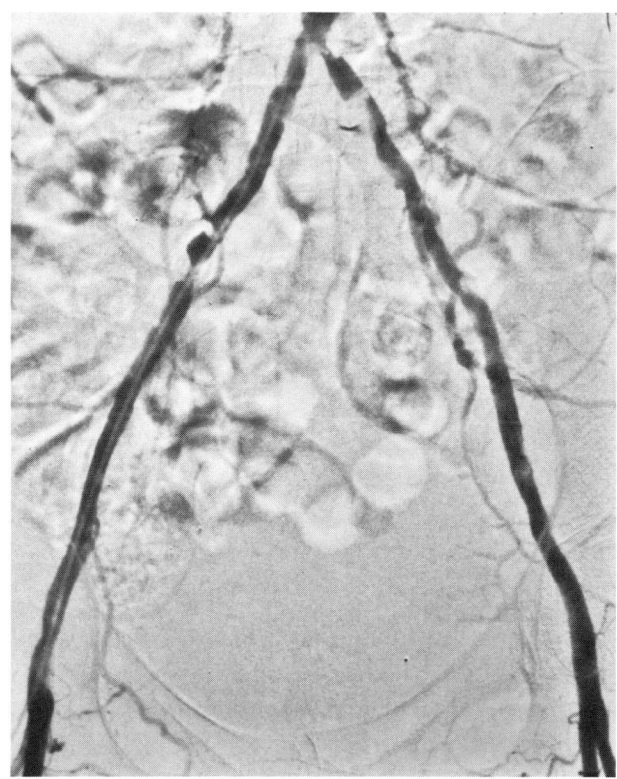

B

Figure 17-13. (A) A scout radiograph of the pelvis demonstrates diffuse calcific disease of the aorta and iliac arteries. (B) Angiography confirmed diffuse disease with multiple stenoses, SCVIR lesion category 4. (C) Category 4 disease is also demonstrated in this patient with iliac artery stenoses that are associated with ulcerated aneurysmal disease of the aorta and common iliac arteries.

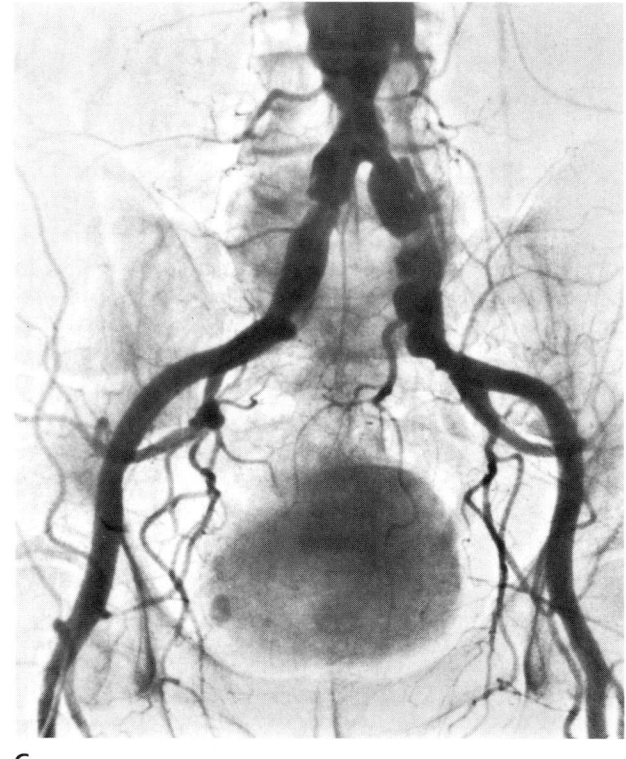

C

a change in hemodynamic patterns within the stenosis. Occasionally, high-grade stenoses may be associated with thrombus below the stenosis. If this is suspected during angiographic evaluation, a trial of thrombolysis may be warranted before dilation to avoid possible intraprocedural embolization.

Impotence may be an indication for aortoiliac intervention.[45,58,142-144] However, there are many causes of impotence, including arterial insufficiency, venous incompetence, and neurogenic etiologies, and a noninvasive vascular study of penile blood flow is useful before an angiographic study is considered. Since supply to the cavernosal arteries is bilateral, either aortic or bilateral iliac disease must be present to produce impotence. A concurrent history of bilateral claudication, particularly if it involves the thighs and/or buttocks, is a strong indicator of this proximal disease. Disease involving the aorta, the common iliac arteries, and/ or the proximal segments of the hypogastric arteries may be amenable to the percutaneous techniques that give the good long-term patency rates associated with

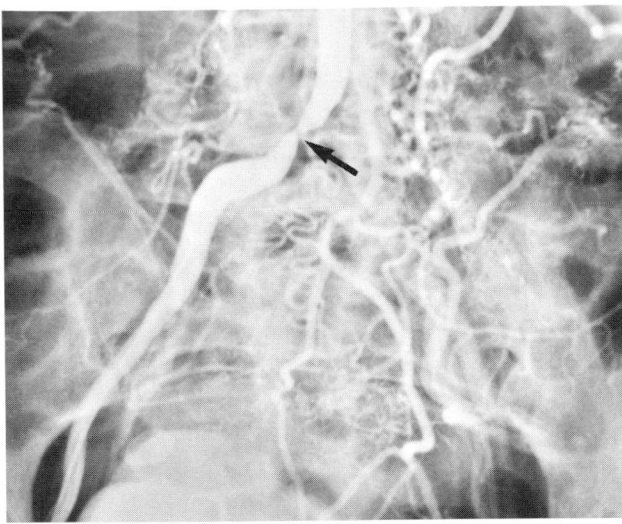

A

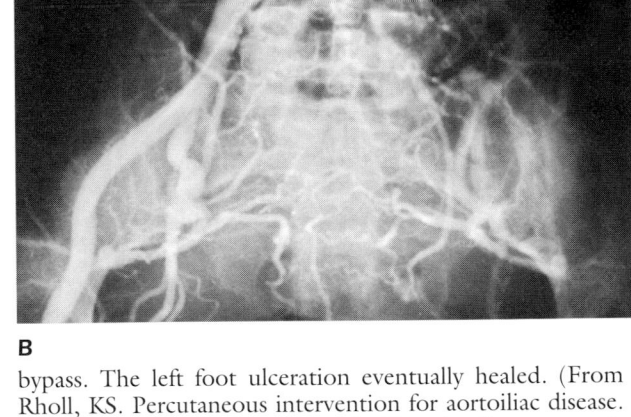

B

Figure 17-14. A 61-year-old man with extensive coronary artery disease and a nonhealing ulcer of the left foot. (A) Diagnostic arteriography revealed left common iliac artery occlusion and a focal severe stenosis of the right common iliac artery (*arrow*). (B) PTA of the right iliac lesion (*arrow*) was successfully performed prior to femorofemoral bypass. The left foot ulceration eventually healed. (From Rholl, KS. Percutaneous intervention for aortoiliac disease. In: Strandness E, van Breda A, eds. Vascular diseases: surgical and interventional therapy. New York: Churchill-Livingstone, 1994. Used with permission.)

larger vessels. Most often, in elderly patients with arteriosclerotic disease, particularly with concurrent diabetes, the disease is located in the smaller distal hypogastric branches, and little benefit is to be offered from either percutaneous or surgical revascularization. A steal phenomenon secondary to an external iliac artery lesion has been reported as a rare cause of arterial impotence; in this instance a history of activity-related impotence was an indicator of the phenomenon.

Finally, hypertension has been reported as a rare indication for aortoiliac intervention.[145] This occurred when an iliac stenosis was proximal to a renal transplant arterial anastomosis, resulting in renal ischemia. Accessory renal arteries may also have their origins from the iliac arteries.

Contraindications to aortoiliac intervention are relative to the clinical situation at hand; there are no absolute contraindications for most of these procedures. The safety of the patient must be considered first and balanced against the possible benefits of the procedure. Although these procedures are generally well tolerated, the extremely debilitated patient may not withstand the strain of even the most benign of procedures. Relative contraindications include severe medical debilitation (such as acute pulmonary edema), irreversible (or untreated) coagulopathy, lack of safe percutaneous access such as with an infected groin, and an uncooperative patient. Severe, limb-threatening ischemia better suited for surgical intervention has histori-

cally been a contraindication, although with advances in percutaneous techniques this situation is becoming less common. Lesion morphology itself can be a relative contraindication to percutaneous intervention. Lesions with extensive exophytic plaque that is likely to result in embolization and involvement of the offending lesion by aneurysmal disease may be better treated by surgical therapy (see Fig. 17-13C). Lesions with a low likelihood of immediate and/or long-term success, such as long-segment occlusive disease or diffuse severe stenotic disease, and for which there is a reasonable surgical alternative may be included in this category. Many occlusions once thought to be the surgical domain are now readily treated by percutaneous alternatives such as thrombolysis and stent placement.

Results

A thorough discussion of the results of a procedure must include not only immediate technical success but also long-term success and clinical implications, complications, and cost-effectiveness. Immediate technical success is easily quantified and has been well documented for most procedures. The long-term success of a procedure, however, is more difficult to quantify. Finally, the direct and indirect costs of a procedure are perhaps the most difficult to quantify but play an important part in the equation of cost-effectiveness of any procedure. Significant cost advantages of PTA over surgical revascularization have been demonstrated in selected groups of patients. These advantages have resulted not only from decreased procedural costs and fees but also from shorter hospitalization and recovery times and avoidance of the costs of general anesthesia.[59,60] Although the cost benefits of other percutaneous procedures are less well documented, it is likely that, used judiciously, procedures such as thrombolysis and intravascular stents may also prove to be cost-effective.

Angioplasty of the Iliac Arteries

Although initial reports suggested that the long-term patency rates for iliac artery angioplasty were in the range of 90 percent at 5 years, subsequent reports have suggested a wide range of "patency" rates: anywhere from 32 to 92 percent at 5 years.[5–42,67,68,117–122,124–127,130–133,146–150] Johnston, in a more recent, rigorous analysis, found the overall 5-year patency rate for PTA of iliac artery stenoses to be 54 percent.[67]

The wide variation in reported results is probably multifactorial, involving differences in patient populations, patient selection, techniques, and, unfortunately, reporting standards. Evolution and improvements in techniques and equipment have contributed to an improved technical success rate. However, the absence of uniform reporting standards has been the greatest limitation to a true assessment of efficacy. Patency rates have generally been expressed as a percentage of technically successful procedures rather than of all PTAs attempted. Authors have justified doing this by arguing that a "failed" PTA rarely results in a worsening of the patient's clinical status, nor does it alter the patient's candidacy for an alternative surgical procedure.[133,151] Undeniably, a failed PTA does not carry the same consequences or implications as a failed surgical procedure. Moreover, it can be difficult to precisely define "failed" PTA as it is frequently performed in concert with an angiographic procedure. In addition, patency rates may be expressed as primary (those remaining patent without further intervention), primary-assisted (those patent although additional intervention was performed to maintain patency), or secondary (those in whom patency needed to be reestablished by a second intervention). Patency rates that are quoted in the literature do not always clearly indicate which of these rates are being used. Finally, the definition of the term *patency* itself can be elusive.

Another problem is that few studies have required rigorous follow-up. Noninvasive testing, most commonly an ankle-brachial index, does not yield information specific to the PTA site. Segmental information from more thorough noninvasive testing still does not specify progression in an adjacent segment from recurrence at the PTA site. Use of the clinical result as an end point, although important to the well-being of the patient, does not give any information specific to the PTA site itself. Recurrence of symptoms does not equate with recurrence of disease at the PTA site. Thorvinger, reporting on the difference between angiographic patency and clinical course, noted that 86 percent of iliac artery PTA sites were angiographically patent in those patients in whom the clinical course had suggested recurrence (Fig. 17-15).[27] Conversely, continued clinical improvement is not always evidence that the PTA site is free of recurrent disease, because there is symptomatic improvement secondary to collateral development.

Given these significant limitations in interpreting the results or outcomes of PTA, a critical review of the literature from 1964 to 1994 reveals an excellent primary success rate averaging 91.9 percent. When data from multiple series are combined, 1-, 3-, and 5-year patency rates have averaged 90.3, 79.8, and 68.7 percent, respectively (Table 17-4). Moreover, the immediate and long-term success rates for iliac PTA (Table 17-4) compare quite favorably with those for surgical aortoiliac reconstruction listed in Table 17-5. The 5- and 10-year patency rates of 80 to 90 percent and 70 to 75 percent were obtained from aggregated reports of surgical series.[130,135,152] When the initial failure rate of PTA was excluded, Wilson et al. found no significant difference in patency rates in a prospective, randomized trial comparing PTA with surgical revascularization.[132] In addition, those patients who failed PTA went on to surgical revascularization without increased morbidity and mortality, in contrast to the group that had initial surgical reconstruction.[132,133,146,151] Johnston et al. reported that only 3.8 percent of patients with a failed iliac PTA had significant worsening of their clinical grade of ischemia,[133] and patients with delayed failure of iliac PTA generally converted back to their initial clinical grade. This characteristic is unique and bears comparison to the corresponding surgical procedures. Although the initial and long-term patency rates are somewhat higher for surgical reconstruction when compared to PTA, the increased morbidity and mortality associated with these surgical procedures are not insignificant.[61,103,132,153,154] Perioperative mortality rates for aortoiliac reconstruction are in the range of 2 to 5 percent.[130,152] Failure of aortoiliac reconstructive surgery can be devastating, as noted by Crawford et al., who reported a 12 percent mortality rate for patients undergoing redo surgery for failed aortoiliac reconstructions.[155] Repeat aortoiliac PTA, however, can be performed with no greater

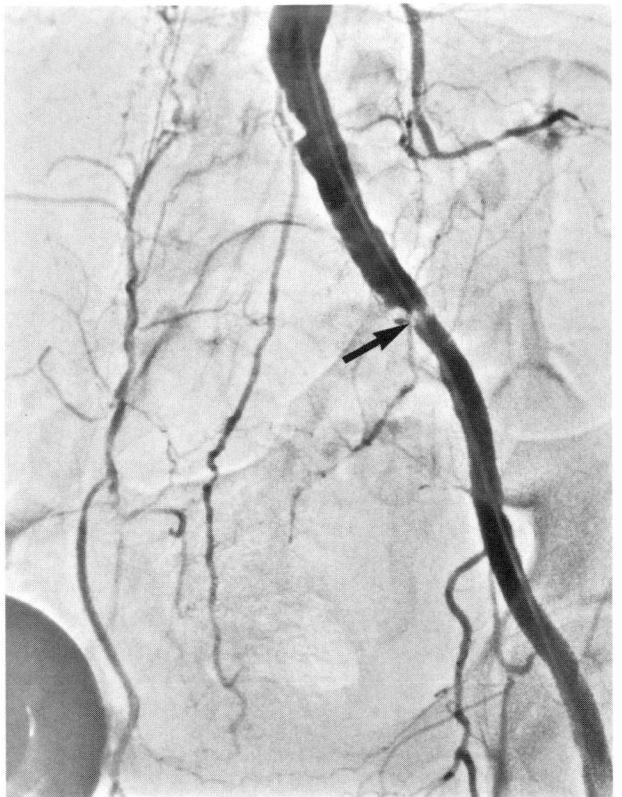

A

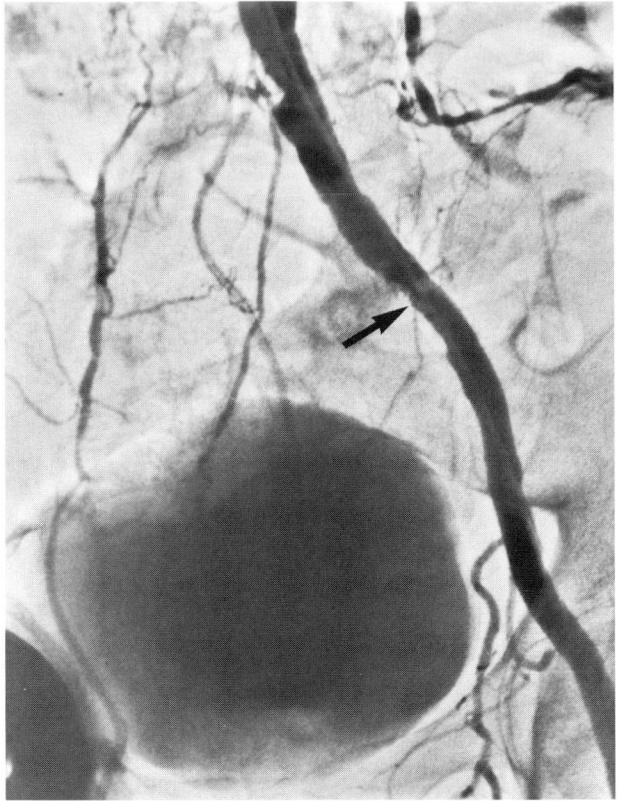

B

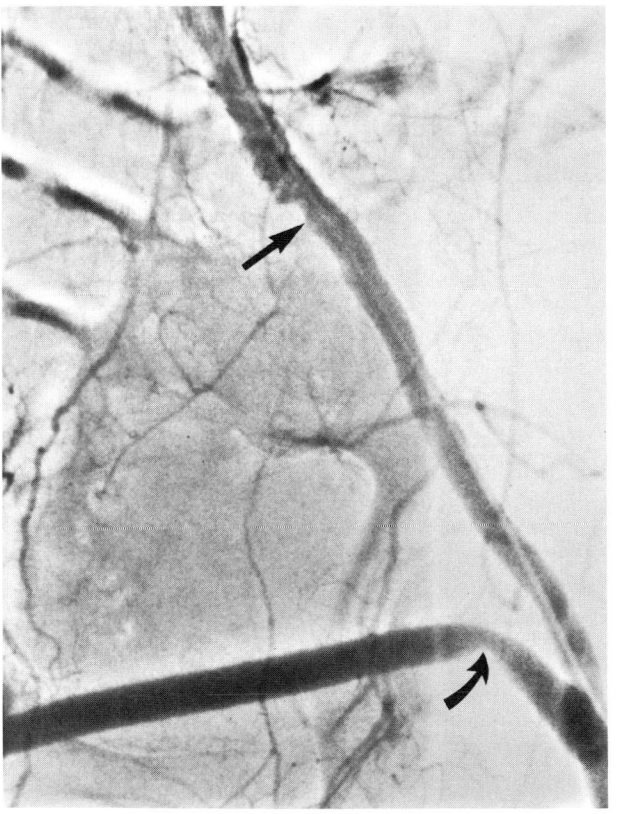

C

Figure 17-15. A 73-year-old man with nonhealing ulceration of the right heel. (A) Diagnostic arteriography revealed a right iliac artery occlusion with focal severe concentric stenosis at the origin of the left external iliac artery (*arrow*). (B) Since aortobifemoral bypass was precluded by severe coronary disease, PTA of the left iliac lesion (*arrow*) was performed prior to a femorofemoral crossover graft. (C) When right lower extremity symptoms recurred despite a clinically patent graft, recurrent stenosis of the left iliac artery PTA site was suspected. Arteriography with intraarterial assessment, however, demonstrated the angioplasty site to be widely patent (*arrow*) with no gradient across the region. A stenosis secondary to kinking of the graft was demonstrated (*curved arrow*) with a significant gradient across this lesion. Revision of the graft was eventually necessary, after which the patient did well.

Table 17-4. Cumulative Iliac PTA Patency Data*

Time	Mean (%)	Range (%)
Primary success	91.9	72–100
1 year	90.3	63–100
3 years	79.8	58–95
5 years	68.7	32–92

* $N = 6610$.
Pooled data from references 5–42, 67, 68, 117–122, 124–127, 130–133, and 146–150. The follow-up period for each of the series was variable; not all series had follow-up data to 5 years.

Table 17-5. Cumulative Aortoiliac Surgical Reconstruction Patency Data

Time	Mean (%)	Range (%)
Primary success	95	80–100
5 years	80–90	68–96
10 years	70–75	62–86

Pooled data from references 130, 135, and 152. The follow-up period for each of the series was variable.

morbidity and mortality than the original procedure (Fig. 17-16).[151]

When considering the success rates of each modality and making appropriate therapeutic decisions, one must keep in mind the life expectancy of this group of patients. The mortality of patients presenting with peripheral vascular disease is 20 to 30 percent at 5 years, and the 10-year mortality approaches 50 to 60 percent, primarily because of coexisting coronary and cerebrovascular disease.[135,152]

Infrarenal Aortic PTA

Since aortic occlusive disease causing lower extremity ischemia is much less common than disease in the iliac arteries, much less information is available in the literature (Fig. 17-17). Nonetheless, as might be expected with large-vessel PTA, the reported results from multiple available series are excellent.[43–58,156–160] The primary technical success rate has averaged 95 percent, and 1-, 3-, and 5-year patency rates have averaged 98, 87, and 80 percent, respectively. These results are closely paralleled by the author's own experience with 12 patients who underwent infrarenal aortic PTA, including PTA for lesions of the aortic bifurcation. On follow-up, a patency rate of 92 percent was demonstrated with an average follow-up of 5.2 years (range, 0.6–9.8 years), indicating the excellent durability of the procedure.[156] Aortic bifurcation lesions frequently extend into the common iliac arteries, necessitating a kissing balloon technique to allow dilation of both iliac arteries and aorta to an appropriate size.[43,45,46,48–50,53–55] The results compare favorably with aortic bypass surgery with a much lower incidence of morbidity and mortality.[130,152] Interestingly, embolization from aortic plaque, which angiographically is frequently exophytic, is seen in less than 1 percent of cases reported.[43–58]

Takayasu aortitis, an uncommon cause of aortic stenosis (Fig. 17-18), has been successfully treated with PTA, although little long-term follow-up is available on these patients.[157–160] Though not supported by a large body of literature, most feel that if dilation is to be performed it should be done during a quiescent

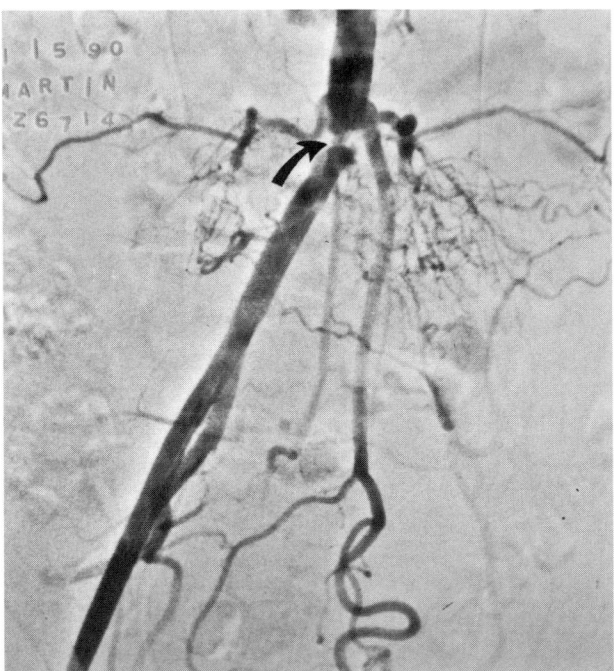

A

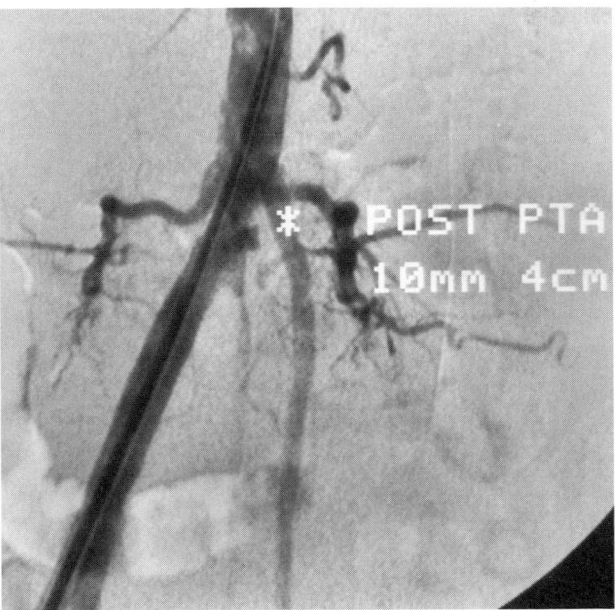

B

Figure 17-16. A patient with bilateral lower extremity claudication and severe digital ischemia, left greater than right. (A) Severe concentric stenosis of the origin of the right common iliac artery (*arrow*) and a chronic left iliac artery occlusion were demonstrated. (B) PTA of the right common iliac artery lesion was performed prior to a planned femorofemoral crossover graft. Both extremities improved, presumably because of transpelvic collaterals, so that the patient was no longer lifestyle-limited and the graft was unnecessary.

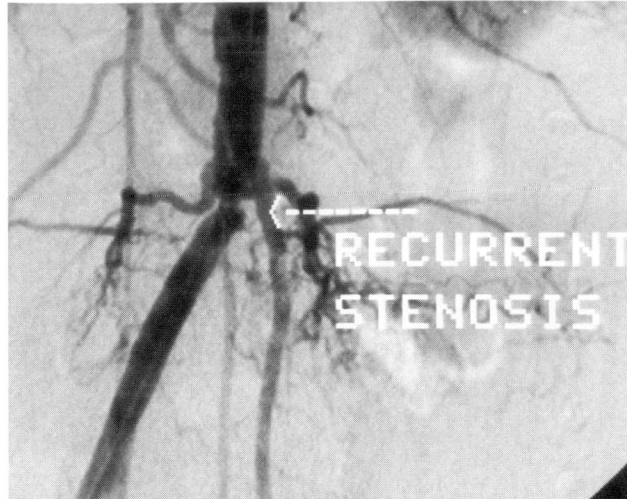

C

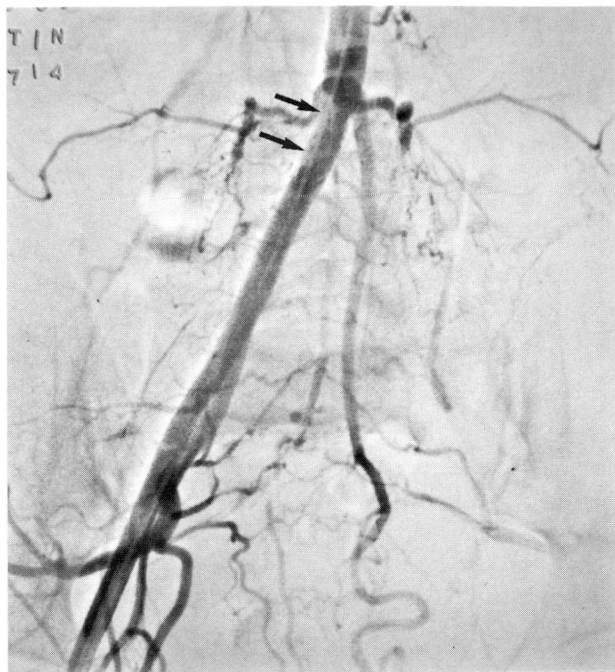

D

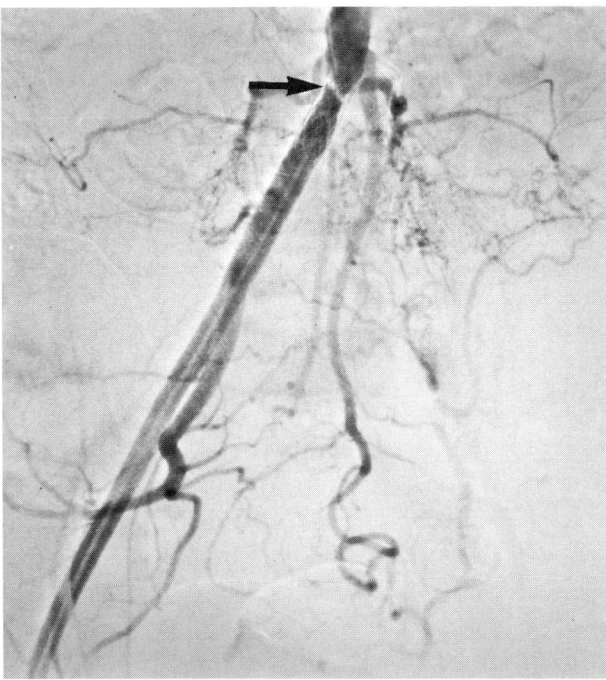

E

Figure 17-16. (continued). (C) One year after treatment, however, the patient returned with increasing recurrent symptoms. Repeat angiography revealed moderate recurrent stenosis at the angioplasty site. (D) A Palmaz stent was deployed in the region of stenosis (*arrows*) with complete resolution of the stenosis and gradient. The patient's symptoms again improved. (E and F) When later the patient again became symptomatic, a recurrent stenosis within the Palmaz stent at the identical site (*arrow*) was demonstrated. Repeat dilation within the stent again resulted in angiographic ablation of the stenosis and relief in the lower extremities. Three

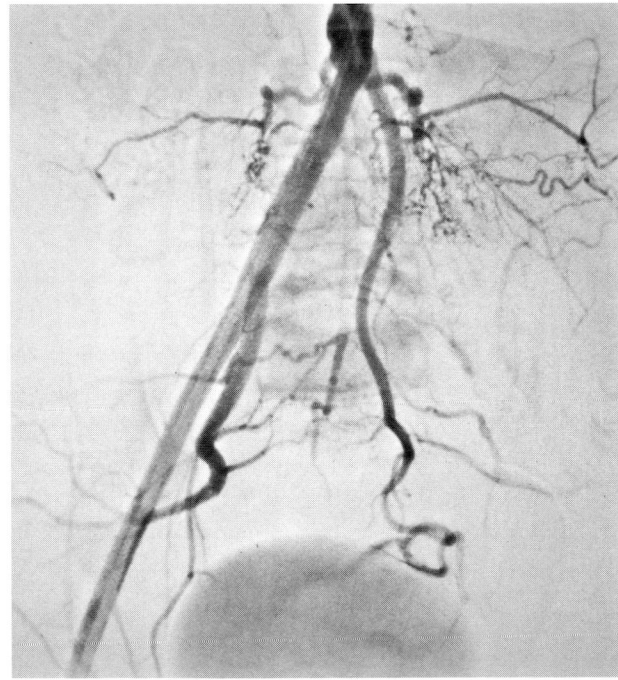

F

years later, the patient remained stable without any recurrent symptoms. (From Rholl, KS. Percutaneous intervention for aortoiliac disease. In: Strandness E, van Breda A, eds. Vascular diseases: surgical and interventional therapy. New York: Churchill-Livingstone, 1994. Used with permission.)

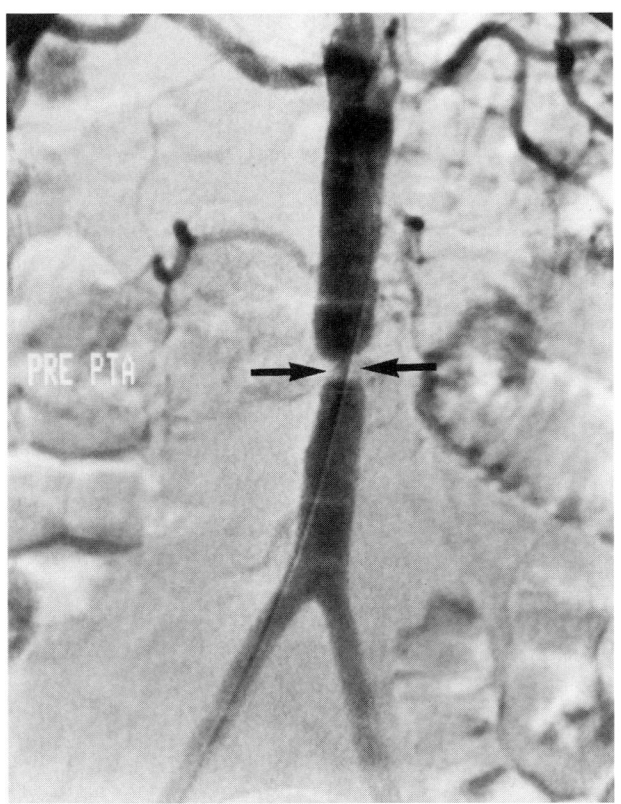

A

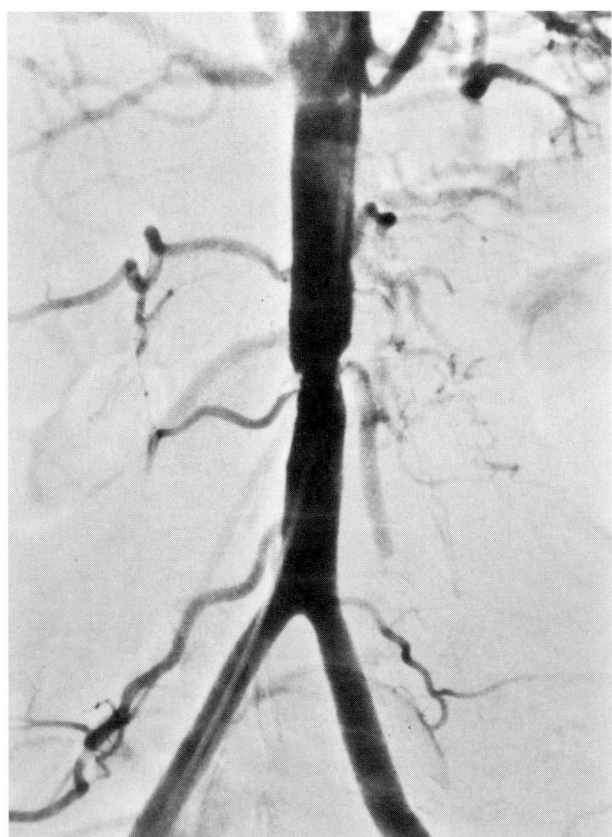

C

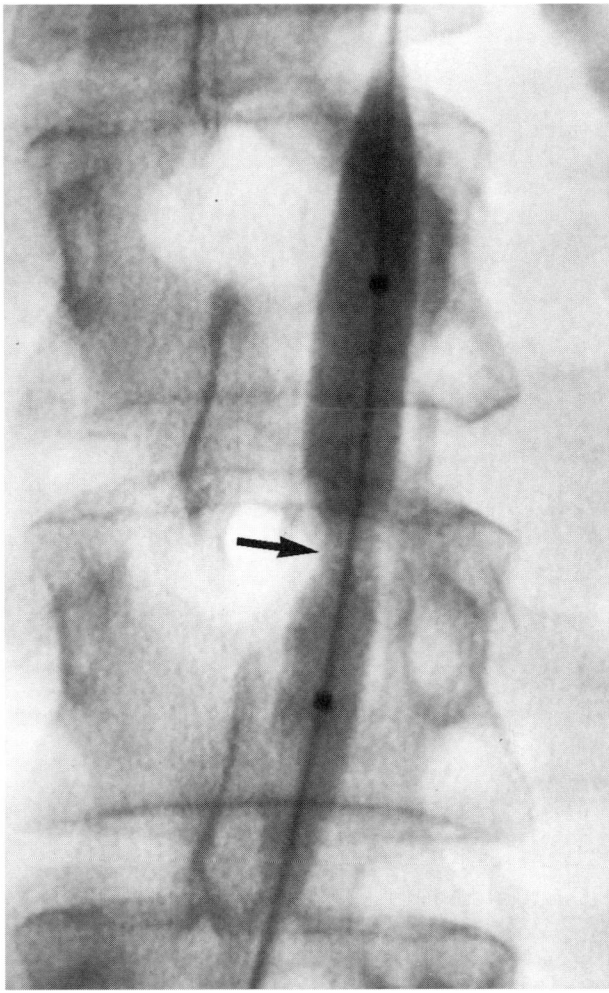

B

Figure 17-17. (A) A focal concentric stenosis (*arrows*) was tient with bilateral buttock, thigh, and calf claudication. (B and C) Balloon dilation of the stenosis was performed, gradually eliminating the balloon waist (*arrow*) with complete resolution of the stenosis and ablation of the transstenotic gradient. Follow-up noninvasive studies at 4 years revealed normal ankle-brachial indices with no return of symptoms. (From Rholl, KS. Percutaneous intervention for aortoiliac disease. In: Strandness E, van Breda A, eds. Vascular diseases: surgical and interventional therapy. New York: Churchill-Livingstone, 1994. Used with permission.)

phase of the disease. Tyagi et al. reported a series of PTA in 36 patients with Takayasu aortitis.[158] Primary technical success was seen in 94 percent. No major complications were reported, including no aneurysm or pseudoaneurysm formation at the site of dilation. Angiography with hemodynamic evaluation at a mean of 7.7 months in 20 patients revealed only 1 restenosis, for a primary patency rate of 95 percent. The single patient with restenosis underwent successful redilation. Rao et al., reporting their experience in

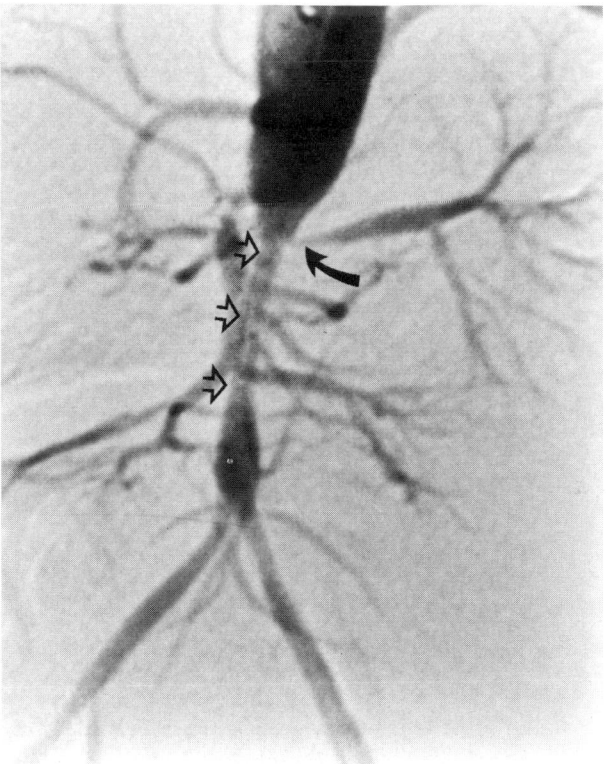

Figure 17-18. Abdominal aortogram in a young patient with severe hypertension and lower extremity claudication. The right renal artery is occluded and there is severe stenosis of the left renal artery (*curved arrow*). Flow to the lower extremities is severely limited by the long, fusiform stenosis (*open arrows*) in this patient with Takayasu aortitis.

16 patients, noted a higher rate of restenosis of 67 percent with a mean follow-up of 21 months.[159] Although additional long-term data are needed, it would appear that judicious use of PTA in these patients may play an important role.

Thrombolysis

Thrombolysis of the iliac arteries can be divided by indication into procedures performed for acute limb-threatening ischemia and procedures performed for an occlusion that is subacute or chronic. In acute ischemia, McNamara has reported excellent results with thrombolytic therapy, even in the face of severe ischemia.[77,80] In acute ischemia with a viable extremity (see Table 17-1), a technical success rate of 100 percent was noted. When limb viability was threatened, a success rate of 84 percent was reported. Even when there was profound ischemia or irreversible ischemia, a positive outcome was noted in 60 percent. McNamara has therefore recommended that percutaneous intraarterial thrombolysis should play a major role in acute

lower limb ischemia. Complications included adult respiratory distress syndrome (ARDS) secondary to reperfusion of a cadaveric limb, acute tubular necrosis (ATN) associated with myoglobinuria, puncture site hemorrhage, development of compartment syndrome, and distal embolization. Given the frequently poor medical condition of this patient group, these events are not surprising. A prospective trial comparing the outcome of thrombolysis versus surgery as a primary therapy in this group of patients suggested that, although short-term outcomes were comparable, long-term outcomes were significantly better in patients undergoing lytic therapy.[161] The cumulative limb salvage for both surgery and thrombolysis was approximately 82 percent at 12 months. However, the cumulative survival rate was significantly higher in the group treated with thrombolysis (84 percent versus 58 percent at 12 months). A nationwide trial currently under way may aid in determining the validity of this initial finding. Without prior thrombolysis, primary PTA or stenting of an acutely thrombosed artery is relatively contraindicated because of the likelihood of embolization of fresh thrombus further compromising the patient's vascular status. The SCVIR guidelines for intervention therefore recommend thrombolysis of acute occlusions before attempted PTA if the percutaneous option is chosen over surgery.[116]

The treatment of chronic iliac occlusive disease has been controversial. Ring et al. suggested that direct recanalization and PTA of iliac artery occlusions should not be attempted because of the low success rate and high frequency of complications, noting that embolization occurred in 40 percent of patients in whom the lesion was successfully traversed and PTA performed.[62] Colapinto, however, indicated that, despite a somewhat lower technical success (78 percent), complications were less frequent than initially suggested and long-term cumulative patency was good (78 percent at 4 years).[63] Thrombolysis of subacute and chronic occlusions prior to intervention may reduce the risk of embolization during the subsequent intervention (Fig. 17-19). Furthermore, though somewhat more costly and time-consuming, conversion of an occlusion to a stenosis may significantly facilitate subsequent PTA.[80,81] Deeter et al. reported the results in 19 iliac artery occlusions of which 11 were chronic (range 1 month to 6 years).[81] The technical success rate for revascularization of the occluded segments was 89 percent, and follow-up at a mean of 1 year showed a patency rate of 85 percent. Minor embolization was noted in 1 patient (5 percent); the embolization was clinically silent and did not require further intervention. No major emboli occurred in this series. Most importantly, failure of the procedure did

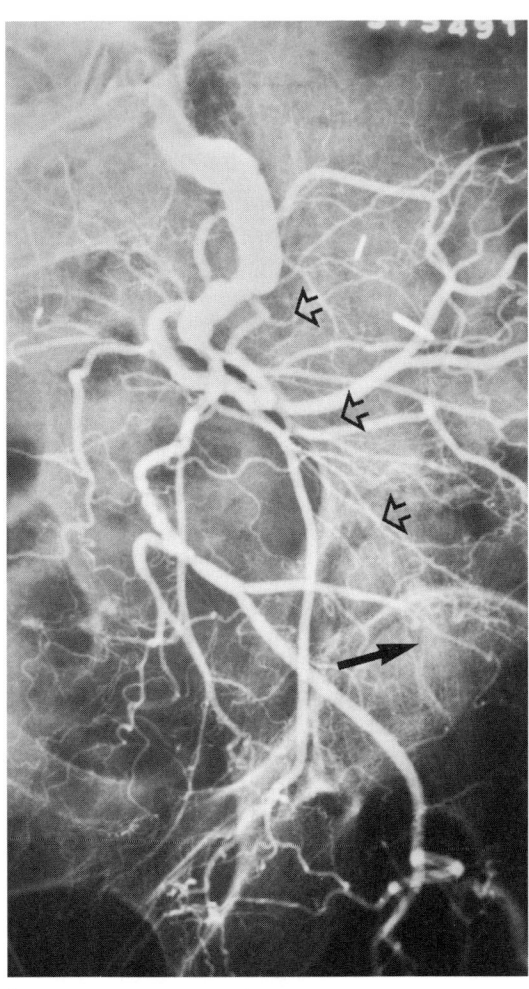
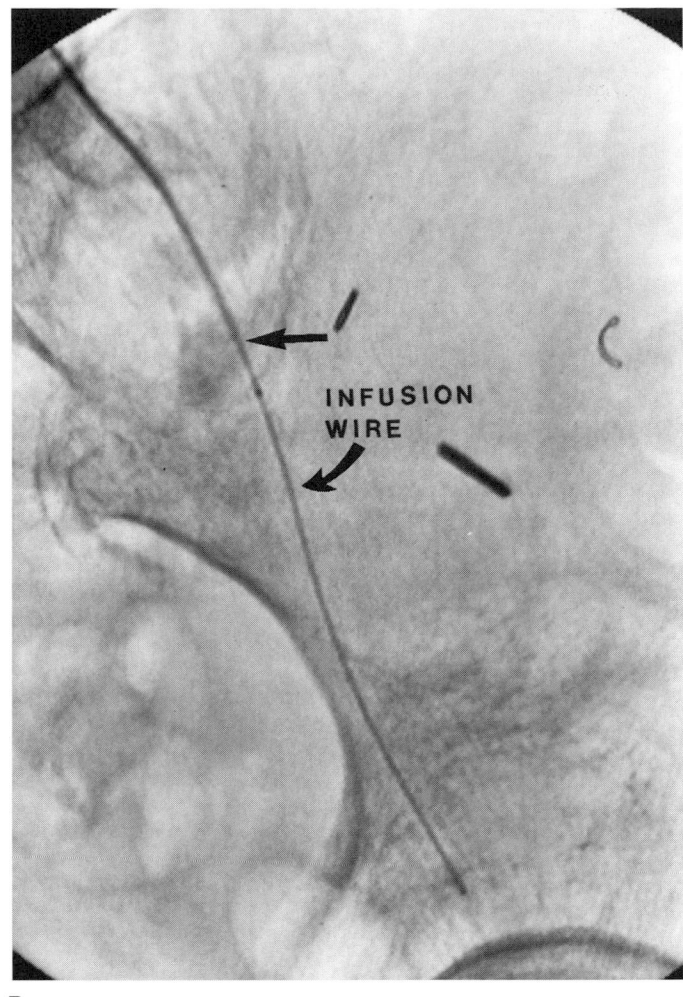

A   **B**

Figure 17-19. A 56-year-old woman with abrupt worsening of claudication 3 months before presentation. (A) Arteriography revealed occlusion of the left external iliac artery (*open arrows*). Reconstitution of the left common femoral artery (*arrow*) is faintly visualized. (B) After the occlusion was traversed, a coaxial infusion system was placed with an infusion wire (*curved arrow*) positioned throughout the occlusion. The 5 French catheter (*arrow*) was positioned at the proximal aspect of the occlusion.

not worsen the vascular status in any patient, nor was any patient precluded from surgical intervention by procedural failure. A review of the literature indicates a 75 to 80 percent overall successful lysis rate in the treatment of iliac occlusions.[69–77,81]

As with angioplasty, proper patient selection is mandatory to ensure the safety and efficacy of thrombolysis in both acute and chronic iliac occlusions. With this proviso, thrombolysis can play an important adjunctive role to either percutaneous or surgical intervention.

Intravascular Stents

Failures of PTA frequently occur during or in the immediate postprocedural period. As noted in Table 17-4, the technical failure rate for iliac PTA is estimated to be in the range of 0 to 27 percent, with an average of 8 percent. Significant elastic recoil of the arterial wall will result in immediate partial restenosis of the vessel on balloon deflation. Calcific and eccentric lesions are prone to elastic recoil and therefore a higher restenosis rate (see Fig. 17-8). Although the mechanism of PTA has been shown to be largely secondary to the creation of an intimal cleft that allows for a larger lumen, occasionally with dilation an extensive dissection results that may significantly compromise flow within the lumen. This can occur not only at the site of dilation; it can also extend proximally and/or distally, resulting in additional obstruction. Finally, even though vasodilators may have been administered, vasospasm occasionally occurs at or about the PTA

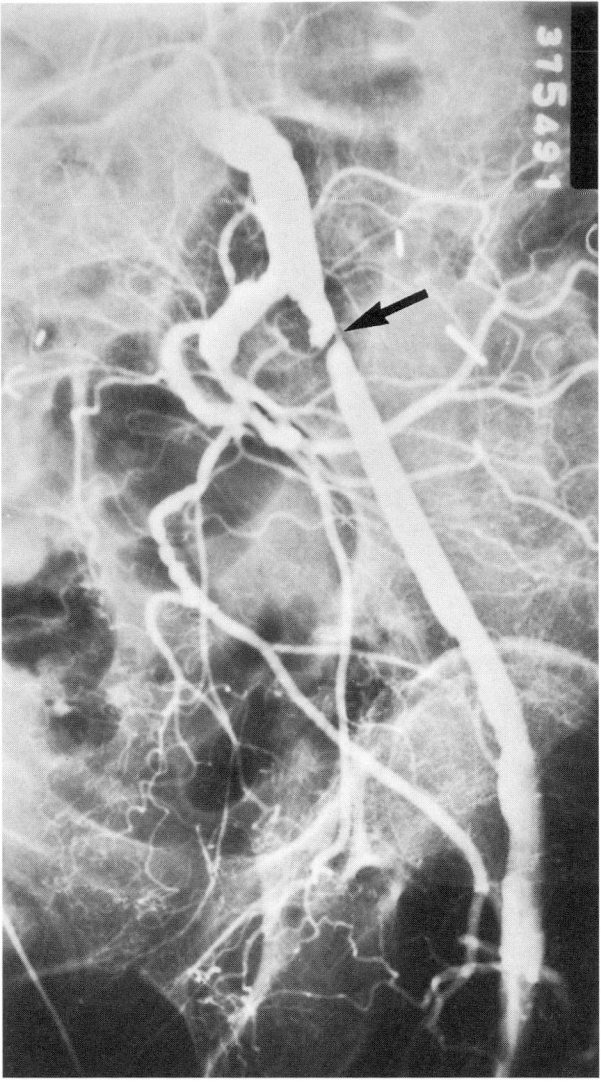

C

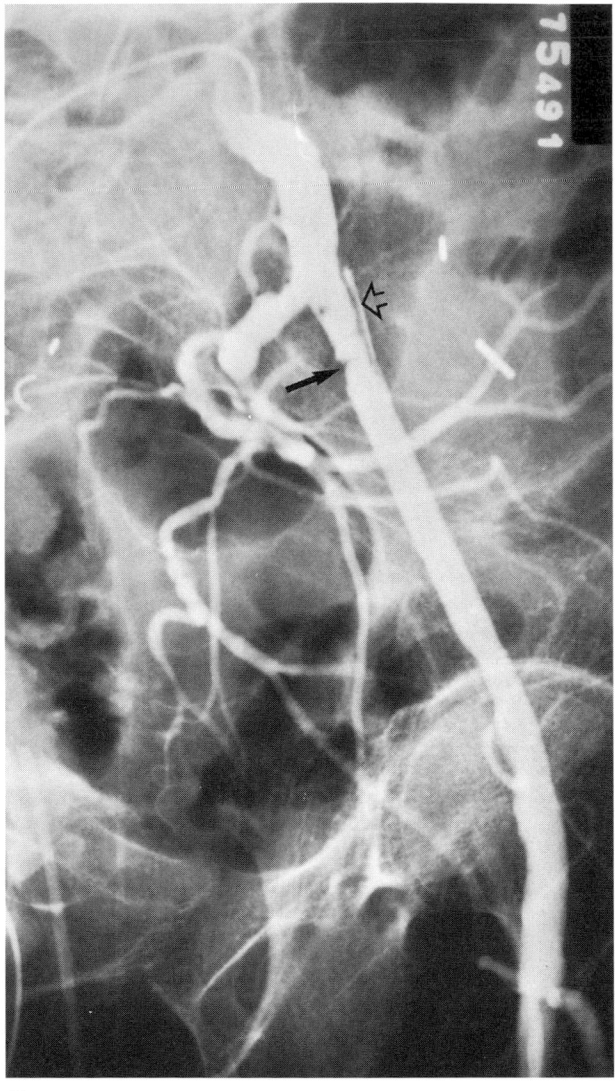

D

Figure 17-19 (continued). (C) After overnight thrombolytic infusion, complete resolution of thrombus revealed an underlying severe eccentric left external iliac artery stenosis (*arrow*). (D) PTA performed from a retrograde ipsilateral approach resulted in marked improvement of the lumen. However, a small dissection (*open arrow*) and moderate residual stenosis (*arrow*) were present. A transstenotic gradient of 20 mmHg following PTA was measured.

site, compromising the lumen. Complete angiographic assessment of the PTA result helps to identify these problems. Equally important is adequate hemodynamic assessment of the vessel after the intervention by intraarterial pressure evaluation, including the use of intraarterial vasodilators to identify possible gradients. Intravascular stents were developed in part to address some of these limitations of angioplasty and have already proved themselves valuable in improving short- and long-term outcomes.[82–89,91,94–96,109,157–171]

The iliac arteries have been the site of most investigations with peripherally placed intravascular stents.

The Palmaz stent (Johnson & Johnson) was the first stent approved in the United States by the FDA for use in the iliac arteries and therefore is the stent with the greatest clinical experience to date. The stent is mounted on a PTA balloon and is delivered in much the same fashion as the original PTA devices, requiring little additional equipment; this feature has aided in its widespread adoption. Palmaz et al. reported the results of a multicenter trail investigating the use of the Palmaz stent in the iliac arteries.[82] The immediate clinical success rate was 99 percent, with 1- and 2-year clinical success rates of 91 and 84 percent, respectively. Inter-

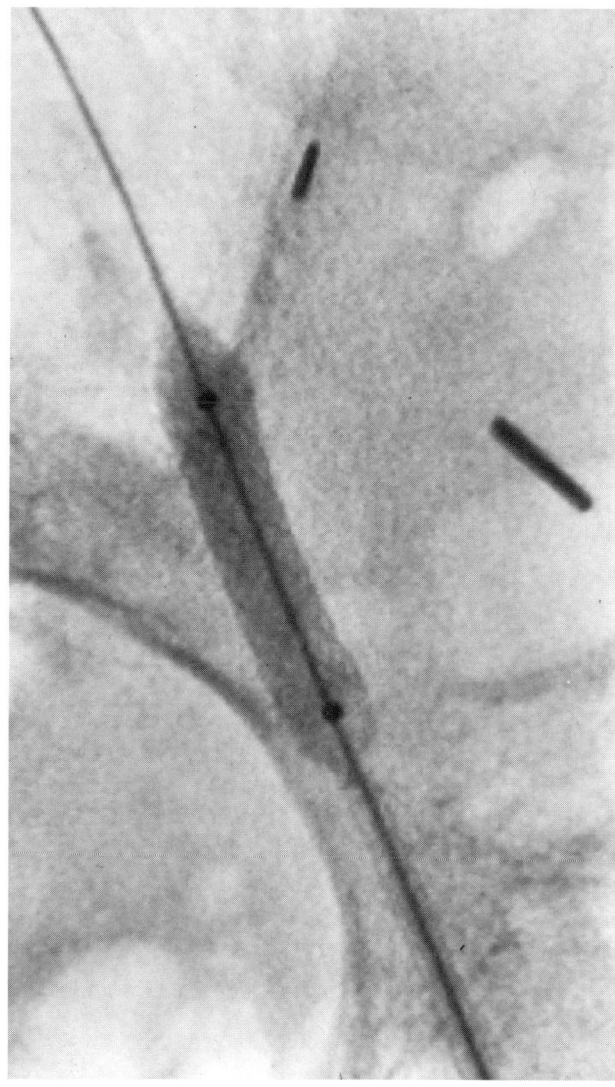

E

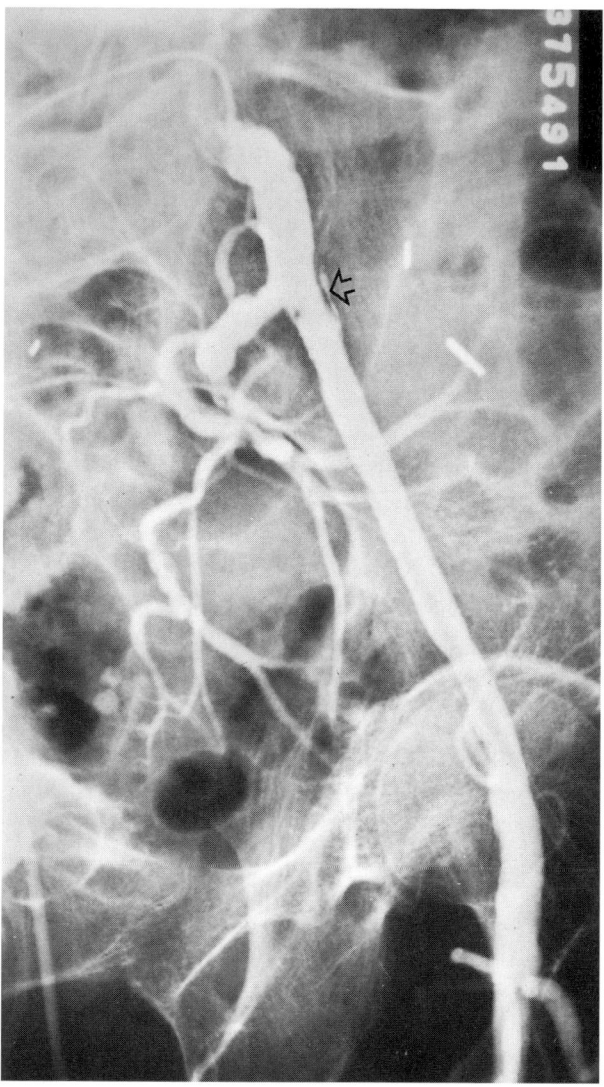

F

Figure 17-19 (continued). (E) A Palmaz stent was deployed through the retrograde sheath at the angioplasty site. (F) Repeat arteriography evaluation revealed complete resolution of the stenosis and transstenotic gradient with minimal residual filling of the intimal crack (*open arrow*). (From

Rholl, KS. Percutaneous intervention for aortoiliac disease. In: Strandness E, van Breda A, eds. Vascular diseases: surgical and interventional therapy. New York: Churchill-Livingstone, 1994. Used with permission.)

estingly, at 3 years the clinical success rate dropped to 69 percent, even though angiographically the stent patency was shown to be much greater, at 92 percent. This results emphasizes the difficulty in defining and determining the long-term durability of any vascular procedure. Most of the patients with clinical evidence of recurrent stenosis instead were found to have a patent stented segment and progression of disease remote to the site as a cause of their recurrent symptoms.

Henry et al. treated 184 iliac arteries with Palmaz stents.[171] At 4-year follow-up, the primary patency rate for the iliac arteries was 86 percent and the secondary

patency rate was 93 percent. Their series, which also included treatment of 126 femoropopliteal arteries, indicated that the length of the lesion and the severity (stenosis versus occlusion) in part determine the long-term durability of stenting, as with balloon PTA. Richter et al. reported the results of a randomized trial comparing PTA to primary stent placement in the iliac arteries in 247 patients.[170] Initial success rates were in conformity with other reports, being 98 percent for stent placement and 91 percent for PTA. Cumulative 5-year patency rates (determined angiographically) showed a marked advantage for stent placement, at

93.6 percent versus 64.6 percent for the group undergoing PTA only. The implication of their study is that long-term durability may be significantly improved in iliac intervention if stents are placed primarily. The cost-effectiveness of this approach remains undetermined. It is also not yet evident whether there might be definable subsets of patients in whom primary stenting might be advantageous, as opposed to those in whom there may be no additional benefit. It is notable that 13 of 19 recurrent stenoses seen after PTA occurred in the external iliac arteries, suggesting that these vessels may not respond as well to PTA as do the common iliac arteries.

The Wallstent has more recently been used for revascularization of the iliac arteries.[91,92,94–96,109,157,162,165,166,168,169] Its advantages include a smaller, more flexible delivery system than was present in the original Palmaz stent. This allows for deployment through a smaller entry sheath and possible delivery to the contralateral iliac artery. The device is self-expanding and inherently flexible, features that may facilitate deployment in tortuous vessels. The wider range of lengths available also allows for deployment of a single stent when treatment of longer lesions is considered. Initial reports of the use of Wallstents in the iliac arteries suggested a technical success rate of 99 percent ($n = 170$). Long-term follow-up was limited but suggested good durability, with 95 percent patency at 1 year and 88 percent at 2 years.[165,168,169] Sapoval et al. has also reported a secondary patency rate at 4.5 years of 80 percent.[172] These early reports led others to expand the investigation of the use of Wallstents to include treatment of arteries not generally suitable for percutaneous techniques. Murphy et al. reported their experience in treating 94 chronically occluded and/or diffusely diseased iliac arteries in 66 patients.[109] In this patient population, they reported a technical success rate of 90 percent, although major complications were noted in 8 percent. The cumulative primary patency rates at 1 and 2 years were 74 and 67 percent, respectively, with a secondary patency rate at 2 years of 86 percent. These results compare quite favorably to the more traditional surgical revascularization in this population, where PTA has been limited by lower success and patency rates and higher complication rates, usually distal embolization. At this point, then, the ultimate place of stents in the treatment of iliac occlusion is still evolving, though it is evident that they will play a significant role, possibly supplanting many surgical procedures.

The use of stents in the infrarenal abdominal aorta and its bifurcation has also been reported.[157,162–164] Since currently available stents are limited in size, stents have generally been used in aortas of smaller caliber. Although the initial Palmaz stent had a maximum optimal working diameter of 12 mm, it has been expanded further (Fig. 17-20). This should be done with some caution because it alters the stent's length and strength and the ratio of metal to endoluminal surface area. The initial Wallstents were limited to a 10-mm diameter; larger diameters are now available but are not approved for aortic placement. Westcott et al. recently compared a series of patients garnered from a multicenter registry with 12 patients undergoing aortic PTA.[173] A 100 percent technical success rate was reported versus 92 percent for patients undergoing PTA. No long-term data were available. Stents may eventually play a significant role in the treatment of aortic stenoses—particularly when there is calcified, eccentric, or exophytic plaque—if increased patency and decreased embolization and elastic recoil can be demonstrated.

Atherectomy

Although there was initial predictable enthusiasm for atherectomy with its theoretical advantages of plaque removal and a resultant smooth lumen, the results of iliac atherectomy have not been significantly different from those of PTA.[30,110–112] Small series suggested a primary success rate averaging only 85 percent with 3-year patency rates ranging widely from 57 to 84 percent. Certainly, no advantage over PTA was demonstrable, even with the selection of focal, noncalcified lesions, which should have better primary success rates and long-term patencies. Coupled with this was a significant increase in the associated complications of the procedure. The complications were largely related to the size of the arteriotomy site, with hematomas at the puncture site noted in 24 percent. Significantly increased costs are also encountered because of the cost of the devices, which ranges from $600 to $800, as well as the cost of increased procedural time. Although atherectomy was described as a means for the removal of obstructing intimal flaps, this function has been replaced by intravascular stents when necessary. Therefore, at the present time, there is no evidence to support the use of atherectomy devices in the iliac arteries.

Complications

When the clinical utility of surgical reconstruction is compared to that of percutaneous revascularization, a dramatic difference in the morbidity and mortality of the two becomes evident. Although surgical revascularization may result in slightly improved long-term durability compared to iliac PTA, the markedly lower

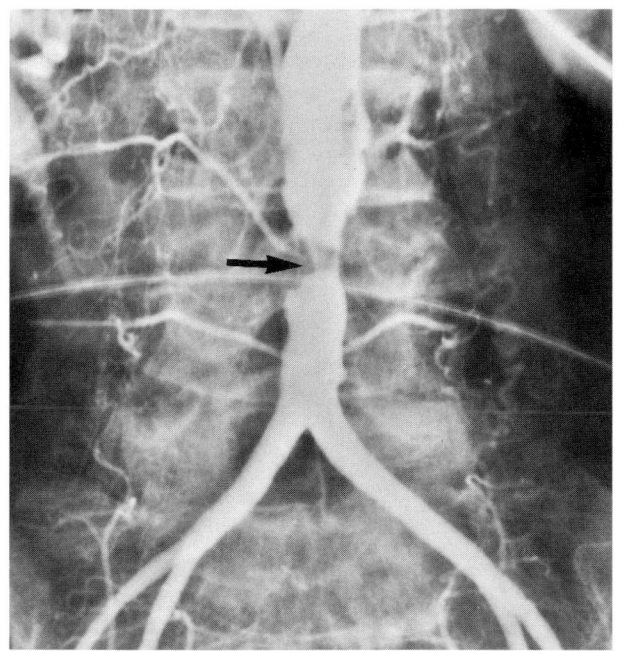

A

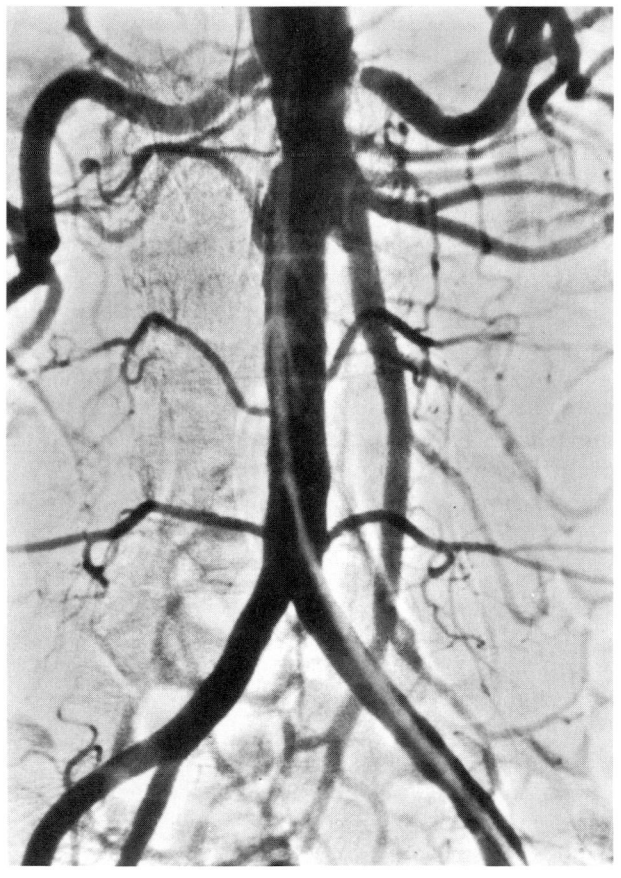

C

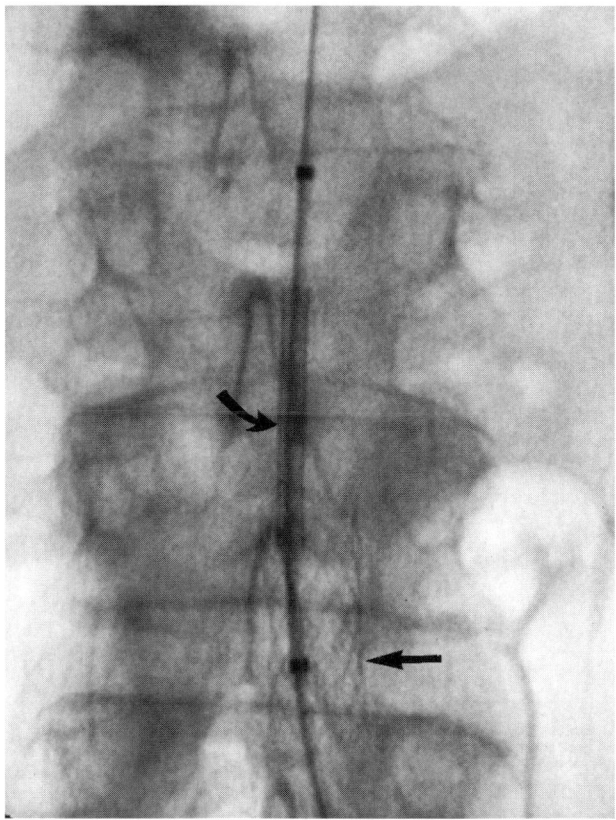

B

Figure 17-20. A 61-year-old woman with bilateral lower extremity claudication and a nonhealing toe ulcer. (A) Diagnostic arteriography revealed an exophytic severe stenosis of the midinfrarenal abdominal aorta (*arrow*). (B) Because of its exophytic appearance, the lesion was primarily stented. Two Palmaz stents were deployed and dilated to 14 mm. *Arrow,* deployed stent; *curved arrow,* undeployed mounted stent. (C) Evaluation after stent placement revealed complete resolution of the stenosis and gradient. Palpable pedal pulses were restored bilaterally.

morbidity and mortality of PTA have led to the general acceptance of PTA as the initial treatment of choice for many patients suffering from aortoiliac disease. Complication rates for patients undergoing aortoiliac PTA are summarized in Table 17-6.[6–13,15–17,19–26,30–32,35–37,39–41,102–104,125,126,133,153,154,174,175] The overall complication rate from this pooled data from series reporting the results of aortoiliac PTA was 8.1 percent. Major complications, however, were noted in only 2.7 percent; only 1.2 percent of patients had complications that required surgical intervention. Finally, the mortality rate that could be attributed to PTA was 0.2 percent, less than one-tenth that attributable to surgical reconstruction.

Coronary artery disease, which accounts for most of the surgical morbidity and mortality, also is respon-

Table 17-6. Complications of Aortoiliac Angioplasty*

Complication	Rate (%)
Type	
Hematoma	2.8
Occlusion (acute)	1.9
Embolization	1.6
Renal dysfunction	0.8
Pseudoaneurysm/arteriovenous fistula	0.5
Arterial rupture	0.3
Mortality	0.2
Limb loss	0.1
Severity	
Overall rate	8.1
Major complications	2.7
Requiring surgery	1.2
Minor complications	5.4

* N = 6676 procedures.
Pooled data from references 6–13, 15–26, 30–32, 35–41, 67, 68, 102–104, 125, 126, 133, 148, 153, 154, 174, and 175.

sible for much of the limited mortality seen with aortoiliac PTA. Complications specific to aortoiliac PTA include arterial rupture, which occurred in 0.3 percent of cases (Fig. 17-21). This complication virtually always requires emergent surgical repair, although conservative management of these patients has been reported.[176] Prompt reinflation of the dilation balloon once the rupture is recognized will generally tamponade hemorrhage until surgical repair can be performed. With the development of covered stents or "stent grafts," percutaneous management of these patients may indeed become possible, reducing the gravity of the complication significantly. Acute arterial occlusion was noted in 1.9 percent of cases. Possible etiologies include vasospasm, dissection, and primary thrombosis. The incidence of acute occlusion can generally be minimized by judicious intraprocedural use of anticoagulation and vasodilators. Similarly, with use of these agents and repeat dilation, a patent lumen can often be restored. In the case of primary thrombosis, a local thrombolytic infusion may also be necessary. With the introduction of stents, salvage of occlusive dissections is almost always possible, generally reducing the necessity for surgical intervention. It is anticipated that this will be reflected in future outcome studies of PTA.

Minor complications occur in 5.4 percent of patients undergoing aortoiliac PTA. Puncture site hematomas account for most of these complications and generally require little if any treatment. Pseudoaneurysms or arteriovenous fistulas are noted in 0.5 percent. Pseudoaneurysm is by far the more common complication; however, with ultrasound-guided compression for ablation, it almost never requires surgical repair and involves little delay in hospital discharge.

A comparison of the complication rates of percutaneous techniques to those seen with surgical recon-

struction is fraught with difficulty because there are no standards or definitions for reporting complications, either surgical or percutaneous. One author may consider a small hematoma at the arteriotomy site a complication, whereas another may feel that it is an expected part of the procedure. Similarly, blood loss requiring a transfusion is generally considered a major complication of PTA, whereas it may be considered routine for the surgical procedure. With the acceptance of aortoiliac PTA has come the expectation of extremely low morbidity and mortality. Reports suggesting that the complication rates for the two procedures are similar clearly do not hold the two procedures to the same standards.[175] However, a review of the literature should leave little doubt as to the large safety margin of aortoiliac PTA over surgical reconstruction.

Conclusions

Since the first percutaneous revascularization performed by Dr. Charles Dotter in 1964, aortoiliac PTA has become one of the most frequently performed procedures in the treatment of peripheral vascular disease. Despite extensive early resistance, it has gained acceptance from both the medical and surgical communities as the initial treatment of choice in patients with focal aortoiliac disease, largely because of its excellent long-term durability and low associated morbidity and mortality. Aortoiliac PTA has been heavily relied upon, not only as a primary therapy for the treatment of peripheral vascular disease, but also as an adjunct to surgical therapy to optimize inflow before an infrainguinal bypass. Excellent patient tolerance and short recovery times have allowed otherwise healthy patients to return to normal activity levels within 1 to 2 days. Although some of surgical reconstructive procedures, such as aortobifemoral bypass, have demonstrated better long-term patency rates, these are more than offset by the differences in morbidity and mortality and the decreased costs secondary to discrepant procedural and professional charges, as well as by the lower cost of hospitalization and recovery.

The excellent safety record of aortoiliac PTA has also led to an expansion of its indication for revascularization beyond the more traditional conservative indications for the corresponding surgical procedures. Unlike the surgical alternatives, failure of PTA, either immediate or delayed, rarely results in worsening of the patient's vascular status. Therefore, patients who do not fit the traditional indications for surgical reconstruction may well meet indications for PTA. Moderate claudication, for instance, is generally not felt to

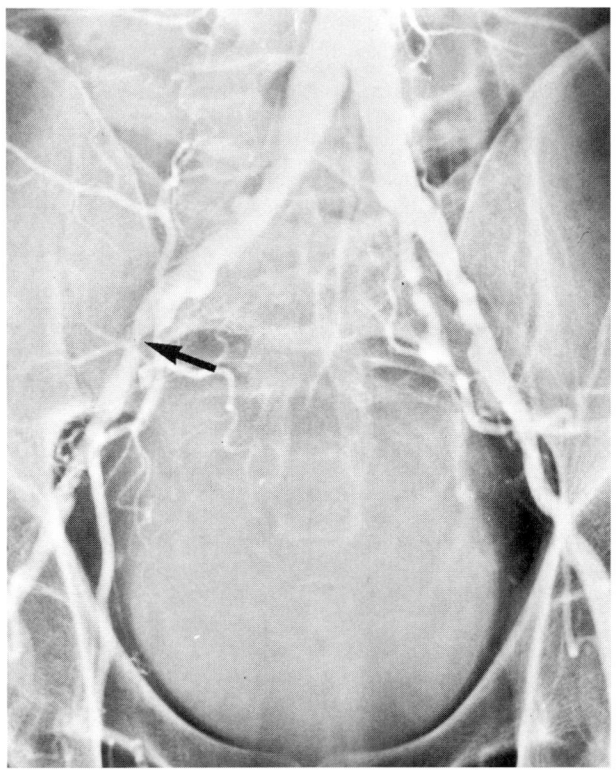

A

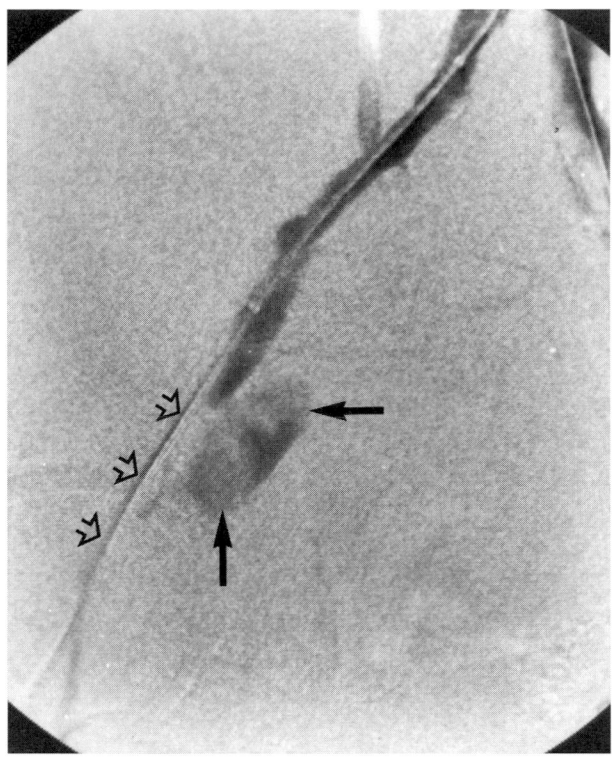

B

Figure 17-21. A 79-year-old man with severe cardiomyopathy secondary to coronary artery disease presented with tissue loss of the right lower extremity. (A) Despite diffuse disease, a severe stenosis with a focal gradient was identified by intraarterial pressure measurements in the right external iliac artery (*arrow*). (B) After dilation, the patient experienced severe pelvic pain. Digital imaging revealed extravasation of contrast from the dilation site (*arrow*), indicating arterial rupture. Severe vasospasm of the artery distal to the rupture was also present (*open arrows*). (C) Prompt reinflation of the balloon resulted in tamponade of the rupture site, allowing emergent surgical repair. (From Rholl, KS. Percutaneous intervention for aortoiliac disease. In: Strandness E, van Breda A, eds. Vascular diseases: surgical and interventional therapy. New York: Churchill-Livingstone, 1994. Used with permission.)

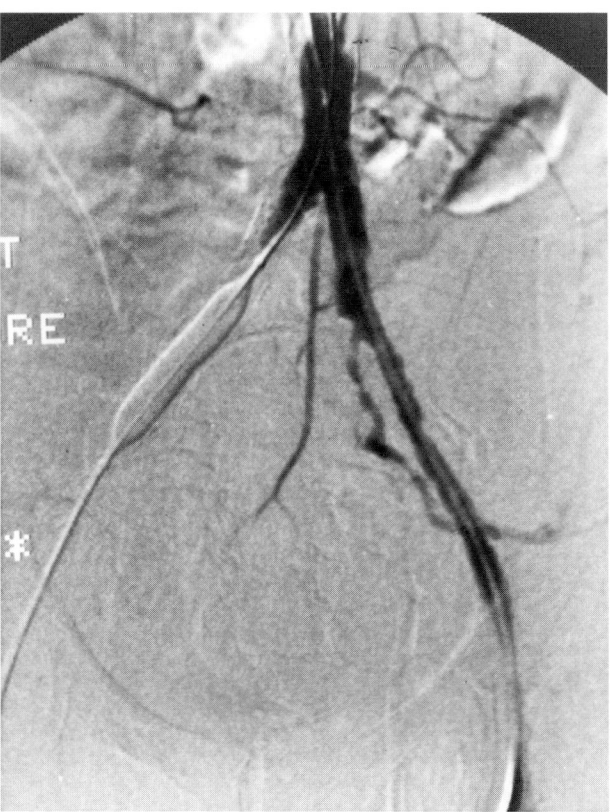

C

be an indication for major surgical revascularization. However, having failed a trial of conservative management, this group may well be appropriately treated with PTA. Furthermore, patients with medical contraindications to surgical revascularization can frequently undergo PTA with a wide margin of safety.

Guidelines for the performance of PTA in vascular disease have been published by the SCVIR and are meant to help distinguish those lesions that respond well to standard PTA from those with a poorer prognosis. However, the safety margin of PTA when compared to surgery has led many to expand the role of percutaneous techniques in the treatment of vascular disease. Thrombolysis has been used successfully to convert occlusions, even those that are chronic, into stenotic disease, which can then be more readily treated by PTA. With the introduction of stents came the ability to "salvage" the suboptimal angioplasty, turning failure into success. Vessels treated by stent placement have already shown excellent long-term patency, although investigation continues. Stents have also been used in the treatment of long-segment occlusions and diffuse disease in the aortoiliac segments, a disease that is otherwise unfavorable for percutaneous treatment. Initial studies in these patients are extremely promising. Continued advances in technology, such as stent grafts, will almost certainly continue to expand the indications for and the success of percutaneous treatment of aortoiliac disease.

References

1. Dotter CT. Transluminal angioplasty: a long view. Radiology 1980;135:561–564.
2. Dotter CT. Cardiac catheterization and angiographic technics of the future. Cesk Radiol 1965;19:217–236.
3. Dotter CT, Judkins MP. Transluminal treatment of arteriosclerotic obstruction: description of a new technic and a preliminary report of its application. Circulation 1964;30:654–670.
4. Gruntzig A. Die perkutane rekavalisation chrovischer artelieller verschlusse (Dotter-Privzip) mit einem nemen doppellumingen dilatationskatheter. Rofo 1976;124(1):80–86.
5. Katzen BT. Percutaneous transluminal angioplasty for arterial disease of the lower extremities. AJR 1984;142:23–25.
6. van Andel GJ, van Erp WF, Krepel VM, Breslau PJ. Percutaneous transluminal dilatation of the iliac artery: long term results. Radiology 1985;156:321–323.
7. Kadir S, White RI, Kaufman SL, Barth KH, Williams GM, et al. Long-term results of aortoiliac angioplasty. Surgery 1982; 94(1):10–14.
8. Freiman DB, Spence R, Gatenby R, Gertner M, Roberts B, et al. Transluminal angioplasty of the iliac and femoral arteries: follow-up results without anticoagulation. Radiology 1981; 141:347–350.
9. Tegtmeyer CJ, Hartwell GD, Selby JB, Robertson R, Kron IL, Tribble CG. Results and complications of angioplasty in aortoiliac disease. Circulation 1991;83(Suppl I):53–60.
10. Katzen BT, Chang J, Knox WG. Percutaneous transluminal angioplasty with the Gruntzig balloon catheter: a review of 70 cases. Arch Surg 1979;114:1389–1399.
11. Spence RK, Freiman DB, Gatenby R, Hobbs CL, Barker CF, Berkowitz HD, Roberts B, et al. Long-term results of transluminal angioplasty of the iliac and femoral arteries. Arch Surg 1981;116:1377–1386.
12. Mosley JG, Gulati SM, Raphael M, Marstron A. The role of percutaneous transluminal angioplasty for atherosclerotic disease of the lower extremities. Ann R Coll Surg Engl 1985; 67:83–86.
13. van Andel GJ. Transluminal iliac angioplasty: long term results. Radiology 1980;135:607–611.
14. Katzen BT, van Breda A. Transluminal angioplasty of the iliac arteries. Semin Intervent Radiol 1985;2(2)(Suppl):196–205.
15. Johnston KW, Rae M, Hogg-Johnston SA, Colapinto RF, Walker PM, Baird RJ, Sniderman KW, Kalman P. Five-year results of a prospective study of percutaneous transluminal angioplasty. Ann Surg 1987;206(4):403–413.
16. Colapinto RF, Harries-Jones EP, Johnston KW. Percutaneous transluminal dilatation and recanalization in the treatment of peripheral vascular disease. Radiology 1980;135:583–587.
17. Kumpe DA, Kempczinski RF. Percutaneous transluminal angioplasty in the selected management of proximal arterial occlusive disease of the lower extremities: a preliminary report. Surgery 1980;87(5):488–493.
18. van Andel GJ. Long-term results of iliac and femoral angioplasty. Ann Radiol 1981;24(5):365–368.
19. Waltman AC, Greenfield AJ, Novelline RA, et al. Transluminal angioplasty of the iliac and femoropopliteal arteries. Arch Surg 1982;117:1218–1221.
20. Gruntzig A, Kumpe DA. Technique of percutaneous transluminal angioplasty with the Gruntzig balloon catheter. AJR 1979;132:547–552.
21. Glover JL, Bendick PJ, Dilley RS, Holden RW, Yune HY, Richmond BC, Klatte EC. Efficacy of balloon catheter dilation for lower extremity atherosclerosis. Surgery 1982;91(5): 560–565.
22. Zeitler E, Richter EI, Roth FJ, Schoop W. Results of percutaneous transluminal angioplasty. Radiology 1983;146:57–60.
23. Korogi Y, Takahashi M, Bussada H, Miyawaki M, Yamashita Y. Percutaneous transluminal angioplasty of the ilio-femoropopliteal arteries: initial and long-term results. Radiat Med 1987;5(3):68–74.
24. In der Maur GAP, de Boo T, Boeve J, Kerdel MC, Braakenburg BA. Angioplasty of the iliac and femoral arteries: initial and long-term results in short stenotic lesions. Eur J Radiol 1990;11:163–167.
25. Lancashire MJR, Torrie EPH, Galland RB. Percutaneous angioplasty in a district general hospital: impact and implications. J R Coll Surg Edinb 1992;37:183–186.
26. Blankensteijn JD, van Broonhoven TJ, Lampmann L. Role of percutaneous transluminal angioplasty in aorto-iliac reconstruction. J Cardiovasc Surg 1986;27:466–468.
27. Thorvinger B, Norgren L, Albrechtsson. Patency after iliac and femoro-popliteal angioplasty: difference between angiographic and clinical results. Acta Radiol 1992;33:29–30.
28. Lynch RD. Percutaneous transluminal angioplasty (PTA) and the community hospital: experience with 126 cases. J AOA 1981;81(3):155–171.
29. Wilson SE, Sheppard B. Results of percutaneous transluminal angioplasty for peripheral vascular occlusive disease. Ann Vasc Surg 1990;4:94–97.
30. Kotb MM, Kadir S, Bennett JD, Beam CA. Aortoiliac angioplasty: is there a need for other types of percutaneous intervention? J Vasc Intervent Radiol 1992;3:67–71.
31. Waltman AC. Percutaneous transluminal angioplasty of the iliac and deep femoral arteries. In: Athanasoulis C, ed. Interventional radiology. Philadelphia: Saunders, 1982:273.
32. Simonetti G, Urigo F. Percutaneous transluminal angioplasty of the iliac arteries. In: Dondelinger RF, Rossi P, Kurdziel JC, Wallace S, eds. Interventional radiology. New York: Thieme, 1990:610.
33. Olbert F, Karnel F. Angioplasty of iliac artery stenoses. In: Kadir S, ed. Current practice of interventional radiology. Philadelphia: Decker, 1991:295.
34. Davies AH, Cole SE, Magee TR, Scott DJA, Baird RN, Horrocks M. The effect of diabetes mellitus on the outcome of angioplasty for lower limb ischemia. Diabetic Med 1992;9: 480–481.
35. Stokes KR, Strunk HM, Campbell DR, Gibbons GW, Wheeler HG, Clouse ME. Five-year results of iliac and femoropopliteal angioplasty in diabetic patients. Radiology 1990; 174:977–982.
36. Johnston KW. Factors that influence the outcome of aortoiliac and femoropopliteal percutaneous transluminal angioplasty. Endovasc Surg 1992;72(4):843–850.
37. Tyagi S, Malhotra A, Khalilullah M. Percutaneous transluminal angioplasty for ischaemic arterial disease of the lower extremities. Indian Heart J 1990;42(6):419–422.
38. Borozan PG, Schuler JJ, Spigos DG, Flanigan DP. Long-term

hemodynamic evaluation of lower extremity percutaneous transluminal angioplasty. J Vasc Surg 1985;2:785–793.

39. Graor RA, Young JR, McCandless M, et al. Percutaneous transluminal angioplasty: review of iliac and femoral dilatations at the Cleveland Clinic. Clevel Clin Q 1984;51:149–154.

40. Gallino A, Mahler F, Probst P, Nachbur B. Percutaneous transluminal angioplasty of the arteries of the lower limbs: a 5 year follow-up. Circulation 1984;70(4):619–623.

41. Motarjeme A, Keifer JW, Zuska AJ. Percutaneous transluminal angioplasty of the iliac arteries: 66 experiences. AJR 1980;135:937–944.

42. Waltman AC. Percutaneous transluminal angioplasty: iliac and deep femoral arteries. AJR 1980;135:921–925.

43. Morag B, Garnick A, Bass A, Schneiderman J, Walden R, Rubinstein ZJ. Percutaneous transluminal aortic angioplasty: early and late results. Cardiovasc Intervent Radiol 1993;16:37–42.

44. Grollman JH, Del Vicario M, Mittal AK. Percutaneous transluminal abdominal aortic angioplasty. AJR 1980;134:1053–1054.

45. Tegtmeyer CJ, Kellum CD, Kron IL, Mentzer RM. Percutaneous transluminal angioplasty in the region of the aortic bifurcation. Radiology 1985;157:661–665.

46. Arbona GL, van Aman ME, Smead WL. Percutaneous transluminal angioplasty of the abdominal aortic bifurcation. South Med J 1983;76(1):22–26.

47. Tadavarthy AK, Sullivan WA, Nicoloff D, Castaneda-Zuniga WR, Hunter DW, Amplatz K. Aorta balloon angioplasty: 9 year follow-up. Radiology 1989;170:1039–1041.

48. Belli AM, Hemingway AP, Cumberland DC, Welsh CL. Percutaneous transluminal angioplasty of the distal abdominal aorta. Eur J Vasc Surg 1989;3:449–453.

49. Morag B, Rubinstein Z, Kessler A, Schneiderman J, Levinkopf M, Bass A. Percutaneous transluminal angioplasty of the distal abdominal aorta and its bifurcation. Cardiovasc Intervent Radiol 1987;10:129–133.

50. Odurny A, Colapinto RF, Sniderman KW, Johnston KW. Percutaneous transluminal angioplasty of abdominal aortic stenoses. Cardiovasc Intervent Radiol 1989;12:1–6.

51. Heeney D, Bookstein J, Daniels E, Warmath M, Horn J, Rowley W. Transluminal angioplasty of the abdominal aorta. Radiology 1983;148:81–83.

52. Mitchell SE, Kadir S, Kaufman SL, Chang R, Williams GM, Kan JS, White RI. Percutaneous angioplasty of aortic graft stenoses. Radiology 1983;149:439–444.

53. Tegtmeyer CJ, Wellons HA, Thompson RN. Balloon dilation of the abdominal aorta. JAMA 1980;244(23):2636–2637.

54. Velasquez G, Castaneda-Zuniga W, Formanek A, et al. Nonsurgical aortoplasty in Leriche syndrome. Radiology 1980;134:359–360.

55. Yakes WF, Kumpe DA, Brown SB, et al. Percutaneous transluminal aortic angioplasty: techniques and results. Radiology 1989;172:965–970.

56. Charlebois N, Saint-Georges G, Hudon G. Percutaneous transluminal angioplasty of the lower abdominal aorta. AJR 1986;146:369–371.

57. Selby JB, Tegtmeyer CJ. Angioplasty of abdominal aortic stenoses. In: Kadir S, ed. Current practice in interventional radiology. Philadelphia: Decker, 1991.

58. Ravimandalam K, Rao VRK, Kumar S, Gupta AK, Joseph S, Unni M, Rao AS. Obstruction of the infrarenal portion of the abdominal aorta: results of treatment with balloon angioplasty. AJR 1991;156:1257–1260.

59. Jeans WD, Danton RM, Baird RN, Horrocks M. A comparison of the costs of vascular surgery and balloon dilatation in lower limb ischaemic disease. Br J Radiol 1986;59:453–456.

60. Kinnison ML, White RI, Bowers WP, Dunlap ED. Cost incentives for peripheral angioplasty. AJR 1985;145:1241–1244.

61. Stanson AW. A perspective of percutaneous transluminal angioplasty. Clin Vasc Dis 1983;13(2).

62. Ring EJ, Freiman DB, McLean GK, Schwarz W. Percutaneous recanalization of common iliac artery occlusions: an unacceptable complication rate? AJR 1982;139:587–589.

63. Colapinto RF, Stronell RD, Johnston WK. Transluminal angioplasty of complete iliac obstructions. AJR 1986;146:859–862.

64. Simonetti S, Rossi G, Passariello R, Caboni M, Caratelli M. PTA in external iliac artery occlusion. Eur J Radiol 1981;1:184–186.

65. Pilla TJ, Peterson GJ, Tantana S, Lang ER, Wolverson MK. Percutaneous recanalization of iliac artery occlusions: an alternative to surgery in the high risk patient. AJR 1984;143:313–316.

66. Graziani L. Percutaneous recanalization of total iliac and femoro-popliteal artery occlusions. Eur J Radiol 1987;7:91–93.

67. Johnston KW. Iliac arteries: reanalysis of results of balloon angioplasty. Radiology 1993;186:207–212.

68. Gupta AK, Ravimandalam K, Rao VRK, Joseph S, Unni M, et al. Total occlusion of the iliac arteries: results of balloon angioplasty. Cardiovasc Intervent Radiol 1993;16:165–177.

69. Dotter CT, Rösch J, Seaman AJ. Selective clot lysis with low dose streptokinase. Radiology 1974;111:31–37.

70. Becker GJ, Rabe FE, Richmond BD, et al. Low dose fibrinolytic therapy: results and new concepts. Radiology 1983;148:663–670.

71. Katzen BT, van Breda A. Low dose streptokinase in the treatment of arterial occlusions. AJR 1981;136:1171–1178.

72. Hess H, Ingrisch H, Mietaschk A, Rath H. Local low dose thrombolytic therapy of peripheral arterial occlusions. N Engl J Med 1982;307:1627–1630.

73. McNamara TO, Fischer JR. Thrombolysis of peripheral arterial and graft occlusions: improved results using high dose urokinase. AJR 1985;144:769–775.

74. McNamara TO, Bomberger RA. Factors affecting initial and 6 month patency rates after intraarterial thrombolysis with high dose urokinase. Am J Surg 1986;152:709–712.

75. van Breda A, Katzen BT, Deutsch AS. Urokinase versus streptokinase in local thrombolysis. Radiology 1987;165:109–115.

76. Auster M, Kadir S, Mitchell SE, Williams GM, Perler BA, Chang R, White RI. Iliac artery occlusion: management with intrathrombus streptokinase infusion and angioplasty. Radiology 1984;153:385–388.

77. McNamara TO. Thrombolysis as an alternative initial therapy for the acutely ischemic lower limb. Semin Vasc Surg 1992;5(2):89–98.

78. Mingoli A, Dimarzo L, Sciacca V, et al. Thrombolysis of graft occlusion using high dose urokinase: an alternative to surgical treatment. Ital J Surg Sci 1989;19(1):79–84.

79. Bookstein JJ, Valji K. Pulse-spray pharmacomechanical thrombolysis. Cardiovasc Intervent Radiol 1992;15:228–233.

80. McNamara TO. Thrombolytic therapy for iliac artery occlusions. In: Kadir S, ed. Current practice of interventional radiology. Philadelphia: Decker, 1991:301.

81. Deeter W, Meranze S, Rholl K, McCarter D, van Breda A. Thrombolytic therapy in iliac artery occlusive disease. Abstract: Society of Cardiovascular and Interventional Radiology, annual meeting, 1991, Washington, DC.

82. Palmaz JC, Laborde JC, Rivera FJ, Encarnacion CE, Lutz JD, Moss JG. Stenting of the iliac arteries with the Palmaz stent: experience from a multicenter trial. Cardiovasc Intervent Radiol 1992;15:291–297.

83. Becker GJ. Intravascular stents: general principles and status of lower extremity arterial applications. Circulation 1991;83(Suppl I):122–136.

84. Palmaz JC, Garcia OJ, Schatz RA, et al. Placement of balloon-expandable intraluminal stents in iliac arteries: first 171 procedures. Radiology 1990;174:969–975.

85. Cikrit DF, Becker GJ, Dalsing MC, Ehrman KO, Llka SG, Sawchuk AP. Early experience with the Palmaz expandable intraluminal stent in iliac artery stenosis. Ann Vasc Surg 1991;5:150–155.

86. Bonn J, Gardiner GA, Shapiro MJ, Sullivan KL, Levin DC. Palmaz vascular stent: initial clinical experience. Radiology 1990;174:741–745.

87. Becker GJ, Palmaz JC, Rees CR, Ehrman KO, Lalka SG, Dalsing MC, et al. Angioplasty-induced dissections in human iliac arteries: management with Palmaz balloon-expandable intraluminal stents. Radiology 1990;176:31–38.

88. Gunther RW, Vorwerk D, Antonucci F, et al. Iliac artery stenosis or obstruction after unsuccessful balloon angioplasty: treatment with a self-expandable stent. AJR 1991;156:389–393.

89. Palmaz JC. Balloon-expandable intravascular stent. AJR 1988;150:1263–1269.

90. Rees CR, Palmaz JC, Garcia O, et al. Angioplasty and stenting of completely occluded iliac arteries. Radiology 1989;172:953–959.

91. Günther RW, Vorwerk D, Bohndorf K, Peters I, El-Din A, Messmer B. Iliac and femoral artery stenoses and occlusions: treatment with intravascular stents. Radiology 1989;172:725–730.

92. Vorwerk D, Günther RW. Mechanical revascularization of occluded iliac arteries with use of self-expandable endoprosthesis. Radiology 1990;175:411–415.

93. Long AL, Gaux JC, Raynaud AC, et al. Infrarenal aortic stents: initial clinical experience and angiographic follow-up. Cardiovasc Intervent Radiol 1993;16:203–208.

94. Murphy KJ, Malloy M. Balloon expandable intravascular stents in iliac artery stenosis: preliminary experience. Clin Radiol 1993;47:189–192.

95. Hausegger KA, Lammer J, Hagen B, et al. Iliac artery stenting: clinical experience with the Palmaz stent, Wallstent, and Strecker stent. Acta Radiol 1992;33:292–296.

96. Dyet JF, Shaw JW, Cook AM, Nicholson AA. The use of the Wallstent in aorto-iliac vascular disease. Clin Radiol 1993;48:227–231.

97. Cronenwett J, Davis J, Gooch J, et al. Aortoiliac occlusive disease in women. Surgery 1980;88:775.

98. Karmody AM, Powers SR, Monaco VJ, Leather RP. Blue toe syndrome: an indication for limb salvage surgery. Arch Surg 1976;111:1263–1268.

99. Rutherford RB, Flanigan DP, Gupta SK, et al. Suggested standards for reports dealing with lower extremity ischemia. J Vasc Surg 1986;4:80–90.

100. Rutherford RB, Becker GJ. Standards for evaluating and reporting the results of surgical and percutaneous therapy for peripheral arterial disease. J Vasc Intervent Radiol 1991;2:169–174.

101. Marinelli MR, Beach KW, Glass MJ, et al. Noninvasive testing vs. clinical evaluation of arterial disease: a prospective study. JAMA 1979;241:2031.

102. Becker GJ. Noncoronary angioplasty. Radiology 1989;170:921–940.

103. Gardiner GA, Meyerovitz MF, Stokes KR, Clouse ME, Harrington DP, Bettmann MA. Complications of transluminal angioplasty. Radiology 1986;159:201–208.

104. Casarella WR. Noncoronary angioplasty. Curr Probl Cardiol 1986;11:138–174.

105. Kashdan BJ, Trost DW, Jagust MB, Rackson ME, Sos TA. Retrograde approach for contralateral iliac and infrainguinal percutaneous transluminal angioplasty: experience in 100 patients. J Vasc Intervent Radiol 1992;3:515–521.

106. Bachman DM, Casarella WJ, Sos TA. Percutaneous iliofemoral angioplasty via the contralateral femoral artery. Radiology 1979;130:617–621.

107. Kumpe DA. Percutaneous dilatation of an abdominal aortic stenosis. Radiology 1981;141:536–538.

108. Cragg AH, Smith TP, Corson JD, Nakagawa N, Castaneda F, et al. Two urokinase dose regimens in native arterial and graft occlusions: initial results of a prospective randomized clinical trial. Radiology 1991;178:681–684.

109. Murphy TP, Lambiase RE, Haas RA, Dorfman GS, Webb MS, et al. Endovascular revascularization of diffusely diseased and chronically occluded iliac arteries with Wallstents. J Vasc Intervent Radiol; in press.

110. Kim D, Gianturco LE, Porter DH, et al. Peripheral directional atherectomy: 4-year experience. Radiology 1992;183:773–778.

111. Clugston RA, Eisenhauer AC, Matthews RV. Atherectomy of the distal aorta using a "kissing-balloon" technique for the treatment of blue toe syndrome. AJR 1992;159:125–127.

112. Hinohara T, Selmon MR, Robertson GC, Braden L, Simpson JS. Directional atherectomy: new approaches for treatment of obstructive coronary and peripheral vascular disease. Circulation 1991;81(Suppl IV):79–91.

113. Maynar M, Reyes R, Cabera V, et al. Percutaneous atherectomy as an alternative treatment for post-angioplasty obstructive intimal flaps. Radiology 1989;170:1029–1031.

114. McAllister FF. The rate of patients with intermittent claudication managed nonoperatively. Am J Surg 1976;132:593–595.

115. Ekroth R, Dahllof AG, Gundevall B, Holm J, Schersten T. Physical training of patients with intermittent claudication: indications, methods, and results. Surgery 1978;84:640–643.

116. Guidelines for percutaneous transluminal angioplasty: standards of Practice Committee of the Society of Cardiovascular and Interventional Radiology. Radiology 1990;177:619–626.

117. Weber G, Kiss T. Intraoperative balloon angioplasty. Eur J Vasc Surg 1989;3:153–157.

118. Wilms G, Nevelsteen A, Baert A, Suy R. Intraoperative angioplasty. Cardiovasc Intervent Radiol 1987;10:8–12.

119. Al-Salman M, Doyle DL, Hsiang YN, Fry PD, Fragoso M. Intraoperative balloon angioplasty: a surgical approach. Can Soc Vasc Surg 1992;35(3):265–268.

120. Spoelstra H, Nevelsteen A, Wilms G, Suy R. Balloon angioplasty combined with vascular surgery. Eur J Vasc Surg 1989;3:381–388.

121. Griffith CDM, Harrison JD, Gregson RHS, Makin GS, Hopkinson BR. Transluminal iliac angioplasty with distal bypass surgery in patients with critical limb ischaemia. J R Coll Surg Edinb 1989;34:253–255.

122. Zeitler E, Raithel D, Gailer H, Nippold AV, Kasprczk. PTA combined with surgical vascular operations in iliac and femoral obstruction. Ann Radiol 1987;30(2):142–144.

123. Olbert F, Weidinger P, Schlegl A, Teiner G, Hagmuller GW, Denck H. Combined transluminal percutaneous dilation and surgical reconstruction of the iliac, femoral and popliteal arteries. Ann Radiol 1981;24(5):369–374.

124. Wilson SE, White GH, Wolf G, Cross AP. Proximal percutaneous balloon angioplasty and distal bypass for multilevel arterial occlusion. Ann Vasc Surg 1990;4:351–355.

125. Walker PJ, Harris JP, May J. Combined percutaneous transluminal angioplasty and extraanatomic bypass for symptomatic unilateral iliac artery occlusion with contralateral iliac artery stenosis. Ann Vasc Surg 1991;5:209–217.

126. Brewster DC, Cambria RP, Darling RC, et al. Long-term results of combined iliac balloon angioplasty and distal surgical revascularization. Ann Surg 1989;210(3):324–331.

127. Kadir S, Smith GW, White RI, et al. Percutaneous transluminal angioplasty as an adjunct to the surgical management of peripheral vascular disease. Ann Surg 1982;195(6):786–795.

128. Motarjeme A, Keifer JW, Zuska AJ. Percutaneous transluminal angioplasty as a complement to surgery. Radiology 1981;141:341–346.

129. Corey CJ, Bush HL, Widrich WC, Nabseth DC. Combined operative angiodilation and arterial reconstruction for limb salvage. Arch Surg 1983;118:1289–1292.

130. Bunt TJ. Aortic reconstruction versus extra-anatomic bypass and angioplasty. Arch Surg 1986;121:1166–1171.

131. Peterkin GA, Belkin M, Cantelmo NL, Guben J, Greenfield AJ, Johnson WC, Menzoian JO. Combined transluminal angioplasty and infrainguinal reconstruction in multilevel atherosclerotic disease. Am J Surg 1990;160:277–279.

132. Wilson SE, Wolf GL, Cross AP. Percutaneous transluminal angioplasty versus operation for peripheral arteriosclerosis. J Vasc Surg 1989;9:1–9.

133. Johnston KW, Colapinto RF, Baird RJ. Transluminal dilation—an alternative? Arch Surg 1982;117:1604–1610.

134. Hallett JW. Trends in revascularization of the lower extremity. Mayo Clin Proc 1986;61:369–376.
135. Brothers TE, Greenfield LJ. Long-term results of aortoiliac reconstruction. J Vasc Intervent Radiol 1990;1:49–55.
136. Whittemore AD, Mannick JA. The ischemic leg. Adv Surg 1981;15:293–316.
137. Daniell SJN, Dacie JE, Lumley JSP. Is percutaneous transluminal angioplasty for common iliac occlusion a safe procedure? J Vasc Intervent Radiol 1987;2:89–95.
138. Ginsburg R, Thorpe P, Bowles CR, Wright AM, Wexler L. Pull-through approach to percutaneous angioplasty of totally occluded common iliac arteries. Radiology 1989;172:111–113.
139. Dolmatch BL, Rholl KS, Moskowitz LB, et al. Blue toe syndrome: treatment with percutaneous atherectomy. Radiology 1989;172:799–804.
140. Kumpe DA, Zwerdzinger S, Griffin DJ. Blue digit syndrome: treatment with percutaneous transluminal angioplasty. Radiology 1988;166:37–44.
141. Brewer ML, Kinnison ML, Perler BA, White RI. Blue toe syndrome: treatment with anticoagulants and delayed percutaneous transluminal angioplasty. Radiology 1988;166:31–36.
142. Castaneda-Zuniga WR, Smith A, Kaye K, et al. Transluminal angioplasty for treatment of vasculogenic impotence. AJR 1962;139:371–373.
143. Van Unnik JG, Marsman JWP. Impotence due to the external iliac steal syndrome treated by percutaneous transluminal angioplasty. J Urol 1984;131:544–545.
144. Becker GJ, Rowe DM, Holden RW, Dalsing MC, Bendick PJ. Percutaneous transluminal angioplasty for vasculogenic impotence. Indiana Med 1986;79:256–262.
145. Weigele JB. Iliac artery stenosis causing renal allograft-mediated hypertension: angiographic diagnosis and treatment. AJR 1991;157:513–515.
146. Clement C, Costa-Foru B, Vernon P, Nicaise H. Transluminal angioplasty performed by the surgeon in lower limb arterial occlusive disease: one hundred fifty cases. Ann Vasc Surg 1990;4:519–527.
147. Harris RW, Dulawa LB, Andros G, Oblath RW, Salles-Cunha SX, Apyan RL. Percutaneous transluminal angioplasty of the lower extremities by the vascular surgeon. Ann Vasc Surg 1991;5:345–353.
148. Cole SEA, Baird RN, Horrocks M, Jeans WD. The role of balloon angioplasty in the management of lower limb ischaemia. J Vasc Surg 1987;1:61–65.
149. Glover JL, Bendick PJ, Dilley RS, Becker GJ, Richmond BC, Yune HY, Holden RW. Balloon catheter dilation for limb salvage. Arch Surg 1983;118:557–560.
150. Kwasnik EM, Siouffi SY, Jay ME, Khuri SF. Comparative results of angioplasty and aortofemoral bypass in patients with symptomatic iliac disease. Arch Surg 1987;122:288–291.
151. Samson RH, Sprayregen S, Veith FJ, Scher LA, Gupta SK, Ascer E. Management of angioplasty complications, unsuccessful procedures and early and late failures. Ann Surg 1984;199(2):234–240.
152. Brewster DC. Clinical and anatomical considerations for surgery in aortoiliac disease and results of surgical treatment. Circulation 1991;83(Suppl I):42–52.
153. Armstrong MWJ, Torrie EPH, Galland RB. Consequences of immediate failure of percutaneous transluminal angioplasty. Ann R Coll Surg Engl 1992;74:265–268.
154. Belli AM, Cumberland DC, Knox AM, Procter AE, Welsh CL. The complication rate of percutaneous peripheral balloon angioplasty. Clin Radiol 1990;41:380–383.
155. Crawford ES, Manning LG, Kelly TF. "Redo" surgery after operations for aneurysm and occlusion of the abdominal aorta. Surgery 1977;81(1):41–52.
156. Hallisey M, Meranze S, Parker BC, Rholl K, Miller W, et al. Percutaneous transluminal angioplasty of the abdominal aorta. Abstract: Society of Cardiovascular and Interventional Radiology, annual meeting, 1993, New Orleans, LA.
157. El Ashmaoui A, Do DD, Triller J, Stirnemann P, Mahler F. Angioplasty of the terminal aorta: follow-up of 20 patients treated by PTA or PTA with stents. Eur J Radiol 1991;13:113–117.
158. Tyagi S, Kaul UA, Nair M, Sethi KK, Arora R, et al. Balloon angioplasty of the aorta in Takayasu's arteritis: initial and long-term results. Am Heart J 1992;124:876–882.
159. Rao SA, Mandalam KR, Rao VR, Gupta AK, Joseph S, et al. Takayasu's arteritis: initial and long-term follow-up in 16 patients after percutaneous transluminal angioplasty of the descending thoracic and abdominal aorta. Radiology 1993;189:173–179.
160. Park JH, Han MC, Lim SH, Oh BH, Park YB, et al. Takayasu arteritis: angiographic findings and results of angioplasty. AJR 1989;153:1069–1074.
161. Ouriel K, Shortell CK, DeWeese JA, Green RM, Francis CW. A comparison of thrombolytic therapy with operative revascularization in the initial treatment of acute peripheral arterial ischemia. J Vasc Surg 1994;19:1021–1030.
162. Vorwerk D, Gunther RW, Bohndorf K, Keulers P. Stent placement for failed angioplasty of aortic stenoses: report of two cases. Cardiovasc Intervent Radiol 1991;14:316–319.
163. Palmaz JC, Encamacion CE, Garcia OJ, Schatz RA, Rivera FJ, et al. Aortic bifurcation stenosis: treatment with intravascular stents. J Vasc Intervent Radiol 1991;2:319–323.
164. Kuffer G, Spengel F, Steckmeier B. Percutaneous reconstruction of the aortic bifurcation with Palmaz stents: case reports. Cardiovasc Intervent Radiol 1991;14:170–172.
165. Vorwerk D, Gunther RW. Stent placement in iliac arterial lesions: three years of clinical experience with the Wallstent. Cardiovasc Intervent Radiol 1992;15:285–290.
166. Rousseau H, Joffre F, Raillat C, Duboucher C, Glock Y, Escourrou G. Iliac artery endoprosthesis: radiologic and histologic findings after 2 years. AJR 1989;153:1075–1076.
167. Long AL, Page PE, Raynaud AC, Beyssen BM, Fiessinger JN, et al. Percutaneous iliac artery stent: angiographic long-term follow-up. Radiology 1991;180:771–778.
168. Zollikofer CL, Antonucci F, Pfyffer M, Redha F, Salomonowitz E, et al. Arterial stent placement with use of the Wallstent: midterm results of clinical experience. Radiology 1991;179:449–456.
169. Raillat C, Rousseau H, Joffre F, Roux D. Treatment of iliac artery stenoses with the Wallstent endoprosthesis. AJR 1990;154:613–616.
170. Richter G, Roeren T, Brado M, Noeldge G. Further update of the randomized trial: iliac stent placement versus PTA—morphology, clinical success rates, and failure analysis. Abstract: Society of Cardiovascular and Interventional Radiology, 1993.
171. Henry M, Amor M, Ethevenot G, Henry M, Allaoui M, et al. Placement of Palmaz stents in the iliac and femoral arteries: four-year follow-up. Abstract: Society of Cardiovascular and Interventional Radiology, annual meeting, 1994, Ft. Lauderdale, FL.
172. Sapoval MR, Long A, Chatellier G, Gaux JC, Raynard A, et al. Reassessment of long-term patency after successful placement of a Wallstent in the iliac artery and multivariate analysis of prognostic factors. Abstract: Society of Cardiovascular and Interventional Radiology, annual meeting, 1994, Ft Lauderdale, FL.
173. Wescott MA, Bonn J. Comparison of conventional angioplasty and angioplasty with stent placement in the treatment of abdominal aortic stenoses from the STAR registry. Abstract: Society of Cardiovascular and Interventional Radiology, annual meeting, 1994, Ft. Lauderdale, FL.
174. Blum U, Gabelmann A, Redecker M, Noldge G, Dornberg W, et al. Percutaneous recanalization of iliac artery occlusions: results of a prospective study. Radiology 1993;189:536–540.
175. Weibull H, Bergqvist D, Jonsson K, Karlsson S, Takolander R. Complications after percutaneous transluminal angioplasty in the iliac, femoral, and popliteal. J Vasc Surg 1987;5:681–686.
176. Joseph N, Levy E, Lipman S. Angioplasty-related iliac artery rupture: treatment by temporary balloon occlusion. Cardiovasc Intervent Radiol 1987;10:276–279.

18

Femoropopliteal Revascularization

ERIC C. MARTIN

Before considering the techniques and results of percutaneous femoropopliteal revascularization, it is important to know the distribution of peripheral vascular disease. A recent multicenter study involving 440 consecutive patients demonstrated that femoropopliteal disease was three times more frequent than iliac disease.[1] Among the patients with femoropopliteal disease, occlusions are about three times more frequent than stenoses, whereas in the iliac system stenoses predominate by about the same factor. Therefore, the majority of patients with significant peripheral vascular disease have femoropopliteal occlusions. When one plots the relative frequency of femoropopliteal lesions against length, the slope for stenoses is approximately asymptotic, with about 80 percent of patients having stenoses 10 cm or less in length. However, only about 20 percent of occlusions are 10 cm or less in length (Fig. 18-1). This would suggest that, because 10 cm is the upper limit of length with good long-term success after angioplasty, only about 35 percent of patients with femoropopliteal disease and significant symptoms are suitable candidates for the procedure.[2] This should be borne in mind when considering angioplasty, and it makes the comparison of angioplasty with surgery unsatisfactory. It is also important to recall these data when considering the role of the newer endoluminal revascularization devices.

History of Angioplasty

In 1964 Dotter and Judkins described the first angioplasty performed in the femoropopliteal system with coaxial systems up to 12 French in diameter.[3] These catheters were later modified by Staple[4] and then by Van Andel, who used serial tapered dilators.[5] However, it was not until Gruntzig and Hopff designed the coaxial balloon catheter, which inflated to a fixed diameter, that angioplasty came to be used with any frequency, particularly in the United States.[6] Nevertheless, Gruntzig and Hopff's balloons were made of polyvinyl chloride and were relatively compliant; that is, they increased their diameter considerably with

pressure. However, above the working pressure of 2 to 6 atm the change was no more than 1 to 2 mm. Since then, less compliant materials, such as polyethylene, have maintained fixed diameters through a wide range of pressures.[7]

There have been significant advances in balloon technology, particularly in size, trackability, and profile, as well as concomitant advances in the pharmacologic adjuncts to angioplasty. This progress, when combined with the improvement in image intensification and digital subtraction imaging, has contributed to the increasing efficacy and safety of the procedure and the gradual increase in the number of procedures performed.[2]

With the acceptance of balloon angioplasty came the development of other methods of recanalization, which will be discussed briefly. Enormous effort went into the development of laser angioplasty in the mid-1980s, and at about the same time the directional atherectomy catheter was described by Simpson et al.[8] Modifications of this device continue to be developed, but few have undergone rigorous testing. The late 1980s saw the development of intravascular stents,[9-12] but to date they have been disappointing in the femoropopliteal position.[13] They have, however, spawned considerable research into covered stents employing polytetrafluoroethylene (PTFE), and preliminary work has been undertaken in the femoropopliteal system.[14]

Technique of Angioplasty

Stenoses

Occasionally, it may be convenient to perform angioplasty of stenoses from the contralateral side, for example, when one is also performing iliac angioplasty, but usually this technique should only be used in short-segment lesions that appear easy to cross. The most frequent use of a contralateral approach is after urokinase perfusion performed around the bifurcation. Otherwise, all femoropopliteal angioplasties are performed with an antegrade puncture. A sheath may be

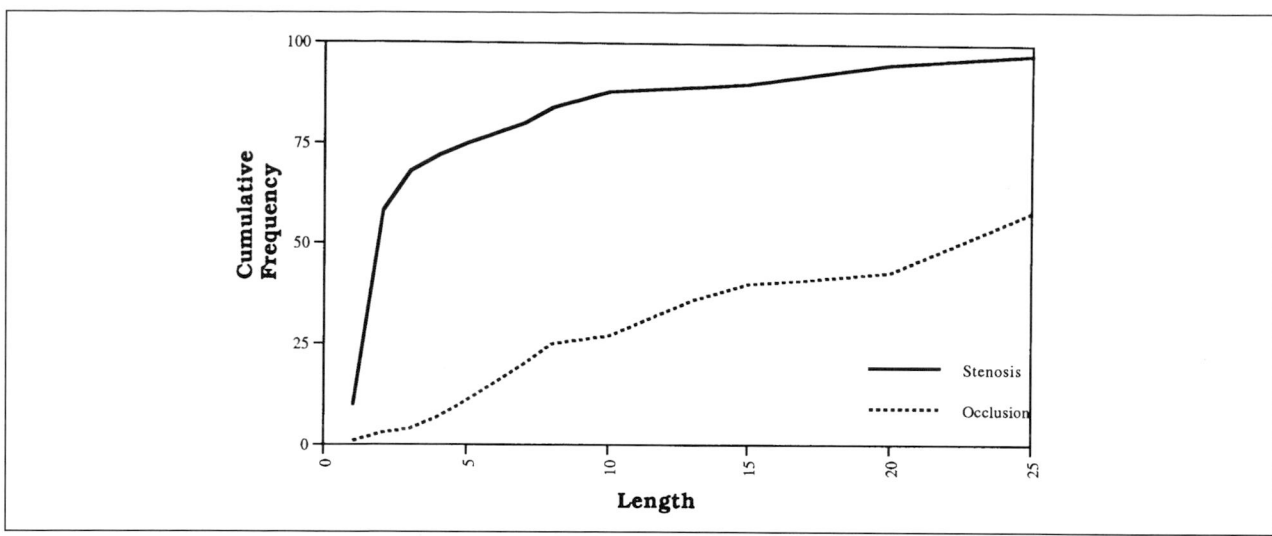

Figure 18-1. Cumulative relative frequency plotted against length for stenoses and occlusions in the femoropopliteal system. (From Martin EC. Transcatheter therapies in peripheral and noncoronary vascular disease. Circulation 1991;83[Suppl I]: 1–5. Used with permission.)

useful, both to reduce trauma to the vessel and to give one the opportunity of injecting through the side arm of the sheath for road-mapping or otherwise delineating the vessel. Nevertheless, although the author feels that sheaths are mandatory for infrapopliteal procedures, they remain optional in the femoropopliteal system.

All patients are heparinized once the catheter is in the vessel, and, in the author's practice, all patients are pretreated with calcium channel blockers. For short-segment stenoses, the balloon catheter is advanced to several centimeters above the stenosis, an image is taken, and the stenosis is crossed with a guidewire. The catheter should be parallel to the line of the vessel when approaching the stenosis. When the superficial femoral artery describes a general curve, the catheter must approximate that curve; otherwise the guidewire will not aim at the center of the stenosis. It may be desirable, therefore, not to use the balloon catheter primarily but to use an appropriately curved catheter and then cross the lesion and exchange over a Rosen wire. For most stenoses, a Newton guidewire is suitable for crossing the lesion, and this may be modified with a slight curve at the tip. Some physicians prefer the softer Bentson wire, and more recently there has been considerable interest in the hydrophilic wires. Nevertheless, for stenoses, great care must be taken not to dissect. The guidewire must be directed through the point of the stenosis no matter how eccentric it is. Once across the obstruction, the balloon catheter is inflated for 1 minute, and some physicians prefer to perfuse the catheter with saline during this

period. When the balloon is deflated, a phasic pressure trace should be observed, but pullback gradients with balloon-mounted catheters in the femoropopliteal system are not reliable. As the balloon is inflated, one should observe the patient for pain, which should be relieved by deflating the catheter. As the balloon is deflated, the appearance of the balloon gives some information; a persistent waist usually indicates an inadequate dilatation. Persistent pain unrelieved by balloon deflation may indicate vessel rupture, but this is seldom catastrophic—unlike in the iliac system.

The catheter is then pulled back above the lesion—over a guidewire if there is a sheath in place—and contrast injected to assess the result. If satisfactory, the runoff is filmed to make sure there has not been distal embolization. If the appearances are unsatisfactory, the lesion is recrossed and the balloon is reinflated. It may be necessary to change to a larger balloon. Most patients with femoropopliteal disease should be dilated with 6-mm balloons, but occasionally 5-, 7-, or even 8-mm balloons will be the primary choice. The balloon should be slightly larger than the normal vessel lumen.

Occlusions

Antegrade punctures are essential for all occlusions, and sheaths are usually used. Once the lesion is filmed and one knows the point of occlusion and reconstitution as well as the shape of the proximal portion of the occlusion, a 5 French Van Andel catheter is positioned 4 or 5 cm above the occlusion, and the lesion is gently probed with a Newton straight wire. Again, as with stenoses, the catheter should be parallel to the vessel just above the occlusion so that the guidewire is centered properly. With a small curve in the distal end of the guidewire, one can change the radius by advancing and retracting the catheter to explore different portions of the occlusion. Nevertheless, exploring the edge of the lesion is likely to lead to a subintimal passage. Again, as in stenoses, a curved catheter may be necessary. If the Newton guidewire is unsuccessful, a hydrophilic wire can be tried and can usually be manipulated through the obstruction. However, these wires are relatively stiff and must be used with caution. Once subintimal dissection has occurred, it is frequently difficult to reenter the lumen. If these two wires are unsuccessful, the so-called snow plow technique may be employed, which is used in about 15 percent of cases in the author's practice. It is occasionally necessary because a collateral arises at the site of the obstruction so that the guidewire always passes down the collateral and the point of obstruction cannot be engaged. With the snow plow technique, a Van Andel catheter is used with a Rosen guidewire just protruding from it so that the tight J of the Rosen wire protects the tip. The catheter and wire are then advanced as a unit across the obstruction into the distal vessel (Fig. 18-2). The disadvantage of this technique is that if a subintimal passage is obtained it is difficult to reenter the true lumen. If the problem is a collateral, one may start with the snow plow technique for the first 2 cm and then switch to the hydrophilic wire technique to complete the crossing.

Once one is in the distal vessel and this is confirmed by a contrast injection, an exchange is made over a Rosen guidewire for the appropriate balloon catheter, and inflation is performed from distal to proximal to cover the length of the lesion. Balloons 4 cm long are usually satisfactory, but for very long lesions 10-cm balloons may be desirable.

For sequential lesions, it is preferable, but not always possible, to cross all lesions and work from distal to proximal. Once dilatation is complete, the operator pulls back over a guidewire and performs a contrast injection. If a sheath has been used, the lesion may then be easily and safely recrossed for reinflation either with the same or a larger balloon. Again, it is important to inject contrast, not only to examine the angioplasty site but also to examine distally for embolization, since emboli will lead to occlusion and usually can be managed with urokinase perfusion.

Because one of the best prognosticators of good long-term patency is a palpable pulse, the author also dilates a single proximal tibial or posterior tibial-peroneal trunk stenosis at the same time as the femoral angioplasty. This is a new addition to the technique and springs from the increasing safety of distal angioplasty. Whereas formerly tibial angioplasty was only recommended for limb salvage, the author feels that a proximal lesion may be dilated with minimal risk and that doing so improves the long-term patency of the femoropopliteal lesion. This belief is still undocumented, and it can only be recommended for centers with extensive experience and low complication rates.

Figure 18-2. Techniques for crossing femoropopliteal lesions. (A) A Newton guide crossing the occlusion. (B) A curved catheter to align the Newton wire. (C) The snow plow technique.

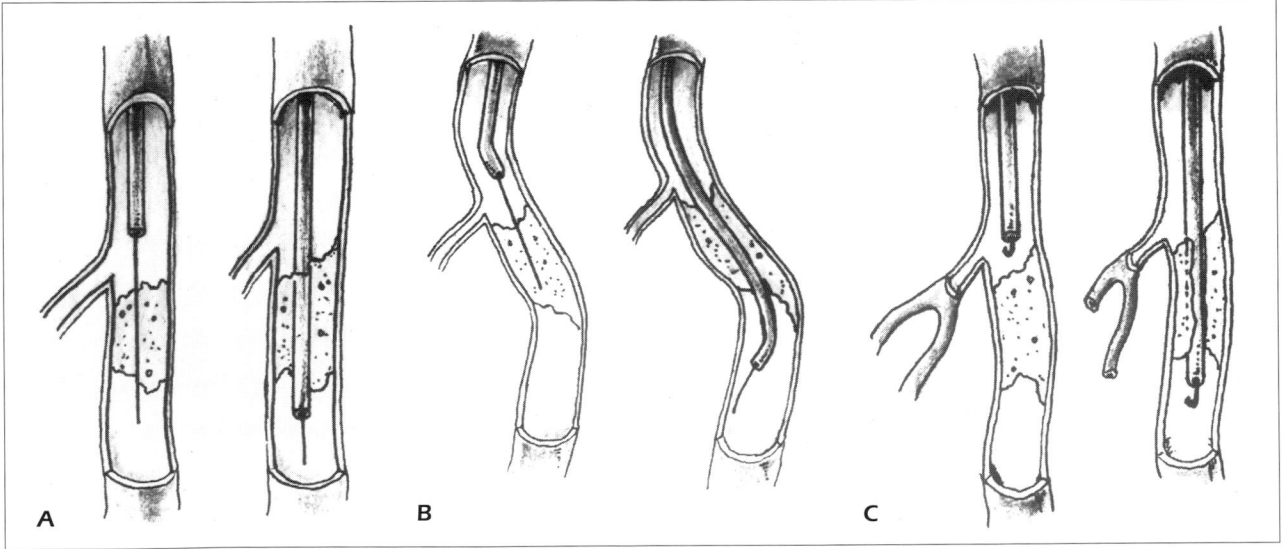

Patient Care During Angioplasty

Standards of care do not differ from those for iliac angioplasty and have been described in Chapter 17. Guidelines published previously[15] and most recently by the American Heart Association (AHA)[16] should be followed.

Criteria for Assessing the Results of Angioplasty

The angioplasty literature has been inconsistent in its reporting, and comparison between studies is difficult. More difficult still is the comparison between angioplasty and surgery, if, indeed, it is warranted because of the different patient populations. Rutherford et al. have attempted to introduce rigid reporting standards, with mixed success.[17] These criteria have recently been modified by Rutherford and Becker for interventional procedures.[18] As Rutherford has said,[19] "One clinician's definition of success or failure may not agree with that of another and who is to say which definition is correct. . . . Overly strict standards are bound to be unpopular. . . . However, it must ultimately be realized that there is more to be gained by compromising and adopting uniform standards."

Interventional radiologists initially reported only successful angioplasties, arguing that these patients were in any case going to have surgery and that, if the radiologist failed to cross the lesion, the intention to treat was not altered. Equally, surgeons have argued that a graft that suffers an immediate postoperative thrombosis that is then successfully reopened should be followed as a primary patency. However, it is important to know both primary and secondary patency rates, and strict reporting standards will achieve this. These standards have yet to be strictly enforced.

An example of the problem in reporting is Johnston et al.'s criteria for a successful iliac angioplasty, which are, not unreasonably, both symptomatic improvement *and* a persistent improvement in the ankle-brachial index.[20] However, over a 5-year period, 15 to 25 percent of patients will develop a new femoropopliteal occlusion and thereby lower their ankle-brachial index. The long-term patency of the angioplasty site will therefore be spuriously low. Under these circumstances, angiographic patency would be more accurate but frequently is unobtainable. Strict reporting standards will make comparisons valid but will not always reflect the absolute truth. The term *long-term patency* is used frequently, yet it is only validly applied to angiographic patency, patency documented at surgery, and, probably now, patency documented by color flow Doppler ultrasound or magnetic resonance angiography. Yet there is obviously a need for clinically derived patency. The Rutherford-Becker criteria supply it.[18] However, to confound the issue further, patients with documented patent grafts may be clinically worse, just as patients with occluded grafts may be symptomatically improved. The Rutherford-Becker criteria for reporting improvement are described below.

Criteria for improvement after percutaneous intervention should be divided into early and late success. Early success should be judged by a combination of clinical, hemodynamic, and angiographic factors, with all three necessary to consider the procedure successful. Clinical improvement should include symptomatic improvement and change in at least one category on the Rutherford scale. Hemodynamic improvement should be defined as an increase in the ankle-brachial index of 0.1 or greater. In the case of diabetic patients with incompressible vessels, the pulse volume recording distal to the revascularization site should increase by 5 mm above preprocedural testing. Angiographic success should result in less than a 30 percent residual stenosis. Changes in the condition of the extremity should be categorized on a scale of +3 to −3 (Table 18-1).

Percutaneous interventions require a modification of the Rutherford criteria to permit a comparison of endovascular techniques. For example, whether an obstruction in the femoral artery is a stenosis or an occlusion is important to the interventionalist but irrelevant

Table 18-1. Changes in the Condition of the Extremity After Percutaneous Intervention

Grade	Clinical Description
+3	Markedly improved: symptoms gone or markedly improved; ABI increased to more than 0.90
+2	Moderately improved: still symptomatic, but at least a single-category improvement; ABI increased by more than 0.10 but not normalized
+1	Minimally improved: greater than 0.10 increase in ABI but no categorical improvement, or vice versa (i.e., upward categorical shift without an increase in ABI of more than 0.10)
0	No change: no categorical shift and less than 0.10 change in ABI
−1	Mildly worse: no categorical shift but ABI decreased by more than 0.10, or downward categorical shift with ABI decreased less than 0.10
−2	Moderately worse: one category worse or unexpected minor amputation
−3	Markedly worse: more than one category worse or unexpected major amputation

Table 18-2. Clinical Categories of Chronic Limb Ischemia

Grade	Category	Clinical Description	Objective Criteria
0	0	Asymptomatic: no hemodynamically significant occlusive disease	Normal treadmill/stress test
1	1	Mild claudication	Completes treadmill exercise, AP after exercise <50 mmHg but >25 mmHg less than BP
	2	Moderate claudication	Between categories 1 and 3
	3	Severe claudication	Cannot complete treadmill exercise; AP after exercise <50 mmHg
2	4	Ischemic rest pain	Resting AP <40 mmHg; flat or barely pulsatile ankle or metatarsal PVR; toe pressure <30 mmHg
3	5	Minor tissue loss: nonhealing ulcer, focal gangrene with diffuse pedal ischemia	Resting AP <60 mmHg; ankle metatarsal PVR flat or barely pulsatile; toe pressure <40 mmHg
	6	Major tissue loss extending above TM level; functional foot no longer salvageable	Same as category 5

Abbreviations: AP = ankle pressure; BP = blood pressure; PVR = pulse volume recording; TM = transmetatarsal.

to the surgeon. Arterial lesions have to be described by location and type, and the length should be quantified. The status of the runoff vessels should also be defined. The clinical categories of chronic limb ischemia are listed in Table 18-2.

Results of Angioplasty

Although there have been numerous reports of the results of femoropopliteal percutaneous transluminal angioplasty (PTA), most do not meet the reporting standards of Rutherford and Becker because their criteria were only recently described. Becker et al. reviewed the combined results of femoropopliteal PTA (including stenoses and occlusions from several clinical series) and found the mean success rate to be 81 percent in 4304 procedures and 89 percent in 1362 cases reported in the previous 6 years.[21] With follow-up on approximately one-third of the original number of patients, the mean 4- to 5-year patency was 67 percent. In a cooperative study from 14 hospitals involving 2337 patients, there was a primary success rate of 87 percent and a 5-year patency rate of 64 percent.[22]

Adar et al. developed a form of metaanalysis called the *confidence profile method* to analyze combined data from 12 selected series. They derived the best estimate of the expected outcome of femoropopliteal angioplasty in patients with intermittent claudication and with more severe limb-threatening ischemia.[23] In this report, the early success rate for angioplasty for claudication was 89 percent, compared with 77 percent for limb salvage. The 3-year patency rate was 62 percent for patients with claudication and 43 percent for those angioplasties performed for limb salvage. The largest decline in patency occurred in the first year. The difference in long-term patency between patients with clau-

dication and those with limb-threatening ischemia was assumed to be caused by the difference in runoff.

In 1989 Wilson et al. reported on a randomized trial of angioplasty against surgery from the Veterans Administration that involved 98 patients with femoropopliteal disease.[24] Fifty-nine percent of the angioplasties were patent at 3 years, a result that was not statistically different from the surgical results. The criticism of this series is that, in order to be randomized, all patients had to be eligible for both angioplasty and surgery; therefore, this group of patients had less severe disease than those in most surgical series. These results mirror an old study from 1981 comparing the results of angioplasty for femoral artery occlusion with surgery in a single institution.[25] The patients were approximately matched for symptoms, the incidence of diabetes, and the runoff. Sixty percent of patients were in Society of Vascular Surgery grades 2 or 3. At 1 year, there was no significant difference between the results of angioplasty and the overall result of bypass grafting. However, the results of saphenous vein bypass grafting were 20 percent better than for angioplasty at 1 year, although only 50 percent of the patients in the surgical group received vein grafts.

Although the majority of patients in angioplasty series have stenoses rather than occlusions, multiple or long-segment stenoses fare particularly badly. In 1987, Murray et al. reported on a group of patients with long-segment stenoses (>7 cm) that had a 6-month patency of 23 percent.[26] Although these results have not been systematically repeated, they are similar to the results of long occlusions (over 10 cm), which have similarly disappointing results.[27]

Fewer studies have drawn attention to the capabilities of angioplasty in total femoropopliteal occlusion. The author and colleagues reviewed the initial results of angioplasty in 116 consecutive patients with complete femoropopliteal artery occlusions who were treated at their institution. Between 1977 and 1980 they performed angioplasty in 46 patients and achieved a technical success rate of 74 percent.[25] In the subsequent study period between 1981 and 1988, angioplasty was performed in 70 patients and the technical success rate increased to 91 percent.[28] During the study period, equipment improved markedly. Balloons now have a lower profile, and 5 French balloons can be used exclusively. In addition, the routine administration of an oral calcium channel blocker (nifedipine) in conjunction with intraarterial nitroglycerin is now a routine part of the angioplasty procedure. Patient selection for angioplasty has also changed as the results have become known. In the first study period, for example, the authors tried to treat occlusions 20 cm in length, whereas in the more recent series no patient had an occlusion longer than 10 cm. During the same period, the skill of the interventionalists also improved. These initial success rates are now standard in recent series, and the procedure is about 20 percent more successful than in series from the early 1980s (Tables 18-3 and 18-4).

Two series deserve further review. The first is a retrospective review of 217 angioplasties performed on 152 patients between 1978 and 1986 at the Hospital of University of Pennsylvania, with the majority of patients being studied in 1979 and 1980.[27] Selection of patients for the series was weighted toward those cases with complete data profiles so that a 10-year follow-up could be obtained. Most patients were therefore dilated with polyvinyl balloons and did not have the benefit of calcium channel blockers or nitroglycerin.

Table 18-3. Technical Success of Angioplasty in Femoropopliteal Occlusion

Angioplasty Study	Published Date	No. of Cases	Initial Success Rate (%)
Zeitler[29]	1980		
SFA[a] occlusions <10 cm		304	81
SFA[a] occlusions >10 cm		133	54
Popliteal occlusions		34	62
Martin et al.[25]	1981	46	74
Waltman et al.[30]	1982	34	76
Tamura et al.[31]	1982	22	86
Krepel et al.[32]	1985		
Occlusions <3 cm		18	89
Occlusions >3 cm		19	26
Murray et al.[26]	1987	77	78
Johnston et al.[20]	1987	79	73–87[b]
Levy et al.[33]	1989	23	91
Morgenstern et al.[28]	1989	70	91
Capek et al.[27]	1991	50	82

[a]SFA = superficial femoral artery.
[b]Depending on status of distal runoff and clinical indication.

Table 18-4. Long-Term Patency of Angioplasty in Femoropopliteal Occlusions

Angioplasty Study	Published Date	No. of Cases	Follow-up Period (yr)	Patency Rate (%)
Martin et al.[25]	1981	46	2.0	68.2[a]
Murray et al.[26]	1987	77	4.5	72.9
Zeitler[29]	1990			
Occlusions <3 cm		58		70.0
		59		66.0
Occlusions 3–10 cm		104		65.0
		88		54.0
Capek et al.[27]	1990	50	7[b]	
(Occlusions)				
<1 cm				64.0[a]
1–3 cm				55.0[a]
3–5 cm				50.0[a]
5–7 cm				37.0[a]
7–10 cm				37.0[a]
Total		482	2–7	64.0[c]

[a]Excluding technical failures.
[b]Mean follow-up 7 years (range 2–11 years).
[c]Mean patency rate.

Follow-up in the series was by segmental Doppler arterial leg pressures and pulse volume recordings initially and thereafter annually for an indefinite period. In patients in whom the ankle-brachial pressure index fell by 0.2 compared to the immediate postangioplasty index, a repeat arteriogram was performed if possible. Repeat arteriography was performed in 71 out of the 152 patients. Most patients were studied for mild to moderate claudication (74 percent), with 26 percent being in SVS grades 2 and 3. Diabetes was present in 33 percent of patients. Forty percent of patients had one- or zero-vessel runoff.

Overall, the 10-year primary patency was 38 percent and the secondary patency was 40 percent, with an initial technical success rate of 90 percent (Fig. 18-3). If one excludes the technical failures from this series, predominantly from 1979, the 5-year patency rises to 58 percent. The prognosis of stenoses appears to be considerably better than for occlusions, but these data are confounded by the primary success of crossing lesions in this series (Fig. 18-4). Failure to cross a stenosis and perform an angioplasty occurred in 7 percent of patients, whereas in 18 percent of occlusions the lesions could not be crossed. Because the life-table curves for stenoses and occlusions are parallel, with the occlusions starting 11 percent lower, it is not unreasonable to assume that with the 91 percent primary success rate expected today these two curves would be superimposed. The data also indicate that angioplasty of an occlusion, if technically successful, carries the same prognosis for long-term patency as angioplasty of a stenosis, an observation previously made by others.[32–35]

This series is valuable for a number of reasons, not least of all in demonstrating the durability of angio-

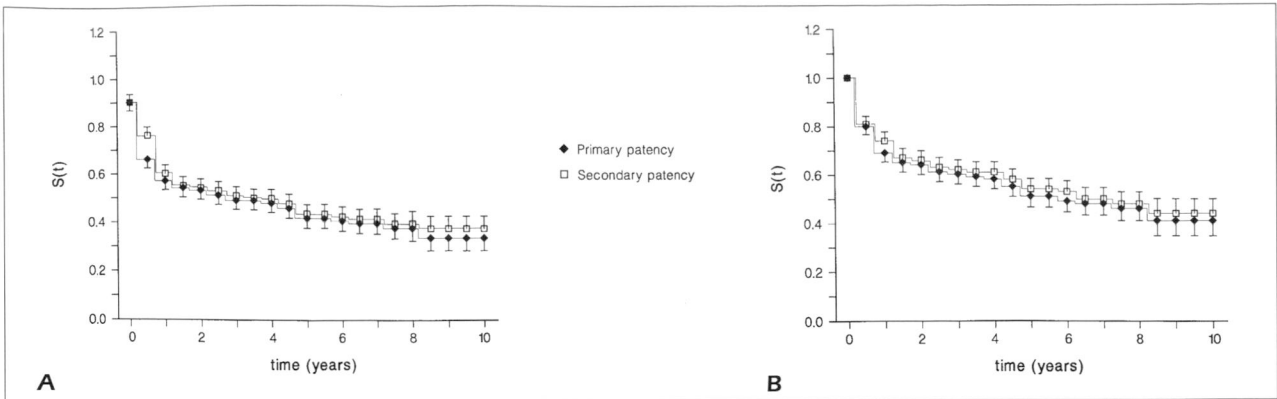

Figure 18-3. Long-term patency of femoropopliteal angioplasty. (A) Includes all patients. (B) Excludes primary treatment failures. (From Capek P, McLean GK, Berkowitz HD. Femoropopliteal angioplasty: factors influencing long-term success. Circulation 1991;83[Suppl II]:70–80. Used with permission.)

plasty after the initial drop in patency at 1 year. It demonstrates that repeat angioplasty carries an identical prognosis to the initial angioplasty. Importantly, it also demonstrates that lesion length correlates with outcome, with shorter lesions doing better than longer lesions. Specifically, the series identified lesions over 10 cm to have only a 20 percent 1-year patency, but among lesions under 10 cm in length no statistical difference was appreciated in long-term patency when stratified for length (Fig. 18-5). Although a superficial glance at the life-table curve would suggest that lesions 0 to 2 cm in length fared better than those 5 to 10 cm in length, when one excludes the confounding variable of the higher incidence of failing to cross the longer lesions, no long-term difference is seen (Table 18-5). The series firmly establishes that the upper limit of length with good long-term success for femoral artery occlusions is 10 cm.

These data conform well with an analysis of 984 consecutive angioplasties by Johnston of which 271 were in the femoropopliteal segment.[20] Again, the majority were performed in the early 1980s. The criteria for success were clinical improvement *and* continued improvement in the ankle-brachial index. The overall 5-year patency in the femoropopliteal position was 40 percent. Again, a difference was seen between the

Figure 18-4. Long-term patency. (A) With technical failures included, stratified by degree of stenosis. Occlusions have a significantly worse prognosis than stenoses ($p = 0.04$). (B) With technical failures excluded. Occlusions fare as well as stenosis ($p = 0.44$). (From Capek P, McLean GK, Berkowitz HD. Femoropopliteal angioplasty: factors influencing long-term success. Circulation 1991;83[Suppl II]; 70–80. Used with permission.)

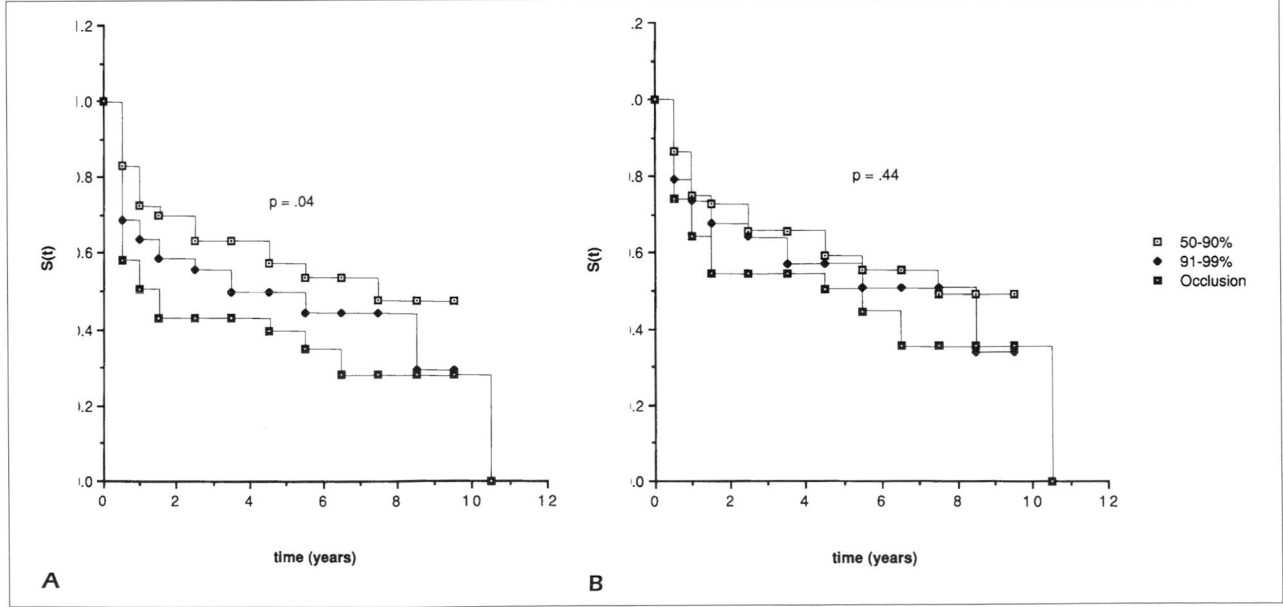

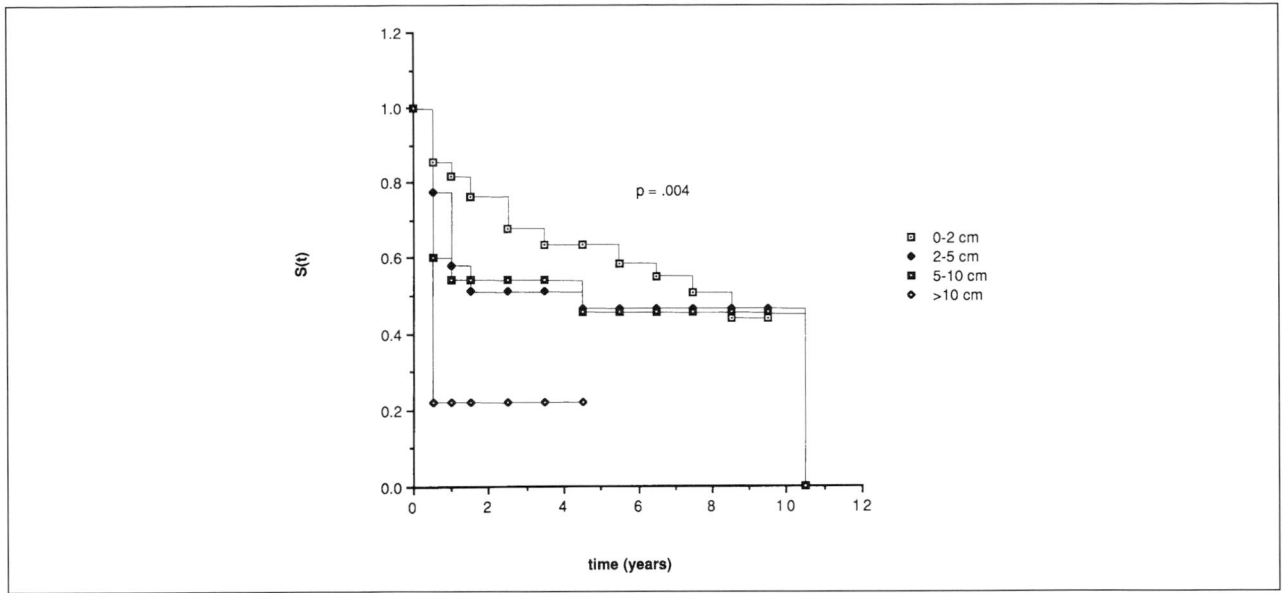

Figure 18-5. Long-term patency stratified for length. (From Capek P, McLean GK, Berkowitz HD. Femoropopliteal angioplasty: factors influencing long-term success. Circulation 1991;83[Suppl II]:70–80. Used with permission.)

long-term patency for stenoses and occlusions, with the curves being parallel. Johnston et al. did not observe that this was due to the difference in primary success rate, but the primary success in patients with claudication was 93 percent and in occlusions 74 percent. Johnston et al. also commented on a significant difference between patients with good runoff and poor runoff, but the patients with poor runoff had a 7 percent lower primary success rate, and, in a modern series with a high technical success rate, it is possible that there might not be a statistically significant difference at 5 years.

In 1992, Johnston reanalyzed the 254 patients with femoropopliteal artery angioplasty.[36] Again, the early (1-month) results demonstrate a significant difference

in primary success between stenoses and occlusions (94 versus 81 percent), which is mirrored in the long-term (5-year) patencies of 40 and 35 percent, respectively (Fig. 18-6). The difference in primary success is

Figure 18-6. Long-term patency of stenoses versus occlusions. The curves are essentially parallel but start at different levels. (From Johnston KW. Femoral and popliteal arteries: reanalysis of results of balloon angioplasty. Radiology 1992; 183:767–771. Used with permission.)

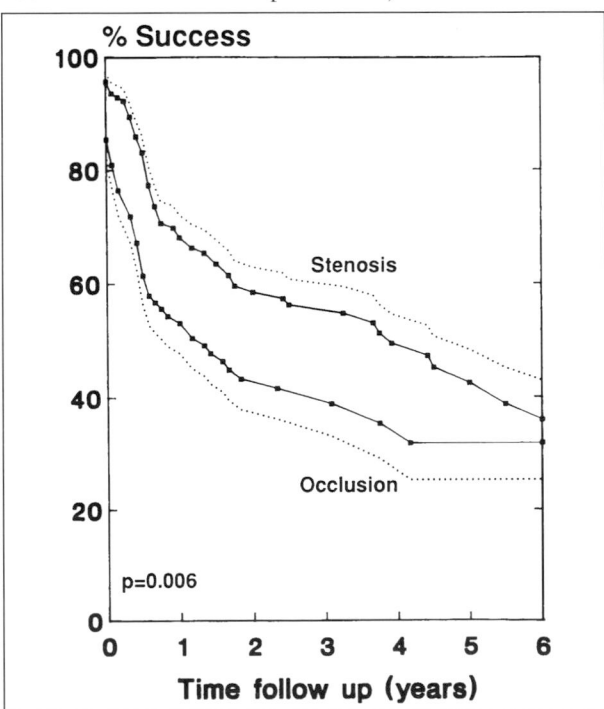

Table 18-5. Effect of Lesion Length on Prognosis

Comparison	*p*	*N*
Overall comparison	0.004*	
0–2 cm		56
2–5 cm		31
5–10 cm		21
>10 cm		9
Comparison between groups		
0–2 vs. 2–5 cm	0.100	
0–2 vs. 5–10 cm	0.060	
2–5 vs. 5–10 cm	0.540	
0–2 vs. >10 cm	0.007*	
2–5 vs. >10 cm	0.015*	
5–10 vs. >10 cm	0.120	

*Statistically significant association.
From Capek P, McLean GK, Berkowitz HD. Femoropopliteal angioplasty factors influencing long-term success. Circulation 1991;83(Suppl II):70–80. Used with permission.

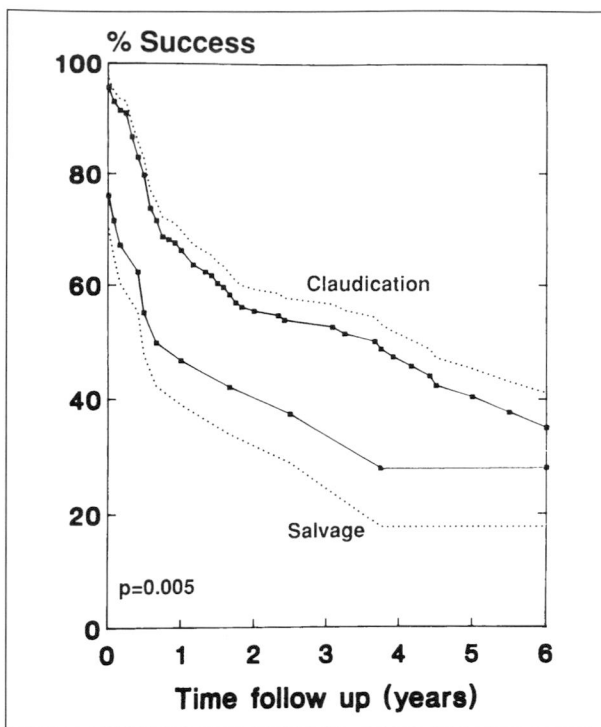

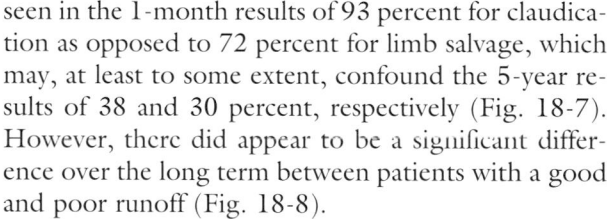

Figure 18-7. Long-term patency of claudication versus limb salvage. (From Johnston KW. Femoral and popliteal arteries: reanalysis of results of balloon angioplasty. Radiology 1992; 183:767–771. Used with permission.)

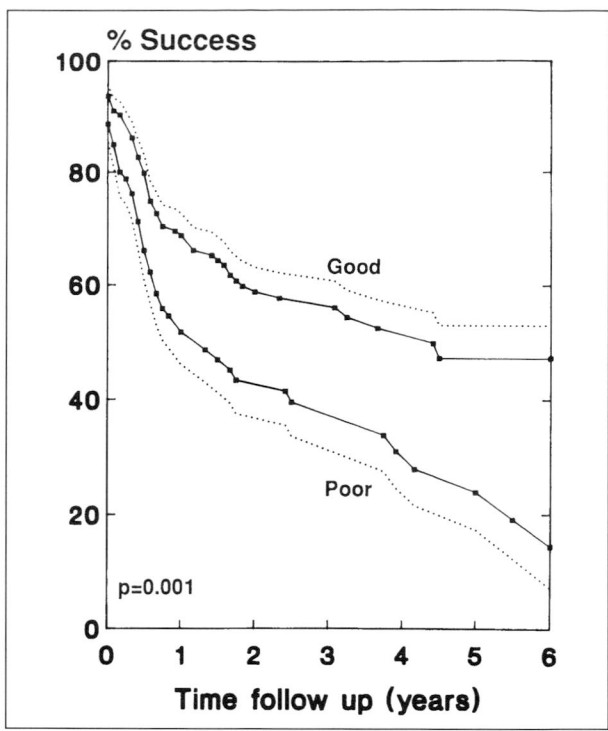

Figure 18-8. Long-term patency of good versus poor runoff. (From Johnston KW. Femoral and popliteal arteries: reanalysis of results of balloon angioplasty. Radiology 1992; 183:767–771. Used with permission.)

seen in the 1-month results of 93 percent for claudication as opposed to 72 percent for limb salvage, which may, at least to some extent, confound the 5-year results of 38 and 30 percent, respectively (Fig. 18-7). However, there did appear to be a significant difference over the long term between patients with a good and poor runoff (Fig. 18-8).

Although extensive comments have been made here about the significance of primary failure, it is important that failures not be excluded from the analysis so that better comparisons may be made from series to series. However, in old series, where the primary success rate may be 20 percent worse than today, some recognition should be given to this fact and its influence as a confounding variable.

No series has met the new Rutherford-Becker criteria, but future studies are planned. For instance, the STAR registry, currently containing nearly 2000 patients with lower extremity angioplasty, is due to report, and the Federal Drug Administration trial of the Wallstent in the femoropopliteal position will use the full Rutherford criteria.

Indications for Angioplasty

Indications depend first on the clinical status of the patient, specifically the symptoms and the comorbidity factors, which influence the risk of therapy.

Asymptomatic Patients

Asymptomatic patients should not have angioplasty because the risks, although small, outweigh the benefits. The exception is to preserve a bypass graft that is in jeopardy.

Symptomatic Patients

All patients in SVS grades 2 or 3 should be considered for angioplasty, although the incidence of patients suitable for angioplasty in this population will be no more than about 30 percent in the femoropopliteal system. The advantages of angioplasty are the low mortality and morbidity compared to surgery,[37] the decreased hospitalization time, and the cost savings.[38,39] Angioplasty should also be considered as an adjunct to surgery so that less surgery may be performed.

Veith et al. recently reviewed 2829 patients with critical lower extremity ischemia, of which 2221 were presenting for the first time.[40] Thirty-five percent were treated by angioplasty, although only 19 percent had angioplasty alone. The remainder also had surgery. This is a good indication of the complementary nature of angioplasty.

Patients who have angioplasty and then have a recurrence are seldom worse than before treatment, and it is unusual for angioplasty to alter the scope of the original surgery that it was planned to replace. This is not true for femoropopliteal bypass grafting because, in a significant percentage of patients, perhaps as high as 25 percent for patients with PTFE grafts, the popliteal artery will occlude when the femoropopliteal artery bypass closes.

Most symptomatic patients being considered for femoropopliteal angioplasty have claudication and are in SVS grade 1. Patients are suitable candidates when the claudication is lifestyle-limiting or when the patient and the physician consider the risk-benefit ratio favorable. This depends on the local interventional experience and the wishes of the patient, which must be considered. Active patients find mild claudication more limiting than patients whose horizons are more limited. Ultimately, the decision depends on the actual risk of angioplasty. In this SVS group of patients, the percentage of patients suitable for angioplasty will rise to 40 to 50 percent.

Patients should be documented to have peripheral vascular disease, which initially is established by noninvasive flow studies. The objective criteria are outlined in the SVS clinical categories of chronic ischemia.[17,18] Grade 1 category 1 (mild claudication) allows patients to complete a treadmill test but to have an ankle pressure after exercise that is greater than 50 mmHg but more than 25 mmHg less than systemic blood pressure. Category 3 (severe claudication) is defined as patients who cannot complete the treadmill test and whose ankle pressure after exercise is less than 50 mmHg. Category 2 patients with moderate claudication fall between these two parameters.

Documentation of the anatomic suitability for angioplasty increasingly will be defined by magnetic resonance angiography, which may become a screening test. In many centers, color Doppler assessment of the vessels is of value. Use of these two methods may reduce the incidence of angiography as a preoperative road map and allow it to become part of the angioplasty procedure. For the moment, however, complete diagnostic arteriography should precede any vascular intervention and should be permanently recorded.[16]

To be judged suitable for angioplasty in the femoropopliteal system, lesions should be less than 10 cm in length, although, very occasionally in patients who are a very high risk for surgery, this may be extended with the knowledge that the angioplasty is destined to close. The Society of Cardiovascular and Interventional Radiology (SCVIR) developed guidelines for the suitability of angioplasty. The SCVIR described four categories,[15] which have since been promulgated by the American Heart Association in guidelines for peripheral transluminal angioplasty of the abdominal aorta and lower extremity vessels.[16] This document is endorsed by the Councils of Cardiovascular Surgery, Cardiovascular Radiology, Clinical Cardiology, and Epidemiology.

- Category 1. Lesions for which PTA alone is the procedure of choice. Treatment of these lesions results in a high technical success rate and will generally result in complete relief of symptoms or normalization of pressure gradients.
- Category 2. Lesions that are well suited for PTA and that will result in complete relief or significant improvement in symptoms, pulses, or pressure gradients. This category includes procedures that will be followed by surgical bypass to treat multilevel vascular disease.
- Category 3. Lesions that may be amenable to percutaneous therapy but, because of disease extent, location, or severity, have a significantly lower chance of initial technical success or long-term benefit when compared to surgical bypass. However, PTA may be performed, generally because of patient risk factors or because of lack of suitable bypass material.
- Category 4. Extensive vascular disease, where percutaneous therapy has a very limited role because of low technical success rate or poor long-term benefit. In very-high-risk patients, or when no surgical procedure is applicable, PTA may have some place.

In the femoropopliteal system, lesions are classified as follows according to these categories.

Category 1
A. Single stenosis, up to 5 cm in length, that is not at the superficial femoral origin or distal portion of the popliteal artery
B. Single occlusion, up to 3 cm in length, that does not involve the superficial femoral origin or distal portion of the popliteal artery

Category 2

A. Single stenosis, 5 to 10 cm in length, that does not involve the distal popliteal artery
B. Single occlusion, 3 to 10 cm in length, that does not involve the distal popliteal artery
C. Heavily calcified stenosis, up to 5 cm
D. Multiple lesions, each less than 3 cm, either stenoses or occlusions
E. Single or multiple lesions where there is no continuous tibial runoff to improve inflow for distal surgical bypass

Category 3

A. Single occlusion, 3 to 10 cm in length, involving the distal popliteal artery
B. Multiple focal lesions, each 3 to 5 cm, that may be heavily calcified

C. Single lesion, either stenosis or occlusion, with a length of greater than 10 cm

Category 4

A. Complete common and/or superficial femoral occlusions
B. Complete popliteal and proximal trifurcation occlusions
C. Severe diffuse disease with multiple lesions and no intervening normal vascular segments

It is important that the decision to proceed with angioplasty is a clinical one and not based exclusively on the anatomy (Figs. 18-9 through 18-14).

Text continues on page 277

Figure 18-9. A femoral stenosis before (A) and after (B) angioplasty showing the typical intimal tear.

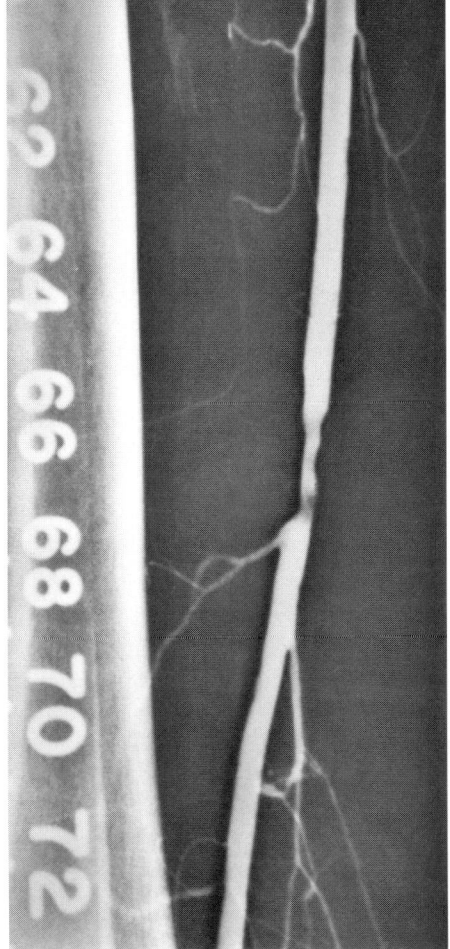

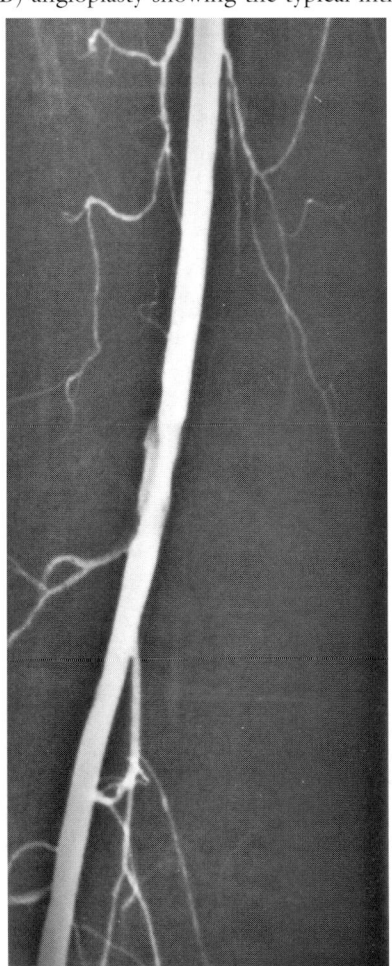

A   B

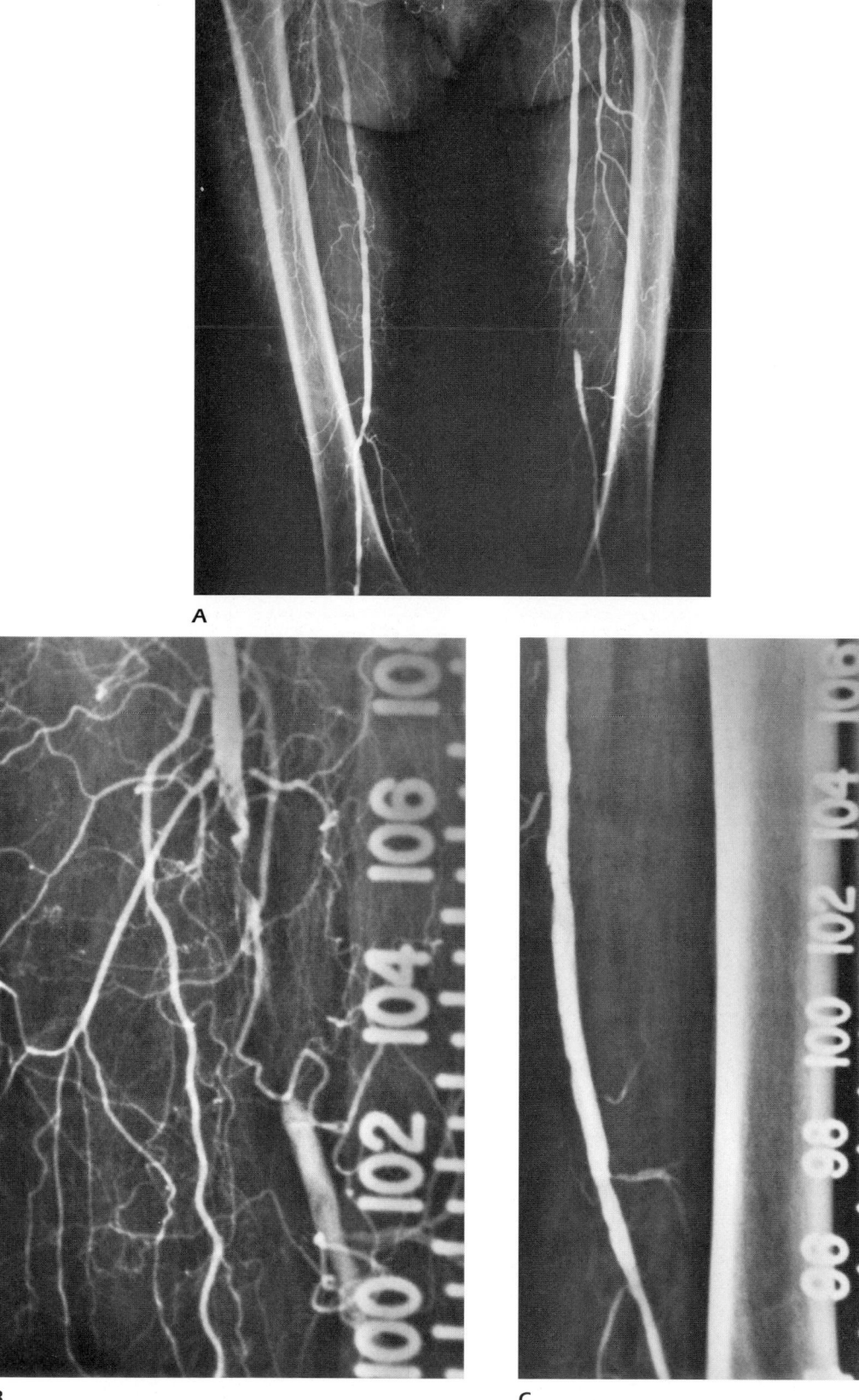

Figure 18-10. (A and B) Pretreatment angiograms in a patient with a 4-week history of claudication. The lesion was treated with urokinase and then angioplasty. (C) After therapy.

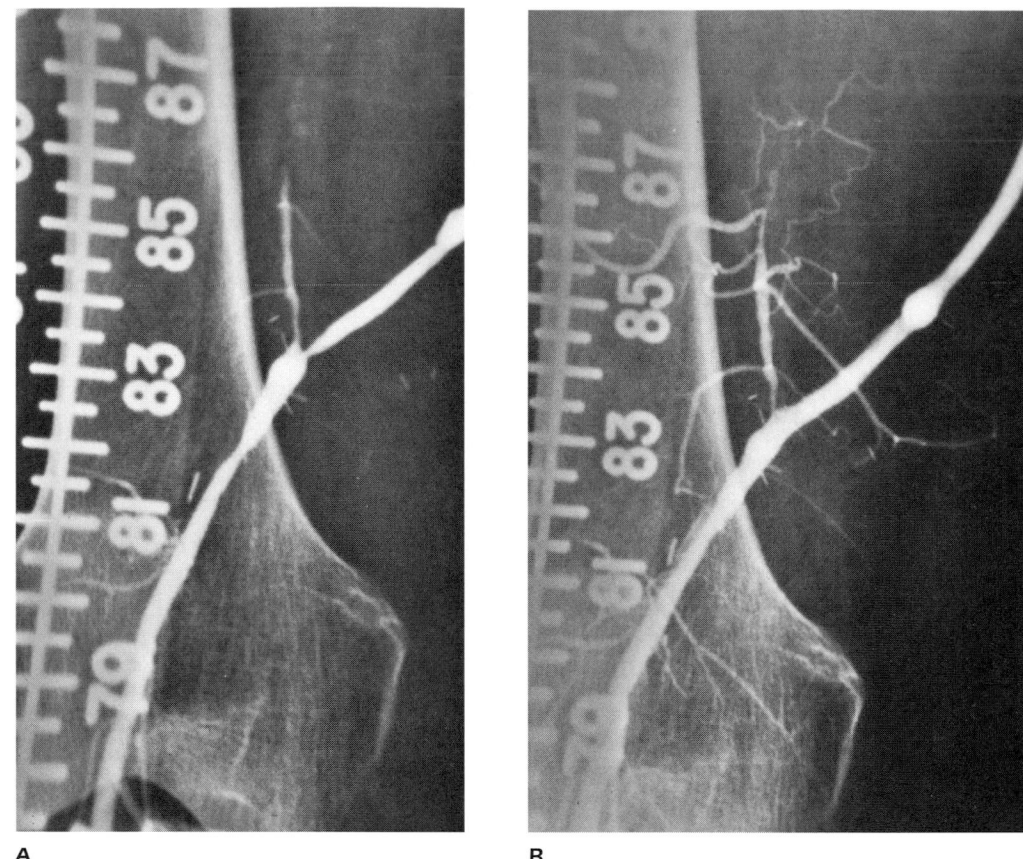

A   B

Figure 18-11. (A) A saphenous vein femoropopliteal bypass with a distal anastomotic stenosis. (B) After treatment with a 6-mm balloon.

Figure 18-12. A short-segment occlusion treated with angioplasty. (A) Before therapy; (B) after therapy.

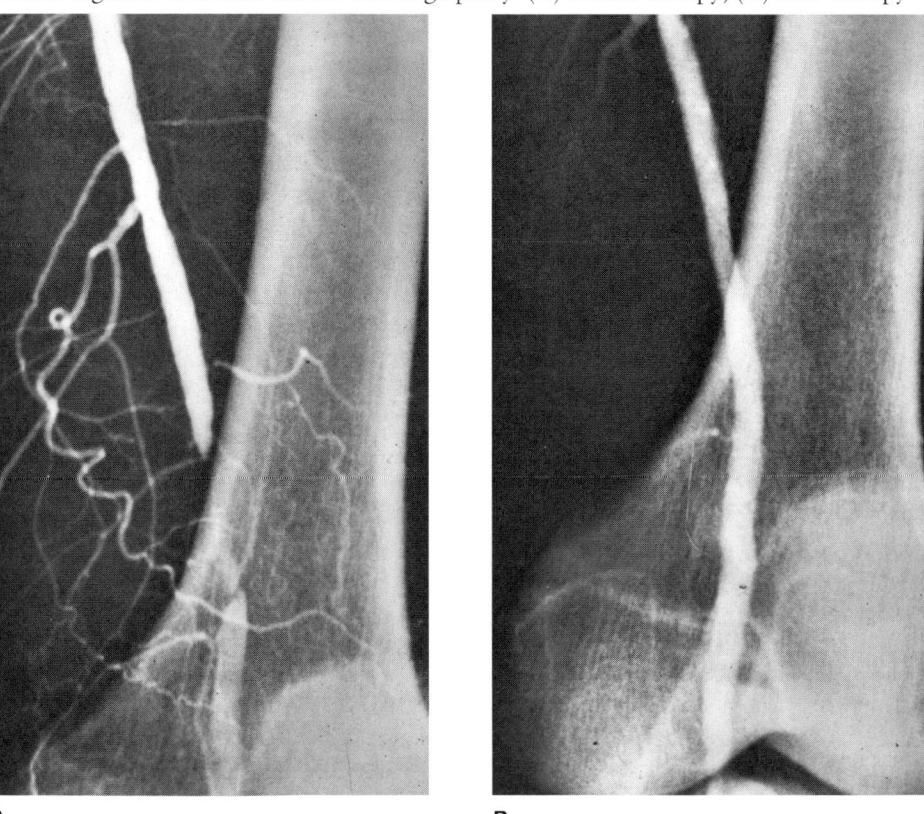

A   B

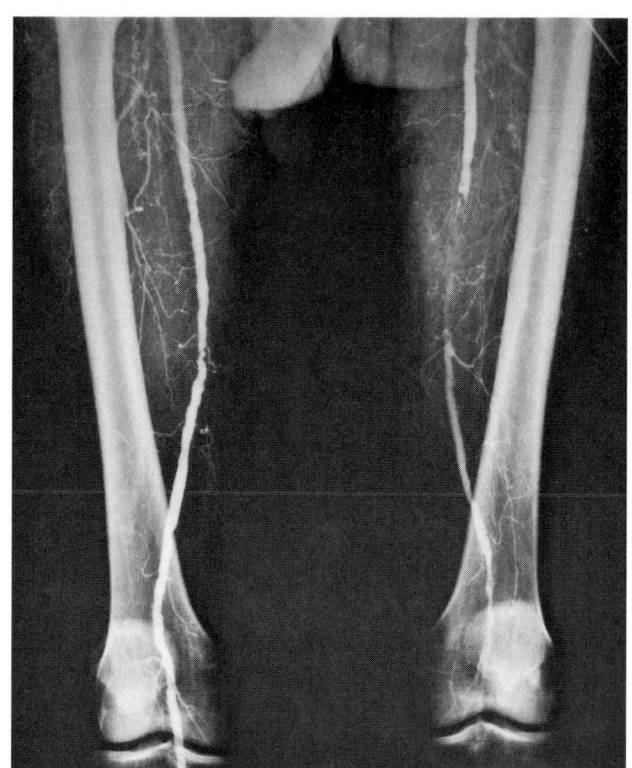

A

Figure 18-13. (A and B) Angiograms of a patient with rest pain and an ABI of 0.37. (C to E) After treatment. The ABI rose to 0.83. Because of the low ABI, the posterior tibial–peroneal trunk was treated at the same time. (F) Two years later with the return of symptoms, there is a restenosis in the posterior tibial–peroneal trunk and a new popliteal stenosis. (G) The original superficial femoral occlusion remains open.

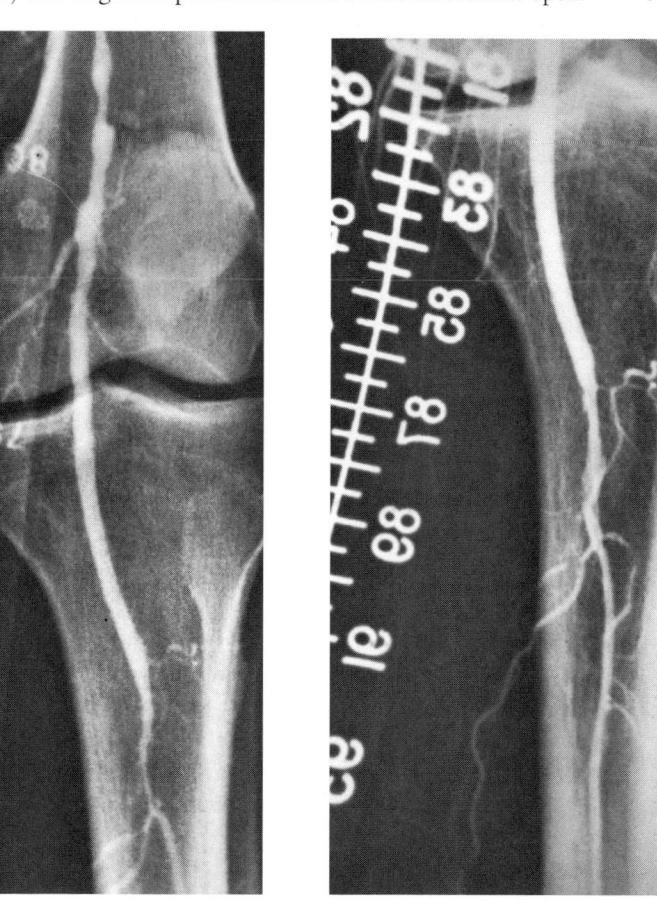

B

C

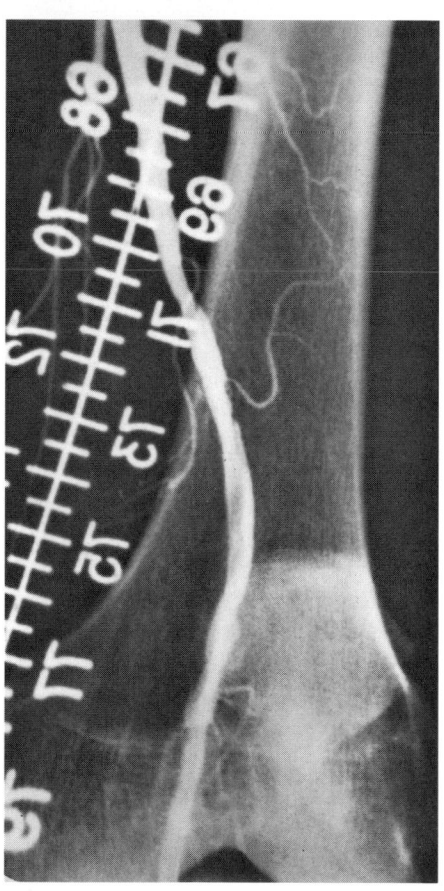

D

275

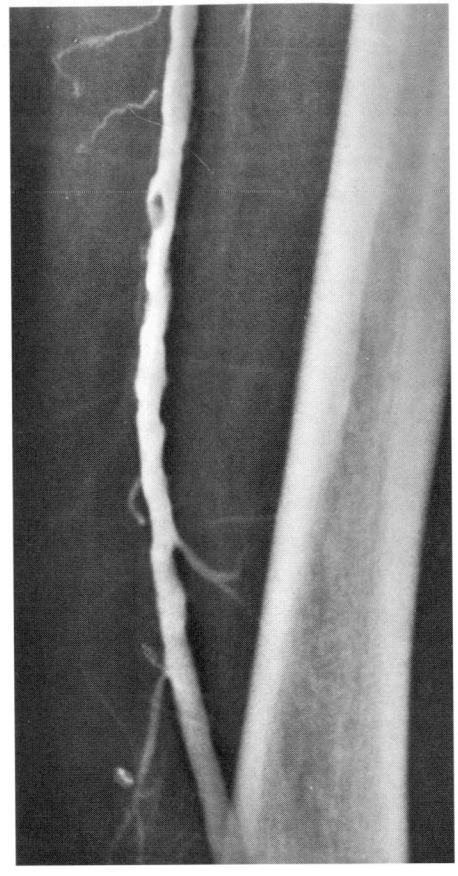

E

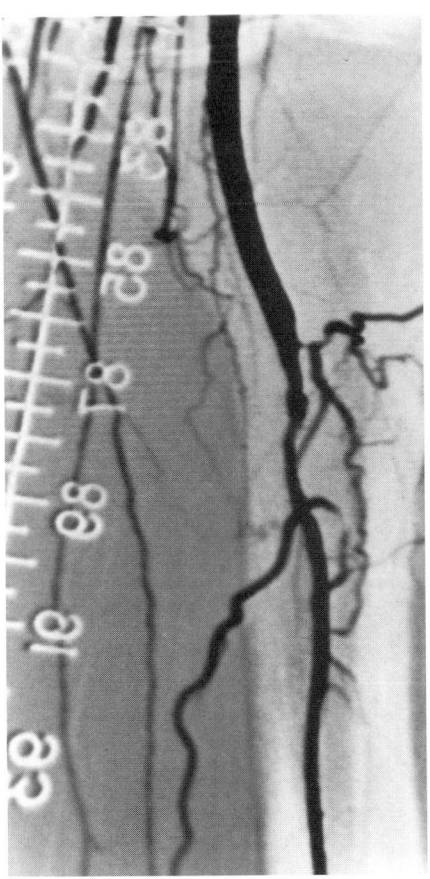

F

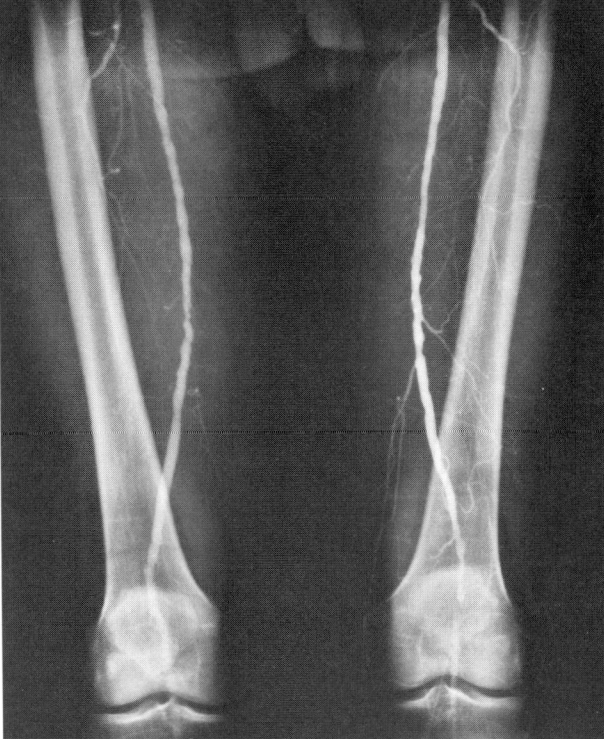

G   **Figure 18-13** (continued).

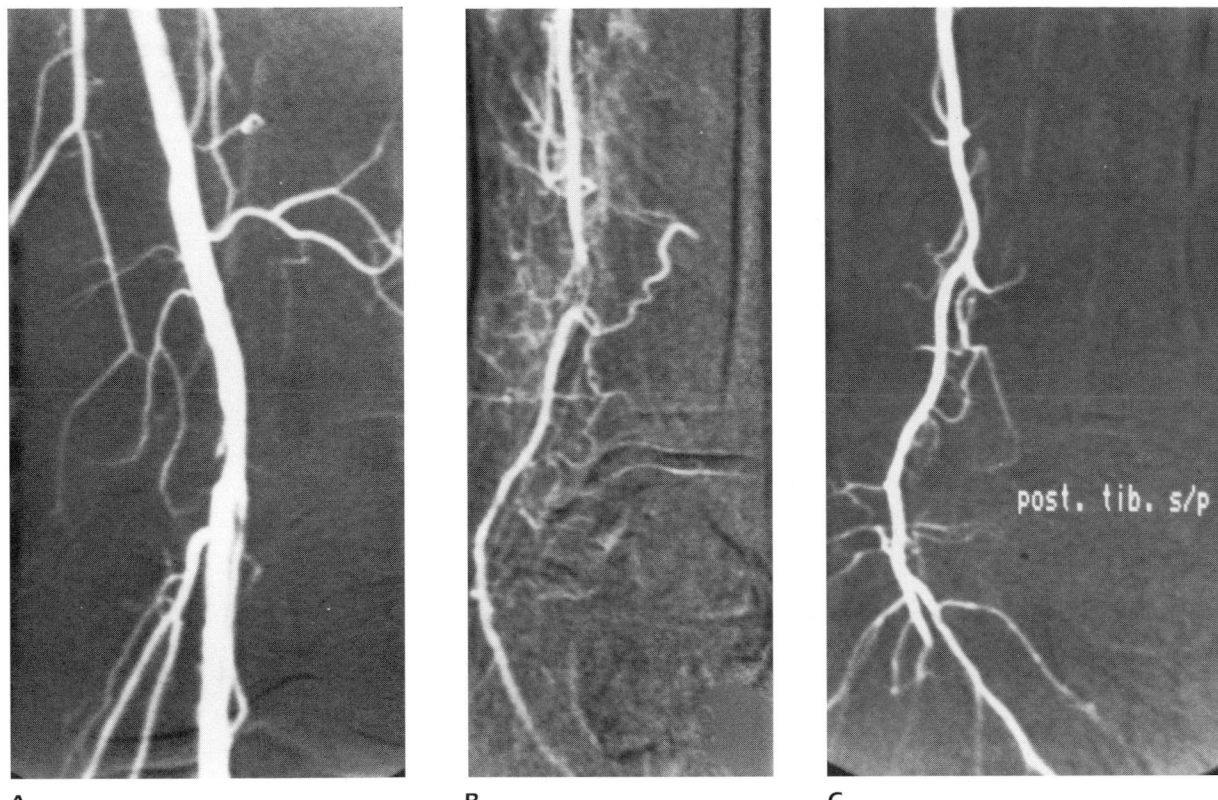

A   **B**   **C**

Figure 18-14. (A) Angiogram after successful angioplasty of a popliteal occlusion. (B) Angiogram showing distal embolization to the posterior tibial artery. (C) After 1 hour of urokinase, 200,000 units.

Complications

The complications of femoropopliteal angioplasty do not differ significantly from those of iliac angioplasty. However, because occlusions have angioplasty more frequently in the femoropopliteal than the iliac system, the embolic risk is higher. In one small series it was 10 percent, although in five of the six symptomatic patients urokinase successfully lysed the thrombus.[25]

Large series do not separate iliac from femoral angioplasties. For 4662 patients gathered from series in the literature (including renal angioplasty), Becker et al. reported a mortality of 0.23 percent; with a 2.5 percent incidence of surgery due to complications of angioplasty.[21] A more recent, and the largest single series, with 1642 patients, reported a mortality of 0.1 percent. Among patients with ischemia the incidence of surgery was 2.8 percent with 0.9 percent requiring bypass, whereas among those with claudication it was 0.7 percent with 0.5 percent requiring bypass.[37]

The recently published guidelines for percutaneous transluminal angioplasty of the abdominal aorta and lower extremity vessels approved by multiple councils of the AHA give thresholds for complications derived from these series (Table 18-6).[16] If the incidence of

Table 18-6. Thresholds for the Incidence of Complications from PTA of the Abdominal Aorta and Lower Extremity Vessels

Complications	Threshold (%)	
Puncture site		
Bleeding	3.4	
False aneurysm	0.5	
Arteriovenous fistula	0.1	
	4.0	
Angioplasty site		
Thrombus	3.2	
Rupture	0.3	
	3.5	
Distal vessel		
Dissection	0.4	
Embolization	2.3	
	2.7	
Systemic		
Renal failure	0.2	
Myocardial infarction	0.2	(fatal)
Cardiovascular accident	0.05	(fatal)
	0.4	
Consequences		
Surgical repair	2.0	
Limb loss	0.2	
Mortality	0.2	

From Pentecost MJ, et al. Guidelines for percutaneous transluminal angioplasty of the abdominal aorta and lower extremity vessels. Circulation 1994; 89:511–531. Used with permission.

complications rises above these levels, the site or the physician should be investigated.

Alternative Methods of Femoropopliteal Recanalization

The major thrust of this chapter has been on angioplasty because it is the most established technique, and certainly the one with the best long-term follow-up. But other, more sophisticated endovascular techniques have been developed. In many instances, these techniques have been driven by the manufacturers, which represents a departure from tradition. Historically, a physician would develop a technique, design a pilot device, test it, and then take it to a manufacturer for refinement and distribution. Today finished products are being thrust on the interventional community by manufacturers, products that have been designed and developed by those not involved in patient care. This matter has been addressed most thoughtfully in an editorial by Ring,[41] who forcefully criticizes the lack of adequate studies surrounding many of these new devices. Another voice of criticism, specifically about lasers, comes from Strandess et al., who see their development more in terms of marketing than of medical progress.[42]

Perhaps because many of these devices were not developed by the medical community, or perhaps because marketing was perceived as important by the end users, their usefulness in peripheral recanalization has not always been seen in perspective. Since femoropopliteal disease is at least three times more prevalent than iliac disease, and since in the femoropopliteal system occlusions predominate over stenoses by a ratio of about 3:1, it is clear that most patients with significant, symptomatic peripheral vascular disease have femoral occlusions. Furthermore, only about 20 percent of these lesions are 10 cm or less in length—that is, suitable for angioplasty.[1,2] One would imagine, therefore, that new devices would be developed to expand the role of angioplasty into the heretofore untreatable patient population. Yet the modern, sophisticated devices have specifically not done so. To date, no device has significantly expanded the patient population suitable for endovascular therapy, although the technique of intravascular bypass grafting proposed by Cragg and Dake[14] may well do so.

Atherectomy

Histologic studies demonstrate that angioplasty, although widening the lumen, leaves large amounts of atheromatous plaque, indeed, nearly the same volume as before.[43] This fact has been confirmed by intravascular ultrasound.[44,45] The concept of excising atheroma and leaving a smooth lumen was therefore attractive, and a suitable device was developed by Simpson et al. in 1985.[46] The Atherocath has a metal housing that contains a window (Fig. 18-15). Opposite this is mounted a balloon that may be inflated to press the window of the catheter into the plaque. A motor then drives a rotating blade through the window, thereby shaving off the atheroma and depositing it in a chamber at the distal end of the catheter. When the chamber is full, the catheter is withdrawn, the chamber is emptied, and the catheter is reinserted through the sheath. Atheroma is shaved off until no more is in the housing; then the catheter is rotated to debulk another 60-degree segment. Percutaneous atherectomy is a relatively time-consuming technique.

Kim et al. reported a 4-year experience involving 68 infrainguinal vessels.[47] Most of these patients had atherectomy alone rather than atherectomy plus angioplasty. In this series, the mean stenosis was reduced from 71 to 14 percent. Mean follow-up was 13.5 months, from which the authors constructed the probability of a 67 percent 2-year patency rate.

In 1991, Dorros et al. reported on 126 patients who had an atherectomy, with 70 percent who had a follow-up angiography.[48] Restenosis was defined as a loss of 50 percent or more of the gain, or an angiographic stenosis of more than 50 percent. Recurrence was seen in 49 percent at 5 months—12 percent among the asymptomatic group and 79 percent among the symptomatic patients. If one looked only at the lesions treated, angiographic restenosis was seen in 52 percent of the stenoses and in 64 percent of the occlusions. These results discouraged many investigators from pursuing atherectomy any further. They have since been confirmed in a careful prospective trial by Katzen et al., who found the 2-year patency to be extremely disappointing.[49]

Nevertheless, atherectomy does have some advantages. First, as initially reported by Maynar et al., it is a useful technique for removing obstructive intimal flaps after balloon angioplasty.[50] Second, it has allowed extensive research into the mechanisms of restenosis because it is an excellent biopsy tool. It has led to the theory that intimal hyperplasia is a nonspecific response to vascular injury. Smooth muscle cell proliferation occurs early after angioplasty or atherectomy, and it is the synthetic smooth muscle cells that are responsible for synthesizing the matrix proteins.[51]

The disadvantages are, however, considerable. Atherectomy is performed through a 9 or 10 French sheath, and Kim et al. reported a 21 percent complication rate.[47] The procedure is time-consuming because the device has to be sequentially rotated to trap the

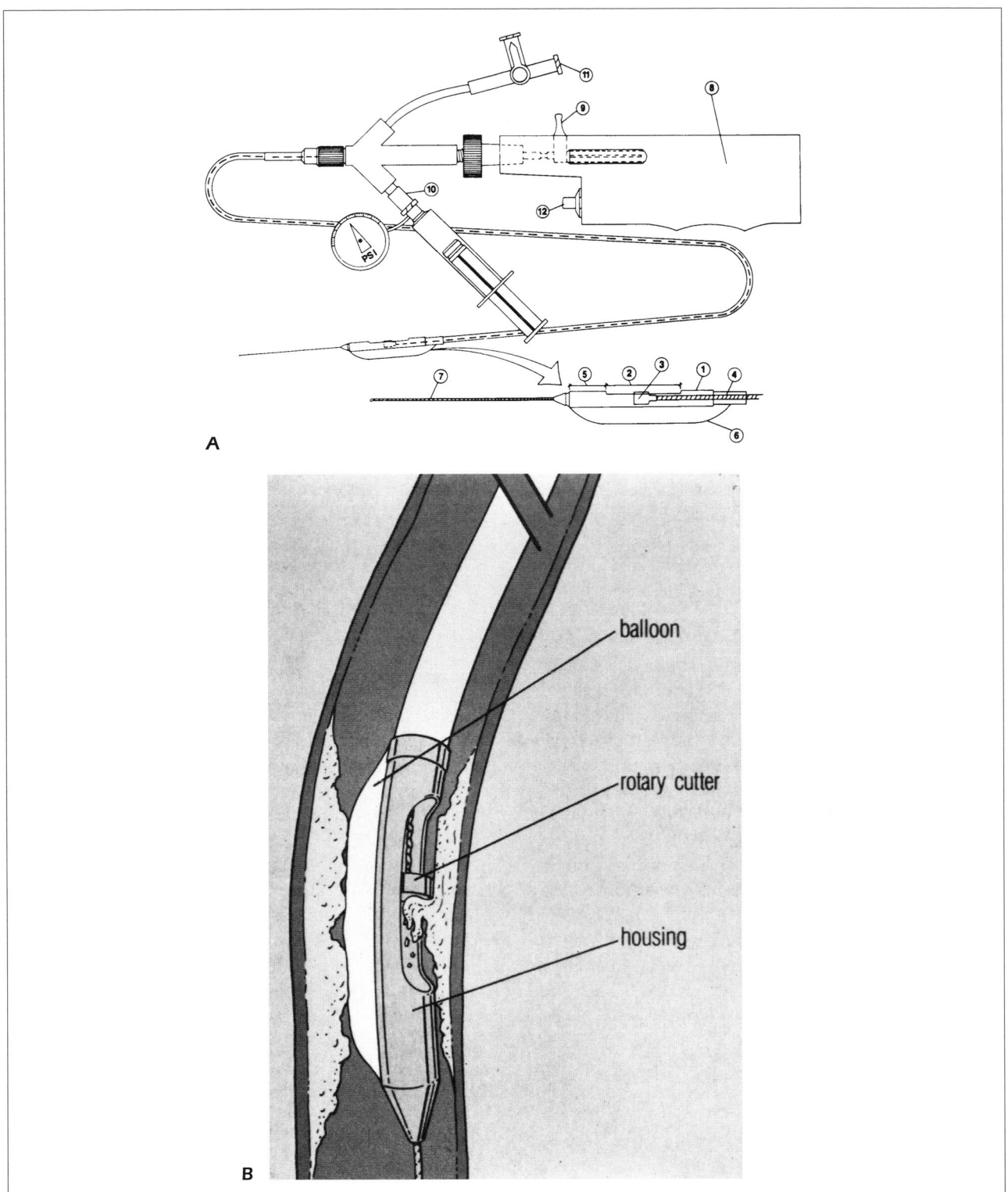

Figure 18-15. (A) Schematic of Simpson Atherocath shows motor drive unit with inset of distal housing. *1,* cylindrical housing; *2,* longitudinal opening; *3,* cutter; *4,* cutter-drive cable (to motor); *5,* specimen collection area; *6,* balloon-support mechanism; *7,* fixed guidewire; *8,* motor; *9,* cutter-advance lever; *10,* balloon-inflation port; *11,* flush port; *12,* on-off switch for motor drive; *PSI,* pounds per square inch. 1 PSI = 6894.7 Pa. (B) The device in use. (From Schwarten D, Katzen B, et al. AJR 1988;150:799–801. Used with permission.)

atheroma in the housing window. This makes it unsuitable for very long stenoses, where it might have a theoretical advantage. It is an unsuitable device for long occlusions because these first have to be crossed, and the Atherocath is not an over-the-wire device. An over-the-wire device has been developed, the Atherotrac, but debulking occlusions is even more time-consuming. It is therefore less useful than balloon angioplasty, whose limitations have already been outlined. Lastly, one might have hoped that, because adjunctive balloon angioplasty is not required, one could achieve better results in longer lesions than with angioplasty. The series of Dorros et al., however, demonstrated a 100 percent restenosis rate in lesions greater than 10 cm.[48] It therefore remains a niche product. A further niche role for the device may be in the "blue toe" syndrome—microembolization from atheromatous plaques.[52]

The initial success reported with atherectomy led to a number of spin-offs working on similar principles. The pullback atherectomy catheter (PAC) is under investigation.[53] It employs a circular cutting blade, and the cut is larger than the catheter; that is, like the Simpson catheter, it has an expansion ratio and does not require adjunctive angioplasty. It is not yet FDA-approved.

The TEC catheter is a commercially available extraction device that is used over a guidewire. It contains two rotating triangular blades driven at 700 rpm. A hollow driveshaft behind the cutting head is on continuous suction to remove debris. The obvious disadvantages are that it is expensive and that it has no expansion ratio; that is, a 3-mm device makes almost a 3-mm lumen—the so-called pilot hole concept. As such, it has been used almost exclusively with adjunctive angioplasty, and there is no valid prospective study available.

A number of truly ablative atherectomy devices have been described. Low-speed rotational angioplasty, which involves a blunt catheter rotating at 200 rpm, has successfully opened up long-segment occlusions.[54] The major disadvantage is that it requires an additional balloon angioplasty and therefore suffers all the limitations of angioplasty in long-segment occlusions.

The Auth Rotablator is an over-the-wire device in which a rotating diamond-studded burr is introduced over a 0.014-inch guidewire. It rotates at up to 190,000 rpm and is the only commercially available ablative device. Again, it has no expansion ratio and therefore requires adjunctive angioplasty except in the tibial vessels. Apparently, all the atheromatous material is ground up into such small fragments that it does no damage and is taken up by the reticuloendothelial system.[55] The lumen thus becomes smooth with no flaps or other irregularities, unless, of course, adjunctive angioplasty is used. Interest in the device has been shown predominantly by the surgical community, but no valid studies have been reported. Zacca et al. reported a 37 percent 6-month patency,[56] and Ahn reported a 44 percent 6-month patency.[57] An interesting complication of the procedure is hematuria, which was seen in 66 percent of patients in one series.[58]

The Kensey catheter has a rotating semicircular cam at the distal end of the catheter powered by a servo-controlled D.C. motor. The cam rotates at 80,000 to 100,000 rpm, and the catheter is lubricated with a perfusate by means of an injection system that delivers a flow rate of about 20 ml a minute. An enthusiastic report by Wholey et al. demonstrated that it could bore through cheese and gelatin,[59] but a subsequent report by Coleman, working in cadavers, demonstrated the fragments to be up to 2 cm in length, which dampened enthusiasm for its use.[60] Like the Auth Rotablator, this device is expensive. It has not achieved FDA approval, although there are isolated reports of its use.[61] It is being tested in the fragmentation of gallstones. An excellent review of atherectomy devices is given by McLean.[62]

Laser Angioplasty

Lasers were first introduced in 1960 and represent monochromatic energy sources in the visible, ultraviolet, and infrared regions of the electromagnetic spectrum. They can operate in a continuous mode or in a pulsed mode with variable pulse lengths and very high repetition rates. The first FDA-approved laser was the hot-tip laser, a hybrid. It uses either argon or neodymium-yttrium aluminum garnet (YAG) laser energy to heat up a ball mounted at the end of the catheter. Although initial reports with the hot-tip laser were encouraging, it rapidly became obvious that the laser was not a stand-alone device but rather required subsequent balloon angioplasty. This led to the "pilot hole" concept, which stated that the device was necessary to cross complete occlusions so that they could have angioplasty. However, because there is a high technical success rate for femoral angioplasty in complete occlusions,[28] and because it is well documented that lesions over 10 cm in length do poorly with angioplasty, the device can add very few patients to those already suitable for PTA, as we have already seen with the atherectomy devices with no expansion ratio.[27] In 1991, Belli et al. reported on a randomized trial of the hot-tip laser against angioplasty and showed no significant difference between the two in primary recanalization,[63] confirming a similar report by Jeans et al. in 1990.[64] The long-term results have been reviewed by Greenfield.[65] Perler et al. reported a 7 percent 15-month patency in patients when the procedure was performed for limb salvage,[66] and similar, poor results have been reported by others.[67,68]

With the rapid demise of the hybrid laser, attention turned to a series of other laser energy sources. Work was done with an excimer laser at 308 nm, and there were some encouraging results,[69] but others were less sanguine.[70] Again, users subscribed to the "pilot hole" project. Nevertheless, the characteristics of excimer laser energy in the treatment of peripheral vascular disease are attractive, with very clean cuts being obtained with a minimum of charring.

Allen et al. reported on direct argon laser energy probes for the recanalization of complete occlusions.[71] The laser light was optically diverged at the fiber tip into a 40-degree cone that had the safety feature that no tissue heating occurred beyond 3 mm from the fiber tip. Nevertheless, despite the divergent energy beam, angioplasty was needed in every patient. No long-term follow-up was reported. Others have used bare fiber argon lasers and reported 1-year patency rates equivalent to angioplasty.[72] Another energy system that was used extensively was the YAG laser in combination with a sapphire lens. Ultimately, a prospective, multicenter trial was initiated with this laser coordinated by Lammer in Austria.[73] He described laser recanalization in 338 patients with femoropopliteal artery occlusions averaging 8.5 cm in length. The initial recanalization rate was 85 percent, and complications were observed in 14 percent of the patients, with emergency surgery required in 1.5 percent. The cumulative long-term patency rate was 57 percent at 3 years; that is, the results were similar to balloon angioplasty.

Experimentation continues with laser energy sources, including the tunable dye laser,[74] solid-state lasers in the deep and near infrared spectrum, and multiple fiber excimer lasers.[75] However, they will probably produce exactly the same myointimal hyperplastic response as any other recanalization device. Nevertheless, one day it may be possible to develop a laser system that does not require adjunctive balloon angioplasty. It will be of value only if it can treat long lesions with a low recurrence rate.

Laser Balloon Angioplasty

Balloon angioplasty increases the luminal diameter by stretching the arterial wall and splitting the atherosclerotic plaque. However, since large cracks and irregularities are thereby created in the intimal lumen, it might be attractive to smooth the lumen at the end of the procedure. Debulking in the form of atherectomy has already been discussed, but the concept of vascular welding derived directly from laser angioplasty techniques. Thermal fusion of dissected portions of the vessel wall was first demonstrated by Hiehle and coworkers in 1985.[76] Laser energy could easily be replaced by radio-frequency energy or even direct heating. Radial delivery of laser energy through an inflated angioplasty balloon was described by Ward[77] and Spears,[78] and the method was refined by Spears into a clinically usable tool.[79] During angioplasty, the plaque is irradiated with a YAG source that produces tissue temperatures of 80°C to 120°C. There are no long-term results of the device in the peripheral vascular system. Although some work has also been done with radio-frequency energy, again, there are no long-term results to substantiate its use.[80]

Few devices have had such a meteoric rise and fall in popularity in so short a time. And just as the literature is replete with papers about laser angioplasty, so, too, is it bereft of long-term data. In the final analysis, there is only the prospective trial by Huppert et al.[70] and one long-term randomized trial by Lammer et al.[73] The two other randomized trials by Belli et al.[63] and Jeans et al.[64] are of the initial results only. The culmination of the enthusiasm was a report by Belli et al. that laser probes may be useful for recanalization but that they may not have to be energized.[81]

Summary

Many millions of dollars have gone into the development of alternatives to balloon angioplasty. By and large they have been unsuccessful. The driving force is first financial—an attempt to capture the lucrative coronary market. A secondary goal is to overcome the very high restenosis rate in the coronary circulation—perhaps 50 percent at 6 months. Yet, despite all the investment, there are very few long-term studies to assess these devices. Current discussions about reducing medical costs have yet to have an impact on this field, and long-term data are seldom collected. Atherectomy shows some promise in the coronary circulation but has been less successful in the periphery. Stents, although improving patency in the iliac system, are not yet superior to angioplasty in the femoral circulation. Lasers of varying outputs have been tried unsuccessfully, but research continues. Intraluminal, stent-supported, bypass grafting may have promise in the femoropopliteal system. One day a suitable device will no doubt emerge, and new devices continue to be developed. For the moment, however, balloon angioplasty with all its limitations remains the procedure of choice except in special situations.

References

1. Martin EC. The impact of angioplasty: a perspective. J Vasc Intervent Radiol 1992;3:511–514.
2. Martin EC. Transcatheter therapies in peripheral and noncoronary vascular disease. Circulation 1991;83(Suppl I):1–5.
3. Dotter CT, Judkins MP. Transluminal treatment of arteriosclerotic obstruction: description of a new technique and a preliminary report of its application. Circulation 1964;30:654–670.
4. Staple TW. Modified catheter for percutaneous transluminal treatment of arteriosclerotic obstructions. Radiology 1968;91: 1041–1043.
5. Van Andel GJ. Percutaneous transluminal angioplasty: the Dotter procedure. A manual for radiologists. Amsterdam: Elsevier, 1976.
6. Gruntzig A, Hopff H. Percutane Rekanalisatin Chronischer Arterieller Verschlusse Mit Einem Neven Dilatations-Katheter. Dtsch Med Wochenschr 1974;99:2502.
7. Abele JE. Technical considerations about balloon catheters and transluminal dilatation. Am J Roentgenol 1980;155:901–909.
8. Simpson JB, Johnson DE, Thapliyal HV, Marks DS, Braden LJ. Transluminal atherectomy: a new approach to the treatment of atherosclerotic vascular disease. Circulation 1985;72(Suppl III):146.
9. Cragg AH, Lund G, Rysavy JA, Salomonowitz E, Castaneda-Zuniga WR, Amplatz K. Percutaneous arterial grafting. Radiology 1984;150:45–49.
10. Maass D, Zolikofer CL, Largiader F, Senning A. Radiological follow-up of transluminally inserted vascular endoprostheses: an experimental study using expanding spirals. Radiology 1984;152:659–663.
11. Charnsangavej C, Wallace S, Wright KC, Carrasco CH, Gianturco C. Endovascular stent for use in aortic dissection: an in vitro experiment. Radiology 1985;157:323–324.
12. Palmaz JC, Sibbitt RR, Reuter SR, Tio FO, Rice WJ. Expandable intraluminal graft: preliminary study. Radiology 1989;156: 73–77.
13. Sapoval MR, Long AL, Raynaud AC, Beyssen BM, Fiessinger JN, Gaux JC. Femoropopliteal stent placement: long-term results. Radiology 1992;184:833–839.
14. Cragg AH, Dake MD. Percutaneous femoropopliteal graft placement. Radiology 1993;187:643–648.
15. Standards of Practice Committee SCVIR. Guidelines for percutaneous transluminal angioplasty. J Vasc Intervent Radiol 1990;1:5–15.
16. Pentecost MJ, Criqui MH, Dorros G, et al. Guidelines for peripheral percutaneous transluminal angioplasty of the abdominal aorta and lower extremity vessels. Circulation 1994;89: 511–531.
17. Rutherford RB, Flanigan DP, Gupta SK, Johnston KW, Karmody A, Whittemore AD, Baker JD, Ernst CB. Suggested standards for reports dealing with lower extremity ischemia. J Vasc Surg 1986;4:80–94.
18. Rutherford RB, Becker GJ. Standards for evaluating and reporting the results of surgical and percutaneous therapy for peripheral arterial disease. J Vasc Intervent Radiol 1991;2:169–174.
19. Rutherford RB. Standards for evaluating results of interventional therapy for peripheral vascular disease. Circulation 1991; 83(Suppl I):6–11.
20. Johnston KW, Rae M, Hogg-Johnston SA, et al. Five-year results of a prospective study of percutaneous transluminal angioplasty. Ann Surg 1987;206:403–412.
21. Becker GJ, Katzen BT, Dake MD. Noncoronary angioplasty. Radiology 1989;170:921–940.
22. Zeitler E. Percutaneous transluminal angioplasty of the femorotibial arteries. In: Dondelinger RF, Rossi P, Kurdziel JC, Wallace S, eds. Interventional radiology. New York: Thieme, 1990:617–624.
23. Adar R, Critchfield GC, Eddie DM. A confidence profile analysis of the results of femoropopliteal percutaneous transluminal angioplasty in the treatment of lower extremity ischemia. J Vasc Surg 1989;10:57–67.
24. Wilson SE, Wolf GL, Cross AP. Percutaneous transluminal angioplasty versus operation for peripheral arteriosclerosis. J Vasc Surg 1989;9:1–9.
25. Martin EC, Fankuchen EI, Karlson KB, Dolgin C, Collins RH, Voorhees AB Jr, Casarella WJ. Angioplasty for femoral artery occlusion: comparison with surgery. Am J Roentgenol 1981; 137:915–919.
26. Murray RR, Hewes RC, White RJ Jr, et al. Long-segment femoropopliteal stenoses: is angioplasty a boon or a bust? Radiology 1987;162:473–476.
27. Capek P, McLean GK, Berkowitz HD. Femoropopliteal angioplasty factors influencing long-term success. Circulation 1991; 83(Suppl II):70–80.
28. Morgenstern BR, Getrajdman GI, Laffey KJ, Bixon R, Martin EC. Total occlusions of the femoropopliteal artery: high technical success rate of conventional balloon angioplasty. Radiology 1989;172:937–940.
29. Zeitler F. Percutaneous dilatation and recanalization of iliac and femoral arteries. Cardiovasc Intervent Radiol 1980;3:207–212.
30. Waltman AC, Greenfield AJ, Noveline RA, et al. Transluminal angioplasty of the iliac and femoropopliteal arteries. Arch Surg 1982;117:1218–1221.
31. Tamura S, Sniderman KW, Beinart C, Sos TA. Percutaneous transluminal angioplasty of the popliteal artery and its branches. Radiology 1982;143:645–648.
32. Krepel VM, Van Andel GJ, vanErp WE, Breslau PJ. Percutaneous transluminal angioplasty of the femoropopliteal artery: initial long-term results. Radiology 1985;156:325–338.
33. Levy JM, Hessel SJ, Horsley WW, Cook GC, Dickey JE. Value of laser-assisted angioplasty in the community hospital. Radiology 1989;170:1017–1018.
34. Hewes RC, White RI Jr, Murray RR, et al. Long-term results of superficial femoral artery angioplasty. Am J Roentgenol 1986;146:1025–1029.
35. Probst P, Cerny P, Owens A, Mahler F. Patency after femoral angioplasty: correlation of angiographic appearance with clinical findings. Am J Roentgenol 1983;140:1227–1232.
36. Johnston KW. Femoral and popliteal arteries: reanalysis of results of balloon angioplasty. Radiology 1992;183:767–771.
37. Belli AM, Cumberland DC, Knoz AM, Procter AE, Welsh CL. The complication rate of percutaneous peripheral balloon angioplasty. Clin Radiol 1990;41:380–383.
38. Kinnison ML, White RI Jr, Bowers WP, Dunlap ED. Cost incentives for peripheral angioplasty. Am J Roentgenol 1985; 145:1241–1244.
39. Jeans WD, Danton RM, Baird RN, Horrocks M. A comparison of the costs of vascular surgery and balloon dilatation in lower limb ischaemic disease. Br J Radiol 1986;59:453–456.
40. Veith FJ, Gupta SK, Wengerter KR, et al. Changing arteriosclerotic disease patterns and management strategies in lower-limb-threatening ischemia. Ann Surg 1990;212:402–412.
41. Ring EJ. New interventional devices and the need for restraint. Radiology 1989;170:945–946.
42. Strandess DE, Barnes RW, Katzen B, Ring EJ. Indiscriminate use of laser angioplasty. Radiology 1989;172:945–946.
43. Castaneda-Zuniga WR, Formanek A, Tadavarthy M, Vlodaver Z, Edwards JE, Zollikofer C, Amplatz K. The mechanism of balloon angioplasty. Radiology 1980;135:565–571.
44. Pandian NC, Kreis A, O'Donnell T. Intravascular ultrasound estimation of arterial stenosis. J Am Soc Echo 1989;2:390–392.
45. Yock PG, Fitzgerald PJ, Linker DT, Angelsen BAJ. Intravascular ultrasound guidance for catheter-based coronary interventions. J Am Coll Cardiol 1991;17(6 Suppl B):39–45.
46. Simpson JB, Zimmerman JJ, Selmon RM. Transluminal atherectomy: initial clinical results in 27 patients. Circulation 1986; 74(Suppl II):203.
47. Kim D, Gianturco LE, Porter DH, et al. Peripheral directional atherectomy: 4-year experience. Radiology 1992;183:773–778.

48. Dorros G, Iyer S, Lewin R, Zaitoun R, Mathiak L, Olson K. Angiographic follow-up and clinical outcome of 126 patients after percutaneous directional atherectomy (Simpson Athero-Cath) for occlusive peripheral vascular disease. Cathet Cardiovasc Diagn 1991;22:79–84.

49. Katzen BT, Becker GJ, Benenati JF. Long-term follow-up of directional atherectomy improvement. J Vasc Intervent Radiol 1992;3:38–39.

50. Maynar M, Reyes R, Cabrera V, et al. Percutaneous atherectomy as an alternative treatment for postangioplasty obstructive intimal flaps. Radiology 1989;170:1029–1031.

51. Strauss BH, Umans VA, vanSuylen RJ, et al. Directional atherectomy for treatment of restenosis within coronary stents: clinical, angiographic and histologic results. J Am Coll Cardiol 1992;20:1465–1473.

52. Dolmatch BL, Rholl KS, Moskowitz LB, Dake MD, vanBreda A, Kaplan JO, Katzen BT. Blue toe syndrome: treatment with percutaneous atherectomy. Radiology 1989;172:799–804.

53. Fischell TA, Fischell RE, White RI. In vivo results using a new pullback atherectomy catheter (PAC). Cathet Cardiovasc Diagn 1990;21:287–291.

54. Vallbracht C, Liermann DD, Prignitz, I, et al. Low-speed rotational angioplasty in chronic peripheral artery occlusions: experience in 83 patients. Radiology 1989;172:327–330.

55. Ahn SS, Auth D, Marcus DR. Removal of focal atheromatous lesions by angioscopically guided high-speed rotary atherectomy. J Vasc Surg 1988;7:292–300.

56. Zacca NM, Raizner AE, Noon GP. Treatment of symptomatic peripheral atherosclerotic disease with a rotational atherectomy device. Am J Cardiol 1989;63:77–80.

57. Ahn SS. The rotablator—high-speed rotary atherectomy: indications, technique, results and complications. In: Moore WS, Ahn SS, eds. Endovascular surgery. Philadelphia: Saunders, 1989:327–335.

58. Dorros G, Lyer S, Zaitoun R. Acute angiographic and clinical outcome of high speed percutaneous rotational atherectomy (Rotablator). Cathet Cardiovasc Diagn 1991;22:157–166.

59. Wholey MH, Smith JAM, Godlewski P, Nagurka M. Recanalization of total arterial occlusions with the Kensey dynamic angioplasty catheter. Radiology 1989;172:95–98.

60. Coleman CC, Posalaky IP, Robinson JD, Payne WD, Vlodaver ZA, Amplatz K. Atheroablation with the Kensey catheter: a pathologic study. Radiology 1989;170:391–394.

61. Triller J, Do DD, Maddern G, Mahler F. Femoropopliteal artery occlusion: clinical experience with the Kensey catheter. Radiology 1992;182:257–261.

62. McLean GK. Percutaneous peripheral atherectomy. J Vasc Intervent Radiol 1993;4:465–480.

63. Belli AM, Cumberland DC, Procter AE, Welsh CL. Follow-up of conventional angioplasty versus laser thermal angioplasty for total femoropopliteal artery occlusions: results of a randomized trial. J Vasc Intervent Radiol 1991;2:485–488.

64. Jeans WD, Murphy P, Hughes O, Horrocks M, Baird RN. Randomized trial of laser-assisted passage through occluded femoro-popliteal arteries. Br J Radiol 1990;63:19–21.

65. Greenfield A. Hot-tip laser results and complications. Circulation 1991;83(Suppl I):94–96.

66. Perler BA, Osterman FA, White RI Jr, Williams GM. Percutaneous laser probe femoropopliteal angioplasty: a preliminary experience. J Vasc Surg 1989;3:351–357.

67. Motarjeme A. Percutaneous laser angioplasty: a 2-year follow-up. Presented at the Scientific Program of the Radiologic Society of North America, November 1988.

68. Wright J, Belkin GM, Greenfield AJ, Guben JK, Sanborn TA, Menzoian JO. Laser angioplasty for limb salvage: observation of early results. J Vasc Surg 1989;10:31–38.

69. Litvack F, Grundfest WS, Ader L, et al. Percutaneous excimer-laser and excimer-laser-assisted angioplasty of the lower extremities: results of initial clinical trial. Radiology 1989;172:331–335.

70. Huppert PE, Duda SH, Helber U, Karsch KR, Claussen CD. Comparison of pulsed laser-assisted angioplasty and balloon angioplasty in femoropopliteal artery occlusions. Radiology 1992;184:363–367.

71. Allen B, Loflin TG, Embry BM, Gaskin TA, Isobe JH, Martin RG. Occluded peripheral arteries: clinical utility of argon laser recanalization. Radiology 1990;176:543–547.

72. Nordstrom LA, Castaneda-Zuniga WR, VonSeggern KB. Peripheral arterial obstructions: analysis of patency 1 year after laser-assisted transluminal angioplasty. Radiology 1991;181:515–520.

73. Lammer J, Pilger E, Karnel F, et al. Laser angioplasty: results of a prospective multicenter study at 3-year follow-up. Radiology 1991;178:335–337.

74. Douek PC, Leon MB, Geschwind H, Cook PS, Selzer P, Miller DL, Bonner RF. Occlusive peripheral vascular disease: a multicenter trial of fluorescence-guided, pulsed dye laser-assisted balloon angioplasty. Radiology 1991;180:127–133.

75. Cothren RM, Hayes GB, Kramer JR, Sacks B, Kittrell C, Feld MS. A multifiber catheter with an optical shield for laser angiosurgery. Lasers Life Sci 1986;1:1–12.

76. Hiehle JF Jr, Bourgelais DBC, Shapshay S, Schoen FJ, Kim D, Spears R. Nd-YAG laser fusion of human atheromatous plaque-arterial wall separations in vitro. Am J Cardiol 1985;56:953–957.

77. Ward H. Laser recanalization of atheromatous vessels using fiber optics. Lasers Surg Med 1984;4:353–363.

78. Spears JR. Percutaneous transluminal coronary angioplasty restenosis: potential prevention with laser balloon angioplasty. Am J Cardiol 1987;60:61B–64B.

79. Spears JR. Percutaneous laser treatment of atherosclerosis: an overview of emerging techniques. Cardiovasc Intervent Radiol 1986;9:303–312.

80. Becker GJ, Lee BI, Waller BF, et al. Potential of radiofrequency balloon angioplasty: weld strengths, dose-response relationship, and correlative histology. Radiology 1990;174:1003–1008.

81. Belli AM, Proctor AE, Cumberland DC. Peripheral vascular occlusions: mechanical recanalization with a metal laser probe after guide wire dissection. Radiology 1990;176:539–541.

19

Infrapopliteal Revascularization

MARCY B. JAGUST
THOMAS A. SOS

Since percutaneous transluminal angioplasty (PTA) of peripheral vessels was first described by Dotter and Judkins[1] in 1964, the procedure has been performed with increasing frequency. Initially, dilatation was performed by passage of progressively larger tapered catheters, which later evolved into the use of balloon catheters. Although initial results were disappointing, advances in catheter and guidewire technology markedly increased success rates. Today, angioplasty of iliac, superficial femoral, and popliteal arteries is a widely accepted and performed procedure.

Early results of infrapopliteal angioplasty were not impressive.[2,3] The higher risks of procedures in this area kept PTA reserved for limb-threatening ischemia and cases in which surgery was not feasible. Manipulation through tibial vessels became easier with the introduction of small-diameter, low-profile balloon catheters and very radiopaque, soft, steerable guidewires originally developed for use in the coronary vasculature. In addition, advances in radiographic equipment that permitted road-mapping allowed radiologists to consider PTA for small, diseased tibial vessels. Angioplasty of the infrapopliteal vasculature has gained increasing popularity over the past few years as technical advances have made tibial PTA safer and more successful.

Patient Selection

Patients with tibial occlusive disease may be minimally symptomatic or asymptomatic. The absence of pedal pulses may be an incidental finding in patients with well-developed collateral vessels or limited activity. Ischemic symptoms must be present before any intervention is considered. Disabling claudication, rest pain, toe ulcers, and gangrene are symptoms of severe, limb-threatening ischemia. These symptoms may be grouped according to a classification outlined by Rutherford et al.[4] Before treatment, the diagnosis of lower extremity ischemia due to tibial vessel disease should be made and other possible etiologies for pain should be excluded. A thorough history and physical examination should be obtained as well as appropriate noninvasive testing, including pulse volume recordings (PVRs) and ankle-brachial pressure indices (ABIs). Ischemic rest pain is associated with ABIs less than 0.5[5] or resting ankle pressures of less than 40 mmHg.[4] Nonhealing ulcers and/or gangrene are associated with ankle pressures of less than 60 mmHg.[4] ABIs are not useful in diabetic patients with calcified noncompressible vessels. PVRs will show marked waveform damping. At the authors' institution, the decision to perform tibial angioplasty is made in conjunction with the vascular surgeon after careful review of the diagnostic arteriogram. Patients with limb-threatening ischemia often have multilevel disease. Depending on the severity of the inflow lesions, the supratibial disease is often treated first. The limb is then reevaluated 4 to 6 weeks later after there has been time for the limb to heal and for collateral vessels to develop.

The type of lesion is also an important determinant in the decision to perform tibial PTA. As in other vessels, long-term patency after dilatation is more favorable for single focal stenoses.[6] Although long-term patency may be limited for diffuscly diseased vessels, short-term patency may be sufficient to heal superficial ulcerations or amputation sites. Occlusions can be crossed and dilated; however, the chance of success decreases with increasing length. The time course for the development of symptoms is also an important consideration. Recent onset of symptoms with an occlusion implies associated thrombus, which should be lysed initially. This may, in turn, reveal underlying stenoses.

Equipment

Balloon Catheters

Tibial angioplasty is performed with 1-mm to 4-mm balloons on catheter shafts of 4.3 French and smaller (Table 19-1). These balloon catheters are available in 90-cm and 120-cm lengths. They accept 0.018-inch

Table 19-1. Balloon Catheters for Tibial Angioplasty

Device	Size	Manufacturer
Schwarten	4.3 French	Peripheral Systems Group, Mountain View, CA
Bard small-vessel PTA catheter	4.3 French	USCI-Bard, Billerica, MA
Sub-4	3.8 French	Medi-Tech, Watertown, MA
Stealth	3.2/3.5 French	Target Therapeutics, Fremont, CA
Viper	3.7 French	Medi-Tech, Watertown, MA
TEGwire*	0.035 inch	Medi-Tech, Watertown, MA
Lobo*	0.035 inch	Mallinckrodt, St. Louis, MO

*Balloons on wires

Table 19-2. 0.018-Inch Wires for Tibial Angioplasty

Device	Manufacturer
Ultraselect nitinol	Microvena, Vadnais, MN
Platinum Plus	Medi-Tech, Watertown, MA
Steerable guidewire (0.016 inch)	USCI, Billerica, MA
Flex-T	Mallinckrodt, St. Louis, MO
Glidewire	Medi-Tech, Watertown, MA
V-18	Medi-Tech, Watertown, MA

guidewires and differ considerably in stiffness and trackability. The catheter shaft should be stiff enough to allow tracking over a guidewire in a small vessel with extensive atherosclerotic disease and increased friction. The authors prefer the Viper balloon catheter (previously Scimed, now Medi-Tech), which has a 3.7 French stiff shaft tapered to 3.1 French at the tip.

Guidewires

The ideal guidewire should be easily visible under fluoroscopy, be torqueable to follow curves and maneuver around plaques, have a relatively floppy tip to avoid dissection, and have a stiff body to allow the balloon catheter shaft to follow. The Flex-T (Mallinckrodt), Platinum Plus (Medi-Tech), and the various hydrophilic guidewires are all useful (Table 19-2). The authors prefer the V-18 Control Wire (previously Scimed, now Medi-Tech), which has a shapeable, soft, radiopaque, hydrophilic tip and a stiff shaft.

Technique

Physical Examination

Before any arteriogram or interventional procedure, it is important to assess the patient's peripheral pulses or Doppler signals as well as extremity color and temperature.

Puncture

The diagnostic arteriogram is usually performed from a retrograde puncture in the groin opposite the affected limb. Vascular access for angioplasty is usually obtained via an antegrade puncture into the common

femoral artery on the symptomatic side with placement of a vascular sheath. Puncture of the common femoral artery below the inguinal ligament is essential to reduce the chance of retroperitoneal hemorrhage. It is also important to make the puncture over the bone so that postprocedure compression is against resistance. In obese patients whose body habitus precludes an antegrade puncture, a retrograde puncture of the contralateral groin may be performed for an up-and-over-the-bifurcation procedure. A retrograde approach may also be helpful in those patients who have had extensive surgery in the ipsilateral groin. Drawbacks to this approach include less control of the catheter and guidewire, inability to reach more distal lesions because of limitations in catheter length, and decreased trackability. The use of guiding catheters or sheaths across the aortic bifurcation helps make the retrograde technique easier.

Because the incidence of puncture site complications increases with increasing catheter size, the authors try to minimize the size of the vascular sheath. If the procedure is limited to the tibial vessels, a 4 French sheath is inserted. If angioplasty of suprapopliteal lesions is also planned, a 5 French sheath is inserted.

Lesion Traversal

Road-mapping may be performed through the balloon catheter or from the side port of the vascular sheath. This capability allows for precise maneuvering through the small diseased tibial vessels. Some authors advocate placing two guidewires when the lesion is close to a bifurcation.[7] The origin of the adjacent vessel may then be dilated if it is narrowed by the first angioplasty. We have rarely found this to be a problem and do not routinely approach bifurcation lesions this way but reserve this approach for severe stenoses at both origins.

An occlusion may be crossed with an 0.018-inch hydrophilic wire. However, on occasion, an 0.018-inch guidewire may not be stiff enough to cross a firm occlusion. In this instance, an 0.035-inch wire is advanced across the lesion followed by a tapered 4 or 5 French straight catheter. We most often use the

Bentson wire, whose floppy tip becomes rigid when only a small length is passed beyond the catheter tip. If the Bentson wire cannot be passed, a straight or angled hydrophilic Terumo guidewire (Medi-Tech) may be used. Care must be taken to avoid subintimal passage because "feedback" is less with the hydrophilic wires. After the catheter is advanced across the lesion, the 0.035-inch guidewire may be exchanged for an 0.018-inch guidewire and the balloon catheter inserted.

In all these maneuvers, gentleness and finesse are used initially and more force is applied only when gentler maneuvers have failed. The platinum tip wires are very visible, easily torqueable, very soft, and therefore atraumatic. However, in vessels with extensive and eccentric disease, the wire tip may become lodged under a plaque. In these cases, it may be impossible to withdraw and redirect the wire as it becomes bent and accordioned at the tip. In these instances, an angled hydrophilic wire may be more useful. In the past, the 0.018-inch Terumo hydrophilic wires were difficult to

see. However, more recent versions have gold tips to make them more radiopaque. The V-18 Control Wire (Medi-Tech) has a very radiopaque hydrophilic tip.

Balloon Selection

In general, 3-mm and 4-mm balloons are used in the proximal to midtibial vessels, 2-mm to 3-mm balloons are used in the mid- to distal tibial vessels, and 1-mm to 2-mm balloons are used in the foot vessels. Balloon size is usually determined by measuring the caliber of the nearest normal segment of vessel. Most operators do not correct for magnification on analogue films. On digital images, the vessel size can be determined by comparison to a known measurement on the image. After many procedures on the same equipment, the authors frequently "eyeball" the balloon size especially when the balloon size can be compared with a real-time road map. The authors usually inflate a balloon for 30 seconds across an infrapopliteal vessel lesion.

Follow-up Arteriography

After angioplasty, the balloon catheter is withdrawn into the popliteal artery and the guidewire is left across the dilated area. The follow-up arteriogram is then performed from the side port of the vascular sheath to avoid having to recross the lesion if further intervention is needed. Successful angioplasty is defined as a residual stenosis of 30 percent or less. If a significant lesion remains, it may be redilated with the same or larger balloon (Figs. 19-1 through 19-4).

Postprocedure Care

After the procedure, patients are brought to the recovery room for observation while the heparin administered is metabolized; we generally do not use protamine to reverse anticoagulation. It is very convenient and almost essential to have a Hemochron (International Technidyne Corporation) machine available to measure the activated clotting time (ACT) to ascertain at what point it is safe to pull the sheath or catheter. The ACT reflects heparin activity and is a means of assessing the anticoagulation status.[8] After the heparin has worn off, the vascular sheath is removed and compression is applied until hemostasis is achieved.

Figure 19-1. (A) Angiogram showing multiple stenoses of the anterior tibial artery, which is the sole runoff vessel. (B) Postangioplasty angiogram. The patient had a palpable dorsalis pedis pulse.

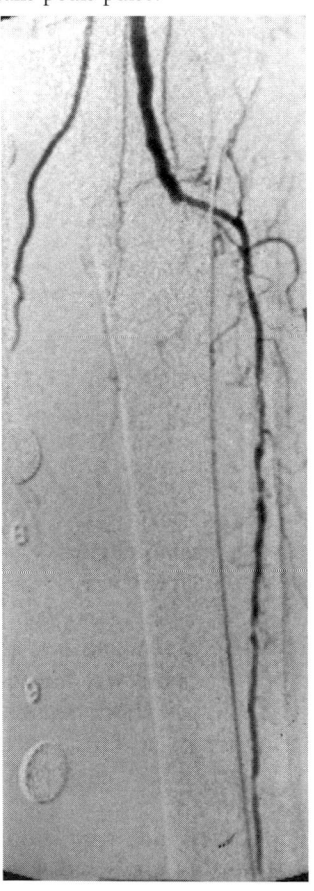
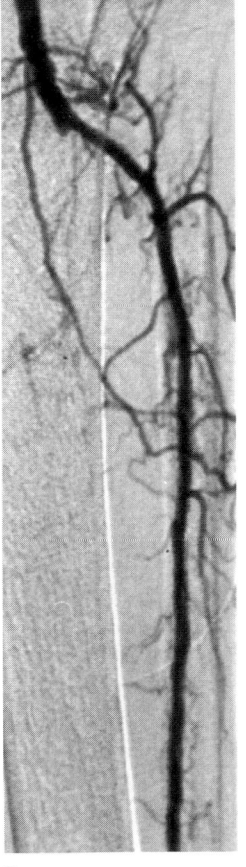

A   B

Figure 19-2. (A) Angiogram showing severe focal stenosis ▶ of the distal left anterior tibial artery. (B) Postangioplasty angiogram. (C) Repeat angiogram 10 months after the procedure when the patient presented with symptoms in the other leg.

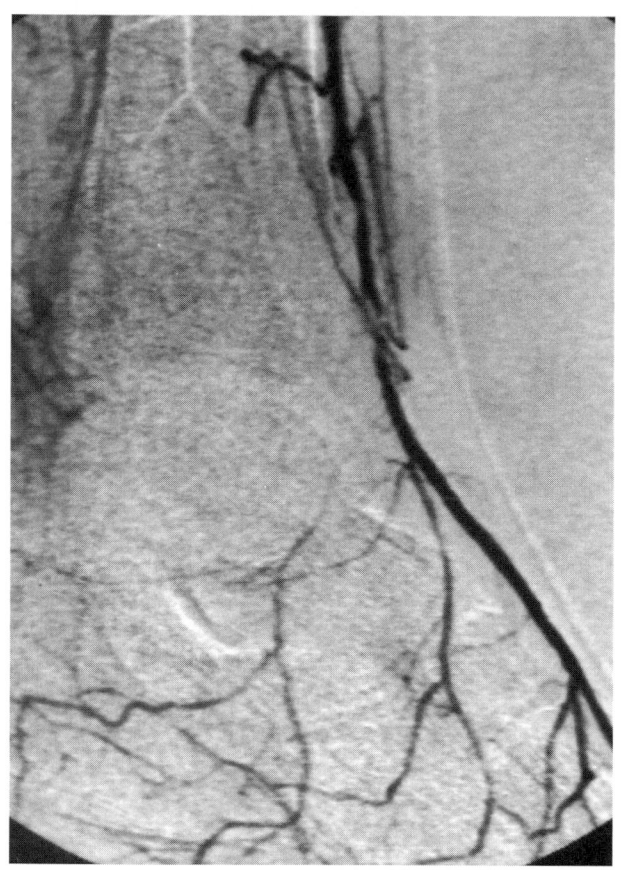

A

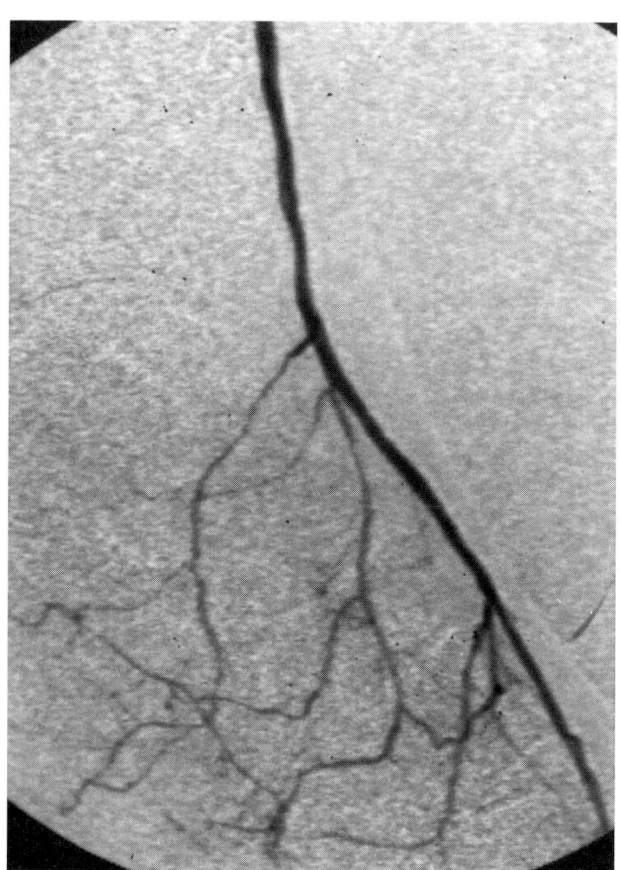

B

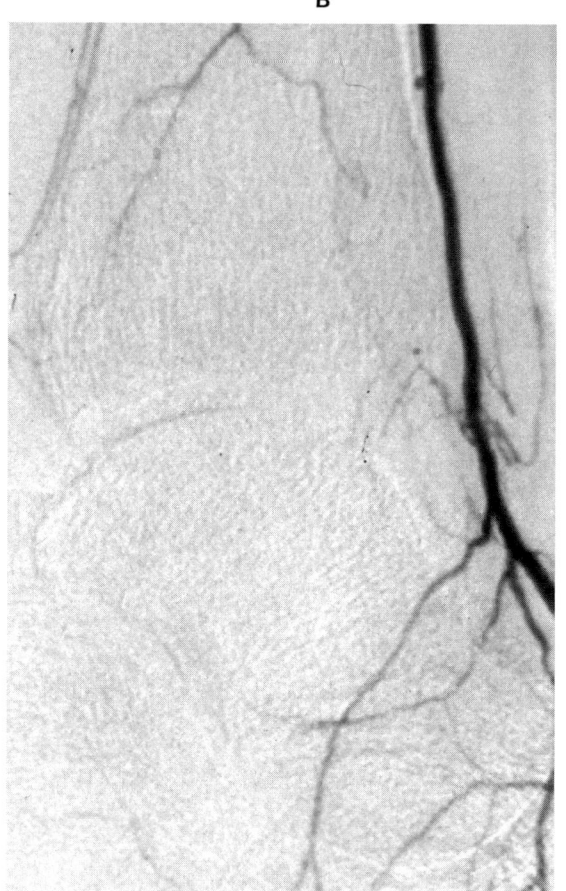

C

287

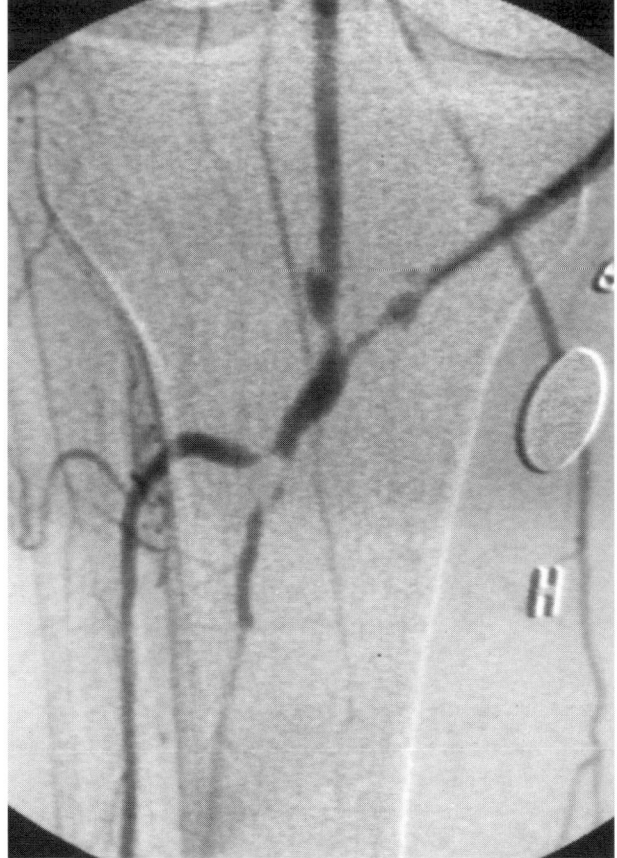

A

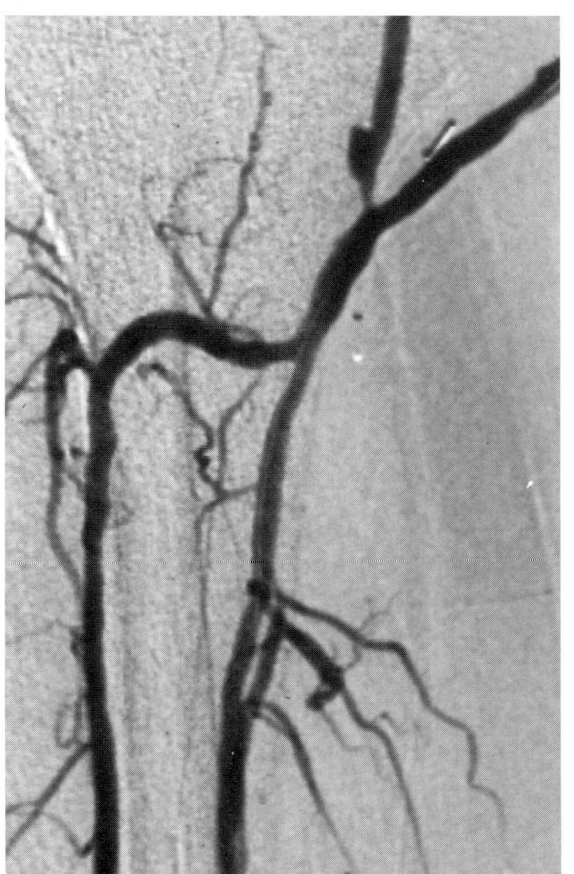

C

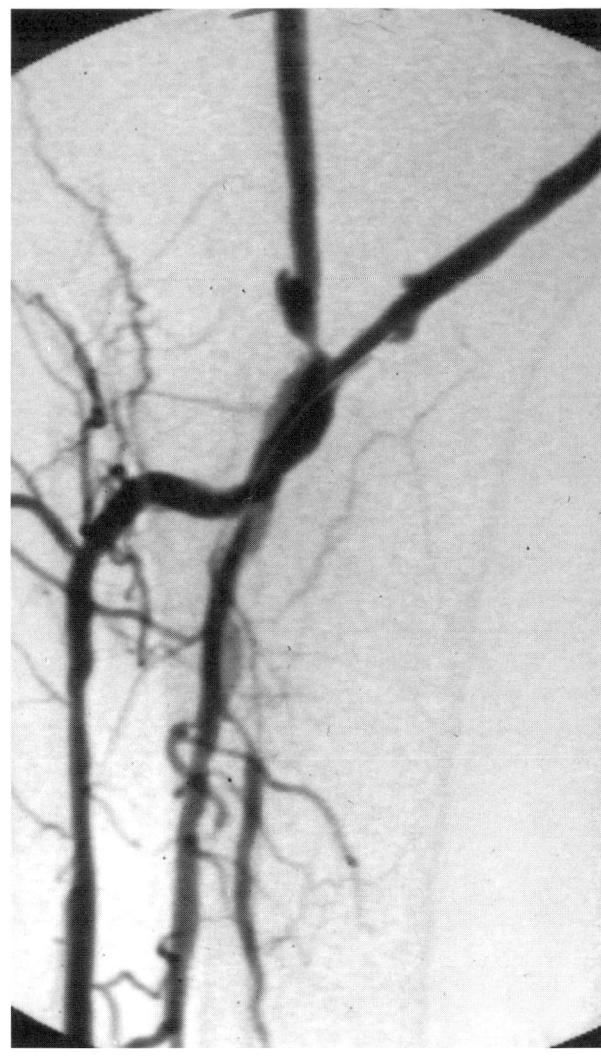

B

Figure 19-3. (A) Angiogram showing severe stenoses at the distal anastomosis of a femoropopliteal bypass graft and at the origins of the anterior tibial artery and tibial peroneal trunk. (B) Postangioplasty angiogram. (C) Angiogram 2 years later after reangioplasty of the distal graft anastomosis. The native vessels remain patent.

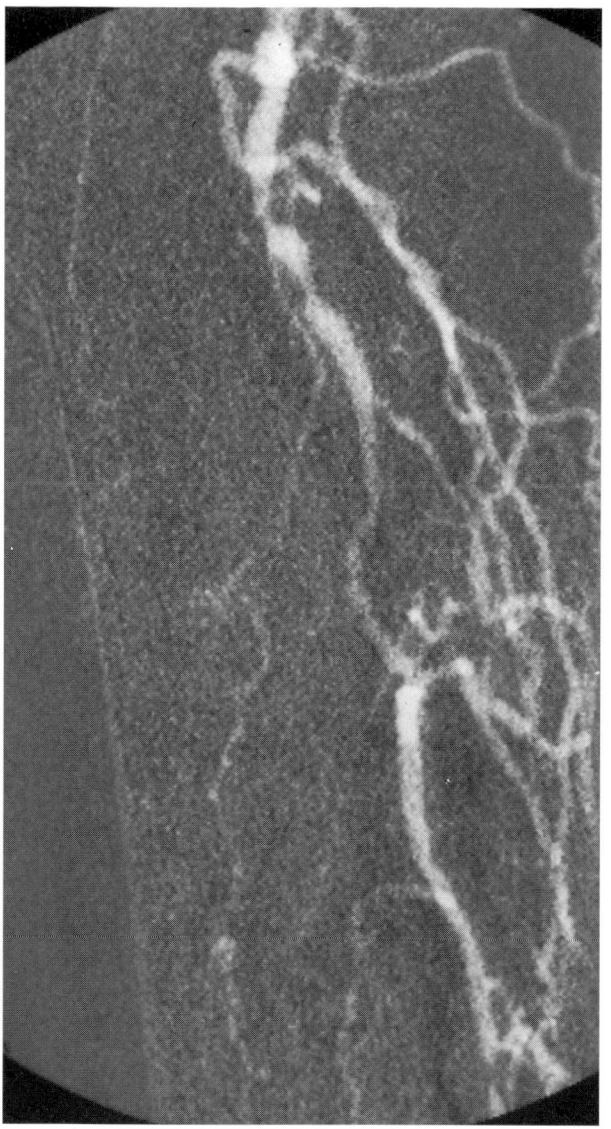

A

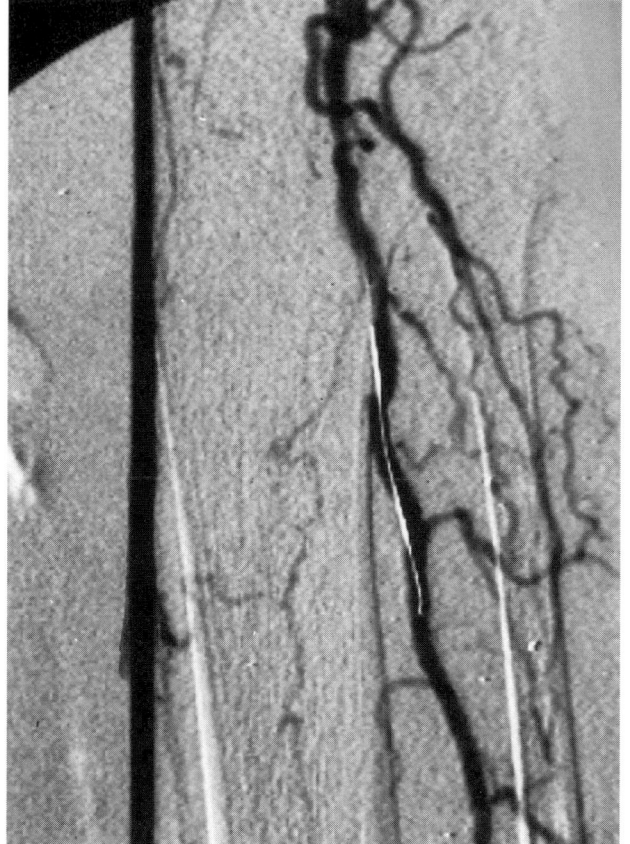

B

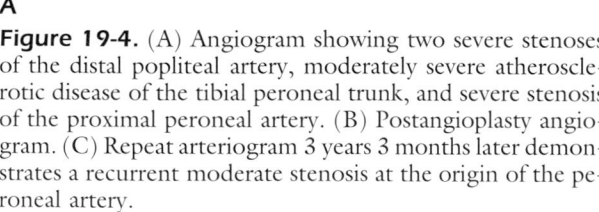

Figure 19-4. (A) Angiogram showing two severe stenoses of the distal popliteal artery, moderately severe atherosclerotic disease of the tibial peroneal trunk, and severe stenosis of the proximal peroneal artery. (B) Postangioplasty angiogram. (C) Repeat arteriogram 3 years 3 months later demonstrates a recurrent moderate stenosis at the origin of the peroneal artery.

C

Patients are not routinely anticoagulated after the procedure. However, patients with a poor initial angiographic result and/or extensive distal atherosclerosis with slow flow are often anticoagulated. After successful angioplasty, chronic antiplatelet therapy with aspirin is recommended. There is no consensus on the correct dosage[9] and either 80 mg daily or 325 mg every other day is recommended.

Pharmacologic Agents

Anticoagulants

After vascular access has been achieved, the patient is systemically anticoagulated. Recommendations for the level of anticoagulation vary. The authors routinely give between 8000 and 10,000 units of heparin, depending on the extent of tibial disease, the length of the procedure, and the size of the patient. If the procedure is prolonged, additional heparin is given. The activated clotting time (ACT) is kept between 260 and 280 seconds.

Antispasmodics and Vasodilators

The tibial vessels, like the coronary arteries, are prone to spasm and occlusion. Patients are usually given 10 mg of nifedipine orally before the procedure. Liberal boluses of 100 to 200 µg of nitroglycerin are also given intraarterially to prevent spasm. Nitroglycerin is administered before passing a wire into a tibial vessel as well as after dilation.

On occasion, significant spasm remains in the tibial vessel after angioplasty despite aliquots of intraarterial nitroglycerin. In this instance, a 30-mg dose of intraarterial papaverine is often helpful. This may be given through the balloon catheter or from the side port of the vascular sheath. The papaverine should be diluted in approximately 20 ml of normal saline to diminish pain and burning on administration.

Complications

The complications of tibial angioplasty are the same as for angioplasty of other vessels and include spasm, thrombosis, subintimal dissection, embolization, perforation, and rupture (Table 19-3).

Thrombosis

Tibial artery thrombosis may occur in situ as the result of slow flow in diseased vessels, as the result of an embolus, or as a complication of angioplasty. In the case

Table 19-3. Complications of Tibial Angioplasty in 511 Patients[a]

Complications	No. of Patients	Percent
Death within 30 days	8	1.6
Myocardial infarction	1	0.2
Pulmonary edema	1	0.2
Acute thrombosis		
Surgical treatment	5	1.0
Lysis	14	2.7
Rethrombosis after primary lysis		
Amputation	1	0.2
Lysis	1	0.2
Renal failure	4	0.8
Distal embolization—clinically significant	1	0.2
Vessel rupture	1	0.2
Major hematoma[b]		
Surgical evacuation	7	1.3
Transfusion	6	1.2
Pseudoaneurysm at puncture site	2	0.4
Vessel perforation	3	0.6
Groin infection	1	0.2
Distal embolization—clinically insignificant	9	1.8
Minor hematoma[b]	18	3.5
Transient renal failure	3	0.6
Spasm	9	1.8
Total	95	18.5

[a]Complications are not divided into major and minor because different authors classify the same complication differently. There is also incomplete reporting of all complications. This table represents the authors' attempt to collect the available data and to present them in a somewhat arbitrary order of decreasing clinical significance.
[b]Four major hematomas and 4 minor hematomas occurred after urokinase administration.
Data from references 7, 11, 14, 15, 16, and 22.

of an acute occlusion, a 3 French catheter or an open-lumen guidewire (Cragg-Medi-Tech, Sos-Bard, etc.) may be passed into the tibial vessel. The vessel is then laced with a bolus of 125,000 to 250,000 units of urokinase. A drip infusion at 250,000 units per hour is started and run from 1 to 2 hours either selectively into a single occluded tibial vessel or from the distal popliteal artery if more than one vessel is involved. If the thrombus has not resolved, an overnight drip may be started to run between 60,000 and 100,000 units per hour. Alternatively, a multi-side-hole open-lumen infusion guidewire (Katzen Infusion Wire, Medi-Tech) or a 3 French multislit catheter (Pulse-Spray, Angiodynamics) may be inserted into the vessel and a pulsed urokinase infusion performed.

Embolization

On occasion, embolization of atherosclerotic plaque or organized thrombus occurs during angioplasty and becomes a persistent filling defect that does not lyse.

A nontapered 5 or 6 French catheter can be used to aspirate this material and is then withdrawn from the vessel under continuous suction through a sheath.[10]

Results

Early studies of tibial angioplasty were not encouraging. In a series from 1980, Sprayregen et al.[2] performed dilatations with tapered catheters. Technical success was achieved in four of six patients, with good clinical results in just two patients at 19 and 22 months after angioplasty. In a series from 1982, Tamura et al.[3] performed tibial dilatation with either tapered catheters or 3-mm and 4-mm balloon catheters after popliteal or superficial femoral artery angioplasty. Of the five tibial angioplasties attempted, only three were technically successful. Of the two that were clinically successful in the short term, symptoms recurred at 3 months in 1 and at 6 months in the other.

Technical success and clinical results have improved with the refinement in catheters and guidewires and improvement in radiographic equipment. Since 1988 a limited number of series of tibial angioplasty patients have concluded that the results are favorable in selected patients (Table 19-4). Recent studies have attempted to define the groups likely to benefit. Clearly, the success of the procedure is influenced by the severity and number of lesions as well as the condition of the distal outflow. Bakal et al.[11] used the term *straight-line flow* to indicate continuous flow to the foot through a tibial vessel whose diameter is narrowed by 75 percent or less. They showed a 97 percent (28 out of 29) clinical response when angioplasty restored straight-line flow to the foot but only a 36 percent (4 out of 11) clinical response when it did not. By life-table analysis, the Bakal series had a 57 percent PTA-assisted limb salvage rate at 2 years with an 82 percent PTA-assisted limb salvage rate at 2 years for patients with straight-line flow to the foot.[12]

One of the largest modern series was reported by Schwarten and Cutliff,[7] who included below-the-knee popliteal dilatations and excluded patients with acute ischemia. Of the 96 patients who had angioplasty with balloon catheters, 97 percent had primary clinical success.[13] By life-table analysis, the cumulative limb salvage at 2 years was 86 percent, which rivals many surgical series. However, only 35 patients were available for follow-up at that interval.

A series by Horvath et al.[14] reported angioplasty procedures on 103 infrapopliteal vessels in 71 patients. The cumulative limb salvage by life-table analysis was 79.8, 75.3, and 64.6 percent at 1, 2, and 3 years, respectively.

In a large series of 168 patients from Austria, Bull et al.[15] also included below-the-knee popliteal arteries and femoropopliteal grafts. By life-table analysis, single stenoses had the greatest cumulative clinical success (83 percent) at 3 years, followed by 76 percent for multilevel lesions, 44 percent after lytic therapy, 36 percent for segmental occlusions, and only 14 percent for anastomotic stenoses. The patients with rest pain had better clinical success than those with tissue necrosis.

Brown et al.[16] found a 79 percent long-term (about 25.8 months) success rate in patients who had angioplasty of only native vessels but only 36 percent success when patients who had infrainguinal bypass grafts were included. Like Bakal et al., Brown et al. found that the success rate was improved when continuous runoff was reestablished. They also found poor results in patients with bypass grafts requiring thrombolysis before PTA and with lesions near the distal anastomoses of bypass grafts, despite good cosmetic results on postprocedure arteriograms. Since atherectomy specimens from such locations yielded myointimal hyper-

Table 19-4. Tibial Angioplasty Results

Series	Number of Patients/Limbs/Vessels	Age (mean)	1° Clinical Success (%)	Cumulative Limb Salvage (%)		
				1 yr	2 yr	3 yr
Schwarten[13]	96/112/146	35–86 (66)	100 (88)	88.0	83.0	NA
Bakal[11,12]	53/57/76	36–96 (70)	28 (78)	60.0	57.0	NA
Horvath[14]	71/NA/103	44–92 (70.2)	63 (92.5)	79.8	75.3	64.6
Bull[15]	168/168/186	44–89 (67.1) F 27–89 (61.6) M	130 (77)	67.0	67.0	NA
Saab[22]	13/14/17	52–83 (67)	10/14 (71)	77.0	77.0	NA
Brown[16]	40/55/NA	(67.6) F (68.7) M	46/55 (84)	60.0	50.0	NA
New York Hosp	70/82/114	34–99 (71.7)	69/82 (84)	72.1	63.5	NA

NA = not available; F = female; M = male.

plasia, the utility of angioplasty in these areas is doubtful.

In the authors' yet unpublished series of tibial angioplasty performed on 82 limbs in 70 patients, there was a limb salvage rate of 64 percent at 2 years. When only the technically successful procedures were included, the limb salvage rate at 2 years was 78 percent, and the results were similar in diabetics and nondiabetics.

Large differences exist between the series in the number of complications reported. Schwarten[7] reported two intraprocedural thromboses after an initial bolus of 5000 units of heparin. These were successfully thrombolysed. Bakal[11] reported three major complications: two puncture site hematomas that required surgical repair, and one death from cardiopulmonary arrest after the procedure. The Horvath series[14] had three major complications: an anterior tibial artery rupture treated by surgical bypass, an intimal flap causing vessel occlusion, and a puncture site hematoma that was evacuated. The Bull series[15] had a much higher incidence of major complications (11.3 percent) than the others. However, 9 cases of spasm were included in this list, as well as 11 cases of thrombosis. This may have been due to inadequate heparinization, since heparin was given at 1000 units per hour but no initial bolus was administered. Although complications occurred in 16 of 55 procedures in the Brown series,[16] 75 percent were associated with primary thrombolysis. The major complications in the present authors' series included three cases of renal failure, one myocardial infarction within 24 hours of the procedure, and two deaths. One death occurred 31 days after the procedure because of multiple cardiac problems, and the other occurred 2 days after redilation of a recurrent stenosis secondary to heart failure. Two intraprocedural thromboses were successfully thrombolysed, and another underwent a surgical bypass. There were also two hematomas requiring transfusions.

Discussion

Because limb loss is a potential consequence of complications of tibial PTA, the patients who were initially chosen for the procedure had to have limb-threatening ischemia with rest pain (grade 2, category 4) or tissue loss (grade 2, category 5). With the increasing success resulting from the continued evolution of catheters and guidewires and the increased experience of the operators, these indications have been expanded by many to include disabling claudication (grade 1, category 3). Indeed, in many institutions, angioplasty has become

the first approach for patients in these categories. Nonetheless, it is important to not jeopardize a potential surgical option with a technically or clinically unsuccessful procedure.

Restoration of continuous flow to the foot has been shown to be highly predictive of a beneficial clinical response. Patients with discontinuous flow do significantly less well. This finding has led some authors to suggest that if an angioplasty procedure will not reestablish straight-line flow, the patient may be better served by going directly to surgery for reconstruction, if possible.[16]

The patient's overall general medical condition is an important consideration when deciding between a surgical or a percutaneous approach to tibial disease. The incidence of cardiac disease in the population with peripheral vascular disease is approximately 60 percent. Previous studies have demonstrated a significant correlation between early death after arterial reconstruction and the presence of trifurcation disease.[17] As with any intervention, the aim is to optimize the risk-benefit ratio.

An additional advantage of angioplasty is that the procedure may be repeated for either recurrent disease or disease progression.

Another consideration is the availability of veins for bypass. Synthetic grafts do poorly when used for infrapopliteal bypass.[18,19] If the vein has been used for coronary bypass grafts, it may be possible in some patients to perform a bypass with synthetic material above the knee and to treat the infrapopliteal disease with angioplasty. Also, tibial PTA may allow a vein to be preserved for future use.

Initial tibial angioplasty results approach those of surgical series, although more long-term follow-up is needed. The associated mortality and morbidity of surgery make PTA an important option in selected patients.

Other Modalities

Although angioplasty remains the primary percutaneous modality for recanalization of the infrapopliteal arteries, many new devices have been developed in recent years for this purpose.[20] Atherectomy was developed to remove plaque from the vessel and was theoretically superior to PTA because it avoided subintimal dissection and would decrease the restenosis rate by reducing the plaque burden. Although some authors advocate atherectomy for eccentric or calcified lesions or occlusions, there is limited experience in the tibial vessels. Directional atherectomy catheters such as the Simpson AtheroCath and AtheroTrack (Peripheral

Systems Group) are best suited for short, eccentric, or calcified lesions.[20] Although complication rates for use in the suprapopliteal vessels are low, there are no significant data from procedures performed in the tibial vessels.

The Kensey atherectomy catheter (Dow-Corning-Wright) has a rotating tip and is designed for occlusions. The catheter is not well suited for the tibial vessels because it has a high perforation rate and has difficulty recanalizing calcified plaque. The Auth Rotablator (Biophysics International) has a rotating metal burr on the catheter tip coated with diamond chips. The Rotablator is limited by an inability to recanalize areas of chronic thrombus and rubbery atherosclerotic intima.[20] The results in superficial femoral and popliteal arteries have been poor and have involved a high incidence of complications. A circumferential atherectomy catheter, the ARROW-Fischell Pullback Atherectomy Catheter (Arrow International Inc.), has undergone clinical trials.

Several studies with hot tip laser probes have not demonstrated improved long-term success over balloon angioplasty.[21] The results in the tibial vessels have been poor. The excimer laser, which uses pulsed wave laser energy (thought to reduce arterial injury), is currently undergoing clinical trials. No studies have yet demonstrated that any of these modalities surpass the clinical success of angioplasty.

References

1. Dotter CT, Judkins MP. Transluminal treatment of arteriosclerotic obstruction: description of a new technique and a preliminary report of its application. Circulation 1964;30:654–670.
2. Sprayregen S, Sniderman KW, Sos TA, Vieux U, Singer A, Veith FJ. Popliteal artery branches: percutaneous transluminal angioplasty. AJR 1980;135:945–950.
3. Tamura S, Sniderman KW, Beinart C, Sos TA. Percutaneous transluminal angioplasty of the popliteal artery and its branches. Radiology 1982;143:645–648.
4. Rutherford RB, Flanigan DP, Gupta SK, et al. Suggested standards for dealing with lower extremity ischemia. J Vasc Surg 1986;4:80–94.
5. Barnes RW. Noninvasive Diagnostic Assessment of Peripheral Vascular Disease. Circulation 1991;83(Suppl I):20–27.
6. Johnston KW, Rae M, Hogg-Johnston SA, et al. Five-year results of a prospective study of percutaneous transluminal angioplasty. Ann Surg 1987;206:403–413.
7. Schwarten DE, Cutliff WB. Arterial occlusive disease below the knee: treatment with percutaneous transluminal angioplasty performed with low profile catheters and steerable guidewires. Radiology 1988;169:71–74.
8. Rath B, Bennett DH. Monitoring the effect of heparin by measurement of activated clotting time during and after percutaneous transluminal angioplasty. Br Heart J 1990;63:18–21.
9. Bochner F, Lloyd J. Is there an optimal dose and formulation of aspirin to prevent arterial thrombo-embolism in man? Clin Sci 1986;71:625–631.
10. Sniderman KW, Bodner L, Saddekni S, Srur M, Sos TA. Percutaneous embolectomy by transcatheter aspiration. Radiology 1984;150:357–361.
11. Bakal CW, Sprayregen S, Scheinbaum K, Cynamon J, Veith FJ. Percutaneous transluminal angioplasty of the infrapopliteal arteries: results in 53 patients. AJR 1990;154:171–174.
12. Bakal CW, Cynamon J, Sprayregen S, Goldsmith J, Raden M, Veith FJ. Infrapopliteal artery angioplasty: followup and factors influencing clinical response. Presented at SCVIR 17th Annual Meeting, April 4–9, 1992.
13. Schwarten DE. Clinical and anatomical considerations for nonoperative therapy in tibial disease and the results of angioplasty. Circulation 1991;83(Suppl I):86–90.
14. Horvath W, Oertl M, Haidinger D. Percutaneous transluminal angioplasty of crural arteries. Radiology 1990;177:565–569.
15. Bull PG, Mendel H, Hold M, Schlegl A, Denck H. Distal popliteal and tibioperoneal transluminal angioplasty: long-term follow-up. J Vasc Intervent Radiol 1992;3:45–53.
16. Brown KT, Moore ED, Getrajdman GI, Saddekni S. Infrapopliteal angioplasty: Long-term follow-up. J Vasc Intervent Radiol 1993;4:139–144.
17. Kallero KS, Bergqvist D, Cederholm C, Jonsson K, Olsson P, Takolander R. Late mortality and morbidity after arterial reconstruction: the influence of arteriosclerosis in popliteal artery trifurcation. J Vasc Surg 1985;2:541–546.
18. Veith FJ, Gupta SK, Ascer E, White-Flores S, Samson RH, Scher LA, et al. Six-year prospective multicenter randomized comparison of autologous saphenous vein and expanded polytetrafluoroethylene grafts in infrainguinal arterial reconstructions. J Vasc Surg 1986;3:104–114.
19. Veterans Administration Cooperative Study Group 141. Comparative evaluation of prosthetic, reversed, and in situ vein bypass grafts in distal popliteal and tibial-peroneal revascularization. Arch Surg 1988;123:434–438.
20. Ahn SS. Status of peripheral atherectomy. Surg Clin North Am 1992;72:869–878.
21. Self SB, Seeger JM. Laser angioplasty. Surg Clin North Am 1992;72:851–869.
22. Saab MH, Smith DC, Aka PK, et al. Percutaneous transluminal angioplasty of tibial arteries for limb salvage. Cardiovasc Intervent Radiol 1992;15:211–216.

20

Renal Angioplasty

CHARLES J. TEGTMEYER
ALAN H. MATSUMOTO
ALLEN M. JOHNSON

There is a documented large population of hypertensive patients in the United States. The United States National Health Examination Survey indicated that hypertension (blood pressure $\geq 160/95$ mmHg) occurs in 10 to 15 percent of the adult population in this country.[1] There are 23 million persons in this group. Of these, approximately 1 million (about 4 percent) have potentially correctable renovascular hypertension.[2] Angiotensinogenic hypertension, the type seen in approximately 4 percent of the correctable hypertensives in the United States, poses the double threat of severe high blood pressure (with its complications of stroke and coronary artery disease) and progressive renal insufficiency.[3,4]

Pharmacotherapy and surgical revascularization, the traditional modes of treatment for renovascular hypertension, have significant shortcomings. In many cases drugs only partially control blood pressure, and when several drugs are used in combination, side effects and poor patient compliance become a problem.[5-7] In addition, if the renal artery is severely stenotic, lowering the blood pressure with drugs further reduces renal blood flow and may lead to ischemic atrophy or even renal infarction. Zierler et al., in a prospective study performed with duplex ultrasonography, showed that in hypertensive patients with known atherosclerotic renal artery lesions, the rate of progression of the renal artery stenosis was approximately 20 percent per year.[8] Hunt et al. proved that surgical correction of renovascular hypertension was superior to medical therapy.[9] In 7 to 14 years of follow-up, 84 percent of the surgically treated patients were alive, in contrast to only 60 percent of those treated medically. Surgery requires general anesthesia, and many of the patients are poor surgical risks because of severe diffuse atherosclerotic disease, renal insufficiency, or both. Moreover, surgical results vary; there is considerable morbidity, and the mortality rate can be as high as 5.9 percent.[10] Therefore, although surgery and medical therapy have significant benefits,[11,12] because of

these shortcomings there is no question that alternate modes of therapy are desirable.

Grüntzig reported the first successful percutaneous transluminal balloon renal angioplasty (PTRA) in 1978.[13] PTRA has evolved into a highly successful method for correcting renal artery stenosis.[14-32] Renal PTRA has become the initial treatment of choice wherever correction of a hemodynamically significant renal artery stenosis is considered.

Etiology of Renal Artery Stenoses

There are many causes of stenoses in the renal arteries. However, the majority of renal artery lesions are atherosclerotic in origin, and most of the remainder are due to fibromuscular dysplasia. Of the 2442 hypertensive patients who were studied in the cooperative study on renovascular hypertension, 884 had renal artery lesions. Atherosclerosis was the etiology in 557 (63.0 percent), fibromuscular hyperplasia in 286 (32.4 percent), and miscellaneous disease entities in 41 (4.6 percent).[11] In the University of Virginia series,[27] atherosclerosis was the etiology of the stenosis or occlusion in 75 patients (66 percent). Fibromuscular dysplasia was the cause in 27 patients (24 percent), and 7 patients (6 percent) had stenoses in the arteries to their renal transplants. Four patients (3 percent) had stenoses or occlusions of their renal saphenous bypass grafts, and 1 patient (1 percent) had renal artery stenoses due to previous irradiation therapy.

Indications for Renal Angioplasty

It is imperative that the angiographer communicates with the referring physician and the patient before attempting renal angioplasty. The potential risks and benefits of the procedure need to be discussed because the expectations of the referring physician and the patient may be different from those of the angiographer. Often the patient and the referring physician expect that successful PTRA will cure the patient. They expect that the patient will be normotensive and off medication with normal renal function. This may indeed be the case in a young woman with the recent onset of hypertension. However, many of the patients referred for renal angioplasty have long-standing hypertension, and suddenly their blood pressure has become difficult to control. In this situation, successful PTRA will correct the angiotensinogenic component of their hypertension, but the underlying essential hypertension will remain. Although the blood pressure will be easier to control, the patient will still have to be maintained on antihypertension medications. He or she will not be cured. If the patient has renal insufficiency and underlying small-vessel disease or renal parenchymal disease, PTRA may stabilize the condition but will not result in a cure. In short, the results of revascularization for treating renal insufficiency are not as good as the results of treatment for hypertension. However, the alternative is often renal dialysis. For these reasons, the goals for the procedure should be individualized for each patient and fully discussed before PTRA is attempted. This discussion prevents unrealistic expectations and dissatisfaction when the desired results cannot be achieved despite a technically successful result.

The indications for renal angioplasty in patients with hemodynamically significant renal artery lesions include the correction of renovascular hypertension or of the angiotensinogenic component in patients with both essential hypertension and renovascular hypertension. Many of the patients in the University of Virginia series had a long history of essential hypertension with recent acceleration due to superimposed renal artery disease. In patients with deteriorating renal function, renal angioplasty may be indicated, because if there are underlying significant renal artery stenoses, correction of these lesions may preserve or improve renal function.

Indications for Renovascular Evaluation

It is not feasible or cost-effective to completely evaluate all hypertensive patients for renovascular disease. The criteria for workup vary from one medical center to another; however, certain patients have an increased risk of renovascular hypertension and should be evaluated:

1. Patients with a documented sudden onset of hypertension
2. Those without a family history of hypertension or other identifiable secondary causes of hypertension
3. Young women who develop hypertension and are not taking oral contraceptives
4. Patients who develop malignant hypertension
5. Those with long-standing hypertension who suddenly develop accelerated hypertension
6. Individuals who are refractory, or who become refractory, to hypertensive drugs other than blockers of the renin-angiotensin system
7. Patients with a flank bruit
8. Those who develop renal insufficiency while taking an angiotensin-converting enzyme (ACE) inhibitor

The workup of patients suspected of having renovascular hypertension is controversial and varies with the institution. A wide range of diagnostic tests is available. However, there is no clear best method for evaluating these patients because the optimal screening test has not been developed yet. A captopril-enhanced radionuclide scan may be obtained, but this test is expensive, time-consuming, and not as sensitive as once believed. Duplex ultrasound is being used in some centers to evaluate the renal arteries, but the study is operator-dependent, the patient must be cooperative, and the presence of bowel gas causes problems. It is also difficult to detect aberrant renal arteries. In expert hands 10 percent of the studies will not be diagnostic. Thus although the study has the advantage of being noninvasive, it is difficult to perform. The simplest test to perform is a captopril-stimulated peripheral renin analysis, which can be done in the doctor's office. If the test is positive, selective renal vein renin samples can be obtained. However, renal vein renin analysis also depends on the laboratory where the samples are analyzed. The authors are not as enthusiastic about selective renal vein renin analysis as they once were, and they now obtain selective renal vein samples only in patients who have arteriographically detected renal artery stenoses in the 50 to 70 percent range.

If the patient is in the increased risk category, as described above, the authors usually proceed directly to arteriography. If a lesion is detected and it is 70 percent or more of the luminal area, PTRA is done. If the lesion is in the range of 50 to 70 percent, selective renal vein renin samples are obtained. If the renin analysis is positive, the renal artery stenosis is dilated. This method works well because the patients referred for renal angioplasty today are highly selected. Most have long-standing hypertension that has suddenly accelerated, blood pressure that has become refractory to antihypertensive therapy, or renal insufficiency that has developed on an ACE inhibitor. This approach is not specific enough for young patients with sudden onset of hypertension, for whom a better screening test is needed.

Mechanism of Angioplasty

The key to successful PTRA is understanding the mechanisms and principles of balloon angioplasty. Experimental studies[33,34] have clarified the mechanism of percutaneous transluminal angioplasty. Atheromatous material is either a solid or a semiliquid; therefore, it is not compressible. In some lesions, however, it may be possible to redistribute a portion of the plaque along the vessel wall. If redistribution is a factor, this can occur only in atheromas that have not undergone significant fibrotic change. Examination of cadaver specimens, animal models, and isolated clinical specimens demonstrates that angioplasty produces a controlled injury in the vessel wall.[35]

With balloon inflation the vessel wall is initially stretched, and there is desquamation of the endothelium and superficial plaque elements. As the pressure in the balloon is increased, dehiscence of the plaque and the intima occurs. There is stretching or splitting of a portion of the media and stretching of the adventitia beyond its elastic recoil. Blood flow and pressure maintain the patency of the lumen. The disrupted arterial layers heal by fibrosis of the media and neointima formation. This is similar to the healing process that occurs after surgical endarterectomy.

Nonatherosclerotic lesions can also be dilated by balloon angioplasty. The mechanism is similar to dilation of atherosclerotic lesions. The intima is disrupted, and the lesions are stretched and/or split. Because angioplasty creates an injury in the vessel wall, it is important to control the location and magnitude of the injury.

Principles of Angioplasty

Crossing the Stenosis

It is extremely important to keep the guidewire and catheter within the lumen of the vessel when crossing the lesion. This requires careful technique and high-resolution fluoroscopy.

Subintimal dilatations frequently do not remain patent and often result in complete occlusion of the vessel. Therefore, it is essential to maintain an intraluminal course. The initial crossing of the lesion should be performed as atraumatically as possible. At some centers, oral antispasmodic medications are administered before angioplasty to prevent spasm. Anticoagulant drugs are injected immediately on introduction of the diagnostic catheter into the proximal renal artery to reduce thrombogenesis. At the University of Virginia, parenteral antispasmodic and anticoagulant medications are given after successful crossing of the lesion but before exchange of the diagnostic catheter for the angioplasty balloon catheter.

A variety of catheters and guidewires are available, and new ones are continually being developed. It is clear, however, that 5 French catheters have a decided advantage over larger selective catheters for crossing tight lesions in the renal arteries. The 5 French catheters still retain the torque control necessary to select the renal arteries, especially in the presence of a tortuous aorta, but they are small enough to be passed across tight lesions in the renal arteries. Larger-diameter catheters select the vessels more easily, but they often cannot be passed across the stenosis, and they may be more injurious to diseased aortas.

Because the Bentson wire is flexible, it is usually the first wire used to cross the lesion. When a slight curve is needed at the tip, the wire can be shaped by drawing it between the tip of the index finger and the thumbnail. If the Bentson wire fails, other guidewires are tried. However, it is prudent to begin with flexible guidewires and to progress to stiffer ones only when necessary to cross the lesion. The 0.014- to 0.018-inch floppy platinum-tipped steerable guidewires used for tibial and coronary angioplasty can be used either by themselves or in a coaxial combination with a 0.038-inch "open-ended," or "interventional," guidewire when other wires have failed.[36] The guidewire may also be helpful in difficult lesions.

Another approach that is often helpful in the renal arteries is to gently advance the appropriate 5 French diagnostic catheter across the stenosis while simultaneously injecting contrast material. The steady flow of contrast material keeps the tip of the catheter off the vessel wall and delineates the lumen of the vessel. If the catheter is advanced slowly and carefully, difficult lesions can often be crossed. Cooperative patients can use deep inspiration and expiration to alter the craniocaudal direction of their renal artery and can be asked to cough to help advance the guidewire through difficult stenoses. A combination of these maneuvers is often necessary to cross long fibromuscular lesions in the renal arteries.

Once the diagnostic catheter has crossed the lesion, the catheter must be exchanged for the appropriate balloon catheter. It is important to avoid trauma to the vessel distal to the lesion during the exchange. Parenteral antispasmodic medications are administered before this catheter exchange. Despite all precautions, however, the tip of the guidewire moves in the vessel during the exchange. It is important, therefore, to use a wire that is flexible at the tip but also stiff enough throughout most of the length to assist the balloon catheter in passing through the lesion. Two basic exchange wires are used: a 0.035-inch, heavy-duty, 1.5-mm movable-core J wire with the core withdrawn 1 to 2 cm, or a 0.035-inch, 1.5-mm J Rosen wire. After the balloon catheter has been inserted and its intraluminal position is confirmed by a test injection, a Y adapter is attached to the catheter and an 0.018-inch, 1.5-mm J guidewire is inserted through the catheter. This allows the guidewire to remain in place across the lesion during the procedure. Contrast material can be injected through the Y adapter to monitor the progress of the dilation while the guidewire is still in position.

Choice of Proper Balloon Diameter

When choosing and inflating the balloon, one should consider several general principles. The balloon should provide a controllable, nearly pure radial force. This radial force reduces the chance of distal embolization because there is no axial component once the balloon is in place. Both the artery to be dilated and the balloon catheter may be considered thin-walled, somewhat elastic cylinders. Thus balloon dilation is governed by the law of Laplace, according to which wall tension (T) in a cylinder is equal to its internal pressure (P) multiplied by its internal radius (R): $T = P \times R$.[37]

Therefore, increasing the radius of the balloon increases the tension on the lesion. If the balloon is undersized, very little force will be applied to the lesion, no matter how much pressure is applied to the balloon. Therefore, selecting the proper-size balloon is critical. Several manufacturers are developing catheters and guidewires with distance markers that can provide and approximate magnification "correction" factors for vessel and balloon sizing. This is especially important when only digital subtraction angiography images are available. The vessel is measured proximal and distal to the stenosis, and the original size of the vessel is estimated in the area of the stenosis. At the University of Virginia, a cut-film arteriogram is obtained. If the artery measures 6 mm in diameter, this is the size of the balloon that is used (Fig. 20-1). Because this does not take into account the magnification factor, the artery is slightly overdilated. When in doubt, one should use a smaller-size balloon initially.

The amount of pain experienced by the patient can indicate whether the proper-size balloon has been used. Patients may normally experience mild to moderate flank or abdominal pain during balloon inflation in the renal arteries. However, the pain should diminish almost immediately following balloon deflation and disappear gradually, usually within a minute. Continued intense pain following balloon deflation is frequently an indication of severe renal artery injury, such as rupture or occlusion. If the patient experiences unusually severe pain during balloon inflation, it is prudent to deflate the balloon immediately. If the pain

Figure 20-1. The balloon catheter is selected to correspond to the original diameter of the stenotic renal artery. Poststenotic dilatation must be taken into account. Because the renal arteries are magnified by 15 to 20 percent on standard angiograms, the arteries will be overdilated by approximately 1 mm. (From Tegtmeyer CJ, Kellum CD, Ayers C. Percutaneous transluminal angioplasty of the renal artery: results and long-term follow-up. Radiology 1984;153:77–84. Used with permission.)

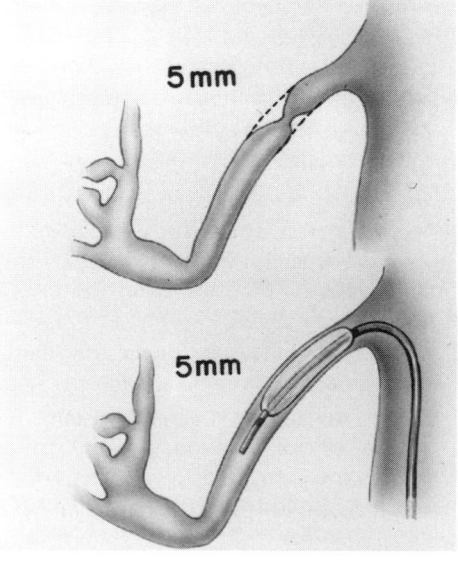
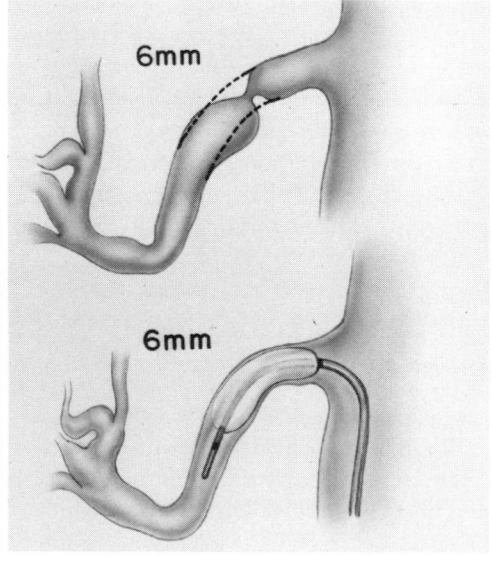

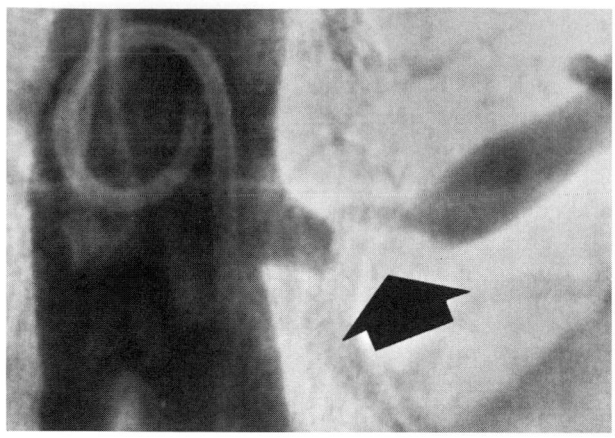

A

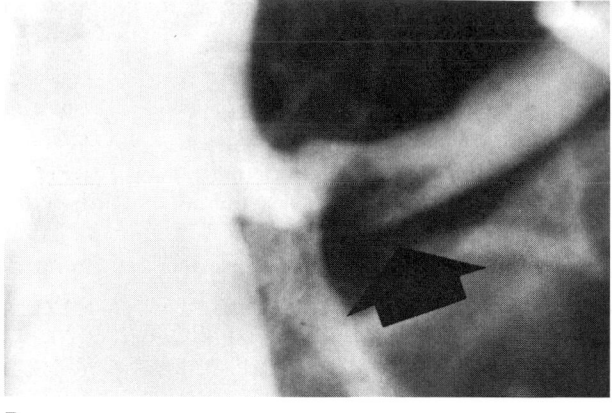

B

C

Figure 20-2. Arteriograms of a 59-year-old hypertensive man with progressive renal failure exacerbated by captopril therapy illustrate the importance of selecting the proper-size balloon. (A) Midstream arteriogram reveals a tight stenosis (*arrow*) in the left renal artery. (B) Arteriogram obtained immediately after dilatation with a 7-mm balloon shows a large subintimal split; however, there is residual stenosis (*arrow*). The patient did not experience any pain when the balloon was inflated. (C) The lesion was immediately redilated with an 8-mm balloon, and the vessel is markedly improved (*arrow*). Comment: The initial balloon was chosen by measuring the artery, as described in the text. This technique is usually successful; however, the lesion was underdilated. In this case a larger balloon was necessary. (From Tegtmeyer CJ, Sos TA. The techniques of renal angioplasty. Radiology 1986;161:577–586. Used with permission.)

disappears rapidly, it is probably safe to reinflate the balloon or use a balloon of the next smaller size. One should proceed with caution, however, because severe pain during inflation of the balloon indicates that the balloon is probably too large. On the other hand, if the patient does not feel any discomfort as the balloon is inflated and the indentation of the plaque on the balloon remains, or during deflation the balloon is re-indented in the region of the original lesion or a test injection shows a residual stenosis, a larger balloon should be used to redilate the lesion (Fig. 20-2). This is done because follow-up studies have shown that if there is greater than 30 percent residual stenosis, the lesion is more likely to recur.[21,26,27]

Choice of Balloon Material and Inflation Pressures

Once the proper-size balloon has been selected, the pressure in the balloon becomes a factor. For a balloon of a given size, an increase in pressure will increase the dilating force in a linear fashion providing there is no change in the lesion. Because most atheromatous lesions are thick-walled, the law of Laplace provides only an approximation. However, the stress on the wall increases as the diameter of the lumen increases and the wall thickness decreases. When the vessel is being dilated, the risk of vessel rupture increases as larger balloons are employed and more pressure is applied. It is also important to remember that normal vessels will rupture more readily at a lower pressure than will thickened atheromatous vessels. However, in practice, normal renal vessels over 5 mm in diameter usually will not rupture if they are overdilated by 1 mm. This fact should be considered when choosing the length of the balloon. Two-centimeter balloons are usually employed for dilating renal lesions. These are long enough to provide proper coverage of the lesion by straddling it without unnecessary damage to adjacent normal portions of the vessel.

The angioplasty balloon catheter is inflated with a mixture of one-half contrast material and one-half saline. This mixture has a concentration of 30 percent. It is dense enough to opacify the balloon yet fluid enough to inflate and deflate the balloon rapidly. The catheter can be inflated either with an automatic pump or by hand. The advantage of the automatic inflation device is that one hand of the operator is available to stabilize the balloon in position during the inflation. There are several basic physical principles governing the choice of syringe. If constant force is applied to the plunger, the pressure is inversely proportional to the syringe diameter. The smaller the diameter of the syringe, the greater the pressure that can be applied. Inflation of a 3-ml syringe with an inner diameter of a 0.78 cm can generate 21 atm of pressure. A 10-ml syringe with a barrel diameter of 1.4 cm is capable of generating only 9.4 atm of pressure.[37] When the syringe is deflated, the reverse is true. The larger the syringe, the greater its volume and therefore the greater the suction produced. Some angiographers use a two-way stopcock and inflate with a small 10-ml syringe and deflate with a larger 60-ml syringe. A 10-ml syringe is the ideal size if only one syringe is employed. This syringe minimizes the likelihood of overinflation of the balloon and at the same time provides enough pressure to easily inflate the balloon to 6 atm.

Inflation of the balloon should usually be monitored with a pressure gauge. Initially, when angioplasty was performed with the compliant polyvinyl chloride balloons, which continued to expand past their nominal diameter and thus gave a continuous tactile and visual feedback, a few angiographers indicated that they could monitor by feel and by fluoroscopic observation the amount of pressure applied, and therefore they did not use a pressure gauge. This is not the case with the standard polyethylene balloons and the high-pressure Mylar (DuPont) balloons. These balloons are less pliable, and they do not continue to expand past their predetermined diameter as the pressure increases. Therefore, there is less tactile and visual warning before balloon rupture. If a pressure gauge is not used with these newer balloons, it is difficult to know how much pressure is being applied.

Given the same pressure, the balloon will exert more pressure on a long lesion than on a short one. At the same pressure, a balloon will exert more force on a tight stenosis than on one that is not as severe. Maintenance of high pressure over a longer period of time weakens the lesion somewhat, resulting in further dilation of resistant lesions. Also, repeated dilatations will stretch the wall of the vessel and the balloon, increasing somewhat the diameter of the vessel in resistant lesions.

The same physical factors that govern the success of the dilation also affect the performance of the balloon. The greater the pressure applied to the balloon, the longer the duration of the pressure applied, and the more times the balloon is inflated, the more likely the balloon will rupture. This was especially true for the early polyvinyl chloride balloons but is less likely with the stronger polyethylene and Mylar balloons currently being used. The larger the diameter of the balloon, the less pressure it takes to rupture the balloon. An 8-mm balloon will rupture at less pressure than a 4-mm balloon. A guidewire must always be in place during the dilation, and the balloon should be inflated slowly, first to 2 atm and then gradually higher. This is because the high-pressure balloons, when fully inflated, become so rigid that they may drive the tip of the balloon through the upper wall of the renal artery when the balloon is inflated in a curved vessel, as is often the case in renal dilation. In addition, the "split" in the vessel wall may be too extensive if the balloon is inflated rapidly. Gradual inflation will usually prevent extensive damage to the vessel.

Pressure measurements are not obtained in the renal arteries at the University of Virginia because it is believed that the end point is the appearance of the artery, not merely the reduction of the pressure gradient. After angioplasty, the deflated balloon catheter should be withdrawn from the renal artery over a guidewire so that the upward deflection of the relatively rigid tip of the catheter does not damage the upper surface of the vessel.

Mindful of these factors, one should approach balloon dilatation cautiously. The size of the balloon is critical: only enough force to fully expand the balloon in the lesion should be used, beginning with 2 to 3 atm. At these low pressures, the impression of the lesion on the balloon allows for proper positioning. Once the balloon has been properly positioned, the pressure can be increased until the balloon expands completely. The balloon should be fixed so it cannot move while it is inflated. Moving the inflated balloon converts the radial force into an axial shearing force and may result in complete disruption of the intima and creation of a large occluding flap and/or distal embolization. Four to 10 atm is adequate to dilate most renal lesions. The balloon should be inflated for 30 to 60 seconds, then deflated. It should also be observed fluoroscopically during deflation, because at reduced pressure and volume it forms a cast of the artery, and therefore a reindentation in the area of the original lesion suggests an incomplete dilatation. Repeat dilatations should be kept as few in number as possible to avoid increased trauma to the vessel and to prevent distal embolization; in most cases, two to three dilatations are adequate. If the lesion does not respond, the pressure and the duration of balloon inflation should be increased. Inflation of the balloon should always be monitored under fluoroscopic control, and a pressure gauge should be used. It is important to remember that only polyvinyl chloride balloons change shape with excess pressure, either "ballooning" eccentrically or lengthening; these are signs of impending rupture. If this occurs, the balloon should be rapidly deflated and not reinflated. Some lesions will not respond completely, but one should remember that *excellent* is the enemy of *good*. In an effort to achieve an excellent result, the renal artery may be ruptured, resulting in a major complication. According to Poiseuille's equation ($Q = \pi P R^4 8 \eta L$), doubling the radius of the vessel produces a 16-fold increase in flow. Therefore, there may be dramatic improvement in flow despite the appearance of the lesion. If a large residual stenosis is left behind, the lesion is more likely to recur,[21,26,27] but this is obviously preferable to rupturing the vessel. Angioplasty produces an injury in the vessel wall, and it is important to keep the injury under control. The easiest way to rupture a vessel is by using a very oversized balloon.

Techniques

Since the introduction of renal balloon angioplasty by Grüntzig et al. in 1978, the technique has been refined and simplified.[38] Nonetheless, renal angioplasty remains more complex than peripheral angioplasty. It is far from innocuous and should be performed only by angiographers who have had considerable experience dilating peripheral vessels. Inflating the balloon is simple, but crossing a tight renal stenosis with a balloon catheter requires technical skill, and selection of the proper-size balloon requires experience.

A high-quality preliminary midstream arteriogram is necessary to determine the optimal approach. Unless an abdominal arteriogram has been obtained within the previous month, the study should always be obtained before selectively catheterizing a renal artery with a stenosis in it. The midstream arteriogram also is helpful for determining the proper angioplasty balloon size.

Six different percutaneous angiographic approaches can be used:

1. Femoral balloon catheter system via a femoral approach
2. Femoral balloon catheter system via an axillary approach
3. Femoral balloon catheter system with the sidewinder approach
4. Guided coaxial balloon catheter system
5. Balloon on a wire system (TEGwire ST system)
6. "Kissing balloon" technique

Femoral Balloon Catheter System

Femoral Approach

This technique involves a modification of the double-lumen balloon catheter designed by Grüntzig for angioplasty of the superficial femoral arteries (Fig. 20-3). Only catheters with a low-profile balloon located close to the catheter tip should be used in the renal arteries. In tight stenoses, it is important not to inflate the balloon before inserting it, because this may interfere with passage through the stenosis.

Originally the Grüntzig-type balloon catheters were only available on a 7 French shaft. Smaller 5 French shaft balloon catheters have become available with balloon diameters ranging from 4 to 10 mm. A 2-cm-long balloon is usually employed for over-the-wire renal angioplasty.

The femoral artery is punctured and the appropriate 5 French diagnostic catheter is advanced into the abdominal aorta using the Seldinger technique. The orifice of the renal artery is carefully selected. Contrast medium is injected to locate the lesion. Under fluoroscopic guidance, a 0.035-inch Bentson guidewire is advanced beyond the stenosis. If this guidewire will not pass, the lesion can often be traversed with a 15-mm J guidewire. It is imperative to avoid subintimal passage of the guidewire. Once the stenosis has been

Figure 20-3. Technique of PTRA with the femoral balloon catheter system using the femoral approach. The renal artery is selected, and the guidewire is passed across the stenosis under fluoroscopic control. After the diagnostic catheter is advanced through the stenosis, it is exchanged for the dilatation catheter over an exchange wire, and the lesion is dilated. (From Tegtmeyer CJ, Sos TA. The techniques of renal angioplasty. Radiology 1986;161:577–586. Used with permission.)

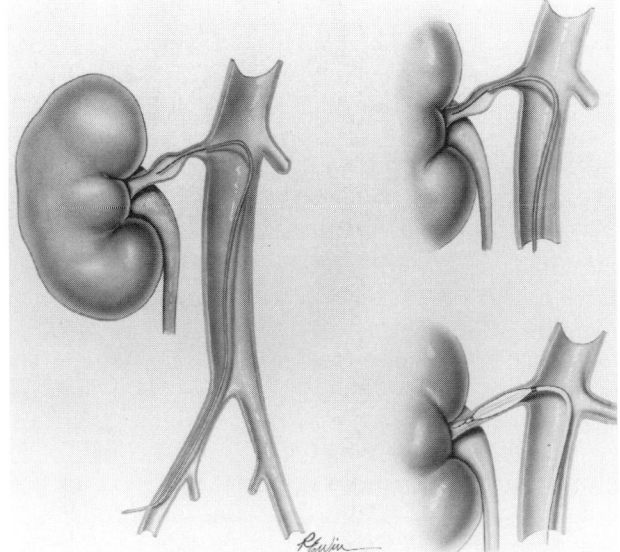

crossed, the 5 French selective catheter should be passed across it to facilitate subsequent passage of the balloon catheter. A small amount of contrast medium is injected to confirm the intraluminal position of the catheter, and 2000 to 5000 IU of heparin and 2.5 mg of verapamil are injected through the catheter. A 1.5-mm, movable-core, type J or Rosen wire is then inserted through the diagnostic catheter beyond the stenosis. The diagnostic catheter is replaced with the appropriate-size renal balloon catheter. The guidewire must not be moved back and forth in the branches of the renal artery when exchanging the catheters, because this may induce spasm or cause occlusion of the segmental branches.

If the balloon catheter will not cross the stenosis, a 3-mm balloon catheter is passed across the lesion and inflated, partially dilating the stenosis. The proper-size balloon catheter can then be advanced easily across the stenosis.

The balloon catheter is positioned across the lesion under fluoroscopic control, and the balloon is inflated either with an inflation device or with a syringe. If a syringe is used, a 10-ml size is probably ideal because it is capable of generating approximately 9.4 atm of pressure during inflation and sufficient negative pressure to deflate the balloon rapidly. A pressure gauge should always be used. The 0.035 inch wire is then replaced with a smaller wire and a Tuohy-Borst connector is attached. An 0.018-inch wire is used with the 5 French balloon catheters. The balloon is first inflated to 2 atm of pressure to determine its position in relation to the stenosis. When it is properly positioned, it is inflated to 4 to 6 atm and left inflated for 30 to 40 seconds. It may be necessary to repeat this process several times. The progress can be monitored by watching the configuration of the balloon as it is inflated and deflated. The balloon is then carefully pulled back over the 0.018-inch wire and contrast medium is injected to assess the results. The balloon catheter can be readvanced if the lesion requires further dilatation. Immediately after angioplasty, an arteriogram is performed to assess the results. Before removing the balloon catheter, it is important to completely deflate the balloon and apply suction as it is being removed from the femoral artery.

The primary advantage of this technique is that only a 5 French arteriotomy is needed in the femoral artery. If the stenosis permits easy passage of the balloon, this is the simplest approach. However, if the stenosis is tight or the renal artery branches from the aorta at an acute angle, the balloon catheter may not follow the guidewire across the lesion, because it has a tendency to buckle in the aorta when pressure has to be applied. This difficulty may often be overcome by advancing,

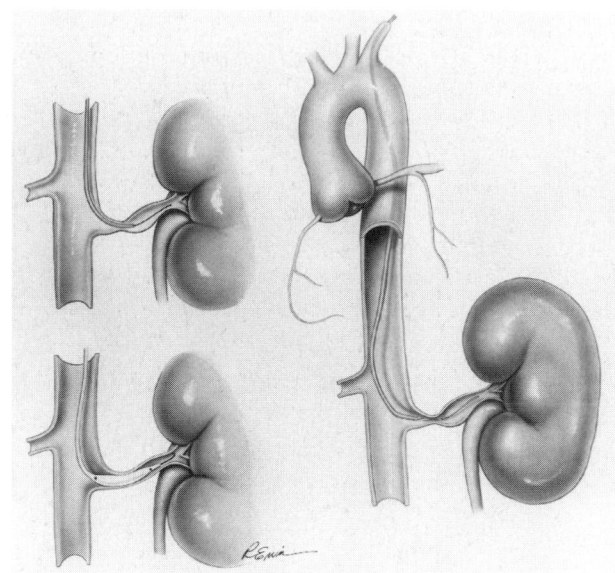

Figure 20-4. Technique of PTRA, axillary approach. The renal artery is selected and the guidewire is gently advanced through the stenosis. The selective catheter is advanced across the lesion, and the diagnostic catheter is exchanged for the balloon catheter. The balloon is then inflated, dilating the lesion. (From Tegtmeyer CJ, Sos TA. The techniques of renal angioplasty. Radiology 1986;161:577–586. Used with permission.)

first, the 5 French diagnostic catheter, and then either a 7 French tapered Van Andel catheter or the 3-mm balloon catheter as described and then reinserting the balloon catheter.

Axillary Approach

The axillary approach may also be used to dilate the renal arteries (Fig. 20-4).[39] This approach greatly simplifies the procedure when the renal arteries originate from the aorta at a sharp angle, because the stenotic artery is easily selected. Once the guidewire is in place across the lesion, the dilatation catheter has a natural tendency to follow its gentle downward curve. Passage of the guidewire and then the catheter through the stenosis is often facilitated by having the patient take a deep breath. The axillary approach is also useful when severe atherosclerotic disease or a bypass graft is present in the pelvic or abdominal vessels.

The technique also uses the double-lumen balloon catheter designed by Grüntzig for superficial femoral artery angioplasty. The balloon is available for renal angioplasty in 4-mm through 10-mm sizes and in several lengths. The 2-cm-long balloon is the most popular. A left axillary approach is usually employed because it offers the straightest approach to the descending aorta and because the catheter has a tendency to buckle in the ascending aorta when the right axillary approach is attempted. The technique is otherwise similar to that of the femoral approach.

Theoretically, there is an increased risk of damage to the smaller axillary artery; however, this can be minimized by using 5 French angioplasty balloons, deflating the balloon carefully, and rotating it as it is being inserted and removed. There is also the possibility of brachial plexus injury, the chances of which can be minimized by using the high brachial approach, in which the artery is entered distal to the axillary crease. The artery is easier to control in this area because it can be compressed against the humerus.

Sidewinder Approach

The sidewinder approach combines the advantages of the femoral and axillary approaches (Fig. 20-5). The same Grüntzig-type double-lumen balloon catheter is used as when the femoral approach is employed. The femoral artery is punctured, but the renal artery is approached from above to take advantage of its natural downward curve. The renal artery is selected with a 5 French "shepherd's crook" or "sidewinder" catheter.[40] The catheter is advanced across the lesion under fluoroscopic control as contrast medium is injected, with care taken to keep the catheter tip within the lu-

men of the artery. Alternatively, a flexible-tip Bentson guidewire is advanced across the stenosis followed by the catheter. Once the catheter is across the lesion, 2000 to 5000 IU of heparin is injected through it. The guidewire is replaced with a movable-core J guidewire or a Rosen wire. Because the diagnostic catheter has crossed the lesion, the balloon catheter will usually cross the stenosis with ease. After dilatation a midstream arteriogram is obtained to document the results.

The principal advantage of this technique is that withdrawing the sidewinder catheter advances the diagnostic catheter across a tight stenosis because the configuration of the catheter exerts considerable downward force as it is withdrawn over the guidewire. This technique is very helpful in traversing tight stenoses.

Guided Coaxial Balloon Catheter System

The Grüntzig-type guided coaxial balloon catheter system uses an 8 or 9 French renal guiding catheter and a 4.3 or 4.5 French coaxial balloon catheter (Fig. 20-6). The renal guiding catheter is available in several configurations. It is inserted by a femoral approach, and the orifice of the renal artery is carefully selected. The small coaxial catheter is then passed through the guiding catheter across the stenosis. The balloon catheter will accept a 0.014- or 0.016-inch guidewire,

Figure 20-5. Technique of PTRA using a shepherd's crook or sidewinder catheter. The orifice of the renal artery is selected, and the guidewire is passed across the lesion. The operator advances the catheter across the stenosis by withdrawing it at the puncture site. The catheter is exchanged for a balloon catheter, and the lesion is dilated. (From Tegtmeyer CJ, Sos TA. The techniques of renal angioplasty. Radiology 1986;161:577–586. Used with permission.)

Figure 20-6. Technique of PTRA with the coaxial balloon catheter system. The orifice of the renal artery is selected with the guiding catheter. The steerable wire is directed into the appropriate branch and across the stenosis. The balloon catheter is then advanced across the stenosis, and the lesion is dilated. (From Tegtmeyer CJ, Sos TA. The techniques of renal angioplasty. Radiology 1986;161:577–586. Used with permission.)

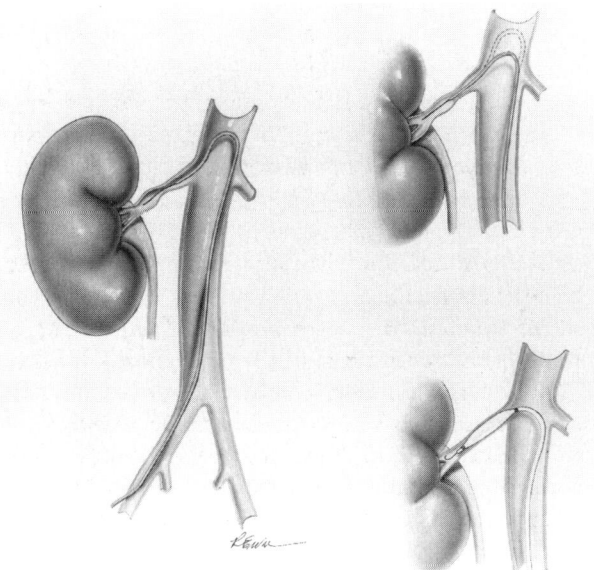

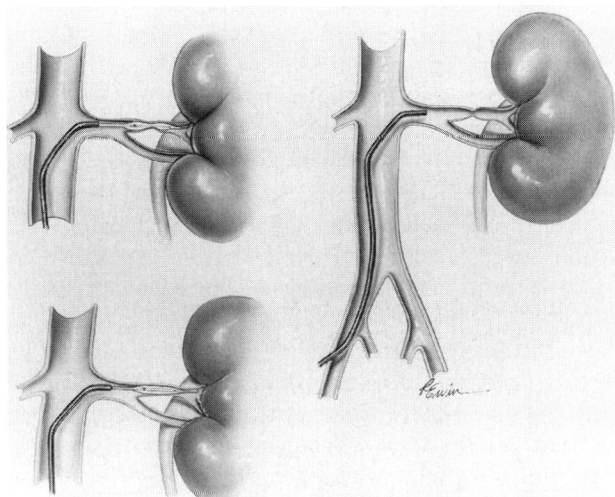

which can be passed across the stenosis before advancing the coaxial catheter to facilitate traversing a tight stenosis. With the advent of the highly visible platinum wires, this is a very effective technique. In the presence of a tortuous renal vessel, a tight stenosis, or a stenosis in a branch, the fine guidewire greatly facilitates passage of the balloon catheter. If the stenosis is not too tight, the coaxial balloon catheter can be advanced across it without the guidewire while a small amount of contrast medium is being injected.

The advantage of this coaxial technique is that the small catheter passes through the tight stenosis more readily than the 5 French balloon catheter. It is also easy to steer this catheter into the branches of the renal artery. Therefore, this catheter system is usually used for a tight stenosis that cannot be traversed by other techniques or for treating distal or branch stenoses. There are several disadvantages to the technique, however. The catheters are expensive, and it is necessary to make a 10 or 11 French puncture wound in the femoral artery because a sheath must be used. Also, the guiding catheter is stiff and may damage the aortic wall. It is inserted over a 0.063-inch guidewire, which is also quite stiff. Balloons are available from 2 to 6 mm.

This technique is more complex than the standard femoral balloon catheter technique. The common femoral artery is punctured, and a long introducer sheath is advanced into the distal abdominal aorta. A 0.063-inch guidewire is advanced into the abdominal aorta as far as the diaphragm. The guiding catheter is then advanced over the guidewire through the sheath and into the abdominal aorta. The guidewire is removed, and the guiding catheter is used to select the renal artery orifice. The balloon catheter is then advanced through the guiding catheter and across the stenosis. The small diameter of the balloon makes it possible to measure pressures across the stenosis. The balloon is inflated with a 1:1 mixture of contrast medium and 0.9 percent saline. Balloon inflation and the progress of the angioplasty can be monitored by injecting contrast medium through either the balloon catheter or the guiding catheter, which is a definite advantage. However, because of the dilatation injury to the intima, caution should be exercised when injecting contrast medium near the dilatation site.

Balloon-on-a-Wire System (TEGwire ST System)

Continuing developments in balloon technology have allowed modifications of the conventional coaxial technique.[41] The development of the angioplasty balloon on a wire has simplified the conventional coaxial technique.

The authors prefer to use the TEGwire ST system for renal angioplasty whenever possible (Fig. 20-7). The system consists of a low-profile polyethylene teraphthalate balloon mounted on a highly torqueable 0.035-inch guidewire shaft. The TEGwire ST has a very flexible, 2-cm-long, 0.014-inch shapeable tip. The balloon is available in 3-, 4-, 5-, and 6-mm diameters. The 3- and 4-mm balloons fit through a 6 French guide. A 7 French guiding catheter is necessary for the 5- and 6-mm balloons. The balloons are available in 1.3- and 2-cm lengths for renal angioplasty.

The appropriately shaped guiding catheter is inserted through a sheath over a 0.035-inch guidewire. The guidewire is removed, and the renal artery is gently selected. The TEGwire 1.3-cm-length balloon is then inserted in the guiding catheter, and the position of the guiding catheter is checked with a gentle injection of contrast material. The TEGwire balloon catheter is passed across the stenosis. Contrast material is injected through the guiding catheter to confirm the position of the balloon. Heparin and verapamil are then injected through the guiding catheter. The balloon is positioned across the stenosis and inflated. The result is checked by performing digital subtraction arteriography through the guiding catheter while the deflated balloon remains across the lesion.

The TEGwire ST system has several advantages. It simplifies renal angioplasty by eliminating the need for guidewire and catheter exchanges. The low-profile balloon on a 0.035-inch shaft is ideal for crossing tight renal artery stenoses and the follow-up renal angiogram is easily obtained through the coaxial guiding catheter while the deflated balloon is still in place across the lesion. A disadvantage of the system is that balloons above 6 mm are not currently available; however, they will be in the near future.

"Kissing Balloon" Technique

This technique, originally described for dilating lesions at the bifurcation of the abdominal aorta,[42,43] has application in selected cases in the renal arteries.[44] If two renal arteries originate from the aorta in proximity or if the lesion involves a major bifurcation in the renal artery (Fig. 20-8A), dilating the lesion may occlude the adjacent vessel. In this situation, catheters are inserted through both femoral arteries, and a catheter is passed across the lesion in the involved branch (see Fig. 20-8B). The origin of the uninvolved branch is usually protected by a diagnostic catheter (see Fig. 20-8C). If the origin of the vessel is involved by the lesion or compromised by the procedure, the catheter is exchanged for a second balloon catheter, and the lesion is dilated. Alternatively, two TEGwires can be used through a 9 French guiding catheter.

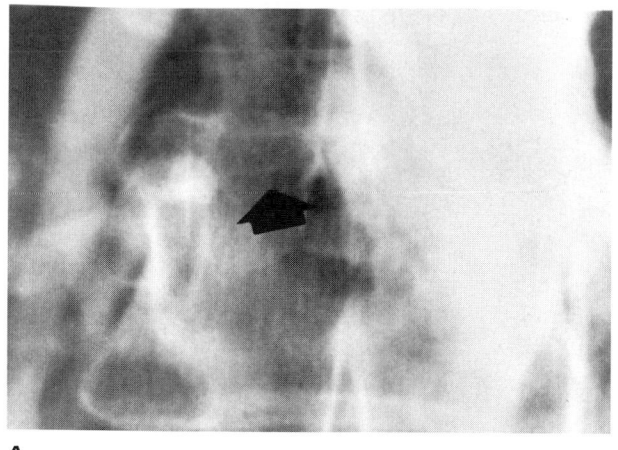

A

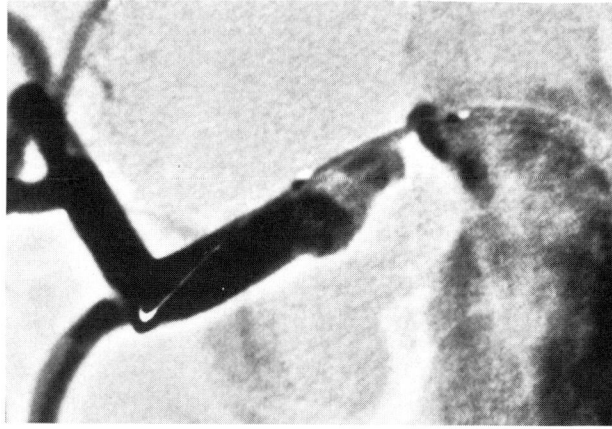

B

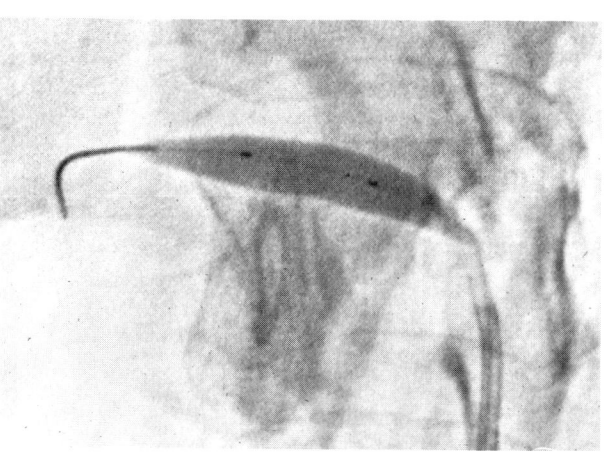

C

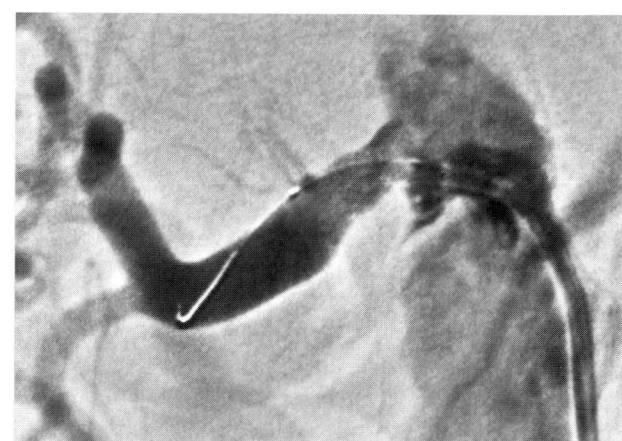

D

Figure 20-7. Technique of PTRA with the TEGwire ST system of balloon on a wire. (A) Midstream arteriogram reveals a threadlike vessel (*arrow*) supplying the distal renal artery. (B) The orifice of the renal artery is selected with the guiding catheter and the TEGwire is passed across the stenosis. (C) The lesion is dilated. (D) The follow-up angiogram is easily obtained through the guiding catheter. The balloon is still across the lesion.

Treatment and Prevention of Vascular Spasm

Spasm of the main renal artery or of a major arterial branch is a frequent occurrence during renal angioplasty (Fig. 20-9).[45] This is usually caused by mechanical stimulation of the vessel wall by the guidewire or catheter and may occur locally or at a distance. If possible, the guidewire should not be placed within the segmental branches of the renal artery. Focal spasm may also be produced in the area adjacent to the angioplasty site or even in distal small branches. Calcium channel blockers are highly effective in preventing and reversing spasm in the renal arteries. At the University of Virginia, patients are prophylactically given 2.5 mg of verapamil hydrochloride intraarterially through the diagnostic or guiding catheter as soon as the lesion is crossed. If spasm is encountered, another 2.5 mg of verapamil is given intraarterially. This protocol has markedly decreased the number of patients experiencing spasm during PTRA.

Alternatively, patients scheduled for renal angioplasty can be pretreated with nifedipine in a dose of 10 to 20 mg orally or sublingually one-half hour before the procedure. If spasm occurs in spite of the calcium channel blockers, nitroglycerin in a dose of 100 to 200 µg is given intraarterially. Nitroglycerin is very effective in relieving spasm, but its mechanism of action differs from that of the calcium channel antagonists. It has an additive effect when given with calcium channel blockers, so it is very effective when spasm is encountered after the blocker has been administered. The authors prefer to use the calcium channel blockers initially because the duration of action is longer than

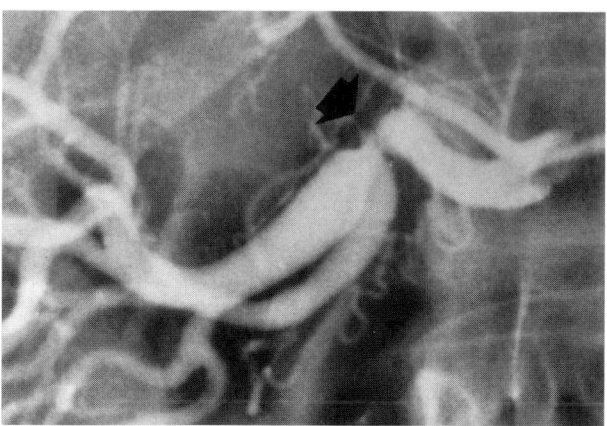

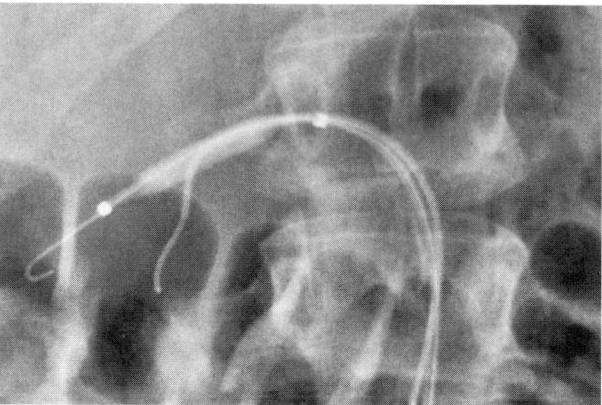

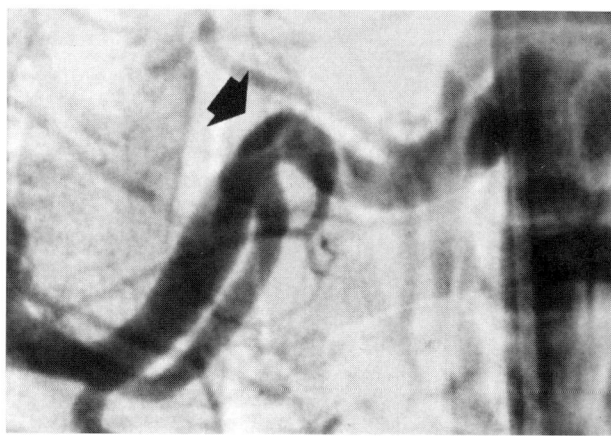

Figure 20-8. "Kissing balloon" technique in the renal arteries. The 28-year-old woman presented with a 2-year history of hypertension. (A) Midstream arteriogram demonstrates a tight stenosis at the junction of the dorsal and ventral branches of the renal artery. (B) A 100-mm spot radiograph shows the balloon inflated in the upper branch, dilating the lesion, and a catheter in the lower artery protecting the orifice of the artery. (C) Immediately after PTRA, the renal artery and both branches are widely patent. (From Tegtmeyer CJ, Sos TA. The techniques of renal angioplasty. Radiology 1986;161:577–586. Used with permission.)

that of nitroglycerin. Verapamil has the advantage of being the only calcium channel blocker available in a liquid parenteral form. Nifedipine, on the other hand, is the most potent vasodilator of the calcium channel blockers available.

Since calcium channel blockers may induce hypotension, they should be used with caution in patients who have known cardiac conduction defects. Verapamil has a greater effect on the heart than the other calcium channel blockers. It is also important to remember that the guidewire is the major cause of spasm and that continued stimulation of the vessel wall will cause spasm to recur. All catheter and guidewire manipulations should be kept to a minimum, and the most effective treatment of spasm is to remove the catheter and guidewire. ·

Patient Management

Proper treatment of candidates for renal angioplasty requires a team approach. The proper selection of patients and the periprocedural management of the blood pressure require the close cooperation of a hypertension specialist. Inadvertent occlusion or rupture of the renal artery may create a surgical emergency. Therefore, the procedure should be performed only when a skilled vascular surgeon is available, because

the complexity of renal reconstruction is increased after PTRA.[46] Before renal angioplasty, the patient's blood pressure should be controlled by angiotensin-converting enzyme inhibitors, such as captopril or enalapril, whenever possible. These agents pharmacologically inhibit the production of angiotensin II, the active hypertensive substance in renin-mediated renovascular hypertension. The pharmacologic action of these agents is physiologically the same as that of a successful renal angioplasty. For this reason, sudden drastic drops of blood pressure due to removal of the renin-angiotensin-aldosterone effect following successful angioplasty are not as pronounced when patients are treated with these drugs.

Because of the complexity of the procedure and the potential for volatile changes in blood pressure after the procedure, renal angioplasty should not be considered an outpatient procedure. The blood pressure must be monitored carefully during the first 24 to 48 hours after PTRA because profound changes may nevertheless occur. If the diastolic pressure rises above 110 mmHg, the blood pressure should be controlled by a repeat dose of captopril or nifedipine, or with a

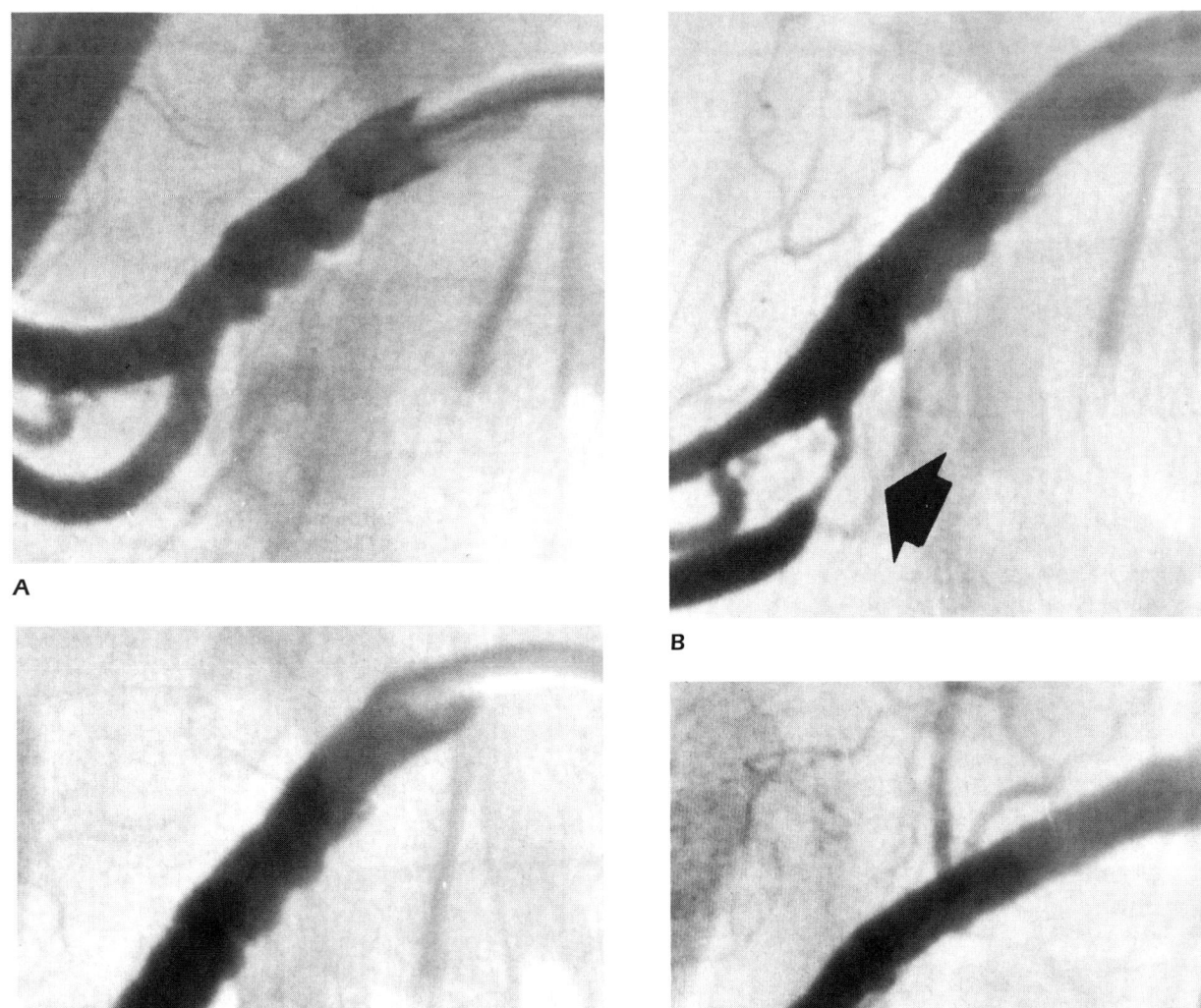

A

B

C

D

Figure 20-9. Renal spasm caused by inflation of the angioplasty balloon. (A) Selective renal arteriogram of this 38-year-old hypertensive woman reveals a "string-of-beads" lesion in the right renal artery. (B) Immediately following dilatation, the lesion is widely patent, but severe narrowing is noted in a branch of the renal artery (*arrow*). (C) Following administration of an antispasmodic agent, the vessel has a more normal appearance (*arrow*), indicating spasm. (D) Arteriogram taken 4½ months later shows that the previously dilated lesion and the spastic branch are both widely patent. (From Tegtmeyer CJ, et al. Radiology 1982;143:631–637. Used with permission.)

rapid and short-acting antihypertensive drug such as labetalol. A drop in blood pressure can usually be controlled by rapid intravenous infusion of normal saline. Therefore, all patients undergoing renal angioplasty should have an intravenous line in place before the procedure.

At the University of Virginia, the patient receives 2000 IU of heparin subcutaneously every 6 hours following PTRA unless it contraindicated. Heparin administration is begun 8 hours after the procedure and continued for 2 days. Patients also receive 75 mg of dipyridamole (Persantine; Boehringer Ingelheim) orally twice a day and 325 mg of aspirin once a day beginning the day of angioplasty and continuing for at least 6 months. Patients are encouraged to stop smoking. After angioplasty, the patient should be checked by a physician who specializes in the control of high blood pressure. Because the patient's blood pressure medication will need to be adjusted after the procedure, blood pressure must be monitored closely. If the blood pressure rises in the ensuing months, repeat arteriography should be performed.

Complications

Complication rates following renal angioplasty vary between 5 and 10 percent. In a recently published metaanalysis of the literature, the complication rate in 1118 patients undergoing PTRA was 9.3 percent.[47] This analysis excluded renal failure. In the University of Virginia series of 109 patients, 12 patients (11 percent) had major complications.[27] Transient exacerbation of chronic renal insufficiency, clearly related to the contrast material, accounted for 6 (50 percent) of these complications. Transient renal failure occurs most often in patients with preexisting renal insufficiency. It also appears to be more severe in patients with a rapidly rising creatinine level than in patients with a stable creatinine level. The severity of this complication can be decreased by making sure the patient is well hydrated. Patients with renal insufficiency are given 500 ml of a 10% mannitol solution intravenously, beginning 4 to 5 hours before the procedure. It is important to attempt to keep the contrast material quantity to a minimum. In high-risk patients the diagnostic angiogram can be performed several days before the angioplasty. Digital subtraction angiography also can be used to decrease the contrast load. Finally, it is prudent to use low-osmolar contrast medium, although the advantages of this contrast agent are unproven in renal insufficiency.

The technical aspect of PTRA that makes it more difficult than peripheral angioplasty is that the lesion in the renal artery is located at an angle of 90 degrees or more from the aorta, making it harder to control the guidewire when crossing the lesion. It is extremely important to avoid subintimal passage of the guidewire, which is a major cause of PTRA failure or complications. It is also important to control the exchange wire when the balloon is inserted because the renal artery branches may be injured during this maneuver. Injury occurs in approximately 2.2 percent of cases.[47] If a small intimal flap occurs when one is attempting to cross the lesion, it will usually heal, but angioplasty should be postponed for 4 weeks.

Thrombosis of the renal artery infrequently follows balloon dilatation. This complication is sometimes treated by infusing a thrombolytic agent into the renal artery, but it is vital that sufficient collateral vessels are present if this approach is selected; otherwise renal ischemia can develop while one is waiting for the enzyme to work. Urokinase is the most widely accepted thrombolytic agent in this setting.

Although rare, another major complication is rupture of the renal artery. This may result from weakening of the wall or from subintimal placement of the balloon catheter. If rupture is noted immediately after deflation of the balloon, the balloon should be reinflated to occlude the proximal renal artery and the patient should be immediately taken to surgery. Distal embolization is an infrequent complication, but a recently occluded renal artery should be approached with caution, because thrombi may be dislodged by the catheter and occlude the segmental branches.

The most frequent minor complication is spasm or occlusion of a renal arterial branch (see Fig. 20-9). This is usually caused by movement of the tip of the guidewire back and forth within the vessel. If possible, the guidewire should not be placed within the segmental branches. Focal spasm may also be produced in the area immediately adjacent to the angioplasty site. The use of antispasmodic drugs has reduced the number of patients experiencing spasm of the main renal artery and its branches during angioplasty, as described in preceding text.

In addition to these complications unique to renal angioplasty, there may be complications at the puncture site. The principal complication is formation of a large hematoma. When using the axillary approach, the operator should be careful to puncture high in the brachial artery and not in the axilla. This technique can decrease the chance of the devastating effects of a brachial plexus injury caused by a large hematoma in the axilla. It is also prudent to use a sheath to avoid the trauma of multiple catheter exchanges.

It is important to remember that because renal angioplasty is a more complicated procedure than peripheral angioplasty, operator experience and judgment are very important. Martin et al.[30] showed in a review of 200 consecutive patients that the complication rate fell from 20 percent in their first 100 patients to 13 percent in their second 100 patients. More significantly, the incidence of complications requiring surgery decreased from 5 to 2 percent.

Results

In experienced hands, renal angioplasty is a highly effective method for correcting renal artery lesions. An initial technical success rate greater than 90 percent should be achieved when dilating renal artery stenoses. Technical failures usually result from an inability to cross the lesion or from insufficient dilatation, usually due to elastic recoil of the lesion or creation of an obstructing intimal flap at the PTRA site.

The long-term results of renal angioplasty can be assessed by its effect on (1) vessel patency, (2) blood pressure, or (3) renal function. Since the referring physician and the patient will assess the results in terms of blood pressure response and improvement in renal function, patient selection is important. Only hemodynamically significant lesions will result in clinical improvement after successful angioplasty. Unfortunately, metaanalyses of the PTRA literature are complicated by a lack of uniformity in reporting. A cure is usually defined as an average diastolic pressure less than or equal to 90 mmHg with a 10-mmHg or more decrease from the procedure level.[48] In Europe 95 mmHg or less is often used. The cooperative study defined *improved* as a 15 percent decrease in diastolic pressure to 110 mmHg or less, but over 90 mmHg. Because this definition depends on how the pre-PTRA blood pressure value was obtained and virtually all patients referred for PTRA today are on multiple antihypertensive medications, the present authors have defined *improved* as diastolic blood pressure less than 110 mmHg and blood pressure easier to control on medications. Failure is anyone who has a diastolic blood pressure over 110 mmHg or whose blood pressure is over 90 mmHg but is not easier to control. Benefit for analysis is anyone who is cured or improved. Analysis of the results is further complicated by the marked improvement in effectiveness of antihypertensive medications in the past few years. Because these new medications are more effective in controlling the blood pressure, patients are being referred for renal artery revascularization later than they once were. Analysis of results based on improvement or stabilization in renal function is even more difficult because of the lack of a clear definition of what constitutes improved or stabilized renal function. What has become clear is that patients with long-standing hypertension or renal insufficiency do not have as dramatic a clinical response following PTRA as patients with a recent onset of hypertension or renal insufficiency.

The effect of the procedure on vessel patency is directly related to the etiology and characteristics of the lesion. The patients can be divided into those with the following five conditions:

1. Atherosclerotic disease
2. Fibromuscular dysplasia
3. Renal allografts
4. Other etiologies
5. Renal insufficiency

Atherosclerotic Disease

Atherosclerotic disease is the most frequent cause of stenoses subjected to renal angioplasty. Most of the patients are in their sixth or seventh decade of life and frequently have associated diffuse vascular disease. The presence of coronary artery, cerebrovascular, and/or peripheral vascular disease complicates the management of these patients. Other risk factors that influence the results are diabetes (approximately 20 percent of the patients), hypercholesterolemia, and smoking. It is becoming clear that treating the lipids and encouraging the patient to stop smoking affects the long-term results. A metaanalysis of prominent papers in the literature (Table 20-1) reveals that PTRA was technically successful in 80 percent of 1032 atherosclerotic patients treated for hypertension. Excluding technical failures, 19 percent of the patients were classified as cured and 56 percent were classified as improved. Therefore, of the 798 reported long-term results, 75 percent of the patients had long-term benefits from the procedure. The analysis also shows that the primary patency rate was 71 percent. However, the patency rate improves to 87 percent when secondary patency, due to redilation, is included. In the University of Virginia series[27] the effect of secondary patency is apparent. Ninety-four percent of the 65 hypertensive patients with atherosclerotic lesions benefited from PTRA. If technical failures are excluded, all the patients benefited, although follow-up was short. If the patients in this series had not been closely followed, the recurrent lesions following PTRA in 13 patients would not have been detected. However, because they were closely followed clinically, all 13 patients underwent redilation with benefit. It is important to follow the patients closely because after PTRA the blood pressure will stabilize on appropriate medications, and a subsequent elevation of the blood pressure or an elevation of the creatinine level therefore usually means that restenosis has occurred. It is also interesting to note that when restenosis occurs it does not have to be as severe as the original lesion to cause elevation in the blood pressure. In the authors' experience a restenosis of 50 percent may cause changes in the blood pressure.

Analysis of the results of PTRA reveals several factors that are important to the success of renal angioplasty. A residual stenosis of 30 percent or more on the postdilatation film is more likely to develop a recurrent lesion.[21,26,27] Therefore, the authors make every effort not to leave behind a 30 percent or greater residual stenosis.

Because the restenosis rate is higher in patients with severe bilateral disease than in patients with unilateral renal artery stenoses,[27] better results are achieved with

Table 20-1. Results of PTRA on Hypertension in Atherosclerotic Disease

Series	No. of Patients	Technical Success	Long-Term Patency 1°	Long-Term Patency 2°	Clinical Results[a] Cure	Clinical Results[a] Improvement	Clinical Results[a] Benefits	Follow-up (mo) Mean	Follow-up (mo) Range
Rodríguez-Pérez 1994[32]	37	30/37 81%	22/30 73%		0/11 0%	10/11 91%	10/11 91%	26	3–96
Baert 1990[49]	165	139/165 84%	76/123 62%		36/123 29%	40/123 33%	76/123 62%	26	6–72
Canzanello 1989[50]	100	73/100 73%	43/73 59%	48/73 66%	4/73 5%	39/73 53%	43/73 59%	29	6–72
Klinge 1989[51]	134	104/134 78%	92/104 88%	103/104 99%	13/104 13%	90/104 87%	103/104 99%	6	
Julien 1989[52]	66	60/66 91%	49/53 92%	50/53 94%	5/50 10%	37/50 74%	42/50 84%	7.5	1–21
Greminger 1989[53]	48	92%[b]	27/48 56%	37/48 77%	11/37 30%	26/37 70%	37/37 100%	26	6–84
Kim 1989[54]	18	15/18 83%	13/15 87%	15/15 100%			15/15 100%	12	
Beebe 1988[55]	38	20/38 53%	13/20 65%	14/20 70%	4/20 20%	10/20 50%	14/20 70%	22	0–72
McDonald 1988[56]	11	9/11 82%	9/11 82%		4/9 44%	5/9 55%	9/9 100%	15	0.5–45
Bell 1987[57]	25	22/25 88%	14/22 64%	16/22 73%	3/22 14%	13/22 59%	16/22 73%	18	1–60
Simonetti 1987[58]	42		35/42 83%		16/42 38%	19/42 45%	35/42 83%	48	
Grim 1986[59]	27		8/27 30%		1/27 4%	7/27 26%	8/27 30%	35	1–60
L. G. Martin 1985[29]	72	60/72 83%	39/60 65%		9/60 15%	30/60 50%	39/60 65%	16	4–40
Miller 1985[60]	34	32/34 94%	20/32 63%		5/32 16%	15/32 47%	20/32 63%	76	9–39
Tegtmeyer 1984[27]	65	61/65 94%	48/61 79%	61/61 100%	15/61 25%	46/61 75%	61/61 100%	24	1–60
Sos 1983[26]	51	34/51 67%			7/34 21%	10/34 29%	17/34 50%	16	4–40
Mahler 1982[61]	8	8/8 100%	7/8 88%	8/8 100%	1/8 13%	5/8 63%	6/8 75%	24	9–33
Flechner 1982[62]	27	13/27 48%	7/13 54%			7/13 54%	7/13 54%	6	2–15
Colapinto 1982[24]	51	44/51 86%	37/44 84%		8/44 18%	29/44 66%	37/44 84%	11	1–36
E. C. Martin 1981[16]	13	6/13 46%			2/13 15%	4/13 31%	6/13 46%	13	4–24
	1032	730/915 80%	559/786 71%	352/404 87%	144/770 19%	442/783 56%	601/798 75%	19	

[a]Initial technical failures are excluded.
[b]Included fibromuscular dysplasia patients.

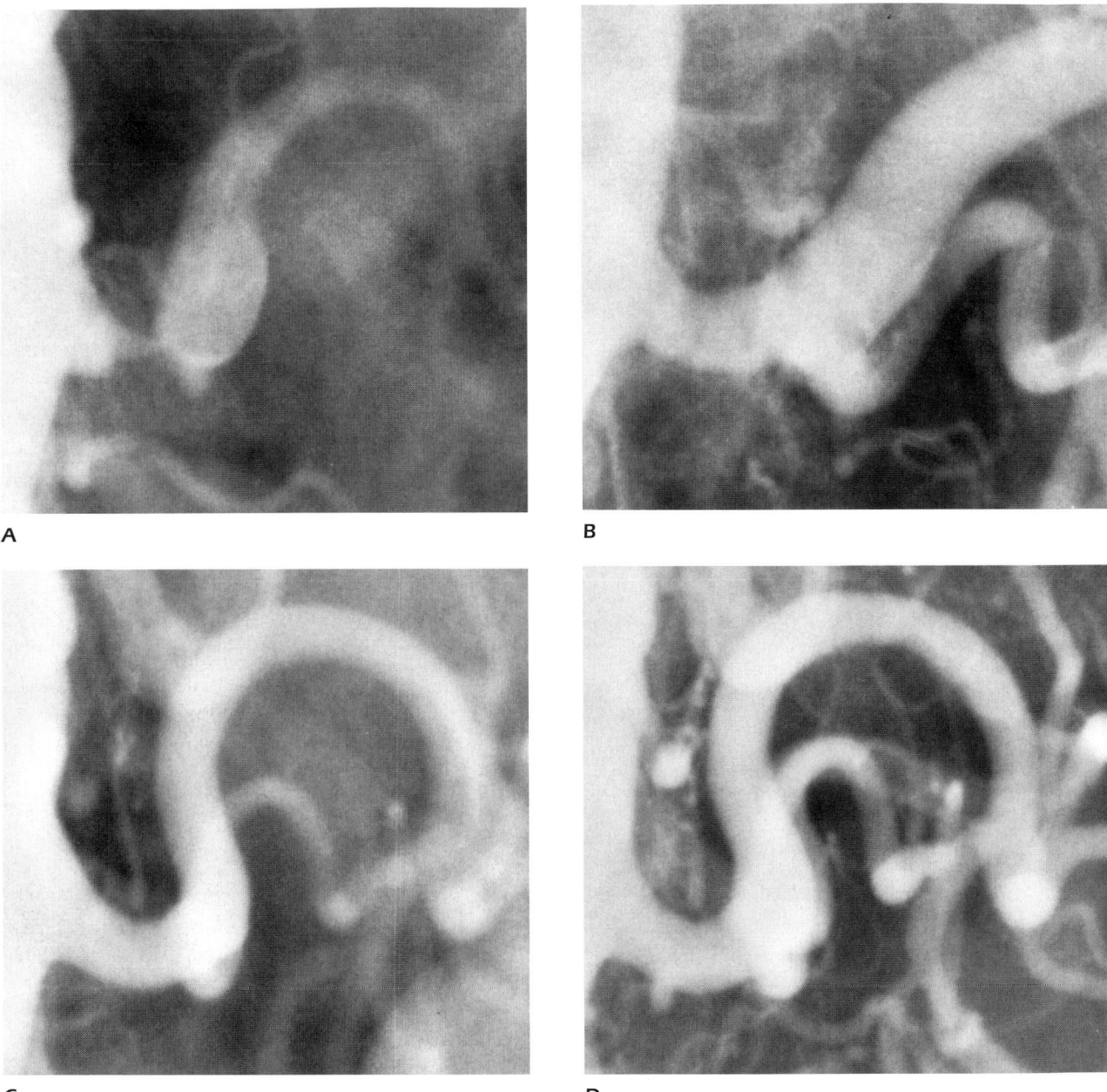

Figure 20-10. Long-term results of PTRA in a 65-year-old woman with a short concentric atherosclerotic lesion in the left renal artery. (A) Midstream renal arteriogram reveals a 99 percent stenosis in the renal artery. (B) Immediately after the latter. PTRA, the vessel is widely patent. (C) Arteriogram obtained 18 months later shows that the vessel is open. (D) Follow-up arteriogram at 53 months demonstrates no evidence of the former lesion.

the latter. Sos et al.[26] and Martin and associates[16] also showed that success was more frequent in patients with unilateral lesions. It is clear that certain lesions are more amenable to balloon dilatation than others. A better result can be expected in short, isolated concentric lesions within the renal artery (Fig. 20-10). However, when the stenosis is caused by a large plaque in the abdominal aorta that engulfs the origin of the renal artery, a so-called ostial lesion, a diminished re-

sponse can be anticipated (Fig. 20-11). Figure 20-12 illustrates the type of lesion in which a diminished response is often obtained. Cicuto et al.,[63] Sos et al.,[26] Schwarten,[64] and Canzanello et al.[50] all reported similar results. The results have prompted some surgeons, Novick[65] and Dean et al.,[46] to recommend that all renal ostial lesions undergo surgical repair, not PTRA. However, Martin et al.[66] recently found in 110 patients with renal ostial stenoses followed for at least 1 year

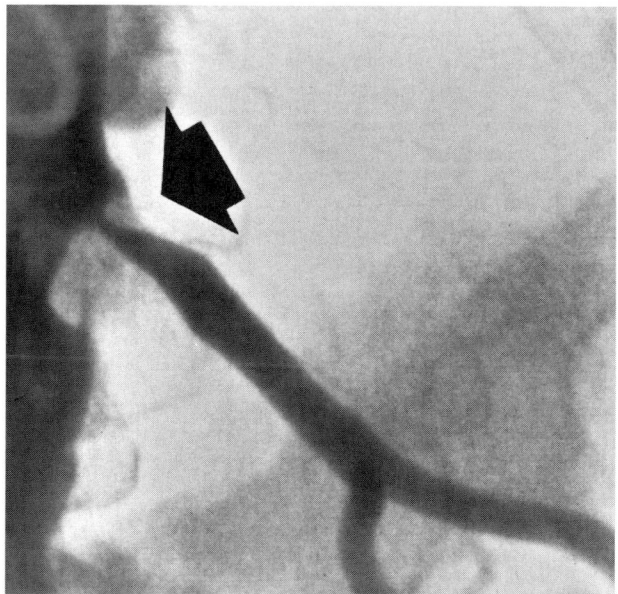

A

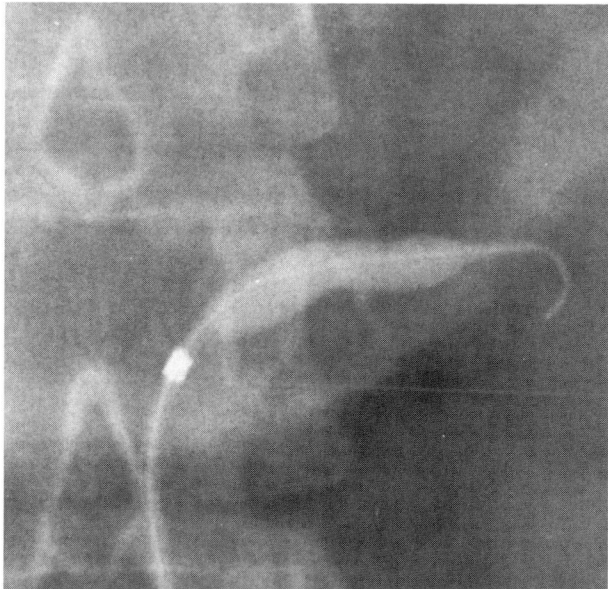

B

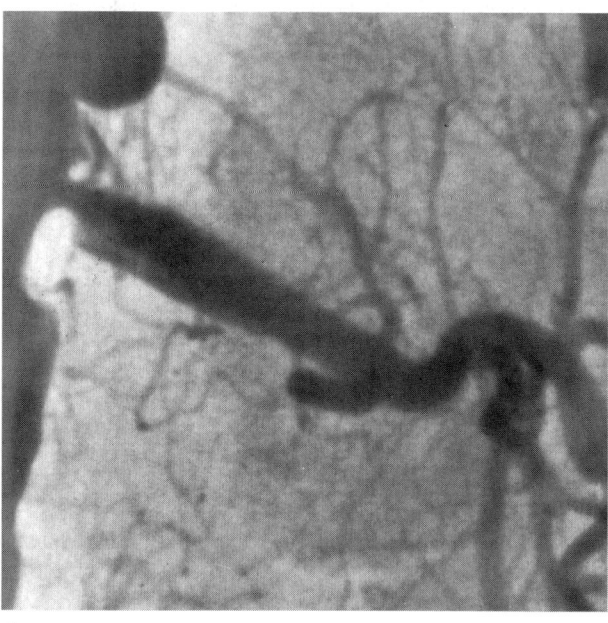

C

Figure 20-11. Diminished response in a renal artery orifice lesion caused by plaques in the abdominal aorta of a 68-year-old woman with long-standing hypertension. (A) Predilatation aortogram shows a tight stenosis at the origin of the left renal artery (*arrow*). (B) A 100-mm spot radiograph shows the 6-mm balloon in place. (The balloon is not completely expanded.) (C) Immediately after PTRA, the artery is improved but residual stenosis remains. (From Tegtmeyer CJ, Kofler TJ, Ayers CA. Renal angioplasty: current status. AJR 1984;142:17–21. Used with permission.)

that 59 percent benefited from renal angioplasty, compared to 69 percent of those with nonstial renal lesions. In the authors' experience, surprisingly good results are obtained in some ostial lesions (Fig. 20-13). Lesions with a very thick aortic plaque do not respond as well as those with a thinner plaque of 2 mm or less. But the outcome based on the appearance of the lesion is not always predictable. Therefore, it is our practice to attempt PTRA and assess the response before recommending surgery. Clearly, the benefits of angioplasty warrant an attempt at angioplasty before recommending surgery.

Complete blocks in the renal artery should be approached with caution. Occlusions are more difficult to dilate than stenoses. Occlusions that are not perfectly straight in the area of the lesion should probably not be attempted because of the risk of perforation. Also, recanalization should only be attempted if the renal artery proximal and distal to the occlusion is clearly identified and if the size of the kidney warrants salvage.

The incidence of restenosis for atheromatous lesions is higher than that for fibromuscular lesions. Martin et al.[47] in a metaanalysis of 518 patients with atheromatous lesions undergoing follow-up angioplasty after PTRA reported a restenosis rate of 30 percent. In the University of Virginia series,[27] there was a 21 percent recurrence rate in atherosclerotic lesions at a mean follow-up of 24 months.

Fibromuscular Dysplasia

The best results with renal angioplasty are achieved in patients with fibromuscular dysplasia (FMD; Fig. 20-14). FMD is the second most common cause of renal artery stenosis. The patients are generally younger

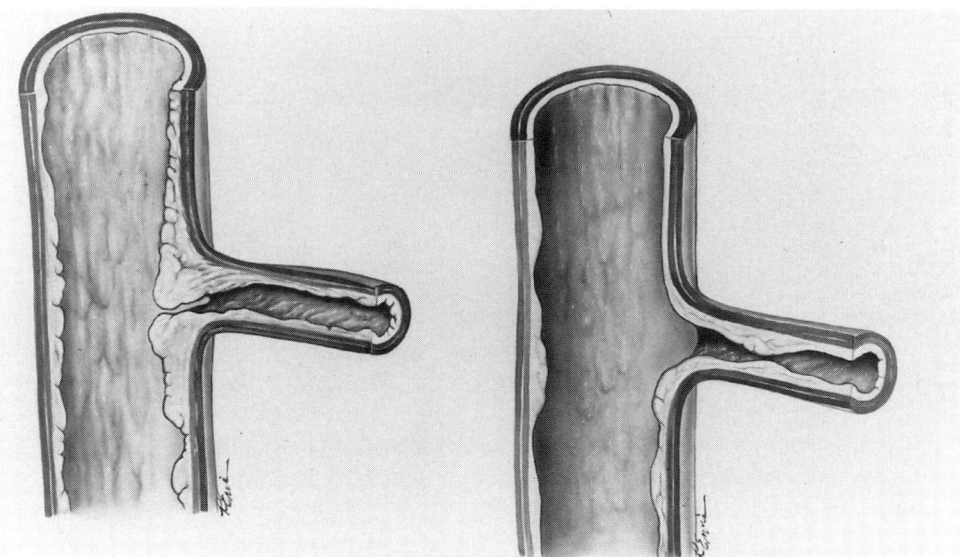

Figure 20-12. The type of atherosclerotic lesion in which a diminished response to balloon dilatation can be anticipated. *Left:* The lesion is caused by atherosclerotic plaque in the abdominal aorta that engulfs the orifice of the renal artery. Occasionally a good result is obtained, but usually the results are poor when compared with results in other types of lesions. *Right:* A good response can be anticipated in short stenoses within the renal artery. (From Tegtmeyer CJ, Kofler TJ, Ayers CA. Renal angioplasty: current status. AJR 1984; 142:17–21. Used with permission.)

than those with atherosclerotic disease and have fewer associated risk factors. In the University of Virginia series,[31] the mean age of the patients was 45 years and the median age was 47 years. The average duration of hypertension was 8.2 years, and the hypertension was refractory to medical management in 46 of the 66 patients. If the patients had been referred for angioplasty earlier, a higher percentage would have been cured.

The disease is frequently bilateral, and in the authors' series 34 of the 66 patients had bilateral lesions of 50 percent or greater.

McCormack et al.[67,68] classified the lesions of FMD according to primary sites of involvement in the arterial wall, and they correlated the histologic findings with angiographic appearances. Their classification includes intimal fibroplasia, medial fibroplasia, fibro-

Figure 20-13. Not all ostial lesions respond the same; a good result is seen in this case. (A) Midstream arteriogram demonstrates a 99 percent stenosis of the left renal artery caused by an aortic plaque. (B) Immediately after angio-plasty, the vessel looks surprisingly good. (From Tegtmeyer CJ, Dyer R, Teates CD, et al. Percutaneous transluminal dilatation of the renal arteries: techniques and results. Radiology 1980;135:589–599. Used with permission.)

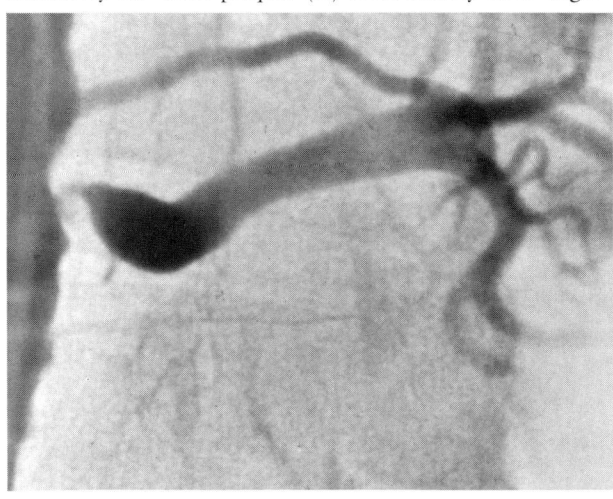

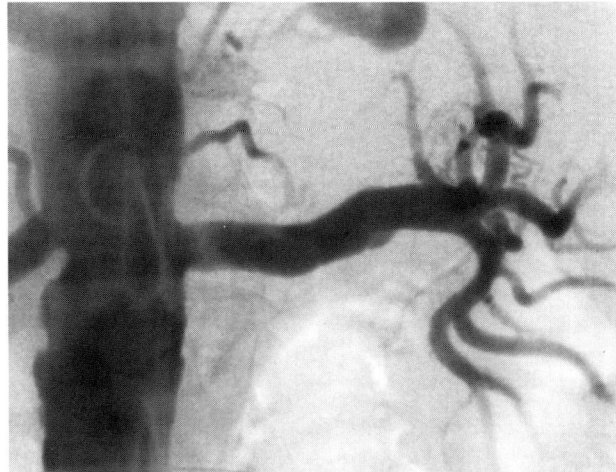

A

B

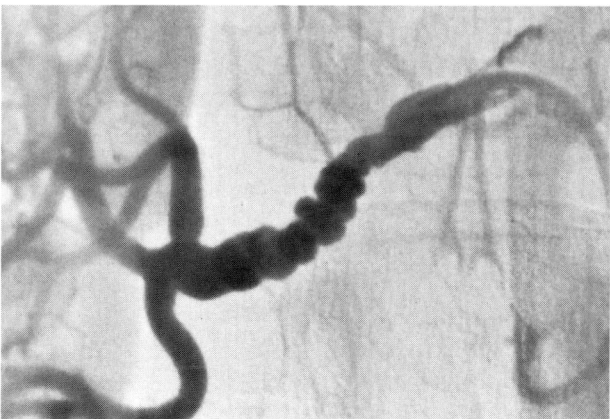

A

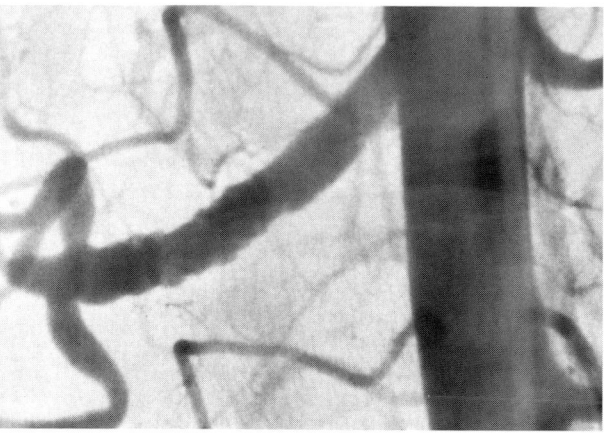

B

Figure 20-14. Long-term results of renal angioplasty in fibromuscular dysplasia are illustrated in a 51-year-old woman with hypertension. (A) Renal arteriogram reveals extensive fibromuscular dysplasia of the right renal artery. (B) Immediately after dilatation with a 5-mm balloon, the vessel appears irregular but there is good flow through it. This appearance is typical immediately after PTRA of fibromuscular dysplasia. (C) Arteriogram obtained 12½ months later shows no evidence of the former lesion. This is the usual long-term appearance after dilatation of fibromuscular lesions. (From Tegtmeyer CJ, Kellum CD, Ayers C. Percutaneous transluminal angioplasty of the renal artery: results and long-term follow-up. Radiology 1984;153:77–84. Used with permission.)

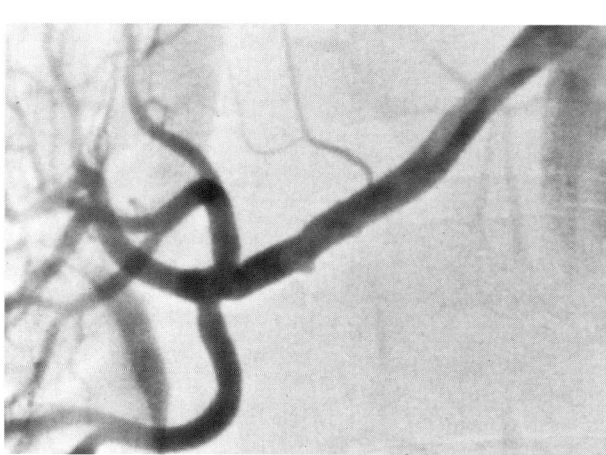

C

muscular hyperplasia, and subadventitial fibroplasia. The classification in the present analysis is based solely on the angiographic appearance of the lesion because histologic material was not available. In this report, intimal fibroplasia consists of symmetric narrowing of the artery with poststenotic dilatation or an irregularly dilated segment. Because there has been considerable difficulty separating intimal fibroplasia from fibromuscular hyperplasia angiographically, these lesions have been grouped together as intimal fibroplasia.[69] Medial fibroplasia consists of the classic "string-of-beads" appearance, with the diameter of the beads exceeding the expected diameter of the renal artery in the affected region. Lesions were classified as subadventitial fibroplasia when they appeared as areas of severe, uneven stenoses. "Beading" may be present in the artery; however, the width of the beads does not exceed the original diameter of the vessel.

Medial fibroplasia was the most common type of FMD seen in the authors' study and was the cause of lesions in 46 patients (70 percent). When localized, intimal fibroplasia involves the proximal third of the renal artery, and it may be difficult to distinguish from other causes of stenoses in the renal arteries. However, the aorta is usually involved in atherosclerotic or Ta-

kayasu disease. Thirteen patients (20 percent) were classified as having intimal fibroplasia. Subadventitial fibroplasia was present in 5 cases (8 percent). One patient was classified as having both medial and intimal fibroplasia, and 1 patient had a combination of medial and subadventitial fibroplasia.

Medial and subadventitial lesions usually respond well to balloon angioplasty. Usually these lesions dilate at pressures of 4 atm or less. Intimal hyperplasia is less predictable, and high atmospheric pressures are often necessary to dilate these lesions. Subadventitial and intimal lesions are generally easy to cross with the guidewire and balloon. Medial lesions, because of their markedly corrugated configuration and lesion length, are harder to cross; however, once crossed, they respond well to PTRA.

A metaanalysis of the literature (Table 20-2) reveals that PTRA was technically successful in 94 percent of 370 fibromuscular patients treated for angiotensinogenic hypertension. Excluding technical failures, 49 percent of the patients were classified as cured, and 43 percent were classified as improved. Therefore, of the

Table 20-2. Results of PTRA on Hypertension in Fibromuscular Dysplasia

Series	No. of Patients	Technical Success	Long-Term Patency		Clinical Results*			Follow-up (mo)	
			1°	2°	Cure	Improvement	Benefits	Mean	Range
Rodríguez-Pérez 1994[32]	27	25/27 92%	19/25 76%	19/25 75%	6/12 50%	3/12 25%	9/12 75%		3–96
Tegtmeyer 1991[31]	66	66/66 100%	60/66 91%	65/66 98%	26/66 39%	39/66 59%	65/66 98%	39	1–121
Baert 1990[49]	22	19/22 86%	15/19 79%		11/19 58%	4/19 21%	15/19 79%	26	6–72
Greminger 1989[53]	34	30/34 88%	23/30 77%	30/30 100%	14/30 47%	16/30 53%	30/30 100%	20	6–48
Klinge 1989[51]	52	47/52 90%		42/47 89%	18/47 38%	26/47 55%	44/47 94%	6	
Beebe 1988[55]	9	9/9 100%	4/9 44%	8/9 89%	3/9 33%	5/9 55%	8/9 88%	23	6–60
Simonetti 1987[58]	25				15/25 60%	6/25 24%	21/25 84%	48	
Bell 1987[57]	8	7/8 88%	7/7 100%		5/7 71%	2/7 29%	7/7 100%	19	12
Kremer Hovinga 1986[70]	10	10/10 100%	7/9 77%					19	4
Grim 1986[59]	26	26/26 100%	24/26 92%		15/26 58%	9/26 35%	24/26 92%	26	1
L. G. Martin 1985[29]	20	20/20 100%	17/20 85%		5/20 25%	12/20 60%	17/20 85%	16	3–36
Miller 1985[60]	15	15/15 100%	13/13 100%		11/13 85%	2/13 15%	13/13 100%		6–36
Sos 1983[26]	31	27/31 87%	25/27 93%		16/27 59%	9/27 33%	25/27 93%	16	4–40
Mahler 1982[61]	6	6/6 100%	4/6 66%	6/6 100%	5/6 83%	1/6 17%	6/6 100%	29	12–47
Colapinto 1982[24]	11	9/11 82%	9/9 100%		4/9 44%	5/9 55%	9/9 100%	11	1–36
E. C. Martin 1981[16]	8	8/8 100%	6/8 75%		5/8 63%	1/8 13%	6/8 75%	13	4–25
	370	324/345 94%	233/274 85%	170/183 93%	159/324 49%	140/324 43%	299/324 92%	22	

*Initial technical failures are excluded.

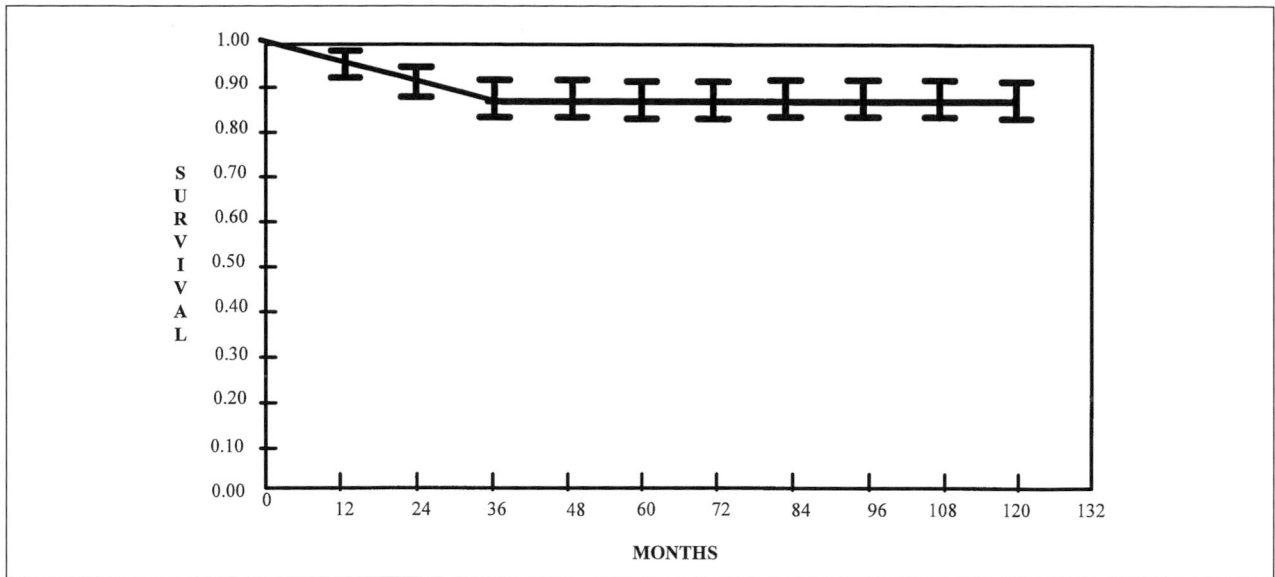

Figure 20-15. Plot of long-term response for 66 patients with fibromuscular disease. Patients were followed for as long as 121 months after renal percutaneous transluminal angioplasty. Life-table method of analysis was used to calculate predicted long-term patency rate. (From Tegtmeyer CJ, et al. Results and complications of angioplasty in fibromuscular disease. Circulation 1991;83(Suppl I):157. Used with permission.)

324 reported long-term results, 92 percent of the patients benefited from the procedure. The primary patency rate was 85 percent, and the secondary patency rate was 93 percent. The durability of PTRA in fibromuscular disease is excellent. In the authors' own series of 66 patients, life-table analyses showed that the 10-year predicted long-term patency rate was 87.07 percent (Fig. 20-15 and Table 20-3). Klinge et al.[51] achieved similar results with a cumulative 5-year patency rate of 89 percent.

The restenosis rate in the authors' series was 8 percent of lesions and 10 percent of patients.[31] Analysis of the six recurrences (Table 20-4) reveals that four lesions were underdilated initially. The underdilated lesions were all due to medial fibroplasia. Selecting the proper balloon size can be difficult because it is sometimes difficult to predict the original size of the artery in extensive disease, since the "beads" in medial fibroplasia are larger than the original size of the artery. It is prudent to be conservative and underdilate the artery rather than overdilate the vessel and rupture it. The authors successfully redilated five of the six recur-

Table 20-3. Long-Term Response: Life-Table Analysis of 66 Fibromuscular Disease Patients

Follow-up Period (mo)	Patent Arteries (*n*)		Recurrences (*n*)	Failure Rate (%)	Patency Rate (%)	Cumulative Patency Rate (%)	SEM of Cumulative Patency Rate (%)
	Beginning of Interval	End Follow-up					
0–12	66	13	2	3.36	96.64	100.00	0.00
12–24	51	12	2	4.44	95.56	96.64	2.34
24–36	37	4	2	5.71	94.29	92.34	3.71
36–48	31	8	0	0.0	100.0	87.07	5.04
48–60	23	7	0	0.0	100.0	87.07	5.04
60–72	16	5	0	0.01	100.0	87.07	5.04
72–84	11	3	0	0.01	100.0	87.07	5.04
84–96	8	2	0	0.0	100.0	87.07	5.04
96–108	6	5	0	0.0	100.0	87.07	5.04
108–120	1	1	0	0.0	100.0	87.07	5.04

SEM, Standard error of the mean.
From Tegtmeyer CJ, Selby JB, Hartwell GD, et al. Results and complications of angioplasty in fibromuscular disease. Circulation 1991;83(Suppl I):158. Used with permission.

Table 20-4. Analysis of Patients with Recurrent Fibromuscular Disease Stenoses

Age (yr)/Sex	Classification of FMD Side	Initial Stenosis (%)	Side Dilated	Time of Recurrence (mo)	Redilated (n)	Long-Term Response (mo)
40/F	Medial R	80	R	3	1	I (112)
	Medial L	25				
50/F	Medial R	Cannot grade	R	0	1	I (36)
	Medial L	Cannot grade	L	27[a]		
66/F	Medial R	Cannot grade	R	27	1 (dilated L)	I (36)
	Medial L	10				
20/F	Intimal R	80	R	6	2	NI (21)
		Small aneurysms	L			
40/F	Medial R[b]	99	R	16[a]	1	I (25)
	Medial L	90	L	16[a]	1	
43/F	Medial L	80	L	15[a]	1	C (18)
		R nephrectomy				

C, cure; I, improved; NI, not improved.

[a]Underdilated initially.

[b]Atherosclerotic lesion also dilated. In one additional patient, one atherosclerotic recurrence was redilated twice.

From Tegtmeyer CJ, Selby JB, Hartwell GD, et al. Results and complications of angioplasty in fibromuscular disease. Circulation 1991;83(Suppl I):158. Used with permission.

rent lesions. The one long-term failure in the University of Virginia series[31] was a case of intimal fibroplasia. The authors have seen other examples of difficulty in dilating intimal fibroplasia since reporting the series. In a metaanalysis of the literature, Martin et al.[47] reported a similar 11.5 percent rate of restenosis.

Clearly PTRA is the treatment of choice in hypertension caused by fibromuscular dysplasia. The restenosis rate is low, and it is easy to redilate the recurrences. The lesion is usually easier to cross the second time because the pleats encountered in medial fibroplasia have been smoothed out by the first dilatation.

Renal Allografts

Stenoses in renal transplant arteries leading to hypertension and/or deterioration of allograft function have been reported in 1.5 to 7.1 percent of recipients.[71-74] This reported incidence is probably low because most patients with dysfunction or hypertension are treated medically and not subjected to angiography. Several factors have to be considered when evaluating transplant patients for PTRA. The incidence of hypertension at 6 months after transplant in patients who retain their native kidneys approaches 80 percent.[75] The etiology of the hypertension is multifactorial. It has been attributed to preexisting essential hypertension, the retained diseased native kidneys, rejection, cyclosporine-induced hypertension, hypercalcemia, steroids, renal insufficiency, and transplant renal artery stenosis. Therefore, it is difficult to assess the physiologic significance of transplant renal artery stenoses. However, it is clear that renal artery stenoses can be responsible for major morbidity, including the intolerable side effects of medications and progressive renal dysfunction.

The causes of transplant renal artery stenoses differ according to the location of the stenosis: preanastomotic (progressive atherosclerosis, vessel trauma caused at surgery), anastomotic (faulty suture technique, perfusion injury, reaction to the suture material), postanastomotic (intimal hyperplasia, immunologic factors that influence the degree of intimal hyperplasia, turbulent flow secondary to malpositioning of the kidney, and arterial kinking, twisting, or compression), and distal (associated with rejection).

Three types of therapy are available for management of transplant renal artery stenoses. The first is medical. However, drug intolerance may be considerable and progressive renal failure may occur.

Surgical correction of transplant stenoses is usually successful. However, the extensive fibrosis that ensues after allograft surgery makes reoperation on these vessels difficult. This requires a transabdominal approach, and there is a high risk of significant injury to the allograft while dissecting the scar tissue. Operating on an immunosuppressed patient has additional risk.

The development of PTRA for treating transplant renal artery stenoses has modified the approach to the treatment of hypertension and renal artery stenoses in the transplant patient. A review of the literature reveals that, in 323 patients treated for transplant renal artery stenosis with percutaneous angioplasty, 82 percent of PTRAs were technically successful (Table 20-5). The blood pressure was reported as improved in 76 percent of the successfully treated patients, and function was stabilized or improved in 86 percent. As anticipated,

Table 20-5. Results of PTRA in Renal Allografts

Series	No. of Patients	Technical Success		Blood Pressure Improved		Allograft Function Stable or Improved		Follow-up (mo) Mean	Range
Rodríguez-Pérez 1994[32]	28	21/28	75%	14/16	88%			12.0	
Fauchald 1992[74]	25	22/25	88%	10/16	63%	14/21	67%	24.0	6–78
Bover 1992[76]	27	25/27	93%	19/25	76%			6.0	
Matalon 1992[77]	18	16/18*	89%	11/18	61%	16/18	89%	11.5	2–32
Benoit 1990[78]	49	34/49	69%	26/34	76%			32.0	1–110
Kirste 1990[79]	32	25/32	78%	25/32	78%				
De Meyer 1989[72]	17	14/17	82%	8/11	73%	13/14	93%	12.0	
Aliabadi 1990[80]	7	7/7	100%	5/7	72%	6/7	86%	30.0	12–96
Greenstein 1987[71]	39	33/39	85%	25/30	83%			30.0	1–72
Raynaud 1986[81]	43	35/43	81%	23/35	66%	33/35	94%	12.0	
Lohr 1986[82]	4	4/4	100%	4/4	100%	4/4	100%	15.0	6–23
Curry 1984[83]	8	5/8	63%	3/5	60%	3/5	60%		
Tegtmeyer 1984[27]	7	6/7	86%	5/6	83%			24.0	5–51
Gerlock 1983[84]	7	7/7	100%	7/7	100%	7/7	100%	7.0	3–12
Sniderman 1980[85]	12	10/12	83%	10/11	91%			9.0	1–15
	323	264/323	82%	195/257	76%	96/111	86%	18.0	

*Includes two patients requiring two attempts at PTRA resulting in initial success.

PTRA proved much easier to perform than surgery and was better tolerated by the patients. However, in a study comparing the results of surgery versus PTRA, De Meyer et al.[72] found in their series that surgery was slightly more successful: bypass in 17 patients failed in 1 patient with graft loss, and PTRA performed in 19 patients was unsuccessful in 3. Recurrent stenoses were noted in 3 PTRA patients. The authors concluded that both methods were equally effective but that PTRA entails a higher rate of initial failure and restenosis. However, because of technical ease and patient tolerance, PTRA should be the first choice of therapy for correction of renal allograft stenoses. Most authors have reached the same conclusion. The exception is Roberts et al.,[73] who concluded that in 25 PTRAs on transplants, only 5 patients were helped. They also found that 7 patients had renal artery injury following PTRA, resulting in thrombosis of the artery in 6 patients and rupture of a renal artery in another patient. This clearly has not been the experience in the authors' series or in the remaining literature. It is clear that

PTRA in renal allografts is effective; however, certain lesions respond better than others. Stenoses caused by twisting, kinking, and poor suture techniques do not respond to PTRA as well as other lesions.

Renal transplant arteries are anastomosed either end to end to the hypogastric artery or end to side to the iliac artery. Often the end-to-side anastomoses include a Carrel patch of donor aorta. Hypogastric anastomoses are best approached with a retrograde contralateral femoral artery puncture or from a high brachial approach. End-to-side anastomoses between transplant arteries and the iliac artery are best approached from the retrograde ipsilateral femoral artery.

The authors obtain a diagnostic arteriogram in multiple views and then assess the etiology and location of the lesion. The films are reviewed with the transplant surgeon, and a decision is made based on the etiology and location of the stenoses. Some lesions are very difficult to reach because of the tortuosity and condition of the feeding arteries. If the vessel is not twisted by the position of the allograft and is not extremely difficult to reach, PTRA is usually the first choice of therapy. If PTRA fails to dilate the lesion, surgery is performed. Because the renal artery allograft is an endartery with no collaterals, it is important not to persist if the lesion cannot be crossed, since repeated trauma to the stenosis may result in thrombosis of the vessel. The use of antispasmodic drugs is extremely important in transplant PTRA. In the future, renal stents will probably be effective in treating kinks and twists in the renal arteries.

Today, surgery in experienced hands is more effective but far more difficult than PTRA for the treatment of allograft stenoses. Because there are no collateral vessels to the allograft, dilatation of lesions in transplant arteries must be performed carefully. If the vessel is occluded during the procedure, open surgery must be undertaken immediately. Therefore, in cases of renal transplant PTRA, a surgeon should be readily available.

Other Etiologies of Renal Artery Stenosis

Takayasu Arteritis

Takayasu arteritis is an uncommon chronic inflammatory stenosing arterial disease that characteristically involves the aorta, its main branches, and the pulmonary arteries. Renal artery stenosis is common and often bilateral. The adjacent aorta is involved in 70 percent of cases. Clinically there are two phases. The early phase is characterized by mild systemic symptoms, arthralgia, fever, night sweats, chest and abdominal pain, and skin rashes. A late occlusive or pulseless phase occurs when the systemic symptoms subside and are replaced by symptoms due to occlusion or stenoses of arteries. Hypertension secondary to renal artery stenosis is common. The disease tends to be chronic and progressive, and the prognosis is poor. Early reports in the literature[86-88] describe the technical difficulties with dilating the lesions. The accompanying severe stenosis in the aorta makes the lesions hard to cross, and the lesions are resistant to dilatation, necessitating high inflation pressures and prolonged dilatation times. The initial results are encouraging. Dong et al.[87] had an initial patency rate of 86.4 percent of hypertensive patients, and Sharma et al.[88] had initial success in 85 percent of patients with renal artery lesions. However, Fava et al.[89] recently reported on 12 patients with renovascular hypertension due to Takayasu arteritis. Although their initial success rate was 83 percent, their 5-year patency rate was only 33.3 percent. Therefore, in Takayasu disease, PTRA may only be a palliative procedure.

Neurofibromatosis

Hypertension in patients with neurofibromatosis may result from coarctation of the aorta, pheochromocytoma, or renal artery stenoses. In elderly patients, the hypertension is often secondary to pheochromocytoma; in younger patients, it is usually due to renal artery stenosis.

The association of vascular lesions and neurofibromatosis occurs most frequently in the abdominal aorta and its branches, especially the renal arteries. There are two basic categories of vascular lesions associated with neurofibromatosis.[90] The first involves larger vessels such as the aorta and proximal renal arteries. The vessels are surrounded by neurofibromatous or ganglioneuromatous tissue. The vessel wall may be involved with changes as well. The second type is seen in the vessel wall and may involve all its layers. These changes are felt to reflect a mesodermal dysplasia.[90] They can occur in multiple arteries and involve small intrarenal branches, making repair difficult. Baxi et al.[91] reported the successful treatment of a renal artery lesion caused by neurofibromatosis by PTRA in 1981. Gardiner et al.[92] reported a delayed response to PTRA leading to a successful clinical response. Millan et al.[93] reported treating five renal artery stenoses in patients with neurofibromatosis. PTRA was only successful in one. Lund et al.[94] attempted without success to treat one patient with neurofibromatosis of the renal artery. Guzzetta et al.[95] attempted to treat one patient with renal artery lesions due to neurofibromatosis and was also unsuccessful.

Because neurofibromatosis is a relatively uncommon condition, experience with PTRA in these patients is infrequent. It is clear that the lesions are difficult to dilate. However, the procedure appears to be successful in a few patients. The authors have treated one patient (Fig. 20-16). After the initial PTRA procedure, the vessel was still narrowed. Repeat PTRA produced improvement in the vessel, but the vessel caliber is not normal. The patient has been normotensive for 35 months since the second procedure. PTRA in this case is being used as a palliative procedure to allow the patient time to grow.

Renal Insufficiency

Renal revascularization, whether by surgery or PTRA, is an accepted treatment for angiotensinogenic hypertension but for renal insufficiency is still controversial.[96] Patients with renal insufficiency are generally sicker than those with renovascular hypertension. Most have diffuse atherosclerotic disease manifested by coronary artery disease, cerebrovascular disease, aortic aneurysms, and peripheral vascular disease. The

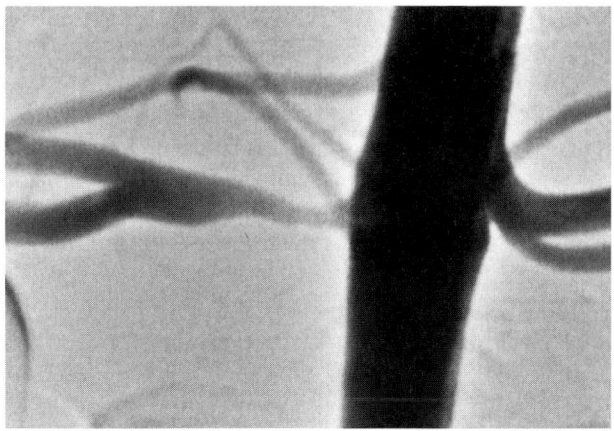

A

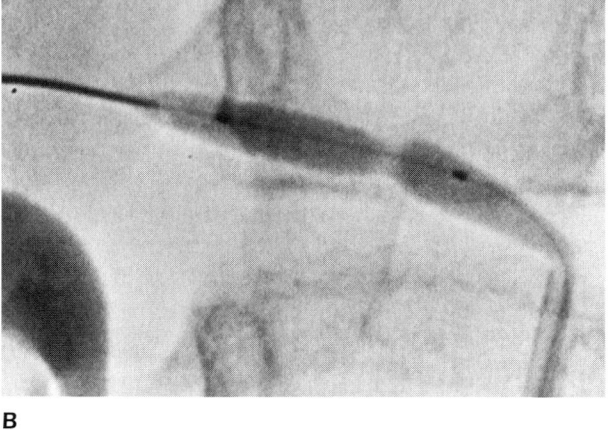

B

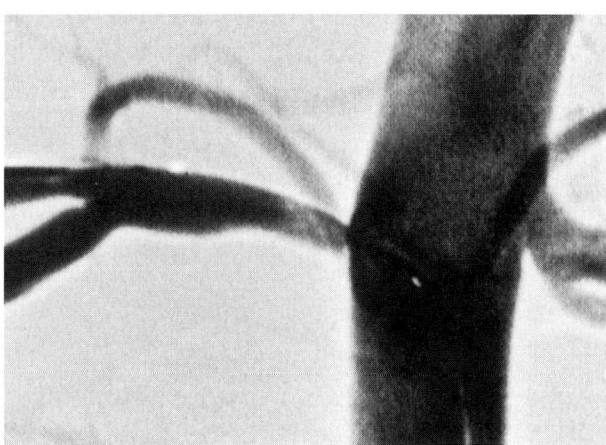

C

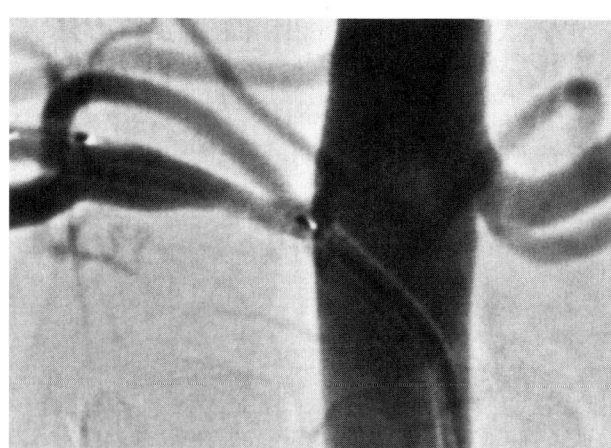

D

Figure 20-16. Results of PTRA in a 9-year-old child with neurofibromatosis. (A) The entire proximal segment of the right renal artery is narrowed. (B) Radiospot shows the persistent narrowing in the balloon despite high pressure. (C) Post-PTRA film demonstrates modest improvement. (D) The 15-month follow-up film reveals improvement in the proximal portion of the lesion but narrowing distally. (E) Following redilatation the vessel is improved, but a residual stenosis remains. The patient was normotensive 50 months after the original procedure.

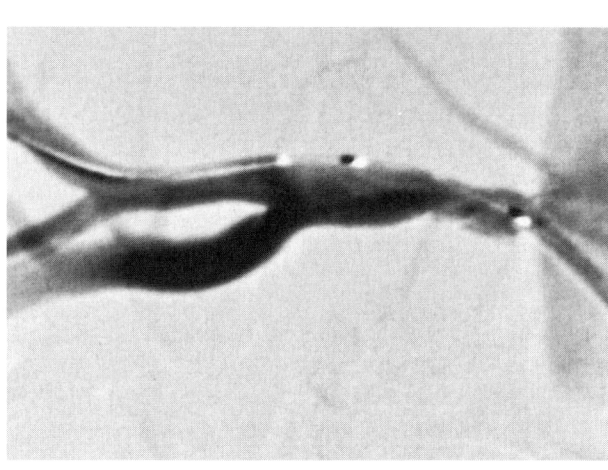

E

operative mortality is also higher for patients with renal insufficiency than for patients with renovascular hypertension. In a series of 652 renovascular operations performed at the Mayo Clinic, Hallett et al.[96] found that the operative mortality was 3.5 percent compared to 7.1 percent for patients with serum creatinine values greater than 2.0 mg/dl. The primary cause of operative death was myocardial infarction. Both Hallett et al.[96] and Novick et al.[97] recommend correction of coronary and carotid artery disease before renovascular operations whenever possible. Hallett et al.[96] found that patients with serum creatinine levels over 3.0 mg/dl tended to have a higher mortality rate. Novick et al.[98] also feel that revascularization to preserve renal function is generally not worthwhile if the patients have a serum creatinine level over 4.0 mg/dl because advanced parenchymal disease prevents improvement in renal function. This is true except in patients with chronic bilateral total occlusion of the renal arteries.

A metaanalysis of 379 patients treated with PTRA for renal insufficiency is shown in Table 20-6. Fifty-five percent of the patients were either stabilized or improved. Martin et al.[101] found that PTRA was more successful in patients who underwent bilateral PTRA (61 percent) than in patients with unilateral procedures (38 percent). The Cornell experience is similar.[102] The surgical experience also demonstrates that patients with revascularization for azotemia have more beneficial results if both kidneys are repaired.[105] Pattynama et al.,[99] however, found no different clinical outcome when the results of bilateral versus unilateral renal angioplasties were compared.

The results of PTRA are not as dramatic in patients treated primarily for renal insufficiency as in patients treated primarily for renovascular hypertension. Nevertheless, they are encouraging, and the alternative is often renal dialysis. In the University of Virginia series,[27] 10 patients were treated primarily for renal insufficiency, all with atherosclerotic lesions. The mean serum creatinine level was 5.2 mg/dl before dilatation. After PTRA, the average decreased to 2.3 mg/dl. Five of the patients responded well to PTRA.

Twenty-nine additional patients treated primarily for hypertension also had renal insufficiency. Of these, 13 improved and 10 did not. Fourteen of the patients with fibromuscular dysplasia treated primarily for hypertension[31] also had renal insufficiency, and 12 of these patients improved their renal function, with 3 having normal blood urea nitrogen (BUN) and creatinine values. In the 2 patients who did not show a decrease, the renal function stabilized and did not continue to deteriorate. In some patients, the improvement was gradual, so that the full benefit of the procedure was not apparent for several months.

Patients with azotemia do not respond as well to revascularization as patients treated primarily for renovascular hypertension. The patients likely to derive the greatest benefit are those in whom the most renal parenchyma is affected by PTRA. Those who benefit the most are those with kidneys 8 cm or more in length and bilateral stenoses in the absence of underlying renal parenchymal disease. Patients with diffuse small-vessel disease within the kidney do poorly. However, in selected patients the benefits outweigh the risks, and PTRA is justified in these high-risk patients.

Table 20-6. PTRA in Renal Insufficiency

Series	No. of Patients	Average Creatinine (mg/dl)		Improved		Stable		Benefits		Follow-up (mo)	
		Pre-PTRA	Post-PTRA							Mean	Range
Pattynama* 1994[99]	40	2.4	2.5			15/25	60%	15/25	60%	12	
Wilms 1989[100]	29			14/29	48%	11/29	38%	25/29	86%		
Canzanello 1989[50]	69	2.4	2.7					36/69	52%	23	
Kim 1989[54]	9			3/9	33%	6/9	66%	9/9	100%	12	
Martin 1988[101]	79			34/79	43%			34/79	43%	11	1–42
McDonald 1988[56]	7	3.8	4.6	3/7	43%			3/7	43%	15	1–49
Simonetti 1987[58]	12	3.8	1.5	12/12	100%			12/12	100%	48	
Pickering 1986[102]	55	3.0		26/55	47%			26/55	47%	36	
Bell 1987[57]	20			8/20	40%	9/20	45%	17/20	85%	18	
Weinberger 1986[103]	14	4.8	5.5	4/14	29%			4/14	29%	16	1–72
Tegtmeyer 1984[27]	33	5.2	2.3	18/33	55%			18/33	55%	7	1–26
Luft 1983[104]	12	4.6	5.3	3/12	25%			3/12	25%	8	1–25
	379			125/270	46%	41/83	49%	202/364	55%	17	1–72

*Includes the use of vascular stents.

Renal Vascular Stents

Several technical problems are associated with renal angioplasty. Elastic recoil, which occurs in some lesions within minutes after PTRA, results in a poor initial result. This happens when the balloon fully expands but the artery recoils and narrows again immediately after PTRA. The recoil is due to very elastic lesions, such as fibrous lesions, in the arterial wall or in the surrounding tissue that yield to the balloon but do not "split." Renal atherosclerotic ostial lesions are also subject to recoil in some cases, especially if the plaque is bulky. The balloon displaces the aortic plaque, but the plaque shifts back after the balloon is deflated. Large splits in the vessel walls may create intimal dissections after angioplasty. These dissections may cause vessel occlusion. Another major problem is restenosis (Fig. 20-17). If a residual stenosis greater than 30 percent remains after PTRA, restenosis is more likely.[21,26,27] The long-term restenosis rate in renal atherosclerotic lesions is probably between 20 and 30 percent. The recurrence rate in fibromuscular lesions is 10 percent.

Renal artery stents have been developed in an effort to solve these problems. The main purposes of the stent are to prevent elastic recoil of the lesion and to cover and tack down intimal flaps. Stents are usually only used after a failed balloon angioplasty. They are deployed percutaneously over a guidewire. The indications for their use are a poor initial result due to elastic recoil, ostial lesions that respond poorly to PTRA, and the need to tack down occluding intimal flaps.

There are several difficulties associated with the placement of stents. Some designs, such as the Palmaz stent, are difficult to insert around the corner and into the renal artery because they are not flexible enough. This difficulty has been partially overcome by inserting the stent inside a guiding catheter and then retracting the catheter once the stent is across the lesion. Another problem, seen in the Wallstent, is that because it must shorten to expand, length is needed distal to the lesion to park the stent before it expands and shortens. This can be a problem in the renal arteries, especially if they branch early. Finally, the stent needs enough radiopacity to be readily detectable for accurate placement. It is extremely important to cover the entire lesion with the stent. Stent misplacement, especially failure to cover the proximal portion of an ostial lesion, has occurred in a considerable number of patients. The Wallstent is not as radiopaque as the other stents, making placement more difficult. However, many of the other stents are difficult to visualize fluoroscopically.

The results of several large renal stent series with angiographic follow-up are presented in Table 20-7.

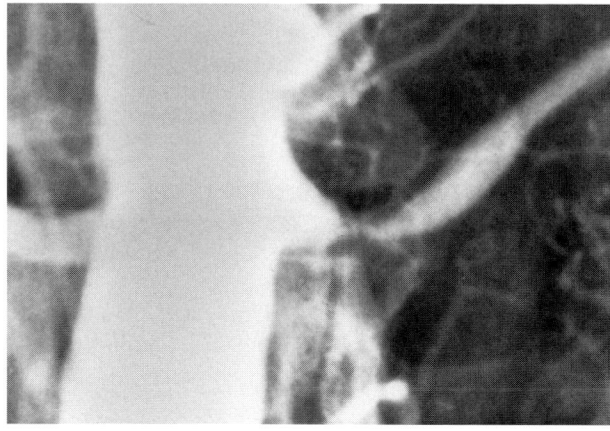

A

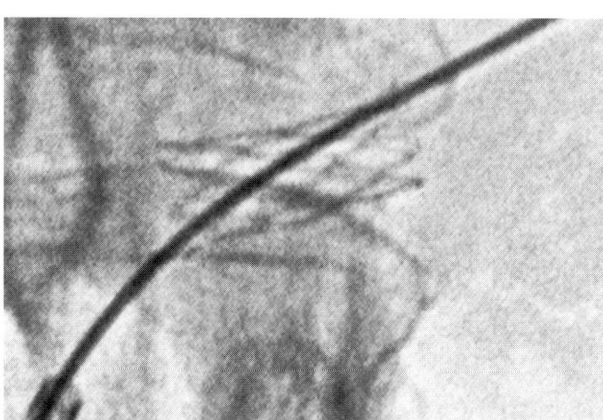

B

C

Figure 20-17. Example of the use of a Palmaz vascular stent to treat a recurrent stenosis. (A) Five months after the initial PTRA, this 73-year-old woman returned with a recurrent stenosis. (B) The Palmaz stent is deployed. (C) Initial follow-up study shows an excellent result.

Table 20-7. Renal Stents—Angiographic Follow-up

Series	No. of Patients	Technical Success		1° Patency		2° Patency		Angiographic Follow-up (mo)	
								Mean	Range
Wallstent									
Hennequin 1994[106]	21	19/21	90%	14/20	70%	18/20	90%	29.0	12–60
Wilms 1991[107]	11	11/11	100%	5/7	71%	6/7	86%	6.7	2–10
Palmaz Stent									
Saeed 1994[108]	50	50/50	100%	24/38	63%			6.0	
Trost 1994[109]	16	15/16	94%	4/9	44%			5.7	3–8.5
Rees 1991[110]	28	27/28	96%	11/18	61%	15/18	83%	7.5	2–18
Strecker Stent									
Kuhn[111] 1992	18	14/18	78%	9/11	82%			12.5	

The secondary patency rate is good. However, the major long-term problem has been the development of myointimal hyperplasia within the stent, necessitating redilatation of the lesion.

In the future, with improvements, stents will become a major factor in the treatment of renal artery lesions. At present, stents are not approved by the FDA for use in the renal arteries. However, it is clear they should be approved for use in recurrent lesions and in lesions where the initial balloon angioplasty results are insufficient.

Conclusions

The results of the University of Virginia experience and other published series show that PTRA of the renal arteries is a versatile and reliable procedure. Excellent results can be obtained in the control of hypertension if the patients are carefully selected. The results of PTRA are not as dramatic in patients treated primarily for renal insufficiency. However, they are encouraging and justify the use of PTRA in these high-risk patients.

In experienced hands, the results of renal angioplasty compare favorably with surgical results in the treatment of renovascular hypertension. The success so far has changed the original skepticism to enthusiasm. If the renal artery remains patent for at least 8 months after PTRA, a good long-term result can be expected. Renal angioplasty should be considered the treatment of choice in patients with hypertension and renal artery stenoses caused by fibromuscular dysplasia or short isolated atherosclerotic lesions. Good results

can also be obtained in patients with stenoses in the arteries of renal allografts.

The procedure is enticing because it offers many advantages. It is relatively simple compared with surgery, and it preserves renal tissue. It avoids general anesthesia and intraabdominal surgery, and the patients experience less pain. The procedure is relatively inexpensive and reduces the hospital stay.[112] Recent refinements in balloon technology and manufacturing, including the development of small balloon catheters and the balloon on a guidewire, have further improved the efficacy of the procedure.

Studies are under way involving new adjunctive technologies, such as atherectomy and intravascular stents. Continued investigation of new innovations can only lead to further improvement in the percutaneous treatment of renal artery stenoses.

Acknowledgments

With grateful appreciation to Tammy Amos for her excellent assistance in the preparation of this manuscript.

References

1. Stokes JB III, Payne GH, Cooper T. Hypertension control—the challenge of patient education. N Engl J Med 1973;289:1369–1370.
2. Gifford RW Jr. Evaluation of the hypertensive patient with emphasis on detecting curable causes. Milbank Mem Fund Q 1969;47:170–186.
3. Kaplan NM. Clinical hypertension. New York: Medcom, 1973:1–45, 173–242.
4. Janeway TC. A clinical study of hypertensive cardiovascular disease. Arch Intern Med 1913;12:755–798.

5. Genest J, Boucher R, Rojo-Ortega JM, et al. Renovascular hypertension. In: Genest J, Koiw E, Kuchel O, eds. Hypertension: physiopathology and treatment. New York: McGraw-Hill, 1977:815–840.

6. Youngberg SP, Sheps SG, Strong CG. Fibromuscular disease of the renal arteries. Med Clin North Am 1977;61:623–641.

7. Dollery CT, Bulpitt CJ. Management of hypertension. In: Genest J, Koiw E, Kuchel O, eds. Hypertension: physiopathology and treatment. New York: McGraw-Hill, 1977: 1038–1068.

8. Zierler RE, Bergelin RO, Isaacson JA, et al. Natural history of atherosclerotic renal artery stenosis: a prospective study with duplex ultrasonography. J Vasc Surg 1993;19:250–258.

9. Hunt JC, Sheps SG, Harrison EG Jr, et al. Renal and renovascular hypertension: a reasoned approach to diagnosis and management. Arch Intern Med 1974;133:988–999.

10. Foster JH, Maxwell MH, Granklin SS, et al. Renovascular occlusive disease: results of operative treatment. JAMA 1975; 231:1043–1048.

11. Veterans Administration Cooperative Study Group on Antihypertensive Agents. Effects of treatment of morbidity in hypertension: results in patients with diastolic blood pressures averaging 115 through 129 mm Hg. JAMA 1967;202:1028–1034.

12. Veterans Administrative Cooperative Study Group on Antihypertensive Agents. Effects of treatment on morbidity in hypertension: results in patients with diastolic blood pressure averaging 90 through 114 mm Hg. JAMA 1970;213:1143–1152.

13. Grüntzig A, Kuhlmann U, Vetter W, et al. Treatment of renovascular hypertension with percutaneous transluminal dilation of a renal artery stenosis. Lancet 1978;1:801–802.

14. Boomsma JHB. Percutaneous transluminal dilation of stenotic renal arteries in hypertension. Groningen, The Netherlands: Drukkerij van Drenderen BV, 1982:103–128.

15. Katzen BT, Chang J, Knox WG. Percutaneous transluminal angioplasty with the Grüntzig balloon catheter: a review of 70 cases. Arch Surg 1979;114:1389–1397.

16. Martin EC, Mattern RF, Baer L, et al. Renal angioplasty for hypertension: predictive factors for long-term success. AJR 1981;137:921–924.

17. Puijlaert CBAJ, Boomsma JHB, Ruijs JHJ, et al. Transluminal renal artery dilation in hypertension: technique, results and complications in 60 cases. Urol Radiol 1981;2:201–210.

18. Schwarten DE. Percutaneous transluminal renal angioplasty. Urol Radiol 1981;2:193–200.

19. Sos TA, Saddekni S, Sniderman KW, et al. Renal artery angioplasty: techniques and early results. Urol Radiol 1982;3:223–231.

20. Tegtmeyer CJ, Dyer R, Teates CD, et al. Percutaneous transluminal dilation of the renal arteries: techniques and results. Radiology 1980;135:589–599.

21. Tegtmeyer CJ, Teates CD, Crigler N, et al. Percutaneous transluminal angioplasty in patients with renal artery stenosis: follow-up studies. Radiology 1981;140:323–330.

22. Tegtmeyer CJ, Brown J, Ayers CA, et al. Percutaneous transluminal angioplasty for the treatment of renovascular hypertension. JAMA 1981;246:2068–2070.

23. Tegtmeyer CJ, Elson J, Glass TA, et al. Percutaneous transluminal angioplasty: the treatment of choice for renovascular hypertension due to fibromuscular dysplasia. Radiology 1982; 143:631–637.

24. Colapinto RF, Stronell RD, Harries-Jones EP, et al. Percutaneous transluminal dilatation of the renal artery: follow-up studies of renovascular hypertension. AJR 1982;139:727–732.

25. Geyskes GG, Puijlaert CBAJ, Oei HY, et al. Follow-up study of 70 patients with renal artery stenosis treated by percutaneous transluminal dilatation. Br Med J 1983;287:333–336.

26. Sos TA, Pickering TG, Sniderman K, et al. Percutaneous transluminal renal angioplasty in renovascular hypertension due to atheroma or fibromuscular dysplasia. N Engl J Med 1983;309:274–279.

27. Tegtmeyer CJ, Kellum CD, Ayers C. Percutaneous transluminal angioplasty of the renal arteries: results and long-term follow-up. Radiology 1984;153:77–84.

28. Kuhlmann U, Greminger P, Grüntzig A, et al. Long-term experience in percutaneous transluminal dilatation of renal artery stenosis. Am J Med 1985;79:692–698.

29. Martin LG, Price RB, Casarella WJ, et al. Percutaneous angioplasty in clinical management of renovascular hypertension: initial and long-term results. Radiology 1985;155:629–633.

30. Martin LG, Casarella WJ, Alspaugh JP, et al. Renal artery angioplasty: increased technical success and decreased complications in the second 100 patients. Radiology 1986;159:631–634.

31. Tegtmeyer CJ, Selby JB, Hartwell GD, et al. Results and complications of angioplasty in fibromuscular disease. Circulation 1991;83(Suppl I):155–161.

32. Rodríguez-Pérez JC, Plaza C, Reyes R, et al. Treatment of renovascular hypertension with percutaneous transluminal angioplasty: experience in Spain. J Vasc Intervent Radiol 1994; 5:101–109.

33. Block PC, Fallon JT, Elmer D. Experimental angioplasty: lessons from the laboratory. AJR 1980;135:907–912.

34. Castaneda-Zuniga WR, Formanek A, Tadavarthy M, et al. The mechanism of balloon angioplasty. Radiology 1980;135: 565–571.

35. Wellons HA Jr, Tegtmeyer CJ, Crosby IK. Balloon catheterization of the iliac artery: results in 34 patients. VA Med Mon 1981;108:598–602.

36. Sos TA, Cohn DJ, Srur M, et al. A new open-ended guidewire/catheter. Radiology 1985;154:817–818.

37. Abele JE. Balloon catheters and transluminal dilatation: technical considerations. AJR 1980;135:901–906.

38. Tegtmeyer CJ, Sos TA. Techniques of renal angioplasty. Radiology 1986;161:577–586.

39. Tegtmeyer CJ, Ayers CA, Wellons HA. The axillary approach to percutaneous renal artery dilatation. Radiology 1980;135: 775–776.

40. Tegtmeyer CJ. A simplified technique for selective and superselective abdominal angiography: technical note. J Assoc Can Radiol 1977;28:224–226.

41. Tegtmeyer CJ. Guide wire angioplasty balloon catheter: preliminary report. Radiology 1988;169:253–254.

42. Tegtmeyer CJ, Kellum CD, Kron IL, et al. Percutaneous transluminal angioplasty in the region of the aortic bifurcation: the two-balloon technique with results and long-term follow-up study. Radiology 1985;157:661–665.

43. Tegtmeyer CJ, Wellons HA, Thompson RN. Balloon dilation of the abdominal aorta. JAMA 1980;244:2636–2637.

44. Baker KS, Sawyer RW, Tisnado J, et al. Percutaneous transluminal angioplasty of the renal arteries: double-catheter technique. Radiology 1986;159:554–555.

45. Beinart C, Sos TA, Saddekni S, et al. Arterial spasm during renal angioplasty. Radiology 1983;149:97–100.

46. Dean RH, Callis JT, Smith BM, et al. Failed percutaneous transluminal renal angioplasty: experience with lesions requiring operative intervention. J Vasc Surg 1987;6:301–307.

47. Martin LG, Rees CR, O'Bryant T. Percutaneous angioplasty of the renal arteries. In: Strandness DE, van Breda A, eds. Vascular diseases: surgical and interventional therapy. New York: Churchill-Livingstone, 1994:721–741.

48. Simon N, Franklin SS, Bleifer KH, et al. Clinical characteristics of renovascular hypertension. JAMA 1972;220:1209–1218.

49. Baert AL, Wilms G, Amery A, et al. Percutaneous transluminal renal angioplasty: initial results and long-term follow-up in 202 patients. Cardiovasc Intervent Radiol 1990;13:22–28.

50. Canzanello VJ, Millan VG, Spiegel JE, et al. Percutaneous transluminal renal angioplasty in management of atherosclerotic renovascular hypertension: results in 100 patients. Hypertension 1989;13:163–172.

51. Klinge J, Mali WPTM, Puijlaert CBAJ, et al. Percutaneous transluminal renal angioplasty: initial and long-term results. Radiology 1989;171:501–506.

52. Julien J, Jeunemaitre X, Raynaud A, et al. Influence of age on the outcome of percutaneous angioplasty in atheromatous renovascular disease. J Hypertens 1989;7(Suppl VI):S188–S189.

53. Greminger P, Steiner A, Schneider E, et al. Cure and improvement of renovascular hypertension after percutaneous transluminal angioplasty of renal artery stenosis. Nephron 1989;51:362–366.

54. Kim PK, Spriggs DW, Rutecki GW, et al. Transluminal angioplasty in patients with bilateral renal artery stenosis or renal artery stenosis in a solitary functioning kidney. AJR 1989;153:1305–1308.

55. Beebe HG, Chesebro K, Merchant F, et al. Results of renal artery balloon angioplasty limit its indications. J Vasc Surg 1988;8:300–306.

56. McDonald DN, Smith DC, Maloney MD. Percutaneous transluminal renal angioplasty in the patient with a solitary functioning kidney. AJR 1988;151:1041–1043.

57. Bell GM, Reid J, Buist TAS. Percutaneous transluminal angioplasty improves blood pressure and renal function in renovascular hypertension. Q J Med 1987;241:393–403.

58. Simonetti G, Urigo F, Sergiacomi GL, et al. Percutaneous transluminal renal angioplasty: follow-up at 48 months. In: Glorioso N, et al., eds. Renovascular hypertension. New York: Raven, 1987:499–509.

59. Grim CE, Yune HY, Donohue JP, et al. Renal vascular hypertension: surgery vs. dilation. Nephron 1986;44(Suppl I):96–100.

60. Miller GA, Ford KK, Braun SD, et al. Percutaneous transluminal angioplasty vs. surgery for renovascular hypertension. AJR 1985;144:447–450.

61. Mahler F, Probst P, Haertel M, et al. Lasting improvement of renovascular hypertension by transluminal dilatation of atherosclerotic and nonatherosclerotic renal artery stenoses: a follow-up study. Circulation 1982;65:611–617.

62. Flechner S, Novick AC, Vidt D, et al. The use of percutaneous transluminal angioplasty for renal artery stenosis in patients with generalized atherosclerosis. J Urol 1982;127:1072–1075.

63. Cicuto KP, McLean GK, Oleaga JA, et al. Renal artery stenosis: anatomic classification for percutaneous transluminal angioplasty. AJR 1981;137:599–601.

64. Schwarten DE. Percutaneous transluminal angioplasty of the renal arteries: intravenous digital subtraction angiography for follow-up. Radiology 1984;150:369–373.

65. Novick AC. Management of renovascular disease: a surgical perspective. Circulation 1991;83(Suppl I):167–171.

66. Martin LG, Cork RD, Kaufman SL. Long-term results of angioplasty in 110 patients with renal artery stenosis. J Vasc Intervent Radiol 1992;3:619–626.

67. McCormack LJ, Poutasse EF, Meaney TF, et al. A pathologic-arteriographic correlation of renal artery disease. Am Heart J 1966;72:188–198.

68. McCormack LJ, Dustan HP, Meaney TF. Selected pathology of the renal artery. Semin Roentgenol 1967;2:126–138.

69. Meaney TF, Dustan HP, McCormack LJ. Natural history of renal arterial disease. Radiology 1968;91:881–887.

70. Kremer Hovinga TK, de Jong PE, de Zeeuw D, et al. Restenosis: prevalence and long-term effects on renal function after percutaneous transluminal renal angioplasty. Nephron 1986;44(Suppl I):64–67.

71. Greenstein SM, Verstandig A, McLean GK, et al. Percutaneous transluminal angioplasty. Transplantation 1987;43:29–32.

72. De Meyer M, Pirson Y, Dautrebande J, et al. Treatment of renal graft artery stenosis: comparison between surgical bypass and percutaneous transluminal angioplasty. Transplantation 1989;47:784–788.

73. Roberts JP, Ascher NL, Fryd DS, et al. Transplant renal artery stenosis. Transplantation 1989;48:580–583.

74. Fauchald P, Vatne K, Paulsen D, et al. Long-term clinical results of percutaneous transluminal angioplasty in transplant renal artery stenosis. Nephrol Dial Transplant 1992;7:256–259.

75. Linas SL, Miller PD, McDonald KM, et al. Role of the renin-angiotensin system in post-transplant hypertension in patients with multiple kidneys. N Engl J Med 1978;298:1440.

76. Bover J, Montaña J, Castelao AM, et al. Percutaneous transluminal angioplasty for treatment of allograft renal artery stenosis. Transplant Proc 1992;24:94–95.

77. Matalon TAS, Thompson MJ, Patel SK, et al. Percutaneous transluminal angioplasty for transplant renal artery stenosis. J Vasc Intervent Radiol 1992;3:55–58.

78. Benoit G, Moukarzel M, Hiesse C, et al. Transplant renal artery stenosis: experience and comparative results between surgery and angioplasty. Transplant Int 1990;3:137–140.

79. Kirste G, Wilms H, Matthias K. Transluminal angioplasty as treatment for renal transplant artery stenosis. Transplantation 1990;50:357.

80. Aliabadi H, McLorie GA, Churchill BM, et al. Percutaneous transluminal angioplasty for transplant renal artery stenosis in children. J Urol 1990;143:569–573.

81. Raynaud A, Bedrossian J, Remy P, et al. Percutaneous transluminal angioplasty of renal transplant arterial stenoses. AJR 1986;146:853–857.

82. Lohr JW, MacDougall ML, Chonko AM, et al. Percutaneous transluminal angioplasty in transplant renal artery stenosis: experience and review of the literature. Am J Kidney Dis 1986;7:363–367.

83. Curry NS, Cochran S, Barbaric ZL, et al. Interventional radiologic procedures in the renal transplant. Radiology 1984;152:647–653.

84. Gerlock AJ Jr, MacDonell RC Jr, Smith CW, et al. Renal transplant arterial stenosis: percutaneous transluminal angioplasty. AJR 1983;140:325–331.

85. Sniderman KW, Sprayregen S, Sos TA, et al. Percutaneous transluminal dilation in renal transplant arterial stenosis. Transplantation 1980;30:440–444.

86. Cook PG, Wells IP, Marshall AJ. Case report: renovascular hypertension in Takayasu's disease treated by percutaneous transluminal angioplasty. Clin Radiol 1986;37:583–584.

87. Dong ZJ, Li S, Lu X. Percutaneous transluminal angioplasty for renovascular hypertension in arteritis: experience in China. Radiology 1987;162:477–479.

88. Sharma S, Saxena A, Talwar KK, et al. Renal artery stenosis caused by nonspecific arteritis (Takayasu disease): results of treatment with percutaneous transluminal angioplasty. AJR 1992;158:417–422.

89. Fava MP, Foradori GB, García CB, et al. Percutaneous transluminal angioplasty in patients with Takayasu arteritis: five-year experience. J Vasc Intervent Radiol 1993;4:649–652.

90. Greene JF Jr, Fitzwater JE, Burgess J. Arterial lesions associated with neurofibromatosis. Am J Clin Pathol 1974;62:481–487.

91. Baxi R, Epstein HY, Abitbol C. Percutaneous transluminal renal artery angioplasty in hypertension associated with neurofibromatosis. Radiology 1981;139:583–584.

92. Gardiner GA Jr, Freedman AM, Shlansky-Goldberg R. Percutaneous transluminal angioplasty: delayed response in neurofibromatosis. Radiology 1988;169:79–80.

93. Millan VG, McCauley J, Kopelman RI, et al. Percutaneous transluminal renal angioplasty in nonatherosclerotic renovascular hypertension: long-term results. Hypertension 1985;7:668–674.

94. Lund G, Sinaiko A, Castañeda-Zúñiga, et al. Percutaneous transluminal angioplasty for treatment of renal artery stenosis in children. Eur J Radiol 1984;4:254–257.

95. Guzzetta PC, Potter BM, Ruley EJ, et al. Renovascular hypertension in children: current concepts in evaluation and treatment. J Pediatr Surg 1989;24:1236–1240.

96. Hallett JW Jr, Fowl R, O'Brien PC, et al. Renovascular opera-

tions in patients with chronic renal insufficiency: do the benefits justify the risks? J Vasc Surg 1987;5:622–627.

97. Novick AC, Ziegelbaum M, Vidt DG, et al. Trends in surgical revascularization for renal artery disease: ten years' experience. JAMA 1987;257:498–501.

98. Novick AC. Current concepts in the management of renovascular hypertension and ischemic renal failure. Am J Kidney Dis 1989;13(Suppl I):33–37.

99. Pattynama PMT, Becker GJ, Brown J, et al. Percutaneous angioplasty for atherosclerotic renal artery disease: effect on renal function in azotemic patients. Cardiovasc Intervent Radiol 1994;17:143–146.

100. Wilms G, Staessen J, Baert AL, et al. Percutaneous transluminal renal angioplasty and renal function. Radiologe 1989;29:195–200.

101. Martin LG, Casarella WJ, Gaylord GM. Azotemia caused by renal artery stenosis: treatment by percutaneous angioplasty. AJR 1988;150:839–844.

102. Pickering TG, Sos TA, Saddekni S, et al. Renal angioplasty in patients with azotaemia and renovascular hypertension. J Hypertens 1986;4(Suppl VI):S667–S669.

103. Weinberger MH, Grim CE, Luft FC, et al. Percutaneous transluminal angioplasty in complicated renal vascular hypertension. Nephron 1986;44(Suppl I):51–53.

104. Luft FC, Grim CE, Weinberger MH. Intervention in patients with renovascular hypertension and renal insufficiency. J Urol 1983;130:654–656.

105. Dean RH, Englund R, Dupont WD, et al. Retrieval of renal function by revascularization: study of preoperative outcome predictors. Ann Surg 1985;202:367–375.

106. Hennequin LM, Joffre FG, Rousseau HP, et al. Renal artery stent placement: long-term results with the Wallstent endoprosthesis. Radiology 1994;191:713–719.

107. Wilms GE, Peene PT, Baert AL, et al. Renal artery stent placement with use of the Wallstent endoprosthesis. Radiology 1991;179:457–462.

108. Saeed M, Schatz RA, Knowles HJ, et al. Experience with Palmaz stents in renal artery stenoses. J Vasc Intervent Radiol 1994;5:46.

109. Trost DW, Sos TA. Palmaz balloon-expandable stents for the treatment of ostial renal artery stenoses. J Vasc Intervent Radiol 1994;5:47.

110. Rees CR, Palmaz JC, Becker GJ, et al. Palmaz stent in atherosclerotic stenoses involving the ostia of the renal arteries: preliminary report of a multicenter study. Radiology 1991;181:507–514.

111. Kuhn von FP, Malms J, Kutkuhn B, et al. Renale stent Implantation. Fortschr Röntgenstr 1992;157:65–71.

112. Doubilet P, Abrams H. The cost of underutilization: percutaneous transluminal angioplasty for peripheral vascular disease. N Engl J Med 1984;310:95.

21

Endovascular Interventions for Chronic Mesenteric Ischemia

ALAN H. MATSUMOTO
CHARLES J. TEGTMEYER
J. FRITZ ANGLE

Despite the frequent involvement of the abdominal aorta and mesenteric arteries with atherosclerosis, chronic mesenteric ischemia is an uncommon manifestation of vascular disease. The rarity of this entity is a reflection of the abundant collateral circulation that exists among the visceral vessels. There is also a difference in opinion as to the degree of mesenteric vascular compromise necessary to cause intestinal angina. Although many authors feel that severe disease in at least two of the three main vessels is necessary to produce symptoms, it is now fairly well accepted that obstruction of one, two, or a combination of the three main visceral vessels can result in intestinal hypoperfusion and mesenteric ischemia. However, gradual progressive stenosis of one or more of the major visceral arteries is generally well tolerated as long as adequate collateralization exists. Indeed, all three main vessels supplying the mesenteric circulation may become totally occluded without creating symptoms.[1] For this reason, there is not always a straightforward correlation between the symptoms of mesenteric ischemia and the degree of narrowing and number of obstructed visceral vessels.

Symptoms of chronic mesenteric ischemia include postprandial abdominal pain and eventually weight loss. The history of "fear of food" can sometimes be elicited. Nausea, vomiting, and diarrhea can also occur but are neither common nor specific to this entity.[2,3] All symptomatic patients should have a biplane abdominal aortogram to thoroughly evaluate the origins of the celiac, superior mesenteric (SMA), and inferior mesenteric (IMA) arteries. If proximal disease is not seen, selective catheterization and filming of each of these arteries is necessary to define the anatomy of the branch vessels (Fig. 21-1).

Patients with signs and symptoms consistent with intestinal angina and a hemodynamically significant stenosis in one or more mesenteric artery are candidates for endovascular intervention. Lesions with at least 70 percent narrowing of the cross-sectional area are hemodynamically significant. Stenoses of 50 to 70 percent, when associated with a peak-to-peak systolic blood pressure gradient greater than 10 mmHg, should be considered significant. Stenoses of less than 50 percent are usually not flow-limiting.

Etiologies

Although atherosclerosis is the most common cause of occlusive mesenteric vascular disease, fibromuscular dysplasia (FMD) and vasculitides can also lead to chronic mesenteric ischemia.[4,5] Intimal hyperplasia can also lead to narrowing of bypass grafts to the mesenteric vessels, resulting in recurrent ischemic symptoms (Fig. 21-2).

Endovascular Techniques

The technique for mesenteric angioplasty is similar to that used in the renal arteries.[6] The femoral artery approach is usually employed. However, in patients with severe weight loss, the mesenteric arteries often originate at a steep caudad angle from the aorta, so that a high left brachial artery approach affords a technical advantage for PTA over the femoral approach.

With the standard over-the-wire balloon system, the high left brachial artery approach provides better control for crossing the stenosis and advancing the balloon. A better result in resistant lesions may also be achieved because the balloon is more parallel to the axis of the mesenteric vessel. In addition, an approach from above allows for easier advancement of metallic stents. The drawback to a high brachial approach is

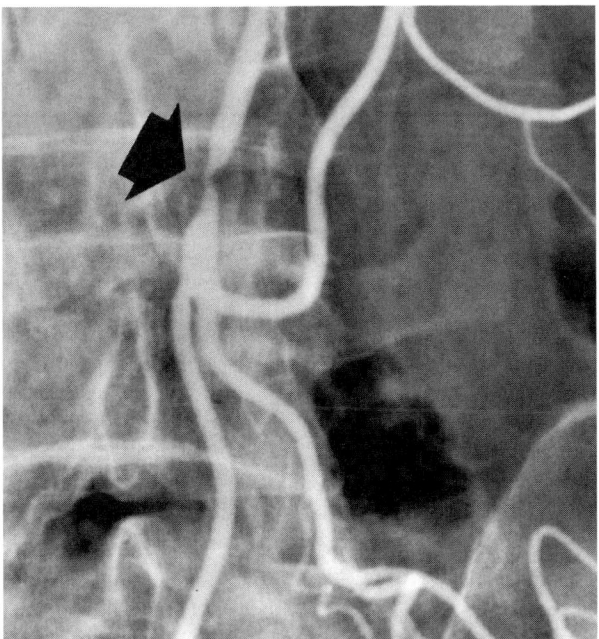

A

Figure 21-1. A 61-year-old man with bright red blood per rectum and endoscopically proven ischemic colitis underwent diagnostic angiography. The proximal celiac artery, SMA, and IMA were widely patent. (A) Selective catheterization and injection of the IMA reveals a tight stenosis of the IMA beyond its origin (*arrow*). (B) A 3-mm TEGwire balloon (*arrow*) was used to treat the lesion. (C) Control arteriogram after the PTA shows a good result (*arrow*). The patient's ischemic colitis resolved after the procedure. (From Tegtmeyer CJ, et al. In: Ernst CB, Stanley JC, eds. Percutaneous transcatheter therapy of visceral ischemia. Current therapy in vascular surgery. 3rd ed. New York: Mosby–Year Book, 1995:689–693. Used with permission.)

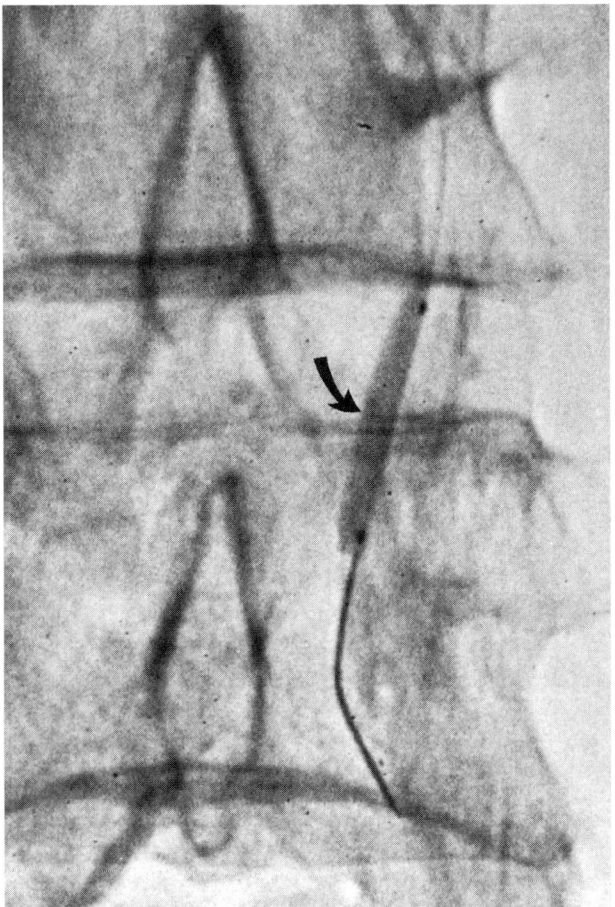

B

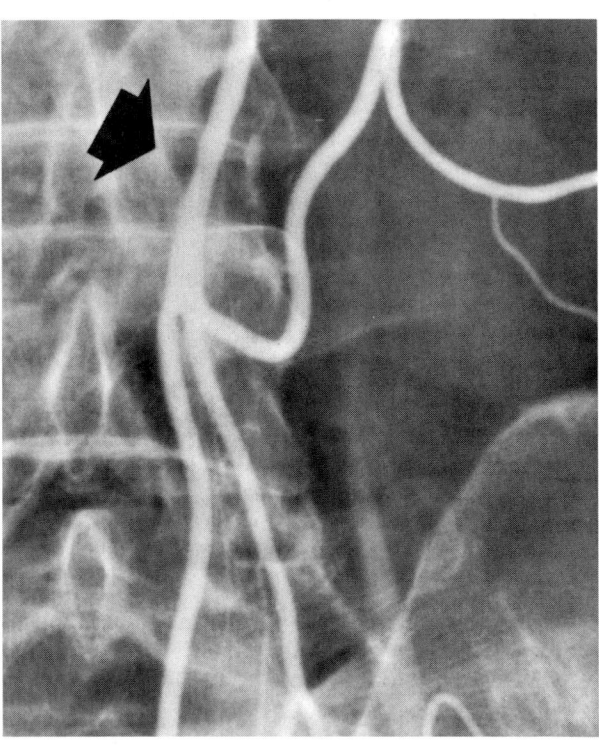

C

the increased risk of damage to the nerves to the upper extremity from a hematoma. The proximal brachial artery also tends to be smaller in diameter than the common femoral artery and may not tolerate the use of a 7 to 8 French introducer sheath.

When one is approaching the lesion from above, a preshaped catheter (multipurpose or H1H shape) is useful. A reverse-curve catheter, such as a shepherd's crook, RC 1, or Simmonds 1, is preferred from the femoral approach. A floppy-tipped guidewire (Bentson wire, Cook, Inc.) or a steerable guidewire (Glidewire, Terumo Corp.) is used to traverse the lesion. Once the guidewire is across the lesion, the diagnostic catheter is advanced beyond the stenosis and contrast is injected to confirm an intraluminal location. The authors routinely give 2000 to 3000 units of heparin during the procedure. If wire-induced spasm is identified, antispasmodic agents are given; otherwise, spasmolytic agents are not routinely used. A 200-cm

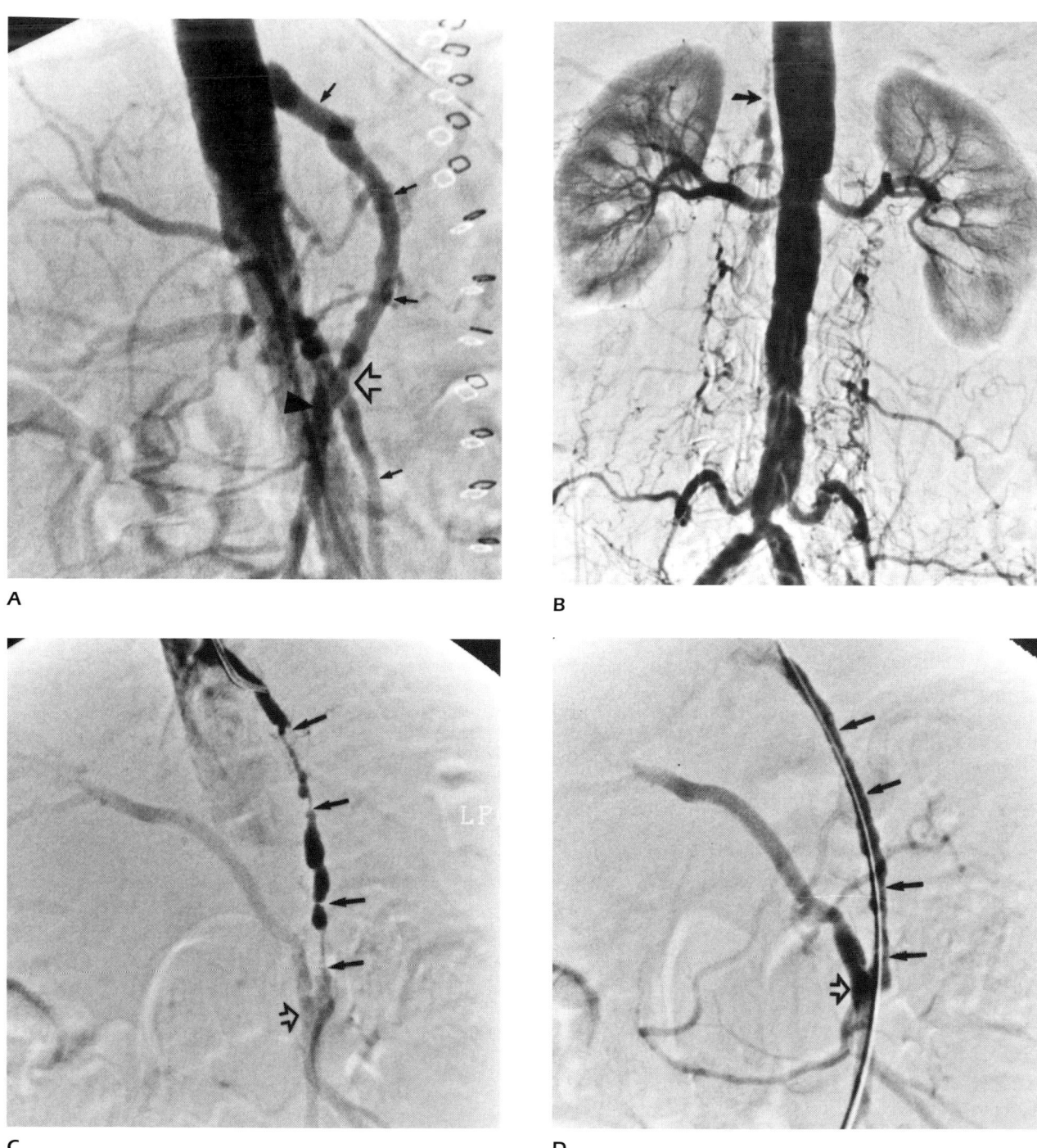

A

B

C

D

Figure 21-2. A 61-year-old woman with postprandial abdominal pain and weight loss had a diagnostic arteriogram that revealed complete occlusion of the celiac artery, SMA, and IMA with reconstitution of these vessels via internal iliac artery collaterals. (A) The patient underwent bypass surgery and a postoperative arteriogram shows the side-to-side anastomosis (*open arrow*) between the venous bypass graft (*small arrows*) and the SMA (*arrowhead*) with extension of the graft to the IMA in an end-to-side fashion. She was asymptomatic for 12 months. (B) The patient presented 15 months after her bypass surgery with a 3-month history of recurrent symptoms, a 10-pound weight loss, and an abdominal bruit. An

aortogram revealed diffuse disease of the bypass graft (*arrow*) with no antegrade flow into the SMA or IMA. The internal iliac arteries reconstituted the mesenteric circulation via collaterals. (C) Selective catheterization of the venous bypass graft demonstrates diffuse disease of the venous conduit (*closed arrows*) to the level of the side-to-side anastomosis with the SMA (*open arrow*). (D) After PTA with a 5-mm-diameter balloon, the venous bypass graft is widely patent (*closed arrows*) and the anastomosis to the SMA (*open arrow*) has a satisfactory appearance. The patient's symptoms resolved and she remained asymptomatic for 8 weeks of follow-up.

Rosen wire (Cook, Inc.) is used for exchanging the diagnostic catheter for an appropriate-size balloon catheter. The balloon diameter is chosen according to the size of the artery on the lateral cut-film arteriogram; no allowance is made for magnification. This results in a slight, but fairly consistent (about 30 percent at the authors' institution) overdilation of the artery. If there is a question about balloon size, it is prudent to use the smaller balloon.

The balloon is inflated for approximately 30 seconds to a pressure sufficient to eliminate any "waist" on the balloon. The patient may experience some abdominal, chest, or back pain during balloon inflation, but the pain should rapidly abate upon balloon deflation. If the pain does not decrease after balloon deflation, a repeat arteriogram should be done immediately to exclude vessel rupture. If the patient experiences severe pain during the process of balloon inflation, a smaller balloon should be used.

A control arteriogram is performed following balloon dilation. An 0.018-inch guidewire is placed through the balloon catheter peripheral to the area of dilatation. The tip of the 0.018-inch wire is left across the lesion and the balloon catheter is withdrawn proximal to the area of dilatation. Contrast is injected through the catheter by using a side-arm adapter. Alternatively, the balloon catheter can be removed and a 6 French nontapered catheter with a radiopaque marker at its tip and a 0.061-inch inner diameter (Microvena Corp.) can be fitted with a side-arm adapter and advanced over the 0.035-inch exchange wire (Fig. 21-3). Although this method requires the use of a 6 French sheath, the authors have found that control arteriograms are of better quality than those obtained with the 0.018-inch guidewire system.

An alternative PTA technique involves the use of a balloon-on-a-wire system (TEGwire, Boston Scientific).[7] A 7 French sheath is placed in the femoral artery and an appropriately shaped 7 French guiding catheter (Schneider, Inc.) is advanced over a 0.035-inch guidewire into the abdominal aorta. The TEGwire is advanced through a side-arm adapter on the hub of the guiding catheter and positioned close to the tip of the guiding catheter. The vessel to be dilated is then selected with the guiding catheter. It should be noted that contrast should not be forcefully injected through a large-lumen guiding catheter without a central wire, because the jet of the contrast material can easily raise an intimal flap and cause abrupt vessel occlusion. The TEGwire, which has a steerable 0.018-inch polyamide or platinum wire tip, is then advanced across the lesion. The lesion is dilated and the results are easily checked by injecting contrast through the side-arm adapter on the hub of the guiding catheter (see Fig.

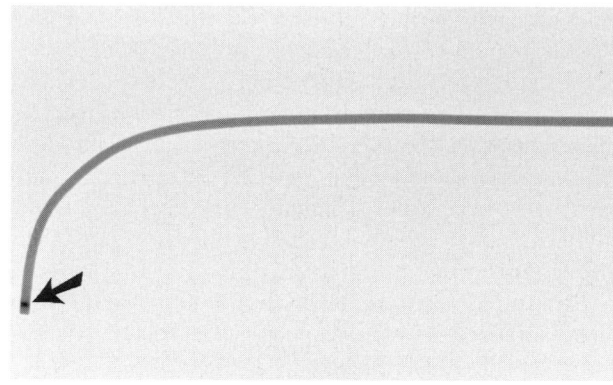

A

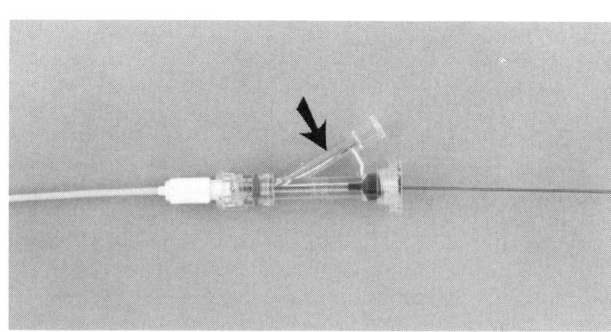

B

Figure 21-3. (A) Magnification view of the tip of the 6 French Microvena catheter (Microvena Corp.) shows the hockey-stick configuration and the radiopaque marker (*arrow*). The catheter costs about $25 and is available in 75-cm and 100-cm lengths. (B) The hub of the catheter is attached to a side-arm adapter (*arrow*) to allow contrast injection around the guidewire.

21-1). The maximum balloon diameter that is currently available on a TEGwire is 6 mm. In addition, in an acutely angled mesenteric vessel, the TEGwire should be used with caution, because if the hypotubing of the TEGwire kinks, the balloon may not easily deflate.

Whenever possible, the end point of the endovascular procedure should be complete ablation of the lesion, because residual stenoses greater than 30 percent or residual gradients greater than 5 to 10 mmHg have been associated with higher recurrence rates. If an appropriate-diameter balloon has been used but elastic recoil or a dissection leads to a suboptimal PTA result, placement of a vascular stent may be helpful. Vascular stents are not currently FDA-approved for use in the mesenteric circulation, but both the Palmaz balloon-expandable stent (Johnson & Johnson Interventional Systems) and the self-expanding Wallstent (Schneider, Inc.) have been used in this vascular bed.

The medium-size Palmaz stent requires the use of an 8 French guiding catheter. The guiding catheter that the authors have found most useful is a hockey stick–shaped guiding catheter (Cordis Corp.) with an 0.086-inch inner diameter. Insertion of a Palmaz stent is facilitated by a high left brachial artery approach, but the accessed artery must be large enough to tolerate insertion of an 8 French introducer sheath. The guiding catheter should be at least 80 cm in length, and the shaft of the balloon catheter on which the Palmaz stent is loaded should be at least 10 cm longer than the length of the guiding catheter. The authors use a 5 French balloon catheter with a balloon made from relatively scratch-resistant material (Opta 5; Cordis Corp. or PE-MT5, Boston Scientific Corp.).

The insertion of a Wallstent requires a 7 French introducer sheath but no guiding catheter. Since the Wallstent is more flexible than the Palmaz stent, it can be inserted from either a femoral or high left brachial artery approach. The delivery catheter for the Wallstent is only 75 cm in length and may be too short to allow its insertion from a high left brachial artery approach. The deployment mechanism of the Wallstent also requires unrestricted retraction of the constraining sleeve to allow exposure and expansion of the stent. If the mesenteric vessel is angled acutely caudad from the abdominal aorta, withdrawal of the constraining sleeve of the delivery device from a femoral artery approach can be problematic secondary to friction.

Results

After the initial description of superior mesenteric artery (SMA) angioplasty in 1980 by Furrer et al.,[8] there have been scattered case reports on the use of PTA for the treatment of mesenteric ischemia.[9-13] More recently, several series have been published on this topic (Table 21-1).[2,14-22] A metaanalysis of these series reveals a mean initial technical success rate of 84 percent (90 of 107 patients). Excluding the initial technical failures, the mean initial clinical success rate (as measured by resolution of symptoms) was 92 percent. The long-term primary and secondary clinical success rates were 75 and 90 percent, respectively. The mean follow-up period varied between 9 to 28 months, with some follow-up as long as 96 months after the procedure. Major complications occurred in 6.5 percent of the 107 patients, and the 30-day mortality rate was 2.8 percent.

Since the authors' initial report,[20] they have treated a total of 27 patients with endovascular therapy; 18

Table 21-1. Summary of Largest Mesenteric PTA Series

Study Authors	No. of Patients Treated	Initial Technical Success	Initial Clinical Success	No. of Patients with Recurrence	Primary Long-term Clinical Success	Successful Repeat PTA	Secondary Long-term Clinical Success	Follow-up (Mo)[a]	Major Complications (deaths)[b]
Matsumoto et al.[20]	19	15 of 19 (79%)	12 of 15 (80%)	2 of 12 (17%)	10 of 12 (83%)	1 of 2 (50%)	11 of 12 (92%)	4–73 (25)	3 of 19 (0)
Sniderman et al.[2]	13	11 of 13 (85%)	11 of 11 (100%)	5 of 11 (45%)	6 of 11 (54%)	3 of 3 (100%)	9 of 11 (82%)	1–96 (N/A)	0 of 13 (1)
Simonetti et al.[19]	22[c]	21 of 22 (95%)	18 of 21 (86%)	2 of 18 (11%)	16 of 18 (89%)	2 of 2 (100%)	18 of 18 (100%)	24–36 (N/A)	0 of 22 (0)
McShane et al.[18]	6	5 of 6 (83%)	5 of 5 (100%)	3 of 5 (60%)	2 of 5 (40%)	2 of 2 (100%)	4 of 5 (80%)	7–24 (16)	0 of 6 (1)
Levy et al.[17]	4	4 of 4 (100%)	4 of 4 (100%)	2 of 4 (50%)	2 of 4 (50%)	2 of 2 (100%)	4 of 4 (100%)	8–42 (25)	0 of 4 (0)
Wilms et al.[16]	8	7 of 8 (88%)	7 of 7 (100%)	0 of 7 (0%)	7 of 7 (100%)	—	—	1–15 (N/A)	1 of 8 (0)
Roberts et al.[15]	4	4 of 4 (100%)	4 of 4 (100%)	2 of 4 (50%)	2 of 4 (50%)	2 of 2 (100%)	4 of 4 (100%)	16–28 (22)	1 of 4 (0)
Rose et al.[22]	8	3 of 8 (38%)	6 of 8 (75%)	2 of 6 (33%)	4 of 6 (67%)	0 of 1 (0%)	4 of 6 (67%)	4–19 (9)	1 of 8 (1)
Hallisey et al.[21]	16	14 of 16 (88%)	14 of 14 (100%)	3 of 12 (25%)	9 of 12 (75%)	3 of 3 (100%)	11 of 12 (92%)	4–60 (28)	1 of 16 (0)
Golden et al.[14]	7	6 of 7 (86%)	6 of 6 (100%)	0 of 6 (0%)	6 of 6 (100%)	—	—	NA–28 (N/A)	0 of 7 (0)
Totals	107	90 of 107 (84%)	87 of 95 (92%)	21 of 85 (25%)	64 of 85 (75%)	15 of 17 (88%)	65 of 72 (90%)	1–96 (N/A)	7 of 107 (3)

N/A = Not available.
[a]Ranges are given, with mean values in parentheses.
[b]Numbers given do not include numbers of deaths, which are given in parentheses.
[c]Includes only patients with chronic mesenteric ischemia.

for classic symptoms of chronic mesenteric ischemia; 5 for symptoms atypical for mesenteric ischemia; and 4 to prevent the development of mesenteric ischemia. In the 18 patients with classic symptoms of chronic mesenteric ischemia, 9 were men and 9 were women. Their mean age was 64 years. Risk factors included smoking, hypertension, diabetes, and coronary artery disease.

The 18 patients with classic symptoms of chronic mesenteric ischemia had postprandial abdominal pain, and either weight loss ($n = 13$; range of weight loss, 6–80 pounds; mean, 24 pounds), surgical or endoscopic findings of ischemic bowel, or angiographic demonstration of greater than 70 percent stenosis in at least 2 of the 3 visceral arteries. The 21 lesions treated in the 18 patients were all stenoses (1 fibromuscular dysplasia, 18 atherosclerotic, and 2 related to intimal hyperplasia in venous bypass grafts).

The initial technical success rate was 89 percent (16 of 18 patients). Initial technical failures were related to the median arcuate ligament in 1 patient and to a combination of the median arcuate ligament and an occult malignancy in the second patient. Excluding the initial technical failures, the initial clinical success rate was 88 percent (14 of 16 patients). In the 2 clinical failures, 1 patient was subsequently diagnosed with an occult carcinoma metastatic to the porta hepatis.

The other patient underwent successful PTA of the celiac artery but had total occlusions of both the SMA and IMA. An IMA endarterectomy at the time of an aortobifemoral bypass graft 4 days after the PTA resulted in complete relief of symptoms. Of the 14 patients who had both a technically and clinically successful PTA, recurrent stenosis occurred in 2 patients. Repeat PTA was successful in 1 of these patients. Therefore, the long-term primary clinical success rate was 86 percent (12 of 14 patients; Figs. 21-4 and 21-5), with a secondary clinical success rate of 93 percent (13 of 14 patients). Clinical follow-up was obtained in all patients, with a mean follow-up of 35 months (range, 1–101 months).

In general, the authors refer most patients with complete mesenteric artery occlusions for surgical revascularization. However, some reports have documented the successful use of endovascular therapy for patients with mesenteric artery occlusions.[10–13,19] Simonetti et al. published a series on 7 patients with acute, chronic, or acute on chronic mesenteric ischemia and complete arterial occlusions.[19] Five of these 7 patients (71 percent) were successfully revascularized with a combination of thrombolysis and balloon angioplasty.

There have also been isolated reports on the use of vascular stents in the treatment of mesenteric arterial disease. The authors have successfully placed

Figure 21-4. A 60-year-old woman presented with postprandial abdominal pain and a 40-pound weight loss. (A) Diagnostic arteriogram reveals an occluded IMA, 50 percent stenosis of the celiac artery, and 95 percent stenosis of the SMA (*arrowhead*). (B) Arteriogram after the PTA shows no residual stenosis at the site of the 95 percent narrowing (*arrowhead*). A residual 30 percent ostial narrowing (*arrow*) is seen. The patient had immediate relief of her pain and had gained 50 pounds at 33 months of follow-up. (From Matsumoto AH, et al. Percutaneous transluminal angioplasty of visceral arterial stenoses: results and long-term clinical follow up. J Vasc Intervent Radiol 1995;6:165–174. Used with permission.)

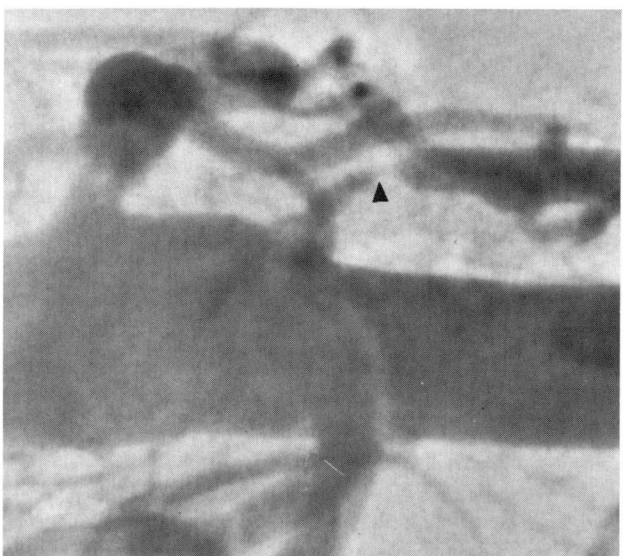

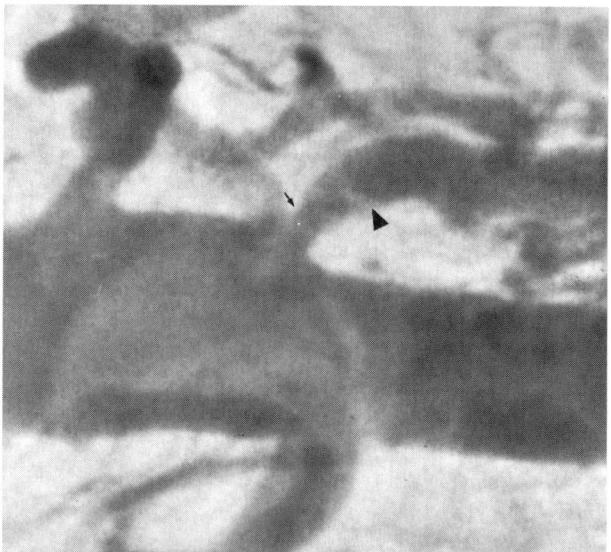

A

B

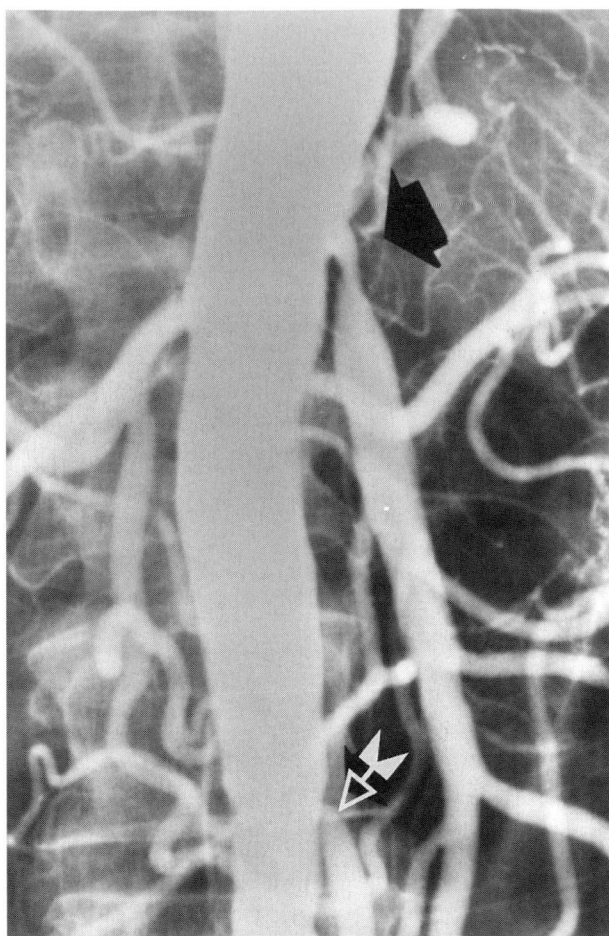

A

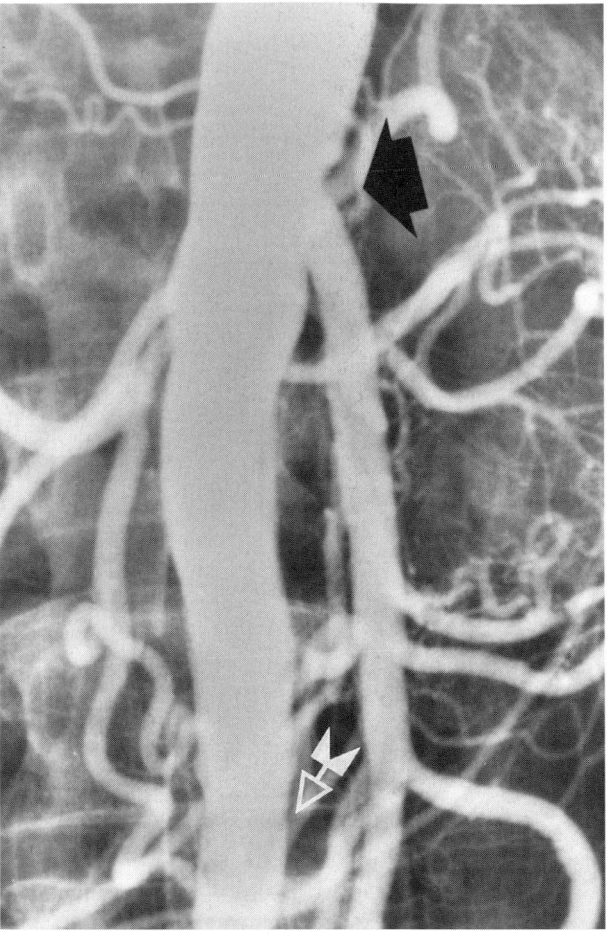

B

Figure 21-5. A 59-year-old woman presented with classic symptoms of chronic mesenteric ischemia. (A) There is a tight stenosis at the origin of the SMA (*black arrow*). The celiac artery is totally occluded and the IMA is stenotic (*white arrow*). After PTA, the patient's symptoms resolved. (B) A follow-up arteriogram 16 months later demonstrates a widely patent SMA (*black arrow*). The IMA is now occluded (*white arrow*). The patient remained asymptomatic. (From Tegtmeyer CJ, et al. In: Ernst CB, Stanley JC, eds. Percutaneous transcatheter therapy of visceral ischemia. Current therapy in vascular disease. 3rd ed. New York: Mosby–Year Book, 1995:689–693. Used with permission.)

mesenteric arterial stents to supplement endovascular therapy in 2 patients with chronic mesenteric ischemia. In both cases, a suboptimal PTA result was the indication for stent placement (Fig. 21-6). Both patients also had a second mesenteric vessel balloon dilated and were asymptomatic at follow-up.

There are relatively few indications for revascularization in patients with asymptomatic mesenteric arterial disease. However, in certain patients with tenuous mesenteric circulation who are undergoing procedures involving the abdominal aorta, prophylactic mesenteric artery revascularization may be indicated as a means to reduce the incidence of postoperative mesenteric ischemia.[23,24] Division of the IMA during reconstruction of the abdominal aorta, in conjunction with disease of the SMA and iliac arteries, predisposes the patient to the development of postoperative mesenteric ischemia.[23] In one study, bowel infarction occurring after reconstructive abdominal aortic surgery was associated with a 100 percent mortality rate.[24]

Although there is little written about prophylactic mesenteric revascularization, the authors have treated four patients with mesenteric artery PTA for this indication. Two of these patients had significant disease of the SMA, IMA, abdominal aorta, and both iliac and internal iliac arteries. Because of concern for the development of mesenteric ischemia after an aortobifemoral bypass graft, the SMA was balloon-dilated in both patients. The third patient had 100 percent occlusion of the SMA, 90 percent stenosis of the celiac artery, and 10 percent stenosis of the IMA and a large abdominal aortic aneurysm. The patient underwent prophylactic PTA of the celiac artery. The abdominal aortic aneurysm was repaired without sequela. The fourth patient

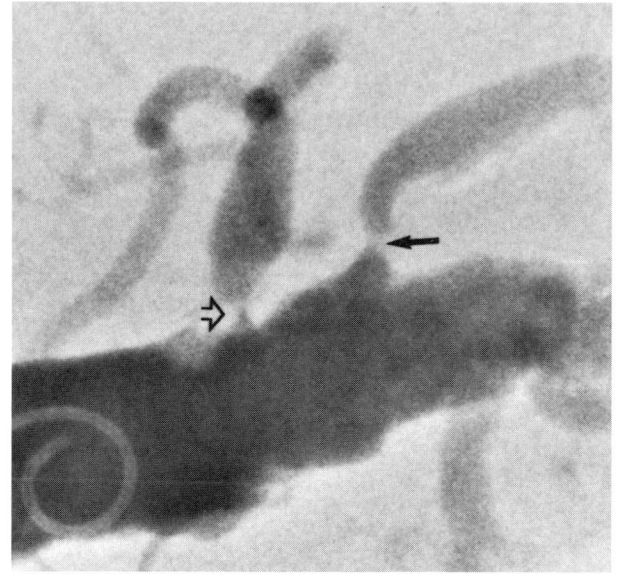

A

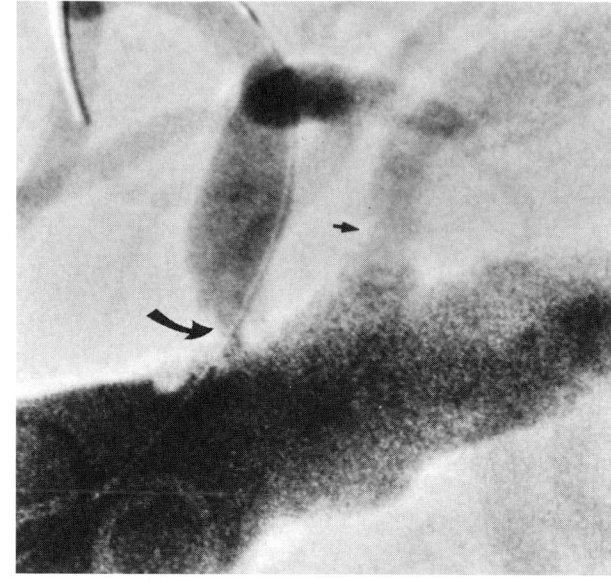

B

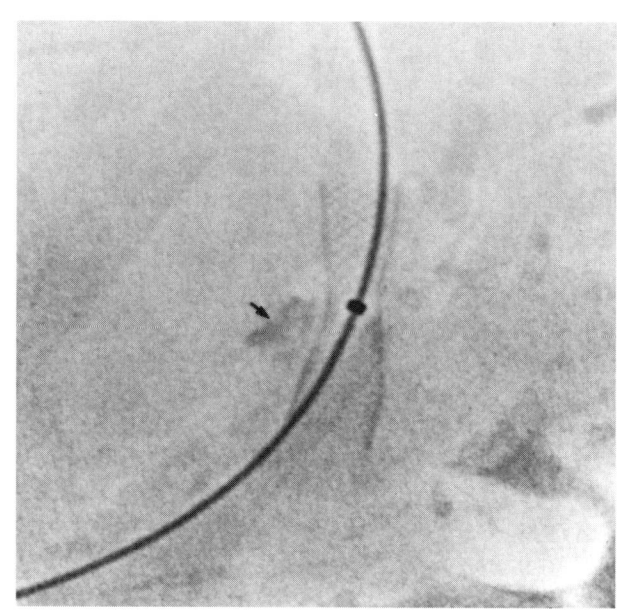

C

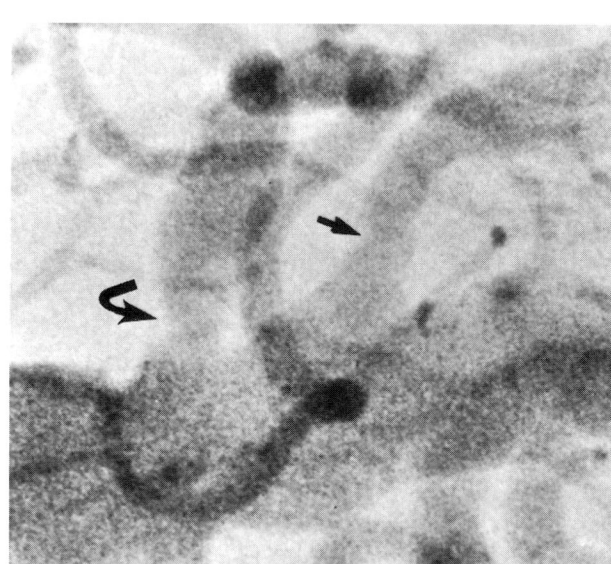

D

Figure 21-6. A 60-year-old woman presented with an 11-pound weight loss and a 4-month history of vague abdominal pain associated with eating solid food. She had had a prior aortobifemoral bypass graft. (A) A diagnostic arteriogram demonstrates an 80 percent stenosis of the SMA (*straight arrow*) and a 95 percent stenosis of the celiac artery (*open arrow*). The IMA is occluded. (B) After balloon dilation of the SMA and celiac artery, the SMA has a satisfactory appearance (*straight arrow*), but the celiac artery remains narrowed (*curved arrow*). (C) The resistant lesion involving the celiac artery was related to a calcified plaque (*arrow*), which was easily visualized at the time of balloon dilation. (D) An 8-mm-diameter, 20-mm-long Wallstent was deployed in the celiac artery and balloon-dilated to 9 mm in diameter. A residual "waist" on the stent secondary to the calcified plaque (*arrow*) could not be completely obliterated. (E) Despite this, the control arteriogram demonstrated a satisfactory appearance to the celiac artery (*curved arrow*) and SMA (*straight arrow*). The patient's symptoms resolved, and she was asymptomatic at 8 months of follow-up.

E

developed complete occlusion at the site of an ostial IMA stenosis after PTA of the abdominal aorta. Balloon dilation was performed on the IMA to reestablish flow in the IMA distribution. None of the four patients developed signs or symptoms of mesenteric ischemia during a follow-up period of 7 to 73 months.

The authors have also treated five patients with a clinical or angiographic presentation that was suggestive of, but not classic for, mesenteric ischemia. Their symptoms usually included atypical abdominal pain unrelated to eating and greater than 70 percent stenosis of at least two visceral arteries. None of these pa-

tients experienced weight loss, and no other etiology for their abdominal pain had been diagnosed. There were two immediate technical failures in this group. Both of these patients had angiographic findings consistent with extrinsic compression of the celiac artery by the median arcuate ligament (Fig. 21-7). After median arcuate ligament release at surgery, both patients had resolution of their symptoms. Of the three immediate technical successes, only one patient had resolution of symptoms. The second patient had abdominal bloating unrelated to meals and neither improved nor deteriorated after angioplasty of the SMA. The third patient had persistent symptoms after a successful SMA angioplasty but became asymptomatic after a surgical bypass of a totally occluded celiac artery. Therefore, of the five patients with symptoms atypical for mesenteric ischemia, only one patient benefited from the endovascular procedure.

In the authors' series, 24 patients intially underwent dilation of a single mesenteric vessel. When the success rates of PTA were evaluated in terms of which visceral vessel was treated, it was found that PTA of 13 of 16 (81 percent) SMAs, 3 of 6 (50 percent) celiac arteries, and 2 of 2 (100 percent) IMAs were both technically and clinically successful (Table 21-2). Two of the 3 failures of celiac artery PTA were secondary to compression by the median arcuate ligament. Although compression of a mesenteric artery by the median arcuate ligament can lead to mesenteric ischemia or cause symptoms that mimic mesenteric ischemia,[25,26] PTA is ineffective in dilating vessels narrowed by extrinsic compression.

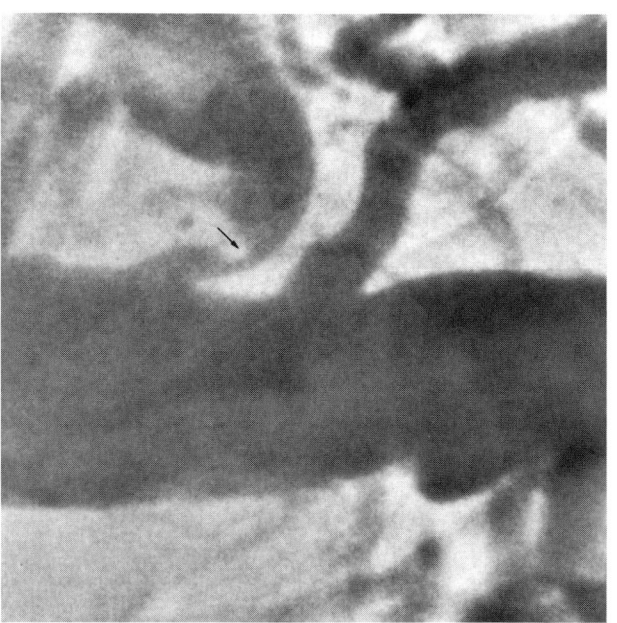

A

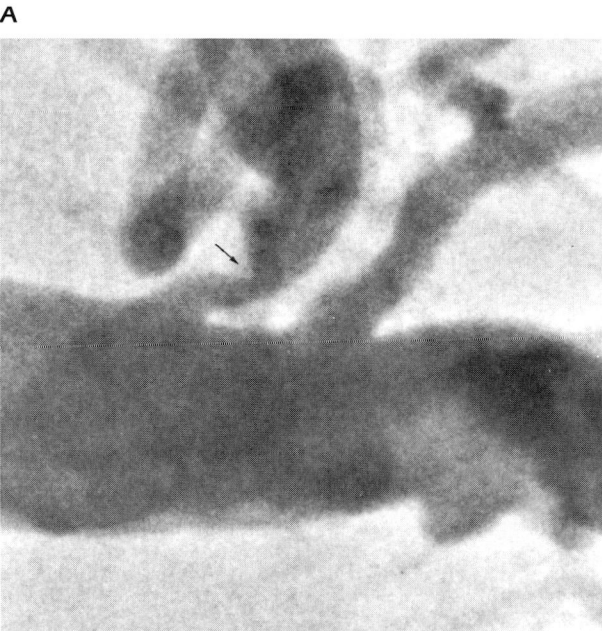

B

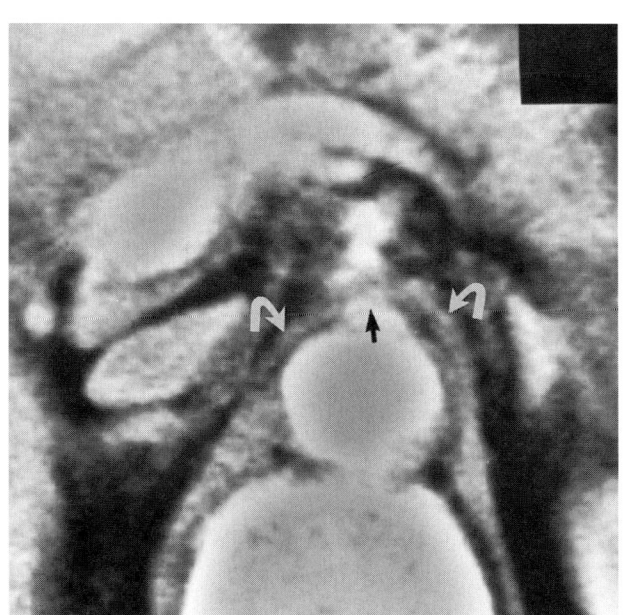

C

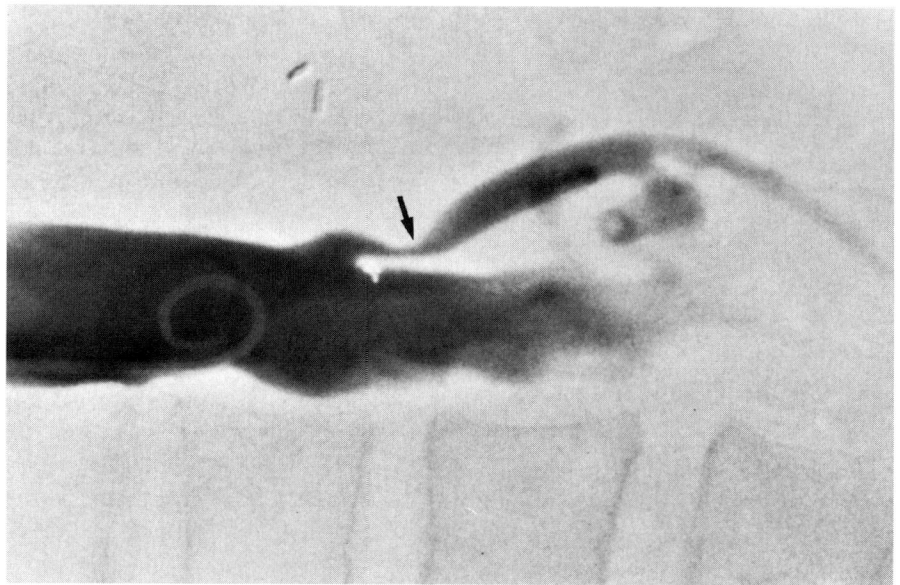

D

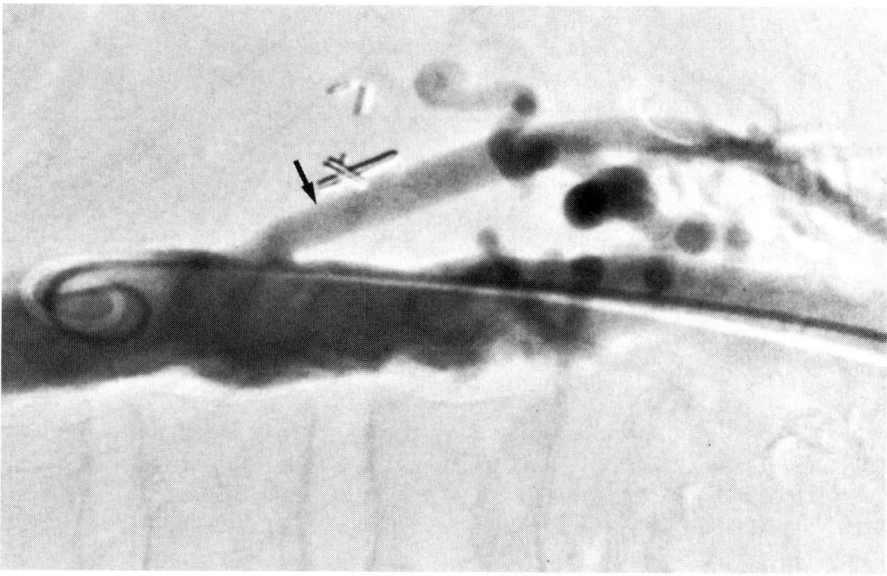

E

Figure 21-7. Narrowing of a mesenteric artery by the median arcuate ligament is characterized by an asymmetric, nonostial stenosis that varies with respiration. (A) On expiration, the celiac artery stenosis is 80 percent (*arrow*). (B) On inspiration, the celiac artery is only 50 percent narrowed (*arrow*). (From Matsumoto AH, et al. Percutaneous transluminal angioplasty of visceral arterial stenoses: results and long-term clinical follow up. J Vasc Intervent Radiol 1995;6:165–174. Used with permission.) (C) A CT scan from a different patient demonstrates the crura of the diaphragm (*curved arrows*) joining centrally to form the median arcuate ligament and compressing the SMA (*straight arrow*). (D) Lateral aortogram from the patient in (C) shows occlusion of the celiac artery and the narrowing of the SMA (*arrow*). (E) Following surgical division of the median arcuate ligament, a follow-up lateral aortogram shows a widely patent SMA (*arrow*). (From Matsumoto AH, et al. Compression of the superior mesenteric artery by the median arcuate ligament: a cause for mesenteric ischemia. Vasc Surg 1994;28:489–493. Used with permission.)

Table 21-2. Technical and Clinical Success in Patients with a Single Dilated Visceral Artery

Patient Group	SMA*	Celiac Artery	IMA
1	10 of 10 (100%)	2 of 4 (50%)	1 of 1 (100%)
2	1 of 4 (25%)	0 of 1 (0%)	—
3	2 of 2 (100%)	1 of 1 (100%)	1 of 1 (100%)
Totals	13 of 16 (81%)	3 of 6 (50%)	2 of 2 (100%)

Group 1: patients with classic presentation for chronic mesenteric ischemia.
Group 2: patients with atypical symptoms for chronic mesenteric ischemia.
Group 3: patients dilated prophylactically.
*Includes two aorta-SMA bypass grafts.

Narrowing of a mesenteric vessel by the median arcuate ligament should be suspected when an asymmetric, nonostial stenosis involving the superior and anterior aspect of either the celiac artery or SMA is present, especially if the stenosis increases with expiration and decreases with inspiration (see Fig. 21-7).[26,27] If balloon inflation in such a lesion is easy but rapid arterial recoil occurs during balloon deflation, extrinsic compression of the mesenteric artery is even more probable. Although stenting such a lesion seems attractive, a Palmaz stent may be permanently deformed by the extrinsic pressure and occlude the vessel. In addition, there is some evidence to suggest that the symptoms caused by the median arcuate ligament are related to compression of the adjacent celiac nerve plexus.[25] Therefore, vascular stents in the treatment of this entity appear to have no current role.

When the results of PTA in the treatment of nonostial versus ostial visceral artery stenoses were compared, there was no statistically significant difference in the clinical success rates (Table 21-3). Although intuitively one might expect nonostial lesions to respond better to PTA, the median arcuate ligament causes a nonostial narrowing. Since the authors treated several lesions that were related to the median arcuate liga-

ment, the data may be biased toward an unfavorable PTA result for nonostial lesions.

Lesions caused by FMD should respond favorably to balloon dilation.[4] The authors have treated one patient with chronic mesenteric ischemia caused by FMD of the SMA. Balloon dilation was successful, and the patient remained asymptomatic at 15 months of follow-up.

The response of vasculitic lesions to PTA is variable. In general, the longer the lesion and the higher the erythrocyte sedimentation rate in a patient with an arteritis, the less favorable is the response to PTA.[5]

The complications from mesenteric PTA are similar to those encountered in patients with diffuse vascular disease who are undergoing peripheral angioplasty.[28] The authors have treated a total of 27 patients and have had 3 (11 percent) major complications. The most serious complication required a patient to undergo an amputation when one limb of a previous aortobifemoral bypass graft occluded at the access site in the femoral artery. Although the authors' 30-day mortality rate was zero, 3 deaths have been reported in the literature in the 107 patients treated (see Table 21-1).

Discussion

Revascularization is indicated in all patients with signs and symptoms of chronic mesenteric ischemia. Unless mesenteric perfusion is restored, patients with critical intestinal ischemia will develop progressive weight loss, food avoidance, and ultimately intestinal infarction.[29]

A variety of surgical techniques have been used to treat mesenteric arterial occlusive disease. The nature of the surgical procedure is determined by the surgeon's experience, the anatomic distribution of the disease, and the institutional bias. The overall technical success rates with surgical revascularization have varied

Table 21-3. PTA Success and Lesion Location

Patient Group	Ostial*	Clinical Success	Nonostial	Clinical Success	Ostial and Nonostial	Clinical Success
1	8	6	11	8	2	2
2	1	1	4	0	—	—
3	1	1	3	3	—	—
Totals	10	8 of 10 (80%)	18	11 of 18 (61%)	2	2 of 2 (100%)

Numbers are based on a total of 30 vessels.
Group 1: patients with classic presentation for chronic mesenteric ischemia.
Group 2: patients with atypical symptoms for chronic mesenteric ischemia.
Group 3: patients dilated prophylactically.
*Stenosis within 5 mm of vessel origin.

from 90 to 98 percent, with long-term clinical success rates of 61 to 100 percent. Morbidity rates range from 20 to 54 percent, with a 30-day mortality rate of 0 to 8 percent.[3,30-34]

Although clinical studies comparing surgical and endovascular techniques in the treatment of mesenteric ischemia are lacking, the authors' experience and a review of the literature indicate that endovascular therapy represents an effective alternative to surgery in patients with chronic mesenteric ischemia. For complete arterial occlusions, surgical revascularization remains the mainstay of therapy. However, patients at high risk for surgery may benefit from an initial attempt at percutaneous therapy.

Since the adequacy of collateral mesenteric blood flow is difficult to determine, the issue of when to perform prophylactic PTA on the mesenteric vessels is hard to define. What is known is that the development of mesenteric ischemia after reconstructive surgery on the abdominal aorta is associated with a high mortality rate.[23,24] Therefore, PTA may be justified in asymptomatic patients with tenuous visceral arterial circulation, especially in patients who will be undergoing revascularization procedures on the abdominal aorta.

Mesenteric PTA in patients with symptoms atypical for ischemia or with an isolated, nonostial stenosis of the celiac artery appears to be less effective. This is partly due to the high prevalence of extrinsic arterial compression by the median arcuate ligament, or less frequently, by an occult malignancy. Since the symptoms of an occult abdominal or retroperitoneal malignancy can mimic the symptoms of chronic mesenteric ischemia, it is important to be alert to this diagnostic possibility. Therefore, an immediate technical or clinical failure of mesenteric artery PTA should raise suspicion for extrinsic vascular compression by the median arcuate ligament or an occult malignancy.[20]

With improvements in fluoroscopic equipment, balloon catheters, and guidewire technology, endovascular techniques have been shown to be useful in the treatment of mesenteric arterial insufficiency. The availability of stents also provides an additional tool for achieving a good technical result, although the long-term efficacy of stents in mesenteric vessels is still unknown. As in other vascular beds, the Palmaz stent should be used cautiously where extrinsic vascular compression (i.e., median arcuate ligament) can cause collapse or distort the stent and lead to abrupt vascular occlusion.

References

1. Fisher D, Fry W. Collateral mesenteric circulation. Surg Gynecol Obstet 1987;164:487–492.

2. Sniderman KW. Transluminal angioplasty in the management of chronic intestinal ischemia. In: Strandness DE, van Breda A, eds. Vascular diseases: surgical and interventional therapy. New York: Churchill-Livingstone, 1994:803–809.

3. Baxter BT, Pearce WH. Diagnosis and surgical management of chronic mesenteric ischemia. In: Strandness DE, van Breda A, eds. Vascular diseases: surgical and interventional therapy. New York: Churchill-Livingstone, 1994:795–802.

4. Tegtmeyer CJ, Selby JB Jr, Hartwell GD, Ayers C, Tegtmeyer V. Results and complications of angioplasty in fibromuscular disease. Circulation 1991;83(Suppl I):155–161.

5. Tanimoto A, Hiramatsu K. Percutaneous transluminal angioplasty for Takayasu's arteritis. Semin Intervent Radiol 1993;10:1–7.

6. Tegtmeyer CJ, Sos TA. Techniques of renal angioplasty. Radiology 1986;161:577–586.

7. Chopra PS, Grassi CJ. Superior mesenteric artery angioplasty with the TEGwire: usefulness and technical difficulties. J Vasc Intervent Radiol 1992;3:523–526.

8. Furrer J, Gruntzig A, Kugelmeier J, Goebel N. Treatment of abdominal angina with percutaneous dilatation of an arteria mesenterica superior stenosis. Cardiovasc Intervent Radiol 1980;3:43–44.

9. Uflacker R, Goldany MA, Constant S. Resolution of mesenteric angina with percutaneous transluminal angioplasty of a superior mesenteric artery stenosis using a balloon catheter. Gastrointest Radiol 1980;5:367–369.

10. Novelline RA. Percutaneous transluminal angioplasty: newer applications. AJR 1980;135:983–988.

11. Birch SJ, Colapinto RF. Transluminal dilatation in the management of mesenteric angina: a report of two cases. J Can Assoc Radiol 1982;33:46–47.

12. Crotch-Harvey MA, Gould DA, Green AT. Case report: percutaneous transluminal angioplasty of the inferior mesenteric artery in the treatment of chronic mesenteric ischaemia. Clin Radiol 1992;46:408–409.

13. Warnock NG, Gaines PA, Beard JD, Cumberland DC. Treatment of intestinal angina by percutaneous transluminal angioplasty of a superior mesenteric artery occlusion. Clin Radiol 1992;45:18–19.

14. Golden DA, Ring EJ, McLean GK, Freiman DB. Percutaneous angioplasty in the treatment of abdominal angina. AJR 1982;139:247–249.

15. Roberts L, Wertman DA, Mills SR, Moore AV, Heaston DK. Transluminal angioplasty of the superior mesenteric artery: an alternative to surgical revascularization. AJR 1983;141:1039–1042.

16. Wilms G, Baert AL. Transluminal angioplasty of superior mesenteric artery and celiac trunk. Ann Radiol 1986;29:535–538.

17. Levy PJ, Haskell L, Gordon RL. Percutaneous transluminal angioplasty of splanchnic arteries: an alternative method to elective revascularisation in chronic visceral ischaemia. Eur J Radiol 1987;7:239–242.

18. McShane MD, Proctor A, Spencer P, Cumberland DC, Welsh CL. Mesenteric angioplasty for chronic intestinal ischaemia. Eur J Vasc Surg 1992;6:333–336.

19. Simonetti G, Lupattelli L, Urigo F, Bars F, Musca S, Mashes F, Guazzaroni M. Interventional radiology in the treatment of acute and chronic mesenteric ischemia. Radiol Med 1992;84:98–105.

20. Matsumoto AH, Tegtmeyer CJ, Fitzcharles EJ, et al. Percutaneous transluminal angioplasty of visceral arterial stenoses: results and long-term clinical follow-up. J Vasc Intervent Radiol 1995;6:165–174.

21. Hallisey MJ, Deschaine J, Illescas FF, et al. Angioplasty for the treatment of visceral ischemia. J Vasc Intervent Radiol 1995;6:785–791.

22. Rose SC, Qurgley TM, Rakev EJ. Revascularization for chronic mesenteric ischemia: comparison of operative arterial bypass grafting and percutaneous transluminal angioplasty. J Vasc Intervent Radiol 1995;6:339–349.

23. Gonzalez LL, Jaffe MS. Mesenteric arterial insufficiency following abdominal aortic resection. Arch Surg 1966;93:10–20.

24. Rogers DM, Thompson JE, Garrett WV, Talkington CM, Patman RD. Mesenteric vascular problems: a 26-year experience. Ann Surg 1982;195:554–565.

25. Tribble CG, Harman PK, Mentzer RM Jr. Celiac artery compression syndrome: report of a case and review of current opinion. Vasc Surg 1986;20:120–129.

26. Matsumoto AH. Meuhle C, Cassada D, Navid F, Tegtmeyer CJ, Tribble CG. Compression of the superior mesenteric artery by the median arcuate ligament: a cause for mesenteric ischemia. Vasc Surg 1994;28:489–493.

27. Reuter SR, Bernstein EF. The anatomic basis for respiratory variation in median arcuate ligament compression of the celiac artery. Surgery 1973;73:381–385.

28. Becker GJ, Katzen BT, Dake MD. Noncoronary angioplasty. Radiology 1989;170:921–940.

29. Kalaya RN, Sammartano RJ, Boley SJ. Aggressive approach to acute mesenteric ischemia. Surg Clin North Am 1992;72:157–182.

30. McMillan WD, McCarthy WJ, Bresticker MR, et al. Mesenteric artery bypass: objective patency determination. J Vasc Surg 1995;21:729–741.

31. Calderon M, Reul GH, Gregoric ID, et al. Long-term results of the surgical management of symptomatic chronic intestinal ischemia. J Cardiovasc Surg 1992;33:723–728.

32. Rheudasil JM, Stewart MT, Schellack JV, Smith RB III, Salam AA, Perdue GD. Surgical treatment of chronic mesenteric arterial insufficiency. J Vasc Surg 1988;8:495–500.

33. Rapp JH, Reilly LM, Qvarfordt PG, Goldstone J, Ehrenfeld WK, Stoney RJ. Durability of endarterectomy and antegrade grafts in the treatment of chronic visceral ischemia. J Vasc Surg 1986;3:799–806.

34. Reul GJ Jr, Wukasch DC, Sandiford FM, Chiarillo L, Hallman GL, Cooley DA. Surgical treatment of abdominal angina: review of 25 patients. Surgery 1974;75:682–689.

22

Extracranial Brachiocephalic Angioplasty

DONALD E. SCHWARTEN

Percutaneous transluminal angioplasty (PTA) is a well-accepted technique for treating arterial occlusive disease in all anatomic territories except the cerebral vascular circulation. The application of PTA to atherosclerotic disease involving the cerebral vessels has lagged behind its application in other territories primarily because of concerns regarding potential risks of embolization to the central nervous system that could result in clinically significant neurologic deficits. We should remember that the same concerns about distal embolization were raised during the development of angioplasty, particularly coronary and renal angioplasty, and the predictions of resultant acute myocardial infarctions and renal failure were seriously overestimated. A review of the brachiocephalic angioplasty literature suggests that the concerns regarding embolization to the neural axis may likewise be exaggerated.[1] A review by Becker et al.[2] included 165 carotid angioplasties with an overall complication rate of 3.6 percent. Casarella[3] reported an angioplasty-related distal embolization rate of 2.5 percent in 3204 patients. In an ironic twist, Kumpe et al.[4] reported the use of angioplasty to successfully treat patients presenting with atheroembolic syndromes.

In the North American Symptomatic Carotid Endarterectomy Trial (NASCET), surgical reconstruction of the carotid bifurcation emerged as the clear-cut treatment of choice in patients with symptomatic greater than 70 percent stenoses of the carotid bifurcation or internal carotid artery origin.[5] In most institutions where morbidity and mortality rates match or surpass those of NASCET, patients are discharged within 48 hours after endarterectomy and expect a relatively prompt return to normal activities with a low risk of recurrent disease and, most importantly, a low risk of subsequent neurologic events, not only in the territory supplied by the operated carotid artery, but also in the contralateral hemisphere and the posterior fossa. With the good results being obtained with carotid endarterectomy, is there a place for carotid bifurcation angioplasty? Reports by Tsai, Higashida, Mathias, and Theron have documented the safety of carotid bifurcation angioplasty.[6-9] Tsai, Higashida, and Mathias perform carotid bifurcation angioplasty using, with minor variations, techniques that are employed in angioplasty of peripheral vessels. In their combined experience, only one clinically significant embolic stroke has occurred in a total of nearly 300 procedures. However, since these series were not randomized and patient selection played a significant role in that patients with angiographic evidence of ulceration were excluded, they cannot be considered comparable to the NASCET. Interestingly, Theron et al.[10] found that when cerebral protection was not used, 10 percent of patients sustained a clinically significant neurologic event associated with the angioplasty procedure.

The North American Cerebral PTA Register[11] was recently concluded, and of patients undergoing PTA of extracranial carotid and vertebral occlusive disease, no incidents of cerebral embolization occurred secondary to angioplasty. The findings were confirmed, not only by rigorous neurologic examination, but also by cross-sectional imaging. Others have documented clinically insignificant emboli during carotid PTA with transcranial Doppler.[1]

Innominate, subclavian, common carotid, and vertebral angioplasty have received at least a modicum of acceptance in the management of patients with symptomatic atherosclerotic disease in these anatomic distributions. In Becker et al.'s[2] review of 423 procedures involving subclavian and innominate arteries, the technical success rate was 92 percent and the central nervous system complication rate was 1 percent.

In this chapter, carotid angioplasty for bifurcation atherosclerosis will serve as the model for the discussion of angioplasty of other extracranial "cerebral" vasculature.

Carotid Artery Angioplasty

Although stroke-related deaths in the United States declined slightly in the decade between 1984 and 1994, stroke remains the third leading cause of death in the United States,[12,13] and among the survivors of stroke, the resulting disability causes an immense burden. It is estimated that the etiology of stroke is at the carotid bifurcation in at least 50 percent of all cases.[14] The NASCET demonstrated that for patients with symptomatic carotid stenoses 70 percent or greater, patients who were randomized to surgical therapy experienced a 17 percent absolute risk reduction for ipsilateral stroke. Similar findings were observed in the European Carotid Surgery Trial (ECST).[15] These randomized trials and others[16] have suggested a strong relationship between the degree of stenosis and the risk of developing an ipsilateral stroke. The Asymptomatic Carotid Artery Surgery (ACAS) Trial[17] has suggested similar although less striking risk reduction for patients with asymptomatic stenoses as little as 60 percent.

In summary, it is clear that the treatment of choice at this time for patients with extracranial carotid occlusive disease at the carotid bifurcation is carotid endarterectomy. Endarterectomy eliminates the plaque with its associated ulcerations, if any, and restores normal luminal caliber to the carotid bulb. The risk of recurrent stenosis is variously reported to range from 6 to 32 percent.[18-20] Most of these recurrences are within the first 2 years after endarterectomy. The finding that recurrent stenoses behave differently than native lesions is somewhat analogous to Meier's[21] report that myocardial infarction attributable to thrombosis at a previous PTCA site is extremely rare. The speculation in both circumstances is that the smooth, elastic, inner lining of the restenosis lesion is much less thrombogenic than that of a native lesion. Neurologic symptoms have been reported to be uncommon after carotid endarterectomy, with symptomatic recurrent stenoses occurring in less than 5 percent of cases.[22] Nichols et al. found no consistent relationship between postoperative neurologic events and recurrent carotid stenoses.[23]

Despite the fact that carotid angioplasty reports lack long-term documentation of efficacy, they have clearly shown that, as in endarterectomy, there is a reduction in stenosis and improvement in flow to the ipsilateral hemisphere, and that the rate of development of permanent neurologic deficits as a result of carotid angioplasty complications is acceptably low. Although it is unknown whether the recurrent stenosis rate will equal or exceed that of carotid endarterectomy, one may theorize that the clinical impact of a recurrent carotid stenosis after angioplasty may be similar if not identical to the findings regarding recurrent disease after endarterectomy.

With exceedingly rare exceptions, carotid angioplasty should be performed only in patients who are appropriately symptomatic. Some patients are at a relatively high risk for surgical intervention for extracranial carotid occlusive disease because of cardiac or pulmonary comorbidity (Fig. 22-1); previous surgical interventions in the neck that predispose the patient to an increased risk (Fig. 22-2), particularly to cranial nerve injury; and difficult surgical access such as that caused by intrathoracic common carotid disease (Fig. 22-3) or an exceptionally high carotid bifurcation, necessitating at the minimum mandibular disarticulation for surgical access. Under any of these circumstances, patients with symptomatic extracranial carotid occlusive disease may be good candidates for percutaneous transluminal angioplasty. If, in the assessment of the vascular surgeon involved with the patient's care, the operative risk is 5 percent or greater, angioplasty is a suitable alternative to surgical intervention.

Preangioplasty Examinations

It is essential that the patient's symptoms and anatomy correlate. This correlation is best documented by a physician skilled in acquiring a complete neurologic history and physical examination. Additional diagnostic examinations are invariably included. Although magnetic resonance angiography (MRA) and spiral CT have been advocated as both screening and definitive procedures in the workup of a patient with cerebrovascular disease, cerebrovascular duplex ultrasound is the most common screening examination employed. In some institutions, B-mode imaging with pulsed Doppler to identify flow disturbances is combined with spectral waveform analysis to categorize the severity of the stenosis; this combination is the primary determinant for proceeding to operative intervention, particularly when spiral CT or MRA is also used to image the intrathoracic and intracranial anatomy.[24] Since carotid duplex examinations are labor-intensive and highly technician-dependent and interlaboratory variability tends to be significant, all patients undergoing percutaneous intervention for extracranial occlusive disease must have a cross-sectional imaging study of the brain. CT and MRI have their advocates, but either is acceptable.

Arteriography remains the gold standard. In patients who are going to be candidates for angioplasty, a complete arch and four-vessel selective cerebrovascular arteriogram is essential. Arch injections with imaging of the intrathoracic and cervical anatomy alone are not adequate. An angiographer who does not possess the skills to perform a selective four-vessel study certainly is not prepared to deal with the technical aspects of carotid angioplasty, let alone the potential pitfalls associated with that procedure. The interventionalist who

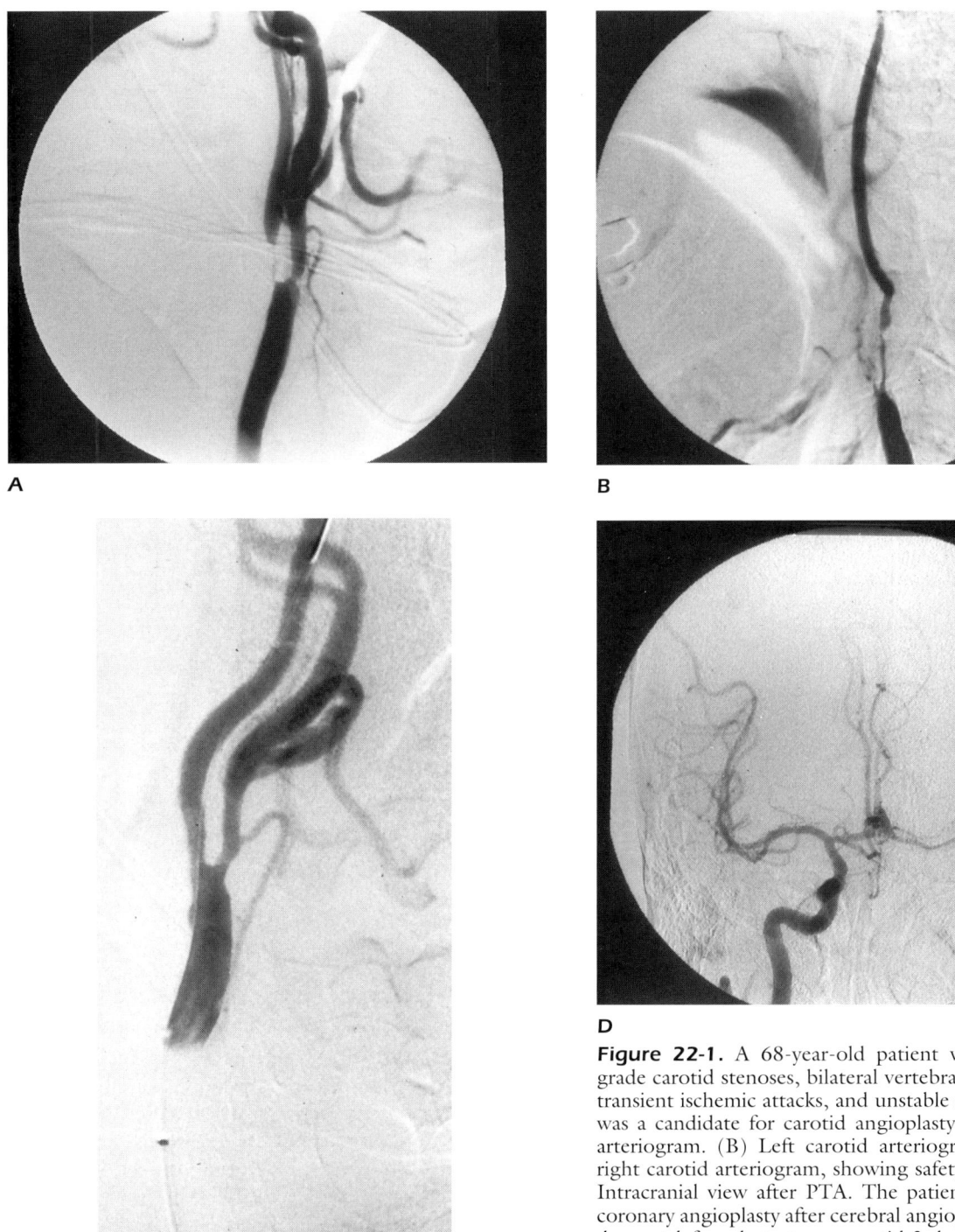

A

B

C

D

Figure 22-1. A 68-year-old patient with bilateral high-grade carotid stenoses, bilateral vertebral disease, crescendo transient ischemic attacks, and unstable angina. The patient was a candidate for carotid angioplasty. (A) Right carotid arteriogram. (B) Left carotid arteriogram. (C) Post-PTA right carotid arteriogram, showing safety wire in place. (D) Intracranial view after PTA. The patient went directly for coronary angioplasty after cerebral angioplasty, and then underwent left endartectomy carotid 2 days later.

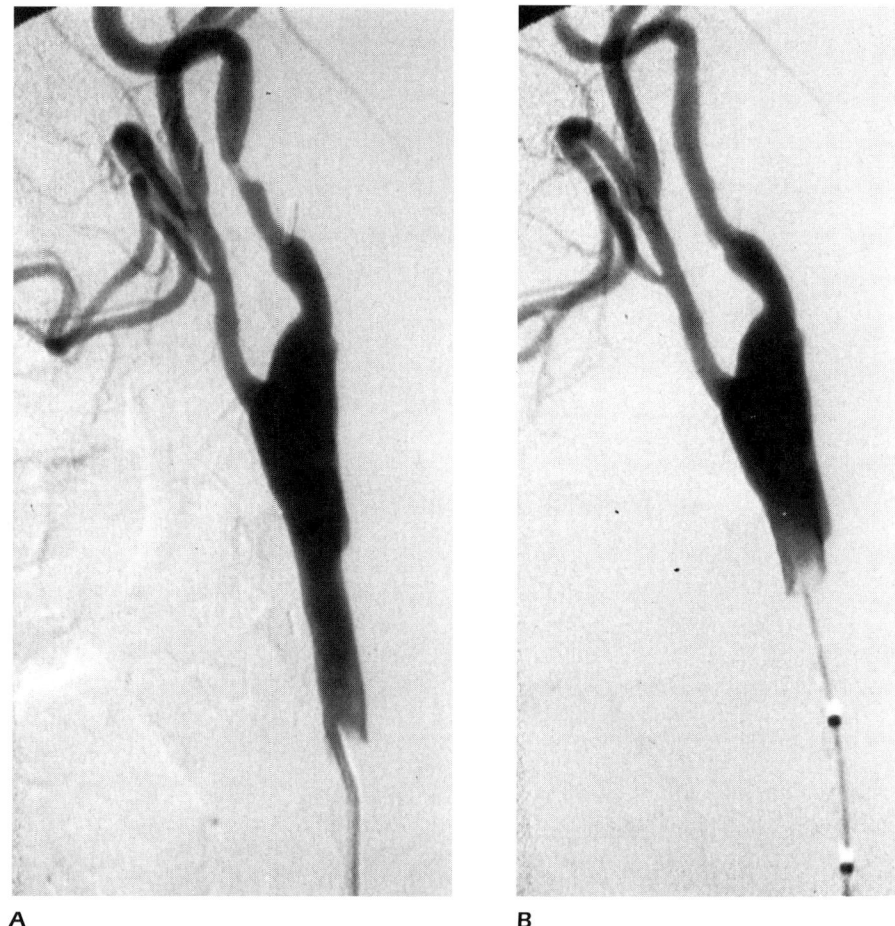

A

B

Figure 22-2. (A) Recurrent stenosis after multiple previous endarterectomies. (B) After PTA.

performs cerebrovascular angioplasty procedures *must* have appropriate training and credentialing in cerebrovascular interventions.

In general, angioplasty of the common carotid artery or the carotid bifurcation is in many ways similar to "guidewire exchange" angioplasty in other anatomic locations, but there are some important differences. Whereas it may be acceptable to perform iliac angioplasty in an unanticoagulated patient, this is not acceptable for carotid angioplasty. Patients should be systemically heparinized with an activated clotting time (ACT) of approximately 300 for the procedure. Heparinization is rarely if ever reversed with protamine sulfate after the procedure. If thrombolysis is employed as part of the procedure or if a substantial intimal cleft is present after PTA, the patient may be maintained on therapeutic doses of heparin for 24 to 72 hours after the angioplasty. Low-molecular-weight dextran may be used in lieu of heparin in patients with a contraindication to heparin use.

Angioplasty in and around the carotid bulb requires the administration of atropine, 0.6 to 1.0 mg, just

prior to catheter manipulation within the bulb to prevent severe bradyarrhythmias.

Vasospasm is typically treated with 100-mcg boluses of intraarterial nitroglycerin and may be supplemented by transdermal nitroglycerin. Although calcium channel antagonists may be used for the management of intraprocedural vasospasm, more commonly these agents are used to treat intraprocedural hypertension. All patients are pretreated with salicylates, and antiplatelet therapy is continued for the patient's lifetime after the procedure.

The procedure is performed under local anesthesia and mild conscious sedation with ECG, pulse oximetry, and automated blood pressure monitoring. Immediately before the procedure a baseline neurologic examination is obtained. During and after the procedure regular neurologic checks are performed.

Since the extracranial carotid artery is of sufficient diameter that microcatheters are not necessary, guiding catheters are also not necessary, and the angioplasty catheters employed include a variety of 5 French catheters designed for use over a 0.035-inch guide-

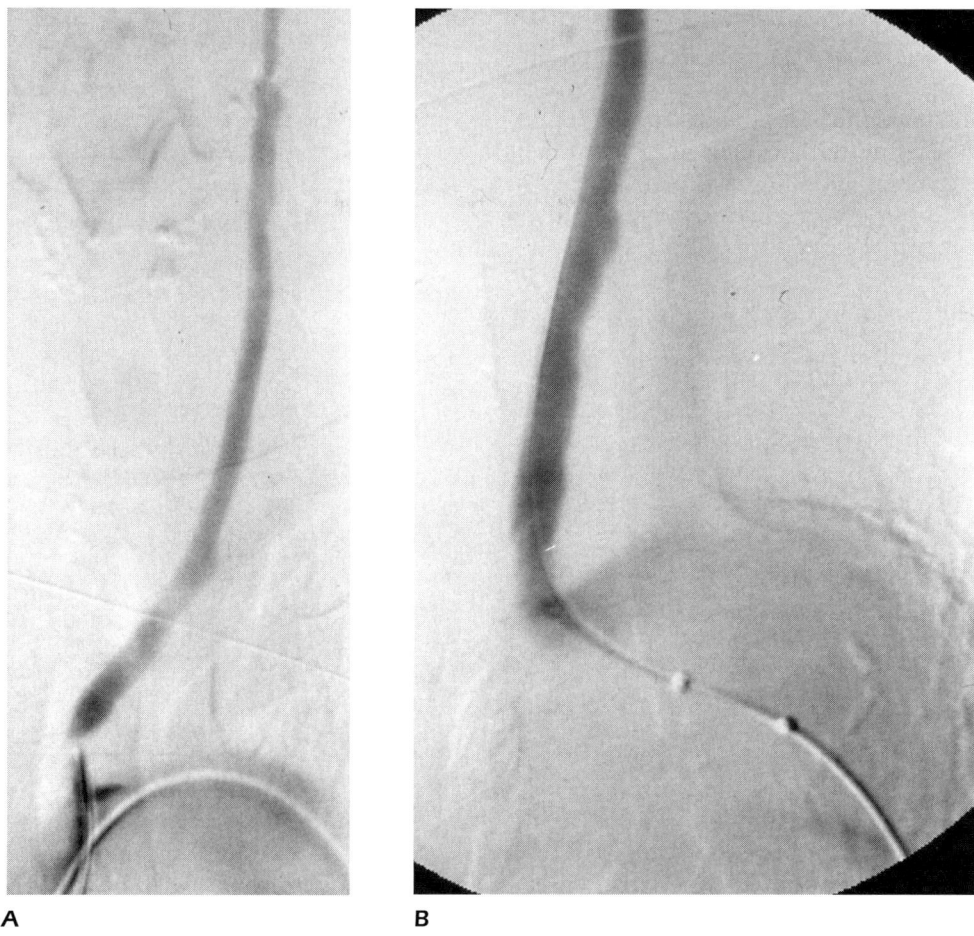

Figure 22-3. (A) Left common carotid stenosis 1 cm inside origin from transverse arch. (B) After PTA.

wire. Noncompliant high-pressure balloons should be avoided. Angioplasty catheters should be used with the balloon as close to the tip of the catheter as possible to ensure that the catheter tip is not placed near the base of the skull or in a tortuous segment of the cervical internal carotid artery.

Most commonly, the retrograde common femoral approach via a sheath is employed; for the occasional patient with extremely tortuous arch anatomy, direct puncture of the common carotid artery in the neck can be used. Unlike angioplasty of subclavian, innominate, and some vertebral arteries, it has not been necessary to use the high brachial or transaxillary approach.

Selective catheterization of the target artery is performed and a preangioplasty study is acquired, both for morphologic assessment of the angioplasty site and for measurement of the nearest adjacent normal-caliber segment of vessel. The measurements may be obtained through a variety of software programs found in digital imaging systems or by acquiring analogue images with a known-diameter large coin or a washer placed in the plane and depth of the target lesion to

permit precise calculation of magnification. The North American CPTA Register protocol permitted the use of a balloon diameter equal to the corrected arterial diameter, a balloon diameter equal to 20 percent greater than the calculated diameter of the target vessel, or a balloon diameter 1 mm greater than the calculated diameter of the target vessel. The smaller-diameter balloon should be used for the first inflation, and if an unacceptable anatomic result is achieved, the next-larger-diameter balloon should be used within the protocol parameters and the angioplasty repeated. The shortest balloon length that permits complete lesion coverage should be selected.

After the vessel diameter is calculated and the appropriate balloon is selected, the images are scrutinized for vessel irregularity at the angioplasty site and for the presence of intraluminal filling defects. If either is discovered or if there has been any change since the most recent diagnostic study, local intraarterial infusion of urokinase is instituted as described by Ferguson.[1] Urokinase is delivered at a rate of 4000 units per minute for 1 hour, and a repeat arteriogram is performed. If there has been no alteration in the appearance of an irregular lesion, the infusion is terminated. If a filling defect was the cause for the institution of the urokinase infusion, the infusion is continued until the filling defect has resolved or the patient has received a total of 500,000 units of urokinase. If, after 500,000 units have been administered, a filling defect is still present but changing, the infusion is continued until the filling defect is resolved, and at this point serum fibrinogen levels are monitored at hourly intervals. If after 500,000 units the filling defect is unchanged in its appearance, it is presumed to be of atheromatous etiology and the angioplasty procedure is undertaken as it would be for an otherwise uncomplicated stenosis.

With the selective catheter positioned proximal to the stenosis, the stenosis is crossed with either a TAD (Mallinckrodt Radiology) guidewire with a docking mechanism or an exchange-length hydrophilically coated guidewire. If a hydrophilically coated guidewire is used, the extended taper design should be used to reduce the risk of subintimal passage of the tip of the guidewire. Once a lesion has been crossed with either of the guidewires, the tip of the guidewire is maintained in the petrosal segment of the internal carotid artery for carotid bifurcation disease or in the distal common carotid artery for common carotid disease, and an exchange is made for the appropriate angioplasty catheter. Abundant bony landmarks are present to assist in precisely localizing the balloon segment within the target stenosis; road-mapping simplifies accurate placement. Once the balloon is positioned within the stenosis, it is inflated to its maximum diameter at its maximum rated pressure. Inflation time need not be exceedingly short. The author has rarely observed transient ischemic events while the balloon is inflated; however, the balloon is inflated only as long as is necessary to resolve the deformity caused by the stenosis or to conclude that the deformity cannot be resolved. This may take only a few seconds or as long as 1 to 2 minutes. After the balloon has been deflated, a guidewire exchange is made, a 0.014- or 0.018-inch guidewire is introduced with a side-arm adapter, the angioplasty catheter is retracted proximal to the stenosis, and a postangioplasty arteriogram is acquired (Fig. 22-4). If a suboptimal anatomic result is achieved, the same balloon may be replaced over the 0.014-inch guidewire, or a guidewire and catheter exchange can be made for an angioplasty catheter with a larger balloon segment. Once the best anatomic result has been achieved, a final arteriogram of the angioplasty site and the distal intracranial circulation is acquired (Fig. 22-5), and if no evidence of anatomic or clinical embolization or complication is present, the procedure is concluded and the patient is transferred from the angiography suite to a holding area. Here the patient is monitored with arterial access maintained for 20 to 30 minutes before access is relinquished. Once hemostasis has been achieved and the patient is stable, the patient is transferred to an environment where aggressive neurologic observation can be maintained.

Management of Complications

Stroke is the most feared and devastating complication of carotid angioplasty. It may occur as the result of distal embolization of either atheromatous material or in situ thrombus. It may be the result of an angioplasty-induced dissection causing a critical compromise in flow, or the result of a dissection or unremitting vasospasm caused by guidewire or catheter trip trauma. Unfortunately, unlike with complications that occur in peripheral angioplasty procedures, the surgeon can rarely "bail out" the interventionalist, and the interventionalist must possess the skills necessary to succeed with what Ferguson[1] terms "neurovascular rescue." The patient must be aggressively treated with oxygen, volume expansion, and therapeutic hypertension if the best outcome is to be achieved. Thus successful carotid and cerebral angioplasty demands that the interventionalist possess the skills necessary to minimize cerebral ischemia in addition to the technical skills necessary for safe catheter manipulation.

It may be impossible to know immediately whether an arterial occlusion is a result of atheromatous embolization or thromboembolism. For that reason, vascular occlusions should be given a trial with vigorous local fibrinolysis. If the site of occlusion is intracranial, a microcatheter should be passed through a guiding catheter with a sufficiently large lumen to permit injection of dilute contrast material for anatomic mapping and monitoring. The microcatheter should be ideally positioned within the occluding material or as close to it as possible, and urokinase should be administered, preferably in small pulsed boluses or in a continuous infusion, at a rate of up to 10,000 units per minute (Fig. 22-6). The infusion is continued until one of the following end points is reached: (1) lysis, (2) total dose of 1 million units of urokinase, (3) a drop in serum fibrinogen below 100 mg/dl, or (4) evidence of intracranial bleeding.

Extensive dissection at the angioplasty site with or without the presence of thrombus can be treated surgically if the dissection is limited to the peri-PTA site in the neck. However, if the dissection is intrathoracic or extends sufficiently far distally that it would compromise the surgeon's ability to gain vascular control, the dissection site may be salvaged by stent deployment if

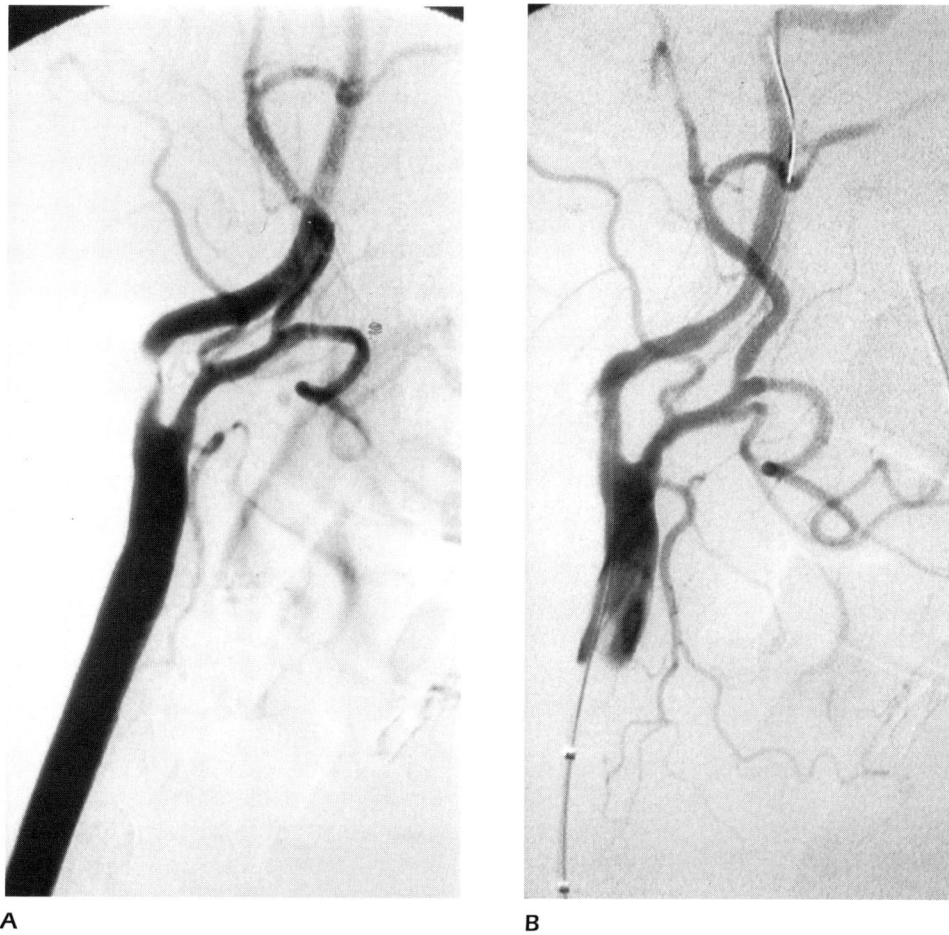

A   B

Figure 22-4. (A) Preangioplasty arteriogram of right internal carotid stenosis. (B) Postangioplasty arteriogram obtained with 0.018-inch guidewire positioned safely across angioplasty site.

no thrombus is present. If thrombus is present, urokinase should be administered and then a stent should be deployed.

Conclusion

Angioplasty for extracranial carotid occlusive disease is controversial, as well it should be, in the face of overwhelming data as to the superiority of carotid endarterectomy over medical therapy in symptomatic patients. The greatest risk associated with carotid angioplasty is the development of a fixed neurologic deficit secondary to distal embolization. This concern has prompted Theron,[10] among others, to protect the cerebral circulation during angioplasty with a second distal balloon that redirects any debris generated by the angioplasty into the external carotid artery. Ferguson[25] sought cerebral protection with a triple-lumen introducer catheter that occludes inflow to the common carotid artery during angioplasty; when the angioplasty balloon is deflated, flow through the circle of Willis provides a sufficient head of pressure to force any debris generated retrograde down the second lumen of the introducer catheter and out a side port of this lumen external to the body.

Other variations of cerebral protection have been advocated; however, a literature review and the experience of the North American Cerebral PTA Register[11] suggest that the incidence of clinical neurologic events secondary to distal embolization associated with cerebral angioplasty is extremely low. Furthermore, the incidence of clinically undetected events discovered on postangioplasty cross-sectional imaging studies is also extremely low.

It appears that the safety of carotid angioplasty may be comparable to that of surgical intervention. It is unknown whether carotid angioplasty can achieve the same reduction in incidence of stroke that has been achieved with endarterectomy. The answer to this awaits randomized controlled clinical trials.

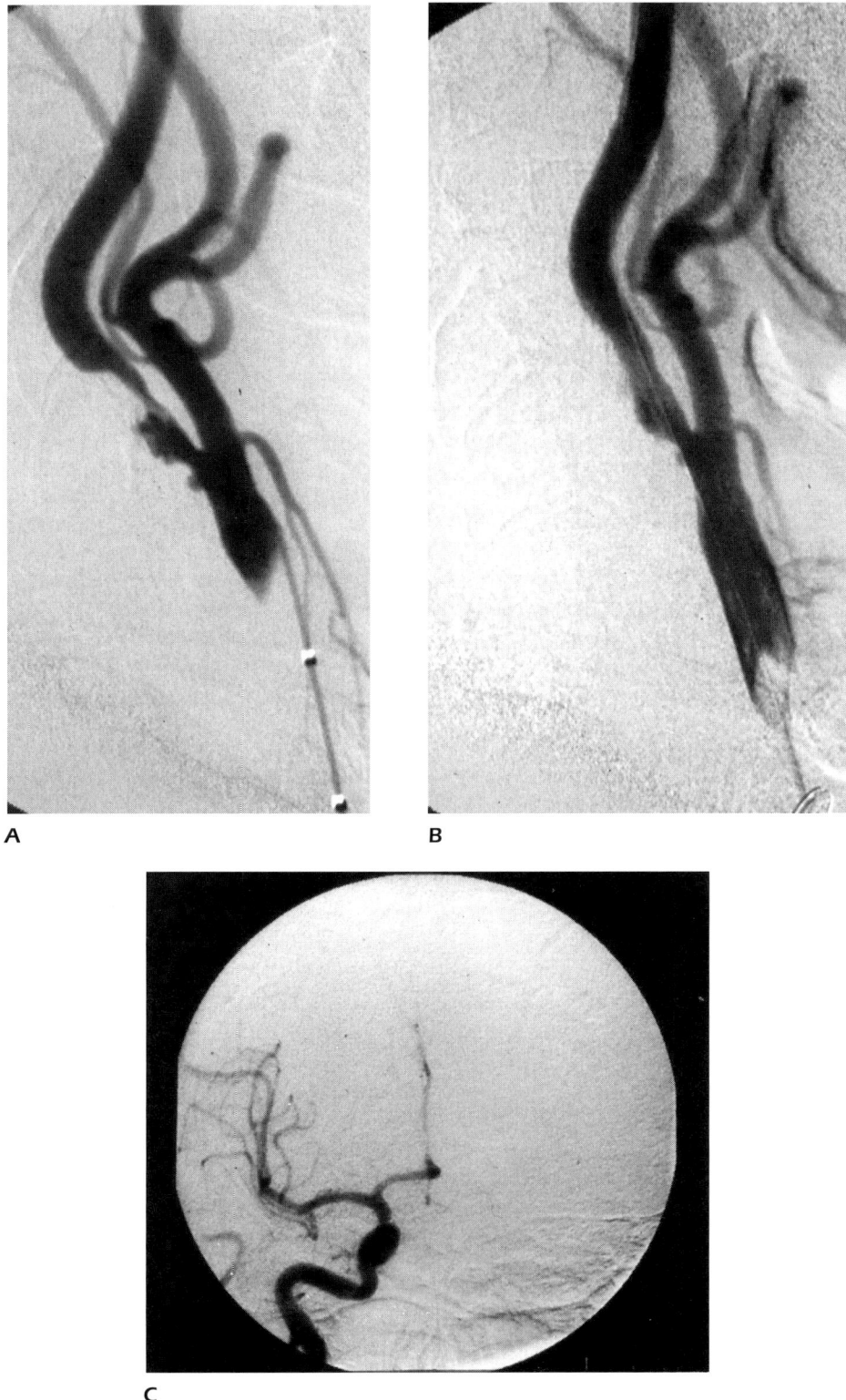

A

B

C

Figure 22-5. (A) Ulcerated stenoses before PTA. (B) After PTA. (C) After PTA, intracranial view.

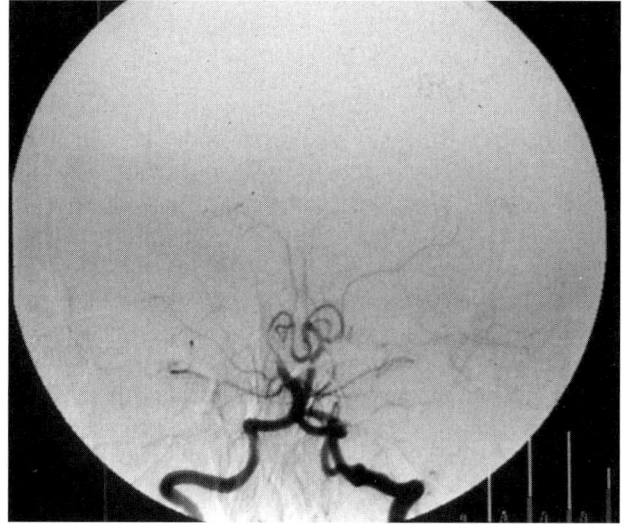

A

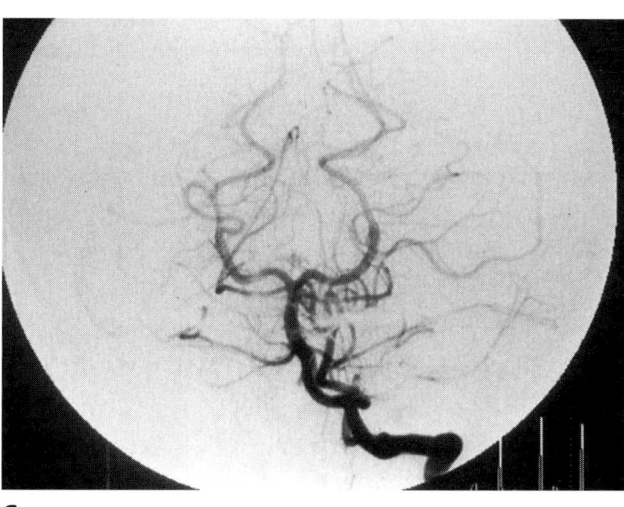

C

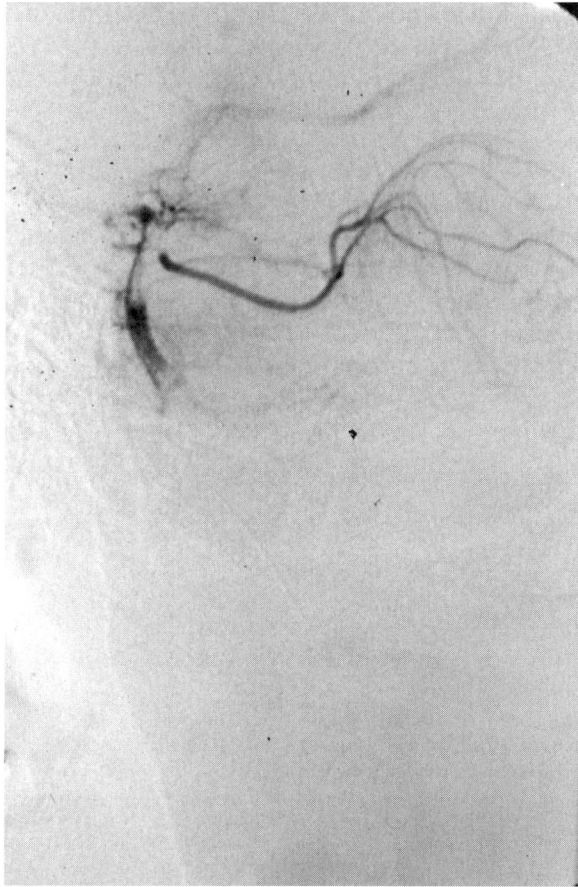

B

Figure 22-6. (A) Basilar occlusion following embolus from vertebral artery dissection flap. (B) Microcatheter in embolus with partial lysis. (C) Complete lysis and restoration of normal anatomy after 1 million units of urokinase.

It is entirely possible that randomized controlled trials of balloon angioplasty and endarterectomy may be sidestepped. Tremendous interest has developed in primary carotid bifurcation stenting, and forthcoming trials may compare primary stenting and surgery rather than angioplasty and surgery.

Vertebral Artery Angioplasty

Patients with the syndrome of vertebrobasilar insufficiency are in significant jeopardy of suffering a stroke within 5 years from the date of diagnosis. The risk has been reported to range from approximately 35 percent[26] to as high as 62 percent.[27] The results of operative intervention for vertebrobasilar disease have not received the rigorous scrutiny that operative intervention for symptomatic carotid artery disease has.[5]

The diagnostic angiographic workup of patients with vertebrobasilar insufficiency must include a full four-vessel cerebral arteriogram. It is essential that both vertebral arteries be examined. Lesions at the origin of the vertebral artery will account for at least 90 percent of vertebral lesions and for about 40 percent of all cases of vertebrobasilar insufficiency. Lesions at the origin and in the more distal segments of the cervical vertebral artery, as well as those within the intracranial segments of the vertebral artery, are amenable to PTA. The management of vertebral disease with PTA has been widely reported,[28-30] if not widely accepted, and the vast majority of vertebral angioplasty procedures have been performed for disease localized to the origin of the vertebral artery where more than 95 percent of the lesions are relatively smooth, concentric, and focal and carry a low risk of distal embolization. One *disadvantage* in PTA of vertebral origin lesions is that, not infrequently, plaque extending from the superior margin of the subclavian artery also encompasses the vertebral artery origin (Fig. 22-7) and may result in a diminished primary technical success rate, as well as a higher recurrence rate, similar to that of "ostial lesions" at the origin of the renal arteries when large volumes of adjacent aortic plaque extend to the orifice of the renal artery. Before a vertebral artery angioplasty is attempted, therefore, it must be documented that the patient's symptoms are the result of the pathologic anatomy to be treated and that there is a reasonable chance that the patient will clinically benefit from the successful angioplasty procedure.

Angioplasty of the Vertebral Artery Origin

Lesions of the origin of the vertebral artery are technically the easiest vertebral lesions on which to perform angioplasty. They may be approached with brachial, high brachial/axillary, or transfemoral catheterization. As with all patients undergoing cerebral angioplasty,

antiplatelet therapy should have been started 24 hours before the angioplasty procedure. The patient should be therapeutically heparinized during the procedure, confirmed with an ACT or a partial thromboplastin time. As with carotid angioplasty, heparinization is not reversed after the procedure. The vertebral artery is more easily stimulated to vasospasm by catheter or guidewire manipulation than the carotid artery but ususally responds well to 100-mcg boluses of intra-arterial nitroglycerin. Some prefer to pretreat patients with transcutaneous nitroglycerin and/or oral or sublingual calcium channel antagonists.

Whichever approach is chosen, lesions at the origin of the vertebral artery may be treated with or without a guiding catheter. The use of a guiding catheter has the disadvantage of requiring a larger sheath at the entry site, but it offers the advantage of sensitive catheter and guidewire control and manipulation and provides for intraprocedural contrast injections and transcatheter pharmacologic manipulation without guidewire removal.

Figure 22-7. (A) Left vertebral stenosis with adjacent subclavian plaque. (B) Postangioplasty result; residual stenosis appears to be caused by subclavian plaque.

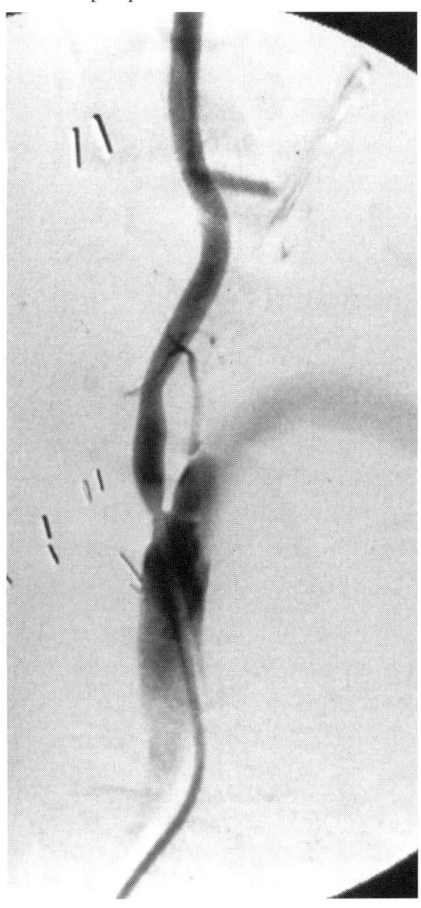
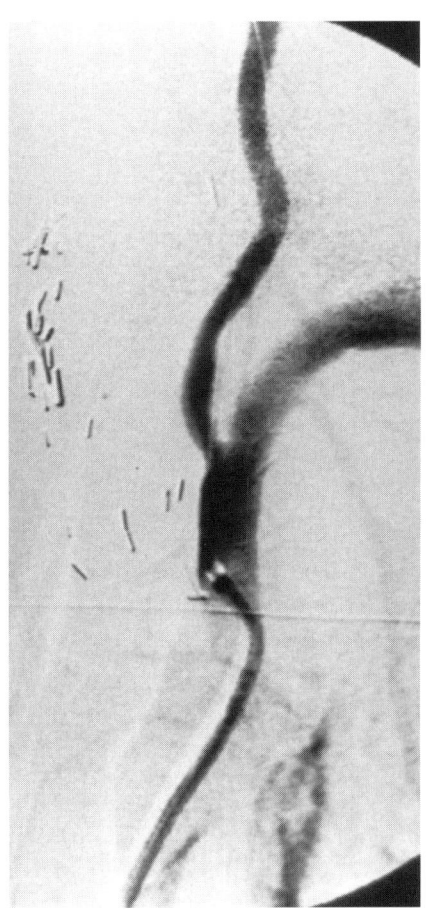

A   B

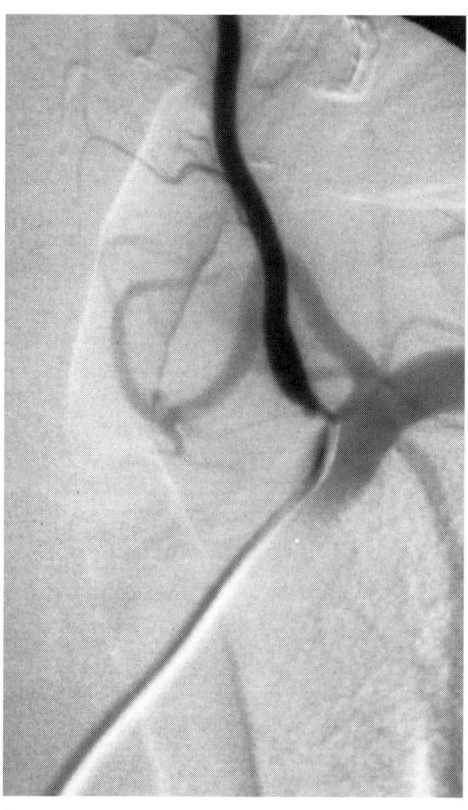

A

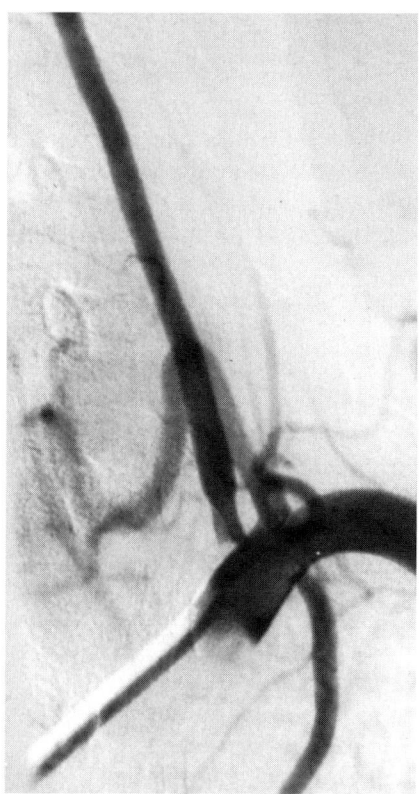

B

Vertebral orifice lesions are usually treated from the femoral approach using a preshaped 7 French (0.074-inch inner diameter) guiding catheter. The angioplasty catheter selected has a balloon segment equal to or slightly less than the diameter of the adjacent normal-caliber vertebral artery measurement, corrected for magnification as with carotid angioplasty. Under no circumstances should one employ an angioplasty catheter with a balloon segment larger than the true diameter of the normal segment of the vertebral artery. Correct sizing of balloon segments is critical in vertebral PTA. Vertebral arteries are very thin-walled, and overdilation carries a high risk of rupture.

Once the true vessel size has been assessed and the shortest balloon to cover the lesion is selected, the guiding catheter is placed adjacent to the orifice of the vertebral artery. The angioplasty catheter is passed over the appropriate guidewire, angioplasty is performed, the balloon is deflated, and the angioplasty catheter is retracted while the guidewire is maintained in position. A postangioplasty study is then acquired. If the anatomic result is acceptable, the angioplasty catheter and guidewire are removed and intracranial views are obtained to document the integrity of the intracranial circulation (Fig. 22-8).

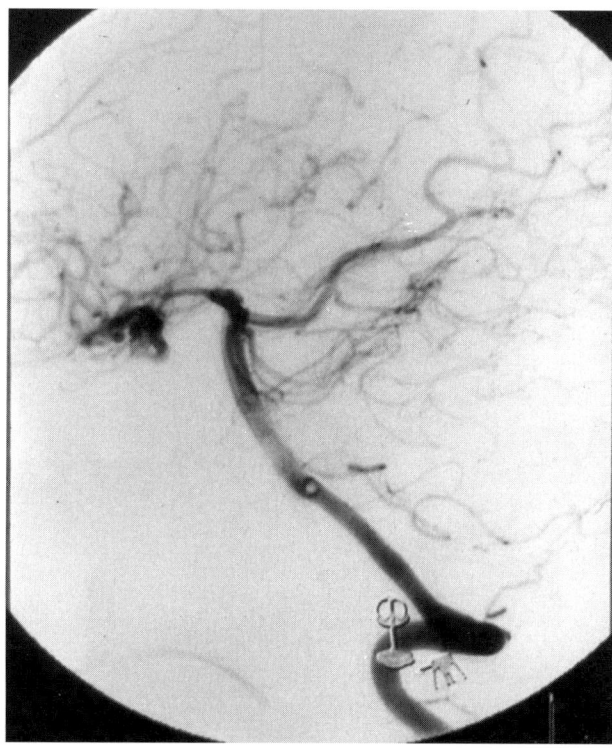

C

Figure 22-8. (A) Left vertebral origin stenosis. (B) Postangioplasty result. (C) Intracranial view after angioplasty. The patient presented with severe multivessel cerebrovascular disease with global ischemic symptoms.

Angioplasty of Nonorifice Cervical Vertebral Stenoses

Approximately 1 to 2 percent of vertebral stenoses are found in this segment of the vertebral artery. Stenoses in the cervical vertebral artery can be managed in the same fashion as orifice lesions (Fig. 22-9). One must be certain that the pathology is intrinsic to the cervical segment of the vertebral artery. MRI or CT imaging is helpful to exclude extravascular causes of an apparent vertebral artery stenosis.

Conclusion

Vertebral artery angioplasty appears to be a relatively safe treatment for atherosclerotic disease in patients with vertebrobasilar insufficiency. A perusal of the literature would indicate that technical success rates greater than 90 percent are the norm, and that more than 80 percent of the patients treated will experience clinical benefit. This literature also indicates that overall complication rates of 5 percent can be expected, with neurologic complications accounting for less than

1 percent. The unknown factor remains the risk of restenosis. In the past 3 years, the author has not seen any restenosis in a lesion distal to the orifice of the vertebral artery. The paucity of medial smooth muscle in vertebral arteries may be one reason.

Subclavian Artery Angioplasty

The subclavian artery is the brachiocephalic artery most commonly involved by atherosclerosis. The left subclavian artery is seven times more frequently involved than the right (a smaller ratio exists for the left common carotid versus the right). Most patients who are candidates for subclavian angioplasty have a high-grade subclavian artery stenosis or occlusion and a clinical subclavian steal phenomenon. Preangioplasty diagnostic studies are the same as for those patients undergoing carotid angioplasty, and intraprocedural aspects are similar except that these patients are not given intravenous atropine. Most patients can be treated from the common femoral approach, although

Figure 22-9. (A) Unusual midcervical atherosclerotic vertebral stenosis. (B) Postangioplasty result.

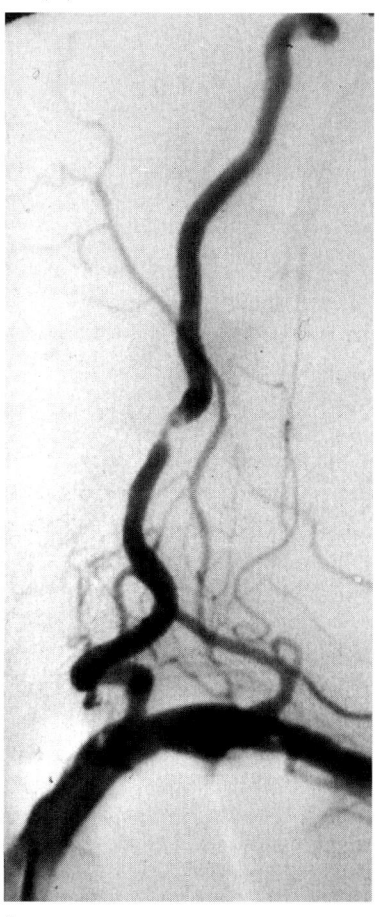
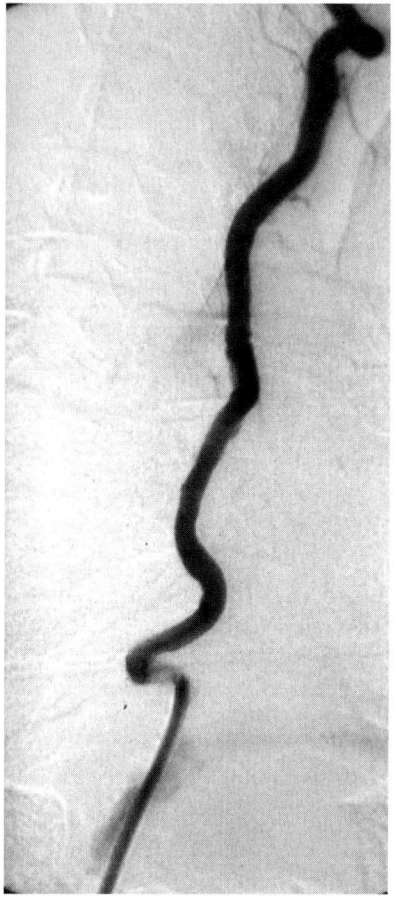

A   B

in patients with subclavian occlusions, the transaxillary approach or a combination of transaxillary and transfemoral approaches may result in a higher technical success rate. If at the time of the procedure the patient does not have angiographically documented retrograde flow in the ipsilateral vertebral artery, every attempt is made to induce retrograde flow during angioplasty by either pharmacologic or mechanical induction of reactive hyperemia in the downstream upper extremity. Placing a blood pressure cuff on the ipsilateral upper extremity, maintaining suprasystolic pressures, and then deflating the cuff immediately before the angioplasty balloon is deflated will produce reactive hyperemia and set the stage for retrograde flow in the ipsilateral vertebral artery. The administration of 30 to 60 mg of papaverine immediately before balloon deflation will also induce reactive hyperemia that may be sufficient to produce retrograde flow in the vertebral artery. If retrograde flow was present before the angioplasty procedure, it has been shown convincingly that this state will be maintained for a sufficiently long period after balloon deflation that embolization to the posterior fossa will not occur.[31] Artificial induction of reactive hyperemia may be most useful in patients who are being treated for subclavian disease that is causing digital ischemia but who do not have a de novo steal phenomenon. Subclavian angioplasty has been used to treat with an internal-mammary-to-coronary bypass steal syndrome.[32]

When the subclavian stenosis encroaches upon the vertebral artery, rendering it at risk from a noncolinear tear at the angioplasty site that may result in dissection of the vertebral artery origin and compromise of this vessel, it may be safest to approach the angioplasty procedure from both a transfemoral and transaxillary access, place a safety guidewire into the vertebral artery from either approach, and at the completion of the subclavian angioplasty, if there is compromise of the vertebral artery origin, place an appropriate-size balloon to "tamp down" on the dissection (Fig. 22-10). Vitek[33] has described angioplasty of proximal subclavian artery stenoses in which the balloon was intentionally or unintentionally placed across the vertebral artery origin during the angioplasty procedure. He concluded that if the vertebral artery originates from a healthy segment of the subclavian artery or from a segment with poststenotic dilatation, the angioplasty balloon can safely extend across the vertebral body origin. If, however, the vertebral artery origin is involved by the subclavian artery stenosis, then subclavian angioplasty would risk the vertebral artery. The author believes that, if the technique described above is used, subclavian angioplasty at any level can be safely performed.

Angioplasty of subclavian occlusions presents a challenge. The reported technical success rate is lower, the embolization rate is higher, and the long-term patency rate is lower than is reported with angioplasty of subclavian stenoses.[34] To optimize results, patients with subclavian artery occlusions should be prepared for angioplasty from both the retrograde femoral and the transaxillary approach. If a selective catheter can be placed into the preoccluded segment of the subclavian artery and the occlusion traversed with a hydrophil-

Figure 22-10. (A) Arch aortogram: subclavian stenosis adjacent to vertebral artery origin steal phenomenon. (B) Angioplasty by combined axillary and femoral approaches.

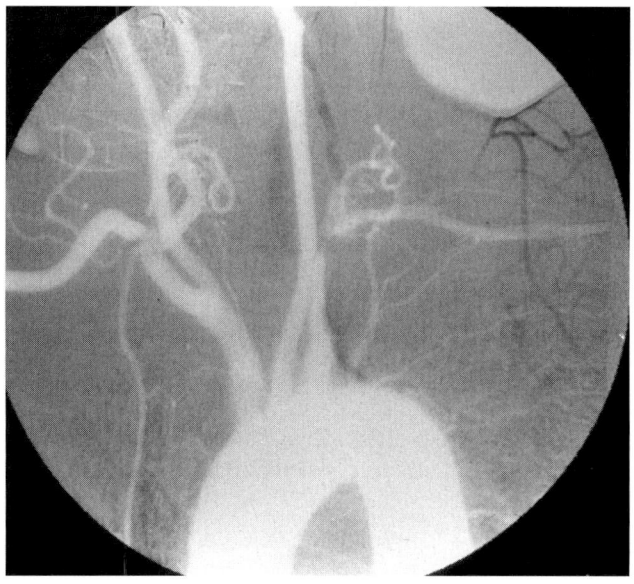

A

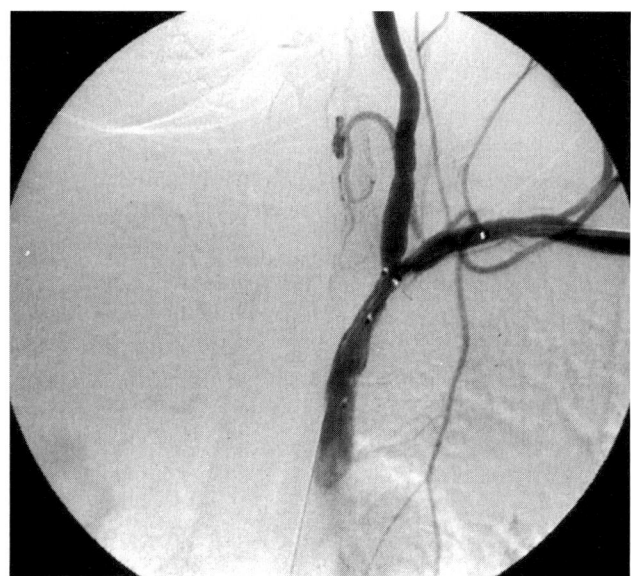

B

ically coated guidewire, a lumen can almost always be created. If the transfemoral approach fails, then the transaxillary approach is attempted. If a guidewire can be placed into the descending aortic true lumen from the transaxillary approach, then angioplasty of the recanalized occluded segment of the subclavian artery will be performed from this approach. Because of the high incidence of recurrent stenosis or occlusion after simple angioplasty of subclavian occlusions, a stent should be placed in recanalized occlusions. If the transaxillary approach was required to achieve recanalization and angioplasty, stents should be deployed from the transfemoral approach to maintain the smallest possible diameter access in the axilla. One should attempt to traverse the recanalized subclavian artery from the transfemoral approach with a hydrophilically coated guidewire or a TAD wire (Mallinckrodt Radiology) while maintaining translesion intraluminal position with a safety wire from the axilla. When transfemoral approach access into the true lumen of the axillary artery has been achieved, one should remove the safety wire from the axillary approach and deploy a stent from the transfemoral approach. Alternatively, if it is difficult to achieve the desired position with a transfemoral wire, a second wire can be passed from the axilla with a loop snare to secure the transfemoral wire and retrieve it into the true lumen of the axillary artery, again allowing stent deployment from the transfemoral approach (Fig. 22-11).

When performing angioplasty of the right subclavian artery, the issue of innominate artery protection and cerebral protection is raised. If the lesion to be angioplastied is truly at the bifurcation of the innominate artery and the right common carotid artery is at risk, one should deploy a second guidewire through the transfemoral sheath as a safety wire for the right common carotid artery. This will protect against dissection-induced occlusion of the right common carotid artery.

Innominate Artery Angioplasty

Neurologic symptoms from innominate artery occlusive disease may be manifest as right hemispheric symptoms, posterior fossa symptoms, or both. A high-grade lesion in the proximal innominate artery may cause reversal of flow in the right common carotid artery as well as in the right vertebral artery. These symptoms may be exacerbated by right upper extremity exercise. Surgical options include endarterectomy, cross-neck bypass grafting, or more commonly grafting from the aortic arch with a bifurcated graft.

The percutaneous management of atherosclerotic disease of the innominate artery is reported less often than angioplasty of the other branches of the aortic arch. Nevertheless, innominate angioplasty may offer the most significant benefits because of the relative complexity of surgical revascularization for innominate occlusive disease and the attendant increased morbidity and mortality for these surgical alternatives.

As with subclavian angioplasty, the favored approach for innominate angioplasty is the retrograde common femoral approach. However, because the angioplasty will be performed at or near a major bifurcation, the patient should be prepared for a high axillary approach as well. When antegrade flow in the right common carotid or right vertebral arteries is present, there is a risk of cerebral embolization. Nonoperative methods to avoid embolization to the right hemisphere have been described and include compression of the right common carotid artery during the angioplasty procedure,[35] the use of a second balloon placed into the right common carotid artery for cerebral protection, and finally,[36] flow augmentation in the right upper extremity during and immediately after angioplasty.

When the stenosis is in proximity to the innominate artery bifurcation, a safety wire should be placed through the right common femoral access sheath into the right common carotid artery to permit prompt access to the origin of the right common carotid artery should it be compromised after the innominate angioplasty.

The normal diameter of the innominate artery is usually 10 mm or greater. Since most angioplasty balloons of this diameter have rather long "shoulders," the balloon segment will extend some distance into either the right common carotid artery or the right subclavian artery during the angioplasty procedure. McNamara[35] has pointed out that it is frequently possible to have a lasting benefit from innominate angioplasty without achieving an optimum lumen in the immediate post-PTA study and that over time further "self-dilation" of the innominate artery may occur. For this reason it is usual to slightly underdilate the innominate artery (Fig. 22-12).

Stents in the Brachiocephalic Arteries

The role of stents in the brachiocephalic arteries has previously been alluded to. Primary stenting of the carotid bifurcation remains a highly charged issue, and there is no scientific documentation as to its efficacy and little documentation as to its safety. Palmaz[37] has expressed concern that balloon-expandable stents can

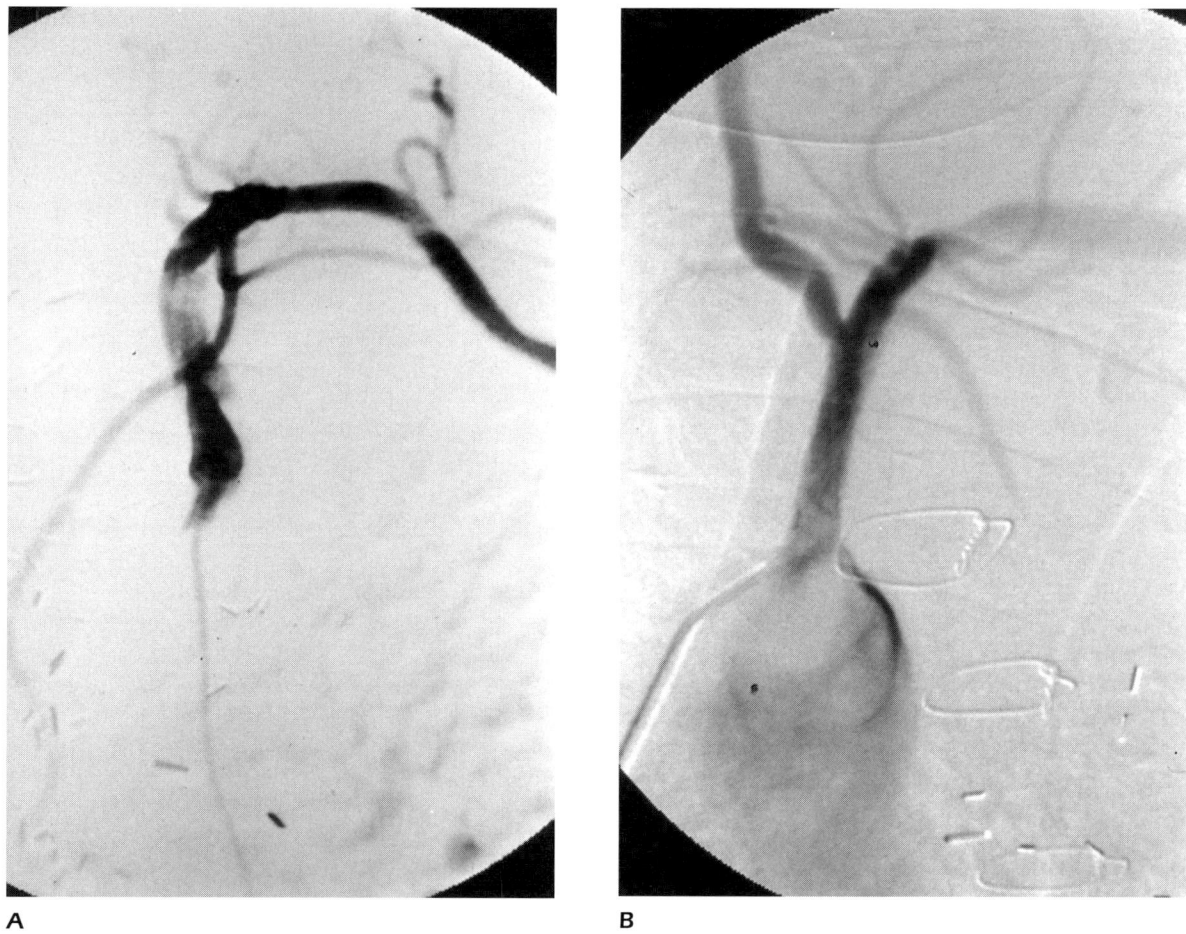

A   B

Figure 22-11. (A) Postangioplasty result after recanalization of an occluded subclavian artery. (B) Appearance after stent deployment.

Figure 22-12. (A) Innominate artery stenosis. The lesion is distant from the bifurcation. (B) Postangioplasty result. Residual stenosis is acceptable in innominate angioplasty.

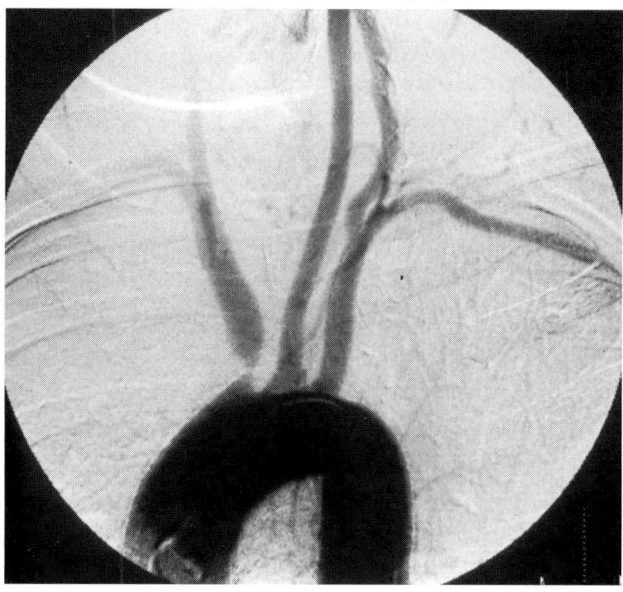
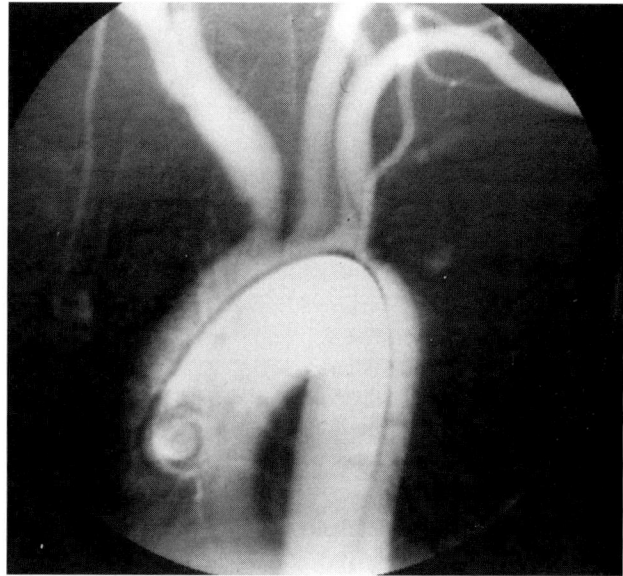

A   B

be deformed significantly by external compression and that deploying them in a position where they may be vulnerable to such compression may therefore be contraindicated. Stents have been used to treat spontaneous and iatrogenic dissections with excellent results (Fig. 22-13).

Stenoses at the origin of vertebral arteries are frequently similar in morphology to renal ostial stenoses and therefore, their response to balloon angioplasty is similar to renal artery ostial stenoses. There is little doubt that stenting of such lesions will accrue the same benefits as stenting of renal artery ostial stenoses. However, unlike the renal artery, the vertebral artery origin is subject to manipulation by external forces. Since the vertebral artery is an extremely thin-walled vessel that is frequently very tortuous in its first 1 to 2 cm as it enters the bony canal, a rigid stent placed under these circumstances may predispose the vessel at the distal margin of the stent to transection. At this time there does not appear to be an ideal stent for deployment in the proximal vertebral artery.

Subclavian stenting is now commonplace and, as described, is used by many routinely in the management of successfully recanalized subclavian occlusions. Stents should also be deployed in subclavian arteries that have substantial intimal dissections or when an optimal angiographic result cannot be obtained from balloon angioplasty.

Future Directions

The role of nonsurgical interventional therapy in the management of the patient with extracranial cerebrovascular disease, particularly carotid bifurcation disease, will remain controversial and may not be resolved without randomized trials. Prospective cohort studies are under way for both percutaneous angioplasty and primary stenting for cerebrovascular disease, and these registers will no doubt lead to prospective randomized trials with carotid endarterectomy if they confirm the safety of percutaneous intervention for extracranial cerebrovascular disease. Refinements in percutaneous techniques and in catheters and related equipment may further enhance the role of percutaneous intervention for extracranial cerebrovascular disease. Finally, if percutaneous intervention is to be a viable therapeutic alternative to surgical intervention, the long-term risk reduction for stroke must be demonstrated.

Figure 22-13. Patient with bilateral spontaneous carotid dissections (total occlusion of the left carotid). (A) Right internal carotid arteriogram demonstrates dissection and false aneurysm with luminal compromise. (B) Immediately after deployment of a Palmaz 294 stent. (C) At 1-year follow-up.

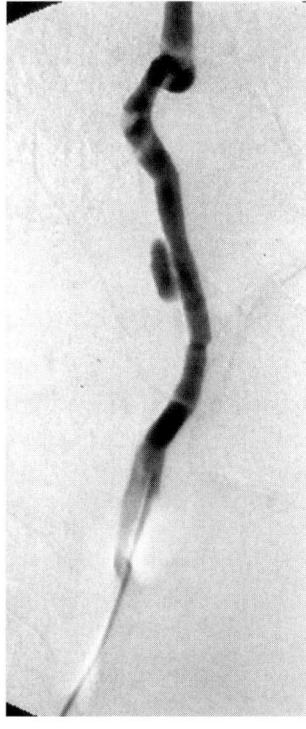
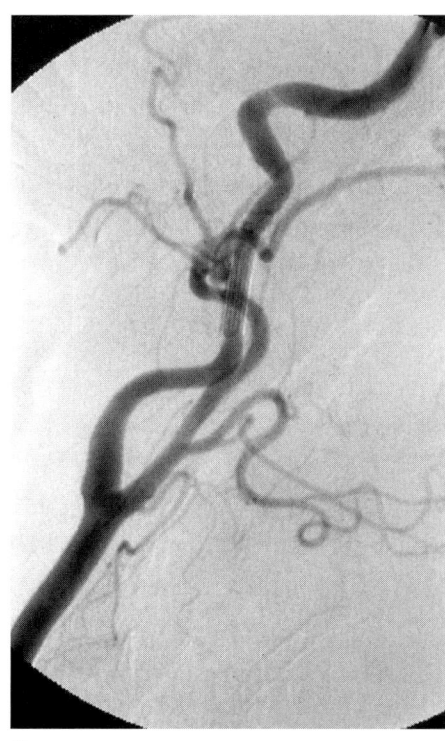

A   B   C

References

1. Ferguson RDG, Lee LI, Connors JJ, et al. Angioplasty of the extracranial and intracranial vasculature. Semin Intervent Radiol 1994;11:64.
2. Becker G, Katzen B, Dake M. Non-coronary angioplasty. Radiology 1989;170:921–940.
3. Casarella WJ. Non-coronary angioplasty: results and complications of percutaneous transluminal angioplasty. Curr Probl Cardiol 1986;11:155–165.
4. Kumpe DA, Zwerdlinger S, Griffin DJ. Blue digit syndrome: treatment with percutaneous transluminal angioplasty. Radiology 1988;166:37.
5. North American Symptomatic Carotid Endarterectomy Trial Collaborators. Beneficial effect of carotid endarterectomy in symptomatic patients with high-grade stenoses. New Engl J Med 1991;325:445–453.
6. Mathias K. Catheter treatment of occlusive disease of supraaortic vessels. Radiology 1987;27:259–264.
7. Tsai FY, Matovich V, Hieshima G, et al. Percutaneous transluminal angioplasty of the carotid artery. Am J Neurol Radiol 1986;7:349–358.
8. Tsai FY, Higashida RT, Matovich V, Alfieri K, Kobayashi S. Seven years' experience with PTA of carotid artery. Neuroradiology 1991;33(Suppl):397–398.
9. Theron J, Courtheoux P, Henriet JP, Pelouze G, Derlon JM, Maiza D. Angioplasty of supra-aortic arteries. J Neuroradiol 1984;11(3):187–200.
10. Theron J, Courtheoux P, Alachkar F, Bouvard G, Maiza D. New triple coaxial catheter system for carotid angioplasty with cerebral protection. AJNR 1990;11:869–874.
11. The North American Cerebral Percutaneous Transluminal Angioplasty Register (NACPTAR). Investigated update of the immediate angiographic results and in-hospital central nervous system complications of cerebral percutaneous transluminal angioplasty. Presented at American Heart 66th Scientific Session, Anaheim, CA, November 14, 1995.
12. Chambers BR, Norris JW, Shurvell BL, Hachinski V. Prognosis of acute stroke. Neurology 1987;37:221–225.
13. Wolf PA, Kannel WB, McGee DI. Epidemiology of strokes in North America. In: Barnett HJM, Stein BM, Mohr JP, Yatsu FM, eds. Stroke: arthrophysiology, diagnosis and management. New York: Churchill Livingstone, 1986:19–29.
14. Strandness DE Jr. Surgical therapy for extracranial arterial disease. In: Strandness DE Jr, VanBreeda A, eds. Vascular diseases: surgical and interventional therapy. New York: Churchill Livingstone, 1994.
15. European Carotid Surgery Trialists Collaborative Group. MRC European Surgery Trial: interim results for symptomatic patients with severe (70% to 99%) or with mild (0% to 29%) carotid stenosis. Lancet 1991;337:1235–1243.
16. Roederer GO, Langlois YE, Jager KA, et al. The natural history of carotid arterial disease in asymptomatic patients with cervical bruits. Stroke 1984;15:605.
17. National Institute of Neurological Disorders and Stroke. Clinical advisory: carotid endarterectomy for patients with asymptomatic internal carotid artery stenosis. Stroke 1994;25:2523–2524.
18. DeGroote RD, Lynch JG, Jamil Z, Hobson RW. Carotid restenosis: long term noninvasive follow up after carotid endarterectomy. Stroke 1987;18:1031.
19. Atnip RG, Wengravitz M, Gittord RR, et al. A rational approach to recurrent carotid stenosis. J Vasc Surg 1990;11:511.
20. Bernstein EF, Torean S, Dilley RB. Does carotid restenosis predict an increased risk of late symptoms, stroke or death? Ann Surg 1990;212:629.
21. Meier B. Long-term results of coronary balloon angioplasty. Annu Rev Med 1991;42:47–59.
22. Zierler RE, Strandness DE Jr. Duplex scan and frequency analysis in the evaluation of recurrent carotid stenosis. In: Bergen JJ, Yao JST, eds. Reoperative arterial surgery. Philadelphia: Grune & Stratton, 1986.
23. Nichols SC, Phillips DJ, Bergelin RO, et al. Carotid endarterectomy: relationship of outcome to early restenosis. J Vasc Surg 1985;2:375.
24. Kadir S, White RI Jr, Kaufman SL, et al. Prevention of thromboembolic complications of angioplasty by critical patient selection. Presented at the 82nd annual meeting of the American Roentgen Ray Society, New Orleans, May 1982.
25. Ferguson R. Getting it right the first time. Am J Neuroradiol 1990;11:875–877.
26. Baker RN, Carroll-Ramseyer J, Schanartz WS. Prognosis in patients with transient ischemic attacks. Neurology 1968;18:1157–1165.
27. Cartlidge NEF, Whisnant JF, Elveback LR. Carotid and vertebral basilar transient cerebral ischemic attacks. Mayo Clin Proc 1977;52:117–120.
28. Motarjeme A, Keifen JW, Zuska AJ. Percutaneous transluminal angioplasty of the vertebral arteries. Radiology 1981;139:715–717.
29. Higashida RT, Hieshima GB, Tsai FY, et al. Transluminal angioplasty of the vertebral and basilar artery. Am J Neurol Radiol 1987;8:745–750.
30. Courtheoux P, Tournade A, Theron J, et al. Transcutaneous angioplasty of vertebral artery atheromatous ostial stricture. Neuroradiology 1985;27:259–264.
31. Theron J, Melancon D, Ethier R. "Pre" subclavian steal syndromes and their treatment by angioplasty. Neuroradiology 1985;27:265–270.
32. Georges NP, Ferretti JA. Percutaneous angioplasty of subclavian artery occlusion for treatment of coronary subclavian steal. AJR 1993;161:399.
33. Vitek JJ. Subclavian artery angioplasty and the origin of the vertebral artery. Radiology 1989;170:407–409.
34. Hebrany A, Maskovic J, Tomac B. Percutaneous transluminal angioplasty of the subclavian arteries: long-term results in 52 patients. AJR 1991;156:1091–1094.
35. McNamara TO. Percutaneous angioplasty of the brachiocephalic arteries, long-term follow up. Presented at the Seventh Annual International Symposium on Vascular Diagnosis and Intervention. Miami, January 25, 1995.
36. Koike M, et al. PTA of supraaortic arteries with temporary balloon occlusion to avoid distal embolism. Neurol Med Chir (Tokyo) 1992;32:140–147.
37. Palmaz JC. Personal communication, July 1995.

23

Transluminal Placement of Endovascular Stent-Grafts for the Treatment of Thoracic Aortic Aneurysms

MICHAEL D. DAKE

The traditional management of thoracic aortic aneurysms is based on surgical graft replacement. Although the results of surgical treatment for thoracic aortic aneurysms have steadily improved over the past 20 to 30 years, a significant perioperative morbidity and mortality do occur, particularly in those patients who have coexisting medical illnesses or who have previously undergone one or more operations for treatment of intrathoracic disease.[1-7] In this regard, a less invasive approach is desirable, especially in patients at high risk for surgery because of preexisting severe neurologic, cardiovascular, pulmonary, or renal dysfunction. In these patients, aortic replacement under general anesthesia and possibly extracorporeal bypass may not be tolerated. Endovascular stent-grafts offer an alternative treatment approach that may be less invasive and less expensive, and that may involve a lower risk and a shorter hospital recuperation than traditional operative therapy.

The concept of transluminally placed endovascular stent-grafts was initially proposed by Dotter.[8] Subsequently, a number of researchers performed feasibility studies using experimental animal models of abdominal aortic aneurysms.[9-15] Recently, the clinical use of endovascular stent-grafts was reported for the management of abdominal aortic aneurysms,[16-23] descending thoracic aortic aneurysms,[24,25] subclavian artery aneurysms,[26,27] iliac artery aneurysms,[28,29] popliteal artery aneurysms,[30] arteriovenous fistulas,[31,32] and peripheral occlusive disease.[33-35] The early application of these new techniques was challenging because of the primitive nature of the devices employed; however, in the relatively short period of time since their introduction, it already appears likely that stent-grafts will play a significant role in the future management of vascular disease. It is anticipated that many of the initial technical difficulties will be overcome with the development of smaller delivery systems for device introduction, newer graft materials customized for endovascular use, and more effective anchoring systems to secure "anastomotic" seals for the isolation of aneurysms.

This chapter explores the use of endovascular stent-grafts for the management of descending thoracic aortic aneurysms. The clinical experience described is preliminary, but the initial results suggest that these less invasive procedures may provide safe and effective therapy for highly selected patients with limited standard surgical alternatives.

Natural History

Thoracic aortic aneurysm is a life-threatening disease associated with damage to the elastic fibers in the medial layer of the vessel, usually because of atherosclerosis. In a retrospective study of 107 cases of thoracic aortic aneurysm, the etiology was thought to be atherosclerotic in 78 percent of the cases.[36] This degenerative process causes progressive weakening of the aortic wall with resultant dilatation. In approximately 80 percent of cases, the dilatation has a fusiform configuration. In about 20 percent of cases, a saccular aneurysm configuration is noted, and 75 percent of these are located in the ascending aorta or transverse arch. Aneurysms with a fusiform configuration, however, are identified in the ascending or transverse arch in 50 percent of cases, and are located in the descending thoracic aorta in the other half.

The formation of a thoracic aortic aneurysm is usually an asymptomatic process, often attracting attention only when the aneurysm is identified as an unsuspected mass on a routine chest radiograph. When symptoms occur, they usually reflect progressive enlargement of the aneurysm, which results in compression of adjacent tissues or rupture. Rupture of a thoracic aortic aneurysm is catastrophic and usually fatal.

Authors describing the natural history of untreated thoracic aortic aneurysm estimate a survival rate of 50 percent at 5 years, and approximately 30 percent at 10 years.[36] The 5-year survival for these patients is worse than that reported for patients with untreated abdominal aortic aneurysms.[37,38] Rupture of a thoracic aortic aneurysm is responsible for 33 to 50 percent of the mortality in these cases.[1,37] Of note, the estimated survival statistics for a subgroup of patients with thoracic aortic aneurysm associated with aortic dissection are exceedingly poor. In one study, a 7.0 percent 5-year survival was observed, compared to a 19.2 percent 5-year survival for thoracic aortic aneurysms not associated with dissection.[37]

Other causes of death are usually related to coexisting medical disease, particularly diffuse cardiovascular pathology often associated with hypertension. It is also important to note that coexisting aneurysms involving adjacent or remote arterial segments are frequently identified. Up to 20 percent of patients are estimated to have a second aneurysm, frequently affecting the abdominal aorta.[2]

Surgical Treatment

Operative therapy is advised if the maximum diameter of the aneurysm is one and a half times greater than the caliber of the adjacent normal aorta, or if the aneurysm is 6 cm in diameter or greater, especially when serial imaging studies show progressive enlargement, or when there is associated sudden onset of aortic regurgitation or acute chest or back pain.[2] The standard operative technique includes surgical resection of the aneurysm and replacement with a segment of prosthetic graft material. If the aneurysm originates distal to the left subclavian artery and terminates above the origin of the celiac axis, surgical resection can often be performed without the need for extracorporeal circulation.[2,39] In a study of 175 patients who underwent surgical treatment of thoracic aortic aneurysms not associated with aortic dissection or syphilis, the hospital mortality following surgical repair was 6.5 percent for patients with ascending aneurysms and 17.7 percent for cases of descending thoracic aortic aneurysms.[3] Even when patients are excellent surgical candidates, there is considerable morbidity, with paraplegia reported in 2 to 12 percent of cases.[2,3,39] In terms of operative morbidity, the above series describing 175 patients reported a 2 percent incidence of paraplegia, a 3 percent incidence of acute myocardial infarction, and a 7 percent incidence of reoperation for bleeding.[3] Using multivariant analysis, a predictive value was demonstrated for two variables in the repair of ascending aortic aneurysms: emergency operation and advanced age. Emergency operation is associated with a 60.0 percent mortality, compared to 4.2 percent for elective operation. Older age (patients over 62 years) is associated with a 14.6 percent mortality, compared to 2.6 percent for younger patients.

Similarly, in patients with descending thoracic aortic aneurysms, emergency operation is associated with a 50 percent mortality, compared to 12 percent for elective repair; preoperative congestive heart failure is associated with a 60 percent mortality, compared to 14 percent for patients without congestive heart failure. The overall experience with both ascending and descending thoracic aortic aneurysms demonstrated six variables associated with an increased in-hospital mortality: emergency operation, age, impaired renal function, rupture, etiology of the aneurysm, and location of the aneurysm. The overall actuarial survival at 10 years after surgical repair of ascending aneurysms was 51 percent, and 38 percent for descending thoracic aortic aneurysms.[3]

Endovascular Therapy

Although these current surgical success rates and complication rates represent significant improvements over those established during the preceding decades, there is a trend toward developing less invasive procedures to repair thoracic aortic aneurysms in an attempt to further reduce operative risks and complications. If successful, these techniques might allow one to extend therapy to high-risk patients with severe coexisting medical illnesses. Stent-graft placement is one such technique that embodies a less invasive surgical approach by combining intravascular stent and prosthetic graft technologies. The first clinical cases of endovascular stent-graft placement for abdominal aortic aneurysms were reported by Parodi and colleagues in 1991.[16] Parodi used polyester graft material sutured to a balloon-expandable stent that was deployed above the aneurysm in its proximal neck.

The author's initial experience with transluminal endovascular stent-graft technology indicates that it can successfully manage highly selected patients with aneurysms of the descending thoracic aorta. Since July 1992, the author's institution has placed endovascular stent-grafts in 71 patients with descending thoracic aortic aneurysms. Most of the aneurysms originated distal to the left subclavian artery and ended above the celiac trunk. A small number of aneurysms involved the origin of the left subclavian artery or the celiac axis. In cases involving the left subclavian artery, antecedent transposition of this vessel to the left carotid artery or graft placement from the left carotid to the left subclavian artery was performed immediately before stent-graft placement under the same general anesthetic. When the aneurysm extended to include the origin of the celiac axis but did not involve the superior mesenteric artery or renal artery origins, transcatheter coil embolization of the proximal celiac trunk was performed before stent-graft placement over the origin of this vessel. All cases were high-risk patients for traditional surgical repair, and most had undergone prior cardiac or aortic surgery. The aneurysms were due to a variety of pathologies, including trauma and dissection (anastomotic and mycotic); however, atherosclerosis was responsible for most of the cases.

Patient Considerations

Since each case has its own unique anatomic considerations, all stent-grafts are custom-fabricated to address the morphology and dimensions of each patient's aorta. Preprocedural imaging is the key to assessing the suitability of an aneurysm for stent-graft repair, including the presence of adequate proximal and distal necks. An extensive preprocedural workup is performed on all patients and includes aortography and spiral CT with axial and three-dimensional reconstructions. The spiral CT data provide the necessary measurements and dimensions to custom-fabricate the stent-graft, including the diameter of the prosthesis (which is based on the caliber of the normal aorta adjacent to the aneurysm) and its overall length. Aortography is performed to precisely define the anatomic relationship between the aneurysm and the left subclavian and celiac arteries, the configuration and relative degree of aortic arch curvature, the number and size of patent intercostal arteries, and the presence of an anterior spinal artery, as well as to assess the size, tortuosity, and any abnormalities of the abdominal aorta and the iliac and femoral arteries.

Ideally, there should be a discrete neck of at least 15 to 20 mm between the distal aspect of the left subclavian artery origin and the aneurysm to prevent inadvertent placement of a stent-graft across this vessel. If the segment of proximal neck is less than desirable, a longer proximal neck may be created by surgically transposing the left subclavian artery onto the left common carotid artery or by placing a bypass graft between the left common carotid artery and the left subclavian artery before stent-graft deployment. In the author's experience, this has been necessary in six cases before placement of the stent-graft. To limit unnecessary occlusion of intercostal arteries, the overall length of the device was calculated to allow extension of only 15 to 20 mm of the stent-graft into both the proximal

and distal necks. In some cases, the pelvic conduit vessels are not of sufficient size to accommodate the introduction of a large stent-graft delivery system. When an adequate femoral access route is not possible, an alternative surgical approach via the distal infrarenal abdominal aorta is used. This access is commonly obtained using a left retroperitoneal exposure. This approach was necessary in seven of the author's cases because of insufficient iliac or common femoral arteries.

Technical Considerations

In general, the technical steps of an endovascular stent-graft procedure, regardless of the exact application, can be reduced to three elements: stents, graft material, and delivery systems. The overall goal of the author's initial work is to develop a strategy that allows the placement of standard surgical graft material into the aorta using basic interventional radiologic techniques to effectively isolate the aneurysm from the circulation by thrombosing the aneurysm sac.

Stents

A stent is a metallic latticelike framework that provides a sutureless means of securing graft material at the proximal and distal necks of aortic aneurysms. Stents are usually manufactured from stainless steel, nitinol, or tantalum and can be divided into two basic designs: balloon-expandable and self-expanding. Although balloon-expandable stents can be placed very accurately within blood vessels, after extensive testing of experimental animal models, the author determined that self-expanding stents are currently better suited for applications in the thoracic aorta. For the most part, this decision is related to the relatively large diameters of the proximal and distal aortic necks observed in patients with atherosclerotic or degenerative thoracic aortic aneurysms. In the author's experience, the mean diameter of the proximal neck measures 36 mm. This is greater than the maximum diameter (25 mm) of valvuloplasty balloons currently marketed in the United States. In addition, during balloon inflation within the thoracic aorta, the significant force associated with blood flow in the aortic arch may cause distal migration of the balloon during initial deployment, and therefore misplacement of the device. Self-expanding devices may be deployed more rapidly within the thoracic aorta and offer less resistance to flow during deployment than a balloon-expandable device. Both of these factors may reduce the likelihood of an inadvertent downstream placement distal to the intended target.

The stents used in the author's clinical experience to date are composed of 0.020-inch surgical-grade stainless steel wire formed into a series of Z-shaped bends (Fig. 23-1). Individual stent bodies are 2.5 cm in length, with variable diameters ranging from 24 to 45 mm. Several stent bodies may be combined to obtain the necessary total length based on dimensions determined from the spiral CT. No. 2-0 polypropylene suture is used to attach individual stent bodies together. The Z-stent endoskeleton serves as a frame to support the entire length of graft material required to bridge the aneurysm from proximal to distal neck. The use of subjacent stents throughout the midportion of the graft, as well as the anchoring ends, provides a midgraft buttress to prevent kinking, buckling, torsion, or collapse of the prosthesis within the aneurysm. The Z-stent design offers the radial force and expansion ratio required to anchor the graft material into position and seal it snugly against the aneurysm necks. No hooks or anchoring wires are required to prevent migration. The mean stent-graft length used in the author's 71 patients is 10.1 cm.

Graft Material

The graft material used in the author's thoracic stent-grafts is woven polyester (Cooley Veri-Soft, Meadox Medical, Inc.). Woven polyester material is resistant to radial stretch, relatively nonporous, and thin. It has been used for many years as a proven prosthetic graft for the surgical treatment of thoracic aortic aneurysms. In preparation of the graft material for attachment to the underlining stent, the crimps are ironed out to reduce the overall diameter of the device. A single piece of tubular graft material is cut to the appropriate length and secured to the Z-stent framework with multiple interrupted 5-0 polypropylene sutures. The

Figure 23-1. Thoracic aortic stent-graft composed of a stainless steel Z-stent framework covered by a woven polyester graft. The graft is attached to the underlying stent at each end with multiple interrupted polypropylene sutures.

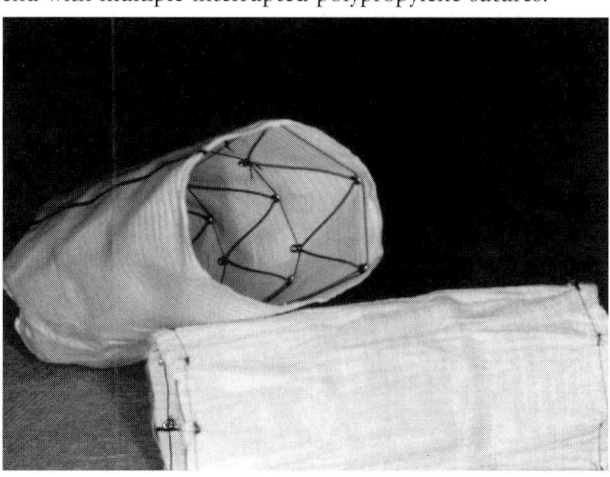

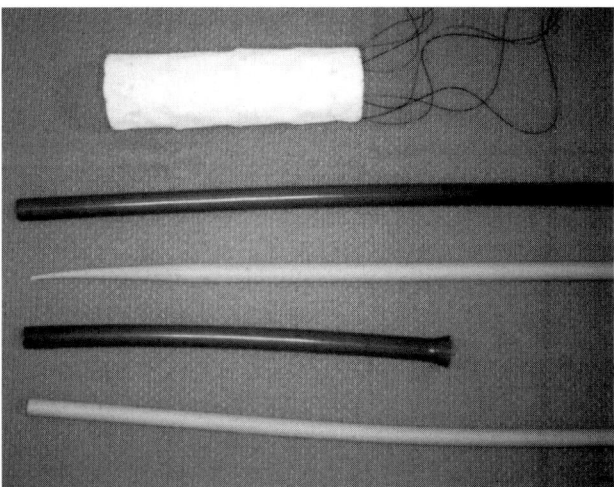

Figure 23-2. Stent-graft (*top*) with delivery system consisting of (*from top to bottom*) a 24 French delivery sheath, a single-piece graduated dilator, a stent-graft loading cartridge, and a solid mandrel pusher to advance the device within the delivery sheath.

cut edges of the graft material are heat-sealed to prevent fraying during handling and insertion. After fabrication is complete, the prosthesis is gas-sterilized using an ethylene oxide process prior to use.

Delivery System

The delivery system used during the introduction and deployment consists of four components (Fig. 23-2): a 20, 22, or 24 French outer-diameter Teflon sheath with an external hemostatic valve apparatus (the exact sheath diameter is determined by the diameter of the stent-graft selected); a gradually tapered single-piece dilator to allow sheath introduction and advancement over a 0.035-inch-diameter extra stiff guidewire; a loading cartridge to facilitate stent-graft introduction into the delivery sheath; and a solid Teflon mandrel that is used to push the stent-graft through the delivery sheath.

Endovascular Procedure

All candidates for thoracic stent-graft placement are evaluated by both the cardiothoracic surgery and interventional radiology teams. Full informed consent is obtained for both conventional surgical and stent-graft procedures. All stent-graft procedures for treatment of thoracic aortic aneurysm are performed in the operating suites, with the patient intubated and under general anesthesia. The patient is prepared and draped as for a left thoracotomy and the operating suite is prepared for an open procedure. After the side with the most favorable pelvic vascular anatomy for introduction of the delivery system is selected, the groin area is prepared for surgical exposure of the femoral artery. After surgical dissection and isolation of the femoral artery, a standard needle puncture and the Seldinger technique allow for the introduction of a soft-tipped guidewire. The guidewire is advanced into the thoracic aorta to facilitate introduction of a 5 French angiographic sheath and a 5 French pigtail catheter for the performance of an initial thoracic aortogram.

High-quality fluoroscopic equipment is essential to ensure accurate placement of the device, and a portable C-arm unit capable of digital acquisition, playback, and "road-mapping" guidance is a minimum requirement. The initial aortogram is replayed and the proximal and distal necks are identified. Their location is marked with external opaque markers or correlated with stationary intrathoracic landmarks. Adjunctive transesophageal ultrasound imaging is often used to further assess the "true" necks of the aneurysm so that arteriographic confusion due to the presence of mural thrombus within the aneurysm can be avoided. The pigtail catheter is removed over an exchange-length (260-cm) 0.035-inch extra stiff guidewire. The patient is anticoagulated with intravenous heparin (300 IU/kg) to prevent thrombus formation associated with the large delivery sheath. A transverse arteriotomy is typically performed, and the dilator and delivery sheath assembly are advanced over the wire under fluoroscopic guidance. Once the delivery sheath is located proximal to the aneurysm neck, the dilator and guidewire are withdrawn. The stent-graft is introduced into the sheath from its loading cartridge using the Teflon pusher. The device is then advanced through the sheath until the stent-graft approaches its tip.

To reduce the likelihood of inadvertent downstream migration of the stent-graft during initial deployment, the arterial blood pressure is lowered to a mean of 50 to 60 mmHg using an intravenous infusion of sodium nitroprusside. With the stent-graft positioned approximately one stent-body above the mouth of the aneurysm, the delivery sheath is rapidly withdrawn while the pusher is maintained in a stationary position. As the sheath is withdrawn, the self-expanding stent-graft deploys. Immediately after stent-graft placement, the nitroprusside infusion is discontinued, allowing the blood pressure to normalize.

The pigtail catheter is reintroduced through the large sheath and a postdeployment aortogram is performed. In conjunction with the arteriographic evaluation, ultrasound imaging is used to look for arteriographically inapparent residual filling of the aneurysm sac. If the stent-graft does not completely cover the length of the aneurysm, a second device may be placed in a similar manner. If there is no perigraft leak evident on the completion aortogram, the delivery sheath is removed, the anticoagulation effects of the heparin are reversed with protamine sulfate, and the common femoral artery is surgically repaired.

Postprocedural Monitoring

Patients usually spend the first 12 to 24 hours after the procedure in the intensive care unit until they are extubated and hemodynamically stable. The next 1 to 2 days are often spent recuperating in the setting of a hospital ward. Patients are usually discharged on the third postoperative day. No postprocedural anticoagulation is administered. Before discharge, all patients undergo a repeat aortogram and spiral CT examination to evaluate the possibility of a perigraft leak and the residual patency of the aneurysm. The patients undergo a repeat spiral CT examination 6 months after stent-graft placement and yearly thereafter.

Clinical Experience

In association with the 71 cases of descending thoracic aortic aneurysm treated by stent-graft placement, the author has identified major complications in 11 patients. Three patients died within 30 days of the procedure, and an additional 3 succumbed during a prolonged postprocedural hospital course. Two of the 3 early deaths were periprocedural within the first 48 hours after stent-graft placement. One death was associated with an iliac artery rupture that occurred during introduction of the delivery sheath, and 1 patient died 36 hours after the procedure from a massive left cerebral hemorrhage. The cause of death in this case was most likely related to the anticoagulation required during the procedure. The other early death occurred in an 83-year-old man 27 days after the procedure, following aspiration and development of bilateral pneumonia and respiratory failure. Three patients developed paraplegia (4.2 percent), and 1 of them died 31 days after the procedure. Four cases of stroke (5.6 percent) occurred. Two resulted in death at 36 hours and 42 days after the procedure. One patient experienced the sudden onset of left hemiparesis 9 hours after the procedure. This 72-year-old woman had multiple bilateral old cerebral infarctions evident on a CT scan. Three months after the stent-graft procedure, she exhibited mild residual left-sided strength deficits. The other case of stroke occurred in a 66-year-old woman who had a large left occipital infarct after undergoing a circulatory arrest procedure for combined surgical resection of a transverse aortic arch aneurysm

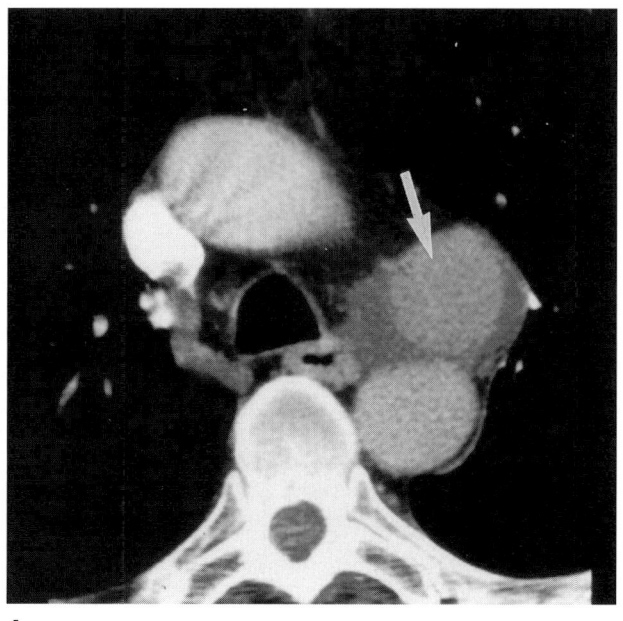

A

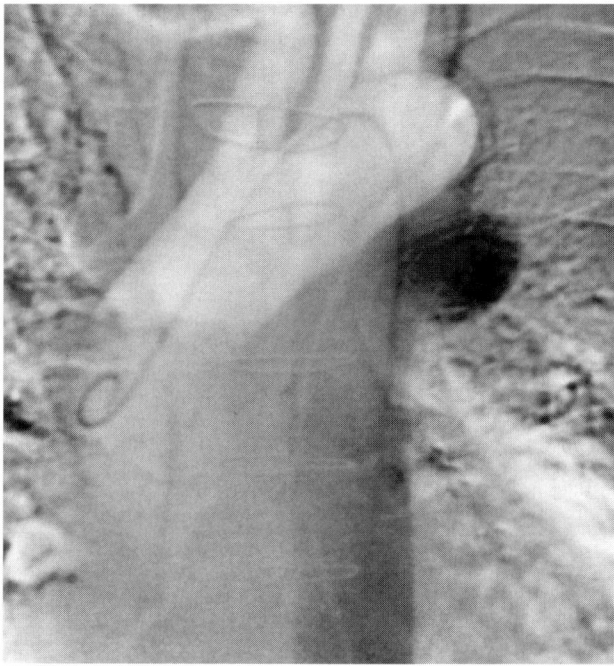

B

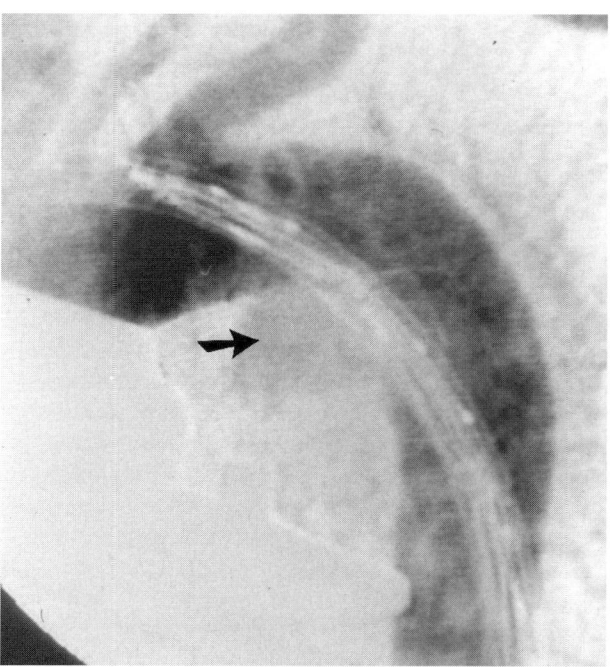

C

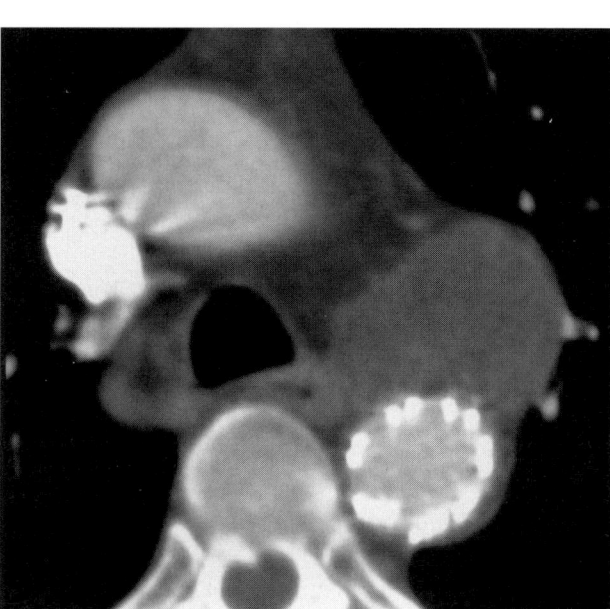

D

Figure 23-3. Endovascular treatment of an aortic ductus diverticulum aneurysm in a 79-year-old man with symptoms of hoarseness. (A) Axial CT scan of the aneurysm (*arrow*) at a level just below the inferior surface of the transverse arch. A rim of mural thrombus is evident within the aneurysm. (B) Frontal projection of a thoracic aortogram shows opacification of the aneurysm, which is protruding beyond the normal contour of the aorta. (C) Intraprocedural aortogram demonstrates the stent-graft within the delivery sheath just prior to deployment across the partially opacified aneurysm (*arrow*). (D) Axial CT image at the same level as the previous procedure scan illustrates a patent stent-graft associated with thrombosis of the aneurysm.

and stent-graft treatment of a descending thoracic aortic aneurysm. There have been no cases requiring immediate or late surgical conversion, distal embolization, or infection. One patient sustained a non-Q-wave myocardial infarction without significant clinical sequelae.

Thrombosis of the aneurysm occurred in 67 of the 71 cases (Figs. 23-3 to 23-5). The mean follow-up

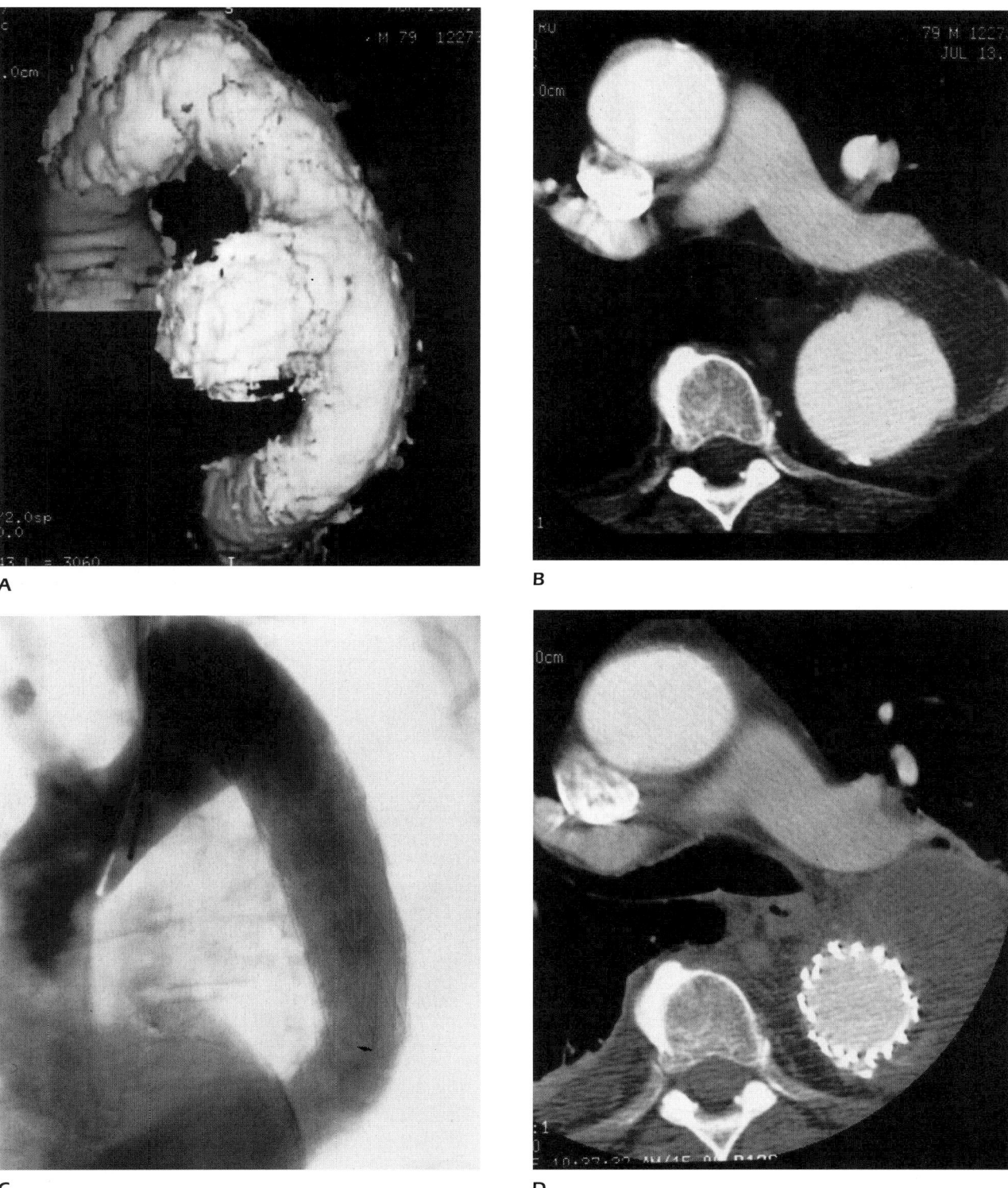

A

B

C

D

Figure 23-4. Stent-graft management of a saccular atherosclerotic descending thoracic aortic aneurysm. (A) Three-dimensional display of a spiral CT scan shows a saccular aneurysm involving the midsection of the descending thoracic aorta. (B) Axial CT scan at the level of the aneurysm identifies a rim of mural thrombus. (C) Completion arteriogram after stent-graft placement demonstrates a patent graft lumen without arteriographic evidence of perigraft leak of contrast material. (D) CT image at the same level as the previous preprocedure scan shows a patent stent-graft associated with thrombosis of the aneurysm sac.

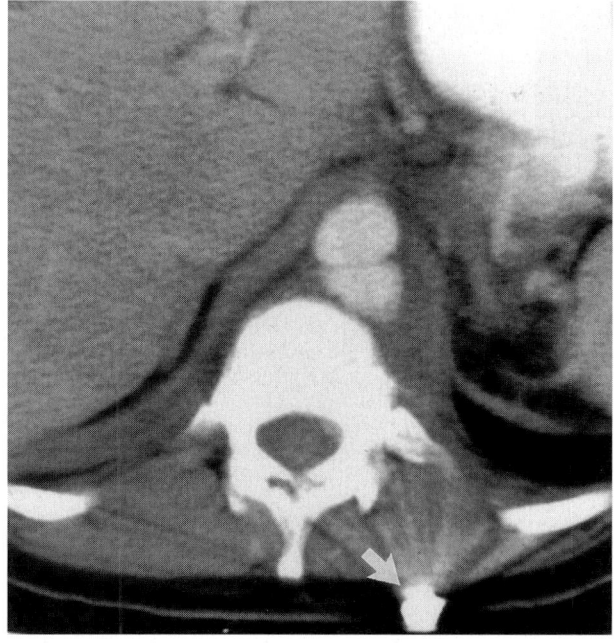

A

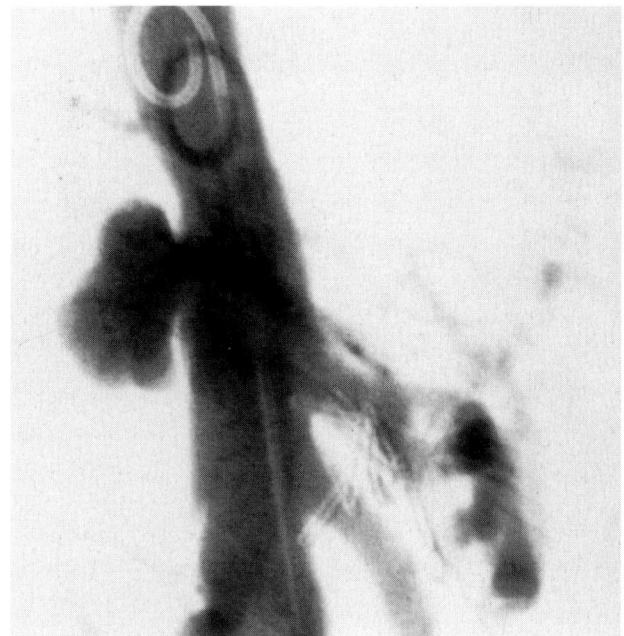

B

C

Figure 23-5. Traumatic false aneurysm of the aorta associated with a gunshot wound. Stent-graft placement was used to manage this lesion after emergency abdominal surgery to treat a traumatically divided pancreas. (A) Axial CT image at a supraceliac level demonstrates a false aneurysm along the posterior aspect of the aorta. The bullet fragment (*arrow*) is noted posteriorly in the subcutaneous tissue. (B) Lateral

D

projection of an abdominal aortogram shows the posterior aneurysm in profile and its relationship to the celiac artery. (C) Lateral aortogram following stent-graft deployment demonstrates successful coverage of the aneurysm with placement of the distal aspect of the device at the superior margin of the celiac trunk origin. (D) After stent-graft placement, an axial CT image at the same level as the preprocedure scan shows a patent aortic stent-graft without contrast filling the aneurysm. Clinically, the patient did well after the procedure.

time for this group is 12.4 months, with a range of 1 to 42 months. Three late deaths occurred 3, 4.5, and 14 months after the stent-graft procedure. The cause of death in two of these patients is unknown; however, in one case a previously thrombosed aneurysm apparently recanalized via a penetrating ulcer located distal to the stent-graft that had been placed 4.5 months before. The patient died after the aneurysm eroded in the esophagus.

The incidence of paraplegia documented in this series is not significantly different from that reported by Svensson in a review of 832 patients surgically treated for diseases of the descending thoracic aorta.[7] Most of these cases were aneurysms managed by operative graft replacement. Although the author does not routinely search for the anterior spinal artery preoperatively, whenever possible the length of the stent-graft is limited to spare any patent intercostal arteries. No patient was excluded from consideration for stent-graft treatment of a descending thoracic aortic aneurysm on the basis of intercostal or spinal artery anatomy.

It should be stressed that these procedures should not be undertaken by individuals without considerable experience in catheter techniques. In the author's experience, a number of devices required adjunctive percutaneous maneuvers after deployment to ensure exclusion of the aneurysm, including embolization of small perigraft leaks (5 patients), balloon angioplasty of the devices, the addition of uncovered stents, and so forth. The morbidity and mortality encountered in the 71 patients compare favorably to results reported for large contemporary surgical series. Clearly, additional studies and long-term follow-up documentation of persistent aneurysm thrombosis, extension of the aneurysm to adjacent aortic segments, intragraft thrombosis, distal embolization, infection, and evolution of the aneurysm size are required; however, the potential for stent-graft treatment of highly selected thoracic aortic aneurysms appears promising. Possible benefits include a reduction in procedural time, blood loss, length of intubation, intensive care unit confinement, total hospital stay, overall complications, and death compared to standards established for traditional surgical management. It is possible that these benefits may first be realized in patients who are considered at high risk for operative repair by virtue of coexisting significant medical disease or prior intrathoracic surgery. In this regard, careful scrutiny of the effects of this type of minimally invasive aortic procedure on these parameters, including documentation of long-term clinical outcome and overall cost savings, presents one of the most important future challenges for this technology.

References

1. Pressler V, McNamara JJ. Thoracic aortic aneurysm: natural history and treatment. J Thorac Cardiovasc Surg 1980;79: 489–798.
2. DeBakey ME, McCollum CH, Graham JM. Surgical treatment of aneurysms of the descending thoracic aorta: long-term results in 500 patients. J Cardiovasc Surg 1978;19:571–576.
3. Moreno-Cabral CE, Miller DC, Mitchell RS, et al. Degenerative and atherosclerotic aneurysms of the thoracic aorta: determinants of early and late surgical outcome. J Thorac Cardiovasc Surg 1984;88:1020–1032.
4. Desanctis RW, Doroghazi RM, Austen WG, et al. Aortic dissection. New Engl J Med 1987;317:1060–1067.
5. Miller DC, Mitchell RS, Oyer PE, et al. Independent determinants of operative mortality for patients with aortic dissections. Circulation 1984;70:153–164.
6. Ergin MA, Galla JD, Lansman S, et al. Acute dissection of the aorta: current surgical treatment. Surg Clin North Am 1985; 65:721–741.
7. Svensson LG, Crawford ES, Hess KR, et al. Variables predictive of outcome in 832 patients undergoing repairs of the descending thoracic aorta. Chest 1993;104:1248–1253.
8. Dotter CT. Transluminally placed coil spring endarterial tube grafts: long-term patency in canine popliteal artery. Invest Radiol 1969;4:329–332.
9. Balko A, Piansecki CJ, Shah DM, Carney WI, Hopkins RW, Jackson BT. Transfemoral placement of intraluminal polyurethane prosthesis for abdominal aortic aneurysms. J Surg Res 1986;40:305–309.
10. Lawrence DD, Charnsangavej C, Wright KC, Gianturco C, Wallace S. Percutaneous endovascular graft: experimental evaluation. Radiology 1987;163:357–360.
11. Yoshioka T, Wright KC, Wallace S, Lawrence DD, Gianturco C. Self-expanding endovascular graft: an experimental study in dogs. AJR 1988;151:673–676.
12. Mirich D, Wright KC, Wallace S, et al. Percutaneously placed endovascular grafts for aortic aneurysms: feasibility study. Radiology 1989;170:1033–1037.
13. Laborde JC, Parodi JC, Clem MF, et al. Intraluminal bypass of abdominal aortic aneurysm: feasibility study. Radiology 1992; 184:185–190.
14. Chuter TAM, Green RM, Ouriel K, Fiore W, DeWeese JA. Transfemoral graft placement. J Vasc Surg 1993;18:185–197.
15. Palmaz JC, Tio FO, Laborde JC, Clem M, Rivera FJ, Murphy KD, Encarnacion CE. Use of stents covered with polytetrafluoroethylene in experimental abdominal aortic aneurysm. J Vasc Intervent Radiol 1995;6:879–885.
16. Parodi JC, Palmaz JC, Barone HD. Transfemoral intraluminal graft implantation for the abdominal aortic aneurysms. Ann Vasc Surg 1991;5:491–499.
17. Moore WS, Vecera CL. Repair of abdominal aortic aneurysm by transfemoral endovascular graft placement. Ann Surg 1994; 220:331–341.
18. May J, White GH, Waugh R, et al. Treatment of complex abdominal aortic aneurysms by combination of endoluminal and extraluminal aortofemoral grafts. J Vasc Surg 1994;19:924–933.
19. May J, Whit GH, Yu W, et al. Endoluminal grafting of abdominal aortic aneurysms: causes of failure and their prevention. J Endovasc Surg 1994;1:44–52.
20. Parodi JC. Endovascular repair of abdominal aortic aneurysms and other arterial lesions. J Vasc Surg 1995;21:549–557.
21. Scott RAP, Chuter TAM. Clinical endovascular placement of bifurcated graft in abdominal aortic aneurysm without laparotomy. Lancet 1994;343:413.
22. Yusuf SW, Baker DM, Chuter TAM, Whitaker SC. Transfemoral endoluminal repair of abdominal aortic aneurysm with bifurcated graft. Lancet 1994;344:350–351.
23. Marin ML, Veith FJ, Cynamon J, et al. Initial experience with

transluminally placed endovascular grafts for the treatment of complex vascular lesions. Ann Surg 1995;222:449–469.

24. Dake MD, Miller DC, Semba CP, et al. Transluminal placement of endovascular stent-grafts for the treatment of descending thoracic aortic aneurysms. New Engl J Med 1994;331:1729–1734.

25. Fann JI, Dake MD, Semba CP, Liddell RP, Pfeffer TA, Miller DC. Endovascular stent-grafting after arch aneurysm repair using the "elephant trunk." Ann Thorac Surg 1995;60:1102–1105.

26. May J, White G, Waugh R, et al. Transluminal placement of a prosthetic graft-stent device for treatment of subclavian artery aneurysm. J Vasc Surg 1993;18:1056–1059.

27. Schmitter SP, Marx M, Bernstein R, Wack J, Semba CP, Dake MD. Angioplasty-induced subclavian artery dissection in a patient with internal mammary artery graft: treatment with endovascular stent and stent-graft. AJR 1995;165:449–451.

28. Razavi MK, Dake MD, Semba CP, Nyman URO, Liddell RP. Percutaneous endoluminal placement of stent-grafts for the treatment of isolated iliac artery aneurysms. Radiology 1995;197:801–804.

29. Marin ML, Veith FJ, Lyon RT, et al. Transfemoral endovascular repair of iliac artery aneurysms. Am J Surg 1995;170:179–182.

30. Marin ML, Veith FJ, Panetta TF, et al. Transfemoral endoluminal stented graft repair of a popliteal artery aneurysm. J Vasc Surg 1994;19:754–757.

31. Marin ML, Veith FJ, Panetta TF, et al. Percutaneous transfemoral insertion of a stented graft to repair a traumatic femoral arteriovenous fistula. J Vasc Surg 1993;18:229–302.

32. Marin ML, Veith FJ, Panetta TF, et al. Transluminally placed endovascular stented graft repair for arterial trauma. J Vasc Surg 1994;20:466–473.

33. Cragg AH, Dake MD. Percutaneous femoropopliteal graft placement. Radiology 1993;187:643–648.

34. Marin ML, Veith FJ, Cynamon J, et al. Transfemoral endovascular stented graft treatment of aorto-iliac and femoropopliteal occlusive disease for limb salvage. Am J Surg 1994;168:156–162.

35. Sanchez LA, Marin ML, Veith FJ, et al. Placement of endovascular stented grafts via remote access sites: a new approach to the treatment of failed aortoiliofemoral reconstructions. Ann Vasc Surg 1995;9:1–8.

36. Joyce JW, Fairbairn JF II, Kincaid OW, et al. Aneurysms of the thoracic aorta: a clinical study with special reference to prognosis. Circulation 1964;29:176–181.

37. Bickerstaff LK, Pairolero PC, Hollier LH, et al. Thoracic aortic aneurysms: a population-based study. Surgery 1982;92:1103–1108.

38. Estes JE Jr. Abdominal aortic aneurysm: a study of 102 cases. Circulation 1950;2:258–264.

39. Crawford ES, Rubio PA. Reappraisal of adjuncts to avoid ischemia in the treatment of aneurysms of the descending thoracic aorta. J Thorac Cardiovasc Surg 1973;66:693–704.

24

Coronary Angioplasty and Related Techniques

HOWARD C. HERRMANN
JOHN W. HIRSHFELD, JR.

History of Coronary Angioplasty

The first coronary angioplasty, performed in 1977 by Andreas Gruentzig at the Kantonspital in Zurich, Switzerland, was the culmination of a decade of creative research directed toward that goal.[1] Gruentzig had carefully studied the work of Dotter and Judkins, which had received relatively little attention.[2] He realized that Dotter's coaxial catheter technique had fundamental shortcomings that limited its efficacy in the peripheral circulation and precluded any attempt to apply it to the coronary circulation. He identified two major problems that needed to be solved to enhance angioplasty in general and to extend it to the coronary circulation: (1) the catheters needed to be miniaturized and the dilation diameter needed to be considerably larger than the catheter shaft diameter; and (2) entirely new techniques were needed to manipulate catheters within the coronary circulation.

To overcome these obstacles, Gruentzig et al. formulated two fundamental concepts that have had far-reaching implications for all interventional radiologic procedures:[3] (1) balloon dilation became the solution to miniaturization and the disparity between catheter shaft diameter and dilation diameter; and (2) the coaxial guide catheter–balloon catheter system provided a means of leading the relatively flexible small balloon catheter to the coronary circulation and provided the axial supporting force needed to advance it into the coronary vessels. This system was later enhanced greatly by the development of the steerable movable guidewire.

Initially, coronary angioplasty was believed to have relatively limited clinical applicability. In the early years after its introduction, articles were written anticipating that coronary angioplasty would be applicable to a maximum of 5 percent of the population of patients with coronary artery disease.[4] These early opinions failed to appreciate the overwhelming attractiveness of a coronary revascularization procedure that did not require thoracotomy. This spawned a prodigious effort on the part of industry and physicians to refine the instrumentation used for coronary angioplasty and to develop techniques to address more complex situations.

The earliest compendium of the results of coronary angioplasty was the National Heart, Lung, and Blood Institute (NHLBI) Percutaneous Transluminal Coronary Angioplasty (PTCA) Registry, which represented procedures performed with crude, early-generation equipment by skilled and experienced diagnostic catheterizers who were learning the techniques of angioplasty "on the job." It demonstrated an acute procedure success rate of only 59 percent and a major complication rate of 18 percent.[5] This modest success rate was achieved in procedures that by current standards would be considered easy and straightforward. Today's exacting standards for operator training and greatly refined radiologic and catheter equipment have yielded acute procedure success rates ranging between 90 and 95 percent with major complication rates of 3 percent.[6]

In response to the striking improvement in the success rate of coronary angioplasty, there has also been a dramatic increase in the number of procedures. The United States National Center for Health Statistics estimated that 331,000 coronary angioplasty procedures were performed in the United States in 1991. In the same year 300,000 coronary bypass operations were performed.[7] Thus, in the United States, coronary angioplasty is now a widely used technique for coronary revascularization and is performed at a frequency comparable to that of coronary bypass surgery.

Differences Between Coronary Angioplasty and Angioplasty in Other Vessels

Coronary Artery Dimensions and Accessibility

A number of important differences between coronary angioplasty and angioplasty in other vascular beds necessitate the use of specific instrumentation, techniques, and monitoring practices. Coronary arteries range in diameter from 2.0 to 4.0 mm. Their small dimensions make thrombosis more likely, and angioplasty-induced dissections are more likely to cause acute occlusion. Their small size also makes restenosis more likely. Because the coronary arteries are also remote from vascular access sites, a large family of instruments and techniques is required to reach target sites within the coronary circulation.

Myocardial Metabolic Rate

The working myocardium, supplied by the coronary circulation, has one of the highest metabolic rates in the body and has limited on-site energy and substrate stores.[8] Consequently, the heart can tolerate only brief (1- to 2-minute) periods of coronary flow disruption. In addition, the heart must support the circulation during the angioplasty procedure. The contractile performance of myocardium deteriorates after less than 1 minute of coronary occlusion.[9] Thus any ischemia caused by a coronary angioplasty procedure must be brief, and its severity must be minimized so that the heart can continue to function while the procedure is performed. Myocardial necrosis begins within 30 minutes of interruption of coronary blood flow.[10] In the event of an angioplasty-induced complete occlusion of a target artery, prompt restoration of flow is essential to prevent myocardial infarction. If the myocardium affected by such an occlusion is an important fraction of the patient's total functioning myocardium, the depression of cardiac contractile performance will cause circulatory deterioration leading to cardiogenic shock. Consequently, the safe performance of interventional cardiac procedures requires that the operator be able to recognize and treat myocardial ischemia and its consequences and also be familiar with the therapeutic agents and devices necessary to support the circulation of a patient who is experiencing an acute myocardial ischemic episode. In addition, as discussed below, patient safety requires the prompt on-site availability of cardiac surgery to restore coronary blood flow in cir-

cumstances that cannot be salvaged by angioplasty techniques.

Monitoring Requirements

Patients undergoing coronary angioplasty have provokable and possibly unstable myocardial ischemia and many have impaired left ventricular contractile function. The overall stress of the procedure, including the administration of a possibly large volume of x-ray contrast agent, may aggravate the patient's condition, particularly if there is extensive coronary disease and impaired left ventricular function. Furthermore, the angioplasty process provokes episodes of myocardial ischemia because the balloon, and at times the guide catheter, transiently occlude the target artery. Consequently, extensive physiologic monitoring is essential for safe, successful coronary angioplasty. Many intraprocedural conduct decisions are based on information about the patient's current condition derived from the monitoring information.

Hemodynamic Monitoring

Proper hemodynamic monitoring enables the operator to recognize and react to impending problems before they become clinically evident. The basics of hemodynamic monitoring begin with the continuous monitoring of aortic pressure. This is accomplished by monitoring the pressure at the tip of the guide catheter. This information discloses not only the patient's systemic arterial pressure but also the degree to which the guide catheter is obstructing the coronary orifice. Guide catheter obstruction of the proximal portion of the target artery may cause ischemic deterioration of cardiac performance and circulatory collapse. Circulatory deterioration must be recognized before circulatory collapse occurs. In addition, in patients who have impaired cardiac performance (seriously reduced left ventricular ejection fraction), concurrent monitoring of pulmonary artery pressure or pulmonary capillary wedge pressure discloses any changes in the patient's circulatory condition that may result from the multiple stresses of the procedure. Central venous access, generally by the femoral route, is important because it makes possible the prompt insertion of a temporary pacemaker or a right heart catheter if needed.

Electrocardiographic Monitoring

Continuous electrocardiographic monitoring has two purposes: (1) the traditional monitoring of cardiac rhythm and conduction and (2) recognition of myocardial ischemia caused by the procedure. Consequently, the electrocardiographic monitoring should include ECG leads that reflect the zone of myocardium supplied by the target artery. In general this would include lead V2 for the left anterior descending artery, lead II for the right coronary artery, and lead I for the circumflex artery.

Coagulation Status Monitoring

Since a fresh angioplasty site is denuded of endothelial cells, adequate anticoagulation is essential to prevent thrombosis at this site. Because individual patients differ in their dose-response characteristics to heparin, real-time monitoring of the degree of anticoagulation is essential. The most frequently used system is the automated measurement of the activated clotting time (ACT),[11] which is essentially an accelerated Lee-White clotting time. Typical values for the conduct of coronary angioplasty are an ACT over 350 seconds. These values should be maintained up to the completion of the procedure.

Requirement for Cardiac Surgical Backup

The ultimate response to angioplasty-induced coronary occlusion with myocardial ischemia that cannot be salvaged by catheter-based techniques is emergent direct surgical revascularization. Accomplishing this effectively requires the rapid response of a skilled team of cardiovascular surgeons, anesthesiologists, and nurses. Executing such a response is particularly demanding when the patient has circulatory instability as a result of the coronary occlusion. Thus the safe performance of coronary angioplasty requires the immediate availability of such a team and the necessary supporting physical facilities within the institution where coronary angioplasty is performed. It is unsafe to perform coronary angioplasty in institutions that do not routinely perform coronary bypass surgery.

Prompt surgical revascularization is impossible in patients who have had previous cardiac surgery because pericardial adhesions preclude rapid thoracotomy and establishment of cardiopulmonary bypass. If a previously operated patient develops an acute occlusion, it is unlikely that revascularization can be accomplished in less than 2 hours and, thus, highly likely that significant myocardial necrosis will occur. This issue should be considered when deciding to perform coronary angioplasty on such patients.

Radiologic Equipment

In coronary angioplasty, as in any radiologic interventional procedure, excellent image quality is essential. The need to resolve fine details of coronary lesion structure and to be able to visualize small instruments in moving vessels in real time has prompted an active effort to enhance the video presentation of fluorographic images. This has led to better image intensifier spatial resolution with a reduction in the x-ray input dose. Concurrently, the development of 1049-line, 25-MHz video chains with enhanced white compression has improved the video display of fluoroscopic and cinefluorographic images. The development of digital video processors that use progressive scan conversion and contrast and edge enhancement software has provided superior live and "road map" images to facilitate instrument manipulation.

Conventional Balloon Coronary Angioplasty

Instrumentation

From the beginning, Gruentzig realized that the complexities of reaching the coronary arteries and manipulating catheters within them meant that coronary angioplasty could not be accomplished with a single catheter. He therefore developed a coaxial catheter system consisting of an outer guide catheter to deliver the dilating catheter system to the coronary orifice and an inner balloon-bearing dilating catheter that could be manipulated into position within the stenosis to be dilated.

Guide Catheters

The guide catheter serves four basic functions: (1) to lead the dilating catheter to the appropriate coronary or graft orifice (Gruentzig's original German designation was *Furungskatheter*, which means "leading catheter"); (2) to inject contrast agent into the target coronary artery to aid in positioning of the dilating catheter; (3) to provide the axial force (or "backup support") needed to advance the dilating catheter against resistance into the coronary artery system and across the target stenosis; and (4) to monitor systemic arterial pressure using an external pressure transducer.

Most guide catheter tip curve designs are derived from the standard Judkins and Amplatz angiographic curves, often with some relaxation of the acuteness of the bends to facilitate passing balloon catheters through them. In addition, there are many specialized tip curves for specific anatomic situations. The minimum acceptable guide catheter lumen diameter is 0.072 inch (1.83 mm), and several manufacturers have designed 7 French guide catheters with 0.072-inch lumina. Most 8 French guide catheters have 0.084-inch (2.13-mm) lumina. Most conventional coronary angioplasty procedures are performed with either 7 or 8

French guide catheters, although 6 French designs are available.

Most guide catheters also incorporate soft, or atraumatic, tips to minimize guide catheter–induced coronary orifice trauma. Some catheters are also constructed with side holes 2 to 3 cm proximal to the tip to enable blood flow into the coronary vessel in the event that the guide catheter tip obstructs the coronary orifice.

Coronary Balloon Angioplasty Catheters and Guidewires

The ideal coronary balloon angioplasty catheter has four attributes: (1) a small shaft diameter to minimize guide catheter lumen diameter requirements; (2) a small deflated balloon profile for crossing tight stenoses; (3) shaft flexibility for negotiating tortuous vascular segments ("trackability"); and (4) shaft axial stiffness so that the catheter can be advanced against resistance ("pushability"). Achieving the optimal combination of these properties in the quest for superior performance requires a number of complex trade-offs and has led to many creative designs employing innovative materials. The typical range of inflated balloon diameters used for native coronary arteries is 2.0 to 4.0 mm. Most commonly used coronary angioplasty catheters have shaft diameters and deflated balloon profiles less than 1 mm.

Two basic types of coronary angioplasty balloon catheters are available: over-the-wire and fixed-wire. Over-the-wire catheters have an inner lumen that reaches to the catheter tip, through which a movable, steerable guidewire is placed. This wire is moved and steered independently of the catheter. The steerable guidewires have highly radiopaque tips that are malleable and so can be shaped into curves. The most popular guidewire diameters are 0.014 inch and 0.018 inch, although 0.010-inch and 0.012-inch designs are available.

There are two types of over-the-wire catheters: (1) standard catheters, in which the wire passes through the entire length of the catheter shaft and exits at the hub; and (2) "monorail" catheters, in which the wire only passes through the distal 20 cm of the catheter and passes along the side of the more proximal portion of the dilatation catheter within the guide catheter. Fixed-wire catheters have a short (2- to 5-cm) malleable wire incorporated into their tips. Although the wire cannot be moved with respect to the catheter, a curve can be imparted to the wire tip, and the entire unit is steerable. With over-the-wire catheters, one can exchange balloon catheters without having to recross the stenosis. Although fixed-wire catheters do not allow this maneuver, their smaller shaft and

deflated balloon diameters enhance their ability to cross very tight stenoses.

One characteristic about which considerable controversy exists is the optimal degree of balloon compliance—the degree to which the balloon expands as its cavity pressure increases. Arguments for noncompliant balloons center around the reliability and stability of inflated balloon dimensions over a large range of inflation pressures.[12] However, there is no convincing demonstration that this property enhances procedure safety or efficacy.[13] Arguments for compliant balloons emphasize that the ability to increase the balloon dimension in a controlled manner by increasing pressure facilitates optimal dilation. Three balloon materials are in common use: (1) polyolefin copolymer—the most compliant, with a 0.5-mm range of inflated balloon dimension over the working pressure range; (2) nylon—intermediate in compliance; and (3) polyethylene terephthalate—the least compliant, with a 0.2-mm range of inflated balloon dimension.

Technique

Preprocedure Pharmacologic Preparation

The cornerstone of pharmacologic preparation for coronary angioplasty is platelet inhibition therapy. An angioplasty site is extremely prothrombotic, and adequate inhibition of platelet function significantly reduces the risk of periprocedure site thrombosis. It is clearly established that preprocedure aspirin therapy is essential. Both retrospective analyses[14] and prospective studies[15] have shown that the acute thrombotic complication rate is considerably greater in patients who are not pretreated with aspirin. Fragmentary data from a retrospective study suggest that the combination of aspirin and dipyridamole confers an even lower risk of acute thrombosis, but this has not been confirmed by a prospective trial.[14] Recently, complete inhibition of platelet aggregation with an antibody to the platelet IIb/IIIa surface receptor has been shown to reduce the frequency of thrombotic complications of PTCA in high-risk patients, at the price of more frequent bleeding complications.[16]

Radiologic Projections

Accurate delineation of the target stenosis and of the related coronary anatomy proximal and distal to it is essential for executing coronary angioplasty successfully. Ideally, the target stenosis should be imaged in two mutually perpendicular radiologic projections. This is not always feasible given the variable geometry and configuration of an individual patient's coronary anatomy. The selected projections should (1) place the stenosis as parallel to the image plane as possible, (2) separate the stenosis from other adjacent opacified vessels, and (3) clearly identify the origin of branches proximal and distal to the target stenosis.

Instrument Selection

Guide Catheter. Selection of the appropriate guide catheter is critical. The ideal guide catheter aligns co-axially with the proximal portion of the target vessel without obstructing it and braces sufficiently against other parts of the aortic root to provide the axial support needed to advance the dilating catheter to the target site. Axial support is particularly important when advancing balloon catheters through tortuous vessels and tight, hard stenoses.

There are no absolute rules for guide catheter selection. Judkins left curves are often optimal for the left anterior descending artery and frequently are satisfactory for the left circumflex artery. Amplatz left curves frequently provide more selective engagement and better axial support but are more difficult to manipulate and more likely to traumatize the proximal left coronary artery. Although Judkins right curves often work successfully for the right coronary artery, the substantial variability of orifice location and direction of the artery's proximal course, together with variations in the shape, diameter, and length of the ascending aorta, requires a large number of different curves. Among the many curves that may be useful in particular situations for the right coronary artery are Amplatz right and left curves, multipurpose A and B curves, and hockey stick, Arani, and Block curves. The orifice location and proximal course of saphenous vein grafts also vary considerably. Most of the curves that are useful for the right coronary artery are also useful for saphenous vein grafts. Several specialized curves for vein grafts have also been designed. The internal mammary artery is generally best engaged with curves specifically designed for that purpose. Curves designed by Stertzer, which are modifications of the original Sones curves for transbrachial coronary arteriography, are used for angioplasty from the brachial approach. Amplatz curves and occasionally Judkins curves may also be used successfully from the brachial approach.

Balloon Catheter. The balloon catheter size should be selected so that the balloon's inflated diameter is between 100 and 110 percent of the diameter of the vessel adjacent to the stenosis. It is difficult to determine the optimal balloon size beforehand, probably because stenosis characteristics such as compliance, geometry, calcification, and other aspects of composition influence the relationship between vessel diameter and the optimal inflation diameter. Statistically, oversizing the balloon to greater than 120 percent of the adjacent

vessel diameter is associated with a greater frequency of dissection with no beneficial influence on either the quality of the immediate result or the likelihood of re-stenosis.[17]

Procedure Conduct

Baseline coronary angiograms are performed in projections selected according to the criteria outlined above. Digital "road maps" of these angiograms are selected for display to guide the operator in crossing the stenosis with the guidewire and positioning the balloon catheter. The guidewire is then advanced across the stenosis and passed as far distally in the vessel as possible (Fig. 24-1A and B). The balloon catheter is advanced over the wire and centered within the target stenosis (Fig. 24-1C). Occlusion of the vessel by the balloon catheter produces a variable degree of myocardial ischemia, depending upon the size of the distribution of the target vessel and the extent of development of intercoronary collaterals. The degree of ischemia provoked determines the allowable duration of balloon-induced vessel occlusion. The balloon is then inflated to dilate the stenosis (Fig. 24-1D). Once the dilation has been completed, the balloon catheter is deflated and withdrawn into the guide catheter and follow-up angiography is performed to assess the effect of the dilation (Fig. 24-1E). This angiogram evaluates the degree of stenosis reduction and the presence or absence of a dissection flap or thrombus. The decision that the procedure is completed is based on the operator's assessment of the degree of stenosis relief and his

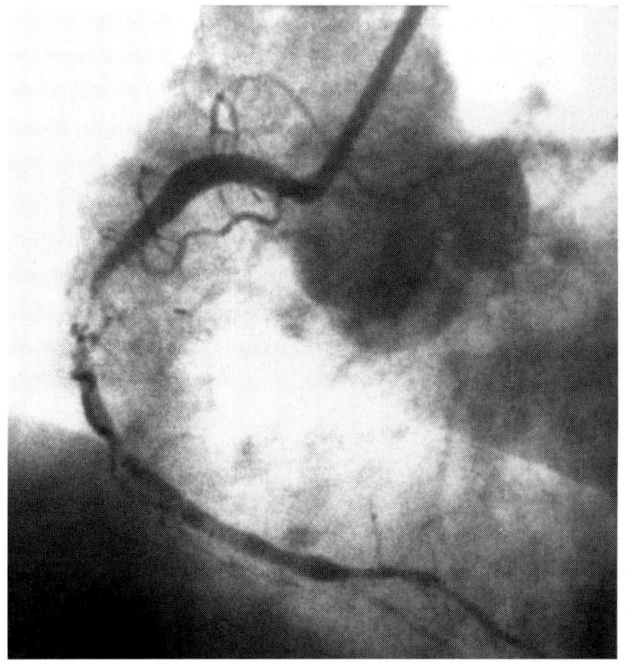

A

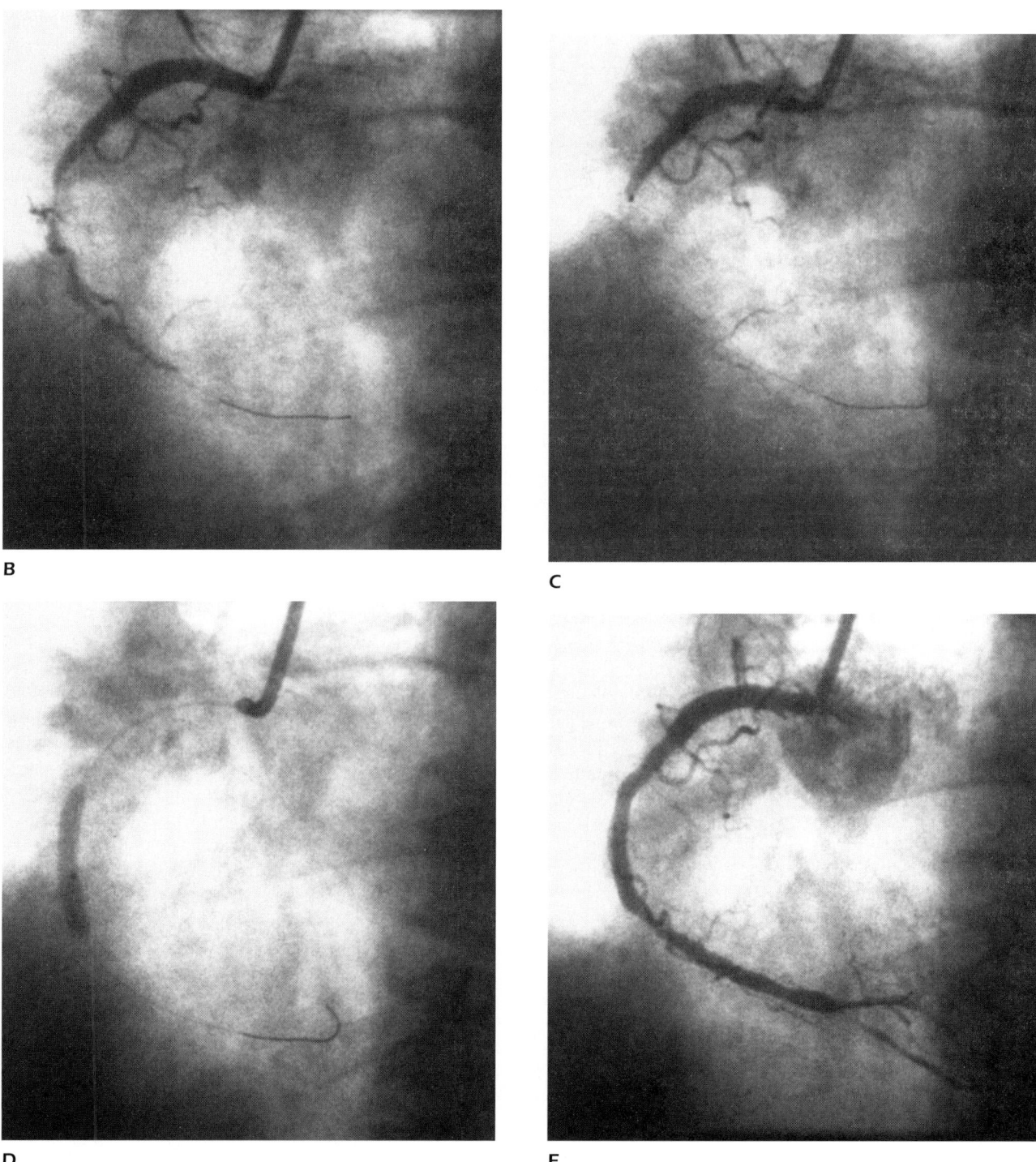

Figure 24-1. Angiograms illustrating the sequential steps of conventional balloon coronary angioplasty. (A) Baseline angiogram in the left anterior oblique projection showing 80 to 90 percent stenosis in the mid–right coronary artery. (B) Angiogram following passage of a coronary guidewire across the stenosis. Only the distal 2 cm of the wire is highly radiopaque. (C) Angiogram with the deflated angioplasty balloon in position within the stenosis. The balloon has a single marker in its center. Note that the balloon obstructs flow to the distal vessel. (D) Cinefluorographic frame showing the balloon inflated during the dilation. (E) Postdilation angiogram showing reduction of stenosis severity to 10 percent. Note the slight haziness at the dilation site.

or her judgment of the presence or absence of dissection at the angioplasty site. Once it is determined that the procedure is completed, the patient is observed in the laboratory with the guidewire remaining across the stenosis for at least an additional 10 minutes, at which time repeat angiography is performed to assess the angioplasty site's stability.

Postprocedure Care

Once it has been ascertained that the angioplasty site is stable, the patient is transferred from the catheterization laboratory to the cardiac care unit. The heparinization is not reversed, and the vascular sheaths are left in place. When the patient arrives in the cardiac care unit, a 12-lead ECG is recorded to assess whether any periprocedural changes have occurred and to serve as a baseline for monitoring. Subsequent anticoagulation management is influenced by the nature of the coronary angioplasty result. In patients with a clean, successful result, free of thrombus or dissection, no further anticoagulation is required. In these patients sheaths can be removed 6 to 12 hours later when the ACT is twice that of control without risk of angioplasty site thrombosis.[18] Patients with dissection flaps or angiographically visible thrombus are treated with intravenous heparin for 12 to 18 hours, after which sheaths are removed. For such patients, many physicians restart heparin after sheath removal and continue it for 24 to 48 hours, believing that it reduces the likelihood of late acute occlusion. The benefit of such a practice has not been established.

Results

Acute Results

The standard definition of acute success for coronary angioplasty is reduction of the target site's diameter stenosis to less than 50 percent without any cardiac ischemic complications. Using this definition, current reported success rates range between 90 and 95 percent.[19,20]

Success rates are heavily influenced by case selection and operator experience and skill. The principal case selection variable is the location and geometric complexity of the stenosis. Stenoses located distal to highly tortuous coronary artery segments may be difficult to reach because of substantial friction between the tortuous vascular segment and both the guidewire and the balloon catheter. A classification of stenosis complexity has been developed,[21] and correlations between increasing complexity and decreasing success rate have been documented.[22] Success rates in crossing and dilating total occlusions are the lowest (30–60 per-

cent).[23,24] Consequently, the prevalence of the total occlusions in any series of procedures has an important impact on the success rate.

Causes of Early Failure and Acute Complications

Causes of early coronary angioplasty failure can be divided into five groups: (1) failure to cross with the guidewire (most common in tortuous vessels, geometrically complex stenoses, and total occlusions); (2) failure to cross a successfully wired stenosis with the balloon (generally caused by excessive stenosis severity and hardness but also by proximal tortuosity); (3) failure of balloon inflation to dilate the stenosis successfully (usually caused by excessive stenosis hardness but occasionally by excessive stenosis elasticity); (4) abrupt vessel closure after a successfully executed dilation (usually caused by dissection, thrombosis, or both, and occasionally by vascular spasm); and (5) injury of the orifice of the target vessel by the guide catheter.

The most severe complications of early angioplasty failure are consequences of myocardial ischemia caused by acute closure of the angioplasty site or guide catheter–induced injury to the target vessel orifice. The severity of ischemia, its clinical importance, and the appropriate response to it are determined by the size of the perfusion territory of the target vessel, the presence of intercoronary collaterals, and the extent and severity of other coronary artery disease. Ischemic complications of coronary angioplasty are reported in 4 to 8 percent of procedures.[25,26]

There are three potential responses to an acute ischemic complication: (1) restoration of flow through a catheter-based technique; (2) emergent aortocoronary bypass surgery; or (3) conservative nonrevascularization therapy. The most appropriate response to a particular ischemic complication is determined by the overall clinical context in which it occurs. Considerations in selecting the optimal response include the severity of the ischemia and the suitability of the patient for the various alternative treatments. Reported frequencies of emergency coronary artery bypass surgery range between 3 and 5 percent.[27] Emergent bypass surgery, although potentially lifesaving, has limited ability to ameliorate the extent of myocardial necrosis unless it is carried out with great rapidity. Both the operative mortality and the perioperative myocardial infarction rate are much greater for emergent bypass surgery conducted to salvage failed coronary angioplasty than for elective bypass surgery.[28]

Most other clinically important early complications of coronary angioplasty are related to vascular access. These include (1) bleeding and hematoma formation, and (2) pseudoaneurysm and arteriovenous fistula formation.[29] The tendency to develop these problems is enhanced by the relatively large catheters needed for vascular access and the aggressive anticoagulation frequently required in the early postangioplasty period.

Late Results

The major deficiency of coronary angioplasty as a treatment for coronary artery disease is the large frequency of restenosis. Although there are several definitions of restenosis in active use, most are similar to the commonly used criterion of a 50 percent diameter stenosis at least 3 months after the procedure.[30] The predominant cause of restenosis is neointimal proliferation, in which media-derived smooth muscle cells proliferate and migrate into the intimal layer of the vessel, reducing the diameter of the lumen.[31] The cause of this process is not understood, but current concepts regard it as a nonspecific response to the physical trauma of the angioplasty process, which, unfortunately, causes the deposition of tissue that occupies space in the vascular lumen, reducing its dimension.[32]

Although the mechanism of restenosis is not known, its frequency, its time course, and correlates of its development have been extensively characterized. Reported angiographic coronary restenosis rates range between 30 and 45 percent.[33,34] So-called clinical restenosis rates are somewhat lower than "angiographic restenosis rates" because a certain fraction of stenoses that are restenotic by angiographic criteria will not cause sufficient myocardial ischemia to provoke clinical symptoms.[35] Nobuyoshi et al. have shown in serial angiographic studies that the process continues for approximately 4 months after the angioplasty procedure and then stabilizes.[36]

Several correlates of restenosis probability have been identified. Most describe the lesion and the quality of the angioplasty result rather than the characteristics of the patient (although some series have reported a greater frequency of restenosis in diabetic patients[37]). Variables that correlate with increased restenosis likelihood include (1) decreasing normal vessel lumen diameter; (2) decreasing stenosis lumen diameter and increasing percent stenosis; (3) increasing stenosis length; (4) increasing stenosis geometric complexity; (5) stenosis located in the left anterior descending artery; (6) stenosis located in saphenous vein grafts; (7) increasing residual stenosis severity following angioplasty; and (8) previous restenosis at the angioplasty site.[33,38] A common theme for many of these variables is the amount of room for the deposition of neointimal proliferative tissue and the aggressiveness with which the process occurs. Thus it is not surprising that restenosis is more common in small vessels with severe long stenoses in which a poor increase in lumen dimension is achieved. This also explains the apparently greater frequency of restenosis in the coronary vascular bed than in other beds in which the vessels have larger diameters.

Use of Angioplasty in Specific Circumstances

Acute Myocardial Infarction and Unstable Angina

The value of early restoration of flow through the occluded infarct artery in acute myocardial infarction is well established. Although this is most commonly accomplished by systemic thrombolysis, direct angioplasty of the infarct artery is also an acceptable strategy. Although success rates are lower than for elective angioplasty of stable lesions, direct angioplasty, when performed by highly experienced, skilled operators, achieves a greater vessel patency rate (85 versus 70 percent) than systemic thrombolysis.[39] This strategy also reduces the frequency of bleeding complications compared to systemic thrombolysis. When performed at facilities that are organized to provide extremely prompt response, direct angioplasty also compares favorably with systemic thrombolysis in terms of the time from presentation to the establishment of reperfusion. However, because of the extreme demands for operator experience and skill and for timely responsiveness, the general applicability of this strategy has not been determined.

The success rate of coronary angioplasty in patients with unstable angina is lower than that for patients with stable angina, primarily because of more frequent thrombotic complications.[40,41] Patients with unstable angina frequently have thrombus at the site of the culprit lesion, and lesions with associated thrombus are more likely to develop angioplasty site thrombosis periprocedurally. Controversy exists as to whether such patients should be treated for a period of time with aggressive antithrombotic therapy before angioplasty.

Multivessel Coronary Artery Disease

The role of coronary angioplasty in single-vessel coronary disease is well established, but the relative roles of angioplasty and bypass surgery in multivessel coronary disease are not as well defined. Multivessel disease increases both the acute complication rate and the restenosis rate. Patients with multivessel disease who require multilesion dilation are more likely to experience acute occlusion of at least one dilated site. These patients, because of their other coronary lesions, are likely to tolerate an acute occlusion at one site more poorly than patients with single-vessel coronary disease. The probability of restenosis at any particular angioplasty site is independent of the other sites. Consequently, when multiple sites are dilated, the probability that at least one site will develop restenosis is high. Gibson et al. found that in patients with three or more sites dilated, the likelihood that at least one site would restenose was greater than 70 percent.[42] Consequently, patients who undergo multilesion coronary angioplasty have a high requirement for repeat revascularization procedures. The Emory Angioplasty Versus Surgery Trial, which randomized patients with multivessel coronary disease to either multilesion angioplasty or bypass surgery, found that 50 percent of patients with multivessel coronary disease who were treated with coronary angioplasty required additional revascularization procedures within the first year after the initial procedure.[43] On the other hand, at 3-year follow-up, the angioplasty cohort had a health status equivalent to that of the bypass surgery cohort, and 80 percent had not required bypass surgery. Thus it seems clear that there is an appropriate role for multilesion angioplasty in patients with multivessel coronary disease.

Deficiencies of Balloon Angioplasty

Acute Closure

Acute closure, occurring either intraprocedurally or in the early postprocedure period, is the principal cause of major complications of coronary angioplasty. Its reported frequency ranges between 4 and 8 percent of procedures.[24] Patients who undergo emergent coronary artery bypass surgery for acute closure have a 25 percent frequency of Q-wave myocardial infarction and a 3 to 12 percent frequency of procedure-related death.[27,44]

Acute closure is most commonly caused by angioplasty-induced dissection at the target site, thrombosis, or a combination of the two. Considerable effort has been directed at developing techniques to recognize impending acute closure, to prevent it, and to salvage vessel patency when it occurs. Techniques that have been employed to restore patency to dissected coronary angioplasty sites include (1) prolonged dilation (10–30 minutes) with specially designed "perfusion balloons" that permit blood flow past the inflated balloon to the distal vessel,[45] (2) stabilization of the dissection by implantation of a stent,[46,47] and (3) excision of the dissection flap by directional atherectomy.[48] If occlusion at a coronary angioplasty site is caused by thrombosis, the thrombus may be disrupted mechanically by repeat balloon inflation within the thrombosed area or lysed by selective infusion of urokinase into the target vessel.[49]

Inadequate Dilation

Certain lesions respond poorly to conventional balloon angioplasty. Some lesions that are heavily calcified and are physically hard cannot be dilated at the inflation pressures that can be achieved with current balloon technology (14–20 atm). Rotational atherectomy has proved to be successful in many such lesions.[50] Other lesions are highly elastic and recoil back to the original lumen dimension after conventional balloon coronary angioplasty. Stenting offers an attractive strategy for managing these lesions.

Total Occlusions

Total occlusions represent a major obstacle to both the short- and long-term success of coronary angioplasty. Acute procedure success rates are lower than for angioplasty of patent vessels because of difficulties in passing guidewires across the total occlusion. The success rates for recent total occlusions (80 percent) are greater than for occlusions known to be present for at least 3 months (40–60 percent).[51] In addition, the restenosis rate is greater for successfully dilated total occlusions (60 percent) than for lesions that were patent at the time of the procedure.[22,23]

Coronary Stenting

Rationale for Stenting

Stenting consists of deploying an expandable endovascular prosthesis at an angioplasty site to attempt to solve the two principal dilemmas of coronary angioplasty: (1) inadequate lumen enlargement of the target site, and (2) acute occlusion due to dissection flaps.

Conventional balloon angioplasty is a controlled injury to the target site. Success requires an optimal degree of lesion stretching. Failure to achieve a satisfactory increase in lumen dimension is associated with a high frequency of inadequate acute results and a high probability of restenosis.[33] Vascular tissue is inherently elastic and recoils after dilation. This presents the angiographer with a dilemma: whereas inadequate dilation or excessive lesion elasticity will cause dilation failure due to elastic recoil of the dilated site, overdilation may create a dissection flap that can cause acute occlusion.[17] The concept of stenting was developed both to oppose elastic recoil and to "scaffold" dissection flaps away from the vascular lumen.

Stent Designs

Four stent designs are currently in various stages of clinical evaluation (Fig. 24-2).

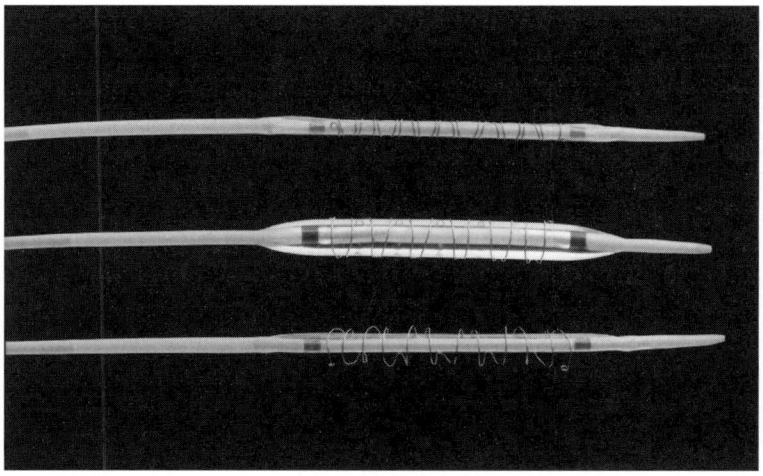

A

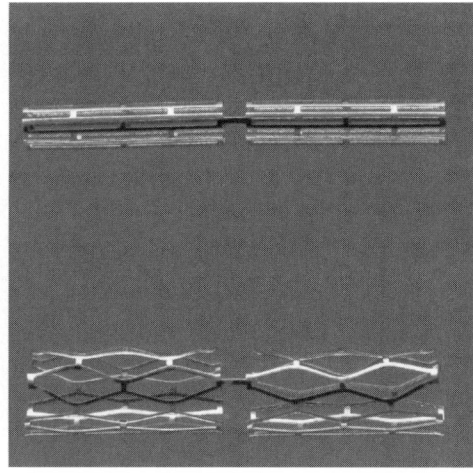

B

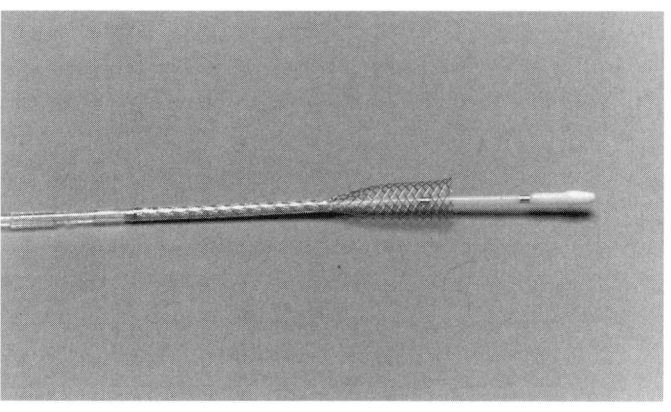

C

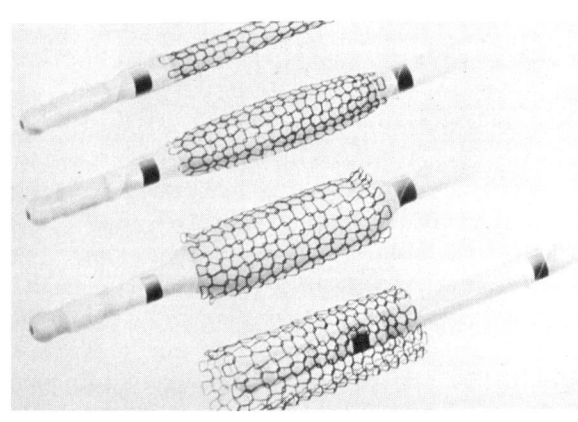

D

Figure 24-2. Illustrations of the four principal coronary stent designs. (A) Gianturco-Roubin stent on delivery catheter collapsed and expanded. (Courtesy of Cook, Inc.) (B) Palmaz-Schatz stent—delivery catheter not shown—collapsed and expanded. (Courtesy of Johnson & Johnson Interventional Systems, Inc.) (C) Wallstent on delivery catheter with the distal portion expanded. (Courtesy of Schneider [USA], Inc.) (D) Strecker stent on delivery catheter collapsed and in different stages of expansion. (Courtesy of Boston Scientific Corp.)

Gianturco-Roubin Stent

The Gianturco-Roubin stent (Cook, Inc.) received FDA approval for marketing in 1993 (see Fig. 24-2A).[52] It is composed of a single piece of malleable stainless steel wire formed into a series of interdigitating curves. It is supplied crimped onto an angioplasty balloon catheter, on which it is delivered to the target site and deployed by expansion of the balloon. Clinical research has focused on its use in salvaging acute angioplasty failures,[47] and it has proved to be highly successful in salvaging angioplasty failure due to dissection. The Gianturco-Roubin design has several shortcomings. (1) Its relatively narrow range of allowable expanded diameters requires accurate selection of the appropriate size. (2) It is relatively rigid and requires a special stiff guidewire to facilitate tracking around bends. (3) In sizes of 3.5 mm or greater, a 9 French guide catheter is required. (4) Its design does

not ensure longitudinal dimensional stability, and "accordioning" of the stent can occur.

Palmaz-Schatz Stent

The Palmaz-Schatz stent (Johnson & Johnson Interventional Systems, Inc.) received FDA approval in 1994 (see Fig. 24-2B). It is a slotted stainless steel tube 15 mm long that is furnished crimped to an angioplasty balloon catheter inside a retractable sheath. The entire delivery system is positioned within the target lesion, after which the sheath is retracted and the stent is deployed by expansion of the balloon. Clinical research with the Palmaz-Schatz stent has focused on (1) its ability to improve the acute outcome (in terms of lumen dimensions) of coronary angioplasty,[53] (2) its ability to salvage failed conventional angioplasties,[46] and (3) its ability to reduce restenosis after angioplasty.[54,55] Success in each area has been demonstrated, although the use to salvage failed angioplasty has been accompanied by a high subacute thrombosis rate (1–14 days after deployment), and the impact of stenting to reduce restenosis has been modest.

The principal advantages of the Palmaz-Schatz stent are its excellent radial strength, its longitudinal dimensional stability, and its stent delivery system, which greatly reduces the risk of stent embolism. Its principal shortcomings are its minimal radiologic visibility; its rigidity, which impairs its trackability; and its associated risk of subacute thrombosis, which is probably comparable to the Gianturco-Roubin stent.[53]

Wallstent

The Coronary Wallstent (Schneider, Inc.) was the first nonballoon coronary interventional device to undergo clinical evaluation and was first implanted in coronary arteries in 1986 (see Fig. 24-2C).[56] At the time of this writing, it is not approved by the FDA. It is an ingenious self-expanding design made of a stainless steel alloy that, unlike other stent designs, is annealed to be springy rather than malleable. Before deployment, the diameter of the device is constrained to a small dimension by a membrane. Upon deployment, the membrane is retracted to allow the device to self-expand to the diameter of the target site. As the device expands it also shortens, a phenomenon that augments its radial strength. After spontaneous expansion, it is frequently further expanded by inflation of a conventional angioplasty balloon within it.

The principal advantages of the Wallstent are that it is flexible, has longitudinal dimensional stability, tracks well, and has a small collapsed diameter, making it easy to deliver. One complexity of positioning it is that the device shortens considerably upon expansion—a phenomenon for which allowance must be made when positioning it for deployment. It has the largest ratio of metal area to tissue area, a property that may make it more prone to thrombosis. Rigorous comparative data are not available, but the reported thrombosis rate of 13 percent for the Wallstent is higher than that reported for the Gianturco-Roubin and the Palmaz-Schatz designs.[57]

Strecker Stent

The Strecker coronary stent (Boston Scientific, Inc.) is a knitted wire mesh tube consisting of multiple interwoven loops of tantalum wire (see Fig. 24-2D). At the time of this writing, it is not approved by the FDA. It is delivered collapsed on a balloon catheter that has special silicone sleeves at each end of the stent to secure it to the delivery catheter and protect against embolization. Like the Gianturco-Roubin and the Palmaz-Schatz designs, it is deployed by balloon expansion.[58]

The principal advantages of the Strecker design are its flexibility and its longitudinal and radial dimensional stability. It is more visible radiologically than other designs because it is made from tantalum rather than stainless steel. This property is simultaneously an advantage and a disadvantage. The greater radiopacity facilitates accurate placement, but it also impairs the ability to detect thrombus within it. The Strecker design, like the Wallstent, may be more prone to thrombosis than the Gianturco-Roubin and Palmaz-Schatz designs, with a reported thrombosis rate of 18 percent.[59]

Equipment and Aspects of Deployment

Most stent designs can be delivered through conventional coronary guide catheters that have lumen diameters of 0.078 inch or greater. Thus currently available 8 French guide catheters are satisfactory. Some of the larger sizes of the Gianturco-Roubin stent require larger lumen dimensions and 9 French guide catheters. Most stent delivery systems are compatible with conventional 0.014-inch angioplasty guidewires, although the recommended guidewire for the Gianturco-Roubin stent is an extra stiff 0.018-inch design.

Three aspects of deployment are critical to success. (1) Accurate positioning is essential because a stent cannot be repositioned once it is deployed. It is undesirable to place a stent across a major side branch, and such positioning should be avoided if possible. (2) Uniform stent expansion with excellent vessel wall contact is important for achieving a satisfactory hydraulic result and for minimizing the risk of thrombosis. (3) The development of any filling defect within a freshly deployed stent signifies the development of thrombus and identifies the patient as being at significant risk for subsequent thrombosis. Stent sites should be observed for at least 10 minutes after deployment and evaluated carefully for the presence of thrombus.

Acute Results

All of the currently available designs perform well acutely, and reported delivery success rates are over 90 percent.[46,47,56] The principal short-term problem is subacute thrombosis, which, depending on the stent used and the circumstances of deployment, occurs in 3 to 13 percent of patients within the first 14 days, with a maximal incidence on the fifth day after stent deployment.[46,47,53,56,58] Subacute thrombosis is two to three times more common in stents deployed for acute occlusion complicating conventional PTCA than for elective placement in stable patients.[46] Therapy to prevent subacute thrombosis has been relatively ineffective to date. The conventional strategy has been to maintain anticoagulation with intravenous heparin until full warfarin anticoagulation (International Normalized Ratio [INR] 2.5–3.0) has been established. Warfarin anticoagulation with concomitant aspirin therapy is conventionally maintained for at least 1 month after stent deployment. Recently reported observations with the Palmaz-Schatz stent suggest that optimal deployment using high-pressure balloons (15 to 18 atm) to ensure uniform expansion and complete stent–vessel wall contact minimizes the likelihood of stent thrombosis.[60]

Late Results

The most important facet of the late performance is the impact of stenting on restenosis. The effectiveness of the Palmaz-Schatz stent in reducing restenosis has been examined in two prospective randomized trials.[54,55] Both have shown that, compared to conventional balloon angioplasty, stenting provides a larger lumen diameter acutely. At 6-month follow-up angiography, the average amount of lumen dimension lost is greater in stented lesions than in lesions treated with conventional balloon angioplasty. However, because the dimension achieved acutely is considerably greater, the net effect is a slightly greater lumen diameter in stented lesions at 6-month angiographic follow-up. In the Stent Restenosis Study, stented lesions had a mean minimal lumen diameter at follow-up of 1.75 ± 0.60 mm, whereas lesions treated with conventional balloon angioplasty had a mean minimal lumen diameter of 1.55 ± 0.56 mm. There was a statistically significantly lower categorical restenosis rate (29.1 versus 42.7 percent) in the stented group.[54]

Summary and Probable Roles

Stenting shows considerable promise in the enhancement of conventional balloon coronary angioplasty. It is clearly effective at improving the acute angiographic outcome of conventional balloon coronary angioplasty and at salvaging threatened and abrupt closure after conventional coronary angioplasty. Limitations of stenting are the difficulties of deploying the device, its expense, the problem of subacute stent thrombosis, the increased frequency of vascular access site complications caused by the currently required aggressive anticoagulation, and the longer hospitalization required by the requirement to establish Coumadin anticoagulation. If the thrombosis and anticoagulation problems are solved, coronary stenting will clearly become an important adjunct to conventional coronary angioplasty.

Atherectomy

The term *atherectomy* encompasses several systems that mechanically destroy, and in some cases remove, atheromatous plaque (Fig. 24-3). These have been developed in an attempt to improve the results obtained with balloon angioplasty. In theory, removal of obstructing atheroma in a coronary artery should provide a better relief of the stenosis, resulting in improved flow, greater predictability of the result, fewer complications (such as dissection), and a lower rate of restenosis than is achieved with conventional balloon angioplasty (PTCA).

Several approaches to the problem of plaque removal are in various stages of development and clinical testing. One such device, the Simpson AtheroCath, was the first to be FDA-approved and has gained widespread acceptance by interventional cardiologists. The use of this device in coronary procedures, called *directional coronary atherectomy* (DCA), will be discussed in detail, and several other atherectomy devices will be commented on briefly.

Equipment

The Simpson AtheroCath (Devices for Vascular Intervention, Inc.) is a catheter-based system with a cylindrical steel cutting blade housed at the distal tip of a rigid cylinder (see Fig. 24-3). The cylinder has a 5- or 10-mm cutting window occupying 25 percent of its circumference, with a compliant balloon on the opposite side. The tip of the catheter is a flexible nosecone that facilitates advancing the device across an obstruction and also stores excised fragments of tissue for retrieval and pathologic analysis. The cutter is connected to a handheld disposable motor drive that rotates it at 2000 rpm. The entire device tracks over a standard 0.014-inch PTCA guidewire.

During atherectomy, the device is advanced over the guidewire and positioned so its cutting window is within the coronary stenosis. By rotating the catheter shaft, one can orient the cutting window under fluoroscopic visualization to cut in any direction. When the desired orientation of the window is achieved, the balloon is inflated to force the window against the atheroma. The motor unit is started, and the spinning cutter is slowly advanced to shave off atheroma and push it into the nosecone for storage. One can make multiple cuts in different orientations by reorienting the device, and one can gradually increase depth by increasing the balloon inflation pressure.

The device is manufactured in several sizes (5–7 French) with two different balloon sizes. Compared to conventional balloon angioplasty catheters, the

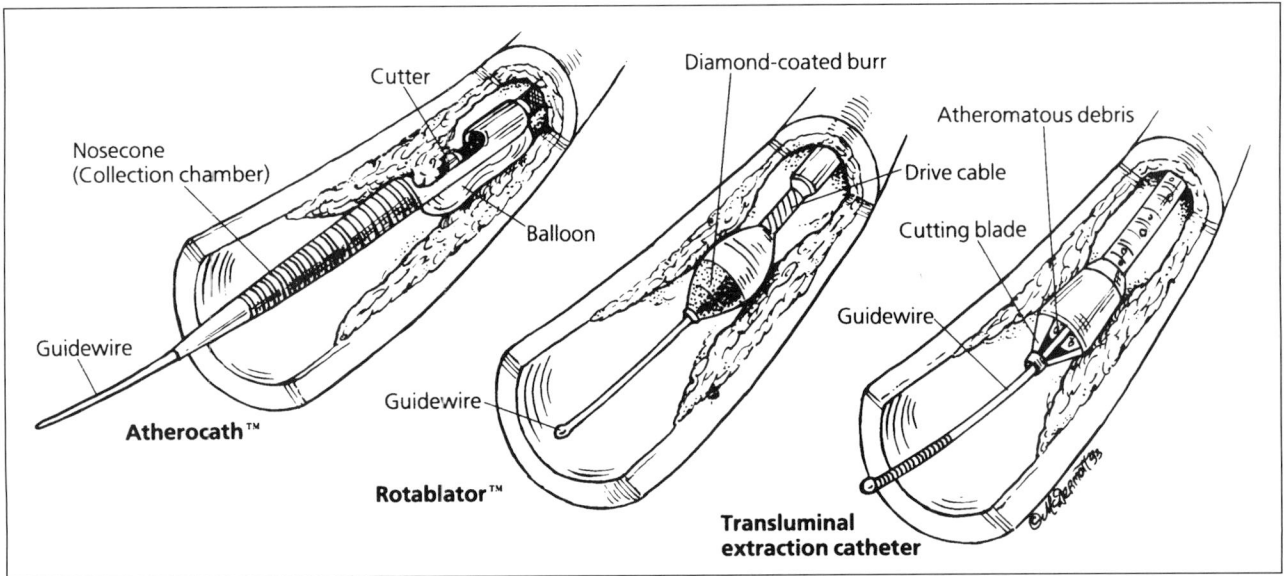

Figure 24-3. Atherectomy devices currently approved for use in coronary arteries. *Left:* The Simpson AtheroCath, used for directional atherectomy. *Middle:* The Rotablator, which ablates tissue using a rotating burr. *Right:* The Transluminal Extraction Catheter, which uses suction to extract debris during cutting.

device is relatively rigid and will not pass through conventional angioplasty guide catheter curves. In addition, it requires considerable axial force to advance it into position within the target lesion. Consequently, special stiff, large-lumen, gently curved guide catheters have been developed in 10 and 11 French sizes. In comparison to conventional PTCA, these limitations have restricted the use of this device to larger and more proximal portions of less tortuous coronary arteries. In some cases, predilation of the lesion with an undersized balloon may be necessary to facilitate passage of the comparatively bulky atherectomy device.

Results

The reported initial success rate of DCA is approximately 90 percent.[61,62] This is similar to current success rates reported for conventional balloon angioplasty. Complications include small incidences of non-Q-wave myocardial infarction and vascular injury requiring surgical repair (3 percent).[61] The reported incidence of non-Q-wave infarction (5–7 percent) is higher than that usually seen in balloon angioplasty, and is more frequent in vein graft procedures.[61,62] Higher success rates were achieved in the less tortuous left anterior descending artery.[62] Transient acute closure occurred in 3.2 percent of atherectomy attempts, similar to the rate with PTCA.[62]

The immediate improvement in lumen diameter

achieved by atherectomy (5–15 percent residual stenosis) is frequently better than that achieved with balloon angioplasty (30–40 percent).[63] In a selected series of 190 patients undergoing DCA, the overall rate of restenosis (defined as >50 percent stenosis at 6-month follow-up angiography) was 32 percent. Predictors of a lower restenosis rate included a larger postprocedure lumen diameter, a lower serum cholesterol level, and recent myocardial infarction.[62]

The recently completed Coronary Angioplasty Versus Excisional Atherectomy Trial (CAVEAT) compared the rates of restenosis after atherectomy with angioplasty.[64] CAVEAT is the first completed randomized trial that has compared balloon angioplasty with any of the newer interventional modalities. More than 1000 patients with de novo coronary lesions were randomized. Patients receiving DCA had higher composite rates of acute complications (11 versus 5 percent, $p<.001$) but slightly lower rates of angiographic restenosis at 6 months (50 versus 57 percent, $p=.06$).[64] Further analysis of these results has demonstrated that the improvement in restenosis was limited to proximal left anterior descending lesions, and that the best predictor of restenosis was the postprocedure lumen diameter; the use of DCA did not influence the rate of restenosis, suggesting that the lower rate of restenosis with DCA was due to the lower postprocedure residual stenosis achieved with the device (29 versus 36 percent). However, the Canadian Coronary Atherectomy Trial failed to show a difference in restenosis rates in proximal left anterior descending artery lesions despite a larger initial gain in lumen size with DCA.[65] At late follow-up, there was a higher rate of late vascular complications and myocardial infarctions in the CAVEAT study atherectomy patients. The high rates of restenosis in both studies were attributed in part to a high incidence of unstable angina and prior myocardial infarction in the study populations.[64,65]

One of the most exciting aspects of DCA has been its ability to obtain atheromatous tissue from primary and restenotic coronary lesions for pathologic analysis. It has allowed investigators to demonstrate the presence of actively proliferating smooth muscle cells in intimal hyperplastic restenotic lesions, and to begin attempts to predict subsequent restenosis based on this initial plaque biopsy.[66]

Summary and Probable Roles

In theory, the controlled removal of obstructing coronary atheroma holds the promise of creating a larger lumen by debulking the lesion without creating tissue dissection flaps. This smoother lumen may be less thrombogenic, which could reduce the risk of abrupt occlusion shortly after the procedure and also reduce the stimulus to restenosis. The most likely mechanism by which directional atherectomy might reduce the restenosis rate compared to conventional balloon angioplasty is by providing a larger residual lumen through a combination of mechanical dilation and tissue removal, so that the intimal hyperplasia that invariably develops after any intervention is less likely to cause a significant obstruction.[67]

In practice, DCA has resulted in similar success and complication rates to PTCA, with a possibly modest improvement in the rate of restenosis. However, DCA is technically more difficult, more expensive, and not as widely applicable as PTCA. This suggests that one of the most important niche uses for this technology will be to improve suboptimal PTCA results. For example, highly eccentric lesions are often dilated poorly with conventional balloon angioplasty because dissection is more frequent with such lesions, and elastic recoil of the normal portion of the artery's circumference is more likely to occur. Similarly, poor results with balloon angioplasty occur in ostial lesions of the left anterior descending artery and in aortocoronary ostial artery lesions. Finally, directional atherectomy may also offer a relative advantage in saphenous vein graft lesions, which may be soft and friable and more prone to distal embolization with conventional PTCA.

Other Atherectomy Techniques

Several other atherectomy devices are under development to address some of the difficulties of directional atherectomy. These include the Transluminal Extraction Catheter (Interventional Technologies), the Rotablator (Heart Technology, Inc.), and the Pullback Atherectomy Catheter (Arrow, Inc.).

The Transluminal Extraction Catheter (TEC) consists of a flexible hollow torque tube with two conical cutting blades at the tip (see Fig. 24-3). The entire device fits over an angioplasty guidewire and can be rotated at 750 rpm by a handheld motor unit. As the rotating device is advanced through a lesion, suction is applied to collect and extract debris, thereby preventing distal embolization. The TEC has been demonstrated to have procedural success, complication, and restenosis rates similar to those of balloon angioplasty in nonrandomized series.[68] In the multicenter experience, a successful result was achieved in 93 percent of patients, although adjunctive balloon angioplasty was used in 75 percent.[68] Good results were also achieved in several subsets of lesions previously identified as high risk for PTCA, including saphenous vein grafts over 3 years old, long lesions, and those containing thrombus, although there was a high incidence of restenosis (69 percent) and late vessel occlusion (29 percent) in saphenous vein grafts.[68] The greatest use of this device is likely to be in ulcerated saphenous vein grafts and in vessels containing thrombus, including patients with evolving myocardial infarction. Because of the frequent use of adjunctive balloon angioplasty after a TEC procedure and the lack of any randomized data, the true role of TEC in interventional cardiology is difficult to assess, but it will probably remain small. The TEC was approved by the FDA in late 1993.

The Rotablator is a mechanical ablation device that consists of diamond chips embedded in an abrasive brass burr (in sizes of 1.0- to 3.0-mm diameter) welded to a flexible driveshaft that tracks over a 0.009-inch guidewire (see Fig. 24-3). The burr is rotated by a turbine at 150,000 to 190,000 rpm and is designed to grind the atheroma into particles small enough (<5 mm) to pass through the coronary capillaries. This device has an advantage over other atherectomy devices in that it is more flexible, can be used with standard 9 French guiding catheters (in smaller burr sizes), and appears to cut even calcified lesions, leaving smooth lumen borders.[69] In the large multicenter registry, procedural success was approximately 95 percent, and major complications included death (1 percent), emergency surgery (2 percent), Q-wave and non-Q-wave myocardial infarction (1 and 5 percent), and a

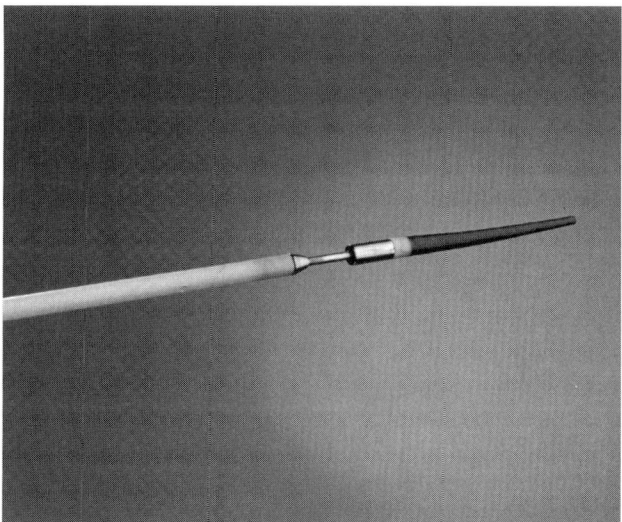

Figure 24-4. The Fischell Pullback Atherectomy Catheter has a rotating nosecone that cuts as it is retracted. This investigational device is undergoing initial clinical evaluation in peripheral arteries.

restenosis rate of 50 percent.[70] The overall results differ from those of conventional PTCA in that the rate of non-Q-wave infarction is higher, possibly because of embolization of particulate matter.[70,71] The results with the Rotablator may be better than with conventional PTCA in calcified lesions, diffusely diseased long lesions, and ostial lesions. The Rotablator was approved by the FDA in 1993.

The Fischell Pullback Atherectomy Catheter (PAC) is the newest atherectomy device and is undergoing initial peripheral arterial evaluation (Fig. 24-4).[72] This device is advanced mechanically across a lesion over a guidewire, and then the distal tip is further advanced to create a gap for cutting. The cutting tip is rotated at 2000 rpm and pulled back toward a hollow collection chamber where atheromatous material is stored. The potential advantages of this system include improved flexibility and coaxial alignment during pullback cutting. Coronary artery evaluation of this device began in 1995.

Laser Ablation Techniques

The hope that mechanical removal or ablation of obstructive plaque would improve the success of PTCA was the initial stimulus for the development of both mechanical atherectomy and laser systems. In the case of lasers, the field has also been driven by a strong public perception that laser energy is inherently a better way to treat almost anything, thus providing a marketing tool for both industries and hospitals investigating

its utility. Initial laser systems used continuous-wave energy delivered through a bare fiber-optic wire, but they caused unacceptable frequencies of arterial perforation and severe thermal injury to adjacent tissue, stimulating a strong hyperplastic response. Current systems use pulsed high-energy waves to ablate plaque with minimal thermal damage to surrounding tissue. The problem of perforation has been largely overcome in a variety of ways, including encapsulation of the tip of the fiber-optic wire with a metal cap, the use of multiple fibers arranged coaxially around a central guidewire, and the use of a balloon catheter to center the fiber-optic light guides within the vessel. However, the success of laser angioplasty is still limited by the small channel size created. The high cost of laser systems and catheters is a further obstacle to the widespread adoption of lasers.

Equipment

Several different types of currently used laser systems are compared in Table 24-1. The LASTAC (GV Medical) continuous-wave argon laser was one of the first systems used in the coronary circulation. The energy is delivered via a bare optical fiber that is centrally aligned in the coronary artery by a balloon angioplasty catheter. In addition, a lens at the catheter tip is used to widen the beam, causing more rapid energy dissipation to limit the risk of perforation.[73]

Unlike the continuous-wave argon laser, most current systems use pulsed-wave energy in either the ultraviolet (308-nm xenon chloride excimer) or infrared (holmium-YAG) spectrums. One excimer laser (Advanced Interventional Systems) is FDA-approved for coronary use. This device delivers high energy via multiple fibers concentrically arranged around a central lumen, and can thus be advanced over a guidewire to minimize the risk of vessel perforation.

Results

The argon laser has been investigated primarily as an aid to crossing chronic total coronary occlusions. In one series of 67 patients with occlusions present for more than 2 months, laser recanalization was successful in 76 percent, allowing placement of a guidewire for subsequent balloon angioplasty.[73] Complications included one perforation, two acute closures, and one myocardial infarction. Restenosis has been high (>50 percent), as is the case with standard PTCA in totally occluded arteries.

Most of the experience with stenosed (not occluded) coronary arteries has been accumulated with the AIS excimer device and is likely to be typical of

Table 24-1. Lasers Employed in the Coronary Circulation

Manufacturers	Type	Fiber Design	Sizes	Possible Uses
AIS, Spectanetics, Technolos	Pulsed excimer, 308-nm xenon chloride (ultraviolet)	Concentric, multifiber, over-the-wire	1.3- to 2.4-mm diameter	Long, calcified, ostial lesions
GV Medical	Continuous-wave argon	Balloon-centered	—	Chronic occlusions
Eclipse Surgical Technologie	Pulsed holmium-YAG (infrared)	Concentric, single ring, over-the-wire	1.5- to 2.0-mm diameter	Same as excimer

other similar over-the-wire systems. The holmium-YAG laser is relatively new, is somewhat bulkier, and has fewer optical fibers, possibly accounting for a lower success rates in early trials.[74] In the multicenter U.S. experience with excimer coronary angioplasty, acute success rates of 84 to 90 percent have been achieved, but adjunctive balloon angioplasty was used in 70 to 95 percent of procedures.[75] Complication rates have been relatively low and resemble those of conventional PTCA. However, vessel perforation with major clinical events has occurred in 1 percent of procedures.[76] More disturbing is that most procedures require adjunctive balloon angioplasty to achieve satisfactory results. In one series of 55 patients, the percentage stenosis decreased from 85 percent to only 44 percent in 32 patients, who then also required balloon angioplasty.[77] Restenosis rates in selected series of excimer laser angioplasty have remained above 50 percent.[73,75,77] In view of the high frequency of adjunctive balloon angioplasty, it is difficult to determine how the laser procedure contributes to either the long-term outcome or to the short-term success rate.

Summary and Possible Roles

Laser coronary angioplasty remains at an early, investigational stage of development. The ability to use laser energy to ablate coronary atherosclerotic plaque in a reasonably safe fashion has been clearly demonstrated. However, no convincing evidence that lasers can improve the success rate and predictability of PTCA, or lower the complication and restenosis rates, has been presented. Furthermore, no randomized trials comparing laser angioplasty to other coronary interventions have been initiated, and data assessment has been limited by the frequent use of adjunctive balloon angioplasty.

One potential niche use for lasers is in total chronic occlusions, where the argon laser may facilitate passage of a guidewire and the excimer laser may be useful to enlarge a channel that cannot be crossed even with a low-profile balloon. Lasers may also be useful in long, ostial, and heavily calcified lesions, in which suboptimal results are often obtained with conventional balloon angioplasty. Cook and his colleagues recently reported on their experience with the excimer laser in lesions considered unfavorable for PTCA.[78] In the least favorable morphologic lesions (type C in the AHA classification), these investigators reported a success rate of 85 percent, whereas the expected balloon angioplasty success rate is usually less than 60 percent.

Future refinements in catheters to improve flexibility and trackability and to increase the number of optical fibers are likely to increase the acute success rate of laser angioplasty. The eventual acceptance of laser angioplasty in the modern cardiac catheterization laboratory will require a convincing demonstration that this very expensive (>$250,000) technology improves the safety or predictability, expands the applicability, or reduces the rates of complications or restenosis associated with conventional balloon angioplasty.[79] Although none of the current laser systems can make this claim, the excimer systems hold the most promise.

Relative Roles of the Different Coronary Angioplasty Techniques and of Catheter-Based Revascularization in the Management of Coronary Artery Disease

Safety and Efficacy of PTCA

Balloon angioplasty remains the mainstay of percutaneous revascularization techniques for the treatment of obstructive coronary artery disease. Success rates generally exceed 90 percent, despite trends in recent years to attempt more complex and distal lesions in patients with multivessel disease. The safety of this procedure is well established, with major complication rates of under 5 percent.[80] Major complications of balloon angioplasty are primarily due to periprocedural acute vessel occlusion, which occurs in 2 to 12 percent of procedures and frequently results in acute myocardial infarction or the need for emergency bypass surgery.[81]

The efficacy of balloon angioplasty in patients with medically refractory unstable angina and acute myocardial infarction has been conclusively demonstrated.[82,83] Its efficacy in symptomatic patients with chronic stable angina is also well documented. A Veterans Administration cooperative study compared the use of PTCA with medical therapy in 212 patients with exercise-induced ischemia and single-vessel coronary disease.[84] Although 15 percent of patients initially receiving balloon angioplasty required a repeat procedure, more of these patients were free of angina at 6 months (64 versus 46 percent, $p < .01$); they also required fewer medications and were able to exercise longer without angina.[84] Complications, including myocardial infarction, were similar in both groups. The investigators concluded that, in this selected group of stable patients with single-vessel coronary artery disease, balloon angioplasty is more successful than medical therapy in relieving symptoms, improving exercise tolerance, and reducing the need for antianginal medication.[84]

Despite the high safety and efficacy of balloon angioplasty, the procedure's major limitation is restenosis. Unlike acute occlusion, which occurs in a small minority of procedures, restenosis may occur in up to 45 percent of dilated lesions, and up to 25 percent of patients with single lesions dilated will develop recurrent symptoms and may require another procedure. The occurrence of restenosis has been a major stimulus to the development of the newer interventional technologies.

Role of Newer Devices

As described in the preceding sections, several devices have proved useful in treating lesions that have not responded well to conventional balloon angioplasty, in preventing acute occlusion, or in reducing the restenosis rate. Stents appear to be most useful for salvaging PTCA procedures that have failed because of large obstructing dissection flaps. They are also useful in opposing vascular recoil and in degenerated saphenous vein grafts, and they are the only devices that have convincingly lowered the restenosis rate. Directional coronary atherectomy may be particularly useful for eccentric lesions, ostial lesions, and saphenous vein grafts. The transluminal extraction catheter will probably be

used in older saphenous vein grafts with long friable thrombus-containing lesions, whereas the Rotablator may yield better results in long and calcified lesions. Finally, lasers may eventually prove helpful in long, heavily calcified, and extremely tight lesions.

Comparison of PTCA with Coronary Bypass Surgery in Multivessel Disease

The role of angioplasty in the treatment of single-vessel coronary artery disease that is refractory to medical therapy is clear. However, most patients undergoing both percutaneous and surgical revascularization have multivessel coronary disease. Three large trials performed more than a decade ago established the usefulness of coronary artery bypass graft surgery (CABG) in prolonging life in patients with significant left main artery stenosis, in patients with severe obstructions of all three major coronary arteries and reduced left ventricular function, and possibly in some other high-risk subsets.[85] The question of whether angioplasty can offer similar survival benefits in such patients and the relative risks of these revascularization procedures are being intensively studied.

The Bypass Angioplasty Revascularization Investigation (BARI) is an NIH-funded randomized comparison of PTCA and CABG as treatment for patients with multivessel disease and severe angina or ischemia. This study has enrolled more than 2000 patients at 14 centers and is following them for 5 years.[86] Long-term follow-up is essential in such a comparison because saphenous vein grafts continue to degenerate over time. No results are available because not all the enrolled patients have reached their 5-year anniversary.

Similar comparative studies have been initiated at Emory University, in Germany, and in Great Britain. The German Angioplasty Bypass Investigation (GABI) randomly compared PTCA and CABG in 358 patients at eight centers with coronary disease in at least two major coronary vessels (mean of 2.5 vessels revascularized per patient) with a primary end point of angina severity. There were no significant differences in baseline characteristics, in-hospital events, or myocardial infarction by 6 months. However, the need for a repeat procedure (either PTCA or CABG) was 50 percent in the group initially treated with PTCA and less than 10 percent in those initially receiving surgery ($p < .001$).[87] Thus, although safety and clinical efficacy were similar, CABG required a longer initial hospitalization but resulted in a lower rate of repeat revascularization procedures in the first year after randomization.

The Revascularization in Treatment of Angina trial (RITA) has a primary end point of death and myocardial infarction at 5 years.[88] A 2.5-year follow-up is available in this comparison, including more than 500 patients in each group treated at 16 British hospitals. No differences have been detected in the primary end points of death, infarction, nonfatal infarction, or combinations of these events. Both treatments effectively reduced angina, although the patients treated with surgery had slightly more improvement with a need for fewer drugs. As in GABI, the need for further revascularization by 2 years was higher in the PTCA group (38 versus 11 percent).

The Emory Angioplasty Versus Surgery Trial (EAST) is a single-center study that has randomized 700 patients suitable for both multivessel PTCA and CABG between the two treatment strategies.[43] At 3-year follow-up, there has been no difference between the two groups in terms of survival, myocardial infarction, or angina severity. However, there was a substantial difference in the requirement for repeat revascularization procedures. Twenty percent of patients assigned to CABG required repeat revascularization procedures, compared to 50 percent of patients assigned to PTCA. The PTCA figure reflects the frequency of restenosis. Virtually all of the revascularization procedures were required within the first year after the initial treatment. Nevertheless, at 3-year follow-up, 80 percent of patients initially assigned to PTCA remained free of the need for CABG.

Thus catheter-based techniques offer many revascularization options for patients with symptomatic coronary artery disease. Percutaneous revascularization devices and techniques are rapidly improving and will continue to extend this option to more patients with more complex anatomic situations considered not suitable for catheter-based revascularization procedures. However, the frequent need for repeat procedures due to restenosis is a major limit to the more widespread application of angioplasty techniques. Comparisons of cost, quality of life, and longer-term follow-up of surgical patients are necessary before a complete comparison of these treatments can be made. A solution to the restenosis problem would alter the landscape dramatically.

References

1. Gruentzig AR, Senning A, Siegenthaler WE. Non-operative dilatation of coronary artery stenosis: percutaneous transluminal coronary angioplasty. N Engl J Med 1979;301:61.
2. Dotter CT, Judkins MP. Transluminal treatment of arteriosclerotic obstruction: description of a new technique and preliminary report of its application. Circulation 1964;30:654.
3. Gruentzig AR, Turina MI, Schneider JA. Experimental percutaneous dilatation of coronary artery stenosis. Circulation 1976;54:81.
4. Berger SM. Candidates for transluminal coronary angioplasty. Am J Cardiol 1981;48(4):810.
5. Holmes DRJ, Holubkov R, Vlietstra RE, et al. Comparison of complications during percutaneous transluminal coronary angioplasty from 1977 to 1981 and from 1985 to 1986: the National Heart, Lung, and Blood Institute Percutaneous Transluminal Coronary Angioplasty Registry. J Am Coll Cardiol 1988; 12:1149.
6. Ellis SG, Cowley MJ, Whitlow PL, et al. Percutaneous transluminal coronary revascularization in 1986–87 and 1991: improved results with initial experience using integrated technologies. JAMA 1995;25:1137–1142.
7. Heart and stroke facts. Dallas: American Heart Association, 1993.
8. Graham TP Jr, Covell JW, Sonenblick EH, Ross J Jr, Braunwald EB. Control of myocardial oxygen consumption: relative influence of contractile state and tension development. J Clin Invest 1968;47:375.
9. Vatner SF. Correlation between acute reductions in myocardial blood flow and function in conscious dogs. Circ Res 1980;47: 201.
10. Jennings RB, Reimer KA, Hill ML, Mayer SE. Total ischemia in dog hearts in vitro: I. Comparison of high energy phosphate production utilization and depletion and of adenine nucleotide catabolism in total ischemia in vitro vs. severe ischemia in vivo. Circ Res 1981;49:892–900.
11. Dougherty KG, Gaos CM, Bush HS, Leachman DR, Ferguson JJ. Activated clotting times and activated partial thromboplastin times in patients undergoing coronary angioplasty who receive bolus doses of heparin. Cathet Cardiovasc Diagn 1992;26: 260–263.
12. Berry KL, Drew TM, McKendall GR, Sharaf BL, Thomas ES, Williams DO. Balloon materials as a risk factor for coronary angioplasty procedural complications. Circulation 1991;84 (Suppl II):130.
13. Mooney MR, Moone JF, Longe TF, Brandenberg RO. Effect of balloon material on coronary angioplasty. Am Heart J 1992; 69:1481.
14. Barnathan ES, Schwartz JS, Taylor L, et al. Aspirin and dipyridamole in the prevention of acute coronary thrombosis complicating coronary angioplasty. Circulation 1987;76:125–134.
15. White CW, Chaitman B, Lassar TA, et al. Antiplatelet agents are effective in reducing the immediate complications of PTCA: results of the ticlopidine multicenter trial. Circulation 1987; 76(Suppl IV):400.
16. The EPIC Investigators. Use of a monoclonal antibody directed against the platelet glycoprotein IIB/IIIA receptor in high-risk coronary angioplasty. N Engl J Med 1994;330:956–961.
17. Roubin GS, Douglas JS, King SBI, et al. Influence of balloon size on initial success, acute complications, and restenosis after percutaneous transluminal coronary angioplasty: a prospective randomized study. Circulation 1988;78:557.
18. Cragg DR, Friedman HZ, Almanay SL, et al. Early hospital discharge after percutaneous transluminal coronary angioplasty. Am J Cardiol 1989;64(19):1270–1274.
19. Myler RK, Shaw RE, Stertzer SH, et al. Lesion morphology and coronary angioplasty: current experience and analysis. J Am Coll Cardiol 1992;19:1641–1652.
20. Kahn JK, Hartzler GO. Frequency and causes of failure with contemporary balloon coronary angioplasty and implications for new technologies. Am J Cardiol 1990;66:858–860.
21. Ryan TJ, Faxon DP, Gunnar RM, et al. Guidelines for percutaneous transluminal coronary angioplasty: a report of the American College of Cardiology/American Heart Association Task Force on Assessment of Diagnostic and Therapeutic Cardiovascular Procedures (Subcommittee on Percutaneous Transluminal Coronary Angioplasty). J Am Coll Cardiol 1988;12:525–545.
22. Ellis SG, Vandormael MG, Cowley MJ, et al. Coronary morphologic and clinical determinants of procedural outcome with

angioplasty for multivessel coronary disease: implications for patient selection. Circulation 1990;82:1193–1202.

23. Bell MR, Berger PB, Brenahan JF, Reeder GS, Bailey KR, Holmes DRJ. Initial and long term outcome of 354 patients following coronary balloon angioplasty of total coronary artery occlusions. Circulation 1992;85:1003–1011.

24. Ivanhoe RJ, Weintraub WS, Douglas JSJ, et al. Percutaneous transluminal coronary angioplasty of chronic total occlusions: primary success, restenosis, and long-term clinical follow-up. Circulation 1992;85:106–115.

25. Lincoff AM, Popma JJ, Ellis SG, Hacker JA, Topol EJ. Abrupt vessel closure complicating coronary angioplasty: clinical, angiographic, and therapeutic profile. J Am Coll Cardiol 1992; 19:926.

26. Kuntz RE, Piana R, Pomerantz RM, et al. Changing incidence and management of abrupt closure following coronary intervention in the new device era. Cathet Cardiovasc Diagn 1992; 27:189.

27. Talley JD, Weintraub WS, Roubin GS, et al. Failed elective percutaneous transluminal coronary angioplasty requiring coronary artery bypass surgery: in-hospital and late clinical outcome. Circulation 1990;82:1203–1213.

28. Craver JM, Weintraub WS, Jones EL, Guyton RA, Hatcher CRJ. Emergency coronary artery bypass surgery for failed percutaneous coronary angioplasty: a 10-year experience. Ann Surg 1992;215:425–434.

29. Wyman RM, Safian RD, Portway V, et al. Current complications of diagnostic and therapeutic cardiac catheterization. J Am Coll Cardiol 1988;12:1400.

30. Beatt KJ, Serruys PW, Hugenholtz PG. Restenosis after coronary angioplasty: new standards for clinical studies. J Am Coll Cardiol 1990;15:491–498.

31. Forrester JS, Fishbein M, Helfant R, Fagin J. A paradigm for restenosis based on cell biology: clues for the development of new preventive therapies. J Am Coll Cardiol 1991;17:758.

32. Libby P, Schwartz D, Brogi E, Tanaka H, Clinton SK. A cascade model for restenosis, a special case of atherosclerosis progression. Circulation 1992;86(Suppl III):47–52.

33. Leimgruber PP, Roubin GS, Hollman J, et al. Restenosis after successful coronary angioplasty in patients with single vessel disease. Circulation 1986;73:710–717.

34. Hirshfeld JW, Schwartz JS, Jugo R, et al. Restenosis after coronary angioplasty: a multivariate statistical model to relate lesion and procedure variables to restenosis. J Am Coll Cardiol 1991; 18:647–656.

35. Popma JJ, van den Berg EK, Dehmer GJ. Long-term outcome of patients with asymptomatic restenosis after percutaneous transluminal coronary angioplasty. Am J Cardiol 1988;62: 1298–1299.

36. Nobuyoshi M, Kimura T, Nosaka H, et al. Restenosis after successful percutaneous transluminal coronary angioplasty: series angiographic follow-up of 229 patients. J Am Coll Cardiol 1988;12:616–622.

37. Margolis JR, Krieger R, Glemser E. Increased restenosis rate in insulin dependent diabetics. Circulation 1984;70(Suppl II): 75.

38. Teirstein PS, Hoover CA, Lignon RW, et al. Repeat coronary angioplasty: efficacy of a third angioplasty for a second restenosis. J Am Coll Cardiol 1989;13(2):291–296.

39. Grines CL, Browne KF, Marco J, et al. Comparison of immediate angioplasty with thrombolytic therapy for acute myocardial infarction. New Engl J Med 1993;328(10):673–679.

40. Laskey MAL, Deutsch E, Hirshfeld JW, Kussmaul WGI, Barnathan ES, Laskey WK. Influence of heparin therapy on percutaneous transluminal coronary angioplasty outcome in patients with coronary arterial thrombus. Am J Cardiol 1990;65:179–182.

41. Laskey MAL, Deutsch E, Barnathan ES, Laskey WK. Influence of heparin therapy on percutaneous transluminal coronary angioplasty outcome in unstable angina pectoris. Am J Cardiol 1990;65:1425–1429.

42. Gibson CM, Kuntz RE, Nobuyoshi M, Rosner B, Baim DS. Lesion-to-lesion independence of restenosis after treatment by conventional angioplasty, stenting, or directional atherectomy: validation of lesion-based restenosis analysis. Circulation 1993; 87(4):1123–1129.

43. King SBI, Lembo NJ, Weintraub WS, and the EAST Investigators. Results from the Emory Angioplasty vs Surgery Trial (EAST) compared to the eligible non-randomized registry. J Am Coll Cardiol 1994;22:469A.

44. Borkon AM, Failing TL, Piehler JM, Killen DA, Hoskins ML, Reed WA. Risk analysis of operative intervention for failed coronary angioplasty. Ann Thorac Surg 1992;54:884.

45. Leitschuh ML, Mills RM, Jacobs AK, Ruocco NA, LaRosa D, Faxon DP. Outcome after major dissection during coronary angioplasty using the perfusion balloon catheter. Am J Cardiol 1991;67:1056.

46. Herrmann HC, Buchbinder M, Clemen MW, et al. Emergent use of balloon-expandable coronary artery stenting for failed percutaneous transluminal coronary angioplasty. Circulation 1992;86:812.

47. Roubin GS, Cannon AD, Agrawal SK, et al. Intracoronary stenting for acute and threatened closure complicating percutaneous transluminal coronary angioplasty. Circulation 1992;85: 916.

48. Vetter JW, Robertson GC, Selmon MR, et al. Use of directional atherectomy for failed PTCA. Circulation 1992;86(Suppl I): 249.

49. Vaitkus PM, Herrmann HC, Laskey WL. Management and immediate outcome of patients with intracoronary thrombus during PTCA. Am Heart J 1992;124:1–8.

50. Tierstein PS, Warth DC, Haq N, et al. High speed rotational atherectomy for patients with diffuse coronary artery disease. J Am Coll Cardiol 1991;18:1694–1701.

51. DiScasio G, Vetrovec GW, Cowley MJ, Wolfgang TC. Early and late outcome of percutaneous transluminal coronary angioplasty in chronic total coronary occlusion. Am Heart J 1986; 111:833–839.

52. Wright KC, Wallace S, Charnasangavej C, Carrasco CH, Gianturco C. Percutaneous endovascular stents: an experimental evaluation. Radiology 1985;156:69–72.

53. Schatz RA, Baim DS, Leon MB, et al. Clinical experience with the Palmaz-Schatz coronary stent: initial results of a multicenter study. Circulation 1991;83:879–885.

54. Fischman DL, Leon MB, Baim D, et al. A randomized comparison of coronary stent placement and balloon angioplasty in the treatment of coronary artery disease. N Engl J Med 1994;331: 496–501.

55. Serruys PW, deJaegere P, Kiemeneij F, et al. A comparison of balloon expandable stent implantation with balloon angioplasty in patients with coronary artery disease. N Engl J Med 1994; 331:489–495.

56. Sigwart U, Puel J, Mirkovitch V, Joffre F, Kappenberger L. Intravascular stents to prevent occlusion and restenosis after transluminal angioplasty. N Engl J Med 1987;316:701–706.

57. Strauss BH, Serruys PW. The coronary Wallstent. In: Topol EJ, ed. Textbook of interventional cardiology. 2nd ed. Philadelphia: Saunders, 1993:687–701.

58. Strecker EP, Liermann D, Barth KH, et al. Expandable tubular stents for treatment of arterial occlusive diseases: experimental and clinical results. Radiology 1990;175:97–102.

59. Hamm CW, Beythien C, Siervert H, et al. First clinical experience with the Strecker-stent for acute coronary occlusions after PTCA. Circulation 1991;84(Suppl II):198.

60. Colombo A, Hall P, Almogar Y, et al. Results of intravascular ultrasound guided coronary stenting without subsequent anticoagulation. J Am Coll Cardiol 1994;21:335.

61. Safian RD, Gelbfish JS, Erny RE, Schnitt SJ, Schmidt DA, Baim DS. Coronary atherectomy: clinical, angiographic, and histologic findings and observations regarding potential mechanisms. Circulation 1990;82:69–79.

62. Fishman RF, et al. Long-term results of directional coronary atherectomy: predictors of restenosis. J Am Coll Cardiol 1992; 20:1101–1110.

63. Hillis DL. Efficacy and safety of coronary balloon angioplasty and directional atherectomy. Circulation 1990;82:305–307.

64. Topol EJ, Leya F, Pinkerton CA, et al. A comparison of directional atherectomy with coronary angioplasty in patients with coronary artery disease. N Engl J Med 1993;329:221–227.

65. Adelman AG, Cohen EA, Kimball BP, et al. A comparison of directional atherectomy with balloon angioplasty for lesions of the left anterior descending coronary artery. N Engl J Med 1993;329:228–233.

66. Simons M, LeClerc G, Safian RD, Isner JM, Weir L, Baim DS. Relation between activated smooth muscle cells in coronary artery lesions and restenosis after atherectomy. N Engl J Med 1993;328:608–613.

67. Kuntz RE, Gibson CM, Nobuyoshi M, Baim DS. Generalized model of restenosis after conventional balloon angioplasty, stenting, and directional atherectomy. J Am Coll Cardiol 1993; 21:15–25.

68. Safian RD, Grines CL, May MA, et al. Clinical and angiographic results of transluminal extraction coronary atherectomy in saphenous vein bypass grafts. Circulation 1994;89:302–312.

69. Mintz GS, et al. Intravascular ultrasound evaluation of the effect of rotational atherectomy in obstructive atherosclerotic coronary artery disease. Circulation 1992;86:1383–1393.

70. Buchbinder M, Reisman M, Fenner J, Gibb MD. High speed rotational ablation in complex calcified lesions. Circulation 1992;86:513.

71. Bertrand ME, Lablanche JM, Leroy F, et al. Percutaneous transluminal coronary rotary ablation with Rotablator (European experience). Am J Cardiol 1992;69:470–474.

72. Fischell TA, Fischell RE, White RI, Chapolini R. Ex-vivo results using a new pullback atherectomy catheter (PAC). Cathet Cardiovasc Diagn 1990;21:287–291.

73. Foschi AE, Myers GE, Flamm MD, Jacobs WC. Laser-enhanced coronary angioplasty: combined early results of direct argon laser exposures in atherosclerotic native arteries and bypass grafts. J Am Coll Cardiol 1990;15:56A.

74. Greschwind HJ, Nakamura F, Kvasnicka J, Dubois-Rande JL. Excimer and holmium yttrium aluminum garnet laser coronary angioplasty. Am Heart J 1993;125:510–522.

75. Litvack F, Eigler N, Margolis J, et al. Percutaneous excimer laser coronary angioplasty: results in the first consecutive 3,000 patients. J Am Coll Cardiol 1994;23:323–329.

76. Bittl JA, Ryan TJ, Keaney JF, et al. Coronary artery perforation during excimer laser coronary angioplasty. J Am Coll Cardiol 1993;21:1158–1165.

77. Karsch KR, Haase KK, Voelker W, Baumbach A, Mauser M, Seipal L. Percutaneous coronary excimer laser angioplasty in patients with stable and unstable angina pectoris. Circulation 1990;81:1849–1859.

78. Cook SL, Eigler NL, Shefer A, Goldenberg T, Forrester JS, Litvack F. Percutaneous excimer laser coronary angioplasty of lesions not ideal for balloon angioplasty. Circulation 1991;84: 632–643.

79. Fischell TA, Stadius ML. New technologies for the treatment of obstructive arterial disease. Cathet Cardiovasc Diagn 1991; 22:205–233.

80. Detre KM, Holmes DR, Holubkov R, et al. Incidence and consequences of periprocedural occlusion: the 1985–1986 National Heart, Lung, and Blood Institute Percutaneous Transluminal Coronary Angioplasty Registry. Circulation 1990;82: 739–750.

81. Herrmann HC, Hirshfeld JW Jr. "Emergent stenting for failed PTCA." In: Herrmann HC, Hirshfeld JW, eds. Clinical use of the Palmaz-Schatz balloon expandable intracoronary stent. Mt. Kisco, NY: Futura, 1993:93–109.

82. Malosky SA, Hirshfeld JW Jr, Herrmann HC. Comparison of the results of intracoronary stenting in patients with unstable vs stable angina. Cathet Cardiovasc Diagn 1994;31:95–101.

83. Eckman MH, Wong JB, Salem DN, Pauker SG. Direct angioplasty for acute myocardial infarction. Ann Intern Med 1992; 117:667–676.

84. Parisi AF, Folland ED, Hartigan P. A comparison of angioplasty with medical therapy in the treatment of single-vessel coronary artery disease. N Engl J Med 1992;326:10–16.

85. ACC/AHA Task Force. ACC/AHA guidelines and indications for coronary artery bypass graft surgery. Circulation 1991; 83:1125–1173.

86. Protocol for the bypass angioplasty revascularization investigation. Circulation 1991;84(Suppl V):1–27.

87. Hann CW, Reimers J, Rupprecht HJ, Ischinger T. Angioplasty versus bypass surgery in patients with multivessel disease: reinterventions and complications during 6 months follow-up. J Am Coll Cardiol 1993;21:72A.

88. RITA investigators. Coronary angioplasty vs. coronary artery bypass surgery: randomized interventional treatment of angina (RITA) trial. Lancet 1993;341:573–580.

III

Interventional Radiology of the Gastrointestinal System

25

Arteriographic Diagnosis and Treatment of Gastrointestinal Bleeding

STANLEY BAUM

Since its introduction in 1963, selective arteriography has become established as an accurate, safe, and important technique for the diagnosis and treatment of gastrointestinal bleeding.[1-3] When this procedure was initially introduced, it was used exclusively for diagnosis. The selective arterial infusion of vasoconstricting drugs through the same catheter used to identify the bleeding site was a natural outgrowth of diagnostic arteriography. This progression from a diagnostic to a therapeutic application of the angiographic catheter was in many ways the beginning of interventional radiology.[4]

In order to use angiography effectively in the emergency management of gastrointestinal bleeding, one must perform it rapidly and efficiently. Well-trained personnel must be available on short notice, 24 hours a day. The indications as well as the limitations of angiography must be well understood by both the radiologist and the attending clinician. About 75 percent of patients requiring hospitalization for gastrointestinal bleeding can be managed conservatively with sedation, bedrest, and replacement of blood volume.[5] These patients are obviously not candidates for emergency angiography. Transcatheter therapy is most useful in patients in whom bleeding does not respond to conservative treatment or those who are poor surgical risks.

Bleeding Site Localization

Although angiography is only one of several methods available for locating sources of gastrointestinal bleeding, it has become a very important and commonly used clinical tool.[6-12] The procedure may be performed on severely ill patients and requires little patient cooperation. The angiographic criteria of bleeding are straightforward, and the examination requires little special preparation and can be performed despite the presence of large amounts of blood in the gastrointestinal tract.

For successful visualization, however, the patient must be bleeding at a rate of at least 0.5 ml per minute. The major limitation of the technique relates to the intermittent nature of gastrointestinal bleeding, which can result in a negative study if the bleeding has temporarily stopped at the time of the injection.[13] Another serious limitation has been the inability of a selective arteriogram to demonstrate venous bleeding. This is also a problem if the patients studied are bleeding massively from esophageal varices.

Experimental gastrointestinal hemorrhage has recently been demonstrated with contrast-enhanced magnetic resonance imaging (MRI).[14] Prior endoscopy can also be of great help to the angiographer. Even if the endoscopist cannot be certain exactly where the bleeding is coming from, the identification of the region of bleeding, such as the duodenum or stomach, is of value in guiding catheterization of the appropriate vessel. If the bleeding is observed coming from esophageal varices, initial therapy is directed toward intravenous vasopressin infusion rather than early angiography. Unfortunately, an accurate endoscopic diagnosis is not always possible because direct visualization is made difficult by active bleeding and blood in the gastrointestinal tract.

The intravenous administration of radionuclides has proven to be a very valuable diagnostic technique for demonstrating active bleeding prior to angiography. This technique is totally noninvasive, simple, and capable of visualizing both arterial and venous bleeding at rates as low as 0.1 ml per minute. The isotope procedure is performed with an intravenous injection of technetium 99m sulfur colloid, a liver-scanning agent.[15] As the isotope reaches the bleeding site, a small amount extravasates. With each additional circulation, more of the isotope leaks into the gut. As activity in the vascular system is removed by the liver and

389

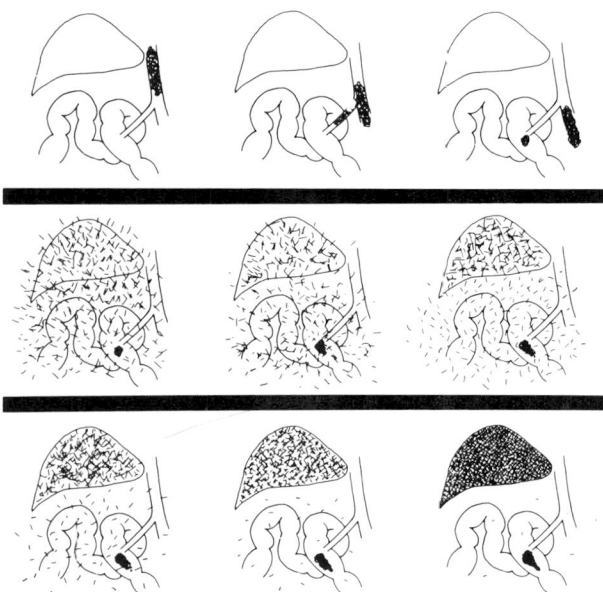

Figure 25-1. ^{99m}Tc sulfur colloid scan for the detection of gastrointestinal bleeding. After the injection of ^{99m}Tc sulfur colloid into a patient who is actively bleeding, the radioactive agent is cleared by the liver and only a fraction of the injected material will extravasate at the bleeding site. This process is repeated each time the blood circulates, adding another, but smaller, fraction to the material already at the site of the hemorrhage. Immediately after the intravenous administration of the radioactive agent, the background activity decreases exponentially, while the activity at the bleeding site increases exponentially.

spleen, a difference is quickly reached between the bleeding site and the background (Figs. 25-1 and 25-2). The extravasated isotope within the gut can usually be demonstrated in the first 5 to 10 minutes after the injection. If sites of bleeding cannot be identified on the early scan, the examination is continued so as to identify activity that moves away from the hepatic or splenic flexure. Such an area may be obscured at first by the activity in the overlying spleen and liver, but as continued peristalsis moves the isotope along the gastrointestinal tract it becomes visible. The technique is frequently used as a screening procedure and enables better selection of patients to be studied by angiography.

With an alternate isotopic technique using tagged red blood cells, bleeding does not have to be occurring at the time of the injection. The tagged red cells are injected and the scans are taken at 1-minute intervals for 1 hour. If the scans are negative, the patient can be sent back to the floor and scans repeated when clinically indicated.[16,17]

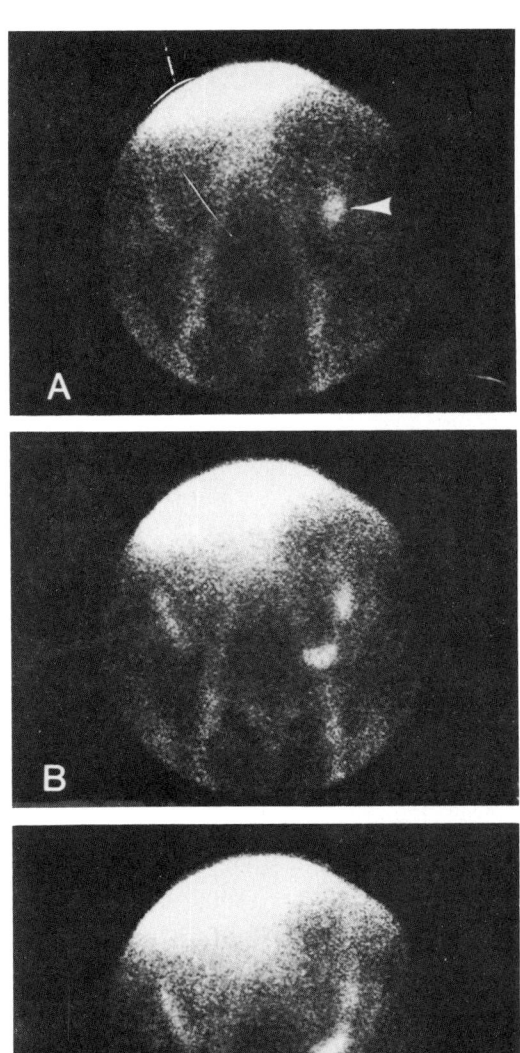

Figure 25-2. Bleeding diverticulum demonstrated with a ^{99m}Tc sulfur colloid scan. (A) Ten minutes after the injection of 10 mCi intravenously, an area of abnormal activity is seen in the left iliac fossa (*arrow*). (B and C) Scans obtained 15 and 30 minutes later demonstrate movement of activity in the lumen of the bowel. The activity outlines a configuration of the descending and proximal sigmoid colons. (D) Twenty minutes after the isotope scan, an inferior mesenteric arteriogram was obtained that demonstrates an area of extravasation (*arrow*) in the descending colon superimposed on the iliac fossa. (E) A late film obtained during inferior mesenteric arteriography shows persistence of extravasated contrast material in the descending colon (*arrow*). The patient was successfully treated by a vasopressin infusion. Before discharge, a barium examination showed the arteriographic abnormality to correspond to a colonic diverticulum.

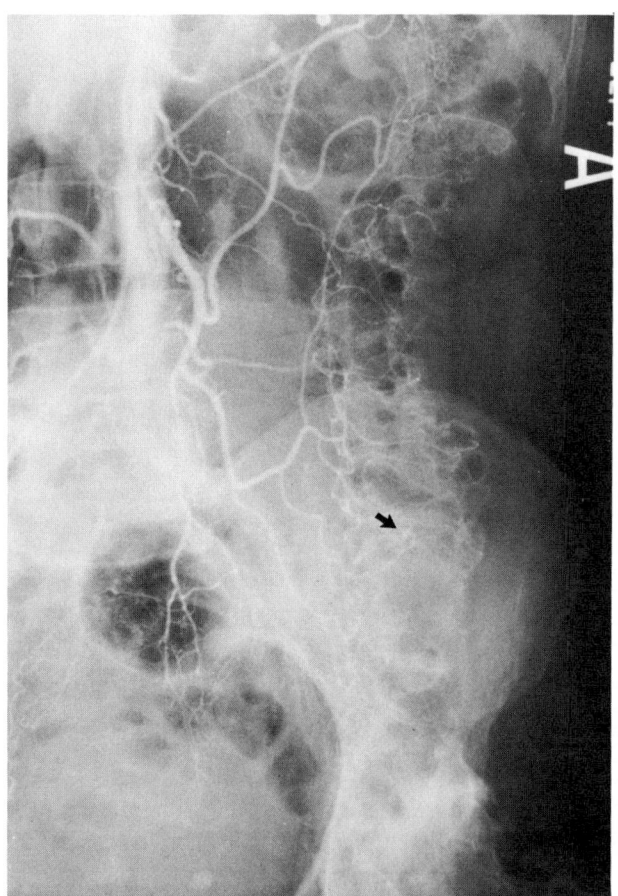

D

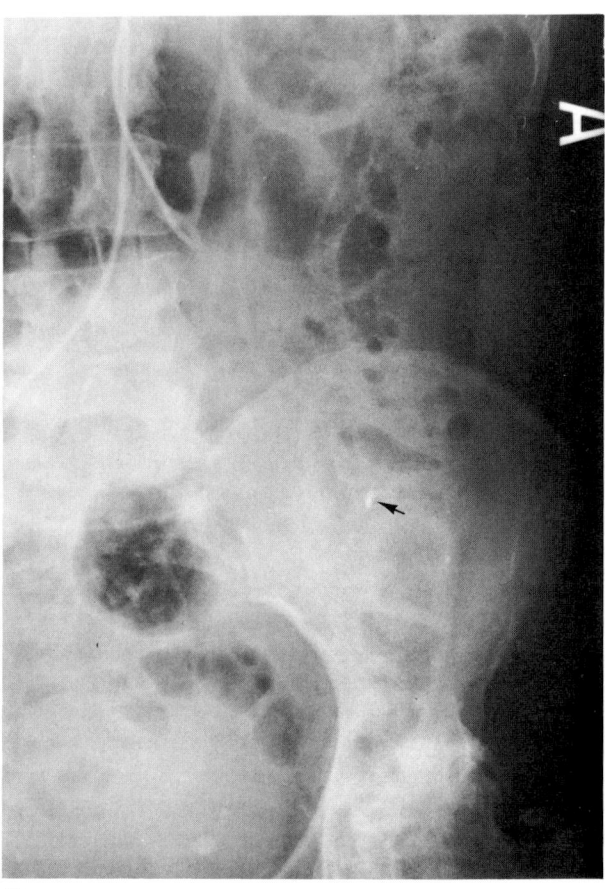

E

Figure 25-2 (continued).

If bleeding occurs, the tagged red cells extravasate into the gastrointestinal tract and can be detected on repeated scans. The disadvantage of this technique is that bleeding may occur in one place, but because the labeled red cells can travel in a retrograde or antegrade fashion, the scan may show the activity in a more distal or proximal site.

The value of emergency barium examinations in patients with severe gastrointestinal bleeding is limited. Large amounts of blood in the gut make upper gastrointestinal barium studies difficult to interpret except in the presence of very large and obvious lesions. Barium enemas are even more limited because of fecal material in the unprepared bowel. If the barium examination is positive, there is no assurance that the detected pathologic processes (e.g., duodenal ulcers, esophageal varices, or colonic diverticular disease) are responsible for the current bleeding episode.[18,19] In addition, the presence of barium in the gastrointestinal tract precludes the possibility of a subsequent angiographic examination and also interferes with direct endoscopic visualization.

Angiographic Appearance of Bleeding

When bleeding is first detected during the arterial phase of a selective arteriogram, it typically appears as a localized puddle of contrast material. As the filming continues, the bleeding becomes increasingly obvious and persists after all the intravascular contrast has washed out. In the presence of very brisk bleeding one may see excellent opacification of the mucosa of the gastrointestinal tract. Small amounts of extravasation appear as localized flecks, which occasionally outline either an ulcer crater (Fig. 25-3) or a colonic diverticulum (Fig. 25-4). If the lumen of the gastrointestinal tract is filled with blood clots, extravasated contrast material will occasionally appear tubular in configuration and resemble a venous structure.[20] This "pseudovein" (Fig. 25-5) is easily distinguished from a vascular malformation because the extravasated contrast persists well beyond the venous phase of the arteriogram.

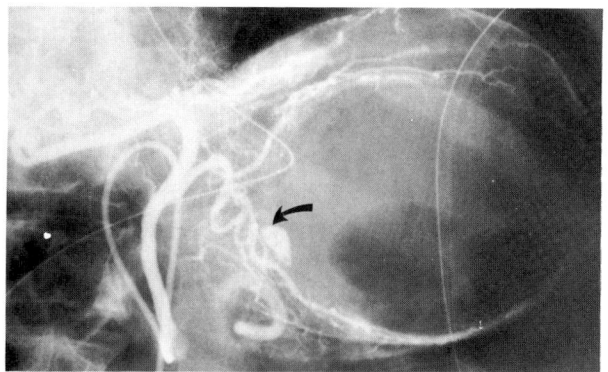

A

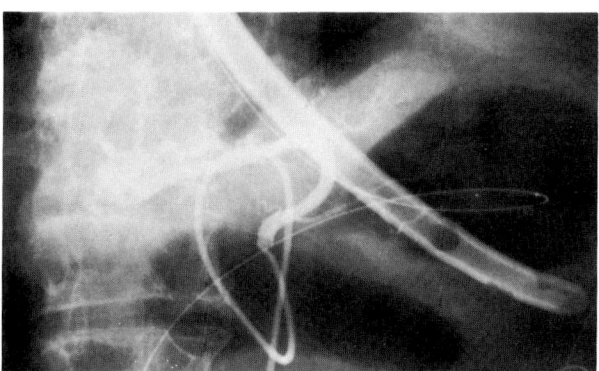

B

Figure 25-3. Bleeding gastric ulcer. (A) Selective left gastric arteriography demonstrates a common left hepatic–left gastric trunk and active bleeding (*arrow*) from a fundal branch of the left gastric artery. (B) Repeat left gastric arteriography during the infusion of vasopressin demonstrates marked vasoconstriction of the left gastric artery without any evidence of continued bleeding. The left hepatic artery branch appears unaffected by the vasopressin. This impression is in keeping with experimental evidence that, although vasopressin causes initial vasoconstriction of the hepatic artery, it does not maintain the vasoconstriction during an infusion. It is generally assumed, therefore, that it is safe to infuse the hepatic artery selectively in patients with normal liver function.

Pitfalls in the Angiographic Diagnosis of Bleeding

The intermittent nature of bleeding in some patients can result in a negative angiographic study if during the injection the bleeding has ceased. Some angiographers have attempted to provoke bleeding in these cases; however, the author's own experience with both heparin and vasodilators such as Priscoline has not been successful. The author has found the isotope technique very helpful in selecting those patients who are actively bleeding, and its use has reduced the number of negative arteriograms.

Venous bleeding is almost never demonstrated an-

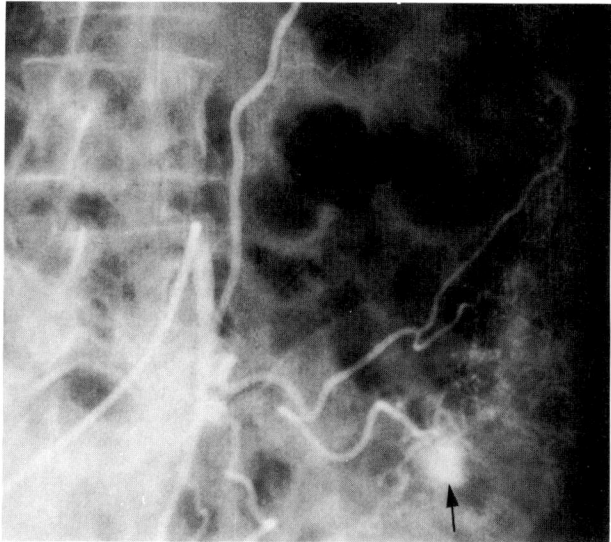

A

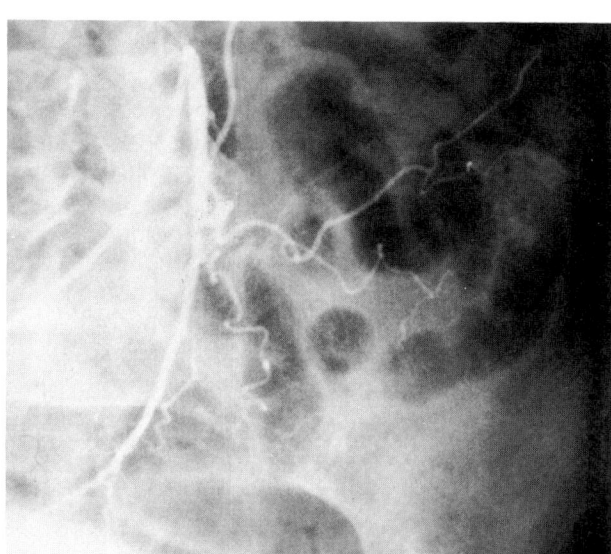

B

Figure 25-4. Bleeding diverticulum in the descending colon outlined with extravasated contrast material. (A) Arterial phase of a selective inferior mesenteric arteriogram shows extravasation of contrast material (*arrow*) in the midportion of the descending colon. The extravasated contrast appears to outline the diverticulum itself. (B) During the infusion of vasopressin at 0.2 unit per minute into the inferior mesenteric artery, a repeat arteriogram demonstrates peripheral vasoconstriction of the arterial branches and cessation of the bleeding. After the patient was weaned from the vasopressin, the bleeding did not recur and the patient was discharged without surgery.

giographically, and the diagnosis of esophageal variceal bleeding is made on angiography only indirectly by demonstrating portal hypertension and excluding all other potential arterial and/or mucosal sites of bleeding.

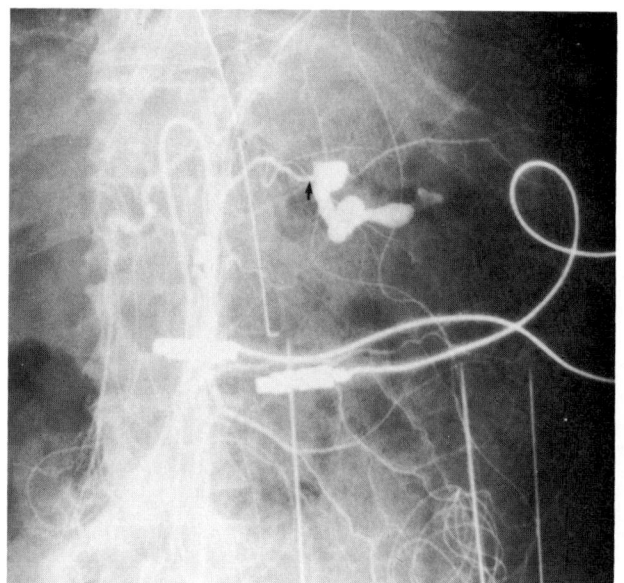

A

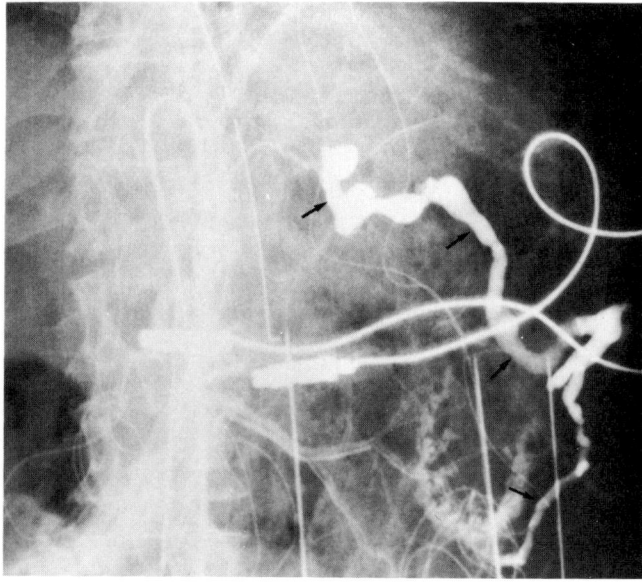

B

Figure 25-5. Pseudovein appearance of extravasated contrast material. (A) Selective left gastric arteriography performed on a patient with an actively bleeding stress ulcer in the fundus of the stomach demonstrates extravasation from a branch of the left gastric artery (*arrow*). (B) A film obtained during the capillary phase of the study demonstrates the ex-travasated contrast material (*arrows*) puddled between clots within a dilated, blood-filled stomach. Although the appearance of the contrast material is that of a vascular structure, this should not be confused with either an arterial or a venous malformation.

False-Negative Examination

Occasionally in a patient actively bleeding from an arterial and/or a capillary site, the arteriogram will not demonstrate an area of extravasation. This is usually the result of injecting the wrong vessel. If there is clinical or endoscopic evidence of upper gastrointestinal bleeding, a complete examination must include opacification of the left gastric, gastroduodenal, pancreaticoduodenal, and splenic arteries. In the absence of a gastrojejunostomy the history of having vomited blood generally indicates that the bleeding is coming from some portion of the gastrointestinal tract proximal to the ligament of Treitz. The history of having passed bright red blood per rectum, however, does not preclude the patient's having a bleeding site in the upper gastrointestinal tract. Examination of the vasculature of the stomach and duodenum should also be carried out if a negative superior and inferior mesenteric arteriogram is obtained in a patient presenting with lower gastrointestinal hemorrhage.

False-Positive Examination

False-positive diagnoses will occasionally be made when normal parenchymal blushes are confused with extravasation. One of the most commonly made errors is the superimposition of a densely opacified left adrenal gland on the gastric fundus (Fig. 25-6). This often occurs when the inferior phrenic arteries originate either as branches of or adjacent to the left gastric artery or celiac axis. The arteriographic parenchymal blush of the adrenal gland resembles a railroad track, being linear in appearance with a radiolucency in the center.

Another instance of a false-positive examination can occur in some patients in whom selective left gastric arteriography demonstrates a marked increase in the size and number of vessels supplying the gastric fundus accompanied by an intense mucosal stain. Although this appearance is similar to that seen in hemorrhagic gastritis, unless one can identify actual points of extravasation the diagnosis of bleeding gastritis should not be made. The hyperemic appearance can be caused by vigorous lavaging of the stomach prior to arteriography in an attempt to stop the bleeding. It must also be remembered that patients bleeding from other causes such as duodenal ulcers or Mallory-Weiss tears of the stomach will frequently have gastritis (Fig. 25-7).

Even after a site of extravasation is identified on the arteriogram, errors can occur in knowing exactly where the bleeding site is within the gastrointestinal tract. In the anteroposterior projection of a superior mesenteric arteriogram, extravasation from a bleeding duodenal ulcer that is being supplied from the inferior pancreaticoduodenal artery may seem to originate in

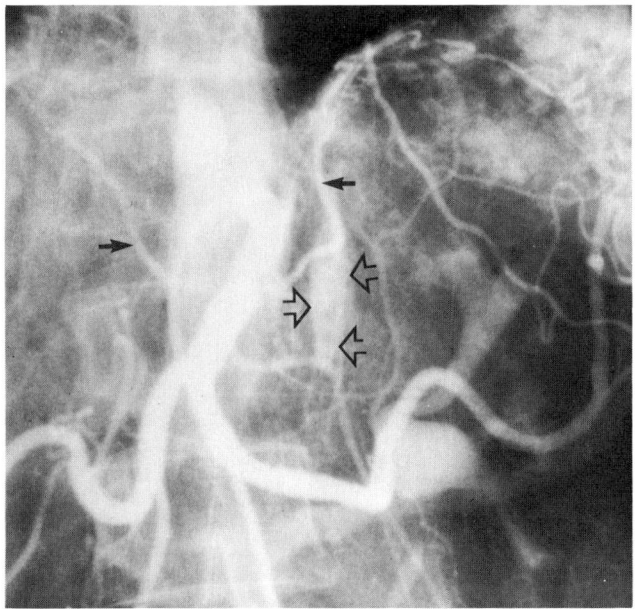

A

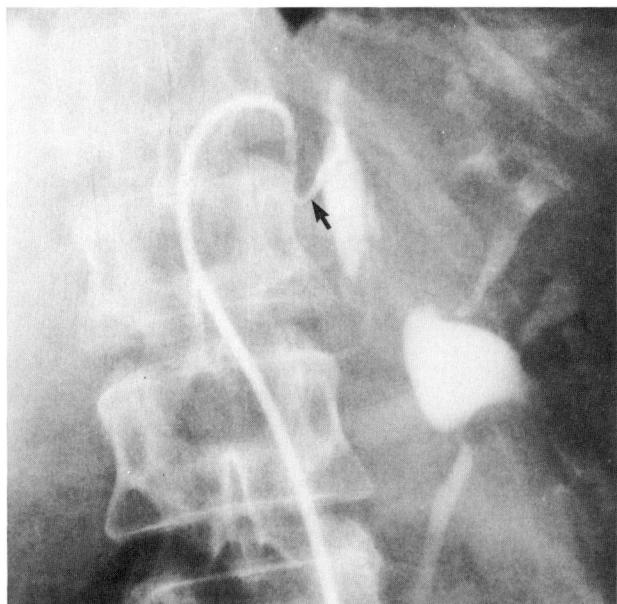

B

Figure 25-6. Left adrenal gland opacification simulating extravasation. (A) Selective celiac arteriography performed on a patient studied for upper gastrointestinal bleeding demonstrates large phrenic arteries coming off as early branches of the celiac axis (*solid arrows*). During the arterial phase of the examination, opacification of the left adrenal gland appears (*open arrows*) as a result of adrenal branches from the inferior phrenic artery. There is no evidence on the celiac arteriogram of arterial extravasation. (B) Intense opacification of the left adrenal gland persists well after the venous phase of the examination and is superimposed on the lesser curvature aspect of the fundus of the stomach. The fact that the tip of the catheter is partially wedged in the left inferior phrenic artery probably accounts for the intense opacification of the adrenal gland and the poor washout of the phrenic artery (*arrow*). The patient did not have any angiographic evidence of arterial or mucosal bleeding.

the transverse colon (Fig. 25-8). The surgeon will therefore be misled unless the angiographer is certain as to the site of extravasation. All doubt can be resolved by repeating the superior mesenteric arteriography with the patient in a right posterior oblique position. Another common error is confusing a prepyloric ulcer that is actively bleeding with a duodenal ulcer. This can also be resolved by repeating the injection with the patient in a left posterior oblique position.

The Precise Localization of Small Bowel Bleeding

During superior mesenteric arteriography it is usually very difficult to be sure which loop of small bowel is bleeding. Athanasoulis has successfully demonstrated the pathologic segment of bleeding in the small bowel by subselectively catheterizing the specific superior mesenteric arterial branch involved immediately prior to the laparotomy.[21] After the small bowel has been surgically exposed, methylene blue or Evans blue is injected into the catheter, resulting in a transient staining of the abnormal bowel. If the patient is actively bleeding at the time of the surgery, the isotopic scanning technique developed by Alavi et al.[15] can be used intraoperatively to localize the bleeding site in the small bowel. A technique that places platinum coils at the time of angiography has also been described.[22]

Angiographic Techniques for the Control of Gastrointestinal Bleeding

After angiography has demonstrated a bleeding site, the catheter can be used to diminish flow and thereby control bleeding. This can be accomplished pharmacologically by selectively infusing a vasoconstrictor such as vasopressin into the vessel supplying the bleeding point. Alternatively, the flow in the vessel can be mechanically obstructed by occluding the lumen with embolic materials.[23]

Pharmacologic Infusion

Vasopressin has had the greatest clinical acceptance as a safe and reliable vasoconstrictor for the angiographic

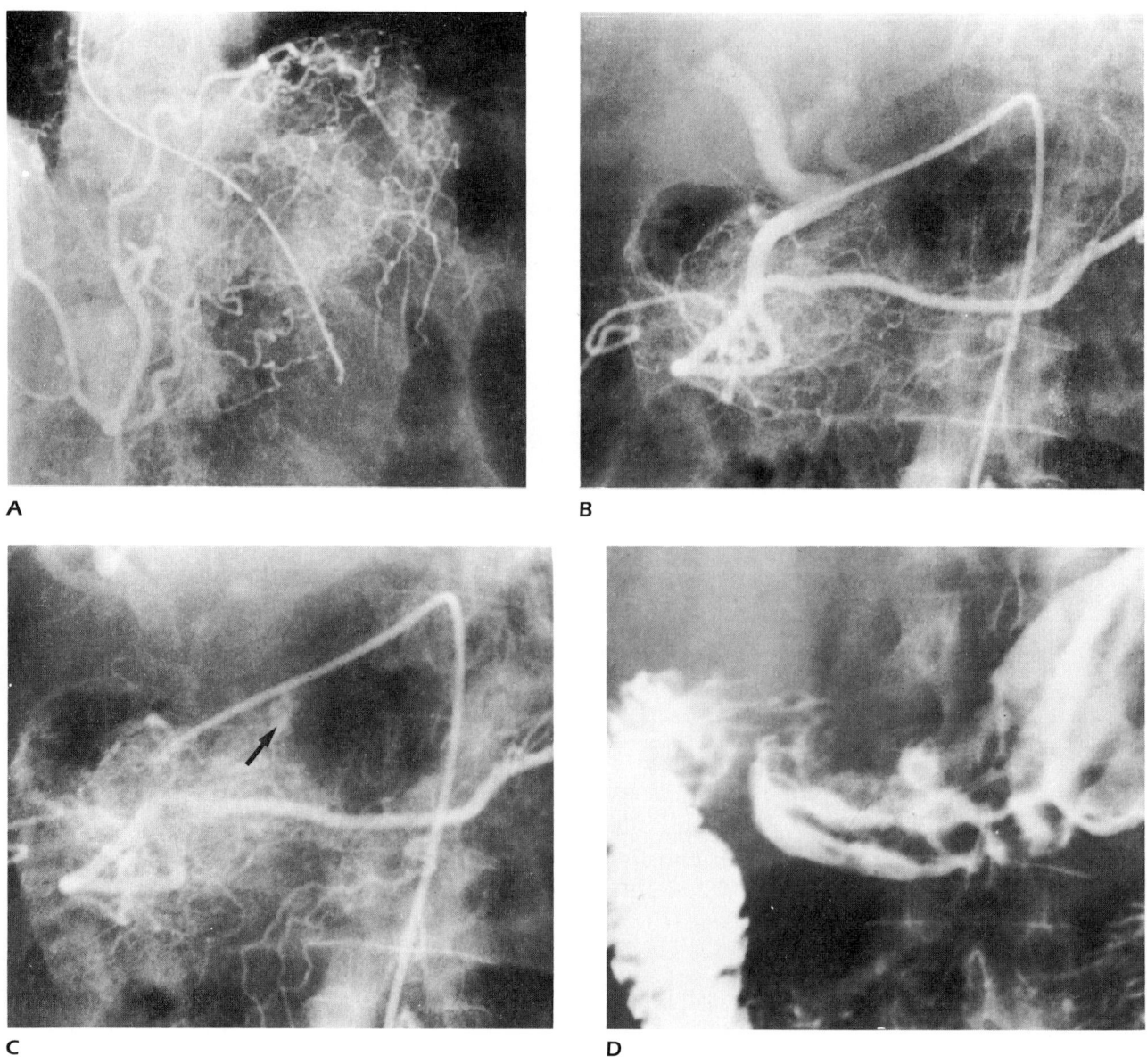

A

B

C

D

Figure 25-7. Fundal gastritis and actively bleeding lesser curvature peptic ulcer in a patient presenting with massive upper gastrointestinal bleeding. (A) Selective left gastric arteriography demonstrates marked hypervascularity in the gastric fundus without any evidence of discrete extravasation. The angiographic appearance is that of gastritis. (B) Early phase of a selective gastroduodenal arteriogram. (C) Late arterial phase of the gastroduodenal arteriogram demonstrates extravasation of contrast material (*arrow*) at the site of an antral ulcer that was seen on a prior upper gastrointestinal series. This bleeding was controlled by infusing vasopressin into the gastroduodenal artery. (D) Upper gastrointestinal series performed 2 weeks earlier demonstrates a lesser curvature ulcer.

control of gastrointestinal bleeding. The vasopressin used for this purpose is an aqueous solution of the pressor principle of the posterior pituitary gland and is relatively free of oxytocic principle. It causes contraction of the smooth muscles of the gastrointestinal tract as well as the vascular bed. These effects are not antagonized by adrenergic blocking agents or prevented by vascular denervation. The antidiuretic properties of vasopressin are important and well known.[24]

Since its introduction, vasopressin has been the preferred drug for transcatheter infusion therapy of gastrointestinal bleeding because of its significant and sustained reduction in splanchnic blood flow.[6-9] More recently the prostaglandins have been investigated but

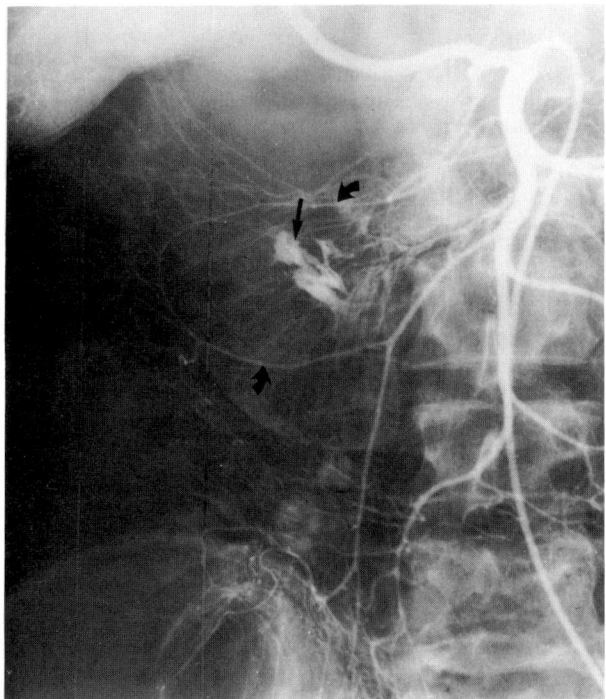

Figure 25-8. Bleeding duodenal ulcer that can be easily confused with bleeding in the proximal transverse colon, seen in an elderly man who presented with bright red rectal bleeding without any history of having vomited blood. Superior mesenteric arteriography demonstrates right-upper-quadrant extravasation (*straight arrow*) surrounded by the right colic (*lower curved arrow*) and the middle colic (*upper curved arrow*) arteries. In view of the clinical history and the proximity of the colic vessels, this duodenal bleed, which actually derived its blood supply from the inferior pancreaticoduodenal artery, could very easily be taken for a bleeding lesion in the proximal transverse colon.

to date have been untried in any large clinical series. Other vasoconstrictors such as norepinephrine were previously evaluated, but since they do not have sustained actions they have never become popular for this form of therapy.

Vasopressin's action is direct and immediate. A repeat arteriogram obtained 20 minutes after the infusion is begun will accurately determine the effectiveness of the therapy. Also, the dose of vasopressin can be modified so as to produce various degrees of vasoconstriction and thereby cause a more controlled and reversible ischemia than that of mechanical embolic therapy.

The selective infusion of vasopressin into a bleeding splanchnic vessel at the dose of 0.2 unit per minute is generally sufficient to stop gastrointestinal arterial or mucosal bleeding. Extensive experimental and clinical experience with this method has shown it to be safe when used in the gastrointestinal tract with little danger of significant organ ischemia. Even direct infusions into the hepatic[25,26] or splenic artery are well tolerated, so that infusion of the celiac axis is a viable alternative when more subselective catheterization of the left gastric artery is not technically possible.

The use of vasopressin is particularly successful in gastric mucosal bleeding when the left gastric artery is selectively infused. If the bleeding is coming from the small or large bowel, the selective infusion of the main superior or inferior mesenteric artery is generally sufficient, obviating subselective catheterization of the specific branch supplying the diseased segment.

Vasopressin diluted in saline or 5 percent dextrose and water is usually infused at a constant rate of 0.2 unit per minute for 20 minutes. Then a repeat arteriogram is obtained to evaluate the success of the therapy. If no further bleeding is demonstrated on the subsequent arteriogram, the infusion is continued at 0.2 unit per minute. If bleeding persists, however, the infusion can be increased to 0.4 unit per minute for another 20 minutes, followed by a repeat arteriogram. Failure to control the bleeding using 0.4 unit per minute indicates that the bleeding is unlikely to be controlled by vasopressin and that alternative methods of therapy should be considered. The angiogram obtained 20 minutes after the start of the infusion is analyzed to be sure that (1) moderate reduction in caliber of the infused vessels has occurred with preservation of good forward flow into the capillary and venous phases, (2) there is still filling of branches in the area of the bleeding point, and (3) there is no further extravasation.

If all these criteria are met, a pressure dressing is applied around the catheter entry site and the patient can be sent back to the intensive care unit for careful monitoring. If there is no clinical evidence of recurrent bleeding, the initial infusion rate is continued for 12 to 24 hours and then reduced by 50 percent for an additional 24 hours. The vasopressin infusion can then be stopped, but the catheter is generally kept in place and its patency maintained by the infusion of either normal saline or dextrose and water for another 12 hours. If the patient remains clinically stable, the catheter can then be removed. If there is recurrent bleeding as the vasoconstrictor dose is being tapered, a return to the initial dose rate usually controls it.

Since vasopressin is also a coronary artery vasoconstrictor, older patients may have nitroglycerin administered sublingually, intravenously, or, more commonly, by a skin patch.[27–31]

The intraarterial infusion of vasopressin at the doses described should be well tolerated by patients. After the initial cramping, which may last for 15 to 30 minutes, the infusion should be pain-free. If the patient complains of continuous abdominal pain during the course of the treatment, the infusion should be stopped and the patient reexamined. Pain may be a result of the catheter tip wedging into a small mesenteric arterial branch or the catheter having slipped into the abdominal aorta.

Role of Angiography in the Management of Esophageal Variceal Bleeding

Before its intraarterial use for gastrointestinal bleeding, vasopressin was injected intravenously in fairly large doses (20 units over 20 minutes) in an attempt to reduce portal pressure during the treatment of variceal bleeding.[32] Although bleeding esophageal varices cannot be constricted by direct infusion of pharmacologic agents, vasopressin is a potent splanchnic vasoconstrictor that causes significant reduction in mesenteric blood flow and consequently portal pressure. Since a relatively large dose of vasopressin given intravenously can be associated with side effects including decreased cardiac output and coronary artery vasoconstriction, the selective mesenteric artery infusion of vasopressin appeared to be an attractive alternative when it was first introduced in 1971.[33] This technique of continuously infusing the superior mesenteric artery with doses of vasopressin at 0.2 unit per minute was highly effective in controlling variceal bleeding and could be maintained for long periods of time without the development of tachyphylaxis. It was less efficacious in controlling bleeding in patients with advanced cirrhosis,[34] probably because of the increased arterialization of the portal system from the hepatic artery in patients with severe liver disease. In 1973 Barr et al.[35] showed that vasopressin, infused intravenously at the same low dose rates used in the superior mesenteric artery, reduces portal pressure by 40 to 50 percent. The systemic side effects with the low-dose intravenous infusions are about the same as those with the intraarterial infusion. Johnson and his associates[36] reported a randomized clinical study confirming that the systemic infusions of vasopressin at low dose rates were as effective as intraarterial infusions at the same rate in controlling variceal bleeding. Therefore, there appears to be no advantage to the selective intraarterial infusion of vasopressin into the superior mesenteric artery in the treatment of bleeding esophageal varices.

The administration of propanolol to lower the portosystemic gradient has been used as a medical therapy for the control of variceal bleeding.[37] Controlled trials have also shown the benefit of long-standing beta blockade for the prophylaxis of variceal bleeding in patients with portal hypertension.[38-40] Further techniques, including endoscopic, surgical, and transjugular intrahepatic portosystemic shunt (TIPS) for the treatment of bleeding esophageal varices, are described in detail in Chapter 33.

The percutaneous transhepatic approach to the portal vein was popularized in 1974 by Lunderquist.[41,42] This technique gives direct access to the portal vein and its tributaries. In the absence of marked ascites the procedure is not technically difficult, and the risk of bleeding from the point of entry is negligible. The more common complication involved in this study is the formation of thrombi in the portal vein as a result of the introduction of the catheter.[43,44] After the catheter has been introduced into the portal vein, the coronary vein can generally be selectively catheterized without too much difficulty. Various embolic materials can then be introduced into the coronary gastric veins to interrupt flow to the varices rapidly and to thereby control the bleeding (Fig. 25-9).[45]

Unfortunately, follow-up studies have shown that varices become patent within 1 to 4 weeks, and permanent occlusion seldom results.[46] Control of the bleeding by this technique is generally temporary and allows the patient to be stabilized and prepared for elective surgery. Various materials have been used for occlusion of the coronary veins, including Gelfoam, steel coils, balloons, and even bucrylate. At the present time, transhepatic variceal embolization is seldom used unless it is combined with transjugular intrahepatic portosystemic shunts (see Chapter 33).

Bleeding Mesenteric Varices

On the parietal surface of the gut, very small, delicate venous communications join the portal branches of the mesenteric vein to the systemic venous channels in the retroperitoneum and abdominal wall. Most varices from portal hypertension occur in the esophagus, rectum, and umbilicus. Some patients, however, have intestinal varices as a result of dilatation of these preexisting intestinal branches—particularly patients who have had previous surgery and have developed adhesions between loops of bowel and the abdominal wall. In patients with portal hypertension the varices may become exceedingly large and capable of bleeding in a manner similar to that of esophageal varices.[47]

Varicosities may also grow across adhesions in the pelvis, allowing for decompression of the portal vein by the gonadal systemic veins. The pelvic adhesions may be the result of either inflammatory disease or previous surgery (Fig. 25-10). Localized varicosities involving the superior mesenteric vein and its branches can occur secondary to pancreatitis or neoplasms of the pancreas that invade the superior mesenteric vein or to neoplasms of the gastrointestinal tract that secondarily occlude mesenteric veins (Fig. 25-11). Intestinal varices have been seen as a result of the extensive

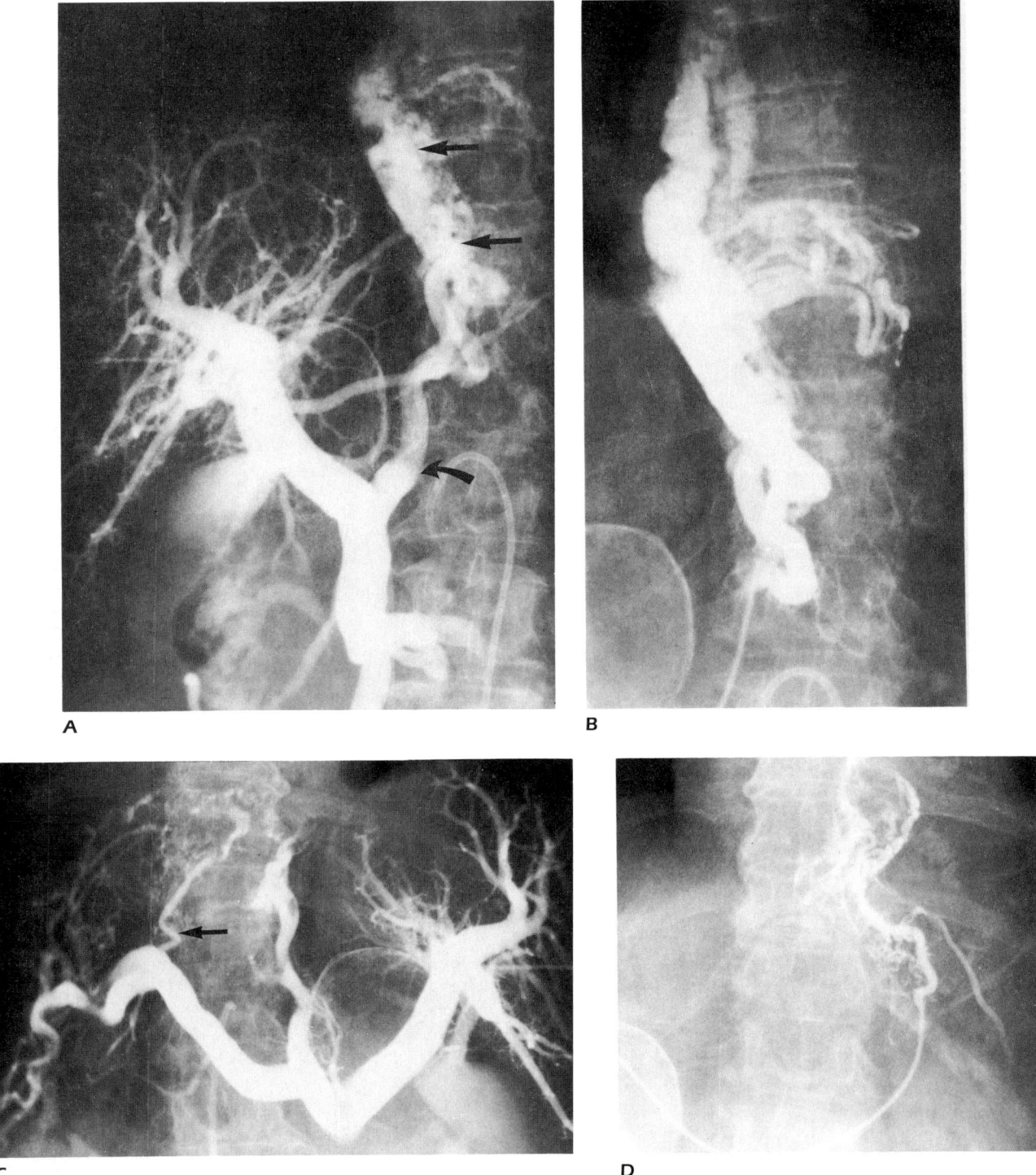

A

B

C

D

Figure 25-9. Bleeding esophageal varices treated by percutaneous transhepatic catheterization of the portal vein and embolization of the coronary veins. (A) Direct portography following percutaneous catheterization of the portal vein demonstrates a large coronary vein (*curved arrow*) supplying large gastric and esophageal varices (*straight arrows*). (B) Selective catheterization of the coronary vein defines with greater clarity the very large gastric and esophageal varices. (C) Following embolization of the coronary vein with Gelfoam, repeat direct portography demonstrates occlusion of the coronary vein. However, there is now filling of a short gastric vein (*arrow*) that appears to be supplying the gastric

varices. (D) Selective catheterization of the short gastric vein demonstrates that it is indeed feeding the gastric and esophageal varices. This vessel was embolized with Gelfoam. After embolization of the coronary and short gastric veins, the patient stopped bleeding. (E) Repeat direct portography performed several days later when the patient's bleeding recurred demonstrates that the coronary vein (*curved arrow*) has remained occluded, as has the short gastric vein (*straight arrow*). Large gastric and esophageal varices (*open arrows*) are now being supplied by multiple gastric veins originating from the splenic vein in the area of the hilus of the spleen.

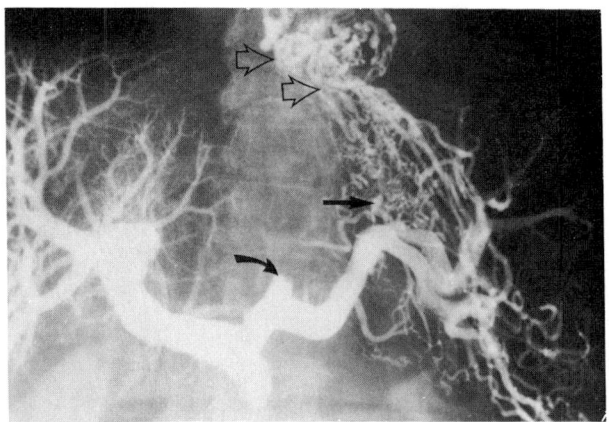

E   **Figure 25-9** (continued).

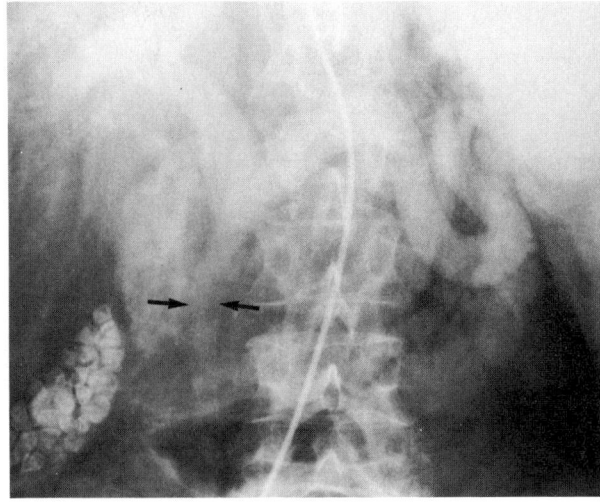

A

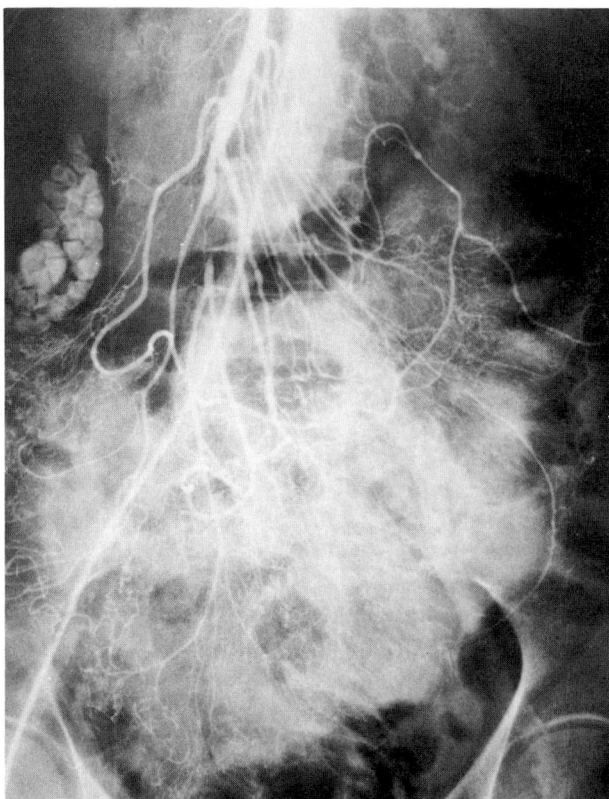

B

Figure 25-10. Bleeding mesenteric varices in a 68-year-old woman with cirrhosis referred for mesenteric arteriography because of lower gastrointestinal bleeding. (A) The venous phase of the selective splenic arteriogram demonstrates patency of the splenic and portal veins. There is retrograde filling of the superior mesenteric vein (*arrows*). (B) A selective superior mesenteric arteriogram fails to demonstrate evidence of an arterial or mucosal bleeding site. (C) During the venous phase of the superior mesenteric arteriogram, retrograde flow is seen in the superior mesenteric vein draining into large pelvic varicosities (*solid arrows*). The pelvic varices

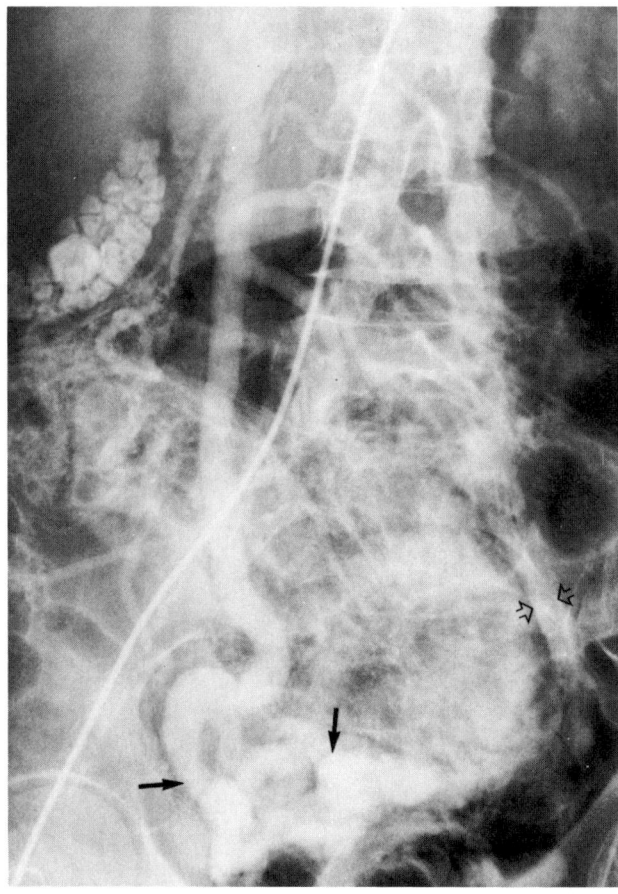

C

decompress the mesenteric vein by the left gonadal vein (*open arrows*). The patient had had pelvic surgery many years earlier. After this examination, the patient was reexplored, and at surgery adhesions containing large varicosities were seen extending between the pelvic organs and the ileal loops of the small bowel. In the resected specimen of the ileum, one of the large mucosal veins was bleeding as a result of an overlying area of mucosal ulceration.

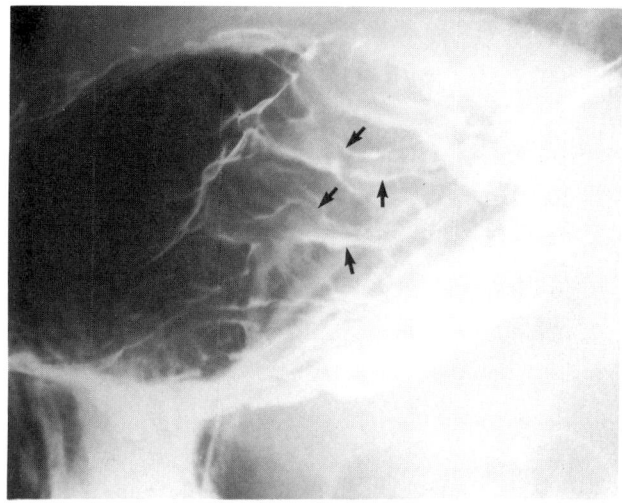

A

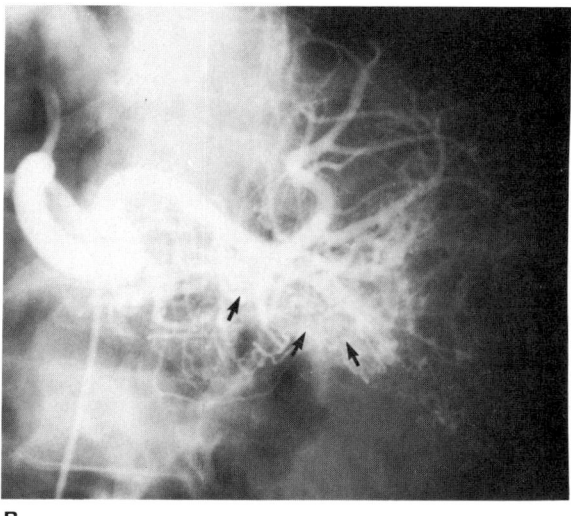

B

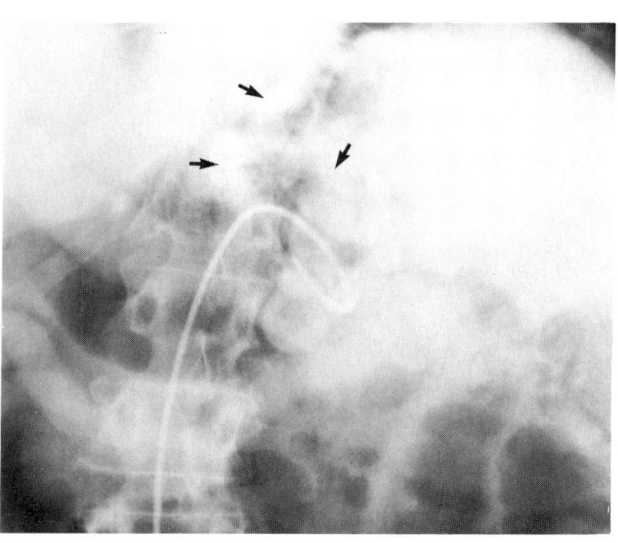

C

Figure 25-11. A 66-year-old man presented with a history of hematemesis. (A) An upper gastrointestinal series with the patient in a steep right posterior oblique position demonstrates gastric varices (*arrows*) without any evidence of esophageal varices. This picture suggested splenic vein obstruction; the patient was referred for angiography. (B) Selective splenic arteriography demonstrates tumor vessels in the distal portion of the pancreas extending into the hilus of the spleen (*arrows*). (C) In the venous phase of the splenic arteriogram, multiple gastric varices (*arrows*) are seen draining into a patent portal vein. The patient had had a left nephrectomy 15 years earlier for a renal cell carcinoma, and the tumor disclosed in the tail of the pancreas on the present examination was renal cell carcinoma metastatic to the pancreas, causing splenic vein occlusion and gastric varices.

desmoplastic reaction that occurs in the root of the mesentery secondary to carcinoid tumors.[48]

Arterial Embolization

Where arterial or capillary bleeding cannot be stopped pharmacologically with the infusion of vasopressin, an alternative approach is to attempt to occlude the supplying artery selectively. The catheter is positioned as close as possible to the site of extravasation, and embolic material is carefully injected through the catheter to block the artery. The very rich collateral arterial supply to the stomach and duodenum usually protects these organs from significant ischemia and infarction after embolization of the bleeding vessel (Fig. 25-12).

Although this method is frequently successful in stopping the bleeding, therapeutic failures may arise

when bleeding takes place in an area that has a dual arterial blood supply.[49] The occlusion of only one limb of such a vascular arcade may result in failure to control bleeding because the abnormal segment continues to be supplied by a second arterial limb (Fig. 25-13). Successful control, therefore, may require individual treatment of each limb, whether by vasopressin infusion or occlusion (Fig. 25-14). A control arteriogram is essential to confirm cessation of previously demonstrated bleeding. If a dual blood supply exists, it may be necessary to embolize both sides of an arcade. Examples of vascular arcades that may be significant in the angiographic management of bleeding include (1) middle colic–left colic artery anastomosis at the splenic flexure of the colon, (2) superior pancreaticoduodenal–inferior pancreaticoduodenal arterial arcades in the duodenum, (3) left gastric–right gastric arcade along the lesser curvature of the stomach, and (4) right gastroepiploic–left gastroepiploic arterial communications along the greater curvature of the stomach.

Various embolic materials have been tried in a search for a safe, effective, and simple agent.[50] Gel-

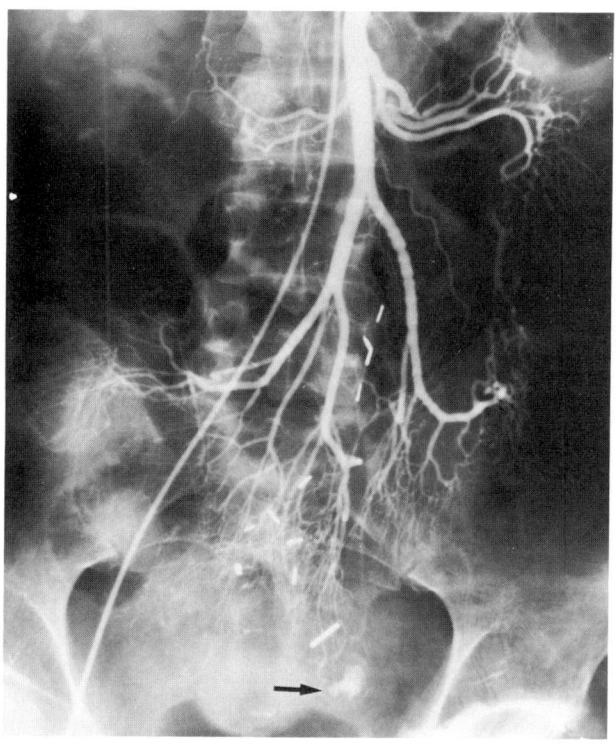

A

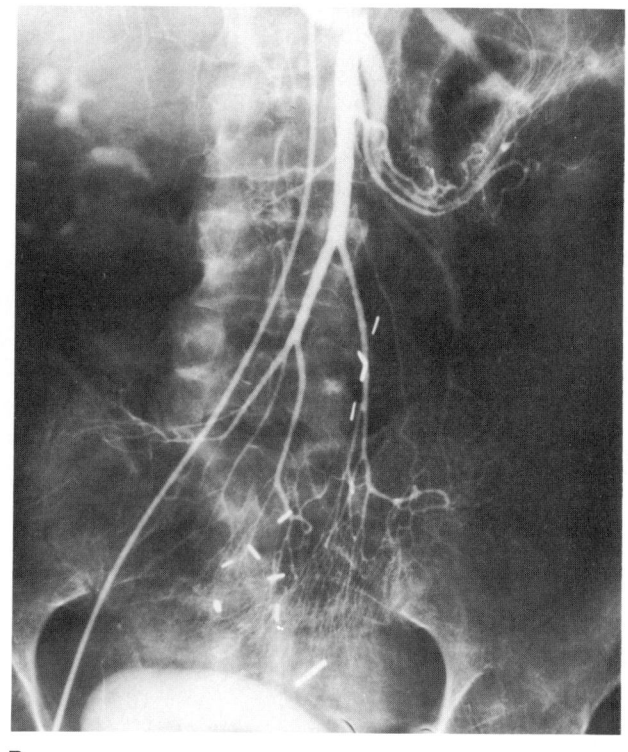

B

Figure 25-12. Bleeding ileitis in a patient with a long-standing history of ileitis and multiple surgical procedures, referred to angiography because of lower gastrointestinal bleeding. Since the pelvic ileal loops were bound together by multiple adhesions, the patient was a very poor surgical candidate. (A) Selective superior mesenteric arteriography demonstrates extravasation of contrast material (*arrow*) from one of the pelvic ileal branches. (B) Bleeding was controlled by the infusion of 0.2 unit of vasopressin per minute into the superior mesenteric artery. There was, however, great difficulty in weaning the patient from the vasopressin, and each time the dose was reduced, the bleeding recurred. (C) Because of the desire of the clinicians to avoid surgery, selective embolization of the bleeding vessel was attempted. The catheter was advanced into the small jejunal artery (*solid arrow*) supplying the bleeding site, and a small hand injection of contrast material once again shows extravasation (*open arrow*). (D) After embolization with a small Gelfoam plug, the bleeding was controlled and repeat arteriography with the catheter partially withdrawn shows very selective occlusion of the small ileal branch (*arrow*). The patient did not rebleed and was discharged from the hospital without having to undergo an operation.

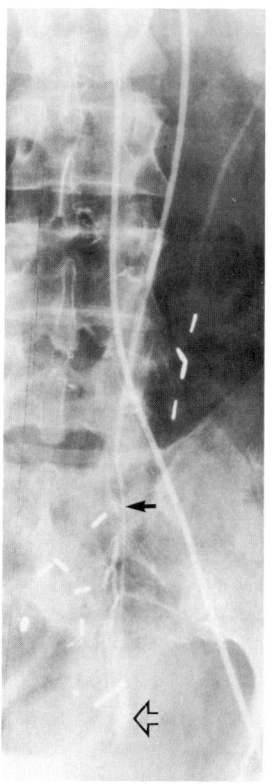

C

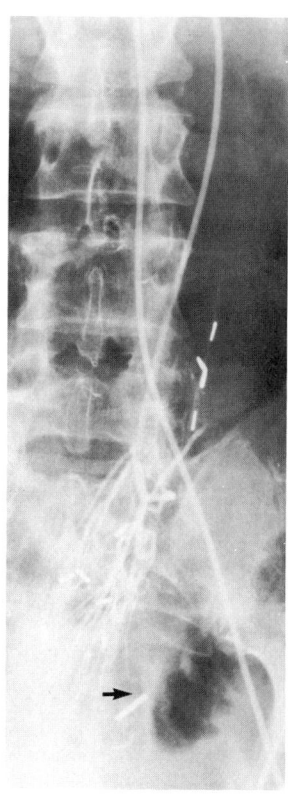

D

foam, a slowly absorbed gelatin sponge, is the most widely used embolic material in the treatment of gastrointestinal bleeding.[51] Although autologous blood clot has the advantage of providing very small emboli that lodge peripherally and thereby lessen the chance of collateral bleeding, this form of control tends to be only temporary because of lysis of the clot, generally within 12 to 14 hours.[52,53] Clots that are pretreated

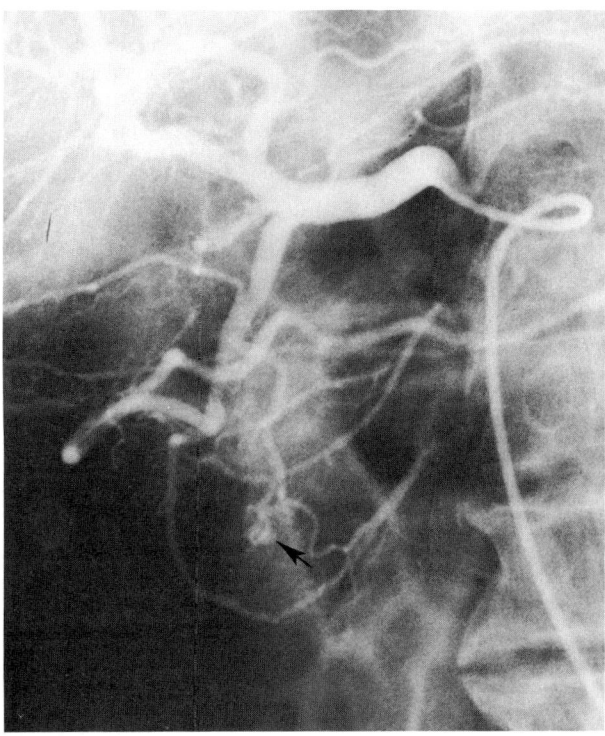

A

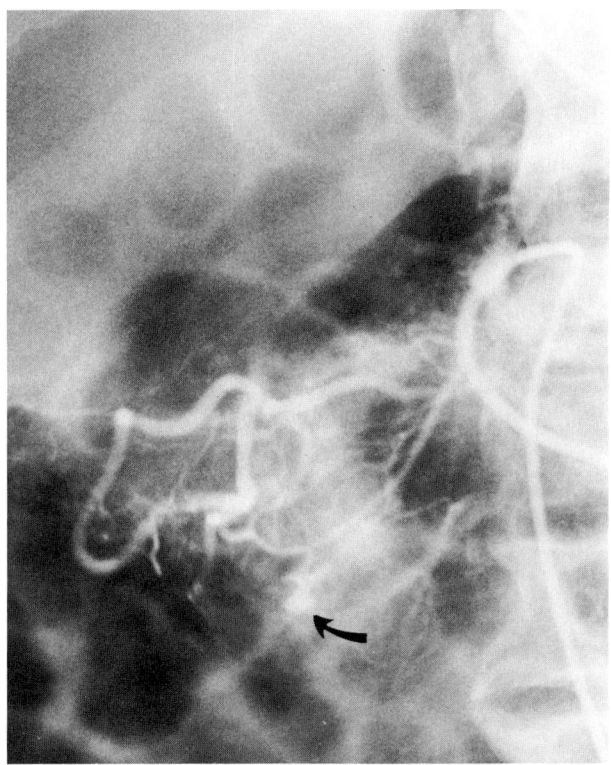

B

Figure 25-13. Dual blood supply of a bleeding duodenal ulcer. (A) After selective hepatic arteriography, extravasation in the duodenum (*arrow*) can be identified as coming from a small branch of the superior pancreaticoduodenal artery. (B) Selective inferior pancreaticoduodenal arteriography

demonstrates the same point of extravasation (*arrow*). In cases like these, infusions into both superior and inferior pancreaticoduodenal arteries may be necessary if angiographic control is attempted.

Figure 25-14. Bleeding duodenal ulcer controlled by angiographically treating both limbs of an arcade. (A) Selective gastroduodenal arteriogram demonstrates massive extravasation of contrast material (*arrows*) into the duodenum from a branch of the superior pancreaticoduodenal artery. (B) A balloon catheter (*curved arrow*) was placed through the angiographic catheter and is occluding the gastroduodenal artery. A second catheter was placed in the inferior pancreat-

icoduodenal branch of the superior mesenteric artery (*straight arrow*), and on injection of this vessel, bleeding is once again demonstrated in the duodenal ulcer (*open arrow*). (C) Embolization of the inferior pancreaticoduodenal artery with small Gelfoam plugs successfully interrupted the inferior pancreaticoduodenal arcade, and the bleeding was controlled.

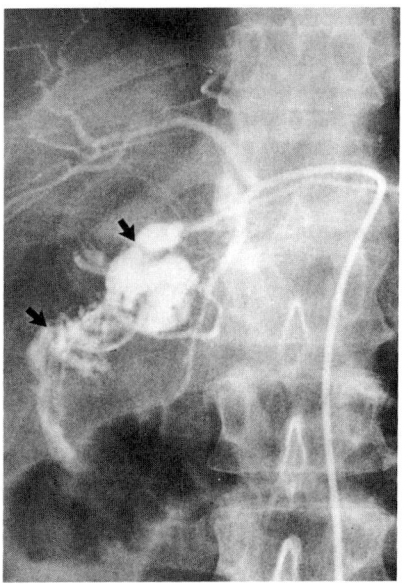

A

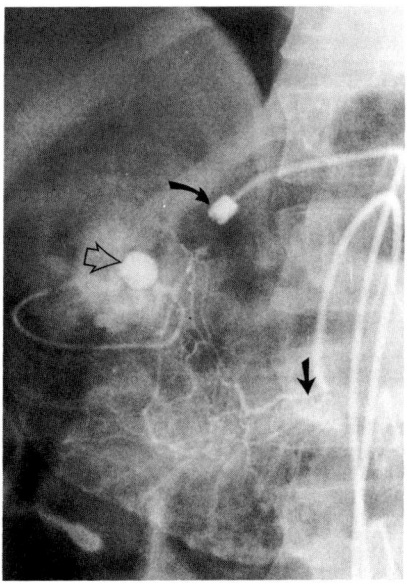

B

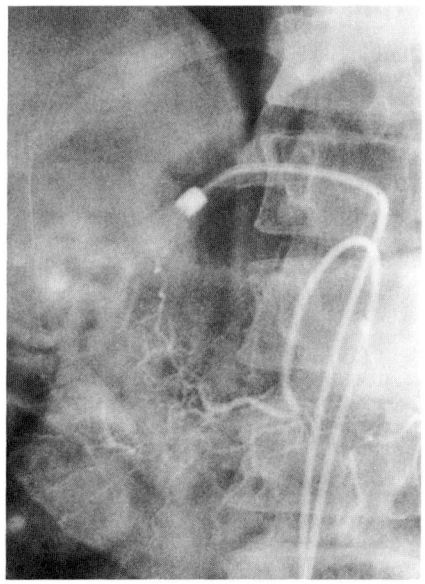

C

with thrombin, aminocaproic acid, or oxidized cellulose (Oxycel) persist for a longer time. Ivalon particles provide even longer-lasting occlusions but are more difficult to use.[54–57]

Rapidly setting tissue adhesives such as isobutyl 2-cyanoacrylate (bucrylate) produce long-term occlusion.[58,59] These rapidly setting glues are liquid monomers that undergo rapid polymerization and solidification when they come in contact with charged ions in the blood. They are difficult to use and must be administered through a coaxial catheter system.

Double-lumen balloon-tipped catheters can be used for the temporary control of gastrointestinal bleeding.[60,61] They can also be of great value with injection of embolic material, preventing possible reflux of emboli to more distant sites.[62] Small detachable balloons are at present under clinical trial.[63] These devices have some advantage in that they are flow-directed and can be retrieved and their position altered if they are not producing the desired effect. They give the angiographer much more control in occluding a vessel, and the danger of inadvertent occlusion, always associated with emboli, is thereby eliminated. One disadvantage of balloon-tipped catheters is that they occlude bleeding vessels much more proximally than do injected embolic materials. Because of the hemodynamics of bleeding in the presence of a rich collateral blood flow, distal occlusion is a desirable feature.

Wool- or nylon-tufted stainless steel coils have been successful in permanently occluding large vessels where Gelfoam emboli are not suitable. Although the original Gianturco coils[64] had to be delivered through a relatively large Teflon catheter, smaller coils are now available that can be delivered through smaller, more versatile catheters (Fig. 25-15); thus their field of application is extended.

In general, mechanical embolization techniques should be used only in patients in whom pharmacologic control has failed or in whom prolonged catheter infusions are not practical. Experience has shown that embolization is much more likely than vasopressin to control duodenal bleeding ulcer disease. However, embolization of the superior or inferior mesenteric arteries is controversial because of the danger of bowel infarction.

Angiographic Control of Gastrointestinal Hemorrhage from Specific Arterial Sites

Esophageal Bleeding

Esophageal tumors, esophagitis, and hiatus hernia rarely cause massive bleeding. When this does occur, however, angiography is able to demonstrate the

Figure 25-15. Hemorrhagic gastritis treated with Gelfoam embolization and proximal occlusion of the left gastric artery with a nylon-tufted steel coil. (A) The patient was referred for angiography because of upper gastrointestinal bleeding following pancreatic surgery. Selective left gastric arteriography demonstrates a marked hyperemia involving the entire upper portion of the stomach consistent with the diagnosis of hemorrhagic gastritis. Oozing around the catheter site in the groin made it impossible to maintain a continuous infusion of vasopressin, and embolization techniques were therefore resorted to. (B) Gelfoam pellets were embolized into the left gastric artery, and the proximal portion of the left gastric artery was occluded by inserting a nylon-tufted Gianturco coil (*arrows*).

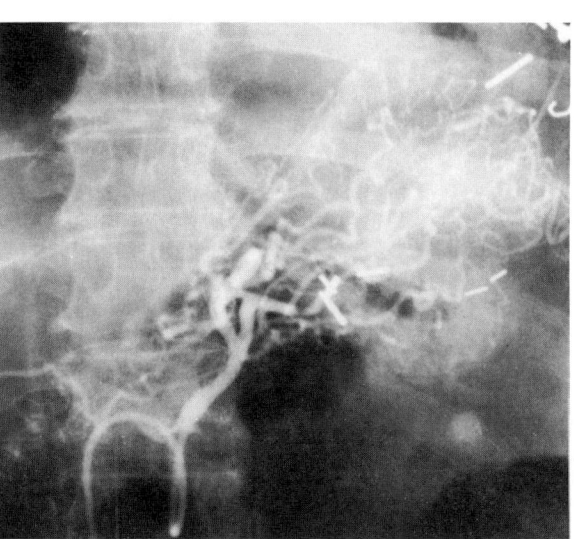

A

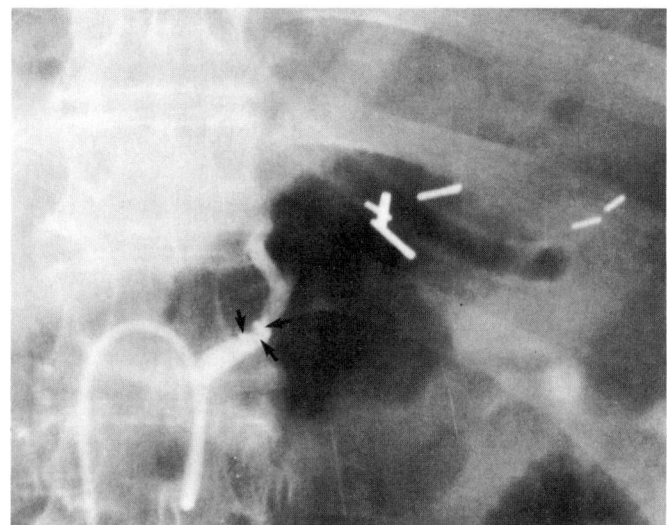

B

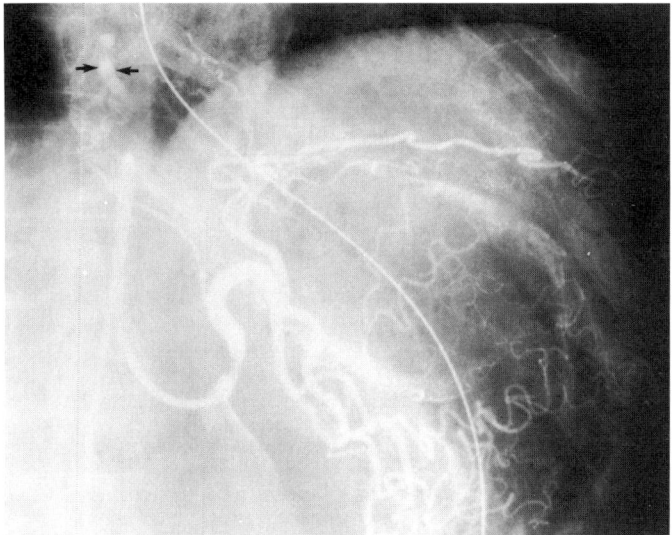

A

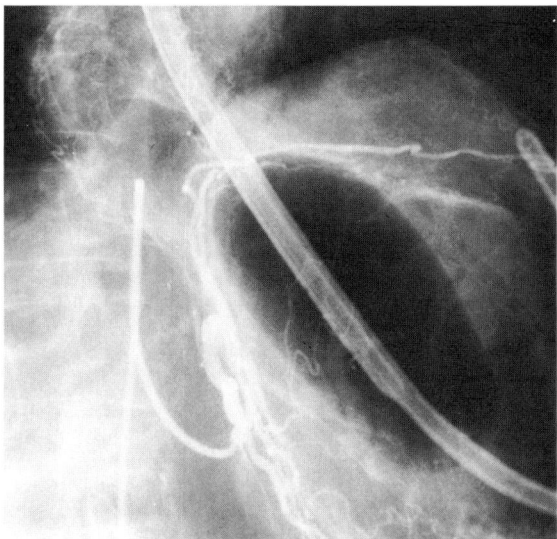

B

Figure 25-16. A 91-year-old man with a long history of a hiatus hernia was referred for arteriography because of massive hematemesis. (A) A selective left gastric arteriogram demonstrates arterial extravasation in the distal esophagus (*arrows*). In addition, there is marked hyperemia of the entire stomach, consistent with a gastritis. (B) Selective left gastric arteriography during infusion of 0.2 unit per minute of vasopressin shows vasoconstriction of the peripheral branches of the left gastric artery and cessation of the bleeding in the distal esophagus. The bleeding was controlled in this patient, and surgery was not required.

bleeding site if the bleeding segment of the esophagus derives its blood supply from branches of the left gastric artery (Fig. 25-16). Bleeding of the upper and middle portions of the esophagus generally cannot be angiographically demonstrated because of the difficulty associated with catheterizing the appropriate vessels. If the bleeding site can be identified angiographically, the selective arterial infusion of vasopressin almost always controls the bleeding. Mallory-Weiss tears at the cardioesophageal junction as well as bleeding esophagitis are readily responsive to vasopressin infusions (Fig. 25-17) and embolic therapy.

Gastric Mucosal Hemorrhage

Acute ulcerations of the stomach and duodenum are frequently the cause of significant gastrointestinal bleeding. These ulcerations may be part of any of the following conditions: (1) stress ulcerations, (2) drug- or alcohol-induced gastritis, (3) idiopathic gastritis, (4) Curling ulcers seen in burn patients, and (5) uremia.

These lesions are being seen less frequently than in the past because of the aggressive use of histamine H2 receptor antagonists by surgeons and gastroenterologists. When gastric acidity is decreased, patients are less prone to develop mucosal ulcerations. When ulcerations do occur, they tend to be acute and multiple

and may be the cause of massive gastrointestinal bleeding.

Patients who develop ulcerations of the gastrointestinal tract following severe physiologic stress usually have ulcers in the stomach, but in some cases they extend up to the esophagus or into the duodenum. The second and third portions of the duodenum may be another site of mucosal ulcerations, and in some patients these may be the only ulcers that are actively bleeding (Fig. 25-18). For reasons that are not completely understood, the ulcers in the second and third portions of the duodenum are seen more often in patients who have had recent cardiac surgery and who are receiving digitalis.[65]

The angiographic appearance of bleeding stress ulceration may be that of massive extravasation in an otherwise normal-appearing stomach (see Fig. 25-3) or duodenum. The bleeding of gastritis, on the other hand, may appear as multiple areas of extravasation in a vascular bed that is diffusely hyperemic (Fig. 25-19).[6]

Since the therapy in all these lesions is directed toward achieving hemostasis, the intraarterial infusion of vasopressin is a very attractive alternative to surgery when patients do not stop bleeding on medical therapy. Despite the theory that stress ulceration is ischemic in origin, experience has been that stress ulcers as well as ulcerations associated with gastritis heal during the infusion of vasopressin, and rebleeding usually

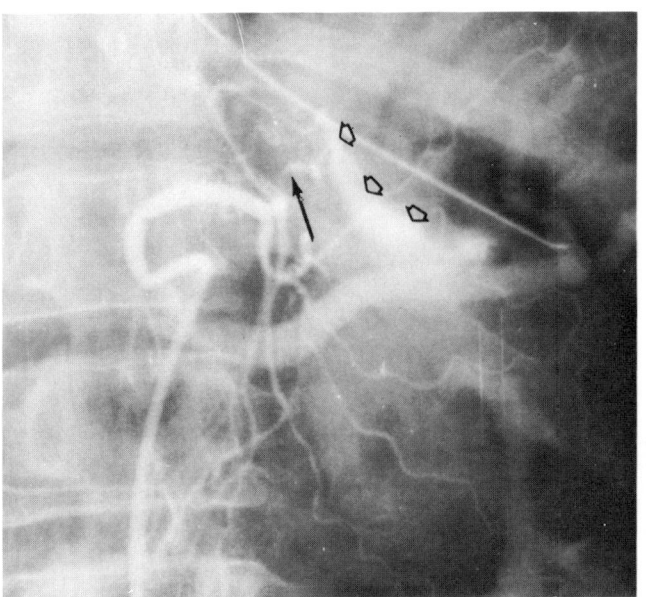

A

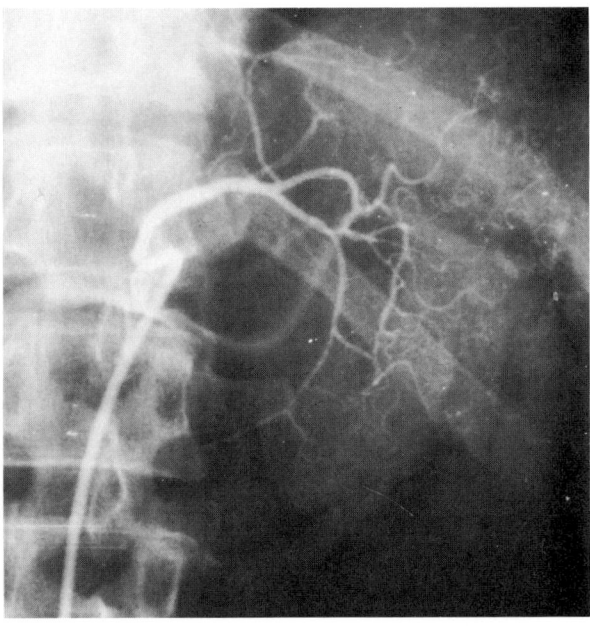

B

Figure 25-17. Bleeding Mallory-Weiss tear at the cardio-esophageal junction controlled by the infusion of vasopressin into the left gastric artery. (A) Selective left gastric arteriography demonstrates extravasation of contrast material from a branch of the left gastric artery (*solid arrow*) into the stomach (*open arrows*). (B) During the infusion of 0.2 unit per minute of vasopressin, repeat arteriogram shows opacifica-tion of the left gastric artery and its branches without any further evidence of extravasation. The patient had an un-eventful recovery with no recurrences of hemorrhage. (From Baum S, Nusbaum M. The control of gastrointestinal hemorrhage by selective mesenteric arterial infusion of vasopressin. Radiology 1971;98:497. Used with permission.)

does not occur. The selective infusion of vasopressin into the left gastric artery has been reported to control bleeding of this sort in more than 80 percent of cases.[66] Of this group about 15 percent of patients have recurrent bleeding after the initial control, and these patients are suitable candidates for repeat treatment.

Peptic Ulceration of the Stomach and Duodenum

Bleeding that is due to an erosion into a small branch vessel can generally be controlled by vasopressin infusion of the left gastric, gastroduodenal, or superior pancreaticoduodenal arteries. Arterial embolization is also successful in these cases. If there is erosion into a main vessel such as a gastroduodenal artery, vasopressin infusion has usually been unsuccessful,[67,68] and in this setting embolization of the bleeding vessel may be necessary to achieve hemostasis (Figs. 25-20 to 25-22).[52]

In most peptic ulcer patients angiography is only a temporary measure to control bleeding and is clearly not the definitive form of therapy. Surgery is still required to deal with the basic problem and prevent recurrence of the disease. Excessive time should not, therefore, be spent on the angiographic procedure unless the patient is unsuitable for surgery. The introduction of histamine antagonists such as cimetidine for the treatment of peptic ulcer disease has caused a reevaluation of the indications for surgery.[69] The angiographic control of bleeding coupled with cimetidine therapy may in fact provide the definitive answer in some patients.

Anastomotic Ulcers

Selective mesenteric arteriography can be used to demonstrate bleeding from an anastomotic ulcer at the site of gastrojejunostomy.[70,71] The bleeding site is usually supplied by a jejunal branch of the superior mesenteric artery (Fig. 25-23) and can frequently be controlled by infusing vasopressin into the superior mesenteric artery. After gastric surgery many collateral vessels are ligated, possibly making embolic therapy dangerous. In addition, embolization requires subselective catheterization of the appropriate feeding vessel, which is difficult to accomplish in this particular group of patients.

Text continues on page 411

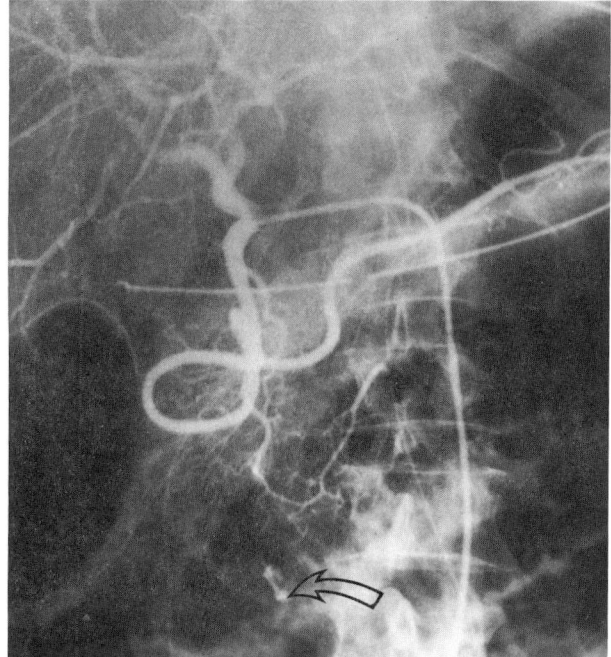

A

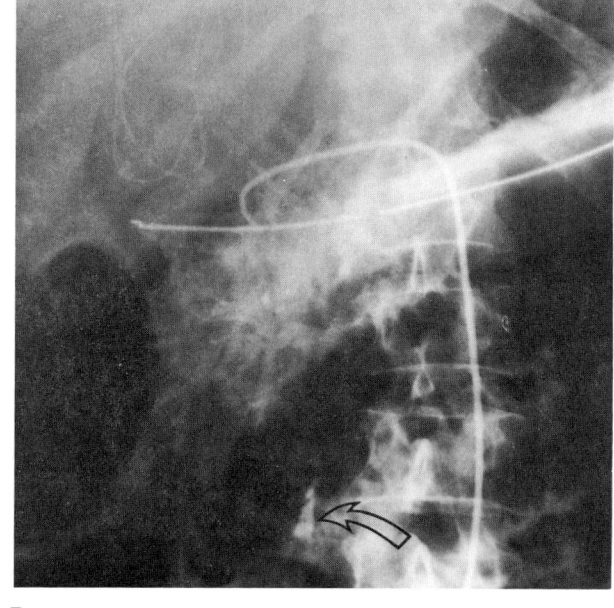

B

C

Figure 25-18. Bleeding stress ulcer at the junction of the second and third portions of the duodenum. (A) Selective gastroduodenal arteriogram of a patient presenting with massive upper gastrointestinal bleeding 4 days after aortic valve replacement demonstrates arterial bleeding at the junction of the second and third portions of the duodenum (*arrow*). (B) During the late capillary phase of the study, persistent contrast material remains (*arrow*), outlining mucosal folds. (C) Control of the bleeding stress ulcer was obtained by the infusion of 0.2 unit of vasopressin per minute into the gastroduodenal artery. Repeat arteriography shows peripheral vasoconstriction without any evidence of extravasation. The patient had no further clinical evidence of bleeding from this site.

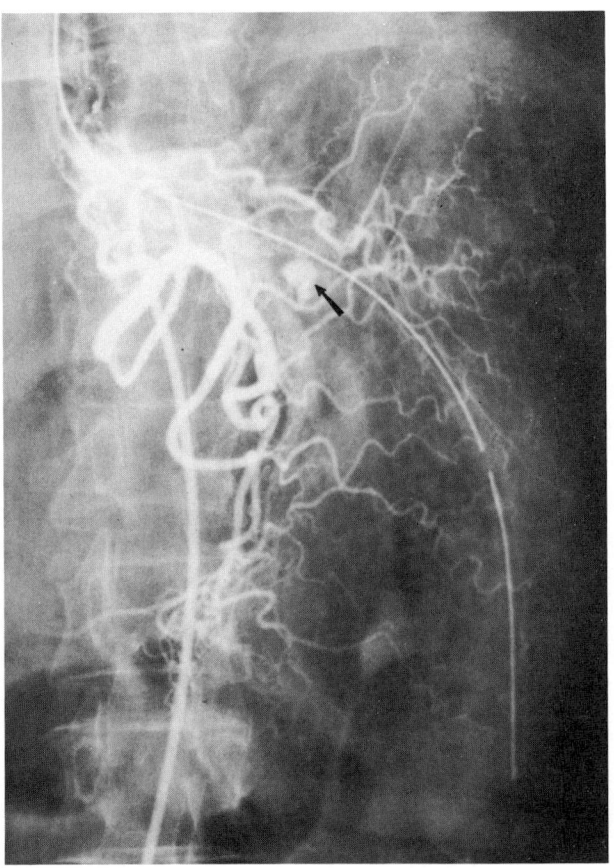

A

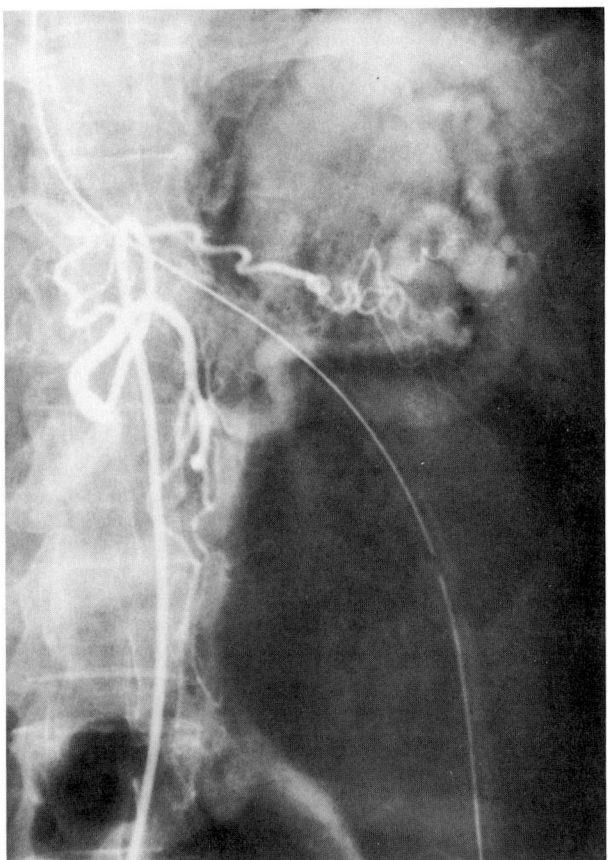

B

Figure 25-19. Bleeding hemorrhagic gastritis in a 60-year-old woman who had had multiple surgical procedures for regional enteritis. Postoperatively the patient began to bleed massively from the gastrointestinal tract. Endoscopy showed several ulcers in the gastric fundus. (A) Selective left gastric arteriography demonstrates extravasation from a branch of the left gastric artery (*arrow*). (B) Repeat left gastric arteriography during the infusion of 0.2 unit per minute of vasopressin shows constriction of peripheral arterial branches without further evidence of extravasation. The infusion was continued for 2 days, and the bleeding was clinically controlled.

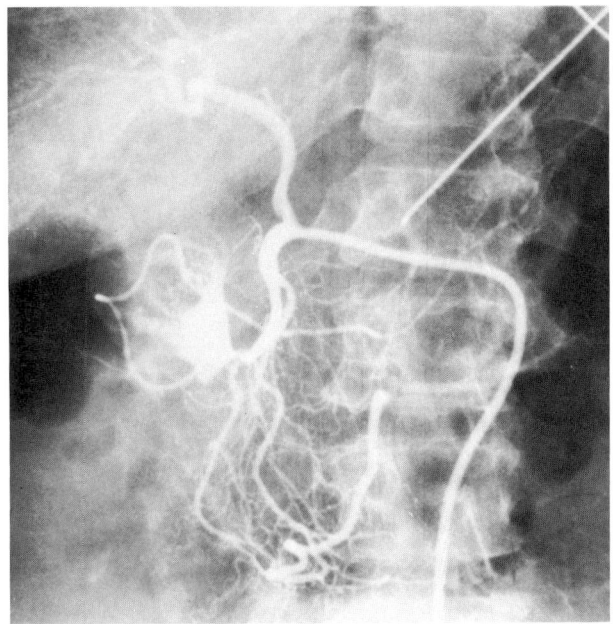

A

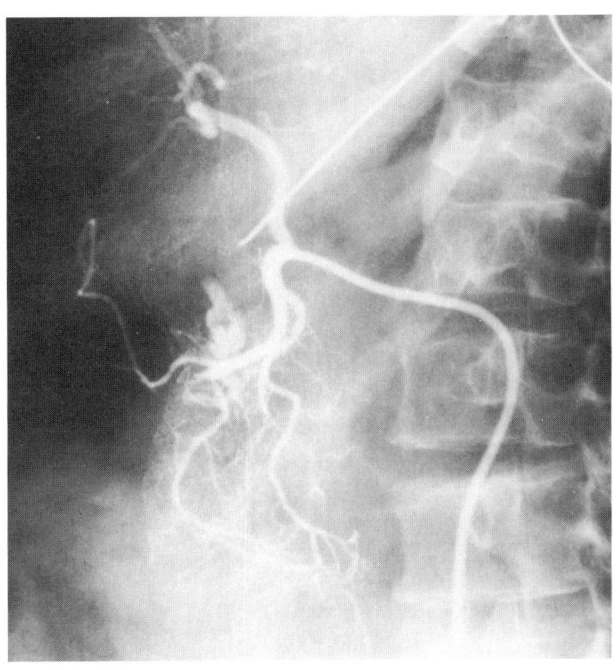

B

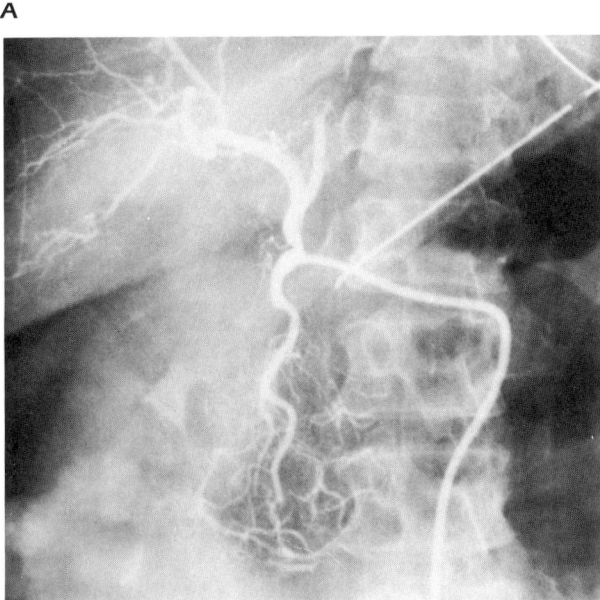

C

Figure 25-20. Actively bleeding duodenal ulcer controlled by the selective embolization of a small amount of autologous blood clot. (A) Arterial phase of a selective gastroduodenal arteriogram shows massive extravasation from a branch of the superior pancreaticoduodenal artery. (B) Infusion of 0.4 unit per minute of vasopressin was unable to stop the bleeding clinically, and on the repeat arteriogram continued extravasation can be seen. (C) Several strands of autologous clot were embolized into both the anterior and the posterior pancreaticoduodenal arcades, thereby disrupting the normal collateralization from the inferior pancreaticoduodenal artery. In addition, the superior pancreaticoduodenal artery was occluded. The bleeding stopped clinically, and a repeat arteriogram failed to show any evidence of extravasation.

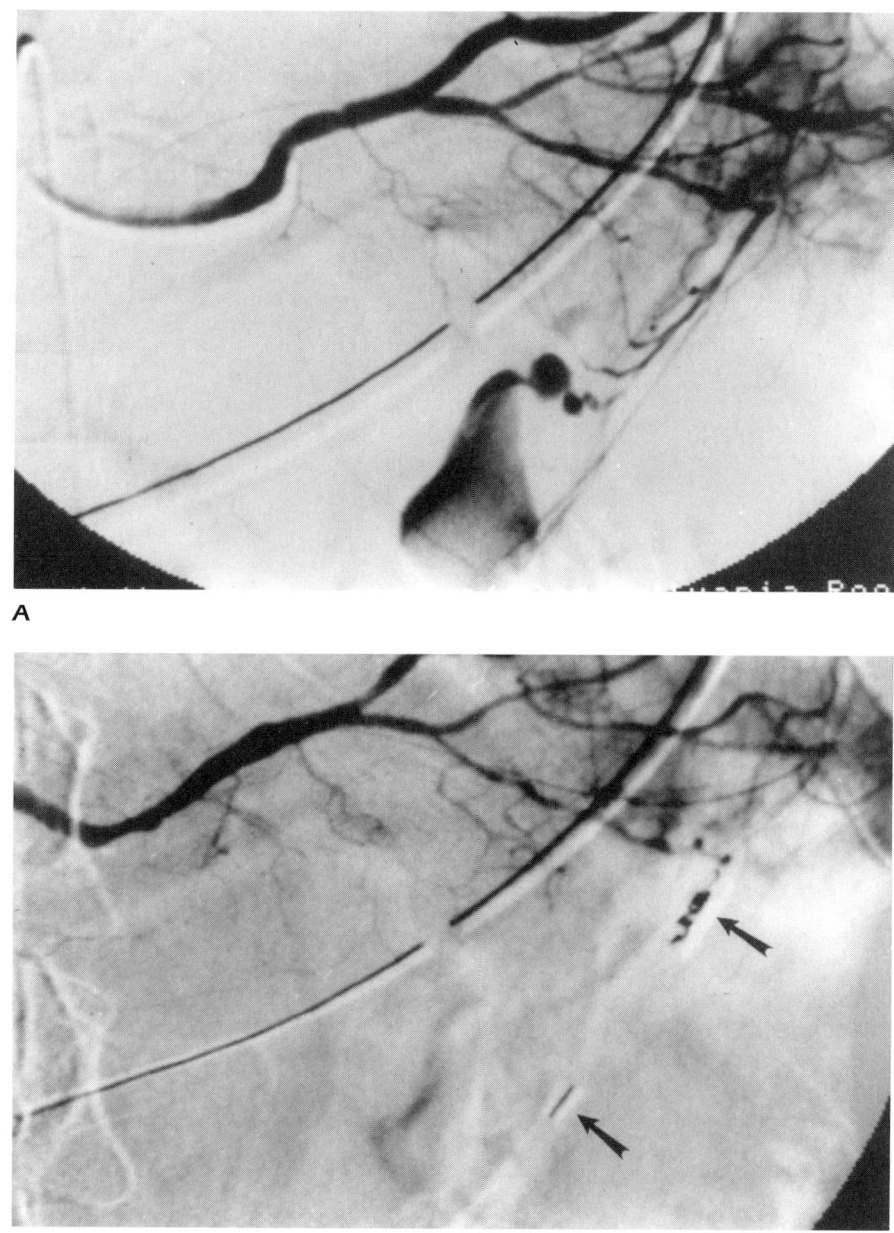

A

B

Figure 25-21. Upper gastrointestinal bleeding from a greater curvature ulcer. The patient had had previous surgery and the gastroduodenal artery was ligated. (A) Selective splenic arteriogram shows massive contrast extravasation from the left gastroepiploic artery. (B) Splenic arteriogram after embolization fails to demonstrate any extravasation. A microcatheter was used to deposit microcoils (*arrows*) in the gastroepiploic artery proximal and distal to the bleeding site. The bleeding stopped and did not recur.

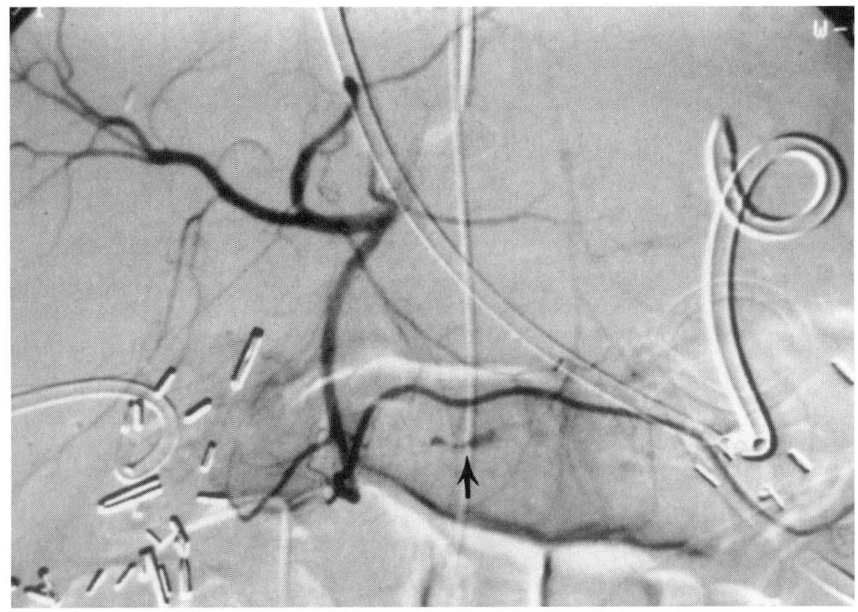

A

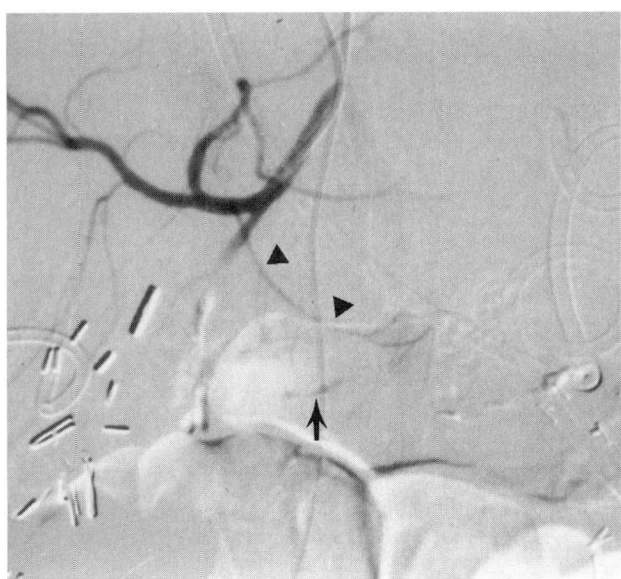

B

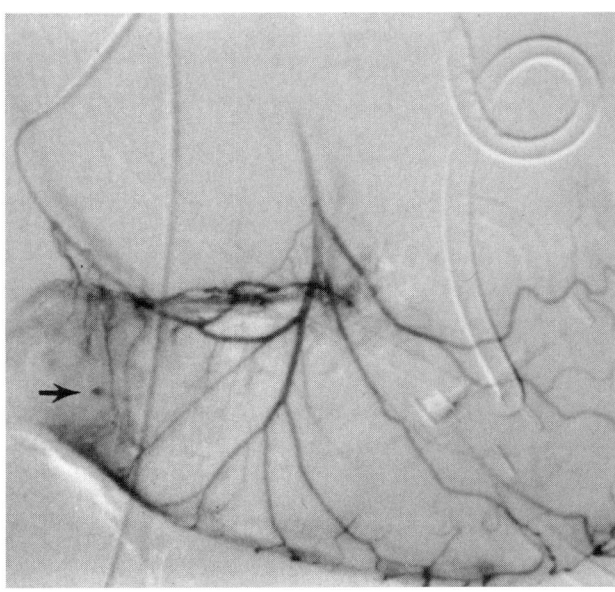

C

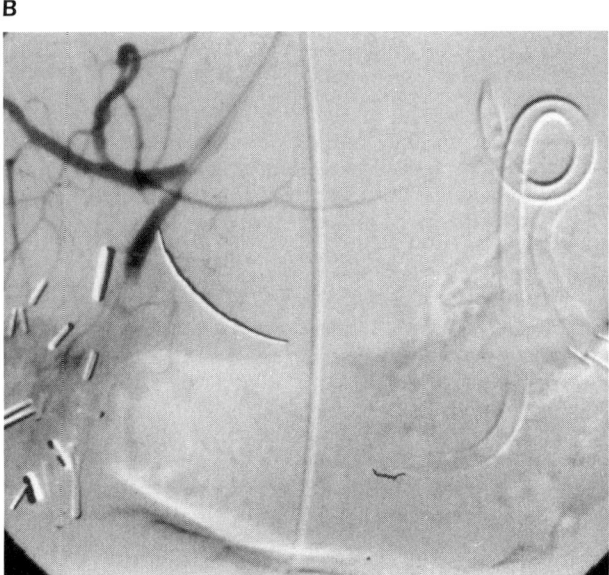

D

Figure 25-22. Upper gastrointestinal bleeding from a pre-pyloric ulcer. (A) Selective gastroduodenal arteriogram shows a bleeding site adjacent to the right gastroepiploic artery (*arrow*). (B) Gastroduodenal arteriogram after emboli-zation of the gastroduodenal artery with Gelfoam shows per-sistent extravasation of contrast (*arrow*) from branches of the right gastric artery (*arrowheads*). (C) Superselective right gastric arteriogram via a 3 French catheter shows the bleed-ing site (*arrow*) and anastomosis to the left gastric artery. (D) After embolization of the right gastric artery proximal and distal to branches feeding the bleeding site, a gastroduo-denal arteriogram shows no further bleeding.

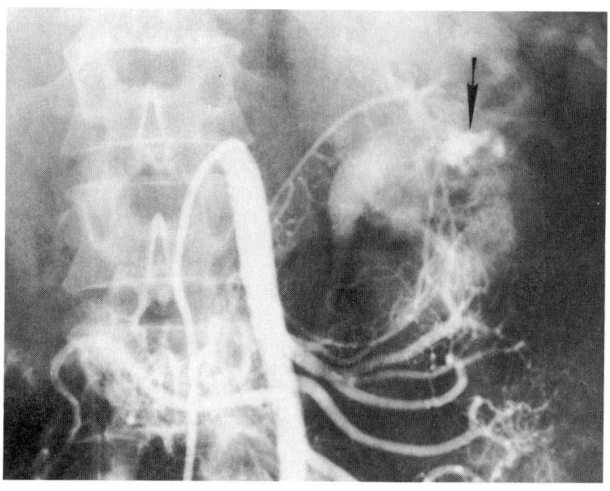

A

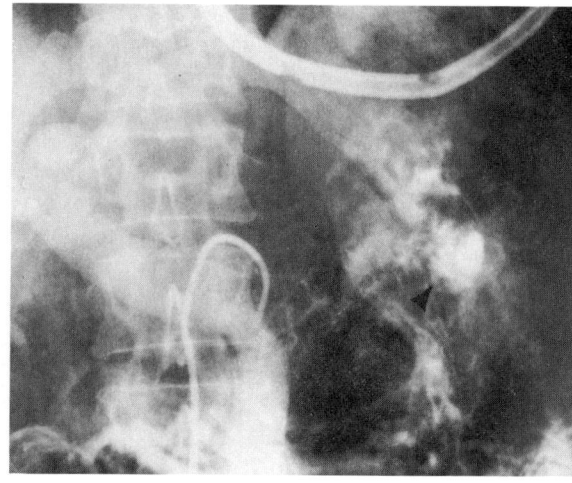

B

Figure 25-23. Bleeding anastomotic ulcer at the site of a Billroth II anastomosis. (A) Selective superior mesenteric arteriography demonstrates extravasation of contrast material (*arrow*) from a jejunal branch at the site of the gastrojejunostomy. (B) Venous phase of the examination shows persistence of contrast material within the jejunum (*arrowhead*). (C) Control of the bleeding was achieved by infusion of 0.2 unit per minute of vasopressin into the superior mesenteric artery.

Postoperative Hemorrhage

Bleeding caused by indwelling tubes or slipped ligatures can often be definitively controlled by vasopressin infusion or embolic therapy, thus avoiding the inconvenience and hazard of reexploration and major abdominal surgery.[72] Further, since most of the patients do not have an underlying disease responsible for the bleeding, the therapy is directed only at controlling the hemorrhage. This method of treatment has also proved helpful after hemorrhage from endoscopic biopsies during colonoscopy (Fig. 25-24).

Diverticular Bleeding

The complication of bleeding has been reported to occur in about 10 to 30 percent of patients with colonic diverticulosis.[73,74] In most patients the blood loss is small and the bleeding stops when the patient is put at rest. Persistent severe diverticular bleeding, however, may require emergency operative treatment. Since this is a disease of the elderly, emergency colectomy carries an extremely high morbidity and mortality.[75]

Establishing the diagnosis of hemorrhage from colonic diverticula by nonarteriographic techniques is difficult and is usually done by exclusion. Emergency

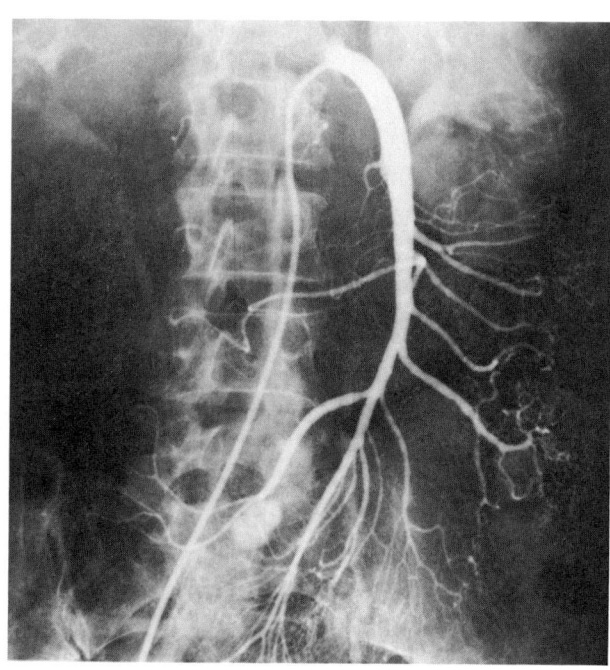

C

mesenteric arteriography during the time of the actual bleeding episode is by far the best method for accurate localization of the bleeding site. The only other nonangiographic technique that has proved of significant value is radionuclide scanning with ^{99m}Tc sulfur colloid (see Fig. 25-1).[15]

Mesenteric arteriography can localize the site of bleeding to the right or left colon (Figs. 25-25 and 25-26). Bleeding demonstrated angiographically is found more commonly in the ascending and transverse colon. In one series 75 percent of patients with massive diverticular bleeding had the bleeding site localized to the right of the splenic flexure.[76,77]

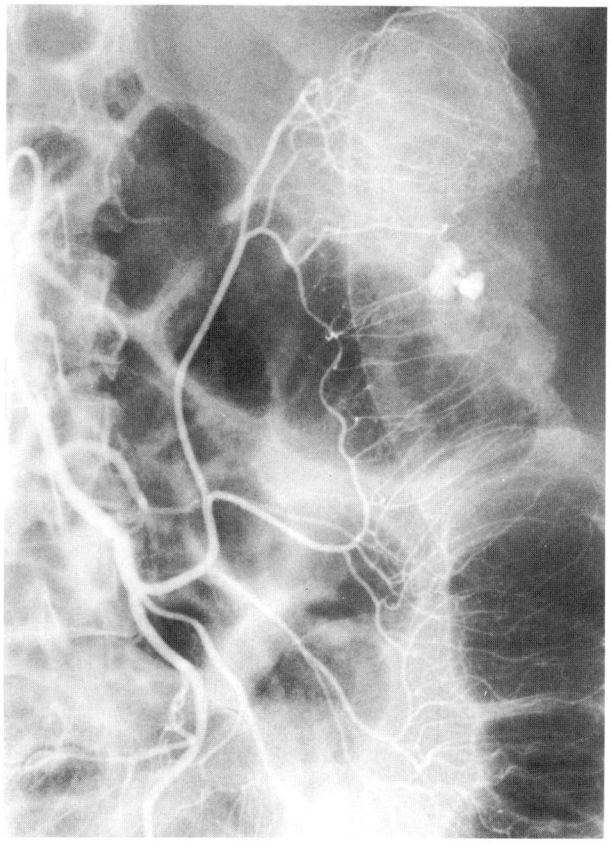

A

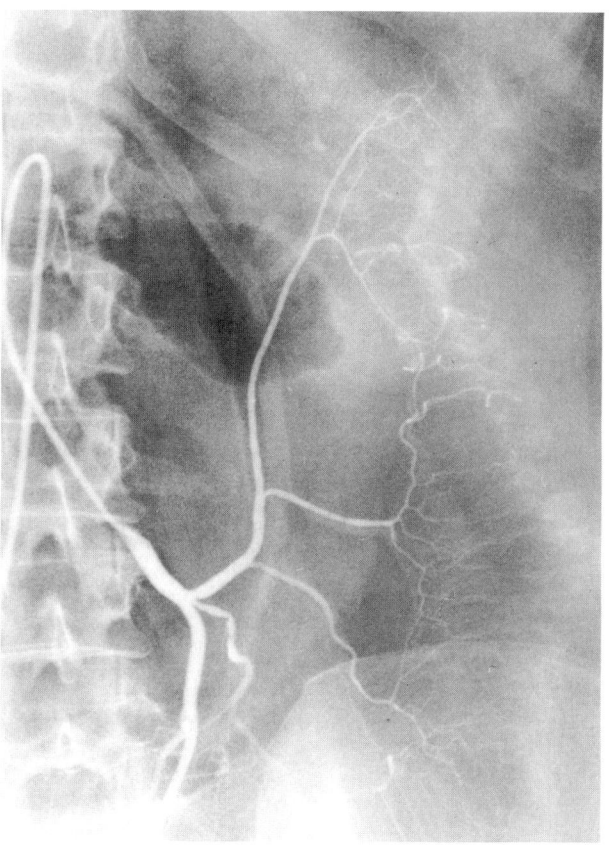

B

Figure 25-24. Lower gastrointestinal bleeding following the colonoscopic removal of a polyp from the descending colon. (A) Arterial phase of a selective inferior mesenteric arteriogram demonstrates bleeding from a branch of the left colic artery at the site of the previous polypectomy. (B) Repeat inferior mesenteric arteriogram 20 minutes after the be-

ginning of an infusion of vasopressin at 0.2 unit per minute. Bleeding can no longer be identified and did not recur. The infusion was continued at the same rate for 12 hours and decreased to 0.1 unit per minute for another 12 hours. The patient was discharged from the hospital without surgery.

Figure 25-25 (*top*). Bleeding diverticulum in the hepatic flexure in an 80-year-old man presenting with massive lower gastrointestinal bleeding. (A) Selective superior mesenteric arteriogram shows extravasation of contrast material from a branch of the right colic artery in the area of the hepatic flexure. (B) Repeat selective superior mesenteric arteriogram

during infusion of 0.2 unit per minute of vasopressin shows ▶ complete cessation of the bleeding. The patient was infused with vasopressin for 72 hours at decreasing dosages, and the catheter was removed at the end of the third day. Bleeding did not recur, and he was discharged from the hospital without surgery.

Figure 25-26 (*bottom*). Bleeding diverticulum in the descending colon in a 73-year-old man with lower gastrointestinal hemorrhage. (A) Selective inferior mesenteric arteriography shows extravasation of contrast material in the sigmoid colon (*arrows*). (B) Repeat arteriogram during infusion of 0.2 unit per minute of vasopressin into the inferior mesenteric artery shows no further extravasation. Note the con-

striction of the peripheral vessels and reflux into the aorta ▶ and iliac vessels (*arrows*) confirming the increase in peripheral resistance. (From Baum S, Rösch J, Dotter CT, Ring EJ, Athanasoulis CA, Waltman AC, Courey WR. Selective mesenteric arterial infusions in the management of massive diverticular hemorrhage. N Engl J Med 1973;288:1269. Used with permission.)

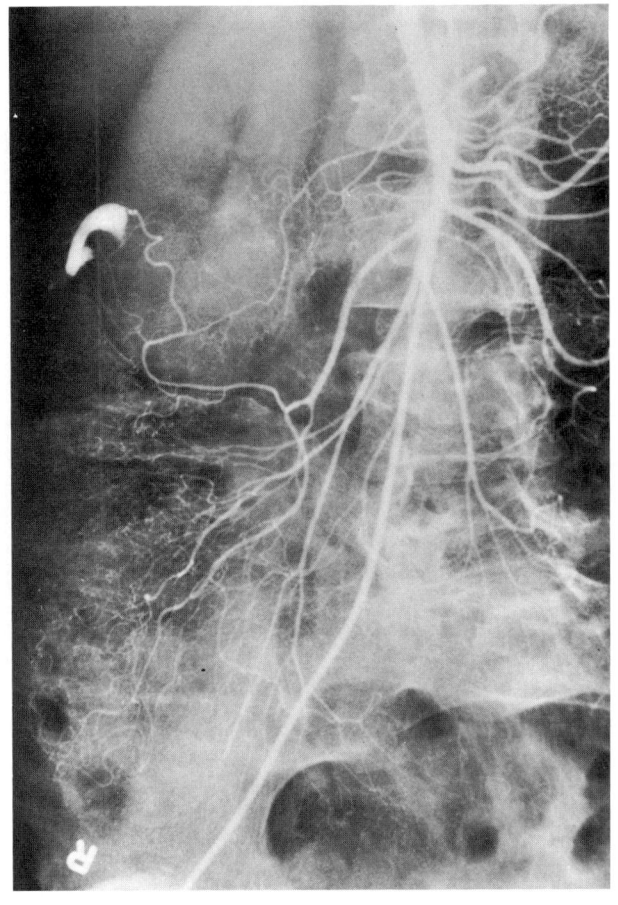

A

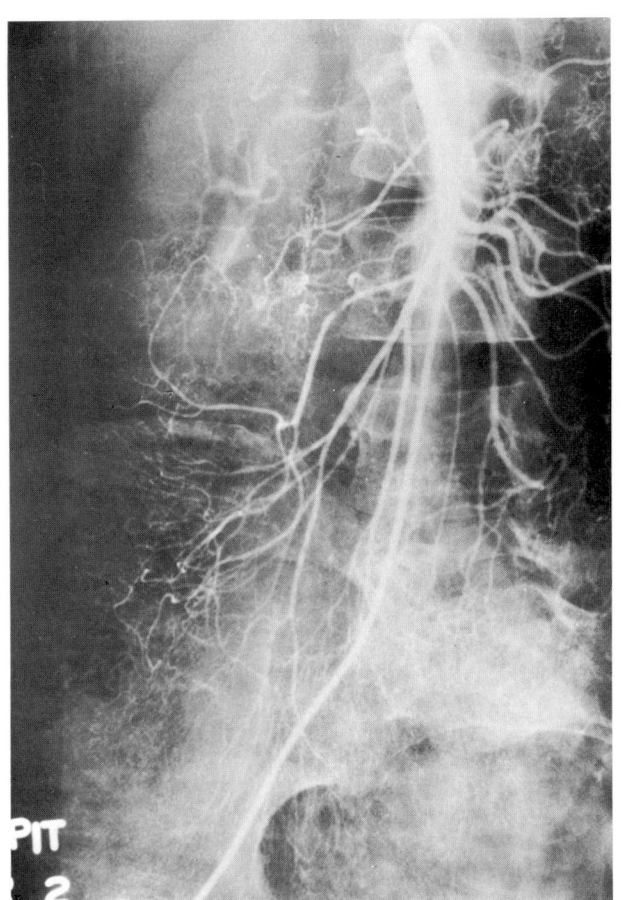

B

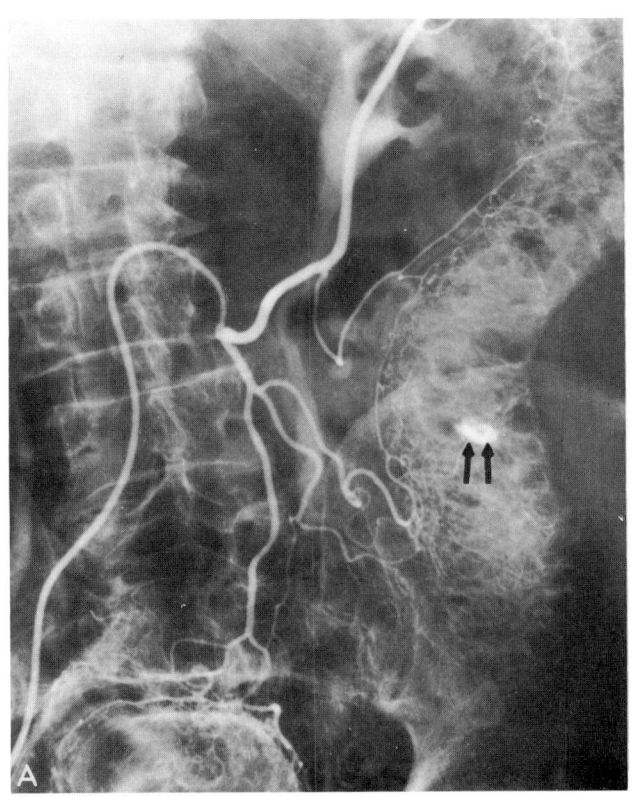

A

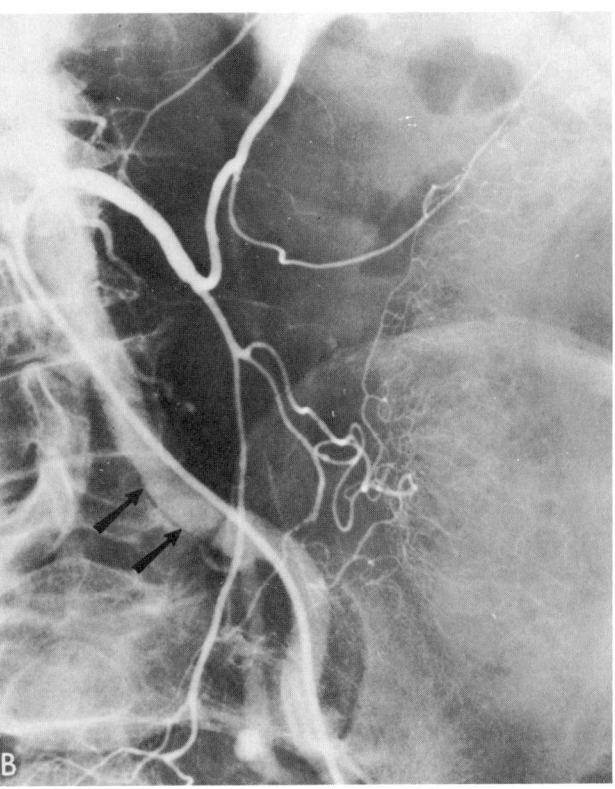

B

413

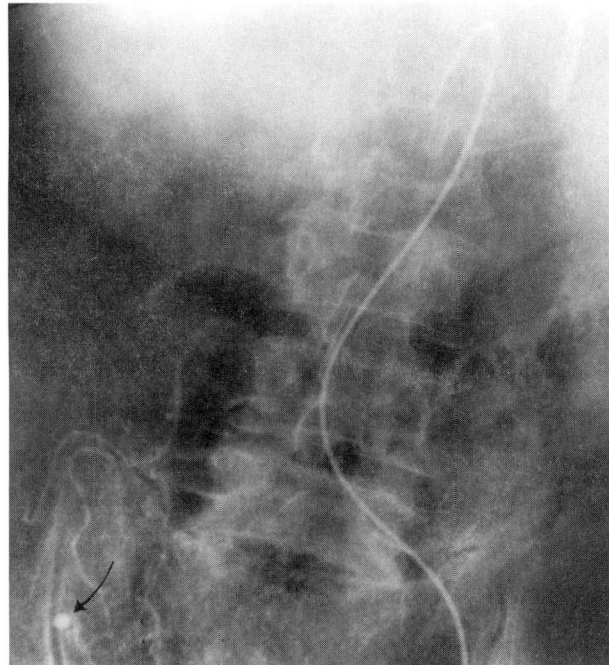

A

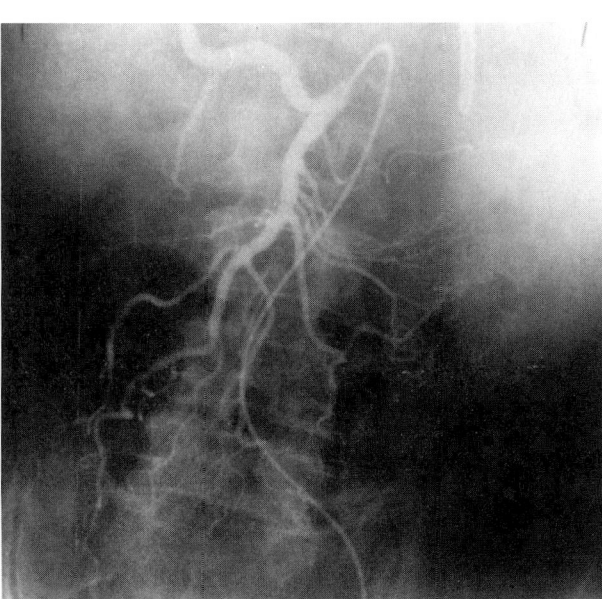

C

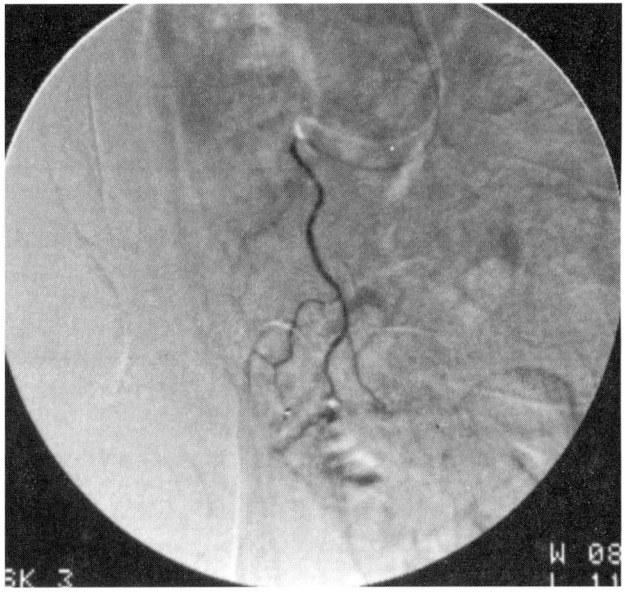

B

Figure 25-27. Bleeding diverticulum in the right colon in an elderly man presenting with massive lower gastrointestinal bleeding. The bleeding was controlled with selective embolization. (A) Selective superior mesenteric arteriography shows the bleeding site in the right colon (*arrow*). (B) Because of preexisting coronary artery disease, the bleeding site was controlled by selective embolization with coils rather than vasopression infusion. (C) Repeat mesenteric arteriogram after embolization fails to demonstrate any further bleeding.

Once the extravasation of contrast material has been demonstrated, infusion of vasopressin into the artery supplying the bleeding point is successful in controlling the bleeding in approximately 90 percent of the patients treated.[77,78] After the bleeding is controlled and the catheter removed, management of the patients remains controversial. If bleeding recurs, it usually does so within the first week after the angiographic treatment. The long-term follow-up of pa-

tients treated by vasopressin infusion suggests that after the first week these patients are probably no more likely to experience recurrent bleeding than those with diverticular bleeding that resolves spontaneously. If, however, it is decided to operate on a patient either because of rebleeding or as prophylaxis, a segmental colonic resection based on the precise localization of the bleeding point can be performed rather than a subtotal colectomy or "blind" hemicolectomy. The initial control of the bleeding episode with vasopressin makes high-risk emergency surgical intervention unnecessary. It allows for preparation of the patient and elective surgery under more favorable circumstances. If the infusion of vasopressin is contraindicated in this group of patients, the deposition of small microcoils at the exact site of the bleeding vessel may also be successful in stopping the bleeding and thus avoiding emergency surgery (Fig. 25-27).

Inflammatory Bowel Disease

Rectal bleeding may at times be the first manifestation of colitis. Some patients are therefore referred for emergency arteriography, and the diagnosis of bleed-

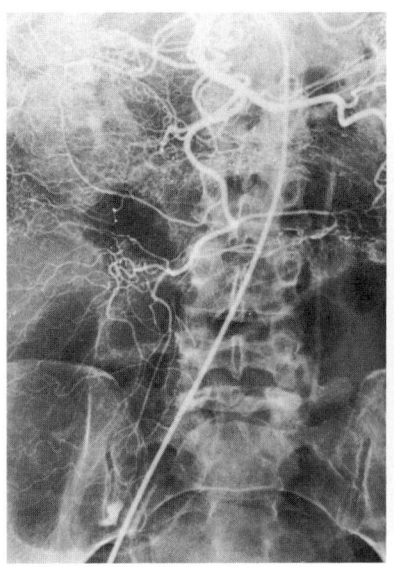
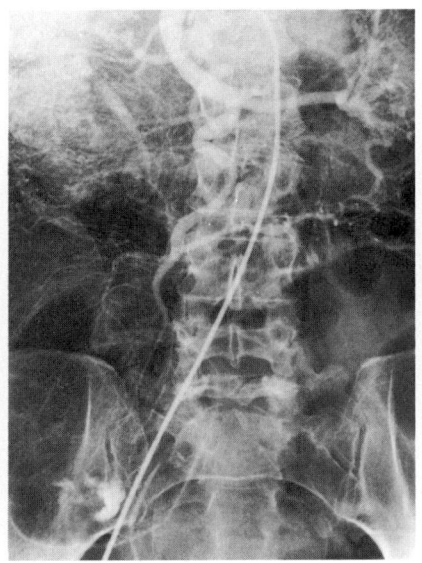
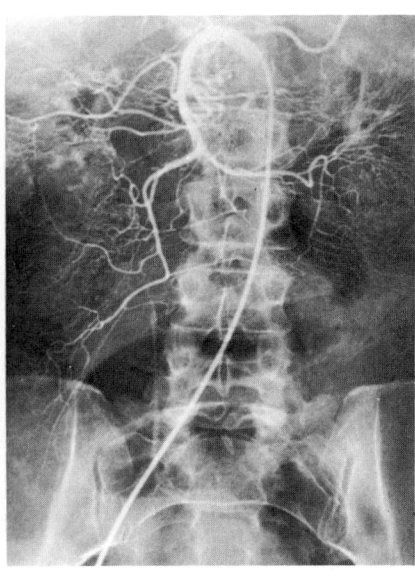

A   **B**   **C**

Figure 25-28. Chronic ulcerative colitis with massive lower gastrointestinal bleeding. (A) Selective superior mesenteric arteriogram shows extravasation from a cecal branch of the ileocecal artery. (B) The extravasated contrast material persists well into the venous phase of the arteriogram. (C) Bleeding stopped during the infusion into the superior mesenteric artery of 0.2 unit per minute of vasopressin. Control of the acute bleeding episode allowed the patient to be adequately prepared and to have a successful elective right colectomy several weeks later.

ing colitis is first made by the angiographer (Fig. 25-28). The infusion of vasopressin in cases of actively bleeding colitis can quickly arrest the bleeding, thereby converting an emergency colectomy to an elective one that allows for much better patient preparation.

Angiodysplasia

Vascular ectasia or angiodysplasia of the colon is a frequent cause of bleeding in elderly patients who have either chronic low-grade or intermittent acute lower gastrointestinal bleeding. The lesions tend to be very small and localized in the cecum, ascending colon, and proximal transverse colon. They generally cannot be detected by barium studies and are only rarely seen on colonoscopy. The surgeon almost never finds these lesions at laparotomy, and the pathologist has difficulty demonstrating them unless guided by preliminary specimen injections.

The clinical manifestation of colonic vascular ectasia or angiodysplasia is usually assumed to be intermittent low-grade lower gastrointestinal bleeding.[79,80] Nevertheless, in at least one series of 34 patients, half the cases presented with acute episodes of massive rectal bleeding.[81] In most of these patients the stool became guaiac-negative between episodes of hemorrhage.

It is difficult to assess the incidence of colonic angiodysplasia among various age groups. The first de-

scription of the entity was probably recorded in 1839.[82] In 1976 Bently collected 234 cases from the literature and added 110 cases from the Mayo Clinic files.[83] These reports, however, include a variety of vascular abnormalities of the intestines, such as congenital arteriovenous malformations and/or vascular neoplasms. Since 1960, when Margulis et al.[84] introduced operative angiography as a tool in the search for gastrointestinal bleeding sites, and 1965, when Baum et al.[85] introduced selective angiography for the preoperative localization of bleeding sites, the unusual character of colonic angiodysplasia has been recognized. These lesions have been reported in many patients with otherwise unexplained gastrointestinal hemorrhage. In one study on autopsy specimens colonic angiodysplasia was demonstrated in 2 percent of asymptomatic elderly patients.[86]

Because colonic angiodysplasia may coexist with other lesions of the gastrointestinal tract, conventional x-ray barium examinations and colonoscopy assume great diagnostic importance. Other pathologic conditions must be excluded before a right colectomy is undertaken. Most patients with angiodysplasia are not studied during periods of active bleeding because the hemorrhage from this condition tends to be more episodic than continuous. Therefore, specific localization of a bleeding site, shown by the extravasation of contrast material, is the exception rather than the rule. Because the surgeon can neither see nor palpate the

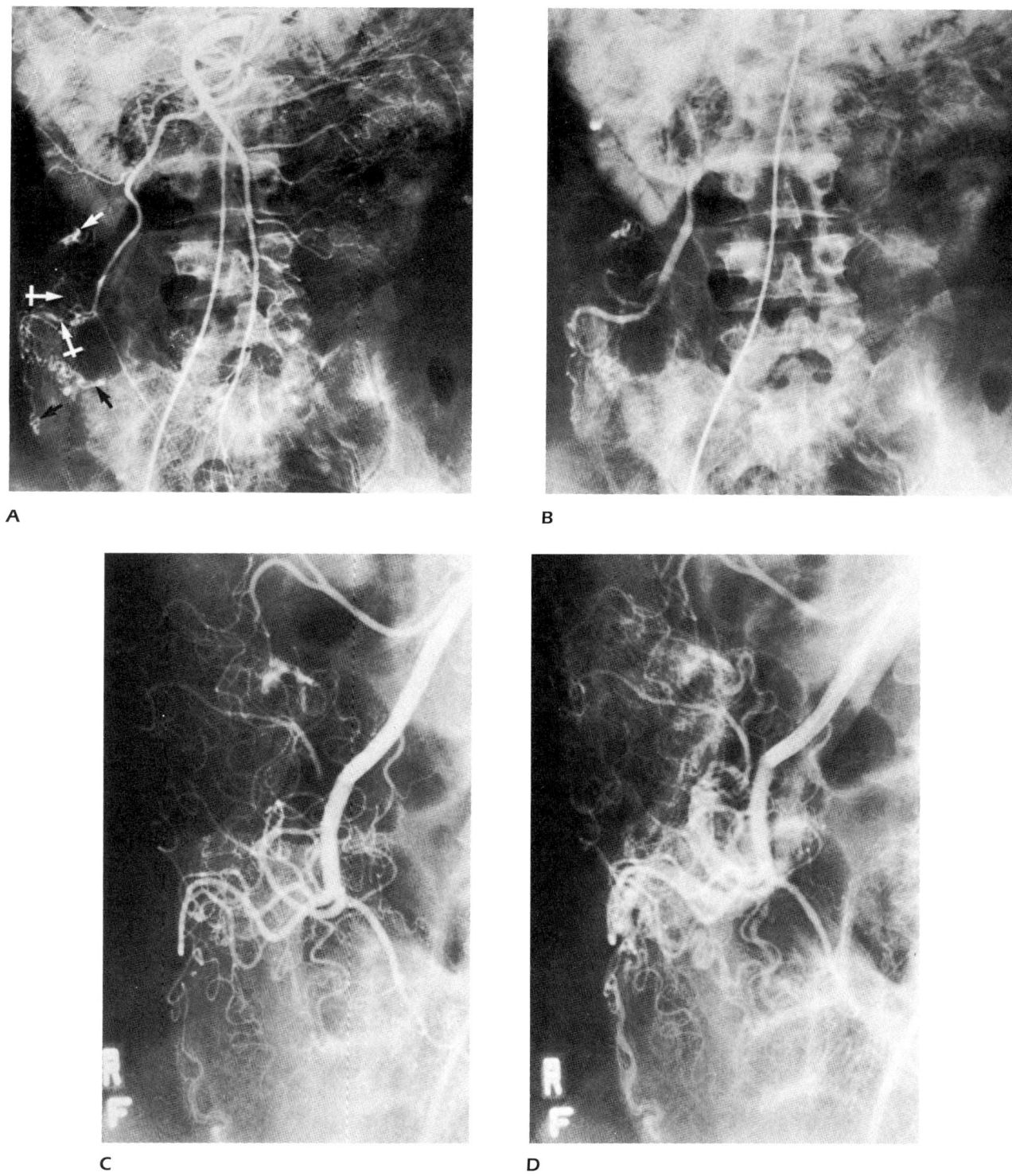

A

B

C

D

Figure 25-29. Angiodysplasia of the cecum and ascending colon. (A) During the arterial phase of a selective superior mesenteric arteriogram, abnormal clusters of small arteries can be identified in the cecum and ascending colon (*solid arrows*) associated with early-draining veins (*barred arrows*). (B) During the capillary phase of the examination, densely opacified colonic veins are seen draining the right colon. (C to E) Direct serial magnification studies of the cecum and ascending colon with a catheter positioned in the ileocecal artery. The changes of angiodysplasia are clearly identified, with most of the increased vascularity and early-draining veins appearing on the antemesenteric border of the colon. The patient underwent a right colectomy, which extended from the cecum to the distal transverse colon. Pathologically, multiple areas of angiodysplasia were identified with large, thin-walled vascular channels in the colonic wall, predominantly in the submucosa and associated with ulceration and thinning of the overlying mucosa.

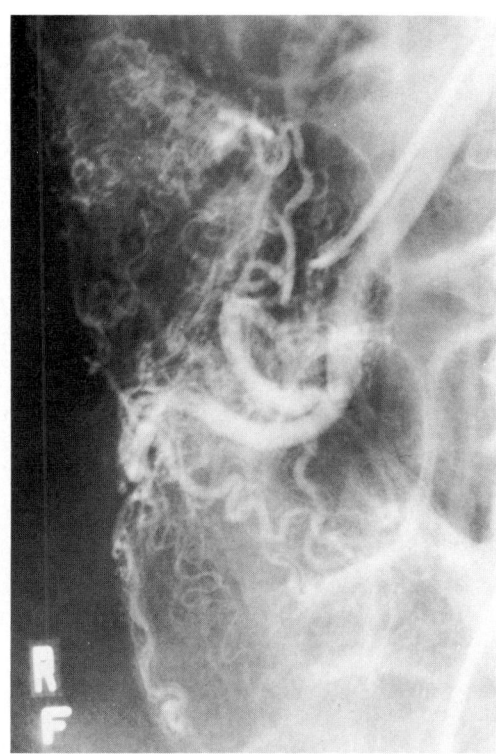

E **Figure 25-29** (continued).

colonic angiodysplasia, the decision to resect the ascending and proximal transverse colon is generally made on the basis of preoperative angiographic findings. Pathologic identification of the lesions in the resected specimen is difficult; lesions are small and focal, and serial sections of the entire specimen are not practical. Hence injection of the right colic artery with silicone rubber is helpful, since this material causes the vessels to remain distended during the tissue fixation. Pathologically angiodysplasia appears as a conglomeration of vascular spaces, often multiple and often coalescent, with adjacent arteries and veins standing out against the homogeneous surface of the normal colonic mucosa. Histologically, the dilated vascular spaces correspond to thin-walled clusters of veins in the submucosa and mucosa.

Angiographically, an increased number of small arteries is seen during the arterial phase of the arteriogram. In the capillary phase of the study an accumulation of contrast material appears in the vascular spaces associated with a very intense opacification of the bowel wall. The veins draining the lesion are identified early in the examination and paradoxically seem to persist late into the venous phase (Figs. 25-29 and 25-30).

The etiology of these angiodysplasias is obscure. It is generally assumed that they are acquired, since they are not seen in children. Some investigators consider the lesions related to a chronic form of ischemic bowel disease that results in poor mucosal perfusion associated with submucosal arterial venous shunting.[81] Other authors have compared them to localized varicosities within the submucosa.[87]

Neoplasms

When bleeding occurs from a neoplasm of the gastrointestinal tract or from an invading contiguous tumor, the bleeding site may be demonstrated angiographically.[88] Vasopressin infusions have not been successful in controlling such bleeding because the tumor vessels themselves do not appear to respond to vasoconstrictors. If the bleeding is life-threatening and surgical intervention is contraindicated, embolization techniques may be employed. Wallace and Goldstein have reported a series of patients with gastrointestinal bleeding secondary to tumors who were successfully handled in this manner.[89]

Complications

Catheter-Related Problems

The risks involved in arteriography are low and well documented.[90] Thrombosis at the puncture site is clearly the most common complication and occurs in about 0.1 percent of studies. Patients studied on account of bleeding seem to have altered coagulability and are less likely to form thrombus around the catheter. Although many studies have shown that a catheter in the vascular system rapidly becomes coated with a fibrin sheath, catheters have been left in place during vasopressin infusion therapy for as long as 7 days without evidence of thromboembolic disease. Mild oozing in the groin and around the catheter may occur. When the catheter is removed, care should be taken not to press on it because this may cause the fibrin sheath that is almost always around the catheter itself to be stripped or to be milked from it and left behind in the femoral artery. Manual compression of the artery after removal of the catheter nearly always stops the bleeding, although it may have to be applied for up to 2 hours.

Problems Related to the Vasopressin Infusion

Almost all patients complain of abdominal cramps when vasopressin is initially infused into the celiac or superior or inferior mesenteric arteries. The pain

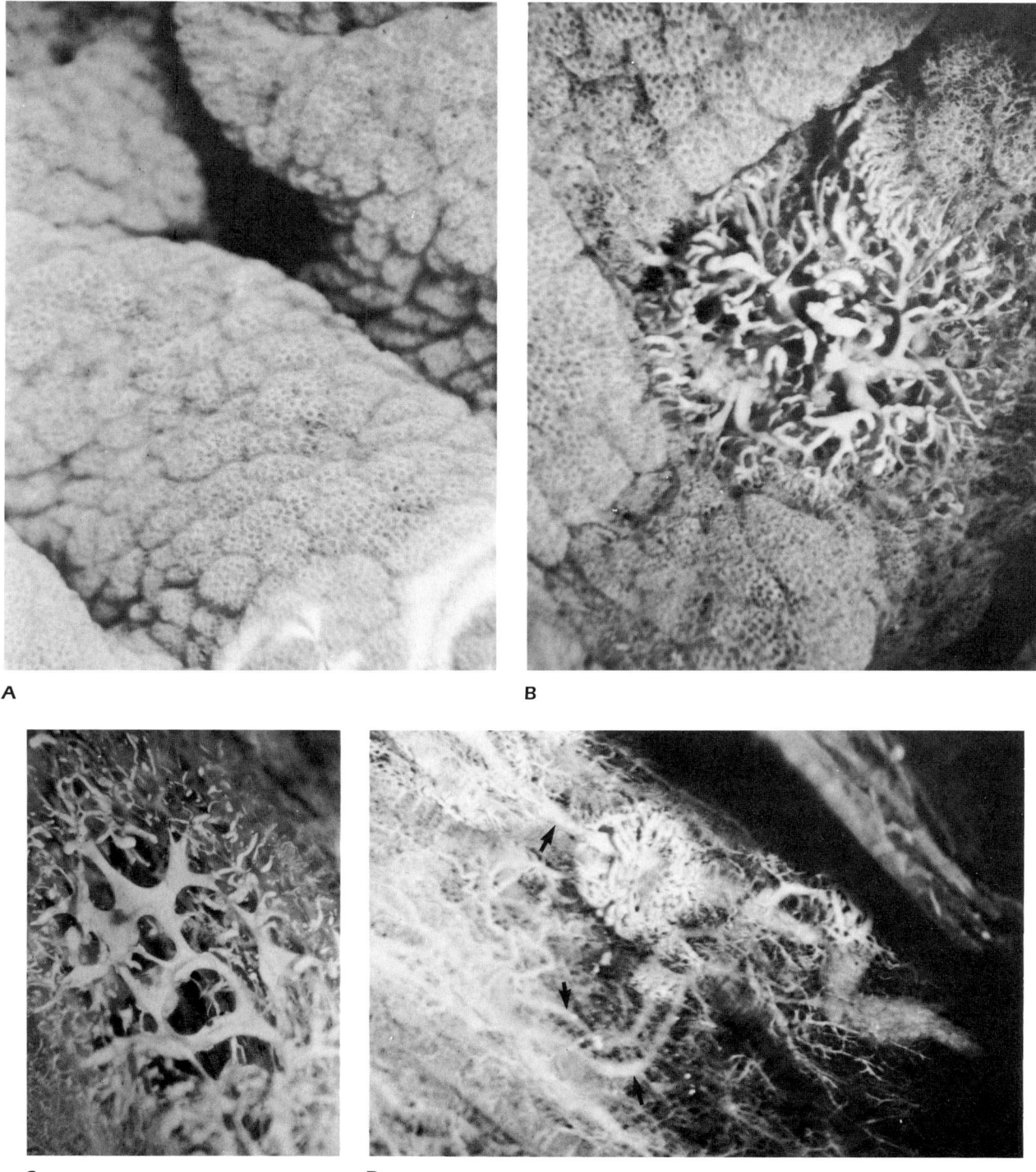

Figure 25-30. Microvascular anatomy of angiodysplasia of the cecum and ascending colon on pathologic specimens. (A) Photograph (×40) of normal colonic mucosa viewed with a dissecting microscope after silicone rubber injection into right colic and ileocolic arteries and tissue clearing using absolute alcohol followed by methyl salicylate. (B to D) Specimens of colonic angiodysplasia as viewed under the dissecting microscope following the tissue-clearing technique. The angiodysplasias appear as clusters of tortuous and dilated vessels against a homogeneous background of normal colonic mucosa. Histologically, these vessels are primarily venules extending from the submucosa into the mucosa. Occasionally, as in (D) (*arrows*), the draining arteries and veins can be identified.

generally subsides within the first 10 to 15 minutes of the infusion and should not recur. It usually has been assumed that the discomfort experienced at first is due to contraction of the bowel itself and the increased peristalsis. Very often patients will evacuate as a sequel to the abdominal cramping. If the catheter tip changes position during the time of infusion and becomes lodged in a small jejunal or colic branch, localized bowel ischemia may result. Persistent severe abdominal cramps suggest ischemia, and the position of the catheter should be checked by repeat arteriography.

Although the dose of vasopressin that is infused intraarterially is quite small, the systemic antidiuretic effect almost always occurs after several hours of continuous infusion. Urinary output and electrolytes must be monitored carefully. Water retention and electrolyte imbalance should be treated by diuretics and suitable electrolyte infusions and not by alteration of the rate or dose of infusion of vasopressin.

Rarely, idiosyncratic reactions to the vasopressin are encountered, and the drug has to be discontinued. Sometimes patients exhibit a marked peripheral vasoconstriction in their extremities, which may have a mottled appearance. Occasionally this is troublesome enough so that the drug has to be discontinued. At the recommended dose rates, reduction in cardiac output is not a frequent problem, but this may depend on the individual cardiac status of the patient. As mentioned earlier, sublingual, intravenous, or, more commonly, a skin patch of nitroglycerin is used during the vasopressin infusion to prevent coronary artery vasoconstriction.

Problems Related to Embolization Techniques

After embolic material is discharged from the catheter tip, the emboli cannot be retrieved. The final position of an embolus cannot be precisely determined before it is injected, and therefore balance between hemostasis and end-organ ischemia is difficult to control. Embolic therapy is much less controllable than are pharmacologic infusions, which can be stopped, slowed, or increased, or balloons, which can be retrieved if they are not in the correct position. Complications that have occurred with the use of particulate emboli include end-organ necrosis[59] and reflux of embolic material from the selected artery with final embolization to unwanted sites. Embolic reflux can be prevented by using a balloon catheter; this is inflated proximally in the artery, and emboli are delivered distally through the lumen.[62]

After Gelfoam embolization, patients may experience a transient rise in temperature to about 39°C (102°F), which may persist for 24 to 36 hours before subsiding spontaneously. Blood cultures in these patients are sterile, and white cell counts tend to be normal.

References

1. Nusbaum M, Baum S. Radiographic demonstration of unknown sites of gastrointestinal bleeding. Surg Forum 1963;13:374.
2. Baum S, Stein GN, Nusbaum M, Chait A. Selective arteriography in the diagnosis of hemorrhage in the gastrointestinal tract. Radiol Clin North Am 1969;7:131.
3. Baum S, Nusbaum M, Clearfield HR, Kuroda K, Tumen HJ. Angiography in the diagnosis of gastrointestinal bleeding. Arch Intern Med 1967;119:16.
4. Baum S. The radiologist intervenes. N Engl J Med 1980;302:1141.
5. Welch CE, Hedberg S. Gastrointestinal hemorrhage: I. General considerations of diagnosis and therapy. Adv Surg 1973;7:95.
6. Athanasoulis CA, Waltman AC, Novelline RA, Krudy AG, Sniderman KW. Angiography, its contribution to the emergency management of gastrointestinal hemorrhage. Radiol Clin North Am 1976;14:265.
7. Conn HO, Ramsby GR, Storer EH. Selective intraarterial vasopressin in the treatment of upper gastrointestinal hemorrhage. Gastroenterology 1972;63:634.
8. Rösch J, Gray RK, Grollman JH, Ross G, Steckel RJ, Weiner M. Selective arterial drug infusions in the treatment of acute gastrointestinal bleeding. Gastroenterology 1970;59:341.
9. Baum S, Athanasoulis CA, Waltman AC, Ring EJ. Angiographic diagnosis and control of gastrointestinal bleeding. In: Hardy JD, Zollinger RM, eds. Advances in Surgery. Chicago: Year Book, 1973:149.
10. Shapiro MJ. The role of the radiologist in the management of gastrointestinal bleeding. Gastroenterol Clin North Am 1994;23:123–181.
11. Shapiro M, Simon D. Angiography in massive UGI bleeding—would you believe better than endoscopy? Am J Gastroenterol 1991;86:1090–1091.
12. Zuckerman DA, Bocchini TP, Birnbaum EH. Massive hemorrhage in the lower gastrointestinal tract in adults: diagnostic imaging and intervention. AJR 1993;161:703–711.
13. Sos TA, Lee JG, Wixson D, Sniderman KW. Intermittent bleeding from minute to minute in acute massive gastrointestinal hemorrhage: arteriographic demonstration. AJR 1978;131:1015.
14. Gupta H, Weissleder R, Bogdanov AA Jr, Brady TJ. Experimental gastrointestinal hemorrhage: detection with contrast-enhanced MR imaging and scintigraphy. Radiology 1995;196:239–244.
15. Alavi A, Dann RW, Baum S, Biery DN. Scintigraphic detection of acute gastrointestinal bleeding. Radiology 1977;124:753.
16. Bentley DE, Richardson JD. The role of tagged red blood cell imaging in the localization of gastrointestinal bleeding. Arch Surg 1991;126:821–824.
17. Orecchia PM, Hensley EK, McDonald PT, Lull RJ. Localization of lower gastrointestinal hemorrhage: experience with red blood cells labeled in vitro with technetium Tc-99m. Arch Surg 1985;120:621–624.
18. Conn HO, Brodoff M. Emergency esophagoscopy in the diagnosis of upper gastrointestinal hemorrhage. Gastroenterology 1964;47:505.
19. McCray RS, Martin F, Amir-Ahmadi H, Sheahan DG, Zamcheck N. Erroneous diagnosis of hemorrhage from esophageal varices. Am J Dig Dis 1969;14:755.
20. Ring EJ, Athanasoulis CA, Waltman AC, Baum S. The pseudovein: an angiographic appearance of arterial hemorrhage. J Can Assoc Radiol 1973;24:242.

21. Athanasoulis CA. Therapeutic applications of angiography. N Engl J Med 1980;302:1117.

22. Schmidt SP, Boskind JF, Smith DC, Catalano RD. Angiographic localization of small bowel angiodysplasia with use of platinum coils. J Vasc Intervent Radiol 1993;4:737–739.

23. Duszak RL, Soulen MC, Shlansky-Goldberg RD, et al. Transcatheter embolization in nonvariceal upper gastrointestinal hemorrhage: laboratory, clinical, and angiographic factors contributing to success. Radiology 1995;197(Suppl):416.

24. Goodman LS, Gilman A. The pharmacological basis of therapeutics. 5th ed. New York: Macmillan, 1975:855.

25. Barr JW, Lakin RC, Rösch J. Vasopressin and hepatic artery: effect of selective celiac infusion of vasopressin on the hepatic artery flow. Invest Radiol 1975;10:200.

26. Simmons JT, Baum S, Sheehan BA, Ring EJ, Athanasoulis CA, Waltman AC, Coggins PC. The effects of vasopressin on hepatic artery blood flow. Radiology 1977;124:637.

27. Tsai YT, Lay CS, Lai KH, et al. Controlled trial of vasopressin plus nitroglycerin vs. vasopressin alone in the treatment of bleeding esophageal varices. Hepatology 1986;6:406–409.

28. Gimson AE, Westaby D, Hegarty J, Watson A, Williams R. A randomized trial of vasopressin and vasopressin plus nitroglycerin in the control of acute variceal hemorrhage. Hepatology 1986;6:410–413.

29. Conn HO. Vasopressin and nitroglycerin in the treatment of bleeding varices: the bottom line. Hepatology 1986;6:523–525.

30. Sirinek KR, Adcock DK, Levine BA. Simultaneous infusion of nitroglycerin and nitroprusside to offset adverse effects of vasopressin during portosystemic shunting. Am J Surg 1989;157:33–37.

31. Bosch J, Groszmann RJ, Garcia-Pagan JC, et al. Association of transdermal nitroglycerin to vasopressin infusion in the treatment of variceal hemorrhage: a placebo-controlled clinical trial. Hepatology 1989;10:962–968.

32. Shaldon S, Sherlock S. The use of vasopressin (Pitressin) in the control of bleeding of oesophageal varices. Lancet 1960;2:222.

33. Baum S, Nusbaum M. The control of gastrointestinal hemorrhage by selective mesenteric arterial infusion of vasopressin. Radiology 1971;98:497.

34. Conn HO, Ramsby GR, Stover EH, et al. Intraarterial vasopressin in the treatment of upper gastrointestinal hemorrhage: prospective controlled clinical trial. Gastroenterology 1975;68:211.

35. Barr JW, Lakin RC, Rösch J. Similarity of arterial and intravenous vasopressin on portal and systemic hemodynamics. Gastroenterology 1975;69:13.

36. Johnson WC, Widrich WC, Ansell JE, Robbins AH, Nabseth DC. Control of bleeding varices by vasopressin: a prospective radiological study. Ann Surg 1977;186:369.

37. LeBrec D, Nouel O, Corbic M, et al. Propanolol, a medical treatment for portal hypertension. Lancet 1980;2:180–182.

38. Lebrec D. Current status and future goals of pharmacologic reduction of portal hypertension. Am J Surg 1990;160:12–25.

39. Greig JD, Garden OJ, Carter DC. Prophylactic treatment of patients with esophageal-varices: is it ever indicated? World J Surg 1994;18:176–184.

40. Pagliaro L, D'Amico G, Sorensen TI, et al. Prevention of first bleeding in cirrhosis: a meta-analysis of randomized trials of nonsurgical treatment. Ann Intern Med 1992;117:59–70.

41. Lunderquist A, Vang J. Transhepatic catheterization and obliteration of the coronary vein in patients with portal hypertension and esophageal varices. N Engl J Med 1974;291:646.

42. Lunderquist A, Vang J. Sclerosing injection of esophageal varices through transhepatic selective catheterization of the gastric coronary vein: a preliminary report. Acta Radiol 1974;15:546.

43. L'Hermine C, Chastanet P, Delemazure O, Bonniere PL, Durieu JP, Paris JC. Percutaneous transhepatic embolization of gastroesophageal varices: results in 400 patients. Am J Roentgenol 1989;152:755–760.

44. Sos T. Transhepatic portal venous embolization of varices: pros and cons. Radiology 1983;148:569–570.

45. Pereiras R, Viamonte M Jr, Russell E, LePage J, White P, Hutson D. New techniques for interruption of gastroesophageal venous blood flow. Radiology 1977;124:313.

46. Lunderquist A, Simert G, Tylén U, Vang J. Follow-up of patients with portal hypertension and esophageal varices treated with percutaneous obliteration of gastric coronary vein. Radiology 1977;122:59.

47. Moncure AC, Waltman AC, Vander Salm TJ, Linton RR, Levine FH, Abbott WM. Gastrointestinal hemorrhage from adhesion-related mesenteric varices. Ann Surg 1976;183:24.

48. Case Records of the Massachusetts General Hospital (Case 1-1973). N Engl J Med 1973;288:36.

49. Ring EJ, Oleaga JA, Freiman D, Husted JW, Waltman AC Jr, Baum S. Pitfalls in the angiographic management of hemorrhage: hemodynamic considerations. AJR 1977;129:1007.

50. White RI Jr, Strandberg JV, Gross GS, Barth KH. Therapeutic embolization with long-term occluding agents and their effect on embolized tissues. Radiology 1977;125:677.

51. Reuter RS, Chuang VP, Bree RL. Selective arterial embolization for control of massive upper gastrointestinal bleeding. AJR 1975;125:119.

52. Eisenberg H, Steer ML. The nonoperative treatment of massive pyloroduodenal hemorrhage by retracted autologous clot embolization. Surgery 1976;79:414.

53. Bookstein JJ, Closta EM, Foley D, Walter JF. Transcatheter hemostasis of gastrointestinal bleeding using modified autogenous clot. Radiology 1974;113:277.

54. Tadavarthy SM, Moller JH, Amplatz K. Polyvinyl alcohol (Ivalon)—a new embolic material. AJR 1975;125:609.

55. Castaneda-Zuniga WR, Sanchez R, Amplatz K. Experimental observations on short- and long-term effects of arterial occlusion with Ivalon. Radiology 1978;126:783.

56. Lang EV, Picus D, Marx MV, Hicks ME, Friedland GW. Massive upper gastrointestinal hemorrhage with normal findings on arteriography: value of prophylactic embolization of the left gastric artery. AJR 1992;158:547–549.

57. Sharma S, Kothari SS, Rajani M, Venugopal P. Life-threatening arterial haemorrhage: results of treatment by transcatheter embolization using home-made steel coils. Clin Radiol 1994;49:252–255.

58. Dotter CT, Goldman ML, Rösch J. Instant selective arterial occlusion with isobutyl 2-cyanoacrylate. Radiology 1975;114:227.

59. Goldman ML, Freeney PC, Tallman JM, et al. Transcatheter vascular occlusion therapy with isobutyl 2-cyanoacrylate (bucrylate) for control of massive upper-gastrointestinal bleeding. Radiology 1978;129:41.

60. Wholey MH. The technology of balloon catheters in interventional angiography. Radiology 1977;125:671.

61. Dotter CT, Rösch J, Lakin PC, Lakin RC, Pegg JE. Injectable flow-guided coaxial catheters for selective angiography and controlled vascular occlusion. Radiology 1972;104:421.

62. Greenfield AJ, Athanasoulis CA, Waltman AC, Le Moure ER. Prevention of embolic reflux using balloon catheters. AJR 1978;131:651.

63. White RI Jr, Ursic TA, Kaufman SL, Barth KH, Kim W, Gross GS. Therapeutic embolization with detachable balloons: physical factors influencing permanent occlusion. Radiology 1978;126:521.

64. Gianturco C, Anderson JH, Wallace S. Mechanical devices for arterial occlusion. AJR 1975;124:428.

65. Baum S, Ward S, Nusbaum M. Stress bleeding from the mid-duodenum: an often unrecognized source of gastrointestinal hemorrhage. Radiology 1970;95:595.

66. Athanasoulis CA, Baum S, Waltman AC, Ring EJ, Imbembo A, Vander Salm TJ. Control of acute gastric mucosal hemorrhage: intra-arterial infusion of posterior pituitary extract. N Engl J Med 1974;290:597.

67. Waltman AC, Greenfield AJ, Novelline RA, Athanasoulis CA. Pyloroduodenal bleeding and intraarterial vasopressin: clinical results. AJR 1979;133:643.

68. Sherman LM, Shenoy SS, Cerra FB. Selective intraarterial vaso-

pressin: clinical efficacy and complications. Ann Surg 1979; 189:298.

69. Fordtran JS, Grossman MI. Third symposium on histamine H$_2$-receptor antagonists: clinical results with cimetidine. Gastroenterology 1978;74:339.

70. Rosenbaum A, Siegelman S, Sprayregen S. The bleeding marginal ulcer: catheterization diagnosis and therapy. AJR 1975; 125:812.

71. Oglevie SB, Smith DC, Mera SS. Bleeding marginal ulcers: angiographic evaluation. Radiology 1990;174:943–944.

72. Athanasoulis CA, Waltman AC, Ring EJ, Smith JC Jr, Baum S. Angiographic management of post-operative bleeding. Radiology 1974;113:37.

73. Behringer GE, Albright NL. Diverticular disease of the colon: a frequent cause of rectal bleeding. Am J Surg 1973;125:419.

74. Welch CE, Hedberg S. Gastrointestinal hemorrhage. In: Hardy JD, Zollinger RM, eds. Advances in surgery. Chicago: Year Book, 1973;7:95.

75. Rigg M, Ewing MR. Current attitudes on diverticulitis with particular reference to colonic bleeding. Arch Surg 1966;92: 321.

76. Casarella WJ, Kanter IE, Seaman WB. Right-sided colonic diverticula as a cause of acute rectal hemorrhage. N Engl J Med 1972;286:450.

77. Athanasoulis CA, Baum S, Rösch J, et al. Mesenteric arterial infusions of vasopressin for hemorrhage from colonic diverticulosis. Am J Surg 1975;129:212.

78. Baum S, Rösch J, Dotter CT, Ring EJ, Athanasoulis CA, Waltman AC, Courey WR. Selective mesenteric arterial infusions in the management of massive diverticular hemorrhage. N Engl J Med 1973;288:1269.

79. Jakab F, Balazs M, Faller J, Kiss S. Gastrointestinal angiodysplasia. Acta Chir Hung 1991;32:57–68.

80. Lau WY, Chu KW, Yuen WK, Poon GP, Li AK. Bleeding angiodysplasia of the gastrointestinal tract. Aust NZ J Surg 1992; 62:344–349.

81. Baum S, Athanasoulis CA, Waltman AC, Galdabini J, Shapiro RH, Warshaw AL, Ottinger LW. Angiodysplasia of the right colon: a cause of gastrointestinal bleeding. AJR 1977;129:789.

82. Phillips B. Letter to the editor. London Med Gaz 1839;1:514.

83. Bently PG. The bleeding caecal angioma: a diagnostic problem. Br J Surg 1976;63:455.

84. Margulis AR, Heinbecker P, Bernard HR. Operative mesenteric arteriography in the search for the site in unexplained gastrointestinal hemorrhage. Surgery 1960;48:534.

85. Baum S, Nusbaum MH, Blakemore SW. The preoperative radiographic demonstration of intra-abdominal bleeding from undetermined sites by percutaneous selective celiac and superior mesenteric arteriography. Surgery 1965;58:797.

86. Baer JW, Ryan S. Analysis of cecal vasculature in the search for vascular malformations. AJR 1976;126:394.

87. Boley SJ, Sammartano RS, Adams A, DiBiase A, Kleinhaus S, Sprayregen S. On the nature and etiology of vascular ectasis of the colon: degenerative lesions of aging. Gastroenterology 1977;72:650.

88. Rösch J, Steckel RJ. Selective angiography of the abdominal viscera. In: Hanafee WN, ed. Selective angiography. Baltimore: Williams & Wilkins, 1972:17.

89. Wallace S, Goldstein HM. Intra-vascular occlusive therapy. Postgrad Med 1976,59:141.

90. Sigstedt B, Lunderquist A. Complications of angiographic examinations. AJR 1978;130:455.

26

Embolotherapy of Hepatic Arterial Injuries

RICHARD G. FISHER
YORAM BEN-MENACHEM

The liver is considered the most commonly injured organ within the peritoneal cavity.[1] The mechanism of injury is either blunt or penetrating trauma. The liver is vulnerable to blunt trauma because of its size, location, architecture, and mobility. It can be injured by direct blows, by compression, or by shearing forces (deceleration) (Fig. 26-1). Each of these mechanisms is a potential factor in the high instance of liver injury in unrestrained motor vehicle drivers and front seat passengers during frontal or lateral impacts. Fractured ribs, particularly on the right, as well as other injuries to the torso, head, and extremities, often accompany blunt hepatic trauma.[2] The large size of the liver and its location in both upper abdominal quadrants also make it especially vulnerable to penetrating injuries from bullets, knives, or shotguns (Fig. 26-2).[2] Demographically, blunt trauma is more common in suburban and rural populations, whereas penetrating injuries dominate in the urban environment. In addition, the frequent application of percutaneous diagnostic and therapeutic hepatic procedures has produced a significant incidence of iatrogenic penetrating injury (Fig. 26-3).[3] Ten percent of all hepatic injuries resulting from street trauma may be fatal. Blunt injuries are potentially more lethal, with a mortality approaching 25 percent, whereas up to 95 percent of patients with penetrating injuries may be salvaged.[1]

A recent reclassification of hepatic injury was proposed by the Organ Injury Scaling Committee of the American Association for the Surgery of Trauma.[2] Categories I through III describe lesser lacerations and hematomas, and categories IV through VI include major lacerations, juxtahepatic venous injuries, and hepatic avulsion (Table 26-1).

Since the initial reported case of surgical treatment of a hepatic gunshot wound by Broons in 1870, surgery has been at the forefront of hepatic trauma management.[2] A variety of techniques, including large resections and hepatic artery ligation, have been followed by a more conservative trend toward direct control of hemorrhage and conservative debridement.[2]

Some propose nonsurgical management of certain patients with hepatic trauma.[4] These usually would be patients in categories I through III, with staging accomplished by ultrasound and CT.[5] In this group as well as in postoperative patients and those with complications from percutaneous procedures, interventional radiology can play a significant role.

Angiography: Interhepatic Arterial Injuries

Angiography was first used for diagnosing hepatic injuries in the 1960s.[6] Reports of interventional techniques used for control of hepatic hemorrhage began appearing in the literature in the 1970s.[7]

The angiographic workup of a hepatic injury typically begins with an aortographic survey of the upper abdomen. This provides information about potential concomitant injuries (renal, splenic) as well as the topography of the blood supply to the liver (Fig. 26-4). The variability of the hepatic arterial supply is discussed later.

Selective angiography is essential for diagnosis because many, if not most, hepatic arterial injuries may not be visible on aortography. A variety of catheter sizes and shapes and an array of guidewire choices are available in today's armamentarium for selective celiac and hepatic angiography. However, even in this enlightened era, an occasional anatomic variation of the celiohepatic complex can humble even the experienced angiographer.

Types of hepatic injury that are amenable to transcatheter therapy include frank extravasation secondary to hepatic branch artery laceration, false aneurysms (Fig. 26-5), and fistulous communications from an artery to the portal or biliary systems (see Fig. 26-3). In the latter, hemobilia may be the dominant clinical finding. Any of these may be accompanied by sizable

Text continues on page 428

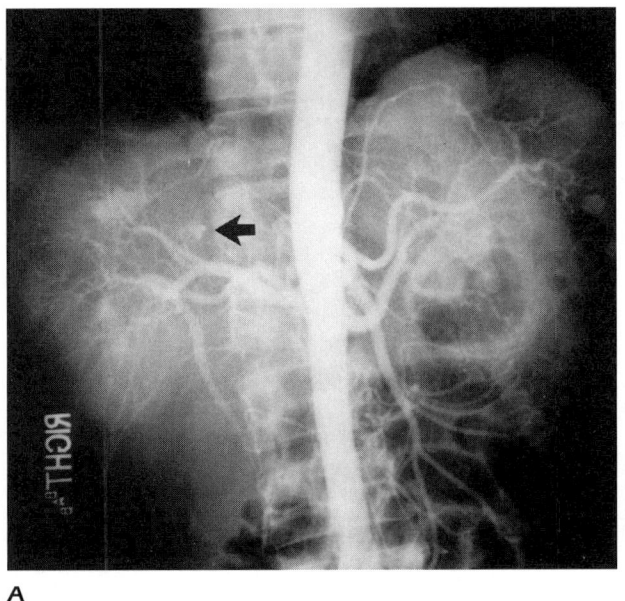

A

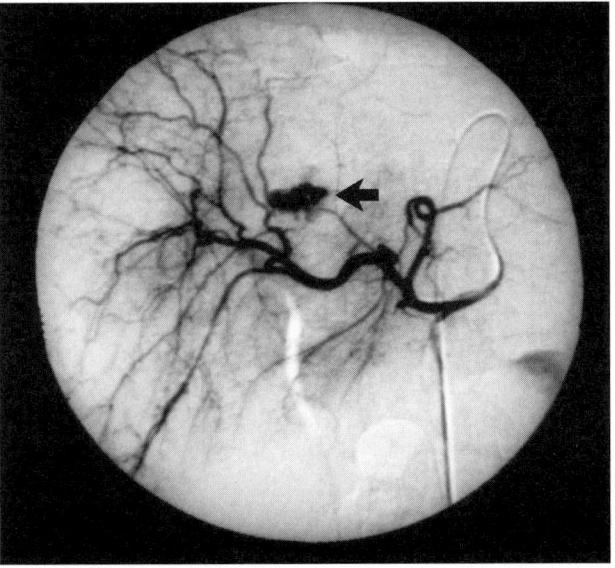

B

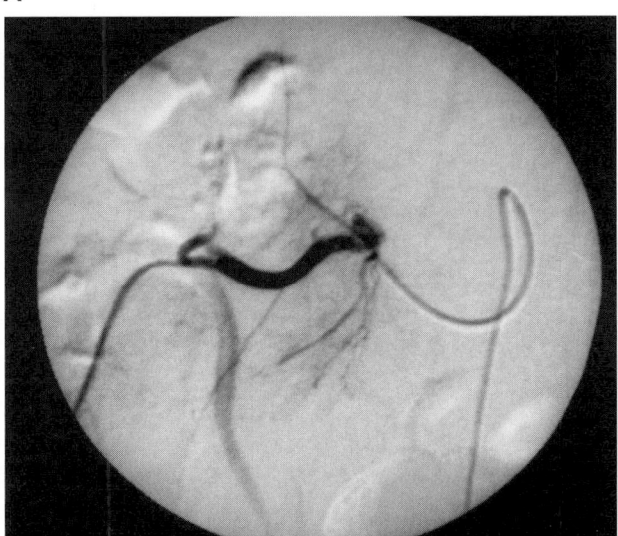

C

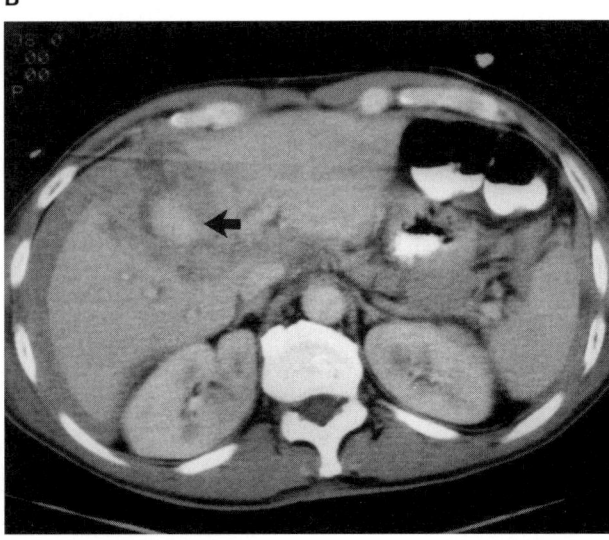

D

Figure 26-1. A 55-year-old male victim of a high-speed motor vehicle accident. Chest x-ray showed multiple rib fractures and mediastinal changes suspicious for hematoma. There were no abdominal symptoms. The aortic arch was normal. (A) Abdominal aortogram obtained as part of the standard trauma evaluation reveals a small area of extravasation in the right lobe of the liver (*arrow*). (B) Selective hepatic digital arteriogram displays a much larger area of extravasation (*arrow*). (C) Subselective right hepatic digital arteriogram after successful embolization with Gelfoam strips shows no further extravasation (peripheral right hepatic branches filled on later images). (D) CT scan done shortly after embolization reveals a large interhepatic and subcapsular hematoma indicative of hepatic laceration. The area of increased density (*arrow*) is extravasated contrast material that occurred before embolization. (E) CT scan of the abdomen 10 days later shows resolution of the subcapsular hematoma and marked diminution and liquefaction of the intrahepatic hematoma. No surgery was required and the patient was ultimately discharged.

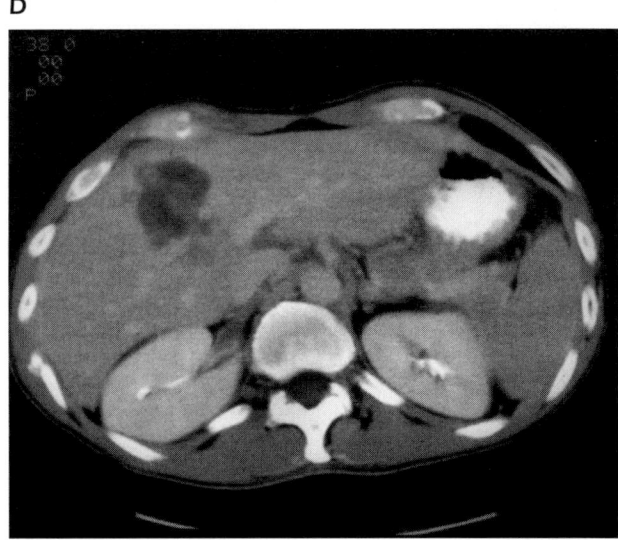

E

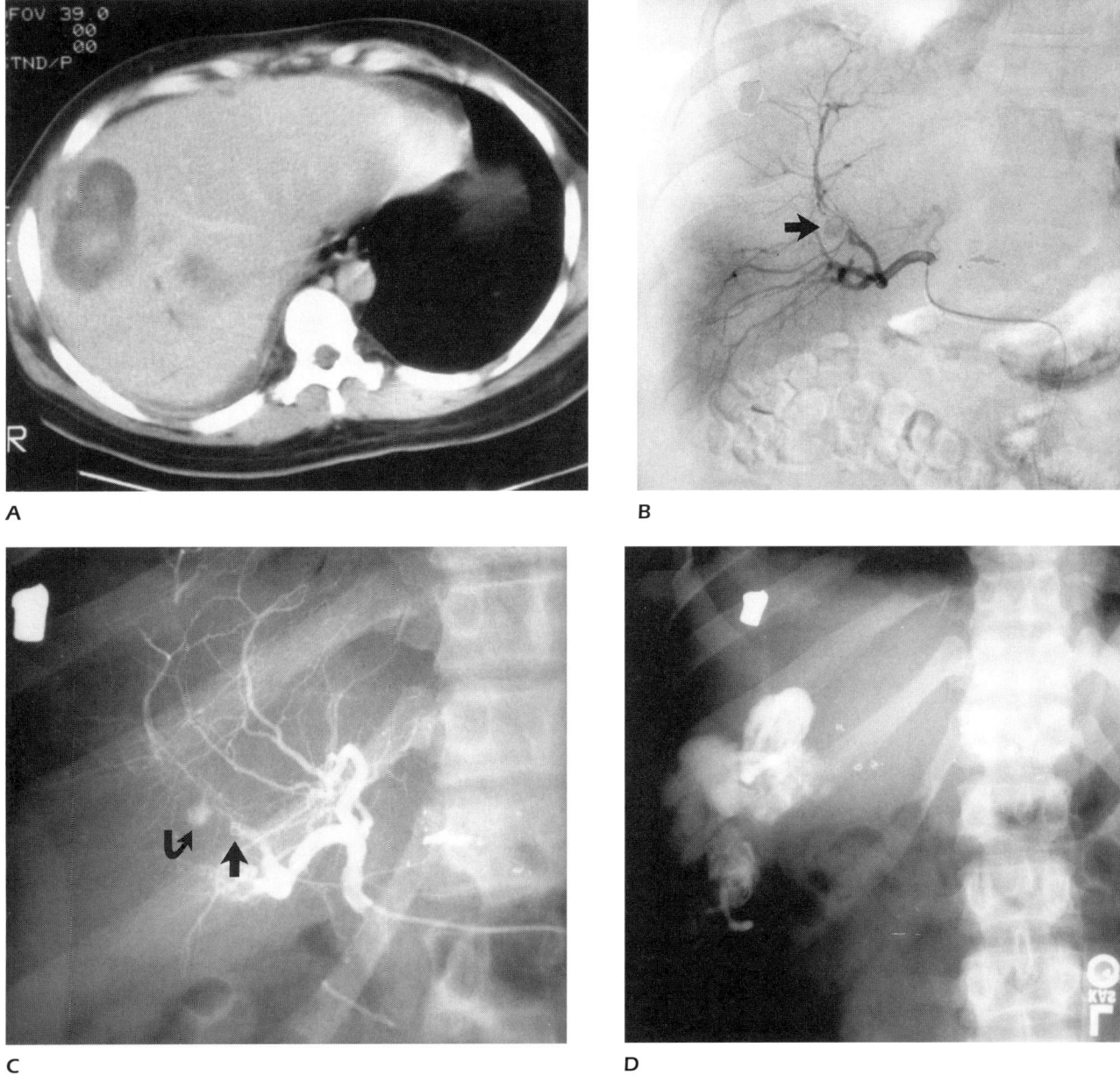

Figure 26-2. A 20-year-old victim of a gunshot wound to the right upper quadrant of the abdomen sustained 1 month previously with resultant T12 paraplegia and a hepatic injury that was initially diagnosed and managed surgically. Over the next 10 days there was moderate elevation of temperature and a slowly dropping hematocrit. (A) CT scan reveals a mixed-density fluid collection in the right lobe of the liver. (B) A difficult access was overcome by using a hydrophilic (slippery) cobra catheter plus a glidewire; selective hepatic arteriography then demonstrated a 1-cm false aneurysm arising from a branch of the right hepatic artery (*arrow*). (C) The vessels feeding the aneurysm were occluded with three Gelfoam strips and three 3-mm steel coils. A postembolization hepatic arteriogram shows the occluding coil(s) (*straight arrow*) and persistent preembolization extravasation (*curved arrow*) but no fresh extravasation. (D) The patient stabilized but subsequently required drainage of a large fluid collection (opacified with contrast media) that proved to be an infected biloma (note embolized coils). Ultimately, the patient recovered.

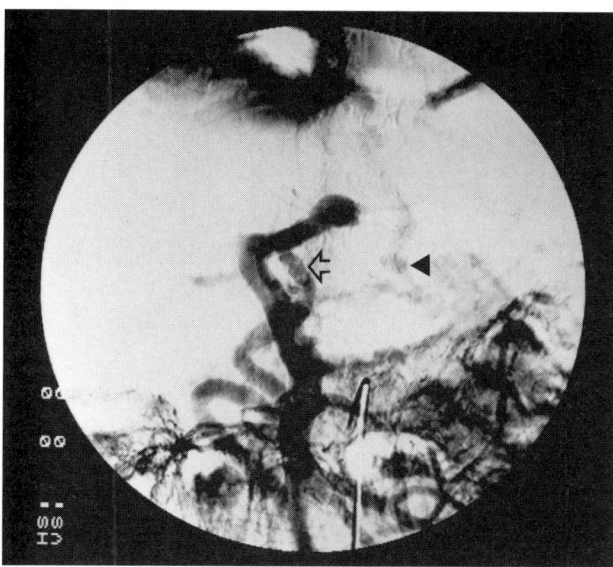

A

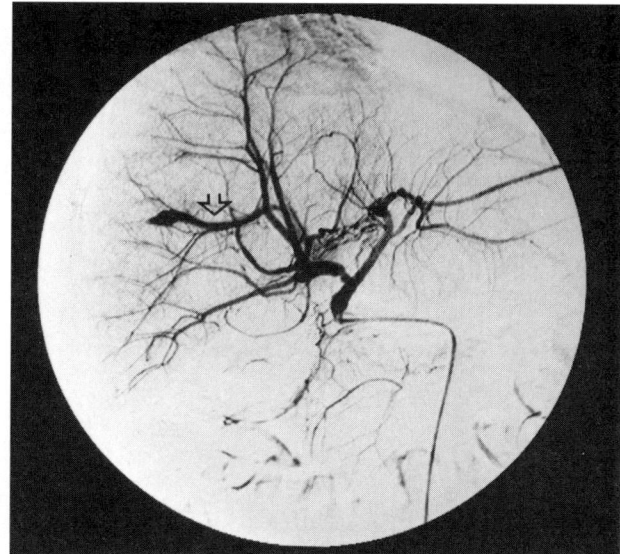

B

Figure 26-3. A 39-year-old woman who reportedly underwent open hepatic biopsy in Brazil. Biopsy diagnosis was hepatic cirrhosis secondary to schistosomiasis. Two months later the patient was admitted to the University of Medicine and Dentistry in New Jersey for a transjugular intrahepatic portosystemic shunt (TIPS) procedure. Hepatic biopsy was repeated, this time by a percutaneous method, and the pathology report indicated normal liver. (A) Transarterial portography obtained after a superior mesenteric artery contrast injection demonstrates no portal flow into the right hepatic lobe. The left portal branch drains into a large umbilical vein (*arrow*). An enlarged left gastric vein and esophageal varices are faintly opacified (*arrowhead*). (B) Selective hepatic arteriogram demonstrates an AVF (*arrow*) arising from a branch of the right hepatic artery that apparently resulted from one of the biopsies. (C) Late phase hepatic arteriogram demonstrates persistent contrast material in the right and central portal venous systems.

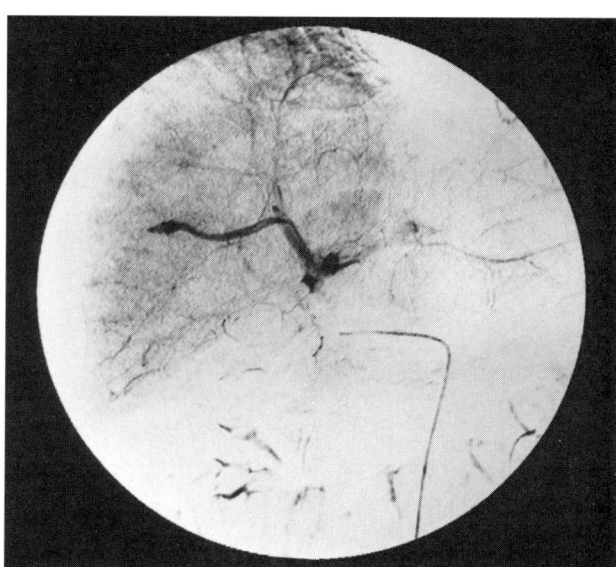

C

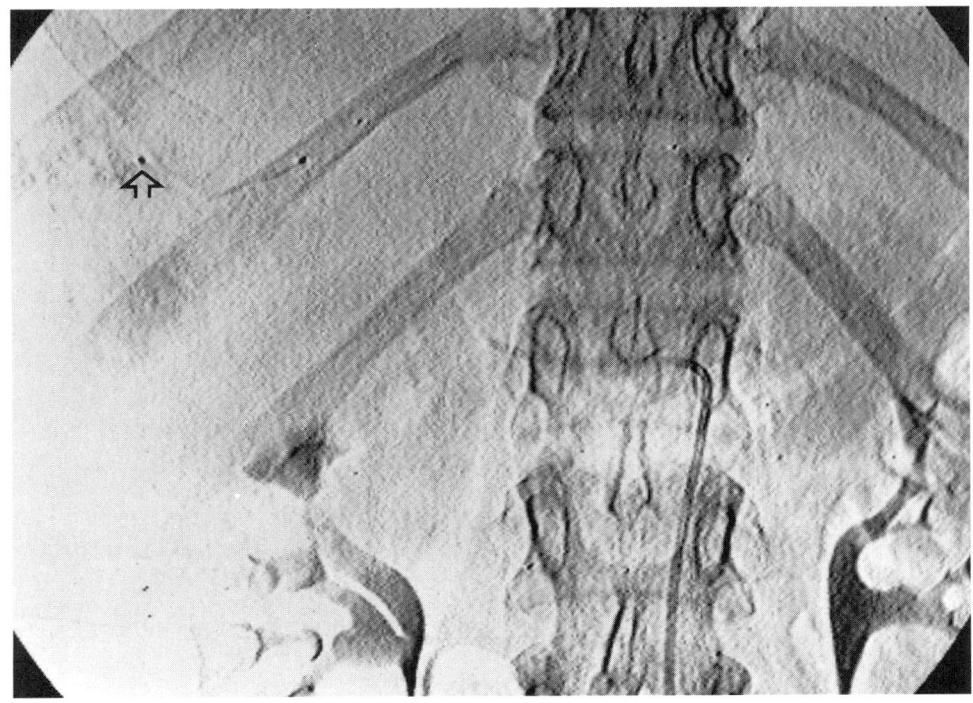

D

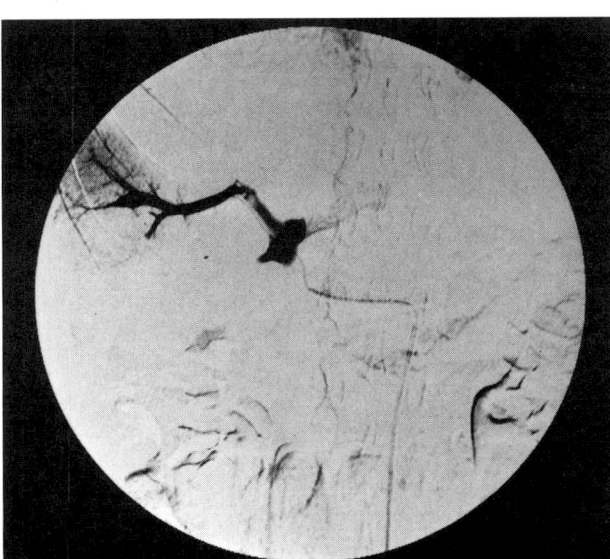

E

Figure 26-3 (continued). (D) The AVF was then accessed with a coaxial catheter (Tracker-18). The tip of the catheter is actually in the portal vein side of the AVF (*arrow*). (E) Contrast injection through the Tracker catheter demonstrates only portal venous filling. (F) Three cloverleaf microcoils were deposited directly in the fistula (*arrow*). (G) Follow-up hepatic arteriogram again shows the coils (*arrow*) and successful occlusion of the AVF. (H) Repeat transarterial portogram, again following superior mesenteric artery injection, now demonstrates normal opacification of the right portal venous system. Embolized coils and persistence of paraumbilical vein filling are again noted. Following embolization, a TIPS procedure was attempted but no hepatic vein was discernible. (I) Transhepatic venography was then done via the right hepatic lobe using a no. 22 needle. Opacification of a right hepatic vein is demonstrated (*arrow*), but communication with the inferior vena cava is occluded. Drainage is occurring by way of a transhepatic collateral vein that enters the left hepatic vein (*curved arrow*), which is also occluded at its orifice. These findings established the diagnosis of Budd-Chiari syndrome.

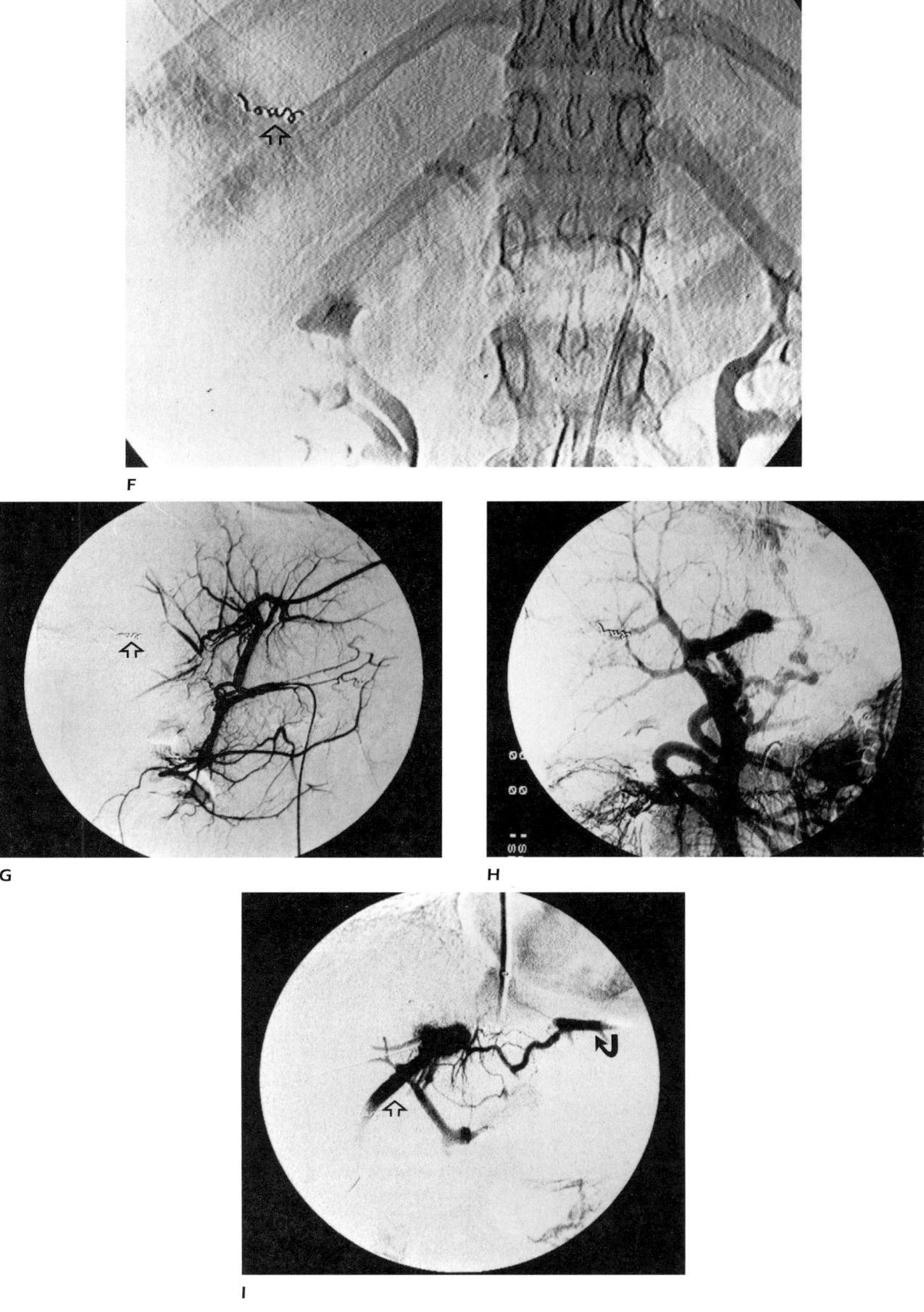

F

G

H

I

Table 26-1. Liver Injury Scale

Grade[a]		Injury Description[b]
I.	Hematoma	Subcapsular, nonexpanding, <10% surface area.
	Laceration	Capsular tear, nonbleeding, with <1 cm deep parenchymal disruption.
II.	Hematoma	Subcapsular, nonexpanding, hematoma 10–50%; intraparenchymal, nonexpanding, <2 cm in diameter.
	Laceration	<3 cm parenchymal depth, <10 cm in length.
III.	Hematoma	Subcapsular, >50% of surface area or expanding; ruptured subcapsular hematoma with active bleeding; intraparenchymal hematoma >2 cm.
	Laceration	>3 cm parenchymal depth.
IV.	Hematoma	Ruptured central hematoma.
	Laceration	Parenchymal destruction involving 25–75% of hepatic lobe.
V.	Laceration	Parenchymal destruction >75% of hepatic lobe.
	Vascular	Juxtahepatic venous injuries (retrohepatic cava/major hepatic veins).
VI.	Vascular	Hepatic avulsion.

[a]Advance one grade for multiple injuries.
[b]Based on most accurate assessment at autopsy, laparotomy, or radiologic study.
Adapted from the Organ Injury Scaling Committee, EE Moore, Chairman, American Association for the Surgery of Trauma, December 1988. Used with permission.

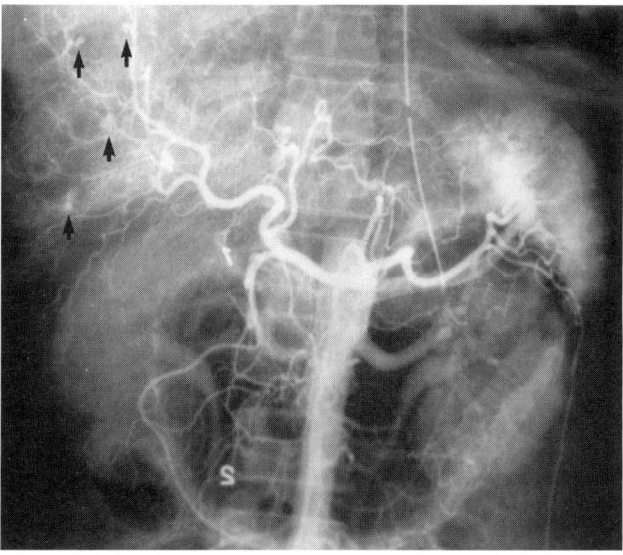

Figure 26-4. A 39-year-old woman who was involved in a motor vehicle accident. (A) An aortogram reveals a large area of extravasation in the spleen and multiple foci of extravasation in the liver (*arrows*).

hematomas that ultimately may require percutaneous drainage. Cross-sectional imaging can show the results of many of these injuries (e.g., hematomas) and may also display some false aneurysms. However, catheter angiography is necessary for definitive localization and for providing the route for embolotherapy.

Timing of Angiography and Embolization

Angiographic diagnosis and subsequent embolotherapy in trauma are potentially urgent procedures,[8] including procedures for hepatic artery branch injuries.[9] A few patients with street trauma have been treated by the authors and others[10] at the time of initial injury, and so have avoided surgery (see Fig. 26-1). However, the patient must be stable during interventional techniques, and many hepatic trauma victims are unstable because of active bleeding and require immediate surgical intervention. As a result, most reported instances of embolotherapy have occurred in the postoperative

patient who has rebled or in those with complications from percutaneous procedures. Rebleeding and/or false aneurysm formation can occur in either of these categories in the immediate postoperative or postprocedure hours, at any time over the next several days, or even months later (Fig. 26-6). These conditions may present as fresh blood in a drain tube and/or a drop in hematocrit or hemobilia. Again, angiography is essential for demonstrating active bleeding and false aneurysm or arteriovenous fistula (AVF) formation. If none of these are seen, the hemorrhage may be venous or parenchymal, and medical management ensues. Consideration may occasionally be given to "preventive embolization" (treatment of an occluded or torn nonbleeding arterial branch) to avoid a potential "3:00 AM emergency embolization syndrome" due to rebleeding.

Embolization

Indications

The primary indication for embolization in hepatic trauma is hemorrhage. Clinically a patient may be hypotensive with a dropping hematocrit; in more stable patients, ultrasound may show fluid collections or CT may display intrahepatic or subcapsular hematomas and/or hepatic lacerations. Others will present with hemobilia, or a bleeding hepatic artery branch may be

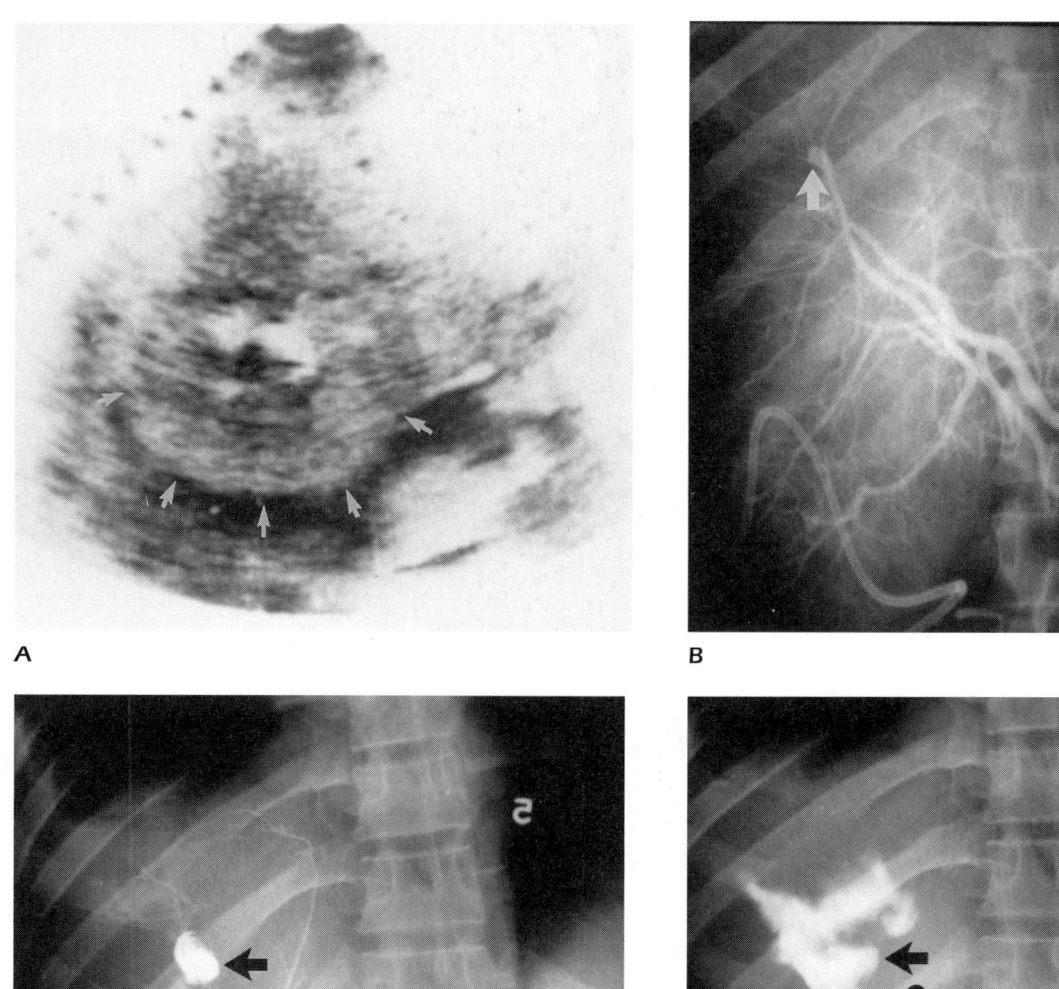

A

B

C

D

Figure 26-5. A 25-year-old man with a gunshot wound to the liver that required emergency surgical management. (A) Postoperative ultrasound reveals a complex mass in the right lobe of the liver (*arrows*) and a subhepatic fluid collection. The latter was drained and proved to be a hematoma. (B) Subsequent common hepatic arteriogram shows two large right hepatic arteries and a subtle false aneurysm in the right lobe of the liver (*arrow*). A drainage catheter is seen in the subhepatic region. (C) Hand-injected subselective arteriogram with the catheter near the site of injury reveals a large false aneurysm (*straight arrow*) and immediate extravasation (*curved arrow*). (D) After prompt embolization with multiple Gelfoam strips, a repeat common hepatic arteriogram shows extensive extravasation (*straight arrow*) that occurred before embolization, and stasis of contrast material in the occluded right hepatic artery branch (*curved arrow*). The hemorrhage ceased and the patient was later discharged in good condition.

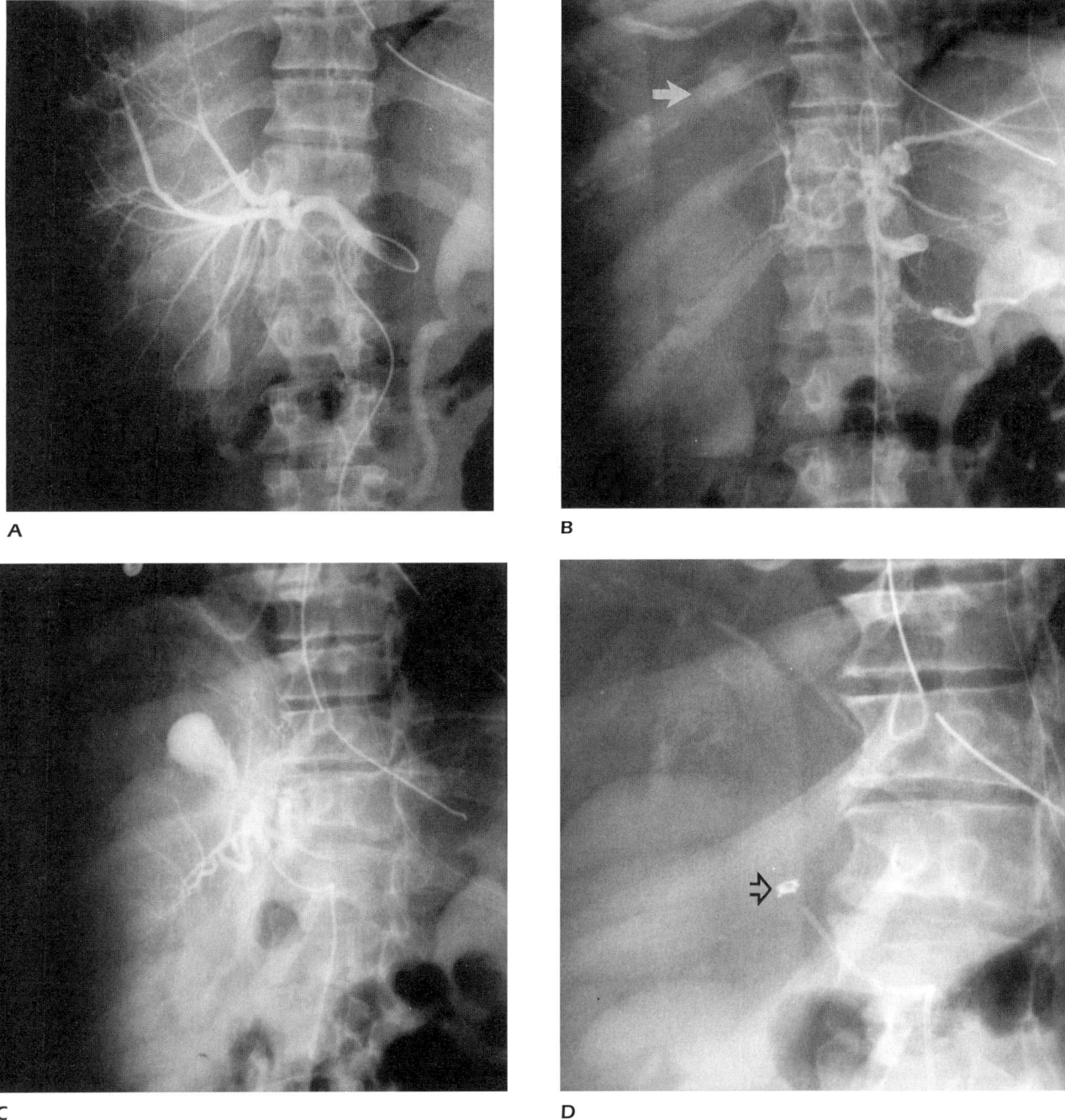

A

B

C

D

Figure 26-6. A 48-year-old man with a right lobe liver laceration resulting from a motor vehicle accident that was repaired surgically. Four weeks later the patient was readmitted with right upper quadrant pain and became hypotensive in the emergency center. Three sequential surgical attempts to contain the hemorrhage were unsuccessful. The patient was ultimately taken to the angiography suite for possible embolization of the right hepatic artery. (A) Aortography revealed an aberrant right hepatic artery, which was selected and shows no abnormality. (B) Subsequent selective celiac arteriography reveals the presence of left and middle hepatic arteries and a faint false aneurysm (*arrow*) arising from the latter. The splenic artery has a separate origin. (C) Subselection of the injured middle hepatic artery branch shows a large and now obvious false aneurysm. (D) Embolization with a single 5-mm steel coil (*arrow*) achieved the desired hemostasis. (E) Follow-up celiac arteriogram shows occlusion of the false aneurysm. The patient recovered.

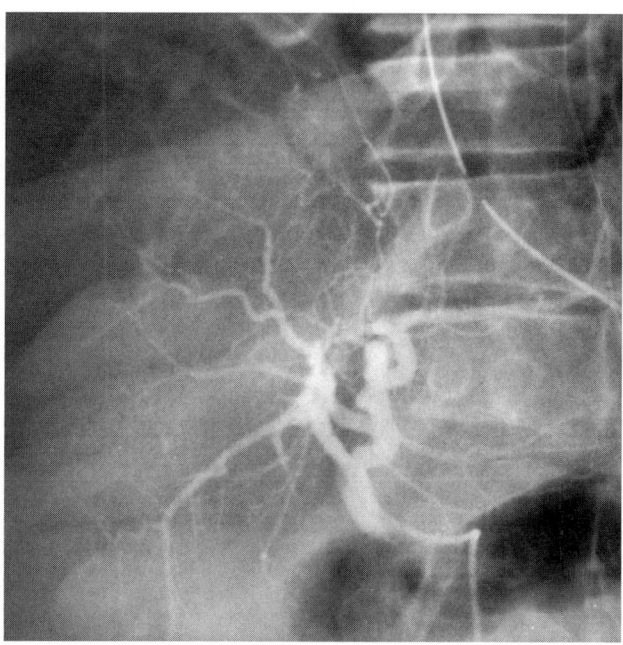

E   **Figure 26-6** (continued).

discovered during the general preoperative angiographic workup of a blunt trauma victim.[8] A demonstrated area of hemorrhage, a false aneurysm, or an arterial portal fistula (APF) can be embolized and the need for surgery thus circumvented (Fig. 26-7). However, most street trauma–induced hepatic injuries are still managed surgically. Therefore, the most common indicator for embolization in this group is, as indicated previously, the postoperative patient who rebleeds (see Fig. 26-6).[9] Apparent surgical hemostasis may convert to breakthrough bleeding as the patient's blood volume is returned to normal in the postoperative period.[9]

Alternatively, hepatic hemorrhage can and does occur as a direct result of percutaneous procedures. The majority of reported patients (1976–1993) in this category with hepatic artery branch injuries have been managed primarily with embolization techniques, with surgery being reserved for treatment failures.[3, 10–20]

Anatomic Considerations

The variability of the arterial blood supply to the liver is well known to the experienced angiographer. The most common alteration is partial or complete replacement of the left hepatic artery by way of the left gastric artery. The next most common alteration is partial replacement of the right hepatic artery with an accessory branch or a situation in which the entire right hepatic artery arises from the superior mesenteric artery. Rarely, the common hepatic artery arises entirely from

the superior mesenteric artery, or there is a common celiomesenteric trunk. Furthermore, the origin of the celiac trunk is variable in that it can extend tangentially out from the aorta, curve abruptly cephalad, or extend abruptly caudad. In some, the celiac trunk may form a tight **S** turn, which can be particularly difficult to negotiate. The anatomic variations of the celiac and superior mesenteric trunks and their branches are well described by Kadir.[21]

Embolization is permissible in the liver because of its unique three-system vascular architecture (the hepatic artery, the portal vein, and the hepatic vein). Portal vein patency is essential when hepatic artery embolization is contemplated. Indeed, portal occlusion or reversed (hepatofugal) flow is a contraindication to embolization.[9] The patency and direction of flow can quickly be established angiographically.

Techniques

A standard sequence of events in the pursuit of a hepatic artery injury is aortography followed by celiac and superior mesenteric arteriography to display the arterial anatomy. The status of the portal vein and its flow direction can be determined at the same sitting by extending the filming sequence through the venous phase. These sequences are followed by selective hepatic arteriography. This procedure can be technically difficult and may require various catheters and guidewires (Fig. 26-8). Available catheter shapes include the standard visceral curve, the cobra curve, the Finck catheter, the left gastric curve, several Simmons curves, and the dedicated hepatic curve (Cook, Inc.). In the authors' experience, the cobra is the most common curve used for subselective placement, especially when embolization is the goal. In difficult cases, precise small-vessel peripheral selection and embolization may be accomplished with the newer Tracker catheter systems (Target Therapeutics) and platinum microcoils (Target Therapeutics and Cook, Inc.) or with small-particle embolization. Guidewires have also evolved over the years from standard straight guidewires to J tips, movable core wires in a variety of longer floppy tips such as the Bentson and Newton catheters (Cook, Inc.). Perhaps the single greatest advance in technology for selective angiography in the authors' parallel experience of over 25 years has been the development of the hydrophilic (slippery) guidewire (Medi-Tech). A similar coating is also available on catheters (Medi-Tech).

Once a hepatic bleeding site, false aneurysm, or APF is identified, the catheter should be advanced as close as possible to the lesion before embolization (see Fig. 26-2). An APF may be quickly recognized or may

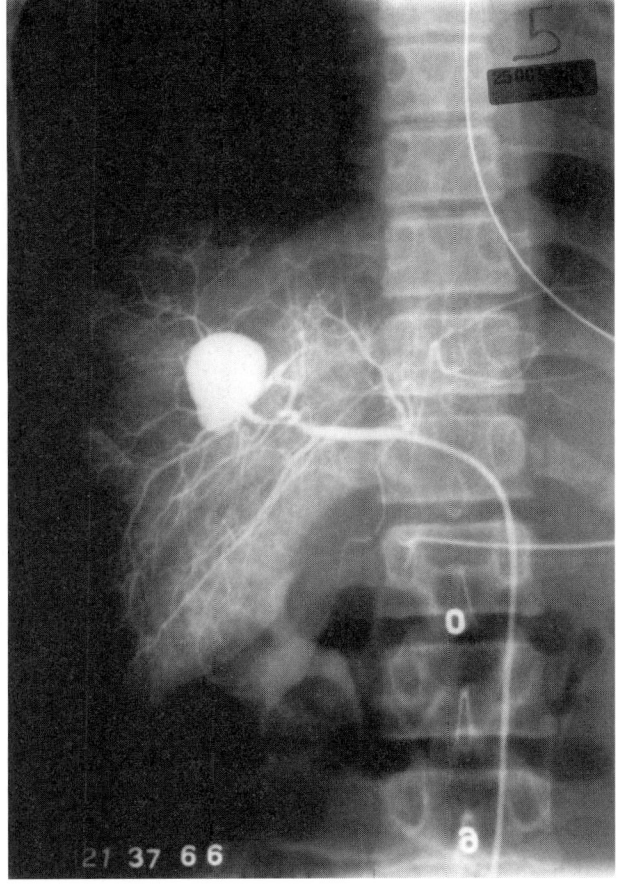

A

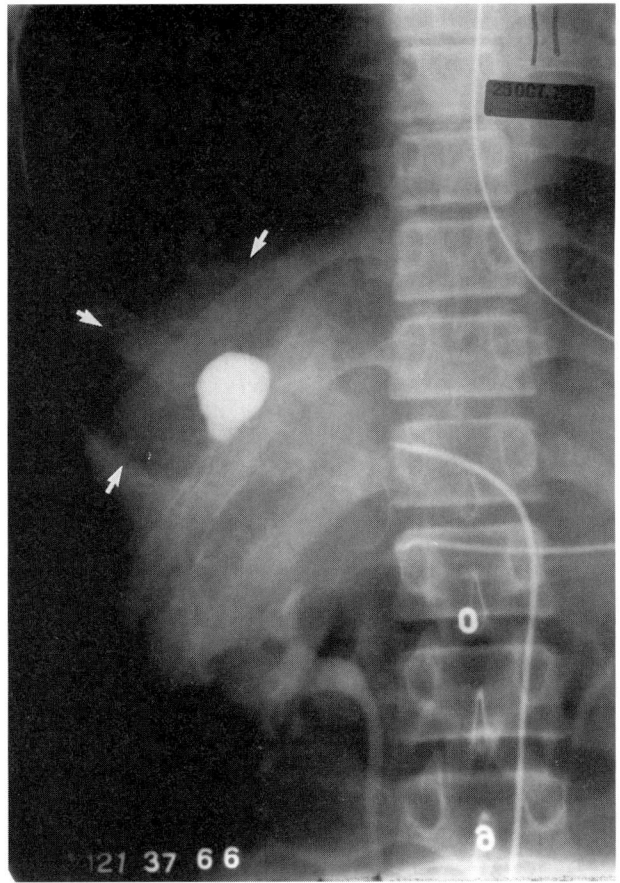

B

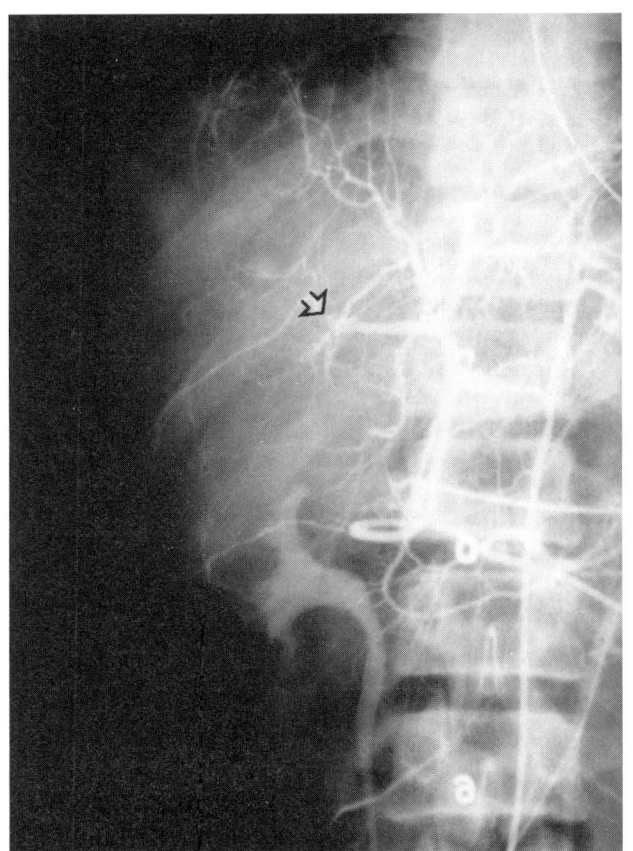

C

Figure 26-7. A 14-year-old boy who fell off his bike 4 weeks previously and who presented with bright red rectal bleeding. Ultrasound revealed a complex intrahepatic mass with a sonolucent center. (A) Selective right hepatic arteriography shows a large false aneurysm and (B) a surrounding lucent halo (*arrows*) indicative of a large hematoma. (C) A single 5-mm coil was placed (*arrow*) to occlude the right hepatic artery and the false aneurysm. The bleeding ceased.

initially present as early portal filling from a particular liver segment, and more specific selection may be needed to pinpoint the site of the actual communication.

A variety of embolic materials have been used to treat traumatic liver lesions: Gelfoam,[10] coils,[10] detachable balloons,[22] balloon occlusion catheters,[17] Amicar plus clot,[23] Silastic beads,[24] cyanoacrylate,[3] platinum microcoils,[25] and Ivalon (Ivalon Inc., San Diego, CA).[18] The authors' preference, especially in trauma patients, is to use Gelfoam when possible (see Fig. 26-5) and to hope for recanalization of vessels later. For large-vessel occlusions, the authors have used coils (see Fig. 26-7). In difficult cases, a combination of materials may be necessary. Figure 26-8 is an example of a huge false aneurysm requiring the use of multiple coils and ultimately thrombin for occlusion. Destructive fluids such as alcohol or phenol must not be used

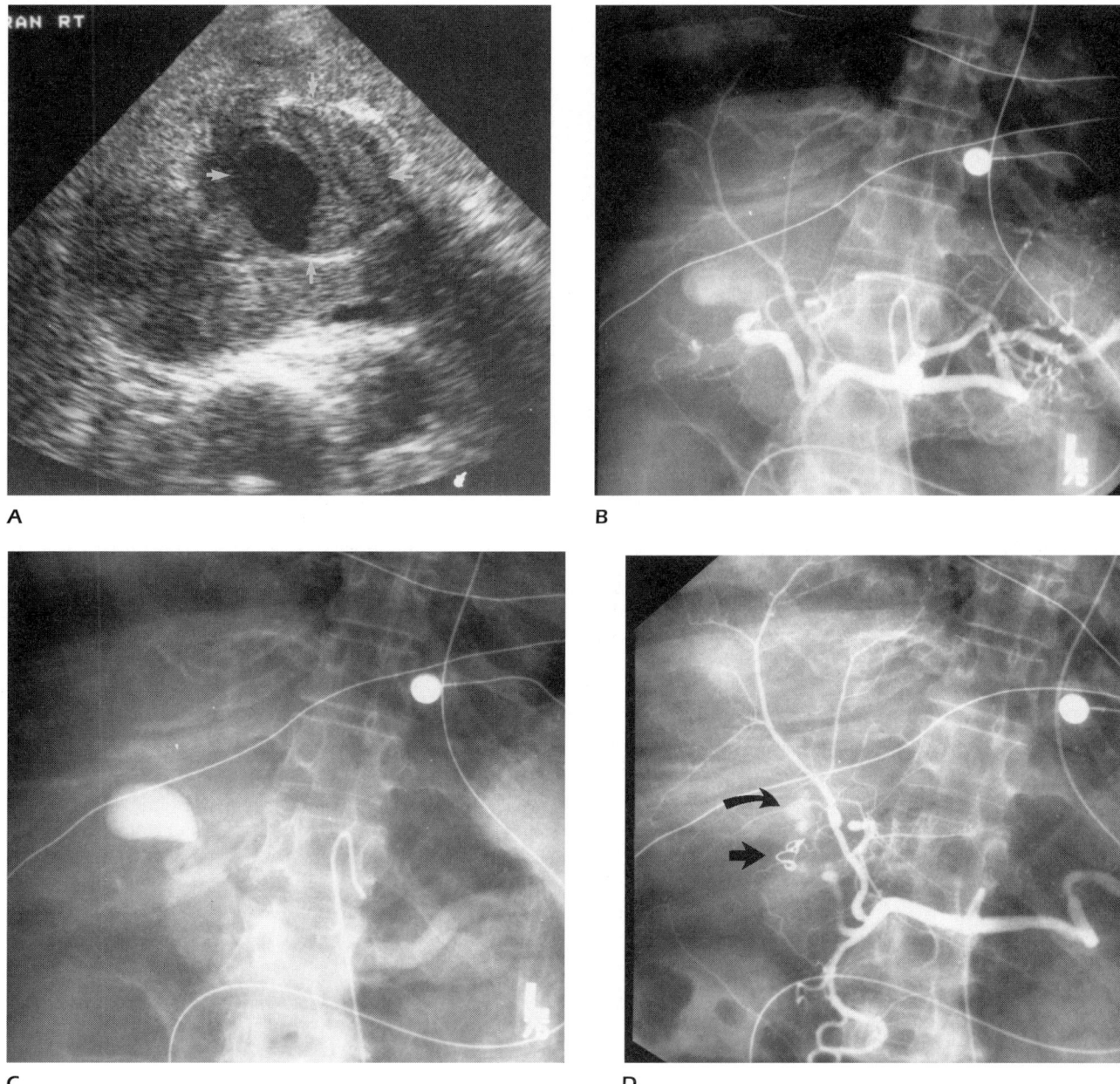

A

B

C

D

Figure 26-8. A 70-year-old woman who presented to an outside hospital with a history of a urinary tract infection and multiple systems complaints. There was no history of trauma, but there was a history of chronic ethanol abuse. (A) A complex intrahepatic mass with a sonolucent core is demonstrated on ultrasound (*arrows*), with corresponding findings on CT. The patient was subsequently referred to the Texas Medical Center for further evaluation. The prior examinations were reviewed and were considered to be most likely representative of a false aneurysm. Angiography with a possibility of embolization was undertaken. The celiac artery was cannulated with a Chung catheter, and a very large false aneurysm was demonstrated: (B) early phase, (C) late phase. A Tracker catheter was then advanced out through the Chung catheter and two microcoils were deposited, but the aneurysm persisted. The catheters were then exchanged for a hydrophilic (slippery) cobra catheter that was advanced

directly to the region of the false aneurysm, and 300 units of thrombin were introduced, successfully occluding the false aneurysm. (D) Follow-up celiac arteriogram shows the coils (*straight arrow*) and a small amount of contrast media (*curved arrow*) trapped in the thrombosed aneurysm. The patient had multiple medical problems (not related to the embolization) and remained hospitalized. Six weeks after embolization, necrosis of the right lobe of the liver developed after a stormy medical course that included hepatic encephalopathy, renal failure, and renal dialysis, as well as gangrene of the toes, presumably due to emboli from a previously demonstrated large aortic aneurysm. The right lobe of the liver was partially resected surgically, but the patient ultimately succumbed to multiple systems failure. (Courtesy of Mary Round, M.D., St. Luke's Episcopal Hospital, Houston, TX.)

because of the risks of hepatic necrosis and biliary fibrosis.[26] APFs, like any fistula in trauma, are a special circumstance and require careful selection of coil size. Despite proper sizing, large APFs may be difficult to occlude and may require repeat embolization[27] or may ultimately result in a treatment failure.[10]

Success and Failure

Despite the availability of embolization techniques for over 20 years, the use of embolization to control posttraumatic hepatic hemorrhage has been sporadic, with approximately 123 cases reported in the literature.[3,4,7,9–20,22–25,27–48] Seventy injuries resulted from street trauma (42 blunt, 27 penetrating). Fifty-four represented complications of medical procedures, 31 of which were percutaneous biliary drainages. Successful embolization with permanent control of hemorrhage occurred in most patients. The overall reported success was 93 percent; however, most reports represent small series (five or fewer) or individual case reports. In a recent larger series (24 patients),[10] hemorrhage was controlled with initial embolization in 88 percent. Failures occurred because of inability to cannulate the bleeding vessel or even the celiac trunk in the face of celiac stenosis.[10] The authors were unable to approach a left hepatic artery false aneurysm because the celiac trunk was occluded, with all of its branches being supplied from the superior mesenteric artery by way of the pancreaticoduodenal/gastroduodenal arcade. Tracker catheters have overcome these difficulties in a few instances.[10,20,25,27] Recurrent hemorrhage has also been described in selected cases, most of which were controlled with reembolization.[3,13,27,33,35] In some cases aggressive and innovative tactics were necessary: direct percutaneous puncture of false aneurysms and occlusion with coils[13,35] or thrombin[12] or multiple collateral vessel occlusions (hepatic artery, left gastric artery, right inferior phrenic artery, and gastroduodenal artery branches) with bucrylate.[27] In the last-mentioned instance, a recurrent hemorrhage months later required a third embolization procedure using Tracker catheters.

Complications

Hepatic necrosis and abscess formation, nontarget embolization, gallbladder infarction, and catheter-induced damage to vessels are uncommon but feared potential complications of hepatic artery embolization. The dual blood supply of the liver provides a relative protection from embolization-induced necrosis because 75 percent of hepatic circulation in a normal liver is by way of the portal vein.[10] Hepatic fibrosis (cirrhosis) with portal hypertension increases the risk potential. As indicated earlier, advanced disease with hepatofugal flow is a contraindication to embolization.[9] Research has also indicated that rapid development of collateralization after hepatic artery occlusion is equally important to hepatic preservation, and that true peripheral embolization is more likely to infarct despite normal portal flow.[49] This is not likely to occur with Gelfoam strips or coils because they generally occlude more proximally.[49]

These factors may help explain why relatively few incidences of hepatic infarction or abscess formation have been reported after embolization.[3,10,31] Hepatic abscess formation after street trauma is also common, making it difficult to assess the specific incidence of embolization-induced necrosis or abscess formation in this group. Schwartz et al.[10] reported 13 incidences of abscesses or phlegmon and 4 incidences of sepsis in 24 embolized patients. However, it is unclear whether any of these were related to embolization or whether they were the result of the primary trauma. Savader et al.[3] recorded 3 abscesses in 13 patients (23 percent) who were embolized for complications of percutaneous biliary drainage. These were more likely embolization-induced. Franklin et al.[31] reported a postembolic infarction that resolved without surgical intervention.

Complications related to selective catheterization have been infrequently reported in hepatic embolization. However, the authors' several years of experience with celiac hepatic angiography has included a small but definite incidence of catheter-induced complication, almost always without serious consequence. Schwartz et al.[10] recorded two such incidences in 24 cases (8 percent). One was a celiac axis dissection and the other an inadvertent gastroduodenal artery occlusion, but apparently neither patient suffered any sequelae and both were successfully embolized.

Gallbladder infarction has been reported in patients who were extensively embolized specifically to control hepatic neoplasms.[50] Precisely locating the origin of the cystic artery before right lobe embolization in the trauma patient can help avoid this potential complication (see Fig. 26-5).[50]

References

1. Pachter HL, Liang HG, Hofstetter SR. Liver and biliary tract trauma. In: Moore EE, Mattox KL, Feliciano DV, eds. Trauma. 2nd ed. Norwalk, CT: Appleton & Lang, 1991.
2. Feliciano DV, Pachter HL. Hepatic trauma revisited. Curr Probl Surg 1989;26:453–524.
3. Savader SJ, Trerotola SO, Marine DS, Venbrux AC, Osterman FA. Hemobilia after percutaneous transhepatic biliary drainage: treatment with transcatheter embolotherapy. J Vasc Intervent Radiol 1992;3:345–352.

4. Richardson A, Simmons K, Gutmann J, Little JM. Hepatic hemobiliary: nonoperative management in 8 cases. Aust N Z J Surg 1985;55:447–451.
5. Foley WD, Cates JD, Kellman GM. Treatment of blunt hepatic injuries: role of CT. Radiology 1987;164:635–638.
6. Boijsen E, Judkins MP, Simay A. Angiographic diagnosis of hepatic rupture. Radiology 1966;86:66–72.
7. Lambeth W, Rubin BE. Nonoperative management of intrahepatic hemorrhage in hematoma following blunt trauma. Surg Gynecol Obstet 1979;148:507–511.
8. Ben-Menachem Y, Fisher TG. Radiology. In: Moore EE, Mattox KL, Feliciano DV. Trauma. 2nd ed. Norwalk, CT: Appleton & Lange, 1991:195–217.
9. Sclafani SJA, Ben-Menachem Y. Embolotherapy in abdominal trauma. In: Neal MP Jr, Tisnado J, Cho S, eds. Emergency interventional radiology. Boston: Little, Brown, 1989:53–77.
10. Schwartz RA, Teitlebaum GP, Katz MD, Pentecost MJ. Effectiveness of transcatheter embolization in the control of hepatic and vascular injuries. J Vasc Intervent Radiol 1993;4:359–365.
11. Beningfield SJ, Bornman PC, Krieg JEJ, Terblanche J. Control of hemobilia by embolization of a false aneurysm and arterioportobiliary fistula of the hepatic artery. AJR 1991;156:1263–1265.
12. Cope C, Zeit R. Coagulation of aneurysms by direct percutaneous thrombin injection. AJR 1986;147:383–387.
13. Clouse ME. Hepatic artery embolization for bleeding and tumors. Surg Clin North Am 1989;69:419–432.
14. Maroney TP. Transcatheter embolization thrives despite controversy. Diagn Imaging 1986:102–106.
15. Merino-de Villasante J, Rodriguez RE, Ortiz J. Management of post-biopsy hemobilia with selective arterial embolization. AJR 1977;128:668–671.
16. Perlberger RR. Control of hemobilia by angiographic embolization. AJR 1977;128:672–673.
17. Sniderman KW, Morse SS, Rapoport S, Ross GR. Hemobilia following transhepatic biliary drainage: occlusion of an hepatoportal fistula by balloon tamponade. Radiology 1985;154:827.
18. Tisnado J, Bezirdjian DR. Transcatheter therapy of iatrogenic vascular injuries to the liver. Semin Roentgenol 1990;7:263–274.
19. Walter JF, Paaso BT, Cannon WB. Successful transcatheter embolic control of massive hematobilia secondary to liver biopsy. AJR 1976;127:847–849.
20. Zajko AB, Chablani B, Bron KM, Jungreis C. Hemobilia complicating transhepatic catheter drainage in liver transplant recipients: management with selective embolization. Cardiovasc Intervent Radiol 1990;13:285–288.
21. Kadir S. Atlas of normal and variant angiographic anatomy. Philadelphia: Saunders, 1991.
22. Ross P Jr, Denny DF Jr, Baker CC. Angiographic embolization of traumatic hepatic artery pseudoaneurysm. Conn Med 1990;54:308–310.
23. Kadir S, Athanasoulis CA, Ring EJ, Greenfield A. Transcatheter embolization of interhepatic arterial aneurysms. Radiology 1980;134:335–339.
24. MacGillivray DC, Valentine RJ. Nonoperative management of blunt pediatric liver injury—late complications: case report. J Trauma 1989;29:251–254.
25. Kaufman SL, Martin LG, Zuckerman AM, Coch SR, Silverstein MI, Barton JW. Peripheral transcatheter embolization with platinum microcoils. Radiology 1992;184:369–372.
26. Doppman JL, Girton ME. Bile duct scarring following ethanol embolization of the hepatic artery: an experimental study in monkeys. Radiology 1984;152:621–626.
27. Larut J, Vauthey N, Triller J, Gertsch PH, Schweiser W. Intrahepatic portal fistula following conservative treatment of a traumatic liver rupture: case report. J Trauma 1992;33:760–764.
28. Baker KS, Tisnado J, Chou S, Beachley MC. Splanchnic artery aneurysms in pseudoaneurysms: transcatheter embolization. Radiology 1987;163:135–139.
29. Bass EM, Crosier JH. Percutaneous control of post-traumatic hepatic hemorrhage by Gelfoam embolization. J Trauma 1977;17:61–63.
30. Fandrich BL, Genanadev D, Jaecks R, Boyle W. Selective hepatic arterial embolization as adjunct to liver packing in severe hepatic trauma: case report. J Trauma 1989;29:1716–1718.
31. Franklin RH, Bloom WF, Schoffstal RO. Angiographic embolization as the definitive treatment of post-traumatic hemobilia. J Trauma 1980;20:702–705.
32. Hashimoto S, Hiramatsu K, Ido K, Yosii H, Motegi M, Yamamoto S. Expanding role of emergency embolization in the management of severe blunt hepatic trauma. Cardiovasc Intervent Radiol 1990;13:193–199.
33. Heimbach DM, Ferguson DS, Harley JD. Treatment of traumatic hemobilia with angiographic embolization. J Trauma 1978;18:221–224.
34. Jander HP, Laws HL, Kogutt MS, Mihas A. Emergency embolization in blunt hepatic trauma. AJR 1977;129:249–252.
35. Lukancic SP, Nemcek AA, Bogelzang RL. Post-traumatic intrahepatic arterial pseudoaneurysm: treatment with direct percutaneous puncture. J Vasc Intervent Radiol 1991;2:335–337.
36. McDougal EG, Mandel SR. Traumatic hemobilia: successful nonoperative treatment in two cases. Am Surg 1984;50:169–170.
37. Mitchell SE, Shuman LS, Kaufman SL, Chang R, Kadir S, Kinnison M, White RI Jr. Biliary catheter drainage complicated by hemobilia: treatment by balloon embolotherapy. Radiology 1985;157:645–652.
38. Pain JA, Karani JB, Heaton NG, Howard ER. Selective arterial embolization for hepatic trauma. Ann R Coll Surg Engl 1991;73:189–193.
39. Pilla TJ, Tantana S, Shields JB. Embolization of blunt trauma in the pediatric patient. Cardiovasc Intervent Radiol 1987;10:153–156.
40. Rosch J, Putman JS, Keller FS. Diagnosis and management of hemobilia. Semin Roentgenol 1988;5:49–60.
41. Rosch J, Petersen BD, Hall LD, Ivancev K. Interventional treatment of hepatic arterial and venous pathology: a commentary. Cardiovasc Intervent Radiol 1990;13:183–188.
42. Rubin BE, Katzen BT. Selective hepatic artery embolization to control massive hepatic hemorrhage after trauma. AJR 1977;129:253–256.
43. Sclafani SJA. Angiographic control of intraperitoneal hemorrhage caused by injuries to the liver and spleen. Semin Intervent Radiol 1985;2:139–147.
44. Sclafani SJA, Nayaranaswami T, Mitchell WG. Radiologic management of traumatic hepatic arterial–portal vein arteriovenous fistula. J Trauma 1981;21:576–580.
45. Tanaka H, Iwai A, Sugimoto H, Yoshioka T, Sugimoto T. Intrahepatic arterial portal fistula after blunt hepatic trauma: case report. J Trauma 1991;31:143–146.
46. Tisnado J, Beachley MC, Cho S. Control of intrahepatic bleeding by super selective embolization of the middle hepatic artery. South Med J 1982;75:70–71.
47. Tobben PJ, Zajko AB, Sumkin JH, et al. Pseudoaneurysms complicating organ transplantation: roles of CT, duplex sonography, and angiography. Radiology 1988;169:65–70.
48. Uflacker R, Mourao GS, Piske RL, Souza VC, Lima S. Hemobilia: transcatheter occlusive therapy and long-term follow-up. Cardiovasc Intervent Radiol 1989;12:136–141.
49. Doppman JL, Girton RT, Kann ER. Proximal versus peripheral hepatic artery embolization: experimental study in monkeys. Radiology 1978;128:577–588.
50. Takayasu K, Moriyama N, Muramatsu Y, et al. Gallbladder infarction after hepatic embolization. AJR 1985;144:135–138.

27

Interventional Therapies for Hepatic Malignancy

MICHAEL J. PENTECOST

The management of the patient with unresectable hepatic malignancy, whether primary or metastatic, represents one of the most difficult problems in cancer care. The interests of interventional radiologists have centered around regional therapies for a group of unresectable tumors that are typically confined to the liver—hepatocellular carcinoma and metastases from colorectal carcinoma, ocular melanoma, and carcinoid and islet cell tumors. Because of the association with chronic hepatitis B in Asia, hepatocellular carcinoma is the most common fatal malignancy worldwide. Colorectal carcinoma claims nearly 60,000 American lives annually; about half of these patients succumb to liver metastases long after the primary malignancy has been successfully resected. Ocular melanoma and carcinoid and islet cell tumors are much less common malignancies; all share a propensity to metastasize exclusively to the liver, where they are notoriously resistant to systemic chemotherapy.

Overall, the results of treating liver tumors with systemic chemotherapy have been disappointing. Response rates to 5-fluorouracil (5-FU), the most common single agent used in treating liver metastases from colorectal carcinoma, seldom exceed 20 percent.[1] Similarly poor results (30 percent response rates) have been reported with hepatocellular carcinoma, and, for the most part, systemic chemotherapy has been abandoned as a treatment option in these patients.[2]

The landmark studies of Clarkson and Sullivan[3,4] opened the door to a number of regional therapies for hepatic malignancies, in these instances the hepatic artery infusion of antineoplastic agents via surgically or percutaneously placed catheters. The aim of these therapies was twofold: to deliver a higher concentration of drug directly to the tumor and to reduce toxicity by lowering the systemic level of agent. Over the past three decades, in the wake of these reports came a number of novel treatments, including the embolization of liver tumors with particulate agents,[5] the isolation of hepatic blood flow during massive infusion of chemotherapy,[6] the concurrent use of hyperthermia

and intraarterial chemotherapy,[7] the direct percutaneous instillation of agents such as ethanol and acetic acid,[8,9] portal vein infusion of chemotherapeutic agents,[10] and the injection of radioactive particles into the hepatic artery.[11]

Among interventional radiologists, the greatest enthusiasm and experience has centered around the marriage of two of these therapies—the simultaneous infusion of particulate and chemotherapeutic agents, or chemoembolization. The rationale of this combination was to provoke tumor ischemia and simultaneously increase the dwell time of the drug. Since the original experiences were described in the early 1980s,[12-14] a myriad different agents in various combinations have been investigated in the management of hepatocellular carcinoma and liver metastases.

Physiologic Basis

Several fortuitous circumstances permit regional hepatic artery infusions to be applied safely and effectively: the dual blood supply of the liver, the blood supply of tumors by the hepatic artery, and the ease of percutaneous catheterization of the hepatic artery.

The liver has a dual blood supply. Depending on body position, satiety, and other factors, the portal vein supplies about three-fourths and the hepatic artery one-fourth of hepatic circulation. This dual circulation allows for occlusion of either vessel without infarction. There have now been decades of experience in surgical and radiologic practice confirming the safety of intentional ligation or embolization of the hepatic artery or portal vein in the management of liver trauma and neoplasia.

Recent experiments have increased the understanding of these circulations. The previously held notion of the liver as a passive recipient of blood flow has been challenged. Lautt et al. observed the ability of the liver to vary oxygen extraction from the portal circulation in the face of a decline in flow in, or occlusion of, the hepatic artery.[15] Using color Doppler sonography, Ralls described the reversibility of portal flow between hepatopetal (toward the liver) and hepatofugal (away from the liver) in patients with cirrhosis.[16] Further, hepatofugal and hepatopetal flow in different branches of the portal vein have been demonstrated in the same patient. Even in patients with chronic hepatitis, cirrhosis, and hepatocellular carcinoma, this reciprocal, autoregulated flow allows hepatofugal flow in the portal vein to revert to hepatopetal in the face of hepatic artery embolization.

The supply of primary and metastatic liver tumors by the hepatic artery was originally described in studies using injection techniques and anatomic sectioning.[17,18] These observations have been confirmed in a number of physiologic studies. Sigurdson et al., with direct observation in surgery, infused fluorodeoxyuridine (FUDR) into the hepatic artery or portal vein prior to biopsy of liver metastases.[19] When radiolabeling techniques were used for assay, significantly higher levels of FUDR were found in specimens where the hepatic artery was injected than where the portal vein was infused. In a study using nitrogen-labeled amino acids, a greater nutrient supply to tumors was observed when the hepatic artery rather than the portal vein was injected.[20]

The dual circulation of the liver and the arterial supply of tumors would be moot points if selective and superselective catheterization of the hepatic artery could not be achieved expeditiously. Lubricious coating materials and microcatheters permit coaxial placement of catheters in the hepatic artery beyond branches to the intestine and gallbladder, even in the face of aberrant circulation or parasitized collateral vessels.

Chemotherapeutic and Embolic Agents

Many pharmacologic agents have been used for hepatic artery infusion (Table 27-1). Most, though not all, are agents that have some demonstrable activity at levels achievable during systemic infusion (e.g., 5-FU, FUDR, doxorubicin, bleomycin, cyclophosphamide, vincristine, mitomycin, and streptozotocin). The most frequently used drugs for chemoembolization are doxorubicin, cisplatin, and mitomycin.

Most agents used for regional infusion have two characteristics. First, when infused into the hepatic artery, the drug must be rapidly cleared by the liver (high "first-pass" clearance); this accounts for the 100- to 400-fold difference in concentration between the liver and systemic circulation of drugs such as 5-fluorouracil and FUDR.[21] Without such clearance, the hepatic ar-

Table 27-1. Cytotoxic Agents for Hepatic Artery Infusion and Chemoembolization

Bleomycin	Epirubicin	Bacille Calmette-Guérin
Carboplatinum	Mitomycin	Cisplatin
Doxorubicin	Mitomycin C	Cyclophosphamide
5-fluorouracil	Nitrogen mustard	Ethanol
Floxuridine	Phenylalanine mustard	Ifosfamide
Methotrexate	Streptozotocin	Interferon
Mitoxantrone	Vinblastine	Interleukin
SMANCS	Vincristine	Tumor necrosis factor
	Vindesine	

tery and systemic levels would be similar and no advantage would be conferred by regional treatment. Second, the drug must be more effective at higher doses (i.e., would have a steep dose-response curve). If the agent worked only in the dose range achieved with systemic infusion, there would be no point in directly injecting the hepatic artery. Added benefit is gained in that regional infusions result in lower systemic levels of drug and thereby less toxicity.

A number of embolic agents have been used to treat liver tumors (Table 27-2). The agents are broadly categorized into mechanical and particulate (further subdivided into permanent and temporary). Mechanical agents such as coils, differing little from proximal surgical ligation of a vessel, have little role in the primary management of liver tumors. The ischemic effect of such agents is, at best, fleeting because collateral flow quickly develops around the point of occlusion.[22] Mechanical coils are used to intentionally occlude vessels ("coil blockade") so that the chemotherapeutic agent or particles will not perfuse a nontarget circulation. Examples include embolization of the gastroduodenal artery when the left hepatic artery arises from the common hepatic artery and surgical ligation of the left hepatic artery before placement of a catheter in the right hepatic artery (so that the left lobe is perfused by intrahepatic collaterals).

In the cancer patient, the most experience has been accumulated with the embolic agents Gelfoam, polyvinyl alcohol, and Lipiodol. Gelfoam is a temporary agent made from gelatin surgical sponge. Experiments in animals demonstrate arterial recanalization after 2 to 6 weeks. Recanalization time in humans is less clear and, given the dwell time of chemotherapeutic agents,

Table 27-2. Embolic Agents Used for Embolization and Chemoembolization

Collagen	[131]I Lipiodol	Gelfoam
Ethylcellulose microspheres	Gianturco coils	Platinum microcoils
Lipiodol	Glass microspheres	Starch microspheres
Polyvinyl alcohol	Liposomes	

probably irrelevant. Polyvinyl alcohol particles, which range in size from 150 to 1000 μ, are also a frequent agent in chemoembolization. Proponents of embolization alone (to be distinguished from chemoembolization) advocate polyvinyl alcohol particles because they provide permanent occlusion. Of course, with the angiogenesis and parasitization of flow that accompanies hepatic malignancies, no embolic agent is truly permanent.

No controlled clinical trial has evaluated embolization or chemoembolization with the only variable being different particles. Therefore, any advantage of one agent over another is only conjecture. Some animal experiments demonstrate an inverse relationship between the tissue concentration of cisplatin and the size of accompanying embolic particle.[23]

Lipiodol is an oily agent that has been used for diagnostic imaging studies of the liver. There is now physiologic evidence to support the combination of Lipiodol and embolic particles in addition to chemotherapeutic agents as the appropriate mixture for chemoembolization. Kan et al.,[24,25] using in vivo microscopy, observed arterioportal shunting of Lipiodol in liver tumors in animals; that is, blood (or Lipiodol) flowed from arteriole to portal venule before entering the tumor bed. Lipiodol was then washed away by incoming higher-pressure arterial flow. They posited that the washout of drug and Lipiodol would be delayed by the addition of embolic particles, which would obstruct arterial flow. This would sandwich the liver tumors between Lipiodol in the portal vein and Gelfoam or polyvinyl alcohol in the hepatic arteries while bathing them in the chemotherapeutic agent; the occlusion of both arterial and portal vessels would interrupt the reciprocal flow to tumors between these two circulations. Two clinical studies support the notion of the synergistic effect of both agents. Takayasu et al.[26] (Table 27-3) observed significantly greater necrosis when both embolic agents were used than when oil alone or oil with doxorubicin was used. Similarly, Nakamura et al.[27] (Table 27-4) described longer survival rates when Lipiodol, Gelfoam, and doxorubicin

Table 27-3. Tumor Necrosis: Histologic Comparison Between Oily Embolization and Chemoembolization

Agent	Complete Necrosis, Main Tumor (%)	Necrosis, Daughter Nodule (%)
Oil	0	0
Oil + doxorubicin	13	6
Oil + doxorubicin + Gelfoam	83	53

Adapted from Takayasu K, Shima Y, Muramatsu Y, et al. Hepatocellular carcinoma: treatment with intraarterial iodized oil with and without chemotherapeutic agents. Radiology 1987;162:345–351.

Table 27-4. Cumulative Survival Rate in Hepatocellular Carcinoma: The Effect of Adding Oil to the Chemoembolic Infusion

Agent	6 Months (%)	1 Year (%)	2 Years (%)	3 Years (%)
Doxorubicin + Gelfoam	67	45	16	4
Doxorubicin + Gelfoam + Lipiodol	82	54	33	18

Adapted from Nakamura H, Hashimoto T, Oi H, et al. Transcatheter oily chemoembolization of hepatocellular carcinoma. Radiology 1989;170:783–786.

were used compared to Gelfoam and doxorubicin alone.

Patient Selection

Regional palliative therapies of liver tumors are predicated on two assumptions. First, the tumor, whether primary or metastatic, should be confined to the liver. One of the premises of regional infusions is the higher concentration of chemotherapeutic agent in the involved organ with a corresponding lower systemic level. Occasional exception is made if extrahepatic tumor burden is minimal or the response uneven (e.g., pulmonary lesions are responding to systemic chemotherapy but liver tumors are not).

Second, the liver tumors should be unresectable. The aim of surgical therapy is curative, not palliative as with regional infusions; indeed, newer techniques permit resection of extensive primary and metastatic tumors. In a recent report, 37 percent of patients with colorectal carcinoma who underwent resection for one liver metastasis and 18 percent with four metastases survived 5 years.[28] New imaging techniques, such as CT portography, have greatly aided in the accurate depiction of the size and location of such liver tumors.[29] In this technique, the injection of contrast into the superior mesenteric artery opacifies the portal vein and the normal hepatic parenchyma. Since liver tumors are supplied by the hepatic artery, they remain conspicuously unopacified. CT portography has been shown to be the most sensitive examination for detecting the number of hepatic lesions and, in so doing, has identified the patients most likely to benefit from resection.

Liver transplantation has also been offered to patients with primary and metastatic tumors; in a report of 383 consecutive transplants, 8.6 percent were for primary malignancy.[30]

The patients most likely to benefit from the regional therapies for hepatic malignancy are those in the earlier stages of disease. Numerous factors affecting response

Table 27-5. Factors Influencing Response or Survival in Patients Treated with Hepatic Chemoembolization

Encephalopathy	Elevated bilirubin, SGOT, SGPT
Cirrhosis	Serum albumin
Ascites	Portal vein invasion
Size of tumor	Oil retention
Grade (Edmondson and Steiner)	Change in alpha-fetoprotein
Biliary obstruction	

or survival have been investigated (Table 27-5). Predictably, patients with normal liver function do better than those with ascites, portal vein invasion, encephalopathy, jaundice, and hypoalbuminemia. Patients with even mild biliary obstruction are at particular risk for lobar infarction after chemoembolization, probably because of alteration in portal flow in the hepatic sinusoids in the presence of bile duct obstruction. With a lesser tumor burden, the response with chemoembolization is more beneficial and the postembolization syndrome less severe.

Technique

A precise definition of the hepatic arterial supply is essential for safe and effective use of the regional vascular therapies. There are several common variations in the arterial supply of the liver. The right hepatic artery is a branch of the superior mesenteric artery in about 15 percent of patients, and the left hepatic artery is a branch of the left gastric artery in about 25 percent. The gastroduodenal artery, the right gastric artery, the duodenal branches of the proper hepatic artery, and the cystic arteries must all be identified to avoid nontarget embolization. In patients with hypervascular liver tumors, there is frequently reversal of flow in the gastroduodenal artery (with filling via inferior pancreaticoduodenal branches of the superior mesenteric artery).

As noted earlier, regional vascular treatments depend on the dual or backup circulation of the liver by the portal vein. Since the hepatic artery is to be intentionally embolized, confirmation of portal vein patency is essential. This can be accomplished with superior mesenteric or splenic artery angiography (Fig. 27-1). This is particularly important in patients with hepatocellular carcinoma, in whom portal vein occlusion can occur in up to 39 percent.[31] Even in the presence of portal vein thrombus, hepatic chemoembolization can be safely performed if collateral flow is adequate (Fig. 27-2).[32] Since cirrhosis and hepatocellular carcinoma frequently coexist in patients with chronic hepatitis, the portal circulation should also be assessed for hepatofugal flow.

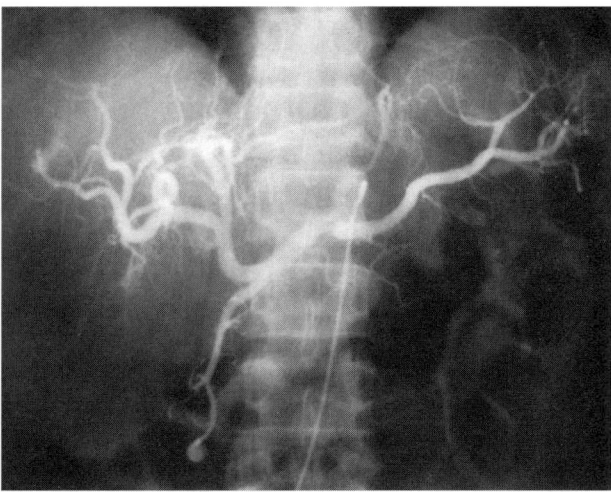

A

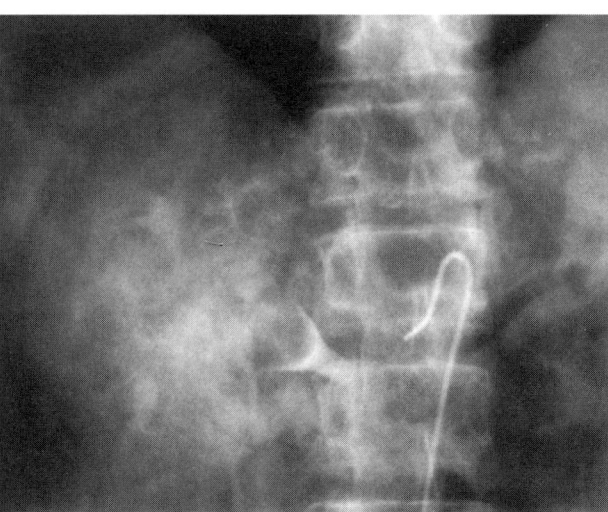

B

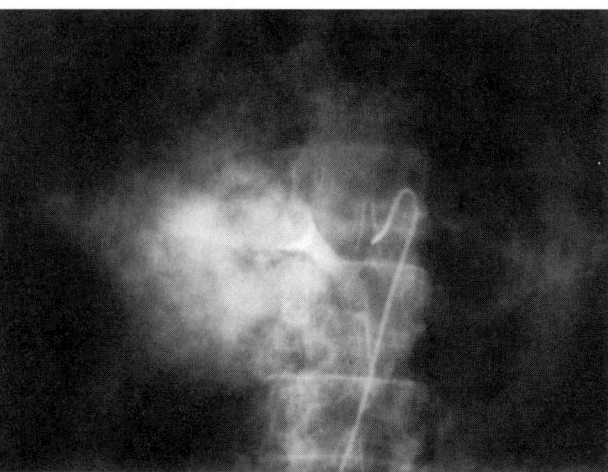

C

Figure 27-1. (A) Celiac angiography in patient with cirrhosis and hepatocellular carcinoma. (B and C) Large tumor thrombus filling and distending the portal vein in the liver hilum. Note the minimal opacification of the liver, mostly the inferior right lobe, from collateral flow.

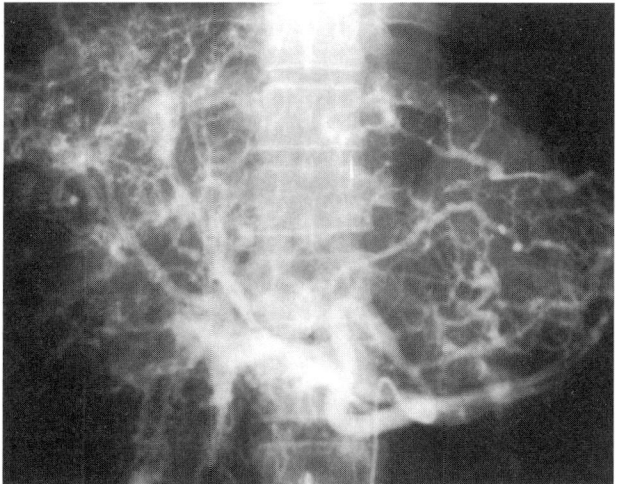

A

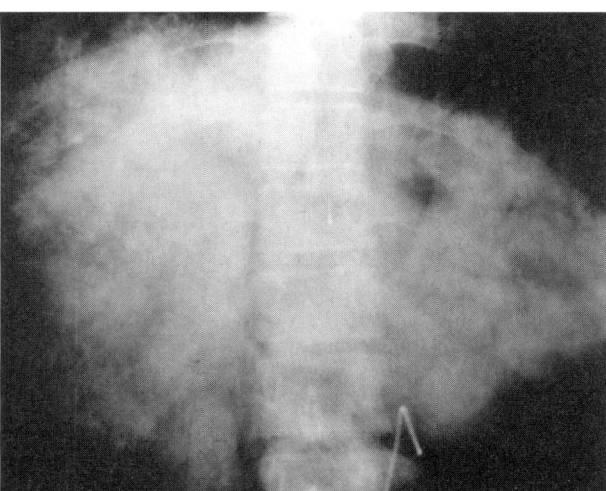

B

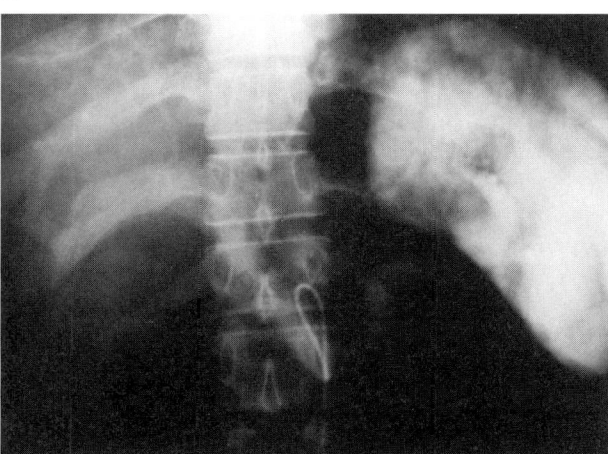

C

Figure 27-2. (A) Hypervascular hepatocellular carcinoma infiltrating entire liver. (B) Tumor thrombus forms a cast of the portal vein on delayed images. Nonetheless, extensive flow around the thrombus permitted safe chemoembolization. (C) Recanalization of the portal vein as tumor thrombus regresses with therapy.

Once the arterial supply of the liver is mapped out and portal vein patency is established, catheterization of the hepatic arteries is undertaken. With the new lubricious coatings, this can usually be accomplished with 5.0 to 5.5 French catheters. Should these efforts be unsuccessful, microcatheters (2–3 French) can be placed coaxially into nearly any vessel supplying the liver—whether native circulation or parasitized collateral (Fig. 27-3). Coaxial catheterization techniques are also helpful when the upper abdominal tumor mass results in distortion or occlusion of native visceral vessels, particularly the celiac axis (Fig. 27-4).

With repeated chemoembolizations, the blood supply of the liver must be continuously reassessed because different flow patterns will emerge over time. This is especially true when repeated embolizations result in obliteration of the native hepatic arteries (Fig. 27-5). Experience has shown that collateral vessels such as the inferior phrenic, adrenal, intercostal, and internal mammary arteries can be safely embolized. On occasion, the development of unusual collateral circulation ("culprit vessels") can cause the paradoxical appearance of growing and responding tumors in the same patient (Fig. 27-6).

Frequently vessels supplying the intestinal viscera are immediately adjacent to the hepatic arteries—such as the left hepatic artery, a branch of the left gastric artery; the right gastric artery, a branch of the proper or left hepatic artery; or the left hepatic off the common hepatic artery (Figs. 27-7, 27-8, and 27-9). This proximity may prevent stable catheterization of the target vessel without placing intestinal tissue at risk. In such cases, "coil blockade," or the intentional mechanical occlusion of the arteries supplying normal organs, can be undertaken (see Fig. 27-7); collateral circulation from distant sites will sustain these tissues while the mechanical coils prevent nontarget embolization (see Fig. 27-8).

Frequently, severe pain—possibly due to stretching of the capsule or embolization of the gallbladder—accompanies these procedures. Effective analgesia with celiac ganglion block and intraarterial lidocaine has been described.[33,34] Chemoembolization can cause sepsis and hepatic abscess, although routine antibiotic coverage has significantly reduced this risk.[35] Ondansetron, a powerful antiemetic, has substantially reduced periprocedural nausea and vomiting. Fever and abdominal pain ("postembolization syndrome") occur commonly after such procedures and can be effectively treated with nonsteroidal anti-inflammatory agents.

Text continues on page 450

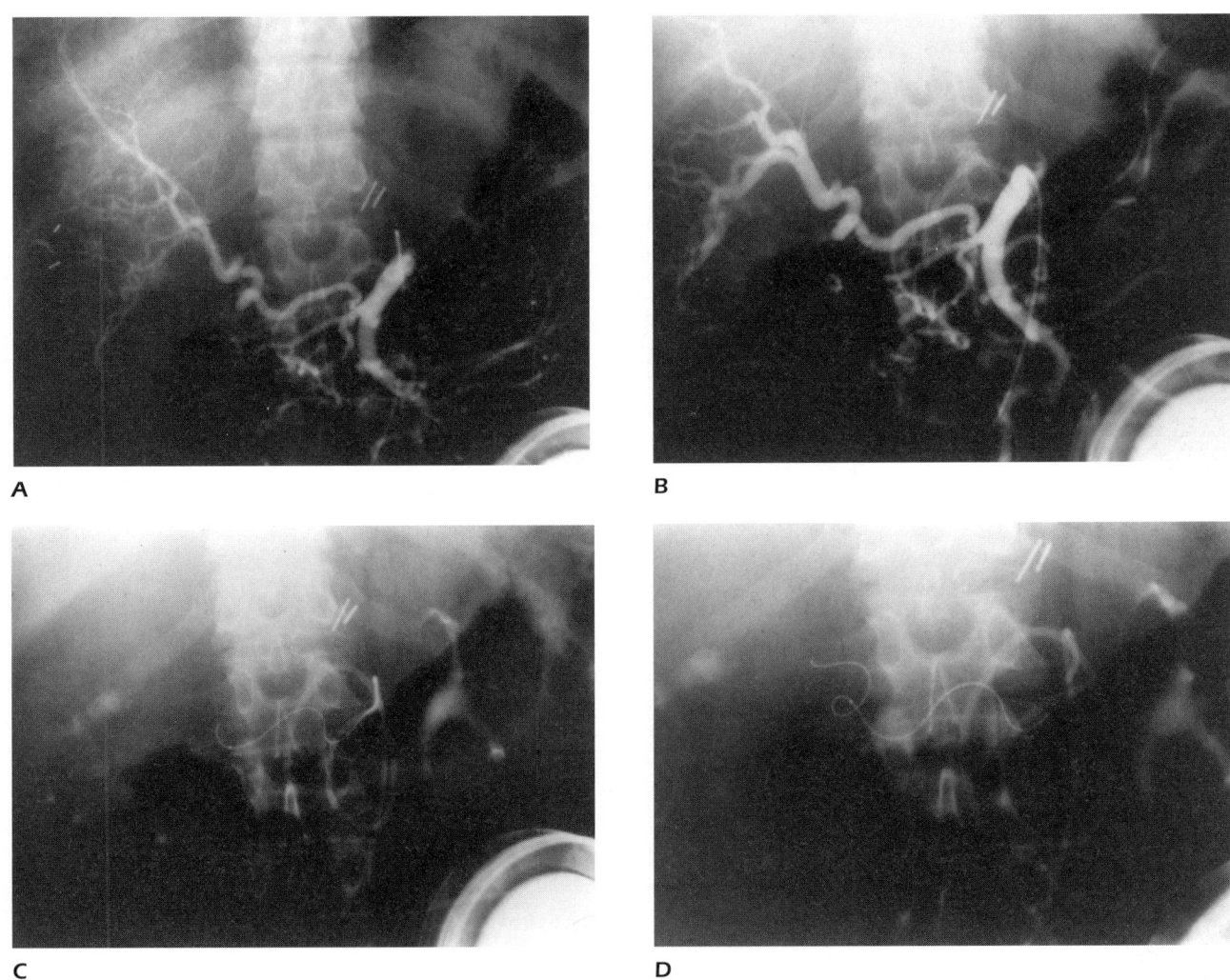

A

B

C

D

Figure 27-3. (A) Patient with metastatic ocular melanoma and occlusion of the hepatic artery by a surgically implanted pump (*reservoir in left lower quadrant*). Arterial supply of the liver is by a collateral branch of the superior mesenteric artery. (B) Narrowing at the origin of the collateral branch prevents safe catheterization with a 5.0 to 5.5 French catheter. (C) A Simmons catheter in the superior mesenteric artery acts as a guide for the microcatheter. (D) Successful placement in the hepatic artery distal to intestinal branches.

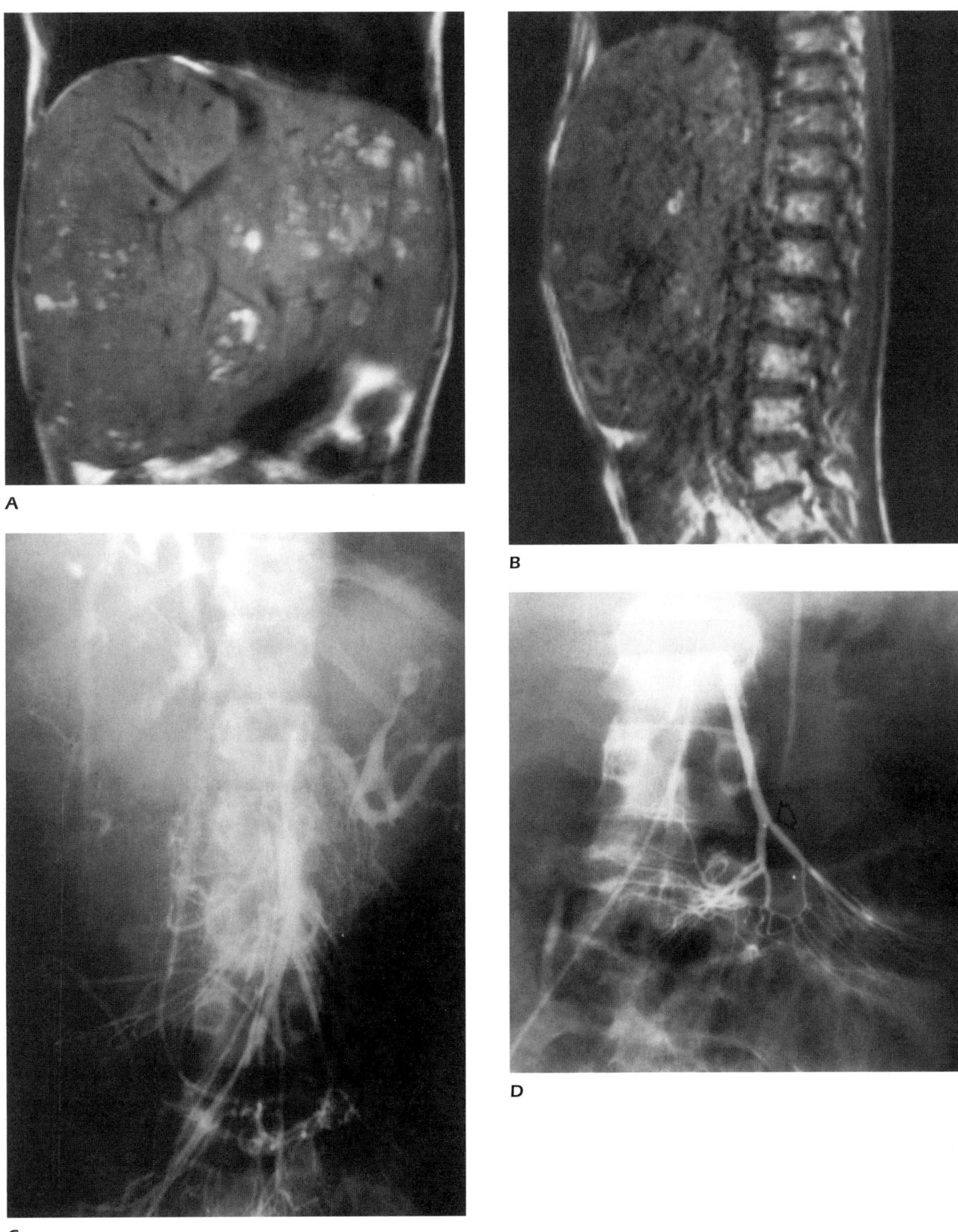

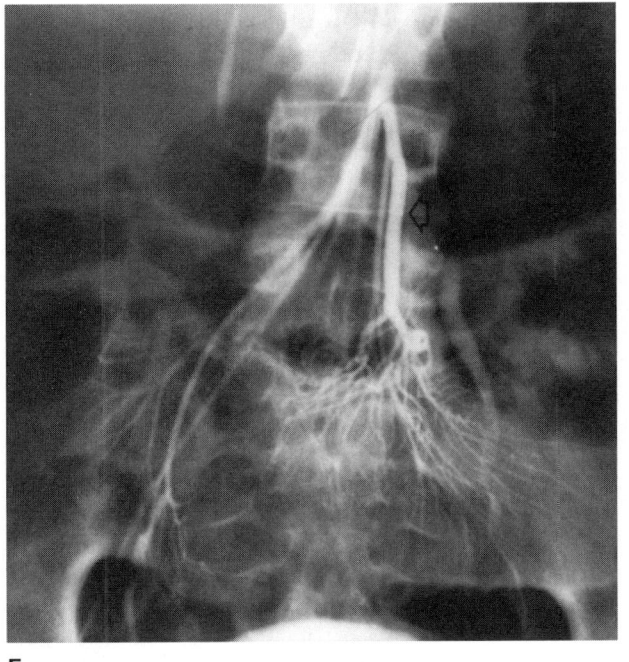

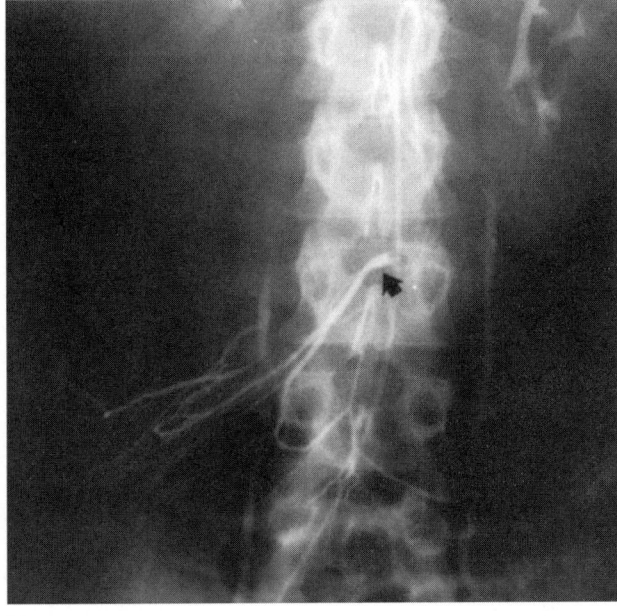

E

F

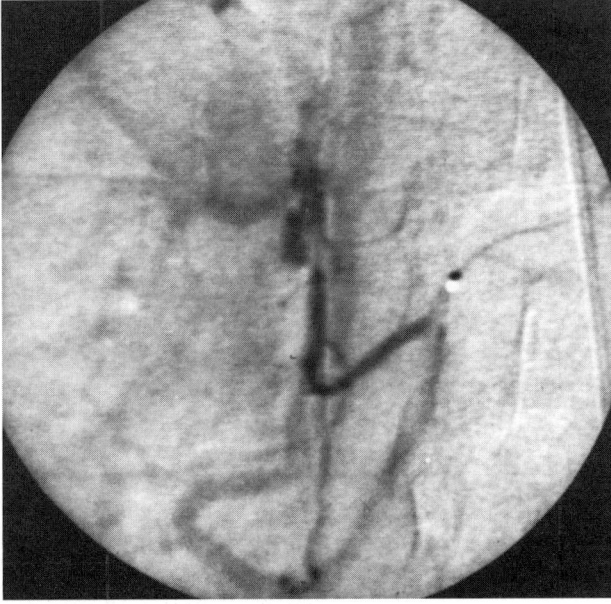

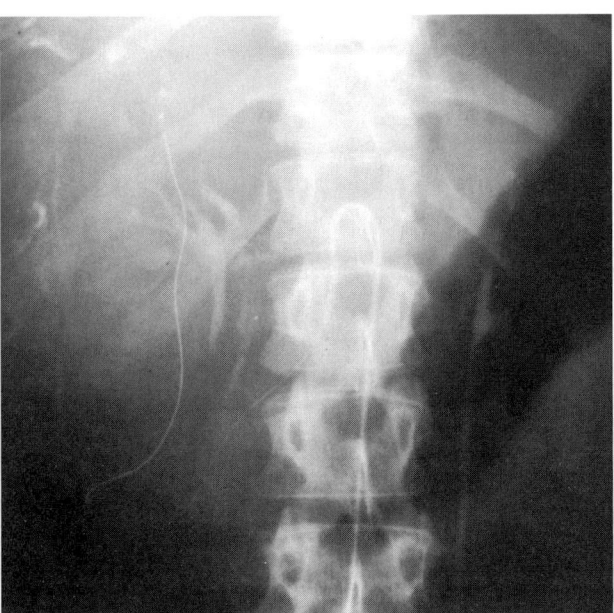

G

H

Figure 27-4. (A and B) Coronal and sagittal MR images demonstrating a large hepatocellular carcinoma filling the upper abdomen of a 15-year-old boy. (C) Occlusion of the celiac axis by the tumor mass (opacification of celiac vessels during superior mesenteric artery injection). (D to F) Sequential angiography of superior mesenteric artery branches with microcatheter (*arrows*) in an attempt to locate a collateral route to the celiac axis. (G and H) Successful catheterization via the inferior pancreaticoduodenal arcade. (I) Proper hepatic artery placement of the tip of a microcatheter (*arrow*). (J) Marked shrinkage of the tumor after repeated chemoembolizations.

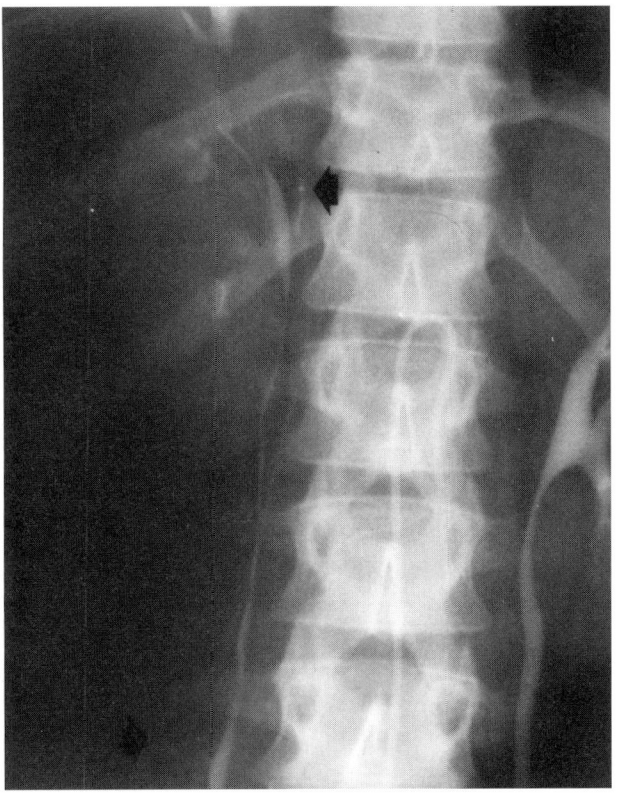

I

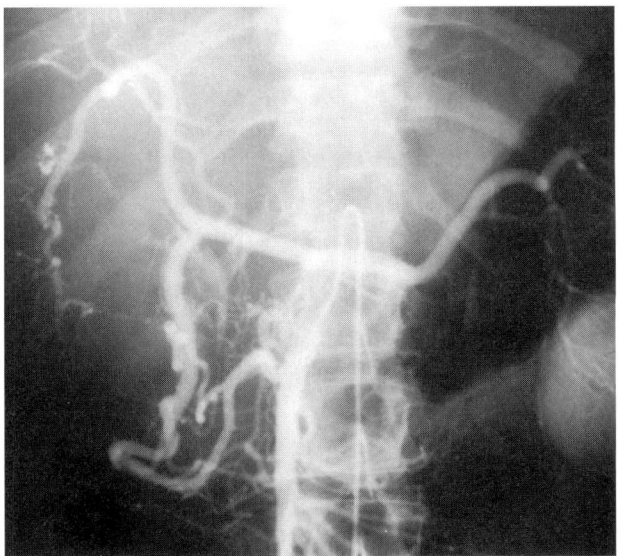

J

Figure 27-4 (continued).

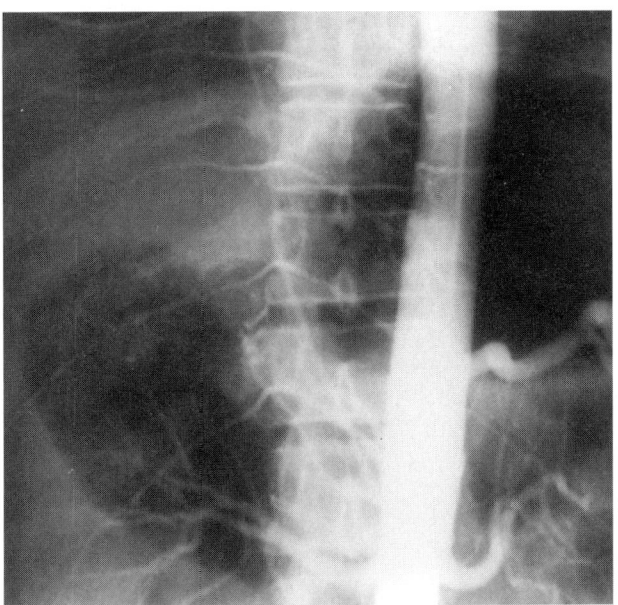

A

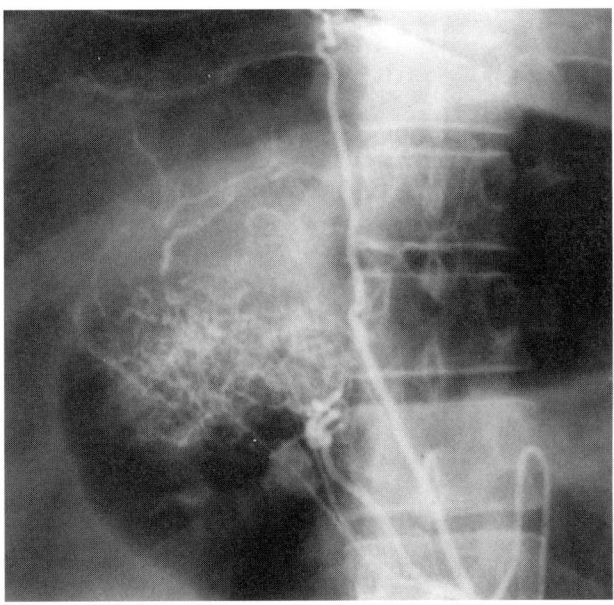

B

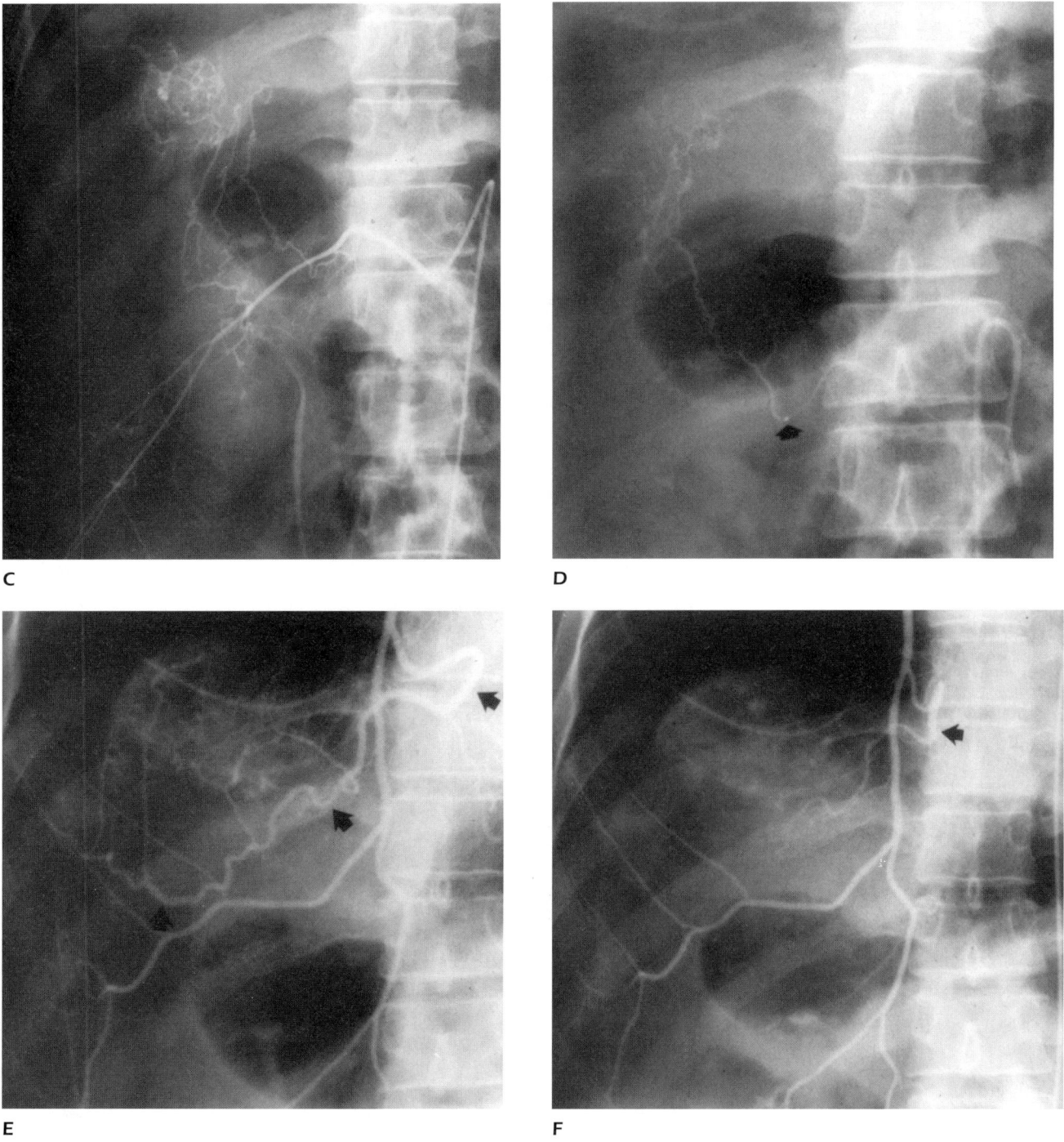

C

D

E

F

Figure 27-5. (A and B) Absence of hepatic artery branches after repeated chemoembolization. The superior adrenal branch of the right inferior phrenic artery supplies the tumor. (C and D) After successful embolization of the adrenal branch, the tumor parasitizes flow from the intercostal artery (*arrow,* D), which is treated. (E and F) The next affected vessel is the right internal mammary artery (*arrows;* pre- and postembolization views).

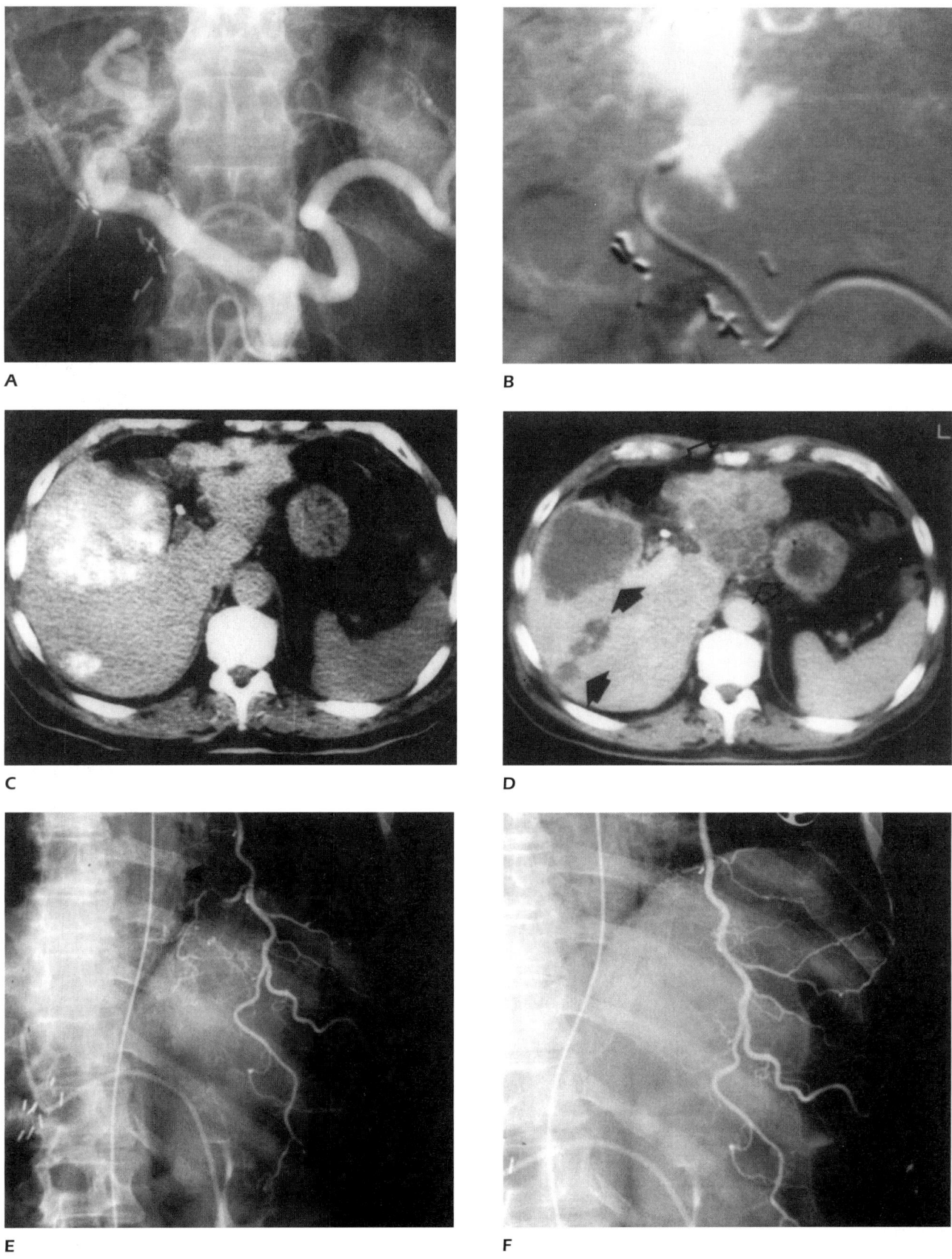

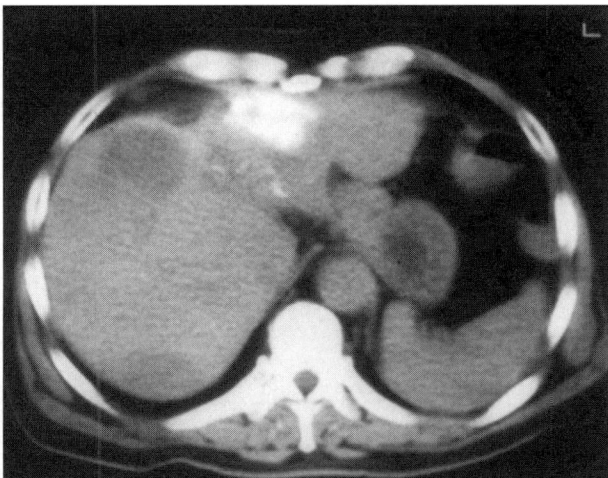

G

Figure 27-6. (A) Surgically implanted pump in the hepatic artery; surgically clipped cystic, gastroduodenal, and right gastric arteries. (B) The catheter has migrated into the left hepatic artery; note the extravasation of contrast into the left lobe of the liver. (C) After chemoembolization, there is deposition of embolic material and contrast into the right lobe of the tumor. (D) Follow-up CT scan reveals shrinkage of the right-lobe tumor (*closed black arrows*) yet marked progression of left-lobe disease (*open arrow*). (E and F) The "culprit vessel" is the left internal mammary artery (pre- and postembolization views). (G) CT scan after embolization with dense staining of the tumor.

Figure 27-7. (A) Prominent right gastric artery (*arrows*) at trifurcation of the proper hepatic artery into right, middle, and left hepatic branches. (B) Selective injection into the right gastric artery with a coaxially placed microcatheter. (C and D) "Coil blockade" of the right gastric artery to prevent nontarget embolization by reflux of chemoembolic particles.

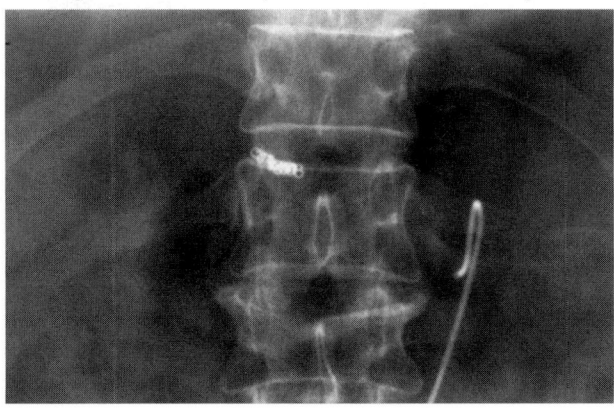

C

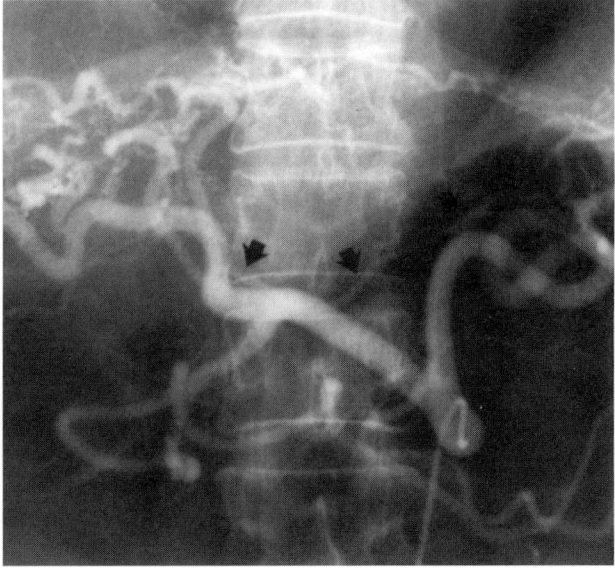

A

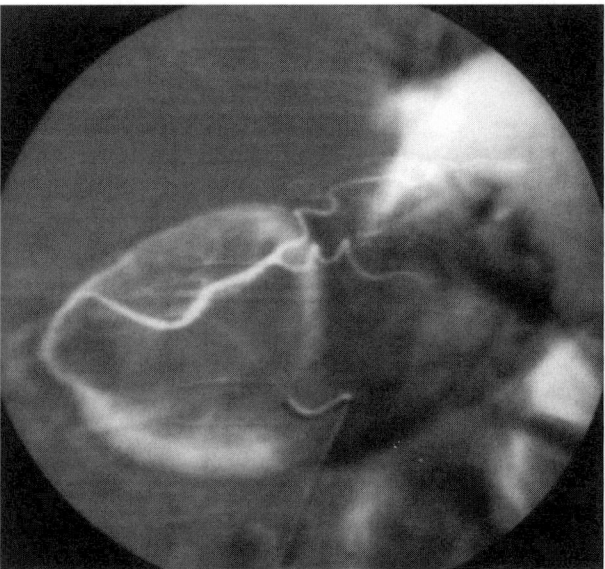

B

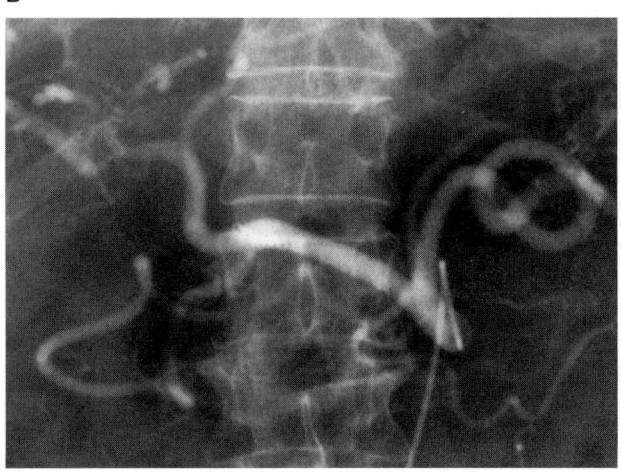

D

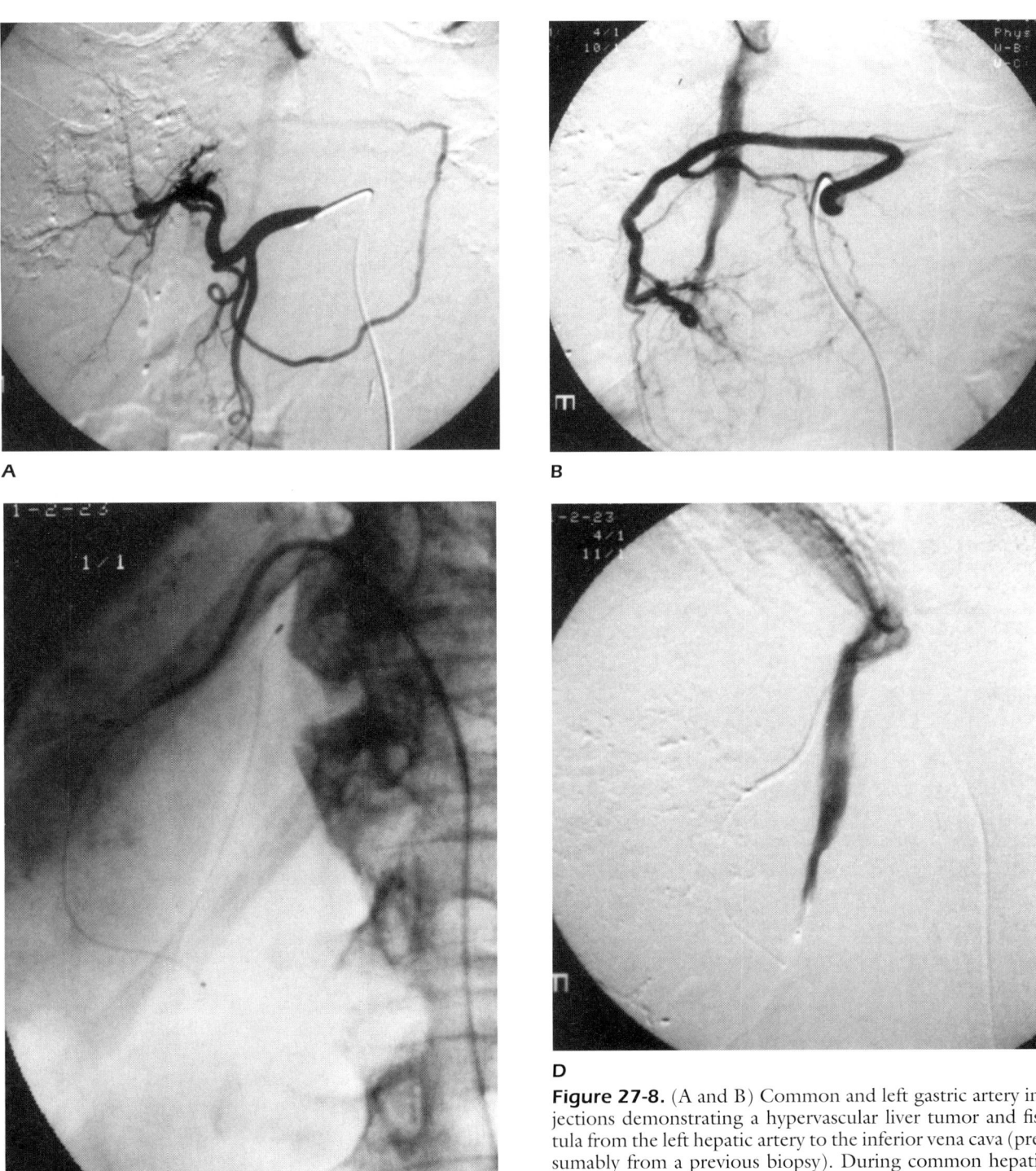

A

B

C

D

Figure 27-8. (A and B) Common and left gastric artery injections demonstrating a hypervascular liver tumor and fistula from the left hepatic artery to the inferior vena cava (presumably from a previous biopsy). During common hepatic injection, note the gastroepiploic-to-left-gastric collateral flow caused by the siphon effect of the fistula. (C and D) Coaxial placement of a microcatheter and guidewire via a Simmons guiding catheter through the fistula and injection of contrast into the vena cava. (E and F) Selective left hepatic artery injection before and after coil embolization (or "coil blockade") to prevent left-to-right shunting during chemoembolization.

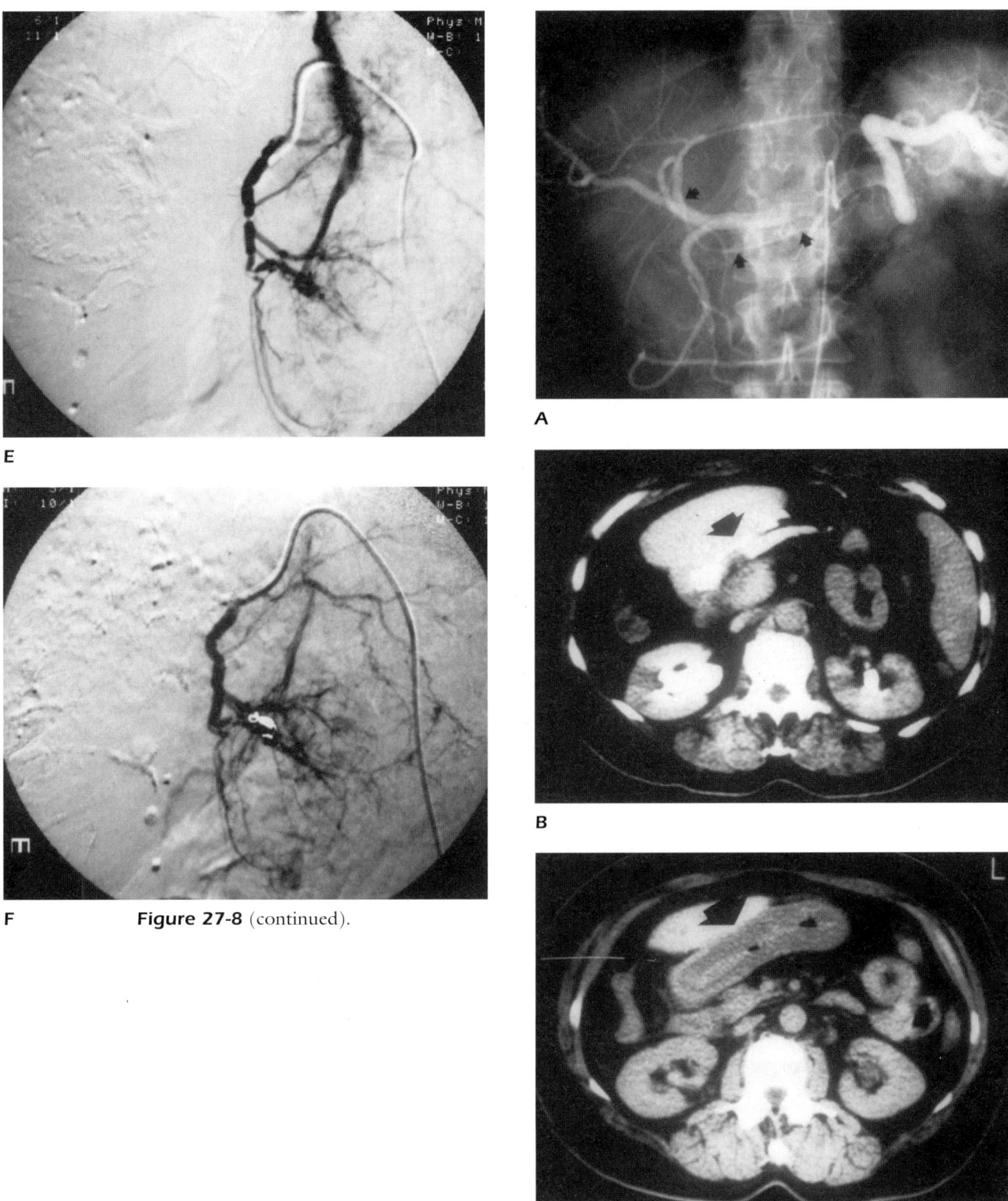

E

F   **Figure 27-8** (continued).

A

B

C

Figure 27-9. (A) Prominent right gastric artery (*arrow*) mistaken for a branch of the left hepatic artery. (B) Deposition of embolic material (*arrow*) in gastric antrum is shown on CT scan immediately after the procedure. (C) Marked thickening (*arrow*) of gastric wall 2 days later.

Results

The results of regional treatments for unresectable liver tumors can be evaluated on the basis of relief of symptoms, shrinkage of tumors or response rate, and prolongation of survival. Embolization and chemoembolization are seldom used for symptomatic relief. In the early stages of development, durable response rates are the standard by which treatments are compared. In liver cancer, such response rates are judged by cross-sectional imaging examinations, although the accuracy of these modalities has been questioned.[36] After some treatments, clear-cut liquefaction of tumor is visible on CT; however, because of the nature of surrounding hepatic parenchyma, the tumor mass may not decrease in size. Prospective studies comparing prolongation of survival are few in number and available mostly for common tumors such as hepatocellular carcinoma and colorectal metastases.

Hepatocellular Carcinoma

Hepatocellular carcinoma is relatively resistant to systemic chemotherapy, with response rates rarely above 30 percent. Hepatic artery chemotherapy infusions have also met with disappointing results. Embolization and chemoembolization have been used widely, particularly in Asia and Europe, and a large body of data has been accumulated. With chemoembolization, response rates from 22 to 75 percent (Table 27-6) have been reported in the larger clinical series. In uncontrolled clinical trials, survival has ranged from 24 to 88 percent at 1 year, 4 to 64 percent at 2 years, and 12 to 51 percent at 3 years (Table 27-7).

Lin et al. evaluated embolization, embolization and systemic chemotherapy, and systemic chemotherapy alone in three groups of patients.[48] Survival with the first two was similar (with both significantly better than chemotherapy alone). Four controlled studies have compared chemoembolization to conservative or supportive therapy (Table 27-8). In each, survival was longer in the treatment arm. However, in the most rigorous and recent study, this survival benefit was not significant.[49]

Table 27-6. Hepatocellular Carcinoma: Response Rates with Chemoembolization in Large Clinical Series

Study	No. of Patients	Response Rate (complete + partial) (%)
Yamada, 1983[37]	120	75
Yamada, 1990[38]	739	75
Yamashita, 1990[39]	85	22
Bismuth, 1992[40]	291	27

Table 27-7. Hepatocellular Carcinoma: Cumulative Survival Rates with Chemoembolization

Study	6 Months (%)	1 Year (%)	2 Years (%)	3 Years (%)
Yamada, 1983[37]		44	29	15
Ohnishi, 1984[41]	65	24		
Yamada, 1990[38]		51	24	12
Yamashita, 1990[39]	70	32	4	
Beppu, 1991[42]		81	64	51
Ikeda, 1991[43]		77	55	41
Nakao, 1991[44]		88	57	42
Taguchi, 1992[45]		54	33	18
Park, 1993*[46]		75	56	40
Nakamura, 1994[47]		56	33	18

*Recurrent tumors after partial hepatectomy.

Ethanol, delivered intravascularly and by direct intratumoral injection, has been recently studied, both alone and in concert with transcatheter embolization.[53,54] The theory behind combining these therapies is that embolization will be more effective against the periphery of the tumor while ethanol will directly fix the tissues in the center. Encouraged by the results of this combination therapy, investigators have treated patients with small (<5 cm) hepatocellular carcinomas with percutaneous ethanol injection alone. Livraghi et al. reported treating 746 patients with ethanol injection. They observed a 5-year survival rate in 47 percent of patients with Childs A cirrhosis and tumors smaller than 5 cm.[55]

Colorectal Hepatic Metastases

For those with colorectal hepatic metastases, the response rate with systemic chemotherapy is poor.[1] Until recently, many patients in whom systemic therapy failed became candidates for one of the regional infusion treatment protocols, typically 5-FU or FUDR.

Using surgically placed infusion pumps, early prospective but uncontrolled trials reported response rates roughly double those of systemic therapy (40 versus 20 percent) with two reporting rates up to 90 percent.[56,57] Five large trials evaluating intraarterial versus systemic treatment (two permitting crossover between the treatment arms and three not) have been recently reported (Table 27-9).[58-62] As with earlier reports, these trials described responses to systemic treatment of 9 to 21 percent and regional therapy of 42 to 62 percent. Despite such a difference, no survival benefit was demonstrated in the reports by Chang, Martin, and Rougier. Survival benefit could not be assessed in the studies that allowed nonresponders in the systemic arm to cross over to regional treatment.

Table 27-8. Results of Controlled Trials Comparing Chemoembolization and Conservative Therapy for Hepatocellular Carcinoma

Study	1 Year (%)		2 Years (%)	
	Control	Chemoembolization	Control	Chemoembolization
Pelletier, 1990[50]	31	24		
Vetter, 1991[51]	0	59		30
Bronowicki, 1994[52]	18	64	6	38
Trinchet, 1995[49]	44	62	26	38

Table 27-9. Systemic Versus Intraarterial Chemotherapy for Colorectal Hepatic Metastases: Results of Randomized Trials

Study	Intraarterial (%)	Systemic (%)	GI Complications (%)	Biliary Complications (%)	Survival Benefit*
Kemeny, 1987[59]	50	20	25	19	Crossover
Chang, 1987[58]	62	12	21	33	N.S.
Hohn, 1989[60]	42	10	0	52	Crossover
Martin, 1990[61]	48	21	13	26	N.S.
Rougier, 1992[62]	43	9	25	37	N.S.

*N.S. = not significant; crossover = crossover permitted, survival benefit could not be evaluated.

Explanations for this lack of survival benefit included a high complication rate from infusate pumps, local toxicity from the infusion, and inappropriate selection of the drug for infusion. Complications and local toxicity were high; Kemeny et al. described ulcer disease (due to nontarget, unintentional intestinal infusion of chemotherapy) in 17 percent of patients and biliary sclerosis (due to FUDR toxicity) in 8 percent.[59] Hohn et al. noted catheter-related complications of 13 percent and biliary toxicity of 52 percent.[60] Many of these nontarget intestinal infusions were the result of catheter migration, pericatheter spasm, and thrombosis, which altered the dynamics of flow to the tumors over time (Figs. 27-6 and 27-10). Thus the clear-cut response difference with regional infusion was offset by the morbidity of catheter insertion and maintenance. Such morbidity and complications can be expected whether the catheters are placed surgically or radiologically.[63]

Given the refractory nature of catheter-related problems, investigators have concentrated on modifying the dose of FUDR and adding other agents to reduce toxicity. Kemeny et al.,[64] in an attempt to reduce the toxicity of intraarterial FUDR, alternated steroid treatment with chemotherapy and found a trend (although not a significant difference) toward increased survival with this new treatment.

Several recent reports have described favorable results with chemoembolization. Lorenz et al.[65] observed responses in 4 of 11 patients treated with degradable starch microspheres and mitomycin C. Hunt et al. conducted a randomized evaluation of support-ive management, embolization, and chemoembolization with 5-FU and starch microspheres.[66] They identified a trend toward prolonged survival in patients with less than 50 percent liver involvement. Martinelli et al. reported responses in 25 percent of patients undergoing embolization or chemoembolization, all of whom had failed systemic chemotherapy.[67] Another recent report observed a 15 percent 3-year survival rate in patients treated with chemoembolization.[68] The mean survival from initiation of intraarterial treatment is usually 18 months.

Carcinoid and Islet Cell Tumors

The management of patients with carcinoid and islet cell carcinoma is among the most difficult in cancer care. These tumors—known collectively as apudomas (amine precursor undergoing decarboxylation)—can secrete serotonin, insulin, gastrin, glucagon, adrenocorticotropic hormone (ACTH), somatostatin, and many other hormones. Typically, systemic manifestations such as the carcinoid syndrome begin as the primary tumor becomes large or, even more commonly, as hepatic metastases develop.

The carcinoid syndrome is rare; the largest clinical series describes less than 100 patients.[69] The largest experience with radiologic management is 18 to 25 patients.[70,71] Most therapies concentrate initially on symptomatic management because most of these tumors have an indolent course (the median survival rate for those patients with liver metastases was 3 years; in

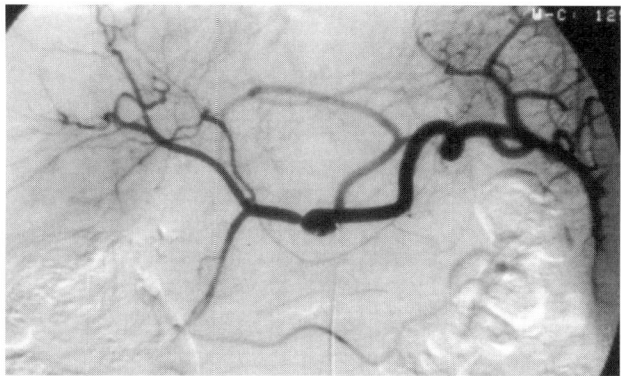

A

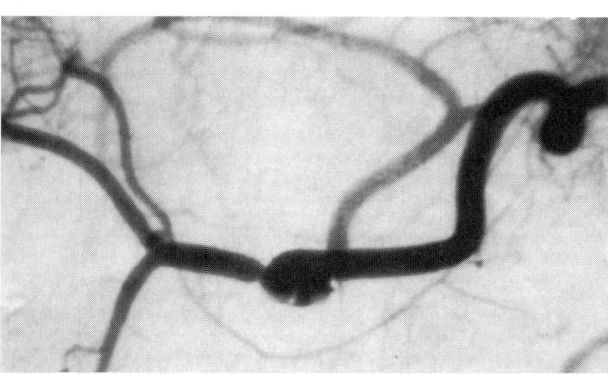

B

C

Figure 27-10. (A) Preliminary celiac angiography demonstrates the left hepatic artery as a branch of the left gastric artery as well as a prominent right gastric artery; otherwise, there is unremarkable hepatic circulation and no evidence of aberrant intestinal circulation. (B) Magnified view of the celiac circulation. (C) Because of spasm at the catheter tip, repeat hepatic angiography was performed. A branch of the right hepatic artery to the intestine is unexpectedly present. Had selective right hepatic angiography not been performed, inexplicable nontarget embolization would have resulted.

the Mayo Clinic series, 30 percent survived 5 years, and 1 patient was alive 41 years after diagnosis).[72] Initially, pharmacologic treatment focuses on the agonist to the particular hormone (e.g., somatostatin analogues in the carcinoid syndrome, H_2 blockers in the Zollinger-Ellison syndrome, etc.). Later, systemic che-

motherapeutic agents such as streptozotocin, 5-FU, and doxorubicin are used. The results with these agents are usually short-lived. The reported response rates with a single agent are typically 30 to 40 percent, and with multiple agents, 50 to 60 percent. The fleeting duration of these responses has led some investigators to skip systemic chemotherapy alone in favor of a combination treatment with embolization.[72]

Transcatheter embolization alone has been used in the management of carcinoid and islet cell tumors. After using Gelfoam, polyvinyl alcohol, and steel coils, Mitty et al. reported a 72 percent objective response rate (i.e., decreased serum levels of serotonin or tryptophan; decreased urinary excretion of 5-hydroxyindoleacetic acid, indoleacetic acid, or tryptamine) in 18 patients with the carcinoid syndrome; 94 percent of patients experienced symptomatic relief.[70] Carrasco et al. described responses in 80 percent of 25 patients undergoing transcatheter embolization for carcinoid hepatic metastases.[71] Marlink et al. reported partial or complete responses in 7 of 10 patients and symptomatic improvement in all patients treated with particulate embolization alone.[73]

Moertel observed a 90 percent success rate in the treatment of carcinoid and islet cell tumors with a combination of systemic chemotherapy (5-FU and streptozotocin) and transcatheter embolization; these responses were also quite durable (24 months for carcinoid; 18 months for islet cell).[72] In another study of transcatheter embolization alone, Ajani et al. described partial remission in 22 patients with islet cell tumor metastatic to the liver.[74]

Ocular Melanoma

Ocular melanoma is quite uncommon, affecting about 2000 Americans annually. The tumor has the unusual tendency of spreading only to the liver, where it is notoriously resistant to systemic chemotherapy (response rates of 4–5 percent). Mavligit et al. have described successful treatment in 14 of 30 patients with a median survival of 11 months (in contrast to the usual 2–6 months).[75]

Complications

Significant complications are described in patients undergoing embolization or chemoembolization (Table 27-10). These include intestinal ischemia, cholecystitis, infection, and hepatic insufficiency. With appropriate antibiotics the rate of liver abscess has been lowered to 2 percent.[35] Postembolization syndrome is so common that it is expected. Some complications, such as nontarget intestinal embolization, are preventable

Table 27-10. Complications of Chemoembolization

Complication	Range (%)
Common	
Ascites	4–20
Cholecystitis	1–11
Death	1–2
Encephalopathy	1–3
GI hemorrhage	1–3
Hepatic abscess	2–5
Intestinal infarction	1–3
Postembolization syndrome	40–90
Renal failure	1–10
Rupture	1–2
Septicemia	1–3
Uncommon	
Variceal bleeding	
Hemoperitoneum	
Tumor lysis syndrome	
Pancreatitis	
Pleural effusion	
Hepatic infarction	
Bile duct necrosis	
Intrahepatic aneurysm	

with meticulous technique. The studies of Martin, Chang, and Rougier have demonstrated that, for the higher response rates of regional treatments to be translated into survival benefit, complications must be minimized.[58,61,62]

Conclusion

Interest in percutaneous regional therapies for unresectable hepatic tumors has grown as technical developments have made their applications feasible and clinical experience has improved their safety and utility. This interest has been fueled by continued disappointments in systemic therapies and the lack of demonstrable survival benefit with therapies delivered by surgically implanted pumps. Large prospective studies may establish the effectiveness of these therapies as appropriate treatment of primary and metastatic liver cancer. Recently reported experiences justify cautious optimism as such trials evolve.

References

1. Wasserman Y, Cornis RL, Goldsmith M, et al. Tabular analysis of the clinical chemotherapy of solid tumors. Cancer Chemother Rep 1975;6:399.
2. Wanebo H, Falkson J, Order S. Cancer of the hepatobiliary system. Philadelphia: J Lippincott, 1989.
3. Clarkson B, Young C, Dierick W. Effects of continuous hepatic artery infusion of metabolites on primary and metastatic cancer of the liver. Cancer 1962;15:472–488.
4. Sullivan RD, Norcross JW, Watkins E. Chemotherapy of metastatic liver cancer by prolonged hepatic-artery infusion. N Engl J Med 1964;270:321–327.
5. Chuang VP, Wallace S. Hepatic artery embolization in the treatment of hepatic neoplasms. Radiology 1981;140:51–58.
6. Behesti MV, Denny DF, Glickman MG, et al. Percutaneous isolated liver perfusion for treatment of hepatic malignancy: preliminary report. J Vasc Intervent Radiol 1992;3:453–458.
7. Hamazoe R, Murakami A, Hirooka Y, et al. A phase II pilot study of the combined application of hyperthermia and intra-hepato-arterial chemotherapy using cisplatinum and 5-fluorouracil. J Surg Oncol 1991;48:127–132.
8. Livraghi T, Bolondi L, Lazzaroni S, et al. Percutaneous ethanol injection of hepatocellular carcinoma in cirrhosis: a study in 207 patients. Cancer 1992;69:925–929.
9. Ohnishi K, Ohyama N, Ito S, et al. Small hepatocellular carcinoma: treatment with US-guided intratumoral injection of acetic acid. Radiology 1994;193:747–752.
10. Tsujitani S, Watanabe A, Kakeji Y, et al. Hepatic recurrence not prevented with low-dosage long-term intraportal 5-FU infusion after resection of colorectal liver metastasis. Eur J Surg Oncol 1991;17:526–529.
11. Order S, Stillwagon GB, Klein J, et al. Iodine[131] antiferritin, a new treatment modality in hepatoma: a Radiation Therapy Oncology Group study. J Clin Oncol 1985;3:1573–1582.
12. Kato T, Nemoto R, Mori H, et al. Arterial chemoembolization with microencapsulated anticancer drug. JAMA 1981;245:1123–1127.
13. Chuang VP, Wallace S, Soo C, et al. Therapeutic Ivalon embolization of hepatic tumors. AJR 1982;138:289–294.
14. Clouse ME, Lee RGL, Duszlak EJ, et al. Peripheral hepatic artery embolization for primary and secondary hepatic neoplasms. Radiology 1983;147:407–411.
15. Lautt WW, Greenway CV. Conceptual review of the hepatic vascular bed. Hepatology 1987;7:952–963.
16. Ralls PW. Doppler sonography of the hepatic artery and portal venous system. AJR 1990;155:517–525.
17. Breedis C, Young G. Blood supply of neoplasms of the liver. Am J Pathol 1954;30:969–985.
18. Healy JE. Vascular patterns in human metastatic liver tumors. Surg Gynecol Obstet 1965;120:1187–1193.
19. Sigurdson ER, Ridge JA, Kemeny N, et al. Tumor and liver drug uptake following hepatic artery and portal vein infusion. J Clin Oncol 1987;5:1836–1840.
20. Ridge JR, Bading JA, Gelbard AS, et al. Perfusion of colorectal hepatic metastases: relative distribution of flow from the hepatic artery and portal vein. Cancer 1987;59:1547–1553.
21. Ensminger W, Gyves J. Regional chemotherapy of neoplastic diseases. Pharmacol Ther 1983;21:277–293.
22. Martin JK, Moertel CG, Adson MA, et al. Surgical treatment of functioning metastatic carcinoid tumors. Arch Surg 1983;118:537–542.
23. Sternlicht M, Sales SF, Daniels JR, et al. Renal cisplatin chemoembolization with Angiostat, Gelfoam, and Ethiodol in the rabbit: renal platinum distributions. Radiology 1989;170:1073–1075.
24. Kan Z, Sato M, Ivancev K, et al. Distribution and effect of iodized poppyseed oil in the liver after hepatic artery embolization: experimental study in several animal species. Radiology 1993;186:861–866.
25. Kan Z, Ivancev K, Lunderquist A, et al. In vivo microscopy of hepatic tumors in animal models: a dynamic investigation of blood supply to hepatic metastases. Radiology 1993;187:621–626.
26. Takayasu K, Shima Y, Muramatsu Y, et al. Hepatocellular carcinoma: treatment with intraarterial iodized oil with and without chemotherapeutic agents. Radiology 1987;162:345–351.
27. Nakamura H, Hashimoto T, Oi H, et al. Transcatheter oily chemoembolization of hepatocellular carcinoma. Radiology 1989;170:783–786.
28. Hughes K, Scheele J, Sugarbaker PH. Surgery for colorectal cancer metastatic to the liver. Surg Clin North Am 1989;69:340–359.
29. Nelson RC, Chezmar JL, Sugarbaker PH, et al. Hepatic tumors: comparison of CT during arterial portography, delayed CT, and MR imaging for preoperative evaluation. Radiology 1989;172:27–34.
30. Haug CE, Jenkins RL, Rohrer RJ, et al. Liver transplantation for primary hepatic cancer. Transplantation 1992;53:376–382.
31. Lai CL, Lam KC, Wong KP, et al. Clinical features of hepato-

cellular carcinoma: review of 211 patients in Hong Kong. Cancer 1981;47:2746–2755.

32. Pentecost MJ, Daniels JR, Teitelbaum GP, et al. Hepatic chemoembolization: safety with portal vein thrombosis. J Vasc Intervent Radiol 1993;4:347–351.

33. Coldwell DM, Lopez KA. Regional anesthesia for hepatic arterial embolization. Radiology 1989;172:1039–1040.

34. Molgaard CP, Teitelbaum GP, Pentecost MJ, et al. Intraarterial administration of lidocaine for analgesia in hepatic chemoembolization. J Vasc Intervent Radiol 1990;1.81–85.

35. Reed RA, Teitelbaum GP, Daniels JR, et al. Prevalence of infection following hepatic chemoembolization with cross-linked collagen with administration of prophylactic antibiotics. J Vasc Intervent Radiol 1994;5:367–371.

36. Venook AP, Stagg RJ, Lewis BJ, et al. Chemoembolization for hepatocellular carcinoma. J Clin Oncol 1990;8:1108–1114.

37. Yamada R, Sato M, Kawabata M, et al. Hepatic artery embolization in 120 patients with unresectable hepatoma. Radiology 1983;148:397–401.

38. Yamada R, Kishi K, Sonomura T, et al. Transcatheter arterial embolization in unresectable hepatocellular carcinoma. Cardiovasc Intervent Radiol 1990;13:135–139.

39. Yamashita Y, Takahashi M, Koga Y, et al. Prognostic factors in liver metastases after transcatheter arterial embolization or arterial infusion. Acta Radiol 1990;31:269–274.

40. Bismuth H, Morino M, Sherlock D, et al. Primary treatment of hepatocellular carcinoma by arterial chemoembolization. Am J Surg 1992;163:387–394.

41. Ohnishi K, Tsuchiya S, Nakayama T, et al. Arterial chemoembolization of hepatocellular carcinoma with mitomycin C microcapsules. Radiology 1984;152:51–55.

42. Beppu T, Ohara C, Yamaguchi Y, et al. A new approach to chemoembolization for unresectable hepatocellular carcinoma using aclarubicin microspheres in combination with cisplatin suspended in iodized oil. Cancer 1991;68.2555–2560.

43. Ikeda K, Kumada H, Saitoh S, et al. Effect of repeated transcatheter arterial embolization on the survival time in patients with hepatocellular carcinoma: an analysis by the Cox proportional hazard model. Cancer 1991;68:2150–2154.

44. Nakao N, Kamino K, Miura K, et al. Recurrent hepatocellular carcinoma after partial hepatectomy: value of treatment with transcatheter arterial chemoembolization. AJR 1991;156:1177–1179.

45. Taguchi T, Nakamura H. Chemoembolization therapy for hepatocellular carcinoma in Japan. J Infusional Chem 1992;2:124–127.

46. Park JH, Han JK, Chung JW, et al. Postoperative recurrence of hepatocellular carcinoma: results of transcatheter arterial chemoembolization. Cardiovasc Intervent Radiol 1993;16:21–24.

47. Nakamura H, Mitani T, Murakami T, et al. Five-year survival after transcatheter chemoembolization for hepatocellular carcinoma. Cancer Chemother Pharmacol 1994;33(Suppl):89–92.

48. Lin D, Liaw Y, Lee T, et al. Hepatic arterial embolization in patients with unresectable hepatocellular carcinoma: a randomized controlled trial. Gastroenterology 1988;94:453–456.

49. Trinchet JC, Rached AA, Mathieu D, et al. A comparison of Lipiodol chemoembolization and conservative treatment for unresectable hepatocellular carcinoma. N Engl J Med 1995;332:1256–1261.

50. Pelletier G, Roche A, Ink O, et al. A randomized trial of hepatic arterial chemoembolization in patients with unresectable hepatocellular carcinoma. J Hepatol 1990;11:181–184.

51. Vetter D, Wenger JJ, Bergier JM, et al. Transcatheter oily chemoembolization in the management of advanced hepatocellular carcinoma in cirrhosis: results of a western comparative study in 60 patients. Hepatology 1991;13:427–433.

52. Bronowicki JP, Vetter D, Dumas F, et al. Transcatheter oily chemoembolization for hepatocellular carcinoma: a 4-year study of 127 French patients. Cancer 1994;74:16–24.

53. Yamakado K, Hirano T, Kato N, et al. Hepatocellular carcinoma: treatment with a combination of transcatheter arterial chemoembolization and transportal ethanol injection. Radiology 1994;193:75–80.

54. Lencioni R, Vignali C, Caramella D, et al. Transcatheter arterial embolization followed by percutaneous ethanol injection in the treatment of hepatocellular carcinoma. Cardiovasc Intervent Radiol 1994;17:70–75.

55. Livraghi T, Giorgio A, Marin G, et al. Hepatocellular carcinoma and cirrhosis in 746 patients: long-term results of percutaneous ethanol injection. Radiology 1995;197:101–108.

56. Balch CM, Urist MM, Soong SJ, et al. A prospective phase II clinical trial of continuous FUDR regional chemotherapy for colorectal metastases to the liver using a totally implantable drug infusion pump. Ann Surg 1983;198:567–573.

57. Niederhuber JE, Ensminger W, Gyves J, et al. Regional chemotherapy of colorectal cancer metastatic to liver. Cancer 1984;53:1336–1343.

58. Chang AE, Schneider PD, Sugarbaker PH, et al. A prospective randomized trial of regional versus systemic continuous 5-fluorodeoxyuridine chemotherapy in the treatment of colorectal liver metastases. Ann Surg 1987;206:685–693.

59. Kemeny N, Daly J, Reichman B, et al. Intrahepatic or systemic infusion of fluorodeoxyuridine in patients with liver metastases from colorectal carcinoma. Ann Intern Med 1987;107:459–465.

60. Hohn DC, Stagg RJ, Friedman MA. A randomized trial of continuous intravenous versus hepatic intraarterial floxuridine in patients with colorectal cancer metastatic to the liver: the Northern California Oncology Group Trial. J Clin Oncol 1989;7:1646–1654.

61. Martin JK, O'Connell MJ, Wieand HS, et al. Intra-arterial floxuridine vs. systemic fluorouracil for hepatic metastases from colorectal cancer. Arch Surg 1990;125:1022–1027.

62. Rougier P, Laplanche A, Huguier M, et al. Hepatic arterial infusion of floxuridine in patients with liver metastases from colorectal carcinoma: long-term results of a prospective randomized trial. J Clin Oncol 1992;10:1112–1118.

63. Yoshikawa M, Ebara M, Nakano T, et al. Percutaneous transaxillary catheter insertion for hepatic artery infusion chemotherapy. AJR 1992;158:885–886.

64. Kemeny N, Seiter K, Neidzwiecki D, et al. A randomized trial of intrahepatic infusion of fluorodeoxyuridine with dexamethasone versus fluorodeoxyuridine alone in the treatment of metastatic disease colorectal cancer. Cancer 1992;69:327–334.

65. Lorenz M, Herrmann G, Kirkow-Reimann M. Temporary chemoembolization of colorectal liver metastases with degradable starch microspheres. Eur J Surg Oncol 1989;15:453–462.

66. Hunt TM, Flowerdew ADS, Birch SJ, et al. Prospective randomized controlled trial of hepatic arterial embolization or infusion chemotherapy with 5-fluorouracil and degradable starch microspheres for colorectal liver metastases. Br J Surg 1990;77:779–782.

67. Martinelli DJ, Wadler S, Bakal CW, et al. Utility of embolization or chemoembolization as second-line treatment in patients with advanced or recurrent colorectal carcinoma. Cancer 1994;74:1706–1712.

68. Lang EK, Brown CB Jr. Colorectal metastases to the liver: selective chemoembolization. Radiology 1993;189:417–422.

69. Davis Z, Moertel CG, McIlrath DC. The malignant carcinoid syndrome. Surg Gynecol Obstet 1973;137:628–644.

70. Mitty HA, Warner RRP, Newman LH, et al. Control of carcinoid syndrome with hepatic artery embolization. Radiology 1985;155:623–626.

71. Carrasco CH, Charnsangavej C, Ajani JA, et al. The carcinoid syndrome: palliation by hepatic artery embolization. AJR 1986;147:149–154.

72. Moertel CG. An odyssey in the land of small tumors. J Clin Oncol 1987;5:1503–1522.

73. Marlink RG, Lokich JJ, Robins JR, et al. Hepatic arterial embolization for metastatic hormone-secreting tumors. Cancer 1990;65:2227–2232.

74. Ajani JA, Carrasco CH, Charnsangavej C, et al. Islet cell tumors metastatic to the liver: effective palliation by sequential hepatic artery embolization. Ann Intern Med 1988;108:340–344.

75. Mavligit GM, Charnsangavej C, Carrasco CH, et al. Regression of ocular melanoma metastatic to the liver after hepatic arterial chemoembolization with cisplatin and polyvinyl sponge. JAMA 1988;260:974–976.

28

Benign Biliary Obstruction

ROY L. GORDON

The most common benign obstructions to the bile duct are those that occur after surgery.[1] This chapter focuses on these lesions and on those of sclerosing cholangitis, the most frequent types of obstruction encountered by the interventional radiologist. The spectrum of other benign causes of biliary obstruction is outlined in Table 28-1. A complete consideration of them is beyond the scope of this chapter, but key references are provided in the table. Obstructions associated with bile duct stones or liver transplantation are covered in Chapters 31 and 32.

Numerous papers have substantiated the predominant causative role of biliary surgery in the etiology of benign strictures.[14,15] In 1971 Warren et al. reviewed 958 patients treated at the Lahey Clinic for benign biliary obstructions.[14] Previous biliary surgery was responsible for the stricture in 918 patients, gastric surgery in 9, and pancreatic surgery in 2. The remaining 29 obstructions were not a result of previous surgery.

The incidence of injury to the bile duct is about 1 in 300 to 500 open operations for gallstones.[1] The recent widespread move from open cholecystectomy to laparoscopic cholecystectomy has increased the incidence of bile duct injury.[16,17] An analysis of a national survey of 77,604 cases of laparoscopic cholecystectomy found bile duct injuries in about 6 out of 1000 cases.[16] The authors of that study suggest that this incidence is likely to decrease as surgeons gain more experience with laparoscopic cholecystectomy.

There is an extensive literature dealing with the types of bile duct injury, the types of surgical repair, and the results of these repairs.[14,15,17–22] In general, the higher or closer to the porta hepatis the injury is, the more difficult is the repair. Better results are achieved with lower lesions. The level of obstruction is described in the Bismuth classification.[22] Type 1 is a low stricture of the common hepatic duct with the hepatic duct stump longer than 2 cm. Type 2 is a midstricture of the common hepatic duct with the hepatic duct stump shorter than 2 cm (Fig. 28-1). Type 3 is a high or a hilar structure without any hepatic duct but with an intact confluence of right and left hepatic ducts (Fig. 28-2). Type 4 is obliteration of the hilar confluence with separation of the right and left hepatic ducts. Type 5 is injury to a right aberrant hepatic duct with or without concomitant injury to the common duct (Fig. 28-3). With the advent of laparoscopic cholecystectomy, injuries have tended to be more complex.[17] Repair is usually performed by construction of a Roux loop that is anastomosed to the remaining bile duct, although other operations are sometimes performed.[1]

The outcome of surgical repair depends on many factors other than the level of injury. Better results are achieved if the injury is recognized immediately and repaired as soon as possible by an experienced surgeon. Results are less good if diagnosis is delayed and if the patient's condition is complicated by cholangitis or periductal infection. The presence of cirrhosis or portal hypertension makes the surgery more difficult and the outcome less satisfactory. Stricture recurrence develops in 10 to 30 percent of patients after initial surgical repair.[19]

Repair of recurrent strictures is even more difficult. Subsequent recurrence following a second repair occurs in 22 percent of patients, even in the most experienced hands.[19] Postoperative morbidity is high, with at least 1 in 10 patients having one or more major nonfatal complications.[1] Operative mortality averages 8.3 percent.[15]

From these statistics, it is clear that the surgery of bile duct lesions presents a formidable challenge, with high rates of recurrence and significant morbidity and mortality. Although surgery is the treatment of choice for benign biliary strictures, interventional techniques such as percutaneous drainage are frequently used as an adjunct to biliary repair. The development of percutaneous balloon dilatation techniques and placement of endoprostheses has provided a valuable treatment alternative when patients are unsuitable for surgery or when nonoperative techniques are chosen after surgical failure.

Table 28-1. Causes of Benign Biliary Obstruction

Postsurgical stricture[1]
Traumatic stricture
Post–liver transplantation: rejection or ischemia[2,3]
Papillary stenosis
Duodenal diverticulum
Biliary atresia
Choledochal cyst[4]
Hepatic cyst, polycystic liver
Sclerosing cholangitis[5]
Oriental cholangiohepatitis[6]
Cholangitis following chemotherapy[7]
AIDS-related cholangitis[8]
Parasitic infection: *Clonorchis sinensis,*[9] *Fasciola hepatica, Ascaris
    lumbricoides, Echinococcus*[10,11]
Tuberculosis
Sarcoidosis
Acute and chronic pancreatitis[12]
Impacted biliary calculus
Mirizzi syndrome[13]

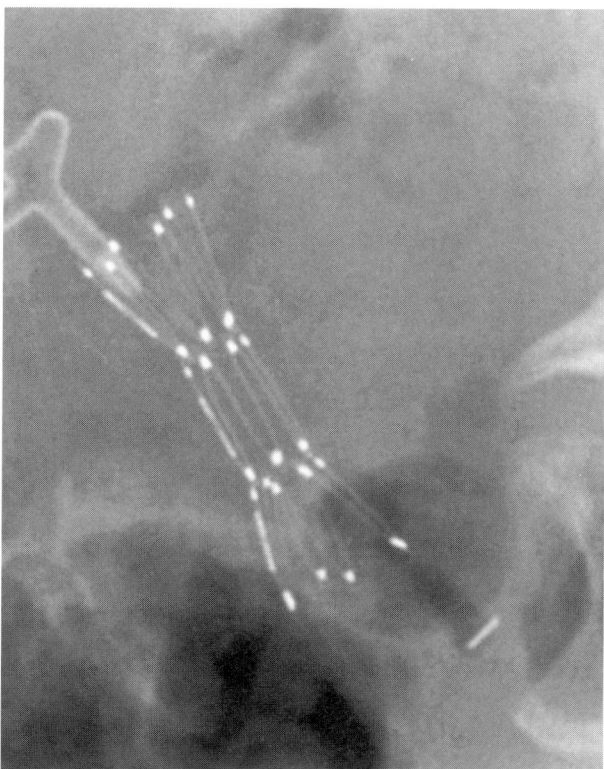

B

Figure 28-1. (A) Cholangiogram of a 53-year-old man with a Bismuth type 2 biliary stricture of the common hepatic duct. A Whipple operation had been performed 2 years earlier because of a small ampullary tumor. (B) A plain film showing three-segment, 8-mm diameter Gianturco stent with "flared" proximal and distal ends for greater stability. (C) The cholangiogram shows the stent is in stable position with good drainage into the Roux loop.

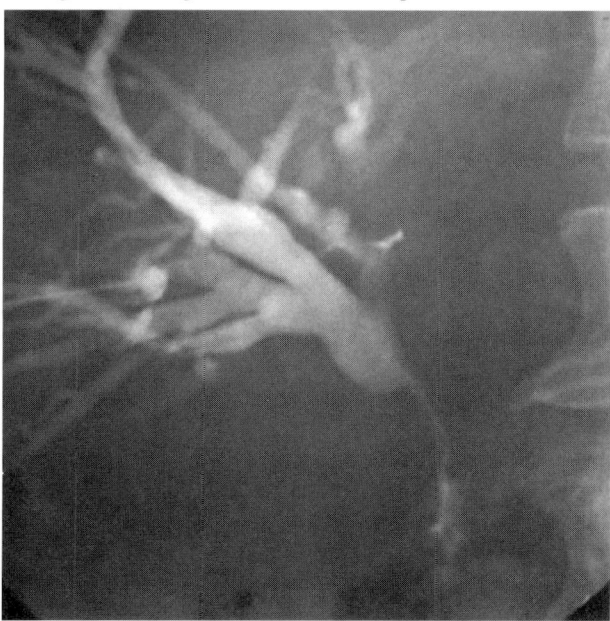

A

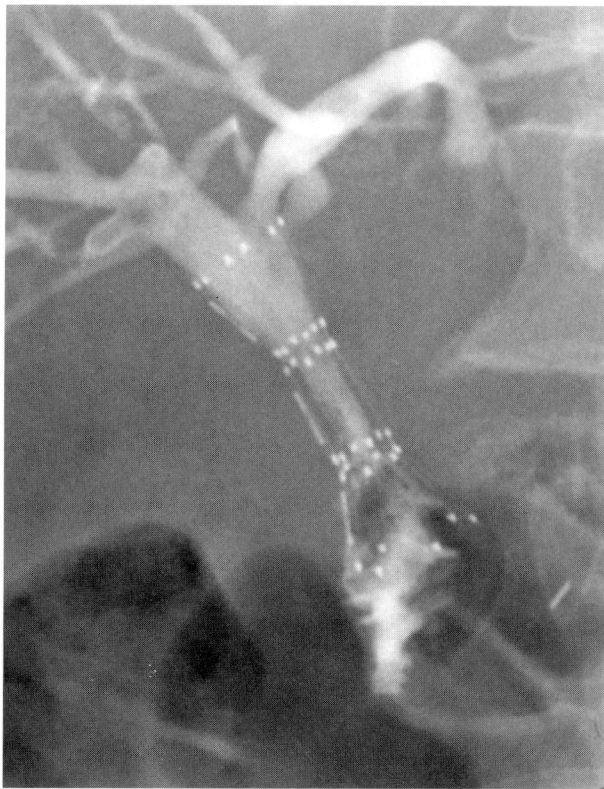

C

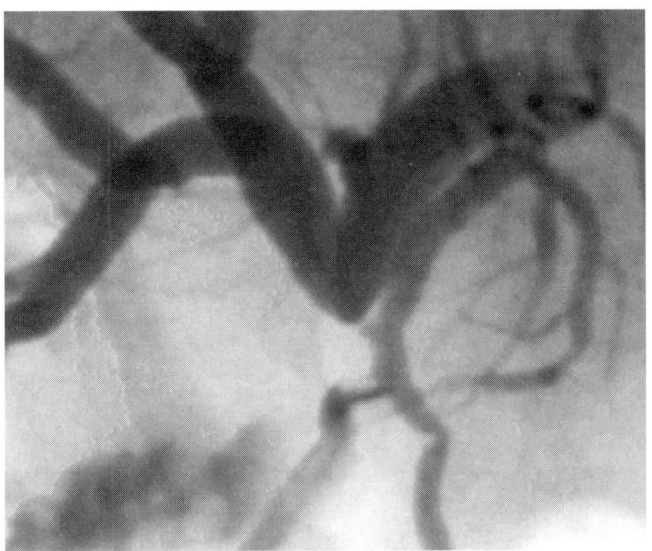

A

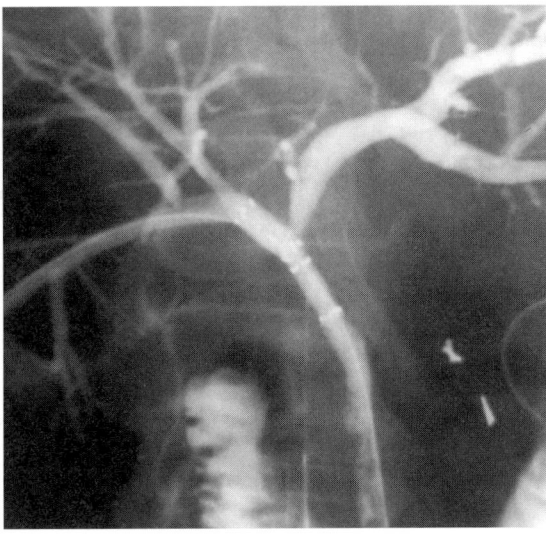

B

Figure 28-2. (A) Cholangiogram of an 80-year-old woman with a complete biliary obstruction of Bismuth type 3. (B) Because of her age, a Gianturco 8-mm stent with two segments was placed by the percutaneous transhepatic route, with excellent results.

Figure 28-3. (A) Cholangiogram of a 42-year-old woman suffering from intermittent bouts of cholangitis following open cholecystectomy for stone disease. On ERCP a clip (*arrow*) is noted on the aberrant right hepatic duct, Bismuth type 5. Note that there are too few ducts seen in the right lobe. (B) Percutaneous transhepatic cholangiography delineates the clipped-off ductal system of the right lobe.

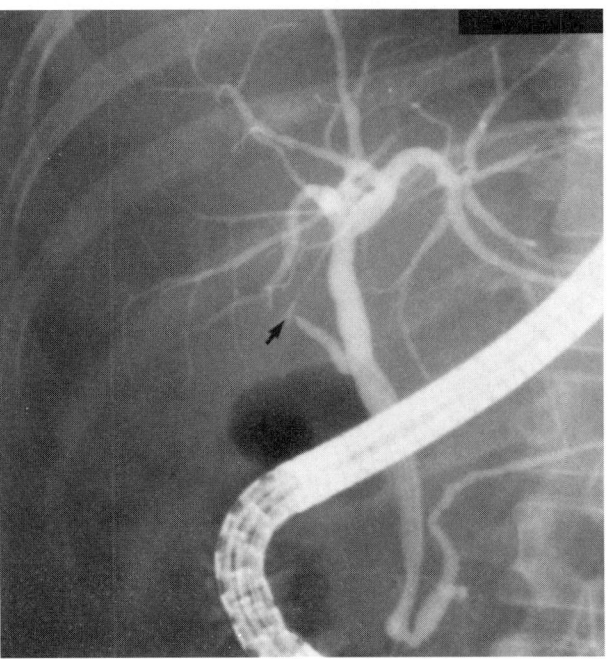

A

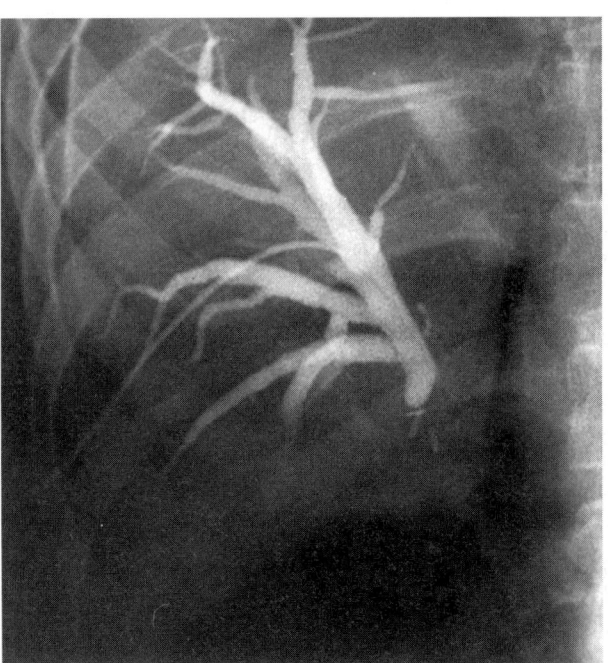

B

Imaging Procedures

Radiology has a very important and noncontroversial role in the diagnostic workup of patients before surgical repair. Ultrasound is an excellent and noninvasive technique for demonstrating ductal dilatation above a stricture or obstruction. A general idea of the level of the lesion may be obtained, but in most cases a more detailed demonstration of the ductal anatomy is required. Ultrasound is of value in demonstrating other intraabdominal fluid collections or hepatic lesions. Intrahepatic ductal dilatation may be absent in spite of biliary obstruction in patients with conditions such as sclerosing cholangitis or with hard, diseased livers such as in advanced cirrhosis. The ultrasound examination may reveal important information on the patency of the portal veins and the presence of venous or arterial collaterals.

Computed tomography (CT) similarly provides general information on ductal dilatation, liver masses, fluid collections, and vascular anatomy. Isotope scanning using hepatic imino diacetic acid (HIDA) provides some functional assessment in cases of incomplete strictures and in the postoperative evaluation of biliary anastomoses. It is a sensitive and specific test for leakage of bile from a damaged biliary tree.[23]

Although these tests are valuable, complete and accurate demonstration of the bile duct obstruction and of the bile ducts above and below the lesion is a key element in the management of bile duct stenoses and obstructions. This will usually require opacification of the bile ducts by percutaneous transhepatic cholangiography (PTC), endoscopic retrograde cholangiopancreatography (ERCP), or injection of contrast through any indwelling catheters such as T tubes.[24]

All branches of the biliary tree should be outlined, with particular care taken to show the confluence of the main right and left ducts at the liver hilus; the level, completeness, and nature of the obstructing lesions; and the status of the extrahepatic bile duct below the stricture. Ducts draining all the areas of the liver should be seen. Intraductal filling defects such as stones should be noted, as should any intrahepatic or extrahepatic narrowings or dilatations. Leaks from the biliary tree should also be identified.

Injection of large volumes of contrast material can lead to overfilling of the ducts. If these obstructed ducts are filled with stagnant infected bile, overdistention may force bacteria or toxins into the bloodstream with resultant sepsis. It is difficult to quantify what constitutes overfilling, but the author has found it safest to use the smallest volume of contrast consistent with obtaining a satisfactory cholangiogram. After a period of drainage, more extensive cholangiograms

can be performed if necessary. Use of a tilting table, cradle, and C arm is helpful in achieving good ductal delineation without overfilling of the system. Alternatively, rolling the patient into suitable oblique or prone positions may achieve the same result.

The least invasive route for contrast injection into the biliary tree is via a preexisting T tube or other surgical drainage tube. This may allow for adequate delineation of the biliary tree. In the absence of such tubes, ERCP is the next choice of access route for contrast cholangiography and is often satisfactory, provided that the biliary stricture is not complete. Adequate filling of the intrahepatic ducts above the narrowing may require the use of an occlusion balloon, especially when there is a sphincterotomy or duct-to-bowel anastomosis. Suitable oblique radiographs are almost always required. In three situations ERCP is of very limited value. (1) If there is a complete obstruction of the bile duct, retrograde injection via ERCP will only show the distal duct. The intrahepatic duct system above the obstruction will require delineation by PTC. (2) Complex hilar lesions are sometimes difficult to evaluate adequately by ERCP. (3) After surgery, such as a Roux-en-Y or Billroth II partial gastrectomy, access to the bile duct by ERCP may be impossible.

When the preceding approaches do not provide adequate information, PTC with a fine needle is used. PTC is often the key examination in the complete evaluation of the ductal system in patients with benign biliary obstruction. It is an effective technique, with success rates in the range of 97 to 100 percent and a low incidence of serious complications.[24-27] In a multiinstitutional survey of 2006 PTCs, the complication rate was 3.4 percent (sepsis 1.4 percent, bile leakage 1.45 percent, intraperitoneal hemorrhage 0.35 percent, death 0.20 percent).[24] In studies from a single institute experienced in biliary work, a negligible complication rate was recorded, which is in keeping with the author's experience.[26] Complete delineation of the ductal system may require separate punctures of individual but noncommunicating segments of the biliary tree. Among the great advantages of PTC compared with ERCP are that it is readily available in most centers, does not require special equipment, and is effective and safe. As with the other techniques, overfilling must be avoided and prophylactic antibiotic coverage is usually indicated.

The diagnostic studies should allow one to classify the lesion according to Bismuth types because the choice of treatment and outcome are influenced by the level of obstruction.[18,19,22] It is of critical importance that the complete biliary tree is opacified. Patients in Bismuth groups 4 and 5 may have isolated segments that may be missed on ERCP or PTC (see Fig. 28-3). To avoid this problem, cholangiograms should be obtained in the LPO (left posterior oblique) projection, which is the best projection to show the whole liver and to identify parts of the liver that appear to lack opacified bile ducts. The standard semiprone position in which ERCP is routinely performed yields an RPO (right posterior oblique) projection cholangiogram. This often superimposes the right and left lobes of the liver and tends to hide areas of the liver without ducts. Repeated passes with a fine needle should be made into these apparently duct-deficient areas to opacify isolated segments (see Fig. 28-3). Correlation with cross-sectional imaging studies may alert one to nonopacified segments.

Treatment

Nonoperative techniques of percutaneous biliary draining and stenting and similar endoscopic techniques are the methods of choice for treatment of inoperable malignant biliary disease.[28] However, treatment of benign biliary strictures is different from the palliative, short-term therapy that is so successfully provided by nonoperative techniques in malignant disease.[28] Patients with benign strictures are often young to middle-aged with a normal life expectancy. Consequently, the stricture treatment should be durable. Studies evaluating and comparing the various treatment options should have follow-up commensurate with the projected life expectancy of the patient and should ideally extend beyond 10 years.

The treatment options include surgery and the recently developed nonoperative approaches. These nonsurgical techniques are based on the retrograde endoscopic route[29] or on the percutaneous transhepatic route.[30,31] In some additional cases, an existing tube or puncture of a Roux or Hutson loop can be used.[32,33] The nonsurgical techniques allow dilatation of the stricture by tapered bougie or dilatation balloon. The dilated stricture may then be temporarily stented or left without a stent. Repeated dilatations may be performed. Patients are usually treated under local anesthetic with intravenous sedation. Frequently, much of the therapy can be undertaken on an outpatient basis. Studies published in 1986 with 73 patients and in 1987 with 74 patients show early success of 67 percent with percutaneous dilatation of biliary strictures.[30,34] They highlight the potential of dilatation therapy for benign lesions. Unfortunately, strictures may recur, even after repeat dilatation. Although dilatation may be satisfactory in the short term, proof of long-term cure has not yet been accumulated in large, well-controlled series. Indwelling internal stents (endoprostheses) are immune to the stricture recurrence associated with dilatation, but their usefulness is limited because all currently available plastic stents become occluded over time.[35] Newer expandable metallic stents are under development with the hope of achieving long-term patency.[36,37]

Dilatation

Early reports showing the feasibility of percutaneous biliary dilatation using balloon dilation catheters include those of Burhenne (1975)[38] via a T-tube tract and of Molnar and Stockum (1978)[39] via the transhepatic route. Since then, various authors have published their experience in dilating benign biliary strictures.[30,34,38–44] Review of this literature unfortunately does not produce an entirely coherent picture because of variation in stricture type, treatment, and follow-up. The method of dilatation used by radiologists is almost always by balloon catheter. Some workers perform multiple inflations, and others use prolonged inflations; the author and many others simply inflate the balloon once or twice until any waist disappears, believing that all that is required is to rupture the fibrous bands of the stricture. No published data are available showing an advantage of one dilatation technique over another, and this appears to be a question of little real importance. The balloon size should match the estimated caliber of the duct on either side of the stricture and is usually in the 4- to 8-mm range. Duct rupture is most unusual with correctly sized balloons even though high pressures (up to 16 atm) are not infrequently needed to dilate the stricture. Stricture dilatation can be very painful, and adequate sedation and pain control are important. Some authors advocate the use of general anesthesia in selected cases.

Management following dilatation varies from center to center. Some centers favor prolonged stenting after dilatation to try to avoid restenosis (Fig. 28-4).[34] They suggest that the stent acts as a scaffold, allowing healing to occur in a mature, stable, and nonstenosed form. This view echoes the arguments of surgeons such as Warren et al.[14] and Pitt et al.[20] in favor of stenting. Others believe stenting has no advantage and may, in fact, be harmful by stimulating further fibrosis.[19] Long-term stenting has an increased rate of infectious complication and has an increased morbidity. Williams et al. reported on dilatation of benign biliary strictures in 74 patients with stenting for 4 to 6 months.[34] Complications related to long-term indwelling stents were common and included tube plugging or dislodgment in 29 patients, intraductal stones in 9 patients, stricture extension in 5 patients, and right portal vein thrombosis in 1 patient. Citron et al., who stented for 3 to 6 months (average 20 weeks), noted that on average

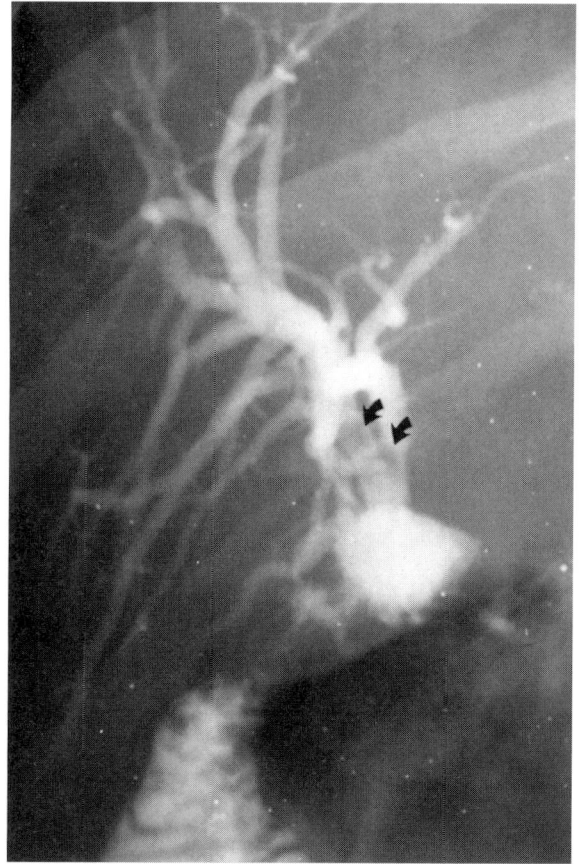

A

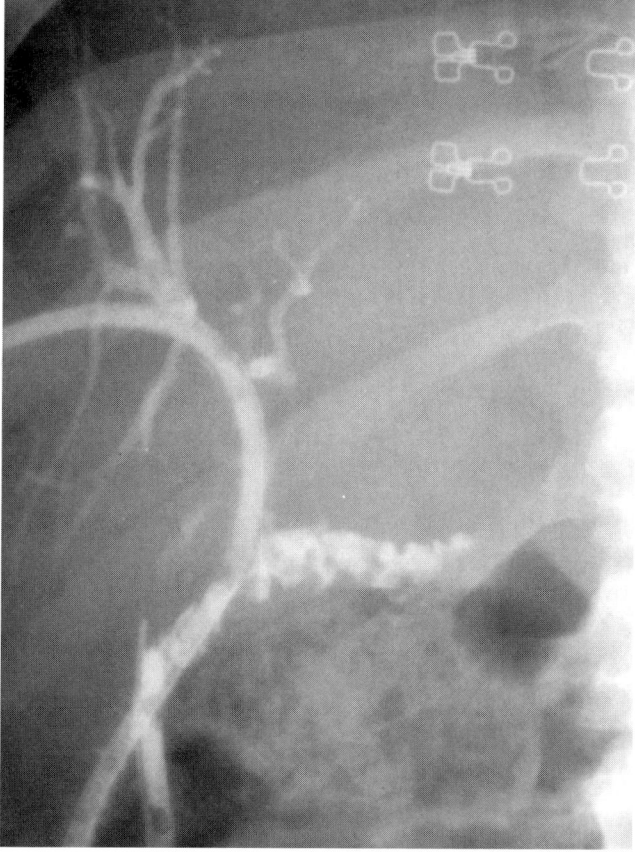

B

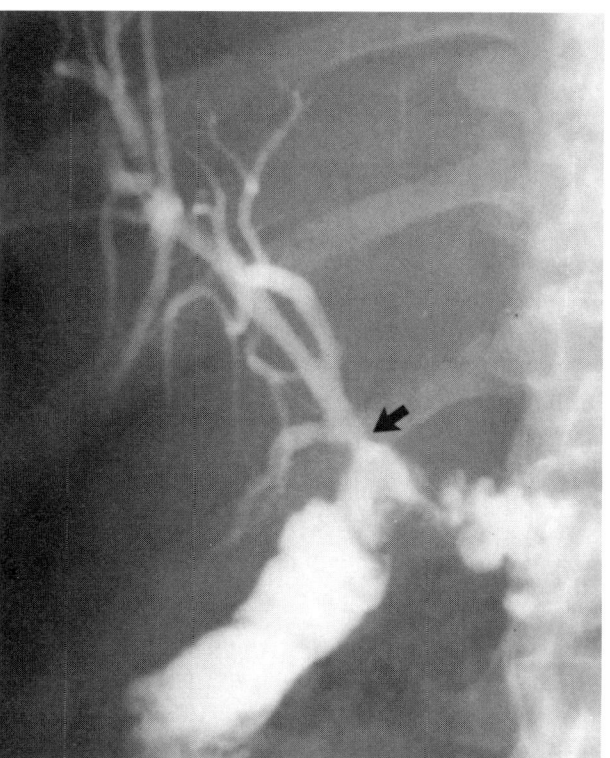

C

Figure 28-4. (A) Cholangiogram of a 60-year-old woman who underwent open cholecystectomy with damage to an aberrant right hepatic duct. This was repaired at the time of injury by anastomosing the right duct to a Roux loop. Eight years later the patient suffered from intermittent attacks of cholangitis, and a PTC showed the right ductal system to be dilated and partially obstructed by stones (*arrows*) above a narrow biliary-enteric anastomosis. (B) The stenosis underwent successful dilatation with a 6-mm balloon. The stones were pushed into the loop and the anastomosis stented with a 14 French Silastic catheter for 6 weeks. (C) The anastomosis (*arrow*) is widely patent and remained so for 4 years until the patient died from colon cancer.

patients required a total of 17 days in the hospital after dilatation at various times.[44] Mueller et al., in their report dealing with 73 patients from four different centers, discussed the controversial question of long-term stenting but did not provide data that were helpful in resolving the issue.[30]

The author's approach has been to inflate the balloon once or twice to efface any balloon waist. A drainage catheter is left across the stricture for six weeks, and then the catheter is positioned in the biliary tree above the stricture. If contrast flows through the dilated stricture, the tube is capped externally and the patient is followed up 2 or 3 weeks later. The tube is removed after this test period if the dilated stricture remains widely patient. If restenosis occurs during the test period, repeat dilatation is performed and the patient is followed for a similar period. Dilatation is considered unsuccessful after two attempts.[19]

The initial results of balloon dilatation are good, with immediate success in the range of 67 to 87 percent. Mueller et al. had a 67 percent patency rate in 73 patients followed up for a minimum of 36 months.[30] They divided their strictures into three groups: 44 patients with anastomotic strictures (choledochojejunostomy or hepaticojejunostomy), 28 patients in an ill-defined group described as "iatrogenic" (presumably bile duct strictures other than those at a biliary-enteric anastomosis), and 17 patients with sclerosing cholangitis. The 36-month patency rates were 67, 76, and 42 percent, respectively. However, 25 patients (34 percent) had recurrent strictures, 16 treated by repeated dilatations and 9 treated by surgery. It is unclear whether these authors' 36-month patency rate refers to primary patency or is an assisted patency rate including those patients treated by repeated dilatations.

The large series of 74 patients with benign biliary obstruction carefully reported by Williams et al. is instructive to consider in detail.[34] Their population does not include sclerosing cholangitis. Initially successful balloon dilatation was performed in 74 patients, but it is not stated if there were any unsuccessful attempts. Forty-nine patients had strictures of a biliary-enteric anastomosis. Forty of these patients had their stenting tubes removed, and 9 retained their stents. Of these 40 patients, 27 (67 percent) had to undergo redilatations before the stents could be removed. After stenting for an average of 8.8 months, 29 or 40 strictures (72.5 percent) were considered to have been successfully dilated. The other group comprised 25 patients with ductal strictures, and these responded better to dilatation. Twenty-four had their stenting tubes removed, and 1 patient remained stented. Ten of 24 patients (42 percent) required redilatation before the stents could be removed. After an average of 4.7 months of stenting, 21 of 24 patients (87 percent) were considered successfully treated. For the whole group, success was 67.5 percent (50 of 74 patients). Follow-up ranged from 1 to 58 months (mean 28 months). Sixty percent of patients (actual numbers are not stated) were without stents at 24 months follow-up, and 38 percent at 36 months or longer. Strictures recurred after stent removal in 14 of 64 patients (22 percent). These posttreatment failures occurred at 1 to 36 months (mean 13.8 months, median 8 months), but 13 of 14 were

successfully treated by repeat dilatations involving additional periods of stenting averaging 9.6 months. This important series proves that benign strictures can be treated in the short term but that they recur frequently. Aggressive management with prolonged stenting and frequent redilatations is essential but results in significant morbidity. Hospitalization time averaged 10 days. Complication rates in both the acute procedure-related category and in the chronic catheter-related category were not insignificant. There is no clear consensus in the literature on whether lesions of the bile duct or those at a biliary-enteric anastomosis respond better to dilatation.

Randomized prospective trials comparing balloon dilatation and surgical repair of strictures are not available, but in 1989 Pitt et al. compared the results of these two techniques in a single institution.[20] They studied 25 patients who were repaired using a Roux loop and compared them with 20 patients treated by balloon dilatation. The two groups were considered similar in many parameters that might have influenced outcome. The authors summarized their findings as follows.

> Twenty-five patients underwent surgical repair with Roux-en-Y choledocho- or hepatico-jejunostomy with postoperative transhepatic stenting for a mean of 13.8 ± 1.3 months. Twenty patients had balloon dilatation a mean of 3.9 times and were stented transhepatically for a mean of 13.3 ± 2.0 months. Mean length of follow-up was 57 ± 7 and 59 ± 6 months for surgery and balloon dilatation, respectively. No patients died after any of the procedures. The same definition of a successful outcome was applied to both groups and was achieved in 88% of the surgical and in 55% of the balloon dilatation patients (p < 0.02). Significant hemobilia occurred more often with balloon dilatation (20% vs. 4%, p < 0.02). The total hospital stay and cost of balloon dilatation was [*sic*] not significantly different from surgery.[20]

Although they concluded that surgery was preferable, they pointed out the value of dilatation for high-risk patients or those unwilling to undergo further surgery. In both groups, patients had the inconvenience of stents for over 13 months, and the study again illustrates the problems involved in adequately treating benign biliary strictures.

Although nonoperative dilatation is not indicated in patients who are candidates for surgical repair, it represents an important treatment option for patients in whom surgical repair is not possible for anatomic reasons, for patients at high surgical risk, for patients with portal hypertension, and for patients unwilling to undergo further surgery. Dilatation is of particular value in patients of advanced age or in those with serious concomitant disease, when the possibility of late recurrence is of less concern. The choice of treatment should, when possible, take into account the current results achieved by operative compared to nonoperative treatment in the institute in which the patient will be treated, rather than by reference to published data from other centers of excellence. Because of the complexity of managing biliary strictures, patients are best referred to centers where both surgery and nonoperative interventions are performed by experienced experts in biliary disease.[45] Modern management of bile duct strictures benefits from the combined use of surgical and nonoperative techniques. The surgical group at UCLA noted a change in their treatment strategies in the period 1953 through 1990.[21] As nonoperative dilatation became available, this was used to correct recurrent anastomotic strictures.

An example of a combined surgical and radiologic approach is that of Hutson, Russell, and colleagues, who cooperated in developing a transjejunal access route to the biliary tree to allow for periodic balloon dilatations of the biliary ducts. A Roux-en-Y loop was constructed and anastomosed to the extrahepatic bile duct. The afferent limb was attached to the abdominal wall, and access to this limb was originally through a surgically created stoma.[32] In later patients, the limb was closed but marked with clips at the site of attachment to the abdominal wall to facilitate percutaneous puncture. This technique provided simple access for periodic bile duct dilatations.[33] In some patients, percutaneous access to a suitably located Roux loop is possible, even if a Hutson loop has not been intentionally constructed.[46]

Endoprostheses

To address the problems of stricture recurrence and the morbidity of chronic indwelling stent catheters, indwelling endoprostheses have been developed. These devices are implanted across the lesion, percutaneously or endoscopically. An endoprosthesis must either remain patent for a long time or be easily exchangeable if it is to offer an advantage over balloon dilatation. Endoprostheses must meet the usual biocompatibility standards, must be safe and easy to insert, and must resist migration. A 12 French plastic endoprosthesis works well for a period of months, but in time will occlude and may migrate, particularly when placed across a biliary-enteric anastomosis.[35] In patients with normal anatomy, stents can be exchanged endoscopically on a routine basis at intervals of about 3 months. This will usually avoid the problems caused by a blocked endoprosthesis. However, such management places considerable burden and expense on the patient and should only be considered in the absence of any better alternative.

Many strictures are at biliary-enteric anastomoses that cannot be reached by the endoscopic route. In these patients, it is almost always possible to place an endoprosthesis via the percutaneous transhepatic route. However, placement of an indwelling plastic endoprosthesis via this route is only a temporary measure because of inevitable clogging of the endoprosthesis. The need for routine percutaneous transhepatic exchanges, although technically feasible, renders the percutaneous plastic stent an unsuitable means of long-term treatment of benign strictures.

Expandable Metallic Stents

The development of expandable metallic stents has provided a new form of implantable endoprosthesis. These stents have the advantage that they can be inserted using small-caliber introducers (7–12 French). Once in position the stents expand to diameters as large as 12 mm. It is hoped that the large bore of these endoprostheses should be more resistant to clogging. In the United States, the most widely used metal endoprostheses are the modified Gianturco-Rösch Z stent (Cook, Inc.), the Wallstent (Schneider), and the Palmaz stent (Johnson & Johnson).[36,47,48] Many other stents, such as the Strecker stent, are either only available for clinical use outside the United States or are in various stages of development and testing.[37]

In 1985, Carrasco et al. published the result of the first experimental use of the Gianturco stent in the extrahepatic bile ducts of dogs, with encouraging results.[36] In 1988, Uchida et al. described modifications to the Gianturco stent achieved by adding circumferential monofilament nylon sutures to limit stent expansion and to allow linking of Gianturco stent chains together.[49] These modifications gave extra length and flexibility without sacrificing resistance to compressibility (Fig. 28-5). These authors emphasized that the expansile force of the stent is controlled by the stent construction. The expansile force increases with the increased diameter of the stainless steel wire used, with the increased number of legs in the stents, with the increased angle of the leg bends, with the decreased length of the stent, and with an increase in the number of the stents used. This modified stent is the type currently available. It is called the modified Gianturco-Rösch Z stent or variations of this name.

A study published in 1989 by Irving et al. summarized the early clinical experience of five hospitals in four European countries using the Gianturco stent.[50] Eleven patients with benign biliary strictures were stented after failure of prior treatment with balloon dilatation or surgical reconstruction. Eight patients had good results and were without jaundice, pruritus, or infection during follow-up of 6 to 21 months. One

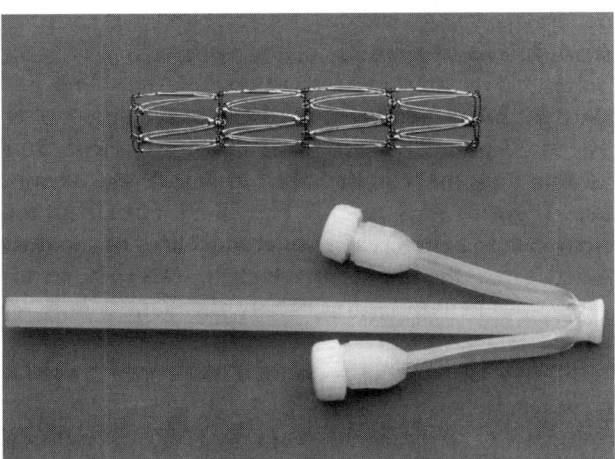

Figure 28-5. A Gianturco stent of 10-mm diameter with four linked segments. The peel-away introducer is shown below the stent.

patient in this group died of carcinoma of the bronchus 4 months after stenting but was asymptomatic from a biliary standpoint. Of the remaining three patients, one had early stent migration and underwent bypass surgery with stent removal, one had stent migration at 4 to 5 months, and one had stent occlusion from epithelial proliferation within the stent after 10 months. This work and similar work by Coons[51] showed the utility of the Gianturco stents in the short-term treatment of benign biliary strictures and led to further clinical use.

In 1990, Rossi et al. published their results using the modified Gianturco stent in 17 patients with benign biliary strictures who had failed repeated previous attempts at surgical correction and dilatation.[52] Fourteen of their 17 patients were symptom-free at an average of 8 months (range 4–12 months) follow-up. These workers continued to follow their patients for an average of 37 months (range 30–41 months), adding 1 patient stented with a Wallstent.[31] Ten of 18 patients (55.5 percent) were asymptomatic, although in 1 patient a stent had migrated into the bowel 6 months after placement. Recurrent symptoms occurred in 5 patients (27.7 percent). Stent obstruction occurred in 3 of these patients after 4, 13, and 22 months, respectively. Stent migration resulted in restenosis in 1 patient, and papillary stenosis caused obstruction in the fifth patient. Three patients died. One patient with Hodgkin disease died 9 months after stent placement. The stent was patent, but there was intrahepatic narrowing from sclerosing cholangitis. A second patient died at 6 months with recurrent jaundice, cholangitis, secondary sclerosing cholangitis, liver failure, and occluded stent. The final patient died with peritoneal spread from a gastric carcinoma resected 10 years previously, but with no sign of bile stasis.

In 1992, Coons summarized his experience with the modified Gianturco-Rösch stent in 54 patients with benign lesions.[53] Eleven had sclerosing cholangitis, leaving a group of 43 patients with benign strictures who had failed previous treatment. The number of patients who were symptom-free were 2 at over 4 years; 2 at over 3 years; 8 at over 2 years; 10 at over 1 year; and 21 at less than 1 year. The overall occlusion rate for the 43 patients was 7 percent. For the 22 followed for more than 1 year it was 13 percent, and for the 4 over 3 years it was 25 percent. For these longer follow-ups, the numbers of patients are too small to draw statistically relevant conclusions.

Six additional papers describe the use of metallic stents in benign strictures in a total of 26 patients, but these series are too small to warrant individual consideration. A review of the current published literature shows a limited experience in using metallic stents in cases of benign lesions. In those cases, the Gianturco stent is the most commonly used type. It provides reasonable results (53 percent patency at 37 months) in the midterm, but appears to be better than plastic stents and of value in patients where surgery and dilatation repeatedly fail.

A few workers have focused on the reaction of the bile ducts to implanted metallic stents to better understand their function. Vorwerk et al. studied the patency of Wallstents placed across experimentally induced benign stenoses in the common bile ducts of 12 dogs.[48] They used silicone-coated Wallstents in three dogs. In two dogs, the coated Wallstents occluded at 3 and 4 months. In one dog, the stent migrated to the bowel within 4 weeks, leaving the common bile duct stenosed. The authors quoted personal communication with H. Rousseau and C. Zollikofer, who always had early migration of coated Wallstents, and they concluded, despite the small numbers, that silicone-coated Wallstents should not be used in clinical applications. However, Alvarado et al. studied 18 dogs using Palmaz stents coated with silicone rubber or segmented polyether-polyurethane and noted no instances of stent migration.[47] Vorwerk suggested that the inflexible rigid nature of the Palmaz stent may have prevented the migration.

In the 10 animals with noncoated Wallstents in Vorwerk's studies, all animals showed significant wall thickening within the stent during the 15- to 24-month follow-up. The thickening was mucosal hyperplasia, with soft, fingerlike hyperplasia protruding through the stent interspaces initially. This led to morphologic high-grade narrowing of the stent lumen but did not result in functional obstruction to bile flow. The mucosal hyperplasia increased within the first year after implantation but leveled off during longer follow-up periods. The hyperplasia was histologically related to stent position within the mucosal or superficial submucosal layer. Once the stent entered deeper into the bile duct wall, mucosal thickening decreased. In the early study by Carrasco et al. using Gianturco stents with shorter follow-up (4–23 weeks), complete stent incorporation, as described above, was not seen.[36] There was mucosal hyperplasia with some pressure necrosis and sloughing, and only partial incorporation.

In their clinical study, Maccioni et al. concluded that the main cause of late stent occlusion was tissue ingrowth.[31] Biopsy specimens collected through a cholangioscope or by intraductal brushing showed hyperplastic epithelium and/or granulation tissue within the stent. CT studies of asymptomatic patients showed a lining of soft tissue density inside the stent of various degrees at different levels without significant changes at subsequent follow-ups, suggesting the presence of reactive, hyperplastic tissue. Maccioni and colleagues believe that tissue ingrowth reaches a certain extent and then stabilizes without completely occluding the stent, and thus allows an unimpeded flow of bile through the stented stricture. The large final diameter of the stent, some six times wider than the common bile duct, easily accommodates this hyperplasia. They could not exclude the possibility that sludge was imaged by the CT scans rather than hyperplasia.

Indications for Stenting

The author's approach has been to use Gianturco stents only after all surgical options have been exhausted and after resolute attempts at balloon dilatation have failed. The Gianturco stent does appear to provide good palliation in some one-half to two-thirds of patients treated over the currently available follow-up. Some patients are now asymptomatic as much as 5 years after stenting. A number of others have returned with cholangitis and stone formation (Fig. 28-6). Reintervention from a percutaneous transhepatic approach has allowed for stone removal and clearing of the ducts, thus prolonging secondary patency. In a small number of cases, a very localized stenosis has recurred within the stent at the same location as the treated stricture (Fig. 28-7). In a personal communication, J. Rösch has suggested that this may be a result of hyperplasia induced by the junctional area between two stent segments. He is developing a spiral stent to try to overcome this problem and to improve other characteristics of the Gianturco-Rösch stent. The author has empirically treated these recurrences by placing a coaxial Wallstent or Palmaz stent within the narrowed Gianturco stent.

Technique

The author's preference for stenting benign lesions is to use the modified Gianturco-Rösch stent. Most ex-

perience in benign lesions has been published with this stent. It is easier to place accurately than the Wallstent because it is much more radiopaque and does not shorten. Biliary stents are available in diameters of 8, 10, or 12 mm. They are made up of individual units 15 mm long that can be linked in flexible chains containing one to five units (see Fig. 28-5). The Gianturco stent covers a smaller circumferential area of the duct mucosa than the Wallstent, which appears to be an advantage in benign lesions, where the stent is only required as a scaffold to prevent stricture formation.

Placement can be performed via a percutaneous transhepatic approach or via an existing T tube. The lesion is crossed using standard techniques, and care is taken to carefully define the upper and lower margins of the stricture. A catheter placed over the wire, with contrast injected through a side-arm adapter, can be helpful at this stage. Accurate delineation is important for selecting the correct stent length and diameter and for positioning the stent. The delivery system, consisting of a sheath with injection side port, radiopaque distal marker, and tapered dilator, is passed over the wire and across the stricture. The dilator is removed, and the small peel-away introducer is loaded on the back end of the wire, followed by the stent (see Fig. 28-5). Care must be taken that the wire passes cleanly through the stent lumen and does not pass through one of the struts of the stent. The stent is carefully loaded into the introducer by manual compression. The introducer and stent are fed through the valve on the external end of the delivery sheath. A blunt-ended pusher then goes over the wire and pushes the stent to the delivery site within the sheath. The introducer is peeled away and, with the stent maintained in the predetermined position with the pusher, the sheath is drawn back, releasing the stent. In most cases, the stent will dilate on its own.

The author does not usually predilate the stricture or dilate the stent after placement, although the retained guidewire allows for postplacement balloon dilatation. A self-retaining catheter is positioned through the stent or in the biliary tree above the stent for check cholangiography the following day. The selection of stent diameter is based on the size of the bile ducts. Single-segment stents are not used because of their marked tendency to migrate. Modified stents with small hooks were once developed and tested in an attempt to prevent migration, but the hooks made the stents difficult to employ and the devices were abandoned. Instead, if there is a short segment stricture, the author places a double stent, with the junction between the stents centered at the narrowest part of the lesion. In some cases, to try to secure a more stable position for the stent, some of the nylon suture links of the leading and/or trailing edges of the stent

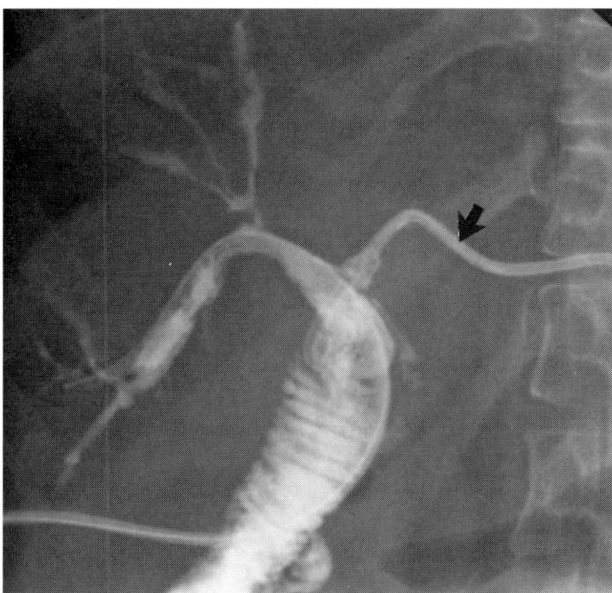

A

Figure 28-6. (A) Cholangiogram of a 54-year-old woman with sclerosing cholangitis and a Roux loop. The right-sided ducts show severe narrowing. There is one percutaneous catheter inserted via the Roux loop into the right-sided bile ducts. A separate percutaneous transhepatic catheter (*arrow*) drains the left ducts. Repeated balloon dilatations provided only transient clinical improvement. (B) The right-sided ducts have been stented with multiple Gianturco stents, leading to marked clinical improvement. (C) Six months later, the patient's clinical situation deteriorated, and a PTC showed blocked stents with numerous stones (*arrows*).

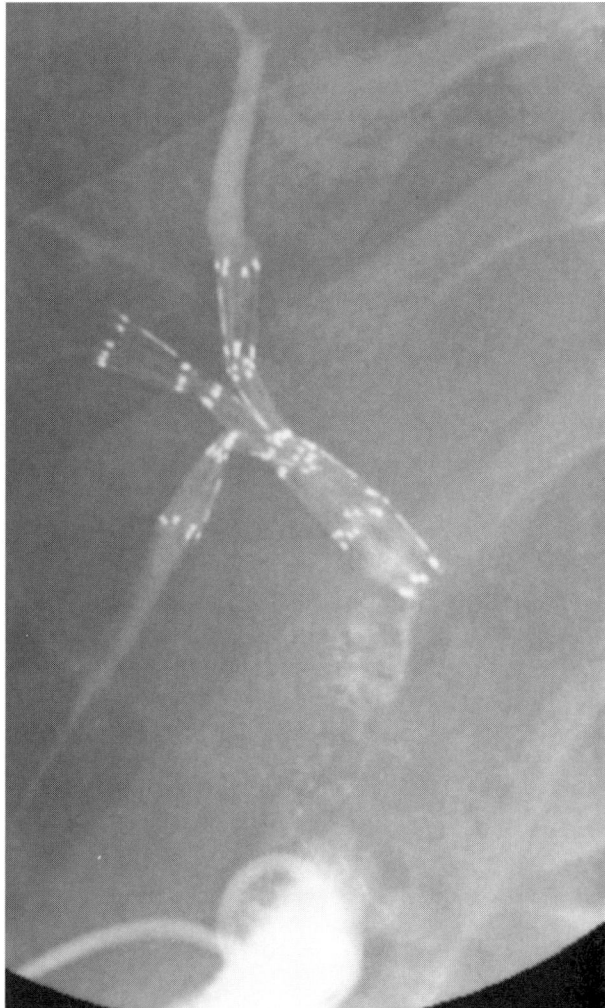

B

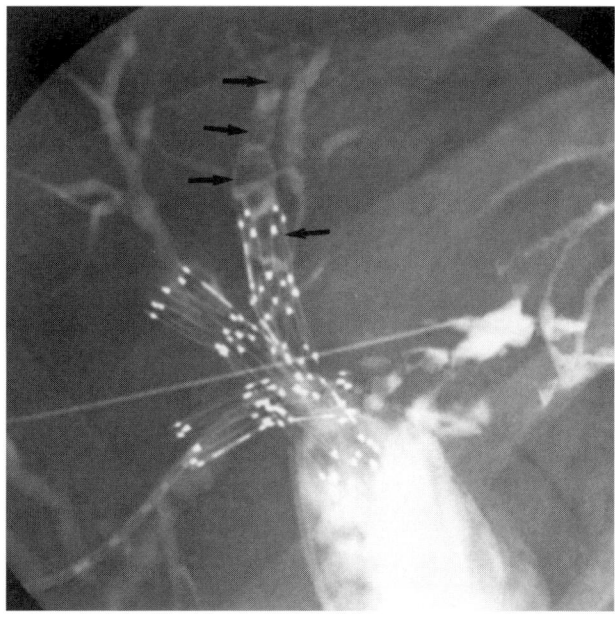

C

are cut. On delivery, these wings flare out, holding the stent more securely in place (see Fig. 28-1B and C). When crossing through a Gianturco stent with a wire, it is important not to inadvertently pass through a side strut or to displace the stent. For this reason, only the original wire is removed when it is clear that no further manipulations are required. If it is necessary to recross a stent, a 3-mm J wire can be helpful.

Primary Sclerosing Cholangitis

Primary sclerosing cholangitis (PSC) is characterized by a cholangiographic picture of multiple diffusely located strictures of intra- and extrahepatic bile ducts. The cause of the syndrome is unknown, but inflammatory bowel disease is present in about two-thirds of patients with PSC. Ulcerative colitis is the main type of bowel disease, with Crohn disease accounting for only about 7 percent of cases (range 1.5–13.0 percent). Men are afflicted most commonly, with a male-female ratio greater than 2:1.[5,54]

Initial presentation occurs between 25 and 45 years

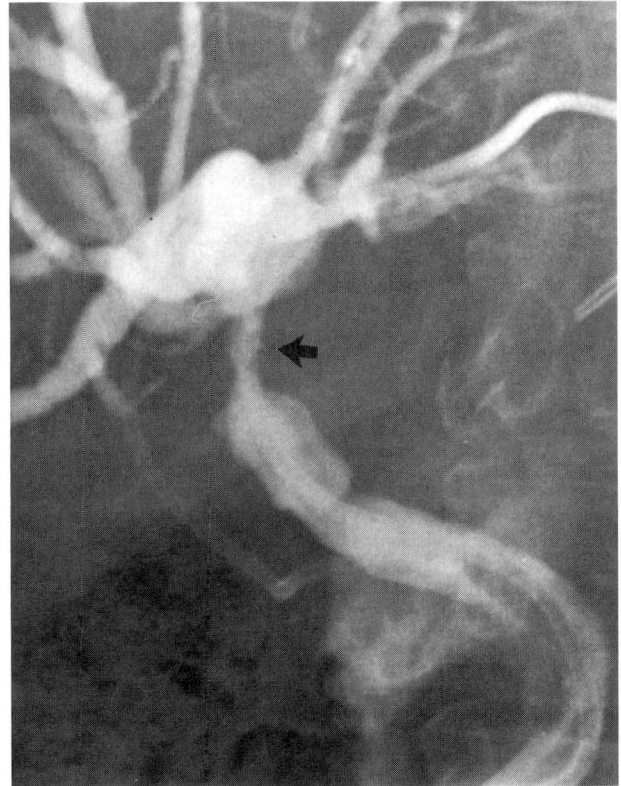

A

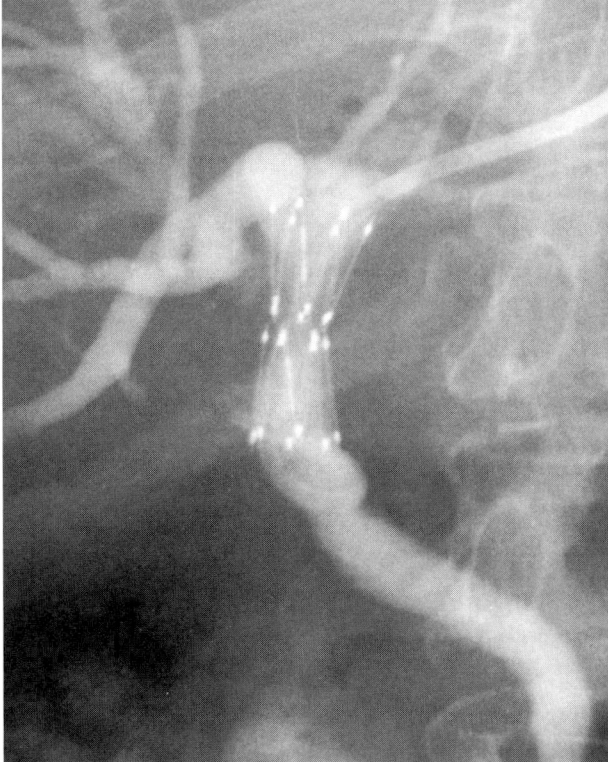

B

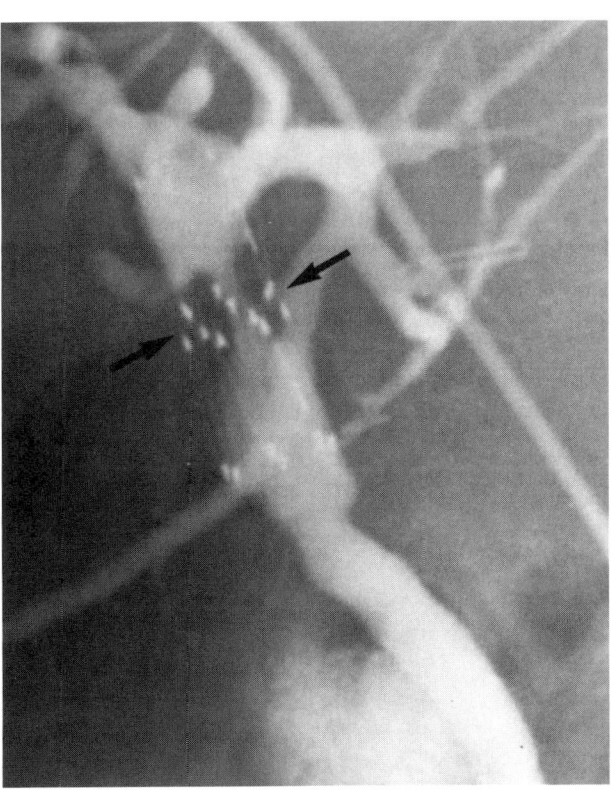

C

Figure 28-7. (A) Cholangiogram of a 54-year-old man with a Bismuth type 2 narrowing (*arrow*) following liver transplantation and thrombosis of the hepatic artery. The stricture did not remain open after balloon dilatation. (B) A good response to stenting with a Gianturco 10-mm stent. (C) Six weeks later the stricture has recurred (*arrows*) in its original location, despite the Gianturco stent.

of age, and more than two-thirds of patients are under 45 years when diagnosed. Typically, the clinical picture is of a gradual onset of progressive fatigue and pruritus, followed by jaundice in a younger male who has inflammatory bowel disease. The syndrome is progressive, following a very unpredictable time course from chronic fibrosing inflammation of the bile ducts, to cirrhosis, portal hypertension, liver failure, and death.

Diagnosis

Diagnosis is usually based on cholangiographic findings by endoscopic retrograde cholangiopancreatography (ERCP) or percutaneous transhepatic cholangiography (PTC). MacCarty et al. described the cholangiographic appearance in 86 patients with PSC.[55] The most common findings were diffuse, multifocal strictures involving both the intra- and extrahepatic biliary ducts. In 20 percent of patients, only the intrahepatic and proximal extrahepatic ducts were involved, and the distal common bile duct was spared. The cystic duct was considered abnormal in 18 percent of 60 patients. However, the spiral valves and complicated anatomic course of the cystic duct make this assessment difficult. The pancreatic ducts were abnormal in 8 percent of 40 patients, but this may be only a coincidental finding. Strictures were typically short (1–2 cm) and annular, alternating with normal or minimally dilated segments, giving a beaded appearance. In more advanced disease, long, confluent strictures were seen. Very short (1- to 2-mm), bandlike strictures were noted in 18 patients (21 percent), most often in the extrahepatic ducts. In 9 patients, these were associated with outpouchings resembling diverticula, which often protruded between adjacent strictures. In 14 patients, similar outpouchings were seen without band strictures. Thirty-eight patients (44 percent) demonstrated mural irregularities that gave a "shaggy" appearance. These varied from a fine "brush border" to coarse filing defects with a frankly nodular appearance and were seen more frequently in the extrahepatic (40 percent) than in the intrahepatic ducts. Focal dilatation of ductal segments between strictures was relatively frequent (42 percent), but diffuse dilatation of the biliary tree was infrequent.

The incidence of cholangiocarcinoma in patients with PSC has been reported as 4 to 9 percent in a number of studies.[5,56] A much higher incidence, 30 to 40 percent, is found at autopsy of patients dying of PSC,[5] and study of excised livers of patients undergoing liver transplantation for PSC shows an incidence of 9 to 33 percent.[5] Diagnosis of cholangiocarcinoma in patients with PSC is difficult. A sudden, unexplained deterioration in clinical condition with rapidly deepening jaundice, weight loss, and abdominal discomfort may suggest cholangiocarcinoma. On the cholangiogram, marked and rapidly progressive ductal dilatation seen on consecutive studies is suggestive of cholangiocarcinoma. A polypoid mass may rarely be seen.[46] Cytologic examination of material obtained by brushing the lumen of the duct has a disappointingly low sensitivity, as does percutaneous biopsy, although specificity is good, about 100 percent, if cells are obtained. CT misses the diagnosis in about 50 percent of cases and is of greater value in more advanced cases where a mass lesion, metastatic invasion of lymph nodes, or liver metastases may be demonstrated.[5]

Treatment

The cause of PSC is unknown, and no specific treatment has proven to be effective. Management is therefore directed at ameliorating the consequences of bile duct narrowing and obstruction using endoscopic, radiologic, or surgical techniques. Because PSC is a progressive disease, it is thought that deterioration in liver function may be aggravated or accelerated by back pressure from dominant strictures and any intraductal debris that may be present. It is hoped that reduction of this obstruction may halt, delay, or even reverse progression to cirrhosis and liver failure.[57] Relief of jaundice, pruritus, and cholangitis by the use of periodic dilatation and antibiotics is of symptomatic value to the patient even if the progression of the disease course is not altered. In patients with end-stage cirrhosis, the benefit to the patients' well-being of arduous dilatation treatments must be carefully considered, and possibly abandoned.

Endoscopic Treatment

In most patients, PSC is diagnosed by ERCP. Dominant strictures can be dilated using standard endoscopic techniques with over-the-wire bougies or dilatation balloon catheters. Dominant strictures in the extrahepatic ducts can usually be dilated successfully by endoscopists.[57] When dominant strictures within the intrahepatic ducts require dilatation, radiologists have often been able to assist their endoscopic colleagues by manipulating torqueable guidewires, such as the Terumo guidewire, through intrahepatic strictures.[45]

Some endoscopists perform a sphincterotomy to allow for easier manipulation of instruments during dilatation and subsequent passage of stone debris. As in the case of stricture dilatation in most parts of the body, there is considerable debate and uncertainty over the value of leaving indwelling stents in the narrowed duct after dilatation. The author's clinical experience with PSC suggests that, wherever possible, plastic stents should not be used.[58] With the characteristically narrow ducts found in PSC, plastic endoprostheses tend to hinder drainage by obturating the whole ductal lumen, compromising drainage from side branches and leading to infection and possible exacerbation of the PSC. If stents are used, they should be removed or exchanged after 2 to 3 months, before they become occluded.

The results of endoscopic management are generally positive, but the published series are somewhat limited by the size of the patient group and the length of follow-up. In 1991, Johnson et al. reported on 35 patients with PSC treated by endoscopic dilatation, with an average follow-up of 24 months.[59] Mean serum bilirubin decreased from 10 to 4 mg/dl in the 19 patients who presented with jaundice. There was a significant decrease in the number of episodes of cholangitis and in the need for hospitalization. Their radiographic evaluation, which assigned numerical scores to pre- and postdilatation strictures seen on the cholangiogram, also showed a significant improvement. Eleven patients were stented. Complications were hemorrhage requiring transfusion following sphincterotomy in one patient, and pancreatitis requiring hospitalization in another.

Cotton and Nickl at Duke University reported on a 3-year experience with 20 patients with symptomatic PSC whom they treated endoscopically.[57] They failed to dilate the dominant stricture in 3 patients, treated 3 others with nasobiliary drainage and lavage, and treated 1 by successfully removing a stone. The remaining 13 were dilated successfully, and in 6 of these indwelling endoprostheses were used. The authors' cautious summary was: "Mean follow-up is so far only 17 months, but more patients have improved clinically and biochemically than have deteriorated."[57]

Percutaneous Radiologic Management

Access to the biliary tree can be achieved by the established percutaneous transhepatic route, or by percutaneous puncture of a subcutaneously located bowel loop in patients with a choledochojejunostomy and Roux-en-Y,[33,58] or by way of a surgically placed T tube or U tube.

Percutaneous transhepatic access can usually be established by an experienced radiologist, but it is more difficult to cannulate the nondilated and strictured ducts found in PSC than it is in other types of obstructive jaundice, which typically have dilated ducts. Once access is achieved, manipulation within the biliary tree can also be difficult because of the multiple strictures.

In 1985, May et al. reported on their experience in balloon-dilating dominant strictures in 14 patients.[60] Access was by percutaneous transhepatic puncture in 9 patients and via a surgically-placed T tube in 5. They achieved initial success in all 14 patients. Their follow-up was 12 to 34 months (mean 16 months). Before dilatation, bacterial cholangitis occurred at 9.3 ± 5.8 episodes per year but decreased significantly after dilatation to 0.5 ± 0.9 episodes per year. Total serum bilirubin decreased significantly from 11.5 ± 9.5 mg/dl before dilatation to 1.8 ± 0.12 mg/dl after dilatation in the 4 patients who had jaundice for less than 6 months before dilatation. In the 5 patients with jaundice for longer than 6 months, no significant change in bilirubin occurred after dilatation. Recurrence of the dominant stricture recurred at 6 to 18 months in 3 patients. Five patients had complications, which were bacteremia and cholangitis requiring hospitalization. Four of 5 patients who showed no symptomatic response died of liver failure.

Skolkin et al. reported on percutaneous balloon cholangioplasty in 14 patients with PSC in 1989.[61] Access was by transhepatic puncture in 12 patients and via a T tube in the remaining 2 patients. They had one failed attempt at transhepatic drainage. Although initial success was achieved in 14 of 15 patients, they reported that PTC, drainage, and cholangioplasty were often technically challenging. Attempts at leaving stents in place for 6 months were successful in only 4 of 14 patients because of septic cholangitis and poor tolerance of the tubes. They had a mean follow-up of 18 to 19 months (range 1–42). Thirteen of 14 patients experienced varying degrees of clinical improvement. Pruritus resolved or decreased in 7 of 7 patients. Malaise and pain were more difficult to assess because of the contribution of the indwelling stent to this symptom complex. They reported only general trends for biochemical response because of the small number of patients and varied patient condition before treatment. Complications included frequent fevers, cholangitis, and sepsis, 1 arterial bleed requiring embolization, 3 patients with pleural effusions as a result of high tube placement across the pleural space, and 1 patient with a subphrenic abscess and 1 with a subcutaneous abscess, both of which were drained percutaneously.

On the basis of this reported experience and the author's own experience, an endoscopic approach is recommended when possible. When balloon dilatation is performed transhepatically or via a T tube, the dilatation is completed without stenting and an effort is made to remove all tubes from the biliary tree as soon as possible.[58] The same principles apply when the approach is retrograde via a percutaneous puncture of the Roux loop. A self-retaining catheter retained in the loop allows for subsequent access to the biliary tree without the infectious complications of an indwelling tube in the biliary tree. All manipulations are performed under antibiotic cover.

The availability of expandable metallic stents has provided additional ways of treating the strictures of PSC. In a few patients who did not respond to periodic dilatations of dominant strictures and who were not yet candidates for liver transplantation, the author has implanted Gianturco stents. Multiple stents can provide an extensive intraductal scaffold to maintain patency, as shown in Figure 28-8. These stents obviously do not represent a permanent treatment option but may be useful as a temporary measure to delay the need for liver transplantation. The author's experience so far is favorable but is too limited at this time to offer any firm data.

Surgical Treatment

Biliary surgery for the treatment of strictures in PSC has largely been replaced by the nonoperative tech-

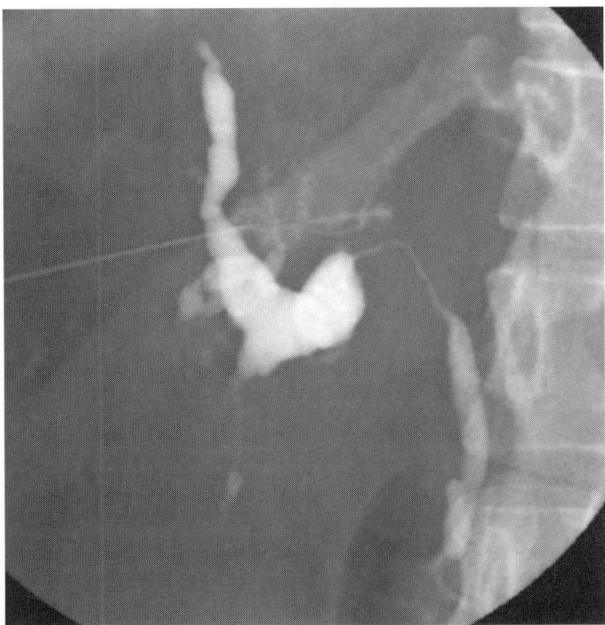

A

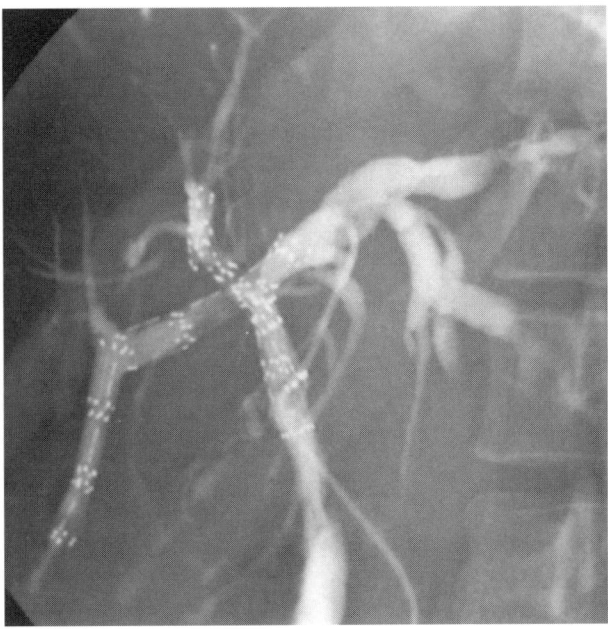

B

Figure 28-8. (A) Cholangiogram of a 34-year-old woman with sclerosing cholangitis and ulcerative colitis. The PTC shows a few irregular dilated ducts on the right, no filling of ducts on the left, and tight stricturing of the common hepatic duct. (B) Multiple Gianturco stents have been placed to keep open the main intrahepatic ducts, with excellent clinical results. Follow-up at 6 months shows maintenance of good health.

niques described above.[62] Although surgeons at Johns Hopkins have advocated resection of the extrahepatic biliary tree, operative intrahepatic dilatation, and hepaticoenteric or choledochoenteric anastomosis with long-term indwelling Silastic stents, there seems to be little support for such an aggressive approach.[62] Periodic dilatations can be achieved much more easily by nonoperative techniques, and the burden and morbidity of indwelling transhepatic tubes can be avoided. Moreover, subsequent liver transplantation is made more difficult by previous biliary surgery of this type.

Anastomosis of the extrahepatic bile duct to a Roux-en-Y loop, with one part tacked up to the abdominal wall, allows for percutaneous puncture and cannulation of the loop.[33] From the loop, radiologists can gain retrograde access to the biliary tree to dilate dominant strictures. This approach eliminates the transhepatic route and the need for indwelling catheters. The loop leading to the ducts should be short and straight for easy percutaneous manipulation. However, increased endoscopic expertise in stricture dilatation and the problems with subsequent liver transplant have also rendered this technique of only occasional value.

The most important operative procedure for PSC is liver transplantation, which is the treatment of choice for patients with end-stage liver disease.[63] Bass

outlines the current indications for transplantation in PSC as patients with (1) complications of portal hypertension; (2) impaired synthetic function of the liver; and (3) severe or worsening cholestasis and cirrhosis on biopsies or recurrent cholangitis refractory to medical or interventional management.[5] The results of liver transplantation for PSC are 3- to 4-year survival rates of 85 to 88 percent. In PSC, the donor duct is anastomosed to a Roux-en-Y loop rather than to the stump of the recipient's common duct, which may be narrow and is always suspect as a site of recurrent PSC. Unfortunately, recent surveys have shown that intrahepatic and nonanastomotic extrahepatic biliary strictures are significantly more common in patients who have undergone liver transplantation for PSC than in patients who receive allografts for other end-stage liver diseases.[2,64] Strictures of the choledochojejunostomy anastomosis occur with equal frequency in both groups. Sheng et al. from Pittsburgh compared 100 transplant patients with PSC to a control group of 543 patients who received choledochojejunostomy biliary anastomoses transplanted for non-PSC liver failure.[64] In the PSC group, intrahepatic strictures were found in 27 percent, compared to 13 percent for the control group, a significant difference. Nonanastomotic extrahepatic strictures were also significantly more frequent: 6 percent compared to 2 percent. Anastomotic strictures were 18 to 15 percent, which was not statistically significant. The long-term implications of these findings have not yet been resolved.

AIDS-Related Cholangiopathy

Some patients with AIDS have been described as suffering from biliary tract abnormalities. It is important that radiologists be familiar with this recently recognized type of biliary obstruction. Cello found a typical presentation of severe right upper quadrant abdominal pain, spiking fevers, markedly elevated serum alkaline phosphatase levels, or any combination of the three findings.[8] In a study of 26 patients, 20 patients (77 percent) had markedly abnormal cholangiograms at ERCP. He recognized four patterns of disease at ERCP: sclerosing cholangitis and papillary stenosis (10 patients); only papillary stenosis (3 patients); only sclerosing cholangitis (4 patients); and long extrahepatic bile duct strictures (3 patients).

Only short-lived, beneficial responses followed endoscopic sphincterotomy. At present, patients suffering from AIDS have a limited life expectancy. Endoprostheses may therefore be of benefit to them until a specific treatment for AIDS is developed.

References

1. Blumgart LH. Benign biliary strictures. In: Blumgart LH, ed. Surgery of the liver and biliary tract. Edinburgh: Churchill Livingstone, 1988;1:721–752.
2. Letourneau JG, Day DL, Hunter DW, Ascher NL, Najarian JS, Thompson WM, Castaneda-Zuniga WR. Biliary complications after liver transplantation in patients with preexisting sclerosing cholangitis. Radiology 1988;167:349–351.
3. Colonna JO, Shaked A, Gomes AS, et al. Biliary strictures complicating liver transplantation. Ann Surg 1992;216:344–352.
4. Savader SJ, Venbrux AC, Benenati JF, et al. Choledochal cysts: role of noninvasive imaging, percutaneous transhepatic cholangiography and percutaneous biliary drainage in diagnosis and treatment. J Vasc Intervent Radiol 1991;2:379–385.
5. Bass NM. Sclerosing cholangitis. In: Sleisenger MH, Fortran JS, eds. Gastrointestinal disease. 5th ed. Philadelphia: Saunders, 1993;2:1868–1890.
6. Kerlan RK, Pogany AC, Goldberg HI, Ring EJ. Radiologic intervention in oriental cholangiohepatitis. AJR 1985;145:809–813.
7. Shea WJ, Demas BE, Goldberg HI, Hohn DC, Ferrell LD, Kerlan RK. Sclerosing cholangitis associated with hepatic arterial FUDR chemotherapy: radiographic-histologic correlation. AJR 1986;146:717–721.
8. Cello JP. Acquired immunodeficiency syndrome cholangiopathy: spectrum of disease. Am J Med 1989;86:539–546.
9. Lin AC, Chapman SW, Turner HR, Wofford JD. Clonorchiasis: an update. South Med J 1987;80:919–922.
10. Uflacker R, Wholey MH, Amaral NM, Lima S. Parasitic and mycotic causes of biliary obstruction. Gastrointest Radiol 1982;7:173–179.
11. McCorkell SJ. Echinococcal cysts in the common bile duct: an uncommon cause of obstruction. Gastrointest Radiol 1985;10:390–393.
12. Yadegar J, Williams RA, Passaro E, Wilson SE. Common duct stricture from chronic pancreatitis. Arch Surg 1980;115:582–586.
13. Becker CD, Hassler H, Terrier F. Preoperative diagnosis of the Mirizzi syndrome: limitations of sonography and computed tomography. AJR 1984;143:591–596.
14. Warren KW, Mountain JC, Midell AI. Management of strictures of the biliary tract. Surg Clin North Am 1971;51:711–731.
15. Blumgart LH, Kelley CJ, Benjamin IS. Benign bile duct stricture following cholecystectomy: critical factors in management. Br J Surg 1984;71:836–843.
16. Deziel DJ, Millikan KW, Economou SG, Doolas A, Ko S, Airan MC. Complications of laparoscopic cholecystectomy: a national survey of 4,292 hospitals and an analysis of 77,604 cases. Am J Surg 1993;165:9–14.
17. Rossi RL, Schirmer WJ, Braasch JW, Sanders LB, Munson JL. Laparoscopic bile duct injuries: risk factors, recognition, and repair. Arch Surg 1992;127:596–602.
18. Pitt HA, Miyamoto T, Parapatis SK, Tompkins RK, Longmire WP. Factors influencing outcome in patients with postoperative biliary strictures. Am J Surg 1982;144:14–21.
19. Pellegrini CA, Thomas MJ, Way LW. Recurrent biliary stricture: patterns of recurrence and outcome of surgical therapy. Am J Surg 1984;147:175–180.
20. Pitt HA, Kaufman SL, Coleman J, White RI, Cameron JL. Benign postoperative biliary strictures. Ann Surg 1989;210:417–425.
21. Millis JM, Tompkins RK, Zinner MJ, Longmire WP, Roslyn JJ. Management of bile duct strictures: an evolving strategy. Arch Surg 1992;127:1077–1084.
22. Bismuth H. Postoperative strictures of the bile duct. In: Blumgart LH, ed. The biliary tract. Clinical surgery international, vol. 5. Edinburgh: Churchill Livingstone, 1982:207–218.
23. Gelman R, Alexander MS, Zucker KA, Bailey RW. The use of radionuclide imaging in the evaluation of suspected biliary damage during laparoscopic cholecystectomy. Gastrointest Radiol 1991;16:201–204.
24. Harbin WP, Mueller PR, Ferrucci JT. Transhepatic cholangiography: complications and use patterns of the fine-needle technique. Radiology 1980;135:15–22.
25. Ferrucci JT, Wittenberg J, Sarno RA, Dreyfuss JR. Fine needle transhepatic cholangiography: a new approach to obstructive jaundice. Am J Roentgenol 1976;127:403–407.
26. Pereiras R, Chiprut RO, Greenwald RA, Schiff ER. Percutaneous transhepatic cholangiography with the "skinny" needle. Ann Intern Med 1977;86:562–568.
27. Mueller PR, Harbin WP, Ferrucci JT, Wittenberg J, van Sonnenberg E. Fine-needle transhepatic cholangiography: reflections after 450 cases. AJR 1981;136:85–90.
28. Gordon RL, Ring EJ, LaBerge JM, Doherty MM. Malignant biliary obstruction: treatment with expandable metallic stents—follow-up of 50 consecutive patients. Radiology 1992;182:697–701.
29. Foerster EC, Hoepffner N, Domschke W. Bridging of benign choledochal stenoses by endoscopic retrograde implantation of mesh stents. Endoscopy 1991;23:133–135.
30. Mueller PR, van Sonnenberg E, Ferrucci JT, Weyman PJ, Butch RJ, Malt RA, Burhenne HJ. Biliary stricture dilatation: multicenter review of clinical management in 73 patients. Radiology 1986;160:17–22.
31. Maccioni F, Rossi M, Salvatori FM, Ricci P, Bezzi M, Rossi P. Metallic stents in benign biliary strictures: three-year follow-up. Cardiovasc Intervent Radiol 1992;15:360–366.
32. Hutson DG, Russell E, Schiff E, Levi JJ, Jeffers L, Zeppa R. Balloon dilatation of biliary strictures through a choledochojejuno-cutaneous fistula. Ann Surg 1984;199:637–647.
33. Russell E, Yrizarry JM, Huber JS, et al. Percutaneous transjejunal biliary dilatation: alternate management for benign strictures. Radiology 1986;159:209–214.

34. Williams HJ, Bender CE, May GR. Benign postoperative biliary strictures: dilation with fluoroscopic guidance. Radiology 1987;163:629–634.

35. Mueller PR, Ferrucci JT, Teplick SK, van Sonnenberg E, Haskin PH, Butch RJ, Papanicolaou N. Biliary stent endoprosthesis: analysis of complications in 113 patients. Radiology 1985;156:637–639.

36. Carrasco CH, Wallace S, Charnsangavej C, Richli W, Wright KC, Fanning T, Gianturco C. Expandable biliary endoprosthesis: an experimental study. AJR 1985;145:1279–1281.

37. Jaschke W, Klose KJ, Strecker EP. A new balloon-expandable tantalum stent (Strecker-Stent) for the biliary system: preliminary experience. Cardiovasc Intervent Radiol 1992;15:356–359.

38. Burhenne HJ. Dilatation of biliary tract strictures: a new roentgenologic technique. Radiol Clin 1975;44:153–159.

39. Molnar W, Stockum AE. Transhepatic dilatation of choledochoenterostomy strictures. Radiology 1978;129:59–64.

40. Salomonowitz E, Castaneda-Zuniga WR, Lund G, Cragg AH, Hunter DW, Coleman CC, Amplatz K. Balloon dilatation of benign biliary strictures. Radiology 1984;151:613–616.

41. Gallagher DJ, Kadir S, Kaufman SL, et al. Nonoperative management of benign postoperative biliary strictures. Radiology 1985;156:625–629.

42. Moore AV, Illescas FF, Mills SR, et al. Percutaneous dilation of benign biliary strictures. Radiology 1987;163:625–628.

43. Trambert JJ, Bron KM, Zajko AB, Starzl TE, Iwatsuki S. Percutaneous transhepatic balloon dilatation of benign biliary strictures. AJR 1987;149:945–948.

44. Citron SJ, Martin LG. Benign biliary strictures: treatment with percutaneous cholangioplasty. Radiology 1991;178:339–341.

45. Gordon RL, Ring EJ. Combined radiologic and retrograde endoscopic and biliary interventions. Radiol Clin North Am 1990;28(6):1289–1295.

46. Maroney TP, Ring EJ. Percutaneous transjejunal catheterisation of Roux-en-Y biliary-jejunal anastomoses. Radiology 1987;164:151–153.

47. Alvarado R, Palmaz JC, Garcia OJ, Tio FO, Rees CR. Evaluation of polymer-coated balloon-expandable stents in bile ducts. Radiology 1989;170:975–978.

48. Vorwerk D, Kissinger G, Handt S, Gunther RW. Long-term patency of Wallstent endoprostheses in benign biliary obstructions: experimental results. J Vasc Intervent Radiol 1993;4:625–634.

49. Uchida BT, Putnam JS, Rösch J. Modifications of Gianturco expandable wire stents. AJR 1988;150:1185–1187.

50. Irving JD, Adam A, Dick R, Dondelinger RF, Lunderquist A, Roche A. Gianturco expandable metallic biliary stents: results of a European clinical trial. Radiology 1989;172:321–326.

51. Coons HG. Self-expanding stainless steel biliary stents. Radiology 1989;170:979–983.

52. Rossi P, Bezzi M, Salvatori FM, Maccioni F, Porcaro ML. Recurrent benign biliary strictures: management with self-expanding metallic stents. Radiology 1990;175:661–665.

53. Coons H. Metallic stents for the treatment of biliary obstruction: a report of 100 cases. Cardiovasc Intervent Radiol 1992;15:367–374.

54. LaRusso NF, Wiesner RH, Ludwig J, MacCarty RL. Current concepts: primary sclerosing cholangitis. N Engl J Med 1984;310:899–903.

55. MacCarty RL, LaRusso NF, Wiesner RH, Ludwig J. Primary sclerosing cholangitis: findings on cholangiography and pancreatography. Radiology 1983;149:39–44.

56. MacCarty RL, LaRusso NF, May GR, Bender CE, Wiesner RH, King JE, Coffey RJ. Cholangiocarcinoma complicating primary sclerosing cholangitis: cholangiographic appearances. Radiology 1985;156:43–46.

57. Cotton PB, Nickl N. Endoscopic and radiologic approaches to therapy in primary sclerosing cholangitis. Semin Liver Dis 1991;11:40–48.

58. Kerlan RK, LaBerge JM, Goldberg HI, Pogany AC, Ring EJ. Interventional radiologic management of sclerosing cholangitis. AJR 1986;147:1002–1006.

59. Johnson GK, Geenen JE, Venu RP, Schmalz MJ, Hogan WJ. Endoscopic treatment of biliary tract strictures in sclerosing cholangitis: a larger series and recommendations for treatment. Gastrointest Endosc 1991;37:38–43.

60. May GR, Bender CE, LaRusso NF, Wiesner RH. Nonoperative dilatation of dominant strictures in primary sclerosing cholangitis. AJR 1985;145:1061–1064.

61. Skolkin MD, Alspaugh JP, Casarella WJ, Chuang VP, Galambos JT. Sclerosing cholangitis: palliation with percutaneous cholangioplasty. Radiology 1989;170:199–206.

62. Lillemoe KD, Pitt HA, Cameron JL. Primary sclerosing cholangitis. Surg Clin North Am 1990;70:1381–1402.

63. Langnas AN, Grazi GL, Stratta RJ, et al. Primary sclerosing cholangitis: the emerging role for liver transplantation. Am J Gastroenterol 1990;85:1136–1141.

64. Sheng R, Zajko AB, Campbell WL, Abu-Elmagd K. Biliary strictures in hepatic transplants: prevalence and types in patients with primary sclerosing cholangitis vs. those with other liver disease. AJR 1993;161:297–300.

29

Malignant Obstruction
of the Hepatobiliary System

ANTHONY C. VENBRUX
FLOYD A. OSTERMAN, JR.

Malignant obstruction of the hepatobiliary system is due to intrinsic occlusion or extrinsic compression of bile ducts. The majority of patients presenting with jaundice due to malignancy have distal common bile duct obstruction.[1] In this group, carcinoma of the pancreas is the most common neoplasm producing extrahepatic biliary obstruction (Fig. 29-1).[2] The survival of patients with pancreatic cancer is variable, and statistics reported in the medical literature vary widely. In one series reported by Cameron et al., 89 patients with carcinoma of the head of the pancreas underwent pancreaticoduodenectomies. The actuarial 5-year survival rate for the 89 patients was 19 percent, with a median survival of 11.9 months. In this series, negative lymph nodes and the absence of blood vessel invasion both favored long-term survival.[3] These results are in contrast to other reports in the literature, in which, despite aggressive surgery, patients with pancreatic carcinoma have a much poorer prognosis. In a series reported by Gudjonsson et al., the 5-year survival rate, even with attempts at curative resection, was less than 1 percent.[4] Other investigators report mean survival after diagnosis of 4 to 7 months.[4–6]

Other causes of malignant biliary obstruction include cholangiocarcinoma and metastatic disease. Cholangiocarcinoma is a slow-growing and uncommon tumor. The peak incidence is in the sixth and seventh decades, and the tumor is two to three times more common in males than in females.[7] It invades hepatic parenchyma and locally invades hepatic arteries and portal veins, making surgical resection difficult.[8] Centrally located cholangiocarcinoma causes obstructive jaundice early,[8] whereas the peripheral type of ductal cholangiocarcinoma originating in a small intrahepatic duct[8,9] causes jaundice at a later stage.

Most cholangiocarcinomas are adenocarcinomas, with a minority being of other histologic types such as squamous cell and anaplastic.[7] Metastatic spread of cholangiocarcinoma, either by lymphatics or blood-borne means, is infrequent and occurs in only 12 percent of patients at the time of clinical presentation.[10] Cholangiocarcinoma growth patterns include (1) infiltrating-scirrhous, (2) nodular, and (3) papillary.[7] The infiltrating-scirrhous pattern is most common[11,12] and characteristically presents as a focal stricture, often without a mass.[13] It may mimic sclerosing cholangitis when extensive.[7] This scirrhous reaction explains the difficulty in obtaining positive preoperative biopsies.[8] Rarely (5 percent), a papilliferous form of growth of adenocarcinoma may occur, expanding the bile ducts and presenting as intraluminal masses.[8,13,14] Patients predisposed to developing cholangiocarcinoma include those with gallstones, ulcerative colitis, choledochal cysts, sclerosing cholangitis, and *Clonorchis sinensis*.[15]

A third major cause of obstructive jaundice is due to metastases, either to nodes in the hilus of the liver or to peripancreatic lymph nodes, the latter causing distal common bile duct obstruction (Fig. 29-2). Rarely, metastases may occlude the bile ducts and appear as filling defects on cholangiography (Fig. 29-3). Direct extension of malignant disease in the gallbladder, stomach, or pancreas may also cause bile duct obstruction. In such tumors, infiltration of the hepatoduodenal ligament results in obstructive jaundice.[15] Short of surgical cure, the clinical course is highly variable.

Malignant obstruction of the biliary system from whatever cause is frequently accompanied by jaundice, malaise, weight loss, anorexia, pruritus, acholic stools, dark urine, abnormal liver function, and other metabolic abnormalities. Relief of obstruction through surgery, endoscopic procedures, percutaneous interventional procedures, or a combination of techniques is the goal of the surgeon, gastroenterologist, and radiologist. In those patients with severe pruritus and metabolic abnormalities due to extrahepatic biliary obstruction, percutaneous biliary drainage alleviates these conditions in 90 percent of patients.[16,17] In the major-

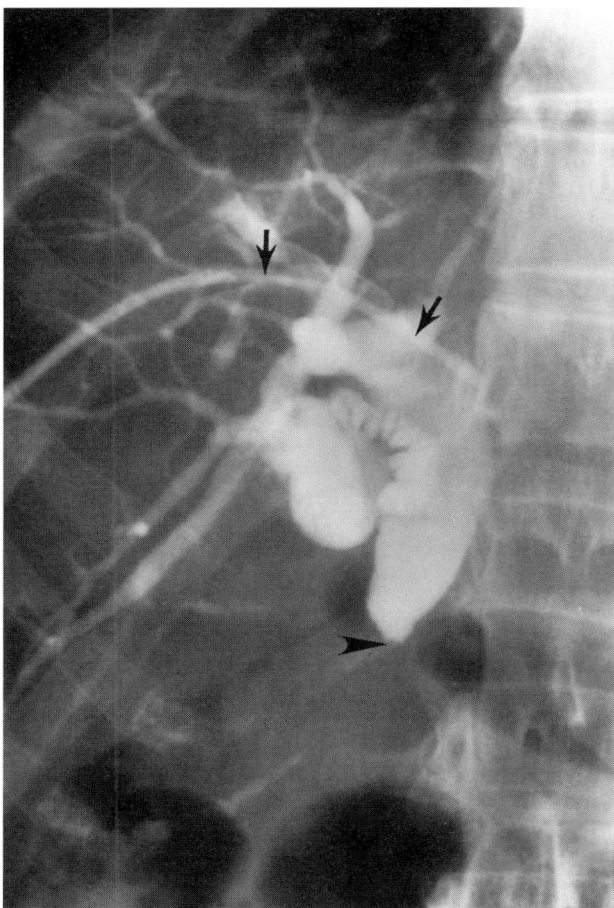

Figure 29-1. Cholangiogram of a 58-year-old woman with painless jaundice and acholic stools. The cholangiogram was taken in the anteroposterior projection after percutaneous transhepatic cholangiography (PTC) and before completion of the percutaneous biliary drainage (PBD) procedure. The common bile duct (CBD) is obstructed (*arrowhead*). There is extrahepatic and intrahepatic bile duct dilation. This cholangiogram was obtained by injecting contrast through the straight sheath (*arrows*) taken from a "one-stick" biliary drainage set (see text). Immediately after this image, the obstruction was crossed with a catheter and a hydrophilic guidewire. The hydrophilic guidewire was exchanged for a stiffer 0.035-inch-diameter guidewire, and the straight sheath and catheter were removed. An internal-external biliary drainage catheter was directed over the stiffer guidewire. Cross-sectional imaging studies demonstrated a large pancreatic head mass consistent with pancreatic adenocarcinoma. The patient was found to be unresectable at exploratory laparotomy.

ity of patients, liver function also improves.[2] Cross-sectional imaging by computed tomography (CT), magnetic resonance imaging (MRI), or ultrasound (US) may suggest the diagnosis. This is generally performed before a more invasive procedure. Cholangiography by percutaneous transhepatic needle placement or by endoscopy best defines the bile duct pathology.

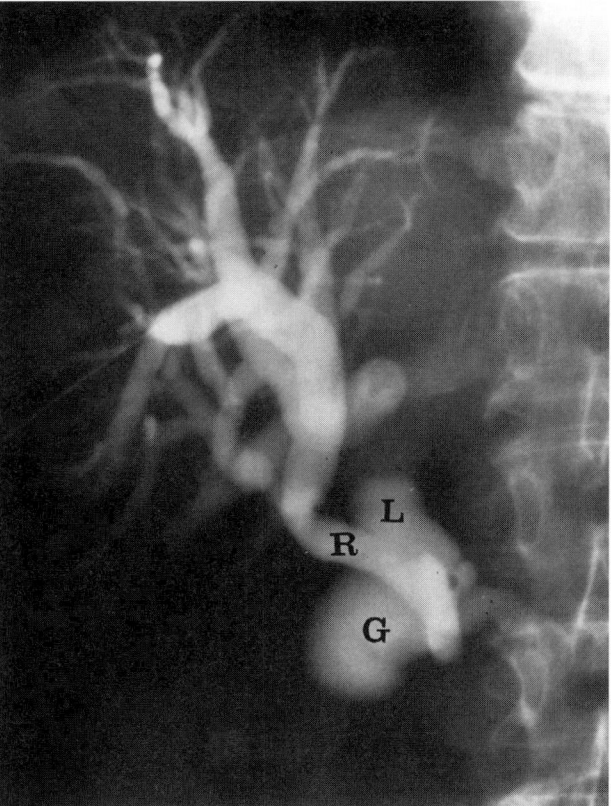

Figure 29-2. Anteroposterior spot film of a 54-year-old man with metastatic colon cancer to the liver and peripancreatic nodes. The film, taken during PTC, demonstrates dilated intrahepatic ducts. There is narrowing of the main right hepatic duct (*R*). Complete obstruction of the biliary system is seen at the level of the proximal CBD. The gallbladder (*G*) is partially filled with contrast. The main left hepatic duct (*L*) is faintly opacified.

Interventional Radiology: Defining Patient Anatomy and Achieving Biliary Drainage

In 1974, Molnar and Stockum first reported the technique of decompressing obstructed bile ducts by transhepatic catheter placement.[16] Bile was diverted into the duodenum to reestablish the enterohepatic bile circulation. The techniques of percutaneous transhepatic cholangiography (PTC) and percutaneous biliary drainage (PBD) have been well described.[2,16–18] Briefly, in those patients who are not clinically septic, intravenous antibiotics are administered on the day of the procedure and continued for 24 hours after the procedure. Intravenous antibiotics are started immediately after admission blood cultures are taken if a patient presents with clinical signs and symptoms of biliary sepsis. A hematocrit, coagulation profile studies, and

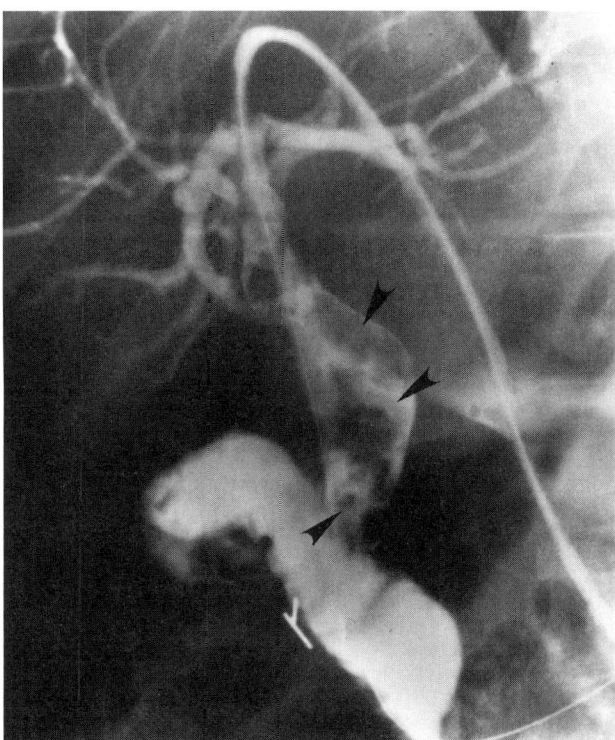

Figure 29-3. This 54-year-old man (different patient than in Fig. 29-2) underwent a right hepatic lobectomy for metastatic colon cancer to the liver. He later presented with obstructive jaundice requiring PBD. On this left anterior oblique spot film taken during a follow-up "over-the-wire" cholangiogram, multiple polypoid filling defects (*arrowheads*) may be seen expanding the lumen of the common hepatic duct (CHD) and CBD. The internal-external biliary drainage catheter, placed percutaneously from the left, was used to palliate this patient's symptoms and to provide access for biopsy. The polypoid lesions proved to be metastatic colon cancer.

liver function tests are drawn as part of the routine preprocedure laboratory evaluation. A coagulopathy that cannot be corrected is a contraindication for PTC or PBD.

The patient is placed supine, and percutaneous access is generally achieved via a right midaxillary approach or slightly anterior to the right midaxillary line, inferior to the costophrenic angle, and above the hepatic flexure of the colon. Local anesthetic is used to anesthetize the skin and subcutaneous tissues before percutaneous transhepatic needle puncture. During infiltration of the local anesthetic and during PTC/PBD, the inferior border of the rib is avoided to prevent possible injury to the neurovascular bundle. Occasionally intercostal nerve blocks may be performed before PTC/PBD in a patient with a low pain threshold.

At the authors' institution, a 22-gauge Chiba needle (Cook, Inc.) is generally used to perform the diagnostic PTC. The Chiba needle is advanced under fluoroscopic guidance into the liver in the coronal plane from the midaxillary line, parallel to the table top, and the tip is directed medially and superiorly. The needle tip is generally not advanced medially into the liver more than approximately one-half inch lateral to the right vertebral bodies. After the stylet of the needle is removed, the hub of the needle is connected to a syringe containing contrast via a flexible connector tubing. As the needle is withdrawn slowly, contrast is injected. If the tip of the needle is in a bile duct, contrast is seen to flow slowly away from the needle tip in a tubular structure. If the needle is in a portal or hepatic vein, contrast flows rapidly away from the needle tip. During opacification of ducts with contrast, images are recorded early and late to define biliary anatomy. If the Chiba needle has punctured a periphral right bile duct, a 0.016-inch-diameter steerable guidewire (Taper Guidewire, Target Therapeutics) is advanced through the 22-gauge Chiba needle and the needle is removed. At the authors' institution, the stiffening dilator/sheath/cannula assembly from a "single-puncture" ("one-stick") system (Fig. 29-4) may then be used to perform a biliary drainage. A "one-stick" system (Jeffrey Wire Guide Exchange Set, Cook, Inc.) is a coaxial system consisting of a small-caliber, platinum tip, 0.018-inch-diameter steerable guidewire (Cope Mandril Wire Guide, Cook, Inc.) and a dilator/sheath/cannula assembly. Such a system allows biliary access via the 21-gauge trocar needle and subsequent conversion to a larger-caliber, stiffer guidewire (e.g., 0.035 inch in diameter or 0.038 inch in diameter; the latter included in the set) for percutaneous biliary catheter placement. Of note, the 0.018-inch-diameter guidewire (Cope Mandril Wire Guide), included in the set in Figure 29-4, will not routinely fit through the lumen of a 22-gauge Chiba needle (but will fit through the 21-gauge trocar needle), and thus the need for the separate 0.016-inch-diameter guidewire. Several "one-stick" or "single-stick" systems are commercially available for PTC/PBD procedures.

If a peripheral duct has not been entered during the diagnostic PTC with the 22-gauge needle, a second "skinny needle" (21 gauge; trocar needle; included in the Jeffrey Wire Guide Exchange Set, Cook, Inc.) may be used to puncture an opacified peripheral bile duct (i.e., two separate punctures). A peripheral puncture is important because it may facilitate later intraductal attempts to cross an obstruction and may decrease the risk of large-vessel injury (e.g., portal vein or hepatic artery). The "one-stick" system (see Fig. 29-4) is then

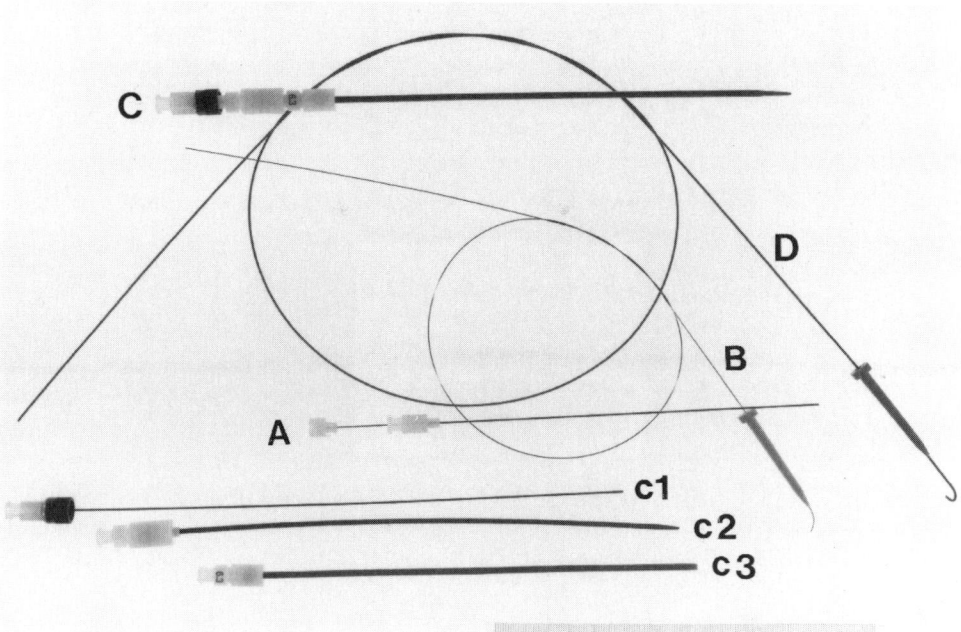

Figure 29-4. "Single-puncture" ("one-stick") system for PTC/PBD (Jeffrey Wire Guide Exchange Set, Cook, Inc.). A 21-gauge trocar needle (*A*) is used to gain access into the biliary system. A radiopaque 0.018-inch-diameter guidewire (Cope Mandril Wire Guide) (*B*) is directed through the needle and the needle is removed. A tapered dilator/stiffening cannula/sheath assembly (*C*) is then directed over the 0.018-inch-diameter guidewire. The dilator and stiffening cannula are removed, leaving the 6.3 French sheath in the biliary system. Through this sheath, a 5 French catheter and guidewire are used to cross the biliary obstruction. A stiffer 0.038-inch-diameter guidewire (*D*) is then directed through the catheter into the bowel. The sheath is removed, and a biliary drainage catheter is advanced over the stiffer guidewire. Other guidewires may be substituted for the 0.038-inch-diameter guidewire. The metal stiffening cannula (*c1*), dilator (*c2*), and 6.3 French sheath (*c3*) are shown disassembled at the bottom of the photograph. When assembled, they constitute a single unit (*C*).

used to gain percutaneous access into the biliary system. The small-caliber, 0.018-inch-diameter Cope Mandril guidewire is used as access for the dilator/sheath/cannula assembly. The lesion is crossed and a larger, stiffer guidewire is directed into the small bowel. An 8.3 French Ring biliary drainage catheter (Cook, Inc.) is frequently used as the drainage catheter to complete the biliary drainage procedure. At the authors' institution, the rather stiff 8.3 French Ring biliary drainage catheter is usually exchanged on the following day (or before discharge) for a softer, more comfortable drainage catheter. Occasionally, if the patient's liver is not too fibrotic or the obstructing biliary lesion is not too severe (i.e., stictured), a softer, more comfortable catheter may be used during the initial drainage procedure. This eliminates having to exchange the stiffer 8.3 French Ring biliary drainage catheter.

A review of the literature indicates a wide range in the prevalence of complications associated with PBD. Patients undergoing PBD for benign and malignant disease have a 4.6 to 25 percent prevalence of major complications and a 0 to 5.6 percent prevalence of procedure-related deaths.[18-23] Major complications include surgical intervention, blood transfusion (for hemorrhage), and cholangitis associated with hypotension. A review of the literature by Yee and Ho combining the results of six groups of investigators (702 patients) reports that the overall percentage of major complications is 8 percent and the percentage of deaths 2 percent. Of the 702 patients, 609 (87 percent) in this combined retrospective review had malignant biliary obstructions.[24] The authors emphasize that the patient's general physical condition is a major determinant of the likelihood of complications. Biliary surgical morbidity and mortality have been correlated with a number of patient characteristics.[25] These include patient age and physical health (nutritional status, whether or not the patient is immunocompromised, etc.). Patients presenting with malignant biliary obstruction are generally more debilitated than those patients presenting with biliary obstruction due to benign causes. This may partly explain the variation in the results reported in the medical literature and the relatively high morbidity and mortality percentages associated with biliary procedures in patients with malignant biliary obstruction.

Interventional Radiology: Confirming the Diagnosis of Malignant Obstruction of the Hepatobiliary System

Once PTC/PBD has been achieved, access into the biliary system is readily available. A number of interventional procedures may be performed. If the etiology of the patient's obstructive jaundice has not been confirmed, percutaneous biliary biopsies may be performed to direct future therapy. With the biliary drainage catheter in place, percutaneous "skinny needle" biopsy of the suspected malignant biliary stricture may be performed using the radiopaque catheter as a guide (Fig. 29-5). Percutaneous fine-needle aspiration biopsy can be performed if a mass is identified on CT, MRI, US, or cholangiography. The sensitivitiy of this technique for malignant obstruction ranges between

50 and 90 percent.[26,27] Since percutaneous access is available, brush biopsy, often performed endoscopically, may also be performed via the transhepatic approach. Brush biopsy yields malignant cells in 50 to 70 percent of malignant cases.[28] Cytology of bile after PBD is inexpensive but detects only 34 percent of malignant biliary strictures.[29] Percutaneous transluminal biopsy of a patient with suspected malignant bile duct stricture using a flexible bioptome is easy to perform and relatively inexpensive if the patient has a biliary drainage catheter (Fig. 29-6). Initial reported results are encouraging. In a paper by Terasaki et al., six of six patients with a history of prior malignancy had biliary stricture bioptome biopsy results positive for malignancy.[30] Such procedures may be performed quickly and easily through an 8 French tract. Other reported percutaneous biopsy techniques for patients with malignant biliary strictures in addition to those described above include the use of a forceps through a T-tube tract[31,32] or through a transhepatic tract,[33] a percutaneous transhepatic "scrape" or "rasp" biopsy,[34] the use of the Simpson Atherocath (Peripheral Systems Group),[35,36] and biopsy of suspicious biliary lesions under direct vision using a choledochoscope.[37,38] With the diagnosis confirmed, appropriate therapy may be instituted.

Figure 29-5. (A) Anteroposterior spot film taken during percutaneous "skinny needle" biopsy in a patient with suspected cholangiocarcinoma at the bifurcation of right and left biliary ducts. A Silastic nonradiopaque right biliary drainage catheter (*arrowhead*) is partially filled with contrast. The left Percuflex biliary drainage catheter and endoscopically placed stent (the latter providing inadequate drainage) are visible. The biliary drainage catheters serve as markers to direct the biopsy. The two radiopaque stents are again seen. (B) Lateral spot film demonstrating depth of percutaneously placed needle for biopsy. Careful fluoroscopic monitoring during biopsy procedures is essential. The partially contrast-filled Silastic right biliary drainage catheter (*arrowhead*) is again noted on this image.

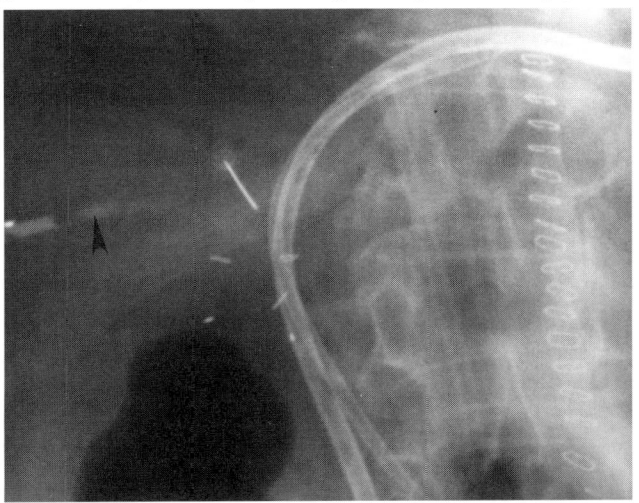

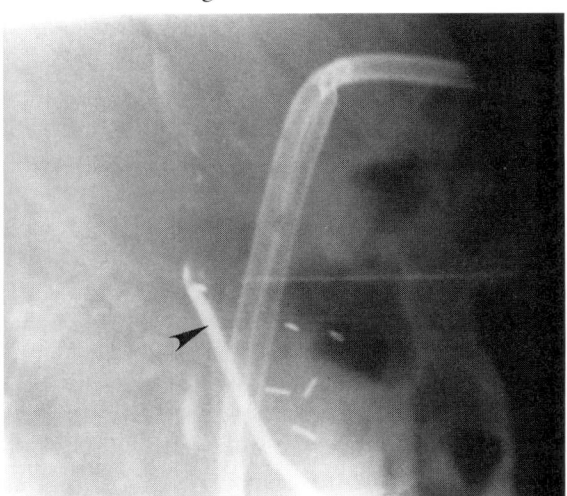

A

B

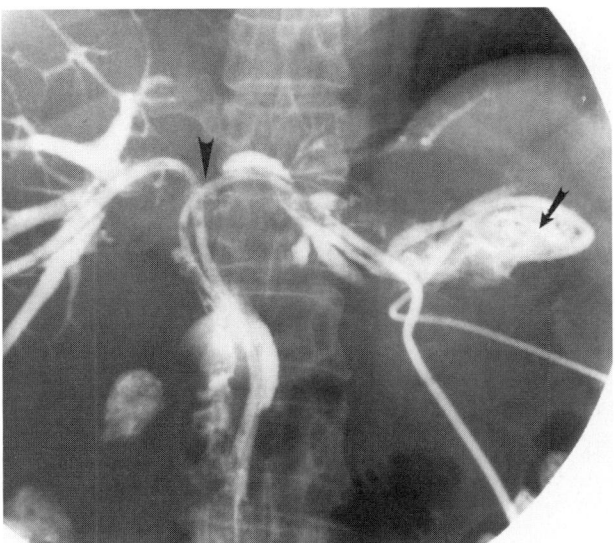

A

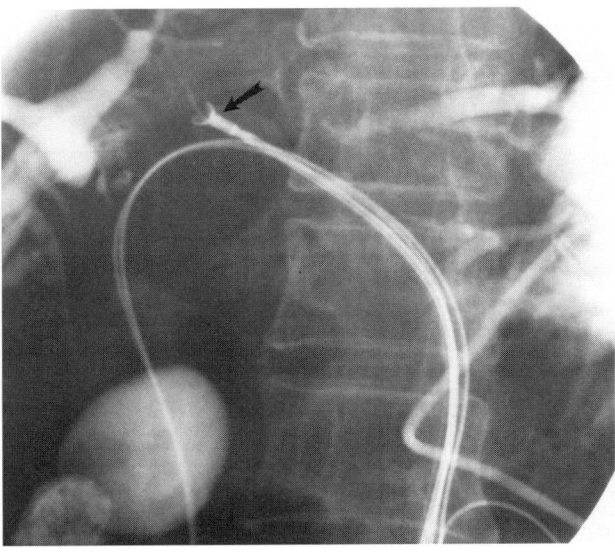

B

Figure 29-6. (A) Anteroposterior spot film taken during a cholangiogram in an adult man who had undergone bilateral PBD procedures and percutaneous drainage of a left hepatic abscess. Contrast was also injected through the tube draining the left hepatic abscess (*arrow*). The site of biliary obstruction is at the bifurcation of right and left ducts (*arrowhead*). (B) Anteroposterior spot film taken during biopsy of the le-

sion at the bifurcation. A bioptome (*arrow*) has been advanced through a transhepatic sheath placed percutaneously from the left. Before biopsy, the left biliary drainage catheter had been removed over a guidewire and a second guidewire (a "safety wire") was advanced into the duodenum. The nonradiopaque Silastic right biliary drainage catheter is still present but not visible on this image.

Management of the Patient with Malignant Obstruction of the Hepatobiliary System

Patients with malignant biliary obstruction, if deemed resectable, may undergo a number of surgical procedures depending on the location of the biliary obstruction. These include a Roux-en-Y hepaticojejunostomy, a choledochoenterostomy, or a Whipple procedure. Palliative surgery for unresectable malignancy of the distal common bile duct may include a cholecystoenterostomy. Preoperative endoscopic or percutaneous transhepatic visualization of the biliary anatomy is the best examination to define the ductal anatomy and to determine the location and extent of biliary obstruction. The cholangiogram helps determine resectability. Biliary decompression through an endoscopically placed stent (i.e., internal drainage) or transhepatically through a percutaneously placed internal-external drainage catheter relieves the patient's obstructive symptoms. This helps to prepare the patient for surgery by (1) preserving hepatocyte function and (2) improving the patient's nutritional status, the latter often combined with hyperalimentation.

At the authors' institution, preoperative biliary decompression is routine. Radical curative or palliative surgical dissection is aided by percutaneous intubation

of the biliary system. Complex biliary-enteric anastomoses are routinely stented during surgery, and the percutaneously placed biliary drainage catheters (stents) facilitate intraoperative ductal intubation. For distal common bile duct or pancreatic tumors, a single 8.3 French Ring biliary drainage catheter is placed to serve as an intraoperative marker during tumor resection. For proximal common bile duct or bifurcation tumors, bilateral percutaneously placed biliary drainage catheters are placed before surgery. Frequently the 8.3 French catheters are converted intraoperatively for larger-diameter Silastic biliary drainage catheters (Heyer-Schulte biliary stent, Bentec). If the patient is not a surgical candidate because of extensive disease or underlying medical conditions, palliative therapy is the goal to improve the patient's quality of life.

Palliation of the Patient with Malignant Obstruction of the Hepatobiliary System

If the patient has undergone percutaneous transhepatic biliary decompression, palliation can be achieved by exchanging the internal-external drainage catheter at periodic intervals. This procedure is generally performed every 2 to 3 months on an outpatient basis.

Intravenous antibiotics should be administered before the cholangiogram and catheter exchange. At the authors' institution, antibiotics are generally not continued after the single initial intravenous dose unless the patient has a history of repreated episodes of cholangitis. If biliary decompression has been achieved endoscopically, the endoscopically placed stent must be periodically exchanged to prevent recurrent obstruction with its associated risks of jaundice and sepsis.

In patients with inoperable biliary obstruction, the use of percutaneously placed biliary endoprostheses has received wider clinical acceptance. In general, such devices should be limited to those patients with limited life expectancy, for example, 6 months or less. A biliary endoprosthesis is an indwelling biliary device constructed of plastic or metal and placed across the site of obstruction. Advantages include (1) restoration of antegrade bile flow and (2) conversion of a percutaneously biliary drainage catheter to an internal device, thereby eliminating the care required for a conventional biliary drainage catheter—tube flushing, dressing changes, leakage at the skin entry site, infection and pain at the catheter skin entry site, and periodic biliary catheter exchanges. Despite these advantages, early clinical studies reported premature occlusion and dislocation of biliary endoprostheses resulting in recurrent jaundice. This was particularly true of early plastic devices. Recent improvements in design, endoprosthesis material composition, and deployment techniques have resulted in greater clinical acceptance for the palliation of patients with malignant biliary obstruction. However, the problem of premature occlusion of both plastic and metallic endoprostheses has not yet been solved. This is an area of ongoing clinical and laboratory investigation.

With percutaneous transhepatic access established in a patient with an inoperable malignant biliary obstruction, a decision must be made as to how to best treat the patient. In general, the authors prefer transhepatic biliary drainage catheters (stents) for palliation. Such stents can be easily changed and can be accurately placed with drainage side holes positioned proximal to complex hilar lesions. Lesions in the distal common bile duct (CBD) or ampulla are best palliated by endoscopically placed stents, which can be changed periodically to maintain adequate drainage.

If the cause of biliary obstruction is cholangiocarcinoma, an endoprosthesis should generally not be used because the patient's life expectancy may exceed the patency of the endoprosthesis. Such patients may benefit from local radiotherapy using an iridium (^{192}Ir) wire placed through the internal-external biliary drainage catheter.[8] In these patients, an endoscopically or percutaneously placed endoprosthesis might not ade-

quately drain the bile ducts, especially if the lesion is complex and located in the hilum, and would also provide no direct access for placement of the iridium wire. In one series reported by Nunnerley et al., 30 patients treated with intraductal radiation survived a mean of 16.8 months, an improvement compared to surgical bypass or endoscopic and radiologic drainage procedures.[8] The use of ^{192}Ir combined with external beam radiotherapy may have some potential in palliating patients with unresectable hilar cholangiocarcinoma. Survival statistics are based on limited numbers of patients. Whether patient survival will improve using radiation therapy alone or combined with surgery and other measures is an active area of ongoing research.

Numerous articles have appeared in the medical literature describing results of patients with malignant obstructive jaundice treated with either plastic or metallic biliary endoprostheses. A variety of plastic (Fig. 29-7) and metal (Fig. 29-8) endoprostheses are commercially available. Since placement of a plastic biliary endoprosthesis generally requires a larger transhepatic tube tract (approximately 10–13 French), the procedure is generally done in two stages: percutaneous biliary drainage followed by tract dilation. A "mushroom" configuration at one end or a subcutaneous anchoring button with an attached suture reduces the chances of endoprosthesis dislocation (see Fig. 29-7). The advantage of a plastic endoprosthesis (i.e., lower cost) may be offset by the two-step procedure.

The formation of occlusive encrustation depends on the mechanical and chemical surface characteristics of the stent material, on the chemical environment, and on the population of bacteria in the patient's bile. After bacteria adhere to the surface of a plastic endoprosthesis, glycoproteins are deposited. Growth of bacteria results in deconjugation of bilirubin and deposition of calcium bilirubinate.[39–42]

Metal endoprostheses are either self-expanding or balloon-expandable. Several metallic biliary endoprostheses are commercially available for biliary applications in the United States (see Fig. 29-8). Examples include the following self-expanding stents: (1) the Wallstent (Schneider [USA], Inc.) and (2) the Gianturco Z stent (Cook, Inc.). A third metallic biliary endoprosthesis is the balloon-expandable Palmaz stent (Johnson & Johnson Interventional Systems). Metallic biliary endoprostheses are considerably more costly than plastic endoprostheses. The Gianturco Z stent is compressed into a 12 French delivery sheath, the Palmaz stent may be delivered through a 7 to 10 French sheath, and the Wallstent may be delivered through a 7 French introducer sheath. Because of the larger size of the delivery sheaths for the Z stent and Palmaz stent, a two-step procedure may also be required. The Wall-

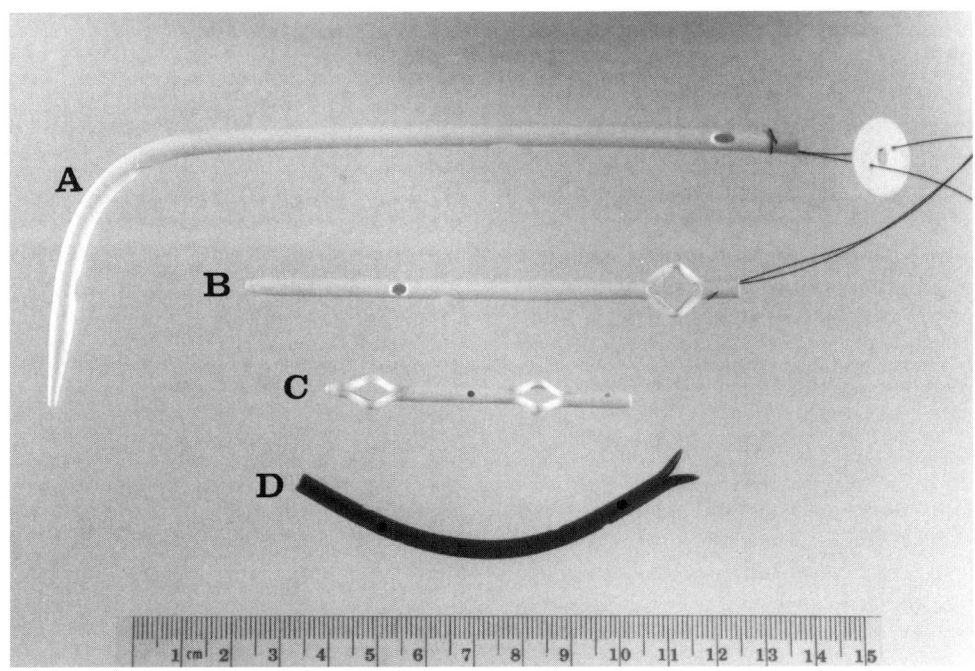

Figure 29-7. Plastic internal biliary stents (endoprostheses): *A*, Carey-Coons (Medi-Tech, Boston Scientific, Watertown, MA); *B*, Ring-Kerlan (Cook, Inc., Bloomington, IN); *C*, Miller Double Mushroom (Medi-Tech); *D*, Ring (Cook, Inc.).

stent may be placed in a single-step procedure if there is no significant bleeding during the initial percutaneous biliary drainage procedure.

Clinical results of patients treated with biliary endoprostheses have varied. In one large series published by Lammer, the results since 1982 of transhepatic placement of biliary endoprostheses in 334 patients are reported.[39] Indications were malignant obstruction in 320 patients and benign stenosis in 14 patients. Plastic endoprostheses were used in 297 patients (289 for malignant obstruction); 102 patients received a Teflon endoprosthesis (9 or 12 French in diameter), 109 patients received a Percuflex (Medi-Tech, Boston Scientific Corp.) endoprosthesis (12 French in diameter), and 86 received a polyurethane endoprosthesis (10 or 12 French in diameter). In this series, stent implantation was successful in all patients in whom the occlusion could be crossed. Fourteen patients died of complications directly related to the procedure, for a mortality rate of 4.7 percent. The 30-day mortality rate in the first 162 patients was 15 percent,[39,43] significantly less than the 24 percent 30-day mortality rate reported in other studies.[44-48] Complications directly related to the procedure included bleeding, bile peritonitis, and intrahepatic, subphrenic, and subhepatic abscesses, cholangitis, ascites, fistula, and duodenal perforation. The overall complication rate in this series

of 297 patients receiving plastic endoprostheses was 9.4 percent. The complication rate reported in the literature is 16.5 percent.[43-48]

In the series by Lammer,[39] premature occlusion of

Figure 29-8. Metallic internal biliary stents (endoprostheses): *A*, Wallstent (Schneider [USA], Inc., Minneapolis, MN); *B*, Gianturco Z stent (Cook, Inc., Bloomington, IN); *C*, Palmaz stent (Johnson & Johnson Interventional Systems Co., Warren, NJ).

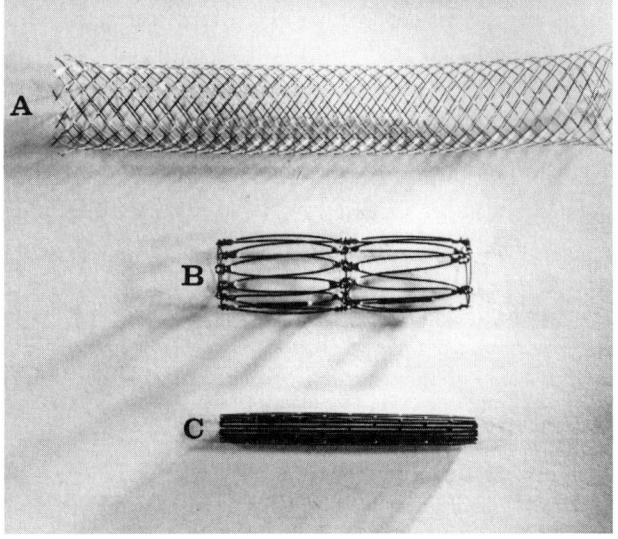

endoprostheses occurred in 25 of 297 patients (8.4 percent). Seven Teflon endoprostheses (7 percent) occluded after 19 to 45 weeks, 13 Percuflex endoprostheses (12 percent) occluded after 9 to 46 weeks, and 5 polyurethane endoprostheses (6 percent) occluded after 10 to 45 weeks. Thus overall stent failure occurred in 36 of 297 plastic stents (12 percent).

In the article by Lammer, 37 patients received metallic biliary endoprostheses since 1988 (31 for malignant biliary obstruction). Two Palmaz stents and 39 Wallstents were inserted in the 37 patients. There were no patient deaths from complications related to metallic endoprosthesis placement. The 30-day mortality rate was 5.4 percent (2 of 37 patients). Complications attributed to the procedure included reflux of bile in 2 patients, causing a biliary effusion and a bile peritonitis. In a third patient, a pseudoaneurysm of a hepatic artery branch caused recurrent hemobilia requiring transcatheter embolotherapy to occlude the injured hepatic artery branch. Reocclusions occurred in 4 of the 31 patients (13 percent) with malignant biliary obstruction treated with a metallic biliary endoprosthesis. Tumor overgrowth was responsible for occlusion in 2 patients, and tumor ingrowth between the metallic struts was reported in 2 additional patients. Because of tumor overgrowth, reported by Lammer et al. and other investigators, it is generally recommended that the malignant obstruction be "overstented" to reduce the incidence of premature endoprosthesis occlusion. This is true for both plastic and metallic biliary endoprostheses. Should occlusion of a metallic endoprosthesis occur, transhepatic (Fig. 29-9) or endoscopic stenting may provide further palliative biliary decompression.

In another published series by Gordon et al., the results of 50 consecutive patients with malignant biliary obstruction treated with the Wallstent endoprosthesis are described.[49] Stent placement was successful in all 50 patients. Follow-up ranged between 9 and 22 months. The overall endoprosthesis patency and patient survival rates were 5.8 months and 7.5 months, respectively. The 30-day mortality rate was 8 percent. The minor complication rate was 18 percent, and the major complication rate was 8 percent. One patient experienced intrahepatic arterial bleeding requiring embolization, another patient developed a right subphrenic abscess, and 2 patients developed transient septic episodes. Stent occlusion requiring a second intervention occurred in 24 percent of patients. There were no reports of stent migration. Long-term patency was comparable to that of plastic endoprostheses. The authors indicate that the ease of placement and the versatility of the Wallstent may offset the high cost of the stent.[49] As mentioned, metal endoprostheses are

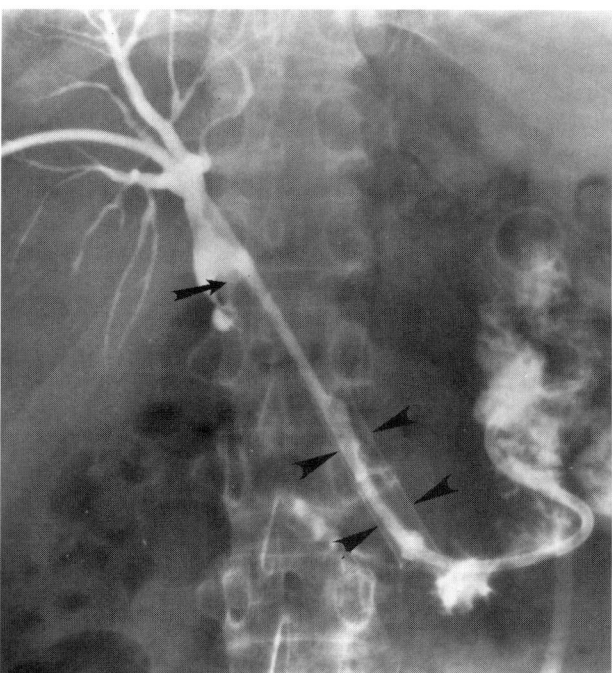

Figure 29-9. Anteroposterior cholangiogram obtained after PBD and placement of an internal-external biliary drainage catheter. This elderly patient initially presented with obstructive jaundice and was found to have unresectable pancreatic adenocarcinoma. As palliation, he received two Wallstents (Schneider [USA], Inc.) (*arrowheads*) placed endoscopically and overlapped slightly. Several months later he again presented with signs and symptoms of biliary obstruction. Attempts at further endoscopic palliation were unsuccessful, and the endoscopic manipulation of the Wallstents resulted in the two stents being pulled toward the ampulla. This was associated with significant shortening of the stents. Therefore, percutaneous transhepatic biliary drainage was performed with relief of symptoms. Note the proximal extent of tumor "overgrowth" (*arrow*). "Overstenting" of malignant hepatobiliary obstruction is important to prevent reocclusion of the biliary system. In this patient, it is unclear whether endoprosthesis occlusion is due to tumor ingrowth (through the stent struts), due to bile salts, bacteria, and biliary debris, or due to both causes.

considerably more expensive than the plastic endoprostheses (approximately 10 times the cost).

The use of the metallic Wallstent endoprosthesis to treat patients with hilar and nonhilar biliary obstruction was reported by Becker et al.[50] Follow-up data in 58 patients with malignant obstructive jaundice who underwent percutaneous palliative treatment with the Wallstent over a 4-year period demonstrated a better long-term patency if common duct obstruction was treated with the endoprosthesis than if hilar obstruction was treated. If the patient had hilar obstruction, the long-term patency of the Wallstent endoprosthesis was significantly lower. These authors further reported that the use of the Wallstent did not result in a lower complication rate compared with the reported results of plastic endoprostheses. Reintervention to restore stent patency was successful in almost all cases. Survival rates of patients with hilar and nonhilar obstruction were similar. The 12-month patency rate of the endoprostheses was 46 percent in patients with hilar obstruction and 89 percent in patients with nonhilar obstruction ($p = .29$). The 6-month survival rate of the 58 patients with malignant obstructive jaundice was 50 percent; the 12-month survival rate was 36 percent.

In an article from the European literature by Salomonowitz et al.,[51] 88 consecutive patients with malignant obstructive biliary stenosis were followed for 18 months and treated with the Wallstent endoprosthesis inserted either percutaneously or endoscopically. Serious complications were observed in 15 percent, including a 10 percent rate of cholangitis with septicemia. No stent migration or occlusion of the endoprostheses was noted. Recurrent jaundice occurred in 17.5 percent of patients because of progressive tumor growth after 3 to 10 months. Of the 88 patients, 34 percent were alive after 2 to 12 months (mean 242 days). Two-thirds of the patients were free of jaundice. Sixty-six percent of the patients died between 3 days and 1.5 years (mean 133 days). The authors indicate that the self-expandable stainless steel endoprostheses provide palliation for patients with malignant biliary obstruction. Given the more lengthy follow-up of patients with limited life expectancy in this series, the results using the metallic endoprosthesis are somewhat encouraging.

The palliation of patients with malignant hilar obstruction using plastic or metal endoprostheses is the subject of considerable debate. A drawback of clinical studies involving the use of endoprostheses for palliation is the lack of patient stratification. Prospective studies are needed based on lesion type, location, and clinical parameters. Such studies should also include randomization to other stents (e.g., internal-external drainage catheters, etc.).

In summary, in patients with hilar obstruction due to malignancy, palliation with internal-external biliary drainage catheters is preferred. This provides access for periodic catheter exchanges and catheter upsizing and for possible brachytherapy. Plastic or metallic biliary endoprostheses provide palliation in those patients with limited life expectancy or in those who psychologically cannot tolerate an external tube. The long-term patency of metallic endoprostheses is similar to that of plastic endoprostheses in most reported series, and metallic endoprostheses are considerably more expensive. However, ease of placement, relative lack of dislodgment or migration, a smaller delivery system

(which reduces patient discomfort during placement), and the ability to potentially place such devices in a single step rather than in a two-step procedure are attractive advantages. The interventional radiologist has a number of therapeutic options to offer the patient with unresectable malignant hepatobiliary obstruction.

References

1. Davids PHP, Groen AK, Rauws EA, Tytgat GN, Huibregtse K. Randomized trial of self-expanding metal stents versus polyethylene stents for distal malignant biliary obstruction. Lancet 1992;340:1488–1492.
2. Kaufman SL. Percutaneous biliary drainage for malignant disease. In: Lang EK, Hasso AN, Crues JV III, eds. Biliary radiology. Philadelphia: JB Lippincott, 1992;1:133–142.
3. Cameron JL, Crist DW, Sitzman JV, Hruban RH, Boitnott JK, Seidler AJ, Coleman J. Factors influencing survival after pancreaticoduodenectomy for pancreatic cancer. Am J Surg 1991; 161:120–125.
4. Gudjonsson B, Livstone EM, Spirto HM. Cancer of the pancreas: diagnostic accuracy and survival statistics. Cancer 1978; 42:2494–2506.
5. Harris GJ, Gaskill HV III, Cruz AB Jr. Carcinoma of the pancreas: a retrospective review. J Surg Oncol 1990;45:184–189.
6. Bornman PC, Harries-Jones EP, Tobias R, et al. Prospective controlled trial of transhepatic biliary endoprosthesis versus bypass surgery for incurable carcinoma of head of pancreas. Lancet 1986;1:69–71.
7. Dachman AH. Primary biliary neoplasia. In: Friedman AC, Dachman AH, eds. Radiology of the liver, biliary tract, and pancreas. St. Louis: Mosby, 1994;611–632.
8. Nunnerley HB, Karani JB. Intraductal radiation in interventional radiology of the biliary tract. Radiol Clin North Am 1990;28:1237–1240.
9. Yamashita Y, Takahashi M, Kanazawa S, Charnsangavej C, Wallace S. Hilar cholangiocarcinoma. Acta Radiol 1992;33:351–354.
10. Wheeler PG, Dawson JL, Nunnerley HB, et al. Newer techniques in the diagnosis and treatment of proximal bile duct carcinoma: an analysis of 41 consecutive patients. Q J Med 1981; 50:247–259.
11. Meyer DG, Weinstein BJ. Klatskin tumors of the bile ducts: sonographic appearance. Radiology 1983;148:803–804.
12. Subramanyam BR, Raghavendra BN, Balthazar EJ, et al. Ultrasonic features of cholangiocarcinoma. J Ultrasound Med 1984; 3:405–408.
13. Schnur MJ, Hoffman JC, Koenigsberg M. Ultrasonic demonstration of intraductal biliary neoplasms. J Clin Ultrasound 1982;10:246–248.
14. Terblanche J, Saunder SJ, Louw JH. U-tube drainage in the palliative therapy of carcinoma of the main hepatic duct junction. Surg Clin North Am 1973;53:1245–1255.
15. Brink JA. Biliary tract imaging: computed tomography and magnetic resonance imaging. Biliary Radiology 1992;1:16–32.
16. Molnar W, Stockum AE. Relief of obstructive jaundice through percutaneous transhepatic catheter: a new therapeutic method. AJR 1974;122:356–367.
17. Ring EJ, Oleaga JA, Freiman DB, et al. Therapeutic applications of catheter cholangiography. Radiology 1978;128:333–338.
18. Mueller PR, vanSonnenberg E, Ferrucci JT Jr. Percutaneous biliary drainage: technical and catheter related problems in 200 procedures. AJR 1982;138:17–23.
19. Carrasco CH, Zounoza J, Bechtel WJ. Malignant biliary ob-

struction: complications of percutaneous biliary drainage. Radiology 1984;152:343–346.

20. Hamlin JA, Friedman M, Stein MG, Bray JF. Percutaneous biliary drainage: complications of 118 consecutive catheterizations. Radiology 1986;158:199–202.

21. Nakayama T, Ikeda A, Okuda K. Percutaneous drainage of the biliary tract: technique and results in 104 cases. Gastroenterology 1980;2:305–314.

22. Ishikawa Y, Oishi I, Miyai M, et al. Percutaneous transhepatic drainage: experience in 100 cases. J Clin Gastroenterol 1980; 2:305–314.

23. Berquist TH, May GR, Johnson CM, Adson MA, Thistle JL. Percutaneous biliary decompression: internal and external drainage in 50 patients. AJR 1981;136:901–906.

24. Yee ACN, Ho CS. Complications of percutaneous biliary drainage: benign vs malignant diseases. AJR 1987;148:1207–1209.

25. Pitt HA, Cameron JL, Postier RG, Gadacz TR. Factors affecting mortality in biliary tract surgery. Am J Surg 1981;141:66–72.

26. Cohan RH, Illescas FF, Braun SD, Newman GE, Dunnick NR. Fine needle aspiration biopsy in malignant obstructive jaundice. Gastrointest Radiol 1986;11:145–150.

27. Teplick SK, Haskin PH, Kline TS, Sammon JK, Laffey PA. Percutaneous pancreaticobiliary biopsies in 173 patients using primarily ultrasound or fluoroscopic guidance. Cardiovasc Intervent Radiol 1988;11:26–28.

28. Mendez G Jr, Russell E, Levi JU, Koolpe H, Cohen M. Percutaneous brush biopsy and internal drainage of biliary tree through endoprosthesis. AJR 1980;134:653–659.

29. Muro A, Mueller JPR, Ferrucci JT, Taft PD. Bile cytology: a routine addition to percutaneous biliary drainage. Radiology 1983;149:846–847.

30. Terasaki K, Wittich GR, Lycke G, Walker R, Nowels K, Swanson D, Lucas D. Percutaneous transluminal biopsy of biliary strictures with a bioptome. AJR 1991;156:77–78.

31. Palayew MJ, Stein L. Postoperative biopsy of the common bile duct via the T-tube tract. AJR 1978;130:287–289.

32. Burhenne JH. Biliary tract. In: Marguilis AR, Burhenne HJ, eds. Alimentary tract radiology. St. Louis: Mosby, 1983:2334–2336.

33. Elyaderani MK, Gabrielle OF. Brush and forceps biopsy of biliary ducts via percutaneous transhepatic catheterization. Radiology 1980;135:777–778.

34. Yip CKY, Leung JWC, Chan MKM, Metrewell C. Scrape biopsy of malignant biliary stricture through percutaneous transhepatic biliary drainage tracts. AJR 1989;152:529–530.

35. Kim D, Porter DH, Siegel JB, Mowschenson PM, Steer ML. Common bile duct biopsy with the Simpson atherectomy catheter. AJR 1990;154:1213–1215.

36. Schechter MS, Doemeny JM, Johnson JO. Biliary ductal shave biopsy with use of the Simpson atherectomy catheter. J Vasc Intervent Radiol 1993;4:819–824.

37. Nishimura A, Otsu H, Hiura T. Forceps biopsy of the bile duct under choledochoscopic control. Endoscopy 1980;12:23–29.

38. Venbrux AC, Robbins KV, Savader SJ, Mitchell SE, Widlus DM, Osterman FA Jr. Endoscopy as an adjunct to biliary radiologic intervention. Radiology 1991;180:355–361.

39. Lammer J. Biliary endoprostheses: plastic versus metal stents. Radiol Clin North Am 1990;28:1211–1221.

40. Groen AK, Out T, Huibregtse K, et al. Characterization of the content of occluded biliary endoprostheses. Endoscopy 1987; 19:57.

41. Leung JWC, Ling TKW, Kung KLS, et al. The role of bacteria in the blockage of biliary stents. Gastrointest Endosc 1988:34; 19–22.

42. McLean GK, Burke DR. Role of endoprostheses in the management of malignant biliary obstruction. Radiology 1989; 170:961.

43. Lammer J, Neumayer K. Biliary drainage endoprostheses: experience with 201 placements. Radiology 1986;159:625.

44. Burcharth F. A new endoprosthesis for non-operative intubation of the biliary tract in malignant obstructive jaundice. Surg Gynecol Obstet 1978;146:76.

45. Coons HG, Carey PH. Large-bore, long biliary endoprostheses (biliary stents) for improved drainage. 1983;148:89.

46. Dooley JS, Dick R, George P, et al. Percutaneous transhepatic endoprosthesis for bile duct obstruction: complications and results. Gastroenterology 1984;86:905.

47. Mueller PR, Ferrucci JT Jr, Teplick SK, et al. Biliary stent endoprosthesis: analysis of complications in 113 patients. Radiology 1985;156:637.

48. Ring EJ, Schwarz W, McLean GK, et al. A simple indwelling biliary endoprosthesis made from commonly available catheter material. AJR 1982;139:615.

49. Gordon RL, Ring EJ, LaBerge JM, Doherty MM. Malignant biliary obstruction: treatment with expandable metallic stents—follow-up of 50 consecutive patients. Radiology 1992; 182:697–701.

50. Becker CD, Glattli A, Maibach R, Baer HU. Percutaneous palliation of malignant obstructive jaundice with the Wallstent endoprostheses: follow-up and reintervention in patients with hilar and non-hilar obstruction. J Vasc Intervent Radiol 1993;4: 597–604.

51. Salomonowitz EK, Adam A, Antonucci F, Stuckmann G, Zollikofer CL. Malignant biliary obstruction: treatment with self-expandable stainless steel endoprosthesis. Cardiovasc Intervent Radiol 1992;15:351–355.

30

Percutaneous Cholecystostomy

CONSTANTIN COPE

Percutaneous trocar decompression of the gallbladder was recorded as far back as 1743 and became used clinically by the end of the nineteenth century.[1] Diagnostic cholecystography by direct percutaneous puncture[2] was first performed in 1922 but was soon replaced by oral cholecystography. Percutaneous cholecystostomy (PC), before the advent of antibiotics and the benefits of localizing imaging techniques, was associated with a high risk of serious or fatal peritonitis due to leakage of infected bile, and consequently was usually only performed by surgeons as an emergency diagnostic or decompression procedure before scheduled surgery.

Percutaneous transhepatic cholangiography (PTC), popularized in this country by Glenn et al.,[3] was introduced to provide a more accurate depiction of the biliary tree than was obtainable by oral cholecystography. The procedure was further refined and rendered safer by Okuda[4] and his colleagues at Chiba University through the use of smaller-gauge 0.7-mm needles, which were introduced via a right intercostal approach. Accidental puncture of the gallbladder was not uncommon during PTC. This was regarded as a potentially serious complication, despite the fact that it did not usually lead to biliary peritonitis as long as the operator aspirated most of the bile before removing the needle or, in cases of common bile duct obstruction, left a smaller catheter in place for external drainage until the patient had surgery.[5] Wannagat demonstrated the potential safety of needle puncture of the gallbladder by performing under laparoscopic control direct needle cholecystography in 2115 patients with only 1 patient developing biliary peritonitis.[6]

Despite the morbid fear instilled over many years by surgical colleagues into interventional radiologists that needling or catheterization of the gallbladder would lead to an unacceptable morbidity, an increasing number of published reports, both experimental and clinical, began to appear, starting in 1979, which demonstrated that PC was in fact generally safe when performed under ultrasound guidance with fine needles and catheters.[7,8] Today's techniques for PC have become fairly standardized and are being applied to a wide variety of clinical diagnostic and therapeutic procedures.

Percutaneous Cholecystostomy: Technical Considerations

The gallbladder is a thin-walled, pear-shaped viscus with a capacity of 50 to 70 ml of bile. It has a remarkable potential for expansion to very large volumes in the face of bile duct obstruction. It lies inferoposteriorly in a fossa of the right hepatic lobe in line with the anatomic division of the liver into right and left lobes. The peritoneum completely covers the sides and posterior surfaces of the body and neck of the gallbladder as well as its fundus, which usually protrudes just beyond the liver edge. The anterior wall of the gallbladder is connected to the liver by fibroareolar tissue to form the bare area, which is quite variable in extent and difficult to recognize by ultrasound examination.[9] Except in unusual congenital anomalies, the anterior relationship of the fundus and body of the normal-sized gallbladder to the liver and anterior abdominal wall is fairly constant. The interventional radiologist should be aware that occasionally the gallbladder may be covered by colon, may be freely movable when anchored by only a mesenteric attachment, or may be located completely within the liver parenchyma.[10] The normal gallbladder position and its relationship to other abdominal viscera may also be significantly altered by tumor, hepatomegaly, and hepatic lobe atrophy.[11] It is important to appreciate these anatomic variants by prior imaging to find the optimal window for safe cholecystostomy.

Patients scheduled to undergo cholecystostomy should have a detailed history and physical examination, baseline studies of serum bilirubin, amylase, lipase, and alkaline phosphatase, and a normal or correctable coagulation profile. Because bile in diseased gallbladders is commonly infected,[12] a broad-spectrum antibiotic should be administered 1 to 4 hours before the diagnostic contrast study or the interventional procedure and continued for another 12 hours or longer in the presence of cholecystitis or cholangitis. When the procedure is elective, cholecystographic tablets and a dose of oral aqueous contrast medium are administered to the patient the night before to opacify a functioning gallbladder and the hepatic flexure of the colon, respectively. This simple measure allows the operator to locate a clear window for puncturing the gallbladder[13] under fluoroscopy. If contrast visualization is not possible, the gallbladder and its relationship to other viscera in direct contact with it are most easily studied by ultrasound. Occasionally, evaluation of gallbladder position may need to be done by computed tomography (CT) when there is marked distortion of the liver or significant interposition of the colon. Despite early predictions based on CT studies[14] that the gallbladder might frequently not be amenable to puncture because of bowel interposition, it is today generally agreed that a fluid-filled gallbladder can always be accessed either trans- or subhepatically. Even when the fundus of the gallbladder is covered by bowel, it may still be possible to puncture it subhepatically by first distending it with fluid through a transhepatic needle. This maneuver can lower the gallbladder fundus sufficiently to expose some wall that is free of bowel adhesions and that can be punctured safely.

A rapidly performed PC for diagnosis or drainage is not a painful procedure when done by an experienced interventionalist. It is usually done under local anesthesia with intravenous sedation administered as required. Intravenous atropine 0.5 mg is given prophylactically to prevent a possible vasovagal reaction, which can be poorly tolerated in older patients with coexistent cardiovascular disease.[15] When percutaneous cholecystostomy is performed only for bile sampling, drainage, or diagnostic opacification of the biliary tree, there is no need to use a needle larger than 21 or 22 gauge for initial puncture or a final catheter size larger than 7 to 8 French for drainage. If the gallbladder is enlarged, tense, and protrudes below the liver, it can be directly punctured transhepatically or subhepatically under real-time ultrasound monitoring with a catheter sheath needle or trocar. Various types of over-the-needle sheaths are commercially available that can be deployed into a locking Cope loop drain with multiple side holes.[16] These provide good drainage and largely diminish the chance of their accidental removal with resulting biliary peritonitis (Fig. 30-1).

When the gallbladder is small to normal in size, it is safer to use the Seldinger technique by initially puncturing it under real-time ultrasound guidance with a 22- or 21-gauge needle using a biopsy guide.[17] The transhepatic route is generally preferred when using small needles or catheters because there is minimal

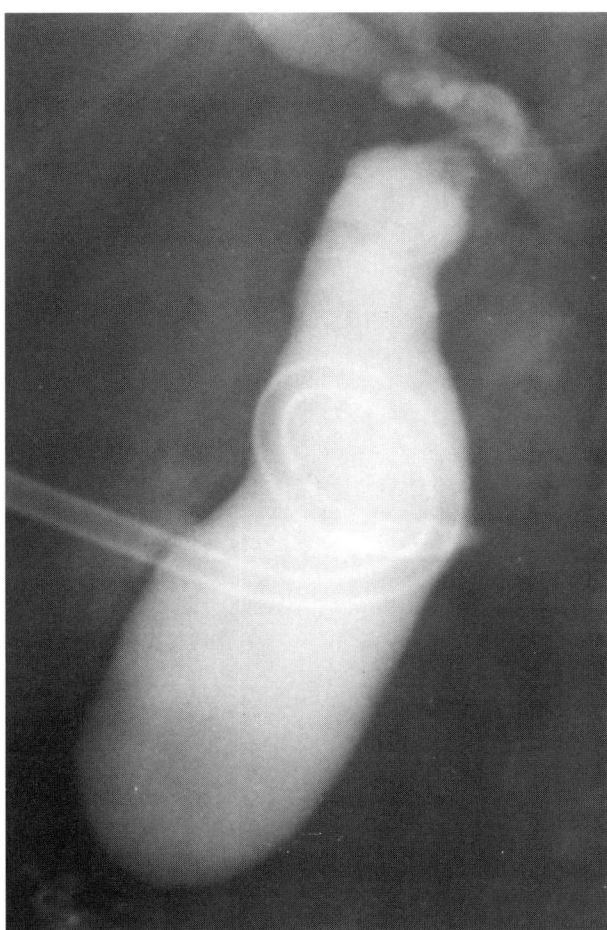

Figure 30-1. An 8 French Cope locking-loop catheter for percutaneous gallbladder drainage.

chance of significant parenchymatous trauma, less hazard of puncturing the colon, and a better likelihood of the liver tamponading the cholecystostomy tract, especially if it passes through the base area of the gallbladder.[9] After 5 ml of bile is aspirated for analysis and culture, the needle is exchanged over an 0.018-inch Mandril guidewire for an Accustick dilator (Medi-Tech) or a Cope Introduction System (Cook, Inc.). Under fluoroscopic monitoring, as much bile as possible is replaced by dilute contrast medium, with care taken not to distend the gallbladder in order to prevent bacteremia and retrograde bile leakage around the needle.

Although the one-step trocar technique[16] is useful for emergency bedside use and theoretically may prevent intraperitoneal bile spillage, it is not always a benign procedure, especially when the gallbladder is not distended[17] or when its wall is chronically thickened. Under these conditions, the gallbladder may become displaced, invaginated, or perforated and further de-

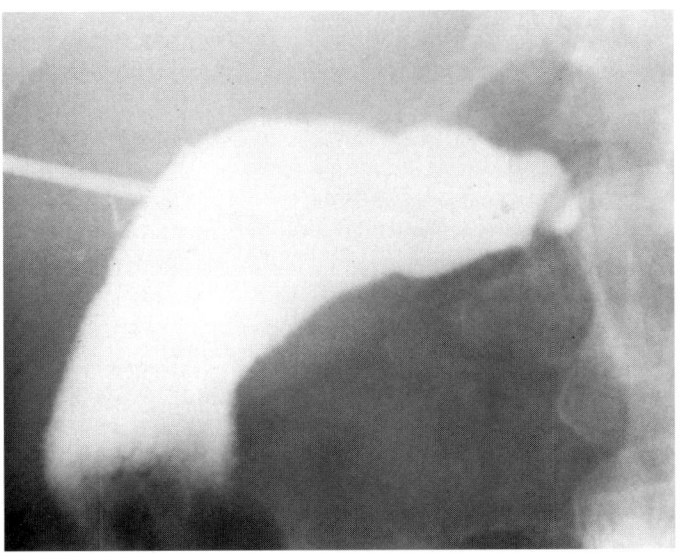
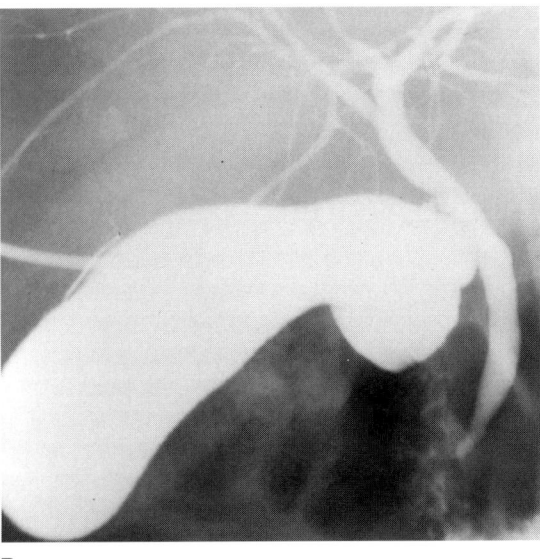

A   **B**

Figure 30-2. PC for acalculous cholecystitis. (A) A locking-loop catheter has been inserted subhepatically into the gallbladder with an anchor. Note occlusion of the cystic duct. (B) After 48 hours, there is good drainage into the common bile duct and duodenum. The retaining anchor is visible.

compressed.[19] When it is difficult to penetrate, further fruitless attempts to enter the gallbladder with the large trocar may lead to liver laceration or perforation of the neighboring bowel. In patients with chronic cholecystolithiasis without distended gallbladders, it may therefore be safer to initially insert a removable anchoring device (Fig. 30-2) through a coaxial 22-gauge/17-gauge needle introducer so that the operator can fixate the fibrotic gallbladder. This precautionary step may prevent loss of the cholecystostomy track or frustrating invagination of the gallbladder wall during the insertion of the cholecystostomy drain.[20]

Because it may take at least 2 weeks for a trans- or subhepatic cholecystostomy tract to form, especially in older, chronically debilitated patients, premature removal of the drain catheter may lead to gallbladder leakage and peritonitis.[21] For this reason, the operator should check the tract for maturity over a safety guidewire by opacifying it with contrast medium before irreversibly removing the drain.

Diagnostic Indications for Percutaneous Cholecystostomy

Bile Sampling

Simple diagnostic procedures of the gallbladder are performed with 21- to 22-gauge needles or Teflon-sheathed 23-gauge needles (Becton, Dickenson) and are useful for chemical,[22] cellular, and bacteriologic analysis. In patients with possible cholecystitis, bile aspirates should be sent to the laboratory for Gram stain, white blood cell count, and bacterial culture. If the bile is light yellow and perfectly clear, the needle may be removed after aspirating as much bile as possible. If the referring physicians still strongly feel on clinical grounds that the patients may have cholecystitis, a 6 to 7 French Cope-type locking loop drain (Cook, Inc.) is inserted immediately or on the next day to further observe the patient over the next 48 hours for signs of clinical improvement.

Cholecystocholangiography

In patients with high serum alkaline phosphatase levels and moderate or intermittent elevation of serum bilirubin due to possible tumor or stones, percutaneous cholecystocholangiography is a very useful procedure for evaluating the biliary tract for incipient partial obstruction, especially when the intrahepatic bile ducts are insufficiently dilated to be easily punctured transhepatically (Fig. 30-3). Once the needle or catheter has been used to empty the gallbladder of bile, 40 to 60 percent contrast medium is injected slowly while the patient is appropriately positioned for optimal opacification of all the major intra- and extrahepatic ducts. Intrahepatic bile duct obstructions may at times be difficult to demonstrate when there is preferential flow of contrast medium into the duodenum.[23] Intravenous administration of 1 to 2 mg of morphine may,

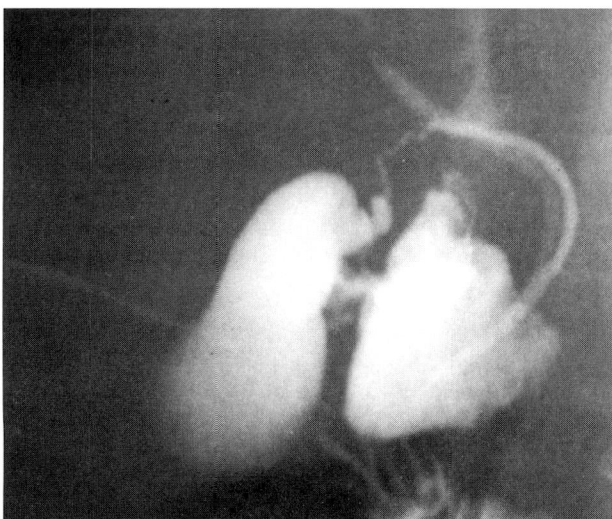

Figure 30-3. Normal transhepatic cholecystocholangiography. A 23-gauge Teflon-sheathed needle was used to opacify the gallbladder and bile ducts in a patient with low-grade bilirubinemia.

by constricting the sphincter of Oddi, help to retain contrast and lead to better intrahepatic filling.

Interventional Indications for Percutaneous Cholecystostomy

Obstructive Jaundice

It is not uncommon to find, in certain patients with complete obstruction of the distal common bile duct, that the intrahepatic ducts are not as proportionally dilated as the gallbladder and the extrahepatic ducts. In fact, intrahepatic ducts may at times remain normal in size or only slightly dilated in the face of a moderately to markedly distended gallbladder. In the presence of minimally enlarged intrahepatic ducts, transhepatic cholangiography and percutaneous transhepatic biliary catheterization may result in a prolonged, frustrating, painful procedure, which sometimes may lead to sepsis and may have to be aborted. Under these conditions, the enlarged gallbladder can become a much easier alternative target for percutaneous drainage.[24] The gallbladder drain can be used either on a temporary basis for decompressing the biliary system before surgery or else for opacifying the intrahepatic ducts so that they can then be more accurately punctured and catheterized under fluoroscopic guidance (Fig. 30-4). In the latter case, the cholecystostomy catheter is, of course, not removed until transhepatic biliary drainage has been firmly established. Patients with biliary sepsis following unsuccessful endoscopic

biliary catheterization or partial common duct obstruction are especially good candidates for drainage from the gallbladder because they often do not have dilated intrahepatic ducts.

Acute Cholecystitis

The primary treatment for acute cholecystitis in ambulatory patients is emergency or elective surgery. Emergency surgery in some elderly and frail patients with severe cardiopulmonary disease can, however, be hazardous, and under these conditions PC may be performed as a temporizing measure until the patient can be stabilized and have a more complete clinical evaluation.[25] Sometime later, when the acute cholecystitis has resolved, the patient can be considered for cholecystectomy or for percutaneous stone extraction. Acute cholecystitis in pregnancy represents another condition for which surgery may be hazardous because it may lead to fetal loss. However, Ginier and McGahan report such a case[26] in whom PC was successfully performed under ultrasound. The patient was managed uneventfully through the rest of her pregnancy with daily irrigation of the cholecystostomy drain.

In hospitalized critically ill patients and especially in those with multiple system disorders after major surgery or trauma, acute cholecystitis is a potentially lethal complication that may go unrecognized. Right upper quadrant pain, fever, leukocytosis, and a palpable gallbladder can be difficult to elicit or differentiate from other organ system diseases. Other tests such as ultrasonography and hepatobiliary scanning are unreliable in these severely sick bedridden patients.[27,28] Gallstones will be absent in a high percentage of trauma patients, who are usually in a younger age group. When present in older postsurgical or in critical medical patients, this may increase the clinical suspicion of acute cholecystitis. Such intensive care patients are usually too ill to undergo open cholecystostomy.[29] In comparison, PC is a safe and atraumatic technique for managing these difficult problem cases.[30] PC can be done at the bedside under real-time ultrasound guidance, either by direct trocar puncture or by the Seldinger technique. The advantages of the percutaneous method over surgery include increased safety, the need for only local anesthesia with little to no sedation, the lack of disruption of tissue planes with resulting less potential for peritonitis, and less risk to the patient if the diagnosis of acute cholecystitis is in error.[31]

It was originally thought that the diagnosis of acute cholecystitis could be made by examining aspirated bile for bacteria and the presence of pus, and/or awaiting a positive culture.[27] The diagnostic specificity for a positive Gram stain and blood culture was re-

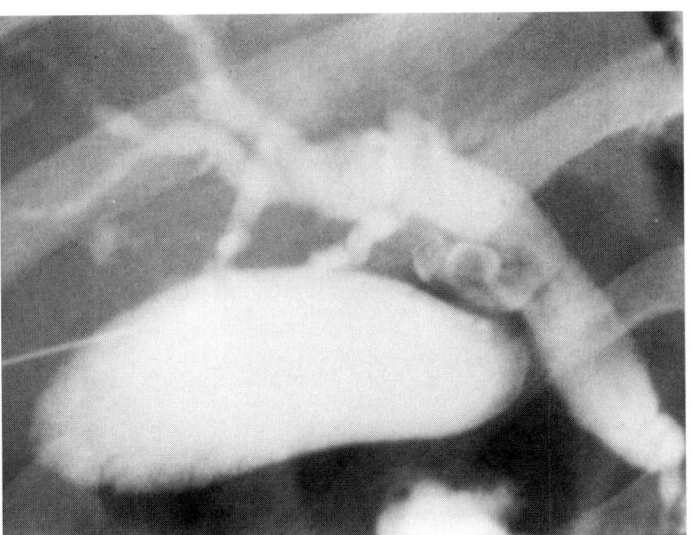

A

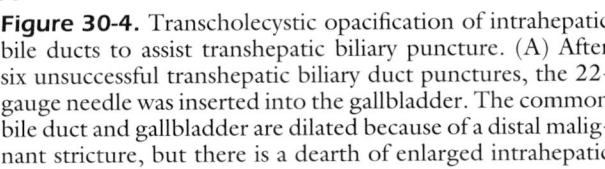

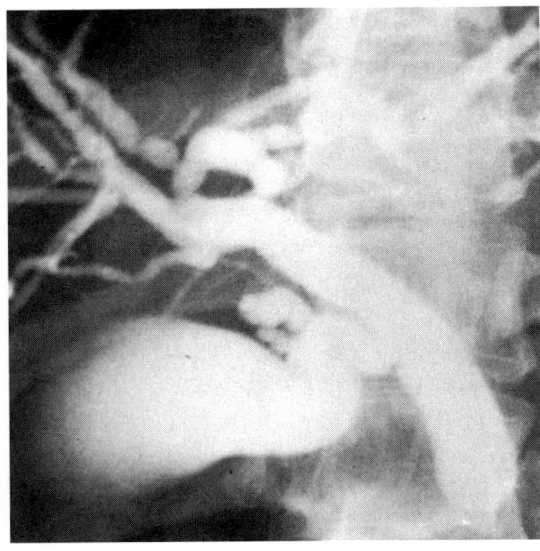

B

Figure 30-4. Transcholecystic opacification of intrahepatic bile ducts to assist transhepatic biliary puncture. (A) After six unsuccessful transhepatic biliary duct punctures, the 22-gauge needle was inserted into the gallbladder. The common bile duct and gallbladder are dilated because of a distal malignant stricture, but there is a dearth of enlarged intrahepatic ducts in the dorsocaudal hepatic lobe, where initial punctures were made. (B) Opacification of ducts allowed for prompt insertion of a transhepatic biliary drain. Note that there is no gallbladder leakage after removal of the skinny needle.

ported as being 87 percent. However, with further experience,[32] McGahan and Lindfors showed that the sensitivity of bile examination is below 50 percent, most probably because the bile has been rendered sterile by potent antibiotics or else the cholecystitis is not primarily due to an infectious process. A negative aspirate of gallbladder bile does not, therefore, exclude the diagnosis of acute cholecystitis. Today, acute cholecystitis is usually diagnosed, even if the bile is not infected, by observing the patient on continued gallbladder drainage for defervescence of fever, normalization of white blood cell count, and marked clinical improvement over a period of 48 hours (see Fig. 30-2). If there is no obvious improvement in clinical signs, a cholangiogram is performed to document patency of the cystic duct. Bile duct strictures may also give rise to sepsis and may be treated by dilatation and more selective drainage through the cystic duct. Gross empyema of the gallbladder is rapidly fatal; however, with early diagnosis and prompt adequate percutaneous drainage, survival rates are high. All patients who are being treated or evaluated for cholecystitis by catheter technique should be considered for immediate cholecystectomy if they develop increasing right upper abdominal pain or peritoneal signs, which can be indicative of a gangrenous or perforated gallbladder.[25]

Some patients[33] present with pericholecystic collections by imaging and yet have no to minimal peritoneal signs and little evidence of sepsis, suggesting that they may have a walled-off infection. Such patients can be managed successfully by simultaneous percutaneous drainage of the gallbladder and of the perforation abscess (Fig. 30-5). The patient can subsequently undergo cholecystectomy or percutaneous gallstone extraction on an elective basis. In some cases, percutaneous drainage and cholecystolithotomy may be the definitive treatment.

Percutaneous Cholecystolithotomy (PCCL)

Although PCCL has been almost completely replaced by laparoscopic cholecystectomy, it still remains an excellent treatment option for the elderly and the debilitated as well as for patients with a limited life expectancy because of greater safety. Elderly patients who present with acute cholecystitis and gallstones and who are initially managed by PC are also good candidates for PCCL 2 to 3 weeks later, once the acute episode has subsided. PCCL is discussed in more detail in Chapter 31.

Cystic Duct Catheterization

Once acute cholecystitis has subsided, and after an adequate period of time on percutaneous drainage, cho-

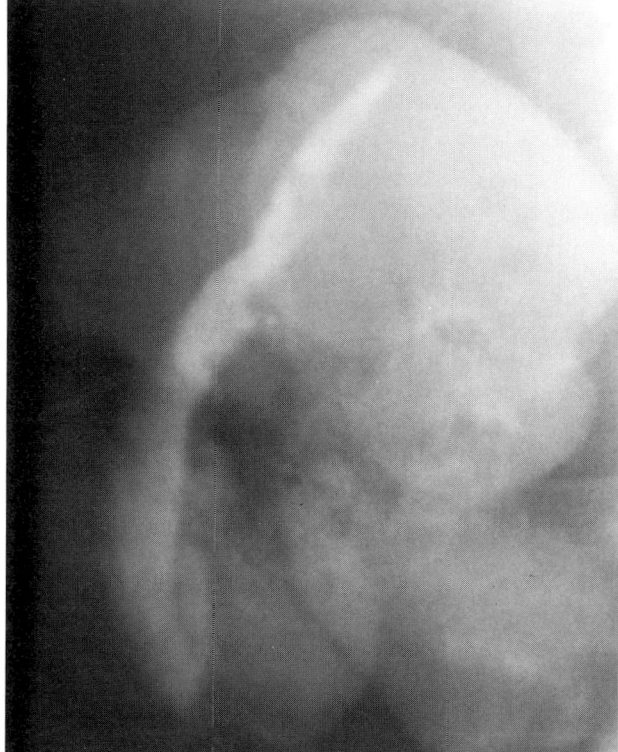

A

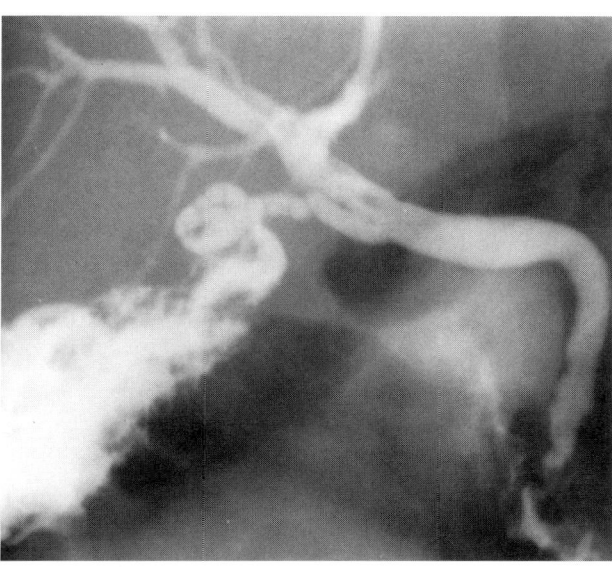

C

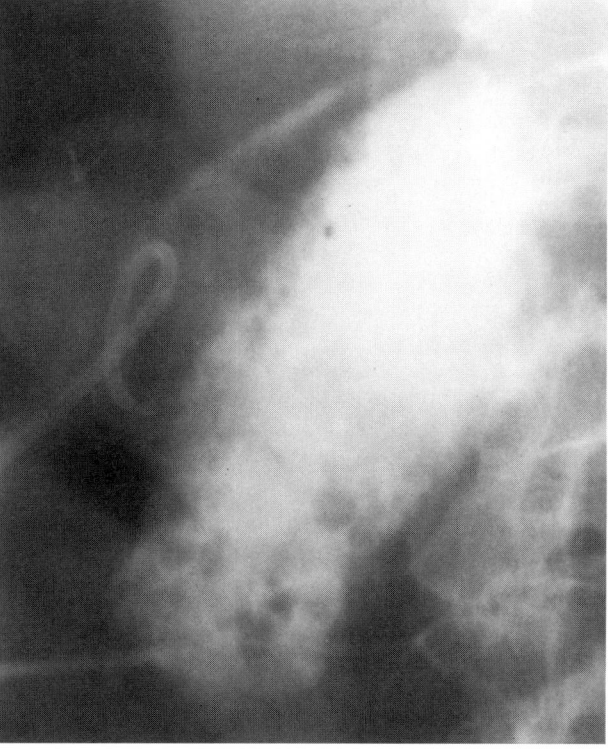

B

Figure 30-5. PC drainage of perforated gallbladder in a postgastrectomy patient. (A) Opacification of pericholecystic collection that contained purulent bile. (B) A 7 French Cope locking-loop drain was inserted in the collection. Opacification of the gallbladder demonstrates multiple gallstones and no drainage through the cystic duct. (C) Two days later, there is good drainage of the gallbladder into the common bile duct, and the bile is clear. Stones were successfully extracted percutaneously after 10 days, and cholecystectomy was performed 4 months later.

lecystography may demonstrate unsuspected disease in the cystic duct or major bile ducts, such as benign and malignant strictures or retained calculi, which can be amenable to interventional treatment. It was once thought that normal or moderately dilated cystic ducts could not be traversed from the gallbladder because of the difficulty in passing a catheter past the valves of Heister. With increasing experience and the introduc-

tion of hydrophilic catheters and guidewires, it is today possible to access the common bile duct in most cases if the cystic duct is patent. The cholecystostomy drain is first removed and replaced with a 7 to 8 French catheter-introducing sheath, which is positioned with its tip against the opening of the cystic duct to prevent coaxial catheters from uselessly coiling within the gallbladder lumen. A 5 French cobra-shaped catheter is passed through the sheath and gently advanced as far as possible into the cystic duct. A hydromer-coated nitinol angled 0.035-inch guidewire (Medi-Tech) is then used to probe the cystic duct with a clockwise-counterclockwise rotary motion while at the same time the catheter is advanced as the guidewire moves forward. Once the guidewire reaches the common duct, the cystic duct will immediately straighten out, making it easy for the catheter to subsequently be maneuvered toward the liver or the duodenum. An alternative technique for crossing the cystic duct, recommended by

Dawson et al.,[33] involves the use of a Tracker-18 system (Target Therapeutics) placed coaxially through a 6.5 French Cobra-1 catheter. A 5 French H-1 catheter (Cook, Inc.) is then passed over the 3 French Tracker catheter into the common duct.

The practical clinical usefulness of reaching the common bile duct from the gallbladder includes possibilities for balloon-dilating duct strictures, inserting internal-external drains or stents[34] in patients with pancreatic malignancies, and expelling retained stones. If the angle of the cystic duct at its junction with the common duct is not too acute, the common hepatic ducts and their intrahepatic branches may also be catheterized for selective drainage, dilatation, and dislodgment of calculi.

Endoscopy

Following PC, it may be difficult to differentiate sludge from small stones contained within sludge. Calculi adherent to the wall can be confused, especially in the chronically diseased gallbladder, with cholesterol or inflammatory polyps, as well as with adenomas. After percutaneous cholecystolithotomy, it may not be possible to visualize small retained stone fragments by cholecystography or to distinguish clots from stones. Endoscopy of the gallbladder is a much more accurate way of identifying small calculi and clearing them out. Likewise, the endoscopic recognition of premalignant or malignant tumors can lead to a prompt curative resection. It is obviously very important not to leave any stone behind,[13] because retained stone fragments may subsequently grow in size, cause new stone formation, or serve as a focus of infection. Rigid or flexible endoscopes under 4 mm in diameter can be readily introduced into the gallbladder through the cholecystostomy tract for inspection, evaluation for retained stones, and, if necessary, biopsy of suspicious mucosal lesions.

Complications of Percutaneous Cholecystostomy

Bile Peritonitis

Bile leakage leading to clinically symptomatic peritonitis is a greatly feared complication of both percutaneous transhepatic biliary drainage and PC. Some patients undergoing percutaneous biliary procedures may develop massive biliary ascites with no immediate ill effects,[35] whereas in others a minor bile leakage may lead to serious biliary peritonitis. Obviously the role of bacterial infection is paramount in the development

of this dreaded complication. It has been shown experimentally in rats that, whereas bile injected intraperitoneally produces no adverse effects, when it is mixed with an inoculum of *Escherichia coli*, the combination gives rise to a much higher mortality rate than when *E. coli* alone is administered.[36] Leakage of infected bile can be minimized by using small needles and catheters and by replacing the gallbladder bile immediately after entry with sterile saline or dilute contrast medium. Preprocedural wide-spectrum antibiotics should be administered to attempt to sterilize the bile before undertaking complex gallbladder interventional procedures, which can lead to intraperitoneal bile leakage[37] when the gallbladder wall is accidentally lacerated or when there is loss of access to the cholecystostomy tract.

Other Complications

In addition to the potential for biliary peritonitis, which can occur intraprocedurally, complicated bile leakage can also occur days or weeks later when the drain-catheter becomes accidentally removed or displaced into the peritoneal cavity[38] or else when the drain is extracted prematurely.[39] It should be remembered that a leak-proof cholecystostomy tract may take 4 to 6 weeks to develop in elderly debilitated patients, and 2 to 3 months or longer in patients receiving immunosuppressive drugs. Other reported complications of PC include hemobilia, severe vasovagal reactions, pneumothorax, intraperitoneal hemorrhage, and sepsis.[17]

Although only minor complications are described in series dealing with simple diagnostic PC using only fine needles and catheters, reviews of larger studies[17,40,41] that include interventional procedures indicate that major complications requiring surgery, transfusions, or vascular pressor therapy can reach values as high as 5.6 to 8.7 percent. Such morbidity is often due to initial operator inexperience, to a higher procedural risk caused by a diseased gallbladder wall, to the use of larger trocars and drains, and to the presence of severe concurrent illness or multisystem failure. The procedure-related mortality rate caused by hemorrhage, gallbladder perforation, and sepsis is under 2 percent and again is often related to patient clinical instability.

Conclusion

In experienced hands PC is a safe procedure for diagnostic bacteriologic and contrast studies. When it is used as an access route for interventional procedures, it is well tolerated and has been found to be especially useful for managing patients with multiple risk factors, either as a temporizing measure or as a definitive treatment.

References

1. Glenn F, Grafe WR Jr. Historical events in biliary tract surgery. Arch Surg 1966;93:848–855.
2. Burckhardt H, Müller W. Versuche über die punktion der Gallenbläse und ihre Röntgendarstellung. Dtsch Z Chir 1921;162:168–171.
3. Glenn F, Evans JA, Mujahed Z, et al. Percutaneous transhepatic cholangiography. Ann Surg 1962;156:451–462.
4. Okuda K, Tanikawa K, Emura T, et al. Non-surgical transhepatic cholangiography: diagnostic significance in medical problems of the liver. Am J Dig Dis 1974;19:21–36.
5. DeMasi CJ, Akdamar K, Sparks RA, Hunter FA. Puncture of the gallbladder during percutaneous transhepatic cholangiography. JAMA 1967;201:225–228.
6. Wannagat L. Laparoskopishe Cholangiographie. Radiologe 1973;13:26–34.
7. Elyaderani M, Gabriele O. Percutaneous cholecystostomy and cholangiography in patients with obstructive jaundice. Radiology 1979;130:601–602.
8. Shaver RW, Hawkins IF Jr, Soong J. Percutaneous cholecystostomy. AJR 1982;138:1133–1136.
9. Nemcek AA Jr, Bernstein JE, Vogelzang RL. Percutaneous cholecystostomy: does transhepatic puncture preclude a transperitoneal catheter route? J Vasc Intervent Radiol 1991;2:543–547.
10. Chuang VP. The aberrant gallbladder: angiographic and radioisotopic considerations. AJR 1976;127:417–421.
11. Gore RM, Ghahremani GG, Joseph AE, et al. Acquired malposition of the colon and gallbladder in patients with cirrhosis: CT findings and clinical implications. Radiology 1989;171:739–742.
12. Farnell MB, van Heerden A, Beart RW. Elective cholecystectomy: the role of biliary bacteriology and administration of antibiotics. Arch Surg 1981;116:537–540.
13. Cope C, Burke DR, Meranze SG. Percutaneous extraction of gallstones in 20 patients. Radiology 1990;176:19–24.
14. Hruby W, Urban W, Stackl W, et al. CT anatomy as the key to safe percutaneous lithotripsy: work in progress. Radiology 1989;173:385–387.
15. van Sonnenberg E, Wing VW, Polard JW, Casola G. Life-threatening vagal reactions associated with percutaneous cholecystostomy. Radiology 1984;151:377–380.
16. McGahan JP. A new catheter design for percutaneous cholecystostomy. Radiology 1988;166:49–52.
17. Teplick SK, Brandon JC, Wolferth CC, et al. Percutaneous interventional gallbladder procedures: personal experience and literature review. Gastrointest Radiol 1990;15:133–136.
18. Klimberg S, Hawkins I, Vogel SB. Percutaneous cholecystostomy for acute cholecystitis in high risk patients. Am J Surg 1987;153:125–129.
19. Kallett MJ, Wickham JEA, Russell RCG. Percutaneous cholecystolithotomy. Br Med J 1988;13:37–40.
20. Cope C. Percutaneous subhepatic cholecystostomy with removable anchor. AJR 1988;151:1129–1132.
21. Miller FJ, Rose SC, Buchi KN, et al. Percutaneous rotational contact biliary lithotrypsy: initial clinical results with the Kensey Nash lithotrite. Radiology 1991;178:781–785.
22. Swobodnik W, Hagert N, Janowitz P, Wenk H. Diagnostic fine needle puncture of the gallbladder with US guidance. Radiology 1991;178:755–758.
23. van Sonnenberg E, Wittich GR, Casola G, et al. Diagnostic and therapeutic gallbladder procedures. Radiology 1986;160:23–26.
24. van Sonnenberg E. The benefits of percutaneous cholecystostomy for decompression of selected cases of obstructive jaundice. Radiology 1990;176:15–18.
25. Werbel GB, Nahrwold DL, Joehl RL, et al. Percutaneous cholecystostomy in the diagnosis and treatment of acute cholecystitis in the high risk patient. Arch Surg 1989;124:782–786.
26. Ginier B, McGahan JP. Percutaneous cholecystostomy for management of acute cholecystitis in pregnancy. J Vasc Intervent Radiol 1992;7:87–89.
27. McGahan JP, Walter JP. Diagnostic percutaneous aspiration of the gallbladder. Radiology 1985;155:619–622.
28. Lee MJ, Saini S, Brink JA. Treatment of critically ill patients with sepsis of unknown cause: value of percutaneous cholecystostomy. AJR 1991;156:1163–1166.
29. Glenn F. Cholecystostomy in the high risk patient with biliary tract disease. Ann Surg 1977;185:185–191.
30. Teplick SK, Brandon JC, Wolferth CC. Percutaneous interventional gallbladder procedures: personal experience and literature review. Gastrointest Radiol 1990;15:133–136.
31. Herbel GB, Nahrwold DL, Voehl RJ, et al. Percutaneous cholecystostomy in the diagnosis and treatment of acute cholecystitis in the high-risk patient. Arch Surg 1989;124:782–785.
32. McGahan JP, Lindfors KK. Acute cholecystitis: diagnostic accuracy of percutaneous aspiration of the gallbladder. Radiology 1988;167:669–671.
33. van Sonnenberg E, D'Agostino HB, Hoyt DB, et al. Gallbladder perforation and leakage: percutaneous treatment. Radiology 1991;178:687–689.
34. Dawson SL, Girard MJ, Saini S, Mueller PR. Placement of a metallic biliary endoprothesis via cholecystostomy. AJR 1991;157:4911–4913.
35. Taormina V, McLean GK. Chronic bile peritonitis with progressive bile ascites: a complication of percutaneous biliary drainage. Cardiovasc Intervent Radiol 1985;8:103–105.
36. Andersson R, Tranberg KG, Bengmark S. Roles of bile and bacteria in biliary peritonitis. Br J Surg 1990;77:36–39.
37. Hwang MH, Mo LR, Chen GD, et al. Percutaneous transhepatic cholecystic ultrasonic lithotripsy. Gastrointest Endosc 1987;33:301–303.
38. Hawkins IF Jr. Percutaneous cholecystostomy. Semin Intervent Radiol 1985;2:97–103.
39. D'Agostino HB, van Sonnenberg E, Sanchez RB. Imaging of the percutaneous cholecystostomy tract: observations and utility. Radiology 1991;181:675–678.
40. Takahashi T, Tada S, Ida M, et al. Complications of percutaneous transhepatic gallbladder drainage. Radiology 1993;189P:307.
41. van Sonnenberg E, D'Agostino HB, Goodacre BW, et al. Percutaneous gallbladder puncture and cholecystostomy: results, complications, and caveats for safety. Radiology 1992;183:167–170.

31

Percutaneous Removal of Biliary Calculi

CONSTANTIN COPE

Although it is estimated that over 20 million people in the United States have gallstones and that 1 to 2 percent of new cases develop each year, the majority of cases are asymptomatic. The prevalence of stones is influenced by race, sex, age, and a diversity of ethnic and cultural backgrounds.[1] The most typical symptom attributable to gallstones is biliary colic, which is defined as severe, steady epigastric or right upper quadrant pain lasting anywhere from 30 minutes to several hours. Bloating, dyspepsia, and nausea are no longer considered sufficiently specific for making the diagnosis.[2] Mild symptoms ascribed to gallstones are thought to occur in 1 to 2 percent of this population over a 20-year period, but significant disease requiring interventional management is estimated to occur in only 1 percent over 20 years.[3] There is, however, an increased incidence of cholecystectomy in subjects who have recurrent cholecystitis. Because the complications and morbidity of gallstones in the asymptomatic population are minimal, treatment is based on the presentation of severe gallbladder colic or on the complications of cholelithiasis, such as cholecystitis, pancreatitis, occlusion, or stricture of bile ducts.

In the past 10 to 15 years, alternatives to traditional cholecystectomy have been introduced, such as oral and contact litholysis, extracorporeal shock wave lithotripsy (ESWL), and percutaneous cholecystolithotomy, in an effort to provide procedures that are safer and better tolerated than surgery, especially in older, more infirm patients and those with limited life expectancy. Laparoscopic cholecystectomy is gradually replacing open cholecystectomy and has supplanted the need for percutaneous procedures in otherwise healthy ambulatory patients.

Retained stones within the bile ducts can also be managed very safely without surgery by extraction through a postcholecystectomy T-tube tract, by percutaneous transhepatic catheterization, by endoscopic retrograde cholangiopancreatic techniques, or by a combination of these techniques with ESWL or litholysis.

Gallstones can be divided into two major types on the basis of their composition: (1) cholesterol stones, which contain more than 60 percent cholesterol by definition, with calcium salts and mucin accounting for the balance; and (2) pigment stones, which contain primarily calcium bilirubinate, smaller amounts of other calcium salts, and little if any cholesterol. Pigment stones can be classified into black stones, which are often found in association with hemolysis, cirrhosis, and old age, and softer, more fatty brown stones, which are found primarily in bile ducts associated with strictures, bile stasis, and infection.

Ten to 15 percent of gallstones are radiopaque on plain film. In the study of 110 patients by Trotman et al.,[4] two-thirds of the grossly calcified stones were pigment and the rest were cholesterol. Conversely, 15 percent of radiolucent stones are made of pigment and therefore unsuitable for bile salt therapy. Large stones that are densely calcified tend to be very hard and difficult to break up with stone baskets and even at times with internal or external lithotriptors.[5] Because stones can form over the long term around retained sutures, metal clips, and catheter fragments or prosthetic stents, it is important to remove all such foreign bodies from the biliary system if possible.

Patient Preparation for Percutaneous Stone Extraction

Ambulatory patients with symptomatic stone disease should have their coagulation, basic liver, pancreatic, and kidney function profiles taken and cardiograms performed on an outpatient basis, whereas those scheduled for transhepatic or transcholecystic stone extraction should be hospitalized. Postcholecystectomy patients with T tubes and retained stones can be scheduled for extraction through the mature sinus track as outpatients or in short-stay units. A single, broad-spectrum antibiotic is administered intravenously usually within 4 hours of the procedure. If the patient is considered to be an unusually high risk for sepsis because of old age, debility, or previous instrumentation, gentamycin is given in addition. Most percutaneous stone extraction procedures can be performed comfortably with intravenous short-acting sedatives and narcotics. The author finds the additional use of epidural anesthesia extremely useful if it is anticipated that the procedure will be unusually painful, as in dilatation of complicating biliary strictures, or will be prolonged, as in extraction of multiple large stones, which sometimes may need to be accomplished over two successive daily sessions. In the hands of a skillful anesthetist, epidural anesthesia is extremely well tolerated in patients with coexisting severe cardiac or pulmonary disease because of the reduced need for sedatives and analgesics, which are all respiratory depressants.[6]

Percutaneous Interventional Management of Bile Duct Stones

The earliest attempts to manage calculi through a postoperative T-tube tract were either too hazardous, as in the use of ether or chloroform for dissolving cholesterol stones, or too unpredictable, as in the use of plain or heparinized saline irrigation. Large red rubber drains were also used to dilate the sphincter and allow the passage of small calculi. The first consistently successful stone extraction technique was practiced by Mazzariello,[7] who used specially designed, low-profile curved forceps that could be inserted through the predilated T-tube tract to break up and retrieve ductal stones. This procedure could, however, be traumatic and was soon replaced by more efficacious basket retrieval techniques. These were popularized in this country by Bean and Mahorner,[7a] who used a simple arterial catheter introduction set, and by Burhenne,[8] who preferred to use a Medi-Tech steerable catheter, which was more convenient but also more expensive.

Stone Extraction Through a T-Tube Tract

Ten to 15 percent of patients undergoing cholecystectomy for cholecystolithiasis in this country have coexisting common duct stones,[9] most of which are thought to have originated from the gallbladder by passing through the cystic duct as small calculi. Larger common duct stones can be diagnosed by ultrasound imaging and removed by retrograde endoscopy before or after surgery. However, small stones can pass into the bile ducts during surgery and may be missed by operative cholangiography, especially when the stones have migrated into the intrahepatic ducts or when the

bile ducts have become partially filled with air or blood clots.

When retained stones are identified on a postoperative T-tube cholangiogram, the patient is requested to come back for stone extraction 5 to 6 weeks later to allow enough time for the intraperitoneal tract to mature. The T tube is then removed over a guidewire, and a selective 7 to 8 French arterial catheter or a 10 French Medi-Tech steerable catheter is advanced in the direction of the stone-bearing duct through the tract. Because stones are usually more easily handled and less given to retrograde migration when they are located in the distal common bile duct, attempts should be made to herd intra- and extrahepatic calculi down to that level. This maneuver can usually be easily accomplished by either flushing saline retrogradely through a small coaxial catheter inserted past the stone or else by passing a small latex balloon catheter beyond the stone and pulling it down after inflating the balloon to the size of the duct. Standard 4-wire spiral or flat wire retrieving stone baskets measuring 15 to 25 mm when expanded are commonly used for trapping, retrieving, and/or fragmenting stones up to 12 to 15 mm in diameter (Fig. 31-1). Nitinol baskets (Cook, Inc.), which have been recently introduced, provide improved stone retrieval capabilities around curves because their basket wire struts will not collapse as readily as those made of stainless steel. Stones in the 6-mm range can be easily retrieved through the T-tube tract. Hard stones that are 8 to 10 mm in diameter can also be extracted by this route if the tract is predilated to that size and a large sheath is also inserted to protect the tract membrane from being lacerated. Generally, to capture calculi it is necessary to use a basket that is a good deal wider in diameter than the stone so that it can be easily snared between the wire struts with short clockwise and counterclockwise movements. During extraction, the basket should be pulled back wide open with the stone lodged in its distal cone. If the operator attempts to close the basket in an attempt to better secure the stone, the calculus will often either be extruded back into the duct or crushed into smaller fragments.

For many years, angiographers preferred to extract stones through the T-tube tract rather than push them through into the duodenum, fearing that the latter maneuver would lead to sepsis, acute pancreatitis, or future duct strictures, complications reported both by surgeons after intraoperative sphincter dilatation with rigid Bakes dilators and by gastroenterologists after retrograde balloon sphincter dilatation.[10] The high incidence of pancreatitis and sepsis after endoscopic sphincteroplasty may be due to difficulties encountered in retrogradely catheterizing the common bile

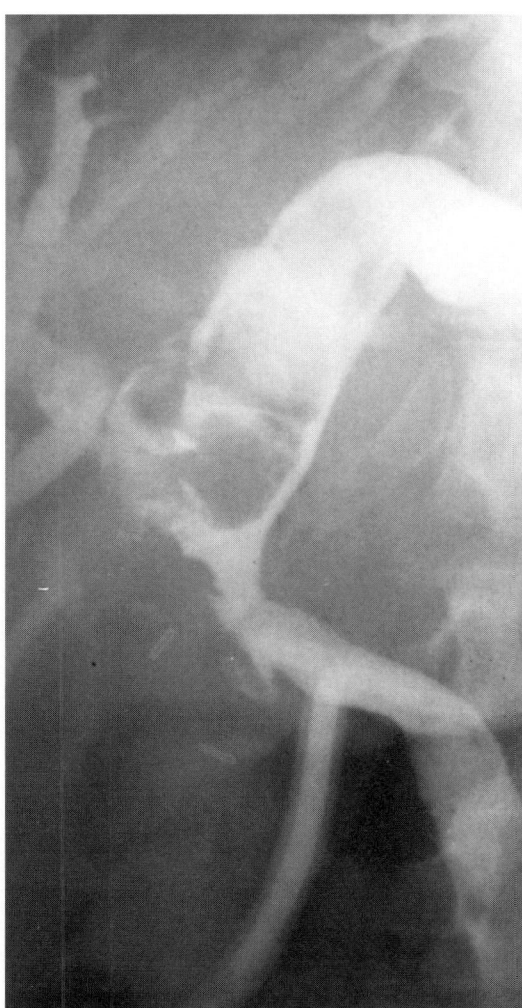

Figure 31-1. Extraction of giant biliary stones. A 24 French cannula was inserted into a T-tube tract after gradual dilatation over several days. The stones were then fragmented with a large four-wire basket, and pieces were retrieved by the basket–balloon occlusion technique. Today, the stones would be fragmented by EHL through a 14 to 16 French sheath.

duct, with concomitant bacterial contamination of the pancreatic duct followed by inadequate drainage with small endoscopic stents through the edematous ampulla. By contrast, interventional radiologists have found that, with increasing experience in the management of bile duct stones and strictures, antegrade dilatation of the sphincter with angioplasty balloons does not generally lead to any clinical complications.[11] The discrepancy in complication rate between antegrade and retrograde sphincter dilatation is due to the fact that catheterization of the ampulla from above is inherently easier and less traumatic than by the retrograde route and does not involve accidental entry into the pancreatic duct. In addition, better internal and external drainage is obtained with large percutaneous

catheters, which can be accurately positioned, monitored, and easily exchanged if occluded. Elevations of serum amylase have been noted after transhepatic biliary drainage, but these are usually transient and only occasionally associated with signs of overt short-lived pancreatitis.[12] There appear to be no contraindications to sphincteroplasty from above except for the presence of an associated duodenal diverticulum, which could be easily ruptured by balloon dilatation, with complicating peritonitis.

One of the disadvantages associated with basketing is that stones may break up into multiple small pieces. These may then escape into intrahepatic ducts and be difficult to identify and retrieve. Many prefer to use the following alternative techniques, which allow direct expulsion of stones and stone fragments from the bile duct into the duodenum (Fig. 31-2).[13]

A 12 or 14 French introduction sheath with a check-flow valve and irrigating side arm is introduced into the T-tube tract to permit opacification of the biliary system and the introduction of various catheter devices. After a long, floppy-tipped guidewire or a Glidewire (Medi-Tech) is passed into the duodenum, the ampulla is predilated with an angioplasty balloon to the size of the largest retained stone but not greater than the diameter of the common duct. After all the stones are directed into the distal duct by irrigation or balloon retrieval, an occlusion balloon catheter is inserted over the guidewire through the T-tube tract, inflated to the diameter of the common duct, and then advanced over the guidewire into the duodenum. This maneuver is repeated until all calculi are swept into the bowel. If the stones are unusually large and hard, they may be first fragmented with a stiffer basket using a powerful stone-crushing device such as the Sohendra kit (Wilson Cook).[5] This consists of a stiff 12 French helical steel spring sleeve that can be threaded over the basket leader wire and a powerful windlass-type handle. The advantage of this device is that the metal spring, in contrast to a plastic catheter, will not accordion as increasing pull is exerted on the stone-bearing basket. Furthermore, the device provides such tremendous crushing power that it will either fragment the stone or break the basket wires. In either case, the operator will not be faced with the embarrassing situation of not being able to retrieve a basket that is irreversibly trapped around a large unbroken stone. Because it is very easy for a stone fragment to escape into intrahepatic ducts during the course of these maneuvers, it is recommended that a safety guidewire or a small occlusion balloon catheter be placed above the cystic duct to prevent retrograde stone migration or allow the subsequent introduction of a catheter for irrigation. In more complicated cases in which the calculi are large,

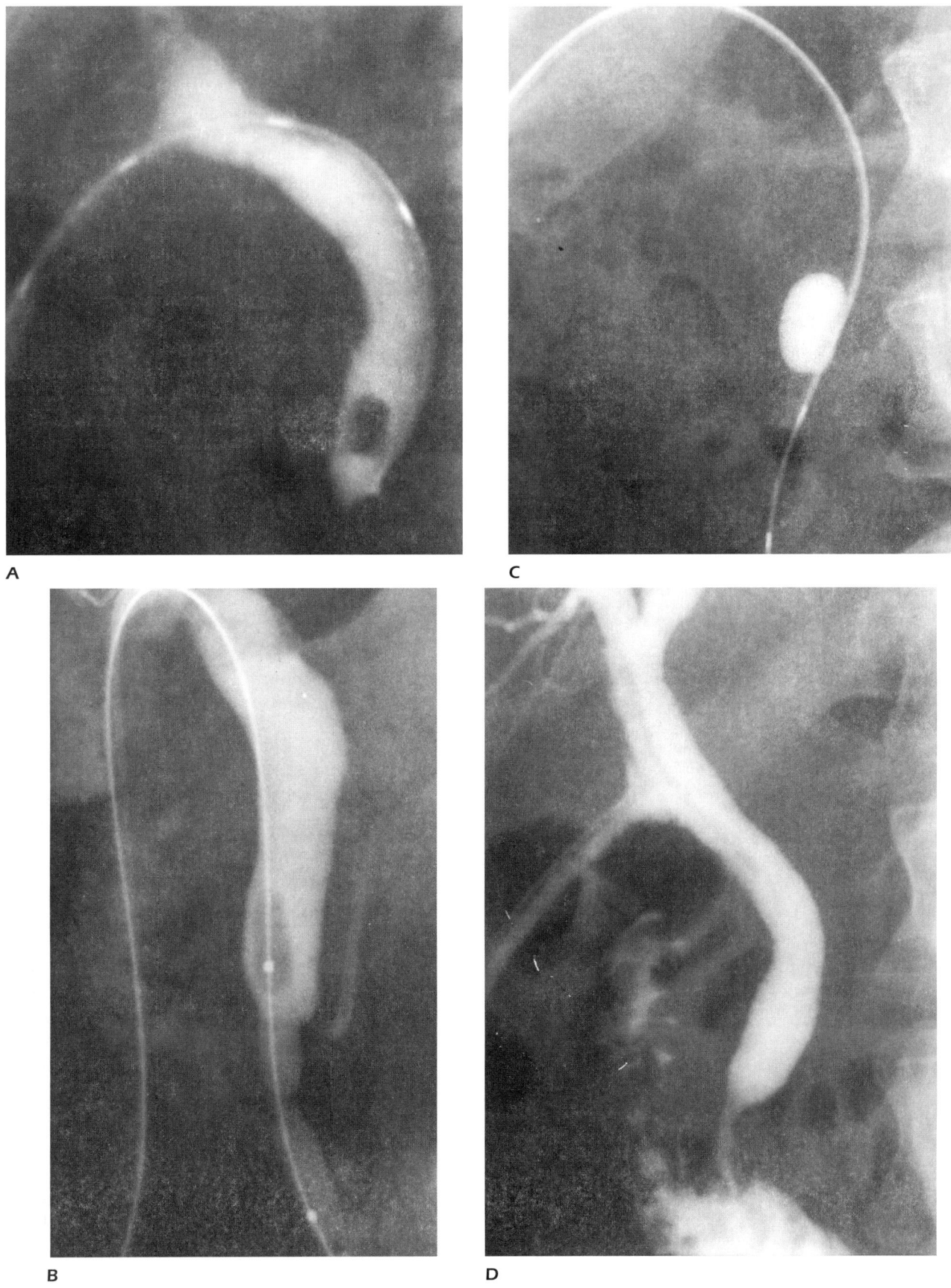

A

B

C

D

multiple, or lodged intrahepatically, the extraction can take several outpatient visits until it is completed. A Silastic or articulated T tube (Cook, Inc.)[14] is easy to reinsert atraumatically for drainage or for maintaining access to the tract between treatments. The success rate for percutaneous extraction of postoperative retained stones is well over 90 percent, with occasional failures due to impacted (Fig. 31-3) or large intrahepatic stones. Patients with sclerosing cholangitis, oriental cholangiohepatitis, Caroli disease, and long-standing large retained stones pose special procedural problems because of recurrent bouts of sepsis and duct stricture.[15–17] Although 72 to 94 percent of these patients can be rendered stone-free over a period of years by using a variety of interventional techniques (see below), the best results over the long term are obtained through a multidisciplinary team approach.[18]

Transhepatic Choledocholithotomy

Although most duct stones are thought to have originally arisen from the gallbladder because of a similar chemical composition, stones can arise de novo from the bile ducts when there is bile stasis or infection. Clinically this problem arises in patients with benign or malignant strictures, sclerosing cholangitis, and oriental cholangiohepatitis. Such patients can present with abdominal crampy pains, fever, and often borderline liver function tests with transient elevations of serum alkaline phosphatase and bilirubin due to intermittent stone obstruction of bile ducts. The diagnosis is then confirmed by retrograde endoscopic cholangiography and the stones are extracted after sphincterotomy. If a gastroenterologic endoscopist is not available or if the endoscopist finds it impossible to catheterize the common bile duct because of anomalies, stricture, or a choledochoenterostomy,[19] the patient is managed by the transhepatic route. A preliminary ultrasound examination of the liver to determine the presence and site of ductal dilatation is useful in assessing the preferred hepatic lobe to puncture. In many cases, the intrahepatic ducts are not enlarged, and it may take repeated transhepatic puncture with a 22-gauge needle to obtain a diagnostic cholangiogram. Once the presence of calculi is documented, an 0.018-inch guidewire is advanced through the needle, maneuvered into the common bile duct, and substi-

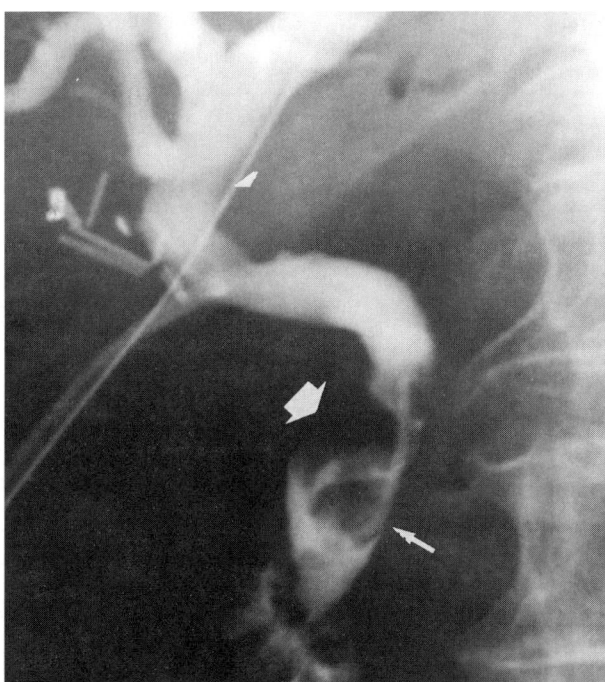

Figure 31-3. Complex common bile duct obstruction. The most distal stone was fragmented and expelled into the bowel (*small arrow*). The proximal filling defect (*large arrow*) was firmly adherent to the wall. On forceps biopsy, it proved to be an unsuspected duct malignancy.

tuted for a standard 0.035-inch guidewire over an intermediary exchange 6.3 French dilator (Cope Introduction System [Cook, Inc.] or Accustick system [Medi-Tech]). This allows for the introduction of a 7 French catheter introducing sheath to the hepatic duct and manipulation of an appropriate catheter and guidewire through the distal duct and bowel. Because it would be too traumatic to extract any but the smallest calculi through the transhepatic tract, a technique must be used that will allow expulsion of stones or stone fragments through the duct into the duodenum. This is performed, as previously described, by dilating the papillary sphincter to the size of the largest stone and then expelling the stones into the duodenum with an occlusion balloon. If the stones are very large, they are first fragmented by the Sohendra basket (Wilson Cook) technique or by electrohydraulic lithotripsy under transhepatic endoscopic control. Small stone fragments located in intrahepatic radicles can usually be

---

◄ **Figure 31-2.** Technique for expelling bile duct stones into bowel. (A) Calculus in the distal common bile duct and poor flow of contrast medium into the duodenum suggest papillary stenosis. (B) Sphincteroplasty is performed with a 6-mm angioplasty balloon. (C) The stone is pushed into the bowel with an occlusion balloon. A T tube is reinserted percutaneously. (D) Forty-eight hours later, the bile ducts are free of stones and there is free flow of contrast medium through the ampulla.

flushed down into the common bile duct with selective catheters. When stones have been cleared, an 8 to 10 French Cope locking-loop or Malecot-type drain is inserted into the common bile duct for external drainage until liver function tests have returned to normal and the associated sepsis has been controlled. The patient is then sent home for 3 to 6 weeks on internal drainage to ensure that there is unobstructed flow of bile into the duodenum. If the patient remains asymptomatic for that period of time, the drain is removed, provided there is no distal duct obstruction or retained stones by cholangiography.

Transjejunal Choledocholithotomy

Patients who have undergone choledochojejunostomy for tumor, bile duct stricture, trauma, sclerosing cholangitis, or oriental cholangiohepatitis are subject to anastomotic strictures with secondary stone formation. Although these stones can often be managed by a standard transhepatic technique, it is often more efficacious to extract them from a transjejunal retrograde approach through a choledochojejunostomy, especially when dealing with diseases associated with recurrent calculi and duct strictures affecting both hepatic lobes. The advantage of this approach is that it allows free access to each hepatic duct with only one catheter entry site and permits monitoring and treatment of long-term recurrent disease without the trauma associated with repeated transhepatic catheterization. Even if the Roux-en-Y loop has not been tacked to the anterior abdominal wall or furnished with a Hutson ostomy, the enteric loop, because of its anterior position, is usually easily accessible to needle puncture and catheterization.[20] It can be punctured with a skinny needle after preliminary opacification by percutaneous transhepatic cholangiography or sometimes by an upper gastrointestinal series. It can also be found by probing over its expected location with a fine needle while injecting puffs of contrast medium under fluoroscopy, although this technique is usually associated with a lower success rate because of the difficulty in locating collapsed bowel lumen. Some workers have successfully catheterized the enteric loop under CT control. To ensure that the colon is not accidentally punctured, the hepatic flexure can be preopacified by having the patient take an oral contrast agent the evening before the procedure. Once the small bowel lumen has been located, the author prefers to insert a metal anchoring device (gastric anchor [Cook, Inc.]) for catheter insertion. This serves two purposes: first, it allows the drain to be easily reinserted if it falls out accidentally before a peritoneal track is well formed, and, second, it provides a useful radiopaque target for recatheterizing the bowel loop at a future date if the choledochoenteric anastomosis needs to be redilated or if stones recur. Once a selective catheter has been inserted into the jejunal loop, it is easy to locate and catheterize the hepatic ducts because of their close proximity to the enterostomy site. The anastomotic strictures are then balloon-dilated and the stones are extracted into the bowel by a combination of techniques involving irrigation, basket snaring, or retrieval with occlusion balloons, with or without endoscopy. In patients with chronic recurrent stones and strictures, it is possible to provide convenient long-term access to the bile ducts for outpatient endoscopic and radiologic procedures through a well-functioning Hutson loop ostomy; however, this entry site can be associated with a 15 percent complication rate.[21]

Complicated Stone Extraction

It is relatively simple, speedy, and safe to extract retained duct stones by standard basket and balloon techniques when these are few in number, mobile, average in size, and easily directable into a main bile duct. However, for patients who have numerous large stones or adherent calculi, recurrent sepsis, and coexisting bile duct strictures, treatment becomes more complex and may require multiple procedures spread over days and months. A close association between the endoscopist and the abdominal surgeon is essential in chronic cases to provide the patient with, if necessary, better routes of access or with tailored segmental hepatectomy in advanced disease. The successful management of stone disease must involve the proper control of infection and attempts at eradicating significant strictures. Sepsis due to cholangitis and coexisting intrahepatic abscesses are first treated with antibiotics and by catheter drainage. Once infection is controlled, it is mandatory to adequately dilate all major strictures to prevent the recurrent cycle of bile stasis–infection–stone formation–stricture. Strictures due to papillary stenoses and some traumatic bile duct strictures can give good long-term patency results with one or two balloon treatment sessions, whereas those resulting from lithiasis, periductal encasement, chronic pancreatitis, choledochoenterostomies, sclerosing cholangitis, and oriental colangiohepatitis require constant vigilance and may need frequent redilatations.[22,23] Although the potential use of expandable metal stents may appear attractive in this setting, their long-term efficacy for treating chronic strictures in the presence of recurrent infections and stones is unknown.[24] The following instruments and techniques, singly or in combination, may need to be used in these difficult cases.

Fogarty Balloon Catheters

Intrahepatic calculi may be found lodged within an ampullary dilatation at a duct confluence. It may not be possible to extract the calculus either with a retrieval basket, because it cannot be sufficiently opened due to the relative stenosis of the efferent main bile duct, or with an occlusion balloon, because the calculus will be extruded into a side duct when it is pulled back. If the calculus is soft, it can be retrieved by blocking one afferent duct within a 2 or 3 French Fogarty balloon and using another similar-size balloon to pull the stone back.

Larger Angioplasty Balloon Catheters

Although there is a natural reluctance to overdilate the ampulla for fear of destroying the terminal sphincter mechanism or tearing the duct, this can be done safely as long as the balloon diameter does not exceed the common duct diameter and there is no duodenal diverticulum. In the presence of giant duct stones and proportionately enlarged common bile ducts, it is possible to dilate the ampulla to 15 mm or, if necessary, even 20 mm with no complications or gross loss of sphincter competence on evaluation of upper gastrointestinal series.[11] However, this is rarely necessary if the stones can first be fractured with electrohydraulic lithotripsy (EHL) (Fig. 31-4) or extracorporeal shock wave lithotripsy.

Litholytic Agents

Monooctanoin is the only agent approved for human use in the United States. Although methyl *tert*-butyl ether is a better solvent of cholesterol stones, it has not achieved widespread application because of its potential toxicity and the difficulties associated with its administration. Monooctanoin is administered through a T-tube tract or a transhepatic drain over 3 to 10 days at a rate of 3 to 5 ml per hour. A second drain should be inserted for venting during the infusion to prevent pressure buildup and systemic absorption of the drug.[25] The majority of cholesterol stones that respond to this agent will become softer or shrink in size and will become more amenable to being crushed with baskets. Only about 30 percent will be completely dissolved. This agent is used to facilitate breaking up of large hard stones only when other modalities have failed. Side effects include diarrhea, nausea, and vomiting, and, if the infusion rate is too high, the patient may develop biliary colic, chills, hypotension, or even pulmonary edema.[26]

Electrohydraulic Lithotripsy

In this procedure, a high-voltage generator is used to create a series of sparks at the tip of a flexible bipolar electrode, which can generate hydraulic shocks of sufficient energy to fragment most calculi.[27] Flexible catheter electrodes are available in sizes varying from 1 to 9 French. The 1 and 3 French probes can be passed through the instrument channel of small flexible endoscopes under 12 French or through the hollow stem of some retrieval baskets. This makes them ideally suited for use in smaller intrahepatic ducts. The best results are obtained by using irrigating solution made up of one-sixth normal saline and by having the electrode tip directly facing the stone at 1 to 2 mm from its surface. Because serious bleeding and perforation can occur if the electrode accidentally comes close to or contacts the wall of the duct, it is safer to steer and monitor the position of the electrode tip under endoscopic control (Fig. 31-5). When, on rare occasions, it is not possible to pass an endoscope into the stone-bearing duct because of excessive angulation, strictures, or space-occupying giant stones, an over-the-guidewire type of Segura basket (Medi-Tech), which allows in-line insertion of an EHL electrode, can be used to capture and fragment the calculus. If this fails, the author has been able to pulverize large stones with EHL by introducing transhepatically an 8 French, malleable steel, blunt-tipped cannula (Cook gastric cannula) to reach the stone. Proper positioning for firing the contained 5 French electrode is ensured when the cannula tip is fluoroscopically centered on the stone and also when a grating sensation is felt when the tip is moved across the surface of the calculus. Some large calcified stones may not break, even when the larger, more powerful, 9 French EHL electrode is used. On these rare occasions, one may find that these are more amenable to treatment with ESWL or laser lithotripsy, if available. Giant stones that cannot be fragmented can be managed with long-term catheter drainage or eventually segmental hepatectomy if the patient can be prepared to tolerate major surgery.

Extracorporeal Shock Wave Lithotripsy (ESWL)

It is sometimes difficult to remove or break up large stones over 15 to 20 mm, especially when they are located intrahepatically. As a calculus grows in size over the years, the duct in which it is contained also locally expands to form a sac. Because the efferent duct of this sac remains of normal caliber or narrows further because of stricture formation, it becomes impossible for the larger stone to pass spontaneously. It is likewise also difficult to introduce and deploy baskets around the stone because of the marked disparity in diameter between the stone-containing sac and the smaller draining intrahepatic duct. Similarly, severe duct angulation, strictures, and lack of maneuvering space around the stone can limit the use of EHL under

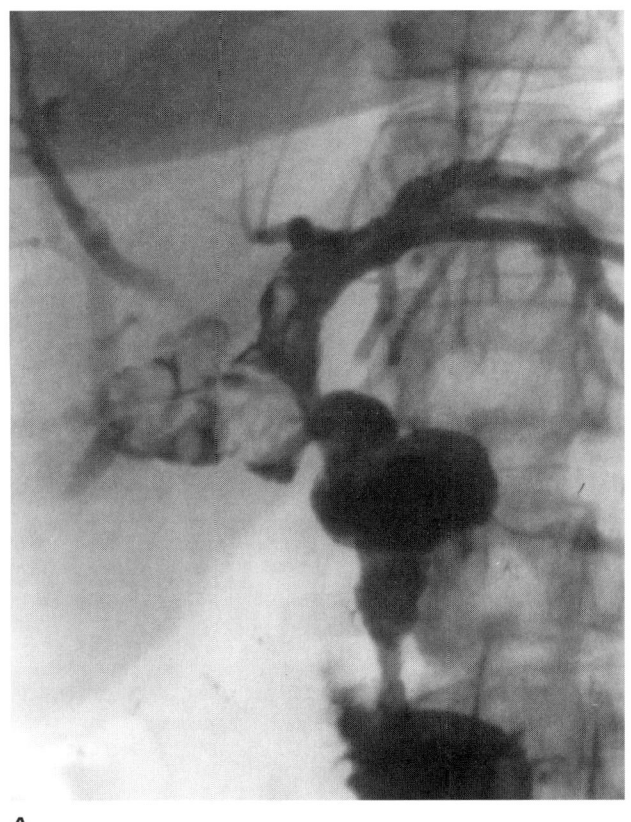

A

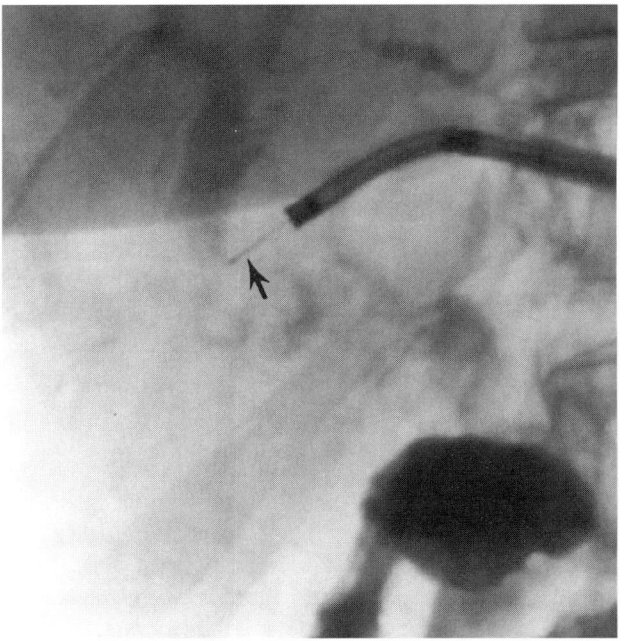

B

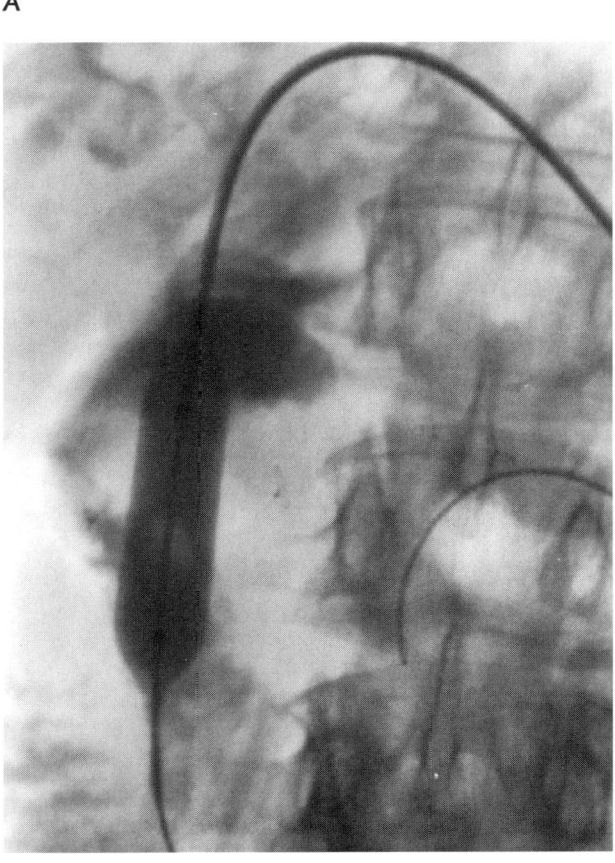

C

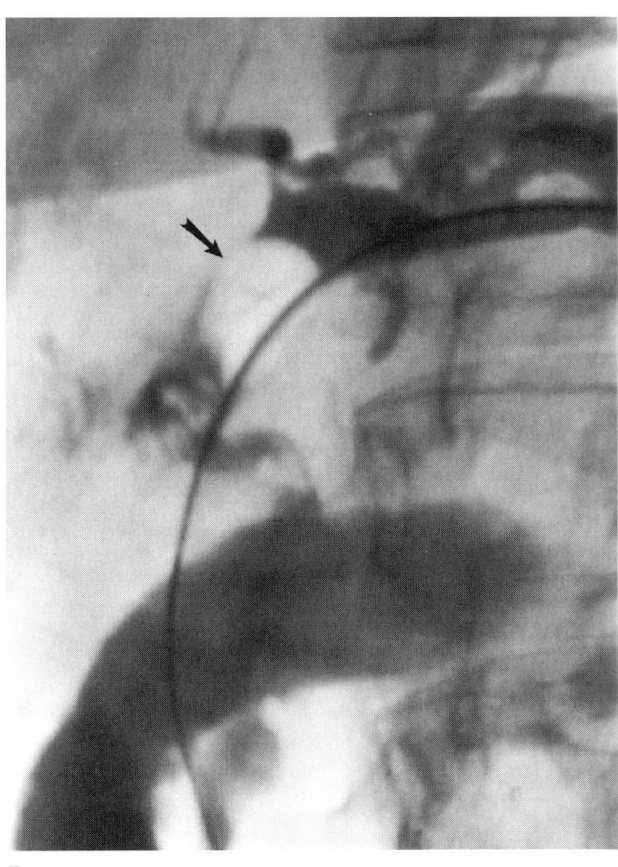

D

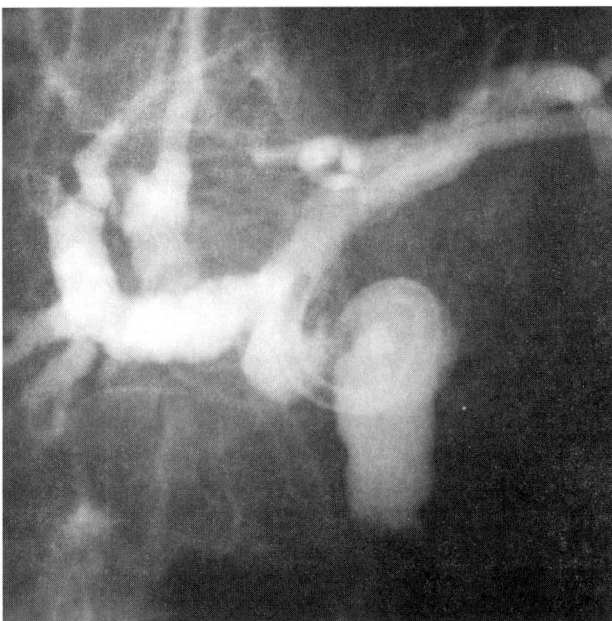

E

Figure 31-4. Technique of transhepatic choledocholithotomy. (A) The patient had possible Caroli disease with a large stone burden. (B) A 16 French sheath was inserted transhepatically into the left lobe. Large stones were fragmented with an EHL electrode (*arrow*) under endoscopic vision. (C) The common hepatic duct and ampulla were dilated with a 15-mm angioplasty balloon to allow passage of stone fragments. (D) After intrahepatic stone fragments were herded into the common bile duct, they were expelled into the bowel with the repeated passage of an occlusion balloon (*arrow*). (E) After three separate sessions, the biliary tract was clear of retained stones.

endoscopic control. When these percutaneous techniques fail and surgery is contraindicated because of coexisting risks or illnesses, ESWL has been shown to be safe and efficacious.[28]

Because ESWL is mostly performed with units that require centering the shock waves under fluoroscopic control, the common bile duct must have a catheter in good position for opacification of the stones. This is performed either through an endoscopic nasobiliary catheter or a percutaneous transhepatic or T-tube tract catheter. Preliminary sphincteroplasty or sphincterotomy must be performed to allow passage of stone fragments. During ESWL the patient must be immobilized with general or epidural anesthesia so that the treatment can be carried out with the patient in the best position for fragmenting the stones safely and efficiently. The patient should be on antibiotic coverage until stone clearance has been achieved. Since ESWL was first described in 1986 for the management of choledocholithiasis, it has been found to be an important method for treating large, irretrievable stones,

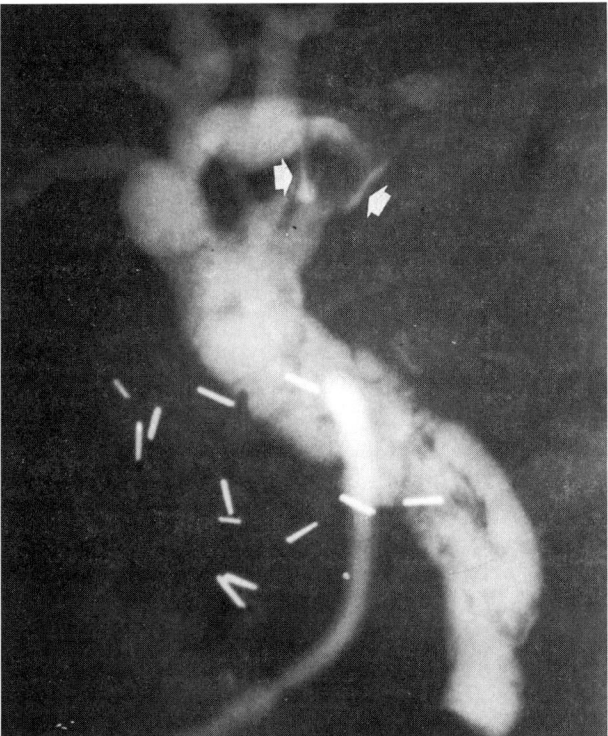

A

B

Figure 31-5. Removal of stone trapped in the left duct. (A) A 1-cm stone could not be snared or retrieved with a balloon catheter. Note that the stone is larger in diameter than the efferent duct (*arrows*). (B) A 6 French loop catheter locked distal to the stone was pulled to bring the stone into view of the endoscope so that it could be fragmented by EHL.

with a fragmentation rate of over 90 percent after one or two sessions.[28] Despite successful fragmentation of these stones in situ, their constituent fragments over 6 mm in diameter will not usually pass spontaneously. In fact, supplemental percutaneous or endoscopic extraction procedures must be performed in as many as 96 percent of patients to achieve complete stone clearance. Complications of ESWL include hemobilia, ileus, pancreatitis, biliary sepsis, hematuria, and abdominal pain, with a 0.9 percent 30-day mortality rate. Contraindications to performing ESWL include vascular aneurysms, calcified vessels, uncorrectable coagulopathy, pacemakers, and inability to safely focus the shock wave beam.

Percutaneous Endoscopy

The use of endoscopy through percutaneous and surgical drain tracts has been under evaluation mostly in the Far East because of the ongoing development and more ready availability of sophisticated smaller Japanese flexible fiberendoscopes with instrument channels and tip deflection capabilities. These instruments, which are now commercially available in 9 to 16 French sizes with matching light sources and recording capabilities on tape or hard copy, are ideally suited to the percutaneous exploration of the biliary tract and for the interventional management of retained calculi.[29] Although surgeons are capable of extracting stones by endoscopy through T-tube tracts or by laparoscopic techniques, many patients are still being referred to the interventional radiologist for removal of small missed stones or for complicated cases that require the integration of careful fluoroscopic techniques with or without the aid of endoscopy.

An increasing number of interventional radiologists with a busy full-time practice[30,31] have fiberendoscopes available in their section. They can be invaluable for visualizing, biopsying, and managing lesions that are difficult to reach or treat solely by radiographic means (Fig. 31-6). Percutaneous endoscopy is useful for distinguishing stone from tumor, clot, or sludge, for finding the opening of unopacified intrahepatic ducts, for biopsy of suspicious ductal lesions, and for the extraction and fragmentation of stones under direct vision with Fogarty balloons or stone baskets or by EHL. The larger, sturdier, 15 French endoscope can be easily passed through a T-tube tract for management of large calculi within the common bile or hepatic ducts, but it is not practical for clearing small impacted intrahepatic stones and for passing acute duct angulations. The author finds the 10.5 French endoscope more convenient for intrahepatic work because it is more flexible, does not require tract overdilatation beyond 12 French, and, despite its smaller size, will

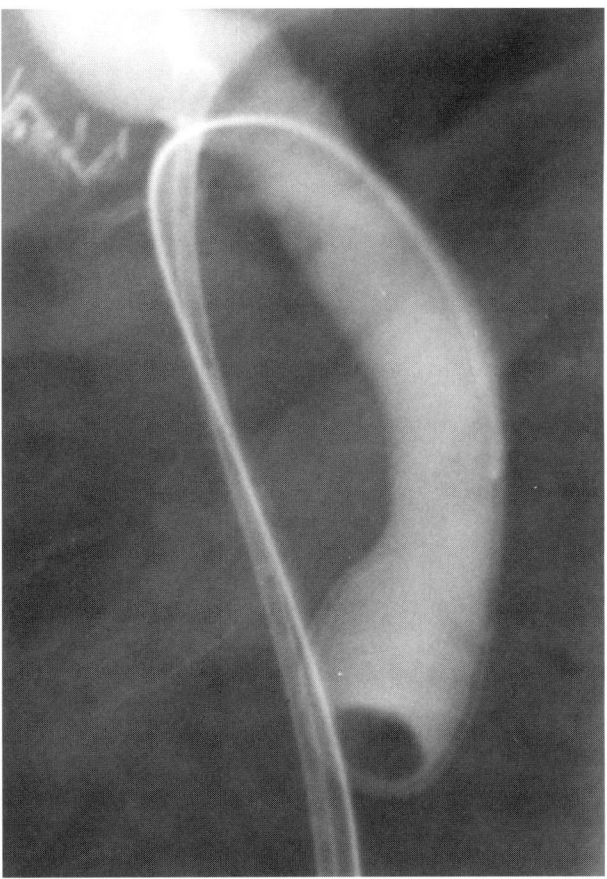

Figure 31-6. Pseudocalculus of the common bile duct. Stone disease was ruled out by flexible endoscopy, and balloon sphincteroplasty was performed to dilate the papillary stricture.

still allow the use of biopsy forceps (Cook, Inc.), EHL electrodes, and small ureteral stone baskets through its 3 French instrument channel. It also permits transhepatic rendezvous procedures to treat stones beyond strictures.[32]

The patient should receive a broad-spectrum antibiotic before any type of complex endoscopic procedure. To obtain a clear field of view, bile ducts must be kept slightly distended by flushing saline through the irrigation channel either by hand or from a bag suspended 15 to 20 cm above the level of the common bile duct. Adherent large blood clots should be removed by flushing through catheters or by suction. It is important that there be free egress of the fluid through the common duct or through a transhepatic catheter introduction sheath to prevent undue pressure elevation, which might give rise to sepsis or leakage of contaminated fluid into the peritoneal cavity.

The tip of the endoscope should always be advanced under direct vision and angled to face the long axis of the duct. The endoscope is directed toward the suspected calculi by endoscopically following a previously placed guidewire and, if necessary, occasionally confirming the correctness of its course by fluoroscopy. In patients with mature access tracts, repeated endoscopy can be performed during outpatient visits for locating and extracting previously overlooked retained calculi.

The small flexible endoscopes used in these procedures are delicate and expensive. The internal quartz fibers used for viewing and illumination are easily fractured if the instrument is hyperflexed during clinical endoscopy or when it is being cleaned and sterilized.

Morbidity and Mortality in Treating Choledocholithiasis

The complication rate associated with the radiologic interventional treatment of choledocholithiasis depends on many factors, which include (1) the size, consistency, number, and intra- or extrahepatic location of stones; (2) the presence of recurring cholangitis and/or intrahepatic abscesses; (3) preprocedural endoscopic or surgical complications; (4) coexisting medical risks associated with old age, advanced cardiopulmonary disease, stroke, and other conditions; (5) the degree of technical complexity required for stone extraction; (6) the need for a percutaneous transhepatic or transjejunal approach; and (7) the presence of sclerosing cholangitis or oriental cholangiohepatitis.

The morbidity rate for simple postoperative stone extraction through a T-tube tract is under 5 percent.[15] This is an outpatient procedure that is generally free of significant complications that might necessitate hospitalization; however, in patients with multiple, large, or intrahepatic calculi, longer and more traumatic intraductal manipulations can lead to sepsis, hemobilia, and pancreatitis, all of which usually respond to conservative management. The T-tube tract can rupture if it is overdilated too quickly or if the operator attempts to extract a large, hard stone through a small tract.

In contrast to the minimal to moderate hazard associated with T-tube stone extraction, there is potentially a much higher morbidity when this is associated with the transhepatic approach because of the additional complications that can occur from the creation of a new tract.[33] In patients with malignant duct obstruction, the immediate morbidity of percutaneous biliary drainage seen in large studies of over 100 patients varies between 5 and 22 percent. Potential serious complications include severe hemobilia requiring blood replacement and/or hepatic arterial embolization or surgery, intrahepatic or subphrenic abscesses, pneumothorax, pleural effusion, peritonitis, and cholangitis

with septic shock. In contrast, the morbidity rate for the transhepatic treatment of benign biliary disease can be much lower. Yee and Ho[34] point out, for example, that in their experience the use of percutaneous transhepatic biliary drainage for the management of biliary strictures, calculi, and fistulas was associated with only 2 percent of major complications, and there were no deaths. The lower morbidity for treating patients with benign biliary obstructive disease is attributed to the fact that these patients are generally younger and healthier and usually require a shorter period of catheter drainage. There was no mortality associated with complex stone extractions in two studies.[18,34] In a third study[35] in which there was a 30-day mortality rate of 3 percent, the deaths were probably not procedurally related.

Percutaneous Cholecystolithotomy (PCCL)

Interventional procedures for PCCL include contact dissolution with a litholytic agent and direct percutaneous extraction of stones and/or removal of stone fragments after internal or external stone fragmentation with electroshock lithotripsy.[36] At this time, PCCL has been reduced to a minor role because of the advent of laparoscopic cholecystectomy (LC), which is fast becoming the accepted manner for managing symptomatic gallstones.[37] However, PCCL may be better tolerated in poor-risk patients and consequently may remain an important therapeutic option in the management of subjects with multiple system diseases who have acute cholecystitis in association with gallbladder calculi or recurrent gallstone colic (Fig. 31-7).[38] The main contraindications to PCCL include gangrenous gallbladder with possible perforation, severely contracted gallbladder with no measurable lumen, large diffusely calcified stones over 3 to 4 cm, porcelain gallbladder, uncorrectable coagulation disorder, and severe allergy to iodinated contrast media. An intrahepatic gallbladder is not a contraindication for PCCL.

Overview of Techniques

Depending on the size of stones and fragments in the gallbladder, the diameter of the cholecystostomy tract that is required for their extraction may vary from 16 French to as large as 30 French. If the transhepatic route is chosen, one should consider the real risk of causing severe hemorrhage from an arterial or liver laceration.[39] Picus et al.[40] access the gallbladder in one step via the transhepatic route. To prevent vascular

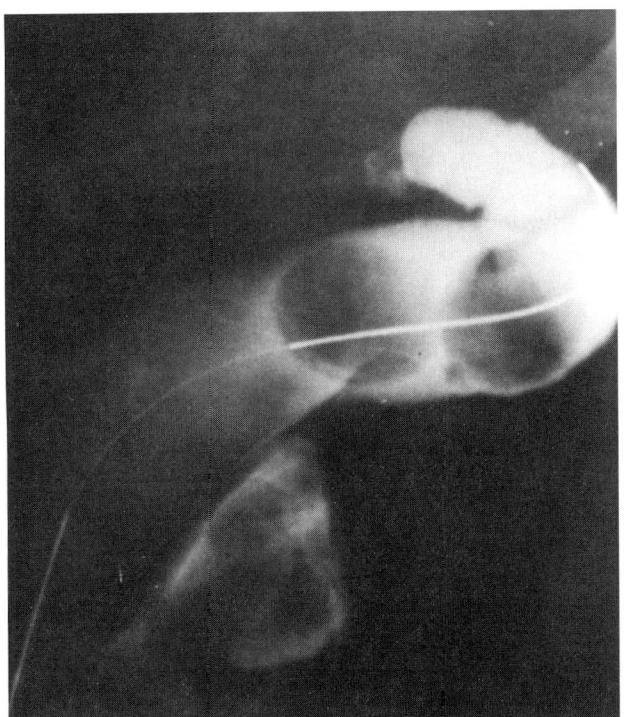

Figure 31-7. PCCL. Two 22-mm stones in a nonfunctioning gallbladder were successfully fragmented mechanically. The patient has remained asymptomatic for 4 years.

complications, they traverse the thin sliver of liver that overlies the body of the gallbladder and dilate the tract coaxially to insert an introduction sheath no larger than 18 French. Others who also prefer this route dilate the transhepatic tract stepwise over a week or longer.[41,42] Many authors prefer to use the direct approach to the gallbladder fundus by a subhepatic transperitoneal route, in line with the long axis of the gallbladder.[43–48] This has the following advantages: (1) it does not require complex retrograde catheter and endoscope maneuvers for reaching and retrieving calculi; (2) very large introduction sheaths can be used with impunity; (3) it is easier to catheterize the cystic duct and common bile duct; (4) it allows the introduction of rigid endoscopes, which have larger instrument channels and better optics and are less expensive than flexible fiberendoscopes; and (5) in contrast to uncertain closure of the transhepatic tract, this approach allows for tamponading of the gallbladder against the abdominal wall to control any bile leakage.

The basic interventions for PCCL used by various authors are the same but vary in detail depending on the approach and technique used to cannulate the gallbladder, the type of instrumentation preferred to break up and retrieve stones, the preferential use of endoscopy versus fluoroscopy or a combination of both, the follow-up, and the timing of drain tube removal. Laparoscopic cholecystolithotomy differs from PCCL in that it requires the induction of a pneumoperitoneum under general anesthesia, whereas PCCL can be performed much more simply with intravenous sedation or epidural anesthesia if desired.

Preferred Methods for Interventional PCCL

The location of the gallbladder and its relationship to the liver and the colon, if not already known from previously performed oral cholecystography, axial tomography, ultrasonography, and barium studies, can be found at the time of the procedure with ultrasound. It is also very useful to have the right hepatic flexure opacified at the time of gallbladder puncture so that the needle can be more safely guided past the large bowel under both fluoroscopic and ultrasound control. Some operators prefer to have the gallbladder also preopacified by oral cholecystography. If it is not functioning, it can be made readily visible by contrast injection through a skinny needle inserted transhepatically. The gallbladder fundus is punctured with a short, vigorous, forward thrust of a sheathed needle. A stiff guidewire is then introduced and used to further dilate the cholecystostomy tract to the usually required size of between 24 and 30 French (Fig. 31-8). A 16 French tract is adequate if the gallbladder contains only small calculi under 6 mm in diameter. Techniques for dilating the cholecystostomy tract include the exchange of serial dilators and the use of angioplasty balloon catheters; many operators prefer to create the tract with metal or plastic coaxial dilators to minimize the chance of gallbladder bile leaking into the peritoneum and of accidentally losing access. The gallbladder wall in chronic cholelithiasis is often thickened and leathery; as a result, tract dilatation may be difficult and can be unsuccessful in 5.3 to 9.0 percent of cases because of wall invagination and/or complete loss of access due to partial decompression of the gallbladder lumen and displacement of guidewires into the peritoneal cavity.[40,46,48,49] This difficulty is especially prevalent with

---

Figure 31-8. PCCL techniques. (A) Opacification of a long sinuous gallbladder full of noncalcified stones. (B) A 24 French introducing sheath was inserted into the gallbladder after percutaneous coaxial balloon dilatation of a second cholecystostomy tract. A removable anchor (*arrows*) was used to prevent invagination of the floating gallbladder. (C) ▶ The stones were removed with crushing forceps. (D) The gallbladder was cleared of all stones after two sessions. A Foley catheter is in place for external drainage.

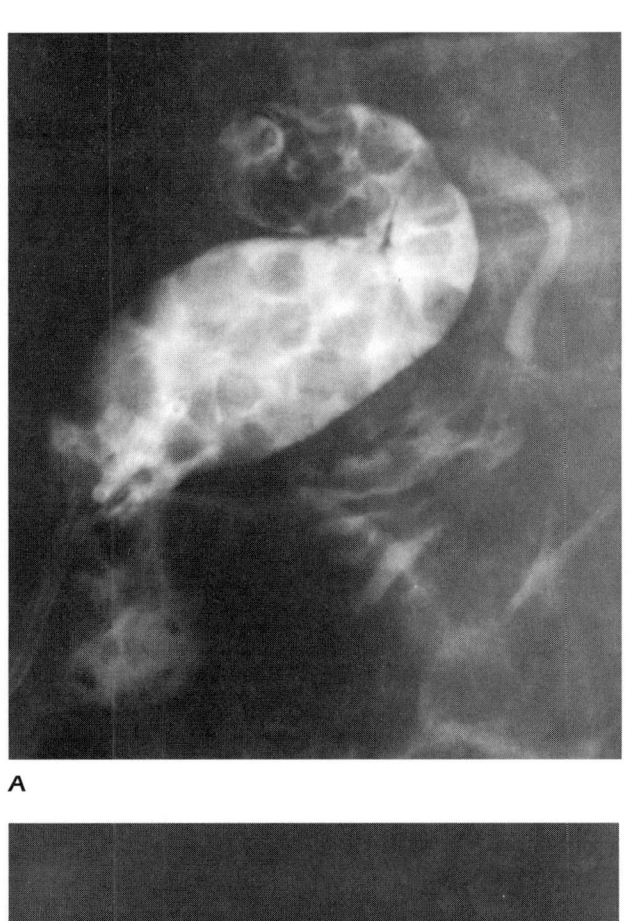

A

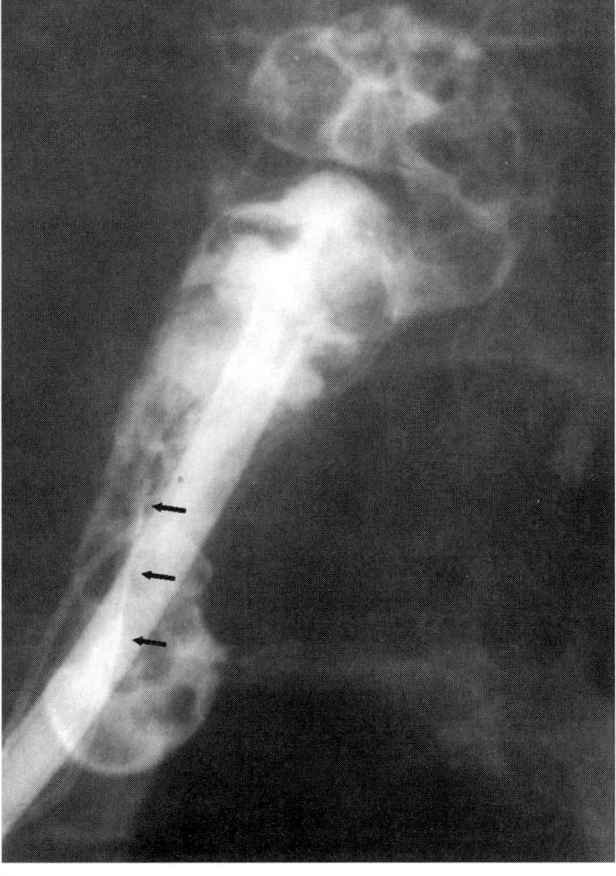

B

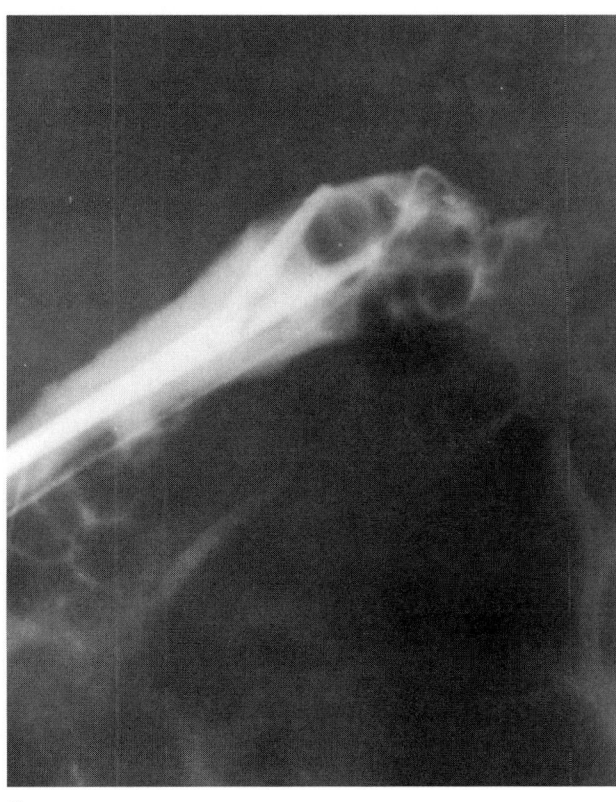

C

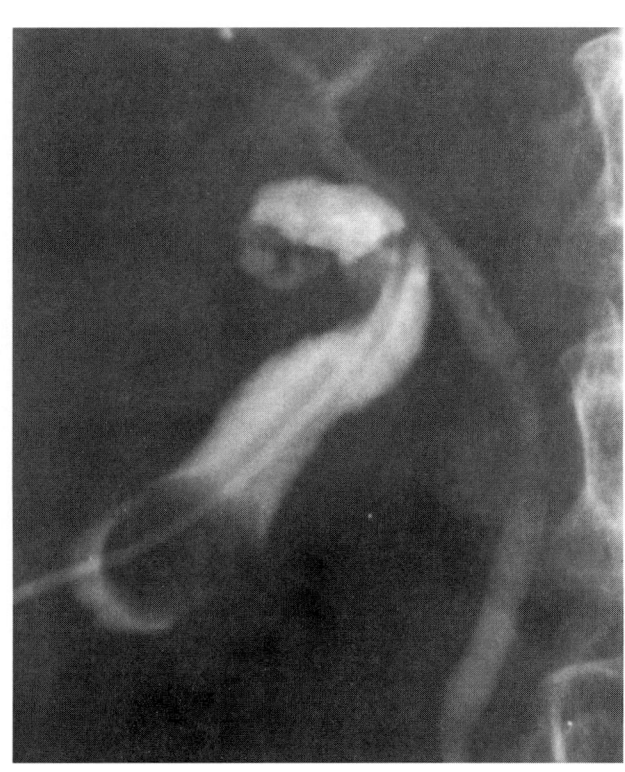

D

floating gallbladders hanging from a mesenteric attachment. This problem can be easily overcome by inserting a removable T anchor (Cook, Inc.) through the initial cholecystostomy needle into the lumen of the gallbladder. This device is used to retract and stabilize the gallbladder against the abdominal wall in order to minimize invagination and bile spillage during the cholecystostomy dilatation process.[50] A transitionless introducer sheath (Cook, Inc.) greatly facilitates entry into such a fibrotic gallbladder because of its stepless profile.[51] It is important to keep the gallbladder slightly distended with fluid during dilatation. A safety wire should be inserted in the tract outside the sheath and advanced to the neck of the gallbladder. In addition, a 5 French catheter or locking-loop catheter can be inserted in parallel through a separate puncture to function as an irrigation port for opacifying the gallbladder, for directing calculi toward the basket, or for flushing stone fragments out through the large cannula.

Once a large cholecystostomy tract has been established, the operator can choose a wide variety of instruments for stone extraction. The most useful are Dormia baskets, nitinol baskets with an instrument channel (Cook, Inc.),[52] the Sohendra kit (Cook, Inc.), and crushing and triradiate forceps. Large stones over 15 mm are best broken up by EHL, ultrasound, or laser lithotripsy. Stone fragments and small calculi can be flushed out by irrigation or extracted with 16 to 20 French Malecot catheters, which are repeatedly passed in and out of the gallbladder with suction. A 16 to 18 French Foley catheter is then inserted into the gallbladder for gravity drainage. The next day, the patient is reevaluated with cholangiography and cholecystoscopy for the extraction of any residual stones from the gallbladder, cystic duct, or common bile duct. Small movable stones that have migrated into the cystic duct are usually simple to extract with small baskets, balloons, or flexible snares. The management of larger stones, which may be impacted in the cystic duct, can be difficult because of the tortuosity and narrow caliber of the duct, which prevents the insertion of rigid forceps and the natural expansion of baskets. The cystic duct is first catheterized and the stone bypassed with the combination of a catheter and a hydromer nitinol guidewire. This will allow the insertion of an extra stiff guidewire within a 7 French catheter, which will cause straightening of the cystic duct and simplify the insertion of instruments. If the duct can be dilated sufficiently to insert a small flexible endoscope, the stone can be pulverized with EHL (Fig. 31-9).

If the T anchor has been used, it should be removed at this time because it may be harder to extract after 10 to 20 days because of tissue ingrowth.[44] The patients are discharged on average in 1 to 3 days after stone extraction or over a longer period, depending on the need for further treatment of their coexisting diseases. The Foley catheter is allowed to drain externally to a bag for 10 to 15 days and then clamped for a week. If, after clamping, there is leakage of bile around the drain indicating delayed cholecystostomy tract formation or common bile duct obstruction, the drain is kept on external drainage for another 1 to 2 weeks, and the test clamping cycle is repeated until tube occlusion is tolerated. It is not uncommon for elderly patients, and especially those who have serious coexisting diseases or are receiving immunosuppressive drugs, to form peritoneal tracts, which can take 1 to 3 months to mature. The patients are reevaluated with both cholangiography and endoscopy at 3 weeks. It is important to endoscope the gallbladder at this time to rule out small retained stones, which can be easily overlooked by cholangiography.[44,48] If there is continued leakage around the Foley catheter, it is important to rule out common bile duct obstruction by stones or papillary stenosis. Both of these conditions can be treated through the cystic duct with balloon catheters, as previously described in the section on choledocholithotomy. Drain catheters can usually be removed between 2 and 4 weeks if a "tractogram" shows no intraperitoneal leakage.

Patients are subsequently followed at regular intervals for stone recurrence both clinically and by ultrasonography. Some are placed on oral ursodeoxycholic acid therapy for several months with the idea that this may dissolve residual cholesterol particles, which could act as foci for recurrent stones.[48,53]

Gallstone Dissolution Therapy

As previously mentioned, two contact solvents have been clinically used for gallstone therapy. Monooctanoin is a relatively poor cholesterol solvent that is rarely used because it requires long-term infusion. It may be useful, however, for softening or dissolving small stones impacted in the cystic duct. Methyl *tert*-butyl ether (MTBE),[54] unlike diethyl ether, is liquid at body temperature and is 50 times more potent than monooctanoin. It can dissolve pure cholesterol stones, irrespective of size and number, usually within a day. Larger stones of more uncertain composition may take 2 to 3 days to completely or partially dissolve. The administration of MTBE is safe if it can be confined within the lumen of the gallbladder. Local extravasation along the tube tract can cause peritonitis or liver necrosis. If it reaches the duodenum in sufficient quantities, it can cause erosions with gastrointestinal bleeding, and its absorption into the bloodstream can lead

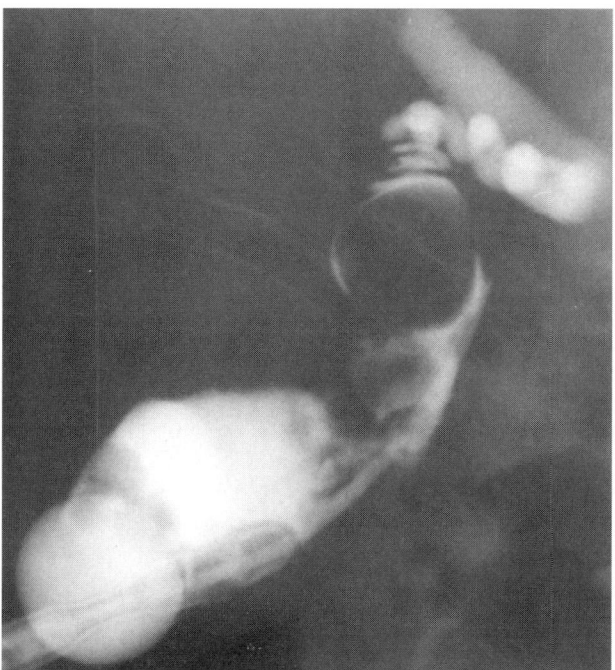

A

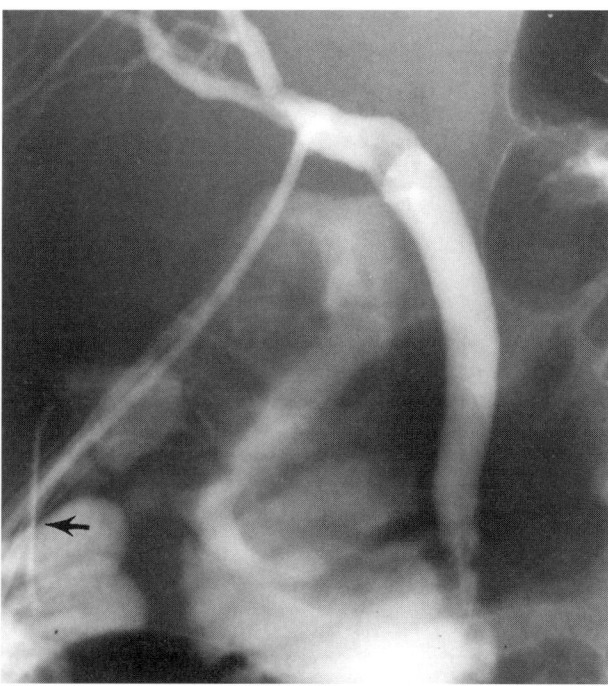

B

Figure 31-9. Removal of impacted infundibular stone. (A) This elderly patient was admitted for acute calculous cholecystitis. After 2 weeks of percutaneous external drainage, about 20 calculi were extracted from the gallbladder. Because of the excessive angulation of the gallbladder, the infundibular stone could not be brought into view endoscopi-

cally. (B) After transcystic catheterization of the common bile duct, the gallbladder axis was straightened with an extra stiff guidewire. The stone could now be easily endoscoped and fragmented with EHL. Note the retaining gallbladder anchor (*arrow*).

to untoward sedation and hemolysis. Although contact stone dissolution with MTBE is generally safe and effective, it requires careful monitoring over many hours, it is operator-dependent, and it may need supplemental basketing for extraction of insoluble residues.[55] MTBE is not approved for general use by the FDA and can only be administered to patients on a compassionate basis. Litholysis is only occasionally performed in complex problems when it is required to replace or complement more standard percutaneous gallbladder procedures.

Gallbladder ESWL

The best stone fragmentation and clearance rates with ESWL of the gallbladder have been obtained in patients bearing small volumes of noncalcified stones and with adjuvant ursodeoxycholic acid administration. A 95 percent clearance rate can be reached with solitary stones under 20 mm in diameter. However, the overall stone clearance rate reached under protocol in the United States has been disappointing, having ranged from 20 to 50 percent at 6 months. ESWL is contraindicated in patients with nonfunctioning gallbladders.

Because of this low efficacy, ESWL of the gallbladder is no longer used as a primary treatment. In those institutions with facilities for kidney stone ESWL, this equipment can be used as an adjuvant for breaking up large gallbladder or cystic duct stones that cannot be extracted by conventional PCCL techniques.

Results

Because of the advent and success of laparoscopic cholecystectomy (LC) in replacing noninvasive or percutaneous gallstone extraction, the greatest activity and experience with PCCL have occurred from 1985 to 1992. Only three PCCL series of over 50 patients have been published.[40,46,48] With such a small pool of study patients available, it is difficult to evaluate the efficacy of this procedure, for it has a 10- to 20-patient "learning curve," which includes not only early complications but also attempts to extract stones with a poor chance of success. The rate of failure or difficulty in accessing the gallbladder with a large introduction sheath could be as high as 27 percent in early studies[49] but varied only between 3 and 7 percent in the larger series.[38,40,42,43,46,48] Catheterization of the gallbladder, when it was successful, led to an immediate stone clearance rate of over 90 percent. The causes of post-PCCL retained stones were due to inadequate endoscopic inspection before the cholecystostomy drain was removed,[38,44] either because the stones could not be extracted from difficult positions within the cystic duct, or because they were too large to break up. It should be emphasized that small retained stones can easily be missed on cholecystography. At the author's institution it was difficult to fully inspect the fundus of the gallbladder by rigid endoscopy; as a result, calculi were missed. Since flexible endoscopy has been used to scan the whole gallbladder at the time of the final cholecystostomy drain removal, there has been no such problem.[53]

The PCCL morbidity has been 9 to 12 percent in the largest series and proportionately higher in studies involving less than 20 patients because of inexperience. The types of complications seen were related to (1) the use of general anesthesia (myocardial infarction, respiratory problems, ileus, deep venous thrombosis)[47]; (2) failure to use atropine (vaso-vagal reaction)[44]; (3) cholecystostomy technique (inability to fully dilate cholecystostomy tract, with resulting peritonitis,[40,46,49] colon puncture with fistula,[46,47] or hepatic or gallbladder hemorrhage[55a]); (4) problems during stone extraction (loss of tract, gallbladder wall perforation, missed retained calculi requiring a second procedure or surgery)[42,43,48]; and (5) post-PCCL bile leakage (immature peritoneal tract, subphrenic collection, leaky transhepatic tract).[40,46,48] Except for problems involving loss of or unsuccessful access to the gallbladder, which necessitated emergency cholecystectomy, most complications were easily resolved by conservative management with antibiotics, fluid replacement, supplemental peritoneal drainage, or recatheterization of the gallbladder. It should be noted, therefore, that, although the incidence of complications involving PCCL can be as high as 10 to 15 percent, most of these are minor and usually occur during the initial learning period. It is important to note that none of these complications, in contrast to LC, are associated with bile duct laceration. Picus et al.[40] found the 30-day mortality to be 3 percent, mostly because of severe coexisting illnesses. One death directly related to PCCL was described in a debilitated patient on steroids who succumbed after laparotomy for unsuspected transhepatic tract bile leak 3 days after removal of the cholecystostomy drain, which had been in place for 29 days.

The main objection to PCCL has to do with failure to remove a diseased organ that may be subject to stone recurrence[56] and a low incidence of carcinoma.[57] Data on long-term stone recurrence are available from series of subjects who have had surgical cholecystoli-

thotomy[58,59] or who were observed after clearance of gallstones following oral bile administration. Reports of gallstone recurrence range widely from 20 to 50 percent over 2 to 20 years.[58,59] In the widely quoted Villanova et al. study,[60] over 50 percent of patients were found to be free of recurrence at 5 years, and 30 percent had remained stone-free by the 11-year observation point.

When PCCL was introduced, it was hoped that the minimal procedural trauma to the gallbladder, combined with endoscopic stone clearance and adjuvant ursodeoxycholic acid therapy, would lead to markedly delayed stone recurrence. It was found, however, on the basis of two studies,[38,53] that retained stone fragments could be missed by rigid endoscopy and that ursodeoxycholic acid did not, as predicted by Villanova, prevent stone formation in the older age group being treated.[53] If the incidence of retained stones was discounted because of potentially remediable endoscopic techniques, these authors found a recurrent stone incidence of about 4 and 22 percent over a mean period of 14 months and 26 months, respectively. In the group described by McDermott et al.,[53] 25 percent died of unrelated causes during the 3-year period of observation. Subjects with recurrent stones had normal gallbladder ejection fractions and were generally asymptomatic. Among the three patients who had recurrent right upper quadrant pain, only one had recurrent calculi. These results suggest that recurrent gallstones appear in the second and third year after PCCL and do not cause any significant problems—an important conclusion that favors the use of this safe procedure in patients who are at high risk, elderly, or with limited life expectancy.

Although the morbidity rates for open and laparoscopic cholecystectomy have been found to be approximately the same, the incidence of significant bile duct complications associated with LC has been much more frequent and often serious enough to require complex biliary-enteric anastomoses.[61] LC may be poorly tolerated in patients who are morbidly obese, elderly, debilitated, or ill with severe cardiopulmonary disease. In such patients pneumoperitoneum and general anesthesia can lead to acute pulmonary and cardiac complications that may be difficult to manage. Unanticipated laparotomy may be likewise poorly tolerated in the 5 percent of patients who have to be converted to open cholecystectomy because of interventional endoscopic difficulties or the presence of profuse intraabdominal adhesions.[62] Unlike LC, PCCL can be performed without general anesthesia and is not associated with any serious bile duct injuries. In experienced hands, PCCL is a safe, efficacious procedure for extracting stones from the gallbladder, cystic duct, and common bile duct.

A gallbladder-sparing procedure has further advantages: (1) it is safe to perform in high-risk patients; (2) it can be repeated for recurrent symptomatic stones; (3) it preserves the gallbladder if the diagnosis of acute cholelithiasis is in error; (4) stones when they recur are usually asymptomatic; (5) gallbladder function is retained or improved after PCCL; and (6) cholecystectomy can be performed at a later date if necessary, when the patient is a better operative risk. For all these reasons, PCCL remains an excellent therapeutic option for managing symptomatic gallstone disease in elderly and critically ill patients with a limited life expectancy.

References

1. Way LW, Pelligrini CA, eds. Surgery of the gallbladder and bile ducts. Philadelphia: Saunders, 1987.
2. Diehl AK, Sugarek NJ, Todd KH. Clinical evaluation for gallstone disease: usefulness of symptoms and signs of diagnosis. Am J Med 1990;89:29–33.
3. Gracie WA, Ransohoff DF. The natural history of silent gallstones. N Engl J Med 1982;307:798–800.
4. Trotman BW, Petrella EJ, Soloway RD, et al. Evaluation of radiographic lucency or opaqueness of gallstones as a means of identifying cholesterol or pigment stones. Gastroenterology 1975;68:1563–1566.
5. Binmoeller KF, Bruckner M, Thonke F, et al. Treatment of difficult bile duct stones using mechanical, electrohydraulic, and extracorporeal shock wave lithotripsy. Endoscopy 1993; 25:201–206.
6. Harshfield DL, Teplick SK, Brandon JC. Pain control during interventional biliary procedures: epidural anesthesia vs IV sedation. AJR 1993;161:1057–1059.
7. Mazzariello R. Review of 220 cases of residual bile calculi treated without reoperation: an eight-year study. Surgery 1973; 73:299–330.
7a. Bean WJ, Mahorner H. Removal of residual stones through the T-tube tract. South Med J 1972;65:377–378.
8. Burhenne HJ. The history of interventional radiology of the biliary tract. Radiol Clin North Am 1990;28:1139–1144.
9. Madden JL. Common duct stones: their origin and surgical management. Surg Clin North Am 1973;53:1095–1100.
10. Guelrud MS, Mendoza S, Viera L. Does somatostatin prevent acute pancreatitis after pancreatic duct sphincter hydrostatic balloon dilatation? Gastrointest Endosc 1987;33:148–151.
11. Berkman WA, Bishop AF, Palagallo GL, et al. Percutaneous dilatation of the distal common bile duct and ampulla of Vater for removal of calculi. Radiology 1988;167:453–455.
12. Savader SJ, Venbrux AC, Robbins AK, et al. Pancreatic response to percutaneous biliary drainage: a prospective study. Radiology 1991;178:343–346.
13. Meranze SG, Stein EJ, Burke DR, et al. Removal of common bile duct stones with angiographic occlusion balloons. AJR 1986;146:383–385.
14. Cope C, Gensburg RS. Drainage of bile ducts with an articulated T-tube. J Vasc Intervent Radiol 1990;1:113–116.
15. Burhenne HJ. Percutaneous extraction of retained biliary tract stones: 661 patients. AJR 1980;134:888–898.
16. Choi BI, Han JK, Han MC. Percutaneous removal of retained intrahepatic stones utilizing a combination of techniques with emphasis on a preshaped angulated catheter: review of 170 patients. Eur J Radiol 1992;2:199–203.
17. Jeng KS, Yang FS, Ohta I, et al. Dilatation of intrahepatic strictures in patients with hepatolithiasis. World J Surg 1990;14: 587–593.
18. Pitt HA, Venbrux AC, Coleman JA, et al. Intrahepatic stones: the transhepatic team approach. Ann Surg 1994;219:527–537.
19. Cotton PB. Endoscopic management of bile duct stones (apples and oranges). Gut 1984;25:587–597.
20. Maroney TP, Ring EJ. Percutaneous transjejunal catheterization of Roux-en-Y biliary-jejunal anastomoses. Radiology 1987;164:151–153.
21. Fan ST, Mok F, Zheng SS, et al. Appraisal of hepaticocutaneous jejunostomy in the management of hepatolithiasis. Am J Surg 1993;165:332–335.
22. Citron SJ, Martin LG. Benign biliary strictures: treatment with percutaneous cholangioplasty. 1991;178:339–341.
23. Gibson RN, Adam A, Yeung E, et al. Percutaneous techniques in benign hilar and intrahepatic strictures. J Intervent Radiol 1988;3:125–130.
24. Rossi P, Salvatori FM, Bezzi M, et al. Percutaneous management of benign biliary strictures with balloon dilation and self-expanding metallic stents. Cardiovasc Intervent Radiol 1990; 13:231–239.
25. Haskin P, Teplick SK. Percutaneous management of biliary stones. Semin Intervent Radiol 1985;2:81–96.
26. Hine LK, Arrowsmith JB, Gallo-Torres HE. Monooctanoin-associated pulmonary edema. Am J Gastroenterol 1988;83: 1128–1131.
27. Picus D. Intracorporeal biliary lithotripsy. Radiol Clin North Am 1990;28:1241–1249.
28. Sauerbruch T, Stern M, and the Study Group for Shock Wave Lithotripsy of Bile Duct Stones. Fragmentation of bile duct stones by extracorporeal shock waves: a new approach to biliary calculi after failure of routine endoscopic measures. Gastroenterology 1989;96:146–152.
29. Hwang MH, Tsai CC, Mo LR, et al. Percutaneous choledochoscopic biliary tract stone removal: experience in 645 consecutive patients. Eur J Radiol 1993;17:184–190.
30. Venbrux AC, Robbins KV, Savader SJ, et al. Endoscopy as an adjuvant to biliary radiologic intervention. Radiology 1991; 180:355–361.
31. Cope C. Needle endoscopy in special procedures. Radiology 1988;168:353–358.
32. Maetani I, Hoshi H, Ohashi S, et al. Cholangioscopic extraction of intrahepatic stones associated with biliary strictures using a rendezvous technique. Endoscopy 1993;25:303–306.
33. Clements WD, Diamond T, McCrory DC, et al. Biliary drainage in obstructive jaundice: experimental and clinical aspects. Br J Surg 1993;80:834–842.
34. Yee ACN, Ho C. Complications of percutaneous biliary drainage: benign vs malignant diseases. AJR 1987;148:1207–1209.
35. Gandini G, Righi D, Regge D, et al. Percutaneous removal of bile stones. Cardiovasc Intervent Radiol 1990;13:245–251.
36. Fache JS. Transcholecystic intervention. Radiol Clin North Am 1990;28:1157–1169.
37. Airan M, Appel M, Berci G, et al. Retrospective and prospective multi-institutional laparoscopic cholecystectomy study organized by the Society of American Gastrointestinal Endoscopic Surgeons. Surg Endosc 1992;6:169–178.
38. Cheslyn-Curtis S, Gillams AR, Russell RCG, et al. Selection, management, and early outcome of 113 patients with symptomatic gallstones treated by percutaneous cholecystolithotomy. Gut 1992;33:1253–1259.
39. Savader SJ, Trerotola SO, Merine DS, et al. Hemobilia after percutaneous transhepatic biliary drainage: treatment with transcatheter embolotherapy. J Vasc Intervent Radiol 1992;3: 345–352.
40. Picus D, Hicks ME, Darcy MD, et al. Percutaneous cholecystolithotomy: analysis of results and complications in 58 consecutive patients. Radiology 1992;183:779–784.
41. Kerlan RK, LaBerge JM, Ring EJ. Percutaneous cholecystolithotomy: preliminary experience. Radiology 1985;157:653–656.
42. Akiyama H, Okazaki T, Takashima I, et al. Percutaneous treatments for biliary diseases. Radiology 1990;176:25–30.
43. Hruby W, Stackl W, Urban M, et al. Percutaneous endoscopic

cholecystolithotripsy: work in progress. Radiology 1989;173: 477–479.

44. Cope C, Burke DR, Meranze SG. Percutaneous extraction of gallstones in 20 patients. Radiology 1990;176:19–24.
45. Griffith DP, Gleeson MJ, Appel MF, et al. Percutaneous chole-cystolithotomy: a minimally invasive alternative to cholecystec-tomy and to shock wave lithotripsy. Arch Surg 1990;125: 1114–1118.
46. Chiverton SG, Inglis JA, Hudd C, et al. Percutaneous cholecys-tostomy: the first 60 patients. Br Med J 1990:300:1310–1312.
47. van Heerden JA, Segura JW, LeRoy AJ, et al. Early experience with percutaneous cholecystostomy. Mayo Clin Proc 1991;66: 1005–1009.
48. Gillams A, Curtis SC, Donald J, et al. Technical considerations in 113 percutaneous cholecystolithotomies. Radiology 1992; 183:163–166.
49. Hwang MH, Mo LR, Chen GD, et al. Percutaneous transhe-patic cholecystic ultrasonic lithotripsy. Gastrointest Endosc 1987;33:301–302.
50. Cope C. Percutaneous subhepatic cholecystostomy with re-movable anchor. AJR 1988;151:1129–1132.
51. Cope C. Improved catheter introducer with recessed sheath. AJR 1989;152:1346–1347.
52. Cope C. Novel nitinol basket instrument for percutaneous cho-lecystolithotomy. AJR 1990;155:515–516.
53. McDermott VG, Arger P, Cope C. Gallstone recurrence and gallbladder function following percutaneous cholecystoli-thotomy. J Vasc Intervent Radiol 1994;5:473–478.
54. Thistle JL, May GR, Bender CE, et al. Dissolution of choles-terol gallbladder stones by methyl tert-butyl ether administered by percutaneous transhepatic catheter. N Engl J Med 1989; 320:633–639.

55. van Sonnenberg E, Casola G, Varney RP, et al. Gallbladder and bile duct stones: percutaneous therapy with primary MTBE dissolution and mechanical methods. Radiology 1988;169: 505–509.
55a. Larsen TB, Gothlin JH, Jensen D, et al. Ultrasonically and flu-oroscopically guided therapeutic percutaneous catheter drain-age of the gallbladder. Gastrointest Radiol 1988;13:37–40.
56. Bass EB, Steinberg EP, Pitt HA, et al. Cost-effectiveness of ex-tracorporeal shock-wave lithotripsy versus cholecystectomy for symptomatic gallstones. Gastroenterology 1991;101:189–199.
57. So CB, Gibney RG, Scudamore CH. Carcinoma of the gall-bladder: a risk associated with gallbladder-preserving treat-ments for cholelithiasis. Radiology 1990;174:127–130.
58. Norrby S, Shonebeck J. Long-term results with cholecystoli-thotomy. Acta Chir Scand 1970;136:711–713.
59. Gibney RG, Chow K, So CB, et al. Gallstone recurrence after cholecystostomy. AJR 1989;153:287–289.
60. Villanova N, Bazzoli F, Taroni F, et al. Gallstone recurrence after successful oral bile acid treatment. Gastroenterology 1989;97:726–731.
61. Keith RG. Is the increasing frequency of laparoscopic bile duct injury justifiable? Can J Surg 1993;36:501–502.
62. Deziel DJ, Millikan KW, Economou SG, et al. Complications of laparoscopic cholecystectomy: a national survey of 4,292 hospitals and an analysis of 77,604 cases. Am J Surg 1993;165: 9–14.

32

Liver Transplantation: Associated Interventions

ALBERT B. ZAJKO
PHILIP D. ORONS

The past 15 years have seen improvements in graft preservation, surgical techniques, immunosuppression therapy, and postoperative care of liver transplant patients. During this time period, 5-year survival rates have increased from 20 to over 70 percent. Accordingly, liver transplantation has become a well-accepted treatment for many patients with irreversible end-stage liver disease. However, hepatic transplantation remains a highly complex surgical procedure that can be associated with technical complications in 30 to 35 percent of patients.[1–12] Technical complications related to the surgical anastomoses involved in biliary tract and vascular reconstructions contribute to the morbidity and mortality of the liver transplant recipient. Early diagnosis and treatment of posttransplantation complications are crucial for patient survival and graft salvage. The mainstay of therapy has traditionally been surgical intervention. However, in recent years, nonsurgical management using interventional radiologic techniques has increasingly been applied, obviating surgery in many cases.[13–27]

For clinically suspected posttransplant biliary and vascular complications, cholangiography and angiography are the definitive diagnostic imaging modalities. In many cases, sonographic screening is employed in patients with nonspecific symptoms and/or elevated liver enzyme levels. In general, sonography is more useful for detecting vascular complications than for detecting biliary problems, especially strictures. In the latter, biliary dilatation is often not present. For this reason, transhepatic cholangiography is often performed in transplant patients with a negative sonogram of the biliary tree, especially if the clinical suspicion of a biliary complication is high.[28] Once a definitive diagnosis is established, the best approach for treatment, surgical or nonsurgical, can be chosen. This chapter reviews the role of nonsurgical interventional techniques in the management of posttransplantation vascular and biliary complications.

Arterial and Venous Reconstruction of the Liver Allograft

Orthotopic liver transplantation generally requires one arterial and three venous anastomoses: one for the portal vein and two for the inferior vena cava (IVC). Additional arterial and/or venous anastomoses (such as with the use of grafts) are occasionally required in cases of complex vascular reconstruction.

Several methods are available for arterial revascularization, depending on the allograft hepatic arterial anatomy. An anomalous recipient hepatic arterial circulation is of little consequence because a vascular interposition graft can be used if a recipient vessel of sufficient caliber is not available to permit adequate arterial flow to the allograft liver.[29] In the donor liver, the celiac axis gives rise to the entire arterial supply in approximately 75 to 80 percent of cases, including those cases in which the left hepatic artery arises wholly or in part from the left gastric artery. In all such cases, the allograft celiac axis with a small aortic patch (Carrel patch) is anastomosed end to end to the recipient hepatic artery.[29] A larger anastomotic lumen can be fashioned if reconstruction is performed at the level of the origin of the recipient gastroduodenal artery. As mentioned previously, if the recipient hepatic artery is not adequate for flow for any reason, a vascular graft using the donor iliac artery is used.[29–31] The proximal anastomosis of the vascular homograft is to the infrarenal aorta, and the distal anastomosis is to the donor celiac axis or common hepatic artery.

Revascularization of an allograft with an anomalous arterial supply requires special consideration. The most commonly encountered anomaly is a right hepatic artery arising from the superior mesenteric artery. In such cases, a single arterial trunk is always created for anastomosis to the recipient. A frequently used method utilizes the splenic artery stump of the donor

509

for anastomosis to the divided end of the right hepatic artery. This method permits a single end-to-end anastomosis to be performed between the allograft celiac axis and the recipient hepatic artery.

In pediatric liver transplantation, direct end-to-end arterial anastomoses (as in adults) are performed when technically possible. If difficulties are encountered, iliac artery vascular grafts are used for rearterialization.

Portal venous revascularization is most often accomplished via an end to end anastomosis between recipient and donor extrahepatic portal veins. If the recipient portal vein is too small or occluded, then the superior mesenteric vein is used. In such cases, a segment of the donor common iliac vein is used as a jump graft between the recipient infrapancreatic superior mesenteric vein (end to side) and the allograft portal vein (end to end).[32]

Reconstruction of the IVC (in patients without anomalies or occlusion) consists of end-to-end anastomoses of the supra- and infrahepatic caval segments of the recipient to their respective allograft counterparts. In small children (those weighing less than 15 kg) or in cases where there is a large discrepancy between the donor and recipient IVC, the IVC anastomosis is often formed in a "piggyback" fashion. The donor infrahepatic IVC is ligated and the recipient hepatic veins are interconnected to form a cloaca. This cloaca or common funnel is then anastomosed to the donor suprahepatic IVC.

Hepatic Artery Complications and Interventions

Technical complications related to rearterialization are a major clinical concern because of possible graft loss and patient mortality.[5–12,33–41] Such complications include hepatic artery stenosis, thrombosis, false aneurysm, and rupture.

Hepatic artery stenosis is a serious posttransplant complication that can cause graft ischemia and dysfunction and that can lead to secondary complications such as hepatic infarction, biloma, abscess, and nonanastomotic biliary strictures. If untreated, stenosis can progress to thrombosis, with subsequent allograft failure and loss.

The authors have recently reported the clinical and cholangiographic findings in 33 patients with angiographically proven hepatic artery stenosis compared with a control group of 58 patients with patent hepatic arteries. Biliary complications were significantly more prevalent in the patients with hepatic artery stenosis with cholangiographic abnormalities present in over 60 percent of cases. The most common biliary abnormality seen was intrahepatic stricture formation, with a prevalence of 42 percent. Bile duct necrosis, although frequently seen in association with hepatic artery thrombosis, was not seen with stenosis alone.[42]

Results of the authors' experience, as well as that of others, revealed an 11 to 13 percent prevalence of hepatic artery stenosis.[6,7] However, with the recent advances in duplex and color Doppler sonography, the prevalence of this complication is considerably higher. Whereas previously, in the authors' experience, most such cases were incidentally detected during angiographic evaluation in patients with suspected thrombosis, hepatic artery stenosis is now initially detected during routine early postoperative sonographic screening and evaluation of patients with graft dysfunction.[43] Presumably, many previously diagnosed cases of thrombosis probably resulted from an undetected underlying significant stenosis.

If a significant hepatic arterial stenosis is identified, treatment options are based on clinical presentation, time of diagnosis, and allograft function. Because of the possible secondary complications due to arterial stenosis, the authors have generally treated most such patients with percutaneous transluminal angioplasty (PTA) (Fig. 32-1). They have recently reported their experience with PTA in a series of 21 allografts.[44] PTA was successful in restoring a normal or near normal lumen in 17 of the allografts, with long-term allograft survival significantly greater in the successful group than those in whom PTA was unsuccessful. However, if significant arterial stenosis is identified, timely intervention is important. Long-term clinical success in these patients appeared to be most meaningfully related to allograft function at time of presentation for PTA. Those with poor allograft function at presentation (based on liver enzyme levels) were much more likely to require eventual retransplantation, regardless of the success or failure of PTA.

Although hepatic artery PTA is generally a safe procedure, the authors have experienced two significant complications, one of which resulted in eventual allograft loss. An extensive hepatic artery dissection occurred during PTA with delayed formation of a large pseudoaneurysm, incidentally detected by ultrasound 14 months later. The aneurysm could not be surgically repaired. Although the patient was asymptomatic, the suspected danger of eventual aneurysm rupture necessitated retransplantation.[45] A second patient developed an arterial leak adjacent to the angioplasty site requiring surgical repair with good result.[44]

Several other authors have also reported their results with hepatic artery PTA, but experience to date has been limited to several case reports.[14–16,41] Cas-

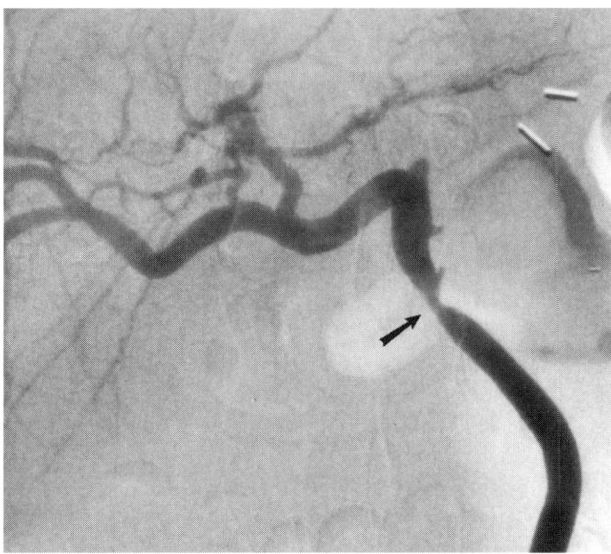

A

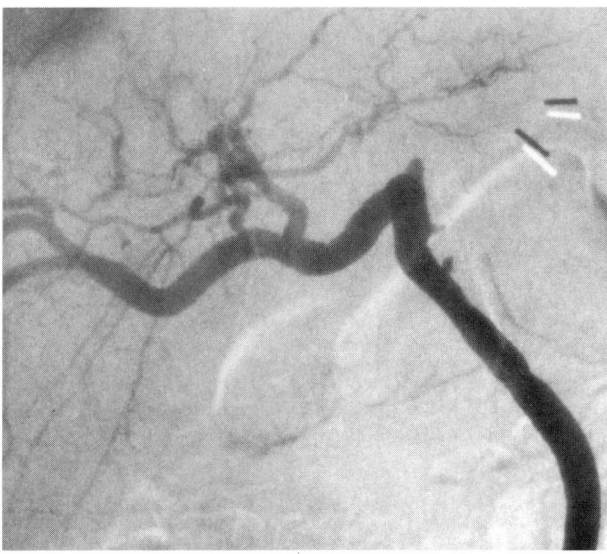

B

Figure 32-1. Hepatic artery angioplasty. (A) Marked stenosis of the hepatic artery anastomosis (*arrow*) is demonstrated on a selective graft arteriogram. In this patient, rearterializa-tion was performed using a donor iliac artery graft between the recipient abdominal aorta and the allograft celiac axis. (B) After PTA, the anastomosis is widely patent.

taneda et al.[14] reported successful PTA in a pediatric patient that resulted in resolution of hepatic infarction and return of liver function to normal. Six-month follow-up demonstrated arterial patency. Abad et al.[15] also reported successful hepatic artery PTA in two cases. The authors have observed recurrent stenosis of the hepatic artery following initially successful PTA, and others have had a similar experience. Two cases of recurrent stenosis (less than 6 months) reported by Raby et al.[16] were successfully redilated with favorable results. As postulated by those authors, perhaps such stenoses respond to PTA in a similar manner as to some cases of renal allograft arterial stenosis. Repeat PTA may result in improved long-term patency.

Hepatic artery thrombosis, reported to occur in 4 to 25 percent of transplant recipients, is a potentially devastating complication.[6,9,10,33,36,37,39,46] Most cases occur within the first 2 months postoperatively; retransplantation is usually required for survival.[6] Thrombosis occurs more commonly in small pediatric patients, probably because of the small arterial size and the technical difficulty of performing the anastomosis.[46]

In the early 1980s, almost all patients underwent repeat retransplantation for hepatic artery thrombosis. Today, the decision to retransplant is based on clinical presentation and synthetic function. Many patients, especially children, have survived without retransplantation. Others have advocated emergent rearterialization to avoid retransplant or to serve as a "bridge" until a suitable donor is available.[38,47,48] The question often asked is, should this complication be treated with thrombolytic therapy? The authors have rarely attempted such treatment,[13] but without clinical success (Fig. 32-2). They are aware of only one report, by Hidalgo et al.,[49] of two successfully treated cases, one of which was a thrombotic complication of PTA. It is the present authors' opinion that, in most cases, thrombolytic therapy for thrombosis of the hepatic artery is not indicated, but it should be considered in selected cases, such as very recent thrombosis, thrombus complicating PTA, and possibly in patients who are not retransplant candidates. In most patients, once the diagnosis is made, hepatic infarction and secondary complications resulting from biliary ischemia are highly likely to develop. The hepatic artery is an end-artery to the allograft liver because all potential arterial collaterals that exist in the peritoneal attachments to the liver have been severed at transplantation. With the allograft biliary tree entirely dependent on the hepatic artery, thrombosis is likely to result in an ischemic biliary problem. Indeed, a study from the authors' institution showed that 84 percent of patients with hepatic artery occlusion had abnormal cholangiographic studies.[34] Cholangiographic abnormalities included nonanastomotic biliary strictures and bile leaks. Hepatic infarction and/or abscesses may also occur.

Despite the complete transection of all potential collateral pathways at recipient hepatectomy, the authors have angiographically observed collateral vessels to the allograft liver in patients with hepatic artery occlusion.[6,41] Such vessels have also been observed at operation in patients undergoing retransplantation for

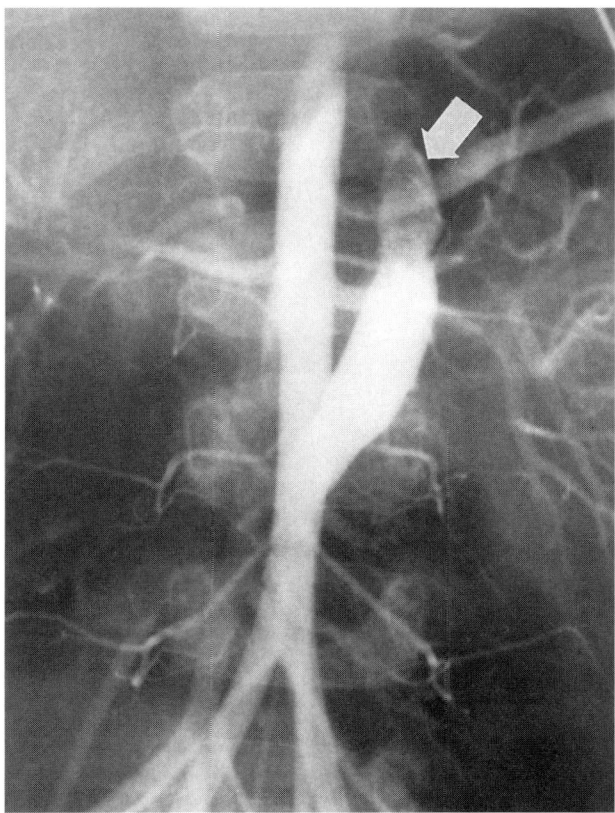

A

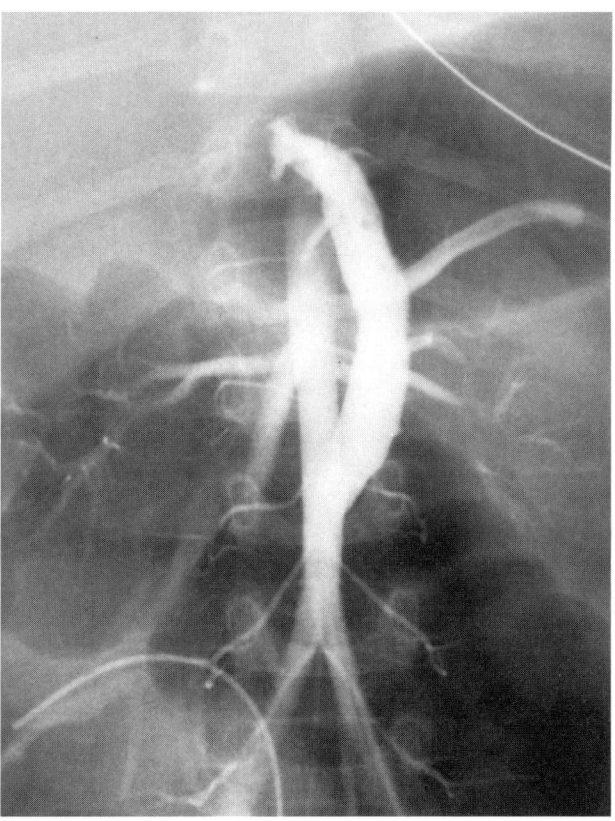

B

Figure 32-2. Attempted thrombolytic therapy for hepatic artery thrombosis. (A) Thrombosis of an aortic graft (*arrow*) is demonstrated on an abdominal aortogram. This patient's intrahepatic arterial tree was patent and filled via collateral vessels via the superior mesenteric artery. (B) After urokinase infusion, the aortic homograft is patent; however, direct flow into the allograft hepatic artery was not established. The patient underwent retransplantation. (From Zajko AB, Bron KM, Orons PD. Vascular complications in liver transplant recipients: angiographic diagnosis and treatment. Semin Intervent Radiol 1992;9:270–282. Used with permission.)

hepatic artery occlusion. Because all potential collaterals have been previously severed, these vessels must arise de novo. The presence of these collaterals, however, does not necessarily protect the dearterialized liver from ischemic injury. In part, this is because it probably takes a considerable amount of time for such collateral circulation to develop. Because these vessels do not form early enough, and because of their collateral nature, they may not be effective in preventing either hepatic or bile ductular ischemic injury. Moreover, because these collaterals produce flow in the intrahepatic arterial tree, they are potentially a source for a false-negative diagnosis of hepatic artery occlusion by sonography.[50] The flow detected on duplex Doppler, however, is not normal but has a characteristic waveform similar to that observed in hepatic artery stenosis.

A pseudo- or false aneurysm of the hepatic artery anastomosis is a rare posttransplant complication. Such aneurysms are extrahepatic and are usually caused by infection or technical failure. Intrahepatic false an-

eurysms may occur following transhepatic interventions, including biopsy, cholangiography, and biliary drainage.[51,52] Rarely, false aneurysms have been seen at the ligated stump of the allograft gastroduodenal artery.[53] Early diagnosis and treatment are crucial to patient survival because of the potential for rupture and fatal hemorrhage. Rupture of the hepatic artery, associated with high patient mortality, has been reported to occur in less than 2 percent of transplants.[7,10,36–38]

The diagnosis of false aneurysm requires a high index of suspicion because many are asymptomatic and incidentally detected during imaging evaluation for other reasons.[35] They can also present with massive gastrointestinal tract bleeding, hemoperitoneum, or hemobilia. False aneurysms appear sonographically as spherical fluid collections that exhibit internal pulsatile flow on Doppler evaluation. To prevent possible hemorrhage, Doppler examination should be applied to all intrahepatic and periportal fluid collections detected

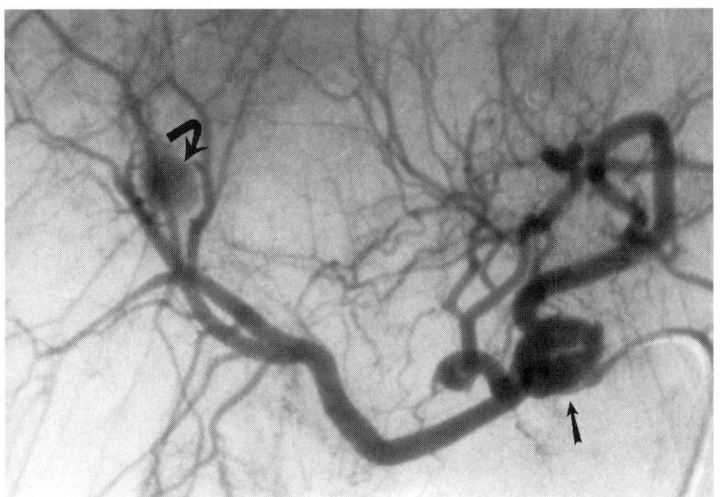

A

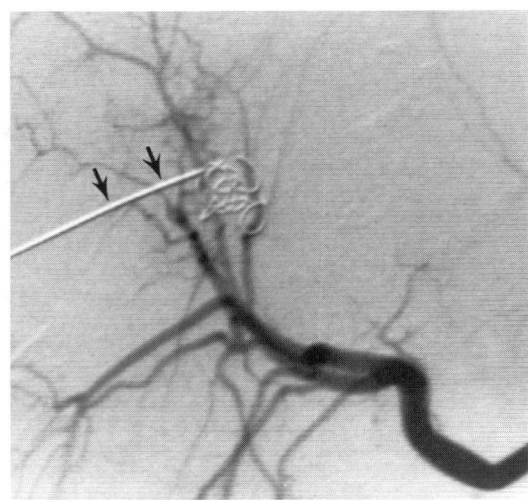

B

Figure 32-3. Direct percutaneous transhepatic embolization of intrahepatic pseudoaneurysm secondary to liver biopsy. (A) An intrahepatic pseudoaneurysm (*curved arrow*) is shown on a hepatic arteriogram in a transplant patient with two severe episodes of gastrointestinal tract bleeding due to hemobilia following biopsy. Because of the severe tortuosity of the proximal allograft hepatic artery (*arrow*), transarterial embolization was technically impossible, even with a coaxial Tracker catheter. (B) Using sonographic guidance, a 22-gauge needle (*arrows*) was inserted transhepatically into the pseudoaneurysm. Embolization with 0.018-inch microcoils and thrombin was performed. Postembolization arteriogram shows complete occlusion of the pseudoaneurysm with preservation of distal arterial flow. Bleeding stopped and the patient was doing well 1 year later. (From Zajko AB, Bron KM, Orons PD: Vascular complications in liver transplant recipients: angiographic diagnosis and treatment. Semin Intervent Radiol 1992;9:270–282. Used with permission.)

on gray scale sonography before diagnostic aspiration.[35]

For the most part, the treatment of posttransplant false aneurysms depends on their location. Transcatheter embolization techniques can usually be used for occluding intrahepatic false aneurysms.[51] However, a tortuous and redundant allograft hepatic artery may make transarterial embolization technically impossible, even with newer coaxial catheter techniques.[13] In such cases, embolization can be performed transhepatically using sonographic guidance to direct a skinny needle into the false aneurysm (Fig. 32-3). Extrahepatic false aneurysms are almost always treated surgically. In a few cases the authors have used hepatic artery embolization as a potentially lifesaving measure in patients with life-threatening bleeding who were not considered surgical candidates.

Venous Complications and Interventions

Venous complications involving the IVC or portal vein are unusual and include stenoses and thromboses.[5,16,19] Overall, such complications occur in less than 3 percent of transplant patients.[5,7,10,38] Stenosis almost always occurs at the donor-recipient anastomosis.

Portal Vein

Clinically, portal vein thrombosis or significant stenosis usually manifests with symptoms of portal hypertension, including variceal bleeding, splenomegaly, and massive ascites.[6] Pleural effusion and hepatic failure may also occur. Occasionally portal venous complications are diagnosed incidentally during angiographic or sonographic evaluation for other reasons. Most stenoses are visible with gray scale and duplex Doppler sonography. However, a negative sonographic study in a transplant patient with upper gastrointestinal tract variceal bleeding should always be angiographically evaluated for a possible portal venous problem.[6]

Symptomatic portal vein stenosis usually requires treatment, which has traditionally been surgical in nature.[54] In recent years, balloon PTA has been employed as the initial therapeutic modality.[13,16,17,55] To date, the authors have used PTA to treat six such patients (Fig. 32-4). Initial success was achieved in five (83 percent). Access to the portal vein was gained via a transhepatic approach, although in one patient an intraoperative approach via the inferior mesenteric vein was used. In this patient, the stenosis could not be traversed transhepatically. Transstenotic gradients are recorded before and after PTA. These patients are

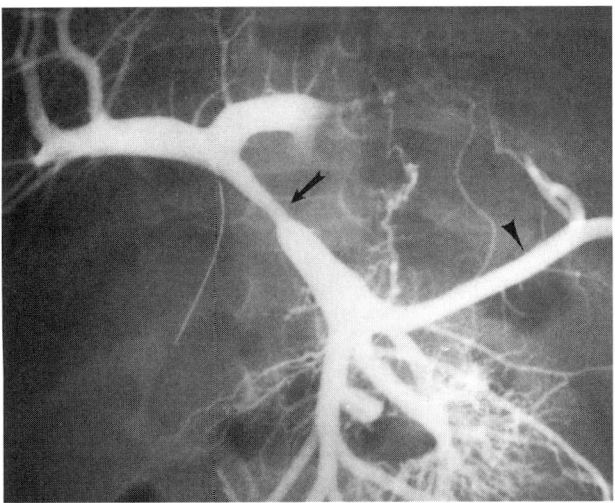

A

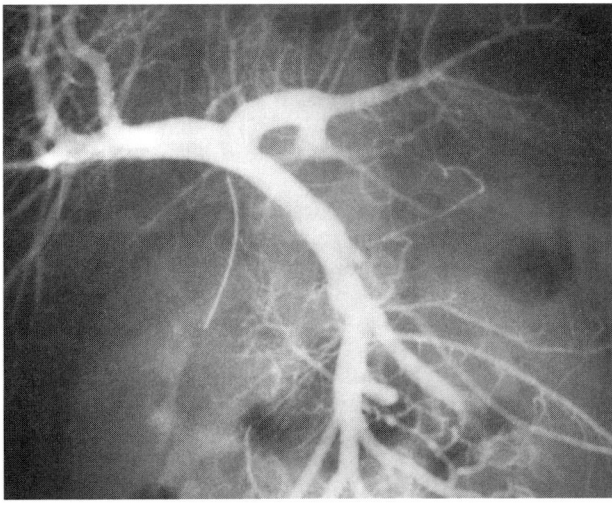

B

Figure 32-4. Portal vein angioplasty. (A) Stenosis of the portal vein anastomosis (*arrow*) is demonstrated on a transhepatic portogram. Note the retrograde flow in the splenic vein (*arrowhead*). (B) The portal vein lumen has been restored to normal after transhepatic balloon angioplasty.

There is no longer retrograde flow in the splenic vein. (From Zajko AB, Sheng R, Bron KM, et al. Percutaneous transluminal angioplasty of venous anastomotic stenoses complicating liver transplantation: intermediate-term results. J Vasc Intervent Radiol 1994;5:121–126. Used with permission.)

then followed clinically and with duplex Doppler sonography.

Documentation of long-term follow-up in transplant patients undergoing portal vein PTA is limited to several case reports. Raby et al.[16] treated two children and one adult who presented with variceal bleeding due to portal vein stenosis. Both children were successfully treated and had no recurrent episodes of bleeding at 1 year. Success was not achieved in the adult patient. Rollins et al.[17] reported two successful cases of portal vein PTA, also in children. Both patients were asymptomatic at 4 and 5 months after PTA. Long-term follow-up in the authors' successfully treated patients has been very good.[55] Four of the five continued to be asymptomatic with follow-up from 8.5 to 30.0 months. The one other patient developed a late portal vein occlusion 1 year after initially successful PTA. Of particular interest is that the four successful portal vein PTA patients were all children. Perhaps a factor responsible for long-term success in portal vein PTA in transplant patients is patient age.

Thrombosis of the portal vein may be partial or complete. Acute complete thrombosis in the early postoperative period has serious consequences, including allograft failure and variceal bleeding.[8] Late portal vein occlusion may be associated with essentially normal liver function, which is perhaps related to the development of hepatopetal venous collaterals. Such periportal collaterals are often demonstrated angio-

graphically and resemble those seen in cavernous transformation.[56] Despite the development of these collaterals, gastroesophageal varices often account for the clinical presentation of bleeding in these patients. Treatment with endoscopic sclerotherapy and occasionally splenorenal shunting has been employed.[6,57] If hepatic failure develops, retransplantation may be required.

The authors have attempted transhepatic thrombolytic therapy in two transplant recipients with partial portal vein thrombosis.[13] Both were unsuccessful. In one case, the clot was removed at surgery and found to be completely organized. There is one report in the literature using transhepatic angioplasty for posttransplant portal vein occlusion.[18] Unfortunately, three of the four treated patients died early from complications unrelated to the angioplasty. Although long-term clinical follow-up was not available, the authors conclude that transhepatic intervention is feasible for portal vein occlusion in transplants. In this same report, the authors successfully placed a metal stent in a transplant patient with portal vein occlusion. The patient died 1 month later of other complications; the stent was patent at autopsy. The present authors have also treated a transplant patient with a portal vein metal stent (Fig. 32-5). In this case, a portal vein stenosis was unresponsive to conventional balloon PTA. After transhepatic placement of a metal stent, the lumen was widely patent. However, after 6 weeks thrombosis developed

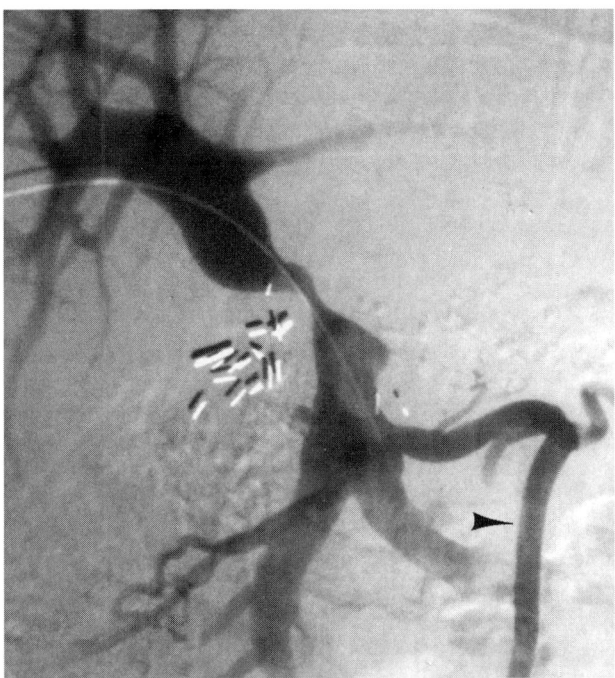

A

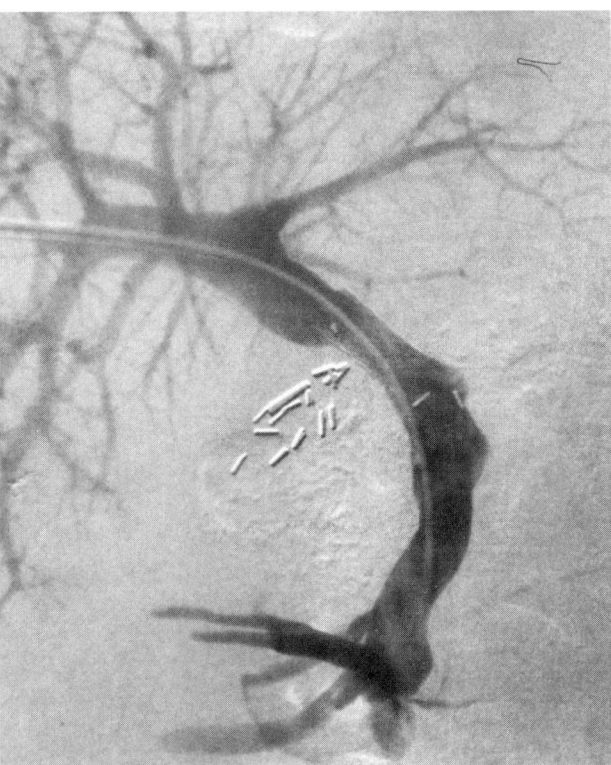

B

Figure 32-5. Metal stent placement for failed balloon angioplasty of the portal vein. (A) Severe stenosis of the portal vein anastomosis is demonstrated on a transhepatic portogram. Following PTA with a 10-mm balloon, there was essentially no change in the stenosis. Note the retrograde flow in the inferior mesenteric vein (*arrowhead*). (B) The portal vein anastomosis is widely patent after placement of a Palmaz stent expanded to 12 mm. There is no longer retrograde flow in the inferior mesenteric vein. (From Zajko AB, Sheng R, Bron KM, et al. Percutaneous transluminal angioplasty of venous anastomotic stenoses complicating liver transplantation: intermediate-term results. J Vasc Intervent Radiol 1994;5:121–126. Used with permission.)

that was unresponsive to transhepatic thrombolytic therapy. The patient eventually underwent retransplantation.

Inferior Vena Cava

Stenosis of the IVC after transplantation is rare and almost always involves the anastomotic sites. A suprahepatic anastomotic stenosis can present clinically as a Budd-Chiari syndrome due to obstruction of hepatic venous drainage.[20] Lower extremity edema may also occur.[16] The authors have seen one case of a pseudostenosis of the upper IVC anastomosis due to extrinsic compression by a large loculated fluid collection.[13] Percutaneous drainage resolved the stenosis (Fig. 32-6). Stenosis of the infrahepatic anastomosis may present with lower extremity edema alone.[21] Rarely, stenosis has been observed in the retrohepatic IVC due to extrinsic compression by hematoma.[13]

Although anastomotic stenoses of the IVC can be treated with PTA, the recurrence rate is high.[55] The

authors have treated six IVC stenosis patients with PTA (Fig. 32-7). Initial angiographic results have been good. Because of the IVC size, more than one balloon may be required for adequate dilatation. Most of the patients have presented with significant ascites, and PTA has resulted in dramatic resolution of ascites in all patients presenting as such. Because of recurrent stenosis, three of the six suprahepatic IVC stenosis patients required several repeat dilatations from 1 to 18 months after initial PTA. In one patient, vena cavography with possible PTA was scheduled every 3 months to maintain patency. In this patient, aggressive interventional radiologic treatment was employed because the patient was not a surgical candidate for revision or retransplantation. Raby et al.[16] also reported recurrent IVC stenosis in one of three treated patients. The reason for the high recurrence rate in this group of patients compared to patients with portal vein stenosis is uncertain. Perhaps suprahepatic IVC stenoses are, at least in part, due to an element of torsion or twisting that leads to early restenosis.

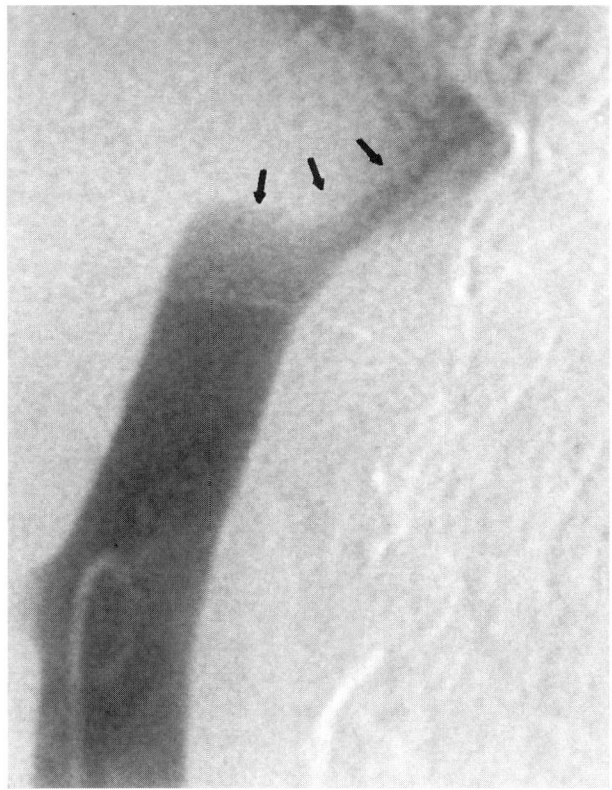

A

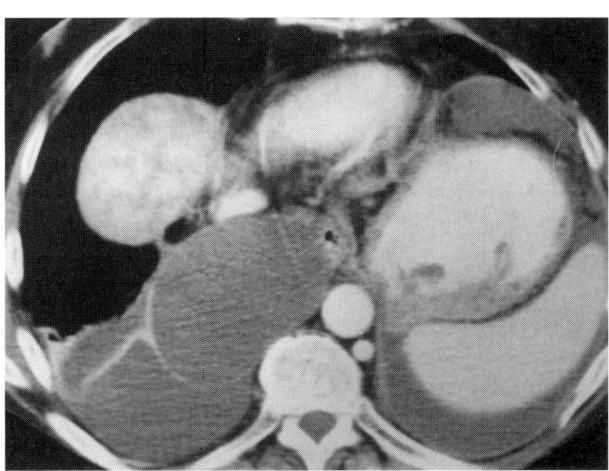

B

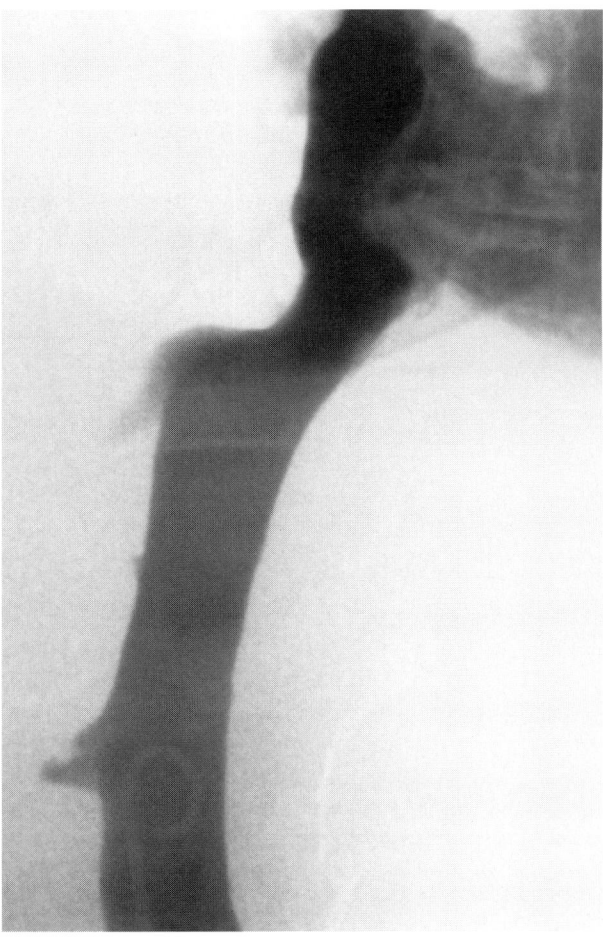

C

Figure 32-6. Percutaneous drainage of fluid collection causing suprahepatic IVC stenosis mimicking an anastomotic stenosis. (A) There is severe stenosis of the suprahepatic IVC caused by an extrinsic mass (*arrows*). (B) Abdominal CT scan shows a large loculated fluid collection adjacent to the suprahepatic IVC. (C) After percutaneous drainage of the fluid collection, the suprahepatic IVC anastomosis is patent, as demonstrated on follow-up vena cavogram. The fluid collection represented loculated ascites. (From Zajko AB, Bron KM, Orons PD: Vascular complications in liver transplant recipients: angiographic diagnosis and treatment. Semin Intervent Radiol 1992;9:270–282. Used with permission.)

Biliary Tract Reconstruction

The preferred method of biliary tract reconstruction is a choledochocholedochostomy, in which an end-to-end anastomosis is formed between the recipient and donor common ducts.[4,58,59] A T tube is left in place through the anastomosis for approximately 3 months after surgery, and this may be used for cholangiography.

An alternative to the choledochocholedochostomy is the choledochojejunostomy in Roux-en-Y.[60] This method is used in patients with diseased extrahepatic ducts (e.g., primary sclerosing cholangitis, biliary atresia) as a means of revising an end-to-end anastomosis, or in pediatric patients, where the small size of the ducts may make end-to-end anastomosis technically difficult. At the authors' institution, an internal stent is placed across the anastomosis. Resorbable sutures

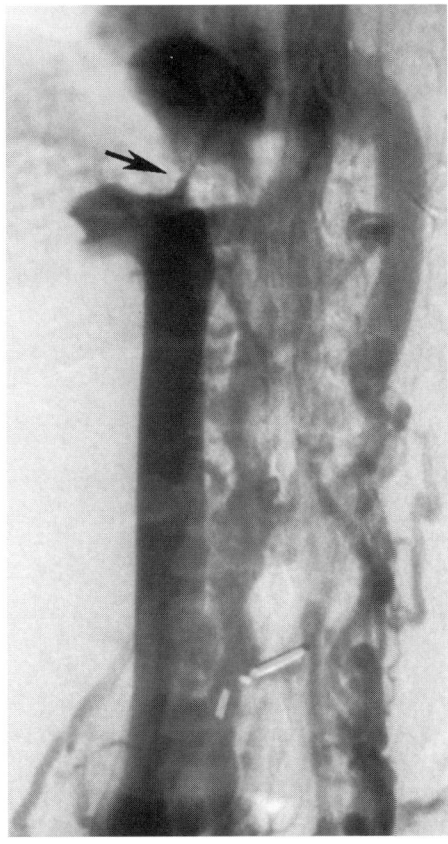

A

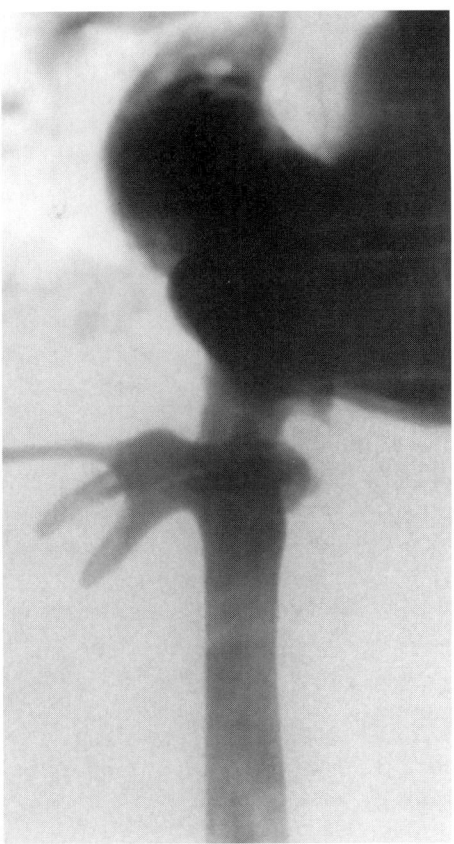

B

Figure 32-7. Angioplasty of suprahepatic IVC anastomosis. (A) Severe stenosis of a suprahepatic IVC anastomosis is demonstrated on a vena cavogram (*arrow*). Note the marked filling of paraspinal collaterals with eventual drainage into the azygos and hemizygous systems. This stenosis represented a recurrent stenosis following successful PTA 9 months earlier. (B) Following repeat PTA with a larger bal-

loon, the suprahepatic IVC anastomosis is widely patent and there is no filling of any collateral veins, as was seen before PTA. (From Zajko AB, Sheng R, Bron KM, et al. Percutaneous transluminal angioplasty of venous anastomotic stenoses complicating liver transplantation: intermediate-term results. J Vasc Intervent Radiol 1994;5:121–126. Used with permission.)

allow the stent to migrate spontaneously into the Roux loop within several weeks.

The gallbladder is generally not used as a conduit between the donor and recipient common ducts (choledocho-cholecysto-choledochostomy) because of the greater tendency toward bile leakage and stricture formation.[59]

Biliary Complications and Interventions

The most common complications encountered after orthotopic liver transplantation are those relating to the biliary tract, with problems occurring in up to 40 percent of patients.[22,24,27,60–64] Most large series have reported an incidence of 10 to 15 percent. Because the clinical presentation may be nonspecific, a high index of suspicion is necessary. Interventional radiologic procedures are crucial to both diagnosis and therapy. Although the diagnostic role of ultrasound, computed tomography, and radionuclide scanning has grown, cholangiography remains the definitive method of evaluation, providing essential information with regard to the location, type, and severity of most biliary complications.[23,65,66]

Bile duct obstruction and bile leakage constitute the two main types of biliary complications.

Bile Duct Obstruction

Bile duct obstruction occurs approximately twice as commonly as bile leakage[24] and is most often secondary to biliary stricture, either anastomotic or nonanastomotic.[22,23,62,64,67] The early identification and treatment of biliary strictures are important because of the potential for the development of sepsis and allograft failure.[63]

Nonanastomotic strictures usually occur within the intrahepatic biliary tree and may signify occult hepatic artery stenosis or thrombosis.[34,42,63] In the authors' early experience, 57 percent of patients with nonanastomotic strictures had hepatic artery occlusion.[34] More recently, the authors have observed a lower prevalence of hepatic artery occlusion (approximately 30 percent) in such patients. Ischemic injury may still be an underlying factor, but its causes may vary. Bile duct ischemia may be due to prolonged cold preservation time.[64,68] Other predisposing factors toward the formation of nonanastomotic strictures may include cytomegalovirus (CMV) infection, acute or chronic rejection, and ABO blood group incompatibility.[64] A recent study from the authors' institution of 693 liver transplant patients over a 10-year period strongly supported a contributory role of pretransplant primary sclerosing cholangitis toward the formation of nonanastomotic intrahepatic strictures.[69] The occurrence of such strictures was significantly higher in patients transplanted for primary sclerosing cholangitis (27 percent) than in those treated for other diseases (13 percent). However, a recent study by Ward et al.[70] refutes the importance of primary liver disease, CMV infection, and allograft rejection. Malignancy as a cause of stricture may be of concern in those patients transplanted for primary sclerosing cholangitis or cholangiocarcinoma.[61,70,71]

Although a duct-to-duct anastomosis is the procedure of choice at most institutions, whether anastomotic strictures occur more commonly after choledochojejunostomy or choledochocholedochostomy remains a matter of debate and is perhaps related to the surgical technique at individual institutions. One recent study of over 700 transplants indicates a higher incidence after choledochojejunostomy,[63] whereas another study of approximately 400 patients suggests a higher incidence of biliary obstruction after choledochocholedochostomy.[12] Mild anastomotic strictures may not be clinically significant, and the need for percutaneous or endoscopic biliary decompression must often be decided on clinical grounds.

The presence of intrahepatic duct dilatation due to stricture is usually a reliable but not the sole indicator of the need for percutaneous drainage. Significant strictures may occur without biliary dilatation.[28] For this reason, transhepatic cholangiography may be performed in transplant recipients with a negative sonogram of the biliary tree.

Nonanastomotic strictures, especially those in the intrahepatic biliary tree, may be impossible to correct surgically and are usually treated with balloon dilata-

tion. Most anastomotic strictures are also treated with balloon dilatation (Fig. 32-8). The authors usually perform three separate sessions 24 to 48 hours apart. A high-pressure balloon is inflated across the strictured segment for three consecutive 10 to 15-minute periods. A 2- to 5-minute decompression interval is given between inflations. The size of the balloon is generally increased by 1 to 2 mm with each session. At the completion of dilatation, a catheter is left in the biliary tree as a stent for 6 to 8 weeks, at which time follow-up cholangiography is performed.

Some data indicate that balloon dilatation is effective in the treatment of biliary strictures in transplants.[63,64,70] Colonna et al.[63] have recently described encouraging results with balloon dilatation in both anastomotic and nonanastomotic strictures. A favorable response to percutaneous management was achieved in 12 of 25 patients (5 anastomotic strictures, 7 intrahepatic strictures). Similar data were presented by Ward et al.,[70] who reported 15 patients with nonanastomotic strictures, 7 of whom maintained duct patency in follow-up as long as 30 months after a combination of balloon dilatation and percutaneous stenting. The remainder underwent retransplantation or died. Ward et al.[72] reported more favorable results with balloon dilatation of anastomotic strictures. Of 14 patients, 13 (93 percent) were successfully treated; all remained patent within a mean follow-up to 2.5 years. One recent study by Sanchez-Urdazpal et al.[73] indicates that balloon dilatation may even have a role in the treatment of ischemic-type biliary strictures. Although generally a poor prognostic sign, ischemic biliary strictures were treated with biliary stents and repeat dilatations, and long-term patency was achieved in 88 percent of patients.[73] Data from 72 patients treated over 5 years at the authors' institution demonstrated an overall patency of 80 percent at 6 months, decreasing to approximately 70 percent at 5 years.[74] Intrahepatic strictures appeared to respond better to balloon dilatation than extrahepatic anastomotic strictures. Several factors have been identified that are predictive of a poor response to balloon dilatation, including hepatic artery thrombosis, stricture formation later than 3 months after transplant, pretransplant primary sclerosing cholangitis, rejection, and CMV infection.[70]

A relatively small amount of data has been published on the use of metallic stents for benign biliary strictures after transplantation. Goertzen et al.[75] reported their results on 36 Gianturco-Rösch Z stents (70 percent anastomotic, 30 percent nonanastomotic) in 21 liver transplant patients. Primary and secondary patency rates of 52 and 90 percent, respectively, were achieved within a mean follow-up of 9.5 months. Diamond et al. recently reported their results using

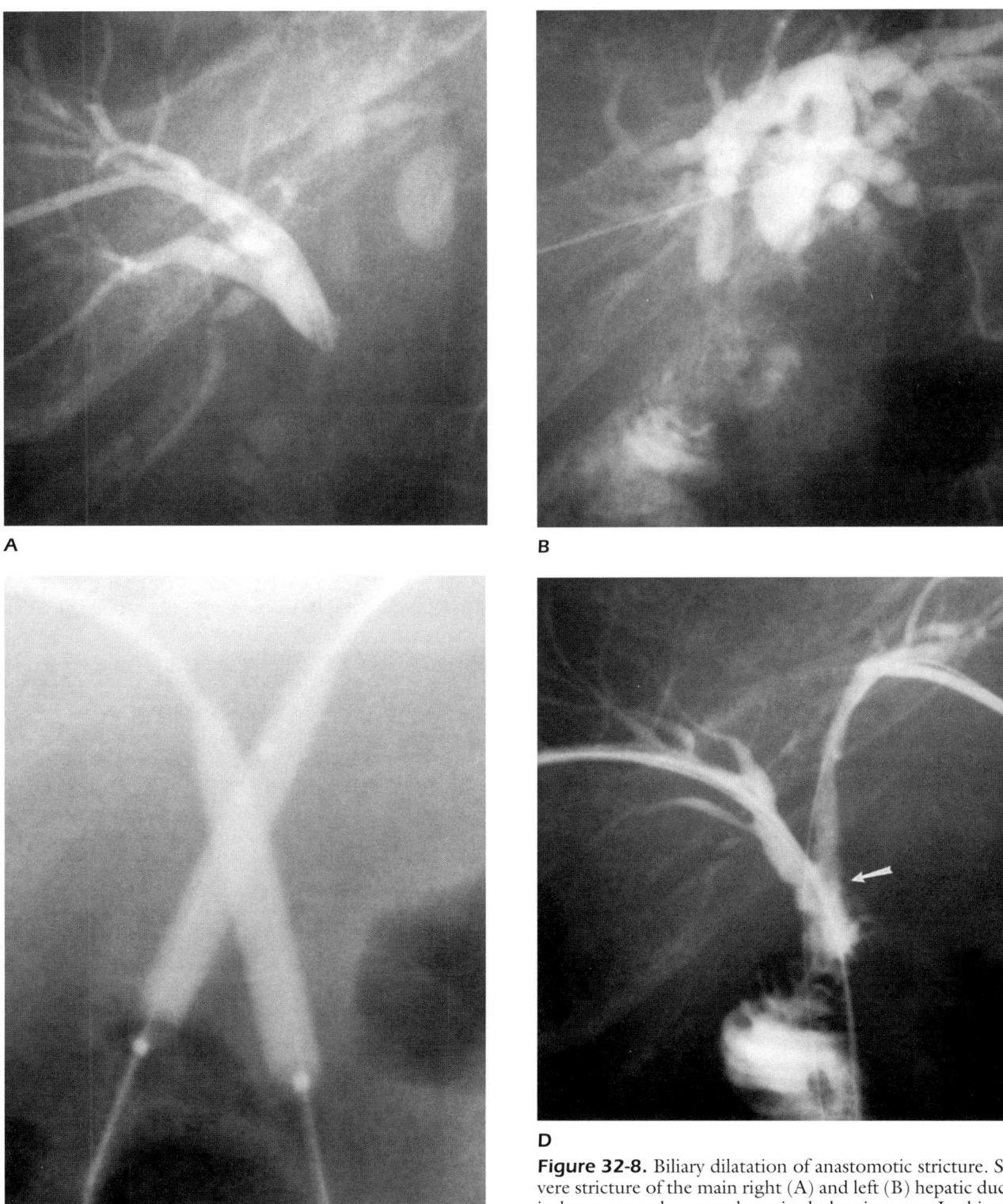

A

B

C

D

Figure 32-8. Biliary dilatation of anastomotic stricture. Severe stricture of the main right (A) and left (B) hepatic ducts is demonstrated on transhepatic cholangiograms. In this patient, a very high anastomosis was performed at the level of the confluence of the right and left ducts. (C) Following bilateral biliary drainage, the stricture was dilated using "kissing" balloons. (D) A widely patent anastomosis (*arrow*) after dilatation is demonstrated on a catheter cholangiogram.

metallic stents in 24 patients with intrahepatic strictures, 12 of whom also had anastomotic strictures.[76] Initial technical success was 100 percent. By life-table analysis, cumulative primary, primary assisted, and secondary patency rates were 50, 61, and 80 percent, respectively, at 18 months.

T tubes or internal stents may become occluded with time, resulting in hyperbilirubinemia and elevated liver enzyme levels secondary to cholestasis or sepsis. T tubes are easily removed, but obstruction by an internal stent that has failed to migrate spontaneously is more problematic. Because the presence of a Roux loop makes endoscopic access to the anastomosis difficult or impossible, a percutaneous transhepatic approach is often necessary. An internal stent that has become encrusted with inspissated bile and is causing biliary obstruction may be grasped and removed to the jejunum with a snare (Fig. 32-9). After standard percutaneous biliary drainage, a working catheter is placed in proximity to the stent. The distal aspect of the stent is then grasped with the snare and pulled into the jejunum.

Less common causes of biliary obstruction include cystic duct remnant mucocele, bile duct kinking due to extrahepatic duct redundancy, and biliary calculi.[22,27,28] Biliary calculi may often be removed to the bowel or crushed with a Dormia basket placed via a transhepatic approach. Surgery is generally necessary for an obstructing mucocele. A cystic duct mucocele forms when the donor cystic duct remnant becomes distended with mucus, causing extrinsic compression of the common bile duct, which leads to cholestasis.[77]

Bile Leakage

Bile leaks usually occur within the first several weeks after transplant and pose a significant risk of infection to the immunocompromised liver transplant patient.[10,23,26,27] Bile leaks may be identified in approximately 2 to 18 percent of patients.[12,67] The authors report a prevalence, as depicted on cholangiography, of 4.3 percent (59 of 1363 grafts).[78] Seepage of bile through abdominal drains, bacteremia, bile peritonitis, and formation of subhepatic fluid collections all represent potential sequelae.[22,26] Ultrasound, computed tomography, and radionuclide imaging may all identify large leaks or perihepatic fluid collections,[63,79] but smaller leaks are more problematic.[65] Cholangiography,

Figure 32-9. Biliary sludge and internal stent removal. (A) Biliary obstruction due to sludge presumed to be related to a retained internal stent is demonstrated on a transhepatic cholangiogram in a transplant patient presenting with cholangitis. (B) After transhepatic biliary drainage, the internal stent was advanced into the jejunum using a snare, and the sludge was irrigated out of the biliary tree. A final cholangiogram shows the biliary tree free of sludge and the anastomosis widely patent. The transhepatic catheter was removed.

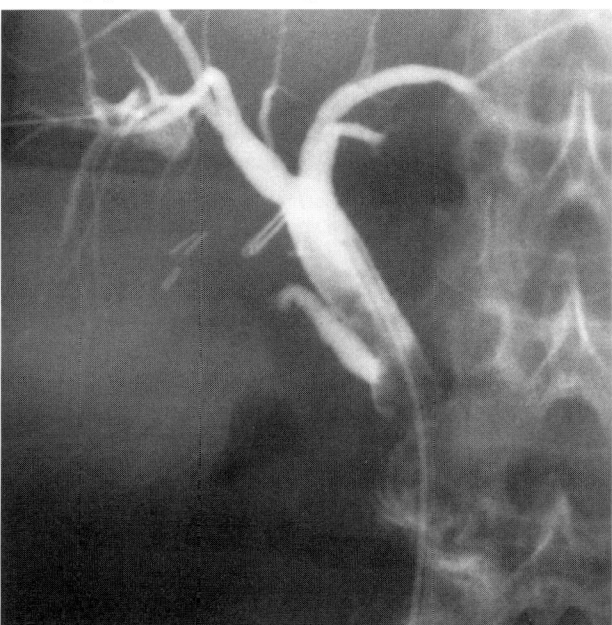

A

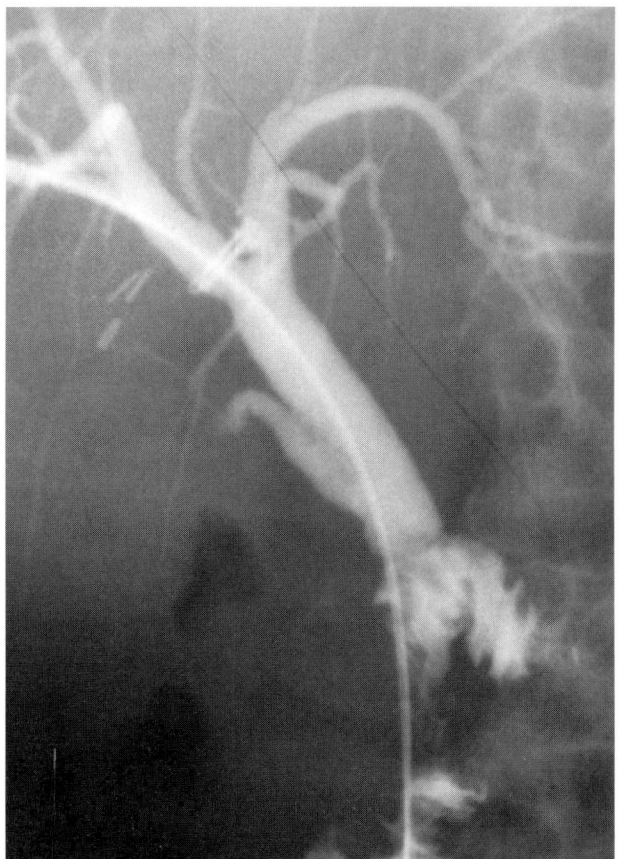

B

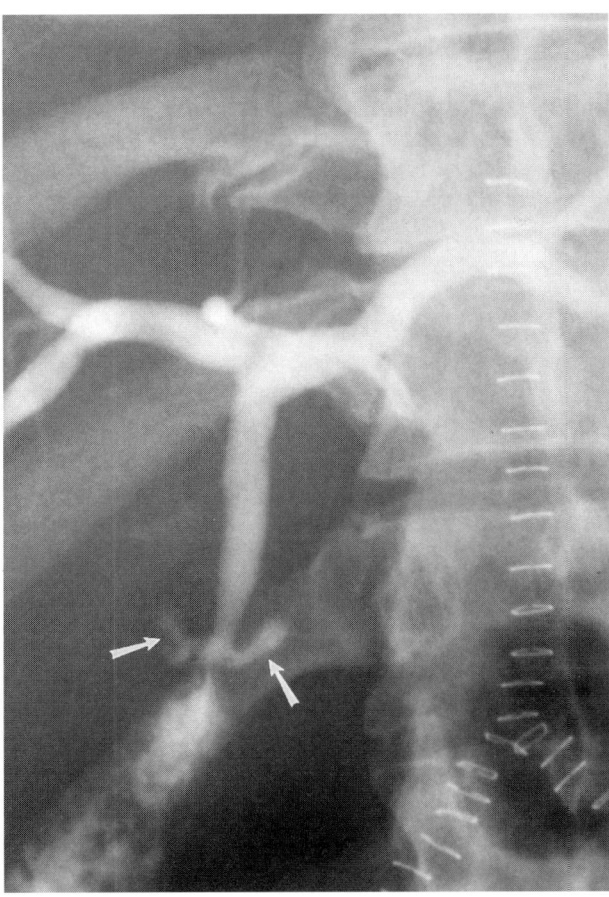

A

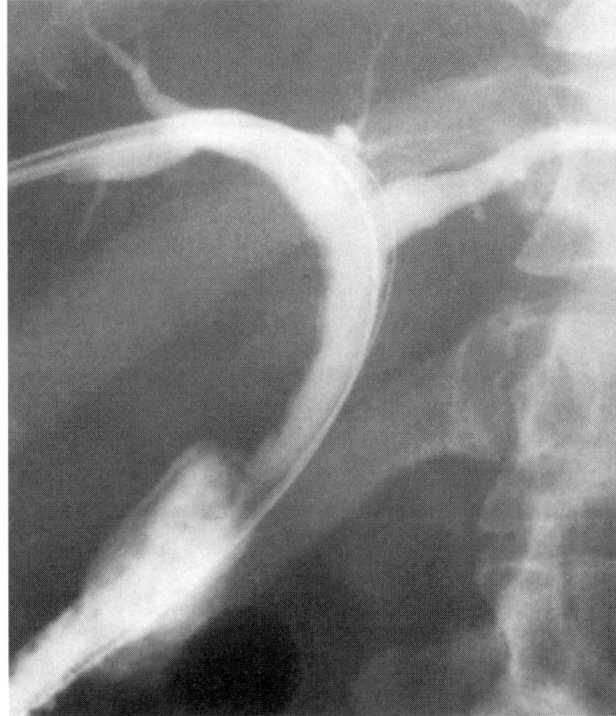

B

Figure 32-10. Biliary drainage for anastomotic bile leak. (A) A small confined anastomotic bile leak (*arrows*) is demonstrated on a catheter cholangiogram after transhepatic external biliary drainage. (B) A catheter cholangiogram after 6 weeks of external drainage shows complete resolution of the leak and free flow into the jejunum. The catheter was removed.

Figure 32-11. Percutaneous drainage of intrahepatic biloma. (A) CT scan shows a large low-attenuation lesion in the left hepatic lobe of an 8-month-old child with hepatic artery occlusion 2 weeks after transplantation. Percutaneous drainage demonstrated an infected biloma that communicated with the biliary tree. (B) CT scan after 6 weeks of catheter drainage shows almost complete resolution of the cavity. The catheter was removed shortly thereafter. This patient

also developed a biliary stricture at the confluence of the right and left hepatic ducts, successfully treated with balloon dilatation. Follow-up at 3 years after transplantation showed that she was doing well. (From Kaplan SB, Zajko AB, Konero B. Hepatic bilomas due to hepatic artery thrombosis in liver transplant recipients: percutaneous drainage and clinical outcome. Radiology 1990;174:1031–1035. Used with permission.)

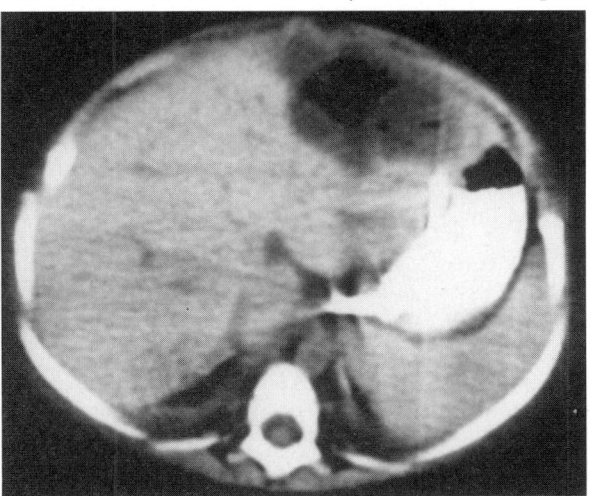

A

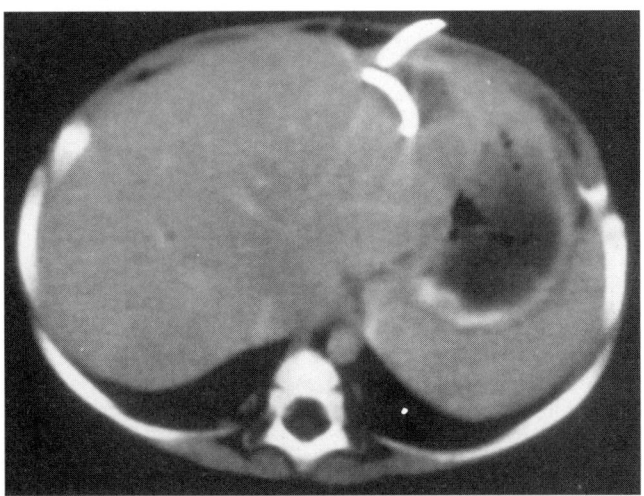

B

either transhepatic or via T-tube or endoscopic cholangiopancreatography, remains the definitive diagnostic modality.[27,28] Commonly seen bile leaks are small linear extravasations from the T-tube choledochostomy in duct-to-duct anastomoses.[27] These small leaks are usually asymptomatic and will resolve with continued T-tube drainage. In the authors' series, 57 percent were successfully treated in this way.[78] Occasionally, these anastomotic leaks persist after T-tube removal and are accompanied by the formation of bilomas or bile ascites, increasing the need for surgical intervention. In the authors' series, 33 percent required surgical repair or drainage. Endoscopic sphincterotomy and percutaneous drainage of the biloma may hasten resolution of persistent leaks and obviate surgery.[25]

Anastomotic leaks occur as commonly as those along the T-tube tract, but they are far more serious. Percutaneous drainage is problematic because the intrahepatic ducts are frequently decompressed. In select cases, external drainage may be curative (Fig. 32-10). However, if leakage persists or increases with drainage, surgical repair is required. In the authors' series, 16 of 21 patients with anastomotic leaks needed 17 surgical repairs.[78]

Intrahepatic bile leaks are serious complications that may indicate biliary necrosis secondary to hepatic artery thrombosis.[34] Extensive biliary necrosis may be accompanied by intrahepatic or hilar bilomas. Although retransplantation is usually necessary, allograft survival may occasionally be prolonged by percutaneous drainage of intrahepatic or hilar collections (Fig. 32-11).[80] An unusual and not well-recognized cause of bile leakage from an intrahepatic bile duct is needle biopsy of the allograft liver.[81] Most such leaks are often associated with increased biliary pressure due to obstruction. Leakage of bile through the biopsy tract and into the peritoneum can occur, resulting in sepsis and peritonitis. Spontaneous resolution is possible if there is no infection or significant biliary obstruction.[81]

Acknowledgments

The authors thank Yvonne Utz for her secretarial assistance in the preparation of this manuscript.

References

1. Gordon RD, Makowka L, Bronsther OL, et al. Complications of liver transplantation. In: Toledo-Pereyra LH, ed. Complications of organ transplantation. New York: Marcel Dekker, 1987:329–354.
2. Iwatsuki S, Shaw BW Jr, Starzl TE. Biliary tract complications in liver transplantation under cyclosporin-steroid therapy. Transplant Proc 1983;15:1288–1291.
3. Iwatsuki S, Starzl TE, Gordon RD, et al. Late mortality and morbidity after liver transplantation. Transplant Proc 1987;19:2373–2377.
4. Lerut J, Gordon RD, Iwatsuki S, et al. Biliary tract complications in human orthotopic liver transplantation. Transplantation 1987;43:47–51.
5. Lerut J, Tzakis AG, Bron K, et al. Complications of venous reconstruction in human orthotopic liver transplantation. Ann Surg 1987;205:404–414.
6. Wozney P, Zajko AB, Bron KM, et al. Vascular complications after liver transplantation: a 5-year experience. AJR 1986;147:657–663.
7. Bechstein WO, Blumhardt G, Ringe B, et al. Surgical complications in 200 consecutive liver transplants. Transplant Proc 1987;19:3830–3831.
8. Koneru B, Tzakis AG, Bowman J III, et al. Postoperative surgical complications. Gastroenterol Clin North Am 1988;17:71–91.
9. Langnas AN, Marujo W, Stratta RJ, et al. Vascular complications after orthotopic liver transplantation. Am J Surg 1991;161:76–83.
10. Lerut JP, Gordon RD, Iwatsuki S, et al. Human orthotopic liver transplantation: surgical aspects in 393 consecutive grafts. Transplant Proc 1988;20:603–606.
11. Wood RP, Rosenlof LK, Shaw BW Jr, et al. Complications requiring operative intervention after orthotopic liver transplantation. Am J Surg 1988;156:513–518.
12. Lebeau G, Yamaga K, Marsh JW, et al. Analysis of surgical complications after 397 hepatic transplantations. Surg Gynecol Obstet 1990;170:317–322.
13. Zajko AB, Bron KM, Orons PD. Vascular complications in liver transplant recipients: angiographic diagnosis and treatment. Semin Intervent Radiol 1992;9:270–282.
14. Castaneda F, So SKS, Hunter DW, et al. Reversible hepatic transplant ischemia: case report and review of literature. Cardiovasc Intervent Radiol 1990;13:88–90.
15. Abad J, Hidalgo EG, Cantarero JM, et al. Hepatic artery anastomotic stenosis after transplantation: treatment with percutaneous transluminal angioplasty. Radiology 1989;171:661–662.
16. Raby N, Karani J, Thomas S, et al. Stenosis of vascular anastomoses after hepatic transplantation: treatment with balloon angioplasty. AJR 1991;157:167–171.
17. Rollins NK, Sheffield EG, Andrews WS. Portal vein stenosis complicating liver transplantation in children: percutaneous transhepatic angioplasty. Radiology 1992;182:731–734.
18. Olcott EW, Ring EJ, Roberts JP, et al. Percutaneous transhepatic portal vein angioplasty and stent placement after liver transplantation: early experience. J Vasc Intervent Radiol 1990;1:17–22.
19. Cardella JF, Castaneda-Zuniga WR, Hunter D, et al. Angiographic and interventional radiologic considerations in liver transplantation. AJR 1986;146:143–153.
20. Zajko AB, Claus D, Clapuyt P, et al. Obstruction to hepatic venous drainage after liver transplantation: treatment with balloon angioplasty. Radiology 1989;170:763–765.
21. Rose BS, Van Aman ME, Simon DC, et al. Transluminal balloon angioplasty of infrahepatic caval anastomotic stenosis following liver transplantation: case report. Cardiovasc Intervent Radiol 1988;11:79–81.
22. Zajko AB, Bron KM, Campbell WL, et al. Percutaneous transhepatic cholangiography and biliary drainage after liver transplantation: a five-year experience. Gastrointest Radiol 1987;12:137–143.
23. Zajko AB, Campbell WL, Bron KM, et al. Cholangiography and interventional biliary radiology in adult liver transplantation. AJR 1985;144:127–133.
24. Letourneau JG, Castaneda-Zuniga WR. The role of radiology in the diagnosis and treatment of biliary complications after liver transplantation. Cardiovasc Intervent Radiol 1990;13:278–282.
25. Ward EM, Wiesner RH, Hughes RW, et al. Persistent bile leak after liver transplantation: biloma drainage and endoscopic ret-

rograde cholangiopancreatographic sphincterotomy. Radiology 1991;179:719–720.

26. Letourneau JG, Hunter DW, Payne WD, et al. Imaging of and intervention for biliary complications after hepatic transplantation. AJR 1990;154:729–733.

27. Zajko AB, Campbell WL, Bron KM, et al. Diagnostic and interventional radiology in liver transplantation. Gastroenterol Clin North Am 1988;17:105–143.

28. Zemel G, Zajko AB, Skolnick ML, et al. The role of sonography and transhepatic cholangiography in the diagnosis of biliary complications after liver transplantation. AJR 1988;151:943–946.

29. Todo S, Makowka L, Tzakis AG, et al. Hepatic artery in liver transplantation. Transplant Proc 1987;19:2406–2411.

30. Starzl TE, Halgrimson CG, Koep LJ, et al. Vascular homografts from cadaveric organ donors. Surg Gynecol Obstet 1979;149:737.

31. Shaw BW Jr, Iwatsuki S, Starzl TE. Alternate methods of arterialization of the hepatic graft. Surg Gynecol Obstet 1984;159:490–493.

32. Tzakis AG, Todo S, Steiber AC, et al. Venous jump grafts for liver transplantation in patients with portal vein thrombosis. Transplantation 1989;48:530–531.

33. Tzakis AG, Gordon RD, Shaw BW Jr, et al. Clinical presentation of hepatic artery thrombosis after liver transplantation in the cyclosporine era. Transplantation 1985;40:667–671.

34. Zajko AB, Campbell WL, Logsdon GA, et al. Cholangiographic findings in hepatic artery occlusion after liver transplantation. AJR 1987;149:485–489.

35. Tobbin PJ, Zajko AB, Sumkin JH, et al. Pseudoaneurysms complicating organ transplantation: roles of CT, duplex sonography, and angiography. Radiology 1988;169:65–70.

36. Hesselink EJ, Slooff MJH, Schuur KH, et al. Consequences of hepatic artery pathology after orthotopic liver transplantation. Transplant Proc 1987;19:2476–2477.

37. Merion RM, Burtch GD, Ham JM, et al. The hepatic artery in liver transplantation. Transplantation 1989;48:438–443.

38. Marujo WC, Langnas AN, Wood RP, et al. Vascular complications following orthotopic liver transplantation: outcome and the role of urgent revascularization. Transplant Proc 1991;23:1484–1486.

39. Blumhardt G, Ringe B, Lauchart W, et al. Vascular problems in liver transplantation. Transplant Proc 1987;19:2412.

40. Tzakis AG. The dearterialized liver graft. Semin Liver Dis 1985;5:375–376.

41. Zajko AB, Bron KM, Starzl TE, et al. Angiography of liver transplantation patients. Radiology 1985;157:305–311.

42. Orons PD, Sheng R, Zajko AB. Hepatic artery stenosis in liver transplant recipients: prevalence and cholangiographic appearance of associated biliary complications. AJR 1995;165:1145–1149.

43. Dodd GD III, Memel DS, Zajko AB, et al. Hepatic artery stenosis in liver transplantation: diagnosis by Doppler sonography. AJR 1993;160:92.

44. Orons PD, Zajko AB, Bron KM, et al. Hepatic artery angioplasty after liver transplantation: experience in 21 allografts. J Vasc Intervent Radiol 1995;6:523–529.

45. Sheng R, Orons PD, Ramos H, et al. Dissecting pseudoaneurysm of the hepatic artery: a delayed complication of angioplasty in a liver transplant. Cardiovasc Intervent Radiol 1995;18:112–114.

46. Esquivel CO, Koneru B, Karrer F, et al. Liver transplantation before 1 year of age. J Pediatr 1987;110:545–548.

47. Langnaş AN, Marujo W, Stratta RJ, et al. Hepatic allograft rescue following arterial thrombosis: role of urgent revascularization. Transplantation 1991;51:86–90.

48. Klintmalm GB, Olson LM, Nery JR, et al. Treatment of hepatic artery thrombosis after liver transplantation with immediate vascular reconstruction: a report of three cases. Transplant Proc 1988;20:610.

49. Hidalgo EG, Abad J, Cantarero JM, et al. High-dose intra-arterial urokinase for the treatment of hepatic artery thrombosis in liver transplantation. Hepatogastroenterology 1989;36:529–532.

50. Hall TR, McDiarmid SV, Grant EG, et al. False-negative duplex Doppler studies in children with hepatic artery thrombosis after liver transplantation. AJR 1990;154:573–575.

51. Zajko AB, Chablani V, Bron KM, et al. Hemobilia complicating transhepatic catheter drainage in liver transplant recipients: management with selective embolization. Cardiovasc Intervent Radiol 1990;13:285–288.

52. Hoevels J, Nilsson U. Intrahepatic vascular lesions following nonsurgical percutaneous transhepatic bile duct intubation. Gastrointest Radiol 1980;5:127–135.

53. Zajko AB, Bradshaw JR, Marsh JW. Gastroduodenal artery mycotic pseudoaneurysm: an unusual cause of lower gastrointestinal tract bleeding following liver transplantation. Transplantation 1988;45:990–991.

54. Scantlebury VP, Zajko AB, Esquivel CO, et al. Successful reconstruction of late portal vein stenosis after liver transplantation. Arch Surg 1989;124:503–505.

55. Zajko AB, Sheng R, Bron KM, et al. Percutaneous transluminal angioplasty of venous anastomotic stenoses complicating liver transplantation: intermediate-term results. J Vasc Intervent Radiol 1994;5:121–126.

56. Zajko AB, Bron KM. Hepatopetal collaterals after portal vein thrombosis following liver transplantation. Cardiovasc Intervent Radiol 1986;9:46–48.

57. Marino IR, Esquivel CO, Zajko AB, et al. Distal splenorenal shunt for portal vein thrombosis after liver transplantation. Am J Gastroenterol 1989;84:67–70.

58. Krom RAF, Kingma LM, Haagsma EB, et al. Choledocho-choledochostomy, a relatively safe procedure in orthotopic liver transplantation. Surgery 1985;97:552.

59. Holland P, Morris E, Buckels J. Cholangiography in liver transplantation: a comparison of two types of biliary reconstruction. Br J Radiol 1991;64:938–989.

60. Tzakis AG, Gordon RD, Makowka L, et al. Clinical considerations in orthotopic liver transplantation. Radiol Clin North Am 1987;25:289–297.

61. Letourneau JG, Day DL, Hunter DW, et al. Biliary complications after liver transplantation in patients with preexisting sclerosing cholangitis. Radiology 1988;167:349–351.

62. Letourneau JG, Hunter DW, Ascher NL, et al. Biliary complications after liver transplantation in children. Radiology 1989;170:1095–1099.

63. Colonna JO, Shaked A, Gomes AS, et al. Biliary strictures complicating liver transplantation. Incidence, pathogenesis, management and outcome. Ann Surg 1992;216:344–350.

64. McDonald V, Matalon TA, Patel SK, et al. Biliary strictures in hepatic transplantation. J Vasc Intervent Radiol 1991;2:533–538.

65. Lantsberg S, Lanchbury EE, Drolc ZA. Evaluation of bile duct complications after orthotopic liver transplantation by hepatobiliary scanning. Nucl Med Commun 1990;11:761–769.

66. Anselmi M, Lancberg S, Deakin M, et al. Assessment of the biliary tract after liver transplantation: T tube cholangiography or IODIDA scanning. Br J Surg 1990;77:1233–1237.

67. Evans RA, Raby ND, O'Grady JG, et al. Biliary complications following orthotopic liver transplantation. Clin Radiol 1990;41:190–194.

68. Sanchez-Urdazpal L, Gores GJ, Ward EM, et al. Ischemic-type biliary complications after orthotopic liver transplantation. Hepatology 1992;16:49–53.

69. Sheng R, Zajko AB, Campbell WL, et al. Biliary strictures in hepatic transplants: prevalence and types in patients with primary sclerosing cholangitis vs those with other liver diseases. AJR 1993;161:297–300.

70. Ward EM, Kiely MJ, Maus TP, et al. Hilar biliary strictures after liver transplantation: cholangiography and percutaneous treatment. Radiology 1990;177:259–263.

71. Herbener T, Zajko AB, Koneru B, et al. Recurrent cholangiocarcinoma in the biliary tree after liver transplantation. Radiology 1988;196:641–642.

72. Ward EM, Mans TP, Sanchez-Urdazpal L. Bile duct strictures after liver transplantation. Presented at the 22nd annual meeting and postgraduate course of the Society of Gastrointestinal Radiologists, Scottsdale, AZ, January 17–22, 1993.

73. Sanchez-Urdazpal L, Gores GJ, Ward EM, et al. Diagnostic features and clinical outcome of ischemic-type biliary complications after liver transplantation. Hepatology 1993;17:605–609.

74. Zajko AB, Sheng R, Zetti GM, et al. Transhepatic balloon dilatation of biliary strictures in liver transplant patients: a 10-year experience. J Vasc Intervent Radiol 1995;6:79–83.

75. Goertzen TC, Lieberman RP, Rantan D, et al. Z stents for treatment of benign biliary strictures following liver transplantation. Presented at the 91st annual meeting of the American Roentgen Ray Society, Boston, MA, May 5–10, 1991.

76. Diamond NG, Lee SP, Niblett RL, et al. Metallic stents for the treatment of intrahepatic biliary strictures after liver transplantation. J Vasc Intervent Radiol 1995;6:755–761.

77. Zajko AB, Bennett M, Campbell WL, et al. Mucocele of the cystic duct remnant in eight liver transplant recipients: findings at cholangiography, CT and US. Radiology 1990;177:691–693.

78. Sheng R, Sammon JK, Zajko AB, et al. Bile leak after hepatic transplantation: cholangiographic features, prevalence, and clinical outcome. Radiology 1994;192:413–416.

79. Oliver JH, Federle MP, Campbell WL, et al. Imaging the hepatic transplant. Radiol Clin North Am 1991;29:1285–1298.

80. Kaplan SB, Zajko AB, Konero B. Hepatic bilomas due to hepatic artery thrombosis in liver transplant recipients: percutaneous drainage and clinical outcome. Radiology 1990;174:1031–1035.

81. Paymani M, Zajko AB, Campbell WL. Bile leakage as a complication of liver biopsy in liver transplants. Abdom Imaging 1993;18:258–260.

33

Interventions in Portal Hypertension

ZIV J. HASKAL

Variceal hemorrhage remains the most feared and lethal complication of portal hypertension. Although there have been significant advances in the understanding of the pathophysiology of portal hypertension, the treatment of bleeding remains a complex and evolving issue that continues to frustrate hepatologists, surgeons, and interventional radiologists. Several forms of therapy have been developed, including pharmacologic therapy, sclerotherapy, variceal band ligation, surgical portosystemic shunts, liver transplantation, transhepatic variceal embolization, and transjugular intrahepatic portosystemic shunts (TIPSs). This chapter reviews the status of these procedures and discusses the development and results of TIPS in the management of portal hypertension.

Pharmacologic Control of Bleeding

Vasopressin was the first medication used to control variceal bleeding and continues to be the mainstay of acute treatment of variceal bleeding.[1-3] It reduces portal venous pressure by constricting the splanchnic arteriolar and venular bed, thereby reducing venous flow to the liver. Vasopressin may also mechanically reduce flow into esophageal varices by directly constricting smooth muscle within the lower esophageal sphincter. Although intravenous vasopressin can lessen acute variceal hemorrhage, it does not improve overall patient survival when compared to placebo infusion, partly because there is a high rate of rebleeding after vasopressin is discontinued. Vasopressin therapy is usually accompanied by simultaneous administration of nitroglycerin by sublingual, topical, or intravenous routes to further reduce portal pressure and prevent the adverse systemic effects of vasopressin, including cerebrovascular and myocardial ischemia.[4-8]

The next major advance in medical therapy of variceal bleeding occurred in 1980 when LeBrec reported the use of propanolol to lower the portosystemic gradient.[9] Beta-receptor blockade with propanolol reduces splanchnic blood flow by blocking vasodilatory beta$_2$ receptors and by lowering cardiac output. Since then, several randomized controlled trials have documented the benefit of long-standing beta blockade for prophylaxis of primary and recurrent variceal bleeding.[10-12] Although an improvement in overall survival has not been shown, propanolol administration is the current initial treatment for primary prevention of bleeding and may be combined with other methods for prophylaxis after an index bleed.

Endoscopic Therapy

Endoscopic therapy for esophageal varices was first reported by Crafoord and Frenckner in 1939.[13] The technique lay fallow until the 1970s and 1980s, when diagnostic and therapeutic flexible fiber-optic endoscopes became available. As the drawbacks of surgical portacaval shunts and devascularization procedures became clear, sclerotherapy became the first-line therapy for patients with acute variceal bleeding. With the current techniques, endoscopic therapy can control acute variceal bleeding in 80 to 90 percent of cases.[14-19]

In this procedure, various sclerosing agents are injected into or adjacent to bleeding esophageal varices. These agents cause variceal thrombosis and sloughing. Intravariceal injection is directed at occluding actual variceal channels, whereas paravariceal injection is aimed at creating a fibrous cover over the varices and thus preventing further bleeding. In practice, a combination of both techniques is often used.

Once the acute bleeding episode has been controlled, elective sessions of sclerotherapy are continued on a weekly basis until the varices are obliterated or complications ensue. The latter include acute, procedural complications such as aspiration, substernal chest pain, mediastinitis, esophageal spasm, and, rarely, esophageal perforation. Injection site ulcers are common; most shallow lesions indicate an effective injection of sclerosant.

Because sclerotherapy does nothing to treat the underlying portal hypertension that causes the bleeding, rebleeding can occur in up to 50 percent of cases. On the other hand, the accelerated liver failure and portosystemic encephalopathy that can accompany portosystemic shunts does not occur. Sclerotherapy has limited application for treatment of gastric varices. Portal hypertensive gastropathy and ectopic intestinal varices that lie beyond the reach of the endoscope must be addressed by other methods. For these reasons, sclerotherapy can provide definitive therapy for only a fraction of patients with recurrent variceal hemorrhage.

Endoscopic variceal band ligation of bleeding varices has more recently been used for the treatment of acute bleeding and for long-term secondary prophylaxis.[20] In one controlled trial comparing sclerotherapy and banding, the latter proved superior with respect to complications, the number of sessions required to obliterate varices, and prevention of recurrent bleeding. A small survival benefit was noted in patients with milder hepatocellular dysfunction (Child classes A and B). These promising results must be confirmed by other studies before the technique is widely adopted.[21,22]

Portosystemic Shunt Surgery

The history of surgical portosystemic shunts traces back over 100 years ago when Eck created the first end-to-side portacaval shunt in dogs.[23] In 1903 Vidal performed this operation in humans.[24] By the mid-1950s, improved surgical techniques and postoperative care allowed routine formation of portacaval shunts. As controlled follow-up data were collected, it became clear that total portal diversion had exchanged excellent prophylaxis against variceal bleeding for high rates of portosystemic encephalopathy (30–70 percent) and liver failure.[25,26]

Warren et al. described selective decompression of the portal system in 1967.[27] The distal splenorenal shunt separates the gastrosplenic and coronary venous system responsible for gastroesophageal variceal bleeding from the higher-pressure mesenteroportal system. The shunt is technically demanding to create and is generally not performed in patients with class C cirrhosis or in patients with acute variceal hemorrhage. It offers a high rate of patency, exceeding 90 percent, and lower rates of encephalopathy and liver failure.[28,29] At 1 year, however, up to three-fourths of patients with alcoholic cirrhosis develop an extensive collateral venous supply between the shunted low-pressure gastrosplenic veins and the high-pressure mesenteroportal system. This may negate the early hemodynamic benefit of selective portosystemic decompression.[30,31]

In 1965, Bismuth introduced side-to-side small stoma shunts as a way of partially decompressing the portal system while preserving a percentage of hepatopetal nutrient portal venous flow.[32,33] In the 1980s, Sarfeh and Rypins modified the technique by using polytetrafluoroethylene (PTFE) graft material to create portacaval interposition grafts with precise, fixed diameters. During that decade, they progressively reduced the size of the portosystemic shunts created to 8 mm in diameter. Their results and those of other investigators have validated the concept and efficacy of partial portal decompression with small-diameter shunts as a viable method of preventing recurrent variceal bleeding with rates of encephalopathy and liver failure that are much lower than those associated with total portacaval shunts.[34–36]

As with all major surgery, the condition of the patient before surgery has a major impact on postoperative morbidity and mortality. Emergency portosystemic shunt surgery is rarely indicated in the setting of acute variceal bleeding, where operative mortality can exceed 50 percent.[37]

Liver transplantation offers the only option that treats both liver failure and variceal hemorrhage.[38,39] In 1988 Iwatsuki et al. reported a 5-year liver transplantation survival rate of 71 percent in 302 patients with a history of variceal bleeding.[40] Although transplantation can provide definitive therapy for portal hypertension and its complications, few patients warrant this on the basis of bleeding alone. In addition, the shortage of donor organs often precludes emergent transplantation.

Percutaneous Management of Portal Hypertension

Transhepatic Variceal Embolization

Percutaneous transhepatic catheterization of the portal vein was first described in 1971 by Weichel.[41] In 1974 Lunderquist and Vang published their initial results with transhepatic catheterization and occlusion of the coronary vein in patients with portal hypertension and esophageal varices.[42] Numerous clinical studies followed reporting the results of transhepatic or transjugular approaches to deliver a number of embolic agents, including autologous clot, Gelfoam sponges soaked in tetradecyl sulfate, stainless steel Gianturco coils, bucrylate, and, most widely, ethanol (Figs. 33-1 and 33-2).[43–62] The last-mentioned had the advantage of causing an intense coagulation of blood cells, disrupting vascular endothelium, and causing vascular thrombosis. As experience with the procedure grew, several significant problems emerged, eclipsing

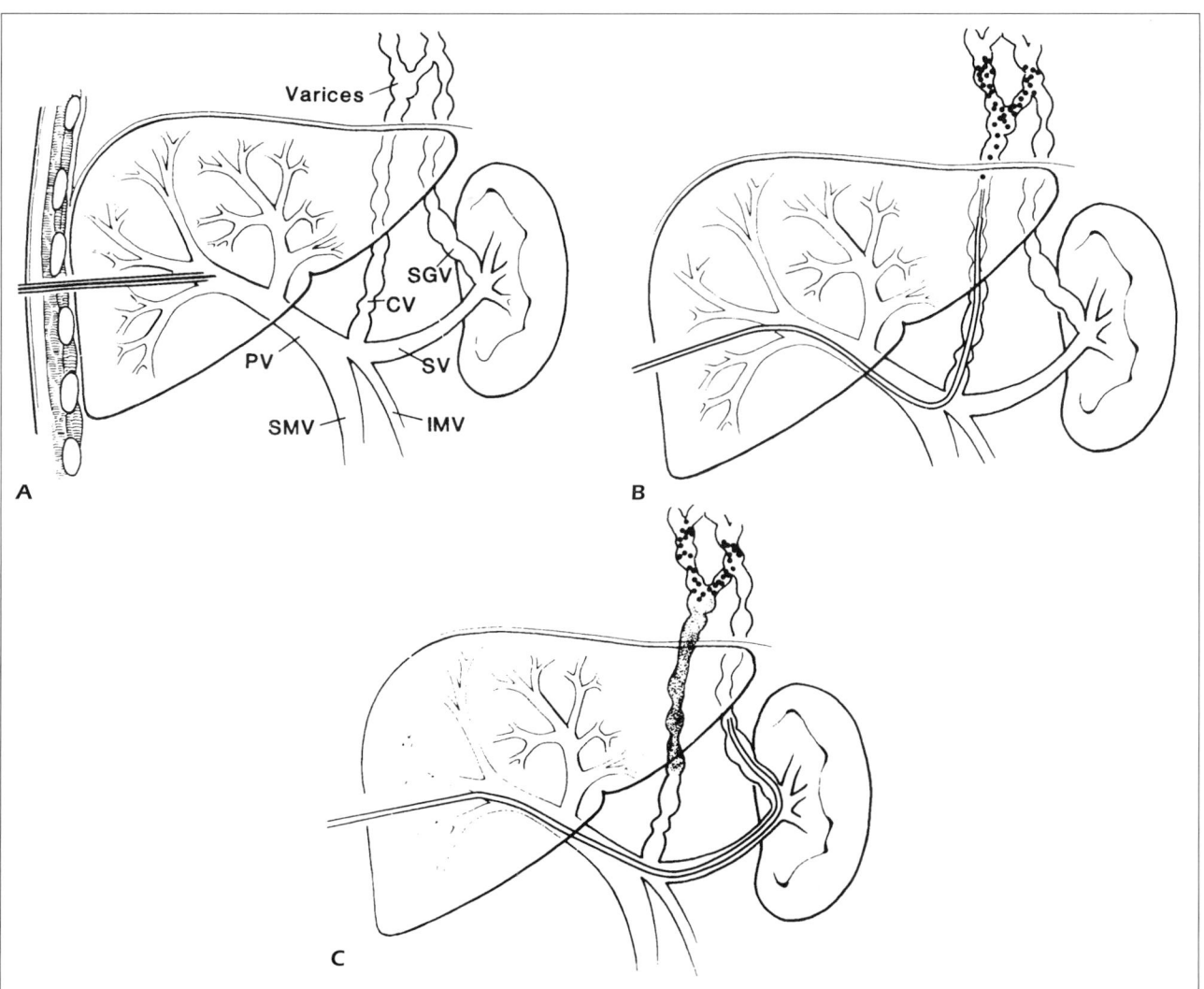

Figure 33-1. Diagrammatic representation of transhepatic embolization of varices. (A) A sheathed needle is percutaneously introduced into the right portal vein. *PV,* portal vein; *SMV,* superior mesenteric vein; *CV,* coronary vein; *SGV,* short gastric vein; *SV,* splenic vein; *IMV,* inferior mesenteric vein. (B) The transhepatic catheter is advanced into the coronary vein and embolic material is delivered into the varices until stasis is achieved. (C) The short gastric vein is similarly catheterized and embolized. (From Athanasoulis et al. Interventional radiology. Philadelphia: Saunders, 1982. Used with permission.)

promising early results. First, recurrent bleeding was common, ranging from 30 to 61 percent. Despite transcatheter occlusion of all demonstrable coronary and short gastric veins, latent veins would enlarge or recanalize to resupply the varices. Second, the procedure led to portal vein thrombosis in 16 to 20 percent of cases because occlusion of the coronary and short gastric veins, which provided the major venous outflow in those patients, led to stagnation of portal flow. Occlusion of the left and short gastric veins, which are the major decompressive channels for patients with portal hypertension, led to stagnation of portal flow and thrombosis.

The largest published experience with transhepatic

variceal embolization was reported by L'Hermine et al. in 1989.[63] Four hundred patients underwent embolization over 7 years. The overall technical failure and complication rates were 9 and 7 percent, respectively. Sixty-five percent of patients had Child class C cirrhosis; 35 percent had class B. Patients were embolized with either ethanol and stainless steel coils or bucrylate. Bleeding was controlled in 83 percent of patients treated emergently. The 10-day survival rate was 76 percent, with 97 deaths from recurrent bleeding or liver failure. Recurrent bleeding occurred in 55 percent of patients at 6 months (38 percent Child class B, 70 percent class C) and in 81 percent at 2 years (71 percent Child class B, 90 percent class C). Half of the

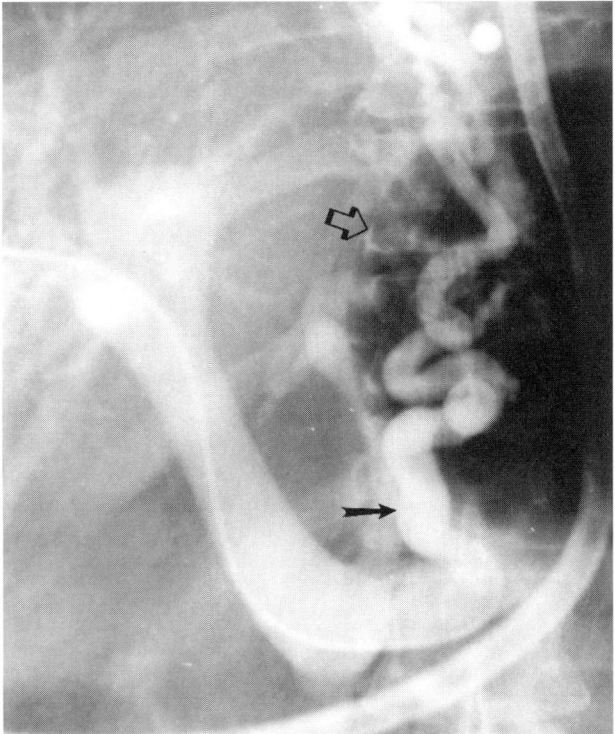

A

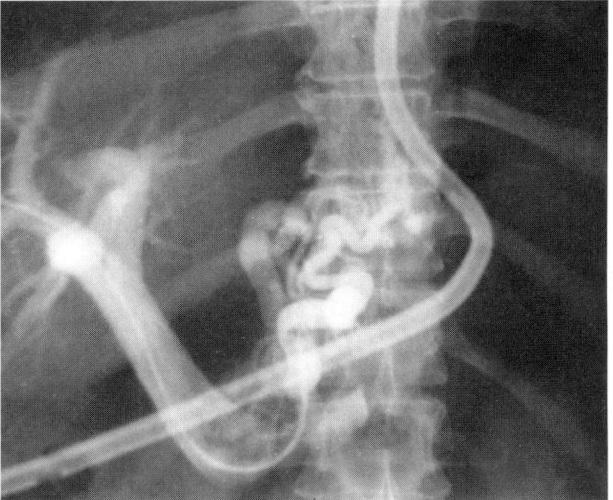

B

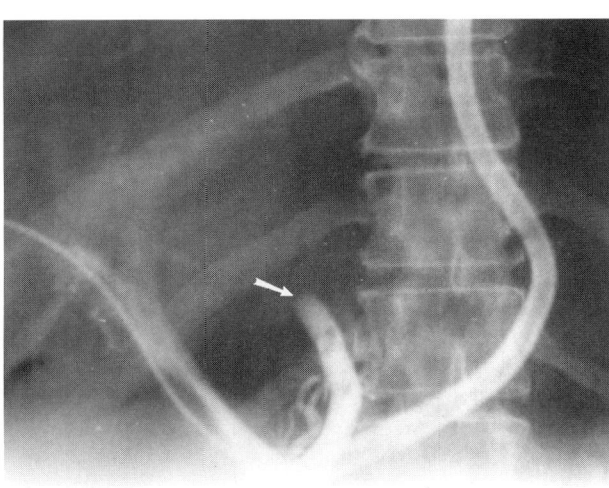

C

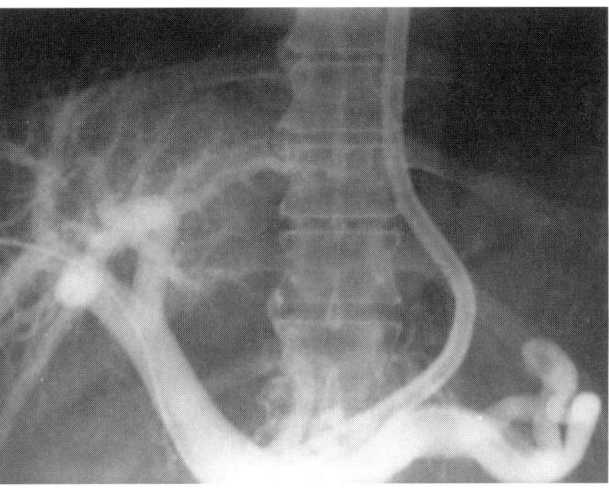

D

Figure 33-2. Transhepatic variceal embolization in a 43-year-old man with uncontrolled variceal bleeding. (A) Transhepatic portography demonstrates hepatofugal filling of varices (*arrow*) despite an inflated balloon tamponade catheter (*open arrow*). (B) The coronary vein is catheterized with a curved angiographic catheter, and contrast venography is performed. (C) Coronary venography after embolization with absolute alcohol demonstrates successful occlusion of the vein (*arrow*). (D) Final splenic venography demonstrates no residual variceal flow. The balloon tamponade catheter has been deflated. (Courtesy of Constantin Cope, MD.)

patients who rebled were controlled with medical therapy. At 1 year, 48 percent were alive; 26 percent were alive at 5 years.

These sobering results, combined with the emergence of flexible endoscopy and the proven efficacy of sclerotherapy, obviated transhepatic embolization in most patients. The procedure has been all but abandoned except when performed in concert with the formation of TIPSs or the treatment of residual or recurrent varices after portosystemic shunt surgery (Fig. 33-3).

Percutaneous Revision of Surgical Portosystemic Shunts

In general, most surgical portosystemic shunts can be readily catheterized from a femoral venous approach. This access makes possible several interventions, including balloon dilatation of stenotic shunts, recanalization of occluded shunts, and transshunt embolization of recurrent or residual varices.

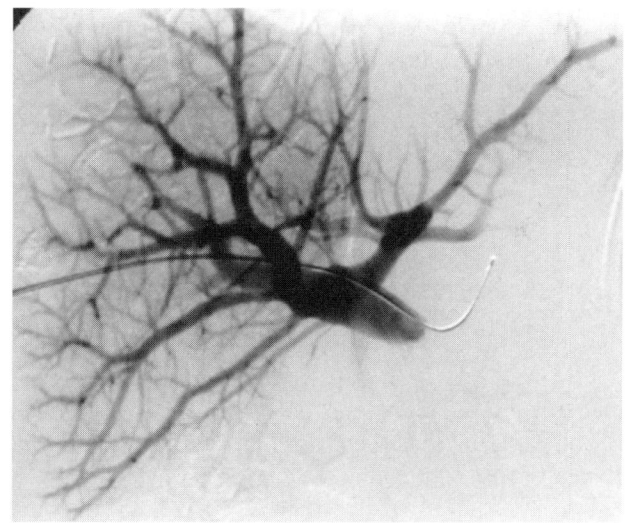

A

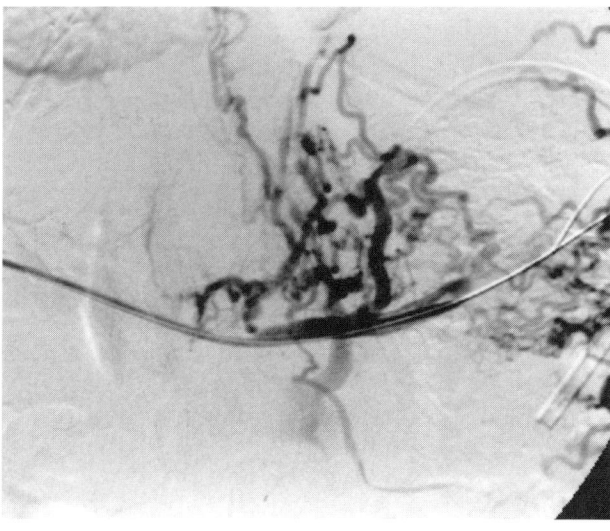

B

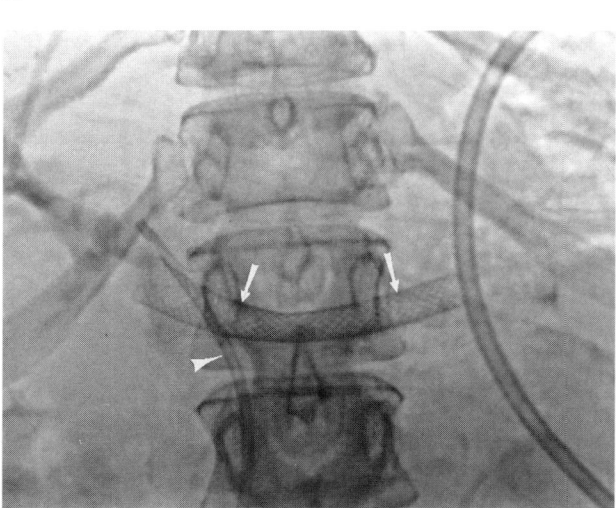

C

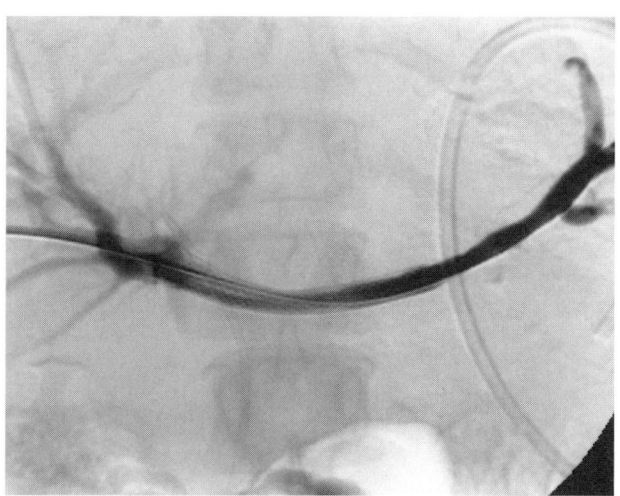

D

Figure 33-3. Percutaneous treatment of prehepatic portal hypertension. Transhepatic recanalization of splenoportal thrombosis in a 39-year-old woman with a history of prior pancreatitis and gastric variceal bleeding. Liver biopsy was normal. (A) Transhepatic portography demonstrates the occlusion of the midportal vein. The intrahepatic portal vein is unremarkable. The portal pressure is 6 mmHg. (B) Hand-injected splenic venography demonstrates hepatofugal flow into multiple short gastric veins leading to gastric varices. The distal splenic vein at the splenoportal confluence is occluded. The splenic vein pressure is 17 mmHg. (C) A Wall-stent has been deployed across the occlusion (*arrows*). A pre-existing endoscopic biliary stent is visible (*arrowhead*). (D) Splenic venography after stent placement demonstrates no residual variceal flow. The splenic and portal vein pressures measure 8 mmHg.

Stenoses due to intimal hyperplasia or technical factors may occasionally limit flow through small-bore surgical shunts. As with most forms of bypass grafts, balloon dilatation can improve luminal diameter, although recurrent stenosis may be frequent.[64–67] The use of metallic stents to lessen the recurrence of stenoses in this setting is an appealing prospect, although current experience is too limited to evaluate it.[68,69]

One can often recanalize completely occluded shunts by probing the anastomosis with standard angiographic catheters. Occlusive thrombus can be macerated using balloon catheters and angioplasty, and stent placement possibly may be used to restore patency. Another approach is that reported by Cope and others, who successfully used fibrinolytic therapy to restore flow through occluded mesocaval and mesoatrial shunts.[70–72]

Transshunt catheterization of the portal system can be used to embolize residual or recurrent varices. Partially decompressive surgical portosystemic shunts often leave residual flow to the varices. Some surgeons routinely request variceal embolization 1 week after the creation of small-bore portacaval shunts. Postoperative transshunt embolization is less likely to cause portal vein thrombosis than transhepatic embolization alone because the shunt provides an alternate low-pressure outlet for portal flow.[66,73] In addition, it may increase the percentage of nutrient flow reaching the intrahepatic portal vein. Variceal embolization is also useful in patients with selective surgical shunts. The distal splenorenal shunt disconnects the splenic–coronary–short gastric pathway responsible for variceal engorgement from the intact mesenteroportal axis and redirects its flow into the left renal vein. Over time, native portosystemic collaterals often develop between the high-pressure mesenteroportal system and the lower-pressure splenorenal system, leading to recurrent varices. These varices can occasionally be treated with transfemoral catheterization of the splenorenal shunt and collateral vein embolization.[30,31]

Finally, intentional coil occlusion of surgical or spontaneous portosystemic shunts has been performed to reverse severe postoperative portosystemic encephalopathy or accelerated liver failure.[66,74–76]

Transjugular Intrahepatic Portosystemic Shunt (TIPS)

The creation of a percutaneous portosystemic shunt was reported in 1969 by Rösch and Hanafee, who used a modified Ross needle to establish communications between hepatic and adjacent portal vein branches in 5 dogs.[77] This intraparenchymal tract was progressively dilated using coaxial Dotter catheters and stented with 12 and 14 French Teflon catheters. Within 2 years, the authors had expanded their series to 34 dogs. Although shunts as large as 8- and 10-mm diameter were established, patencies were limited to several weeks. Shunt thrombosis often occurred when the stent tubing migrated out of its intrahepatic position, allowing the surrounding liver parenchyma to recoil.[78] Subsequent investigations focused on other methods of creating durable shunt tracts, including balloon catheter techniques[79] and cryoprobes.[80]

In 1982, Colapinto et al. reported the first human application of the technique.[81] Using balloon catheters, shunts were created in six patients with advanced cirrhosis and uncontrolled variceal bleeding. To improve shunt patency, the angioplasty catheters were kept inflated within the liver for as long as 12 hours. Four out of six patients had recurrent variceal bleeding, despite an initial reduction of the portal venous pressures by 10 to 15 mmHg. One year later, these investigators reported results in a larger series of patients in whom variceal bleeding was controlled in each case. Unfortunately, only 2 out of 15 shunts were patent at 6-month follow-up.

The TIPS technique lay fallow for several years until metallic stents became available. These devices serve as scaffolds that support the intrahepatic parenchymal tract and prevent its collapse from elastic recoil of the surrounding tissue. In one experimental study, Rösch et al. created shunts using self-expanding Gianturco stents in 30 nonhypertensive pigs, and these maintained patency for 4 to 6 weeks.[82] Palmaz et al. used balloon-expandable stents to line shunts in 12 dogs with experimentally induced portal hypertension. These shunts remained patent for an average of 48 weeks.[83]

In 1990, Richter et al. reported the first creation of TIPSs with stents in humans.[84] In these early cases, a combined transjugular and transhepatic approach was used. A transjugular needle was passed out of a hepatic vein toward a Dormia basket that had been transhepatically placed in the portal vein. The resulting shunt tract was balloon-dilated and stented with Palmaz stents. Three patients with advanced class C cirrhosis and uncontrolled hemorrhage were thus treated. Portal decompression was achieved in each case. Two patients had sufficient metabolic improvement to be upgraded to Child class A. In a later article, this experience was expanded to nine patients.[85]

Since then, thousands of TIPSs have been created worldwide as the procedure has been widely disseminated. The technique has undergone several technical refinements, and many centers have reported their results.[86–115]

TIPS Technique

A number of different TIPS catheter and needle systems can be used to create shunts; in general, all are used in a similar fashion (Fig. 33-4). The specific method the author uses for creating a TIPS is described below.

Preprocedure preparation includes recent esophagogastroduodenoscopy to confirm the presence of varices and to exclude concomitant peptic sources of upper gastrointestinal bleeding. Baseline encephalopathy testing is performed.[116] Doppler hepatic sonography is used to assess portal vein patency. If sonography fails to demonstrate flow, selective visceral angiography is performed.

Actively bleeding patients are stabilized as much as possible before TIPS with blood transfusions, vasopressin, nitrates, and fluid resuscitation. The author generally defers placement of balloon tamponade catheters unless the TIPS procedure cannot be begun

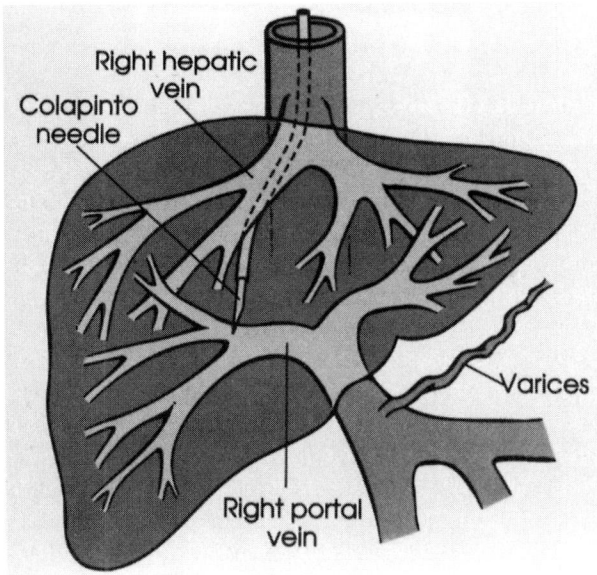

A

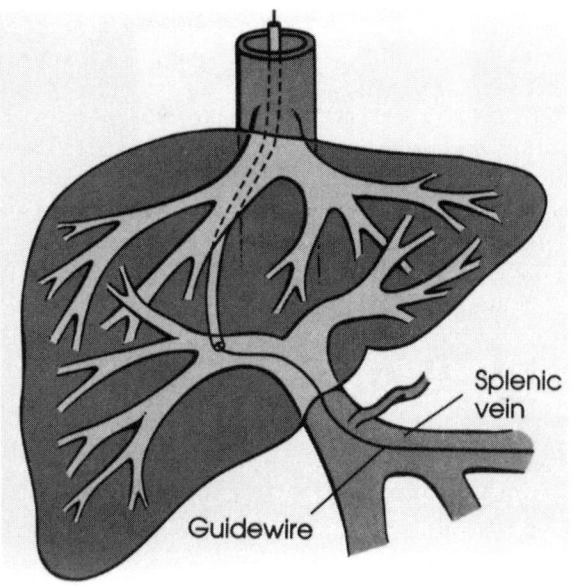

B

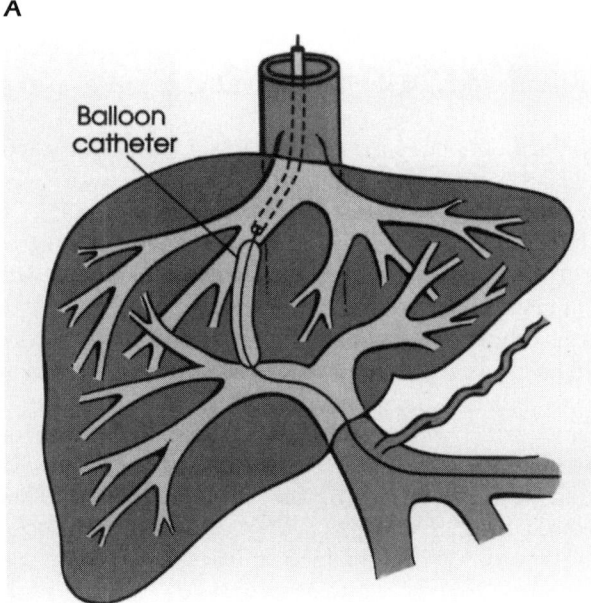

C

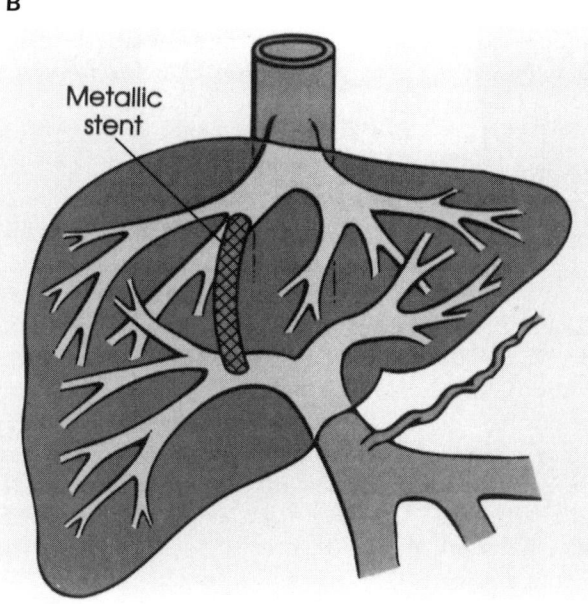

D

Figure 33-4. Diagrammatic representation of TIPS placement. (A) The sheathed Colapinto needle is advanced out of a hepatic vein into a portal vein branch. Varices are present. (B) A guidewire is advanced through the needle sheath into splenic vein. (C) The parenchymal liver tract is dilated using a balloon angioplasty catheter. (D) The metallic stent is deployed within the shunt tract. (E) If numerous varices remain after the stent is fully dilated and the portosystemic gradient remains elevated, then a second, parallel TIPS is constructed. (From Haskal ZJ, Ring EJ. Current techniques in interventional radiology (Cope C, ed.). Philadelphia: Current Science, 1994. Used with permission.)

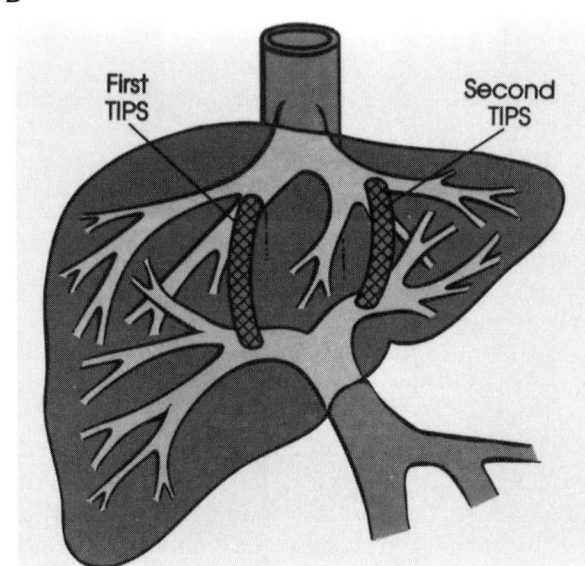

E

promptly. No specific effort is made to correct most coagulopathies because procedure-related bleeding is uncommon.

The procedure is performed under intravenous conscious sedation, using a combination of narcotic and anxiolytic medications such as midazolam, fentanyl, and droperidol. The last-mentioned potentiates the effect of the narcotic agent and provides an antiemetic effect. A broad-spectrum antibiotic, such as cefazolin, is given before TIPS. Supplemental oxygen is provided through nasal prongs. The right internal jugular approach is used in most cases because it provides direct, straight-line needle access to the liver. TIPS can also be created from external jugular, left internal jugular, and femoral vein approaches.[117]

A long 9 French hemostatic sheath is advanced into the right atrium, and initial atrial pressures are recorded. The sheath is threaded into the inferior vena cava, and a 5 French diagnostic catheter is passed through it and used to select a suitable hepatic vein. A right hepatic vein is used in most cases because it is readily catheterized and because it lies cephalad and posterior to the anterosuperior branches of the right portal vein. This anatomic relationship allows an anterocaudal pass of the portal puncture needle to reach the right portal vein. If the right hepatic vein is occluded or too stenotic to support TIPS, a middle or left hepatic vein can be used. In unusual circumstances where no suitable hepatic veins are present, a transcaval intrahepatic portosystemic shunt can be created.

Once free hepatic venography has been used to map the hepatic vein, wedged contrast venography can be used to attempt to visualize the intrahepatic portal vein. This provides satisfactory opacification of the portal vein in half of cases. In contrast, Rees et al. achieved excellent visualization of the intrahepatic portal vein in most cases by performing wedged hepatic venography with carbon dioxide.[118] A number of other techniques have been reported to aid transjugular portal vein catheterization, including transhepatic portal vein catheterization,[84] anteroposterior and lateral angiographic portal mapping,[88] and real-time ultrasound guidance.[105] Others have used sonographic guidance to place platinum guidewires or microcoils adjacent to the intended site of portal vein entry,[119,120] have placed temporary marker guidewires in the hepatic artery as an indirect marker of the portal vein,[121] or have used sonographic guidance to pass a marker wire through the paraumbilical vein into the portal vein.[122] One group performed surgical minilaparotomies to pass transmesenteric venous catheters into the portal vein for fluoroscopic localization during TIPS.[123]

The multiplicity of these techniques reflects the continuing absence of a definitive method of reliably finding the portal vein. In the author's experience, the portal vein can be punctured using fluoroscopic guidance alone, based on its expected location. This method was been rapid and reliable in over 150 cases. Transhepatic portal vein catheterization and recanalization are reserved for cases of extensive portal vein thrombosis.[96,124]

Once a suitable hepatic vein is identified, the diagnostic catheter is exchanged for a 50-cm-long, 16-gauge curved Colapinto needle and its surrounding 45-cm-long Teflon sheath. The relatively large diameter of this stiff needle allows its controlled passage through even hard cirrhotic liver parenchyma. The needle and sheath are rotated ventrally and passed approximately 3 to 4 cm caudally into the liver parenchyma. A contrast-filled syringe is attached to its hub and aspirated as the needle is slowly withdrawn. Contrast is hand-injected when blood return is noted in the syringe. When an appropriate portal vein branch has been entered, a long flexible guidewire is threaded through the needle into the main portal vein. The needle is held in place, serving as a stiffening cannula, and its sheath is advanced into the main portal vein. The needle is removed, and a 5 French catheter is threaded over the guidewire into the splenic vein.

Portal venous pressures are recorded through the catheter, and hand-injected splenic venography is performed. In the case of bleeding intestinal varices, superior or inferior mesenteric venography is performed. These provide real-time assessment of the portosystemic gradient, the direction of portal flow, and the extent of variceal filling.

The catheter is exchanged for an 8-mm balloon angioplasty catheter, which is used to dilate the parenchymal tract between the hepatic and portal veins. A focal waist is usually identified at the hepatic vein exit site and portal vein entry site. The shunt tract is lined with overlapping metallic stents, which are progressively enlarged with 8-, 10-, and 12-mm balloon angioplasty catheters until venography no longer demonstrates variceal flow and the portosystemic gradient has been reduced below 12 mmHg (Figs. 33-5 and 33-6).

TIPSs have been created using a variety of metallic stents, including Palmaz,[88,93,95] Strecker,[113] and Gianturco stents.[106,125] At present, the Wallstent (Schneider USA) is used to line most shunts. This springlike device is composed of monofilament strands of biomedical-grade superalloy (Elgiloy) woven into a helical braid configuration. Its advantages include a flexible low-profile 7 French delivery catheter. The ability to introduce the stent around even the most tortuous shunt tracts has simplified the TIPS proce-

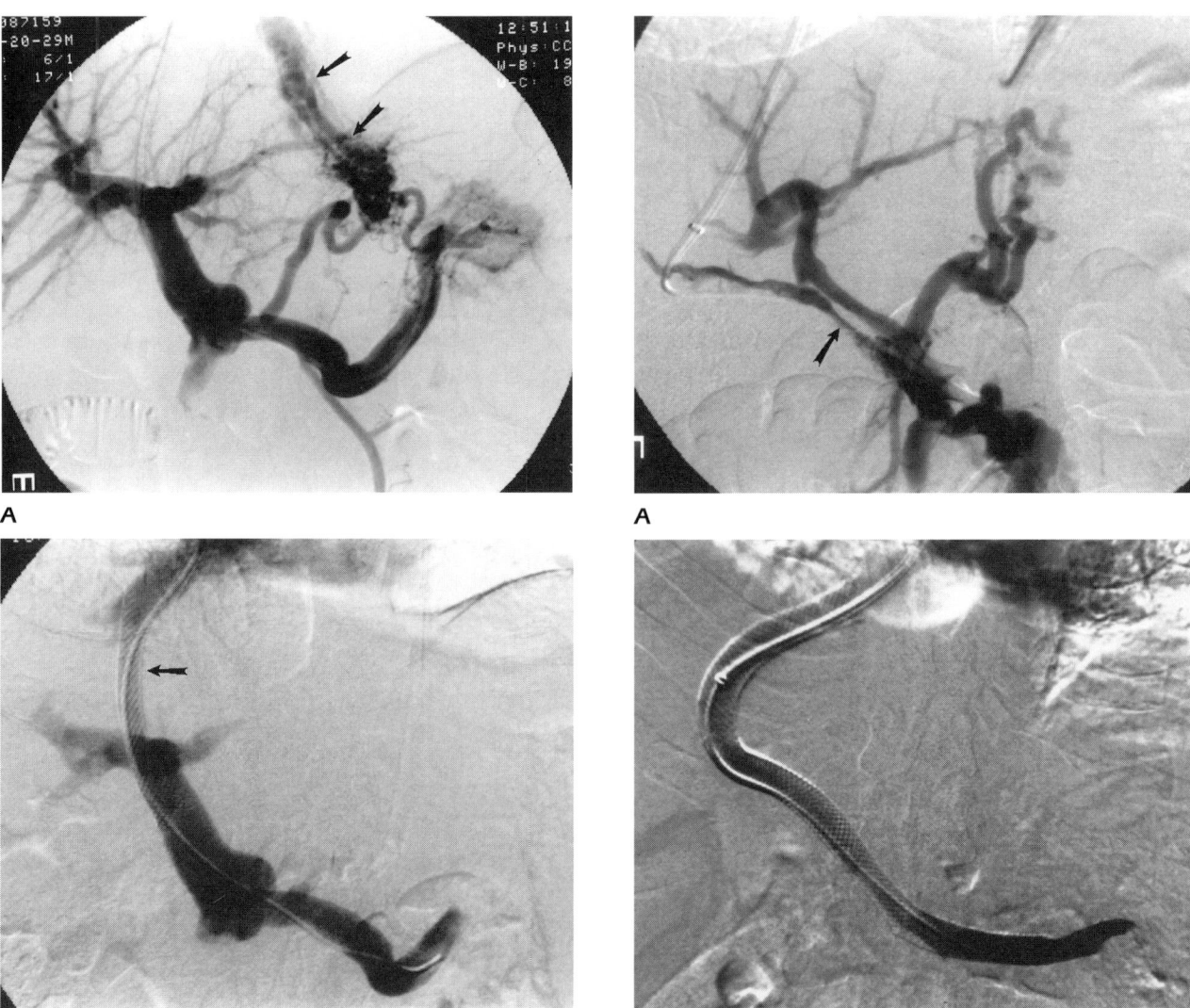

A

B

Figure 33-5. TIPS placement in a patient with a patent portal vein. A 36-year-old man presented for elective TIPS after repeated episodes of esophageal variceal hemorrhage despite three episodes of sclerotherapy. (A) Initial transjugular splenic venography demonstrates hepatopetal portal flow with fugal flow into the coronary, short gastric, and inferior mesenteric veins. The esophageal varices are visible (*arrows*). The portosystemic gradient is 18 mmHg. (B) Transjugular portogram after placement of a 10-mm right-hepatic-to-right-portal-vein TIPS (*arrow*) demonstrates flow through the shunt into the hepatic vein. There is no residual variceal flow. The portosystemic gradient is 9 mmHg.

dure by allowing the operator to create a shunt from almost any portal entry site. Once deployed and dilated, the stent maintains a cylindrical lumen around even the sharpest bends. Its disadvantages include relatively poor radiopacity and marked shortening during deployment. The latter characteristic makes precise stent deployment more difficult than with the Palmaz or Gianturco stents.

A

B

Figure 33-6. TIPS formation in the setting of distal splenic and portal vein thrombosis. A 52-year-old woman with alcoholic cirrhosis and seven episodes of gastric and esophageal variceal bleeding. Preshunt sonography demonstrated no flow in the portal vein. (A) Portography after transjugular recanalization of the chronically occluded portal vein. After balloon fragmentation of the thrombus, there is some hepatopetal flow in the portal vein (*arrow*). Hepatofugal variceal flow is present. The initial portosystemic gradient was 28 mmHg. (B) Splenic venography after recanalization of the splenic and portal veins and creation of a 12-mm-diameter TIPS. The stents extend from the occluded splenic vein into the right hepatic vein. No variceal flow remains. The portosystemic gradient is 12 mmHg.

In some cases, residual varices can be selectively catheterized and embolized with stainless steel coils and/or ethanol. Persistent variceal filling usually indicates that insufficient decompression has been achieved and that the shunt must be enlarged further. In the vast majority of cases, a 10-mm-diameter shunt

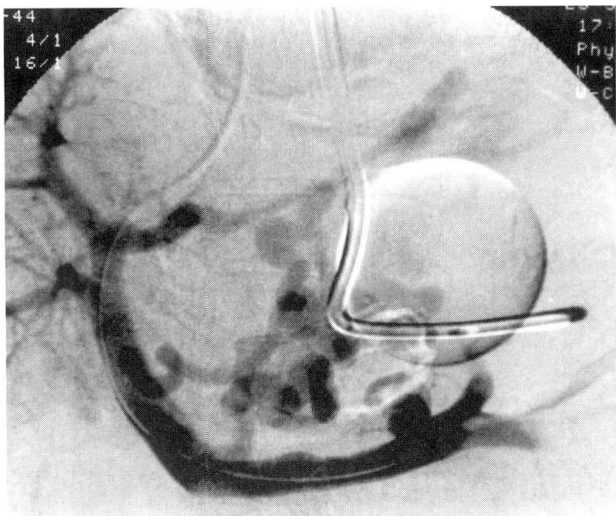

A

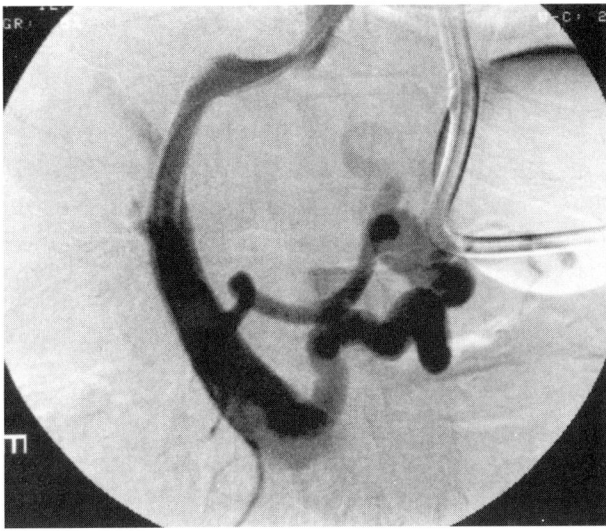

B

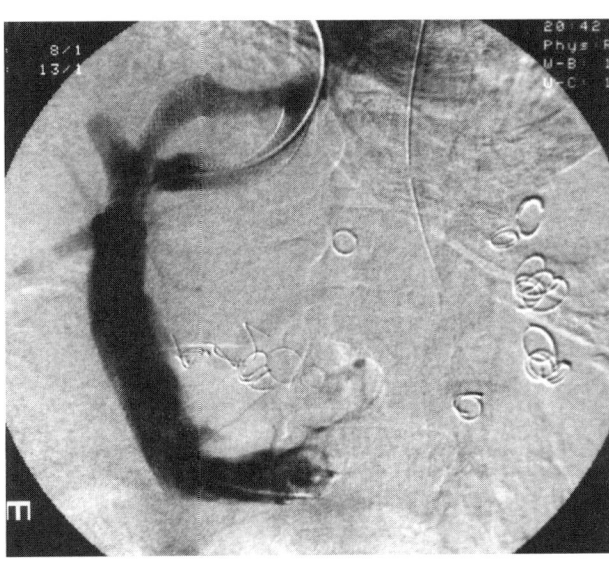

C

Figure 33-7. Parallel shunt formation. A 42-year-old man presented with uncontrolled gastric variceal bleeding despite inflation of a balloon tamponade catheter. (A) Initial transjugular portography demonstrates filling of multiple variceal trunks despite the inflated balloon tamponade catheter. The portosystemic gradient is 32 mmHg. (B) After formation of a right-hepatic-to-right-portal-vein TIPS, the portosystemic gradient has been reduced to 20 mmHg. Apparent narrowing of the outflow hepatic vein is partly due to inflow from other right hepatic veins. (C) No variceal flow remains after creation of a left-hepatic-to-left-portal TIPS. Variceal embolization has been performed. The portosystemic gradient is 11 mmHg. The balloon tamponade catheter has been deflated.

is sufficiently large to lower the portosystemic gradient below the bleeding threshold. If a 10-mm-diameter stent has been maximally dilated and significant portal hypertension remains, a second parallel shunt can be created between another hepatic vein and portal vein branch (Fig. 33-7).[126] This allows for the option of intentional, selective shunt occlusion should excessive encephalopathy develop. In addition, many patients with advanced cirrhosis have diminutive hepatic veins that are incapable of supporting the flow of a single 12-mm-diameter shunt. In these cases, a parallel shunt is the only percutaneous option for achieving additional portal decompression.

Final systemic venous pressures are measured during withdrawal of the jugular sheath. The patients are observed overnight in an intensive care or intermediate care unit for postsedation recovery. A color flow Doppler TIPS sonogram is obtained before discharge to document blood velocities in the main portal vein and shunt. These provide a baseline study for comparison with follow-up assessments of shunt patency. Patients undergoing elective TIPS placement are typically discharged the morning after the procedure. Arrangements are made for outpatient assessment of continued shunt patency and encephalopathy.

Results of TIPS

As with any relatively novel therapy, much of the early published literature on TIPS describes results in large and small uncontrolled patient series, technical advances and modifications, and new applications of the procedure. As experience with TIPS continues, data from large, externally funded, prospective randomized trials of TIPS versus other treatment options will be forthcoming. This section reviews the results from several larger TIPS series and highlights notable findings from selected smaller reports.

Pooled data from the University of California, San Francisco (UCSF), the Freiburg, Germany, group, and the University of Pennsylvania are included in Tables 33-1 through 33-6.[86,93,111] These results demonstrate that shunts can be created with a technical success rate of over 90 percent. The ability to create shunts in patients with new or chronic portal system thromboses illustrates the versatility of the TIPS technique. In the UCSF series, 7 of 10 patients with portal vein thrombosis underwent successful shunt placement (70 percent technical success); at the University of Pennsylvania, TIPSs were successfully formed in 25 cases of portal, splenic, and/or superior mesenteric thrombus (100 percent technical success). Patients with portal vein thrombosis were excluded from the Freiburg study.

TIPSs have proven very effective at lowering portal pressure. The use of real-time fluoroscopic and hemodynamic monitoring allows shunts to be progressively enlarged with balloon catheters until the portosystemic gradient has been satisfactorily reduced. In over

Table 33-1. Clinical Features of Patients Undergoing TIPS

	Univ Penn (*n* = 100)[111]	Freiburg (*n* = 100)[93]	UCSF (*n* = 100)[86]
Gender (M/F)	64/36	67/33	64/36
Age			
Mean	53.8	57	50
Range	20–84	18–84	5–84
Child-Pugh class			
A	9%	27%	10%
B	39%	51%	35%
C	52%	22%	55%

Table 33-2. Etiology of Liver Disease

	Univ Penn	Freiburg	UCSF
Alcoholic	59	68	56
Postnecrotic	21	19	26
Cryptogenic	14	9	15
Primary biliary cirrhosis	4	3	—
Budd-Chiari	2	—	1
Other	—	1	2

Table 33-3. Indications for TIPS Placement

	Univ Penn	Freiburg	UCSF
Bleeding	90	100	94
Acute	51	10	32
Chronic	39	83	62
Ascites or pleural effusion	8	—	3
Hepatorenal	—	—	2
Preoperative	2	—	1

Table 33-4. Hemodynamic and Technical Results of TIPS

	Univ Penn	Freiburg	UCSF
Technical success (%)	100	93	96
Pre-TIPS (mmHg)			
Portal vein	35.8	—	34.5
Right atrium	12.1	—	—
Portosystemic gradient	24.0	21.5	—
Post-TIPS (mmHg)			
Portal vein	26.1	—	24.5
Right atrium	15.3	—	—
Portosystemic gradient	11.0	9.2	10.4

Table 33-5. Procedural Complications of TIPS

	Univ Penn	Freiburg	UCSF
Bleeding (no. of patients)			
Intraabdominal	3	6	1
Hemobilia	0	4	1
Fever (no. of patients)	13	—	10
Renal failure (no. of patients)	—	—	3
Encephalopathy (%)			
New or worse	23	25	17
Uncontrolled	5	7	3

Table 33-6. Effect of TIPS on Ascites

	Univ Penn	Freiburg	UCSF
Improved/resolved	34/44 (77%)	47/53 (89%)	49/59 (83%)

90 percent of cases, shunts formed with 10-mm-diameter stents will adequately lower the portosystemic gradient to below 12 mmHg. Twelve-millimeter-diameter shunts can be created in patients with extremely high portal pressures. Alternatively, a smaller, parallel shunt can be created between different hepatic and portal vein branches to provide additional decompression.[126] Because flow is proportional to the fourth power of the radius of the shunt (Poiseuille law), the rate of portosystemic encephalopathy can be substantially greater than 12-mm- versus 10-mm-diameter shunts.[127,128] Creating smaller parallel shunts provides the option of selective shunt size reduction by occlusion of a single shunt, should excessive encephalopathy develop.[129] In addition, the hepatic veins are often shrunken in size in cirrhotic patients. Thus individual hepatic veins are often too small in caliber to support the flow of a single 12-mm-diameter TIPS.

Reduction of the portosystemic gradient below the generally accepted bleeding threshold of 12 to 15 mmHg can be achieved in almost every case. This accounts for the nearly universal control of acute variceal bleeding after creation of a satisfactory shunt. In the

UCSF series, bleeding was controlled in 30 of 32 patients. In 2 cases, repeat upper endoscopy revealed a duodenal ulcer and oozing sclerotherapy ulcer. In the author's experience, 47 out of 51 actively bleeding patients stopped bleeding during or shortly after TIPS. TIPS provided prompt control of variceal bleeding from all enteric sources, including esophageal, gastric, and large and small intestinal sites.[109] Repeat endoscopy was performed in 5 patients with continued oozing after TIPS. In 3 cases, this revealed interim variceal decompression and duodenal, gastric, and sclerotherapy ulcers. In 2 patients, the varices were only partially decompressed. These shunts were further enlarged with balloon catheters, after which bleeding stopped completely.

The overall 30-day mortality was 3, 13, and 30 percent in the Freiburg, UCSF, and University of Pennsylvania series, respectively. Not surprisingly, these differences are directly attributable to differing patient populations. One end of the spectrum is illustrated by the Freiburg data, wherein 78 percent of patients had Child A or B cirrhosis and 90 percent of the patients underwent elective TIPS. In contrast, the patient group at the University of Pennsylvania consisted of 100 consecutive, unselected patients—that is, "all-comers." Fifty-two percent of patients had class C cirrhosis, and 39 percent had class B cirrhosis. Fifty-one patients were actively bleeding during the TIPS procedure. All of these patients were receiving blood transfusions during the procedure; 47 were receiving vasopressin; 33 were mechanically ventilated; and 25 had balloon tamponade catheters in place. Death within 30 days of TIPS resulted from incipient multiorgan failure, aspiration pneumonia, cardiac arrhythmia, and preexisting adult respiratory distress syndrome. In fact, in all three series, the 30-day mortality was approximately 30 percent for patients with active variceal hemorrhage. In the author's patient group, Child class C disease conferred a 4-fold increased risk of early demise compared with Child class A and B disease. To better stratify survivors and nonsurvivors after TIPS, the author prospectively calculated pre-TIPS APACHE II (Acute Physiology and Chronic Health Evaluation) scores for 130 consecutive patients.[111,130] A pre-TIPS APACHE II score of 20 conferred a nearly 20-fold risk of early death, independent of Child class. A pre-TIPS APACHE II score of 20 or greater correctly predicted mortality within 30 days of TIPS with 84 percent accuracy. In contrast, the early mortality rate in patients undergoing elective TIPS at the University of Pennsylvania was 2 percent. Once patients survived the morbidity of the acute hemorrhage, 1-year survival leveled off for all Child classes. At 1 year, only 7 additional patients had died; causes of death included congestive heart failure, pneumonia, liver failure, pulmonary hemorrhage, and advanced age.

Longer-term survival was examined by LaBerge et al. in a report of 90 patients who underwent TIPS for treatment of variceal bleeding.[87] The mean follow-up period was 1.0 ± 1.2 years (range 1 day to 3.3 years). During follow-up, 31 patients survived without liver transplantation (mean survival 2.2 years $\pm$ 5.1 months), 34 patients died (mean time to death 4.9 months $\pm$ 6.6 months), and 22 patients underwent liver transplantation (3.0 months $\pm$ 5.2 months). Cumulative survival rates for Child A, B, and C patients were 75, 68, and 49 percent at 1 year and 75, 55, and 43 percent at 2 years, respectively. Survival differences between Child C and A or B patients were not statistically significant. However, when Child C patients were subdivided into those with Child-Pugh scores of 10 or 11 and those with scores of 12 to 15, significant survival differences emerged. Patients with Child A, B, or low-C class disease had significantly longer survival than Child C patients with high Child-Pugh scores ($p = 0.0001$). Nearly all of the high Child C deaths occurred within 1 month of TIPS. Twenty patients died more than 30 days after TIPS, in most cases (13/20) from liver failure. In 2 cases, death was caused by recurrent variceal bleeding. This fact emphasizes the sobering inexorable course of advanced liver disease. Although TIPS may prolong survival by removing the morbidity of recurrent variceal bleeding, ultimately enhancement of long-term survival depends on the availability of liver transplantation.

One of the incidental benefits of TIPS in patients treated for variceal hemorrhage is a marked improvement of ascites in 75 to 85 percent of cases[86,93] and cirrhotic pleural effusions.[131] This is not surprising, because TIPSs function as side-to-side surgical portosystemic shunts, which are effective in treating ascites. Accordingly, a number of centers are evaluating TIPS as a primary therapy for patients with refractory ascites (Fig. 33-8). Relatively few prospective studies have been published reporting the results of TIPS for this indication. Ferral et al. reported a series of 14 Child B and C patients with tense ascites who underwent TIPS.[112] TIPS creation succeeded in 13 cases (93 percent technical success). Seven patients (50 percent) had complete resolution of ascites. Five of the patients who did not respond had Child-Pugh scores of greater than 11, leading the authors to suggest that these patients should not undergo the procedure.

Ochs et al. reported more encouraging results in a larger prospective study of 50 out of 62 consecutive patients with refractory ascites.[99] In this uncontrolled study, refractory ascites was defined as no drop in body weight after 4 weeks of sodium restriction; spironolactone doses of 300 to 400 mg per day; furosemide 120 mg per day; or treatment intolerance, manifested by a serum sodium concentration of less than 125 mmol per liter, a serum creatinine level greater than 2.4 mg/dl, or medication allergy. The patients were followed for a mean (± standard deviation [SD]) of 426 = 333 days after TIPS placement. The severity of liver disease in the cohort was 36 percent Child class B and 62 percent class C. Shunts were successfully created in all cases, lowering the portosystemic gradient from a mean (± SD) of 22 ± 7 mmHg to 8 ± 4 mmHg. In sharp contrast to Ferral's early experience, Ochs et al. found a 74 percent total and 18 percent partial remission of ascites within 3 months of TIPS. Hepatic encephalopathy was present in 40 percent of patients before TIPS and in 50 percent after TIPS. In 8 cases, the postshunt encephalopathy was severe and was associated with rapid, lethal liver failure. Twenty procedural complications developed in 16 patients. Two patients died within 2 weeks of TIPS. During the remainder of the follow-up period, 29 additional patients died, 10 from progressive liver failure and 19 from other causes. Although these promising results clearly support ongoing evaluation of TIPS for treatment of refractory ascites, eventual patient mortality from liver failure and underlying disease will likely remain substantial without liver transplantation.

In a small but elegant study, Somberg et al. performed extensive hormonal and renal function testing before and after creating TIPSs in five patients with refractory ascites.[91] Four out of five patients had a marked improvement in their ascites; one patient experienced crippling encephalopathy and liver failure and underwent accelerated liver transplantation 36 days later. At 2 weeks after TIPS, the four responders demonstrated marked increases in urine sodium excretion, free water clearance, glomerular filtration rate, and urine flow rates. There was concomitant normalization of the plasma renin activity and serum aldosterone levels. In another study, Quiroga et al. reported similar results as well as a significant reduction in plasma norepinephrine levels.[132] The reductions in the overactivity of the renin-aldosterone axis and sympathetic nervous system, and improvement in renal tubular sodium handling support the theory that portal decompression with a TIPS improves the "effective plasma volume" in patients with severe ascites. TIPS had limited effectiveness in patients with serum creatinine levels greater than 2.0 mg/dl, presumably because of a significant component of irreversible renal insufficiency. The ultimate role of TIPS in the treatment of refractory ascites must be clarified in randomized controlled trials of TIPS versus large-volume paracentesis and possibly peritoneovenous shunts.

Procedural Complications and Hepatic Encephalopathy

Complications of TIPS creation can be divided into two groups: those specifically attributable to the TIPS procedure, and those shared by all portosystemic shunts, such as hepatic encephalopathy and the potential for accelerated liver failure. With respect to procedural complications, creating a TIPS is one of the more technically demanding procedures performed by interventional radiologists. Not surprisingly, there is a steep learning curve, and a broad range of complications have been reported.[133] With increasing operator experience, however, serious complications occur in less than 5 percent of cases[86,87,133] and can be managed conservatively in most instances. Certain complications, including inadvertent hepatic artery puncture during transjugular portal vein localization, are shared with all transhepatic procedures, including liver biopsy and percutaneous biliary drainage. Although the complication is potentially lethal, it is unusual and can in some cases be treated angiographically.[134,135] In a prospective study of 50 patients undergoing TIPS at the University of Pennsylvania, hepatic angiograms were performed before and after TIPS to identify the rate of asymptomatic but angiographically demonstrable hepatic artery lesions. Despite several recognized arterial punctures with large and small portal puncture systems, no arterial pseudoaneurysms, arteriovenous fistulas, or arterial occlusions were identified, indicating that hepatic arterial injuries after TIPS are rare. Other reported complications of TIPS include contrast-induced renal failure, allergic contrast reactions, fever, myocardial ischemia, hemobilia, and pulmonary edema.[86,93,94,130,136]

Hepatic encephalopathy and accelerated liver failure are the most significant adverse effects of all methods of portosystemic diversion. Early experience with TIPS suggested that portosystemic encephalopathy (PSE) might occur less frequently than with surgical shunts because the size of the TIPS could be tailored to the portal hemodynamics of the individual. This finding has not been borne out, partly because of the difficulty of comparing encephalopathy rates among surgical and even radiologic series because of varying methods of assessing and reporting encephalopathy data. For example, some centers prescribe prophylactic oral lactulose therapy for all TIPS patients, whereas others reserve it for those patients who develop spontaneous encephalopathy. In general, new or worsened encephalopathy develops in 18 to 30 percent of patients who undergo TIPS for treatment of variceal bleeding.[86,93,136,137] Severe encephalopathy occurs in only 4 to 7 percent of cases, all other patients being well controlled with oral lactulose, dietary protein restriction, or antibiotic therapy. Furthermore, encephalopathy diminishes over time as the metallic stent is incorporated within a layer of pseudointimal and collagenous tissue.[110,137,138] This process usually reduces the shunt lumen by a minimum of 1 to 2 mm, lessening the degree of portosystemic diversion. In a prospective randomized trial of TIPS versus sclerotherapy, the portosystemic encephalopathy index in patients undergoing TIPS rose markedly within 7 days of TIPS and slowly decreased thereafter to a 6-month level that remained significantly higher than that of the sclerotherapy group.[136] In this and other studies, the strongest predictor for the development of encephalopathy after TIPS was its presence before the procedure.

The rate of encephalopathy in patients undergoing TIPS for refractory ascites is less well defined. These patients often have a significantly worse baseline liver function and may thus be more susceptible to postshunt encephalopathy. As noted earlier, in the largest published series, Ochs et al. created TIPS in 20 patients with a history of encephalopathy. Twenty-five patients manifested encephalopathy after TIPS; in 8 cases there was no prior history of encephalopathy. More notably, 8 out of 25 patients (32 percent) developed debilitating encephalopathy, liver failure, and death.

In cases of rapidly progressive liver failure or uncontrolled encephalopathy after TIPS, accelerated liver transplantation may be necessary. In some cases, encephalopathy can be reversed by intentional thrombosis of the shunts. Thrombosis can be achieved by overnight placement of an inflated balloon catheter within the shunt, which creates a dead space within the shunt that promptly occludes. This technique allows for sub-

sequent shunt recanalization should recurrent bleeding occur.[129] Alternatively, effective shunt flow can be reduced by placing an hourglass-shaped stent within the TIPS. This provides a measure of continued portal decompression and prophylaxis against bleeding or ascites (Fig. 33-9).[139,140]

Another adverse effect of TIPS is worsening of the hyperdynamic circulatory state that most cirrhotics maintain.[132] Azoulay et al. reported an immediate and persistent elevation in central venous pressures, cardiac output, and cardiac index and a decrease in systemic vascular resistance after TIPS.[141] At 1 month, the mean cardiac index had risen from 4.5 ± 1.3 to 7.4 ± 1.4 L/min-m². These are recognized complications of other forms of portosystemic diversion, accounting for the surgical dictum of fluid restriction after portacaval shunt surgery. Although these findings may have little clinical relevance in most patients undergoing TIPS, patients with limited cardiac reserve are at risk of cardiac failure and severe pulmonary edema after TIPS, making these preconditions a nearly absolute contraindication for the procedure.

Several relative contraindications to TIPS placement have been suggested, including portal and hepatic vein thrombosis and the presence of malignancies or other causes of distorted hepatic anatomy, such as polycystic liver disease. In the author's experience,

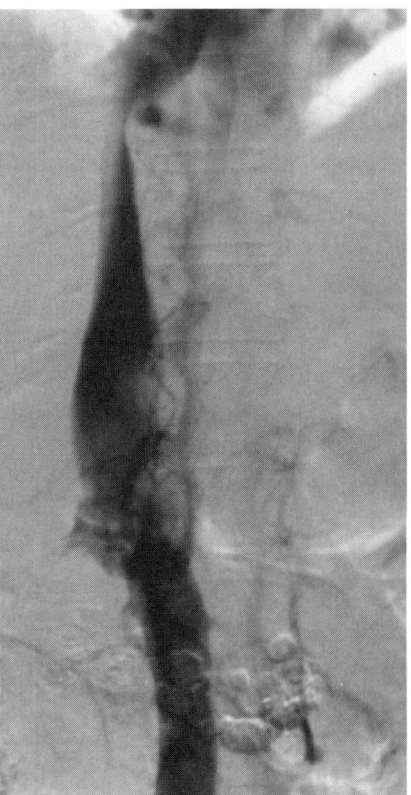

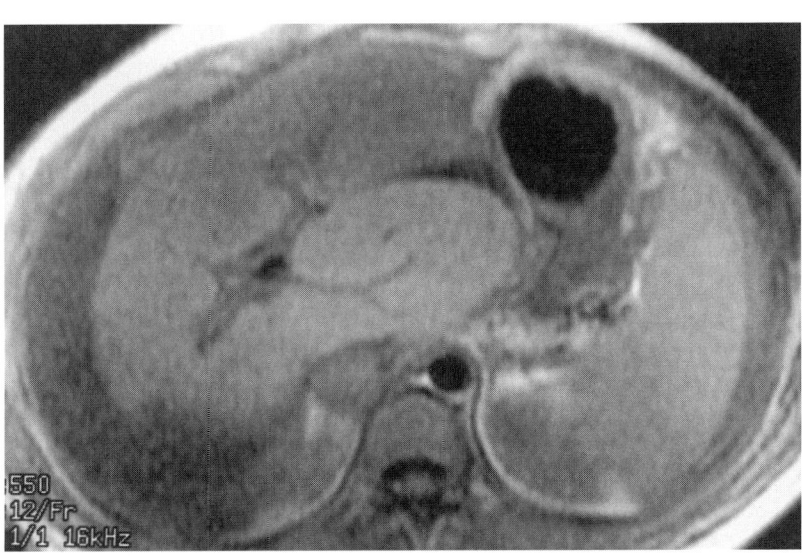

A

B

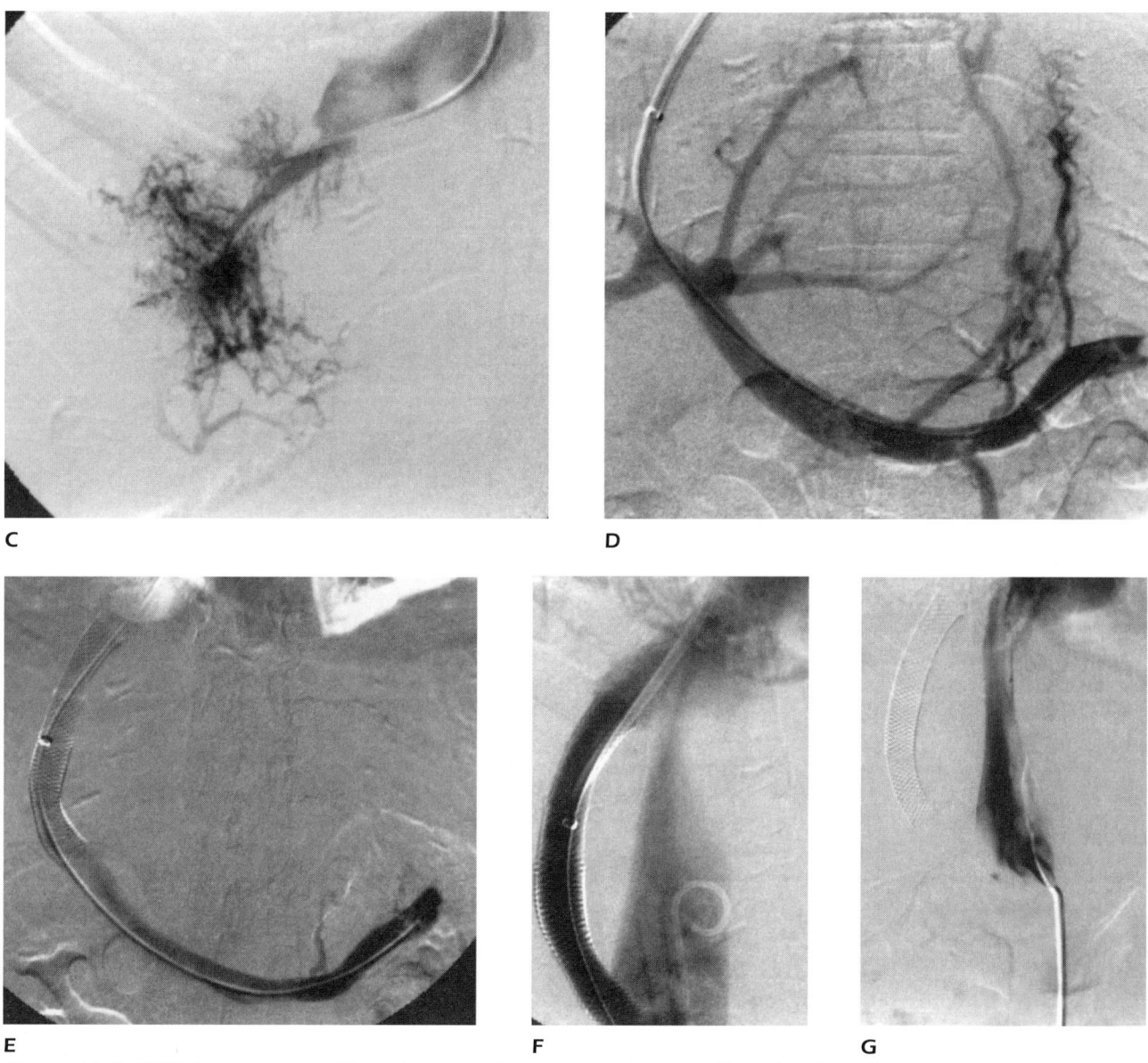

C   D

E   F   G

Figure 33-8. TIPS for treatment of hepatic venoocclusive disease (Budd-Chiari syndrome). A 27-year-old woman presented with hypotension, variceal bleeding, massive ascites, hepatosplenomegaly, and lower extremity edema. Subsequent bone marrow biopsy revealed a myeloproliferative disorder. Within 1 week of TIPS, the patient spontaneously diuresed 16 kg of fluid; her ascites and pedal edema completely resolved. At 2-year follow-up, she was fully functional and remained free of symptoms. Her liver function was normal. (A) Upper abdominal magnetic resonance image demonstrates marked enlargement of the caudate lobe and ascites. (B) Inferior vena cavogram demonstrates marked narrowing of the intrahepatic cava and collateral filling of the paravertebral veins. A 28-mmHg gradient was measured across the caval narrowing. (C) Wedged hepatic venography demonstrates irregularity of the right hepatic vein. Racemose he-patic vein collaterals indicate hepatic venoocclusive disease. (D) Initial transjugular portography demonstrates hepatofugal flow within the coronary, short gastric, and inferior mesenteric veins. The initial portosystemic gradient was 40 mmHg. A markedly enlarged caudate branch of the portal vein is present. (E) After TIPS placement, the portosystemic gradient was reduced to 11 mmHg. (F) Simultaneous injection of contrast into the TIPS and inferior vena cava demonstrates decompressive flow of the TIPS into the suprahepatic vena cava cephalad to the level of caval compression. (G) Inferior vena cavogram performed during 4-month surveillance TIPS venography. The intrahepatic vena cava is no longer compressed because the hepatic congestion has resolved. The inferior-vena-cava-to-right-atrium gradient was 4 mmHg. The TIPS was widely patent (not shown).

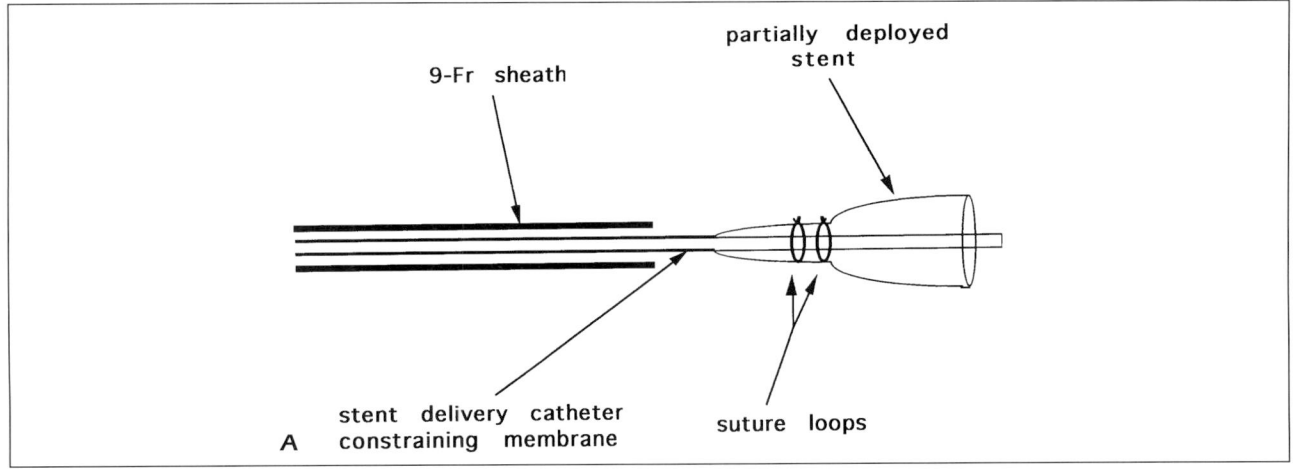

A

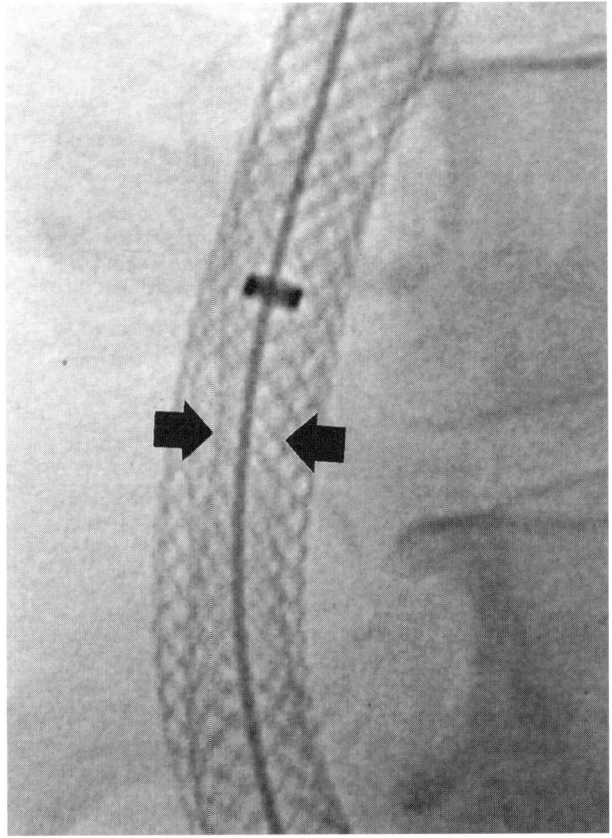

B

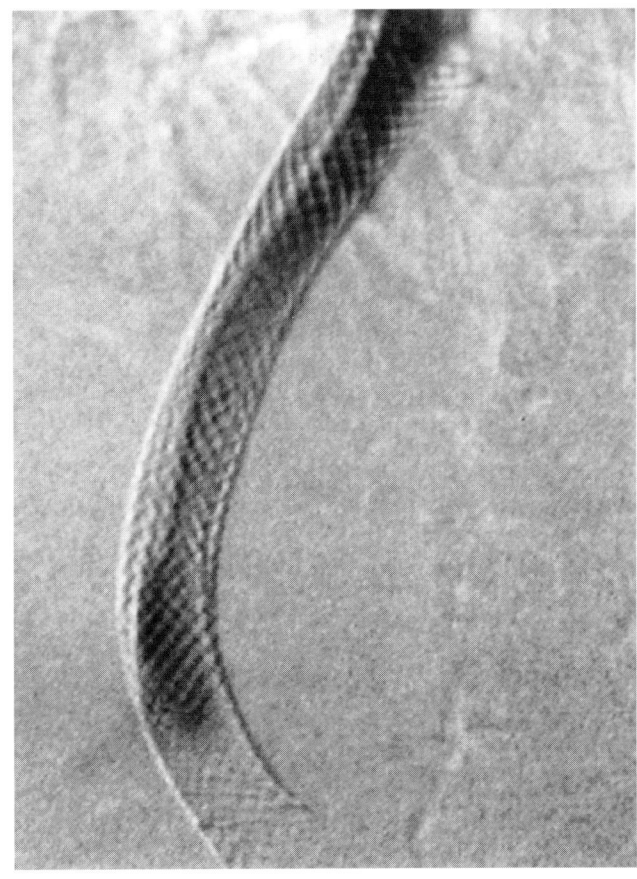

C

Figure 33-9. Creation of an hourglass-shaped stent to reduce flow in patients with excessive portosystemic encephalopathy after TIPS. (A) Diagrammatic representation of the stenotic stent assembly. Two suture loops are fixed around a partially deployed Wallstent. The stent is then enclosed within the 9 French vascular sheath, which had been backloaded over the stent delivery catheter. (B) Spot radiograph of the stenotic stent within the previously created shunt (*arrows*). The radiopaque band marks the leading end of the 9 French delivery sheath. (C) TIPS venogram after stent placement demonstrates flow through both the stent and, to a lesser degree, its interstices. (From Haskal ZJ, Middlebrook MR. Creation of a stenotic stent to reduce transjugular intrahepatic portosystemic shunt flow. J Vasc Intervent Radiol 1994;5:827–830. Used with permission.)

shunts have been successfully created in 25 out of 25 patients with hepatic, portal, mesenteric, and/or segmental splenic vein thrombosis. Although these conditions complicate the procedure, with experience, shunts can be created in almost all such cases.

Shunt Biology and Patency

LaBerge et al. published the first detailed descriptions of TIPS histology in 1991. The explanted livers of seven liver transplant patients who had undergone TIPS were examined. At 4 days after TIPS, fresh thrombus was adhered to the mesh of the stents. By 3 weeks, the shunt lumen was lined with a 400- to 600-μ-thick layer of pseudointimal tissue. At 3 months, the stents were enveloped within a layer of dense collagen.[138]

In most instances, smooth muscle cell activity and tissue proliferation continue unchecked within the shunt tract or the outflow hepatic vein, leading to a reduction of the effective shunt lumen and recurrent portal hypertension and symptoms. A number of authors have emphasized the need for close follow-up to ensure shunt patency. Because there is no consensus on methods of shunt surveillance (e.g., Doppler ultrasound versus venography), intervals of surveillance, and definitions of patency, markedly different patency data have been reported from different centers, ranging from 15 to 50 percent.[87,100,108,110,142] In general, most investigators agree that a significant percentage of patients will develop hemodynamically significant shunt stenoses within 6 to 12 months of TIPS (Fig. 33-10). In the author's experience with a prospective surveillance shunt venography study in 75 patients, by 6 months approximately 25 percent of TIPSs developed stenoses leading to recurrent elevation of the portosystemic gradient above 15 mmHg (75 percent 6-month primary shunt patency). At 1 year, half of the

Figure 33-10. Development of outflow hepatic vein stenosis after TIPS. (A) Initial "free" hepatic venogram before TIPS demonstrates a widely patent right hepatic vein. (B) Hepatic venogram at 6-month surveillance shunt study demonstrates interim stenosis of the outflow hepatic vein near its ostium (*arrows*). (C) The hepatic vein is reexpanded after placement of an overlapping Wallstent (*arrow*).

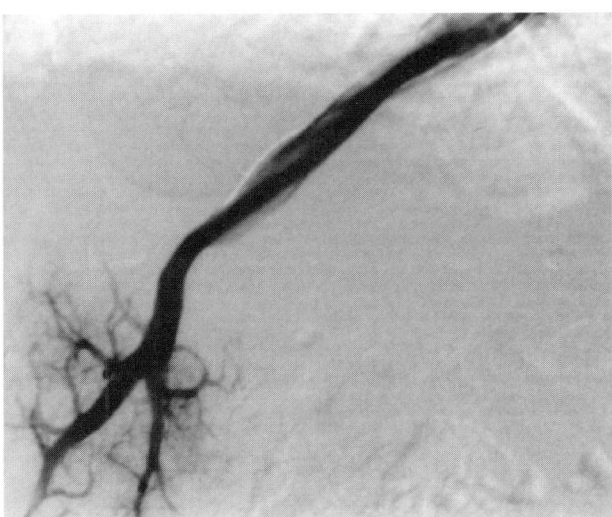

A

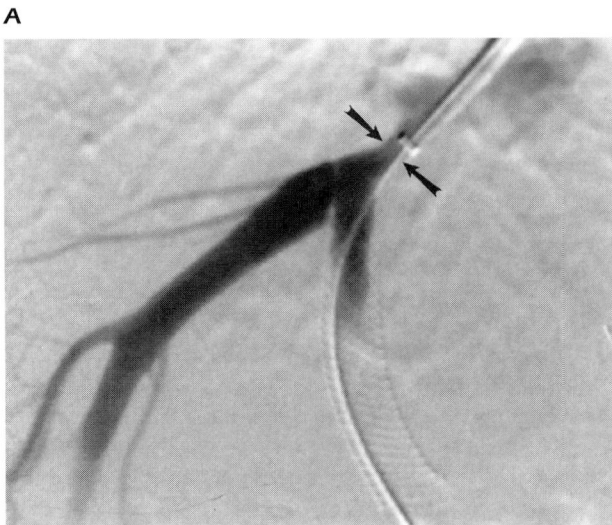

B

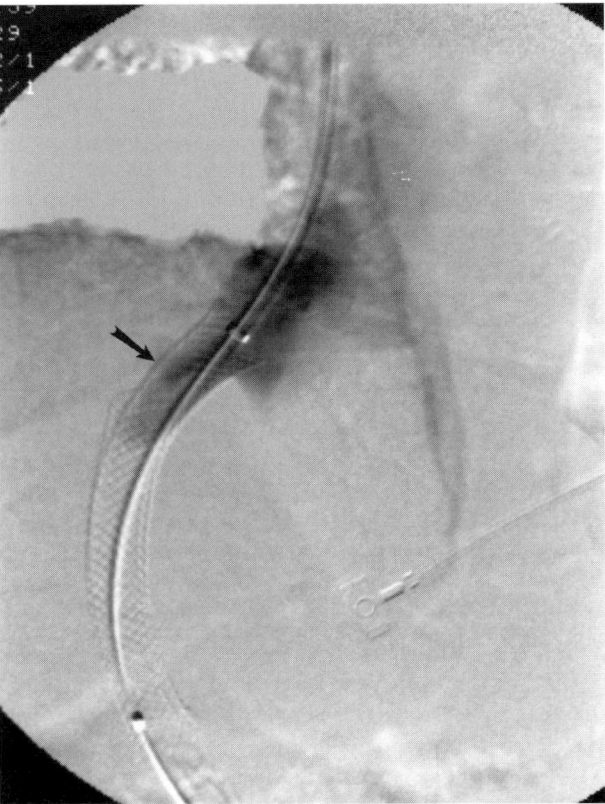

C

patients had developed significant shunt stenoses. On the other hand, shunt revision provided 1- and 2-year assisted or secondary patencies of nearly 90 percent. LaBerge et al. reported similar patency results using a combination of sonographic and venographic follow-up. Primary patency at 1 and 2 years was 66 and 42 percent, respectively, whereas primary-assisted and secondary patencies were 83 and 79 percent and 96 and 90 percent at 1 and 2 years, respectively.[87]

Two years later, the same investigators described the histopathologic findings in a series of patients with stenotic and occluded shunts. Bile staining of several occluded shunts was present, suggesting that the inflammatory effect of biliary leakage into the shunt contributed to thrombus accumulation and occlusion.[143] These findings have been clinically corroborated by others.[110,144] In the author's experience, nine patients with demonstrable biliary-to-TIPS fistulas had repeated shunt thromboses at rates double that of the larger population of TIPS patients (Fig. 33-11). In several instances, near-occlusive thrombus repeatedly developed adjacent to the site of the fistula, ultimately requiring that the shunt be abandoned in favor of a new TIPS. This problem, however, accounts for only a portion of shunt failures. In many cases, narrowing of the outflow hepatic vein accounts for the flow-limiting stenosis. In one prospective study of the natural development of TIPS stenosis, all hepatic veins shrank an average of 50 percent in diameter in response to TIPS.[110] Advances in shunt technology may eventually solve these problems, particularly stents combined with microporous graft material. All TIPS patients should undergo evaluations of shunt patency at 6-month intervals until the stability of shunt diameter has been demonstrated. Shunt stenoses or occlusions can be treated on an outpatient basis with balloon angioplasty or with placement of additional stents within the narrowed segments. With regular follow-up and periodic revisions, it appears that assisted shunt patency may be preserved almost indefinitely.

Conclusion

The treatment of portal hypertension remains a complex clinical challenge that is best approached with a multidisciplinary group consisting of interventional radiologists, hepatologists, and surgeons. Although TIPS clearly represents a landmark therapy for portal hypertension, it is too early to determine what final impact it will have on the treatment of portal hypertension. Clearly, TIPSs provide a relatively safe method of quick and reliable partial portal decompression and are as effective as surgical shunts at arresting acute

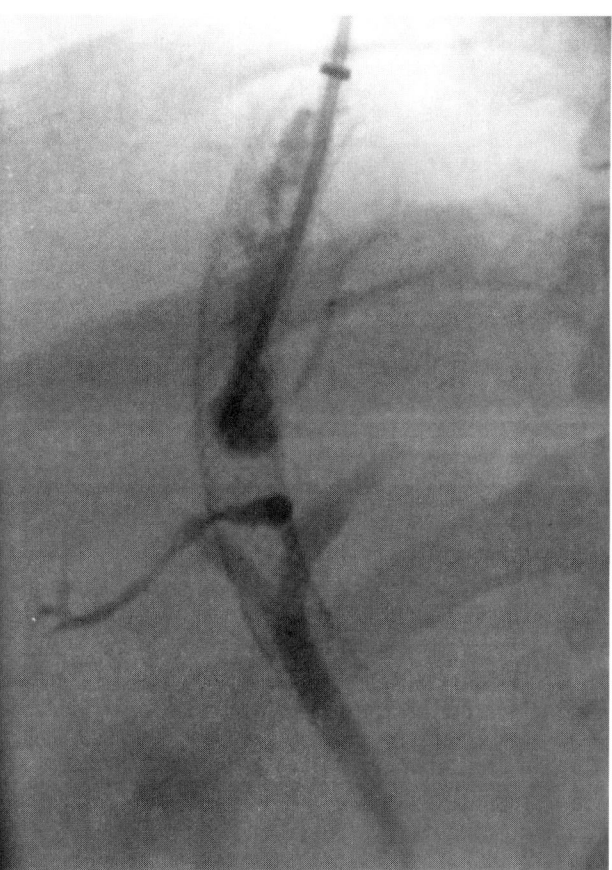

Figure 33-11. Bile-duct-to-TIPS fistula causing accelerated shunt stenosis and occlusion. Three shunt occlusions developed within 10 months in a 53-year-old woman who underwent TIPS for variceal bleeding. Gentle injection of contrast into the midportion of the occluded TIPS demonstrates immediate filling of the biliary tree.

variceal hemorrhage. Long-term prophylaxis against bleeding appears to be entirely related to maintenance shunt patency. Shunt stenosis remains a significant, albeit manageable, problem. However, it is likely that upcoming developments in endovascular graft technology will reduce the need for close surveillance and intervention. Stents lined with surgical graft material or imbued with agents that limit intimal hyperplasia may lessen the neointimal stenoses and allow TIPS to become a more durable treatment for patients with portal hypertension.

References

1. Johnson WC, Widrich WC. Efficacy of selective splanchnic arteriography and vasopressin perfusion in diagnosis and treatment of gastrointestinal hemorrhage. Am J Surg 1976; 131:481–489.
2. Nusbaum M, Baum S, Sakiyalak P, et al. Pharmacologic control of portal hypertension. Surgery 1967;62:299–310.
3. Johnson WC, Widrich WC, Ansell JE, Robbins AH, Nabseth

DC. Control of bleeding varices by vasopressin: a prospective randomized study. Ann Surg 1977;186:369–376.

4. Tsai YT, Lay CS, Lai KH, et al. Controlled trial of vasopressin plus nitroglycerin vs. nasopressin alone in the treatment of bleeding esophageal varices. Hepatology 1986;6:406–409.

5. Gimson AE, Westaby D, Hegarty J, Watson A, Williams R. A randomized trial of vasopressin and vasopressin plus nitroglycerin in the control of acute variceal hemorrhage. Hepatology 1986;6:410–413.

6. Conn HO. Vasopressin and nitroglycerin in the treatment of bleeding varices: the bottom line. Hepatology 1986;6:523–525.

7. Sirinek KR, Adcock DK, Levine BA. Simultaneous infusion of nitroglycerin and nitroprusside to offset effects of vasopressin during portosystemic shunting. Am J Surg 1989;157:33–37.

8. Bosch J, Groszmann RJ, Garcia-Pagan JC, et al. Association of transdermal nitroglycerin to vasopressin infusion in the treatment of variceal hemorrhage: a placebo-controlled clinical trial. Hepatology 1989;10:962–968.

9. LeBrec D, Nouel O, Corbic M, et al. Propanolol, a medial treatment for portal hypertension. Lancet 1980;2:180–182.

10. Pagliaro L, D'Amico G, Sorensen TI, et al. Prevention of first bleeding in cirrhosis: a meta-analysis of randomized trials of nonsurgical treatment. Ann Intern Med 1992;117:59–70.

11. Greig JD, Garden OJ, Carter DC. Prophylactic treatment of patients with esophageal-varices: is it ever indicated? World J Surg 1994;18:176–184.

12. LeBrec D. Current status and future goals of pharmacologic reduction of portal hypertension. Am J Surg 1990;160:19–25.

13. Crafoord C, Frenckner P. New surgical treatment of varicose veins of the esophagus. Acta Oto-laryngol 1939;27:422.

14. Paquet KJ, Kalk JF, Koussouris P. Immediate endoscopic sclerosis of bleeding esophageal varices: a prospective evaluation over five years. Surg Endosc 1988;2:18–23.

15. Terblanche J, Northover J, Bornman P, et al. A prospective controlled trial of sclerotherapy in the long term management of patients after oesophageal variceal bleeding. Surg Gynecol Obstet 1979;148:323–333.

16. Terblanche J, Burroughs AK, Hobbs KEF. Controversies in the management of bleeding esophageal varices (first of two parts). N Engl J Med 1989;320:1393–1398.

17. Terblanche J, Burroughs AK, Hobbs KEF. Controversies in the management of bleeding esophageal varices (second of two parts). N Engl J Med 1989;320:1469–1475.

18. Cello JP, Grendall JH, Cross RA, et al. Endoscopic sclerotherapy versus portacaval shunt in patients with severe cirrhosis and variceal hemorrhage. N Engl J Med 1984;311:1589–1600.

19. Infante-Rivard C, Esnaola S, Villeneuve JP. Role of endoscopic sclerotherapy in the long-term management of variceal bleeding: a meta analysis. Gastroenterology 1989;96:1594–1600.

20. Goff JS, Reveille RM, Stiegmann GV. Endoscopic sclerotherapy versus endoscopic variceal ligation: esophageal symptoms, complications, and motility. Am J Gastroenterol 1988;83:1240–1244.

21. Stiegmann GV, Goff JS, Michaletz-Onody PA, et al. Endoscopic sclerotherapy as compared with endoscopic ligation for treatment of bleeding esophageal varices. N Engl J Med 1992;326:1527–1532.

22. Terblanche J, Stiegmann GV, Krige JE, Bornman PC. Long-term management of variceal bleeding: the place of varix injection and ligation. World J Surg 1994;18:185–192.

23. Child C. Eck's fistula. Surg Gynecol Obstet 1953;96:375–376.

24. Vidal E. Traitment chirurgical des ascites. Presse Med 1903;11:747.

25. Kanel CC, Kaplan MM, Zawacki JK, Callow AD. Survival in patients with post-necrotic cirrhosis and Laennec's cirrhosis undergoing therapeutic portacaval shunt. Gastroenterology 1977;73:679–683.

26. Reynolds T, Donovan AJ, Mikkelson WP, Redeken AG, Turrill FL, Weiner JM. Results of a 12-year randomized trial of portacaval shunt in patients with alcoholic liver disease and bleeding varices. Gastroenterology 1981;80:1005–1011.

27. Warren WD, Zeppa R, Forman JJ. Selective transsplenic decompression of gastroesophageal varices by distal splenorenal shunt. Ann Surg 1967;166:437–455.

28. Warren WD, Millikan WJ, Henderson JM, et al. Ten years of portal hypertensive surgery at Emory. Ann Surg 1982;195:530–542.

29. Rikkers LF, Rudman D, Galambos JT, et al. A randomized, controlled trial of the distal splenorenal shunt. Ann Surg 1978;188:271–282.

30. Henderson JM, Gong-Liang J, Galloway J, Millikan WJ, Sones PJ, Warren WD. Portaprival collaterals following distal splenorenal shunt: incidence, magnitude, and associated portal perfusion changes. J Hepatol 1985;1:649–661.

31. Widrich WC, Robbins AH, Johnson WC, Nabseth DC. Long-term follow-up of distal splenorenal shunts: evaluation by arteriography, shuntography, transhepatic portal venography, and cinefluorography. Radiology 1980;134:341–345.

32. Bismuth H, Csillag MJ, Benhamou JP, Fauvert R. L'anastomose portocave chez le rat normal: IV. Influence du calibre de l'anastomose. Rev Fr Etud Clin Biol 1965;10:1087–1092.

33. Bismuth H, Franco D, Hepp J. Portal-systemic shunt in cirrhosis: does the type of shunt decisively influence the clinical result? Ann Surg 1974;179:209–218.

34. Collins JC, Rypins EB, Sarfeh IJ. Narrow-diameter portacaval shunts for management of variceal bleeding. World J Surg 1994;18:211–215.

35. Rypins EB, Sarfeh IJ. Small-diameter portacaval H-graft for variceal hemorrhage. Surg Clin North Am 1990;70:395–404.

36. Johansen K. Partial portal decompression for variceal hemorrhage. Am J Surg 1989;157:479–482.

37. Sarfeh IJ, Carter JA, Welch HF. Analysis of operative mortality after portal decompressive procedures in cirrhotic patients. Am J Surg 1981;140:306–311.

38. Iwatsuki S, Starzl TE, Todo S, et al. Experience in 1,000 liver transplants under cyclosporine-steroid therapy: a survival report. Transplant Proc 1988;20:498–504.

39. Ewaga H, Keeffe EB, Dort J, Concepcion W, Esquivel CO. Liver transplantation for uncontrollable variceal bleeding. Am J Gastroenterol 1994;89:1823–1826.

40. Iwatsuki S, Starzl TE, Todo S, et al. Liver transplantation in the treatment of bleeding esophageal varices. Surgery 1988;104:697–705.

41. Weichel KL. Tekniken vid perkutan transhepatisk portapunton (PTP). Nord Med 1971;86:912.

42. Lunderquist A, Vang J. Transhepatic catheterization of the coronary vein in patients with portal hypertension and esophageal varices. N Engl J Med 1974;291:646–649.

43. Lunderquist A, Borjesson B, Owman T, Bengmark S. Isobutyl 2-cyanoacrylate (bucrylate) in obliteration of gastric coronary vein and esophageal varices. Am J Roentgenol 1978;130:1–6.

44. Ansell JE, Widrich WC, Johnson WC, et al. Gelfoam and autologous clot embolization: effect on coagulation. Invest Radiol 1978;13:115–120.

45. Uflacker R. Percutaneous transhepatic obliteration of gastroesophageal varices using absolute alcohol. Radiology 1983;148:621–625.

46. Widrich WC, Srinivasan M, Johnson WC, et al. Transhepatic embolization of gastroesophageal varices: analysis of results in 90 patients. Semin Intervent Radiol 1988;5:76–84.

47. Sos T. Transhepatic portal venous embolization of varices: pros and cons. Radiology 1983;148:569–570.

48. Vinel JP, Scotto JM, Levade M, et al. Embolization of esophageal varices by the transjugular route in severe digestive hemorrhage in cirrhotic patients: prospective study of 83 patients. Gastroenterol Clin Biol 1985;9:814–818.

49. Menu Y, Gayet B, Nahum H. Bleeding duodenal varices: diagnosis and treatment by percutaneous portography and

transcatheter embolization. Gastrointest Radiol 1987;12: 111–113.

50. Ozaki CK, Hansen M, Kadir S. Transhepatic embolization of superior mesenteric varices in portal hypertension. Surgery 1989;105:446–448.
51. Samaraweera RN, Feldman L, Widrich WC, et al. Stomal varices: percutaneous transhepatic embolization. Radiology 1989;170:779–782.
52. Benner KG, Keefe EB, Keller FS, Rösch J. Clinical outcome after percutaneous transhepatic obliteration of esophageal varices. Gastroenterology 1983;85:146–153.
53. Bengmark S, Borjersson B, Hoevels J, et al. Obliteration of esophageal varices by percutaneous transhepatic embolization: follow-up of 43 patients. Ann Surg 1979;190:549–554.
54. Widrich WC, Robbins AH, Nabseth DC. Transhepatic embolization of varices. Cardiovasc Intervent Radiol 1980;3:298–303.
55. Keller FS, Dotter CT, Rösch J. Percutaneous transhepatic obliteration of gastroesophageal varices: some technical aspects. Radiology 1978;129:327–332.
56. Widrich WC, Robbins AH, Nabseth DC, Johnson WC, Goldstein SA. Pitfalls of transhepatic portal venography and therapeutic coronary vein occlusion. Am J Roentgenol 1978; 131:637–643.
57. Viamonte MJ, Pereiras R, Russell E, Le Page J, Hutson D. Transhepatic obliteration of gastroesophageal varices: results in acute and nonacute bleeders. Am J Roentgenol 1977;129: 237–241.
58. Ellman BA, Curry TI, Glotzbach RE, Simpson PR. Systemic embolization as a complication of transhepatic venography. Radiology 1981;141:67–71.
59. Johnson WC, Nabseth DC, Widrich WC, Bush HJ, O'Hara ET, Robbins AH. Bleeding esophageal varices: treatment with vasopressin, transhepatic embolization and selective splenorenal shunting. Ann Surg 1982;195:393–400.
60. Terabayashi H, Ohnishi K, Tsunoda T, et al. Prospective controlled trial of elective endoscopic sclerotherapy in comparison with percutaneous transhepatic obliteration of esophageal varices in patients with nonalcoholic cirrhosis. Gastroenterology 1987;93:1205–1209.
61. Funaro AH, Ring EJ, Freiman DB, Oleaga JA, Gordon RL. Transhepatic obliteration of esophageal varices using the stainless steel coil. Am J Roentgenol 1979;133:1123–1125.
62. Durham JD, Kumpe DA, Van Stiegmann G, Goff JS, Subber SW, Rothbarth LJ. Direct catheterization of the mesenteric vein: combined surgical and radiologic approach to the treatment of variceal hemorrhage. Radiology 1990;177:229–233.
63. L'Hermine C, Chastanet P, Delemazure O, Bonniere PL, Durieu JP, Paris JC. Percutaneous transhepatic embolization of gastroesophageal varices: results in 400 patients. Am J Roentgenol 1989;152:755–760.
64. Cope C. Dilatation of mesocaval shunts. Ann Radiol 1986; 29:178–180.
65. Grosso M, Spalluto F, Rossato D, Capello S, Fava C. Percutaneous unblocking of porto-systemic shunts: personal experience with 11 cases. Radiol Med 1990;80:334–338.
66. Ruff RJ, Chuang VP, Alspaugh JP, Casarella WJ, Tuten TU, Gaylord GM. Percutaneous vascular intervention after surgical shunting for portal hypertension. Radiology 1987;164: 469–474.
67. Soyer P, Roche A, Breittmayer F. Percutaneous transluminal angioplasty of portosystemic shunts. Gastroenterol Clin Biol 1991;15:280–284.
68. Soyer P, Levesque M, Zeitoun G. Treatment of mesocaval shunt stenosis with a metallic stent. Am J Roentgenol 1992; 158:1251–1253.
69. Hausegger KA, Klein GE, Fluckiger F, Planinz W, Wildling R, Sternthal HM. Stenosis of a surgical portosystemic shunt: treatment with angioplasty and placement of a Wallstent. Cardiovasc Intervent Radiol 1993;16:243–244.
70. Cope C. Balloon dilatation of closed mesocaval shunts. Am J Roentgenol 1980;135:989–993.

71. Savader SJ, Venbrux AC, Klein AS, Osterman FA. Percutaneous intervention in portosystemic shunts in Budd-Chiari syndrome. J Vasc Intervent Radiol 1991;2:489–495.
72. Cope C. Percutaneous dilatation of closed mesocaval shunts. In: Castaneda-Zuniga WR, ed. Transluminal angioplasty. New York: Thieme, 1983:165–172.
73. Coldwell DM, Moore AD, Ben-Menachem Y, Johansen KH. Bleeding gastroesophageal varices: gastric vein embolization after partial portal decompression. Radiology 1991;178:249–251.
74. Uflacker R, d'Albuquerque LA, de Oliveira e Silva A, de Freitas JM, Gama-Rodrigues JJ. Embolization to reverse severe recurrent hepatic encephalopathy. Arq Gastroenterol 1988; 25:21–25.
75. Uflacker R, de Oliveira e Silva A, d'Albuquerque LA, Piske RL, Mourao GS. Chronic portosystemic encephalopathy: embolization of portosystemic shunts. Radiology 1987;165: 721–725.
76. Henderson JM. Treatment of post-shunt portal systemic encephalopathy by embolization of the shunt. Hepatology 1989;9:164–165.
77. Rösch J, Hanafee WN, Snow H. Transjugular portal venography and radiologic portacaval shunt: an experimental study. Radiology 1969;92:1112–1114.
78. Rösch J, Hanafee W, Snow H, Barenfus M, Gray R. Transjugular intrahepatic portacaval shunt: an experimental work. Am J Surg 1971;121:588–592.
79. Burgener FA, Gutierrez OH. Nonsurgical production of intrahepatic portosystemic venous shunts in portal hypertension with the double lumen balloon catheter. Rofo 1979;130: 686–688.
80. Reich M, Olumide F, Jorgensen E, Eisman B. Experimental cryoprobe production of intrahepatic portacaval shunt. J Surg Res 1977;23:14–18.
81. Colapinto RF, Stronell RD, Gildiner M, et al. Formation of intrahepatic portosystemic shunts using a balloon dilatation catheter: preliminary clinical experience. Am J Roentgenol 1983;140:709–714.
82. Rösch J, Uchida BT, Putnam JS, Buschman RW, Law RD, Hershey AL. Experimental intrahepatic portacaval anastomosis: use of expandable Gianturco stents. Radiology 1987;162: 481–485.
83. Palmaz JC, Sibbitt RR, Reuter SR, Garcia F, Tio FO. Expandable intrahepatic portacaval shunt stents: early experience in the dog. Am J Roentgenol 1985;145:821–825.
84. Richter GM, Noeldge G, Palmaz JC, et al. Transjugular intrahepatic portacaval stent shunt: preliminary clinical results. Radiology 1990;174:1027–1030.
85. Richter GM, Noeldge G, Palmaz JC, Roessle M. The transjugular intrahepatic portosystemic stent-shunt (TIPSS): results of a pilot study. Cardiovasc Intervent Radiol 1990;13: 200–207.
86. LaBerge JM, Ring EJ, Gordon RL, et al. Creation of transjugular intrahepatic portosystemic shunt (TIPS) with the Wallstent endoprosthesis: results in 100 patients. Radiology 1993; 187:413–420.
87. LaBerge JM, Somberg KA, Lake JR, et al. Two-year outcome following transjugular intrahepatic portosystemic shunt for variceal bleeding: results in 90 patients. Gastroenterology 1995;108:1143–1151.
88. Zemel G, Katzen BT, Becker GJ, Benenati JF, Sallee DS. Percutaneous transjugular portosystemic shunt. JAMA 1991; 266:390–393.
89. Woodle E, Darcy M, White H, et al. Intrahepatic portosystemic vascular stents: a bridge to hepatic transplantation. Surgery 1993;113:344–351.
90. Vinel JP, Rousseau H. Transjugular intrahepatic portacaval shunts (TIPS). Indian J Gastroenterol 1992;11:159–161.
91. Somberg K, Lake J, Tomlanovich S, et al. Transjugular intrahepatic portosystemic shunts for refractory ascites: assessment of clinical and hormonal response and renal function. Hepatology 1995;21:709–716.

92. Rousseau H, Vinel JP, Bilbao H, et al. Transjugular intrahepatic portosystemic shunts using the Wallstent prosthesis: a follow-up study. Cardiovasc Intervent Radiol 1994;17: 7–11.

93. Rossle M, Haag K, Ochs A, et al. The transjugular intrahepatic portosystemic stent-shunt procedure for variceal bleeding. N Engl J Med 1994;330:165–171.

94. Ring EJ, Lake JR, Roberts JP, et al. Using transjugular intrahepatic portosystemic shunts to control variceal bleeding before liver transplantation. Ann Intern Med 1992;116:304–309.

95. Richter GM, Roeren T, Roessle M, Palmaz JC. Transjugular intrahepatic portosystemic stent shunt. Baillieres Clin Gastroenterol 1992;6:403–419.

96. Radosevich PM, Ring EJ, LaBerge JM, et al. Transjugular intrahepatic portosystemic shunts in patients with portal vein occlusion. Radiology 1993;186:523–527.

97. Peltzer MY, Ring EJ, LaBerge JM, Haskal ZJ, Radosevich PM, Gordon RL. Treatment of Budd-Chiari syndrome with a transjugular intrahepatic portosystemic shunt. J Vasc Intervent Radiol 1993;4:263–267.

98. Ochs A, Sellinger M, Haag K, et al. Transjugular intrahepatic portosystemic stent-shunt (TIPS) in the treatment of Budd-Chiari syndrome. J Hepatol 1993;18:217–225.

99. Ochs A, Rossle M, Haag K, et al. The transjugular intrahepatic portosystemic stent-shunt procedure for refractory ascites. N Engl J Med 1995;332:1192–1197.

100. Nazarian GK, Ferral H, Castaneda-Zuniga WR, et al. Development of stenoses in transjugular intrahepatic portosystemic shunts. Radiology 1994;192:231–234.

101. Maynar M, Cabrera J, Pulido-Duque JM, et al. Transjugular intrahepatic portosystemic shunt: early experience with a flexible trocar/catheter system. Am J Roentgenol 1993;161: 301–306.

102. Martin M, Zajko AB, Orons PD, et al. Transjugular intrahepatic portosystemic shunt in the management of variceal bleeding: indications and clinical results. Surgery 1993;114: 719–726.

103. Simpson KJ, Chalmers N, Redhead DN, Finlayson ND, Bouchier IA, Hayes PC. Transjugular intrahepatic portosystemic stent shunting for control of acute and recurrent upper gastrointestinal haemorrhage related to portal hypertension. Gut 1993;34:968–973.

104. Menegaux F, Baker E, Keeffe EB, Monge H, Egawa H, Esquivel CO. Impact of transjugular intrahepatic portosystemic shunt on orthotopic liver transplantation. World J Surg 1994; 18:866–870.

105. Longo JM, Bilbao JI, Rousseau HP, et al. Color Doppler ultrasound guidance in transjugular placement of intrahepatic portosystemic shunts. Radiology 1992;184:281–284.

106. Krajina A, Hulek P, Elias P, et al. Transjugular intrahepatic portosystemic shunt with spiral Z stents: first clinical experience in 20 patients. Eur Radiol 1993;4:425–429.

107. Kerns SC, Sabatelli FW, Hawkins IF. Fine-needle transjugular portal venous access system. J Vasc Intervent Radiol 1994;5: 835–837.

108. Hausegger KA, Sternthal HM, Klein GE, Karaic R, Stauber R, Zenker G. Transjugular intrahepatic portosystemic shunt: angiographic follow-up and secondary interventions. Radiology 1994;191:177–181.

109. Haskal ZJ, Scott M, Rubin RA, Cope C. Intestinal varices: treatment with the transjugular intrahepatic portosystemic shunt. Radiology 1994;191:183–187.

110. Haskal ZJ, Pentecost MJ, Soulen MC, Shlansky-Goldberg RD, Baum RA, Cope C. Transjugular intrahepatic portosystemic shunt stenosis and revision: early and midterm results. Am J Roentgenol 1994;163:439–444.

111. Haskal ZJ, Cope C, Shlansky-Goldberg RD, Soulen MC, Baum RA, Pentecost MJ. Transjugular intrahepatic portosystemic shunts: early and midterm efficacy into 100 patients. Radiology 1994;193:130.

112. Ferral H, Bjarnason H, Wegryn S, et al. Refractory ascites: early experience in treatment with transjugular intrahepatic portosystemic shunt. Radiology 1993;189:795–801.

113. Echenagusia AJ, Camunez F, Simo G, et al. Variceal hemorrhage: efficacy of transjugular intrahepatic portosystemic shunts created with Strecker stents. Radiology 1994;192: 235–240.

114. Conn HO. Transjugular intrahepatic portal-systemic shunts: the state of the art. Hepatology 1993;17:148–158.

115. Helton WS, Belshaw A, Althaus S, Park S, Coldwell D, Johansen K. Critical appraisal of the angiographic portacaval shunt (TIPS). Am J Surg 1993;165:566–571.

116. Conn HO. Quantifying the severity of hepatic encephalopathy. In: Conn H, Bircher J, eds. Hepatic encephalopathy: syndromes and treatment. Bloomington, IL: Medi-Ed, 1994: 13–26.

117. LaBerge JM, Ring EJ, Gordon RL. Percutaneous intrahepatic portosystemic shunt created via a femoral vein approach. Radiology 1991;181:679–681.

118. Rees CR, Niblett RL, Lee SP, Diamodn NG, Crippin JS. Use of carbon dioxide as a contrast medium for transjugular intrahepatic portosystemic shunt procedures. J Vasc Intervent Radiol 1994;5:383–386.

119. Teitelbaum GP, Van Allan RJ, Reed RA, Hanks S, Katz MD. Portal venous branch targeting with a platinum-tipped wire to facilitate transjugular intrahepatic portosystemic shunt (TIPS) procedures. Cardiovasc Intervent Radiol 1993;16:198–200.

120. Harman JT, Reed JD, Kopecky KK, Harris VJ, Haggerty MF, Strzembosz AS. Localization of the portal vein for transjugular catheterization: percutaneous placement of a metallic marker with real-time US guidance. J Vasc Intervent Radiol 1992;3:545–547.

121. Warner D, Owens C, Hibbein J, Ray C. Indirect localization of the portal vein during a transjugular intrahepatic portosystemic shunt procedure: placement of a radiopaque marker in the hepatic artery. J Vasc Intervent Radiol 1995;6:87–89.

122. Wenz F, Nemcek AAJ, Tischler HA, Minor PL, Vogelzang RL. US-guided paraumbilical vein puncture: an adjunct to transjugular intrahepatic portosystemic shunt (TIPS) placement. J Vasc Intervent Radiol 1992;3:549–551.

123. Rozenblitt G, Del Guercio LR. Combined transmesenteric and transjugular approach for intrahepatic portosystemic shunt placement. J Vasc Intervent Radiol 1993;4:661–666.

124. Haskal ZJ. Percutaneous recanalization and transjugular intrahepatic portosystemic shunt (TIPS) placement for treatment of portal, mesenteric, or splenic vein thrombosis. Am J Roentgenol 1994;163:107.

125. Rösch J, Uchida B, Putnam J, Buschman R, Law R, Hershey A. Experimental intrahepatic portacaval anastomosis: use of expandable Gianturco stents. Radiology 1987;162:481–485.

126. Haskal ZJ, Ring EJ, LaBerge JM, et al. Role of parallel transjugular intrahepatic portosystemic shunts in patients with persistent portal hypertension. Radiology 1992;185:813–817.

127. Sarfeh IJ, Rypins EB, Conroy RM, Mason GR. Portacaval H-graft: relationships of shunt diameter, portal flow patterns and encephalopathy. Ann Surg 1983;197:422–426.

128. Sarfeh IJ, Rypins EB, Mason GR. A systematic appraisal of portacaval H-graft diameters. Ann Surg 1986;204:356–363.

129. Haskal ZJ, Cope C, Soulen MS, Shlansky-Goldberg RD, Baum RA, Redd DR. Intentional reversible thrombosis of transjugular intrahepatic portosystemic shunts. Radiology 1995;195:485–488.

130. Rubin R, Haskal ZJ, O'Brien C, Cope C, Brass C. Transjugular intrahepatic portosystemic shunt: decreased survival for patients with high APACHE II scores. Am J Gastroenterol 1995;90:556–563.

131. Haskal ZJ, Zuckerman J. Resolution of hepatic hydrothorax after transjugular intrahepatic portosystemic shunt (TIPS) placement. Chest 1994;106:1293–1295.

132. Quiroga J, Sangro B, Nunez M, et al. Transjugular intrahepatic portal-systemic shunt in the treatment of refractory ascites: effect on clinical, renal, humoral, and hemodynamic parameters. Hepatology 1995;21:986–994.

133. Freedman AM, Sanyal AJ, Tisnado J, et al. Complications of transjugular intrahepatic portosystemic shunt: a comprehensive review. Radiographics 1993;13:1185–1210.

134. Haskal ZJ, Pentecost MJ, Rubin RA. Hepatic arterial injury after transjugular intrahepatic portosystemic shunt placement: report of two cases. Radiology 1993;188:85–88.

135. Kerlan RKJ, LaBerge JM, Gordon RL, Ring EJ. Inadvertent catheterization of the hepatic artery during placement of transjugular intrahepatic portosystemic shunts. Radiology 1994;193:273–276.

136. Sanyal AJ, Freedman AM, Shiffman ML, Purdum P3, Luketic VA, Cheatham AK. Portosystemic encephalopathy after transjugular intrahepatic portosystemic shunt: results of a prospective controlled study. Hepatology 1994;20:46–55.

137. Somberg KA, Riegler JL, LaBerge JM, et al. Hepatic-encephalopathy after transjugular intrahepatic portosystemic shunts: incidence and risk-factors. Am J Gastroenterol 1995;90:549–555.

138. LaBerge JM, Ferrell LD, Ring EJ, et al. Histopathologic study of transjugular intrahepatic portosystemic shunts. J Vasc Intervent Radiol 1991;2:549–556.

139. Hauenstein KH, Haag K, Ochs A, Langer M, Rossle M. The reducing stent: treatment for transjugular intrahepatic porto-systemic shunt-induced refractory hepatic encephalopathy and liver failure. Radiology 1995;194:175–179.

140. Haskal ZJ, Middlebrook MR. Creation of a stenotic stent to reduce transjugular intrahepatic portosystemic shunt flow. J Vasc Intervent Radiol 1994;5:827–830.

141. Azoulay D, Castaing D, Dennison A, Martino W, Eyraud D, Bismuth H. Transjugular intrahepatic portosystemic shunt worsens the hyperdynamic circulatory state of the cirrhotic patient: preliminary report of a prospective study. Hepatology 1994;19:129–132.

142. Lind CD, Malisch TW, Chong WK, et al. Incidence of shunt occlusion or stenosis following transjugular intrahepatic portosystemic shunt placement. Gastroenterology 1994;106:1277–1283.

143. LaBerge JM, Ferrel LD, Ring EJ, Gordon RL. Histopathologic study of stenotic and occluded transjugular intrahepatic portosystemic shunts. J Vasc Intervent Radiol 1993;4:779–786.

144. Stout LC, Lyon RE, Murray NG, Barth MH. Pseudointimal biliary epithelial proliferation and Zahn's infarct associated with a 6$\frac{1}{2}$-month-old transjugular intrahepatic portosystemic shunt. Am J Gastroenterol 1995;90:126–130.

34

Percutaneous Gastrostomy and Gastrojejunostomy

DANIEL PICUS
ERIC S. MALDEN

Direct enteral feeding can be given by a variety of techniques. Tube feedings by the nasogastric, orogastric, or nasojejunal route are simple. However, these tubes are uncomfortable for the patient and are poorly tolerated for long-term nutrition. In addition, nasojejunal tubes, because of their long length and relatively small caliber, frequently clog and require replacement. For long-term enteral nutrition, direct gastrostomy or gastrojejunostomy tubes are the most straightforward and best methods available.[1]

A variety of different techniques are available for the placement of gastrostomy and gastrojejunostomy tubes. Each uses a different guidance method. *Surgical gastrostomy* is performed through a laparotomy incision and uses direct visualization of the stomach for catheter placement. This technique has been available for over 100 years. Surgical gastrostomy requires an abdominal incision and therefore is usually performed under general anesthesia. For this reason, this technique can be associated with significant morbidity and expense.[2]

The most recent trend is toward less invasive methods for gastrostomy placement. *Percutaneous endoscopic gastrostomy (PEG)* uses endoscopic guidance to direct a needle and then a catheter into the stomach in either an antegrade or retrograde fashion. *Percutaneous gastrostomy,* as performed by interventional radiologists, uses fluoroscopic guidance and the standard Seldinger technique to percutaneously place a feeding tube into the stomach and, if necessary, direct it into the jejunum. Because percutaneous gastrostomy does not require either a surgical incision or endoscopy, it rarely requires significant amounts of intravenous sedation and is the least invasive method for direct placement of catheters into either the stomach or jejunum.

This chapter reviews the indications for and techniques of percutaneous fluoroscopically guided gastrostomy and gastrojejunostomy. The results and complications with these techniques are reviewed and compared to those obtained with both the surgical and endoscopic gastrostomy techniques.

Indications

The most common indication for percutaneous gastrostomy and gastrojejunostomy is long-term nutritional support in adults and children.[1,3–10] Such patients include those unable to swallow because of esophageal obstruction secondary to head and neck cancer, or because of central nervous system diseases including strokes and organic brain syndrome. Another group of patients is those predisposed to aspiration because of advanced neurologic diseases, including amyotrophic lateral sclerosis, multiple sclerosis, and muscular dystrophy. Finally, more unusual indications include enteral nutrition in patients with esophageal perforation, advanced malignancy, or unusual psychiatric problems such as anorexia nervosa or severe depression.[3,4,6,11]

Intestinal decompression is a less common but excellent indication for percutaneous gastrostomy.[3,6,11–14] For patients who require long-term decompression, a gastrostomy tube is much more comfortable than a nasogastric tube. In addition, gravity drainage through a gastrostomy tube is usually sufficient for decompression, whereas nasogastric decompression requires mechanical suction.[12] The most common indication for decompressive gastrostomy in the authors' practice is in patients with bowel obstruction from peritoneal carcinomatosis secondary to gynecologic malignancies. Decompressive gastrostomy can also be valuable in patients with postoperative anastomotic obstructions and diabetic gastroparesis.

Gastrostomy Versus Gastrojejunostomy

Whenever possible, the authors prefer to place a gastrostomy rather than a gastrojejunostomy tube. Technically, gastrostomy tube placement is much simpler than gastrojejunostomy placement in that it requires much less manipulation. Moreover, because gastrojejunostomy tubes are longer than gastrostomy tubes and usually of a smaller caliber, they become clogged

547

more often and so require more frequent tube changes.[15] Finally, with gastrostomy tube feedings the function of the stomach is preserved, and therefore almost any type of diet can be used. Since gastrojejunostomy tubes bypass the stomach, delivering feedings directly into the jejunum, they require a more expensive elemental diet, as well as the use of an infusion pump with slower, more prolonged infusions.

The authors reserve gastrojejunostomy tube placement for patients with either poor gastric emptying or those at high risk for gastroesophageal reflux.[15,16] Poor gastric emptying is seen in patients with diabetic gastroparesis or partial gastric outlet obstruction. Significant gastroesophageal reflux can accompany a wide variety of neurologic problems. However, pulmonary aspiration in these patients is more often due to problems with swallowing rather than reflux.[15]

One clear advantage of the percutaneous technique over other techniques for enteral tube placement is the ability to easily convert from a gastrostomy tube to a gastrojejunostomy tube if problems develop.[17] The authors generally wait 5 to 7 days for the percutaneous tract to mature before converting a gastrostomy tube to a gastrojejunostomy catheter.[17,18]

Contraindications

There are few absolute contraindications to percutaneous gastrostomy tube placement. The most important absolute contraindication is the lack of a safe access route to the stomach. Rarely, the colon blocks access to the stomach. Although the authors routinely place gastrostomy catheters through the transverse mesocolon, occasionally they are unable to access the stomach because of overlying transverse colon. Insufflation of the stomach almost always pushes the transverse colon inferiorly, allowing safe access to the stomach. If the colon is still in the way, overnight placement of either a nasogastric tube or rectal tube may create sufficient colonic decompression to allow for a safe access route. Rarely, small bowel projects over the stomach on fluoroscopy. Simple rotational fluoroscopy is extremely useful in these cases and almost always shows small bowel to lie posterior to the stomach.

Relative contraindications to percutaneous gastrostomy include coagulopathy, gastric varices, ascites, and gastric carcinoma. Coagulopathy is usually correctable with appropriate blood products or vitamin K. In patients with ascites, preprocedural paracentesis and the use of T fasteners may prevent ascitic fluid leakage around the catheter (see below).[13] Placement of a percutaneous gastrostomy tube through a gastric carcinoma may result in bleeding and failure of tract matu-

ration. Therefore, in patients with gastric or peritoneal malignancy, a preprocedural CT scan may be helpful to allow selection of an appropriate window for gastrostomy tube placement.

The authors do not consider partial gastrectomy to be a contraindication to gastrostomy tube placement.[19] The previous surgical procedure may even make percutaneous gastrostomy easier because of the adhesions that develop between the stomach and abdominal wall. However, placement of a percutaneous gastrostomy tube in a patient with a previous partial gastrectomy may require modifications in the standard technique, including more frequent insufflation of the stomach, use of compound angles with C-arm fluoroscopy, and use of a longer needle (see below).

Technique

A variety of techniques are used for percutaneous gastrostomy and gastrojejunostomy.[1,3–7,9,17,19–21] The following sections describe the authors' standard approach to these procedures, and then discuss several modifications.

Percutaneous Gastrostomy

Preferably, patients have nothing by mouth or nasogastric tube beginning the night before the examination. A nasogastric tube is placed before the patient arrives in the radiology department. This tube is best placed to suction for several hours before the procedure. If a nasogastric tube placement is unsuccessful, a small 5 French angiographic catheter can usually be placed under fluoroscopic guidance in the interventional radiology suite.

Intravenous sedation, when necessary, can be given during the procedure (e.g., morphine sulfate, midazolam, and so forth). Intravenous sedation is usually required for gastrostomy tube placement in children but is rarely needed in adults.

Fluoroscopy is used to evaluate the abdomen before selecting a skin entry site. It is critical to avoid puncturing overlying transverse colon. In addition, the access must be below the costal margin. Usually a site is easily selected in the upper abdomen to the left of the midline. This skin site is then prepared in a sterile fashion.

Before air insufflation, the authors routinely administer glucagon (1 mg IV push) to decrease gastric peristalsis and emptying. Generally, 250 to 400 cc of air is sufficient to bring the anterior wall of the stomach to the anterior abdominal wall, separate the anterior and posterior gastric walls, and force the transverse colon inferiorly. Fluoroscopic guidance is used to monitor the appropriate volume of gastric distention. Distention of the stomach is critical to provide an appropriate counterforce to the passage of the needle, dilators, and the gastrostomy catheter.

A site is selected over the midbody of the stomach (Fig. 34-1A). It is important to avoid the greater and lesser curvatures of the stomach because this is the location of the large arterial vessels. Lidocaine is used to anesthetize both the skin and the peritoneum.

For routine percutaneous gastrostomy placement the authors use a standard kit modified to specifications (Mallinckrodt Institute Gastrostomy Set, Cook, Inc.) (Fig. 34-2). This kit contains everything necessary for percutaneous gastrostomy placement, including the needle, guidewire, dilators, and catheter.[3]

A 7.5-cm, 18-gauge, Teflon-sheathed needle is directed vertically into the stomach under fluoroscopic guidance. Frequently, tenting of the anterior wall of the stomach is observed under fluoroscopy, ensuring an intragastric location of the needle tip (see Fig. 34-1B). The metal stylet is removed, and air is aspirated. Contrast injection should outline rugal folds as the contrast flows freely away from the tip of the Teflon sheath (see Fig. 34-1C). If the tip of the sheath is in the retroperitoneum, the contrast will extravasate into the retroperitoneal tissue in a typical pattern. The intraperitoneal position is obvious as the contrast outlines the peritoneal space. If the sheathed needle is not positioned appropriately, it is either advanced or withdrawn so that it lies within the stomach.

Once the intragastric position of the Teflon sheath is confirmed, a 0.38-inch Amplatz extra stiff guidewire is coiled within the fundus of the stomach (see Fig. 34-1D). The tract is then dilated, first with a 7–12 French transition dilator and then with a 14 French dilator. As the dilators are advanced into the stomach, it is important to fluoroscopically observe tenting of the anterior wall of the stomach. Often additional air must be added to the stomach to provide an appropriate counterforce. It is absolutely critical to confirm that each dilator adequately passes through the anterior wall of the stomach into the gastric lumen. The stomach tends to back away from the dilator. Often a forceful twisting thrust is necessary to enter the gastric lumen.

A variety of percutaneous gastrostomy catheters are used by different authors, all requiring some type of retention device. Traditionally a modified pigtail catheter is used (Fig. 34-3A). This large-caliber (14 French) gastrostomy catheter has extra large side holes and a standard Cope loop retention mechanism. The authors prefer a recently developed 14 French catheter (Cook, Inc.), which does not have a straight segment distal to the pigtail (Fig. 34-3B). The straight distal catheter segment may be related to a small number of gastric perforations (Kanterman, unpublished data). In addition, this new 14 French catheter is stronger, allowing larger side holes along the pigtail portion (Fig. 34-3C). The catheter is placed with the use of a flexible stiffening cannula. To prevent partial extragastric or intraperitoneal placement, one must be certain that the catheter is well positioned into the stomach before forming the Cope loop. Proper intragastric placement is confirmed by contrast injection. The authors do not pull the catheter back against the anterior wall of the stomach; this is not necessary for gastrostomy tract maturation. If the tube is pulled back too forcefully, there is a risk that one of the side holes in the pigtail portion may be pulled into the peritoneal cavity, leading to peritonitis.

The authors prefer to secure the catheter in place with a single no. 0 Prolene suture. It is important to secure the catheter to the anterior abdominal wall. If the catheter is not adequately secured, it may be carried by peristalsis into the duodenum. This can lead to duodenal perforation and/or obstruction.

The catheter is initially placed to external drainage overnight. The patient is seen the next morning, and, if the abdominal examination is benign, feedings may begin.

Percutaneous Gastrojejunostomy

The initial steps outlined above (to the point of puncture site selection) are similar for percutaneous gastrojejunostomy placement. Passage of a catheter through the stomach into the jejunum is facilitated by directing the puncture downhill toward the pylorus. Therefore, it is advantageous to select an entry site slightly higher on the body of the stomach with the needle angled toward the antrum.

Because of the additional manipulations necessary to access the jejunum, the authors routinely place a T fastener before accessing the stomach (see below). The same access used for the T fastener can be used for catheter placement.

Once the T fastener is in the stomach, a catheter is advanced over the T fastener wire to seek out the duodenum. A variety of tip configurations may help facilitate passage through the pylorus. The authors routinely use an angled multipurpose configuration. A Headhunter or Cobra catheter may also be useful. Either a floppy-tipped wire (e.g., Bentson) or a hydrophilic angled wire (e.g., Terumo) is used in combination with the catheter to access the jejunum.

Once the guidewire is manipulated into the jejunum, the tract is dilated and an appropriately sized peel-away sheath is placed. The use of a peel-away

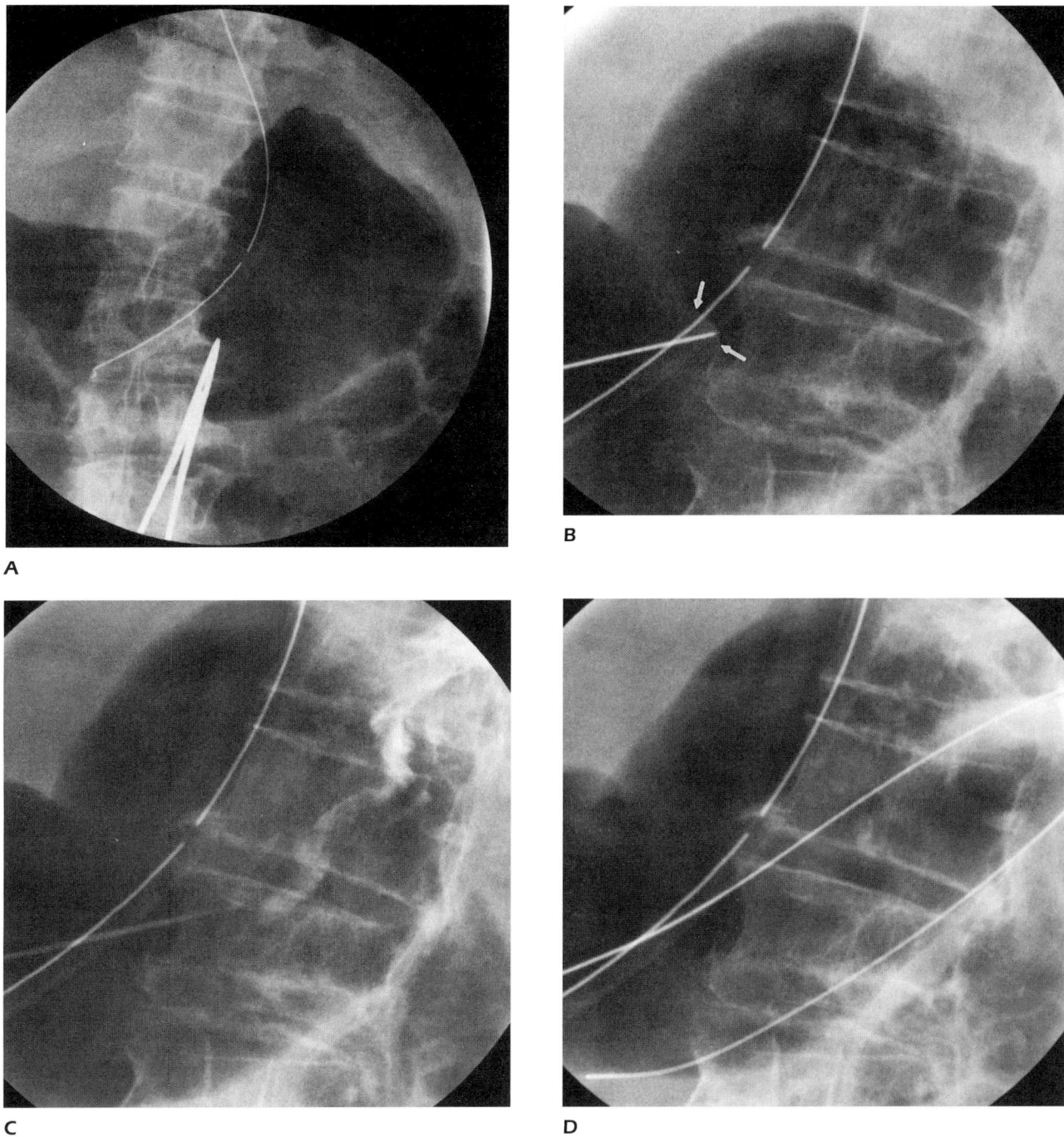

A

B

C

D

Figure 34-1. Technique of percutaneous gastrostomy tube placement. (A) Following insufflation of the stomach a safe access path into the gastric body is marked. Access should be in the middle of the body of the stomach. (B) While the 18-gauge needle is being advanced, the gastric wall "tents" as the needle enters the stomach (*arrows*). (C) Contrast is injected through the needle to confirm intragastric position. (D) A guidewire is advanced through the access needle and coiled within the fundus of the stomach. (E) After tract dilatation, the 14 French gastrostomy tube and flexible stiffening cannula are placed generously within the stomach. (F) After the stiffening cannula and the guidewire are removed, the Cope loop is formed by pulling the external string. A final contrast injection is done to confirm intragastric placement.

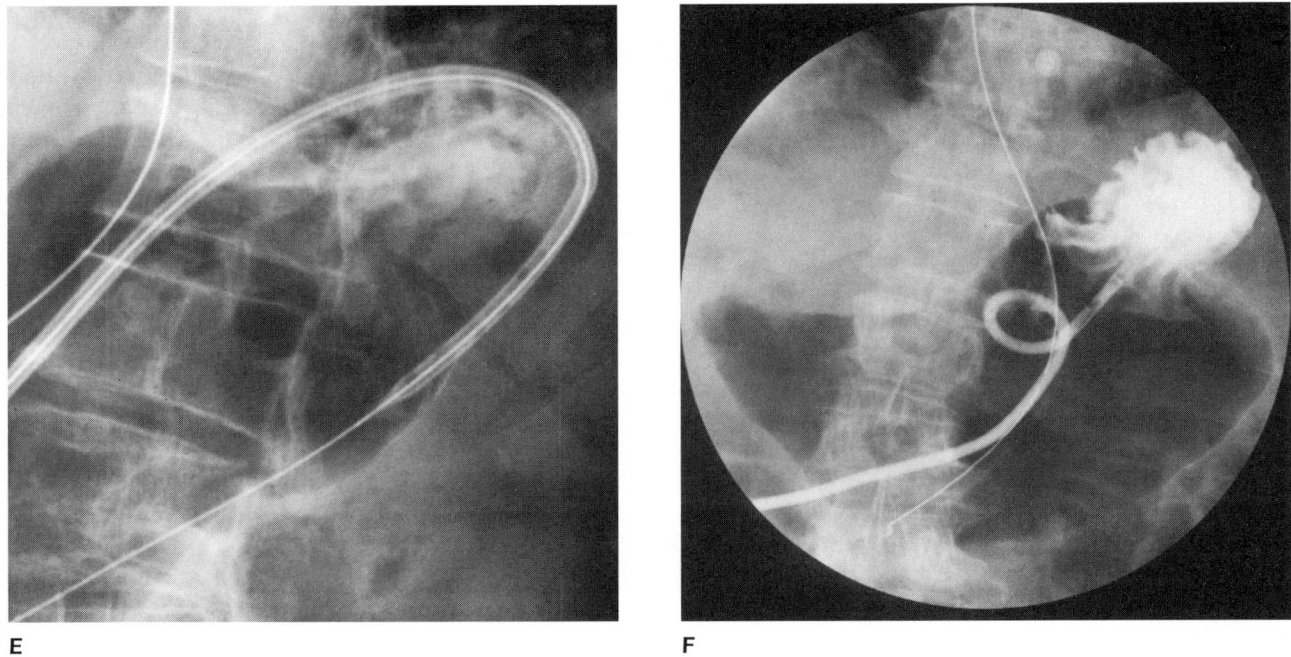

E F

Figure 34-1 (continued).

Figure 34-2. The Mallinckrodt Institute Gastrostomy Set contains (*from top to bottom*) an 18-gauge Teflon sheath needle, a 7 to 12 French transition dilator, a 14 French dilator, a 14 French gastrostomy tube, a flexible stiffening cannula, and a 100-cm Amplatz extra stiff guidewire.

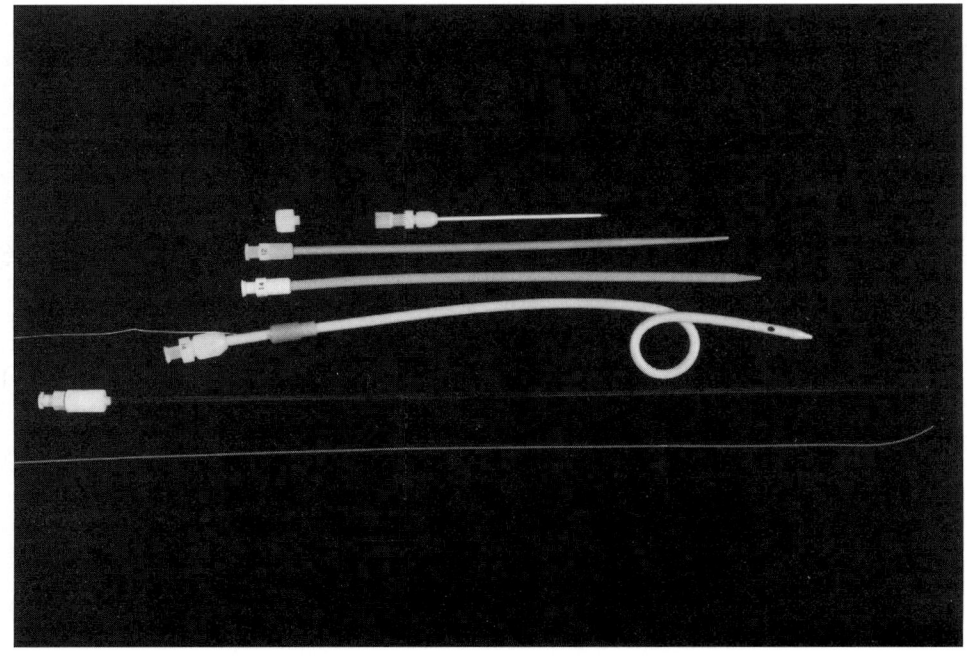

sheath decreases the resistance to catheter passage through the abdominal wall, allowing for easier placement of the catheter into the jejunum. In addition, the authors prefer to use a large nontapered end-hole gastrojejunostomy catheter, feeling that these catheters are less prone to plugging. Because these catheters are not tapered to the guidewire, they require placement through a peel-away sheath.

The authors' standard gastrojejunostomy tubes have either a Cope loop or a friction lock Mallecot retention mechanism (Fig. 34-4). The tip of the gastrojejunostomy catheter is placed in the proximal jejunum distal to the ligament of Treitz (Fig. 34-5). The

retention mechanism is formed in the stomach after the peel-away sheath is removed.

Unlike with gastrostomy tubes, feeding through the gastrojejunostomy catheters is begun immediately after the procedure. Because these tubes are prone to plugging, they should be irrigated liberally with water after each use.

Procedural Modifications

A variety of alternative catheters are available for both percutaneous gastrostomy and gastrojejunostomy tube placement. Some authors prefer Foley balloon catheters for percutaneous gastrostomy. The authors have found the complication rate with Foley catheters to be significantly higher than with Cope loop catheters and prefer not to use them.[3,22]

Occasionally, patients require gastric decompression as well as jejunal feedings. For this purpose a double-lumen gastrojejunostomy tube is used. For this tube to decompress the stomach adequately, the gastric port must be in the fundus of the stomach. Therefore, this catheter must be looped in the fundus of the stomach before passing into the jejunum (Fig. 34-6). This can be done either during the initial access procedure or once access into the jejunum is obtained.

Figure 34-3. The 14 French gastrostomy tube has a short tube length distal to the Cope loop, which contains multiple large side holes. (A) The Cope loop is formed by pulling on the retention suture (*arrow*). Here the loop is almost entirely formed. (B) New 14 French gastrostomy tube without a straight segment distal to the pigtail. (C) New catheter side hole arrangement.

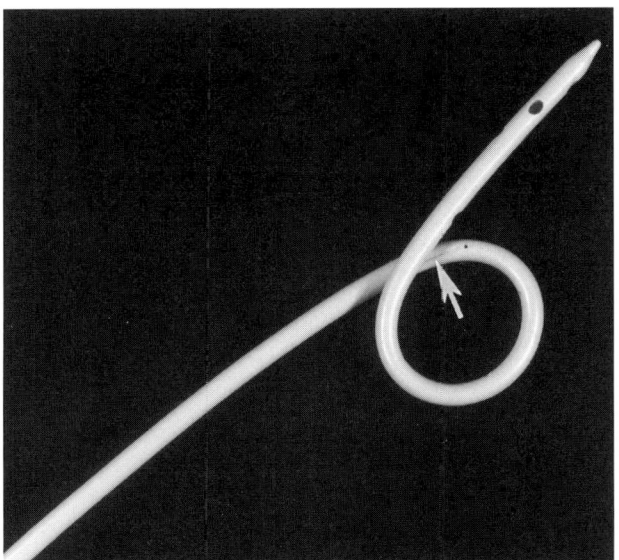

A

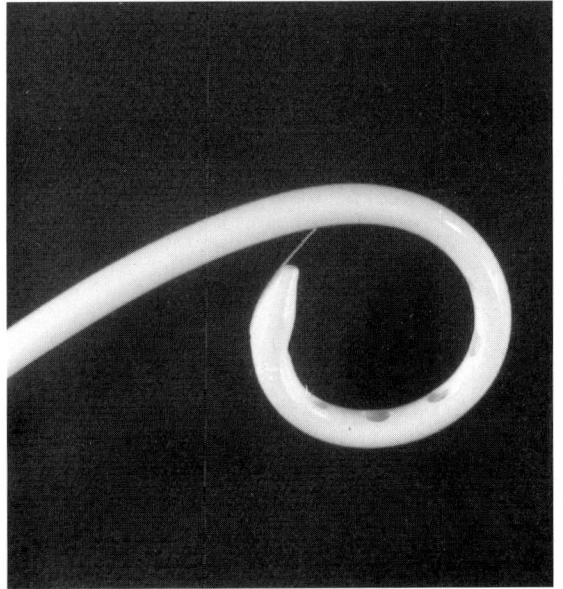

B

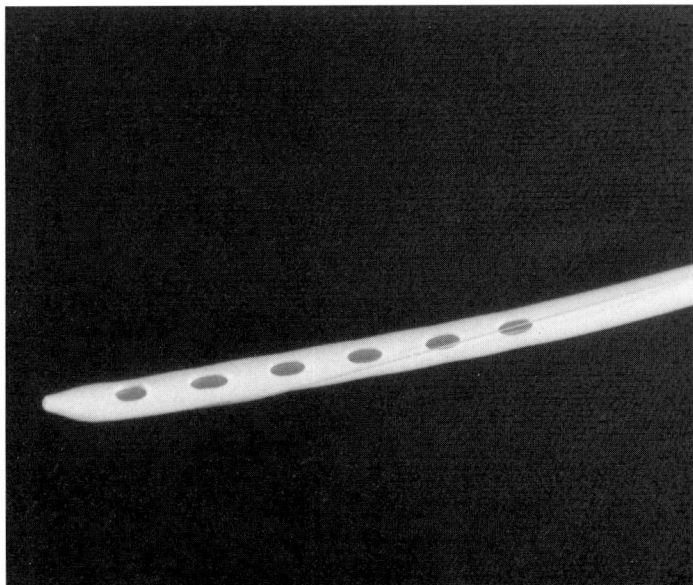

C

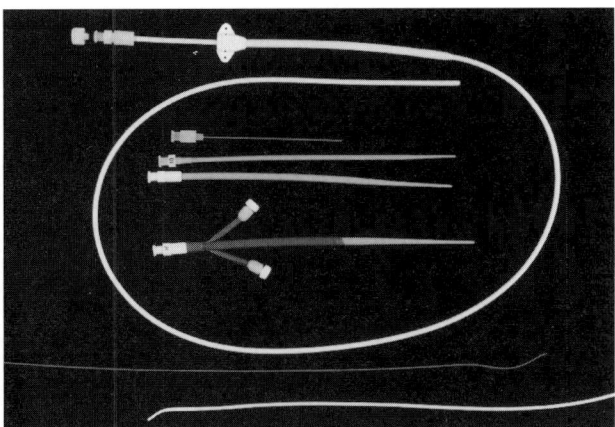

Figure 34-4. The Carey-Alzate-Coons Gastrojejunostomy Set (Cook, Inc.) contains (*from top to bottom*) the 15 French to 10.2 French gastrojejunostomy catheter, an 18-gauge needle, a 10 French and 14 French dilator, a 16 French peel-away introducer, a 0.038-inch, 260-cm guidewire, and a 7 French seeking catheter. The set also contains a Cope suture anchor set (see Fig. 34-7).

Several authors have described a variety of devices to simulate surgical apposition of the stomach to the anterior abdominal wall. These devices are called T fasteners or suture anchor devices (Fig. 34-7A).[23–25] T fasteners are placed with a large-bore needle (16 or 18 gauge) either as a single fixation point or at the corners of a triangle with the gastrostomy tube placed in the middle (see Fig. 34-7B). Advocates of this technique feel that it encourages adequate tract maturation and minimizes leakage of gastric contents into the perito-

neal cavity. However, many series have reported no such problems with percutaneous gastrostomy and gastrojejunostomy even when T fasteners were not used routinely, and some authors feel that the routine use of T fasteners may actually be disadvantageous.[26,27] The increased number of punctures necessary to place these devices may increase the risk of bleeding during the procedure, and the suture may lead to an increased infection rate. The authors prefer to use T fasteners for selected indications in which it may be more important to ensure apposition between the stomach and the anterior abdominal wall. Examples include patients with ascites, uncooperative patients, and patients in whom extensive manipulations will be necessary (e.g., in gastrojejunostomy tube placement).

Placement of a percutaneous gastrostomy tube in a patient with partial gastrectomy may require modifications of the standard technique.[19] Often the adhesions that form between the stomach and the anterior abdominal wall after gastric surgery are advantageous for percutaneous placement. However, because the gastric remnant is small, frequent insufflation of air during the procedure may be necessary to keep the stomach distended. In addition, the gastric remnant may lie high underneath the costal margin, and complex angulation may be necessary to direct the needle into the stomach. Such complex angulation is facilitated by the use of C-arm fluoroscopy. Finally, a relatively long tract may be needed to access the stomach,

Figure 34-6. Double-lumen gastrojejunostomy catheter. Contrast has been injected through the gastrostomy port into the gastric fundus. The feeding lumen extends into the proximal jejunum.

Figure 34-5. Percutaneous gastrojejunostomy catheter. Note the downhill orientation of the gastric access, which facilitates transpyloric manipulation.

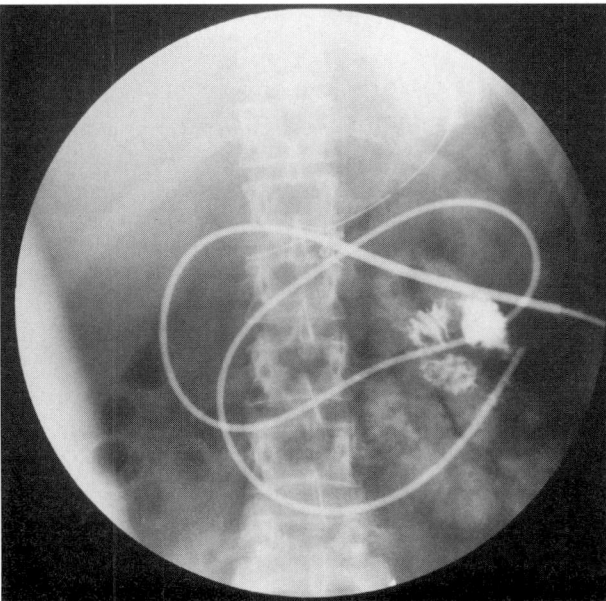

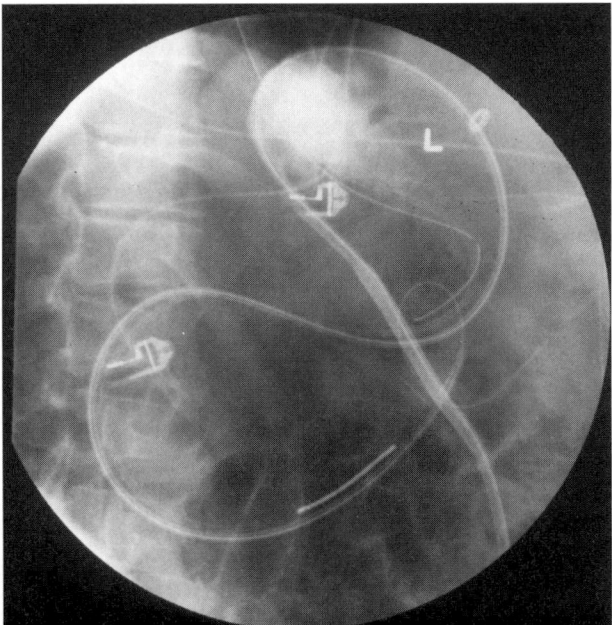

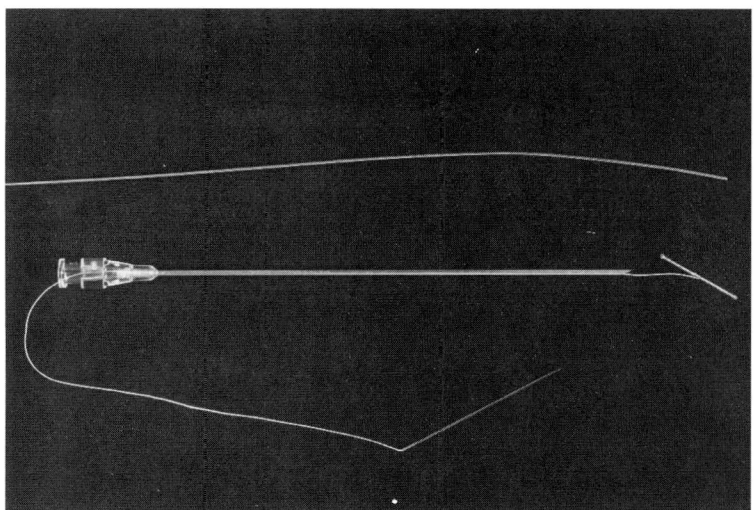

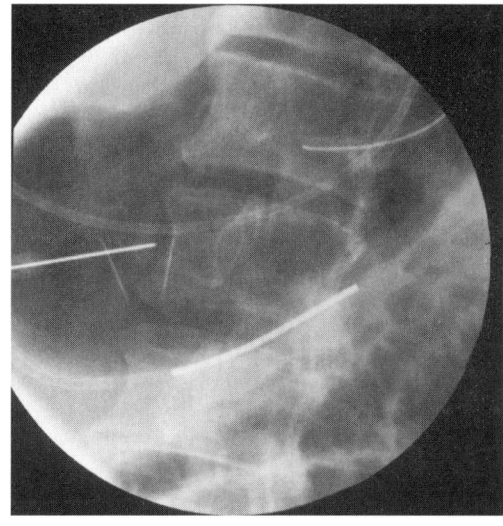

A   **B**

Figure 34-7. (A) The Cope suture anchor (Cook, Inc.). Initially the anchor is within the needle housing. After the needle has been inserted into the stomach, the guidewire is coaxially advanced to extrude the anchor. The needle is then removed, and the suture is sewn to the skin. (B) Anterior gastropexy has been performed with two T fasteners. The 18-gauge needle is advanced between the T fasteners.

particularly in a subcostal location. This may require the use of a longer 15- to 30-cm needle.

When a standard nasogastric tube cannot be placed, it is usually possible to manipulate a small 5 French catheter into the stomach using standard guidewire techniques and fluoroscopic guidance. Occasionally, however, even this is not possible in patients with high-grade esophageal obstructions. In these patients, if a gastric air collection can be seen with fluoroscopy, the stomach can be entered directly with a 22-gauge needle. This 22-gauge needle can then be used for air insufflation as described above. In these patients it may be helpful to place a T fastener, because access to the stomach may be tenuous.

Occasionally, CT guidance is helpful in directing percutaneous gastric access, particularly in patients with gastric malignancies or abdominal masses that require careful gastric access.[28] The authors prefer to either mark an appropriate access route on the abdominal wall or place a needle into the stomach under CT guidance and then transfer the patient to the fluoroscopy suite for the completion of the procedure. The use of fluoroscopy is extremely helpful to ensure that both the dilators and gastrostomy catheter are appropriately positioned into the stomach.

The presence of ascites presents a particular challenge for percutaneous gastric access. The authors routinely use ultrasound to evaluate all patients with ascites before gastrostomy tube placement. Occasionally, a window can be found to the stomach where no ascites is present. If this is not found, a percutaneous peritoneal catheter can be placed to withdraw ascitic fluid

to better allow apposition of the anterior gastric wall with the anterior abdominal wall. T fasteners may also be helpful to draw the wall of the stomach to the anterior abdominal wall and decrease ascitic fluid leakage after gastrostomy tube placement.[13]

Management

To minimize complications, it is essential that the interventional radiologist takes care of the short-term and long-term management of gastrostomy tube patients. Immediately after the procedure the percutaneous gastrostomy catheter is left to external drainage. This permits evaluation for postprocedural bleeding and decreases short-term gastric distention after tube placement. The patient is visited the next morning, and if he or she is afebrile with a benign abdominal examination, feedings may begin. Gastric feedings are begun initially at a slow rate to see how the patient tolerates them. It is also important to check for residuals before each feeding. If the patient has a large amount of residual intragastric material, the subsequent feedings should be held. In the authors' experience most major complications occur within 5 days of gastrostomy tube placement (Hicks ME, Malden ES, unpublished data). Therefore, these patients are routinely seen on a daily basis for at least 5 days after the procedure.

If the patient develops large residuals or symptoms of reflux, he or she should be fed in a semierect position and kept in this position for at least 30 minutes

How to Care for the Feeding Tube
(Gastrostomy Tube)
  I. Dressing changes—every 1–2 days.
     A. Clean around tube with hydrogen peroxide.
     B. Dress with gauze pads and tape.
        Position tube so it does not kink.
 II. Showers—no tub baths.
     A. Cover dressing with a double layer of plastic
        wrap and tape edges.
     B. Remove plastic wrap and change dressing
        after you shower.
III. Activities—no specific restrictions.
 IV. Feedings.
     A. Use water to flush the tube after each feed-
        ing.
     B. Use liquid forms of medication if possible.
     C. Ask your doctor or nurse to provide you
        with specific information about feedings or
        medications.
  V. Problems with the tube.
     Please call the appropriate number listed for any
     of the following problems.
     A. Leakage of feedings around the tube.
     B. Signs of infection such as swelling, tender-
        ness, redness, or drainage of pus around the
        tube.
     C. If the tube falls out completely, call immedi-
        ately. The tube usually can be easily replaced
        if it is done within 24 hours from the time
        it fell out. Waiting longer could mean that a
        separate new tube will have to be placed.
 VI. Call us anytime if the tube plugs up or if you have
     any questions or problems regarding the tube.

Figure 34-8. Each patient, family, or caregiver is provided with a tube care sheet. The sheet includes specific directions on dressing changes, feedings, and a number to call with any questions or problems.

after feeding. If large residuals continue to be a problem or the patient develops signs or symptoms of aspiration, the gastrostomy tube can be converted to a gastrojejunostomy catheter.

Long-term management is also important. All patients and their caregivers receive a gastrostomy care sheet (Fig. 34-8) and are instructed to contact the interventionalist directly with any difficulties or questions. The authors do not perform routine gastrostomy tube changes. However, catheter changes are frequently required 4 to 6 months after placement because of tube malfunctions. This is easily done as an outpatient procedure using fluoroscopic guidance.

If gastrostomy tube removal is indicated, it is important to be certain the percutaneous tract is mature before it is removed. Tract maturation usually occurs 1 to 3 weeks after tube placement.[18] If integrity of the tract is a concern, contrast may be injected into the tract while a guidewire is left in the stomach to preserve access.

Gastrostomy Button Placement

A variety of skin-level gastrostomy devices are available from different manufacturers (e.g., Bard, Inc., Medical Innovations, Inc.) (Fig. 34-9). Their main advantage is that they are less intrusive than a standard gastrostomy catheter and may be more cost-effective in the long term.[29,30] This may be particularly important in an ambulatory patient, a child, or patients receiving physical therapy. The patient's self-image may also be improved with the use of these skin-level devices.

The authors generally wait 2 to 3 months after the initial gastrostomy tube placement before attempting placement of a gastrostomy button. The percutaneous tract must be well healed before manipulation. The button devices are 18 or 24 French in size. Because the gastrostomy tube may not be that large, the tract usually must be dilated before button placement. This may be done by placing gastrostomy catheters of increasingly larger size at weekly intervals. Alternatively, standard Teflon dilators may be used to dilate the tract using the Seldinger technique.

Before button placement, it is critically important to accurately measure the length of the percutaneous tract to the stomach.[31] Percutaneous gastrostomy tracts tend to be longer than surgical tracts. This obviously requires the use of a longer device for button placement in patients with percutaneous gastrostomy tubes. In addition, if the button is too long, it will move in and out at the skin site. Such excessive movement can stimulate exuberant granulation tissue.

Figure 34-9. Gastric buttons: the Bard Button (*left*) and the MIC-Key Button (*right*). Note the balloon retention device on the MIC-Key button.

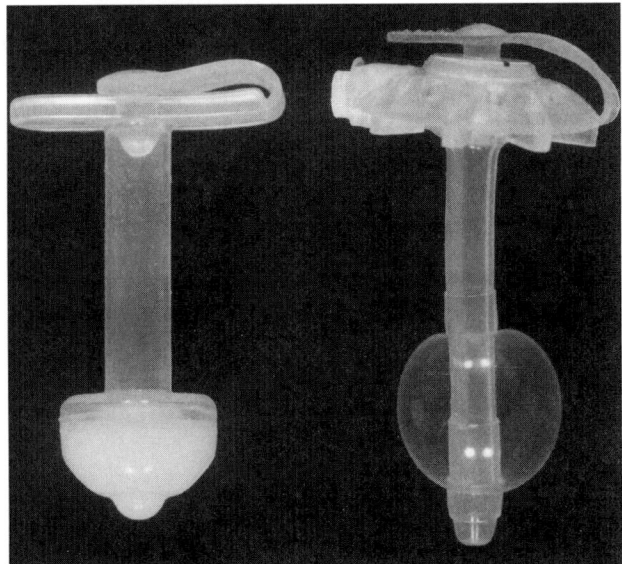

The authors prefer to place buttons under fluoroscopic guidance with a guidewire protecting the tract. If the device cannot be advanced into the stomach for any reason, a gastrostomy catheter can be easily replaced over the guidewire. Fluoroscopic guidance is helpful to be certain that the button is appropriately placed within the gastric lumen. Once the button is in place, injection of contrast should be performed to document appropriate position.

The authors prefer buttons with a balloon type of retention mechanism (MIC-Key, Medical Innovations) (see Fig. 34-9). These balloon buttons are lower-profile devices and therefore easier to place. Buttons with a mushroom type of retention device are more commonly placed by surgeons. These devices are slightly less expensive but often require considerable force to advance into the tract.

All buttons have a one-way valve in the lumen to prevent reflux of gastric contents after feeding. These valves eventually fail. Patients and their caregivers should be given instructions to return for button replacement when the device begins to leak. In the case of balloon buttons, the caregivers often are able to replace the button when it malfunctions.

Results

Percutaneous gastrostomy is associated with a high technical success rate, generally ranging from 98 to 100 percent.[1] Failure is usually due to lack of a safe access route—most commonly because of overlying transverse colon. Other causes for technical failure include massive ascites, gastric cancer, peritoneal carcinomatosis, large overlying open abdominal incisions, and previous gastric surgery.

Occasionally, access to the stomach is lost during attempts at tract dilatation. In most cases, this should not result in technical failure. If access can be promptly established through a new puncture, significant complications usually do not occur.

Complications

Most authors report a relatively low rate of major and minor complications associated with percutaneous gastrostomy. Ho and Yeung reviewed the complication rates from the four largest reported series of percutaneous gastrostomy tube placements (635 patients).[1] Pooling these data, they showed a 5 percent major and a 5 percent minor complication rate for percutaneous gastrostomy.[1,3–6]

Comparison between the complication rate resulting from percutaneous gastrostomy and that seen with both percutaneous endoscopic and surgical gastrostomy is difficult.[1] Various authors classify complications differently, and most series include different patient populations. In general terms, however, most series of endoscopic or surgical gastrostomy tube placements report minor complications ranging from 5 to 10 percent and major complications ranging from 3 to 10 percent.[1,2,32–35]

The most common minor complication associated with percutaneous gastrostomy tube placement is skin site infection.[1,3,8] Early stomal infection usually occurs 3 to 5 days after tube placement. These infections can almost always be treated with local skin care, but occasionally they require antibiotics.

Another minor tube site problem is fluid leakage around the catheter, which usually represents ascitic fluid. Such an ascitic fluid leak can become a difficult management problem and is best treated by trying to decrease the amount of ascites. Feedings can leak out through the tract if the catheter erodes a larger hole through the skin. Feeding can be differentiated from ascites by placing food coloring in the patient's feedings.

Other late minor tube complications include tube malfunction and displacement of the gastrostomy catheter. In patients with a mature gastrostomy tract, such problems are easily managed by simply changing for a new tube. However, if the tube falls out and the tract closes before the catheter is replaced, a new access may be required.

The most serious major complication associated with percutaneous gastrostomy tube placement is peritonitis. Patients requiring gastrostomy tube placement are often severely debilitated, and peritonitis in these elderly, debilitated patients can result in major morbidity and even death. Peritonitis associated with percutaneous gastrostomy is extremely unusual. When it does occur, it usually results from tube displacement in a patient with an immature tract. This displacement may be subtle, resulting from a single side hole of the catheter that pulls back into the peritoneal cavity. Perforation of the stomach or duodenum also can result in peritonitis. Frank perforation can occur from erosion by the tip of the gastrostomy catheter.[3] In patients in whom peritonitis is suspected, tube feedings should be held. Usually, fluoroscopically guided contrast injection into the gastrostomy catheter can quickly clarify the situation. Patients with peritonitis usually require immediate operative intervention.

Significant bleeding associated with percutaneous gastrostomy is rare but is most often related to an underlying coagulopathy. Once the coagulopathy is corrected, the bleeding should stop. If patients continue to bleed through the gastrostomy catheter, gastritis or gastric ulceration should be suspected. These conditions can usually be treated with medical therapy but may require endoscopy for diagnosis.

Aspiration pneumonia can occur from reflux of gastric feedings. The use of food coloring in the feedings can be helpful to differentiate aspiration pneumonia secondary to reflux of feedings from pneumonia due to other causes. If the patient develops symptoms of aspiration, consideration should be given to converting the gastrostomy tube to a gastrojejunostomy catheter.

Pneumoperitoneum is frequently seen after percutaneous gastrostomy and is not considered a complication.[36] Free air in the peritoneum after the procedure is not clinically significant unless it is increasing in volume or is associated with signs of peritoneal irritation.

Advantages and Disadvantages of Various Approaches

Surgical gastrostomy has little advantage over the less invasive techniques unless it is done at the time of another major surgical procedure. Since it requires a laparotomy incision to expose the stomach, it usually requires general anesthesia and this introduces additional morbidity to the procedure.[2,37] In addition, the performance of gastrostomy in the operating room is more expensive than either endoscopic or radiologic placement.[37,38] Recently, there have been several reports of laparoscopic placement of gastrostomy tubes,[39,40] but the utility of this procedure is questionable and far from proven. It is more invasive and expensive than either the endoscopic or fluoroscopic alternative. There appears to be little indication for laparoscopic gastrostomy unless it is done in conjunction with another laparoscopic procedure.

There have been no randomized trials comparing percutaneous endoscopic gastrostomy with fluoroscopically guided gastrostomy. However, in individual studies reporting results from these techniques, the results and complication rates are similar.[1,3,4-6,34,35,41] The endoscopic technique can be performed at the bedside in critically ill patients who are unable to come to the radiology department. This technique also allows endoscopic inspection of the esophagus and stomach in patients in whom such an examination is indicated. However, the endoscopic technique has several distinct disadvantages when compared to fluoroscopically guided gastrostomy tube placement. Because it requires upper endoscopy, significantly more sedation is needed than for the fluoroscopic technique.[34] The endoscopic technique also requires two operators and carries the risk of respiratory distress and aspiration during introduction of the endoscope.[34,41] In patients

with esophageal obstruction it may be difficult or even impossible to pass the endoscope into the stomach; however, using fluoroscopy, it is almost always possible to place a small 5 French catheter to insufflate the stomach. Finally, most endoscopically placed gastrostomy catheters have a bumper (fixation device for anterior gastropexy) in the stomach, which requires repeat endoscopy for tube changes.

Fluoroscopically guided gastrostomy tube placement is the least invasive of the three alternatives. Because it does not require the use of either the operating room or endoscopy, it is the least expensive of the three alternatives. In most patients, percutaneous gastrostomy requires minimal to no sedation, and, because it uses direct fluoroscopic control, there is little risk of placing the tube through the colon or small bowel. Fluoroscopically guided gastrostomy can be performed rapidly by one operator. In addition, with standard guidewire and catheter techniques it is usually a simple matter to place a catheter into the jejunum at the time of initial gastrostomy tube placement. A percutaneous gastrostomy usually can be easily converted to a gastrojejunostomy if problems with aspiration develop. The same cannot be said for surgical or endoscopic access.[17]

Conclusions

Percutaneous fluoroscopically guided gastrostomy and gastrojejunostomy provide safe, effective, and economical access to the intestinal tract for either enteral nutrition or decompression. The technique is useful in patients of all ages and in almost all clinical circumstances. The skills required for this procedure are identical to those in common use by interventional radiologists for all types of drainage and organ access procedures. This technique should be a standard part of all interventional radiology practices.

References

1. Ho C-S, Yeung EY. Percutaneous gastrostomy and transgastric jejunostomy. AJR 1992;158:251–257.
2. Shellito PC, Malt RA. Tube gastrostomy: techniques and complications. Ann Surg 1985;201:180–185.
3. Hicks ME, Surratt RS, Picus D, et al. Fluoroscopically guided percutaneous gastrostomy and gastroenterostomy: analysis of 158 consecutive cases. AJR 1990;154:725–728.
4. Halkier BK, Ho C-S, Yee ACN. Percutaneous feeding gastrostomy with the Seldinger technique: review of 252 patients. Radiology 1989;171:359–362.
5. Saini S, Mueller PR, Gaa J, et al. Percutaneous gastrostomy with gastropexy: experience in 125 patients. AJR 1990;154:1003–1006.
6. O'Keeffe F, Carrasco CH, Charnsangavej C, et al. Percutaneous drainage and feeding gastrostomies in 100 patients. Radiology 1989;172:341–343.

7. van Sonnenberg E, Wittich GR, Cabrera OA, et al. Percutaneous gastrostomy and gastroenterostomy: 2. Clinical experience. AJR 1986;146:581–586.

8. Malden ES, Hicks ME, Picus D, et al. Fluoroscopically guided percutaneous gastrostomy in children. J Vasc Intervent Radiol 1992;3:673–677.

9. Towbin RB, Ball WS, Bissett GS. Percutaneous gastrostomy and percutaneous gastrojejunostomy in children: antegrade approach. Radiology 1988;168:473–476.

10. Ho C-S, Yee CN, McPherson R. Complications of surgical and percutaneous nonendoscopic gastrostomy: review of 233 patients. Gastroenterology 1988;95:1206–1210.

11. Wills JS, Oglesby JT. Percutaneous gastrostomy. Radiology 1988;167:41–43.

12. Picus D, Marx MV, Weyman PJ. Chronic intestinal obstruction: value of percutaneous gastrostomy tube placement. AJR 1988;150:295–297.

13. Lee MJ, Saini S, Brink JA, et al. Malignant small bowel obstruction and ascites: not a contraindication to percutaneous gastrostomy. Clin Radiol 1991;44:332–334.

14. Herman LL, Hoskins WJ, Shike M. Percutaneous endoscopic gastrostomy for decompression of the stomach and small bowel. Gastrointest Endosc 1992;38:314–318.

15. Olson DL, Krubsack AJ, Stewart ET. Percutaneous enteral alimentation: gastrostomy versus gastrojejunostomy. Radiology 1993;187:105–108.

16. Gray RR, St. Louis EL, Grosman H. Percutaneous gastrostomy and gastro-jejunostomy. Br J Radiol 1987;60:1067–1070.

17. Lu DSK, Mueller PR, Lee MJ, et al. Gastrostomy conversion to transgastric jejunostomy: technical problems, causes of failure, and proposed solutions in 63 patients. Radiology 1993;187:679–683.

18. van Sonnenberg E, Wittich GR, Brown LK, et al. Percutaneous gastrostomy and gastroenterostomy: techniques derived from laboratory evaluation. AJR 1986;146:577–580.

19. Stevens SD, Picus D, Hicks ME, et al. Percutaneous gastrostomy and gastrojejunostomy after gastric surgery. J Vasc Intervent Radiol 1992;3:679–683.

20. Gehman KE, Elliott JA, Inculet RI. Percutaneous gastrojejunostomy with a modified Cope loop catheter. AJR 1990;155:79–80.

21. Alzate GD, Coons HG, Elliott J, et al. Percutaneous gastrostomy for jejunal feeding: a new technique. AJR 1986;147:822–825.

22. O'Keefe KP, Dula DJ, et al. Duodenal obstruction by a nondeflating Foley catheter gastrostomy tube. Ann Emerg Med 1990;19:1454–1457.

23. Wills JS, Oglesby JT. Controlled percutaneous gastrostomy: nylon T-fastener for fixation of the anterior gastric walls [letter]. Radiology 1986;160(1):278.

24. Brown AS, Mueller PR, Ferrucci JT. Controlled percutaneous gastrostomy: nylon T-fastener for fixation of the anterior gastric wall. Radiology 1986;158(2):543–545.

25. Cope C. Suture anchor for visceral drainage. AJR 1986;146:160–161.

26. Moote DJ, Ho C-S, Felice V. Fluoroscopically guided percutaneous gastrostomy: is gastric fixation necessary? Can Assoc Radiol J 1991;42:113–118.

27. Deutsch L-S, Kannegieter L, Vanson DT, et al. Simplified percutaneous gastrostomy. Radiology 1992;184:181–183.

28. Sanchez RB, van Sonnenberg E, D'Agostino HB, et al. CT guidance for percutaneous gastrostomy and gastroenterostomy. Radiology 1992;184:201–205.

29. Malki TA, Langer JC, Thompson V, et al. A prospective evaluation of the button gastrostomy in children. Can J Surg 1991;34:247–250.

30. Gauderer MWL, Olsen MM, Stellato TA, et al. Feeding gastrostomy button: experience and recommendations. J Pediatr Surg 1988;23:24–28.

31. McQuaid KR, Little TE. Two fatal complications related to gastrostomy "button" placement. Gastrointest Endosc 1992;38:601–603.

32. Taylor CA, Larson DE, Ballard DJ, et al. Predictors of outcome after percutaneous endoscopic gastrostomy: a community-based study. Mayo Clin Proc 1992;67:1042–1049.

33. Rogers DA, Bowden TA. Gastrostomy: operative or nonoperative? Surg Clin North Am 1992;72:515–524.

34. Larson DE, Burton DD, Schroeder KW, et al. Percutaneous endoscopic gastrostomy: indications, success, complications and mortality in 314 consecutive patients. Gastroenterology 1987;93:48–52.

35. Ponsky JL, Gauderer WL, Stellato TA. Percutaneous endoscopic gastrostomy: a review of 150 cases. Arch Surg 1983;118:913–914.

36. Wojtowycz MM, Arata JA, Micklos TJ, et al. CT findings after uncomplicated percutaneous gastrostomy. AJR 1988;151:307–309.

37. Grant JP. Comparison of percutaneous endoscopic gastrostomy with Stamm gastrostomy. Ann Surg 1988;207:598–603.

38. Stiegmann GV, Goff JS, Silas D, et al. Endoscopic versus operative gastrostomy: final results of a prospective randomized trial. Gastrointest Endosc 1990;36:1–5.

39. Morris JB, Mullen JL, Yu JC, et al. Laparoscopic guided jejunostomy. Surgery 1992;112:92–96.

40. Duh QY, Way LW. Laparoscopic gastrostomy using T-fasteners as retractors and anchors. Surg Endosc 1993;7:60–63.

41. Gibson SE, Wenig BL, Watkins JL. Complications of percutaneous endoscopic gastrostomy in head and neck cancer patients. Ann Otol Rhinol Laryngol 1992;101:46–50.

IV

Interventional Radiology of the Genitourinary System

35

Nephroureteral Obstruction

PARVATI RAMCHANDANI

Radiologically directed interventional uroradiologic procedures are indispensable in the management of obstructive uropathy. The procedures are widely available and are applicable in the treatment of urinary obstruction due to virtually any cause. This chapter addresses percutaneous nephrostomy, ureteral stenting, and dilation and interventions in obstructed renal transplants.

Percutaneous Nephrostomy (PCN)

Since the first description by Goodwin et al.[1] and Fowler et al.,[2] PCN has evolved to become the cornerstone of interventional procedures in the urinary tract. Levin et al.[3] reported that in 1992 upper urinary tract decompressions were performed by radiologists in 74 percent of cases, with most of the remainder being performed by urologists. PCN has established itself as a safe and effective alternative to surgical nephrostomy, which it has almost completely supplanted. Although the procedure was initially developed as a therapeutic technique for the relief of urinary tract obstruction, it is now increasingly used to provide access to the collecting system and is therefore the first step in a variety of other interventional procedures in the kidney and ureter.

The indications for PCN vary depending on the referral patterns and the patient population in an individual institution. They include the following:

1. To gain rapid relief of urinary obstruction, whether acute or more long-standing. This subject will be considered further in this chapter.
2. To gain access to the collecting system for a wide array of therapeutic and diagnostic procedures. These include the treatment of renal or ureteral calculi (stone fragmentation, removal, or chemolysis) (Fig. 35-1), ureteral interventions such as stricture dilation or stent placement, retrieval of foreign bodies (e.g., fractured stent fragments) that are inaccessible ureteroscopically, nephroscopic surgery such as endopyelotomy for ureteropelvic junction obstruction, and brush biopsy or therapy of urothelial tumors (Figs. 35-2 and 35-3). The list of possible procedures that can be performed through a PCN track continues to expand as radiologists and urologists gain mastery of the available equipment that can be adapted for percutaneous use. This application of PCN is the most frequent indication for the procedure in many institutions,[4,5] particularly where the urologists are active in endourologic therapy.
3. Urinary diversion to allow closure of a ureteral fistula or a dehiscent urinary tract anastomosis. In most cases, PCN drainage alone is unsuccessful in totally diverting the urine output from the kidney and necessitates the addition of either ureteral stenting or ureteral occlusion (the latter in patients with intractable vesicovaginal fistulas). Urine diversion by percutaneous nephrostomy alone has been used with some success to treat patients with intractable hemorrhagic cystitis.[6]
4. To assess residual function in a chronically obstructed kidney that appears to be either nonfunctioning or poorly functioning. Temporary renal drainage by PCN may allow assessment of residual recoverable function so that one can determine whether a kidney is worth salvaging. Kidneys that contribute 15 to 20 percent of overall renal function after relief of obstruction are usually deemed to be worth salvaging. A substantial increase in renal plasma flow within 10 days after decompression of an obstructed kidney is a reliable predictor of recovering renal function. The presence of renal parenchymal atrophy on computed tomography (CT) or renal ultrasonography does not always portend a poor potential for functional recovery after a PCN.

PCN is most often requested in patients after imaging studies demonstrate hydroureteronephrosis. These studies may also indicate the etiology as well as the anatomic level of the obstruction. The obstruction

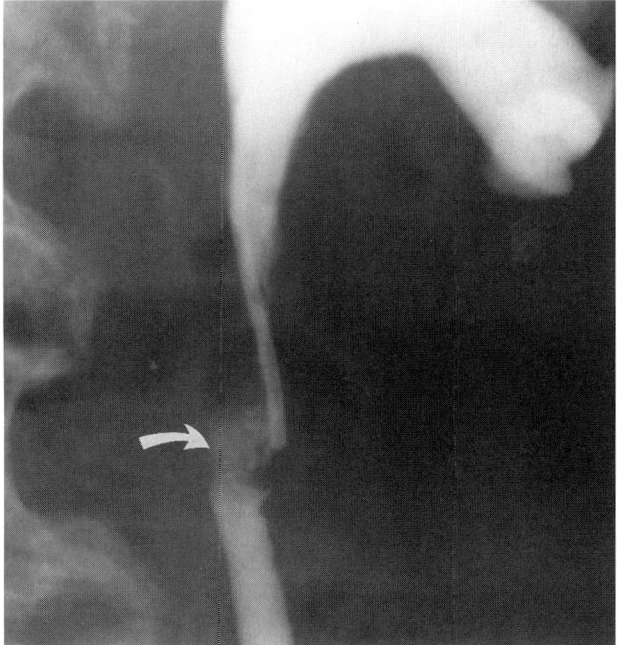

A

Figure 35-1. (A) Obstructing proximal ureteral calculus (*arrow*). Although a 5 French catheter was negotiated past the calculus (B), the stone could not be trapped within a basket or fragmented with extracorporeal shock wave lithotripsy because of embedding in the ureteral wall. The patient underwent open ureterolithotomy.

can be acute (e.g., obstructing ureteral calculi, complications of recent surgical or endoscopic procedures) or can be due to a more chronic process such as a tumor (primary urothelial neoplasms or extrinsic compression by primary or metastatic retroperitoneal or pelvic malignancies). It is important to attempt or at least consider the retrograde approach for renal drainage before resorting to the percutaneous route; the latter should ideally be reserved for patients in whom retrograde attempts are either unsuccessful or not feasible.

Technique

Preprocedural evaluation in patients being considered for percutaneous nephrostomy should include a clinical history to identify a potential bleeder as well as a hemostatic evaluation consisting of measurement of prothrombin time, partial thromboplastin time, and platelet count.[7-9] A baseline hemoglobin, blood urea nitrogen, and serum creatinine level should also be obtained. If the patient is taking aspirin or other drugs known to interfere with platelet function, a planned elective procedure can either be postponed for 3 to 10 days after the last dose of aspirin or the bleeding time can be used as a guide with the procedure being de-

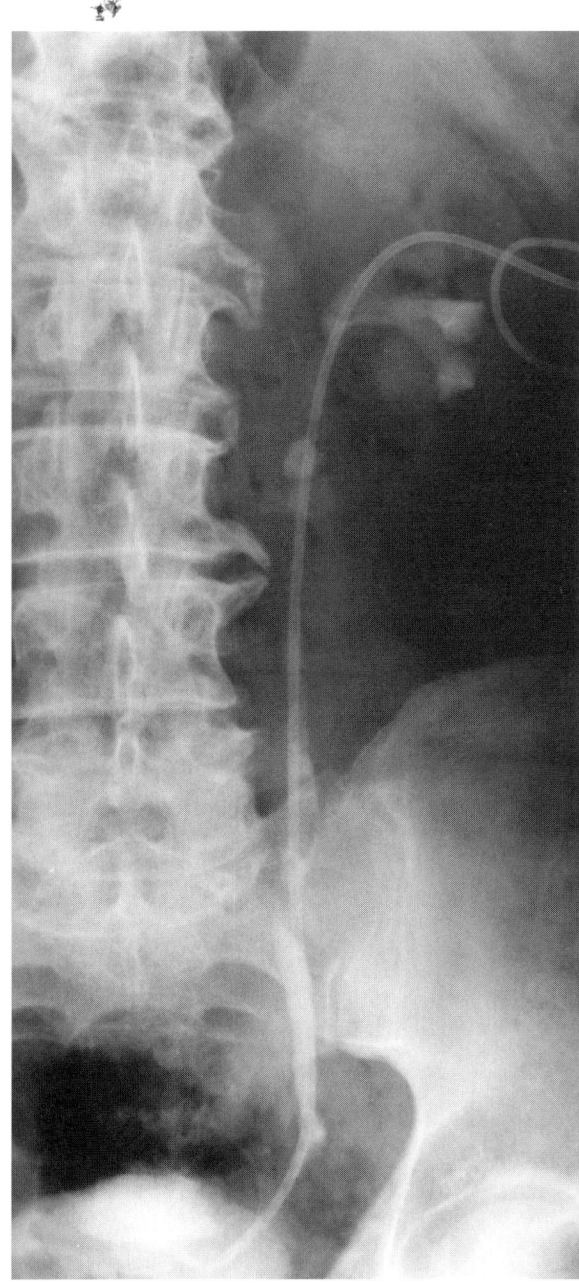

B

layed if the bleeding time exceeds the upper range of normal.[9] When coagulation values are abnormal, fresh-frozen plasma or platelets are given to correct them.

Urinalysis and urine culture with susceptibility results should be performed before elective PCN, and antibiotic therapy should be instituted if infection is present. The procedure should be postponed until the infection has cleared. In patients with obstruction and overt clinical infection in whom a specific organism has not yet been identified, broad-spectrum antibiotics such as an aminoglycoside (e.g., gentamycin) in con-

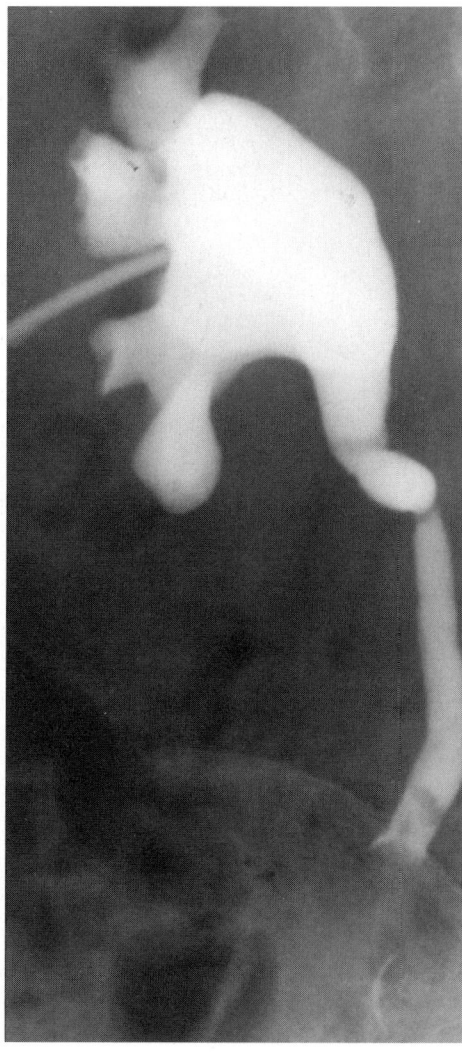

A

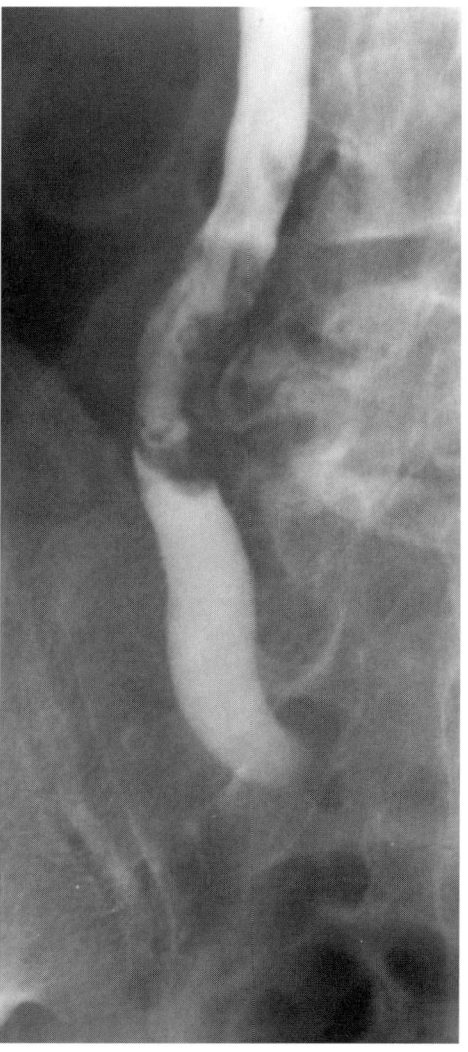

B

Figure 35-2. (A) Percutaneous nephrostomy (PCN) for right renal obstruction in a patient with a history of bladder cancer. (B) Selective contrast injection into the ureter dem-onstrates a large filling defect in the right ureter. Subsequent brush biopsy via the nephrostomy tract demonstrated transitional cell carcinoma.

junction with ampicillin should be started before the procedure[8,10] and continued after the procedure. Cochran et al.[8] reported that prophylactic antibiotics were beneficial in decreasing the development of sepsis in both high-risk patients (e.g., those with struvite stones, diabetes, urinary tract obstruction, indwelling catheters, previous manipulation, or instrumentation of the urinary tract) and in patients with a low risk for developing sepsis. They recommended that the antibiotics be administered in such a way that maximum blood levels would be attained during the procedure and that the antibiotics be continued for 24 to 48 hours in low-risk groups and for 48 to 72 hours in high-risk groups.

Percutaneous nephrostomies are most safely per-formed as an inpatient procedure. When performed on an outpatient basis, 25 percent of patients may require admission to the hospital after the procedure because of sepsis[8] even if they appear to be in a low-risk group and good candidates for an outpatient procedure.

Continuous electrocardiogram monitoring during the procedure is advisable. Large-bore and secure in-travenous access should be routinely established be-fore the procedure so that intravenous sedation and analgesia can be administered during the procedure and intravenous access is readily available if other med-ications need to be administered. Intravenous sedation combined with local anesthesia is sufficient to keep most patients comfortable; such patients require trans-cutaneous oximetry. The author has occasionally used

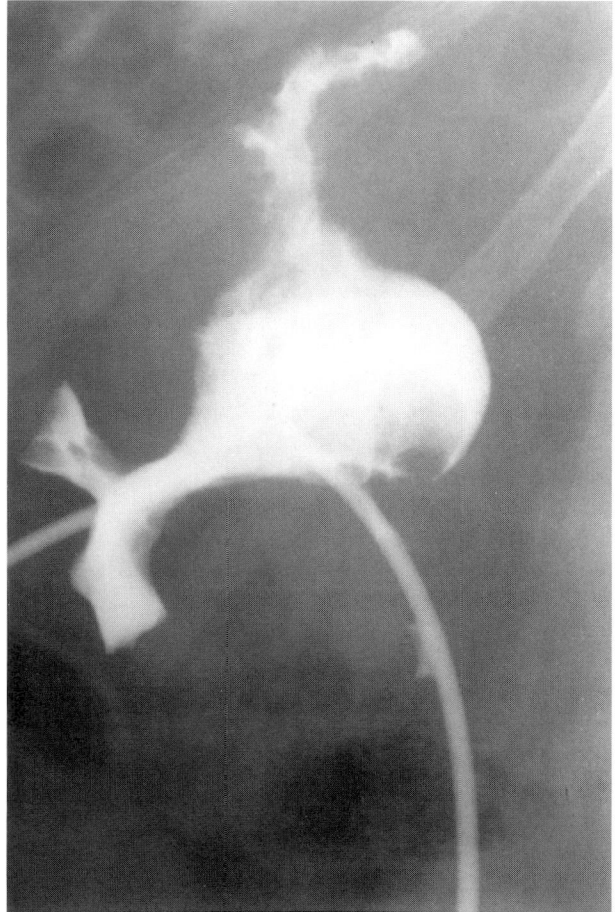

Figure 35-3. Percutaneous nephrostomy for obstructing transitional cell carcinoma in renal pelvis of solitary kidney. The patient underwent nephroscopic resection of the tumor.

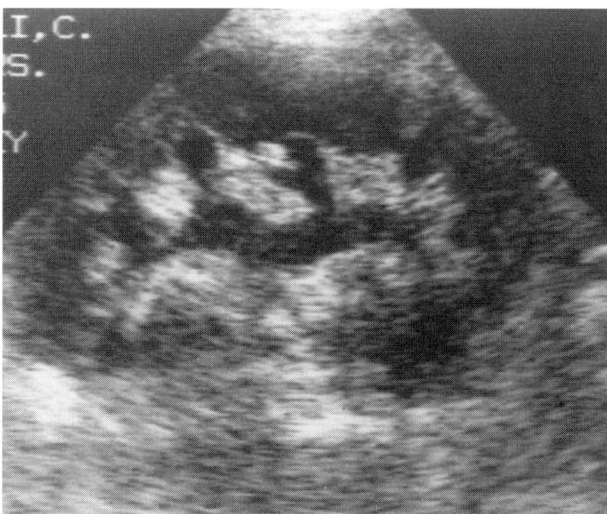

A

B

Figure 35-4. Ultrasound guidance for nephrostomy placement. (A) Ultrasonogram of a renal transplant demonstrates hydronephrosis. (B) Electronic lines define the track into the collecting system. The needle tip is visualized as an echogenic focus (*arrow*).

epidural anesthesia in patients with renal calculi who are to undergo stone removal through the nephrostomy track either on the same day or on the following day; in these cases a flexible epidural catheter is placed in the epidural space through which local anesthetic agents can be instilled. This serves to keep patients comfortable for both the percutaneous nephrostomy and the subsequent track dilatation and percutaneous nephrostolithotomy.

The patients are positioned in either a prone or a prone oblique position with the ipsilateral side elevated 20 to 30 degrees; however, if the patient cannot lie prone, the procedure can be performed in a supine oblique position.

The collecting system is localized using either fluoroscopy or ultrasound (US) guidance (Fig. 35-4). The former is used if a prior urographic study is available for guidance, if there is an opaque caliceal calculus that can serve as the target for puncture, or if the collecting

system can be opacified with contrast (either by excretion after intravenous administration or by means of a retrograde catheter). If renal function is poor (the usual case with obstruction) or if contrast cannot be administered, US guidance is used, which provides a precise measurement of the depth of the pelvocaliceal system and directs puncture into the optimal calix. The author's preference is to use real-time ultrasound (either a portable scanner or a unit housed in the fluoroscopy suite) and a transducer-mounted needle guide. The transducer is covered with a sterile sleeve, and the needle tip is followed with real-time scanning

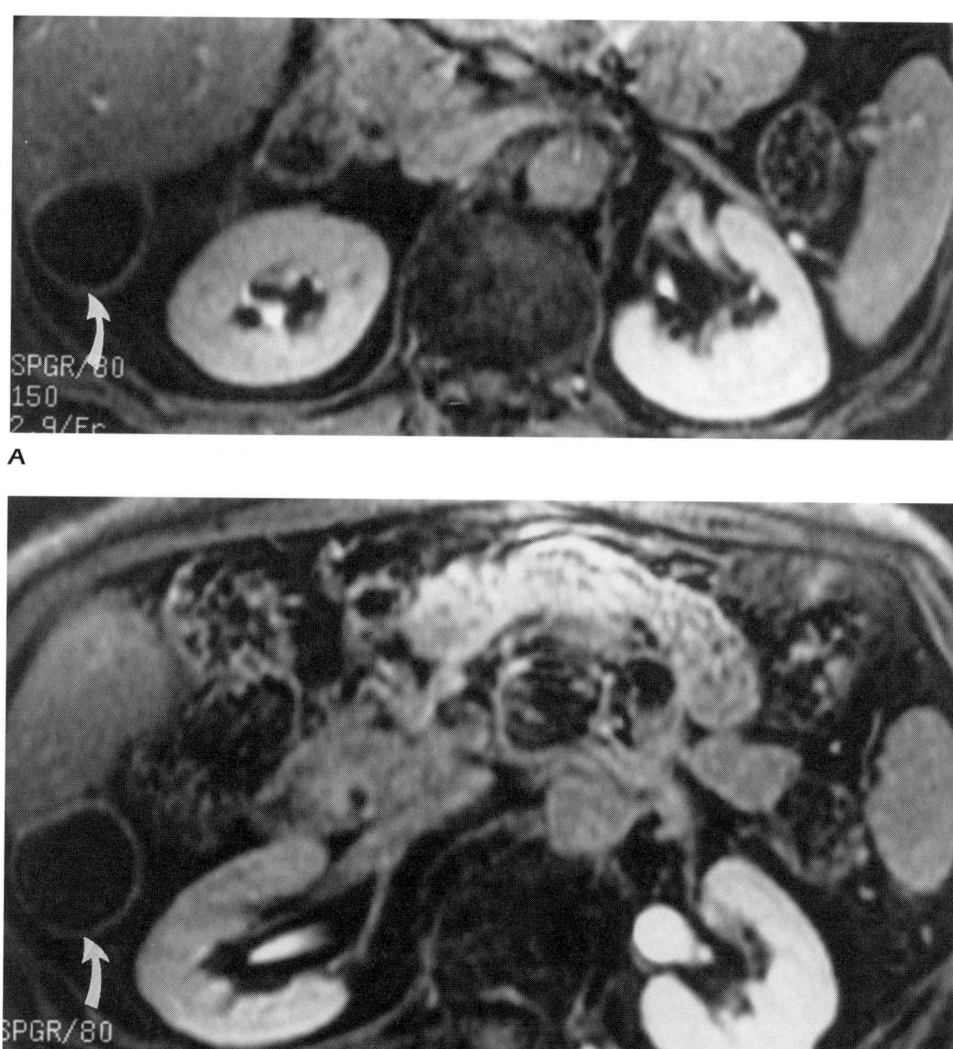

Figure 35-5. MRI demonstration of relationship of spleen and gallbladder to kidneys. Higher section (A) and lower section (B) demonstrate the proximity of the spleen and dis-tended gallbladder (*arrow*) to the kidneys. Both these organs are likely to be inadvertently entered by a puncture that is too far lateral.

as it enters the retroperitoneum, kidney, and then the collecting system (see Fig. 35-4). Once the collecting system has been entered, the remainder of the procedure is performed with fluoroscopic guidance. Thus US and fluoroscopy are complementary rather than competitive. Rarely, CT or MR scanning is necessary in patients with aberrant anatomy (e.g., severe scoliosis, congenital abnormalities) or in obese patients in whom US guidance is not possible, so that the relationship of the kidney to the liver, spleen, colon, gallbladder, and pleural space can be determined (Fig. 35-5).

Numerous techniques have been described for PCN placement,[11-14] all of which entail imaging and puncturing the collecting system, dilating the tract, and then placing a catheter. Planning the puncture site is the most crucial step in the procedure because a poorly placed puncture can make the track dilation technically arduous and fraught with complications.

The skin puncture site is chosen so that it enters the flank in the posterior axillary line, approximately 5 to 7 fingerbreadths lateral to the midline. The track should course subcostally, well below the inferior margin of the 12th rib. This placement minimizes the chances of injury to the intercostal artery and also decreases the chances of intercostal nerve irritation, which can be very painful. If the intercostal space between the 11th and 12th ribs is used, care should be taken to stay close to the superior aspect of the 12th rib to avoid the neurovascular bundle. The puncture should be advanced at an angle of approximately 45 degrees and should traverse the renal parenchyma before entering a posteriorly directed calix. This approach results in an oblique (posterolateral) nephrostomy tract that passes lateral to the paraspinous muscles and medial and posterior to the peritoneum and colon and that enters the renal parenchyma at the relatively avascular posterolateral plane of the kidney (Brödel line), minimizing the risk of entering the large vessels in the renal hilum. Such a track is more likely to be comfortable for a patient in the supine recumbent position, and the risk of catheter kinking is minimized. All nephrostomy catheters should traverse the renal parenchyma before entering the collecting system so that the parenchyma can provide a secure seal around the catheter.

If PCN is being performed for drainage alone, an interpolar or lower polar posterior calix is chosen for access. However, if PCN is to be followed by ureteral stent insertion, an interpolar caliceal entry is preferable so that the vector of pushing forces can be directed toward the ureteropelvic junction. Access through the upper pole calices may be required in patients with stones, in which case an intercostal tract may be needed.

Once the puncture site is chosen, local anesthesia is liberally administered into the skin site and throughout the proposed track to the level of the renal fascia. A variety of puncture sets using coaxial needles and/or sheaths are commercially available for the procedure. Two widely available sets (and used in the author's practice) are the Neff set (Cook, Inc.) and the Accustick set (Medi-Tech).

After localization, the collecting system is initially punctured with thin-walled, flexible, 21- or 22-gauge needles. A sample of urine is withdrawn and sent for culture if necessary. A small amount of contrast is then injected to confirm the needle position and to determine the caliceal entry site. In a dilated and obstructed collecting system, an attempt should be made to partially decompress the collecting system before contrast injection, with care being taken to inject a lesser volume of contrast than the volume of urine aspirated to avoid overdistention and possible sepsis. The purpose of contrast injection is merely to confirm the position of the needle. If the initial entry point into the collecting system is not optimal, a second puncture is performed into the desired calix with either a second 21-gauge needle (the first needle is not removed to avoid decompression of the collecting system through the needle site and to provide a route for continuing opacification) or an 18-gauge trocar stylet needle. In pa-

tients undergoing nephrostomy for subsequent stone removal, the author has found that puncture with 18-gauge needles is preferable because they are less flexible and thus easier to direct into the desired calix. Puncture of the renal infundibula or pelvis should be avoided because there is a high risk of injury to the interlobar vessels and the major segmental branches of the renal artery and vein. Sampaio and associates found that punctures through the caliceal fornix were highly unlikely to cause renal arterial injury, whereas infundibular punctures lacerated interlobar or segmental arteries in 23 percent of cases and direct renal pelvic punctures caused injury to a large retropelvic vessel in 33 percent of cases.[15]

If a 21-gauge needle has been used for the puncture, the introducer sets are used to eventually place a 0.038-inch (0.87-mm) guidewire into the collecting system. If an 18-gauge needle has been used, the 0.038-inch guidewire can be directly advanced through the needle. The nephrostomy track is then dilated with fascial dilators and a nephrostomy catheter placed. A self-retaining catheter is preferable, and these may be of a pigtail, accordion, Malecot, or Foley type. A "self-retaining" loop-type catheter (Cope loop catheter) in used in most cases and is less prone to being inadvertently withdrawn than are the Malecot and Foley catheters. Initially, even these catheters are best secured to the skin with a suture to prevent accidental withdrawal. With well-developed nephrostomy tracks, skin sutures are rarely necessary. The tubes are held to the skin with either gauze and adhesive tape or clear skin dressing. The self-retaining loop catheters are also available with a hydrophilic coating, which should theoretically facilitate catheter insertion. However, with proper tract selection and guidewire use, the placement of nephrostomy catheters in most cases is straightforward. Thus the value of hydrophilic coating on these catheters remains unproven.

Contraindications

These have to be considered in the context of the potential risks and benefits for each individual patient. The only absolute contraindication is the presence of an uncorrectable bleeding disorder; however, if the bleeding diathesis is due to a coagulopathy caused by urosepsis, urinary drainage will be necessary before the bleeding abnormality can be corrected. If there are severe electrolyte changes because of the obstructive uropathy (e.g., hyperkalemia with serum potassium levels above 7 mEq/liter), emergency hemodialysis and/or ion exchange therapy should be considered before PCN to quickly correct the electrolyte abnormalities, since the cardioplegia associated with hyperkalemia can be refractory to all therapy.

Results

Percutaneous nephrostomy is almost universally successful in draining obstructed dilated kidneys and allows for immediate renal decompression.[16] In nondilated systems or in complex stone cases, 85 to 90 percent success has been reported.[11] Lee et al.[17] analyzed the outcomes of emergency nephrostomies performed by radiologists with different levels of experience; all operators performed a minimum of 10 PCNs a year. Although all the operators successfully placed drainage catheters on an emergent basis, mean procedure and fluoroscopy times were significantly longer for the more inexperienced radiologists (fluoroscopy and procedure times 2 minutes and 25 minutes for experienced operators and 10 minutes and 42 minutes for inexperienced operators). Furthermore, 20 to 33 percent of the procedures performed by inexperienced operators were repeated the next day because of catheter dislodgment or malposition.

When obstruction is complicated by urosepsis or azotemia, the response to renal decompression is marked and often immediate. In one series,[18] PCN decreased the mortality from gram-negative septicemia from 40 to 8 percent in patients with urinary obstruction complicated by infection. Although pyonephrosis mandates emergent drainage, percutaneous manipulations themselves can readily precipitate septicemia (manifested as shaking chills and fever) in these patients. It is important that these patients be treated with intravenous antibiotics before the attempted nephrostomy. In addition, forceful opacification of the collecting system to visualize the site and cause of obstruction should be deferred until the collecting system has been adequately decompressed. The addition of contrast to an already distended, infected system may force bacteria into the peripapillary veins and induce urosepsis (Fig. 35-6).[18,19] The author generally defers antegrade nephrostograms until the patient has drained for 24 to 48 hours and is afebrile. In patients with fungal urinary infections, topical antibiotics can be directly infused into the kidneys if systemic toxicity prevents one from achieving effective therapeutic levels by parenteral administration; in addition, obstructing fungus balls can be extracted through the nephrostomy track.[20]

In patients with azotemia secondary to obstruction, PCN provides rapid amelioration of impending renal failure with return of renal function to normal or near normal levels.[21] As such, the procedure can be a temporizing measure to improve or at least preserve renal function while other therapies such as radiation or chemotherapy are given time to reverse the underlying obstruction. PCN drainage may also be required to optimize renal function before definitive surgery or to

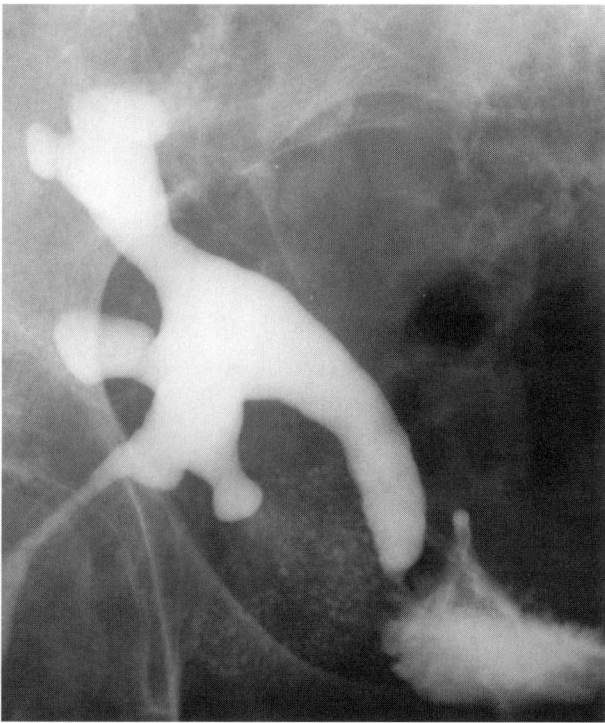

Figure 35-6. Overly vigorous nephrostogram in a renal transplant with a distal ureteral stricture. There is retrograde opacification of the collecting ducts in both the upper and lower poles. This degree of overdistention can result in sepsis.

allow the administration of nephrotoxic drugs such as cisplatin.

In patients with terminal malignancies where the obstruction is irremediable, the need for nephrostomy drainage will likely be permanent. This poses ethical and moral dilemmas that have to be frankly and openly discussed with the patient and the family. The physical and financial burdens posed by the presence of a drainage catheter have to be weighed against the benefit of extending life for a few months. Even with careful patient selection, 32 percent of patients are unable to achieve any improvement in the quality of life after percutaneous nephrostomy.[22] Long-term survival after palliative diversion for malignant ureteral obstruction is poor, with only 25 percent of patients alive at 1 year[23] in one series. If a PCN is performed in these circumstances, only unilateral drainage is usually required and bilateral nephrostomies confer no benefit.[24] As a group, patients with hormone-responsive prostate carcinoma tend to live longer than those with hormone-resistant prostate cancer or other pelvic malignancies.[25] Bilateral drainage may be a preferable option in these patients, particularly if the patient is young (Fig. 35-7), so that maximum renal function can be preserved.

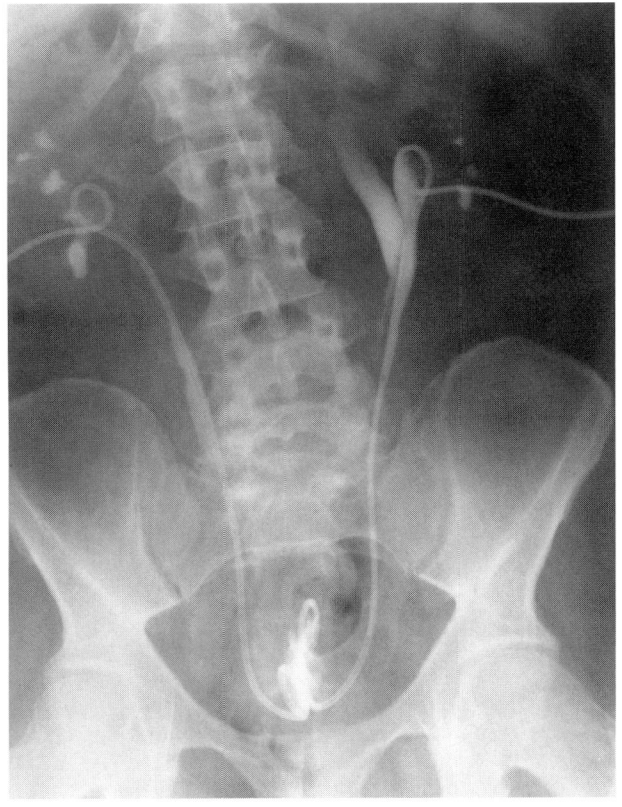

◀ **Figure 35-7.** Bilateral nephroureteral catheters in a 40-year-old man with advanced prostate cancer. The proximal loops of the catheters are self-retaining (Cope loops). Although malignant ureteral obstruction is usually well managed with a unilateral nephrostomy, bilateral drainage catheters were placed in view of the patient's age.

Complications

The overall serious complication rate of PCN is low, with a mortality of 0.2 percent compared to a surgical mortality of 6.0 percent.[14] Complications related to percutaneous nephrostomy can be divided into major procedure-related complications (4–6 percent incidence)[14,26,27] and minor complications (10 to 28 percent incidence). Major complications include hemorrhage and sepsis.

Hemorrhage requiring transfusion or other therapy is a complication in 1.0 to 2.4 percent of patients[26–28] and is related to renal arterial pseudoaneurysms or arteriovenous fistulas due to laceration of lobar arteries (Fig. 35-8). Using fine needles and small-bore cathe-

Figure 35-8. Pseudoaneurysm following percutaneous stone removal. Early phase (A) and late phase (B) films from a selective renal arteriogram demonstrate a pseudoaneurysm in the nephrostomy track. If no vascular injury is demonstrated with the nephrostomy catheter in place, the catheter should be removed over a guidewire and the injection repeated to counteract the possible tamponading effects of the nephrostomy catheter.

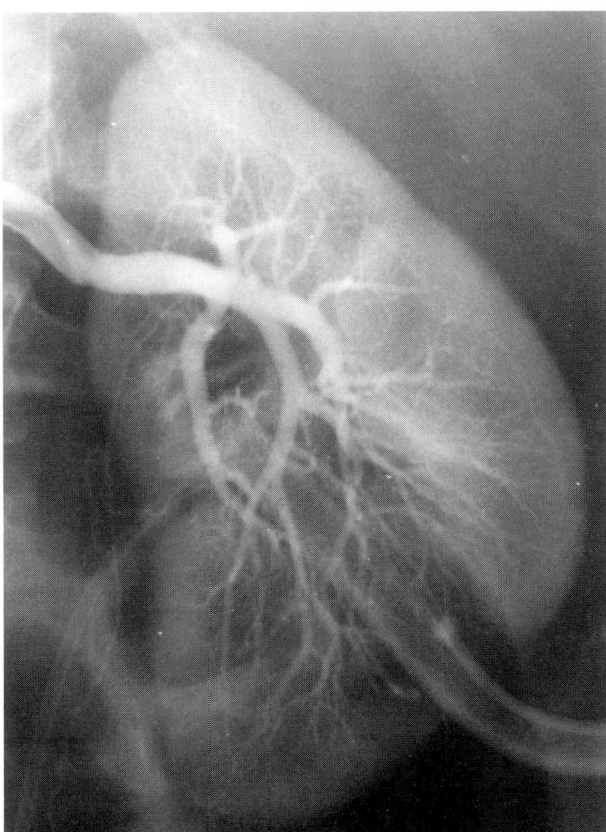

A

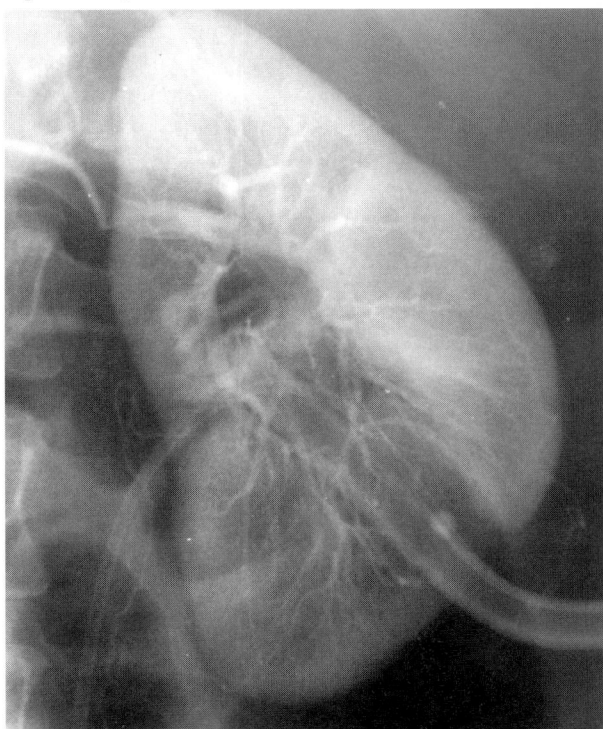

B

ters and avoiding puncture of the anteromedial renal vessels may decrease the incidence of this complication. Most hemorrhage associated with nephrostomy placement is transient and self-limited; it is not uncommon to have pink or slightly bloody urine drainage for several days after a nephrostomy, and this is not considered a complication. If the urine is grossly bloody or large clots are seen on the nephrostogram, repeated irrigation with cold saline and/or placement of a slightly larger catheter to tamponade the bleeding vessel are usually effective in controlling the bleeding (Fig. 35-9). Serious vascular trauma is suspected if the urine continues to be grossly bloody after 3 to 5 days, if new intrapelvic clots are observed on nephrostograms, or if there is a significant drop in the hematocrit. If the drop in the hematocrit is out of proportion to the urine blood loss, a retroperitoneal hematoma should be suspected and a CT scan obtained (Fig. 35-10). Therefore, angiography and possible arterial embolization should be considered in patients who have significant continuous or recurrent bleeding longer than 4 to 5 days after PCN placement.[28] Unsuspected retroperitoneal hematomas not requiring treatment have been reported in 13 percent of patients on CT scans performed after nephrostomy tube placement.[29] If the initial angiogram fails to show a source of bleeding, the study should be repeated immediately after the drainage catheter is removed over a guidewire so that the tamponading effect of the catheter is relieved and the bleeding site can be angiographically localized (see Fig. 35-8).[30] Although unusual, development of a perirenal hematoma has been described after a nephrostomy catheter was removed that had been in place for 3 months.[31]

The incidence of sepsis after nephrostomy tube placement has been reported as 1.4 to 21.0 percent.[8,18,26,27] This wide variance is likely due to the differing definitions of sepsis in different series. Cochran et al.[8] considered fever and shaking chills to be signs of sepsis and noted them in 21 percent of patients. Lee et al.[26] defined sepsis as fever over 101°F (38.4°C) with shaking chills and noted its occurrence in less than 3.6 percent of their patients who underwent emergent drainage. All 160 patients in their series developed a transient increase in body temperature, which usually lasted less than 6 hours. Fifteen percent of patients undergoing nephrostomy drainage for pyonephrosis develop postprocedure fever, and 7 percent develop septic shock[19] despite the use of aminoglycoside prophylaxis.

The use of antibiotic-bonded nephrostomy catheters appears to have no influence on the overall incidence of infective complications associated with nephrostomy drainage.[32]

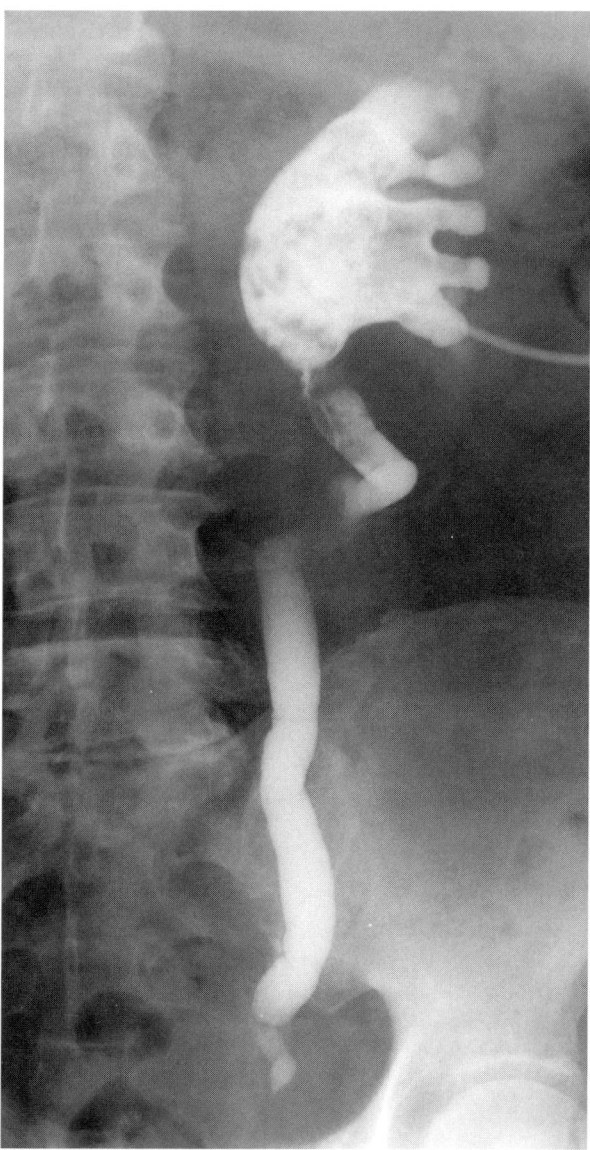

Figure 35-9. Large blood clots appearing as filling defects in the opacified collecting system. The patient was clinically stable and the urine cleared within a week after the procedure.

Minor complications that may occur are catheter dislodgment, urine extravasation or leak due to renal pelvic perforation, pneumonia, and/or atelectasis, pleural effusion, and accidental puncture of adjacent viscera. Inadvertent puncture of the spleen can cause severe hemorrhage or even a splenic abscess in patients with infected urine.[33] A renoduodenal fistula has been reported in a patient with xanthogranulomatous pyelonephritis who underwent PCN.[34] An intercostal approach (often required for access to the upper poles of the kidneys) causes more thoracic complications than a

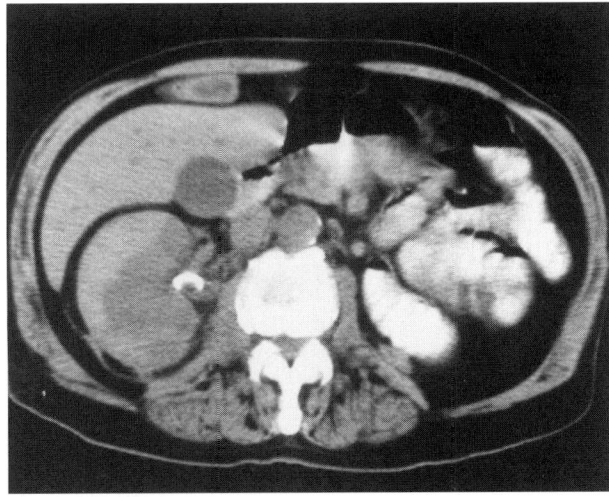

A

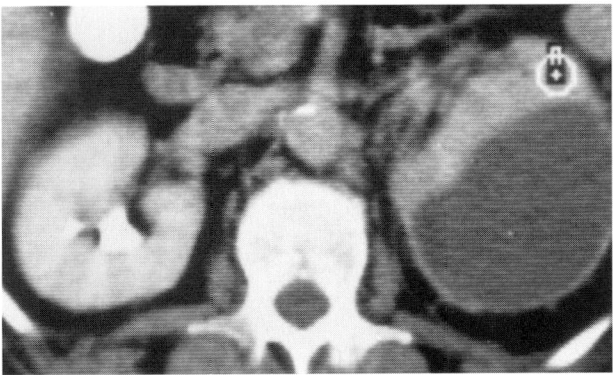

B

Figure 35-10. Subcapsular hematomas following PCN in two different patients. (A) Unenhanced CT scan. The hematoma is denser than the renal parenchyma. (B) On contrast-enhanced CT, the hematoma appears to be of low attenuation compared to the enhancing renal parenchyma.

subcostal puncture.[35] In expiration, a posterior intercostal approach between the 11th and 12th ribs poses little risk of injury to the spleen and liver,[36] but the lungs remain vulnerable to puncture in many patients. The right lung is in the path of the needle in 29 percent and the left lung in 14 percent of patients in expiration. During maximal inspiration, the lung would be in the needle path in most patients in whom an intercostal puncture is performed.

Follow-up

Most PCN drainage catheters are replaced every 3 to 6 months on an outpatient basis (Fig. 35-11). Occasionally, catheter changes need to be more frequent in patients in whom the lumen occludes in 6 to 8 weeks. A dissolving-tip nephrostomy catheter (Temp-Tip, Medi-Tech) is available commercially. The tip of the catheter dissolves shortly after insertion into the collecting system and results in a larger end hole. The major advantage is in facilitating catheter exchange over a guidewire.

Blocked or dislodged nephrostomy tubes can pose a challenge. With blocked catheters, intraluminal encrustation prevents passage of a guidewire. Maneuvers that may be useful in such a situation are advancing a sheath over the nephrostomy catheter (the sheath is selected to be slightly larger than the nephrostomy catheter, such as a 9 French sheath for an 8.3 French nephrostomy catheter) until the tip of the sheath is within the collecting system and then withdrawing the nephrostomy catheter through it.[37] A parallel guidewire method has also been described to replace blocked tubes,[37] as well as puncture of the occluded catheter within the pelvocaliceal system with an 18-gauge needle.[38] The author has found that hydrophilic guidewires can often be successfully negotiated through an encrusted catheter that does not allow the passage of a standard Teflon-coated guidewire. If the encrustations trap the retention string, the loop on the self-retaining catheters will not open and the catheter may have to be withdrawn in a loop configuration through a large sheath. With Malecot catheters, tissue may occasionally grow through the wings of the catheter, making them resistant to removal.[39] Stewart et al. believe that if nephrostomy tube drainage is required for longer than a few weeks, Malecot-type winged catheters should not be used to avoid this complication.[39]

When the catheters are completely extruded, the first step is to inject contrast medium into the skin opening to determine if the track is still patent. Failure to define a track into the renal pelvis usually indicates that the catheter has been dislodged for more than 48 hours and may necessitate a fresh nephrostomy. If the track can be opacified, an 8 French pediatric feeding tube or a 4 French angiographic sheath can usually be

Figure 35-11. Patient with chronic nephrostomy catheter placement for ureteral stricture with flank pain. (A) Well-formed Cope loop within the renal pelvis immediately after a routine catheter change. (B and C) Two days later, the loop has retracted into the lower pole infundibulum, causing great flank discomfort. Catheter retraction into an infundib-

ulum is an extremely common event, and most patients are asymptomatic with it. (D) The locking Malecot nephrostomy catheter was replaced because there is no foolproof method of ensuring that the catheter loop will remain within the renal pelvis. The Malecot catheter distended the infundibulum less and the patient's flank pain resolved. ▶

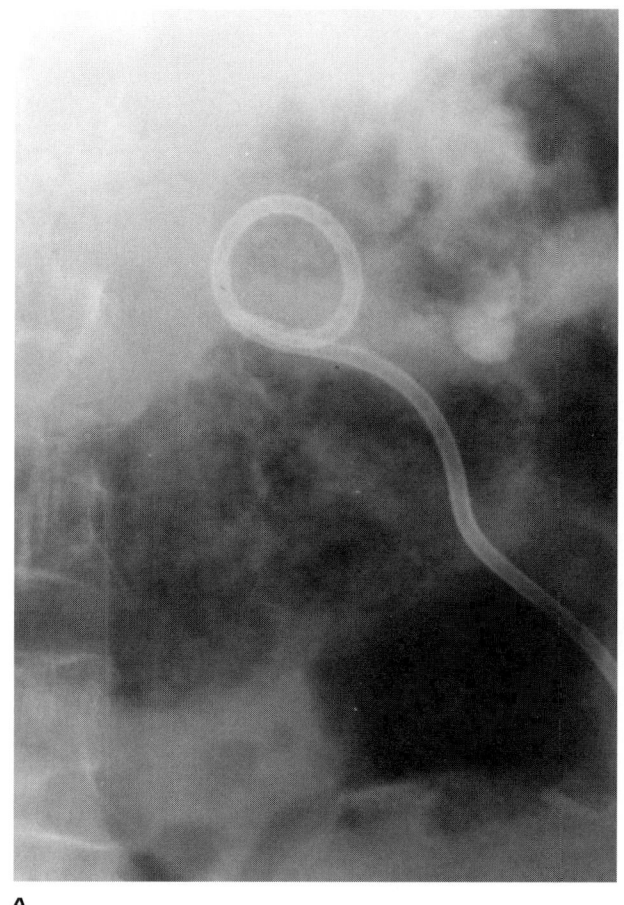

A

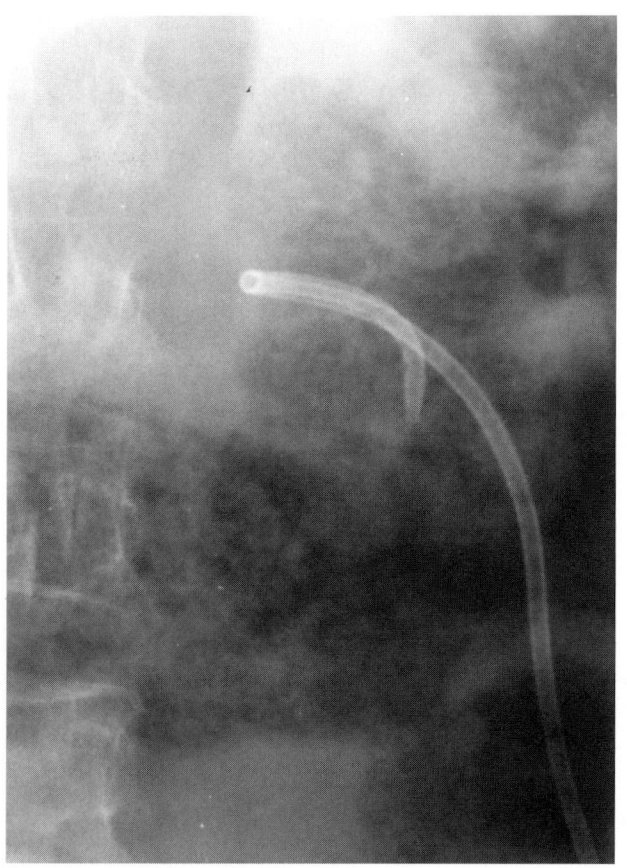

B

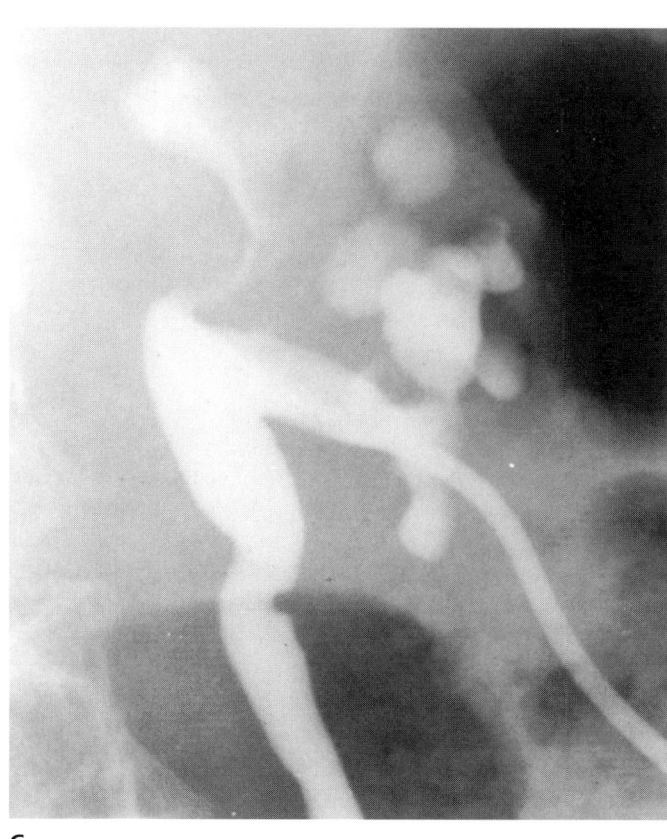

C

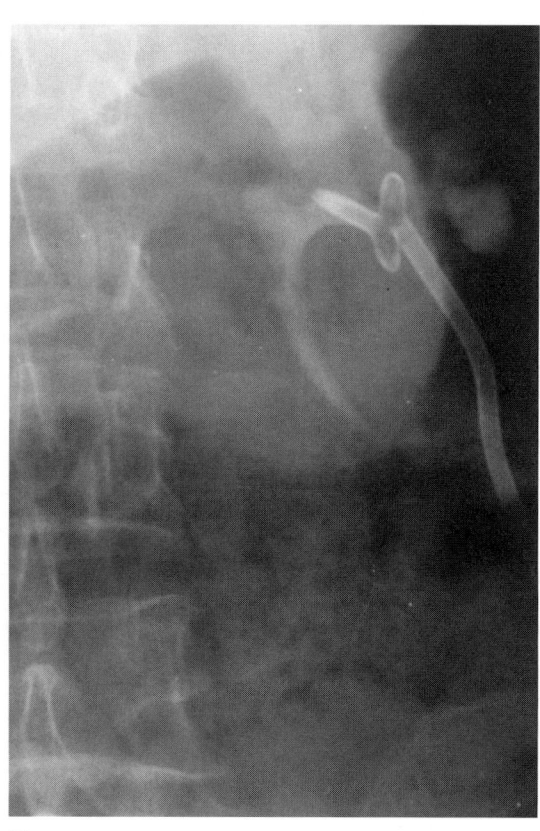

D

negotiated through the track over a straight or angled-tip guidewire. Hydrophilic guidewires are extremely useful when the track is particularly tortuous. An alternative approach proposed by some urologists is to use a rigid ureteroscope to recannulate the nephrostomy track after catheter dislodgment,[40] with the purported advantage being the ability to perform the entire replacement in the urology suite. In an occasional patient who is disoriented or confused, accidental tube dislodgment can become a frequent occurrence. A U-shaped nephrostomy tube may be a consideration in such cases.

The presence of a nephrostomy tube invariably causes bacteriuria, candiduria, or pyuria within 9 weeks of initial nephrostomy tube drainage.[41] However, antibiotic prophylaxis is unnecessary in routine catheter exchanges when the catheters have been draining adequately and, in fact, fails to prevent bacteremia.[41,42] Cronan et al.[41,42] found that asymptomatic bacteremia occurred in 11 percent of routine tube changes and that preprocedural antibiotics were unsuccessful in preventing bacteremia. This has implications for patients at risk for endocarditis, in whom routine tube changes should be preceded by antibiotic therapy with the aim of eradicating bacteriuria. Antibiotics should be chosen for activity against the organisms isolated in the urine. Cronan et al.[41,42] also advocate that after bacteriuria has been eliminated an antibiotic regimen recommended in the American Heart Association guidelines for genitourinary procedures be administered in conjunction with an elective nephrostomy tube change.

In patients who are not at risk for endocarditis, antibiotic prophylaxis prior to elective tube change should be considered if the catheter is occluded, if urine drainage has been suboptimal (indicating impending catheter occlusion), or if the patient is febrile (in which case the antibiotics should be continued for 24 to 48 hours). Defervescence of fever usually occurs when free drainage is established.[8]

The author generally does not flush the nephrostomy catheters between tube changes. Catheter flushing at home, whether by visiting nurses or the patient, does little to favorably influence the incidence of tube encrustation.

Nephrostograms in patients who have long-term nephrostomy catheters often demonstrate changes of pyelitis cystica (Fig. 35-12), probably related to chronic irritation. If renal CT scans are performed after catheter removal, surprisingly few morphologic changes are evident.[43] Hruby and Marberger[43] reported slight capsular fibrosis at the puncture site in 22 percent of patients, slight perirenal scarring in 28 percent, a 1-cm cortical scar at the puncture site in one patient, and no signs of loss of renal function. Thus

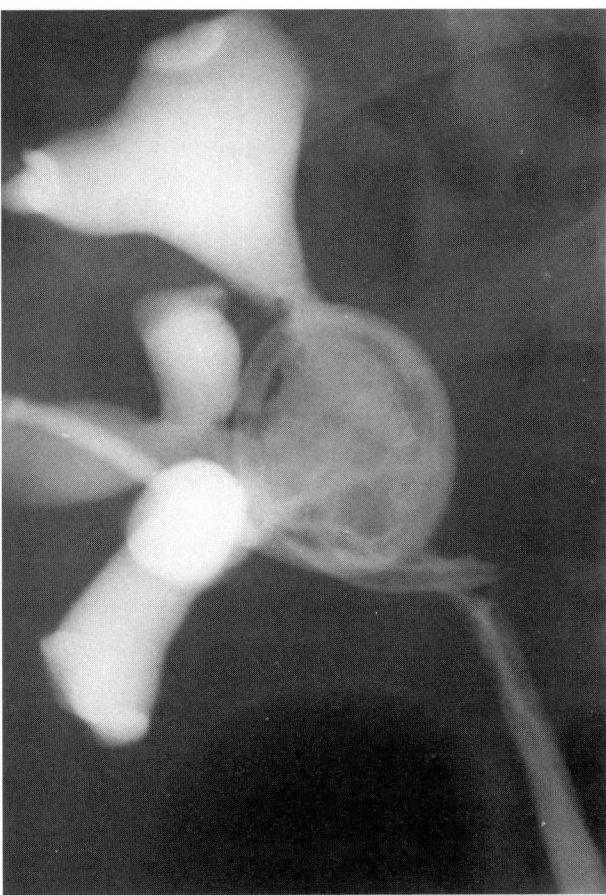

Figure 35-12. Pyelitis cystica in a patient with nephrostomy catheter drainage for 6 years. These changes can occur as early as a few weeks after catheter placement. The multiple filling defects represent submucosal cysts.

PCNs produce no significant late effect on renal morphology or function.

Ureteral Stenting

Ureteral intubation is an essential component in the management of patients with nephroureteral obstruction or other ureteral problems such as fistulas, in patients undergoing open ureteral surgery, and prior to extracorporeal shock wave lithotripsy (ESWL).

Stent Materials

The ideal ureteral stent should be easy to insert and retrieve (and therefore easy to change), resist encrustation and occlusion, be strong yet flexible (and resist buckling during insertion), have low surface friction, be radiopaque (for ease of insertion and subsequent plain film evaluation of position), be biocompatible and chemically stable (biodurable), resist migration, and have good flow characteristics so that urine flow can be effectively restored and maintained. A number of materials have been used in the quest to produce an ideal ureteral stent, but there is no material available[44,45] that satisfies all the above-mentioned criteria.

At first, polyurethane and polyethylene stents were widely used by radiologists because the stent design permitted insertion over a standard guidewire, making percutaneous antegrade placement feasible. Both materials tended to become brittle in urine and have been abandoned in favor of newer materials. Polyurethane is a generic class of condensation polymers that are derived from polyisocyanate and a polyol.[45] They are highly versatile and inexpensive materials and popular for stent manufacture. Polyurethane tends to be a stiff, rubbery, and elastomeric material: that is, it can reform to an original configuration after substantial deformity. Polyethylene, on the other hand, is a waxlike polymer that was used extensively to fabricate stents but was phased out in favor of polyurethane stents because of anecdotal reports of stent fracture in patients whose polyethylene stents were left indwelling beyond the maximum recommended 6-month period.[46–48] Although both are adequate stent materials for short-term drainage, stents made of these materials can be left in no longer than 6 months because encrustation and occlusion are problems with extended use.[49] Furthermore, when Marx et al.[50] evaluated stents within canine ureters, polyurethane stents caused epithelial erosions and ulcers in all cases, whereas other stent materials rarely did so. Mardis et al.[45] speculate that the poor biocompatibility of polyurethane may be related to its irregular surface, best demonstrated by electron microscopy.

Ureteral stents made of silicone, C-Flex, and Percuflex are also in wide clinical use and are offered by many manufacturers. Silicone stents retain their flexibility and elasticity even 10 years after placement, which is an advantage. However, silicone has several disadvantages: (1) inherently low tensile strength, which limits the inner diameter of the stents as well as the size of the side holes, thus reducing the functional efficacy of the stent; (2) a high coefficient of surface friction, which hampers stent insertion and requires placement through a peel-away sheath; and (3) weak coil strength, which allows the pigtail configuration of the coiled ends of the stent to straighten easily, making the stents prone to spontaneous migration. Silicone is also poorly radiopaque, making fluoroscopic monitoring during insertion difficult. For these reasons, silicone is not the preferred choice of material for stents, particularly indwelling ureteral stents.

Percuflex is a proprietary biocompatible olefinic copolymer material from Boston Scientific Corporation (Medi-Tech, Microvasive) that has high tensile strength (and therefore the largest available inner lumen for a given outside diameter); an intrinsic low coefficient of friction, which facilitates stent placement; and long-term biodurability with resistance to fracture and migration.[51] Although the manufacturer recommends replacing the stents every 6 months, Rackson et al.[51] found that the Percuflex stents remained patent for a mean period of 10 months. Of all currently available stent materials, Percuflex may represent one of the most balanced materials.

C-Flex is a proprietary silicone-modified copolymer from Concept Polymer Technologies that was designed to be urine-compatible. Although not as strong as Percuflex or polyurethane, the material has sufficient tensile strength to allow good flow rates and coil strength. The stents resist both migration and fracture,[52] are less rigid than polyurethane stents, and demonstrate an overall patency of 80 percent. The external surface of the stent is slippery, a property that enhances resistance to stent encrustation and also makes stent placement easier.

To summarize, at the current time, stents made of C-Flex and Percuflex appear to confer the most advantages with regard to patency, flexibility, resistance to migration, good urine flow rates, and resistance to fracturing. The manufacturers recommend stent exchange at 6 months for both stents, although in certain clinical situations, such as terminal malignancy, stent replacement can be deferred for a longer period if the stent is functioning well.

Endoureteral implantation of self-expanding metal stents was a natural offshoot of experience with metal stent use in the biliary tract and urethra. The stents have been used primarily in patients with malignant ureteral obstruction[53–55] as an alternative to conventional double pigtail ureteral stents, with the hope that ureteral patency could be maintained for a longer period. The potential incorporation of the stent into the ureteric wall with covering by urothelium should theoretically avoid calcium encrustation, infection, and risk of migration. However, the stents have demonstrated no greater beneficial effect than conventional plastic stents. Hyperplasia of the urothelium leading to stent occlusion, encrustation, and hematuria have been reported, and the role of metal stents in the treatment of malignant ureteral obstruction is yet to be established. Because the biocompatibility of metallic devices in the urinary tract is unknown, as also the effects of the corrosive action of urine and extracellular fluids on the metal, most researchers have been reluctant to use metal stents in ureteral obstruction due to benign disease.[44,56–58]

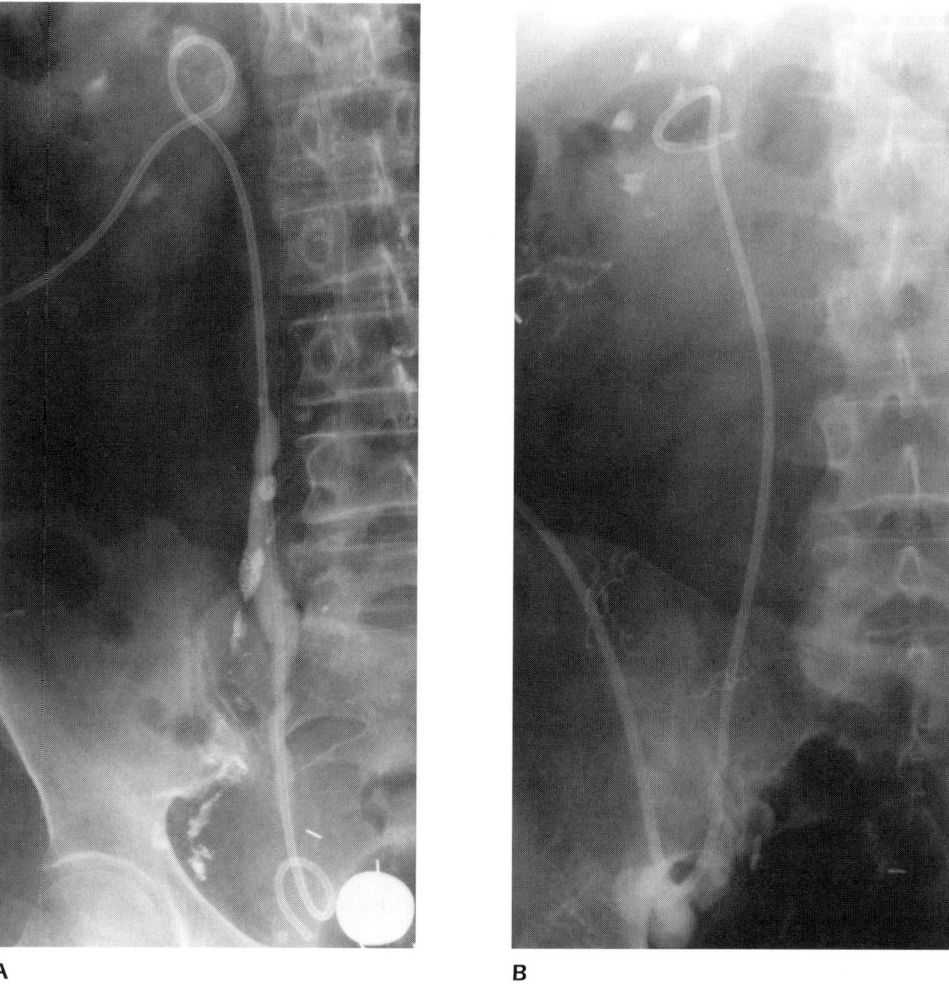

Figure 35-13. Ureteral stents. (A) Nephroureteral catheter placed in an antegrade fashion. (B) Transconduit retrograde placement of a nephrostomy catheter through an ileal conduit.

Technique

Ureteral stents can be inserted in one of three ways (Fig. 35-13): (1) percutaneously (antegrade), (2) per urethral (retrograde), and (3) transconduit (retrograde). The transconduit approach will be discussed in Chapter 38. In difficult cases, a combined approach may be required. Regardless of the route used for insertion, ureteral stent placement provides the benefits of urine drainage and diversion without the inconvenience of a drainage bag with its attendant cosmetic problems and the risk of inadvertent dislodgment. If the urinary bladder is markedly contracted or diseased (as with neoplastic invasion, radiation cystitis, or tuberculosis) or in patients with incontinence, drainage via a percutaneous nephrostomy is preferable to ureteral stenting.

Antegrade Ureteral Stenting

Percutaneous antegrade stent insertion is performed when retrograde insertion fails or is not possible. Antegrade ureteral stenting requires percutaneous access to the collecting system, preferably through an interpolar or upper pole calix because this approach allows the pushing forces to be directed toward the ureteropelvic junction. A guidewire is then maneuvered across the ureteral obstruction using a combination of preshaped catheters (cobra, multipurpose) and guidewires. Hydrophilic-coated guidewires ("glidewires") are particularly helpful in crossing tight strictures. The use of transrenal Teflon sheaths (peel-away or non-peel-away) also facilitates the placement of stents by preventing buckling in the subcutaneous tissues and in the renal pelvis[49,59] because the stent encounters high

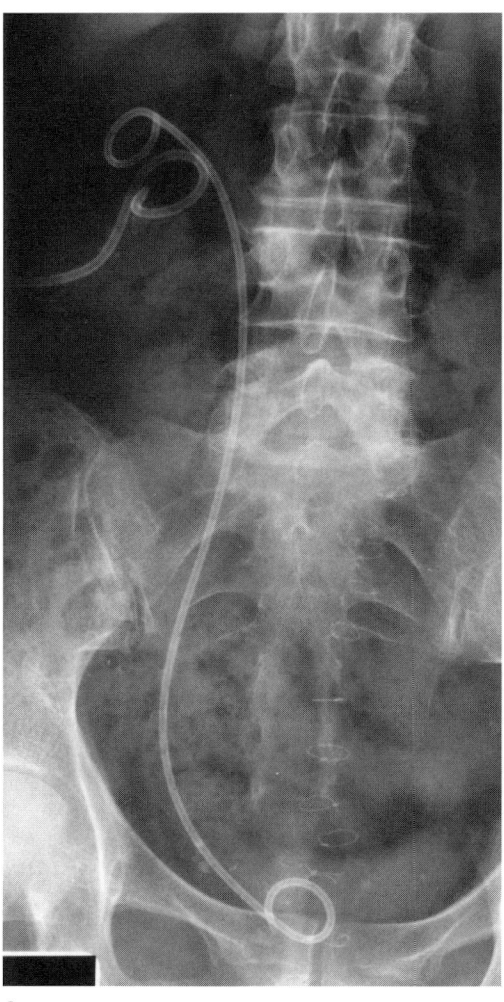

A

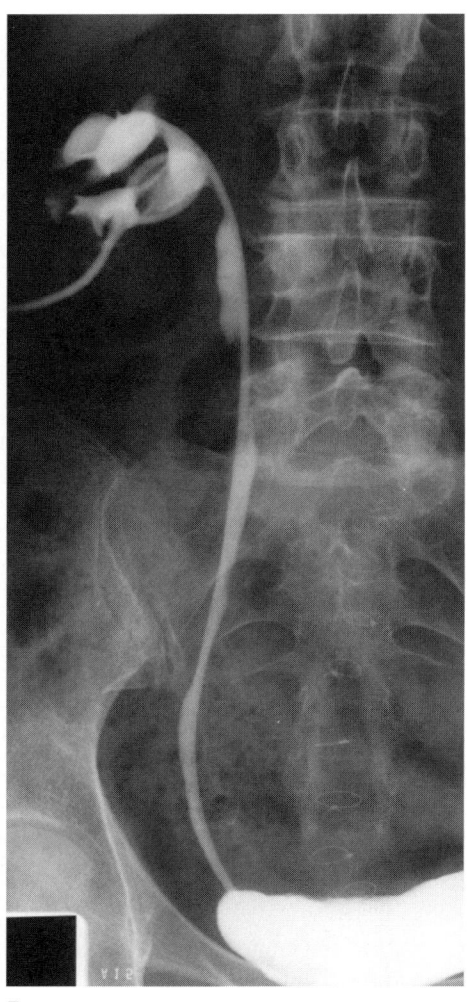

B

Figure 35-14. Internalized double-pigtail ureteral stent. (A) A nephrostomy catheter is left in place for continuing access. (B) Contrast injection through the nephrostomy catheter demonstrates satisfactory stent function with contrast draining readily into the urinary bladder. The nephrostomy catheter was then removed.

resistance in the area of a tight stricture. In difficult cases, a guidewire can be passed antegrade through the urethra so that it can be grasped at both ends and the stent can be advanced by pushing and pulling.[60,61] If the urine draining from the nephrostomy is bloody or infected, stent placement should be deferred until the urine clears.

Two kinds of ureteral stents can be inserted in an antegrade fashion: an internal stent (double J or double pigtail) and an external stent (nephroureteral). External-internal stents (nephroureteral stents) are introduced percutaneously and advanced into the urinary bladder or bowel (see Fig. 35-13A). A segment of the stent remains protruding from the flank and is capped externally to allow antegrade urine drainage. Side holes at the level of the renal pelvis allow urine to drain distally through the stent. External stents are

easily exchanged percutaneously and can be irrigated to maintain patency. External stents are used in patients in whom the stent placement is only for a short period (as after stone removal or ureteral dilation). They are also indicated in patients in whom retrograde stent exchange would be difficult because of bladder disease or distortion.

Completely internalized ureteral stents do not protrude from the flank, an obvious cosmetic and nursing advantage. A nephrostomy tube should be left in for 24 hours after stent placement so that antegrade pyelography can be performed to confirm stent patency before the nephrostomy catheter is removed (Fig. 35-14). It is important to use fluoroscopic guidance when removing the nephrostomy catheter to prevent inadvertent extraction of a double-pigtail ureteral stent that may be trapped by the nephrostomy catheter.[62]

If the urine is bloody, nephrostomy catheter drainage should be maintained until the urine clears.

Per Urethral (Retrograde) Ureteral Stenting

The retrograde route is a familiar one for most urologists for access to the kidneys or ureters. When the endoscopic retrograde approach is unsuccessful in placing a stent or a guidewire, a percutaneous nephrostomy is usually performed followed by stent placement (Fig. 35-15). However, an unsuccessful or incomplete retrograde procedure can often be successfully completed with fluoroscopy and the use of guidewires and catheters.[63]

Primary retrograde catheterization of the ureter without cystoscopic assistance has been reported.[64-66]

Figure 35-15. Antegrade ureteral stent placement for distal ureteral perforation that occurred during ureteroscopic stone extraction. Retrograde placement of a ureteral stent was unsuccessful. A pigtail catheter (without side holes in the ureteral limb) and a nephrostomy catheter were left in place. The patient eventually developed a stricture at the site of perforation that was successfully treated with balloon dilation.

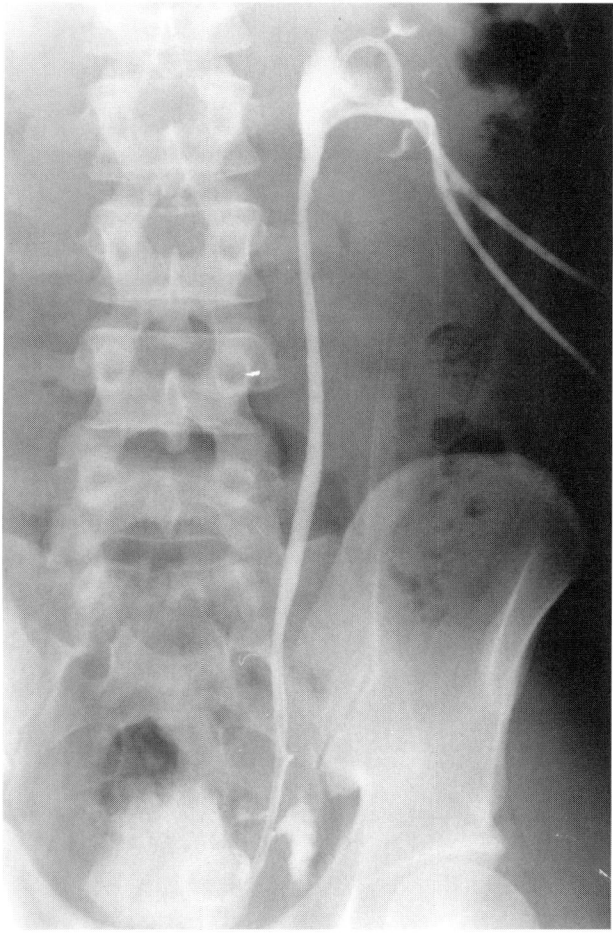

The procedure was successful in 70 percent of cases in a small series,[64] with patients requiring only mild intravenous sedation and with fluoroscopy times averaging less than 3 minutes. The trigone is identified by cystography, and the ureteral orifice is cannulated using a combination of angled-tip glidewires and angled hockey-stick catheters. Replacement of ureteral stents using fluoroscopic control (as opposed to cystoscopy) has been reported with successful exchange in 97 percent of cases.[67,68] The bladder end of the stent is grasped with a snare or lasso, withdrawn through the urethra, and then replaced over a guidewire using standard technique. The technique is most easy in female patients, although it has also been used in a few male patients.

Results and Complications

Antegrade ureteral stenting is successful in 70 to 80 percent of cases. Failure of placement is usually related to marked ureteral angulation or encasement by tumor or fibrosis. Technical failures can be minimized by placing the nephrostomy in a favorable calix so as to provide the best vector for stent advancement, liberally using transrenal sheaths as a buttress and using appropriately stiff guidewires. If stenting cannot be accomplished at the initial sitting, attempts following nephrostomy drainage for a few days are often successful because of a decrease in ureteral tortuosity and/or edema related to ureteral obstruction.

In patients with impassable ureteral strictures, two novel approaches have been described. Cornud et al.[69] created a neotract between the ureter and bladder using electrocautery, and Lang[70] used a perforating guidewire to create a ureteroneocystostomy. Fistulas to the alimentary tract were a serious (and fatal) complication in Cornud's series.[69]

Bilbao et al.[71] described direct translumbar puncture of the ureter with subsequent stent placement in patients in whom ureteral laceration or rigid ureteral kinking prevented stent placement. The interested reader is referred to the original source for details regarding the technique.

The single most frequent complication encountered is occlusion of stents due to encrustation, which is an unpredictable phenomenon and depends on the degree of crystalloid supersaturation in the urine. Sixty-eight percent of stents that were indwelling for 9 weeks have been found to be obstructed with mucus and microcalculi when they were removed.[72,73] Therefore, patients should be encouraged to maintain a high fluid intake after stent placement, and routine follow-up should be mandatory. Patients should undergo evaluation at 3 months to confirm that the stent is functioning optimally, and if necessary, cystography, excretory urography, or radionuclide urography may be performed. If pyelocaliectasis persists after placement of an internal ureteral stent, intrarenal Doppler sonography can be used to distinguish between patency and obstruction. Platt et al.[74] reported that obstructed stents were associated with increased mean resistive indices (0.78) whereas patent stents were associated with a resistive index of less than 0.70.

Stents should be changed every 6 months, whether cystoscopically by urologists or in a retrograde per urethral fashion by radiologists.

Stent migration can lead to perforation of the renal pelvis,[75] which can cause formation of a urinoma or even catastrophic exsanguination due to erosion of the stent tip into a renal vessel.

Fistulas between the iliac artery and the ureter have been reported in patients with pelvic surgery, irradiation, and indwelling ureteral stents.[76] The condition is rare, with only approximately 35 reported cases in the literature. The primary predisposing factor is compromise of the vascular supply of the ureter with a fistula occurring where the ureter crosses the iliac artery. Primary abnormalities of the iliac artery (i.e., an aneurysm) are an additional risk factor. Prompt diagnosis requires an awareness of the condition, selective or subselective arterial injections in multiple projections, and provocative maneuvers such as stent removal or manipulation during angiography if the angiogram is being performed in a quiescent period. Unsuspected and undiagnosed ureteroarterial fistulas are associated with a 52 percent mortality, whereas a correct preoperative diagnosis allows 89 percent of patients to be successfully discharged from the hospital.[77]

Stones can form on indwelling ureteral stents, particularly if the stents are not replaced regularly in a timely fashion. Stents that have migrated up into the kidney above a lower ureteral stricture or anastomosis can be extracted through a nephrostomy track under fluoroscopic guidance (Fig. 35-16). A second approach is to use ureteroscopy to reposition the caudal end of the stent within the bladder. If ureteroscopy is not available, a catheter can be placed through the

Figure 35-16. Malpositioned left ureteral stent. This complication is usually related to poor positioning of the stent at the time of placement rather than to retraction. (A) The distal end of the stent is within the distal ureter and not the urinary bladder. (B) Following a nephrostomy the stent was snared with a tip-deflecting guidewire and removed through the nephrostomy track. Another option would have been ureteroscopic repositioning of the distal end within the urinary bladder.

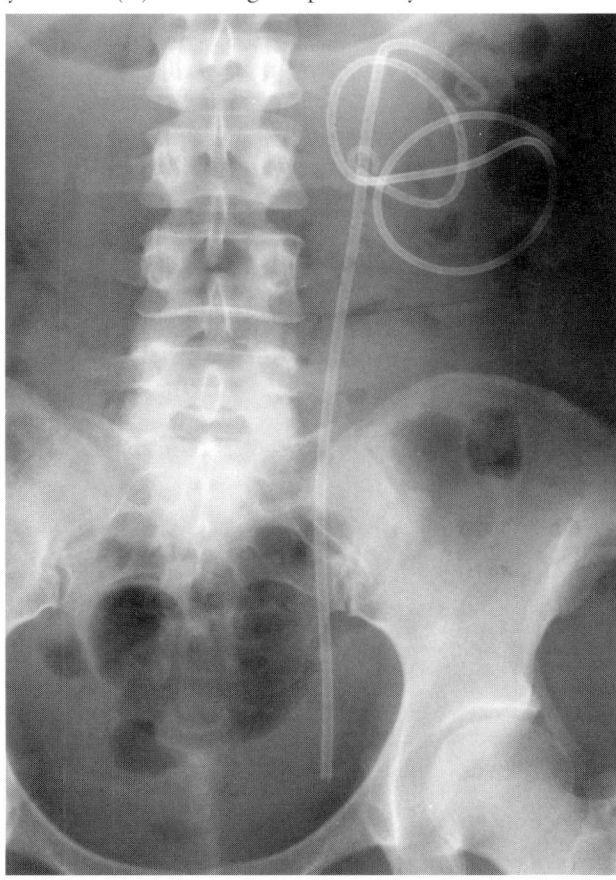

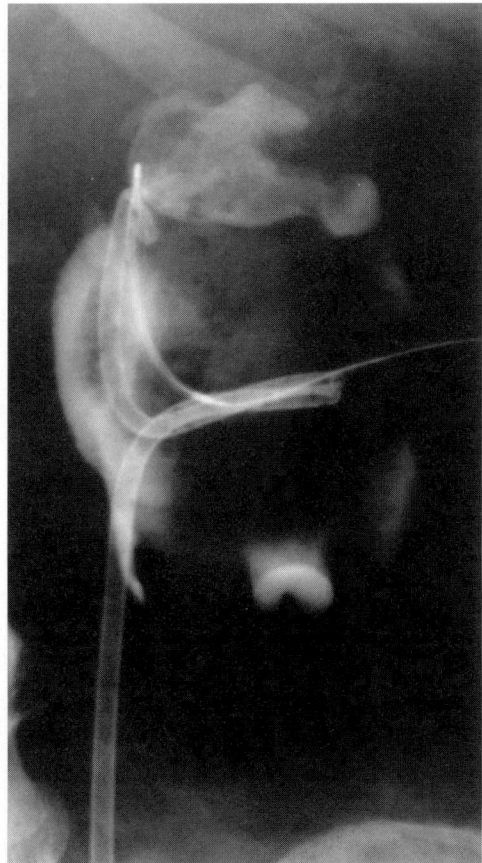

A

B

urethra (cystoscopically or fluoroscopically) and a basket used to reposition the distal pigtail within the urinary bladder. A stent that is positioned too far cephalad (so that the distal end is no longer within the urinary bladder) is usually related to placement of too short a stent rather than to cephalad migration. Stents that have fractured are best approached with a combined percutaneous-endoscopic technique. Although the stent fragments can be removed percutaneously, the fragments tend to be brittle and refracture into smaller pieces when they are grasped with forceps or baskets. Therefore, removal under endoscopic guidance is most likely to result in complete extraction.[48] Distal migration is more common than proximal migration and may be a result of inappropriate positioning.

A vexing complication with an indwelling stent is discomfort in the flank or the pelvis, which can range from severe pain to a mild annoyance. A long intravesical segment can cause significant dysuria and bladder spasms due to irritation of the trigone, and may necessitate removal of the stent. However, most patients can be managed with antispasmodics. Intolerance to ureteral stents is neither material- nor design-specific— Pryor et al.[78] found no significant differences in patient symptoms in an analysis of stents made of polyurethane, silicone, Silitek, and C-Flex. In cases of extreme discomfort, changing to a different stent can sometimes ameliorate the patient's symptoms.

Ureteral Stricture Dilation

The management of ureteral strictures has been dramatically altered by the introduction and subsequent refinement of interventional and endourologic techniques. Iatrogenic causes predominate in the development of ureteral strictures. Gynecologic and general surgical procedures are widely considered to be common causes of ureteral trauma and stricture formation, but recent series describing endourologic management of ureteral strictures indicate that endourologic procedures (such as ureteroscopy of ureterolithotomy), which facilitate less invasive management of many conditions, may paradoxically cause ureteral injury (see Fig. 35-15) and account for 70 to 80 percent of the strictures now being treated.[79-81]

Some other urologic procedures that have been implicated in ureteral stricture formation are transurethral resections, radical prostatectomy (Fig. 35-17), ureteral meatotomy, traumatic ureteral catheterization, ureteroneocystostomy, and renal transplantation. Gynecologic procedures that have been associated with strictures are hysterectomy (for benign or malignant disease), cesarean sections, and tubal ligations.

Surgical procedures that may cause ureteral trauma and stricture formation are abdominal aortic aneurysm repair, bowel resection, and pelvic exenterations. Ureteroenteral anastomotic strictures associated with urinary diversion are considered in Chapter 38.

Ureteral strictures can also develop in patients with chronic calculous disease as well as after penetrating abdominal trauma, particularly high-velocity gunshot wounds. Urinary extravasation and ureteral ischemia may contribute to scar formation in these cases and in postoperative strictures.

With malignant strictures, the goal of treatment is to provide drainage (percutaneous or internal) so that renal function can be improved. Chronic stenting is often an appropriate and the most reasonable option for these patients. For benign strictures, stenting alone is not the optimal therapy, and attempts are made to relieve the obstruction, with balloon dilation often being the initial mode of therapy. If successful, balloon dilation obviates the use of chronic indwelling stents or additional open surgery.

Ureteral dilation can be performed through either an antegrade or retrograde approach or a combination of these two approaches. The antegrade approach is the preferred route, for several reasons. Many strictures that may be impassable by a retrograde approach can be negotiated in an antegrade fashion (Fig. 35-18). More importantly, once dilation and stenting have been completed, the remaining nephrostomy tube can be used to assess the results of the dilation as well as to perform urodynamic tests (such as the Whitaker test) for more physiologic evaluation. The only disadvantage of the antegrade route is the invasiveness of establishing a percutaneous access track.

The retrograde approach is the least invasive method of management. Access can be gained by either cystoscopy or ureteroscopy and a retrograde catheter inserted, which can then be exchanged for guidewires and balloon dilators.

For dilation, reinforced high-pressure balloon catheters are used with inflated balloon diameters ranging between 4 and 10 mm. A "waist" deformity is seen in the balloon on initial inflation and should disappear with continued or subsequent inflations. There is no consensus in the literature regarding the most effective method of dilation, whether it be the optimal size of balloon to be used or the inflation period for the balloon. In experimental studies,[82] twofold dilation of the ureter was well tolerated but threefold dilation produced changes ranging from hydronephrosis to complete rupture. The time that the balloon is inflated varies from 1 minute to as long as 1 to 16 hours in different series. Similarly, there is no uniformity regarding the number of inflations that should be performed. The various technical approaches have been

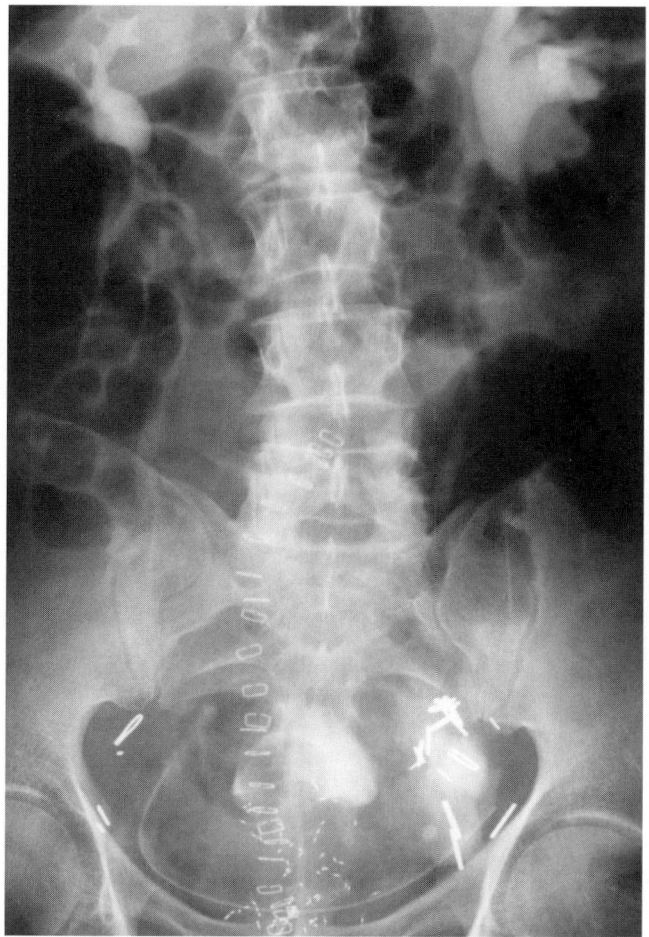

A

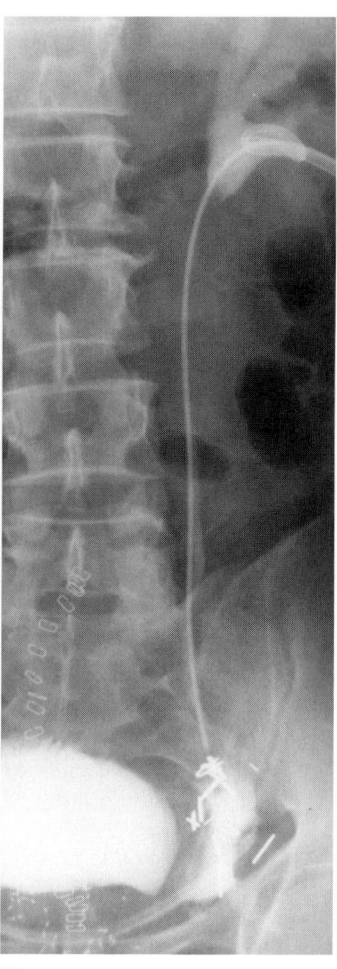

B

Figure 35-17. Left ureteral transection during radical prostatectomy. (A) Intravenous urogram 2 days after surgery demonstrates contrast extravasation on the left side. (B) A nephrostomy was performed. Attempts at traversing the transected ureteral segment with a guidewire were unsuccessful. The patient underwent ureteral reimplantation. Note that a ureteral catheter was positioned as far distally in the ureter as possible to facilitate identification at surgery.

summarized in reviews by Meretyk et al. and Chang et al.[83,84]

After dilation, there is no consensus regarding the necessity for stenting, with some authors leaving in stents for several days to months and others avoiding stenting altogether. Laboratory studies of ureteral healing demonstrate reepithelialization in 7 to 10 days and muscular healing in 6 to 8 weeks. Thus 6 weeks of postprocedural stenting appears prudent, because the stent serves as a scaffold for organized reepithelialization and smooth muscle growth.[85] The ultimate outcome may depend more on the nature (and etiology) of the stricture rather than on the technical nuances of dilation.

The author's approach is to perform balloon dilation through the preferred antegrade route. After dilation, a ureteral stent is placed (7–10 French size in native ureters, 6–8 French size in transplanted ureters) and left in place for at least 6 weeks to allow muscular healing while the ureteral caliber is maintained. Nephroureteral stents (external-internal stents) are preferred; they are initially left to gravity drainage and can then be capped. The patient is asked to uncap the tube if flank pain, fever, or drainage around the catheter develops. The stent is exchanged for a nephrostomy catheter at the end of 6 to 8 weeks. The efficacy of the dilation can then be assessed by nephrostograms and urodynamic studies before catheter removal. The tube can be safely removed if the opening pressures are low (less than 14 cm of water), the renal pelvic residual volumes are low, and the stricture itself appears to be anatomically improved, with satisfactory flow through the previously strictured segment. If the studies demonstrate a recurrent stricture, a second attempt at redilation is usually made. Subsequent failures are managed with either open surgical repair or chronic stenting, depending on the circumstance.

When balloon dilation is apparently successful,

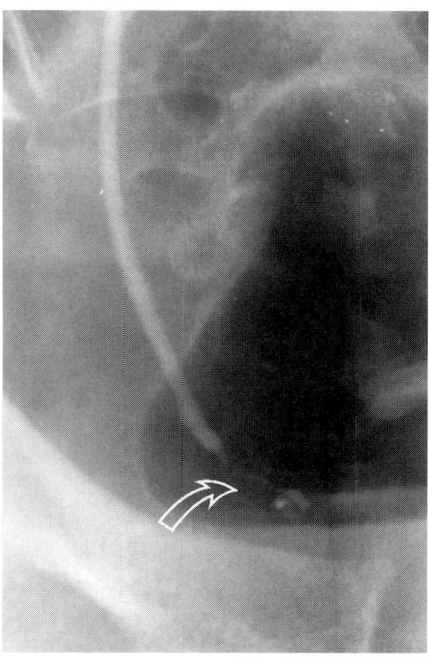
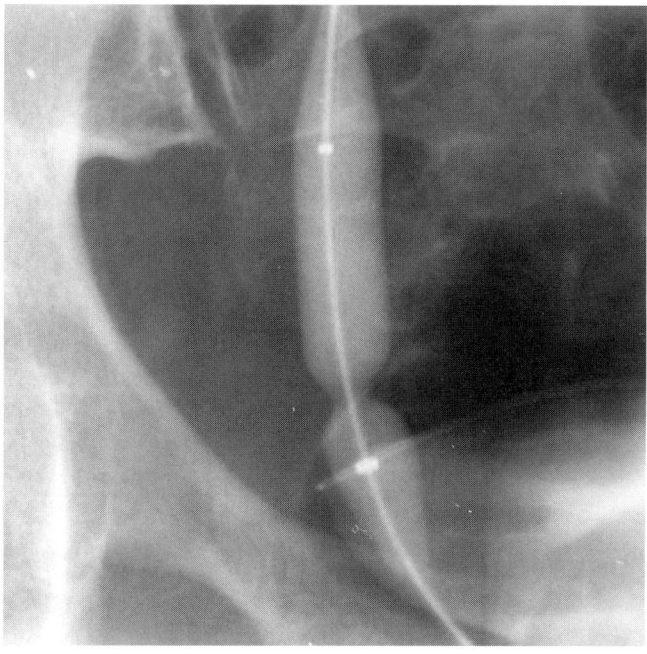

A   **B**

Figure 35-18. (A) Distal ureteral stricture that developed after hysterectomy and radiation therapy for cervical cancer. The stricture (*arrow*) could not be crossed by the retrograde approach. (B) Balloon dilation with deformity at the site of the stricture. The stricture could not be dilated despite maximal inflation of a high-pressure balloon.

follow-up intravenous urography or renal scans are performed at 1, 6, and 12 months and then periodically, as indicated, to check on the continuing patency of the ureter.[86]

As previously mentioned, percutaneous ureteroneocystostomy and direct percutaneous ureteral puncture are other techniques that have been used in the management of impassable ureteral strictures. Electrocautery and rotational atherolytic devices have also been used to recanalize occluded ureters and stenotic ureteropelvic junctions,[87-89] but their efficacy remains to be proven.

Results

The response of strictures to balloon dilation is influenced by factors such as the etiology of the stricture, the length and location of the stricture, the duration of time that the stricture has been present, and the presence of ischemia or dense fibrosis (as in patients who have undergone radical extirpative surgery or have had radiation therapy).

Overall, 50 percent of all benign strictures respond favorably to one attempt at balloon dilation. Lang and Glorioso[90] reported that 91 percent of strictures less than 3 months old responded to dilation, compared to 53 percent of strictures that were treated more than 3 months later. In the presence of ischemia or fibrosis,

only 21 percent of strictures were successfully dilated, whereas 70 percent of strictures not associated with vascular compromise responded. In a small series, Kim et al.[91] found that balloon dilation and stenting were successful in dilating tuberculous strictures in 75 percent of cases with good long-term results. Chang et al.[84] reported 100 percent success in dilating strictures less than 1.5 cm in length, and O'Brien et al.[92] reported no difference in the outcomes whether the interval between ureteral injury and dilation was short or long. They reported 65 percent overall success in dilating benign ureteral strictures. Kwak et al.[93] found that multiple dilations were of no benefit in prolonging or maintaining ureteral patency.

Strictures related to ureterolithotomy, ureteral endoscopy, and gynecologic surgery responded in 100, 71, and 62 percent of cases, respectively, in Van Arsdalen and Banner's series.[81] However, strictures associated with radical hysterectomy or retroperitoneal fibrosis responded poorly (33 and 0 percent, respectively).

Balloon dilation and stenting have been used to treat ureteropelvic junction obstruction (both primarily as an alternative to pyeloplasty and in secondary obstruction following pyeloplasty), although experience to date is limited. The reported success rate varies from 64 to 86 percent.[86,94,95] The minimal morbidity, short operative time, and hospitalization are attractive advantages as compared to open pyeloplasty or endopy-elotomy. However, long-term results in a large series are not available yet to assess the ultimate role of this procedure. In the series reported by Snow et al.,[94] resolution of the waist in an inflated balloon was accompanied by a successful outcome in 75 percent of cases, whereas persistence of the waist was associated with success in only 43 percent of cases. The procedure may be more efficacious in relieving primary ureteropelvic junction (UPJ) obstruction and less effective for secondary obstructions occurring after a pyeloplasty.[96] After dilation, the renal component of the stent placed across the UPJ should be 12 to 14 French in size so that wide-caliber regeneration of the UPJ can occur. Such stents taper to a 5 to 7 French ureteral segment.

Obstructed Renal Transplants

Urologic complications occur in 2 to 10 percent of renal transplant recipients, with ureteral complications accounting for the majority. Actuarial data predict that the rate of posttransplant ureteral stenosis is 9.7 percent at 5 years.[97] Ureteric strictures can be related to one or more of the following: postoperative urine leak with periureteric fibrosis, ureteric ischemia with resultant necrosis, selective ureteric rejection, and surgical technique used to harvest the ureter as well as to create the ureteroneocystostomy.[98,99] Ureteric obstruction due to intraluminal pathology such as a blood clot, fungus ball, or calculus is less common, as is extrinsic compression by the spermatic cord. Other complications that can affect renal transplants are renal artery stenosis and perirenal fluid collections, which can occur in the early or late postoperative periods. These complications are addressed in other chapters.

Urinary obstruction is suspected if the urinary output is poor, if the serum creatinine levels increase, or if renal ultrasonography or radioisotope renal scan (including diuretic renography) suggest hydronephrosis. In such cases, antegrade pyelography is first performed to confirm the presence of obstruction, localize the site, and establish an etiology, if possible (Fig. 35-19). Antegrade pyelography can be followed by therapeutic nephrostomy, if deemed necessary.

Technique for Percutaneous Urinary Interventions in Renal Transplants

As for a nontransplant nephrostomy, preprocedural preparations include a check of clotting parameters and antibiotic prophylaxis. When planning the puncture, it is important to avoid entry into the peritoneum by staying lateral to the lateral border of the transplant

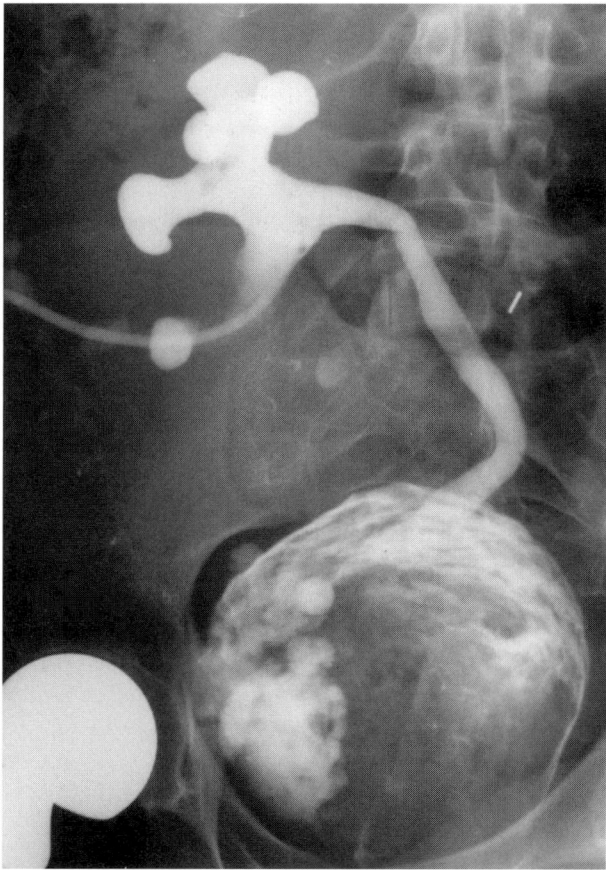

Figure 35-19. Obstruction due to large clots in the urinary bladder in a renal transplant patient with hemorrhagic cystitis. Antegrade pyelography is of great value in this patient population in confirming the presence and site of obstruction.

and the skin sutures. Real-time ultrasound is useful in directing puncture into an anterolateral calix with a minimal number of sticks.

Once obstruction is confirmed, a nephrostomy catheter can be placed after track dilation. Through the nephrostomy access, definitive interventions such as ureteral dilation and stenting or calculus extraction can then be performed. Internalized stents are preferred over stents that project externally in order to minimize infection complications in this immunocompromised group of patients (Fig. 35-20). Surgical management of ureteral obstructions is reserved for those cases when the stricture cannot be traversed with a wire or the radiographic findings strongly suggest extrinsic compression by vascular structures or the spermatic cord (Fig. 35-21). In these cases, the nephrostomy serves as a diagnostic tool as well as a temporizing measure to improve renal function preoperatively.

Balloon dilation of transplant ureteral strictures has

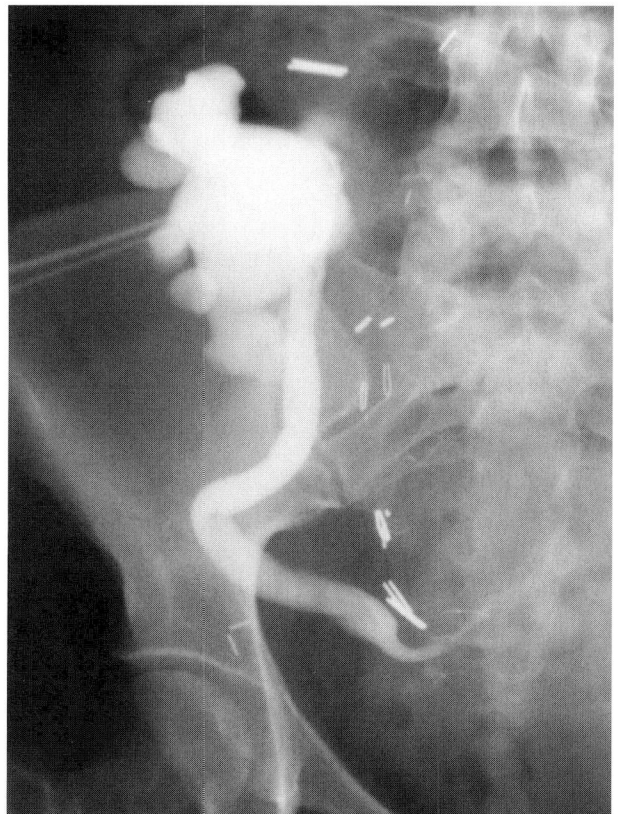

A

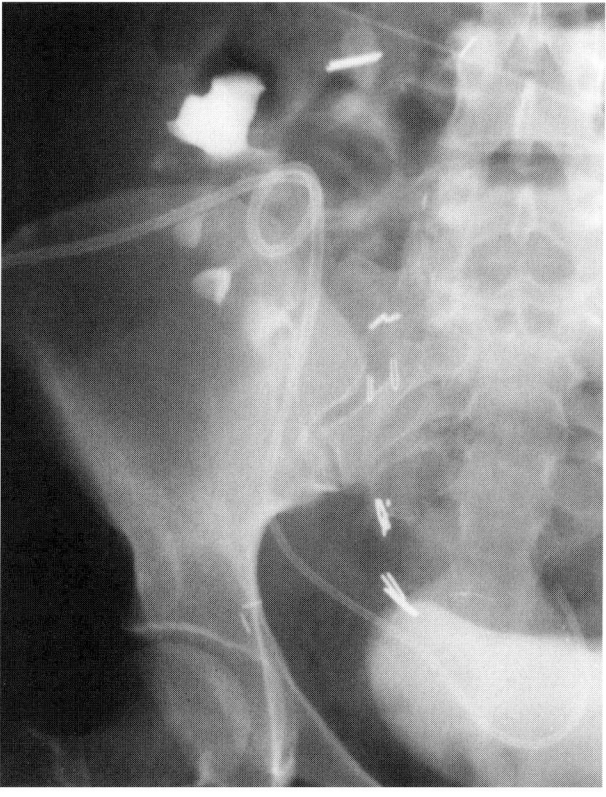

B

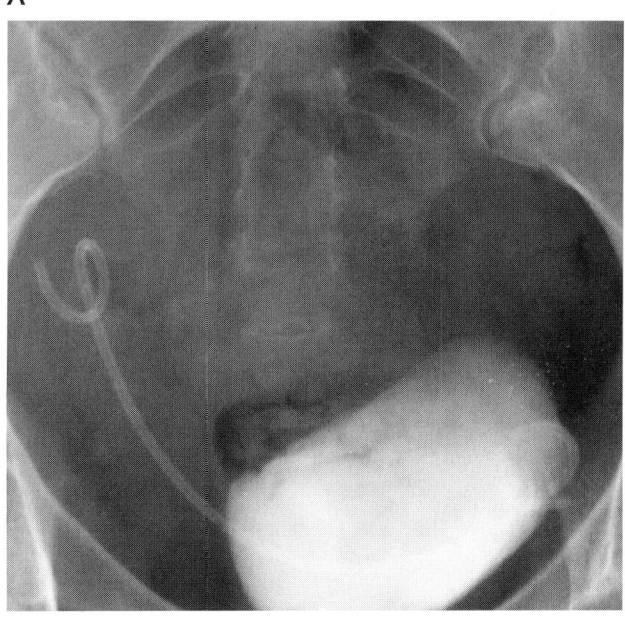

C

Figure 35-20. (A) Ureteral stricture at ureteroneocystostomy site following renal transplant. The stricture was balloon-dilated. (B) A nephroureteral catheter was initially placed and followed by an internalized stent (C). The latter was removed cystoscopically after 8 weeks.

been reported to be effective in 40 to 78 percent of patients.[97–102] Initial technical success in dilating the stricture does not translate into long-term success. Failure of balloon dilation becomes evident usually within weeks of the stent removal; Streem and colleagues[102] found that all failures presented within 12 months of dilation.

Strictures that develop at the ureteroneocystostomy site appear to respond better to balloon dilation than strictures at other sites in the ureter (see Fig. 35-20). This may be related to the fact that strictures in the proximal and middle ureter are more likely to be ischemic in nature, whereas strictures at the ureteral anastomotic site are related to either errors in surgical technique (for strictures that present in the early postoperative period) or to periureteral fibrosis in the later period. Some series have also reported a higher rate of success for strictures that have been present for less than 3 months than for more chronic lesions[100]; however, other series have not had this result.[101] In the author's experience, strictures developing in association

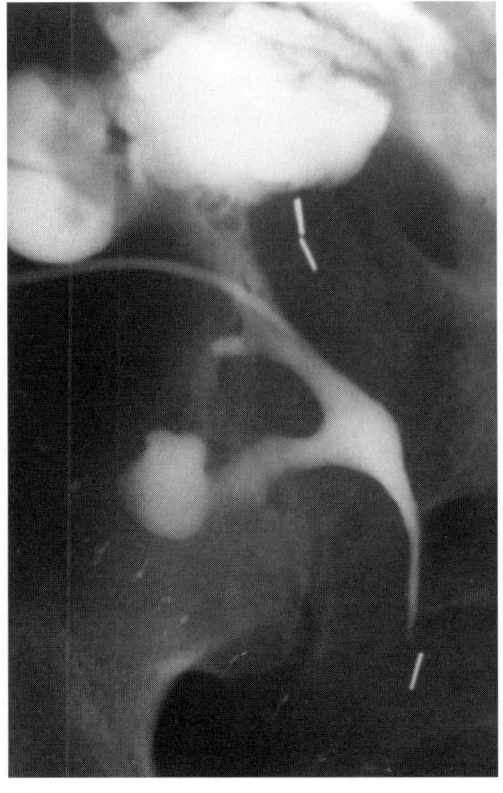

A

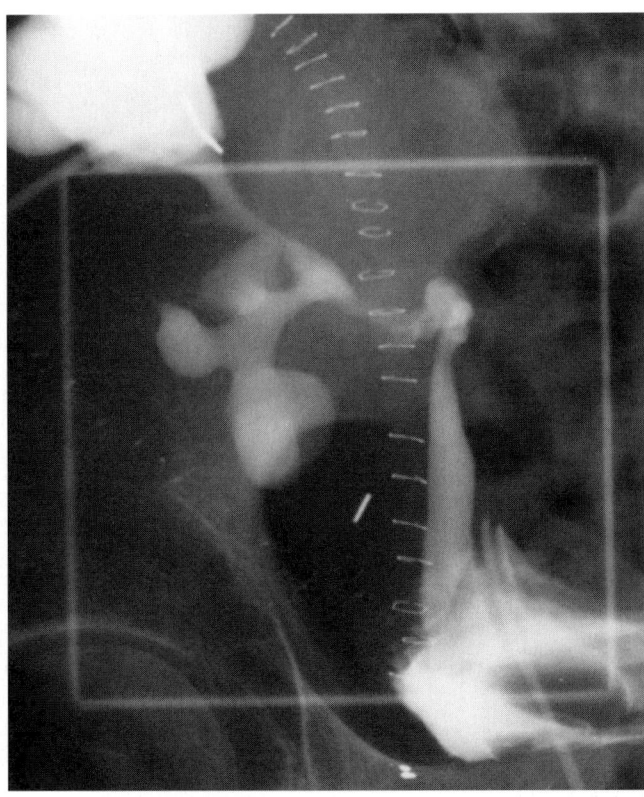

B

Figure 35-21. Midureteral stricture in renal transplant 16 years after the transplant. (A) Antegrade nephrostogram demonstrates a high-grade stricture in the ureter that could not be traversed with a guidewire. Note the contrast leakage from the dilated upper pole calix due to spontaneous rupture of the calix. (B) The patient underwent ureteroureterostomy (native ureter anastomosed to transplant ureter proximal to stricture). Nephrostogram demonstrates good contrast flow through the ureteral anastomotic site into the urinary bladder.

Figure 35-22. Dehiscence at ureteroneocystostomy site. (A) Antegrade pyelogram demonstrates marked extravasation at ureteral anastomotic site with no contrast entering the urinary bladder. (B) A guidewire was successfully advanced into the bladder and a stent was placed. *C,* extravasated contrast; *B,* bladder.

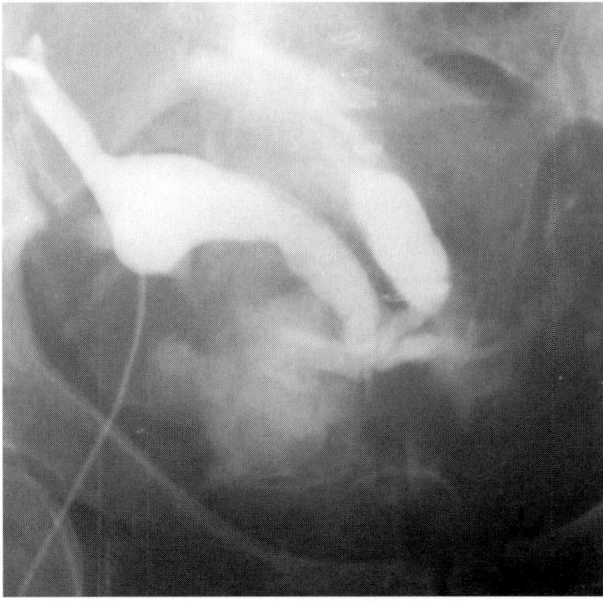

A

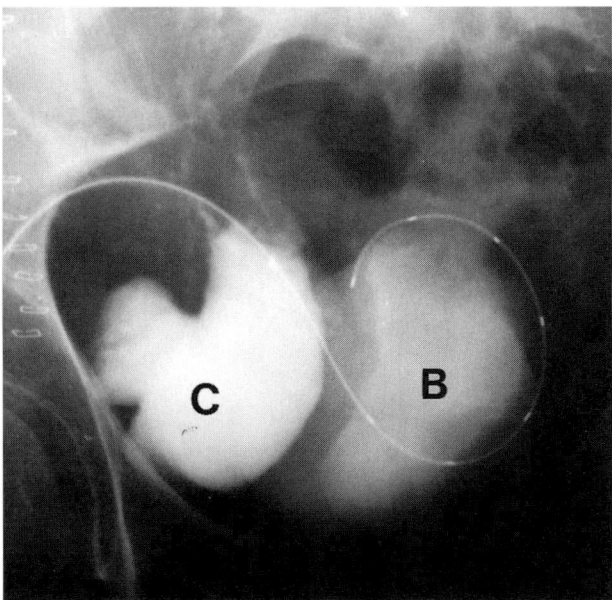

B

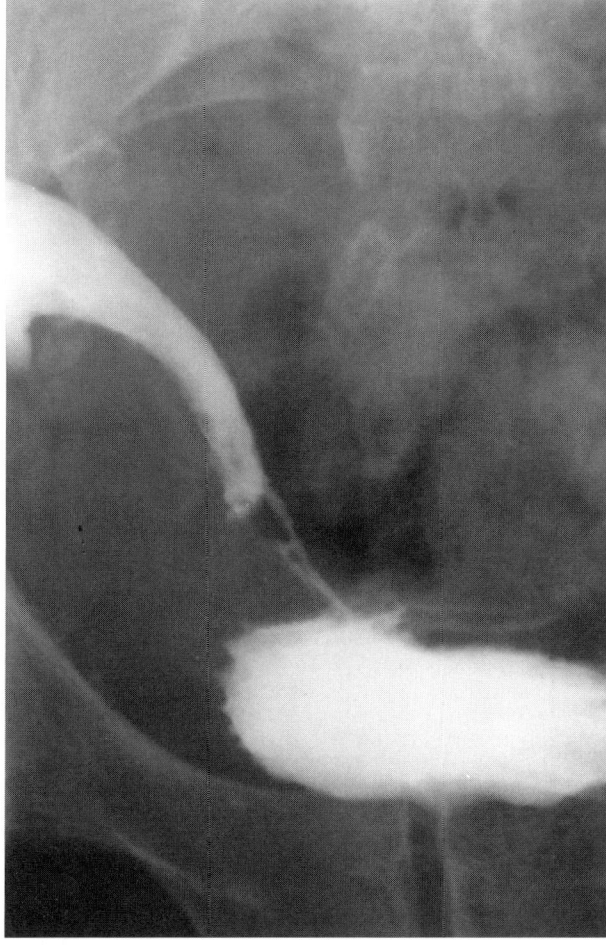

C

Figure 35-22 (continued). (C) Two months later, a high-grade stricture is seen in the distal ureter that was unresponsive to balloon dilation.

with dehiscence at the ureteroneocystostomy site are generally resistant to balloon dilation and require surgery for definitive therapy (Fig. 35-22).

The only complication that is unique to the transplant nephrostomy is intraperitoneal leak of contrast due to inadvertent puncture of the peritoneum. This problem usually resolves spontaneously without event. Because the patients are immunocompromised, special vigilance is required to avoid precipitating septicemia when percutaneous interventions are performed.

References

1. Goodwin WE, Casey WC, Woolf W. Percutaneous trocar (needle) nephrostomy in hydronephrosis. JAMA 1955;157: 891–894.
2. Fowler JS, Meares EM Jr, Goldin AR. Percutaneous nephrostomy: techniques, indications and results. Urology 1975;6: 428.
3. Levin DC, Flanders SJ, Spettell CM, et al. Participation by radiologists and other specialists in percutaneous vascular and nonvascular interventions: findings from a seven-state database. Radiology 1995;196:51–54.
4. Fritzsche P. Antegrade pyelography: therapeutic applications. Radiol Clin North Am 1986;24:573–586.
5. Barbaric ZL. Percutaneous nephrostomy for urinary tract obstruction. AJR 1984;143:803–809.
6. Zagoria RJ, Hodge RG, Dyer RB, et al. Percutaneous nephrostomy for treatment of intractable hemorrhagic cystitis. J Urol 1993;149:1449–1451.
7. Silverman SG, Mueller PR, Pfister RC. Hemostatic evaluation before abdominal interventions: an overview and proposal. AJR 1990;154:233–238.
8. Cochran ST, Barbaric ZL, Lee JJ, Kashfian P. Percutaneous nephrostomy tube placement: an outpatient procedure. Radiology 1991;179:843–847.
9. Rapaport SI. Assessing hemostatic function before abdominal interventions. AJR 1990;154:239–240.
10. Spies JB, Rosen RJ, Lebowitz AS. Antibiotic prophylaxis in vascular and interventional radiology: a rational approach. Radiology 1988;166:381–387.
11. Reznek RH, Talner LB. Percutaneous nephrostomy. Radiol Clin North Am 1984;22:393–406.
12. Newhouse JH, Pfister RC. Percutaneous catheterization of the kidney and perinephric space: trocar technique. Urol Radiol 1981;2:157–164.
13. Hawkins IF Jr, Hunter P, Leal G, et al. Retrograde nephrostomy for stone removal—combined cystoscopic/percutaneous technique. AJR 1984;143:299–304.
14. Stables DP. Percutaneous nephrostomy: techniques, indications and results. Urol Clin North Am 1982;9:15–29.
15. Sampaio FJB, Zanier JFC, Aragao AHM, Favorita LA. Intrarenal access: 3-dimensional anatomical study. J Urol 1992; 148:1769–1773.
16. Leroy AJ. Percutaneous nephrostomy: techniques and instrumentation. In: Pollack HM, ed. Clinical urography. Philadelphia: Saunders, 1990:2726.
17. Lee WJ, Mond DJ, Patel M, et al. Emergency percutaneous nephrostomy: technical success based on level of operator experience. J Vasc Intervent Radiol 1994;5:327–330.
18. Lang EK, Price ET. Redefinitions of indications for percutaneous nephrostomy. Radiology 1983;147:419–426.
19. Yoder IC, Pfister RC, Lindfors KK, Newhouse JH. Pyonephrosis: imaging and intervention. AJR 1983;141:735–740.
20. Bell AD, Rose SC, Starr NK, et al. Percutaneous nephrostomy for nonoperative management of fungal urinary tract infections. J Vasc Intervent Radiol 1993;4:311–315.
21. Gadducci A, Madrigali A, Facchini V, Fioretti P. Percutaneous nephrostomy in patients with advanced or recurrent cervical cancer. Clin Exp Obstet Gynecol 1994;21:71–73.
22. Hoe JWM, Tung KH, Tan EC. Reevaluation of indications for percutaneous nephrostomy and interventional uroradiological procedures in pelvic malignancy. Br J Radiol 1993;71: 469–472.
23. Markowitz DM, Wong KT, Laffey KJ, Bixon R, Nagler HM, Martin EC. Maintaining quality of life after palliative diversion for malignant ureteral obstruction. Urol Radiol 1989;11: 129–132.
24. Chapman ME, Reid JH. Use of percutaneous nephrostomy in malignant ureteric obstruction. Br J Radiol 1991;64:318–320.
25. Dowling RA, Carrasco CH, Babaian RJ. Percutaneous urinary diversion in patients with hormone refractory prostate cancer. Urology 1991;37:89–91.
26. Lee WJ, Patel U, Patel S, et al. Emergency percutaneous nephrostomy: results and complications. J Vasc Intervent Radiol 1994;5:135–139.
27. Stables DP, Ginsberg NJ, Johnson ML. Percutaneous nephrostomy: a series and review of the literature. AJR 1978; 130:75–82.
28. Cope C, Zeit RM. Pseudoaneurysms after nephrostomy. AJR 1982;139:255–261.

29. Cronan JJ, Dorfman GS, Amis ES, Denny DF Jr. Retroperitoneal hemorrhage after percutaneous nephrostomy. AJR 1985; 144:801–803.

30. Routh WD, Tatum CM, Lawdahl RB, et al. Tube tamponade: potential pitfall in angiography of arterial hemorrhage associated with percutaneous drainage catheters. Radiology 1990; 174:945–949.

31. Merine D, Fishman EK. Perirenal hematoma following catheter removal—an unusual complication of percutaneous nephrostomy. Clin Imaging 1989;13:74–76.

32. Nosher JL, Ericksen AS, Trooskin SZ, et al. Antibiotic bonded nephrostomy catheters for percutaneous nephrostomies. Cardiovasc Intervent Radiol 1990;13:102–106.

33. Reinberg Y, Moore LS, Lange PH. Splenic abscess as a complication of percutaneous nephrostomy. Urology 1989;34: 274–276.

34. Morris DB, Siegelbaum MH, Pollack HM, et al. Renoduodenal fistula in a patient with chronic nephrostomy drainage: a case report. J Urol 1991;146:835–837.

35. Picus D, Weyman PJ, Clayman RV, McClennan BL. Intercostal space nephrostomy for percutaneous stone removal. AJR 1986;147:393–397.

36. Hopper KD, Yakes WF. The posterior intercostal approach for percutaneous renal procedures: risk of puncturing the lung, spleen and liver as determined by CT. AJR 1990;154: 115–117.

37. Pollack HM, Banner MP. Replacing blocked or dislodged percutaneous nephrostomy and ureteral stent catheters. Radiology 1982;145:203–205.

38. Cazenave FL, Glass-Royal MC, Barth KH. Exchange of an obstructed loop nephrostomy catheter: technical note. Cardiovasc Intervent Radiol 1990;13:327–328.

39. Stewart LH, Kernohan RM, Loughridge WG. Nephrostomy tubes resistant to removal. Br J Urol 1992;70:213–214.

40. Vaccaro JA, Davis R, Hansberry K. Replacement of nephrostomy tube using ureteroscopes. J Urol 1993;149:334.

41. Cronan JJ, Marcello A, Horn DL, et al. Antibiotics and nephrostomy tube care: preliminary observations: Part I. Bacteriuria. Radiology 1989;172:1041–1042.

42. Cronan JJ, Horn DL, Marcello A, et al. Antibiotics and nephrostomy tube care: preliminary observations: Part II. Bacteremia. Radiology 1989;172:1043–1045.

43. Hruby W, Marberger M. Late sequelae of percutaneous nephrostomy. Radiology 1984;152:383–385.

44. Holmes SAV, Kirby RS, Whitfield HN. Urinary tract prostheses and their biocompatibility. Br J Urol 1993;71:378–383.

45. Mardis HK, Kroeger RM, Morton JJ, et al. Comparative evaluation of materials used for internal ureteral stents. J Endourol 1993;7:105–115.

46. Mardis HK, Kroeger RM. Ureteral stents: materials. Urol Clin North Am 1988;15:471.

47. El-Faqih SR, Shamsuddin AB, Chakrabarti A, et al. Polyurethane internal ureteral stents in treatment of stone patients: morbidity related to indwelling times. J Urol 1991;146:1487.

48. Leroy AJ, Williams HJ, Segura JW, et al. Indwelling ureteral stents: percutaneous management of complications. Radiology 1986;158:219–222.

49. Mitty HA, Dan SJ, Train JS. Antegrade ureteral stents: technical and catheter related problems with polyethylene and polyurethane. Radiology 1987;165:439–443.

50. Marx M, Bettman MA, Bridges S, et al. The effects of various indwelling ureteral catheter materials on the normal canine ureter. J Urol 1988;139:180.

51. Rackson ME, Mitty HA, Lossef SV, et al. Biocompatible copolymer ureteral stent: maintenance of patency beyond 6 months. AJR 1989;153:783–784.

52. Cardella JF, Castaneda-Zuniga WR, Hunter DW, et al. Urine-compatible polymer for long term ureteral stenting. Radiology 1986;161:313–318.

53. Pauer W, Lugmayr H. Metallic Wallstents: a new therapy for extrinsic ureteral obstruction. J Urol 1992;148:281–284.

54. Lugmayr H, Pauer W. Self expanding metal stents for palliative treatment of malignant ureteral obstruction. AJR 1992; 159:1091–1094.

55. Flueckiger F, Lammer J, Klein GE, et al. Malignant ureteral obstruction: preliminary results of treatment with metallic self expandable stents. Radiology 1993;186:169–173.

56. van Sonnenberg E, D'Agostino HB, O'Laoide R, et al. Malignant ureteral obstruction: treatment with metal stents—technique, results and observations with percutaneous intraluminal US. Radiology 1994;191:765–768.

57. Cussenot O, Bassi S, Desgrandchamps F, et al. Outcomes of non-self-expandable metal prostheses in strictured human ureter: suggestions for future developments. J Endourol 1993;7:205–209.

58. Desgrandchamps F, Cussenot O, Cochand-Priollet B, et al. Strecker stent as ureteral stent: experimental study. J Endourol 1992;6:433–437.

59. Lee MJ, Lu DS, Papanicolaou N, Girard M Jr, Yoder IC, Slater GJ. Antegrade ureteral stents: proposed solutions to technically difficult problems. Radiology 1993;189(P):371.

60. Mitty HA. Ureteral stenting facilitated by antegrade transurethral passage of guide wire. AJR 1984;142:831–832.

61. D'Souza R, Tait P, Thomson RW, et al. Case report: an alternative approach to stenting the ureter. Br J Radiol 1993;66: 460–461.

62. Greenstein A, Shoval Y, Chen J, et al. Incidental extraction of double pigtail catheter during nephrostomy removal. Urol Radiol 1989;11:121–122.

63. Amendola MA, Banner MP, Pollack HM, Gordon RL. Fluoroscopically guided pyeloureteral interventions by using a perurethral transvesical approach. AJR 1989;152:97–102.

64. Babel SG, Winterkorn KG. Retrograde catheterization of the ureter without cystoscopic assistance: preliminary experience. Radiology 1993;187:547–549.

65. Huang T-Y, Perkins T, Mader G. Retrograde placement of internal double-J ureteral stents by using cystographic guidance. AJR 1994;163:371–372.

66. Babel SG, Winterkorn KG. Primary retrograde placement of ureteral stents by radiologists. AJR 1995;164:1555.

67. deBaere T, Denys A, Pappas P, et al. Ureteral stents: exchange under fluoroscopic control as an effective alternative to cystoscopy. Radiology 1994;190:887–889.

68. Yedlicka JW, Aizpuru R, Hunter DW, et al. Retrograde replacement of internal double-J ureteral stents. AJR 1991;156: 1007–1009.

69. Cornud FE, Casanova JP, Bonnel DH, et al. Impassable ureteral strictures: management with percutaneous ureteroneocystostomy. Radiology 1991;180:451–454.

70. Lang EK. Percutaneous ureterocystostomy and ureteroneocystostomy. AJR 1988;150:1065–1068.

71. Bilbao JI, Longo JM, Martin-Palance A, et al. Direct percutaneous ureteral approach for the treatment of ureteral stenosis or obstruction. J Vasc Intervent Radiol 1992;3:553–555.

72. Thomas R. Indwelling ureteral stents: impact of material and shape on patient comfort. J Endourol 1993;7:137–140.

73. Ramsay JWA, Crocker RP, Ball AJ, et al. Urothelial reaction to ureteric intubation: a clinical study. Br J Urol 1987;60:504.

74. Platt JR, Ellis JH, Rubin JM. Assessment of internal ureteral stent patency in patients with pyelocaliectases: value of renal duplex sonography. AJR 1993;161:87–90.

75. Salazar JE, Johnson JB, Scott RL. Perforation of renal pelvis by internal ureteral stents. AJR 1984;143:816–818.

76. Quillin SP, Darey MD, Picus D. Angiographic evaluation and therapy of ureteroarterial fistulas. AJR 1994;162:873–878.

77. Keller FS, Barton RE, Routh WD, et al. Gross hematuria in two patients with ureteral ileal conduits and double-J stents. J Vasc Intervent Radiol 1990;1:69–79.

78. Pryor JL, Langley MJ, Jenkins AD. Comparison of symptom characteristics of indwelling ureteral catheters. J Urol 1991; 145:719.

79. Netto NR, Ferreira U, Lemos GC, et al. Endourological management of ureteral strictures. J Urol 1990;144:631.

80. Kramolowsky EV, Tucker RD, Nelson CMK. Management of benign ureteral strictures: open surgical repair or endoscopic dilation. J Urol 1989;141:285.

81. Van Arsdalen KN, Banner MP. The management of ureteral and anastomotic strictures. Probl Urol 1992;6:420–432.

82. Selmy G, Hassovna M, Begin LR, et al. Effect of balloon dilation of ureter on upper tract dynamics and ureteral wall morphology. J Endourol 1993;7:211–219.

83. Meretyk S, Albala DM, Kavoussi LR, et al. Endosurgery: non calculus applications in the upper urinary tract. In: Clayman RU, ed. Monographs in urology. Florida: Medical Directions, 1991:68–89.

84. Chang R, Marshall FF, Mitchell S. Percutaneous management of benign ureteral strictures and fistulas. J Urol 1987;137: 1126.

85. Lee CK, Smith AD. Role of stents in open ureteral surgery. J Endourol 1993;7:141–144.

86. Beckmann CF, Roth RA, Bihrle W. Dilatation of benign ureteral strictures. Radiology 1989;172:437–441.

87. Chandhoke PS, Clayman RV, Stome AM, et al. Endopyelotomy and endoureterotomy with the Acucise ureteral cutting balloon device: preliminary experience. J Endourol 1993;7: 45–51.

88. Cardella JF, Hunter DW, Castaneda-Zuniga WR, et al. Electrolysis for recanalization of urinary collecting system obstructions: a percutaneous approach. Radiology 1985;155:87–90.

89. Uflacker R, Wholey MH. A new low-speed rotational atherolytic device for ureteral recanalization. AJR 1988;151:1157–1158.

90. Lang EK, Glorioso LW III. Antegrade transluminal dilatation of benign ureteral strictures: long-term results. AJR 1988; 150:131–134.

91. Kim SH, Yoon HK, Park JH, et al. Tuberculous stricture of the urinary tract: antegrade balloon dilation and ureteral stenting. Abdom Imaging 1993;18:186–190.

92. O'Brien WM, Maxted WC, Pahira JJ. Ureteral stricture: experience with 31 cases. J Urol 1988;140:737.

93. Kwak S, Leef JA, Rosenblum JD. Percutaneous balloon catheter dilation of benign ureteral strictures: effect of multiple dilation procedures on long-term patency. AJR 1995;165:97–100.

94. Snow TM, Wells IP, Hammonds JC. Balloon rupture and stenting for pelviureteric junction obstruction: abolition of waisting is a prognostic marker. Clin Radiol 1994;49:708–710.

95. Gerber GS, Lyon ES. Endopyelotomy: patient selection, results and complications. Urology 1994;43:2–10.

96. McClinton S, Steyn JH, Hussey JK. Retrograde balloon dilatation for pelviureteric junction obstruction. Br J Urol 1993; 71:152–155.

97. Kinnaert P, Hall M, Janssen F, et al. Ureteral stenosis after kidney transplantation: true incidence and long term follow up after surgical correction. J Urol 1985;133:17.

98. Thrasher JB, Temple DR, Spees EK. Extravesical versus Leadbetter-Politano ureteroneocystostomy: a comparison of urological complications in 320 renal transplants. J Urol 1990;144:1105–1109.

99. Swierzewski SJ III, Konnak JW, Ellis JH. Treatment of renal transplant ureteral complications by percutaneous techniques. J Urol 1993;149:986–987.

100. Voegeli ER, Crummy AB, McDermott JC, et al. Percutaneous dilation of ureteral strictures in renal transplant patients. Radiology 1988;169:185–188.

101. Kim JC, Banner MP, Ramchandani P, et al. Balloon dilation of ureteral strictures after renal transplantation. Radiology 1993;186:717–722.

102. Streem SB, Novick AC, Steinmuller DR, et al. Long-term efficacy of ureteral dilation for transplant ureteral stenosis. J Urol 1988;140:32–35.

36

Renal Calculus Disease

PARVATI RAMCHANDANI

The first percutaneous nephrostomy performed expressly for the purpose of stone removal was in 1975.[1] In the ensuing 2 decades, interventional management of renal calculus disease has come to be regarded as the therapeutic model for minimally invasive therapy, with a high level of patient and physician acceptance. With few exceptions, almost all renal calculi can be successfully managed with either extracorporeal shock wave lithotripsy (ESWL) or percutaneous nephrostolithotomy (PCNL) with success rates that rival open surgery but with significantly decreased morbidity and cost. Open surgical procedures for stone disease are currently required in only 1 to 2 percent of cases.[2] Although primary percutaneous procedures are most apt to be used in patients who are not candidates for ESWL (approximately 10–20 percent of patients with upper urinary tract calculi), they can also be successfully used as a salvage technique for ESWL or ureteroscopic failures or complications. Conversely, ESWL may follow or be combined with PCNL so that all stone material can be successfully eliminated.

Percutaneous Stone Removal (PCNL)

Indications

Percutaneous methods of stone removal have indisputable advantages compared to open surgical techniques; however, the widespread worldwide availability of ESWL, its efficacy, and its relative noninvasiveness compared to PCNL make it the treatment of choice for most renal and ureteral calculi. Nonetheless, there are many situations where percutaneous stone removal is the primary procedure of choice. Table 36-1 lists the current indications where percutaneous techniques should be considered to be the first line of treatment. In all of these clinical situations, ESWL suffers from certain disadvantages and is less effective than PCNL in complete stone removal. These indications are discussed below.

Stone Size

In patients with large calculi, ESWL has a poor chance of complete success, a high probability of requiring adjunctive therapy, and a significant incidence of complications. As the size of stones increases to over 2 to 3 cm, the fragmentation efficiency with ESWL decreases, necessitating multiple ESWL attempts before complete breakup occurs.[3] Correspondingly, stone-free rates drop and the number of ancillary procedures required to aid in the passage of calculus particles increases.[3,4] Some calculi that are 3 cm or larger but are of low radiographic density (e.g., struvite, apatite) may respond to multiple ESWL treatments, but for most large stones (including staghorn calculi) ESWL is not the treatment of choice. With stones larger than 2.5 to 3.0 cm, only 30 to 35 percent may be rendered stone-free with ESWL, compared to 70 to 90 percent of those treated with PCNL. Furthermore, 60 to 75 percent of patients with stones over 2.5 cm in size treated with ESWL require additional procedures such as repeat ESWL, PCNL, ureteroscopy, percutaneous nephrostomy, or stone manipulation, compared to 30 percent of patients treated primarily with PCNL.[3] Roth et al. reported that only 38 percent of patients with stones larger than 3 cm were treated successfully with ESWL monotherapy; additional ESWL increased success to 43 percent, and subsequent percutaneous procedures raised success rate only to 64 percent.[5] In the same series, initial PCNL of these large calculi was successful in 83 percent of patients with adjunctive therapy (such as ESWL), increasing the overall success rate to 90 percent.

There is also a direct correlation between the size of the stone being treated with ESWL and the subsequent accumulation of stone fragments (steinstrassen) in the distal ureter.[6] Fedullo et al.[6] reported that the prevalence of steinstrassen was 17 percent when the calculi being treated were smaller than 10 mm, 26 percent when stones were 10 to 19 mm, 61 percent when stones were 20 to 29 mm and 57 percent when stones were 30 mm or larger in size (Fig. 36-1). Therefore, it appears prudent to treat all stones that are greater

Large stones (>2–3 cm)
Staghorn calculi
Stone + urinary obstruction or compromised urine drainage
    (includes stones in dependent calices and in caliceal diverticula)
Cystine calculi
Abnormal body habitus
Symptomatic stones during pregnancy
Certain removal of all calculous material important
Stones for which other treatment modalities have failed

than 2.5 cm in size with PCNL, while recognizing that the urologist's personal preference, the stone composition, the availability of personnel skilled in interventional techniques, and the patient's size are additional factors that influence the mode of therapy that is finally adopted. It should be noted that a single stone larger than 25 to 30 mm is of a different significance than several stones that are each 5 mm in diameter; the former is initially better managed with percutaneous techniques, whereas ESWL is better for multiple smaller stones that are scattered throughout the collecting system and therefore less accessible to percutaneous techniques. Although each stone may easily be targeted for ESWL, the presence of multiple stones does decrease the efficiency of ESWL and the stone-free rate as compared to a single small stone.

Staghorn Calculi

Staghorn calculi are most commonly composed of struvite and are associated with recurrent urinary tract infections. Complete stone removal is essential in these patients because failure to do so allows persistence of infection and the eventual regrowth of the stone (Fig. 36-2). Other stones that may occasionally have a staghorn configuration are cystine stones (Fig. 36-3), uric acid stones, and, rarely, calcium oxalate monohydrate stones. Staghorn calculi can range in size from a surface area that is less than 250 mm^2 to over 5000 mm^2;[4] more than 60 percent of staghorn calculi treated by Lingeman et al.[4] ranged between 500 mm^2 to 1500 mm^2.

The treatment of staghorn calculi remains highly controversial, with treatment philosophies ranging from monotherapy with ESWL or PCNL alone to a varying combination of the two modalities. Branched stones that fill the majority of the collecting system pose special problems because stones may be located deep in calices that are difficult to reach.

The most efficacious method of treating staghorn calculi is by the so-called sandwich technique.[7,8] PCNL is initially used to rapidly remove large volumes of easily accessible stone with ultrasonic or electrohydraulic lithotripsy ("debulking"). If caliceal fragments are inaccessible from the nephrostomy tract using the usual

endourological techniques, ESWL is used to break up the small volumes of remaining stones, followed by PCNL to remove the residual fragments (see Fig. 36-2). Some advocate a second percutaneous procedure to remove the stone gravel, because stone fragments have a tendency to remain in dilated collecting systems for prolonged periods. Others allow the stone fragments to pass spontaneously after adjunctive ESWL.[9,10]

In patients with partial staghorn calculi, monotherapy with ESWL is an option (Fig. 36-4). Lingeman[4] reported that patients with staghorn calculi that were less than 500 mm^2 in size and with no dilatation of the collecting system could be made stone-free in over 90 percent of cases with ESWL alone. They cautioned, however, that such small-volume staghorn calculi are uncommon and made up only 3 percent of the staghorn stones treated in their series. An additional indication for ESWL monotherapy of staghorn calculi is the presence of a partial or complete staghorn calculus in a nondilated collecting system (see Fig. 36-4).[10] It is recommended that ESWL be performed with an indwelling ureteral catheter in such cases. In Lingeman's series,[4] if all staghorn calculi were considered, stones treated with ESWL monotherapy tended to be smaller, with a mean surface area of 693 mm^2 (range, 161–5907 mm^2) compared to stones treated with initial PCNL, which tended to be larger and have a mean surface area of 1378 mm^2 (range, 302–6028 mm^2). Furthermore, ancillary procedures to facilitate the passage of stone fragments were required much more frequently in patients undergoing ESWL monotherapy than in those being treated with PCNL or PCNL with ESWL (30.5 percent versus 3.4 percent, respectively).

In another series,[11] ESWL monotherapy of complete staghorn calculi, without stents, had a reported stone-free rate of 44 percent at 6 months. With incomplete staghorn calculi, ESWL monotherapy without ureteral stents resulted in a stone-free rate of 48 percent at 6 months. In patients with indwelling ureteral stents, the results were appreciably better, with a stone-free rate of 85 percent.

If staghorn calculi are considered as a group, reported stone-free rates for PCNL alone vary from 71 to 86 percent,[12,13] compared to 84.2 percent for PCNL with or without ESWL.[4] Even though the addition of ESWL at first glance appears to confer no advantage over PCNL alone as far as the stone-free success rate is concerned, the combination of the two procedures minimizes or eliminates the need for multiple renal accesses as well as for secondary endourologic procedures. The latter advantage simplifies the otherwise technically arduous goal of complete stone removal in extensive bulky staghorn calculi and also decreases the risks inherent in establishing multiple access tracks.

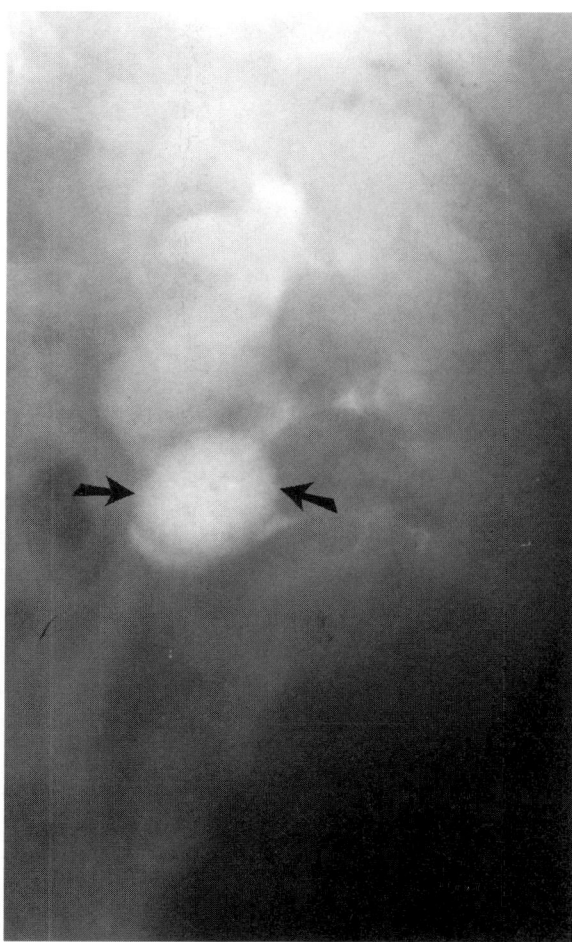

A

B

Figure 36-1. Extracorporeal shock wave lithotripsy (ESWL) of left renal calculus. (A) Image demonstrates a 2.5-cm calculus in the left renal pelvis (*arrows*) with upper pole hydronephrosis. The stone is at the upper limits of the ideal size for ESWL. (B) After ESWL, stone fragments (steinstrassen) are seen in the pelvicaliceal system and proximal ureter. Note the large lead fragment (*arrow*), which impedes the passage of other smaller calculus fragments. (C) A few days later, the column of steinstrassen moved spontaneously to the distal ureter. Although many patients can pass the calculus fragments, this patient required ureteroscopic extraction of the lead fragment preceded by ureteral meatotomy.

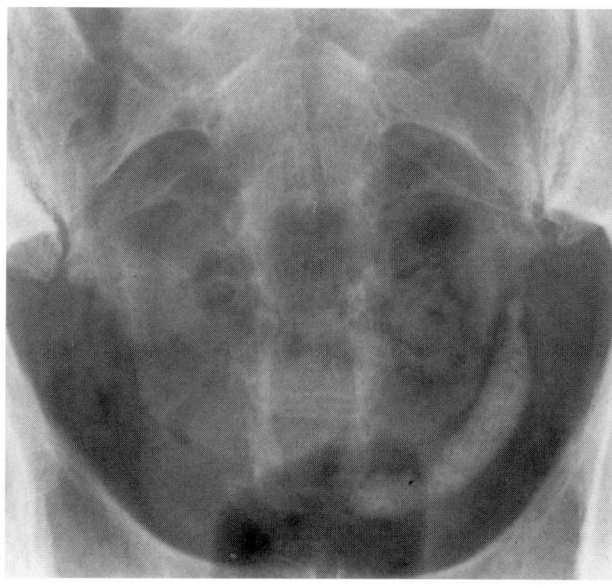

C

Only a minority of staghorn calculi require the addition of ESWL to PCNL. During initial PCNL, efforts should be made to remove as much stone material as possible; if residual stone material is unavoidable, efforts should be directed toward removing enough stone material so that the residual stone burden is less than 2.0 to 2.5 cm in diameter (and thus more effectively treated with ESWL).

To summarize, the effectiveness of ESWL monotherapy in treating staghorn stones is directly proportional to the stone burden,[14] with stone-free rates of 91.7 percent for staghorn stones smaller than 500 mm^2 and 51.2 percent for larger stones.[15] In contrast,

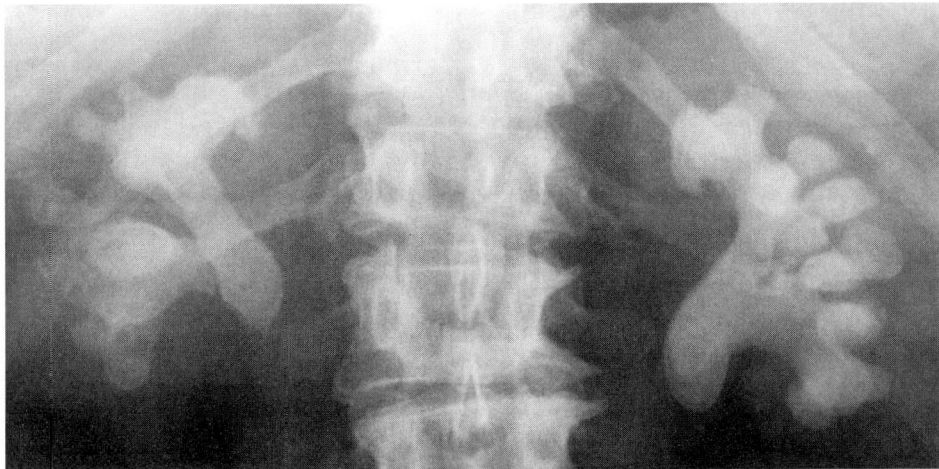

Figure 36-2. Bilateral staghorn calculi. Note the laminations in the stones, indicating that they represent infection stones. Percutaneous nephrostolithotomy (PCNL) for debulking followed by ESWL was performed on both sides to render the patient stone-free.

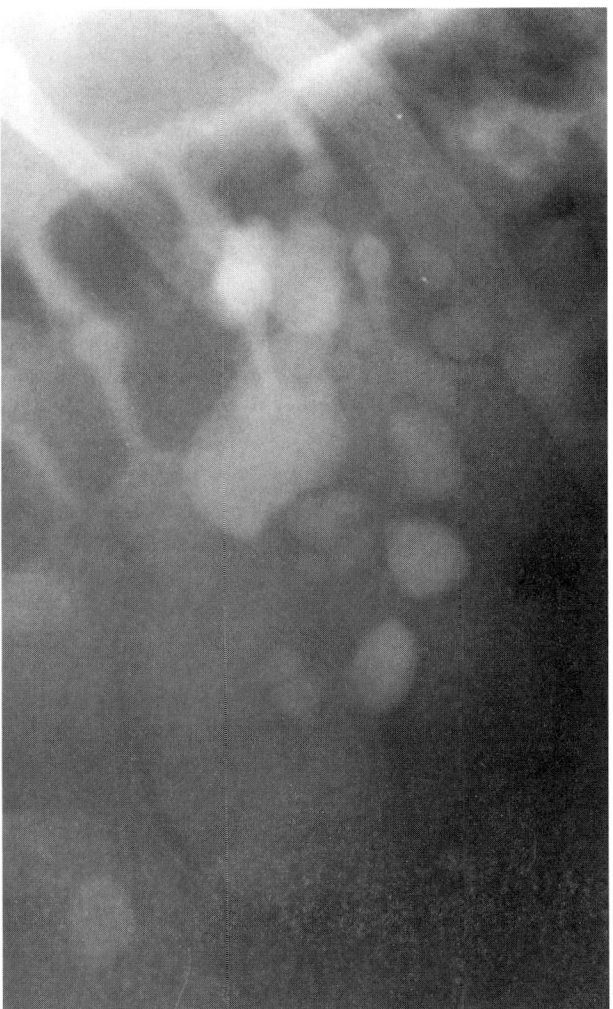

the efficacy of PCNL is excellent independent of stone size until extremely large staghorn calculi (>2500 mm^2) are treated, with stone-free rates of approximately 85 percent (Fig. 36-5). In addition, with ESWL monotherapy it can take as long as a year before the final stone-free rate is achieved.

Urinary Obstruction, Compromised Urinary Drainage

Urinary stasis can predispose to calculus formation. Although ESWL can successfully break up the symptomatic calculi, the fragments are unlikely to be able to successfully pass in the face of continuing obstruction. Furthermore, ESWL does not treat the underlying anatomic abnormality. Therefore, the presence of an anatomic abnormality that would prevent spontaneous passage of stone fragments should be considered a contraindication to shock wave lithotripsy. The most common examples of stones in association with obstruction are in ureteropelvic junction (UPJ) obstruction (Figs. 36-6 and 36-7) and caliceal diverticula. Other examples are stones in dilated lower pole calices (see Fig. 36-7), malrotated kidneys, ectopic kidneys, horseshoe kidneys, and obstruction due to renal cysts or other renal masses. Changes in ureteral caliber or course due to congenital anomalies (retrocaval ureter, crossed ectopia), previous surgery (ureterolithotomy, ureteral reimplantation), and chronic obstruction with

◀ **Figure 36-3.** Cystine staghorn stone with additional proximal ureteral calculus in a 19-year-old woman. The homogeneous, smooth ("ground glass") opacity of the stone suggests its composition. These stones respond poorly to ESWL but fragment readily with ultrasonic lithotripsy, making PCNL the treatment of choice.

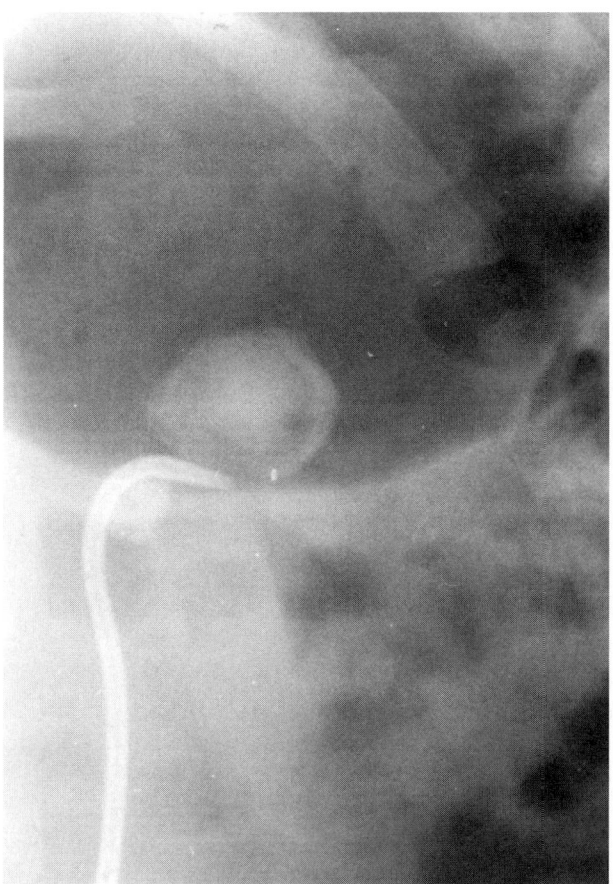

A

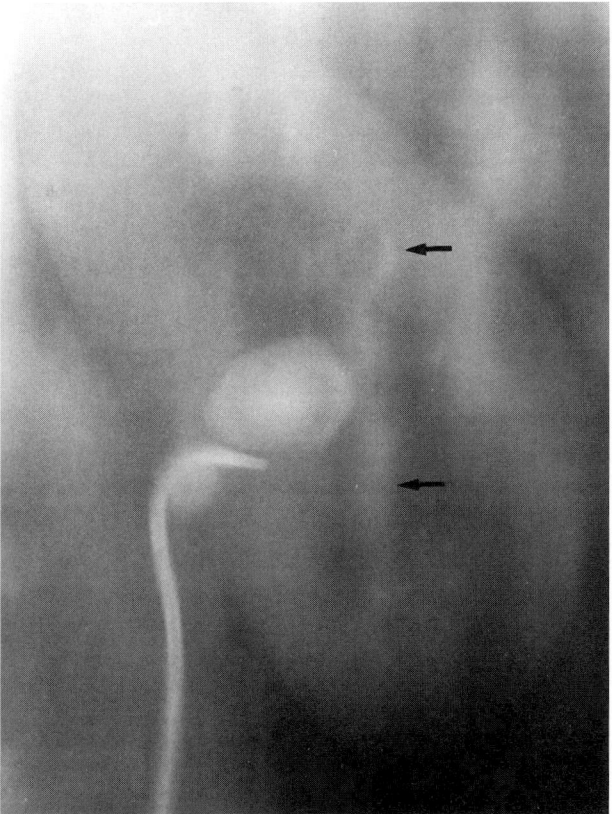

B

Figure 36-4. Staghorn calculus treated with ESWL. (A) Plain film demonstrates a laminated calculus in the renal pelvis. (B) Tomography demonstrates the faintly opaque caliceal and infundibular components of the stone (*arrows*) that could not be appreciated on the plain film. (C) After ESWL, calculus fragments are seen to coat the collecting system, with a denser concentration in the lower pole infundibula and calices. The lower pole is the most common site for residual fragments to accumulate.

resultant tortuosity or retroperitoneal processes (retroperitoneal fibrosis, tumors) that impede ureteral drainage are also rightfully considered to be relative contraindications to ESWL, because the ureteral abnormality may preclude passage even of adequately fragmented stone debris.

In all of the above situations, PCNL is the treatment modality of choice because the percutaneous removal of the calculi circumvents the anatomic abnormalities that prevent stone passage.

In patients with UPJ obstruction, the PCNL is often combined with an endopyelotomy. Briefly, incisions are made along the posterior and lateral margins of the UPJ, with the incisions extending through the ureteral wall into the periureteric fat. Such an approach avoids the vascular structures that are usually located

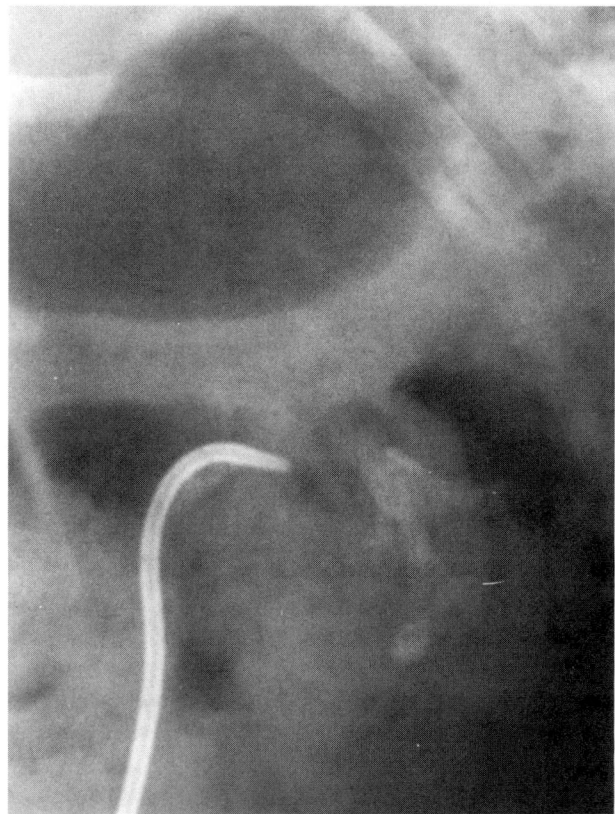

C

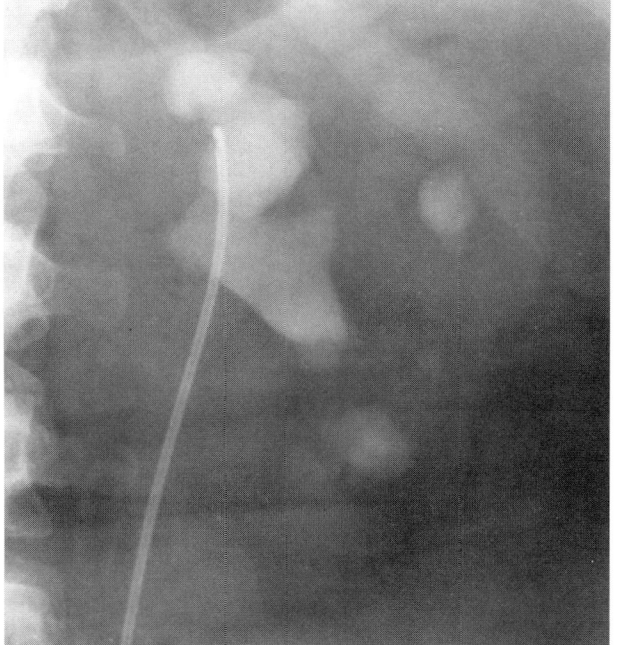

A

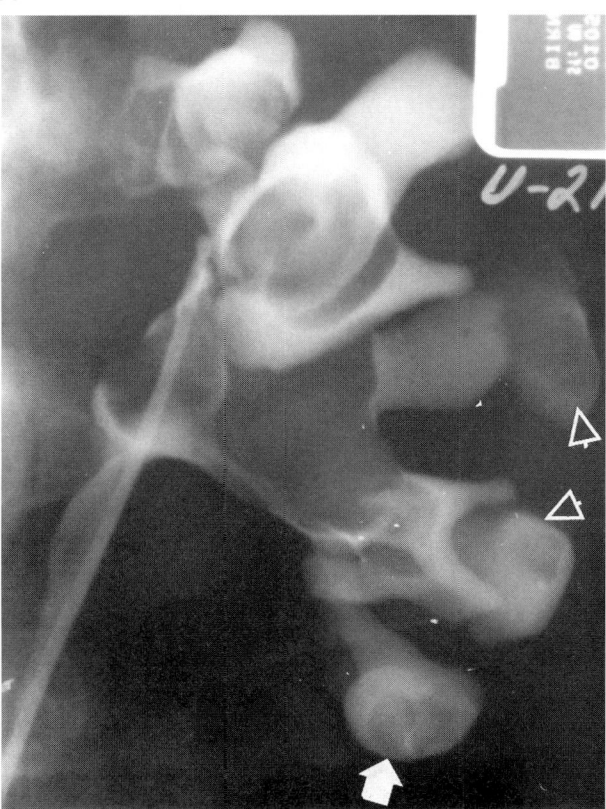

B

Figure 36-5. Staghorn calculus with multiple detached caliceal fragments. (A) Plain film and (B) retrograde pyelogram demonstrate a staghorn calculus with discontinuous caliceal fragments in interpolar and lower pole calices. The collecting system is hydronephrotic, making PCNL the therapy of choice. After access was gained through the medial lower pole calix (*arrow*, B), the renal pelvis and upper and lower pole components of the stone were removed. ESWL was used to fragment the calculi in the interpolar and lateral lower pole calix (*arrowheads*, B).

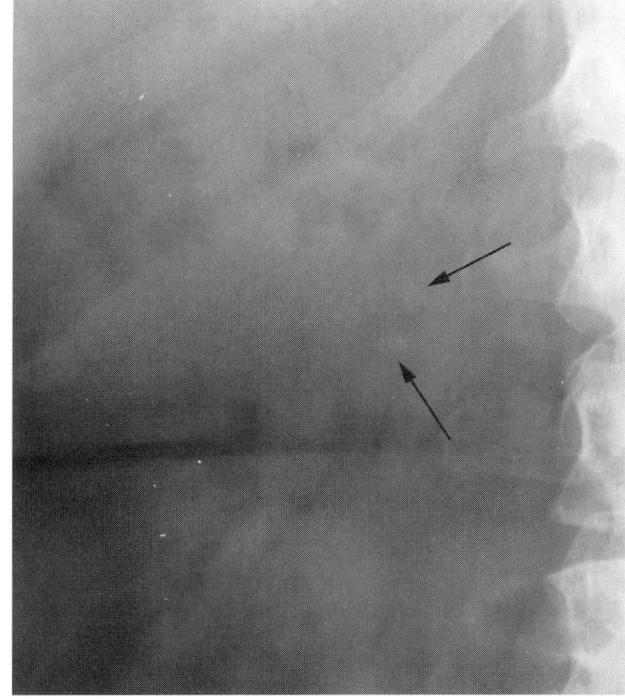

A

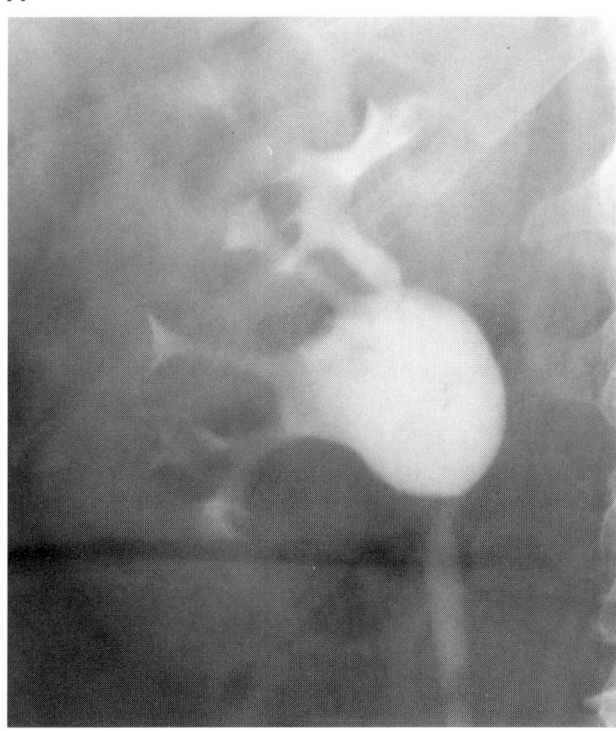

B

Figure 36-6. Small uric acid calculi in a patient with congenital ureteropelvic junction (UPJ) narrowing. (A) Plain film demonstrates very faintly opaque calculi in the right renal pelvis (*arrows*). (B) Urogram demonstrates a prominent extrarenal pelvis with poor funneling of the UPJ. The calculi are obscured by the densely opacified renal pelvis. Although the calculi would respond well to ESWL (because they are small and composed of uric acid), the fragments are unlikely to pass in toto. The patient underwent PCNL.

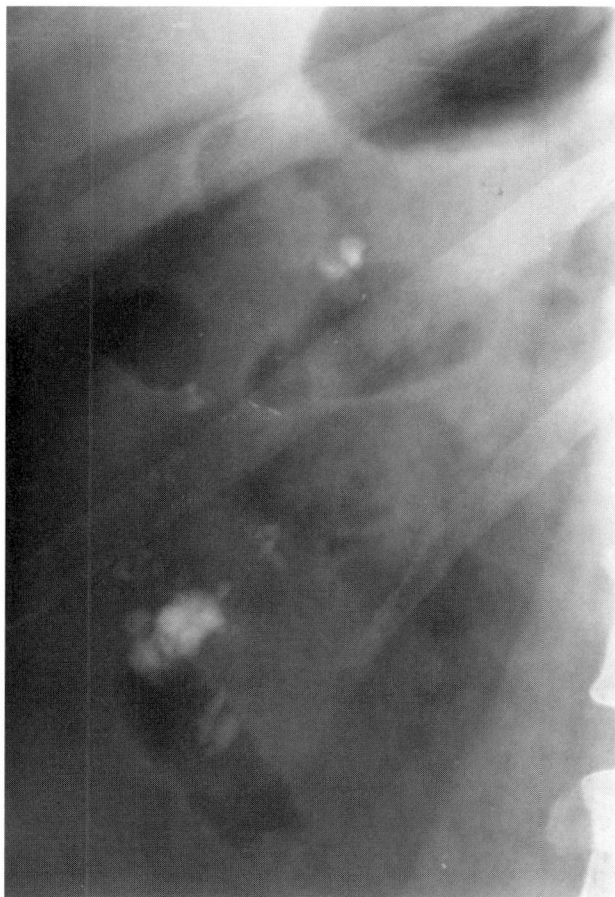

A

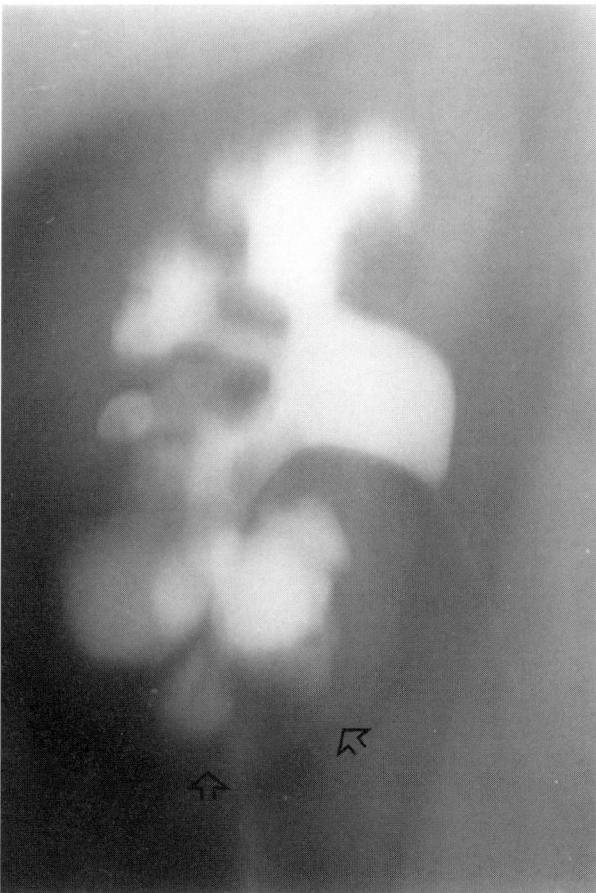

B

Figure 36-7. Renal calculi in conjunction with lower pole hydronephrosis and UPJ narrowing. (A) Plain film demonstrates multiple calculi with the largest in the lower pole. The patient had undergone ESWL in the past and had a long history of stone disease. (B) Tomogram after contrast administration shows selective hydronephrosis in the lower pole with marked parenchymal atrophy (*arrowheads* outline cortical margin). There is also narrowing of the right UPJ. The patient underwent PCNL through the stone-bearing lower pole calix. Other lower pole calculi were flushed out during stone removal.

anteriorly and medially. After the procedure, the ureter is stented for 6 to 8 weeks with a large-bore stent. The reported success for relief of obstruction varies from 64 to 86 percent.[16,17] When an endopyelotomy is planned, PCNL access through a posterior interpolar calix or upper polar calix provides the most direct and straight access to the UPJ.

Calculi occur in about 40 percent of caliceal diverticula and are usually asymptomatic and of little clinical significance. However, they may be associated with flank pain and/or chronic urinary tract infections.[18,19] Open surgery with either marsupialization or excision of the diverticulum and fulguration or closure of the narrow neck is highly successful.[20] Occasional patients may also be treated with partial or, rarely, total nephrectomy.

ESWL of stones within caliceal diverticula may alleviate symptoms temporarily. However, ESWL does not address the underlying stasis within the diverticu-

lum, the narrow neck of which can prevent adequate passage of calculus fragments, which consequently remain in situ within the diverticulum (Fig. 36-8). Not surprisingly, the results of ESWL are poor, and stone-free rates of only 20 to 25 percent have been reported[21-23] with ESWL; curiously, relief of symptoms can occur even if the patient is not rendered stone-free. Residual fragments do eventually grow and become symptomatic again. Moreover, 65 percent of patients with caliceal diverticula and urinary tract infections continue to have persistent infection after ESWL.[24]

For the above reasons, percutaneous procedures are being increasingly advocated[25,26] as the safe and effective alternative for the management of symptomatic caliceal diverticular calculi. Retrograde ureteroscopic techniques[27] as well as a combined technique using both retrograde flexible ureteroscopy and simultaneous caliceal puncture[18] have also been used.

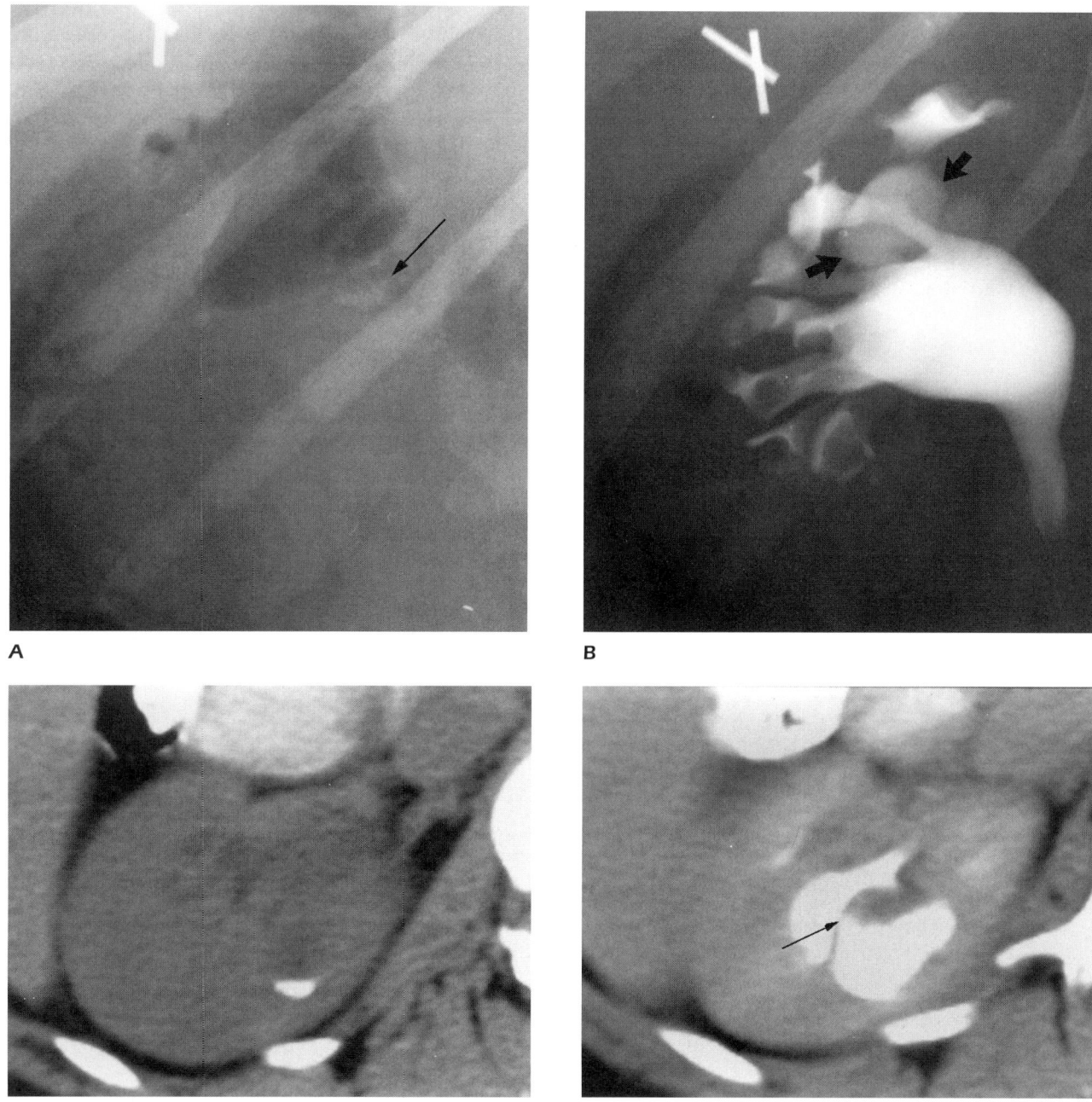

A

B

C

D

Figure 36-8. Calculus in caliceal diverticulum. (A) Plain film and (B) urogram demonstrate calculi (*arrow*, A) in a caliceal diverticulum (*arrows.* B). The calculus had been previously treated with ESWL, but the patient remained symptomatic. (C) Unenhanced CT scan demonstrates layering of the calculus fragments. (D) After contrast administration, the diverticulum fills with contrast through a narrow neck (*arrow*). CT confirmed that the diverticulum could be safely accessed percutaneously.

The percutaneous technique consists of direct puncture of the symptomatic diverticulum[25,26] followed by tract dilation to 24 to 34 French and nephroscopic stone extraction. Subsequently, either the neck of the diverticulum is dilated to 18 to 34 French to enlarge its connection to the collecting system or the diverticular cavity is obliterated by electro-coagulation. Direct puncture into the diverticulum offers the advantage that a rigid nephroscope can be used for the procedure and calculus extraction can be accomplished without accessing the diverticular neck, should it prove to be difficult. Wire placement across the neck of the diverticulum is often easiest after the calculus has been removed nephroscopicly.

The treatment of stones within anteriorly positioned diverticula can be technically challenging. Direct puncture of these diverticula results in an acute angle, such that the neck of the diverticulum cannot be negotiated with either an endoscope or a guidewire. Therefore, the neck of these diverticula cannot be dilated, although the stone within the diverticulum can be extracted, after which the diverticulum can be fulgurated.[26] If direct puncture of the symptomatic diverticulum is technically unfeasible, the diverticulum can be approached indirectly by puncturing a distant calix, dilating the diverticular neck, and then flushing the stones into the collecting system for extraction.[25] Lang has described the creation of a new communication between the renal pelvis and a caliceal diverticulum or obstructed calix ("percutaneous infundibuloplasty") in cases where the infundibulum is stenotic and impassable.[28] The neoinfundibulum reportedly remained patent in 67 percent of the patients for 2 to 7 years.

Percutaneous techniques result in a stone-free rate of 95 to 100 percent,[25,26] with obliteration of the diverticulum in 80 percent of patients and a marked decrease in size in the remaining 20 percent.[26] These results are far superior to those obtainable by ESWL and justify the use of PCNL as a preferred treatment, despite its greater invasiveness.

In an effort to overcome the shortcomings of percutaneous techniques in treating anterior caliceal diverticula as well as small-volume symptomatic diverticula, Grasso et al.[18] have recently described the use of retrograde, actively deflectable, flexible ureteroscopy in four patients. This was combined with simultaneous percutaneous puncture in patients with a caliceal diverticular stone burden greater than 1 cm. The technique was successful in all of their four patients, and symptoms resolved. When a standard retrograde approach was employed, Fuchs et al. described great difficulty in entering the necks of lower pole diverticula,[29] all of which then had to be treated percutaneously. Further, 23 percent of patients in whom a retrograde approach to a caliceal diverticulum was used required a second retrograde or percutaneous approach. Another concern with using the retrograde approach is the creation of ureteral strictures because of the extended procedural time[26,30] required to find the neck of the diverticulum in a retrograde fashion. It should be noted that Grasso et al.[18] reported that procedural times for flexible retrograde ureteroscopy averaged only 2.5 hours, and they believe it to represent a more efficient technique than standard retrograde ureteroscopy.

The clearance of stone fragments from the dependent calices, that is, the lower pole of the kidneys, is variable, unpredictable, and problematic after ESWL.

If stones occur in association with lower pole hydronephrosis, the clearance of fragments can be expected to further diminish (see Fig. 36-7). Lingeman et al.[31] reported stone-free rates of 90 percent for PCNL versus 59 percent for ESWL and also noted that results of ESWL correlated inversely with the stone burden treated whereas the results of PCNL were independent of the stone burden. The results reported by Lingeman et al. were also substantiated by a metaanalysis of other series that reported stratified data for lower pole stone treatment with ESWL and PCNL.[31] The stone-free rate for ESWL of lower pole calculi overall was 60 percent, compared to 90 percent for PCNL; patients with stones less than 1 cm in size had a stone-free rate of 74 percent for ESWL, compared to 100 percent for PCNL. With stones that were 1 to 2 cm in size or larger than 2 cm, stone-free rates with ESWL were 56 and 33 percent, compared to 89 and 94 percent, respectively, for PCNL.

There is a tendency for the fragments of lower pole calculi to remain within the dependent calices after ESWL. These retained stone particles in the lower pole can serve as a nidus for stone growth; stone recurrence rates in the lower pole following ESWL range from 22 to 58 percent (Fig. 36-9).[32,33] When the stone burden is small and located in a nondilated collecting system, stone fragments are more likely to be propelled and expelled out of the lower dependent calices by the coaptation of the nondilated calices and infundibula during normal peristalsis (Fig. 36-10).[31] Coaptation of the calices and infundibula is less likely in hydronephrotic collecting systems where peristalsis is often diminished or absent, thus contributing to the retention of calculi and calculus fragments (see Fig. 36-9).

The American Urologic Association Guidelines Panel Review[31] suggests that an increasing percentage of stones currently being treated with ESWL are located in the lower pole. Two percent of the treated stones in 1984 were in the lower pole, compared to 48 percent in 1991. There has been a corresponding decrease in the incidence of renal pelvic calculi treated with ESWL during the same period, from 87 to 26 percent. Although ESWL continues to be the initial therapy for lower pole stones, the proven success and efficacy of PCNL in treating these calculi would argue for PCNL being the therapeutic modality of choice.

PCNL has been successfully applied in the treatment of calculous disease in anomalous kidneys such as crossed-fused renal ectopia,[34] horseshoe kidneys,[35] and pelvic kidneys.[36,37] These complicated cases call for extensive preprocedural planning. With pelvic kidneys, laparoscopy in conjunction with retrograde[36] and antegrade nephrostomy[37] has been used by some. A posterior approach to a pelvic kidney reportedly led to

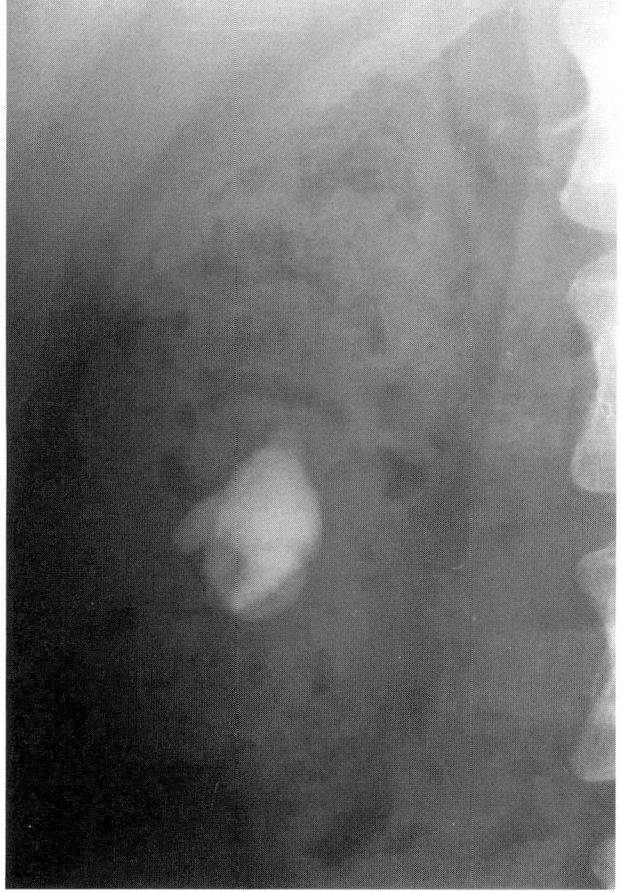

A

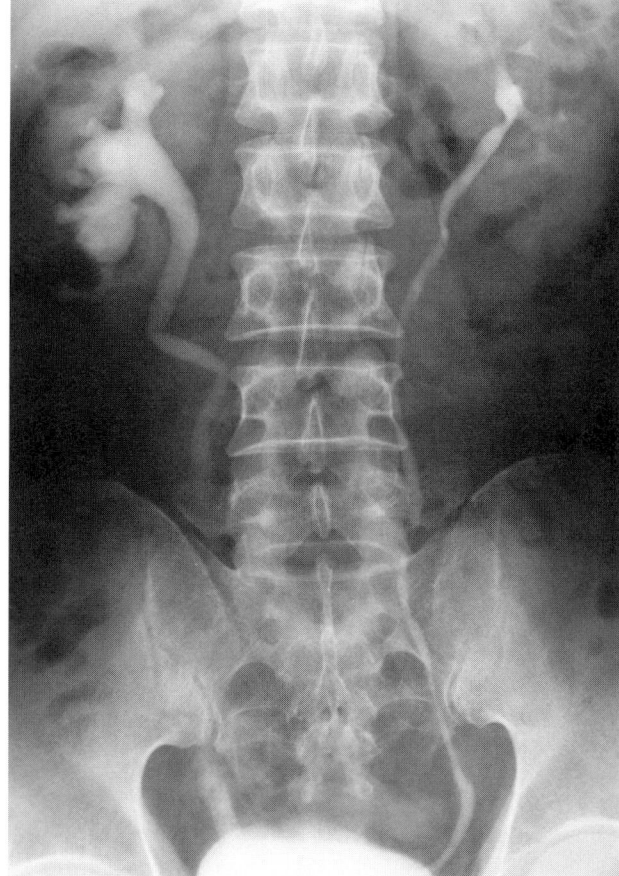

B

Figure 36-9. Lower pole calculus, treated with ESWL. (A) Plain film and (B) urogram demonstrate a large lower pole calculus with hydronephrosis of the lower pole calices. (C) After ESWL, a plain radiograph demonstrates that fragments remain in the lower pole and fail to clear. The patient developed a recurrent lower pole stone within a short time.

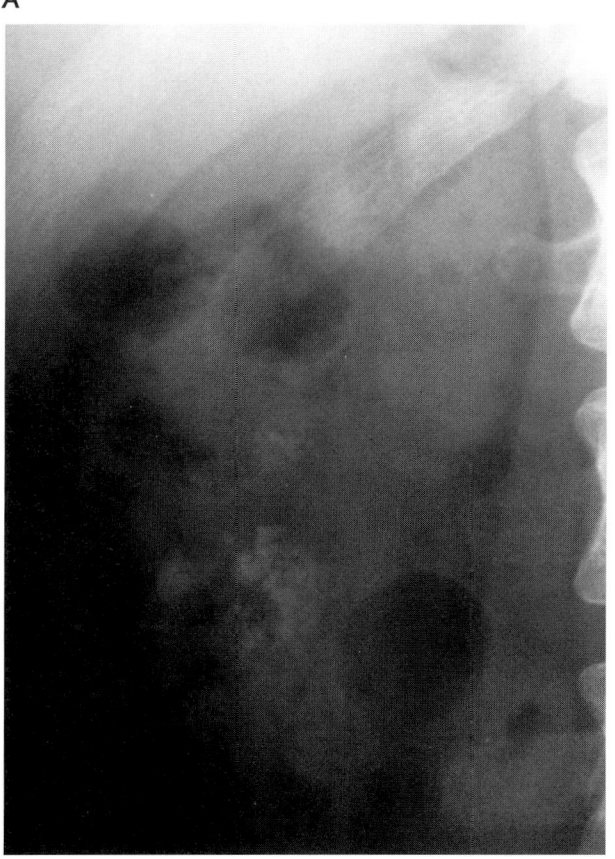

C

femoral neuropathy in one patient[38]; the authors speculated that direct trauma occurred to the dorsal divisions of the lumbar plexus (which form the femoral nerve) lying along the psoas muscle.

Stone Composition

The composition of a given calculus is critical when one is deciding on the best method of management. Certain calculi are readily fragmented by ultrasonic lithotripsy but are refractory to ESWL (e.g., cystine calculi), making PCNL the treatment of choice. On the other hand, uric acid calculi respond well to ESWL but not to ultrasonic lithotripsy.

Cystine calculi fragment unreliably with ESWL, requiring a greater number of treatments and total number of shocks compared to other calculi.[39] Since many of these patients are plagued with multiple stone events, which have required multiple previous interventions and can be anticipated to do so again, a trial

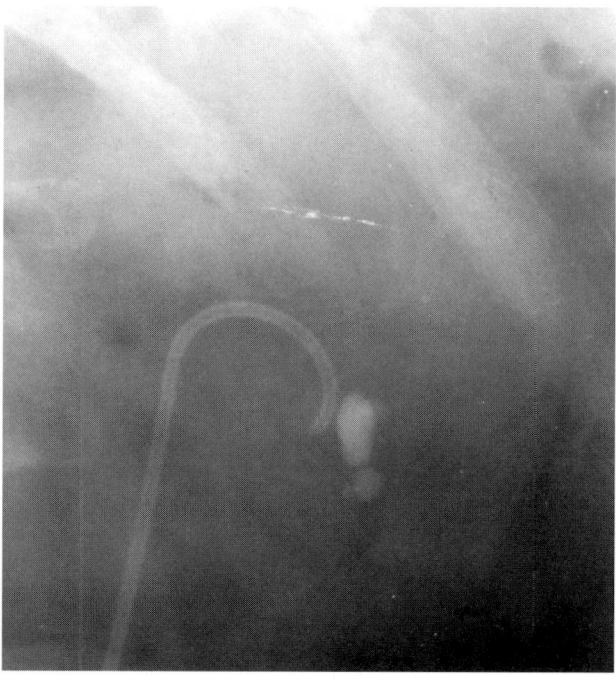

A

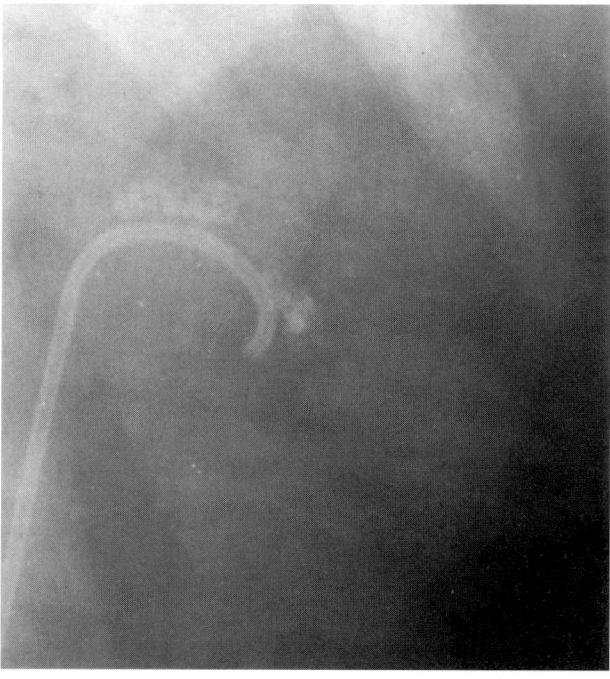

B

Figure 36-10. Small lower pole calculi in a nondilated collecting system, treated with ESWL. (A) Plain film before ESWL demonstrates small lower pole calculi. The ureteral stent was placed for an obstruction due to migration of a calculus into the ureter; the stone was displaced back into the kidney during stent placement. (B) After ESWL, fragments are dispersed in the renal pelvis and lower pole. The patient was rendered stone-free by ESWL.

of ESWL for stones less than 2 cm in size is reasonable. Rough, spiculated cystine stones that have recently formed respond better to ESWL than do homogeneous, smooth, long-standing stones.[40] High-power machines such as the HM-3 also appear to be more effective.

For stones larger than 2 cm, proceeding directly to PCNL is the best option (see Fig. 36-3). All stone material must be removed at the time of the percutaneous procedure to ensure that the patient will remain stone-free.

Medical treatment (acetyl cysteine) has been unreliable in removing residual fragments,[41] but its efficacy may be improved by infusing the drugs through percutaneously placed catheters. Since cystine calculi characteristically break into chunks with ESWL, further pulverization requires additional ESWL sessions, percutaneous extraction, and/or ultrasonic lithotripsy or chemical dissolution (see above).

Stones composed of calcium oxalate dihydrate and struvite break up well with ESWL or any other form of power lithotripsy, whereas stones composed either partially or completely of calcium oxalate monohydrate do not respond well to ESWL. With these stones, the volume of the stone is the main determinant of the most desirable mode of therapy.

Anatomic Abnormalities and Abnormal Body Habitus

A misshapen body habitus such as that caused by scoliosis or, more commonly, morbid obesity may make ESWL unfeasible because the patients cannot be positioned so that the stone is in the focal point of the machine. PCNL may also be technically demanding in these patients but carries fewer risks than open surgery would. A preprocedural CT scan is helpful in such patients to evaluate the anatomy and plan an access route that avoids bowel and other viscera (Fig. 36-11).

Certainty of Final Results

If the presence of residual fragments and the attendant uncertainties related to their passage are unacceptable to the patient for psychological or occupational reasons (airline pilots being the classic example), PCNL is an optimal option because of its superior stone-free rate of 95 to 98 percent.

Symptomatic Stones During Pregnancy

Renal colic affects 1 in 1500 pregnancies, usually during the second and third trimesters. Many believe stones may be more frequent in multiparous women than in primiparous patients, although this is not

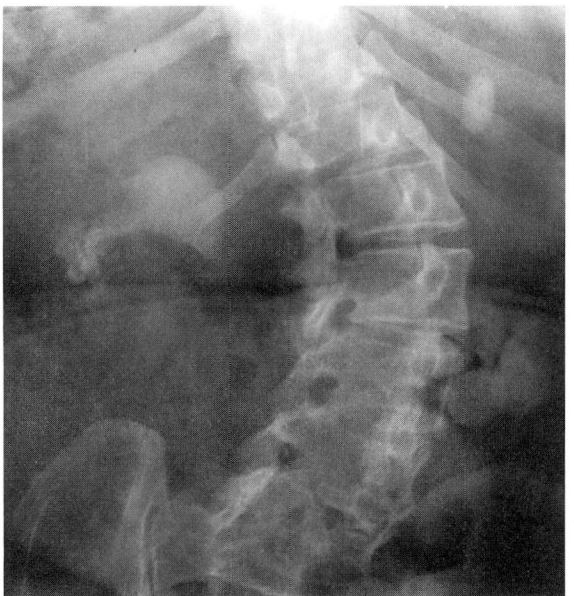

A

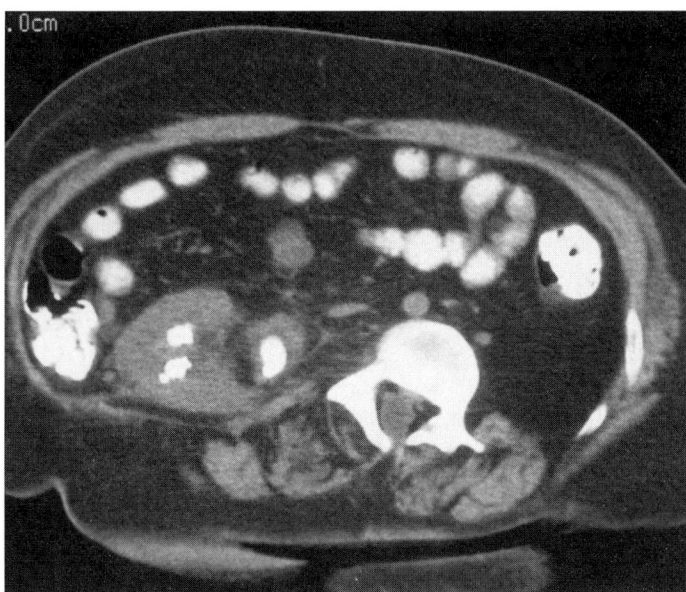

B

Figure 36-11. Renal calculi in a patient with scoliosis and myelomeningocele. (A) Plain film demonstrates right staghorn calculus, left renal calculus, marked scoliosis, and spinal dysraphism. (B) CT scan demonstrates that access to the lower pole of the right kidney can be safely achieved. The patient underwent successful PCNL.

universally agreed upon.[42] Symptomatic stones are usually located in the mid or distal ureter, with flank pain, microhematuria, and urosepsis being the common presenting symptoms. The diagnosis can be confirmed by a limited intravenous urogram or sonography. However, it should be recognized that both these studies may be challenging to interpret in pregnant patients because of the difficulty in differentiating between upper tract dilation due to progressive hydronephrosis of pregnancy (a common and expected change) from that due to obstruction by a stone.[43,44]

Conservative treatment consisting of analgesia and hydration is effective in most patients, and the renal calculi pass spontaneously in 75 percent of patients.[45] More aggressive therapy is required in patients with refractory pain, sepsis, renal insufficiency (particularly if there is a solitary kidney), and colic-induced preterm labor.

Therapeutic interventions during pregnancy are restricted to drainage of the affected collecting system by either a ureteral stent placed in a retrograde fashion or a percutaneous nephrostomy (Fig. 36-12). Ureteral stents can be placed with local anesthesia and are usually well tolerated during pregnancy.[46,47] Endoluminal ultrasound has been used to place a ureteral stent,[48] thus avoiding the potential risks of radiation exposure. Wolf et al.[48] used a 20-MHz transducer (through a 6.2 French catheter) for stent placement in a 27-week gravid patient. If stent placement fails, percutaneous nephrostomy is performed. The necessity for periodic stent changes during pregnancy is controversial. Some authors believe that there is accelerated stent encrustation during pregnancy[49] and that stents should be changed every 8 to 12 weeks to avoid this complication.[47] Others are of the opinion that stents can be left in place for 3 to 9 months without a change being necessary.[46,50]

ESWL as well as ultrasonic and laser lithotripsy are contraindicated during pregnancy. Other definitive therapy for the calculus is best postponed until 6 weeks postpartum. PCNL, ureteroscopic stone extraction, and open surgery (pyelolithotomy or ureterolithotomy) have all been performed during pregnancy,[46] and general anesthesia can safely be administered during pregnancy.[51] Since radiologic monitoring during ureteroscopy is not essential and can be eliminated, it is preferred over PCNL if stone extraction is deemed necessary. However, even with the current refinement of techniques, ureteroscopy is still associated with a potential risk of ureteral perforation, sepsis, and possible fetal injury. Therefore, conservative management should be regarded as the most prudent management until after delivery.

Technique

Two primary components in the percutaneous therapy of upper urinary tract calculi are the establishment of an access tract and the actual stone removal itself. These are further discussed below. The technical de-

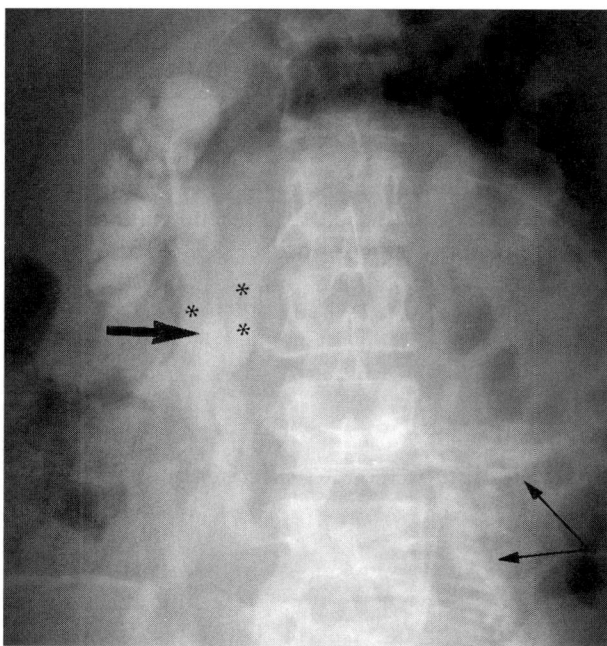

Figure 36-12. Obstructing ureteral calculus in pregnant patient. Urogram demonstrates contrast extravasation in the retroperitoneum (*asterisks*) due to a proximal ureteral calculus (*large arrow*). Note the fetal skull and skeleton (*long arrows*). A percutaneous nephrostomy was performed for drainage. The patient passed the calculus spontaneously when she was postpartum.

tails of the procedure cannot be addressed here but have previously been described.[52–54]

Access to the upper urinary tract can be obtained either percutaneously or in a retrograde fashion. The percutaneous route is used most frequently to approach renal and upper ureteral calculi. Although a team approach is advocated by and practiced in many institutions,[55] including the author's, many endourologists believe that the nephrostomy track placement is rightfully performed by the urologist,[4,56,57] preferably in the operating room.

Accurate access is the essential underpinning of a successful PCNL; a well-placed access track can simplify a complex procedure, and, conversely, a poorly placed track may make it impossible to remove even the most accessible of calculi. Fluoroscopic control is usually preferred for the procedure, especially if the calculi are radiopaque. CT or sonography is occasionally useful in preprocedural planning, especially in patients with aberrant anatomy, so that the liver, spleen, colon, and pleural space can be avoided by the proposed track (see Fig. 36-11).

If the calculus is located in a calix or diverticulum, access should be obtained through that particular calix or diverticulum. For large-volume calculi, a lower pole or interpolar caliceal puncture through a subcostal approach offers the advantages of avoiding the pleura while being certain to clear the dependent lower pole calices of calculi. The necessity for gaining access to the kidney via an intercostal track is controversial because a stone-free rate of over 95 percent can be achieved using a subcostal approach.[52] An intercostal puncture is required to access an upper pole calix, usually to extract upper pole staghorn calculi and occasionally for concurrent endopyelotomy (although the latter can usually be successfully accomplished via a posterior interpolar access).

Two representative series that reported on results using an intercostal approach[58,59] are summarized. Narasimhan et al.[58] used an intercostal approach in 24 percent of their cases. In two of the three patients with access above the 11th rib, thoracic complications requiring treatment (hydrothorax, pneumothorax) occurred. The authors recorded no clinically significant complications in cases where the puncture was below the 11th rib and into a middle or lower calix. Fuchs et al.[59] used an intercostal approach in 30 percent of their patients, of whom 5 percent had a major thoracic complication. The authors of both series[58,59] recommend that access above the 11th rib be avoided. Hopper et al.[60] performed CT on prone patients to estimate the risks associated with a puncture between the 10th and 11th ribs and found that an 11th–12th rib intercostal approach would puncture the right lung in 14 percent of patients and the left lung in 29 percent of patients in expiration; the risk of puncturing the liver and spleen was minimal in full expiration. However, the risk to the lungs was considered to be prohibitive with a 10th–11th intercostal approach, regardless of the degree of respiration.

Puncture of the desired calix can be performed with either a skinny 21- or 22-gauge needle (with conversion to a larger guidewire using commercially available introducer systems) or directly with an 18-gauge needle. The rigidity of the latter needle facilitates precise placement into the targeted calix, a task that can be more difficult with the flexible 21-gauge needles. In most cases where the calculus is radiopaque (and can therefore serve as a target for puncture), contrast opacification of the collecting system before puncture is unnecessary, as long as a previous intravenous urogram or retrograde pyelogram is available to evaluate the anatomy of the pyelocaliceal system. If the calculi are faintly opaque or the collecting system is not dilated, placement of a retrograde catheter is a useful adjunct to both opacify and distend the collecting system. At the author's institution, local anesthesia and intravenous sedation are generally used for establishing the track. Occasionally, if the stone removal is to follow immediately afterwards, epidural anesthesia has been

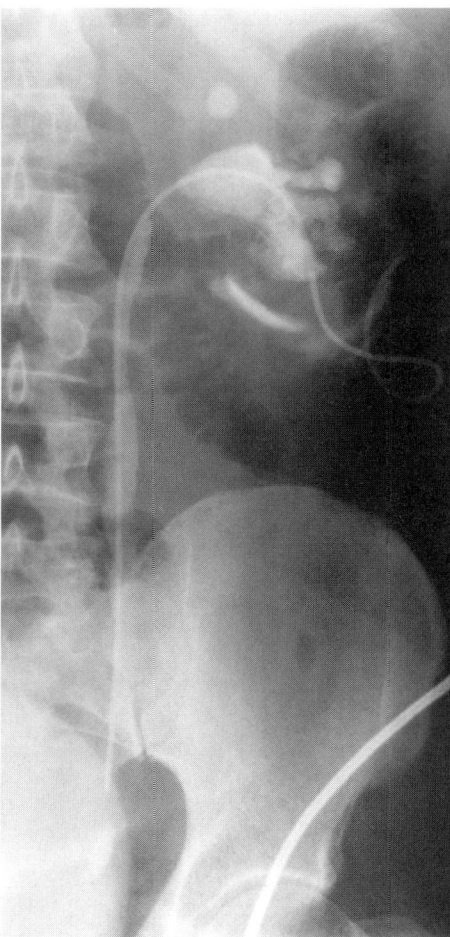

Figure 36-13. Ureteral access catheter placed percutaneously in a patient with a large left staghorn calculus. Since the collecting system was not obstructed, a separate nephrostomy catheter was not placed. Note that access is through the lower pole.

used for both the percutaneous nephrostomy and the subsequent track dilation and stone removal.

The technique for access in a retrograde fashion is briefly described here.[61,62] Using a transurethral retrograde route, a catheter is placed coaxially over a wire into the exact calix picked for puncture. A sharp wire or needle is then passed through the catheter under fluoroscopic control, through the calix, kidney, and flank, and out the skin. The wire is captured at the skin, and dilation is performed as outlined when a track is established percutaneously. The purported advantage of this technique is a greater degree of control over track placement and the ability to perform it in a standard cystoscopy suite.[3] However, this technique of access has not gained popularity because it is technically arduous and, in fact, may not be as precise as a percutaneously placed track.

After the puncture is made, a 0.038-inch guidewire is placed into the collecting system and maneuvered into the ureter. Depending on the circumstances unique to the institution, track dilation may be performed at the same sitting, in the radiology suite, or in the operating room immediately after the nephrostomy,[52,63] with the urologists extracting the calculus under nephroscopic guidance. At the author's institution, a 6 French ureteral access catheter is placed with its tip in the midureter after the nephrostomy is performed (Fig. 36-13). An additional nephrostomy catheter is placed to drain the collecting system if there is obstruction. The subsequent track dilation and stone removal are performed by the urologists in the operating room, usually on the following day. A decade of experience has amply proven that tracts can be dilated acutely to 24 to 30 French with no adverse effects; this approach considerably shortens hospitalization and physician time.[63] In most cases, bleeding associated with the track dilation does not hamper visibility enough to require postponing the procedure.

Track dilation is a painful procedure and requires that the patient be under either general anesthesia (preferably) or regional anesthesia. The dilation can be performed with tapered-tip fascial dilators of 10 to 30 French size or high-pressure track balloons measuring 10 cm in length and 10 mm in width when inflated. It is essential to securely place a sturdy superstiff guidewire from the flank into the urinary bladder to prevent inadvertent withdrawal of the guidewire from the collecting system, which will cause either loss of access or perforation of the collecting system. Track dilation should be performed under fluoroscopic monitoring, with care being taken to avoid perforating the medial aspect of the renal pelvis when the stiff dilators are advanced.

Depending on the size and complexity of the stone, multiple access tracts may be necessary to remove the stone in its entirety.[64,65] The addition of ESWL to PCNL can reduce the number of tracks required, with ESWL being used to fragment the residual stone and the fragments being extracted through the existing nephrostomy track. Simultaneous bilateral PCNL has been described for bilateral staghorn calculi.[66]

Small calculi can be directly extracted through the sheath using forceps or a basket. For larger calculi, some form of lithotripsy is used to break the stone into smaller fragments. Ultrasonic lithotripsy is frequently used: the vibrating probe breaks up the calculus and the fragments are aspirated through the hollow probe (Fig. 36-14). For particularly hard stones, electrohydraulic lithotripsy or laser is used. Flexible nephroscopy is valuable in identifying and breaking up caliceal and ureteral fragments.

After the procedure, the collecting system is inspected to ensure a stone-free state. A straight catheter is placed down the ureter, and a nephrostomy tube is placed through the track into the collecting system.

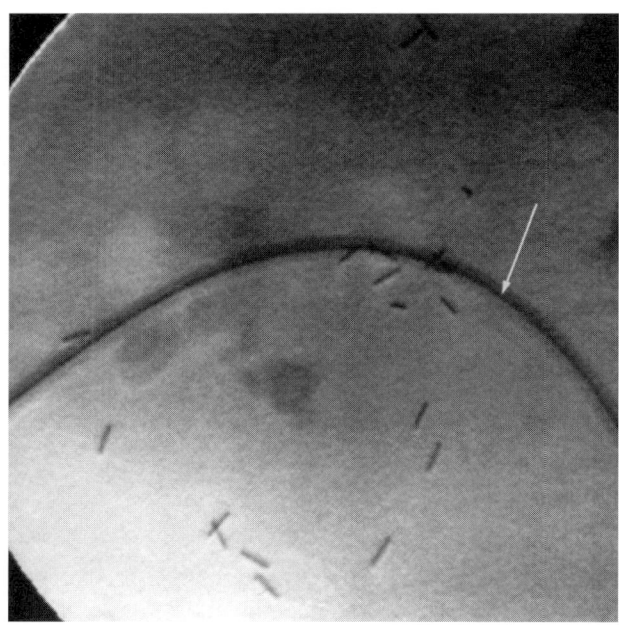

A

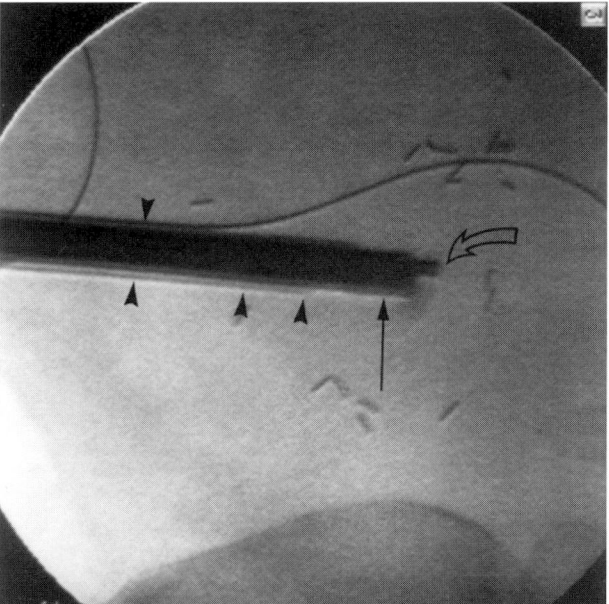

B

Figure 36-14. Stone removal. (A) Intraoperative spot film before track dilation demonstrates a staghorn calculus in a patient who had had previous open surgery for stone disease. A guidewire is in place within the ureteral access catheter (*arrow*). (B) After track dilation, a 30 French sheath (*arrowheads*) was placed. Note the nephroscope (*long arrow*) and ultrasonic lithotripsy probe (*open arrow*). Most of the stone has been removed. The safety guidewire is visible outside the sheath. (C) After stone removal, contrast injection demonstrates no extravasation. A Malecot catheter and straight ureteral catheter were placed.

The author generally uses 20 to 24 French Malecot catheters for this purpose, but Foley catheters have also been used. The author prefers to leave the nephrostomy catheter in for a week or two after stone removal to ensure healing. Others obtain a nephrostogram 48 hours after the procedure, and if no leaks are seen, the nephrostomy tube is clamped. If this is well tolerated, the nephrostomy tube is removed before discharge.[3]

Contraindications

An uncorrected bleeding diathesis is the only absolute contraindication. The procedure should not be performed if a stone-bearing kidney is uninfected and nonfunctioning. A relative contraindication is the inability to establish a safe access track.

Complications

Bleeding

Significant arterial bleeding occurs in 0.5 to 1.5 percent of patients.[67] Stoller et al.[68] reported an average

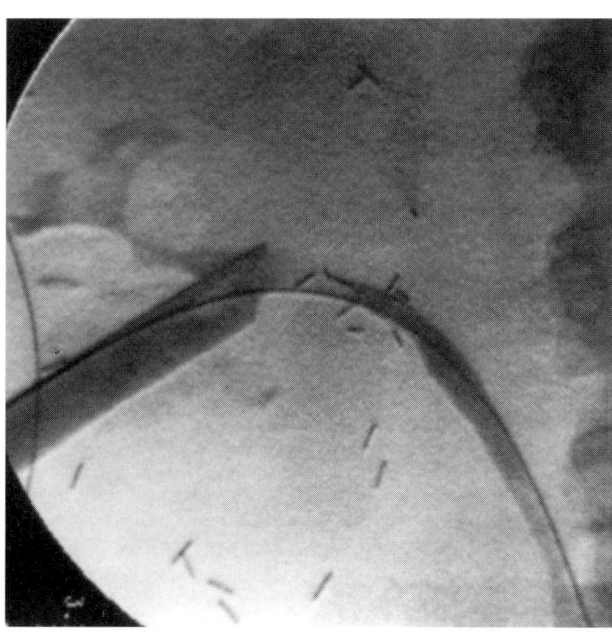

C

blood loss of 2.8 g/dl hemoglobin for an uncomplicated one-stage, single-puncture PCNL. A twofold increase in blood loss occurred in complicated staghorn calculi, which required multiple punctures, and in cases with renal pelvic perforation. Total blood loss was not affected by the presence of hypertension, the type of fascial dilation, previous open surgery, or ESWL. Interestingly, mature nephrostomy tracks bled half as frequently as fresh tracks.

Vascular injury during the placement of the access track or track dilation can lead to pseudoaneurysms, arteriovenous fistulas, perinephric hematomas, and loss of functional parenchyma.[69] Initial puncture into a calix rather than an infundibulum or the renal pelvis is preferable and the least likely to cause major vascular injury. If bleeding appears to be excessive during or after PCNL, the nephrostomy tube can be clamped to tamponade the track and the collecting system. If that fails, a larger nephrostomy catheter can be placed, which will tamponade the track better and also allow blood clots as well as residual calculus fragments to pass. Forced diuresis by means of intravenous mannitol administration and vigorous hydration may help by causing the kidney to swell within its capsule and thus tamponade.[68] Selective angiography and embolization should be considered if the above measures fail.[70,71]

Injury to Adjacent Organs

The colon can be nicked if it is positioned posterior to the kidney. In one series, CT scanning showed that the ascending colon was more posterior than the mid right kidney in 39.4 percent at the level of the lower pole, and the descending colon was more posterior in 30.6 percent at the level of the left lower pole.[72] Furthermore, in 75 percent of patients, the colon moved more posteriorly in the prone position. The colonic injury may not be obvious until the postprocedure nephrostogram demonstrates colonic filling with contrast. If the nick is small, the injuries can be managed conservatively by draining the kidneys with a double-pigtail ureteral stent placed from below, pulling the nephrostomy tube into the colon, and leaving it to drainage to act as a colostomy tube. The track usually seals in a few days.[73] If a more serious injury occurs, open repair may be required.[74]

Injury to the duodenum is uncommon and occurs if the large-bore dilators perforate the medial aspect of the right renal pelvis and then enter the duodenum during track dilation. Conservative management with nasogastric tube drainage has been reportedly effective.[3]

Injury to the liver and spleen is uncommon, and especially so if puncture is performed in full expiration.

Pleural and lung injuries have been previously discussed. The injury is usually recognized when the nephrostogram is done. A chest tube may be required if a large amount of pleural fluid accumulates.

Candidemia

Segura[3] described candidemia in four patients who underwent stone removal. All patients had an indwelling nephrostomy tube and had been on antibiotics. There was overgrowth of candida in the urinary tract related to the presence of the tube and the antibiotic administration. The urine of such patients should be sterilized before stone removal is attempted.

Sepsis

A rise in temperature is common after stone removal. Preoperative urine cultures will identify the patients who should be treated before the procedure, particularly those with infected stones. The author generally uses prophylactic antibiotics, usually a cephalosporin, in all patients undergoing stone removal.

Perforation

During the process of stone removal, the renal pelvis can be perforated by a sharp fragment of stone or by one of the instruments, such as the ultrasound probe. Most such perforations heal within 12 to 24 hours as long as good urine drainage is maintained. Serial nephrostograms will show that even sizable renal pelvic and ureteral lacerations heal in a few days without stricture formation.

A calculus can extrude through a urothelial tear (Fig. 36-15). If it is not recognized at endoscopy, it will usually become obvious on postprocedural radiographs.[75] Extruded calculi will be closely related to the collecting system and ureter yet be outside these structures on different projections. Renal pelvic extrusions should be treated with nephrostomy drainage, whereas ureteral tears should be treated with stenting for a few weeks. In the absence of infection, extrusion of calculus material into the perinephric and periureteral tissues appears to be of no clinical consequence.[75]

Entrapped Nephrostomy Tube

Malecot tubes are often placed after PCNL to allow residual fragments to drain. If the renal pelvis is small and intrarenal, tissue bridges can grow through the wings of the Malecot tube, making it resistant to removal.[76-78] Therefore, it is unwise to place a Malecot type of nephrostomy catheter for more than 2 to 3 weeks in patients with small, intrarenal pelves.

Nephroscopy is usually required to incise the anchoring tissue bridges. Forceful removal of the catheter is unwise because it may result in either incomplete removal or significant renal injury.

Extracorporeal Shock Wave Lithotripsy (ESWL)

ESWL is one of the most significant advances in modern urologic history. It is the treatment of choice for uncomplicated, small (up to 2 cm) upper urinary tract calculi (renal and ureteral), with stone-free rates of about 70 percent for a broad range of stone patients and rates of more than 90 percent in selected series of small renal pelvic or upper ureteral stones. About 97

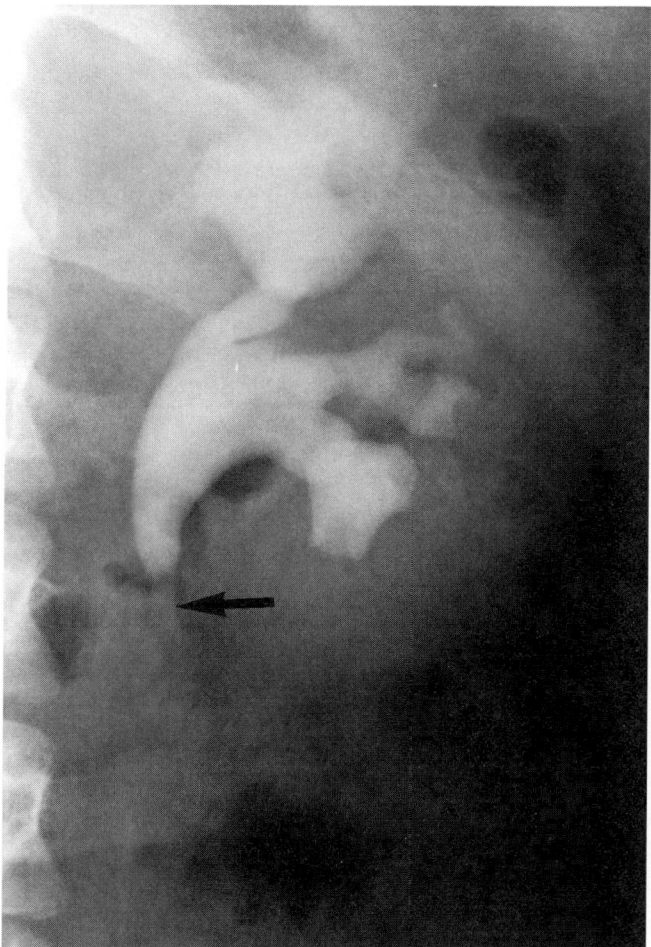

A

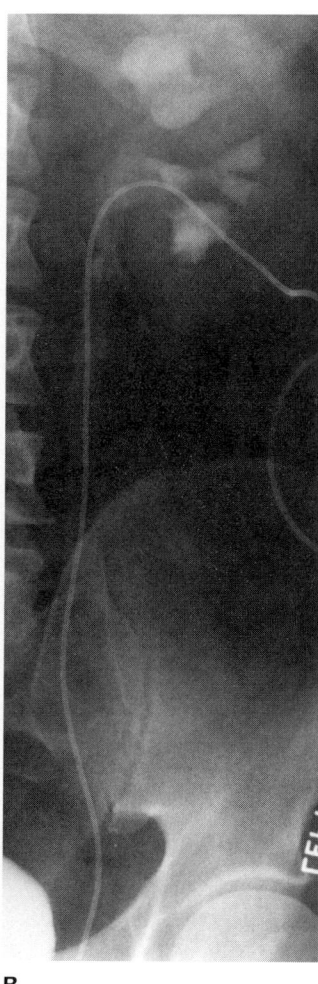

B

Figure 36-15. Extrusion of ureteral calculus. (A) Urogram demonstrates obstruction and hydronephrosis due to a 6-mm proximal ureteral stone (*arrow*). (B) Percutaneous nephrostomy was performed and a ureteral catheter placed past the calculus. Attempts at fluoroscopically guided basket extraction of the stone were unsuccessful.

percent of stones are effectively fragmented with one ESWL treatment, and an additional 2 percent are fragmented with a second treatment.[79]

Principles

The history and theory of ESWL as well as details of the many different varieties of lithotripters available cannot be discussed here. The reader is referred to several publications on this subject.[80,81]

The basic premise of ESWL is that kidney stones will break up when exposed to a series of relatively low energy shock waves. A shock wave is produced by an electric spark in water and then focused on the kidney stone by an ellipsoid reflector. The shock waves can be produced by a spark gap, piezoelectricity, electromagnetic shock wave generation, or microexplosive techniques. The original Dornier HM-3 lithotripter (Dornier Company) uses the spark gap technique for shock wave generation.

The shock waves are transmitted to the kidney either through a water bath in which the patient is immersed or through a fluid-filled cushion coupled to the patient's body. The trend is toward eliminating the cumbersome water bath and instead using more compact coupling devices and lower-power shock waves to allow for therapy with little or no anesthesia.

In most instances the stones are localized with biplane fluoroscopy. For localizing nonopaque or poorly opaque stones, contrast instillation is a necessity, requiring the placement of ureteral catheters. Many newer lithotripters use ultrasound to localize calculi. However, ultrasound limits the effectiveness of these machines in treating ureteral calculi because they often cannot be identified accurately. Some machines have both fluoroscopy and ultrasound[80] available for stone localization.

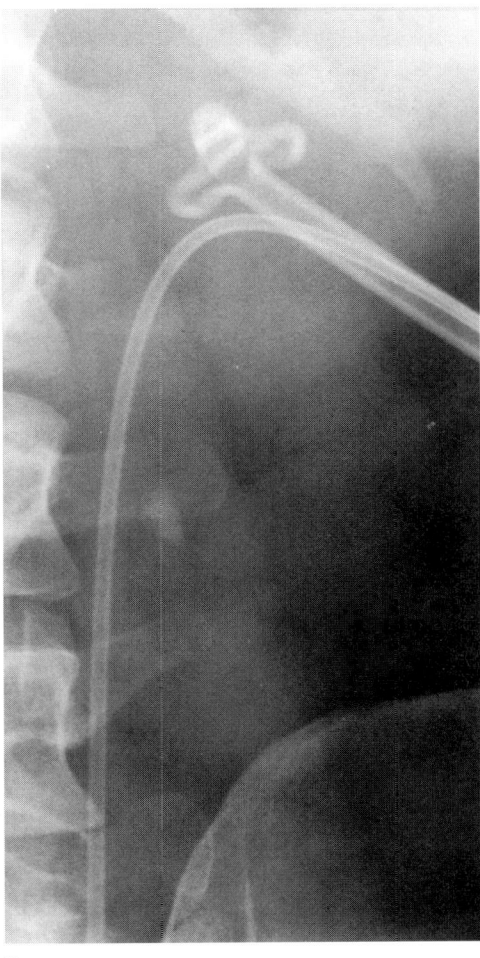

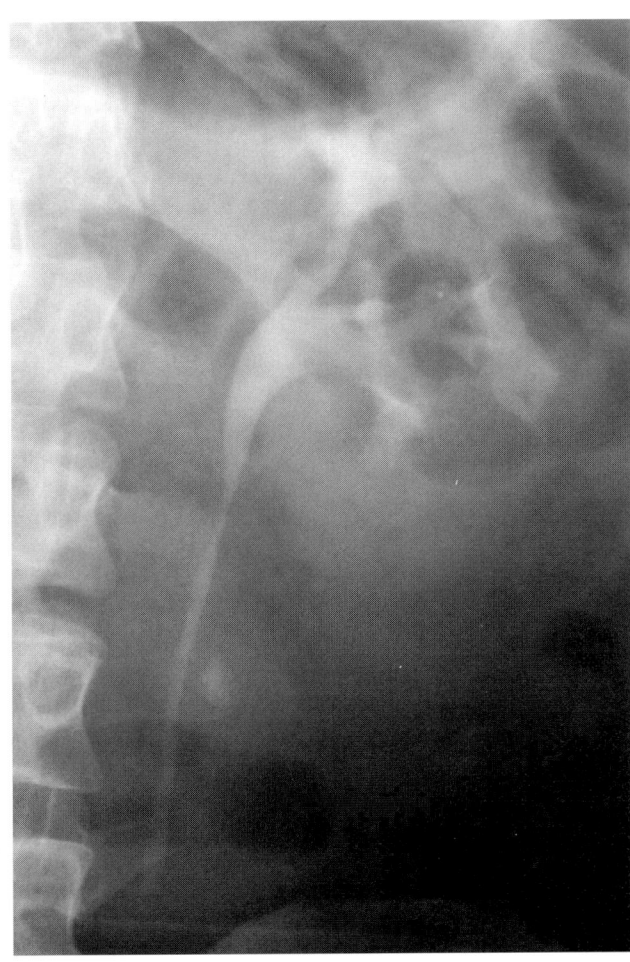

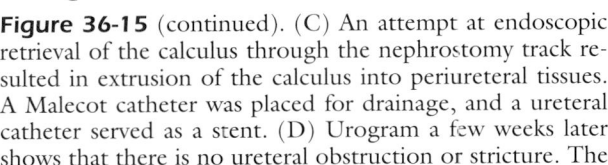

C   D

Figure 36-15 (continued). (C) An attempt at endoscopic retrieval of the calculus through the nephrostomy track resulted in extrusion of the calculus into periureteral tissues. A Malecot catheter was placed for drainage, and a ureteral catheter served as a stent. (D) Urogram a few weeks later shows that there is no ureteral obstruction or stricture. The calculus is clearly extraureteral. Most perforations of the renal pelvis or ureter heal without event as long as there is good urine drainage. If the extruded calculus is infected, however, attempts should be made to remove it to prevent recurrent retroperitoneal abscesses.

Results

A stone-free state should be the most important yardstick for any therapy for urinary calculi. However, the widespread application of ESWL and the inevitable generation of fragments by shock wave therapy have led some to adopt the phrase "clinically insignificant residual fragments." There is great confusion and controversy over what size fragment can be construed to be clinically insignificant. Some investigators believe that stone fragments 4 mm or less in size are insignificant because they have about an 85 percent chance of spontaneously passing.[3,80] However, since calculi of this size can cause both ureteral obstruction and symptoms as they pass down the ureter, others believe that the goal of any therapy for stone disease should be to achieve a stone-free state.

To assess whether a patient is or is not stone-free, it is best to wait and allow sufficient time for the fragments to pass. Most investigators believe that if fragments are still present at 3 months, they are unlikely to pass[80]; they also bode poorly for recurrent stone disease. Residual stone fragments are associated with a 2- to 3-fold increase in the incidence of stone recurrence within 2 years of treatment (17–22 percent versus 7 percent if the patient was stone-free). Persistent stone fragments in patients with a history of urinary tract infections cause a 10-fold increase in recurrent urinary tract infections (84 versus 6 percent if stone-free).[82]

Treatment results are influenced by many factors[83,84]: (1) stone size, (2) stone location, (3) stone composition, (4) efficacy and quality of stone disintegration, (5) urinary tract anatomy, and (6) metabolic stone management.

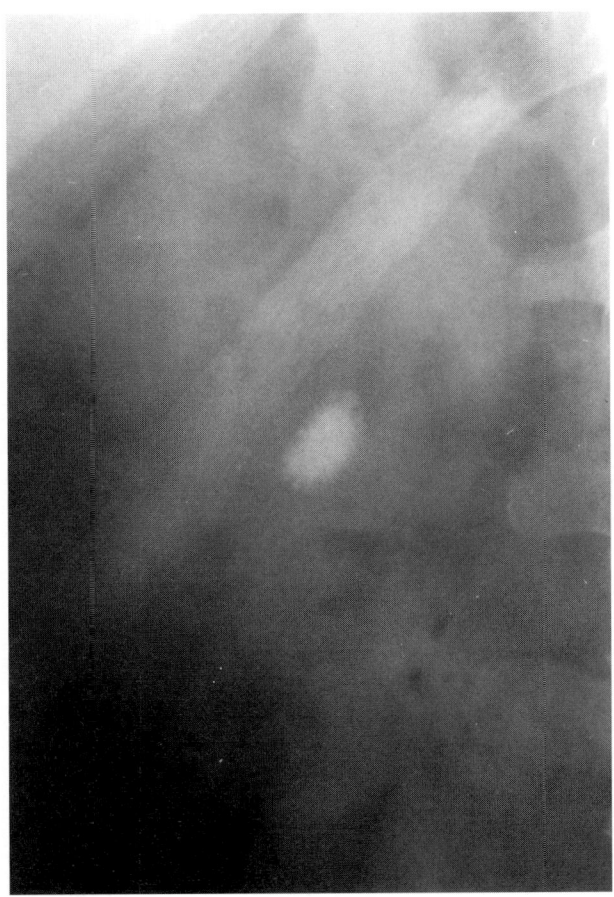

A

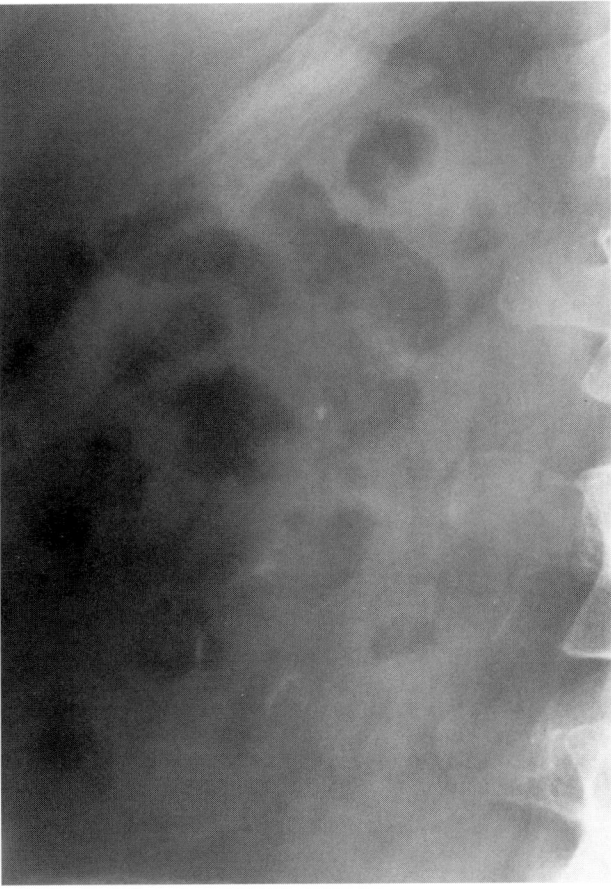

B

Figure 36-16. Satisfactory results with ESWL. (A) Plain film before ESWL demonstrates a 1.5-cm spiculated calcium dihydrate stone in the renal pelvis. (B) After ESWL, only tiny fragments coat the lower pole calices. Fragments can be completely eliminated in a few days or a few weeks. If fragments are still present 3 months after ESWL, they are unlikely to pass.

The choice of therapy as it pertains to stone size has been previously discussed. Stone-free success is greatly influenced by the stone size, with stones that are 1 cm or less in size representing the ideal for ESWL (Fig. 36-16). Riehle[83,84] reported a stone-free rate of 87 percent for stones that were 1 to 2 cm in size, and Graff et al.[85] reported that with stones 1.5 cm or less in size, 85 percent were stone-free at 3 months.

For stones over 2.5 to 3.0 cm in size, PCNL is the preferred treatment in the United States. If large stones are being treated with ESWL monotherapy, many urologists place an indwelling double-pigtail ureteral stent to facilitate the passage of stone fragments and to ensure that the kidney remains unobstructed.

Stone location affects treatment results. Primary ureteral stones rarely (17 percent) have residual fragments after treatment, with most of the fragments accumulating in the lower calices. In most series reporting on ESWL, the lower calices are the most common site for fragment retention. The relative efficacies of ESWL and PCNL in treating lower pole calculi have been previously discussed. Stone-free rates for patients with calculi in the lower calices are less than 60 percent, compared to 75 to 80 percent for stones in the middle and upper calices.

In patients with metabolically active stone disease, fragmentation of a solitary stone into multiple fragments creates multiple niduses for subsequent stone growth.[86,87] In these patients, vigorous treatment of the underlying metabolic abnormality is clearly of prime importance in achieving a long-term stone-free state.

The presence of multiple stones decreases the efficacy of ESWL and the stone-free rate. In one study, the stone-free rate in patients with four or more stones dropped to 30 percent (for comparison, in the same study, the stone-free rate was 82 percent for single stones less than 1 cm in size and 53 percent for 2- to 3-cm stones).[88]

The effect of stone composition on ESWL efficacy has been previously mentioned. Calcium oxalate dihydrate, struvite, and uric acid stones fragment easily with ESWL. Cystine stones, calcium oxalate monohydrate, hydroxyapatite and brushite stones are more resistant to fragmentation with ESWL and thus more likely to produce large fragments that may require either repeat ESWL or endourologic procedures for removal.

Contraindications

The accumulation of clinical experience with ESWL and the availability of advanced lithotripters have greatly minimized the number of absolute and relative contraindications to ESWL. At present, only pregnancy and uncontrolled or uncorrectable coagulopathic conditions are considered to be the absolute contraindications to ESWL. Uncorrected bleeding disorders predispose to intraparenchymal or subcapsular hematomas if ESWL is employed. Therefore, hematologic abnormalities should be corrected prior to ESWL. Anticoagulants, antiinflammatory drugs, and aspirin should be discontinued before the procedure.[89] Several patients with hemophilia have been successfully treated.[90]

Shortly after its introduction, ESWL was believed to be contraindicated in a few clinical situations, which are discussed below. Clinical experience has proven that ESWL can safely be performed in these patients.

Renal arterial aneurysms and aortic aneurysms in proximity to a stone that required treatment were previously regarded to be relative contraindications to ESWL. However, ESWL can be safely performed in such patients without incurring an increased risk of rupture[91,92] and should be considered the treatment of choice if these patients have stones that require treatment and that are suitable for ESWL. Calcification of the renal artery or aorta adjacent to a symptomatic stone is not a contraindication to ESWL because the shock wave energy does not affect arterial calcifications.[10] Similarly, vascular clips in the vicinity of treatment are of no consequence.[93]

Patients with cardiac pacemakers can be treated safely with ESWL. Such patients should be monitored by a cardiologist so that, if necessary, a temporary transvenous pacemaker can be inserted or a pacemaker reprogrammed if it malfunctions as a result of the shock waves.[93-95]

The standard HM-3 lithotripter had traditionally been used with general or epidural anesthesia, which made ESWL a relative contraindication in patients who were at high risk for anesthesia complications. This is no longer a significant factor in most patients because intravenous sedation can be successfully used to treat patients, even with the HM-3 lithotripters.[96] Newer lithotripters may also require less anesthesia because the shock waves are less powerful.[80]

Obese patients present special problems. For the Dornier HM-3 lithotripter, the weight limit is 130 kg. With other machines, although there is no set weight limit, the ability to image and effectively fragment the stone is compromised in obese patients because the stone may be difficult to position in the focal range.

Children who are less than 4 feet in height or 20 pounds in weight can be successfully treated with gantry modifications. In children, care is taken to avoid inadvertently traumatizing tissues near the kidney and ureter (such as bone, lung, gonad, or pancreas). ESWL has not been shown to adversely affect renal growth in children.[97]

A relative contraindication is the coexistence of calculi with obstruction (e.g., ureteral strictures, ureteropelvic junction obstruction) as previously discussed in the section on PCNL. Ureteral obstruction distal to a stone can be managed with ureteral stents or catheters.

Active urinary tract infections require treatment before, during, and after ESWL. Similarly, patients with struvite stones should have their urine cultured and should be treated with antibiotics prior to ESWL.

Complications

ESWL is well tolerated by most patients, and major complications are rare. The complications can be divided into several categories: (1) complications related to the effects of the shock waves on the kidney and adjacent organs; (2) residual stone fragments (see above); (3) complications related to ureteral obstruction due to the passage of stone fragments; and (4) anesthetic and cardiac complications.

Mechanical Effects of Shock Waves

Renal Parenchymal Damage. The number of shock waves that the kidney can safely tolerate at a given kilovoltage is unknown. Shock wave–induced renal parenchymal damage does not cause a measurable reduction in renal function, as judged by serum creatinine and creatinine clearance or excretory urography. There is a transient increase in urinary excretion of enzymes that are specific markers for renal injury, such as gamma-glutamyl transferase, beta-galactosidase, and N-acetyl-beta-glucosaminidase.[98] Some immediate decrease in renal plasma flow has been reported[99] in 30 percent of kidneys treated with ESWL, but no abnormalities were seen on ^{131}I hippurate scans done 4 years after ESWL.[100]

Nearly 100 percent of patients treated with ESWL

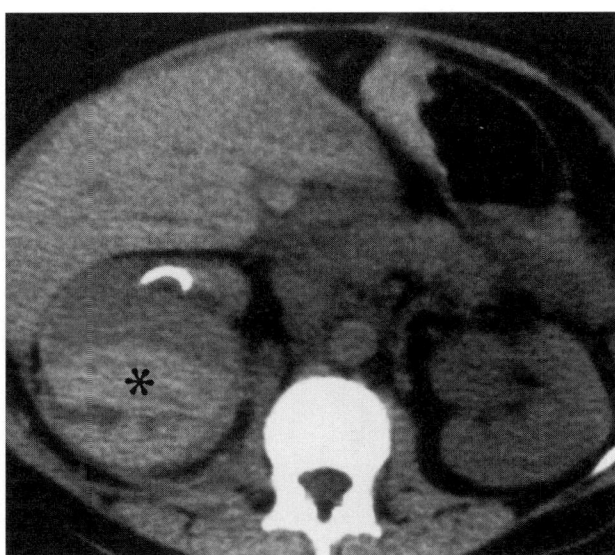

Figure 36-17. Unenhanced CT scan demonstrates a high-density subcapsular hematoma on the posterior aspect of the right kidney (*asterisk*) after ESWL. Note the proximal end of the ureteral stent in the renal pelvis.

have hematuria for the first 24 hours. This reaction is thought to be related to trauma to the renal parenchyma and not to injury to the urothelium by the calculus fragments.

Clinically significant subcapsular or perinephric hematomas have been reported in 0.5 to 2.5 percent of patients and represent the most common, serious extrarenal complication.[101,102] CT is the best modality to evaluate these complications (Fig. 36-17). CT demonstrates[103] perinephric soft tissue stranding and fascial thickening in 70 percent of patients, subcapsular hematomas in 15 percent, and intrarenal contusions in 4 percent. Scans done several months later showed resolution of the hematomas. Similarly, MRI shows swelling of the kidney and fluid in the perinephric, subcapsular, and intraparenchymal regions,[104,105] with changes reverting to normal in 3 months. MRI demonstrates abnormalities in 85 percent of patients[106] treated with ESWL; they consist of loss of the corticomedullary junction in 52 percent of patients, intrarenal hemorrhage in 18 percent, and perinephric changes in 64 percent. Lower-power piezoelectric lithotripters, in contrast, cause demonstrable morphologic changes in only 5 percent of patients (edema in the perinephric space), suggesting that lower-power, small-focal-region piezoelectric lithotripters may induce less acute renal parenchymal damage than higher-power electrohydraulic lithotripters,[107] even though the former require a larger number of shocks to be equally effective in stone fragmentation.

Injury to Adjacent Organs. Damage to neighboring organs is not unexpected after renal ESWL. Sporadic

cases of pancreatitis,[88] bowel hematomas (intramural and mucosal), and transient gastrointestinal erosions with mucosal bleeding have been reported. Colonic ileus is a frequent but transient occurrence after ESWL and usually resolves in 24 to 48 hours.

Pulmonary hemorrhage due to lung damage may be seen if the lower lung is included in the high-shock-wave energy field. This usually occurs with aberrant anatomy such as in myelodysplastic infants and in children. Gallstones have been inadvertently shattered during renal ESWL.

Iliac vein and iliac arterial thrombosis have been reported after ESWL of lower ureteral calculi.

Cutaneous bruising can occur at the shock wave entry site.

Hypertension After Lithotripsy. The occurrence of ESWL-associated hypertension is a source of debate and controversy. Initial reports suggested the new onset of hypertension one or more years after ESWL. Subsequent large series suggest that there is no increased incidence of hypertension after ESWL.[108]

Ureteral Obstruction

Ureteral colic, obstruction, or urosepsis can result from the passage of calculus fragments into the ureter. The fragments can line up in the ureter, simulating the appearance of a cobblestoned street, and are referred to as *steinstrasse*. This complication occurs in 1 to 5 percent of cases, and intervention is required in 6 to 35 percent of cases.[6] Frequently, a larger lead fragment is responsible for the obstruction and the subsequent piling up of fragments proximally. Steinstrasse occurs 75 percent of the time in the distal ureter, 18 percent in the proximal ureter, and 6 percent in the midureter. Fragments can often pass spontaneously, and interventions are reserved for patients with pain, total obstruction, particularly of a solitary kidney, urosepsis, and failure to pass fragments (Fig. 36-18). It is not uncommon for patients to be asymptomatic despite urinary obstruction and impaired renal function, the obstruction being diagnosed on a routine post-ESWL urogram. If intervention is required, ureteroscopic removal of the lead fragment, ureteral meatotomy, or ureteroscopic lithotripsy followed by stenting is helpful. Another option is to drain the kidney by means of a percutaneous nephrostomy and allow the fragments to pass spontaneously (which they often do). For large steinstrasse (greater than one-third ureteral length), a combined percutaneous and ureteroscopic approach may be required. Upper ureteral steinstrasse may also be treated by repeat ESWL to the "lead" fragment.

Prophylactic ureteral stenting is often used before ESWL to prevent ureteral obstruction when large stones are being treated. Until recently, it was generally believed that ureteral stents increased the speed of stone fragment passage while reducing the incidence of colic. It appears that stents are useful for preventing obstruction and sepsis after lithotripsy but do not necessarily facilitate the passage of stone fragments.[109]

Sepsis. Zero to 1.5 percent of patients may develop septic complications after ESWL.[5] Aggressive treatment of urinary tract infections prior to ESWL can reduce the incidence of this complication. In addition, patients with large infection stones (staghorn stones) should be treated with ureteral stenting or percutaneous nephrostomy after or preferably before ESWL to prevent the large volume of fragments from precipitating a urinary obstruction. Rarely, lithotripsy of an infected stone can lead to the development of a perinephric abscess.[110]

Cardiac and Anesthetic Complications

Anesthetic complications are self-evident. Arrythmias can be provoked by the effect of the shock waves on the myocardium, especially at high treatment voltages. Use of a gating system so that shock waves discharge only during the refractory period of the heart, following the R wave, can prevent arrythmias[5] by preventing aberrant electrical stimulation.

Body warming due to immersion in the water bath of the HM-3 unit can cause vasodilation, central blood pooling, and cardiac stress in patients with severe heart disease.

Treatment of Ureteral Calculi

Management of ureteral calculi is largely determined by their location.

Proximal Ureteral Calculi

Stones in the upper ureter can be treated by ESWL either in situ in the ureter or after displacement into the kidney (by forceful retrograde injection of saline or contrast or sometimes by simple advancement of a retrograde catheter). The success rate of fragmentation is higher, with stone-free rates approaching 100 percent when upper ureteral stones are pushed into the kidney and treated with ESWL.[85,111,112] In contrast, in situ therapy is successful in 60 to 85 percent of cases. In situ ESWL of ureteral calculi generally requires a higher kilovoltage and more shock waves than for kidney stones.

Upper and midureteral calculi can also be approached in a percutaneous, antegrade fashion. In one series,[113] 35 of 37 proximal ureteral calculi and 20 of 20 midureteral calculi were successfully removed by flexible nephroscopy. The stones were removed under direct vision, basketed under fluoroscopy, or frag-

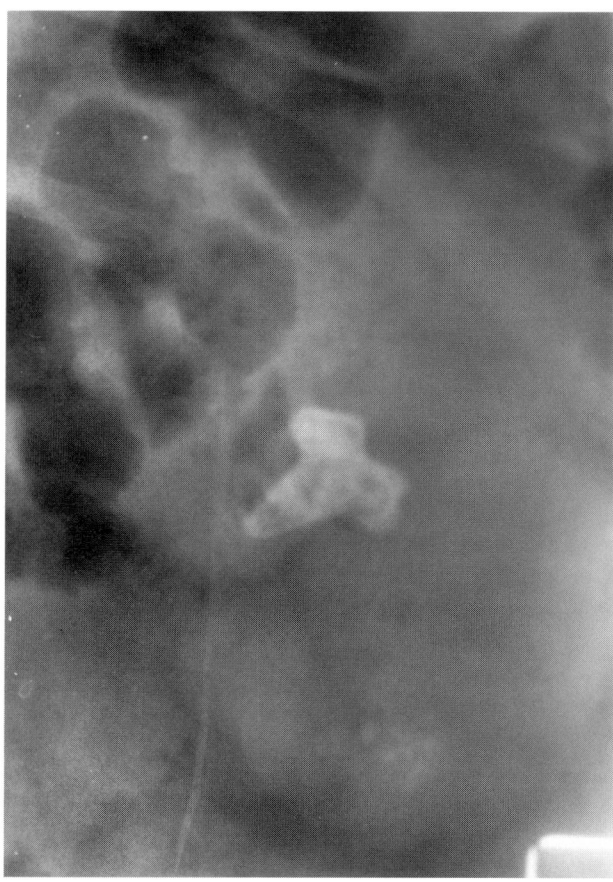

A

Figure 36-18. Obstructing steinstrasse after ESWL. (A) Plain radiograph shows a partial left staghorn calculus in a patient with a solitary kidney. The patient was treated with ESWL. (B) One week later, the serum creatinine level was found to be markedly elevated, to 17 mg. The patient was asymptomatic. Radiograph demonstrates ureteral steinstrasse and residual lower pole fragments. (C) An emergent percutaneous nephrostomy was performed for renal decompression. The ureteral fragments eventually cleared spontaneously.

mented with ultrasonic or electrohydraulic lithotripsy and then removed.

Midureteral Calculi

When ureteral stones overlie the pelvic bones, ESWL has to be performed in the prone position so that the shock waves do not have to traverse the pelvic bones. The prone position can also be used to treat some horseshoe kidneys, pelvic kidneys,[114,115] and calculi in the distal ureter or at the ureterovesical junction.

Distal Ureteral Calculi

The optimal therapy for lower ureteral calculi is the subject of considerable debate and controversy, centered primarily on whether ureteroscopy or ESWL is

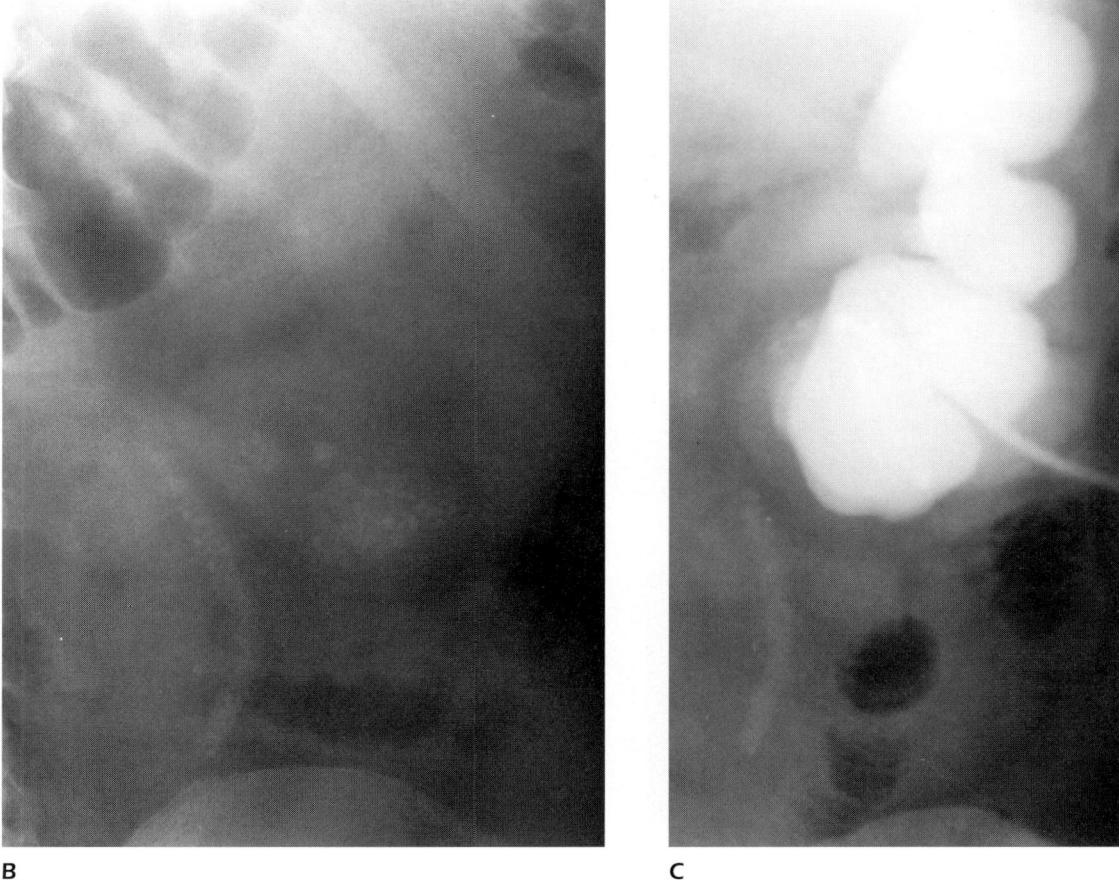

B

C

Figure 36-18 (continued).

the better modality. Transurethral ureteroscopy is a natural extension of ureteroscopic techniques and is being increasingly used by urologists for both diagnostic and therapeutic purposes, largely because of the current availability of smaller, more flexible ureteroscopes that can easily be maneuvered even into the proximal and midureter. Rigid ureteroscopes, in contrast, are difficult to advance past the iliac vessel crossing and are therefore limited in their application on a routine basis (except for calculi lodged at the ureterovesical junction). In the United States, ureteroscopic removal of distal ureteral calculi is favored, whereas European urologists more often use ESWL in these patients. Ureteroscopy has a higher initial success rate than ESWL in the treatment of distal ureteral stones, with reported success rates of greater than 95 percent. However, ureteroscopy is more invasive, has a higher complication rate (primarily ureteral avulsion or perforation and ureteral stricture formation due to trauma caused by the ureteroscope or the stone fragmentation device[116]), and is extremely operator dependent. The success of ureteroscopic stone retrieval decreases the higher the stone is in the ureter; reported success rates

are 38 percent for upper ureteral calculi, 50 percent for stones in the midureter, and 96 percent for the distal ureter.[117] The converse is true for ESWL.

Small stones that are less than 5 mm in diameter are removed under direct ureteroscopic guidance with baskets or instruments. It is important to note that the very small working channel (2–4 French) of flexible ureteroscopes limits the size of the instruments that can be used for stone extraction. Larger stones (>5 mm) are often difficult to grasp with small baskets or forceps and require fragmentation with direct contact fragmentation devices (pulsed dye laser lithotripsy or electrohydraulic lithotripsy) for successful stone removal. Blind passage of cystoscopically guided baskets into the ureter in a retrograde fashion is rare today because of the availability of ureteroscopy (Fig. 36-19).

The necessity for placement of ureteral stents when treating ureteral calculi with ESWL is also controversial, with many authors believing that ureteral stones can be treated just as successfully without stents bypassing the stone. When a stent is placed past a stone, it allows urine to surround the calculus and thus

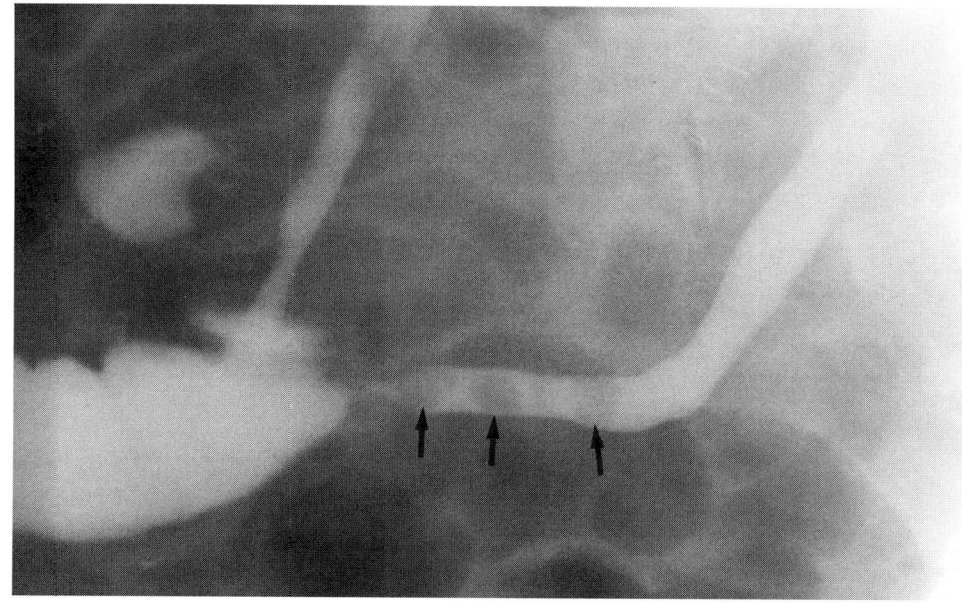

A

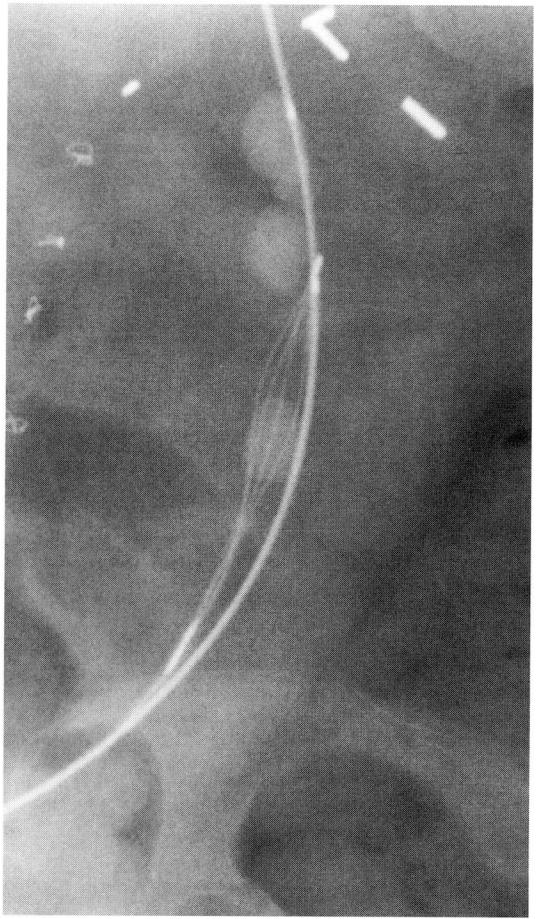

B

C

Figure 36-19. Distal ureteral calculi in a patient with ileal conduit urinary diversion. (A) Loopogram demonstrates three calculi (*arrows*) in the left ureter, just proximal to the ureteroileal anastomosis. (B) Sheath and guidewire placed proximal to the calculi. (C) The calculi were removed by bas-keting under fluoroscopy. Diverted ureters are difficult to approach by ureteroscopy but can be easily catheterized with fluoroscopic guidance if the ureteroileal anastomoses are not strictured.

creates a fluid-filled expansion chamber around the stone. This is thought to facilitate stone fragmentation by allowing the disintegrated outer fragments to fall away while the shock waves disintegrate the core of the calculus. Previous reports had suggested that only 78 percent of ureteral calculi treated in situ without a stent were completely disintegrated, compared to 90 percent of stones when bypass stent placement was possible.[118] Dretler et al.[119] reported 60 percent successful disintegration in situ without a stent and 100 percent after stent placement. However, other reports[120,121] suggest that ureteral calculi can be successfully fragmented without stent placement with high rates of success—77 percent after one treatment and 97 percent overall.

Summary

ESWL is the treatment of choice for upper ureteral calculi and has higher success rates if the stone can be pushed back into the kidney. These calculi can also be approached in a percutaneous, antegrade fashion. In the midureter, most authors favor ureteroscopic extraction of calculi or retrograde displacement of the calculus into the kidney followed by ESWL. ESWL with the patient prone is yet another option. For distal ureteral stones, ureteroscopic extraction is probably the technique of choice[122] because of its high initial success rate, the rare need for secondary treatments and postureteroscopic interventions, and the low complication rate of ureteroscopy in the distal ureter. However, the treatment of choice for distal ureteral calculi is not settled, and there are many institutional and individual variations.

Ureterolithotomy for stone removal is unusual because there are so many other viable treatment options. Rarely, stones that are impacted or embedded in the ureter may require open surgical removal. ESWL has been successfully used to fragment stones that were entrapped within stone baskets[123] and also to fragment calculus encrustations on indwelling ureteral stents, thus permitting their removal.[124]

References

1. Fernstrom I, Johannson B. Percutaneous pyelolithotomy: a new extraction technique. Scand J Urol Nephrol 1976;10:257.
2. Segura JW. Surgical management of urinary calculi. Semin Nephrol 1990;10:53–63.
3. Segura JW. Percutaneous nephrolithotomy: technique, indications and complications. AUA Update Series 1993;12:154–159.
4. Lingeman JE. Staghorn stones: the continued challenge. AUA Update Series 1993;12:146–151.
5. Roth RA, Beckmann CF. Complications of extracorporeal shock wave lithotripsy and percutaneous nephrolithotomy. Urol Clin North Am 1988;15:155.
6. Fedullo LM, Pollack HM, Banner MP, et al. The development of steinstrassen after ESWL: frequency, natural history and radiologic management. AJR 1988;151:1145–1147.
7. Streem SB, Lammert G. Long term efficacy of combination therapy for struvite staghorn calculi. J Urol 1992;147:563.
8. Schulze H, Hertle L, Kutlar A, et al. Critical evaluation of treatment of staghorn calculi by percutaneous nephrolithotomy and ESWL. J Urol 1989;141:822–825.
9. Miller K, Bachor R, Sauter T, et al. Percutaneous nephrolithotomy/ESWL vs stent/ESWL for large stones and staghorn calculi: what have we learned? J Endourol 1989;3:287.
10. Chaussy CG, Fuchs GJ. Current state and future developments of noninvasive treatment of human urinary stones with extracorporeal shock wave lithotripsy. J Urol 1989;141:782.
11. Constantinides C, Recker F, Jaegar P, et al. Extracorporeal shock wave lithotripsy as monotherapy of staghorn renal calculi: 3 years' experience. J Urol 1989;142:1415.
12. Chibber PJ. Percutaneous nephrolithotomy for large and staghorn calculi. J Endourol 1993;7:293–295.
13. Patterson DE, Segura JW, LeRoy AJ. Long term follow up of patients treated by percutaneous ultrasonic lithotripsy for struvite staghorn calculi. J Endourol 1987;1:777.
14. VanDeursen H, Baert L. Extracorporeal shock wave lithotripsy monotherapy for staghorn stones with the second generation lithotripters. J Urol 1990;143:252.
15. Lingeman JE, Coury TA, Newman DM, et al. Comparison of results and morbidity of percutaneous nephrostolithotomy and extracorporeal shock wave lithotripsy. J Urol 1987;138:485.
16. Beckmann CF, Roth RA, Bihrle W. Dilatation of benign ureteral strictures. Radiology 1989;172:437–441.
17. Gerber GS, Lyon ES. Endopyelotomy: patient selection, results and complications. Urology 1994;43:2–10.
18. Grasso M, Lang G, Loisides P, et al. Endoscopic management of the symptomatic caliceal diverticular calculus. J Urol 1995;153:1878–1881.
19. Middleton AW, Pfister RC. Stone containing pyelocalyceal diverticulum: embryogenic, anatomic, radiologic and clinical characteristics. J Urol 1974;111:2–6.
20. Wulfsohn MA. Pyelocaliceal diverticula. J Urol 1980;123:1–8.
21. Psihramis KE, Dretler SP. Extracorporeal shock wave lithotripsy of caliceal diverticula calculi. J Urol 1987;138:707–711.
22. Ritchie AWS, Parr NJ, Moussa SA, et al. Lithotripsy for calculi in caliceal diverticula? Br J Urol 1990;66:6–8.
23. Hendrikx AJM, Bierkens AF, Bos R, et al. Treatment of stones in caliceal diverticula: extracorporeal shock wave lithotripsy versus percutaneous nephrolitholapaxy. Br J Urol 1992;70:478–482.
24. Streem SB, Yost A. Treatment of caliceal diverticular calculi with extracorporeal shock-wave lithotripsy: patient selection and extended follow up. J Urol 1992;148:1043–1046.
25. Ellis JH, Patterson SK, Sonda LP, et al. Stones and infection in renal caliceal diverticula: treatment with percutaneous procedures. AJR 1991;156:995–1000.
26. Bellman GC, Silverstein JI, Blickensderfer S, et al. Technique and follow up of percutaneous management of caliceal diverticula. Urology 1993;42:21–25.
27. Pang K, David R, Fuchs GJ. Treatment of stones in caliceal diverticula using retrograde endoscopic approach: critical assessment after 2 years (abstr). J Endourol 1992;6:(Suppl) F-15.
28. Lang EK. Percutaneous infundibuloplasty: management of calyceal diverticula and infundibular stenosis. Radiology 1991;181:871–877.

29. Fuchs AM, David RD, Fuchs GJ. Treatment of stones in caliceal diverticuli using retrograde endoscopic approach. J Endourol 1990;4:109.

30. Meretyk I, Meretyk S, Clayman RV. Endopyelotomy: comparison of ureteroscopic retrograde and antegrade techniques. J Urol 1992;148:775–783.

31. Lingeman JE, Siegel YI, Steele B, et al. Management of lower pole nephrolithiasis: a critical analysis. J Urol 1994;151:663–667.

32. Graff J, Diederichs W, Schulze H. Long-term follow up in 1003 extracorporeal shock wave lithotripsy patients. J Urol 1988;140:479.

33. McCullough DL. Extracorporeal shock wave lithotripsy and residual stone fragments in lower calices: letter to the editor. J Urol 1989;141:140.

34. Siegel YI, Lingeman JE. Percutaneous transilial access for stone removal in crossed fused renal ectopia. Urology 42:82–85, 1993.

35. Segura JW, Patterson DE, LeRoy AJ, et al. Percutaneous removal of kidney stones: review of 1000 cases. J Urol 1985;134:1077–1081.

36. Lee CK, Smith AD. Percutaneous transperitoneal approach to the pelvic kidney for endourologic removal of calculus: three cases with two successes. J Endourol 1992;6:133–135.

37. Toth C, Holman E, Pasztor I, et al. Laparoscopically controlled and assisted percutaneous transperitoneal nephrolithotomy in a pelvic dystopic kidney. J Endourol 1993;7:303–305.

38. Monga M, Castaneda-Zuniga WR, Thomas R. Femoral neuropathy following percutaneous nephrolithotomy of a pelvic kidney. Urology 1995;45:1059–1061.

39. Hockley NM, Lingeman JE, Hutchinson CL. Relative efficacy of extracorporeal shock wave lithotripsy and percutaneous nephrostolithotomy in the management of cystine calculi. J Endourol 1989;3:273.

40. Motola JA, Smith AD. Therapeutic options for the management of upper tract calculi. Urol Clin North Am 1990;17:191.

41. Knoll LD, Segura JW, Patterson DE. Long term follow up in patients with cystine urinary calculi treated by percutaneous ultrasonic lithotripsy. J Urol 1988;140:246.

42. Horowitz E, Schmidt JD. Renal calculi in pregnancy. Clin Obstet Gynecol 1985;28:324–338.

43. MacNeily AE, Goldenberg SL, Allen GJ, et al. Sonographic visualization of the ureter in pregnancy. J Urol 1991;146:298–301.

44. Loughlin KR. Management of urologic problems during pregnancy. Urology 1994;44:159.

45. Cass AS, Smith CS, Gleich P. Management of urinary calculi in pregnancy. Urology 1986;28:370–372.

46. Drago JR, Rohner TJ, Chez RA. Management of urinary calculi in pregnancy. Urology 1982;20:578–581.

47. Loughlin KR, Bailey RB Jr. Internal ureteral stents for conservative management of ureteral calculi during pregnancy. N Engl J Med 1986;315:1647–1649.

48. Wolf MC, Hallander JB, Salisz JA, et al. A new technique for ureteral stent placement during pregnancy using endoluminal ultrasound. Surg Obstet Gynecol 1992;175:575–576.

49. Goldfarb RA, Neerhut GJ, Lederer E. Management of acute hydronephrosis of pregnancy by ureteral stenting: risk of stone formation. J Urol 1989;141:921–922.

50. Spirnak JP, Resnick MI. Stone formation as a complication of indwelling ureteral stents: a report of 5 cases. J Urol 1985;134:349–351.

51. Shnider SM, Webster GM. Maternal and fetal hazards of surgery during pregnancy. Am J Obstet Gynecol 1965;92:891–900.

52. Bush WH, Brannen GE, Burnett LL, et al. Ultrasonic renal lithotripsy: single stage percutaneous technique and adjuvant radiological procedures. Radiology 1984;152:387–390.

53. LeRoy AJ, May GR, Segura JW, et al. Percutaneous ultrasonic lithotripsy. Radiol Clin North Am 1984;22:427–432.

54. Lingeman JE, Smith LH, Woods JR, et al. Percutaneous procedures. In: Urinary calculi: ESWL, endourology and medical therapy. Philadelphia: Lea & Febiger, 1989:322–359.

55. Feagins BA, Preminger GM. Options in stone management. In: Stein BS, ed. Clinical urologic practice. New York: Norton, 1995:523.

56. Mahaffey KG, Bolton DM, Stoller ML. Urologist directed percutaneous nephrostomy tube placement. J Urol 1994;152:1973–1976.

57. Smith AD. Percutaneous punctures—is this the endourologist's turf? J Urol 1994;152:1982–1983.

58. Narasimhan DL, Jacobsson B, Vijayan P, et al. Percutaneous nephrolithotomy through an intercostal approach. Acta Radiol 1991;32:162–165.

59. Fuchs EF, Forsyth MJ. Supercostal approach for percutaneous ultrasonic lithotripsy. Urol Clin North Am 1990;17:99–102.

60. Hopper KD, Yakes WF. The posterior intercostal approach for percutaneous renal procedures: risk of puncturing the lung, spleen and liver as determined by CT. AJR 1990;154:115–117.

61. Hosking DH. Retrograde nephrostomy: experience with two techniques. J Urol 1986;135:1146.

62. Hunter PT, Hawkins IF, Finlayson B, et al. Hawkins-Hunter retrograde transcutaneous nephrostomy: a new technique. Urology 1983;23:583–587.

63. LeRoy AJ, May GR, Segura JW, et al. Rapid dilatation of percutaneous nephrostomy tracks. AJR 1984;142:355–357.

64. Lang EK, Glorioso LW. Multiple percutaneous access routes to multiple calculi, calculi in caliceal diverticula and staghorn calculi. Radiology 1986;158:211–214.

65. Mercado S, Hunter DW, Castaneda-Zuniga WR. The double puncture: an effective percutaneous technique for removing complex, multiple renal calculi. Radiology 1986;158:207–209.

66. Regan JS, Shang Lam H, Lingeman JE. Simultaneous bilateral percutaneous nephrolithotomy. J Endourol 1992;6:245–247.

67. Patterson DE, Segura JW, LeRoy AJ, et al. The etiology and treatment of delayed bleeding following percutaneous lithotripsy. J Urol 1985;133:447.

68. Stoller ML, Wolf JS, St Lezin MA. Estimated blood loss and transfusion rates associated with percutaneous nephrolithotomy. J Urol 1994;152:1977–1981.

69. Clayman RV, Surya V, Hunter D, et al. Renal vascular complications associated with the percutaneous removal of renal calculi. J Urol 1984;132:228.

70. Kernohan RM, Johnston LC, Donaldson RA. Bleeding following percutaneous nephrolithotomy resulting in loss of the kidney. Br J Urol 1990;65:657.

71. Kalash SS, Young JD Jr. Serious complications associated with percutaneous nephrolithotomy. Urology 1987;29:290.

72. Hopper KD, Sherman JL, Williams MD, et al. The variable anteroposterior position of the retroperitoneal colon to the kidneys. Invest Radiol 1987;22:298–302.

73. LeRoy AJ, Williams HJ, Bender CE, et al. Colon perforation following percutaneous nephrostomy and renal calculus removal. Radiology 1985;155:83–85.

74. Vallancien G, Capdeville R, Veillon B, et al. Colonic perforation during percutaneous nephrolithotomy: case report. J Urol 1985;134:1185.

75. Verstandig AG, Banner MP, VanArsdalen KN, et al. Upper urinary tract calculi: extrusion into perinephric and periureteric tissues during percutaneous management. Radiology 1986;158:215–218.

76. Sardina JI, Bolton DM, Stoller ML. Entrapped Malecot nephrostomy tube: etiology and management. J Urol 1995;153:1882–1883.

77. Stewart LH, Kernohan RM, Loughbridge WGG. Nephrostomy tubes resistant to removal. Br J Urol 1992;70:213.

78. Koolpe HA, Lord B. Eccentric nephroscopy for the incarcerated nephrostomy. Urol Radiol 1990;12:96.

79. Lingeman JE, Newman D, Mertz JHO, et al. Extracorporeal

shock wave lithotripsy: the Methodist Hospital of Indiana experience. J Urol 1986;135:1134.

80. McCullough DL. Extracorporeal shock wave lithotripsy. In: Walsh PC, Retik AB, Stamey TA, et al, eds. Campbell's urology. Philadelphia: Saunders, 1992:2157–2182.

81. Chaussy CG, Fuchs GJ. Extracorporeal shock wave lithotripsy (ESWL) for the treatment of upper urinary tract stones. In: Gillenwater JY, et al, eds. Adult and pediatric urology. Chicago: Year Book, 1987, chapter 20.

82. Clayman RV, McClennan BL, Garvin TJ, et al. An electromagnetic acoustic shock wave unit for extracorporeal lithotripsy. J Endourol 1989;3:307.

83. Riehle RA, Naslund EB, Fair W, et al. Impact of shock wave lithotripsy on upper urinary tract calculi. Urology 1986;28:261.

84. Riehle RA, Naslund EB. Patient management and results after ESWL. In: Riehle RA, Newman DM, eds. Principles of extracorporeal shock wave lithotripsy. New York: Churchill-Livingstone, 1989:121.

85. Graff J, Pastor J, Funke PJ, et al. Extracorporeal shock wave lithotripsy for ureteral stones: a retrospective analysis of 417 cases. J Urol 1988;139:513.

86. Segura JW. Role of percutaneous procedures in the management of renal calculi. Urol Clin North Am 1990;17:207.

87. Fine JK, Pak CYC, Preminger GM. Residual fragments following ESWL—the role of medical management. J Urol 1992;2(147):79.

88. Drach GW, Dretler S, Fair W, et al. Report of the United States cooperative study of extracorporeal shock wave lithotripsy. J Urol 1986;135:1127.

89. McCullough DL. Complications of ESWL. Probl Urol 1988; 1:604.

90. Christensen JG, McCullough DL, Cline WA Sr. Extracorporeal shock wave lithotripsy in hemophiliac patient. Urology 1989;33:424.

91. Deliveliotis CH, Kostakopoulos A, Stavropoulose E, et al. Extracorporeal shock wave lithotripsy in 5 patients with aortic aneurysm. J Urol 1995;154:1671–1672.

92. Thomas R, Cherry R, Neal DW Jr. The use of extracorporeal shock wave lithotripsy in patients with aortic aneurysms. J Urol 1991;146:409.

93. Abber JD, Langberg J, Mueller SC, et al. Cardiovascular pathology and extracorporeal shock wave lithotripsy. J Urol 1988;140:408.

94. Asroff SW, Kingston TE, Stein BS. Extracorporeal shock wave lithotripsy in patient with cardiac pacemaker in an abdominal location: case report and review of the literature. J Endourol 1993;7:189–192.

95. Drach GW, Weber C, Donovan JM. Treatment of pacemaker patients with extracorporeal shock wave lithotripsy: experience from 2 continents. J Urol 1990;143:895.

96. Petterson B, Tiselius HG, Anderson A, et al. Evaluation of extracorporeal shock wave lithotripsy without anesthesia using a Dornier HM-3 lithotripster without technical modification. J Urol 1989;142:1189.

97. Adams MC, Newman DM, Lingeman JE. Pediatric ESWL: long-term results and effects on renal growth. J Endourol 1989;3:245.

98. Assimos DG, Boyce WH, Gurr EG, et al. Selective elevation of urinary enzyme levels after extracorporeal shock wave lithotripsy. J Urol 1989;142:687.

99. Kaude JV, Williams CM, Millner MR, et al. Renal morphology and function immediately after extracorporeal shock wave lithotripsy. AJR 1985;145:305.

100. Chaussy CG, Fuchs GJ. Extracorporeal shock wave lithotripsy. Monogr Urol 1987;4:80.

101. Krysiewicz S. Complications of renal extracorporeal shock wave lithotripsy reviewed. Urol Radiol 1992;13:139–145.

102. Papanicolaou N, Stafford SA, Pfister RC, et al. Significant renal hemorrhage following extracorporeal shock wave lithotripsy: imaging and clinical features. Radiology 1987;163:661–664.

103. Rubin JI, Arger PH, Pollack HM. Kidney changes after extracorporeal shock wave lithotripsy: CT evaluation. Radiology 1987;162:21.

104. Baumgartner BR, Dickey KW, Ambrose SS, et al. Kidney changes after extracorporeal shock wave lithotripsy: appearance on MR imaging. Radiology 1987;163:531.

105. Dyer RB, Karstaedt N, McCullough DL, et al. Magnetic resonance imaging evaluation of immediate and intermediate changes in kidneys treated with extracorporeal shock wave lithotripsy. J Lithotripsy Stone Dis 1990;2:302.

106. Knapp PM, Scott JW. Magnetic resonance imaging following extracorporeal shock wave lithotripsy with the Dornier HM-3 lithotripter. J Urol 1987;132:287A.

107. Wilson WT, Miller G, Morris JS, et al. Morphologic renal changes following piezoelectric and spark gap lithotripsy. In: Lingeman JE, Newman DM, eds. Shock wave lithotripsy II: urinary and biliary. New York: Plenum, 1989.

108. Lingeman JE, Newman DM, Mosbaugh PG, et al. The risk of hypertension following various forms of treatment for urolithiasis. J Urol 1989;141:241A.

109. Banner MP. Extracorporeal shock wave lithotripsy: selection of patients and long term complications. Radiol Clin North Am 1991;29:543–556.

110. Karamalegos AZ, Diokno AC, Moylan DF. Formation of perinephric abscess following extracorporeal shock wave lithotripsy. Urology 1989;34:277.

111. Lingeman JE, Shirrell WL, Newman DM, et al. Management of upper ureteral calculi with extracorporeal shock wave lithotripsy. J Urol 1987;138:720.

112. Fuchs GJ, Chaussy CG, Stenzl A. Current management concepts in the treatment of ureteral stones. J Endourol 1988;2:107.

113. Kahn RI. Endourological treatment of ureteral calculi. J Urol 1986;135:239–243.

114. Locke DR, Newman RC, Sternbock GS, et al. Extracorporeal shock wave lithotripsy in horseshoe kidneys. Urology 1990;35:407.

115. Jenkins AD, Gillenwater JY. Extracorporeal shock wave lithotripsy in the prone position: treatment of stones in the distal ureter or anomalous kidney. J Urol 1988;139:911.

116. Kramolowsky EV. Complications of ureteroscopy. Semin Urol 1989;7:39–42.

117. Kostakopoulos A, Sofras F, Karayiannis A, et al. Ureterolithotripsy: report of 1000 cases. Br J Urol 1989;63:243.

118. Lingeman JE, Smith LH, Woods JR, et al. Percutaneous procedures. In: Urinary calculi: ESWL, endourology and medical therapy. Philadelphia: Lea & Febiger, 1989:198.

119. Dretler SP, Weinstein A. A modified algorithm for the management of ureteral calculi: 100 consecutive cases. J Urol 1988;140:732–736.

120. Barr JD, Tegtmeyer CJ, Jenkins AD. In situ lithotripsy of ureteral calculi: review of 261 cases. Radiology 1990;174:103–108.

121. Becht E, Mohl V, Neisius D, et al. Treatment of prevesical ureteral calculi by extracorporeal shock wave lithotripsy. J Urol 1988;139:916.

122. Banner MP, VanArsdalen KN, Pollack HM. Extracorporeal shock wave lithotripsy of ureteral calculi. Radiology 1990;174:12–14.

123. Durano AC, Hanosh JJ. A new alternative for entrapped stone basket in the distal ureter. J Urol 1988;139:116.

124. Flam TA, Brochard M, Zerbib M, et al. Extracorporeal shock wave lithotripsy to remove calcified ureteral stents. Urology 1990;36:164.

37

The Lower Genitourinary Tract

FLAVIO CASTAÑEDA
JOSÉ M. HERNANDEZ-GRAULAU

*I*n recent years, we have witnessed a proliferation of interventional radiologic techniques and procedures, largely because of impressive technological advances and the continuous search for simpler, less invasive, and less costly procedures. These advances have reduced costs and significantly decreased the morbidity and mortality associated with the surgical procedures used to treat various conditions.

This technologic revolution has affected the management of lower genitourinary tract disease. Many old therapeutic techniques have been replaced, improved, or combined with surgical techniques, resulting in better outcomes. The development of transrectal ultrasound is one of these major advances. In the late 1960s, the experimental work of Watanabe et al.[1] on the diagnostic application of transrectal ultrasound set the stage for the development of high-resolution axial and sagittal imaging of the prostate. This technology has produced significant advances in the early detection and staging of prostatic cancer because its high sensitivity allows for directed biopsies of abnormal or equivocal areas. Transrectal ultrasound has also helped in the imaging and intervention of other perineal structures, such as the seminal vesicles, bladder, and rectum.

Balloon catheter technology has also progressed, from the early Gruntzig design to the current designs that provide almost limitless accessibility. This technology has allowed for access to anterior urethral strictures that were previously impassable or inaccessible by either an antegrade or retrograde approach. This therapeutic modality is less traumatic than the use of bougies, which are sometimes impossible to advance through the more severe strictures. Special large balloons with small profiles have been developed for prostatic urethroplasty, one of the nonsurgical treatments of benign prostatic hyperplasia (BPH).[2-6]

Metal stent technology, initially used intravascularly and later applied to almost all body systems, has also been applied to the genitourinary system. *Hyperthermia,* used initially for tumor shrinking and ablation, is now being tried in humans for BPH and carcinoma. *Hypothermia,* used for carcinoma, is yielding excellent preliminary results in the prostate. Because interventional radiologists either conceptualized or developed most of these advances, they have assumed an ever-increasing role in the management of lower urinary tract disease.

The Bladder

The bladder is the end point of almost all upper genitourinary interventions that drain or bypass upper collecting or ureteral obstructions. It also serves as a temporary reservoir for stones or other foreign bodies that cannot be removed through the nephrostomy tracts. However, there are very few specific indications for direct bladder access.

Interventional Procedures in the Bladder

Although voiding cystourethrograms (VCUGs) are performed most satisfactorily with the use of a urethral catheter in the vast majority of patients, the suprapubic route has been advocated as a way of avoiding ascending infection and for use in patients in whom transurethral catheterization is either difficult or contraindicated.[7] This is exactly the same access used in a suprapubic cystostomy for temporary or permanent bladder drainage. Percutaneous puncture is made 2 to 3 fingerbreadths above the symphysis pubis in the midline, after the area is infiltrated with a local anesthetic. To enter the bladder, a 19-gauge sheathed needle (such as the Amplatz needle, Becton-Dickinson Co.) is directed 10 degrees cranially to avoid damage to the bladder neck. Once the bladder has been entered, contrast material can be injected to fill the bladder to perform the VCUG, or a straight floppy-tip guidewire can be advanced and coiled in the bladder and a 10 to 12 French self-retaining pigtail catheter deployed over the guidewire, after dilation of the tract, if a cystostomy catheter is needed. To prevent urine leakage, taut tension is placed on the catheter until the tract matures. If longer catheters are needed, Councill catheters of the desired caliber can be placed either through peelaway sheaths or with the Councill stiffening rods.

The Urethra

The Male Urethra

The male urethra is a fibroelastic structure that extends from the internal urethral orifice at the vesical neck to the external urethral meatus at the tip of the glans penis. It is divided by the urogenital diaphragm into three parts: prostatic, membranous, and penile (Fig. 37-1). The prostatic urethra is the widest, and about

3 cm long in normal adults. The lumen of the urethra is distensible but normally is obliterated by elastic fibers that cause apposition of its anterior and posterior walls. In prostatic lateral lobe hyperplasia, the urethral wall is changed into a wide anteroposterior fissure by encroachment of the enlarged lateral lobes on the urethra.

The urethral crest extends along the posterior floor of the urethra from its origin on the vesical trigone to its bifurcated end. The prostatic sinus is a depressed fossa on each side of the crest and has many orifices from prostatic ducts. The seminal colliculus or verumontanum is the greatest prominence of the urethral crest, and the prostatic utricle opens in its central surface. The finer, slitlike orifices of the ejaculatory ducts open beside the prostatic utricle.

Figure 37-1. Schematic representation of the male lower genitourinary tract (A) showing its relationships with the pelvic organs and structures and (B) showing in more detail the different structures and portions of the urethra and bladder.

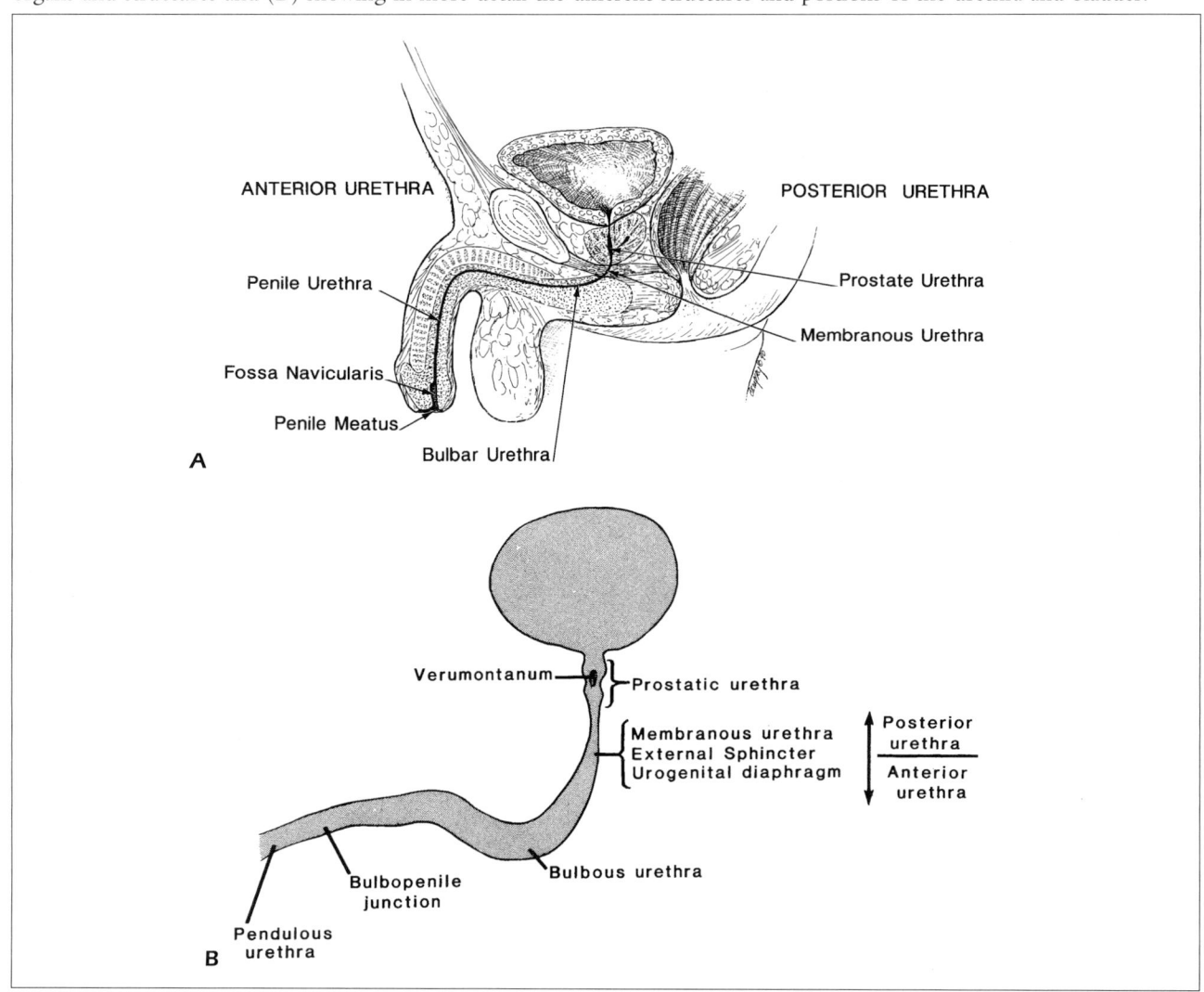

The membranous urethra is the shortest, about 1.5 cm long, and passes through the urogenital diaphragm between its superior and inferior layers of fascia. This part of the urethra has no proper surrounding tissue but contains the circular fibers of the deep transverse perineal muscle, called the external urethral sphincter. This is a voluntary muscle controlled by the perineal branch of the internal pudendal nerve.

Behind the membranous urethra, close to the inferior layer of the urogenital diaphragm, lie the bulbourethral glands of Cowper, which open into the penile urethra at its bulbous part on each side.

The penile urethra is the longest segment and is surrounded by the spongy body. It is about 15 cm long when the penis is flaccid and has a right-angled curve at the penoscrotal junction. The bulbous urethra is dilated and forms the perineal curve. Openings of the bulbourethral glands of Cowper lie at its posterior wall. On the floor of the penile urethra are numerous small lacunae and mucosal glands, known as the glands of Littre. The external meatus is the narrowest part of the urethra. The preterminal urethra, next to the meatus, has a dilated lumen known as the fossa navicularis. The function of the fossa navicularis may be to convert the energy of the narrow, but faster, urinary stream in the distal urethra into a slower stream, but with higher pressure. The result is increased velocity as the stream passes through the narrow meatus; the increased velocity provides a jet for directing the stream to prevent self-contamination. The arterial supply to the urethra is derived from branches of the internal pudendal and inferior vesical arteries. Veins drain into the pudendal and perivesical plexuses. Lymphatic drainage is to the inguinal nodes and lymphatic glands along the iliac vessels.

The membranous urethra is involved in urinary incontinence and control of ejaculation of semen. The remainder of the urethra serves two different functions: one is to allow the free passage of urine during urination, and the other is to assist the expulsion of the semen during ejaculation. The glands of Littre are responsible for lubricating the urethra before ejaculation.

The male urethra can be visualized readily either by retrograde urethrography (RUG) studies or by voiding films. The delineation of its three main segments usually can be easily made radiographically (Fig. 37-2).

The Female Urethra

The female urethra is approximately 4 to 5 cm long and begins at the internal urethral orifice or vesical neck. It follows a slightly curved course downward and

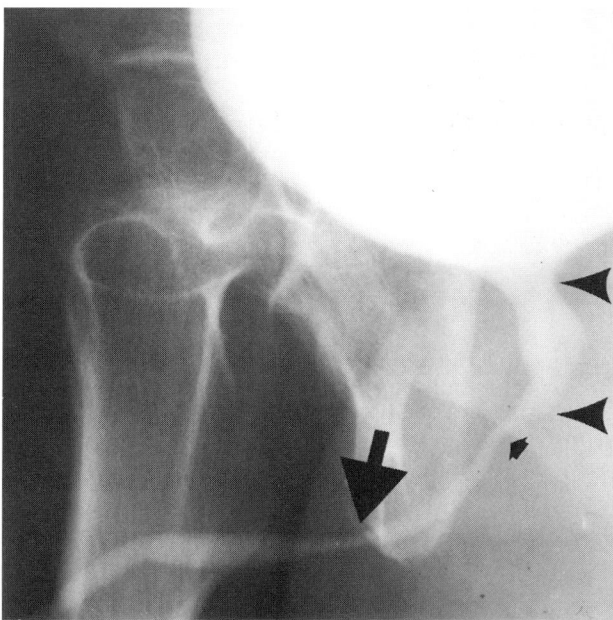

Figure 37-2. Normal voiding cystourethrogram in a male patient showing the appearance of the prostatic urethra (*arrowheads*); the location of the membranous urethra, which corresponds with the location of the external sphincter or urogenital diaphragm (*small arrow*); and finally the anterior or pendulous urethra (*large arrow*).

forward and terminates at the external urethral meatus on the roof of the vestibule.

The epithelium of the female urethra is squamous in its distal portion and transitional in its proximal segment. Numerous periurethral glands are embedded in the submucosal layer; the largest are the glands of Skene, which open just inside the meatus.

The longitudinal smooth muscle layer of the bladder neck is prolonged to encase the urethra, but at the portion that pierces the urogenital diaphragm, it is surrounded by striated sphincter muscle, as in the man. The urethra also passes through the levator ani muscle before traversing the diaphragm and is supported by bulbocavernous muscle under the diaphragm.

Because the female urethra is short and its diameter is only 6 mm, care must be taken not to damage the urethral wall in operative or interventional procedures. (The female urethra represents the entire sphynteric mechanism for the bladder.) A distinct sphincter action is not always demonstrable in a woman. The female urethra is much more readily dilatable than that of the male. The entire female urethra receives innervation from both divisions of the autonomic nervous system and from the somatic system. Parasympathetic cholinergic nerve endings, as well as adrenergic nerve endings, especially alpha-adrenergic, are found throughout the entire length of the urethra. Somatic fibers coming from the pudendal nerve supply the striated external sphincter in both sexes.

The radiographic anatomy of a normal female urethra is well visualized during a VCUG. Radiographically, the female urethra is a uniform, smooth, wide, tubular structure with gentle ventral curvature, adequate lumen throughout, and relative narrowing right at the meatus.

Urethral Strictures

A urethral stricture is a scar that is usually the result of tissue injury caused by urethral trauma, pelvic fracture, inflammatory disease, or neoplasia. As this scar heals, it contracts and creates fibrotic narrowing composed of dense collagen and fibroblasts. Fibrosis usually extends into the surrounding corpus spongiosum, causing spongiofibrosis. Urethral strictures can be congenital, traumatic, inflammatory, or neoplastic.

Congenital Strictures

Congenital lesions are found most commonly at the external urethral meatus, often associated with hypospadias orifices,[8] but the membranous urethra and the penoscrotal junction frequently are involved. They are seen in both sexes but are more common in men.

Traumatic Strictures

Traumatic lesions are the result of tears or ruptures of the urethra caused by blows to the perineum or by pelvic fracture, or they are iatrogenic. They can occur anywhere in the anterior or the membranous urethra, but they probably are most common in the bulbomembranous portion (Fig. 37-3). Chemical strictures, which are considered to be traumatic, usually occur in the anterior urethra. Iatrogenic strictures are a common form of traumatic stricture of the urethra in children and adults, secondary to instrumentation. Traumatic strictures usually develop much more rapidly than inflammatory strictures. They also tend to be dense and longer because of more ischemic necrosis.

Inflammatory Strictures

Inflammatory strictures may be caused by gonorrhea, tuberculosis, syphilis, or nonspecific infections. Although gonococcal urethritis is seldom a cause of stricture, infection remains a major cause, particularly infection from long-term use of indwelling urethral catheters. Large catheters and instruments are more likely than small ones to cause ischemia and internal trauma. Approximately 75 percent of inflammatory strictures occur at the bulbomembranous junction.

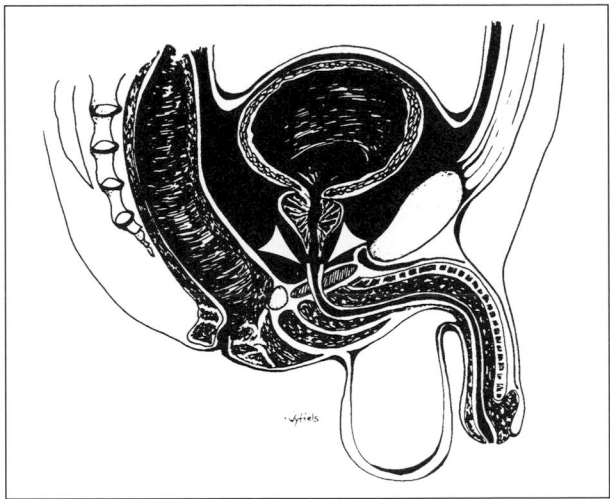

Figure 37-3. After bulbomembranous urethral ruptures (*arrowheads*) blood and urine tend to collect extraperitoneally, displacing and elevating contiguous structures.

The strictures caused by infection tend to be more diaphragmlike and short. Tuberculosis is spread from another focus, usually higher up in the urinary tract and most likely from the prostate. The urethra appears to be particularly resistant to tuberculous infection, but when these strictures occur, they are intractable and often associated with fistula formation and abscesses.

Neoplastic Strictures

Neoplastic strictures are the result of primary urethral carcinoma or are secondary from the bladder or the prostate. They may occur at any place in the urethra but are most common in the bulbomembranous area. Recurrent stricture disease of the urethra, even in the absence of hematuria, demands periodic RUG to rule out the possibility of a clinically occult urethral cancer. Transitional cell carcinoma of the urethra may be associated with a bladder cancer. This possibility must be ruled out before the urethral lesion is addressed.

Signs and Symptoms

The patient with urethral stricture usually has symptoms of bladder outlet obstruction, which are described in detail below under BPH. Gross observation of the urinary stream may reveal a decrease in the usual force and caliber, as well as multiple streams. Obstruction from BPH may coexist with a previously undiagnosed stricture, and the effect may be additive. Stricture occasionally may be suggested by a careful palpation of the urethra. Induration may be present, more so with posttraumatic stricture than with strictures from instrumentation or gonococcal urethritis.

Radiologic Findings

VCUGs best demonstrate dilatation behind a stricture, but RUGs best demonstrate the stricture itself. Although strictures may be diagnosed by the insertion of a cystoscope into the urethra, important information, such as length, caliber, location, and multiplicity, cannot be obtained without the use of urethrograms.

Strictures of the urethra appear as narrowed segments, which can vary in length and appearance from valvelike structures to long constrictions. Approximately 10 percent are multiple. The congenital type is single, usually short, and regular in appearance. The inflammatory stricture may be single or, more commonly, multiple; it may be short or long. It usually appears more irregular than either the congenital or traumatic stricture. The traumatic stricture can be single or multiple but is more commonly single. It may be long or short and is usually smooth. Neoplastic strictures are irregular and long and tend to occur with fistulous formation.

Complications

The most common complication of urethral stricture is significant lower urinary tract obstruction. Over time, the obstruction leads to characteristic changes in the bladder and upper urinary tract. These changes may be observed cystoscopically as well as radiologically. Bladder trabeculation or hypertrophy of the detrusor muscle causes the individual muscle fascicles to become prominent beneath the vesical mucosa. The interureteric ridge (Bell muscle) also participates in this process of hypertrophy, as does the bladder neck. Hypertrophy of the vesical neck causes an acute angulation between the trigone and the prostatic urethra.

Cellule formation can also be a complication of long-standing stricture disease. Extreme degrees of trabeculation allow the vesical mucosa to be pushed between the muscle fibers of the bladder wall, forming small pockets called *cellules.*

Diverticulum formation or herniation of the vesical mucosa through the detrusor muscle constitutes a bladder diverticulum. Acquired bladder diverticula contain no muscular components and are therefore prone to poor emptying, even if the bladder is emptied by catheterization. Because of a stasis of urine within the diverticula, they are likely to harbor infection, stones, and urothelium cancer. A diverticulum near the ureteric orifice (Hutch diverticulum) may cause vesicoureteral reflux.

Bladder calculi form most commonly as a result of outflow obstruction, residual urine, stasis, and infection. The presence of a bladder calculus is strong evidence of a long-standing bladder outflow obstruction.

The most common mineral constituent of these stones in developed countries is calcium oxalate.

Patients with urethral strictures frequently accumulate residual urine. The integrity of the upper urinary tract may be jeopardized by the lower tract obstruction. With hypertrophy and thickening of the detrusor muscle, increased work is required to transport the urinary bolus from the ureter into the bladder. This process results in ureteral muscle hypertrophy, which is analogous to bladder hypertrophy. In the early stages, the condition appears, radiologically, as a mild dilatation of the distal segment, elongation, and some tortuosity of the ureter. Later, there is more marked dilatation of the entire ureter, attenuation of the ureteral wall, and marked tortuosity.

Periurethral abscess is closely related in its development to that of urinary extravasation. Periurethral abscess may cause multiple urethrocutaneous fistulas in the perineum, buttocks, and thighs.

Role of Interventional Radiology in Urethral Lesions

The urethra offers such an easy access for direct endoscopic procedures that interventional radiology has only a limited role in managing lower urinary tract problems; however, such a limited role can be lifesaving on many occasions. For example, when cystoscopy is not possible because of urethral stricture, bladder contracture, malformation of the urethra, or trauma-related changes, interventional radiology may offer an alternative form of treatment. Interventional radiology of the urethra depends on gaining access by percutaneous catheter or needle and on monitoring the events by fluoroscopy, ultrasonography, or computed tomography (CT).

As mentioned above, radiologic assistance is seldom required in performing a simple transurethral catheterization; however, with a stricture or urethral trauma, when the urethral continuity has been violated, major developmental abnormalities are present, or if multiple urethral false passages are present, RUG may give useful information before catheterization.

Cases of urethral trauma or disruption can be treated atraumatically by using a coaxial catheter-guidewire system under fluoroscopy after administering local anesthesia (1 percent lidocaine jelly; uro-jet, IMS Ltd.). When the transurethral route is not accessible, a transvesical approach provides good access for various interventional procedures. Percutaneous puncture is made 2 to 3 fingerbreadths above the symphysis pubis in the midline, after the area is infiltrated with a local anesthetic. To enter the bladder, a 19-gauge, sheathed needle (such as the Amplatz needle) is directed 10 degrees cranially to avoid damage to the bladder neck. Once the bladder has been entered, a straight floppy-tip guidewire can be advanced and coiled in the bladder. A 5 to 7 French curved catheter (Headhunter, hockey stick, or cobra curve) with good torque properties can then be advanced over the guidewire into the bladder for directing the guidewire into the bladder neck and subsequently into the urethra. Even with complete, hard obstructions, this can be performed without much difficulty, especially with the new hydrophilic guidewires. Once the wire is out of the urethral meatus, a Councill catheter can be placed over this through-and-through wire for restoration of urethral continuity in cases of urethral trauma or disruption. This wire can provide an easy access for placing balloons to dilate difficult urethral strictures.

Balloon Dilation of Strictures

The method used most commonly by urologists for treating urethral strictures is dilation with different calibrated sounds. This method, although acceptable in many situations, has certain disadvantages, one of which is that the patients have to be treated at regular intervals over many years. Dilation is a blind technique and may result in urethral trauma with formation of false passages. Also, besides the obvious discomfort, infection may complicate its course. Therefore, dilation of urethral strictures is not usually curative, but it fractures the scar tissue of the stricture and temporarily enlarges the lumen. Dilation of the urethra must be a process of gradual stretching because forceful disruption of this stricture area will lead to further scarring and subsequent worsening of the situation. It is not advisable to dilate a urethral stricture beyond 30 French or 10 mm in a male patient. Rather, the patient should be asked to return at weekly intervals. If dilation is going to be an acceptable modality, the eventual interval between visits should be every 6 to 12 months.

Balloon dilation has several theoretical advantages related to the radial forces of dilation by the balloon catheter. In theory, these forces should produce less tissue trauma and scarring and fewer complications (such as urethral and periurethral perforations and false passages) compared with the longitudinal shearing forces applied by bouginage.

A baseline RUG or VCUG is performed to assess the exact location and extent of the stricture. Under fluoroscopic guidance, a guidewire is advanced through the urethra into the bladder. If the stricture is tight, angiographic techniques using different catheters and guidewires are usually successful in most cases. Once the stricture is traversed with the guidewire, and after the right balloon has been chosen (balloons not exceeding 8 to

10 mm in diameter with the smallest profile possible and of adequate length), dilation is carried out until the initial balloon waist disappears. Prolonged dilations are avoided to prevent further ischemic damage to the urothelium and adjacent tissues. All manipulations should be performed with abundant lubricating jelly or viscous lidocaine to minimize trauma.

Preliminary results are encouraging,[9,10] but reports of long-term follow-ups are lacking. Unfortunately, the consensus is that repeated dilations are required to maintain adequate flows. However, this technique is very useful, especially in tight or impassable strictures that can be converted to traversable lesions.[11,12] These lesions may then be candidates for internal urethrotomy, which produces better long-term results. Bleeding and pain are the major problems caused by bougie or sound dilation, as well as perforation of the urethral wall and creation of false passages, which are avoided by balloon dilation.

Urethral Stents

As described above, the treatment for urethral strictures, either by surgery or by dilation, is still far from ideal. Recurrences, difficulty in performing the urethroplasty procedures and the specialized surgical skills required, morbidity of the procedures, and difficult management have hampered the success of such procedures.

The search for new techniques in the treatment of this common problem is ongoing. Recent technical developments in metallic stent technology, initially developed for intravascular[13–15] and biliary[16,17] use, have precipitated its use in the urinary system for the treatment of urethral strictures.[18]

The metallic stent most commonly used for this purpose is the Wallstent (Medinvent S.A.),[18] which is a self-expandable, stainless steel, woven wire tube that can be manufactured to different diameters and lengths (Fig. 37-4). The stent comes loaded on a small-diameter (7 French) delivery catheter (Fig. 37-5) and is constrained in its compressed form by a coaxial restraining sleeve that is pulled back while the delivery catheter is held in place across the area of the stricture (Fig. 37-6). As the stent is being deployed, it expands to fit the luminal diameter, and because of the elastic properties of the mesh, it will hold against the wall of the urethra and thus will not migrate or dislodge.

It is of crucial importance to measure the desired caliber and length of the area to be stented to select the most appropriate stent. It should be noted that the deployed length of the stent is shorter than when it is loaded in its collapsed state. Long strictures can be bridged by several stents placed in tandem.

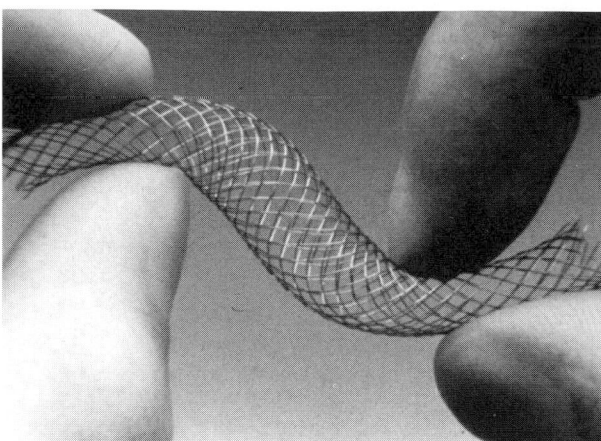

Figure 37-4. The Wallstent is a very flexible, self-expanding metallic stent that accommodates well to the ureteral contours and that has sufficient strength to keep the urethral lumen patent without causing significant discomfort.

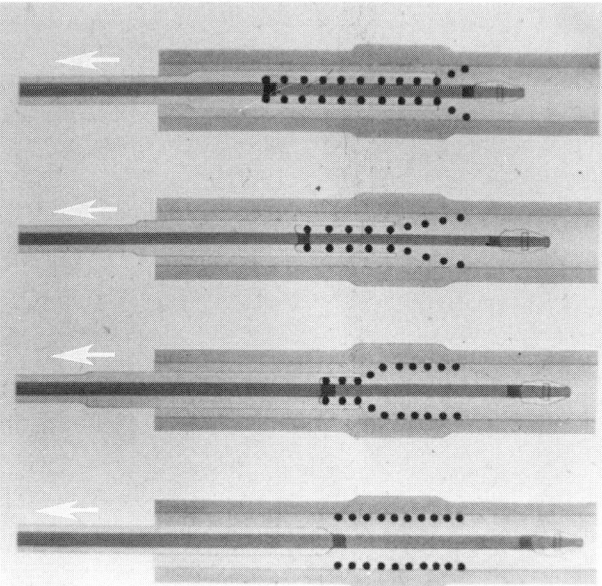

Figure 37-6. As the restraining catheter is pulled back (*arrows*) while the inner coaxial delivery catheter is held in place across the desired location, the stent is deployed and the self-expanding device conforms to the diameter and shape of the urethra.

Technique. After the urethra has been catheterized and a guidewire has been placed in the bladder, the site of the stricture is dilated to diameters of up to 10 mm with complete resolution of the balloon waist, and the balloon catheter is removed. Assurance is made that the site of the stricture is well marked, and the guidewire is left in place. Over the guidewire, the stent

Figure 37-5. The 7 French delivery catheter and introduction system that allows an almost atraumatic placement. The *arrows* show the location of the compressed and restrained stent before deployment.

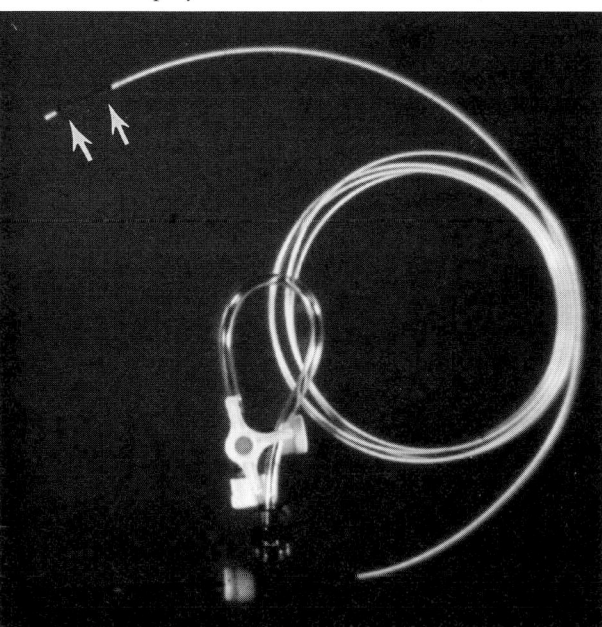

delivery system is advanced to the desired location, taking into consideration the shortening of the stent that will occur after deployment. Once in position, the delivery catheter is held securely in position and the restraining catheter is then slowly pulled back to allow adequate delivery and expansion until the stent is fully deployed. If more stents are required, the same procedure is repeated until the entire length of the stricture is covered. There should be a slight overlap between the stents at the ends to avoid restenosis in these areas.

All patients are covered prophylactically with broad-spectrum antibiotics for about a week, starting the day of the procedure. There is no need to leave indwelling draining catheters either transurethrally or suprapubically, because all patients are able to empty the bladder. The patient, relatives, and medical personnel are instructed to avoid retrograde catheterization in the immediate poststenting period because it may cause dislodgment. If such catheterization becomes necessary, caution should be exercised; the procedure should be performed preferably under fluoroscopic guidance using angiographic catheterization technique. Patients are also advised to avoid sexual intercourse for 1 month after stent placement.

A device has been developed (Fig. 37-7) for cystoscopic stent placement. However, excessive bleeding

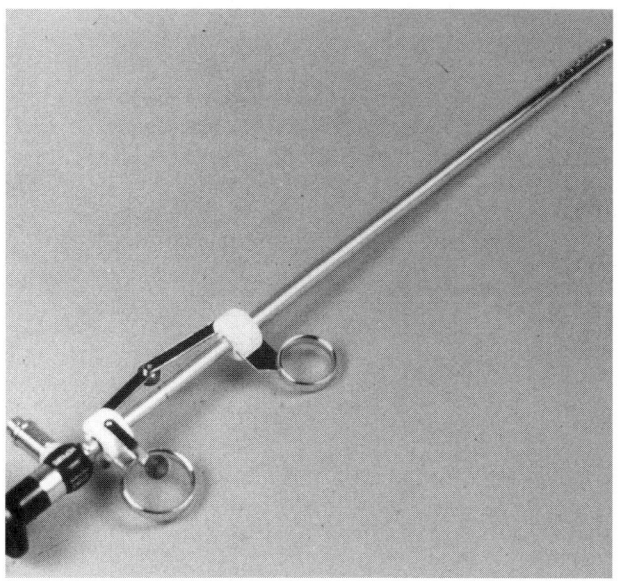
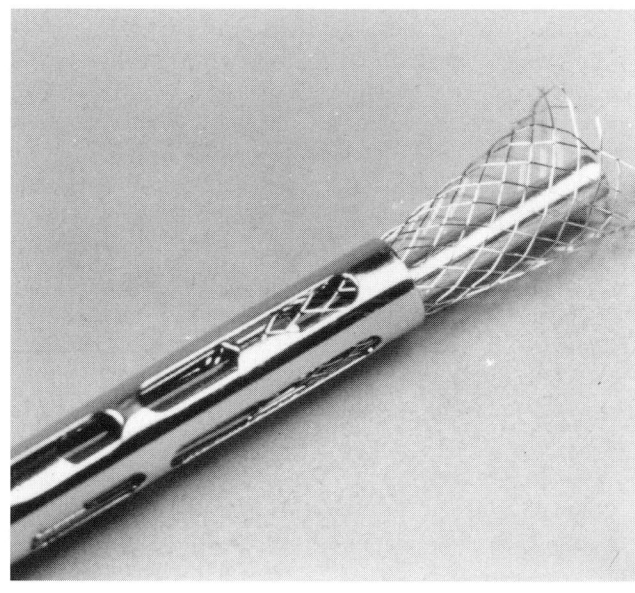

A   **B**

Figure 37-7. (A) This endoscopic delivery tool, developed specifically for the urologist, has a 24 French diameter and incorporates some of the features of the urologic endoscopic tools. (B) Closeup view of the distal end, with the stent partially deployed, shows its mechanism of action in better detail.

after stricture dilation may preclude successful cystoscopic operation. This does not occur when fluoroscopy is used because a guidewire is always in the lumen and the stricture location is always known from previous radiologic localization. Also, when fluoroscopy is used, the deployment systems are much smaller (7 French) than the systems specifically designed for the cystoscope (24 French). Another advantage of the small delivery system is that, when several stents are necessary, it is easier to move in and out of previously placed stents with less risk of migration or dislodgment.

Results. In all the reported cases,[18] the procedure has been successful and free from complications for up to 2 years without evidence of recurrence. The general trend has been significant improvement in the obstruction and urine flow without alteration of sexual function or ejaculation. The stents have been covered completely and incorporated by urothelium in 4 to 6 months. This result seems to prevent the infection and incrustations seen with other types of stents placed in the urinary system.

The most common complaint has been transient discomfort at the site of the stent, which usually resolves in 2 to 3 weeks. In a few patients, mild postmicturition dribbling has also been noted, and this resolves after the stent is completely covered with urothelium.

The Prostate

Surgical Anatomy

The prostate is a chestnut-shaped, multilobular, glandular, fibromuscular organ that surrounds the first part of the urethra between the bladder neck and the urogenital diaphragm, or external sphincter. It is traversed throughout its length by the posterior urethra and is fixed to the pelvic floor by investments of the parietal and endopelvic fascial. Two dense condensations of the endopelvic fascia, which affixes the prostate to the pubis, are the puboprostatic ligaments. Anteriorly, the prostate is separated from the symphysis pubis by the extraperitoneal, prevesical (retropubic) space of Retzius. The prostatic venous plexus and the puboprostatic ligaments are found in this space. Posteriorly, the prostate is separated from the rectum by Denonvilliers fascia, which represents the connective tissue remaining from the obliterated peritoneal cul-de-sac between the rectum and the prostate. The prostate is covered by a firm, fibrous capsule.

Traditionally, the prostate is divided into five lobes: anterior, posterior, median, and two lateral lobes. The lateral lobes constitute the major portion of the gland. These lobes are a frequent site of benign adenomas. The posterior aspect of the prostate is traversed by the terminal portions of the vas deferens, which exit in the ejaculatory ducts and the posterior urethra. The posterior urethra, which traverses the prostate, houses a small mound on the dorsal aspect, termed the *verumontanum*. This part of the prostate is readily palpable by digital rectal examination and is a frequent site of cancer of the prostate. In the middle portion of the verumontanum is a small pit called the *utricle*. The ejaculatory ducts exit on the verumontanum. The middle lobe lies between the urethra and the ejaculatory ducts and is intermittently related to the vesical neck. Because of this anatomic relationship, even small adenomas in this lobe may obstruct the vesical outlet. The anterior lobe of the prostate is formed by approximately 13 tubules that grow out from the anterior wall of the prostatic urethra. After first becoming large and multibranched, these tubules decrease in both size and number; at birth, there are rarely more than two present. Usually it is impossible to identify the anterior lobe in the gland of the adult, but occasionally it persists.

The blood supply of the prostate is primarily derived from the prostatic artery, which is derived from the inferior vesical artery. There are two main groups of arteries: a capsular group and a urethral group. Some accessory vessels to the prostate are supplied by the middle, hemorrhoidal, and internal pudendal arteries. The venous drainage of the prostate is through a prostatic plexus that joins the venous drainage of the penis in Santorini plexus and then drains into the hypogastric veins. It is important to note that the prostatic plexus connects with the prevertebral veins, also called *Batson plexus*.

The innervation of the prostate is through sympathetic fibers from L1 and L2 and from the third and fourth sacral nerves through the sacral plexus.

Prostatic lymphatics egress via vesical, hypogastric, external iliac, and sacral lymph nodes.

Zonal Anatomy

As described above, traditional concepts of prostate anatomy emphasized the lobar nature of the gland. More recently, extensive histopathologic studies have led to a description of anatomic zones of the prostate, each with a distinct histologic character.[19-22]

The pioneering work of McNeal[19] and others[20-22] on the histology of the prostate has led to the concept of four major categories of tissue within the gland: the periurethral, the transitional (or preprostatic), the fibromuscular, and the acinar glandular regions (Fig. 37-8). The periurethral zone is a small region referred to by some as the *internal gland* and is composed of glands that line the urethra from the bladder neck to the verumontanum. The transitional, or preprostatic,

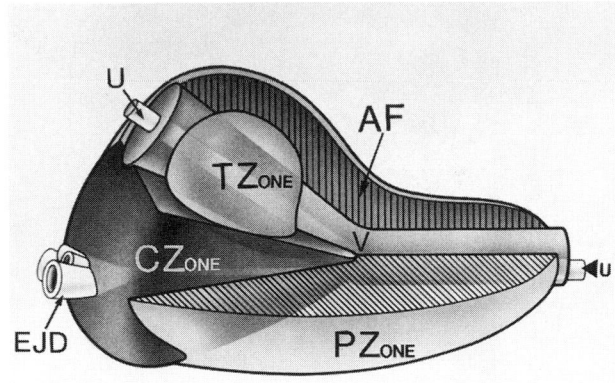

Figure 37-8. Three-dimensional schematic representation of the prostate gland with its different tissue characteristics as well as the structures coursing through its parenchyma. *U*, urethra; *EJD*, ejaculatory ducts; *AF*, anterior fibromuscular region; *T Zone*, transitional zone; *C Zone*, central zone; *P Zone*, peripheral zone.

zone is histologically similar to the glandular peripheral zone. It is typically small, situated between the anterior fibromuscular zone and the peripheral zone, and related to the preprostatic sphincter above the verumontanum. The anterior fibromuscular tissue is located anterior to the urethra along the entire craniocaudad extent of the gland. It is least prominent at the prostatic apex and widens maximally at the level of the midprostate. It has both smooth and striated muscle components.

The central glandular region lies posterior to the urethra and is broadest at the base of the gland, tapering toward the apex. It is through this region that the ejaculatory ducts course obliquely downward and anteriorly into the verumontanum in the prostatic urethra. However, the predominant glandular region in the normal prostate is the peripheral zone, which comprises approximately 75 percent of the acinar tissue of the prostate. It is situated primarily posterolaterally but also extends anterolaterally, especially in the more cranial aspects of the gland. The peripheral zone is somewhat funnel-shaped and surrounds the central glandular tissue. It is the tissue that composes most of the prostatic apex.

The seminal vesicles are paired, saccular, elliptical organs that lie immediately cephalad to the prostate. The ejaculatory ducts join with the ampullae of the vas deferens to course through the central glandular region of the prostate to the verumontanum.

The normal anatomic regions of the prostate can be defined to a variable degree by sophisticated high-resolution imaging modalities. Axial and longitudinal transrectal sonography is capable of defining some

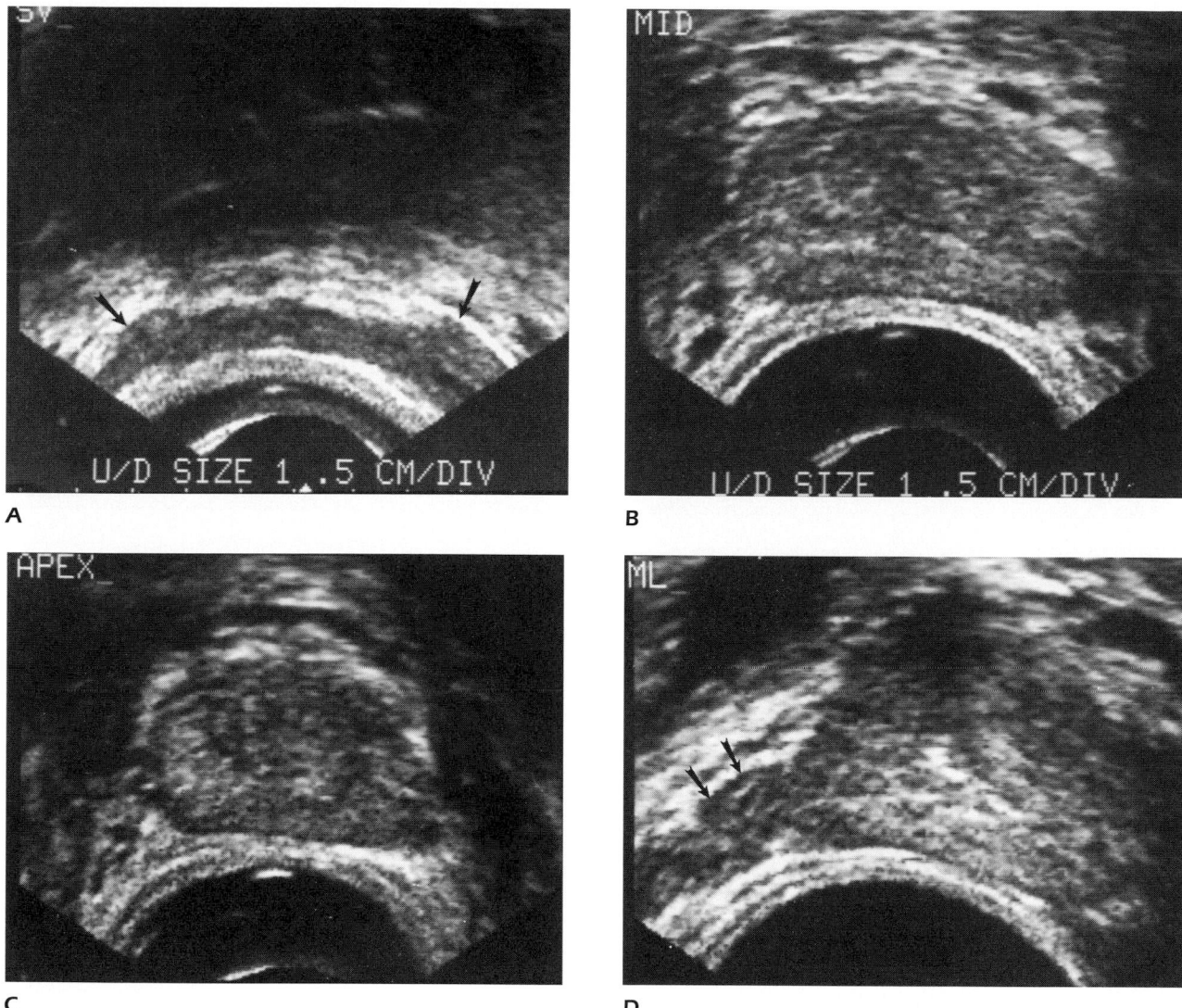

A

B

C

D

Figure 37-9. Normal anatomy of the prostate gland, shown by transrectal ultrasound using a 7.0-MHz probe. (A) Transverse view of the seminal vesicles (*arrows*). (B) Transverse view of midprostate showing more central and peripheral zones. (C) Transverse view at apex also showing the peripheral zone distant from the other anatomic zones of the prostate. (D) Longitudinal view of the right side of the prostate at the right seminal vesicle (*arrows*).

zonal anatomy of the normal prostate (Fig. 37-9).[23] The periurethral region is characterized by a slightly hypoechoic region surrounding the curvilinearly coursing urethra. The tissue of the central and peripheral glandular zones produces a medium level of echogenicity, with the two areas often not sonographically distinct. Distinction between the central regions and the peripheral acinar regions can also occasionally be made by CT. More recently, magnetic resonance imaging (MRI) with high field strengths and T2-weighted sequences has shown improved capabilities for defining zonal prostate anatomy (Fig. 37-10).[24–27] The lower signal intensity of the anterior fibromuscular region can be differentiated easily from the inter-mediate intensity of the central glandular region and the higher intensity of the peripheral zone.

Pathologic Anatomy

The zonal anatomy of the prostate relates directly to the pathologic processes that affect the gland.[22] Histopathologic studies reveal that malignancy and inflammation principally involve the peripheral glandular zone.[22] It is thought that 80 percent of prostate cancer arises in the peripheral zone (Fig. 37-11). However, this figure also implies that a small proportion of prostate cancer does originate in more central regions, the transitional zone and the central glandular zone.

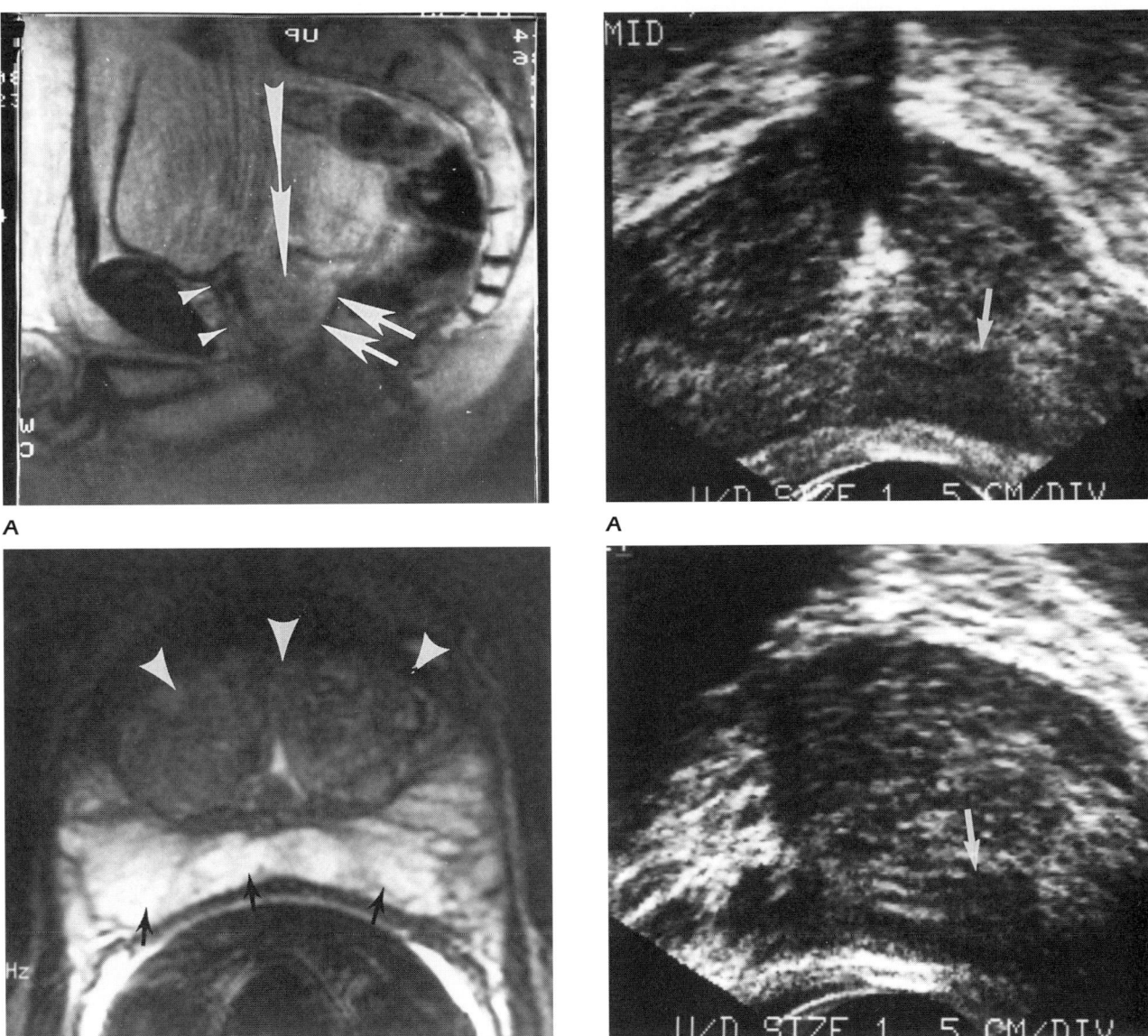

A

B

A

B

Figure 37-10. (A) T2-weighted image of the prostate performed with a pelvic multicoil array showing the different signal intensities of the different regions. The anterior fibromuscular zone (*arrowheads*) has a lower intensity than the peripheral zone (*short arrows*). The central, more adenomatous region (*long arrow*) is characterized by a more inhomogeneous midrange intensity. (B) Transverse T2-weighted image of the prostate performed with a high-resolution endorectal coil. The peripheral zone is hyperintense (*arrows*). The central gland appears hypointense with some areas of increased signal (*arrowheads*).

Figure 37-11. Adenocarcinoma of the prostate. Transverse view (A) and sagittal view (B) from transrectal ultrasound show a hypoechoic adenocarcinoma in the left peripheral zone (*arrow*). The diagnosis was proven by ultrasound-guided needle biopsy. Note the calcification and adenomatous change centrally.

Prostatitis is also principally a process of the peripheral zone[22]; however, with severe infections of the gland, inflammation extends throughout the prostate, making differentiation of the various regions by sonography difficult.

BPH primarily affects the transitional and, to a lesser extent, the periurethral zones of the gland (Fig. 37-12).[22] In extreme cases, the massive enlargement of these regions compresses the central glandular tissue and displaces it posteriorly.

As described above, different disease processes selectively affect different regions of the prostate. New high-resolution imaging techniques provide noninvasive means of understanding both the normal prostate and the pathologic processes that affect it.

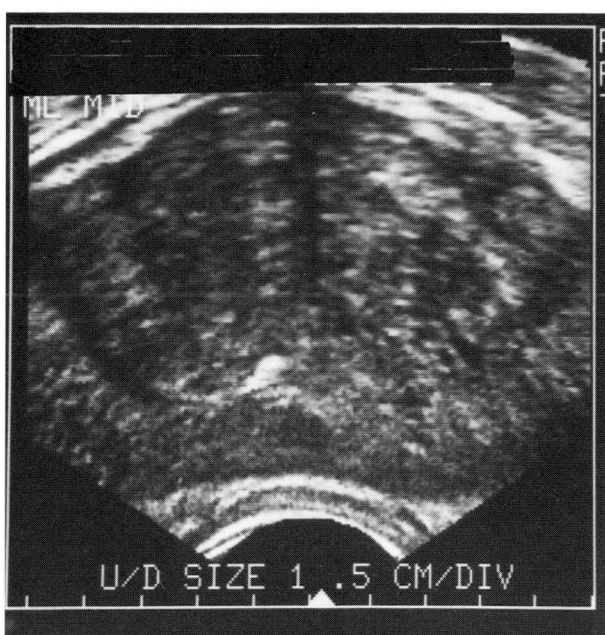

Figure 37-12. Transverse view from transrectal ultrasound shows an enlarged gland with calcification and adenomatous change in the central gland—characteristics of benign prostatic hypertrophy.

Examination of the Prostate

Examination of the prostate is best performed with the patient standing, bent over the examining table or bed, and supported on his elbows. An alternative and less desirable position is the lateral decubitus position, with one leg drawn up toward the abdomen. The examiner's gloved, generously lubricated index finger is inserted slowly into the rectum. The purpose of the prostatic examination is to gain information regarding prostatic size, symmetry, consistency, and motility; to assess anal tone; and to determine the presence of rectal masses. A lax anal sphincter that the patient cannot contract may indicate peripheral neuropathy.

The average prostate is about 4 cm in length and width. It is widest superiorly, at the bladder neck. As the gland enlarges, the lateral sulci become relatively deeper and the median furrow becomes obliterated. The prostate may also elongate.

The clinical importance of clinical hyperplasia is measured by the severity of symptoms and the amount of residual urine, not by the size of the gland. Normally, the consistency of the gland is similar to that of the contracted thenar eminence of the thumb. It is rather rubbery. It may be mushy if congested (due to chronic infection with impaired drainage), indurated (due to chronic infection with or without calculi), or stony-hard (due to advanced carcinoma). The normal prostate has a weight of approximately 18 to 20 g. Any

areas of induration are termed *suspicious prostate nodules* and should be biopsied.

The differential diagnosis of a prostate nodule includes prostate cancer, asymmetric benign prostatic hypertrophy, prostatic calculi, and granulomatous prostatitis. Approximately 50 percent of prostate nodules discovered on rectal examination are proven to be carcinoma on biopsy.

Functions of the Prostate

The functions of the prostate can be summarized as follows:

1. The prostate produces approximately 1 ml of cloudy fluid daily, which is carried out in the urine.
2. The prostate is responsible for about half of the semen volume of ejaculation.
3. The prostatic fluid facilitates fertilization by acting as a vehicle for spermatozoa and as an aid to semen liquefaction through the enzyme fibrinolysin.

Benign Prostatic Hyperplasia

BPH represents a nonmalignant neoplasm of the prostate. BPH as a cause of urinary dysfunction has been known for several centuries. It was mentioned in the Egyptian papyri as early as 1500 B.C. and was discussed by Hippocrates 1000 years later. Hyperplasia describes an increase in the number of individual tissue elements, whereby the bulk of the organ is increased. Hypertrophy describes a general increase in the bulk of an organ through an increase in size, but not in number, of the individual tissue elements. BPH is a hyperplastic process because there is a net growth of the epithelial and stromal elements of the prostate. The natural history of BPH involves two phases. The first, the pathologic phase, involves two stages, microscopic and macroscopic BPH, neither of which produces clinical symptoms. Nearly all men worldwide eventually develop microscopic BPH if they live long enough. In only about one-half of these men, however, will microscopic BPH grow to produce a macroscopic enlargement of the gland, suggesting that additional factors are required for the progression of microscopic to macroscopic BPH.

The second, or clinical, phase involves the progression of pathologic BPH to clinical BPH, in which the patient develops symptomatic dysuria. Only about one-half of men with macroscopic BPH progress to clinical BPH requiring therapeutic intervention. Thus approximately 25 percent of all men eventually require some type of treatment for clinical BPH.

Pathogenesis

Although the pathogenesis of BPH remains unknown, it is universally accepted that a source of circulating androgens is required for the development of BPH, because males castrated before puberty do not develop BPH. Regression of the prostate has also been reported after castration in adults. BPH can be produced by hormones in animal models. BPH is also associated with abnormal accumulation of the hormone dihydrotestosterone. The precise role of the testes in the pathogenesis of BPH, however, is controversial. There is no convincing evidence that alteration of serum or prostatic androgen levels are related to the development of BPH. It is important to note that there is no relation between BPH and cancer of the prostate.

Prevalence of BPH

The prevalence of BPH in the aging male population has been estimated from histologic examination of prostates obtained at autopsy. A comprehensive review of such autopsy data is described by Berry et al.[28] These data show that BPH rarely occurs in men younger than 40 years and that approximately 50 percent of men have histologic evidence of BPH by the age of 60 years. It is known that there is a slow increase in prostatic size from birth until puberty. For the prostate to reach the adult size of 20 to 25 g, two factors are necessary: time and testes. There is a rapid increase in the size of the prostate from puberty to age 20. The size remains constant until about age 45, at which time the prostate either atrophies and progressively decreases in size, or develops BPH.

Spectrum of Clinical Manifestations

The clinical manifestations of BPH are related primarily to obstruction caused by prostatic enlargement. Prostatism, the symptom complex associated with BPH, is a syndrome composed of obstructive and irritative symptoms. The obstructive symptoms include hesitancy and straining to urinate, a diminished caliber and interrupted urinary stream, and postmicturition dribbling. The irritative symptoms include urinary frequency, nocturia, dysuria, and urgency to urinate. As the severity of the obstruction progresses, bladder hypertrophy is unable to compensate for the obstruction, resulting in incomplete bladder emptying. The incomplete bladder emptying exacerbates the symptoms of prostatism and further disposes the patient to urinary tract infections. Complete urinary retention is one of the most severe sequelae of bladder outlet obstruction secondary to BPH; the other is chronic renal insufficiency. Hematuria represents the only clinically significant manifestation of BPH not related to bladder outlet obstruction.

Diagnosis of BPH

The diagnostic approach to patients suspected of having outflow obstruction should include an orderly, well-planned assessment to determine whether there is objective evidence of obstruction and, if so, the level of the obstruction and the effect on the more proximal urinary tract. The assessment should begin with a careful history and physical examination.

To facilitate the assessment of the patient's symptoms, the American Urological Association (AUA) has developed a symptom score evaluation form, and most urologists follow a simple algorithm to treat bladder outflow obstruction (Fig. 37-13). Laboratory tests should include urinalysis, urine culture, complete blood count, and levels of serum creatinine, blood urea nitrogen, serum electrolytes, and prostate-specific antigen (PSA).

Indications for Intervention

The indications for surgical or nonsurgical treatment of BPH are highly variable. An absolute indication requires immediate attention. Urinary retention, recurrent urinary tract infections, renal insufficiency secondary to BPH, and/or persistent gross hematuria are generally accepted as absolute indications for treatment. Relative indications for intervention include moderate postvoid residual urine, bothersome symptoms of prostatism, and urodynamic evidence of obstruction. Cystoscopic evidence of BPH should be considered a weak indication for intervention of BPH.

The decision to intervene surgically, medically, or by interventional (minimally invasive) techniques in a man with relative indications should reflect the impact of the symptoms on his quality of life, his expectations and treatment preference, his general medical condition, and the relative effectiveness and morbidity of available treatment options.

Surgical Therapy: Transurethral Resection

Transurethral resection of the prostate (TURP) is one of the most common urologic operations performed.[29] In 1985, 350,000 were performed. It was the second most costly operation after cataract extraction under Medicare, accounting for 1.4 percent of the total allowable charges. In 1987, a survey of urologists revealed that TURP accounted for 38 percent of major urologic operations. Interestingly, the rate at which TURP is performed shows great regional and even international variability.[30,31] This probably reflects, at least in part, the perceived utility of this treatment. With an aging population, therefore, one should expect a further increase in the number of these operations performed, with a corresponding impact on

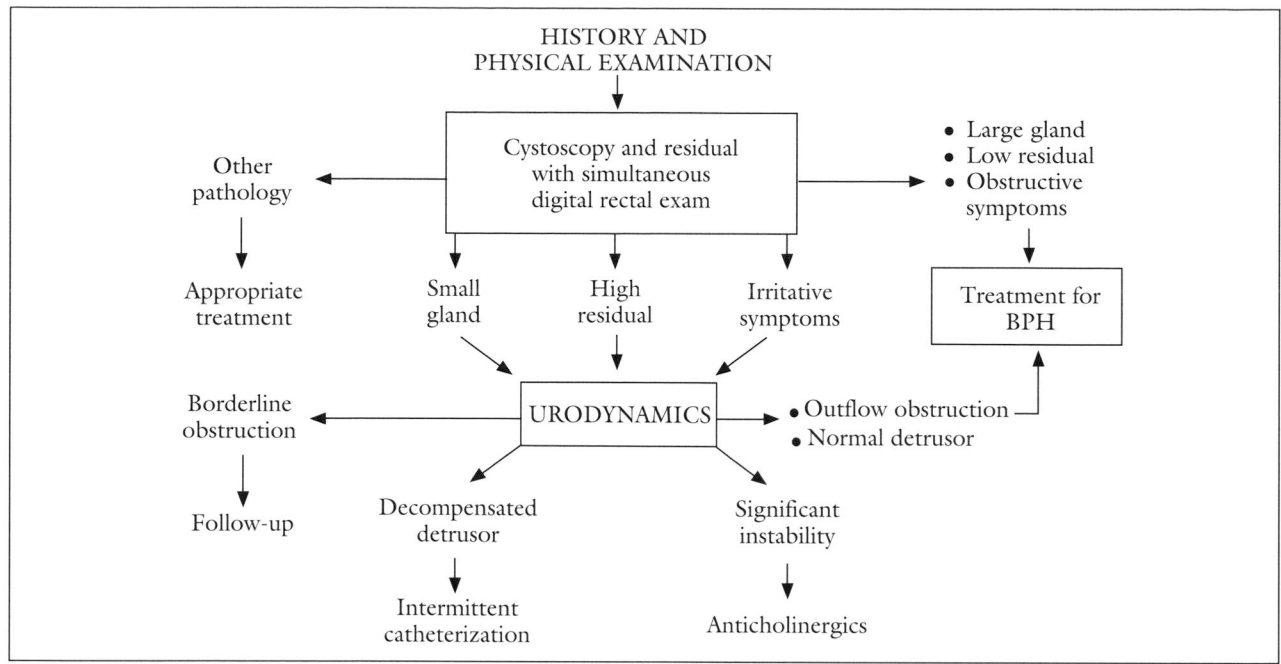

Figure 37-13. Diagnostic algorithm for bladder outflow obstruction.

money spent for medical care.[32] Although TURP has been associated with a low surgical mortality rate and a good outcome, the need to control rising medical costs has led to a reevaluation of prostatectomy with regard to the indications for therapeutic intervention and the long-term, as well as short-term, results. Although most patients undergoing TURP experience long-term improvement in symptoms and quality of life, short-term complications, such as clot retention, and occasional long-term complications, such as incontinence and impotence, may occur.[33,34]

In the United States, mortality is adversely correlated to surgical volume.[35] Mortality is also nearly two times higher in smaller hospitals and more than three times higher in nonuniversity hospitals.[36] For a given age group, a man undergoing TURP is almost three times more likely to die the same year as a man not having TURP.[31] Nearly two-thirds of post-TURP deaths occur in the first 3 months after discharge.[36,37] Compounding the initial risk is a 20 percent 8-year probability of reoperation.[36] With advancing age, operative mortality may increase by almost six times.[37] Age also determines postoperative ability to void, complications, and length of stay.[38]

Notwithstanding the above, the overall mortality and morbidity associated with TURP have decreased over the past 3 decades.[38] Better recognition and management of individual risks factors, preoperative prophylaxis, and advances in instrumentation have been responsible.

Medical Therapy

Clinical Trials with Alpha Blockers

The first clinical study using an alpha blocker was published by Caine et al.[39] In this study, 49 patients received 10 mg of phenoxybenzamine twice a day. Administration of the drug resulted in improvement in daytime and nighttime frequency and overall symptomatic improvement. Two other studies, by Abrams et al.[40] and Brooks et al.,[41] were not able to identify urodynamic or symptomatic improvement in patients receiving phenoxybenzamine. Because blockers using phenoxybenzamine have caused side effects, such as hypotension (orthostatic), nasal congestion, or absence of ejaculation, and because they have been associated with intestinal malignancy in rats, trials of several other blockers, mostly selective alpha$_1$ blockers, have been undertaken.

Results. Clinical trials of alpha blockers are of short duration with no long-term follow-up, and some are not placebo-controlled or blinded. The number of patients is often small, and the criteria for including patients are seldom well defined. Therefore, definite conclusions are difficult to draw at this time.

Hormonal Treatment with Antiandrogens

A number of different approaches have been used in the hormonal treatment of BPH. One group of antiandrogen drugs works centrally and prevents production of testosterone. Another group acts peripherally on the prostatic cell. This peripherally acting group prevents transformation of testosterone to dihydrotestosterone (5-alpha-reductase inhibitor) or competes for binding to the androgen receptor. Peters and Walsh[42] demonstrated a positive effect of medical castration using a centrally acting antiandrogen, a luteinizing hormone–releasing hormone (LH-RH) analogue. The prostate size regressed by approximately 25 percent based on ultrasound measurement. Biopsy from the prostate confirmed that regression was in the glandular tissue. There was no change in stromal tissue. Gabrilove et al.[43] describe the use of the analogue leuprolide.

These centrally working drugs have many side effects, including impotence, and drugs that do not substantially alter sexual function would be more desirable.

In a study by Stone[44] investigating flutamide, which blocks the uptake of dihydrotestosterone by the cytoplasmic androgen receptor, 84 patients were randomized into equal drug and placebo groups. Twelve patients were studied for 6 months, and 58 were studied 12 or more weeks. At 6 weeks, peak urinary values had increased by 12 percent in the placebo group and by 30 percent in the drug group. However, symptom reduction was identical in both groups. The study is not completed, but at this time, it can be concluded that antiandrogens should be taken for a prolonged period of time to achieve maximum efficacy.

Geller et al.[45] described the effect of megestrol acetate in the treatment of BPH. A total of 61 patients were randomized into placebo and megestrol acetate groups and studied over a 5-month period. Improvement in symptoms of prostatism was similar in both groups. Seventy percent of the drug-treated patients reported a reduction of libido. Sexual side effects have kept the steroidal antiandrogens, such as megestrol, from being used widely for BPH.

A large, prospective, randomized clinical trial comparing a 5-alpha-reductase inhibitor with a placebo is being conducted in the United States and abroad. Results of this investigation are not available, but preliminary reports suggest that the administration of synthetic alpha$_1$-reductase inhibitor causes regression of prostate size on a magnitude similar to that with LH-RH analog administration. Very few side effects, including impotence, have been reported.

Results. Prevention of contraction of the smooth muscle should, from a theoretical point of view, provide the patient relief from obstruction. However, there is an important factor that has not been considered. Stereometric studies by Bartsch[46,47] and Ohrh and Bartsch[48] demonstrated that although the prostate is usually considered to be a glandular organ, it contains a large quantity of fibromuscular stroma. In normal prostates, the ratio of stroma to epithelium is

2:1, whereas in BPH it is approximately 5:1. The stroma consists of smooth muscle and intermuscular components, such as collagen. The extractability of collagen is the limiting factor in the contraction and release of the smooth muscle. The effect of the alpha blockers will therefore depend on nonmuscular components. At the present time, very little is known about age-related changes in these components.

Hormonal treatment of BPH has resulted largely in regression of the epithelial component; there is no apparent effect on the stroma. It is important to keep in mind that prostate involution because of regression of the epithelial part may not necessarily decrease urethral resistance and therefore may not reduce the symptoms of prostatism. Again, BPH is characterized by more stromal than epithelial enlargement.

Interventional Therapy

Prostatic Urethroplasty

Prostatic urethroplasty with a balloon catheter is meant to be an entirely outpatient procedure, performed under topical anesthesia aided by mild intravenously administered sedation. Its morbidity is minimal,[2–6,49–54] and no mortality is expected. The procedure is relatively simple in skilled hands, and few guidelines have to be followed to avoid complications such as incontinence from dilating the external urinary sphincter. This procedure should markedly reduce the cost of treatment of BPH and should lead to greater patient acceptance. It can be performed on almost any patient regardless of his medical condition.

Technique. For this procedure, the patient is placed in a supine position on the table. Optimal imaging and guidance are obtained in either oblique projection. The desired oblique position can be obtained by placing a sponge wedge on either side of the patient, or, if a C-arm fluoroscopy unit is available, the tube can be rotated either way. The latter method is preferable since the patient is more comfortable in a flat supine position.

An intravenous line is started before the procedure for the administration of antibiotics and sedatives or for emergency medication if it should become necessary. Broad-spectrum prophylactic antibiotics, such as cephalosporin, ampicillin, or a combination of sulfamethoxazole and trimethoprim, are started before the procedure and continued orally for 5 to 7 days, after completion of the procedure.

The penis is prepared and draped as it would be for a surgical procedure. Transureteral topical 2 percent viscous lidocaine is applied generously in the urethra. All catheter and guidewire maneuvers are performed under fluoroscopic guidance.

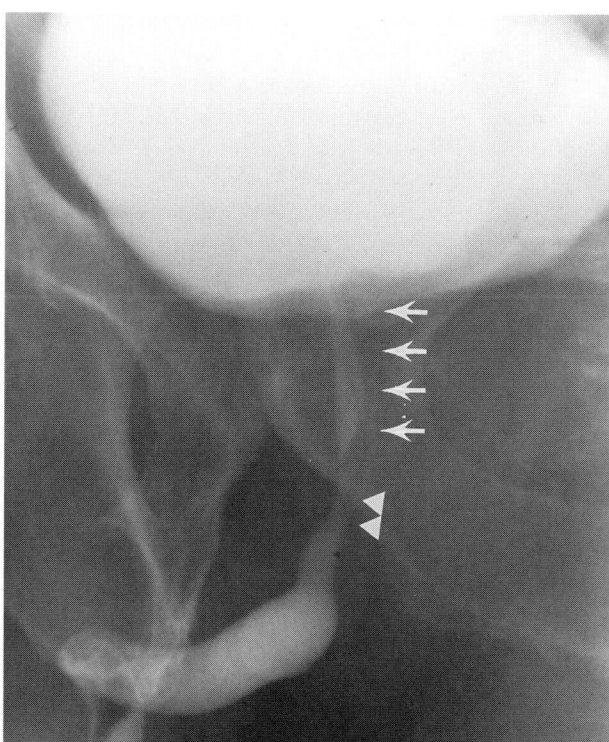

Figure 37-14. RUG showing the length and caliber of the prostatic urethra (*arrows*) as well as the location of the membranous urethra that corresponds to the external sphincter (*arrowheads*).

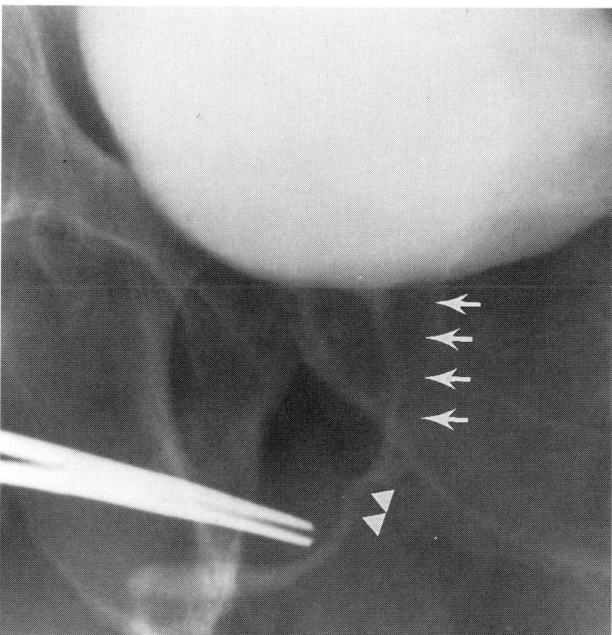

Figure 37-15. VCUG in the same patient showing the length and different morphologic appearance of the prostatic urethra (*arrows*) obtained in this dynamic study as well as the location of the external sphincter (*arrowheads*).

A baseline RUG is performed to assess the degree of obstruction and to determine the landmarks that will be followed throughout the procedure, such as the position of the external sphincter, the length of the prostatic urethra, and the position of the bladder floor and neck. This baseline RUG is performed by advancing a 20 to 22 French Councill catheter to the midanterior urethra or just beyond the meatus; the balloon is filled with 1 or 2 ml of dilute contrast material. This ensures snug occlusion of the urethra so that forceful injection of contrast material can be accomplished to achieve maximal distention of the anterior and posterior urethra without retrograde reflux. The catheter can be positioned at the midanterior urethra or just beyond the meatus so that the partially inflated balloon lodges in the fossa navicularis.

Once the urethra has been occluded, a RUG is performed with a 60-ml catheter tip syringe (Fig. 37-14). The catheter tip ensures that the connections are snug and leakproof. The operator then determines and marks the position of the external sphincter, either by putting a small-gauge needle through the skin directed toward and overlapping the position of the external sphincter or by rotating the C arm so that the position of the external sphincter is overlapped by a known bony landmark, such as the inferior margin of the inferior pubic ramus. From this point on, the tube angle

and the patient should remain as stable as possible so that the landmarks remain unchanged.

The length of the prostatic urethra is determined so that it may be dilated in its entirety. Some contrast material should be kept in the bladder to identify the bladder base because this is where most of the prostatic bulk lies, and it is extremely crucial to dilate this area adequately. Once this has been accomplished, the Councill catheter balloon is deflated, and the catheter is advanced into the bladder. A guidewire is advanced through the lumen of the Councill catheter and curled in the bladder. At this point, the Councill catheter is removed from the bladder and penis. Although not essential, a VCUG can be performed on the table (Fig. 37-15), especially if the patient feels like voiding. This helps to confirm the landmarks.

A generous amount of lubricant is applied to the prostatic urethroplasty balloon catheter before it is advanced over the guidewire. The catheter is advanced so that the proximal balloon marker is placed beyond the external sphincter. The authors use a balloon diameter of 30 mm (Fig. 37-16) (Cook, Inc.); smaller balloons do not decrease the morbidity and might be less effective. At this point, and especially if the patient or the C-arm arc has moved, a repeat RUG can be performed using a small (6 French) pediatric feeding tube, which should be advanced *alongside* the shaft of the catheter to approximately the midanterior urethra. Compression should be applied to the penis so that the proximal urethral channel is occluded adequately

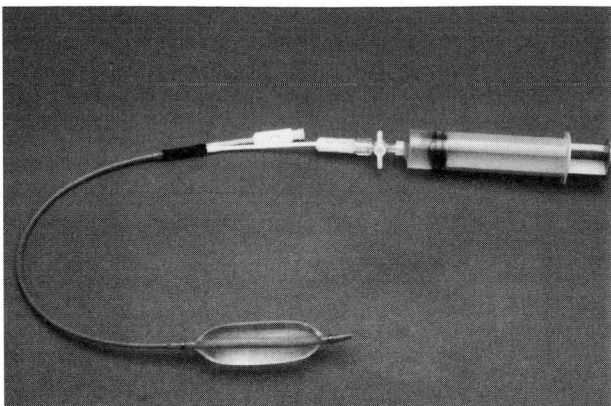

Figure 37-16. The 30-mm-diameter prostatic urethroplasty balloon catheter used by most investigators.

and no reflux of contrast material can occur. A repeat injection of contrast material will determine the relationship of the external sphincter to the proximal balloon marker. These repeat RUGs can be performed at any time during the dilation procedure, even when the balloon is fully inflated, to ensure that the landmarks have remained unchanged.

The balloon catheter is inflated slowly to its maximal diameter and pressure (Fig. 37-17). Because the patient experiences the most discomfort during the

Figure 37-17. Image showing the balloon fully inflated in the prostatic urethra, including the bladder neck (*arrows*) and the entirety of the prostatic urethra.

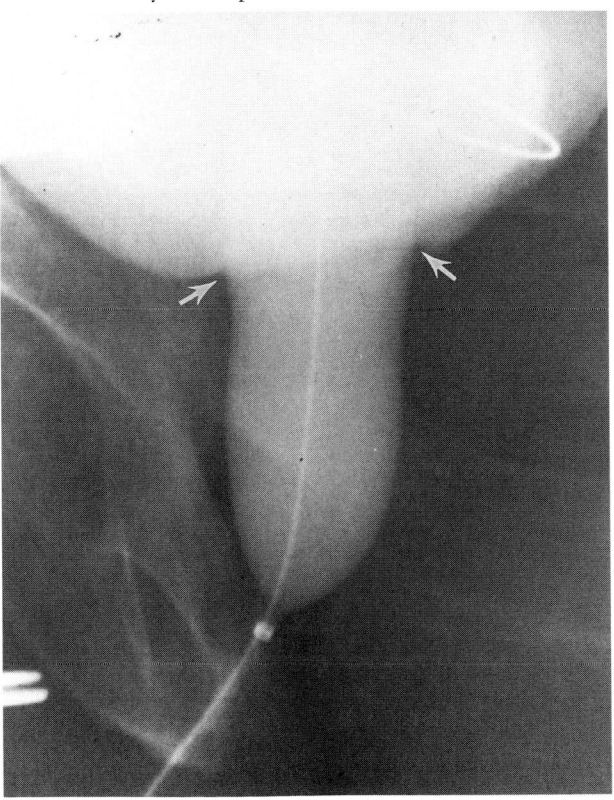

initial inflation, adequate intravenously administered sedation should be available. More intense than the pain is the extreme urge to void, which results from the stretching of the muscle and nerve fibers of the bladder neck. Because the balloon has a strong tendency to migrate into the bladder, the place of least resistance, strong tension should be applied on the catheter while the balloon is being inflated. If at any point the balloon has migrated into the bladder or distal in the prostatic urethra, it should be deflated and repositioned so that adequate dilatation of the entire prostatic urethra, including the apex, may be accomplished. If there is any doubt about the position of the external sphincter, a repeat RUG with the feeding tube should be performed. The balloon may appear as if it is being pulled proximal to the external sphincter and anterior urethra. However, the pelvic floor is formed by a group of muscles, tendon attachments, and soft tissues, and the external sphincter is a very strong muscular structure that most likely will not allow the balloon to go through when fully inflated. If there is any doubt, a repeat RUG will show that the relationships are still the same and it is merely the pelvic floor that is being pulled. After a few minutes of full balloon inflation, the tension required on the catheter shaft will decrease as the compliance of the prostatic and periprostatic tissues increases with the forces applied by the balloon. The balloon should be left in place for approximately 10 minutes.

In some instances the prostatic urethra is so long that the balloon has to be repositioned more distally to dilate the entire urethra, including the bladder neck. If this is necessary, an extra 5 to 10 minutes of dilation should be adequate.

At the completion of the dilation, the balloon is fully deflated and removed and the guidewire left in place. During balloon catheter removal, the shaft of the catheter should be turned continuously in the same direction in which the balloon was originally folded so that the catheter collapses as much as possible, thus avoiding more trauma to the anterior urethra.

The next step is to repeat the RUG (Fig. 37-18) to assess the results. The same 20 to 22 French Councill catheter is advanced *alongside* the guidewire to the midanterior urethra. Again, the Councill catheter balloon is partially inflated with 1 to 2 ml of dilute contrast material to ensure snug occlusion of the urethra. (Note: If the Councill catheter is advanced *over* the guidewire, the seal between the syringe and the injecting port of the Councill catheter will be faulty, allowing leakage of contrast material and precluding a good forceful injection to distend the anterior and posterior urethra adequately.) The RUG is performed in an oblique projection to evaluate the prostatic urethra. If no significant dilatation has been obtained, re-

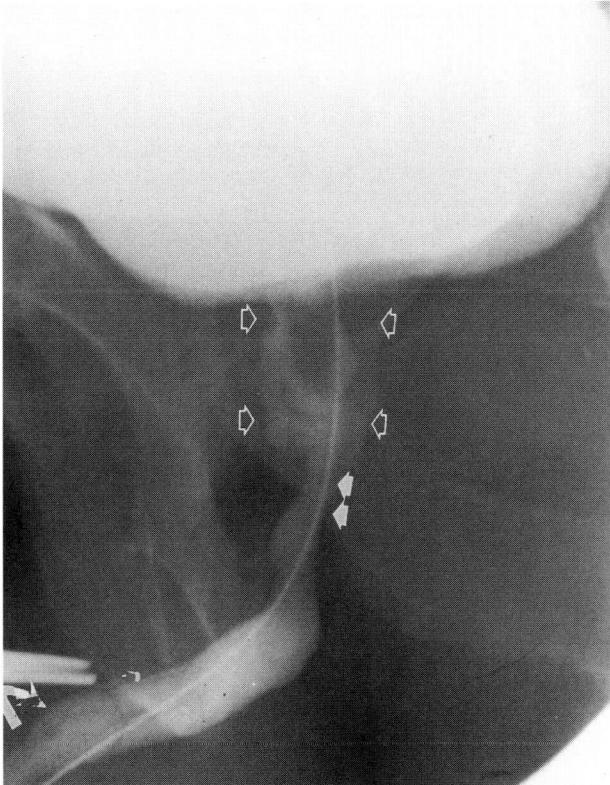

Figure 37-18. RUG immediately after balloon dilation while the guidewire is still in place and curling the bladder. Note the significant increase in the prostatic urethra caliber (*open arrows*) after dilation and the intactness of the external sphincter (*solid arrows*). The Councill catheter balloon has been partially inflated to ensure snug occlusion of the urethra for the adequate performance of the RUG (*curved arrow*).

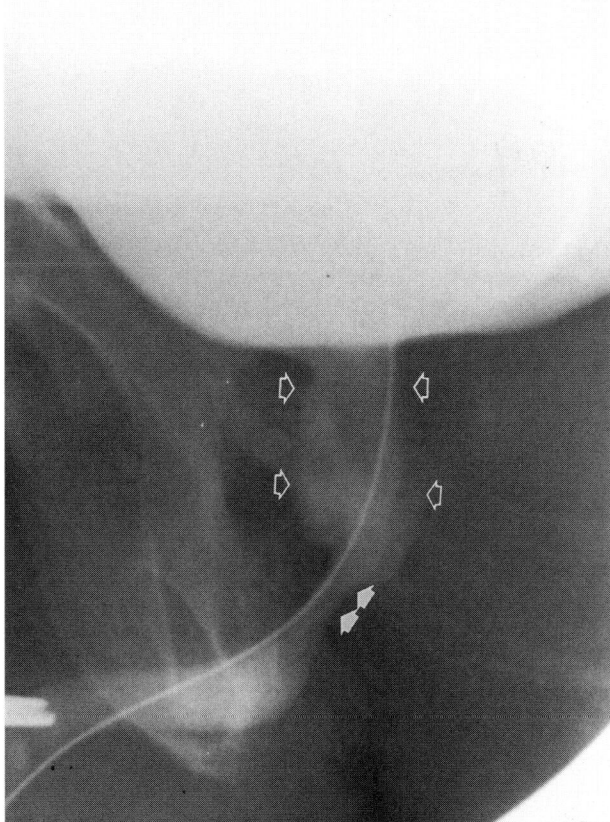

Figure 37-19. VCUG obtained immediately after balloon dilation while the guidewire is still in place. Again, note the significantly increased prostatic urethra caliber (*open arrows*) as well as the intactness and preservation of the external sphincter (*solid arrows*).

peat dilation will be necessary. Increased incidence of hematuria or complications because of repeat dilations have not been described. Again, a VCUG can be obtained on the table (Fig. 37-19), although this is not mandatory.

To verify that the prostatic commissures have been disrupted, the RUG is repeated in a straight anteroposterior projection. This radiographic impression will show a much narrower prostatic urethra than the oblique projection because the anterior and posterior commissures have been disrupted, allowing an increase in the anteroposterior caliber but not in the transverse diameter because of the opposing prostatic lobes. The increase in the anteroposterior caliber by disruption of the prostatic commissures, plus the stretching of the prostatic capsule, is enough to allow the creation of a larger lumen so that the bladder outlet resistance decreases.

If the dilation is adequate, the partially inflated Councill catheter balloon is deflated and removed to be advanced later *over* the guidewire into the bladder. At this point, the guidewire is removed and the 5-ml Councill catheter balloon is inflated with 20 ml of very

dilute contrast material or saline. The balloon usually will not rupture at this volume because it is made of latex, which is very distensible. Tension on the catheter from the inflated balloon will prevent it from falling into the traumatized prostatic fossa, which might produce significant discomfort and bleeding once the local anesthesia has worn off.

The bladder is irrigated vigorously, and all blood and clots are removed. The catheter should be left in place, with slight tension applied to the end to decrease the amount of subsequent hematuria. Most of the hematuria occurs during catheter manipulations, especially during balloon inflation. The hematuria may seem excessive, but once the bladder has been well irrigated and the clots have been removed, the urine will usually have only a light red tint. If the hematuria remains significant, the 20 to 22 French Councill catheter should be exchanged over a guidewire for a larger one, perhaps 26 to 30 French, so that the small capillary bleeding is tamponaded. Continuous tension at the end of the catheter should also help to decrease the hematuria, which should be minimal by 24 hours.

The patient is instructed to be relatively sedentary the rest of the day so that the hematuria does not recur or continue. In most instances, the Councill catheter is removed the following morning. The patient's bladder is fully filled before catheter removal. The patient is instructed to void after removal to ensure that he can void and will not go into retention at home. In a few instances a patient has developed delayed retention and required recatheterization. This has occurred in patients with very large prostates in whom the superimposed edema has resulted in retention. If this situation seems likely, the drainage catheter should be left for longer periods of time (48–72 hours).

Results. As more procedures are performed and longer follow-ups are available, it has become clear that the procedure is not for everyone; but when the indications are followed and the patients are carefully selected, satisfactory results should occur in approximately 75 to 85 percent of cases.[50–52,54–62] These results have been fairly consistent among the different published series, even in those in which patient selection has been suboptimal. Improvement is noted on both the obstructive and irritative symptoms. An approximately 50 percent improvement in average and peak uroflows, a 75 percent increase in average uroflow volumes, and a 300 percent average decrease in postvoid residuals have been noted after prostatic urethroplasty in a nonrandomized, nonselective study.[62]

All the studies that made special note of the presence of an enlarged middle lobe have reported a significant decrease in the success rate.[60,62,63] Therefore, this group of patients should be carefully screened and excluded if possible, especially if there are other options for these patients.

Patients with bladder dyssynergic problems, large residuals, or atony are also not good candidates, because adequate detrusor function is required for emptying of bladder contents and therefore the relief of prostatism and associated complications. This group of patients probably would not benefit from other procedures, such as TURP, either.

Complications. Although prostatic urethroplasty with a balloon catheter is an easy procedure to perform, certain guidelines must be followed to avoid complications, such as damage to the external sphincter with resulting incontinence. All postdilation manipulations over a guidewire must be done under fluoroscopic or direct vision to avoid the creation of false passages that could result in a perineal abscess(es),[64] bleeding, or further trauma to the already lacerated and disrupted prostatic urethra and commissures. In none of the studies in which these guidelines have been strictly followed has incontinence as the result of external sphincter injury been seen.

There has been one case of a perineal abscess that developed after a difficult blind bladder recatheterization in a patient with a significantly enlarged prostate and previous retention who was confined to catheter drainage before balloon urethroplasty and who remained in retention after catheter removal. As previously stated, this type of complication can easily be avoided if the guidelines are followed.

There have been no significant long-term complications. Prolonged hematuria requiring hospital admission is seen in approximately 4 percent of cases[50,52,62] and is associated mainly with concomitant coagulopathy or severe hypertension. In none of the reported series has this complication required a blood transfusion; it can be managed by catheter traction and bladder irrigations in approximately 24 hours.

Urinary retention is another possible complication that is rarely seen, usually in patients with very large prostates, in whom the slightest amount of edema tips the patient into retention. This complication is managed by careful recatheterization and drainage for 48 to 72 hours.

If the procedural guidelines are followed, if proper antibiotic coverage is given before and after the procedure, if coagulopathies are corrected or foreseen before the procedure, if prostatic size is taken into consideration, and if prolonged catheterization is used prophylactically, the procedure should be complication-free.

Summary. Prostatic urethroplasty is a relatively new procedure for which we are still gathering data, but so far it has been shown to provide symptomatic improvement in 75 to 85 percent of a carefully selected group of patients (Tables 37-1 and 37-2). It is meant to be an outpatient procedure performed under local

Table 37-1. Characteristics of the Prostate and Requirements for Best Results of Balloon Dilation

Bilobar prostatic enlargement
Prostatic size less than 50 g
Prostatic urethral length between 2.5 and 4.5 cm
Moderate symptoms of prostatism
Adequate detrusor function

Table 37-2. Absolute and Relative Contraindications for the Performance of Balloon Dilation of the Prostate

Absolute Contraindications
  Localized prostatic malignancy
  Obstructing median lobe
  Decompensated detrusor
  Very large prostate (>60–70 g)
Relative Contraindications
  Multiple large prostatic calculi
  Chronic bacterial prostatitis
  High residual urine (>50% of total bladder capacity)
  Urethral strictures

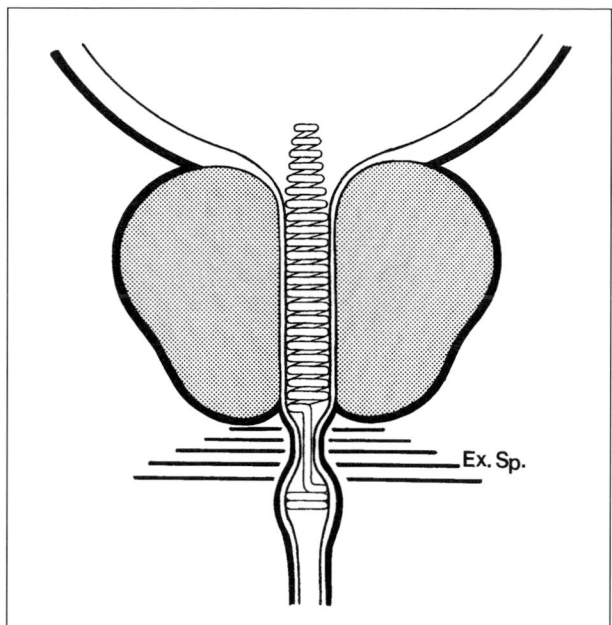

Figure 37-20. Diagrammatic presentation of the Fabian stent and anatomic relationships. *Ex.Sp.,* external sphincter.

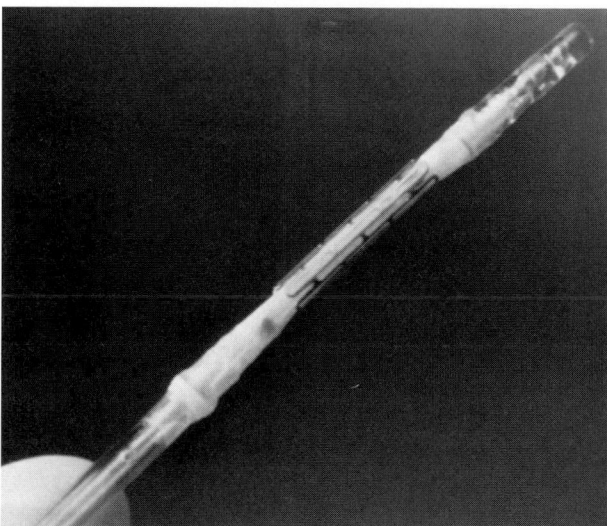

Figure 37-21. Titanium prostatic stent crimped over the deployment balloon catheter.

anesthesia and intravenously administered sedation and therefore should decrease medical costs significantly.

The higher recurrence rate, as compared with TURP, is a real issue and should be weighed against the higher morbidity and side effects associated with TURP in relatively healthy patients, although it probably should not be an issue in high-risk patients.

Prostatic Stents

Four stents have found the most clinical applications in Europe: the double-helix or Fabian stent, the Wallstent (Medinvent) tubular mesh stent, the balloon-expandable titanium stent, and the Double Mallecot intraurethral plastic stent. All of these devices can be placed with cystoscopic or fluoroscopic guidance. The procedure is similar to the ones described above. Cystoscopy or radiographic studies are performed to determine anatomic landmarks, to measure the length of the prostatic urethra, and to exclude other abnormalities. The patients receive antibiotics for about a week. The introduction and placement of the device are monitored closely for correct deployment. The patients are also instructed to avoid retrograde urethral catheterizations.

Double-Helix or Fabian Stent. This intraurethral prosthesis (Fig. 37-20) (Uromed, Kurt Drews) is made of stainless steel and consists of three parts: a body formed by spiral loops very close to one another that will remain in the prostatic urethra and include the bladder neck; a neck, 2 cm long, that will remain in the membranous urethra; and a head formed by two

spiral loops that should remain in the bulbous urethra. Four lengths are available: 45, 55, 65, and 75 mm; the size is selected according to the prostatic urethral length plus 1 cm so that the proximal portion of the body surpasses the cervical adenomatous border.

The prosthesis can be placed under fluoroscopic, sonographic, or cystoscopic guidance with subsequent radiographic confirmation. The new prostheses are gold-plated to reduce contact allergy and incrustation. They can be removed, if desired, for repositioning. Because of the tight winding of the coils, there is no incorporation of the stent by urothelium. For this reason, it was originally recommended that the stent be changed yearly; however, follow-up studies have reported patients with no infections, incrustations, or stent migration for close to 2 years.[65–69]

Wallstent or Tubular Wire Mesh. This stent has been discussed under urethral stents. Its advantage is that, because of the spaces between the mesh, the stent is completely incorporated into the adjacent tissues within 4 to 6 months, and infectious incrustation or migration is therefore avoided. The proximal portion of the placed stent should avoid the external sphincter to preclude incontinence or irritation but should include the bladder neck.[70]

Balloon-Expandable Titanium Stent. This stent[71] comes collapsed and mounted over a high-pressure balloon (Fig. 37-21) that deploys it to its full diameter; therefore, secondary dilations are not needed (Fig. 37-22). It is available in several lengths from 22 to 58 mm.

The insertion is simple and similar to the techniques previously mentioned. This stent also becomes incorporated into the urethral and periurethral tissues.

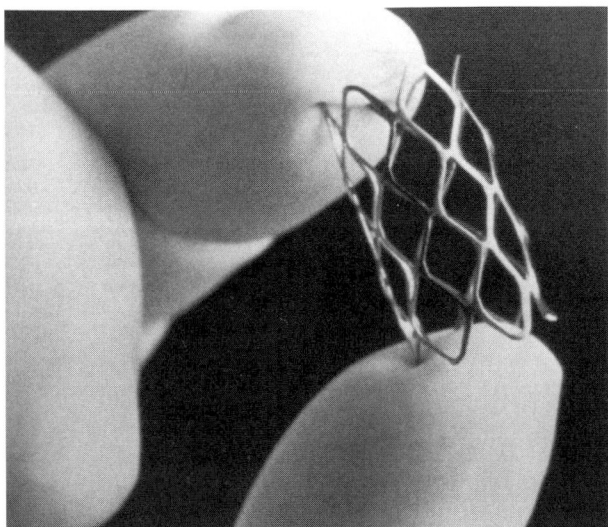

Figure 37-22. Appearance of the fully-expanded titanium stent, which resembles the Palmaz vascular stent.

Double Mallecot Plastic Urethral Stent. This stent (Angiomed, Germany) is made of a plastic polymer (Fig. 37-23A) and comes in special kits (Fig. 37-23B) for cystoscopic or fluoroscopic placement. The stent consists of a larger intravesical "basket" that localizes to the bladder neck and a smaller basket that localizes just proximal to the verumontanum and proximal to the external sphincter. These baskets are bridged by a 16 French catheter of various lengths, depending on the prostatic urethral length. The distal end of the catheter has a suture that allows withdrawal and repositioning and is removed after the procedure is completed. Like other plastic stents or drainage catheters elsewhere in the urinary system, this stent requires periodic changes.

Summary. Temporary prostate stents inserted under local anesthesia offer a useful alternative for the short-term relief of urinary retention and prostate symptoms in patients who have limited life expectancy or who are awaiting prostate surgery. Because of problems with incrustation and infection, the stents cannot be left in place for a long period of time and must be changed. If long-term results confirm the early successes with these devices, permanent prostate stents, such as the Wallstent and Palmaz stents, which are known to be incorporated by epithelium (Fig. 37-24) while holding open the prostatic urethra, will offer a simple and effective alternative to prostate surgery for many patients.

Prostatic Hyperthermia

Hyperthermia is the central elevation of tissue temperature. The concept that hyperthermia has some cura-

Figure 37-23. (A) Cone-down magnified view of the Double Mallecot prostatic urethral stent. (B) Components of the deployment kit.

A

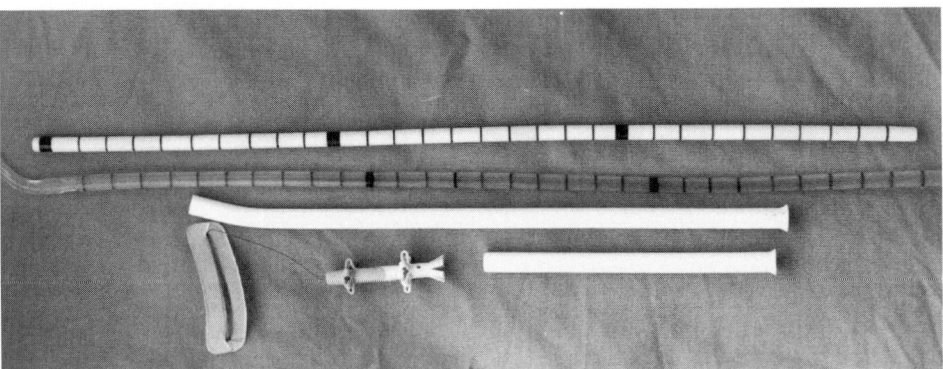

B

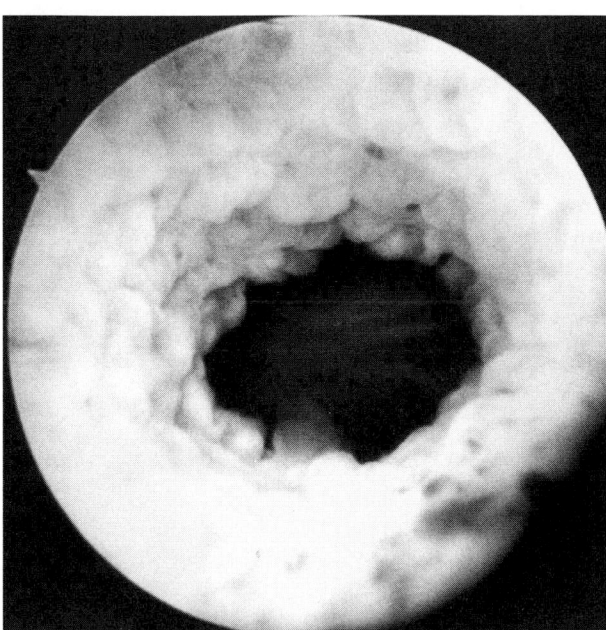

Figure 37-24. Cystoscopic follow-up 6 months after prostatic urethral Wallstent placement. The extrudent and overgrown urothelium through the stent mesh gives the typical cobblestone appearance while keeping the prostatic urethral caliber wide open.

tive benefits has been known for millennia. This idea developed from the observation that after a high fever many ailments resolved or improved. In 1866, Busch[72] published the first scientific report of the complete regression of a histologically proven sarcoma after a bout of erysipelas with high fever. In 1877, Bruns[73] reported the complete cure of a patient terminally ill with multiple recurrent melanomas after erysipelas. In 1893, Coley[74] reported a series of patients with advanced cancer who were either cured or significantly improved by accidental or deliberate exposure to erysipelas. Many other reports followed, with similar results after natural exposure or injection of filtered extracts of highly pyrogenic toxins.[75,76] By the same principle, others reported cure or significant improvement after deliberate hyperthermia exposure locally or of the whole body.[75,77-86] It is well known that some bacteria and viruses adapted to body temperatures find it difficult to proliferate at temperatures only a few degrees higher.

In the past few years, there has been a revival of interest in the effects of hyperthermia on biologic systems, particularly for the treatment of cancer. Investigations have focused on hyperthermia as the sole treatment or combined with radiotherapy with or without cytotoxic drugs.

Hyperthermia alone has the capacity to kill cells selectively. Temperatures from 42°C to 45°C cause selective death of tumor cells.[87] One of the factors that make cancer cells more susceptible than normal cells is the defective heat dissipation by neoplastic tissue due to the poor blood supply and decreased vasodilation capacity of the neovascular bed in response to the thermal load. Other factors known to influence tumor cell sensitivity to heat include nutritional factors, pH, and O_2 concentration, all of which are also related to tumor perfusion.[88-90] These effects are potentiated by both radiation and chemotherapy.

Hyperthermia may be applied externally or interstitially. External techniques include radiofrequency current fields, ultrasound, and microwave. Interstitial techniques include radiofrequency current between implanted electrodes, microwave heating with needle-shaped implanted antennas, implanted ferromagnetic seeds or needles heated by radiofrequency magnetic induction, hot water circulated through implanted hollow tubes, and conductive heating catheters.[91-96] This expanding knowledge of hyperthermia benefits has motivated its use in almost every system and organ in the body, including the prostate. Hyperthermia has been used for both malignant tumors and BPH.[97-104]

There are two basic delivery methods of hyperthermia: transrectally, as used by Servadio and others,[95,101,103,105] Yerushalmi et al.,[97,102] and Mendecki et al.[98]; and transurethrally, as used by Astrahan et al.[104] All of these techniques have used temperatures in the range of 42°C to 46°C and require a prolonged series of treatments ranging from 6 to 18. The preferred course for best results is 12 to 15 treatments. The treatments are 1 hour each one or two times a week. The reported early clinical results are encouraging, although most lack objective documentation, such as uroflow, urodynamic, and prostate volumetric data before and after treatments.

It is the authors' opinion that this protracted course of treatments will not replace either completely or in specific instances the conventional mode of BPH therapy. To compete with transurethral resection, a procedure would have to be safer, less expensive, less involved, and accomplished in a single treatment on an outpatient basis.

With these premises as background, the authors' research has completely changed the previously established clinical and experimental protocols. The goal of this therapy is to produce central prostatic tissue ablation (Fig. 37-25), with subsequent debulking (Fig. 37-26) of the periurethral adenomatous tissue, by a retrograde transurethral approach that uses much higher temperatures—in the range of 80°C to 90°C—for a single exposure period ranging from 15 to 60 minutes.

The current prototype is a 7 French, computer-controlled, heat-emitting catheter that has only been used in experimental animals. With this catheter, the depth

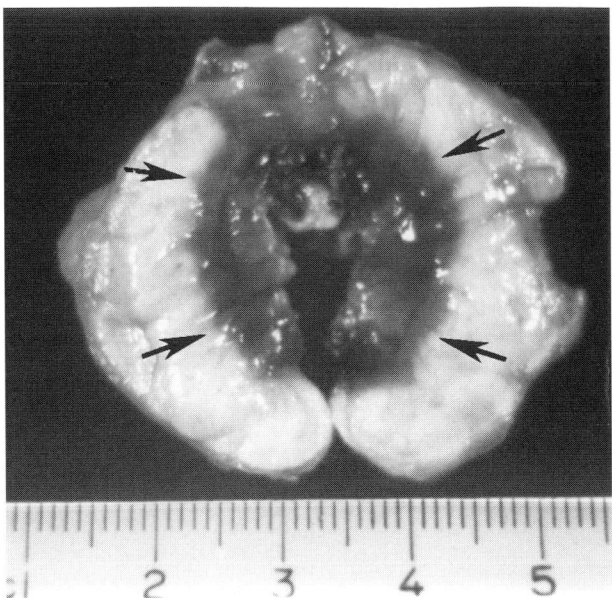

Figure 37-25. Transverse microscopic section of the prostate at its midportion showing the clear-cut demarcation between the area of acute coagulative necrosis (*arrows*) and the healthy surrounding peripheral prostatic tissue after exposure to conductive hyperthermia at 95°C.

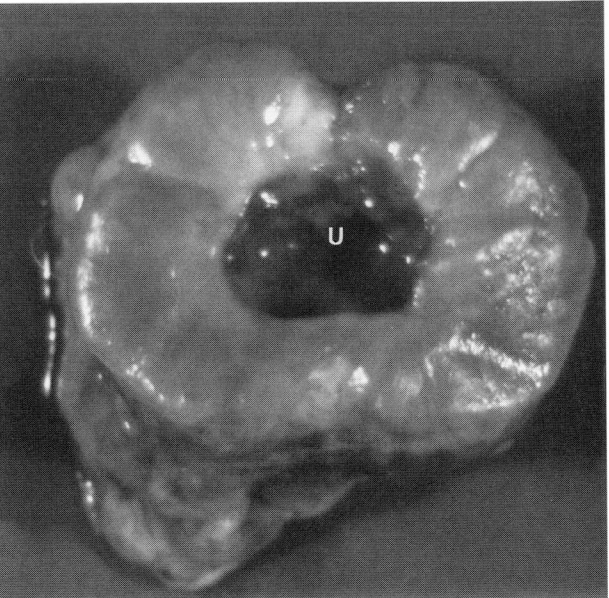

Figure 37-26. One-month posttreatment gross prostatic specimen transversely sectioned showing the much larger central prostatic urethral lumen once the necrosed tissue has sloughed off. *U*, urethral channel.

and amount of tissue to be ablated and subsequently debulked from the central periurethral adenoma can be adequately controlled.

Histopathologic findings have shown coagulative necrosis that extended to different depths, depending on the treatment and length of exposures used. After treatment and complete resolution of the initial inflammatory response, reepithelialization, widening of the prostatic urethra, atrophy of the periurethral prostatic tissue glands, maintenance of the normal architecture of the periurethral prostatic tissue glands, and maintenance of the normal architecture of the periurethral connective tissue were seen on subsequent follow-ups.

With this technique, it is possible to ablate periurethral prostatic tissue completely with resultant debulking. Experimentally this produces a large central lumen in the bladder outlet obstruction caused by central adenomatous tissue (Fig. 37-27). This limited resection of a central channel has been proposed by some urologists[106] in high-risk patients in an effort to limit the intervention. The technique suggested here accomplishes the goal in a single treatment, and because it is easy to control and selectively ablate the desired amount of periurethral tissue, the chances of complications are diminished. The authors doubt that other complications, such as strictures, would develop because of the normal appearance of the regenerated tissues. Because the major nerve networks are more

toward the periphery, impotence, another condition that might be of concern, probably will not occur if the ablation is only deep enough to open a reasonable channel. This procedure may be performed on an outpatient basis, because there is no bleeding or need for external drainage. The necrosed tissue sloughs off gradually, without sequelae. The procedure would require regional anesthesia because of the higher temperatures used.

Some of the clinical issues involved with this procedure will be resolved only when the clinical trial begins. However, experimental animal studies suggest that this technique may be a nonsurgical, minimally invasive way of debulking the central prostatic adenoma. The ongoing clinical series using low temperatures have not produced results comparable to those of transurethral resection of the prostate, the standard mode of BPH treatment. Although the proposed high-temperature debulking of the periurethral central adenoma has not reached the clinical stage, it has many theoretical advantages over previous methods.

Prostatic Biopsy

Sonography-guided transrectal prostatic biopsy is usually performed as an outpatient procedure. The medical history is reviewed, and a physical examination is performed. Biopsy is contraindicated in patients who have coagulopathy, who are on anticoagulant therapy, or who have acute prostatitis.

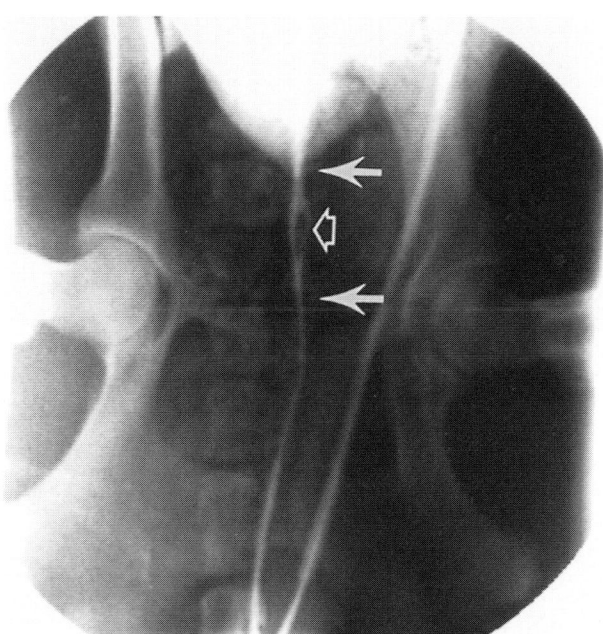

A

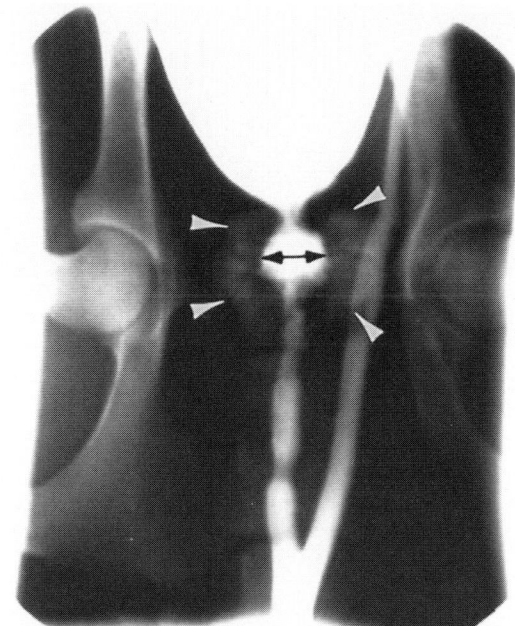

B

Figure 37-27. (A) Baseline RUG of male canine showing the length of the prostatic urethra (*solid arrows*) and the location of the verumontanum (*open arrow*). (B) Two weeks after prostatic conductive hyperthermia there is a much larger prostatic urethral lumen (*double black arrow*) as compared to baseline. At this time, there is still evidence of generalized prostatic swelling, as evidenced by the contra reflux into the periphery of the prostatic glands (*arrowheads*). (C) After 1 month there is further increase of the central prostatic urethral channel (*double black arrow*) from further tissue sloughing.

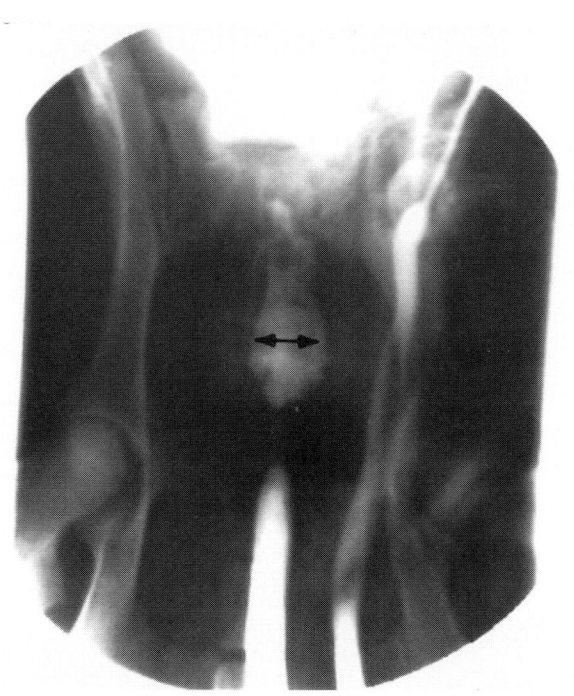

C

Sedation is not required except in patients with severe anxiety or pain. Because the biopsy will be performed through the rectal wall and in order to prevent infectious complications, a broad-spectrum antibiotic is given immediately before and for 3 to 5 days after the procedure. Local anesthesia is achieved with topical intrarectal 2 percent lidocaine jelly or 1 percent lidocaine (Xylocaine; Astra Pharmaceutical) injected through a fine needle into the rectal wall. Sonographic artifacts related to air or feces in the rectum are minimized by a preprocedural cleansing enema. The patient is scanned in the left lateral decubitus knee-chest position. Having the patient maintain a partially distended urinary bladder aids in imaging the base of the prostate.

Biplanar imaging of the prostate is performed with a high-frequency transducer (5–7 MHz). The probe should have a needle channel and an electronic targeting guide for precise transrectal needle positioning (Fig. 37-28). A condom is placed over each probe to decrease the risks of contamination and infection. An acoustic window is provided by interfacing water in

the protecting condom between the transducer and the rectal wall.

After application of local anesthesia in the periprostatic tissues, an 18-gauge needle is advanced through the biopsy channel of the linear-array probe. The biopsy needle is placed in an automatic spring-loaded biopsy gun (Biopty; Bard Urologic). The needle is advanced under continuous direct sonographic guidance so that the echogenic tip is placed adjacent to, but not

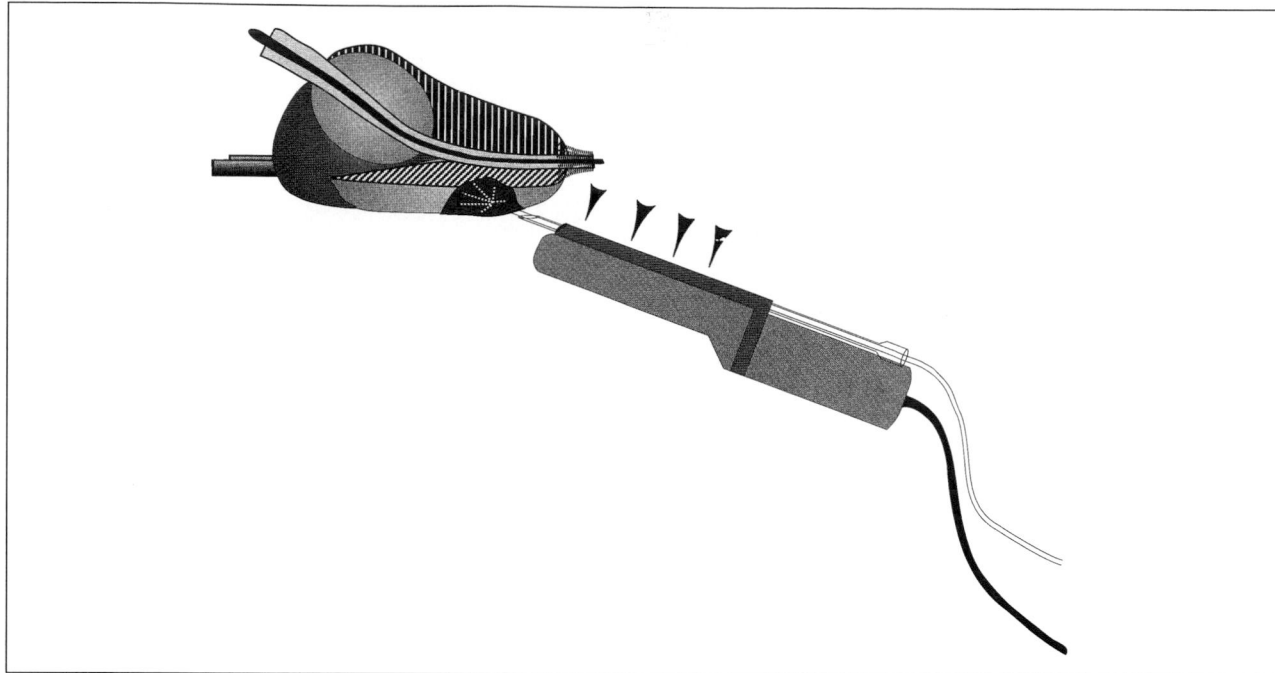

Figure 37-28. Diagram highlighting the biopsy channel of needle (*arrowheads*) for the accurate performance of prostatic biopsies done through the transrectal prostatic ultrasound probe.

at, the area to be biopsied. (One must be aware that no sample is obtained from the 5 mm of tissue immediately adjacent to the needle tip.) The biopsy gun is fired, sampling the tissue of interest with a histologic core. The biopsy tract can be seen sonographically as an echogenic line within the prostatic parenchyma (Fig. 37-29).

Typically, the authors obtain two to three histologic cores from the area with abnormal sonographic features and an additional sample of sonographically normal contralateral prostatic lobe as a control biopsy. It is desirable to include the prostatic capsule and, if possible, a sample of the adjacent seminal vesicle in the biopsy specimen. The cores are submerged in formaldehyde for analysis.

After the procedure, the patient is briefly reexamined to rule out formation of periprostatic fluid collections, suggesting hemorrhage. Vital signs are compared with the values obtained before the biopsy. Only a few patients complain of pain during or after the procedure and are usually discharged, requiring only the antibiotic therapy and conditional analgesics.

Results

The reader is referred to the latest works of McNeal[19] and Lee,[24] pioneers and primary researchers of this technology, which is constantly changing and being updated. Sonography offers the most sensitive evaluation of the prostate, with predictive values equivalent

to those of the digital rectal examination (DRE). The use of DRE and prostate-specific antigen (PSA) results further increases the positive predictive value of transrectal ultrasound (TRUS), which may help in the

Figure 37-29. Longitudinal transrectal ultrasound image of the prostate showing a large hypoechoic nodule (*long white arrows*) in the base of the prostate extending into the seminal vesicles (*SV*), suspicious for a carcinoma. The needle (*short white arrows*) is noted sampling the center of the suspicious nodule. *B*, bladder.

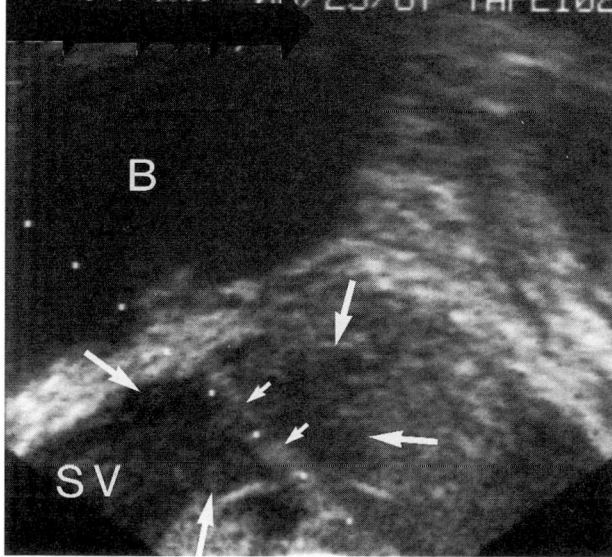

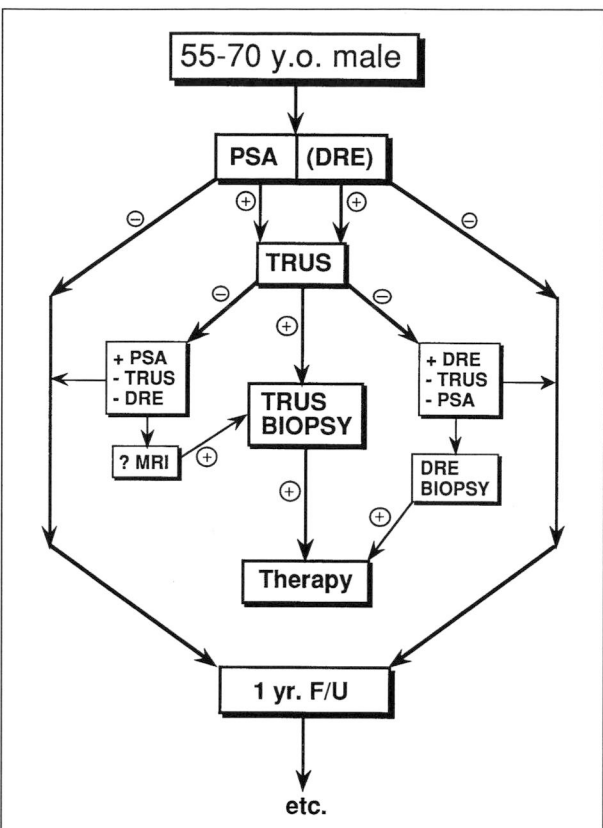

Figure 37-30. Prostate cancer screening algorithm showing the sequence of events according to the results obtained on digital rectal examination (*DRE*), prostate-specific antigen (*PSA*) levels, and transrectal ultrasound (*TRUS*) imaging.

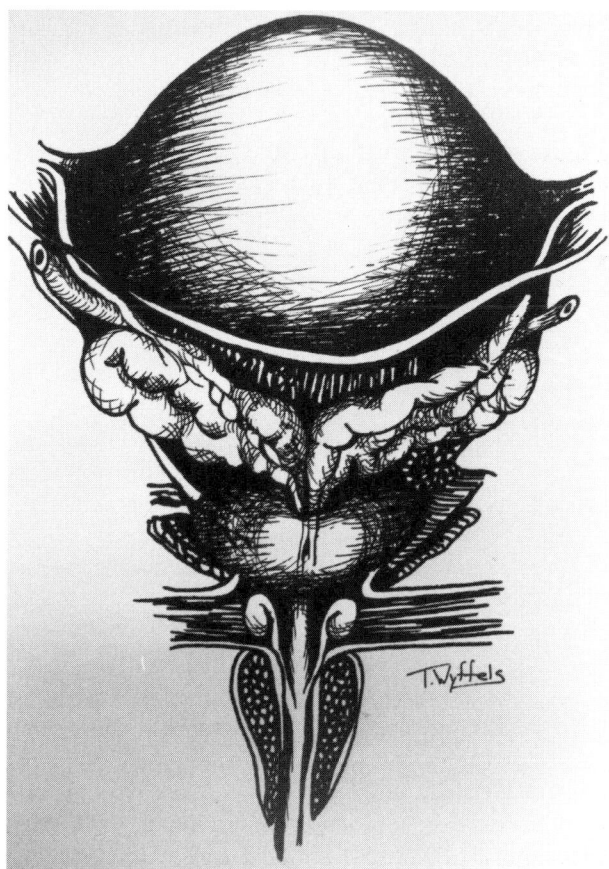

Figure 37-31. Diagram showing the relationship and location of the seminal vesicles and the pelvic floor.

management of TRUS-positive small lesions. The currently accepted "standard of care" for early detection, the DRE, must be expanded to include the use of TRUS and PSA.

The current lack of definitive data should not prevent the cost-effective use of appropriate technology in the early detection of prostate cancer. Littrup and Lee[107] have devised a clinical algorithm for efficacious patient care (Fig. 37-30), which, if followed, should increase early cancer detection.

The Seminal Vesicles and Ejaculatory Ducts

Surgical Anatomy

The seminal vesicles (Fig. 37-31) are two sacculated and contorted tubes between the posterior surface of the bladder and the rectum. Each vesicle is about 5 cm long and is somewhat pyramidal in form, the base being directed backward, upward, and laterally. Each seminal vesicle consists of a single tube coiled upon itself and giving off several irregular diverticula; the separate coils, as well as the diverticula, are connected together by fibrous tissue. The tube has a diameter of 3 to 4 mm, and its length, when uncoiled, varies from 10 to 15 cm. It ends above in a cul-de-sac; its lower extremity becomes constricted into a narrow straight duct that joins with the corresponding deferential duct to form the ejaculatory duct. The arteries supplying the seminal vesicles are derived from the inferior vesical and middle rectal arteries. The veins and lymph vessels accompany the arteries. The nerves are derived from the pelvic plexuses.

The ejaculatory ducts, one on each side of the median plane, are formed by the union of the duct of a seminal vesicle with a terminal part of a different duct and are nearly 2 cm long. They arise at the base of the prostate, run anteroinferiorly between the median and right (or left) lobes, pass along the sides of the prostatic utricle, and end on the colliculus seminalis in a slitlike orifice on or just within the margins of the opening of the utricle. The ducts diminish in size and also converge toward their termination.

The spermatic cord is composed of arteries, veins,

link vessels, nerves, and the deferential duct, connected together by areolar tissue. The arteries of the spermatic cord are the testicular, cremasteric, and deferential. The nerves are the genital branch of the genitofemoral nerve, the cremasteric nerve, and the testicular plexus of the sympathetic nerve, joined by filaments from the pelvic plexus that accompany the deferential artery.

Important Affections of the Seminal Vesicles

Important affections of the seminal vesicles include nonspecific seminal vesiculitis or seminal vesicle inflammation, which is usually a secondary inflammatory process associated with prostatitis[108]; gonococcal vesiculitis; tuberculosis; calculi; calcification; cysts; benign tumors; primary carcinoma; sarcoma; and secondary carcinoma. Of these, the only one discussed in this chapter is seminal vesicle inflammation.

Inflammation of the seminal vesicle in the absence of an inflamed prostate is unusual, but it may occur. Ultrasonography may show enlarged, echogenic seminal vesicles. This appearance is best appreciated by endorectal ultrasonography, which may also demonstrate seminal vesicle or ejaculatory duct calculi.[109] CT demonstration of cystic dilatation of an inflamed seminal vesicle has also been reported.[110,111] It is very important to treat seminal vesiculitis because it may lead to seminal vesicle abscess.[108]

In general, inflammatory conditions of the prostate and seminal vesicles are usually diagnosed by clinical symptoms and the physical examination. Imaging studies are often complementary and may guide appropriate intervention. Since seminal vesiculitis and prostatitis can be challenging conditions to treat clinically, an interventional procedure has been developed that can be beneficial in treating these inflammatory processes.

Interventions in the Seminal Vesicles

Candidates for seminal vesicle aspiration and injection are patients with chronic prostatitis unresponsive to standard medical therapy in whom seminal vesiculitis is suspected. Patients with bleeding disorders or acute prostatitis are excluded. After cleansing enemas, a standard biplanar transrectal ultrasound examination of the seminal vesicles is performed with the patient in the left lateral decubitus knee-chest position. The probe needs to have a channel and electronic guidance for direct transrectal needle puncture. This channel is also used to administer local anesthesia and as a port

for the transrectal diagnostic aspiration or therapeutic injection of the seminal vesicles.

After sonographic evaluation of the size and internal sonographic pattern of the seminal vesicles, the lateral aspect or more distended portion of the seminal vesicles is localized. Local anesthesia is accomplished with a 22-gauge needle and 1 percent lidocaine. The seminal vesicles are then punctured with an 18-gauge needle under continuous sonographic monitoring. Accurate positioning of the needle is verified with imaging of the echogenic needle tip in the seminal vesicles and by the aspiration of seminal vesicle fluid. Thick secretions often do not permit the easy acquisition of a fluid sample despite an accurate needle position. It is then necessary to inject 1 to 2 ml of sterile nonbacteriostatic saline before again attempting aspiration. Fluid samples are submitted for aerobic, anaerobic, chlamydial, and ureaplasmal cultures.

After diagnostic aspiration of the seminal vesicles, the needle can be reinserted for therapeutic injection. Each seminal vesicle is injected with 2 ml of 1 percent lidocaine and 20 to 40 mg of gentamycin. Accurate delivery of these drugs is confirmed by observing expansion of the seminal vesicles during the injection and the dispersion of small echogenic foci within the seminal vesicles, related to movement of microbubbles of air from the injected material.

As with transrectal prostatic biopsy, a broad-spectrum antibiotic is given orally immediately before and for 3 to 5 days after the seminal vesicle puncture to minimize infection related to the procedure.

Results

The only series available reports the results of seminal vesicle aspirations and injections performed in 19 men ages 28 to 70 years (mean, 44.5 years) with symptoms of chronic prostatitis unresponsive to therapy for periods ranging from 1 to 40 years (mean, 11 years).[112] These patients underwent seminal vesicle aspiration, injection, or both for suspected seminal vesiculitis.

The sonographic pattern of the seminal vesicles is variable. Normally, the seminal vesicles display a homogeneous low level of echogenicity in comparison with the adjacent prostatic parenchyma (Fig. 37-32). Although the seminal vesicles appeared normal in some patients in this series, diffuse cystic changes or inhomogeneous increased echogenicity within the glands were also seen. The seminal vesicles were enlarged in 11 of the patients; some degree of asymmetry was frequently noted.

Aspiration yielded material for microbiologic culture in 18 of 23 attempts (12 bilateral, 6 unilateral; 78 percent), and 15 of those aspirates yielded positive

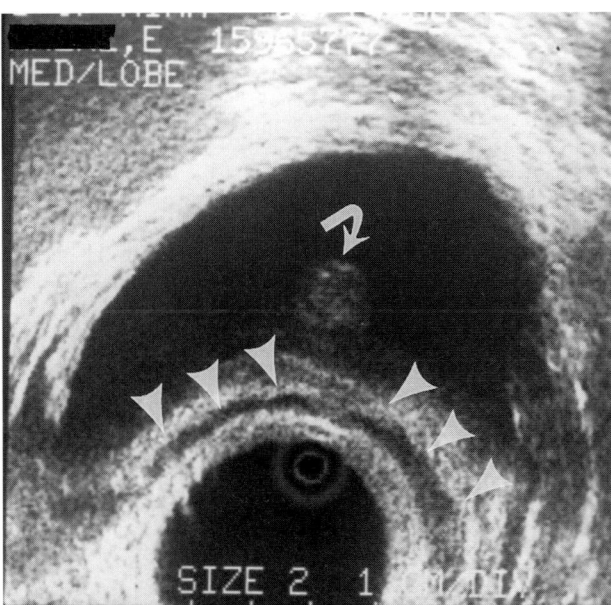

Figure 37-32. Transverse transrectal ultrasound image of the seminal vesicles (*arrowheads*) showing their normal characteristic hypoechogenicity. Incidentally noted is the presence of a prostatic middle zone protruding and elevating the bladder floor (*curved arrow*).

cultures. Except for 2 instances, all positive cultures revealed multiple bacteria, including both aerobes and anaerobes. *Pseudomonas paucimobilis* was cultured in the 2 aspirates showing a single organism. No cases of *Chlamydia* or ureaplasma were found.

A total of 21 seminal vesicle injections were performed in 18 patients; all but 1 were bilateral. Temporary relief of symptoms (range, 2 days to 6 months) was reported in association with 10 procedures (48 percent), and no change was seen following the other 9 (43 percent). Adequate follow-up was not available in the remaining cases.

Summary

Transrectal sonography provides a means of directly imaging the seminal vesicles and also of localizing those structures for direct puncture. Diagnostic aspiration and therapeutic injection of the seminal vesicles are technically easy procedures that may reflect new areas of clinical application of transrectal sonography, providing us with a potentially powerful tool for evaluating infectious processes of the seminal vesicles.

The temporary relief of symptoms after therapeutic seminal vesicle injection in patients with chronic prostatitis may reflect a contribution by seminal vesiculitis to the clinical manifestations classically ascribed to chronic prostatic infection. In this setting, therapeutic

seminal vesicle injection may represent a means of treating seminal vesiculitis; however, more long-term follow-up is necessary to evaluate the role of this procedure.

The Scrotum

Surgical Anatomy

The scrotum is a cutaneous and fibromuscular contractile sac containing the testes and the lower parts of the spermatic cords. It is dependent below the pubic symphysis, in front of the upper parts of the thighs. It is divided on its surface into right and left halves by a cutaneous ridge or raphe, which is continued ventrally to the inferior surface of the penis and dorsally along the middle line of the perineum to the anus; the left usually descends a little more than the right, in correspondence with the greater length of the left spermatic cord. The raphe indicates the bilateral origin of the scrotum from the genital swellings. The scrotum consists of the skin and the dartos muscle, together with the external spermatic, cremasteric, and internal spermatic fascia, already described in connection with the spermatic cord. The inner surface of the internal spermatic fascia is loosely attached to the parietal layer of the tunica vaginalis.

The arteries supplying the scrotum are the external pudendal branches of the femoral artery, the scrotal branches of the femoral cutaneous nerve. The anterior third of the scrotum is supplied mainly from the first lumbar segment of the spinal cord (through the ilioinguinal and genitofemoral nerves), whereas the posterior two-thirds are supplied mainly from the third sacral segment (through the perineal and posterior femoral cutaneous nerves).

The Scrotum and the Role of Ultrasonography in Interventional Techniques

High-resolution, high-frequency ultrasound images of the scrotum have assumed a significant role in the evaluation of both acute and chronic scrotal lesions. This safe and rapid technique produces information that is complementary to the clinical history and examination and to physiologic studies such as radioisotope scanning or Doppler ultrasonography. Successful images can be obtained with dynamic or static scanning and can be performed using either contact scanning of the scrotum or a water bath, to permit the transducer to stand off from the scrotum. Frequencies between 7.5 and 20 MHz are generally employed.

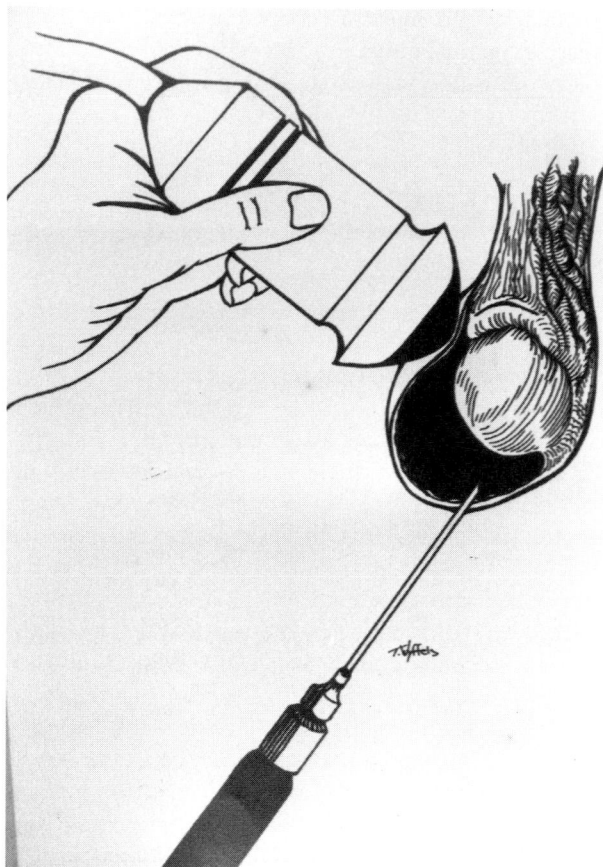

Figure 37-33. Diagram showing the technique for real-time ultrasound-guided hydrocele diagnostic puncture and drainage.

The testes are identified sonographically as homogeneously echogenic structures. The lobes of the testes cannot be defined sonographically. The head, body, and tail of the epididymis can be identified as contiguous with the testes. This structure is at least as brightly reflected as the testes. The multiple, individual layers of the scrotal skin are generally seen as a single echogenic band; differences in skin thickness between the two sides are an important sonographic finding. Among the small structures that are frequently seen are the normal veins of the pampiniform plexus, as well as the appendix of the testis or epididymis, which may be identified as a punctate echogenic focus.

Although interventional techniques in the scrotum using ultrasonography are limited, they can be important in the evaluation of patients with hydrocele. Aspirations of hydroceles are not commonly performed; however, this procedure may be the treatment of choice in patients who refuse surgical treatment or in patients with multiple medical problems who are not candidates for surgical drainage. It can also be used in the evaluation of patients with hydrocele, secondary

to an underlying lesion, to provide a better physical examination of the testicle.

The technique is rather simple. The authors prefer to use a 22-gauge needle attached to a 10-ml syringe. The scrotal skin is cleaned either with Betadine or alcohol. The skin is penetrated with a needle in the most dependent part of the scrotum, without injuring the testicle itself or the epididymis. This can obviously be accomplished under ultrasound guidance (Fig. 37-33).

In the past, the use of sclerosing agents like tetracycline has been advocated for the treatment of recurrent hydrocele. However, this technique is rarely used in today's practice.

References

1. Watanabe H, Kato H, Kato T. Diagnostic application of the ultrasonotomography to the prostate. Jpn J Urol 1968;59: 273–279.
2. Castaneda F, Lund G, Larson BW, et al. Prostatic urethra: experimental dilation in dogs. Radiology 1987;163:649–654.
3. Castaneda F, Johnson S, Hulbert J, et al. Urethroplasty with balloon catheter in prostatic hypertrophy. AJR 1987;149: 313–314.
4. Castaneda F, Reddy P, Wasserman N, et al. Benign prostatic hypertrophy: retrograde transurethral dilation of the prostatic urethra in humans. Work in progress. Radiology 1987;163: 649–654.
5. Castaneda F, Reddy P, Hulbert J, et al. Retrograde prostatic urethroplasty with balloon catheter. Semin Intervent Radiol 1987;4:115–121.
6. Castaneda F, Isorna S, Hulbert J, et al. The importance of separation of prostatic lobes in relief of prostatic obstruction by balloon catheter urethroplasty: studies in dogs and humans. AJR 1989;153:1301–1304.
7. Amis ES, Pfister RC, Yoder IC. Interventional radiology of the adult bladder and urethra. Semin Roentgenol 1883;18:322.
8. Lattimer JK. Similar urogenital anomalies in identical twins. Am J Dis Child 1944;67:199–200.
9. Mohammed SH, Wirima J. Balloon catheter dilatation of urethral strictures. AJR 1988;150:327–330.
10. Russinovican LK, Griggs W, Jander P. Balloon dilatation of urethral strictures. Urol Radiol 1980;2:33–37.
11. Hare W, McOmish D, Nunn I. Percutaneous transvesical antegrade passage of urethral strictures. Urol Radiol 1981;3: 107–112.
12. Scales F, Katlen B, vanBreda A, et al. Impassable urethral strictures: percutaneous transvesical catheterization and balloon dilation. Radiology 1985;157:59–61.
13. Palmaz JC, Ritcher GM, Noelge G, et al. Intraluminal stents in atherosclerotic iliac artery stenosis: preliminary report of a multicenter study. Radiology 1988;168:727–731.
14. Sigwart U, Puel J, Mirkovitch V, et al. Intravascular stents to prevent occlusion and restenosis after transluminal angioplasty. N Engl J Med 1987;316:701–706.
15. Rousseau H, Puel J, Joffre F, et al. Self-expanding endovascular prosthesis: an experimental study. Radiology 1987;164: 709–714.
16. Coons H. Self-expanding stainless steel biliary stents. Radiology 1989;170:979–983.
17. Irving DJ, Adam A, Dick R, et al. Gianturco expandable metallic biliary stents: results of a European clinical trial. Radiology 1989;172:321–326.
18. Milroy E, Chapple C, Eldin A, et al. A new stent for the treat-

ment of urethral strictures: preliminary report. Br J Urol 1989;63:392–396.

19. McNeal JE, Bostwick DG, Kindrachuk RA, et al. Patterns of progression in prostate cancer. Lancet 1986;1:60–63.
20. Kaufman JJ, Schultz JI. Needle biopsy of the prostate: a reevaluation. J Urol 1962;87:164–168.
21. Golimbu M, Morales P, Al-Askari SA, et al. CAT scanning in staging of prostatic cancer. Urology 1981;18:305–308.
22. Pollack HM. Clinical imaging of prostatic carcinoma. Prog Clin Biol Res 1987;239:643–657.
23. Watanabe H. Historical perspective on the use of transrectal sonography of the prostate. Prog Clin Biol Res 1987;237:5–13.
24. Lee F, Gray JM, McLeary RD, et al. Transrectal ultrasound in the diagnosis of prostate cancer: location, echogenicity, histopathology, and staging. Prostate 1985;7:117–129.
25. Rifkin MD, Friedland GW, Shortliffe L. Prostatic evaluation by transrectal endosonography: detection of carcinoma. Radiology 1986;158:85–90.
26. Griffiths GJ, Clements R, Jones DR, et al. The ultrasound appearances of prostatic cancer with histological correlation. Clin Radiol 1987;38:219–227.
27. Lee F. Transrectal ultrasound in the diagnosis, staging, guided needle biopsy and screening for prostatic cancer. Prog Clin Biol Res 1987;237:73–109.
28. Berry SJ, Coffey DS, Walsh PC, et al. The development of human benign prostatic hyperplasia with age. J Urol 1984;132:474–479.
29. Rutkow IM. Urological operations in the United States. J Urol 1986;135:1206–1208.
30. McPherson K, Wennberg JE, Hovind OB, et al. Small-area variations in the use of common surgical procedures: an international comparison of New England, England, and Norway. N Engl J Med 1982;307:1310–1314.
31. Wennberg J, Gittelsohn A. Variations in medical care among small areas. Sci Am 1982;246:120–134.
32. Holtgrewe HL, Mebost WK, Dowd JB, et al. Transurethral prostatectomy: practice aspects of the dominant operation in American urology. J Urol 1989;141:248–253.
33. Bruskewitz RC, Larsen EH, Madsen PO, et al. Three-year follow-up of urinary symptoms after transurethral resection of the prostate. J Urol 1986;136:613–615.
34. Fowler F, Wennberg JE, Timothy RP, et al. Symptom status and quality of life following prostatectomy. JAMA 1988;259:3008–3022.
35. Riley G, Lubitz J. Outcomes of surgery among the Medicare aged: surgical volume and mortality. Health Care Finance Rev 1985;7:37–47.
36. Wennberg JE, Roos N, Sola L, et al. Use of claims data systems to evaluate health care outcomes: mortality and re-operation following prostatectomy. JAMA 1987;257:933–936.
37. Lubitz J, Riley G, Newton M. Outcomes of surgery among the Medicare aged: mortality after surgery. Health Care Finance Rev 1985;6:103–105.
38. Mebust WK, Holtgrewe HL, Cockett ATK, et al. Transurethral prostatectomy: immediate and postoperative complications. A cooperative study of 13 participating institutions evaluating 3,885 patients. J Urol 1989;141:243–247.
39. Caine M, Perlberg S, Meretyk S. A placebo-controlled double-blind study of the effect of phenoxybenzamine in benign prostatic obstruction. Br J Urol 1978;50:551.
40. Abrams PH, Shah PJR, Stone R, et al. Bladder outflow obstruction treated with phenoxybenzamine. Br J Urol 1982;54:527.
41. Brooks ME, Sidi AA, Hanani Y, et al. Ineffectiveness of phenoxybenzamine in treatment of benign prostatic hypertrophy: a controlled study. Urology 1983;21:474–478.
42. Peters CA, Walsh PC. The effect of nafarelin acetate, luteinizing hormone/releasing hormone agonist on benign prostatic hyperplasia: a placebo-controlled study. N Engl J Med 1987;317:599.
43. Gabrilove JL, Levine AC, Kireschenbaum A, et al. Effect of long-acting gonadotropin-releasing hormone analog (leuprolide) therapy on prostatic size and symptoms in 15 men with benign prostatic hypertrophy. J Clin Endocrinol Metab 1989;68:461.
44. Stone N. Flutamide in the treatment of benign prostatic hypertrophy. Urology 1989;34(Suppl):64.
45. Geller J, Nelson CG, Albert JD, et al. Effects of megestrol acetate on uroflow rates in patients with benign prostatic hypertrophy. Urology 1979;14:467.
46. Bartsch D. Electron microscopic stereological analysis of the normal human prostate and of benign prostatic hyperplasia. J Urol 1979;122:481.
47. Bartsch D. Light microscopic stereological analysis of the normal human prostate and of benign prostatic hyperplasia. J Urol 1979;122:487.
48. Ohrh P, Bartsch D. Human benign prostatic hyperplasia: stroma disease. New prospective by quantitative morphology. Urology 1980;16:625.
49. Klein L, Lemming B. Balloon dilation for prostatic obstruction: long-term follow-up. Urology 1989;33:198–201.
50. Goldenberg L, Perez-Marrero R, Lee L, et al. Endoscopic balloon dilation of the prostate: early experience. J Urol 1990;144:83–88.
51. Dowd J, Smith J. Balloon dilation of the prostate. Urol Clin North Am 1990;17:671–677.
52. Daughtry J, Rodan B, Bean W. Balloon dilation of prostatic urethra. Urology 1990;36:203–209.
53. Grado G, Larson T, McKee G. Urethral dilation in prostatic malignancies for obstructive uropathy secondary to radiation-induced edema. Presented at the Radiological Society of North America, Chicago, IL, 1990.
54. Lopatin W, Martynik M, Hickey DP, et al. Retrograde transurethral balloon dilation of prostate: innovative management of abacterial chronic prostatitis and prostatodynia. Urology 1990;36:508–510.
55. Abrams P, Lewis P, Gillatt D, et al. Balloon dilatation in BPH under endoscopic control. Presented at meeting of the American Urological Association, Dallas, TX, 1989.
56. Hernandez-Graulau J, Goldberg H, Choudhury M, et al. Transurethral prostate divulsion for treatment of benign hyperplasia: New York Medical College preliminary report. Presented at meeting of the American Urological Association, Dallas, TX, 1989.
57. Klein LA, Perez-Marrero R, Bowers GW, et al. Balloon dilatation of the prostate: a multicenter study with one-year follow-up. Presented at meeting of the American Urological Association, Dallas, TX, 1989.
58. McCullough DL, Herrera M, Harrison LH, et al. Transurethral balloon dilatation of the prostate (TUBDP)—alternative to transurethral resection of the prostate. Presented at meeting of the American Urological Association, Dallas, TX, 1989.
59. Perez-Marrero RA, Emerson L. Urodynamic changes after prostatic balloon dilatation for outflow tract obstruction. Presented at meeting of the American Urological Association, Dallas, TX, 1989.
60. Reddy PK. Role of balloon dilation in the treatment of benign prostatic hyperplasia. Prostate (Suppl) 1990;3:39–48.
61. Wasserman NF, Reddy PK, Zhang G, et al. Experimental treatment of benign prostatic hyperplasia with transurethral balloon dilation of the prostate: preliminary study in 73 humans. Radiology 1990;177:485–494.
62. Winfield HN, Castaneda F, Richardson K. Transurethral balloon dilation: University of Iowa experience. In: Castaneda F, Smith A, Castaneda-Zuniga W, eds. Therapeutic alternatives in the management of benign prostatic hyperplasia. New York: Thieme, 1993:65–103.
63. Machan L, Gill KP, Abel P, et al. Prostatic urethroplasty: results at the Royal Postgraduate Medical School. Semin Intervent Radiol 1989;6:65–71.
64. Castaneda F, Hulbert JC, Letourneau JG, et al. Perineal abscess after prostatic urethroplasty with balloon catheter: report of a case. Radiology 1990;174:49–50.

65. Vicente J, Chechile G, Salvador J, et al. Long-term follow-up of patients with intraurethral prostheses. Semin Intervent Radiol 1989;6:82–89.

66. Reuter JH, Oettinger M. Las primeras experiencias con la espiral de acero en lugar del cateter permanente. Arch Esp Urol 1986;39:65–68.

67. Fabian KM. Der intraprostatische, partielle katheter (urologische spirale). Urologe 1980;19:236–238.

68. Fabricius PG, Matz M, Zepnick H. Die endourethralspiraleeine alternative zum daverkatheter? Arztl Fortbild (Jena) 1983;77:482–485.

69. Yachia D, Lask D, Rabinson S. Self-retaining intraurethral stent: an alternative to long-term indwelling catheters or surgery in the treatment of prostatism. AJR 1990;154:111–113.

70. Milroy E. Self-expandable metallic prostatic urethral stents. In: Castaneda F, Smith A, Castaneda-Zuniga W, eds. Therapeutic alternatives in the management of benign prostatic hyperplasia. New York: Thieme; in press.

71. Perez-Marrero R, Emerson LE. Balloon expandable titanium prostatic urethral stents. In: Castaneda F, Smith A, Castaneda-Zuniga W, eds. Therapeutic alternatives in the management of benign prostatic hyperplasia. New York: Thieme, 1993:145–150.

72. Busch W. Ober den Einfluss welchen Heftigere Erysipeln Zuweilen auf Organisierte Neubildugen Ausuben. Verh Naurh Preuss Rhein Westphal 1866;23:28–30.

73. Bruns P. Die heilwirkung des Erysipels auf Geschwulste. Beitr Klin Chir 1877;3:443–466.

74. Coley WB. The treatment of malignant tumors by repeated inoculations of erysipelas—with a report of ten original cases. Am J Med Sci 1893;105:487–511.

75. Rohdenburg GL. Fluctuations in the growth of malignant tumors in man, with special reference to spontaneous recession. J Cancer Res 1918;3:193–225.

76. Nauts HC, Fowler GA, Bogatko FH. A review of the influence of bacterial infections and bacterial products (Coley's toxin) on malignant tumors in men. Acta Med Scand (Suppl) 1953;267:1–103.

77. Westermark F. Ober die Behandlung des Ulcerirenden Cervixcarcinomas. Mittel Konstanter Warme. Zentralbl Gynaekol 1898:1335–1339.

78. Gottschalk S. Zur Behandlung des Ulcerirenden inoperablen Cervixcarcinomas. Zentralbl Gynaekol 1899:79–80.

79. Vidal E. Travaux de la Deuxieme Conference Internationale pour l'Etude du Cancer. Paris, 1911:160.

80. Percy JF. Heat in the treatment of carcinomas of the uterus. Surg Gynecol Obstet 1916;22:77–79.

81. Goetz O. Ortliche Homogene Oberwarmung Gesunder und Kranker Gliedmassen. Dtsch Z Chir 1932;234:577–589.

82. Warren SL. Preliminary study of the effect of artificial fever upon hopeless tumor cases. AJR 1935;33:75–87.

83. Woodhall B, Prickrill KL, Georgiade NG, et al. Effect of hyperthermia upon cancer chemotherapy—application to external cancer of head and face structures. Ann Surg 1960;151:750–759.

84. Crile G Jr. Selective destruction of cancers after exposure to heat. Ann Surg 1962;156:404–407.

85. Shingleton WW, Bryan FA, O'Quinn WL. Selective heating and cooling of tissue in cancer chemotherapy. Ann Surg 1962;156:408–416.

86. Kirsch R, Schmidt D. Erste Experimentelle and Klinische Erfahrungen mit der Gaszkorper-Extrem-Hyperthermie. In: Doerr W, Linder F, Wagner G, eds. Aktuelle Probleme aus dem Gebiet der Cancerologie. Heidelberg: Springer-Verlag, 1966:53–70.

87. Cavaliere R, Cioczotto EC, Giovanella BC, et al. Selective heat sensitivity of cancer cells. Cancer 1967;20:1251–1381.

88. Bicher HI, Hetzel FW, Sanhu T, et al. Effects of hyperthermia on normal and tumor microenvironment. Radiology 1980;137:523–530.

89. Song CS, Kang MS, Rhee JG, et al. The effect of hyperthermia on vascular function, pH, and cell survival. Radiology 1980;137:795–803.

90. Emami B, Song CW. Physiological mechanisms in hyperthermia: a review. Int J Radiat Oncol Biol Phys 1984;10:289–295.

91. Astrahan MA, Norman A. A localized current field hyperthermia system for use with 192-iridium interstitial implants. Med Phys 1982;9:419–424.

92. Samaras GM. Intracranial microwave hyperthermia: heat induction and temperature control. IEEE Trans Biomed Eng 1984;31:63–69.

93. Strohbehn JW, Trembly BS, Douple EB. Blood flow effects on temperature distributions from an invasive microwave antenna array used in cancer therapy. IEEE Trans Biomed Eng 1982;29:649–661.

94. Lyons BE, Britt RH, Strohbehn JW. Localized hyperthermia in the treatment of malignant brain tumors using an interstitial microwave antenna array. IEEE Trans Biomed Eng 1984;31:53–62.

95. Stauffer PR, Cetas TC, Jones RC. Magnetic induction heating of ferromagnetic implants for inducing localized hyperthermia in deep seated tumors. IEEE Trans Biomed Eng 1984;31:235–251.

96. Brezovich IA, Atkinson WJ, Lilly MB. Local hyperthermia with interstitial techniques. Cancer Res 1984;44 (Suppl):4752s–4756s.

97. Yerushalmi A. Localized, non-invasive deep microwave hyperthermia for the treatment of prostatic tumors: the first 5 years. Recent Results Cancer Res 1988;107:140–146.

98. Mendecki J, Firedenthal E, Botstein C. Microwave applicators for localized hyperthermia treatment of cancer of the prostate. Int J Radiat Oncol Biol Phys 1980;6:1583–1588.

99. Kaver I, Ware J, Koontz W. The effect of hyperthermia on human prostatic carcinoma cell lines: evaluation in vitro. J Urol 1989;141:1025–1027.

100. Lindner A, Golomb J, Siegel Y, et al. Local hyperthermia of the prostate gland for the treatment of benign prostatic hypertrophy and urinary retention: a preliminary report. Br J Urol 1987;60:567–571.

101. Servadio C, Lieb Z, Lev A. Diseases of the prostate treated by local microwave hyperthermia. Urology 1987;30:97–99.

102. Yerushalmi A, Fishelovitz Y, Singer D, et al. Localized deep microwave hyperthermia in the treatment of poor operative risk patients with benign prostatic hyperplasia. J Urol 1985;133:873–886.

103. Servadio C, Lieb Z, Lev A. Further observations on the use of local hyperthermia for the treatment of diseases of the prostate in man. Eur Urol 1986;12:38–40.

104. Astrahan MA, Sapozink MD, Cohen D, et al. Microwave applicator for transurethral hyperthermia of benign prostatic hyperplasia. Int J Hyperthermia 1989;5:283–296.

105. Lieb Z, Rothem A, Lev A, et al. Histopathological observations in the canine prostate treated by local microwave hyperthermia. Prostate 1986;8:93–102.

106. Blandy JP. The history and current problems of prostatic obstruction. In: Blandy JP, Lytton BJ, eds. The Prostate. Chicago: Butterworths, 1986:17–18.

107. Littrup PJ, Lee F. Screening for prostate cancer: state of the art. Semin Intervent Radiol 1989;6:10–19.

108. Lee SB, Lee F, Solomon MH, et al. Seminal vesical abscess: diagnosis by transrectal ultrasound. J Clin Ultrasound 1986;14:546.

109. Littrup PJ, Lee F, McLeary RD, et al. Transrectal US of the seminal vesicles and ejaculatory ducts: clinical correlation. Radiology 1988;168:625.

110. Patel PS, Wilbur AC. Cystic seminal vesiculitis: CT demonstration. J Comput Assist Tomogr 1987;11:1103.

111. Rifkin MD. Ultrasound of the Prostate. New York: Raven, 1988.

112. Llerena J, Letourneau JG. Other prostatic interventions: seminal vesicles. Semin Intervent Radiol 1989;6:102–107.

38

Interventions in Urinary Diversions

PARVATI RAMCHANDANI

Background

Urinary diversion is performed in patients who have undergone cystectomy and in those with dysfunctional or nonfunctioning urinary bladders. The technique has evolved from the surgical creation of cutaneous fistulas such as nephrostomy, pyelostomy, or ureterostomy for urinary drainage to the use of the intestinal tract to divert and reconstruct the urinary tract.

In the early days of urinary diversion, the ureters were anastomosed to an intact sigmoid colon that was in continuity with the fecal stream (ureterosigmoidostomy) (Fig. 38-1). This procedure was the most common form of urinary drainage into the bowel when it was first introduced, but the frequent occurrence of complications such as pyelonephritis, upper tract deterioration, and carcinoma at the site of the ureteral anastomosis led to decreasing enthusiasm for this form of urinary diversion.[1,2]

Currently, ureters are implanted into bowel segments that are isolated from the intestinal and fecal streams. Two primary forms of such urinary diversion are the ileal conduit and the continent urinary diversion.

Ileal conduits (ileal loop, ureteroileostomy, Bricker loop) were introduced by Bricker in 1950[3] and are an important form of permanent supravesical urinary drainage. A 15- to 25-cm loop of distal small bowel is isolated and its proximal end is brought to the lower abdominal wall as a stoma while the distal end (the "butt" end) is closed. The ureters are anastomosed in an end-to-side fashion to the ileal segment to permit free retrograde reflux of ileal segment contents into the ureters (Fig. 38-2). Ileal conduits are relatively easy to construct and are the gold standard by which all urinary diversions are judged. However, the necessity for a stomal appliance to collect the urine and a significant rate of long-term complications, including reflux-induced deterioration in renal function, have led to the increasing popularity of continent urinary diversions.[4] These are constructed from either small

bowel alone or from a combination of small and large bowel and can either open onto the abdominal wall (cutaneous) or be anastomosed to the urethra (orthotopic) (Fig. 38-3). The ureteroenteral anastomosis is nonrefluxing in these cases. The many variations in surgical technique and the radiologic imaging cannot be addressed in this chapter, but the interested reader is referred to elegant reviews on the subject.[5-7] Both the cutaneous and orthotopic continent diversions have been enthusiastically accepted by patients because of the singular advantage that no stomal collection device is necessary. The long-term results and effects on renal function, if any, remain to be determined.

Complications of Urinary Diversion

The complications of ureteroileostomies and continent diversions are considered together because they necessitate similar interventions. The complications for which no interventional procedures are applicable, such as metabolic alterations, are not considered in this chapter.

Early complications, occurring less than 30 days postoperatively, can be separated into two main groups: general postoperative complications and complications related to the urinary pouch (ileal conduit or colonic reservoir) or the ureteral anastomotic site. General complications include those related to the wound and collections in the cystectomy bed, such as hematomas and infection. Infected hematomas and abscesses are best diagnosed by computed tomography (CT) and, as in other sites, can be successfully treated by CT- or ultrasound-guided aspiration and drainage.[8,9]

Complications related to the urinary pouch or the ureteroenteral anastomosis usually result in urinary extravasation, which is the most common urologic complication in the early postoperative period. It usually occurs at one or more of the suture lines. Patients may present with abdominal pain, prolonged ileus,

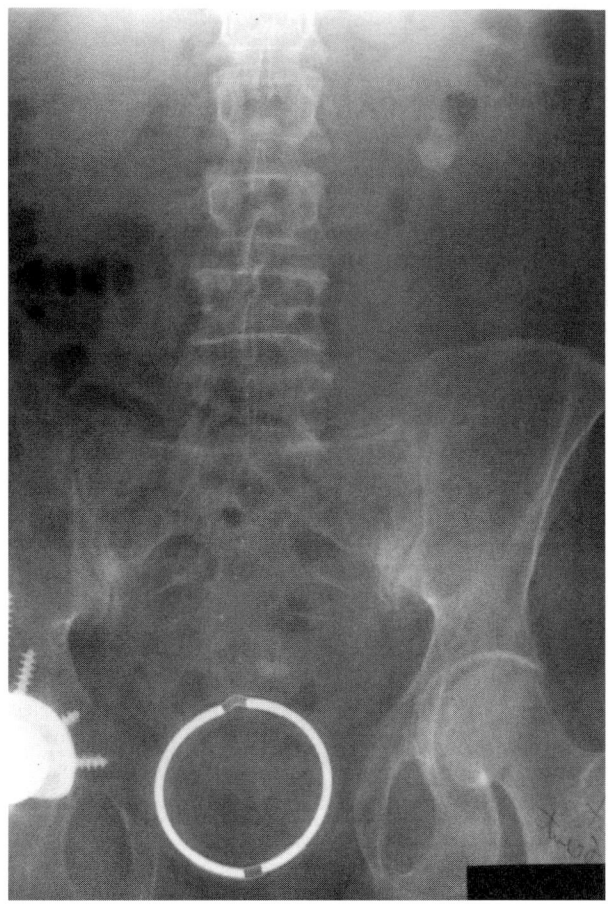

A

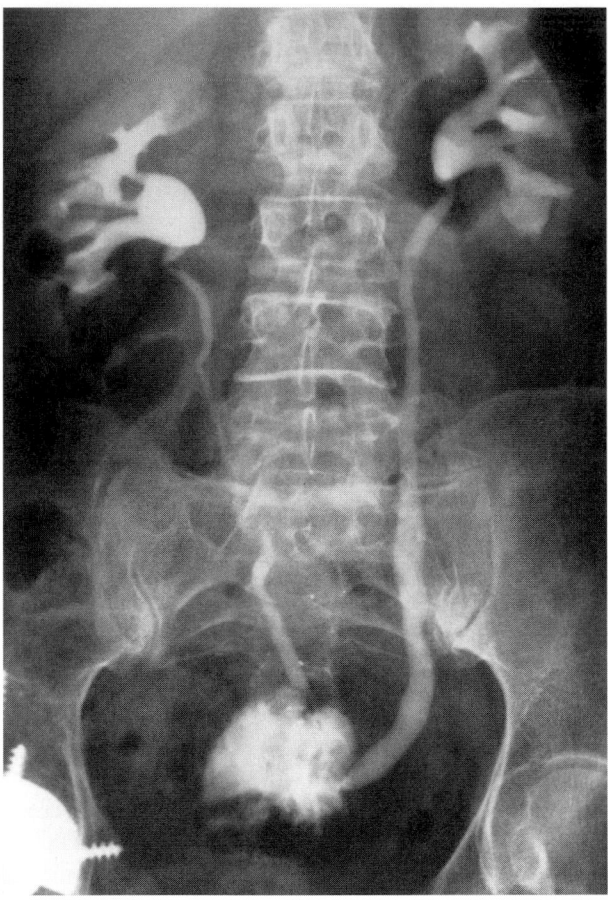

B

Figure 38-1. Ureterosigmoidostomy in patient with bladder exstrophy. (A) Plain film demonstrating calculus in lower pole of left kidney and in distal left ureter. (B) Intravenous urogram (IVU) demonstrating ureteral insertion into sigmoid colon. The renal and ureteral calculus were removed percutaneously.

Figure 38-3. Continent urinary diversion, normal appearance. (A) Cutaneous diversion (Indiana pouch) with ureters draining into a colonic pouch in the right upper abdomen. (B) Orthotopic pouch (hemi-Kock). This pouch is anastomosed to the native urethra. The patient has a right ureteral calculus (*arrow*) with proximal hydronephrosis. The patient was treated with extracorporeal lithotripsy after percutaneous ureteral stenting (percutaneous stone extraction was unsuccessful). ▶

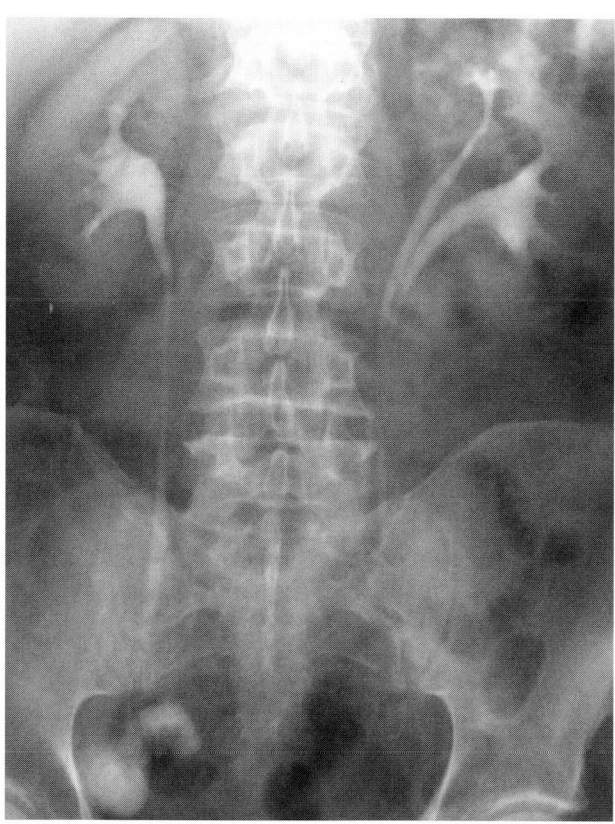

A

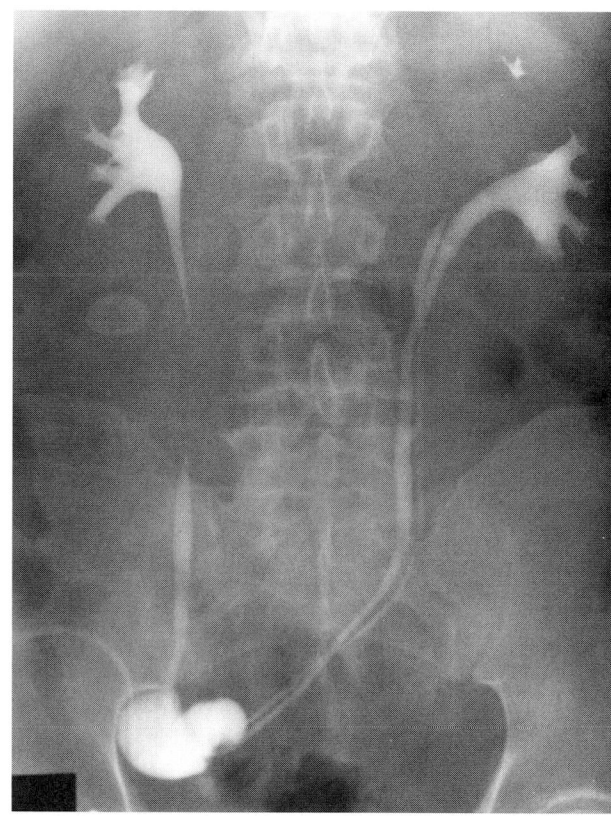

B

Figure 38-2. Ureteroileostomy. IVU (A) and loopogram (B) demonstrate the expected normal appearance. Note the free bilateral ureteral reflux on the loopogram (B).

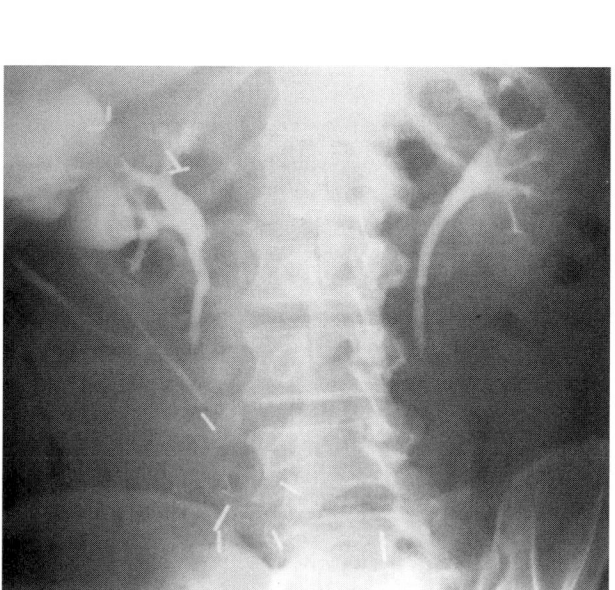

A

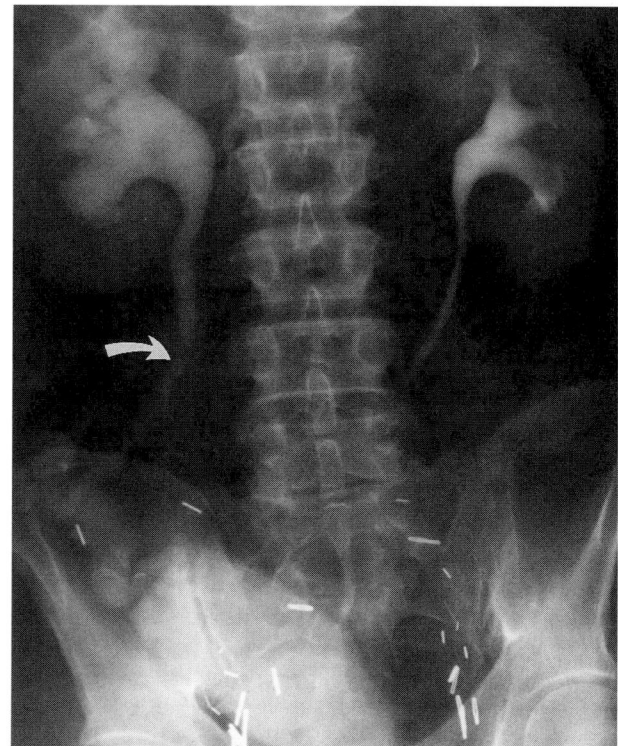

B

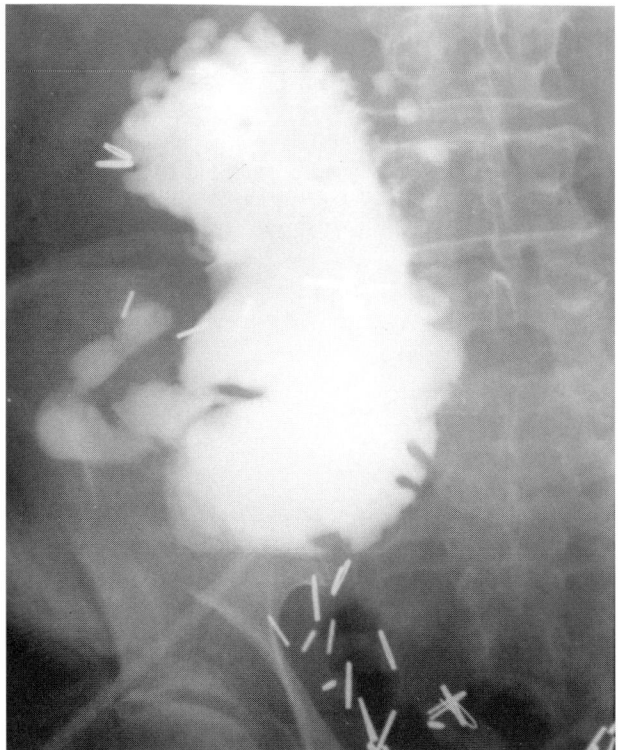

A

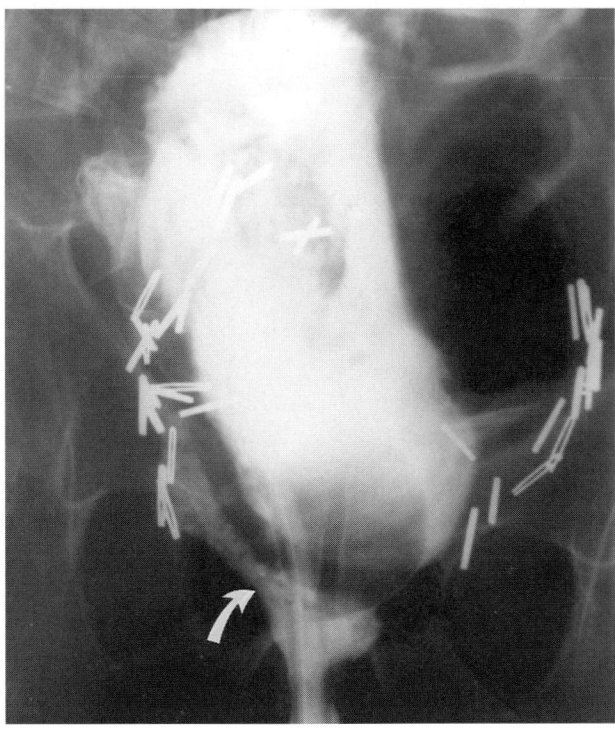

B

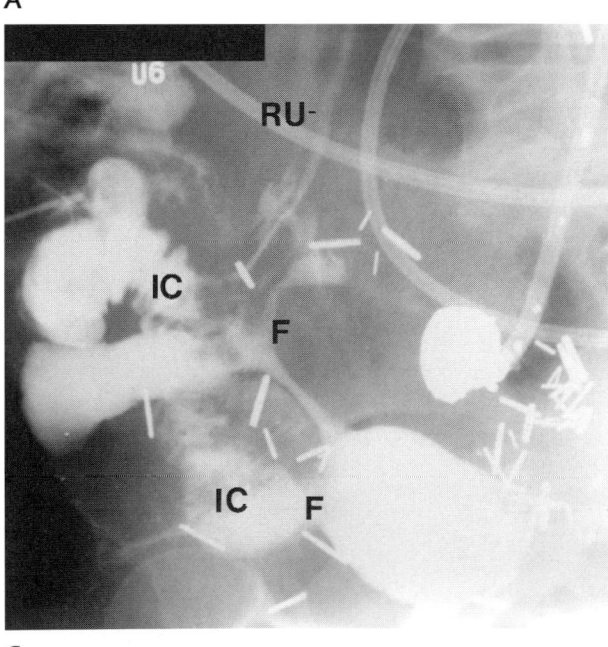

C

Figure 38-4. Contrast studies of urinary pouches. (A) Normal appearance of an Indiana pouch. Contrast was injected through a catheter left in the pouch postoperatively. (B) Extravasation from anastomosis of hemi-Kock pouch to urethra (*arrow*), successfully managed with prolonged Foley catheter drainage of pouch. (C) Enteroenteral fistulas after ureteroileostomy. *IC*, ileal conduit; *RU*, right ureter; *F*, fistulas.

decreasing urine output from the reservoir or ileal conduit (with concomitant increased drainage from surgical drains in the operative site), and an increase in blood urea nitrogen (BUN) level out of proportion to the serum creatinine level. Definitive diagnosis is made by contrast study of the ileal conduit or reservoir (Fig.

38-4). Most patients can be successfully treated with continuing catheter drainage,[10] with catheters being placed both within the urinary pouch and extraluminally at the leak site. Rarely, open surgical repair is required if leakage persists despite optimal catheter drainage in an adequately nourished patient.

Extravasation at the ureteroileal-ureteroenteric anastomosis is clinically indistinguishable from leaks emanating from the conduit or reservoir. The diagnosis is usually made by contrast studies of the ureteral stents left in postoperatively (a common surgical practice for both ureteroileostomies and continent diversions) (Fig. 38-5). Most such leaks will heal spontaneously if the ureteral stents are left in place until complete healing occurs. Percutaneous nephrostomy and ureteral stenting are required if the leaks develop after the stents have already been removed. Occasionally, extravasation at the anastomosis is related to actual detachment of the ureter. Anastomotic leaks appear to be more prevalent in highly irradiated ileal conduit patients, probably because of radiation injury

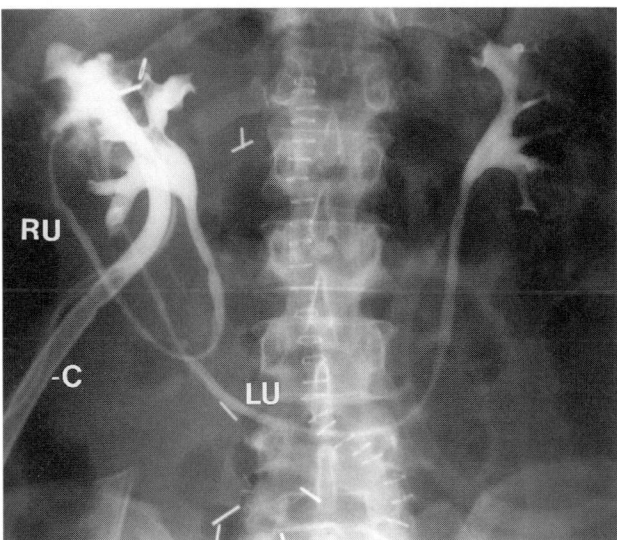

Figure 38-5. Normal contrast study performed through ureteral stents in patient with Indiana pouch. No extravasation is seen. *RU,* right ureter; *LU,* left ureter; *C,* drainage catheter in pouch.

to the distal ureters in patients with pelvic neoplasms.[11] A higher rate of extravasation has been reported in patients with ileal conduits than with continent diversions.[11]

Although minor and occasionally even large degrees of extravasation at the anastomotic site can often be successfully treated with ureteral stenting with no untoward sequelae,[12] extravasation can predispose to later stricture formation[13] in the ureter or at the ureteroenteric anastomosis.

Late complications (defined as those occurring 30 days or more after surgery) can be related either to the ileal conduit or continent bowel reservoir or to the ureteroenteral anastomosis. It is important to emphasize that significant complications that can adversely affect renal function may develop silently and not be apparent clinically (Fig. 38-6). Periodic radiologic evaluation of these patients is therefore mandatory, with the first postoperative urogram being obtained at 3 months and subsequent studies being performed annually if the patient remains asymptomatic.[10,13]

Figure 38-6. Ureteroileal anastomotic stricture. (A) IVU demonstrates left hydronephrosis and stricture at ureteroileal anastomotic site. (B) Loopogram 2 weeks after IVU demonstrates no reflux through the stenotic left anastomosis and ready reflux on the right side.

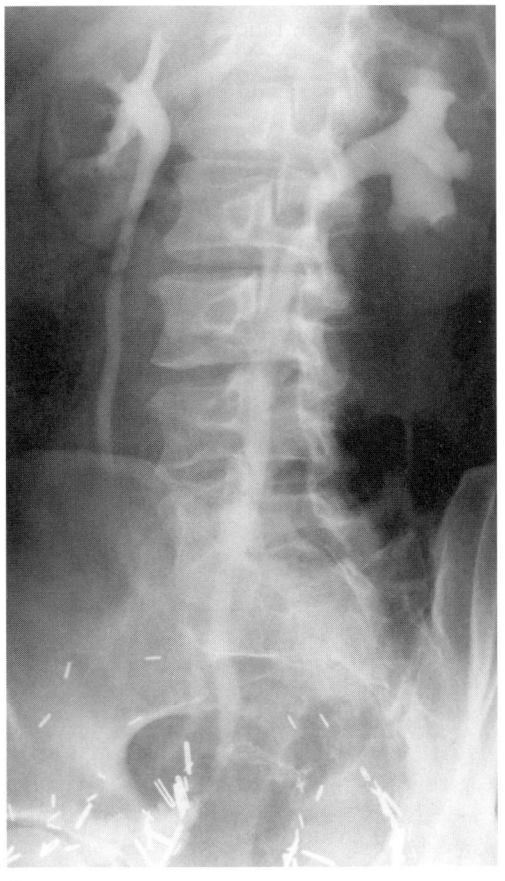

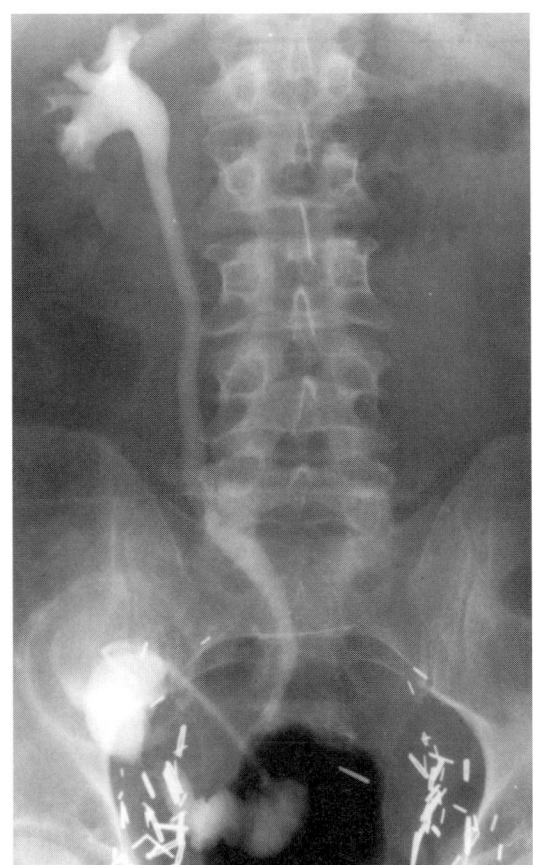

A

B

Ureteroileal Anastomotic Strictures

Benign obstructive strictures at the ureteroenteral anastomosis reportedly occur in 4 to 10 percent of patients.[14,15] One study that compared complications in the different forms of urinary diversion[15] reported the incidence of ureteroenteric strictures in ileal conduits to be 6.5 percent, compared to 10.0 percent in the continent reservoir group and 13.6 percent in patients who underwent ureterosigmoidostomy. The predisposing factors are ischemic necrosis and subsequent fibrosis and stricture due to excessive mobilization and skeletonization of the ureter. Preoperative radiation therapy appears to have a compounding effect. Other causes are poor surgical technique with improper anastomotic construction, inflammation due to abscess formation with scarring and stricturing, extravasation at the anastomosis with subsequent scarring, and, rarely, recurrent tumor in the ureter. Stenoses tend to be more prevalent on the left side, probably because of the necessity for high mobilization of the left ureter (to ensure a gradual course to the right), which often requires the middle ureteric artery to be sacrificed.[16] Rarely, ureteral obstruction can be due to extrinsic compression by a crossing vessel or to compression at the site where the left ureter is brought through the sigmoid mesocolon into the peritoneal cavity to be anastomosed to the ileal conduit.[13] Strictures can predispose patients to urinary infections, stone formation, and loss of renal function, which can often be clinically silent.

Surgical revision of anastomotic strictures is fraught with technical difficulty because of fibrotic adhesions from prior surgery and, frequently also, prior radiation therapy. Nonoperative interventional therapy has been embraced as an alternative, but results to date have been disappointing and not equivalent to those of surgical repair. However, the lower morbidity of interventional techniques and the ability to perform open repair if the interventional procedures are a failure justify the continuing primary application of interventional and endourologic procedures.

The diagnosis of an anastomotic stricture is made when an intravenous urogram demonstrates progressive hydronephrosis and/or a loopogram demonstrates absence of ureteral reflux in a patient in whom the diagnosis of a stricture is being entertained (Figs. 38-6 and 38-7). Ultrasound examination in this situation, although highly sensitive, demonstrates a specificity of only 50 percent because of the high prevalence of dilated collecting systems that are not obstructed in patients with ureteroileostomies.[17] Both antegrade and retrograde studies are performed in an attempt to define the site, length, degree of narrowing, and possible

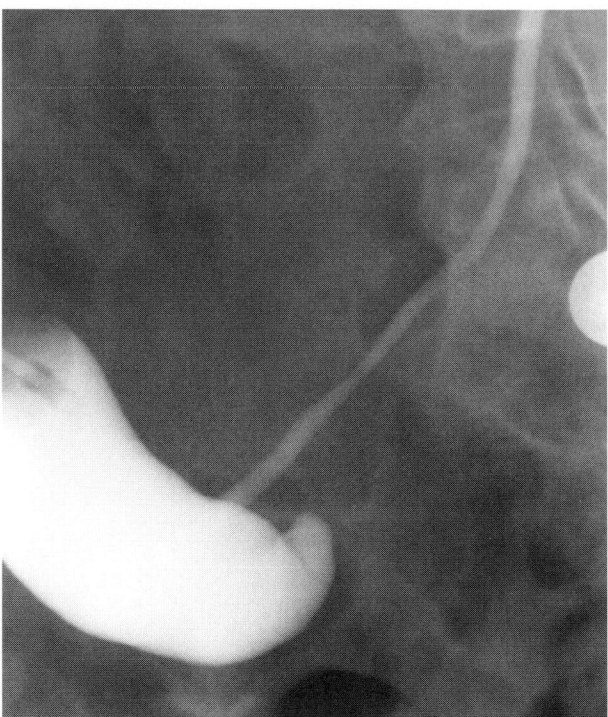

Figure 38-7. Loopogram demonstrates no reflux through stenotic right ureteroenteral anastomosis and ready reflux on the left side.

etiology of the stricture. Brush biopsies are performed if there is a concern that the stricture may be malignant. There is a consensus that malignant obstruction is best treated by ureteral stenting and drainage. As previously mentioned, with benign strictures, the frequency and severity of complications associated with repeat surgery for repair of the strictures have led to the acceptance of percutaneous interventions as the primary modality of treatment.

Ureteroenteral anastomotic stricture dilation is best performed through an antegrade percutaneous approach. Nonrefluxing strictured anastomoses are difficult to catheterize in a transconduit fashion, even though this route is usually successful in catheterizing patent ureteroileal anastomoses (Fig. 38-8).[18] Fluoroscopic retrograde catheterization of patent anastomoses can be performed in 85 percent of patients. The procedure is usually performed to provide drainage for partially obstructing ureteral strictures, extraction of renal or ureteral calculi in patients who would otherwise require a percutaneous nephrostomy, and for brush biopsies of filling defects in the collecting systems. Endoscopy of the conduit is usually unsuccessful in identifying or catheterizing the ureteroenteral anastomosis.

The technique of dilation consists of performing a

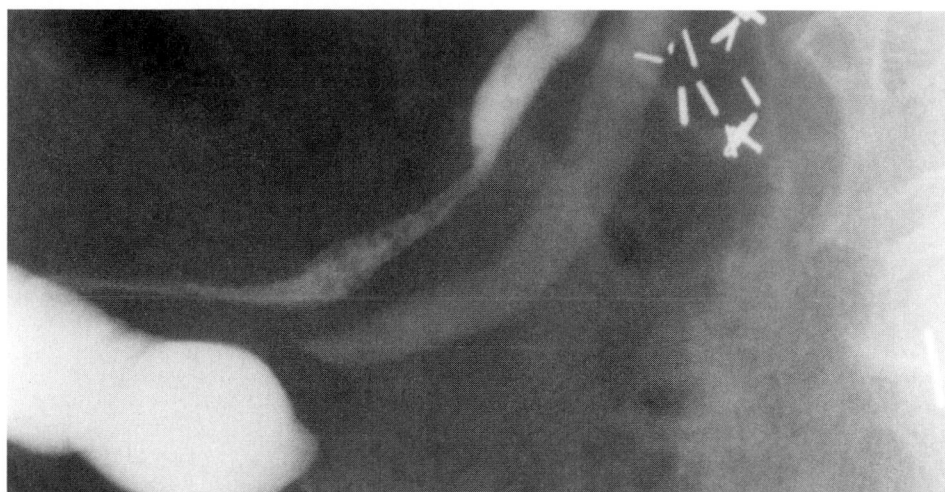

A

Figure 38-8. (A) Patent ureteroenteral anastomosis with bilateral reflux. Multiple filling defects were seen in the distal portion of the right ureter, which was easily catheterized in a retrograde fashion (B) for brush biopsy. Filling defects proved to be due to ureteritis cystica and not tumor recurrence.

nephrostomy; maneuvering a guidewire across the anastomotic stricture, through the ileal conduit, and out the stoma; and then advancing a balloon catheter to the site of the stricture. High-pressure reinforced balloons of 8- to 10-mm diameter and 4- to 10-cm length are preferable. As with balloon dilation of other benign ureteral strictures, there is no consensus on the size of the balloon, the ideal period of balloon inflation, the necessity or desirability or repeated inflations, and, lastly, the size of the catheter used to stent the newly dilated anastomosis.

The ureteral stent placement following balloon dilation is performed in a retrograde transconduit fashion. The author's preference is to place a stent that has a large lumen with side holes only in the renal pelvis and that is long enough to extend beyond the stoma into the ileostomy drainage bag (Fig. 38-9). This approach is advocated so that intestinal mucus does not reflux into the renal pelvis and predispose to occlusion of drainage holes,[19] although other authors[20] have reported no problems with catheter occlusion even with side holes positioned within the conduit. The catheter is left in place for roughly 6 weeks, after which a nephrostogram is performed. If the stricture appears persistent, a second attempt at balloon dilation is made. Because of the high recurrence rate of ureteral strictures after apparently successful balloon dilation, close follow-up is essential to detect stricture recurrence before renal function deteriorates.

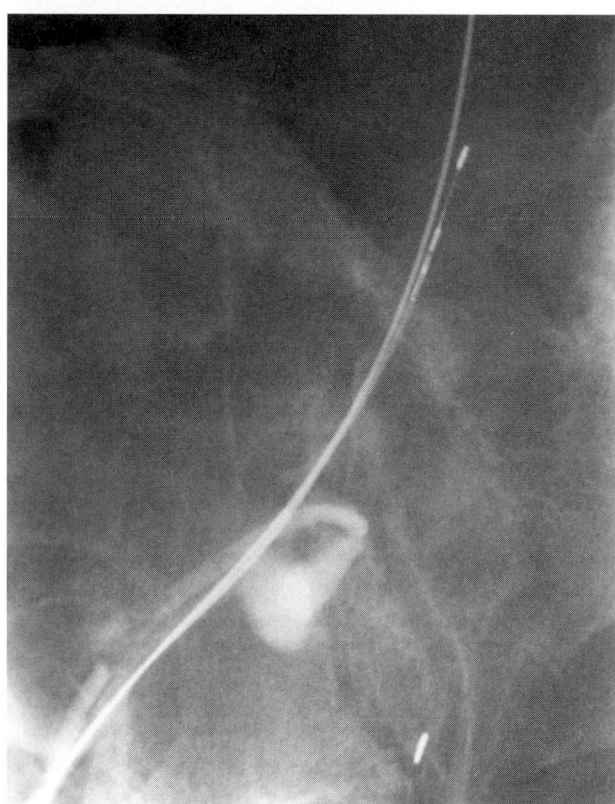

B

The long-term results of balloon dilation of ureteroenteral anastomotic strictures are poor, indicating that the strictures are resistant to nonoperative therapy. Shapiro et al.[21] reported a patency rate of only 30 percent at 6 months and 16 percent at 1 year. Similarly, Chang and Kramolowsky[22,23] reported patency rates of 20 to 38 percent at 1 year. Recently, Kwak et al.[20] reported a 9-month success rate of 18 percent for continuing patency of balloon-dilated anastomotic

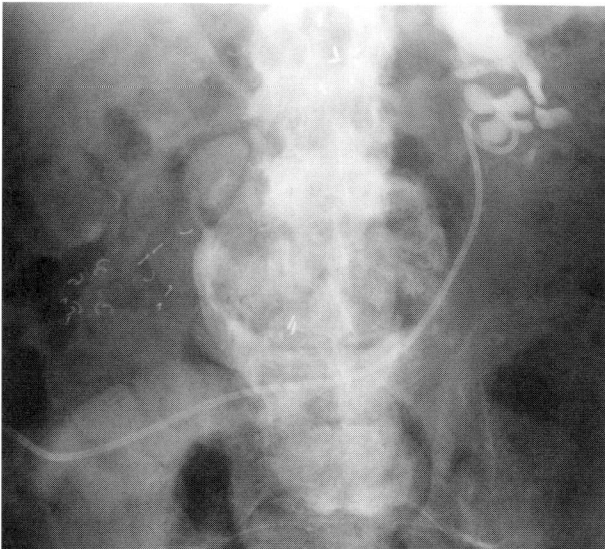

Figure 38-9. Placement of a drainage catheter in a retrograde, transconduit fashion through an ileal loop. The distal end of the catheter drains into a bag attached to the stoma.

strictures. They found that multiple dilations were of no benefit in maintaining ureteral patency.

The addition of endoscopic electroincision of the stricture to balloon dilation may improve patency rates to 42 to 71 percent[19,24,25] (average follow-up 16–28 months). Pollak et al.[26] recently reported that even metallic stents (Wallstent endoprostheses) are ineffective in keeping benign ureteroileal strictures patent. Only one of six stents remained patent at 11 months, with the remainder becoming occluded by hyperplastic tissue growth within the stent.

Ureteroenteral Anastomotic Strictures in Continent Diversions

Rates of ureteral obstruction vary depending on the type of pouch and ureteral anastomosis, with a reported 3 percent incidence for Kock reservoirs[27] and a 10 percent incidence for the modified Indiana pouch,[28] the difference being attributed to the obstructive effects of a tunneled anastomosis in the latter (the tunneling is performed in an attempt to prevent ureteral reflux). Wilson et al.[28] reported dismal results with combined therapy of balloon dilation and incision of strictures. The failure rate of percutaneous therapy was 83 percent, whereas subsequent ureteral reimplantation was successful in 91 percent. They also reported an increased risk for stricture complications in patients who received preoperative radiation therapy, whereas Frazier et al.[15] reported no increase in the risk of long-term complications with radiation therapy.

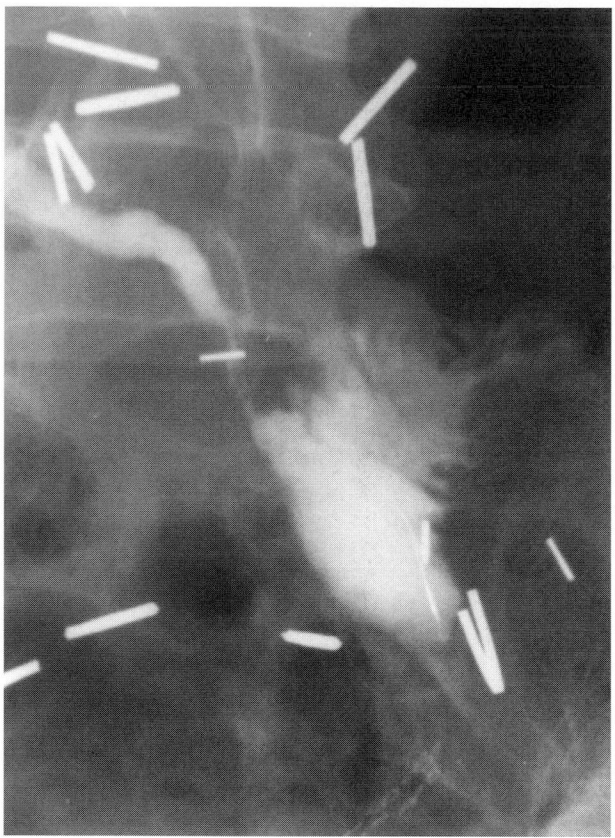

A

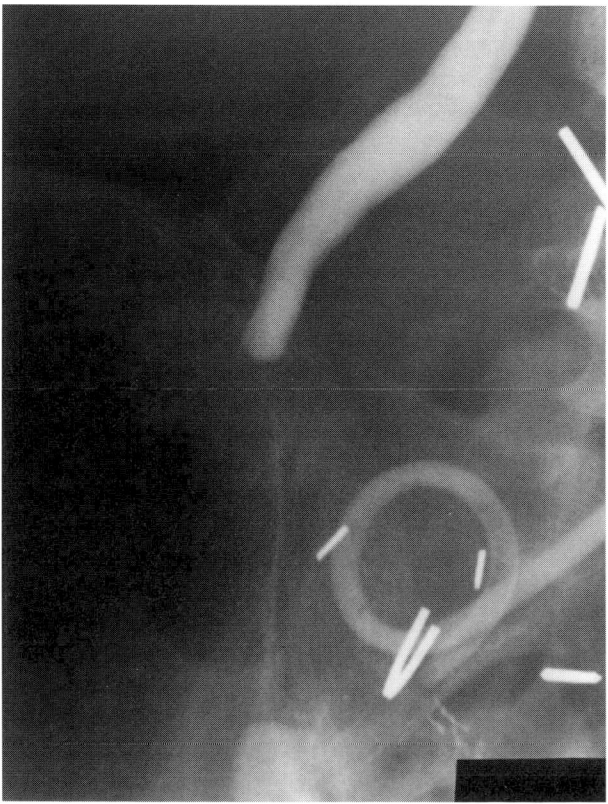

B

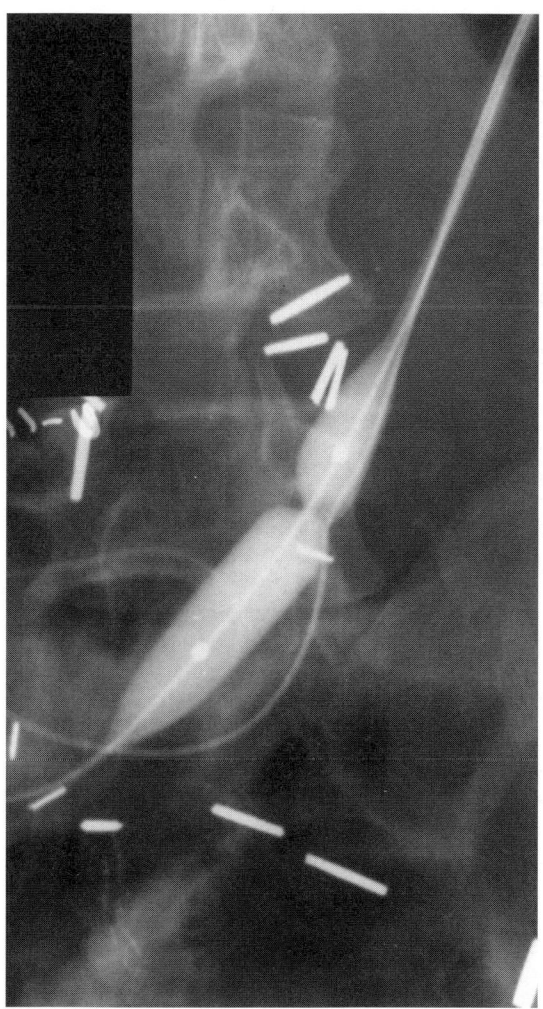

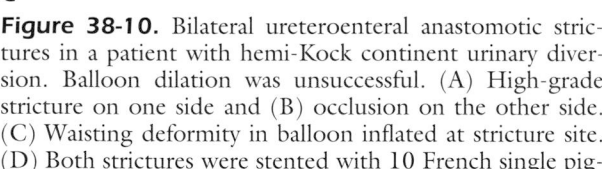

C

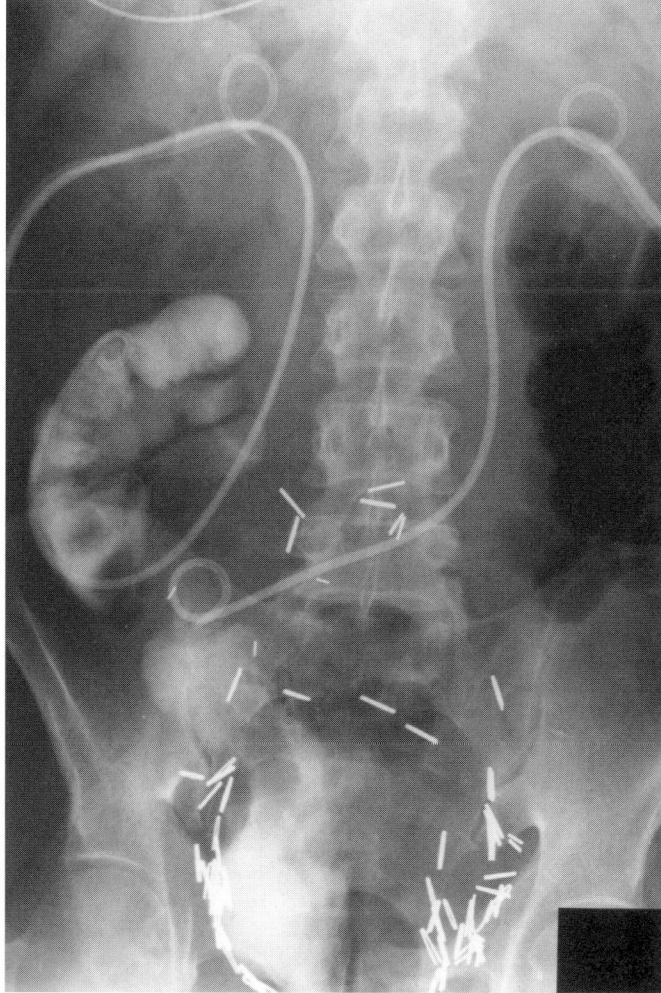

D

Figure 38-10. Bilateral ureteroenteral anastomotic strictures in a patient with hemi-Kock continent urinary diversion. Balloon dilation was unsuccessful. (A) High-grade stricture on one side and (B) occlusion on the other side. (C) Waisting deformity in balloon inflated at stricture site. (D) Both strictures were stented with 10 French single pig-tail catheters after balloon dilation. The ureteral catheters were capped externally and the kidneys were drained by nephrostomy catheters. (E) Nephrostogram 1 week after ureteral stent removal shows no passage of contrast into the urinary pouch. The patient underwent successful surgical repair.

A few technical points need to be emphasized at this juncture. The antegrade route is the safest and most practical approach for stricture dilation because there is no reported experience regarding the feasibility and safety of cannulating nonrefluxing ureterocolonic anastomoses. After dilation, an 8 to 10 French stent is placed across the anastomosis with its distal end in the colonic pouch and the proximal end obturated to prevent intrarenal reflux of mucus. In addition, a nephrostomy catheter is placed within the renal pelvis to facilitate drainage of the kidney. There are no reports regarding the effect of balloon dilation on the antireflux properties of the anastomosis, but the au-

thor's own experience indicates no significant ureteral reflux when the balloon dilation is successful. After a 6- to 8-week period of stenting, the ureteral stent is removed and the effects of balloon dilation are assessed by a nephrostogram performed via the remaining nephrostomy catheter (Fig. 38-10). When open surgical repair of the anastomotic stricture becomes necessary, the preoperative placement of a stent across the stricture (through a nephrostomy access) is helpful because it facilitates identification of the ureter.[28] If the stricture is impassable, a catheter is placed as distally as possible within the ureter.

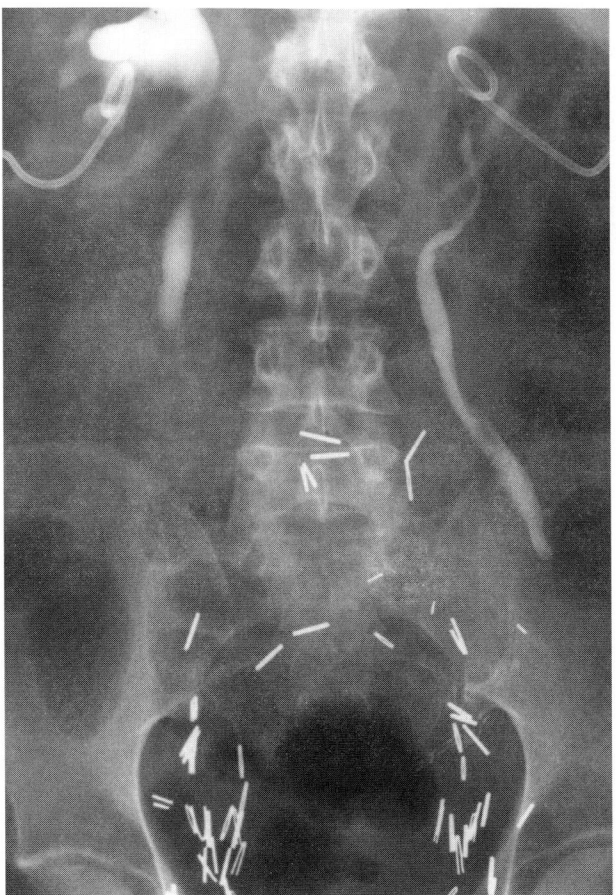

E

Figure 38-10 (continued).

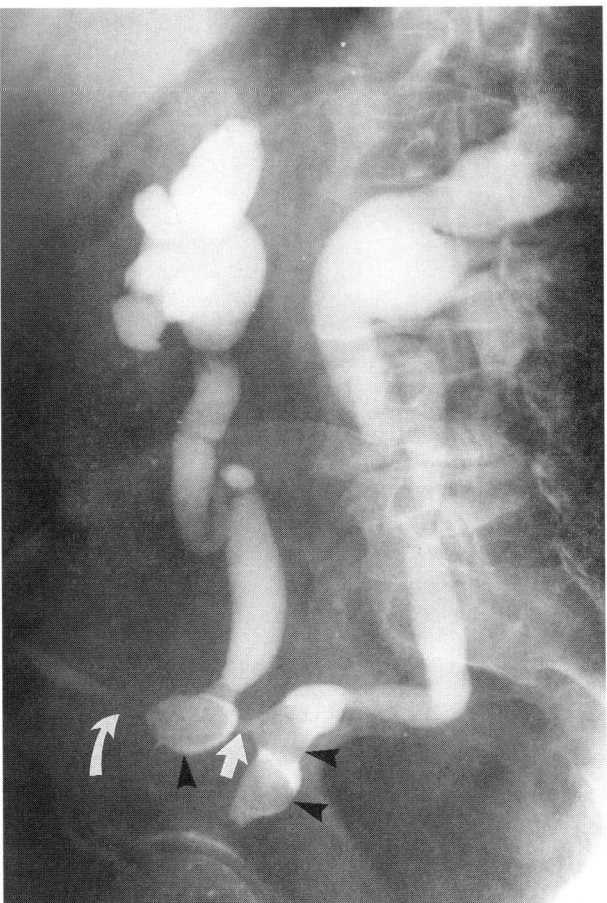

Figure 38-11. Multiple stenotic segments (*arrows*) in ileal conduit with stones (*arrowheads*) seen as filling defects in the opacified conduit. Note the bilateral hydronephrosis. Conduit stenoses respond poorly to balloon dilation and generally require surgical revision.

Complications Related to the Conduit

Ileal Conduit

Patients with ureteroileostomies can develop parastomal hernias, volvulus of the conduit (usually due to an excessively long ileal segment), fistulas (often enteroenteric), and conduit malfunction. In addition, stenoses and calculi can form in the conduit (Fig. 38-11). Interventional procedures have no significant role in managing conduit-related complications other than for the calculi. The stenoses are characterized histologically by a chronic inflammatory reaction in the mucosa and submucosa; such stenoses respond poorly to balloon dilation. Conduit stenoses can occur at the level of the stoma, or the fascia or can involve the ileal segment (Figs. 38-11 and 38-12).

Stones in a conduit usually occur in relation to strictures within the conduit or on exposed metallic staples.[29] The incidence of staple-related calculi is 3 to 7 percent, with the stones forming in the first 3 postoperative years. Most calculi can usually be managed by endoscopically directed electrohydraulic lithotripsy, whereas the stenoses require surgical revision. If calculi develop within the ureters, they can be approached through the ileal conduit in a retrograde fashion (Fig. 38-13), whereas renal calculi require a percutaneous approach or extracorporeal shock wave lithotripsy, depending on stone and patient characteristics (Fig. 38-14). Sutures and staples can migrate to the renal pelvis and then serve as a nidus for calculus formation.[30]

Continent Diversions

Most interventional procedures related to the reservoir in continent urinary diversion are for the management of calculi. Kock pouches appear to be particularly vulnerable to this complication because of the use of metallic staples, which act as a foreign-body nidus.[31] The reported incidence varies from 3 to 33 percent. Urolithiasis has not been a problem with the Indiana pouch.[28] Most stones can be successfully treated by en-

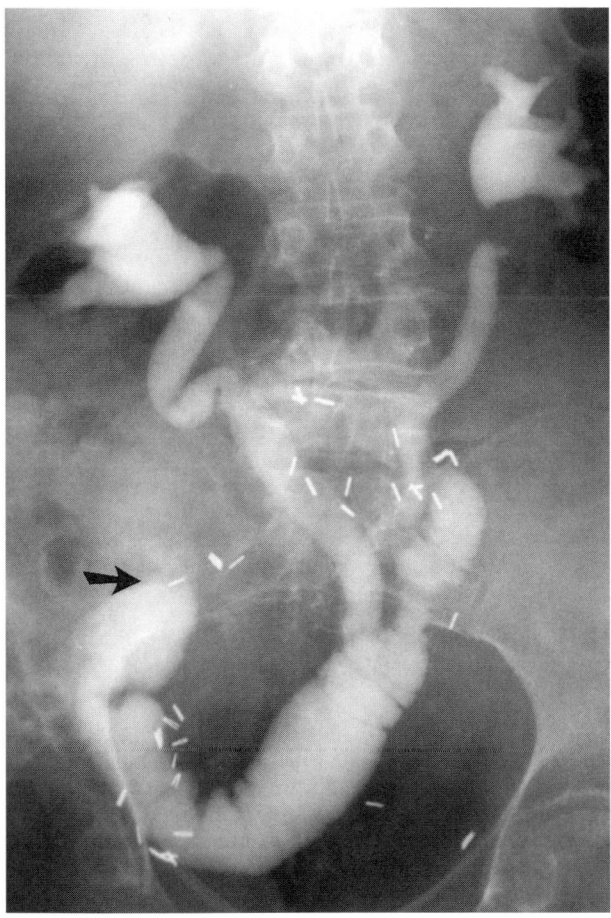

A

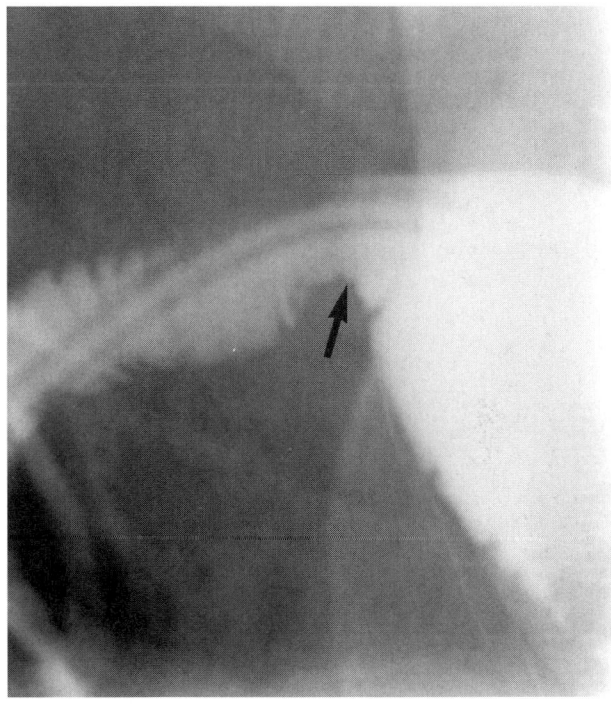

B

Figure 38-12. Stenosis at fascial level causing obstruction of ileal conduit. (A) Loopogram demonstrates dilation of conduit proximal to fascial stenosis (*arrow*). (B) The conduit distal to the stenosis (*arrow*) is of smaller caliber.

doscopic stone removal. Extracorporeal shock wave lithotripsy has a more peripheral role for these calculi.[31] Endoscopy can be performed either through the stoma (and the efferent limb) or by establishing a percutaneous track into the neobladder.[32]

Sutures and metallic staples can migrate to the renal pelvis in a retrograde fashion and simulate a urothelial neoplasm.[33]

If the stoma or the efferent limb of a cutaneous continent diversion becomes stenotic, fluoroscopy and standard interventional techniques can be used to negotiate the stenotic limb and place a drainage catheter into the pouch. If these attempts fail, percutaneous puncture of the pouch can be performed using ultrasound or fluoroscopic guidance (if contrast can be instilled into the pouch through the stoma).

Figure 38-13. Loopogram demonstrating multiple calculi in distal left ureter. Calculi are seen as filling defects (*arrows*) in the opacified ureter. They were removed in a transconduit retrograde fashion with a basket.

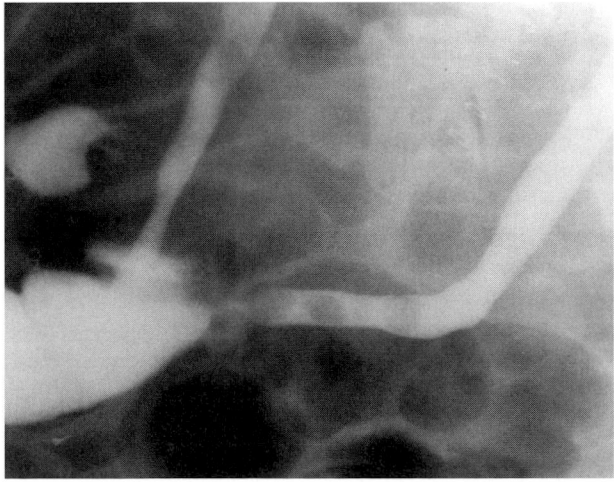

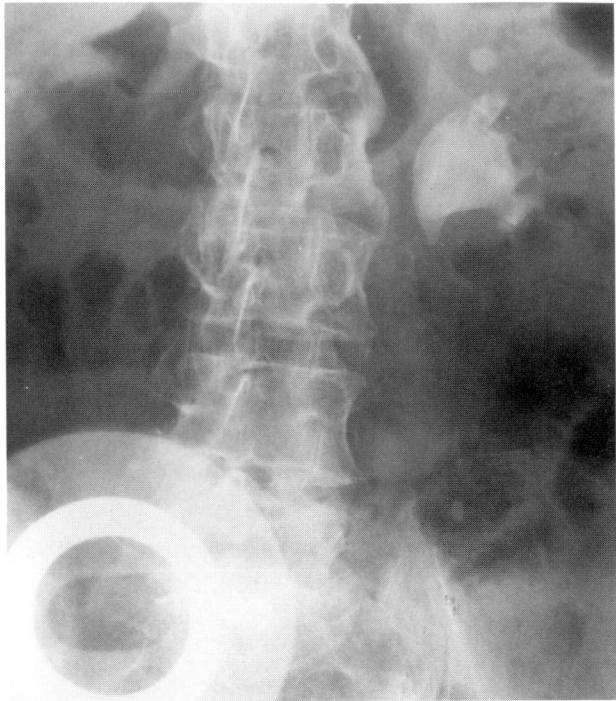

A

B

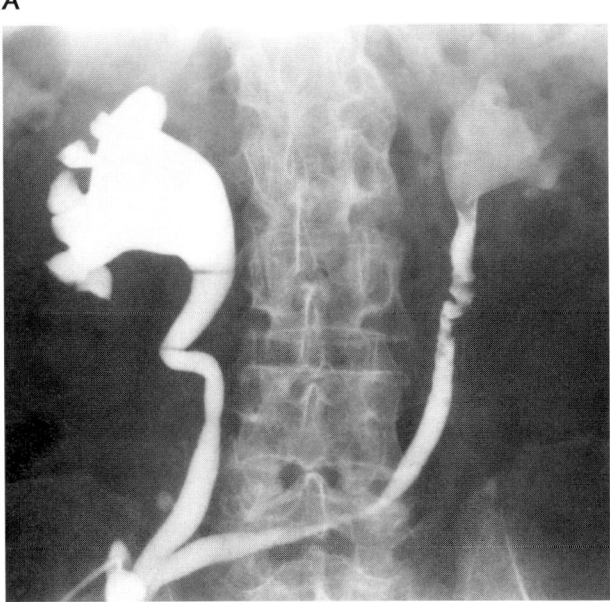

C

Figure 38-14. Staghorn calculus in patient with ileal conduit urinary diversion. Plain film (A) and IVU (B) demonstrate a large left staghorn calculus. (C) Loopogram demonstrates no stricture at the ureteroenteral anastomosis. The patient was treated with percutaneous stone removal.

References

1. Clarke BG, Leadbetter WF. Ureterosigmoidostomy: collective results in 2897 reported cases. J Urol 1955;73:999–1008.
2. Sooriyaarachchi GS, Johnson RO, Carbone PP. Neoplasms of the large bowel following ureterosigmoidostomy. Arch Surg 1977;112:1174–1177.
3. Bricker EM. Bladder substitution after pelvic evisceration. Surg Clin North Am 1950;30:1511–1521.
4. Middleton AW Jr, Hendren WH. Ileal conduits in children at the Massachusetts General Hospital from 1955 to 1970. J Urol 1976;115:591.
5. Amis ES, Newhouse JH, Olsson CA. Continent urinary diversions: review of current surgical procedures and radiologic imaging. Radiology 1988;168:395–401.
6. Goldwasser B, Webster GD. Continent urinary diversion. J Urol 1985;134:227–236.
7. Spring DB, Deshon GE. Radiology of vesical and supravesical urinary diversions. In: Pollack HM, ed. Clinical urography. Philadelphia: Saunders, 1990:296–310.
8. Lee JKT, McClennan BL, Stanley RJ, et al. Use of CT in evaluation of postcystectomy patients. AJR 1981;136:483–487.
9. Spring DB, Moss AA. Computed tomography of ideal loop urinary diversion in adults. J Comput Assist Tomogr 1984;8:866–870.
10. Rowland RG. Monitoring the silent complications of continent urinary diversion. Contemp Urol 1995;7:17–27.
11. Ahlering TE, Weinberg AC, Razor B. A comparative study of the ileal conduit, Kock pouch and modified Indiana pouch. J Urol 1989;142:1193–1196.

12. Bettmann MA, Murray PD, Perlmutt LM, et al. Ureteroileal anastomotic leaks: percutaneous treatment. Radiology 1983; 148:95–100.
13. Banner MP, Pollack HM, Bonavita JA, et al. The radiology of urinary diversions. Radiographics 1984;4:885–913.
14. Schmidt JD, Hawtrey CE, Flocks RH, et al. Complications, results and problems of ileal conduit diversions. J Urol 1973; 109:210–216.
15. Frazier HA, Robertson JE, Paulson DF. Complications of radical cystectomy and urinary diversion: a retrospective review of 675 cases in 2 decades. J Urol 1992;148:1401–1405.
16. Vandenbroucke F, Van Poppel H, Vandeursen H, et al. Surgical versus endoscopic treatment of non malignant uretero-ileal anastomotic strictures. Br J Urol 1993;71:408–412.
17. Cronan JJ, Amis ES, Scola FH, et al. Renal obstruction in patients with ileal loops: US evaluation. Radiology 1986;158:647–648.
18. Banner MP, Amendola MA, Pollack HM. Anastomosed ureters: fluoroscopically guided transconduit retrograde catheterization. Radiology 1989;170:45–49.
19. Van Arsdalen KN, Banner MP. The management of ureteral and anastomotic strictures. Probl Urol 1992;6:420–432.
20. Kwak S, Leef JA, Rosenblum JD. Percutaneous balloon catheter dilation of benign ureteral strictures: effect of multiple dilation procedures on long-term patency. AJR 1995;165:97–100.
21. Shapiro MJ, Banner MP, Amendola MA, et al. Balloon catheter dilation of ureteroenteric strictures: long-term results. Radiology 1988;168:385–387.
22. Chang R, Marshall FF, Mitchell S. Percutaneous management of benign ureteral strictures and fistulas. J Urol 1987;1237:1126–1131.
23. Kramolowsky EV, Clayman RV, Weyman PJ. Endourological management of ureteroileal anastomotic strictures: is it effective? J Urol 1987;137:390–394.
24. Kramolowsky EV, Clayman RV, Weyman PJ. Management of ureterointestinal anastomotic strictures: comparison of open surgical and endourological repair. J Urol 1988;139:1195–1198.
25. Cornud F, Mendelsberg M, Chretien Y, et al. Fluoroscopically guided percutaneous transrenal incision of ureterointestinal anastomotic strictures. J Urol 1992;147:578–581.
26. Pollak JS, Rosenblatt MM, Egglin TK, et al. Treatment of ureteral obstructions with the Wallstent endoprosthesis: preliminary results. J Vasc Intervent Radiol 1995;6:417–425.
27. Freeman JA, Skinner DG. Orthotopic urinary diversion. Contemp Urol 1995;6:29–41.
28. Wilson TG, Moreno JG, Weinberg A, et al. Late complications of the modified Indiana pouch. J Urol 1994;151:331–334.
29. Brenner DO, Johnson DE. Ileal conduit calculi from stapler anastomosis: a long term complication? Urology 1985;26:537–540.
30. McCarthy P, Cheung L, Hanno P, et al. Metallic staples refluxing to the upper urinary tract: a source of renal calculi in patients with ileal conduit urinary diversion. Br J Radiol 1991;64:467–469.
31. Young PR, Weinreth JL. Endoscopic management of calculi in Kock pouch continent urinary diversion. Probl Urol 1992;6:392–398.
32. Faerber GJ, Wan J, Bloom DA, et al. Percutaneous extraction of calculi from continent augmentation cystoplasty. J Endourol 1992;6:417–419.
33. Klotz LH, Egerdie RB, Herschorn S. Migrating suture masquerading as a renal pelvic carcinoma: an unusual complication of the Kock pouch. Urol Radiol 1989,11:100–101.

39

Renal Cysts and Urinomas

MICHAEL D. DARCY

Renal cysts and urinomas are frequently encountered genitourinary fluid collections occurring outside the main collecting system. Cysts and urinomas differ significantly in their etiology, composition, and therapy and therefore are discussed separately.

Renal Cysts

Types of Renal Cysts

The appropriate application of interventional techniques requires an understanding of the different types of renal cystic lesions. By far the most common is the *simple cortical cyst,* which is a cavity lined by a single layer of benign cuboidal epithelium. It has been estimated that simple cysts account for 80 to 85 percent of all space-occupying lesions in the kidneys.[1] In adults, cysts are extremely common. Autopsy studies have shown that more than half of patients over 50 years of age have renal cysts. Simple cysts are much less common in the pediatric population, being seen in 0.22 to 0.55 percent.[2,3] Although their etiology is unclear, the age distribution suggests that they are acquired lesions. It has been postulated that they may result from focal infarcts or inflammation or may represent a response to accumulated toxins.[4,5]

Another type of renal cyst amenable to interventional therapy is the *parapelvic cyst.* Parapelvic cysts account for 5 percent of all renal cysts in adults but, like simple cysts, are rare in children.[6] Parapelvic cysts arise in the parenchyma adjacent to the renal sinus and extend into the sinus. These cysts may not be completely surrounded by renal parenchyma as are simple cortical cysts, but their etiology is probably similar. The major difference in their management from the management of simple cortical cysts is that one must pay close attention to their location to avoid damaging the main renal vessels or the renal pelvis. Parapelvic cysts need to be distinguished from *peripelvic cysts,* which are small, multiple confluent cysts that arise primarily in the renal sinus. These may arise either from a congenital embryologic remnant or from acquired lymphatic obstruc-

tion, and are much less likely to cause cyst-related symptoms.[7] Peripelvic cysts rarely require interventional treatment.

Multilocular renal cysts are rare, benign, unilateral, solitary, multiloculated cysts.[8] Although follow-up studies of these cysts have not shown any potential to develop into a malignancy, they should be managed by surgical exploration because they are difficult to differentiate from cystic malignancy.[9] Cysts occurring in *polycystic kidneys* or *multicystic dysplastic kidneys* are also not usually treated with interventional techniques except when a specific complication develops such as infection or pain due to intracyst hemorrhage. Distinguishing which cyst is the source of problems can be difficult in patients with polycystic disease. Comparison to older cross-sectional imaging studies is vital for finding changes in cyst density, internal structure, size, or contrast enhancement. Infection or hemorrhage into a cyst can lead to increases in cyst size and density. Enhancement of the cyst wall on computed tomography (CT) may indicate cyst infection. [111]Indium-labeled leukocyte scans have also been used to help determine which cyst might be infected.[10] The presence of perirenal fluid detected by ultrasound or CT may indicate cyst rupture but will not necessarily point out which cyst needs to be treated.

Symptoms and Diagnosis

Studies of the natural history of cysts have shown that in most patients cysts do not significantly increase in size as the patient ages; rather, the number of cysts tends to increase.[2,11] Also, because most cysts never cause symptoms, the mere presence of a cyst does not mandate intervention. However, cysts may cause significant symptoms, with pain being the most common problem. Pain probably results from distention of the renal capsule but may also be a secondary effect due to obstruction of the collecting system. Parapelvic cysts may obstruct the ureter or low pelvis (Fig. 39-1), whereas peripheral cortical cysts can obstruct infundibuli or calices. Cysts cause some degree of collecting system obstruction in 2.5 to 16.0 percent of

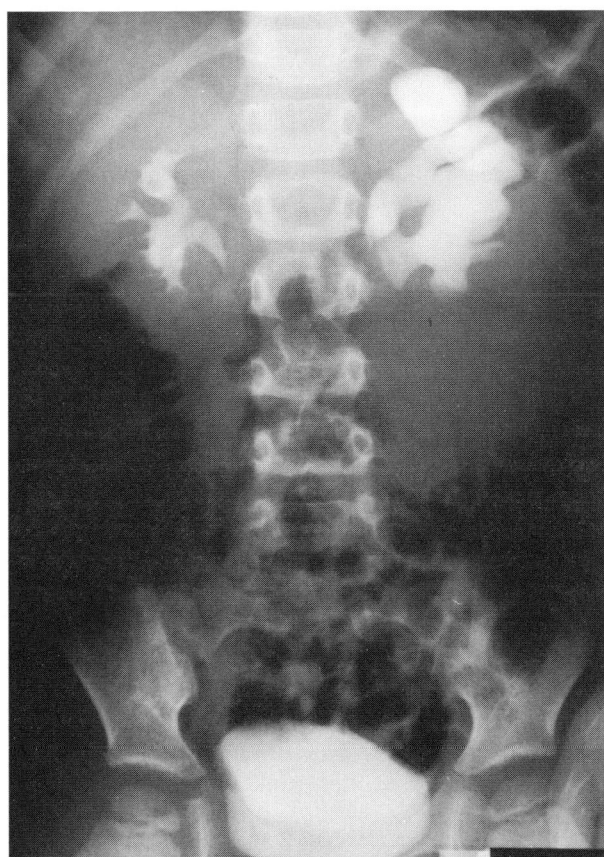

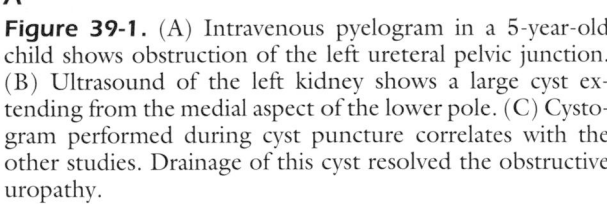

A

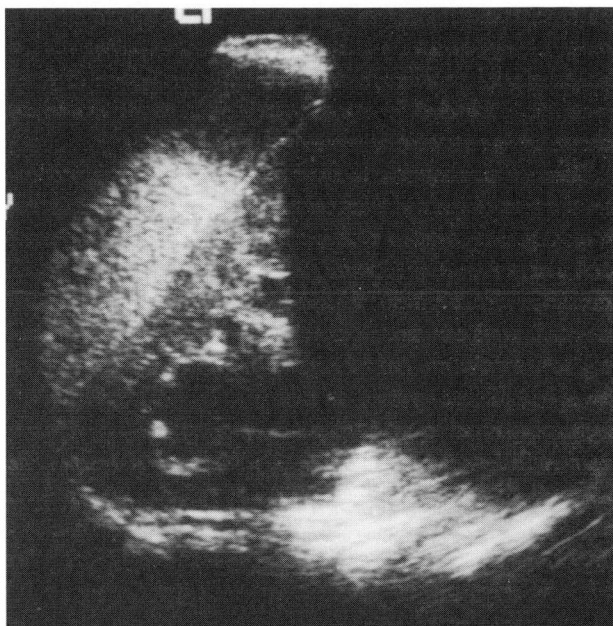

B

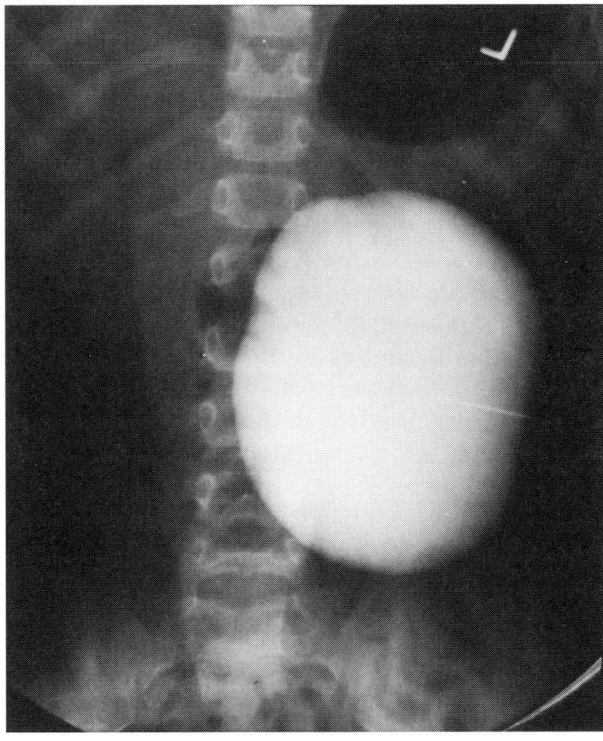

C

Figure 39-1. (A) Intravenous pyelogram in a 5-year-old child shows obstruction of the left ureteral pelvic junction. (B) Ultrasound of the left kidney shows a large cyst extending from the medial aspect of the lower pole. (C) Cystogram performed during cyst puncture correlates with the other studies. Drainage of this cyst resolved the obstructive uropathy.

cases.[6,7] Hypertension is another reported result of the compressive effects of cysts. Compression of the surrounding parenchyma can induce a hyperreninemic state. Drainage of cysts has been shown to cure documented hyperreninemic hypertension in some cases.[12]

Infection of cysts occurs in approximately 2.5 percent of cases.[13] This can result from either hematogenous spread of bacteria or from local extension of pyelonephritis. In addition to pain, patients generally present with elevated white blood cell counts and fever. Pain caused by infected cysts can be severe enough to mimic an acute abdomen.[13] When cysts are infected, the initial management is similar to that of an abscess.

Another cyst symptom is pain induced by rupture. Rupture can occur spontaneously because of increases in pressure within the cyst (due to intracyst hemorrhage or infection) or because of trauma. Hematuria

is seen in 64 to 84 percent of patients with cyst rupture.[14] In over half of cases, this is partially due to cyst rupture into an adjacent calix.[14] Less commonly, cysts may rupture through the renal capsule, causing a perirenal urinoma or hemorrhage.[15] Therapy may be necessary if there is persistent hematuria. Drainage of the perirenal collection may also be required to relieve pain, compression, or infection. In cases of perirenal hemorrhage, it is important that the presence of a tumor be excluded because tumor is a more common cause of spontaneous perirenal hemorrhage.[15]

Before attempting to obliterate a cyst with interventional techniques, it is important to determine that one is not dealing with a malignancy. Four percent of renal cell carcinomas are cystic. Simple cysts and renal cell carcinomas have been found to coexist in the same kidney in 2 to 3 percent of cases, although carcinoma arising within the cyst itself is rare.[16–19] The cross-sectional imaging differentiation of benign cyst from cystic malignancy or other conditions such as caliceal diverticulum is fairly straightforward. Ultrasound relies on the identification of a thin-walled cavity containing fluid of low echogenicity with good through transmission and no internal echoes. The cyst wall should be regular with no mass effects. Fine strandlike septations may be present but should be less than 1 mm thick and have no associated solid mass component. Similarly, CT should demonstrate a thin-walled, fluid-filled cyst with no mass effect or wall irregularity. Cyst fluid should be of low attenuation (in the range of 0–20 HU). Hyperdense benign cysts have been described with fluid attenuation in the range of 60 to 100 HU (possibly resulting from prior intracyst hemorrhage).[1,20,21] These should meet all the other criteria for a simple cyst.

There is some controversy about the diagnostic value of calcium within a lesion. Bosniak[22] felt that the type of calcification is important and that a small amount of thin, smooth calcification in a cyst wall is acceptable. Although central, thick, or irregular calcification is certainly the most suggestive of malignancy, approximately 20 percent of peripherally calcified lesions are malignant.[23] In polycystic kidneys, this is an even less helpful distinguishing point because calcification can be seen in up to 75 percent of cysts.[20] Contrast enhancement of the cyst wall is another sign that is worrisome for the presence of malignancy. This may also occur in infected cysts, but these should be distinguishable by clinical symptomatology and white blood cell count.

Using the described criteria, ultrasound and CT are accurate at distinguishing simple benign cysts from other processes such as cystic malignancies. The accuracy is generally felt to be over 90 percent.[11,24–26] There have been reported cases of malignancies that appeared to be benign cysts by all standard ultrasound or CT criteria,[27,28] but this is a rare event. Magnetic resonance imaging (MRI) has not added much to the diagnostic workup of cysts. In one study,[26] MRI was not able to distinguish between carcinoma and cysts with hemorrhage in 32 percent of cases.

Cyst Puncture and Aspiration

For the 5 to 7 percent of renal masses that are indeterminate after complete cross-sectional imaging evaluation, cyst puncture with aspiration cytology and contrast cystography is the next logical step. Before cyst puncture, one needs to take the precautions one usually takes before an interventional procedure. Clotting parameters and platelet count need to be checked. Inquiry must be made about the patient's contrast allergy history and any other medical conditions that could be exacerbated by the procedure (e.g., angina).

Choosing a skin entry point for the puncture requires some of the same considerations used in choosing a nephrostomy access. For most peripheral cortical cysts, the puncture should be started around the lateral border of the major erector muscles of the back. Starting much further lateral than that increases the risk of hitting nontarget organs such as colon, liver, or spleen. Choosing a more medial entry point is acceptable if there is no plan to leave a drainage tube in place. A medial entry for a drainage tube is not advised. It is uncomfortable for the patient because it goes through more muscle mass, and it is more difficult to avoid lying on the tube in this location. An exception to these general guidelines is puncture into a parapelvic cyst. Here a more medial puncture is acceptable because entering along the lateral border of the erector muscles would cause the tract to excessively traverse renal parenchyma.

Localization of the cyst can be achieved in several ways. Ultrasound is most commonly used because it generally allows easy visualization of the cyst and also provides real-time guidance of the needle. The portability of ultrasound is advantageous because it can be used in the interventional suite, and fluoroscopy can then be used to monitor subsequent guidewire and catheter manipulations. An alternate method of localization is to give the patient an intravenous bolus of iodinated contrast and to then visualize the cyst fluoroscopically once there is an adequate nephrogram (Fig. 39-2). This requires that the cyst be large enough to either appreciably deviate the collecting system or cause a significant defect in the nephrogram. This technique is therefore not applicable to patients with poor renal function (and hence a poor nephrogram) or in patients with cysts that are too small to cause an appreciable defect.

CT is rarely needed to guide cyst puncture. Circumstances in which it may be helpful are when trying to hit a very small cyst, or in obese patients in whom there is poor ultrasound penetration. CT guidance is also helpful when it is necessary to puncture one specific cyst in a patient with polycystic or multicystic disease.

A 21- or 22-gauge needle is generally sufficient for aspiration and a cystogram. If a drainage catheter is

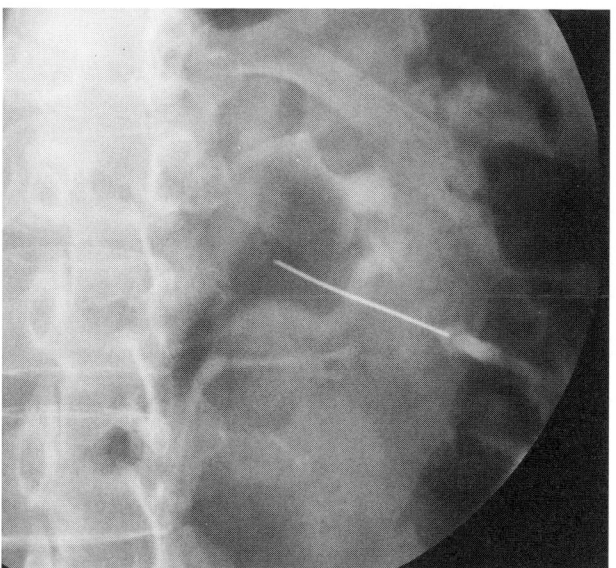
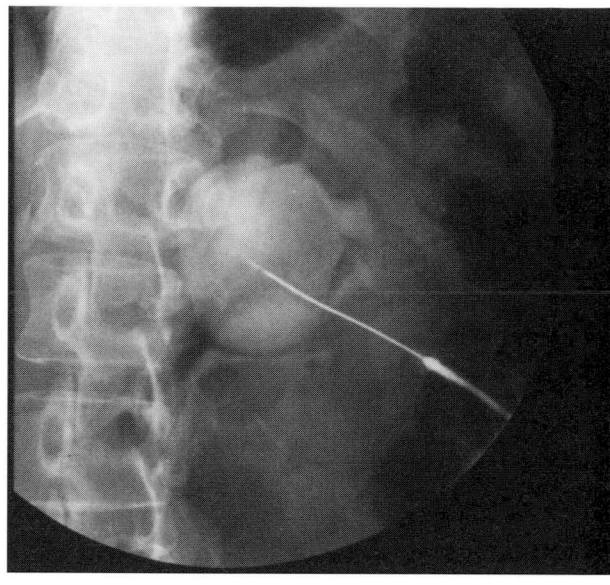

A   **B**

Figure 39-2. (A) After administration of intravenous contrast, the distortion of the collecting system is used to guide cyst puncture. The collecting system is displaced inferiorly and laterally around a large cyst. (B) Contrast injection into the cyst after successful puncture.

definitely planned, an 18-gauge needle may be more beneficial because its greater stiffness decreases the chance of needle deviation during its passage. In addition, the 18-gauge needle will accept a standard-size guidewire (0.035–0.038 inch). Thus one can avoid having to initially use a flimsy 0.018-inch guidewire and then go through the extra step of using a transition dilator to scale up to a 0.035-inch guidewire.

The cyst should be punctured as atraumatically as possible because the consistency of the fluid provides some information. The fluid in a benign simple cyst should be clear or slightly yellowish. A small amount of blood in the fluid that clears during the drainage indicates a traumatic tap. Bloody fluid that does not become more serous is suggestive of a tumor.[29,30] Some cystic malignancies, however, may contain clear fluid.[18] The aspirated fluid should be sent for cytologic evaluation, which in some series has been a technique with good sensitivity for malignancy.[17] However, other authors have indicated that a negative cytology does not exclude malignancy.[19,31] In fact, Kleist et al.[31] found that cytology failed to detect malignant cells in 9 of 11 cystic malignancies that they studied. To improve the ability to detect malignancy, some authors have recommended analyzing the lipid content of the aspirated fluid, which in cystic malignancies is approximately five times higher than that seen in benign cysts.[31] However, both false-positive and false-negative lipid analyses are possible.[18]

A cystogram should be performed after the cyst fluid is aspirated. This may be done using a single con-

trast technique in which the cyst fluid is replaced with dilute contrast. Contrast must be diluted to avoid obscuring details of the cyst wall. Double contrast techniques have also been described[30] in which 50 percent of the aspirated volume of the cyst is replaced with air and 25 percent of the volume is replaced by contrast. The remaining 25 percent is cyst fluid. The cyst walls in a simple benign cyst should be perfectly smooth. Any irregularity of the wall raises the possibility of tumor (Fig. 39-3). Internal septations or lobulations may be seen in up to 19 percent of cases,[32] but in these situations the cyst wall should still be smooth.

Incomplete distention of the cyst may cause some wall irregularity that presents a pitfall in the interpretation of the cystogram. A similar pitfall can occur when the cyst has previously ruptured into a calix and has partially collapsed, lending an irregular appearance to the wall. Organized or adherent thrombus from prior hemorrhage may also mimic malignancy. With the combination of cyst fluid analysis and cystogram, the accuracy of cyst aspiration for exclusion of malignancy has been reported to be around 95 to 98 percent.[1,33] The accuracy of these techniques decreases in the setting of hemorrhagic cysts or highly septated cysts.

Aside from helping to differentiate malignancy from simple cyst, cyst aspiration can be used to confirm if a cyst is infected or not. If infected, cyst drainage is valuable because some antibiotics do not penetrate into cyst fluid even when the cyst wall is inflamed.[34] Other indications for drainage are when the cyst causes pain, urinary obstruction, or hypertension or when the

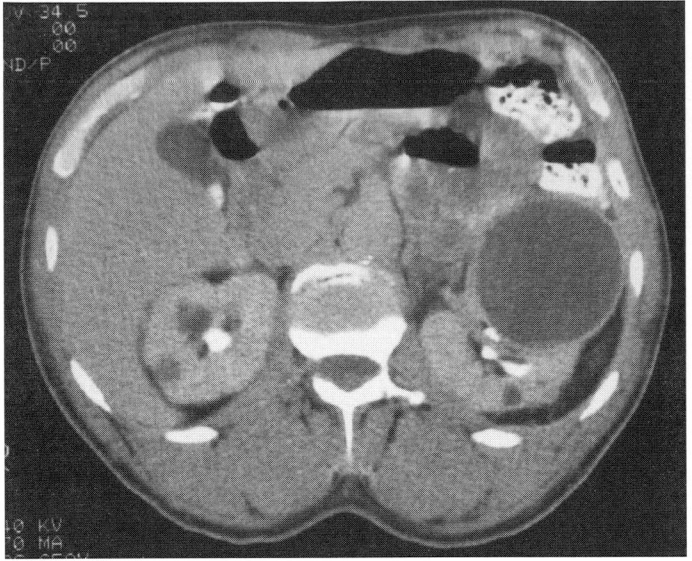

A

B

Figure 39-3. (A) CT scan in an elderly man showing a large cyst in the left kidney. Although the cyst wall is slightly thick in places, there is nothing specific to allow a diagnosis of malignancy. (B) Cyst puncture in the same patient shows a very irregular cyst wall with a mass (*arrow*) protruding from the caudal aspect of the cyst. Pathology confirmed this to be a renal cell carcinoma.

patient has unexplained hematuria. Cyst drainage may be used to initiate therapy or as a diagnostic trial to see if it eliminates the symptoms.

Simple needle aspiration of cysts can be done with a great degree of safety. Major complications have been reported to occur in the range of 0.75 to 3.00 percent.[35,36] The most common complication is perirenal hemorrhage, which occurs in 0.18 to 0.30 percent of cases when 20- to 22-gauge needles are used. Other complications that have been reported include pneumothorax, arteriovenous fistula, infection, formation of urinomas, and inadvertent puncture of adjacent bowel. Pneumothorax occurs most frequently with punctures of upper pole cysts, particularly in the left kidney. Aside from these immediate procedural complications, the only long-term problem that has been noted is tumor seeding along the tract after aspiration of a cystic malignancy. However, this is a rare complication, with only a few case reports in the literature.[24,37] The downfall of simple aspiration is the high recurrence rate, since the cuboidal epithelium of cysts can rapidly produce cyst fluid and refill the cyst.[38] Recurrence of renal cysts after simple aspiration occurs in anywhere from 30 to 100 percent of cases in the series reported.[39–42]

Sclerosis

To decrease the incidence of cyst recurrence, sclerosis was introduced as an adjunct to drainage. Simple cath-

eter drainage (without sclerosis) has not been used and is not likely to be successful because of the active secretion of cyst fluid. Although sclerosis could theoretically be performed via the aspirating needle, sclerotherapy can generally be more safely and effectively performed after placement of a catheter within the cyst. Using a catheter has several advantages. With the catheter in place it is possible to get delayed cystograms after initial drainage, which allows one to detect communications with the collecting system that were not apparent at the time of initial drainage (Fig. 39-4). Subsequent cystograms allow one to monitor the collapse of the cyst cavity as it is sclerosed. The volume of fluid draining from the cyst is also useful information in deciding whether the cyst has been adequately sclerosed. In addition, the catheter will help drain some of the debris produced by sloughing of cyst lining in response to the sclerosant. The fibrous tract that forms around a drainage catheter is beneficial in that sclerosant leaking from the cyst will drain along the tract rather than freely extravasate into the perirenal space.

Both trocar and Seldinger techniques can be used to place catheters within renal cysts. Each technique has its advantages and disadvantages. With the Seldinger technique, it may be difficult to coil a significant amount of guidewire within the cyst if the cyst is not particularly large. In addition, the cyst may decompress into the perirenal space during exchanges between dilators and drainage catheters. This can poten-

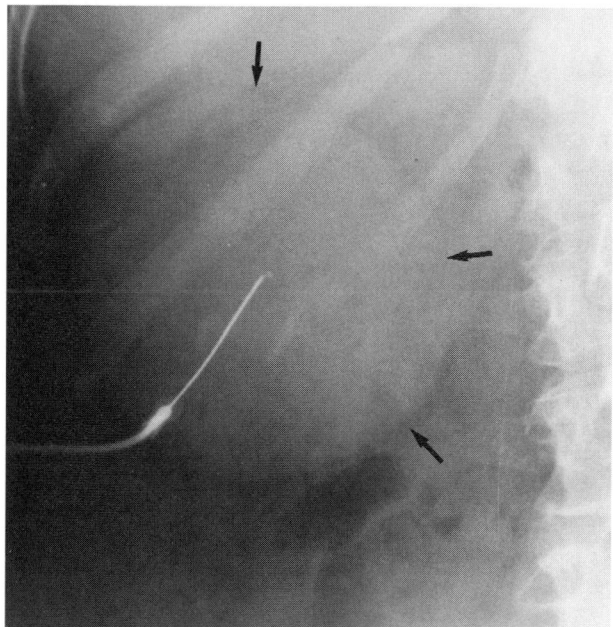

A

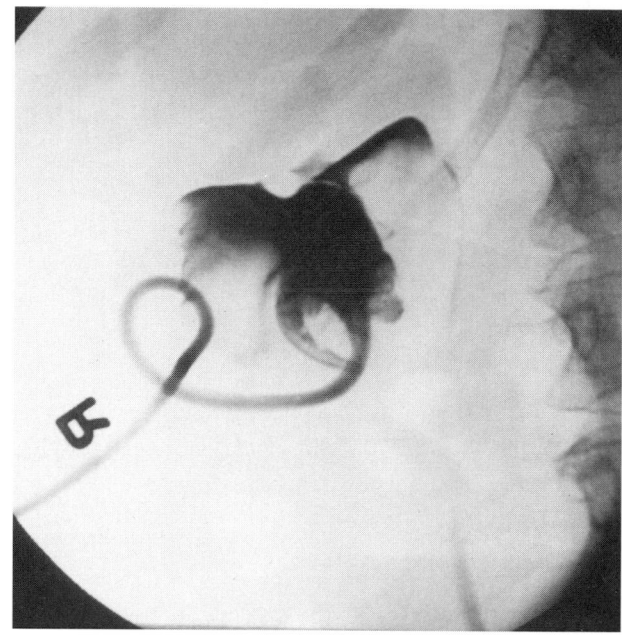

B

Figure 39-4. (A) This large cyst (*arrows*) of the right kidney was punctured and drained, relieving the patient's flank pain. A cystogram performed immediately after this puncture showed no communication with the collecting system.

(B) After drainage, sclerosis of the cyst was planned. Immediately before sclerosing the cyst, a repeat nephrostogram shows clear communication with the collecting system. Thus sclerosis could not be performed.

tially make it difficult to pass the catheter through the nondistended cyst wall. Although trocar techniques avoid some of these problems, most ultrasound biopsy guides are not adaptable for use with larger trocar systems and instead require initial placement of a bare needle into the cyst.

Once the catheter has been positioned in the cyst, it is important to perform a thorough cystogram to ensure that there is no communication with the collecting system. Of cysts that partially or completely rupture, 52 percent rupture into the caliceal system. These communications may partially seal, allowing the cyst to redistend but to still maintain communication with the collecting system.[14] Clearly, injection of sclerosing agent that could flow freely into the collecting system would be contraindicated. Moreover, if the cyst appears infected, it should be completely drained until the infection clears before one initiates sclerosis. Sclerosis of an infected cyst could theoretically lead to an increased chance of bacteremia or cause loculation of infected material.

After complete drainage of the cyst fluid, replacement with contrast allows one to estimate the cyst volume to determine how much sclerosant to use. Extravasation of contrast along the catheter into the perirenal space should be noted. If this occurs freely without overdistention of the cyst, it is advisable to continue catheter drainage until a fibrous tract forms around the

catheter. The volume of sclerosant used should approximate 25 to 50 percent of the volume of the cyst estimated by the injection of contrast.

Multiple agents have been used to sclerose cysts, including glucose, phenol, Pantopaque, tetracycline, bismuth, and Betadine.[3,41,43-45] Absolute alcohol is probably the most commonly used sclerosant. Bean[42] showed experimentally that although the cyst wall epithelium becomes nonviable after 1 to 3 minutes of exposure to alcohol, it takes approximately 4 to 12 hours for alcohol to penetrate the cyst capsule. Thus this agent can safely defunctionalize the secreting cells of the cyst without affecting adjacent renal parenchyma. Alcohol also has the advantages of being inexpensive and readily available.

Once alcohol is instilled, the patient should be turned at intervals onto each side and onto both prone and supine positions to expose all portions of the cyst wall to the alcohol. Some have recommended aspirating the alcohol and replacing it with a fresh aliquot midway through the sclerosis session. The catheter is then placed back to drainage. Repeat sclerosis can be done in subsequent sessions until the drainage from the cyst becomes negligible. It is also advisable to continue drainage until the cavity has contracted down around the drainage catheter. When one is attempting to sclerose very large cysts, the cyst walls may adhere to themselves and form separate loculated compartments

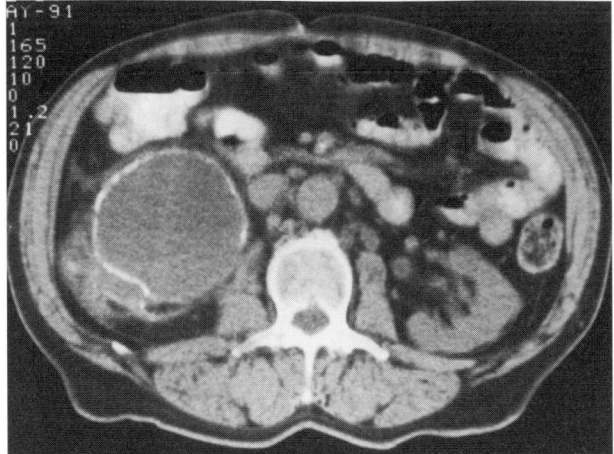

A

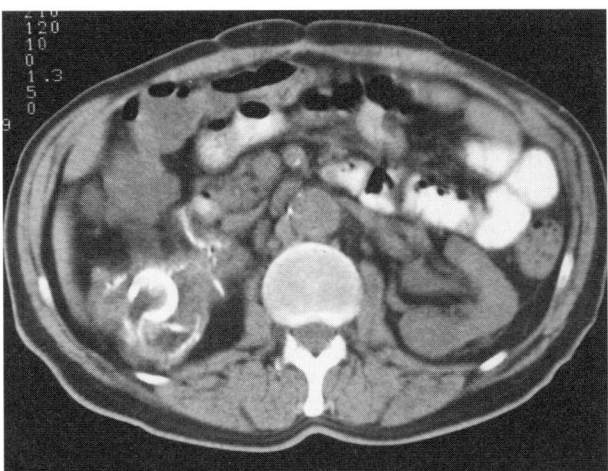

C

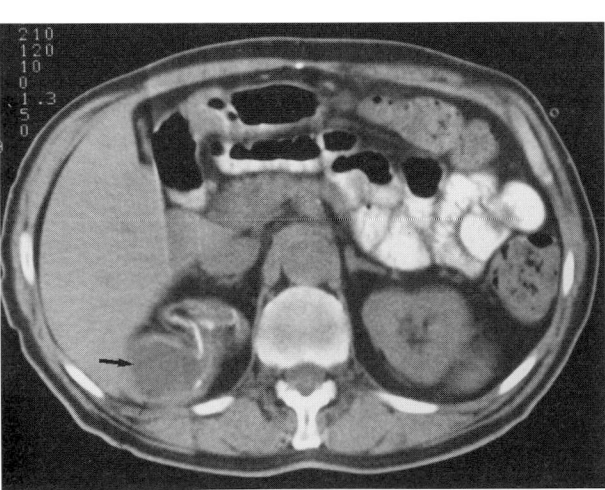

D

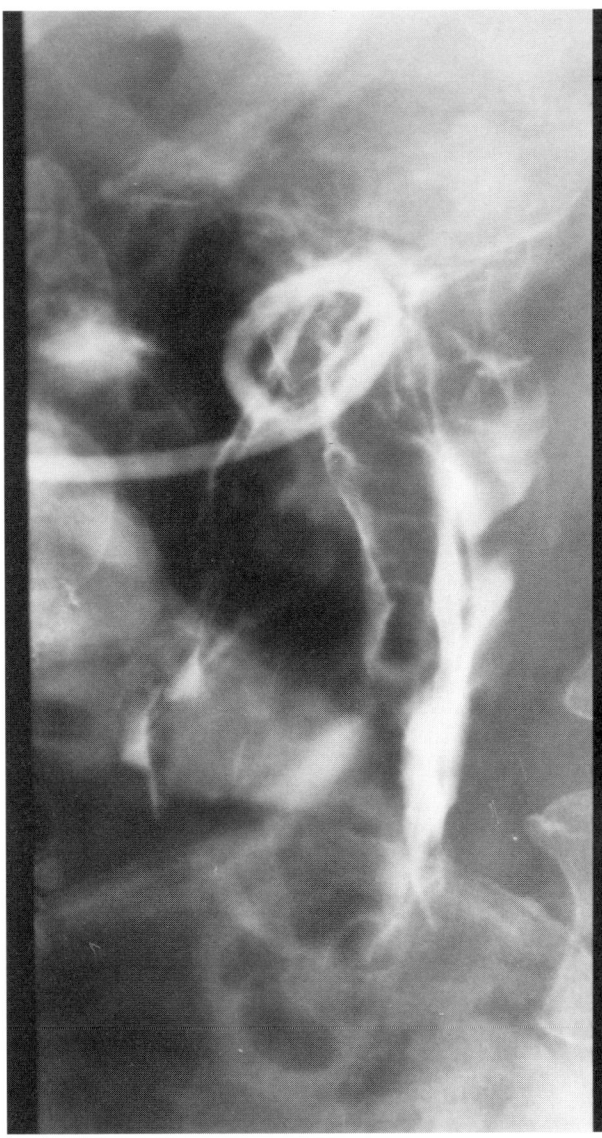

B

Figure 39-5. (A) CT scan shows a large cyst in a dysplastic right kidney. Drainage and sclerosis were planned because of the patient's right flank pain. (B) Contrast injection into the cyst 1 week after the initial injections of alcohol shows a very irregular cyst cavity with the walls of the cyst starting to adhere to themselves. (C) CT slice after several sclerotherapy sessions shows that most of the cavity has collapsed down around the drainage catheter. (D) CT slice at a more cephalad level shows that a portion of the cyst has formed a separate loculation (*arrow*) as the cyst walls have collapsed together. This separate loculation required placement of an additional drainage catheter.

(Fig. 39-5). This may require manipulating the catheter into the loculations or even placing an additional drainage catheter.

Although some pain or fever may occur, significant complications are infrequent with cyst sclerosis. Bean[42] reported microscopic hematuria in 2 of 29 patients (6.9 percent) but had no major complications. Gelet et al.,[45] on the other hand, reported infectious-type complications in 2 of 10 patients (20 percent) after Betadine sclerosis. One patient developed sepsis after the procedure, and 1 patient developed delayed infection of a residual cyst cavity 3 months after sclerosis. The more typical incidence of infectious complication is 0 to 0.5 percent.[42,46] No other major complications have been described for peripheral cysts. Sclerosis of para- and peripelvic cysts carries the additional theoretic risk of damage to adjacent hilar structures. Ureteral pelvic obstruction caused by sclerosis-induced fibrosis has been described in one case.[46]

The effectiveness of sclerotherapy appears to vary with the sclerosing agent used. Series in which tetracycline or ethanol were used have all reported a high degree of technical success with minimal recurrences (Fig. 39-6).[3,40,42,47] Bean noted 1 recurrence out of 34 cysts (2.9 percent), and this 1 recurrence occurred in a patient who had a giant cyst with an initial volume of approximately 2 liters.[42] Other series using agents such as Betadine, Pantopaque, or bismuth to attempt sclerosis have shown incomplete obliteration of cyst cavities in 30 to 56 percent of cases.[41,43,45]

Surgical therapy has been proposed as a better way of dealing with cysts because (1) it allows for direct inspection of the cyst to more confidently exclude malignancy, (2) it can eliminate the problem in one step rather than requiring return visits for sclerosant installation, and (3) surgical specimens of the cyst wall can be obtained for pathologic examination. However, the standard open surgical cyst unroofing is associated with a morbidity of 8 to 16 percent, and the hospital stay averages 9 days for this procedure.[36,48] Laparoscopy has recently been used to surgically unroof cysts in a less invasive fashion.[48–51] Only a few cases have been reported, but the results have generally been successful. One large retroperitoneal hematoma was reported in a series of three patients as a result of this procedure.[50]

Another surgical alternative is to marsupialize the cyst into the collecting system. This can be combined

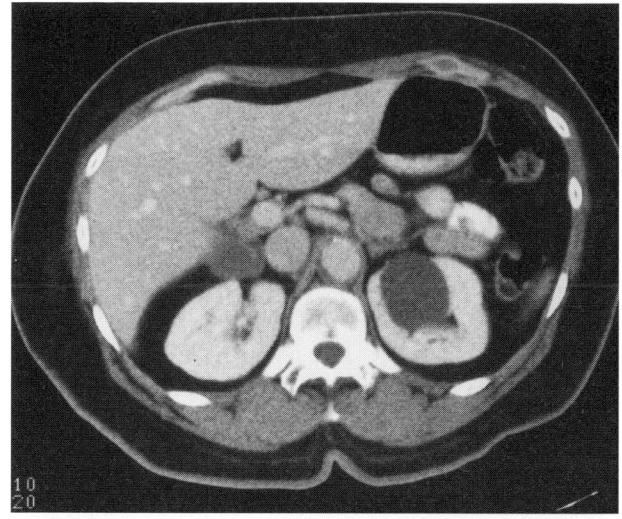

A

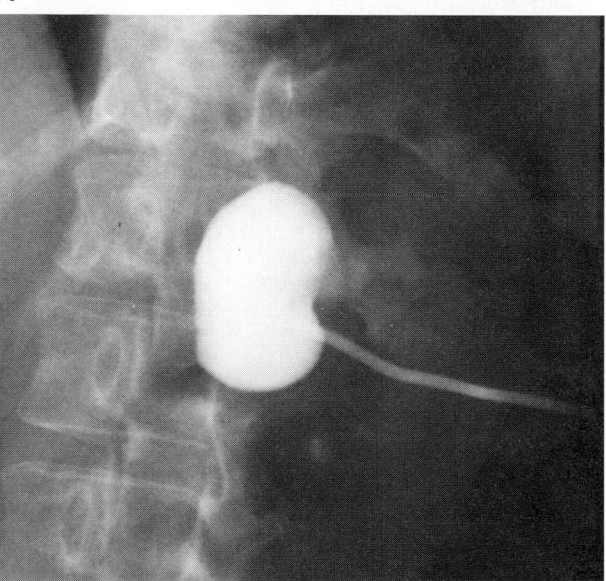

B

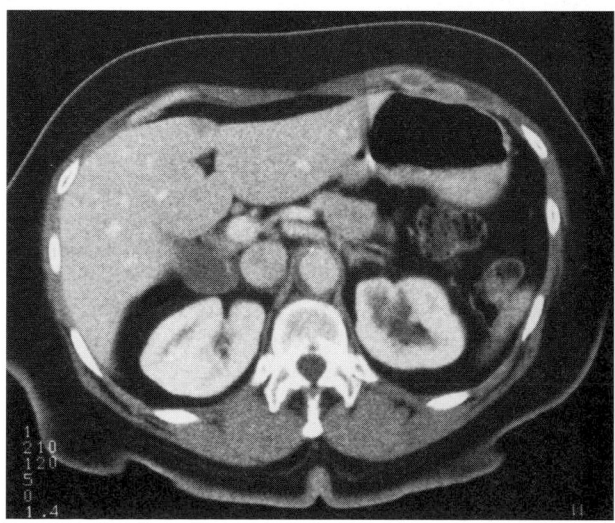

C

Figure 39-6. (A) Left parapelvic cyst that was causing left flank pain. (B) A drainage catheter was placed into the cyst, which relieved the patient's symptoms. (C) CT scan obtained for follow-up 6 months after the course of sclerosis shows complete resolution of the cyst.

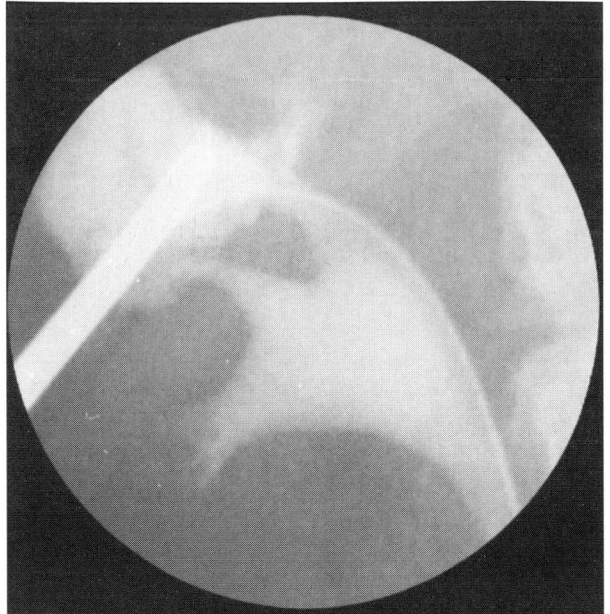

A

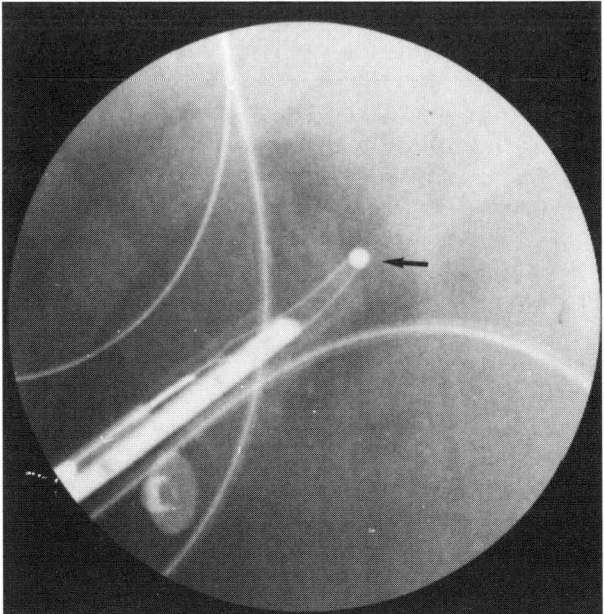

B

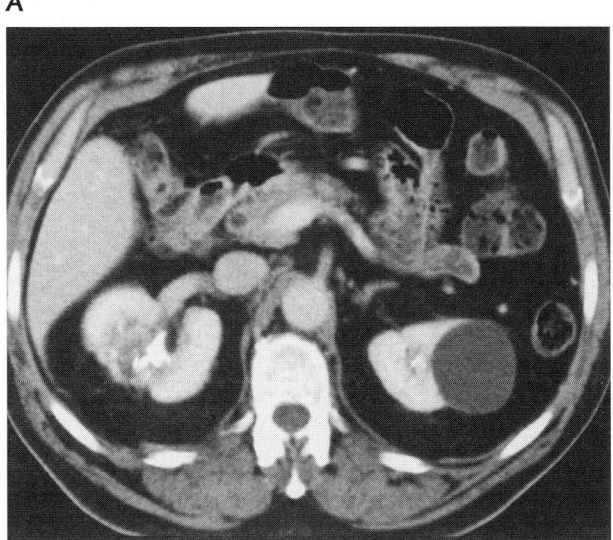

C

Figure 39-7. (A) Endoscopic marsupialization of a cyst into the collecting system. A sheath was percutaneously placed into the cyst, and an endoscope with a cutting electrode was used to create a communication into the collecting system. (B) The lining of the cyst is then endoscopically fulgurated using a roller-ball electrode (*arrow*). This is done to devitalize the cyst lining and to cause it to close through scarring. (C) CT scan obtained several months later shows complete resolution of the cyst. A moderate parenchymal defect indicates where the cyst once was.

with fulguration of the cyst wall to cause the cavity to close through scarring (Fig. 39-7). Although this has been done entirely via a retrograde approach with a ureteroscope,[33] the more common access is via a percutaneous tract into the cyst.[52] This requires placement of a 24 to 30 French sheath to provide access large enough for the endoscope. The technique used to place these sheaths is similar to those described for providing access for stone removals. Although laparoscopic and endourologic cyst procedures are generally effective, complete cyst obliteration may not be possible in all cases. In one series only 60 percent of cysts

totally resolved even though the cyst-related symptoms initially resolved in all cases.[45] Recurrent symptomatology did occur in one of six cysts in this series.

The success rates of surgical therapy and cyst sclerosis are fairly comparable. Cyst sclerosis, however, has multiple advantages. Sclerotherapy can easily be incorporated as an extension of an initial diagnostic procedure. Even the initial catheter placement can be performed with local anesthesia and does not require the general anesthetic needed for surgical techniques. Since no operating room fee or anesthesia charge is incurred, the procedure costs less. Moreover, sclerosis can be accomplished with a single 8 to 10 French catheter, which is considerably smaller than the hole created for an endourologic sheath. Even if treated laparoscopically, four small incisions are required for the various ports used for visualization and manipulation. Thus cyst sclerosis via a catheter is less complex and carries lower risks because of the smaller access used.

Urinomas

Urinomas are perinephric collections of urine that are seen in a variety of conditions. They may arise from obstruction of the ureter or collecting system with subsequent forniceal rupture. This can occur in any age range. In neonates obstruction from posterior urethral valves may cause localized urinomas,[53–55] and in adults obstructions due to stones or malignancies are potential causes.[56,57] Urinomas may also occur secondary to rupture of cortical cysts, leading to communication between the collecting system and the perirenal space. They are a common occurrence after renal transplants. Ureteral leak in conjunction with ureteral obstructive problems accounts for 95 percent of transplant urologic complications.[58,59] The cause of a peritransplant urinoma may be suspected on the basis of the time frame. A leak that occurs within the first week after transplant is most likely due to a technical error with dehiscence of the neoureterocystotomy. After the first week or two, ischemia of the ureter with perfora-

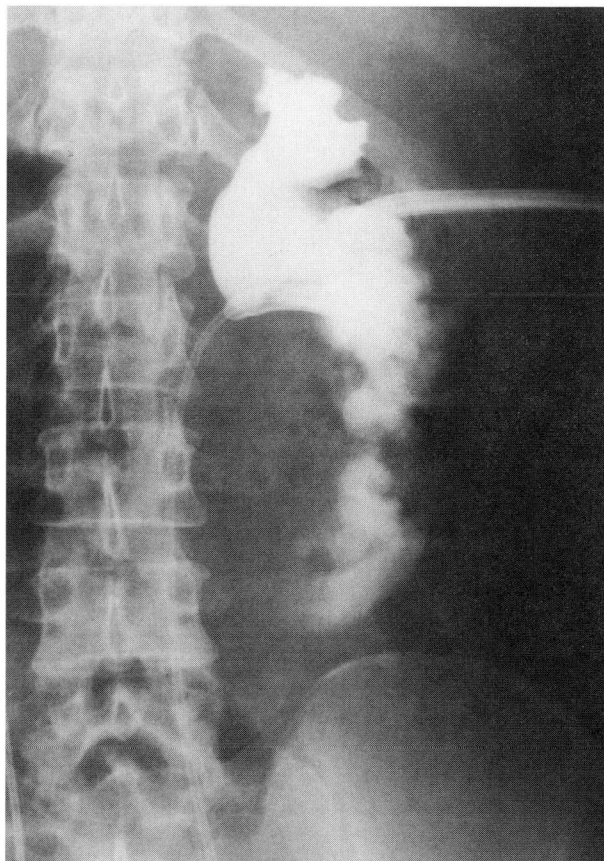

Figure 39-9. Iatrogenic urinoma occurring after percutaneous stone removal. Nephrostogram shows free extravasation of contrast around the drainage catheter into a large perinephric urinoma.

Figure 39-8. Iatrogenic urinoma caused by ureteral injury during placement of an aortobifemoral bypass graft. Contrast is seen to extravasate from the midureter. The urinoma was successfully treated by internal stenting.

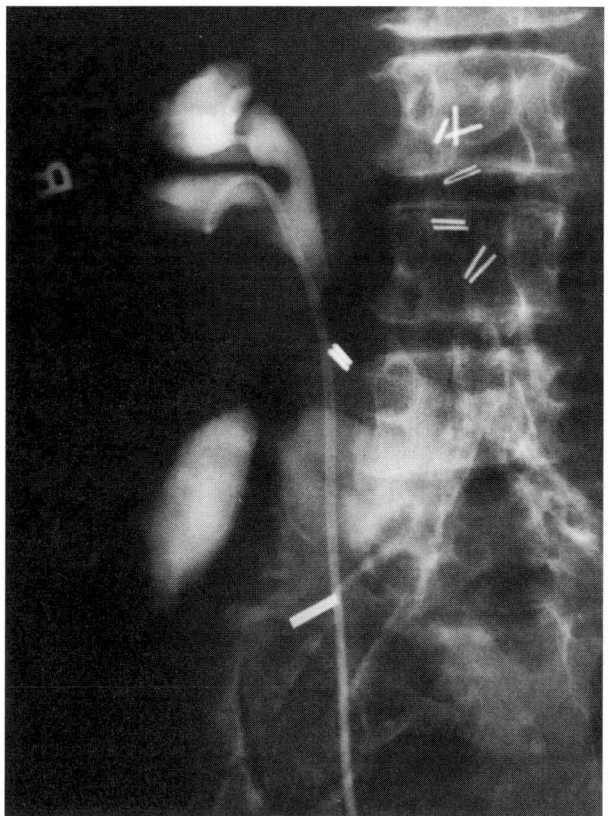

tion is more likely. Blunt or penetrating trauma to the kidney may either give rise to a urinoma by direct disruption of the pelvis or ureter, or may occur in a delayed fashion secondary to parenchymal necrosis and degeneration of nonviable tissue. Surprisingly, traumatic disruptions of the pelvis or ureter often go unrecognized initially.[60] Surgical trauma to the ureter may also lead to urinoma formation (Fig. 39-8). Finally, minimally invasive procedures are another potential source for urinomas. Urinomas have been reported after percutaneous nephrostomy (Fig. 39-9), stone basketing, cystoscopy, transurethral prostate resection, and extracorporeal shock wave lithotripsy.[61–65]

The symptoms that lead to the discovery of urinomas are most often related to the mass and pressure effects. Distention of the perinephric space or displacement of adjacent organs may lead to pain. Pain may also result secondarily from hydronephrosis due to ureteral obstruction. In pediatric cases, the mass effect from urinomas can lead to significant compromise of

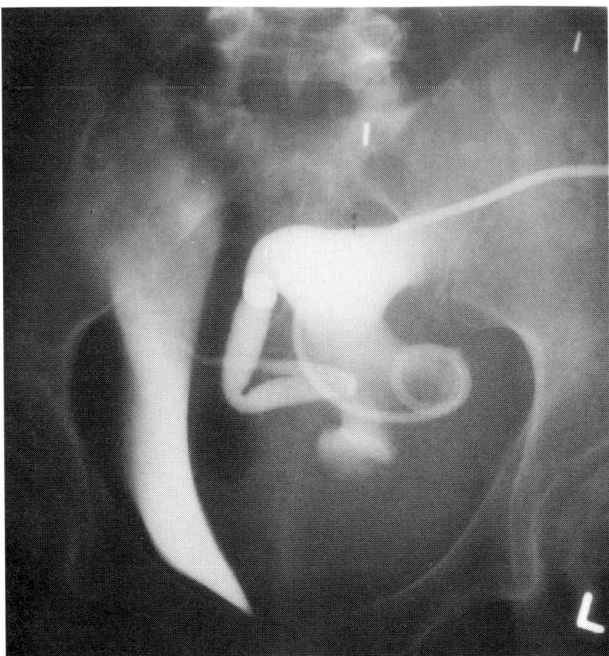

Figure 39-10. Large transplant urinoma causing compression of the bladder and distal ureteral obstruction. In addition to the nephrostomy, a drainage catheter into the urinoma was required to relieve the distal ureteral obstruction.

the diaphragm, including pulmonary compression. This may be severe enough to cause respiratory distress.[53,55,66] As mentioned, the mass effect may lead to ureteral obstruction (Fig. 39-10), which in the transplant patient may be manifested by rising creatinine levels or decreased urine output. If the transplant was recent, the urinoma may extend to the surgical incision and urine may leak out the incision. Fever or an elevated white count can herald a urinoma in patients in whom the urinoma becomes infected.

Diagnosis

The proper diagnosis of urinomas may require multiple techniques. Intravenous pyelography is generally not of great use. Although extravasation of contrast into a urinoma may be detected, it is rarely possible to define the point of leak with enough precision to direct the therapy. Both CT and ultrasound can accurately detect urinomas when the urine forms a well-defined collection. However, this may be a problem in renal transplants because the urine may not collect locally (i.e., it may leak out the surgical incision) (Fig. 39-11). In addition, the volume of urine leakage may be small enough that the urine can readily be resorbed by the surrounding tissues. Thus a defined urinoma collection may not be seen in 23 to 33 percent of renal

transplants in which there is a ureteral leak.[67,68] The other pitfall of ultrasound and CT is their specificity. Although fluid may be detected, it is generally not possible to distinguish a urinoma from a lymphocele, which is more commonly seen after transplants. Nuclear scintigraphy has been proposed as a more sensitive method of detecting urine extravasation; however, in two series scintigraphy failed to detect urinary leak in 50 to 67 percent of cases.[67,68] This most likely was due to decreased renal function and masking of a leak by overlying bladder.

Antegrade nephrostograms may be useful tests in the diagnosis of urinomas. This will generally allow accurate assessment of the location of a urinary leak, which in turn makes it easier to plan the appropriate therapy. Renal transplants are the only population in which the accuracy of antegrade nephrostograms has been assessed. In these patients, a leak may not be detected in 17 to 43 percent of cases.[67,68] False-negative studies are often due to the coexistence of ureteral obstruction. Although antegrade nephrostograms can be performed with a high degree of technical success, the procedure tends to be more difficult in patients with active urinary leak because the collecting system may be decompressed. Nevertheless, significant complications are uncommon.[68,69] Self-limited minor hematuria is usually the only sequela seen.

Because of the problems with noninvasive diagnosis, needle aspiration plays an important role in the diagnosis of urinomas. Aspiration of the fluid and analysis of the cell counts and the creatinine level can

Figure 39-11. Ultrasound examination failing to demonstrate a urinoma in a patient with documented gross urinary extravasation from the ureter. Only a minimal amount of fluid is seen immediately beneath the abdominal musculature. Most of the urine was leaking out of the transplant incision.

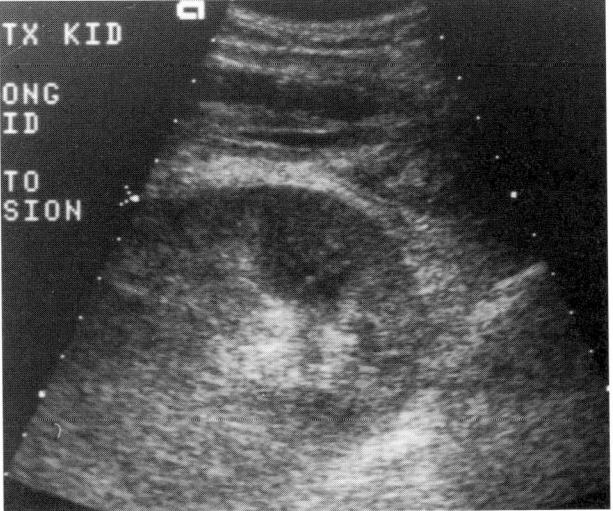

definitively distinguish between urinoma and other fluid collections. Aspiration may also be diagnostically useful to obtain material for culture, particularly for peritransplant urinomas, which may be infected 60 percent of the time.[70] In addition, these patients may not manifest normal signs of infection because of their immunosuppressive therapy. Aspiration can generally be performed with a 22- or 21-gauge needle passed under CT or ultrasound guidance. In most cases an unobstructed access to the collection can be easily found.

Therapy

The main therapy for a urinoma should actually be tailored to treat the underlying problem that led to the urinoma. When the urinoma has resulted from obstruction, the obstructing lesion (whether it is posterior ureteral valves or a ureteral stone) must be dealt with. With malignant obstructions percutaneous nephrostomy and/or ureteral stenting should be provided to relieve the obstruction. Iatrogenic urinary leaks should be treated with decompression of the collecting system and/or diversion of urine past the leak point by means of a stent. This diversion needs to be maintained until the breach in the urothelium heals. The same principle applies to leaks that result from blunt trauma. After trauma, surgical removal of devitalized tissue may be necessary when the urinary leak results from tissue necrosis. Finally, therapy in transplants should first involve drainage of the collecting system to decrease the amount of urine flow to the urinary leak. An internal-external ureteral stent may be used to further divert urine away from the leak, which most often arises from the distal ureter (Fig. 39-12). A ureteral stent has the additional advantage of helping to hold open the ureteral obstruction, which is a frequent concomitant condition. When percutaneous methods are used, ureteral transplant leaks will seal in 54 to 100 percent of cases, although sometimes prolonged stenting is required.[71–73]

Drainage of urinomas often takes a secondary role compared to definitive treatment of the underlying problem. In fact, if the primary problem is corrected, urinomas may spontaneously resolve and not require drainage. However, when the urinoma is large, drainage helps resolve the symptoms more quickly. Urinoma drainage is definitely indicated when the urinoma causes significant discomfort or compressive effects, such as obstruction of the ureter in a renal transplant or respiratory compromise in pediatric urinomas. Infection of the urinoma is also an indication for drainage. Even if definitive surgical therapy is ultimately required to treat the urinary leak, preoperative

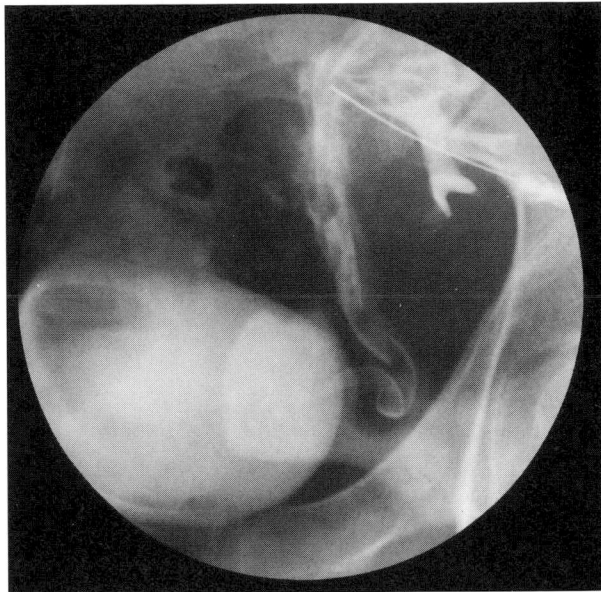

Figure 39-12. Transplant patient with elevated creatinine levels. Antegrade nephrostogram shows extravasation of contrast from the distal ureter tracking into the right pelvis.

drainage of infected urinomas can allow the patient to be stabilized and allow for the institution of appropriate antibiotics.

Before a urinoma is drained, the patient should be evaluated. The evaluation should include the usual history and physical examination. Coagulation factors and platelet count should be assessed to help prevent bleeding complications. Pretherapy assessment with CT or ultrasound is essential in helping one choose a safe access and avoid hitting adjacent structures such as bowel or the kidney. Cross-sectional imaging may also reveal extension of the urinoma into unusual places such as the chest or mediastinum, which may alter the drainage procedure. Antibiotic coverage is indicated if there is any fever or elevation of the leukocyte count. All renal transplants should probably receive predrainage antibiotics because of the high incidence of urinoma infection in this population.[70]

Drainage of a urinoma may be achieved by a simple needle aspiration, which suffices in some cases as long as the primary problem is sufficiently addressed.[57,74] Catheter drainage has several advantages. Generally more complete drainage can be obtained, and having the catheter in place allows the degree of urine leak to be monitored. This monitoring reveals the adequacy of the therapy for the underlying problem. In addition, it may not be possible by visual inspection of the fluid to determine the nature of the fluid collection and whether it is infected, and placement of a catheter maintains access into the collection until the fluid analysis has been completed.

Urinomas can be drained with a high degree of technical success and low morbidity. They are generally superficial, and access can usually be obtained without risk of puncture to adjacent structures. Since significant septations or loculations are not common and urine is not viscous, a single small-bore catheter will suffice to drain most urinomas. Although urinoma drainage has been described in several papers, there are no larger series that detail the technical success rate. No failed drainages have been reported, and no significant complications related to urinoma drainage have been described. This is not surprising, because the drainage pathway usually only crosses some subcutaneous fat and minimal abdominal musculature. Theoretically, if the urinoma is infected, bacteremia could result. This should be preventable by using prophylactic preprocedural antibiotics and by avoiding vigorous contrast injections until adequate drainage has occurred.

Summary

Although urinomas and renal cysts vary significantly in both their incidence and etiologies, each condition can benefit both diagnostically and therapeutically from interventional radiologic techniques.

References

1. Lang EK. Renal cyst puncture studies. Urol Clin North Am 1987;14:91–102.
2. McHugh K, Stringer DA, Hebert D, et al. Simple renal cysts in children: diagnosis and follow-up with US. Radiology 1991; 178:383–385.
3. Reiner I, Donnell S, Jones M, et al. Percutaneous sclerotherapy for simple renal cysts in children. Br J Radiol 1992;65:281–282.
4. Bretan P Jr, Novick AC, Steinmuller DR, et al. Ultrasonographic prospective pretransplant screening in 100 patients for acquired renal cysts and renal cell carcinoma. Transplant Proc 1989;21:1974–1975.
5. Mosli H, MacDonald P, Schillinger J. Caliceal diverticula developing into simple renal cyst. J Urol 1986;136:658–661.
6. Patel K, Caro PA, Chatten J. Parapelvic renal cyst causing UPJ obstruction: investigation by IVP, ultrasound and CT. Pediatr Radiol 1988;19:2–5.
7. Amis EJ, Cronan JJ. The renal sinus: an imaging review and proposed nomenclature for sinus cysts. J Urol 1988;139:1151–1159.
8. Egerdie RB, Buckspan MB, Klotz PG, et al. Bilateral multilocular renal cysts. J Urol 1986;135:346–348.
9. Castillo OA, Boyle ET, Kramer SA. Multilocular cysts of kidney: a study of 29 patients and review of literature. Urology 1991;37:156–162.
10. Fortner A, Taylor AJ, Alazraki N, et al. Advantage of indium-111 leukocytes over ultrasound in imaging an infected renal cyst. J Nucl Med 1986;27:1147–1149.
11. Dalton D, Neiman H, Grayhack JT. The natural history of simple renal cysts: a preliminary study. J Urol 1986;135:905–908.
12. Pearl M, Klein S. Simple renal cyst and hypertension. Ann Radiol 1986;29:421–423.
13. de Lichtenberg MH, Nielsen OS. Infected renal cyst simulating acute abdomen: case report. Acta Chir Scand 1989;155:135.
14. Papanicolaou N, Pfister RC, Yoder IC. Spontaneous and traumatic rupture of renal cysts: diagnosis and outcome. Radiology 1986;160:99–103.
15. Davis JD, McLaughlin AP. Spontaneous renal hemorrhage due to cyst rupture: CT findings. AJR 1987;148:763–764.
16. Emmett JL, Levine SR, Woolner LB. Co-existence of renal cyst and tumor: incidence in 1,007 cases. Br J Urol 1963;35:403–410.
17. Lang EK. The differential diagnosis of renal cysts and tumors: cyst puncture, aspiration, and analysis of cyst content for fat as diagnostic criteria for renal cysts. Radiology 1966;87:883–888.
18. Lang EK. Coexistence of cyst and tumor in the same kidney. Radiology 1971;101:7–16.
19. Ljungberg B, Holmberg G, Sjodin JG, et al. Renal cell carcinoma in a renal cyst: a case report and review of the literature. J Urol 1990;143:797–799.
20. Meziane MA, Fishman EK, Goldman SM, et al. Computed tomography of high density renal cysts in adult polycystic kidney disease. J Comput Assist Tomogr 1986;10:767–770.
21. Coleman BG, Arger PH, Mintz MC. Hyperdense renal masses: a computed tomographic dilemma. AJR 1984;143:291–294.
22. Bosniak MA. The current radiological approach to renal cysts. Radiology 1986;158:1–10.
23. Weyman PJ, McClennan BL, Lee JKT. CT of calcified renal masses. AJR 1982;138:1095–1099.
24. Clayman R, Surya V, Miller RP, et al. Pursuit of the renal mass: is ultrasound enough? Am J Med 1984;77:218–223.
25. McClennan BL, Stanley RJ, Melson GL, et al. CT of the renal cyst: is cyst aspiration necessary? AJR 1979;133:671.
26. Marotti M, Hricak H, Fritzsche P, et al. Complex and simple renal cysts: comparative evaluation with MR imaging. Radiology 1987;162:679–684.
27. Sarma DP, Weilbaecher TG, Waggenspack GA. Renal cell carcinoma presenting as a single large cyst. J Surg Oncol 1986;32:30–31.
28. Hartman DS, Weatherby ED, Laskin WB, et al. Cystic renal cell carcinoma: CT findings simulating a benign hyperdense cyst. AJR 1992;159:1235–1237.
29. Newhouse JH, Pfister RC. Renal cyst puncture. In: Anthasoulis CA, Pfister RC, Greene RE, Roberson GH, eds. Interventional radiology. Philadelphia: Saunders, 1982:409–425.
30. Sandler CM. Renal cyst puncture and percutaneous drainage of perirenal fluid. In: Kadir S, ed. Current practice of interventional radiology. Philadelphia: Decker, 1991:662–668.
31. Kleist H, Jonsson O, Lundstam S, et al. Quantitative lipid analysis in the differential diagnosis of cystic renal lesions. Br J Urol 1982;54:441–445.
32. Amis ES, Cronan JJ, Yoder IC, et al. Renal cysts: curios and caveats. Urol Radiol 1982;4:199–209.
33. Kavoussi LR, Clayman RV, Mikkelsen DJ, et al. Ureteronephroscopic marsupialization of obstructing peripelvic renal cyst. J Urol 1991;146:411–414.
34. Ohkawa M, Motoi I, Hirano S, et al. Biochemical and pharmacodynamic studies of simple renal cyst fluids in relation to infection. Nephron 1991;59:80–83.
35. Lang EK. Renal cyst puncture and aspiration: a survey of complications. AJR 1977;128:723–727.
36. Zelch J. Complication of renal cyst exploration versus renal mass aspiration. Urology 1976;7:244.
37. von Schreeb T, Arner O, Skovsted G, et al. Renal adenocarcinoma: is there a risk of spreading tumour cells in diagnostic puncture? Scand J Urol Nephrol 1967;1:270–276.
38. Jacobsson L, Lindqvist B, Michaelson G, et al. Fluid turnover in renal cysts. Acta Med Scand 1977;202:327.
39. Wahlqvist L, Grumstedt B. Therapeutic effect of percutaneous puncture of simple renal cyst: follow-up investigation of 50 patients. Acta Chir Scand 1966;132:340–347.
40. Ozgur S, Cetin S, Ilker Y. Percutaneous renal cyst aspiration

and treatment with alcohol. Int Urol Nephrol 1988;20:481–484.

41. Holmberg G, Hietala SO. Treatment of simple renal cysts by percutaneous puncture and instillation of bismuth-phosphate. Scand J Urol Nephrol 1989;23:207–212.
42. Bean WJ. Renal cysts: treatment with alcohol. Radiology 1981;138:329–331.
43. Raskin MM, Poole DO, Roen SA, et al. Percutaneous management of renal cysts: results of a four-year study. Radiology 1975;115:551.
44. Pfister RC, Schaffer D. Percutaneous ablation of renal cysts. AJR 1979;132:1031.
45. Gelet A, Sanseverino R, Martin X, et al. Percutaneous treatment of benign renal cysts. Eur Urol 1990;18:248–252.
46. Camacho MF, Bondhus MJ, Carrion HM, et al. Ureteropelvic junction obstruction resulting from percutaneous cyst puncture and intracystic isophendylate injection: an unusual complication. J Urol 1979;124:713.
47. van der Ent CK, van Dalen A, Enterman JH. Antibiotic sclerotherapy for renal cysts. Rofo 1989;150:339–341.
48. Nieh PT, Bihrle W. Laparoscopic marsupialization of massive renal cyst. J Urol 1993;150:171–173.
49. Morgan C Jr, Rader D. Laparoscopic unroofing of a renal cyst. J Urol 1992;148:1835–1836.
50. Hulbert JC, Shepard TG, Evans RM. Laparoscopic surgery for renal cystic disease. J Urol 1992;147:433A.
51. Amar AD, Das S. Surgical management of benign renal cysts causing obstruction of renal pelvis. Urology 1984;24:429.
52. Hulbert JC, Hunter D, Young AT, et al. Percutaneous intrarenal marsupialization of a perirenal cystic collection—endocystolysis. J Urol 1988;139:1039.
53. Feinstein KA, Fernbach SK. Septated urinomas in the neonate. AJR 1987;149:997–1000.
54. Fernbach SK, Feinstein KA, Zaontz MR. Urinoma formation in posterior urethral valves: relationship to later renal function. Pediatr Radiol 1990;20:543–545.
55. Connor JP, Hensle TW, Berdon W, et al. Contained neonatal urinoma: management and functional results. J Urol 1988;140:1319–1322.
56. McClinton S, Richmond P, Steyn JH. Spontaneous extravasation and urinoma formation secondary to cervical carcinoma. Br J Urol 1989;64:100–101.
57. Spurlock JW, Burke TW, Dunn NP, et al. Calyceal rupture with perirenal urinoma in a patient with cervical carcinoma. Obstet Gynecol 1987;70:511–513.
58. Mundy AR, Podesta ML, Bewick M. The urological complications in 1000 renal transplants. Br J Urol 1981;53:397–402.
59. Loughlin KR, Tilney NL, Richie JP. Urologic complications in 718 renal transplant patients. Surgery 1984;95:297–302.
60. Boone TB, Gilling PJ, Husmann DA. Ureteropelvic junction disruption following blunt abdominal trauma. J Urol 1993;150:33–36.
61. Braf ZF, Morag B, Many M. Spontaneous peripelvic extravasation of urine after transurethral resection of bladder tumor. Urology 1983;21:570.
62. Alkibay T, Karaoglan U, Gundogdu S, et al. An unusual complication of extracorporeal shock wave lithotripsy: urinoma due to rupture of the renal pelvis. Int Urol Nephrol 1992;24:11–14.
63. Portela LA, Patel SK, Callahan DH. Pararenal pseudocyst (urinoma) as complication of percutaneous nephrostomy. Urology 1979;13:570.
64. Rajendran MS, Rao MS, Bapna BC. Peripelvic extravasation and formation of perinephric urinoma after cystoscopy. Urology 1980;16:199.
65. Thompson IM, Ross G, Ezzard J. Experiences with 16 cases of pararenal pseudocyst. J Urol 1976;116:289.
66. Hoffer FA, Winters WD, Retik AB, et al. Urinoma drainage for neonatal respiratory insufficiency. Pediatr Radiol 1990;20:270–271.
67. Cullmann HJ, Prosinger M. Necrosis of the allograft ureter: evaluation of different examination methods in early diagnosis. Urol Int 1990;45:164–169.
68. Smith TP, Hunter DW, Letourneau JG. Urine leaks after renal transplantation: value of percutaneous pyelography and drainage for diagnosis and treatment. AJR 1988;151:511–513.
69. Turner AG, Howlett KA, Eban R, et al. The role of antegrade pyelography in the transplant kidney. J Urol 1980;123:812–814.
70. Kinnaert P, Hall M, Janssen F. Ureteral stenosis after kidney transplantation: true incidence and long-term follow up after surgical correction. J Urol 1985;133:17–20.
71. Darcy MD. Radiologic diagnosis and management of urologic complications of renal transplantation. Semin Intervent Radiol 1992;9:246–255.
72. Lieberman RP, Glass NR, Crummy AB. Nonoperative percutaneous management of urinary fistulas and strictures in renal transplantation. Surg Gynecol Obstet 1982;155:667–672.
73. Matalon TAS, Thompson MJ, Patel SK. Percutaneous treatment of urine leaks in renal transplantation patients. Radiology 1990;174:1049–1051.
74. Lang EK, Glorioso LD. Management of urinomas by percutaneous drainage procedures. Radiol Clin North Am 1986;24:551–559.

40

Selective Salpingography and Fallopian Tube Recanalization

AMY S. THURMOND

Proximal Tubal Obstruction

Anatomy and Pathophysiology

The intramural portion of the fallopian tube is an average of 1 cm in length and has a luminal diameter of about 1 mm. Its course is straight or slightly curved in 60 percent of cases and convoluted or tortuous in 40 percent.[1] A large number of pathologic conditions can affect this part of the tube, and their relative frequency varies depending on the patient population. Infection and subsequent inflammation or fibrosis are leading causes of proximal tubal occlusion and are frequently the consequence of chlamydial or gonococcal salpingitis or postpartum endometritis.[2] About half of patients with well-documented bilateral proximal tubal obstruction have localized disease with no pelvic adhesions.[3]

The circular muscle layer of the proximal tube and its innervation have been of interest for a number of years. Hysteroscopists have noted a spasmodic opening and closing of the tubal ostium, and it has long been postulated that some cases of proximal tubal obstruction are due to tubal spasm. Although many agents, including cyclic adenosine monophosphate, indomethacin, beta$_2$ agonists, and alpha-adrenergic antagonists, have been demonstrated to relax the circular muscle layer in vitro, their in vivo effects are variable or uncertain, and no reliable antispasmodic, including general anesthesia, has been discovered.[4]

Alternative Therapies

Microsurgical tubocornual anastomosis for proximal tubal obstruction, first described in 1977 by Gomel[5] and Winston,[6] has supplanted tubouterine implantation because it has fewer complications and improved results, with a long-term pregnancy rate of about 58 percent and a tubal pregnancy rate of about 4 percent.[7]

In vitro fertilization, an alternative therapy that bypasses the tubes altogether, results in an approximately 15 percent term pregnancy rate per successful embryo transfer.[8] Both of these treatments are expensive and time-consuming and should be reserved for patients who fail transcervical tubal catheterization. Which of these alternative treatments are used will depend on the clinical circumstances. Absence of concomitant distal tubal disease and young age may favor surgical therapy.

Patient Selection

Patients with unilateral or bilateral obstruction of the fallopian tube within the first 1 to 2 cm of the tube by hysterosalpingography (HSG) or laparoscopy are candidates for transcervical fallopian tube catheterization. The procedure can be accomplished using fluoroscopic or hysteroscopic and laparoscopic guidance. The patient selection process will vary from one institution to another and will depend somewhat on individual levels of expertise and the degree of cooperation between radiologists and gynecologists in a given practice setting.

If a patient has not had laparoscopy and has a history of pelvic inflammatory disease, proximal tubal obstruction (PTO) may be best evaluated using combined hysteroscopy and laparoscopy.[9] Also, if there is a uterine cavity mass that may interfere with catheterization or fertility and that could be removed hysteroscopically, then a hystersopically guided procedure is warranted.

If the patient has had prior laparoscopy that showed absent or minimal pelvic disease, or if there is low suspicion for concomitant pelvic disease, the procedure may be best carried out using fluoroscopic guidance. Fluoroscopic guidance also appears technically advantageous if the obstruction is in the isthmic part of the tube, 3 to 5 cm from the tubal ostium.

Technique

A variety of instruments and techniques for fluoroscopic fallopian tube catheterization, selective salpingography, and recanalization have been described.[10-15] The procedure is performed during the follicular phase of the menstrual cycle, using sterile technique and with antibiotic prophylaxis (usually doxycycline 100 mg orally bid for 5 days). Small doses of intravenous sedation and pain medication may be given but are usually not necessary. It is not necessary to dilate the cervix or give paracervical anesthesia.

The author's method (Fig. 40-1) consists of gaining access to the uterus with a vacuum cup hysterosalpingography device (Thurmond-Rösch Hysterocath, Cook, Inc., or Cook, OB/Gyn). This provides a sterile conduit through which a series of coaxial catheters and guidewires can be introduced and allows traction on the uterus without the application of a tenaculum. Conventional HSG with diluted water-soluble contrast medium is performed initially to localize the uterine cornua without obscuring the catheters. A coaxial catheter system (9 French Teflon sheath and 5.5 French polyethylene catheter) is advanced over a 0.035-inch-diameter (0.089-cm) J guidewire. The 5.5 French catheter is wedged in the uterine cornu. This coaxial system of three devices is advantageous in that it creates the flexibility to catheterize the ostia in flexed or distorted uteri (Fig. 40-2). The guidewire is removed, and full-strength contrast agent is injected (selective salpingography). If proximal tubal obstruction persists, a 0.015-inch-diameter (0.038-cm) guidewire with a flexible platinum tip and a 3 French Teflon catheter (Cook, Inc., or Cook, OB/Gyn) are advanced together into the fallopian tube and an attempt is made to recanalize the obstruction with gentle probing movements of the guidewire. If there is an acute angulation in the tube at the site of the obstruction, or if the obstruction is in the isthmic portion of the tube, a softer tapered guidewire and catheter are used (Tracker-18 and Taper guidewire, Target Therapeutics). When the guidewire passes the obstruction, the guidewire is removed and contrast agent is injected through the 3 French catheter. Once the recanalization is completed, the 3 French catheter is removed, and contrast agent is injected through the 5.5 French catheter still wedged in the tubal ostium to better delineate the tube and visualize the site of recanalization. A postrecanalization HSG can then be performed if desired. The patient can usually be dismissed within 30 minutes of concluding the procedure.

The principles and equipment for transcervical fallopian tube catheterization by hysteroscopy are the same as for fluoroscopic catheterization. The catheter system is adapted to pass through the operating channel of a hysteroscope with a gas-tight seal around the catheters.[9]

Results

Fluoroscopic fallopian tube catheterization clearly improves tubal diagnosis. Using a variety of techniques, the ability to gain access to the fallopian tube is greater than 95 percent in most series. The ability to establish proximal tubal patency is 80 to 85 percent.[12,15-25] Approximately one-third of patients who undergo successful fluoroscopic fallopian tube recanalization for unilateral or bilateral PTO have normal-appearing tubes after the procedure. Another one-third have patent tubes; however, the appearance of the tubes and the peritoneal spill suggest peritubal adhesions. Of the remaining patients, approximately 10 percent have patency with a small dilatation at the site of the obstruction, approximately 10 percent have patency with salpingitis isthmica nodosa, and approximately 10 percent have proximal patency but distal occlusion with hydrosalpinx (Fig. 40-3).[26]

Most investigators agree that tubal catheterization is also a treatment for infertility. This is more difficult to prove, however, because of the many clinical variables involved in achieving pregnancy.[27] Thurmond and Rösch evaluated the therapeutic effect of fallopian tube recanalization in 20 carefully selected patients in whom proximal tubal obstruction was thought to be the primary or sole cause of infertility.[16] All had bilateral proximal tubal obstruction by at least two hysterosalpingograms and by laparoscopy, with no distal tubal disease identified by laparoscopy. The average duration of infertility was 4 years. Seven of the couples had additional infertility factors. All 20 patients had been recommended for tubal microsurgery or in vitro fertilization but underwent catheter recanalization instead. Recanalization of one or both tubes was successful in 19 women (95 percent). By 1 year after the procedure, 58 percent of the women had conceived without receiving any other therapy, and all pregnancies were intrauterine. In a more heterogeneous group, including women with unilateral obstruction and peritubal adhesions, one may expect a lower short-term intrauterine pregnancy rate in the 20 to 30 percent range and an approximately 3 percent tubal pregnancy rate.[12,15-25]

The tubal reocclusion rate is difficult to determine because it depends partly on time. In patients who do not conceive by 6 months, it appears that about 50 percent of the tubes are reoccluded. If one assumes

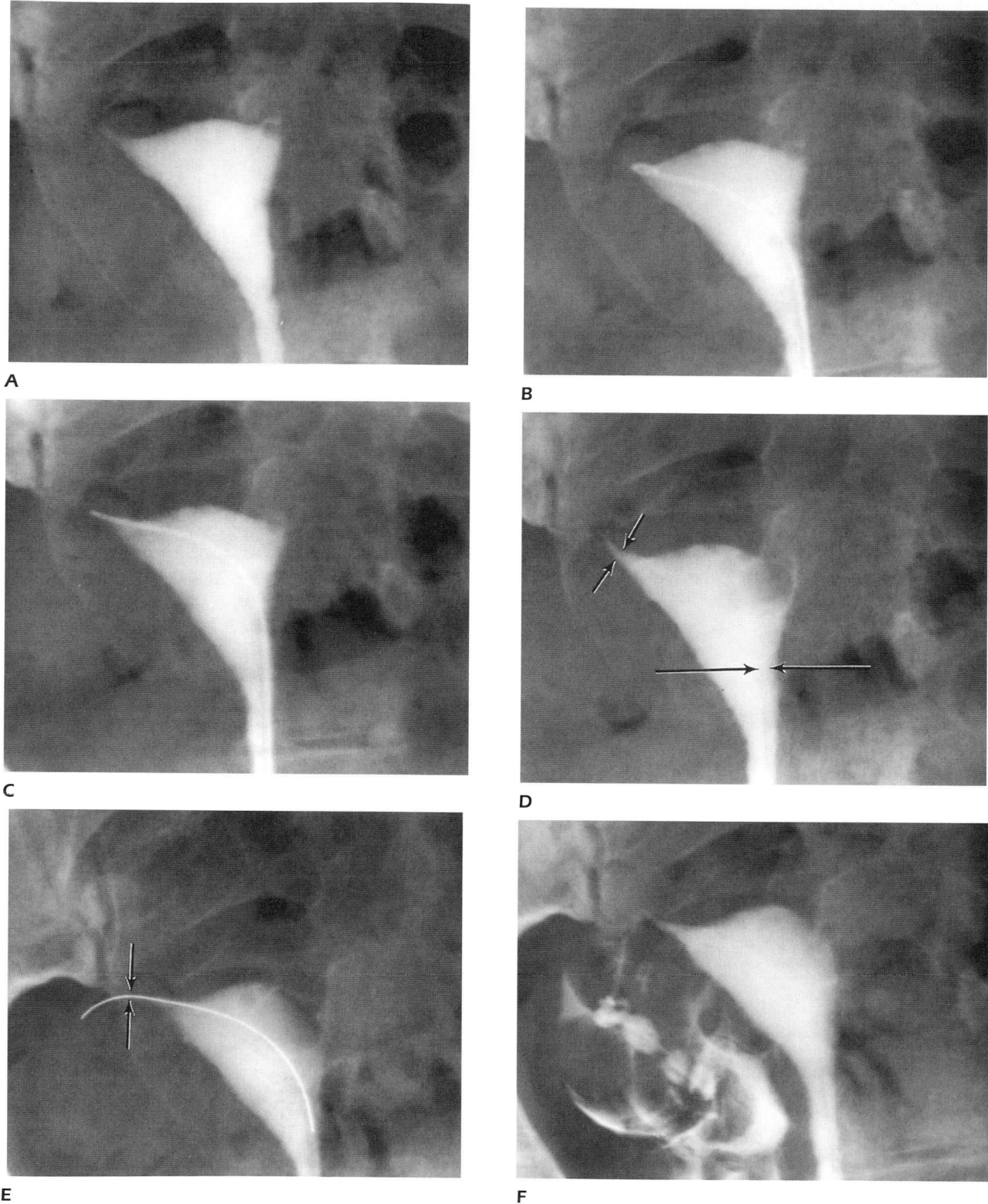

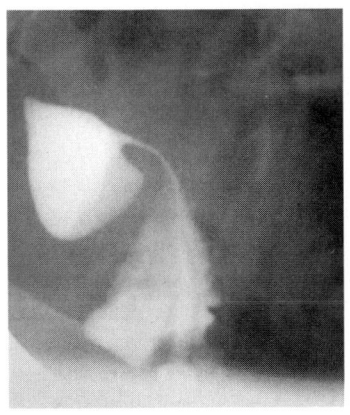
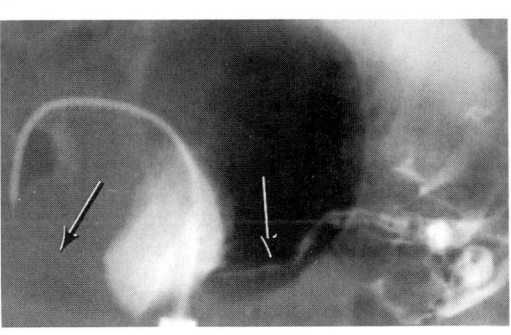
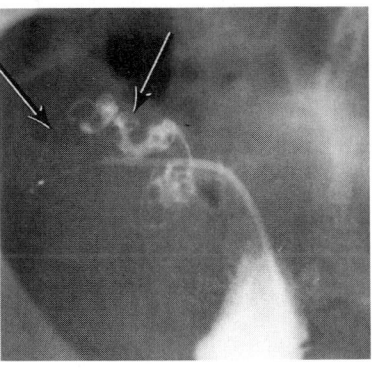

A **B** **C**

Figure 40-2. The described technique for catheterizing the fallopian tubes is applicable even to severely flexed or deviated uterine cavities. (A) Initial hysterosalpingogram shows bilateral proximal tubal obstruction and a uterine cavity that is retroflexed and deviated to the right. (B) Use of the 0.035-inch-diameter J-tipped and straight-tipped guidewires permits accurate placement of the 5.5 French catheter in the left tubal ostium. Selective salpingography reveals a normal-appearing left tube (*arrows*). (C) On the right side, advancement of the small catheter and guidewire through the 5.5 French catheter was necessary, and injection through the 2.7 French catheter (tip indicated by a radiopaque bead) reveals a normal-appearing right tube (*arrows*). (From Gleicher N, ed. Tubal catheterization procedures. 1st ed. New York: Wiley-Liss, 1992:91. Used with permission.)

that the tubes are patent in the patients who conceive, this gives an approximate reocclusion rate of 25 percent.[12,15–17,19–21,24] Repeat catheter recanalization is possible, and pregnancies have resulted after the second or even third procedure.

Complications

Mild uterine cramping and vaginal bleeding usually occur with fallopian tube catheterization. Intravenous sedation can be used but is usually not necessary.

Perforation occurs in about 2 percent of tubes and has not required additional monitoring or treatment.[12,15–25]

There has been one instance of a guidewire tip breaking in the tube during falloposcopy, and this was retrieved without further complication.[28] There has

also been one case of tuboovarian abscess necessitating salpingectomy and ovariectomy following catheterization without imaging guidance. This patient had not received prophylactic antibiotics.[29]

The radiation dose to the ovaries during fluoroscopic catheterization has been documented to be less than 1 rad (10 Gy).[30] This is in the same range as the radiation dose delivered during a barium enema or an intravenous pyelogram (IVP). The dose, of course, varies depending on the equipment and the amount of fluoroscopy used as well as the number of radiographs exposed.

Discussion

A variety of techniques for fallopian tube catheterization have emerged, with the differences centering

---

◄ **Figure 40-1.** A 35-year-old woman with a history of left salpingectomy for tubal pregnancy 3 years previously. Two recent HSGs and one laparoscopy showed right proximal tubal obstruction and an otherwise normal pelvis. She conceived shortly after this procedure and delivered a healthy baby. (A) Initial hysterosalpingogram shows bilateral proximal tubal obstruction. (B) The 0.035-inch J-tipped guidewire is advanced into the right cornu, and the 5.5 French catheter and 9 French sheath are advanced over it. The use of the J-tipped guidewire allows for atraumatic catheterization of the uterine cornu even when the uterine cavity is large or unusually shaped. (C) The 0.035-inch J-tipped guidewire is exchanged for a 0.035-inch straight wire, which allows one to carefully wedge the 5.5 French catheter into the tubal os-

tium. (D) Injection through the 5.5 French catheter wedged in the right tubal ostium confirms an obstruction approximately 5 mm from the uterine cavity. The tip of the 5.5 French catheter is indicated by *short arrows,* and the tip of the 9 French sheath is indicated by *long arrows.* (E) The 0.015-inch guidewire, supported by the 3 French catheter, is advanced through the 5.5 French catheter, and the guidewire is used to carefully probe the obstruction. The tip of the guidewire is visible as a metallic density; the tip of the 3 French catheter (*arrows*) is not easily visible. (F) After the guidewire passes the obstruction, it is removed and contrast agent is injected, initially through the 3 French catheter and then through the 5.5 French catheter (shown here), to document tubal anatomy.

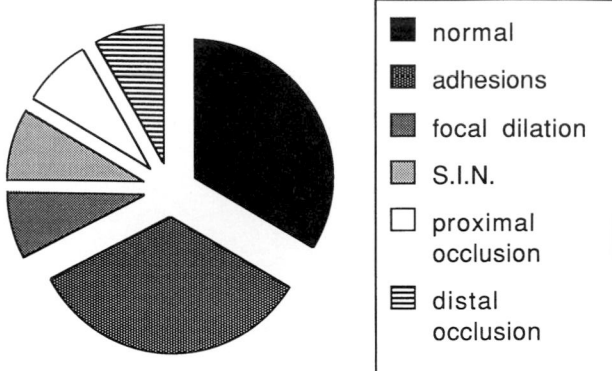

Figure 40-3. Tubal findings after selective salpingography and tubal recanalization in 100 consecutive patients evaluated for proximal tubal obstruction. (From Thurmond AS. Selective salpingography and fallopian tube recanalization. AJR 1991;156:33–38. Used with permission.)

around (1) the imaging guidance used, either fluoroscopy, hysteroscopy, ultrasound, or no imaging (tactile); (2) the device for uterine access, either a cervical vacuum cup, a cervical tenaculum, or an intrauterine balloon; (3) the tubal ostium access, either a coaxial catheter and guidewire, a balloon catheter and guidewire, or a ball-tipped catheter; and (4) the fallopian tube access, usually a small-caliber catheter and guidewire or a small scope. More than 20 centers have published their experiences, with some centers authoring several publications detailing their experience with a variety of imaging systems or catheter assemblies.[12,15-25]

Imaging guidance by ultrasound is advocated by some because of the absence of radiation exposure and the ability to perform the procedure in a gynecology office.[31] However, these benefits are outweighed by the risks of inadequate tubal visualization,[32] which precludes the diagnosis of salpingitis isthmica nodosa, fimbrial phimosis, or other tubal changes that may be relevant to patient management. With ultrasound it is also impossible to know when one has perforated the tube. Perforation can lead to continued attempts at catheterization and unacceptable tubal damage or complications. The same limitations exist for tactile guidance of fallopian tube catheterization and office hysteroscopy without simultaneous laparoscopic guidance.

Under fluoroscopic guidance, all systems appear to allow about the same success rate for tubal catheterization, and the choice of a system depends on individual preferences. The author prefers to avoid using a tenaculum and prefers a tubal catheterization system that can be adapted to a range of uterine shapes and sizes (see Fig. 40-2).

Transcervical access to the fallopian tube can lead to a number of interventions in addition to the improved diagnosis and treatment of proximal tubal obstruction described above. Other applications that have been tried include intratubal placement of gametes or embryos,[33] falloposcopy for a variety of reasons,[34] or miscellaneous interventions such as tubal sterilization[35,36] or treatment of tubal pregnancy.[37] These applications show promise and are still in the developmental stages. Selective salpingography and tubal recanalization, however, are no longer considered experimental and have been advocated by the American Fertility Society in patients with proximal tubal obstruction, before tubal microsurgery or in vitro fertilization is tried.[38]

FDA Approval

Catheters and guidewires from one manufacturer, Conceptus, Inc., were approved by the Food and Drug Administration (FDA) for transcervical placement in the fallopian tube in July 1995. Additional devices from other companies, which have been approved by the FDA for intravascular use, are being used in the fallopian tubes and have been described in the literature.[11-13,19] These catheters and guidewires are also likely to gain FDA approval for use in the female reproductive system.

Conclusion

Selective salpingography and catheter recanalization are indicated in patients with proximal tubal obstruction by HSG or laparoscopy. The procedure is an extension of conventional HSG and uses standard angiographic equipment and technique. The primary goal is to improve diagnosis and to visualize both fallopian tubes. This allows the patient and her gynecologist to determine the most effective management plan. In some patients who have isolated proximal tubal obstruction as a cause for infertility, the procedure is therapeutic and allows natural conception to occur.

References

1. Merchant RN, Prabhu SR, Chougale A. Uterotubal junction—morphology and clinical aspects. Int J Fertil 1983;28:199–205.
2. Musich JR, Behrman SJ. Surgical management of tubal obstruction at the uterotubal junction. Fertil Steril 1983;40:423–441.
3. Sulak PJ, Letterie GS, Coddington CC, et al. Histology of proximal tubal occlusion. Fertil Steril 1987;48:437–440.
4. Thurmond AS, Novy M, Rösch J. Terbutaline in diagnosis of interstitial fallopian tube obstruction. Invest Radiol 1988;23:209–210.

5. Gomel V. Tubal reanastomosis by microsurgery. Fertil Steril 1977;28:59–65.
6. Winston RML. Microsurgical tubocornual anastomosis for reversal of sterilisation. Lancet 1977;1:284–285.
7. Marana R, Quagliarello J. Proximal tubal occlusion: microsurgery versus IVF—a review. Int J Fertil 1988;33:338–340.
8. Society for Assisted Reproductive Technology of the American Fertility Society. Assisted reproductive technology in the United States and Canada: 1991 results from the Society of Assisted Reproductive Technology generated from the American Fertility Society Registry. Fertil Steril 1993;59:956–962.
9. Novy MJ, Thurmond AS, Patton PE, et al. Diagnosis of cornual obstruction by transcervical fallopian tube cannulation. Fertil Steril 1988;50:434–440.
10. Thurmond AS, Uchida BT, Rösch J. Device for hysterosalpingography and fallopian tube catheterization. Radiology 1990;174:571–572.
11. Thurmond AS, Rösch J. Fallopian tubes: improved technique for catheterization. Radiology 1990;174:572–573.
12. Confino E, Tur-Kaspa I, DeCherney A, et al. Transcervical balloon tuboplasty—a multicenter trial. JAMA 1990;264:2079–2082.
13. LaBerge JM, Ponec DJ, Gordon RL. Fallopian tube catheterization: modified fluoroscopic technique. Radiology 1990;176:283–284.
14. Meyerovitz MF. Hysterosalpingography and fallopian tube cannulation: use of a double-balloon introducing catheter. Radiology 1991;181:901–902.
15. Lisse K, Sydow P. Fallopian tube catheterization and recanalization under ultrasonic observation: a simplified technique to evaluate tubal patency and open proximally occluded tubes. Fertil Steril 1991;56:198–201.
16. Thurmond AS, Rösch J. Nonsurgical fallopian tube recanalization for treatment of infertility. Radiology 1990;174:371–374.
17. Segars JH, Herbert CM III, Moore DE, et al. Selective fallopian tube cannulation: Initial experience in an infertile population. Fertil Steril 1990;53:357–359.
18. Kumpe DA, Zwerdlinger SC, Rothbarth LJ, et al. Proximal fallopian tube occlusion: diagnosis and treatment with transcervical fallopian tube catheterization. Radiology 1990;177:183–187.
19. Lang EK, Dunaway HE Jr, Roniger WE. Selective osteal salpingography and transvaginal catheter dilatation in the diagnosis and treatment of fallopian tube obstruction. AJR 1990;154:735–740.
20. Capitaneo GL, Ferraiolo A, Croce S, et al. Transcervical selective salpingography: a diagnostic and therapeutic approach to cases of proximal injection failure. Fertil Steril 1991;55:1045–1050.
21. Kelekis D, Papageorgiou G, Fezoulidis I, et al. Selective transcervical recanalization of fallopian tubes: a method for diagnosis and treatment of infertility. J Intervent Radiol 1992;7:37–40.
22. Maubon A, Rouanet JP, Cover S, et al. Fallopian tube recanalization by selective salpingography: an alternative to more invasive techniques? Hum Reprod 1992;7:1425–1428.
23. Sato M, Yamada R, Kimura M, et al. Transvaginal fallopian tube catheterization: diagnostic and therapeutic usefulness. Radiat Med 1993;11:49–52.
24. Hayashi N, Kimoto T, Sakai T, et al. Selective fallopian tube catheterization: limited value in the treatment of fallopian tube diseases. Radiology 1994;190:141–143.
25. Hovsepian DM, Bonn J, Eschelman DJ, et al. Fallopian tube recanalization in an unrestricted patient population. Radiology 1994;190:137–140.
26. Thurmond AS, Rösch J, Patton PE, et al. Fluoroscopic transcervical fallopian tube catheterization for diagnosis and treatment of female infertility caused by tubal obstruction. RadioGraphics 1988;8:621–640.
27. Thurmond AS. Interpretation of pregnancies after selective salpingography. Radiology 1994;190:11–13.
28. Kerin J, Daykhovsky L, Grundfest W, et al. Falloposcopy: a microendoscopic transvaginal technique for diagnosing and treating endotubal disease incorporating guide wire cannulation and direct balloon tuboplasty. J Reprod Med 1990;35:606–612.
29. Pratt DE, Bieber E, Barnes R, et al. Transvaginal intratubal insemination by tactile sensation: a preliminary report. Fertil Steril 1991;56:984–986.
30. Hedgpeth PL, Thurmond AS, Fry R. Radiographic fallopian tube recanalization: absorbed ovarian radiation dose. Radiology 1991;180:121–122.
31. Stern JJ, Peters AJ, Coulam CB. Transcervical tuboplasty under ultrasonographic guidance: a pilot study. Fertil Steril 1991;56:359–360.
32. Thurmond AS, Patton PE, Hector DM, et al. US-guided fallopian tube catheterization. Radiology 1991;180:571–572.
33. Jansen RPS, Anderson JC. Transvaginal versus laparoscopic gamete intrafallopian transfer: a case-controlled retrospective comparison. Fertil Steril 1993;59:836–840.
34. Kerin JF, Williams DB, San Ramon GA, et al. Falloposcopic classification and treatment of fallopian tube lumen disease. Fertil Steril 1992;57:731–741.
35. Ross PL, Thurmond AS, Jones MJ, et al. Transcatheter tubal sterilization in rabbits: techniques and results. Invest Radiol 1994;29:570–573.
36. Maubon A, et al. Tubal sterilization by selective catheterization: preliminary study of 3 occluding materials in an animal model. Radiology 1994;193:721–723.
37. Risquez F, Confino E. Transcervical tubal cannulation, past, present, future. Fertil Steril 1993;60:211–225.
38. American Fertility Society. Guideline for tubal disease. Am Fertil Soc 1993: February 15.

41

Varicocele

RICHARD SHLANSKY-GOLDBERG

The relationship between sperm count and infertility has been recognized since the 18th century; however, it was not until the late 19th century that the effect of varicocele on seminal parameters was demonstrated.[1] In 1885 Barwell reported his experience with the "subcutaneous wire loop" ligation of 100 varicoceles,[2] and in 1889 Bennett reported improvement in semen quality in a patient with bilateral varicoceles "after one side had been cured" by surgery.[3] Not until the early 1950s, when Tulloch in Britain reported the production of sperm after varicocele ligation in a previous azoospermic man that resulted in a pregnancy, did the implication of varicocele causing infertility become apparent.[4] In 1962, Charny was the first in the United States to publicize the effects of varicocele on fertility.[5] Finally, MacLeod studied the semen analyses from 200 men with varicocele because of the developing reports of improvement in semen characteristics after surgical ligation.[6] He defined the "stress pattern," which is an increased number of immature cells and tapered forms with decreased motility with or without a decrease in concentration, confirming the effect of varicoceles on sperm quality. Although this pattern may be seen with other conditions, such as congenital adrenal hyperplasia and alcohol abuse, and following a febrile or viral episode, it is best known for its association with varicocele. Iaccarino, in 1977, and Lima et al., in 1978, published the first reports of percutaneous therapy for the correction of varicoceles with a sclerosing agent.[7,8]

Percutaneous treatment of varicocele for infertility has become popular as a primary treatment or as an adjuvant to failed surgery.[9,10] Other indications for varicocele correction include pain and swelling, in addition to testicular atrophy in the pediatric or adolescent population.[11] In the adolescent population, correction is recommended for varicoceles associated with decreased testicular mass, particularly when the left testicle is smaller than the right by at least 5 mm, or for failure of testicular growth that does not correspond with the level of puberty.[12]

Definition and Incidence

Varicocele is an abnormal degree of venous dilatation of the pampiniform plexus that may extend from the spermatic veins up to the level of the left renal vein or inferior vena cava. Rarely, the varicocele can also be associated with dilated intratesticular veins or subcutaneous varices.[13,14] The incidence of varicocele in healthy males is 8 to 23 percent, with the left side involved in 70 to 100 percent of cases, the right side involved in 0 to 9 percent of cases, and both sides involved in 0 to 23 percent of cases.[15–18] The incidence of varicocele rises at the onset of puberty and is 16.2 percent at the ages of 10 to 19.[15] It is considered an important factor in infertility in approximately 21 to 41 percent of infertile men visiting infertility clinics, with 20 to 25 percent of these men seeking percutaneous or surgical correction.[15–17,19]

Anatomy

Venous drainage of the testicle is by several routes (Fig. 41-1). The spermatic venous plexus, also called the *pampiniform plexus,* is formed by multiple dilated and tortuous venous sinuses in the scrotum.[20] Opposite the head of the femur, the veins coalesce and unite to form the internal spermatic vein, which is the major draining vein.[20] The internal spermatic vein usually drains into the left renal vein on the left and into the infrarenal inferior vena cava (IVC) on the right with conventional anatomy (Fig. 41-2).[21] In a left-sided vena cava, the left spermatic vein drains directly into the vena cava.[22] There are three additional routes of venous drainage from the scrotum and testicle: the external pudendal, vasal, and cremasteric veins.[20,23] The external pudendal vein, also named the *superficial external pudendal vein,* originates from the pampiniform plexus at the level of the inferior pubic ramus and travels superolaterally to terminate in the long saphenous vein, which drains into the femoral vein. The vasal

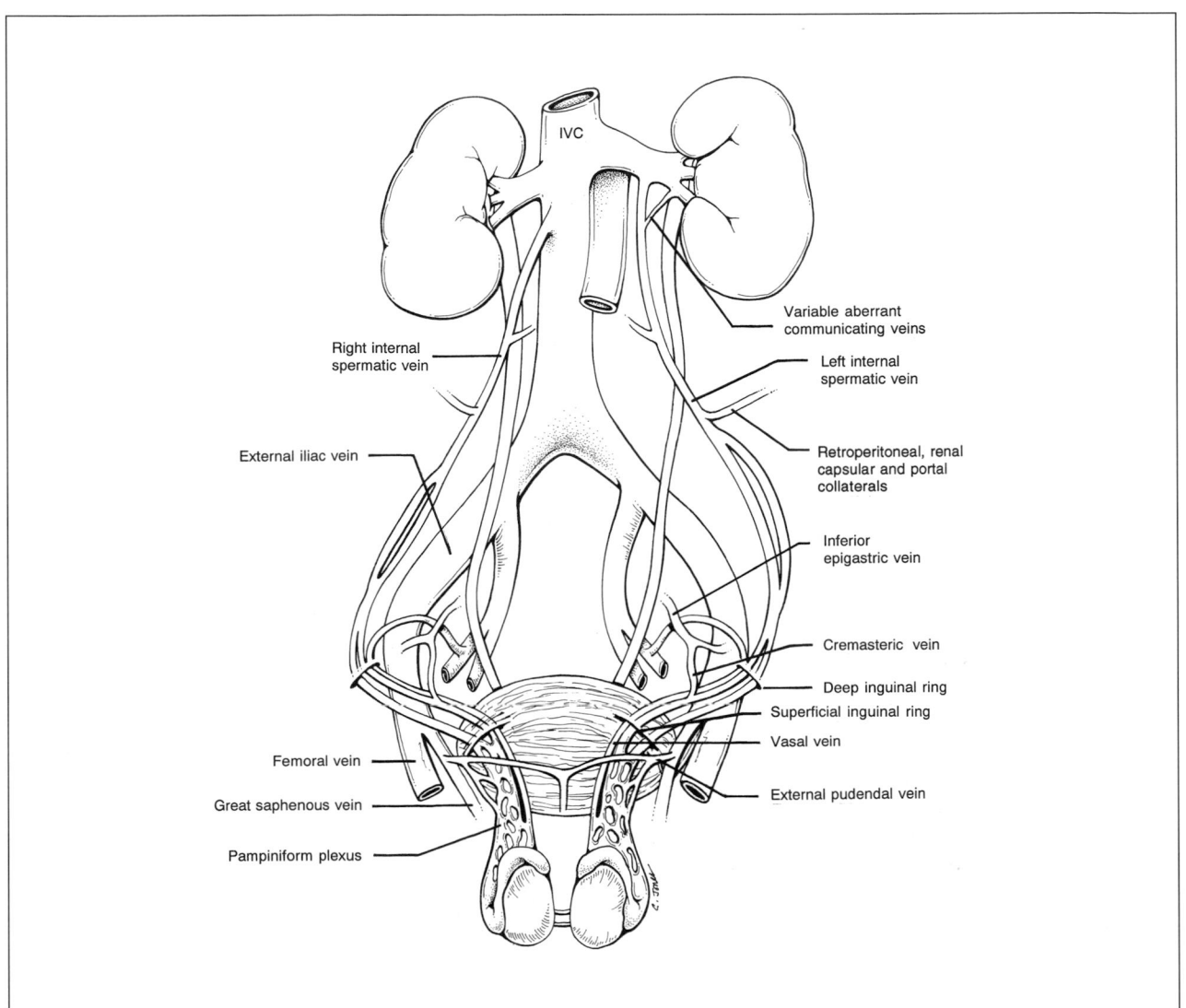

Labels on figure:

IVC

Right internal spermatic vein

External iliac vein

Femoral vein

Great saphenous vein

Pampiniform plexus

Variable aberrant communicating veins

Left internal spermatic vein

Retroperitoneal, renal capsular and portal collaterals

Inferior epigastric vein

Cremasteric vein

Deep inguinal ring

Superficial inguinal ring

Vasal vein

External pudendal vein

Figure 41-1. Classic gonadal venous drainage for both the right and left testicles. The main drainage of the testicle involves several veins that originate from the pampiniform plexus as the spermatic, cremasteric, pudendal, and vasal veins. The left gonadal vein enters the left renal vein, and the right renal vein enters the inferior vena cava below the right renal vein.

vein, also named the *ductus deferens vein,* is a small vessel that arises near the testis and passes upward to join the internal iliac vein. The cremasteric vein, also called the *external spermatic vein,* arises at the level of the superior pubic ramus and passes laterally and superiorly to anastomose to the external iliac vein via the inferior epigastric vein. Although typically the internal spermatic vein is involved in the formation of the varicocele, the cremasteric vein may also be involved.[24] After embolization or ligation, the external pudendal vein most often provides the major drainage from the scrotum followed by the cremasteric vein.[20,25]

The spermatic venous anatomy has been described by several investigators using postmortem specimens or venography. Unfortunately, there are considerable differences in the descriptions of venous collaterals, cross-scrotal collaterals, and venous valves.[20,21,23,26–30] Lechter et al. analyzed 200 spermatic veins from 100 cadavers and found that the classic pattern was present 78 percent of the time on the right and 79 percent of the time on the left (Fig. 41-3).[21] The spermatic vein

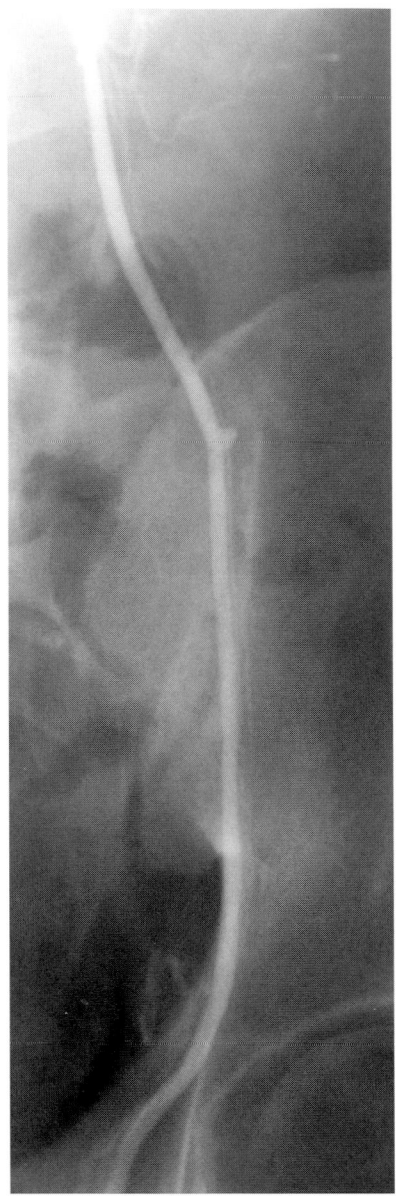

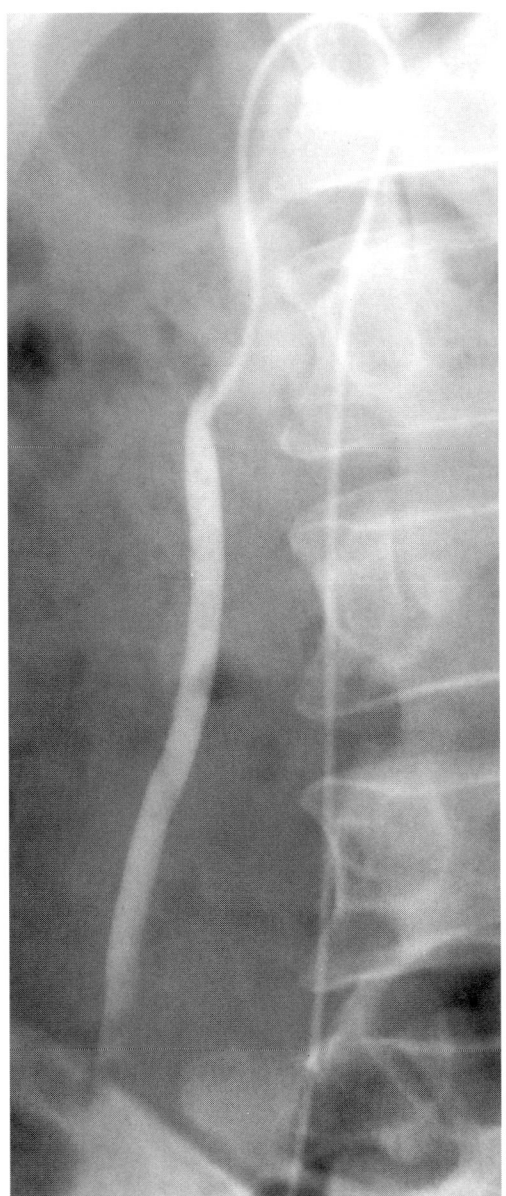

A   **B**

Figure 41-2. Typical spermatic venogram seen with varicocele demonstrating reflux of contrast without evidence of valves. (A) Left gonadal venogram with catheter advanced through the left renal vein with the tip in the left gonadal vein demonstrates reflux of contrast down the spermatic vein. (B) Right gonadal venogram with a Simmons catheter through the IVC with the tip of the catheter in right gonadal vein, also demonstrating reflux of contrast down the spermatic vein.

may terminate in the right renal vein in 8 percent of cases. Double or multiple terminations may be found in 16 percent of cases on the right and in rare instances may enter above the right renal vein. On the left, there is a double system going to the renal vein in 19 percent of cases and a triple system in 1 percent of cases; rarely, the system has accessing branches that may also enter the IVC on the left (see Fig. 41-3).[21]

Analysis of the spermatic vein trunks usually demonstrates one to six trunks originating in the lower one-third as they ascend and merge to form fewer trunks in the upper third of the spermatic vein.[21] In some cases, there is one trunk in the lower third that ascends into multiple veins (Figs. 41-4 and 41-5).[21]

There may be zero to three valves distributed along the course of the spermatic vein, with some investigators finding more veins valvulated on the left and others finding more on the right (Fig. 41-6).[21,26] Analyses

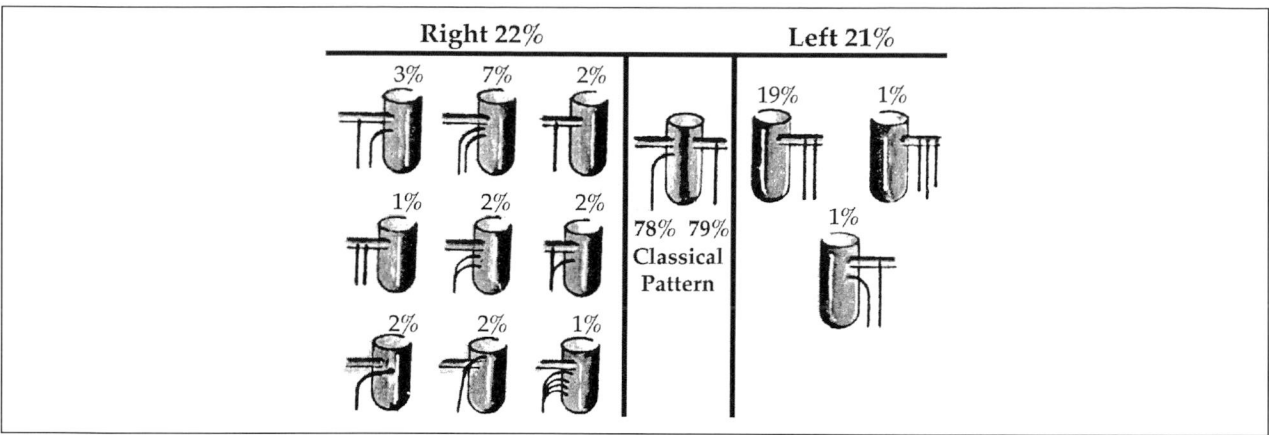

Figure 41-3. Anatomic variation in the termination of the right and left gonadal veins with the percentages of each variation as seen in 200 gonadal veins. The classic pattern of a single left spermatic vein entering the left renal vein is seen in 79 percent of cases, and that of a single right spermatic vein entering into the inferior vena cava below the right renal vein is seen in 78 percent of cases as determined by Lechter et al. (From Lechter A, Lopez G, Martinez C, et al. Anatomy of the gonadal veins: a reappraisal. Surgery 1991;109:735–739. Used with permission.)

by other investigators have demonstrated no valves at all; Wishahi failed to find valves in a post-mortem review of 40 men.[29]

There are several descriptions of collateral vessels around the spermatic vein that create anastomoses to

Figure 41-4. Number of venous trunks as they ascend from the pampiniform plexus, with the percentage seen in 200 gonadal veins as determined by Lechter et al. (From Lechter A, Lopez G, Martinez C, et al. Anatomy of the gonadal veins: a reappraisal. Surgery 1991;109:735–739. Used with permission.)

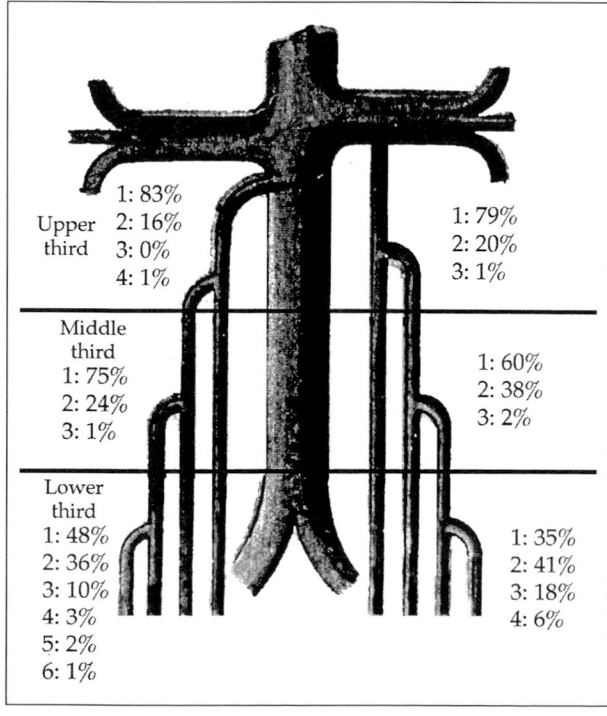

the systemic circulation at the cremasteric, pudendal, vasal, retroperitoneal, ureteral, peritoneal, renal, right testicular, and adrenal veins, in addition to the IVC, and to the portal system through the splenic, superior mesenteric, and sigmoid colonic veins (Figs. 41-7 through 41-9).[20,21,28–30] Lechter et al. found that 67 percent of the left-side veins and 49 percent of the right-side veins demonstrated collaterals, with those in the upper third of the vein coming from Gerota's perirenal fat and the lower third coming from the retroperitoneum.[21] Examining autopsy specimens, Wishahi noted that the spermatic vein divided at L4 into medial and lateral divisions (Fig. 41-10). The medial division was the largest terminating in the left renal vein on the left and in the IVC on the right. At the level of L3, multiple veins emerge from the medial division to anastomose with the veins of the bladder, ureter, and pelvis of the kidney. The lateral division terminates in the perinephric fat. Multiple venules extend from the lateral division toward the lateral border of the kidney to join the renal capsular vessels and the colonic veins of the portal system (see Fig. 41-8).[29] Wishahi found no cross-communication between the left and right systems in the scrotal, retropubic, or pelvic areas on venography but found cadaver evidence of communication at the L3 level between the medial spermatic vein divisions in 55 percent of cases. Others have demonstrated scrotal cross-collaterals (Fig. 41-11).[31] Sofikitis et al. found the gonadal vein to bifurcate into medial and lateral divisions, as described by Wishahi, in only 45 percent of cases, with cross-lumbar collaterals in 4 percent of specimens.[30]

Text continues on page 686

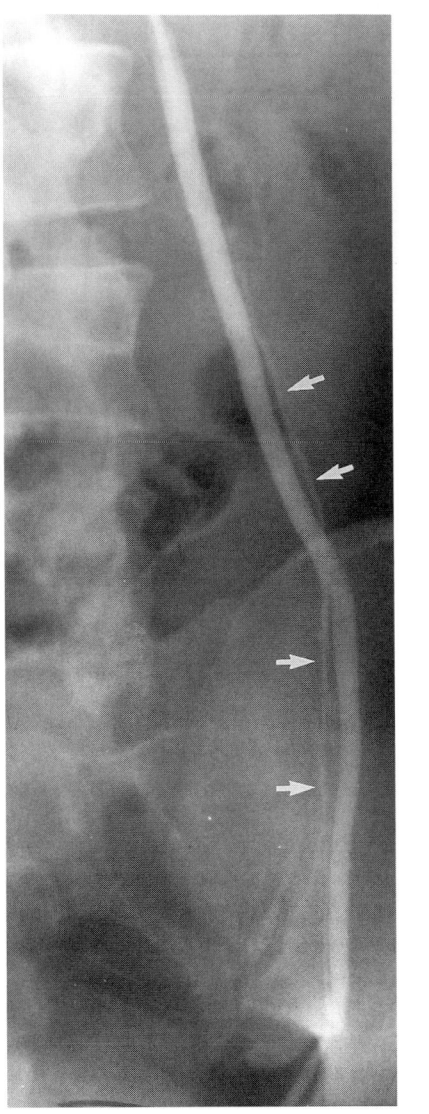

A

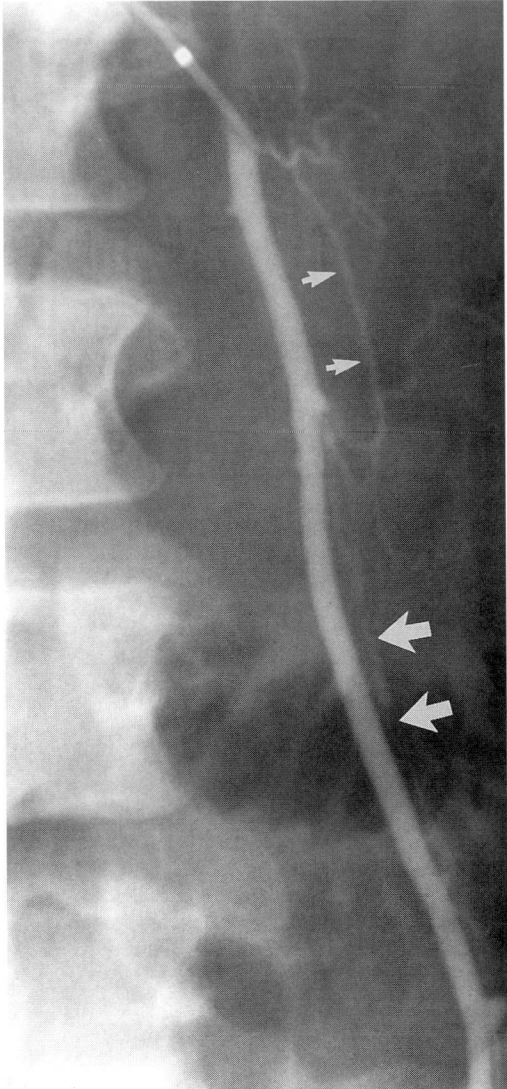

B

Figure 41-5. Two left gonadal venograms demonstrating multiple venous trunks. (A) Two venous trunks: one large trunk and an additional smaller parallel trunk (*arrows*).

(B) Several small trunks: one in the cephalad portion of the vein (*small arrows*) and additional ones in the inferior portion (*large arrows*).

Figure 41-7. Venograms demonstrating communication to the systemic circulation. (A) Left spermatic vein injection demonstrating filling of the internal iliac vein without filling of the varicocele. (B) Left spermatic venogram demonstrat-

ing filling of the varicocele that communicates with the internal iliac vein, most likely through the vasal veins. Note the cross-sacral venous collaterals. ▶

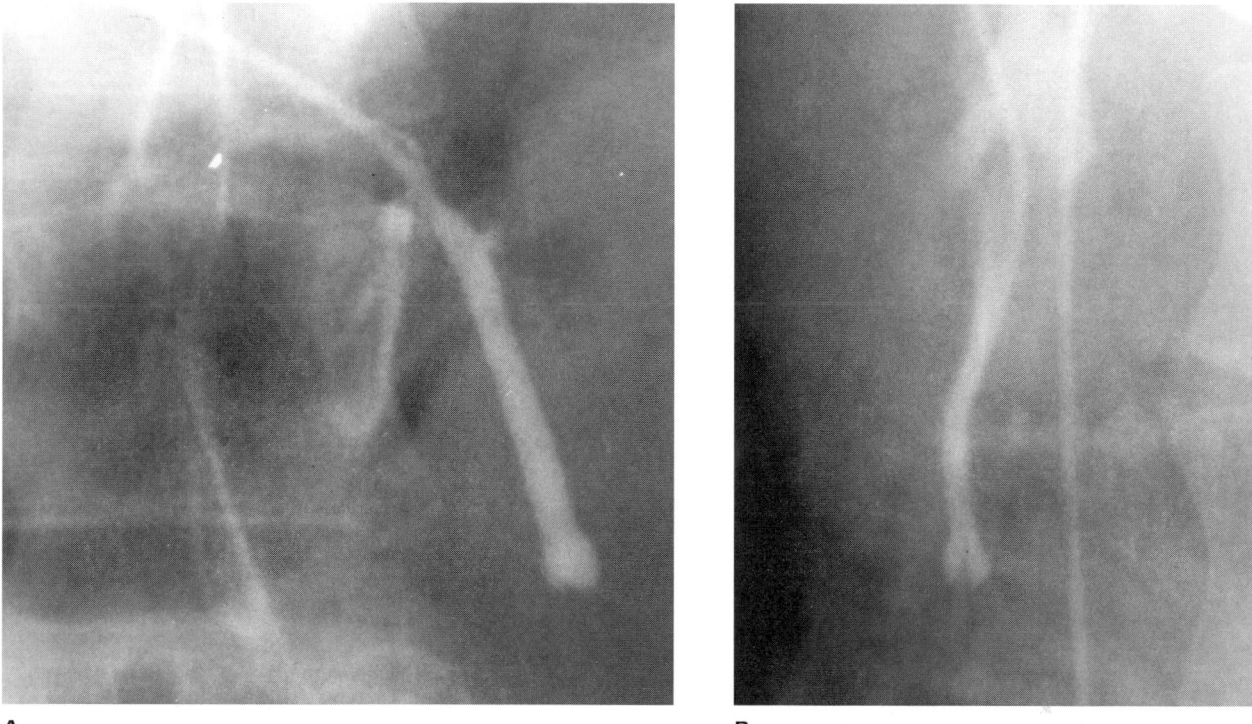

A   B

Figure 41-6. Normal competent venous valves. (A) Left spermatic vein with valve near entrance into left renal vein. (B) Right spermatic vein with valve near entrance into inferior vena cava.

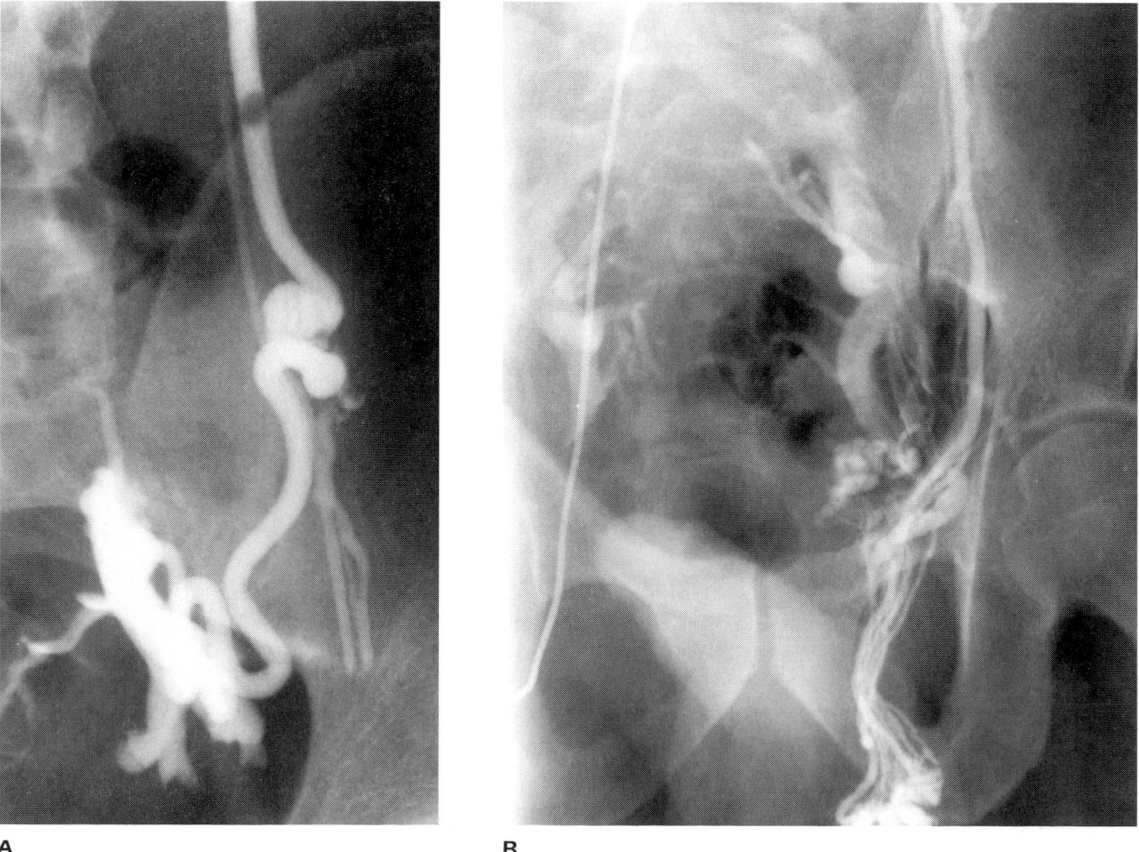

A   B

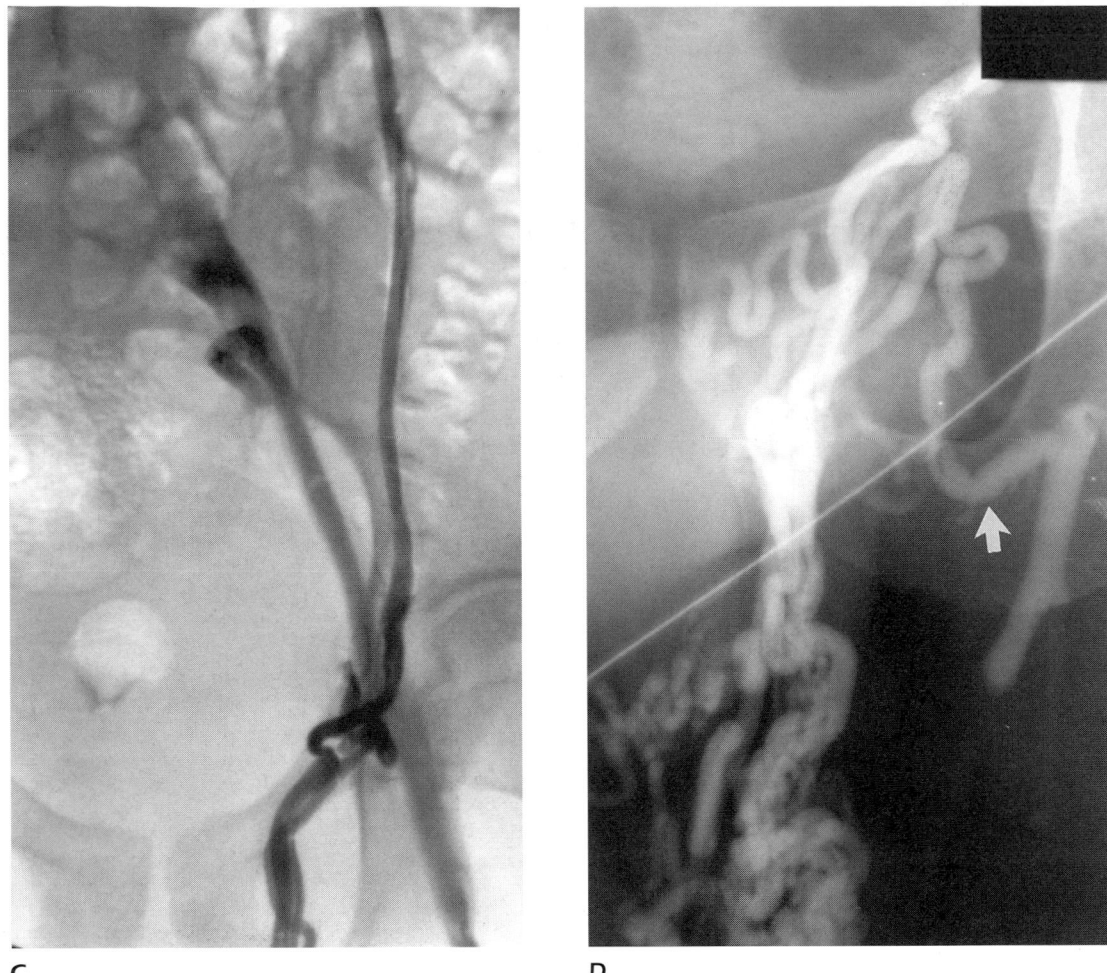

C   D

Figure 41-7 (continued). (C) Left spermatic venogram demonstrating filling of the varicocele and the left external iliac vein, via the cremasteric or pudendal veins. (D) Left spermatic venogram demonstrating filling of the greater saphenous vein via the external pudendal vein (*arrow*).

Figure 41-8. Left spermatic venograms demonstrating retroperitoneal collaterals. These have the appearance of the medial and lateral divisions as described by Wishahi et al.[29] (A) Left spermatic vein with major medial division and smaller lateral division (*arrows*), which communicates with the retroperitoneal and the renal capsular veins. Note the smaller parallel venous trunks of the medial division. (B) Left spermatic venogram demonstrating another example of retroperitoneal collaterals (*large arrow*) and a small parallel trunk in the caudal portion of the spermatic vein (*small arrows*). ▶

Figure 41-9. Left spermatic venograms demonstrating communication with the portal circulation. (A) Venogram demonstrating filling of superior mesenteric vein branches (*arrows*). (B) Venogram demonstrating filling of the colonic vein branches (*arrows*) from the inferior mesenteric vein. ▶

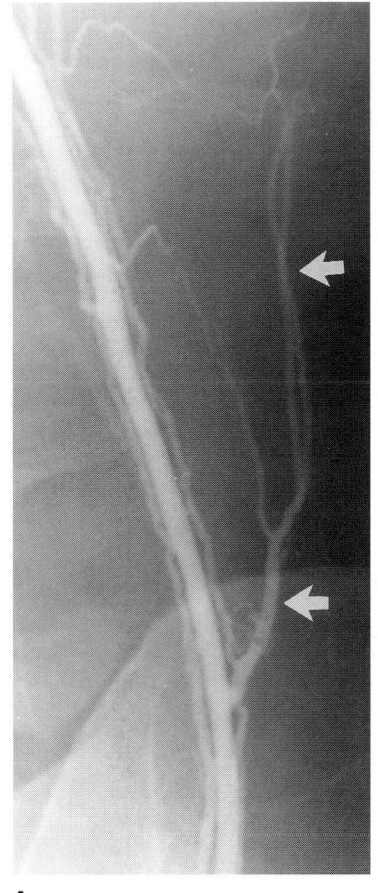

A

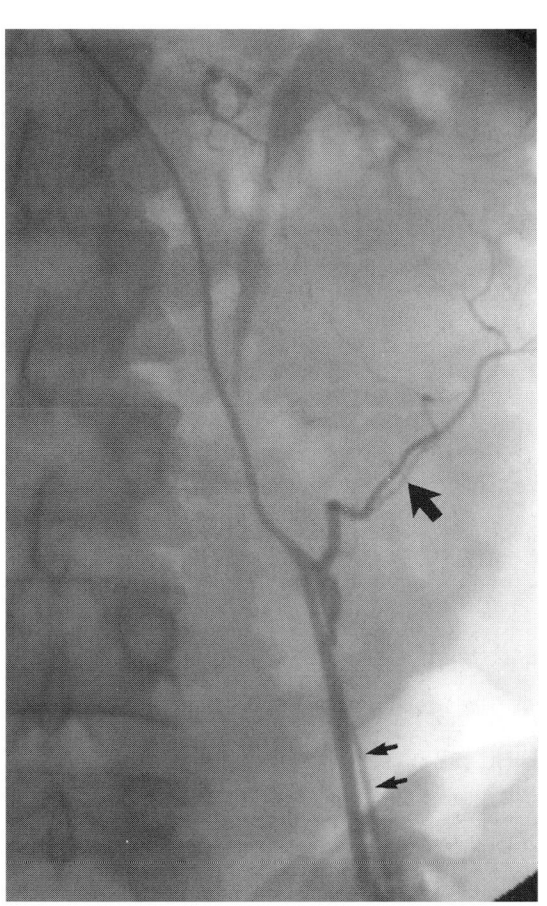

B

Figure 41-8

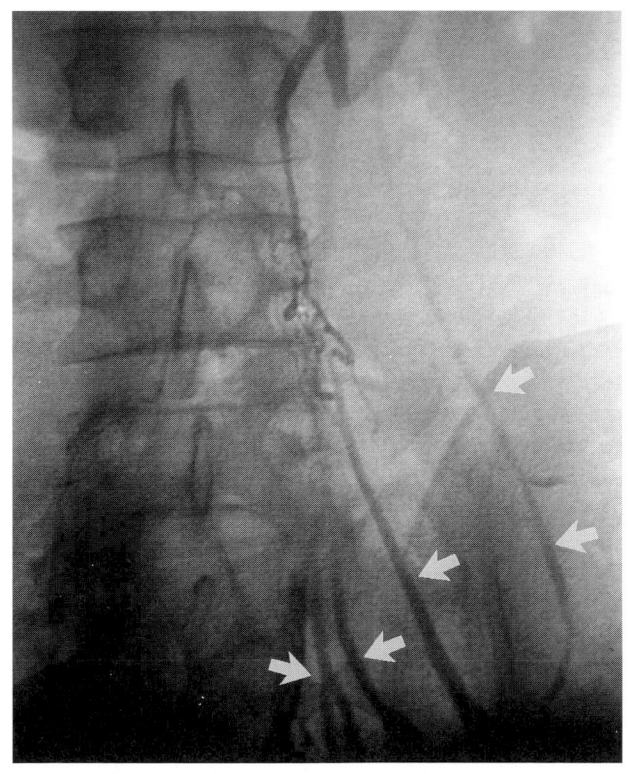

A

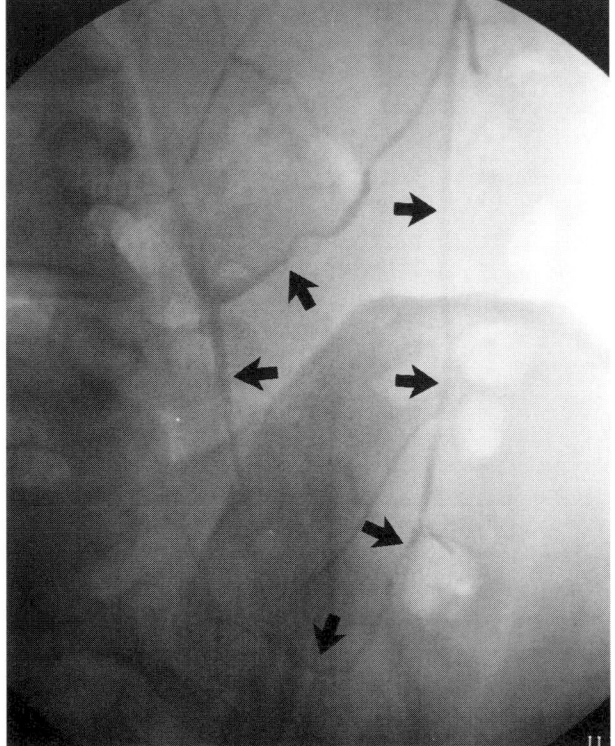

B

Figure 41-9

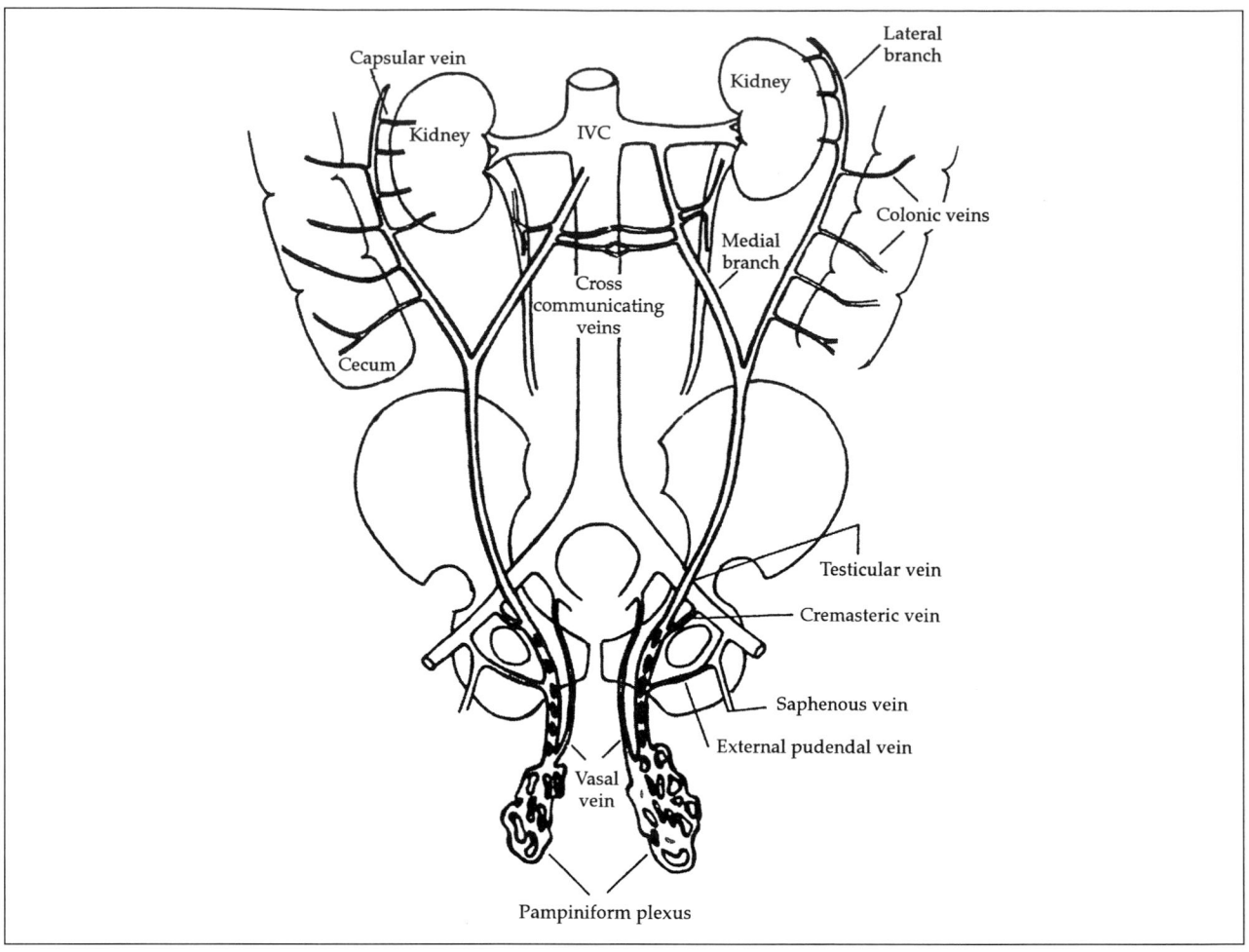

Figure 41-10. Anatomy of the left and right gonadal vein as described by Wishahi. Note the presence of the medial and lateral branches in addition to portal venous and systemic collaterals. (Modified from Wishahi MM. Anatomy of the venous drainage of the human testis: testicular vein cast, microdissection and radiographic demonstration. A new anatomical concept. Eur Urol 1991;20:154–160. Used with permission.)

Many of these described collaterals or divisions cause bypassing anastomoses that create aberrantly fed varicoceles, as described by Marsman in 17 to 19 percent of patients, making successful percutaneous embolization more difficult with a lower technical success rate (Fig. 41-12).[32] Typically, these high parallel or renal collaterals cause recurrences for patients treated with embolization, and middle and low vessels cause recurrences for patients treated with surgical ligation.[33,34] Other recurrences are due to transcrotal collaterals.[34] The surgical recurrences may be treated easily by embolization, whereas embolization recurrences are more difficult to successfully retreat.[35]

Pathophysiology

Varicoceles may be either primary or secondary. Secondary causes of varicocele are compression of the veins draining the pampiniform plexus due to pelvic and abdominal tumors, such as lymphoma, and metastasis from renal cell adenocarcinoma. These cases may

Figure 41-12. Left spermatic venograms demonstrating tortuous veins and bypassing anastomoses, which make embolization difficult. (A) Two vessels entering into different branches of the renal vein. (B) Another example of two vessels entering the renal vein, with one entering the main renal vein and the other entering a branch. (C) Venogram demonstrating multiple collaterals extending into the renal vein. ▶

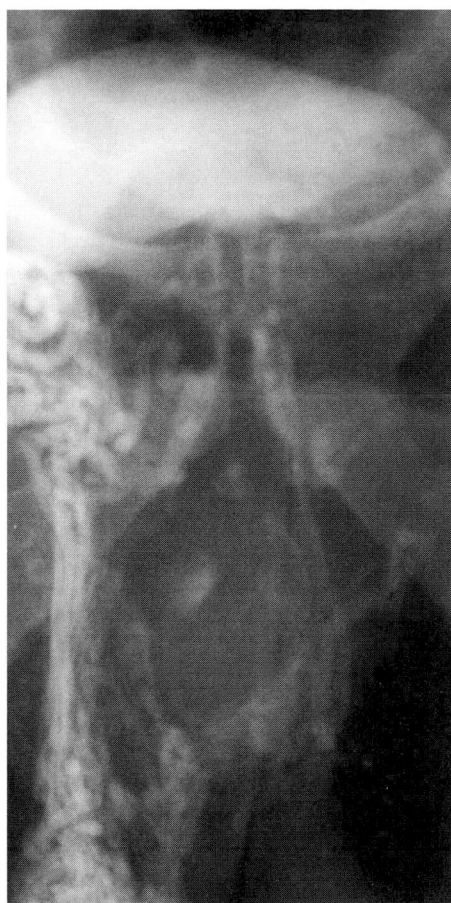

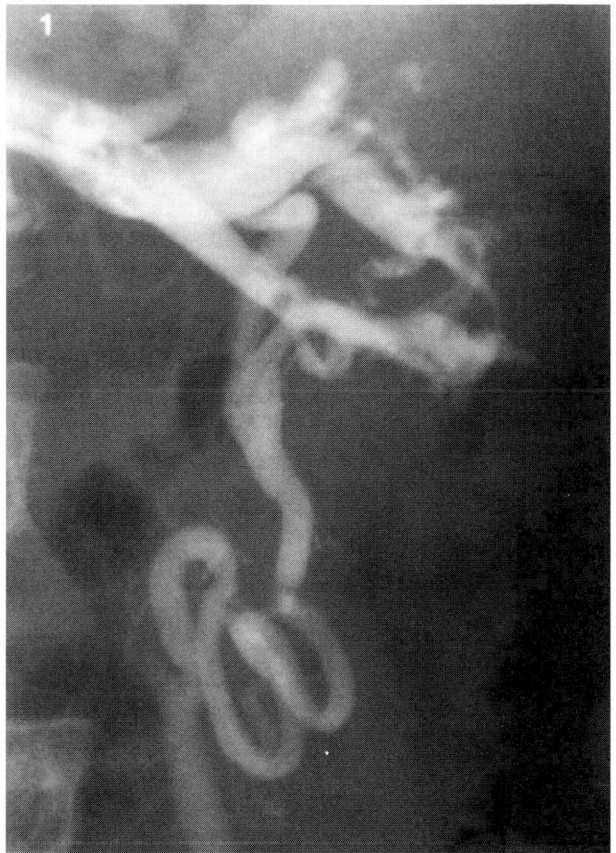

A

Figure 41-11. Left spermatic venogram demonstrating filling of the varicocele and cross-scrotal and pelvic collaterals.

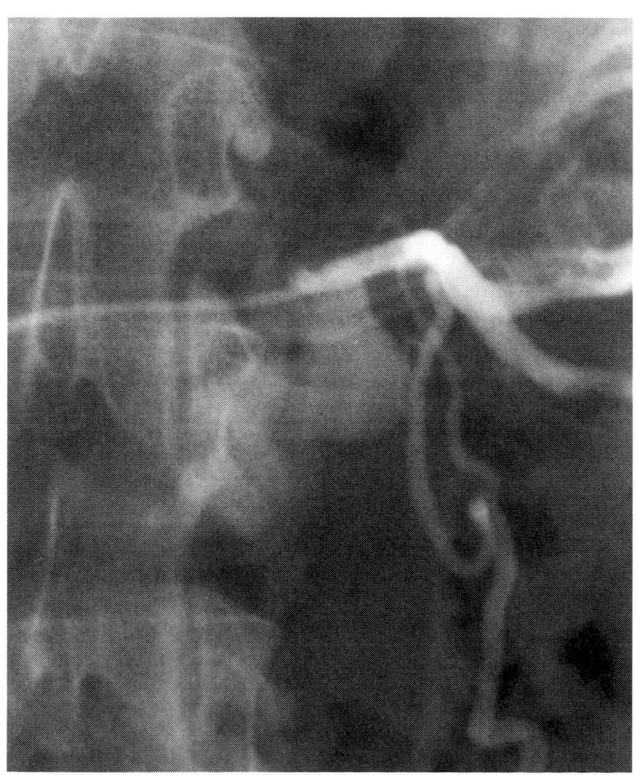

B

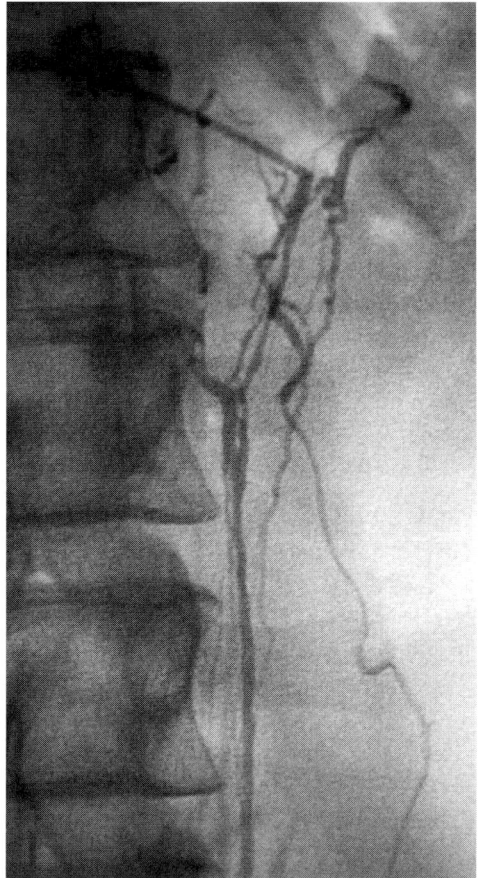

C

present as an isolated right varicocele.[36,37] Cases of rupture of an aortic aneurysm into the renal vein causing left-sided varicocele, and compression by a false aneurysm from an aortic graft causing a right varicocele, have also been described.[38,39] Another cause of solitary or predominantly right-sided varicocele is situs inversus.[40]

Most varicoceles, especially those associated with infertility, are primary. There are several hypotheses for the etiology of primary varicocele. One is that there is a lack of venous valves in the spermatic vein or an abnormality of the vein that transmits hydrostatic pressure from the IVC.[41] This hypothesis alone cannot explain the cause of varicocele, because individuals without varicocele may lack valves. In addition, valvular incompetence may be secondary to the internal spermatic vein dilatation rather than the cause of the dilatation.[42]

Another suspected cause of varicocele is the "nutcracker phenomenon."[43] This theory maintains that the left renal vein is compressed between the aorta and the superior mesenteric artery, particularly when a patient is erect, causing increased pressure in the gonadal vein that results in the dilatation. Other causes of left renal vein compression are also possible.[43] This phenomenon includes not only renal vein compression but also compression of the iliac vein by the iliac artery, the so-called lower nutcracker.[44] Several studies have supported this theory using anatomic and pressure measurements.[43,45–48] Other theories concerning the etiology of varicocele suspect that it may be due to anatomic differences between the left and right renal veins. The left spermatic vein is longer and enters the left renal vein at a right angle, across from the orifice of the adrenal vein, possibly causing turbulence and valvular dysfunction.[42] Another theory, disproved by Sayfan et al., suggested that the cause was a defect in the cremaster muscles, resulting in diminished tension of the fasciomuscular tube of the spermatic cord and therefore decreased venous return and venous congestion, the so-called cremasteric pump mechanism.[49–51]

Etiology of Infertility

Several theories have postulated the effect of varicoceles on testicular function, and more than one theory may be correct. The two most plausible hypotheses are elevated testicular temperatures and reflux of toxic metabolites causing testicular dysfunction and infertility.

Some investigators believe that the varicocele causes increased scrotal temperature, possibly by interfering with the normal countercurrent heat exchange.[5,17] Elevated testicular temperature is known to have an adverse effect on spermatogenesis.[52] In experimental animal models, Kay et al. in rhesus monkeys and Saypol et al. in dogs and rats demonstrated that an increase in blood flow and temperature within the scrotum is associated with varicoceles.[53,54] Normal scrotal temperature is lower than body core temperature, with the difference between core body temperature and scrotal temperature being smaller in men with varicocele.[55] Several studies have demonstrated higher scrotal temperatures in patients with varicocele.[7,52,55,56] The average temperature is 0.3°C higher on the side with the varicocele compared to the normal side, with the greatest difference obtained with the patient standing.[52] Using a device to lower testicular temperature in men with varicocele has improved semen quality, resulting in pregnancies.[57]

Reflux of renal and adrenal metabolites has also been hypothesized to cause testicular dysfunction. The compounds reach the testicles by backflow into the spermatic vein from the renal vein and by venous crossover to the contralateral testis. A few investigators have reported catecholamine concentrations in patients with varicoceles to be higher than in patients without.[58,59] Others have found that cortisol and renin levels are not different.[58,60] Charny and Baum in 1968 found no significant difference in adrenal steroid concentrations from peripheral blood samples, compared to spermatic vein samples in patients with varicocele.[61] Presently, data suggest that prostaglandins (PG) E_2 and $F_{2\alpha}$, produced in the kidneys, reflux into the gonadal vein, causing impaired spermatogenesis due to vasoconstriction and inhibition of luteinizing hormone.[55,62] Higher levels of PGE_2 and $PGF_{2\alpha}$ have been found in the gonadal vein of varicocele patients than in peripheral blood, and phospholipase A_2 levels in semen decrease after varicocele correction.[55]

Another etiology includes an alteration in the hypothalamic-pituitary-testicular axis.[63] Hudson et al. described a population of varicocele patients whose gonadotropin response to gonadotropin-releasing hormone (GnRH) was excessive. These patients had improvement in their semen and normalization of their response to GnRH after correction. The authors suggested that there is an abnormality in the pantesticular hormone synthesis and spermatogenesis in some men with varicocele, which, after correction, undergoes some improvement.[63] Other explanations for the abnormality in spermatogenesis include Leydig cell dysfunction, hypoxia due to venous stasis, and alterations in the thickness of intratesticular blood vessels resulting in changes in nutrient transfer and edema.[64–68]

Diagnosis

Varicoceles are generally diagnosed by palpation and graded. A varicocele is considered to be grade I or small if it is palpable with a Valsalva maneuver. A moderate varicocele or grade II is present if it is palpable without a Valsalva maneuver. A grade III or larger is visible without palpation.[69]

Subclinical varicoceles are those that cannot be palpated, but the patient is infertile and demonstrates in a sperm analysis "stress-forms" that are consistent with a varicocele.[69] Subclinical varicoceles can also be diagnosed by Doppler stethoscope, thermography, duplex and color Doppler, scintigraphy, radionuclide scrotal imaging, and magnetic resonance imaging in addition to spermatic venography (Figs. 41-13 and 41-14).[37,70]

Conventional duplex scanning using a high-resolution, dedicated small-parts transducer (5–10 MHz) is diagnostic for varicocele with a dilated pampiniform plexus greater than 2 mm, whereas color Doppler allows demonstration of venous reflux into the varicosity.[71-73] Performing a Valsalva maneuver in the supine and erect positions aids the diagnosis of a small varico-

cele. Petros demonstrated ultrasound to detect 93 percent of the venographically evident subclinical varicoceles when compared to physical examination, which only detected 71 percent of the venographically evident varicocele.[74] Sigmund et al. have described two different types of hemodynamic patterns in varicoceles as determined by bidirectional Doppler flow studies and confirmed by venography, called *stop-type* and *shunt-type* varicoceles (Fig. 41-15).[75] The stop-type varicocele refluxes only into the spermatic vein. The shunt type first refluxes into the spermatic vein and then has physiologic retrograde and orthograde flow

Figure 41-13. Duplex ultrasound demonstrating varicoceles. (A) A moderate-size varicocele seen with hypoechoic tubular structures (*arrows*) behind the testicle (*T*), representing veins of the dilated pampiniform plexus. (B) A large varicocele behind the testicle (*T*) fills most of the scrotum. (C) Another view of the varicocele seen in (B) demonstrating the large hypoechoic varicosities.

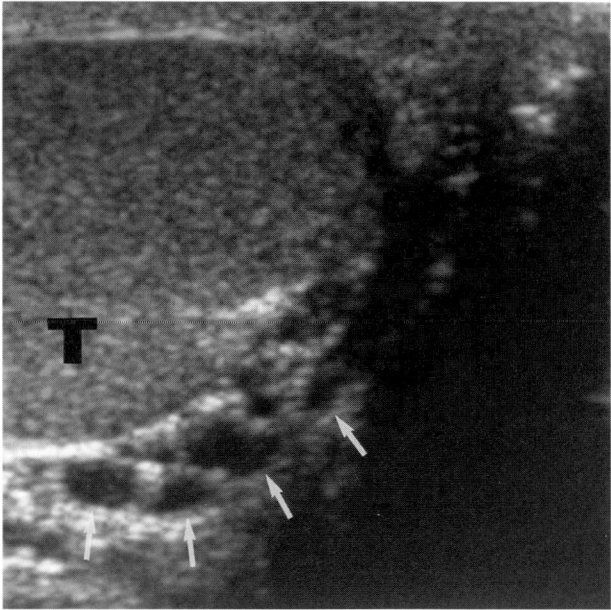

A

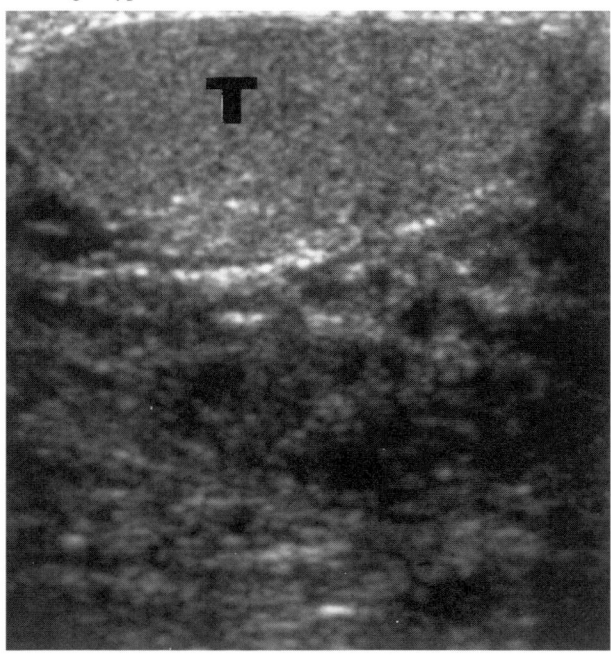

B

C

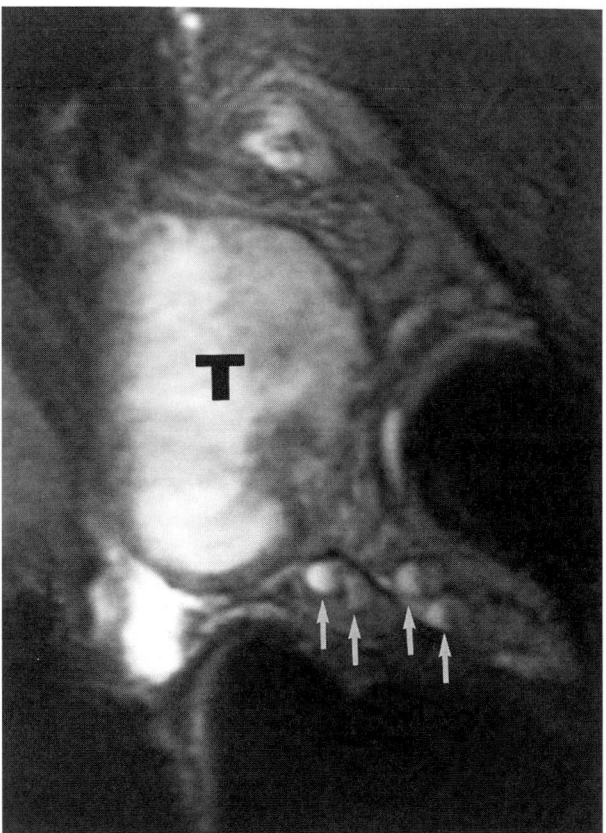

Figure 41-14. Sagittal magnetic resonance image (TR/TE: 5000/150 msec) of the scrotum demonstrating a high-intensity testicle (*T*) with dilated veins (*arrows*) of the pampiniform plexus. Note the slow flow within the varicocele, causing a "hematocrit effect."

in the cremasteric or deferential veins or both, thus providing a shunt or venous bypass.[75] The pathophysiology is explained by incompetence of the venous valves in the region of the pampiniform plexus and the communicating veins. The shunt type was more frequent and felt to be a precondition for medium and large varices.

Spermatic venography, first described by Ahlberg in 1966, is generally considered the gold standard for demonstrating reflux into the gonadal vein.[76,77] One concern about the diagnosis of varicocele by venography is that the diagnosis of venous reflux is made under conditions of variable injection pressure and catheter tip placement, which may be beyond the valves or disrupt them and may not represent normal physiologic conditions.[10] In addition, injecting into the renal vein may not represent true physiologic conditions under which the patient may reflux into the spermatic vein, especially if the patient is not fully erect.

Although the size of varicocele can be graded, studies have demonstrated that this parameter does not in-

Figure 41-15. Schematic diagram of stop-type (A) and shunt-type (B) varicocele demonstrating reflux (*arrows*) with bidirectional Doppler recording below each diagram as described by Sigmund et al. In the stop-type varicocele, reflux is stopped by competent valves within the pampiniform plexus above the level of the communicating veins (vasal and cremasteric veins), resulting in only spermatic vein dilatation. In the shunt-type varicocele, because of absent or incompetent valves within the pampiniform plexus, blood flow is shunted to the communication veins. This causes bidirectional blood flow, which increases with Valsalva as demonstrated by Doppler. (From Sigmund G, Gall H, Bahren W. Stop-type and shunt-type varicoceles: venographic findings. Radiology 1987;163:105–110. Used with permission.)

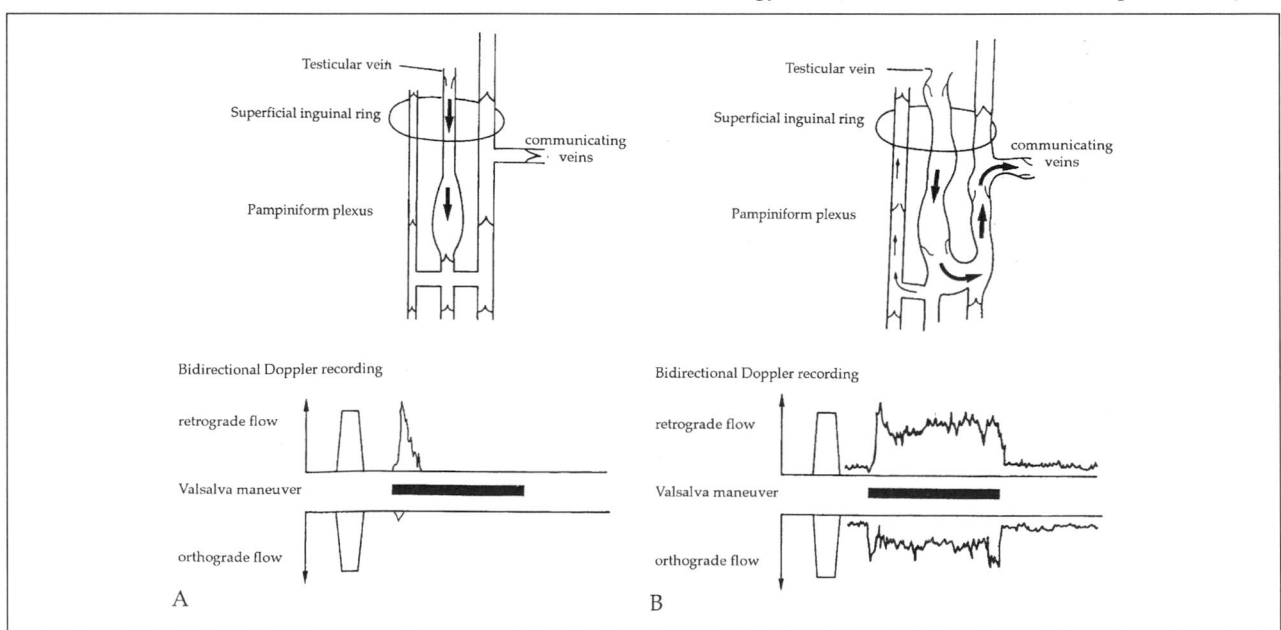

Surgical Correction

Before the advent of percutaneous therapy, surgical correction of varicocele was the main treatment option. The three major surgical procedures currently performed vary by the level at which the spermatic vein is ligated (Fig. 41-17). The modified Palomo procedure, or retroperitoneal approach, involves an incision approximately 3 cm medial and 5 to 6 cm below the anterior portion of the iliac crest.[80] This allows access to the retroperitoneal space so that one can ligate one or more of the branches of the internal spermatic veins immediately superior to the inguinal ring.[37,69] A lower retroperitoneal approach, the Ivanissevich procedure, is carried out through an inguinal incision so that one can ligate the internal spermatic vein or its tributaries at the level of the internal ring.[37,69,81] More recently, Marmar et al. described a subinguinal approach requiring microdissection at the external inguinal ring; this technique requires only a subcutaneous incision and does not disturb fascial planes.[82] It is performed with local anesthesia on an outpatient basis and requires only a few days of recovery time. The recovery time for inguinal or retroperitoneal approaches is generally longer, with patients returning to work within a few days and to full activity in 3 to 4 weeks.[37]

The main purpose of surgery is to interrupt the dilated spermatic vein while preserving the testicular artery and lymphatics to prevent testicular atrophy and formation of a hydrocele (Fig. 41-18). Newer techniques include the use of laparoscopic procedures compared to standard surgical therapies to correct varicoceles.[83] Surgery

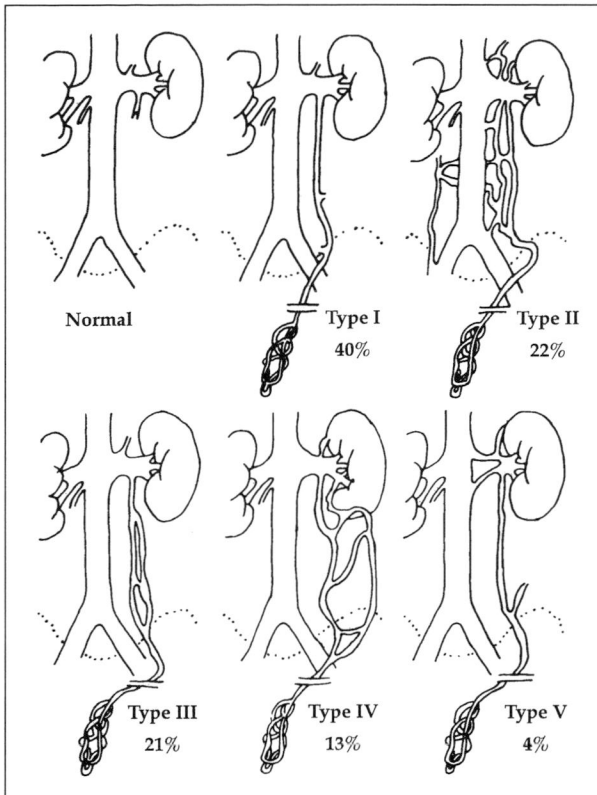

Figure 41-16. Venographic classification of the course of the left renal vein with percentages in a study population of 259 left-sided varicoceles as described by Porst et al. *Type I:* Single renal vein without valves, the most common type. *Type II:* Collateral retroperitoneal vessels to ascending lumbar vein or retroaortal to caval vein. *Type III:* Duplicated internal spermatic vein with cross-connecting vessels. *Type IV:* Collaterals to renal or capsular veins. *Type V:* Retroaortic bifurcated renal vein. (From Porst H, Bahren W, Lenz M, et al. Percutaneous sclerotherapy of varicoceles: an alternative to conventional surgical methods. Br J Urol 1984;56: 73–78. Used with permission.)

fluence the improvement seen after varicocele correction by either surgery or percutaneous embolization.[78] Marsman demonstrated that the venographic differences between clinical and subclinical varicoceles were in the degree of reflux, with about equal spermatologic improvement after percutaneous embolization.[78] He classified the degree of reflux into grades of 0 to 5, with grade 0 representing no reflux and grades 1 to 5 representing reflux into the upper lumbar, lower lumbar, upper pelvic, lower pelvic, or inguinal portion of the spermatic veins, respectively. Other classification systems deal with the venographic findings of varicocele and their collaterals. Porst et al. established a classification based on five venographic patterns (types I–V).[79] Some types were more frequent than others and easier to percutaneously embolize with sclerotherapy (Fig. 41-16).

Figure 41-17. Schematic drawing demonstrating location of incisions for the three types of surgical corrections for varicocele. (From La Nasa JA Jr, Lewis RW. Varicocele and its surgical management. Urol Clin North Am 1987;14:127–136. Used with permission.)

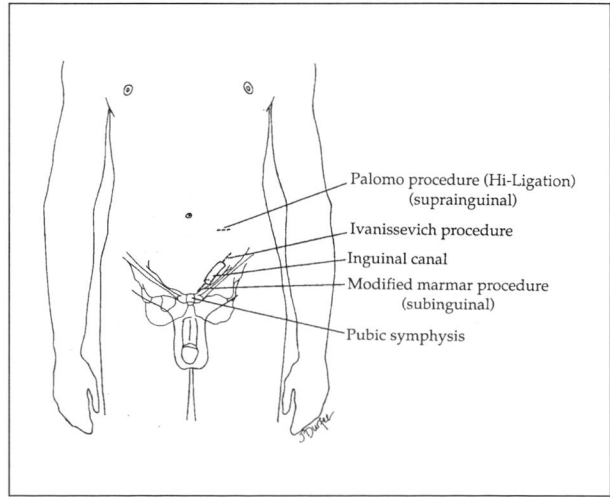

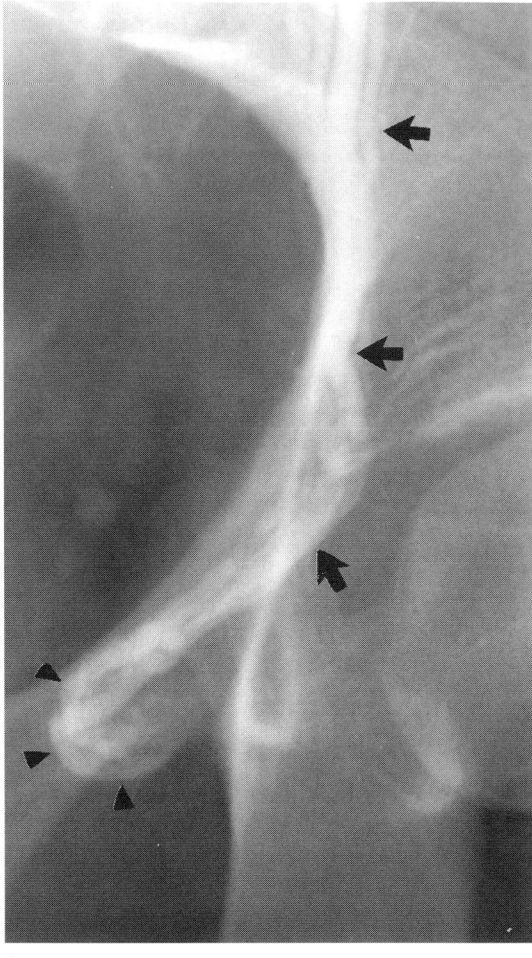

A

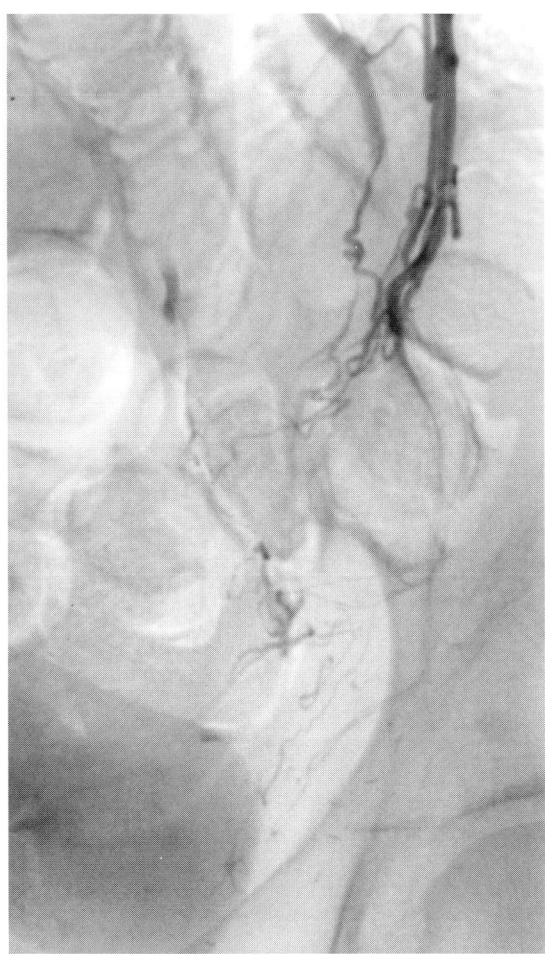

B

Figure 41-18. Left spermatic venogram after surgical ligation. (A) Venogram demonstrating the spermatic vein (*arrows*) filling just below the femoral head, where it terminates abruptly (*arrowheads*), consistent with surgical liga- tion. (B) Left spermatic venogram demonstrating filling of the gonadal vein, which terminates relatively high in the pelvis with the filling of a few very small collaterals.

for varicocele generally carries a low morbidity and the usual complications associated with any operation, including hematoma and wound infections. In a review of varicocelectomy in 986 men, Dublin and Amelar reported a rate of hematoma, infection, and hydrocele of 1.0, 0.7, and 3.0 percent, respectively.[84] The pregnancy rates and semen improvement rates reported from various surgical papers have varied from 0 to 63 percent and 0 to 92 percent, respectively.[84,85] Surgical studies generally report pregnancy rates and semen analysis improvements rather than recurrence rates. In the studies that report recurrences, the rate is 0 to 37 percent, which is higher than the percutaneous rate.[51,84,86,87] Although the recurrence rate for surgery tends to be higher than the percutaneous rate, some urologists advocate percutaneous therapy only for surgical failures, because they feel that the technical success rate for surgery is higher than for percutaneous embolization.[12]

Some surgeons advocate the use of venography during surgical ligation of the gonadal vein to better isolate the spermatic vein and its tributaries, particularly in the pediatric patient, whereas others use a sclerosing agent during their surgical procedure.[88-91] Venography performed after ligation has demonstrated several routes of recurrence. After high ligation of left varicocele, Morag et al. studied 40 patients who had recurrence or persistence. Over 50 percent of the patients still demonstrated a left varicocele, and other patients demonstrated a right varicocele.[9] There were three patterns of persistent varicocele filling after surgical ligation. The first was filling of the varicocele via collateral veins bypassing the site of ligation (Fig. 41-19). The second pattern was by a large additional branch of the spermatic vein, which was not ligated (Fig. 41-20). The third pattern of varicocele filling was direct filling due to the ligature slipping or the sperma-

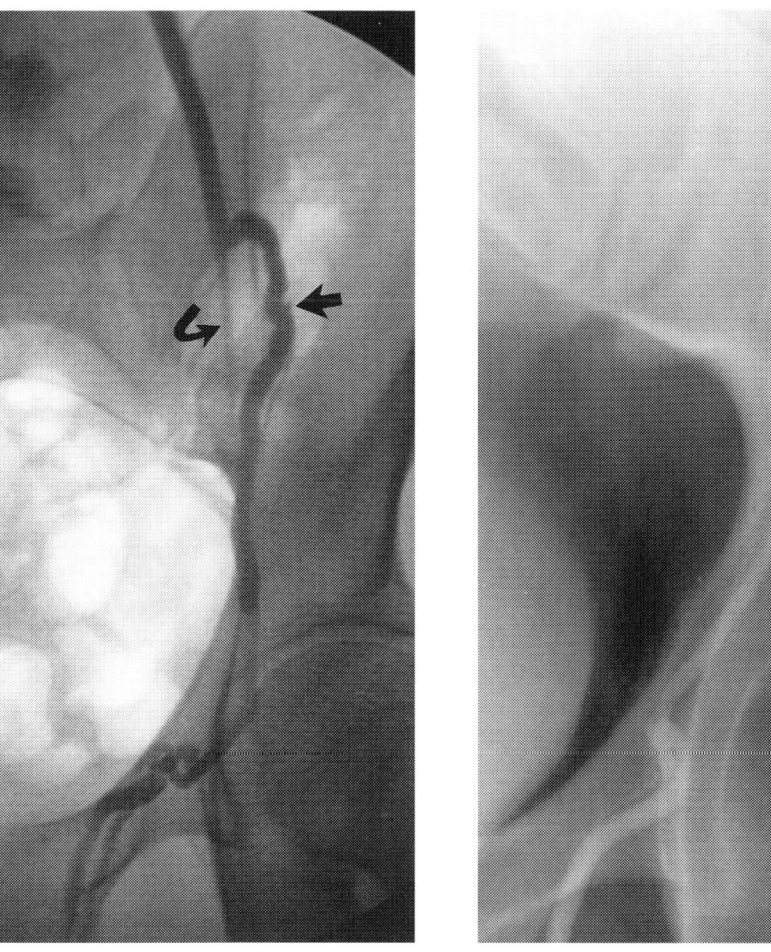

A   B

Figure 41-19. Venogram demonstrating recurrence after surgical ligation due to collateral vessels. (A) Left spermatic venogram reveals a large collateral vein (*arrow*) that bypasses the site of surgical ligation (*curved arrow*). (B) A smaller collateral vein bypasses the site of surgical ligation.

tic vein being misidentified (Fig. 41-21). Kaufman et al. studied five patients after surgery with varicocele recurrence, all of whom had collaterals that were not ligated.[33] Some recurrences may also be due to cross-filling from an undetected right varicocele.[9,33] Both Morag and Kaufman treated recurrences with embolotherapy.[9,33]

Percutaneous Embolization

Percutaneous embolization is typically performed as an outpatient procedure with intravenous conscious sedation and analgesia, unless the patient has a severe bleeding diathesis or previous life-threatening reaction to contrast.[35] Embolizations in the 1970s initially were performed using sclerotherapy but later utilizing metal coils.[8,92,93] The author typically uses the transjugular approach originally described by Formanek et al. in

1981 because of the simplicity and safety of gaining access into the gonadal vein (Fig. 41-22).[94] Morag et al. reported a greater success rate for right gonadal vein occlusion via the jugular vein (89.0 percent) than via the femoral vein access (62.5 percent).[95] Kuroiwa et al. reported a greater success rate with the basilic vein than with the femoral vein access.[96] More recently, several authors have reported using guiding catheters or coaxial systems with the transfemoral approach as an aid to performing embolizations with balloons or coils.[97–100]

Because of the variations in collaterals, varicocele embolization is performed at several levels along the internal spermatic vein. Unembolized communications with large collaterals may result in immediate failure with little improvement, whereas small collaterals may increase in size with time, resulting in a recurrence. Fobbe et al. evaluated the success of treatment with a sclerosing agent with regard to the location of occlusion of the gonadal vein.[101] They had a 68 percent

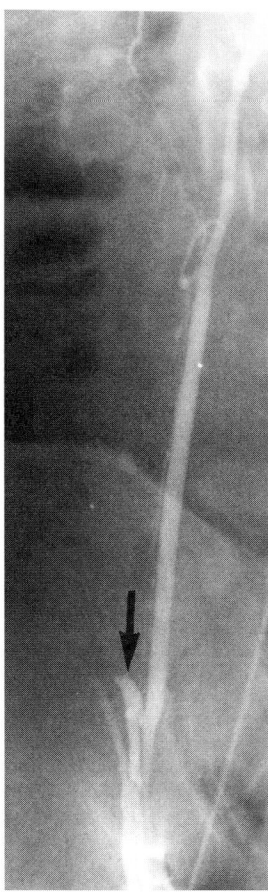

Figure 41-20. Right spermatic venogram demonstrating the remains of a main large gonadal vein after surgical ligation. A remnant of the parallel double vein that was ligated is seen low in the pelvis.

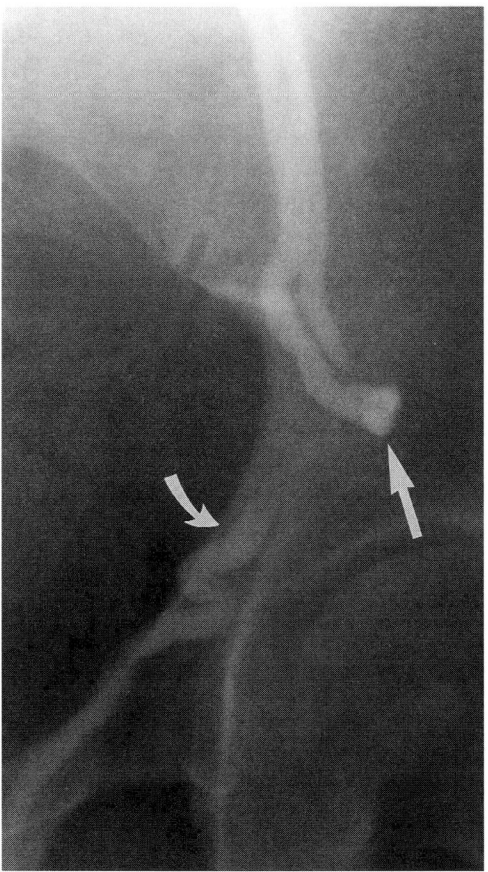

Figure 41-21. Left spermatic venogram during a hard Valsalva maneuver in a weightlifter who had a recurrence after surgical ligation. The surgical ligation site is identified by termination of the vein (*arrow*); however, contrast is still able to pass through the ligation site (*curved arrow*).

technical success rate, determined 3 months after treatment, when the occlusion was performed in the cranial portion of the vein, as opposed to an 82 percent success rate when the vein was occluded at the caudal extent near the inguinal ring, thus eliminating many of the collateral vessels.

The author's approach to varicocele embolization is as follows. The patient is given intravenous sedation, such as midazolam hydrochloride and fentanyl citrate, in addition to nifedipine 10 mg sublingually, to reduce potential venous spasm in the gonadal vein. A 5.01 microvascular set (Cook, Inc.) with a 21-gauge needle is generally used to puncture the internal jugular vein, exchanging the 0.018-inch wire to a 0.038-inch guidewire to gain access to the inferior vena cava. A long 30-cm, 6 French sheath (Medi-Tech) is introduced, through which a 5.5 French H1H (Cook, Inc.) or 5.0 French Bernstein (Medi-Tech) catheter is used to catheterize the renal veins, usually with the aid of an angled Glidewire (Terumo Corporation). If the right common femoral vein approach is used, a 5 French straight catheter (Cook, Inc.) with a tip-deflecting wire (Cook, Inc.) is generally used to access the left gonadal vein, and a 5.5 French Simmons 3 catheter (Cook, Inc.) is used for the right gonadal vein.

The patient is placed in reverse Trendelenburg position, and a left renal venogram is performed to look for reflux into the gonadal vein. The left gonadal vein is catheterized, and a gonadal venogram is performed to look for reflux and filling of systemic and portal collaterals. Care is taken to minimize exposure of the testicles by using shielding or adequate collimation. Direct filming of the varicocele is not necessary and increases the radiation dose to the gonads. The operator advances the catheter to the region of the inguinal canal, avoiding imaging over the scrotum. Generally 5-mm and 8-mm Gianturco coils (Cook, Inc.) are used because of their ease of placement and low cost, and an attempt is made to block all collaterals that could result in a recurrence. One must avoid deploying a coil partially into the renal vein or sizing the coil too small in diameter, especially if the vein is in spasm,

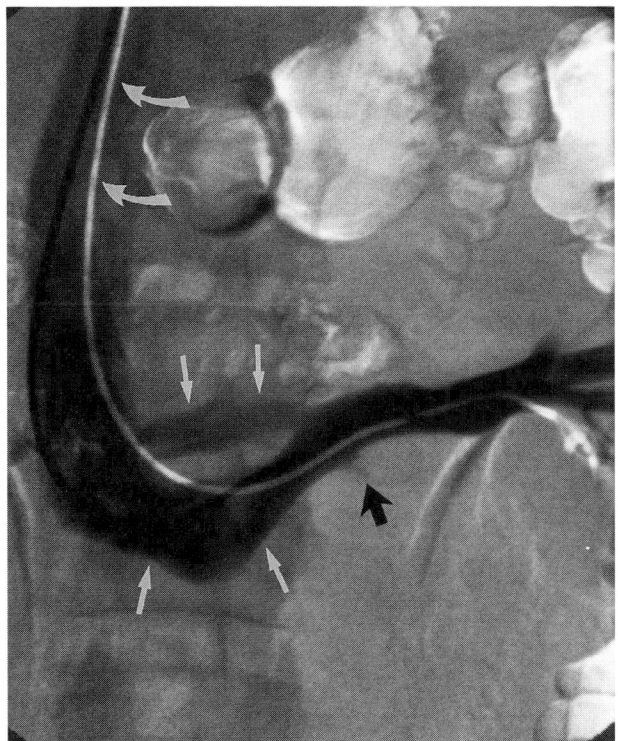

Figure 41-22. Left renal venogram performed from the right internal jugular approach. Catheterization of the gonadal vein is facilitated by being able to advance the catheter (*curved white arrows*) in one direction deep into the spermatic vein. The appearance of double catheters is from subtraction artifact. The circumaortic renal vein (*straight white arrows*) is demonstrated with a competent valve (*black arrow*) preventing reflux into the left gonadal vein.

since these errors might result in coil migration to the lungs. If spasm is encountered, 1-ml aliquots of nitroglycerin (100 μg/ml) can be given to reverse it.

After embolization of the left gonadal vein, an attempt is made to selectively catheterize the right gonadal vein. If the vein is competent, no embolization is performed. If incompetent, embolization is performed as with the left renal vein. The patient is discharged 4 to 6 hours after the procedure and told to refrain from physical activity for 24 hours. Postprocedure symptoms include testicular and back pain in addition to low-grade fever, which can be treated with nonsteroidal anti-inflammatories.

Multiple studies have been published on the use of different agents for embolization or even multiple agents. Success rates can be given for correction of the varicocele but can vary depending on the imaging modality used to detect the failures or recurrences. In reviewing their 11-year experience using various types of embolic agents, including balloons, coils, and different sclerosing agents, Zuckerman et al. did not find a statistical difference in the type of embolic agent used.[102] They had a technical failure rate of 4.3 percent. Their reasons for failure included inability to cannulate the left gonadal vein or to pass through a partially competent valve, too many collaterals, origin of the vein from the upper pole of the kidney at too acute an angle, a balloon catheter too large for the gonadal vein, a stenotic vein, a circumaortic renal vein, spasm of the

Figure 41-23. Left renal venograms demonstrating renal vein variants, which may make catheterization of the renal vein difficult. (A) Venogram revealing circumaortic renal vein (*large arrows*). Note the faint reflux into the left spermatic vein (*small arrows*). (B) Venogram demonstrating two veins, with the catheter in the upper vein and the spermatic vein entering into the lower vein along with possible bypassing collaterals.

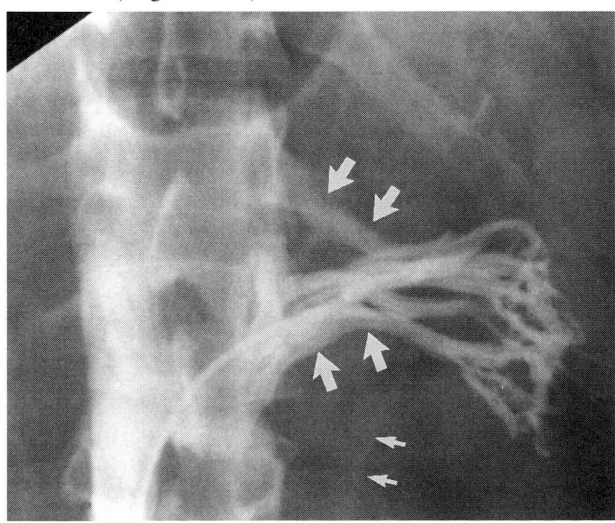

A

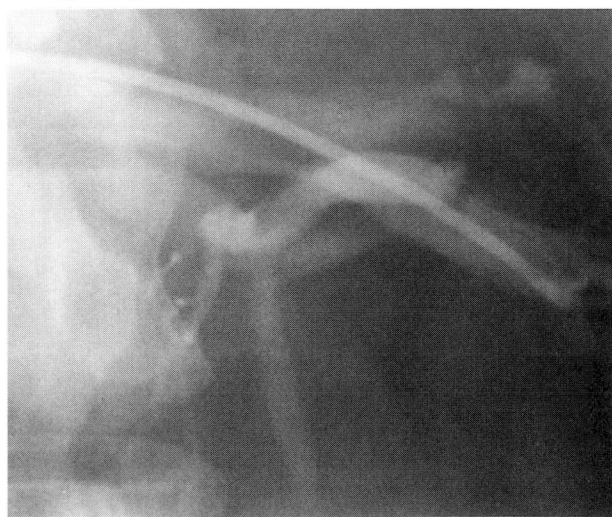

B

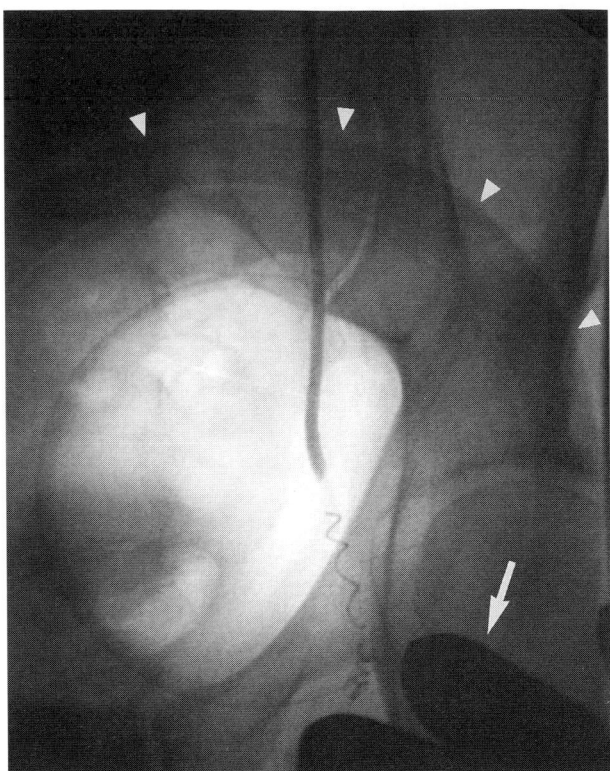

A

Figure 41-24. Embolization of left gonadal vein with ethanol. (A) Left spermatic venogram demonstrating contrast injection terminating in the pelvis. A coil has been placed in the lower portion of the vein to prevent reflux into the pampiniform plexus. Note the circular compression device (*ar-*

B

rowheads) and the shielded hand (*arrow*) pressing the abdomen at the inguinal ligament to prevent reflux into the scrotum. (B) Ethanol is injected, washing out contrast from the vein.

gonadal vein, and bradycardia (Figs. 41 12 and 41 23). Although the left spermatic vein is most often embolized, solitary right embolizations are performed for several reasons. In a report by Shuman et al., 10 out of 227 patients had only a right varicocele embolized. One patient had a solitary right varicocele, 6 had an accompanying left varicocele but competent left valves, and 3 had recurrent varicoceles with a previously successful left embolization.[103]

Initial experience with percutaneous embolization involved the use of sclerosing agents (Fig. 41-24). Several milliliters of the agent are injected, usually with an occlusion balloon in the gonadal vein. One agent used in multiple studies in Varikocid (Combustinwerk, Seefel/Obb), which is sodium morrhuate (55 mg/ml) and benzyl alcohol (20 mg/ml).[79,101,104–107] Another agent, used less frequently, is Aethoxysklerol (Kreussler and Co., Chemische Fabrik), which is polidocanol.[107–110] Other agents include hypertonic glucose (70–80 percent), monoethanolamine and absolute ethanol.[108] The sclerosing agent is injected and usually allowed to remain in contact with the vein for

several minutes. Manual compression at the inguinal canal may be performed to prevent reflux into the scrotum. Complications associated with a sclerosing agent are usually due to flow of the sclerosing agent into the pampiniform plexus, which can lead to painful scrotal swelling, phlebitis, and testicular damage, with possible temporary depressions of sperm count or testicular atrophy. A plastic compression device has been used by some investigators to prevent sclerosant from flowing into the scrotum.[111]

Investigators have used Gianturco steel coils in sizes of 3, 5, 8, and 12 mm because of their low cost, safety, and ability to be easily placed in multiple locations (Fig. 41-25).[93,95,96,112–114] Some authors have implicated coils in producing chronic inflammation that results in pain.[112,115] Retrieval of malpositioned coils from the lung using flexible intravascular forceps has been reported by Chomyn et al.[116]

Other investigators advocate the use of detachable silicone balloons through a guiding sheath (e.g., Miniballoon, Becton-Dickinson; Detachable Silicone Balloon, Interventional Therapeutics). They claim that a

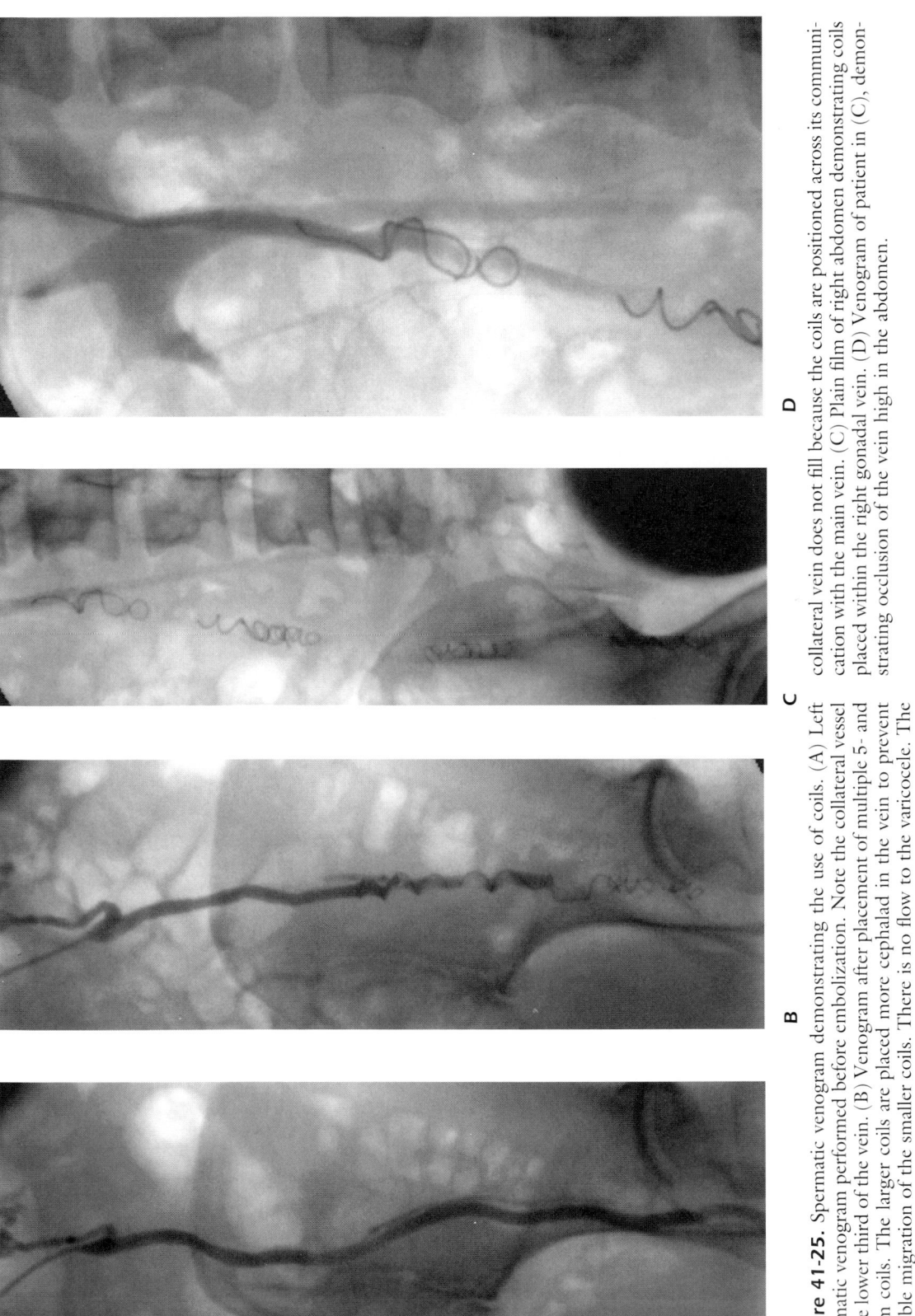

A   **B**   **C**   **D**

Figure 41-25. Spermatic venogram demonstrating the use of coils. (A) Left spermatic venogram performed before embolization. Note the collateral vessel in the lower third of the vein. (B) Venogram after placement of multiple 5- and 8-mm coils. The larger coils are placed more cephalad in the vein to prevent possible migration of the smaller coils. There is no flow to the varicocele. The collateral vein does not fill because the coils are positioned across its communication with the main vein. (C) Plain film of right abdomen demonstrating coils placed within the right gonadal vein. (D) Venogram of patient in (C), demonstrating occlusion of the vein high in the abdomen.

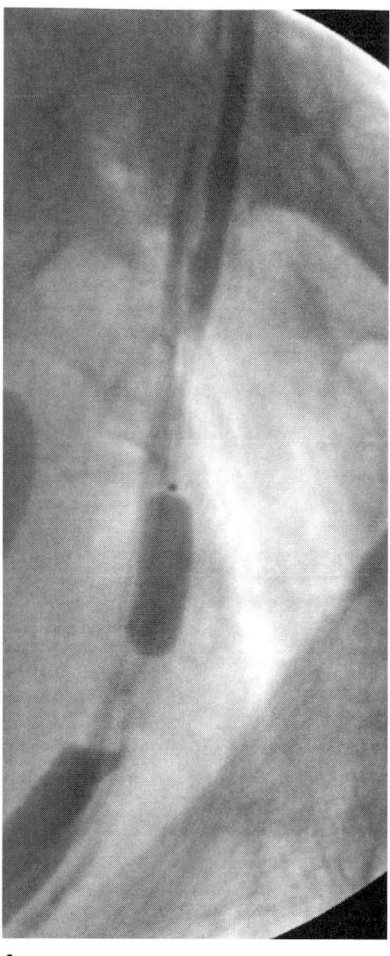

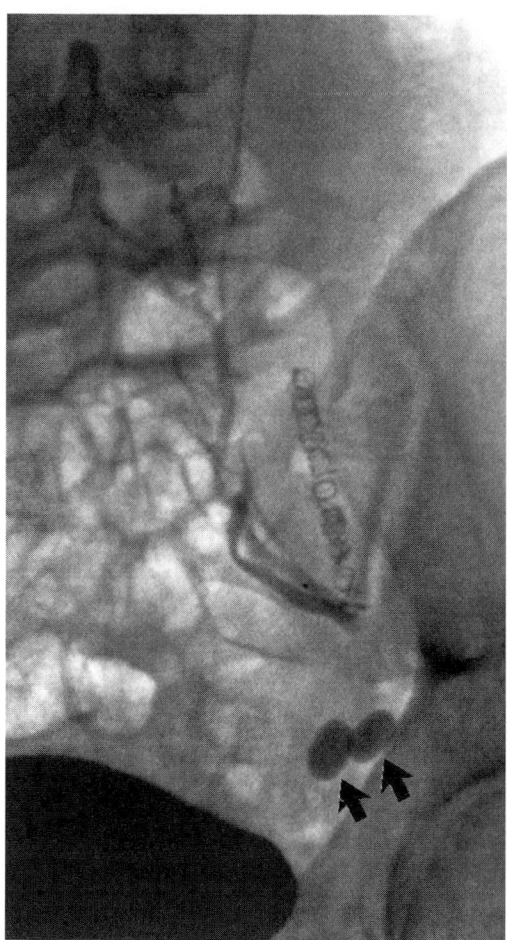

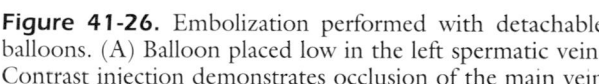

Figure 41-26. Embolization performed with detachable balloons. (A) Balloon placed low in the left spermatic vein. Contrast injection demonstrates occlusion of the main vein before detachment. Another balloon is seen lower in the pelvis. (B) Two balloons (*arrows*) are present low in the pelvis with coils above the balloons.

balloon can be optimally positioned in the internal spermatic vein because it can be inflated and contrast can be infused to visualize potential collaterals before permanent deployment (Fig. 41-26).[115,117,118] In addition, there is no need for superselective catheterization of the gonadal vein, because a guiding sheath is used and test occlusions can be performed before the balloons are detached.[115] Shuman et al.'s series of right internal spermatic vein embolizations with balloon occlusions demonstrated an 89 percent success rate with only an 11 percent technical failure rate.[103] Other benefits are that a single device rather than multiple coils are used to obstruct the whole vein and a sclerosing agent can be trapped below the balloon if desired.[118] Makita et al. reported the use of a guidewire-directed balloon, which they feel can be more effectively delivered than conventional flow-directed balloons.[119] The problems with balloons include cost, availability, and

the possibility that they may become dislocated or deflated, resulting in embolization to the lungs.[115,118]

Other agents used for percutaneoous embolization have included hot iodinated contrast medium and isobutyl 2-cyanoacrylate (Bucrylate, Ethicon Inc.). Smith et al. reported the use of hot contrast to obliterate varicoceles.[120] They suggested that the advantage of hot contrast as opposed to mechanical devices is that it is readily available, creating no additional expense, and also creates an occlusion of both the main channel and collateral vessels similar to sclerotherapy. Thrombosis of the gonadal veins by injection of hot contrast (average 25.8 ml on the left and 21.4 ml on the right) resulted in a pregnancy rate of 40.5 percent with only minor complications. Other mechanical types of agents have included compressed Ivalon plugs (Scientific Apparatus Shop, University of Minnesota), which are polyvinyl alcohol sponges that expand to obstruct the vein, and "spiderlons" (Scientific Apparatus Shop, University of Minnesota, MN), which is a combination of an Ivalon plug and steel spider to provide occlusion.[94]

Results of Percutaneous Varicocele Correction

The reported technical success rate of percutaneous embolization ranges from 50 to 100 percent, with the most recent rates greater than 90 percent and a recurrence rate of 2 to 12 percent.[11,12,102] The etiology of recurrences after embolization is similar to that of surgical recurrences, as previously discussed, and usually is related to the enlargement of small collateral vessels that were not originally embolized. Kaufman et al. reported an 11 percent rate of recurrence when the spermatic vein was embolized at the L3 or L4 level, and recommended that embolization be performed in the inguinal portion of the vein below the level of the collaterals.[33]

Complications are generally minor, except for non-

target embolization to the lungs with embolic agents, although these are usually asymptomatic. Minor complications include extravasation of contrast, contrast reactions, testicular thrombophlebitis from sclerosing agents, pain, venous spasm, and complications associated with the venous puncture (Fig. 41-27). Rates of these complications range from 1 to 30 percent.[11,12,102] Radiation exposure has been reported to be low. Walsh et al. reported a mean testicular dose of 26 mrad with shielding, whereas Weissbach et al. reported a rate of 1350 mrad without.[112,117]

Semen Analysis

Semen analysis is critical in the evaluation of the infertile male. As previously described, MacLeod introduced the concept of stress pattern, defined as greater than 15 percent of tapered forms.[6,121] Other characteristics include immature cells of the germinal line, especially spermatids and severe oligospermia.[6,121] Although first described with varicocele, this pattern is not pathognomonic for varicocele and may be seen in

Figure 41-27. Complications associated with varicocele embolization. (A) Left gonadal venogram demonstrating venous spasm. The cephalad portion of the gonadal vein is narrowed (*arrow*) compared to the caudal portion, making catheterization more difficult. (B) Left spermatic venogram demonstrating focal narrowing due to spasm (*arrow*). (C) Left spermatic venogram demonstrating extravasation of contrast in the lower portion of the vein.

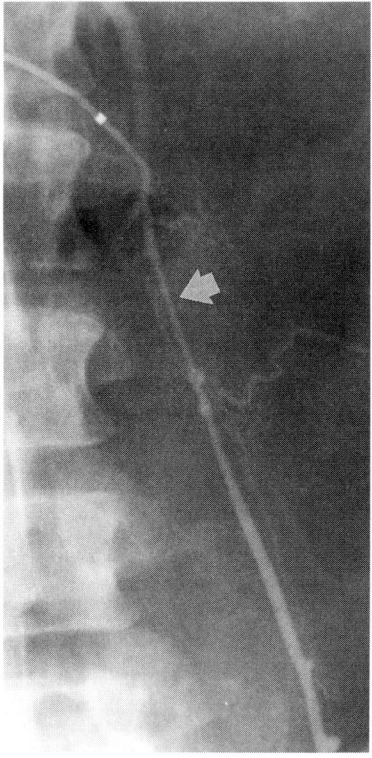
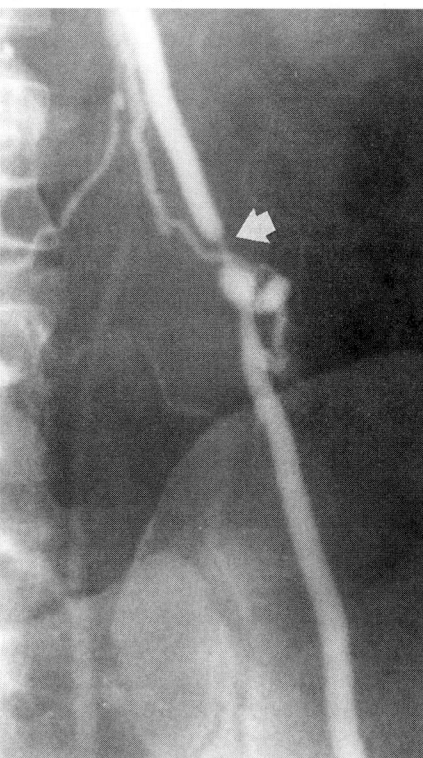
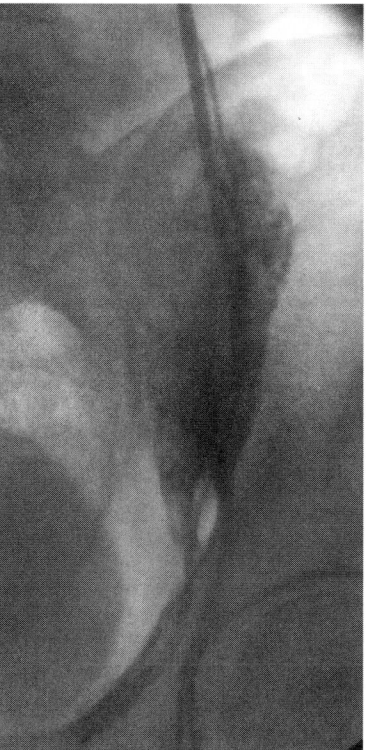

A   B   C

males without varicocele who are infertile for other reasons.[12] Seminal parameters studied for infertility, evaluated before and after varicocele correction, include sperm density, motility, and morphology. The reports of multiple studies, including both surgical and percutaneous techniques, have demonstrated improvements in density, motility, and morphology ranging from no significant change to a dramatic improvement in the various parameters.[122] Schlesinger et al. performed an extensive review of treatment outcome after varicocelectomy to determine the efficacy of treatment.[122] Although the results varied, they concluded that varicocelectomy does improve sperm density. The improvement is more pronounced when initial densities are greater than 10 million/ml. In addition, they describe a "ceiling effect," with less response when the preprocedure sperm density is greater than 40 million/ml. In spite of anecdotal reports of azoospermic patients improving, the authors do not support varicocele correction for these patients.

Motility and morphology may improve significantly after correction when associated with a rise in density. Isolated improvements in motility or morphology may occur, but generally there must be a significant improvement in density. From their review, Schlesinger et al. concluded that, despite the report of an occasional study that varicocele correction does not improve fertility, the majority of the literature supports the efficacy of correction in improving fertility. Improvement in semen quality ranges from 24 to 84 percent after surgical correction and from 27 to 78 percent after percutaneous embolization.[12,102,106,109,123]

Pregnancy Rates

The most important outcome variable in assessing the efficacy of spermatic embolization is the pregnancy rate. However, there is considerable difficulty in reviewing studies that are not well controlled, because

Figure 41-28. Gonadal venogram performed in a woman with pelvic pain due to venous congestion, treated with embolization. (A) Left gonadal venogram demonstrating reflux into the gonadal vein and cross-pelvic collateral filling consistent with an ovarian varicocele. (B) Successful treatment with percutaneous embolization of the ovarian varicocele.

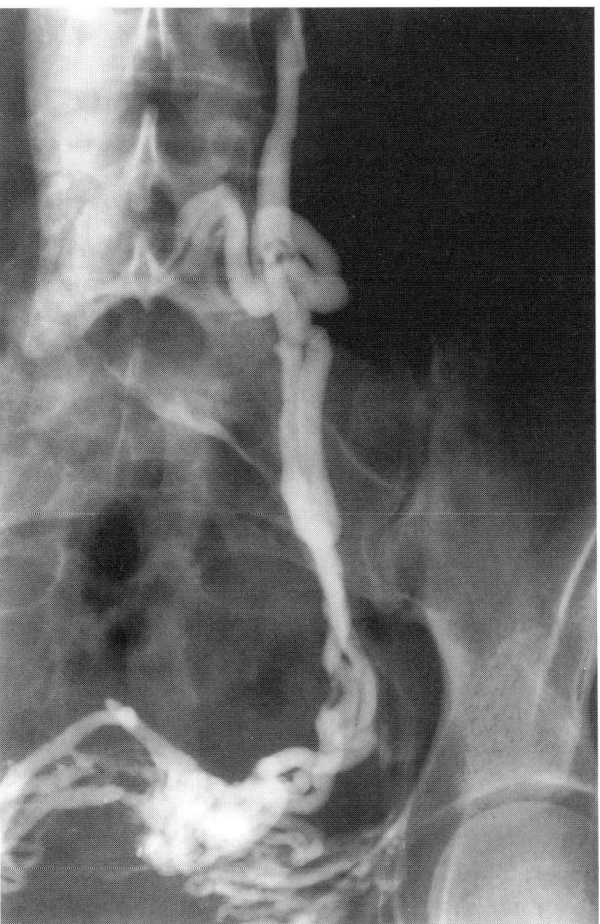

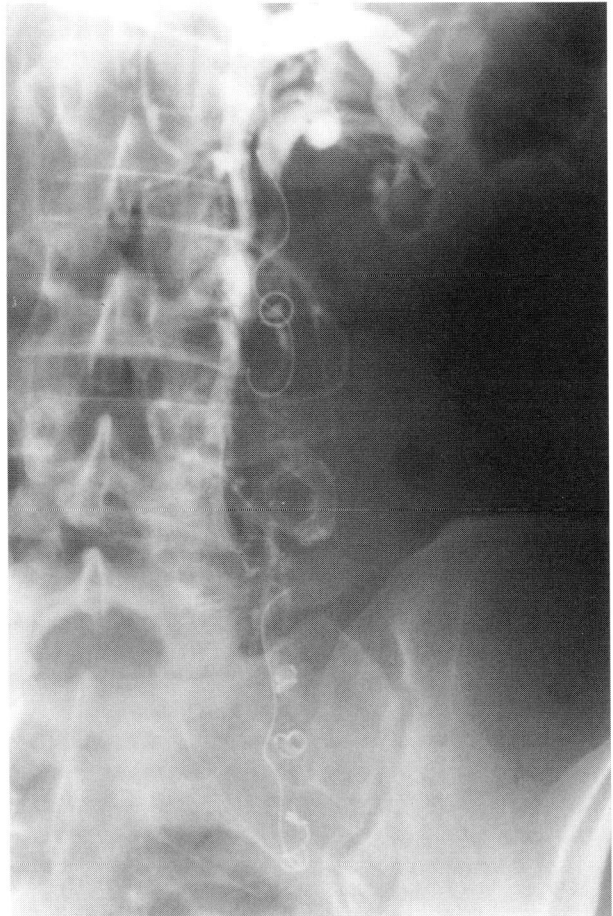

A

B

fertility and pregnancy are multifactorial when both the man and woman are undergoing therapy. In addition, the percutaneously treated population of men is heterogeneous; different-size varicoceles are involved, and some men are already fertile and others are being treated for recurrences after previous surgery. Until the pathophysiology of varicoceles is understood and prospective randomized controlled studies are performed, it will not be known whether treatment is truly beneficial, even though the majority of evidence supports varicocele correction as an aid to infertility. Pregnancy rates after varicocele correction vary from 0 percent to as high as 70 percent.[12,102,122,124,125] Comhaire et al. evaluated the factors affecting the probability of pregnancy embolization with bucrylate and found that 50.5 percent of couples achieved pregnancy, with a constant probability of conception of 3.9 percent per cycle determined by life table analysis. The factors found to predict success for pregnancy from varicocele embolization were the coincidence of other disease in the man or woman interfering with fertility, serum follicle-stimulating hormone concentration, total testicular volume, and pretreatment semen quality, with the probability of conception ranging from 8 to 80 percent.[126] For all members in the study by Zuckerman et al., the average time to pregnancy after percutaneous occlusion was 17.2 months ± 15.8 months, whereas the time was shorter for individuals who were treated with embolization only.[102] The reported improvement in pregnancy rate due to surgical ligation or percutaneous embolization is similar, with few prospective studies to compare the two techniques.[37] Some studies suggest that there is a difference in pregnancy outcome from surgery compared to percutaneous techniques, whereas others show no difference.[108,122,127-129] Yavetz et al. and Nieschlag et al. performed randomized prospective studies comparing surgery to embolization. Although neither demonstrated an advantage of percutaneous embolization over surgery in improving pregnancy rates, both demonstrated greater patient acceptance with shorter hospital stays and less discomfort with embolization.[128,129]

Ovarian Varicocele

Percutaneous embolization has also been suggested to treat gonadal varices in females. Pelvic pain syndrome or pelvic congestion syndrome can be due to ovarian vein reflux causing a "female varicocele syndrome," which produces chronic pain.[130,131] The suspected etiology of this syndrome is venous reflux in dilated, incompetent ovarian veins. Recent reports suggest that embolization is a safe and effective treatment to provide symptomatic pain relief (Fig. 41-28).[132,133]

Acknowledgments

I would like to thank many of my colleagues for their contribution to the text and illustrations: Constantin Cope, M.D., Michael C. Soulen, M.D., Harvey Nisenbaum, M.D., Evan Siegelman, M.D., Scott Savader, M.D., and Lindsay Machan, M.D.

References

1. Zorgniotti A. The spermatozoa count: a short history. Urology 1975;5:672–673.
2. Barwell R. One hundred cases of varicocele treated by subcutaneous wire loop. Lancet 1885;1:978.
3. Bennett W. Varicocele, particularly with reference to its radical cure. Lancet 1889;1:261–265.
4. Tulloch W. Consideration of sterility factors in the light of subsequent pregnancies: subfertility in the male. Trans Edinb Obstet Soc 1952;59:29–34.
5. Charny C. Effect of varicocele on fertility: results of varicocelectomy. Fertil Steril 1962;13:47–56.
6. MacLeod J. Seminal cytology in the presence of varicocele. Fertil Steril 1965;16:735–757.
7. Iaccarino V. Trattamento conservativa del varicoceles: flebografia selecttiva e scleroterapia delle vene gonadiche. Riv Radiol 1977;17:107–117.
8. Lima S, Castro M, Costa O. A new method for the treatment of varicocele. Andrologia 1978;10:103–106.
9. Morag B, Rubinstein ZJ, Madgar I, et al. The role of spermatic venography after surgical high ligation of the left spermatic veins: diagnosis and percutaneous occlusion. Urol Radiol 1985;7:32–34.
10. Demas BE, Hricak H, McClure RD. Varicoceles: radiologic diagnosis and treatment. Radiol Clin North Am 1991;29:619–627.
11. Reyes BL, Trerotola SO, Venbrux AC, et al. Percutaneous embolotherapy of adolescent varicocele: results and long-term follow-up. J Vasc Intervent Radiol 1994;5:131–134.
12. Pryor JL, Howards SS. Varicocele. Urol Clin North Am 1987;14:499–513.
13. Van der Sluiszen PL, Leguit P, Sanders FB. Subcutaneous varices of the scrotum: a possible presentation of varicocele. Eur J Radiol 1990;10:198–200.
14. Weiss AJ, Kellman GM, Middleton WD, et al. Intratesticular varicocele: sonographic findings in two patients. AJR 1992;158:1061–1063.
15. Steeno O, Knops J, Declerck L, et al. Prevention of fertility disorders by detection and treatment of varicocele at school and college age. Andrologia 1976;8:47–53.
16. Comhaire F. Varicocele infertility: an enigma. Int J Androl 1983;6:401–404.
17. Turner T. Varicocele: still an enigma. J Urol 1983;129:695–699.
18. Meacham RB, Townsend RR, Rademacher D, et al. The incidence of varicoceles in the general population when evaluated by physical examination, gray scale sonography and color Doppler sonography. J Urol 1994;151:1535–1538.
19. Gorelick JI, Goldstein M. Loss of fertility in men with varicocele. Fertil Steril 1993;59:613–616.
20. Wishahi MM. Anatomy of the spermatic venous plexus (pampiniform plexus) in men with and without varicocele: intraoperative venographic study. J Urol 1992;147:1285–1289.
21. Lechter A, Lopez G, Martinez C, et al. Anatomy of the gonadal veins: a reappraisal. Surgery 1991;109:735–739.

22. Wilms G, Oyen R, Baert AL. Left spermatic vein in left-sided vena cava. Cardiovasc Intervent Radiol 1987;10:258–260.
23. Turner TT, Howards SS. The venous anatomy of experimental left varicocele: comparison with naturally occurring left varicocele in the human. Fertil Steril 1994;62:869–875.
24. Hill J, Green N. Varicocele: a review of radiological and anatomical features in relation to surgical treatment. Br J Surg 1977;64:747–752.
25. Hill J, Hirsh A, Pryor J, et al. Changes in the appearance of venography after ligation of a varicocele. J Anat 1982;135:47–52.
26. Ahlberg N, Bartley O, Chidekel N, et al. Right and left gonadal veins: an anatomical and statistical study. Acta Radiol 1966;4:593–601.
27. Shafik A, Moftah A, Olfat S, et al. Testicular veins: anatomy and role in varicocelogenesis and other pathologic conditions. Urology 1990;35:175–182.
28. Wishahi MM. Anatomy of the venous drainage of the human testis: testicular vein cast, microdissection and radiographic demonstration. A new anatomical concept. Eur Urol 1991;20:154–160.
29. Wishahi MM. Detailed anatomy of the internal spermatic vein and the ovarian vein. Human cadaver study and operative spermatic venography: clinical aspects. J Urol 1991;145:780–784.
30. Sofikitis N, Dritsas K, Miyagawa I, et al. Anatomical characteristics of the left testicular venous system in man. Arch Androl 1993;30:79–85.
31. Erturk E, Sheinfeld J, Cockett AT. Male infertility due to communicating bilateral varicoceles. Urology 1984;24:390–391.
32. Marsman JW. The aberrantly fed varicocele: frequency, venographic appearance, and results of transcatheter embolization. AJR 1995;164:649–657.
33. Kaufman S, Kadir S, Barth K, et al. Mechanisms of recurrent varicocele after balloon occlusion or surgical ligation of the internal spermatic vein. Radiology 1983;147:435–440.
34. Murray RR Jr, Mitchell SE, Kadir S, et al. Comparison of recurrent varicocele anatomy following surgery and percutaneous balloon occlusion. J Urol 1986;135:286–289.
35. Halden W, White RI Jr. Outpatient embolotherapy of varicocele. Urol Clin North Am 1987;14:137–144.
36. Roy CR, Wilson T, Raife M, et al. Varicocele as the presenting sign of an abdominal mass. J Urol 1989;141:597–599.
37. Thomas AJ Jr, Geisinger MA. Current management of varicoceles. Urol Clin North Am 1990;17:893–907.
38. Linsell JC, Rowe PH, Owen WJ. Rupture of an aortic aneurysm into the renal vein presenting as a left-sided varicocoele. Case report. Acta Chir Scand 1987;153:477–478.
39. Corlett MP, Gwynn BR, Hamer JD. Right-sided varicocele caused by false aneurysm from aortic graft. Br J Urol 1992;70:204–205.
40. Wilms G, Oyen R, Casselman J, et al. Solitary or predominantly right-sided varicocele: a possible sign of situs inversus. Urol Radiol 1988;9:243–246.
41. Kohler FP. On the etiology of varicocele. J Urol 1967;97:741–742.
42. Verstoppen G, Steeno O. Varicocele and the pathogenesis of the associated subfertility: a review of the various theories. I: Varicocelogenesis. Andrologia 1977;9:133–140.
43. Mali WP, Oei HY, Arndt JW, et al. Hemodynamics of the varicocele: Part II. Correlation among the results of renocaval pressure measurements, varicocele scintigraphy and phlebography. J Urol 1986;135:489–493.
44. Bomalaski MD, Mills JL, Argueso LR, et al. Iliac vein compression syndrome: an unusual cause of varicocele. J Vasc Surg 1993;18:1064–1068.
45. Sayfan J, Halevy A, Oland J, et al. Varicocele and left renal vein compression. Fertil Steril 1984;41:411–417.
46. Mali WP, Oei HY, Arndt JW, et al. Hemodynamics of the varicocele: Part I. Correlation among the clinical, phlebo-

graphic and scintigraphic findings. J Urol 1986;135:483–488.
47. Kim SH, Park JH, Han MC, et al. Embolization of the internal spermatic vein in varicocele: significance of venous pressure. Cardiovasc Intervent Radiol 1992;15:102–107.
48. Carl P, Stark L, Ouzoun N, et al. Venous pressure in idiopathic varicocele. Eur Urol 1993;24:214–220.
49. Shafik A, Khalil A, Saleh M. The fasciomuscular tube of the spermatic cord: a study of its surgical anatomy and relation to varicocele. A new concept for the pathogenesis of varicocele. Br J Urol 1972;44:147–151.
50. Shafik A. The cremasteric muscle: role in varicocelogenesis and in thermoregulatory function of the testicle. Invest Urol 1973;11:92–97.
51. Sayfan J, Halevy A, Shperber Y, et al. The role of the spermatic cord layers in the development of varicoceles. J Urol 1985;133:223–224.
52. Zorgniotti A, MacLeod J. Studies in temperature, human semen quality and varicocele. Fertil Steril 1973;24:854–863.
53. Kay R, Alexander N, Baugham W. Induced varicoceles in rhesus monkeys. Fertil Steril 1979;31:195–199.
54. Saypol D, Howards S, Turner T, et al. Influence of surgically induced varicocele on testicular blood flow, temperature, and histology in adult rats and dogs. J Clin Invest 1981;68:39–45.
55. Takihara H, Sakatoku J, Cockett ATK. The pathophysiology of varicocele in male infertility. Fertil Steril 1991;55:861–868.
56. Ali JI, Weaver DJ, Weinstein SH, et al. Scrotal temperature and semen quality in men with and without varicocele. Arch Androl 1990;24:215–219.
57. Zorgniotti AW, Sealfon AI. Scrotal hypothermia: new therapy for poor semen. Urology 1984;23:439–441.
58. Comhaire F, Vermeulen A. Varicocele sterility: cortisol and catecholamines. Fertil Steril 1974;25:88–95.
59. Cohen M, Plaine L, Brown J. The role of internal spermatic vein plasma catecholamine determinations in subfertile men with varicoceles. Fertil Steril 1975;26:1243–1249.
60. Lindholmer C, Thulin L, Eliasoon R. Concentrations of cortisol and renin in the internal spermatic vein of men with varicocele. Andrologie 1973;5:21–22.
61. Charny C, Baum S. Varicocele and infertility. JAMA 1968;204:75–78.
62. Ito H, Fuse H, Minagawa H, et al. Internal spermatic vein prostaglandins in varicocele patients. Fertil Steril 1982;37:218–222.
63. Hudson RW, Perez-Marrero RA, Crawford VA, et al. Hormonal parameters of men with varicoceles before and after varicocelectomy. Fertil Steril 1985;43:905–910.
64. Donohue R, Brown J. Blood gases and pH determinations in the internal spermatic veins of subfertile men with varicocele. Fertil Steril 1969;20:365–369.
65. Rodriguez-Rigau L, Weiss D, et al. A possible mechanism for the detrimental effect of varicocele on testicular function in man. Fertil Steril 1978;30:577–585.
66. Spera G, Alei G, Coia L, et al. Histological lesions in the testis of infertile men with varicocele. Arch Androl 1979;2:335–339.
67. Chakraborty J, Hikim AK, Jhunjhunwala J. Stagnation of blood in the microcirculatory vessels in the testes of men with varicocele. J Androl 1985;6:117–126.
68. Sharpe R. Paracrine control of the testis. Clin Endocrinol Metab 1986;15:185–207.
69. La Nasa JA Jr, Lewis RW. Varicocele and its surgical management. Urol Clin North Am 1987;14:127–136.
70. Gonda RLJ, Karo JJ, Forte RA, et al. Diagnosis of subclinical varicocele in infertility. AJR 1987;148:71–75.
71. Rifkin MD, Foy PM, Kurtz AB, Pasto ME, Goldberg BB. The role of diagnostic ultrasound in varicocele evaluation. J Ultrasound Med 1983;2:271–275.
72. Wolverson MK, Houttuine E, Heiberg E, Sundaram M,

Gregory J. High resolution real-time sonography of scrotal varicocele. AJR 1983;141:775–779.

73. Aydos K, Baltaci S, Salih M, et al. Use of color Doppler sonography in the evaluation of varicoceles. Eur Urol 1993;24: 221–225.

74. Petros JA, Andriole GL, Middleton WD, Picus DA. Correlation of testicular color Doppler ultrasonography, physical examination and venography in the detection of left varicoceles in men with infertility. J Urol 1991;145:785–788.

75. Sigmund G, Gall H, Bahren W. Stop-type and shunt-type varicoceles: venographic findings. Radiology 1987;163:105–110.

76. Ahlberg N, Bartley O, Chidekel N, et al. Phlebography in varicocele scroti. Acta Radiol 1966;4:517–528.

77. Comhaire F, Kunnen M. Selective retrograde venography of the internal spermatic vein: a conclusive approach to the diagnosis of varicocele. Andrologia 1976;8:11–24.

78. Marsman JW. Clinical versus subclinical varicocele: venographic findings and improvement of fertility after embolization. Radiology 1985;155:635–638.

79. Porst H, Bahren W, Lenz M, et al. Percutaneous sclerotherapy of varicoceles: an alternative to conventional surgical methods. Br J Urol 1984;56:73–78.

80. Palomo A. Radical cure of varicocele by a new technique. J Urol 1949;61:604–607.

81. Ivanissevich O. Left varicocele due to reflux: experience with 4470 operative cases in 42 years. J Int Coll Surg 1960;34: 742–755.

82. Marmar JL, DeBenedictis TJ, Praiss D. The management of varicoceles by microdissection of the spermatic cord at the external inguinal ring. Fertil Steril 1985;43:583–588.

83. Enquist E, Stein BS, Sigman M. Laparoscopic versus subinguinal varicocelectomy: a comparative study. Fertil Steril 1994; 61:1092–1096.

84. Dubin L, Amelar RD. Varicocelectomy: twenty-five years of experience. Int J Fertil 1988;33:226–228, 231–235.

85. Mordel N, Mor-Yosef S, Margalioth EJ, et al. Spermatic vein ligation as treatment for male infertility: justification by postoperative semen improvement and pregnancy rates. J Reprod Med 1990;35:123–127.

86. Mozes M, Bogokowsky H, Antebi E. Surgical treatment of varicocele. J Int Coll Surg 1965;44:44–46.

87. Comhaire F, Kunnen M, Nahoum C. Radiologic anatomy of the internal spermatic vein(s) in 200 retrograde venograms. Int J Androl 1981;4:379–387.

88. Levitt S, Gill B, Katlowitz N, et al. Routine intraoperative post-ligation venography in the treatment of the pediatric varicocele. J Urol 1987;137:716–718.

89. Zaontz MR, Firlit CF. Use of venography as an aid in varicocelectomy. J Urol 1987;138:1041–1042.

90. Hart RR, Rushton HG, Belman AB. Intraoperative spermatic venography during varicocele surgery in adolescents. J Urol 1992;148:1514–1516.

91. Tauber R, Johnsen N. Antegrade scrotal sclerotherapy for the treatment of varicocele: technique and late results. J Urol 1994;151:386–390.

92. Riedl P. Selektive phlebographie und katheterthrombosierung vena testicularis bei primarer varikocele. Wein Klin Wochenschr 1979;99(Suppl):3–20.

93. Thelen M, Weissbach L, Franken T. Die behandlung der idiopathischen varkozele durch transfemorale spiralokklusion der vena testicularis sinistra. Rofo 1979;131:24–29.

94. Formanek A, Rusnak B, Zollikofer C, et al. Embolization of the spermatic vein for treatment of infertility: a new approach. Radiology 1981;139:315–321.

95. Morag B, Rubinstein ZJ, Goldwasser B, et al. Percutaneous venography and occlusion in the management of spermatic varicoceles. AJR 1984;143:635–640.

96. Kuroiwa T, Hasuo K, Yasumori K, et al. Transcatheter embolization of testicular vein for varicocele testis. Acta Radiol 1991;32:311–314.

97. Berkman WA, Price RB, Wheatley JK, et al. Varicoceles: a co-axial coil occlusion system. Radiology 1984;151:73–77.

98. Berger T, Sorensen R. Varicoceles: distal occlusion with coaxial catheter system. Radiology 1987;162:271.

99. Takeyama M, Honjoh M, Kodama M, et al. Testicular steroids in spermatic and peripheral veins after single injection of hCG in patients with varicocele. Arch Androl 1990;24: 207–213.

100. Trerotola SO, Venbrux AC, Savader SJ, et al. Guiding catheter for varicocele embolization. J Vasc Intervent Radiol 1993; 4:433–434.

101. Fobbe F, Hamm B, Sorensen R, et al. Percutaneous transluminal treatment of varicoceles: where to occlude the internal spermatic vein. AJR 1987;149:983–987.

102. Zuckerman AM, Mitchell SE, Venbrux AC, et al. Percutaneous varicocele occlusion: long-term follow-up. J Vasc Intervent Radiol 1994;5:315–319.

103. Shuman L, White RI Jr, Mitchell SE, et al. Right-sided varicocele: technique and clinical results of balloon embolotherapy from the femoral approach. Radiology 1986;158:787–791.

104. Seyferth W, Jecht E, Zeitler E. Percutaneous sclerotherapy of varicocele. Radiology 1981;139:335–340.

105. Sigmund G, Bahren W, Gall H, et al. Idiopathic varicoceles: feasibility of percutaneous sclerotherapy. Radiology 1987; 164:161–168.

106. Bach D, Bahren W, Gall H, et al. Late results after sclerotherapy of varicocele. Eur Urol 1988;14:115–119.

107. Pisco JM, Basto I, Batista AM, et al. Percutaneous sclerotherapy of varicocele. Acta Med Port 1992;5:477–481.

108. Belgrano E, Puppo P, Quattrini S, et al. The role of venography and sclerotherapy in the management of varicocele. Eur Urol 1984;10:124–129.

109. Riedl P, Kumpan W, Maier U, et al. Long-term results after sclerotherapy of the spermatic vein in patients with varicocele. Cardiovasc Intervent Radiol 1985;8:46–49.

110. Salgarello G, Cagossi M, Salgarello TL, et al. Transvenous sclerotherapy of the gonadal veins for treatment of varicocele: long-term results. Angiology 1990;41:427–431.

111. Hunter DW, Bildsoe MC, Amplatz K. Aid for safer sclerotherapy of the internal spermatic vein. Radiology 1989;173:282.

112. Weissbach L, Thelen M, Adolphs H. Treatment of idiopathic varicoceles by transfemoral testicular vein occlusion. J Urol 1981;126:354–356.

113. Pochaczevsky R, Lee WJ, Mallett E. Management of male infertility: roles of contact thermography, spermatic venography, and embolization. AJR 1986;147:97–102.

114. Rooney MS, Gray RR. Varicocele embolization through competent internal spermatic veins. Can Assoc Radiol J 1992;43: 431–435.

115. White R, Kaufman S, Barth K, et al. Occlusion of varicoceles with detachable balloons. Radiology 1981;139:327–334.

116. Chomyn JJ, Craven WM, Groves BM, et al. Percutaneous removal of a Gianturco coil from the pulmonary artery with use of flexible intravascular forceps. J Vasc Intervent Radiol 1991; 2:105–106.

117. Walsh P, White R. Balloon occlusion of the internal spermatic vein for the treatment of varicoceles. JAMA 1981;246:1701–1702.

118. Pollak JS, Egglin TK, Rosenblatt MM, et al. Clinical results of transvenous systemic embolotherapy with a neuroradiologic detachable balloon. Radiology 1994;191:477–482.

119. Makita K, Furui S, Tsuchiya K, et al. Guide-wire-directed detachable balloon: clinical application in treatment of varicoceles. Radiology 1992;183:575–577.

120. Smith TP, Hunter DW, Cragg AH, et al. Spermatic vein embolization with hot contrast material: fertility results. Radiology 1988;168:137–139.

121. MacLeod J. Further observations on the role of varicocele in human infertility. Fertil Steril 1969;20:545–563.

122. Schlesinger MH, Wilets IF, Nagler HM. Treatment outcome after varicocelectomy: a critical analysis. Urol Clin North Am 1994;21:517–529.

123. Braedel HU, Steffens J, Ziegler M, et al. Out-patient sclerotherapy of idiopathic left-sided varicocele in children and adults. Br J Urol 1990;65:536–540.

124. Vermeulen A, Vandeweghe M. Improved fertility after varicocele correction: fact or fiction? Fertil Steril 1984;42:249–256.

125. Breznik R, Vlaisavljevic V, Borko E. Treatment of varicocele and male fertility. Arch Androl 1993;30:157–160.

126. Comhaire FH, Kunnen M. Factors affecting the probability of conception after treatment of subfertile men with varicocele by transcatheter embolization with bucrylate. Fertil Steril 1985;43:781–786.

127. Parsch EM, Schill WB, Erlinger C, et al. Semen parameters and conception rates after surgical treatment and sclerotherapy of varicocele. Andrologia 1990;22:275–278.

128. Yavetz H, Levy R, Papo J, et al. Efficacy of varicocele embolization versus ligation of the left internal spermatic vein for improvement of sperm quality. Int J Androl 1992;15:338–344.

129. Nieschlag E, Behre HM, Schlingheider A, et al. Surgical ligation vs. angiographic embolization of the vena spermatica: a prospective randomized study for the treatment of varicocele-related infertility. Andrologia 1993;25:233–237.

130. Beard R, Reginald P, Wadsworth J. Clinical features of women with chronic lower abdominal pain and pelvic congestion. Br J Obstet Gynaecol 1988;95:153–161.

131. Giacchetto C, Cotroneo G, Marincolo F, et al. Ovarian varicocele: ultrasonic and phlebographic evaluation. J Clin Ultrasound 1990;18:551–555.

132. Edwards R, Robertson I, MacLean A, et al. Case report: pelvic pain syndrome—successful treatment of a case by ovarian vein embolization. Clin Radiol 1993;47:429–431.

133. Machan L, Hurwitz T, Fry P, et al. Ovarian vein embolization as treatment for pelvic congestion syndrome. Presented at the 81st Scientific Assembly and Annual Meeting of the Radiological Society of North America, Chicago, Illinois, 1995.

42

Penile Vascular Catheterization in Diagnosis and Therapy of Erectile Dysfunction

JOSEPH J. BOOKSTEIN
KARIM VALJI

Penile vascular catheterization refers to catheterization of the penile arterial supply for arteriography or angioplasty, needle access of the lacunar spaces of the corpus cavernosum for cavernosometry or cavernosography, and catheterization of the penile veins for transcatheter venoablation. The purpose and rationale of these procedures simultaneously reflect and augment current understanding of penile erection and erectile dysfunction.

Physiology of Erection

Current understanding of the physiology of penile erection may be summarized as follows. Various psychogenic or sensory stimuli lead to activation of autonomic nerve fibers within the spinal nuclei at the S2–S4 and the T10–L2 levels.[1] From these nuclei, autonomic impulses pass via the pelvic plexus and the cavernosal nerves to release neurotransmitters of smooth muscle relaxation.[2] Although these neurotransmitters have not yet been identified with certainty, there is evidence to suggest the presence of several relaxant agents, including acetylcholine, vasoactive intestinal polypeptide,[2,3] and endothelium-derived relaxation factor (EDRF, now thought to be nitric oxide).[4]

The corpora cavernosa, the major erectile structures of the human penis, consist largely of vascular spaces termed *lacunae* (or sinusoids) that are lined by smooth muscle. They receive arterial flow via a central artery, but there exists no central cavernosal vein. Instead blood percolates peripherally through the cavernosa to drain through a plexus of veins situated just beneath the unyielding tunica albuginea. Tiny emissary veins perforate the tunica at intervals to form an external venous drainage system consisting primarily of deep dorsal and crural veins that drain secondarily into internal pudendal, preprostatic, and vesical veins.

The cavernosal relaxant neurotransmitters relax lacunar smooth muscle, as well as the smooth muscle of arteries and arterioles (termed *helicine arterioles*). The arterial and arteriolar relaxation enables markedly augmented cavernosal arterial blood flow during the initial phases of erection. Simultaneously, relaxation of lacunar musculature enables lacunar dilatation and penile tumescence. As the lacunae distend, they mechanically compress peripheral venules against the unyielding fibrous layer surrounding the corpora (the tunica albuginea). This venous compression mechanically obstructs venous drainage from the penis, providing the mechanism of venoocclusion (Fig. 42-1).[5] Thus muscular relaxation of the lacunae, arteries, and arterioles is the common denominator of penile erection, yielding increased arterial flow, venoocclusion, and penile tumescence and rigidity.

Based on the physiologic interplay of nerves, arteries and arterioles, lacunar musculature, and pericavernosal veins, the erectile process may be divided into the following phases.[3]

Flaccid Phase. Strong tonic sympathetic tone maintains lacunar muscular contraction, arteriolar contraction, and minimal arterial and venous flow.

Filling Phase. Arteriolar relaxation combined with early activation of the venoocclusive mechanism produces penile tumescence.

Erection Phase. Tumescence gradually merges into rigidity as the corpora cavernosa distend forcefully against the rigid tunica albuginea. Mean intracavernosal pressure at this stage is about 85 mmHg, secondarily slowing cavernosal arterial flow toward control levels.

Rigid Erection Phase. As a result of contraction of the ischiocavernosus muscles with the approach of

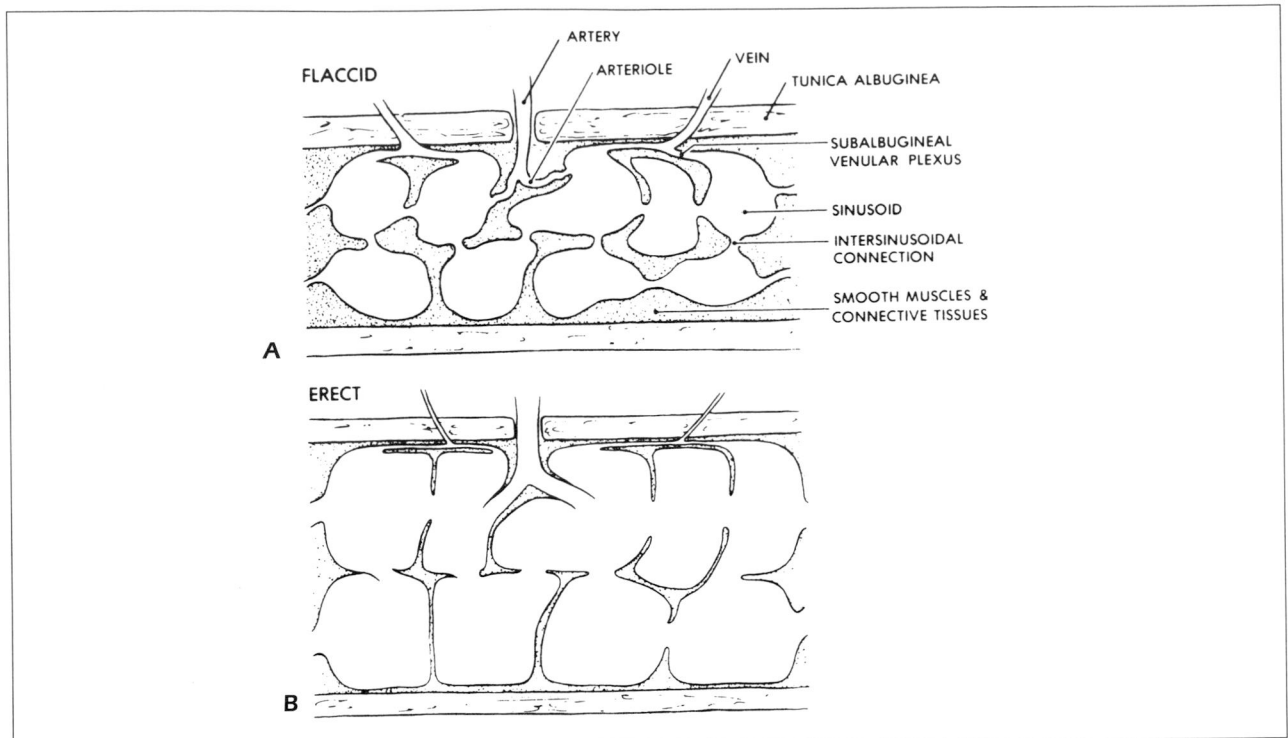

Figure 42-1. Current favored theory of venoocclusive mechanism. (A) In the flaccid state, the sinusoidal vascular space and arterial inflow are limited by wall tonus. Venous outflow is unimpeded. (B) After neurostimulation or intracavernosal injection of a smooth muscle relaxant, sinusoidal smooth muscle relaxes and distended sinusoids compress and obstruct peripheral venules against the tunica albuginea. Simultaneously, resistance to arterial flow decreases until cavernosal pressures approach systemic pressures. (From Fournier GR, Juenemann KP; Lue TF, Tanagho EA. Mechanisms of venous occlusion during canine penile erection: an anatomic demonstration. J Urol 1987;137:163–167. Used with permission.)

orgasm, the intracavernous pressure can temporarily reach high suprasystolic levels. Simultaneously, contraction of the bulbocavernosus muscle augments turgor of the corpus spongiosum and glans.

Detumescent Phase. After ejaculation or cessation of stimulation, tonic sympathetic tone returns, causing contraction of arteries and arterioles and terminating cavernosal filling. Simultaneously, the lacunar musculature contracts, shrinking the cavernosa and releasing the venoocclusive mechanism.

Pharmacologic Erection

In addition to the above-described physiologic erection, artificial penile erection can be produced by intracavernosal (IC) injection of many smooth muscle relaxants, including papaverine, prostaglandin E_1 (PGE_1), nitroglycerin, phenoxybenzamine, and verapamil.[6] The corollary is also true; erection can be reversed by intracavernosal injection of a smooth muscle constrictor, such as epinephrine or norepinephrine, as when treating priapism.

Understanding of penile erection was greatly aug-

mented by Virag's discovery in 1982 of the erectogenicity of IC papaverine.[7] That single discovery contributed in rapid succession to the following developments:

1. IC papaverine was recognized and widely accepted as an effective drug for the treatment of impotence.[8]
2. IC papaverine and other smooth muscle relaxants provided useful animal models for the study of erectile physiology and contributed to current understanding of erectile hemodynamics and the venoocclusive mechanism.[5,9]
3. IC injection of the alpha blocker phentolamine was found to augment the therapeutic efficacy of papaverine.[6]
4. IC injection of papaverine led to the development of penile pharmacoarteriography, which, when combined with selective magnification techniques, enabled consistent visualization of penile arterial structures through the level of the cavernosal arteries and the helicine arterioles.[10]
5. The ability to achieve consistent activation of the

venoocclusive mechanism via IC papaverine and/ or other IC smooth muscle relaxants made possible clinically practical methods for quantitating venoocclusive incompetence.[11] The major external routes of abnormal venous leakage could be identified via pharmacocavernosography.[12]

6. Prostaglandin E_1, alone or in combination with papaverine and phentolamine, was found to further augment the therapeutic efficacy of IC relaxant regimens.[13]

7. IC relaxants, as well as developments in ultrasonic instrumentation, enabled duplex sonographic evaluation of the cavernosal arteries.[14]

8. Adrenergic and cholinergic mechanisms failed to adequately explain cavernosal smooth muscle relaxation. Other (nonadrenergic and noncholinergic, or NANC) relaxant neurotransmitter(s) were sought. Endothelium-derived relaxation factor (EDRF), now known with reasonable certainty to be similar or identical to nitric oxide, is the current putative NANC.[4,15]

9. The above described advances in the diagnosis of vasculogenic impotence provided strong impetus for the further development and evaluation of specific corrective therapeutic procedures. New bypass operations and transluminal angioplasty were developed for arterial insufficiency, and new methods of venous ligation and transluminal venoablation were developed to treat excessive cavernosal leak. Except for posttraumatic impotence, however, clinical results of these specific therapeutic procedures have been discouraging. The limited clinical benefit has stimulated reexamination of the erectile paradigm. Failure of arteriolar dilatation as an etiologic factor in impotence is receiving renewed emphasis.[16]

Causes of Impotence

Impotence should be considered a continuum of erectile dysfunction. It is commonly accepted as clinically significant when rigidity is insufficient for vaginal penetration in most attempts over a period of several months. With regard to the physiologic events described above, impotence may be secondary to dysfunction of any component of the erectile process: (1) cerebral dysfunction (psychogenic impotence), (2) nerve conduction (neurogenic impotence), (3) arterial (arteriogenic) impotence, (4) failure of the venoocclusive mechanism (venogenic impotence), (5) deficiency of EDRF, and (based on the authors' own experience) (6) organic or functional failure of arteriolar dilatation. For many years impotence was considered largely psychogenic in origin. More recently, circulatory abnor-

malities, usually either incompetence of the venoocclusive mechanism or arterial atherosclerosis, have been found in most impotent patients and have been presumed to play an etiologic role. It must be pointed out, however, that these circulatory abnormalities might be secondary to another cause of erectile dysfunction rather than primary etiologic factors. Penile trauma is a common cause of impotence, as a result of arterial damage or damage of the tunica albuginea leading to venoocclusive incompetence.

Diagnostic Penile Vascular Catheterization

Background

Because penile erection is largely a circulatory phenomenon, it was assumed that penile angiography would be easily applicable and reliable in the study of erectile function and dysfunction. Penile angiography and vascular catheterization, however, proved to be of limited value until the erectogenic potential of IC smooth muscle relaxants, such as papaverine, was appreciated. Until that time, arteriography on conscious patients enabled only poor visualization of the dorsal penile arteries, and virtually never adequately demonstrated the cavernosal arteries or the helicine arterioles. Although arteriography after spinal anesthesia provided much better visualization,[17] the requirement for anesthesia severely limited the applicability of penile arteriography. Thus, before pharmacoarteriography there was no practical gold standard for the diagnosis of "arteriogenic impotence." Likewise, before the advent of pharmacocavernosometry, results of cavernosometry were totally unreliable, and there was no accepted standard for diagnosis of "venogenic impotence."

It was only after the effects of IC relaxants were recognized and exploited that penile vascular catheterization began to provide consistent and reliable arteriographic and cavernosometric data. Our early pharmacoarteriographic experience of the 1980s showed that atherosclerotic obstruction of penile arteries existed alone or combined with venoocclusive insufficiency in approximately 50 percent of an unselected group of impotent patients undergoing penile vascular catheterization. For obscure reasons, the proximal cavernosal or the distal internal pudendal arteries proved to be sites of strong atherosclerotic predilection.[18,19] In addition, venoocclusive insufficiency of the corpus cavernosum (variously termed *venous leak*, *venosinusoidal leak*, or *venogenic impotence*) was observed in approximately 50 percent of impotent

Table 42-1. Vascular Status: 280 Penile
Vascular Catheterizations

Diagnosis	No. of Cases	Percent
Normal arteries and manometry	65	23.2
Arterial insufficiency only	62	22.1
Venoocclusive insufficiency only	71	25.4
Combined arterial and venoocclusive disease	68	24.3
Arteriolar dysfunction only (last 145 cases only)	6	2.1 (4.1)*
Endothelial dysfunction only (last 93 cases only)	8	2.9 (8.6)*

*Compared to evaluated cases.

patients (Table 42-1). More recently, we have developed methods for evaluating arteriolar patency and cavernosal endothelial production of EDRF (see below).

The prevalence of vascular abnormalities in impotence greatly stimulated interest in revascularization procedures for arterial obstruction[20,21] and in venous ligation for venoocclusive insufficiency.[22,23] The initial reported results of these specific vascular therapeutic procedures were encouraging and provided support for the following new paradigm of erectile dysfunction:

> Impotence is frequently caused by arterial or venoocclusive insufficiency. Identification of these conditions by morphologic and physiologic methods makes possible a specific diagnosis of venogenic or arteriogenic impotence. A specific diagnosis often enables rational and specific corrective vascular surgical or transluminal therapy.

This paradigm has now been tested for over a decade. Unfortunately, the expected therapeutic yield has not materialized. Arterial revascularization or therapeutic venous obstruction fails to restore potency in at least half of those so treated,[16,24,25] casting doubt on the relevance and validity of the diagnostic tests, as well as on the precepts of the paradigm. Possible reasons for failure of the paradigm and an alternative paradigm are presented at the conclusion of this chapter.

Overview of Methodology

We perform penile vascular catheterization on an outpatient basis under mild sedation and local anesthesia. The procedure requires 75 to 90 minutes and consists of the following elements.

1. Pharmacoarteriography.
   A. Survey pelvic arteriograms in 30-degree oblique projection.

B. Relaxation of the corpora cavernosa, usually with papaverine (60 mg) admixed with phentolamine (1 mg); as an alternative, a mixture of 8 μg PGE_1, 12 mg papaverine, and 1 mg phentolamine has proven slightly more potent.
   C. Selective internal pudendal arteriography, using highly concentrated nonionic contrast agent, direct 2× magnification, and 30-degree oblique projections.
   D. Supplementary complex projections as needed.
2. Pharmacocavernosometry.
   A. Determination of pharmacologic maintenance erectile flow (PMEF), using the same IC relaxant injection as for arteriography.
   B. Observation of the amplitude of cavernosal pressure pulses.
   C. Evaluation of endothelial function via the papaverine/ACh (acetylcholine) PMEF method[26,27] (see below).
3. Pharmacocavernosography. Performed after pharmacocavernosometric demonstration of excessive venoocclusive insufficiency, only if venoablative therapy is an option. Dilute (14 percent iodine) nonionic hydrophilic contrast agent (Ioversol, Mallinckrodt Inc.) is used.

Yield of Penile Vascular Catheterization

The basic expected yield of penile vascular catheterization is (1) visualization of the penile arterial blood supply from the aorta through and including the cavernosal arteries, (2) quantitation of cavernosal venous leak, and (3) identification of major routes of venous drainage, if surgical or transcatheter interruption of venous drainage is a therapeutic consideration. In addition, we believe that our methods can be exploited to (4) evaluate the patency of the helicine arteriolar bed by visualizing these vessels on magnification arteriography, estimating the density of the cavernosal stain, and demonstrating the amplitude of the cavernosal pressure pulse[16]; and (5) evaluate endothelial production of EDRF via the papaverine/ACh method.[26]

Indications for Penile Vascular Catheterization

Our experience to date has demonstrated a poor predictive value of all screening tests for arterial insufficiency or venoocclusive incompetence, including duplex ultrasound.[14,28] We therefore do not rely on screening methods to determine eligibility for penile vascular catheterization. Instead we accept any patient with impotence of over 3 months' duration who desires a definitive determination of a possible vasculogenic cause, usually with the intent to undergo a specific vascular corrective procedure should vasculogenic impotence be demonstrated. All candidates for penile vascular catheterization are made aware of the less-than-satisfactory results of current vascular corrective procedures.

Methodology

To maximize the usefulness of injected pharmacologic agents, and for other logistic reasons, the elements of examination are not performed in the order indicated under "Overview of Methodology," but rather in the following order:

Step 1. The penile vascular catheterization procedure is begun with bilateral 30-degree oblique pelvic arteriograms to assess the major arteries and to identify the course and patency of the internal pudendal arteries for subsequent selective catheterization. Contrast is injected through a pigtail catheter at the aortic bifurcation (about 25 ml in 2 seconds, iodine concentration about 30 percent, filming one per second for 9 seconds). In the 30-degree anterior oblique projection, the ipsilateral internal pudendal artery is easily identified as the vessel that crosses the obturator foramen en route to the penis. It is also advisable to look for supplemental cavernosal arteries that most frequently course just lateral to the pubic symphysis. The remainder of the arteriogram is then delayed until later in the course of study.

Step 2. The root of the penis is then anesthetized in preparation for later passage of cavernosal needles. Five ml of 2 percent lidocaine is injected on each side of the dorsum of the penile root, about 4 mm to each side of the midline, and to a depth of approximately 4 mm. To our knowledge, we have never pierced a dorsal penile artery or nerve.

Step 3. The pigtail catheter is then exchanged for a long-reversed catheter, which is ideal for selective internal pudendal catheterization (Cordis, Inc.).[29] The reversed curve is usually reformed around the aortic bifurcation after a guidewire is maneuvered through the pigtail catheter into the contralateral common iliac artery. If that maneuver fails, a deflector wire (Cook, Inc.) can be used. The reversed-curve catheter is manipulated into the anterior division of an internal iliac artery and left there during the next several steps.

Step 4. A 21-gauge butterfly needle is placed within each corpus cavernosum for pharmacocavernosometry/-ography. The glans is bent down over the left index finger by the thumb of the operator, and the needle is passed straight into a corpus via the coronal sulcus, entering about 4 mm to each side of the midline. Ideally, blood should be aspiratable, but if not,

then a small amount of saline can be injected while palpating the needle tip for evidence of fluid accumulation. If no fluid is felt to accumulate, the needle is probably properly situated in the corpus cavernosum. If there is question, a small amount of dilute contrast medium (Ioversol) can be injected, and the characteristic cavernosal spongy network and septum observed. The needles are then connected by flexible tubing to a pump (Cavro-pump, Life-Tech) specifically designed for cavernosometry, and the lines are completely cleared of air. One needle is connected to the infusion source, and the second to a manometer.

Step 5. At our institution, cavernosometric evaluation of endothelium-derived relaxation factor (EDRF), an experimental procedure, is performed at this time.

The principles of the cavernosal EDRF estimation have been previously described.[26] To recapitulate: relaxation of vascular smooth muscle by acetylcholine (ACh) depends on release of a factor(s) from the endothelium, termed *endothelium-derived relaxation factor (EDRF)*, now thought to be nitric oxide. In other words, ACh is an endothelium-dependent relaxant. In the presence of dysfunctional endothelium, ACh produces reduced smooth muscle relaxation or even muscular contraction. Papaverine, on the other hand, is a direct relaxant of smooth muscle, independent of endothelial presence or function. Since the venoocclusive mechanism is a manifestation of smooth muscle relaxation, the degree of cavernosal venous leak can serve as an index of the degree of cavernosal smooth muscle relaxation. By comparing the changes in maintenance erectile flow from control levels after IC infusion of the endothelium-dependent agent ACh (640 µg) with the response of an equimolar dose of the endothelium-independent agent papaverine (1.2 mg), one can estimate the endothelial release of EDRF. If, for example, the response to papaverine is near normal and the response to ACh grossly deficient, then one can infer deficient endothelial production of EDRF.

We have used this method in 93 patients to date. Results suggest deficient EDRF in over 30 percent of cases. The method remains experimental in humans, and further consideration of methodology and results is beyond the scope of this chapter.

Step 6. Selective magnification arteriography is performed next. The long-reversed catheter resting in the anterior division of the internal iliac artery is advanced into the pudendal artery. A preliminary magnification film is obtained in 30-degree anterior ipsilateral oblique projection, with the penis overlying the contralateral thigh.

Through one of the cavernosal needles the vasodilator regimen is then injected, usually consisting of 60 mg papaverine admixed with 1 mg phentolamine, diluted in 10 ml nonheparinized saline. (Caveat: Papaverine and heparin yield a precipitate.) The fluid should be manually massaged by the operator between both corpora (the corpora communicate freely via the septum in almost all patients). An umbilical tape is applied around the base of the penis for one minute to provide temporary intracavernosal retention. Cavernosal pressure is monitored. After 3 minutes, or when the cavernosal pressure reaches 30 mmHg (whichever occurs first), the arteriogram is performed. If cavernosal pressure exceeds 30 mmHg, it is necessary to drain blood from the penis before arteriography through at least one of the needles; otherwise cavernosal artery and helicine arteriolar visualization will be impaired.

A nonionic contrast medium (preferably hydrophilic, i.e., Ioversol, Mallinckrodt Inc.) containing 350 to 370 mg iodine per ml is injected at 3 ml per second for 18 ml. The filming sequence is two films per second for 3 seconds and one film per 2 seconds for 14 seconds.

If the first side studied is completely normal, the cavernosal artery is well seen, and there is no evidence of anomaly or collateral circulation, then unilateral arteriography is considered sufficient. Otherwise, the contralateral internal pudendal artery is selectively catheterized via the same long-reversed catheter, and contralateral internal pudendal arteriography is performed.

Step 7. Cavernosometric determination of the pharmacologic maintenance erectile flow (PMEF) is then obtained. At our institution, the PMEF is defined as the rate of saline infusion required to maintain the IC pressure at 150 mmHg.[11] At this pressure level, virtually no arterial inflow occurs, and the rate of infusion equals the rate of leak. Pressure rate and flow are conveniently determined via the dedicated Life-Tech peristaltic pump.

The PMEF is obtained between 5 and 10 minutes after the papaverine-phentolamine injection, while the vasorelaxant effects are still strong.

Step 8. The next step is determining the cavernosal pulse amplitude (CPA). Pressure pulsations with an amplitude of 0.5 to 6.0 mmHg are regularly observed during pharmacocavernosometry, presumably reflecting transmission of the pulse wave through the arterioles into the lacunae.[11] With our system (Hewlitt-Sanborn monitor, 21-gauge needles, K-50 tubing), the normal peak amplitude of pulsation appears to be more than 4.5 mmHg, although a sizable series of normals has not been systematically evaluated. The pressure lines should be observed carefully to be certain that air bubbles have been completely eliminated. If the pulse amplitude is diminished, needle apposition

against a lacunar wall can be excluded by rotating the needle to another position or by obtaining the pulse amplitude via the contralateral needle. Artificial augmentation of the pulse amplitude by a pendulum swing of the penis can be eliminated by manually stabilizing the penis during pulse measurement.

In patients with bilateral hemodynamically significant arterial obstruction, the CPA is diminished.

Step 9. Pharmacocavernosography is performed in patients with increased venous leak if surgical or transluminal venoablation is a therapeutic possibility. Through one of the two intracavernosal needles, contrast medium is injected at a rate approximating the PMEF. The injection is made within 15 minutes of the IC injection of papaverine/phentolamine used for arteriography and cavernosometry. The contrast medium is of the nonionic hydrophilic type (Ioversol) diluted to 14 percent iodine. Heparin, 1000 units in 1 ml of solution, is instilled intracavernosally beforehand to help protect the cavernosal endothelium, and the contrast is washed out after the injection with a slow infusion of several hundred ml of isotonic saline. Imaging is performed in frontal and both 30-degree oblique projections, and is recorded on full-size or 100-mm film.

Interpretation

A final diagnosis of our case material is given in Table 42-1. The diagnosis of arteriogenic impotence requires arteriographic demonstration of bilaterally hemodynamically significant obstruction of the cavernosal arterial supply. Diagnosis of venoocclusive insufficiency is based on a PMEF of over 20 ml per minute, and diagnosis of venogenic impotence on a PMEF of over 45 ml per minute. Diagnosis of arteriolar dysfunction is based on poor arteriographic visualization of helicine arterioles and amplitude of the cavernosal pulse less than 4.6 mmHg, in the presence of adequate patency of central arteries by arteriography. In cases of arteriolar dysfunction studied with duplex ultrasound, duplex ultrasound has usually demonstrated markedly diminished peak systolic velocity of cavernosal arterial flow and diminished peak acceleration.[28]

Arteriography

A diagnostic penile arteriogram must demonstrate the arterial anatomy from the aorta through at least one cavernosal artery. The initial aortic bifurcation arteriogram is intended to demonstrate the patency of major arteries and to serve as a road map for selective internal pudendal catheterization. The size, patency, and anatomy of the inferior epigastric arteries also should be noted in the event that these arteries may be considered for inferior epigastricodorsal penile arterial bypass.

The major purposes of arteriography is to demonstrate cavernosal arterial patency, and the examination cannot be considered complete or technically adequate until at least one normal or both cavernosal arteries are well demonstrated, along with their arterial sources. Even in the presence of bilaterally hemodynamically significant stenoses or occlusions of the penile arterial supply, the cavernosal arteries are almost always demonstrable via collateral flow if the arteriogram is properly performed. Failure to visualize the cavernosal artery on one or both sides suggests an anomalous origin of the cavernosal arteries and the need for a less selective injection site.

The following arterial anatomy should be observed. The internal iliac arteries divide into anterior and posterior rami. The anterior rami generally divide into three major branches, the obturator, the inferior gluteal, and the internal pudendal arteries. The internal pudendal artery courses laterally within the pelvis, crosses the obturator fossa within Alcock's canal, and after giving origin to the anterior and posterior scrotal

branches becomes the common penile artery. Typically, the branches of each common penile artery (Fig. 42-2) are the bulbar, the dorsal penile, and most importantly, the cavernosal. A single dominant cavernosal artery, sometimes accompanied by a small supplemental artery, is usually visible in the pendulous portion of each corpus cavernosum. In addition, a branch is usually visible within each crus (the cavernosal root that is attached to the ischium).

In normal individuals, a bottle-brush-like profusion of fine arterioles can be visualized arising at right angles from the cavernosal artery, reflecting helicine arterioles approximately 200 μ in diameter (Fig. 42-3). In many patients the helicine arterioles are not well visualized (Fig. 42-4), a feature consistent with functional or organic arteriolar disease. About 5 seconds after onset of the injection, a prominent stain of the corpora cavernosa may be seen, and individual opacified lacunae may be identified on magnification studies. Caveat: As stated previously, helicine arterioles are not well visualized if IC pressure is greater than about 35 mmHg during the arteriogram.

Anatomic variants are common. Supplemental cavernosal or pudendal arteries may arise from the obturator artery, the anterior division of the internal iliac artery, the inferior gluteal artery, or the inferior

Figure 42-2. Diagram of penile artery anatomy. Note that the right internal pudendal artery crosses the obturator foramen in 30-degree anterior oblique projection, a useful iden-

tifying feature. Also note the unlabeled helicine branches of the cavernosal artery and the distal communication of the dorsal penile and cavernosal branches.

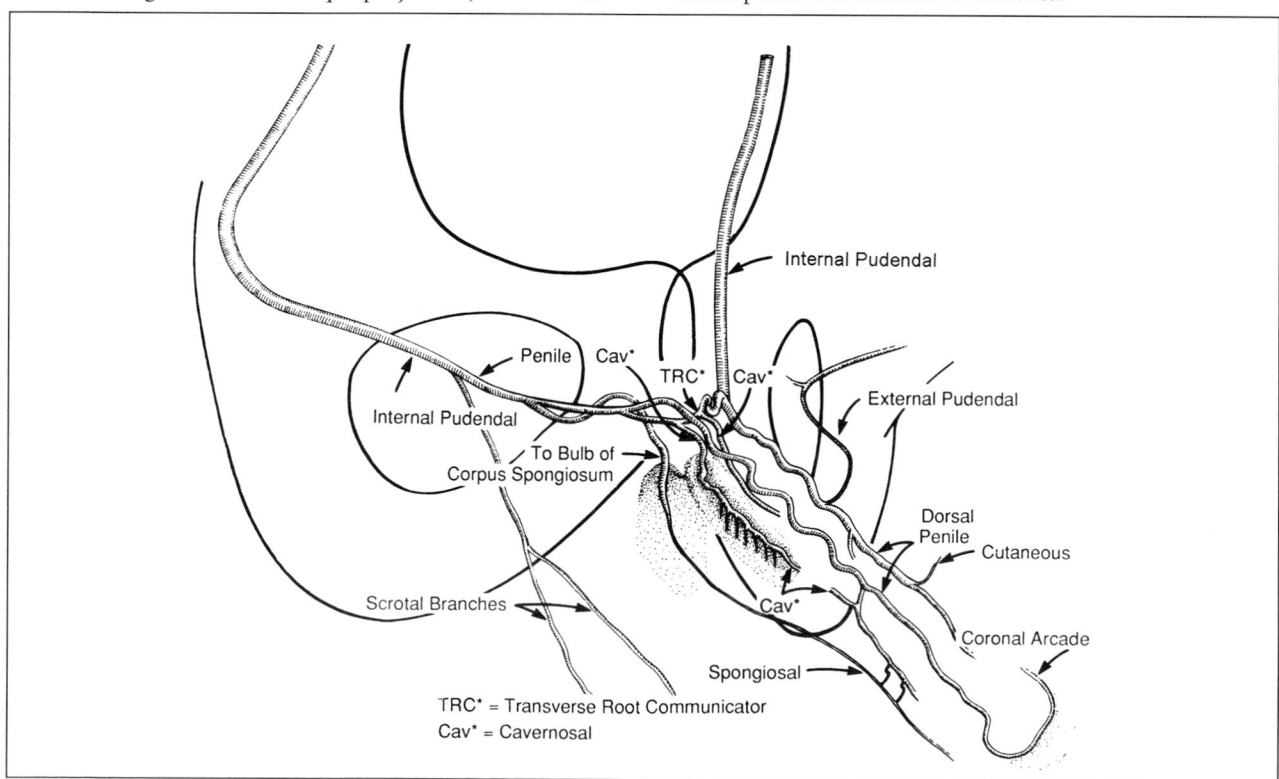

TRC* = Transverse Root Communicator
Cav* = Cavernosal

epigastric artery. Much or all of the cavernosal supply may originate from one common penile artery, in which case the distal ipsilateral dorsal penile artery is often hypoplastic. It is common for a cavernosal artery to supply only the central or crural portion of a corpus cavernosum, whereas the distal corpus may be supplied by a branch from the contralateral cavernosal artery or from a dorsal penile artery. One can distinguish between the cavernosal arterial variant and collateral flow beyond a cavernosal obstruction by noting whether a disproportion exists between the size of the feeding vessel and the recipient cavernosal artery. Gradual uniform tapering of visualized arteries reflects an anatomic variant; tortuous feeders and distal arteries larger than feeders indicate collateral inflow. Whether some cav-

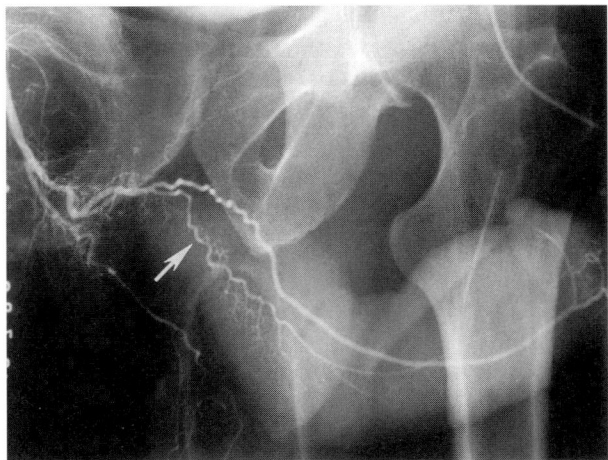

A

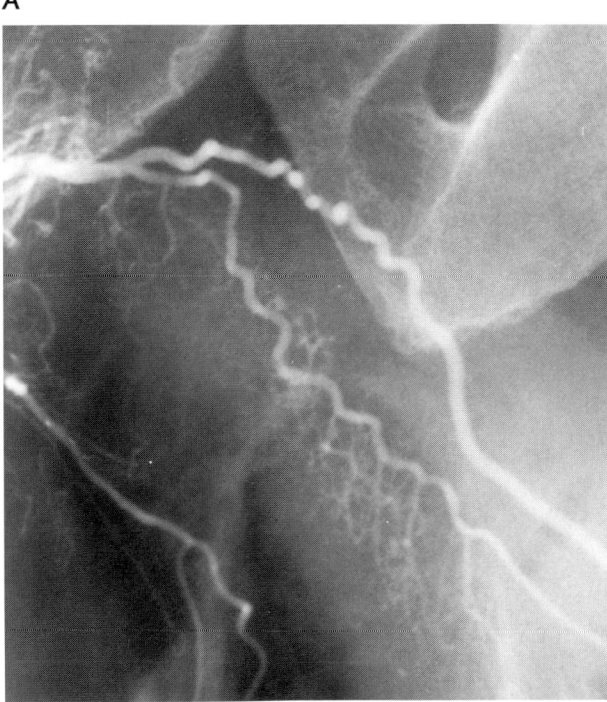

B

ernosal arteries arise from the distal dorsal penile artery, and whether direct communication exists between cavernosal and dorsal penile arteries beyond a central obstruction, may be of critical importance if bypass surgery to the deep dorsal artery is being considered.

Arterial obstruction is evident in over 50 percent of our impotent patients. The obstruction is most frequent in the cavernosal arteries (Fig. 42-5), particularly near their origins, and in the distal internal pudendal artery beyond the origin of the scrotal branches (Figs. 42-6 and 42-7). Not infrequently, the entire cavernosal artery is reduced in caliber, without focal stenoses, possibly reflecting the presence of chronically reduced blood flow.

Collateral arterial flow to the penis and corpora occurs in the presence of penile arterial occlusions (see Figs. 42-6 and 42-7). Relatively central arterial obstructions commonly generate collaterals from the obturator arteries or scrotal branches of the internal pudendal artery, and less commonly from supplemental arteries or the external pudendal artery. Obstructions of the cavernosal arteries at or near their origins generate intrapenile collaterals, such as dorsocavernosal, cavernosal-cavernosal, or urethrocavernosal vessels.

Figure 42-3. Normal selective magnification penile pharmacoarteriogram in a patient with venogenic impotence. (A) Note the large single cavernosal artery (*arrow*) and the prominent branches (helicine arterioles). The dorsal penile artery passes with minimal tapering to the glans. In this case a distal communication between the dorsal penile and cavernosal arteries is not present. (B) Closeup of the central portion of the cavernosal artery seen in (A), better demonstrating the helicine arterioles. (C) Normal mottled cavernosal stain from contralateral injection, reflecting overlapping opacified lacunae. The dorsal penile artery is hypoplastic, a common variant.

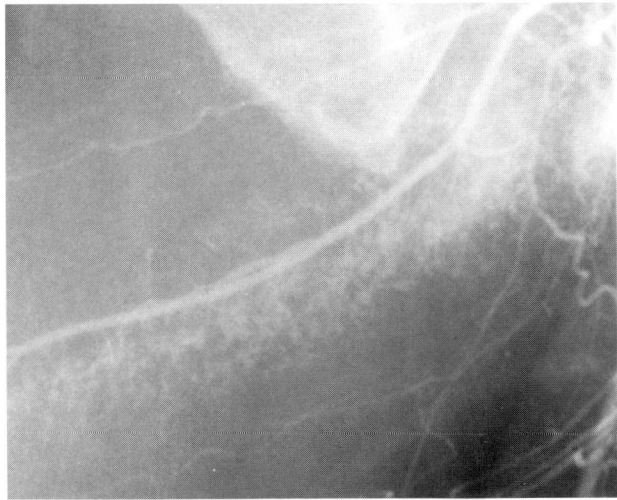

C

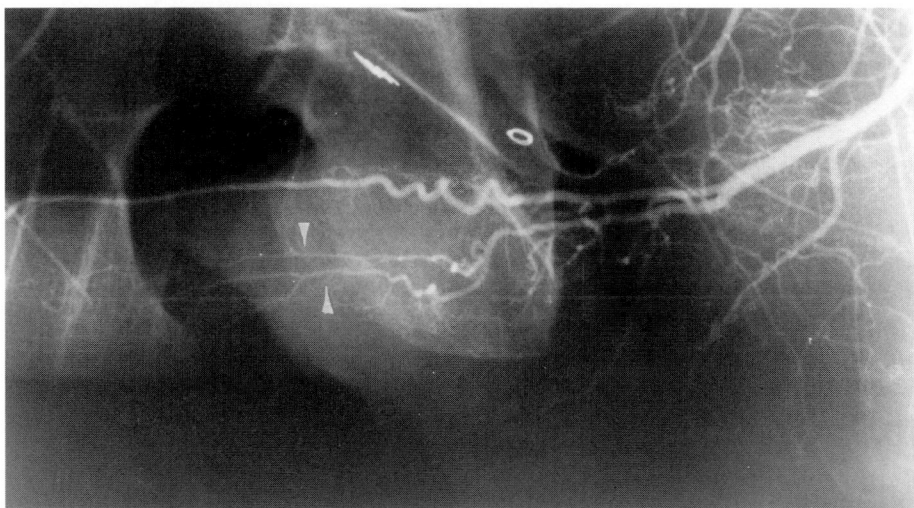

Figure 42-4. Arteriolar dysfunction (suspected arteriolar impotence). The two cavernosal arteries (one in each corpus) arise from the cavernosal trunk, which arises from the left internal pudendal artery (*arrowheads*). Note the narrow caliber of the cavernosal arteries and the absence of visible helicine arterioles.

Figure 42-5. Presumed arteriogenic impotence from cavernosal arterial stenoses (*arrow*) in a 17-year-old rodeo rider. Comparable cavernosal arterial stenoses were present contralaterally. *CP*, common penile; *Bu*, bulbar; *DP*, dorsal penile; *Ca*, cavernosal; *Sp*, spongiosal; *Sc*, scrotal.

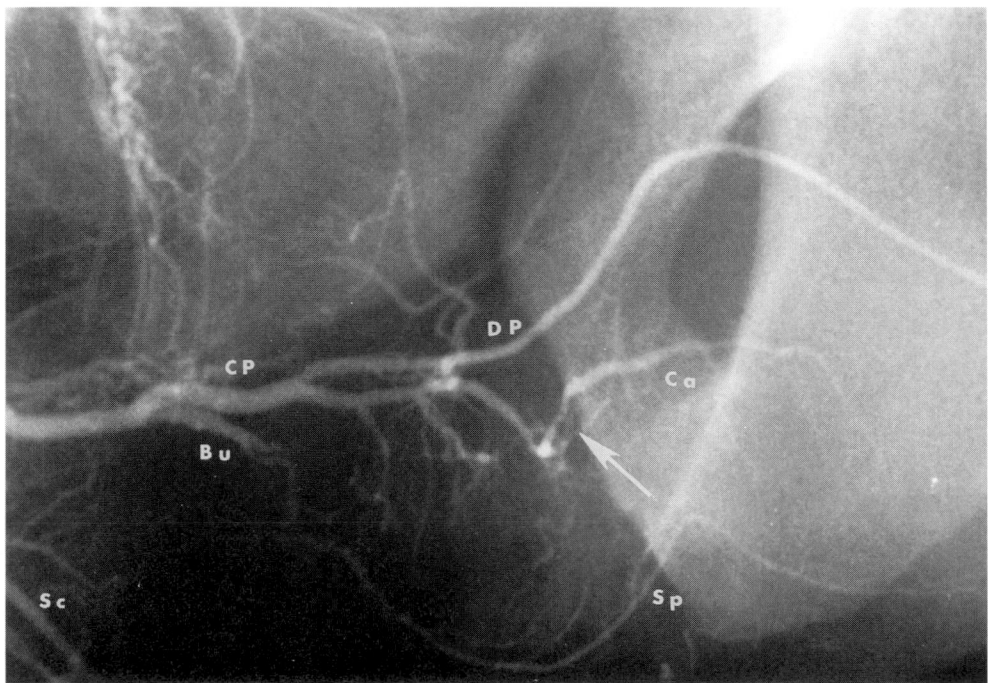

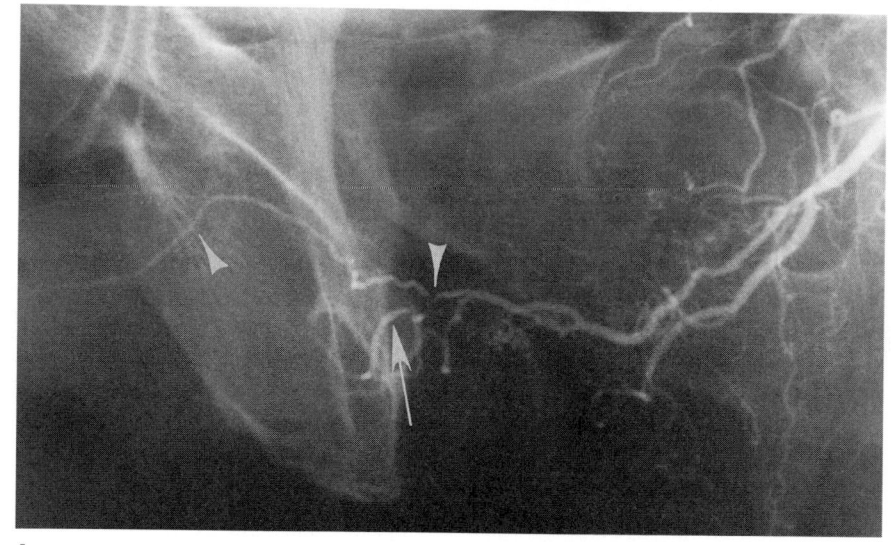

A

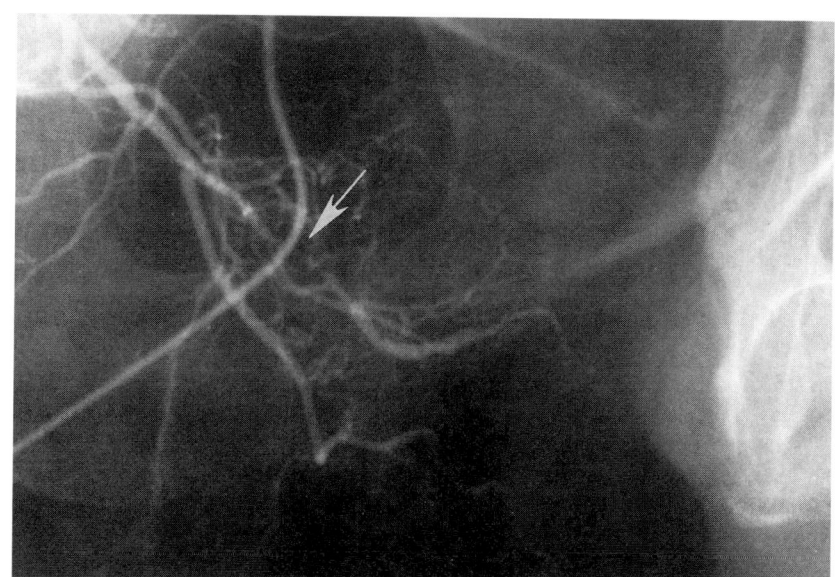

B

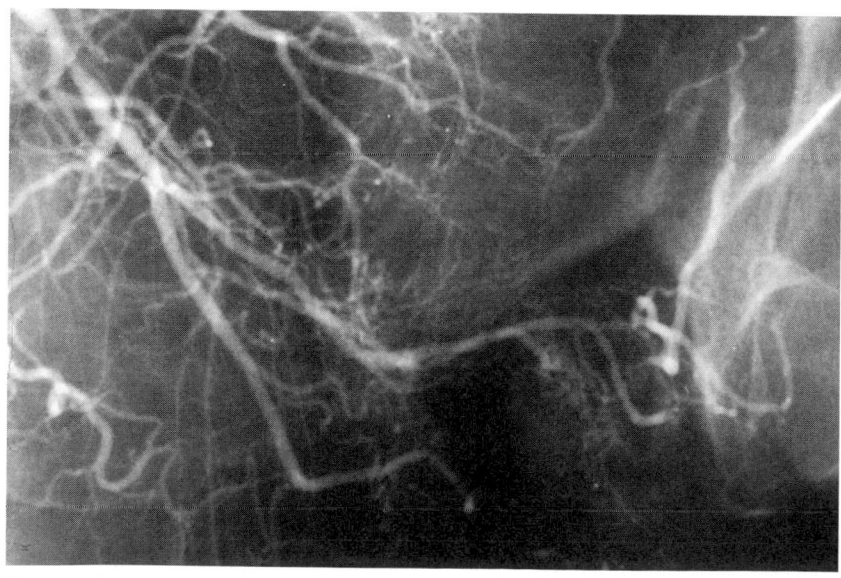

C

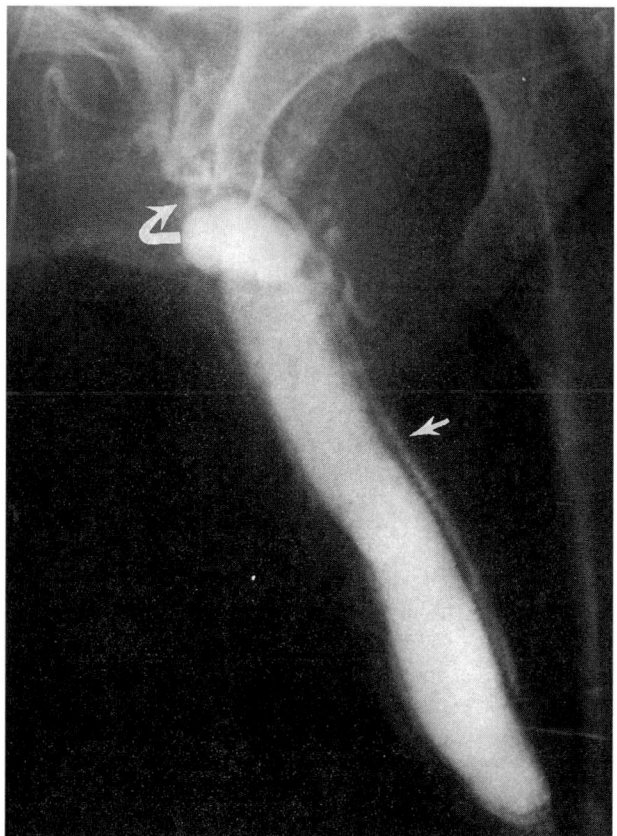

A

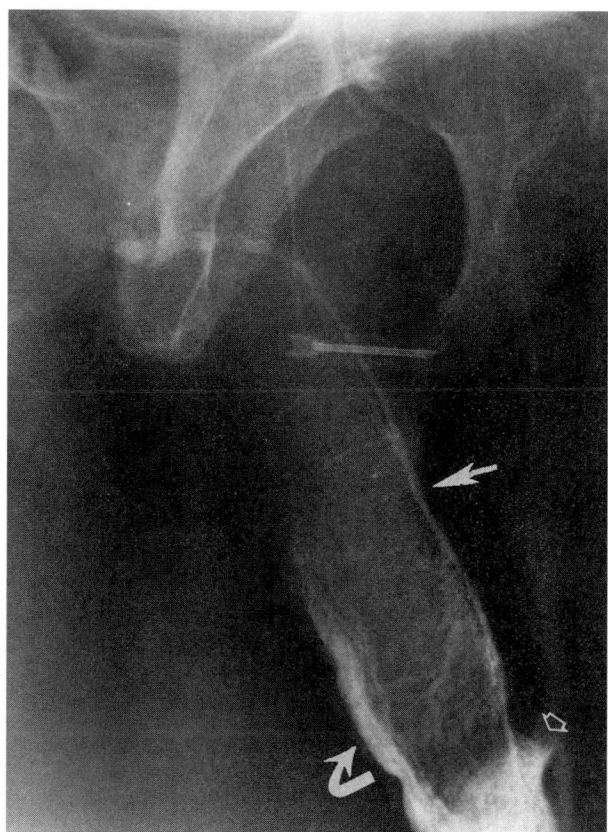

B

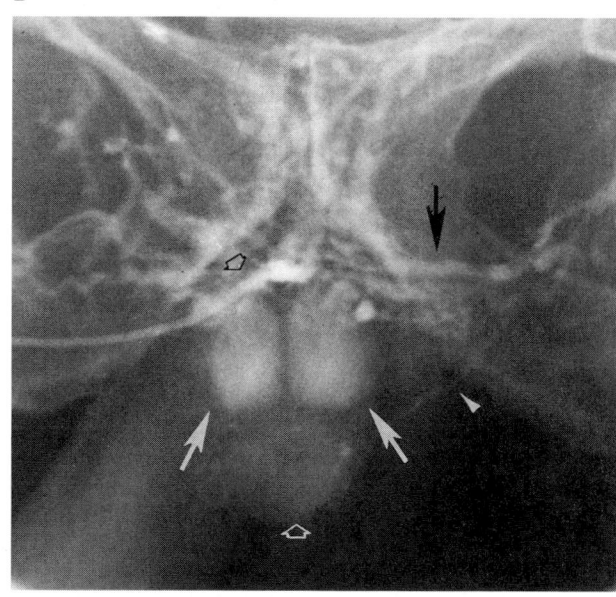

C

Figure 42-7. Elderly man with venogenic and arteriogenic impotence. The estimated PMEF was 240 ml per minute. (A) Pharmacocavernosography demonstrates that leakage occurs via the deep dorsal penile vein (*straight arrow*), and possibly also via crural veins (*curved arrow*). (B) A glansogram was performed to enter the dorsal penile vein percutaneously. (Percutaneous entry was accomplished, although only the operative approach is used currently.) The glans (*open arrow*) drains primarily into the deep dorsal penile vein (*straight arrow*). Also note the corpus spongiosum (*curved arrow*) communicating with the glans, and circumferential veins (unmarked) joining the dorsal penile vein. (C) Injection of contrast into the confluens of the dorsal penile and internal pudendal veins demonstrates the innumerable veins draining the penis and the impracticality of occluding all these veins by coils alone. Thus the anatomic justification for the use of liquid sclerosants such as Sotradecol or alcohol. This venogram, obtained during a Valsalva maneuver, demonstrates reflux of contrast into both corpora (*straight white arrows*) as well as into the corpus spongiosum (*open white arrow*). Note the spongiosal vein draining into the internal pudendal vein (*arrowhead*), the catheter in the dorsal penile vein (*open black arrow*), the internal pudendal vein (*solid black arrow*), and the extensive preprostatic plexus (unmarked).

◀ **Figure 42-6.** Transluminal angioplasty for presumed arteriogenic impotence with excessive cavernosal leakage in a 64-year-old man. (A) Selective left internal pudendal arteriogram demonstrates collateral flow from the small left cavernosal artery to the right (*arrow*), a prominent cavernosal branch from the left deep dorsal penile artery (*upward arrowhead*), and a focal stenosis of the dorsal penile artery (*downward arrowhead*). (B) Right internal pudendal arteriogram demonstrates virtual occlusion of the common penile artery (*arrow*). (C) After angioplasty with a 2-mm balloon, the internal pudendal artery is widely patent. Potency did not improve, however, perhaps because of the associated moderate amount of venous leak. The patient elected not to try venoablation.

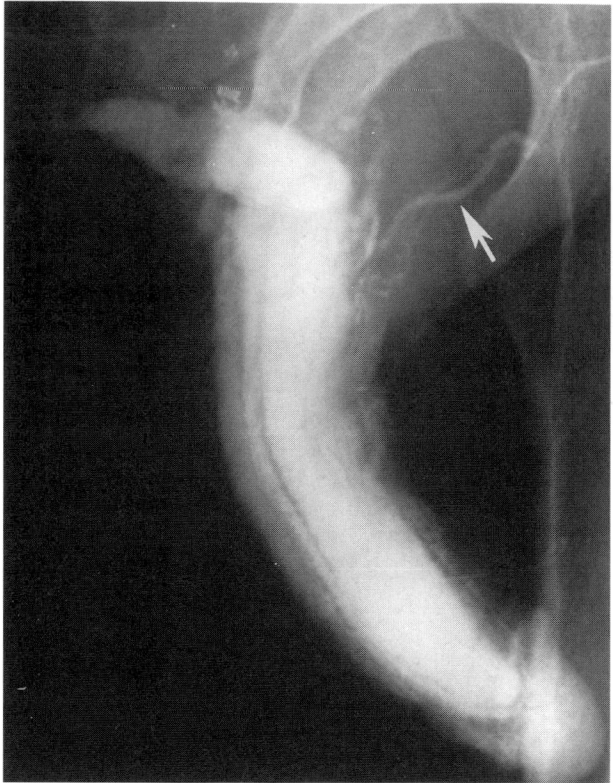

D

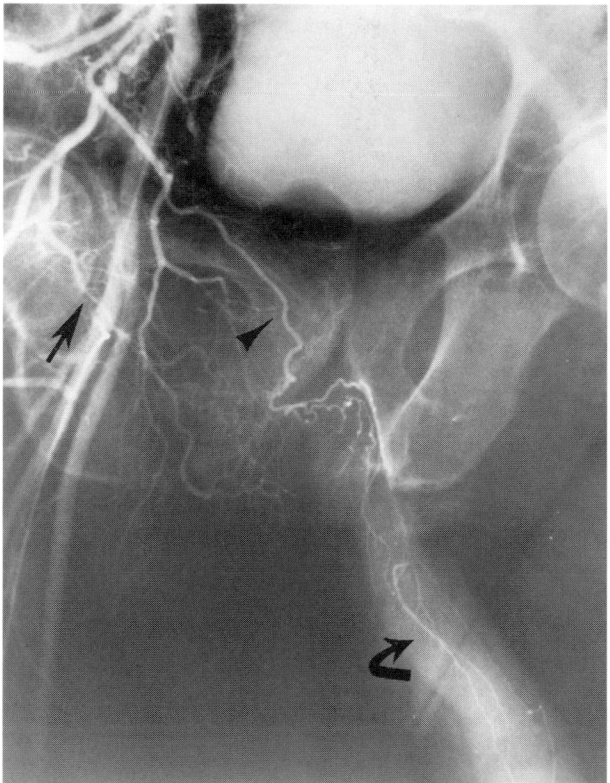

E

Figure 42-7 (continued). (D) Potency improved for a very short time after venoablation. A follow-up study at 8 days indicated decreased leakage. Cavernosography now shows absent opacification of the deep dorsal and crural veins, but the external pudendal vein is now seen (*arrow*). (E) Classic appearance of arteriogenic impotence. The internal pudendal artery on this side is occluded (*straight arrow*), as well as on the contralateral side. Collateral circulation is identified from the obturator artery via a supplemental cavernosal artery (*arrowhead*), which opacified central cavernosal arteries and then, via collaterals, distal cavernosal arteries (*curved arrow*). (From Bookstein JJ, Lurie AL. Transluminal penile venoablation for impotence: a progress report. Cardiovasc Intervent Radiol 1988;11;253–260. Used with permission.)

Pharmacocavernosometry

The primary purpose of cavernosometry is quantitation of the rate of leakage from the corpus cavernosum after pharmacologic relaxation. Two major methods are used in the United States, the pharmacologic maintenance erectile flow (PMEF) method developed by ourselves, and the dynamic infusion cavernosometry method developed by Goldstein.[30] Both methods evaluate cavernosal leakage after pharmacologic cavernosal relaxation. We prefer the PMEF method, in which leakage is expressed in terms of milliliters per minute. In this method, the PMEF equals the infusion rate required to maintain IC pressure at 150 mmHg. Our clinical experience suggests that the normal PMEF is less than 10 ml per minute. Young patients often have rates as low as 2 to 6 ml per minute. Reliable data regarding the significance of leaks at various rates are not available. From limited numbers of normal volunteers, and from limited data indicating responses to arterial revascularization despite some venous leak, we believe that leaks of less than 20 ml per minute are not clinically significant in the absence of coexistent arterial or arteriolar disease, and that leaks of more than 45 ml per minute will always produce venogenic impotence.

Some investigators determine the PMEF at 80 mmHg, a more physiologic erection pressure than we use. Based on a very few records, the normal PMEF at this level is probably less than 5 ml per minute. Others determine the PMEF at IC pressure of 100 or 125 mmHg, where the normal PMEF is presumably between 5 and 10 ml per minute. Some investigators express cavernosal venoocclusive function in terms of cavernosal resistance, a parameter derived from the PMEF.[31]

The method of dynamic infusion cavernosometry quantifies leakage in terms of the rate of fall of the cavernosal pressure after abrupt cessation of the IC infusion.[30] A pressure decrement of less than 1.5 mmHg per second at an IC pressure of about 100 mmHg is considered normal. Results are influenced by a number of variables other than the amount of venous leak, such as the amount of arterial inflow or the coefficient of elasticity of the tunica albuginea. We have found the method correlates imperfectly with the PMEF.

All pharmacologic manometric methods make two basic assumptions: (1) there is free communication between the two corpora so that relaxant injected into one corpus diffuses into the other, and (2) the dose of relaxant injected is sufficient to achieve maximal relaxation of the cavernosal musculature, regardless of anxiety or other psychologic parameters. Our experience indicates that assumption 1 is valid. Free communication is almost always evident on cavernosography, except in patients with hypospadias or epispadias. Lack of free communication can be recognized when only one corpus becomes rigid after unilateral saline infusion.

With regard to assumption 2, experience indicates that this assumption is not completely justified. The standard dose of 60 mg of papaverine admixed with 1 mg of phentolamine has been assumed to produce full pharmacologic relaxation. The adequacy of this dose is suggested by the fact that a dose of only 1/45 this amount, namely, 1.2 mg of papaverine alone, as given during our investigational low-dose studies, produces about two-thirds as much venoocclusion as the full dose of papaverine plus phentolamine.[27] In a few patients in whom venoocclusion was measured after both 60 and 120 mg of papaverine, no significant further venoocclusive competency occurred. However, in several patients in whom the PMEF after the usual dose of papaverine/phentolamine was compared with the PMEF after a much smaller dose of papaverine/phentolamine admixed with 10 μg of prostaglandin E$_1$ (PGE$_1$), significant further reduction of leakage was observed. We also suspect that extremely nervous patients are resistant to IC smooth muscle relaxants, and for this reason the patients are mildly sedated with midazolam during the procedure. In canine experiments,[27] it was observed that intravenous infusion of norepinephrine in doses that raised blood pressure only 20 mmHg significantly inhibited the venoocclusive effects of 5 mg IC papaverine. Thus there is substantial evidence that the standard dose of papaverine/phentolamine may fail to produce maximal venoocclusion.

Cavernosal Pulse Amplitude

Observation of the cavernosal pulse amplitude (CPA) yields useful information when cavernosometry is performed by PMEF methods (Fig. 42-8). Although the significance of diminished pulsations has not been well studied, we have concluded by deduction that the pulse amplitude reflects the degree of arterial patency from the aorta through the helicine arterioles. Certain pitfalls, mentioned above, must be avoided. Correlation between final diagnosis and CPA is indicated in Table 42-2. The CPA is often unobtainable in patients with marked venous leak, a fact which explains the paucity of patients with venoocclusive insufficiency included in Table 42-2.

The CPA is useful primarily when interpreted in conjunction with the arteriogram. For example, a normal CPA in the presence of a central arterial stenosis suggests that the stenosis is not hemodynamically significant. A diminished CPA in the presence of arteriographically normal central arteries and diminished prominence of helicine arterioles offers further evidence in support of a diagnosis of arteriolar dysfunction.

Cavernosography

Injection of contrast medium into the corpus cavernosum without prior injection of vasorelaxant will usually demonstrate free flow into all external draining veins, and little or no diagnostic information is provided. Thus cavernosography performed for evaluation of impotence should almost always mean pharmacocavernosography.

Pharmacocavernosography is primarily used to demonstrate the routes of cavernosal leakage in the event that surgical or transluminal venoablative therapy is planned. This anatomy is depicted diagrammatically in Figure 42-9. It must be emphasized that pharmacocavernosometry, not pharmacocavernosography, is the method for determining the presence and amount of cavernosal venoocclusive insufficiency. Prolonged contrast injections at a rate equal to the PMEF will result in opacification of venous drainage even in normal individuals. Thus mere visualization of venous drainage during pharmacocavernosometry does not necessarily indicate abnormal venoocclusive competence.

As performed clinically, cavernosography does not ordinarily enable one to identify individual leaking emissary (perforating) venules, although these can be demonstrated by retrograde venous catheterization when they are incompetent (Figs. 42-10 and 42-11). But the larger external (secondary) routes of venous drainage, that is, the dorsal penile vein, crural veins, and internal pudendal, preprostatic, and vesical veins, as well as superficial penile and external pudendal veins, can be readily identified in patients with

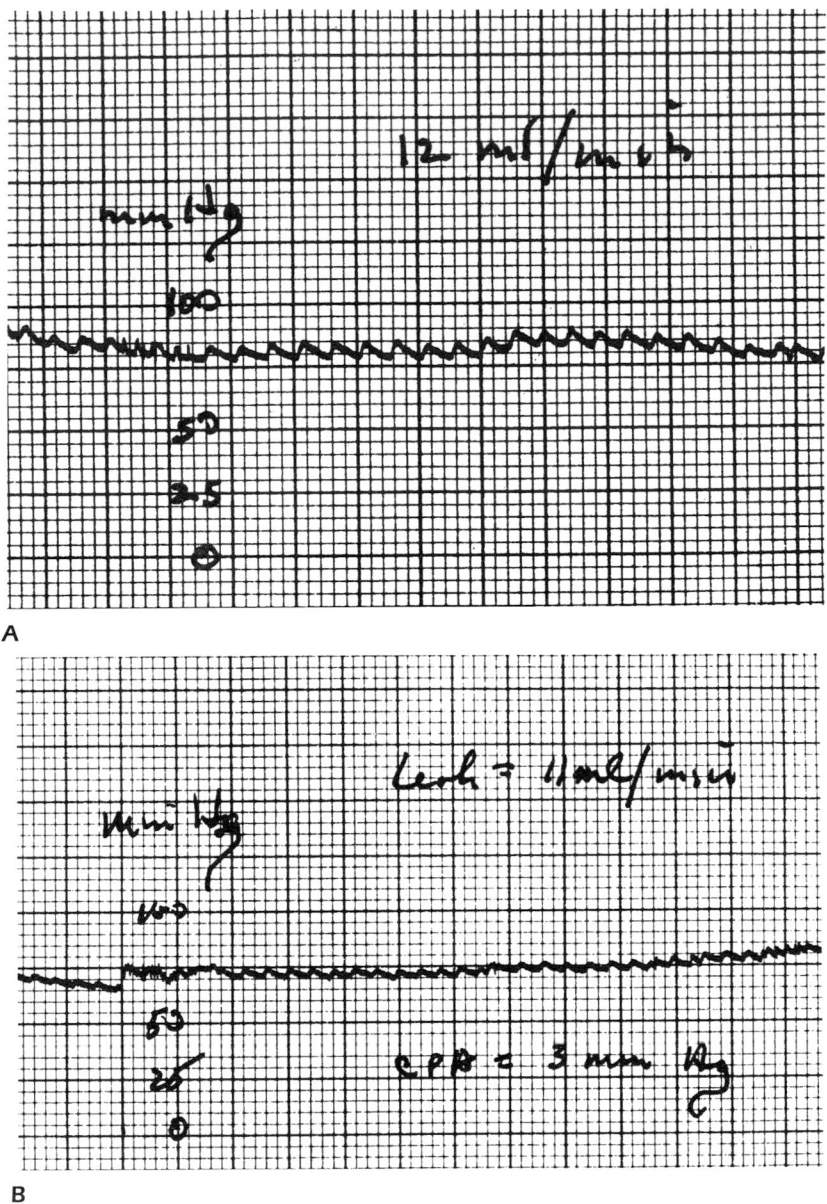

A

B

Figure 42-8. Cavernosal pulse amplitudes. (A) Normal 5-mm pulse amplitude in a patient with mildly increased venous leak (PMEF = 12 ml per minute). The amplitude is determined at IC pressure of about 85 mmHg, the level at which the pulse amplitude is usually maximal. (B) Diminished pulse amplitude (3 mm) in a patient with arteriolar dysfunction (same patient as Fig. 42-3), as well as a PMEF elevated to 11 ml per minute.

Table 42-2. Cavernosal Pulse Amplitude

Final Diagnosis	Amplitude Cavernosal Pulse	No. of Cases
Normal	4.6 ± 0.8 mmHg	9
Arterial insufficiency	2.5 ± 1.5 mmHg*	27
Venoocclusive insufficiency	2.6 ± 1.4 mmHg*	5
Arteriolar dysfunction	1.3 ± 1.6 mmHg*	11
Endothelial dysfunction	2.9 ± 1.7 mmHg*	14

*$p < .05$ from normal values.

significant leak. Demonstration of the major external routes of drainage helps determine the approach to be used for transluminal or operative venoablation. When warranted, the best demonstration of penile venous anatomy is achieved by selective venography, as employed routinely during transluminal venoablation (see below).[32]

In patients with significant venoocclusive insufficiency, more than one route of external drainage is usually visible. Drainage via both crural and dorsal penile routes is evident in most cases. The crural veins

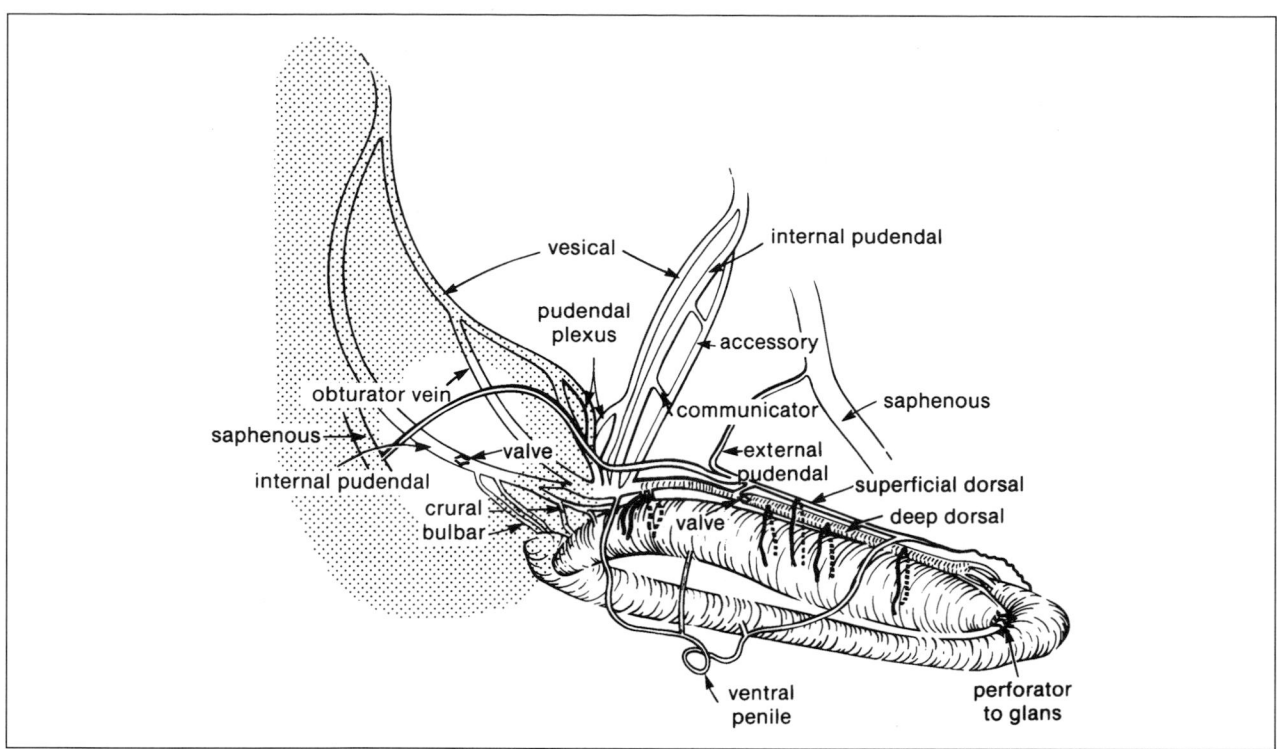

Figure 42-9. Diagram of the external penile venous anatomy. (From Bookstein JJ, Lurie AL. Selective penile venography: anatomical and hemodynamic observations. J Urol 1988;140:55–60. Used with permission.)

(see Figs. 42-9 and 42-10) can usually be faintly identified draining into the internal pudendal veins, and then centrally to the preprostatic plexus, or laterally to the internal iliac veins. Surgical ablation of this venous route is possible but requires deep and extensive dissection and ligation of many deep venules.

The midline deep dorsal penile vein is usually easily recognized on cavernosography (see Figs. 42-7 and 42-11) paralleling the superior surface of the corpus cavernosum and draining into the preprostatic plexus. Surgical obstruction of this route of flow is easily accomplished by simple ligation, often supplemented by venous excision and ligation of circumflex veins. Cavernosal leakage may be partially or predominantly into the corpus spongiosum, a situation that has been treated by the heroic procedure of spongiolysis, in which ligation of all cavernosal-spongiosal veins is attempted. Finally, abnormal leakage may occur predominantly via superficial penile and external pudendal veins (see Fig. 42-11). In addition to operative ligation, transluminal venoablation also enables obstruction of crural, dorsal penile, internal pudendal, preprostatic, and superficial venous routes. No transluminal method is known for ablating cavernosal-spongiosal routes.

Duplex Sonography

Modern duplex sonographic instrumentation now makes possible visualization of the cavernosal arteries, providing a relatively noninvasive method for evaluating the cavernosal arterial supply, and perhaps also venous leakage.[14,30] The critical determinant of arterial adequacy is generally considered to be the peak systolic velocity of cavernosal arterial flow after IC injection of a vasorelaxant such as 60 mg papaverine or 10 μg prostaglandin E_1. Acceleration has also been identified as a useful criterion. Peak linear velocity over 25 cm per second or (in our experience) acceleration over 400 cm per second per second[28] has been considered the threshold of arterial adequacy. Unfortunately, sonographic-clinical[33] or sonographic-arteriographic[34] correlations have been poor in some reports, and the accuracy of sonographic indices has not been well established.

We performed a study correlating cavernosal sonography with selective magnification pharmacoarteriography in 30 patients.[28] Using the above threshold for peak systolic velocity, duplex sonography was only 35 percent sensitive and 61 percent specific in diagnosing *arterial* obstruction. Acceleration was more reliable, with a sensitivity of 100 percent and a specificity

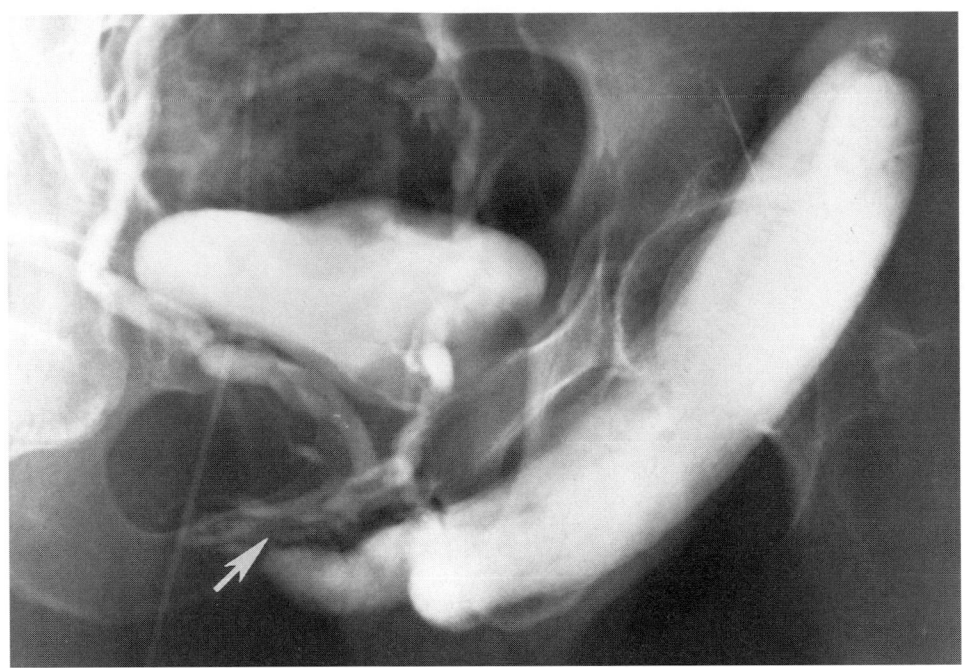

A

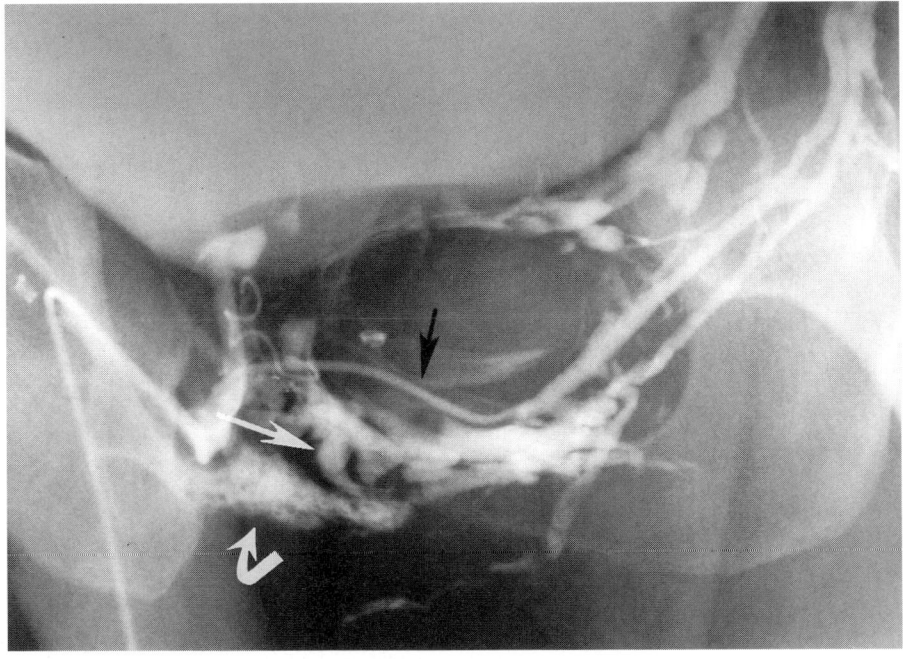

B

Figure 42-10. A 28-year-old man with excessive venous leak (PMEF = 60 ml per minute). (A) Cavernosography demonstrates a leak primarily via the crural veins (*arrow*), which drain via the internal pudendal veins into the preprostatic plexus veins. (B) Selective oblique internal pudendal venogram taken during a Valsalva maneuver more clearly demonstrates the anatomy of the crural drainage. Note the catheter in one of the two internal pudendal venae comitantes (*black arrow*), one of multiple short crural veins (*straight white arrow*), and reflux into the crus of the corpus cavernosum (*curved white arrow*). (C) Cavernosography after 1 week shows multiple coils in place, only minimal venous drainage via a right obturator vein (*arrow*), and obliteration of the preprostatic plexus. Erectile function had improved clinically.

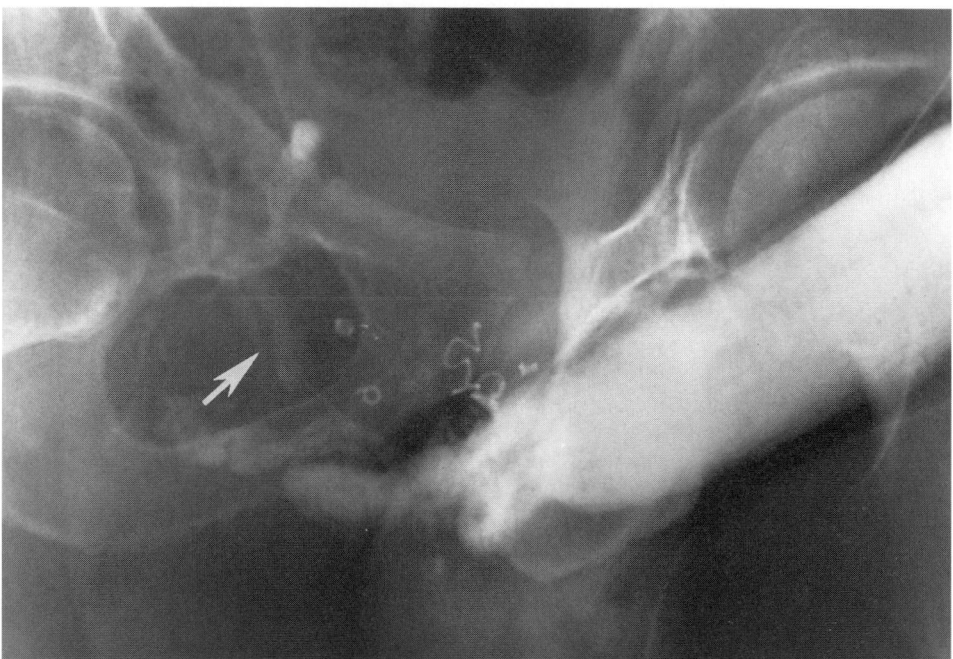

C   **Figure 42-10** (continued).

of 46 percent. However, neither index enabled one to reliably differentiate *arterial* from *arteriolar* insufficiency. Thus duplex sonography showed some promise as a screening method but did not reliably differentiate between potential surgical disease (i.e., central arterial obstruction) and nonsurgical arteriolar insufficiency. In conjunction with penile vascular catheterization, however, duplex sonography proved helpful in confirming the presence of arteriolar disease (i.e., diminished flow despite normal arteries) or in confirming the significance of central arterial obstruction.

A more comprehensive discussion of cavernosal duplex sonography, including its possible role in identifying venoocclusive insufficiency, is beyond the scope of this chapter.

Transluminal Therapy

Prior Reported Experience

To date, no large-scale study has shown the value of either angioplasty of the iliac or internal pudendal artery or transcatheter venoablation for the treatment of impotence. In our recent review of published experience after angioplasty for impotence,[35] favorable responses were reported in 27 of 47 (68 percent) cases after iliac angioplasty, and 7 of 17 (41 percent) cases after angioplasty of the internal pudendal artery. However, these reports were largely anecdotal and objective confirmation of improved erectile function was not provided.

Figure 42-11. A 29-year-old man who developed impotence after being struck in the penis by a recoiling cable. Cavernosography demonstrates a localized leak into superficial penile veins (*arrows*) that drain via the external pudendal veins into the saphenous veins. Note the minimal opacification of the deep dorsal penile vein (*open arrow*) and no opacification of the deep pelvic veins (internal pudendal or preprostatic). The patient was cured by ligation of the deep dorsal penile vein and several nearby superficial veins. (From Lurie AL, Bookstein JJ, Kessler WO. Post-traumatic impotence: angiographic evaluation. Radiology 1987;165:115–119. Used with permission.)

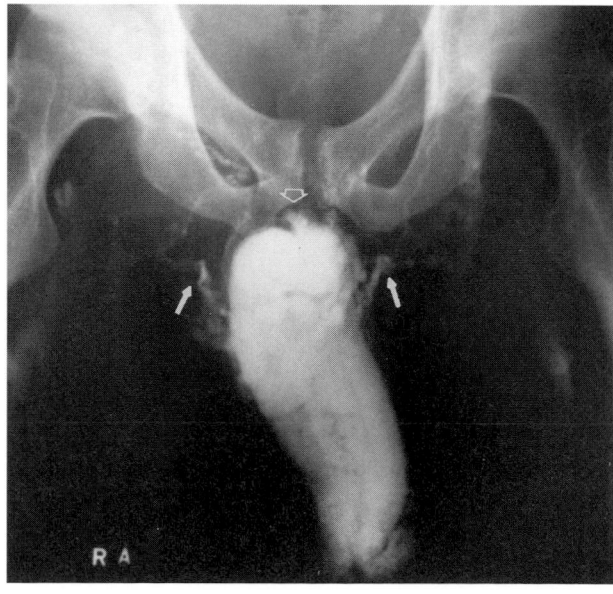

After transcatheter venoablation success was reported in 65 to 84 percent in four small series of cases.[36-39] Again, objective documentation of improvement was not provided.

Transluminal Angioplasty

Case Selection

We believe the following diagnostic criteria should be met before transluminal angioplasty (TLA) is considered.

1. Arteriograms must be of excellent quality and performed by pharmacoangiographic methods.
2. There must be arteriographic evidence of bilateral hemodynamically significant obstructions of the vascular supply to the corpora cavernosa, as defined in earlier sections.
3. The anatomy must be suitable for catheterization and angioplasty on at least one side. Involved vessels should not be less than 1.5 mm in diameter, obstructions should be shorter than 2.5 cm, and the midcavernosal artery should be at least 0.6 mm in diameter after correction for magnification.
4. The distal cavernosal arteries should be patent, and the helicine arterioles should appear normally prominent.
5. The venoocclusive mechanism must be relatively competent (PMEF <30 ml/minute).

Methodology for Distal Penile TLA

At our institution, angioplasty is performed on an inpatient basis at a session separate from the diagnostic study. Because of the small size of the target artery and the limited arterial flow during the sexually quiescent posttherapeutic state, the risk of arterial thrombosis is high, and anticoagulant and antiplatelet therapy is indicated during and after the procedure. Patients are pretreated with aspirin (300 mg/day) and dipyridamole (75 mg tid) for 2 days before the procedure, and for 3 months thereafter. Heparin is administered during the procedure and for 18 hours afterward. Nifedipine and low-molecular-weight dextran can also play a role. In an effort to inhibit restenosis, alpha-omega-3 fish oil supplements have been administered in the last six cases. The evidence supporting the value of fish oils for this purpose is inconclusive.[40]

Relatively standard angioplasty techniques are used for dilating larger arteries such as the internal or common iliac arteries. For transluminal angioplasty of small arteries, such as the distal internal pudendal, common penile, or proximal cavernosal arteries, special methods are required. Balloon catheters as small as 1.5 to 2.0 mm in diameter are available (Probe catheter, USCI; Scimed) that will pass through a 5.3 French diagnostic catheter (Cordis, Inc.). Special sheaths, guiding catheters, and torqueable guidewires are frequently required. Detailed consideration of this methodology is beyond the scope of this chapter. It is also possible to dilate the internal pudendal artery via a retrograde approach from a dorsal penile cutdown, an approach that was used in one patient undergoing simultaneous transluminal venoablation.

Results

At our institution, 10 impotent patients with disease of small penile arteries have undergone 12 angioplasty sessions to date on 16 arteries. An example is shown in Figure 42-6. The arteries dilated in the 10 patients were the internal pudendal (3), common penile (8), cavernosal origin (4), and the dorsal penile (1). From the technical point of view, at least one artery was successfully dilated in 8 of 12 sessions. Complete technical failures were attributable to inability to pass a stenosis in two cases, inability to penetrate an occluded cavernosal artery origin in one case, and production of obstructive dissection in one case.

Marked improvement was reported by the patient in five instances, and moderate improvement in one instance (in association with venoablation). Of the five instances of marked improvement, relapse occurred after 3 months in the three instances in which fish oil supplements had not been administered. In the remaining three instances of marked or moderate improvement, fish oil supplements had been administered, and improvement had persisted 6, 18, and 47 months as of last follow-up.

Transluminal Penile Venoablation

At our institution, penile venoablation has been performed in 48 patients, with PMEF ranging from 10 to 300 ml per minute (see Figs. 42-7 and 42-10). Except for 2 patients in whom both angioplasty and venoablation were performed, these patients had essentially normal arteriograms. The methodology has been previously reported.[36] In most patients the procedure was performed via a dorsal penile cutdown under local anesthesia on an outpatient basis. Caveat: Differentiation of the dorsal penile artery from vein by visual inspection can be difficult or impossible, and fluoroscopic documentation of venous catheterization via a small injection of contrast medium through a butterfly needle is advisable if any question exists to avoid accidental catheterization or even sclerosis of the arterial system. A 4.5 French catheter with a short "hockeystick" distal curve is passed via the deep dorsal penile vein into the confluens of the deep dorsal, internal pudendal, crural, and preprostatic veins. After control venography from the confluens, the major draining veins are selectively catheterized. A curved low-friction guidewire is of great value. As each major vein is catheterized, it is occluded by deposition of one or more Gianturco coils (Cook, Inc.), usually 3 to 5 mm in diameter. The crural veins cannot usually be directly catheterized, and these veins, along with innumerable small others, are obstructed by sclerosants injected in their vicinity: 3 percent sodium tetradecyl sulfate (Sotradecol, Elkin-Sinn), absolute alcohol, or boiling contrast agent. *Warning: Temporary damage of the dorsal penile nerve occurred in one case after transcatheter injection of hot contrast medium, probably due to inadvertent approximation of catheter and nerve.* We have found that moderate doses of fentanyl and midazolam produce adequate anesthesia for injection of alcohol or boiling contrast agent, and Sotradecol injection is painless. When cavernosography has demonstrated prominent drainage via the superficial veins, these veins are also ablated with sclerosants. Our results are presented in Table 42-3.

In seven patients in whom the dorsal penile vein had been previously occluded by surgery or transcatheter methods, the confluens was catheterized in retrograde fashion via the femoral and internal iliac veins.

Multiple parameters were evaluated in an effort to identify indices predictive of therapeutic results: cause of impotence, age, duration of impotence, amplitude of cavernosal pulse, and PMEF. Lower PMEF, younger age, and higher amplitude of cavernosal pressure pulse were marginally favorable factors, but no indices could be found that reliably predicted success or failure of venoablation.

Follow-up pharmacocavernosometry and pharmacocavernosography were performed in 24 patients 1 to 12 months after transluminal venoablation. Correlation between absolute or increased cavernosal resistance and clinical response was poor (Table 42-4).

Table 42-3. Transcatheter Venoablation: 48 Patients with over 3-Month Follow-up

Return of potency with or without drugs	26/48 (54%)
Return of potency without drugs	22/48 (46%)
Erections considered good	8/22 (36%)
Erections considered adequate	14/22 (64%)
Loss of potency after cure at 3, 4, 7, 9, 14 months	5/22 (23%)
Improved nocturnal erections	29/48 (60%)
Continued potency without drugs	17/48 (35%)
Duration improvement last follow-up	3–35 months
Diminution of potency	2/17 at 7 months

From Bookstein JJ, Valji K. Transluminal therapeutic interventions in vasculogenic impotence. In: Papanicolaou N, ed. Radiology of impotence and infertility. Philadelphia: Lippincott, 1992:631–644. Used with permission.

Table 42-4. Follow-up Cavernosal Studies: 24 Cases 1 to 12 Months After Transluminal Venoablation

Parameter	Potent (*n* = 14)	Not Potent (*n* = 10)
Resistance (p/PMEF) pre-Rx	7.2 ± 12.7 mmHg/ml	1.5 ± 2.3 mmHg/ml
Resistance post-Rx	8.1 ± 12.6	2.1 ± 2.2
Mean change in resistance	1.0 ± 1.9	0.6 ± 1.4
Occluded deep veins on cavernosography (1–4+)	3.5	3.1

p = pressure; PMEF = pharmacologic maintenance erectile flow.
From Bookstein JJ, Valji K. Transluminal therapeutic interventions in vasculogenic impotence. In: Papanicolaou N, ed. Radiology of impotence and infertility. Philadelphia: Lippincott, 1992:631–644. Used with permission.

Implications of Suboptimal Results of Transcatheter Therapy

The specific diagnosis of arterial or venoocclusive insufficiency by the above criteria does not appear to lead to consistently specific and effective therapy. These suboptimal therapeutic results could be due to limitations of the therapeutic methods themselves. The arterial bypasses may fail to remain patent, or prompt development of venous collaterals may obviate the benefit of venoablative procedures.

But perhaps the problem lies with the basic penile paradigm itself. It is well known that chronic slowing of renal arterial blood flow, as, for example, flow to atrophic glomerulonephritic kidneys, will produce accelerated atherosclerosis of the main and segmental renal arteries. Perhaps the arterial obstructions observed angiographically in impotent patients are not the primary cause of impaired flow, but instead reflect accelerated atherosclerosis due to chronically slowed penile blood flow *secondary to* impotence. The possibility also must be considered that venoocclusive insufficiency is only part of a more global functional deficiency of smooth muscle relaxation that involves cavernosal arterioles as well as cavernosal lacunae.

As indicated above, there is considerable reason to suspect that the primary site of dysfunction is frequently at the arteriolar level.[16] By simple logic, erectile dysfunction may be attributed to arteriolar obstruction if after IC injection of smooth muscle relaxant (1) the venoocclusive mechanism is found to be competent, (2) the arteries are fully patent arteriographically, and (3) erection does not develop. More objective evidence in support of an arteriolar dysfunctional component in impotence is the following.

1. Many patients show diminished cavernosal pulse amplitude despite angiographically normal central arteries.

2. These patients usually demonstrate inconspicuous helicine arterioles on magnification cavernosal arteriography.

3. These patients usually demonstrate diminished peak systolic velocity of cavernosal arterial flow and diminished peak acceleration by ultrasonography.[28]

The microscopic basis of arteriolar dysfunction has not been clarified. Although several descriptions of pads or polsters in the helicine arterioles have been published that could account for diminished arteriolar patency,[37-39] the existence of such structures is not uniformly accepted.[40] The lack of clear histologic evidence of arteriolar disease suggests that the arteriolar constriction might be functional. Perhaps the lack of arteriolar dilation is related to the recently identified deficiency of EDRF in many impotent patients.[4,15,27] It is apparent that concepts regarding erectile insufficiency are in a state of flux and await further guidance from well-conducted experimental and clinical studies and advances in the basic science of erectile physiology.

Summary

Understanding of erectile physiology has advanced considerably over the past decade. Along with this advance, and contributing importantly to it, have been advances in penile angiography and penile vascular catheterization. These recent advances led to the development of a new paradigm of erectile dysfunction that has largely replaced the old psychogenic paradigm. The new paradigm attributes much of the problem of impotence to dysfunction of vascular components. It was hoped and expected that identification of these vascular components would lead to specific vascular corrective procedures. But the vascular corrective procedures developed to date have not resulted in a high rate of therapeutic success. The lack of therapeutic success prompts the development of further concepts regarding erectile dysfunction and may lead to an alternative paradigm that emphasizes functional or organic arteriolar disease.

References

1. Lue TF, Zeineh SJ, Schmidt RA, Tanagho EA. Neuroanatomy of penile erection: its relevance to iatrogenic impotence. J Urol 1984;131:273–280.
2. Steers WD. Neural control of penile erection. Semin Urol 1990;8:66–79.
3. Aboseif SR, Lue TF. Fundamentals and hemodynamics of penile erection. Cardiovasc Intervent Radiol 1988;11:185–190.
4. Rajfer J, Aronson WJ, Bush PA, Dorey FJ, Ignarro LJ. Nitric oxide as a mediator of relaxation of the corpus cavernosum in response to nonadrenergic, noncholinergic neurotransmission. N Engl J Med 1992;326:90–94.
5. Fournier GR, Juenemann KP, Lue TF, Tanagho EA. Mechanisms of venous occlusion during canine penile erection: an anatomic demonstration. J Urol 1987;137:163–167.
6. Brindley GS. Pilot experiments on the actions of drugs injected into the human corpus cavernosum penis. Br J Pharmacol 1986;87:495–500.
7. Virag R. Intracavernous injection of papaverine for erectile failure. Lancet 1982;2:938.
8. Zorgniotti AW, Rossi G, Padula G, Makovsky RD. Diagnosis and therapy of vasculogenic impotence. J Urol 1980;123:674–676.
9. Lue TF, Takamura T, Umraiya M, Schmidt RA, Tanagho EA. Hemodynamics of erection in the monkey. J Urol 1983;130:1237–1241.
10. Bookstein JJ, Valji K, Parsons L, Kessler W. Pharmacoarteriography in the evaluation of impotence. J Urol 1987;137:333–337.
11. Bookstein JJ, Fellmeth B, Moreland S, Lurie AL. Pharmacoangiographic assessment of the corpora cavernosa. Cardiovasc Intervent Radiol 1988;11:218–224.
12. Bookstein JJ. Cavernosal venoocclusive insufficiency in male impotence: evaluation of degree and location. Radiology 1987;164:175–178.
13. Lue TF. Intracavernous drug administration: its role in diagnosis and treatment of impotence. Semin Urol 1990;8:100–106.
14. Lue TF, Hricak H, Marich KW, Tanagho EA. Vasculogenic impotence evaluated by high-resolution ultrasonography and pulsed Doppler spectrum analysis. Radiology 1985;155:777–781.
15. Saenz de Tejada I, Goldstein I, Azadzoi K, Krane RJ, Cohen RA. Impaired neurogenic and endothelium-mediated relaxation of penile smooth muscle from diabetic men with impotence. N Engl J Med 1989;320:1025–1030.
16. Bookstein JJ, Valji K. The arteriolar component in impotence: a possible paradigm shift. AJR 1991;157:932–934.
17. Ginestie J-F, Romieu A. Radiologic exploration of impotence. The Hague: Martinus Nijhoff, 1978.
18. Bookstein JJ. Penile angiography: the last angiographic frontier. AJR 1988;150:47–54.
19. Rosen MP, et al. Arteriogenic impotence: findings in 195 impotent men examined with selective internal pudendal angiography. Radiology 1990;174:1043–1048.
20. Michal V, Kramar R, Pospicahl J. Arterial epigastric cavernous anastomosis for the treatment of sexual impotence. World J Surg 1977;1:515–520.
21. Michal V, Kramar R, Hejhal L. Revascularization procedures of the cavernous bodies. In: Zorgniotti AW, Rossi G, eds. Vasculogenic impotence. Springfield, IL: Charles C Thomas, 1980:239–255.
22. Wespes E, Schulman CC. Venous leakage: surgical treatment of a curable cause of impotence. J Urol 1985;138:796–798.
23. Lewis RW, Puyau FA, Bell DP. Another surgical approach for vasculogenic impotence. J Urol 1986;136:1210–1212.
24. Sharlip ID. The incredible results of penile vascular surgery. Int J Impotence Res 1991;3:1–6.
25. Goldstein I. Overview of types and results of vascular surgical procedures for impotence. Cardiovasc Intervent Radiol 1988;11:240–244.
26. Bookstein JJ, Vandeberg J, Machado T. The cavernosal acetylcholine/papaverine response—a practical in vivo method for quantification of endothelium-dependent relaxation: rationale and experimental validation. Invest Radiol 1990;25:1168–1174.
27. Bookstein JJ. Unreported clinical data.
28. Valji K, Bookstein JJ. Diagnosis of arteriogenic impotence: efficacy of duplex sonography as a screening tool. AJR 1993;160:65–69.
29. Fellmeth BF, Bookstein JJ, Lurie A. Ultralong, reversed-curve angiographic catheter. Radiology 1989;172:872–873.
30. Rosen MP, Schwartz AN, Levine FJ, Greenfield AJ. Radiologic

assessment of impotence: angiography, sonography, cavernosography, and scintigraphy. AJR 1991;157:923–931.

31. Freidenberg DH, Berger RE, Chew DE, Ireton R, Ansell JS, Schwartz AN. Quantitation of corporal venous outflow resistance in man by corporal pressure flow evaluation. J Urol 1987; 138:533–538.

32. Bookstein JJ, Lurie AL. Selective penile venography: anatomical and hemodynamic observations. J Urol 1988;140:55–60.

33. Meuleman EJH, Bemelmans BLH, VanAsten WNJC, Doesburg WH, Skotnicki SH, Debruyne FMJ. The value of combined papaverine testing and duplex scanning in men with erectile dysfunction. Int J Impotence Res 1990;2:87–98.

34. Rajfer J, Canan V, Dorey FJ, Mehringer M. Correlation between penile angiography and duplex scanning of the cavernous arteries in impotent men. J Urol 1990;143:1128–1130.

35. Dehmer GJ. Another piece of the fish-oil puzzle. Circulation 1990;82:639–642.

36. Bookstein JJ, Valji K. Transluminal therapeutic interventions in vasculogenic impotence. In: Papanicolaou N, ed. Radiology of impotence and infertility. Philadelphia: Lippincott, 1992: 631–644.

37. von Ebner V. Uber Klappenartige vorrichtungen in den Arterien der Schewellkorper. Anat Anz 1900;18:79–81.

38. Conti G, Virag R, von Niederhausem W. The morphological basis for the polster theory of penile vascular regulation. Acta Anat 1988;133:209–212.

39. Ruzbarsky V, Michal V. Morphologic changes in the arterial bed of the penis with aging. Invest Urol 1977;15:194–199.

40. Benson GS. Polsters: function structure or atherosclerotic changes? J Urol 1981;125:800–803.

43

Recanalization of Dialysis Fistulas

ANNE C. ROBERTS
KARIM VALJI

The maintenance of hemodialysis access is an important but sometimes frustrating challenge. Large numbers of patients depend on hemodialysis; in 1992 approximately 128,000 individuals in the United States were receiving hemodialysis for end-stage renal disease (ESRD).[1] The survival rate of patients with ESRD has been steadily increasing, and there has also been a trend toward treating older patients and more patients with diabetes.[1] As a result of these trends, the prevalence of treated ESRD is growing at approximately 11 percent per year.[1] The number of older patients (>65 years old) treated with hemodialysis has also increased dramatically. The annualized change in treated ESRD in 1986 through 1988 versus 1989 through 1991 was 11.5 percent in patients age 65 to 74 and 15 percent in patients over age 75.[1] In 1991, 45 percent of patients being treated for ESRD were over 65.

Because older patients are not usually candidates for renal transplantation, the number of patients on hemodialysis will increase even more dramatically as the population continues to age. In some centers, as few as 10 percent of the patients on dialysis are transplant candidates.[2] Even those patients who are transplant candidates may need dialysis access for a considerable period of time because of the limited availability of donor organs. The number of patients awaiting transplantation has continued to increase steadily. In 1992 there were almost 22,000 patients awaiting transplantation, and this number has been increasing by about 2000 patients per year.[1] Thus for patients with ESRD, hemodialysis access is their "life-line."

The frustrations with access maintenance are due to the many problems associated with hemodialysis grafts, the most common being progressive stenoses and eventual thrombosis. Vascular access placement and the complications associated with vascular access account for approximately one-quarter of all admissions and hospitalization days for hemodialysis patients.[3–5]

The placement of a hemodialysis access is the first challenge. An endogenous arteriovenous (AV) fistula is the preferred access because it provides the greatest chance for long-term function. The Brescia-Cimino fistula is usually constructed with a side-to-side anastomosis of the cephalic vein and radial artery at the wrist. Such fistulas usually require 6 to 8 weeks for resolution of edema, wound healing, dilation of the vein, and hypertrophy of the vein wall before they can be used for dialysis. Creation of an autologous fistula is difficult or impossible in many patients. Reports indicate an inability to construct an autologous fistula in 10 to 68 percent,[6–8] failure of the fistula at 1 month in 24 to 35 percent,[9] failure at 6 months in 71 percent,[7] and a 2-year extended patency of initially functional fistulas in about 65 to 75 percent.[6,9] Failures are particularly common in elderly and diabetic patients. As the number of these patients in the dialysis population has increased, the percentage of patients who are candidates for autologous fistulas has decreased. Consequently, in most centers, less than 30 percent of the dialysis population currently have native AV fistulas.[5]

Patients who are not candidates for an endogenous AV fistula have fistulas created from polytetrafluoroethylene (PTFE) graft material. The PTFE grafts mature in only 2 weeks, which allows for earlier dialysis than with endogenous fistulas. However, these grafts are plagued by relatively frequent failures, with patency rates at 1 year varying from 55 to 75 percent.[7,9,10] The average life span of a PTFE graft has been estimated at less than 2 years.[11] The most common reason for failure is the development of a stenosis in the outflow veins and subsequent thrombosis of the graft.

Vascular access patency and adequate flow for dialysis depend on fistula blood flow, which may reach as high as 800 ml per minute in normal grafts,[12] and at least 300 ml per minute is essential for successful long-term dialysis.[13] Insufficient graft flow increases the risk of thrombosis and decreases dialysis efficacy by limiting extracorporeal blood flow. As neointimal hyperplasia and subsequent stenoses begin to develop, the graft flow decreases and the risk of thrombosis increases.

Causes and Treatment of Graft Dysfunction

Thrombosis is the most common cause of vascular access loss and is almost always associated with stenoses, usually in the venous outflow tract. Thrombosis occurring in the first weeks to a month after placement of the access is usually due to a technical error in the creation of the fistula. Occasionally, venous stenoses develop rapidly within the first month.[14] Thrombosis developing later than 1 month is most commonly due to stenosis in the venous outflow. Less frequently, arterial inflow stenoses are responsible for thrombosis, but in one series this occurred in less than 2 percent of thrombosed grafts.[15] Rarely, no underlying anatomic lesion can be identified; these patients may have had excessive postdialysis compression, hypotension, hypovolemia, compression of the graft due to sleeping position, or a hypercoagulable state, any of which may lead to thrombosis.[5]

Neointimal hyperplasia occurring in the venous outflow leads to the development of venous stenoses. The phenomenon of neointimal hyperplasia is complex and not well understood. The hyperplasia and resulting stenoses develop near the venous anastomosis most likely as a response to turbulent blood flow and vibration resulting from placement of the fistula.[16] Other mechanical factors, such as compliance mismatch between graft materials and the vein,[17] or angulation and stretching of the vein, may be important.[18] When treated with either angioplasty or surgical revision, stenoses inevitably recur, because the conditions that caused the original stenoses are unchanged.[19,20] These lesions are the most common cause for thrombosis of the dialysis grafts, and the long-term durability of any procedure to improve the venous outflow is constrained by the development of such stenoses.

Because access sites for dialysis fistulas are limited, it is important to extend the life of each fistula as long as possible. The standard therapy for thrombosis has been surgical thrombectomy with graft revision as necessary. Thrombectomy alone is generally not curative because the thrombosis is usually a consequence of perianastomotic stenosis, most frequently at the venous end of the graft. Therefore, if a surgical approach is used to treat thrombosed grafts, a patch angioplasty or interposition graft must be performed to ensure prolonged patency. When the graft is treated operatively, an intraoperative angiogram or blind exploration is essential after thrombectomy to identify the cause of thrombosis. Graft longevity after operative repair is significantly reduced; the 1-year secondary patency for revised PTFE grafts is 60 to 70 percent.[9,21] Most grafts require additional procedures to maintain patency, and patients with PTFE grafts average a revision of one per 1.0 to 1.5 graft-years.[9] In approximately 40 percent of patients with graft thrombosis, salvage is not possible and shunt replacement is necessary.[6] Revision of the outflow is limited by anatomic considerations because there is limited vein available for sequential revisions. If grafts are replaced rather than revised, the possible vascular access sites will be rapidly exhausted.

Because of the significant drawbacks to the surgical management of dialysis grafts, there has been increasing interest in a percutaneous approach to failed grafts. Thrombosed dialysis grafts are also uniquely suited to percutaneous therapy. These grafts are readily accessible and can easily be punctured directly. The clot within the graft is fresh because patients are usually no longer than 2 to 3 days from their last dialysis session. This fresh clot is very susceptible to thrombolytic therapy. The closed system of the graft, with only a single inflow and outflow, means that the thrombolytic agent administered into the clot will be less likely to diffuse into the systemic circulation until lysis has been achieved.

There has been an interest in performing thrombolysis of occluded dialysis shunts and grafts for almost 30 years.[22-24] The equipment, technique, and approach to malfunctioning grafts have continued to improve. Early reports of thrombolytic therapy for dialysis grafts were discouraging.[25] Initial experience using streptokinase and percutaneous infusion techniques reported long infusion times of 7 to 44 hours requiring days of hospitalization for lysis and monitoring,[26] high doses of thrombolytic agents, and low success rates.[27] Other reports were also pessimistic because of long infusion times, the need for operative repair in a high percentage of patients, and significant bleeding complications.[25]

Subsequent reports, particularly those in which urokinase was used, were more encouraging.[24,28,29] Refinements of the technique included the development of the crossed two-catheter technique, which allowed for deposition of thrombolytic agent throughout the graft[30]; clot maceration, which increased the surface area available to the thrombolytic agent; and angioplasty of the usual venous stenosis, which improved the speed of lysis and prevented rethrombosis.[30] Further refinements of the technique included the pulse-spray catheters, which permitted more homogeneous intrathrombic infusion. This method increased the area of interface between clot and fibrinolytic agent.[31] Higher concentrations of urokinase were rapidly administered directly into the graft, eliminating the need for prolonged lower-dose infusions. These improvements further decreased the time required for lysis.[15,32]

Acceptance of transcatheter therapy had to await the development of a practical percutaneous therapy that could serve as an alternative to the standard surgical approach. Such an approach now exists, although evolution of the techniques will undoubtedly continue. Techniques for thrombolysis and angioplasty now allow for rapid and consistent graft recanalization with acceptable long-term results.

There are a number of methods for treating thrombosed dialysis grafts. A current, popular method of thrombolysis is pulse-spray pharmacomechanical thrombolysis (PSPMT).[15,31,33–36] This technique is characterized by the high-pressure delivery of small aliquots of highly concentrated thrombolytic agents via a multi-side-hole catheter. The PSPMT technique allows for the homogeneous and simultaneous distribution of concentrated thrombolytic agent throughout the entire length of the occlusion. Injecting thrombolytic agent throughout the clot enhances the diffusion of activator into the clot, and the mechanical disruption of the clot matrix increases the surface area exposed to the thrombolytic agent. Because almost all of the fibrinolytic agent is incorporated into the clot and not freely circulating, the risk of bleeding complications is decreased. This technique results in the rapid restoration of graft patency with a minimal dose of thrombolytic agent. Angiography is performed immediately after lysis to demonstrate the anatomic factors contributing to the thrombosis. The entire graft, including the proximal arterial inflow and the complete venous outflow, can be evaluated, and the usual venous anastomotic stenosis can then be treated with transluminal angioplasty. Because the entire procedure is performed in a single session in the angiographic facility, the patient does not have to be transferred to and from an intensive care unit and the expense is decreased. The procedure is performed on an outpatient basis, and the patient is discharged to the dialysis unit or to home at the conclusion of the examination. In addition, the grafts are functional and available for dialysis immediately following the recanalization procedure, precluding the need for temporary subclavian catheters for dialysis access. Avoiding the use of temporary subclavian catheters decreases expense and eliminates the complications of such devices, particularly the risk of central venous stenoses.

Patient Selection

PTFE grafts are the most common type of vascular access to be treated with the percutaneous approach, but endogenous AV fistulas can also be treated with this technique. Many AV fistulas present with dialysis difficulties, such as problems with punctures or increased venous pressure, and are less likely to present with thrombosis. Thrombosis of a recently constructed graft is usually due to a technical problem. Thrombolysis can be performed to establish the nature of the problem, with the understanding that there is some risk of bleeding from the anastomotic sites. A surgical revision of the graft will usually be required.

The criteria for excluding a patient from thrombolysis are the same as those for any thrombolytic procedure. Absolute contraindications to thrombolytic therapy are recent neurologic processes, including intracranial bleeding, stroke, or neurologic surgery, and the presence of active gastrointestinal bleeding. Relative contraindications include recent major surgery, severe hypertension, and pregnancy. A contraindication that is more unique to thrombosed dialysis access is the presence of a graft infection; this requires primary surgical therapy. Infected clot is relatively resistant to thrombolysis; more importantly, lysis of infected thrombus is potentially life-threatening because it may precipitate a bacteremia and lethal sepsis.[30]

Determining infection in a graft may be difficult. The classic signs of infection or inflammation include redness, tenderness, warmth, and fluctuance around the graft. These signs may be blunted in uremic patients. A fever or the presence of leukocytosis may be of diagnostic help, but some patients may not manifest such a response. Purulent discharge or skin breakdown around the graft is a clear sign of an infectious process but is rarely present. Needle aspiration of the graft clot for Gram stain and culture, or of perigraft fluid collections found on ultrasound evaluation, may be helpful in diagnosing graft infections.[36] Any patient with signs of infection must be treated with antibiotics and referred for surgical removal of the graft.

Technique of Pulse-Spray Thrombolysis

Access

A crossed-catheter technique is used in all patients undergoing thrombolysis of dialysis grafts.[31,34,35,37,38] This allows for simultaneous access to both the arterial and venous ends of the graft. The graft is first punctured with a one-wall needle (Cook, Inc.) at the junction of the proximal and middle thirds of the graft (the arterial end of the graft) and directed toward the venous end of the graft (Fig. 43-1A). The graft is grasped between the thumb and index finger and held while the puncture is made by the needle. When the graft wall has been punctured, there is usually a popping sensation as the needle traverses the PTFE material. Successful entry into the graft is indicated by easy passage of a guidewire through the graft or sometimes by the return of a small amount of dark blood. The guidewire should go through the graft quite easily despite the presence of clot. Injection of contrast material through the needle is not usually performed to determine if the graft has been entered. If the needle is not in the graft and contrast agent is injected into the soft tissues, the appearance may be misleading. Early in the injection it may appear as if the graft has been entered, but with continued injection it will become evident that the contrast material is in the tissues and not within the graft. Unfortunately, by this point, the graft is often obscured and remains obscured for the remainder of the procedure.

After the guidewire has been placed into the graft, a 5 French dilator or catheter is passed over the guidewire. The guidewire is then used to traverse the venous anastomosis (see Fig. 43-1B). The venous anastomosis is occasionally difficult to cross because of the presence of a venous stenosis, and in such cases an angled Glidewire (Terumo, Inc., Medi-Tech) can be very useful. It is important to confirm the passage of a wire into the venous outflow before proceeding with further punctures or thrombolysis. If the venous outflow cannot be cannulated, thrombolysis is not performed. Thrombolysis without venous outflow results in reestablished blood flow with no outlet for the blood except through puncture sites. This leads to bleeding from previous puncture sites and possibly the development of hematomas. Patients in whom the venous anastomosis cannot be crossed are referred for surgical thrombectomy and revision of the anastomosis.

If the guidewire can be passed into the venous outflow, the dilator or catheter is placed over it into the outflow tract. While small amounts of contrast material are injected, the catheter is withdrawn until the upper extent of the thrombosis is identified. The length of the thrombosed segment can be estimated. If a more precise measurement is required, the operator places a wire through the dilator to the point of free flow of contrast and then withdraws it to the site of the graft puncture. The length of the occlusion determines the length of the subsequent pulse-spray catheter side-hole segment. A second puncture is then made at the junction of the middle third and the distal third of the graft (the venous end of the graft), and the guidewire is directed toward the arterial end (see Fig. 43-1C). The length of this occluded segment is determined and a catheter is placed with the length of the side-hole segment corresponding to the length of the occlusion. The end hole of the catheter is again placed just beyond the clot. The crisscross nature of the catheterization allows the entire clot to be treated simultaneously and permits access to both sides of the graft for possible angioplasty or other transcatheter therapy (see Fig. 43-1D). It is important that catheter or wire manipulations are done gently at the arterial end of the graft because vigorous movement of the wire or forceful contrast injections can cause the embolization of clot from the arterial anastomosis into the artery.

This procedure is identical for both straight and loop grafts. In the loop graft (Fig. 43-2), there will be more overlap of the catheters, which will usually need to be repositioned during the pulse-spray procedure so that the entire graft receives the thrombolytic agent.

Equipment

A variety of commercial pulse-spray catheter systems suitable for use in clotted dialysis grafts are available. The catheters used most often are the multi-side-hole infusion catheter (Cook, Inc.) and the side-slit catheter (Angiodynamics, Inc.). These catheters have multiple, tiny side holes or slits over a length of 4 to 30 cm. A wire with a bead is used to occlude the end hole of the catheter. These systems come prepackaged with a hemostatic Y adapter to allow injections around the wire.

A suitable delivery system can also be fashioned from standard angiographic materials. One can create multiple side holes in a commonly used 5 French polyethylene catheter by puncturing the catheter every 5 mm with the tip of a 27- or 30-gauge needle. The side holes are placed in a spiral pattern around the catheter, and the length of the segment with side holes varies with the length of the occlusion. With this type of catheter the length of the side-hole segment should probably not exceed 15 cm. With the commercially manufactured catheters with side slits, the length of the catheter segment with side slits may be up to 30 cm, and the catheter end hole is occluded by a 0.032-inch tip-occluding wire (Cook, Inc.). A hemostatic Touhy-Borst or Y adapter is placed over the wire and attached to the catheter. The gasket of the adapter is tightened down over the end of the tip-occluding wire, and a three-way stopcock is placed on the side arm of the adapter.

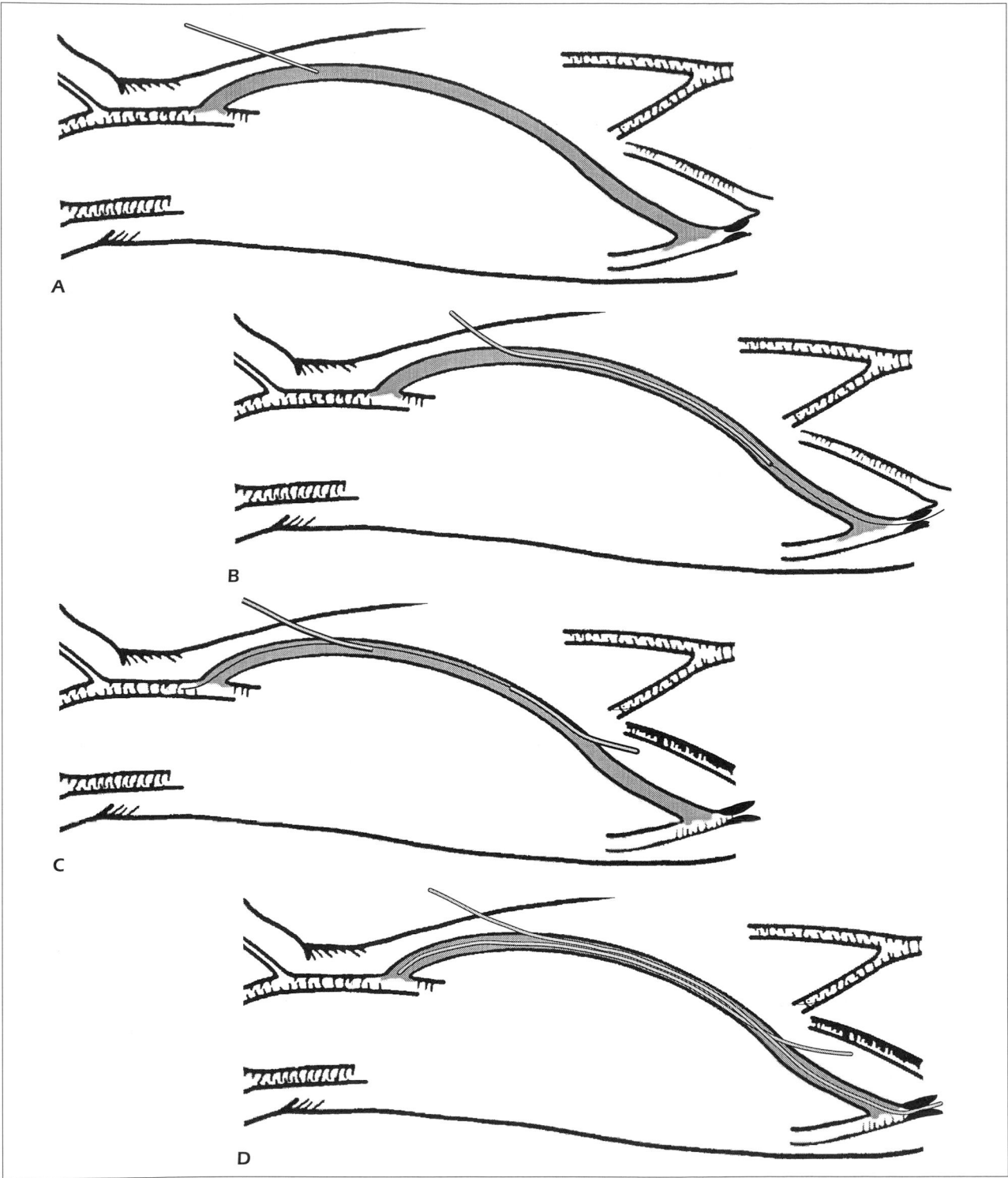

Figure 43-1. (A) The graft is punctured with a one-wall needle at the junction of the proximal and middle thirds of the graft (the arterial end of the graft) and directed toward the venous end of the graft. (B) The guidewire is placed through the needle and the needle is exchanged for a 5 French dilator or catheter. The guidewire is then used to traverse the venous anastomosis. (C) A second puncture is then made at the junction of the middle third and the distal third of the graft (the venous end of the graft), and the guidewire is directed toward the arterial end. (D) Crisscross catheters allow the entire clot to be treated simultaneously and permit access to both sides of the graft for possible angioplasty or other transcatheter therapy.

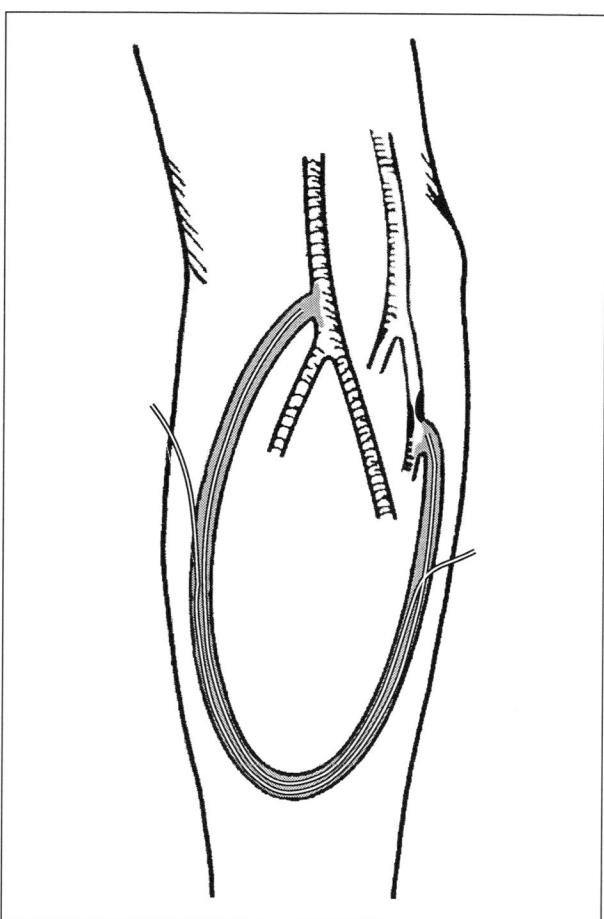

Figure 43-2. Loop grafts are accessed in a similar manner. Because of the length of the graft, there is more overlap of the catheters.

Thrombolytic Agents

The most commonly used thrombolytic agent is urokinase. The contents of a 250,000-unit vial of urokinase (Abbokinase, Abbott Laboratories) are dissolved in sterile water. Typically 9 ml of sterile water is added to the vial, plus 1 ml of heparin solution (in a dilution of 5000 units/ml). This yields a concentration of 25,000 units of urokinase and 500 units of heparin per milliliter of solution. Heparin is only added to the first vial of urokinase; any additional urokinase is dissolved in 10 ml of sterile water without heparin. A 2000- to 3000-unit bolus of heparin is usually given intravenously when the thrombolytic procedure begins. If the procedure extends for longer than an hour, heparin is administered at a rate of 1000 units per hour. If the patient has no contraindications to aspirin therapy, a soluble aspirin tablet (325 mg) is administered orally before the procedure is begun.

Tissue plasminogen activator (tPA) is less frequently used for this procedure because of its cost and the bleeding complications associated with tPA. For pulse-spray application, tPA is used in a concentration of 0.5 mg/ml with heparin admixed with the first 5 mg to a concentration of 500 units/ml.[39] The protocol for tPA administration is the same as for urokinase.

Thrombolytic Procedure

After the pulse-spray catheters have been positioned and their end holes securely occluded, the hemostatic valves are tightened around the wires. The urokinase solution is divided equally into two syringes, which will act as urokinase reservoirs. One of these syringes is attached to the side port of the Y adapter (commercially available system) or to the side port of a three-way stopcock of the catheter directed toward the arterial end. The other syringe is attached to the catheter directed toward the venous end. A tuberculin syringe is connected to the other leg of the side port or to the third port of the stopcock. The tuberculin syringe is used to inject the urokinase solution, in 0.2-ml increments, as forcefully as possible through the catheter. This forceful injection is designed to maximize penetrance of urokinase into the clot. If the injection is not performed forcefully, the urokinase will simply dribble from the catheter, negating the mechanical aspect of the procedure. Injections are repeated every 20 to 30 seconds (Fig. 43-3A). When the active catheter length is shorter than the length of clot to be treated, the catheter is advanced or withdrawn as needed to expose the entire clot to urokinase (see Fig. 43-3B). After 250,000 units of urokinase have been introduced into the graft, contrast material is injected to assess clot dissolution. Because of their greater clot volume, loop grafts may require more urokinase than straight grafts, and 500,000 units of urokinase may be needed for these grafts. Contrast agent is injected through the catheter and directed toward the arterial anastomosis. The contrast injection usually demonstrates an anatomic abnormality, most commonly a venous stenosis, that is responsible for the thrombosis.

In most cases, clot lysis is almost complete after 250,000 units of urokinase are delivered. However, graft flow may be slow and the graft pulse may be faint. Several possibilities should be considered in this situation. If a critical venous anastomotic stenosis, which prevents outflow, is present, balloon angioplasty will be required before clot lysis is completed. Other causes for poor flow include resistant thrombus at the arterial anastomosis, incomplete delivery of urokinase to the entire thrombus, inadequate heparin administration, or infected thrombus that is resistant to lysis.

Once the urokinase has been placed into the clot,

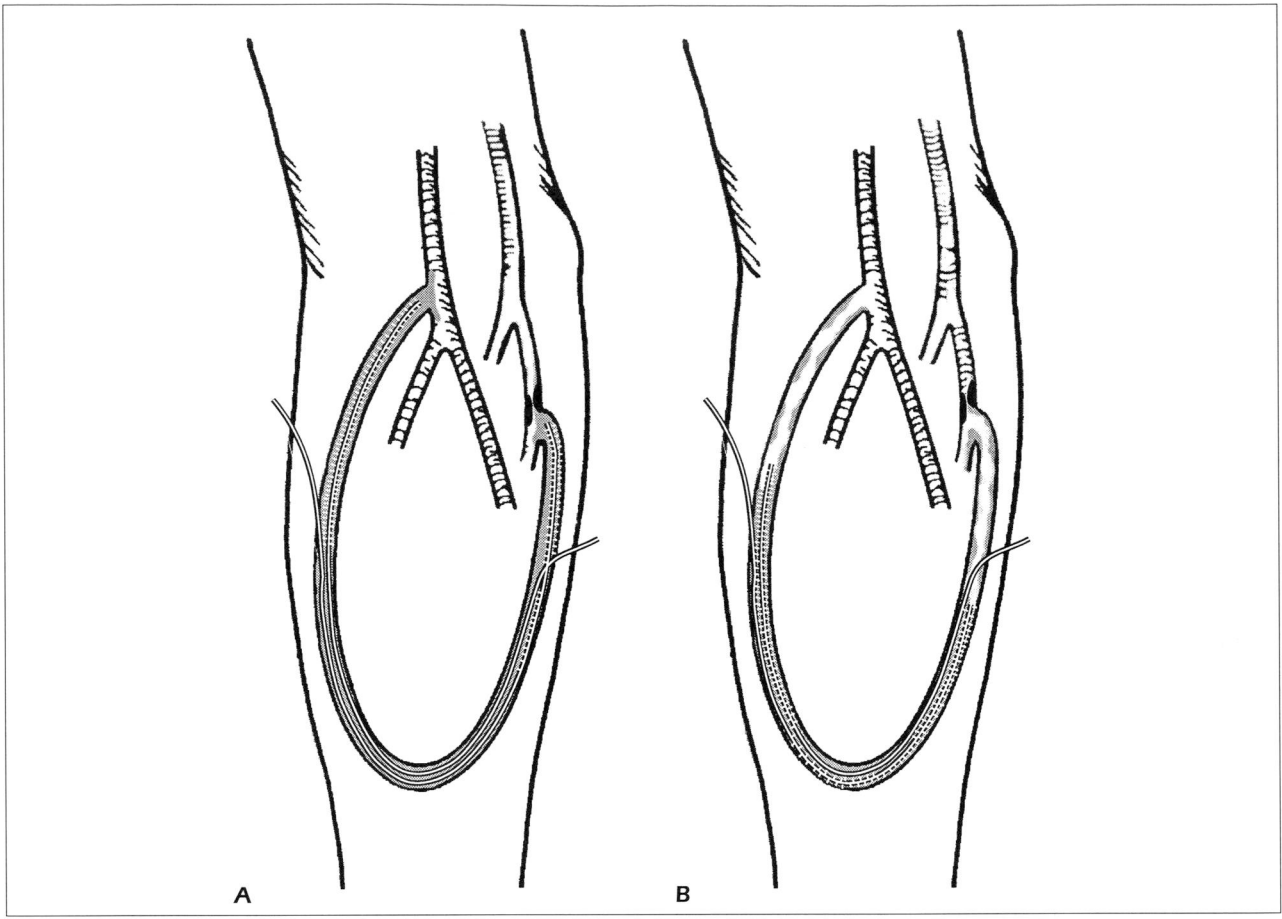

Figure 43-3. (A) After the catheters are positioned, pulse-spray thrombolysis is begun using a tuberculin syringe to make forceful injections through the catheters. (B) When the active catheter length is shorter than the length of clot to be treated, the catheter is withdrawn as needed to expose the entire clot to urokinase.

relatively aggressive methods can be used to reestablish flow. Attention should first be directed to the venous outflow. A venous anastomotic stenosis is usually found. If a stenosis is present, the first intervention should be dilatation with an angioplasty balloon (Fig. 43-4). Relatively small amounts of residual clot in the graft can then be compressed and broken up with the same angioplasty balloon catheter (Fig. 43-5). If a large clot burden remains, further therapy with urokinase will be required. Early venous angioplasty is also necessary if bleeding develops around the catheters or through recent dialysis puncture sites. The reestablishment of inflow in the setting of a tight venous outflow stenosis invariably leads to bleeding from puncture sites in the graft. This is most easily handled by dilatation of the venous stenosis and gentle compression of the bleeding sites.

Angiographic evaluation is performed to assess the arterial inflow, the body of the graft, and the venous outflow to the level of the superior vena cava. After the treatment of any underlying abnormalities, a final angiogram is obtained to document graft patency and flow. To assess the anticoagulation status, an activated clotting time (ACT) may be obtained before the catheters are removed. When the catheters are removed, gentle digital compression is applied to the puncture sites until hemostasis is obtained. Upon completion of the procedure, the patients are sent to the dialysis unit or are discharged home. Patients are continued on daily aspirin (325 mg) if they have no contraindications to such therapy.

Resistant Arterial Clots

After lysis, a residual plug of lysis-resistant clot may remain at the arterial anastomosis (Figs. 43-6A and 43-7A). In one series these plugs were present in almost 60 percent of patients treated with PMPST,[40] and they have also been noted by surgeons performing graft embolectomy.[21] When these plugs are removed

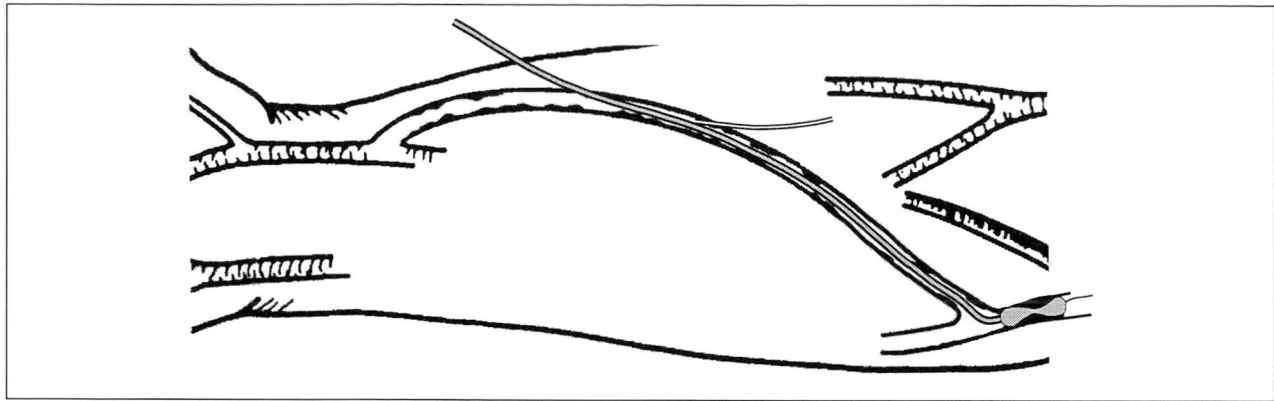

Figure 43-4. After initial pulse-spray thrombolysis, contrast is injected and the graft is evaluated. A venous anastomotic stenosis is usually present, and the first intervention should be dilatation with an angioplasty balloon.

surgically, they seem to have a consistency different from that of clot removed from the remainder of the graft. They are believed to represent platelet-rich "white clots" formed because of persistent exposure

Figure 43-5. Relatively small amounts of residual clot in the graft can then be compressed and broken up with the same angioplasty balloon catheter.

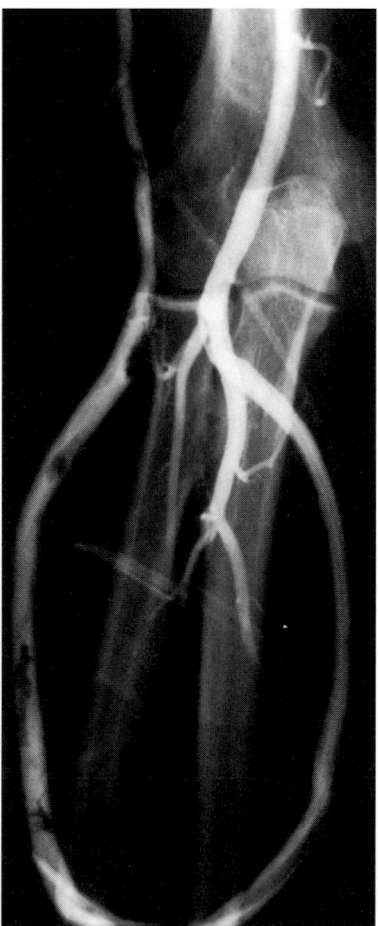

of the leading edge of clot to arterial blood flow and tend to be relatively resistant to thrombolysis.

The plugs can usually be removed with an 8.5-mm occlusion balloon catheter (Medi-Tech, Inc.). The thrombolysis catheter, which is directed toward the arterial anastomosis, is exchanged for an occlusion balloon catheter (Fig. 43-6B). The catheter is positioned with the balloon beyond the clot in the distal artery. Using dilute contrast material, the balloon is inflated and the catheter is pulled back, dragging the clot into the graft. It is important not to overinflate the balloon while it is in the native artery. As the balloon is pulled up against the clot, the balloon is more firmly inflated in order to dislodge the clot. If the clot is not dislodged on the initial pass (Fig. 43-7B), repeated passes can be performed as needed (Fig. 43-7C). If the displaced clot becomes trapped in the graft (Fig. 43-7D), it can be crushed with an angioplasty balloon. This thrombectomy procedure is preferred over initial angioplasty of these plugs because angioplasty of the plug at the arterial anastomosis may lead to the embolization of clot fragments into the distal arterial circulation. Since this material tends to be more resistant to thrombolysis, a potentially more hazardous embolization may occur.

Specific Technical Aspects

Venous Anastomotic Stenoses

Significant narrowing in the venous outflow is present in 75 to 90 percent of failed grafts, either alone or in combination with other sources for thrombosis.[15,32,35] Because these types of stenoses are so common, it is important to carefully evaluate the venous anastomotic site. If there are multiple outflow channels, the

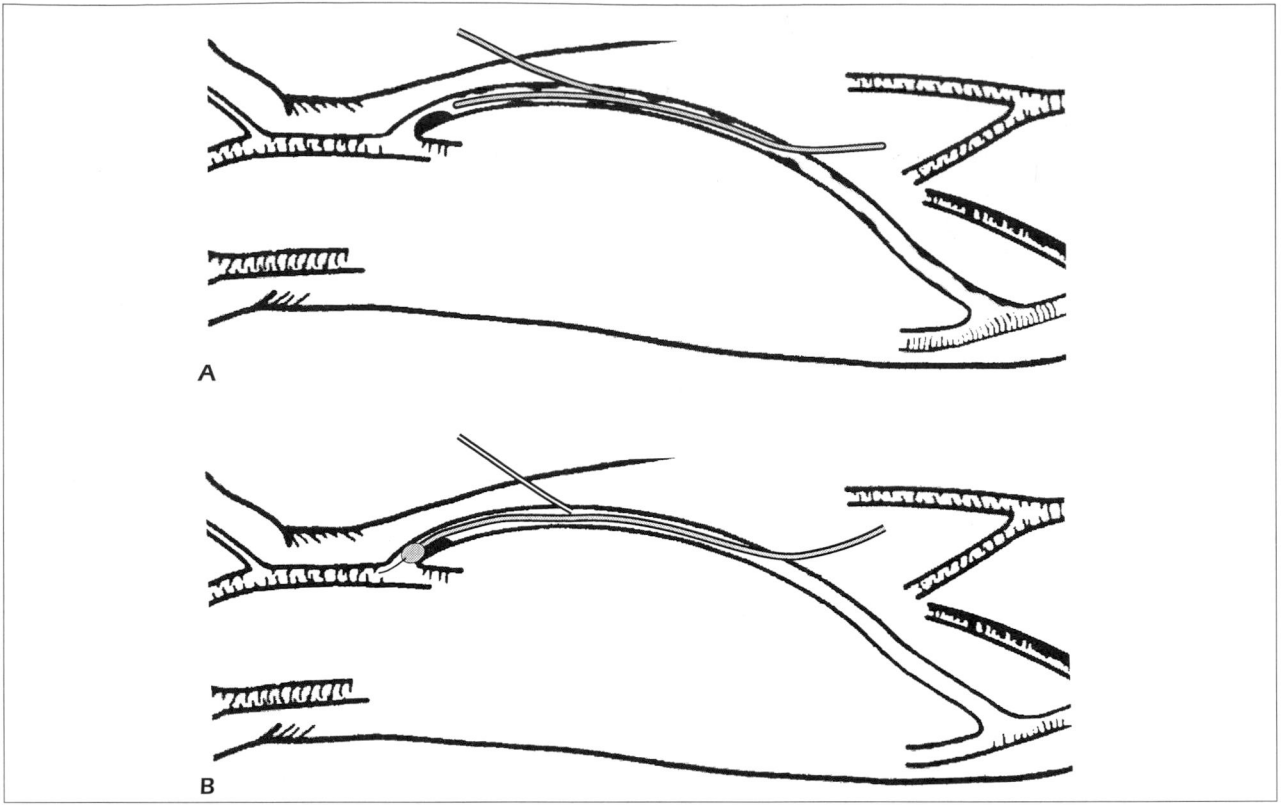

Figure 43-6. (A) After lysis, a residual plug of lysis-resistant clot may remain at the arterial anastomosis. (B) The thrombolysis catheter is exchanged for an occlusion balloon catheter. The catheter is positioned with the balloon beyond the clot in the distal artery. Using dilute contrast material, the balloon is inflated and the catheter is pulled back, dragging the clot into the graft.

offending stenosis may not be visualized easily and a number of different angiographic projections may be required for visualization. The presence of multiple collaterals is a clue to the presence of a significant venous outflow obstruction. Venous stenoses respond relatively well to balloon dilatation, at least in the short term (Fig. 43-8). Selection of the proper balloon size is based on the diameter of the PTFE graft and the size of the draining vein. In most cases a 6-mm balloon is appropriate, but sizes from 5 to 8 mm are not uncommon. The balloon is centered across the stenosis and inflated, and the inflation is held for 2 minutes. An inflation device such as a Leveen inflator (Medi-Tech, Inc.) is helpful for maintaining the inflation. Multiple prolonged inflations may be required to completely expand the balloon at the site of stenosis. A high-pressure balloon is useful in overcoming resistant lesions. In some cases with a very resistant lesion, an oversized balloon will be needed. After angioplasty, if there is a residual stenosis of greater than 50 percent, directional atherectomy with a Simpson device should be considered.[41]

Arterial Inflow Stenoses

Significant stenoses in the feeding artery requiring treatment are found in less than 15 percent of treated grafts.[15,20,35,40,42] However, these lesions often result in inadequate flow for dialysis or in early rethrombosis. To visualize the arterial anastomosis, the catheter directed toward the arterial anastomosis is advanced until it is positioned just at the anastomosis, and an injection of contrast is made at that position. If good flow has been reestablished, visualization of the proximal artery may be difficult. Visualization can be improved by briefly compressing the graft or by inflating a blood pressure cuff above the shunt to occlude outflow. Because of the geometry of the anastomosis, multiple views may be necessary to adequately assess the anastomosis and the arterial inflow. If a significant stenosis is identified, balloon angioplasty may be an effective alternative to surgical revision. It is often possible to pass a wire through the anastomosis from the graft and to perform an angioplasty in the same session as the thrombolysis. If angioplasty cannot be performed be-

A

B

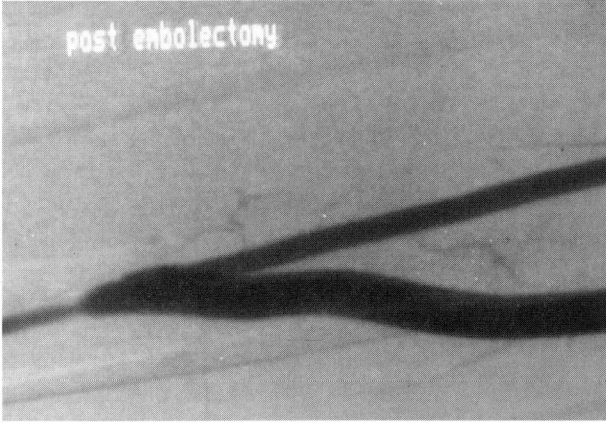

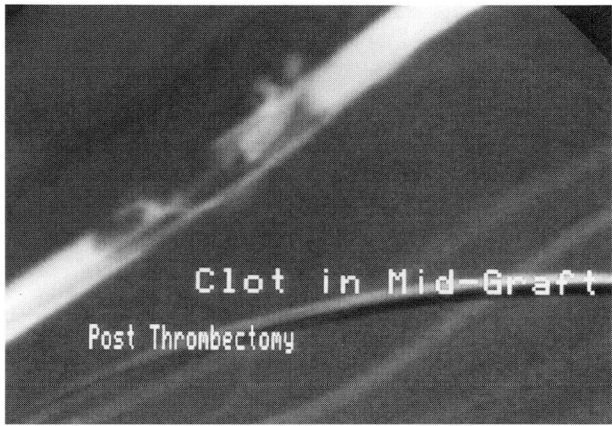

C

D

Figure 43-7. (A) Residual clot at the arterial anastomosis. (B) After the first pass with the occlusion balloon, there is an improved appearance but still residual thrombus. (C) Second pass with occlusion balloon and clearing of plug. (D) The clot is now caught in midgraft and treated with an angioplasty balloon.

cause of an unfavorable angle at the anastomosis, an additional procedure with direct puncture of the supplying artery will be necessary.

Intragraft Stenoses

Significant intragraft stenoses are uncommon, but they do occur. The cause of these stenoses is not clear. They may represent hypertrophy of the neointima that lines the luminal surface of PTFE grafts[43] or may represent organized mural thrombus lining the graft, particularly in the area of multiple previous punctures. Such stenoses can usually be treated with balloon angioplasty, but occasionally a Simpson atherectomy device will be required for resistant lesions (Fig. 43-9).[44]

Central Venous Stenoses

The venous outflow should be examined to the level of the superior vena cava because stenoses may develop anywhere along the venous outflow. The most com-

mon site of stenoses is the venous anastomosis site, but stenoses may develop in the axillary region and as far proximal as the subclavian and brachiocephalic veins. Subclavian stenoses are most often the result of venous injury from previous temporary dialysis access catheters (Fig. 43-10).[45–47] However, a subclavian stenosis or occlusion may not be the cause of dialysis access thrombosis. If there are well-developed collaterals around the subclavian stenosis or occlusion, this lesion is less likely to be the cause of the thrombosis. If there is another lesion, such as an anastomotic stenosis, then the anastomotic stenosis is likely to be the culprit and treatment of that lesion should be sufficient to restore function. New subclavian stenoses, or those without well-developed collaterals, can be treated with balloon angioplasty or with stent placement.[48,49] The significant aspect of these stenoses is their potential role in compromising outflow in future dialysis access.[50] An argument for prompt thrombolytic therapy, allowing immediate dialysis, is to avoid the use of temporary subclavian catheters, which cause subclavian vein stenoses.

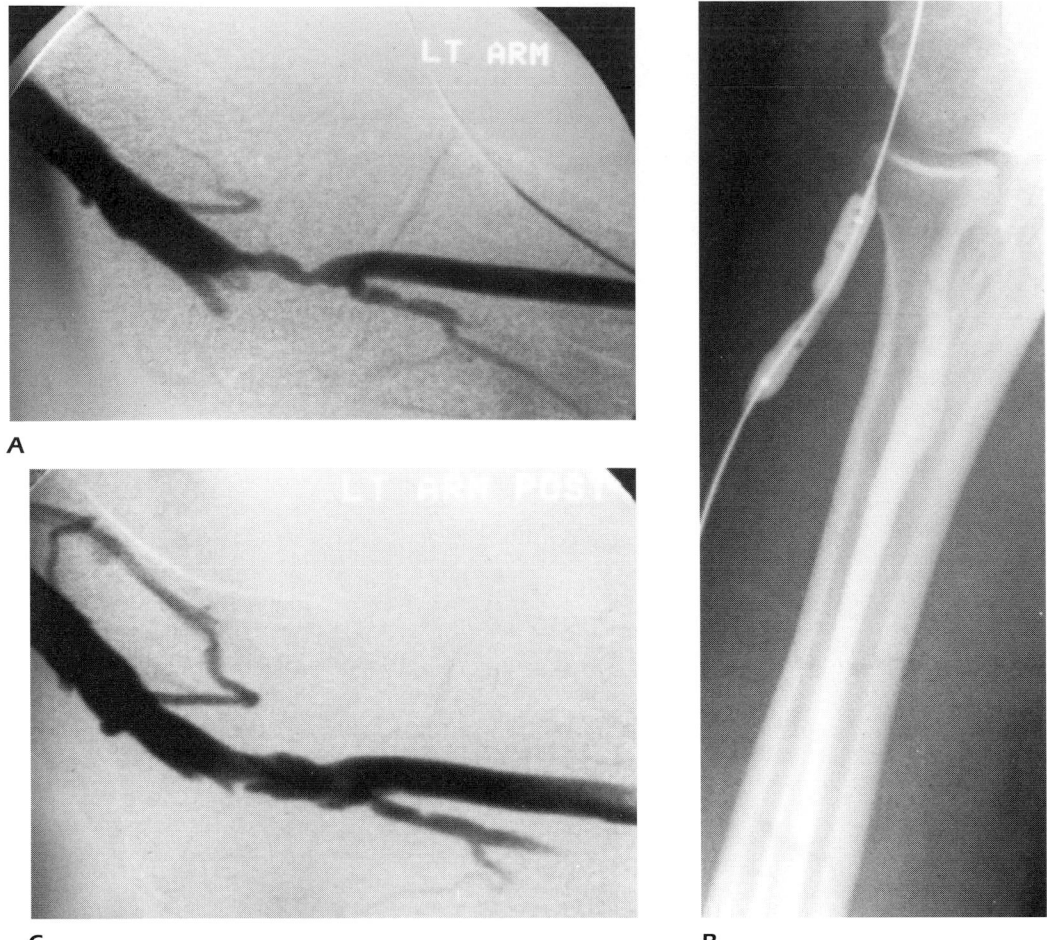

Figure 43-8. (A) Tight stenosis of outflow vein, just at the venous anastomosis. (B) Balloon inflation. Balloons should be fully inflated for 2 minutes. Inflation is usually repeated at least once. (C) After dilatation. Although the appearance is slightly irregular, the vein remained patent for approximately 15 months.

Complications

Complications of the PSPMT method have been uncommon. In 276 grafts undergoing this therapy, there were 27 complications, 8 of which were serious enough to compromise the graft or require additional therapy.[32] One patient who received tPA for treatment of a graft thrombosis and subclavian venous outflow occlusion developed a significant retroperitoneal hemorrhage. Another patient who had a distal embolization required a surgical embolectomy. A large perigraft hematoma prompted cessation of therapy in 1 patient, and extravasation from the graft prompted termination of the procedure in another case. Vein damage, including 1 vein rupture and 3 vein dissections, occurred after angioplasty in 4 patients. Less severe complications occurred in 4 patients who had distal embolization: 1 required no further treatment, 1 was successfully treated with further thrombolysis, and the other 2 had the embolus pulled back into the graft with an occlusion balloon. Nine patients developed small perigraft hematomas for which they required no further therapy. There was limited extravasation from 3 grafts: shearing of a catheter by an access needle, with subsequent percutaneous retrieval of the fragment, in 1 patient; and adverse reaction to contrast material in 2 patients.[32] Other reported complications associated with thrombolysis of dialysis grafts (but not with the pulse-spray method) include gastrointestinal bleeding, extravasation from the graft, and sepsis when an unrecognized infected graft was treated with thrombolysis.[30,35,51]

Rarely, distal arterial embolization of clot occurs. It seems to be somewhat more common with the forearm loop grafts, perhaps because of the size of the brachial artery and/or the geometry of the anastomosis.

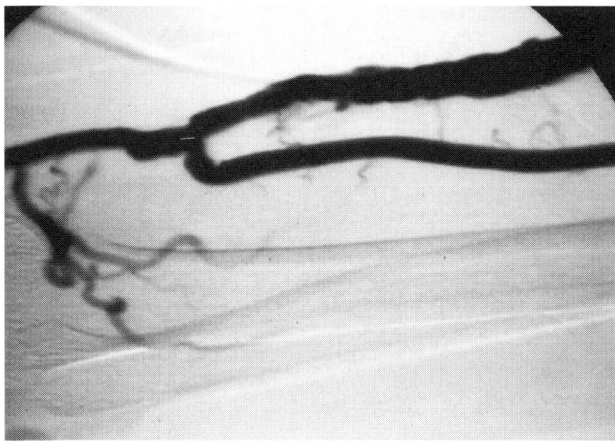

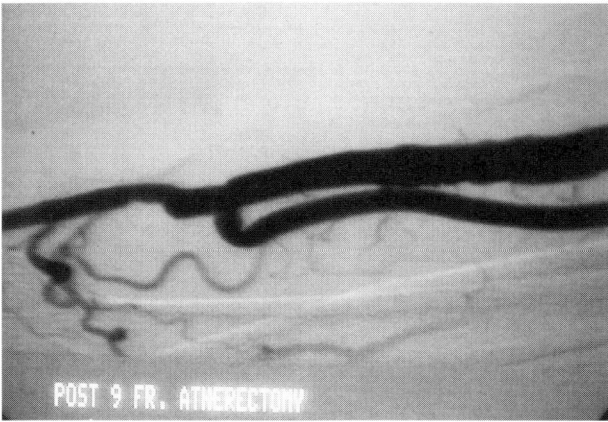

Figure 43-9. (A) Irregular appearance of graft after angioplasty. (B) After treatment with atherectomy device.

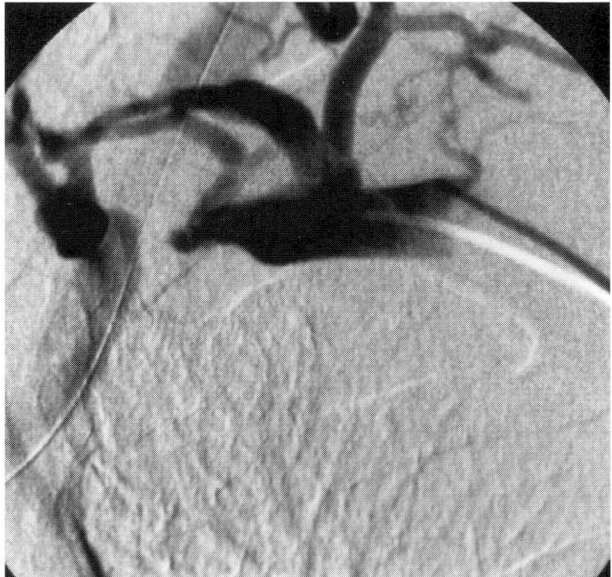

Figure 43-10. Occlusion of left subclavian vein after subclavian catheter placement for hemodialysis. The patient had developed massive arm swelling after placement of an upper arm graft.

Careful technique is important, and manipulation of guidelines and catheters at the arterial anastomosis should be performed gently and carefully. Angioplasty of clot directly at the arterial anastomosis should be avoided. If distal embolization occurs, the catheter may be placed against the clot and urokinase administration can be attempted. Unfortunately, clot that embolizes tends to be more resistant to lysis. If lysis cannot be achieved, placement of an occlusion balloon past the clot and gentle displacement of the clot back into the graft may be the best approach. This embolectomy technique is similar to a surgical embolectomy. Performing this maneuver in the angiographic suite has the advantage of fluoroscopic guidance, an embolectomy catheter that is placed over a wire, and immediate angiographic evaluation, which is preferable to a blind operative procedure.

Results

PSPMT in conjunction with balloon angioplasty allows for rapid, consistent, and safe restoration of graft patency. Almost all grafts can be treated in this manner, provided the anastomoses can be traversed with a wire. The combination of rapid thrombolysis time and high success rate represents a substantial improvement over early reports on thrombolysis in dialysis grafts. A study comparing a single catheter infusion technique with a cross-catheter lacing technique demonstrated marked improvement in success rates and a significant decrease in bleeding complications.[51] Lysis time has now been decreased to an average of 23 minutes, at which time flow has been reestablished and angioplasty can be instituted. Procedure times are now consistently less than 2 hours. Technically successful lysis can be achieved in 96 percent of cases, with a clinical success rate (defined as the ability to dialyze) of 92 percent.

Recent clinical and laboratory evidence highlighting the problem of concurrent rethrombosis during thrombolysis[38] has led to further modifications of the procedure. Heparin is now admixed with the thrombolytic agent for intrathrombic administration, and oral aspirin is administered before the procedure is begun. If thrombolysis is proceeding more slowly than usual, evaluation of the degree of anticoagulation (activated clotting time) by an automated device (Hemochron) may demonstrate heparin resistance or inadequate anticoagulation.

The procedure time has been decreased by mechanical disruption of thrombus within the graft early in the procedure and by early angioplasty of the venous anastomosis. Early and aggressive maceration of clot with an angioplasty balloon helps to speed the procedure. Resistant clot at the arterial end of the graft is quite common. Initially angioplasty of such plugs had been performed, but with refinement of the technique it now appears preferable to pull the clot into the graft and then crush it with an angioplasty balloon, to reduce the risk of arterial embolism. Aggressive displacement of this arterial clot is important for rapid treatment of the graft. Reestablishment of flow will promote lysis of any remaining thrombus.

Future directions include the development of a mechanical pulse injector to deliver the rapid, forceful pulse of thrombolytic agent automatically. There may be some improvement in thrombolytic agents as research continues into methods to make thrombolytic agents more fibrin-specific, more resistant to inactivation, more efficient, and safer.[52–54] More effective use of adjuvant anticoagulation and antiplatelet therapy is also an area of active investigation.[55]

Few studies have evaluated the long-term patency of clotted dialysis grafts treated with percutaneous therapy. Primary patency at 1 year has been reported at 11 to 26 percent.[35,51,56] Secondary patency at 1 year has been reported at 51 and 69 percent.[35,51] These results are very similar to surgical patency rates.[9,21] Studies that have directly compared surgical thrombectomy with thrombolysis have found that the patency rates are similar.[57,58] These findings suggest that the method for opening the graft is less important than the underlying cause of the thrombosis. The poor long-term patency rates indicate that recurrent therapeutic procedures will be required. The need for repeated treatments does not indicate failure of the technique, but instead represents the chronic physiologic abnormality that produces restenosis.

An Approach to the Poorly Functioning Graft

The greatest challenge in the long-term maintenance of dialysis grafts is, of course, the problem of stenosis and restenosis. Although it is clear that graft patency can be rapidly restored by percutaneous thrombolytic techniques, early detection and treatment of a developing stenosis with angioplasty or surgical revision appear to be more cost- and time-effective than delaying therapy until thrombosis has developed. Various clinical criteria can be used to identify grafts with developing stenoses that are at risk for thrombosis. These criteria include elevated venous pressures,[14,59] increased recirculation,[17] difficulty with needle placement, increased bleeding following needle removal, and frequent physical examination of the dialysis graft.[2,13]

Access patency can be assessed by measuring the pressure in the venous return line of the dialyzer circuit, the venous dialysis pressure (VDP). Persistently elevated venous pressures can identify patients at high risk for significant venous stenosis.[59] Patients with stenoses detected by venous pressure screening have had an approximately 10 times higher risk of thrombosis (1.40 patients per year) than patients with treated stenoses (0.15 patient per year). The measurement of venous pressures at low blood flow rates (200–250 ml per minute) allows for detection of venous stenoses, but at high blood flow rates (400 ml per minute) this method does not appear to differentiate as accurately between patients with and without stenoses.[17]

Direct recirculation of dialyzed blood through the extracorporeal circuit reduces effective urea clearance. Elevated recirculation ratios identify patients with significant venous stenoses.[60] However, other factors can affect the urea recirculation, including needle placement, extracorporeal blood flow, hypotension, decreased cardiac output, intravascular volume depletion, and arterial stenosis.[5]

Physical examination of the graft involves auscultation of the graft, particularly at the region of the venous anastomosis. When a stenosis is present, there is often a high-pitched, harsh, or discontinuous bruit at the site of the stenosis. Palpation of a discontinuous or water-hammer pulse within the graft usually indicates an outflow stenosis. A thrill may also be palpated at the venous anastomosis or in the early venous outflow tract at the level of the stenotic lesion. Careful physical examination is accurate in detecting significant lesions. In a recent study, angiographically significant abnormalities were found in 92 percent of patients referred for angiographic evaluation after an abnormality was found on physical examination.[61]

Ultrasound evaluation with color flow technique may be useful for detecting stenoses. This technique is accurate in identifying and characterizing stenoses of the venous anastomotic site in patients with grafts.[62,63] Ultrasonography is much less accurate in evaluating autologous AV fistulas and in detecting stenoses in the subclavian veins.[62,63] In most centers, ultrasound studies are not routinely used for the evaluation or surveillance of dialysis access fistulas.

If an inflow lesion is suspected, an angiographic evaluation of the entire length of the feeding artery should be performed to visualize the artery from its origin to the arterial anastomosis. Many of the dialysis patients are elderly and/or diabetic and are prone to the development of atherosclerosis anywhere along the course of the supplying artery. If such a lesion is identified, it can usually be successfully treated with angioplasty.

If clinical evaluation suggests a possible venous stenosis, the graft and the venous outflow may be easily evaluated angiographically after dialysis using a dialysis needle left in place. If a stenosis is discovered, angioplasty can be immediately performed and the patient discharged home after the procedure is completed.

Early correction of venous stenoses with angioplasty or fistula revision reduces thrombosis rates and prolongs access viability.[59] The durability of angioplasty versus surgical revision is currently under study. One study comparing angioplasty with surgical revision in the treatment of thrombosed grafts found no statistical differences in initial success, primary patency, or secondary patency.[11] One-year cumulative patency rates of 60 to 70 percent following surgical revision have been reported.[9,21,64,65] Secondary patency rates for balloon angioplasty have been reported in the range of 31 to 51 percent at 1 year.[10,20,21,35] Many of these studies contain patency data on grafts that have thrombosed, as well as on those that are dysfunctional on the basis of other criteria, and also include grafts with arterial and intragraft stenoses. A recent study followed 106 grafts suspected on clinical examination to have a venous stenosis.[61] These grafts were studied angiographically, and any venous stenoses were treated with balloon angioplasty. The technical success rate for angioplasty was 98 percent. The primary patency at 1 year was 23 percent for PTFE grafts. Repeated angioplasty significantly improved the patency rates, for a primary assisted patency rate of 68 percent at 1 year and 51 percent at 2 years. A combination of thrombolysis and repeated angioplasty further improved patency, with secondary patency rates at 1 year of 82 percent and at 2 years of 65 percent.[61] Aggressive therapy for failing dialysis grafts does seem to be useful.

Approximately one-half of treated stenoses recur before 6 months.[20,61] Lesions developing in the venous outflow almost always recur at the same anatomic site. These recurrent lesions should not be considered failures of the procedure but rather symptoms of the underlying pathophysiology. Redilatations allow for easy and safe maintenance for months and even years,[2] and gaining these months of patency can be extremely valuable in elderly dialysis patients.[61] Rapidly recurring stenoses frequently involve patients with limited surgical options because these patients may have already had previous grafts fail because of such quickly forming stenoses.[19] An advantage of angioplasty is that loss of more proximal vein does not occur, in contrast to a surgical interposition graft. Because both angioplasty and surgical techniques may have similar secondary patency rates, the number of treatments required to achieve those results and the loss of future sites become important issues.

Newer recanalization devices have become available for percutaneous use and have some applicability to the treatment of dialysis grafts. Atherectomy devices have been used for treating intragraft stenoses and venous stenoses that do not respond to angioplasty.[41,66,67] A disadvantage of this technique is that it requires a sheath that is considerably larger than the 5 to 7 French angioplasty balloon catheters. It also is considerably more expensive than angioplasty. Although the technical success rate is about 80 percent, the longer-term (6-month) clinical patency rate has been reported as 50 percent for intragraft stenoses, 67 percent for subclavian occlusions, and 38 percent for venous outflow occlusions.[67] Even excluding the initial technical failures, the 6-month clinical patency rate was only 56 percent, similar to the historically reported clinical patency rate after balloon angioplasty.[67] These results suggest that atherectomy should not be used as a primary modality and should be reserved for use when a very resistant stenosis is present that does not respond to angioplasty.

Stents are another modality used in the treatment of dialysis fistulas. A number of different stents have been used, including the Gianturco self-expanding stent,[68,69] the Strecker stent,[70] and the Wallstent.[71-75] The study by Beathard[68] randomized 58 patients, all of whom had 50 percent or greater stenosis at the PTFE graft-vein anastomosis, to stent or angioplasty groups. Gianturco Z stents were placed in 28 patients, and angioplasty was performed in the other 30 patients. Data on these patients demonstrated no significant difference in long-term follow-up. The primary patency rate (no further interventions) at 1 year was 19 percent for the stent group and 28 percent for the angioplasty group. Several studies using Wallstents for venous stenoses have been reported.[72,73,75] In most cases, the stent was placed when the result of a balloon dilatation was considered insufficient. Stents were placed in multiple venous channels, including the immediate venous outflow (anastomosis or slightly distal), or in the central veins, including the subclavian, innominate, and iliac veins. The success rate of stent placement was very high—96 to 100 percent. Complications included early rethrombosis, migration of the stent, and a pseudoaneurysm related to the stent.[75] An important complication related to the migration of two stents to the pulmonary artery after placement of a central line into the stented subclavian vein.[75] The primary patency rates at 6 months were 46 and 56 percent, and at 1 year 20 and 30 percent.[72,75] With reintervention the patency rates improved to 33 and 86 percent at 1 year.[72,75] The restenoses within the stent were treated largely by atherectomy (treating one technology's complication with another technology), although balloon angioplasty was also used. The primary stenoses occurred just above the previously placed stent. This raises the concern for losing vein sites that could be used to perform graft interpositions, and thus losing potential access site. One of the advantages of percutaneous transluminal angioplasty is that it does not preclude surgery at a later date. At this time stenting has been largely used for failed angioplasty as a secondary procedure, where the graft would otherwise be abandoned. Primary stenting of venous stenoses raises other issues. One important consideration is the expense of stent placement. If placing stents decreased the need for angioplasty or other interventions for a significant period, then the expense would be justified. If, however, the stents require the same degree of reintervention as an angioplasty, then placing a stent is disadvantageous.

Despite the poor results of stents in the peripheral veins, the results in the central veins appear more promising.[48,49,71,72] In dialysis patients, the vast majority of lesions in the proximal veins are caused by previous central line placement, usually temporary dialysis access catheters.[48,50,76] Angioplasty of these stenoses is effective, but the long-term patency is diminished because of restenosis.[42,77] Stenting seems to improve long-term patency. An additional consideration is that other options for treatment in this area are very poor. Wallstents, Gianturco stents, and Palmaz stents have been used in the central veins. All stents are subject to compression by musculoskeletal forces, and both the Palmaz stent and the Wallstent have been reported to undergo deformation.[48] Restenosis occurs in the central vein stents primarily in 6 to 12 months after placement. The high rate of restenosis in that period is consistent with hyperplasia developing in the stent.[72] When a stent is placed in a subclavian vein, the internal jugular vein origin should not be crossed unless absolutely necessary. This avoids compromising the jugular vein, allowing it to be used as another access site.[75] The considerations of cost of the stent and of reinterventions and the lack of long-term follow-up and randomized trials must be weighed before making the decision to go beyond an angioplasty procedure.

Conclusion

Revascularization of dialysis grafts remains a frustrating problem. In the last 20 years, there have been enormous advances in our understanding and approach to these grafts. Lysis of thrombosed grafts is faster and more economical than it was previously, and we have the ability to achieve excellent technical success. However, long-term success continues to elude us, and we need to continue to refine our approach to dialysis access. We need to better understand when to use angioplasty, atherectomy, stents, or surgical revision. Ultimately, our ability to achieve long-term success with dialysis access will await advances in mechanisms to prevent neointimal hyperplasia and subsequent restenosis. Once we are able to control that process, many of our present frustrations will only be of historical interest.

References

1. System USRD. U.S. renal data system annual data report. Bethesda, MD: National Institutes of Health, National Institute of Diabetes and Digestive and Kidney Disease, 1994.
2. Ziegler TW, Safa A, Amarillis K, Callihan V, Roberts AC, Valji K, et al. Prolonging the life of difficult hemodialysis access using thrombolysis, angiography and angioplasty. Adv Renal Replacement Ther 1995;2:52–59.
3. Besarab A, Dorrell S, Moritz M, Sullivan K, Michael H. What can be done to preserve vascular access for dialysis? Semin Dial 1991;4:155–156.
4. Carlson D, Duncan D, Naessens J, Johnson W. Hospitalization in dialysis patients. Mayo Clin Proc 1984;59:769–775.
5. Fan PY, Schwab SJ. Vascular access: concepts for the 1990s. J Am Soc Nephrol 1992;3:1–11.
6. Wilson S. Complications of vascular access procedures. In: Vascular Access Surgery. Chicago: Yearbook 1988:285.
7. Ballard JL, Bunt TJ, Malone JM. Major complications of angioaccess surgery. Am J Surg 1992;164:229–232.
8. Windus DW, Audrain J, Vanderson R, Jendrisak MD, Picus D, Delmez JA. Optimization of high-efficiency hemodialysis by detection and correction of fistula dysfunction. Kidney Int 1990;38:337–341.
9. Palder S, Kirkman R, Whittemore A, Hakim R, Lazarus J, Tilney N. Vascular access for hemodialysis. Ann Surg 1985;202:235–239.
10. Beathard G. Percutaneous transvenous angioplasty in the treatment of vascular access stenosis. Kidney Int 1992;42:1390–1397.
11. Schwartz C, McBrayer C, Sloan J, Meneses P, Ennis W. Thrombosed dialysis grafts: comparison of treatment with transluminal angioplasty and surgical revision. Radiology 1995;194:337–341.
12. Rittgers S, Garcia-Valdez C, McCormick J, Posner M. Noninvasive blood flow measurement in expanded polytetrafluoroethylene grafts for hemodialysis access. J Vasc Surg 1986;3:635–642.
13. Beathard GA. Physical examination of AV grafts. Semin Dial 1992;5:74.
14. Zeit RM. The problems and management of hemodialysis accesses. In: Castaneda-Zuniga W, Tadavarthy S, eds. Interventional radiology. Baltimore: Williams & Wilkins, 1992:422–437.

15. Roberts A, Valji K, Bookstein J, Hye R. Pulse-spray pharmaco-mechanical thrombolysis for treatment of thrombosed dialysis access grafts. Am J Surg 1993;16:221–226.

16. Fillinger M, Reinitz E, Schwartz R, Resetarits D, Paskanik A, Bruch D, et al. Graft geometry and venous intimal-medial hyperplasia in arteriovenous loop grafts. J Vasc Surg 1990;11: 556–566.

17. Windus DW. Permanent vascular access: a nephrologist's view. Am J Kidney Dis 1993;21:457–471.

18. Malchesky P, Koshino I, Pennza P, Kiraly R, Nose Y. Analysis of the segmental venous stenosis in blood access. Trans Am Soc Artif Intern Organs 1975;21:310–319.

19. Turmel-Rodrigues L, Pengloan J, Blanchier D, Abaza M, Birmele B, Haillot O, et al. Insufficient dialysis shunts: improved long-term patency rates with close hemodynamic monitoring, repeated percutaneous balloon angioplasty, and stent placement. Radiology 1993;187:273–278.

20. Kanterman RY, Vesely TM, Pilgram TK, Guy BW, Windus DW, Picus D. Dialysis access grafts: anatomic location of venous stenosis and results of angioplasty. Radiology 1995;195: 135–139.

21. Etheredge E, Haid S, Maeser M, Sicard G, Anderson C. Salvage operations for malfunctioning polytetrafluoroethylene hemodialysis access grafts. Surgery 1983;94:464–470.

22. Hartley L, Ellis F, Rendall D, Cameron J, Ogg C. The use of urokinase in Scribner shunts. Br J Urol 1972;42:246–249.

23. Hargrove WCI, Barker CF, Berkowitz HD, et al. Treatment of acute peripheral arterial and graft thromboses with low-dose streptokinase. Surgery 1982;92:981–993.

24. Zeit R. Clearing of clotted dialysis shunts by streptokinase injection at multiple sites. AJR 1983;141:1053–1054.

25. Young A, Hunter D, Castaneda-Zuniga W, et al. Thrombosed synthetic hemodialysis access fistulas: failure of fibrinolytic therapy. Radiology 1985;154:639–642.

26. So S, Hunter D. Vascular access for long-term hemodialysis: preoperative evaluation and the management of failing and thrombosed accesses. In: Castaneda-Zuniga W, Tadavarthy S, eds. Interventional radiology. Baltimore: Williams & Wilkins, 1992:437–450.

27. Rodkin R, Bookstein J, Heeney D, Davis G. Streptokinase and transluminal angioplasty in the treatment of acutely thrombosed hemodialysis access fistulas. Radiology 1983;149:425–428.

28. Zeit R. Arterial and venous embolization: declotting of dialysis shunts by direct injection of streptokinase. Radiology 1986; 159:639–641.

29. Docci D, Turci F, Baldrati L. Successful declotting of arteriovenous grafts with local infusion of urokinase in hemodialyzed patients. Artif Organs 1986;10:494–496.

30. Davis G, Dowd C, Bookstein J, Maroney T, Lang E, Halasz N. Thrombosed dialysis grafts: efficacy of intrathrombic deposition of concentrated urokinase, clot maceration, and angioplasty. AJR 1987;149:177–182.

31. Bookstein J, Fellmeth B, Roberts A, Valji K, Davis G, Machado T. Pulsed-spray pharmacomechanical thrombolysis: preliminary clinical results. AJR 1989;152:1097–1100.

32. Valji K, Bookstein JJ, Roberts AC, Oglevie SB, Pittman C, O'Neill MP. Pulse-spray pharmacomechanical thrombolysis of thrombosed hemodialysis access grafts: long-term experience and comparison of original and current techniques. AJR 1995; 164:1495–1500.

33. Bookstein JJ, Valji K. Pulse-spray pharmacomechanical thrombolysis. Radiology 1993;187:273–278.

34. Roberts A, Bookstein J. Dialysis fistula occlusion: treatment by thrombolysis. In: Kadir S, ed. Current practice of interventional radiology. Philadelphia: Decker, 1991:291–294.

35. Valji K, Bookstein JJ, Roberts AC, Davis GB. Pharmacomechanical thrombolysis and angioplasty in the management of clotted hemodialysis grafts: early and late clinical results. Radiology 1991;178:243–247.

36. Valji K, Roberts A, Bookstein J. Thrombosed hemodialysis access grafts: management with pulse-spray thrombolysis and bal-

loon angioplasty. In: Strandness D, Van Breda A, eds. Vascular diseases: surgical and interventional therapy. New York: Churchill-Livingstone, 1994:1087–1095.

37. Bookstein JJ, Valji K. Pulse-spray pharmacomechanical thrombolysis. J Vasc Intervent Radiol 1992;3:505–510.

38. Bookstein J, Valji K. Pulse-spray pharmacomechanical thrombolysis: updated clinical and laboratory observations. Semin Intervent Radiol 1992;9:174–182.

39. Bookstein JB, Valji K, Roberts AC. Pharmacomechanical thrombolysis in the peripheral vasculature (pulse-spray technique). In: Comerota AJ, ed. Thrombolytic therapy for peripheral vascular disease. Philadelphia: Lippincott, 1995:297–312.

40. Valji K. Transcatheter treatment of thrombosed hemodialysis access grafts. AJR 1995;164:823–829.

41. Zemel G, Katzen BT, Dake MD, Benenati JF, Lempert TE, Moskowitz L. Directional atherectomy in the treatment of stenotic dialysis access fistulas. Nephrol Dial Transplant 1991;6: 5–10.

42. Saeed M, Newman GE, McCann RL, Sussman SK, Braun SD, Dunnick NR. Stenoses in dialysis fistulas: treatment with percutaneous angioplasty. Radiology 1987;164:693–697.

43. Puckett J, Lindsay S. Midgraft curettage as a routine adjunct to salvage operations for thrombosed polytetrafluoroethylene hemodialysis access grafts. Am J Surg 1988;156:139.

44. Zemel G, Katzen BT, Dake MD, Benenati JF, Lempert TE, Moskowitz L. Directional atherectomy in the treatment of stenotic dialysis access fistulas. J Vasc Intervent Radiol 1990;1: 35–38.

45. Okadome K, Komori K, Fukumitsu T, Sugimachi K. The potential risk for subclavian vein occlusion in patients on haemodialysis. Eur J Vasc Surg 1992;6:602–606.

46. Kerstein K. End-stage renal disease with venous occlusion in both upper extremities. South Med J 1993;86:1229–1232.

47. Davis D, Peterson J, Feldman R, et al. Subclavian vein stenosis: a complication of subclavian dialysis. JAMA 1984;252:3404.

48. Shoenfeld R, Hermans H, Novick A, Brener B, Cordero P, Eisenbud D, et al. Stenting of proximal venous obstructions to maintain hemodialysis access. J Vasc Surg 1994;19:532–538.

49. Matthews R, Clugston R, Eisenhauer A, Dake M, Schatz R, Feinstein E. Balloon expandable stents to treat central venous stenoses in hemodialysis patients. Am J Nephrol 1992;12:451–456.

50. Surratt R, Picus D, Hicks M, Darcy M, Kleinhoffer M, Jendrisak M. The importance of preoperative evaluation of the subclavian vein in dialysis access planning. AJR 1991;156:623–625.

51. Cohen MAH, Kumpe DA, Durham JD, Zwerdlinger SC. Improved treatment of thrombosed hemodialysis access sites with thrombolysis and angioplasty. Kidney Int 1994;46:1375–1380.

52. Collen D, Lijnen H. Molecular mechanisms of thrombolysis: implications for therapy. Biochem Pharmacol 1990;40:177–186.

53. Collen D. Designing thrombolytic agents: focus on safety and efficacy. Am J Cardiol 1992;69:71A–81A.

54. Lijnen H, Collen D. New strategies in the development of thrombolytic agents. Blut 1988;57:147–162.

55. Fareed J, Bacher P, Messmore H, et al. Pharmacological modulation of fibrinolysis by antithrombotic and cardiovascular drugs. Prog Cardiovasc Dis 1992;34:379–398.

56. Sands JJ, Patel S, Plaviak D, Miranda CL. Pharmacomechanical thrombolysis with urokinase for treatment of thrombosed hemodialysis access grafts: a comparison with surgical thrombectomy. ASAIO J 1994;40:M886–M888.

57. Summers S, Drazan K, Gomes A, Freischlag J. Urokinase therapy for thrombosed hemodialysis access grafts. Surg Gynecol Obstet 1993;176:534–538.

58. Schuman E, Quinn S, Standage B, Gross G. Thrombolysis versus thrombectomy for occluded hemodialysis grafts. Am J Surg 1994;167:473–476.

59. Schwab SJ, Raymond JR, Saeed M, Newman GE, Dennis PA, Bollinger RR. Prevention of hemodialysis fistula thrombosis: early detection of venous stenoses. Kidney Int 1989;36:707–711.

60. Collins D, Lambert M, Middleton J, et al. Fistula dysfunction: effect on rapid hemodialysis. Kidney Int 1992;41:1292–1296.

61. Safa AA, Valji K, Roberts A, Ziegler T, Oglevie SB, Hye RJ. Prolongation of dialysis graft survival by balloon angioplasty of venous anastomosis stenoses detected by clinical surveillance. Radiology 1996;199(3):653–657.

62. Middleton WD, Picus DD, Marx MV, Melson GL. Color doppler sonography of hemodialysis vascular access: comparison with angiography. AJR 1989;152:633–639.

63. Dousset V, Grenier N, Douws C, Senuita P, Sassouste G, Ada L, et al. Hemodialysis grafts: color Doppler flow imaging correlated with digital subtraction angiography and functional status. Cardiovasc Intervent Radiol 1992;15:228–233.

64. Kumpe DA, Cohen MA. Angioplasty/thrombolytic treatment of failing and failed hemodialysis access sites: comparison with surgical treatment. Prog Cardiovasc Dis 1992;34:263–278.

65. Dapunt O, Feurstein M, Rendl K, Prenner K. Transluminal angioplasty versus conventional operation in the treatment of haemodialysis fistula stenosis: results from a 5 year study. Br J Surg 1987;74:1004–1005.

66. Vorwerk D, Guenther RW. Removal of intimal hyperplasia in vascular endoprostheses by atherectomy and balloon dilatation. AJR 1990;154:617–619.

67. Gray RJ, Dolmatch BL, Buick MK. Directional atherectomy treatment for hemodialysis access: early results. J Vasc Intervent Radiol 1992;3:497–503.

68. Beathard GA. Gianturco self-expanding stent in the treatment of stenosis in dialysis access grafts. Kidney Int 1993;43:872–877.

69. Quinn SF, Schuman ES, Hall L, Gross GF, Uchida BT, Standage BA, et al. Venous stenoses in patients who undergo hemodialysis: treatment with self-expandable endovascular stents. Radiology 1992;183:499–504.

70. Petar B, Tomislav I, Miodrag I, Snezana A. Strecker stent in stenotic hemodialysis Brescia-Cimino arteriovenous fistulas. Cardiovasc Intervent Radiol 1992;15:217–220.

71. Zollikofer CL, Antonucci F, Stuckmann G, Mattias P, Bruhlmann WF, Salomonowitz EK. Use of the Wallstent in the venous system including hemodialysis-related stenoses. Cardiovasc Intervent Radiol 1992;15:334–341.

72. Vorwerk D, Guenther RW, Mann H, Bohndorf K, Keulers P, Alzen G, et al. Venous stenosis and occlusion in hemodialysis shunts: follow-up results of stent placement in 65 patients. Radiology 1995;195:140–146.

73. Vorwerk D, Gunther RW, Bohndorf K, Kistler D, Gladziwa U, Sieberth HG. Follow-up results after stent placement in failing arteriovenous shunts: a three-year experience. Cardiovasc Intervent Radiol 1991;14:285–289.

74. Vorwerk D, Gunther RW, Bohndorf K, Kistler D, Handt S, Mann H, et al. Percutaneous vascular endoprostheses for occlusions or stenoses of hemodialysis shunts. Rofo Fortschr Geb Rontgenstr Nuklearmed 1990;153:239–245.

75. Gray RJ, Horton KM, Dolmatch BL, Rundback JH, Anaise D, Aquino AO, et al. Use of Wallstents for hemodialysis access-related venous stenoses and occlusions untreated with balloon angioplasty. Radiology 1995;195:479–484.

76. Schwab SJ, Quarles LD, Middleton JP, Cohan RH, Saeed M, Dennis VW. Hemodialysis-associated subclavian vein stenosis. Kidney Int 1988;33:1156–1159.

77. Landwehr P, Lackner K, Gotz R. Dilatation and balloon-expandable stents for the treatment of central venous stenosis in dialysis patients. Cardiovasc Intervent Radiol 1992;15:228–233.

V

Interventional Radiology of the Central Nervous System

44

Revascularization in the Central Nervous System

ROBERT W. HURST

Because of the widespread prevalence of cerebro-vascular disease, ischemic brain damage represents an immense medical problem with both individual and public health consequences. Recent developments in neuroradiologic intervention have made possible the revascularization of regions of the central nervous system (CNS) that have been deprived of adequate blood flow. Revascularization procedures encompass various methods for restoring and/or increasing blood flow in symptomatic CNS ischemia. Procedures include intraarterial thrombolysis, pharmacologic dilation or balloon angioplasty of intracranial vasospasm, and angioplasty of brachiocephalic vessels. These procedures permit possible salvage of CNS tissue and function in the face of ischemia. Through the use of these techniques, the potential exists to prevent or ameliorate a significant portion of damage resulting from acute cerebral infarction, the third leading cause of mortality in the developed world. In addition, revascularization techniques have been shown to have a significant role in the treatment of delayed ischemic deficits caused by post-subarachnoid-hemorrhage vasospasm. Ischemic deficits resulting from vasospasm are responsible for the majority of delayed morbidity and mortality in patients surviving aneurysmal subarachnoid hemorrhage.

Acute Intraarterial Thrombolytic Therapy in the Central Nervous System

The term *stroke* refers to a sudden-onset nonconvulsive neurologic deficit of cerebrovascular origin. Etiologies of stroke include a heterogeneous group of cerebrovascular disorders ranging from ischemia to intracranial hemorrhage. Eighty to 90 percent of ischemic strokes result from atherothrombotic or thromboembolic events.[1] Most often, emboli originate from the extracranial carotid arteries or the heart. In patients studied angiographically within 6 hours of ischemic stroke onset, an occlusive vascular lesion correlating with the clinical deficit has been found in over 75 percent.[2,3] The need for rapid effective treatment in ischemic stroke is highlighted by the dismal outcome of affected patients when managed conservatively. Despite recent improvements in short-term survival, largely due to improved supportive care, over 15 percent of patients admitted to hospital with ischemic stroke will be dead within 30 days. The long-term prognosis for return to normal life is also poor because even 1 year later less than half of patients suffering major ischemic stroke can live independently.[4] In cases of stroke caused by thromboembolic occlusion of vessels supplying the central nervous system, acute treatment with intraarterial thrombolysis is based on the premise that timely reopening of vessels with consequent restoration of blood flow to the affected regions may result in significant resolution of neurologic deficits. Because of the high frequency of thromboembolic occlusive lesions in patients with ischemic stroke, thrombolysis holds tremendous therapeutic potential in this devastating disease.

The first investigation into the use of thrombolytic agents for the treatment of acute stroke was reported in 1958.[5] Later trials during the pre-CT era were hampered by an inability to diagnose the cause of acute neurologic deficit before intravenous thrombolytic treatment. In these early studies, limited angiographic diagnosis of vessel occlusion and infrequent follow-up angiography impaired confirmation of vascular pathology and vessel reopening. With the introduction of CT scanning, diagnosis was improved, particularly with regard to the exclusion of intracranial hemorrhage. Nevertheless, the intravenous use of thrombolytic agents resulted in systemic fibrinolytic effects and discouraging numbers of hemorrhagic complications.[6]

Intraarterial injection of thrombolytic agent was found to be useful in the treatment of vascular disease involving both peripheral and coronary circulations. However, the application of these methods to the central nervous system lagged behind. By the 1980s, advances in superselective arterial catheterization made possible the local infusion of fibrinolytic agent directly into occluded vessels of the CNS. Since smaller amounts of fibrinolytic medication were needed, systemic effects were minimized. In addition, angiographic studies suggested that stagnation of flow proximal to an occlusion might prevent delivery of fibrinolytic agent to the blockage unless the agent was infused locally into the obstructed vessel. Since 1988, multiple studies have reported successful reopening of occluded CNS vessels with good resolution of deficits and minimal hemorrhagic complications.[7-9]

Before one uses intraarterial fibrinolytic agents, one must accurately diagnose the etiology of the neurologic deficit and evaluate the potential contraindications. Understanding the pathophysiology of embolic infarction is essential to appreciating the potential complications and contraindications to acute intraarterial fibrinolytic therapy in the treatment of stroke.

Pathophysiology

Acute occlusion of an artery supplying CNS tissue results in ischemic injury to the neuronal tissue supplied by the vessel. Experimental studies of focal ischemia suggest that the severity of injury depends on both the time and completeness of the ischemic insult. At least two critical thresholds of blood flow exist. At blood flows below 15 and 17 ml per 100 g per minute, cessation of neuronal electrical activity occurs but cell viability is maintained and activity may be restored to normal with increases in blood flow. As flow rates decrease further, below about 10 ml per 100 g per minute, failure of ion pumps occurs with disruption of the cell membrane and irreversible cell death. The area of ischemic brain receiving blood flow between the two thresholds—the upper threshold of electrical failure and the lower threshold of pump failure and cell death—represents a zone of injured but potentially viable tissue that surrounds the most severely affected region of irreversible ischemic damage. This surrounding area, known as the *ischemic penumbra,* appears capable of functional recovery after restoration of blood flow.[10] Clinical studies in humans with embolic stroke have confirmed the existence of an ischemic penumbra. The studies also suggest that a finite interval exists after occlusion after which ischemic damage is most likely irreversible. Chances for return of function within the ischemic penumbra are therefore greater with earlier reperfusion.[11]

Multiple clinical features of the embolic episode in addition to the time of occlusion are important in determining the severity and amount of ischemic dam-age. The site and completeness of occlusion as well as the availability of collateral flow also directly affect the degree of ischemia. In the anterior circulation, emboli most commonly occlude the middle cerebral artery (MCA), a vessel whose distribution has limited effective collateral supply. Proximal MCA occlusion often blocks the territory of the lenticulostriate arteries, a region with even more limited collateral availability. Because severe ischemia results, irreversible injury tends to occur relatively early.[12] In the vertebrobasilar circulation, multiple potential collaterals often permit longer viability of marginally perfused tissue after embolic occlusion.

Embolic occlusion of a vessel is often followed by fragmentation of the embolus and distal migration. In addition, physiologic fibrinolytic mechanisms act to lyse the obstructing clot. Although over 90 percent of embolic occlusions eventually show angiographic reopening, less than 20 percent recanalize within 24 hours of stroke onset.[1,13] Spontaneous recanalization within the substantially shorter interval needed to preserve cerebral tissue and restore function is even less common.[14,15] The speed and extent of physiologic mechanisms of clot lysis are therefore unpredictable and often do not permit reperfusion within sufficient time to prevent infarction. Intraarterial infusion of thrombolytic agent dissolves obstructing clot and accelerates reopening of the vessel in an effort to salvage ischemic but still viable tissue.

With lysis or distal migration of the embolus, reperfusion may expose a recently ischemic area to the force of arterial blood pressure. Distention and congestion of the capillary bed follow with possible extravasation of red cells into ischemic areas, a phenomenon known as *hemorrhagic transformation.* The occurrence of red cell extravasation is related to the volume of tissue affected as well as the extent and severity of ischemic damage. If present, hemorrhagic transformation is most often mild, with only microscopic or petechial hemorrhage into part of the infarcted area. Some degree of hemorrhagic infarction is common and is reported in 10 to 43 percent of patients in CT studies of embolic infarction.[16-20] Although hemorrhagic infarction is frequently seen in patients who are clinically stable or improving, its clinical significance is uncertain. With large amounts of bleeding into an area of infarction, transformation into frank parenchymal hemorrhage may occur. Virtually always associated with clinical deterioration, parenchymal hemorrhage represents solid clot with mass effect that may displace, damage, or destroy the involved area as well as adjacent brain. Although the risk factors predisposing to this condition are incompletely understood, parenchymal hemorrhage appears more commonly in patients treated with anticoagulants. Fortunately, parenchymal hemorrhage following ischemic stroke is uncommon, with an incidence of less than 5 percent.[19]

The time course of hemorrhagic transformation has important therapeutic implications. Spontaneous hemorrhagic transformation in the anterior circulation is uncommon before 6 hours after occlusion and is identified in only 5 percent of cardioembolic strokes within the first 24 hours. Most instances occur even later, with nearly one-quarter occurring later than 1 week after the ictus.[21] The usual delay in the occurrence of hemorrhagic transformation implies the existence of a therapeutic window during which vessel reopening may be accomplished with minimal chance of clinically significant hemorrhage into the ischemic area.

Any therapy designed to reperfuse ischemic CNS tissue also has the potential for causing or worsening hemorrhagic transformation of the ischemic area. The result may be clinically insignificant hemorrhagic infarction or, uncommonly, parenchymal hemorrhage. In each case the risk of hemorrhagic transformation of damaged tissue must be balanced against the potential for regaining CNS function. Successful early thrombolytic recanalization has been shown to actually decrease the amount of hemorrhagic transformation.[8] Early treatment of appropriately selected patients may therefore provide the best protection against hemorrhagic complications in addition to offering potential restoration of CNS function.

Pharmacologic agents useful for fibrinolysis in the CNS have been widely studied for use in peripheral and coronary circulations. They include urokinase, streptokinase, and tissue plasminogen activator (tPA). All clinically available thrombolytic agents act by enhancing conversion of plasminogen to plasmin, a serine protease that degrades fibrin and fibrinogen as well as factors II, Va, and VIIIa. Although the thrombolytic effects are comparable for all three agents, there are significant differences in relative clot selectivity, plasma half-life, dose, and cost. A complete comparison of the characteristics of these and other agents is beyond the scope of this chapter and is more fully covered elsewhere in this volume.

Pretreatment Evaluation

Guidelines for acute intraarterial fibrinolytic therapy in stroke must focus primarily on rapid and thorough neurologic evaluation to select appropriate patients. Patients most likely to benefit include those with severe acute-onset neurologic deficits secondary to thromboembolic occlusion. Exclusion of intracranial hemorrhage is paramount and can usually be accomplished without difficulty using CT. Patients with stroke secondary to lacunar infarction, global hypoperfusion, or diffuse intracranial vascular disease have no large-vessel occlusive lesion and will not benefit from intraarterial thrombolysis. Differentiating between these potential causes for stroke may be challenging, requiring expert neurologic consultation and frequently angiographic evaluation.

A careful history and physical examination are necessary to exclude potential contraindications to thrombolytic therapy. Any condition predisposing to an increased risk of hemorrhage must be actively sought and may exclude patients from consideration. Potential contraindications include intracranial aneurysm, arteriovenous malformation, recent surgery, or biopsy. Other systemic conditions such as peptic ulcer disease, diverticulosis, coagulation defect, uncontrolled hypertension, or conditions associated with an expected shortened survival (malignancy, hepatic disease, coma) may also exclude fibrinolytic therapy. Baseline coagulation parameters, including prothrombin time (PT), partial thromboplastin time (PTT), fibrinogen level, and platelet count, are evaluated.

In the anterior circulation, it is important to accomplish fibrinolytic therapy within 6 to 8 hours after the onset of the clinical deficit. Later therapy may be less effective in restoring function and may also expose the patient to an increased risk of hemorrhagic transformation of a previously infarcted area. In the vertebrobasilar circulation, the safety and effectiveness of fibrinolysis after longer intervals of occlusion have been demonstrated. With basilar occlusion, additional sources of collateral circulation may delay irreversible clinical deterioration and minimize the potential for hemorrhagic transformation. In addition, the devastating and frequently fatal outcome of vertebrobasilar embolism justifies later treatment of these patients. Intraarterial fibrinolytic treatment at up to 24 hours in patients with partial deficits of brain stem function has resulted in good resolution of clinical deficits. Several clinical features of vertebrobasilar ischemia portend a poor outcome, however, and represent contraindications to thrombolysis. These include coma lasting more than 6 hours, decerebration, and angiographic evidence of chronic occlusion.[7]

An unenhanced CT scan is obtained immediately before starting fibrinolytic treatment. Any CT evidence of intracranial hemorrhage is an absolute contraindication to the use of fibrinolytic agents. Large hypodense infarcts and mass effect on CT have been found to predict the development of later hemorrhagic transformation.[16,19,20] Although uncommon within the first 6 to 7 hours of embolic stroke, these imaging findings are also relative contraindications to the use of thrombolytic therapy. MRI cannot exclude hyperacute hemorrhage with sufficient confidence to proceed with fibrinolytic therapy on the basis of MRI alone. Although MR angiography may detect the abrupt vessel cutoff that suggests embolic occlusion, it does not eliminate the need for angiography and delays the initiation of therapy. Therefore, MRI is not currently incorporated into the evaluation of patients being considered for urgent intracranial fibrinolytic therapy.

At present, conventional angiography represents not only the means for delivering therapy but also the diagnostic method of choice for confirming and localizing the site of vessel occlusion. Local anesthesia is used when possible so that the patient's neurologic condition can be monitored throughout the procedure. A high-resolution digital angiography unit with road-mapping capability is essential for identifying the lesion and navigating within intracranial vessels. The transfemoral approach is used. Injection of the symptomatic vessel distribution is performed, including appropriate oblique views to confirm occlusion as the etiology of the clinical deficit and to localize the site of vessel occlusion (Fig. 44-1). Diagnostic angiography of other vessel distributions may also be necessary. Evaluation of the contralateral carotid artery, for example, is important to demonstrate cross-filling of the intracranial circulation, especially in cases of complete carotid occlusion.

After the occlusion is localized, selective catheterization of the occluded vessel is accomplished using a variable-stiffness microcatheter such as a Tracker-18 (Target Therapeutics Inc.). A variable-stiffness microcatheter is necessary rather than a flow-directed microcatheter because of stagnant or very slow flow occurring proximally in the obstructed vessel. The microcatheter is placed within the occluded vessel as closely as possible to the site of obstruction, and infusion of fibrinolytic agent is started (Fig. 44-2). If infusion just proximal to the obstruction fails to lyse the blockage, the catheter tip may be embedded in the obstruction and infusion continued. In some cases, gentle advancement of a flexible guidewire and catheter past the embolus may be possible with initial injection of agent distal to the clot. The catheter is then withdrawn through the clot while continued injection perfuses the clot with thrombolytic agent. Infusion is continued into and proximal to the obstruction. Reported rates of urokinase infusion have varied from 2000 to over 13,000 units per minute, with total doses of up to 750,000 units. Infusion is terminated after 2 hours or when recanalization occurs (Fig. 44-3).[9,22,23]

Heparinization is instituted during the angiogram after the arterial puncture. After the procedure, depending on the etiology of the occlusion, heparinization may be continued for a short period (2–3 days) or stopped. Long-term therapy with anticoagulants or antiplatelet agents is based on the etiology of the obstructive lesion and the potential for recurrence. Follow-up values of PT, PTT, fibrinogen, and platelet counts are checked.

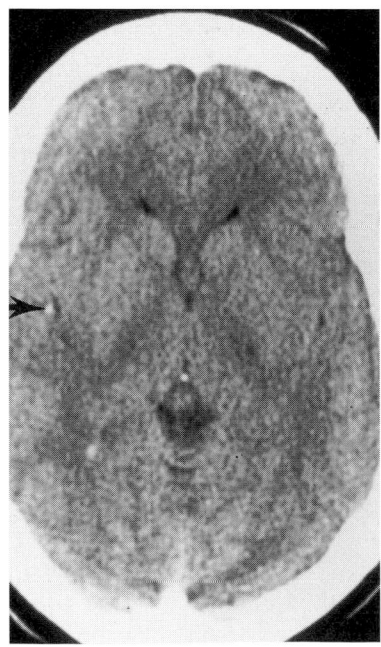

A

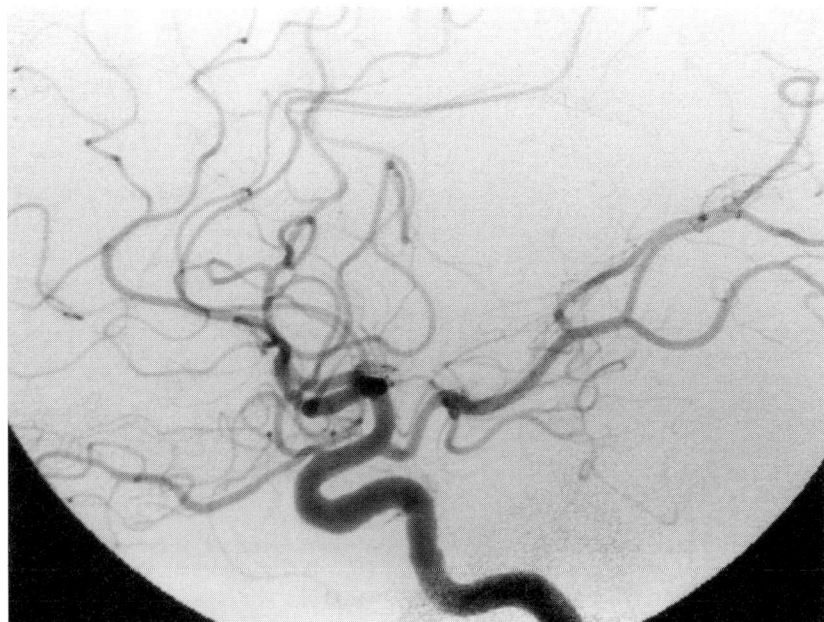

B

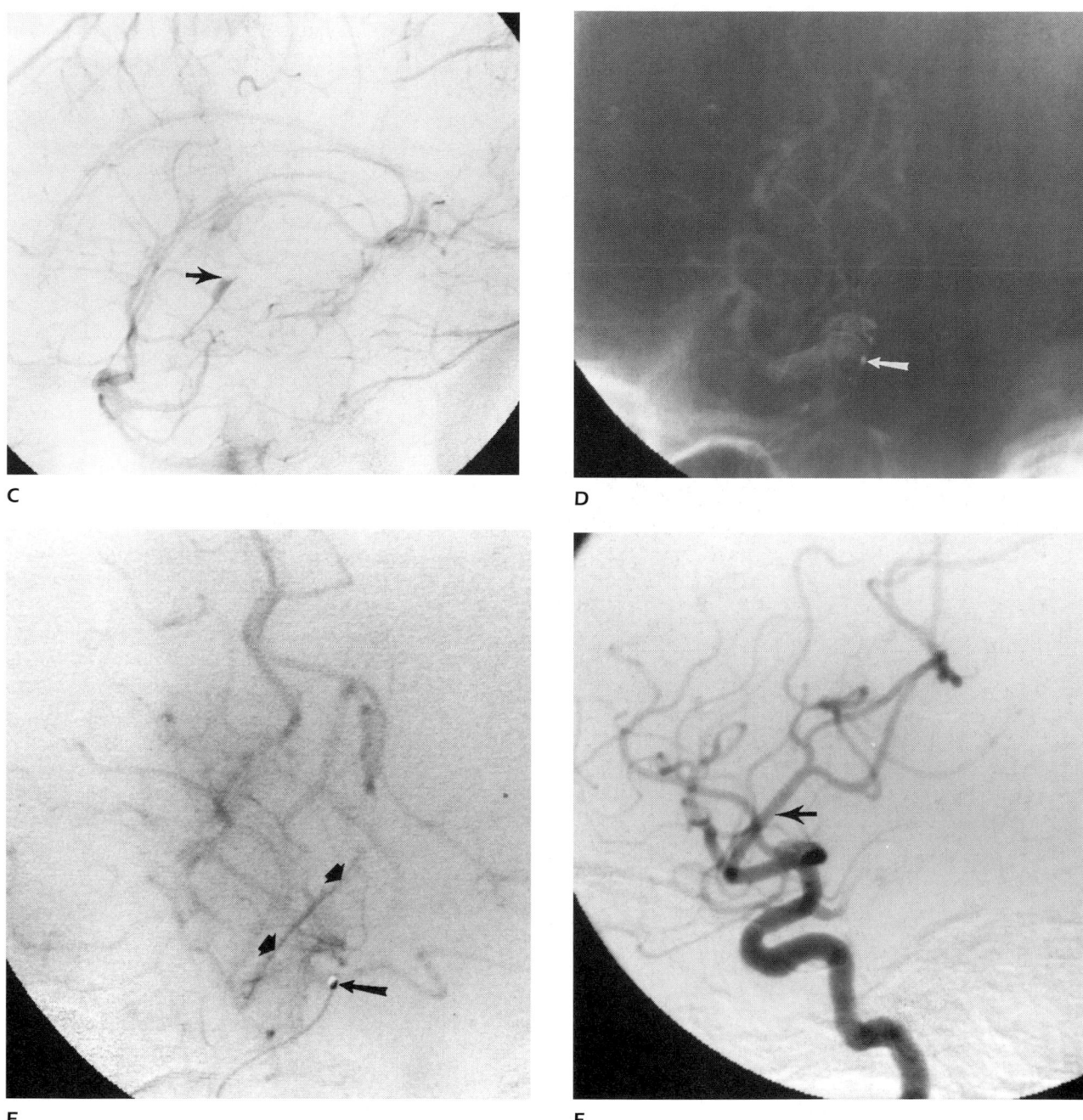

C

D

E

F

Figure 44-1. (A) A 28-year-old woman with new-onset left hemiparesis, left sensory deficits, and left hemianopsia. CT scan 3 hours after onset of neurologic deficit shows hyperdensity in the right sylvian fissure compatible with embolus within a branch of the MCA (*arrow*). (B) Lateral right internal carotid artery injection (early arterial phase) demonstrates no filling of the inferior trunk of the right MCA. (C) Venous phase shows gradual filling of the inferior trunk of the right MCA with abrupt meniscus cutoff at the site of the embolic occlusion (*arrow*). Unsubtracted (D) and subtracted (E) film of selective right MCA injection shows filling of the obstructed branch (*short arrows*) prior to superselective catheterization and urokinase infusion (*arrow* shows catheter tip). (F) Right internal carotid injection after thrombolysis shows filling of the previously occluded branch (*arrow*). The patient made a full recovery. Evaluation showed a cardiac source of the embolus.

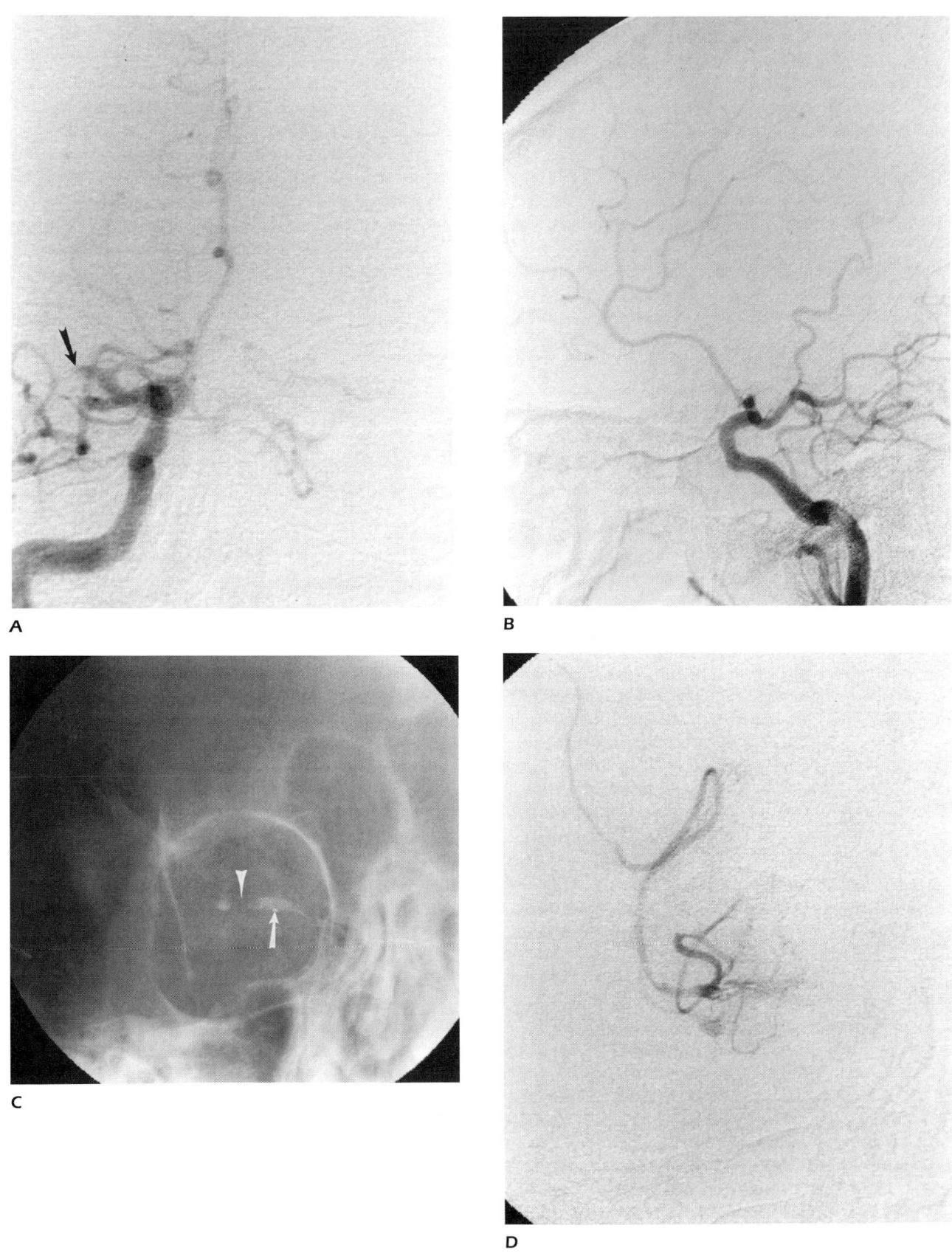

A

B

C

D

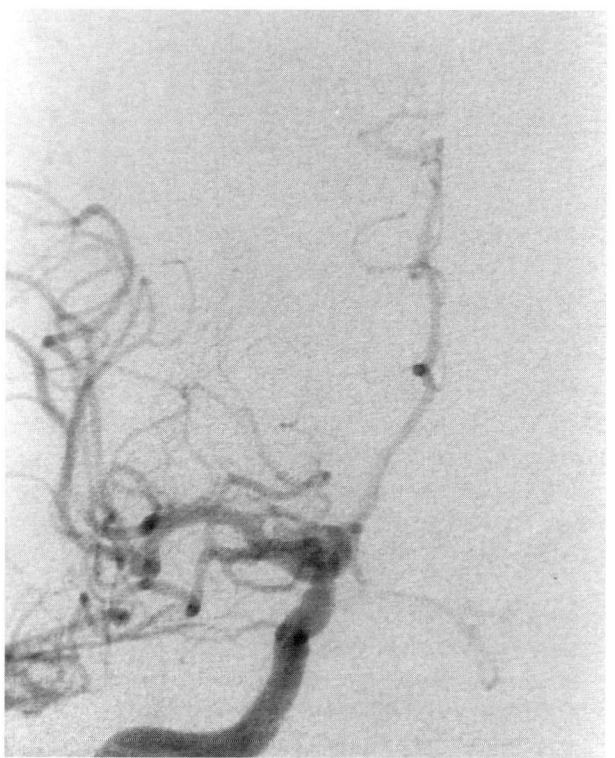

E

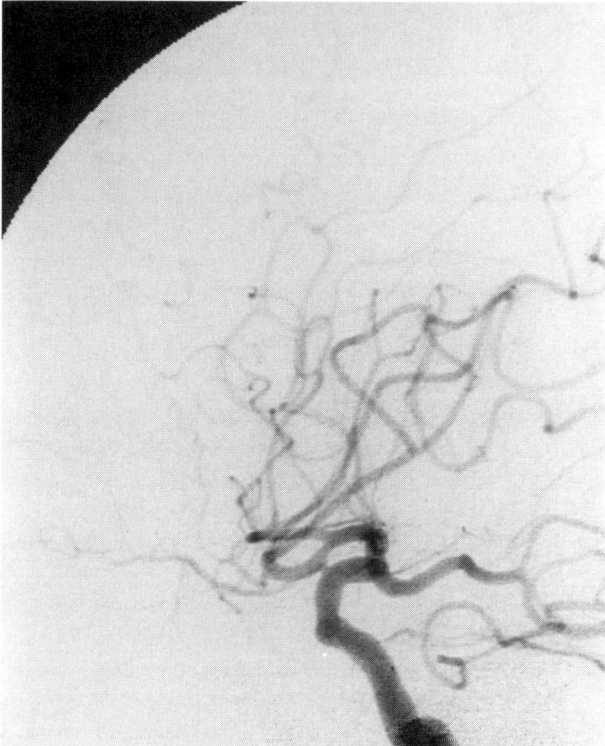

F

Figure 44-2. Anteroposterior (A) and lateral (B) views demonstrate acute right MCA occlusion (*arrow*, A). (C) Unsubtracted view with microcatheter tip (*arrow*) adjacent to embolus (*arrowhead*). There is no distal filling of distal MCA branches. (D) Anteroposterior subtracted view. After lysis of the embolus, there is filling of distal branches of the MCA. Anteroposterior (E) and lateral (F) views of right internal carotid artery (RICA) injection after urokinase infusion demonstrate reperfusion of distal MCA branches.

Results

The ultimate place of fibrinolytic therapy in the management of acute stroke will be known with complete certainty only after large clinical trials have been conducted with sound methodology.[24] Recent studies of local intraarterial infusion of thrombolytic agents have suggested both the safety and effectiveness of the procedure. In 94 patients treated for carotid territory occlusions using either streptokinase or urokinase, recanalization of the obstructed artery was accomplished in 75 percent. The rate of intraparenchymal hemorrhage, not all of which was symptomatic, was less than 10 percent.[9,12,25] In the vertebrobasilar circulation, treatment of a total of 86 patients has been reported in three separate studies. Recanalization was accomplished in 51 percent with a rate of hemorrhage of only 3.5 percent.[25-27]

Although impressive, the angiographic results are not nearly as important an end point as the clinical benefits resulting from treatment. Successful recanalization of anterior circulation occlusive lesions, most involving the MCA, resulted in clinical improvement of 75 percent of patients.[9,12] These results assume even more significance when considered in light of the poor outcome of embolic stroke using conventional treatment methods. Over 80 percent of patients with stroke secondary to occlusion of the middle cerebral artery will be dead or manifest severe persistent neurologic deficits 3 months after the ictus.[28] The potential for benefit in posterior circulation events is also striking. A retrospective comparison of patients whose vertebrobasilar occlusions were successfully recanalized using intraarterial fibrinolysis to a group treated with conventional anticoagulant therapy has been reported. The results revealed significant clinical benefits, with survival in nearly 70 percent of those whose vessels were recanalized compared to a 13 percent survival in patients treated conventionally.[27]

Most studies reported to date have included patients in whom treatment was started at relatively long intervals after onset of the neurologic deficit. Continued efforts to institute therapy as early as possible after the onset of neurologic deficit would be expected to result in even fewer complications and more significant clinical benefit.[23,29]

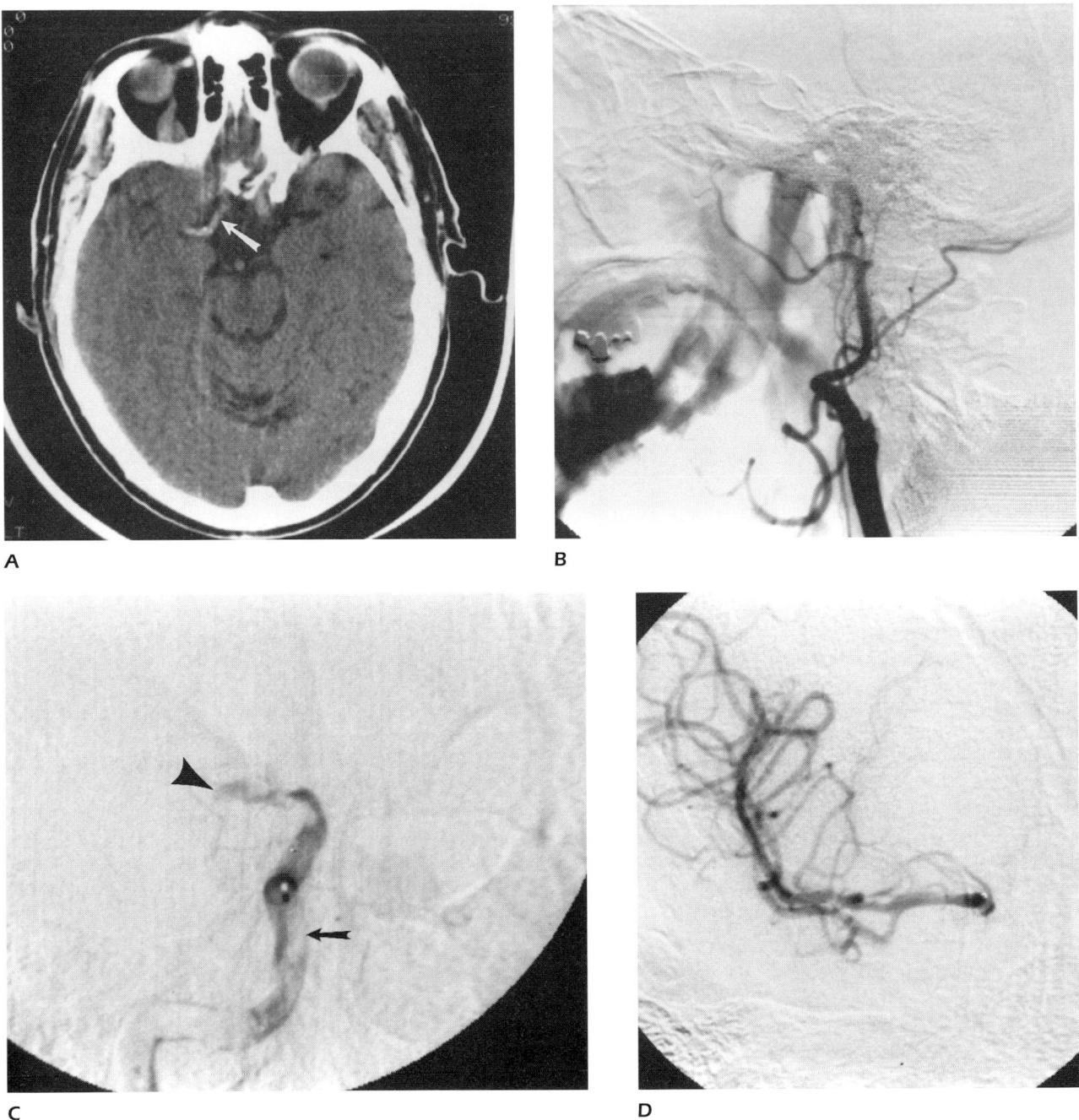

A

B

C

D

Figure 44-3. (A) A 75-year-old man with acute-onset left hemiparesis, hemianopsia, and neglect. CT shows acute clot within the supraclinoid internal carotid artery (ICA) extending into the MCA (*arrow*). (B) Right common carotid artery injection shows acute occlusion of the right internal carotid artery. (C) Anteroposterior angiogram with microcatheter in cavernous ICA during thrombolysis. Considerable residual clot remains within the ICA (*arrow*) with com-plete obstruction distally (*arrowhead*). (D) Anteroposterior angiogram during thrombolysis after opening of the middle and anterior cerebral arteries. (E) Proximal ICA injection following thrombolysis shows tight atherosclerotic stenosis at the origin of the reopened ICA (*arrow* shows catheter tip). The patient improved neurologically during the thrombolysis procedure. Endarterectomy was performed, and there were no neurologic deficits 24 hours later.

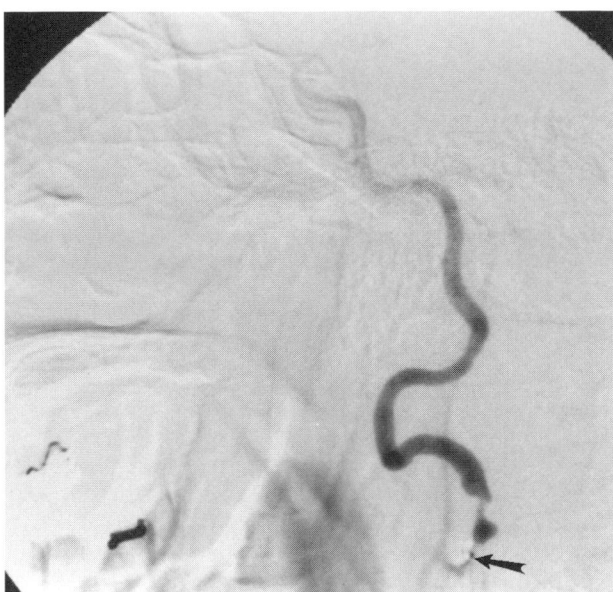

E   **Figure 44-3** (continued).

Intracranial Angioplasty and Pharmacologic Vasodilation in Post-Subarachnoid-Hemorrhage Vasospasm

Intracranial aneurysm rupture is responsible for nearly 80 percent of nontraumatic subarachnoid hemorrhages. In the United States, aneurysmal subarachnoid hemorrhage affects over 26,000 patients a year, with estimates of mortality as high as 50 to 65 percent. The prognosis for survivors of aneurysmal subarachnoid hemorrhage is equally grim. Of those patients well enough to be discharged from the hospital, nearly two-thirds never regain the quality of life experienced before rupture.[30] After aneurysmal rupture, the risk of recurrent rupture is high: up to 2 percent per day for the first 2 weeks, with mortality of up to 60 percent associated with rebleeding. Modern techniques of microneurosurgery usually permit surgical clipping of ruptured aneurysms, thereby minimizing rebleeding as a cause of significant morbidity. The leading contributor to both morbidity and mortality in patients surviving aneurysmal subarachnoid hemorrhage is delayed ischemic damage caused by intracranial vasospasm.

Although incompletely understood, the pathophysiology of post-subarachnoid-hemorrhage vasospasm is initiated by the presence of blood in the subarachnoid space. Vasoactive substances resulting from the presence of subarachnoid blood act on the vessel wall to cause abnormal contraction of vascular smooth muscle and narrowing of luminal diameter. Evidence has implicated a number of substances, including oxyhemo-globin, released from erythrocytes in the subarachnoid space, as potential spasmogens engendering this contraction.[31] The narrowed vessel lumen decreases delivery of blood to the cerebral parenchyma with consequent ischemia and infarction.

Over time a spectrum of morphologic change develops in the vessel wall. Histologic findings include the occurrence within days of intimal and medial swelling. By 1 to 6 weeks, intimal proliferation and myonecrosis are present with associated luminal narrowing. Medial fibrosis and enlargement of luminal diameter have been found to develop after 3 to 6 months. The arteriopathic response of the cerebral arteries after exposure to subarachnoid blood appears to be both time- and dose-dependent.[32]

Estimates of the incidence of angiographically visible vasospasm after subarachnoid hemorrhage range as high as 76 percent. Less frequent but more important clinically is the incidence of symptomatic vasospasm giving rise to ischemic deficits. Delayed ischemic deficits resulting from vasospasm are reported with a frequency of about 30 percent from major referral centers.[31] Clinically significant vasospasm (vasospasm resulting in delayed ischemic deficit) is therefore not equivalent to angiographic vasospasm. Treatment modalities are directed only toward those patients who manifest symptoms of cerebral ischemia.

Clinically symptomatic vasospasm usually presents between the 4th and 12th day after subarachnoid hemorrhage. New-onset headache or exacerbation of previously present headache most often heralds the development of symptomatic vasospasm. Impairment of consciousness invariably develops, often accompanied by the appearance of focal neurologic signs. Progression is usually rapid, reaching a peak within a few hours to a day.

The focal neurologic features of symptomatic vasospasm reflect not only the anatomy of the most significantly involved vascular territories but also the adequacy of the potential collateral circulation and the cerebral autoregulatory capacity. Thus the involvement of intracranial vessels by vasospasm is often far more extensive than is suggested by the focal neurologic deficits. The clinical localization of a vascular territory responsible for a given deficit is important, however, because it permits therapy to be directed toward areas of clinically significant ischemia. Involvement of the MCA results in hemiparesis, often with aphasia or contralateral neglect, depending on whether the dominant or nondominant hemisphere is involved. If unilateral, anterior cerebral artery (ACA) involvement results in contralateral leg weakness. Commonly bilateral, ACA spasm may cause diplegia in company with abulia, mutism, akinesia, incontinence, and frontal

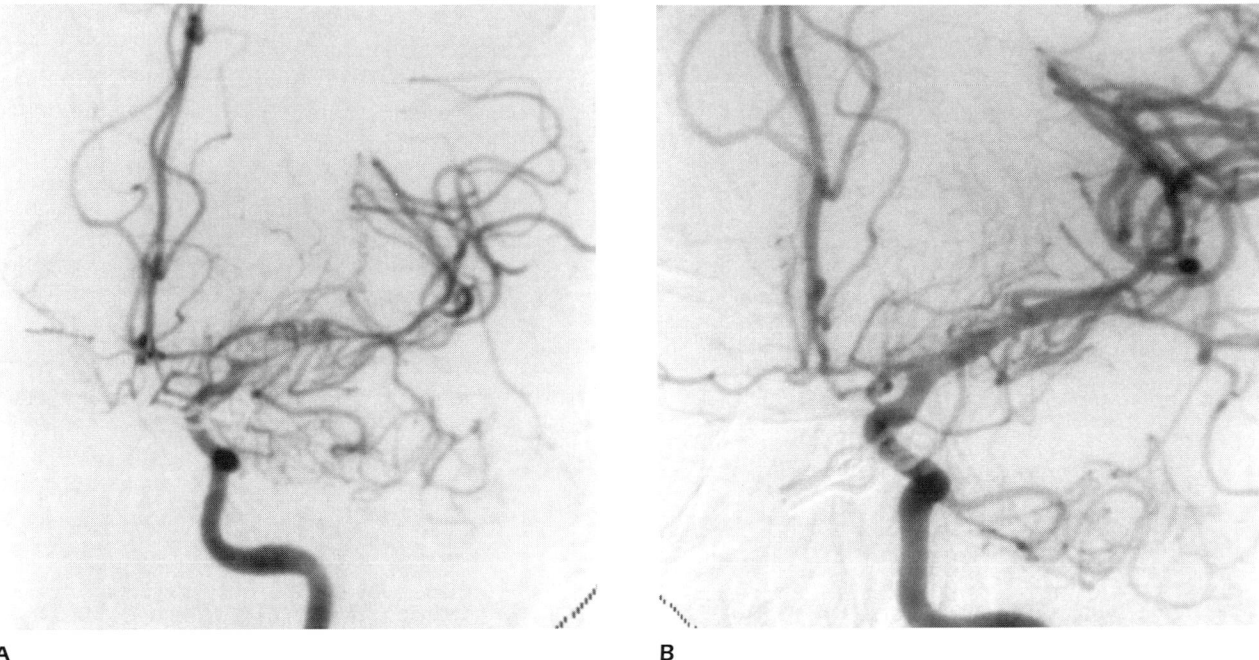

A **B**

Figure 44-4. (A) Anteroposterior left ICA injection with diffuse spasm in a 40-year-old woman with new-onset aphasia and right hemiparesis 2 days after aneurysm clipping. (B) After angioplasty of the left MCA, there is improved filling of the MCA and distal branches.

release signs. Posterior cerebral artery (PCA) spasm may manifest hemianopsia in addition to obtundation, bilateral ptosis, and memory deficits suggesting rostral basilar artery embolism. With involvement of the posterior fossa vasculature, deficits referrable to the brain stem are often the most prominent clinical features. Dysconjugate gaze and skew deviation may occur, often accompanied by coma. Autonomic derangements may be present and include alterations of blood pressure, temperature, and respiration.[33]

The amount of blood present on early CT scan is the most accurate predictor of a high risk of subsequent vasospasm. Localized clot surrounding a vessel or a layer of blood greater than 1 mm thick suggests a particularly high risk (Fig. 44-4). The distribution and severity of vasospasm have been found to correlate closely with the clot distribution on CT scan.[34,35]

Transcranial Doppler (TCD) provides a means of noninvasively evaluating flow velocities within the major intracranial arteries at the base of the brain. Narrowing of the vessel lumen with the onset of vasospasm results in a proportional increase in flow velocity as long as constant flow is maintained.

Daily serial assessment of flow velocities with TCD is performed in patients after subarachnoid hemorrhage. With the development of vasospasm, increasing flow velocities are seen. Because increased flow velocities on TCD precede the development of clinical ischemic deficits, identification of high-risk patients is

often possible before the development of clinically significant vasospasm. Because of the limited collateral networks supplying the territory of the middle cerebral arteries, close correlation is often found between the amount of MCA narrowing angiographically and increases in flow velocities measured by TCD. Normal blood flow velocities in the proximal MCA range between 30 and 80 cm per second, with a mean of 62 cm per second. Velocities greater than 120 cm per second usually correlate with angiographically visible spasm, and velocities greater than 200 cm per second usually reflect severe spasm with greater than 50 percent vessel narrowing. Increased velocities may also be found in the supraclinoid internal carotid artery, the ACA, the PCA, and the basilar arteries if they are involved by vasospasm.

Serial TCD assessment has indicated that patients who develop velocities indicative of severe spasm on or before the fifth day after hemorrhage are at high risk of developing subsequent infarction.[36] The early identification of high-risk patients permits close observation and rapid institution of therapy as soon as clinical signs of vasospasm develop.

Medical Treatment

Reversal of ischemic neurologic deficits secondary to vasospasm was first documented in 1967 after therapy with induced hypertension.[37] Also in 1976, Kosnik and

Hunt reversed vasospasm-associated neurologic deficits in 6 of 7 patients using a combination of induced hypertension and volume expansion.[38] Later studies have confirmed the usefulness of volume expansion and pharmacologically induced hypertension to increase perfusion to ischemic areas in the face of impaired autoregulation. Fluid status is monitored via a Swan-Ganz catheter, and pressor agents are added if neurologic deficits persist in the face of volume expansion. Reversal of neurologic deterioration may be seen in over 80 percent of patients so treated. Reasons for faiure of therapy include preexisting infarct, rebleeding, or inability to induce hypertension. Complications have included rebleeding from unclipped aneurysm, pulmonary edema, hyponatremia, coagulopathy, and myocardial infarction. Conversion of bland infarcts into hemorrhagic infarcts has not been reported with mean blood pressures in the range of 150 mm.[39]

Recent data have also confirmed the usefulness of the calcium channel blocker nimodipine in ameliorating the effects of vasospasm-induced ischemia.[40] Patients treated with nimodipine demonstrate decreases in morbidity and mortality of 30 percent in comparison to placebo-treated patients.[41] Nimodipine treatment also decreases the incidence of angiographically visible vasospasm.[42]

Current vasospasm management protocols include treatment with calcium channel blockers as well as presurgical supportive measures. After aneurysm clipping, volume expansion and induced hypertension may be instituted if clinical spasm occurs. Failure of maximal medical treatment to resolve vasospasm-induced ischemic deficits should prompt early consideration of interventional neuroradiologic therapy.

Interventional Neuroradiologic Treatment

Angioplasty of vasospastic intracranial vessels with an inflatable intravascular balloon catheter results in mechanical dilation of the vessel lumen with concomitant increase in blood flow. This treatment was first reported in 1984 by Zubkov et al., and multiple series have confirmed the clinical usefulness of intracranial angioplasty in the treatment of selected patients with symptomatic vasospasm.[43-46]

Vasospasm-induced neurologic deficits that persist in the face of maximal medical therapy constitute the major indication for interventional neuroradiologic treatment of vasospasm. Before angioplasty, patients must meet criteria to ensure that the procedure is performed only when necessary in those most likely to benefit. Patients must be symptomatic with new-onset neurologic deficits after subarachnoid hemorrhage. The deficits must not have reversed with maximal

medical therapy. Abnormal flow velocities on TCD should be present but are not sufficient in the absence of symptoms to initiate therapy. Recent CT scan must be available to exclude the most common differential causes for new-onset deficits, including rehemorrhage, hydrocephalus, and infarction. Most importantly, angiographic vasospasm in the vessel distribution responsible for the clinical deficit must be present.

As with any treatment modality for cerebral ischemic deficit, angioplasty should be performed as soon as possible after the onset of symptoms. The most dramatic recovery is usually seen after treatment instituted within 6 to 12 hours after the deficit, although recovery may occur after later angioplasty.

Angiography is performed via the transfemoral approach on a high-resolution digital angiography unit with road-mapping capability. Local anesthesia is used whenever possible to permit neurologic examination throughout the procedure. An initial four-vessel study determines the extent of vasospasm, the severity of narrowing, the sources of collateral circulation, and the presence of residual aneurysm. In patients whose aneurysms have been clipped, heparinization is used during the procedure and reversed immediately thereafter using protamine sulfate.

Intracranial arteries involved by vasospasm usually demonstrate smooth angiographic narrowing of the contrast column. Distal widening of a vessel or the presence of a branch with a diameter greater than the parent vessel also indicates a high probability of involvement by vasospasm. Irregular discontinuous areas of spasm may also be seen, and on occasion a more beaded appearance is present. With severe spasm, slowing of flow through the involved vessel distributions may necessitate prolonged filming sequences. Spasm may involve only a localized area adjacent to the aneurysm or may be distributed diffusely and extensively throughout the intracranial circulation.[47,48]

Comparison with prior angiograms is very useful in determining the extent of vasospastic narrowing in an individual vessel. Previously present intracranial atherosclerotic disease should be identified as well as areas of vessel hypoplasia. Hypoplasia of the A_1 segment is particularly common in patients with aneurysms of the anterior communicating artery complex and must be excluded before attempting angioplasty of this segment.

Intracranial dilation using angioplasty or pharmacologic means is performed only in vessel distributions that do not harbor an unclipped previously ruptured aneurysm. Increasing blood flow through an unprotected aneurysm may result in hemorrhage with potentially fatal consequences.

Several types of microballoons are available for

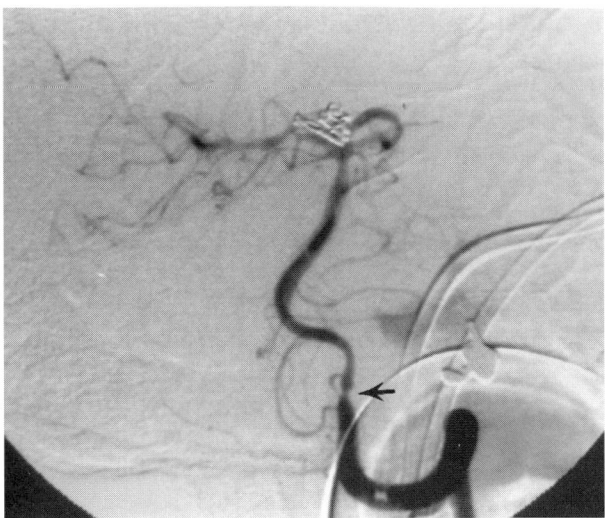

A

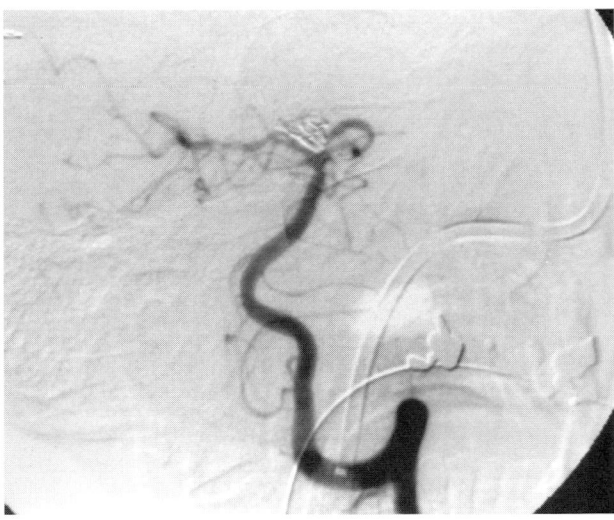

B

Figure 44-5. (A) A 64-year-old man with new-onset cranial nerve deficits and decreased level of consciousness 2 days after clipping of a basilar tip aneurysm. Left vertebral artery injection shows spasm of the intracranial vertebral artery (*arrow*) and proximal basilar artery. (B) After angioplasty, there is return of normal caliber.

intracranial angioplasty. A silicone balloon catheter has a low inflation pressure and elongates within the vessel lumen, thereby minimizing the risk of vessel rupture (Interventional Therapeutics Corporation, Inc.). It is important to select the proper size of balloon to avoid overdilating the vessel, since overdilation may lead to rupture. A calibrated leak latex balloon catheter exerts transient pressure on the vessel wall with each inflation (Balt Corporation). Immediate deflation occurs through the distal leak in the balloon. Either catheter may be used without a guidewire, thereby reducing the risk of vessel injury. The catheters are advanced into the involved vessel with gentle inflation and deflation of the balloon. However, it is often helpful to use a guidewire when entering the A_1 segment, especially in the face of decreased flow from vessel narrowing. A polyethylene balloon catheter is also available and may prove useful, particularly when relatively prolonged spasm has resulted in more rigidity of the vessel wall, requiring a higher pressure for dilation (Target Therapeutics Corporation, Inc.). This catheter also uses a guidewire for steerability.

The technique of angioplasty for intracranial vasospasm reflects the underlying pathology of the vessel wall. The mechanism of dilation in vasospasm is believed to be stretching and disruption of connective tissue, which abnormally proliferates in the vessel wall in response to subarachnoid blood. This mechanism of vessel dilation is in marked contrast to the mechanism of angioplasty of vessels affected by atherosclerosis. In atherosclerotic disease, high intraluminal pressure is needed to fracture intraluminal plaque and dilate the vessel. In vasospasm, only transient, low dila-

tion pressures are necessary to accomplish angioplasty, and high pressures or overdilation of the vessel is to be avoided. After intracranial angioplasty for vasospasm, no angiographic evidence of dissection or anatomic disruption of the vessel wall should occur (Figs. 44-5 and 44-6). Restoration of normal luminal diameter and configuration is seen throughout the treated portion of the vessel. After treatment by angioplasty, no recurrence of vasospasm has been observed in treated segments of the vessel.[49]

Intracranial angioplasty is performed in involved vessel distributions responsible for clinical deficits. Dilation using angioplasty is limited to the larger intracranial vessels, including the supraclinoid ICA, the intracranial vertebral arteries, the basilar artery, and proximal segments of the anterior, middle, and posterior cerebral arteries. Attempts to perform angioplasty in more distal segments incur a high risk of vessel rupture with currently available balloon catheters. Angioplasty in the immediate vicinity of an aneurysm clip is also to be avoided because of the potential for clip dislodgment as well as the possibility of angiographically invisible wall defects, which might predispose to rupture.[50]

Postangioplasty angiographic evaluation is performed to ensure that all segments of the involved vessel distribution amenable to angioplasty have been dilated. This requires filming the vessel in both anteroposterior and lateral views. Any residual segments involved by vasospasm are then dilated. After angioplasty of proximal vessels, improved filling of the more distal portions of the distribution is frequently present.

Reported results of intracranial angioplasty indicate

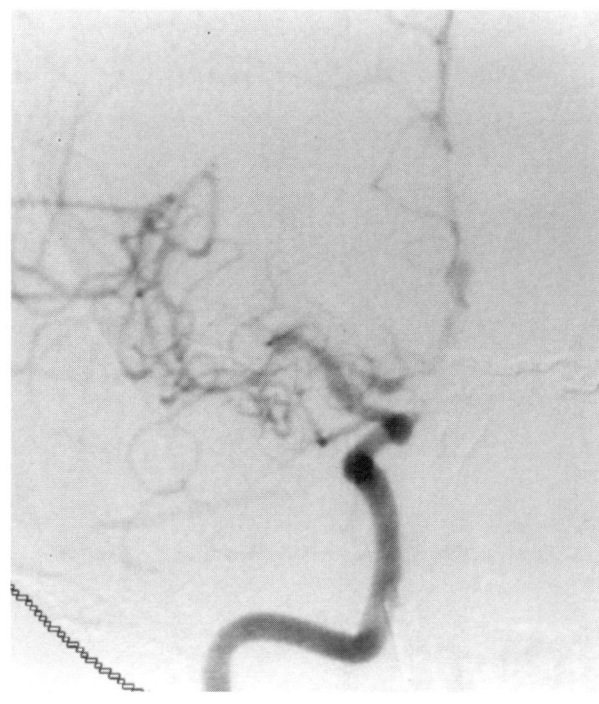

A

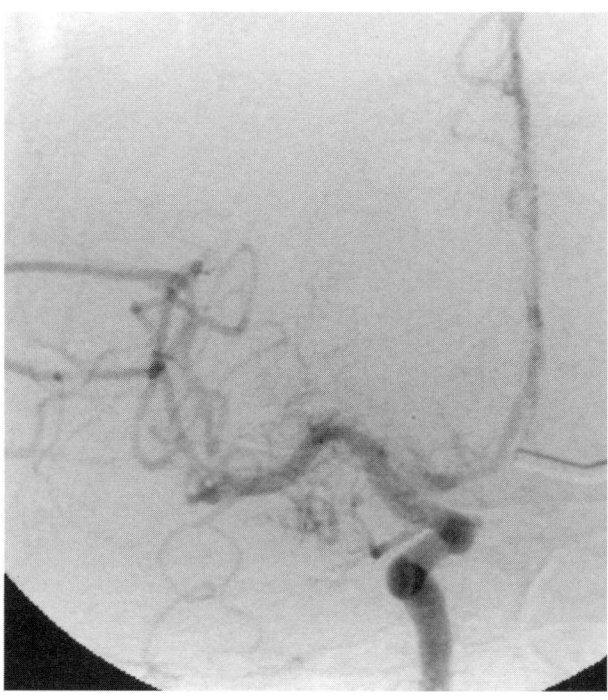

B

Figure 44-6. (A) 45-year-old woman with new-onset left upper extremity and left facial paresis 4 days after clipping of an anterior communicating artery aneurysm. Anteroposte-rior right internal carotid artery injection shows diffuse spasm. (B) After angioplasty, there is dilation of A_1 and M_1 segments with improved filling of distal branches.

that significant clinical improvement may be expected in over 60 percent of patients treated. Several instances of complications, including rare vessel rupture, have been reported, particularly if more distal portions of vessels are treated.[44–46] After the procedure, patients are monitored in the intensive care unit, and hypertensive hypervolemic therapy is continued. Follow-up TCD is performed to confirm decreased flow velocity after dilation. Increases in flow velocity seen on follow-up TCD studies may indicate the development of new areas of spasm in previously uninvolved portions of the vessel.[51]

In some cases vasospasm involves arterial branches that cannot be selectively catheterized or more distal branches where angioplasty is unsafe. Under these circumstances, intraarterial infusion of vasodilating medication may be performed. A number of studies have documented the effectiveness and safety of intraarterial papaverine infusion for the treatment of vasospasm following subarachnoid hemorrhage.[52,53] Selective infusion is performed directly into the involved vessel through a microcatheter (Fig. 44-7). A dose of 300 mg of papaverine in 100 ml of normal saline is infused over 20 minutes to 1 hour. Results indicate a 65 to 90 percent success rate in dilating arterial distributions involved by vasospasm. No significant blood pressure alterations or toxicity has been reported. A transient

10 to 20 percent increase in heart rate may occur, however, during the infusion. Unlike intracranial angioplasty, the effects of papaverine infusion are not necessarily permanent, and recurrent symptomatic vasospasm may develop in treated vessel distributions, requiring retreatment.

Interventional neuroradiologic treatment offers significant benefit to large numbers of patients with intracranial vasospasm who fail to respond to medical treatment. These patients would otherwise be expected to sustain severe neurologic deficits, which in many cases would result in permanent disability. Early consideration and application of these methods are important for the optimal management of appropriately selected patients with post-subarachnoid-hemorrhage vasospasm.

Angioplasty of Brachiocephalic Vessels for Cerebral Ischemia

Occlusive disease, most often of atherosclerotic origin, involving the brachiocephalic vessels may result in impairment of blood flow to either the internal carotid artery distribution or to the vertebrobasilar distribution. Consequently, symptomatic ischemia referable to

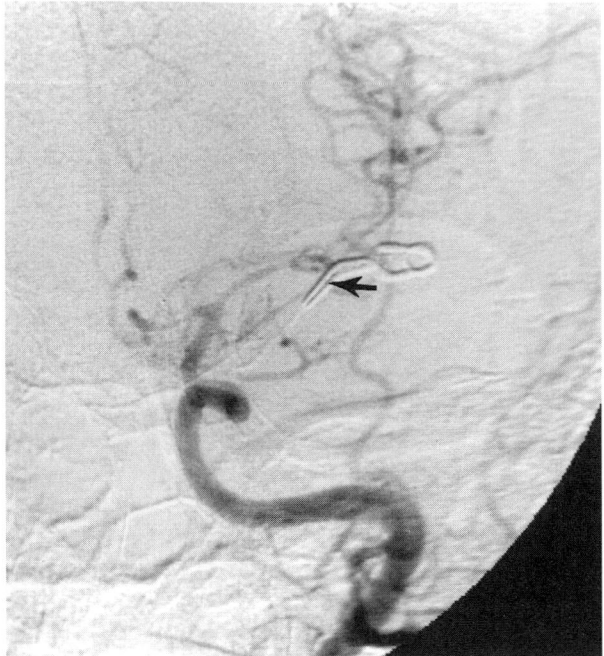

A

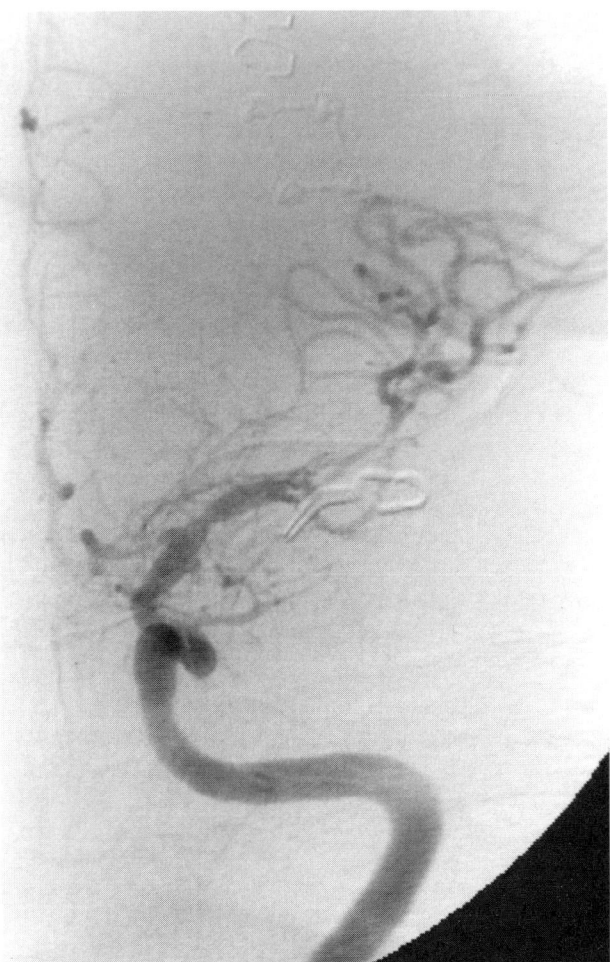

Figure 44-7. (A) A 38-year-old woman with new-onset right hemiparesis and aphasia 7 days after subarachnoid hemorrhage and 6 days after clipping of a left MCA bifurcation aneurysm. Anteroposterior left internal carotid injection shows diffuse spasm involving ACA and MCA distributions (*arrow* shows clip). (B) After angioplasty of the M_1 segment proximal to the clip followed by papaverine infusion into distal branches, there is improved filling.

B

either cerebral distribution may arise from occlusive disease involving the major branches of the aortic arch. In general, symptomatic occlusive lesions of the internal carotid artery, common carotid artery, and innominate artery give rise to neurologic deficits referable to the internal carotid vascular distribution.[54] Most commonly, symptoms include amaurosis or deficits resulting from compromise of the ipsilateral cerebral hemisphere (Fig. 44-8). Symptomatic lesions of the vertebral or subclavian arteries may cause deficits referable to the vertebrobasilar circulation, including dysfunction of the brain stem, cerebellum, or occipital lobes.

Since the pioneering studies of percutaneous transluminal angioplasty (PTA) in 1964, the technique has found wide application in the management of vascular occlusive disease in many locations throughout the body. Successful dilation in over 90 percent of cases with a complication rate of approximately 5 percent has made PTA the treatment of choice in many lower extremity and coronary vessel locations. Extension of the procedure to treatment of stenotic lesions involving vessels of the upper extremity and neck has pro-

ceeded much more cautiously, however. There are several reasons for the less frequent application of PTA to brachiocephalic vessels. First, these vessels are less often involved by atherosclerotic disease, the major indication for PTA in vessels of the lower extremity. Consequently, much less emphasis has been placed on brachiocephalic vessel dilation in the past, and less experience with PTA is available. In addition, the often complex relationship of a given vascular lesion to clinical neurologic symptoms and concern for the procedural risks have inhibited the use of PTA in brachiocephalic vessels.

Stenotic lesions in the brachiocephalic vessels are frequently found in asymptomatic patients. Even when symptoms are present, the relationship of stenosis to cerebral ischemic symptoms is often unclear. Consequently, the mere presence of an occlusive lesion involving the major blood supply to a symptomatic region of the brain does not constitute definite evidence that the lesion is causative. This fact is particularly true in the vertebrobasilar circulation, with its multiple

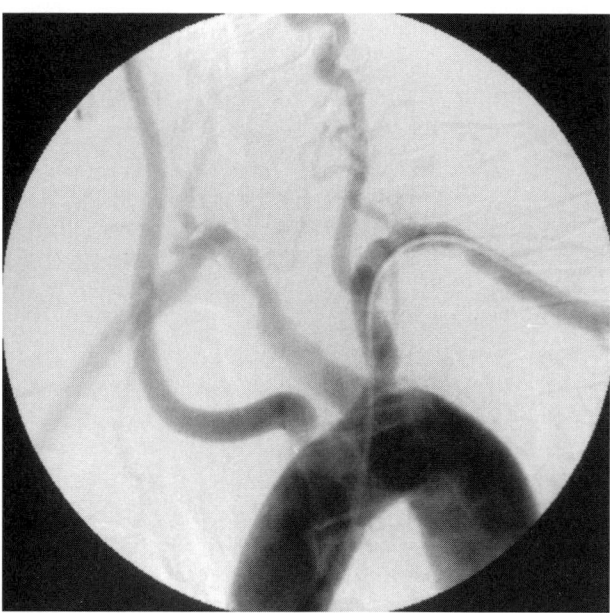

A

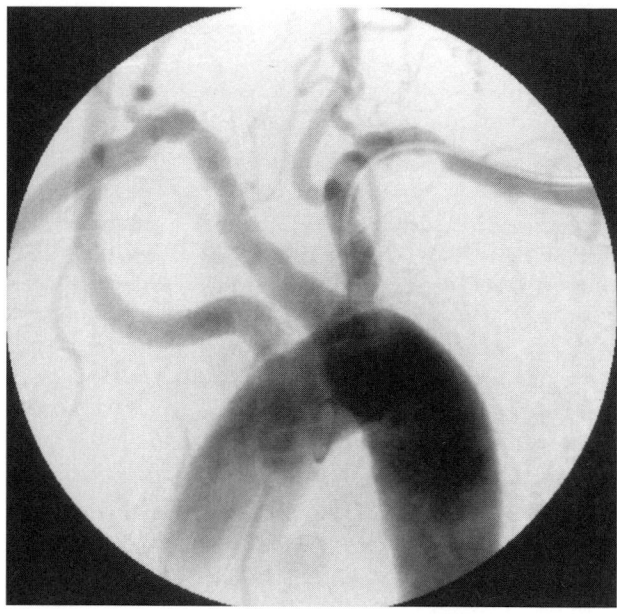

B

Figure 44-8. (A) Aortic arch injection in a 75-year-old woman with stenosis at the origin of the right common carotid artery, which originates directly from the aortic arch. The left common carotid artery was completely occluded. Symptoms included right amaurosis and transient ischemic attacks (TIAs) referable to the right cerebral hemisphere. (B) After angioplasty, the TIAs resolved.

pathways of potential collateral circulation. In each case, specific clinical symptomatology, potential collateral pathways, the location and severity of the obstruction, the natural history of the lesion, and associated vascular lesions must all be considered when identifying a lesion as the cause of neurologic symptoms. Only after this often complex process is completed can a decision be made to proceed with treatment. At that point the relative risks of potential therapy, including medical management, PTA, and surgical therapy, should be evaluated to determine appropriate treatment.

A final but significant factor that has hampered more widespread application of PTA to the treatment of extracranial occlusive disease relates to the concern for potential complications, especially the possibility of cerebral embolization. This concern must be addressed through a better understanding of the frequency of significant neurologic complications associated with the procedure. Despite the infrequent application of PTA for the treatment of cerebral ischemia in the past, considerable data are accumulating to suggest its safety as an alternative to surgical endarterectomy or bypass in selected patients with occlusive disease of the brachiocephalic vessels.

Any of the major branches of the aortic arch may be involved by atherosclerotic occlusive disease. The relative frequency of atherosclerotic involvement of the brachiocephalic vessels has been evaluated in sev-

eral large series of patients with cerebrovascular insufficiency.[55,56] Obstructive lesions are most often found to involve the carotid bifurcation, with an incidence of slightly greater than 30 percent on each side. Frequent involvement of the more distal internal carotid artery and involvement of the common carotid artery contribute to the potential for compromise of the anterior circulation. After the carotid bifurcation in frequency of involvement are the proximal vertebral arteries, affected in nearly 20 percent on each side. Stenosis of the subclavian and innominate arteries occurs with lower but still significant frequency. An extremely important and often confounding factor in determining the clinical significance of involvement of these vessels by occlusive disease is the presence of multiple lesions in over two-thirds of patients studied.

Several characteristics of stenotic lesions have been noted to increase the chance for good results following balloon dilation. These are similar to lesion characteristics delineated in other vascular beds and include short lesion length, smooth lesion configuration, and an absence of extensive calcification. In contrast, a number of features of the lesion represent relative contraindications to the use of PTA. These include ulcerations, presence of fresh thrombus, and complete arterial occlusion. Arterial narrowing secondary to extrinsic compression from tumor is not amenable to treatment with PTA, and narrowing associated with considerable tortuosity also represents a relative contraindication.[57] Reports have also appeared on the use of PTA in nonatherosclerotic vascular disease involving the vessels of the aortic arch including the ICA.[58]

Carotid Artery

As the most common brachiocephalic location of atherosclerotic involvement, stenosis involving the internal carotid artery has long been of interest as an area for preventive treatment of stroke. Surgical endarterectomy for occlusive disease of the internal carotid artery has been employed for this purpose since 1954 with varying degrees of enthusiasm. Several recent randomized trials of medical treatment alone versus endarterectomy with medical treatment have been conducted in patients with symptomatic carotid stenosis. All have concluded that patients with carotid stenosis equal to or greater than 70 percent with symptoms referrable to the territory of the narrowed vessel do better with a combination of surgical and medical treatment than with medical treatment alone.[59-61] Perioperative complication rates in the studies ranged from 2.1 to 7.5 percent.

The randomized study results provide a sound basis for anatomic correction of symptomatic internal carotid stenosis in appropriately selected patients. However, controversy remains surrounding the role and risks of PTA in the management of internal carotid disease. Reasons for optimism that the carotid artery PTA risk may be within an acceptable range are found in the data for peripheral PTA, which show rates of embolization, most asymptomatic, of approximately 3 to 5 percent.[62] Although any embolus to vessels of the CNS may result in significant symptoms, these relatively low rates at least provide a basis for trials comparing PTA to surgical therapy in symptomatic patients.

Several investigators have studied the potential for distal blockade of the internal carotid artery during angioplasty to prevent cerebral embolization. No complications have been reported.[63] Although the necessity for carotid blockade and the potential drawbacks of the technique are presently unresolved, the technique does offer a potential solution to the risk of embolic stroke.[64]

Angioplasty is generally performed via a transfemoral approach using an arterial sheath. Intravenous sedation with benzodiazepines is used, but patients must be arousable for neurologic testing. Diagnostic angiography is performed in at least two planes to completely visualize the lesion. Visualization of the intracranial carotid artery is important to exclude more distal stenotic lesions. The characteristics of the stenotic region are evaluated to exclude potential contraindications to PTA. After the size of the distal cervical

ICA is carefully evaluated, an appropriate balloon catheter is selected. Balloons are generally 1.5 to 2.0 cm in length with a 3- to 6-mm diameter. Careful purging of air from the balloon is imperative to prevent air embolus in the event of balloon rupture.

The lesion is carefully crossed under fluoroscopic guidance using a straight, soft-tipped guidewire, and exchange is made for the angioplasty catheter. Care must be taken to avoid advancing the wire above the C1-C2 level to minimize the chance of spasm. The balloon is positioned in the midportion of the lesion, and several inflations not exceeding 30 seconds each are made. Several authors recommend perfusing the distal internal carotid artery with heparinized blood during balloon inflation to prevent transient ischemia. Blood is withdrawn through the femoral sheath and immediately injected through the distal lumen of the angioplasty catheter during the dilation.[57,65] After dilation the balloon catheter is withdrawn, with the wire left across the lesion. A postangioplasty angiogram is performed in two projections to confirm the success of the dilation.

During the procedure, the patient is anticoagulated using 5000 to 10,000 units of heparin. Postprocedure care recommendations vary and include short periods (2–3 days) of heparinization followed by oral anticoagulants or antiplatelet agents alone.

Recent and ongoing studies have begun to provide data on the results of PTA in internal carotid stenosis.[63,66-70] To justify the use of the procedure in patients who would otherwise be surgical candidates, a complication rate in similarly selected patients that is equal to or lower than that of surgery must be attainable. A recent review identified 123 published cases of angioplasty for atherosclerotic disease of the internal carotid artery from 10 different centers. The results showed an overall complication rate of 9.7 percent and a rate of permanent neurologic complications of only 0.81 percent.[71] Results from the largest single series of both common and internal carotid artery angioplasty indicate a complication rate of 6.8 percent.[72] These rates compare favorably with those reported for carotid endarterectomy in both large randomized trials and other surgical series.[73] They suggest the usefulness of PTA in some patients who might be considered candidates for endarterectomy and emphasize the need for further evaluation in this patient population. In addition, more distal ICA lesions not amenable to surgical therapy may be treated by PTA. Alternatively, the performance of PTA under local anesthesia without open surgery makes it potentially beneficial for patients who present excessive risks for surgical therapy. This might include patients with multiple medical problems, severe pulmonary disease, or ischemic heart disease. The improved social and cost advantages from the shorter hospital stay associated with PTA would be an added benefit in appropriate patients.

Although present experience is limited and the small numbers of reports undoubtedly reflect selected results, larger trials of PTA in the treatment of carotid artery stenosis should be expected to justify a much larger role for the procedure in the future. Meanwhile, meticulous attention to procedural detail and careful selection of appropriately symptomatic patients cannot be overemphasized when performing PTA of the carotid artery.

Subclavian, Innominate, and Vertebral Artery Occlusive Disease

Occlusive disease affecting the vertebrobasilar circulation may occur at a number of locations within the large brachiocephalic vessels, including the innominate artery, the proximal subclavian arteries, or the vertebral arteries. Nevertheless, despite the multiple locations of potentially symptomatic lesions, large-vessel occlusive disease is much less frequently responsible for ischemic symptoms in the vertebrobasilar circulation than is the case in the carotid circulation. Several anatomic features account for this difference. A larger portion of the posterior circulation is fed by small (80- to 200-μ diameter) penetrating vessels than is the case in the anterior circulation.[74] This results in a prevalence of small-vessel disease as an etiology for vertebrobasilar ischemia. In addition, multiple pathways of collateral flow are available to the vertebrobasilar circulation, particularly in occlusion by proximal large-vessel lesions. Because of the unique anatomy of the paired vertebral arteries, for example, which join to form the larger basilar artery, a unilateral stenosis or even a complete occlusion of one vertebral artery is much less likely to be symptomatic than a lesion of equal hemodynamic effect involving an internal carotid artery. In general, the more distally located a vascular lesion along the vertebral artery, the more likely it is to cause infarction.[74] Intracranial disease of the vertebrobasilar system is therefore much more likely to be responsible for infarction than extracranial occlusive disease. This is in contrast to the case of the internal carotid artery, in which occlusive lesions precipitating infarction are frequently located extracranially.[75]

The numerous potential collaterals make determination of a causative relationship between an occlusive vertebrobasilar lesion and symptoms of CNS ischemia much more problematic than with the carotid artery. Thorough neurologic evaluation is important, and usually a trial of medical therapy is warranted before consideration of a patient for PTA. The difficulty of relating vertebrobasilar symptoms to arterial stenotic lesions has been apparent for many years. In a 1972 study of 1114 patients with subclavian or innominate stenosis or occlusion, only 15 percent demonstrated angiographic features of subclavian steal. Over 80 percent of patients had multiple lesions, often with disease of the vertebral arteries and retrograde collateral circulation via the thyrocervical trunk.[76] Recent studies have indicated the often benign course of angiographic subclavian steal syndrome and further highlight the importance of correlating the lesion with significant neurologic symptoms. In one group of 45 asymptomatic patients with severe disease of the subclavian artery, only 11 percent developed symptoms, and none had a stroke during a 4-year prospective follow-up period.[77] Another investigation of 96 patients with severe subclavian artery disease and symptoms of subclavian steal syndrome revealed spontaneous remission of symptoms in 50 percent within 2 years.[78] These studies document the frequent disparity between severe anatomic abnormalities and the often benign clinical course of patients with disease of the subclavian, innominate, and vertebral arteries. Nevertheless, some data have suggested that transient ischemic attacks (TIAs) of the vertebrobasilar system may be as ominous a predictor of stroke as TIAs involving the internal carotid artery distribution.[79] Because occlusive disease of the vertebrobasilar system may result in devastating neurologic deficits or death, thorough evaluation of patients with symptoms suggestive of vertebrobasilar ischemic disease is imperative. In addition, higher risks are often associated with surgical correction of vertebrobasilar lesions than with internal carotid artery stenoses.[80] Surgical therapy is therefore much less frequently performed for the treatment of vertebrobasilar ischemic symptoms. These facts emphasize the importance of careful patient evaluation and selection, especially when treatment is directed toward a chief complaint of neurologic symptoms in the face of minimal or no upper extremity claudication (Fig. 44-9).

Complete angiographic evaluation of the innominate, subclavian, and vertebral arteries often requires oblique projections to best profile the lesion. Both right and left anterior oblique projections are often necessary to demonstrate stenosis of the innominate and subclavian arteries. Because vertebral artery stenosis most often occurs at the origin, selective innominate or subclavian injections are best for visualization. The left anterior oblique projection is often necessary for the right vertebral origin, whereas the right anterior oblique projection may be needed to best evaluate the right vertebral origin. In the face of a symptomatic lesion with stenosis of 50 percent or more, angioplasty should be considered.

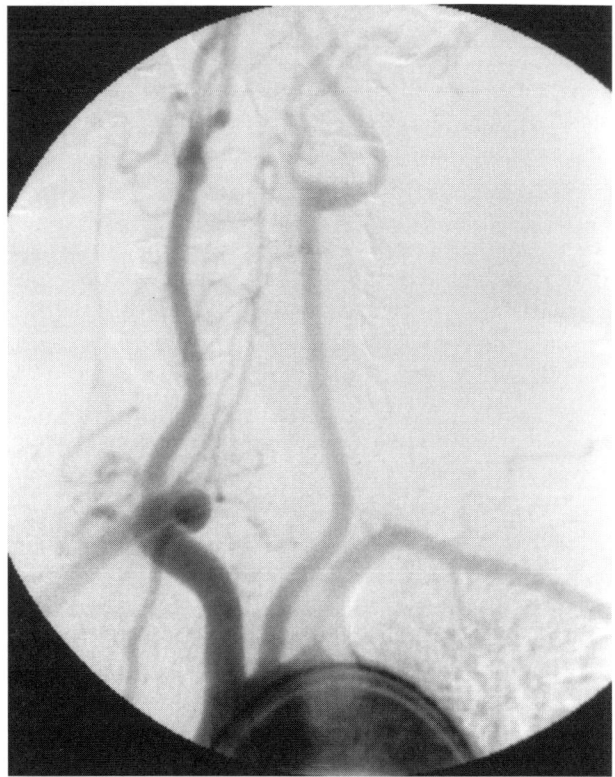

A

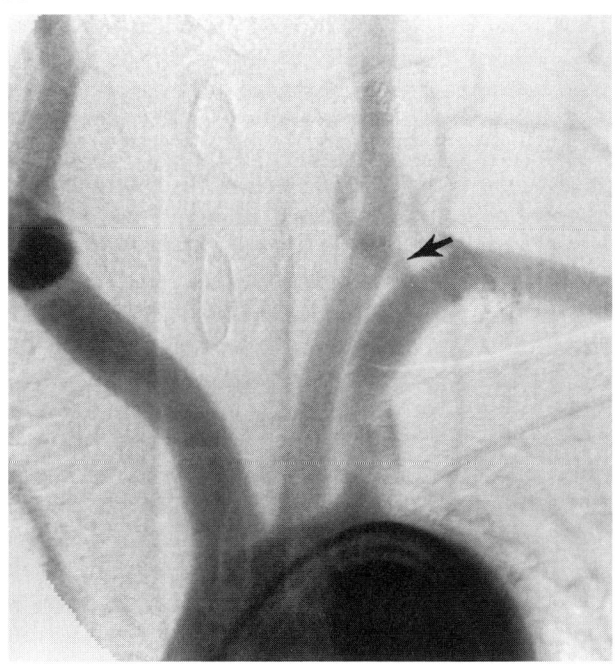

C

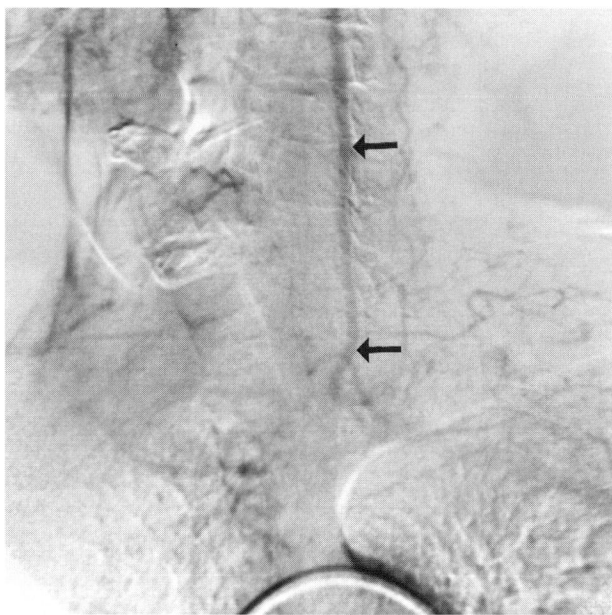

B

Figure 44-9. A 60-year-old man with left arm claudication and episodic vertigo accompanied by transient left hemiparesis. (A) Aortic arch injection, early view, shows stenosis of the origin of the left subclavian artery with no filling of the left vertebral artery. (B) Later view shows retrograde filling of the left vertebral artery (*arrows*). (C) After angioplasty, the stenotic area is dilated with early antegrade filling of the left vertebral artery (*arrow*). The symptoms resolved after angioplasty.

After an appropriate lesion is identified, an estimation of vessel diameter is made. Exact measurement of the vessel diameter may be difficult, and if doubt exists, a smaller-diameter balloon is used initially. Heparin, 5000 units, is given before crossing the lesion. A soft-tipped guidewire is used to cross the lesion, and ex-

change is made for the angioplasty balloon catheter. The Olbert Catheter System (Meadox Surgimed Inc.) is a low-profile balloon catheter that has been useful for PTA of brachiocephalic vessels. One to three inflations, each lasting 10 to 20 seconds, are performed. The result of the dilation is evaluated by either a selective contrast injection or an aortic injection through a pigtail catheter.

Several series have evaluated PTA of the innominate, subclavian, and vertebral arteries. Neurologic complications have not been reported in association with PTA of the subclavian artery, and emboli to the digital arteries have occurred in only a few cases. Resolution of neurologic symptoms reportedly occurred after the procedure with no recurrence with follow-up.[81-83] Only one study has compared patients treated with PTA to a group treated with surgical reconstruction of the subclavian artery.[84] Complication rates were similar, but a tendency toward late restenosis was observed in patients treated with PTA compared to those treated surgically. Angioplasty of the innominate artery has been infrequently reported, possibly because of the relatively infrequent involvement of this vessel with atherosclerotic disease. The high risks associated with surgical correction of innominate artery lesions and a lack of reported complications from PTA, however, suggest an expanded role for angioplasty in this location. Angioplasty of the vertebral arteries has been the subject of study by several investigators.[65,85,86] Reported results are favorable, with a success rate of 85 to 95 percent and clinical improvement in 80 percent of cases. Complications in the range of 5 percent have been reported.

Extracranial angioplasty designed to revascularize ischemic areas of the CNS has been neglected as a method of treatment in the past. Well-documented results in other vascular systems as well as initial studies suggest a high potential for benefit in occlusive disease of the brachiocephalic vessels and emphasize its potential value. The often high risks associated with surgical therapy of these vessels further suggest an expanded role for PTA. An understanding of the complex pathophysiology of extracranial occlusive disease by the interventional neuroradiologist and application of this knowledge by careful patient selection are prerequisites to ensure complete and proper application of this technique in the future.

Summary

Interventional neuroradiologic procedures, including thrombolysis, angioplasty, and pharmacologic vasodilation, may be of immense benefit in restoring blood flow to ischemic regions of the CNS. Although still evolving, these procedures promise to expand therapeutic alternatives in areas where therapy in the past has been extremely limited.

References

1. Mohr J, et al. The Harvard cooperative stroke registry: a prospective registry. Neurology 1978;28:754–762.
2. Fieschi C, et al. Clinical and instrumental evaluation of patients with ischemic stroke within the first six hours. J Neurol Sci 1989;91:311–321.
3. Sloan M. Thrombolysis and stroke. Arch Neurol 1987;44:748–768.
4. Coull B, Briley D. Outcome and rehabilitation in ischemic stroke. In: Awad I, ed. Cerebrovascular occlusive disease and brain ischemia. Cleveland: American Association of Neurological Surgeons, 1992:265–280.
5. Sussman B, Fitch T. Thrombolysis with fibrinolysin in cerebral arterial occlusion. JAMA 1958;167:1705–1709.
6. Meyer J, et al. Anticoagulants plus streptokinase therapy in progressive stroke. JAMA 1964;189:373.
7. Hacke W, et al. Intra-arterial thrombolytic therapy improves outcome in patients with acute vertebrobasilar occlusive disease. Stroke 1988;19:1216–1222.
8. Mori E, et al. Intracarotid urokinase with thromboembolic occlusion of the middle cerebral artery. Stroke 1988;19:802–812.
9. del Zoppo G, et al. Local intra-arterial fibrinolytic therapy in acute carotid territory stroke. Stroke 1988;19:307–313.
10. Astrup J, Siesjo B, Symon L. Thresholds in cerebral ischemia: the ischemic penumbra. Stroke 1981;12:723–725.
11. Skyhoj-Olson T, et al. Blood flow and vascular reactivity in collateral perfused brain tissue: evidence of an ischemic penumbra in patients with acute stroke. Stroke 1983;14:332–341.
12. Theron J, Courtheoux P, Casasco A. Local intraarterial fibrinolysis in carotid territory. AJNR 1989;10:753–756.
13. Teal P, Pessin M. Hemorrhagic transformation. Neurosurg Clin North Am 1992;3:601–610.
14. Liebeskind A, Chinichian A, Schechter M. The moving embolus seen during serial cerebral angiography. Stroke 1971;2:440–443.
15. Dalal P, et al. Cerebral embolism: angiographic observations in spontaneous clot lysis. Lancet 1965;1:61–64.
16. Lodder J, CT-detected hemorrhagic infarction: relation with the size of the infarct and the presence of midline shift. Acta Neurol Scand 1984;70:329–335.
17. Okada Y, Yamaguchi T, Minematsu K. Hemorrhagic transformation in cerebral embolus. Stroke 1989;20:598.
18. Pessin M, del Zoppo G, Estol CJ. Thrombolytic agents in the treatment of stroke. Clin Neuropharmacol 1990;13(4):271–289.
19. Hornig C, Dorndorf W, Agnoli A. Hemorrhagic cerebral infarction: a prospective study. Stroke 1986;17:174–185.
20. Weisberg L. Nonseptic cardiogenic cerebral embolic stroke: clinical-CT correlations. Neurology 1985;35:896.
21. Levine S, Brott T. Thrombolytic therapy in cerebrovascular disorders. Prog Cardiovasc Dis 1992;34:235–262.
22. Jungreis C, Wechsler L, Horton J. Intracranial thrombolysis via a catheter embedded in the clot. Stroke 1989;20:1578–1580.
23. Zeumer H, et al. Local intraarterial thrombolysis in acute vertebrobasilar occlusion. Neuroradiology 1989;31:336–340.
24. Wardlaw J, Warlow C. Thrombolysis in acute ischemic stroke: does it work? Stroke 1992;23:1826–1839.
25. Matsumoto K, Satoh K. Topical intraarterial urokinase infusion for acute stroke. In: Hacke W, del Zoppo G, Hirschberg M, eds. Thrombolytic therapy in acute ischemic stroke. Berlin: Springer-Verlag, 1991:207–212.
26. Mobius E, et al. Local thrombolytic therapy in acute basilar artery occlusion: experience in 18 patients. In: Hacke W, del Zoppo G, Hirschberg M, eds. Thrombolytic therapy in acute ischemic stroke. Berlin: Springer-Verlag, 1991:213–215.
27. Hacke W, et al. Intraarterial thrombolytic therapy improves outcome in patients with acute vertebrobasilar occlusive disease. Stroke 1988;19:1216–1222.
28. Saito I, Segawa H, Shiokawa Y. Middle cerebral artery occlusion: correlation of computed tomography and angiography and clinical outcome. Stroke 1987;18:863–868.
29. Harper G, et al. Factors delaying hospital admission after stroke in Leicestershire. Stroke 1992;23:835–838.
30. Mohr J, et al. Intracranial aneurysms. In: Stroke pathophysiology, diagnosis and management. New York: Churchill Livingstone, 1986:643–677.
31. Findlay J, MacDonald RL, Weir B. Current concepts of pathophysiology and management of cerebral vasospasm following aneurysmal subarachnoid hemorrhage. Cerebrovasc Brain Metab Rev 1992;3:336–361.
32. Mayberg M, Okada T, Bark D. Morphologic changes in cerebral arteries after subarachnoid hemorrhage. Neurosurg Clin North Am 1990;1:417–432.
33. Barker F, Heros R. Clinical aspects of vasospasm. Neurosurg Clin North Am 1990;1(2):277–288.
34. Kistler J, et al. The relation of cerebral vasospasm to the extent and location of subarachnoid blood visualized by CT scan: a prospective study. Neurology 1983;33:424–436.
35. Adams H, et al. Predicting cerebral ischemia after aneurysmal subarachnoid hemorrhage: influences of clinical condition, CT results, and antifibrinolytic therapy. Neurology 1987;37:1586–1591.
36. Seiler R, et al. Cerebral vasospasm evaluated by transcranial ultrasound, correlated with clinical grade and CT visualized subarachnoid hemorrhage. J Neurosurg 1986;64:594–600.

37. Farhat S, Schneider R. Observations on the effect of systemic blood pressure on intracranial circulation in patients with cerebrovascular insufficiency. J Neurosurg 1967;24:441–445.

38. Kosnik E, Hunt W. Postoperative hypertension in the management of patients with intracranial arterial aneurysms. J Neurosurg 1976;45:148–153.

39. Kassell N, et al. Treatment of ischemic deficits from vasospasm with intravascular volume expansion and induced arterial hypertension. Neurosurgery 1982;11:337–343.

40. Grotta JC, Clinical aspects of the use of calcium antagonists in cerebrovascular disease. Clin Neuropharmacol 1991;14:373–390.

41. Pickard J, Murray G, Illingworth R. Effect of oral nimodipine on cerebral infarction and outcome after subarachnoid hemorrhage: British aneurysm nimodipine trial. Br Med J 1989;298:636–642.

42. Haley E, et al. Nimodipine ameliorates angiographic vasospasm following subarachnoid hemorrhage. Neurology 1991;41(Suppl I):346.

43. Zubkov Y, Nikiforov B, Shustin V. Balloon catheter technique for dilation of constricted cerebral arteries after aneurysmal subarachnoid hemorrhage. Acta Neurochir 1984;70:65–79.

44. Newell D, et al. Angioplasty for the treatment of symptomatic vasospasm following subarachnoid hemorrhage. Neurosurgery 1989;71:654–660.

45. Higashida R, et al. Intravascular balloon dilation therapy for intracranial arterial vasospasm: patient selection, technique, and clinical results. Neurosurg Rev 1992;15:89–95.

46. Higashida R, et al. Transluminal angioplasty for treatment of intracranial arterial vasospasm. J Neurosurg 1989;71:648–653.

47. Kwak R, et al. Angiographic study of cerebral vasospasm following rupture of intracranial aneurysms: Part 2. Relation between the site of aneurysm and the occurrence of vasospasm. Surg Neurol 1979;11:263–267.

48. Kwak R, et al. Angiographic study of cerebral vasospasm following rupture of intracranial aneurysms: Part 1. Time of appearance. Surg Neurol 1979;11:257–261.

49. Yamamoto Y, Smith R, Bernanke D. Mechanism of action of balloon angioplasty in cerebral vasospasm. Neurosurgery 1992;30:1–6.

50. Linskey M, et al. Fatal rupture of the intracranial carotid artery during transluminal angioplasty for vasospasm induced by subarachnoid hemorrhage. J Neurosurg 1991;74:985–990.

51. Hurst R, et al. Role of transcranial doppler in neuroradiological treatment of vasospasm. Stroke 1993;24:299–303.

52. Kaku Y, et al. Superselective intra-arterial infusion of papaverine for the treatment of cerebral vasospasm after subarachnoid hemorrhage. J Neurosurg 1992;77:842–847.

53. Kassell N, et al. Treatment of cerebral vasospasm with intra-arterial papaverine. J Neurosurg 1992;77:848–852.

54. Robicsek F. Atherosclerotic occlusive disease of the innominate and subclavian arteries. In: Robicsek F, ed. Extracranial cerebrovascular disease. New York: Macmillan, 1986:359–386.

55. Hass W, et al. Joint study of extracranial arterial occlusion. JAMA 1968;203:961–968.

56. Diethrich E, et al. Occlusive disease of the common carotid and subclavian arteries treated by carotid subclavian bypass. Am J Surg 1967;114:800–808.

57. Kachel R. Angioplasty of neck and intracranial vessels. In: Kadir S, ed. Current practice of interventional radiology. Philadelphia: Decker, 1991:127–134.

58. Hasso A, et al. Fibromuscular dysplasia of the internal carotid artery: percutaneous transluminal angioplasty. AJNR 1981;2:175–180.

59. ECST Collaborative Group. MRC European carotid surgery trial: interim results for symptomatic patients with severe (70–99%) or with mild (0–29%) carotid stenosis. Lancet 1991;337:1235–1243.

60. Mayberg M, et al. Carotid endarterectomy and prevention of cerebral ischemia in symptomatic carotid stenosis. JAMA 1991;266:3289–3294.

61. North American Symptomatic Endarterectomy Trial Collaborators. Beneficial effect of carotid endarterectomy in symptomatic patients with high grade carotid stenosis. N Engl J Med 1991;325:445–453.

62. De Segni R, et al. Angioplasty: general principles and mechanisms. In: Kadir S, ed. Current practice of interventional radiology. Philadelphia: Dekker, 1991:51–57.

63. Theron J, et al. New triple coaxial catheter system for carotid angioplasty with cerebral protection. AJNR 1990;11:869–874.

64. Ferguson R. Getting it right the first time. AJNR 1990;11:875–877.

65. Tsai F, Higashida R, Meoli C. Percutaneous transluminal angioplasty of extracranial and intracranial arterial stenosis of the head and neck. Neuroimaging Clin North Am 1992;2(2):371–384.

66. Theron J, et al. Percutaneous angioplasty of atherosclerotic and postsurgical stenosis of carotid arteries. AJNR 1987;8:495–500.

67. Kachel R, et al. Percutaneous transluminal angioplasty (PTA) of supraaortic arteries especially the internal carotid artery. Neuroradiology 1991;33:191–194.

68. Bockenheimer S, Mathias K. Percutaneous transluminal angioplasty in arteriosclerotic internal carotid artery stenosis. AJNR 1983;4:791–792.

69. Wiggli U, Gartzl O. Transluminal angioplasty of stenotic carotid arteries: case reports and protocol. AJNR 1983;4:793–795.

70. Brown M, et al. Feasibility of percutaneous transluminal angioplasty for carotid artery stenosis. J Neurol Neurosurg Psychiatry 1990;53:238–243.

71. Brown M. Balloon angioplasty for cerebrovascular disease. Neurol Res 1992;14(Suppl II):159–163.

72. Munari L, et al. Carotid percutaneous angioplasty. Neurol Res 1992;14(Suppl II):156–158.

73. Callow A. Cerebrovascular insufficiency. In: Haimovici H, ed. Vascular surgery. New York: Appleton & Lange, 1991:719–749.

74. Caplan L. Stroke, a clinical approach. Stoneham, MA: Butterworth-Heinemann, 1993:547.

75. Fisher C. Occlusion of the vertebral arteries causing transient basilar symptoms. Arch Neurol 1970;22:13–19.

76. Fields W, Lemak N. Joint study of extracranial arterial occlusion. JAMA 1972;222:1139–1143.

77. Hennerici M, Klemm C, Rautenberg W. The subclavian steal phenomenon: a common vascular disorder with rare neurologic deficits. Neurology 1988;38:669–673.

78. Ackerman H, et al. Ultrasonographic follow up of subclavian stenosis and occlusion: natural history and surgical treatment. Stroke 1988;19:431–435.

79. Whisnant J, Cartlidge N, Elveback L. Carotid and vertebral-basilar transient ischemic attacks: effect of anticoagulants, hypertension, and cardiac disorders on survival and stroke occurrence—a population study. Ann Neurol 1978;3:107–115.

80. Spetzler R, Hadley M. Revascularization of the brain stem and posterior fossa. In: Samii M, ed. Surgery in and around the brain stem and the third ventricle. Berlin: Springer-Verlag, 1986:262–269.

81. Burke D, et al. Percutaneous angioplasty of subclavian arteries. Radiology 1987;164:699–704.

82. Tsai F, Hieshima G, Higashida R. Percutaneous transluminal angioplasty for the treatment of stroke. In: Fischer M, ed. Medical therapy of acute stroke. New York: Marcel Dekker, 1989:203–237.

83. Vitek J, et al. Brachiocephalic artery dilation by percutaneous transluminal angioplasty. Radiology 1986;158:779–785.

84. Farina C, et al. Percutaneous transluminal angioplasty versus surgery for subclavian artery occlusive disease. Am J Surg 1989;158:511–514.

85. Higishida R, et al. Transluminal angioplasty of the vertebral and basilar artery. AJNR 1987;8:745–749.

86. Courtheoux P, et al. Transcutaneous angioplasty of vertebral artery atheromatous ostial stricture. Neuroradiology 1985;27:259–264.

45

Neurointerventional Radiology: Intraaxial Embolotherapy of the Central Nervous System

TONY P. SMITH
RANDALL T. HIGASHIDA

*I*nterventional neuroradiology of intraaxial lesions primarily encompasses the treatment of two major clinical entities: cerebral aneurysms and arteriovenous malformations (AVMs). Although the techniques of endovascular intervention are in a continuous state of development and evolution, many of the principles and goals of therapy remain the same. This chapter evaluates the current therapy being used at medical centers specializing in the treatment of complex neurovascular disorders by interventional neuroradiology.

Patient Management

For embolotherapy involving the central nervous system, in addition to the standard history and physical examination, a complete neurologic examination must also be performed by the interventional neuroradiologist before the procedure. It is imperative to know the patient's baseline neurologic examination so that even subtle changes can be detected and evaluated during and after the procedure.

All the patient's prior imaging studies must be evaluated. In addition, high-quality diagnostic cerebral angiography is essential before embolotherapy. It is preferable to perform a complete four-vessel diagnostic cerebral arteriogram in a separate session rather than at the time of treatment. This allows additional time to review the films for more detailed planning and better understanding of the procedure.

Particularly with neurologic procedures, the patient and family must be given a complete explanation of the benefits and risks of the procedure and be given adequate time to ask questions so that they can make a truly informed decision.

As with all interventional procedures, patients should receive standard monitoring, including continuous ECG, heart rate, blood pressure, and pulse oximetry tests. Many procedures can be performed under local anesthesia using intravenous sedation. However, general anesthesia sometimes may be used, especially in the pediatric population and when patients may not be able to fully cooperate. The disadvantage of general anesthesia is that it precludes direct neurologic testing during the procedure. In these cases, hemispheric or brain stem function can be monitored using electroencephalographic analysis and/or evoked potentials (acoustic or somatosensory).[1-3]

Systemic anticoagulation is often used during intracranial embolization procedures at many centers. The disadvantage of using anticoagulation is that if a hemorrhage occurs during the procedure, the bleeding complications will be more severe. However, it is well known that thromboembolic complications increase with catheter size and the duration of the procedure.[4] Because most procedures require relatively large catheters and long procedure times, systemic anticoagulation is routinely used at most centers. Several centers have reported large numbers of cases performed without systemic heparinization, with only local perfusion of heparinized saline flushes between coaxial catheters and guidewires, and have reported no difficulty from catheter-induced thrombosis. Conversely, large numbers of cases have been performed in patients who recently experienced intracranial hemorrhage and no additional hemorrhagic complications were noted with systemic anticoagulation.[5]

Debrun et al. reported on 57 patients who were pretreated with aspirin and received anticoagulation for neurointerventional radiology procedures and 25 subsequent patients who received only continuous heparinized flushing of the catheter systems.[6] There were no complications in the first group, either hemorrhagic or thrombotic, whereas the second group had two embolic (7 percent) and two thrombotic (7 percent) complications. The first group, however, did not include patients with acute or recent subarachnoid hemorrhage. If systemic anticoagulation is used, one must be prepared to immediately reverse the heparinization with protamine sulfate if a bleeding complication arises.

The principles of patient care immediately after interventional therapy are similar to the postoperative surgical management for the particular disorder being treated. Therefore, the neurointerventionalist must be familiar with standard postprocedure management and potential complications. After embolization, the patients' original symptoms may become worse, and patients may complain of moderate to severe headaches. Transient worsening of symptoms in patients who present with focal deficits is not uncommon and is usually due to local edema, swelling, and acute inflammation from thrombosis. In most cases, with conservative treatment, these symptoms improve to their baseline and usually continue to improve over the preembolization state. Headache is also a common complaint following embolization, especially with AVM therapy. The etiology of the pain is not well understood, but it is probably also due to the acute thrombosis and associated edema with inflammatory response. Both headaches and worsening of symptoms may continue for several days to weeks following treatment.[7] However, the patient's symptoms should only be attributed to thrombosis induced by the embolization treatment if more ominous etiologies such as hemorrhage or cerebral ischemia have been eliminated.

Equipment and Materials

As with all interventional procedures, high-quality radiographic equipment is essential. For interventional neuroradiology procedures, the highest-resolution images, using small focal-spot tubes, are a necessity. One must have digital imaging with road-mapping capability, and rapid-sequence film timing of at least four images per second is required. Biplane imaging with stereoscopic capability during both fluoroscopy and filming improves the safety of treatment and the quality of the study. Finally, the radiographic equipment should not be so cumbersome as to prevent easy access to the patient for monitoring and performing frequent neurologic examinations.

Catheter Systems

In interventional neuroradiology, most procedures are performed using coaxial catheterization techniques. The outer guiding catheters vary in size from 5.0 to 8.0 French. Through the guiding catheter, microcatheters from 1.5 to 3.2 French are coaxially placed. There are two basic catheter designs: one uses guidewires (0.018 inch or less) and is directed using conventional guidewire catheter techniques; the second catheter system uses extremely thin compliant tubing without a guidewire and depends exclusively on blood flow to direct and carry the catheter to the desired site. The advantages of the flow-directed catheters include rapid and very distal placement. However, because these catheters have very small internal lumina, their use with embolic materials is limited. The flow-directed catheters are used almost exclusively for distal catheterization of high-flow AVMs.

All coaxial catheter systems should be used with continuous heparinized saline flushing to prevent thrombus formation. Once the catheter has been placed, superselective angiography is performed to assess more clearly the anatomy and associated pathology.[8]

Embolic Agents

A complete description of the different embolic materials is given in Chapter 4. Only several agents that are commonly used in the central nervous system are discussed here. Some of these agents are under clinical investigation in the United States and require institutional review board approval before use.

Platinum microcoils are available in a variety of sizes and shapes. They produce a relatively permanent occlusion and can be easily placed either by injection or by conventional pushing with a special introducing guidewire to the desired location. Coils are used in the treatment of large fistulous connections in AVMs. In addition, newer coils that are electrolytically or mechanically placed are becoming the agent of choice in the treatment of certain types of aneurysms. The electrolytic and mechanical detachable coils give the interventionist better control of the coil during placement because the coil cannot be released until optimal placement is confirmed. The electrolytic coils have recently received approval for use in the United States.

Detachable balloons are available in two basic varieties: latex and silicone. Both are available with self-sealing valves and can be detached from microcatheters.[9] Latex is impermeable but in vivo may start to deflate within 2 to 3 weeks after placement. Silicone balloons are semipermeable and therefore must be inflated with solutions, usually metrizamide, that are isotonic to blood.[10] Silicone balloons tend to deflate at a much slower rate and have been shown to be inflated beyond 3 years.[11] If permanent inflation is needed, the balloons can be filled with 2-hydroxyethyl methacrylate (HEMA).[12] These balloons can stay inflated indefinitely. HEMA should only be used with silicone balloons because it may cause fissuring and rupture of latex balloons.[12–14]

In the early 1980s, isobutyl-2-cyanoacrylate

(IBCA) was used as a liquid embolic material, but since 1988 it has been replaced by *N*-butyl-2-cyanoacrylate (NBCA) because of a question of weak mutagenicity in animal models.[15] Both agents polymerize upon contact with isotonic solutions (blood, contrast, saline flush, etc.), and therefore the catheters and entire system need to be thoroughly flushed with a nonionic solution, usually 5 percent dextrose, before use. Polymerization times may be controlled by adding iophendylate to the cyanoacrylate. Although both cyanoacrylate solutions are considered to be permanent agents, some reports state that recanalization may occur even with the use of these liquid embolic agents.[16]

There is no ideal embolic material for use in treating cerebral AVMs or aneurysms. Continued work is necessary, and virtually all available agents could be improved upon by further development.

Complications

Two major complications are associated with interventional neuroradiologic procedures: hemorrhage and ischemia (embolic and/or thrombotic). Hemorrhage may occur from perforation of a vessel or aneurysm by the catheter or guidewire; alternatively, the vessel, aneurysm, or AVM may rupture as a result of changes in flow characteristics.

Acute hemorrhage is often due to perforation of a small distal intracerebral artery. In 1200 endovascular procedures to treat cerebral disorders, Halbach et al.[17] reported 15 (1.25 percent) vessel perforations. The treatment is to reverse the anticoagulation (if given), seal the perforation, and support the patient clinically, which may require intubation and surgical intervention. The perforation can be sealed with coils if the catheter is still through the site, or the entire compartment (aneurysm, AVM, etc.) can be immediately occluded. Either method must take into consideration the site of perforation and the patient's clinical status.

Hemorrhage, with or without edema, can complicate the excision and/or embolization of AVMs and has been recently termed *occlusive hyperemia*.[18,19] This development was initially thought to occur from normal perfusion pressure breakthrough[20] and was believed to be due to shunting of blood to an AVM and away from normal vessels, the latter losing the ability to autoregulate. Once greater flow is returned to the normal vessels after embolization or surgery of the AVM, the lack of autoregulation allows for edema and hemorrhage in normal areas of the brain. This phenomenon has been reported after surgery of high-flow AVMs[21] and may occur after embolization. Recently it has been postulated that edema and hemorrhage may

be the result of abrupt venous occlusion, particularly if embolization of the distal draining veins, without complete treatment of the AVM, results in a venous overload. The exact mechanisms are still unclear but may represent a combination of both venous occlusion and normal perfusion pressure breakthrough.[19] It is known that these complications, although rare, do occur, and therefore larger AVMs should be embolized in multiple stages to prevent sudden venous occlusions and large hemodynamic shifts. Occlusive hyperemia based on venous occlusion can result in acute hemorrhage or delayed hemorrhage after the procedure and is based on the rate and degree of venous restriction as well as the amount of residual flow to the AVM.

Thrombotic and embolic complications may result from the inadvertent placement of embolic agents into normal vessels or inadvertent thromboemboli arising from the catheter systems. Treatment is based on the clinical situation and may include hydration, volume expansion, anticoagulation, and thrombolysis in selected situations. Treatment should be individualized to the particular patient and the underlying medical condition.

Vasospasm can occur, especially during distal catheterization of small intracerebral vessels. Nitroglycerin ointment in paste form (nitropaste) placed on the patient's skin has been used both to prevent spasm and to relieve it.[22] Nifedipine and other calcium channel blockers have also been used sublingually for vasospasm.[23] Direct intraarterial injection of vasodilators, particularly papaverine, has been used for catheter-induced spasm in a small number of cases with encouraging early results.[24]

Aneurysms

Since the initial reports in the early 1970s, embolization therapy has continued to evolve as a definitive therapy for both ruptured and unruptured intracranial aneurysms. Most centers still consider surgical clipping to be the preferred treatment. In North America, the criteria for treating patients are as follows:

1. Unsuccessful attempted neurosurgical clipping
2. Difficult surgical access (cavernous, midbasilar)
3. Broad-based aneurysms with a wide or no definable neck
4. Heavily calcified aneurysms that would not sustain clipping
5. Health reasons that do not permit craniotomy

McCormick and Nofzinger[25] reported on five large autopsy series involving 1026 saccular aneurysms.

Approximately 90 percent were in the anterior circulation and 10 percent in the posterior circulation. In the anterior circulation, the most common sites were the middle cerebral artery (29 percent), the anterior cerebral and anterior communicating arteries (26 percent), and the internal carotid and posterior communicating arteries (20 percent).

The endovascular treatment of aneurysms falls into two categories: (1) occlusion of the parent artery from which the aneurysm originates (*vessel occlusion*); and (2) treatment of the aneurysm proper with preservation of the parent vessel (*direct therapy*). Direct aneurysm therapy is the *preferred* treatment for aneurysms with a well-defined neck. The most common aneurysms treated by endovascular means include those usually requiring vessel occlusion (petrous carotid, cavernous carotid) and those of the posterior fossa that are deemed surgically difficult; these will be discussed in detail.

Parent vessel occlusion is often performed by endovascular techniques. The vessel is tested before permanent occlusion to determine if any neurologic consequences develop. Although this can be performed in any vessel to be occluded, the procedure is best delineated for the internal carotid artery (ICA). For the carotid artery, occlusion is based on the Matas test,[26] which involves manual compression and occlusion of the common carotid artery and evaluation by neurologic testing. Today, test occlusion is performed under systemic anticoagulation with a nondetachable balloon system and is more accurate for producing complete vessel occlusion for a specified period of time.

A number of methods of analysis have been used to determine the patient's tolerance to vessel occlusion, particularly in the carotid artery. All patients are tested throughout the occlusion period by direct neurologic examination. Stable xenon-enhanced computed tomography cerebral blood flow measurements can also be performed during the test occlusion.[27,28] This technique appears to be a relatively accurate way to determine cerebral blood flow, but its exact predictiveness for carotid ligation is still unknown.[29] Other imaging studies, including [99m]technetium-labeled hexamethylpropyleneamine oxine (^{99m}Tc HMPAO), have been used.[30] In addition, electroencephalographic monitoring can detect changes attributable to inadequate blood flow and has been used in conjunction with test occlusion.[31] Test occlusions, particularly of the ICA, are usually done with double-lumen balloon catheters, and therefore distal occlusion arterial pressures can be measured. Older data generated from arterial stump pressures during carotid occlusion suggested that occluded arterial back-pressures of 40 mmHg or greater were required to prevent ischemia.[32–34] However,

stump pressures have also been noted to be inaccurate in predicting subsequent neurologic compromise.[35] Barker et al.[36] correlated data in 70 patients who underwent test occlusion with back-pressures and found large overlaps in pressures and patient outcomes. The results therefore did not allow the pressure changes to be used as a completely accurate predictor of cerebral blood flow or of stroke risk in individual patients.

The available embolic agents for the direct treatment of aneurysms are still under investigation. In a review by Taki et al., 19 patients were treated with balloons, coils, or a liquid polymer. Complete aneurysmal ablation was achieved in only 4 of 7 cases, and 11 cases underwent parent artery occlusion.[37] The authors concluded that endovascular treatment of aneurysms, particularly giant ones, remains difficult because of the irregular shape of the base, the size, and the presence of intraluminal thrombus.[38,39] In an effort to improve on the results of endovascular occlusion, other embolic materials are being developed. Conventional platinum coils have been used, but the potential for coil misplacement is high.[40] Methods to control coil placement for intraaneurysmal therapy are under investigation at major neurovascular centers in the United States, Europe, and Japan.

Petrous Carotid Artery Aneurysms

Petrous aneurysms are rare and usually present with symptoms of mass effect. In addition, epistaxis, bloody otorrhea, pulsatile tinnitus, hearing loss, vertigo, hoarseness, or dysphagia can occur. If the aneurysms are large and partially thrombosed, transient ischemic attacks may occur from distal embolization. A review by Halbach et al. in 1990[41] states that only 30 cases had been reported in the literature up to that time. These aneurysms were treated by primary resection (aneurysmectomy) with primary carotid artery reconstruction or grafting.[42] However, because of its invasive nature, primary surgical repair has not become the treatment of choice. In addition, extension superiorly above the foramen lacerum, thus preventing distal exposure, has made primary surgical repair of these aneurysms difficult. Other forms of surgical treatment are wrapping of the aneurysm or trapping by surgical exposure above and below the aneurysm.[43]

Carotid occlusion has become the treatment of choice for aneurysms in this location, and carotid occlusion by endovascular techniques has been demonstrated to be effective (Fig. 45-1). Detachable balloon embolotherapy for occlusion of the carotid artery has become the primary treatment for these patients. In the largest reported series,[41] seven symptomatic patients were treated: five by carotid occlusion, one by

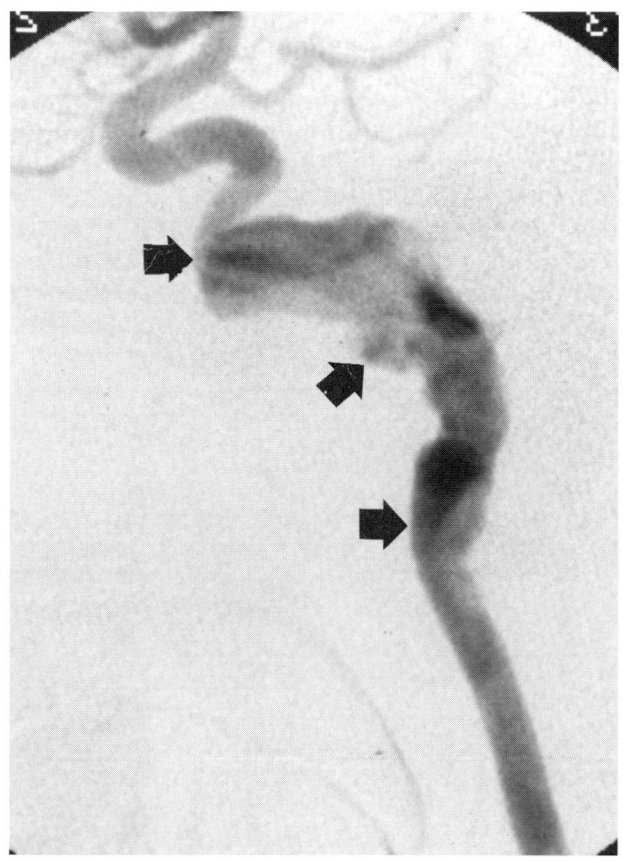

A

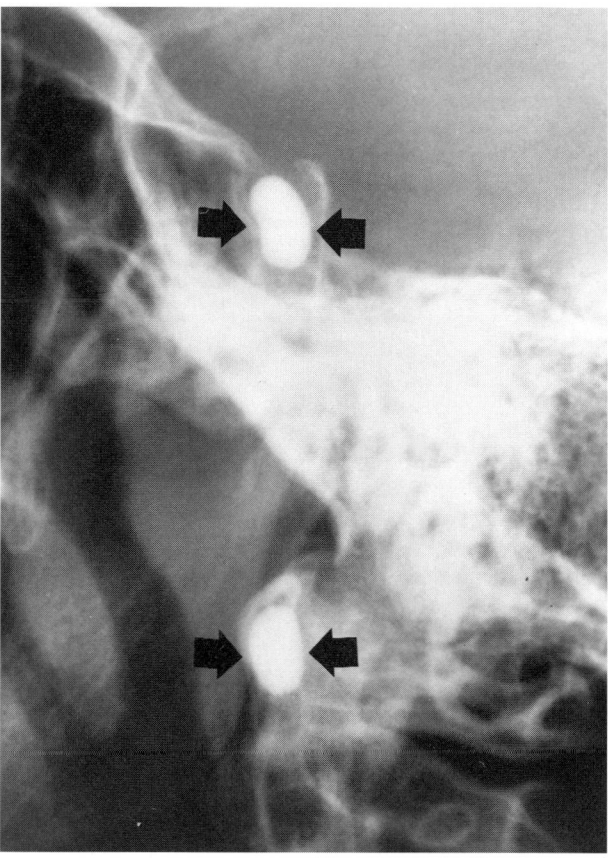

B

Figure 45-1. Petrous carotid artery aneurysm. (A) Lateral carotid artery angiogram demonstrates an irregular, partially thrombosed, giant aneurysm involving the cervical carotid artery and extending into the petrous segment (*arrows*). (B) Occlusion of the carotid artery with detachable balloons (*arrows*). Note that the aneurysm has been "trapped" by placing a balloon above and below the aneurysm. Follow-up angiography showed complete internal carotid artery occlusion.

ICA ligation, and one by direct balloon occlusion of the aneurysm with preservation of the parent artery. Only one complication occurred, consisting of transient visual loss in a hypercoagulable patient who fully recovered. In patients whose preoperative evaluation demonstrates unlikely tolerance of carotid artery occlusion, external-carotid-to-internal-carotid bypass grafting, before balloon occlusion, is the treatment of choice.[44]

Carotid-Cavernous Artery Aneurysms

Patients with intracavernous aneurysms usually present with signs and symptoms of mass effect on the cavernous sinus structures. Rupture of a cavernous aneurysm is not common, and these patients may have symptoms of a carotid-cavernous fistula. Rarely, in appropriately 7 percent of cases, an intracavernous aneurysm may project superiorly, and rupture can result in subarach-

noid hemorrhage. This is more common with giant aneurysms, which have a greater chance of projecting above the dural covering.[45] If the aneurysm projects medially, eroding adjacent bone, massive epistaxis can be the clinical presentation. As with petrous aneurysms, transient ischemic attacks may occur from distal embolization of clot material within a partially thrombosed aneurysm.

Localization of the aneurysm to the cavernous sinus can be difficult angiographically. Although the roof of the cavernous sinus is usually at the level of the ophthalmic artery origin, the ophthalmic artery may arise within the cavernous sinus (in up to 15 percent of cases).[46] Therefore, even localizing the aneurysm and determining its extent and subsequent risks for subarachnoid hemorrhage can be difficult.

Consideration for treatment depends on the clinical presentation of the patient. Kupersmith et al.[47] followed 79 patients with only 1 rupture (1.3 percent) into the subarachnoid space and concluded that an aneurysm of the carotid-cavernous artery was rarely associated with life-threatening symptoms. Also in the same series, all initially asymptomatic aneurysms remained so within an average follow-up of 2.8 years. The authors did confirm that progression of cranial nerve palsies and retroorbital pain does occur and eventually required treatment in 36 of the 79 patients (46 percent). Therefore, patients with more acute or marked symptoms of a cavernous sinus syndrome or with more ominous signs such as transient ischemic attacks, subarachnoid hemorrhage, or epistaxis should certainly undergo treatment.

In a review of 20 intracavernous aneurysms that did not undergo initial treatment, Linskey et al.[48] concluded that, although clinical progression does occur, symptomatic intracavernous carotid artery aneurysms may also spontaneously improve. They agreed that therapeutic intervention should be reserved for patients with aneurysms arising at the anterior genu of the carotid siphon and/or extending into the subarachnoid space, where subarachnoid hemorrhage is most likely. Therefore intervention should be reserved for those cases with the potential for subarachnoid hemorrhage or epistaxis, or for patients who present with severe facial or orbital pain, radiographic evidence of enlargement, progressive ophthalmoplegia, or progressive visual loss.

Surgical treatment of cavernous internal carotid artery aneurysms consists of either exposure of the cavernous sinus with direct repair of the aneurysm or cervical carotid artery occlusion. Direct surgical exposure of the cavernous internal carotid artery, packing of the cavernous sinus, and techniques for microsurgery in the cavernous sinus continue to be explored and refined.[49–51] However, direct surgical access to the cavernous sinus continues to carry high operative risk and remains a technically difficult procedure.[52] In fact, treatment may require more than one approach.[50] Therefore, most surgical therapy has centered around occlusion of either the common or internal carotid artery. This occlusion has been by abrupt ligation or placement of a clamp around the carotid artery. Surgical clamping theoretically allows for collaterals to form and provides the ability to reverse occlusion if signs of cerebral ischemia develop. However, it has been shown that an alteration in either blood pressure or flow rate is not noted until the cross-sectional area of the occluded vessel is decreased by 90 percent.[53] Therefore, most of the carotid occlusion occurs in the last turn of the clamp. Literature reports have noted no difference in complication rates between the two methods of ligation.[54,55] Furthermore, release of the occlusion by the clamp failed to clear an induced neu-

rologic deficit in 44 percent of affected patients.[54] For these reasons, there does not appear to be any advantage to gradual vessel occlusion.

The treatment of ICA aneurysms has been shown to be successful by carotid occlusion techniques either with surgery or embolization (Fig. 45-2) Kak et al.[55] reported on 106 patients, 84 of whom presented with subarachnoid hemorrhage. Carotid ligation was performed in most cases by abrupt surgical closure. The success rates for ruptured and unruptured aneurysms were 77 percent and 82 percent, respectively. No patients in the series experienced acute rehemorrhage from their ICA aneurysm after treatment. Follow-up of 57 patients demonstrated an acute morbidity and mortality of 29 percent. Long-term follow-up on 39 of these patients demonstrated a complication rate of 26 percent, including 3 patients with delayed subarachnoid hemorrhage.

Scott and Skwarok[56] reported on a large series of their patients and also reviewed the literature of patients receiving surgical carotid ligation. There was an 11 percent complication rate with an 11 percent mortality rate following common carotid artery ligation and a 22 percent and 6 percent rate, respectively, for ICA ligation. The authors noted that the most important consideration was proper patient selection for carotid ligation, including toleration of the Matas test, normotension, absence of vasospasm angiographically, and a stable clinical condition such that adequate neurologic evaluation could be obtained. For all anterior circulation aneurysms treated by surgical ligation, rebleeding rates decreased, and 50 percent or more of these aneurysms did not fill on follow-up angiography when this technique was employed.[54,57]

With the ease and success of detachable balloon placement for carotid occlusion and the possibility of direct aneurysm treatment by endovascular means, it is not surprising that endovascular techniques have replaced surgery in many institutions as the treatment of choice for intracavernous aneurysm therapy (Fig. 45-3). Endovascular treatment has been advocated over surgery for two main reasons: (1) direct exposure of the carotid artery is unnecessary, and (2) a test occlusion can be easily performed just before carotid occlusion.

Treatment by endovascular techniques—by carotid occlusion and direct aneurysm treatment—has been shown to be successful since it was first introduced. In 1974, Serbinenko[58] reported on 82 patients who were successfully treated by occlusion of the carotid siphon with detachable balloons. In 1982, Romodanov and Shcheglov[59] reported on 67 patients treated with endovascular balloon embolization of ICA aneurysms. In 49 of these cases direct aneurysm therapy with

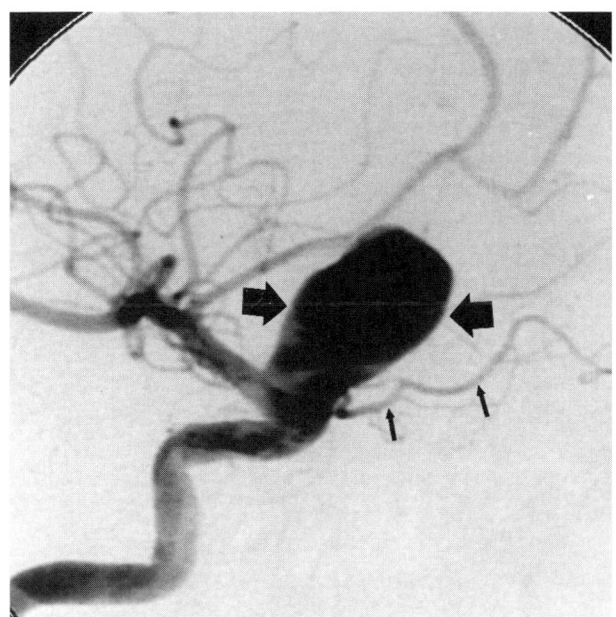

A

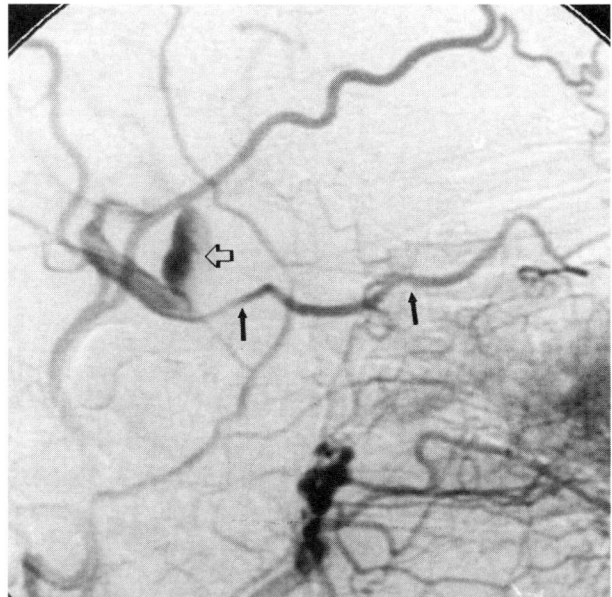

B

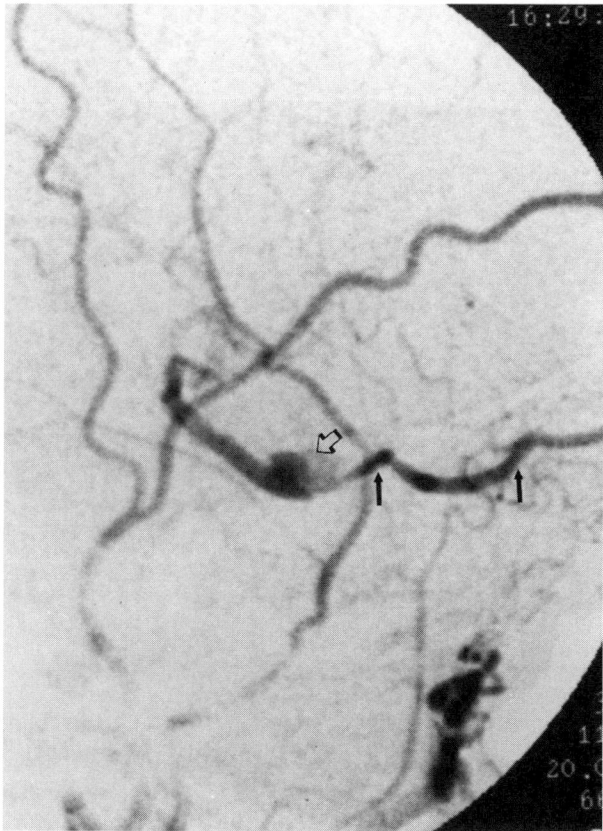

C

Figure 45-2. Large carotid-ophthalmic aneurysm. (A) Oblique view of left internal carotid artery demonstrates a large aneurysm (*large arrows*) in the region of the ophthalmic artery (*small arrows*). The aneurysm originates in the cavernous region (below the carotid artery) with extension well above the level of the cavernous sinus. Because of its wide neck, this aneurysm was treated by carotid occlusion therapy. (B) After occlusion of the internal carotid artery, there is a small amount of filling of the aneurysm (*open arrow*) from the ophthalmic artery (*small arrows*) as seen on this lateral external carotid artery injection. Collateral flow through the ophthalmic artery may keep an aneurysm patent. (C) Follow-up, left external carotid artery injection, 7 days after embolization, demonstrates virtually no filling of the aneurysm (*open arrow*) and some residual filling of the supraclinoid carotid artery from the ophthalmic artery (*arrows*). Slow flow within the aneurysm after occlusion of the internal carotid artery allows thrombosis.

preservation of the carotid artery was performed. More recently, Fox et al.[60] reported on 37 patients with infraclinoid aneurysms treated by proximal artery occlusion using detachable balloons. All patients were deemed to have complete obliteration of the aneurysm. Eleven of these patients (41 percent) had an associated bypass procedure before occlusion. Three patients had transient ischemic events, and two had transient worsening of their cavernous sinus symptoms.

Higashida et al.[61] reported on 87 patients with intracavernous aneurysms treated with endovascular balloon embolization. In 68 of these patients, occlusion of the ICA was performed. Nineteen patients had direct aneurysm therapy with preservation of the parent artery. Of these 19 patients, total occlusion of the an-

eurysm was achieved in 12 patients (63.2 percent) and partial occlusion (>85 percent) in the remaining 7 cases. Complications in the carotid occlusion group included transient ischemia in 7 cases and stroke in 3 patients. Complications in the direct therapy group included transient ischemia in 2 patients and thrombo-

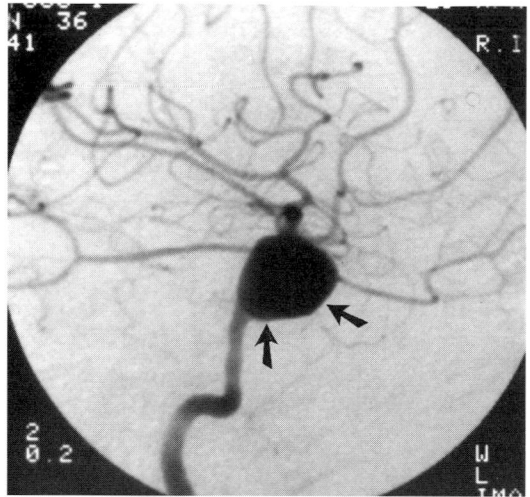

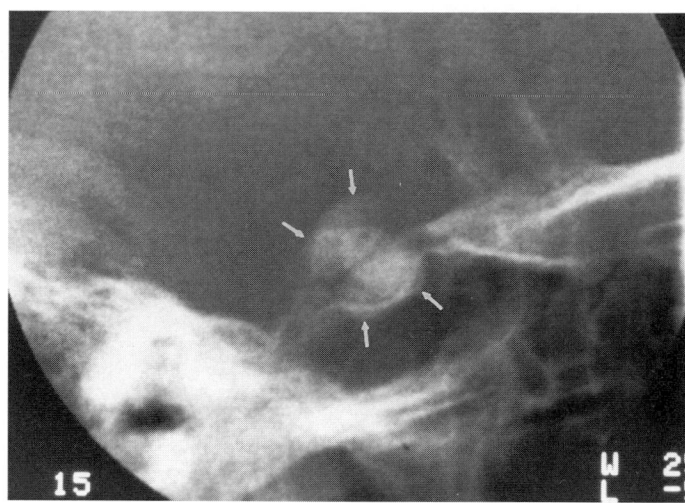

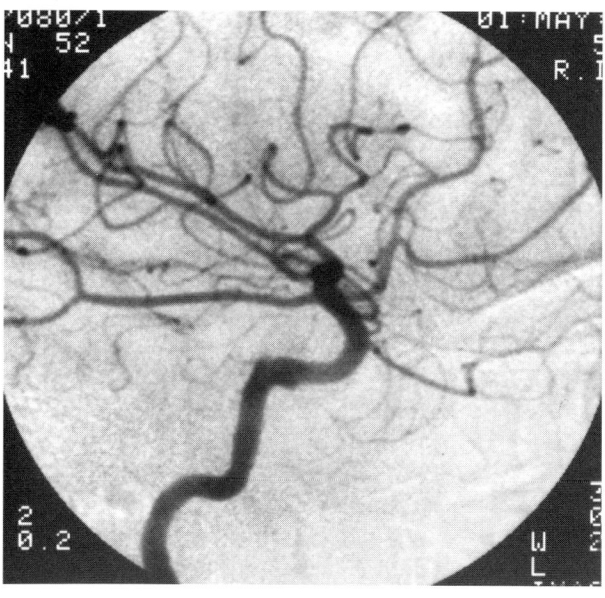

Figure 45-3. Carotid-cavernous artery aneurysm treated by direct occlusion with detachable balloons. (A) Lateral view of right internal carotid artery demonstrates a cavernous aneurysm (*arrows*). (B) Lateral view of the skull shows two detachable silicone balloons placed within the aneurysm (*arrows*). (C) After embolization, lateral view, a right internal carotid artery angiogram demonstrates complete occlusion of the aneurysm with preservation of the parent artery.

the endovascular patients were worse symptomatically, and the majority of patients were improved.

Following carotid occlusion, aneurysm size tends to decrease, relieving many of the patient's symptoms.[63] Giannotta et al.[64] treated 21 cases of ICA aneurysms, including 9 cavernous, 8 ophthalmic, and 4 supraclinoid, with 85 percent of the patients experiencing relief or marked improvement in their symptoms. In addition, they had no patients with ischemic symptoms after instituting volume expansion and induced hypertension as adjuncts to the graded carotid occlusion.

Bilateral cavernous aneurysms occur in up to 21 percent of cases,[48,52] causing a unique treatment problem. One does not wish to treat a cavernous aneurysm by carotid occlusion on one side if there is an aneurysm on the other. Because most collateral flow to the occluded side originates from the untreated carotid artery, there is resulting greater flow through the untreated carotid artery. If the second aneurysm becomes symptomatic, treatment by carotid occlusion is not possible without prior surgical bypass. Treatment must therefore be individualized for each particular patient and the clinical situation.

Vertebral and Basilar Artery Aneurysms

The incidence of vertebral and basilar artery aneurysms has been reported to be as high as 10 percent by

embolic symptoms in 1 case. There were no deaths. Four patients had a shift in balloon placement at follow-up angiography and required placement of at least one additional detachable balloon (Fig. 45-4). Higashida et al.[62] updated their data in 1991, in which there were 102 cavernous internal carotid artery aneurysms with essentially the same results.

Linskey et al.[51] reported on the treatment of 19 intracavernous carotid artery aneurysms; 8 treated surgically and 11 by endovascular techniques. The surgeries included aneurysm clipping, primary repairs, or trapping with associated bypass grafting. Endovascular techniques included either carotid occlusion or direct aneurysm treatment with preservation of the parent artery. All aneurysms were occluded on follow-up studies. Clinically 3 of the surgical patients and none of

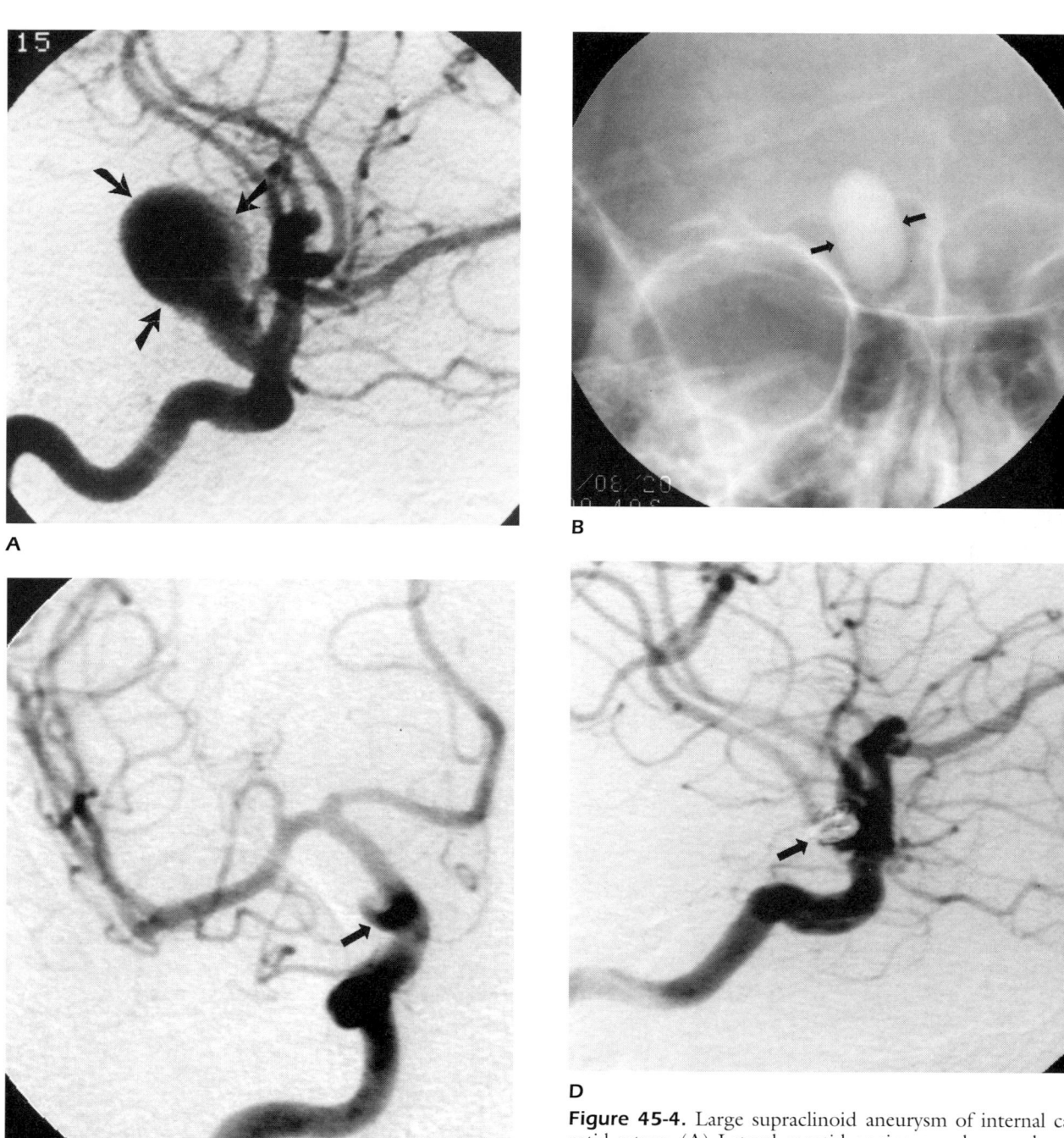

Figure 45-4. Large supraclinoid aneurysm of internal carotid artery. (A) Lateral carotid angiogram shows a large, partially thrombosed, giant aneurysm (*arrows*). (B) Single detachable silicone balloon (*arrows*) within aneurysm. The aneurysm was completely treated following balloon placement. (C) Follow-up angiogram demonstrates a residual neck (*arrow*) of the aneurysm after the balloon settled into thrombus. (D) Residual neck treated with electrolytically detachable coils (*arrow*). Only a small residual neck remains. Because shifting and repositioning of embolic materials may be a problem in aneurysms with intraluminal thrombus, follow-up angiograms are essential in these cases.

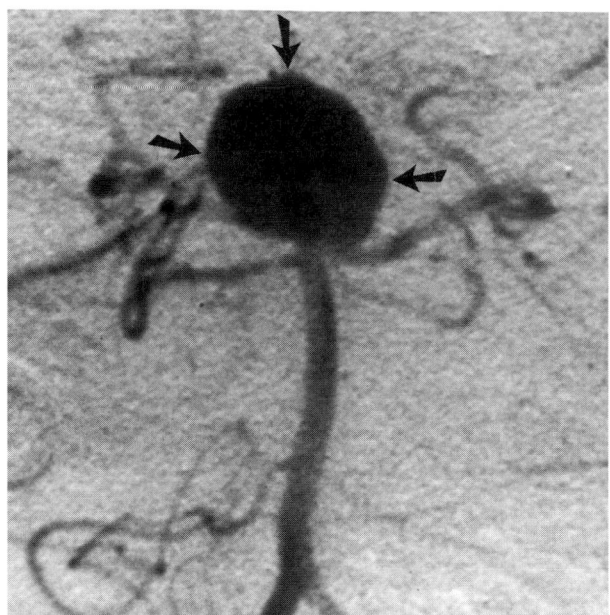
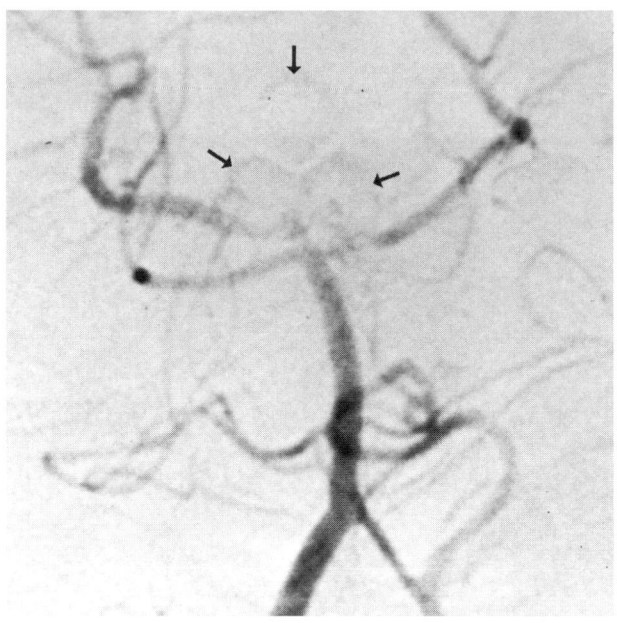

A   **B**

Figure 45-5. Basilar bifurcation aneurysm. (A) Preembolization angiogram demonstrates a large aneurysm (*arrows*). (B) After embolization with three detachable silicone balloons (*arrows*), the aneurysm is completely triated.

autopsy series.[25] The most common location is the basilar bifurcation. These aneurysms can present with subarachnoid hemorrhage or mass effect referable to the posterior fossa. Once hemorrhage has occurred, the rebleed rate may be as high as 50 percent within 5 years.[65]

The initial operative morbidity and mortality of posterior fossa aneurysms have been extremely high. An early series by Jamieson[66] of successive operations of the vertebrobasilar system demonstrated a mortality in 10 of 19 patients (52.6 percent) receiving surgery. In that series and later ones,[67] the morbidity and mortality rates appear to correlate most closely with aneurysm size, being up to 50 percent for aneurysms larger than 25 mm. The surgical data have improved somewhat, but a recent series of 11 posterior cerebral artery aneurysms still had only 7 (63.6 percent) favorable outcomes.[68]

Therefore, even in the best of circumstances, treatment of these aneurysms is difficult. As with aneurysms in all locations, the treatment may consist of vessel occlusion or direct aneurysm therapy with parent vessel preservation. Test occlusion is extremely important in the vertebrobasilar system when considering vessel occlusion. Small perforating branches from the basilar artery, if occluded, can be devastating. Occlusion of the posterior inferior cerebellar artery (PICA) (Wallenberg syndrome), anterior inferior cerebellar artery (AICA), and/or the superior cerebellar artery (SCA) may also

result in severe consequences. Test occlusion is usually based on the direct neurologic examination. In addition, evaluation of collateral flow from the anterior circulation via the posterior communicating arteries is essential. Brain stem evoked potentials and transcranial Doppler may also have a role in evaluation.

Endovascular treatment with detachable balloons offers an alternative to surgery (Fig. 45-5). Higashida et al.[69] reported on 26 aneurysms in 25 patients. The aneurysms involved the distal vertebral artery (5), the midbasilar artery (6), the distal basilar artery (11), and the posterior cerebral artery (4). In 9 cases occlusion of the parent vessel was necessary, and 15 patients had direct aneurysm treatment with preservation of the parent vessel. In an average follow-up interval of 22.5 months, there were 11 complications (44 percent): 3 cases of transient ischemia, 3 cases of stroke, and 5 deaths due to aneurysm rupture. Six patients in this series were judged to have poor results due to subtotal occlusion of the aneurysm. This most certainly is a reflection of the difficulty in handling aneurysms in this location.

Aymard et al.[70] reported on 21 patients with vertebrobasilar aneurysms who were treated with unilateral or bilateral occlusion of the vertebral artery. The distribution included the intracranial vertebral artery (3), the vertebrobasilar junction (3), the PICA (1), the midbasilar artery (7), the SCA (3), and the basilar bifurcation (3). On follow-up, 13 patients had no angiographic demonstration of aneurysm filling, and 6 were partially thrombosed. As expected, the cures were mainly confined to the vertebral and midbasilar aneurysms.

Electrolytically detachable coils have been used to alleviate the technical difficulties with detachable balloons. Guglielmi et al.[71] reported on treatment of 42 patients with 43 aneurysms in the posterior fossa using these coils. With a maximum follow-up of 18 months, there was complete occlusion of the aneurysm in 17 cases and partial occlusion (70–98 percent) in 25 cases. A single aneurysm could not be treated. One patient died from aneurysm rupture, and there was a single stroke. Coil migration occurred in one case but produced no untoward consequences. These data are preliminary but certainly show that more promising results are achievable using endovascular occlusion techniques.

Arteriovenous Malformations

An arteriovenous malformation (AVM) is an abnormal shunting between arterial inflow and venous outflow that bypasses the normal capillary network. Radiographically, two major types of shunts are possible:

1. *Plexiform nidus,* which represents a collection of small vessels with arteriovenous shunting
2. *Fistula(s),* which represent single-hole communications between an artery and vein

Although this classification is often used, in practice there is often a mixture of these two types, and most of the information presented here under nidus AVMs is also applicable to fistulous types. This is often apparent during embolization, particularly with particles such as polyvinyl alcohol (PVA) sponge. Smaller particles may simply traverse the fistulous sites, necessitating the use of larger embolic materials.

Cerebral AVMs may also be radiographically divided into three types—*dural, pial,* or *mixed*—depending on topography and blood supply.

Nidus Arteriovenous Malformations

Parenchymal AVMs are congenital in origin, arising from primitive arterial and venous connections.[72] Because of lowered resistance, there is increased blood flow through the developing malformation, and the nidus may continue to grow in size. The feeding arteries and draining veins may also increase in size. The AVM produces symptoms based primarily on one or a combination of two factors:

1. Hemorrhage
2. Mass effect and vascular steal from surrounding brain tissue[73]

Intracranial hemorrhage from an AVM is estimated to be between 1 and 4 percent per year. Following one bleed there is approximately a 6 to 10 percent increased incidence of a rebleed in the first year.[74,75] The risk of neurologic deficit following hemorrhage is also comparatively high and is between 20 and 30 percent.[76-78]

High-quality, rapid-sequence cerebral angiography is essential for treatment planning with AVMs. Evaluation must include the size of the nidus, the number of feeding arteries, the amount of flow through the lesion, the location, the accessibility for treatment, the eloquence of the surrounding brain, and the patterns of venous drainage. Several grading systems have been devised to classify AVMs and to predict treatment outcomes in patients. These systems have varied from the number of arteries supplying the AVM,[79] to systems that take into account the size, pattern of venous drainage, and neurologic eloquence of adjacent brain.[80] All of these factors must be addressed by pretreatment angiography.

The risks of hemorrhage may be determined by angiography and include the presence of nidus aneurysms, the degree of venous stenoses, and venous occlusion.[81,82] Several reports state that small AVMs (<3 cm) have almost five times an increased risk for hemorrhage,[75] whereas others note little difference in the rate of hemorrhage based on size.[82] There has been strong correlation reported between nidus aneurysms and hemorrhage (Fig. 45-6).[83] Marks et al.[84] reviewed 125 patients with AVMs; 15 had intranidal aneurysms, and all had a history of hemorrhage. Garcia-Monaco et al.[85] reviewed 189 patients with AVMs that had hemorrhaged. Fifteen (8 percent) of these had pseudoaneurysms, and the authors stressed the importance of embolization with liquid adhesives to occlude nidus aneurysms. These aneurysms should be differentiated angiographically from feeding artery aneurysms, which may also increase the risk of hemorrhage (see Fig. 46-6).[86] There are some reports of feeding artery aneurysms decreasing in size following treatment of the AVM, but this opinion is not shared by others.[87-90]

Venous outflow restriction refers to alteration in the normal pattern of venous drainage, with areas of stenosis and/or occlusion (Fig. 45-7). Vinuela et al.[91] suggested a relationship between an increased incidence of intracranial bleeding and impaired venous outflow, particularly for deep-seated cerebral AVMs. There appears to be a statistical correlation between severely impaired venous drainage and the risk of

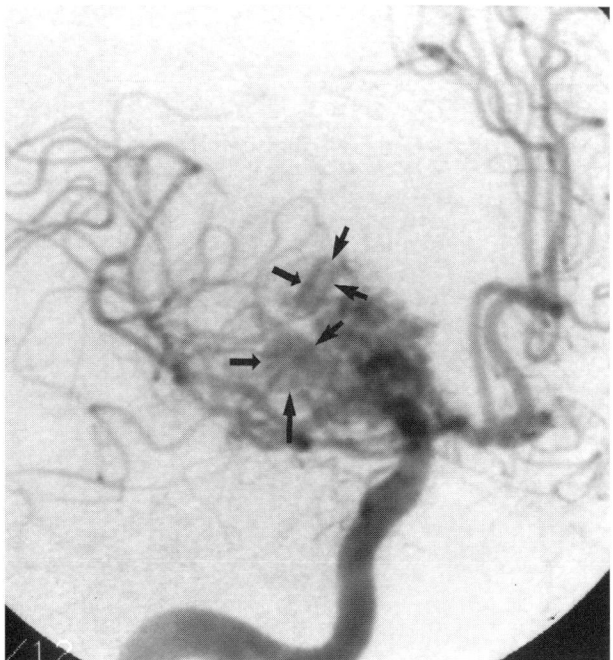

A

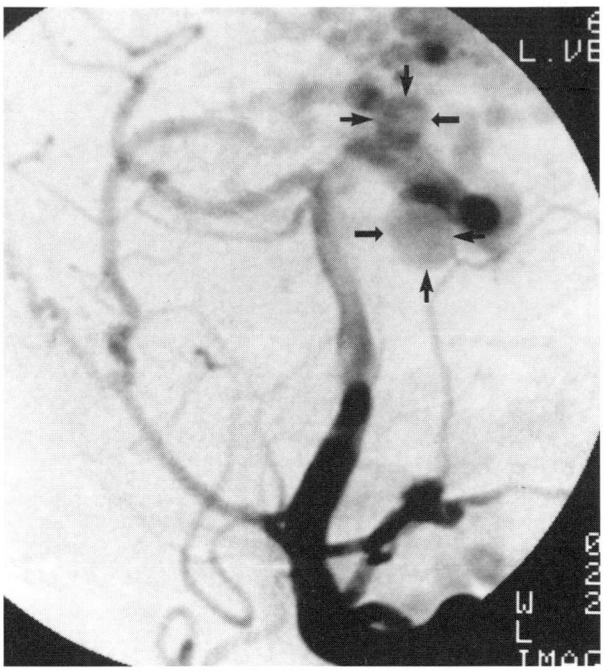

B

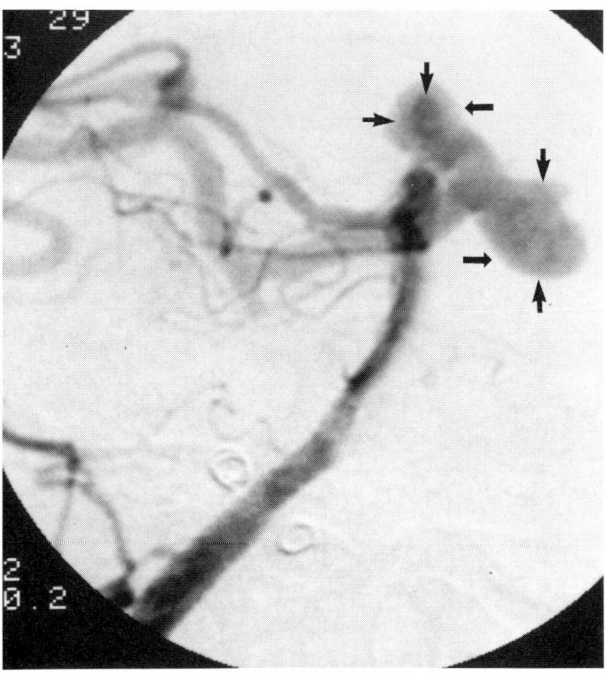

C

Figure 45-6. Aneurysms associated with AVMs. (A) Frontal view of right internal carotid artery demonstrates a thalamic AVM with nidus aneurysms (*arrows*). (B) Parietooccipital AVM with feeding artery aneurysms (*arrows*) arising from the posterior cerebral artery. Frontal view of left vertebral artery injection. (C) Parietooccipital AVM with feeding artery aneurysms (*arrows*) from the left posterior cerebral artery. Lateral view of left vertebral artery.

cerebral hemorrhage.[92] There is also a correlation between hemorrhage, central venous drainage, and the presence of a small number of draining veins, particularly when only one vein is present.[83,92]

After an acute hemorrhage an AVM may not be demonstrated angiographically, may be displaced, or may be separated by the adjacent hematoma.[93] Therefore, additional imaging studies are important, particularly MRI because it gives a three-dimensional view of the AVM and better defines its location.

After subselective angiography and before AVM embolization, it is useful to perform provocative testing to predict any functional loss from vessel occlusion (Fig. 45-8). This is performed by injecting a short-acting barbiturate, sodium amobarbital, superselectively at the site of proposed embolization.[94] This test is a selective version of the intracarotid Wada and Rasmussen test[95] for lateralization of cerebral speech dominance; it also tests for motor, sensory, and visual symptoms. The dose of Amytal varies according to vessel size and flow and is usually in the range of 25 to 50 mg per vessel. The Amytal is injected at the same rate as blood flow, and neurologic and EEG examinations are performed. The most accurate assessment of neurologic function is in the awake, cooperative patient. Rauch et al.[96] found that of 23 positive Amytal examinations in 109 superselective vessels, only 12 were positive by neurologic examination alone. The remainder were positive only on EEG. There were 3 positive examinations by neurologic examination only, suggesting that both methods of evaluation should be

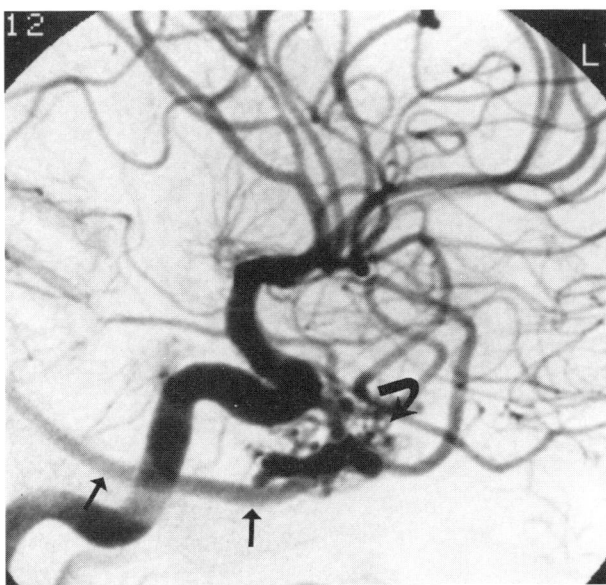

A

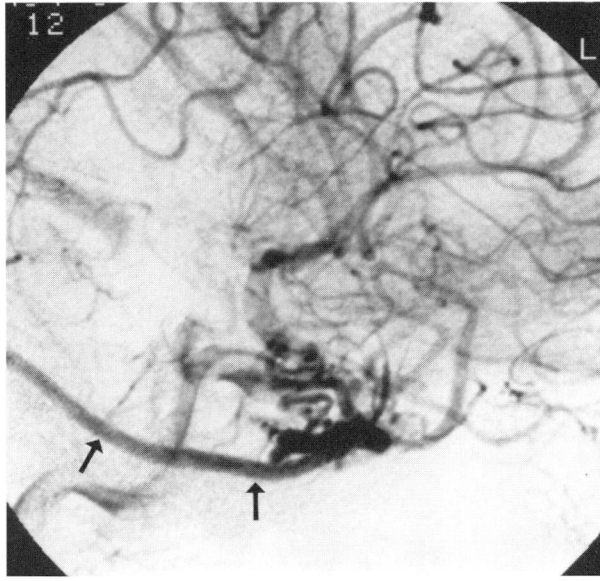

B

Figure 45-7. Temporal lobe AVM (*curved arrow*) demonstrated on lateral internal carotid artery angiograms. Note that the only venous drainage is via the sphenobasal sinus (*arrows*) and therefore represents a severe restrictive pattern.

The *pattern* of drainage may indicate restriction, as opposed to the more commonly recognized venous *narrowing*, which represents venous restrictive disease. (A) Early arterial phase. (B) Late arterial phase.

used. In a follow-up study, Rauch et al.[97] embolized five vessels with positive studies resulting in neurologic complications in two. In neither of the above studies were there complications from the Amytal.

In theory, Amytal testing represents the expected result of distal embolization with liquid adhesive agents. Larger particles, such as PVA sponge, may not penetrate to small vessels, and more proximal vessel occlusive agents, such as microcoils, may therefore result in what appears to be a false-positive test. Functional imaging has improved over the past few years and may become a reliable method of predicting neurologic deficits that may result from embolization and possibly from subsequent surgery.[98] One method combines the use of amobarbital with [99m]technetium-labeled hexamethyl-propyleneamine oxine (^{99m}Tc HMPAO) with single photon emission computed tomography (SPECT).[99]

The results of embolization of AVMs can be divided into its adjunctive role to surgery and radiosurgery and as a sole treatment modality. Preoperative embolization has been reported to empirically decrease operative blood loss and may make large, previously unresectable AVMs surgical candidates.[100] Jafar et al.[101] reported on a comparison of two groups receiving surgery for AVMs, with one receiving preoperative embolization. The embolized group had significantly larger AVMs (3.9 cm versus 2.3 cm), and there was no statistical difference between groups for operative times or blood losses.

Figure 45-8. Superselective injection of left middle cerebral artery branch demonstrates a posterior frontal AVM (*curved arrow*). There is also filling of normal branches (*arrows*) posterior to the AVM. Although the Amytal examination was negative, the patient experienced transient aphasia after embolization. Although provocative testing is useful, there may be false-negative testing.

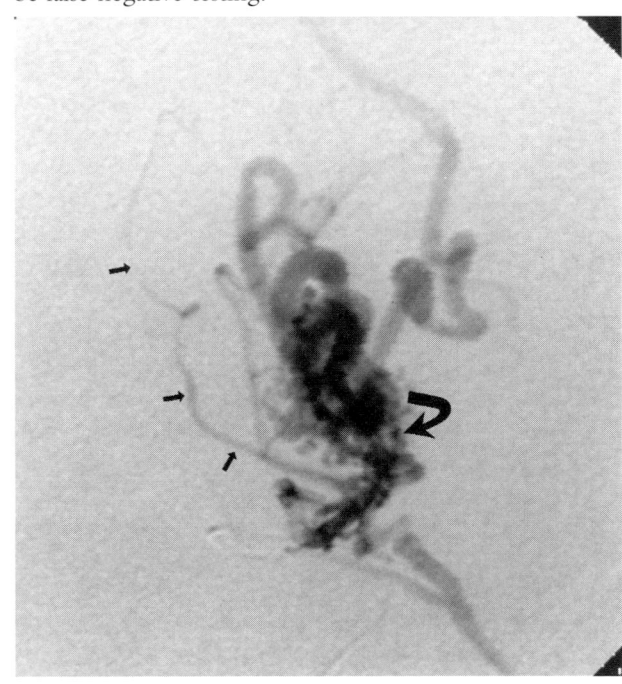

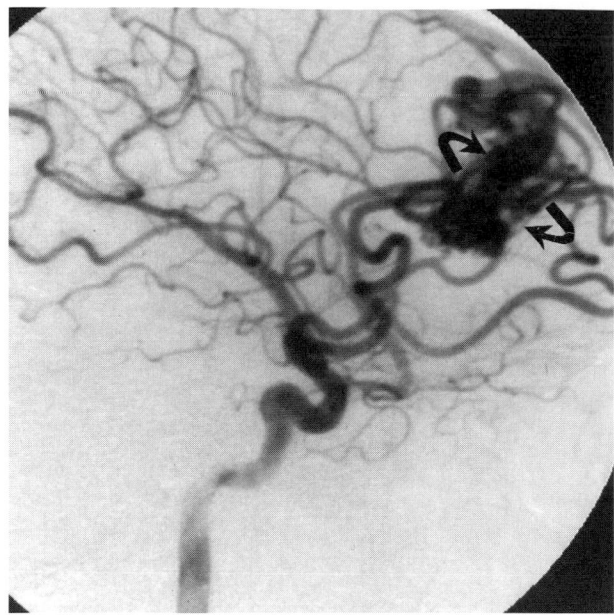
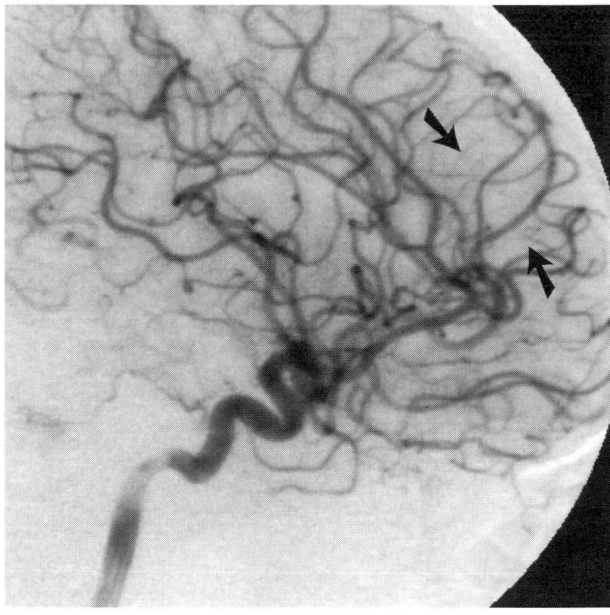

A

B

Figure 45-9. Lateral internal carotid angiograms of a frontal AVM. (A) Preembolization AVM (*arrows*). (B) After embolization with PVA sponge particles there is virtually no filling of the AVM (*arrows*). The patient underwent complete surgical resection of the AVM.

The overall goal of embolotherapy, as an adjunct to surgery, is to diminish the arteriovenous shunt and to embolize arterial feeders that are difficult to access surgically (Fig. 45-9). The surgical approach to AVMs varies according to location. Eloquent areas of the brain must be spared. Deep-seated AVMs are often adjacent to ventricles. In general, the feeding arteries are initially approached; then coagulation of the nidus is undertaken, followed by clipping of the draining veins and resection of the AVM. Surgical results have improved dramatically over the past 2 decades because of the operating microscope and the technical advances made in preoperative embolization. Yamada et al.[102] reported on 56 patients who had resection of their AVMs in functional areas of the cerebral hemisphere (sensory, motor, visual, speech) using microsurgical techniques. They reported 2 significant complications (4 percent) and 18 temporary postoperative deficits (32 percent). There were no mortalities, and of these patients 55 resumed their preoperative occupation. Heros et al.[103] reported their long-term results of surgical excision and noted that none of their 153 patients had delayed hemorrhage within a mean follow-up of 3.8 years. They had an overall immediate morbidity in 37 patients (24.2 percent), with this number decreasing to 12 patients (7.8 percent) at long-term follow-up. There were 3 deaths (0.6 percent) in their series.

A relatively large number of studies have been published on the results of embolization preoperatively since the initial case by Luessenhop and Spence in 1960.[104] Halbach et al.[105] treated arterial feeders to AVMs in 29 patients with detachable balloons preoperatively and concluded that this was a valuable surgical adjunct. However, they realized that such proximal occlusion plays little role in long-term treatment because of collateral circulation. In an effort to achieve better surgical hemostasis from the nidus, more distal embolic agents have been used.

Debrun et al.[106] treated 39 of 46 patients with liquid adhesives using calibrated leak balloons; a number of their cases were performed intraoperatively. They reported complete obliteration of the AVM in 9 and partial obliteration in 30 patients. Twelve of their patients underwent complete surgical resection. There were 14 complications (27 percent), including 1 death from intracranial hemorrhage. Long-term follow-up was not given.

Purdy et al.[107] reported on 54 patients with AVMs embolized using PVA sponge particles and platinum microcoils. The average AVM size was 3.9 cm. The authors reported 1 death and a complication rate of 21 percent with selective catheterization and embolization, which was performed in 39 of the 54 patients. This included patients experiencing transient neurologic difficulties and arterial perforations in which the patients remained asymptomatic. In addition, the same authors[108] reviewed 108 embolized and surgically resected AVMs and concluded that PVA for distal occlusion and microcoils for proximal occlusion appeared to be superior choices with fewer complications when compared to other embolic agents.

Vinuela et al.[109] reported on 101 patients who underwent surgical resection of their AVMs after embolization. Fifty-seven of these malformations were greater than 5 cm in size. Ninety of their patients were embolized with liquid adhesives, 6 with PVA alone and 28 with a combination of PVA, Avitene, and 30 percent ethanol. Complete surgical removal and subsequent cure were reported in 97 patients (96 percent). The authors reported 12 complications (12 percent) and a single death (1 percent). Vinuela[2] updated his series with 283 patients, 270 of whom were embolized with liquid adhesives either alone or in combination with other agents. He achieved complete cures in only 20 cases (7 percent), and in all these cases the AVMs were small (<3 cm in diameter). There were 131 cases of surgical removal, with complete excision in 127 cases (97 percent). Hemorrhage, either subarachnoid or parenchymal, occurred in 15 patients (5 percent). There were 4 cases of arterial rupture, all due to overinflation of a calibrated leak balloon. There were 7 deaths (2.4 percent), 5 of which were 6 or more months after embolization, all due to hemorrhage.

Higashida et al.[110] treated 100 patients with a combination of surgery and embolization and with complete obliteration of the AVM in 99 patients (99 percent). They used PVA sponge particles in combination with larger hand-cut pieces of PVA, silk suture, detachable balloons, and platinum microcoils for larger shunts. There were 12 transient neurologic deficits (12 percent), 3 permanent neurologic deficits (3 percent), and a single death (1 percent) due to intracranial hemorrhage.

The success and avoidance of complications vary with the experience of the team. The location of the AVM, its size, and whether it has previously bled are all important factors in considering patients for therapy.

Most studies list the location of the AVMs as a percentage of the whole. The largest portion of these are in the frontal, temporal, and parietal lobes. However, none of the larger studies have attempted to define the location of the AVM in relationship to success or complications. Vinuela et al.[111] reported embolization of 16 patients with AVMs in the dominant hemisphere with liquid adhesives. Although early complications were common (50 percent), only 3 patients (19 percent) had mild permanent deficits at 6 months.

Concerning AVM size, Spetzler et al.[112] reported on 20 patients with giant AVMs (>6 cm) embolized preoperatively with PVA sponge particles. Complete surgical excision was achieved in 18 of these patients (90 percent). However, long operative times were still necessary for excision.

Radiosurgery for AVMs

Radiosurgery is an option over surgical excision for an AVM. The criteria for radiosurgery[113] are as follows:

1. AVM unresectable by surgery (usually related to location and/or size)
2. High risks of surgery due to patient condition
3. Residual AVM after surgery and/or embolotherapy
4. Patient preference

Several forms of radiosurgery are available for treating cerebral AVMs. These include partial brain irradiation, linear accelerator-based radiosurgery, gamma knife radiosurgery, and Bragg peak therapy. Radiation therapy induces many changes, the most important of which is intimal proliferation, which results in gradual vascular lumen obliteration. A review of the four more widely used forms of radiotherapy showed that the incidence of hemorrhage during the first 2 years after treatment was not different from the observed natural history of AVMs.[114] Therefore, the vascular changes secondary to radiation may not completely confer protection until at least 2 years after treatment or when the AVM is completely obliterated.

Because of the ability to concentrate the higher doses of radiation to smaller areas, smaller AVMs respond much better to radiation therapy than larger lesions. There is a reported 80 to 95 percent complete angiographic obliteration for lesions less than 3.7 cm in diameter 3 years after treatment.[115]

Embolization has two main goals as an adjunct to radiosurgery: (1) to decrease the size of the AVM volume; and (2) to embolize areas that are at high risk to bleed, such as nidus aneurysms. Therefore, excellent-quality angiography must be performed and an in-depth analysis made before proceeding with embolization. The target areas of potential hemorrhage sites should be initially approached and treated. To decrease the size of the AVM nidus, vessels that supply the periphery of the lesion should be targeted to decrease the volume for treatment. Embolizing the center of the AVM does not necessarily decrease the volume for radiation therapy. Most centers use permanent agents for embolization because the areas embolized may not be subjected to radiation. Liquid adhesives have been used by most centers, often in combination with coils.[116]

Incomplete treatment of AVMs, especially larger ones, is common with radiosurgery.[117,118] Steiner et al.[119] found that the protective effect of radiation against hemorrhage in incompletely treated AVMs was not any greater (3.7 percent per year) than the natural history of the disease for at least 5 years after radiosurgery. Embolotherapy of intracranial AVMs may therefore also have a role *after* radiosurgery to assist in the management of unresponsive or incompletely responsive lesions.[120]

AVMs with a defined nidus are rarely cured by

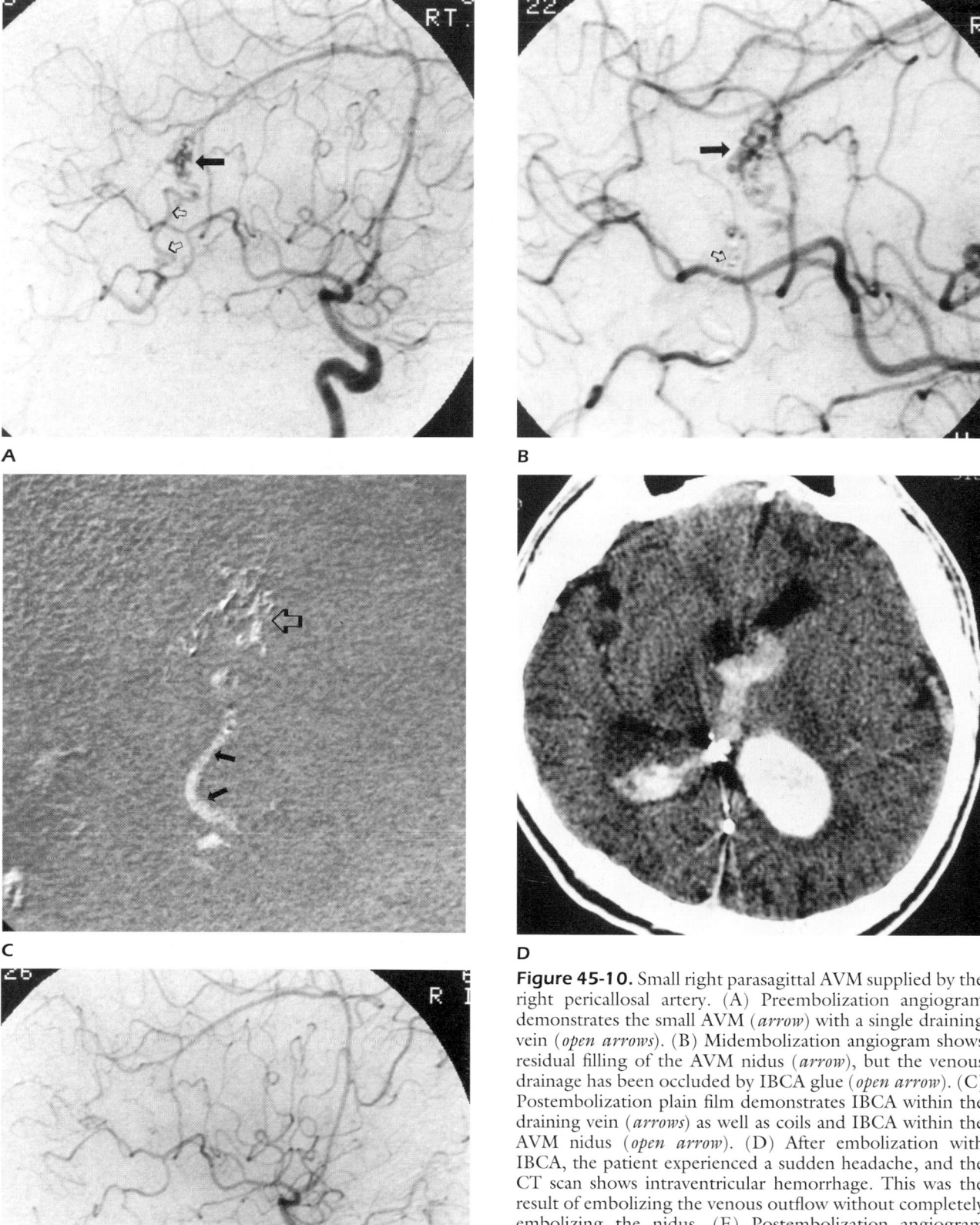

Figure 45-10. Small right parasagittal AVM supplied by the right pericallosal artery. (A) Preembolization angiogram demonstrates the small AVM (*arrow*) with a single draining vein (*open arrows*). (B) Midembolization angiogram shows residual filling of the AVM nidus (*arrow*), but the venous drainage has been occluded by IBCA glue (*open arrow*). (C) Postembolization plain film demonstrates IBCA within the draining vein (*arrows*) as well as coils and IBCA within the AVM nidus (*open arrow*). (D) After embolization with IBCA, the patient experienced a sudden headache, and the CT scan shows intraventricular hemorrhage. This was the result of embolizing the venous outflow without completely embolizing the nidus. (E) Postembolization angiogram demonstrates no visualization of the AVM, representing a complete cure. The patient recovered fully from the hemorrhage.

endovascular means as a sole therapy[121] (Fig. 45-10). The indications for treatment are usually based on size, location, and patient symptoms. The symptoms may range from hemorrhage to mass effect and vascular steal from the surrounding normal brain. Vascular steal may account for seizure activity and motor and/ or sensory deficits and is still somewhat controversial.[122] Embolization has been shown to produce significant clinical improvement in a number of cases. The exact mechanism for this improvement is still unknown. As with preradiation, the main goal of embolization is to target the suspected bleeding site(s) and to occlude those areas with a permanent agent.

The results of embolization as sole therapy have also been reported. An early study of embolization alone using Silastic spheres resulted in reduced headache frequency in patients but did not alter their neurologic deficits.[123] Vinuela et al.[124] followed 30 large AVMs partially embolized with IBCA and demonstrated the importance of embolization of the nidus as opposed to the arterial feeders alone. However, in that series, only 2 of 30 cases (7 percent) were cured, and 28 (93 percent) were either larger or unchanged in size. Fournier et al.[125] reported on 33 patients who were treated with liquid adhesives alone and followed with angiography at 2 years, with clinical follow-up from 2 to 6 years. A morphologic cure was obtained in 7 (21.2 percent) of these patients; however, 3 of these were single-hole fistulas. Two patients had delayed bleeding from subtotal occlusion.

Direct Arteriovenous Fistulas

Intracerebral direct arteriovenous connections without an associated nidus are relatively rare. They consist of one or more major arteries emptying directly into a large vein, often a varix. Halbach et al.[126] reported 5 fistulas out of 320 AVMs. Lownie et al.[127] presented the experiences of two institutions (14 cases) as well as a literature review (35 cases) for a total of 48 patients. The clinical presentation ranged from hemorrhage, mass effect, and seizures to congestive heart failure in large fistulas.

The treatment of these fistulas involves interruption of the fistulous site, which can be accomplished with either surgery or embolization (Fig. 45-11). In the 48 total patients reported by Lownie et al.,[127] 25 had neurosurgical correction of their fistulas with excellent results in 22 (88 percent).

Transarterial occlusion with balloons or platinum coils can also be curative in these cases. Treatment is based on positioning the embolic material at the fistulous connection. Out of 14 patients in their institution, Lownie et al.[127] treated 5 patients with balloons

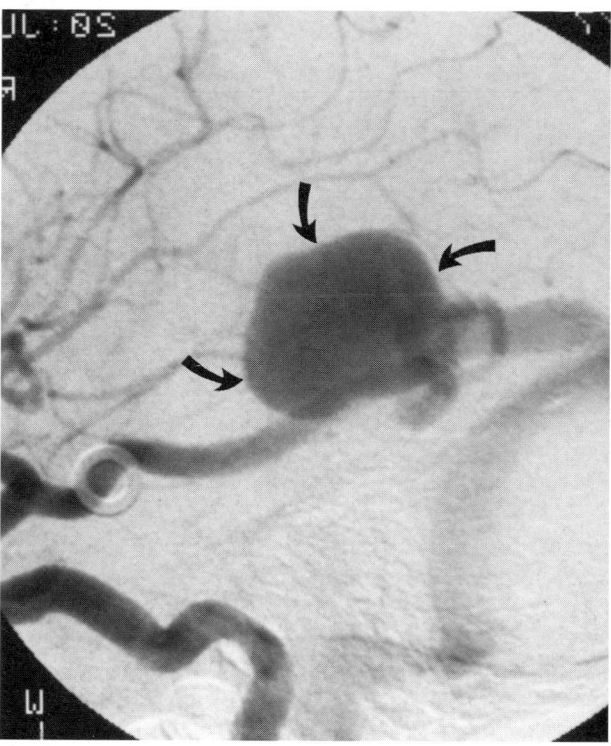

A

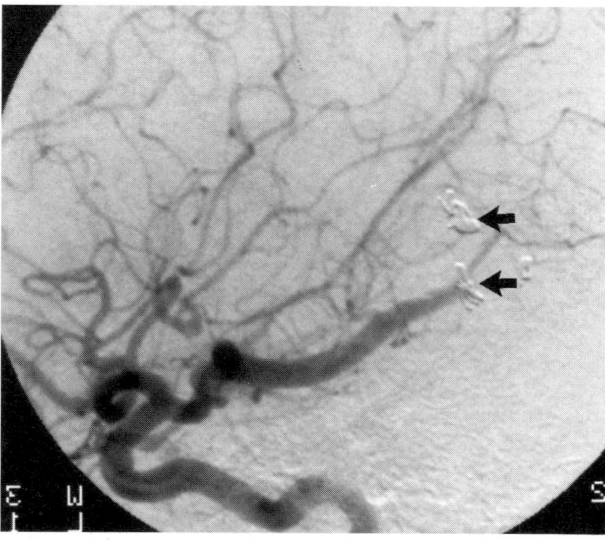

B

Figure 45-11. Direct arteriovenous fistula. (A) Direct fistula with large varix (*arrows*). (B) After embolization with coils there is nonfilling of the fistula (*arrows*). This type of single-hole arteriovenous fistula can be completely cured by intravascular embolization techniques.

with excellent results in 4. Halbach et al.[126] treated five patients using balloons or coils and silk suture. Surgical intervention was necessary in only one of their cases because of embolization of an arterial feeder too proximal to the fistula site.

Vein of Galen Malformations

An unusual type of arteriovenous malformation of the fistulous type is the vein of Galen aneurysm or malformation. These disorders have in common a midline dilated venous structure, the vein of Galen.[128] Garcia-Monaco et al.,[129] after a review of 100 cases, described two main types:

1. Vein of Galen aneurysmal malformation (VGAM)
2. Vein of Galen aneurysmal dilatation

The vein of Galen aneurysmal dilatation represents fistulous connections to the true vein of Galen, which also drains normal brain tissue. Although there are various subtypes, they all represent fistulous arteriovenous malformations and can be treated by endovascular techniques.

The vein of Galen aneurysmal malformation (VGAM) is different. It represents the persistence of the embryologic prosencephalic vein of Markowski, which only drains the arteriovenous shunt and does not drain normal brain tissue.[130] The true vein of Galen fails to develop. In addition, there is retention of fetal anatomic features and frequent occlusions of the dural sinuses of the posterior fossa. These result in other associated anomalies of venous drainage, including a persistent falcine sinus, occipital sinuses, and marginal sinuses. The draining prosencephalic vein is usually stenotic along its course, causing the aneurysmal dilatation.

The arteriovenous fistula may be a single- or multiple-hole connection, and the location of the site divides the VGAM into mural and choroidal types, the latter usually presenting in neonates with congestive heart failure. The treatment in these patients depends on their clinical condition. If they can be stabilized medically, treatment may be deferred until there has been interval somatic growth and the vascular systems are easier to access. However, acute clinical deterioration may necessitate more urgent intervention, particularly in cases of severe and uncontrollable congestive heart failure, acute hydrocephalus, or deterioration in the patient's neurologic status.

Definitive treatment requires interruption of the arteriovenous shunt (Fig. 45-12). Surgical therapy for this condition has been universally poor in the neonatal period.[131] Ciricillo et al.[132] reported on 13 neonates in which all 5 treated surgically died in the perioperative period, whereas 6 of 8 (75 percent) treated with endovascular techniques survived.

Embolotherapy has become the treatment of choice for VGAMs. Embolization can be performed from either the arterial or venous route and should be performed with permanent agents such as microcoils or liquid tissue adhesives (Figs. 45-12 and 45-13). Garcia-Monaco et al.[129] reported on 39 cases of embolization in which 26 patients (67 percent) were either normal or had mild manifestations (stable macrocephaly or asymptomatic cardiomegaly) after embolotherapy. Lylyk et al.[133] treated 28 patients with vein of Galen malformations using a combination of transfemoral and transarterial approaches. The results were an immediate improvement in the patient's clinical status in 23 (82 percent) with good long-term clinical outcomes in 17 patients (61 percent). There were 5 deaths (18 percent) in this series.

Larger fistulous sites may be occluded using balloons, coils, or silk suture. If a transvenous route is used, arterial embolization can be performed of the largest feeder(s) before transvenous embolization to decrease flow into the dilated vein. The transvenous route can be femoral or jugular or via a retrograde catheterization from the torcula (see Fig. 46-13).[134,135] The transtorcular approach allows direct access to the dilated venous structure. Venous access also enables one to measure pressures within the dilated veins during embolization.[136]

Transvenous embolization should begin at the fistulous portions and continue posteriorly. Because by definition VGAMs do not drain normal brain, the entire vein can be occluded. The transvenous route usually uses coils and/or detachable balloons. The choice of transfemoral versus transtorcular approach depends on the size of the fistulous flow and the venous anatomy. The placement of large numbers of coils and/or the frequent association of venous anomalies must be a consideration for the route taken.

During embolization, two aspects are important considerations: coil size and the starting site for embolization. Coils or balloons must be carefully chosen for size because with very rapid flow undersized embolic agents can be carried out with the blood flow. Although the agent may be trapped in the lungs, given the cardiodynamic status of these patients, a right-to-left cardiac shunt is possible. Therefore the embolic agent may end up in the systemic circulation. Embolization should begin at the anteriormost portion of the vein and/or at the fistula site(s). Regardless of the route used, embolization may take more than one session. This approach may be preferable for large shunts to prevent rapid changes in the cardiovascular equilibrium.

Postembolization Care

After embolization therapy, the two most dreaded delayed consequences are *hemorrhage* and *ischemia*. De-

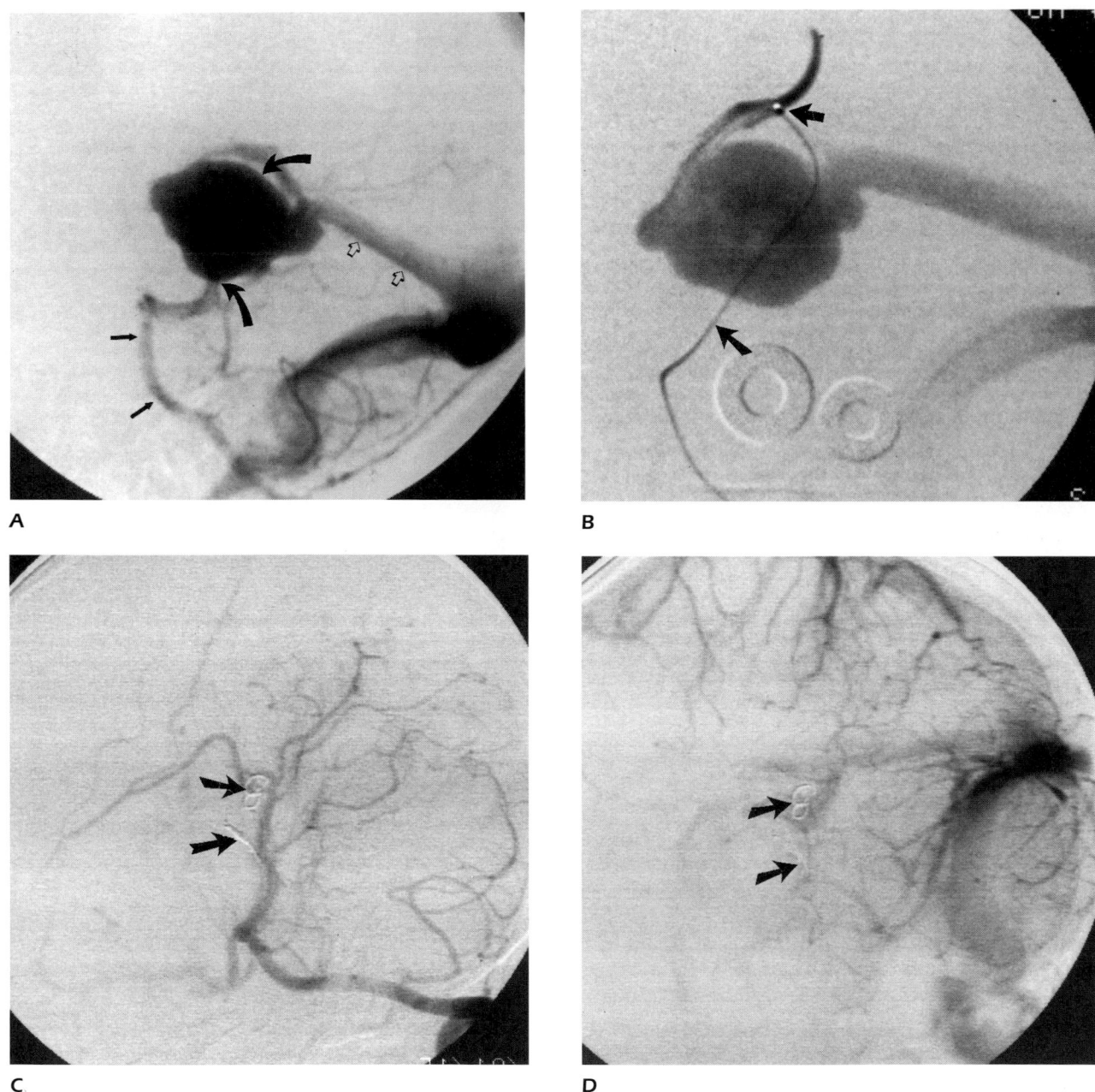

Figure 45-12. Vein of Galen malformation. (A) Vertebral artery injection shows large vein of Galen malformation (*curved arrows*) draining into the straight sinus (*open arrows*). Supply is from the posterior circulation via the basilar artery (*arrows*). (B) Transarterial catheter (*arrows*) placed selectively into the posterior lateral choroidal artery for arterial embolization with coils. (C) Frontal view of left vertebral artery after embolization. The malformation is completely embolized by the coils (*arrows*). (D) Lateral view of left vertebral artery (venous phase) after embolization with coils (*arrows*). The malformation is completely embolized. The patient was completely cured.

layed hemorrhage of an AVM may be the result of changes in the hemodynamics after embolotherapy. The patient is particularly at risk if the venous outflow to the AVM is occluded without complete arterial occlusion. It is in these settings that arterial pressures measured before and after embolization are important. Patients with markedly high pressures without com-

plete embolization of the nidus are at a higher risk for delayed hemorrhage. Postembolization edema is also believed to be produced by a combination of sudden removal of the AVM sump effect and a lack of regional vascular autoregulation of the surrounding normal brain (normal perfusion pressure breakthrough phenomenon).[20] This same phenomenon can also lead to

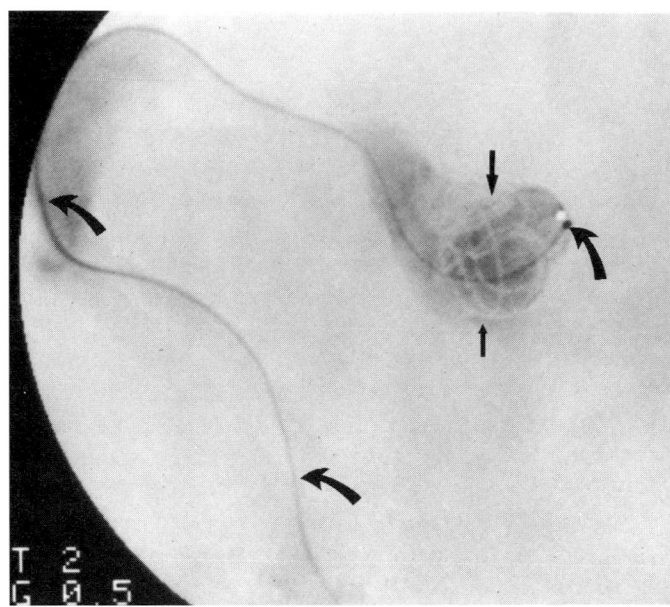

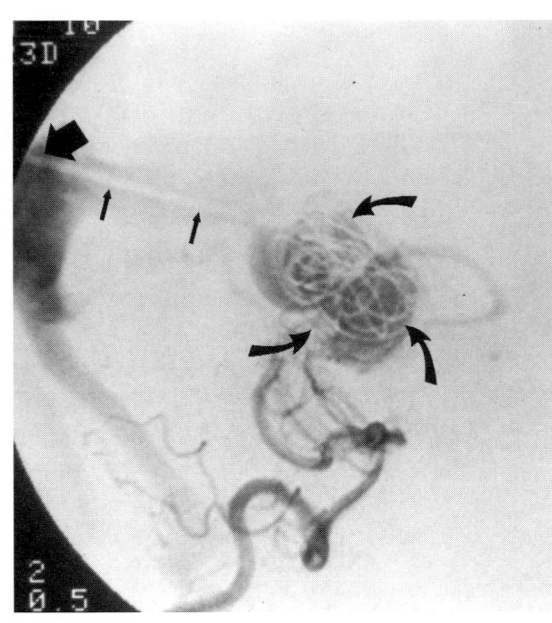

Figure 45-13. Vein of Galen malformation. (A) Transvenous approach. Note the catheter through the venous sinus system (*curved arrows*) into the malformation, where coils (*straight arrows*) have been placed. (B) Transtorcular approach. A sheath (*small arrows*) has been placed through a surgical exposure of the torcula (*large arrow*). Coils have been placed into the malformation (*curved arrows*).

hemorrhage. Direct intraoperative punctures of vessels supplying AVMs have shown blood pressure elevations as the distal runoff was decreased by surgery.[137] These same pressure changes have been noted during embolization of feeding arteries.[138] It has been shown that AVMs with higher feeding artery pressures have a greater tendency to present with hemorrhage. The authors postulate that hemorrhage after embolization may be related to this increase in feeding artery pressures.[139] Therefore, one must keep these principles in mind when embolizing large AVMs.

For surgical series, the postoperative complications of perioperative edema and/or hemorrhage have correlated positively with preoperative angiographic steal, the diameters of the feeding vessels, and the recruitment of perforating vessels.[140] As with staged surgical resection, only a portion of larger AVMs should be embolized in a single session.

Delayed ischemia is most often due to arterial or venous thrombosis that may continue to occur after embolization.[141] The theory is that arteries thrombose where they feed the AVM but remain patent where there are open side branches to normal tissue. Retrograde arterial thrombosis has been shown to occur after surgical removal of AVMs and has been correlated in a small series with advanced patient age, large

AVM size, and markedly dilated and elongated arterial feeding arteries.[142] These data are also applicable to patients after embolotherapy.

Summary

The treatment of intracerebral vascular lesions by interventional neurovascular techniques has made tremendous advances in the past two decades. As further innovations, improved technology, and basic science research in this area continue, the indications for treating patients by these techniques will continue to broaden. Currently, treatment of patients with cerebral aneurysms is technically feasible by interventional techniques. However, long-term follow-up and which patients are ideally suitable for therapy are unresolved issues. Treatment of patients with a cerebral AVM by embolization techniques has been established as efficacious for larger AVMs preoperatively and for selected preradiosurgery candidates. Continuing advances in the development of embolic materials, microcatheters and guidewires, and functional testing will improve the overall morbidity associated with these procedures and improve patient outcome.

References

1. Hacke W, Zeumer H, Berg-Dammer E. Monitoring of hemispheric or brainstem functions with neurophysiologic methods during interventional neuroradiology. AJNR 1983;4: 382–384.
2. Vinuela F. Functional evaluation and embolization of intracranial arteriovenous malformations. In: Vinuela F, Halbach VV, Dion JE, eds. Interventional neuroradiology: endovascular therapy of the central nervous system. New York: Raven, 1992;77–86.
3. John ER, Chabot RJ, Prichep LS, et al. Real-time intraoperative monitoring during neurosurgical and neuroradiological procedures. J Clin Neurophysiol 1989;6:125–158.
4. Formanek G, Frech R, Amplatz K. Arterial thrombus formation during clinical percutaneous catheterization. Circulation 1970;41:833–839.
5. Barnwell SL, Dowd CF, Higashida RT, et al. Endovascular therapy for cerebral arteriovenous malformations. In: Apuzzo MLJ, ed. Brain surgery complication avoidance and management. New York: Churchill Livingstone, 1993:1225–1242.
6. Debrun GM, Vinuela FV, Fox AJ. Aspirin and systemic heparinization in diagnostic and interventional neuroradiology. AJNR 1982;3:337–340.
7. Vinuela FV, Fox AJ, Debrun GM, et al. Progressive thrombosis of brain arteriovenous malformations after embolization with isobutyl 2-cyanoacrylate. AJNR 1983;4:1233–1238.
8. Willinsky R, TerBrugge K, Montanera W, et al. Micro-arteriovenous malformations of the brain: superselective angiography in diagnosis and treatment. AJNR 1992;13:325–330.
9. Higashida RT, Halbach VV, Dormandy BS, et al. Endovascular treatment of intracranial aneurysms with a new silicone microballoon device: technical considerations and indications for therapy. Radiology 1990;174:687–691.
10. Hawkins TD, Szaz KF. The permeability of detachable latex rubber balloons: an in vitro study. Invest Radiol 1987;22: 969–972.
11. Dion JE. Principles and methodology. In: Vinuela F, Halbach VV, Dion JE, eds. Interventional neuroradiology: endovascular therapy of the central nervous system. New York: Raven, 1992:1–15.
12. Taki W, Handa H, Yamagata S, et al. Radiopaque solidifying liquids for releasable balloon technique: a technical note. Surg Neurol 1980;13:140–142.
13. Monsein LH, Debrun GM, Chazaly JR. Hydroxyethyl methylacrylate and latex balloons. AJNR 1990;11:663–664.
14. Forsting M, Sartor K. HEMA and latex: a dangerous combination? Neuroradiology 1991;33:338–340.
15. Brothers MF, Kaufmann JCE, Fox AJ, et al. N-butyl 2-cyanoacrylate—substitute for IBCA in interventional neuroradiology: histopathologic and polymerization time studies. AJNR 1989;10:777–786.
16. Rao VRK, Mandalam KR, Gupta AK, et al. Dissolution of isobutyl 2-cyanoacrylate on long-term follow-up. AJNR 1989;10:135–141.
17. Halbach VV, Higashida RT, Dowd CF, et al. Management of vascular perforations that occur during neurointerventional procedures. AJNR 1991;12:319–327.
18. Al-Rodhan NRF, Sundt TM, Piepgras DG, et al. Occlusive hyperemia: a theory for the hemodynamic complications following resection of intracerebral arteriovenous malformations. J Neurosurg 1993;78:167–175.
19. Wilson CB, Hieshima GB. Occlusive hyperemia: a new way to think about an old problem. J Neurosurg 1993;78:165–166.
20. Spetzler RF, Wilson CB, Weinstein P, et al. Normal perfusion breakthrough theory. In: Congress of Neurological Surgeons, eds. Clinical surgery. Baltimore: Williams & Wilkins, 1978: 651–672.
21. Batjer HH, Devous MD, Meyer YJ, et al. Cerebrovascular hemodynamics in arteriovenous malformation complicated by normal perfusion pressure breakthrough. Neurosurgery 1988;22:503–509.
22. Erba M, Jungreis CA, Horton JA. Nitropaste for prevention and relief of vascular spasm. AJNR 1989;10:155–156.
23. Allen GS, Ahn HS, Preziosi TJ, et al. Cerebral arterial spasm: a controlled trial of nimodipine in patients with subarachnoid hemorrhage. N Engl J Med 1983;308:619–624.
24. Eckard DA, Purdy PD, Girson MS, et al. Intraarterial papaverine for relief of catheter-induced intracranial vasospasm. AJR 1992;158:883–884.
25. McCormick WF, Nofzinger JD. Saccular intracranial aneurysms: an autopsy study. J Neurosurg 1965;22:155–159.
26. Matas R. Testing the efficiency of the collateral circulation as a preliminary to the occlusion of the great surgical arteries. Ann Surg 1911;53:1–43.
27. Erba SM, Horton JA, Latchaw RE, et al. Balloon test occlusion of the internal carotid artery with stable xenon/CT cerebral blood flow imaging. AJNR 1988;9:533–538.
28. de Vries EJ, Sekhar LN, Horton JA, et al. A new method to predict safe resection of the internal carotid artery. Laryngoscope 1990;100:85–88.
29. Stringer WA. Accuracy of xenon CT measurement of cerebral blood flow. AJNR 1991;12:86–87.
30. Eckard DA, Purdy PD, Bonte FJ. Temporary balloon occlusion of the carotid artery combined with brain blood flow imaging as a test to predict tolerance prior to permanent carotid sacrifice. AJNR 1992;13:1565–1569.
31. Morioka T, Matsushima T, Fujii K, et al. Balloon test occlusion of the internal carotid artery with monitoring of compressed spectral arrays (CSAs) of electroencephalogram. Acta Neurochir 1989;101:29–34.
32. Sweet WH, Sarnoff SJ, Bakay L. A clinical method for recording internal carotid pressure: significance of changes during carotid occlusion. Surg Gynecol Obstet 1950;90:327–334.
33. Heyman A, Tindall GT, Finney WHM, et al. Measurement of retinal artery and intracarotid pressures following carotid artery occlusion with the Crutchfield clamp. J Neurosurg 1960;297–305.
34. Miller JD, Jawad K, Jennett B. Safety of carotid ligation and its role in the management of intracranial aneurysms. J Neurol Neurosurg Psychiatry 1977;40:64–72.
35. Kelly JJ, Callow AD, O'Donnell TF, et al. Failure of carotid stump pressures: its incidence as predictor for a temporary shunt during carotid endarterectomy. Arch Surg 1979;114: 1361–1366.
36. Barker DW, Jungreis CA, Horton JA, et al. Balloon test occlusion of the internal carotid artery: change in stump pressure over 15 minutes and its correlation with xenon CT cerebral blood flow. AJNR 1993;14:587–590.
37. Taki W, Nishi S, Yamashita K, et al. Selection and combination of various endovascular techniques in the treatment of giant aneurysms. J Neurosurg 1992;77:37–42.
38. Heilman CB, Kwan ESK, Wu JK. Aneurysm recurrence following endovascular balloon occlusion. J Neurosurg 1992; 77:260–264.
39. Miyachi S, Negoro M, Handa T, et al. Histopathological study of balloon embolization: silicone versus latex. Neurosurgery 1992;30:483–489.
40. Numaguchi Y, Pevsner PH, Rigamonti D, et al. Platinum coil treatment of complex aneurysms of the vertebrobasilar circulation. Neuroradiology 1992;34:252–255.
41. Halbach VV, Higashida RT, Hieshima GB, et al. Aneurysms of the petrous portion of the internal carotid artery: results of treatment with endovascular or surgical occlusion. AJNR 1990;11:253–257.
42. Glassock ME, Smith PG, Bond AG, et al. Management of aneurysms of the petrous portion of the internal carotid artery by resection and primary anastomosis. Laryngoscope 1983; 93:1445–1453.

43. Stallings JO, McCabe BF. Congenital middle ear aneurysm of internal carotid. Arch Otolaryngol 1969;90:65–69.
44. McGrail KM, Heros RC, Debrun G, et al. Aneurysm of the ICA petrous segment treated by balloon entrapment after EC-IC bypass. J Neurosurg 1986;65:249–252.
45. Linskey ME, Sekhar LN, Hirsch W, et al. Aneurysms of the intracavernous carotid artery: clinical presentation, radiographic features, and pathogenesis. Neurosurgery 1990;26: 71–79.
46. Tran-Dinh H. Cavernous branches of the internal carotid artery: anatomy and nomenclature. Neurosurgery 1987;20: 205–210.
47. Kupersmith MJ, Hurst R, Berenstein A, et al. The benign course of cavernous carotid artery aneurysms. J Neurosurg 1992;77:690–693.
48. Linskey ME, Sekhar LN, Hirsch WL, et al. Aneurysms of the intracavernous carotid artery: natural history and indications for treatment. Neurosurgery 1990;26:933–938.
49. Parkinson D. A surgical approach to the cavernous portion of the carotid artery: anatomical studies and case report. J Neurosurg 1965;23:474–483.
50. Inoue T, Rhoton AL, Theele D, et al. Surgical approaches to the cavernous sinus: a microsurgical study. Neurosurgery 1990;26:903–932.
51. Linskey ME, Sekhar LN, Horton JA, et al. Aneurysms of the intracavernous carotid artery: a multidisciplinary approach to treatment. J Neurosurg 1991;75:525–534.
52. Johnston I. Direct surgical treatment of bilateral intracavernous internal carotid artery aneurysms. J Neurosurg 1979; 51:98–102.
53. Tindall GT, Odom GL, Cupp HB, et al. Studies on carotid artery flow and pressure: observations in 18 patients during graded occlusion of proximal carotid artery. J Neurosurg 1962;19:917–923.
54. Nishioka H. Report on the cooperative study of intracranial aneurysms and subarachnoid hemorrhage: results of the treatment of intracranial aneurysms by occlusion of the carotid artery in the neck. J Neurosurg 1966;25:660–682.
55. Kak VK, Taylor AR, Gordon DS. Proximal carotid ligation for internal carotid aneurysms: a long-term follow-up study. J Neurosurg 1973;39:503–513.
56. Scott M, Skwarok E. The treatment of cerebral aneurysms by ligation of the common carotid artery. Surg Gynecol Obstet 1961;113:54–61.
57. Galbraith JG, Clark RM. Role of carotid ligation in the management of intracranial carotid aneurysms. Clin Neurosurg 1973;21:171–181.
58. Serbinenko FA. Balloon catheterization and occlusion of major cerebral vessels. J Neurosurg 1974;41:125–145.
59. Romodanov AP, Shcheglov VI. Intravascular occlusion of saccular aneurysms of the cerebral arteries by means of a detachable balloon catheter. In: Krayenbuhl H, ed. Advances and technical standards in neurosurgery. New York: Springer Verlag 1982;9:25–49.
60. Fox AJ, Vinuela F, Pelz DM, et al. Use of detachable balloons for proximal artery occlusion in the treatment of unclippable cerebral aneurysms. J Neurosurg 1987;66:40–46.
61. Higashida RT, Halbach VV, Dowd C, et al. Endovascular detachable balloon embolization therapy of cavernous carotid artery aneurysms: results in 87 cases. J Neurosurg 1990;72: 857–863.
62. Higashida RT, Halbach VV, Dowd CF, et al. Intracranial aneurysms: interventional neurovascular treatment with detachable balloons—results in 215 cases. Radiology 1991;178: 663–670.
63. Tytus JS, Ward AA. The effect of cervical carotid ligation on giant intracranial aneurysms. J Neurosurg 1970;33:184–190.
64. Giannotta SL, McGillicuddy JE, Kindt GW. Gradual carotid artery occlusion in the treatment of inaccessible internal carotid artery aneurysms. Neurosurgery 1979;5:417–421.
65. Troupp H. The natural history of aneurysms of the basilar bifurcation. Acta Neurol Scand 1971;47:350–356.
66. Jamieson KG. Aneurysms of the vertebrobasilar system. J Neurosurg 1964;21:781–797.
67. Drake CG. Giant intracranial aneurysms: experience with surgical treatment in 174 patients. Clin Neurosurg 1979;26:12–95.
68. Sakata S, Fujii K, Matsushima T, et al. Aneurysm of the posterior cerebral artery: report of eleven cases—surgical approaches and procedures. Neurosurgery 1993;32:163–168.
69. Higashida RT, Halbach VV, Cahan LD, et al. Detachable balloon embolization therapy of posterior circulation intracranial aneurysms. J Neurosurg 1989;71:512–519.
70. Aymard A, Gobin P, Hodes JE, et al. Endovascular occlusion of vertebral arteries in the treatment of unclippable vertebrobasilar aneurysms. J Neurosurg 1991;74:393–398.
71. Guglielmi G, Vinuela F, Duckwiler G, et al. Endovascular treatment of posterior circulation aneurysms by electrothrombosis using electrically detachable coils. J Neurosurg 1992;77:515–524.
72. McCormick WF. The pathology of vascular ("arteriovenous") malformations. J Neurosurg 1966;24:807–816.
73. Luessenhop AJ. Natural history of cerebral arteriovenous malformations. In: Wilson CB, Stein BM, eds. Intracranial arteriovenous malformations. Baltimore: Williams & Wilkins, 1984;12–23.
74. Ondra SL, Troupp H, George ED, et al. The natural history of symptomatic arteriovenous malformations of the brain: a 24-year follow-up assessment. J Neurosurg 1990;73:387–391.
75. Graf CJ, Perret GE, Torner JC. Bleeding from cerebral arteriovenous malformations as part of their natural history. J Neurosurg 1983;58:331–337.
76. Forster DMC, Steiner L, Hakanson S. Arteriovenous malformations of the brain: a long-term clinical study. J Neurosurg 1972;37:562–570.
77. Heros RC, Tu YK. Is surgical therapy needed for unruptured arteriovenous malformations? Neurology 1987;37:279–286.
78. Aminoff MJ. Treatment of unruptured cerebral arteriovenous malformations. Neurology 1987;37:815–819.
79. Luessenhop AJ, Gennarelli TA. Anatomical grading of supratentorial arteriovenous malformations for determining operability. Neurosurgery 1977;1:30–35.
80. Spetzler RF, Martin NA. A proposed grading system for arteriovenous malformations. J Neurosurg 1986;65:476–483.
81. Dobbelaere P, Jomin M, Clarisse J, et al. Interet pronostique de l'etude du drainage veineux des anevrysmes arterio-veineux cerebraux. Neurochirurgie 1979;25:178–184.
82. Crawford PM, West CR, Chadwick DW. Arteriovenous malformations of the brain: natural history in unoperated patients. J Neurol Neurosurg Psychiatry 1986;49:1–10.
83. Marks MP, Lane B, Steinberg GK, et al. Hemorrhage in intracerebral arteriovenous malformations: angiographic determinants. Radiology 1990;176:807–813.
84. Marks MP, Lane B, Steinberg GK, et al. Intranidal aneurysms in cerebral arteriovenous malformations: evaluation and endovascular treatment. Radiology 1992;183:355–360.
85. Garcia-Monaco R, Rodesch G, Alvarez H, et al. Pseudoaneurysms within ruptured intracranial arteriovenous malformations: diagnosis and early endovascular management. AJNR 1993;14:315–321.
86. Brown RD, Wiebers DO, Forbes GS. Unruptured intracranial aneurysms and arteriovenous malformations: frequency of intracranial hemorrhage and relationship of lesions. J Neurosurg 1990;73:859–863.
87. Hayashi S, Arimoto T, Itakura T, et al. The association of intracranial aneurysms and arteriovenous malformation of the brain: case report. J Neurosurg 1981;55:971–975.
88. Koulouris S, Rizzoli HV. Coexisting intracranial aneurysm and arteriovenous malformation: case report. Neurosurgery 1981;8:219–222.
89. Shenkin HA, Jenkins F, Kim K. Arteriovenous anomaly of the brain associated with cerebral aneurysm: case report. J Neurosurg 1971;34:225–228.

90. Batjer H, Suss RA, Samson D. Intracranial arteriovenous malformations associated with aneurysms. Neurosurgery 1986; 18:29–35.
91. Vinuela F, Nombela L, Roach MR, et al. Stenotic and occlusive disease of the venous drainage system of deep brain AVMs. J Neurosurg 1985;63:180–184.
92. Miyasaka Y, Yada K, Ohwada T, et al. An analysis of the venous drainage system as a factor in hemorrhage from arteriovenous malformations. J Neurosurg 1992;76:239–243.
93. Wilson CB, U HS, Domingue J. Microsurgical treatment of intracranial vascular malformations. J Neurosurg 1979;51: 446–454.
94. Peters KR, Quisling RG, Gilmore R, et al. Intraarterial use of sodium methohexital for provocative testing during brain embolotherapy. AJNR 1993;14:171–174.
95. Wada J, Rasmussen T. Intracarotid injection of sodium Amytal for the lateralization of cerebral speech dominance: experimental and clinical observations. J Neurosurg 1960;17:266–282.
96. Rauch RA, Vinuela F, Dion J, et al. Preembolization functional evaluation in brain arteriovenous malformations: the superselective Amytal test. AJNR 1992;13:303–308.
97. Rauch RA, Vinuela F, Dion J, et al. Preembolization functional evaluation in brain arteriovenous malformations: the ability of superselective Amytal test to predict neurologic dysfunction before embolization. AJNR 1992;13:309–314.
98. Martin N, Grafton S, Vinuela F, et al. Imaging techniques for cortical functional localization. Clin Neurosurg 1990;38: 132–165.
99. Jeffery PJ, Monsein LH, Szabo Z, et al. Mapping the distribution of amobarbital sodium in the intracarotid Wada test by use of Tc-99m HMPAO with SPECT. Radiology 1991;178: 847–850.
100. Pelz DM, Fox AJ, Vinuela F, et al. Preoperative embolization of brain AVMs with isobutyl-2 cyanoacrylate. AJNR 1988;9: 757–764.
101. Jafar JJ, Davis AJ, Berenstein A, et al. The effect of embolization with *N*-butyl cyanoacrylate prior to surgical resection of cerebral arteriovenous malformations. J Neurosurg 1993;78: 60–69.
102. Yamada S, Brauer FS, Knierim DS. Direct approach to arteriovenous malformations in functional areas of the cerebral hemisphere. J Neurosurg 1990;72:418–425.
103. Heros RC, Korosue K, Diebold PM. Surgical excision of cerebral arteriovenous malformations: late results. Neurosurgery 1990;26:570–577.
104. Luessenhop AJ, Spence WT. Artificial embolization of cerebral arteries: report of use in a case of arteriovenous malformation. JAMA 1960;172:1153–1155.
105. Halbach VV, Higashida RT, Yang P, et al. Preoperative balloon occlusion of arteriovenous malformations. Neurosurgery 1988;22:301–307.
106. Debrun G, Vinuela F, Fox A, et al. Embolization of cerebral arteriovenous malformations with bucrylate. J Neurosurg 1982;56:615–627.
107. Purdy PD, Samson D, Batjer HH, et al. Preoperative embolization of cerebral arteriovenous malformations with polyvinyl alcohol particles: experience in 51 adults. AJNR 1990;11: 501–510.
108. Purdy PD, Batjer HH, Risser RC, et al. Arteriovenous malformations of the brain: choosing embolic materials to enhance safety and ease of excision. J Neurosurg 1992;77:217–222.
109. Vinuela F, Dion JE, Duckwiler G, et al. Combined endovascular embolization and surgery in the management of cerebral arteriovenous malformations: experience with 101 cases. J Neurosurg 1991;75:856–864.
110. Higashida RT, Hieshima GB, Halbach VV. Advances in the treatment of complex cerebrovascular disorders by interventional neurovascular techniques. Circulation 1991;83(Suppl I):196–206.
111. Vinuela FV, Debrun GM, Fox AJ, et al. Dominant-

hemisphere arteriovenous malformations: therapeutic embolization with isobutyl-2-cyanoacrylate. AJNR 1983;4:959–966.
112. Spetzler RF, Martin NA, Carter LP, et al. Surgical management of large AVMs by staged embolization and operative excision. J Neurosurg 1987;67:17–28.
113. Lunsford LD, Flickinger J, Lindner G, et al. Stereotactic radiosurgery of the brain using the first United States 201 cobalt-60 source gamma knife. Neurosurgery 1989;24: 151–159.
114. Ogilvy CS. Radiation therapy for arteriovenous malformations: a review. Neurosurgery 1990;26:725–735.
115. Steinberg GK, Fabrikant JI, Marks MP, et al. Stereotactic heavy-charged-particle Bragg-Peak radiation for intracranial arteriovenous malformations. N Engl J Med 1990;323:96–101.
116. Dawson RC, Tarr RW, Hecht ST, et al. Treatment of arteriovenous malformations of the brain with combined embolization and stereotactic radiosurgery: results after 1 and 2 years. AJNR 1990;11:857–864.
117. Friedman WA, Bova FJ. Linear accelerator radiosurgery for arteriovenous malformations. J Neurosurg 1992;77:832–841.
118. Lunsford LD, Flickinger J, Coffey RJ. Stereotactic gamma knife radiosurgery. Arch Neurol 1990;47:169–175.
119. Steiner L, Lindquist C, Adler JR, et al. Clinical outcome of radiosurgery for cerebral arteriovenous malformations. J Neurosurg 1992;77:1–8.
120. Marks MP, Lane B, Steinberg GK, et al. Endovascular treatment of cerebral arteriovenous malformations following radiosurgery. AJNR 1993;14:297–303.
121. Wilson CB, Hieshima GB, Higashida RT, et al. Interventional radiologic adjuncts in cerebrovascular surgery. Clin Neurosurg 1989;37:332–352.
122. Wade JPH. Neurological deficit from an inoperable arteriovenous malformation: an indication for therapeutic embolization? Arch Neurol 1986;43:508–509.
123. Wolpert SM, Barnett FJ, Prager RJ. Benefits of embolization without surgery for cerebral arteriovenous malformations. AJNR 1981;2:535–538.
124. Vinuela F, Fox AJ, Pelz D, et al. Angiographic follow-up of large cerebral AVMs incompletely embolized with isobutyl-2-cyanoacrylate. AJNR 1986;7:919–925.
125. Fournier D, TerBrugge KG, Willinsky R, et al. Endovascular treatment of intracerebral arteriovenous malformations: experience in 49 cases. J Neurosurg 1991;75:228–233.
126. Halbach VV, Higashida RT, Hieshima GB, et al. Transarterial occlusion of solitary intracerebral arteriovenous fistulas. AJNR 1989;10:747–752.
127. Lownie SP, Duckwiler GR, Fox AJ, et al. Endovascular therapy of nongalenic cerebral arteriovenous fistulas. In: Vinuela F, ed. Interventional neuroradiology: endovascular therapy of the central nervous system. New York: Raven, 1992:87–106.
128. Yasargil MG. Anatomical locations of AVMs from the surgical viewpoint. In: Microneurosurgery. Stuttgart: Thieme, 1988; 38:3–11.
129. Garcia-Monaco R, Lasjaunias P, Berenstein A. Therapeutic management of vein of Galen aneurysmal malformations. In: Vinuela F, Halbach VV, Dion, JE, eds. Interventional neuroradiology: endovascular therapy of the central nervous system. New York: Raven, 1992:113–127.
130. Raybaud CA, Strother CM, Hald JK. Aneurysms of the vein of Galen: embryonic considerations and anatomical features relating to the pathogenesis of the malformation. Neuroradiology 1989;31:109–128.
131. Johnston IH, Whittle IR, Besser M, et al. Vein of Galen malformation: diagnosis and management. Neurosurgery 1987; 20:747–758.
132. Ciricillo SF, Edwards MSB, Schmidt KG, et al. Interventional neuroradiological management of vein of Galen malformations in the neonate. Neurosurgery 1990;27:22–28.
133. Lylyk P, Vinuela F, Dion JE, et al. Therapeutic alternatives

for vein of Galen vascular malformations. J Neurosurg 1993; 78:438–445.

134. Mickle JP, Quisling RG. The transtorcular embolization of vein of Galen aneurysms. J Neurosurg 1986;64:731–735.

135. Dowd CF, Halbach VV, Barnwell SL, et al. Transfemoral venous embolization of vein of Galen malformations. AJNR 1990;11:643–648.

136. Casasco A, Lylyk P, Hodes JE, et al. Percutaneous transvenous catheterization and embolization of vein of Galen aneurysms. Neurosurgery 1991;28:260–266.

137. Barnett GH, Little JR, Ebrahim ZY, et al. Cerebral circulation during arteriovenous malformation operation. Neurosurgery 1987;20:836–842.

138. Jungreis CA, Horton JA. Pressure changes in the arterial feeder to a cerebral AVM as a guide to monitoring therapeutic embolization. AJNR 1989;10:1057–1060.

139. Spetzler RF, Hargraves RW, McCormick PW, et al. Relationship of perfusion pressure and size to risk of hemorrhage from arteriovenous malformations. J Neurosurg 1992;76:918–923.

140. Batjer HH, Devous MD, Seibert GB, et al. Intracranial arteriovenous malformation: relationship between clinical factors and surgical complications. Neurosurgery 1989;24:75–79.

141. Duckwiler GR, Dion JE, Vinuela F, et al. Delayed venous occlusion following embolotherapy of vascular malformations in the brain. AJNR 1992;13:1571–1579.

142. Miyasaka Y, Yada K, Ohwada T, et al. Retrograde thrombosis of feeding arteries after removal of arteriovenous malformations. J Neurosurg 1990;72:540–545.

46

Neuroendovascular Therapy of Intracranial, Extraaxial Lesions

PETER KIM NELSON
AVI SETTON
ALEJANDRO BERENSTEIN

*I*n recent years, neuroradiology has witnessed the development of therapeutic endovascular procedures for the treatment of central nervous system (CNS) and maxillofacial lesions.[1-3] These developments have been facilitated by improvements in angiographic methods, microcatheter technology, and embolic agents, as well as by advancements in the understanding of the functional vascular anatomy of the head and neck.[4]

To be successful, the endovascular management of CNS and maxillofacial lesions must involve a multidisciplinary approach to the unique clinical needs of each patient. Neuroradiologists performing endovascular therapies should be skilled in the use of microcatheters and embolic agents. They must also have a thorough understanding of the pathologic entities and specific neurovascular anatomy involved in each case. Regardless of the technique employed, however, the ultimate degree of success in treatment is strongly dependent on appropriate patient selection and the precise definition of therapeutic goals.

Intracranial, extraaxial lesions amenable to endovascular therapy can be divided into two categories: (1) vascular disorders, including vasculopathies affecting dural vessels or the extradural internal carotid artery (ICA), as well as traumatic lesions resulting in vessel injury, and (2) neoplasms of the dura and calvarium. Therapeutic procedures directed toward lesions of the head and neck are best performed under general anesthesia, except when patient cooperation, as in carotid or vertebral occlusion or cranial nerve testing, is required.[2]

In most cases, it is possible to perform the angiographic workup and embolization in one session. This process is generally facilitated by preoperative planning based on information provided by CT and MRI studies (see Figs. 46-2 through 46-6). The diagnostic angiogram should follow a specific protocol and must delineate the arterial supply, including collateral circulation, arterioarterial anastomoses with critical vascular territories, and potential vascular supplies to cranial nerves and cutaneous tissues. The angioarchitecture and vascular compartmentalization (see Figs. 46-5 and 46-6) of the lesion should be defined, as well as the prevailing cortical or dural venous drainage and any alterations in the normal cerebrofacial venous system.

Although various preshaped catheters are used in diagnostic angiography, embolizations often require special guiding catheters that permit the coaxial introduction of microcatheters of various sizes during the superselective phase of angiography and embolization. For neurointerventional procedures requiring catheterization of distal branches arising from the external carotid artery, variable-stiffness microcatheters[5] employing a selection of specially designed guidewires are preferred because of their improved ability to negotiate tortuous distal vascular segments previously regarded as inaccessible even during slow-flow states. From a technical perspective, four principal factors determine the success of embolization: (1) the intrinsic complexity of a specific lesion, (2) the accessibility of its vascular supply, (3) the technical quality and selectivity of the superselective catheterization, and (4) the choice of embolic material.[6]

Functional Embolization

Selective catheterization of the distal vascular supply to a lesion presents obvious advantages because it improves the effectiveness of embolization while reducing complications due to nonselective embolization of normal tissues.[2] The level to which a catheter may be advanced, however, is theoretically limited by the inner diameter of the artery in question relative to the outer diameter of the microcatheter, ignoring additional problems related to vessel tortuosity that increase resistance to catheter motion and promote kinking. Furthermore, attempts at deploying microcatheters distally within branches of the external carotid artery are often frustrated by the development of vasospasm or vessel injury during the catheterization. The reduction of antegrade flow beyond the distal tip of the catheter during vasospasm impedes the flow-assisted deposition of particulate agents into the vascular bed of a more distally located lesion. In certain situations, flow arrest may be desirable in achieving reversal of flow through critical anastomoses or in establishing a stagnant conduit through which liquid embolic agents may be more effectively delivered to a distal target site.[7,8] However, with particulate agents such as Gelfoam powder or polyvinyl alcohol (PVA), free-flow embolization from a more proximal catheter position may be preferable, in that the emboli are better carried into the selected target by an unimpeded bloodstream. Unfortunately, embolizations from proximal catheter positions are often confounded by the wider distribution of emboli into a more extensive vascular territory that includes the lesion in question as well as normal tissues.

During embolization, normal tissues are placed at risk, depending on the specific anatomic disposition, (1) by virtue of their vascularization directly from a branch continuation of the parent artery supplying a given lesion, or (2) through anastomotic connections with vessels supplying the lesion (see Figs. 46-3H and I and 46-5H). Either of these conditions may necessitate some precautions to ensure safe embolization. The most obvious precaution requires advancement of the microcatheter selectively into distal vessels directly vascularizing the lesion. If this is not possible because multiple small feeding vessels are supplying a lesion or because the distal branches irrigating a lesion cannot be catheterized atraumatically, the parent artery may be temporarily occluded with an inflatable balloon distal to the origin of the target vessels. The lesion is then embolized with microparticles from a proximal position. Parent vessel occlusion is designed to protect the normal tissues distal to the occluded segment while preserving free-flow embolization into the lesion. This assumes adequate collateral supply to the protected vascular territory. In the extreme example, the protected vascular territory may be the brain, as in cavernous sinus or clival lesions supplied by C4 or C5 branches (Fischer classification)[9] of the internal carotid artery. These lesions may be embolized with microparticles after temporary balloon occlusion of the distal supracavernous segment, assuming adequate collateral circulation at the level of the circle of Willis. Moreover,

in this specific instance, to avoid embolization of microparticles into the cerebral vasculature, multiple aspirations and exchange rinsing of the occluded carotid segment with heparinized saline should be done before balloon deflation.[10] Alternatively, in cases where tumor involvement of the petrous or cavernous internal carotid artery has been suggested by axial imaging studies, temporary occlusion of the internal carotid artery may be converted to permanent occlusion, if collateral supply to the brain is adequate.

Under conditions where anastomoses have been shown between the supply to a lesion and a critical vascular territory, it may be possible to occlude the anastomotic channel with a coil or strip of Gelfoam before embolizing the primary arterial feeder. When the anastomotic connection is too small to be catheterized, embolization of the lesion may be attempted using flow reversal across the anastomosis.[2] The desired reversal of flow occurs when the arterial pressure differential across the anastomosis results in the flow of blood from the region of concern (e.g., the orbit) into the channel supplying the target lesion, thereby protecting the normal tissues. Reversal of flow may be facilitated by inducing a state of flow arrest within the main feeding pedicle proximal to the anastomosis, either by wedging the microcatheter or, in selected cases, by using a proximal occlusion balloon. Under ideal conditions, flow reversal may permit initial embolization with small microparticles or liquid adhesives. However, microparticulate embolization usually requires a change to a particulate size larger than the anastomotic channels during the later stages of the procedure as reflux becomes more likely. To reduce the risk of the procedure, the larger particulate sizes are preferred in embolizations of meningeal vessels suspected of supplying cranial nerves and other critical anastomoses. The larger particles should also be used in embolizations involving supplying arteries arising from scalp vessels to avoid necrosis in the territories fed by the cutaneous branches.

Another adaptation of functional embolization may be employed in cases where anastomoses between divisions of the external carotid artery (ECA) and internal carotid artery (ICA) are in hemodynamic balance in the supply to a dural lesion. This condition exists in lesions dually supplied by the inferolateral trunk (ILT) of the cavernous internal carotid artery as well as by dural branches arising from the accessory meningeal artery, middle meningeal artery, and artery of the foramen rotundum (see Fig. 46-3A and C). Temporary balloon occlusion of the cavernous ICA across the origin of the ILT may permit embolization of the lesion from one of the above-mentioned ECA branches, thereby exploiting the anatomic anastomoses between these meningeal vessels and the temporarily occluded ILT.

Alternatively, in situations where flow arrest within a supplying ECA branch is achieved by way of a wedged microcatheter, a lesion supplied by meningeal arteries anastomosing with dural branches of the ICA may be embolized using the inflow from the ICA to carry particles introduced by way of the ECA axis into the target vascular territory (see Fig. 46-5). Under these conditions, however, extreme caution must be exercised in avoiding reflux of emboli into the ICA.

Embolic Agents

The choice of embolic agent depends on the goal of the procedure, the selectivity accomplished during catheterization, the vascular anatomy, and the pathologic entity.[2,3,11] The following are commonly used embolic materials for embolization of extraaxial lesions.

Polyvinyl Alcohol (PVA) Foam. PVA is a nonabsorbable, biocompatible sponge material. Particulate forms useful in the embolization of extraaxial lesions vary in size from 150 to 500 μm in diameter and are easily injected through an appropriately sized microcatheter. As a general rule, microparticles are preferred to fluid materials for the preoperative embolization of extraaxial tumors. They are easier and safer to use and, when employed in dilute suspensions, can reach the intratumoral vasculature, where they obstruct small arteries.

Gelfoam. Gelfoam represents an alternative to microparticulate PVA embolization. It is available in powder form with particles ranging in size from 40 to 60 μm in diameter. Because of their smaller size, Gelfoam microparticles are carried more distally into the microvasculature, promoting more complete embolic occlusion of a vascular bed. However, the smaller size increases the possibility of inadvertent embolization through dangerous anastomoses or the development of cranial nerve palsy when embolization is performed too proximally. For this reason, the larger PVA particulate sizes are preferred in embolizations of meningeal vessels that are also supplying cranial nerves or coupled with cutaneous arteries.[2,12]

Large strips of Gelfoam sponge can be used for proximal occlusion of feeding vessels in a manner analogous to the deposition of metallic coils. Although this approach is not advocated for the primary embolization of arterial pedicles involved in the supply to dural-based lesions, such strips may be used advantageously to protect vascular territories in which the deposition of microparticles is undesirable. They may also be used to effect an endovascular ligation of an artery after

traumatic vascular injury or to control a major arterial pedicle after microparticulate embolization of a more distally placed lesion.

N-Butyl-Cyanoacrylic Acid (NBCA). NBCA[13] is a low-viscosity liquid that polymerizes rapidly after coming in contact with the electrolytic environment of the blood. The polymerization time may be delayed by diluting the NBCA in oil-based iodinated contrast materials such as Lipiodol so that a target distal to the site of injection can be reached before final solidification. In addition, tantalum powder may be added for increased viscosity, depending on the lesion in question and the rate of blood flow through the embolized pedicle. Although of considerable use in the embolizations of dural arteriovenous malformations, NBCA generally is less preferable to microparticles for the embolization of extraaxial tumors. Its use should be carefully controlled to avoid inadvertent embolization through dangerous anastomoses or penetration into normal vascular territories, where it may cause ischemia or necrosis of vital tissues. Skill with the use of such agents is also important to avoid gluing the catheter tip within the arterial lumen.

Ethanol. The potent sclerosing effect and relatively benign metabolism of ethanol make it an effective embolic material. As with other liquid agents, however, if it is inadvertently introduced into a normal vascular territory, serious complications related to the necrosis of normal tissues may result.[2]

Coils. Metallic coils are supplied in a variety of lengths and configurations and may contain materials such as cotton or Dacron to promote thrombosis. They are easily introduced through size-matched microcatheters with the assistance of a guidewire/coil pusher and, as with Gelfoam strips, may be used to protect normal vascular territories, as well as to provide endovascular ligation of traumatized vessels or pedicles previously embolized with microparticles.

Anatomic Considerations

Extraaxial lesions may be subdivided into distinct locations by virtue of their characteristic vascular supply: the calvareal convexity, the falx cerebri, the floor of the anterior cranial fossa, the sphenoid wings, the cavernous sinus and parasellar regions, the tentorium cerebelli and adjacent dural sinuses, or the posterior fossa, including the cerebellar convexity, the cerebellar pontine angle, and the foramen magnum.[11]

Lesions of the Convexity

Extraaxial lesions of the convexity and parasagittal surfaces of the skull vault predictably derive their vascular

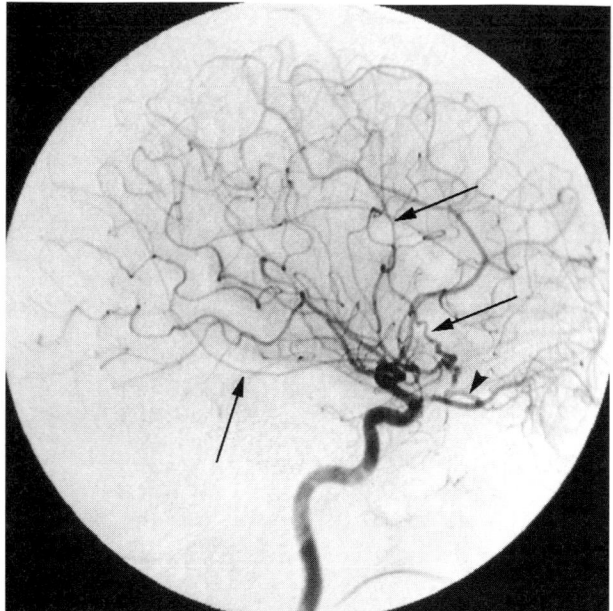

A

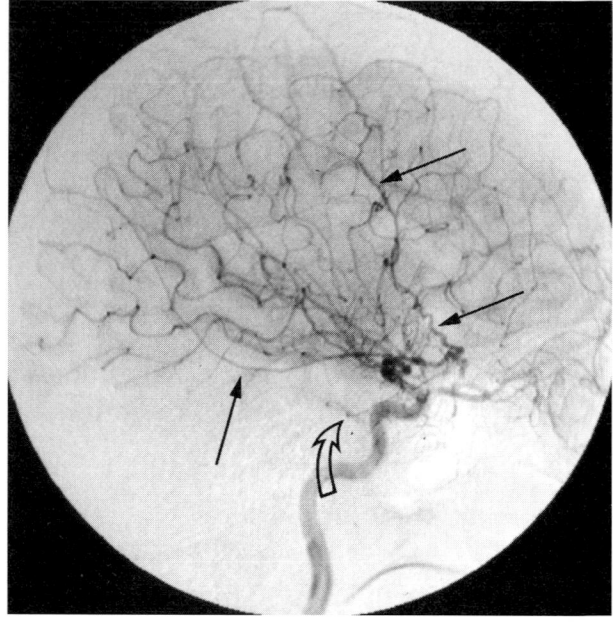

B

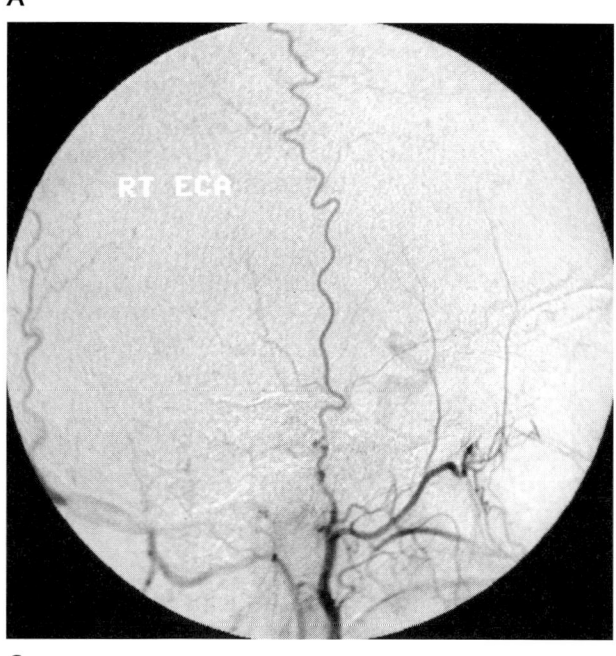

C

Figure 46-1. Anatomic variation in the dural blood supply. Lateral digital subtraction angiographic (DSA) images from a right internal carotid angiogram, middle (A) and late (B) arterial phase. The right middle meningeal artery (*arrows*) originates from the intraorbital right ophthalmic artery by way of a recurrent meningeal segment (*arrowhead,* A). The petrous territory of the right middle meningeal artery is supplied directly by way of the posterior branch of the inferolateral trunk (*open curved arrow,* B) arising from the cavernous segment of the right internal carotid artery. (C) An accompanying right external carotid angiogram confirms the absence of a middle meningeal segment proximal to the foramen spinosum.

supply from branches of the middle meningeal or anterior ethmoidal arteries. The middle meningeal artery (MMA) most frequently originates from the ipsilateral internal maxillary artery (IMA) and enters the skull base through the foramen spinosum. It subsequently gives rise to several important branches vascularizing the dura of the skull base and middle cranial fossa before reaching the convexity. Although variable in their predominance, several branches are commonly recognized as supplying the cranial convexity. Anterior and posterior frontal branches may supply the frontal and anterior parietal regions of the convexity, originating most commonly from the continuation of the MMA through the foramen spinosum or, more infrequently, from the ophthalmic or the intraorbital lacrimal artery by way of a recurrent course through the superior orbital fissure (Fig. 46-1). A parietooccipital trunk may be identified as supplying the meninges of the posterior parietal and occipital regions of the supratentorial convexity. A petrosquamosal trunk is usually seen coursing within a groove defined by the petrous and squamous portions of the temporal bone. In addition to supplying the meninges throughout this region, this trunk gives tentorial branches to the basal edge of the tentorium cerebelli and may be used instead of the petrosal branch of the MMA to more safely embolize lesions involving the petrous ridge and petroclinoid region, thereby decreasing the likelihood of iatrogenic seventh cranial nerve palsy.

Two considerations must be addressed in the angiographic workup and embolization of lesions involving the parasagittal region. First, in addition to the ipsilateral meningeal vascular supply, potential contribution from the corresponding contralateral middle meningeal branches must be evaluated. The participation of contralateral supply occurs as a result of anastomoses along the extent of the superior sagittal sinus. The frontal parasagittal region may also include supply from the artery of the falx cerebri, which arises from the anterior ethmoidal arteries. Proper pre- and postembolization angiographic evaluation of these lesions includes thorough assessment of the possible ipsilateral as well as contralateral middle meningeal supplies. A second consideration of importance concerns convexity and parasagittal lesions arising anteriorly along the frontal convexity. This area may derive vascular supply from meningeal branches of the anterior ethmoidal arteries and requires angiographic evaluation of potential contribution from the ophthalmic arteries.

The dural structures of the middle cranial fossa receive arterial branches from sphenoidal and middle cranial fossa divisions of the MMA. Embolization in this territory should avoid potential intervascular communications between these branches of the MMA and (1) the cavernous internal carotid artery by way of anastomoses between the recurrent tentorial artery and the inferolateral or meningohypophyseal trunks, and (2) the orbit by way of meningolacrimal or meningoophthalmic anastomoses.

Lesions Involving the Falx Cerebri

Lesions arising from the falx cerebri are supplied by distal branches of the MMA that reach the midline and participate in the vascularization of the superior sagittal sinus and the falx cerebri. These vessels anastomose among themselves and potentially with their corresponding contralateral arteries as well as with transosseous branches arising from the superficial temporal artery. Lesions affecting the falx cerebri anteriorly may also be expected to receive supply from the artery of the falx cerebri, which, as previously mentioned, may arise from anterior ethmoidal branches of the ophthalmic artery. As with lesions of the convexity, in those cases where transosseous supply from scalp vessels can be demonstrated, embolization must take into consideration maintenance of continued viable vascularization of the affected scalp. Infrequently, falceal lesions may receive direct supply from the meningeal branches of the callosomarginal, pericallosal, and posterior cerebral arteries.

Lesions of the Anterior Cranial Base

Lesions involving the floor of the anterior cranial fossa can be subdivided into lateral and medial groups. Those involving the supraorbital regions are generally vascularized by anterior frontal branches of the MMA and meningeal branches of the ophthalmic artery. Conversely, midline lesions most typically are supplied by meningeal branches of the anterior and posterior ethmoidal arteries that participate in a rich anastomotic network to supply the floor of the anterior cranial fossa throughout the midline. In addition to the expected anastomoses with corresponding contralateral ethmoidal arteries, the posterior ethmoidal arteries anastomose with meningeal branches of the internal carotid artery as well as with medially directed branches arising from the sphenoidal and frontal divisions of the MMA. Complete angiographic study of these lesions requires thorough selective angiographic evaluation of the internal carotid artery, the sphenopalatine artery, and the MMA. The study should specifically address potential anastomoses among dural vessels originating from the horizontal segment of the carotid-cavernous artery, the ophthalmic artery, and distal branches of the sphenopalatine and middle meningeal arteries. Additionally, because these lesions occur near the midline, attention must be paid to the possibility of bilateral vascular supply when performing and evaluating embolization.

For both classes of lesions, attention must be directed during embolization to the anastomosis with the ophthalmic artery, which directly supplies the anterior and posterior ethmoidal arteries and may communicate with the sphenoidal division of the MMA via a recurrent meningeal branch arising from the second portion (lateral division) of the intraorbital ophthalmic artery.

Greater Sphenoid Wing Lesions

The vascular supply to lesions involving the greater wing of the sphenoid is often provided by sphenoidal branches of the MMA, either directly or by way of a recurrent meningeal vessel arising from the ophthalmic artery. Before embolization, attention must be directed toward the possibility of a dominant meningoophthalmic supply to the orbit, or a less readily identifiable anastomosis between the middle meningeal and ophthalmic arteries occurring either across the superior orbital fissure or via the Hyrtl canal. In subtle cases, the demonstration of these anastomoses often requires superselective angiography and may not be fully disclosed by less selective angiography of the external or internal carotid arteries.

Lesions Involving the Cavernous Sinus and Parasellar Region

The vascular supply to the parasellar region, including the posterior clinoid, cavernous sinus, and petroclinoid ligament, is often complex because of extensive regional anastomoses between meningeal branches of the internal carotid, middle meningeal, and accessory meningeal arteries, and also because of contribution from the distal internal maxillary artery via the artery of the foramen rotundum. As mentioned previously, the ophthalmic artery may participate indirectly via a tentorial branch of the recurrent meningeal artery. From the perspective of angiographic workup and embolization, these lesions may be divided conceptually into two groups: (1) an anterolateral group, arising from the orbital apex and lateral cavernous sinus, and (2) a posterior group, including the posterior cavernous sinus, petroclinoid ligament, and dorsum sellae.

The meningeal supply to anterior division lesions may be considered to reflect the hemodynamic balance between branches arising from the horizontal (C4) segment (Fischer classification)[9] of the cavernous internal carotid artery, most notably the inferolateral trunk (ILT) and meningeal branches of the internal maxillary artery. This latter group includes cavernous and recurrent tentorial branches of the MMA, cavernous meningeal branches of the accessory meningeal artery, and the artery of the foramen rotundum (see Fig. 46-3C). As expected, embolization of these meningeal arteries should be preceded by superselective angiographic analysis to prevent inadvertent embolization into the internal carotid artery or possible damage to the orbit or regional cranial nerves.

The supply to posterior division lesions is derived primarily from medial and lateral clival branches arising from the C5 segment of the internal carotid artery and their potential anastomotic connections with branches of the ascending pharyngeal and middle meningeal arteries (see Fig. 46-5). These most notably include the ascending clival and inferior petrosal arcades, derived from the hypoglossal and jugular divisions of the ascending pharyngeal artery, respectively; the posterior cavernous branches of the MMA; and the basal tentorial arcade supplied by the petrosal and the petrosquamosal branches of the MMA.

Three critical points should be considered before embolization of lesions involving this territory. (1) The vascular supply to the intrapetrous facial nerve should be determined. This may come primarily from the petrous branch of the MMA. For this reason, petroclinoid lesions supplied by the basal tentorial arcade should be embolized preferentially from the petrosquamosal branch of the MMA, thereby avoiding the proximal petrosal artery. (2) Potential contribu-

tions from the contralateral internal carotid and ascending pharyngeal arteries via transclival anastomoses should be evaluated, particularly in lesions involving the dorsum sellae. (3) Because embolization of upper clival and petroclinoid lesions may involve the hypoglossal or jugular division of the ascending pharyngeal artery, attention must be directed to the possibility of iatrogenic lower cranial neuropathy when using NBCA, ethanol, or Gelfoam microparticles. Midline lesions requiring aggressive embolization of supplies from both ascending pharyngeal arteries should be performed as a staged procedure on different days, specifically to avoid development of bilateral hypoglossal nerve deficits.

Lesions of the Tentorium Cerebelli

Lesions involving the tentorium cerebelli are characteristically supplied by the marginal tentorial and basal tentorial arteries, depending on location. The basal insertion of the tentorium cerebelli is supplied by a vascular arcade paralleling the superior petrosal sinus. It receives supply from the basal tentorial branches of the petrosal and petrosquamosal divisions of the MMA, as well as potentially from the lateral clival branch of the ICA. Infratentorial supply may also be derived from the transmastoid branch of the occipital artery, as well as from meningeal contributions from the ascending pharyngeal, vertebral, or posterior inferior cerebellar arteries.

Extraaxial lesions arising from the free margin of the tentorium cerebelli typically receive supply from the marginal tentorial branch of the meningohypophyseal trunk (Fischer C5 branch of the ICA).[9] Additional sources may include the inferolateral trunk via its superior division, and a recurrent tentorial arcade variably supplied by branches of the middle meningeal and accessory meningeal arteries, as well as recurrent meningeal collaterals arising from the ophthalmic artery. Anatomically, this arcade follows the lesser wing of the sphenoid, curving posteriorly along the free margin of the tentorium. Because vessels supplying this arcade also participate in the vascular supply of cranial nerves III to VI, attention must be directed to the potential for cranial nerve deficits during embolization. Provocative testing with lidocaine may be of some benefit before devascularization of these lesions.[14]

Lesions of the Posterior Fossa

Extraaxial lesions occurring in the posterior fossa may be grossly classified as convexity, cerebellar pontine angle, and foramen magnum or lower clival lesions. Depending on location, the sources of vascular supply usually originate from meningeal branches of the ascending pharyngeal, occipital, and vertebral arteries as well as from posterior fossa branches of the MMA. For lesions of the cerebellar pontine angle, the middle meningeal supply is primarily derived from branches contributing to the basal tentorial arcade. Lesions arising from the cerebellar pontine angle, depending on the specific hemodynamic balance, may also be expected to derive vascular supply from meningeal vessels arising from the transmastoid branch of the occipital artery, the subarcuate branch of the anterior inferior cerebellar artery, and the jugular division of the ascending pharyngeal artery. Lesions arising over the cerebellar convexities more characteristically are supplied by dural branches of the transmastoid artery, which participates in anastomotic balance with posterior meningeal branches of the vertebral artery. Lesions occurring more closely to the transverse sinus, or midline, may also receive supply from the artery of the falx cerebelli (variably arising from the occipital artery, the vertebral artery, or the posterior inferior cerebellar artery [PICA]); there may also be a transosseous contribution from the occipital arteries at the level of the torcular herophili. In all cases, connection with the vertebral arteries via meningeal anastomoses must be considered before embolization to avert possible vertebrobasilar crisis.

Lesions involving the foramen magnum are typically vascularized from the hypoglossal division of the ascending pharyngeal artery (APA) and meningeal branches of the vertebral arteries. Embolizations involving this territory must consider the potential supply to cranial nerve XII derived from the hypoglossal division of the APA, in addition to the anastomoses of this vessel, over the odontoid arch arcade, with the vertebral artery at the C3 neuroforamen. Moreover, anastomoses between branches of the occipital artery and the ipsilateral vertebral artery exist throughout the upper cervical spaces (see Fig. 46-5H), permitting accidental vertebrobasilar embolization during procedures involving the occipital artery.

Pathologic Lesions

Dural Arteriovenous Malformations

Approximately 10 to 15 percent of all clinically apparent intracranial arteriovenous malformations (AVMs) are of the dural type.[15] These lesions are characterized by discrete fistulas involving the intracranial venous sinuses or dural veins and are typically classified by location of the involved sinus or shunt[2,4] as well as by the pattern of venous drainage.[16] Although the precise etiology of dural arteriovenous fistulas (DAVFs) is unknown, there is evidence that fistula formation is preceded in some instances by trauma resulting in skull fracture or by an episode of thrombosis involving the adjacent dural sinus.[17,18] It has been postulated that during recanalization a pathologic fistula develops, possibly from degenerative changes involving a normal physiologic arteriovenous shunt or from the triggering of a latent congenital dural AV shunt that ultimately progresses to a clinically and angiographically apparent syndrome.[19,20] The disease, with the exception of those shunts localizing to the posterior fossa, is more prevalent in women and is usually diagnosed in patients between the ages of 30 and 80 years.[21]

The clinical features associated with DAVFs generally depend on the location of the lesion, the extent of the AV shunting, and associated abnormalities of venous drainage (Figs. 46-2 and 46-3).[4,22] Symptoms may be indistinguishable from those associated with pial brain arteriovenous malformations and may include headache, diplopia, blurred vision, or neurologic dysfunction.[23] Focal neurologic deficits and seizures may develop in relation to disturbances in regional cortical venous drainage resulting from the redirection of venous flow from the shunt into pial veins, the congested venous territory of which may be remote from the site of the shunt (see Fig. 46-2B and C).[24] In patients with severe compromise of the deep venous drainage of the brain or with diffuse intracranial hypertension resulting from the obstruction of both sigmoid sinuses, the clinical presentation may include dementia.[2] Closure of the arteriovenous shunts may successfully reverse this state only when there are adequate venous channels available for the normal venous drainage of the brain. Focal symptomatology may worsen or change as a result of the redirection of venous outflow from a DAVF.[22,24] For example, progressive thrombosis and occlusion of the inferior and superior petrosal sinuses may be associated with worsening of signs in a patient with a cavernous sinus DAVF drainage anteriorly through the ipsilateral opthalmic veins. If contralateral drainage is available, the venous sinus hypertension may be transmitted to the contralateral cavernous sinus, leading to development of bilateral orbital symptomatology.

The signs and symptoms of increased intracranial pressure occasionally complicate cases of DAVFs.[25] In certain cases this can be attributed to diminished CSF absorption through the arachnoid villi resulting from the transmission of increased venous pressure throughout the superior sagittal sinus.[23] Alternatively, obstruction of the cerebral aqueduct secondary to compression of the mesencephalon by an ectatic draining vein may occur, leading to obstructive hydrocephalus.

Text continues on page 800

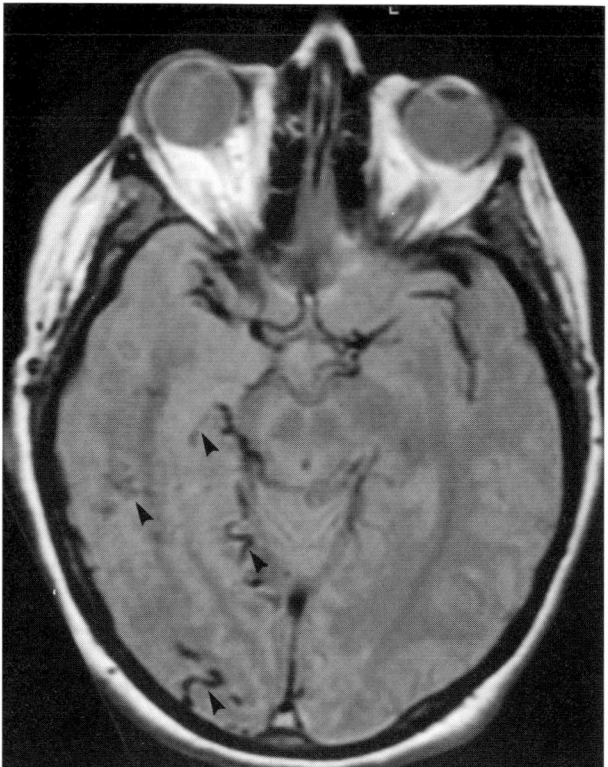

A

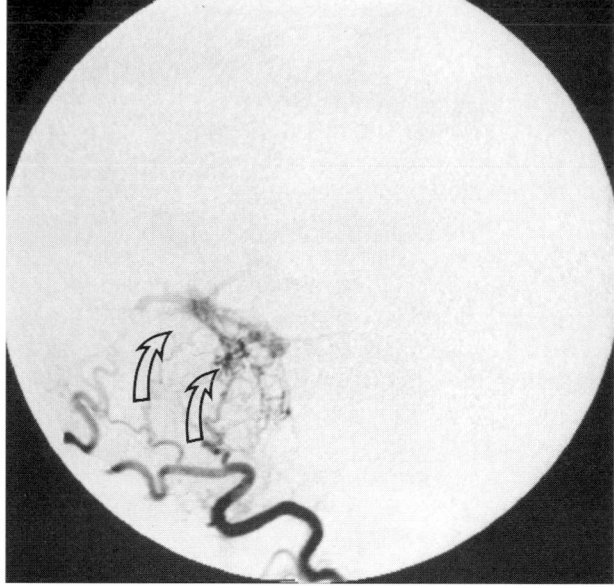

B

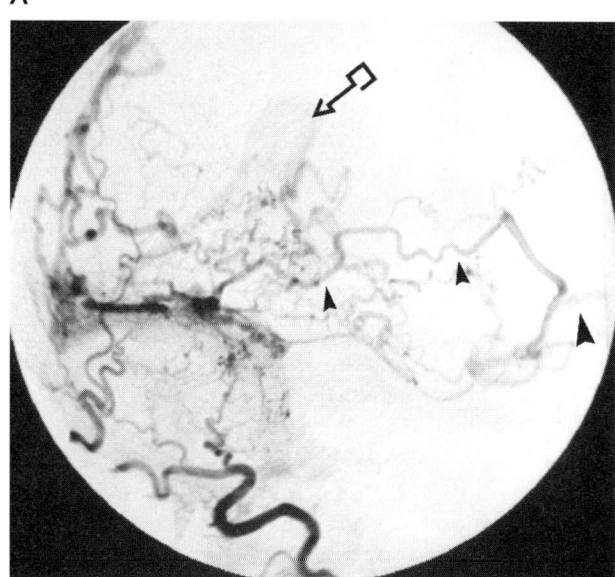

C

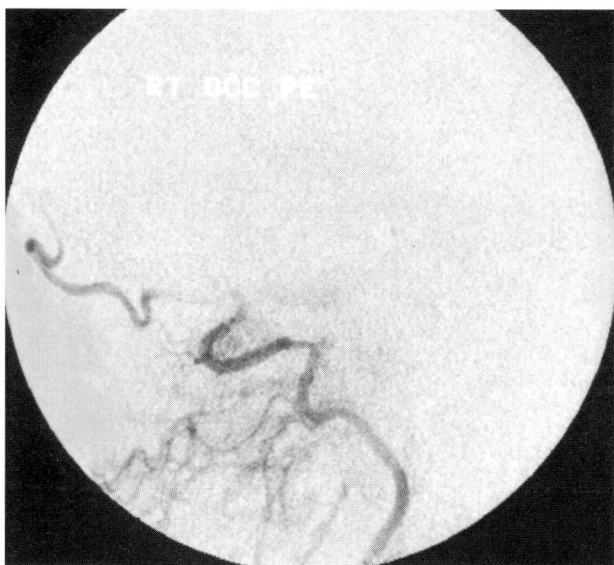

D

Figure 46-2. Transverse sinus dural arteriovenous malformation (AVM) with pial venous drainage. (A) Transaxial proton density spin-echo magnetic resonance image through the level of the temporal lobes demonstrates multiple serpiginous signal voids (*arrowheads*), representing engorged veins, throughout the right temporal-occipital lobe and along the margin of the tentorium. The subsequent angiographic investigation reveals a dural AVM involving the right transverse sinus that is supplied by the right occipital artery (B and C), the right ascending pharyngeal artery (E and F), the right middle meningeal artery (G), and the meningohypophyseal trunk of the right internal carotid artery (H). Early (B) and late (C) arterial phase lateral DSA images from a right occipital angiogram demonstrate the transosseous supply (*open curved arrows,* B) to the dural AVM. The transmastoid as well as at least two additional emissary arteries are

demonstrated to supply the malformation. The late arterial phase image (C) reveals the extensive venous congestion of the deep and superficial veins draining the right temporal and occipital lobes. The patient's symptoms of proptosis and scleral injection correlated with the anteriorly directed venous drainage through the right vein of Labbé (*small arrowheads,* C) and the superficial sylvian system toward the right cavernous sinus, and ultimately into the right ophthalmic veins (*large arrowhead,* C). The late arterial phase image also reveals opacification of the vein of Galen, confirming drainage into the deep venous system (*open straight arrow,* C). The right sigmoid sinus is occluded. (D) Mid-arterial-phase lateral angiogram of the right occipital artery after selective embolization with a combination of NBCA and PVA, which abolished supply to the shunt from this axis. Early (E) and late (F) arterial phase lateral DSA images from a right ascending pharyngeal angiogram. The shunt (*asterisk,* E) is supplied primarily by meningeal collaterals arising from the jugular division (*solid curved arrow*) of the neuromeningeal trunk and a posterior meningeal branch (*solid acutely curved arrow*), in this case arising from the ascending pharyngeal artery. Note the cortical venous drainage (*small arrowheads,* F) reproducing the pattern demonstrated previously in the

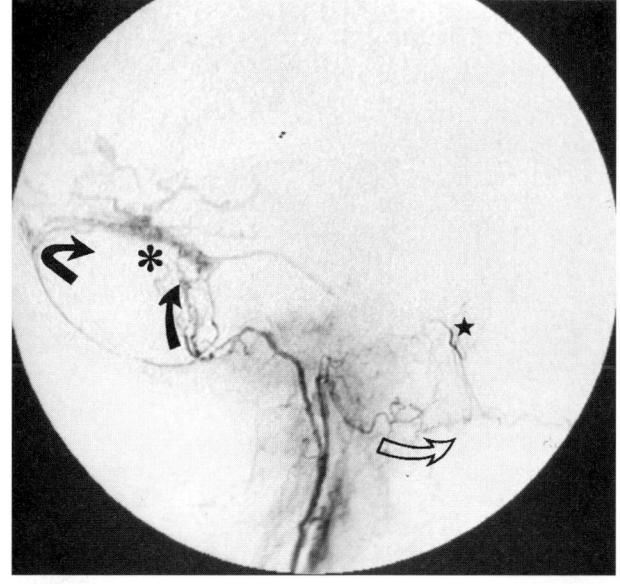

E

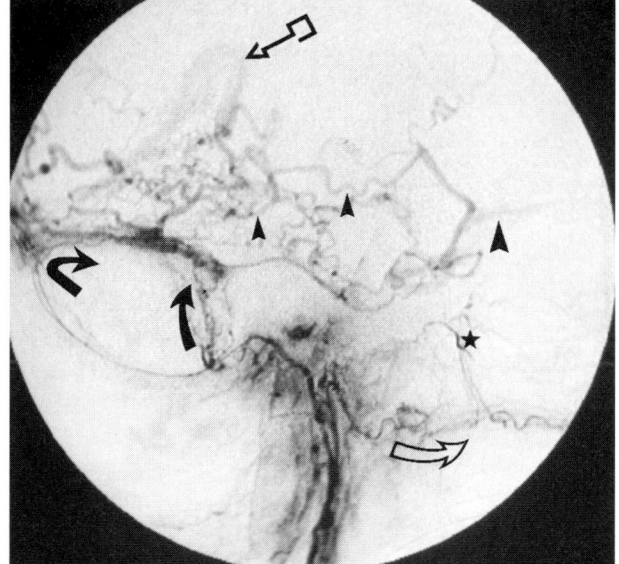

F

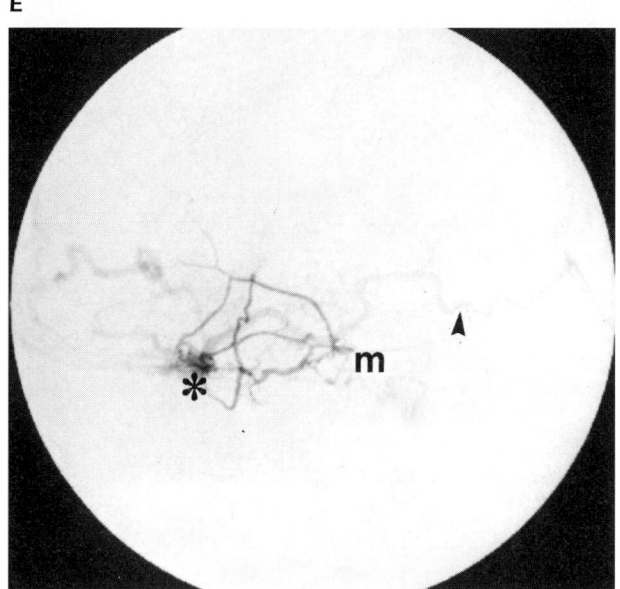

G

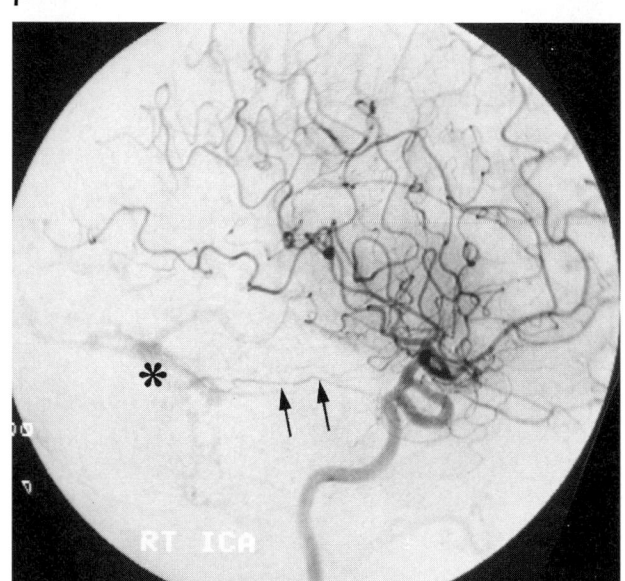

H

right occipital angiogram. Again, note the anterior drainage toward the ophthalmic veins (*large arrowhead,* F) and vein of Galen (*open straight arrow,* F). Incidentally seen is retrograde opacification of the descending palatine artery (*star*) by way of anastomotic connection with the middle pharyngeal branch of the ascending pharyngeal artery through the soft palate (*open curved arrow*). (G) Mid-arterial-phase lateral DSA image from a superselective angiogram within the right middle meningeal artery. The superselective angiogram is performed through a microcatheter (*m*) located within the petrosquamosal branch of the right middle meningeal artery and discloses the contribution of these vessels to the shunt (*asterisk*). Note the superficial cortical venous drainage over the surface of the right temporal lobe (*arrowhead*), as seen on the previous right occipital and ascending pharyngeal angiograms. (H) Late arterial phase lateral DSA image from a right internal carotid angiogram documents the contribution of the meningohypophyseal trunk (*straight arrows*) to the transverse sinus dural AVM (*asterisk*). (I) A lateral plain film of the skull demonstrates the radiopaque NBCA cast.

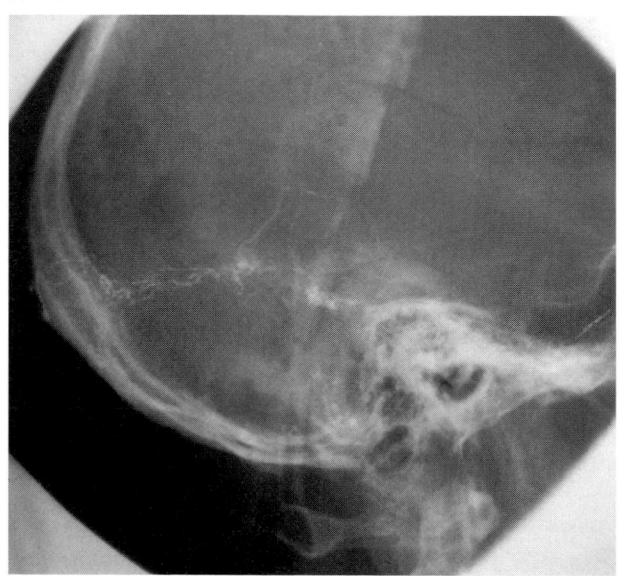

I

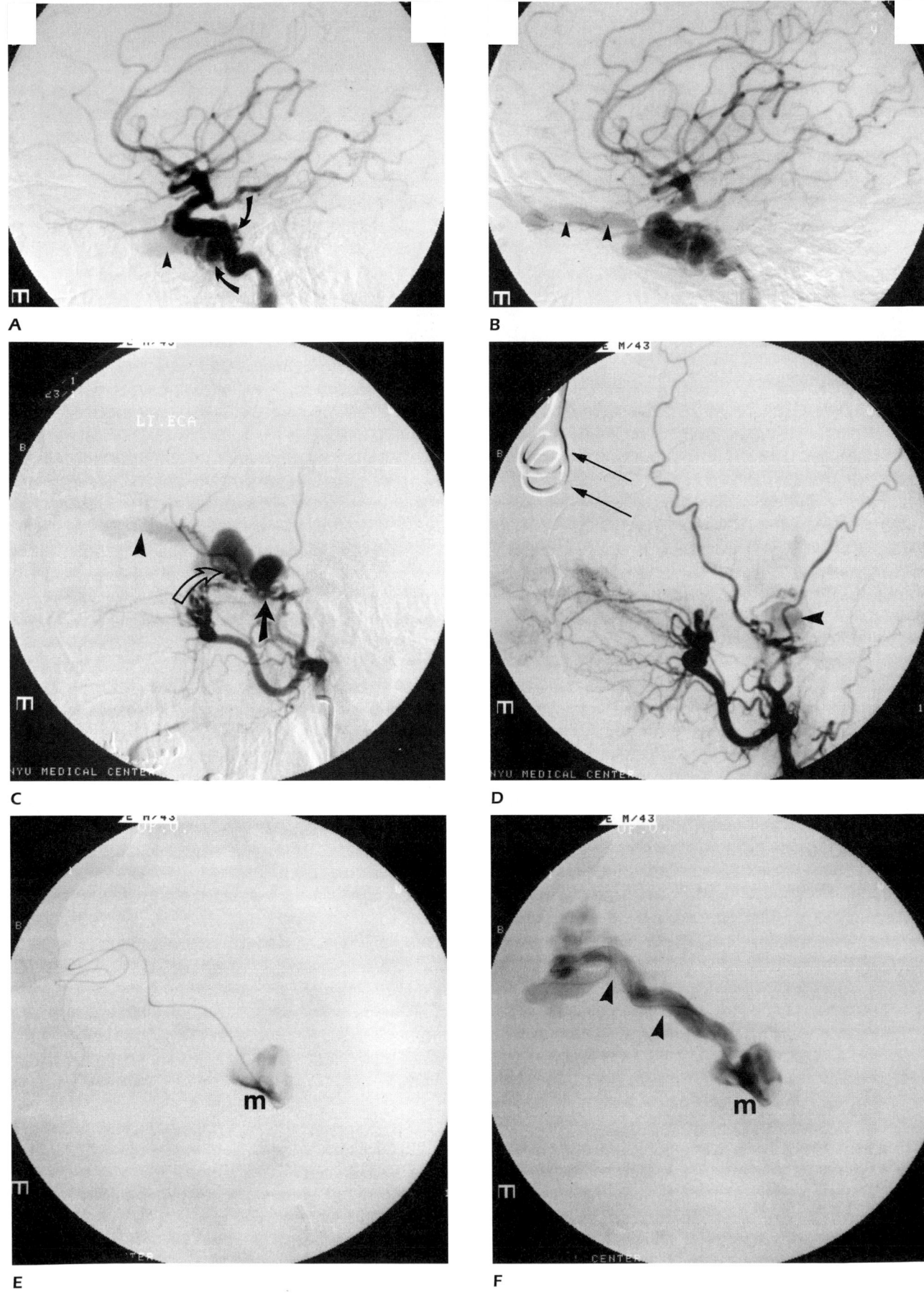

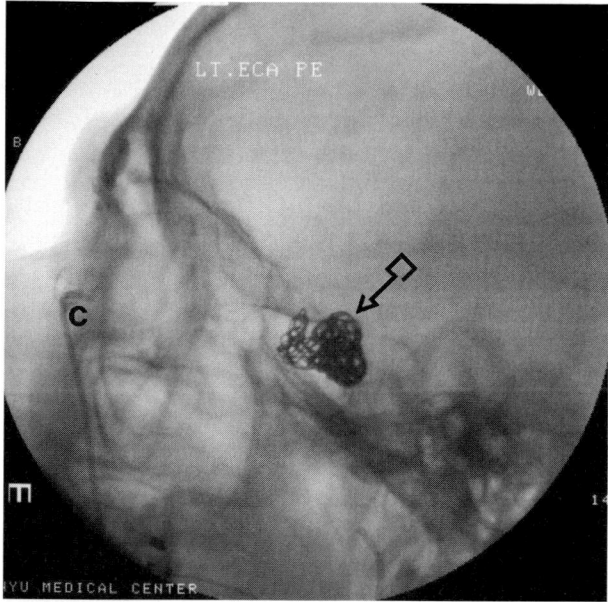

G

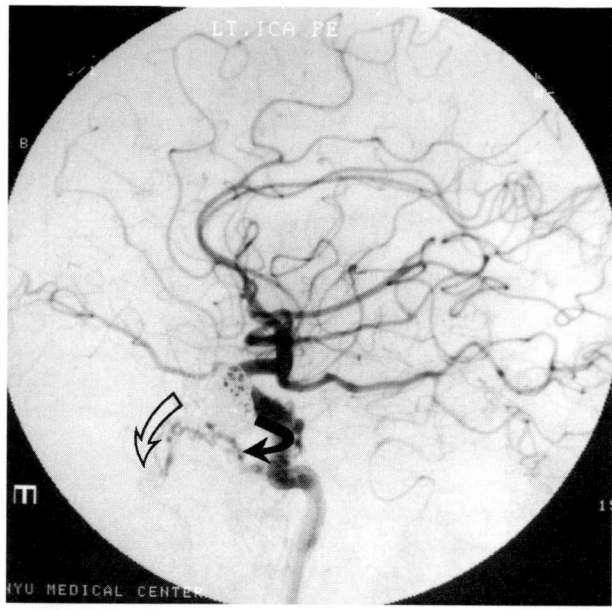

H

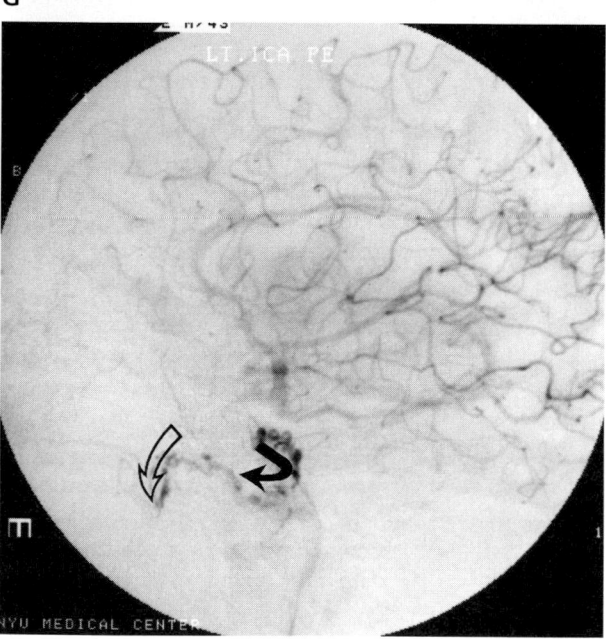

I

J

Figure 46-3. Dural AVM involving the left cavernous sinus. Early (A) and late (B) arterial phase lateral DSA images from a left internal carotid angiogram. The dural AVM receives supply from the left carotid-cavernous segment primarily by way of an enlarged inferolateral trunk (*solid curved arrows,* A). Note that the entire venous drainage of the AVM is conducted anteriorly through the left cavernous sinus into an enlarged superior ophthalmic vein (*arrowheads*). (C) Early arterial phase lateral DSA image from a left external carotid angiogram discloses the external carotid contribution to the shunt by way of the artery of the foramen rotundum (*open curved arrow*) and cavernous branches of the left middle meningeal artery (*solid straight arrow*). Again visible is the exclusive drainage of the cavernous sinus malformation into the left superior ophthalmic vein (*arrowheads*). (D) Mid-arterial-phase lateral DSA image from a left external carotid angiogram after a compressive maneuver to obstruct the left superior ophthalmic vein at the orbital margin. The external

compression is employed to assess the potential for diversion of the shunt drainage into cortical veins once the ophthalmic outlet is occluded. The compressive device is evident as a metallic subtraction artifact (*straight arrows*) and, when applied, results in the marked reduction of AV shunting, confirming the feasibility of a venous approach. The minimal persistent shunting suggested by the slight opacification of the cavernous sinus in this angiogram (*arrowhead*) results from incomplete occlusion of the left superior ophthalmic outlet and was noted not to drain by an alternate route. (E and F) Serial digital subtraction venogram performed through a microcatheter (*m*) positioned within the left cavernous sinus. The microcatheter has been introduced into the left cavernous sinus by way of retrograde catheterization through the left superior ophthalmic vein (*arrowheads*) after advancement of a guiding catheter into the distal left facial vein. (G) Lateral unsubtracted image documenting the deposition of metallic coils within the left cavernous sinus (*open*

Legend continues on page 800

Moreover, aneurysmal venous ectasia may unusually cause symptomatic mechanical compression of adjacent neurologic structures, most commonly in dural AVMs draining into pial veins of the posterior fossa.[26]

Approximately 20 to 33 percent of patients with symptomatic DAVFs present with an intracranial hemorrhage.[4,27,28] This most frequently is encountered in lesions involving the floor of the anterior cranial fossa or the tentorium cerebelli; however, it may occur in any case associated with cortical venous drainage. More rarely, cranial neuropathy or unilateral visual phenomena may arise secondary to arterial steal without evidence of associated venous hypertension.[4,22]

As alluded to previously, DAVFs commonly involve specific sites related to the intracranial venous sinuses and dural veins. From a clinicoanatomic perspective, fistulas may be classified as those involving the cavernous sinus (see Fig. 46-3), transverse (see Fig. 46-2) and sigmoid sinuses, superior sagittal sinus, petrosal sinus, torcular, tentorial incisura, and anterior cranial base.

Approximately one-third of symptomatic intracranial DAVFs involve the transverse and sigmoid sinuses.[29] The patients often present with a subjective bruit as the first clinical manifestation. The tinnitus is synchronized to arterial pulsations and results from turbulence associated with the shunting of blood into the sigmoid or transverse sinuses. Auscultation over the retroauricular area usually reveals the pulsatile bruit. As with the other DAVFs, additional neurologic symptoms and findings generally depend on the pattern of venous drainage encountered in the individual patient. Symptoms may include chronic signs of increased intracranial pressure potentially leading to papilledema[30] and optic atrophy in addition to disturbances related to balance and hearing. In progressive cases, associated with obstruction of the ipsilateral jugular outflow (see Fig. 46-2), redirected venous drainage into pial veins of the posterior fossa may result in brain stem or cerebellar dysfunction as well as posterior fossa hemorrhage. Rerouting of drainage into the supratentorial cortical venous compartment may be associated with the development of focal neurologic deficit or seizures as well as increased risk of intracranial hemorrhage.

DAVFs of the cavernous sinus (see Fig. 46-3) generally are associated with signs and symptoms related to the orbit that fluctuate depending on alterations in the orbital venous outflow that develop secondary to thrombosis and changes in head position.[31-33] Patients typically present with the gradual onset of focal or diffuse chronic eye redness distinguishable from uveitis in that close inspection will reveal dilated tortuous conjunctival and epibulbar vessels that exhibit an acute angulation near the ocular limbus.[34] These lesions are often associated with an elevation of episcleral venous pressure leading to a persistent rise in intraocular pressure in the affected eye, potentially resulting in the development of glaucoma.[35,36] If both cavernous sinuses become involved in the venous drainage because of a change in the ipsilateral venous outflow of the affected cavernous sinus, the ocular findings may become bilateral. The patient may complain of pulsatile tinnitus, and in 25 percent of cases a bruit can be auscultated over the orbit.[32,33] Cranial neuropathies, most commonly involving the sixth nerve, frequently lead to ocular motor dysfunction, which also may be exacerbated by orbital venous congestion and proptosis.[31,37] More important to the planning of embolization are the hypoxic ischemic retinal changes that develop in approximately 15 percent of patients.[32] Rarely, if thrombosis in the cavernous sinus is extensive, abnormal drainage into cerebral veins may occur, increasing the likelihood of an intracranial hemorrhage or venous infarction.

DAVFs involving the superior sagittal sinus,[38] tentorial incisura,[39] petrosal sinuses,[40] and anterior cranial base[41-43] occur less frequently than DAVFs involving the transverse, sigmoid,[44] or cavernous sinuses.[31] In these lesions, symptoms typically depend on the route of abnormal venous drainage and associated pattern of venous hypertension, and may include dysphasia, hemiparesis, hemisensory deficits, and abnormal visual phenomena. Several specific features deserve particular attention. (1) Dural fistulas involving the floor of the anterior cranial fossa are usually associated with drain-

---

Figure 46-3 (continued). *arrow*). The position of the guiding catheter (*c*) within the distal left facial vein is demonstrated. Early (H) and late (I) arterial phase lateral DSA images from the postembolization left internal carotid angiogram. Note the obliteration of arteriovenous shunting. The metallic coils within the left cavernous sinus are evident as a subtraction artifact projecting over the distal cavernous segment of the left internal carotid artery. Note the retrograde opacification of the artery of the foramen rotundum (*open curved arrow*) by way of anastomoses with the prominent inferolateral trunk (*solid acutely curved arrow*). These highly developed anastomoses persist after the shunt is eliminated and illustrate the potential danger of cerebral embolic events during transarterial embolizations of external carotid branches that anastomose with meningeal branches of the internal carotid artery. (J) Mid-arterial-phase lateral DSA image from the postembolization left external carotid angiogram illustrates complete obliteration of the left cavernous sinus dural shunt by transvenous embolization.

age into ectatic parasagittal cortical veins and often present with intracranial hemorrhage.[41,43] Moreover, these patients may exhibit unilateral visual loss secondary to arterial steal from the ophthalmic circulation into ethmoidal and recurrent meningeal supplies to the shunt.[41] (2) DAVFs of the petrosal sinuses or tentorial incisura may occasionally drain inferiorly into perimedullary veins of the spinal cord, resulting in progressive myelopathy similar to that encountered in spinal dural AVMs.[13,45] Assuming the venous sinus drainage of the brain is otherwise unimpaired, these symptoms usually respond well to endovascular or surgical closure of the shunt.

Neuroimaging of Intracranial DAVFs

Although computed tomography (CT) or magnetic resonance imaging (MRI) is usually obtained in all patients with symptoms related to DAVFs, the studies commonly are normal or present subtle findings. Occasionally, dilated or thrombosed venous structures may be seen, particularly in dural fistulas with associated cortical venous drainage (see Fig. 46-2A). In patients presenting with intracranial hemorrhage, obvious findings will be evident in both CT and MRI studies. Focal or generalized atrophy of the brain, possibly accompanied by hydrocephalus, is a nonspecific secondary finding that may be appreciated. The chronic enlargement of meningeal branches of the external carotid or carotid-cavernous artery may be demonstrated by imaging studies. More recently, several reports have suggested a role for magnetic resonance angiography (MRA) in the delineation of abnormal AV shunting secondary to dural fistulas.[46]

The angiographic evaluation usually includes selective studies of the internal and external carotid arteries bilaterally as well as of both vertebral arteries when evaluating lesions of the posterior fossa or tentorium.[2] The pretherapeutic examination must be tailored to the clinically suspected location of the fistula and must disclose the entire arterial supply as well as any anastomoses between the supplying vessels and arterial distributions to the orbit, brain, or cranial nerves. This usually requires superselective arterial catheterization and angiography before the use of embolic materials. The venous anatomy must be studied with respect to the pattern of drainage from the fistula, and the adequacy of normal venous drainage of the brain must be assessed.

Therapeutic Approaches to DAVFs

An understanding of the natural history of the disease, the treatment options, and the risks and benefits of those therapies is important in the development of a treatment plan. Although spontaneous resolution of

clinical signs related to DAVFs has been reported,[47,48] most notably in patients with cavernous sinus lesions, most symptomatic DAVFs require some form of treatment. This is most urgent in those fistulas accompanied by cortical venous drainage and venous ectasias. The goals of therapy should be tailored to each individual patient and may include relief from symptoms or complete occlusion of the DAVF.[2] The efficacy and safety of the treatment must be considered in conjunction with the patient's presentation and prognosis.

Carotid-Jugular Compression. Patients with Djindjian type I transverse or sigmoid sinus DAVFs or with fistulas of the cavernous sinus with otherwise normal ophthalmologic examinations may be treated conservatively. Intermittent manual compression of the carotid artery may be effective in eliminating DAVFs involving the ipsilateral cavernous sinus in patients with mild findings and no evidence of carotid vascular disease or other contraindications to carotid compression.[31,32] The ipsilateral carotid artery is compressed, using the contralateral hand, for approximately 5 minutes every waking hour for 1 to 3 days. If this is tolerated, the compression time is increased to 10 to 15 minutes of compression per waking hour. The compression, if properly performed, produces concomitant partial obstruction of the ipsilateral carotid artery and jugular vein. This results in the transient reduction of arteriovenous shunting by decreasing arterial inflow while simultaneously increasing the outlet venous pressure, thereby promoting spontaneous thrombosis within the nidus. When applied to highly motivated patients with cavernous sinus DAVFs, it is approximately 30 to 40 percent effective in eliminating the shunt.[31,32]

Embolization. The development of improved superselective angiographic catheter systems and embolic agents has increased the role of interventional neuroradiology in the management of these lesions, both primarily and preoperatively. Two strategies may be employed, depending on the location and complexity of the lesion as well as its vascular features. In transarterial embolization, selective catheterization of individual feeding vessels is required (see Fig. 46-2).[2,27,31,49] As mentioned previously, superselective angiography is performed to evaluate the vascular supply to the fistula, particularly with respect to potential anastomosis with the orbit or cerebral vasculature. It is important to understand that such anastomoses may not be demonstrable on the initial angiograms; however, they may become manifest after alterations in flow within the target vascular territory occur during embolization. For ease of catheterization, guidewire-directed microcatheters are employed in the microcatheterization of those meningeal branches supplying such lesions. The embolic agents employed are usually liquid cyanoacrylate (NBCA), polyvinyl alcohol foam (PVA), or ethanol. When possible, liquid acrylic agent is the first choice for embolic therapy because it is capable of permeating the supplying complex and providing permanent occlusion of the nidus by way of the feeding pedicles. This degree of permeation is not possible when using particulate agents that lodge within supplying arterioles at a point proximal to microcollateral networks, which may at some future time reestablish flow through the nidus complex.

Nevertheless, PVA may find use in several situations. First, the initial use of PVA in embolizing the less favorable arterial supplies to a multipedicle fistula may facilitate more complete embolization later with liquid cyanoacrylate by way of the safest pedicle. The embolization of competing supplies to the shunt in this situation permits the undiluted permeation of the nidus by the liquid embolic agent without fragmentation of the liquid stream. PVA may also be useful in reducing flow through low-velocity shunts, thereby facilitating thrombosis through these fistulas. This may be particularly applicable in managing cavernous sinus DAVFs, where embolization of meningeal branches of the ECA can be combined with manual compression in treating lesions also supplied by dural branches of the ipsilateral ICA, which usually cannot be embolized conservatively. In certain situations, partial embolization of dural fistulas may be performed in an attempt to ameliorate symptoms. For instance, partial embolization of a cavernous sinus DAVF may be performed to reduce intraocular pressure in a patient suffering acute deterioration of visual acuity secondary to the fistula. Partial embolization may also be advocated in patients presenting with new-onset dementia or in those patients with severe tinnitus. Lastly, PVA and liquid embolic agents are used in the preoperative devascularization of dural fistulas proceeding to surgical excision.[50] In this situation, particulate emboli, because of their low morbidity, are generally preferred and should be applied 1 to 2 days before surgery. Regardless of the embolic agent (NBCA or PVA), when the nidus is not obliterated because of proximal occlusion of feeding vessels, the fistula will often reconstitute by way of unembolized collaterals.

Transvenous embolization with metallic coils or detachable balloons has been advocated in the treatment of DAVFs involving the transverse, sigmoid,[44] or cavernous sinus.[51–53] The technique involves a transfemoral or intraoperative approach to the affected sinus (see Fig. 46-3). Several features are critical in appropriate patient selection for this method of treatment. (1) The segment of sinus to be occluded must be in proximity to the fistula and receive its entire venous drainage. (2) The sinus to be occluded should not be essential to the normal venous drainage of the brain. In this connection, the cerebral venous drainage must be thoroughly evaluated before embolization to determine the potential alternate pathways for cerebral venous drainage. (3) The target sinus must be completely occluded throughout the involved segment to avoid diversion of the fistula drainage into pial veins after embolization by way of a trapped sinus segment.

Carotid-Cavernous Fistulas

Carotid-cavernous fistulas (CCFs) are acquired lesions involving an abnormal vascular communication between the cavernous portion of the internal carotid artery and the enveloping cavernous sinus. The fistula most commonly results from traumatic injury to the internal carotid artery proper or a cavernous branch and generally leads to extensive, rapid arteriovenous shunting.

In 20 percent of cases, the fistula develops spontaneously without a history of trauma.[2,54] Specific disorders associated with vascular deficiencies can be identified in approximately 60 percent of such cases.[54] These include Ehlers-Danlos syndrome,[55] pseudoxanthoma elasticum, fibromuscular dysplasia,[56] aneurysm of the carotid-cavernous artery, a persistent embryologic trigeminal artery, and other nonspecific angiodysplasias. The recognition that a carotid-cavernous fistula has arisen spontaneously is essential to the proper management of the shunt and the underlying disorder.

Although the clinical signs and symptoms of CCFs may fluctuate, in general, the clinical diagnosis is not difficult to establish. The patient may complain of visual blurring, diplopia, headache, orbital pain, and a subjective bruit.[2] After extensive trauma, however, additional injuries may complicate the diagnosis and delay treatment of the underlying fistula. Signs of orbital congestion may be noted after head trauma but may be inaccurately ascribed to local orbital damage. In addition, a small pseudoaneurysm may develop after traumatic injury to the cavernous ICA and subsequently rupture after an asymptomatic period of days to weeks. In CCFs, the congestion of orbital contents results from increased flow into the superior and inferior ophthalmic veins, which contributes to orbital venous hypertension and ultimately the elevation of intraocular pressure, chemosis, and edema throughout the eyelids.[54,57] The pronounced venous congestion generally leads to proptosis with the globe displaced downward and laterally. Isolated third or sixth nerve palsies or combinations of third, fourth, and sixth nerve dysfunctions are common[33,54] and occasionally may be associated with first- and second-division trigeminal nerve sensory deficits. Trigeminal motor dysfunction is almost never attributable to the CCF but may be a manifestation of traumatic neuropathy acquired during the precipitating event. Likewise, traumatic cases are often associated with direct injury to the third, fourth, sensory fifth, and sixth nerves as well as with cranial neuropathies of the seventh and eighth nerves resulting from accompanying basilar skull fractures.[33]

Intraocular pressure is elevated in most patients with CCFs in whom the venous drainage is conducted anteriorly from the cavernous sinus into the ophthalmic veins. This may result in the development of visual changes, or, less commonly, in central retinal artery occlusion in severe untreated cases.[58] These changes are typically unilateral; however, if the opposite cavernous sinus is affected because of the shunting of blood across the intercavernous coronary sinus, both eyes may exhibit signs of orbital congestion and elevated intraocular pressure. Optic neuropathy, commonly with a mild reduction in visual acuity, dyschromatopsia, an afferent pupillary defect, and a generally constricted visual field, may occur.[54] In these cases, the fundus may appear normal, suggesting a retrobulbar process, most likely related to compression of the optic nerve by a distended superior ophthalmic vein.

Diagnostic Imaging of CCFs

In patients presenting with CCF secondary to head trauma, CT is often the first imaging modality of evaluation. Enlargement of the ophthalmic veins, most often the superior division, may be demonstrated readily in axial or coronal views of the orbit by contrast-enhanced CT. Orbital congestion is easily appreciated by CT as a diffuse increase in the attenuation of orbital fat, and is often associated with swelling of the extraocular muscles and lacrimal gland. The ipsilateral cavernous sinus is often dilated, resulting in the convex bulging of the lateral cavernous sinus wall. Exophthalmos may be appreciated by CT; however, it is usually more easily apparent by clinical inspection. In cases associated with cortical venous drainage, dilatation of one or more cerebral veins and/or the sphenoparietal sinus may be noted. CT often reveals other stigmata of head injury, including fractures involving the skull base or paranasal sinuses and additional intracranial lesions such as epidural, subdural, or intracerebral hematomas. Of particular importance is the detection of sphenoid sinus fracture, which, when associated with a traumatic pseudoaneurysm of the carotid-cavernous artery, places the patient at risk for catastrophic epistaxis.[59] Potentially life-threatening conditions resulting from intracranial injury should be attended to before definitive treatment for the CCF is initiated. By comparison, facial and orbital fractures are probably best treated after closure of this fistula, thereby permitting a reduction in the venous congestion and associated soft tissue swelling of the orbit.

Although CT is superior to MRI in the evaluation of head trauma, MRI may demonstrate changes within the cavernous sinus and orbit suggestive of the diagnosis. In addition, MRI and MRA may be helpful in following posttreatment results and complications.

Despite the features of transaxial imaging that may suggest the presence of a CCF, the diagnosis is primarily confirmed by angiography.[60] The angiographic evaluation should include several specific objectives. First, the fistula site should be precisely identified. This is usually accomplished by rapid sequential angiography of the ipsilateral internal carotid artery employing frame rates between 6 and 15 frames per second. If this approach fails to disclose the precise site of the fistula, the angiogram may be repeated employing a double-lumen occlusive balloon catheter placed within the cervical internal carotid artery. Under systemic heparinization, the balloon is inflated, and contrast material is injected into the occluded ICA at a low, sustained injection rate. The dilution of the contrast column by retrograde nonopacified blood flow identifies the fistula site. As an alternative, in cases presenting with a competent ipsilateral posterior communicating artery, a vertebral angiogram with or without manual compression of the affected internal carotid artery can pinpoint the exact site of the fistula (Fig. 46-4H).

Second, the anatomic competence of the circle of Willis should be thoroughly evaluated by angiography. The potential collateral arterial supply to the ipsilateral hemisphere must be identified if the shunt cannot be closed without sacrificing the involved ICA. Of additional importance is the identification of potential transsellar anastomoses with the contralateral ICA in cases employing a trapping procedure as a therapeutic solution. This is necessary to avoid the creation of a persistent shunt between the occlusion balloons supplied by the contralateral ICA.

Selective angiography of the external carotid artery must be performed to determine if the external carotid artery provides collateral contribution to the AV shunt (Fig. 46-4I). This potential contribution is usually derived from the natural collaterals of C4 and C5 segment branches (Fischer classification)[9] of the affected ICA and includes cavernous branches of the middle meningeal or accessory meningeal arteries, the artery of the foramen rotundum, and the ascending pharyngeal artery, depending on the precise location of the internal carotid injury.

The angiogram will also disclose the direction of drainage away from the cavernous sinus (Fig. 46-4A to C) as well as indicate the presence of partial thrombosis or aneurysmal ectasia of the cavernous sinus and draining veins.

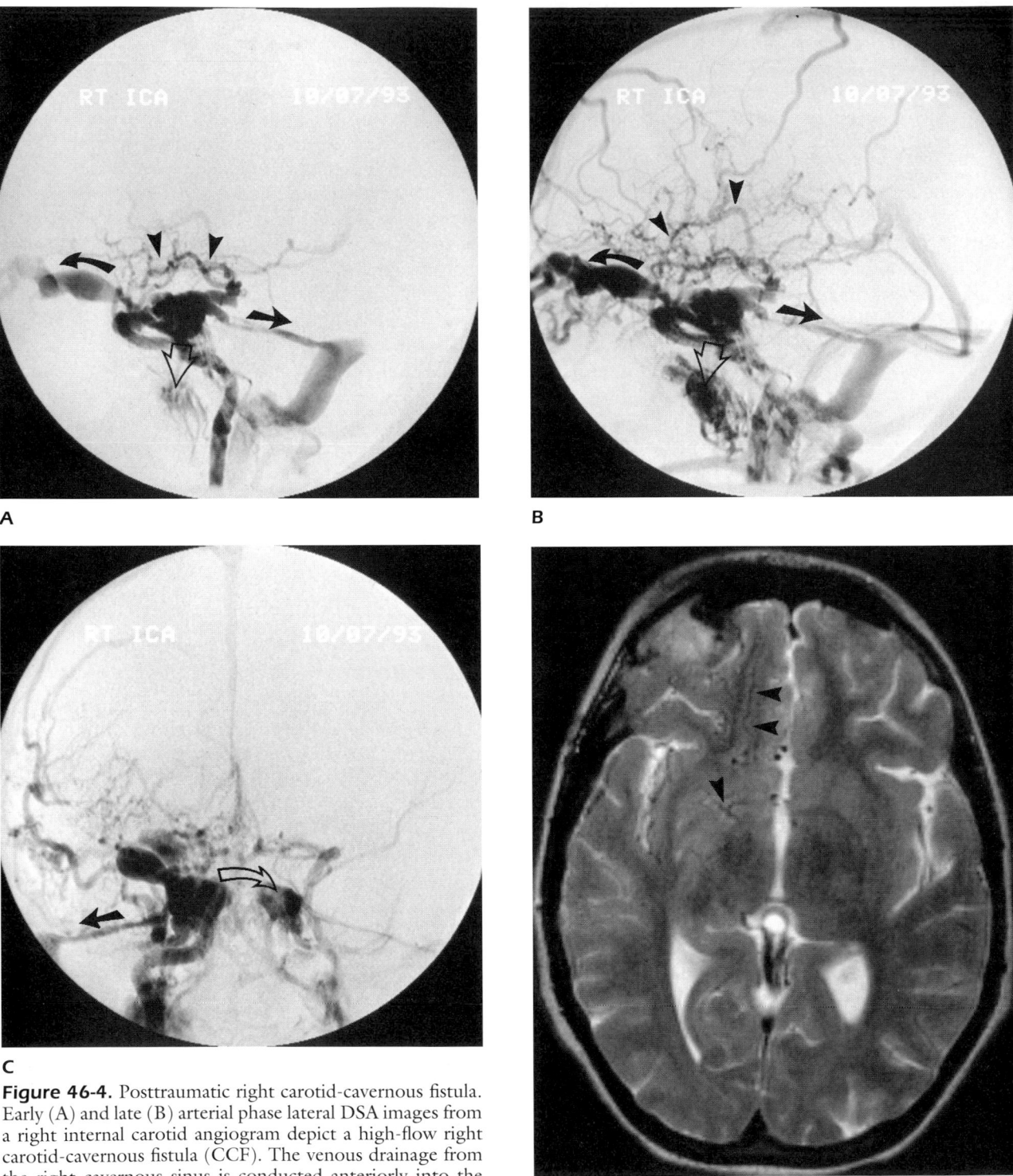

A

B

C

D

Figure 46-4. Posttraumatic right carotid-cavernous fistula. Early (A) and late (B) arterial phase lateral DSA images from a right internal carotid angiogram depict a high-flow right carotid-cavernous fistula (CCF). The venous drainage from the right cavernous sinus is conducted anteriorly into the superior ophthalmic vein (*solid curved arrow*), inferiorly through the foramen ovale into the pterygoid plexus of veins (*open straight arrow*), posteriorly into the superior petrosal sinus (*solid straight arrow*), and superiorly into cortical veins (*arrowheads*). Note the extensive cortical venous drainage that is conducted superficially toward the superior sagittal sinus and into the deep venous system that empties through the vein of Galen and straight sinus. (C) The accompanying frontal DSA image illustrates the contralateral drainage re-

sulting in the opacification of the left cavernous sinus (*open curved arrow*). Note the posterior drainage from the right cavernous sinus into the right superior petrosal sinus (*solid straight arrow*) in the frontal projection. (D) Transaxial T2-weighted spin-echo magnetic resonance image demonstrates multiple serpiginous signal voids (*arrowheads*), reflecting engorged pial veins. (E) Frontal DSA image illustrates an arterial dissection of the left internal carotid artery (*solid white*

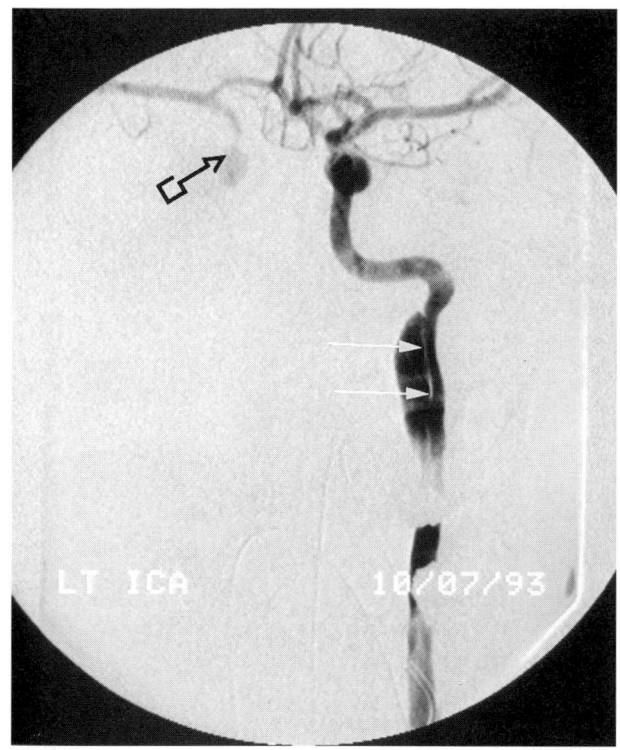

E

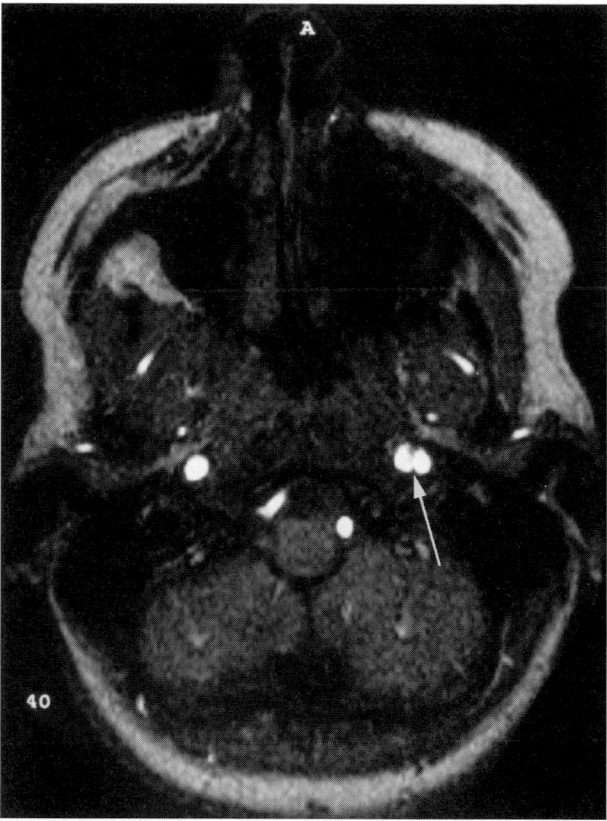

F

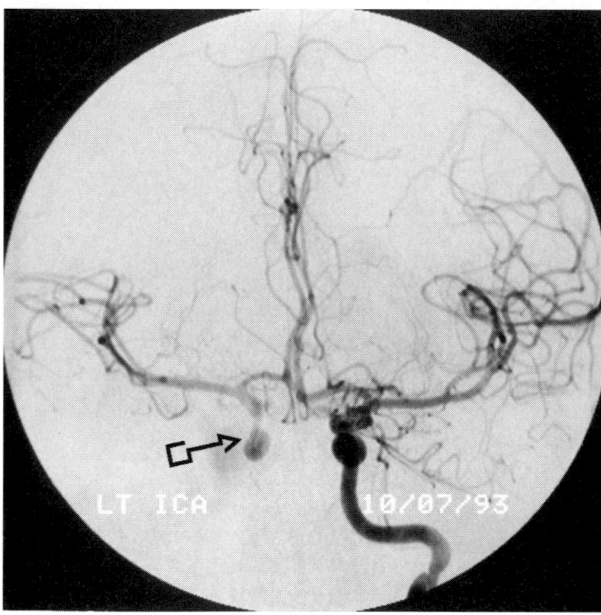

G

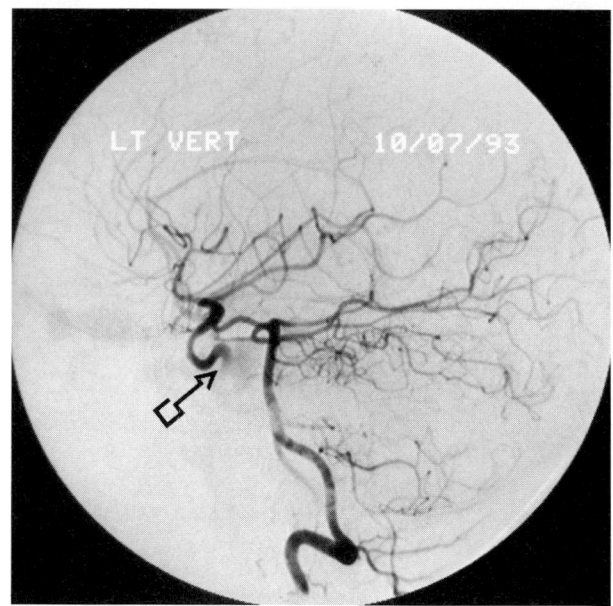

H

arrows) and retrograde opacification of the right carotid-cavernous fistula (*open straight arrow*). (F) An accompanying transaxial gradient-echo MR image through the level of the skull base shows the dissection of the left internal carotid artery along with an intimal flap and accompanying pseudoaneurysm (*solid white arrow*). (G to I) Retrograde opacification of the right CCF (*open straight arrow*) obtained during angiography of the left internal carotid artery (G, frontal DSA image), left vertebral artery (H, lateral DSA

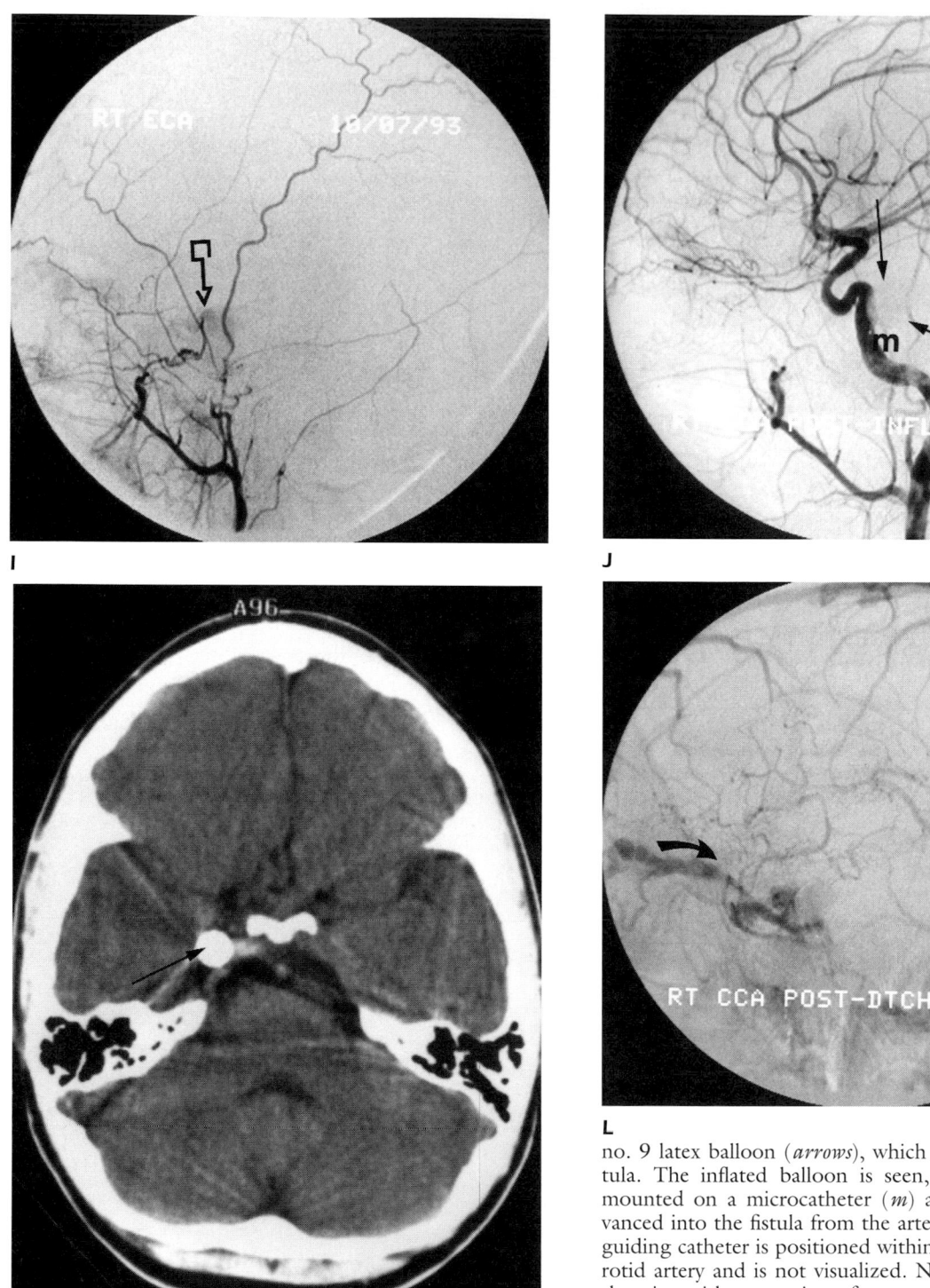

Figure 46-4 (continued). image), and right external carotid artery (I, lateral DSA image). The opacification of the fistula from the right external carotid artery occurs through anastomoses between the artery of the foramen rotundum and the inferolateral trunk of the left carotid-cavernous artery. (J) Lateral mid-arterial-phase DSA image from a right common carotid angiogram obtained after inflation of a no. 9 latex balloon (*arrows*), which has obliterated the fistula. The inflated balloon is seen, prior to detachment, mounted on a microcatheter (*m*) and was previously advanced into the fistula from the arterial side. The 8 French guiding catheter is positioned within the right common carotid artery and is not visualized. Note the absence of AV shunting with restoration of antegrade sequential opacification of the right hemispheric vasculature. (K) A postembolization transaxial CT scan through the level of the cavernous sinus depicts the contrast-inflated balloon (*arrow*). (L) Venous phase lateral DSA image of the postembolization right internal carotid angiogram. Note the normal venous pattern of drainage and reestablishment of centripetal flow within the right superior ophthalmic vein directed toward the cavernous sinus (*curved arrow*). When this image is compared to the lateral DSA images depicted in (A) and (B), the right superior ophthalmic vein is clearly reduced in size.

Because of the association of CCFs with traumatic injury to the head and neck, the angiographic study should include evaluation of all cervical and intracranial vessels, including the vertebrobasilar system (Fig. 46-4E). Other traumatic injuries to these vessels, including vessel dissection or AV fistulas involving the ophthalmic, internal carotid, or vertebral artery, may cause persistent symptoms after closure of the CCF and may affect the treatment strategy if known prospectively. Secondary shunts may become apparent on angiography only after the dominant CCF is occluded. Cerebral angiography may also uncover those cases of cavernous origin of the ophthalmic artery. This variation may be associated with a deficiency of collateral circulation to the distal ophthalmic artery and may argue against occlusion of the internal carotid artery at the cavernous level because of the risk of blindness.

The clinical signs and symptoms related to CCFs can usually be explained by angiographic analysis of the arterial inflow, the location of the fistula, and the venous outflow.[54] Each of these factors influences the abnormal hemodynamic condition and may evolve, resulting in fluctuating symptoms. The nature and degree of dysfunction depend to some degree on the extent and location of thrombosis within the cavernous sinus and draining veins as well as on the location of the compartment of the cavernous sinus directly involved with the AV shunt.

The contralateral cavernous sinus may receive arterialized flow via the anterior and posterior limbs of the coronary venous plexus, ultimately leading to orbital congestion and cranial neuropathy on the side opposite a particular shunt (Fig. 46-4C). Bilateral signs of varying severity are found in approximately 20 percent of cases but are usually the result of a unilateral fistula. Bilateral traumatic fistulas have been described but occur in fewer than 1 percent of cases.[54]

Most CCFs come to clinical attention as a result of orbital congestion, which can be quite impressive, particularly when the outlet venous drainage is conducted exclusively anterior into the ophthalmic venous system. Alternatively, when the venous drainage is directed posteriorly into the petrosal sinuses, patients may have few or no orbital findings related to the CCF, and a sixth nerve paresis or a retroauricular bruit may be the only presenting sign.[54] When the drainage from the cavernous sinus is conducted into the sphenoparietal sinus or the deep sylvian veins, cortical venous hypertension may result, predisposing the patient to an intracranial hemorrhage[61] or signs of increased intracranial pressure.

Cases in which the accompanying circle of Willis is incompetent may be associated with ischemic infarct in the distribution of the ipsilateral internal carotid artery secondary to complete "steal" through the fistula.

Therapeutic Approaches to CCFs

The urgency of intervention in the treatment of CCFs is determined by several considerations.[62,63] Although emergent embolization is required in fewer than 30 percent of presenting cases, spontaneous closure of the high-flow CCF is unlikely. Visual loss, related to persistent glaucoma, retinopathy, optic neuropathy, or corneal ulcerations, evolving to complete unilateral blindness, has been reported in 26 to 89 percent of untreated patients.[64,65] Moreover, in patients without severe visual loss, diplopia secondary to associated cranial neuropathies has been frequently reported as a persistent finding.[54] From the standpoint of treatment, recent reviews have established the efficacy of early intervention in cases complicated by the onset of transient ischemic attacks, increased intracranial pressure, cortical venous drainage, epistaxis, and loss of vision or sudden increase in intraocular pressure uncontrolled by antiglaucoma medications.[54,62,63,66]

The goal of therapy is to occlude the untoward shunt, preferably with preservation of the involved internal carotid artery. Obviously, the symptoms due to the CCF must be considered in relation to the patient's overall clinical status, particularly as it relates to multisystem trauma. Moreover, with respect to the orbit, the management of intraocular pressure by temporizing pharmacologic methods may assume importance in the preembolization period.

Neurointerventional Management of CCFs

In recent years, transarterial embolization has become the preferred means of treating CCFs.[2,60,66,67] The primary method employs a detachable balloon mounted on a microcatheter that is introduced coaxially through an 8 or 9 French guiding catheter positioned proximally within the involved internal carotid artery (Fig. 46-4J). The microcatheter is flow-guided into the lesion from the arterial side by hemodynamic conditions associated with the rapid arteriovenous shunting present. Once positioned on the venous side of the fistula, the balloon is inflated, thereby occluding the shunt, ideally without compromising the internal carotid artery. The balloon is then detached, and the microcatheter is removed. An assortment of easily mounted latex or silicone balloons is available, differing in size and shape.[2,60] In general, they retain their original characteristics after multiple inflations and deflations, a feature that may be necessary in optimally positioning the balloon before detachment. In most cases, the balloon is filled with half-strength contrast to facilitate visualization during the procedure and in the postembolization follow-up. Over the course of several weeks, the balloon normally deflates; however, it generally provides an adequate interval of occlusion during which thrombosis of the fistula occurs. Premature deflation or change in the position of the balloon, either at the time of the procedure or within 1 to 2 days, is usually associated with recurrence or exacerbation of symptoms coinciding with an observable change in the disposition of the balloon on plain skull film. When appropriate, treatment failure is usually followed by a second attempted transarterial closure. If the fistula cannot accommodate a balloon, an open-ended microcatheter may be used to deliver microcoils into the fistula. If the carotid artery must be sacrificed, it is important to occlude the entire segment involved in the fistula to prevent reconstitution of the shunt through anastomoses with the ipsilateral external carotid artery, generally through C4 or C5 branches of the cavernous ICA or by way of the ophthalmic artery. Care should also be taken to avoid occlusion of the internal carotid artery proximal to the fistula, thereby allowing persistent filling of the fistula from the supraclinoid segment of the internal carotid circulation. As mentioned previously, under conditions of anticipated internal carotid sacrifice, preembolization angiography must establish the adequacy of collateral circulation through the circle of Willis.

Various agents that induce thrombosis may be introduced directly into the cavernous sinus to effect successful closure of a CCF. If a transarterial approach cannot be performed because of traumatic vessel occlusion, vasculopathy, or a failed trapping procedure, venous access to the cavernous sinus may be considered.[60,67–70] The technique involves either direct cannulation of the superior ophthalmic vein or femoral transvenous catheterization of the cavernous sinus by way of access through the inferior petrosal sinus or ophthalmic vein. Metallic coils are the preferred embolic agent by this route and should be deposited in a fashion that results in thrombosis of the cavernous sinus without diverting the drainage of the fistula into cortical veins.

After closure of the shunt, there is immediate resolution of the objective bruit, which can be used to confirm clinically the occlusion of the CCF in the postembolization period. Recurrence of the bruit, in the absence of luminal compromise of the internal carotid artery, suggests reestablishment of the shunt even in the absence of additional symptoms. After shunt closure, elevations in intraocular pressure usually normalize within 48 to 72 hours.[54] Other signs of orbital congestion generally resolve within days to weeks, with concomitant improvement in the associated cranial neuropathies not secondary to direct traumatic paresis.

Complications related to the embolization of CCFs are uncommon. Stroke, secondary to the premature or inadvertent deployment of embolic agents, is relatively infrequent because of the propensity of the released

device to enter the fistula and lodge within the venous side.[71] Cranial neuropathies that are present at the time of embolization may worsen because of the transient mass effect of the inflated balloon, which may compress cranial nerves within the cavernous sinus.[72] This usually improves with the subsequent spontaneous deflation of the balloon over several weeks after treatment. The incidence of symptomatic venous pouches developing at the site of balloon deflation ranges from 2.4 to 21.0 percent.[66] If symptoms persist, closure of the venous pouch with a second detachable balloon or microcoils may be contemplated. More commonly, the symptoms resolve spontaneously over several weeks to months and may be associated with shrinkage of the venous pouch as demonstrated by serial MRI following the course of the venous aneurysm.

Embolization of Intracranial, Extraaxial Neoplasms

Neuroendovascular therapy is a useful approach to the preoperative or palliative management of extraaxial and calvarial vascular neoplasms. When coupled with contemporary microsurgical methods, selective presurgical embolization can facilitate the removal of tumor by significantly reducing intraoperative blood loss and by increasing the frequency of complete tumor resection.[73–76]

Regardless of the tumor type or location, the preferred goal of tumor embolization is to devascularize the tumor capillary bed while preserving normal arterial distributions.[77] Moreover, adjunctive techniques such as permanent balloon occlusion of the internal carotid artery, when feasible, may enable more radical excision of tumors extensively involving the skull base.[2]

The diagnosis of intracranial neoplasm is usually established by correlating the clinical history with transaxial imaging by CT and MRI. Formal angiography is generally reserved for those cases in which the information gained may be useful diagnostically or in planning therapeutic intervention. The angiographic evaluation should assess the arterial supply, specifically the vascular territory involved and its anatomic pattern, the mix of dural and pial supply, and should also define regional arterial anastomoses and likely supplies to cranial nerves or cutaneous structures. The venous drainage of the lesion and the surrounding brain should be documented, and any abnormalities pertaining to venous structures identified. Of particular importance in planning the embolization of an extraaxial tumor is the angiographic delineation of the unique vascular compartmentalization of the lesion.

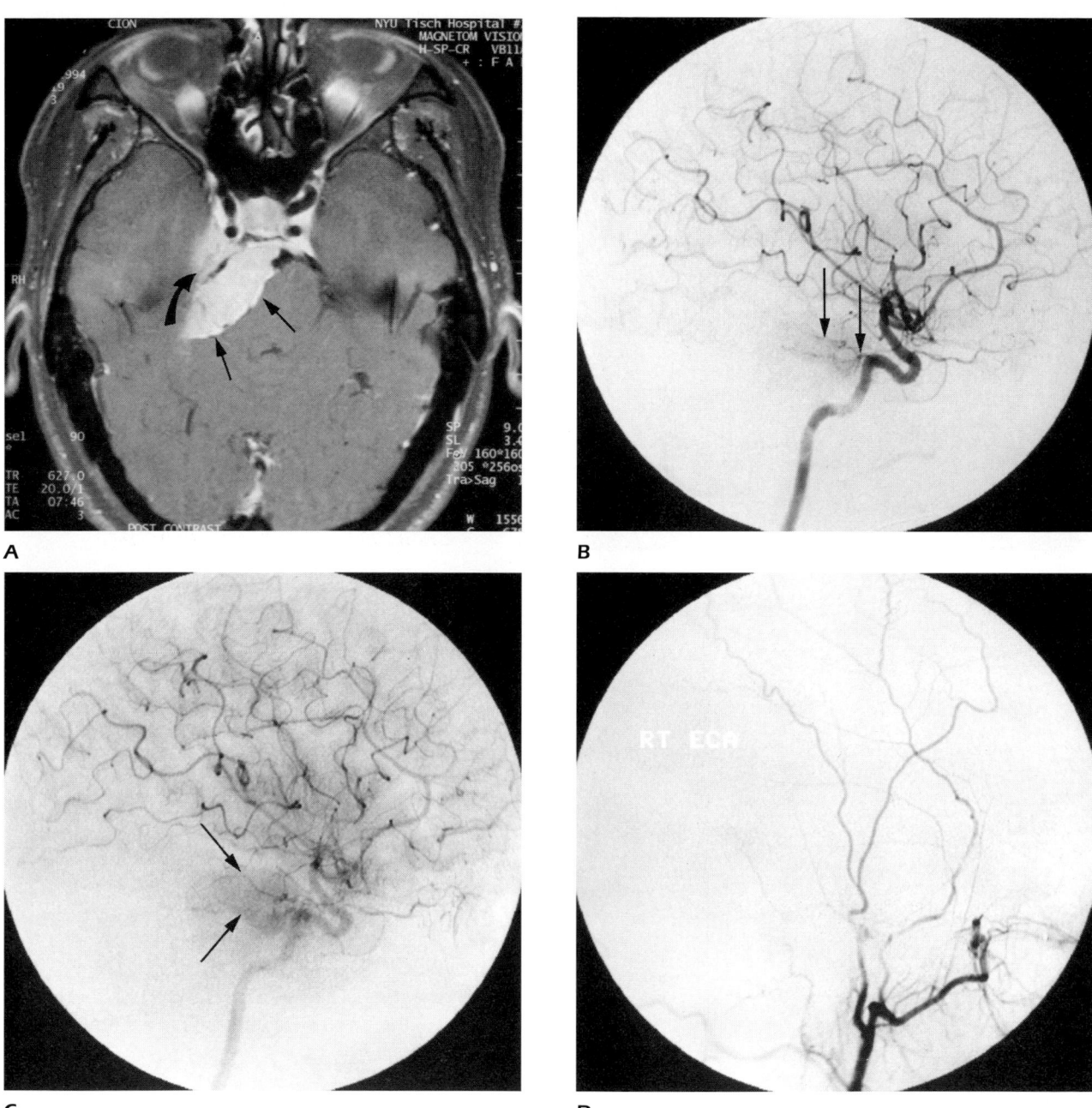

Figure 46-5. Monocompartmental right petroclival meningioma. (A) Gadolinium-enhanced transaxial T1-weighted MR image with fat suppression demonstrates an enhancing right petroclival tumor (*straight arrows*). The mass extends inferiorly along the clivus, displacing the brain stem toward the left, and is seen to extend through Dorello's canal (*curved arrow*), possibly explaining the patient's right sixth nerve palsy. Early (B) and late (C) arterial phase lateral DSA image of the right internal carotid artery. Note the abnormal tumor blush developing as a result of contribution from the right internal carotid artery by way of its meningohypophyseal trunk (*arrows*). (D) The subsequent DSA of the distal right external carotid artery failed to disclose evidence of middle or accessory meningeal contribution to the lesion, consistent with monocompartmental C5 segmental supply.

Extraaxial tumors may be distinguished angiographically as mono- or multicompartmental with respect to their hemodynamic composition.[70,75] Each type of lesion may receive vascular contribution from several arterial sources, depending on the precise anatomic origin and the ultimate pattern of extension of the mass. Monocompartmental tumors may be opacified in their entirety by supraselective angiography of any one of the supplying arteries (Fig. 46-5). The embolization of such lesions should therefore be performed from the safest vascular approach with respect to risk to cranial nerve damage or cerebral

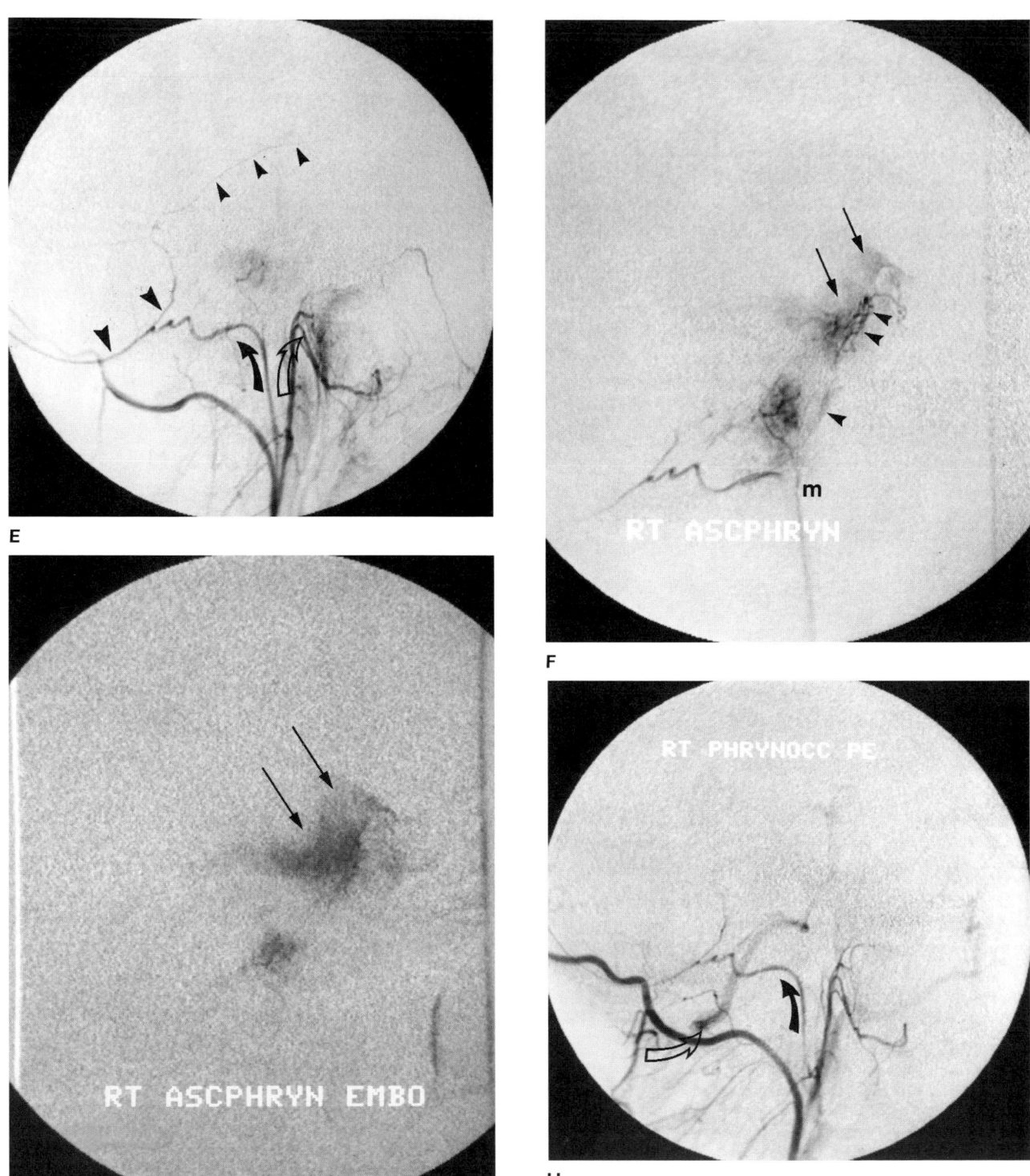

E

F

G

H

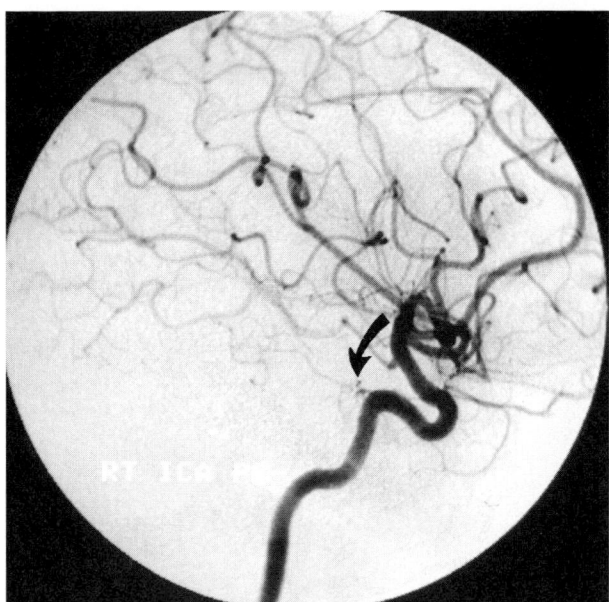

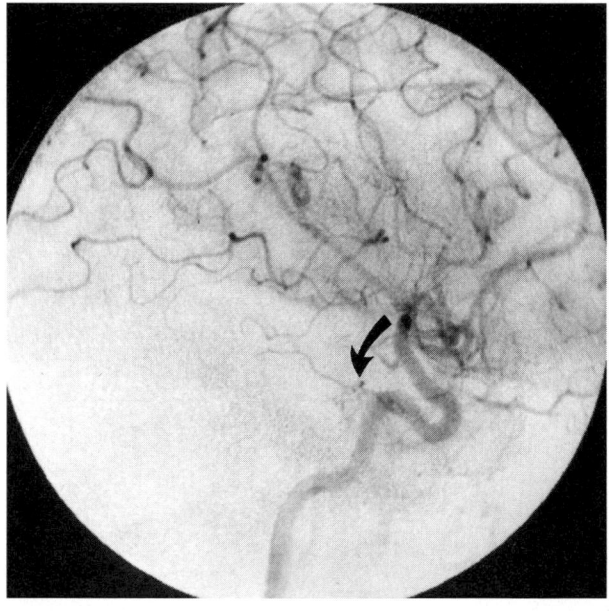

I

J

Figure 46-5 (continued). (E) Lateral DSA image of the right ascending pharyngeal artery depicts subtle supply to the lesion from the neuromeningeal trunk (*solid curved arrow*) of the ascending pharyngeal artery. Note the origin of the posterior meningeal supply to the cerebellar fossa (*large arrowheads*), which anastomoses with the right middle meningeal artery, opacifying the petrosquamosal division (*small arrowheads*). The pharyngeal division of the right ascending pharyngeal artery is also depicted (*open curved arrow*). (F) Lateral superselective DSA image from the neuromeningeal trunk of the right ascending pharyngeal artery. A microcatheter (*m*) has been advanced to the origin of the ascending clival branches, which constitute the natural collaterals in hemodynamic balance with the clival divisions of the meningohypophyseal trunk. The subsequently obtained superselective angiogram more fully discloses the extent of the clival supply (*arrowheads*) to the mass (*arrows*). The pattern of supply suggests a monocompartmental tumor deriving contribution from the anastomotic balance between the clival arcade and the meningohypophyseal trunk of the right cavernous carotid artery. (G) Stagnant contrast within the meningioma (*straight arrows*) is seen during Gelfoam powder embolization from the clival division of the right ascending pharyngeal artery. (H) Postembolization lateral DSA image of the right pharyngooccipital trunk documents obliteration

of the ascending pharyngeal contribution to the meningioma. The neuromeningeal trunk is preserved (*solid curved arrow*). Note the transient opacification of the right vertebral artery by way of C1 anastomosis with the right occipital artery (*open curved arrow*). This finding illustrates the potential risk of vertebrobasilar embolization during procedures involving the occipital artery axis. Middle (I) and late (J) arterial phase lateral DSA images from the postembolization right internal carotid angiogram depict the prominent segment of the right meningohypophyseal trunk (*curved arrow*) but fail to disclose evidence of the tumor blush demonstrated in the preembolization angiogram of (B) and (C). The single-pedicle embolization has successfully devascularized this right petroclival meningioma from the ascending pharyngeal artery without necessitating direct catheterization of the meningohypophyseal trunk of the right internal carotid artery. Extreme caution, however, must be exercised during such a procedure to avoid inadvertent embolization of the right internal carotid artery with microparticles passing retrogradely from clival feeders through the meningohypophyseal trunk. This could occur with a forceful injection of embolic agent and increases in likelihood as the preferential runoff into the tumor mass diminishes during the later stages of embolization.

embolization, thereby avoiding complications that may arise from a procedure conducted by way of a competing, more dangerous route. By comparison, multicompartmental tumors are composed of distinct vascular territories, each supplied by a separate arterial source (Fig. 46-6). Complete devascularization of such lesions requires catheterization and embolization of several distinct supplying arteries. This implies increased risk of the procedure related to the multiplicity of potential complications unique to the separate embolizations of each vascular territory.

The therapy of choice for most extraaxial tumors is surgical removal. The introduction of surgical micro-

technique and preoperative embolization has significantly improved the completeness of tumor resection while minimizing morbidity. Although a variety of extraaxial and calvarial neoplasms may satisfy specific criteria for embolic therapy, certain general principles apply to their embolization. The specific techniques employed are similar to those required in the treatment of other extraaxial lesions. Individual supplying arteries are selectively catheterized and embolized after superselective angiography to verify microcatheter position and margin of safety. Where feasible, small particulate agents such as Gelfoam powder (40–60 μm) or PVA (150–250 μm) are preferred for tumor

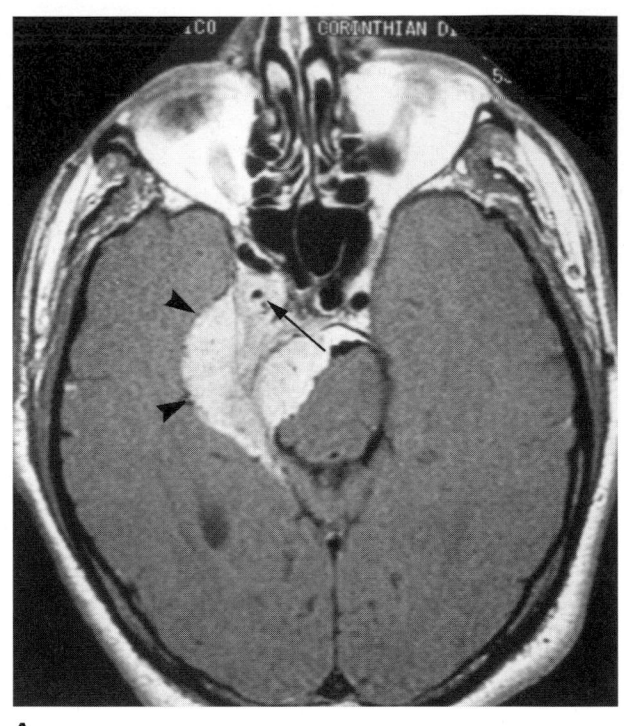

A

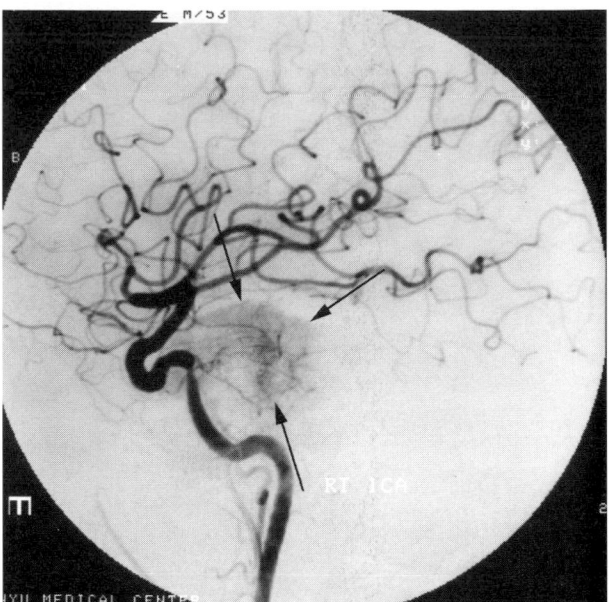

B

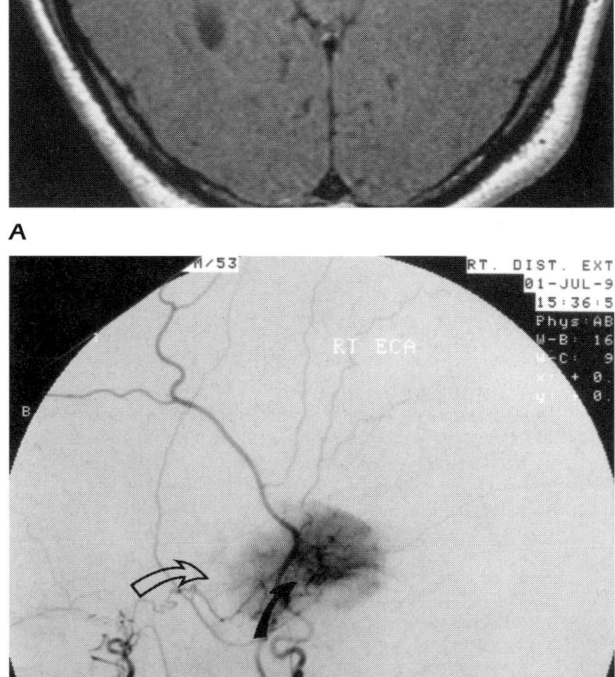

C

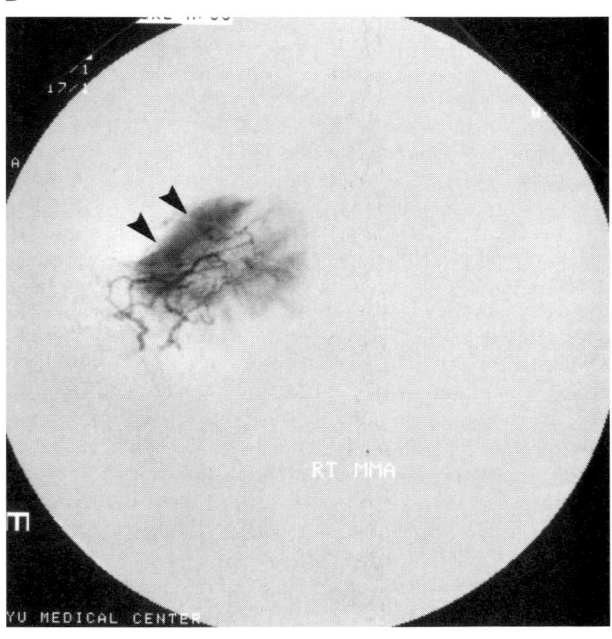

D

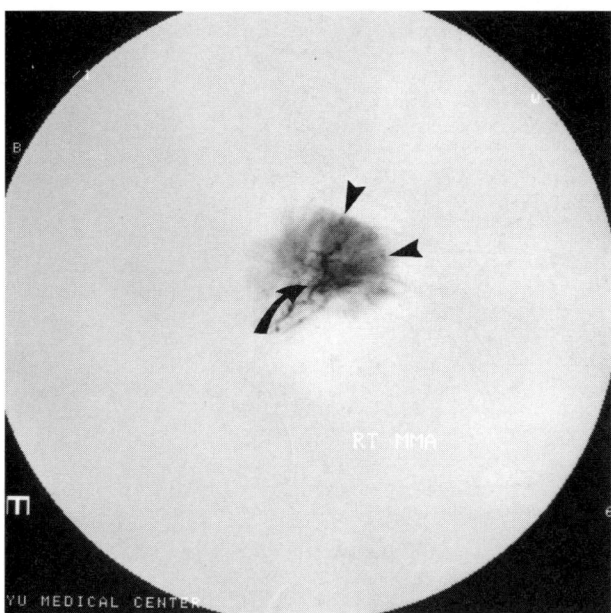

E

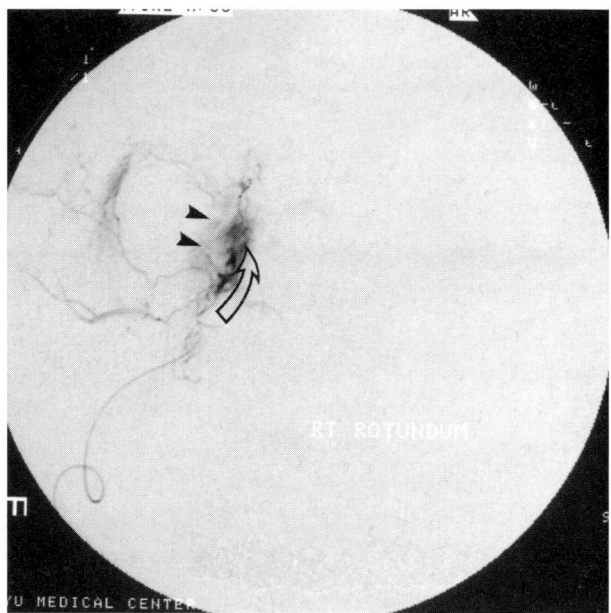

F

Figure 46-6. Right petroclival meningioma with supply from multiple pedicles. (A) Gadolinium-enhanced T1-weighted spin-echo MR image through the level of the cavernous sinuses depicts a right petroclival meningioma (*arrowheads*). The mass extends into the right cavernous sinus and circumferentially narrows the C5 segment of the right carotid-cavernous artery (*arrow*). (B) Lateral mid-arterial-phase DSA image of the right internal carotid artery demonstrates an abnormal tumor blush (*arrows*) supplied primarily by the meningohypophyseal (C5 segment) and inferolateral (C4 segment) branches of the right internal carotid artery, consistent with a mass comprising at least two hemodynamically independent compartments. As suggested by MRI, the C5 segment of the carotid-cavernous artery is seen to be narrowed circumferentially. (C) Lateral right external carotid artery DSA image illustrates an abnormal tumor blush developing within the anterolateral compartment of the mass. The external carotid contribution to the lesion has two components: (1) a contribution to the posterolateral compartment derived from petrosal and cavernous branches of the right middle meningeal artery (*solid curved arrow,* C and E) and (2) a contribution from the artery of the foramen rotundum (*open curved arrow*), which supplies the anteromedial aspect of the mass. (These separate compartmental supplies are more clearly depicted in the superselective angiograms of D to G). Frontal (D) and lateral (E) DSA images from the superselective right middle meningeal (*curved arrow,* E) angiogram clearly depict the segmental supply to the posterolateral compartment of the mass (*arrowheads*). The multicompartmental angiographic appearance of this lesion differs from that of the petroclival meningioma presented in Figure 46-5 and complicates the interventional approach to embolization of this specific mass. (F and G) This is easily recognized from the subsequent superselective angiogram of the artery of the foramen rotundum performed after Gel-

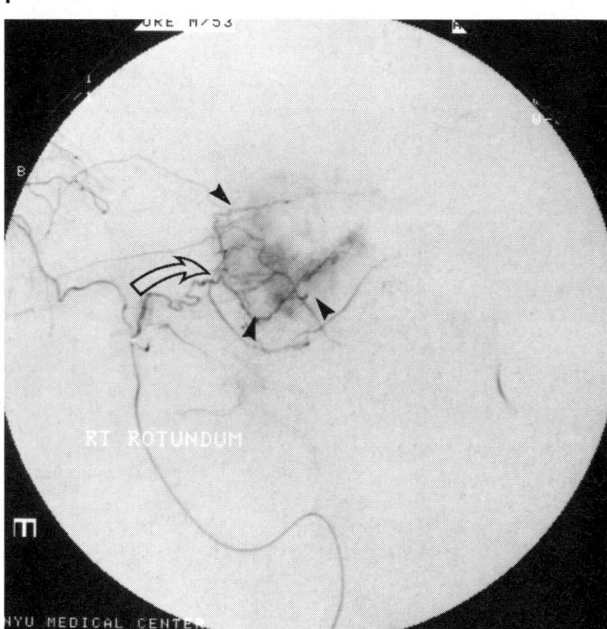

G

foam powder embolization of the middle meningeal supply. Frontal (F) and lateral (G) projection DSA images illustrate the residual supply to the cavernous portion of the meningioma (*arrowheads,* F and G), which represents the vascular territory supplied by the unembolized artery of the foramen rotundum (*open curved arrow*). The postembolization right internal carotid angiogram also showed persistent supply to the posteromedial compartment of the mass, which remains supplied by the meningohypophyseal trunk (not shown).

embolization. The use of small particles permits more distal penetration of the tumor vascular bed, precluding revascularization of the mass during the interval before surgery by collateral meningeal supply. A small aliquot of particles is diluted into contrast material, occasionally mixed with 10 to 30 percent ethanol (if performed under general anesthesia), and subsequently injected into the arterial feeder via the microcatheter. Strict attention is paid to avoiding extensive reflux of the embolic agent, which becomes more likely as the procedure progresses due to curtailment of antegrade runoff into the tumor vascular bed. Other particulate agents frequently used in tumor embolization include the larger sizes of PVA (250–1000 μm), Gelfoam sponge strips, and platinum fiber coils. The latter two materials find use in sealing pedicles after PVA or Gelfoam powder embolization, particularly after embolizations of the MMA, where proximal occlusion is helpful in reducing bleeding from the level of the foramen spinosum during the subsequent craniotomy. As previously mentioned, Gelfoam sponge strips or coils may be used to occlude potentially dangerous anastomoses before microparticulate embolization of meningiomas in certain territories.

Although the use of smaller PVA sizes is advocated for the embolization of most extraaxial tumors, the larger particulate sizes are preferred for the embolization of tumor feeders also supplying cranial nerves or other eloquent anastomoses to reduce the risk of the procedure. The larger particles may also be helpful in embolizing vessels arising from scalp arteries to avoid necrosis in territories fed by cutaneous branches.

With respect to large skull base tumors, two specific situations deserve particular attention. In patients in whom the cavernous sinus or carotid canal is involved by tumor, and in whom the collateral circulation via the circle of Willis adequately supports the ipsilateral cerebral hemisphere, balloon occlusion of the internal carotid artery distal to the horizontal cavernous segment may be used for more effective embolization of supplies derived from cavernous or petrous branches of the ICA. Balloon occlusion of the ipsilateral internal carotid artery is also felt to reduce the risks of pericarotid tumor removal, permitting a more radical tumor resection. Second, tumors with intradural extension, especially within the posterior fossa, are almost never amenable to complete embolization because of the variable pial supply.

Complications

If performed properly, embolization of calvarial or extraaxial masses is associated with a high degree of effectiveness and a low complication rate. Most complica-

Table 46-1. Vascular Supply to Cranial Nerves

I. Internal carotid artery (dural branches)
  A. Inferolateral trunk
    Anterolateral branch—V2
    Anteromedial branch—III, IV, VI, V1
    Posterior branch—V3, Vmotor, VII
    Superior branch—III, IV
  B. Meningohypophyseal branch
    Lateral clival artery
      Medial branch—VI
      Lateral branch—III, IV, V
    Marginal tentorial artery—III, IV, VI
II. External carotid artery
  A. Ascending pharyngeal artery
    Neuromeningeal trunk
      Jugular branch—VI, IX, X, XI
      Hypoglossal branch—XII
    Inferior tympanic—Jacobson's nerve
    Musculospinal artery—XI
  B. Middle meningeal artery
    Cavernous branches—Vmotor, V3
    Petrosal branch—VII
    Orbital branches—orbit
  C. Accessory meningeal artery—V2, V3, Vmotor
  D. Artery of foramen rotundum—V2

tions pertain to cranial nerve palsies, particularly when one is embolizing skull base lesions or posterior fossa masses vascularized by the ascending pharyngeal artery or those lesions supplied by a dominant accessory meningeal artery with liquid acrylic or ethanol (Table 46-1).[2,11] In addition, facial paralysis may complicate embolization involving the stylomastoid or petrosal distributions to the temporal bone. Attention should also be directed to any potential risk of cerebral embolization by way of anastomoses between meningeal branches of the ECA and ICA or vertebrobasilar circulations. Several investigators have also reported complications related to intratumoral,[78] perilesional, or subarachnoid hemorrhage in addition to acute exacerbation of mass effect secondary to postembolization swelling of the tumor. These complications emphasize the importance of postembolization monitoring and may necessitate emergent surgical intervention. The patient should be warned in advance of these potential complications. When liquid embolic agents are used in these vascular territories, provocative testing with intraarterial lidocaine may be recommended.

References

1. Dion JE. Principles and methodology. In: Vinuela F, Halbach VV, Dion JE, eds. Interventional neuroradiology: endovascular therapy of the central nervous system. New York: Raven, 1992: 1–15.
2. Lasjaunias P, Berenstein A. Surgical neuroangiography: Vol. 2. Endovascular treatment of craniofacial lesions. Berlin: Springer-Verlag, 1987.

3. Valavanis A. Interventional neuroradiology. Berlin: Springer-Verlag, 1993.

4. Lasjaunias P, Ming C, Ter Brugge K, Atul T. Neurological manifestations of intracranial dural arteriovenous malformations. J Neurosurg 1986;64:724–730.

5. Berenstein A. Brachiocephalic vessels: selective and superselective catheterization. Radiology 1983;148:437–441.

6. Berenstein A, Kricheff II. Catheter and material selection for transarterial embolization: technical considerations. Part II. Materials. Radiology 1979;132(3):631–639.

7. Berenstein A, Lasjaunias P, Kricheff II. Functional anatomy of the facial vasculature in pathologic conditions and its therapeutic applications. AJNR 1983;5:149–153.

8. Lasjaunias P, Berenstein A, Doyon D. Normal functional anatomy of the facial artery for superselective angiography. Radiology 1979;133:631–638.

9. Fischer E. Die Lageabweichungen der vorderen Hirnarterie im Gefassbild. Zentralbl Neurochir 1938;3:300–312.

10. Theron J, Cosgrove R, Melanson D, Ethier R. Embolization with temporary balloon occlusion of the internal carotid and vertebral arteries. Neuroradiology 1986;28:246–253.

11. Lasjaunias P, Berenstein A. Surgical neuroangiography: Vol. 1. Functional anatomy of the craniofacial arteries. Berlin: Springer-Verlag, 1987.

12. Berenstein A, Russell EJ. Gelatin sponge in therapeutic neuroradiology: a subjective review. Radiology 1981;141:145.

13. Berenstein A, Lasjaunias P. Surgical neuroangiography: Vol. 5. Endovascular treatment of spine and spinal cord lesions. Heidelberg: Springer-Verlag, 1992.

14. Horton JA, Kerber CW. Lidocaine injection in the external carotid branches: provocative test to preserve cranial nerve function in therapeutic embolization. AJNR 1986;7:105–108.

15. Newton TH, Cronqvist S. Involvement of dural arteries and intracranial arteriovenous malformations. Radiology 1969;93:1071–1078.

16. Djindjian R, Cophignon J, Theron J. Embolization by superselective arteriography from the femoral route; review of 60 cases: technique and indications, complications. Neuroradiology 1973;6:20–26.

17. Chaudhary M, Sachdev VB, Cho SH, Weitzner I, Puljic S, Huang YP. Dural arteriovenous malformation of the major venous sinus, an acquired lesion. AJNR 1982;3:13–19.

18. Houser OW, Campbell JK, Campbell RJ, Sundt TM. Arteriovenous malformations affecting the transverse dural sinus—an acquired lesion. Mayo Clin Proc 1979;54:651–661.

19. McCormick WF, Boulter TR. Vascular malformations ("angiomas") of the dura mater: report of 2 cases. J Neurosurg 1966;25:309–311.

20. Vidyasagar C. Persistent embryonic veins in the arteriovenous malformations of the dura. Acta Neurochir 1979;48:199–216.

21. Houser OW, Baker HL, Rhoton AL, Okazaki H. Dural arteriovenous malformations. Radiology 1972;105:55–64.

22. Vinuela F, Fox AJ, Pelz DM, Drake CG. Unusual clinical manifestations of dural arteriovenous malformations. J Neurosurg 1986;64:554–558.

23. Kosnik EJ, Hunt WE, Miller DA. Dural arteriovenous malformations. J Neurosurg 1974;40:322–329.

24. Laurent A, Guimarens L, Rufenacht D, Riche MC, Merland JJ. Five cases of unilateral exophthalmos associated with abnormalities in the lateral sinus area. J Neuroradiol 1986;13:125–136.

25. Lamas E, Loboto RD, Esparza J. Dural posterior fossa AVM producing raised sagittal sinus pressure: case report. J Neurosurg 1977;46:804–810.

26. Albright AL, Latchaw RE, Price RA. Posterior dural arteriovenous malformations in the infancy. Neurosurgery 1983;13:129–135.

27. Halbach VV, Higashida RT, Hieshima GB, Goto K, Norman D, Newton TH. Dural fistulas involving the transverse sigmoid sinuses: results of treatment in 28 patients. Radiology 1987;163:443–447.

28. Obrador S, Soto M, Sileva J. Clinical syndromes of arteriovenous malformations of the transverse sigmoid sinus. J Neurol Neurosurg Psych 1975;38:436–451.

29. Picard L, Bracard S, Malaet J, Per A, Glacobbe HL, Roland J. Spontaneous dural arteriovenous fistulas. Semin Intervent Radiol 1987;4:219–240.

30. Gelwan MJ, Choi IS, Berenstein A, Pile-Spellman JM, Kupersmith MJ. Dural arteriovenous malformations and papilledema. Neurosurgery 1988;22:1079–1084.

31. Halbach VV, Higashida RT, Hieshima GB, Reicher M, Norman D, Newton TH. Dural fistulas involving the cavernous sinus: results of treatment in 30 patients. Radiology 1987;163:437–442.

32. Kupersmith MJ, Berenstein A, Choi IS, Warren F, Flamm E. Management of nontraumatic vascular shunts involving the cavernous sinus. Ophthalmology 1988;95:121–130.

33. Kupersmith MJ, in collaboration with Berenstein A. Neurovascular neuro-ophthalmology. Heidelberg: Springer-Verlag, 1993.

34. DeKeizer RJW. Spontaneous carotico-cavernous fistulas: the importance of the typical limbal vascular loops for the diagnosis, the recognition of glaucoma and the uses of conservative therapy in this condition. Doc Ophthalmol 1979;46:403–412.

35. Grove AS. The dural shunt syndrome: pathophysiology and clinical course. Ophthalmology 1983;90:31–44.

36. Newton TH, Hoyt WF. Dural arteriovenous shunts in the region of the cavernous sinus. Neuroradiology 1970;1:71–81.

37. Hawke SHB, Mullie MA, Hoyt WF, Hallinan JM, Halmagyi CM. Painful ocular nerve palsy due to dural-cavernous sinus shunt. Arch Neurol 1989;46:1252–1255.

38. Halbach VV, Higashida RT, Hieshima GB, Cahan L, Rosenblum M. Treatment of dural arteriovenous malformations involving the superior sagittal sinus. AJNR 1988;9:337–343.

39. Halbach VV, Higashida RT, Hieshima GB, Wilson CW. Treatment of dural fistulas involving the deep cerebral venous system. AJNR 1989;10:393–399.

40. Barnwell SL, Halbach VV, Dowd CF, Higashida RT, Hieshima GB. Dural fistulas including the inferior petrosal sinus. AJNR 1990;11:511–517.

41. Halbach VV, Higashida RT, Hieshima GB, Wilson CW, Barnwell SL, Dowd CF. Dural arteriovenous fistulas supplied by ethmoidal arteries. Neurosurgery 1990;25:816–823.

42. Ito J, Imamura H, Kobayashi K, et al. Dural arteriovenous malformations of the base of the anterior cranial fossa. Neuroradiology 1983;24:149–154.

43. Kobayashi H, Hayashi N, Noguchi Y, Tsuji T, Handa Y, Caner HH. Dural arteriovenous malformations in the anterior cranial fossa. Surg Neurol 1988;30:396–401.

44. Halbach VV, Higashida RT, Hieshima GB, Mehringer CM, Hardin CW. Transvenous embolization of dural fistulas involving the transverse sigmoid sinuses. AJNR 1989;10:385–392.

45. Versari PP, D'Aliberti G, Talamonti G, Branca V, Boccardi E, Collise M. Progressive myelopathy caused by intracranial dural arteriovenous fistula: report of 2 cases and review of the literature. Neurosurgery 1993;33(5):914–919.

46. DeMarco JK, Dillon W, Halbach VV, Tsuruda JS. Dural arteriovenous fistulas: evaluation with MR imaging. Radiology 1990;175:193–199.

47. Endo S, Koshu K, Kodama N, Okada H. Spontaneous regression with posterior fossa dural arteriovenous malformations. Neurol Surg 1979;7:1001–1004.

48. Magidson MA, Weinberg DE. Spontaneous closure of a dural arteriovenous malformation. Surg Neurol 1976;6:107–110.

49. Vinuela F, Fox AJ, Debrun GM, Peerless SJ, Drake CG. Spontaneous carotid-cavernous fistulas: clinical, radiological, therapeutic considerations. Experience with 20 cases. J Neurosurg 1984;6:976–984.

50. Barnwell SL, Halbach VV, Higashida RT, Hieshima GB, Wilson CB. Complex dural arteriovenous fistulas: results of a new combined neurosurgical and interventional neuroradiology treatment in 16 patients. J Neurosurg 1989;7:352–358.

51. Halbach VV, Higashida RT, Hieshima GB, Hardin CW, Privam H. Transvenous embolization of dural fistulas involving the cavernous sinus. AJNR 1989;10:377–384.

52. Mullen S. Treatment of carotid cavernous fistulas by cavernous sinus occlusion. J Neurosurg 1979;50:131–144.

53. Takahashi A, Yoshimoto T, Kawakami K, Sugawara T, Suzuki J. Transvenous copper wire insertion for dural arteriovenous malformations of the cavernous sinus. J Neurosurg 1989;70:751–754.

54. Kupersmith MJ, Berenstein A, Flamm E, Ransohoff J. Neuro-ophthalmologic abnormalities and intravascular therapy of traumatic carotid cavernous fistulas. Ophthalmology 1986;93:906–912.

55. Graf CJ. Spontaneous carotid-cavernous fistula: Ehlers-Danlos syndrome and related condition. Arch Neurol 1965;13:662–672.

56. Kaufman HH, Lind TA, Mullen S. Spontaneous carotid-cavernous fistula with fibromuscular dysplasia. Acta Neurochir 1978;40:123–129.

57. Henderson JW, Schneider RC. The ocular findings in carotid cavernous fistula in a series of 17 cases. Am J Ophthalmol 1959;48:585–597.

58. Sanders MD, Hoyt WF. Hypoxic ocular sequelae of carotid-cavernous fistulae: study of the causes and failure before and after neurosurgical treatment in a series of 25 cases. Br J Ophthalmol 1969;53:82–97.

59. Maurer JJ, Mills M, German WJ. Triad of unilateral blindness, orbital fracture and massive epistaxis after head trauma. J Neurosurg 1961;45:837–840.

60. Debrun GM. Endovascular management of carotid cavernous fistulas. In: Valavanis A, ed. Interventional neuroradiology. Berlin: Springer-Verlag, 1993:23–34.

61. Turner DM, VanGilder JC, Mojthedi S, Dierson EW. Spontaneous intracerebral hematoma in carotid cavernous fistula. J Neurosurg 1983;59:680–686.

62. Debrun GM, Vinuela F, Fox AJ, Davis KR, Ahn HS. Indications for treatment and classification of 132 carotid-cavernous fistulas. Neurosurgery 1988;22:285–289.

63. Halbach VV, Hieshima GB, Higashida RT, Reicher M. Carotid cavernous fistula: indications for urgent treatment. AJNR 1987;8:627–633.

64. deSchweinitz GA, Holloway TB. Pulsating exophthalmos. Philadelphia: Saunders, 1908:11–120.

65. Palastine AG, Younge BR, Piepgras DG. Visual prognosis in carotid-cavernous fistulas. Arch Ophthalmol 1981;99:1600–1603.

66. Debrun G, Lacour P, Vinuela F. Treatment of 54 traumatic carotid-cavernous fistulas. J Neurosurg 1981;55:678–692.

67. Debrun GM, Nauta HJ, Miller NR, Drake CG, Heros RC, Ahn HS. Combining the detachable balloon technique and surgery in managing CCFs. Surg Neurol 1989;38:3–10.

68. Halbach VV, Higashida RT, Hieshima GB, Hardin CW, Yang BJ. Transvenous embolization of direct carotid cavernous fistulas. AJNR 1988;9:741–747.

69. Manelfe C, Berenstein A. Treatment of carotid cavernous fistulas by venous approach. J Neuroradiol 1980;7:13–21.

70. Moret J, Lasjaunias P. Vascular architecture of tympano-jugular glomus tumor. In: Vignaud J, Jardic C, Rosen L, eds. The ear. Paris: Masson, 1986:289–303.

71. Barrow DL, Fleischer AS, Hoffman JC. Complications of detachable balloon technique in the treatment of traumatic intracranial arteriovenous fistulas. J Neurosurg 1982;50:396–403.

72. Kendall B. Results of treatment of arteriovenous fistulas with the Debrun technique. AJNR 1983;4:405–408.

73. Halbach VV, Hieshima GB, Higashida RT, David CF. Endovascular therapy of head and neck tumors. In: Vinuela F, Halbach VV, Dion JE, eds. Interventional neuroradiology: endovascular therapy of the central nervous system. New York: Raven, 1992:17–28.

74. Manelfe C, Lasjaunias P, Ruscalleda J. Preoperative embolization of intracranial meningiomas. AJNR 1986;7:963–972.

75. Valavanis A. Embolization of intracranial and skull base tumors. In: Valavanis A, ed. Interventional neuroradiology. Berlin: Springer-Verlag, 1993:63–92.

76. Wakhloo AK, Juengling FD, Delthoven VV, Schumacher M, Hennig J, Schwechheimer K. Extended preoperative polyvinyl alcohol microembolization of intracranial meningiomas: assessment of two embolization techniques. AJNR 1993;14:571–582.

77. Valavanis A. Preoperative embolization of the head and neck: indications, patient selection, goals and precautions. AJNR 1986;7:943–952.

78. Suyama T, Tamaki N, Fujiwara K, et al. Peritumoral and intratumoral hemorrhage after gelatin sponge embolization of malignant meningioma: case report. Neurosurgery 1987;21:944–946.

VI

Interventional Radiology
of the Thorax

47

Transcatheter Bronchial Artery Embolization for Inflammation (Hemoptysis)

MATTHEW A. MAURO
PAUL F. JAQUES

Massive hemoptysis, defined as 300 to 600 ml per 24-hour period, carries a 50 to 85 percent mortality with conservative treatment and has traditionally been the principal indication for bronchial artery embolization. Asphyxiation and less commonly exsanguination are the usual causes of death.[1] Aggressive therapeutic maneuvers are required to manage these emergencies. Surgical resection of the bleeding source is the initial treatment of choice for those patients with isolated abnormalities and adequate pulmonary reserve. However, patients with chronic lung disease and limited pulmonary reserve are often considered unacceptable surgical risks, and this group may benefit from palliative bronchial artery embolization. In addition, there is some evidence that the surgical mortality rate may be lowered by preoperative bronchial artery embolization in those patients who are actively bleeding. It is well established that safe and rapid control of massive hemoptysis can often be obtained by therapeutic transcatheter embolization of the bronchial arteries.

More recently, moderate hemoptysis (greater than or equal to three episodes of 100 ml of blood per day within 1 week) and even mild hemoptysis (chronic or slowly increasing hemoptysis) are considered indications for transcatheter therapy.[2] Recurrent nonmassive hemoptysis is particularly common in patients with cystic fibrosis, where these recurrent bleeds are debilitating and preclude routine postural drainage of other lung regions. Bronchial artery embolization for mild or moderate bouts of hemoptysis has been shown to play a valuable role in the management of this group of patients.[2-4] The availability of lung transplantation has also stimulated a more aggressive approach to the management of mild to moderate hemoptysis in the cystic population.

Clinical Considerations

Severe hemoptysis most commonly presents in patients with a history of chronic inflammatory lung disease. Tuberculosis with associated aspergillosis remains the most common worldwide etiology.[5] In the United States, complicated pulmonary sarcoid, cystic fibrosis, and other types of bronchiectasis are the most common causes of hemoptysis that may benefit from transcatheter therapy. The chronicity of the disease is an important aspect in patient selection. It is in this clinical setting that bronchial artery hypertrophy occurs, facilitating transcatheter therapy. Without hypertrophy, bronchial artery embolization is less likely to be of benefit. In most cases, severe hemoptysis results from a systemic arterial source rather than the pulmonary circulation, and tends to be episodic. Initial management includes resuscitation, sedation, coagulation profile, chest x-ray, and early bronchoscopy. If embolotherapy is being considered, localization of the bleeding to a single lung or lobe is helpful because it will guide the angiographer to concentrate on the affected region. Bronchoscopy may localize the source of bleeding and guide the use of selective intrabronchial balloon tamponade if massive hemorrhage continues. Bronchoscopy has been shown to be of increased value when obtained early in patient management. Saumench et al. found the site of the hemorrhage in 91 percent of patients when bronchoscopy was performed early, compared to 50 percent of patients when bronchoscopy was performed later in the clinical course.[6] A review of previous and current chest radiographs and computed tomograms (if available) may also help in determining the probable site of bleeding. Patients often experience a gurgling sensation and may be able to locate the source of bleeding themselves. If surgical treatment has been permanently or temporarily excluded, patients should undergo emergent angiography, preferably during a quiescent phase to maximize the chances of a technically successful procedure.

Patients with cystic fibrosis frequently present with a recurrent crescendo type of bleeding rather than a singular massive bleed and are more likely to have recurrent bleeds even after successful transcatheter therapy.[2-4] There is a rich anastomosis between many of the mediastinal structures and the bronchial arterial circulation. Patients who have undergone previous bronchial artery embolization procedures should not be excluded from subsequent attempts at palliative embolization. Recurrent hemorrhages are secondary to recanalization of embolized vessels or hypertrophy of collateral vessels from other systemic supplies.[7]

Significant bleeding of pulmonary arterial origin is rare and secondary to erosive pseudoaneurysms in association with cavitary aspergillosis, cavitary tuberculosis, or pyogenic abscesses. A pulmonary arterial source should be considered in addition to the more common systemic supply in settings of destructive lung disease. Suggestive chest x-ray findings include a necrotic cavity, a cavity closely related to a central pulmonary artery, or replacement of a cavity with a rapidly growing nodule or mass.[8] A pulmonary arterial source should also be considered when bleeding continues after technically successful bronchial artery and nonbronchial systemic arterial embolization.

Anatomy

Bronchial arteries most commonly arise from the thoracic aorta at the T3 to T8 level and supply the trachea, bronchi, vagus nerve, posterior mediastinum, and esophagus. A number of anatomic variations in bronchial artery origin have been described. Cauldwell, in 1948, described four common variations: type 1—two left and single right bronchial arteries (41 percent); type 2—single bronchial arteries bilaterally (21 percent); type 3—two left and two right bronchial arteries arising separately or in various combinations (21 percent); and type 4—single left and two right bronchial arteries (10 percent).[9] In 1985, Uflacker and colleagues reported the four most frequent bronchial artery variations as single right intercostobronchial trunk with single left artery (31 percent), single right intercostobronchial trunk and right and left bronchial arteries sharing a common trunk (25 percent), single right intercostobronchial trunk and two left bronchial arteries (13 percent), and single right intercostobron-

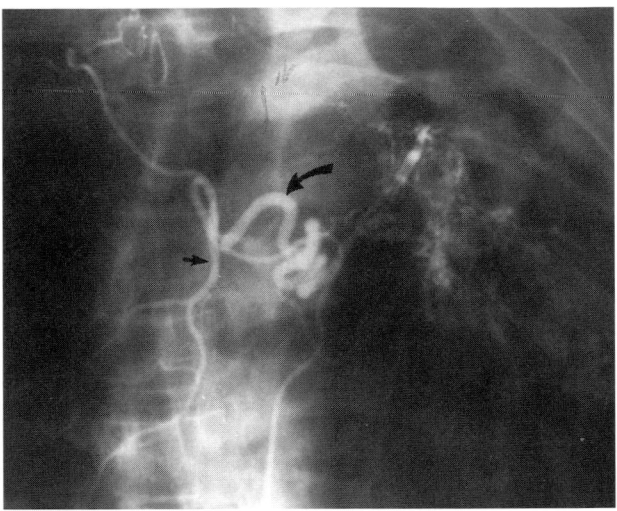

Figure 47-1. Common bronchial trunk. Left and right bronchial arteries arise from a common trunk. The right bronchial artery (*straight arrow*) appears normal, whereas the left bronchial artery (*curved arrow*) is enlarged and tortuous. Note the superior intercostal artery arising from the right bronchial artery. (From Mauro MA, Jaques PF, Morris S. Bronchial artery embolization for control of hemoptysis. Sem Intervent Radiol 1992;9(1):46. Used with permission.)

chial trunk with separate bronchial arteries bilaterally (11 percent) (Figs. 47-1 through 47-3). In this series, 43 percent of patients had common bronchial trunks.[10] No left intercostobronchial trunks were identified, whereas the right bronchial arteries frequently shared origins with superior intercostal arteries. Nearly 80 percent of all bronchial arteries arise at the T5 to T6 level. Right bronchial or intercostobronchial artery trunks typically arise from the right lateral or anterolateral surface of the descending thoracic aorta. The left bronchial arteries usually arise from the more anterior surface of the aorta or the concavity of the arch. As many as 20 percent of bronchial arteries have anomalous origins from sites other than the aorta, and approximately 10 percent originate from the concave or convex surfaces of the aortic arch. Other aberrant origins of the bronchial arteries include the subclavian, thyrocervical, internal mammary, innominate, pericardiophrenic, superior intercostal, abdominal aorta, and inferior phrenic arteries.[11-13]

Cohen et al. reported a higher prevalence of aberrant origins of bronchial arteries (35 percent) among 20 patients with cystic fibrosis. In addition, they found a tenfold higher incidence of radicular supply from the bronchial arteries.[3] The authors suggest that lifelong bronchial wall inflammation causes enlargement of the existing extensive and anastomotic network that interconnects the bronchial circulation with mediastinal, head, neck, and spinal arteries.

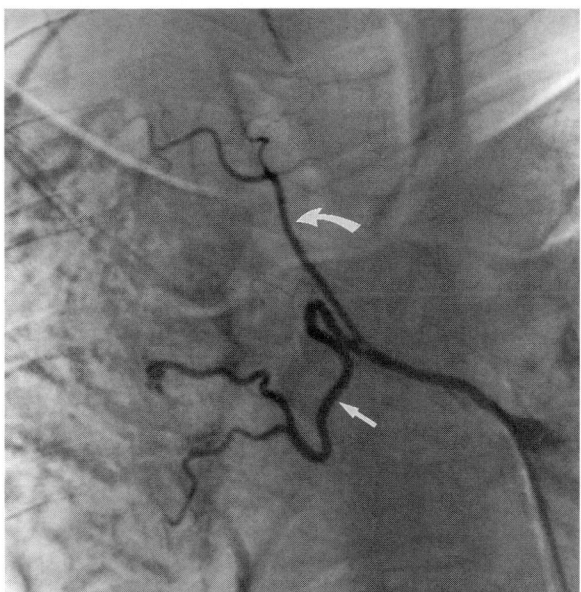

A

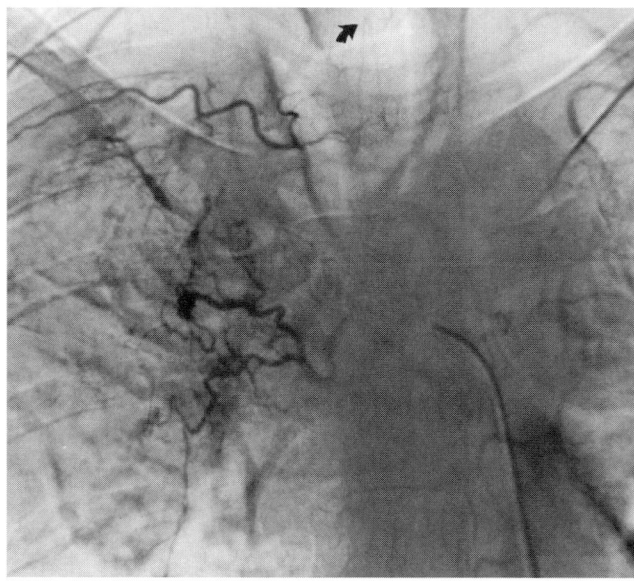

B

Figure 47-2. Right intercostal-bronchial trunk. (A) The right bronchial artery (*straight arrow*) and superior intercostal artery (*curved arrow*) arise from a common trunk. (B) Film later in the run shows characteristic hairpin loop (*arrow*) of spinal artery branch originating from the superior intercostal artery. Embolization of the right bronchial artery was performed by placing a catheter distal to the origin of the intercostal artery. (From Mauro MA, Jaques PF, Morris S. Bronchial artery embolization for control of hemoptysis. Sem Intervent Radiol 1992;9(1):47. Used with permission.)

The bronchial arteries extend along the bronchi to the level of the respiratory bronchiole, where they anastomose with the pulmonary circulation. Branches supply the vasa vasorum of the pulmonary vasculature as well as the diaphragmatic and mediastinal portions of the visceral pleural, the middle third of the esophagus, and lymph nodes. Most of the venous return occurs through the pulmonary veins by way of bronchial pulmonary anastomoses.[14] There is an extensive potential anastomotic network between the bronchial

Figure 47-3. Two right bronchial arteries. (A) Right upper bronchial arteriogram reveals hypervascularity, enlargement, and tortuosity. (B) Right lower bronchial arteriogram shows similar hypervascularity and, in addition, an area of contrast extravasation (*arrow*). Both arteries were successfully embolized. (From Mauro MA, Jaques PF, Morris S. Bronchial artery embolization for control of hemoptysis. 1992;9(1):48. Used with permission.)

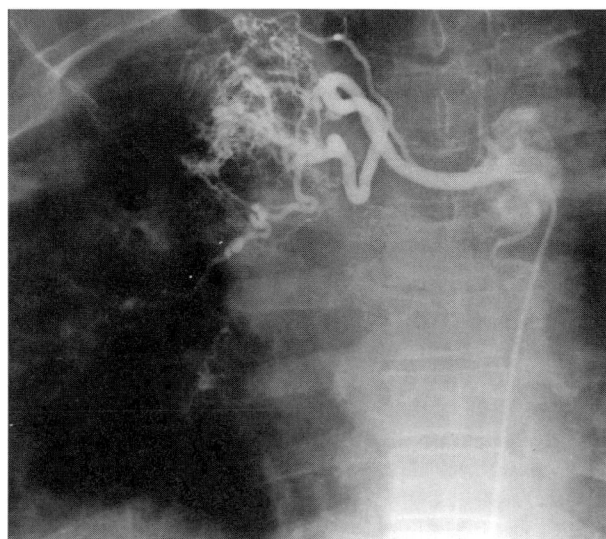

A

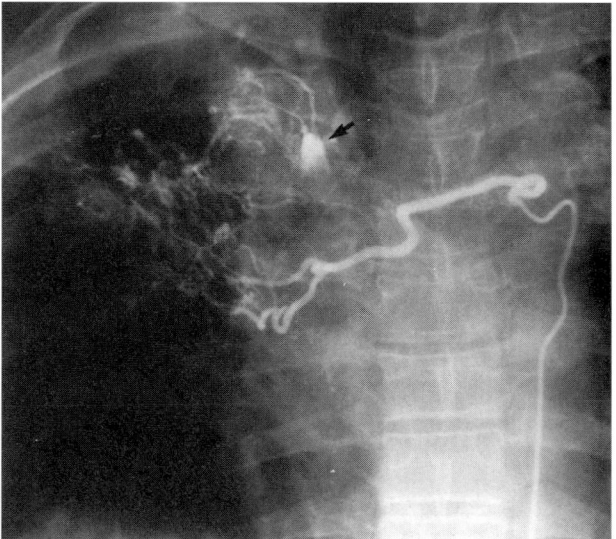

B

arteries and other structures in the mediastinum, spine, head, and neck. These bronchial pulmonary arterial anastomoses may become prominent in the abnormal lung, reflecting either chronic inflammation or pulmonary hypertension.[15,16] Transpleural systemic collaterals from intercostal, internal mammary, phrenic, and thyrocervical arteries, as well as from branches of the axillary artery, provide pulmonary bronchial supply in these situations and may be responsible for hemoptysis.[16] Tanaka et al. reviewed bronchial artery drainage in patients undergoing bronchial artery embolization or chemoinfusion. They discovered four types of venous drainage: type 1—direct drainage into the pulmonary vein (42 percent); type 2—direct drainage into the pulmonary artery (19 percent); type 3—direct drainage into the pulmonary artery with retrograde flow (19 percent); and type 4—direct drainage into the bronchial vein (4.8 percent).[14]

When one is performing bronchial artery arteriography and embolization, careful consideration must be given to the arterial supply to the spinal cord. The anterior spinal artery supplies the anterior portion of the cord and runs in the ventral median sulcus. The anterior spinal artery originates from branches of the intracranial segments of the vertebral arteries and receives supply from anterior radiculomedullary branches of intercostal and lumbar arteries along its length.[17] As many as six to eight contributing branches to the anterior spinal artery may exist, and each has a characteristic course resembling a hairpin loop. The largest anterior medullary branch (the artery of Adamkiewicz) has a variable origin from the T5 to L5 level but is most commonly found at the T8 to L1 level. In approximately 5 percent of the population, a right intercostobronchial artery contributes to or arises with the artery of Adamkiewicz. The right superior intercostal artery and right bronchial artery may share a common trunk and supply a branch to the anterior spinal artery (see Figure 47-2). Left bronchial arteries rarely supply the anterior spinal artery. The posterior portion of the cord is supplied by a pair of posterior spinal arteries that course along the posterolateral surface of the spinal cord. These vessels are fed by posterior radicular arteries arising from intercostal and lumbar arteries and are much shorter and smaller than the anterior radiculomedullary arteries.

Technique

Angiography

A brief neurologic examination should be performed to establish a baseline before the angiographic and embolization procedure. This will often be repeated throughout the course of the procedure to monitor the patient's neurologic status, particularly in relation to sensory and strength changes of the lower extremities. Several authors have recommended the use of somatosensory evoked potentials to monitor ischemic spinal cord changes during the embolization procedure.[18] This is cumbersome and far from routine and in general is not necessary.

A descending thoracic aortogram can be initially performed before selective catheterization to provide a road map. If this is the first episode of hemoptysis, the involved bronchial arteries are often enlarged and catheterization is usually straightforward. Therefore, routine thoracic aortography may not be required and direct subselective catheterization of the bronchial arteries may be initially performed. If, however, successful catheterization of the bronchial arteries is not promptly achieved, the selective catheter can be easily replaced with a pigtail catheter to perform descending thoracic aortography.

Arterial access is most commonly achieved via common femoral artery puncture through which a sheath is inserted. An axillary or high brachial artery approach is occasionally necessary to define and embolize vessels arising from subclavian artery branches. A 6 or 7 French vascular sheath connected to an infusion system is routinely used at the authors' institution. If the patient is obese or if the iliac vessels are markedly tortuous, a long sheath is used that extends into the aorta. A variety of selected catheter curves can be used for subselective catheterization. The authors usually begin with a reverse-curve catheter: a Mikaelsson, Simmons 1, or shepherd's hook. However, when there is a low aortic arch or if the bronchial artery originates from the arch, a reverse-curve catheter may fail to adequately probe the aortic wall. The apex of the reverse-curve catheter will lie partially within the transverse arch, tilting the catheter and making catheterization of more proximately located bronchial arteries impossible. In these circumstances, forward-looking catheters, such as the cobra, H1H, or RC shapes, can be used successfully. In general, 5.0 or 5.5 French catheters are initially used, reserving the larger 6.5 to 7.0 French catheters for a particularly tortuous vascular system where increased steerability is required.

The bronchial artery search is begun at the T5 to T6 level.[9] The air-filled left main stem bronchus serves as a convenient fluoroscopic landmark for this general location of bronchial artery origin. The catheter tip is initially directed laterally to anterolaterally when one is searching for the right bronchial artery or intercostobronchial trunk. A left lateral to anterolateral direction is used for left bronchial artery catheterization. Catheter occlusion of a bronchial artery, particularly a right intercostobronchial trunk, should be avoided because this may result in spinal cord ischemia if spinal artery branches are present.

Before embolization, a selective arteriogram must be performed. Bronchial arteries have characteristic branches that follow the course of the main stem bronchi toward the hila and can be easily differentiated from intercostal arteries, which have an initial cephalic course and then travel laterally along the undersurface of a rib (see Fig. 47-2). Coughing may be elicited during a bronchial artery injection, whereas a pure intercostal artery injection may be painful but will not initiate coughing. Nonionic contrast media should be used for all injections. The coughing response is less severe, and the risk of transverse myelitis may be lower.

Standard cut-film techniques or digital subtraction arteriography can be used when performing subselective bronchial artery injections. The injection volumes and rates must be sufficient to identify any spinal artery branches that may exist. The spinal artery can be identified by its characteristic cephalic course with a hairpin bend in the midline within the spinal canal (see Fig. 47-2B). When conventional filming is used, subtractions may be required for this identification. If there is some doubt concerning a midline branch on an anteroposterior film, an oblique film should be obtained to identify whether this branch does indeed enter the spinal canal. Tracheal and esophageal branches also originate from the bronchial artery and may appear midline on anteroposterior films but do not feature the hairpin loop. In cases of chronic inflammation, the bronchial arteries are hypertrophied and tortuous (see Figs. 47-1 and 47-2). Other signs include hypervascularity, systemic-to-pulmonary artery or venous shunting, and bronchial artery aneurysms. Frank contrast extravasation into a bronchus at angiography is rare (see Fig. 47-3).[19-24] When abnormal bronchial arteries are not identified, arch aortography and selective subclavian arteriography must be performed to search for anomalous bronchial arteries, nonbronchial systemic arterial supply, or both.[17,25-27] The search for a nonbronchial systemic supply is particularly urgent in patients with recurrent bleeding after previous bronchial artery embolization, particularly if proximal coil occlusion has been performed. Vessels responsible for recurrent bleeding might include a bronchial artery not previously embolized (aberrant or nonaberrant), a recanalized bronchial artery, or nonbronchial systemic collaterals (Figs. 47-4 and 47-5). If lower-lobe disease is present, an abdominal aortogram and examination of the inferior phrenic arteries should also be performed. If no systemic (bronchial or nonbronchial) arterial supply is identified, selective pulmonary arteriography should be performed in an attempt to identify a pulmonary arterial source such as a pseudoaneurysm or arteriovenous fistula.[8,19,23,28-31]

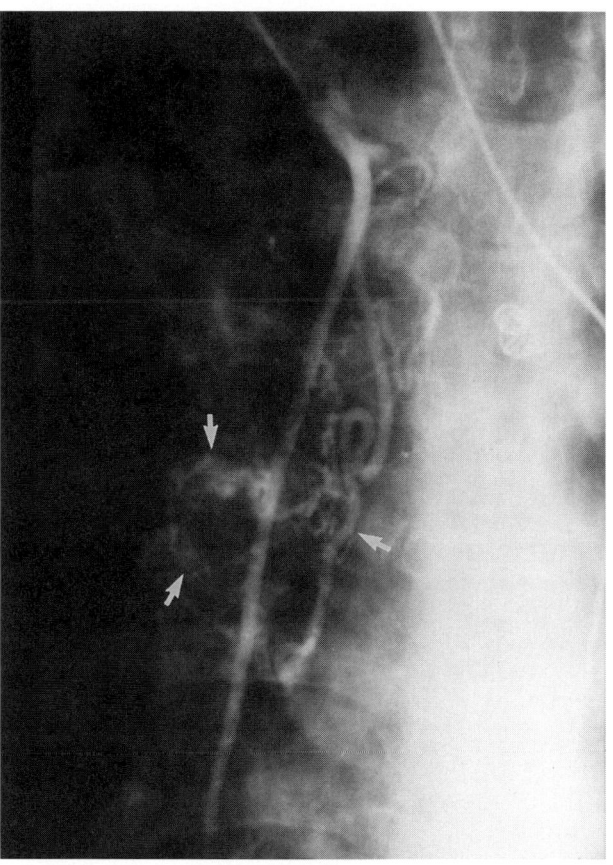

A

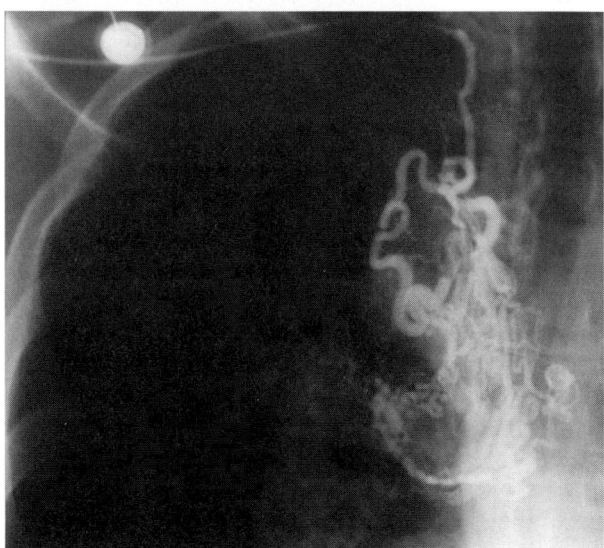

B

Figure 47-4. Nonbronchial systemic collaterals in a patient with recurrent hemoptysis. (A) Right internal mammary arteriogram shows hypervascularity (*arrows*) in right hilum. (B) Superselective injection of thyrocervical trunk branch shows massive collateral supply in a patient who had undergone previous bronchial artery embolization. (From Mauro MA, Jaques PF, Morris S. Bronchial artery embolization for control of hemoptysis. 1992;9(1):48. Used with permission.)

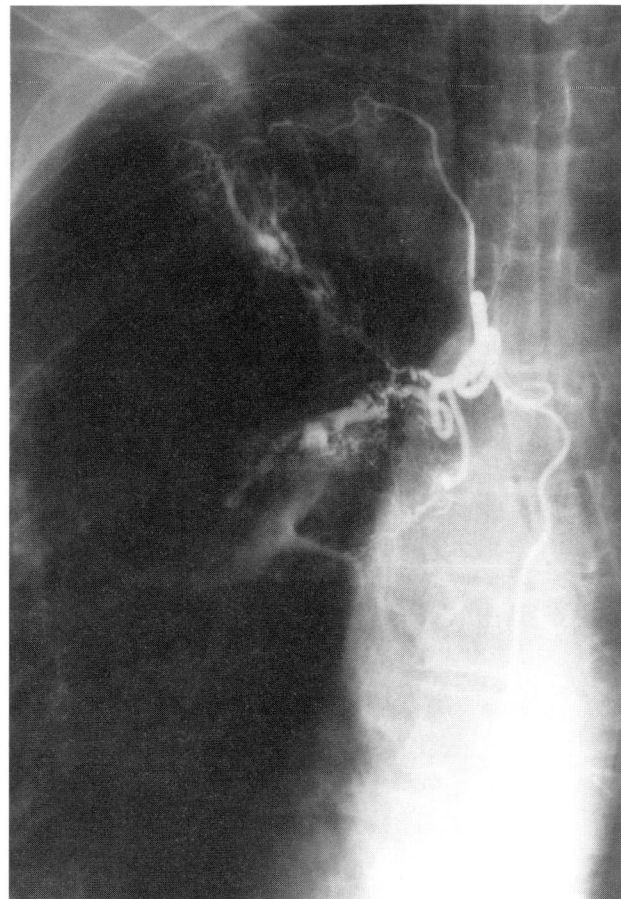

A

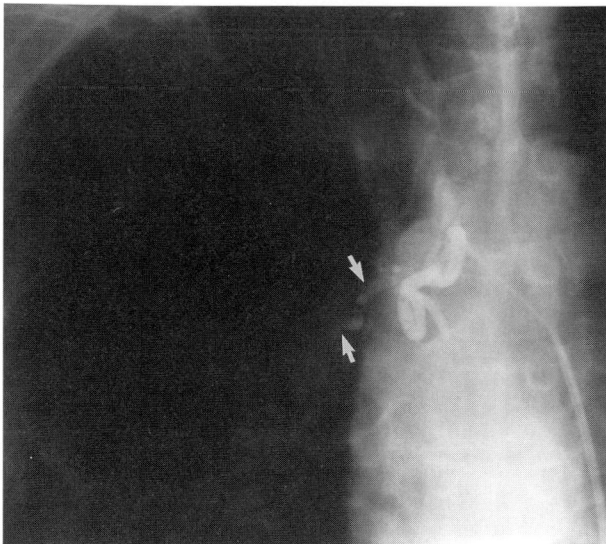

B

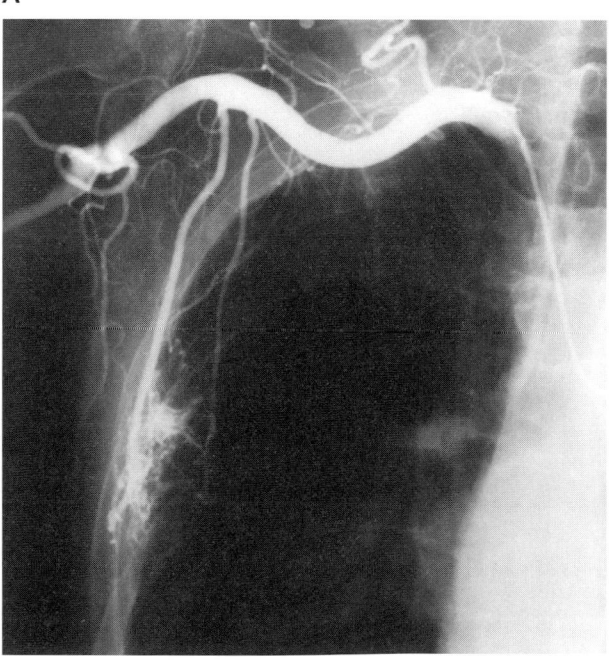

C

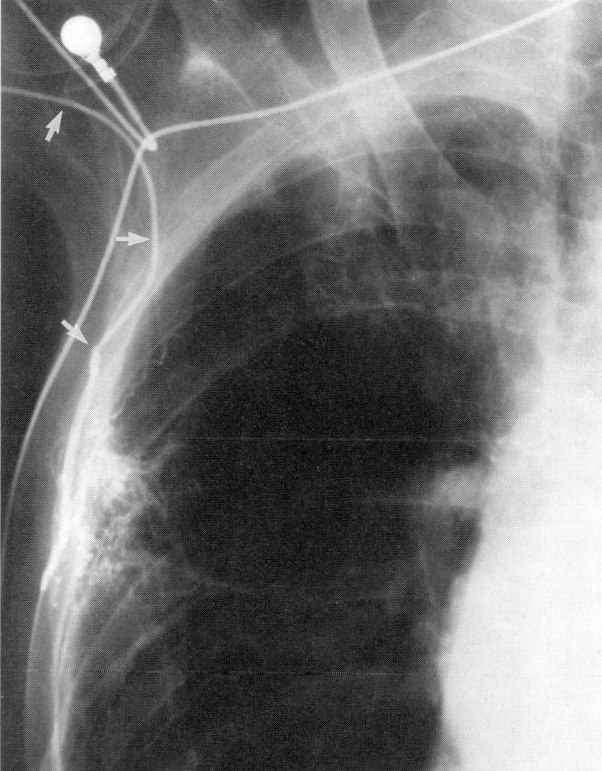

D

Figure 47-5. Recurrent hemoptysis in a patient with pleural disease. (A) Right bronchial arteriogram shows hypervascularity and tortuosity. (B) Successful embolization with a Gelfoam slurry mixture (*arrows*). Note the pleural disease along the lateral chest wall. (C) Subclavian arteriogram 2 years later shows hypervascularity along the lateral chest wall. (D) Selective catheterization of subscapular artery via the brachial approach (*arrows*) for embolization. (From Mauro MA, Jaques PF, Morris S. Bronchial artery embolization for control of hemoptysis. Sem Intervent Radiol 1992;9(1):50. Used with permission.)

Embolization

The goal of the embolization procedure varies, depending on whether the bleeding site has been located with some degree of reliability and whether there have been previous embolization procedures. If the site of hemorrhage is known, attention can be confined to embolization of bronchial arteries and collaterals supplying that area. Otherwise bronchial artery embolization of both lungs must be attempted. In the presence of previous bronchial artery embolization, collateral pathways will require special attention, although one should remember that principal bronchial arteries embolized with Gelfoam and even coils may recanalize.

When possible, any abnormal bronchial artery supplying the site(s) of hemorrhage should be embolized. The dominant feeding vessels should be embolized in all cases. It is important to realize that not all abnormally appearing vessels need to be embolized to obtain a clinically beneficial therapeutic response. Recurrent hemorrhage at a future date, however, may be more likely to occur and occur earlier if nondominant vessels are not treated. Embolization of a bronchial artery with a documented spinal artery contribution is controversial and depends on operator experience and the risk-benefit ratio of bronchial artery embolization (i.e., the clinical status of the patient) (see Fig. 47-2). Boushy et al. performed intraarterial embolization in dogs and found hind limb paralysis with small (29- to 100-μm) microspheres and only transient weakness when larger particles (200 μm) were used.[32] This suggests that particles greater than 200 to 250 μm are too large to enter the spinal feeders and therefore can be used for embolization.[3,5,10] Clearly a catheter position distal to the spinal artery origin is preferential and is often achievable with modern coaxial systems. Occasionally, a spinal artery branch will only be identified after partial distal embolization when the resistance of that vascular bed is elevated and smaller proximal branches are better opacified.[3] Some authors have advised the use of an intraarterial barbiturate as a provocative test in searching for an occult spinal artery contribution before bronchial artery embolization.[33,34] A short-acting barbiturate, amobarbital, temporarily produces the symptoms of spinal cord ischemia when injected into a vascular bed with arterial supply to the spinal cord. Lidocaine solutions can also be used in a similar fashion. After hand injections of either of these substances, a repeat physical examination evaluating lower extremity strength is performed. When no neurologic changes are identified, one can be more comfortable that there are no significant arterial contributions to the spinal cord. Transverse myelitis associated with this procedure has more commonly been associated with the use of ionic contrast media.[35,36] Nonionic contrast agents should be routinely used.

Transcatheter embolization requires a stable catheter position. When reverse-curve catheters are used, the tip can often be advanced deeper into the vessel by simply withdrawing the catheter at the groin. Because particulate materials used for embolization require brisk forward flow of blood to be propelled distally into the vascular bed, flow occlusion by catheter wedging must be avoided.

Standard catheterization for embolization is performed with 5.0 to 5.5 French tapered catheters. When a stable catheter position cannot be obtained with these catheters, coaxial catheterization can be performed. Several coaxial systems are commercially available. An inexpensive system involves the use of a 3 French Teflon catheter (T3S, Cook, Inc.) that is tapered to 0.025-inch diameter and can be placed within a tapered guiding catheter having a 0.038-inch lumen. This catheter is available with a radiopaque tip to aid in visualization but is rather stiff and difficult to advance around acute angles. The Cragg injectable wire (Medi-Tech) is also compatible with a 0.038-inch tapered diagnostic catheter and is available in a fixed or removable hub configuration. This injectable wire is designed to be used with a 0.025-inch Terumo Glidewire. An open-end guidewire (0.035 or 0.038 inch) can also be used for distal embolization (Fig. 47-6). The Tracker catheter (Target Therapeutics) has become the authors' standard coaxial system. The Tracker-18 catheter has a very flexible 2.2 French tip with a distal radiopaque marker and a 3 French proximal shaft. It can be conveniently used through any tip or diagnostic catheter that has a 0.035- to 0.038-inch tapered tip. The Tracker-18 catheter is used with a 0.014- to 0.016-inch platinum-tipped steerable or gold-tipped glidewire. Although small, this device will permit embolization with particulates (Gelfoam, polyvinyl alcohol), slurry, glue, and even coils (Target, Cook-Hilal).[3,37] A high-flow infusion tracker is available that has a slightly larger internal diameter and will allow larger particulates.

Distal embolization should be performed whenever possible. If permanent proximal occlusion alone is performed, distal collaterals will invariably develop, and future access to the main bronchial artery may be lost. The most commonly used embolic materials for bronchial artery embolization include Gelfoam and polyvinyl alcohol (PVA) particles.[3,4,7,20,22,24] Liquids such as ethanol or fine particles (Gelfoam powder) should be avoided because they produce very distal embolization with occlusion of the capillary bed, leading to potential tissue infarction. Although cyanoacrylate has been used successfully, it is not commercially available and requires significant operator experience.[38]

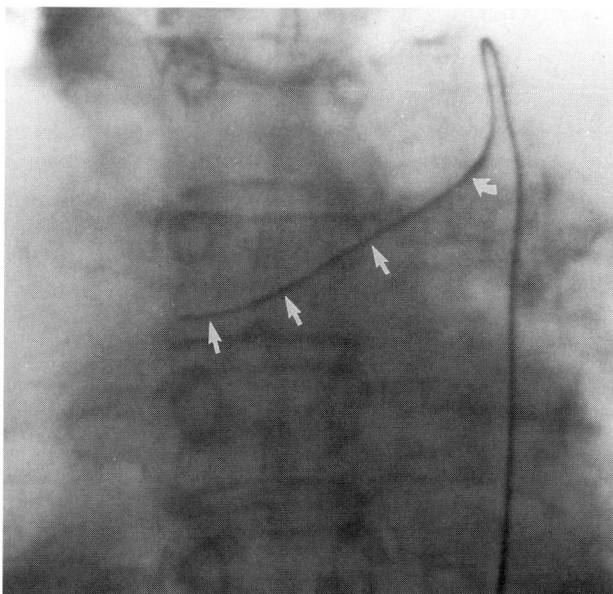

Figure 47-6. Coaxial embolization. Open-end guidewire (*straight arrows*) is placed through tip (*curved arrow*) of Mikaelsson catheter. Embolization was achieved with PVA particles.

Gelfoam (gelatin sponge) is the most commonly used material. It is a readily available, slowly resorbable material that can be used as individual pledgets, torpedoes, or part of a slurry. For initial distal occlusion, 0.5- to 2.0-mm cubes can be used followed by 3- to 4-mm pledgets or torpedoes for more proximal occlusion. Gelfoam pledgets are mixed with dilute contrast within a 1- or 3-ml syringe. Since the Gelfoam pledgets float within the contrast saline solution, the tip of the syringe should be pointed upward. A theoretical disadvantage of Gelfoam particles is that their resorption may lead to more rapid recanalization and recurrent bleeding.[39] A Gelfoam slurry mixture composed of Gelfoam shavings, dextrose 50, Pantopaque, and epsilon aminocaproic acid may also be used and will produce a more lasting occlusion (see Fig. 47-5).[40] This mixture is instilled in small (0.25- to 0.50-ml) amounts using a 3- or 1-ml syringe with a standard or coaxial catheter, respectively.

Polyvinyl alcohol (PVA) is the other commonly used particulate embolic material that is permanent in nature and available in several particle sizes. Particles greater than 250 μm should be used to avoid tissue ischemia or neurologic damage. PVA is available in various packaged sizes, depending on the manufacturer. Particles in the 300- to 500-μm range and 500- to 700-μm range are compatible with coaxial systems and are used routinely in the authors' practice. With 5 French or larger catheters, a 3- or 5-ml syringe is used for particle instillation, whereas a 1-ml syringe is

preferable when using coaxial catheters or injectable wires. After the particle size is selected, the contents of the bottle are placed in a 20-ml syringe with the plunger removed. After the plunger is replaced, a solution of diluted contrast (50:50 nonionic contrast with saline) is placed into the 20-ml syringe with the PVA particles. One degasses the solution by removing the air in the syringe, placing a finger over the top, withdrawing the plunger, and shaking vigorously. After this maneuver, the solution is degassed and particles are diffusely distributed within the 20-ml syringe, which serves as the particle reservoir. This is connected via flexible tubing to a three-way stopcock connected to the catheter and injection syringe. Before instillation, the particles are remixed with multiple in-and-out aspirations between the injection syringe and the 20-ml reservoir syringe. Because of the contrast solution, the embolization procedure can be visually monitored. Whenever there is slowing of the contrast/PVA column, the catheter should be immediately cleared of residual particulate matter with a saline injection and a formal contrast injection performed. This delivery system allows for quick, accurate, and safe delivery of PVA particles. When forward flow is markedly reduced, further embolization should be terminated. After distal embolization with small PVA particles, some authors advocate the use of Gelfoam cubes or torpedoes for more proximal embolization. These Gelfoam particles should be placed one at a time until flow all but ceases. When there is a major bronchial-artery-to-pulmonary-vein shunt, larger particulate particles are used initially to avoid systemic embolization.

Enormous bronchial arteries with high flow and large systemic-to-pulmonary shunts are sometimes encountered in cystic fibrosis and may require the use of coil embolization for safe and adequate occlusion (Fig. 47-7).[32,41] Coils should be 15 to 25 percent larger than the vessel diameter to avoid retrograde dislodgment, and the catheter should be well seated.[42] This type of proximal coil occlusion should not be a routine practice and should be used only when other methods fail or are contraindicated, or when the patient's clinical condition demands very rapid control.

Complications

Spinal cord infarction with transverse myelitis is the most feared complication of bronchial artery embolization, but the literature suggests that this is more a potential than a real problem.[11] Transverse myelitis has been reported after diagnostic bronchial arteriography with the use of ionic hyperosmolar contrast agents.[35,36] This complication should be significantly reduced by

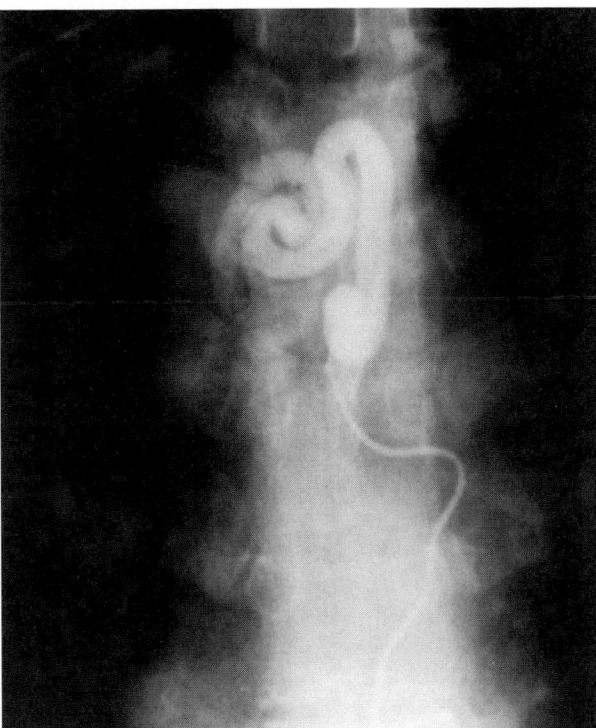

Figure 47-7. Enormous bronchial artery in a patient with cystic fibrosis with first episode of hemoptysis. Occlusion required coils in addition to PVA particles. (From Mauro MA, Jaques PF, Morris S. Bronchial artery embolization for control of hemoptysis. Sem Intervent Radiol 1992;9(1):50. Used with permission.)

the use of nonionic contrast and the avoidance of catheter occlusions. The single reported case of paralysis after embolization for severe hemoptysis actually involved the left seventh intercostal artery and not a bronchial artery.[43] Nevertheless, it is mandatory to perform preembolization angiography to identify any dominant radicular branch to the anterior spinal artery. Such a branch will usually involve a common intercostal bronchial artery anatomic variant.

Two cases of frank bronchial infarction after bronchial artery embolization have been reported, one of which was fatal.[19,44] Liquid sclerosing agents (10 percent sodium chloride in one, ethanol in the other) were used in each case because a stable catheter position could not be obtained for a particulate embolization. The current coaxial catheter systems should overcome this difficulty, and liquid agents should be avoided. Bronchoesophageal fistulas have been reported when very small particulate agents were used and there was concomitant bronchial and esophageal ischemia.[45,46] Chest pain and dysphagia commonly occur approximately 2 to 7 days after embolization procedures and are self-limiting. These are thought to occur secondary to the supply of the posterior mediastinum and esophagus by the bronchial arteries.

Results

Bronchial artery embolization has been shown to be a very effective technique for the immediate control of hemoptysis of inflammatory origin. Rabkin et al. reported the results of 306 bronchial artery embolizations in which there was immediate control of hemoptysis in 91 percent of patients.[19] Uflacker, Rémy, and Hayakawa have published series reporting immediate control of hemoptysis in 77, 84, and 86 percent of patients, respectively.[5,7,10] In a review of 63 patients, Hayakawa reported a complete remission of bleeding in 50 percent, partial remission in 22 percent, and recurrent hemoptysis in 28 percent of patients. The recurrent bleeding rate increased to 46 percent after repeat embolization.[7] In general, the long-term control rate of hemoptysis is approximately 70 to 80 percent and is largely determined by the natural progression of the underlying disease. Repeat embolization may be required, particularly for those younger patients with longer prognoses. Recurrent bleeding is also more commonly seen in patients with advanced pleural disease and is more difficult to control because of multiple nonbronchial systemic collateral pathways. Tamura et al. demonstrated long-term hemostasis in 70 percent of patients without documented pleural thickening, whereas this was achieved in only 29 percent of patients with significant pleural thickening.[47] Therefore, pleural abnormalities negatively affect the long-term effectiveness of bronchial artery embolization (see Fig. 47-5).

Bronchial artery embolization may be of particular benefit in patients with cystic fibrosis. Fellows et al. reported immediate control in 12 of 13 patients, and Cohen et al. reported immediate control in 19 of 20 patients with cystic fibrosis.[3,4] Palliation is extremely important to these young patients as lung transplantation programs become more prevalent.

Conclusion

Bronchial artery embolization is a well-established, worthwhile, palliative control of severe as well as recurrent mild hemoptysis secondary to inflammatory disease. Indications for embolization have expanded to include not only severe and massive bouts of hemoptysis but also mild to chronic and intermittent episodes of hemoptysis as well. The procedure should be performed promptly when indicated, and, when good embolization techniques are used, complications are infrequent.

References

1. Wholey MH, Chamorro HA, Rao G, et al. Bronchial artery embolization for massive hemoptysis. JAMA 1976;236:2501–2504.
2. Tonkin ILD, Hanissian AS, Boulden TF, et al. Bronchial arteriography and embolotherapy for hemoptysis in patients with cystic fibrosis. Cardiovasc Intervent Radiol 1991;14:241–246.
3. Cohen AM, Doershuk CF, Stern RC. Bronchial artery embolization to control hemoptysis in cystic fibrosis. Radiology 1990;175:401–405.
4. Fellows KE, Khaw KT, Schuster S, et al. Bronchial artery embolization in cystic fibrosis: technique and long-term results. J Pediatr 1979;95:959–963.
5. Rémy J, Arnaud A, Fardou H, et al. Treatment of hemoptysis by embolization of bronchial arteries. Radiology 1977;122:33–37.
6. Saumench J, Excarrabill J, Padró L, et al. Value of fiberoptic bronchoscopy and angiography for diagnosis of the bleeding site in hemoptysis. Ann Thorac Surg 1989;48:272–274.
7. Hayakawa K, Tanaka F, Torizuka T, et al. Bronchial artery embolization for hemoptysis: immediate and long-term results. Cardiovasc Intervent Radiol 1992;15:154–159.
8. Rémy J, Lemaitre L, Lafitte JJ, et al. Massive hemoptysis of pulmonary arterial origin: diagnosis and treatment. AJR 1984;143:963–969.
9. Cauldwell EW, Siekert RG, Lininger RE, et al. The bronchial arteries: an anatomic study of 150 human cadavers. Surg Gynecol Obstet 1948;86:395–412.
10. Uflacker R, Kaemmerer A, Picon PD, et al. Bronchial artery embolization in the management of hemoptysis: technical aspects and long-term results. Radiology 1985;157:637–644.
11. Tan RT, McGahan JP, Link DP, et al. Bronchial artery embolisation in management of haemoptysis. J Intervent Radiol 1991;6:67–76.
12. McPherson S, Routh WD, Nath H, et al. Anomalous origin of bronchial arteries: potential pitfall of embolotherapy for hemoptysis. J Vasc Intervent Radiol 1990;1:86–88.
13. Cohen AM, Antoun BW, Stern RC. Left thyrocervical trunk bronchial artery supplying right lung: source of recurrent hemoptysis in cystic fibrosis. AJR 1992;158:1131–1133.
14. Tanaka F, Hayakawa K, Satoh Y, et al. Evaluating bronchial drainage pathways in patients with lung disease using digital subtraction angiography. Invest Radiol 1993;28:434–438.
15. Roberts AC. Bronchial artery embolization therapy. J Thorac Imaging 1990;5:60–72.
16. Keller FS, Rösch J, Loflin TG, et al. Nonbronchial systemic collateral arteries: significance in percutaneous embolotherapy for hemoptysis. Radiology 1987;164:687-692.
17. Stoll JF, Bettmann MA. Bronchial artery embolization to control hemoptysis: a review. Cardiovasc Intervent Radiol 1988;11:263–269.
18. Schrodt JF, Becker GJ, Scott JA, et al. Bronchial artery embolization: monitoring with somatosensory evoked potentials. Radiology 1987;164:135–139.
19. Rabkin JE, Astafjev V, Gothman LN, et al. Transcatheter embolization in the management of pulmonary hemorrhage. Radiology 1987;163:361–365.
20. Bookstein JJ, Moser KM, Kalafer ME, et al. The role of bronchial arteriography and therapeutic embolization in hemoptysis. Chest 1977;72:658–661.
21. Osada H, Kawada T, Ashida H, et al. Bronchial artery aneurysm. Ann Thorac Surg 1986;41:440–442.
22. Harley JD, Killien FC, Peck AG. Massive hemoptysis controlled by transcatheter embolization of the bronchial arteries. AJR 1977;128:302–304.
23. Muthuswamy PP, Akbik F, Franklin C, et al. Management of major or massive hemoptysis in active pulmonary tuberculosis by bronchial arterial embolization. Chest 1987;92:77–82.
24. Vujic I, Pyle R, Hungerford GD, et al. Angiography and therapeutic blockade in the control of hemoptysis. Radiology 1982;143:19–23.
25. Jardin M, Rémy J. Control of hemoptysis: systemic angiography and anastomoses of the internal mammary artery. Radiology 1988;168:377–383.
26. Parke WW, Michels NA. The nonbronchial systemic arteries of the lung. J Thorac Cardiovasc Surg 1965;49:694–707.
27. Moore LB, McWey RE, Vujic I. Massive hemoptysis: control by embolization of the thyrocervical trunk. Radiology 1986;161:173–174.
28. Ferris EF. Pulmonary hemorrhage: vascular evaluation and interventional therapy. Chest 1981;80:710–714.
29. Rémy J, Smith M, Lemaitre L, et al. Treatment of massive hemoptysis by occlusion of a Rasmussen aneurysm. AJR 1980;135:605–606.
30. Renie WA, Rodeheffer RJ, Mitchell S, et al. Balloon embolization of a mycotic pulmonary artery aneurysm. Am Rev Respir Dis 1982;126:1107–1110.
31. Davidoff AB, Udoff EJ, Schonfeld SA. Intraaneurysmal embolization of a pulmonary artery aneurysm for control of hemoptysis. AJR 1984;142:1019–1020.
32. Boushy SF, Helgason AH, North LB. Occlusion of the bronchial arteries by glass microspheres. Am Rev Respir Dis 1971;103:249–263.
33. Lois JF, Gomes AS, Smith DC, et al. Systemic-to-pulmonary collateral vessels and shunts: treatment with embolization. Radiology 1988;169:671–676.
34. Doppman JL, Girton M, Oldfield EH. Spinal WADA test. Radiology 1986;161:319–321.
35. Kardjiev V, Symeonov A, Chankov I. Etiology, pathogenesis, and prevention of spinal cord lesions in selective angiography of the bronchial and intercostal arteries. Radiology 1974;112:81–83.
36. Feigelson HH, Ravin HA. Transverse myelitis following selective bronchial arteriography. Radiology 1965;85:663–665.
37. Matsumoto AH, Suhocki PV, Barth KH. Technical note: superselective Gelfoam embolotherapy using a highly visible small caliber catheter. Cardiovasc Intervent Radiol 1988;11:303–306.
38. van Heesch HA, Tjan GT, Lampmann LE. Treatment of haemoptysis by embolisation of the systemic arteries with isobutyl-2 cyanoacrylate: technique and long term results. J Intervent Radiol 1988;3:63–68.
39. Fairfax AJ, Ball J, Batten JC, et al. A pathological study following bronchial artery embolization for haemoptysis in cystic fibrosis. Br J Dis Chest 1980;74:345–352.
40. Mauro MA, Jaques PF. Transcatheter embolisation with a Gelfoam slurry. J Intervent Radiol 1987;2:157–159.
41. Fuhrman BP, Bass JL, Castaneda-Zuniga W, et al. Coil embolization of congenital thoracic vascular anomalies in infants and children. Circulation 1984;70:285–289.
42. Nancarrow PA, Fellows KE, Lock JE. Stability of coil emboli: an in vitro study. Cardiovasc Intervent Radiol 1987;10:226–229.
43. Vujic I, Pyle R, Parker E, et al. Control of massive hemoptysis by embolization of intercostal arteries. Radiology 1980;137:617–620.
44. Ivanick MJ, Thorwarth W, Donohue J, et al. Infarction of the left main-stem bronchus: a complication of bronchial artery embolization. AJR 1983;141:535–537.
45. Hélénon CH, Chatel A, Bigot JM, et al. Fistule œsophago-bronchique gauche après embolisation bronchique. Nouv Presse Med 1977;6:4209.
46. Munk PL, Morris DC, Nelems B. Left main bronchial-esophageal fistula: a complication of bronchial artery embolization. Cardiovasc Intervent Radiol 1990;13:95–97.
47. Tamura S, Kodama T, Otsuka N, et al. Embolotherapy for persistent hemoptysis: the significance of pleural thickening. Cardiovasc Intervent Radiol 1993;16:85–88.

48

Interventional Radiology of Thoracic Abscesses

GILES W. BOLAND
STEVEN L. DAWSON

The surgical management of intrathoracic abscess collections has largely been superceded in the past 15 years by the development of image-guided percutaneous catheter placement. Radiologic intervention in the thoracic collections is a direct extension of the principles and techniques used in abdominal intervention and developed rapidly once abdominal interventional techniques were established. The ability of ultrasound and computed tomography (CT) to detect intrathoracic disease has made possible accurate placement of drainage catheters into abscess collections. This chapter outlines the principles of percutaneous catheter drainage of thoracic abscesses, including lung abscess, empyema, and mediastinal abscess.

Lung Abscess

Lung abscess is a necrotizing process in the pulmonary parenchyma that often progresses to cavitation and that is enclosed by a visceral pleural envelope. During the preantibiotic era, lung abscess carried a mortality rate from 35 to 70 percent, with fewer than half the survivors being "cured."[1] Despite advances in antibiotic therapeutic regimens, there remains a significant mortality rate approaching 30 percent even with aggressive therapy.[2]

Lung abscesses are defined as either primary or secondary. The main predisposing factor in the development of primary lung abscess is aspiration. Primary abscesses usually arise in patients with altered states of consciousness from anesthesia, CNS-related disorders, or alcoholism. Other conditions associated with aspiration pneumonia and subsequent abscess include hiatus hernia and other esophageal conditions where gastroesophageal reflux may occur. Another important contributing factor is poor oral and dental hygiene. Abscesses most frequently involve bronchial segments, which are dependent when the patient is in the supine or lateral decubitus position.

The bacteriology of primary lung abscess closely resembles that of aspiration pneumonia. Anaerobic organisms account for 85 to 90 percent of lung abscesses.[3] Aerobic streptococci are the most common aerobic pathogens. Gram-negative rods and staphylococci are frequently cultured in nosocomially acquired infections.

Secondary lung abscess is defined as abscess formation in areas of preexisting infection or disease, or as a result of hematogenous spread from a remote site. These abscesses are usually caused by secondary abscess formation in patients with preexisting aerobic pneumonias, the most important cause of which is underlying bronchial malignancy. Other predisposing factors include septic emboli, inhaled foreign bodies, bronchoesophageal fistula, emphysematous and other lung cysts, and pulmonary infarction.[4] Immunocompromised hosts are susceptible to certain opportunistic infections, including tuberculosis and fungal and parasitic infections, which can lead to secondary abscess formation.

The diagnosis of lung abscess is usually made by findings of cavitary, necrotizing inflammation on conventional chest radiography in conjunction with the appropriate clinical setting. CT has become an extremely important tool for diagnosing lung abscess and in differentiating these lesions from empyema and bronchopleural fistula.[5]

Up to 90 percent of patients with lung abscess can be treated with supportive measures, postural drainage, and antibiotics. Bronchoscopic placement of transtracheal drainage catheters may facilitate removal of pus and secretions, although there are limited reports in the literature. Surgical intervention is reserved for those patients who do not respond to medical management and antibiotics. A review of the surgical series demonstrated a need for surgery in 11 to 21 percent of patients with lung abscess.[4] Surgical therapy may result in bronchopleural fistula, empyema, bleeding, and spillage of pus into the tracheobronchial tree with subsequent dissemination of infection. Postoperative mortality has been reported to be 11 to 16 percent.[4]

Several studies have demonstrated that percutaneous radiologic catheter placement is a safe and effective alternative to surgery.[2,4,5] Furthermore, quoted complication rates are lower after percutaneous drainage than after surgery, even though patients tend to be sicker in the former group.

Indications and Contraindications

The indications for catheter drainage of lung abscess are similar to those for surgical intervention, namely, sepsis that fails to respond to antibiotics and postural drainage. In addition, abscesses larger than 4 cm are generally better treated by drainage.[6] When standard medical therapy is unlikely to be effective, as in bronchial obstructive lesions with an absent cough reflex, percutaneous or surgical drainage is indicated. Finally, patients requiring persistent mechanical ventilatory support usually require drainage.

Contraindications to catheter drainage include an uncorrectable bleeding diathesis and uncooperative patients, although with effective intravenous sedation most uncooperative patients can be successfully treated. Although catheter drainage of lung abscess through normal lung is generally considered safe,[2,7,8] transparenchymal drainage has led to infected bronchopleural fistulas; for this reason, whenever possible, the catheter should traverse only contiguous abnormal lung and pleura en route to the abscess.[4]

Image Guidance

Initial reports of percutaneous catheter placement for lung abscess used plain radiographs and fluoroscopy for guidance.[2,9,10] Fluoroscopy has the advantage of wide availability and cheaper cost. More recently, CT has been advocated as the primary imaging modality complemented by fluoroscopic guidance when necessary.[4,11] CT allows for precise assessment of the abscess cavity and delineates the optimum transpleural route that avoids intervening normal lung. It is effective in demonstrating loculations that may require placement of more than one catheter. Fluoroscopy is more useful when real-time observation is necessary to manipulate guidewires and catheters into the abscess cavity or to reposition previously placed catheters.

Technique

Regardless of the radiologic guidance system used, initial access to the abscess cavity is obtained with a small-gauge needle, which allows for aspiration of pus for Gram stain and culture. Either the trocar or the Seldinger technique can be used for catheter placement, depending on personal preference. If the trocar technique is used with CT guidance, localization should be done with a guiding needle to reduce the risk of incorrect catheter position. When either fluoroscopic or CT guidance is used, the contralateral lung must not be dependent during catheter placement. Aspiration of pus into the normal lung is associated with markedly increased morbidity and mortality. Up to 22 percent of deaths can be attributed to aspiration of infected material into uninfected ipsilateral or contralateral lung.[12] As long as the contralateral lung is not dependent, drainage can be performed with the patient supine, prone, decubitus, or in the oblique position. Consideration should also be given to how the patient will lie after catheter insertion. Since most lung abscesses are in the lower lobes, catheter placement should be via a posterior route. To avoid subsequent patient discomfort and catheter kinking, the catheter should be placed through a more lateral posterior axillary approach. Occasionally a true posterior approach is required, and special care with catheter dressing will be necessary to prevent kinking of the catheter.

Adequate local anesthesia with infiltration of the periosteum of the adjacent rib and parietal pleura helps reduce unnecessary pain. The lung is entered using aseptic technique. Whenever a catheter is placed via an intercostal approach, the tube should be placed through the midportion of the intercostal muscle, avoiding the neurovascular bundle of the rib above and also avoiding constant rubbing of the catheter on the periosteum of the rib below. The character of the initial aspirated material dictates catheter selection. Generally, 12 to 16 French catheters are required because of the viscous nature of infected material found in lung abscesses.

After catheter placement, the contents of the abscess cavity should be evacuated as completely as possible. Gentle irrigation of completely walled-off cavities is then performed with normal saline to remove the more viscous pus and to help evacuate loculated areas within the abscess cavity. The catheter is secured by "flagging" the tube with cloth adhesive tape, which is then sutured to an ostomy disk (Hollister) and connected to a standard three-bottle water-seal drainage system (Pleur-evac, A4005; Deknatel). In-hospital drainage with suction at 20 cm of water is required for all patients.

An important part of the overall management is the follow-up of patients by members of the interventional radiology team. This is essential to evaluate the clinical response to drainage, to assess tube function and the amount of drainage, and to inspect the catheter insertion site for possible loosening. Goldberg et al. found catheter-related problems in 59 percent of patients with thoracic and abdominal percutaneous catheters. Most catheter-related problems (71 percent) were successfully managed at the bedside.[12] If the catheter occludes, the radiologist can irrigate the catheter and the drainage system with sterile saline, which is usually sufficient to restore patency. Otherwise, the patient will need to be brought to the radiology department for further catheter assessment and manipulation.

Follow-up CT can be performed 3 to 5 days after catheter insertion to evaluate outcome. If the abscess cavity has collapsed and there are no undrained loculations and the catheter drainage has decreased to less than 10 ml per day with a good associated clinical response, the catheter can be withdrawn in two stages. On the first day, the drainage system is disconnected from wall suction and placed on water seal for 12 to 24 hours. If no pneumothorax is present on a chest radiograph obtained the following day, the chest tube is removed and a pressure bandage is applied. If no clinical improvement occurs after catheter insertion, or if there is a deterioration in clinical status, CT is performed earlier (within 12–48 hours) to check catheter position and assess for further undrained collections or dissemination of infection.

Results and Complications

Percutaneous catheter drainage of lung abscesses is usually successful, and surgery can usually be avoided. The mean duration of drainage is approximately 10 days.[4] Reasons for failure include multiloculated or poorly defined abscesses or thick-walled cavities that cannot collapse.[13] Secondary lung abscesses are unlikely to resolve unless the underlying illness is treated. In these instances, the patient will require surgical resection.

Complications occur in approximately 2 percent of cases.[11] Sepsis or bacteremia is more common if the abscess is not adequately drained. Bleeding may occur in the presence of a bleeding diathesis or from injury to adjacent vascular structures such as the intercostal or internal mammary artery.

Thoracic Empyema

An empyema is an infection involving the pleural space that may result from secondary spread from pulmonary infection, thoracic trauma, a foreign body, bronchiectasis, esophageal perforation, or infradiaphragmatic disease. Light et al.[14–16] helped define the pathophysiology of empyema, which must be understood for successful treatment. The first or exudative stage results when a focus of infection contiguous to the pleura causes an exudative pleural effusion. The fluid has normal pH and glucose levels and a mild exudate of polymorphonuclear leukocytes. Effusions at this stage may not require drainage because many spontaneously resolve with appropriate antibiotic treatment. However, once this sterile effusion is contaminated with bacteria, the glucose and pH fall, resulting in the second or fibrinopurulent stage. Light et al. suggest that this is chemically recognized when the pH is at or below 7, the glucose level is at or below 40 mg/dl (2.2 mmol/liter), and the LDH level is at or below 1000 units/liter. This second-stage effusion becomes more viscous as polymorphonuclear cells and debris accumulate. Finally, in the third stage, fibrin is deposited and an inner elastic membrane, or pleural peel, forms. Once a pleural peel forms, open thoracostomy and decortication are generally required. Although percutaneous drainage of empyema early in the third stage may be effective, the highest chance of success occurs during the second stage.

Indications and Contraindications

Any thoracentesis resulting in positive Gram stain or culture requires drainage. However, because the initial Gram stain may be inconclusive and because cultures take at least 24 hours, the decision to drain a collection is often based on Light's criteria (outlined above) in the correct clinical setting (fever, persistence of symptoms, or increasing effusion despite appropriate antibiotic therapy).

Contraindications are similar to those for all percutaneous catheter placements: uncontrollable bleeding diathesis and an uncooperative patient despite intravenous sedation.

Image Guidance

Traditionally, surgical empyema drainage was performed at the bedside using the chest radiograph as a reference. In some institutions this is still commonly practiced. However, surgical series suggest that the mortality of this technique may be as high as 5 percent,[17] with as many as 35 percent of patients requiring open chest tube drainage or decortication.[18] In addition, incorrect tube placement can occur in up to 80 percent of blind tube thoracostomies,[19] with complications including fibrothorax, bronchopleural fistula, prolonged hospitalization, and death.[20,21] Therefore, image-guided catheter drainage of thoracic empyemas has become more common and is the procedure of choice in the authors' institution.

Ultrasound guidance is preferred for catheter insertion, particularly for large or free-flowing empyemas.

Ultrasound is very sensitive in detecting and localizing collections and provides real-time monitoring of catheter insertion and efficacy of drainage. It also allows for immediate assessment of undrained collections. For loculated or less accessible collections, CT is the modality of choice. CT demonstrates the wall characteristics, pleural separation, and lung compression of empyemas and can adequately distinguish them from lung abscesses, which may respond to conservative measures.[22]

Fluoroscopy is now rarely used as the sole guidance system, although it may be used in combination with either ultrasound or CT for Seldinger insertion of pleural catheters or as the sole guidance method for catheter exchanges.

Technique

The patient should be seated over the side of the stretcher facing away from the radiologist. The patient is encouraged to lean forward onto a bedside table with the arms folded to provide greater access for catheter placement. If the patient cannot sit up, then he or she is positioned in the decubitus manner with the affected side up. An image-guided thoracentesis is usually performed initially on all patients, and, when the diagnosis of empyema or complicated parapneumonic effusion is confirmed according to the established criteria, a drainage catheter is inserted.

Usually, 16 to 24 French catheters are required. Specifically designed empyema catheters (Mueller Empyema Catheters, Cook, Inc.) are suitable for most collections. These catheters are designed for trocar insertion and have a stylet-cannula assembly. They have a soft, curved tip with distal side holes and are made of polyvinylchloride that is sufficiently rigid to prevent catheter compression by adjacent ribs. Occasionally, larger 24 French catheters (Thal-Quick Chest Tube, Cook, Inc.) are required for thick purulent collections. Except for the 24 French catheters, which are inserted with Seldinger technique, the trocar technique is preferable, because the Seldinger technique is more likely to introduce air and result in pneumothorax. Furthermore, with a Seldinger insertion it is occasionally difficult to advance the catheter intercostally through the intercostal muscles and thickened pleura without buckling the guidewire or catheter.

After catheter placement, the empyema fluid is aspirated completely. The catheter is secured either to the skin or to an ostomy disk (Hollister) and connected to a water-seal pleural drainage system (Pleur-evac, Pfizer). Drainage with 20-cm water suction is essential. All patients are followed daily by members of the interventional radiology team to assess catheter func-

tion and to ensure that the catheter is securely fastened to the skin.

Usually a CT scan is performed to assess treatment outcome, and catheters remain until fluid drainage has decreased to less than 10 ml per day. Catheters can then be removed at the bedside in a single step, without the need for progressive removal of wall suction, water seal, and follow-up chest films, as is necessary with lung abscesses.

Loculated empyemas may require multiple catheters for complete drainage. However, fibrin deposition and locule formation can make closed percutaneous drainage of empyema difficult, and until recently open surgical drainage has been the only alternative treatment. However, recent reports have demonstrated successful and safe use of intrapleural urokinase (Abbott) to lyse locules.[23,24] Generally, up to four treatments of 80,000 to 100,000 units (1000 units/ml) of urokinase are injected every 8 hours through the indwelling catheter, which is then clamped for 1 to 2 hours before suction drainage is restored (Fig. 48-1). If urokinase fails, then open surgical drainage is indicated (Fig. 48-2).

Results and Complications

Lee et al. reviewed the five main series in the radiologic literature and found an average success rate of 77 percent for percutaneous catheter drainage compared to a 35 to 71 percent success rate for conventional surgical tube thoracostomy.[25] Failure occurs because of thick, viscous pus that is not amenable to drainage with standard empyema catheters. Therefore, larger 24 French catheters are used when viscous pus is encountered at thoracentesis.

Complications are uncommon and are quoted at less than 2 percent.[25] The most significant, although fortunately rare, complication is cardiopulmonary arrest during catheter placement[26] and transient bacteremia.[27]

Mediastinal Abscess

Mediastinal abscess formation usually occurs after esophageal perforation, which may occur spontaneously (Boerhaave syndrome) or iatrogenically after esophageal endoscopy. Mediastinal abscess is also a well-recognized complication after median sternotomy (Fig. 48-3). Patients with mediastinitis and abscess formation are usually severely ill, with a high fever, sepsis, and leukocytosis, and are often poor surgical candidates. Acute mediastinitis carries a high mortality and is considered a surgical emergency.

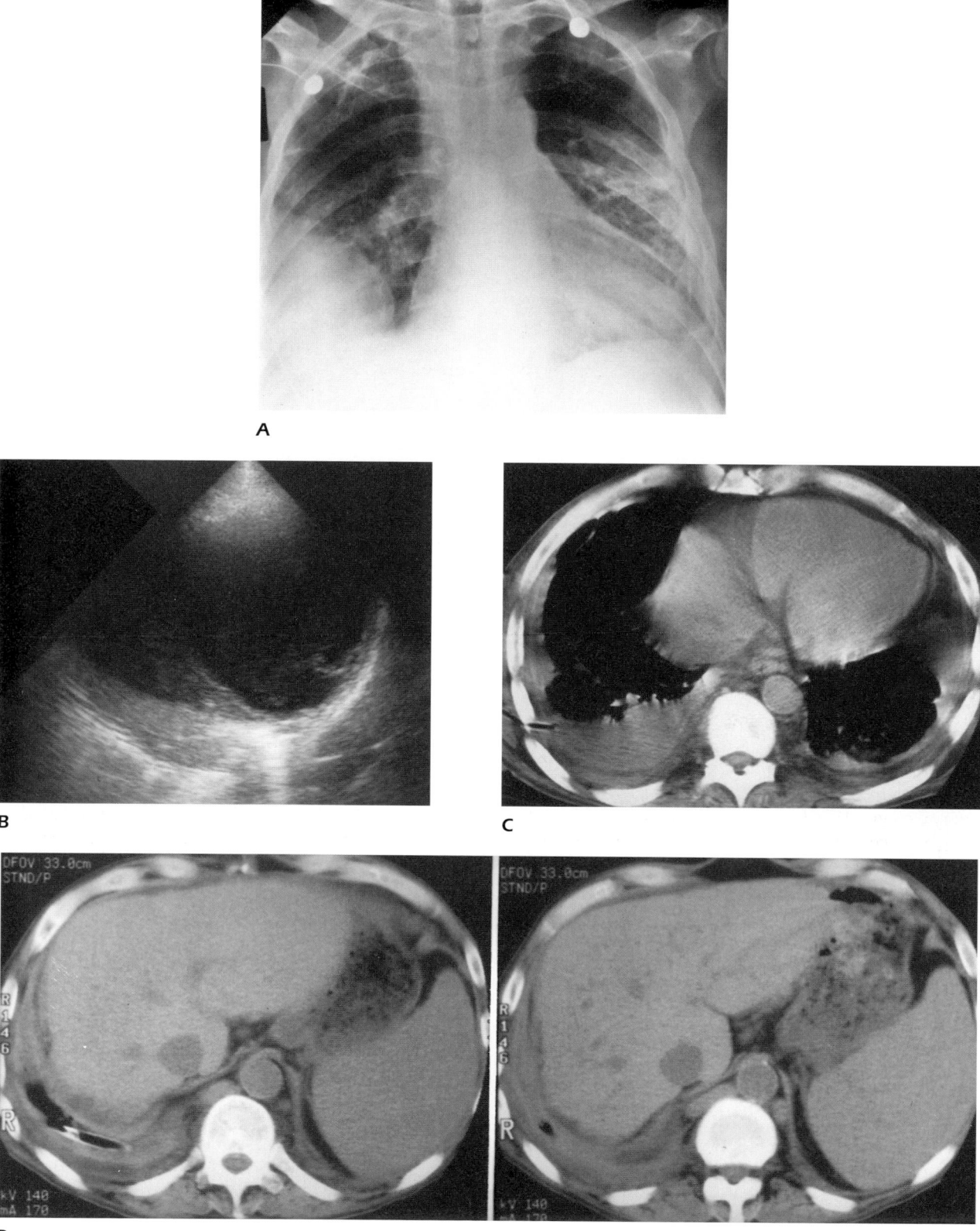

Figure 48-1. A 74-year-old man with a history of chronic lymphocytic lymphoma and prior tuberculosis. (A) Chest film shows a right basilar lateral pleural collection with changes of old granulomatous disease. (B) Ultrasound of the right pleural collection shows loculations and low-level echoes. (C) Ultrasound-guided chest tube placement yielded 2000 ml of pus, but follow-up CT shows residual fluid following chest tube placement. (D) Intracavitary urokinase was used to dissolve the residual debris, and follow-up CT shows complete resolution of the empyema with residual pleural thickening secondary to chronic inflammation.

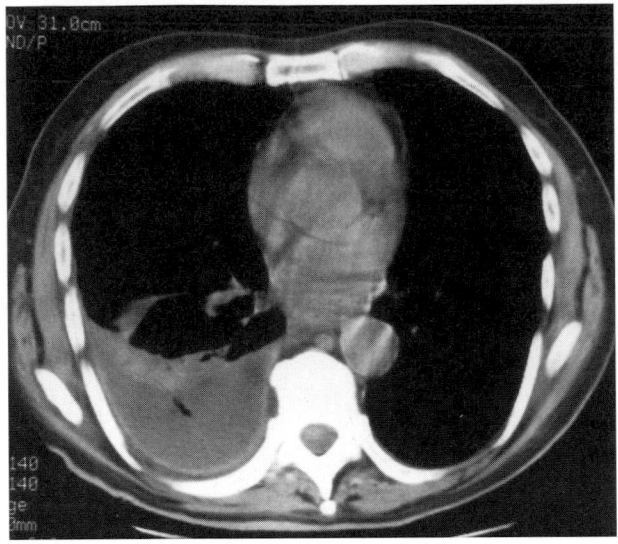

A

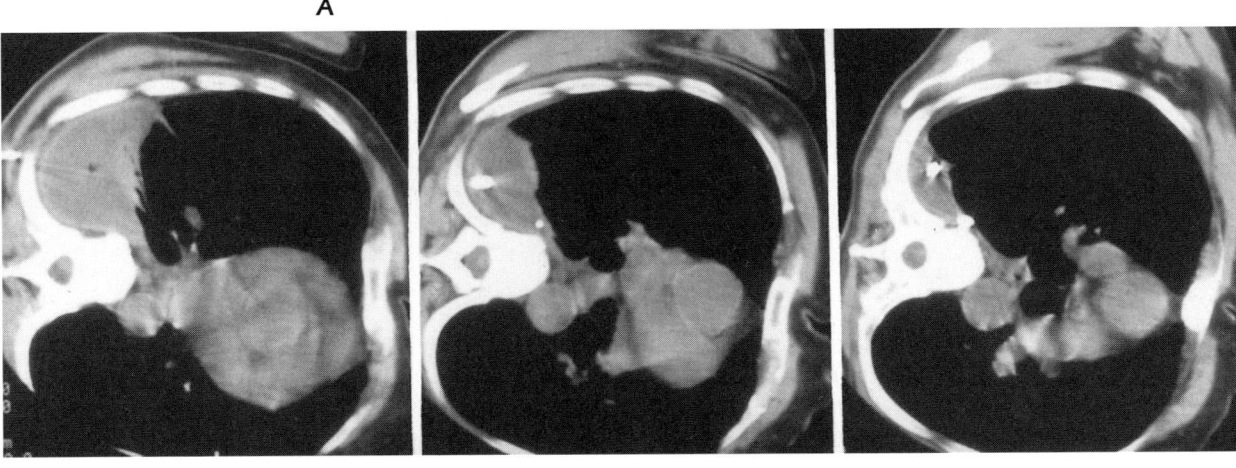

B

Figure 48-2. A 67-year-old man with fever and right pleural abnormality. (A) CT scan showing a right posterior pleural collection and associated air space disease. Despite the patient's fever, drainage of the pleural collection was not attempted initially. (B) After 2 weeks, right chest tube placement was performed using a right lateral decubitus approach. Although a 16 French catheter was placed, drainage was not successful because of the fibrinous organization of the collection (see text). The patient subsequently had surgical decortication and evacuation of the pleural collection.

Radiologically guided percutaneous drainage techniques are beneficial in this group of patients. Surgical repair is usually required for esophageal leaks, and percutaneous drainage permits the patient to undergo elective surgery in an improved physiologic state.

Indications and Contraindications

Percutaneous drainage of a mediastinal abscess should be considered in any severely ill patient, particularly if the collection is situated superficially. Deeply sited collections may be difficult to access and therefore require surgical drainage. Contraindications to the technique are similar to those of other radiologic percutaneous techniques and include uncorrectable bleeding diathesis and an uncooperative patient.

Image Guidance

Computed tomography (CT) is the image guidance modality of choice. CT is able to demonstrate mediastinal widening, infiltration of mediastinal fat, extent of disease, and low-density abscess collections with or without gas formation. CT is essential to delineate the relation of the abscess to vital cardiovascular and tracheobronchial structures so that catheters can be placed accurately via a safe extrapleural route.

Technique

Drainage can be performed either by an anterior or posterior approach. Regardless of which route is chosen, whenever possible the catheter should be placed

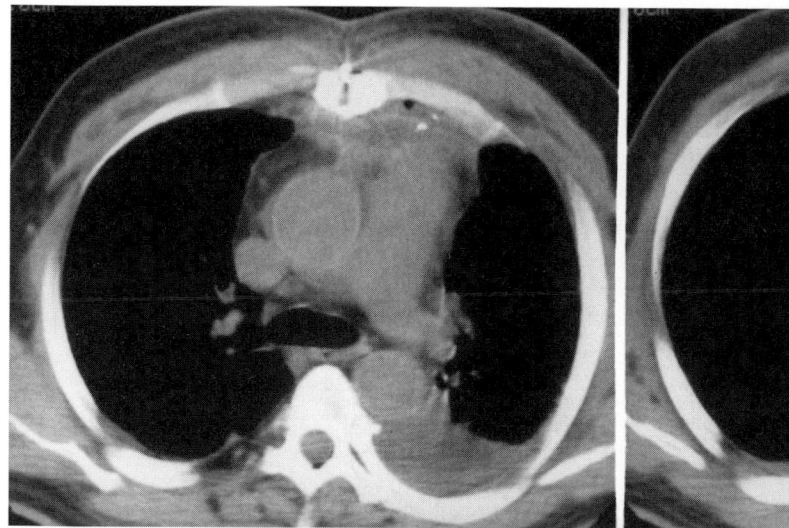
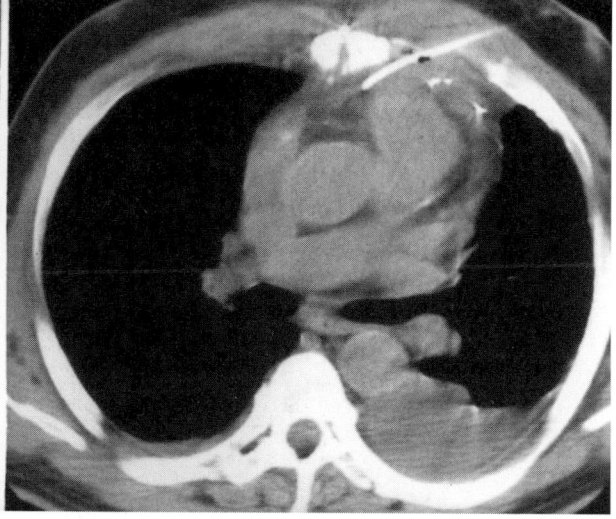

A
B

Figure 48-3. A 63-year-old man with fever for 5 days following median sternotomy and coronary artery bypass graft (CABG). (A) CT scan shows a small retrosternal fluid collection just anterior to the main pulmonary artery, with a small bubble of air anteriorly. (B) A left parasternal approach has been used to place an 8 French catheter into the retrosternal abscess. In retrosternal collections, thin CT slices and angling of the gantry may help to demonstrate a bone-free soft tissue window into the retrosternal mediastinum. Meticulous technique is necessary to avoid the great vessels.

directly into the mediastinum or through the pleura without traversing normal lung. Anterior mediastinal collections are usually drained via a parasternal approach, with care taken to avoid the internal mammary artery. Posterior collections are drained paravertebrally.

The technique for CT-guided catheter placement is identical to that of catheter placement elsewhere in the chest. After initial CT scanning has localized the abscess, the precise site of entry through the skin is marked and an initial localizing needle is inserted to a predetermined depth and location, avoiding vital organs such as the lung, heart, and great vessels. The needle should be advanced in a plane perfectly parallel to the central beam. In this way the needle tip is clearly identified as an abrupt end to the needle with a black metallic artifact projecting beyond the needle. Angulation out of the plane of the x-ray beam will create difficulties in identifying the needle tip and multiple CT slices, and needle repositionings may be required to determine the correct angle and depth of insertion. An angled needle shaft is recognized by its tapering shape rather than an abrupt end and does not have an associated artifact. Occasionally an oblique path to the abscess is specifically chosen to avoid vital organs. Once a satisfactory pathway has been identified, catheter placement can be performed either via a Seldinger or a trocar technique. If the abscess is relatively superficial or large, a trocar technique is preferable. However, the Seldinger technique allows for more precise catheter placement and may be necessary for deeply sited collections. The catheter size depends on the size of the

abscess; small collections can be drained with 8 French catheters (see Fig. 48-3).

One report has suggested that periesophageal collections may be drained via a transesophageal approach under fluoroscopic guidance, particularly if there is no safe access route to the abscess.[28]

Results and Complications

Percutaneous abscess drainage of mediastinal collections has been performed with similar results to percutaneous drainage of empyema and lung abscess. However, because there are limited reports in the literature,[28-31] the occurrence of major complications is difficult to assess, although injury to major cardiovascular structures and the lung is possible. In addition, the position of the internal mammary artery should be considered in any percutaneous parasternal approach because injury to this structure is associated with significant hemorrhage. However, since CT guidance permits accurate assessment of the position of the internal mammary artery and other vital structures, these complications should be avoidable.

References

1. Estrera AS, Melvin RP, Mills LJ, et al. Primary lung abscess. J Thorac Cardiovasc Surg 1980;79:275–282.
2. Parker LA, Melton JW, Delany DJ, et al. Percutaneous small bore catheter drainage in the management of lung abscess. Chest 1987;92:213–218.

3. Pennza PT. Aspiration pneumonia, necrotizing pneumonia, and lung abscess. Emerg Med Clin North Am 1989;7:279–307.

4. van Sonnenberg E, D'Agostino HB, Casola G, et al. Lung abscess: CT guided drainage. Radiology 1991;178:347–351.

5. Lorenzo RL, Bradford BF, Black J, et al. Lung abscesses in children: diagnostic and therapeutic needle aspiration. Radiology 1985;157:79–80.

6. Bernhard WF, Malcolm JA, Wylie RH. Lung abscess: a survey of 148 cases due to aspiration. Chest 1963;43:620.

7. Mengoli L. Giant lung abscess treated by tube thoracostomy. J Thorac Cardiovasc Surg 1985;90:186–194.

8. Lawrence GH, Rubin SL. Management of giant lung abscess. Am J Surg 1978;136:134–139.

9. Rice TW, Ginsberg RJ, Todd TJ. Tube drainage of lung abscess. Ann Thorac Surg 1987;44:356–359.

10. Yellin A, Yellin EO, Lieberman Y. Percutaneous tube drainage: the treatment of choice of refractory lung abscess. Ann Thorac Surg 1985;39:3, 266–270.

11. Moore AV, Zuger JH, Kelley MJ. Lung abscess: an interventional radiology perspective. Semin Intervent Radiol 1991;8:1, 36–43.

12. Goldberg MA, Mueller PR, Saini S, et al. Importance of daily rounds by the radiologist after interventional procedures of the abdomen and chest. Radiology 1991;180:767–770.

13. Kosloske AM, Ball WS Jr, Butler C, et al. Drainage of pediatric lung abscess by cough, catheter or complete resection. J Pediatr Surg 1986;21:596–600.

14. Light RW. Management of parapneumonic effusions. Chest 1976;70:325–326.

15. Light RW, Girard WM, Jenkinson SG, et al. Parapneumonic effusions. Am J Med 1980;69:507–512.

16. Light RW. Parapneumonic effusions and empyemas. Clin Chest Med 1985;6:55–61.

17. Sherman MM, Subramanian V, Berger RL. Management of thoracic empyema. Am J Surg 1977;133:474–478.

18. Varkey B, Rose HD, Kesavan Kutty CP, et al. Empyema thoracis during a ten year period. Arch Intern Med 1981;141:1771–1776.

19. Stark DD, Federle MP, Goodman PC. CT and radiographic assessment of tube thoracostomy. AJR 1983;141:253–258.

20. Maurer JR, Friedman PJ, Wing VW. Thoracostomy tube in an interlobar fissure: radiologic recognition of a potential problem. AJR 1982;139:1155–1161.

21. Webb WR, Laberge J. Major fissure tube placement. AJR 1983;140:1039.

22. Stark DD, Federle MP, Goodman PC, et al. Differentiating lung abscess and empyema: radiography and computed tomography. AJR 1983;141:163–167.

23. Moulton JS, Moore PT, Mencini RA. Treatment of loculated pleural effusions with transcatheter intracavitary urokinase. AJR 1989;153:941–945.

24. Lee KS, Im J-G, Kim YH, et al. Treatment of thoracic multiloculated empyemas with intracavitary urokinase: a prospective study. Radiology 1991;179:771–775.

25. Lee MJ, Saini S, Brink JA, et al. Interventional radiology of the pleural space: management of thoracic empyema with image-guided catheter drainage. Semin Intervent Radiol 1991;8:1, 29–35.

26. Merriam MA, Cronin JJ, Dorfman GS, et al. Radiographically guided percutaneous catheter drainage of pleural fluid collections. AJR 1988;151:1113–1116.

27. van Sonnenberg E, Nakamato SK, Mueller PR, et al. CT and ultrasound guided catheter drainage of empyemas after chest-tube failure. Radiology 1984;154:349–353.

28. Meranze SG, LeVeen RF, Burke DR. Transesophageal drainage of mediastinal abscesses. Radiology 1987;165:395–398.

29. Stavas J, van Sonnenberg E, Casola G, et al. Percutaneous drainage of infected and noninfected thoracic fluid collections. J Thorac Imaging 1987;2:80–87.

30. Ball WS Jr, Bisset GS III, Towbin RB. Percutaneous drainage of chest abscess in children. Radiology 1989;171:431–434.

31. Neff C, Lawson DW. Boerhaave syndrome: interventional radiologic management. AJR 1985;145:819–820.

49

Pulmonary Arteriovenous Malformations

ROBERT I. WHITE, JR.
JEFFREY S. POLLAK

Congenital pulmonary arteriovenous malformations (PAVMs) are direct low-pressure connections between a pulmonary artery (PA) and a pulmonary vein (PV) without an intervening capillary bed.[1] As a result, deoxygenated blood is shunted from the pulmonary to the systemic circulation, leading to low arterial blood oxygen, dyspnea, and fatigue. Because the lung also no longer serves as a filter of small bland emboli and bacteria, patients often sustain transient ischemic attacks (TIAs), strokes, and brain abscesses. The neurologic manifestations may be the first and predominant symptoms in many patients with one or two PAVMs that are not large enough to cause significant arterial hypoxemia.[2]

PAVMs were originally described by Churton in 1897, but it was not until 1938 that a significant association between PAVMs and hereditary hemorrhagic telangiectasia (HHT) was documented by Rodes.[3,4] In all patients with HHT, it is estimated that 6 to 15 percent of them have PAVMs.[5] In a large series described from the Mayo Clinic, it was determined that 40 percent of PAVMs occur spontaneously and that 60 percent are associated with HHT.[6] The present authors' own experience in 159 patients treated and followed between 1978 and 1992 suggests a much higher association between PAVM and HHT, partly because the expression of PAVM in asymptomatic family members with HHT appears much higher than previously reported.[7,8]

Successful surgical resection of PAVMs by pneumonectomy with relief of cyanosis and dyspnea was first performed in 1940 and reported in 1942.[9] Ultimately techniques for lobectomy, wedge resection of lung, and surgical ligation of the arterial pedicle were developed to reduce the amount of lung removed with lobectomy.[10-14] Unfortunately, in patients with multiple bilateral PAVMs, surgical repair required bilateral thoracotomies or median sternotomy.[15] In addition, because small PAVMs are known to enlarge with time, serial thoracotomies needed to be considered over a lifetime.[16,17]

In 1977, Porstmann described a transcatheter technique for occluding PAVMs using personally designed metal coils.[18] Shortly thereafter, single patients were reported with closure of their PAVMs using conventional stainless steel coils and detachable balloons.[19,20] Since 1980, multiple reports of successful transcatheter closure of PAVM have accumulated. This chapter describes in detail some of the clinical aspects and technical approaches to PAVM closure.

Acquired PAVMs and aneurysms associated with Swan-Ganz balloon injury, overwhelming infection, and superior vena cava–pulmonary artery surgical shunts may account for pulmonary hemorrhage, cyanosis, and dyspnea.[21-30] Approaches to treatment of these conditions by transcatheter embolotherapy are similar to techniques for closure of congenital PAVMs. Specific clinical details associated with these lesions are referred to in the references at the end of the chapter.[21-30]

Symptoms and Signs of PAVM

Tables 49-1 and 49-2 list the common presentations, symptoms, and signs of patients with PAVMs coming to medical attention. Medical textbooks portray the classical patient as cyanotic and dyspneic with multiple masses present on the chest radiograph. The authors' experience suggests that patients with PAVMs present more commonly with neurologic symptoms or with the hemorrhagic symptoms of HHT predominating.[2,8] They also have pursued an aggressive screening program in families affected by HHT. When one family member with HHT has PAVM, it is not unusual to discover 20 to 30 percent of other family members with HHT who also have PAVM and are not yet symptomatic. These asymptomatic patients are at risk for stroke, brain abscess, and pulmonary hemorrhage.[2,8]

Several review articles are available detailing the varied presentation of patients with HHT.[31-33] HHT is an autosomal dominant disorder that affects predominantly five organ systems: the skin, gastrointestinal

Table 49-1. Clinical Presentations of Patients with PAVM

Pulmonary presentations
  Dyspnea, cyanosis, fatigue
  Spontaneous hemoptysis or hemothorax
  Asymptomatic "lung mass or infiltrate"
  Lung tumor or inflammatory disease
  Congenital heart disease
Neurologic presentations
  Stroke or transient ischemic attack (TIA)
  Brain abscess
  Subarachnoid or intracerebral hemorrhage associated with cerebral AVM
  Epilepsy
  Alzheimer disease, multistroke dementia
  Migraine headache disorder
Presentations associated with HHT
  Recurrent epistaxis
  Iron deficiency anemia
  Polycythemia
  Gastrointestinal bleeding
  Pseudohemophilia

Table 49-2. Signs Associated with PAVM and HHT

Cyanosis

Clubbing

Bright red, pinhead- to pea-size telangiectasia on lips, palate, buccal mucosa, tongue, conjunctiva, ears, cheeks, and fingers

Systolic murmur over large PAVM, "spilling" over into diastole in 50 percent

Table 49-3. Diagnostic Techniques for PAVM

Chest radiography or fluoroscopy

Arterial blood gases (ABG), room air and 100% oxygen

Contrast ("bubble") echocardiography

Radionuclide shunt study

High-resolution helical-computed tomography without contrast material

Magnetic resonance imaging

Pulmonary angiography

tract, nervous system, lung, and nose. Because the symptoms are so varied, many different specialists become involved in the patient's care during the course of the disease. Radiologic consultants also include the general and chest radiologist, the abdominal imager, the neuroradiologist, and the interventional radiologist. The first radiologist or family practitioner or internist to see the patient is in a unique position to suggest the diagnosis of PAVM when reviewing chest radiographs of patients presenting with epistaxis, gastrointestinal bleeding, unexplained neurologic symptoms, or asymptomatic chest masses.

Diagnosis

The common radiologic and nonradiologic methods for establishing the diagnosis of PAVM are discussed in Table 49-3 and in a recent review article.[34] Despite the vast array of diagnostic tests available, it has not been practical to determine the sensitivity, specificity, and accuracy of each in patients with HHT. The authors have adapted a simple algorithm for screening based on their experience over the past 15 years.

Chest radiography and baseline arterial blood gases

(ABGs) are useful, and ABGs are a low-cost method of following patients after diagnosis and treatment of PAVMs.[34] Noncontrast standard, high-resolution, and spiral CT with three-dimensional reconstruction have recently been popularized by the Remys and may offer the best noninvasive imaging method for determining the size of the arterial pedicle and the morphology of PAVMs short of performing pulmonary angiography.[35-37] Bubble echocardiography, magnetic resonance imaging (MRI), and radionuclide shunt determinations are alternative techniques that may have value.[34,38-44] ABGs and/or radionuclide shunt determinations are relatively simple methods for quantifying the shunt and following patients after embolotherapy. Because small unoccluded PAVMs grow with time, it is important that all patients are followed up at 3- to 5-year intervals.[34]

Pulmonary angiography is important to perform before therapy to determine the number, type, and size of PAVMs and to determine which require closure. Pulmonary angiography also provides assessment and selection of the best projection for performing therapeutic occlusion.

Diagnostic pulmonary angiography includes standard anteroposterior film changer radiography of selective right and left pulmonary artery injections, supplemented by oblique intraarterial digital subtraction angiography (IADSA) views of both lungs. At the time of embolotherapy, superselective IADSA is performed before selective balloon or coil occlusion to determine the exact position in the arterial pedicle for safe placement of the occluding device.

Anatomic Types of PAVM

Individual PAVMs are conveniently divided into simple and complex types (Figs. 49-1 through 49-3).[45] Additionally, in approximately 5 percent of patients, the PAVMs are diffuse, arising from almost all segmental lower lobe pulmonary artery branches. In this latter variation, both simple and large PAVMs may occur (see Fig. 50-3).

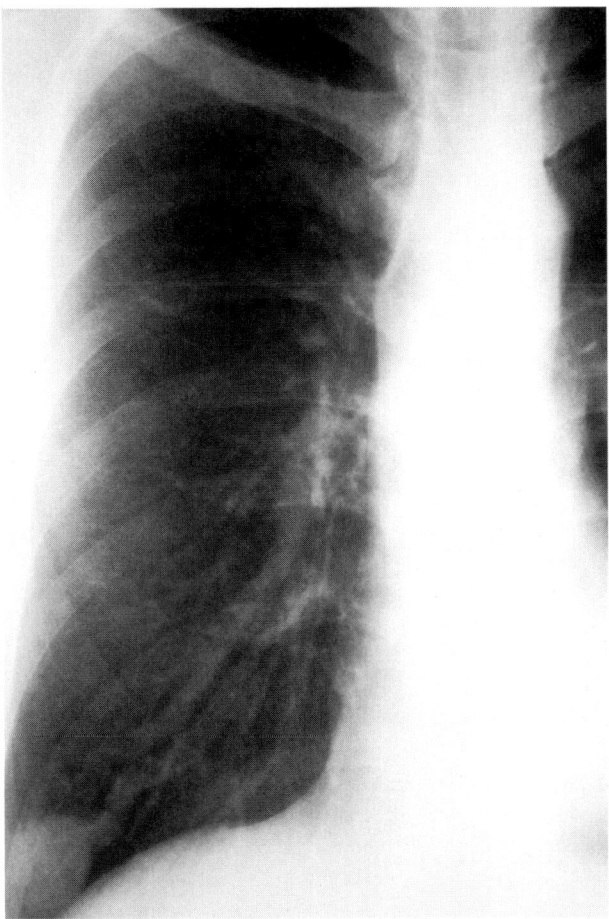

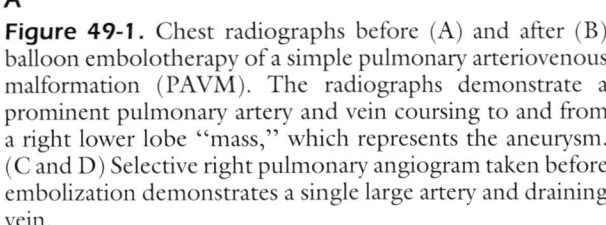

A

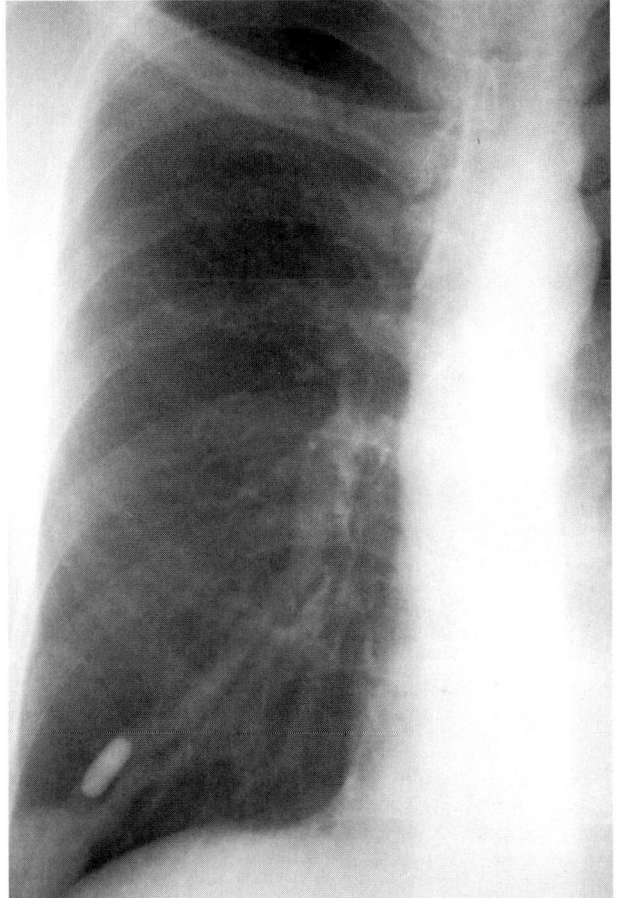

B

Figure 49-1. Chest radiographs before (A) and after (B) balloon embolotherapy of a simple pulmonary arteriovenous malformation (PAVM). The radiographs demonstrate a prominent pulmonary artery and vein coursing to and from a right lower lobe "mass," which represents the aneurysm. (C and D) Selective right pulmonary angiogram taken before embolization demonstrates a single large artery and draining vein.

Simple PAVMs consist of a single pulmonary artery (PA) in the arterial pedicle supplying the malformation and one draining vein (PV) (see Fig. 49-1). The PA and PV are connected through an aneurysm that is smooth-walled but occasionally is racemose with many intertwining connections.[45] Complex PAVMs consist of two or more PA branches in the arterial pedicle supplying the malformation and frequently two or more draining veins.[45] The number of PA branches supplying the malformation may be as many as four or five (see Fig. 49-2). The exact number of PA branches in the pedicle to the malformation may not be apparent from the diagnostic angiogram but will become more apparent on the IADSA done after the largest arterial

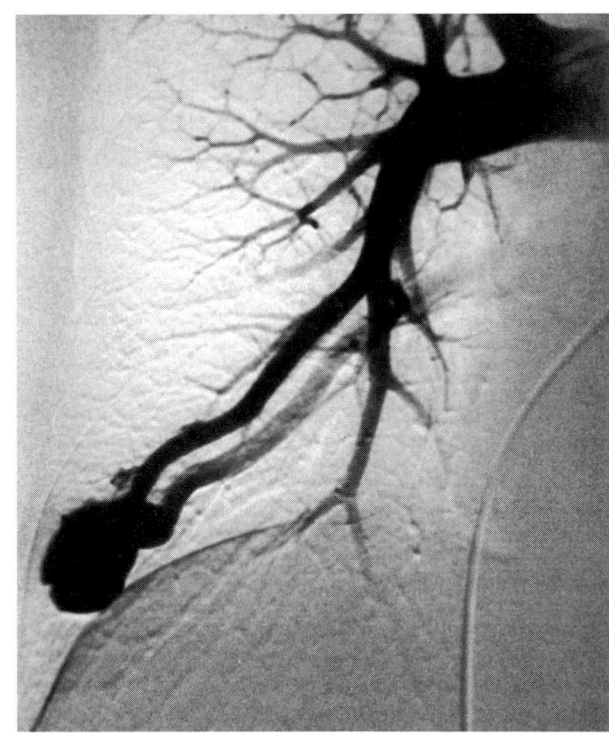

C

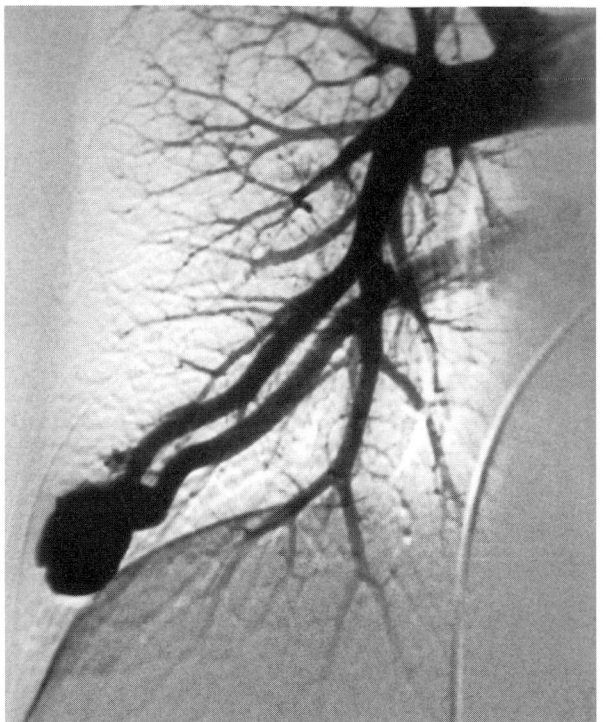

D

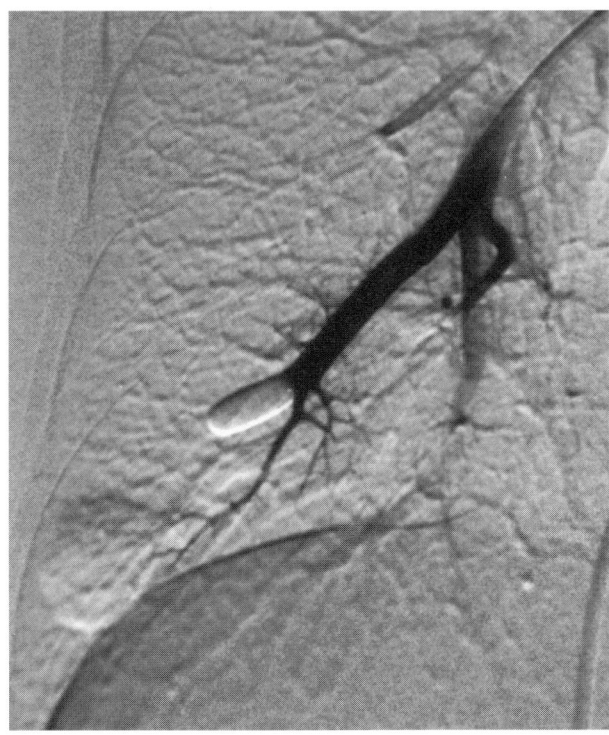

E

Figure 49-1 (continued). In (D) the pulmonary vein is seen entering the left atrium directly. (E) The detachable balloon, also shown in (B), is placed distally in the artery supplying the aneurysm as far beyond all normal branches as possible while still ensuring a secure fit in the artery. (From Guttmacher AE, Marchuk DA, White RI Jr. Hereditary hemorrhagic telangiectasia. N Engl J Med 1995;333:918–924. Used with permission.)

feeder is occluded. It is extremely important to perform a proximal (left or right) pulmonary angiogram after therapy because up to 10 percent of accessory arteries to a PAVM may be left unoccluded.[35]

In an earlier study of 276 PAVMs occluded in 76 patients reported in 1988, the authors found that approximately 80 percent were simple and 20 percent were complex.[7] The complex variety is particularly important to recognize because this form will lead to persistence of the PAVM if all PA branches are not occluded (see Fig. 49-2).[35–37] Since 1990, the authors have modified their postocclusion follow-up to include a chest radiograph and ABGs 30 days and 1 year after occlusion.[14] Persistence of the aneurysm unchanged in size at 1 year, early deflation of a balloon (<21 days), or a drop in the arterial PO_2 from the 24-hour postocclusion level should suggest continued patency of the primary arterial feeder or enlargement of nonoccluded secondary arterial feeders not occluded initially.[35,36] These patients should be restudied, and any remaining feeding vessels should be occluded.

The observation that up to 10 percent of PAVMs may persist after occlusion is different from the authors' earlier experience as reported in 1988. In 1988 it was determined that all 16 patients restudied had permanent occlusion (Fig. 49-4).

The diffuse type consists of small PAVMs arising from each terminal basilar branch, much like a "sprinkling can" (see Fig. 49-3). These terminal PAVMs are preferentially located in the lower lobes; selective injection of each lower lobe segmental artery will reveal them. The arterial oxygen tension usually varies between 35 and 45 mmHg in patients with the diffuse type. Larger, simple, and complex PAVMs may also coexist in patients with diffuse PAVM. Of 159 patients treated by the authors, 8 (6 percent) have had the diffuse variety.

Occasionally, patients with diffuse malformations will have them confined exclusively to either the right or left lung or to both lower lobes. In these patients, some interesting options for management exist, including a more global, lobar embolization to redistribute blood flow to the more normal lung (see Fig. 49-3).[46]

Text continues on page 845

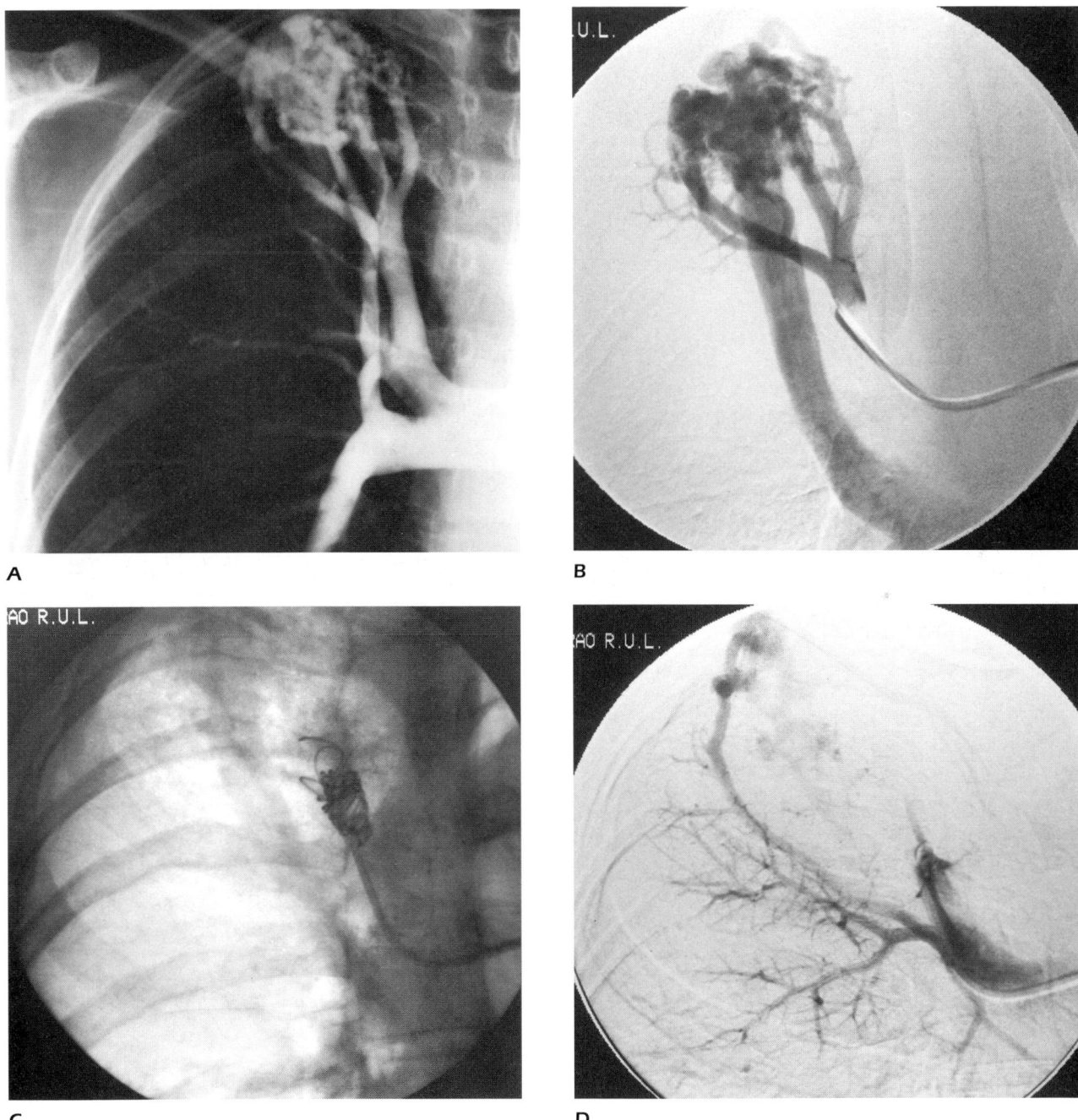

Figure 49-2. Complex right upper lobe PAVM with two primary and five secondary pulmonary artery branches. (A) Right pulmonary angiogram demonstrates two primary right upper lobe branches arising from the right pulmonary artery. (B) Selective injection in the largest branch demonstrates that it trifurcates into three branches supplying a cir-soid aneurysm with a large draining pulmonary vein into the left atrium. After the large trunk was occluded with a nest of 10-, 8-, 5-, and 3-mm-diameter coils (C), the large right upper lobe branch with the trifurcating arteries became occluded and a secondary feeder (D) is demonstrated.

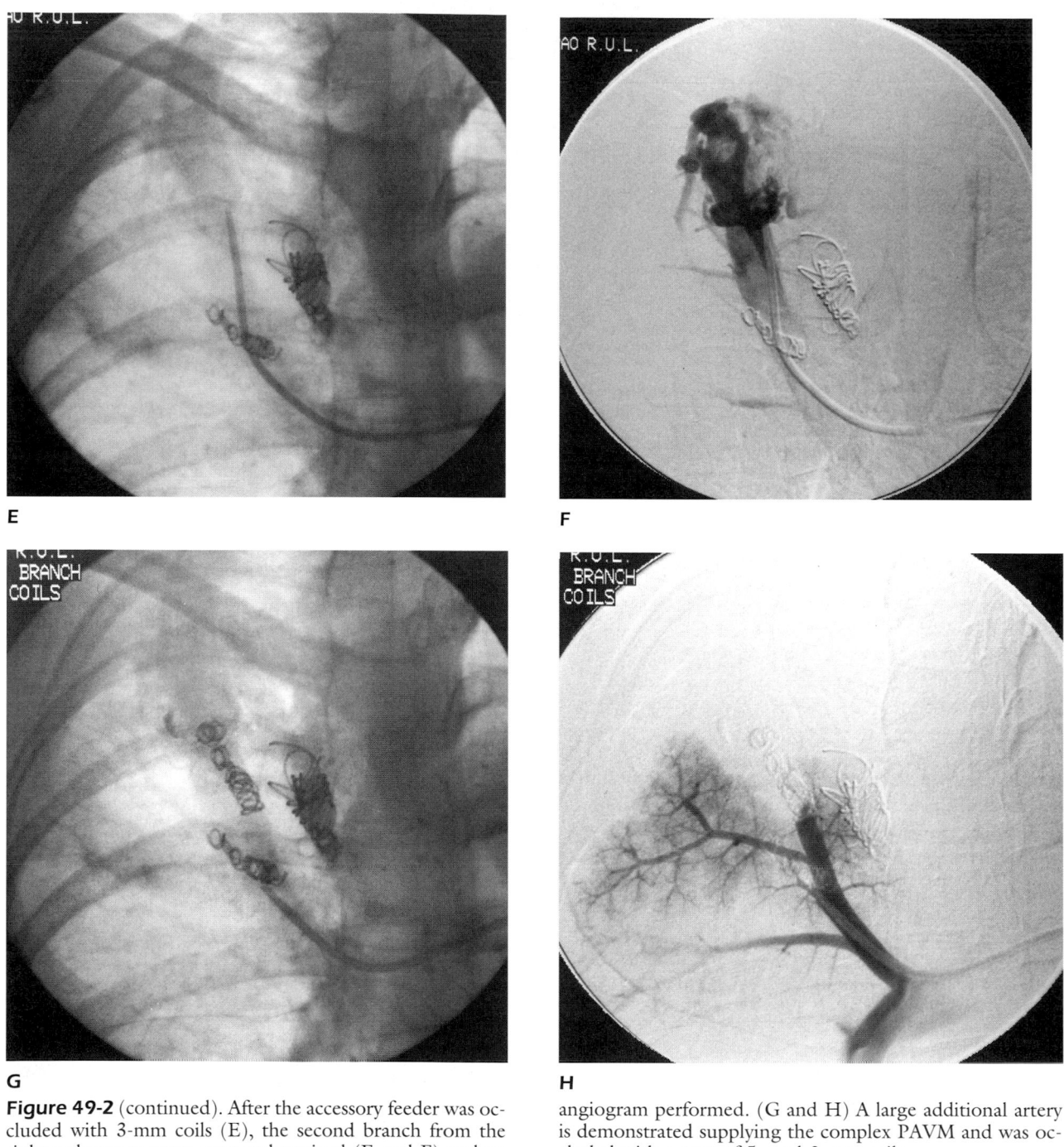

E

F

G

H

Figure 49-2 (continued). After the accessory feeder was occluded with 3-mm coils (E), the second branch from the right pulmonary artery was catheterized (E and F) and an angiogram performed. (G and H) A large additional artery is demonstrated supplying the complex PAVM and was occluded with a nest of 5- and 3-mm coils.

Figure 49-3. (A) A 16-year-old girl with diffuse right lower lobe PAVMs and one large simple PAVM. The large simple PAVM was occluded at age 16 and remained occluded despite deflation of the balloon at age 19 (not shown). The patient's arterial PO_2 sitting fell from 58 mmHg at age 16 to 51 mmHg at age 23. Selective right and left pulmonary angiograms at age 23 (B and C) demonstrate marked progression of right lower lobe diffuse PAVMs with relative sparing of the left lower lobe. (D) At age 25, during temporary occlusion of the right lower lobe with a 17-mm balloon catheter, the arterial PO_2 rose from 44 to 60 mmHg. (E) Permanent occlusion of the right lower lobe with a nest of 15- to 8-mm-diameter coils was performed at age 25. The patient's arterial PO_2 rose to 60 mmHg in the sitting position after the occlusion, and the cyanosis and dyspnea were significantly relieved at 6-month follow-up. ▶

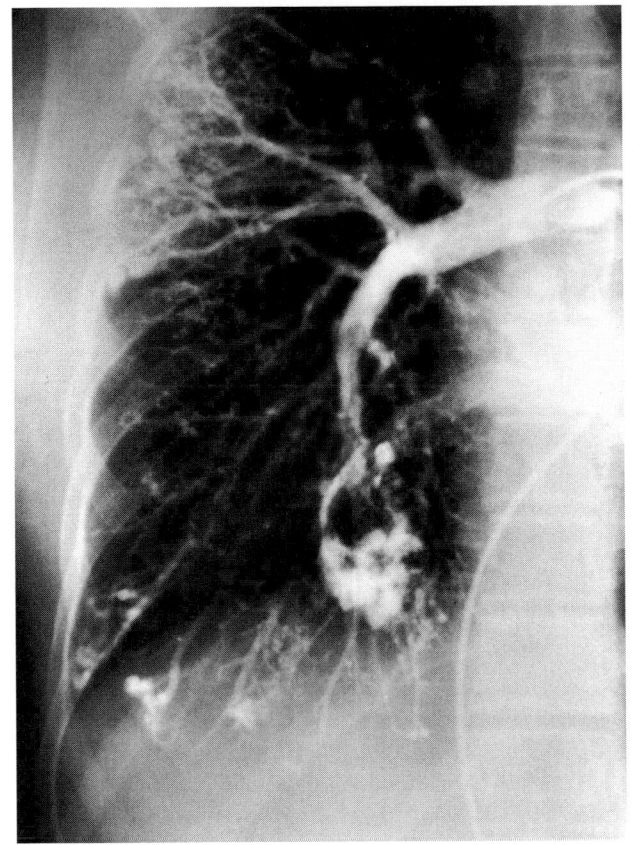

A

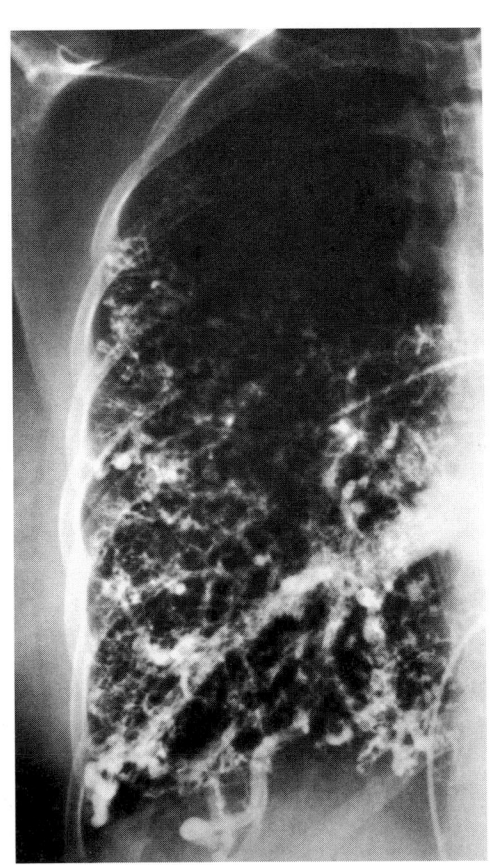

B

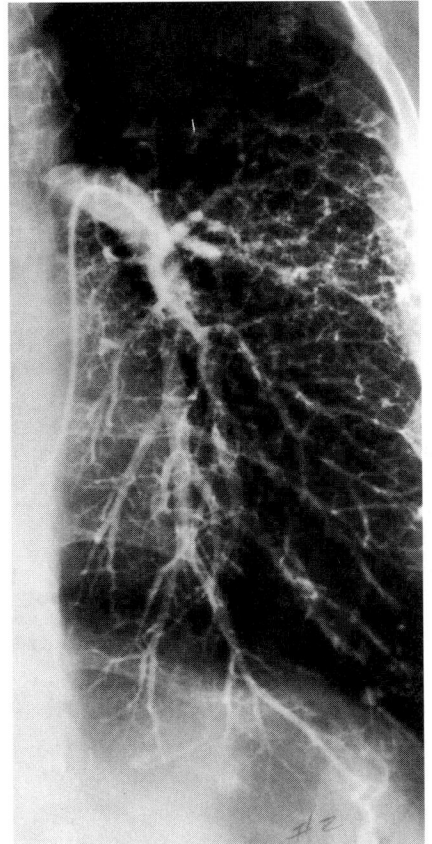

C

843

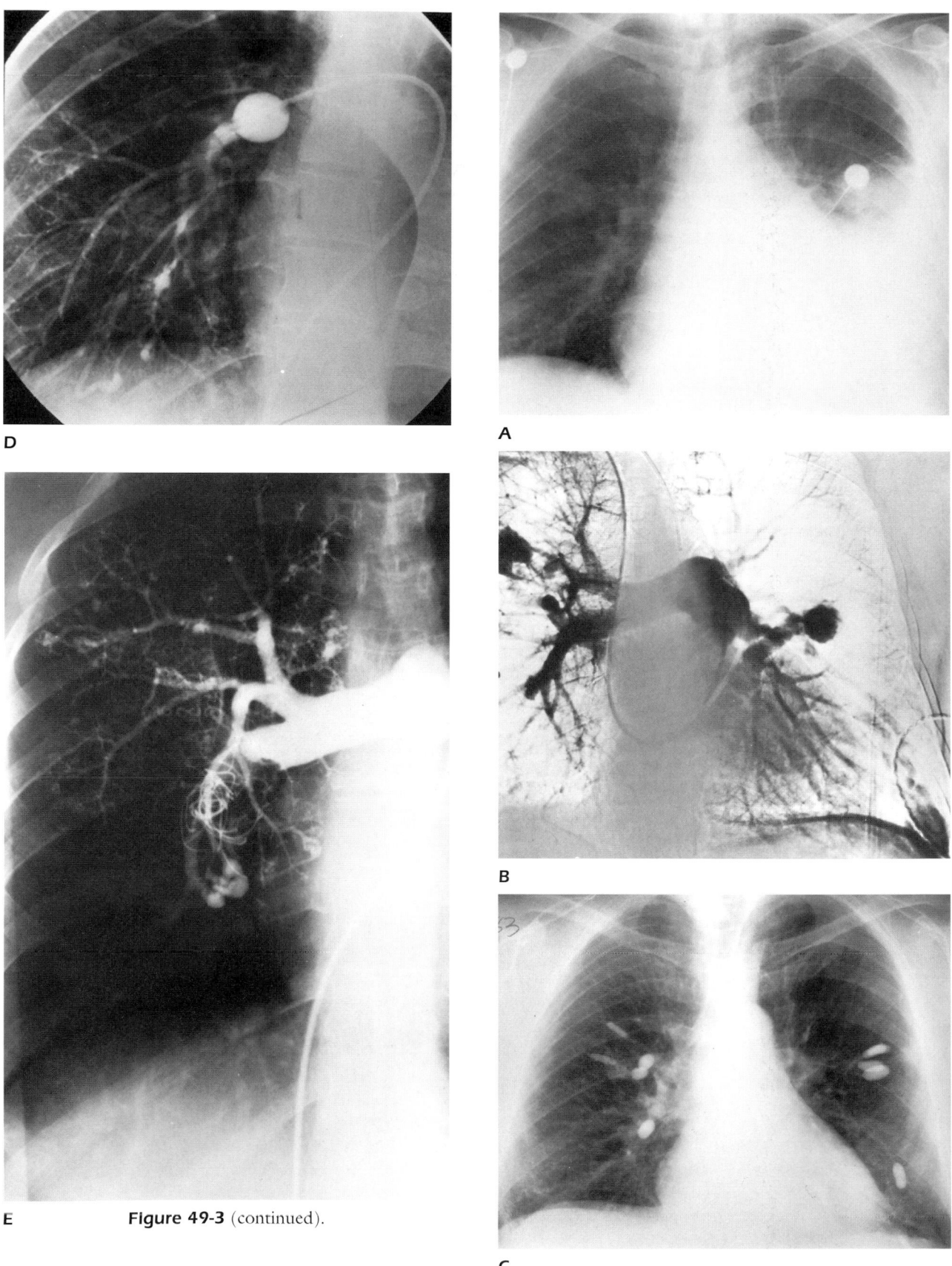

Figure 49-3 (continued).

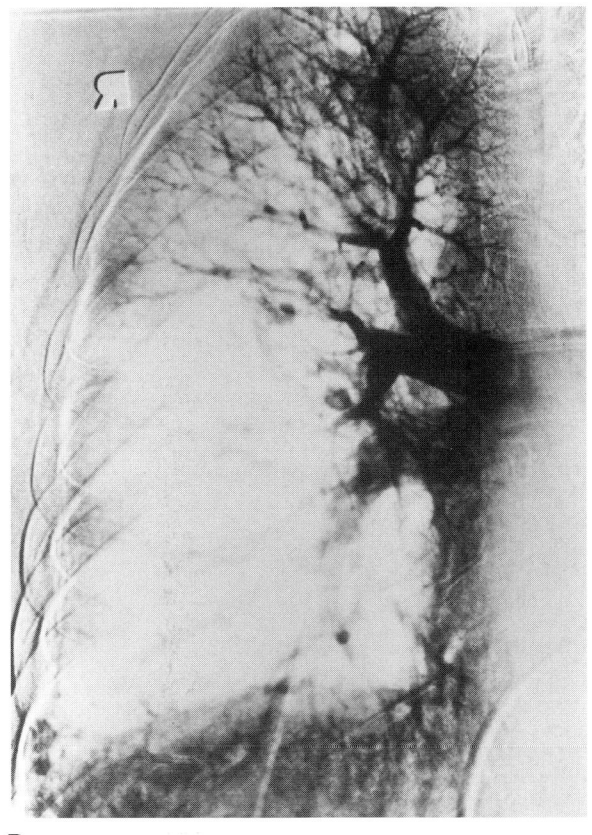

D

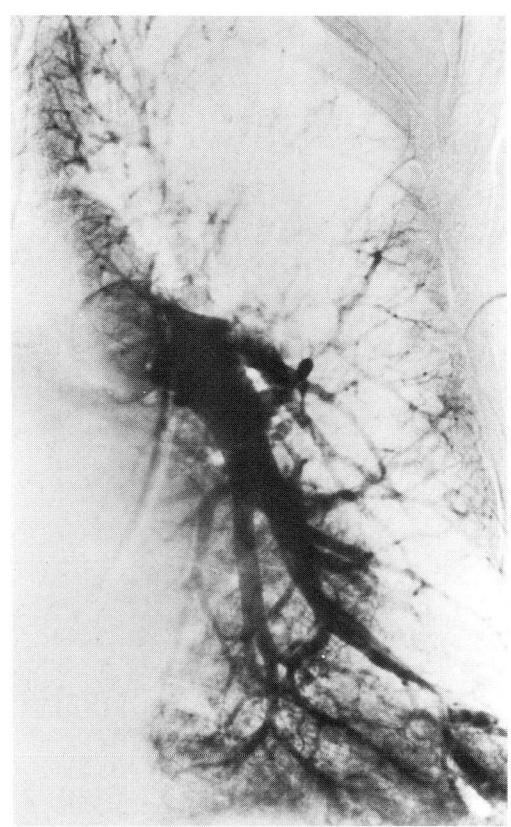

E

Figure 49-4. (A) A 63-year-old man who presented with massive left hemothorax and multiple PAVMs. (B) Central pulmonary angiogram 2 months after the hemothorax was evacuated demonstrates multiple PAVMs. (C) Detachable balloons were placed in all large PAVMs. (D and E) Repeat left and right selective pulmonary angiograms were performed 10 years later. Despite deflation of all balloons over the 10-year period of follow-up, all PAVMs remained occluded and the patient was asymptomatic. (Ference BA, Shannon TM, White RI Jr, et al. Life-threatening pulmonary hemorrhage associated with pulmonary arteriovenous malformations and hereditary hemorrhagic telangiectasia. Chest 1994;106:1387–1390. Used with permission.)

Technique of Embolotherapy

Goals of Therapy

Between 1978 and 1984, the authors' goals were to raise the arterial PO$_2$ to levels greater than 60 mmHg to achieve arterial oxygen saturation levels that would relieve dyspnea and return patients to a more "normal" life.[2] By 1984, it was realized that paradoxical embolization with clinical stroke was still occurring through large unoccluded PAVMs.[2] Since 1984, the authors have encouraged 3- to 5-year follow-up of all patients, including return visits and repeat pulmonary angiography for those patients with a 20 percent reduction in arterial oxygen tension.[14,47] In 1992, Rosenblatt demonstrated clinical stroke events in 4 of 17 patients with single PAVMs and arterial feeders 3 mm or larger in diameter.[48] Since this study the authors have occluded all PAVMs with arteries 3 mm or larger in diameter. In patients with multiple PAVMs in both lungs, this may require two or three short admissions over a 6-month period.

Although the authors believe that embolotherapy protects patients against further clinical stroke or TIA, it does not appear to protect them against brain abscess. Beginning in 1984, they recognized a striking association between brain abscess and dental manipulation. Others have also recognized this association.[49,50] In patients with HHT, many tiny, even microscopic malformations will remain after treatment. Because the authors are unable to relieve all shunting through small unoccluded PAVMs, they recommend that patients receive prophylactic oral antibiotics 1 hour before and 6 hours after dental work per the guidelines of the American Heart Association for the remainder of their lives.

Diagnostic Study

The authors prefer to perform a separate diagnostic study with multiple oblique projections, as described earlier. A tailored evaluation of the arterial pedicle to each PAVM in multiple projections is important because the arteries may enlarge immediately before entering the aneurysm of the PAVM. This needs to be recognized so that the occluding device can be placed proximal to the terminal enlargement of the PA branch, thus avoiding the potential for paradoxical embolization of the device. The diagnostic study also provides the best fluoroscopic angle for viewing the malformation, which is then used the next day during embolotherapy. The diagnostic study is usually performed via a left femoral vein approach.

Selective Catheterization

The transcatheter embolotherapy procedure is performed from the right femoral vein using an 8 French sheath. After a 7 French multipurpose end-hole catheter is placed in the right or left pulmonary artery, a variety of guidewires are used to selectively enter the branches to be occluded. A floppy "Bentson" wire is preferred, followed by a Terumo glidewire or a TAD (torsional attenuating diameter) wire. The multipurpose catheter serves well for selective catheterization of most basilar and upper lobe branches. Occasionally, an internal mammary artery catheter, with a steam-shaped proximal curve, is helpful for catheterization of the lingula and right middle lobe arteries.

A catheter should not be flushed unless it can be aspirated. Because of selective positioning of end-hole catheters, there is a tendency for catheters to become wedged. This problem can be overcome by either repositioning the multipurpose catheter or having the patient deeply inspire. This will move the end hole away from the artery wall or "unwedge" it so that blood can be aspirated gently before flushing or injecting contrast material. Flushing of a wedged catheter or passing of a detachable coil will introduce intravascular air, which can cause significant angina, bradycardia, and arrhythmias due to passage of air through the left side of the heart and into the coronary circulation.

When the major arterial feeder supplying the malformation is entered, hand injection IADSA is performed in the best projection possible to provide a view of the artery entering the aneurysm. At this point, depending on the branching pattern, the length of the artery supplying the malformation, and the size of the artery, the decision is made to either embolize the feeding artery with a nest of coils or to exchange for a larger catheter to introduce a balloon for occlusion. Often, in smaller malformations with 3- to 5-mm feeding arteries, a position distally in the artery cannot be achieved without wedging the selective catheter and risking air embolus. In these instances, an exchange can be made for a nontapered, soft, straight end-hole catheter for use with coils or balloons. Alternatively, if the larger 8 French balloon introducer catheter is in place, a detachable balloon can be advanced to the more distal position without the danger of air embolus (Fig. 49-5). Also, 5 French, 100- to 110-cm H1H or Berenstein-shaped catheters can be easily advanced through the 8 French introducer catheter for selective positioning in the feeding artery if coils are used later in the procedure. At the present time, the authors favor flow-directing a detachable balloon to the site of occlusion in order to avoid air embolus (see Fig. 49-5).

Embolization Devices

Most PAVMs may be safely occluded using detachable balloon techniques; in fact, in smaller vessels where wedging of catheters is a problem, proximal placement of the introducer catheter with distal balloon placement avoids the problem of air embolism (see Fig. 49-5). Detachable balloons also allow for temporary inflation and repeat IADSA views before detachment. The balloon position before detachment may be adjusted depending on the anatomy in an effort to preserve most of the normal branches of a large segmental feeder supplying the PAVM.

If the feeding artery is less than 2 or 3 cm in length, it may be difficult to achieve a safe position with the introducing catheters for the delivery of balloons or coils. In this instance or in extremely large vessels with high flow, occlusion balloon catheters (Medi-Tech, Arrow) with 0.035- to 0.038-inch inner diameters may be used to temporarily occlude the proximal portion of the artery and thus allow for the safe introduction of coils (Fig. 49-6). In very large PAVMs with arterial feeders greater than 10 mm in diameter, the risk of premature release of a detachable balloon potentially exists because of the large drag forces on the balloon. In this situation, flow can be reduced by inflating an occlusion balloon in the more proximal portion of the vessel. The occlusion balloon is introduced from one femoral vein while the introducer catheter for the detachable balloon is placed from the other femoral vein (Fig. 49-7).[46,51,52]

To achieve permanent closure of large PAVMs with coils, a nest of 4 to 12 coils is required. Using the IADSA selective injection at the time of embolotherapy or the diagnostic film-screen angiogram obtained

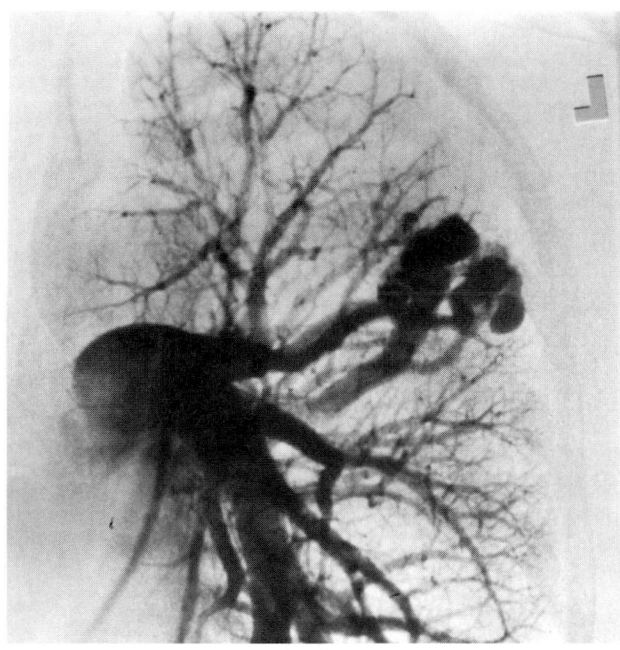

A

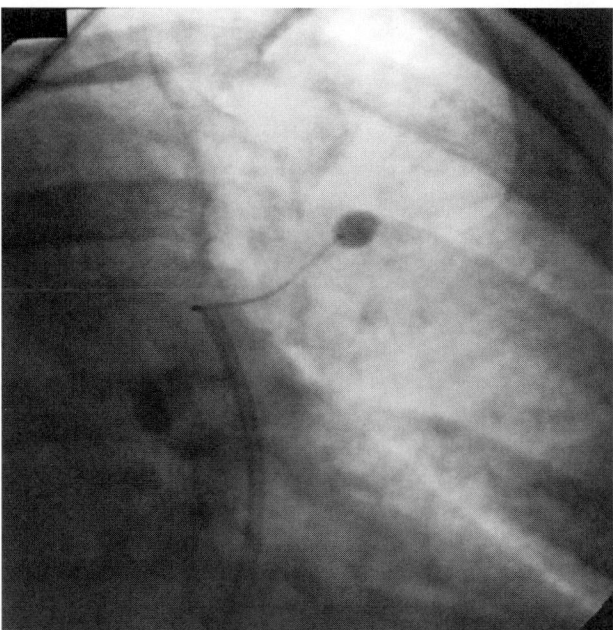

B

Figure 49-5. (A) Large simple left upper lobe PAVM with two aneurysmal components. (B) After multiple attempts to get the 8 French thin-walled introducer catheter into the feeding artery and the 5 French selective catheter through the 8 French catheter in a stable position, a still attached, detachable balloon was flow-directed into the artery. The 8 French catheter is placed at the origin of the left upper lobe. (C) After the balloon was further inflated, it was detached and a completion angiogram obtained. Note that the apical and posterior segmental branches are spared while selective occlusion of the anterior segmental branch to the PAVM is achieved.

earlier, a coil with a 2-mm-larger diameter than the feeding artery is placed initially. After two large coils are placed, others with progressively smaller diameters are chosen until the nest is formed. The authors have rarely seen persistent patency of PAVMs in patients referred after placement of three or more coils in the artery to a PAVM.

Detachable balloons are placed through the larger 8 French introducer catheter. At least 2 cm of relatively uniform diameter of the feeding artery needs to be present for safe placement of the balloons and 3 cm for coils. Rarely, with a very short feeding artery, the authors have resorted to occluding the aneurysm with oversized coils (Fig. 49-8).[53] In the one patient in which this technique was required, penetration of the aneurysm wall occurred after placement of the first coil. One needs to be ready to proceed quickly to finish the occlusion by introducing other coils to avoid significant hemorrhage under these circumstances. This patient did well with further embolization of the aneurysm.

C

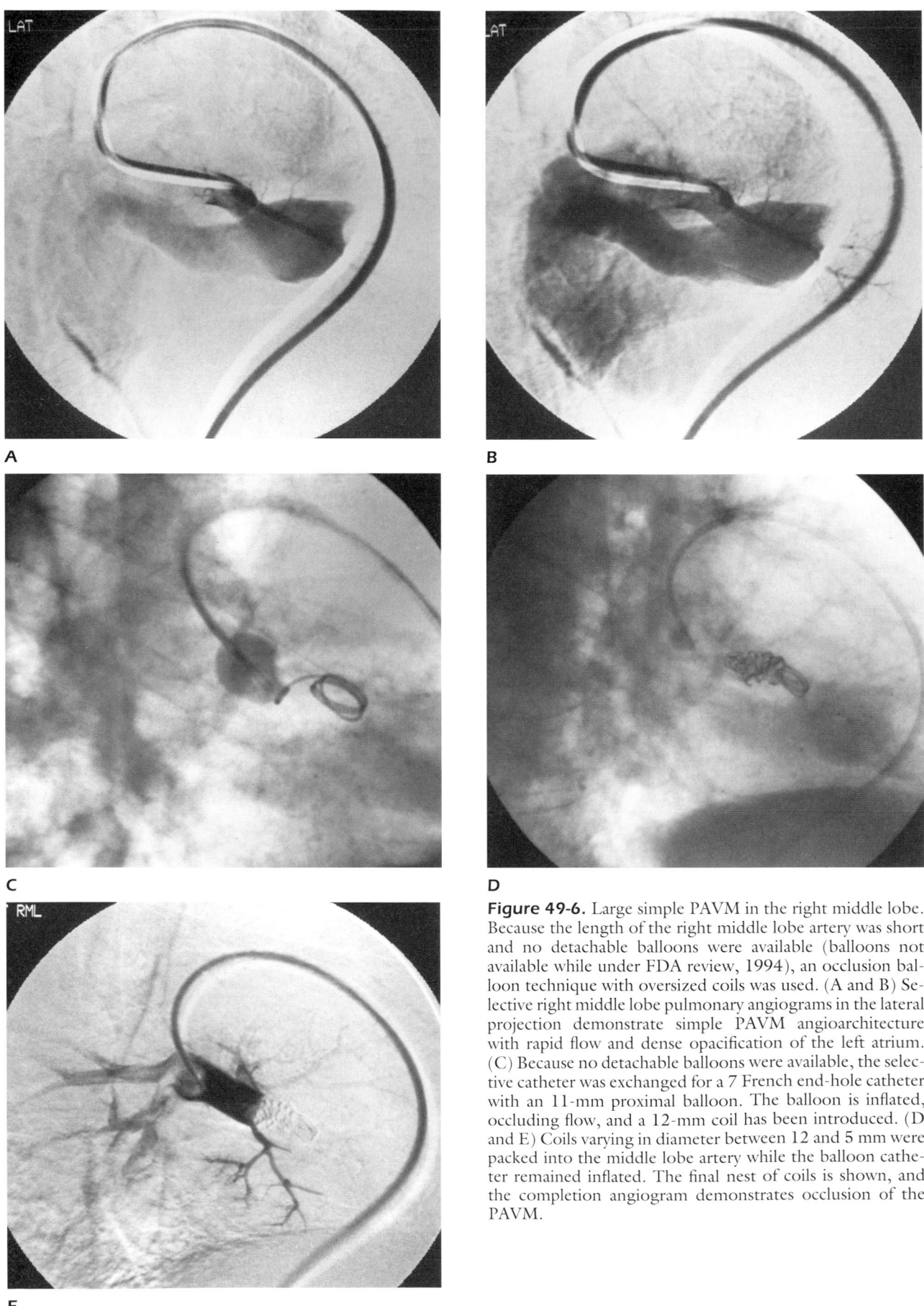

A

B

C

D

Figure 49-6. Large simple PAVM in the right middle lobe. Because the length of the right middle lobe artery was short and no detachable balloons were available (balloons not available while under FDA review, 1994), an occlusion balloon technique with oversized coils was used. (A and B) Selective right middle lobe pulmonary angiograms in the lateral projection demonstrate simple PAVM angioarchitecture with rapid flow and dense opacification of the left atrium. (C) Because no detachable balloons were available, the selective catheter was exchanged for a 7 French end-hole catheter with an 11-mm proximal balloon. The balloon is inflated, occluding flow, and a 12-mm coil has been introduced. (D and E) Coils varying in diameter between 12 and 5 mm were packed into the middle lobe artery while the balloon catheter remained inflated. The final nest of coils is shown, and the completion angiogram demonstrates occlusion of the PAVM.

E

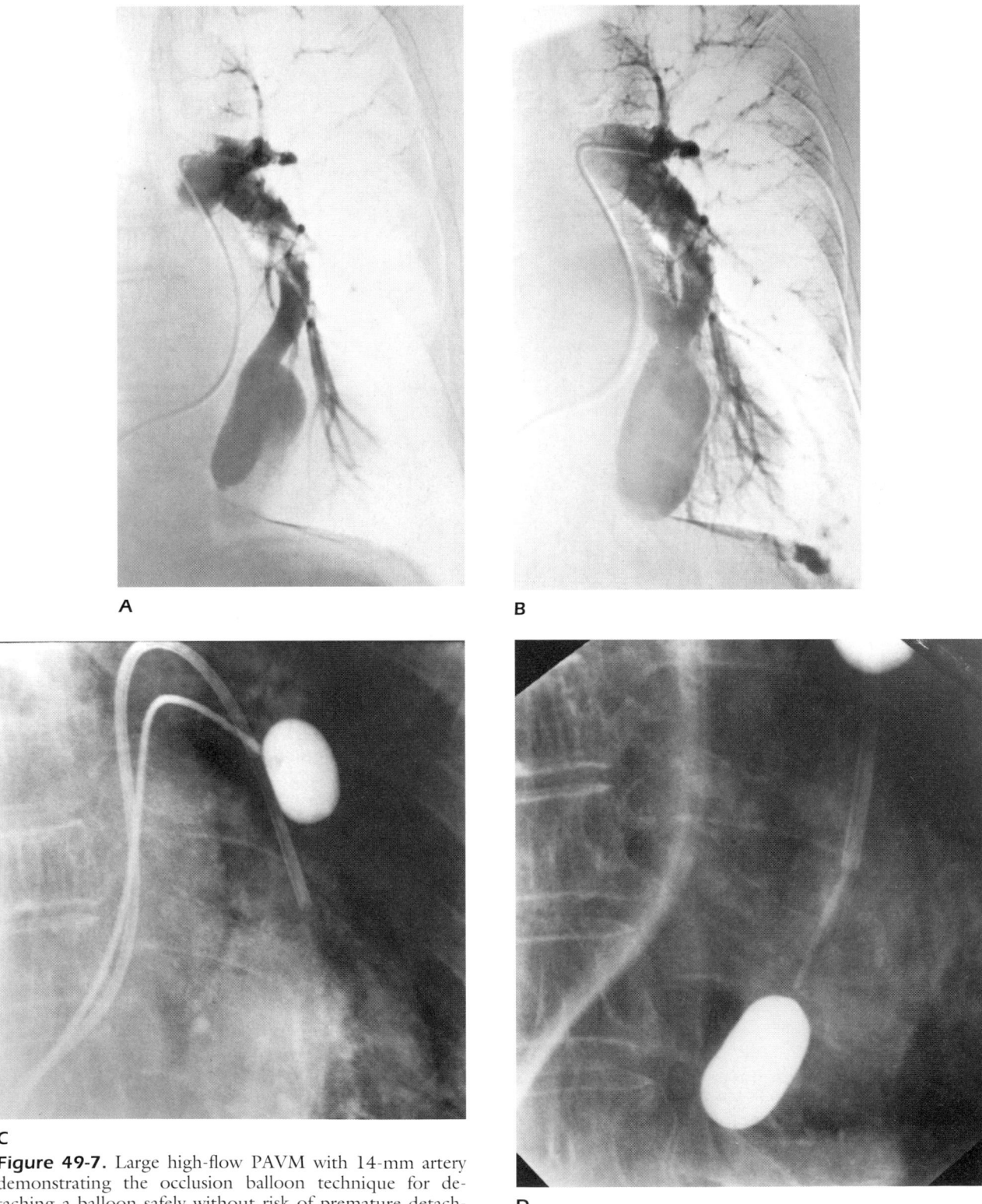

A

B

C

D

Figure 49-7. Large high-flow PAVM with 14-mm artery demonstrating the occlusion balloon technique for detaching a balloon safely without risk of premature detachment. (A and B) Selective left pulmonary angiogram, early and later phases, demonstrates a large artery, an aneurysm, and the draining vein of a "simple" PAVM. (C) To temporarily occlude the supplying artery while placing a detachable balloon distally in the artery, a 17-mm Boston Scientific occlusion balloon was placed proximally from one femoral vein and a 9 French introducer catheter was placed distally, beyond the balloon occlusion catheter, from the other femoral view. A distal balloon was placed coaxially (D) just above the aneurysm (*legend continues on page 850*)

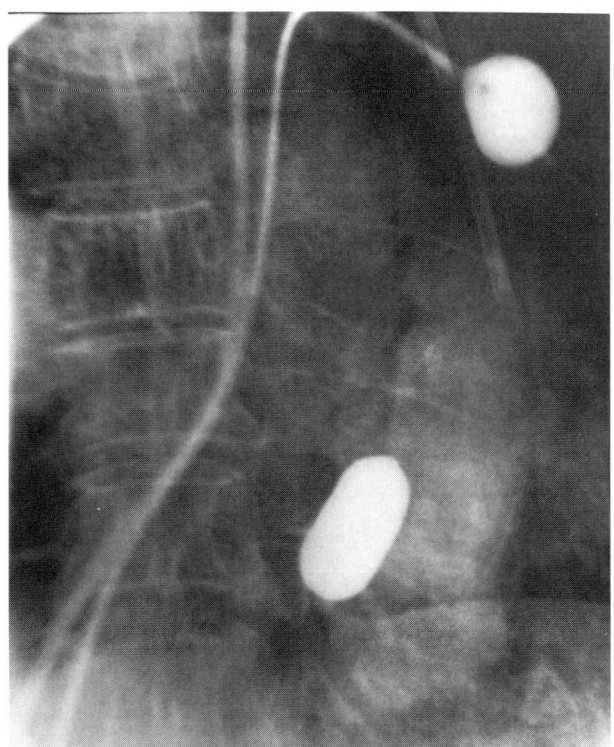
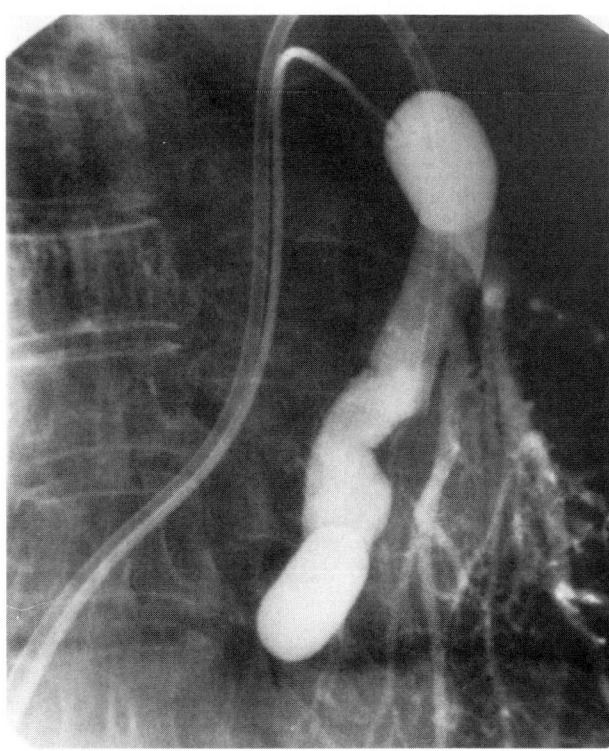

E

F

Figure 49-7 (continued). and detached (E). A conclusion pulmonary angiogram (F) demonstrates satisfactory occlusion of the artery to the PAVM. Before the proximal occlusion balloon was removed, a second detachable balloon was placed above the first one (not shown).

Complications of Embolotherapy

Paradoxical Embolization of Balloon or Coils

The authors have had two instances of paradoxical embolization of a balloon early in their experience,[7] and other patients have been referred to them because of paradoxical embolization of balloons or coils. To avoid device migration through the PAVM, it is important to have an accurate angiographic image of the feeding artery diameter and morphology in the preaneurysmal segment of the artery. If coils traverse the aneurysm and escape into the systemic circulation, they may be retrieved by intravascular snares. When a balloon is trapped in a nonessential systemic artery, it is easily punctured percutaneously with a 22-gauge needle, as long as distal migration of the small balloon shell does not have the potential for causing symptomatic ischemia. If a balloon does migrate into an essential artery like the carotid, surgical removal is required.

Air Embolus

This complication occurs when air is inadvertently introduced during selective angiography or balloon and

coil positioning. Small amounts of air traverse the aneurysm, pulmonary vein, left atrium, and ventricle to selectively enter the right coronary artery (RCA). The "RCA" ostium arises anteriorly from the right sinus of Valsalva and is in a nondependent position when the patient is supine. It is presumed that air emboli traverse the aorta and during diastole may flow rather selectively into the anteriorly located right sinus of Valsalva and right coronary artery ostium. The patient immediately experiences chest pain or chest tightness associated with bradycardia and multiple premature ventricular contractions, which may last up to 20 minutes. Sublingual nitroglycerin is administered and intravenous atropine (0.5–1.0 mg) is injected. After 20 minutes, the authors proceed with the rest of the procedure if all the symptoms and electrocardiographic changes have disappeared. They have not recorded any permanent electrocardiographic changes or noted cardiac enzyme elevation the following day. This reaction is frightening to the patient and potentially very dangerous if a large bolus of air is inadvertently injected.

In the authors' original series of 76 patients reported in 1988, 5 percent of patients experienced anginal-type symptoms during one of their catheterizations.[7] During 1988 to 1992, 4 out of 83 patients

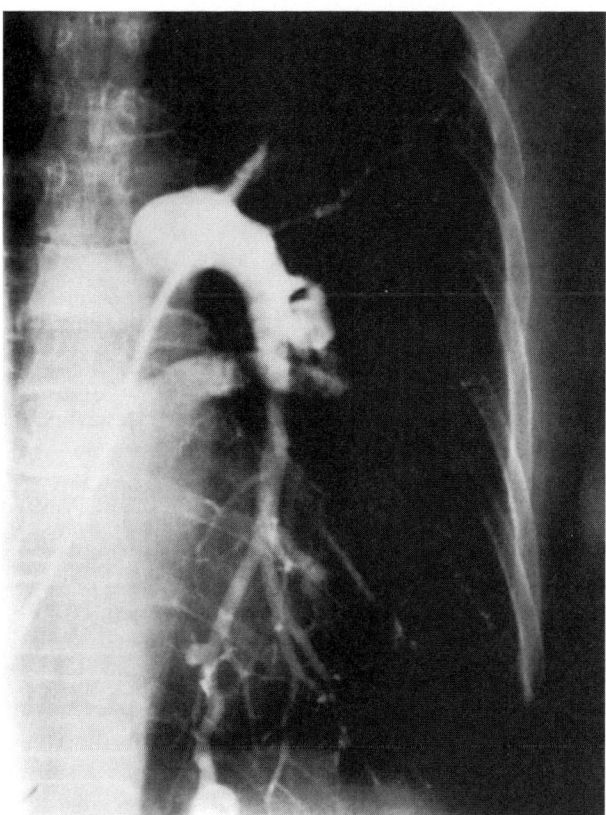

A

B

Figure 49-8. Large simple PAVM with short feeding artery arising from the superior segmental artery to the left lower lobe. Selective left pulmonary angiogram in the anteroposterior (A) and right posterior oblique (B) position demonstrates the anatomy. Because a safe position for balloon or coil deposition in the feeding artery could not be obtained, the aneurysm was occluded instead. (C) During placement of the first oversized coil, the patient began coughing. The final radiography demonstrates the occluded aneurysm with alveolar hemorrhage around it. The patient had no sequelae, but because aneurysms are so thin-walled, the authors prefer to always occlude the artery rather than the aneurysm. (From Denny DF, Markowitz DM, Pollak JS, Yoselevitz M. Thoracic vascular interventional procedures. Semin Intervent Radiol 1991;8:51–77. Used with permission.)

(5 percent) have also experienced mild anginal symptoms during coil placement.[47] These episodes were of much shorter duration and severity than those experienced by patients in the authors' original series. As discussed in the section on technique, to prevent air embolization, no catheter is flushed or coil introduced unless there is clear return of blood. One may spend up to 30 to 60 minutes gaining a satisfactory position for embolization, only to discover that the catheter cannot be aspirated. If a coil or balloon is introduced at that time, air often accompanies it. It is for this reason that leaving an introducer catheter more proxi-

C

mally placed where it is easily aspirated and flow-directing a balloon to the distal occlusion site are often preferred over superselective positioning in small and tortuous arterial pedicles.

Venous Complications

Thrombophlebitis occurred in one early patient after three venous catheterizations during the same admission through the right femoral vein.[7] The authors have not experienced an episode of phlebitis since alternating femoral vein catheterization sites. All patients receive intravenous heparinization (4000–5000 units plus 1000 units per hour) during embolization procedures.

Delayed Pleurisy

In 16 (20 percent) of the authors' last 83 patients, mild to moderate pleurisy has occurred 48 to 72 hours after embolotherapy. This syndrome consists of pleuritic chest pain that may be accompanied by fever as high as 102°F and that is believed to be caused by pulmonary infarction. Pleurisy often occurs after the patient has been discharged and usually lasts 3 to 5 days. It is readily managed by acetaminophen or ibuprofen and by reassuring the patient of the self-limited nature of the symptoms. Oral narcotics are rarely needed. In 2 patients in which coils were used, high fever and pleurisy 2 weeks after occlusion necessitated oral antibiotics with resolution.

Remy et al. have studied this phenomenon more completely with chest radiographs and CT and have reached similar conclusions.[35,36] The present authors have all patients use a handheld incentive spirometer every hour while awake for the first 4 or 5 days after the occlusion and at home. Although not proven, it appears that keeping the lung expanded maximally during the first week after embolotherapy minimizes pleurisy in the 20 percent of patients who experience it. In addition, it is felt that spending the necessary time to place the occluding device beyond all PA branches to normal lung minimizes this self-limited pulmonary infarction. The authors believe that pleurisy is more common after coil embolization or when the aneurysm is pleural based.

Reperfusion

Remy and associates have recently emphasized that up to 10 percent of patients will have persistence or recurrence of the PAVM after initial embolotherapy.[35-37] This phenomenon has also recently been described by Puskas et al. in the summary of experience at the Massachusetts General Hospital.[13,14] The present authors' experience at Johns Hopkins Hospital appeared to differ in that all 16 of 76 patients restudied through 1987 had permanent occlusion of their PAVM. However, since beginning study of a new balloon in 1990 at Yale–New Haven Hospital, the authors have performed chest radiology and ABGs 30 days after occlusion in all patients.[47] From these data, they concur with Remy that 10 percent of patients do have persistent perfusion or reperfusion of the PAVM as a result of continued patency of the arterial feeder or of an accessory branch to a complex PAVM that was missed during the initial embolotherapy. In addition, Remy and Laffey have described the development of systemic transpleural collaterals that maintain the aneurysm and account for a reperfusion phenomenon.[37,54] In most instances, reperfusion can be treated by a repeat 24-hour admission to occlude the remaining arterial feeders.

Figure 49-9. Right middle lung field pulmonary aneurysm in a 53-year-old woman, which doubled in size between 1973 (A) and 1988 (B).

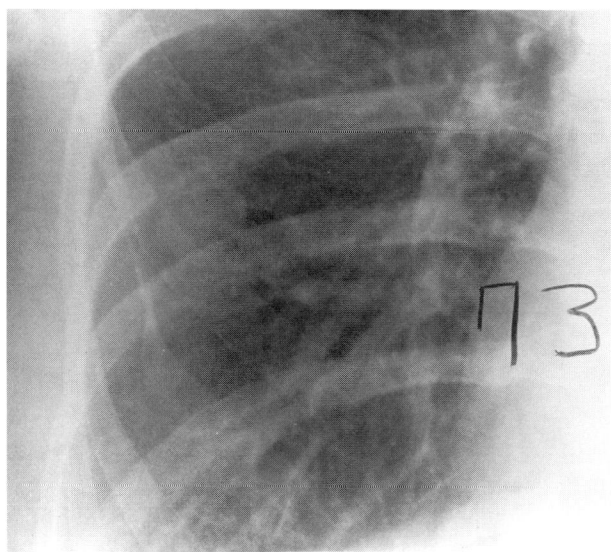

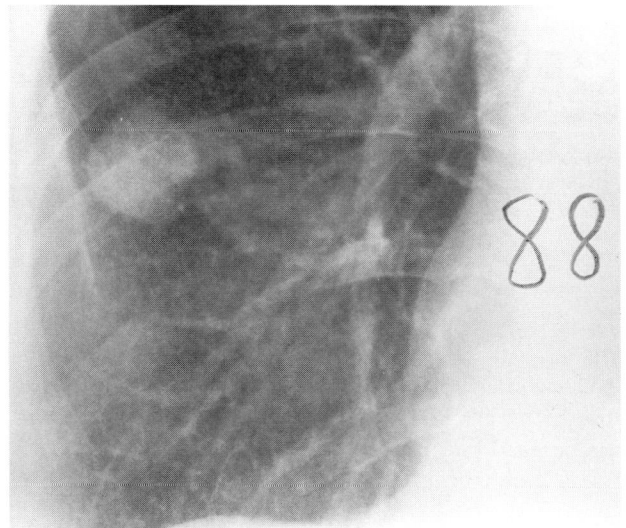

A

B

Serial Growth of PAVMs and Long-Term Follow-up After Embolotherapy

Vase and associates emphasize that unoccluded PAVMs grow slowly, and the authors have noted this as well (Fig. 49-9).[16] It is important for all patients with PAVMs, whether they undergo treatment or not, to have serial evaluations every 3 to 5 years. This evaluation includes measurement of ABGs on room air and 100 percent oxygen as well as a chest radiograph. When the feeding arteries of unoccluded PAVMs exceed 3 mm in diameter, patients should be treated because of the risk of paradoxical embolization.[48]

In summary, PAVMs appear to occur more commonly in patients with HHT than was previously recognized. Furthermore, if one family with HHT has a family member with PAVM, the expression of PAVM in other asymptomatic family members will be much more common than previously reported.[8] As is so common in patients with rare disorders, a large series comparing surgical and radiologic outcomes is not available. From the authors' own data and that of Hughes and Allison,[55] transcatheter embolotherapy still appears to be the treatment of choice for PAVMs.[55] In the small group of patients who have persistence or recurrence, the technique can be readily performed again as part of a short-stay admission.

Finally, the varying presentations of patients with HHT and PAVM provide a challenge for many specialists and generalists. With the discovery of the chromosome for HHT and the promise of improved genetic diagnosis, more patients with this disorder will undoubtedly be identified, allowing for earlier treatment of those affected by PAVM.[56–58]

References

1. Burke CM, Safai C, Nelson DP, Raffin TA. Pulmonary arteriovenous malformations: a critical update. Am Rev Respir Dis 1986;134:334–339.
2. Hewes RC, Auster M, White RI Jr. Cerebral embolism: first manifestation of pulmonary arteriovenous malformation in patients with hereditary hemorrhagic telangiectasia. Cardiovasc Intervent Radiol 1985;8:151–155.
3. Churton T. Multiple aneurysms of pulmonary artery. Br Med J 1897;1:1223.
4. Rodes CB. Cavernous hemangiomas of lung with secondary polycythemia. JAMA 1938;110:1914–1915.
5. Hodgson CH, Burchell HB, Good CA, Claggett OT. Hereditary hemorrhagic telangiectasia and pulmonary arteriovenous fistula; study of a large family. N Engl J Med 1959;26:625–636.
6. Dines DE, Arms RA, Bernatz PE, Gomes MR. Pulmonary arteriovenous fistulas. Mayo Clin Proc 1974;49:460–465.
7. White RI Jr, Lynch-Nyhan A, Terry P, et al. Pulmonary arteriovenous malformations: technic and long term outcome of embolotherapy. Radiology 1988;169:663–669.
8. Ference BA, Shannon TM, White RI Jr, et al. Life threatening pulmonary hemorrhage associated with pulmonary arteriovenous malformations and hereditary hemorrhagic telangiectasia. Chest 1994;106:1387–1390.
9. Hepburn J, Dauphine JA. Successful removal of hemangioma of lung followed by disappearance of polycythemia. Am J Med Sci 1942;204:681–687.
10. Lindskog EE, Liebow AA, Kausel H, Jenzen A. Pulmonary arteriovenous aneurysm. Ann Surg 1950;132:591–610.
11. Packard GB, Waring JJ. Arterio-venous fistula of the lung treated by ligation of the pulmonary artery. Arch Surg 1945;56:724–740.
12. Bosher LH Jr, Blake DA, Byrd BR. An analysis of the pathologic anatomy of pulmonary arteriovenous aneurysms with particular reference to the applicability of local excision. Surgery 1959;45:91–104.
13. Puskas JD, Allen MS, Moncure AC, et al. Pulmonary arteriovenous malformations: therapeutic options. Ann Thorac Surg 1993;56:253–258.
14. White RI Jr, Pollak JS. Pulmonary arteriovenous malformations: options for management. Ann Thorac Surg 1994;57:519–521.
15. Brown SE, Wright PW, Renner JW, et al. Staged bilateral thoracotomies for multiple pulmonary arteriovenous malformations complicating hereditary hemorrhagic telangiectasia. J Thorac Cardiovasc Surg 1982;83:258–289.
16. Vase P, Holm M, Arendreys P. Pulmonary arteriovenous fistulas in hereditary hemorrhagic telangiectasia. Acta Med Scand 1985;218:105–109.
17. Teragaki M, Akioka K, Yasuda M. Case report: hereditary hemorrhagic telangiectasia with growing pulmonary arteriovenous fistulas followed for 24 years. Am J Med Sci 1988;295:545–547.
18. Porstmann W. Therapeutic embolization of arteriovenous fistula by catheter technique. In: Kelop O, ed. Current concepts in pediatric radiology. Berlin: Springer, 1977:23–31.
19. Taylor BG, Cockerill EM, Manfredi F, Klatte EC. Therapeutic embolization of the pulmonary artery in pulmonary arteriovenous fistula. Am J Med 1978;64:360–365.
20. Terry PB, Barth KH, Kaufman SL, White RI Jr. Balloon embolization for treatment of pulmonary arteriovenous fistulas. N Engl J Med 1980;302:1189–1190.
21. Cloutier A, Ash JM, Smallhorn JF, Williams WG, Trusler GA, Rowe RD, Rabinowitz M. Abnormal distribution of pulmonary blood flow after the Glenn shunt or Fontan procedure: risk of development of arteriovenous fistulae. Circulation 1985;72:471.
22. Moore JW, Kirby WC, Madden WA, Gaither NS. Development of pulmonary arteriovenous malformations after modified Fontan operations. J Thorac Cardiovasc Surg 1989;98:1045–1050.
23. Kopf GS, Laks H, Stansel HC, Hellenbrand WE, et al. Thirty-year follow-up of superior vena cava–pulmonary artery (Glenn) shunts. J Thorac Cardiovasc Surg 1990;100:662–671.
24. von Scheidt W, von Arnim T, Schneider B, Erlmann E. Balloon embolization of a pulmonary arteriovenous fistula after cavopulmonary anastomosis in tricuspid atresia. Am Heart J 1988;116:182–185.
25. Bartter T, Irwin RS, Nash G. Aneurysms of the pulmonary arteries. Chest 1988;94:1065–1075.
26. Stricker H, Malinverni R. Multiple, large aneurysms of pulmonary arteries in Behcet's disease: clinical remission and radiologic resolution after corticosteroid therapy. Arch Intern Med 1989;149:925–927.
27. Bartter T, Irwin RS, Philips DA, Benotti JR, Worthington-Kirsch RL. Pulmonary artery pseudoaneurysm: a potential complication of pulmonary artery catheterization. Arch Intern Med 1988;148:471–473.
28. Carlson TA, Goldenberg IF, Murray PD, Tadavarthy M, Walker M, Gobel FL. Catheter-induced delayed recurrent pul-

monary artery hemorrhage: intervention with therapeutic embolism of the pulmonary artery. JAMA 1989;262:1943–1945.

29. Smart FW, Husserl FE. Complications of flow-directed balloon-tipped catheters. Chest 1990;97:227–228.

30. Renie WA, Rodeheffer RJ, Mitchell S, Balke WC, White RI Jr. Balloon embolization of a mycotic pulmonary aneurysm. Am Rev Respir Dis 1982;126:1107–1110.

31. Perry WH. Clinical spectrum of hereditary hemorrhagic telangiectasia (Osler-Weber-Rendu disease). Am J Med 1987;82:989–997.

32. Plauchu H, de Chadarevian JP, Bideau A, Robert JM. Age-related clinical profile of hereditary hemorrhagic telangiectasia in an epidemiologically recruited population. Am J Med Genet 1989;32:291–297.

33. Porteous MEM, Burn J, Proctor SJ. Hereditary haemorrhagic telangiectasia: a clinical analysis. Med Genet 1992;29:527–530.

34. White RI Jr. Pulmonary arteriovenous malformations: how do we diagnose them and why is it important to do so? Radiology 1992;182:633–635.

35. Remy-Jardin M, Wattinne L, Remy J. Transcatheter occlusion of pulmonary arterial circulation and collateral supply: failures, incidents, and complications. Radiology 1991;180:699–705.

36. Remy J, Remy-Jardin M, Wattinne L, Deffontaines S. Pulmonary arteriovenous malformations: evaluation with CT of the chest before and after treatment. Radiology 1992;182:809–816.

37. Remy J, Remy-Jardin M, Giraud F, Wattinne L. Angioarchitecture of pulmonary arteriovenous malformations: clinical utility of three dimensional spiral CT. Radiology 1994;191:657–664.

38. Terry PB, White RI Jr, Barth KH, et al. Pulmonary arteriovenous malformations: physiologic observations and results of therapeutic balloon embolization. N Engl J Med 1983;308:1197–1210.

39. Chilvers ER, Peters AM, George P, et al. Effect of percutaneous transcatheter embolization on pulmonary function, right-to-left shunt, and arterial oxygenation in patients with pulmonary arteriovenous malformations. Am Rev Respir Dis 1990;142:420–425.

40. Chilvers ER, Peters AM, George P, et al. Quantification of right-to-left shunt through pulmonary arteriovenous malformations using $^{99}Tc^m$ albumin microspheres. Clin Radiol 1988;39:611–614.

41. Chub C, Tajik AJ, Seward JB, Dines DE. Detecting intrapulmonary right-to-left shunt with contrast echocardiography. Mayo Clin Proc 1976;51:81–84.

42. Barzilai B, Waggoner AD, Spessert C, Picus D, Goodenberger D. Two-dimensional echocardiography in the detection and follow-up of congenital pulmonary arteriovenous malformations. Am J Cardiol 1991;68:1507–1510.

43. Dinsmore BJ, Gefter WB, Hatabu H, Kressel HY. Pulmonary arteriovenous malformations: diagnosis by gradient refocused MR imaging. J Comput Assist Tomogr 1990;14:918–923.

44. Bergin CJ, Pualy JM, Macovski A. Lung parenchyma: projection reconstruction MR imaging. Radiology 1991;179:777–781.

45. White RI Jr, Mitchell SE, Barth KH, et al. Angioarchitecture of pulmonary arteriovenous malformations: an important consideration before therapy. AJR 1983;140:681–686.

46. Shannon T, Pollak JS, White RI Jr. Redistribution of pulmonary blood flow by embolotherapy: a new method for improving oxygenation in patients with diffuse pulmonary arteriovenous malformations. Am Rev Respir Dis 1992;145(Suppl):A600.

47. Pollak JS, Egglin TK, Rosenblatt MM, et al. Clinical results of transvenous systemic embolotherapy with a neuroradiological balloon. Radiology May 1994;191:477–482.

48. Rosenblatt M, Pollak JS, Fayad PB, Egglin TE, White RI Jr. Pulmonary arteriovenous malformations: what size should be treated to prevent embolic stroke? Radiology 1993;186:937.

49. White RI Jr. Case 16-1990: Brain abscess and pulmonary arteriovenous malformation. N Engl J Med 1991;324:1439–1440.

50. Mohler ER, Monahan B, Canty MD, Flockhart DA. Cerebral abscess associated with dental procedure in hereditary haemorrhagic telangiectasia. Lancet 1991;338:507–509.

51. Florentine M, Wolfe RR, White RI Jr. Balloon embolization to occlude a Blalock-Taussig shunt. J Am Coll Cardiol 1984;3:200–202.

52. White RI, Mitchell SE, Kan J. Interventional procedures in congenital heart disease. Cardiovasc Intervent Radiol 1986;9:286–298.

53. Denny DF, Markowitz DM, Pollak JS, Yoselevitz M. Thoracic vascular interventional procedures. Semin Intervent Radiol 1991;8:51–77.

54. Laffey KS, Thomashaw A, Jaretzki A, Martin EC. Systemic supply to a pulmonary arteriovenous malformation: a relative contraindication to surgery. AJR 1985;145:720–722.

55. Hughes JMB, Allison DJ. Pulmonary arteriovenous malformations: the radiologist replaces the surgeon. Clin Radiol 1990;41:297–298.

56. McDonald MT, Papenberg KA, Ghosh S, Glatfelter AA, et al. A disease locus for hereditary haemorrhagic telangiectasia maps to chromosome 9q33-34. Nature Genetics 1994;6:197–204.

57. Shovlin CL, Hughes JMB, Tuddenham EGD, Temperley I, et al. A gene for hereditary haemorrhagic telangiectasia maps to chromosome 9q3. Nature Genetics 1994;6:205–209.

58. Guttmacher AE, Marchuk DA, White RI Jr. Hereditary hemorrhagic telangiectasia. N Engl J Med 1995;333:918–924.

VII

Interventional Radiology
of Trauma

50

Arteriography and Transcatheter Treatment of Extremity Trauma

MICHAEL D. KATZ
SUE E. HANKS

When traumatic injuries to vascular structures are suspected, prompt and accurate diagnosis is essential to minimize adverse sequelae. Arteriography is an important part of the management of patients with suspected vascular injury, both for diagnosis and for treatment. With the rise in trauma related to increasing urban violence, the interventional radiologist is increasingly called on to diagnose and treat acute arterial injuries.

History of Extremity Trauma Management

The principles of diagnosis and therapy for civilian trauma have evolved largely from military experience. During World War II, most extremity arterial injuries were treated by ligation. This treatment resulted in a high rate of limb amputation.[1] During the Korean and Vietnam wars, primary vascular repair was performed for arterial injuries. This therapy markedly decreased the amputation rate, from 48 to 62 percent down to 7 to 13 percent, and a policy of mandatory surgical exploration was adopted.[2,3]

This military experience with high-velocity extremity wounds was extrapolated to civilian trauma, leading to a large number of negative surgical explorations. Since the late 1970s arteriography has replaced surgical exploration in most patients, reducing negative explorations from 84 to 3 percent.[4] Accumulated experience has shown arteriography to be a safe and accurate means of diagnosing vascular injury.[5–8] Concern has recently focused on the resultant large number of negative arteriograms rather than on negative explorations.

Indications for arteriography for extremity trauma remain controversial. The increasing endorsement of expectant management of minor vascular injuries has caused surgeons and radiologists alike to question whether diagnosis of such injuries is necessary. The utility of arteriography, however, goes beyond diagnostic purposes. Arteriography can also be used therapeutically to guide transcatheter embolization, which can be definitive therapy for suitable lesions.

Indications for Arteriography

The clinical situation, physical findings, and mechanism of injury play a large role in directing trauma management. In all forms of trauma—penetrating, iatrogenic, and blunt—physical examination is central to patient selection. Not all patients require arteriography for extremity trauma. For example, a patient with a through-and-through gunshot wound in the distal thigh, an expanding hematoma, and no distal pulses clearly has a superficial femoral artery injury, precisely localized by the wound. This injury requires prompt surgical repair rather than arteriography. Arteriography is indicated when an injury is suspected but not certain, when there are multiple potential vascular injury sites, when the location of injury is not clear (e.g., involves a long path through the limb), or when an injury might be amenable to transcatheter therapy.[9]

Significant clinical findings in extremity trauma that increase suspicion for arterial injury include pulse deficit, bruit, expanding hematoma, a history of hypotension or significant bleeding, and possibly neurologic deficit. Pulse deficit, the most important finding, indicates arterial injury in 56 to 87 percent of cases.[10–12] Although uncommon, the presence of a bruit or thrill, suggestive of an arteriovenous fistula (AVF), yields a positive arteriogram rate of nearly 100 percent.[10,11] An expanding hematoma is associated with arterial injury in 38 percent.[11] Patients who present with these findings should therefore undergo emergency arteriography for suspected vascular injury. A neurologic deficit has been found to be associated with a high percentage of vascular injuries in some studies, but this finding has not been confirmed by others.[10,12-14] Other physical signs, such as long bone fracture or large areas of soft tissue injury, are of lesser yield.[10,11]

Controversy exists as to the need for arteriography for wounds near major neurovascular bundles.[14-23] A proximity wound is usually defined as within 1 cm of the expected location of the vessels concerned. Recent studies have led to a declining interest in obtaining arteriography for proximity. Although injuries will be detected by proximity arteriography, they are most likely to be of small branches or nonaxial arteries. Many of these asymptomatic injuries do not require surgical or radiologic intervention, but rather heal spontaneously.[19,20,24] Finally, missed injuries requiring delayed intervention may not be as difficult to repair, nor complications as frequent, as previously thought.[19,24]

Efforts have been directed toward identifying subgroups of proximity wounds that are at higher risk for vascular injury. The Doppler-derived ankle-brachial index (ABI) or wrist-brachial index (WBI) has been adopted at several centers for this purpose.[13,25] At one trauma center, an ABI or WBI of less than 1.00 has been associated with a positive arteriography rate of 30 percent.[13] Such arteriograms need not be performed on an emergent basis but can be delayed up to 24 hours unless surgical intervention is planned earlier for another indication.[20] Doppler examinations will miss lesions that do not decrease distal flow: nonaxial arterial injuries, small AVFs, and nonobstructing arterial defects. The adoption of Doppler indices remains controversial primarily because the natural history of such arterial lesions, particularly small injuries, is unknown. Further investigation is required to determine which type or degree of injury will become clinically significant.

Alternatively, some trauma specialists believe that because major vascular injuries can result in limb loss and functional disability in characteristically young victims, diagnosis and repair of all injuries are critical. The cost and legal ramifications of a missed diagnosis motivate some surgeons to request arteriography on all penetrating trauma patients.[16,23] But although arteriography is both sensitive (98 percent) and specific (98 percent), occult injuries do, in fact, occur and may have a delayed presentation.[5] Even surgical exploration does not identify all injuries.[26,27] Although long-term delays in treatment may result in huge AVFs or large pseudoaneurysms, which complicate treatment, most delays are of short duration and definitive therapy is not usually more difficult.[24,28] Review of the recent lit-

erature indicates that, for most trauma specialists, proximity is no longer an indication for arteriography.[10,12,15,19-22]

The mechanism of injury is also an important factor in the decision to perform arteriography. All high-velocity wounds, such as those from assault weapons and rifles, should undergo exploration or arteriography because of the greater force and possibility of remote concussive damage. High-speed missiles are preceded by a shock wave and followed by an area of decreased pressure, the temporary cavity, which can produce extensive damage. Such high-velocity wounds have the highest incidence of arterial injury, followed in decreasing order by gunshot wounds and stab wounds, which must penetrate the vessel directly.[19] Shotgun wounds have a high rate of arterial injury (46-62 percent) because of the multiplicity of projectiles and the larger area of trauma from pellet scatter (Fig. 50-1).[19] Recently, dog bites have been recognized as having a high rate of vascular injury. These wounds, a result of both blunt and penetrating

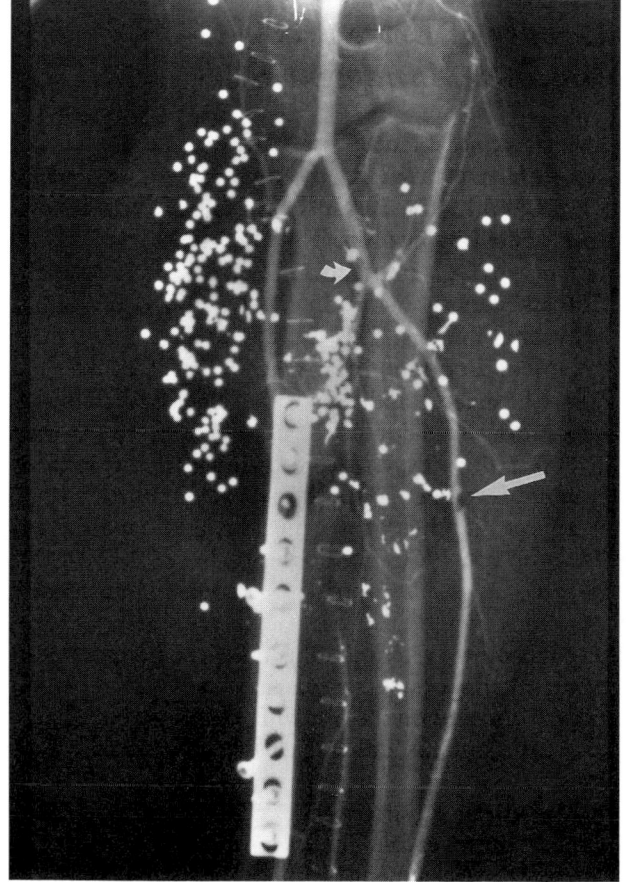

Figure 50-1. Arteriogram following upper extremity shotgun wound. Pellet scatter has caused multiple intimal injuries to the ulnar artery (*arrows*) as well as segmental occlusion of the interosseous artery.

Table 50-1. Predictors of Arterial Injury

High Suspicion	Moderate Suspicion	Low Suspicion
Pulse deficit	Proximity with	Normal physical
Bruit	ABI/WBI < 1	Normal Doppler
Expanding hema-	Shotgun blast	
toma	Dog bite injury	
Neurologic deficit?		
High-velocity mis-		
sile		

	Action	
Emergency angi-	Urgent angiog-	Observation
ography	raphy	

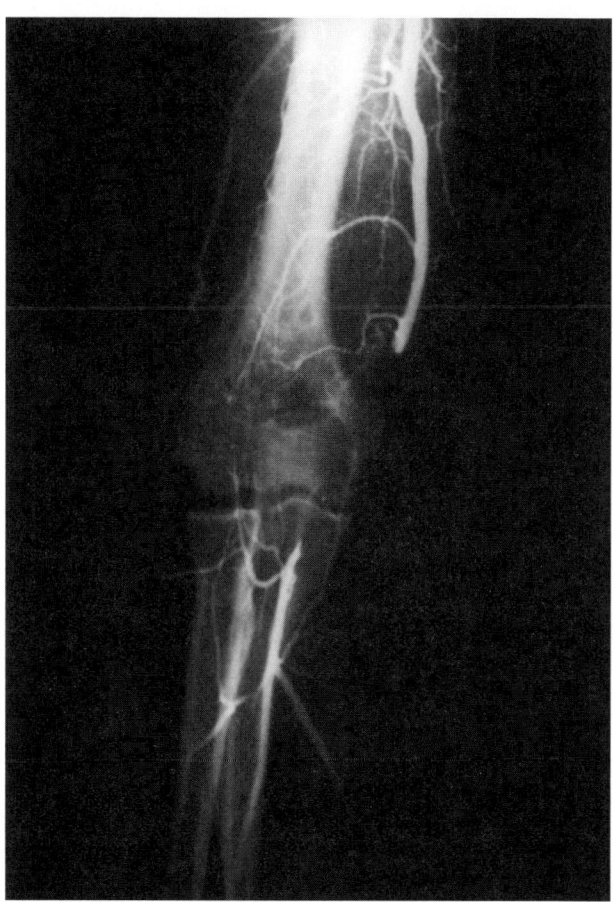

Figure 50-2. Arteriogram following elbow dislocation demonstrates segmental occlusion of the brachial artery.

trauma, are associated with a 24 percent rate of vascular injury.[29] Findings predictive of arterial injury are summarized in Table 50-1.

Although in urban centers most extremity arterial injuries are due to penetrating trauma, blunt trauma can also cause significant vascular injuries and accounts for 17 percent of arterial injuries.[30] Knee dislocations carry a 23 to 43 percent rate of popliteal artery injury.[31–34] Dislocations produce stretch injuries, which may cause isolated intimal damage. As with other forms of trauma, it remains controversial whether arteriography is indicated in all patients with knee dislocation or only in those with physical or Doppler signs of injury.[31–33] Open elbow dislocations and supracondylar humeral fractures also have a high incidence of vascular injury (Fig. 50-2). Long bone fracture, however, is a poor indicator of arterial injury. Among patients with fractures requiring admission, there is only a 0.3 percent arterial injury rate.[30] Blunt injury to the distal extremities is more likely to produce significant arterial injury than more proximal injuries because of the smaller quantity of surrounding soft tissues. Complex fractures of the tibia and fibula are frequently associated with vascular injury. Blunt trauma may produce internal penetrating injury from fracture fragments. Identification of these injuries is important because isolated tibial arterial injuries, when associated with extensive soft tissue damage, should be repaired to avoid limb loss, nonunion of fractures, and poor wound healing.[35]

Guidelines for Conservative Management

Initially all patients with abnormal arteriograms underwent surgical exploration without regard for the type of angiographic abnormality. Even small injuries were explored because of fear of subsequent thrombosis and possible distal embolization. Experience with angioplasty and anecdotal reports have brought into question such practices. Large and even multisegmental injuries heal after angioplasty. Small AVFs often close. Accordingly, doubt exists regarding the necessity to explore or treat small arterial injuries. Minor arterial injuries are being followed conservatively at many centers, and clinical deterioration has rarely occurred. There have been no instances of major vessel thrombosis or recurrent hemorrhage noted in several studies.[24,28,36] Resolution of this controversy depends on the difficult task of obtaining adequate follow-up in a largely noncompliant, unreliable patient population.

When observation is the chosen management, clinical follow-up is essential because of the unpredictability of injury healing. Areas of segmental narrowing and small intimal flaps are best suited to such follow-up. Small pseudoaneurysms (<2–5 mm) and small AVFs can also be managed conservatively. Angiography is usually performed one to several weeks after the initial injury. Observation needs to be maintained until the injury completely heals or until definitive therapy is provided. Therefore, improving but incompletely healed or stable injuries require serial follow-up examinations.[11,24] One center uses platelet inhibitors in these patients because of concern for thrombosis.[37]

An alternative method for follow-up, in selected patients, is color Doppler ultrasound. If an injury is to be treated expectantly, and it can be well identified by ultrasound, this modality can be used to monitor wound healing. Ultrasound is less sensitive at diagnosing vascular injury, in part because it is operator-dependent. In addition, casts, splints, and dressings may prevent adequate imaging in trauma patients.[38]

Technique of Arteriography

The site of arterial access depends on clinical evaluation of the patient. For isolated extremity trauma, the preferred access is femoral. With lower extremity injuries, the contralateral common femoral artery is most often used to allow for possible transcatheter intervention. For multiple trauma or hypotensive patients in military antishock treatment (MAST) suits, an axillary approach may be required.

Arteriography may be performed with conventional serial cut films or with digital subtraction arteriography (DSA).[39] The field of view, the number of sites to be evaluated, and the number of foreign bodies that may cause artifacts on DSA should be considered. DSA may not identify very small intimal injuries but is more sensitive than cut film for extravasation. Windowing to "see through" the contrast is useful for identifying small intraluminal defects.[40] Uncooperative patients are best studied by conventional film technique.

Sequential images are essential, with early rapid images required to identify the site of a high-flow AVF, whereas delayed images are needed to identify sites of extravasation. Since each trauma site deserves attention in this manner, runoff-type filming should be avoided. Two views, preferably orthogonal, should be obtained to exclude injury. When large foreign bodies are present, fluoroscopy and test injections can allow positioning of the vessel of interest away from obscuring metallic material. An area 10 to 15 cm proximal and distal to the potential injury site should be evaluated.

Careful positioning of the catheter is important so that all arteries in the potential injury path are evaluated. Knowledge of both the entrance and exit wounds is therefore required. The catheter should be positioned proximal enough to the injury site to allow for common anatomic variants (e.g., high take-off of the radial artery).

Significant findings on extremity arteriography for

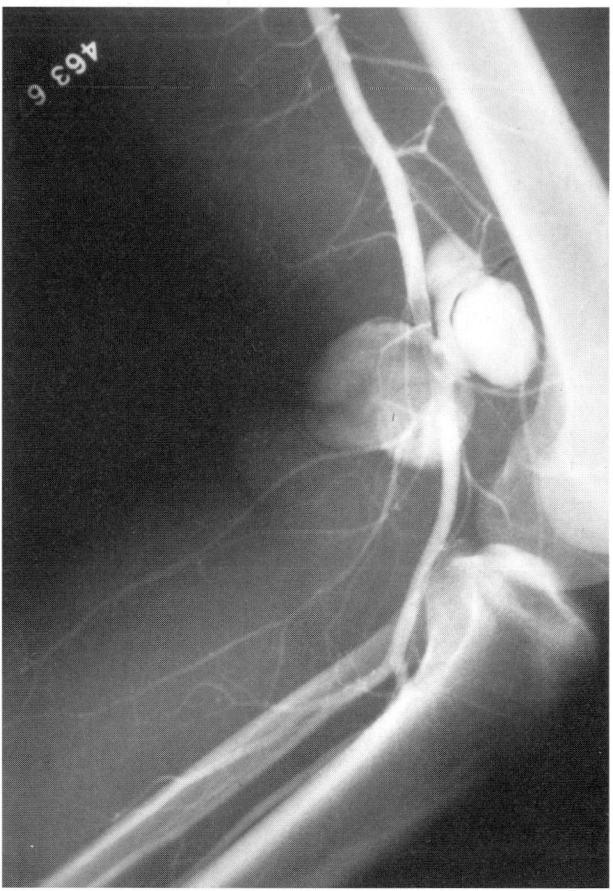

A

Figure 50-3. (A) Large, lobulated popliteal artery pseudoaneurysm following gunshot injury. (B) Large arteriovenous fistula and pseudoaneurysm of the profunda femoris artery following gunshot injury. (C) Active extravasation from the ulnar artery. The ulnar artery is retracted, indicating complete transection (*arrow*). (From Hanks SE, Pentecost MJ. Angiography and transcatheter treatment of extremity trauma. Semin Intervent Radiol 1992; 9(1): 20–25. Used with permission.)

trauma include extravasation, which indicates active bleeding, pseudoaneurysms, and AVFs (Fig. 50-3). Occlusions may be caused by extrinsic vessel compression, or thrombosis associated with arterial laceration or intimal flap. Luminal narrowing may be secondary to arterial spasm, intramural hematoma, extrinsic compression, or atherosclerosis. Intraluminal filling defects indicate nonocclusive thrombi or intimal injuries. Intimal flaps appear as a thin strip or globule attached to the arterial wall in at least one view (Fig. 50-4).[41] The vessel course may be altered because of hematoma or associated long bone fracture displacement. Slow flow is an important finding and may be the sole arteriographic indication of a compartment syndrome.[41]

Of the many findings seen arteriographically, luminal narrowing is the most difficult to evaluate because

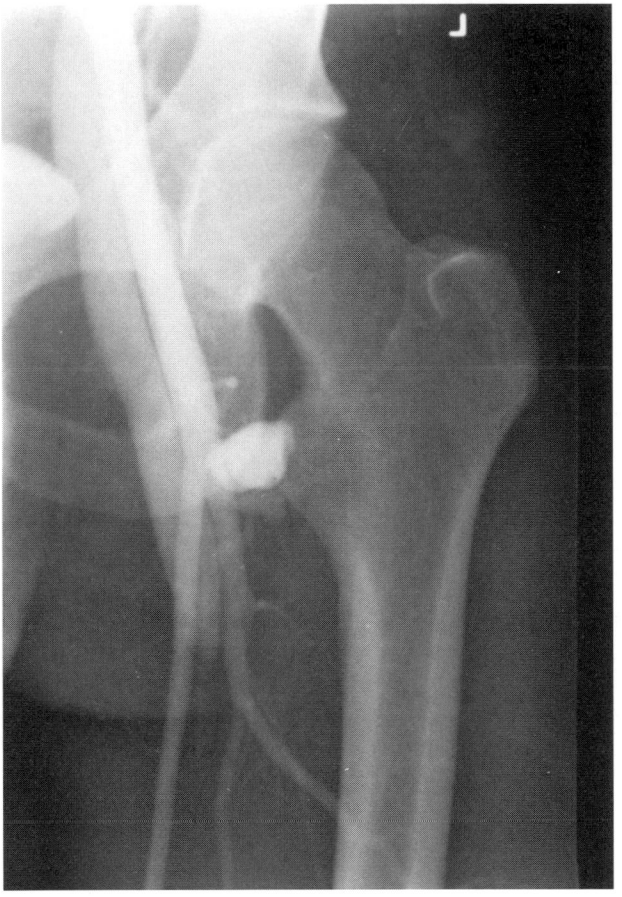

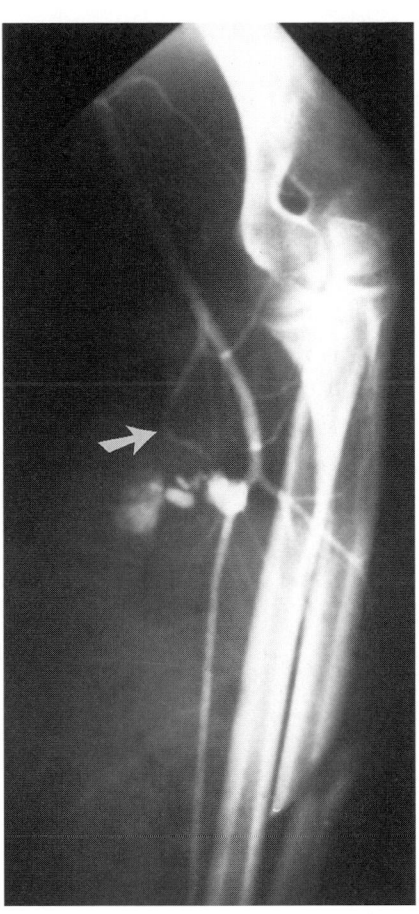

B　　　　　　　　　　　　　　　　　　　**C**

Figure 50-3 (continued).

Figure 50-4. Two appearances of intimal flaps: a linear band (*arrow*) or a globule attached to the vessel wall (*curved arrow*). (From Hanks SE, Pentecost MJ. Angiography and transcatheter treatment of extremity trauma. Semin Intervent Radiol 1992; 9(1): 20–25. Used with permission.)

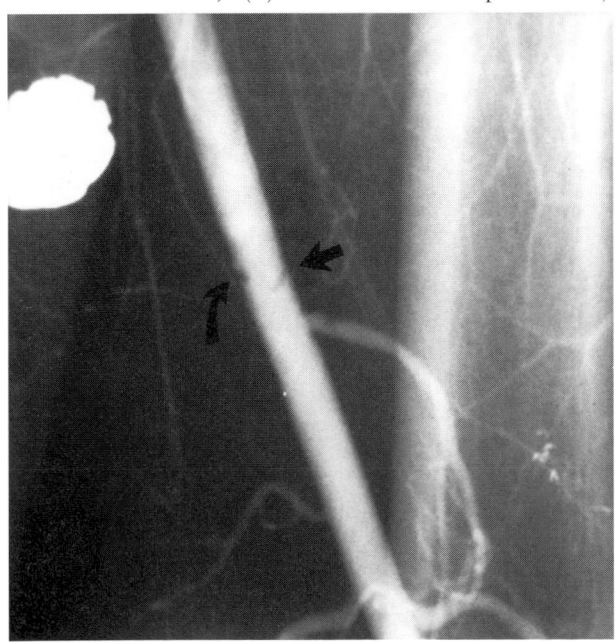

vasospasm and intimal injury may be impossible to differentiate. Luminal narrowing may be due to arterial spasm, which appears as a focal area of smooth concentric narrowing and is particularly prevalent in pediatric patients.[42] Some authors recommend the use of vasodilators when such lesions are encountered to exclude more significant lesions. Calcium channel blockers such as nifedipine, as well as tolazoline and papaverine, have been used as vasodilators, although their effectiveness is unreliable.[42] Areas of narrowing that are not concentric should raise concern for intimal injury.

Transcatheter Management of Arterial Injuries

Before undertaking transcatheter therapy for arterial lesions, it is important to understand the surgical alternatives for treatment and their risks and benefits. Arteries may be ligated, primarily repaired, patched by vein, bypassed by vein, or, rarely, bypassed by prosthetic graft.

Radiologic management is primarily limited to embolotherapy, the intentional occlusion of a vessel.

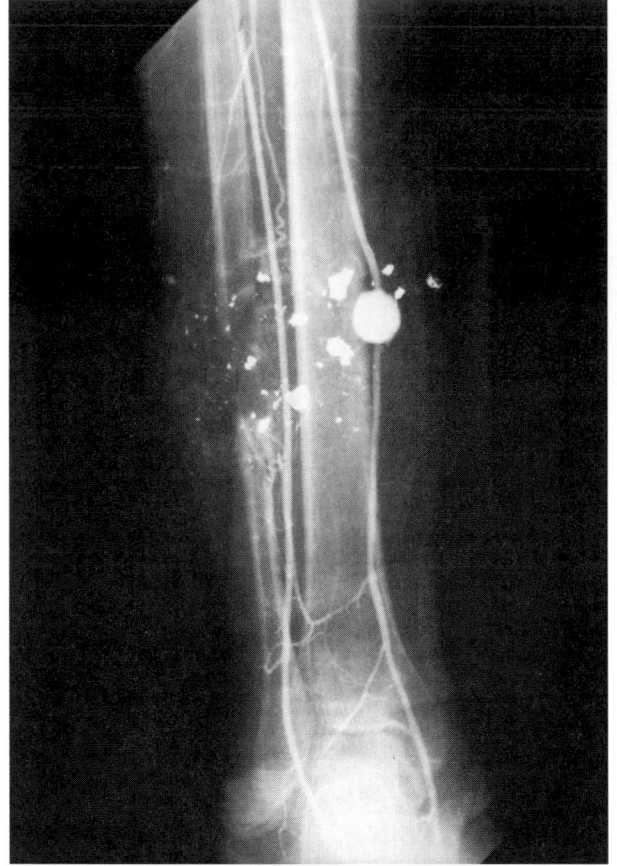

A

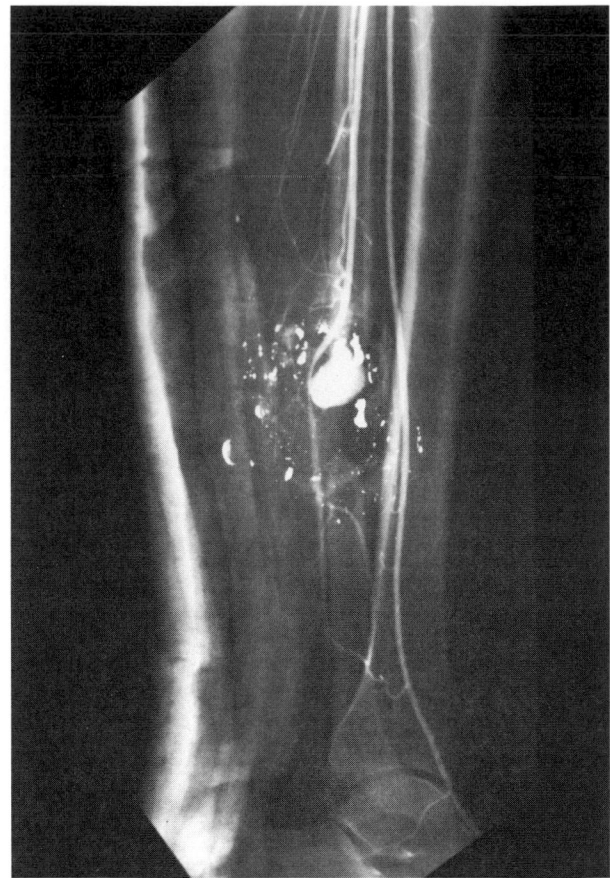

B

Figure 50-5. (A,B) Lower extremity arteriogram performed for persistent bleeding 1 week following gunshot injury, surgical exploration, peroneal artery ligation, and fasciotomy demonstrates a pseudoaneurysm of the posterior tibial artery. (C) Post-embolization arteriogram demonstrates coils both distal and proximal to the now occluded pseudoaneurysm. A single coil is lodged inside the pseudoaneurysm. The anterior tibial artery supplies the foot and reconstitutes the distal posterior tibial artery.

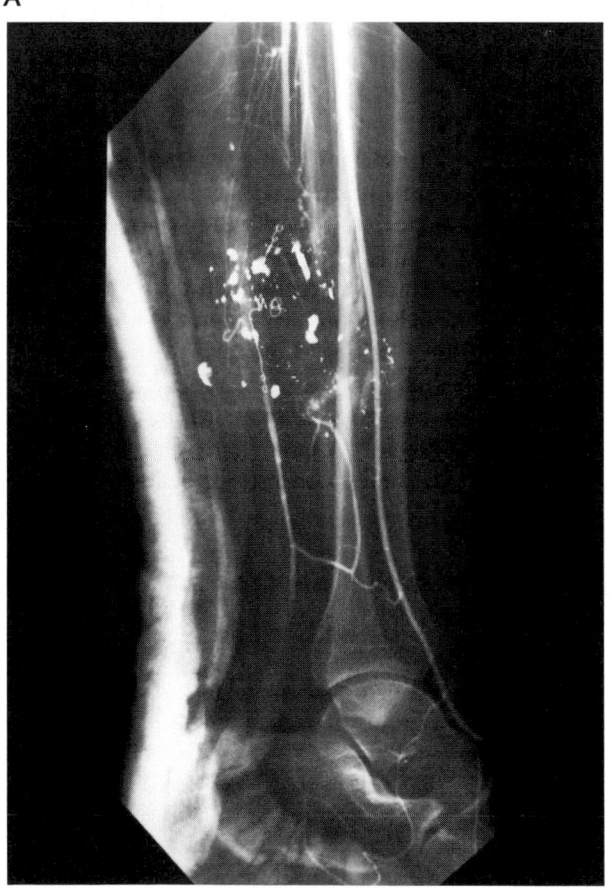

C

Vessels to be treated by percutaneous means must, therefore, be expendable. These are vessels that are likely to be ligated surgically as an alternative treatment. Transcatheter techniques are usually used for nonaxial arteries (e.g., profunda femoris artery, geniculate artery, etc.) or distal axial arteries that are multiple (e.g., tibial arteries).

Transcatheter therapy of many of these injuries is preferable to surgical intervention where access or vascular control would be difficult (e.g., distal profunda femoris artery).[43] In such cases, surgical dissection may require division of additional collateral vessels. Each patient and each injury need to be considered individually. It is fortunate that the majority of extremity trauma patients are young and without significant atherosclerosis. In older individuals caution should be exercised to avoid obliterating important collaterals.

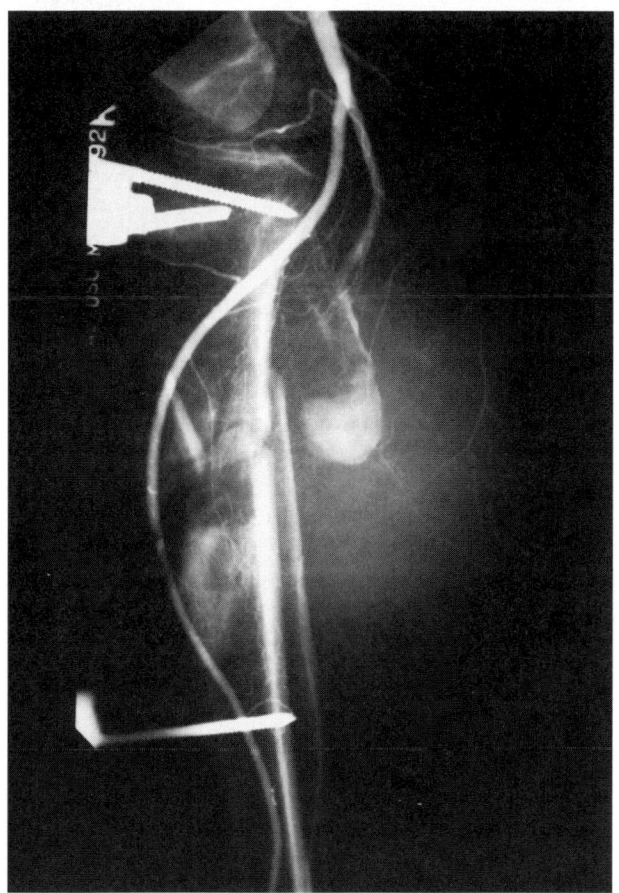

A

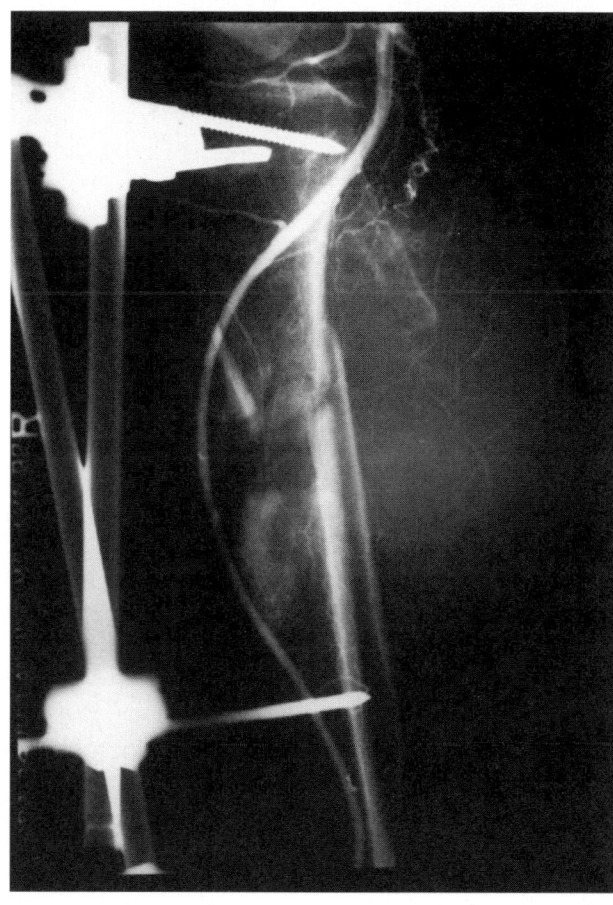

B

Figure 50-6. (A) Lower extremity arteriogram following gunshot injury demonstrates a large pseudoaneurysm of the tibioperoneal trunk with occlusion of the distal arterial segment. (B) Successful embolization of the tibioperoneal trunk with steel coils in the proximal arterial segment.

The technique of embolization depends on the type and location of the vascular lesions. In general, the extremities have an extensive collateral network. For pseudoaneurysms and especially AVFs, it is important, therefore, to embolize both proximal and distal to the injury to prevent retrograde arterial filling or recruitment of collaterals (Fig. 50-5). Occlusion of the proximal segment is satisfactory if the distal artery is thrombosed (Fig. 50-6). For very peripheral branch arteries, embolization of the proximal portion of the injured artery may be sufficient (Fig. 50-7).[43]

A variety of materials are available for embolization. Choice of an agent is often based on personal preference and experience. In trauma, a temporary occluding agent such as gelatin sponge is theoretically advantageous because many of these lesions will heal. Alternatively, fibered coils, although permanent, offer the advantage of speed and precise positioning. In the extremities, exact placement is usually of foremost concern, and therefore coils, both Gianturco steel coils and platinum microcoils, are favored. Gianturco coils are 0.038- or 0.035-inch wire segments, and microcoils are 0.018- or 0.010-inch platinum wire segments. These coils have polyester fibers attached to increase thrombogenicity and are available in multiple sizes and in straight, curved, and complex configurations. Detachable balloons and tissue adhesives are possible alternatives but are not currently available pending FDA approval. Regardless of the embolic agent chosen, the use of an arterial sheath is recommended to preserve arterial access in the event embolic material lodges within the guiding catheter.

Embolization requires placement of a catheter at the injury site. After identification of an arterial injury suitable to transcatheter embolization, a diagnostic catheter must be manipulated to the target vessel. Achieving adequate catheter position can be the limiting factor for embolization success. Once the guiding

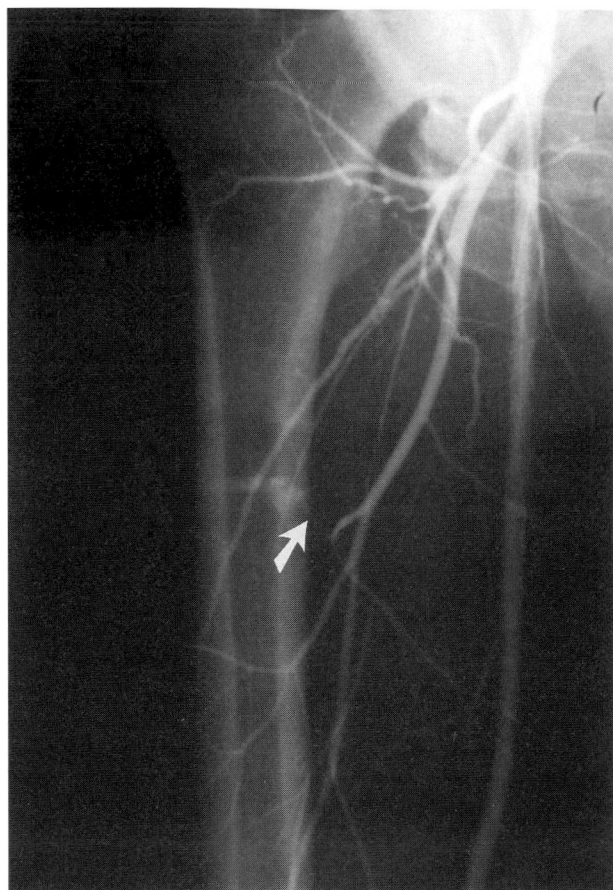

A

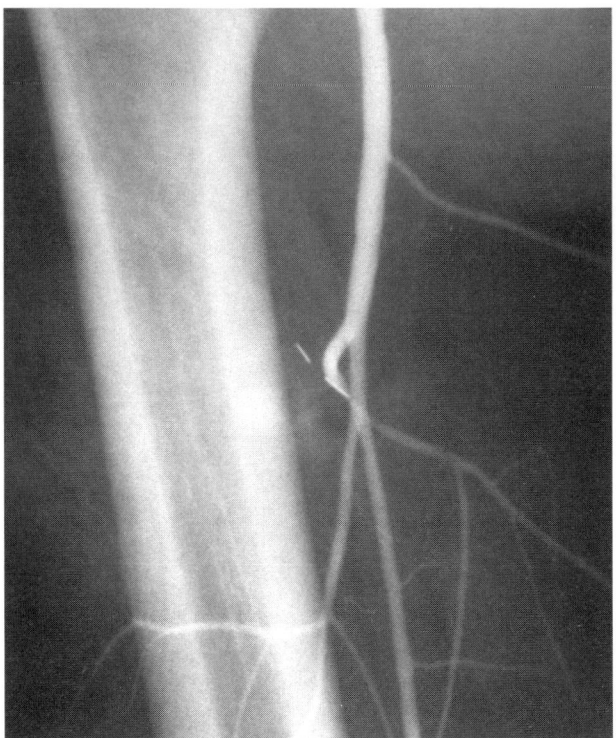

B

Figure 50-7. (A) Lower extremity arteriogram following thigh stab wound demonstrates extravasation from a distal branch of the profunda femoris artery (*arrow*). (B) Successful superselective embolization of the bleeding muscular branch with two straight platinum microcoils.

Figure 50-8. Diagrammatic representation of ideal coil placement for occlusion of an arteriovenous fistula. The coils are placed both distal and proximal to the AVF with no intervening arterial branches.

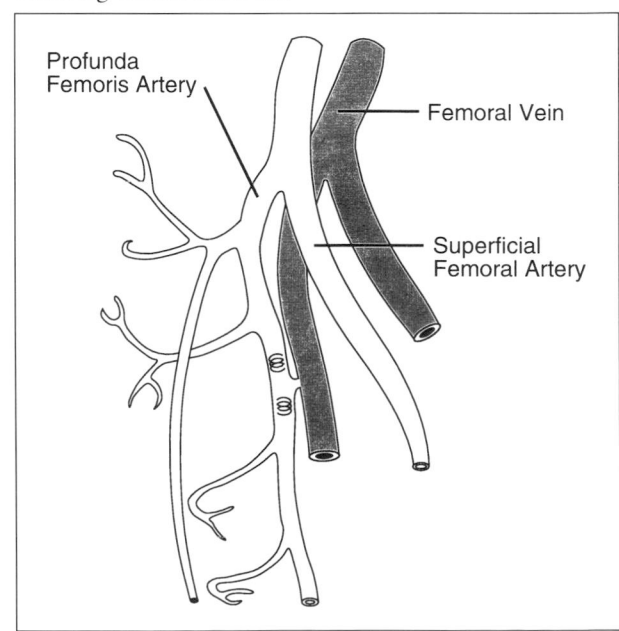

catheter is in a good position for embolization, a soft guidewire should be passed to the catheter tip to check for stability. If the catheter is stable, Gianturco coils of an appropriate size may be used.

Care should be taken in selecting the size of coils to match the target vessel. Too large a coil will not reform and will instead push the catheter out of the target vessel and risk embolization of a nontarget site. Too small a coil will pass too far distally, possibly compromising additional tissue or passing through an AVF, and will be ineffective at occluding the injured vessel at the appropriate site.

For AVFs or pseudoaneurysms, coils should be placed so there are no arterial branches between the coils and the injury site. It is not necessary to occlude the pseudoaneurysm or AVF itself, but rather the artery proximal and distal to the injury (Figs. 50-8 and 50-9). Coils may be placed directly across the injury, beginning distally and progressing more proximally (Fig. 50-10). Initial placement of a large coil can provide a network for retaining smaller coils.[44] If the artery distal to the injury is patent and access to this distal

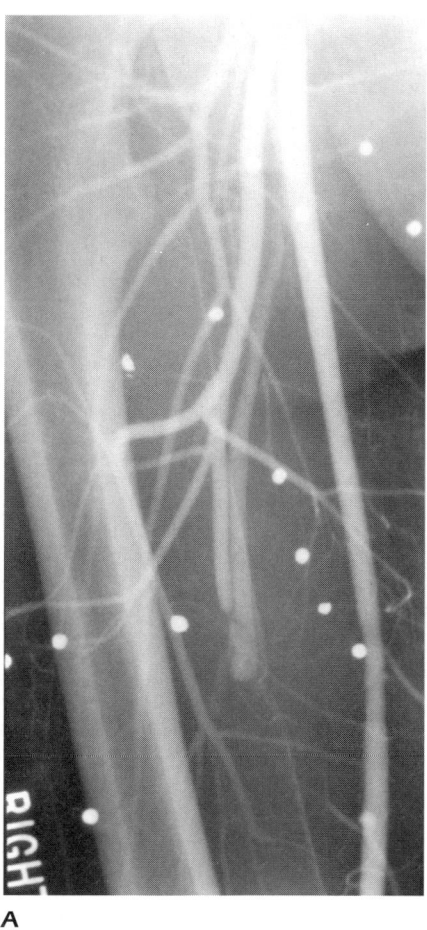
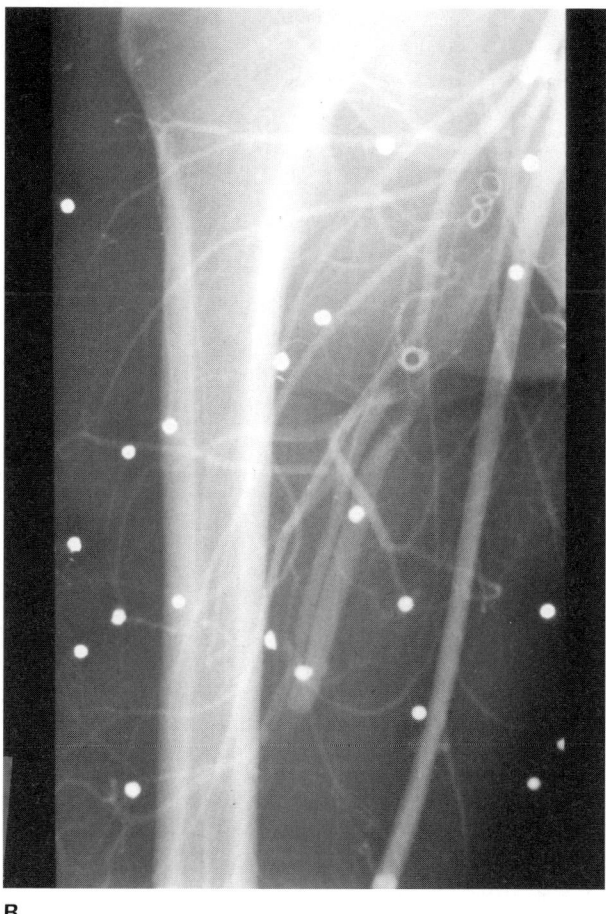

A **B**

Figure 50-9. (A) Lower extremity arteriogram following shotgun injury demonstrates arteriovenous fistula from the distal profunda femoris artery. (B) Arteriogram following poor placement of occlusion coils. Isolated proximal placement of the coils has allowed for distal reconstitution of the distal profunda femoris artery and persistence of the AVF. Distal occlusion could have been accomplished with a microcatheter. (From Hanks SE, Pentecost MJ. Angiography and transcatheter treatment of extremity trauma. Semin Intervent Radiol 1992; 9(1): 20–25. Used with permission.)

segment cannot be achieved from the proximal vessel, alternative strategies should be employed to prevent distal retrograde filling. For pseudoaneurysms, small Gelfoam pledgets can be used to occlude the distal arterial segment. For AVFs, a transvenous approach or direct percutaneous puncture of the distal artery can be performed.

It may be unsafe to embolize too near essential arteries. If the target vessel is small or tortuous or if the diagnostic catheter is unstable, a microcatheter can be placed coaxially. Microcatheters allow for rapid catheterization of branches that are unreachable by diagnostic catheters (Fig. 50-11). They minimize vasospasm and the risk of nontarget embolization by providing added stability. Superselective coaxial systems maximize the amount of preserved blood supply.[45–47]

The success rate for transcatheter embolization has been reported to be between 85 and 100 percent.[43,45,47–49] These high rates can safely be achieved with modern catheters and coaxial systems. Complications from transcatheter embolization are identical to those of diagnostic arteriography, but also include nontarget embolization. With careful technique and, when necessary, the use of microcatheters and microcoils, nontarget embolization is infrequent.[47,48] If coil maldeployment occurs, multiple retrieval devices have been developed to enable coil removal. Infection following embolization rarely occurs. Significant limb ischemia should not occur with appropriate lesion selection. Local infarction of tissue can be avoided by using gelatin sponge or coils, and by avoiding liquid or powder agents.

For injuries to arteries which cannot be safely sacrificed by embolic occlusion, operative intervention remains typical. Occasionally massive hemorrhage may be identified from an essential artery (e.g., superficial femoral artery). If the clinical situation is appropriate, an occlusion balloon can be used for short-term

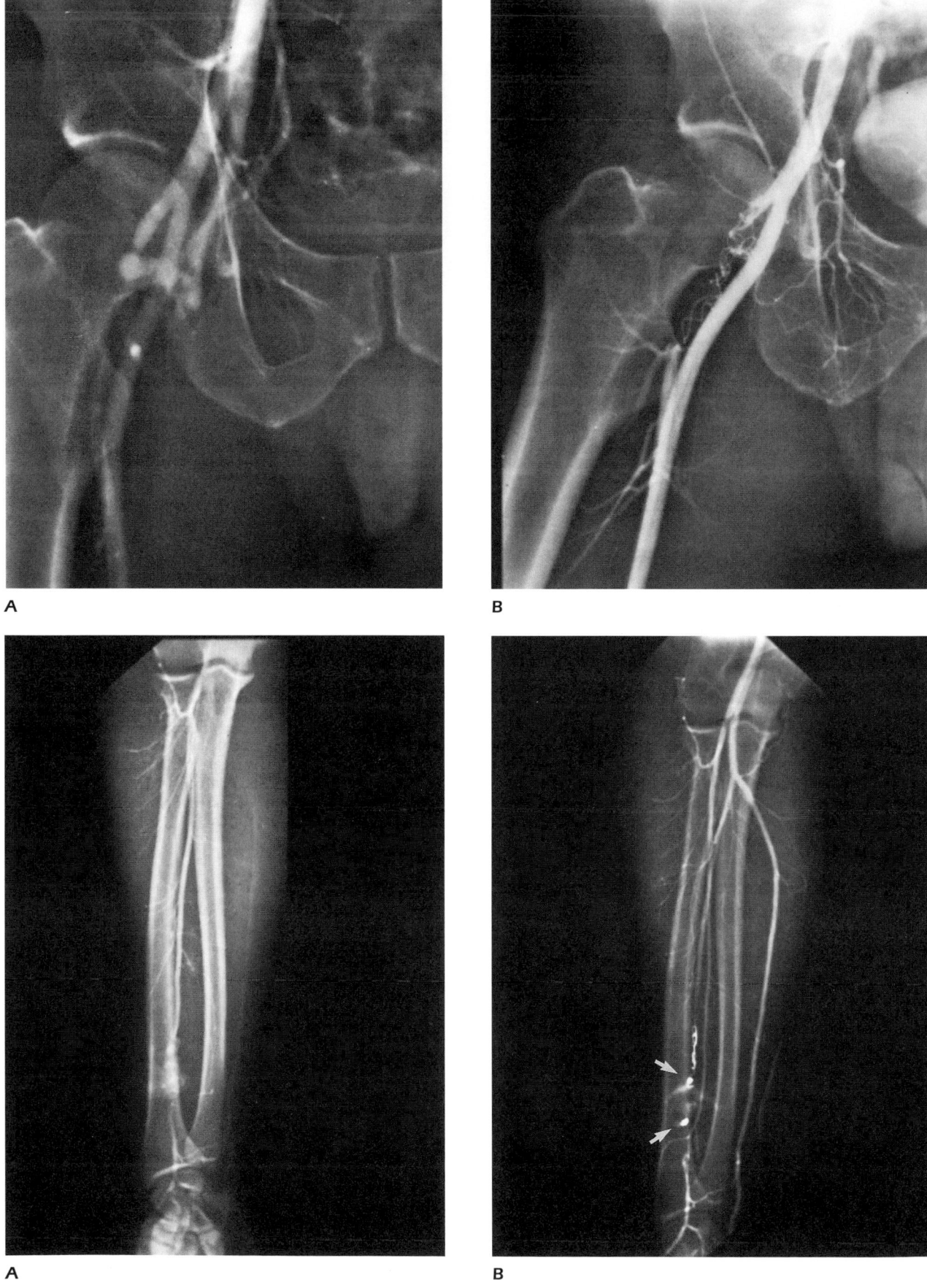

A

B

A

B

occlusion to decrease blood loss during transit to the operating room.[50] Alternatively, recent investigation suggests that covered stents can successfully treat pseudoaneurysms and AVFs where embolization would be inappropriate.[51-54] Metallic stents covered by polytetrafluoroethylene have been used investigationally to manage selected arterial injuries to the subclavian, axillary, iliac, common, or superficial femoral arteries. A suitable delivery system is not yet commercially available and clinical outcomes have not yet been confirmed by prolonged follow-up.

Conclusion

The management of extremity trauma continues to evolve as the natural history of nonsurgically treated arterial injuries is reported. Clinical findings and arteriography form the basis for extremity trauma management. Arteriography is both sensitive and specific for the diagnosis of arterial injury. The role of nonoperative management, by both observation and transcatheter embolization, continues to expand. Transcatheter embolization is effective and safe, and can be definitive therapy for suitable arterial injuries. For vessels where embolization is contraindicated, the role of transcatheter management can be expected to expand if covered stents are determined to be effective.

References

1. DeBakey ME, Simeone FA. Battle injuries of the arteries in World War II: an analysis of 2,471 cases. Ann Surg 1946;123: 534–579.
2. Inui FK, Shannon J, Howard JM. Arterial injuries in the Korean conflict: experiences with 111 consecutive injuries. Surgery 1955;37:850–857.
3. Rich NM, Baugh JH, Hughes CW. Acute arterial injuries in Vietnam: 1,000 cases. J Trauma 1970;10:359–369.
4. Geuder JW, Hobson RW, Padberg FT, et al. The role of contrast arteriography in suspected arterial injuries of the extremities. Am Surg 1985;51:89–93.
5. Rose SC, Moore EE. Emergency trauma angiography: accuracy, safety, and pitfalls. AJR 1987;148:1243–1246.
6. Reid JDS, Redman HC, Weigelt JA, et al. Wounds of the extremities in proximity to major arteries: value of angiography in the detection of arterial injury. AJR 1988;151:1035–1039.
7. Snyder WH, Thal ER, Bridges RA, et al. The validity of normal arteriography in penetrating trauma. Arch Surg 1978;113: 424–428.
8. Jebara VA, Haddad SN, Ghossain MA, et al. Emergency arteriography in the assessment of penetrating trauma to the lower limbs. Angiology 1991;42:527–532.
9. Lipchik EO, Kaebnick HW, Beres JJ, et al. The role of arteriography in acute penetrating trauma to the extremities. Cardiovasc Intervent Radiol 1987;10:202–204.
10. Weaver FA, Yellin AE, Bauer M, et al. Is arterial proximity a valid indication for arteriography in penetrating extremity trauma? A prospective analysis. Arch Surg 1990;125:1256–1260.
11. Trooskin SZ, Sclafani S, Winfield J, et al. The management of vascular injuries of the extremity associated with civilian firearms. Surg Gynecol Obstet 1993;176:350–354.
12. McCorkell SJ, Harley JD, Morishima MS, et al. Indications for angiography in extremity trauma. AJR 1985;145:1245–1247.
13. Schwartz MR, Weaver FA, Bauer M, et al. Refining the indications for arteriography in penetrating extremity trauma: a prospective analysis. J Vasc Surg 1993;17:116–124.
14. Henderson V, Nambisan R, Smith ME, et al. Angiographic yield in penetrating extremity trauma. West J Med 1991;155: 253–255.
15. Kaufman JA, Parker JE, Gillespie DL, et al. Arteriography for proximity of injury in penetrating extremity trauma. J Vasc Intervent Radiol 1992;3:719–723.
16. King TA, Perse JA, Marmen C. Utility of arteriography in penetrating extremity injuries. Am J Surg 1991;162:163–165.
17. Anderson RJ, Hobson RW, Lee BC, et al. Reduced dependency of arteriography for penetrating extremity trauma: influence of wound location and noninvasive vascular studies. J Trauma 1990;30:1059–1065.
18. Anderson RJ, Hobson RW, Padberg FT, et al. Penetrating extremity trauma: identification of patients at high-risk requiring arteriography. J Vasc Surg 1990;11:544–548.
19. Dennis JW, Frykberg ER, Crump JM. New perspectives on the management of penetrating trauma in proximity to major limb arteries. J Vasc Surg 1990;11:84–93.
20. Frykberg ER, Crump JM, Vines FS, et al. A reassessment of the role of arteriography in penetrating proximity extremity trauma: a prospective study. J Trauma 1989;29:1041–1052.
21. Gomez GA, Kreis DJ, Ratner L, et al. Suspected vascular trauma of the extremities: the role of arteriography in proximity injuries. J Trauma 1986;26:1005–1008.
22. Smyth SH, Pond GD, Johnson PL, et al. Proximity injuries: correlation with results of extremity arteriography. J Vasc Intervent Radiol 1991;2:451–456.
23. Cikrit DF, Dalsing MC, Bryant BJ, et al. An experience with upper-extremity vascular trauma. Am J Surg 1990;160:229–233.
24. Stain SC, Yellin AE, Weaver FA, et al. Selective management of nonocclusive arterial injuries. Arch Surg 1989;124:1136–1141.
25. Johansen K, Lynch K, Paun M, et al. Non-invasive vascular tests reliably exclude occult arterial trauma in injured extremities. J Trauma 1991;31:515–522.
26. Richardson JD, Vitale GC, Flint LM. Penetrating arterial trauma. Arch Surg 1987;122:678–683.

◄ **Figure 50-10** (*top*). (A) Pelvic arteriogram following gunshot injury demonstrates a large arteriovenous fistula from the profunda femoris artery. (B) Arteriogram following successful embolization of the profunda femoris artery with steel coils. The coils were placed, beginning distally, directly across the AVF.

◄ **Figure 50-11** (*bottom*). (A) Upper extremity arteriogram following multiple stab wounds demonstrates active extravasation from a lacerated radial artery. (B) Upper extremity arteriogram following successful embolization with platinum microcoils, both distal and proximal to the injury (*arrows*).

27. Feliciano DV, Cruse PA, Burch JM, et al. Delayed diagnosis of arterial injuries. Am J Surg 1987;154:579–584.

28. Frykberg ER, Crump JM, Dennis JW, et al. Nonoperative observation of clinically occult arterial injuries: a prospective evaluation. Surgery 1991;109:85–96.

29. Snyder KB, Pentecost MJ. Clinical and angiographic findings in extremity arterial injuries secondary to dog bites. Ann Emerg Med 1990;19:983–986.

30. Sturm JT, Bodily KC, Rothenberger DA, et al. Arterial injuries of the extremities following blunt trauma. J Trauma 1980;20:933–936.

31. Treiman GS, Yellin AE, Weaver FA, et al. Examination of the patient with a knee dislocation. Arch Surg 1992;127:1056–1063.

32. Kaufman SL, Martin LG. Arterial injuries associated with complete dislocation of the knee. Radiology 1992;184:153–155.

33. Applebaum R, Yellin AE, Weaver FA, et al. Role of routine arteriography in blunt lower-extremity trauma. Am J Surg 1990;160:221–225.

34. Bunt TJ, Malone JM, Moody M, et al. Frequency of vascular injury with blunt trauma–induced extremity injury. Am J Surg 1990;160:226–228.

35. Shah DM, Corson JD, Karmody AM, et al. Optimal management of tibial arterial trauma. J Trauma 1988;28:228–234.

36. Frykberg ER, Vines FS, Alexander RH. The natural history of clinically occult arterial injuries: a prospective evaluation. J Trauma 1989;29:577–583.

37. Sclafani SJA. Nonoperative management of arterial trauma. Presented at SCVIR 18th Annual Scientific Meeting, March 3, 1993:101–103.

38. Schwartz M, Weaver F, Yellin A, Ralls P. The utility of color flow Doppler examination in penetrating extremity arterial trauma. Am Surg 1993;59:375–378.

39. Howard CA, Thal ER, Redman HC, et al. Intra-arterial digital subtraction angiography in the evaluation of peripheral vascular trauma. Ann Surg 1989;210:108–111.

40. Sibbitt RR, Palmaz JC, Garcia F, et al. Trauma of the extremities: prospective comparison of digital and conventional angiography. Radiology 1986;160:179–182.

41. Rose SC, Moore EE. Angiography in patients with arterial trauma: correlation between angiographic abnormalities, operative findings, and clinical outcome. AJR 1987;149:613–619.

42. Sclafani SJA, Cooper R, Shaftan GW, et al. Arterial trauma: diagnostic and therapeutic angiography. Radiology 1986;161:165–172.

43. Sclafani SJA, Shaftan GW. Transcatheter treatment of injuries to the profunda femoris artery. AJR 1982;138:463–466.

44. Butto F, Hunter DW, Castaneda-Zuniga W, et al. Coil-in-coil technique for vascular embolization. Radiology 1986;161:554–555.

45. Kaufman SL, Martin LG, Zuckerman AM, et al. Peripheral transcatheter embolization with platinum microcoils. Radiology 1992;184:369–372.

46. Morse SS, Clark RA, Puffenbarger A. Platinum microcoils for therapeutic embolization: nonneuroradiologic applications. AJR 1990;155:401–403.

47. Teitelbaum GP, Reed RA, Larsen D, et al. Microcatheter embolization of non-neurologic traumatic vascular lesions. J Vasc Intervent Radiol 1993;4:149–154.

48. Levey DS, Teitelbaum GP, Finck EJ, et al. Safety and efficacy of transcatheter embolization of axillary and shoulder arterial injuries. J Vasc Intervent Radiol 1991;2:99–104.

49. Clark RA, Gallant TE, Alexander ES. Angiographic management of traumatic arteriovenous fistulas: clinical results. Radiology 1983;147:9–13.

50. Ben-Menachem Y. Embolotherapy in extremity trauma. In: Neal MP, Tisnado J, Cho SR, eds. Emergency interventional radiology, Boston: Little, Brown, 1989:79–90.

51. Marin ML, Veith FJ, Panetta TF, et al. Percutaneous transfemoral insertion of a stented graft to repair a traumatic femoral arteriovenous fistula. J Vasc Surg 1993;18:299–302.

52. Marin ML, Veith FJ, Cynamon J, et al. Transfemoral endoluminal repair of a penetrating vascular injury. J Vasc Intervent Radiol 1994;5:592–594.

53. Marin ML, Veith FJ, Panetta TF, et al. Transluminally placed endovascular stented graft repair for arterial trauma. J Vasc Surg 1994;20:466–471.

54. Schmitter SP, Marx M, Bernstein R, et al. Angioplasty-induced subclavian artery dissection in a patient with internal mammary artery graft: treatment with endovascular stent and stent-graft. AJR 1995;165:449–451.

51

Angiographic Management of Hemorrhage in Pelvic Fractures

JOHN A. KAUFMAN
ARTHUR C. WALTMAN

Retroperitoneal arterial bleeding from pelvic trauma is ideally suited for management with angiographic embolization techniques. Uncontrolled pelvic hemorrhage is associated with a high mortality rate despite aggressive transfusion.[1,2] Open surgical procedures are extremely difficult because of the confined space of the pelvis and difficulty localizing bleeding vessels in the presence of an extensive retroperitoneal hematoma.[3-5] Proximal ligation of the hypogastric arteries is frequently unsuccessful because of the rich collateral arterial supply within the pelvis.[1,6,7] Furthermore, incision of the retroperitoneum with evacuation of the hematoma can be counterproductive, because release of the tamponading effect of the contained thrombus permits more bleeding and may predispose to infection.[8]

Angiographic localization and embolization of pelvic arterial bleeding in blunt trauma were first described by Margolies et al. in 1972.[9] Angiography permits rapid, precise identification of arterial injury without disruption of the retroperitoneum. Transcatheter embolization effectively controls bleeding, with success rates that approach 90 percent.[10] This technique is now generally accepted as the treatment of choice in patients with pelvic trauma and uncontrolled retroperitoneal bleeding.[11-25]

Hemorrhage in Pelvic Fracture

Exsanguination into the retroperitoneum has long been recognized as a major problem in patients with pelvic fractures.[1,2] Historically, 60 percent of early deaths in patients with crush injuries of the pelvis were attributed to bleeding.[2,16] Recent studies indicate that most patients with pelvic fractures can be managed successfully with pelvic fixation devices, with mortality rates that approach 10 to 20 percent.[26-29] However, 5 to 15 percent of all patients with pelvic fractures continue to require angiographic intervention to control pelvic hemorrhage.[11,12,30,31]

The etiology of retroperitoneal hemorrhage in patients with pelvic fracture is multifactorial. Bleeding may be from fractured cancellous bone, severed arterial and venous structures, secondary to coagulopathic states induced by massive transfusion, or due to iatrogenic lesions created during resuscitation of the patient.[11,32-34] Arterial injury can occur from shearing of a vessel against a fixed ligamentous structure, avulsion of a vessel attached to a displaced pelvic segment, or penetrating injury from a shard of bone.[11] In a postmortem study of 27 individuals who had died from pelvic fractures, Huittinen et al. found retroperitoneal extravasation of contrast material from internal iliac artery injections in 23 cases.[32] Leakage was unilateral in 6, bilateral in 17, and from multiple vessels in 14.[32] However, discrete sources of arterial extravasation could be identified at dissection in only 14 cases, and the remaining 9 hematomas were attributed to bleeding from fractured cancellous bone.[32]

Internal iliac artery ligation was suggested in the early 1960s in response to the dismal outcomes noted with supportive management of patients with obvious hemodynamic instability due to retroperitoneal hemorrhage.[35] This technique was extrapolated from experience in elective pelvic surgery during which bilateral internal iliac artery ligation was performed with a low incidence of ischemic injury to the pelvic viscera or soft tissues.[35-37] Successful outcomes were described in several small trauma series, but the technique did not achieve lasting popularity.[12,35-37] Not only was it difficult to perform in the setting of a massive retroperitoneal hematoma and active bleeding, but serious concerns were expressed regarding the utility of the technique and the morbidity of disturbing the retroperitoneal hematoma.[4,38,39] In particular, critics of proximal ligation of both internal iliac arteries argued that it would not stop hemorrhage from vessels that had uninterrupted collateral supply from lumbar, femoral, and inferior mesenteric arteries, and that the risk of infection of the pelvic hematoma was increased.[6]

The potential value of angiography in the evaluation and management of hemodynamically unstable patients with pelvic trauma was suggested in 1971 and described in a small series in 1972.[9,40] In the first reported case, autologous blood clot was used to embolize the right obturator artery after a pitressin infusion failed to control bleeding in an elderly patient.[9] Although two of the three patients in this series died of multiorgan system failure, there was dramatic hemodynamic stabilization immediately after embolization.[9] The clinical utility of the technique was confirmed in a larger series from the same institution, which showed that early embolization markedly reduced transfusion requirements in patients with pelvic fractures.[19] Embolization was successfully applied by several other authors, with similarly encouraging results.[8,10,20,24] In some centers, angiographic evaluation assumed an early and primary role in the management of patients with pelvic fractures.[17] However, it was recognized that angiographic techniques had limitations in that the bleeding sites could not be identified in as many as 29 percent of patients, and embolizations could not be performed in 10 percent of patients in whom bleeding was visualized because of technical difficulties.[10,17]

Early stabilization of pelvic fractures to control pelvic bleeding and facilitate recuperation was proposed because of evidence suggesting that a large amount of the bleeding was due to fractured cancellous bone.[32] This technique has since become a basic component of the management of pelvic fractures. Initial studies employed the pneumatic antishock garment (the "MAST-suit" or "G-suit").[14] This apparatus was supplanted in the 1980s by externally or internally applied fixation devices.[26–29] Early fixation is believed to reduce the bleeding associated with pelvic fractures by reapproximating bone fragments and reducing the volume of the bony pelvis.[11,12] A 3-cm diastasis of the symphysis pubis is estimated to double the potential volume of the pelvis to 8 liters.[11] In addition to reducing transfusion requirements, pelvic fixation has other benefits, such as early and simpler mobilization of the patient, which decreases overall morbidity.[28,29] Rapid application of pelvic fixation has dramatically improved the mortality and morbidity rates associated with pelvic fracture when compared to the conservative management techniques of the 1960s.

Despite the application of early pelvic fixation, some patients continue to exsanguinate from their fractures. Between 5 and 15 percent of all patients with pelvic fractures will still have uncontrolled retroperitoneal bleeding after pelvic fixation.[11,12,15,30,31] Several studies have shown that the patients at risk for continued bleeding can be identified by the mechanism of pelvic fracture.[12,30,31,41] Pelvic fractures are caused by (1) lateral compression, (2) anteroposterior compression, (3) vertical shear, and (4) combined mechanisms.[12,31,40] In civilian trauma, the mechanism of injury in 65 percent of patients is lateral compression.[11,40] With the application of lateral force, the side of the pelvis folds inward, preserving the pelvic ligaments.[40] In general, this is a stable injury with a reduced pelvic volume and intact ligaments that contain the retroperitoneal hematoma.[30] Transfusion requirements are low, with angiographic intervention needed in only 1 percent of patients.[31] An uncommon, but severe form of lateral compression injury in which the contralateral side of the pelvis rotates externally, the so-called wind-swept pelvis, typically results in greater blood loss, with embolization necessary in 7 percent.[31]

Anteroposterior compression, vertical shear, and combined force injuries to the pelvis are less common than lateral compression fractures but typically result in more unstable injuries.[12,30,31,40] Anteroposterior injuries may involve disruption of the sacrotuberous, sacrospinous, and sacroiliac ligaments in addition to widening of the symphysis pubis and/or pubic rami fractures.[31] Vertical shear injuries involve symphysial diastasis or fracture of the pubic rami, rupture of the sacroiliac ligaments and/or a vertical fracture through the sacrum or ilium, and vertical displacement of the affected hemipelvis.[40] Combined injuries involve multiple force vectors, but usually one predominates.[31]

Patients with these mechanisms of injury are more likely to be hemodynamically unstable than patients with lateral compression fractures.[30] The potential volume of the pelvis is increased because of the disrupted ligaments, allowing unchecked retroperitoneal bleeding.[11] As a group, these patients have a higher transfusion requirement than patients with lateral compression fractures.[30] Percutaneous embolization is required in addition to early pelvic fixation in 18 to 22 percent of patients with anteroposterior compression, vertical shear, and combined force injuries.[12,30,31]

The current management of hemodynamically unstable patients with pelvic fractures involves vigorous fluid resuscitation, rapid assessment to determine the sources of bleeding, and rapid intervention.[4,11] This process is complicated by the fact that patients with severe pelvic fractures are frequently multiply injured because of the high energy of the trauma.[4,5,12,15,17,42] Because intraabdominal injury is common, peritoneal lavage or abdominal computed tomography (CT) is performed early in the evaluation of patients with pelvic fractures.[11] If the lavage or CT is positive for intraperitoneal hemorrhage, the patient proceeds to emergent laparotomy.[4,10,11] Pelvic fixation is performed as soon as possible, frequently at the time of laparotomy.[28,29] If

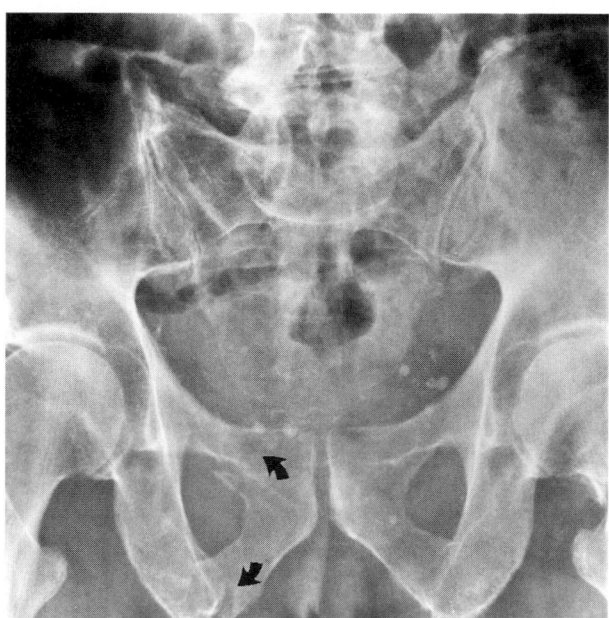

A

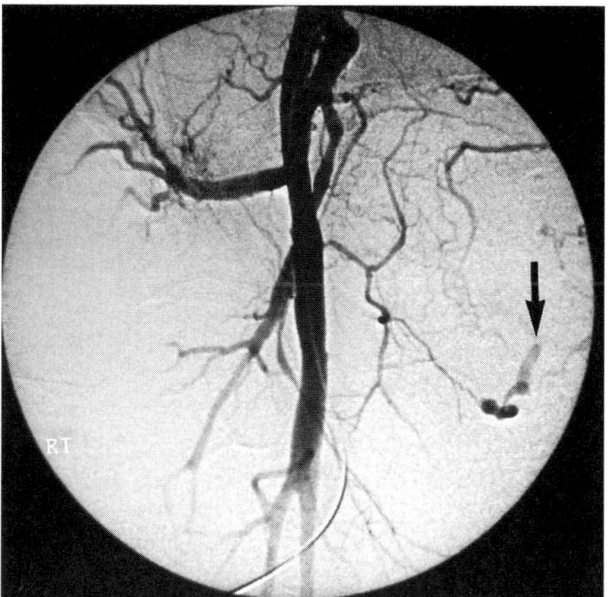

B

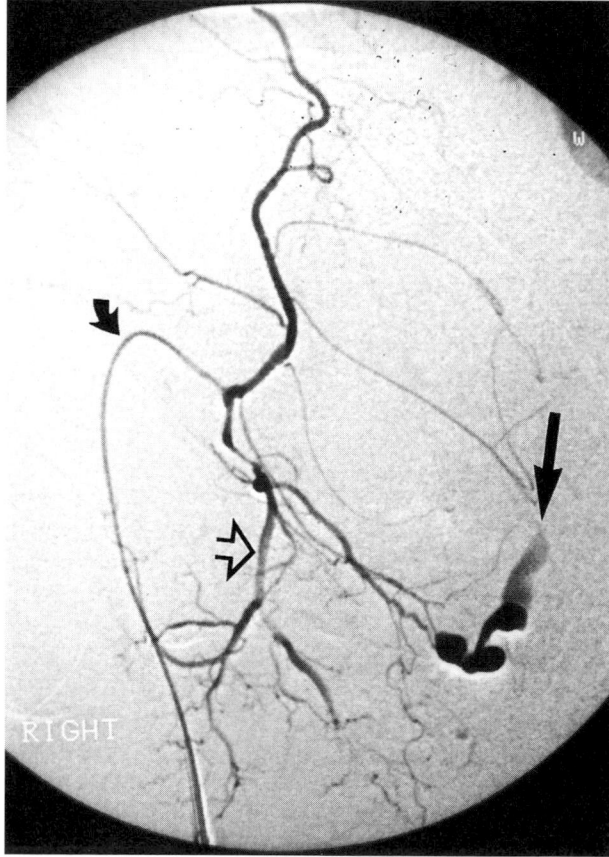

C

Figure 51-1. Examination of the plain films may predict the site of bleeding. Elderly man with a stable pelvic fracture but a massive pelvic hematoma. (A) Plain film of the pelvis shows fractures of the right pubic rami (*arrows*). (B) Digital subtraction angiogram of the right common iliac artery (left posterior oblique) shows extravasation in the region of the fractures (*arrow*). (C) Selective right inferior epigastric artery injection shows extravasation from the external pudendal artery (*straight arrow*). In this patient the obturator artery is replaced to the inferior epigastric artery (*open arrow*). The injection was performed through a 5 French Cobra-2 catheter from the ipsilateral approach (*curved arrow*).

the patient remains hemodynamically unstable or has a transfusion requirement that exceeds 4 to 6 units in 24 hours, angiography is performed emergently as both a diagnostic and therapeutic procedure.[10–12,19] Many authors recommend angiography before CT scans, urethrograms, or cystograms because spillage of contrast into the pelvis from ruptured viscera may obscure arterial extravasation at angiography.[12,14,17,18] A more important reason for early angiography is that the embolization can be performed before the patient develops a coagulopathic diathesis secondary to massive transfusion.[12,19]

Angiography

Angiography in hemodynamically unstable patients with pelvic fractures has two goals: (1) rapid but thorough diagnostic evaluation of potential sources of arterial bleeding, and (2) expeditious embolization of bleeding vessels. Whenever possible, plain films and CT scans of the pelvis should be reviewed to identify

the location of fractures and ligamentous injuries, because the sites of arterial trauma may be suggested by the pattern of pelvic injury (Fig. 51-1).[15,30,31] Available abdominal and chest studies should be reviewed to determine if angiographic evaluation of the abdomen or

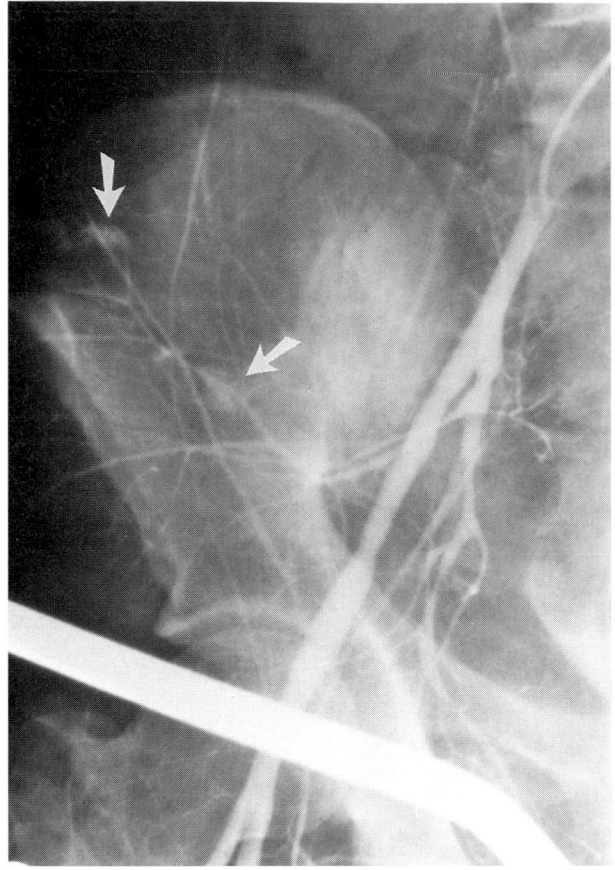

A

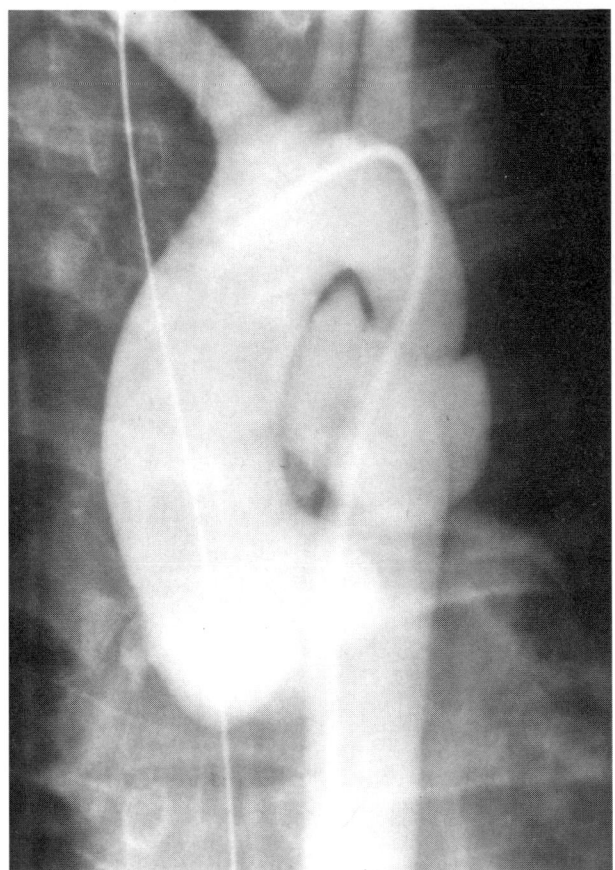

B

Figure 51-2. Patients with pelvic fractures frequently have multiple injuries. Young man involved in a high-speed motor vehicle accident with pelvic fractures and a widened mediastinum on chest x-ray. (A) Right common iliac artery angiogram shows diffuse spasm and multiple sites of extravasation in the region of the right iliac fracture (*arrows*). These were successfully embolized with Gelfoam pledgets. (B) Thoracic aortogram in the same patient performed after the embolization shows an aortic transection.

thorax is also indicated (Fig. 51-2). Angiography is indicated in the absence of a fracture in patients with blunt pelvic trauma if there is evidence of uncontrolled retroperitoneal bleeding. Arterial injury in the pelvis without bony injury has been reported.[43,44]

The internal iliac branches that are most commonly injured are (in descending order of frequency) the superior gluteal; the internal pudendal; the obturator; the inferior gluteal; the lateral sacral; and the iliolumbar arteries (Figs. 51-3 through 51-5).[12,17,19] Complete transection of the internal iliac artery trunk occurs less frequently than injury to a branch vessel.[17]

Less common bleeding sites include lumbar arteries (particularly in patients with vertical shear injuries); branches of the inferior epigastric artery such as accessory or replaced obturator and external pudendal arteries; and the iliac circumflex arteries.[19] Spasm is commonly observed in the external iliac artery due to either vasoconstriction or trauma, but the predominant injury to this vessel is intimal tear rather than transection.[17,45]

The full range of arterial injuries occurs in patients with pelvic trauma, including complete transection, partial transection, intimal disruption, intramural

Figure 51-4. Young man with pelvic injury including disruption of the symphysis pubis and left sacroiliac joint. (A) Left common iliac angiogram shows generalized spasm of the hypogastric artery, occlusion of the branches of the superior gluteal artery (*curved arrows*), and extravasation from the inferior pudendal artery (*straight arrow*). The external iliac artery is narrowed because of spasm, extrinsic compression by hematoma, or both. (B) After successful embolization with Gelfoam, both the internal pudendal and the inferior gluteal arteries are occluded. ▶

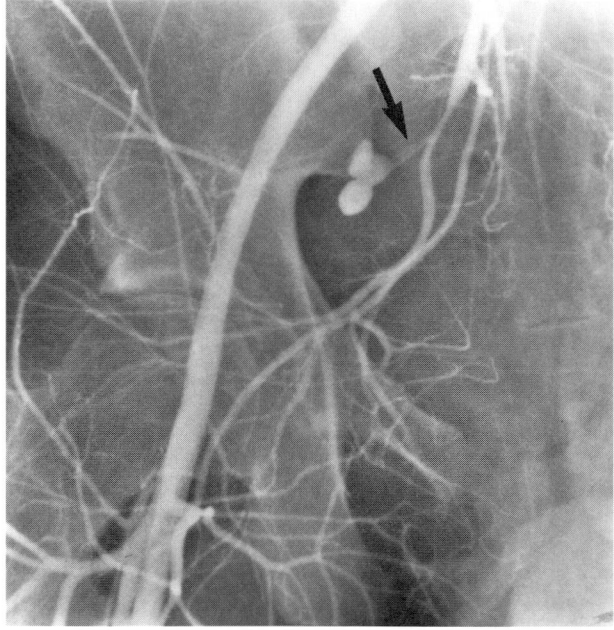

A

Figure 51-3. Patient with fractures of the right pubic rami and right ilium. (A) Extravasation is present from a transected right superior gluteal artery (*arrow*). (B) Selective injection of the gluteal arteries shows massive extravasation (*arrows*).

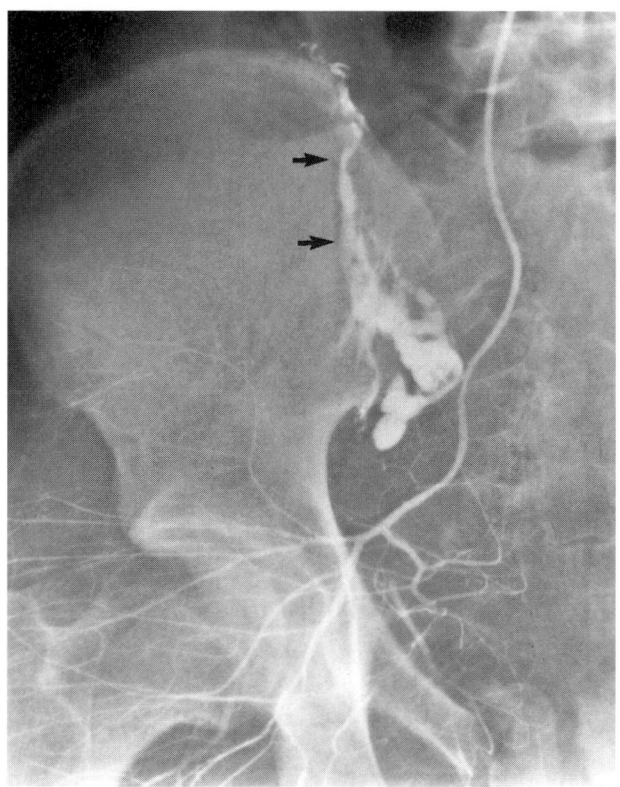

B

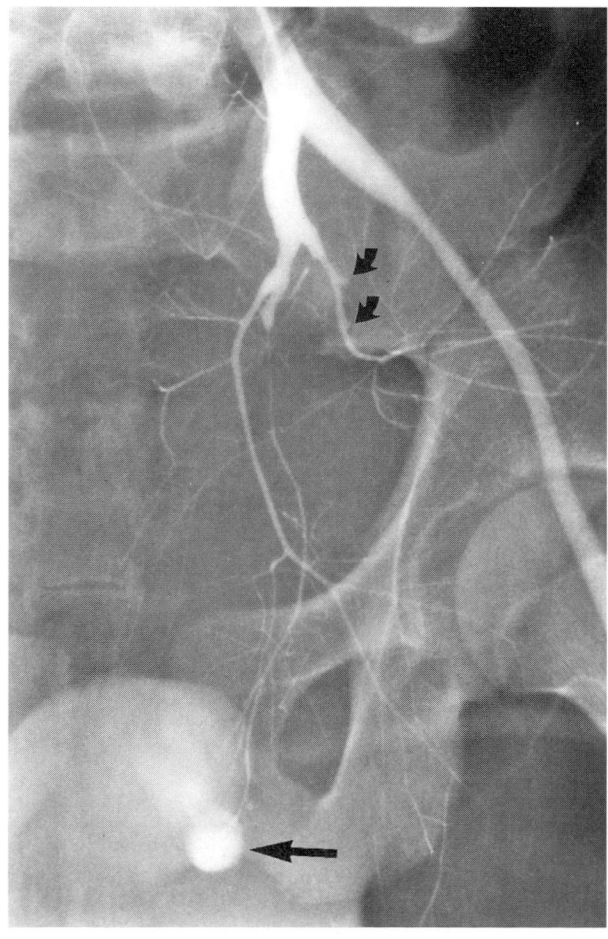

A

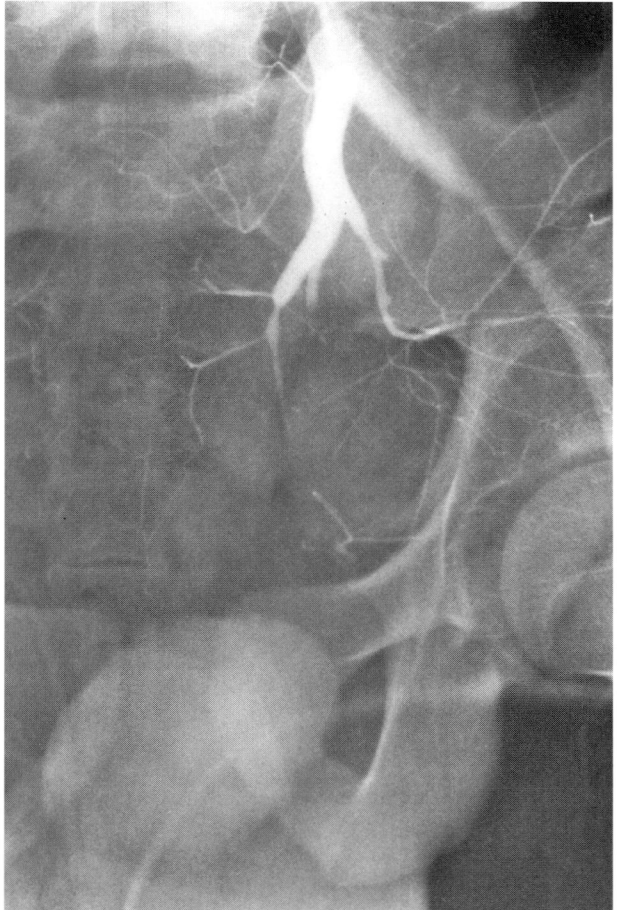

B

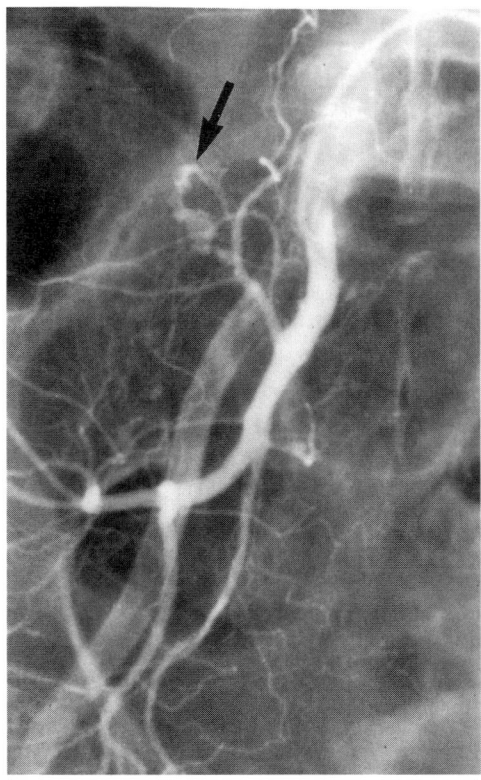

Figure 51-5. Extravasation from the right iliolumbar artery (*arrow*) in a patient with a pelvic fracture.

hematoma, acute arteriovenous communication, and spasm. These injuries manifest angiographically as free extravasation, contained extravasation or pseudoaneurysm, abrupt vessel occlusion, intimal flap, arteriovenous fistula, and focal arterial spasm (Figs. 51-6 and 51-7).

Angiography should be performed from the femoral approach if possible.[12-25] The short distance from the femoral access site to the internal iliac arteries facilitates selective catheterization. In some patients, a femoral pulse may not be palpable because of overlying soft tissue swelling, vasospasm, or hypotension. In these instances, fluoroscopically guided puncture over the middle third of the femoral head may achieve arterial access.[10] If the femoral vein is inadvertently punctured, an angiographic guidewire should be inserted. This guidewire can then be used as an indirect guide to fluoroscopically localize the femoral artery for a more lateral puncture. The axillary approach may be necessary in patients with extensive soft tissue trauma to the groins.[12,18,25] In this instance, the left axillary approach is preferred to minimize the risk to the great vessels and to provide the most direct access to the descending thoracic aorta. Regardless of the approach, insertion of an angiographic sheath is recommended early in the procedure to protect the arterial access during catheter exchanges and the embolization procedure.[12]

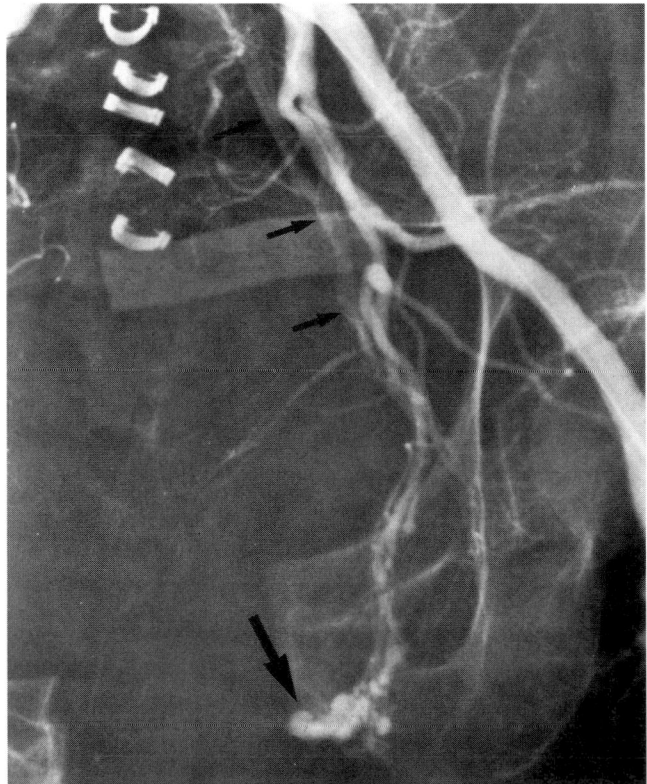

A

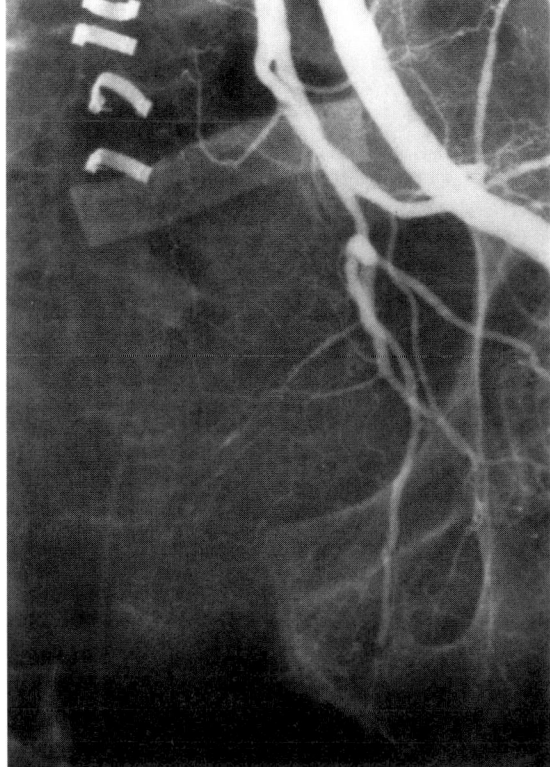

B

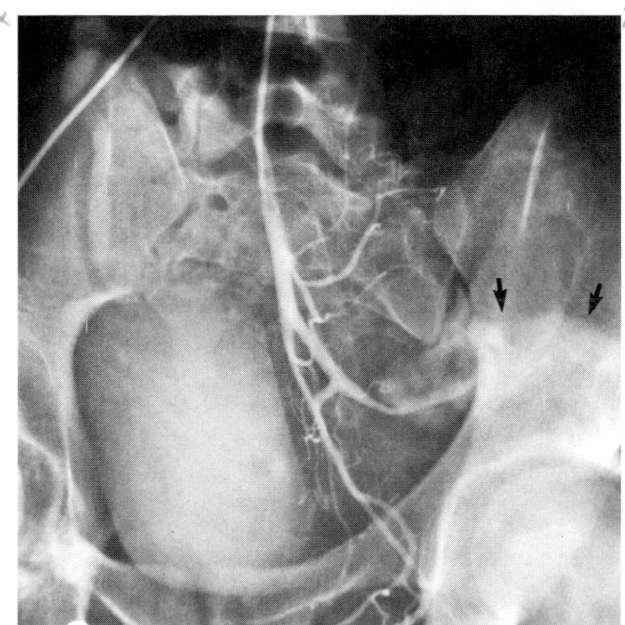

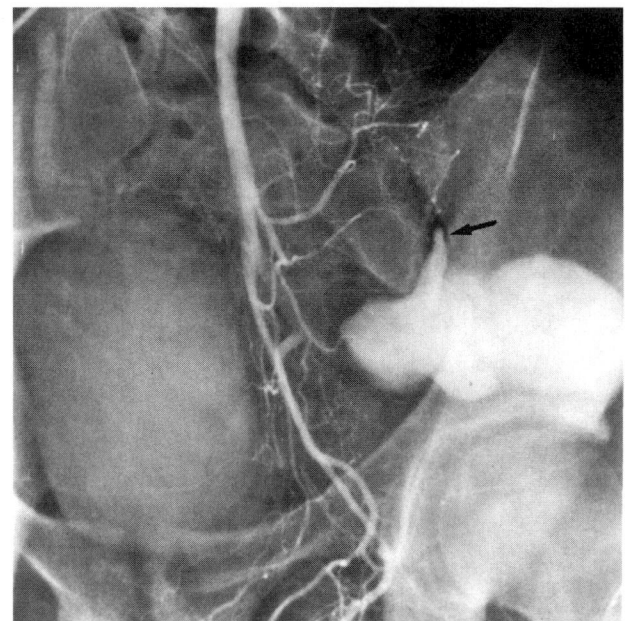

A **B**

Figure 51-7. Patient with bilateral pelvic fractures and a large hematoma on the left. (A) Left hypogastric artery angiogram shows filling of a large pseudoaneurysm (*arrows*) from the superior gluteal artery. Note the medial displacement of the hypogastric artery. (B) Later image from the same injection shows extension of the pseudoaneurysm into the disrupted sacroiliac joint (*arrow*). (C) Postembolization angiogram shows occlusion of the superior gluteal artery. The pseudoaneurysm does not opacify.

Drainage of the bladder by a Foley catheter or a cystostomy tube is helpful to prevent a contrast-filled bladder from obscuring the pelvic vessels during the angiogram. However, this is frequently not feasible before angiography in hemodynamically unstable patients with suspected urethral injury. The potentially lifesaving angiographic procedure should not be delayed in order to drain the patient's bladder.[12,18,19]

An initial pelvic arteriogram should be performed with a 5 or 6 French pigtail catheter positioned at the aortic bifurcation. Contrast material should be injected at a rate of 8 to 12 ml per second for 3 to 4 seconds. The purpose of the pelvic arteriogram is to determine the arterial anatomy and to detect extravasation. Therefore, adequate volumes of contrast and extended filming are essential. Important arterial variants, such as obturator arteries replaced to the inferior epigastric artery, and occlusive disease in older patients, may be detected on the pelvic arteriogram.

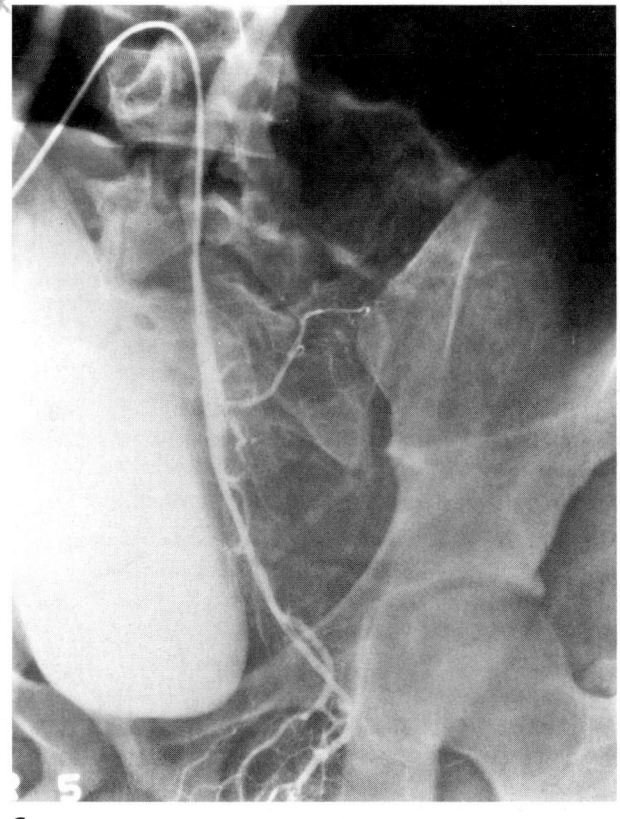

C

◄ **Figure 51-6.** Pelvic fracture due to crush injury with severe widening of the symphysis pubis and a posttraumatic arteriovenous fistula. (A) Pelvic angiogram shows a traumatic fistula fed by the internal pudendal artery (*large arrow*). Faint filling of the internal iliac vein is present (*small arrows*). (B) Postembolization angiogram shows occlusion of the fistula.

Brisk arterial bleeding from an internal iliac artery branch can frequently be visualized from injection in the distal aorta, but the absence of this finding on the pelvic angiogram does not exclude its presence.

Selective bilateral internal and external iliac artery angiograms should be routinely performed in patients with pelvic trauma.[12] A selective catheter should be positioned in the proximal internal iliac artery. Angiograms in both the posterior and anterior oblique projections should be obtained with injection of contrast material at a rate of 5 to 8 ml per second for 3 seconds. In some cases, selective anterior and posterior division injections may be required to evaluate questionable areas of extravasation. Multiple views are commonly necessary to completely evaluate patients with external pelvic fixation because of the bulky metal components of the device.

The importance of selective angiography in patients with pelvic trauma cannot be overstated (Fig. 51-8). Selective arteriography is necessary before embolization when extravasation is present on the initial pelvic angiogram to precisely localize the bleeding. When extravasation is not demonstrated on the initial pelvic an-

giogram, selective arteriography is essential to conclusively exclude arterial injury. Lastly, selective injections are required to evaluate extravasation that occurs in a site supplied by multiple vessels such as the sacrum and the iliac wing (Fig. 51-9).

There are several techniques for performing selective internal iliac artery angiography.[10,12,18,25] From the femoral approach, the authors favor a looped 5 French braided Cobra-2 catheter for both the ipsilateral and contralateral arteries.[10] The precise torque control and cephalad angle of the tip of the looped catheter permit rapid selection of the internal iliac artery trunk and the branches of the anterior and posterior divisions. Alternatively, an angled selective catheter can be used to cross the bifurcation and select the contralateral internal iliac artery directly. The use of a hydrophilic-coated guidewire greatly facilitates this process. In patients with a steep aortic bifurcation or tortuous iliac arteries, a long curved sheath placed over the aortic bifurcation improves the stability and control of the selective catheter. The same selective visceral catheter may be used to select the ipsilateral internal iliac artery if the common iliac artery bifurcation is not too acute, although

Figure 51-8. Selective internal iliac artery injections should be performed whenever possible when evaluating patients for posttraumatic pelvic bleeding. Patient with severe injury to the bony pelvis following a motor vehicle accident. (A) Late film from the flush pelvic angiogram demonstrates bilateral extravasation from the lateral sacral arteries

(*arrows*). (B) Selective right internal iliac artery injection shows extravasation from the lateral sacral artery (*straight arrow*). In addition, extravasation from the internal pudendal artery is visualized that was not shown on the flush pelvic angiogram (*curved arrow*).

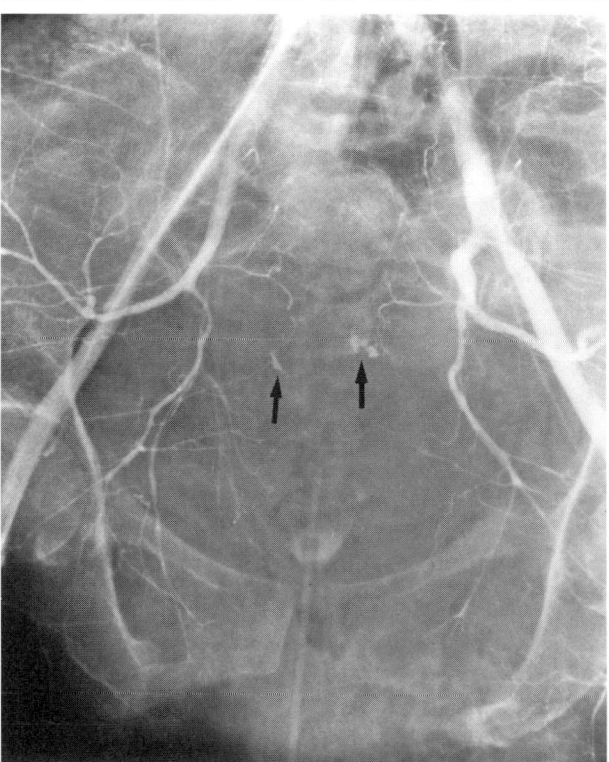

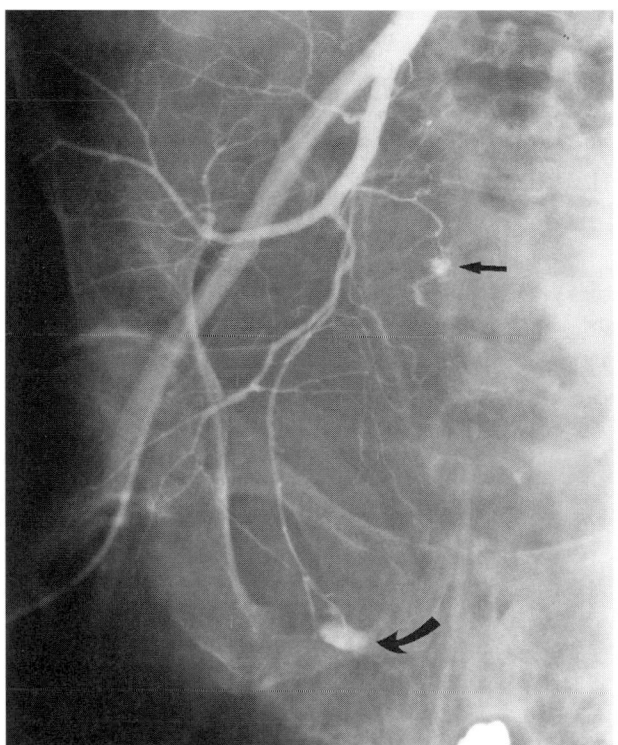

A

B

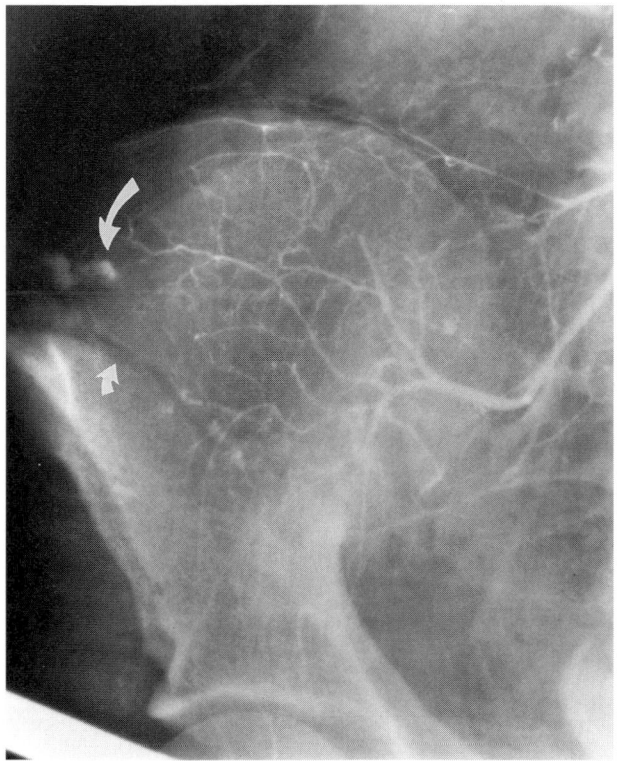

A

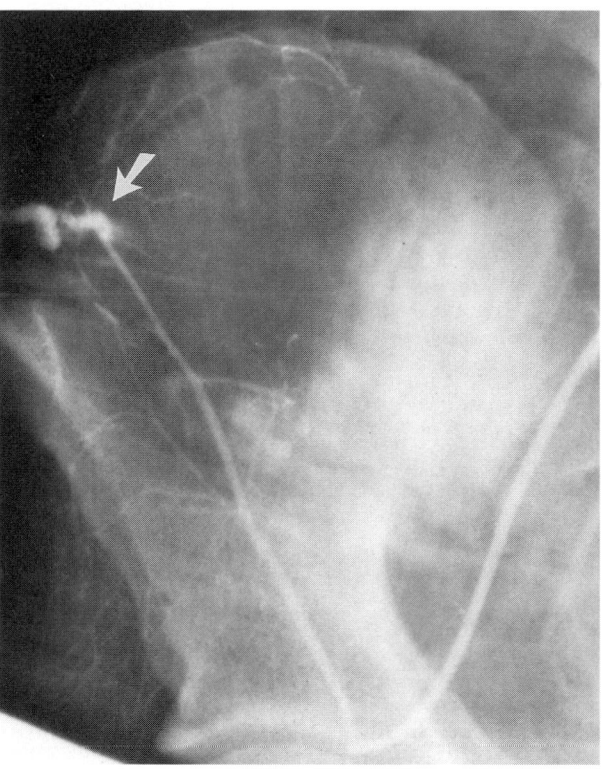

B

Figure 51-9. Selective injection of multiple vessels may be necessary to evaluate bleeding that occurs in territories with shared blood supply. Young man with right iliac wing pelvic fracture after a motor vehicle accident (same patient as Fig. 51-2). (A) Selective injection of the iliolumbar artery shows extravasation of contrast (*long arrow*). The fracture of the iliac wing is also seen (*short arrow*). (B) After embolization of the iliolumbar and superior gluteal arteries with Gelfoam pledgets, the patient had clinical evidence of continued bleeding. Injection of the right deep iliac circumflex artery showed extravasation in the same location as seen from the iliolumbar artery (*arrow*).

a Simmons 1 or 2 catheter will usually be necessary.[18] Bilateral femoral artery punctures with bilateral selection of the contralateral internal iliac artery may be required in patients with tortuous or diseased iliac arteries. The catheterization from the axillary approach requires a long angled catheter such as a Headhunter-1.[25]

Extended filming over 20 seconds may be necessary to visualize pelvic arterial extravasation.[18,25] Subtraction angiography is particularly helpful when extravasation occurs over bone, behind the bladder, or in an area of prior extravasation from another source such as a ruptured bladder (Fig. 51-10). Intraarterial digital subtraction angiography (IADSA) improves the conspicuity of extravasation and allows for rapid examination of hemodynamically unstable patients.[18] An important pitfall of IADSA is pseudoextravasation caused by misregistration artifacts from bowel gas, ureteral peristalsis, and patient movement. Careful selection of the mask, pixel shifting, or review of the unsubtracted digital angiogram may reveal the true nature of the suspected extravasation. With both cut-film or IADSA techniques, neither the normal uterine blush in menstruating women nor the stain at the base of the penis in males should be confused with extravasation.[46]

Embolization

Once bleeding has been identified, a selective catheter should be securely positioned to allow embolization of the target vessel. The primary goal of embolization in patients with pelvic fractures is to expeditiously decrease or arrest the flow of arterial blood to the injured vessel to allow hemostasis to occur.[12] Supraselective catheterization should be used judiciously in patients who are unstable because the time spent manipulating a microcatheter into a small vessel may unnecessarily prolong the procedure and limit the operator to small embolic materials. Rapid embolization of the entire anterior or posterior division is preferable to an elegant but long supraselective embolization. Complete occlusion of the internal iliac artery is an acceptable alternative to exsanguination.

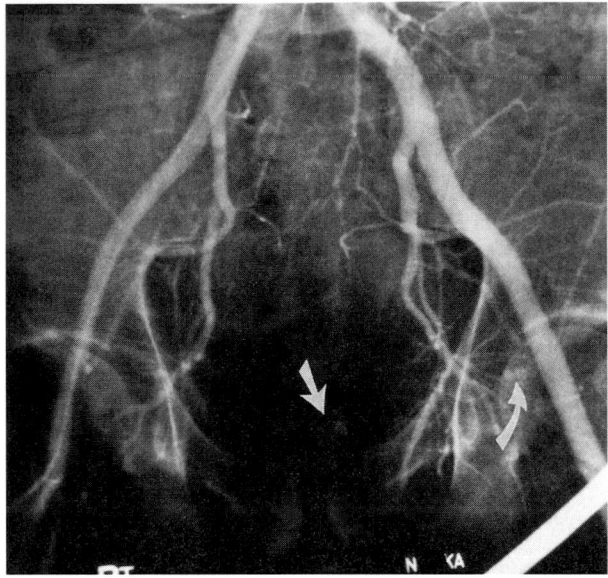

A

B

Figure 51-10. Subtraction techniques are very useful in the evaluation of pelvic arterial trauma. Young man with a pelvic fracture after a motorcycle accident. (A) Extravasation of contrast is seen faintly above the symphysis pubis (*straight arrow*) and over the femoral head (*curved arrow*) on the cut-film pelvic angiogram. (B) The areas of extravasation are more obvious on the subtracted image. Digital subtraction angiography was not available at the time that this patient was studied, but would have been similarly useful.

The embolic material should be easy to use, widely available, and able to rapidly occlude medium-size arteries. Temporary occlusion on the order of several weeks is ideal because this allows recanalization of the vessel after healing of the injury.[12] Materials that are difficult to use, such as tissue adhesives, are inappropriate because of the emergent nature of the procedure. Materials that embolize the terminal arterial branches, such as Gelfoam powder or other fine particles, should not be used because of the risk of ischemia to the pelvic viscera, soft tissues, and nerves.[47,48] Absolute alcohol is contraindicated because of tissue necrosis and poor control of the liquid embolic agent within the richly anastomotic pelvic circulation. The original pelvic embolizations for trauma employed autologous blood clot formed in a sterile bowl during the procedure.[9] This is no longer a first-line agent because it is difficult to control the size of the emboli and recanalization can occur within days. In addition, formation of clot can take a long time in coagulopathic patients, requiring the use of topical thrombin.[22]

The agent of choice in pelvic trauma is Gelfoam (Upjohn) cut into pieces to match the vessel to be embolized.[10,12,17,18,25] Gelfoam is readily available, easy to use, quickly tailored to the individual patient, partially directed by the increased flow through the injured vessel, and a temporary agent that permits later recanalization. The dimensions of the pledget should be sized to the diameter of the vessel at the bleeding site. Proximal embolization of the vessel may allow continued bleeding via collateral supply. Typical pledget dimensions range from 1-mm cubes to 1 mm × 2 mm × 5 mm rectangles. Long Gelfoam strips up to 5 cm in length may be necessary for large vessels.[12] The Gelfoam pledget is first soaked in contrast, then loaded into a 1-ml Luer-Lok syringe. Embolization is accomplished by injection of the pledget through the selective catheter. Use of tuberculin syringes should be avoided because they lack Luer-Loks and dislodge from the catheter during injection of the embolus. Large strips of Gelfoam are injected using 5- to 10-ml Luer-Lok syringes, and must be injected through 5 French or larger catheters.[12] Multiple pledgets of varying sizes may be required depending on the progress of the embolization. Embolization continues until extravasation is no longer visualized.

When numerous bleeding sites are present, or selection beyond the internal iliac trunk cannot be accomplished, the "scatter" technique described by Ben-Menachem et al. may be used.[12] Numerous 2-mm Gelfoam cubes suspended in contrast material are injected in a pulsatile fashion into the internal iliac artery, resulting in occlusion of multiple vessels.[18] The low resistance within the bleeding vessels favors distribution of the Gelfoam emboli to these branches.

Coils are useful adjuncts in pelvic embolization procedures. When large vessels are transected, the Gelfoam may be swept through the rent into the retroperitoneum. Coils can provide an intravascular substrate on which Gelfoam pledgets can be packed. In patients with pseudoaneurysms or arteriovenous fistulas, where a precise embolization may be desirable, coils can be the embolic material of choice. In contrast to Gelfoam pledgets, which are injected in a relatively uncontrolled manner, coils can be pushed through the catheter with a floppy wire and deposited in a more deliberate fashion. In patients with pelvic hemorrhage, some authors have used proximal coil blockade to protect normal vessels during injection of small pieces of Gelfoam.[10] This practice is only suitable in stable patients in whom the pace of the embolization can be slower, and is of unproven benefit. A large variety of coil sizes and shapes are available for both standard selective and supraselective microcatheters. In most cases, however, coils are not the primary embolization material in hemodynamically unstable patients because of the time needed for careful placement and occasional incomplete vascular occlusion.[12]

Balloon occlusion catheters positioned in the internal iliac artery can temporarily control hemorrhage in exsanguinating patients.[9,12,18,25,49] Embolization can then be performed through the lumen of the occlusion catheter using sub–3 French microcatheters. Balloon occlusion techniques may also be useful when hemorrhage is discovered from a vessel that cannot be safely embolized, such as the common or external iliac arteries. The balloon remains inflated while the patient is transferred to the operating room for open repair.

The role of embolization in the management of traumatic occlusions of internal iliac artery branches is not well defined. These occlusions may represent thrombosed arterial transections or areas of spasm.

Differentiation is impossible from the diagnostic angiograms because both lesions appear as abrupt arterial cutoffs. Probing of the occlusion with a guidewire is ill advised because of the risk of converting an intact but spastic artery into a perforated vessel. Some authors recommend prophylactic embolization of the occluded vessels to prevent possible future hemorrhage, particularly in patients who are hemodynamically unstable.[12,18] This may be technically difficult if only a short stump of the vessel remains patent. In this instance, placement of a coil is preferred to the less controlled injection of Gelfoam pledgets. An alternative management strategy in hemodynamically stable patients is to follow transfusion requirements without embolization, with prompt return to the angiographic suite for evidence of resumed bleeding (transfusion of more than 4 to 6 units of packed red cells in less than 24 hours). Patients who are not embolized should be monitored carefully because the rate of clot lysis is unpredictable.

Successful embolization is frequently clinically evident with sudden improvement in the patient's hemodynamic status during the procedure. Angiographically, extravasation ceases, and vasospasm improves (Fig. 51-11). Completion angiography is necessary to document cessation of bleeding and to screen for

Figure 51-11. The hemodynamic status of the patient may improve dramatically after successful embolization. Young man with a pelvic fracture and persistent hemodynamic instability despite placement of an external fixation device. (A) Cut-film angiogram of the pelvis shows massive extravasation from the right superior gluteal artery (*solid arrow*). There is severe spasm of the right external iliac artery (*open arrow*), which is virtually obturated by the 5 French catheter. (B) Postembolization digital subtraction angiogram shows occlusion of most of the branches of the right hypogastric artery and marked improvement of the external iliac artery spasm. With embolization, the patient immediately became hemodynamically stable.

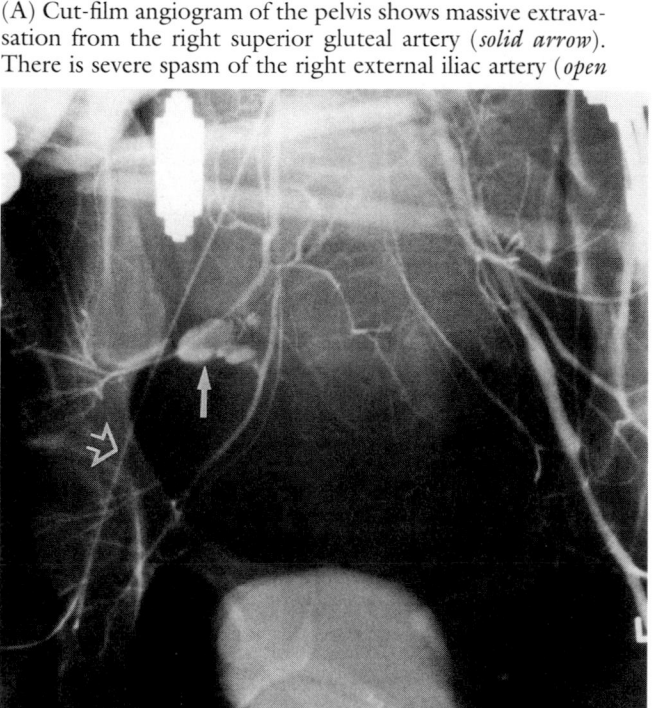

A

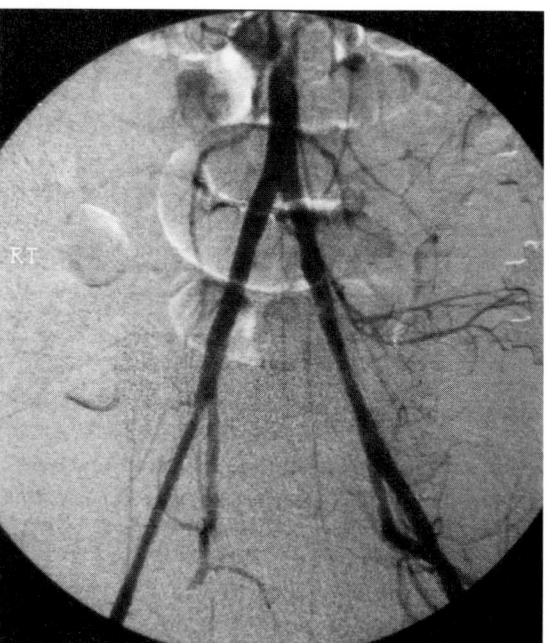

B

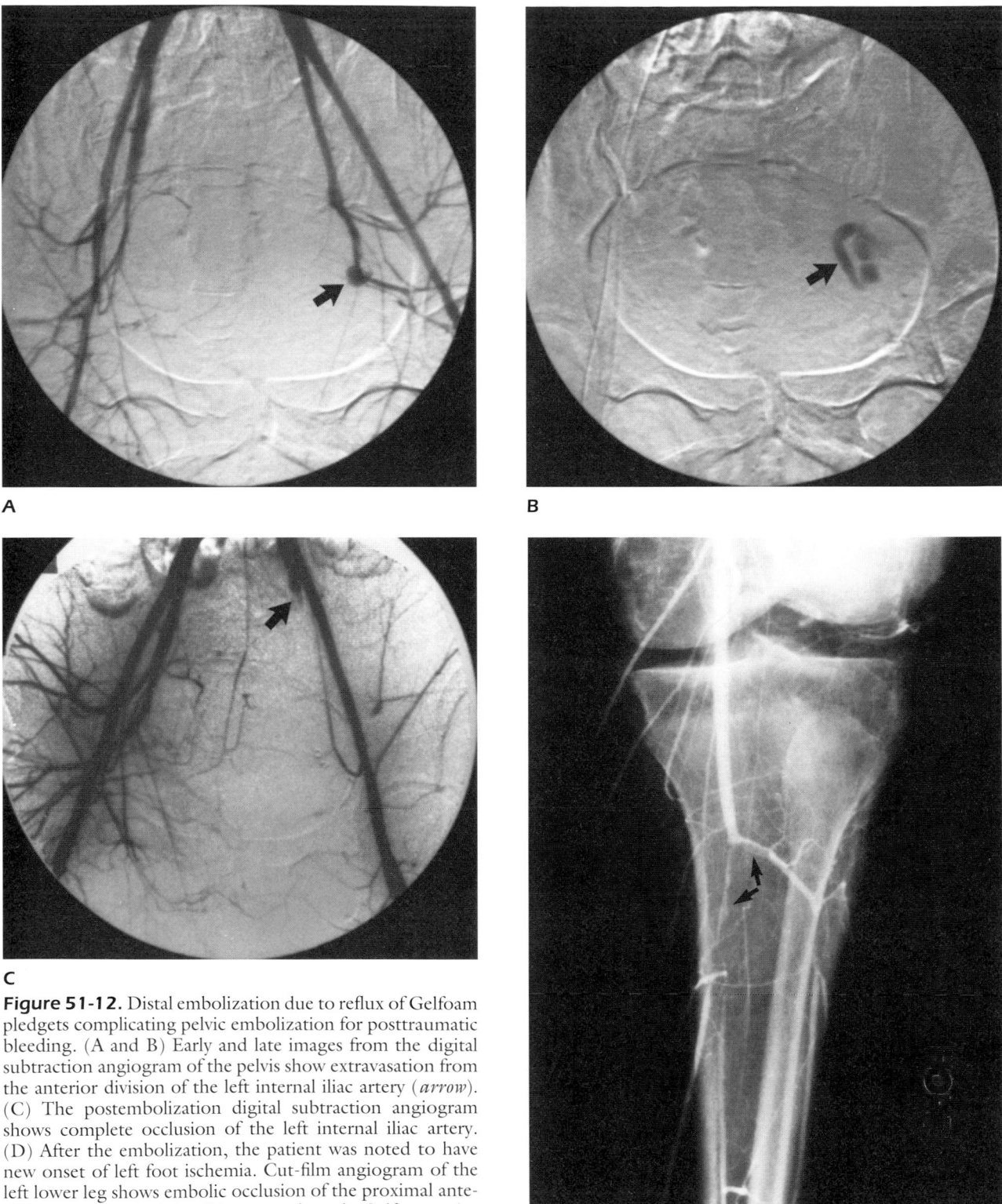

Figure 51-12. Distal embolization due to reflux of Gelfoam pledgets complicating pelvic embolization for posttraumatic bleeding. (A and B) Early and late images from the digital subtraction angiogram of the pelvis show extravasation from the anterior division of the left internal iliac artery (*arrow*). (C) The postembolization digital subtraction angiogram shows complete occlusion of the left internal iliac artery. (D) After the embolization, the patient was noted to have new onset of left foot ischemia. Cut-film angiogram of the left lower leg shows embolic occlusion of the proximal anterior tibial artery and the tibioperoneal trunk. Gelfoam strips and thrombus were recovered at surgery.

previously unsuspected sites of extravasation or collateral supply. A pelvic angiogram is mandatory. If extravasation was only visualized with selective injections, these should be repeated. Bilateral internal iliac angiograms should be performed if extravasation was from a midline vessel. When embolization in the pelvis is complete but the patient remains hemodynamically unstable, angiographic evaluation of the abdomen or thorax for another source of bleeding may be warranted.[12]

The complications of percutaneous embolization of bleeding in pelvic trauma should be compared to the morbidity associated with attempted operative repair or conservative management with massive transfusion.[24] Patients should never be considered "too unstable" to undergo this procedure if the suspected etiology of hemodynamic collapse is uncontrolled pelvic hemorrhage. Concerns regarding contrast material such as renal failure are legitimate but should never prevent the procedure. Patients who undergo angiography for diagnosis and treatment of pelvic bleeding are dying. Most complications are acceptable outcomes of a lifesaving intervention.

Nontarget embolization is an important procedure-specific complication of pelvic embolization. Fortunately, the most common site of nontarget embolization is another branch of the internal iliac artery. This is usually of little clinical consequence because the bladder, rectum, and pelvic soft tissues have multiple sources of blood supply, including the opposite internal iliac artery and sources originating outside the anatomic boundaries of the pelvis. As long as the embolic material is of appropriate size and composition, ischemic complications are rare.[47,48] Reflux of embolic material into the ipsilateral lower extremity can occur if the catheter is not well seated in the internal iliac artery or the pledget is injected with excessive force. Emboli that lodge in the profunda femoris artery or other muscular branches are usually clinically silent unless these are sources of collateral supply to the lower limb. Occlusion of a runoff vessel such as the superficial femoral or popliteal artery may result in a severely ischemic limb that requires urgent revascularization (Fig. 51-12).[19]

Impotence in men and inability to achieve pregnancy in women may be perceived as potential complications of embolization by referring physicians. Before the widespread application of percutaneous embolization in pelvic trauma, impotence was closely linked to urethral injury, with an incidence of 30 to 50 percent.[50,51] The etiologies of impotence following pelvic fracture are predominantly vascular and neurologic insults that occur at the time of the original trauma.[52,53] In women, conception with successful pregnancies has been documented after surgical devascularization of the uterus and ovaries.[54] The use of a temporary embolic agent such as Gelfoam may permit future recan-

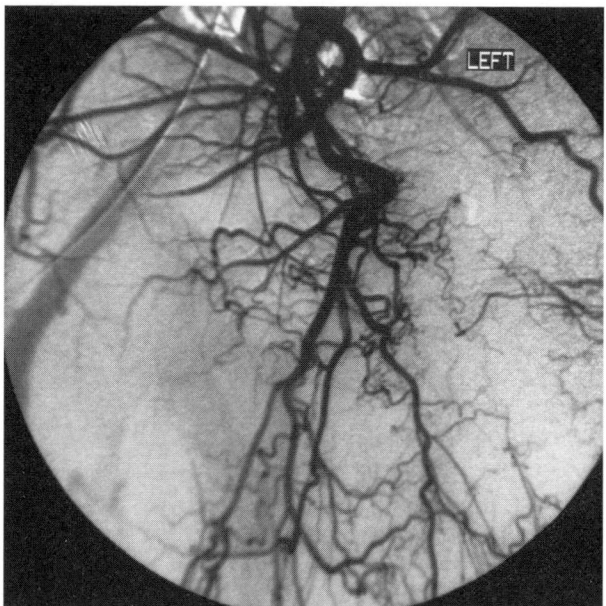

Figure 51-13. Recanalization of embolized vessels is common when temporary agents such as Gelfoam are used. Digital subtraction angiogram of the right hypogastric artery (right posterior oblique projection) of the same patient as Fig. 51-11, obtained 1 year later. The embolized vessel is now patent.

alization of pudendal, uterine, and ovarian arteries (Fig. 51-13). However, there are no studies that prove that pelvic embolization in trauma does not cause impotence in men or infertility in women. These concerns should be weighed against the immediate needs of an exsanguinating patient.

Other Applications

Retroperitoneal pelvic hemorrhage can occur after penetrating trauma, orthopedic surgery, obstetric procedures, and percutaneous interventions.[7,18,25,55–57] The techniques and principles that apply to hemorrhage in pelvic fractures can be employed in these situations as well (Fig. 51-14). Intraoperative embolization of the internal iliac artery to control bleeding from stab wounds and fractures has been reported.[58] In most instances, pelvic embolization is best performed in a fully equipped angiographic suite with optimal imaging and the full range of angiographic materials.

Conclusion

Percutaneous embolization of uncontrolled retroperitoneal pelvic hemorrhage is a lifesaving technique for which no adequate alternative procedure exists. Early intervention in hemodynamically unstable patients

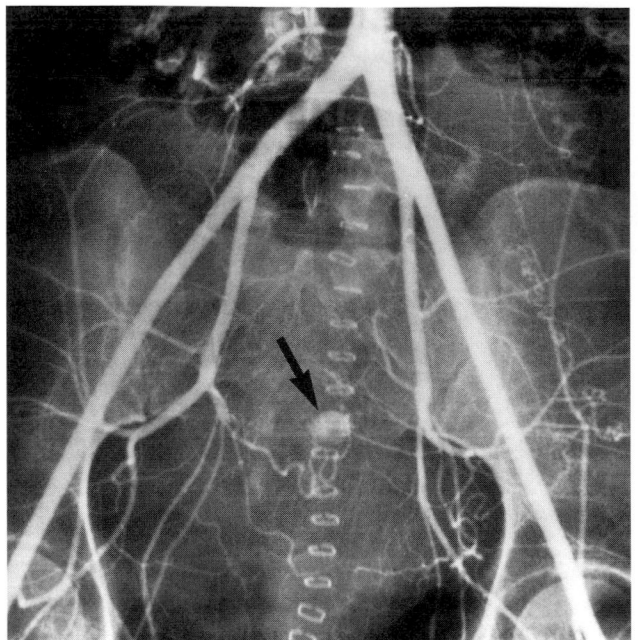

A

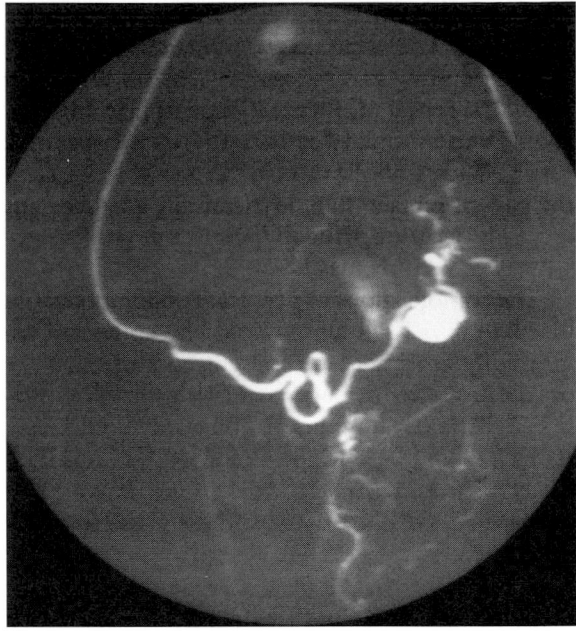

B

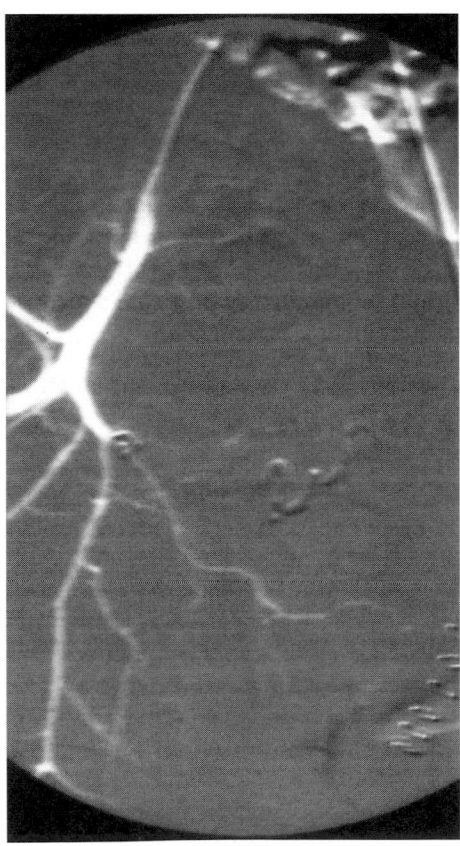

C

Figure 51-14. Embolization techniques used in pelvic fractures can be applied to hemorrhage from other types of pelvic trauma. Young woman with uterine bleeding after cesarean section. (A) Cut-film angiogram of the pelvis shows extravasation of contrast centrally in the pelvis (*arrow*). (B) Digital subtraction angiogram of the right uterine artery localizes the extravasation. (C) Selective digital subtraction right internal iliac artery angiogram after embolization with Gelfoam pledgets and a single coil shows cessation of bleeding. (Courtesy of Edwin Kim, M.D.)

References

1. Patterson FP, Morton KS. The cause of death in fractures of the pelvis: with a note on treatment by ligation of the hypogastric (internal iliac) artery. J Trauma 1973;13:849–856.
2. Rothenberger DA, Fischer RP, Strate RG, Velasco R, Perry JF Jr. The mortality associated with pelvic fractures. Surgery 1978; 84:356–361.
3. Ravitch MM. Hypogastric artery ligation in acute pelvic trauma. Surgery 1964;56:601–602.
4. Mucha P, Farnell MN. Analysis of pelvic fracture management. J Trauma 1984;24:379–386.
5. Reed RA, Teitelbaum GP, Katz MD, Pentecost MJ. Early management of the trauma patient with pelvic fracture: a medical perspective. Semin Intervent Radiol 1992;9:1–3.
6. Brotman S, Soderstrom CA, Oster-Granite M, et al. Management of severe bleeding in fractures of the pelvis. Surg Gynecol Obstet 1981;153:823–826.
7. Yellin AE, Lundell CJ, Finck EJ. Diagnosis and control of posttraumatic pelvic hemorrhage: transcatheter angiographic embolization techniques. Arch Surg 1983;118:1378–1383.
8. Ayella RJ, DuPriest RW Jr, Khaneja SC, et al. Transcatheter embolization of autologous clot in the management of bleeding associated with fractures of the pelvis. Surg Gynecol Obstet 1978;147:849–852.
9. Margolies MN, Ring EJ, Waltman AC, Kerr WS, Baum S. Arteriography in the management of hemorrhage from pelvic fractures. N Engl J Med 1972;287:317–321.
10. Panetta TP, Sclafani SJA, Goldstein AS, Phillips TF, Shaftan GW. Percutaneous transcatheter embolization for massive bleeding from pelvic fractures. J Trauma 1985;25:1021–1029.

with pelvic fractures is essential to reduce the morbidity of the injury. Embolization can be quickly and safely performed using widely available embolic materials. Angiography is likely to continue to have an important role in the management of pelvic trauma.

11. Agnew SG. Hemodynamically unstable pelvic fractures. Orthop Clin North Am 1994;25:715–721.
12. Ben-Menachem Y, Coldwell DM, Young JWR, Burgess AR. Hemorrhage associated with pelvic fractures: causes, diagnosis, and emergent management. AJR 1991;157:1005–1014.
13. Brown JJ, Greene FL, McMillan RD. Vascular injuries associated with pelvic fractures. Am Surg 1984;50:150–154.
14. Evers BM, Cryer HM, Miller FB. Pelvic fracture hemorrhage: priorities in management. Arch Surg 1989;124:422–424.
15. Flint LW, Brown A, Richardson JD, Polk HC. Definitive control of bleeding from severe pelvic fractures. Ann Surg 1979; 189:709–714.
16. Gilliland MD, Ward RE, Barton RM, Miller PW, Duke JH. Factors affecting mortality in pelvic fractures. J Trauma 1982; 22:691–693.
17. Kam J, Jackson H, Ben-Menachem Y. Vascular injuries in blunt pelvic trauma. Radiol Clin North Am 1981;19:171–186.
18. Katz MD, Teitelbaum GP, Pentecost MJ. Diagnostic arteriography and therapeutic transcatheter embolization for post-traumatic pelvic hemorrhage. Semin Intervent Radiol 1992;9: 4–12.
19. Matalon TSA, Athanasoulis CA, Margolies MN, et al. Hemorrhage with pelvic fractures: efficacy of transcatheter embolization. AJR 1979;133:859–864.
20. Maull KI, Sachatello CR. Current management of pelvic fractures: a combined surgical-angiographic approach to hemorrhage. South Med J 1976;69:1285–1289.
21. Poole GV, Ward EF, Muakkassa FF, et al. Pelvic fracture from major blunt trauma: outcome is determined by associated injuries. Ann Surg 1991;213:532–538.
22. Ring EJ, Athanasoulis CA, Waltman AC, Margolies MN, Baum S. Arteriographic management of hemorrhage following pelvic fracture. Radiology 1973;109:65–70.
23. Ring EJ, Waltman AS, Athanasoulis CA, Smith JC, Baum S. Angiography in pelvic trauma. Surg Gynecol Obstet 1974;139: 375–380.
24. Smith K, Ben-Menachem Y, Duke JH Jr, Hill GL. The superior gluteal: an artery at risk in blunt pelvic trauma. J Trauma 1976; 16:273–279.
25. Stock JR, Harris WH, Athanasoulis CA. The role of diagnostic and therapeutic angiography in trauma to the pelvis. Clin Orthop Relat Res 1980;151:31–40.
26. Davidson BS, Simmons GT, Williamson PR, Buerk CA. Pelvic fractures associated with open perineal wounds: a survivable injury. J Trauma 1993;35:36–39.
27. Riemer BL, Butterfield SL, Diamond DL, et al. Acute mortality associated with injuries to the pelvic ring: the role of early patient mobilization and external fixation. J Trauma 1993;35: 671–677.
28. Latenser BA, Gentilello LM, Tarver AA, Thalgott JS, Batdorf JW. Improved outcomes with early fixation of skeletally unstable pelvic fractures. J Trauma 1991;31:28–31.
29. Goldstein A, Phillips T, Sclafani SJA, et al. Early open reduction external fixation of the disrupted pelvic ring. J Trauma 1986; 26:325–333.
30. Cryer HM, Miller FB, Evers BM, Rouben LR, Seligson DL. Pelvic fracture classification: correlation with hemorrhage. J Trauma 1988;28:973–979.
31. Burgess AR, Eastridge BJ, Young JWR, et al. Pelvic ring disruptions: effective classification system and treatment protocols. J Trauma 1990;30:848–856.
32. Huittinen V-M, Slätis P. Postmortem angiography and dissection of the hypogastric artery in pelvic fractures. Surgery 1973; 73:454–462.
33. Motsay GJ, Manlove C, Perry JF. Major venous injury with pelvic fracture. J Trauma 1969;9:343–346.
34. Ben-Menachem Y. Delayed, exsanguinating pelvic hemorrhage after blunt trauma without bony fracture: case report. J Trauma 1991;31:1018.
35. Seavers R, Lynch J, Ballard R, Jernigan S, Johnson J. Hypogastric artery ligation for uncontrollable hemorrhage in acute pelvic trauma. Surgery 1964;55:516–519.
36. Horton RE, Hamilton SGI. Ligature of the internal iliac artery for massive haemorrhage complicating fracture of the pelvis. J Bone Joint Surg 1968;50-B:376–379.
37. Fleming WH, Bowen JC. Control of hemorrhage in pelvic crush injuries. J Trauma 1973;13:567–570.
38. Ger R, Condrea H, Steichen FM. Traumatic intrapelvic retroperitoneal hemorrhage: an experimental study. J Surg Res 1969;9:31–34.
39. Ravitch MM. Hypogastric artery ligation in acute pelvic trauma. Surgery 1964;56:601–602.
40. Athanasoulis CA, Duffield R, Shapiro JH. Angiography to assess pelvic vascular injury. N Engl J Med 1971;285:1539.
41. Young JWR, Resnik CS. Fracture of the pelvis: current concepts and classification. AJR 1990;155:1169–1175.
42. Ochsner MG, Hoffman AP, DiPasquale D, et al. Associated aortic rupture-pelvic fracture: an alert for orthopedic and general surgeons. J Trauma 1992;33:429–434.
43. Brumback RJ. Traumatic rupture of the superior gluteal artery, without fracture of the pelvis, causing compartment syndrome of the buttock. J Bone Joint Surg 72-A;1990:134–137.
44. Baumgartner F, White GH, White RA, et al. Delayed, exsanguinating pelvic hemorrhage after blunt trauma without bony fracture: case report. J Trauma 1990;30:1603–1605.
45. Birchard JD, Pichora DR, Brown PM. External iliac artery and lumbosacral plexus injury secondary to open book fracture of the pelvis: report of a case. J Trauma 1990;30:906–908.
46. Schrumpf JD, Sommer G, Jacobs RP. Bleeding simulated by the distal internal pudendal artery stain. AJR 1978;131:657–659.
47. Braf ZF, Koontz WW Jr. Gangrene of the bladder: complication of hypogastric artery embolization. Urology 1977;9:670–671.
48. Hare WSC, Holland CJ. Paresis following internal iliac artery embolization. Radiology 1983;143:47–51.
49. Paster SB, Van Houten FX, Adams DF. Percutaneous balloon catheterization: a technique for the control of arterial hemorrhage caused by pelvic trauma. JAMA 1974;230:573–575.
50. Gibson GR. Impotence following fractured pelvis and ruptured urethra. Br J Urol 1970;42:86–88.
51. King J. Impotence following fractures of the pelvis. J Bone Joint Surg 975;57-A:1107–1109.
52. Ellison M, Timberlake GA, Kerstein MD. Impotence following pelvic fracture. J Trauma 1988;28:695–696.
53. Sharlip ID. Penile arteriography in impotence after pelvic trauma. J Urol 1981;126:477–481.
54. Mengert WF, Burchell RC, Blumstein RW, Daskal JL. Pregnancy after bilateral ligation of the internal iliac and ovarian arteries. Obstet Gynecol 1969;34:664–666.
55. Mitty HA, Sterling KM, Alvarez M, Gendler R. Obstetric hemorrhage: prophylactic and emergency arterial catheterization and embolotherapy. Radiology 1993;18:183–187.
56. Yamashita Y, Harada M, Yamamoto H, et al. Transcatheter arterial embolization of obstetric bleeding: efficacy and clinical outcome. Br J Radiol 1994;67:530–534.
57. Malden ES, Picus D. Hemorrhagic complication of transgluteal pelvic abscess drainage: successful percutaneous treatment. J Vasc Intervent Radiol 1992;3:323–328.
58. Saueracker AJ, McCroskey BL, Moore EE, Moore FA. Intraoperative hypogastric artery embolization for life-threatening pelvic hemorrhage: a preliminary report. J Trauma 1987;27: 1127–1129.

52

Transcatheter Arterial Embolization in the Management of Splenic Trauma

GEORGE I. GETRAJDMAN
SALVATORE J. A. SCLAFANI

Background

The spleen has been an organ of mystery for centuries. Its role and purpose have been debated, and contradictory conclusions as to its value have been reached. Aristotle, more than 2000 years ago, declared that the spleen served no purpose.[1] Pliny, in the first century A.D., suggested that its absence might cause loss of a sense of humor or an inability to laugh.[2] Maimonides proposed that the organ might function to purify the blood.[3] With time the esteem of the spleen rose significantly, and by the 17th century it was judged to be essential for the sustenance of life.

However, with the advent of splenectomy in the 1600s, the spleen's vaulted position was again questioned. In fact, documentation of the potential for normal life after splenectomy seemed to suggest rather firmly that the spleen was an accessory organ unnecessary for normal human function. Combined laparotomy and splenectomy was established as the treatment of choice for all splenic trauma regardless of the degree of injury identified at operation.

The standing of the spleen began to improve again in the 20th century when its roles in the immune response were recognized and elaborated. King and Schumacker[4] provided an important clue when they described a possible causal relationship between prior splenectomy and overwhelming lethal infections in children, manifested by fulminant pneumonia, meningitis, septicemia, coagulopathy, and death.

Nonoperative management of selected splenic injuries in children was therefore attempted and reported successfully by Upadhyaya and Simpson as early as 1968.[5] With the continued demonstration of the healthful function of the spleen and elucidation of its role in the immune response, surgical support for splenectomy eroded further. The focus of management of splenic trauma, even in the adult population, eventually moved to procedures such as splenorrhaphy, partial splenectomy, splenic reimplantation, and splenic artery ligation.[6–22]

It is this shift in the attitude from mandatory splenectomy to more conservative therapies that has created an environment conducive to the use of interventional radiologic techniques in the management of some splenic injuries.

Immunologic Considerations

Overwhelming Postsplenectomy Infection

The rationale for a conservative approach to the injured spleen is based on the uncommon but real lifelong risk of death from overwhelming sepsis observed after splenectomy (overwhelming postsplenectomy infection, or OPSI). In children who had had splenectomy, Singer[23] reported a prevalence of sepsis 58 times greater than that of the general population. O'Neal and McDonald[24] documented death from sepsis in 2.7 percent of adult patients who had had their spleen removed. This is a prevalence more than 500 times greater than in the population at large. Green et al.,[25] after extensive follow-up of patients who had had splenectomy, detected a 5.9 percent incidence of significant delayed septic complications.

Immunologic Function of the Spleen

The primary immunologic role of the spleen is protection from blood-borne infections, especially opsonized encapsulated bacteria. Several immunologic abnormalities have been noted that render patients susceptible to overwhelming infection after their spleens have been removed. Neither asplenic rats nor humans are able to mount a normal antibody response.[26–28] IgM levels drop considerably,[29] and there is a failure to switch from IgM to IgG synthesis after secondary immunization.[30] In addition to changes in antibody production, the polymorphonucleocytes and macrophages of patients without spleens show impaired chemotactic function.[31] Decreased function is also seen in helper T cells.[32] Furthermore, the activity of tuftsin, a circulating polypeptide that stimulates phagocytosis by acting directly on blood-borne leukocytes, has been shown to be absent within 6 to 8 weeks of removal of the spleen.[33] Impairment of immune response is not limited to intravascular phenomena. The spleen appears to be a source of mediators that help regulate certain cell populations in other organs. Changes in Kupffer cell function have been noted after splenectomy[34]; there is decreased clearance of bacteria from the lungs after aerosol challenge with streptococcal pneumonia.[35-37]

Indications for Nonoperative Therapy

Patient Selection

Patients who are to be considered candidates for nonoperative therapy must meet certain clinical criteria. Although these criteria may vary between institutions, the majority of studies generally agree on certain parameters:

1. Patients must be hemodynamically stable or easily and rapidly stabilized before they are transported to imaging facilities. The determination of stability is dynamic and depends on variables such as the patient's age, general conditions, and associated injuries.

    The systolic blood pressure should generally be above 100 mmHg, although the preinjury blood pressure of children may be lower and that of the elderly may be much higher. Medications such as beta blockers may blunt the response to hypovolemia. The pulse rate should be less than 120 beats per minute.

    Arterial pH and other laboratory determinants of metabolic acidosis caused by hypovolemia and hypoperfusion from blood loss are very sensitive indicators of hemodynamic instability. The arterial pH should be greater than 7.30.

2. Only minimal peritoneal findings should be present on physical examination. Although any degree of hemoperitoneum may result in peritoneal irritation, tenderness to palpation is usually mild. Severe peritonitis manifested by rebound tenderness and severe abdominal distention usually suggest that

other injuries to the hollow viscera have also occurred. Exploratory laparotomy is indicated when severe peritonitis is present.

3. There should be no intraabdominal injuries that require urgent laparotomy. These include hollow viscus injury, pancreatic fracture, and major vascular injuries (such as to the renal artery).

4. The patient should be examinable and therefore should have a level of consciousness that will allow assessment of pain and other factors. Ideally the patient should have an intact mental status.

5. The requirements for blood transfusion should be limited, depending on other injuries, age, and other such factors.

6. Underlying coagulopathy should be considered carefully. The risks and benefits of a nonoperative approach must be tailored to the underlying condition causing the clotting problems. Correction of the coagulation should be attempted.

Diagnosis

At the authors' institution candidates for nonoperative therapy are first evaluated by diagnostic peritoneal lavage (DPL), CT scanning, or both, depending on age, clinical suspicions, hemodynamic status, and so forth. DPL remains the least expensive, most expeditious, and most reliable screening procedure in patients with blunt abdominal trauma. A negative DPL excludes most significant abdominal injuries. A DPL positive for white blood cells, particulate matter, bacteria, or bilirubin suggests a hollow viscus injury and mandates laparotomy. In the authors' current algorithm, a DPL positive for blood no longer requires immediate laparotomy. It has become an indication for CT scanning.

The value of contrast-enhanced CT scanning in the evaluation of blunt abdominal trauma is well documented.[38-43] CT scanning has a number of diagnostic advantages when compared to DPL.[44-46] CT can delineate the specific injury causing the intraperitoneal hemorrhage as well as look for associated injuries, including those in the retroperitoneum. It is particularly valuable in demonstrating splenic injuries,[47-49] and has a sensitivity and specificity above 96 percent. CT scanning can also help characterize the type, location, and extent of splenic injury.

A number of studies have attempted to correlate CT findings with the successful outcome of nonsurgical treatment. Various classifications and scoring systems have been proposed in an attempt to predict the natural history of an injured spleen.[50-53] While confirming CT's accuracy in detecting and often quantifying splenic injury, many studies have shown that the extent of injury illustrated by CT does not necessarily correlate with the need for surgical intervention or the expected outcome of observational therapy.[54-60] The studies have shown that low-grade "observable" injuries, as classified by CT, often require operative intervention. At the other end of the spectrum, high-grade "surgical" injuries have very frequently been observed nonoperatively with good clinical outcomes.

CT has consistently underestimated the degree of splenic injury found at celiotomy.[50,60,61] It may not adequately evaluate the extent of longitudinal fractures of the spleen that may tear across the larger segmental arteries within the splenic parenchyma. Such bleeding is not likely to stop spontaneously. Inconsistency in imaging protocols, variations in interpretive skills of the radiologist, and the subjective nature of the CT grading systems limit their usefulness. For example, failure to recognize a congenital cleft may lead to diagnostic errors. Single small parenchymal injuries without capsular disruption may be classified as high as class II in Buntain's system (Table 52-1). Difficulties in differentiating perihilar from nonperihilar lacerations are another deficiency. Another interpretive difficulty is the infarcted spleen. As infarcted spleen clearly indicates blood vessel involvement (class III or IV), yet a patient without parenchymal laceration or capsular tear is not classified by Buntain. In the Resciniti grading system (Table 52-2), problems arise in trying to differentiate perisplenic and subcapsular fluid.

The most significant limitation of both the CT scoring systems and DPL remains their inability to determine whether bleeding is still active or whether spontaneous hemostasis has occurred. This shortcoming makes observational therapy more hazardous and less predictable.

The authors have used diagnostic arteriography to provide this information. Arteriography was frequently

Table 52-1 CT Classification of Splenic Injury

Class	Description
Class I	Localized capsular disruption or subcapsular hematoma without significant parenchymal injury.
Class II	Single or multiple capsular and parenchymal disruptions, transverse or longitudinal, that do not extend into the hilum or involve major vessels. Intraparenchymal hematoma may or may not coexist.
Class III	Deep fractures, single or multiple, transverse or longitudinal, extending into the hilum and involving major blood vessels.
Class IV	Completely shattered or fragmented spleen, or separated from its normal blood supply at the pedicle.

Data from Buntain WL, Gould HR, Maull KI. Predictability of splenic salvage by computed tomography. J Trauma 1988;28:24–31.

Table 52-2. CT Scoring System of Splenic Injury

Region	Score
Splenic parenchyma	0 = intact 1 = laceration (linear defects) 2 = fracture (thick, irregular defects) 3 = shattered
Splenic capsule	0 = intact 1 = perisplenic fluid present
Abdominal fluid	0 = none 1 = any intraabdominal intraperitoneal fluid except perisplenic fluid
Pelvic fluid	0 = none 1 = any intraperitoneal pelvic fluid
Total	Sum of parenchymal, capsular, abdominal fluid, and pelvic fluid scores

Adapted from Resciniti A, Fink MP, Raptopoulos V, Davidoff A, Silva WE. Nonoperative treatment of adult splenic trauma: development of computed tomographic scoring system that detects appropriate candidates for expectant management. J Trauma 1988;128:828–831.

used in the past to image splenic injuries, and its value in illustrating splenic arterial anatomy and bleeding is well documented.[62-64] Although currently having shortcomings as a screening tool, arteriography has been used in the past to classify the severity of splenic injury.[65] The current role of arteriography in the management of blunt splenic trauma should be viewed as a dual one: diagnostic and therapeutic. Diagnostic arteriography can be used to better determine the degree of splenic injury and to predict with more confidence the success of observation by excluding active arterial hemorrhage. Therapeutically, splenic artery embolization can extend and refine the indications for nonsurgical treatment of splenic injuries by stopping active bleeding.

In the authors' institution, arteriography is used to further analyze all splenic injuries diagnosed by CT as long as the patient remains hemodynamically stable (Figure 52-1). A selective study of the celiac artery is done initially. This allows simultaneous assessment of the liver and the spleen as well as evaluation of the status of the potential collateral vessels if splenic artery embolization is considered. Selective splenic arteriography must be done, especially if the evidence of extravasation is equivocal. Two views of the spleen are the minimum requirement; they include the frontal celiac arteriogram and at least one oblique view. The right posterior oblique view of the left upper quadrant, which projects the splenic flexure medially and separates it from the spleen, is helpful because it is common for the splenic flexure of the colon to become opacified by the gastrointestinal contrast used for the CT scan and to obscure the spleen in the frontal or left posterior oblique views.

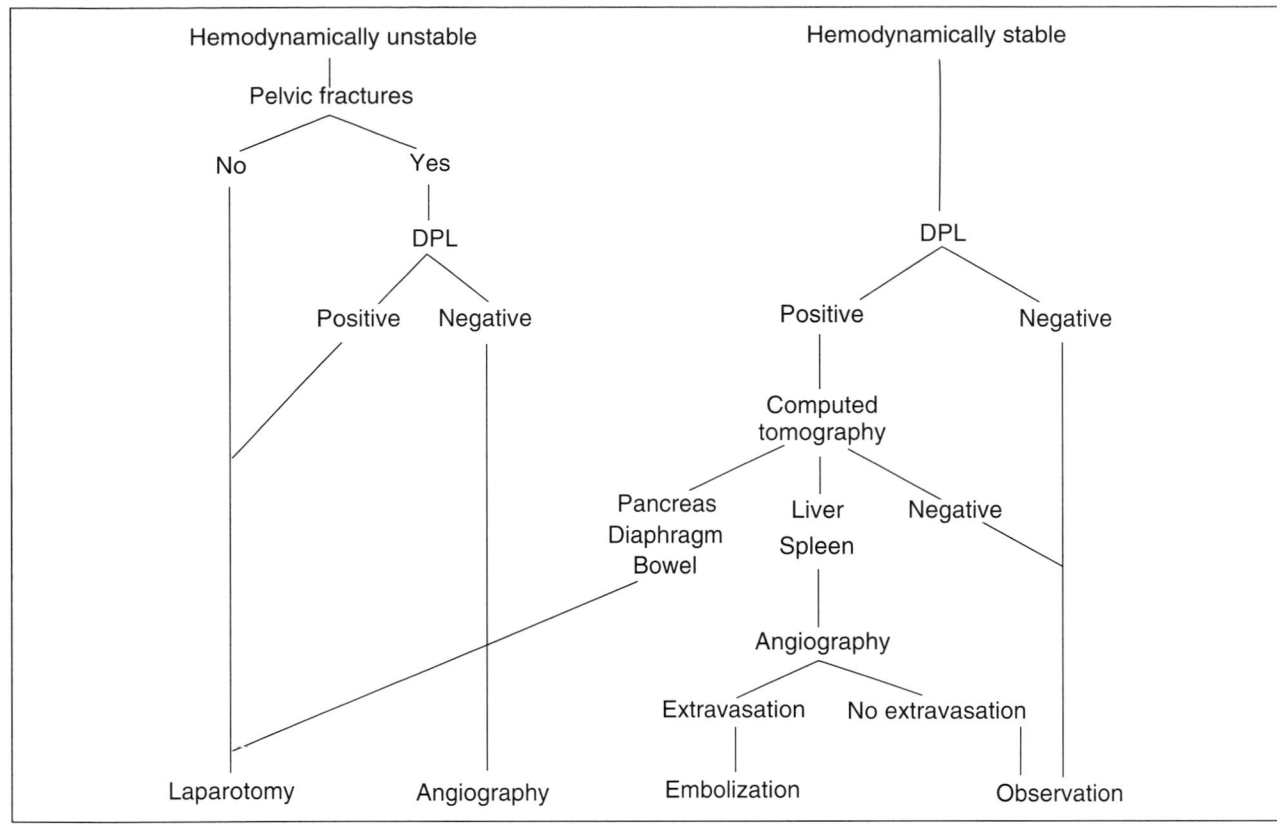

Figure 52-1. Algorithm for the management of blunt abdominal trauma.

If no arterial extravasation is seen at arteriography (Fig. 52-2), successful nonsurgical treatment can be anticipated. Filling defects, mass effect, and subcapsular compression also are not indications for embolization because they do not signify continuous bleeding.

It is the authors' belief that extravasation indicates ongoing, pulsatile, intrasplenic hemorrhage, which results in an expanding splenic hematoma, recurrent bleeding, and, in some patients, delayed rupture requiring laparotomy. Arterial extravasation is seen early in the arteriogram and should persist into the parenchymal phase. It may vary from large focal accumulations to diffuse irregular swirls of contrast material. Extravasation may be from a single vessel or, more frequently, from multiple vessels (Fig. 52-3). Fine, punctate, and uniform accumulations of contrast material ("Seurat spleen"[66]) are considered a minor finding for which the authors do not embolize. Arteriovenous shunts are only embolized if they are large and located in the splenic hilum.

Embolization Techniques

Principles

The goal of embolization in splenic trauma is to stop active bleeding while preserving as much splenic tissue as possible. The more conventional technique of splenic embolization—that is, particulate embolization of the spleen as is employed in clinical conditions like hypersplenism—is not suited for trauma situations. In hypersplenism the goal is permanent reduction of splenic substance.[67,68] The philosophy behind trauma embolization is temporary reduction in splenic blood flow and splenic arterial pressure in order to preserve splenic viability while allowing the formation of a secured clot at the site of injury. These goals are achieved by embolizing the proximal splenic artery and allowing collateral flow in the distal vessel.[64,65]

Ellison and Fabri[69] suggest that at least one-third of splenic mass must be conserved to maintain splenic

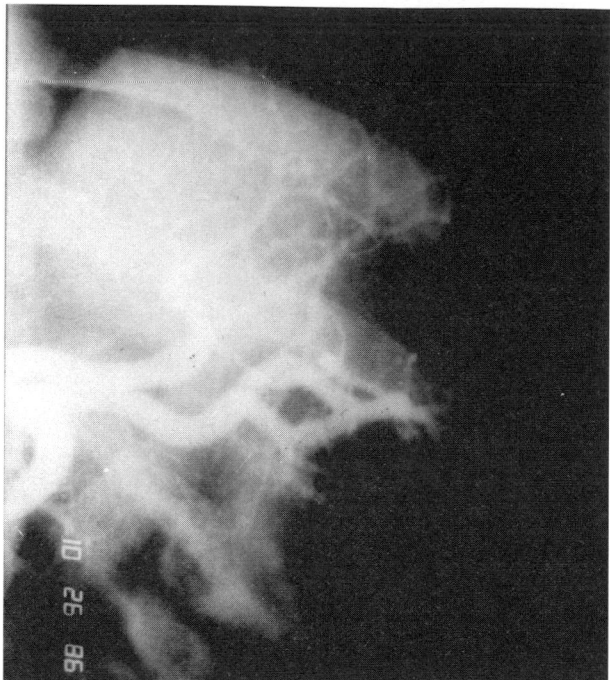

A

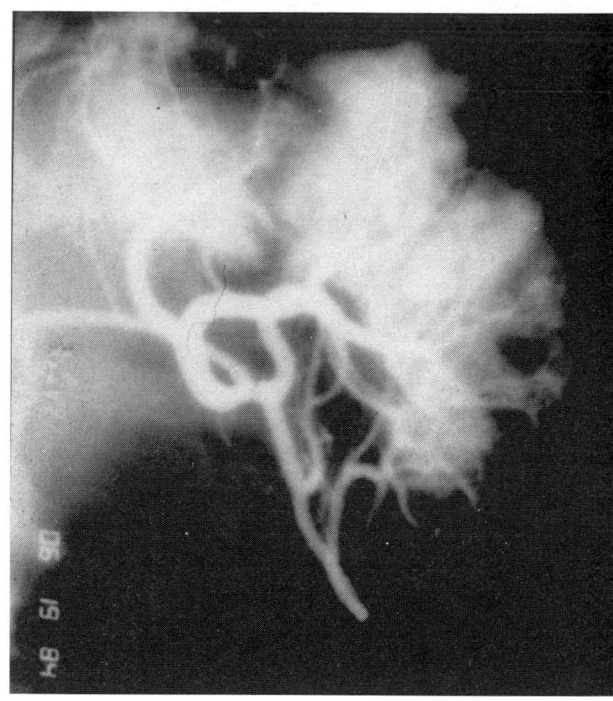

B

Figure 52-2. Nonbleeding splenic injuries. (A) This 32-year-old pedestrian was struck by a motor vehicle and was admitted with stable vital signs. Paracentesis was positive for blood, and a CT scan showed hemoperitoneum and a laceration of the spleen with intraparenchymal hematoma. Splenic arteriogram shows displacement of intrasplenic vessels but no arterial extravasation. The patient was treated by bedrest and observation, and recovery was uneventful. (B) This 23-year-old man was a driver involved in a high-speed motor vehicle accident. He stabilized after fluid resuscitation and blood transfusions. Peritoneal tap was negative, but lavage was positive (180,000 RBC/ml). A CT scan showed extensive fractures of the spleen. Angiogram demonstrates separation of multiple splenic fragments and filling defects consistent with intraparenchymal hematomas. However, no arterial contrast extravasation is seen. The patient was observed without laparotomy, and follow-up was uneventful.

immune function. Greco and Alvarez,[70] on the other hand, have shown that the spleen does undergo hypertrophy, and as much as 80 percent can be removed; although supplied only by short gastric collaterals, this amount can still protect against delayed sepsis. Both Horton et al.[71] and Scher et al.[72] demonstrated that bacterial clearance is diminished after splenic artery ligation. However, as Scher also noted, the majority of evidence supports the contention that splenic artery ligation has a significant immune advantage compared to splenectomy or splenic autotransplantation.

Technique

The status of the collateral vasculature of the spleen must be confirmed before embolization. The catheter may then be advanced for embolization into a position in the splenic artery approximately 1 to 5 cm distal to the origin of the dorsal pancreatic artery, which is used as a major collateral circuit for splenic blood flow after embolization (Fig. 52-4). The catheter should be sufficiently distal within the splenic artery so that the coil cannot protrude into the celiac axis if the coil does not completely reform. This is occasionally a problem because of the size mismatch in the diameters of conventional coils (5-mm or 8-mm helical diameter) and the splenic artery (often 6 or 7 mm).

Stainless steel coils are the authors' preferred embolic material. They are relatively safe, fast, easy to use, and inexpensive. They allow precise occlusion of the splenic artery without obliterating parenchymal blood flow. The coil selected should be of sufficient diameter not to migrate distally into the hilum and cause splenic infarction. Therefore, it is preferable to use larger coils that may not completely reform in the splenic artery rather than smaller coils, which may migrate. Incompletely reformed coils can be augmented by packing smaller coils at the site of embolization to lead to rapid occlusion.

In cases of massive extracapsular extravasation from third- and fourth-order branches of the splenic artery, superselective catheterization of specific intrasplenic arteries can be considered. This is rarely necessary if appropriate clinical triage is performed. Active intraperitoneal hemorrhage usually results in hemodynamic

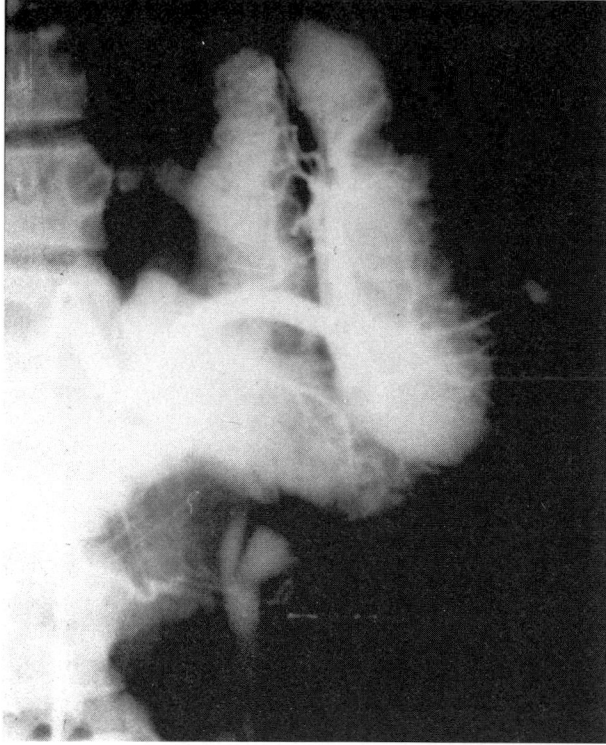

A

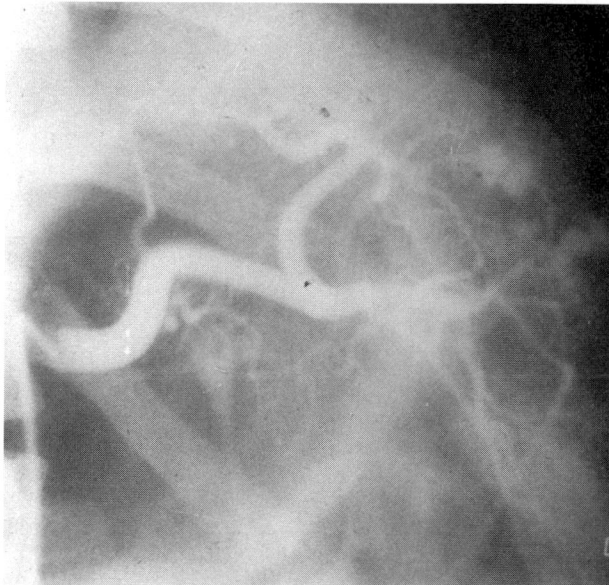

B

Figure 52-3. Splenic injuries with arterial extravasation. (A) This 28-year-old man was a passenger involved in a high-speed motor vehicle accident. He did not go to the hospital at that time, but arrived several hours later after he passed out at home. DPL was not done; CT showed a large subcapsular hematoma of the spleen. Angiogram shows a large subcapsular hematoma manifested by lateral indentation on the spleen. This was caused by arterial hemorrhage from an intrasplenic branch of the splenic artery (*arrow*). The splenic artery was occluded proximally with a steel coil. The patient had an uneventful recovery; the splenic subcapsular hematoma slowly resolved over several months. (B) An 18-year-old boy was struck by a motor vehicle and sustained multiple injuries to the extremities, pelvis, and chest. DPL was marginally positive (100,000 RBC/ml). He stabilized after blood transfusions. An arteriogram was performed to evaluate pelvic hematoma. Pelvic arteriography was normal but splenic arteriography shows multiple irregular collections of contrast extravasation within the spleen. Coil occlusion was performed, and no further blood transfusions were required.

Figure 52-4. Technique of embolization. The catheter has been positioned distal to the dorsal pancreatic artery and proximal to pancreatica magna branches so that pancreatic collaterals pathways can be used. (A) Postembolization arteriogram shows the position of the coil and occlusion of the proximal splenic artery. (B) A later film shows excellent and rapid filling of the distal splenic artery. The presence of persistent extravasation does not indicate failure of the technique; healing of the spleen without recurrent hemorrhage has always occurred even when extravasation persists. Additional embolization should be based on clinical parameters rather than on the presence of continued extravasation.

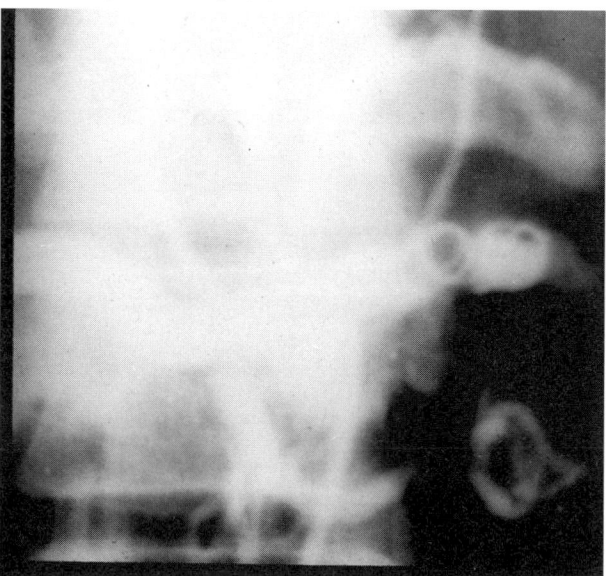

A

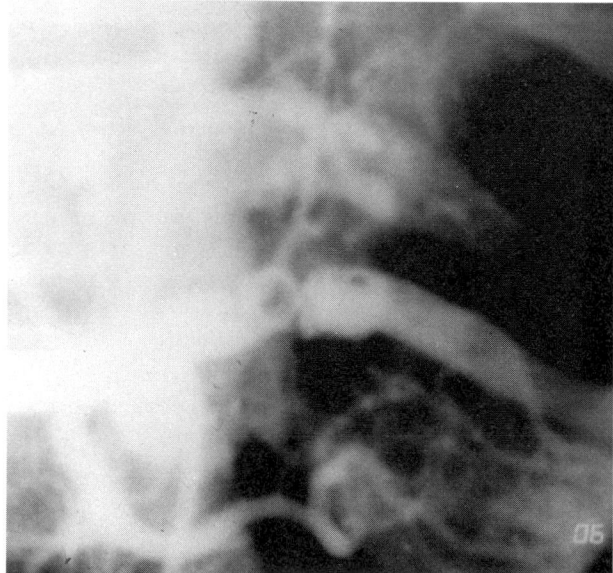

B

instability, and such patients rarely undergo nonoperative management.

Coaxial techniques may be used to selectively catheterize and occlude specific bleeding vessels. However, such techniques may require significantly more time. If selective catheterization of specific bleeding branches is not easily and expeditiously accomplished, only proximal splenic artery embolization may be performed.

After the splenic artery has been occluded, celiac arteriography is repeated to confirm the presence of collateral flow. The end point of embolization is occlusion of the splenic artery, not cessation of arterial extravasation. It is not unusual to see persistent intrasplenic extravasation immediately after embolization. The authors do not consider this a failure of embolization because patients with these findings have not required delayed laparotomy. It takes some time for intrasplenic extravasation to resolve. Angiograms performed 2 to 3 weeks after embolization do not show any extravasation.

Postembolization Care

Postprocedural observation is critical to the success of this technique. Patients must be carefully observed to identify persistent or recurrent hemorrhage, peritonitis, or sepsis, which would necessitate exploratory laparotomy.

The patient is placed in the intensive care unit for 24 to 72 hours. If the patient remains hemodynamically stable and does not have worsening clinical parameters, limited ambulation is begun. After an additional 24 to 48 hours the patient is allowed to walk freely. Discharge from the hospital may be considered after a week, depending on patient reliability, the extent of the injury, and associated injuries.

A CT scan performed before discharge is used as a baseline for subsequent comparison. Dulchavsky and coworkers,[73] studying the efficacy of wound healing by secondary intent in the canine and porcine models, have shown that by 6 weeks the wound's breaking strength equals that of the uninjured spleen. Full activity, including contact sports, is allowed only after complete resolution of splenic injury is documented by CT. Outpatient CT scans are performed every 6 to 10 weeks until complete resolution is documented.

Conclusion

By taking advantage of the benefits of DPL, CT, angiography, and splenic artery embolization, the authors have successfully managed nonoperatively more than 100 patients with splenic injury, including patients who arrived at the emergency room hypotensive, patients with extensive hemoperitoneum, and patients with severely fractured spleens and lacerations extending into the splenic hilum.[65] Absence of arterial extravasation has successfully predicted successful nonoperative care in all cases. More than 95 percent of patients with arterial extravasation have been successfully managed nonoperatively after splenic artery embolization, and none have required laparotomy for persistent or recurrent hemorrhage.[74]

References

1. Aristotle. Parts of animals, book III. Peck AL, trans. Cambridge: Harvard University Press, 1955, ch. 12.
2. Sherman R. Perspectives in management of trauma to the spleen: 1979 presidential address, American Association for the Surgery of Trauma. J Trauma 1980;20:1.
3. Quoted in Rosner F. The spleen in the Talmud and other early Jewish writings. Bull Hist Med 1972;46:82.
4. King H, Shumacker HB Jr. Splenic studies 1: susceptibility to infection after splenectomy performed in infancy. Ann Surg 1952;136:239.
5. Upadhyaya P, Simpson JS. Splenic trauma in children. Surg Gynecol Obstet 1968;126:781.
6. Mishalany H. Repair of ruptured spleen. J Pediatr Surg 1974; 9:175.
7. Shackford SK, Sise MJ, Virgilio RW, et al. Evaluation of splenorrhaphy: a grading system for splenic trauma. J Trauma 1981; 21:538.
8. Feliciano DV, Bbitondo CG, Moore GE, et al. A four-year experience with splenectomy versus splenorrhaphy. Ann Surg 1985;201:568.
9. Moore FA, Moore EE, Moore GE, et al. Risk of splenic salvage after trauma: analysis of 200 adults. Am J Surg 1984;148:800.
10. Buntain WL, Lynn HB. Splenorrhaphy: changing concepts for the traumatized spleen. Surgery 1979;86:748.
11. Burrington JD. Surgical repair in children: a report of eight cases. Arch Surg 1977;112:417.
12. Giviliano HE, Lim RC. Is splenic salvage safe in the traumatized patient? Arch Surg 1981;116:651.
13. Ratner MH. Surgical repair of the injured spleen. J Pediatr Surg 1977;12:1019.
14. Barrett J, Sheab C, Abuadon S, et al. Splenic preservation in adults after blunt and penetrating trauma. Am J Surg 1983; 145:313.
15. Chadwick SJ, Huizinga WK, Baker LW. Management of splenic trauma: the Durban experience. Br J Surg 1985;72:634.
16. Millikan JS, Moore EE, Moore GE, et al. Alternatives to splenectomy in adults after trauma: repair, partial resection, and reimplantation of splenic tissue. Am J Surg 1982;144:711.
17. Patcher HL, Hofstetter SR, Spencer FC. Evolving concepts in splenic surgery: splenorrhaphy versus splenectomy and postsplenectomy drainage. Experience in 105 patients. Ann Surg 1981;194:262.
18. Traub AC, Perry JF. Splenic preservation following trauma. J Trauma 1982;22:496.
19. Conti S. Splenic artery ligation for trauma: an alternative to splenectomy. Am J Surg 1980;140:44.
20. Hadley GP. Splenic artery ligation: an adjunct to splenorrhaphy in children. S Afr Med J 1984;88:578.
21. Hoivik B, Soldheim K. Splenic artery ligation in splenic injuries. Injury 1983;15:1.
22. Schwalke MA, Crowley P, Spencer P, et al. Splenic artery liga-

tion for splenic salvage: clinical experience and immune function. J Trauma 1991;31(3):385.

23. Singer DB. Post splenectomy sepsis. In: Rosenberg HS, Bolander RP, eds. Perspectives in pediatric pathology. Chicago: Year Book, 1973:285.
24. O'Neal B, McDonald JC. The risk of sepsis in the asplenic adult. Ann Surg 1981;194:775.
25. Green JB, Shackford SR, Sise MJ, et al. Late septic complications in adults following splenectomy for trauma: a prospective analysis in 144 patients. J Trauma 1986;26:999.
26. Rowley DA. The effect of splenectomy on the formation of circulating antibody in the adult male albino rat. J Immunol 1950;64:289.
27. Sullivan JL, Och HD, Schiffman G, et al. Immunoresponse after splenectomy. Lancet 1978;1:178.
28. Hosea SW, Burch CG, Brown EJ, et al. Impaired immune response of splenectomized patients to polyvalent pneumococcal vaccine. Lancet 1981;1:804.
29. Schumacker MJ. Serum immunoglobulin and transferrin levels after childhood splenectomy. Arch Dis Child 1979;45:114.
30. Liende M, Santiago-Delpin EA, Laverene J. Immunological consequences of splenectomy: a review. J Surg Res 1986;40:85.
31. Simon M Jr, Djaware D, Hornstein OP. Mikro-Und Makrophagen Funktion Sprufungenn Bei Patienten Mit Lichen Ruber Planus. Z Hautkr 1984;59:89.
32. Kreuzpelder E, Obertacke U, Erhard J, et al. Alternations of the immune system following splenectomy in childhood. J Trauma 1991;31(3):358.
33. Constantopoulos A, Najjar VA, Wish JB, et al. Defective phagocytosis due to tuftsin deficiency in splenectomized subjects. Am J Dis Child 1973;125:663.
34. Billiar TR, West MA, Hyland BJ, et al. Splenectomy alters Kupffer cell response to endotoxin. Arch Surg 1988;123:327.
35. Shennib H, Chin RC, Mulder DS. The effects of splenectomy and splenic implantation on alveolar macrophage function. J Trauma 1983;23:7.
36. Lau HT, Hardy MA, Altman RP. Decreased pulmonary alveolar macrophage bactericidal activity in splenectomized rats. J Surg Res 1983;34:568.
37. Herbert JC. Pulmonary antipneumococcal defenses after hemisplenectomy. J Trauma 1989;28:1217.
38. Federle MP, Crass RA, Jeffrey RB, et al. Computerized tomography in blunt abdominal trauma. Arch Surg 1982;117:645.
39. Kaufman RA, Towbin R, Babcock DS, et al. Upper abdominal trauma in children: imaging evaluation. AJR 1984;142:449.
40. Wing VW, Federle MP, Morris JA Jr, et al. The clinical impact of CT for blunt abdominal trauma. AJR 1985;145:1191.
41. Peitzman AB, Makaroun MS, Slasky BS, et al. Prospective study of computerized tomography in initial management of blunt abdominal trauma. J Trauma 1986;26:585.
42. McCort JJ. Caring for the major trauma victim: the role for radiology. Radiology 1987;163:1–9.
43. Wolfman NT, Bechtold RE, et al. Blunt upper abdominal trauma: evaluation by CT. AJR 1992;158:493.
44. Goldstein AS, Sclafani SJA, Kupferstein NH, et al. The diagnostic superiority of computerized tomography. J Trauma 1985;25:938.
45. Gomez GA, Alvarez R, Plasencia G, et al. Diagnostic peritoneal lavage in the management of blunt abdominal trauma: a reassessment. J Trauma 1987;27:1.
46. Powell RW, Green JB, Ochsner MG, et al. Peritoneal lavage in pediatric patients sustaining blunt abdominal trauma: a reappraisal. J Trauma 1987;27:6.
47. Federle MP, Griffiths B, Minagi H, Jeffrey RB. Splenic trauma: evaluation with CT. Radiology 1987;162:69.
48. Mall JC, Kaiser JA. CT diagnosis of splenic laceration. AJR 1980;134:265.
49. Jeffrey RB, Laing FC, Federle MP, Goodman PC. Computed tomography of splenic trauma. Radiology 1981;141:729.

50. Buntain WL, Gould HR, Maull KI. Predictability of splenic salvage by computed tomography. J Trauma 1988;28:24–31.
51. Resciniti A, Fink MP, Raptopoulos V, Davidoff A, Silva WE. Nonoperative treatment of adult splenic trauma: development of computed tomographic scoring system that detects appropriate candidates for expectant management. J Trauma 1988;128:828–831.
52. Scatamacchia SA, Raptopoulos V, Fink MP, Silva WE. Splenic trauma in adults: impact of CT grading on management. Radiology 1989;171:725–729.
53. Mirvis SE, Whitley NO, Gens DR. Blunt splenic trauma in adults: CT-based classification and correlation with prognosis and treatment. Radiology 1989;171:33–39.
54. Pickhardt B, Moore EE, Moore FA, et al. Operative splenic salvage in adults: a decade perspective. J Trauma 1989;29:1386.
55. Brick SM, Taylor GA, Potter BM, et al. Hepatic and splenic injury in children: role of CT in the decision for laparotomy. Radiology 1987;165:643.
56. Buckman RF, Dunham CM, Kerr TM, et al. Hypotension and bleeding with various anatomic patterns of blunt splenic injury in adults. Surg Gynecol Obstet 1989;169:206.
57. Mahon PA, Sutton JE. Nonoperative management of adult splenic injury due to blunt trauma: a warning. Am J Surg 1985;149:716.
58. Taylor GA, Fallat ME, Potter BM, et al. The role of computerized tomography in blunt abdominal trauma in children. J Trauma 1988;28:1660.
59. Jeffrey RB. CT diagnosis of blunt hepatic and splenic injuries: a look into the future. Radiology 1989;171:17.
60. Umlas S, Cronan JJ. Splenic trauma: can CT grading systems enable prediction of successful nonsurgical treatment? Radiology 1991;178:481.
61. Malangoni MA, Cue JI, Fallat ME, et al. Evaluation of splenic injury by computerized tomography and its impact on treatment. Ann Surg 1990;211(5):592.
62. Ward RE, Miller P, Clark DG, et al. Angiography and peritoneal lavage in blunt abdominal trauma. J Trauma 1981;21:848.
63. Stein HL. The diagnosis of traumatic laceration by selective angiography, direct serial magnification angiography, and intraarterial epinephrine. Radiology 1969;93:367.
64. Sclafani SJA. The role of angiographic hemostasis in salvage of the injured spleen. Radiology 1981;141:645.
65. Sclafani SJA, Weisberg A, Scalea TM, et al. Blunt splenic injuries: nonsurgical treatment with CT, arteriography, and transcatheter arterial embolization of the splenic artery. Radiology 1991;181:189.
66. Kass JB, Risher RG. The Seurat spleen. AJR 1979;132:683.
67. Owman T, Lunderquist A, Alwmark A, et al. Embolization of the spleen for the treatment of splenomegaly and hypersplenism in patients with portal hypertension. Invest Radiol 1979;14:457.
68. Spigos DG, Jonasson O, Mozes M, et al. Partial splenic embolization in the treatment of hypersplenism. AJR 1979;132:777.
69. Ellison EC, Fabri PJ. Complications of splenectomy: etiology, prevention, and management. Surg Clin North Am 1983;63:1313.
70. Greco RS, Alvarez FG. Protection against pneumococcal bacteremia by partial splenectomy. Surg Gynecol Obstet 1981;152:67.
71. Horton J, Ogden ME, Williams S. The importance of splenic blood flow in clearing pneumococcal organisms. Ann Surg 1982;195:172.
72. Scher KS, Scott-Conner C, Jones C, et al. Methods of splenic preservation and their effect on clearance of pneumococcal bacteria. Ann Surg 1985;202(5):595.
73. Dulchavsky SA, Lucas CE, Ledgerwood AM, et al. Wound healing of the injured spleen with and without splenorrhaphy. J Trauma 1987;27:1155.

53

Arteriography and Transcatheter Embolization in the Management of Renal Trauma

SUE E. HANKS
MICHAEL D. KATZ

The radiologic evaluation of patients with renal trauma is critical to their subsequent management. A combination of intravenous pyelography, computed tomography (CT), and renal arteriography may be necessary to fully assess the extent of renal injury. In addition, therapeutic embolization of traumatic renal arterial injuries has become the definitive treatment in many cases. This chapter discusses the evaluation of renal trauma and the role of interventional radiology for both diagnosis and treatment.

Anatomy

A thorough knowledge of renal and retroperitoneal anatomy is necessary to accurately stage renal injuries. The kidneys are retroperitoneal structures protected from injury by the lower ribs, Gerota fascia, and surrounding perirenal fat. At the level of the kidneys, the retroperitoneum may be divided into three compartments. The anterior pararenal space is bounded anteriorly by parietal peritoneum and posteriorly by Gerota fascia. The perirenal space, surrounded by Gerota fascia, contains the kidney, adrenal gland, and perirenal fat. The posterior pararenal space is bounded anteriorly by Gerota fascia and posteriorly by transversalis fascia.[1,2]

Classification of Renal Injuries

Several systems have been used to classify the extent of renal injury.[3,4] Classification systems relate the class of injury to the degree of renal disruption and the clinical implication of the injury. Class I injuries, therefore, are minor in nature and include parenchymal contusions, subcapsular hematomas, and superficial cortical lacerations not extending into the collecting system. Class II injuries are more severe lacerations that extend into the collecting system. Class III injuries involve complete disruption of the kidney, also called shattered kidneys. Class IV injuries are injuries to the vascular pedicle (Fig. 53-1).

Renal trauma management is based on this classification system. Class I injuries are treated conservatively, since almost all renal contusions and minor lacerations heal spontaneously. Management of class II injuries is controversial. The trend is to be as conservative as possible and to closely monitor the patient for hypotension, dropping hematocrit, sepsis, or other signs that require intervention. Class III and IV injuries require emergent surgical intervention. To successfully revascularize a renal pedicle injury, one should perform surgery within 12 hours.[5]

Mechanism of Renal Injuries

Renal injuries must be categorized as blunt or penetrating in order to be properly evaluated and managed. Blunt renal trauma is much more common than penetrating trauma, except in a few urban trauma centers.[6] Blunt injuries rarely require intervention, with only 5 to 10 percent being class III or IV. Penetrating injuries are much more likely to require intervention, with as many as 70 percent causing major injury.

The mechanism of injury in blunt trauma may be a direct blow, laceration by adjacent ribs, or an acceleration-deceleration injury. Automobile accidents account for most blunt trauma. Because of the kidney's protected position, the force required to cause renal injury must be extreme; therefore, associated injuries are common and are found in approximately 20 percent of blunt trauma patients.[7,8]

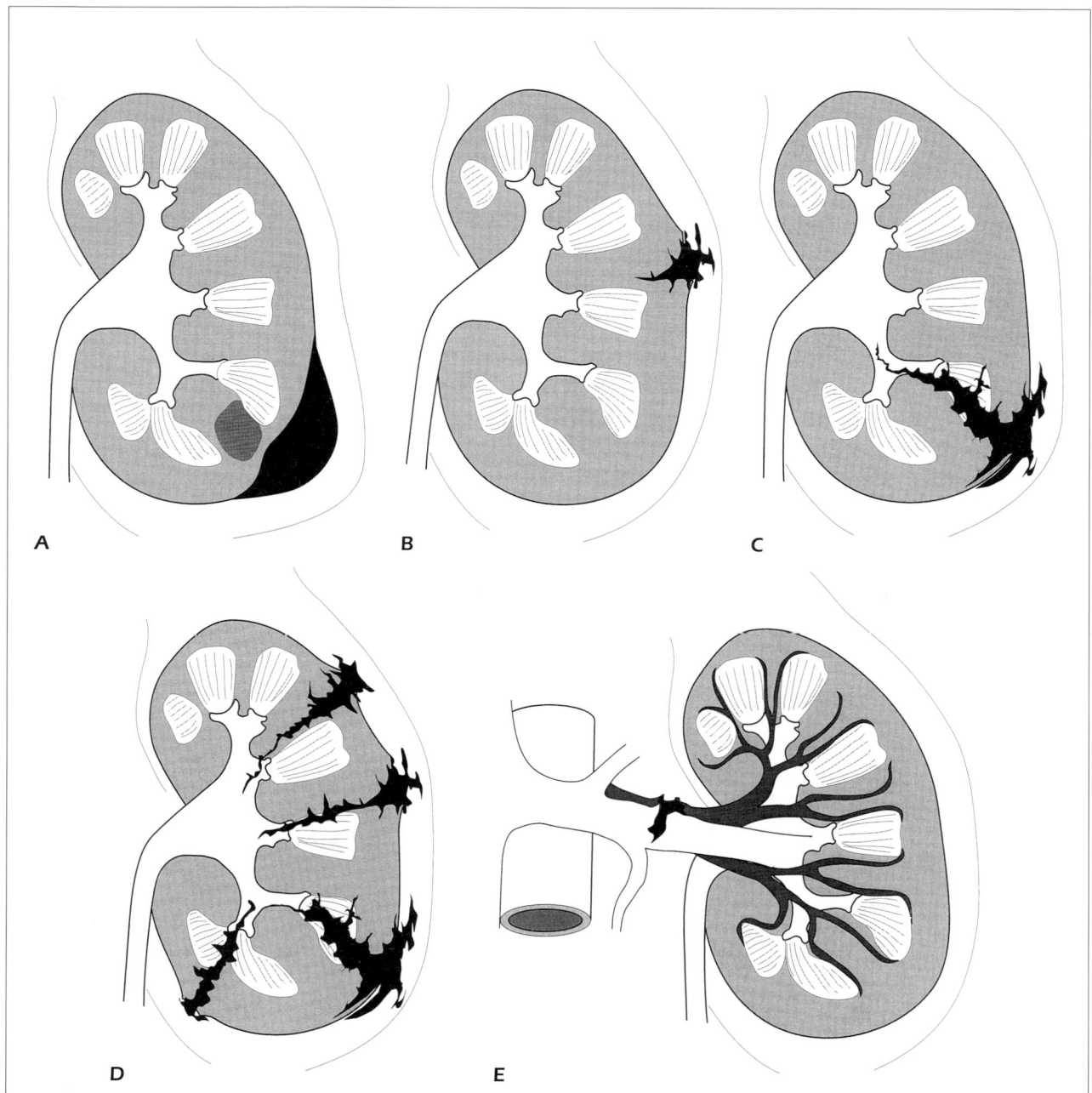

Figure 53-1. (A) Class I renal injury. Subcapsular hematoma (*black*) with an underlying contusion (*dark gray*). (B) Class I renal injury. Superficial cortical laceration. (C) Class II renal injury. Laceration extending into the collecting system. (D) Class III renal injury. Completely disrupted, "shattered" kidney. (E) Class IV renal injury. Vascular pedicle injury.

In the polytraumatized patient, emergent surgical exploration for abdominal injuries is often the required management. Workup of renal trauma may then be limited to an abbreviated "one-shot" intravenous pyelogram (IVP) done in the emergency department or the operating room. The information gained from this procedure is enough to establish the position, perfusion, and functional status of the kidneys. The overriding concern for these patients is frequently the associated injuries, not the renal injury itself. Cass and Luxenberg correlated the severity of renal trauma with the number of associated injuries. They found that patients with more severe renal trauma had more than two associated injuries.[9]

Initial Radiologic Evaluation of Blunt Renal Trauma

The indications for radiologic workup in stable patients with blunt renal trauma has been controversial. In the past, all patients with hematuria underwent radiologic studies. Mee and McAninch reviewed this subject and compiled the results of several large series.[10–12] Of 1671 patients who had microhematuria and no history of shock, they found only 7 significant renal injuries. Five of these would have required radiologic studies for nonrenal injuries, and 1 minor laceration was managed conservatively. Thus only 1 significant injury in 1671 patients (0.05 percent) would have been missed. The authors advocate using either gross hematuria or microhematuria with a history of hypotension (systolic blood pressure <90 mmHg) at any time after the injury as an indicator for further studies.

The choice of which radiologic study to obtain depends primarily on the clinical situation. For a stable patient suspected of having an isolated renal injury, an IVP remains the study of choice. If the IVP is normal, then the greatest injury likely to be present is a contusion.[13] Information obtained from the IVP is sufficient to properly manage patients in 70 to 95 percent of cases.[14–16]

Patients with more severe trauma, not isolated to the kidney, should be evaluated by CT, since parenchymal disruption is better defined with this study. The extent of a perirenal hematoma is also clearly demonstrated, and small amounts of extravasation can be identified.[17,18] In addition, the evaluation of the entire retroperitoneum and abdomen in those patients suspected of having associated injuries can be invaluable.[19] CT scanning can more accurately identify renal pedicle injuries by demonstrating nonvisualization of a kidney with or without a rim of enhancement from capsular collaterals (Fig. 53-2).[20]

Preexisting pathology makes a kidney more susceptible to injury. Trivial trauma may cause hematuria out of proportion to the degree expected when an anomalous or abnormal kidney is present. CT scanning is superior to an IVP in delineating the exact nature of the preexisting condition.[21] Hydronephrosis, cysts, and tumors in normally positioned kidneys may become manifest after only minor trauma. Ectopic or horseshoe kidneys are less protected and therefore are more subject to lacerations.[18,22] This is particularly true in pediatric patients, in whom up to 20 percent with renal injuries have preexisting abnormalities.[23,24]

Children are more susceptible to renal trauma, even without preexisting pathology. Almost 90 percent of renal pedicle injuries occur in children and young adults.[5] In children, the kidney is the most frequently injured organ as a result of abdominal trauma.[25] As in adults, conservative management is the preferred approach.

Initial Radiologic Evaluation of Penetrating Renal Trauma

Penetrating trauma to the kidney differs considerably from blunt trauma. The number of associated injuries is much higher, especially after gunshot wounds. Sur

Figure 53-2. (A) CT scan of a 25-year-old woman pedestrian who was struck by a train. The scan demonstrates nonfunction of the right kidney. (B) Abdominal aortogram demonstrates occlusion of the main right renal artery (*arrow*).

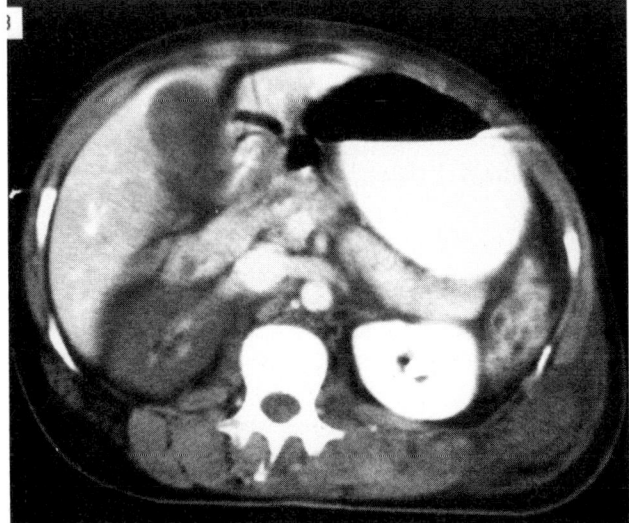

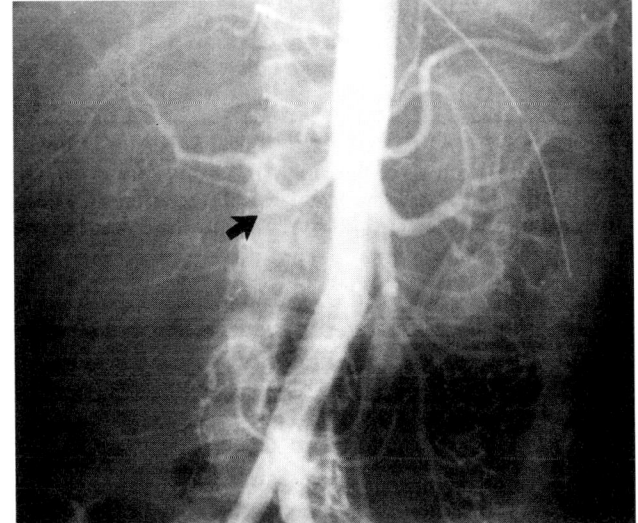

A

B

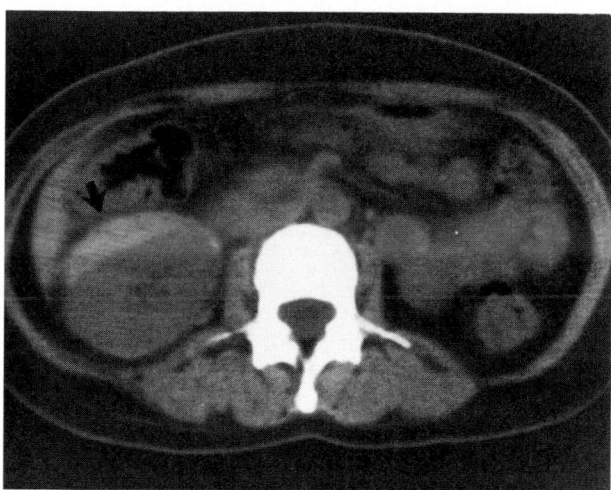

Figure 53-3. CT scan of high-density perirenal hematoma following a renal biopsy.

gical exploration is required in as many as 42 percent of stab wounds and 76 percent of gunshot wounds.[7] If the wound is from the anterior abdomen, almost all patients require exploratory celiotomy to exclude bowel injuries.

Back and flank wounds do not always require urgent exploration, particularly if intraperitoneal injury has been excluded by peritoneal lavage and there are no peritoneal signs on physical examination.[26] CT should be used for evaluating stable patients because of the frequency of associated injuries. Philips et al. recommend CT using a contrast enema in addition to oral contrast to exclude colonic injury.[27]

Iatrogenic trauma is another common cause of penetrating renal injury. Percutaneous renal biopsy causes some degree of hemorrhage in up to 90 percent of cases (Fig. 53-3),[28] and arteriovenous fistulas in up to 15 percent.[29] The majority of these can be managed conservatively. Serious vascular trauma occurs in 1 to 2 percent of percutaneous nephrostomy tube placements.[30] Dilatation of a tract for percutaneous nephrostolithotomy also may cause renal damage ranging from arteriovenous fistulas to renal rupture (Fig. 53-4).[31] The first report of transcatheter management of an arteriovenous fistula, by Bookstein and Goldstein, was in a patient following a renal biopsy.[29]

Diagnostic Renal Arteriography

The most frequent indications for renal arteriography are persistent or recurrent hematuria. A large retroperitoneal hematoma found during surgical exploration or seen on CT may also require arteriography.

Occasionally there may be a need for a preoperative arteriogram to define the arterial anatomy before a segmental renal resection. Evaluation of hypertension that has developed after renal trauma may include arteriography.

The initial arteriographic evaluation should begin with aortography, for several reasons. Multiple renal arteries are common, occurring in approximately 30 percent of patients.[32] Since associated injuries are also common, the additional information regarding adjacent structures may prove to be significant.[33] For example, a retroperitoneal hematoma may be caused by a lumbar artery laceration. In addition, injury to the renal vascular pedicle can be identified on the aortogram, and selective catheterization of the injured vessel can then be avoided. Once the renal pedicle has been evaluated, variants in anatomy have been identified, and other major arterial injuries have been excluded, a selective renal arteriogram should be performed. An alternative approach is recommended by Sclafani and Stein, who advocate beginning the examination with a selective renal injection. Minimizing contrast in the collecting system helps one identify arteriocaliceal communication.[34]

Selective renal arteriography is performed with a preshaped catheter such as a Simmons 1 or Cobra catheter. Two or more projections are usually necessary to adequately evaluate the entire kidney. An ipsilateral anterior oblique projection shows the renal parenchyma to best advantage. Either cut-film or digital arteriography may be used. Digital arteriography is particularly efficient during embolization procedures and can significantly decrease the procedure time. Rapid filming sequences are necessary to identify arteriovenous fistulas or the vessel of origin of pseudoaneurysms, whereas delayed films are necessary to reveal subtle extravasation.

Findings that may be demonstrated on arteriography include intrarenal hematomas, which can be identified by displacement or splaying of vessels. Subcapsular hematomas may be demonstrated as concave or flattened areas of parenchyma best seen in the nephrogram phase. Perirenal hematomas may be large enough to cause significant displacement of the kidney. In blunt injury, in particular, there may be single- or multiple-branch artery occlusions. Follow-up of these occlusions has shown them to be of little clinical consequence.[35]

Additional arteriographic findings include extravasation, arteriovenous fistulas, and pseudoaneurysms (Fig. 53-5). Arterial extravasation may be difficult to distinguish from urinary extravasation, and careful examination of all phases of the arteriogram is necessary. Arteriovenous fistulas are identified by the presence of

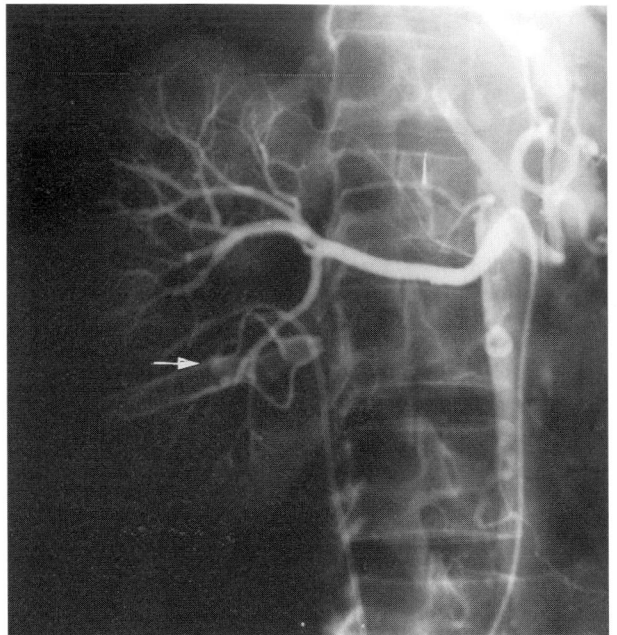

A

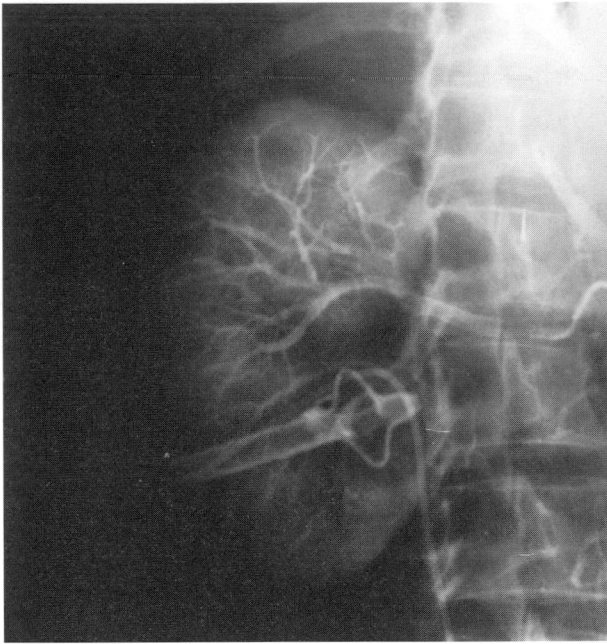

B

Figure 53-4. Early (A) and late (B) selective renal arteriograms demonstrate a pseudoaneurysm of a lower pole branch after placement of a 24 French Malecot catheter. (C) Successful embolization of the injured lower pole branch with a single steel coil.

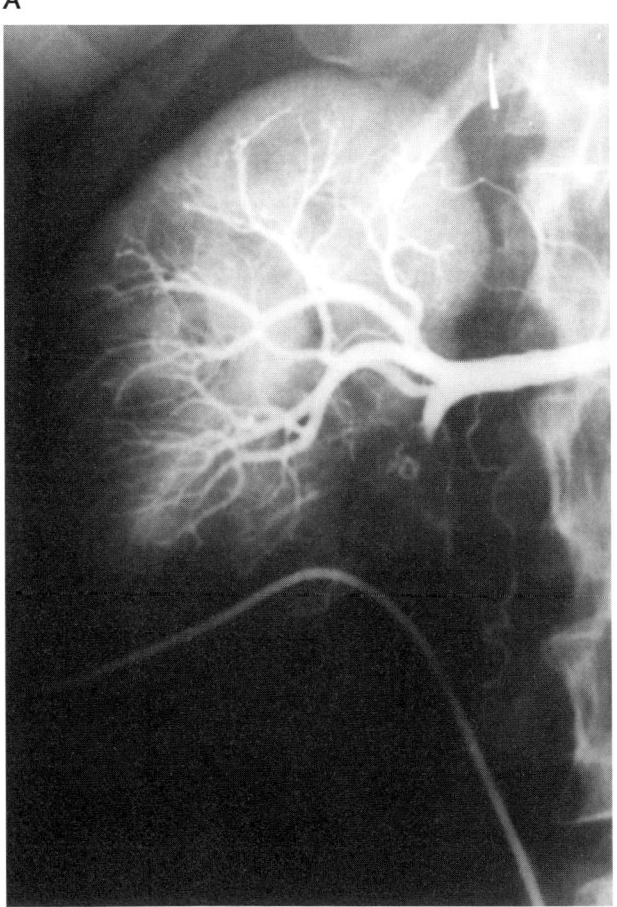

C

an early-draining vein. Pseudoaneurysms are demonstrated as focal areas of extravascular contrast that may show delayed washout. Identification of these renal injuries is particularly important because they may be appropriate for embolization.

Transcatheter Renal Embolization

Important factors to consider before embolizing any vessel include whether the vessel can be sacrificed and the alternative methods of treatment. The kidney is an end-artery organ with small collaterals from capsular branches. Occlusion of renal branch vessels will cause parenchymal infarction congruent to the size of the vessel. Improvements in catheter technology and the availability of microcatheters now make it possible to cannulate 1- to 2-mm vessels. Although it may not be necessary in every case, the use of a coaxial microcatheter can facilitate cannulation of more distal or tortuous vessels, preserving the maximum amount of renal parenchyma (Fig. 53-6). The alternative surgical treatment would result in at least equal and usually greater tissue loss.[36,37] In addition, surgical treatment is much more invasive and has the associated risks and morbidity of a major surgical procedure under general anesthesia.

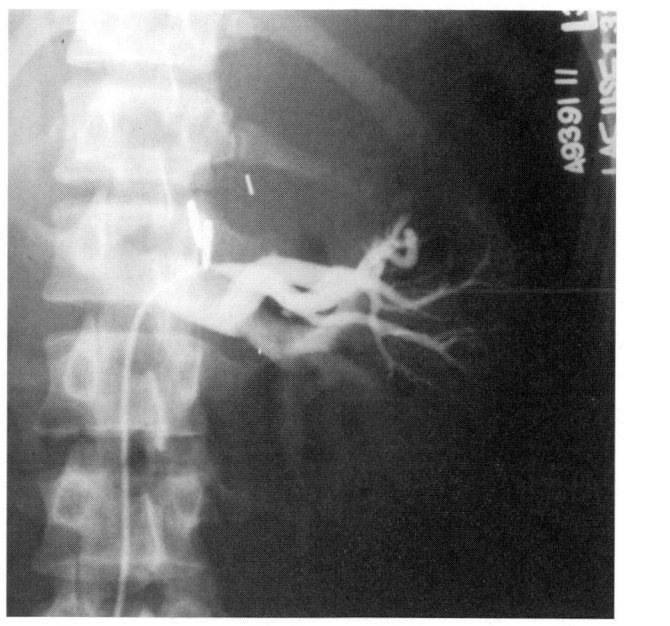
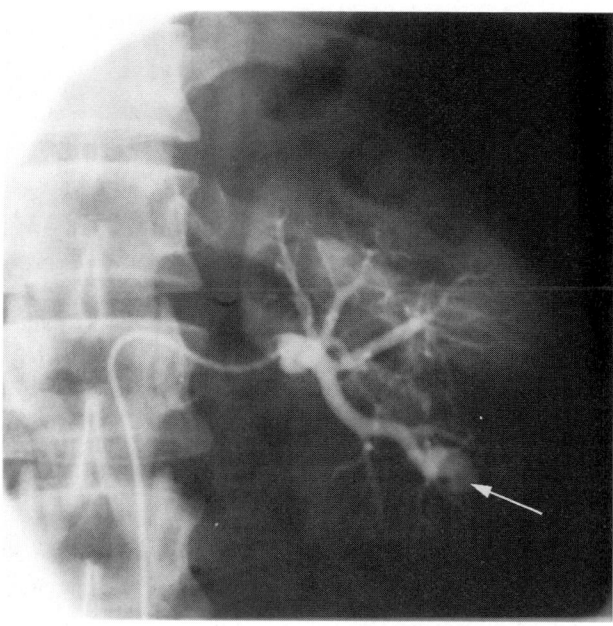

A **B**

Figure 53-5. (A) Arteriovenous fistula of an upper pole branch secondary to a stab wound in a patient with multiple renal arteries. (B) Pseudoaneurysm of lower pole branch (*arrow*).

Historically, many agents have been used to occlude abnormal vessels, including autologous clot,[29] cotton pellets,[33] detachable balloons,[38] cyanoacrylate,[39] and polyvinyl alcohol.[40] Gelatin sponge (Gelfoam, Upjohn Co.) and coils are the most commonly used agents.[19,26,36,37,41–45] Gelfoam can be cut into pledgets that closely match the diameter of the vessel to be oc-

cluded and can be delivered through diagnostic or coaxial catheter systems. Platinum microcoils may be used for distal small-vessel injuries (Fig. 53-7). Stainless steel coils work well in occluding more proximal arteriovenous fistulas and pseudoaneurysms. Particular care should be taken when choosing a coil to occlude an arteriovenous fistula. The coil size should match the

Figure 53-6. (A) Digital arteriogram through a coaxial catheter demonstrates a pseudoaneurysm and extravasation from a distal renal artery branch following a biopsy. (B) Postembolization arteriogram demonstrates occlusion of the injured branch by two microcoils placed distally.

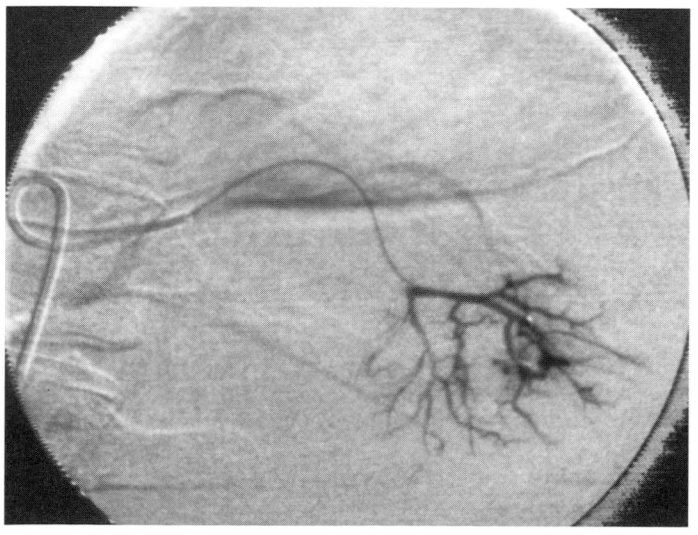
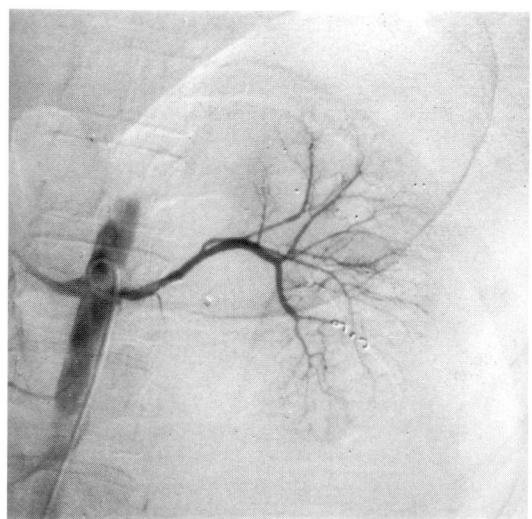

A **B**

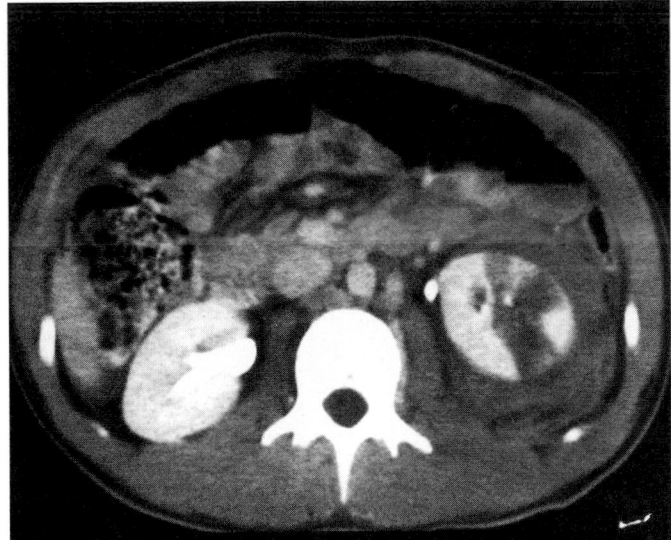

A

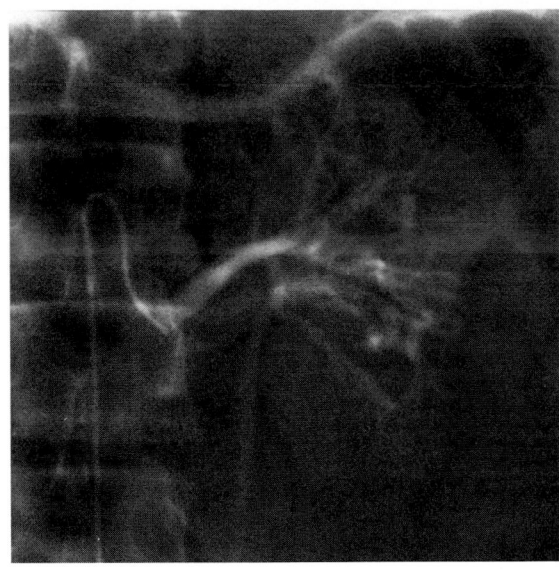

B

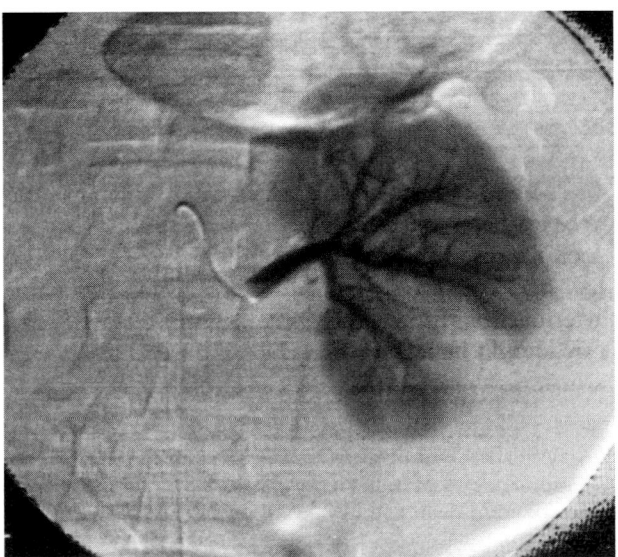

C

Figure 53-7. (A) A 25-year-old man with a stab wound to the left flank. CT scan demonstrates perirenal hematoma and nephrographic defects. (B) Early phase arteriogram demonstrates an arteriovenous fistula with thrombus present in the draining vein in a patient following a stab wound. (C) Post-embolization arteriogram demonstrates a small wedge-shaped defect after placement of a single straight coil, with most of the kidney preserved.

vessel size as closely as possible. If the coil chosen is too small, it could pass through the fistula and possibly embolize to the lungs.

The position of the catheter should be as close to the injury as possible when deploying either coils or Gelfoam to minimize parenchymal infarction. Transcatheter treatment of renal artery branch injuries has a high success rate. Studies report both radiologic and clinical success rates between 84 and 100 percent.[36,41,42]

The complication rate of transcatheter embolization is low. Nontarget embolization causes the most concern. The majority of studies report no incidents of coil misplacement.[26,37,38,41,46] There are a few reports

of nontarget embolization, including a case of embolization of the main renal artery that caused uncontrollable hypertension requiring nephrectomy.[47] Misplaced coils can now be retrieved with snares designed for either microcoils or steel coils.[48,49] A complication unique to renal embolization is the rare occurrence of transient hypertension, which can be easily controlled with medication.[35] Most studies do not report any cases of hypertension after embolization.[26,35,36,38,46] Approximately 10 percent of patients may develop post-embolization syndrome, experiencing transient pain, leukocytosis, and low-grade fever.[26,44] This condition is self-limited and resolves without treatment. Small infarcts are usually asymptomatic.

Conclusion

Blunt, penetrating, or iatrogenic trauma may result in significant renal arterial injuries. The most conservative treatment possible is favored in managing an injured kidney. Arteriography is typically reserved for those patients who have failed conservative treatment and require intervention. This philosophy has resulted in an increased use of renal artery branch embolization to treat traumatic arterial injuries. Transcatheter embolization has a high success rate and a low complication rate, and also minimizes parenchymal loss. The alternative surgical procedure frequently results in more parenchymal loss and is more invasive. Transcatheter embolization, therefore, is the preferred method of therapy in many patients with traumatic renal artery branch injuries.

References

1. Love L, Meyers MA, Churchill RJ, et al. Computed tomography of extraperitoneal spaces. AJR 1981;136:781–789.
2. Dodds WJ, Darweesh RMA, Lawson TL, et al. The retroperitoneal space revisited. AJR 1986;147:1155–1161.
3. Federle M. Evaluation of renal trauma. In: Pollack HM, ed. Clinical urography. Philadelphia: Saunders, 1989:1472–1494.
4. Carroll PR, McAninch JW. Staging of renal trauma. Urol Clin North Am 1989;16:193–201.
5. Cass AS. Renovascular injuries from external trauma: diagnosis, treatment, and outcome. Urol Clin North Am 1989;16:213–219.
6. Peters PC, Sagalowsky AI. Genitourinary trauma. In: Walsh PC, Retik AB, Stamey TA, Vaughn ED Jr, eds. Campbell's urology. 6th ed. Philadelphia: Saunders, 1992:2571–2594.
7. McAninch JW, Carroll PR. Renal exploration after trauma: indications and reconstructive techniques. Urol Clin North Am 1989;16:203–211.
8. Federle MP, Kaiser JA. The role of computed tomography in renal trauma. Radiology 1981;141:455–460.
9. Cass AS, Luxenberg M. Conservative or immediate surgical management of blunt renal injuries. J Urol 1983;130:11–16.
10. Mee SL, McAninch JW. Indications for radiographic assessment in suspected renal trauma. Urol Clin North Am 1989;16:187–192.
11. Cass AS, Luxemberg M, Gleich P, et al. Clinical indications for radiographic evaluation of blunt renal trauma. J Urol 1986;136:370.
12. Hardemann SW, Husmann DA, Chinn HKW, et al. Blunt urinary tract trauma: identifying those patients who require radiological diagnostic studies. J Urol 1987;138:99–101.
13. Bergren CT, Chan FN, Bodgin H. Intravenous pyelogram results in association with renal pathology and therapy in trauma patients. J Trauma 1987;27:515.
14. Lang EK, Sullivan J, Frentz G. Renal trauma: radiological studies. Comparison of urography, computed tomography, angiography, and radionuclide studies. Radiology 1985;154:1–6.
15. Mahoney SA, Persky L. Intravenous drip nephrotomography as an adjunct in the evaluation of renal injury. J Urol 1968;99:513–516.
16. Erturk E, Sheinfeld J, DeMarco PL, et al. Renal trauma: evaluation by computerized tomography. J Urol 1985;133:946–949.
17. Sandler CM, Toombs BD. Computed tomographic evaluation of blunt renal injuries. Radiology 1981;141:461–466.
18. Pollack HM, Wein AJ. Imaging of renal trauma. Radiology 1989;172:297–308.
19. Scalfani SJA, Becker JA, Shafton GW, et al. Strategies for the radiologic management of genitourinary trauma. Urol Radiol 1985;7:231–244.
20. Steinberg DL, Jeffrey RB, Federle MP, et al. The computerized tomographic appearance of renal pedicle injury. J Urol 1984;132:1163–1164.
21. Rhyner P, Federle MP, Jeffrey RB. CT of trauma to the abnormal kidney. AJR 1984;142:747–750.
22. Brower P, Paul J, Brosman SA. Urinary tract abnormalities presenting as a result of abdominal trauma. J Trauma 1978;18:719–722.
23. Cass AS. Blunt renal trauma in children. J Trauma 1983;23:123–127.
24. Mertz HF, Wishard WN Jr, Nouse MH, et al. Injury of the kidney in children. JAMA 1963;183:730–733.
25. Morse TS. Renal injuries. Pediatr Clin North Am 1975;22:379.
26. Kantor A, Sclafani SJA, Scalea T, et al. The role of interventional radiology in the management of genitourinary trauma. Urol Clin North Am 1989;16:255–265.
27. Philips T, Sclafani SJA, Goldstein A, et al. Use of the contrast enhanced CT enema in the management of penetrating trauma to the flank and back. J Trauma 1986;26:593–601.
28. Ralls PW, Barakos JA, Kaptein EM, et al. Renal biopsy related hemorrhage: frequency and comparison of CT and sonography. J Comput Assist Tomogr 1987;11:1031–1034.
29. Bookstein JJ, Goldstein HM. Successful management of postbiopsy arteriovenous fistula with selective arterial embolization. Radiology 1973;109:535–536.
30. Cope C, Zeit RM. Pseudoaneurysms after nephrostomy. AJR 1982;139:255–261.
31. Lang EK. Percutaneous nephrostolithotomy and lithotripsy: a multi-institutional survey of complications. Radiology 1987;162:25–30.
32. Kadir S. Kidneys. In: Kadir S, ed. Atlas of normal and variant angiographic anatomy. Philadelphia: Saunders, 1991:387–434.
33. Lang EK. Arteriography in the assessment of renal trauma: the impact of arteriographic diagnosis on preservation of renal function. J Trauma 1975;15:553–566.
34. Sclafani SJA, Stein K. Arteriographic management of traumatic arteriocalyceal fistula. Urol Radiol 1981;3:177–179.
35. Bertini JE Jr, Flechner SM, Miller P, et al. The natural history of traumatic branch renal artery injury. J Urol 1986;135:228–230.
36. Clark RA, Gallant TE, Alexander ES. Angiographic management of traumatic arteriovenous fistulas: clinical results. Radiology 1983;147:9–13.
37. Heyns CF, vanVollenhoven. Increasing role of angiography and segmental artery embolization of renal stab wounds. J Urol 1992;147:1231–1234.
38. Kadir S, Marshall FF, White RI Jr, et al. Therapeutic embolization of the kidney with detachable silicone balloons. J Urol 1983;129:11–13.
39. Kerber CW, Freeney PC, Cromwell L, et al. Cyanoacrylate occlusion of a renal arteriovenous fistula. AJR 1977;128:663–665.
40. Pilla TJ, Tantana S, Shields JB. Embolization of blunt trauma in pediatric patients. Cardiovasc Intervent Radiol 1987;10:153–156.
41. Uflacker R, Paolini RM, Lima S. Management of traumatic hematuria by selective renal artery embolization. J Urol 1984;132:662.
42. Fisher RG, Ben-Menacham Y, Whigham C. Stab wounds of the renal artery branches: angiographic diagnosis and treatment by embolization. AJR 1989;152:1231–1235.
43. Teigin CL, Venbrux AC, Quinlan DM, et al. Late massive hematuria as a complication of conservative management of blunt renal trauma in children. J Urol 1992;147:1333.
44. Corr P, Hacking G. Embolization in traumatic intrarenal vascular injuries. Clin Radiol 1991;43:262–264.
45. Richman SD, Green WM, Kroll R, et al. Superselective transcatheter embolization of traumatic renal hemorrhage. AJR 1977;128:843–844.
46. Chuang VP, Reuter SR, Walter J, et al. Control of renal hemorrhage by selective arterial embolization. AJR 1975;125:300–306.
47. Eastham JA, Wilson TG, Larsen DW, et al. Angiographic embolization of renal stab wounds. J Urol 1992;148:266–270.
48. Cekirge S, Weiss JP, Foster RG, et al. Percutaneous retrieval of foreign bodies: experience with the nitinol goose neck snare. J Vasc Intervent Radiol 1993;4:805–810.
49. Graves VB, Rappe AH, Smith TP, et al. An endovascular retrieving device for use in small vessels. AJNR 1993;14:804–808.

VIII

Pediatric Interventional Radiology

54

Pediatric Interventional Angiography

J. A. GORDON CULHAM

*I*nterventional procedures in pediatric patients have a long history. In the nonvascular area, reduction of intussusception has been carried out under radiologic guidance for many years but was first performed before the discovery of the x-ray. Early cardiovascular intervention included the balloon atrial septostomy for cyanotic congenital heart disease. Many of the newer vascular techniques have been delayed in being applied to children because of the conservative nature of pediatric practitioners, the shortage of trained physicians, and the need for minification of equipment appropriate for pediatric use.

Interventional nonvascular, vascular, and cardiac procedures are commonly performed in tertiary pediatric centers. In all pediatric patients, particularly neonates and infants, special consideration must be given to choice of sedation or anesthesia, maintenance of temperature control, fluid balance, radiation safety, and equipment selection. A skilled team of personnel that includes the pediatric radiology nurse, x-ray technologist, and hemodynamic technologist is required to handle the patient, prepare the room, and assist in the efficient performance of the procedure. Excellent imaging systems are needed to provide diagnostic angiography quickly and to monitor the interventions. High-resolution digital systems are valuable in acquiring and processing data quickly, providing on-line vessel measurement and image subtraction, and reducing contrast load. Reference images and road-mapping functions are also useful.

Patient Preparation

Indications

Interventional procedures are performed when they offer some advantage over conventional therapy or when there are no reasonable alternatives.

Consent

Informed consent is obtained from the parent, guardian, and, when possible, from the child. Care must be taken to provide an unbiased view of the procedure and the alternatives. Possible and rare but serious complications must be revealed.

Coagulation

Routine blood work is obtained as required for hospital admission and anesthesia. Coagulation studies are obtained when there is a bleeding disorder, risk of hemorrhage, or a plan to perform systemic thrombolysis. Blood is matched only for occurring or possible major blood loss. Heparin is given during the procedure in the flush solution and when the arterial circulation has been entered. The dose given is 50 to 100 units/kg. The larger dose is given for retrograde arterial balloon dilatation procedures.

Anesthesia

The choice of anesthesia or sedation is made in conjunction with the anesthesia department with consideration being given to the physiologic needs of the test and the need for immobilization. The author's institution is fortunate to have anesthesia coverage for all angiographic procedures. Most diagnostic studies are carried out with intravenous sedation. Difficult interventions such as device implantation or particularly painful procedures are done under general anesthesia. Some patients, such as children with advanced cystic fibrosis, are poor anesthetic risks and are examined with the least possible medication. The anesthetist acts as an advocate for the child and participates in the decisions about how best to handle the patient and when a procedure should be discontinued. In other centers the angiographers perform their own sedation.[1,2] The patient must be monitored carefully throughout the procedure.

Patient Immobilization

Smaller children are immobilized on a restraining board. Older children will have hand and leg restraints but, if uncooperative, will be anesthetized.

Temperature Control

Neonates and particularly premature babies are likely to become hypothermic if care is not taken to maintain a warm environment. The room temperature should be increased, radiant heaters used as required, and care taken to cover the infant quickly when the infant is being prepared and draped. The use of plastic drapes over the operative site helps to keep the patient warm and dry.

Diet and Medications

Patients are kept NPO for an appropriate time as determined by age and normal diet. The preparation is the same for sedation or anesthesia. Routine antibiotics are not prescribed except for high-risk procedures such as splenic embolization. Anxious children may receive a preoperative sedative or anxiolytic agent. Emla cream is applied to the expected intravenous site if a good intravenous line is not already established.

Dose of Radiation and Fluids

All fluids and medications must be scaled to the patient size. It is easy to administer an excessive amount of local anesthetic, fluid, or contrast material. As interventional procedures become more complicated, one must try to minimize the radiation exposure to individuals who will live for many years and who are believed to be more sensitive to radiation. Digital systems are helpful in reducing the volume of contrast material and in speeding up procedures but probably do not reduce radiation exposure. At the author's institution, the dedicated pediatric facility has been altered in several ways to reduce radiation exposure. Fluoroscopy is performed at the lowest dose possible and is done with the scatter grids removed. In addition, rare earth filters have been installed in the x-ray tubes to further reduce radiation. These approaches allow fluoroscopy doses to be far below radiation standards.

Postoperative Care

Care for the patient who has undergone an interventional procedure continues as long as the child is in the hospital. The radiologist is best suited to advise the pediatric medical or surgical staff of the anticipated effects or possible complications of the procedure. Continued monitoring of the child's progress also allows the radiologist to assess the efficacy of the procedure and to be aware of any complications that arise.

Techniques

Embolization

Percutaneous transcatheter embolization has become a common procedure in centers with trained personnel. It replaces surgery for many problems and provides a treatment alternative for patients in whom surgery has little to offer. Equipment and techniques have evolved to a point where most vascular abnormalities can be treated by one or another of many approaches. Microsystems permit small vessels and territories to be treated that were previously inaccessible. These microsystems, which were developed particularly for adult neurointervention, are ideal for pediatric applications. New hydrophilic coated steerable guidewires permit the catheterization of complex turns without provoking spasm or dissection (Radiofocus guidewire, Terumo).

Embolization procedures are more risky than diagnostic angiography and should only be performed by experienced physicians familiar with the equipment and technical alternatives. Pediatric surgical support for the procedure and backup is essential. The choice of agent to be used is determined by the rheology of the vascular bed to be treated. Therapy may be directed to large vessels, high-flow arteriovenous communications, small arterioles, or the matrix of a vascular malformation. Introducer sheaths should be used to preserve vascular access in the event that the delivery catheter has to be removed. They may also protect against thrombosis.[3]

Particles

Small vessels are frequently treated with particles of gelatin sponge (Gelfoam, Upjohn Co.) or polyvinyl alcohol foam. Gelfoam is slowly resorbed and should be used for temporary occlusion. Ivalon is a more permanent occlusive agent. Both agents tend to plug the delivery catheter, which may then have to be replaced. Nontapered catheters introduced through a sheath are less likely to obstruct, and newer, specially shaped and sized particles also seem less likely to aggregate and obstruct the catheter (Contour emboli, Interventional Therapeutics Corporation). Particles come in sizes from 150 to 1000 μ. These agents are used to treat bleeding and to preoperatively devascularize tumors. Small particles may be delivered through catheters as small as 2.6 French (Tracker catheter, Target Therapeutics).

An arterial sheath is always available either in the groin or on the catheter to protect vascular access. When extensive manipulation and multiple catheter exchanges are needed, a sheath, although larger, is less likely to result in femoral thrombosis. Arterial heparinization is used except when active bleeding has occurred.

Indications. Particulate embolization is most frequently used to control bleeding or to devascularize a tumor, malformation, or organ. Bleeding may be gastrointestinal, pulmonary, posttraumatic, or anticipated at surgery. Posttraumatic bleeding may necessitate urgent surgery if the patient is unstable, but if the child can be stabilized, embolization control may be more selective and may result in more tissue preservation. Embolization of gastrointestinal bleeding is done after failure of endoscopic sclerotherapy or vasopressin infusion, and limited and selective embolization of bowel can be effective.[2] Bleeding from pelvic fractures is difficult to control surgically but can be embolized.[4] If extensive groin hematomas are present, a brachial approach may be required.

Hemoptysis from cystic fibrosis tends to occur in young adults with long-standing disease but is also seen in children (Fig. 54-1).[5,6] Treatment is best using Ivalon particles injected through a 4 to 5 French catheter. Careful preembolization angiography and monitoring of the procedure are required to prevent inadvertent occlusion of vessels supplying the spinal cord or brain. The central dilated bronchial vessels should not be occluded with coils or balloons to permit future treatment if bleeding recurs.

Devascularization may be done preoperatively for lesions such as nasopharyngeal angiofibroma or to provide definitive therapy for control of cardiac failure in hepatic hemangioendothelioma or vascular malformation. Infantile hepatic hemangioendothelioma is a benign neoplasm that will involute spontaneously provided the child does not succumb to congestive cardiac failure or consumptive coagulopathy.[7] Treatment is directed to control these symptoms, not to ablate the tumor. Particulate embolization may carry an increased risk of hepatic infarction, and coil or balloon occlusion may be preferred.[7]

Aneurysmal bone cysts may be treatable with embolization alone or in combination with injection sclerotherapy.[8,9] Organ ablation has been done combining particles with alcohol to treat hypertension from native kidneys in end-stage renal disease or in renal transplant patients.[10] At the author's institution, particles soaked in antibiotics are used to perform subtotal splenectomy in patients with hypersplenism.[11] These children will have considerable pain and fever after tissue infarction (Fig. 54-2).

Vascular malformations must be carefully evaluated before treatment, and the goals of therapy must be defined and the risks assessed. High-flow lesions may require particles or devices. Although slow-flow lesions

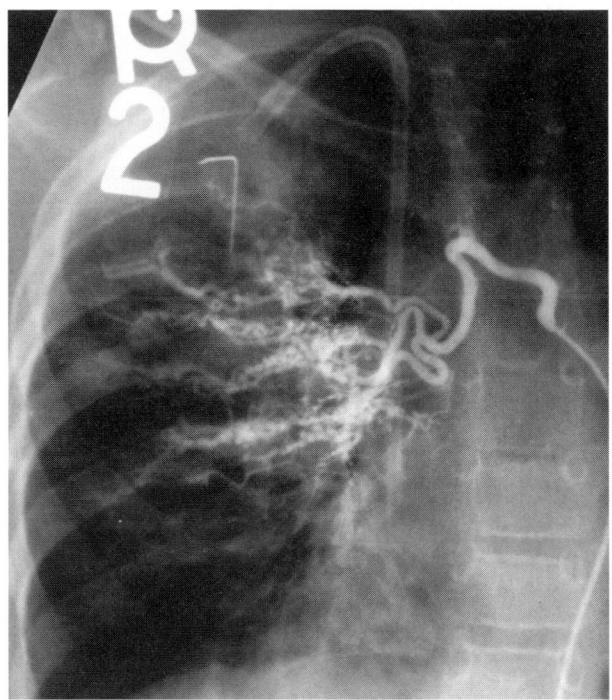

A

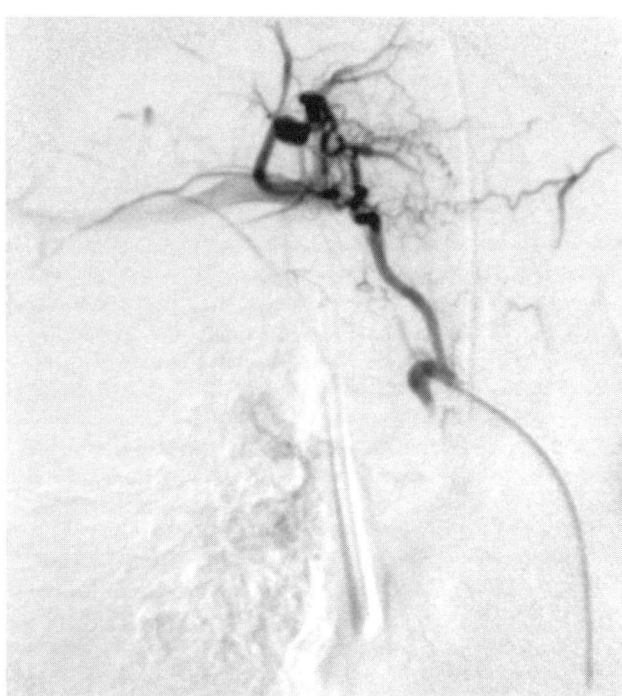

B

Figure 54-1. (A) Selective bronchial arteriogram in a 9-year-old girl with advanced cystic fibrosis shows extensive collateral flow between an enlarged right bronchial artery and the pulmonary artery. (B) After embolization with particles and marked attenuation of flow in the bronchial artery, there is filling of extensive mediastinal arteries and collateral flow into the right subclavian and right vertebral arteries, emphasizing the risks of these procedures.

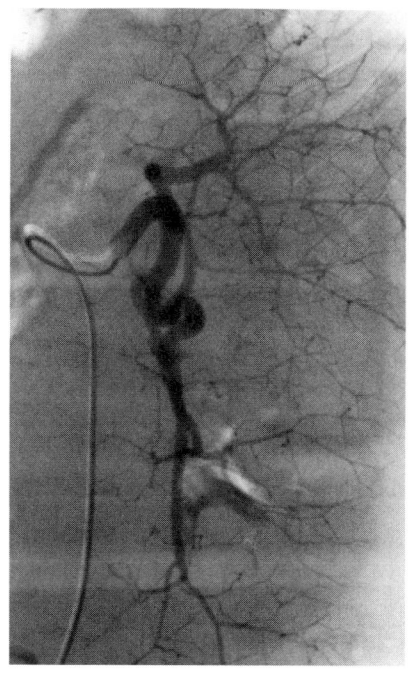
A

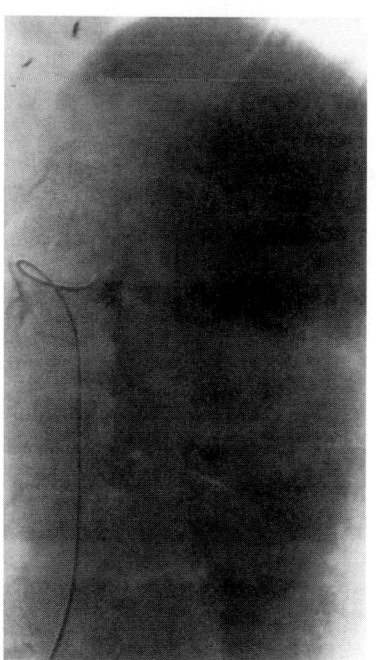
B

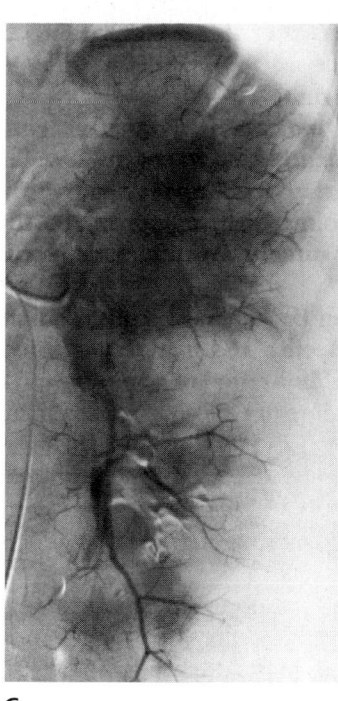
C

Figure 54-2. Selective splenic arteriogram shows marked enlargement of the spleen (A) and a homogeneous parenchymal phase (B). (C) After subtotal splenic embolization with polyvinyl alcohol particles, the arterial phase is prolonged and the parenchymal phase is patchy and inhomogeneous.

may be treatable with small permanent particles, alcohol extends farther into the bed and is preferred alone or combined with particles. In Europe, Ethibloc is a popular material for embolization of vascular malformations.[12] Large-vessel devices should not be used in vascular malformations except to treat large arteriovenous connections because they will not be effective. Capillary or venous malformations may require direct injection and multiple procedures. Finally, it is important to differentiate between vascular tumors and vascular malformations.[13]

Liquids

Ethanol, sodium tetradecyl sulfate, and cyanoacrylate adhesive have all been used to treat small-vessel abnormalities, particularly when the goal is to ablate the matrix of a vascular malformation or the parenchyma of an organ or tumor. Alcohol is the most popular agent and can be used through a catheter or injected directly into the lesion. The adhesives are more difficult to prepare and to use, and they have an uncertain biocompatibility. Furthermore, the aggressive nature of these agents, although desirable for the lesion, can also cause necrosis of normal tissues such as skin or nerves. Care must also be taken to isolate the vascular bed with selective catheterization, balloon occlusion, and test injections to quantify the size and flow rate in the vascular bed. Overflow of alcohol into a larger vessel is quickly diluted and well tolerated. The author opacifies absolute alcohol with metrizamide to monitor the distribution of the alcohol, and others have mixed Ethiodol with the alcohol.[14] These agents may also be delivered through microcatheters (2.6 French).

Indications. Liquid agents are used to treat low-flow vascular malformations as they penetrate the matrix of the lesion.[15] Occlusion of the feeding vessels alone will often fail to improve a vascular malformation and will result in loss of the best route to the lesion for other endovascular therapy.[2,16,17] In vascular malformations without enlarged feeding vessels, alcohol is injected directly (Fig. 54-3). Similarly, if tumor necrosis or organ ablation is desired, liquids are the agents of choice and may be used to treat tumors preoperatively or for metastatic disease. Renal ablation for hypertension is performed using alcohol.[18]

Devices

The occlusion of large or high-flow vessels often requires the use of devices such as coils, detachable latex or silicone balloons, or double-umbrella occluders.[19-21] Stainless steel or platinum coils can be used to occlude a wide range of vessels as long as the vascular branching pattern or a distal stenosis protects from distal embolization. Where no such protection exists, control can be achieved by placing an endovascular spider to anchor the coils or by using an umbrella

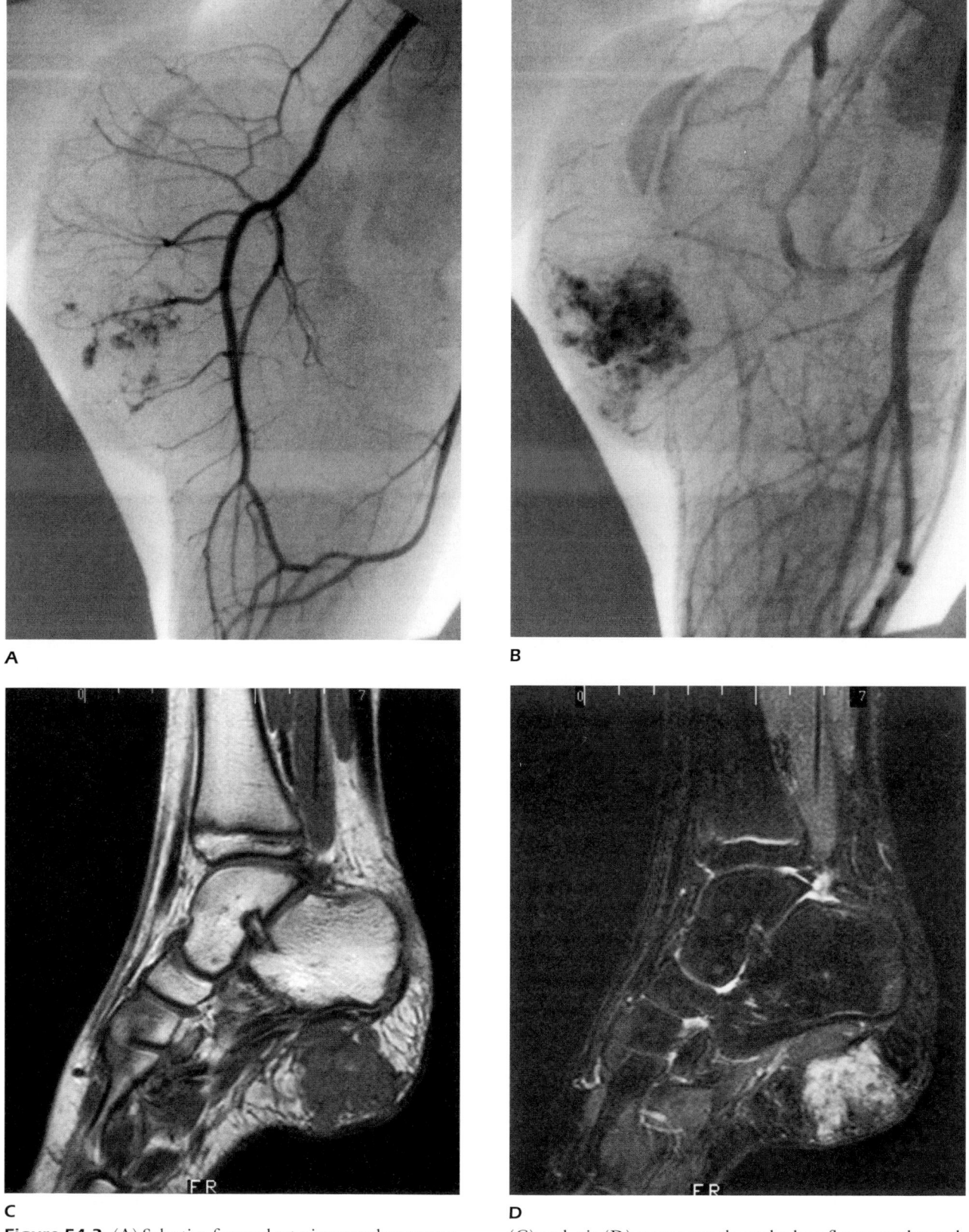

A

B

C

D

Figure 54-3. (A) Selective femoral arteriogram shows a vascular malformation of the heel pad with arterial supply from two small vessels. (B) Venous phase shows delayed puddling of contrast material in small cavernous spaces. T1-weighted (C) and stir (D) sequences show the low-flow vascular malformation within the heel pad. (E) Alcohol (100 percent) opacified with metrizamide was injected directly into the vascular malformation.

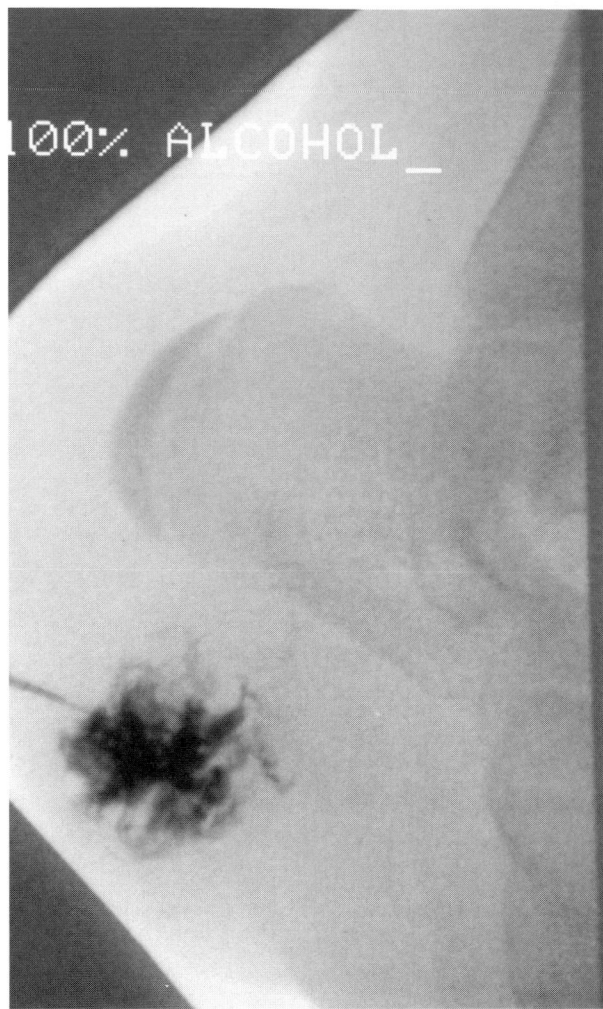

E   **Figure 54-3** (continued).

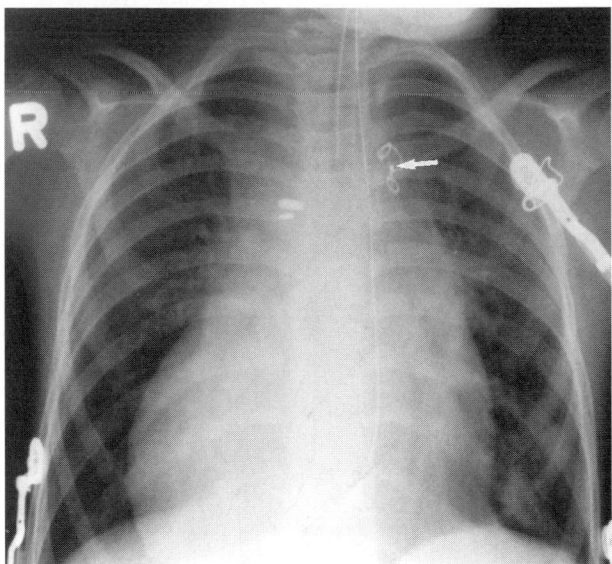

Figure 54-4. Chest film in a child with complex congenital heart disease shows a thrombogenic coil positioned in a left-sided Blalock-Taussig (BT) shunt to control congestive heart failure. The coil has been positioned on top of an intravascular spider (*arrow*).

occluder (Rashkind device) (Fig. 54-4).[22] Short communications such as arteriovenous fistulas (AVFs) and fenestrations in surgical baffles require the umbrella approach. Detachable balloons have been used extensively in neuroradiology but have found limited use elsewhere in the body.[23] They are expensive and difficult to use, and high-flow lesions can result in uncontrolled detachment.

Coils can be delivered through microcatheters or more commonly 4 to 5 French systems. Care must be taken to select the appropriate-sized coil and then to properly position it.[24] A coil that is too long or too large for the vessel may fail to coil properly and protrude proximally or even embolize inadvertently, whereas one that is too small may pass through a vessel or malformation. The operator should also be familiar with retrieval systems to remove coils or devices that migrate (see below).

The umbrella device requires 8 to 11 French delivery systems and is not appropriate in the arterial circu-

lation of pediatric patients. The venous route to the PDA has been successful in many centers (see Chapter 16 in *Abrams' Angiography,* 4/e, Vol. I).

Indications. Thrombogenic coils are used to occlude a variety of larger vessels. Anomalous systemic arteries to normal or abnormal lung segments and aortopulmonary collateral vessels in pulmonary atresia are commonly treated.[25,26] The author's institution has also treated Blalock-Taussig shunts that are too large or that persist after surgical ligation (see Fig. 54-4).[27] High-flow vascular malformations and AVFs can often be treated (Fig. 54-5), and false aneurysms and bleeding following trauma or biopsy are suitable for coil embolization. Coils or detachable balloons have been used to treat pulmonary arteriovenous malformations, patent ductus arteriosus, and hepatic hemangioendotheliomas (Fig. 54-6).[7,28]

Complications

Embolization procedures may be complicated by inadvertent embolization of a vascular territory due to stray particles or liquids that pass through a lesion or overflow out of the supplying artery. Devices may also pass through a fistula or a PDA or may be malpositioned during implantation. Another complication is extensive tissue ablation, which may produce unwanted necrosis of organs, nerves, or skin. Finally, long, difficult procedures may result in fluid or contrast overload, excessive radiation exposure, hypothermia, and femoral thrombosis.

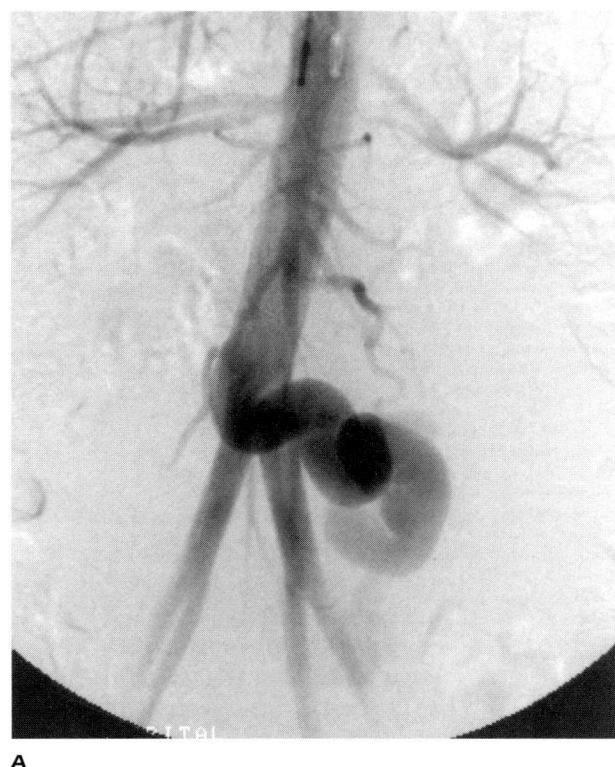

A

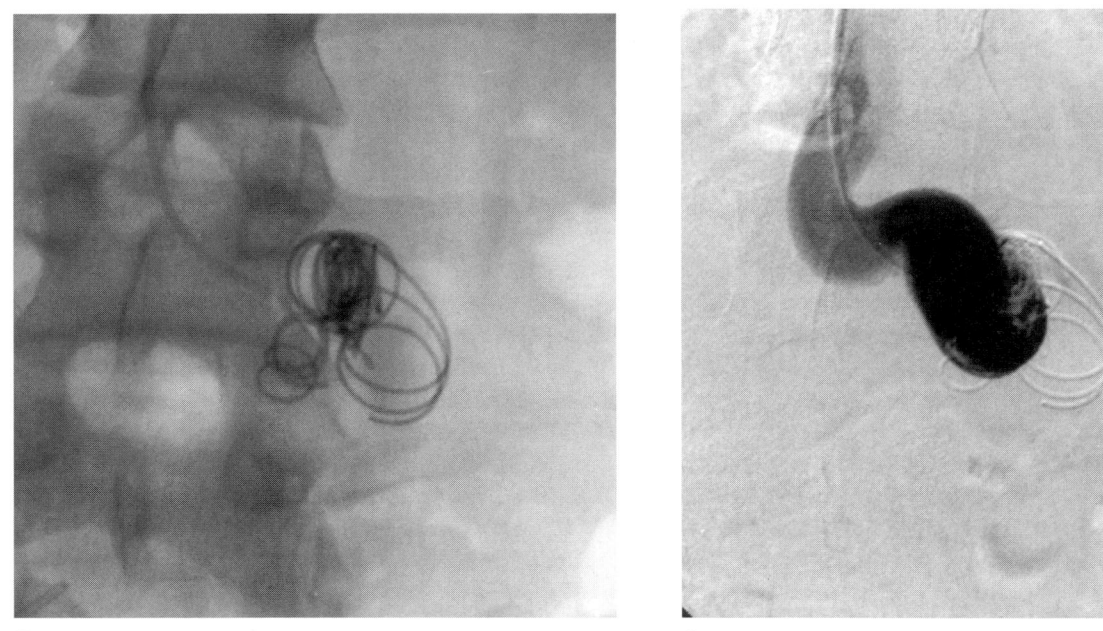

B   C

Figure 54-5. (A) Abdominal aortogram performed from a left brachial approach shows a huge artery supplying a lumbar arteriovenous fistula. Treatment with an assortment of large and medium coils (B) resulted in complete occlusion (C).

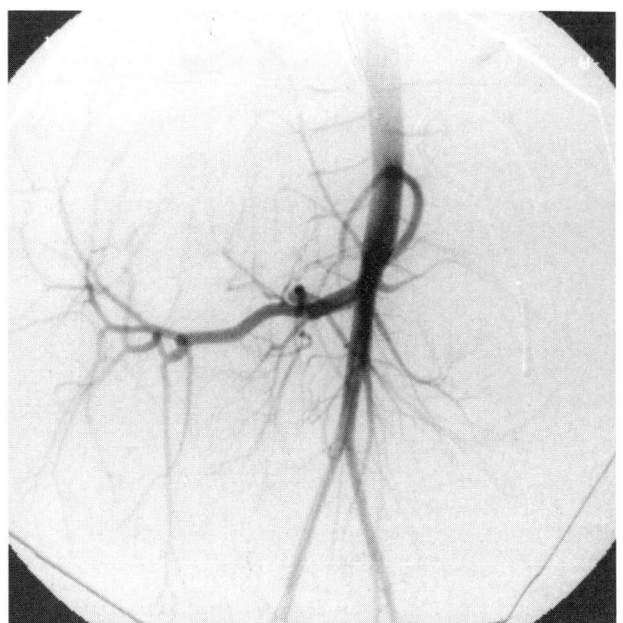

A

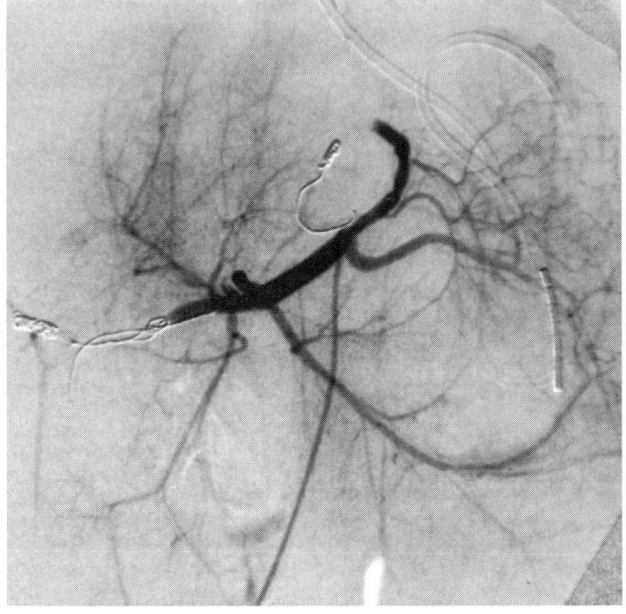

B

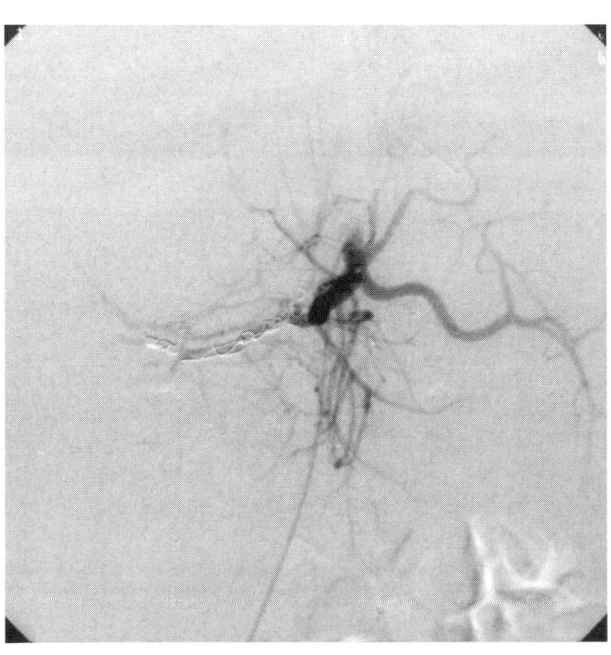

C

Figure 54-6. A 6-month-old baby with a massive hepatic hemangioendothelioma. (A) Abdominal aortogram shows supply to the liver from enlarged right and left hepatic arteries. (B) Embolization using microcoils delivered through a 2.6 French Tracker catheter resulted in occlusion of the right hepatic artery and the left hepatic artery arising from the left gastric artery. (C) A subsequent procedure resulted in further obliteration of supply to the liver by occlusion of the middle hepatic artery and the right gastroepiploic artery.

Angioplasty

The techniques of balloon dilatation of vascular stenoses are the same for children as for adults. With the new balloon catheter systems, balloon dilatation can be carried out safely even in small children and can permit access to peripheral stenoses. The nature of the lesions to be treated varies, as do the results. Many cardiac lesions are now primarily treated by balloon dilatation. This chapter is limited to vascular lesions and does not discuss balloon valvotomy.

Small balloon diameters (2 mm) and small-shaft catheters (3.8 French) can be used with 4 French delivery systems. Small steerable guidewire systems are helpful in crossing small distal stenoses. For most applications, low-profile balloons up to 10 mm in diameter are used on 5 French catheters. Larger balloons up to 20 mm in size are used to treat recurrent coarctation and peripheral pulmonary stenosis. High-pressure balloons (17 atm) are available in small sizes to treat fibrous lesions.

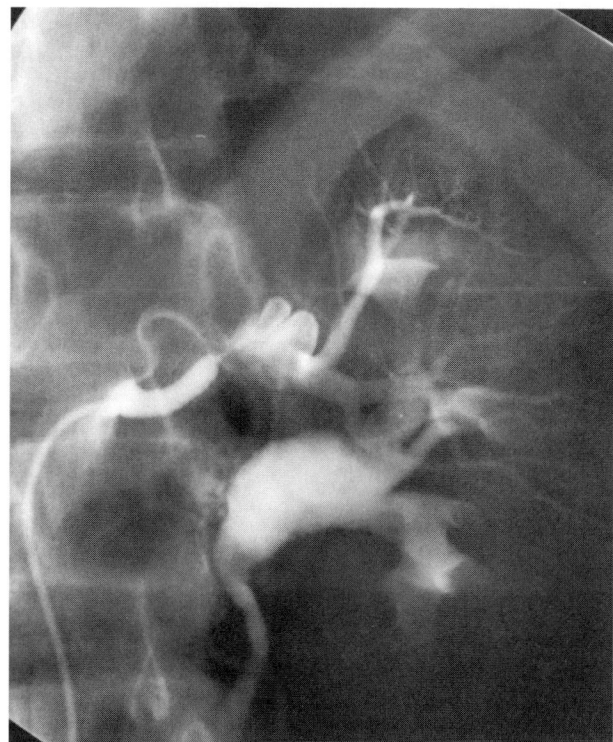

A

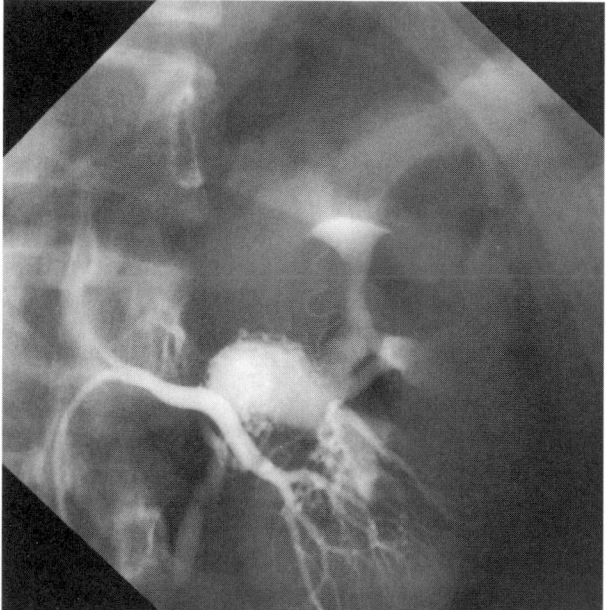

B

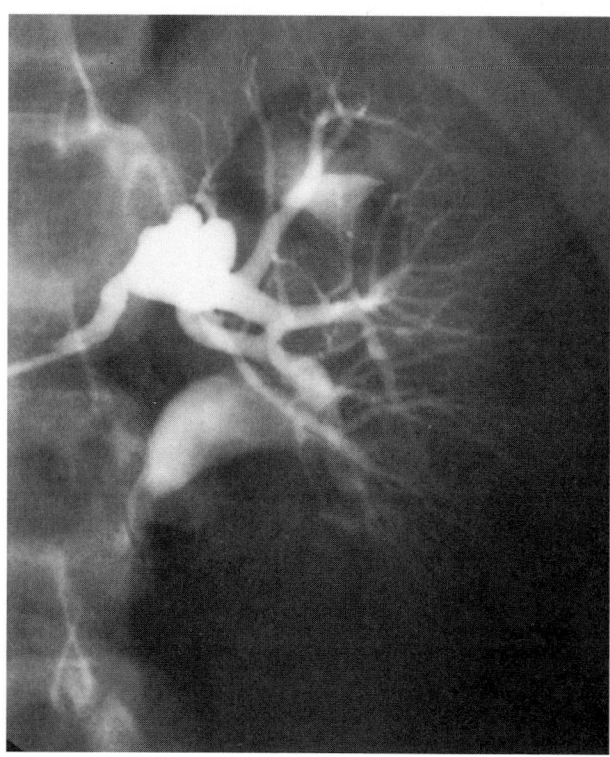

C

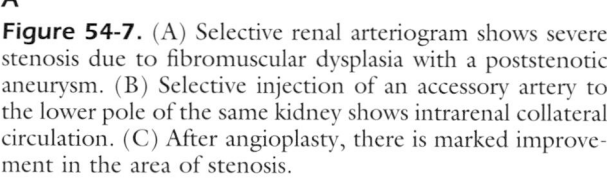

Figure 54-7. (A) Selective renal arteriogram shows severe stenosis due to fibromuscular dysplasia with a poststenotic aneurysm. (B) Selective injection of an accessory artery to the lower pole of the same kidney shows intrarenal collateral circulation. (C) After angioplasty, there is marked improvement in the area of stenosis.

Indications

Balloon dilatation is the treatment of choice for renal artery stenosis in children, most of which is due to fibrodysplasia and responds well to treatment (Fig. 54-7).[2,29,30] Peripheral lesions in segmental branches can be dilated, but more distal lesions require embolization or surgical resection (Fig. 54-8). Once the lesion is crossed, heparin is given to prevent thrombosis on the guidewire. The author uses 100 units/kg body weight. The correct balloon size is determined by measuring the normal vessel proximal to the stenosis or beyond an area of poststenotic dilatation. A balloon is chosen with a diameter slightly larger than the normal vessel. A digital system with adjustable table height allows for direct measurement. Those that use conventional filming have recommended a balloon equal in size to the mildly magnified vessel on the film. The children are given acetyl salicylic acid and dipyridamole for 3 months to decrease platelet adhesiveness. In children with vasculitis or vascular dysplasia associated with neurofibromatosis, Takayasu arteritis, Williams

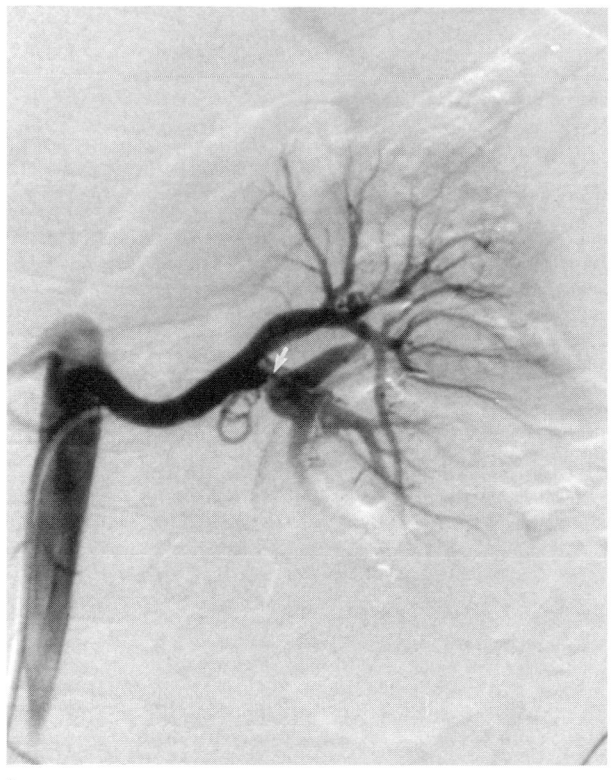

A

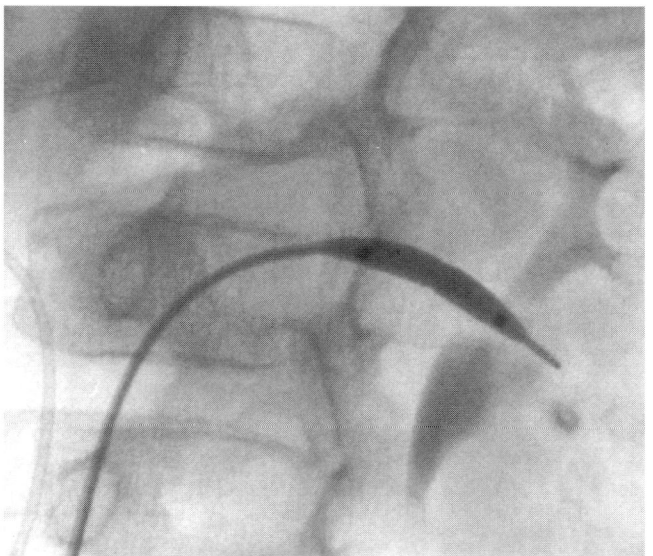

B

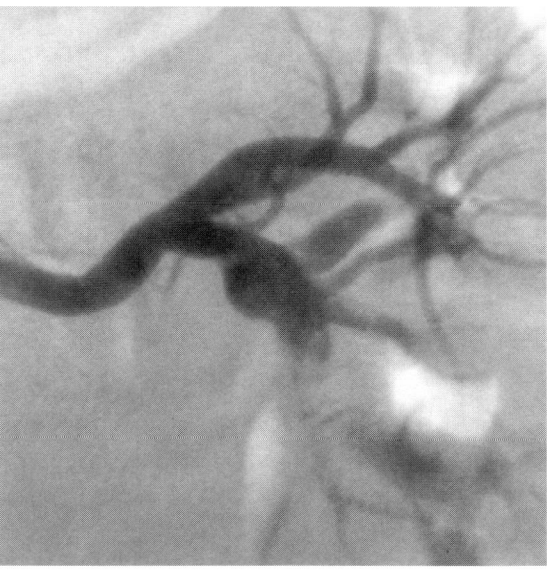

C

Figure 54-8. (A) Selective renal arteriogram shows a severe stenosis of the segmental artery to the lower pole of the left kidney (*arrow*). Intrarenal collaterals are evident. (B) Balloon dilatation was carried out. (C) After dilatation, the area of stenosis is markedly improved.

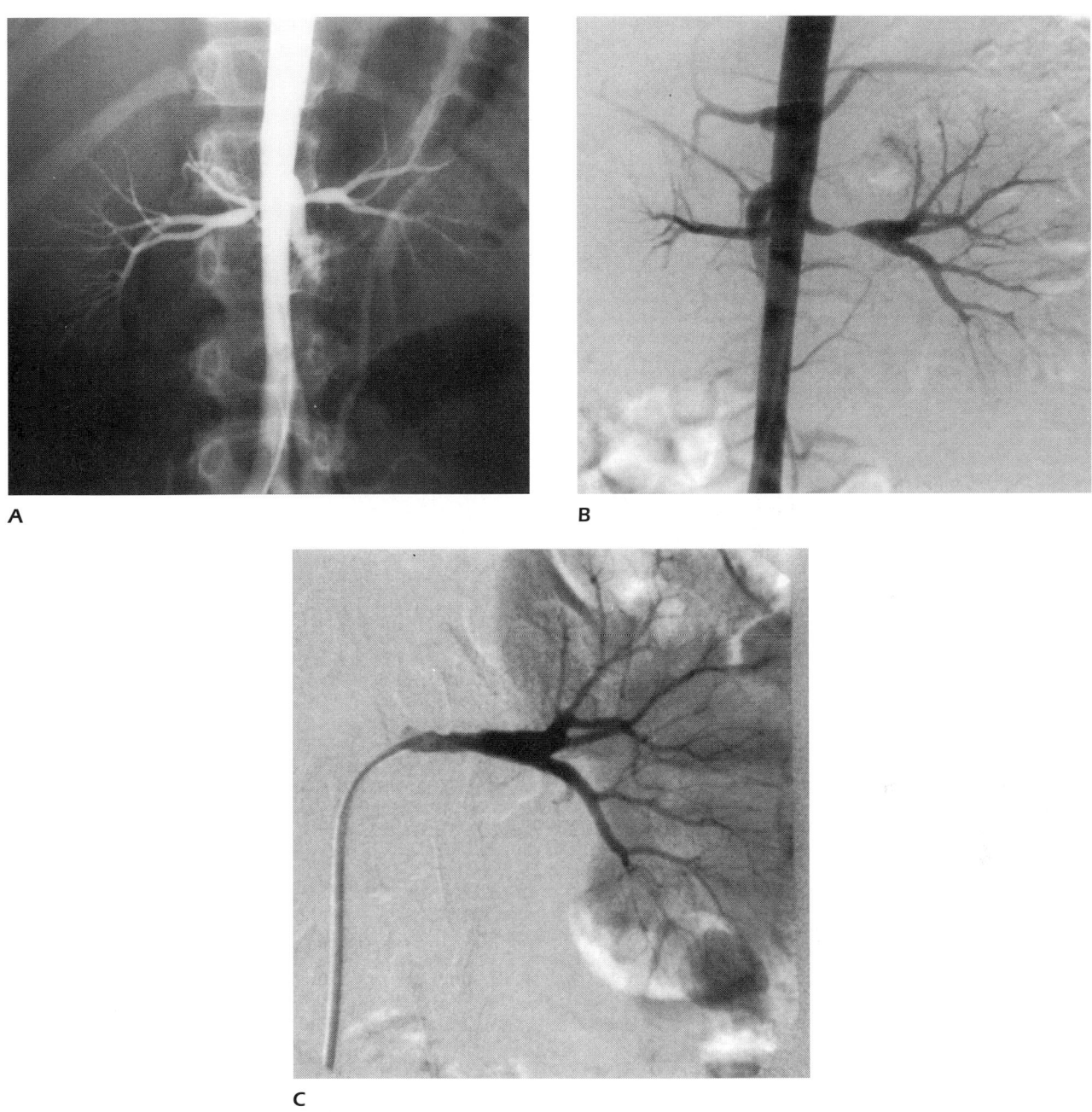

Figure 54-9. (A) Abdominal aortogram shows bilateral ostial renal artery stenoses. (B) In another patient, an ostial lesion was repaired surgically and restenosis developed in the grafted area. (C) This lesion responded well to balloon dilatation.

syndrome, or abdominal coarctation, the results are less gratifying even with high-pressure balloons, particularly for ostial lesions (Fig. 54-9). Arterial stenosis associated with renal transplantation can often be improved.[31,32] These obstructions may be at or beyond the suture line. It is important to evaluate the hemodynamic significance of the proximal stenosis because in some of these patients extensive peripheral disease due to rejection nullifies the proximal lesion.

Other uses for balloon dilatation include the treatment of venous stenosis such as the Budd-Chiari syndrome or venous baffle stenosis (Figs. 54-10 and 54-11), dilatation of an adjustable pulmonary artery band, and treatment of branch pulmonary artery stenosis, aortopulmonary shunts, dialysis fistulas, splenorenal shunts, or recurrent coarctation of the aorta (for a discussion of coarctation, see Chapter 17 of *Abrams' Angiography*, 4/e, Vol. I). Peripheral pulmonary artery

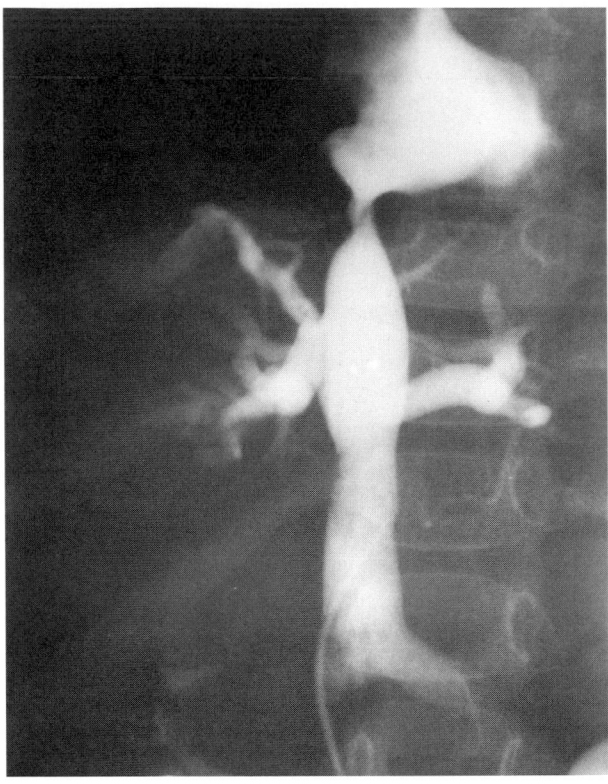

A

B

C

Figure 54-10. (A) Vena cavogram shows stenosis of the inferior vena cava just below its point of entry into the right atrium and reflux into dilated and tortuous hepatic veins. (B) Balloon dilatation at low inflation pressure shows a marked waist, subsequently dilated to almost the full diameter of a 20-mm balloon (C).

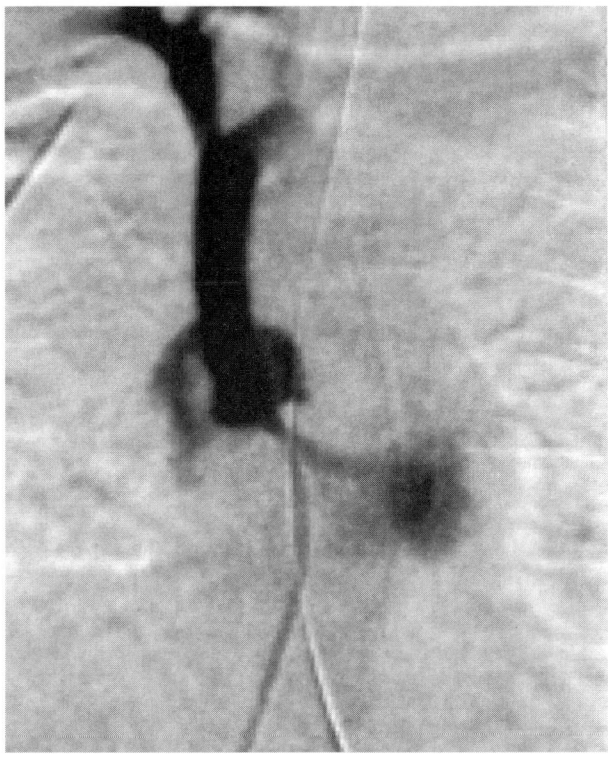

A

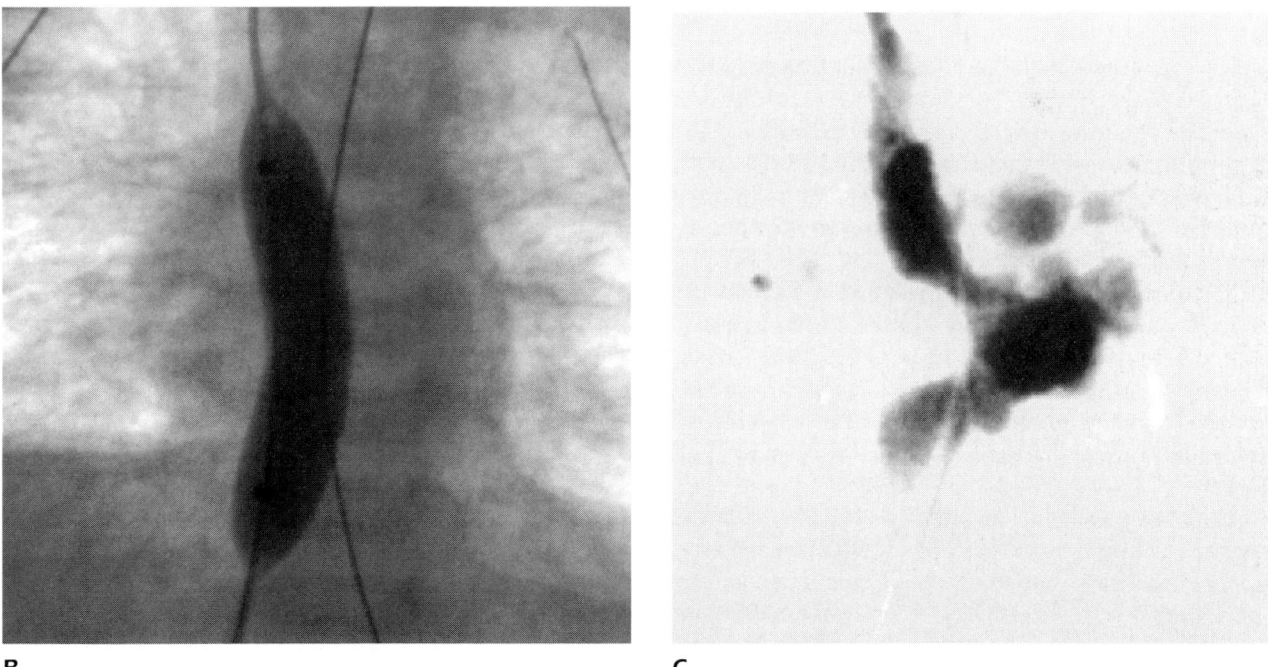

B   C

Figure 54-11. An infant underwent repair of transposition by Mustard procedure in the neonatal period. (A) Superior vena cava injection shows severe obstruction in the superior baffle limb. Balloon dilatation (B) produced marked improvement in the superior baffle stenosis (C).

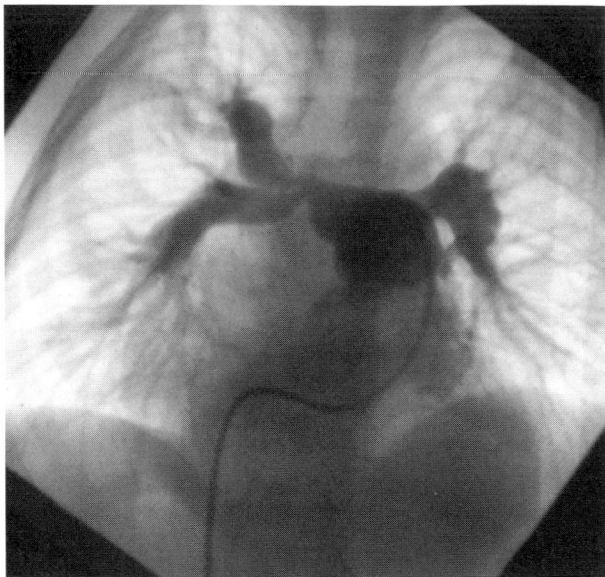

A

B

Figure 54-12. A 4-year-old girl who had undergone repair of tetralogy of Fallot. (A) Injection in the main pulmonary artery shows narrowing of the left pulmonary artery and the origins of the right upper lobe and descending branch of the right lower lobe pulmonary arteries. (B) Balloon dilatation was carried out using a large-diameter balloon.

stenosis can sometimes be treated effectively but at moderate risk. Because of the elasticity of pulmonary arteries, these lesions require large balloons for small increases in artery size (Fig. 54-12). Arterial rupture can occur, resulting in death. Because there are no surgical options to treat these lesions, balloon dilatation is the procedure of choice when treatment is clinically indicated.[33] Stenting is a safer and more effective approach to these lesions.[34]

The author's center has developed a balloon expandable device for banding the pulmonary artery. This device can be adjusted as the child grows, allowing for proper banding in infancy and precluding the need for early corrective surgery or other palliative procedures when the band becomes too small (Fig. 54-13).[35]

After the modified Blalock-Taussig (BT) shunt is placed, stenoses may develop in the subclavian artery, the proximal or distal anastomosis, the graft, or the pulmonary artery. All of these may be treated except for the graft stenoses. The author has had the best success in improving pulmonary blood flow in those patients with a traditional BT shunt where the subclavian artery has been directly connected to the pulmonary artery. Most BT shunts are performed using Gor-tex grafts, which limit the amount of stretching of the stenoses. Narrowing within the graft is probably caused by kinking, thrombosis, or fibrointimal proliferation.

Complications

Vascular spasm can occur, particularly in renal artery angioplasty, and may in turn provoke thrombosis and segmental infarction. To minimize thrombosis, an initial dose of heparin, 100 units/kg, is given, and more may be required in prolonged procedures. Monitoring of heparinization with measurements of the activated clotting time is helpful.[36] Effective heparinization has been shown to decrease the incidence of femoral thrombosis during catheterization,[37] and spasm may be treated with direct intraarterial injection of papaverine or nitroglycerin (0.25 to 1.00 µg/kg/min[2]).

Thrombosis may occur at the angioplasty site or at the groin; if it does occur, thrombolytic therapy is given. Intimal dissection is part of many angioplasty procedures but usually does not cause vascular obstruction. If an intimal flap obstructs the vessel, stents may be used. Vascular rupture is always a concern but can usually be avoided with proper balloon selection. When one is treating peripheral pulmonary artery stenosis, rupture may occur because of the large balloons needed to dilate these elastic stenoses.

Thrombolysis

Experience with thrombolysis in children is limited but has increased because of the need to treat the complications of cardiac catheterization and systemic arterial

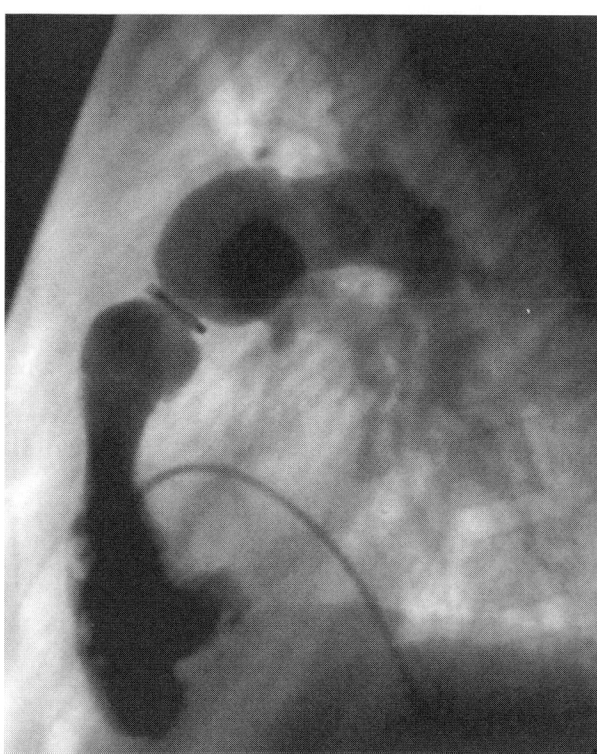

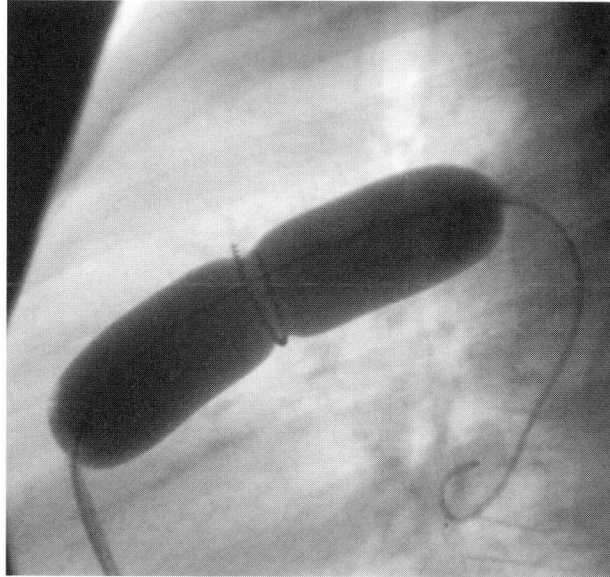

B

A

Figure 54-13. (A) Right ventricular injection in lateral projection shows a band in place on the main pulmonary artery consisting of a balloon-dilatable fatigued helix. (B) Balloon dilatation expanded the pulmonary artery band and decreased the obstruction to pulmonary blood flow.

intervention.[38] Agents used include streptokinase, urokinase, and rtpa. Effective dose schedules for children have been extrapolated from adult studies. Coagulation and fibrinolysis are probably different, particularly in neonates. Plasminogen levels are known to be low in neonates, and it has been proposed that plasminogen or fresh plasma be given to enhance fibrinolytic therapy.[36] Most centers favor urokinase as the most cost-effective approach, and this may be locally delivered via a selective catheter or may be given systemically. Local low-dose therapy is unlikely to produce systemic changes in coagulation, whereas systemic therapy will and therefore has greater risk and more contraindications. The dose of urokinase for local low-dose infusion is 300 to 500 IU/kg/hr. Systemic therapy is 10 times this dose, or 3000 to 5000 IU/kg/hr. In all systemic therapy, the fibrinogen level, thrombin time, prothrombin time, and activated partial thromboplastin time are monitored at regular intervals, and the children are observed in an intensive care unit or neonatal nursery. Systemic therapy with heparin is recommended for indwelling catheters, but its role in the

neonate is uncertain. The trend in thrombolytic therapy is toward higher-dose, shorter-duration treatment given locally, which often produces rapid clearing of thrombus. Failures may relate to delays in implementing therapy, resulting in maturation of the thrombus.[39]

Indications

The most common lesion treated in the author's center is femoral artery thrombosis complicating catheterization, especially for balloon angioplasty of the aortic arch or aortic valve. These procedures require the insertion of large balloons, which are currently mounted on large shafts. Initially a local low-dose approach from the opposite groin was preferred, but now systemic therapy is frequently used if there are no contraindications.[1] Local low-dose thrombolysis is used for thrombosis of BT shunts, dialysis fistula, pulmonary artery thrombosis (Fig. 54-14), iliofemoral thrombophlebitis, aortic thrombosis in neonates,[40,41] and brachial artery occlusion after supracondylar fracture (Fig. 54-15).[42]

Complications

Bleeding is the most serious complication of thrombolytic therapy. Cerebral hemorrhage is a concern in the neonate, and in this group the author chooses local low-dose treatment. One patient suffered a cerebral hemorrhage during the first hours of a local low-dose infusion of streptokinase into a BT shunt. The catheter became displaced and probably perfused the vertebral bed. The child probably also had a coagulation disorder associated with cyanotic congenital heart disease

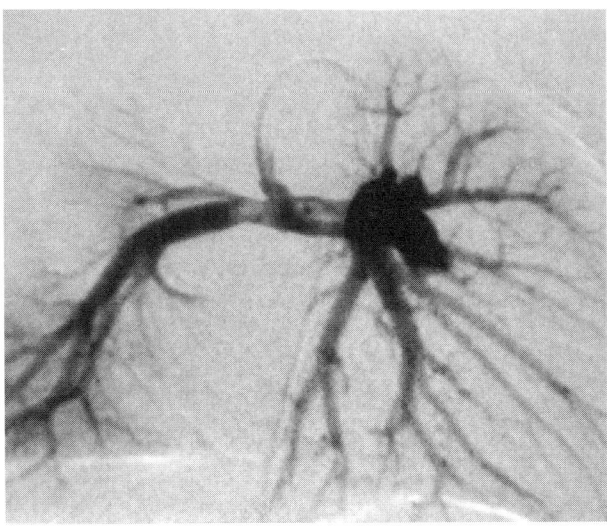

A

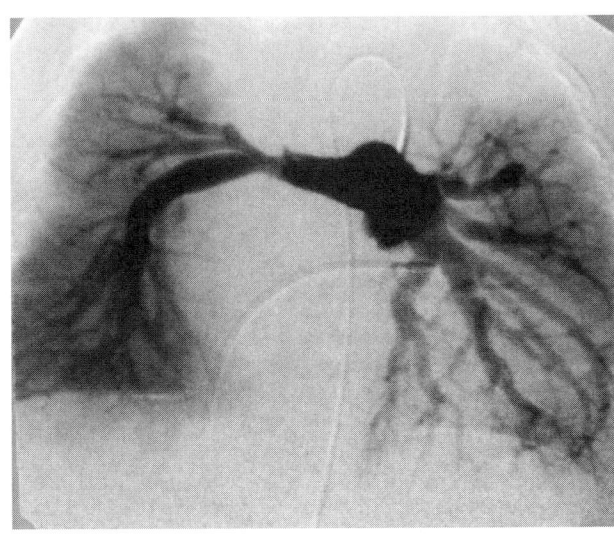

B

Figure 54-14. (A) Pulmonary angiogram performed via a right modified BT shunt shows extensive thrombosis within the lower end of the shunt and in the right pulmonary artery. (B) After thrombolysis, there is a marked improvement in the amount of thrombus within the pulmonary artery. Some residual narrowing is present in the right pulmonary artery, and there is a very small amount of residual thrombus along the upper surface of the proximal right pulmonary artery.

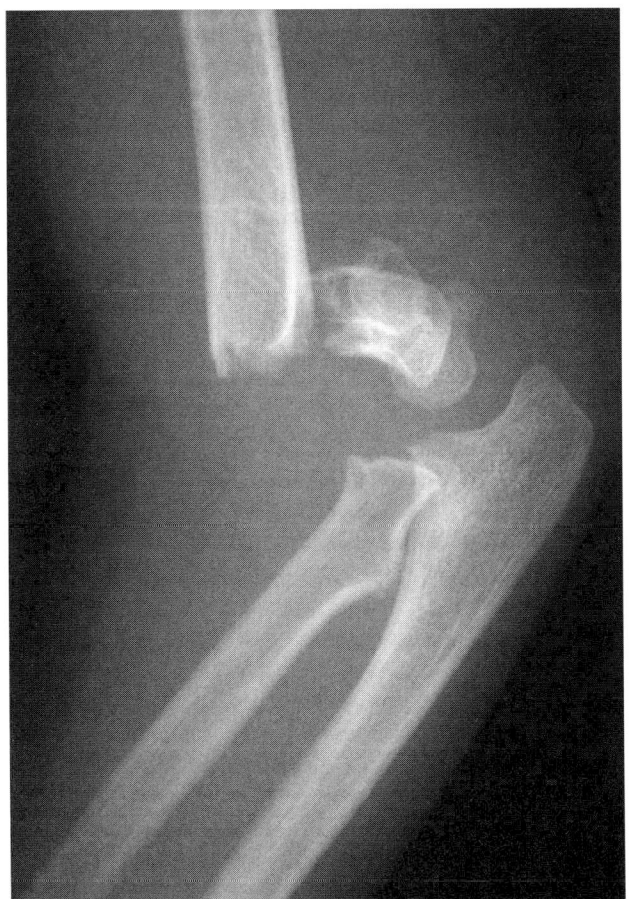

A

B

Figure 54-15

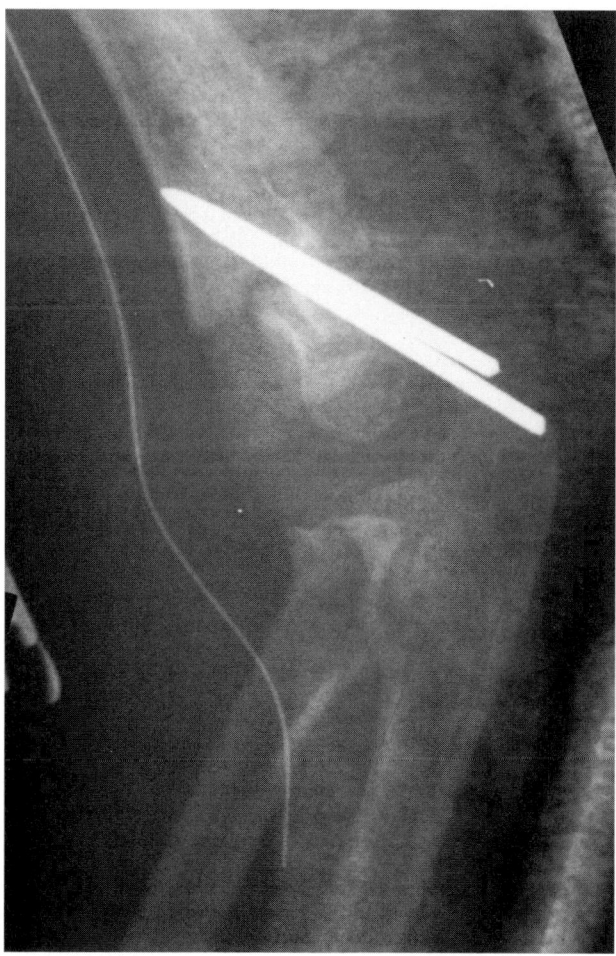

C

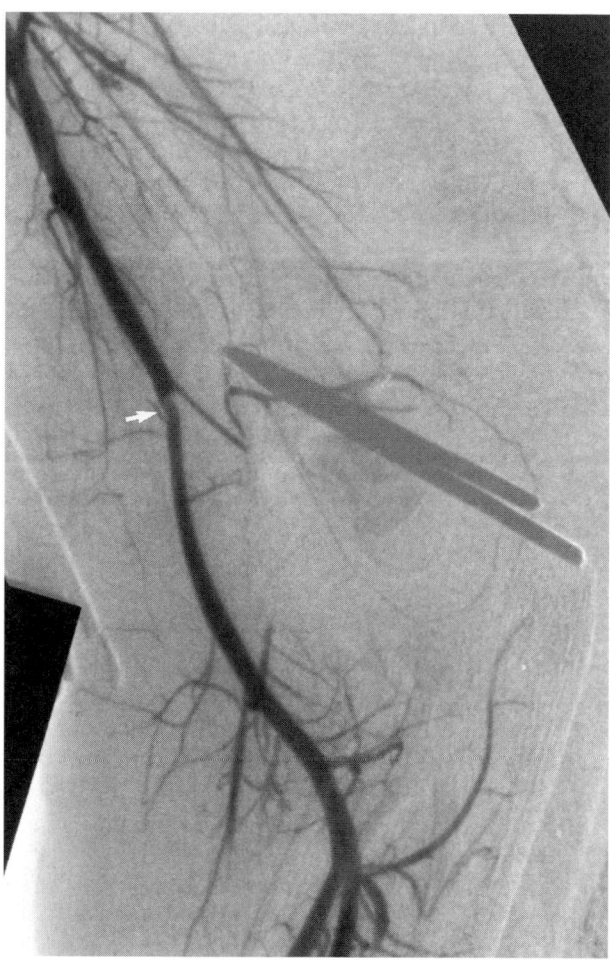

D

Figure 54-15. (A) Severely displaced supracondylar fracture. (B) Selective left brachial arteriogram after closed reduction and internal fixation of the fracture shows an occluded distal brachial artery (*arrow*) with collateral circulation about the elbow reconstituting the distal vessels. (C) The occluded segment was carefully crossed with a small-caliber wire and then an infusion catheter. (D) Uroki-

nase infusion resulted in lysis of the thrombosis and reperfusion of the forearm via the brachial artery despite the presence of an intimal injury (*arrow*). (From Cairns RA, MacKenzie WG, Culham JAG. Urokinase treatment of forearm ischemia complicating supracondylar fracture of the humerus in three children. Pediatr Radiol 1993;23:391–394. Used with permission.)

and extensive pulmonary artery thrombosis. There has also been bleeding from recent surgical sites infused locally, but the occluded vessel was opened despite this expected complication. Thrombosis can occur around the indwelling catheters and is the major argument in favor of concurrent heparinization.

Foreign-Body Removal

Modern medicine, with its complex monitoring systems, indwelling catheters, and interventional radiology, is associated with an increase in intravascular foreign bodies. These may be catheter fragments, pieces of guidewires, electrodes, or ventriculoatrial shunt

tubing. Large intravascular fragments are believed to pose a risk of thrombosis, hemorrhage, and arrhythmia. Snares, deflectable guidewires, wire baskets, and intravascular forceps may be used to retrieve these objects.[43,44]

Complications: General Considerations

Complications that relate to a specific technique are dealt with in the appropriate sections. Since any interventional procedure may be difficult and prolonged, care must be taken to prevent hypothermia, overhydration with fluids, or excessive doses of contrast or anesthetic agents. Most infants can tolerate 4 ml/kg of contrast, whereas children over 6 months can tolerate 6 ml/kg if it is delivered as several injections spread out over time. Hydration should be maintained with intravenous fluids if doses this large have been used. A child with a kidney replaced by tumor is likely to develop tubular injury in the healthy kidney with smaller doses because it is subjected to the bulk of the contrast load. Fortunately, few of these children require angiographic investigation. Prolonged procedures are associated with an increased likelihood of vascular thrombosis or embolism.

Children are probably more susceptible to radiation and will carry the risk through their reproductive years and beyond. Care must therefore be taken to minimize radiation exposure. However, this is seldom considered in the design of catheterization laboratories or in the risks of interventional procedures.

Devices or materials implanted into children may be there for 70 or 80 years and therefore must be biologically safe. New materials or those with uncertain safety should be used with caution and then only for strong indications when no alternative exists. For these reasons, the author is reluctant to use cyanoacrylate adhesives in children; these substances also pose a hazard to the staff in the laboratory.

New Directions

Since the last edition of this book there have been dramatic changes in diagnostic imaging and intervention, and it is impossible to predict even the near future. Procedures currently being evaluated in adults and in experiments will probably become adapted to children, including the percutaneous insertion of central lines and the creation of portocaval anastomoses. Endovascular stents will become more useful as smaller sizes and better-tolerated materials are developed, and these will be particularly useful in making pulmonary artery dilatation a safer and more effective procedure.[34] Atherectomy devices or lasers will probably be used for lesions such as the fibrointimal proliferation that develops on vascular grafts or in stents and may also be applicable to coarctation or recoarctation of the aorta once wall structure is better understood with the aid of intravascular ultrasound. Endovascular stenting of the neonatal ductus may replace the surgical creation of aortopulmonary anastomoses. The future is indeed bright for new and creative approaches to the catheter-related diagnosis and treatment of disease.

References

1. Hubbard AM, Fellows KE. Pediatric interventional radiology: current practice and innovation. Cardiovasc Intervent Radiol 1993;16:267–274.
2. Towbin RB, Ball WS. Pediatric interventional radiology. Radiol Clin North Am 1988;26:419–440.
3. Burrows PE. Variations in the vascular supply to infantile hepatic hemangioendotheliomas. Radiology 1991;181:631–632.
4. Barlow B, Rottenberg RW, Santulli TV. Angiographic diagnosis and treatment of bleeding by selective embolization following pelvic fracture in children. J Pediatr Surg 1975;10:939–942.
5. Cohen AM, Doershuk CF, Stem RC. Bronchial artery embolization to control hemoptysis in cystic fibrosis. Radiology 1990;175:401–405.
6. Fellows KE, Khaw KT, Schuster S, et al. Bronchial artery embolization in cystic fibrosis: technique and long term results. J Pediatr 1979;95:959–963.
7. Fellows KE, Hoffer FA, Markowitz RI, et al. Multiple collaterals to hepatic hemangioendotheliomas and arteriovenous malformations: effect on embolization. Radiology 1991;181:813–818.
8. Radanovic B, Simunic S, Stojanovic J, et al. Therapeutic embolization of aneurysmal bone cyst. Cardiovasc Intervent Radiol 1990;12:313–316.
9. DeRosa GP, Graziano GP, Scott J. Arterial embolization of aneurysmal bone cyst of the lumbar spine: a report of two cases. J Bone Joint Surg 1990;72:777–780.
10. Keller FS, Coyle M, Rosch J, et al. Percutaneous renal ablation in patients with endstage renal disease: alternative to surgical nephrectomy. Radiology 1986;159:447–451.
11. Kumpe DA, Rumack CM, Pretorius DH, et al. Partial splenic embolization in children with hypersplenism. Radiology 1985;155:357–362.
12. Dubois JM, Soban GH, DeFrost Y, et al. Soft-tissue venous malformations in children: percutaneous sclerotherapy with Ethibloc. Radiology 1991;180:195–198.
13. Burrows PE, Mulliken JB, Fellows KE, et al. Childhood hemangiomas and vascular malformations: angiographic differentiation. AJR 1983;141:483–488.
14. Wright KC, Loh G, Wallace S, et al. Experimental evaluation of ethanol-Ethiodol for transcatheter renal embolization. Cardiovasc Intervent Radiol 1990;13:309–313.
15. Takebayashi S, Hosaka M, Ishizuka E, et al. Arteriovenous malformations of the kidneys: ablation with alcohol. AJR 1988;150:587–590.
16. Gomes AS, Mali WP, Oppenheim WL. Embolization therapy in the management of congenital arteriovenous malformations. Radiology 1982;144:41–49.
17. Widlus DM, Murray RR, White RI, et al. Congenital arteriovenous malformations: tailored embolotherapy. Radiology 1988;169:511–516.
18. Nanni GS, Hawkins IF Jr, Orak JK. Control of hypertension by ethanol renal ablation. Radiology 1983;148:51–54.
19. Anderson JH, Wallace S, Gianturco C, et al. "Mini" Gianturco stainless steel coils for transcatheter vascular occlusion. Radiology 1979;132:301–303.
20. White RI, Kaufman SL, Barth KH, et al. Embolotherapy with detachable silicone balloons: technique and clinical results. Radiology 1979;131:619–627.
21. Lock JE, Cockerham JT, Keane JF, et al. Transcatheter umbrella closure of congenital heart defects. Circulation 1987;75:593–599.
22. Castaneda-Zuniga WR, Galliani CA, Rysavy J. "Spiderlon": a new device for simple, fast arterial and venous occlusion. AJR 1981;136:627–628.
23. Janik JS, Culham JAG, Filler RM, et al. Balloon embolization of a bleeding gastroduodenal artery in a one year old child. Pediatrics 1981;67:671–674.

24. Lock JE, Keane JF, Fellows KE. Diagnostic and interventional catheterization in congenital heart disease. Boston: Martinus Nijhoff, 1987:126–133.
25. Lois JF, Gomes AS, Smith DC, et al. Systemic-to-pulmonary collateral vessels and shunts: treatment with embolization. Radiology 1988;169:671–676.
26. Perry SB, Keane JF, Lock JE. Interventional catheterization in pediatric congenital and acquired heart disease. Am J Cardiol 1988;61:109G–117G.
27. Culham JAG, Izukawa T, Burns JE, et al. Embolization of a Blalock-Taussig shunt in a child. AJR 1981;137:413–415.
28. Goergen SK, Sacharias NR. Pulmonary arteriovenous malformations: pathology, clinical features and treatment with balloon and coil occlusion. Australas Radiol 1992;36:222–229.
29. Stanley P, Hieshima G, Mehringer M. Percutaneous transluminal angioplasty for pediatric renovascular hypertension. Radiology 1984;153:101–104.
30. Robinson L, Gedroyc W, Reidy J, et al. Renal artery stenosis in children. Clin Radiol 1991;44:376–382.
31. McMullin ND, Reidy JF, Koffman CG, et al. The management of renal transplant artery stenosis in children by percutaneous transluminal angioplasty. Transplantation 1992;53:559–563.
32. Raynaud A, Bedrossian J, Remy P. Percutaneous transluminal angioplasty of renal transplant arterial stenoses. AJR 1986;146:853–857.
33. Rothman A, Perry SB, Keane JF, et al. Balloon dilation of branch pulmonary artery stenosis. Semin Thorac Cardiovasc Surg 1990;2:46–54.
34. O'Laughlin MP, Perry SB, Lock JE, et al. Use of endovascular stents in congenital heart disease. Circulation 1991;83:1923–1929.
35. Vince DJ, Culham G, Taylor G. Development of a prosthesis for banding of an artery capable of staged dilatation by intraluminal balloon dilator: an experimental investigation. J Thorac Cardiovasc Surg 1987;93:628–631.
36. Andrew M. Anticoagulation and thrombolysis in children. Tex Heart Inst J 1992;19:168–177.
37. Freed MD, Keane JF, Rosenthal A. The use of heparinization to prevent arterial thrombosis after percutaneous cardiac catheterization in infants and children. Circulation 1974;50:565–569.
38. Ino T, Benson LN, Freedom RM, et al. Thrombolytic therapy for femoral artery thrombosis after pediatric cardiac catheterization. Am Heart J 1988;115:633–639.
39. Ryan CA, Andrew M. Failure of thrombolytic therapy in four children with extensive thromboses. Am J Dis Child 1992;146:187–193.
40. Pritchard SL, Culham JAG, Rogers PC. Low dose fibrinolytic therapy in infants. Pediatrics 1985;106:594–598.
41. Smith PK, Miller DA, Lail S, et al. Urokinase treatment of neonatal aortoiliac thrombosis caused by umbilical artery catheterization: a case report. J Vasc Surg 1991;14:684–687.
42. Cairns RA, MacKenzie WG, Culham JAG. Urokinase treatment of forearm ischemia complicating supracondylar fracture of the humerus in three children. Pediatr Radiol 1993;23:391–394.
43. Selby JB, Tegtmeyer CJ, Bittner GM. Experience with new retrieval forceps for foreign body removal in the vascular, urinary, and biliary systems. Radiology 1990;176:535–538.
44. Yedlicka JW Jr, Carlson JE, Hunter DW, et al. Nitinol gooseneck snare for removal of foreign bodies: experimental study and clinical evaluation. Radiology 1991;178:691–693.

IX

Abscess Drainage

55

Percutaneous Treatment
of Abdominal Abscesses

PETER J. EISENBERG
STEVEN L. DAWSON

Etiology of Abdominal Abscesses

Abscess formation represents one of three possible outcomes in a patient with acute bacterial peritonitis.[1] If the size of the bacterial innoculum is relatively small or the patient's host defense mechanisms are effective, then peritonitis may occur followed by complete resolution of the acute inflammatory process. If there is massive bacterial contamination or if the patient is immunocompromised, fulminant peritonitis and death may occur. Abscess formation may be thought of as a "draw" between the host's defense mechanisms and the bacterial contaminants.

Abscess formation is the result of a specific set of events occurring within the abdomen. The physiologic flow of fluid spreads the contaminants throughout the abdomen and toward the diaphragm, allowing exposure to the greatest surface area of cell-mediated host defense mechanisms. As noted by Fry et al., the diaphragmatic fenestrations are the lymphatic channels by which macromolecules are resorbed from the peritoneum.[1] If the volume of bacteria-laden fluid exceeds the body's capability for effective clearance, then the infected fluid gravitates toward well-defined regions within the abdomen, including the subphrenic, subhepatic, and pelvic spaces, thus explaining the most common locations for abdominal abscesses.

Approximately two-thirds of abdominal abscesses occur after abdominal operations, and nearly one-third are caused by a perforated viscus (Fig. 55-1).[2]

Therapy: Surgical and Medical

Traditionally, there have been two methods of therapy for intraabdominal abscesses. Medical therapy based on antibiotic use alone is associated with a mortality rate in excess of 50 percent.[3] Although antibiotics play an important adjunctive role in the treatment of abdominal infection, they must not be the sole method of therapy and must not prevent primary surgical or radiologic drainage when signs of sepsis and clinical deterioration persist.

As noted by Gerzof et al., "percutaneous nonoperative catheter drainage is a significant departure from universally accepted but heretofore unchallenged surgical methods of operative incision and drainage for therapy of abdominal abscess."[4] The basic tenets of surgical abscess drainage were stated by Ochsner, DeBakey, and Murray in 1938: drainage should be direct, simple, and avoid unnecessary contamination of uninvolved areas.[5] Image-guided abscess drainage provides a rapid means of therapy,[6] and percutaneous drainage routes usually closely parallel the specific operative approaches suggested for abscesses in similar locations.

Percutaneous catheter therapy and open surgical drainage should not be considered as two mutually exclusive therapies. Percutaneous drainage is the treatment of choice for abdominal abscesses, but when surgery will still be required, preoperative catheter drainage will allow improvements of the patient's condition to permit surgery in the most favorable physiologic condition.

Percutaneous Therapy

Percutaneous therapy of abdominal abscesses begins with establishing the diagnosis of an abscess. Although this may seem obvious, it is not a simple matter, particularly in the postoperative patient, in whom signs and symptoms of infection from any of several anatomic sites are common and not specific. Computed tomography (CT) and ultrasound characteristics of abscesses are well known but not specific. In fact, the differential diagnosis may include other processes, such as hematoma, seroma, biloma, lymphocele, primary and

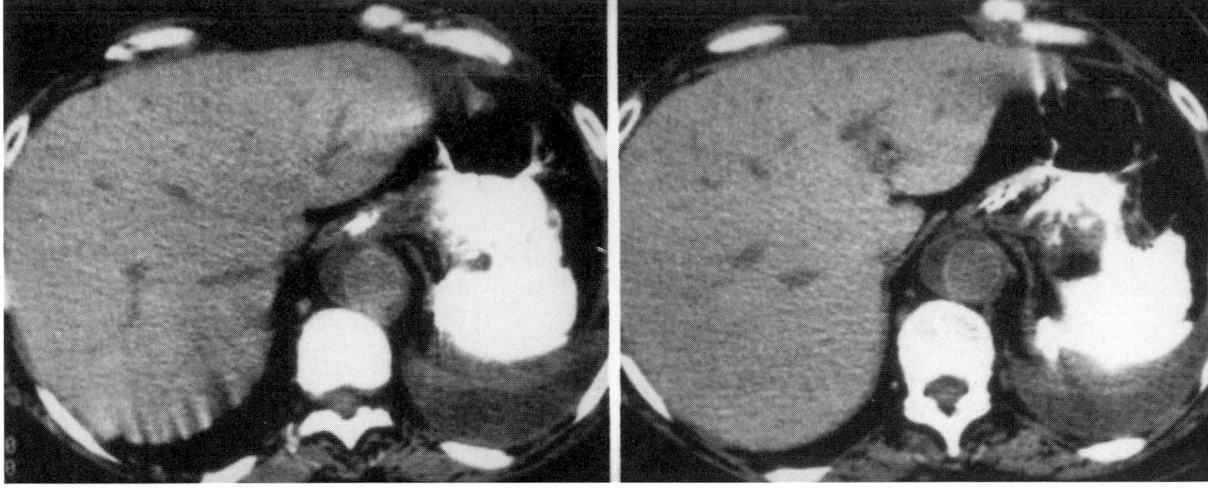

A

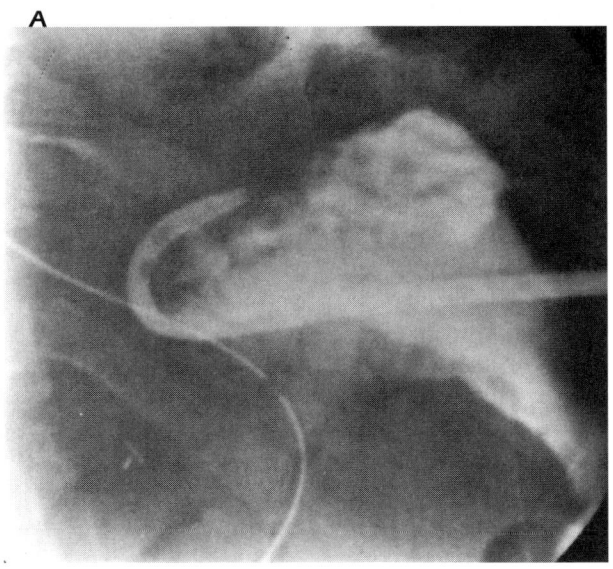

B

Figure 55-1. This 54-year-old woman developed a subphrenic abscess after repair of a thoracoabdominal aneurysm, with splenectomy. (A) CT scans obtained 5 days after surgery. The *left* image shows contrast leaking from the gastric fundus into the subphrenic space. On the *right*, a widely patent gastric perforation is seen in the posterior fundal wall with accumulation of dense gastrograffin in the left subphrenic space. (B) A 16 French catheter was placed into the collection, and contrast injection shows the left subphrenic space. (C) Lateral (*left*) and anteroposterior (*right*) films after contrast injection show opacification of the stomach via the posterior fundal perforation, with the catheter in good position. The patient was maintained on bowel rest using hyperalimentation and nasogastric suction with subsequent gastrostomy tube placement. (D) Right posterior oblique spot film 3 months after the initial study shows a smaller communication with the gastric fundus with no residual abscess collection in the subphrenic space. Drainage ceased and the communication closed 10 days after this film. The catheter was removed.

secondary malignancies, pancreatic pseudocysts, and fluid-filled loops of bowel.

Fever and elevated white count are seen in postoperative infections in the immunocompetent patient. Physical examination may be localizing but can be limited because antibiotic therapy in the febrile patient with an elevated white count can mask findings of early infection, causing a delay in the clinical diagnosis.[2]

Radiologic diagnosis of abdominal abscess has improved with the introduction of ultrasound, magnetic resonance imaging (MRI), and CT. However, conventional radiologic methods continue to be used in the patient with clinical suspicion of intraabdominal infection. The plain abdominal film is of limited value but docs provide important clinical information. One study has reported that over 70 percent of upper abdominal abscesses in 82 patients were visible in retrospect on plain abdominal radiographs but were cor-

rectly diagnosed prospectively in only 51 percent.[7] Upright views reveal the presence of intraperitoneal free air and may demonstrate extraluminal air–fluid levels. Additionally, abdominal films may demonstrate retroperitoneal air or an abdominal fluid collection with adjacent mass effect. Contrast examinations of the gastrointestinal tract are generally of limited usefulness.

The two most useful examinations to diagnose abdominal abscess are ultrasound and CT. Ultrasound has been reported to be as effective as other imaging methods in the evaluation of the abdominal abscess[3] and has the added advantages of being inexpensive, portable, quick, and free of ionizing radiation. Patients who are obese, who have an ileus, or who have extensive surgical wounds may be difficult to examine.[2] Ultrasound is better than CT in evaluating the subphrenic and perihepatic spaces, and it is the screening

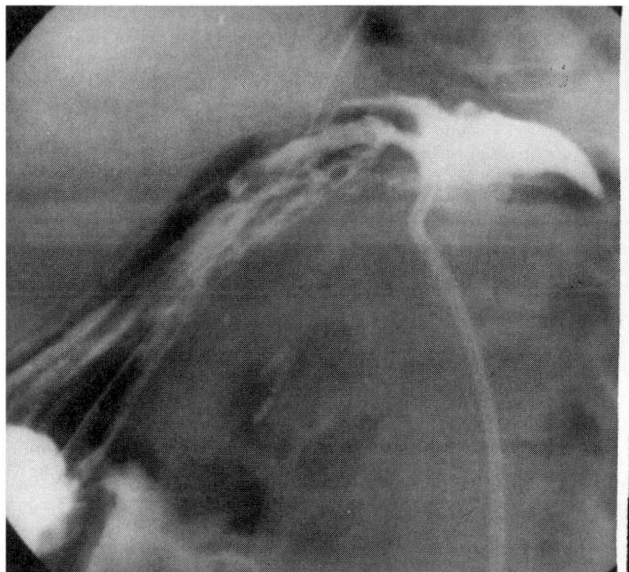
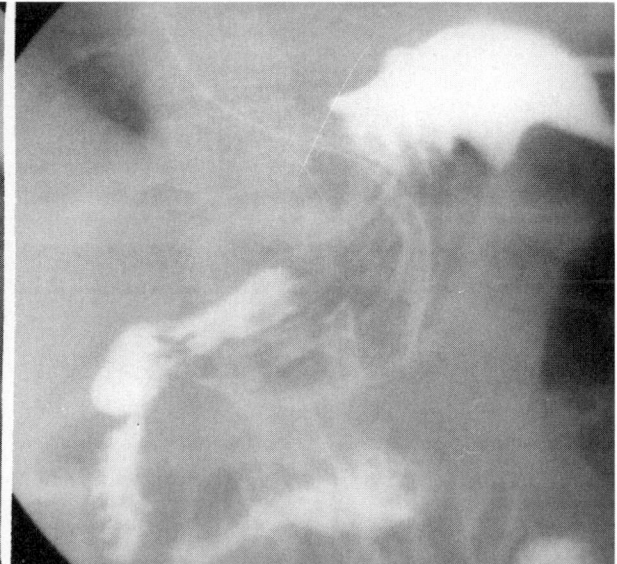

C

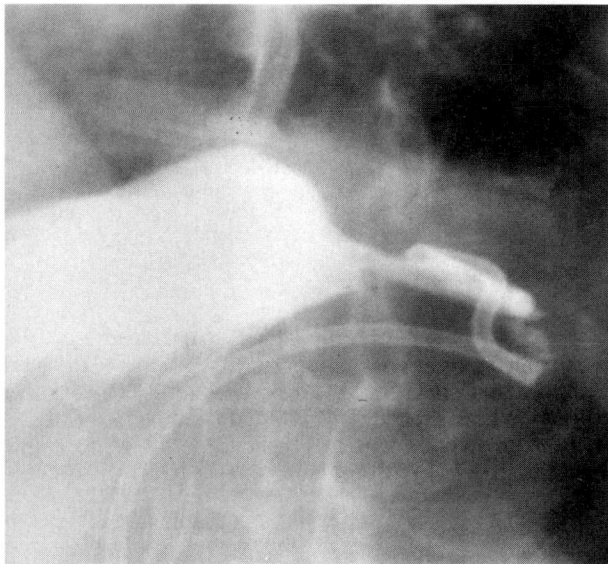

D

modality of choice in thin patients, in children, and in those with vague, nonlocalizing clinical findings.[8]

Sonographically, some abscesses appear anechoic with good posterior through transmission. However, bloody or cellular fluid can appear as mixed echogenicity, or the collection may actually appear highly echogenic.[9]

Ultrasound is particularly useful in evaluating multiloculated collections. Real-time sonographic monitoring has been advocated to document complete or nearly complete evacuation of the abscess after initial drainage. In 33 percent of patients with complex or multiseptated abscesses, sonography revealed residual fluid that required an additional drainage catheter for complete evacuation.[10]

Although ultrasound is particularly useful in selected cases, CT is the preferred method to diagnose abdominal abscesses. With complete bowel opacification, accurate diagnosis is possible in over 95 percent of patients with abscesses.[11] In addition, because CT allows for the guidance of percutaneous drainage, it is an important therapeutic tool.

The appearance of an abscess on CT depends to some extent on location. In the liver, for example, abscesses may be low attenuation with respect to either nonenhanced or enhanced liver parenchyma, with Hounsfield measurements ranging from 2 to 36, reflecting their varying contents.[12] However, abscesses may appear of homogeneous soft tissue attenuation.[13] In fact, the composition and maturity of any abdominal fluid collection are so variable that, unless an extraluminal air–fluid level is seen, there are no absolute indications that a collection is infected. Any extraluminal collection is potentially an abscess.

Imaging studies should be considered complementary to diagnostic needle aspiration. Needle aspiration can confirm the presence of a collection, determine whether that collection is infected, and determine whether the material present in the collection is amenable to catheter drainage.[14]

As an example, consider the case of a large symptomatic hematoma (Fig. 55-2). The ability to achieve successful catheter drainage depends on the fluidity of the blood, which may not be accurately portrayed by CT or ultrasound images. The decision to pursue catheter drainage must be based on the results of needle aspiration.[14]

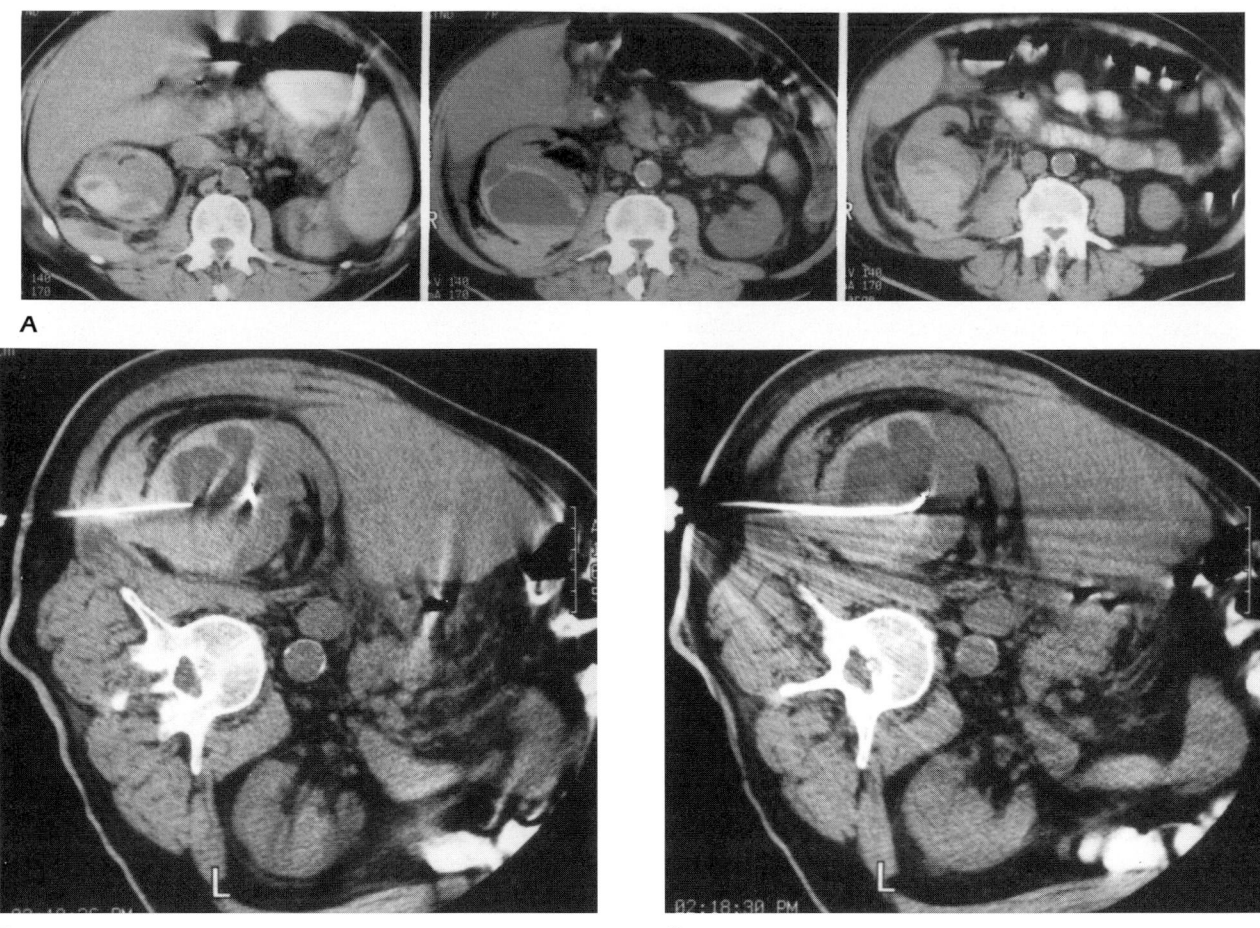

Figure 55-2. (A) A 52-year-old patient on anticoagulants, with complex right renal and posterior perirenal hematoma demonstrated on CT scan. The collection is loculated and consists of both fluid and fresh blood components, with associated perirenal edema. Temperature and white count were elevated. (B) With the patient in the left lateral decubi-

tus position, the right renal cortical collection was aspirated using a 22-gauge needle, and frank pus was obtained. (C) After diagnostic aspiration, a percutaneous drainage was performed via a posterolateral approach, with aspiration of bloody pus. Drainage continued for 8 days, after which the catheter was removed. (Courtesy of Michael J. Lee, M.D.)

This chapter considers sites and etiologies of specific intraabdominal abscesses and discusses interventional techniques specific to these conditions. Broadly applicable descriptions of the appropriate imaging guidance for abscess drainage, tools and techniques, catheter care, and management of fistulas can be found in Chapter 56, "Percutaneous Drainage of Pelvic Abscesses and Fluid Collections."

Morbidity and Mortality: Comparative Results

Despite the development and use of powerful antibiotics, intraabdominal abscesses are still associated with high morbidity and mortality. Delayed diagnosis and subsequent multisystem organ failure, inadequate localization of the abscess before drainage, and poor host defense mechanisms are cited as the etiologies for the failure of decline in morbidity and mortality.[1] Clinical results of large published series indicate that percutaneous abscess drainage results in a better overall outcome with fewer complications, lower morbidity, and lower mortality compared with surgery. Johnson et al. evaluated 27 patients treated with percutaneous abscess drainage and 43 patients treated with surgical drainage and noted that the rate of complications (4 versus 16 percent), the rate of inadequate drainage (11 versus 21 percent), and the duration of drainage (17 versus 29 days) were lower in those patients treated percutaneously than in those treated surgically.[15]

There are a number of reasons why percutaneous

catheter drainage may be associated with a lower rate of complications and shorter postdrainage hospitalization than traditional open surgical drainage. As noted by Brolin et al., patients treated with open surgical drainage had their abscesses diagnosed via imaging studies (CT or ultrasound) in only 51 percent of cases, as compared with 100 percent of those patients treated via percutaneous catheter drainage.[3] In addition, open surgical drainage via midline incision has a greater potential for spreading contamination throughout the abdomen than does percutaneous drainage via the direct retroperitoneal approach suggested for treatment of subphrenic and other abdominal abscesses.

With percutaneous drainage a shorter posthospitalization stay would also be anticipated. Patients are able to recuperate faster because they have not had general anesthesia and can be discharged from the hospital with small catheters in place, which can be cared for on an outpatient basis.[3] Other contributing factors may include the more rapid institution of appropriate antibiotic regimens in those patients who have their abscesses diagnosed via percutaneous means.[2,16]

Liver Abscesses

In the 1938 review by Ochsner et al., the most frequent cause of pyogenic hepatic abscess was pyelophlebitis secondary to acute appendicitis. Mortality was high because surgical drainage transgressed either the pleural or peritoneal space.[5] Pyogenic liver abscess now more commonly results from prior abdominal surgery, trauma, neoplastic disease, biliary tract disease, or bacteremia in immunocompromised patients.[17] Percutaneous therapy of pyogenic liver abscesses is considered the treatment of choice.[15]

The ultrasound appearance of hepatic abscesses is variable, ranging from anechoic with marked posterior acoustic enhancement to echogenic with posterior shadowing. The walls may be well defined or indistinct and may be irregular, thick, or imperceptible.[18] Septations, fluid–fluid levels, and debris have all been noted.

The CT appearance is equally varied and may be nonspecific. Only when gas is detected within an intrahepatic fluid collection can a definitive imaging diagnosis of abscess be made, but this occurs in only approximately 19 percent of pyogenic liver abscesses.[19,20] Pyogenic liver abscesses tend to be of lower attenuation than surrounding liver, but some peripheral enhancement may occur because of an inflammatory rind surrounding the abscess. The abscess may be more easily detected and unsuspected additional abscesses may be discovered after contrast administration; however,

according to Halvorsen et al., no abscess was detected on scans performed only after contrast administration.[19]

Immunosuppressed patients may have multifocal, tiny abscesses resulting from unusual organisms such as *Candida*. These collections generally are not amenable to percutaneous catheter drainage and typically are associated with a poor prognosis.[21]

The differential diagnosis of hepatic abscess includes simple and complicated cysts, necrotic malignancies, echinococcal cysts, hematoma, and primary or metastatic cystadenocarcinoma.[18]

Superficial abscesses in the left lobe and caudal aspect of the right lobe may be easily approached perpendicularly in the axial plane. Abscesses located high in the dome of the liver may require cephalocaudal angulation to avoid the pleura and may be approached with real-time ultrasound guidance or by CT using the triangulation approach.[22] The entry site for aspiration and drainage is chosen according to the location of the abscess. Treatment begins with diagnostic needle aspiration using a 22-gauge needle. In some collections, the fluid is too viscous for aspiration through a 22-gauge needle. If no fluid is obtained and the needle is in the proper location, an 18-gauge needle is used.

After the skin and subcutaneous tissue are infiltrated with 1 percent Xylocaine, the needle is inserted in a sterile fashion. A small amount of fluid is removed and sent for Gram stain, culture, and sensitivity. Gram stain should reveal both white blood cells and bacteria if an abscess is present. If bowel has inadvertently been entered or if the patient is severely immunocompromised, bacteria without white blood cells will be seen on Gram stain. White cells without bacteria implies a "sterile abscess." These collections should be drained if they are symptomatic.

Once the presence of an abscess has been confirmed, catheter placement may be accomplished using either the modified Seldinger or trocar technique. If the Seldinger technique is chosen, a floppy-tipped guidewire is coiled within the cavity and the percutaneous tract is enlarged using fascial dilators. The trocar technique requires specifically designed catheters that include a sharp metal stiffener (Fig. 55-3). Catheter insertion is monitored by CT, ultrasound, or fluoroscopy as the catheter is coiled within the abscess cavity in as dependent a position as possible.[10]

To reduce inadvertent contamination of intervening spaces, all catheter side holes must be within the cavity. Pneumothorax and empyema may be avoided by locating the pleural reflection in its anterior and lateral margins (usually the 8th and 10th intercostal spaces, respectively).[17] Once the catheter is in satisfactory position, the cavity is lavaged gently with saline

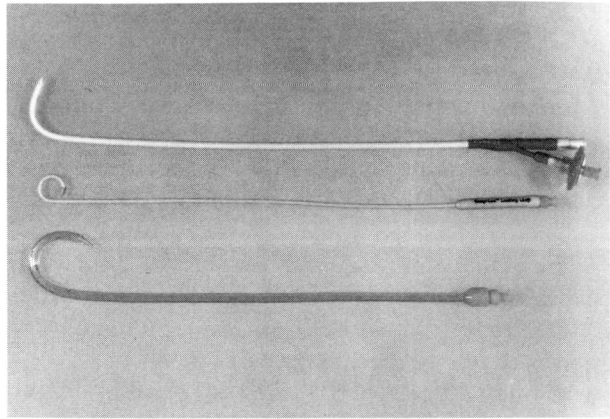

A

B

Figure 55-3. Representative catheters for percutaneous abscess drainage. (A) *Top:* 14 French vanSonnenberg sump catheter (Medi-Tech). *Middle:* 8.5 French Dawson-Mueller drainage catheter (Cook, Inc.). *Bottom:* 16 French Mueller drainage catheter (Cook, Inc.). (B). Closeup of the catheter tips shown in (A) showing the design of the tip and the insertion stiffener and stylet used for trocar insertion. Each of the catheters is designed for primary trocar insertion but can be used in the Seldinger fashion if the central needle is removed. The vanSonnenberg catheter (*right*) is nonlocking but contains a sump lumen and is available in 12 and 14 French sizes. The Dawson-Mueller catheter (*middle*) is a Cope loop self-retaining catheter and is currently available in 8.5 through 14 French sizes. The Mueller catheter (*left*) is non-self-retaining and does not have a sump lumen. It is available in 8 to 16 French sizes.

to remove residual debris. The catheter is then attached to gravity drainage.

An alternative form of therapy consisting of needle aspiration combined with systemic antibiotic treatment without the use of an indwelling drainage catheter was first described in 1953 and has more recently been proposed as an effective form of therapy for he-

patic abscesses.[23,24] In a series of 24 patients treated by this method, Baek et al. reported that unilocular and mostly hypoechoic abscesses were more likely to heal completely (86 and 77 percent, respectively).[23] Fifty-six percent of multiloculated abscesses were treated effectively in this way, although they required a slightly greater average number of aspirations than unilocular abscesses.

Although the duration of drainage is longer in hepatic abscesses that communicate with the biliary tree than in those without intrahepatic biliary communication, there is no significant difference in the cure rate between these groups of patients.[25]

Numerous studies have demonstrated both the efficacy and safety of percutaneous catheter drainage for pyogenic hepatic abscess. Success rates range from 81 to 90 percent.[26-28] Fifty percent of patients treated percutaneously have a shorter hospital stay than patients treated surgically.[29] A number of factors contribute to unsuccessful treatment, including the presence of large amounts of viscous material, attempted drainage or infected metastases,[10] the presence of multiple intraabdominal as well as intrahepatic abscesses, retained intrahepatic foreign bodies, and undrained loculated collections.

Numerous authors have noted that multiseptated abscesses are amenable to percutaneous drainage because many of the locules intercommunicate. In fact, true septations are felt to be rare in liver abscesses.[27] In the series by Bernadino et al., 83 percent of patients were successfully treated using a single catheter, with no patient requiring more than two simultaneously placed catheters.[29] Mortality following percutaneous drainage of a solitary abscess is generally in the range of 3 to 4 percent. This figure compares favorably to that of surgery, which has an associated mortality of approximately 9 percent in the case of a solitary abscess and a 36 percent mortality for multiple abscesses.[27]

Echinococcal Abscesses

Echinococcus granulosis causes the most common form of hydatid disease in humans, resulting in benign cystic disease of the liver. Until recently, percutaneous treatment of echinococcal cysts was considered to be contraindicated because spillage or leakage of the cyst contents into the peritoneal cavity could result in anaphylactic shock or the dissemination of viable scolices throughout the peritoneum.[13]

Because of the widespread occurrence of hydatid disease and the occasional absence of a pathognomonic imaging appearance (multiloculated cysts with daughter cysts and scolices), there have been a number of inadvertent as well as intentional aspirations of hydatid cysts.[30] Mueller et al. first reported the successful drainage of a recurrent hepatic hydatid cyst.[31]

Although aspiration and catheter drainage are not suggested as the primary means of diagnosis or treatment in hydatid disease, they may be indicated if there is suspicion of recurrent disease after surgery or in complex type IV lesions.[30] Using ultrasound or CT for guidance, a transparenchymal approach should be used to minimize the chance of leakage of cyst contents. After microscopic demonstration of scolices, the cyst cavity may be gently aspirated and then irrigated with a scolicidal agent such as hypertonic saline, 80 percent alcohol, or 0.5 percent silver nitrate.[32] Formalin is not suggested as a sclerosant because of the risk of systemic toxicity and the risk of sclerosing cholangitis in the case of bile duct communication.[30] Sclerotherapy has successfully been performed using 95 percent alcohol with no major complications and no cyst recurrence during a 12-month follow-up.[33] Although hydatid cysts may be treated with needle aspiration and sclerosants, drainage catheters may be left in situ and removed when repeat cyst fluid analysis reveals no living parasites.

Amebic Abscesses

Amebic abscess, caused by the parasite *Entamoeba*, represents the most frequent nonenteric manifestation of amebiasis and is seen in up to 9 percent of patients with amebiasis,[34] accounting for 42 percent of hospital admissions in this group. The diagnosis of amebiasis may be established with serologic studies in more than 90 percent of cases.

Medical therapy using metronidazole or chloroquine is effective therapy in virtually all cases of hepatic amebic abscess.[35] However, percutaneous catheter drainage of amebic liver abscess may be done to differentiate a pyogenic from an amebic abscess, as adjunctive therapy in the 5 to 15 percent of patients refractory to medical therapy,[36] in the case of persistent pain and imminent rupture, because of deterioration while on medical therapy, in the 2 to 15 percent of patients with initially negative serologies, in the patient who is noncompliant with medical therapy, and in the patient with a left lobe abscess (where rupture into the pleura, bronchi, or pericardium may occur and is associated with a mortality of 30 percent).[34] Dramatic cure may be accomplished in well over 90 percent of these patients. An additional indication for percutaneous catheter therapy is in the patient with a perforated amebic abscess, which is associated with a mortality of 23 to 42 percent.[37–39]

In pregnant patients, in whom antiamebic drugs can cross the placenta, the role of catheter drainage is uncertain because percutaneous drainage alone, without concurrent amebicidal therapy, has not been shown to be curative.[35]

Fluid aspiration alone frequently is not diagnostic of amebic abscess. The classic anchovy-paste-colored material is recovered in only 50 percent of patients, and purulent material is obtained in the remainder. Gram stain usually reveals abundant white cells without organisms, simulating a sterile pyogenic abscess. Biopsy of the wall may demonstrate active trophozoites in the capsule but not within the abscess cavity.[34]

Amebicidal drugs are given to supplement catheter drainage. If the abscess is located cephalad within the right lobe, the most frequent site for a solitary amebic abscess, it may be safest to perform the drainage under CT guidance with the patient in the prone position using the triangulation technique to avoid transgressing the pleura.[22]

Splenic Abscesses

Splenic abscess is a relatively uncommon clinical problem. Chun et al.[40] group the various etiologies into four categories: (1) pyogenic infections, most frequently related to endocarditis, (2) traumatic causes, (3) sickle cell disease, and (4) secondary to spread of inflammation from an adjacent focus. The clinical manifestations are nonspecific and include left upper quadrant pain and tenderness, splenomegaly, fever, and leukocytosis. Localizing signs may be present, but the classic triad of fever, splenic enlargement, and left upper quadrant pain is seen in less than 50 percent of cases. If the infectious process does not involve the capsule of the spleen, only vague symptoms may predominate.

The ultrasound and CT appearances of splenic abscesses are variable. On ultrasound, collections may be hypo- to hyperechoic.[41] On CT, abscesses are usually low attenuation.[42] Untreated splenic abscesses are associated with an 80 to 100 percent mortality rate.[43,44] Surgical drainage or splenectomy is associated with a 14 to 30 percent mortality rate.[42,45] Because of the concern about infection and subsequent sepsis in asplenic patients, percutaneous drainage is a desirable form of therapy because it preserves the spleen.[46] Yet, before 1986, only eight percutaneous splenic drainages had been reported (Fig. 55-4).[47]

Because of the vascularity of the spleen, clotting abnormalities should be corrected before interventional procedures are done.[47] The access route must avoid transgressing surrounding structures such as colon, kidney, pleura, diaphragm, pancreas, and surrounding vascular structures. It is crucial to determine the

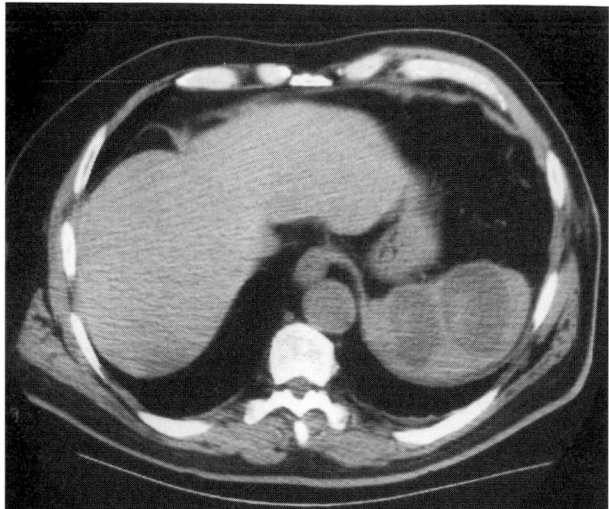

A

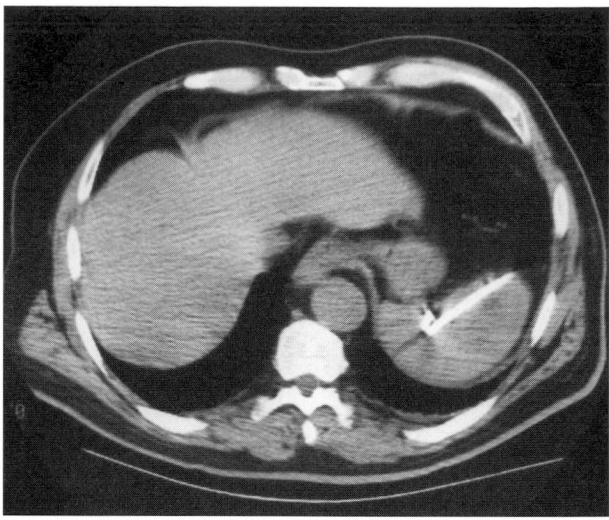

B

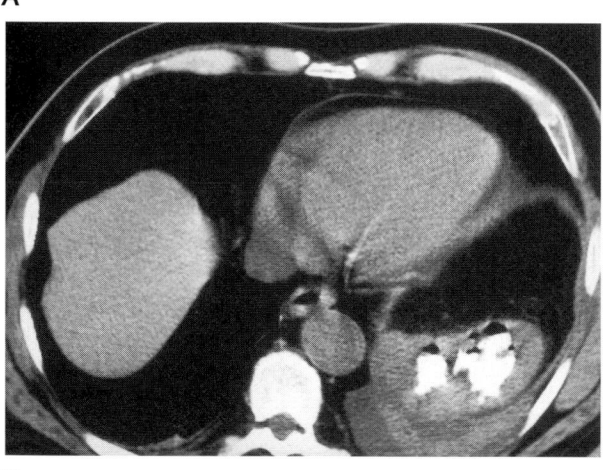

C

Figure 55-4. A 74-year-old man with severe bilateral carotid stenoses and three-vessel coronary disease. Fever to
106°F developed while he was awaiting carotid surgery.
(A) CT scan shows a bilobed central splenic collection. Diagnostic aspiration, without drainage, revealed *Propionibacte-
rium* sp. The collection recurred within 4 days, and catheter
drainage was performed using a transsplenic trocar technique. (B) An 8.5 French self-retaining catheter was placed.
(C) CT image slightly cephalad to (B) obtained 5 days after
drainage shows communication of the two locules. The patient did well, and the catheter was removed on the 10th
postdrainage day. Carotid and coronary surgery was performed after the abscess resolved. The etiology of this unusual infection was hematogenous spread from psoriasis.

position of the lung in full inspiration before drainage
to avoid pleural contamination or pneumothorax.[41] In
general, one should choose the route that traverses the
least amount of normal splenic tissue. However, if the
collection is very peripheral, use of this approach may
not provide secure catheter purchase; in these cases,
aspiration using a small trocar catheter can still be performed.

After diagnostic aspiration, drainage may be accomplished with either the Seldinger or trocar technique.
After a drainage catheter is placed, the abscess cavity
may be manually decompressed and placed to gravity
drainage. The catheter is removed when the drainage
has decreased to 3 to 5 ml per day.

The rate of successful percutaneous drainage of the
spleen is slightly lower than that reported for drainage
in other organs (76 versus 80 to 90 percent). These
lower rates may be related to multiloculation of the
abscess and the associated phlegmon.[47] Drainage of a
unilocular hematogenous splenic abscess carries low
morbidity. However, complex splenic abscesses more

often require surgery for successful treatment.[48] Mi-
croabscesses related to fungal disease in immunocompromised patients and tuberculosis are less amenable
to percutaneous therapy.

Pancreatic Disease

One of the most serious complications of pancreatitis
is sepsis as a result of infected parenchymal necrosis,
or secondary infection of a phlegmon, fluid collection,
or pseudocyst.[49] Mortality is directly related to the
form of therapy chosen and approaches 100 percent
when adequate and early therapy is not employed.
Mortality rates of 0 percent in patients treated surgically with less than 30 percent gland necrosis and up
to 67 percent in patients with total or near total gland
necrosis have been reported.[50] The success of percutaneous drainage depends to a large extent on the form
of complicated pancreatic disease present. Although
few doubt that survival is unlikely in patients with ex-

tensive necrosis unless some form of operative intervention is undertaken,[51] patients with loculated fluid collections and pseudocysts are effectively treated with percutaneous drainage. However, in many cases, pancreatic abscess drainage is used to improve the patient's status before subsequent surgery.

Pseudocysts

Percutaneous drainage of pseudocysts, which are reported to occur in 2 to 18 percent of cases of pancreatic inflammatory disease, remains controversial.[52] Although pseudocysts resolve spontaneously in up to 20 percent of cases, the numbers that do so decrease after the first 6 weeks after formation. Approximately 20 percent of patients may develop severe complications such as rupture, hemorrhage, infection, or obstruction. Infected pseudocysts are treated emergently and are considered to be abscesses associated with fistulas.[53] Indications for draining noninfected pseudocysts are more complex but include persistent abdominal pain, biliary or intestinal obstruction, pseudocysts over 5 cm in diameter, and increase in size or failure to decrease in size over a 2- to 6-week period of observation.[52,54]

Imaging alone does not allow one to distinguish between infected and uninfected collections. Infected pancreatic fluid collections and pseudocysts are well marginated, homogeneous masses of low attenuation. Bubbles of gas may be seen on 50 percent of cases, but this does not necessarily signify infection because gas may arise from fistulazation to the gastrointestinal tract.[55]

Whereas the thickness of the pseudocyst wall is of prognostic significance in surgical therapy, this is not the case in percutaneous treatment, and a thin wall should not be considered a contraindication to percutaneous drainage.

Catheter insertion may be accomplished using either tandem needle trocar insertion or the Seldinger techniques. The choice of catheter size and whether to use a single- or double-lumen sump catheter for drainage are determined by the viscosity and consistency of the aspirated fluid. Broad-spectrum antibiotics are employed either before or immediately after aspiration.

Although most patients with pseudocysts can be treated effectively with a single catheter, the radiologist should not hesitate to place additional catheters when follow-up imaging studies reveal residual fluid collections (Fig. 55-5).[53]

The choice of drainage route is controversial. The "conventional" route is a direct transperitoneal or retroperitoneal approach.[56] However, pseudocysts are frequently surrounded by bowel, liver, spleen, kidney, and vascular structures, which necessitate the use of other access routes. Numerous authors have demonstrated the safety and efficacy of the transgastric, transduodenal, transhepatic, and transsplenic routes for achieving prompt external decompression and drainage with equally successful drainage.[53,57]

Various authors have performed "short-term drainage" (defined as evacuation of pseudocyst contents without placement of an indwelling drainage catheter) in patients with both infected and noninfected pseudocysts. The recurrence rate of this technique ranges from 50 to 90 percent, and this is no longer advocated as a primary mode of therapy.[52,58,59] In addition, simple aspiration may allow some pseudocyst fluid to leak from the puncture site, with resultant localized retroperitoneal, intraperitoneal, or pleural inflammatory reaction.

The success of long-term catheter drainage of pseudocysts varies from 67 percent to greater than 90 percent.[52,53] Treatment failure may be attributed to undetected and undrained remote collections, subsequent development of new collections and unrecognized loculi,[49] or an unrecognized pseudocyst-pancreatic duct fistula, resulting in recurrence after catheter removal. Freeny et al. suggest that patients who are stable and being treated nonemergently should be evaluated with endoscopic retrograde cholangiopancreatography (ERCP) in an attempt to define the relationship between the pancreatic duct and the fluid collection. Operative intervention is preferable when there is a high risk of pancreaticocutaneous fistula, such as when the fluid collection communicates with the pancreatic duct and the normal route of transpapillary drainage is compromised by stone or stricture.

Complications in pseudocyst drainage occur in approximately 13 percent of cases and consist of bacterial superinfection or colonization, minor bleeding, pleural effusion, empyema, and pneumothorax.[49,52,53] These results compare favorably with those of surgery, which is associated with a mortality of 19 to 25 percent and a major complication rate of 46 to 75 percent in acutely ill patients treated with operative external drainage and a rate of 2 to 9 percent in those patients treated on an elective basis.[54] The 10 percent rate of failed percutaneous catheter drainage compares favorably with the recurrence rate following surgery of 9 to 11 percent.[53]

The timing of catheter removal depends on clinical as well as imaging criteria. If an uninfected pseudocyst does not communicate with the pancreatic duct and drainage is over 10 ml per day, the tube is clamped for 2 to 3 days. If there is no reaccumulation, the catheter is removed.[49,58]

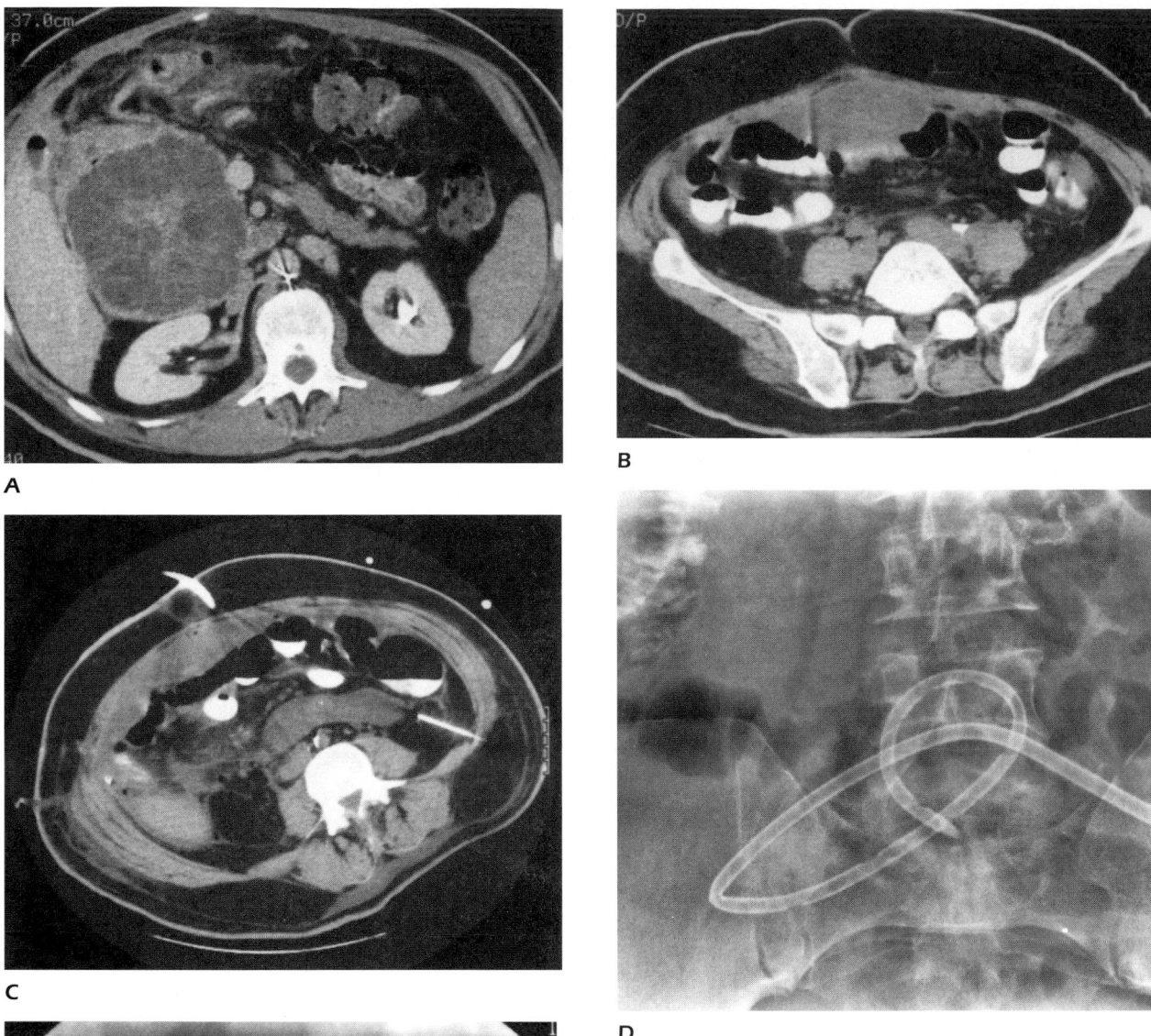

A

B

C

D

E

Figure 55-5. A 64-year-old man with a 10-cm pancreatic head mass. (A) CT arterial portography shows the complex pancreatic head mass with little obvious adjacent invasion. The patient underwent a Whipple resection. Postoperatively (not shown), the patient developed signs of abdominal infection, and CT showed five intraabdominal abscesses, all of which were treated percutaneously. (B) CT scan shows an elliptical anterior abdominal collection measuring 7 by 4 cm and displacing the adjacent bowel. (C) After catheter drainage of the anterior abdominal collection, the patient was placed into a right posterior oblique position and a left posterolateral approach was made into a pancreatiform collection in the lesser sac. The needle and catheter were directed along the axis of the collection, using the only available safe access route. (D) Postdrainage film of the catheter in the lesser sac collection shows that the tube is kinked upon itself proximal to the most proximal side hole. If the tube is left in this position, no drainage will occur, since all side holes are beyond the kink. (E) One week after initial drainages, contrast injection into the lesser sac collection shows a peripheral limb of abscess extending toward the right upper

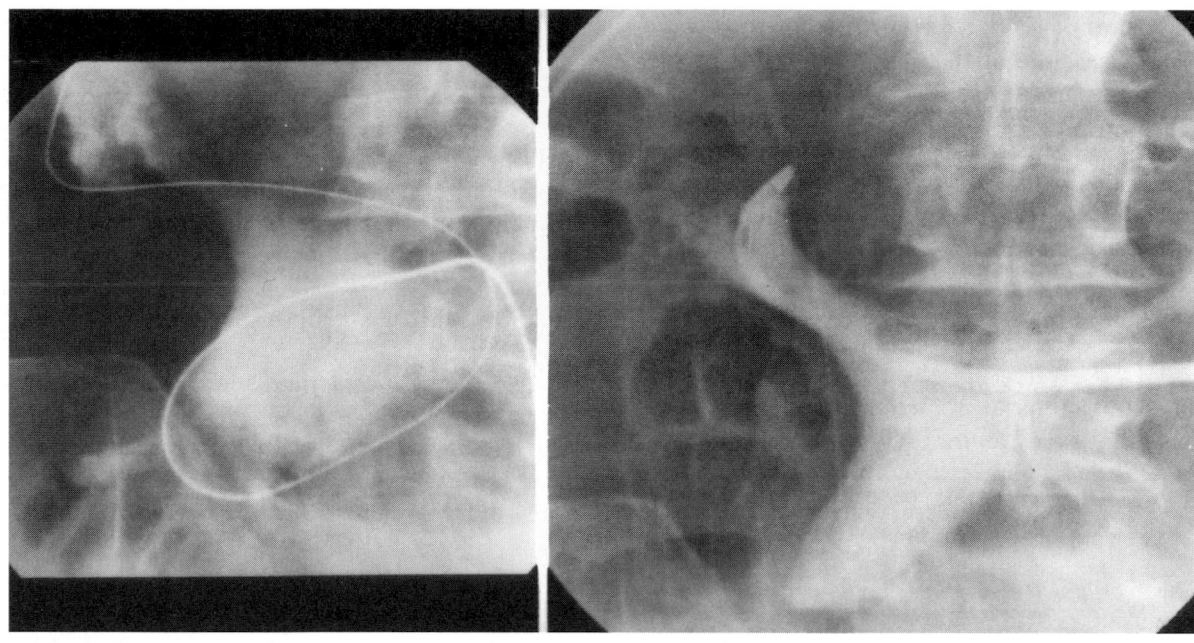

F

Figure 55-5 (continued). quadrant, with the majority of the catheter in the lesser sac collection, which is smaller. The patient was doing better but still had elevated white count and occasional fevers. (F) Guidewire manipulation into the more superior portion of the lesser sac collection allows placement of the catheter into the most superior and dependent recess. The collection completely drained from this catheter position. This case demonstrates the value of aggressive management and close clinical follow-up by the interventional team to successfully treat a seriously ill patient who was deemed unfit for further surgical exploration after his original Whipple procedure and the development of multiple intraabdominal abscesses.

Pancreatic Abscesses

Pancreatic abscesses are the greatest challenge to successful percutaneous therapy. These collections are multiseptated and multilocular and are often associated with fistulas and extensive necrotic debris.[56] Some combination of percutaneous drainage and surgical debridement is usually necessary. The patient's overall clinical status may improve after drainage of infected fluid, allowing the patient to undergo definitive surgery on an elective basis. Alternatively, surgery may be performed as the initial therapy with percutaneous drainage of residual or postoperative collections.

On CT, areas of decreased parenchymal enhancement following contrast administration correlate with surgically proven regions of necrotic pancreatic tissue.[60] Needle aspiration of these areas is performed to evaluate for infection and to choose appropriate preoperative antibiotics. Patients with infected pancreatic necrosis should be treated surgically even in the presence of drainable fluid. In the subset of patients who are too ill for surgery, significant benefit may be derived from percutaneous catheter drainage.[49]

The reported mortality rate from pancreatic abscess treated with extensive surgical debridement ranges from 0 to 67 percent, depending on the amount of necrotic pancreatic tissue present and the aggressiveness of surgical debridement.[49,56,58] Postoperative recurrence approaches 19 percent.[61] Factors such as acute respiratory distress syndrome (ARDS), pulmonary emboli, and pleural fluid collections contribute to the mortality associated with pancreatic abscess.[62]

There are multiple reasons for failure in percutaneous pancreatic abscess drainage. One of these is failure to correctly differentiate between pancreatic abscess and phlegmon. Percutaneous drainage should not be performed in the presence of phlegmon if a clearly defined abscess is not present.[63] Additional reasons for unsuccessful drainage include the use of an inadequate number of catheters to evacuate all of the loculated abscess compartments present. Lee et al. noted that in cases of complicated pancreatitis patients required an average of 1.4 catheters during their course of treatment (range, 1–10).[64]

As noted by Steiner et al., pancreatic abscesses may not only exist within the pancreatic bed itself but may extend into the lesser sac, peripancreatic, and pericolic areas.[65] The rate of successful drainage depends on where the collection resides in relation to the pancreas. Primary percutaneous drainage in central areas such as the pancreas and lesser sac is associated with a success rate of 17 percent, compared to nearly 60 percent when the collection is in peripheral areas such as the pararenal space or paracolic gutter.[64] The authors prefer to use percutaneous methods to drain peripheral collections, leaving central collections for surgical treatment. The use of larger-bore catheters (24–28 French) is essential to allow adequate evacuation of the thick fluid, pus, and debris that may collect dependently in infected pancreatic collections.[49] After surgical debridement, percutaneous drainage may be used if debridement is incomplete or if fluid reaccumulates.

Successful interventional treatment of infected pancreatic collections requires aggressive early therapy, diligence in follow-up care, and prompt evaluation of unfavorable clinical changes.[64,65] Failure of percutaneous drainage of pancreatic abscesses results from inadequate drainage of all locules, removal of the catheter before complete liquefaction of the collection, or attempted drainage of the phlegmon that is seen in acute pancreatitis but that may not be associated with drainable fluid collection.[63,64] Higher rates of success are seen when central necrotic collections are treated surgically and peripheral peripancreatic and lesser sac collections are treated percutaneously.[64]

Lesser Sac Abscesses

Lesser sac abscesses can be therapeutically challenging because of the surrounding liver, stomach, spleen, and bowel.[66] Because these structures surround a large potential space where abscesses can sequester themselves, percutaneous drainage will usually require traversing one of these organs, preferably the liver.[66]

Several principles guide transhepatic drainage of the lesser sac. The first is that the catheter should traverse the most peripheral portion of the liver, compatible with adequate drainage of fluid, preferably the left lobe. The second is that this access route should not be attempted in patients with obstructed bile ducts or in patients with large, dilated, tortuous vessels, as occur in portal hypertension. The third is that the cavity should be evacuated as completely as possible at the time of catheter placement, and the fourth is that care should be taken to ensure that all of the catheter's side holes are within the collection and none are within the hepatic parenchyma.

Adherence to these principles has allowed successful drainage of this anatomic space with no evidence of spread of infection to the liver parenchyma, or of hematoma or biloma. It has also been used successfully in patients with lesser sac bowel and biliary fistulas.

Perirenal Abscesses

The perirenal space lies between the anterior and posterior portions of Gerota fascia and contains the kidneys, adrenal glands, and associated connective tissues. Small perirenal abscesses may respond to antibiotic therapy alone, but large or persisting collections are best treated by percutaneous catheter drainage. In those few cases that do not respond completely to percutaneous management, surgery is often simplified by prior catheter placement.[67]

Perirenal infection may arise from the kidney or from the spread of infection from adjacent structures.[68] CT findings in perirenal infections include perirenal fluid and gas collections, distortion of the renal contour, and thickening of the Gerota fascia. Ultrasound may reveal a relatively sonolucent mass with low-level internal echoes and good through transmission. Occasionally no through transmission is seen because of intraabscess gas–fluid interfaces. Additionally, if a large number of small gas bubbles are present, the mass may be of increased echogenicity and appear solid.[69] Ultrasound suffers from its inability to detect fascial thickening or subtle alteration in the perinephric fat.[70]

Perirenal aspiration and drainage may be accomplished using fluoroscopy, ultrasound, CT, or a combination of these methods. A direct extraperitoneal approach will avoid contamination of the peritoneum.[69] Lang et al. have noted that, in general, the size of the catheter required to adequately drain perirenal abscesses is larger than that required to treat intrarenal abscess because of the more viscous and debris-laden fluid present.[67] However, the choice of catheter type and size is a matter of personal preference. One of the causes for failure in perirenal drainage is placement of an inadequate number of catheters in a septated abscess, but septation is no longer considered a contraindication to percutaneous treatment.[68] Septa can be broken up with guidewires during initial catheter placement.[71] Signs of complete drainage are resolution of fever and leukocytosis and reduction of output through a patent drainage catheter to less than 5 to 10 ml per day. In complicated collections, follow-up imaging should be performed before catheter removal.

Psoas Abscesses

Psoas infections may present with nonlocalized abdominal pain, varied gastrointestinal complaints, and constitutional symptoms such as fever, chills, sweats, and malaise. Patients with psoas abscess may complain of pain referred to the hip, groin, or knee.[72] Most commonly, patients complain of unilateral hip, back, or flank pain, which is exacerbated by extension of the ipsilateral leg because this causes stretching of the psoas muscle fibers. These vague signs combined with the relative rarity of psoas infection make the diagnosis of psoas abscess a difficult challenge to both clinicians and radiologists.[73]

The causes of psoas abscess are varied and may be related to direct extension from the kidneys, ureters, pancreas, and retroperitoneal portions of the bowel, or may be secondary to adjacent disk infections and spinal osteomyelitis.[74] Diverticulitis and complicated appendicitis are reported as the most common etiologies of psoas abscess.[74] Necrotic tumors may mimic true psoas abscesses (see Fig. 56-4).

Mueller et al. have noted that some pyogenic iliopsoas abscesses are related to suppuration of iliac lymph nodes that drain the peritoneum, buttocks, and pelvic areas. These nodes lie between the muscle bundles posteriorly and the peritoneum anteriorly within the iliac fossa.[75]

CT is the best method to define psoas infection and guide treatment. Asymmetrical muscular enlargement with a central low-attenuation collection is characteristic.[75] In psoas hematomas, high-attenuation fresh blood may be seen. Drainage of fresh hematomas is usually not successful, but aspiration for culture and Gram stain can still be performed. If the collection is within the confines of the bony pelvis, aspiration and drainage are done from an anterior approach. The aspirating needle is directed over the anterior iliac spine and then caudally and posteriorly into the psoas, taking care to avoid bowel. After the presence of pus is confirmed, a multi-side-hole, large-lumen catheter is inserted. If the collection is confined mostly to the lower lumbar regions as opposed to the pelvis, drainage may be performed using a posterior approach, which avoids transgressing the peritoneum.[75] These collections tend to contain thick, viscous debris, necessitating the use of the largest drainage catheters available.[75]

References

1. Fry DE, Garrison RN, Heitsch RC, et al. Determinants of death in patients with intraabdominal abscess. Surgery 1980;88:517–522.
2. Fry DE, Clevenger FW. Reoperation for intra-abdominal abscess. Surg Clin North Am 1991;71:159–173.
3. Brolin RE, Nosher JL, Leiman S, et al. Percutaneous catheter versus open surgical drainage in the treatment of abdominal abscesses. Am Surg 1984;50:102–108.
4. Gerzof SG, Robbins AH, Birkett DH, et al. Percutaneous catheter drainage of abdominal abscesses guided by ultrasound and computed tomography. AJR 1979;133:1–8.
5. Ochsner A, DeBakey M, Murray S. Pyogenic abscess of the liver: II. An analysis of 47 cases with review of the literature. Am J Surg 1938;40:292–319.
6. Ferrucci JT. Percutaneous drainage of abdominal abscesses and fluid collections. M Sinai J Med 1984;51:547–551.
7. Connell TR, Stephens DH, Carlson HC, et al. Upper abdominal abscess: a continuing and deadly problem. AJR 1980;134:759–765.
8. Nguyen KT, Sauerbrei EE, Nolan RL. The peritoneum and the diaphragm. In: Rumack CM, Wilson SR, Charboneau JW, eds. Diagnostic ultrasound. St. Louis: Mosby–Year Book, 1991:365–382.
9. Kressel HY, Filly RA. Ultrasonographic appearance of gas-containing in the abdomen. AJR 1978;130:71–73.
10. Jeffrey RB Jr, Wing VW, Laing FC. Real-time sonographic monitoring of percutaneous abscess drainage. AJR 1985;144:469–470.
11. Knochel JQ, Koehler PR, Lee TG, et al. Diagnosis of abdominal abscesses with computed tomography, ultrasound and [111]indium leukocyte scans. Radiology 1980;137:425–432.
12. Baron RL, Freeny PC, Moss AA. The liver. In: Moss AA, Gamsu G, Genant HK, eds. Computed tomography of the body: with magnetic resonance imaging. 2nd ed. Philadelphia: Saunders, 1992:735–821.
13. Sones PJ. Percutaneous drainage of abdominal abscesses. AJR 1984;142:35–39.
14. Mueller PR, vanSonnenberg E, Ferrucci JT Jr. Percutaneous drainage of 250 abdominal fluid collections. Part II. Current procedural concepts. Radiology 1984;151:343–347.
15. Johnson RD, Mueller PF, Ferrucci JT Jr, et al. Percutaneous drainage of pyogenic liver abscesses. AJR 1985;44:463–467.
16. Johnson WC, Gerzoff SG, Robbins AH. Treatment of abdominal abscesses: comparative evaluation of operative drainage versus percutaneous catheter drainage guided by computed tomography or ultrasound. Ann Surg 1981;194:510–519.
17. Silver S, Weinstein A, Cooperman A. Changes in the pathogenesis and detection of intrahepatic abscess. Am J Surg 1979;137:608–610.
18. Kuligowska E, Connor SK, Shapiro JH. Liver abscess: sonography in diagnosis and treatment. AJR 1982;138:253–257.
19. Halvorsen RA, Korobkin M, Foster WL, et al. The variable CT appearance of hepatic abscesses. AJR 1984;141:941–946.
20. Robinson HA, Isikoff MB, Hill MC. Diagnostic imaging of hepatic abscesses: a retrospective analysis. AJR 1980;135:735–740.
21. Bernadino ME. Space occupying lesions of the liver. In: Taveras J, Ferrucci JT Jr, eds. Radiology: diagnosis—imaging—intervention. Philadelphia: Lippincott, 1992:1–13.
22. vanSonnenberg E, Wittenberg J, Ferrucci JT Jr, et al. Triangulation method for percutaneous needle guidance: the angled approach to upper abdominal masses. AJR 1981;137:757–761.
23. Baek SY, Lee MG, Cho KS, et al. Therapeutic percutaneous aspiration of hepatic abscesses: effectiveness in 25 patients. AJR 1993;160:799–802.
24. McFadzean AJS, Chang KPS, Wong CC. Solitary pyogenic abscess treated by closed aspiration and antibiotics: fourteen consecutive cases with recovery. Br J Surg 1953;41:141–152.
25. Do H, Lambiase RE, Deyoe L, et al. Percutaneous drainage of hepatic abscesses: comparison of results in abscesses with and without intrahepatic biliary communication. AJR 1991;157:1209–1212.
26. Bertel CK, van Heerden JA, Sheedy PF. Treatment of pyogenic hepatic abscesses: surgical vs percutaneous drainage. Arch Surg 1986;121:554–558.
27. Gerzof SG, Johnson WC, Robbins AH, et al. Intrahepatic pyogenic abscesses: treatment by percutaneous drainage. Am J Surg 1985;149:487–493.
28. Attar B, Levendoglu H, Causay NS. CT-guided percutaneous aspiration and catheter drainage of pyogenic liver abscesses. Am J Gastroenterol 1986;81:550–555.
29. Bernadino ME, Berkman WA, Plemmons M, et al. Percutane-

ous drainage of multiseptated hepatic abscess. J Comput Assist Tomogr 1984;8:38–41.

30. Bret PM, Fond A, Bretagnolle M, et al. Percutaneous aspiration and drainage of hydatid cysts in the liver. Radiology 1988;168:617–620.

31. Mueller PR, Dawson SL, Ferrucci JT Jr, et al. Hepatic echinococcal cyst: successful percutaneous drainage. Radiology 1985;155:627–628.

32. Acunas B, Rozanes I, Acunas G, et al. Hydatid cyst of the liver: identification of detached cyst lining on CT scans obtained after cyst puncture. AJR 1991;156:751–752.

33. Simonetti G, Profili S, Sergiacomi GL, et al. Percutaneous treatment of hepatic cysts by aspiration and sclerotherapy. Cardiovasc Intervent Radiol 1993;16:81–84.

34. vanSonnenberg E, Mueller PR, Schiffman HR, et al. Intrahepatic amebic abscesses: indications for and results of percutaneous catheter drainage. Radiology 1985;156:631–635.

35. Ralls PW, Barnes PF, Johnson MB, et al. Medical treatment of hepatic amebic abscess: rare need for percutaneous drainage. Radiology 1987;165:805–807.

36. Thompson JE, Forlenza S, Verma R. Amebic liver abscess: a therapeutic approach. Rev Infect Dis 1985;7:171–179.

37. Eggleston FC, Handa AK, Verghese M. Amebic peritonitis secondary to amebic liver abscess. Surgery 1982;91:46–51.

38. Adams EB, MacLeod IN. Invasive amebiasis: amebic liver abscess and its complications. Medicine 1977;56:325–334.

39. Ken JG, vanSonnenberg E, Casola G, et al. Perforated amebic liver abscess: successful percutaneous treatment. Radiology 1989;170:195–197.

40. Chun CH, Raff MJ, Conteras L, et al. Splenic abscess. Medicine 1980;59:50–65.

41. Chou YH, Hsu CC, Tiu CM, et al. Splenic abscess: sonographic and percutaneous drainage or aspiration. Gastrointest Radiol 1992;17:262–266.

42. van der Laan RT, Verbeeten B Jr, Smits NJ, et al. Computed tomography in the diagnosis and treatment of solitary splenic abscesses. J Comput Assist Tomogr 1989;13:71–74.

43. Lerner RM, Spataro RF. Splenic abscess: percutaneous drainage. Radiology 1984;153:643–645.

44. Karlson KB, Martin EC, Fankuchen EI, et al. Nonsurgical drainage of intraabdominal and mediastinal abscess: a report of 12 cases. Cardiovasc Intervent Radiol 1981;4:170–176.

45. Berkman WA, Harris SA, Bernadino ME. Nonsurgical drainage of splenic abscess. AJR 1983;141:395–396.

46. Schwartz PE, Sterioff S, Mucha P, et al. Postsplenectomy sepsis and mortality in adults. JAMA 1982;248:2279–2283.

47. Quinn SF, vanSonnenberg E, Casola G, et al. Interventional radiology in the spleen. Radiology 1986;161:289–291.

48. Pruett TL, Simmons RL. Status of percutaneous catheter drainage of abscesses. Surg Clin North Am 1988;68:89–105.

49. Freeny PC, Lewis GP, Traverso LW, et al. Infected pancreatic fluid collections: percutaneous catheter drainage. Radiology 1988;167:435–441.

50. Beger HG, Bittner R, Block S, et al. Bacterial contamination of pancreatic necrosis: a prospective study. Gastroenterology 1986;91:433–438.

51. Bittner R, Block S, Buchler M, et al. Pancreatic abscess and infected pancreatic necrosis: different local septic complications in acute pancreatitis. In: Beger HG, Buchler M, eds. Acute pancreatitis. Berlin: Springer-Verlag, 1987:216–223.

52. Torres WE, Evert MB, Baumgartner BR, et al. Percutaneous aspiration and drainage of pancreatic pseudocysts. AJR 1986;147:1007–1009.

53. vanSonnenberg E, Wittich GR, Casola G, et al. Percutaneous drainage of infected and noninfected pancreatic pseudocysts: experience in 101 cases. Radiology 1989;170:757–761.

54. Matzinger FRK, Ho CS, Yee AC, et al. Pancreatic pseudocysts drained through a percutaneous transgastric approach: further experience. Radiology 1988;167:431–434.

55. Banks PA, Gerzof SG. Indications and results of fine needle aspiration of pancreatic exudate. In: Beger HG, Buchler M, eds. Acute pancreatitis. Berlin: Springer-Verlag, 1987:171–174.

56. vanSonnenberg E, D'Agostino HB, Casola GC, et al. Percutaneous abscess drainage: current concepts. Radiology 1991;181:617–626.

57. Kuligowska E, Olsen WL. Pancreatic pseudocysts drained through a percutaneous transgastric approach. Radiology 1985;154:79–92.

58. vanSonnenberg E, Wittich GR, Casola G, et al. Complicated pancreatic inflammatory disease: diagnostic and therapeutic role of interventional radiology. Radiology 1985;155:335–340.

59. Grosso M, Gandini G, Cassinis MC, et al. Percutaneous treatment (including pseudocystogastrostomy) of 74 pancreatic pseudocysts. Radiology 1989;173:493–497.

60. Maier W. Early objective diagnosis and staging of acute pancreatitis by contrast-enhanced computed tomography. In: Beger HG, Buchler M, eds. Acute pancreatitis. Berlin: Springer-Verlag, 1987:132–140.

61. Altemeier WA, Alexander JW. Pancreatic abscess. Arch Surg 1963;87:80–89.

62. Bittner R, Block S, Buchler M, et al. Pancreatic abscess and infected pancreatic necrosis: difficult local septic complications in acute pancreatitis. Dig Dis Sci 1987;32:1082–1087.

63. Lang EK, Springer RM, Glorioso LW, et al. Abdominal abscess drainage under radiologic guidance: causes of failure. Radiology 1986;159:329–336.

64. Lee MJ, Rattner DW, Legemate DA, et al. Acute complicated pancreatitis: redefining the role of interventional radiology. Radiology 1992;183:171–174.

65. Steiner E, Mueller PR, Hahn PF, et al. Complicated pancreatic abscesses: problems in interventional management. Radiology 1988;167:443–446.

66. Mueller PF, Ferrucci JT Jr, Simeone JF, et al. Lesser sac abscesses and fluid collections: drainage by transhepatic approach. Radiology 1985;155:615–618.

67. Lang EK. Renal, perirenal, and pararenal abscesses: percutaneous drainage. Radiology 1990;174:109–113.

68. Sacks D, Banner MP, Meranze SG, et al. Renal and related retroperitoneal abscesses: percutaneous drainage. Radiology 1988;167:447–451.

69. Gerzof SG, Gale ME. Computed tomography and ultrasonography for diagnosis and treatment of renal and retroperitoneal abscesses. Urol Clin North Am 1982;9:185–193.

70. Hoddick W, Jeffrey RB, Goldberg HI, et al. CT and sonography of severe renal and perirenal infections. AJR 1983;140:517–520.

71. Lieberman RP, Hahn FJ, Imray, et al. Loculated abscesses: management by percutaneous fracture of septations. Radiology 1986;161:827–828.

72. Jeffrey RB, Callen PW, Federle MP. Computed tomography of psoas abscesses. J Comput Assist Tomogr 1980;4:639–641.

73. Ralls PW, Boswell W, Henderson R, et al. CT of inflammatory disease of the psoas muscle. AJR 1980;134:767–770.

74. Mendez G Jr, Isikoff MB, Hill MC. Retroperitoneal processes involving the psoas demonstrated by computed tomography. J Comput Assist Tomogr 1980;4:78–82.

75. Mueller PR, Ferrucci JT Jr, Wittenberg J, et al. Iliopsoas abscess: treatment by CT-guided percutaneous catheter drainage. AJR 1984;142:359–362.

56

Percutaneous Drainage of Pelvic Abscesses and Fluid Collections

GREGORY J. SLATER
STEVEN L. DAWSON

Percutaneous drainage of pelvic abscesses was a late addition to the list of interventional procedures established in the 1980s. Before the revolutionary advances in cross-sectional imaging of the 1970s, the deep location and complicated anatomic relations of typical pelvic abscesses rendered them undiagnosable and undrainable except by laparotomy. Subsequently they were able to be accurately characterized and localized, but safe access routes frequently were not recognized, and the misconception persisted that abscesses complicated by fistulas were not suitable for percutaneous abscess drainage (PAD).

Only in the latter half of the 1980s were the indications for PAD widened to include "complicated" abscesses, and innovative access routes to deep pelvic abscesses were established. Percutaneous PAD in the pelvis is now accepted as a safe and effective therapy that may variously result in cure, delay of surgery in a seriously ill patient until the underlying medical condition has been stabilized, or "downstaging" of a subsequent surgical procedure. These benefits are achieved with lower morbidity and cost than traditional alternatives, success and complication rates that are at least similar, and greater patient acceptance.

Common Sites and Etiologies

Pelvic fluid collections may be intra- or extraperitoneal. Knowledge of the anatomy of the pelvic peritoneum is necessary to understand the paths of dissemination of sepsis.

The pelvic peritoneal space extends from the pelvic brim, iliac vessels, and pelvic mesocolon superiorly to the peritoneal reflection from the anterior rectal wall inferiorly. The peritoneal reflection extends anteriorly to cover the seminal vesicles and bladder in men and the vagina, uterus, and bladder in women. In women,

the reflection lies more caudally and is divided into the rectouterine and uterovesical fossae by the uterus, vagina, and broad ligament. Laterally the peritoneum is reflected toward the pelvic wall and forms the shallow pararectal and paravesical fossae. There is free communication of the pelvic cavity with the abdominal peritoneum, including both its supra- and infracolic portions. The most common site of pelvic abscess formation is the cul-de-sac, which is the most dependent portion of the abdominal cavity.

The pelvic extraperitoneal space and its compartments are more complex and are less well known than their retroperitoneal counterparts.[1] The anterior extraperitoneal fat is divided by the umbilicovesical fascia into the prevesical and perivesical spaces. The perivesical space contains the bladder, umbilical arteries, and urachus. The prevesical space, also known as the space of Retzius in its retropubic portion, is a large potential space extending superiorly to the umbilicus. Fluid in the prevesical space has a "molar-tooth" shape on axial scans, with the "roots" separating the bladder posteriorly from the cecum and sigmoid colon laterally.[2] The "roots" are often asymmetric, resulting in displacement of the bladder from the midline. The prevesical space also communicates directly with the rectus sheath, femoral sheath, presacral space, and infrarenal peritoneal compartment, allowing for collections of fluid such as blood, urine, or pus from these sites of origin.

Common initiating causes of pelvic abscesses are surgery or trauma to the gastrointestinal tract. Appendicitis, diverticulitis, and Crohn disease are also frequent antecedents. Perianal abscesses may dissect into the retroperitoneum. These conditions share the common etiology of loss of integrity of the bowel wall as a barrier to the spread of infection. A different pathway exists in women, in whom tuboovarian abscesses may result from ascending sexually acquired infection of the genital tract.

Leakage of urine from surgery, trauma, or instrumentation of the lower urinary tract may result in very large collections that may become infected. Hematomas may result from trauma, surgery, anticoagulant medication, or angiography. Renal transplants may be complicated by various fluid collections, including urinoma, hematoma, lymphocele, abscess, or seroma. Pancreatic transplants may also be associated with pancreatitis or pseudocysts. Infected necrotic tumors are an uncommon but easily overlooked cause of pelvic abscess.

Efficacy and Rationale of Pelvic PAD

Undrained abdominal abscesses result in a distressingly high mortality rate of 50 to 80 percent despite modern antibiotic therapy.[3]

The principles of therapy are as follows:

1. *Complete evacuation of pus.* Whether achieved surgically or radiologically, the major benefit of intervention occurs at the time of the procedure when the cavity contents are completely evacuated. This can result in the recovery of an unstable, critically ill patient in a matter of hours. Continued external drainage adds to the therapeutic effect, but the major benefit occurs immediately.[4]
2. *Early diagnosis and intervention.* Early drainage forestalls the development of a multiorgan dysfunction syndrome, which is associated with a much worse prognosis.
3. *Accurate anatomic localization.* This allows a suitable access route to be chosen and defines loculations that will require a further drainage tube or more extensive surgery to prevent failure.
4. *Diagnosis of any underlying cause.* An underlying enteric connection must be identified and allowed to heal before the drainage tube can be successfully removed.
5. *Imaging follow-up to document resolution.* Minimal tube drainage alone does not necessarily equate with resolution because the tube may be blocked, malpositioned, or too small to drain the abscess contents.

Cross-sectional imaging techniques have revolutionized the treatment of abscesses by allowing assessment of these fundamentals. Success rates for PAD of selected unilocular uncomplicated abscesses range from 90 to 100 percent. Complicated abscesses in the pelvis result from factors such as recent surgery, urine leaks, or enteric communication. These abscesses have a lower cure rate than uncomplicated abscesses, in the range of 65 to 95 percent. Their management is more prolonged than for simple abscesses, often requiring CT both at diagnosis and follow-up and multiple catheters for loculated abscesses. Over 90 percent of peridiverticular abscesses may be drained successfully percutaneously.[5,6] Periappendiceal abscesses are drained successfully in approximately 90 percent of patients,[7,8] and the success rate for PAD in Crohn disease is from 70 to 100 percent.[9-11] Postoperative pelvic abscesses can be cured by PAD in 80 to 85 percent of cases.[12]

A number of studies have shown PAD to have a higher success rate with lower morbidity and mortality than surgical drainage.[13,14] Johnson et al., in a study comparing surgical and percutaneous drainage, found a mortality rate of 11 percent and a complication rate of 4 percent for percutaneous drainage, compared with 21 and 16 percent, respectively, for surgery.[15] Other studies have shown no difference.[16] Because a randomized prospective trial has never been performed, it is not valid to compare the success rates of PAD and surgical drainage. Such a trial would be unethical now that PAD has been so widely adopted as the initial therapy of choice.

Success rates for percutaneous drainage depend on the definition of cure. Cure is most completely defined as defervescence, disappearance of the abscess, avoidance of surgery, and lack of recurrence in the long term. However, even if all these objectives are not achieved, it does not mean the treatment has failed to be of benefit to the patient. Often the patient is gravely ill at the time of diagnosis for such reasons as advanced age, concurrent medical conditions, or recent surgery. Surgery in this setting may be life-threatening, particularly for complicated abscesses where the prognosis is dismal. PAD in this setting has a temporizing effect, delaying surgery until risks have been minimized.

PAD frequently reduces the extent of subsequent surgery. Once inflammation and mass effect have resolved, the task of the surgeon may be much easier than otherwise. More definitive surgery may be possible at the initial operation than would otherwise be contemplated. For example, in a patient with a pericolonic diverticular abscess, separate operations to drain the abscess and create a defunctioning colostomy, resect the diseased segment, and subsequently close the diversion may be unnecessary. Surgery may thus be "downstaged" from a two- or three-stage procedure to a one- or two-stage procedure. This is the major goal of PAD in enteric abscesses, where subsequent surgery will usually be required.[14]

To summarize, PAD is a nonoperative intervention performed under local anesthesia with success rates, morbidity, and mortality as good as or better than surgery, a major intervention that is accompanied by the risks of general anesthesia. PAD also encompasses the other major attributes of temporization and down-staging of subsequent surgery when this is required. Its role was summed up in an authoritative surgical review that referred to PAD as "clearly one of the great advances in abdominal surgery in the past few years."[15]

What to Drain and What Not to Drain

Sigmoid Peridiverticular Abscesses

Sigmoid diverticulosis is a common entity in Western countries that may affect more than half of Americans over 60 years of age.[16] Diverticulitis eventually develops in 15 to 30 percent of these cases, and in 1983 resulted in over 200,000 hospitalizations and 50,000 surgical procedures in the United States.[17,18]

Although uncomplicated acute diverticulitis will resolve with appropriate antibiotic therapy, surgery is indicated for bleeding, bowel obstruction, perforation, or abscess formation. The aims of pericolonic abscess surgery are to drain the abscess, resect the diseased segment, and restore colonic continuity.[19–21] Depending on whether all these entities can be performed at the initial procedure, surgery may be performed as a one-stage procedure, two stages with delayed closure of the diverting colostomy, or three stages with delayed resection and delayed closure.

In a review of diverticular abscesses, Hinchey[22] classified them according to size and containment. Type A abscesses are small and lie in the contiguous mesentery; type B abscesses result from a large perforation with a well-defined mesenteric or pelvic abscess; type C abscesses result from a free perforation into the adjacent mesentery or pelvis without fecal contamination; type D results from gross perforation with contamination of the peritoneum and pelvis from free fecal spillage. In type A abscesses, percutaneous drainage is unnecessary because the diseased segment can be removed en bloc in a single-stage procedure, whereas in type D percutaneous drainage is ineffective. PAD is best reserved for large localized abscesses in the mesentery or pelvis, without fecal contamination (types B and C).

The optimal timing of surgery after PAD is unclear. Frequently the diseased segment is removed early, after the clinical signs have abated, but with the catheter still in place. The patient may be sent home with the catheter still in place if early surgery is not contemplated. Surgery may not be necessary in all patients following successful PAD. Some elderly patients have not undergone subsequent resection and have remained well. Selection of suitable candidates for conservative follow-up may be possible with further experience.[4]

Periappendiceal Abscesses

Periappendiceal abscesses may complicate acute appendicitis or appendectomy. Abscess formation complicates acute appendicitis in 2 to 3 percent of cases,[21,22] resulting from a gangrenous or perforated appendix. Often these patients present with a palpable "appendix mass," which may be due to an abscess, a phlegmonous thickening of omentum and small bowel loops, or a combination of both. The differential diagnosis includes lymphadenitis, Meckel diverticulitis, perforated cecum (tumor, foreign body, diverticulitis), Crohn disease, or ovarian pathology.[8] Clinical diagnosis is imprecise, and 45 percent of a series of 42 patients undergoing surgical drainage for an appendix mass had phlegmons without significant abscess formation.[23] There is also a high morbidity of 24 to 28 percent for attempted early appendectomy and drainage of periappendiceal abscesses, compared to only 5 percent if an unperforated appendix is removed intact.[24,25] The more frequent complications include wound infection, abscess formation, fecal fistula, pylephlebitis, and intestinal obstruction.[26,27]

CT with intravenous contrast can reliably stage complicated appendicitis and postappendectomy inflammation, allowing for rational selection of medical, surgical, or percutaneous therapy. A periappendiceal phlegmon is a mass of soft tissue density, 20 Hounsfield (HU) units or more, after contrast. A periappendiceal abscess is a well-defined fluid collection (<20 HU). The presence of a calcified appendicolith in the phlegmon or abscess is diagnostic of an inflammatory etiology and is detected much more frequently on CT than on plain radiographs (Fig. 56-1).

Jeffrey et al. reviewed 70 periappendiceal inflammatory masses in patients with clinically suspected appendiceal perforation.[28] Patients with phlegmons or small abscesses less than 3 cm in diameter (category 1) responded rapidly to intravenous antibiotic therapy without surgical or percutaneous drainage. In these patients, CT-guided diagnostic aspiration may occasionally be useful for isolation of an organism for antibiotic sensitivity testing. Patients with larger well-defined abscesses (category 2) were treated with intravenous antibiotics in combination with percutaneous drainage. In both categories the cure rate was approximately 90 percent. Fistulas to the tip of the appendix or cecum were demonstrated at routine sinography in 46 percent of category 2 patients. These required a longer period of catheter drainage, up to 3½ weeks,

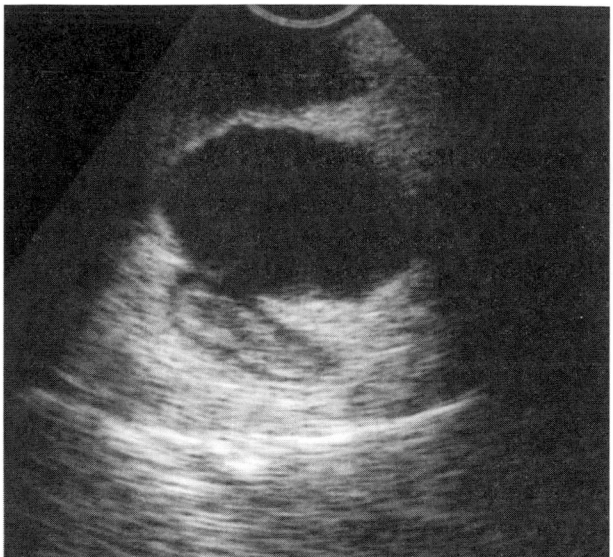

A

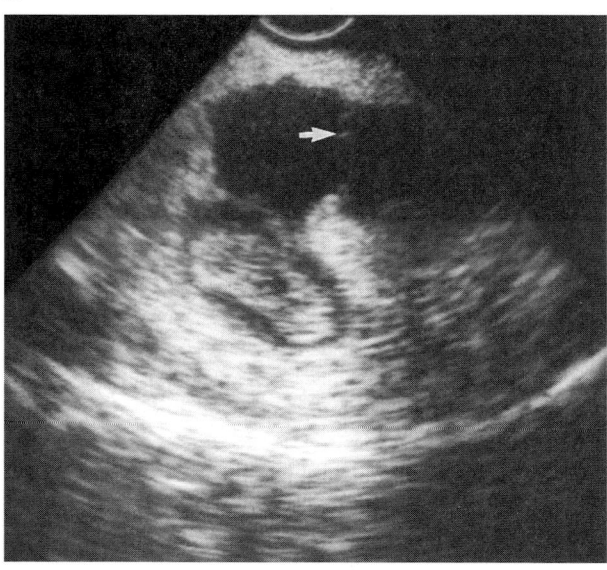

C

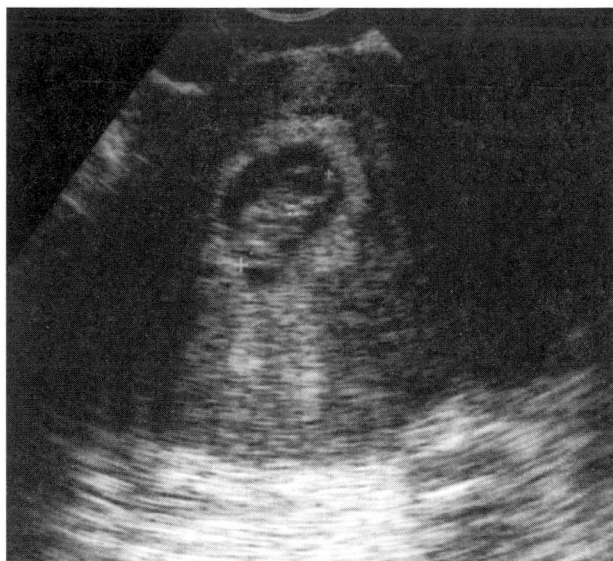

B

Figure 56-1. A 20-year-old regnant woman with right lower quadrant pain, fever, and elevated white count. (A) Transvaginal ultrasound shows a 5 × 3 cm collection between the vagina and a collapsed rectosigmoid. (B) Transvaginal ultrasound of the uterus shows a single fetus of 9 weeks' gestational age. Fetal heart motion was seen. (C) Transvaginal drainage of the cul-de-sac collection was performed using an 18-gauge needle inserted under direct ultrasound guidance through the vaginal vault into the collection (*arrow*). A guidewire and self-retaining catheter were placed into the collection and remained for 4 days, during which time the patient's clinical symptoms markedly improved, with no further collection identified on follow-up imaging. The pregnancy continued uneventfully and the patient subsequently had interval appendectomy.

but all fistulas closed. Patients were discharged from the hospital for outpatient follow-up and sinograms once their clinical signs had returned to normal.

Patients with extensive, poorly defined abscesses with pelvic, extraperitoneal, or interloop extension (category 3) were treated with early surgery in this study. Other causes of a periappendiceal inflammatory mass, such as perforated cecal lymphoma, diverticulitis, and ruptured ovarian cyst, were also present in this group, mimicking appendiceal abscess.

Patients with postappendectomy abscesses also respond favorably to PAD. Catheter drainage for several weeks is required in this group to allow the fistula that is usually present to heal.[27]

Elective appendectomy may be unnecessary after PAD for a periappendiceal abscess.[28] After surgical drainage of periappendiceal abscess without appendectomy, 80 to 95 percent of patients remain asymptomatic.[29,30] If removed electively, the appendix frequently shows no sign of inflammation[31] or may be impossible to find, having been destroyed by inflammation at the time of the abscess.[32] The 19 percent complication rate of interval appendectomy is also high in this situation.[26]

The length of hospitalization for PAD for periappendiceal abscess averaged 8 days, comparing favorably with 6½ to 17 days for operative therapy.[8]

Crohn Disease

Crohn disease is complicated by abscess formation in 20 to 24 percent of patients, with approximately equal incidence spontaneously and postoperatively.[32,33] Mechanisms include direct extension from involved bowel, hematogenous seeding, and peritoneal contamination or anastomotic breakdown after surgery.

Diagnosis may be delayed because of masking or

clinical signs by concurrent corticosteroid therapy, and CT is invaluable in making the diagnosis and differentiating abscess from phlegmon. Management by whatever means is fraught with difficulty, reflecting the transmural nature of the underlying disease. There is a high incidence of cutaneous fistula formation following surgical drainage, up to 85 percent.[34] To avoid the considerable morbidity and mortality associated with bypass surgery in the presence of a coexisting abscess, a two-stage approach is advocated, consisting of abscess drainage and subsequent resection of the diseased segment and fistulectomy (when present) 6 weeks later.

The roles of PAD in Crohn disease are temporization and a decrease in the scope of subsequent surgery, with an increase in the proportion of patients undergoing a successful one-stage operation. Although both surgical and percutaneous drainages are well tolerated, PAD is preferred as the less invasive technique (Fig. 56-2).

In patients without enteric communication of the abscess, PAD has been shown to be an effective therapy.[10] When communication is present, PAD is also effective in helping to resolve the abscess, although success rates are lower than when no communication exists, and a longer period is required for the fistula to close. Aggressive adjunctive medical therapy with intravenous antibiotics and total parenteral nutrition (TPN) is necessary and may allow resolution of the fistula. The fistula is likely to recur if the underlying bowel disease is severe and there are marked stenosis and strictures, and these patients benefit from elective resection. The recurrence rate is low in patients with

mild underlying disease, and these patients may be observed. The extent of the underlying disease may be assessed with a barium study once resolution has occurred.

Postoperative abscesses in Crohn disease are due to an anastomotic leak and occur in 10 to 15 percent of patients. They respond well to PAD, in common with other postoperative abscesses with biliary or enteric communication, where there is an 80 percent cure rate.[35,36]

No iatrogenic enterocutaneous fistula has occurred as a complication of PAD for Crohn disease abscesses in series totaling 40 patients, despite its frequency following surgical drainage.[9,37,38]

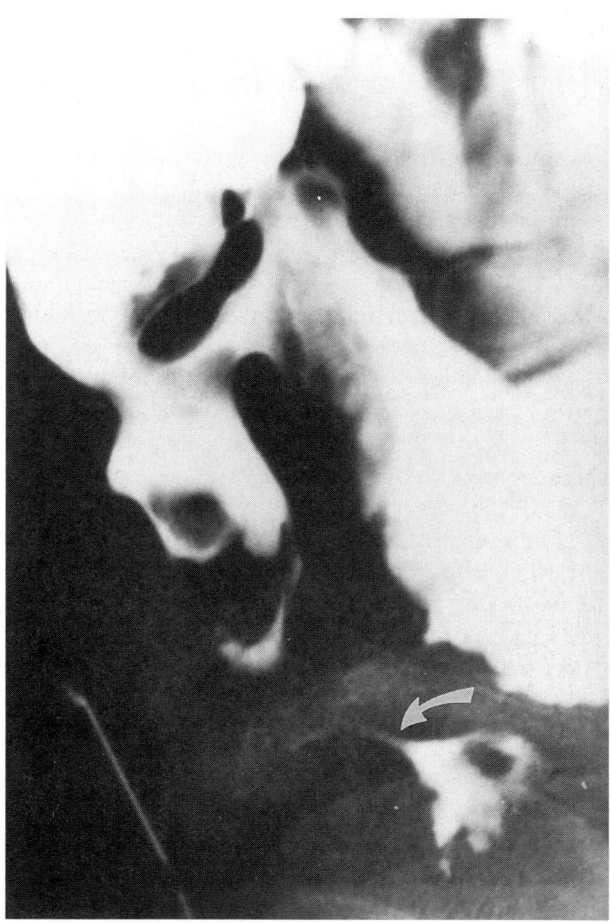

A

Figure 56-2. A 23-year-old woman with a 7-year history of Crohn disease. (A) Spot film from a small bowel follow-through shows irregularity of the terminal ileum with narrowing of the cecum and a fistulous communication to a right lower quadrant collection (*curved arrow*). (B) Three images from the CT examination show thickening of the cecum (*left image*), with air–fluid level and contrast opacifying the fistulous tract (*center image*). The collection tracks into the superficial right lower quadrant. Although percutaneous drainage of Crohn abscesses and long-term management of fistulas is possible (see text), in this case the patient was managed surgically and percutaneous drainage was not performed.

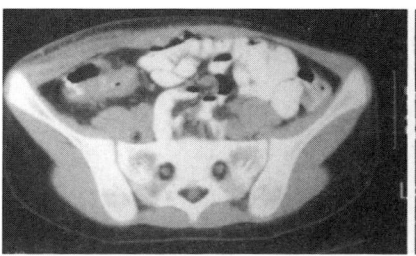 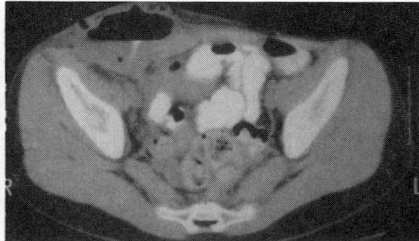 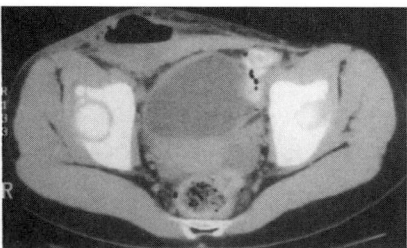

B

Tuboovarian Abscesses (TOAs)

Approximately 85,000 women develop tuboovarian abscesses each year in the United States.[38] Management has traditionally been with intravenous antibiotics or surgery, which may range from colpotomy to total abdominal hysterectomy and bilateral salpingo-oophorectomy. Several series have documented success with PAD for TOAs, with cure rates of approximately 90 percent.[39,40] Complications are few and minor. Some patients suffer recurrence some months after the initial abscess and require repeat PAD, but the long-term avoidance of surgery is over 80 percent.

Although most TOAs are diagnosed with ultrasound, CT is generally the preferred modality for guidance of the drainage to avoid transgression of bowel, blood vessels, or bladder. Access is obtained by the transabdominal, transgluteal, or transvaginal routes, depending on the location of the abscess. If the transvaginal route is selected, transvaginal ultrasound may be used for guidance, and a commercial or simply manufactured biopsy guide is used for needle insertion.

It has been suggested that abscesses larger than 7 cm may be best treated by a combination of antibiotics and PAD as initial therapy, but that smaller abscesses should be drained only if medical treatment fails.[41] Abscesses smaller than 3 to 4 cm in diameter can be aspirated but often cannot be catheterized, although needle aspiration alone can be therapeutic in this instance.[42] The exact role and timing of aspiration, drainage, and surgery await further elucidation. PAD has the potential to reduce the early morbidity and mortality associated with major surgery, to reduce costs of hospital treatment, and to avoid surgical sterilization and premature menopause in young women.

Infected Tumors

Percutaneous drainage of infected tumors is an uncommon interventional procedure, constituting less than 1 percent of a series of more than 2500 percutaneous abscess and fluid drainages.[42] Central tumor necrosis occurs after a neoplasm outgrows its blood supply. Infection is more likely in debilitated patients (Fig. 56-3).

Large catheters are effective in bringing about defervescence and clinical improvement in 75 percent of patients, but in most cases the tumor persists, with the relatively thick, nonpliable wall preventing collapse of the cavity. These patients require either surgery to resect the tumor or lifelong catheter drainage. Patients remained alive with catheter drainage for up to 1 year in the study.[43] Catheter changes were usually performed every 2 to 3 months on an outpatient basis, affording significant palliation in patients who were unresectable.

Although the diagnosis of tumor has usually been established before the drainage procedure, infection may be the presenting manifestation of an underlying neoplasm. Clues that this is the case include nodularity of the wall, persistence of drainage, persistent hemorrhagic aspirate, failure of resolution, or recurrence following catheter withdrawal. Needle biopsy may be falsely negative for tumor, as has happened in all eight patients biopsied in the above series.[43] However, cytology of aspirated fluid or image-guided biopsy of a mural nodule may be valuable in selected cases.

Fluid Collections

Patients who are febrile and have a new fluid collection or a collection of unknown duration require diagnostic aspiration with a small-bore needle. If the collection is determined to be infected by inspection or on Gram stain of the aspirate, PAD should be performed if a safe route exists and coagulation parameters are acceptable. Noninfected fluid collections require drainage only if they are thought to be symptomatic.

Lymphoceles

Lymphoceles complicate major abdominal vascular operations, up to 18 percent of renal transplantations,[41] and 30 percent or more of radical pelvic lymphadenectomies.[43] Although frequently asymptomatic and requiring no treatment, they may cause pain, tenesmus, urinary frequency, ureteral obstruction, compression of the vascular pedicle of renal transplants, bowel obstruction, leg edema, or deep venous thrombosis, or they may become infected.[44,45] They result from leakage from lymphatics in the retroperitoneum or in the transplant, and typically do not manifest until 2 to 3 weeks after surgery. Heparin prophylaxis is an important promoter of lymphocele formation by preventing lymph coagulation. Corticosteroids, diuretics, extensive retroperitoneal dissection, and transplant rejection all increase lymph production and may also predispose to lymphocele formation, and immunosuppression significantly delays healing of transected lymphatics.

Surgery has been considered the therapy of choice in the past, with cure rates of over 90 percent for peritoneal marsupialization. However, this is an extensive procedure with attendant risks, particularly in an immunosuppressed transplant recipient. Needle aspiration has a recurrence rate of 80 to 90 percent because of the persistence of leaking lymphatics. These require repeated aspirations, which are associated with an in-

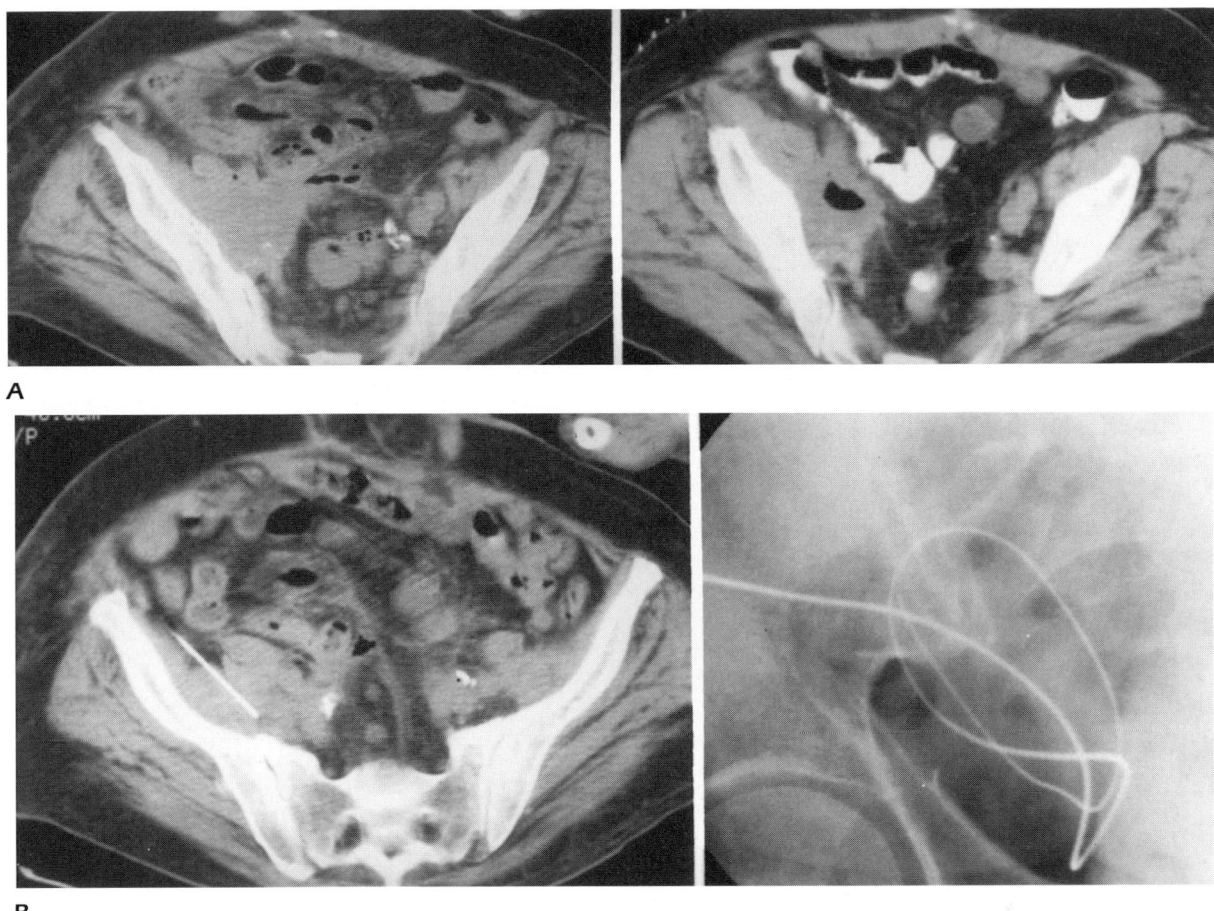

A

B

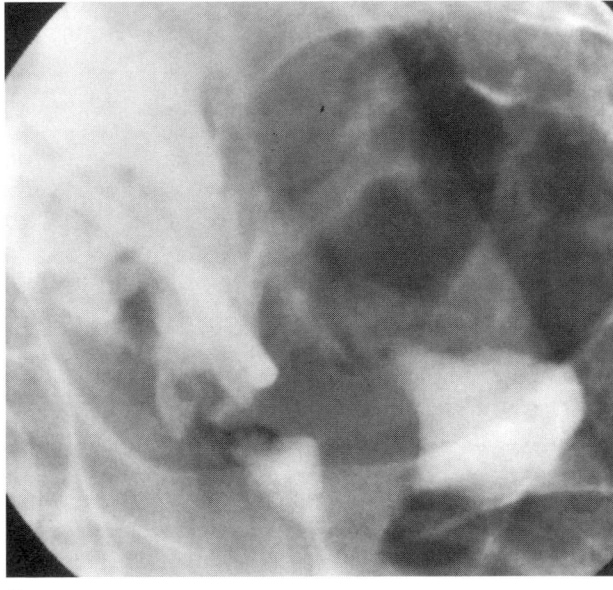

C

Figure 56-3. A 74-year-old man with a history of transitional cell carcinoma who presented to the emergency room with fever. (A) CT scan shows a large air-containing fluid collection in the right iliacus muscle, with adjacent opacified and unopacified bowel. The preliminary diagnosis was diverticulitis with bowel communication and abscess. (B) CT and fluoroscopic guidance were used to place a catheter into the iliacus muscle. The initial needle placement was performed under CT guidance, avoiding loops of bowel in the right lower quadrant. The patient was then transferred to fluoroscopy for further guidewire and catheter manipulations. (C) After catheter placement, contrast injection shows a fistulous communication with a loop of bowel deep in the pelvis. Bacteriology showed mixed flora consistent with bowel communication. Cytology of the aspirated fluid showed transitional cell carcinoma metastatic to the iliacus. Because this collection represents necrotic metastasis with bowel communication, the catheter remained in place until the patient's death 5 months later.

fection rate of 25 to 50 percent.[46,47] Percutaneous catheter drainage alone has been shown to be successful, but drainage may be prolonged—more than 1 month in duration.

The duration of catheter drainage may be decreased and success rates increased to equal those of peritoneal marsupialization by the transcatheter installation of sclerosants, which inflame and seal the feeding lymphatics. These may be used if drainage persists after 1 week of catheter drainage alone.[48] Agents used for sclerosis include povidone-iodine, ethanol, bleomycin, tetracycline, sodium salt solutions, bismuth, and talc. The lymphocele should not communicate with the peritoneal cavity if sclerosants are to be used. Multiple installation sessions are frequently required. Surgery should be reserved for patients in whom percutaneous therapy has failed repeatedly, because recurrences often respond to repeat drainage and sclerosis.

Renal biopsy should be performed when a lymphocele requires drainage in a renal transplant recipient because rejection frequently coexists, which if treated may facilitate resolution of the lymphocele.[49] Cystic ovarian neoplasms may be indistinguishable from lymphoceles on all imaging studies and on biochemical analysis of aspirate, and require a high index of suspicion for their recognition. For this reason, cytologic examination should be obtained on any aspirate from a pelvic cystic mass. Ovarian neoplasms are treated by resection and should not be aspirated because peritoneal dissemination may ensue.

Urinomas

Urinomas may occur in the setting of trauma, after surgery or renal transplantation, or because of obstruction, most commonly due to a ureteral calculus. Small urinomas resorb spontaneously once drainage of the urinary tract is established. Large urinomas or those causing obstruction or symptomatic compression require separate drainage as well. Resorption may be accompanied by elevation of the serum creatinine level.

Choice of Imaging Method

Cross-sectional imaging has been responsible for the improved localization of abscesses and has been followed by an impressive reduction in their mortality.[50,51] Ultrasound (US) is usually the most readily available modality, is relatively inexpensive and portable, and is the most reliable modality for the identification of fluid. For these reasons it is particularly useful in intensive care or postoperative patients. However, an abscess may be obscured by overlying gas in the bowel or peritoneal cavity, or sometimes within the abscess itself. Sinuses, stomas, wounds, or dressings may also impede US diagnosis. The examiner must be experienced and thorough, using a methodical technique such as that described by Baker et al.[52] An understanding of the anatomy of the peritoneal and extraperitoneal spaces will assist in the identification of abscesses remote from the site of original sepsis. A full bladder will be required if the pelvis is to be adequately examined transabdominally.

The classic US appearance of an abscess as an ovoid or round anechoic mass with posterior acoustic enhancement is only seen in half of all abdominal cases.[53] Abscesses may contain internal echoes mimicking solid lesions or gas simulating a loop of bowel. The absence of typical features should not dissuade one from aspiration where it is otherwise indicated.

The advantages of US have led some to advocate its use as the initial diagnostic modality when an abdominal abscess is suspected.[52] However, the superior sensitivity and specificity of CT have been documented in a number of studies[54] and approach 100 percent. Many also consider it to be the most cost-effective imaging investigation.[3] It, too, has occasional pitfalls. Optimal opacification of the bowel with contrast material is necessary to distinguish between an unopacified loop and an abscess. Metallic hip prostheses and surgical clips may also hinder interpretation. The radiation dose burden is considerable and should be remembered in those requiring follow-up imaging. In practice, the choice between US and CT will depend on availability and the type of abscess suspected.

Radionuclide scanning is a sensitive method of detecting inflammation and abscesses, but it lacks the ability of CT and US to demonstrate exact anatomic relationships. Gallium 67 has been supplemented by the white blood cell–labeling agents indium 111 and Tc-HMPAO. Gallium is inexpensive but requires 24 to 48 hours from administration for diagnostic imaging. Its interpretation may be difficult because of activity in the colon, liver, and spleen. Indium, unlike gallium, is not commonly taken up by tumors, and thus is more specific for infective processes. Results are available in 3 hours. Tc-HMPAO is less well established than indium as a white blood cell–scanning agent, and its interpretation is more difficult because of renal and biliary excretion. The labeling of white cells is time-consuming and requires skill, and false-negative results may occur when cells are damaged in labeling. False-positive uptake may occur in tumors, noninfected hematomas, and recent surgical wounds.

Isotope scanning is best reserved for the uncommon situation where US and CT are negative but the clinical suspicion of an abscess remains high. In this instance, isotope scanning may reveal a focus of increased uptake, which should be followed by a targeted reexamination with US or CT under optimal conditions. An unsuspected focus remote from the pelvis may also be identified. However, "clinically useful serendipitous findings are rare."[55]

MRI can detect abscesses, but, like other modalities, it is unable to differentiate between infected and noninfected fluid collections.[56] Relatively long scan times, expense, inaccessibility of the patient inside the magnet, and metal-induced artifact from drainage needles have limited its use in PAD.

The choice of imaging modality for diagnosis also depends on the underlying pathologic condition. CT is indispensable in staging periappendiceal and peridiverticular abscesses and in determining the most appropriate therapy. US is frequently the preferred modality in the diagnosis of appendicitis and periappendiceal abscess in children, where it is desirable to avoid ionizing radiation. Similar considerations apply in assessing pelvic pathology in women of childbearing age, where US is widely used in the diagnosis and follow-up of pelvic inflammatory disease. US is also widely used in the assessment of fluid collections complicating transplantation surgery. Without these specific indications, however, "CT is usually the *only* special radiologic test that should be performed to localize a suspected intraabdominal abscess."[57]

For guidance of PAD, US and especially CT allow a safe access route to be chosen. Deep abscesses may be obscured by overlying bowel gas on US, and collapsed loops of bowel may be difficult to recognize. US is most useful in guiding drainage of superficial abscesses or those that can be accessed by the transvaginal or transrectal routes, and at the bedside in intensive care or postoperative patients. The early approach to PAD as a two-step procedure with diagnosis at CT or US followed by fluoroscopically guided drainage has largely given way to one-step PAD, with the entire procedure performed expeditiously at CT or US. Post-procedure CT or US is performed immediately after evacuation of the cavity to confirm the adequacy of drainage or the need for catheter repositioning or additional catheters. The main role of fluoroscopy is to establish the presence of internal communication with bowel or other organs. This is best established at about 3 days after catheter insertion.

Barium studies may be required to exclude an underlying neoplasm in patients with a peridiverticular or periappendiceal abscess. These studies must be performed subsequent to CT and drainage; otherwise valuable time may be lost waiting for barium to be cleared from the bowel before the diagnosis is made and drainage instituted. CT is the initial diagnostic imaging modality of choice in these adult patients.

Tools and Technique

The decision to proceed to PAD requires that a safe access route is available, that coagulation parameters are acceptable, and that appropriate parties give informed consent. No patient is too sick for PAD.

Consultation

Consultation with clinicians and surgeons involved in the care of the patient is important in making the deci-

sion to proceed to PAD. Ongoing communication is necessary for a satisfactory outcome, and the adjustment of catheter position, placement of additional catheters, or surgical intervention may need to be addressed. The patient and relatives must never be neglected in the decision-making process.

Intravenous Drugs

Intravenous access should be established for the administration of antibiotics and analgesics. Broad-spectrum antibiotics covering multiple organisms, including anaerobes, can be administered during the procedure to combat bacteremia resulting from catheter manipulation and irrigation. They are continued until culture results permit selection of a more appropriate agent.

Adequate sedation is important for the safe and accurate placement of the drain and for patient comfort through the procedure. It is now possible to achieve conscious sedation, which, in combination with the generous administration of local anesthetic, results in safe, reliable analgesia in virtually all patients, and amnesia for the procedure in most.[58] This requires the presence of a specially trained and experienced nurse or doctor to administer frequent small intravenous doses of drugs such as midazolam and fentanyl in combination. The patient's vital signs, electrocardiogram (ECG), and blood oxygen saturation must be monitored continuously during the procedure and for a suitable period thereafter.

Diagnostic Aspiration

Diagnostic needle aspiration precedes catheter placement and achieves three purposes. It confirms the presence of a fluid collection, it determines whether the collection is infected, and it determines whether the viscosity of the contents is sufficiently low to allow successful drainage.[4] Signs of an abscess such as the presence of gas or a hypervascular rim on contrast-enhanced CT are not frequently present, and drainable abscesses can appear "solid" on both CT and US, whereas lymphoma or fibrous scar can appear sonolucent.

The authors perform the initial aspiration with a 22-gauge needle because of its safety. If no fluid can be aspirated from the lesion, an 18-gauge needle is used. A Gram stain should be immediately performed if the fluid aspirated is not frankly purulent. If a layered collection is present, the dependent sediment should be sampled, because the supernatant fluid may yield false-negative results. Lack of free-flowing fluid aspirate through an 18-gauge needle indicates that a drainable collection is unlikely to be present. In this instance, biopsy for histologic examination may be performed.

Only 2 to 3 ml of fluid should be aspirated for Gram

stain and culture. Withdrawal of larger volumes will result in partial collapse of the abscess, making insertion of a drainage catheter more difficult. Abscess fluid contains abundant leukocytes and bacteria on Gram stain. The presence of abundant leukocytes but no bacteria in a patient receiving prior antibiotic therapy indicates a sterile abscess, and drainage should proceed if the collection is causing symptoms. Abundant bacteria with scanty leukocytes indicate that bowel contents have been aspirated or that the patient has an abscess and is immunocompromised.

Figure 56-4. A 10-year-old child with cerebral palsy and spina bifida with an indwelling ventriculoperitoneal shunt. (A) Pelvic CT scan shows an air–fluid level anteriorly within the bladder, with a right lower quadrant thick-walled, septated fluid density collection. (B) Right lower quadrant ultrasound shows a large multiloculated superficial collection. No bowel is seen between the skin surface and the collection. Trocar catheter placement and drainage were performed. Laboratory studies revealed typical characteristics of a cerebral spinal fluid collection that had walled off at the tip of the ventriculoperitoneal shunt. (C) Five days after catheter

Choice of Access Route

Transabdominal

The advantages of transabdominal drainage are convenience for the operator, a comfortable position for the patient during the procedure, and easy and secure skin fixation (Fig. 56-4). The disadvantages include the possibility of damage to the external iliac or inferior epigastric vessels because of the lateral approach required to avoid trangressing bowel, uterus, or bladder; the potential for contaminating the peritoneal cavity;

placement, no residual fluid collection is seen and the right lower quadrant is now filled with opacified bowel and minimal residual fatty inflammatory change. This case demonstrates the value of correlative imaging before abscess drainage. Although the CT scan appears to show a relatively simple collection, the multiple septa that were visible on the ultrasound could have deterred percutaneous treatment. However, all of the septa were easily broken with a guidewire during catheter placement, and the patient did well with percutaneous management and intravenous antibiotics. The shunt was subsequently replaced.

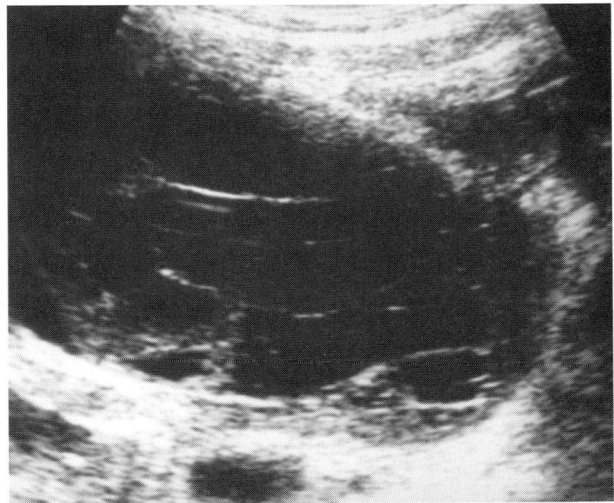

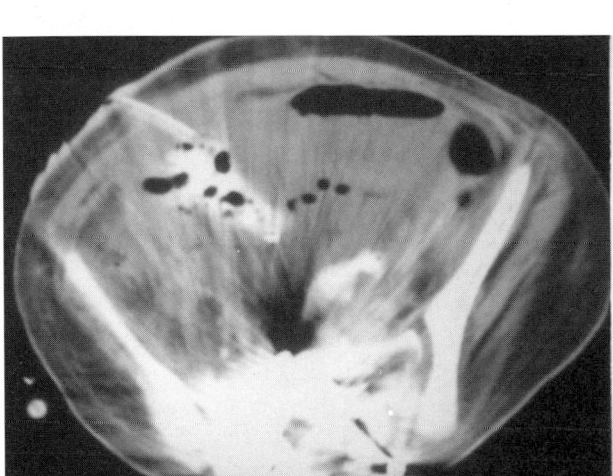

A

B

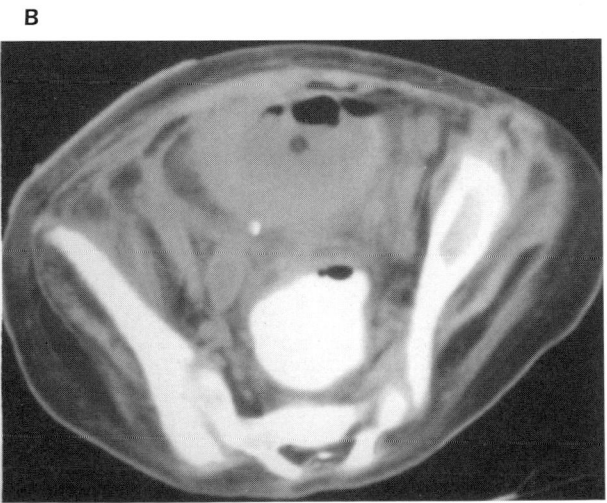

C

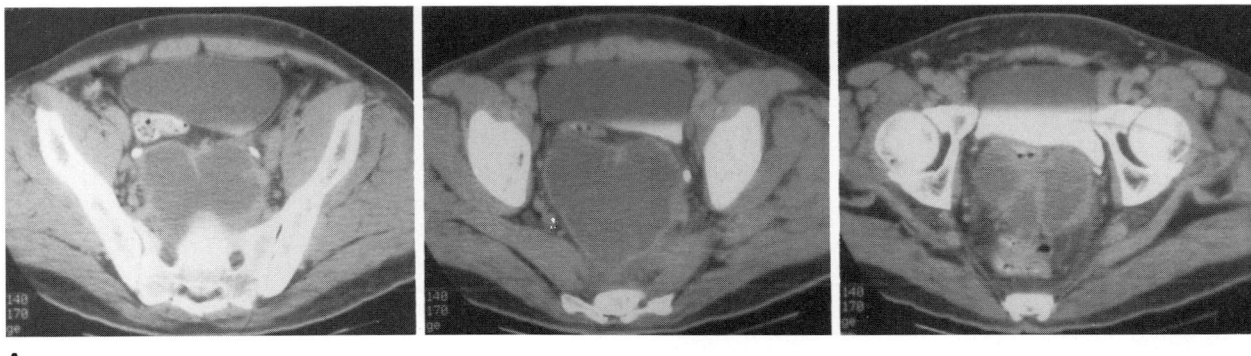

A

Figure 56-5. A 33-year-old HIV-positive man with a tender mass palpated on rectal examination. (A) Three CT images through the pelvis following intravenous contrast and oral contrast administration show a septated thin-walled fluid collection in the pouch of Douglas. Anterior access routes are obscured by the iliac vasculature and the urinary bladder. (B) The patient was placed prone and a right transgluteal approach was made. Images of the initial needle can be seen in the pelvic musculature, but the tip of the needle used for drainage is seen within the cavity with the typical black artifact projecting from the tip. A relatively posterior approach is preferred for transgluteal drainage to avoid the sciatic nerve and neurovascular bundle, which are closely related to the ischial spine. (C) Six days after percutaneous transgluteal drainage, after symptoms resolved, repeat scanning with the patient supine shows no residual collection and normal position of the sigmoid and bladder.

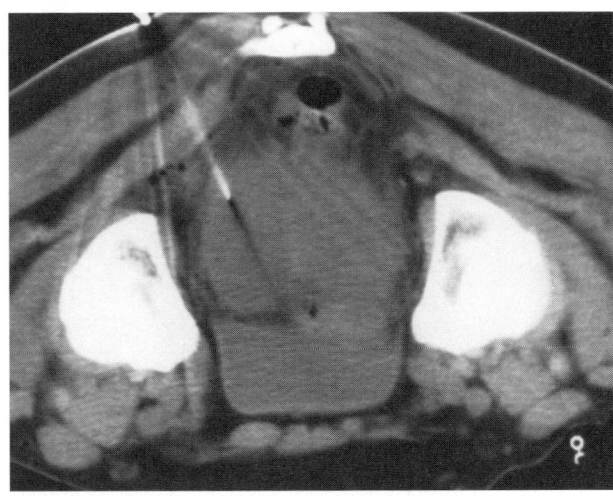

B

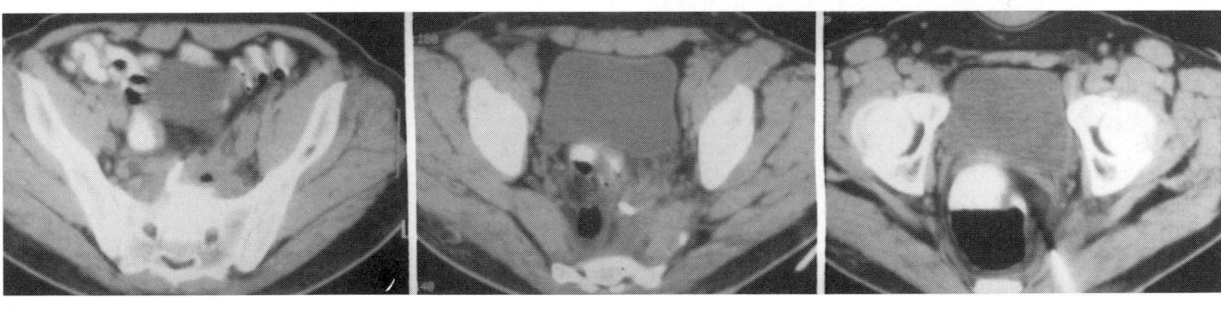

C

and the length of the track. Despite CT guidance, this route is often not feasible in the pelvis.

Transgluteal

This route offers an alternative to surgery when a transabdominal approach is not possible. It requires precise catheter placement under CT guidance and a familiarity with the regional anatomy (Fig. 56-5).

The greater sciatic foramen is crossed by the piriformis muscle, the sciatic nerve, the superior and inferior gluteal vessels, the superior gluteal nerve, the posterior cutaneous nerve of the thigh, the nerve to the obturator internis, and the internal pudendal vessels. The sci-

atic nerve is formed from the inferior continuation of the sacral plexus and exits the greater sciatic foramen in its anterior third, passing posterior to the sacrospinous ligament at its attachment to the ischial spine. The ideal trangluteal entry site to the pelvis is through the sacrospinous ligament medially, which avoids injury to the neurovascular structures of the greater sciatic foramen (Fig. 56-6). The sacrospinous ligament is thin and is usually easily distinguished from the piriformis on CT. In a few patients the location of the pelvic collection will necessitate puncture through the piriformis.[55] The sacral plexus and sciatic nerve can still be avoided in these patients by entry as close to the

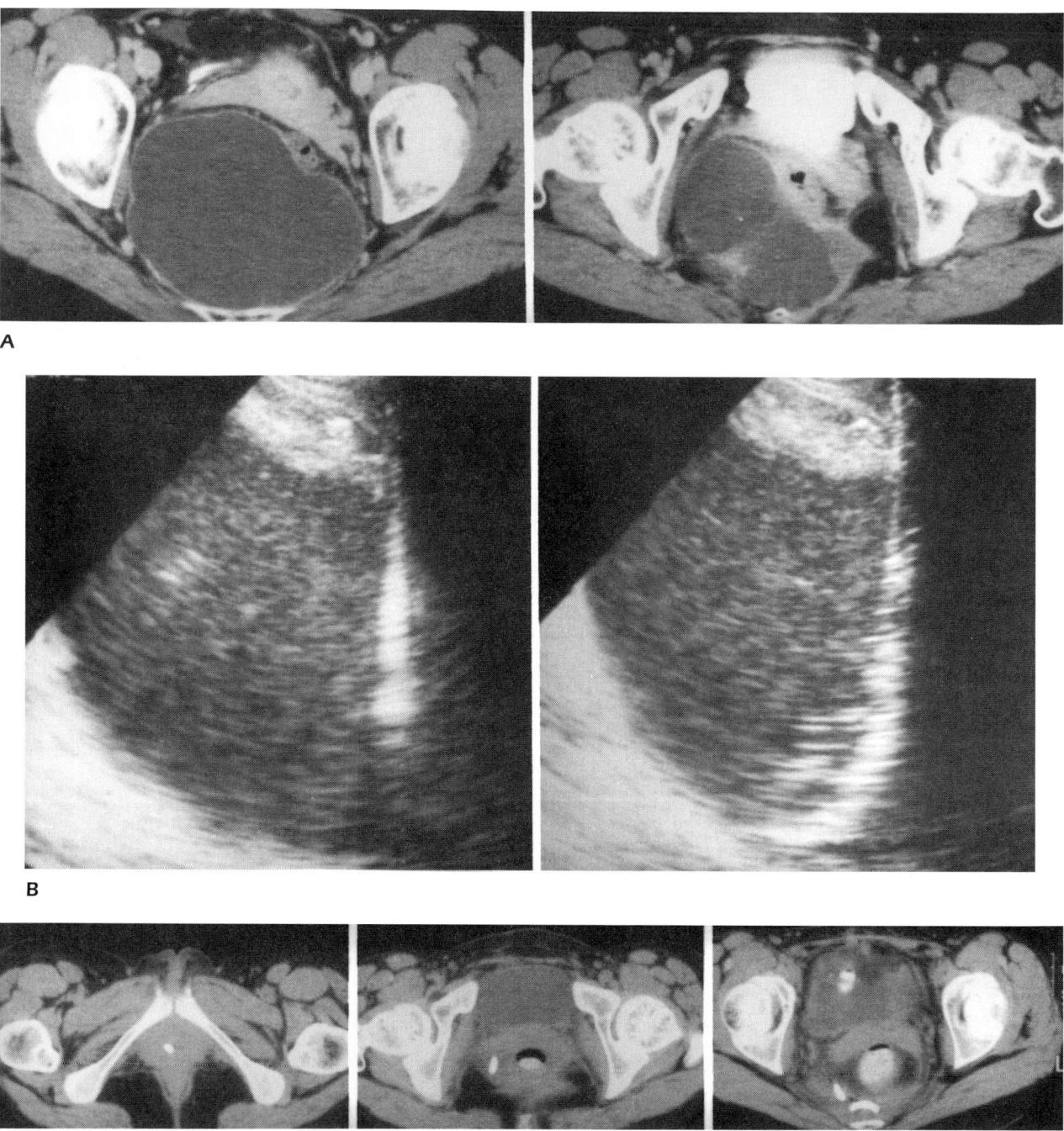

Figure 56-6. A 43-year-old woman with a 10-year history of benign presacral teratoma. Previous surgical resection attempts were unsuccessful and incurred large blood losses. Because of her religious beliefs, the patient refused further surgery, given the probable need for transfusion. (A) CT scan shows a large loculated mass adherent to the sacrum, displacing the rectum and bladder anterolaterally. (B) Transvaginal needle placement. The fluid shows uniform low-level echoes, with bright linear echoes corresponding to the needle position. (C) After complete aspiration of the collection and placement of a self-retaining 10 French catheter, follow-up CT shows no residual collection, with the catheter entering the presacral space via a right superior lateral transvaginal approach. Nine months later the collection had recurred and was again treated with transvaginal drainage. The patient declined further surgery.

sacrum as possible, although the gluteal vasculature may still be at risk. A single case of major hemorrhage from the internal pudendal artery has been described in a patient undergoing transgluteal PAD through the greater sciatic foramen under guidance by fluoroscopy alone.[59]

The most common complication of the transgluteal route is postprocedure pain, which may occur locally or deep in the pelvis or may radiate down the leg. It is associated with catheter placement through the piriformis and the sacral plexus, and in the authors' experience is most commonly mild and resolves within 24 hours. Soft catheters are better tolerated than those made from stiffer materials but are more difficult to insert through the large gluteal muscle bulk. Adequate dilation and dissection of the track help in this regard, as does the trocar technique, which increases stiffness of the catheter insertion system. Kinking of the catheter may occur in patients who lie supine or sit up.

Transvaginal

Surgical drainage of pelvic abscesses by the transvaginal route is well established and of proven benefit,[60] but is limited in most instances to collections that displace the vaginal wall.[61] Drainage may be readily performed under US guidance, which allows accurate needle or catheter placement within a collection that abuts but need not deform the vaginal vault.

Initial reports of transvaginal abscess drainage used transabdominal US for guidance.[62] Transvaginal US, with its increased resolution, increases the sensitivity of diagnosis and allows for more precise catheter placement. It is not necessary to perform the procedure in the operating room, and the procedure may be combined with fluoroscopy to assist in catheter positioning if the Seldinger technique is used. A curved array transducer is the most suitable because of the wide field of view, which permits visualization of the needle close to the probe.

A vaginal speculum is unnecessary. The patient's bladder is emptied, she is placed in the lithotomy position, and the vagina is swabbed with a disinfectant solution, while the cervix is displaced and stabilized with a long clamp. Local anesthetic is administered directly through the long initial puncture needle. Intravenous sedation may also be required. A biopsy guide is attached to the probe, although a plastic tube will suffice. A custom-made guide has been described.[63] If a drain has to be inserted, a small slit is made with a long scalpel in the vaginal vault, since it is sometimes difficult to penetrate the vaginal wall. Catheters with an inner metal stiffener are advantageous. A self-locking catheter eliminates the need for suturing to the vaginal wall or thigh for catheter retention.

In early studies and in the authors' own experience, transvaginal abscess drainage is safe and effective, with a success rate comparable to that of transabdominal drainage, if a little more difficult technically. It is relatively painless and well tolerated. The place of needle aspiration alone in small nonviscous collections is yet to be determined.[64]

Transrectal

Abscesses in contact with the rectum may be drained transrectally. Surgical drainage by the transrectal route is well established but generally requires general anesthesia and an abscess that is palpable rectally. Image-guided drainage overcomes these problems and may be guided by a number of modalities. Fluoroscopically guided drainage has been described with needle insertion through an anoscope[65] or a modified enema tip.[66] CT guidance may also be used.[67,68] Sonographic guidance was initially transabdominal[69] but more recently has been described transrectally, and may be combined with fluoroscopy.

Abscesses anterior or posterior to the rectum may be drained transrectally. The abscess need not be palpable. The patient is placed in the left lateral decubitus position and the needle, which is withdrawn a short distance into its sheath, is inserted into the rectum under imaging control. A gloved finger, plastic tube, or biopsy guide attached to a transrectal probe may be used to direct the needle, depending on the imaging method employed. The procedure is almost painless and is remarkably well tolerated. Local anesthesia and intravenous sedation are usually unnecessary. Skin fixation is unnecessary if locking catheters are used, but should be used if the patient is ambulatory.

A drawback of this technique is early expulsion of the catheter, which may occur during defecation. Reaccumulation of the abscess may result but usually is cured by repeat transrectal drainage. Lomas et al.[69] have postulated that the use of large catheters will help maintain track patency in the event of catheter expulsion, but this is unproven. Overall success rates have been comparable with those of transabdominal drainage.

Catheter Selection

Large-bore catheters such as the 12 to 14 French van Sonnenberg sump (Medi-Tech) or the 16 French Mueller Drainage Catheter (Cook, Inc.) are used if the contents are viscous or the estimated volume exceeds 100 ml. The large lumen allows for drainage or aspiration of tenacious pus and particulate matter. The smaller lumen of sump catheters allows for circulation of room air to the collection through a filter, preventing adherence of the abscess wall to the side holes and allowing efficient introduction of irrigants. The efficiency of sump drainage is said to be two to four times that of closed drainage systems.[70]

Medium-bore nonsump catheters include most standard biliary and nephrostomy catheters such as the VTC Nephrostomy or Biliary Systems (Medi-Tech) or the Cope Biliary Loop (Cook, Inc.), and are suitable for drainage or nonviscous fluids. The smaller diameter of the lumen and side holes limits their effectiveness in patients with thick pus or necrotic material. Small-bore catheters (9 French and less) such as the Dawson-Mueller Ultrathane Drainage Catheter (Cook, Inc.) or the McGahan Multipurpose Catheter (Cook, Inc.) are effective for limited drainages of small nonviscous collections, or as secondary catheters in tandem with double-lumen sumps for draining locules that are not decompressed by the main catheter.

Self-retaining catheters with locking loops or other devices to prevent dislodgment should be used where possible. They are particularly useful for transvaginal and transrectal drainages. Fixation of non-self-retaining catheters to the skin with sutures is giving way to the use of various adhesive and locking devices that improve patient comfort and decrease the incidence of skin infection.[71] A practical method of catheter fixation is to anchor the catheter to the plastic rim of a stoma disk with adhesive tape and sutures.

Catheter Insertion

The Seldinger technique may be used if the access route is difficult or the abscess is located immediately adjacent to a vital organ, and is probably safer than the trocar technique in inexperienced hands. It is particularly useful in transrectal and transvaginal drainages where combined US-fluoroscopic guidance is used. Following diagnostic needle puncture, an 18-gauge sheathed needle is introduced into the abscess and a 0.038-inch wire is introduced through the outer sheath. A "single-stick" method using commercially available introducer systems such as Accustik (Medi-Tech) or Neff (Cook) in which an 0.018-inch wire is initially passed through the diagnostic 22-gauge puncture needle may be used when additional safety is required.

When transabdominal or transgluteal catheter insertion is being performed via a safe track under CT guidance, the authors generally prefer the tandem trocar technique because of its speed and simplicity, since the patient does not have to be moved to the fluoroscopy suite. The 22-gauge diagnostic needle is left in place to indicate the correct path, and the catheter with internal trocar and stiffener is placed alongside.

Catheter Management

Cavity Lavage and Catheter Irrigation

Immediate cavity lavage is performed in the radiology department after aspiration of the drainable contents of the abscess. Multiple aliquots of normal saline are injected and aspirated until the irrigant is clear. The volume of fluid in each aliquot depends on the size of the collection that has been drained: 20- to 30-ml injections can be used in large cavities during the initial lavage, whereas 10-ml volumes are adequate in smaller cavities. A total volume of several hundred milliliters may be required.

Catheter irrigation is performed at the bedside. Initially 10 to 20 ml of saline is injected every 8 hours by the patient's nurse, tapering to once daily over a few days. Further irrigation is performed on interventional rounds if catheter blockage is suggested by persistent symptoms and unexpectedly low drainage.

Although low suction continues to be used in a number of institutions, continuous suction alone or through sump or double-catheter systems has not been convincingly shown to increase success rates over gravity drainage alone.[72,73] Instillation of antibiotics has been unrewarding, and the proteolytic agent N-acetylcysteine lacks significant in vivo activity at the physiologic pH found within abscesses.[74] However, intracavitary urokinase appears to be of significant value in liquefying clot and increasing success rates in the drainage of infected hematomas that do not respond to catheter drainage alone. It may also assist in breaking down fibrinous septations in other loculated collections resistant to drainage. For a large hematoma, abscess, or empyema, the authors use a schedule of 80,000 units in 50 ml of normal saline, instilled every 8 hours for 3 days. The catheter is clamped and the patient is placed in different positions for 30 minutes after instillation, following which drainage is recommended. Proportionately smaller doses are used for smaller collections.

Catheter Withdrawal

Criteria for catheter withdrawal include the volume of daily drainage, the clinical status of the patient, the size of the abscess cavity, and the character of the drained fluid.

Satisfactory progress toward cure is indicated by a progressive decrease in the volume of drainage. Daily drainage should be less than 10 ml before the catheter is removed. Daily volumes that are not decreasing or that suddenly increase suggest the likelihood of internal fistulization. Similarly, the character of the drainage should progress from purulent to nonpurulent. A progressive change to resemble feces, urine, or lymph will be seen where a fistula exists, and can be confirmed by chemical or microscopic examination of the fluid or definitively by abscessography.

Fever may continue for 4 to 5 days in certain patients, although defervesence typically occurs by 48 hours. Persisting sepsis at this time should prompt a search with CT for an undrained abscess or locule. If progress is satisfactory, follow-up imaging with abscessography or US can be performed to document resolution, but imaging is often not required in patients in whom the clinical response is appropriate and when the drained collection was simple. As experience is gained, less follow-up imaging is required, making PAD especially cost-effective. However, when in doubt, it is better to reimage than to prematurely remove a catheter and allow the patient to have a clinical recurrence. Although a small infected collection may only require drainage for 3 or 4 days, a larger abscess may require 3 to 4 weeks. The drain should not be removed until drainage has effectively ceased and the patient's clinical condition has returned to normal.

Abscess-Fistula Association

Enteric abscesses occur in the setting of surgical enterotomy or anastomotic leakage or result from intestinal perforation in inflammatory disorders, particularly diverticulitis, appendicitis, and Crohn disease. Enteric communication, loosely termed *fistulization,* can be demonstrated in many of these patients if it is searched for. It is important to identify its presence because premature removal of the abscess drainage catheter will be followed by recurrence of the abscess unless the communication has been allowed to heal. Diagnosis of the communication is also important in determining the cause of the abscess, in providing correct catheter placement for healing of the communication, and in determining appropriate nutritional support. Enteric abscesses can be cured in 70 to 90 percent of cases with meticulous technique.[73]

CT signs of enteric communication are the presence of gas, extraluminal oral or rectal contrast or a long gas–liquid level within the collection, proximity to bowel, and the presence of known gastrointestinal disease. Diagnosis is confirmed by abscessography at 3 to 5 days after catheter insertion, by which time the cavity can be distended with contrast without risk of bacteremia. Injection by appropriate positioning of the catheter and gentle probing of any areas of "beaking" of the cavity will often demonstrate a communication that would otherwise be overlooked.[4] Occasionally, communications may not be apparent for up to 2 weeks.

The majority of enteric abscesses, including those due to postoperative bowel injury, anastomotic leaks, appendicitis, and diverticulitis, are associated with a low-output "fistula" draining less than 100 ml per day. These abscesses respond well to PAD as long as the underlying bowel is healthy and capable of healing. The catheter should be placed with its side holes as close as possible to the opening of the communication, but the dependent portion of the abscess should also be drained. In most cases this can be achieved with a single catheter, but sometimes two catheters will be necessary.[37] Patients may be discharged once defervescence has occurred, and outpatient abscessograms may be obtained at 7- to 14-day intervals until the communication and abscess have healed. Patients should keep a record of catheter output while at home.

PAD of high-output "fistulas" requires a longer and more intensive period of therapy and is associated with a lower success rate. An underlying neoplastic cause must be ruled out, and distal bowel obstruction must be excluded with an appropriate luminal contrast study. Control of bowel secretions is obtained by gastrostomy or by nasogastric or nasojejunal intubation. Nutrition may be instituted enterally if the communication arises in the proximal small bowel and a jejunal feeding tube can be placed with its tip distal to the communication so that no reflux occurs into the fistula. Otherwise total parenteral nutrition should be begun. Electrolyte balance and metabolic status must be closely monitored. PAD is achieved by placing a large-bore sump drain in a dependent portion of the cavity and another at the opening of the fistula, or preferably within it, occluding the tract. Subsequently this catheter is replaced by smaller-bore catheters, which are slowly retracted to permit healing.[75,76] A protracted period of catheter drainage will be required, with cure occurring as late as 12 weeks after drainage commenced. Patients with immunosuppression associated with solid organ transplantation can be successfully treated but usually require longer drainage times.[77] In those patients in whom PAD is unsuccessful and surgery is required, worthwhile temporization and improvement of clinical status are still achieved.

Interventional Rounds

Catheter-related problems are common, occurring in 59 percent of inpatients in one study.[77] Early identification of problems allows for their timely correction, maximizing the success rate of PAD and decreasing the length of hospital stay. The radiologist's familiarity with catheter problems, management, and imaging follow-up makes him or her the ideal person for the task.

The most common problem is that the catheter is

not draining. This may be due to intrinsic obstruction such as a blood clot, to extrinsic obstruction such as kinking, or to inadequate drainage of the collection. Other problems are pericatheter leakage, improper catheter fixation, change in catheter position, local skin or wound complications, and distant complications such as peritonitis. Most of these problems can be successfully managed at the bedside. In the eyes of the referring physician, "increased participation in patient care elevates the status of the interventional radiologist from a technician to a valued consultant."[78]

Complications and Failures

Hemorrhage is usually minor and self-limiting but occasionally is major and life-threatening. Embolization of a perforated bleeding artery may rarely be necessary and has been described via the original needle track.[61] Bacteremia with "shaking chills" is common, but septicemia with hypotension is rare. Both are minimized by using adequate cover with broad-spectrum antibiotics and by avoiding overdistention of the abscess with contrast or saline during irrigation, and both suggest an undrained locule or cavity if they persist.

Catheter insertion into or through the bowel should be avoided. Inadvertent diagnostic needle puncture of the bowel is usually innocuous, but a fistula has been described as a result of PAD of an interloop abscess. The fistula resolved with conservative management.[79] Accidental catheter insertion into or through the bowel should be treated by leaving the catheter in situ for 1 to 2 weeks to allow the formation of a mature track and then slowly withdrawing it.

Failure of PAD is avoidable in many cases. Failures are due to errors in diagnosis or to technical errors. The principal cause of failure of both PAD and surgical drainage is misdiagnosis relating to the magnitude, extent, complexity, location, or response of the abscess. Meticulous preprocedural characterization of the abscess is necessary. Phlegmon and organized hematoma should be recognized as undrainable, whereas an underlying neoplasm can be treated by PAD if it is infected but cannot be cured. Undrained locules or abscesses and enteric communications should be aggressively pursued when the clinical course is indicative.

The most common technical error is premature withdrawal of the catheter. Another is the improper selection of the route or entry site to the abscess, which results in the dependent portion remaining undrained. The catheter position should be corrected if it is unsatisfactory on follow-up imaging, as was the case in 26 percent of patients in one series.[37] Additional catheters may be necessary, and multiple catheters were necessary in 31 percent of patients in that series.[37]

References

1. Korobkin M, Silverman PM, Quint LE, et al. CT of the extraperitoneal space: normal anatomy and fluid collections. AJR 1992;159:933–941.
2. Auh YH, Rubenstein WA, Schneider M, et al. Extraperitoneal paravesical spaces: CT delineation with US correlation. Radiology 1986;159:319–328.
3. Cook DE, Walsh JW. Computed tomography- and ultrasound-guided drainage of abscesses or other fluid collections. In: Pinson Neal M Jr, Tisnado J, Cho Shao-Lu, eds. Emergency radiology. Boston: Little, Brown, 1989:343–368.
4. Mueller PR, van Sonnenberg E, Ferrucci JT Jr. Percutaneous drainage of 250 abdominal abscesses and fluid collections: Part II. Current procedural concepts. Radiology 1984;151:343–347.
5. Neff CC, van Sonnenberg E, Casola G, et al. Diverticular abscesses: percutaneous drainage. Radiology 1987;163:15–18.
6. Mueller PR, Saini S, Wittenberg J, et al. Sigmoid diverticular abscesses: percutaneous drainage as an adjunct to surgical resection in 24 cases. Radiology 1987;164:321–325.
7. Jeffrey RB Jr, Tolentino CS, Federle MP, et al. Percutaneous drainage of periappendiceal abscesses: review of 20 patients. AJR 1987;149:59–62.
8. van Sonnenberg E, Wittich G, Casola G, et al. Periappendiceal abscesses: percutaneous drainage. Radiology 1987;163:23–26.
9. Casola G, van Sonnenberg E, Neff CC, et al. Abscesses in Crohn disease: percutaneous drainage. Radiology 1987;163:19–22.
10. Safrit HD, Mauro MA, Jaques PF. Percutaneous abscess drainage in Crohn disease. AJR 1987;148:859–862.
11. Saini S, Mueller PR, Wittenberg J, et al. Percutaneous drainage of diverticular abscess: an adjunct to surgical therapy. Arch Surg 1986;121:475–478.
12. Johnson CM. Drainage of retroperitoneal and pelvic abscesses and fluid collections. In: Kadir S, ed. Current practice of interventional radiology. Philadelphia: Decker, 1991:727–734.
13. Glass CA, Cohn I Jr. Drainage of intra-abdominal abscesses: a comparison of surgical and computerized tomography guided catheter drainage. Am J Surg 1984;147:315–317.
14. Aeder M, Jacqueline L, Wellman J, et al. Role of surgical and percutaneous drainage in the treatment of abdominal abscesses. Arch Surg 1983;118:273–280.
15. Johnson RD, Mueller PR, Ferrucci JT Jr, et al. Percutaneous drainage of pyogenic liver abscesses. AJR 1985;144:463–467.
16. Olak J, Christou N, Stein LA, et al. Operative versus percutaneous drainage of intra-abdominal abscesses. Arch Surg 1986;121:141–146.
17. Welch CE, Malt RA. Abdominal surgery (three parts). N Engl J Med 1983;308:753–760.
18. Cotran RS, Kumar V, Cotran RR. Robbins pathologic basis of disease. Philadelphia: Saunders, 1989:884.
19. Williams I, Schnyder P. Diverticula. In: Margulis AR, Burhenne JH, eds. Alimentary tract radiology. 3rd ed. St. Louis: Mosby, 1983:1090–1112.
20. Asch MJ, Markowitz AM. Diverticulitis coli: a surgical appraisal. Surgery 1967;62:239–247.
21. Jeffrey RB Jr. Enteric abscesses: imaging and intervention. Syllabus, Categorical Course in Interventional Radiology, 77th Scientific Assembly and Annual Meeting of the Radiological Society of North America, Chicago, 1991.

22. Hinchey EJ, Schaal PGH, Richards GK. Treatment of perforated diverticular disease of the colon. Adv Surg 1978;12:85–109.

23. Stafford ES, Sprong DH Jr. The mortality from acute appendicitis in the Johns Hopkins Hospital. JAMA 1940;115:1242–1245.

24. Cooperman M. Complications of appendectomy. Surg Clin North Am 1983;63:1233–1247.

25. Jordan JS, Kovalcic PJ, Schwab CW. Appendicitis with a palpable mass. Ann Surg 1981;193:227–229.

26. Bradley EL, Isaacs L. Appendiceal abscess revisited. Arch Surg 1978;113:130–132.

27. Paul DL, Bloom GP. Appendiceal abscess. Arch Surg 1982; 117:1017–1019.

28. Jeffrey RB Jr, Federle M, Tolentino CS. Periappendiceal inflammatory masses: CT directed management and clinical outcome in 70 patients. Radiology 1988;167:13–16.

29. Peer A, Strauss S. Percutaneous drainage of postappendectomy abscess complicated by enteric communication. Cardiovasc Intervent Radiol 1991;14:106–108.

30. Nunez D, Huber JS, Yrizarry JM, et al. Nonsurgical drainage of appendiceal abscesses. AJR 1986;146:587–589.

31. Barnes BA, Behringer GE, Wheelock FC, et al. Treatment of appendicitis at the Massachusetts General Hospital, 1932–1959. JAMA 1962;180:122–126.

32. Mosegard A, Nielson OS. Interval appendectomy: a retrospective study. Acta Chir Scand 1979;145:109–111.

33. Homans J, Powers LH. Appendiceal abscess: treatment of the appendix. N Engl J Med 1928;199:319–321.

34. Greenstein AJ, Sacher DB, Greenstein RJ, et al. Intraabdominal abscess in Crohn's (ileo) colitis. Am J Surg 1982;143:727–730.

35. Keighley MRB, Eastwood D, Ambrose NS, et al. Incidence and microbiology of intraabdominal and pelvic abscess in Crohn's disease. Gastroenterology 1982;83:1271–1275.

36. Steinberg DM, Cooke WT, Alexander-Williams J. Abscess and fistulae in Crohn's disease. Gut 1973;14:865–869.

37. Papanicolaou N, Mueller P, Ferrucci JT, et al. Abscess-fistula association: radiologic recognition and percutaneous management. AJR 1987;143:811–815.

38. Doemeny JM, Burke DR, Meranze SGO. Percutaneous drainage of abscesses in patients with Crohn's disease. Gastrointest Radiol 1988;13:237–241.

39. Millward SF, Ramswak W, Fitzsimons P, et al. Percutaneous abscess in Crohn's disease. Gastrointest Radiol 1986;11:289–290.

40. Ginsburg DS, Stern JL, Hamod KA, et al. Tubo-ovarian abscess: a retrospective review. Am J Obstet Gynecol 1980;138:1055–1058.

41. Tyrrel RT, Murphy FB, Bernadino ME. Tubo-ovarian abscesses: CT-guided percutaneous drainage. Radiology 1990;175:87–89.

42. Casola G, van Sonnenberg E, D'Agostino HB, et al. Percutaneous drainage of tubo-ovarian abscesses. Radiology 1992;182:399–402.

43. Mueller PR, White EM, Glass-Royal M, et al. Infected abdominal tumors: percutaneous catheter drainage. Radiology 1989;173:627–629.

44. Braun WE, Banowsky LH, Saffron RA, et al. Lymphoceles associated with renal transplantation: report of 15 cases and review of the literature. Am J Med 1974;57:714–729.

45. Ilacheran A, Monaghan JM. Pelvic lymphocyst—a 10-year experience. Gynecol Oncol 1988;29:333–336.

46. Gilliland JD, Spies JB, Brown SB, et al. Lymphoceles: percutaneous treatment with povidone-iodine sclerosis. Radiology 1989;171:227–229.

47. Conte M, Panici PB, Guariglia L, et al. Pelvic lymphocele following radical para-aortic and pelvic lymphadenectomy for cervical carcinoma: incidence rate and percutaneous management. Obstet Gynecol 1990;76:268–271.

48. White M, Mueller PR, Ferrucci JT Jr, et al. Percutaneous drainage of postoperative abdominal and pelvic lymphoceles. AJR 1985;145:1065–1069.

49. van Sonnenberg E, Wittich GR, Casola G, et al. Lymphoceles: imaging characteristics and percutaneous management. Radiology 1986;161:593–596.

50. van Sonnenberg E. Advances in percutaneous abscess drainage. Syllabus, Categorical Course in Interventional Radiology, 77th Scientific Assembly and Annual Meeting of the Radiological Society of North America, Chicago, 1991:56–72.

51. Cohan RH, Saeed M, Sussman SK, et al. Percutaneous drainage of pelvic lymphatic fluid collections in the renal transplant patient. Invest Radiol 1987;22:865–867.

52. Baker ME, Binder RA, Rice RP. Diagnostic imaging of abdominal fluid collections and abscesses. Crit Rev Diagn Imaging 1986;25:233–278.

53. Saini S, Kellum JM, O'Leary MP, et al. Improved localization and survival in patients with intra-abdominal abscesses. Am J Surg 1983;145:136–142.

54. Schwerk WB, Durr HK. Ultrasound grey-scale pattern and guided aspiration puncture of abdominal abscesses. J Clin Ultrasound 1981;9:389.

55. Dobrin PB, Gully PH, Greenlee HB, et al. Radiologic diagnosis of an intra-abdominal abscess: do multiple tests help? Arch Surg 1986;121:41–46.

56. Joseph AEA, Macvicar D. Ultrasound in the diagnosis of abdominal abscesses. Clin Radiol 1990;42:154–156.

57. Haaga JR. Imaging intraabdominal abscesses and nonoperative drainage procedures. World J Surg 1990;14:204–209.

58. Brown JJ, van Sonnenberg E, Gerber KH, et al. Magnetic resonance relaxation times of percutaneously obtained normal and abnormal body fluids. Radiology 1985;154:727–731.

59. Lind LL, Mushlin PS. Sedation, analgesia and anesthesia for radiologic procedures. Cardiovasc Intervent Radiol 1987;10:247–253.

60. Butch RJ, Mueller PR, Ferrucci JT Jr, et al. Drainage of pelvic abscesses through the greater sciatic foramen. Radiology 1986;158:487–491.

61. Malden ES, Picus D. Hemorrhagic complication of transgluteal pelvic abscess drainage: successful percutaneous treatment. J Vasc Intervent Radiol 1992;3:323–328.

62. Walker AP, Malangoni MA. Peritonitis and intraabdominal abscesses. In: Schwartz SI, ed. Principles of surgery. 5th ed. New York: McGraw-Hill, 1989:1459–1489.

63. Nosher JL, Winchman HK, Needell GS. Transvaginal pelvic abscess drainage with US guidance. Radiology 1987;165:872–873.

64. Graham D, Sanders RC. Ultrasound-directed transvaginal aspiration biopsy of pelvic masses. J Ultrasound Med 1982;1:279–280.

65. VanDerKolk HL. Small deep pelvic abscesses: definition and drainage guided with an endovaginal probe. Radiology 1991;181:283–284.

66. van Sonnenberg E, D'Agostino HB, Casola G, et al. US-guided transvaginal drainage of pelvic abscesses and fluid collections. Radiology 1991;181:53–56.

67. Mauro MA, Jaques PF, Mandell VS, et al. Pelvic abscess drainage by the transrectal catheter approach in men. AJR 1985;144:477–479.

68. Bennett JD, Kozak RI, Taylor BM, et al. Deep pelvic abscesses: transrectal drainage with radiologic guidance. Radiology 1992;185:825–828.

69. Lomas DJ, Dixon AK, Thomson HJ, et al. CT guided drainage of pelvic abscesses: the perianal transrectal approach. Clin Radiol 1992;45:246–249.

70. Gazelle GS, Haaga JR, Stellato TA, et al. Pelvic abscesses: CT guided transrectal drainage. Radiology 1991;181:49–51.

71. Nosher JL, Needell GS, Amorosa JK, et al. Transrectal pelvic abscess drainage with sonographic guidance. AJR 1986;146:1047–1048.

72. Castenada-Zuniga WR, Tadavarthy SM, Letourneau JG, et al. Drainage of abdominal abscesses. In: Castenada-Zuniga WR,

Tadavarthy SM, eds. Interventional radiology. 2nd ed. Baltimore: Williams & Wilkins, 1992:1311–1356.

73. van Sonnenberg E, D'Agostino HB, Casola G, et al. Percutaneous abscess drainage: current concepts. Radiology 1991;181: 617–626.

74. van Sonnenberg E, Schiffman HR, Casola G, et al. Simplified solvent infusion and drainage in closed systems: double-lumen single-catheter method. AJR 1985;144:259–260.

75. Edwards KC, Katzen BT, Woods C. Continuous gentle suction apparatus for abscess drainage. Radiology 1982;145: 537.

76. Dawson SD, Mueller PR, Ferrucci JT Jr. Mucomyst for abscesses: a clinical comment. Radiology 1984;151:342.

77. Schuster MR, Crummy AB, Wojtowycz MM, et al. Abdominal abscesses associated with enteric fistulas: percutaneous management. J Vasc Intervent Radiol 1992;3:359–363.

78. Goldberg MA, Mueller PR, Saini S, et al. Importance of daily rounds by the radiologist after interventional procedures of the abdomen and chest. Radiology 1991;180:767–770.

79. Lambiase RE, Cronan JJ, Dorfman GS, et al. Postoperative abscesses with enteric communication: percutaneous treatment. Radiology 1989;171:497–500.

X

Miscellaneous Applications of Interventional Radiology

57

Percutaneous Vascular and Nonvascular Foreign Body Retrieval

FREDERICK S. KELLER
JOSEF RÖSCH
RICHARD A. BAUM

The first transluminal recovery of an intravascular foreign body, as well as the first such recovery done percutaneously, can be credited to Porstmann,[1] in connection with his 1967 catheter technique for ductal closure. That Porstmann's foreign body was a guide-spring deliberately passed across the ductus into the right heart and securely held at its other end rather than an accidentally embolized fragment of guidewire or tubing does not detract from his technical accomplishment. As far as is known, all transluminally recovered foreign bodies have gotten into, as well as out of, the vascular system through man's doing. Unlike Porstmann's, however, most of them were turned loose by mishap rather than design; and unlike Porstmann's, they posed a serious risk to their hosts.

This chapter deals specifically with the relatively noninvasive transluminal removal of unwanted errant foreign bodies lodged in the depths of the cardiovascular system. The first such removal was done in 1964 by Thomas, who used bronchoscopic forceps passed through a saphenous vein cutdown.[2] In 1968, Henley and Ballard accomplished a similar removal percutaneously.[3] In 1971, it was possible to report a total of 29 guided transvascular foreign-body retrievals, 6 done percutaneously.[4] By now, there has appeared a seemingly unending series of reports describing a host of methods used to extricate unwanted foreign bodies from various parts of the vascular system. The impulse to publish is understandable, since the presence of such debris poses significant threats to patients, especially the risks of surgical removal or, alternatively, the potential consequences of nonremoval, among which are sepsis and death. Nonremoval or surgical removal is potential grounds for malpractice action and a source of embarrassment to the presumably responsible physician or manufacturer.

The veritable plethora of related reports also reflects the excitement of the actual procedure and the nearly universal feeling of triumph at the moment of success. Thus, editors of scientific journals can expect to continue to receive manuscripts with reviews of the general subject and case reports illustrating minor variations on the many technical wrinkles already described in print. By now, hundreds of foreign bodies have been removed percutaneously from the vascular system, sparing hundreds of patients from surgery or the serious complications of doing nothing. As in dealing with retained bile stones, there is little wonder that image-guided catheter removal has now become the standard therapeutic approach.

Cardiovascular Foreign Bodies— What and Where?

Extensive 1977 reviews on the nonsurgical retrieval of intravascular foreign bodies include the review by Fisher and Ferreyro[5] and Bloomfield's report[6] of an international survey dealing with types and sites of lodgment of some 180 foreign bodies. Of these 180 foreign bodies, 143 were cut-off bits of plastic tubing used for measuring central venous pressure (Fig. 57-1). In addition, Bloomfield reported the recovery of 6 fragments of diagnostic catheters, 6 broken-off guidewires, 7 pacing catheters damaged during pacemaker replacement, 12 errant ventricular-jugular shunt tubes, and 6 other items, ranging from bullets (presumably not iatrogenic) to a Swan-Ganz catheter that had been sewn to the right atrial wall during prior surgery and broken during attempted withdrawal! As detailed in Table 57-1, all but 6 objects came to lie in the veins, right heart chambers, or pulmonary arteries. The 6 exceptions were guidewire fragments that had

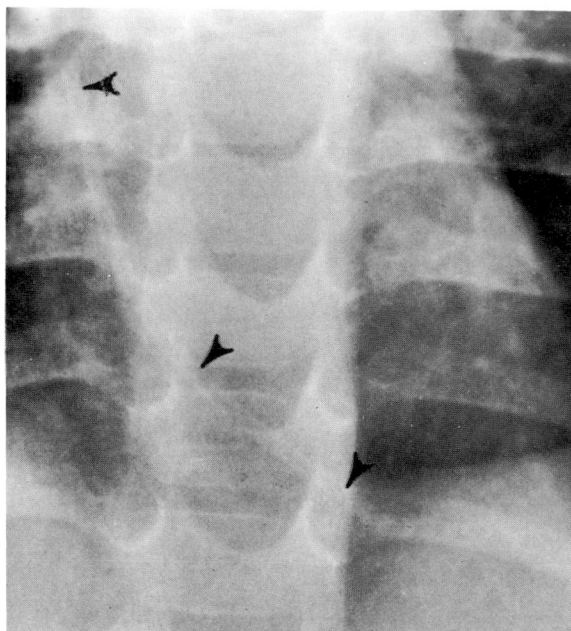

Figure 57-1. Detail of a chest film showing an 8-cm fragment of a central venous pressure catheter (*arrowheads*) lodged in the right atrium and extending into the right ventricle of a 3-year-old patient; its radiopacity and position allowed its prompt retrieval with a homemade loop snare.

Table 57-1. Distribution of Lodging Sites in the Right Heart of 180 Catheter Fragments

Site	Proximal (Cut) End	Distal (Leading) End
Subclavian vein	11	1
Internal jugular vein	2	1
Superior vena cava	36	6
Right atrium	46	22
Right ventricle	1	38
Pulmonary artery	33	35
Inferior vena cava	9	6
Hepatic vein	—	4
Umbilical vein	1	1

The proximal, most accessible, end of a foreign-body fragment can be expected to lie no more central in the circulation than the right atrium unless the entire fragment passes to the pulmonary artery. The only instance of a right ventricular lodging site occurred when a polyethylene catheter doubled over on itself with both ends in the ventricle and the midsection looped in the pulmonary artery. (Adapted from Bloomfield DA. The nonsurgical removal of intracardiac foreign bodies—an international survey. Cathet Cardiovasc Diagn 1978;4:1.)

lodged in peripheral arteries. If Bloomfield's collection were brought up to date, it would include several instances of Gianturco spring coil occluders being retrieved following their malplacement or subsequent displacement. These and other objects used in the transluminal therapeutic production of vascular—usually arterial—occlusion can get into the wrong places and become the opposite of therapeutic. Fortunately, they are usually susceptible to transluminal, nonoperative disposal. It seems clear that future progress in interventional radiology will bring both the promise of new therapeutic techniques and the problems of unintended, misplaced, or migrant intravascular foreign bodies requiring nonoperative extraction.

Transluminal Retrieval Techniques

There are many ways of finding, visualizing, moving, and, with skill and luck, removing foreign bodies from the heart and blood vessels.[7-13] Fortunately, surgery is a rarely needed last resort. Though details have varied from one report to the next, in general, angiographers rely upon image guidance—usually fluoroscopy—and the use of the following basic retrievers: (1) loop-snare catheters, (2) hook-tip guidewires or catheters, (3) basket retrievers, and (4) grasping forceps or catheters (Fig.

57-2). Tip deflectors[14] and sheath "introducers"[15] can be useful aids. The tools and techniques must be chosen in accordance with individual circumstances. How to remove the foreign body depends on what is to be removed and on where and how it has come to rest. Loose-ended radiopaque tubing can usually be caught in commercially available (Cook) or improvised loop-snare catheters.

Loop-Snare Catheters

Loop-snare catheters[16-26] are the catheters through which a flexible, double length of guidewire or thin tubing or monofilament can be passed so as to form a variable loop extending from the central orifice of the introducing catheter. The size, configuration, and orientation of the loop and the introducing catheter are exploited so as to pass the loop over an accessible, free end of the usual embolized length of polyethylene tubing. Naturally, this is greatly facilitated if the foreign body is radiopaque, as is usually the case. Common sense, manipulative skill, and a bit of luck usually result in a successful lassoing. The snare is then drawn into the end of the guiding catheter so as to lock tightly to the foreign body, and both catheter and foreign body are removed together (Fig. 57-3). This approach in one or another of its many reported variations works equally well with guidewire fragments, provided again that at least one end of the guidewire is free to be snared. Loop-snare catheters have been responsible for most retrievals (Figs. 57-4 through 57-8). Porstmann's successful use of the loop-snare method in nearly 200 consecutive patients undergoing

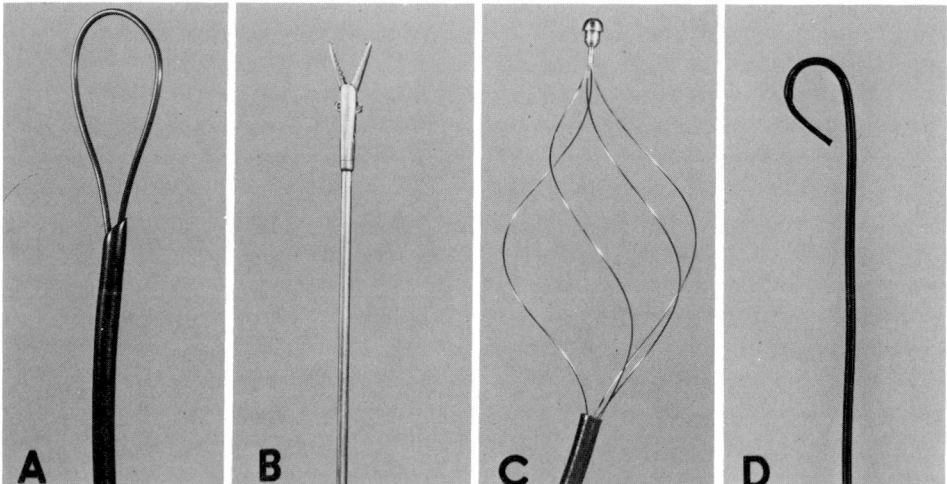

Figure 57-2. Four transluminal retrieval devices used in the cardiovascular system. (A) Loop snare. (B) Grasping forceps. (C) Basket retriever. (D) Hook-tip catheter.

transluminal ductual closure offers convincing confirmation of the value of the approach. In accomplishing the fifth and sixth reported percutaneous foreign-body retrievals,[4] the present authors found that the use of a compound, convoluted loop (see Fig. 57-3C) facilitated fishing for a loose end in the right atrium. Within limits, if one loop could do it, more loops did it

sooner, especially when poor visibility impeded precise three-dimensional control of the snaring maneuver. Closed loops are unlikely to be effective when there is no free end to snare. The shape-memory nitinol "gooseneck" snare (Microvena) has a unique 90-degree loop that allows for accurate sizing and control (see Figs. 57-4 through 57-8).

Figure 57-3. Mechanics of transluminal retrieval by loop-snare techniques. (A) A fragment of broken central venous pressure catheter in the right atrium and hepatic vein. (B) A homemade loop-snare system with a 12 French Teflon outer catheter and a 4 French Teflon loop. (C) One convolution of a deliberately redundant loop has engaged the foreign body. (D) A fragment securely held and ready to be withdrawn via the inferior vena cava and the femoral vein.

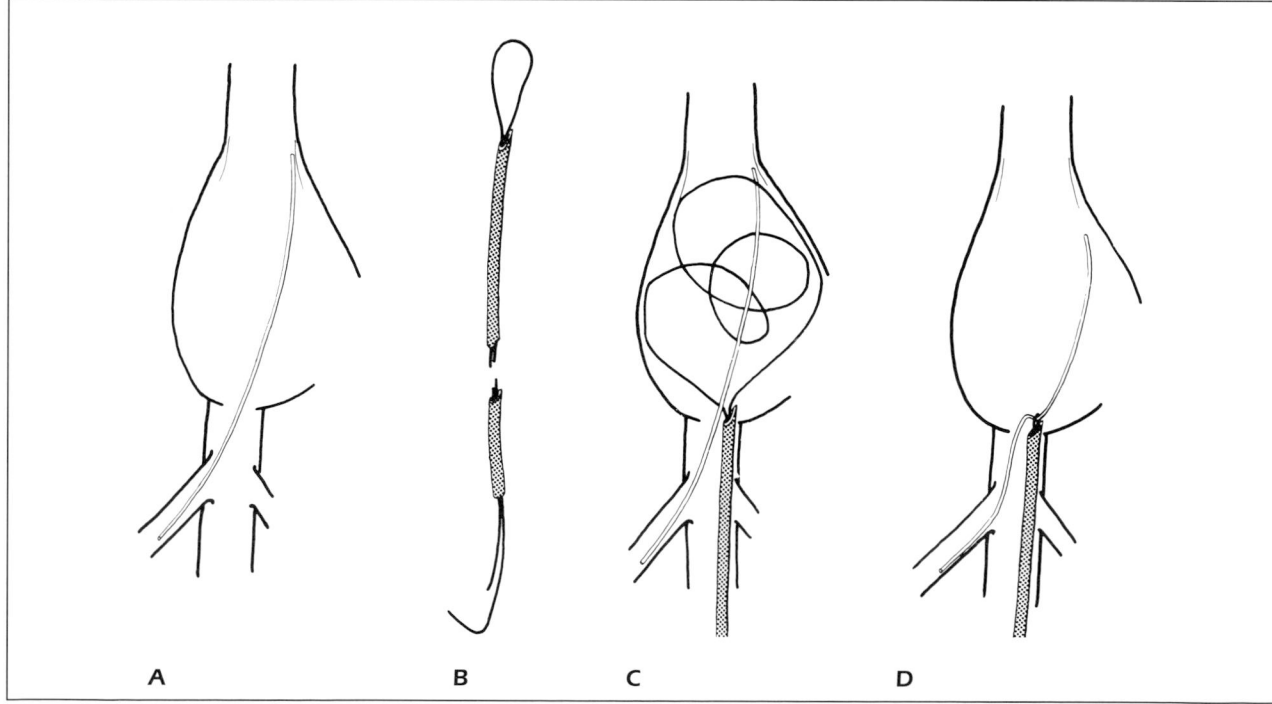

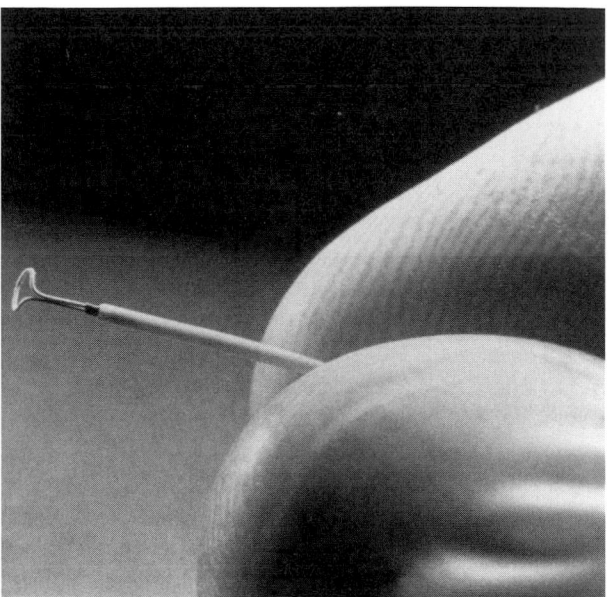

A

B

Figure 57-4. (A) A nitinol snare catheter. The wire snare goes through the catheter and conforms to a predetermined shape. (B) Many different sizes are available.

Hook-Tip Guidewires or Catheters

Hook-tip guidewires or catheters[19,26–31] can be formed ad hoc and used to engage lengths of intravascular debris lacking an accessible free end. Hooked over the offender, they can be used to pull it into a position favorable for snaring; they can be used to twist and thereby engage and withdraw lengths of tubing

Figure 57-5. A nitinol snare catheter being used to retrieve a urethral stent.

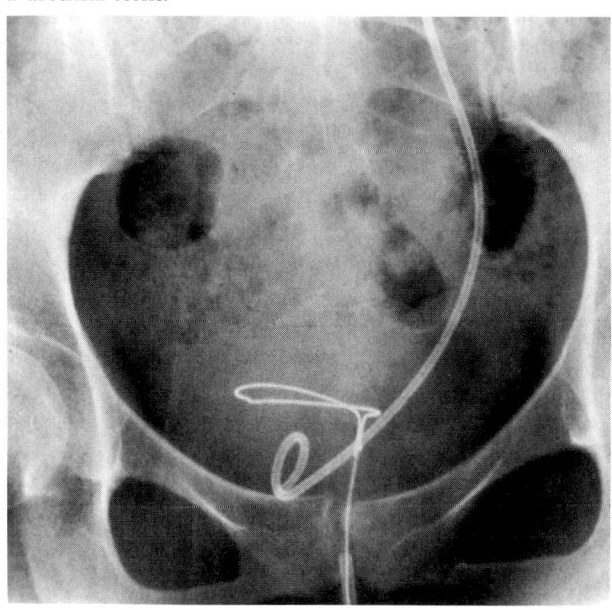

with ends embedded or otherwise out of reach. Tip-deflector guide systems can be useful, although final removal from the vein of access has usually required a cutdown and venotomy.

Basket Retriever Catheter Systems

Wire catch baskets similar to those Dormia used for ureteral stones and Burhenne used for retained gallstones work well in the entrapment of tubing lying within such blood vessels as the pulmonary artery or the vena cava.[20,32–36] In one of the authors' patients, an hour's time was wasted trying to throw a loop snare over a piece of shunt tubing lying within the right pulmonary artery. A basket catheter opened up adjacent to the tubing and rotated slightly before its closure managed the removal on the first try and in less than a minute (Fig. 57-9). A basket retriever system designed for intravascular use is commercially available (Cook). Used and maintained with care, one such catheter can serve several times. For obvious reasons, basket retrievers are used through and in conjunction with larger outer catheters. It is convenient to employ sheaths for their introduction. Since baskets can be expanded to embrace the entire vascular lumen, they necessarily contact and usually can entrap a contained foreign body, be it a bullet or a long length of radiolucent tubing lying flat along the vessel wall. Baskets are best not expanded within cardiac chambers lest trabeculae or valves be unintentionally caught and damaged.

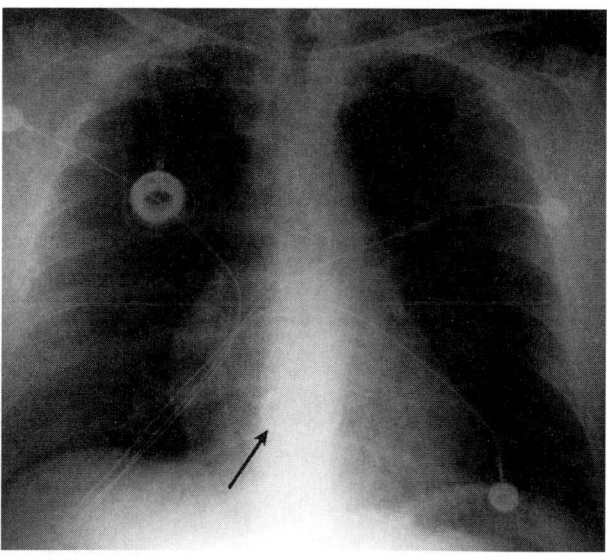

A

Grasping Forceps or Catheters

Bronchoscopic forceps are of limited value because of their rigidity and short length. They have been used with success in several transluminal retrievals, generally necessitating cutdowns.[34,37–39] Ranniger[40] devised a flexible catheter with three grasping prongs that successfully recovered a fragment of guidespring from a right ventricle.

Balloon Catheters

Simple balloon-tipped catheters can be used percutaneously to move intravascular foreign bodies into more favorable positions for conventional catheter recovery. Balloons can also be used to prevent undesired distal embolization of foreign bodies during their recovery from pulmonary or systemic arteries. Their planned percutaneous use in removing unwanted material from blood vessels[41] promises to exceed their past value in connection with "blind" surgical embolectomy.

Nonvascular Foreign-Body Retrieval

Although the vascular tree harbors numerous iatrogenic foreign bodies, many end up in the extravascular space. As with the cardiovascular system, foreign bodies removed percutaneously from extravascular tissue will escape the morbidity and mortality associated with open surgical removal. Biliary, bronchial, gastrointestinal, pleural, subcutaneous, and intraperitoneal spaces are all potential spaces in which foreign bodies may

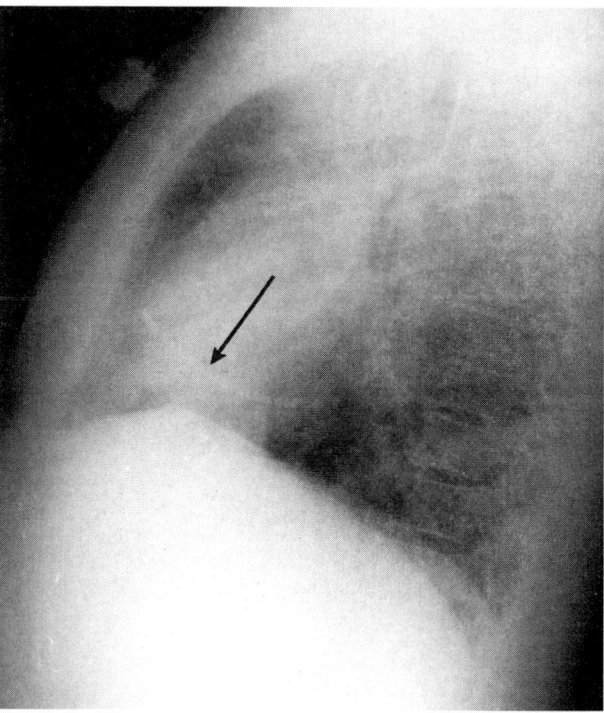

B

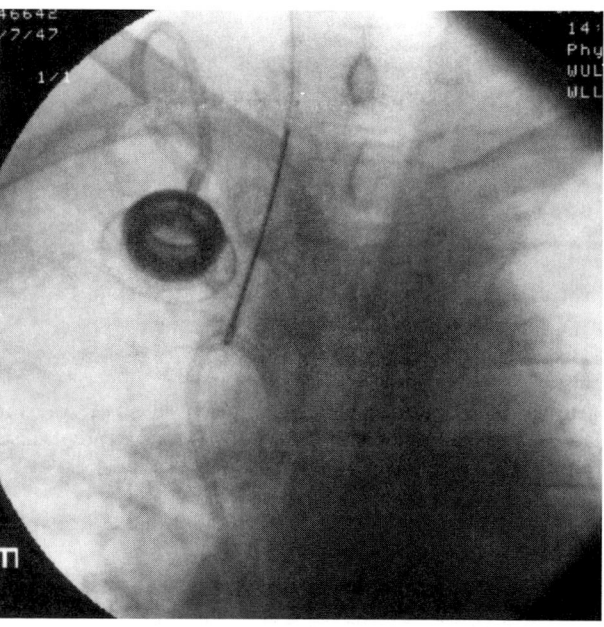

C

Figure 57-6. Retrieval of a fractured Portacath. Anteroposterior (A) and lateral (B) views of the chest reveal a fracture of the midportion of a Portacath (*arrow*). The fragment is seen lying within the right ventricle of the heart. (C) The catheter is successfully retrieved using a snare.

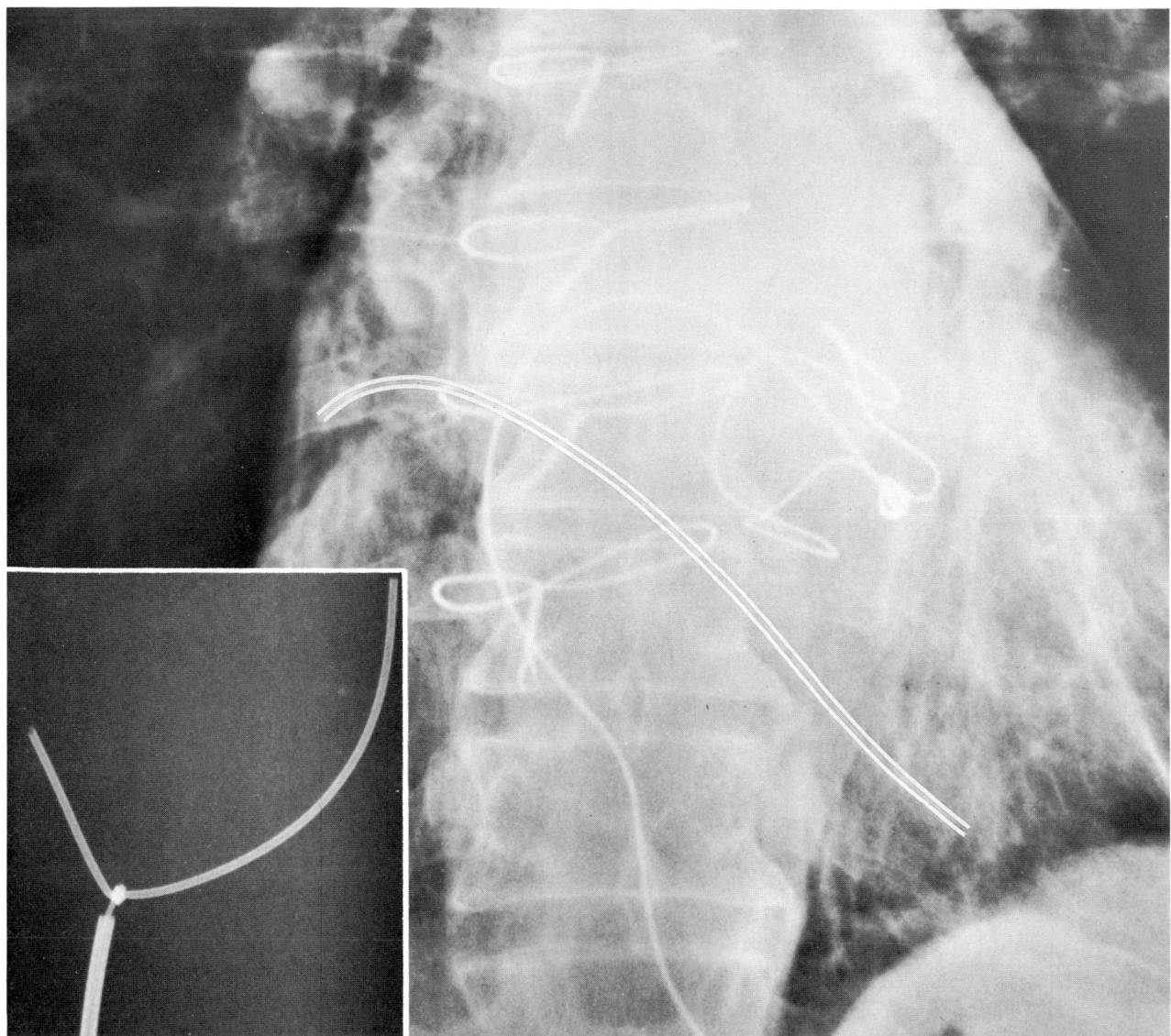

Figure 57-7. Fragment of a broken central venous pressure catheter (retouched) crosses the tricuspid valve with its distal end in the right ventricular apex and its proximal end in the right atrium. Inset at the same scale: a radiograph of 12.5-cm-long central venous pressure catheter fragment after successful retrieval by a loop snare.

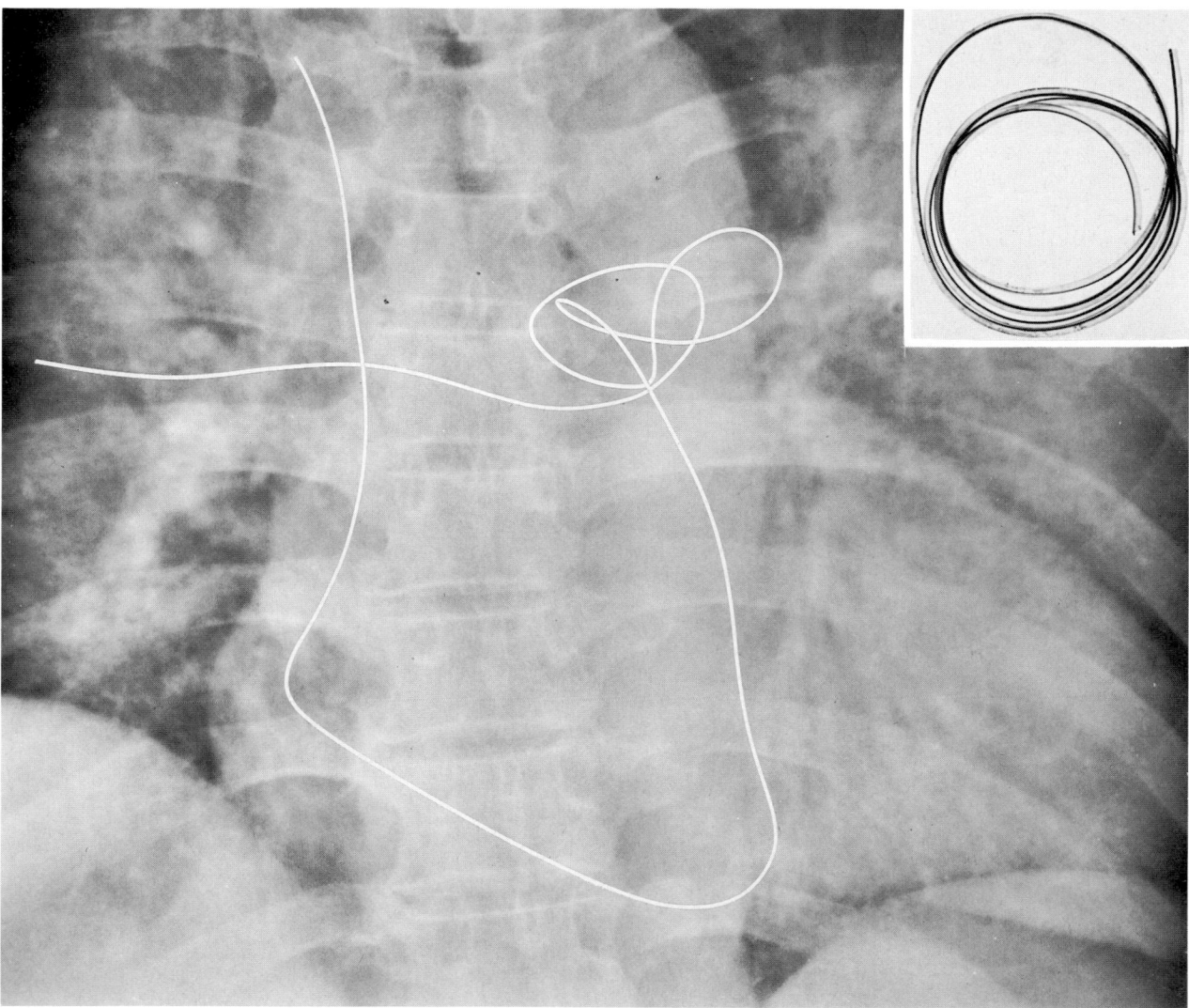

Figure 57-8. Long (5-cm) fragment of a broken central venous pressure catheter (retouched), extending from the superior vena cava through the right atrium, right ventricle, and main pulmonary artery, with its distal end in the right pulmonary artery. Inset at the same scale: a 65-cm-long central venous pressure catheter fragment after successful retrieval with a loop snare.

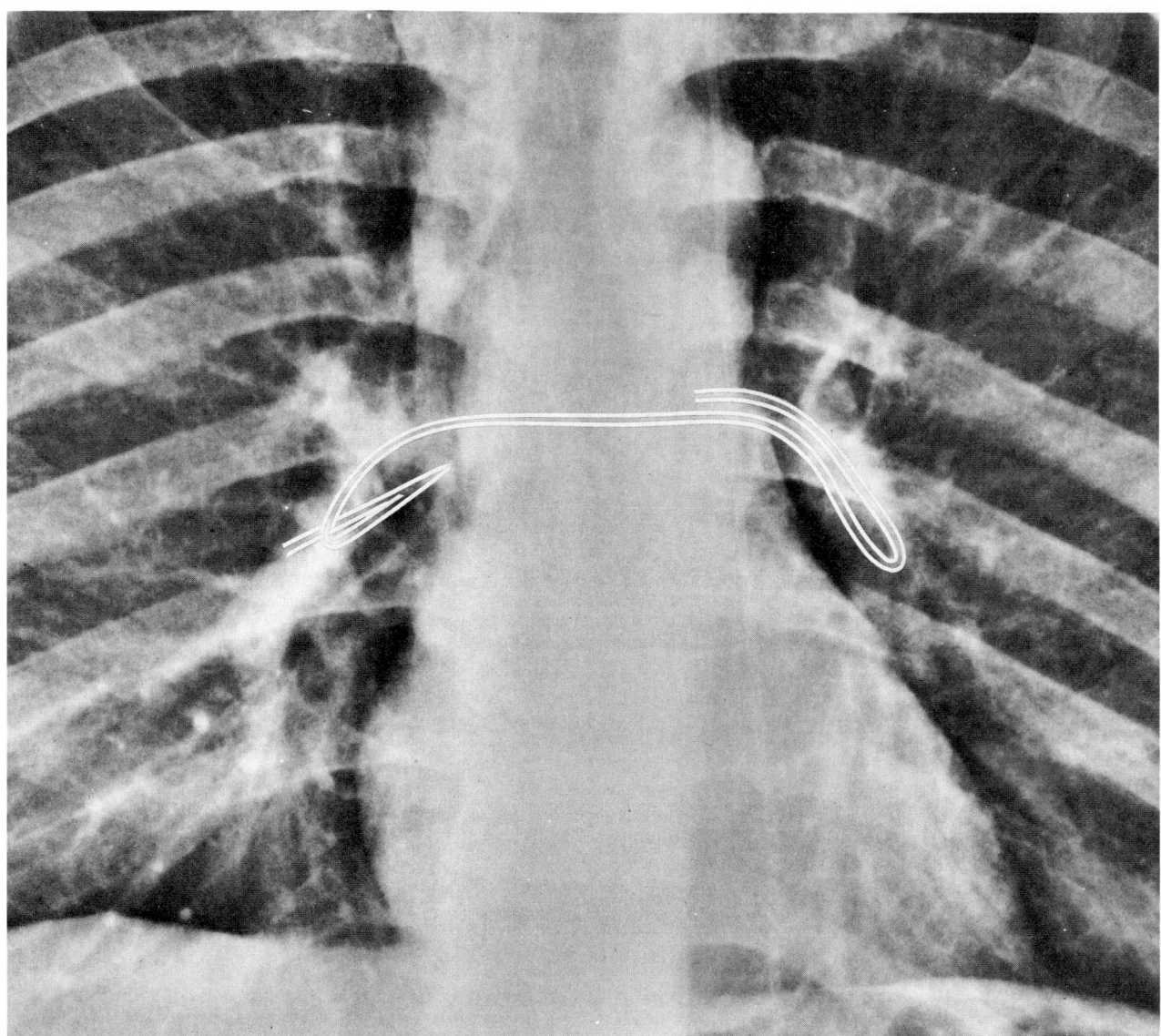

Figure 57-9. Embolized fragment of a ventriculoatrial shunt (retouched) looped across the pulmonary artery confluence with coiled ends in the left and right pulmonary arteries. A new ventriculoperitoneal shunt is already in place. After an hour's failure with loop snares, the shunt was grasped and retrieved within a minute using a basket retriever.

lodge. Removal depends on access to the site as well as the space allowed for catheter manipulation. Snares, baskets, and retrieval forceps are most commonly used.[8,42-53] In addition, endoscopy is an invaluable tool in guidance and localization, and with specific attachments may be the primary mode of retrieval.[54-56] In some cases the combination of endoscopic and fluoroscopic techniques facilitates extraction.

Complications of Percutaneous Foreign-Body Removal

Considering that most angiographers have learned to retrieve objects by actually performing transcatheter retrievals, the complication rate is remarkably low. Katzen reported minor pulmonary embolization after removing a pacemaker wire that had been embedded for 5 years.[57] Two patients experienced transient arrhythmias when the end of a fragment being removed impinged on the right ventricle wall. In view of its extensive and generally successful use, catheter retrieval is clearly indicated wherever feasible.

Discussion

The percutaneous catheter removal of undesired foreign bodies by techniques selected to suit the individual circumstances is an invaluable aid to modern medical practice. Every facility engaged in vascular catheterization for diagnostic, monitoring, or feeding purposes should have the simple equipment needed to effect transluminal retrievals. The manufacturers of vascular catheters, guidewires, and tubing have done their best to design relatively foolproof products, but their progress in this direction can only reduce, never eliminate, the basic problem. The most carefully prepared instructions and warnings can be overlooked by physician or nurse; the patient, especially when asleep or unconscious, can undo the best of prophylactic efforts. Therapeutically placed vascular occlusive devices can be dislodged, with potentially calamitous results. The prompt transluminal removal of mislodged or displaced spring-coil occluders has reportedly been done at least three times.[33,58,59]

Extrapolation

We can accidentally or intentionally place a variety of foreign bodies within the body. Surgeons have been installing prosthetic grafts and valves for years. Thus far, when these chanced to become a problem, their removal necessitated further major surgery. As Postmann has already shown, the radiologist may some day offer alternatives to the surgical placement of prosthetic devices. In the percutaneous transluminal retrieval of unwanted foreign bodies from the cardiovascular, biliary, and gastrointestinal systems, radiologists not only have increased the safety of medicine for many patients but have also pointed the way to further progress, both in the removal of foreign bodies and in the deliberate therapeutic placement of foreign bodies (perhaps in the latter context the term *prosthetic* is more suitable). Percutaneous retrieval is an accomplished fact; its success has broad implications for the future of relatively noninvasive image-guided transluminal catheter techniques for accomplishing objectives that today involve the greater pain, risk, cost, and disability inherent in even the most modern surgery. One patient's complication can point the way to another's therapeutic benefit.

References

1. Porstmann W, Wierny L, Warnke H. Closure of persistent ductus arteriosus without thoracotomy. German Med Monthly 1967;12:1.
2. Thomas J, Sinclair-Smith B, Bloomfield D, Davachi A. Nonsurgical retrieval of broken segment of steel spring guide from right atrium and inferior vena cava. Circulation 1964;30:106.
3. Henley FT, Ballard JW. Percutaneous removal of flexible foreign body from the heart. Radiology 1969;92:176.
4. Dotter CT, Rösch J, Bilbao MK. Transluminal extraction of catheter and guide fragments from the heart and great vessels; 29 collected cases. AJR 1971;111:467.
5. Fisher RG, Ferreyro R. Evaluation of current techniques for nonsurgical removal of intravascular iatrogenic foreign bodies. AJR 1978;130:541.
6. Bloomfield DA. The nonsurgical retrieval of intracardiac foreign bodies—an international survey. Cathet Cardiovasc Diagn 1978;4:1.
7. Egglin TK, Dickey KW, Rosenblatt M, et al. Retrieval of intravascular foreign bodies: experience in 32 cases. AJR 1995;164:1259–1264.
8. Lan RS. Non asphyxiating tracheobronchial foreign bodies in adults. Eur Respir J 1994;7:510–514.
9. Yang FS, Ohta I, Chiang HJ, et al. Nonsurgical retrieval of intravascular foreign body: experience of 12 cases. Eur J Radiol 1994;18:1–5.
10. Weigele JB, Sheline ME, Cope C. Expandable intravascular catheter: percutaneous use for endoluminal retrievals. Radiology 1992;185:604–606.
11. Dondelinger RF, Lepoutre B, Kurdziel JC. Percutaneous vascular foreign body retrieval: experience of an 11-year period. Eur J Radiol 1991;12:4–10.
12. Morse SS, Strauss EB, Hashim SW, et al. Percutaneous retrieval of an unusually large, nonopaque intravascular foreign body. AJR 1986;146:863–864.
13. Uflacker R, Lima S, Melichar AC. Intravascular foreign bodies: percutaneous retrieval. Radiology 1986;160:731–735.
14. McSweeney WJ, Schwartz DC. Retrieval of a catheter foreign body from the right heart using a guide wire deflector system. Radiology 1971;100:61.

15. Soo CS, Chuang VP, Wallace S. Nonsurgical retrieval of a severed catheter from femoral artery using a mylar sheath. AJR 1980;135:400.
16. Bett JHN, Anderson ST. Plastic catheter embolism to the right heart: a technique of non-surgical removal. Med J Aust 1971; 2:854.
17. Curry JL. Recovery of detached intravascular catheter or guide wire fragments: a proposed method. AJR 1969;105:894.
18. Enge I, Flatmark A. Percutaneous removal of intravascular foreign bodies by the snare technique. Acta Radiol 1973;14:747.
19. Fisher RG, Romero JR. Extraction of an embolized central venous catheter using percutaneous technique. Radiology 1975; 116:735.
20. Grand M, Harry G, Rémy J, Doyon D. Extraction non chirurgicale de corps étrangers iatrogènes intravasculaires. J Radiol Electrol 1978;59:479.
21. Khaja F, Lakier J. Foreign body retrieval from the heart by two catheter technique. Cathet Cardiovasc Diagn 1979;5:263.
22. Massumi RA, Ross AM. Atraumatic, nonsurgical technique for removal of broken catheters from cardiac cavities. Med Intell 1967;277:195.
23. Miller RE, Cockerill EM, Helbig H. Percutaneous removal of catheter emboli from the pulmonary arteries. Radiology 1970; 94:151.
24. Miller RE. Internal jugular pulmonary arteriography and removal of catheter emboli. Radiology 1972;102:200.
25. Picard L, Roland J, Sigiel M, Schwartz JF, André JM, Montaut J, Lepoire J. Transluminal retrieval of ventriculoatrial shunt catheters from the heart and great vessels: a new method. Neuroradiology 1975;10:159.
26. Randall PA. Percutaneous removal of iatrogenic intracardiac foreign body. Radiology 1972;102:591.
27. Zollikofer C, Nath PH, Castaneda-Zuniga WR, Probst P, Barreto A, Tadavarthy SM, Amplatz K. Nonsurgical removal of intravascular foreign bodies. ROEFO 1979;130:590.
28. Maxwell DD, Anderson RE. Transfemoral retrieval of an intracardiac catheter fragment, using a simple hood-shaped catheter. Radiology 1972;103:213.
29. Mullen JL, Oleaga J, Ring EJ. Catheter migration during home hyperalimentation. JAMA. 1977;238:1946.
30. Padula G. Hook and snare technique for intravascular retrieval. Radiology 1979;133:529.
31. Rossi P. "Hook catheter," technique for transfemoral removal of foreign body from right side of the heart. AJR 1970;109: 101.
32. Bessler VW. Transvenöse Entfernung embolisierter Katheter. ROEFO 1977;127:164.
33. Chuang VP. Nonoperative retrieval of Gianturco coils from abdominal aorta. AJR 1979;132:996.
34. Hasse J, Buckart F, Grädel E. Behandlung der iatrogenen transvenösen Fremdkörperembolie. Schweiz Med Wochenschr 1978;108:1470.
35. Lassers BW, Pickering D. Removal of an iatrogenic foreign body from the aorta by means of a ureteric stone catheter. Am Heart J 1967;73:375.
36. Ort VJ, Kolář J, Bruthans J. Erfolgreiche Entfernung eines kurzen Führungsdrahtbruchstückes aus der rechten Herzkammer. ROEFO 1978;128:495.
37. King JF, Manley JC, Zeft HJ, Auer JE. Nonsurgical removal of foreign body from right heart. J Thorac Cardiovasc Surg 1976;71:785.
38. Millan VG. Retrieval of intravascular foreign bodies using a modified bronchoscopic forceps. Radiology 1978;129:587.
39. Smyth NPD, Boivin MR, Bacos JM. Transjugular removal of foreign body from the right atrium by endoscopic forceps. J Thorac Cardiovasc Surg 1968;55:594.
40. Ranniger K. An instrument for retrieval of intravascular foreign bodies. Radiology 1968;91:1043.
41. Dotter CT. Interventional radiology—review of an emerging field. Semin Roentgenol 1981;6:7.
42. Yen PT, Tsai MH, Huang TS. Retrieval of a pin from the airway: a case report. Chang Gung Med J 1995;18:275–279.
43. Falchetti D, Salucci P, Alterti D, et al. Endoscopic retrieval of a large gastric foreign body with a home-made fishing net. Endoscopy 1995;27:408.
44. Downey RJ, Libutti SK, Gorenstein L, et al. Airway management during retrieval of the very large aspirated foreign body: a method for the flexible bronchoscope. Anesth Analg 1995; 81:186–187.
45. Cekirge S, Weiss JP, McLean GK. Percutaneous retrieval of a surgical laparotomy sponge from the peritoneal cavity. Cardiovasc Intervent Radiol 1995;18:59–61.
46. Mangal BD, Mangal Y, Pandey RP. Retrieval of foreign body from upper GI tract by flexible fibreoptic endoscope—an experience. J Assoc Physicians India 1993;41:11–13.
47. Nosher JL, Siegel R. Percutaneous retrieval of nonvascular foreign bodies. Radiology 1993;187:649–651.
48. Fulginiti J III, Dedhia HV, Kizer J, et al. Retrieval of an aspirated bullet fragment by flexible bronchoscopy in a mechanically ventilated patient. Chest 1993;103:626–627.
49. Ellis JH, Brodeur FJ Jr, Marx MV, et al. Superelastic guidewire snare for removal of foreign bodies from the urinary tract. Radiology 1992;183:871–873.
50. Crysdale WS, Sendi KS, Yoo J. Esophageal foreign bodies in children: 15-year review of 484 cases. Ann Otol Rhinol Laryngol 1991;100:320–324.
51. Selby JB, Tegtmeyer CJ, Bittner GM. Experience with new retrieval forceps for foreign body removal in the vascular, urinary, and biliary systems. Radiology 1990;176:535–538.
52. Stankiewicz JA, Consiglio AR. Retrieval of the large, round foreign body from the airway. Laryngoscope 1986;96:327–328.
53. Case WG, Mayer AD, Benson EA. Retrieval of an unusual foreign body from the second part of the duodenum. Br J Surg 1985;72:711.
54. Bertoni G, Pacchione D, Sassatelli R, et al. A new protector device for safe endoscopic removal of sharp gastroesophageal foreign bodies in infants. J Pediatr Gastroenterol Nutr 1993; 16:393–396.
55. Maretyk S, Clayman RV, Myers JA. Retroperitoneoscopy: foreign body retrieval. J Urol 1992;147:1608–1611.
56. Kurtz CP, Sakurai H, Yoo OH. Successful retrieval of fractured tracheostomy cannula by flexible fibreoptic bronchoscopy. Mt Sinai J Med NY 1990;57:371–373.
57. Katzen BT. Personal communication, 1980.
58. Radojkóvić S, Kamenica S, Jašović M, Draganić M. Catheter-aided extraction of a steel coil accidentally lodged in the right ventricle. Cardiovasc Intervent Radiol 1980;3:153.
59. Weber J. A complication with the Gianturco coil and its non-surgical management. Cardiovasc Intervent Radiol 1980;3: 156.

58

Venous Access

MATTHEW A. MAURO
PAUL F. JAQUES

The indications for the placement of central venous catheters are continually expanding. The rapid growth of hemodialysis services, transplantation programs, and oncologic centers has contributed to the need for maintaining patients who require parenteral nutrition, hemodialysis, plasmapheresis, blood transfusions, blood sampling, and long-term chemotherapy for various neoplastic and infectious diseases. In addition, the desire for outpatient treatments has spurred the development of catheter materials that are compatible with long-term in-home use while being relatively free from infectious and thrombotic complications.[1,2]

There are three basic categories of several venous catheters: nontunneled catheters, tunneled catheters, and implantable subcutaneous ports. Nontunneled catheters are most commonly placed via the central veins (subclavian and internal jugular) by blinded percutaneous techniques at the bedside. Peripherally inserted central catheters (PICCs) are designed to be placed into the superior vena cava via an upper extremity vein. Nontunneled catheters are sutured or taped into position and are primarily used for short-term access. PICCs and the nontunneled, nontapered, silicone centrally placed Hohn catheter (Bard Access Systems) are used for intermediate access (weeks to months).

Tunneled catheters are most commonly constructed of medical-grade silicone material and a Dacron cuff bonded to the catheter that is positioned in a subcutaneous tunnel for stabilization. These catheters are externally accessed and designed for long-term home use. Tunneled and nontunneled catheters are available in single-, dual-, or triple-lumen varieties. Implantable subcutaneous ports use the same catheter materials as do tunneled catheters but are attached to a domed access reservoir (port) that is buried subcutaneously for stabilization (Fig. 58-1). This type of device is accessed with a percutaneously placed noncoring needle and is intended for long-term use. Most available subcutaneous ports are designed for chest wall placement. Several products are available, and more are expected that can be subcutaneously placed in the upper arm or forearm. Single- and dual-port devices are available that are MRI-compatible. A nonreservoir, subcutaneously buried device is now available (Cath-Link, Bard Access Systems) that allows direct access to the catheter with the use of a 20-gauge angiocath. The Cath-Link is also available in two sizes, allowing chest wall and extremity placement.

Radiologic Placement

Tunneled catheters and subcutaneous ports have traditionally been placed by surgeons within the operating room. These devices can also be placed by percutaneous radiologic techniques using high-quality fluoroscopy and ultrasound. Percutaneous radiologic placement of these long-term devices requires three basic procedural steps: (1) establishment of central venous access, (2) formation of a subcutaneous tunnel or pocket, and (3) placement of the catheter into the central venous system.

Standard sites of venous access for central venous catheters include the internal jugular vein (IJV), subclavian vein (SCV), axillary vein, brachial vein, and basilic vein. Unconventional access sites include the infrarenal inferior vena cava (IVC), the suprarenal IVC, hepatic veins, and collateral veins. The selection of venous access site depends on the catheter being placed but more importantly on the patency of venous pathways to the heart.

Venous Access Techniques

Axillary and Subclavian Veins

Standard Approach

The standard percutaneous access technique to the SCV uses an infraclavicular puncture approximately 2 cm inferior to the junction of the medial and middle

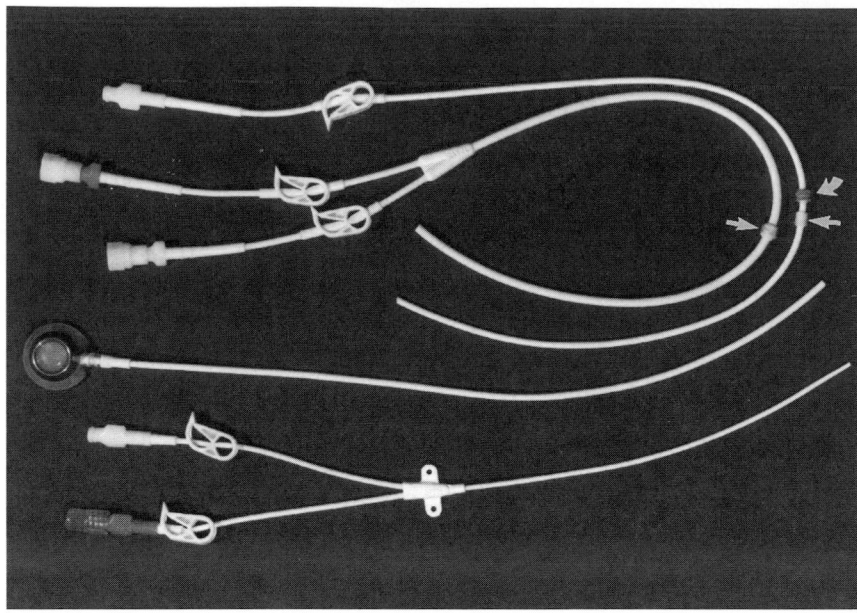

A

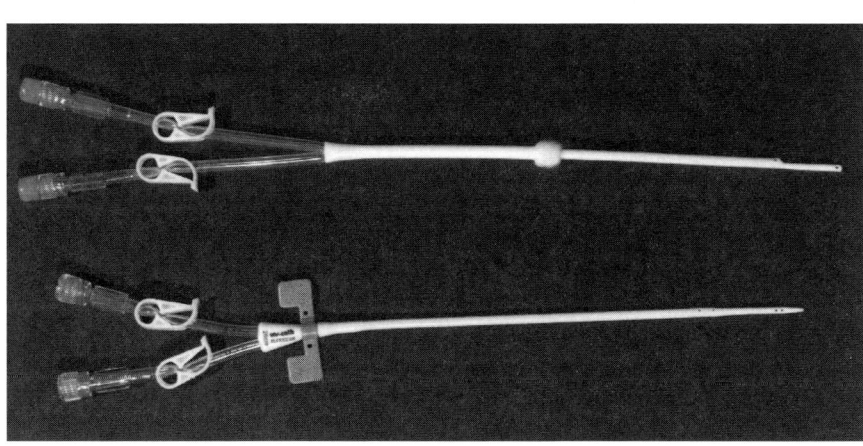

B

Figure 58-1. (A) Central venous catheters. *From top to bottom:* Single-lumen tunneled Hickman catheter with Dacron cuff (*straight arrow*) and VitaCuff (*curved arrow*); dual-lumen tunneled Leonard catheter with Dacron cuff (*straight arrow*); subcutaneous port; and dual-lumen, nontunneled Hohn catheter. (B) Dual-lumen dialysis catheters. *Top:* Nontapered tunneled catheter with Dacron cuff. *Bottom:* Tapered nontunneled catheter.

thirds of the clavicle. The needle is advanced medially and cephalad to a point slightly behind a fingertip firmly placed in the suprasternal notch. The needle is advanced in a horizontal plane with respect to the table to minimize an inadvertent pleural puncture. A 21-gauge 7-cm needle (Cook, Inc.) is the authors' choice for access needle, although 18-gauge needles are available in most commercial kits. Small-gauge needles with stylets roughened to enhance echogenicity are also available. The 21-gauge needle is attached to a 20-ml syringe with a short flexible tubing. Intermittent gentle suction is applied during needle advancement. Once free blood is obtained, contrast material may be injected to document a successful entry, although this is not usually necessary. An 0.018-inch

steerable mandrel guidewire is inserted and easily guided into the right atrium. This guidewire has a gentle curve at its tip that will allow it to be directed away from the internal jugular vein or contralateral innominate vein. After guidewire placement into the right atrium, the needle is removed and a transition dilator is placed, which will then accommodate a larger 0.035- or 0.038-inch working guidewire.

Fluoroscopic Guidance

The subclavian vein reliably crosses the first rib just inferior to its most lateral aspect. The needle is initially passed along a tract with a fairly shallow angle until the tip overlies the lateral margin of the first rib. The angle is then steepened and an abrupt pass is made to strike the first rib. The needle is withdrawn while simultaneously aspirating. If the pass is unsuccessful, the needle path is redirected caudally or cranially 5 to 10 degrees and another pass made.[3] Neither ultrasound nor peripheral contrast medium administration is required.

Direct puncture of the axillary or subclavian vein can be made under direct fluoroscopic vision after contrast administration into an extremity vein. After a venous puncture is made in an extremity vein (preferably in a median basilic vein), initial contrast injections are performed to select the site of vascular access. After a suitable site is selected, local anesthesia is administered and a skin incision is made. A second contrast injection is performed, and the needle is advanced directly under real-time fluoroscopic control. The vein should be approached from an anterior or inferior direction because the artery lies superior to the vein. After blood is aspirated, guidewire and catheter insertions are performed in a standard fashion.[4–6]

Occasionally, standard techniques are unsuccessful and an intravenous catheter cannot be placed in the upper extremity. In these circumstances, a transfemoral puncture can be made and either a guidewire or catheter can be placed in the subclavian vein or axillary vein. Using the guidewire as a target, the subclavian or axillary vein can then be punctured under direct fluoroscopic guidance. This technique can also be used when there is subclavian vein occlusion but a patent innominate vein. The transfemorally inserted guidewire can then be placed into the lateral aspect of the innominate vein, which is then directly punctured under fluoroscopic guidance.

Ultrasound Guidance

Ultrasound guidance is the authors' standard and preferred method for venous access into the axillary or subclavian venous segment. Ultrasound guidance localizes the vein, confirms its patency, and allows a more peripheral venous entry. A peripheral venous entry minimizes the chance of a pneumothorax and ensures an intravenous catheter position proximal to the space bordered by the clavicle and first rib, thereby avoiding potential catheter compression or fracture.[7–9] As noted previously, the subclavian artery and vein lie close to each other in their lateral aspects, unlike in their medial positions, where they are separated by the anterior scalene muscle. Therefore, safe peripheral entry requires a direct guidance technique. Using ultrasound, the needle, vein, and surrounding tissues are simultaneously imaged and the needle can be seen directly entering the vein, avoiding surrounding structures.

A 7.5-MHz linear transducer is most commonly used for vascular access. In large patients, a 5-MHz probe may be needed for added penetration. The linear transducer is usually placed with its medial edge against the patient's clavicle. The SCV/axillary segment is typically imaged in a longitudinal plane, although the transverse plane, which images the artery and vein together, can also be used. The SCV is easily identified because of its easy compressibility and respiratory variation. The artery that courses just superior to the vein will not be easily compressed and will demonstrate characteristic pulsations.[10] A skin dermatomy is placed at the lateral aspect of the linear transducer. The needle is inserted parallel to the transducer, and its entire course to the vein can be monitored.[10] A 7-cm 21-gauge needle is again used for this access. The needle is advanced under real-time imaging, and when the vein is indented by the needle, a short thrust is made for venous entry. After free return of blood, an 0.018-inch guidewire is inserted and guided into the right atrium (Fig. 58-2). Contrast injection is generally not necessary because the course of the guidewire will easily determine successful placement into the venous system. A transition-type catheter will then be placed over the mandrel guidewire. It is not unusual to see the vein completely collapse during needle insertion. In these circumstances, the needle may be passed through the vein and withdrawn with gentle aspiration until blood is returned. An inadvertent arterial puncture generally has no adverse sequelae because a small-gauge needle is used in an easily compressible, peripheral location.

Internal Jugular Vein

Standard Approach

Posterior, central, and anterior approaches have been described for percutaneous access to the IJV. The anterior approach is most commonly used by radiologists. The carotid artery is palpated and retracted medially. The needle is inserted at a point midway between the angle of the mandible and clavicle and directed toward the ipsilateral nipple. After return of blood, guidewire insertion and venous catheterization proceed as usual.

Ultrasound Guidance

Ultrasound guidance is used routinely for IJV punctures. Using this system, successful entry is obtained on the first pass in most cases. The 7.5-MHz linear transducer is placed in transverse orientation at a point midway between the clavicle and the angle of the mandible. The IJV and the adjacent carotid artery are easily identified (Fig. 58-3).[10] The transducer should be oriented so that the vein and artery are side by side. A 4-cm 18- or 21-gauge needle is used. The needle is

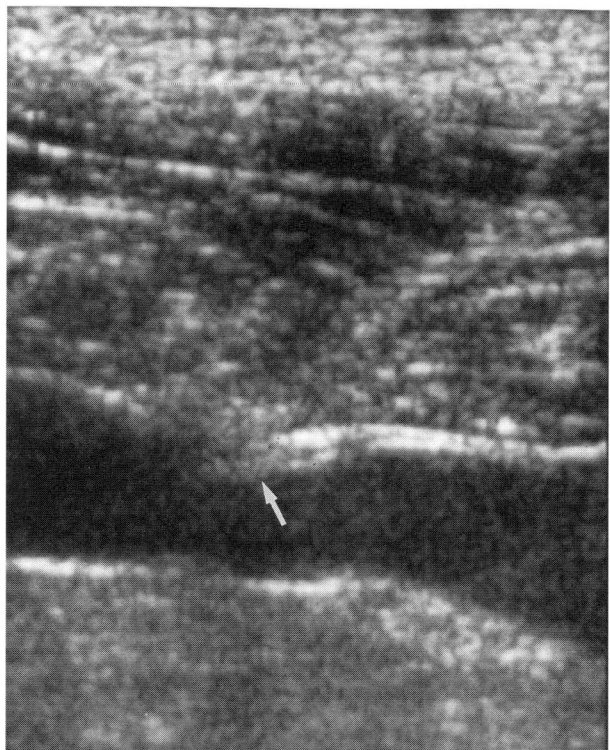

A

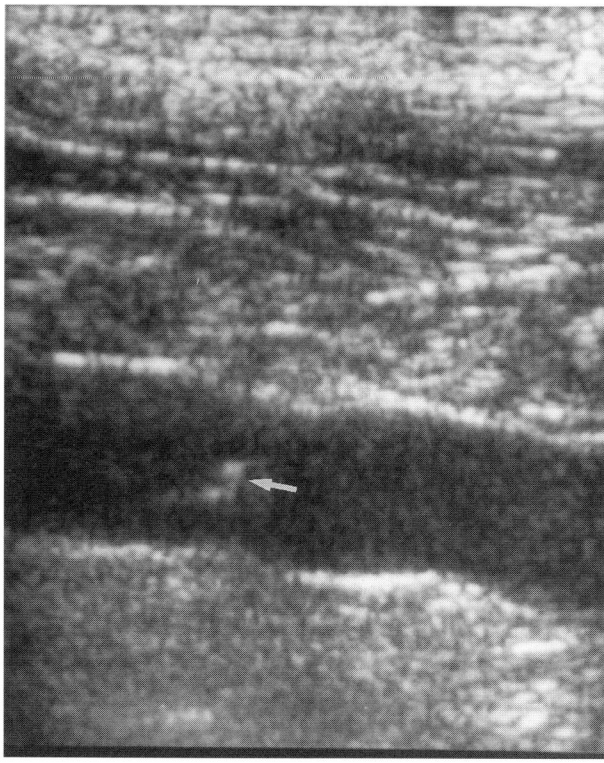

B

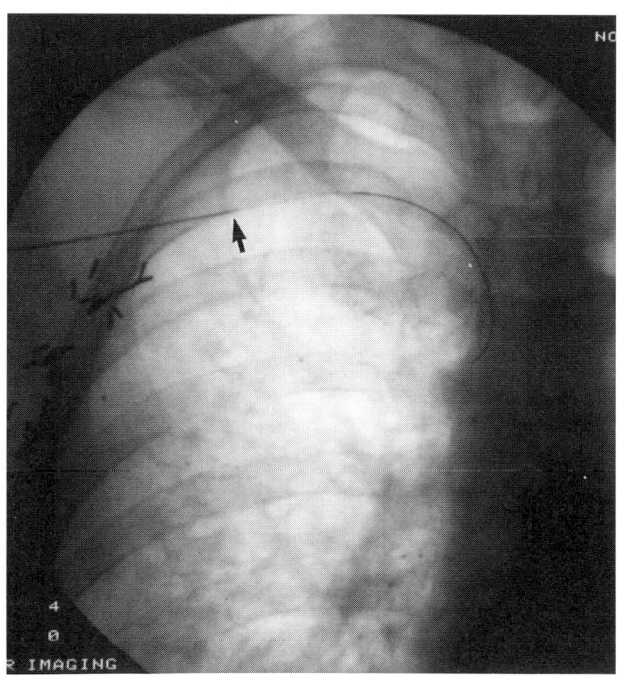

C

Figure 58-2. Subclavian/axillary venous access with ultrasound guidance. (A) Longitudinal view of axillary vein with needle indenting anterior wall (*arrow*). (B) Needle tip within lumen (*arrow*). (C) Digital film shows tip of 21-gauge entry needle (*arrow*) overlying second anterior rib and tip of mandrel guidewire entering the SVC. (From Mauro MA, Jaques PF. Radiologic placement of long-term central venous catheters: a review. J Vasc Intervent Radiol 1993;4:127–137. Used with permission.)

needle is passed through the vein. The needle tip, IJV, and carotid artery are simultaneously imaged while the needle is advanced to indent the anterior wall of the vein. A short, brisk thrust is then made to enter the vein. Not uncommonly, the vein completely collapses and a through-and-through puncture is made.[10] Once free aspiration of blood is obtained, guidewire and catheter insertions are performed.

Upper Extremity Veins

Venous access devices inserted via the upper extremity use the basilic, cephalic, brachial, or axillary veins. Palpation may suffice if access to an antecubital median cephalic or basilic vein is desired. More commonly, access is preferred in the upper arm where simple palpation is not possible. In these cases, access can be guided by ultrasound or fluoroscopy during contrast venography.

placed just superior to the midportion of the transducer directly over the vein. A gentle up-and-down motion of the needle is used to confirm its location. The side-to-side artery-vein orientation ensures that an inadvertent carotid puncture cannot occur if the

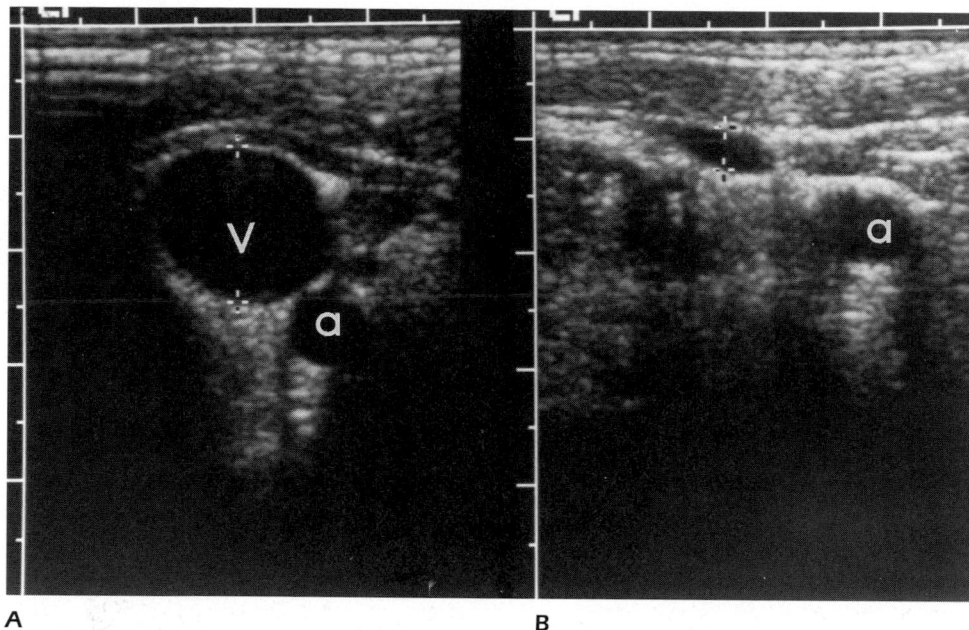

A

B

Figure 58-3. Internal jugular vein access. (A) Transverse ultrasound image of internal jugular vein (*V*) without compression (*a,* carotid artery). (B) Collapsed vein with mild compression (*a,* carotid artery). (From Mauro MA, Jaques PF. Radiologic placement of long-term central venous catheters: a review. J Vasc Intervent Radiol 1993;4:127–137. Used with permission.)

For fluoroscopic guidance, a venipuncture is made within a superficial vein of the hand, forearm, or antecubital space. A contrast injection is initially performed to identify the access site. After skin anesthesia and skin nick, venous entry is made into the opacified vein during a second contrast injection.[4,6,11] Venous entry can be made with a 21- or 20-gauge needle, which accommodates an 0.018-inch guidewire, or a 19-gauge thin-walled needle, which allows a 0.035-inch wire to be initially inserted.

Venous localization can also be accomplished with ultrasound. This is particularly useful in a swollen edematous arm where an initial venipuncture is impossible.[10] The venous segments to be finally accessed are imaged in both longitudinal and transverse orientations, and the most suitable position is selected for real-time needle guidance. Following blood return, administration of nitroglycerin (100–200 μg) is helpful to avoid venospasm.

Inferior Vena Cava

When central access via the superior vena cava is impossible because of venous occlusions, catheter placement to the central venous system can still be accomplished via the IVC. A transfemoral approach to the IVC is not suitable for long-term care because the catheter hinders free ambulation, there is an increased

likelihood of catheter trauma, kinking, or fracture, and groin placement leads to increased catheter infection rates. The IVC can be approached by a direct translumbar approach into the infrarenal IVC or a transhepatic approach into the suprarenal IVC.[12–15] All conventional access routes should be reevaluated before an unconventional route is chosen because recanalization may occur quickly, particularly in children.

A translumbar IVC cannulation is somewhat analogous to translumbar aortography. A preprocedural CT scan is useful to detect any venous anomalies, to identify the location of the left renal vein, and to identify any structures (colon or ptotic kidney) that may be in the catheter path. The patient is placed in a prone or prone oblique position with the right side elevated 30 to 45 degrees. The L3 vertebral body on the right is the usual level of insertion. However, the CT scan may identify a more optimal site. A skin site is chosen to allow a 45-degree medial and slight cranial angulation of the needle. In average or thin patients, a 21-gauge diamond-tipped needle (Cook, Inc.) is advanced until it hits the L3 vertebral body. The needle then is retracted and redirected anteriorly at increasing angles until a pass is made anterior to the vertebral body.[12,14] At this time the stylet is removed and the needle is withdrawn until blood is freely returned. Contrast injection can be used to confirm the needle's location, and this will be followed by an 0.018-inch mandrel

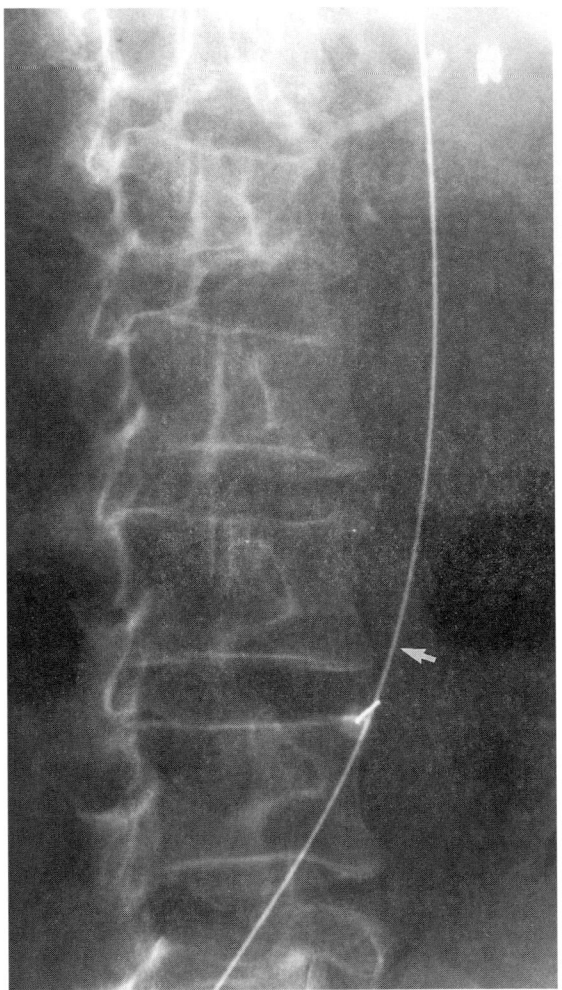

A

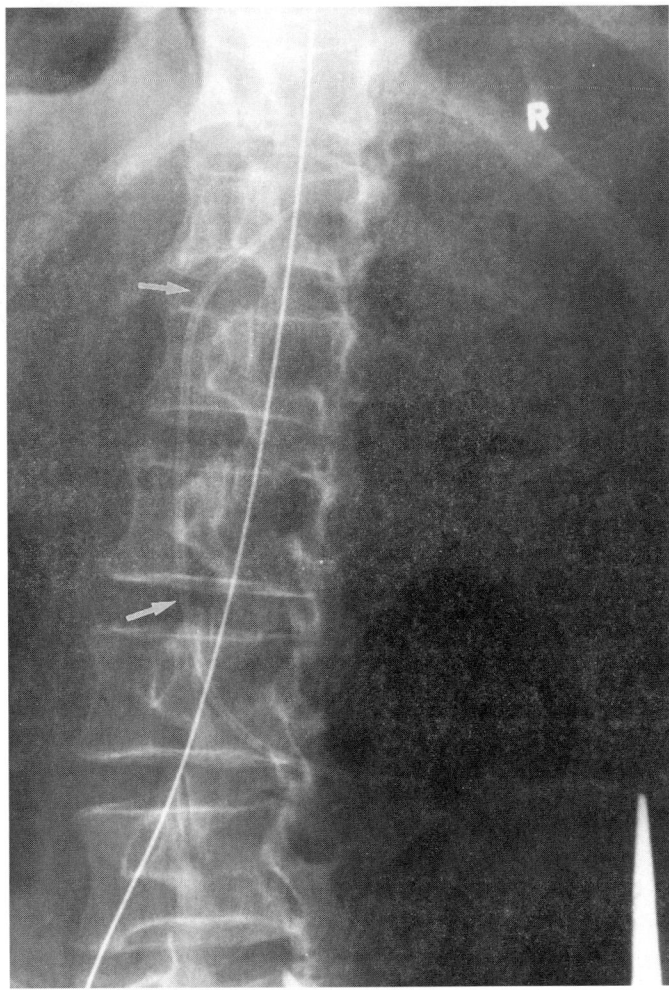

B

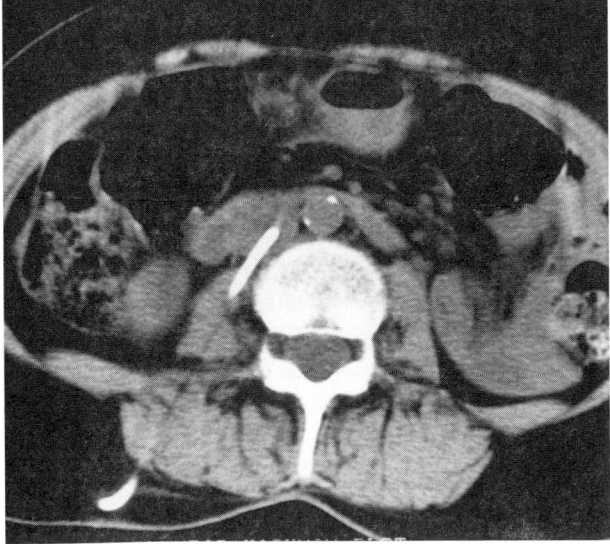

C

Figure 58-4. Translumbar IVC access. (A) With a guidewire (*arrow*) inserted transfemorally into the IVC, a 21-gauge needle is inserted into the IVC with right posterior oblique fluoroscopy. (B) Transition dilator (*arrows*) is inserted into the IVC with left posterior oblique fluoroscopy. Hemostat marks skin site. (C) Postprocedural CT scan shows catheter entering the IVC. (From Mauro MA, Jaques PF. Radiologic placement of long-term central venous catheters: a review. J Vasc Intervent Radiol 1993;4:127–137. Used with permission.)

guidewire and transition catheter. In larger patients, a sturdier 18-gauge diamond-tipped or Turner needle may be used, which can be followed by a heavier-duty guidewire.

If the common femoral veins are patent, the authors prefer to place a guidewire via a transfemoral approach to serve as a fluoroscopic marker for the IVC. The patient is then placed prone, and, with oblique fluoroscopy, the needle is inserted directly into the IVC using fluoroscopic guidance (Fig. 58-4). In very thin adults or children, the IVC is easily visualized with ultrasound using standard 3.0- or 3.5-MHz transducers.

In these circumstances, entry can be guided by using an ultrasound biopsy guide. Computed tomography can also be used for initial caval access.

Suprarenal caval access can be performed when there is infrarenal IVC occlusion. A transhepatic approach is used by either a subcostal or intercostal approach. A subcostal approach using direct ultrasound guidance is the authors' preferred method for suprarenal caval access. In most patients, the liver and IVC can be suitably imaged with ultrasound using a subcostally positioned transducer. The initial ultrasound study is performed with an attached biopsy guide to determine the skin site that will allow a direct transhepatic approach to the IVC without traversing major structures.[16] Under direct real-time guidance, a 21-gauge, diamond-tipped, 15-cm needle can be directly advanced into the cava. The stylet is removed and the needle is withdrawn until free flow of blood is returned. The mandrel wire and transistor dilator are then placed. The subcostal approach avoids the pleura and rib space and is well tolerated by patients. The intercostal approach is reserved for those patients with high-riding livers in whom safe access to the cava cannot be accomplished via a subcostal approach. In these cases, the needle is advanced via a right lateral approach under fluoroscopic control similar to that used for transhepatic cholangiography.[13]

Hepatic Veins

An additional access pathway to the central venous system via the suprarenal IVC is by initial catheterization of a hepatic vein.[17] The authors have used this approach mostly in small children with short gut syndrome who require long-term venous access for nutrition. Because of the long-term nature of this problem, conventional access sites, including the internal jugular veins, subclavian veins, and even infrarenal IVC, have become occluded. A hepatic vein entry maximizes the intravascular catheter length in these small children. With adequate nutrition, these children experience rapid growth, and catheters that are externally anchored may migrate out of the vascular system if a significant intravascular length is not placed.

For very young children, these procedures are performed under general anesthesia. Ultrasound with biopsy attachment is used for guidance. An initial examination is performed to identify a suitable hepatic vein for entry. The middle hepatic vein is usually selected because of its relative anterior course within the main interlobar fissure of the liver. The right and left hepatic veins, however, can also be employed. A subcostal approach is again used to avoid the intercostal space, pleura, and lung. Using the biopsy guide, a 21-gauge

diamond-tipped needle is directly inserted into the peripheral aspect of the hepatic vein. After successful aspiration of blood and contrast material documentation, a guidewire and transition catheter are placed in the standard fashion.[17]

Collateral Veins

In patients with bilateral internal jugular and subclavian venous occlusion, collateral veins are often able to be identified with ultrasound. This is particularly true in children. These collateral channels can be accessed with a needle using ultrasound guidance. A venogram is then performed to identify a pathway to the heart. These collateral pathways can often be catheterized using steerable hydrophilic guidewire and catheter combinations, ultimately allowing central access.

Tunneling and Catheter Placement

Tunneled Catheters

Tunneled catheters are available in either an end-hole variety (Hickman-type catheters, Bard Access Systems) or a tip-occluded valved catheter (Groshong type, Bard Access Systems). Both types are externally accessible catheters that require subcutaneous tunneling.[18,19] Tunneling is performed as a second part of the procedure following venous access. The skin exit site of the externalized portion of the catheter requires careful choosing. If the patient is to care for the catheter himself or herself, the skin exit site must be placed in an easily accessible position. For catheters placed via the axillary or subclavian veins, a parasternal site in the upper chest wall is usually chosen. The site should not interfere with undergarments.[17] For translumbar IVC catheters, the skin exit site is usually placed on the lower anterior abdominal wall or the lower chest wall.

The skin exit site is infiltrated with local anesthesia, and a dermatotomy is made with a no. 11 blade. Hemostats are used to spread the skin and enter the subcutaneous space. The entire subcutaneous tunnel (skin exit site to venous access site) is then infiltrated with local anesthesia using a 15-cm, 22-gauge Chiba-type needle. This needle must remain in the subcutaneous plane. For end-hole catheters, a blunt plastic tunneling tool (supplied in kit) is then inserted into the skin exit site and maneuvered through the subcutaneous tissues to the venous access site. With the Groshong-type catheter, the subcutaneous tunnel is formed in the reverse direction. The tunneling tool is inserted into the venous access site and is brought through to exit out of the skin exit site. Both types of catheters have a Dacron cuff that should be positioned within the tunnel to allow stabilization once fibrosis occurs. In the authors' practice, this cuff is positioned approximately 1 to 2 cm from the exit site to allow for easier subsequent catheter and cuff removal. Catheters are also available with a second cuff of silver-impregnated collagen (VitaCuff, Vitaphore), which serves as an antimicrobial barrier. When present, the VitaCuff is placed just within the skin exit site.

The catheter length from the venous access site to its final tip position can be accurately determined by first inserting a guidewire through the indwelling venous catheter. The tip of the guidewire is placed in the distal superior vena cava or proximal right atrium, and the guidewire is kinked. The guidewire is then withdrawn until its tip is at the venous access site, and a clamp is placed on the guidewire. The length between the kink and the clamp represents the length of catheter required to be inserted into the patient. Catheters placed more proximally into the brachiocephalic vein or proximal superior vena cava often do not function as well. Distal placement into the right atrium may allow the catheter to contact the tricuspid valve and septum and should be avoided. With translumbar caval catheters, the tip should be ideally placed just inferior to the renal veins to help avoid renal vein thrombosis if pericatheter thrombosis occurs. However, to ensure an adequate intravascular length of catheter, this is usually not possible. The catheter tip should then be placed at the level of the hepatic veins. After measurement, the end-hole-type catheters are cut to the appropriate length. Groshong-type catheters should not be cut at their tips. The catheter length is adjusted after the catheter is placed into the venous system, and the catheter is trimmed from its proximal aspect.

After tunnel formation, a 0.038-inch guidewire is inserted through the transition catheter and functions as the final working wire. For axillary, subclavian, or jugular approaches, the guidewire should be placed well into the IVC if possible. Guidewire placement into the IVC adds stability to the system and eliminates the possibility of guidewire slippage into the right atrium during tract dilatation. The tract is dilated using a fascial dilator, and an appropriately sized peel-away sheath is then inserted. For the standard 9.6 or 10.0 French Hickman-type catheters, a 10 French sheath (supplied in kit) is used. The dilator and guidewire are removed, followed immediately by insertion of the catheter into the venous system. The patient should carefully be instructed to suspend respirations during this step. For uncooperative patients, pinching the sheath between the fingertips between dilator removal and catheter insertion is necessary to avoid inadvertent air embolism. The final catheter placement is fluoroscopically checked, and, when satisfactory, the sheath is removed while a finger is placed on the cathe-

ter for stabilization. Minor adjustments to position can then be made. For the Groshong catheter, the proximal portion of the catheter is cut to length and an attachment is applied to assemble the hub.[18]

Difficulty in passing the soft silicone catheter into the SVC may occur if there are any unusual venous junction angles present. For example, a catheter inserted via the right subclavian vein may preferentially enter the left innominate vein during insertion via the peel-away sheath. This occurs less commonly from a left-sided approach because of the obliquely angled left innominate vein. A forceful injection of saline may produce catheter recoil into the appropriate position. Alternatively, the catheter tip can be beveled, and rotation may overcome this problem. With tunneled catheters, this problem can also be managed by passing a hydrophilic guidewire through the catheter and steering it into the superior vena cava. This convenient guidewire technique, however, is not applicable with fixed-hub subcutaneous ports. Refractory cases may require long peel-away sheaths or a femoral venous approach to snare the catheter.

A skin suture is placed at the venous access site as well as the skin exit site. The suture at the skin exit site closes the skin but also is wrapped around the catheter for added initial stability. This suture should only gently dimple the catheter as it is being secured. The catheter is then heparinized, and an external dressing is applied (Fig. 58-5).

Implantable Subcutaneous Ports

Following venous access, placement of implantable subcutaneous ports requires formation of the subcutaneous pocket.[20] For chest wall ports, a site inferior and medial to the original venous access site is chosen where there is ample subcutaneous tissue to support the port. A cutdown tray contains all of the required surgical tools. Lidocaine with epinephrine is used for anesthesia. A straight skin incision approximately 5 cm long is made with a no. 15 blade and can be located inferior or superior to the subcutaneous pocket to be created. The incision is made through the dermis and into the subcutaneous space, which is easily identified by the presence of fatty tissue. The pocket is formed using blunt dissection. Fibrous bands within the subcutaneous space will need to be cut with small scissors. The subcutaneous pocket should be just large and deep enough to allow opposition of the skin margins at the incision adjacent to but not overriding the port. If the pocket is too large, port migration is more likely to occur. In these cases, two or three absorbable sutures can be used to fixate the port to the deep fascia. When a snug fit is present, the stabilizing sutures may not be necessary. The pocket is visually inspected, and

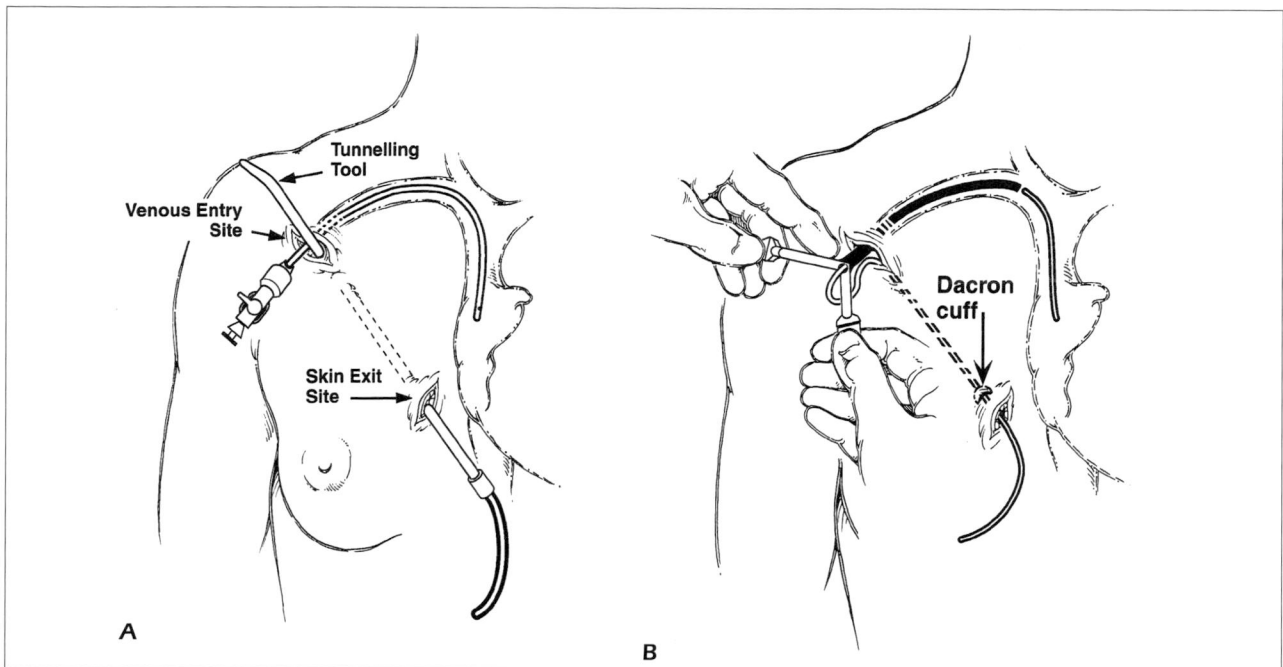

A

B

Figure 58-5. (A) Schematic of tunneling tool for subcutaneous tunnel. (B) Schematic of the Hickman catheter held in place while the sheath is split and peeled out. (From Robertson LJ, Mauro MA, Jaques PF. Radiologic placement of Hickman catheters. Radiology 1989;170:1007–1009. Used with permission.)

gauze pads are placed in the pocket to ensure that it is dry with no bleeding. A short subcutaneous tunnel is then placed from the superior lateral aspect of the subcutaneous pocket to the venous access site. The direction of tunneling will be determined by the type of catheter tip. After the catheter is brought through the tunnel, the port is situated into the pocket. At this time, the port can be accessed using the right-angled Huber needle (available in kit) attached via flexible tubing to a syringe with heparinized saline. Huber needle placement allows for stabilization of the port within the pocket during suturing and permits subsequent catheter flushing. The pocket is closed with interrupted absorbable subcutaneous sutures followed by interrupted skin sutures. The catheter is then cut to the appropriate length and inserted via a peel-away sheath into the appropriate final position as described earlier.[16,20] Blood is withdrawn through the Huber needle and flushed. The venous access site can then be closed, and the port can be flushed with normal saline followed by heparin. When a Groshong catheter is chosen, the proximal end of the catheter is brought through the subcutaneous tunnel and the distal tip is positioned via the peel-away sheath into the venous system. The proximal end of the catheter is cut to length and secured to the port, which is placed into the pocket; the pocket is then closed.

For upper extremity ports, a small (2.5-cm) transverse incision is made at the site adjacent to the initial venous access that can accommodate the port. For up-per arm placements, this incision often includes the initial skin nick. A small subcutaneous pocket is formed by blunt dissection. The catheter is then placed into the superior vena cava via a peel-away sheath (contained in kit) cut to length and attached to the port. If the subcutaneous pocket is placed away from the initial entry site, a short tunnel will be needed.[6,11,16] Once the catheter is attached to the infusion port, the port is accessed, blood is aspirated, and the system is flushed. The port is then secured with a two-layered closure.

Dialysis Catheters

Dialysis catheters are dual-lumen catheters that are available in cuffed (tunneled) and noncuffed (nontunneled) varieties. They are therefore available in fixed lengths that are designed for left- and right-sided SCV or IJV access in the average adult or pediatric patient. In many circumstances, the catheter length can be chosen so that the cuff can be placed in the subcutaneous space just at the venous access site. However, it may be necessary to form a short (2- to 5-cm) tunnel to accommodate the catheter that is slightly too long.

In any patient in whom an upper extremity arteriovenous fistula or shunt is a possibility, the subclavian veins are avoided at all cost and the catheter is placed via the jugular routes. The subcutaneous tunnels are either placed in a supraclavicular location or brought over the clavicle to exit in the upper chest wall. An appropriately sized catheter must be selected so that the tip can be placed in the appropriate location (distal SCV, proximal right atrium) and the cuff can be located in the tunnel, preferably near the catheter exit site (allows easier removal).

Instead of a single large-bore, dual-lumen, staggered-tip catheter, two smaller-bore (10 French), single-lumen catheters with end and multiple side holes are also available (Twin Catheters, Medcomp). These catheters are typically placed in the IJV approximately 1 cm apart, and dual parallel tunnels are created. The venous catheter is placed in the right atrium and the arterial catheter is placed approximately 4 cm proximal in the SVC.[21] The catheters need not be placed in the same vein. The major potential advantages are that the incidence of catheter dysfunction is lowered and higher flow rates can be accommodated.

Many of the dual-lumen dialysis catheters are made of a slightly stiffer silicone material than the conventional Hickman catheters. In average or thin patients, these nontapered catheters may be placed without the use of a peel-away sheath. When the tract is dilated with a dilator 1 French larger than the outer diameter of the catheter, the dialysis catheter can often be simply advanced over a stiff guidewire directly into the vein. When this is not possible, an appropriately sized peel-away sheath must be used in the standard fashion. The noncuffed tapered dual-lumen dialysis catheters, which are designed for more short-term use, are inserted using standard Seldinger techniques. All catheters should be heparinized according to manufacturers' recommendations because the amount of heparin varies with catheter length.

Nontunneled Catheters

Nontunneled catheters are available in tapered or nontapered varieties and can be placed via central access or peripheral venous access. The standard tapered catheters placed via the central veins are for in-hospital use and are placed using standard needle guidewire techniques.

The Hohn catheter (Bard Access Systems) is a nontapered silicone catheter designed for long-term in-hospital or intermediate-term home use. It is commonly used for fluid and blood product administration, parenteral nutrition, chemotherapy, and blood withdrawal. Single 5 French or dual 7 French catheters are available. They are either sutured or taped to the skin for stabilization. These catheters cannot be trimmed and do not require the placement of a tunnel. Access is obtained in the standard fashion using a 21-gauge needle followed by an 0.018-inch mandrel guidewire. The catheter is designed to be placed over a 0.025-inch standard guidewire, which is available in

the kit; however, the authors have found this guidewire too flimsy for routine use. In most cases, the initial 0.018-inch mandrel guidewire is used followed by dilation with the 7 French dilator available in the kit. The catheter then can be inserted over the 0.018-inch guidewire directly into the venous system. When this is not possible, the 0.018-inch mandrel guidewire can be replaced with a 0.025-inch heavy-duty guidewire by the use of a transition dilator. When the heavy-duty 0.025-inch guidewire will not suffice, a 0.038-inch guidewire can be inserted using the transition dilator followed by placement of an 8 French peel-away sheath. The 7 French dual-lumen Hohn catheter can then be simply placed via the 8 French peel-away sheath even in very large patients.

Peripherally inserted central catheters are 3 to 5 French catheters available in end-hole or Groshong-type tips. After venous access is achieved using techniques previously described, the length of catheter required is measured with an intravascular guidewire and the catheter is cut to an appropriate length.[4] The catheter is then inserted via an appropriately sized peel-away sheath (included in the kit) and advanced into the superior vena cava. The wings of the catheter hub are then sutured in place, and the catheter is heparinized.

Catheter Management and Removal

A specialized nursing team that supervises routine catheter management has been shown to significantly reduce local and systemic infection and catheter thrombosis rates. Strict adherence to sterile techniques during catheter use, daily dressing changes, and proper heparinization are mandatory for successful long-term catheter survival and cannot be overemphasized.[22]

Catheter removal is the responsibility of the service that initially placed the catheter. Tunneled catheters can usually be removed with gentle continuous traction. In many cases this will leave the cuff within the subcutaneous tissues. Removal of the cuff will require a separate incision under local anesthesia or blunt dissection from the catheter exit site if the cuff was initially placed adjacent to that area. Removal of a subcutaneous port requires a more extensive dissection under a full sterile prep. The previous incision site is used for cosmetic purposes. Long-term subcutaneous ports develop a white, tough vascular capsule that must be incised for port removal. The subcutaneous pocket that is left behind must be closed with deep sutures to avoid the presence of a hematoma or seroma, which will increase the likelihood of a wound infection. These patients require careful follow-up and daily dressing changes.

Catheters may become inadvertently cracked or otherwise damaged. When this occurs, catheter repair or replacement should be performed as soon as possible. In many cases, the catheters can be repaired with the use of commercially available repair kits specifically designed to replace a damaged hub or segment of catheter. Radiologists who place these long-term catheters should have these repair kits available and understand their usage.

Complications

Procedural Complications

With the use of radiologic guidance, central venous catheters of all types can be successfully placed in over 98 percent of cases.[11,18,20] Blinded percutaneous placements have reported 5.0 to 8.9 percent access failures.[7,23] A final catheter malposition complicates blinded insertion techniques in 1.2 to 2.5 percent of cases.[7,23,24] During radiologic insertion, any malposition is immediately detected and corrected so that virtually no patient leaves the suite with a malpositioned catheter. The major procedural complications that may occur during radiologic catheter insertion include inadvertent arterial puncture with hematoma, pneumothorax, and air embolism during placement of the silicone catheter through the peel-away sheath.

Hematomas may be the result of an inadvertent needle entry into the subclavian or axillary artery or bleeding within the subcutaneous tunnel or pocket in patients with bleeding disorders. The use of a 21-gauge needle and an ultrasonically directed peripheral puncture in a compressible region has virtually eliminated a clinically significant hematoma secondary to an arterial puncture.[7,14,18,20] Careful visualization of the guidewire course will allow one to determine whether the venous or arterial system has been entered. A venous puncture will direct the guidewire into the right atrium, whereas an inadvertent arterial puncture will have the guidewire proceed more centrally into the aorta. A simple injection of contrast can also be performed after needle entry to determine a proper puncture. Patients who are to receive tunneled catheters or implantable ports should have normal blood coagulation studies, and, if abnormal, they should be corrected before catheter placement.

An ultrasound-guided peripheral puncture has lowered the pneumothorax rate to 2 percent or less.[7,18,20] A pneumothorax may still occur with ultrasound guidance, particularly in cachectic patients, when visualization of the needle tip or target vein is lost and continued needle advancement occurs. Most pneumothoraces resulting from a 21-gauge needle are small

and resolve spontaneously. If not, a small-bore tube can easily be placed in the apex under fluoroscopic guidance and connected to an underwater suction device.

Air embolism may occur if the patient takes a deep inspiration when the dilator of the peel-away sheath and guidewire are removed while the operator is preparing to pass the silicone catheter. This risk is minimized if the patient is instructed to stop breathing during this procedure and if the sheath is gently squeezed shut between removal of the dilator and insertion of the silicone catheter.[16] In the authors' experience, if air embolism does occur, the air will pass into the outflow tract of the right ventricle. The patient should be left in a supine position until the air is absorbed, which may take up to 20 minutes. Oxygen should be administered nasally, and vital signs should be continuously monitored.

Late Complications

Catheter-related infections resulting from the placement of venous access devices include exit site infections, subcutaneous tunnel or pocket infections, and catheter-related bacteremia.[18] Exit site infections (tunneled or nontunneled catheters) are local infections manifested by induration and/or drainage confined to the catheter exit site. Induration, drainage, and tenderness extending into the subcutaneous tunnel or involving a pocket represent a tunnel or pocket infection, respectively. Catheter-related bacteremia is suspected and assumed when persistent fevers exist without another source of infection, when there is resolution of fevers and leukocytosis after catheter removal, or when positive blood cultures are obtained for an organism not localized to another site. Catheter-related bacteremia is definitively diagnosed when the same organism is isolated from both the catheter and peripheral blood.[18,25–27]

Several theories have been suggested for the pathogenesis of catheter-related infections. One theory suggests that colonization at the skin-catheter interface occurs first and the pathogens later migrate along the catheter surface to reach the venous circulation.[27] Another theory believes that excessive manipulation of the catheter hub is a major source of organisms, which then travel down the catheter lumen.[28,29] External catheters, multilumen catheters, and increased duration of catheter placement increase the risk of catheter-related infections.

Catheter-related infection rates have been shown to be comparable and no higher for those procedures performed in a radiologic interventional suite than for those performed in the operating room.[7,18–20,24,30–33] In addition to sterile insertion techniques, the quality of subsequent nursing care regarding wound and catheter management has been shown to be directly related to the rate of local and systemic infections.[22]

Because of the importance of these indwelling catheters, every effort should be made to treat exit site and subcutaneous tunnel and pocket infections with local care and antibiotics in an attempt to avoid premature removal. Catheter-related bacteremias can also be treated aggressively with antibiotics, and the catheter can be removed only when there is no clinical response. For severe subcutaneous infections, incision and drainage of the tunnel or pocket will be required in addition to catheter removal.

Two basic types of catheter thrombosis occur: a circumferential fibrin-sleeve thrombosis, which encircles the catheter, and mural thrombosis affecting the catheter and vein. The development of a circumferential fibrin sleeve occurs commonly on all catheter materials and may form as early as 24 hours after insertion.[34-36] The fibrin sleeve may interfere with catheter function and can be treated with low-dose intracatheter urokinase, stripped intravascularly with the use of a gooseneck retrieval system placed transfemorally, or simply exchanged. Many of these silicone catheters can be exchanged over a superstiff hydrophilic guide, particularly when they have been in place for over 4 weeks.

Mural thrombosis may partially or totally occlude the catheter and vessel lumen. Luminal occlusion is directly related to the duration and size of the indwelling catheter.[36,37] Catheter thrombosis rates of radiologically inserted devices are similar to those inserted by surgeons.[7,11,18-20,30,31] Clots developing within or around the catheter tip adversely affect catheter function. This is often heralded by inability to withdraw blood while still being able to inject. Careful adherence to the manufacturer's heparin volumes, strengths, and protocols is essential for maintaining catheter function. A low-dose urokinase infusion specifically designed for catheter occlusions is usually successful in restoring patency. If this fails, catheter stripping or exchange is advised.

All veins subjected to continuous catheter trauma for a sufficient length of time will eventually thrombose. Although common, thrombosis of central veins used for access is infrequently symptomatic. Nonoccluding thrombus is generally asymptomatic, whereas an occlusive thrombus will be symptomatic in approximately 30 percent of patients.[18,38,39] The treatment of catheter-related venous thrombosis heavily depends on the patient's presentation, need for access, and availability of other sites. In the asymptomatic patient, the catheter can be removed if the need for access is low, but heparinization is indicated when the need is high. If the patient has pain and swelling, removal and heparin are indicated when the need is low, but only heparin followed by warfarin may be tried in those patients with limited access. For very symptomatic patients or those with the SVC syndrome, catheter removal and heparin are in order.[40] If access must be saved, thrombolytic infusion can be used. A routine low-dose warfarin protocol may reduce the thrombotic complications associated with indwelling catheters.[41] A localized fibrotic stenosis may also occur at the site of venous entry following catheter removal.[42] This occurrence is particularly troublesome in dialysis patients who will receive a hemodialysis access shunt in that same extremity.

Repeated clamp trauma at the hub may cause eventual catheter fracture and leakage. These fractures can often be repaired with commercially available kits. If this is unsuccessful, the catheter must be replaced. Catheters that lie outside the vein at the clavicle–first rib junction are subject to continuous trauma, which may result in compression, fracture, separation, and fragment embolization.[9] This problem can easily be avoided by using a peripheral venous puncture to ensure an intravascular location at the clavicle–first rib junction.

Catheter malpositions may occur during catheter placement or weeks to months after a successful procedure. Catheter malpositions can easily be corrected by transfemoral relocation. If the malposition is recurrent, the catheter should be exchanged for one with a longer, more stable intravenous limb. Transhepatic catheters that become malpositioned because of respiratory motion are difficult to reposition and often require replacement.

Summary

Placement of long-term central venous catheters has traditionally been performed by surgeons in the operating rooms with acceptable procedural and late complication rates. However, surgical placement remains relatively expensive, often requiring the services of both the operating surgeon and an anesthesiologist as well as costly operating room time. In addition, operating room availability often limits prompt service. Procedural complication rates for radiologic placement are similar or lower when compared to surgical placement. Late complications, including infections, have been shown to be the same and depend heavily on postplacement catheter management. In most institutions, radiologic facilities can accommodate a request within 24 hours and do not carry the heavy overheads of the operating and recovery rooms or anesthesia facilities. Most cases can be handled within 45 minutes, which includes patient preparation, procedure time, and wound dressing. Most patients require no postoperative recovery. These features result in a procedure that is significantly more cost-effective than standard surgical placement. However, catheter placement is only part of a radiologist's responsibility in patient care. The radiologist must become familiar with and involved in postprocedural catheter care, patient follow-up, and the management of complications.

References

1. Hickman RO, Buckner CD, Clift RA, et al. A modified right atrial catheter for access to the venous system in marrow transplant recipients. Surg Gynecol Obstet 1979;148:871–875.
2. Broviac JW, Cole JJ, Scribner BS, Scribner BH. A silicone rubber atrial catheter for prolonged parenteral alimentation. Surg Gynecol Obstet 1973;136:602–606.
3. Jaques PF, Campbell WE, Dumbleton S, Mauro MA. The first rib as a fluoroscopic marker for subclavian vein access. J Vasc Intervent Radiol 1995;6:619–622.
4. Andrews JC, Marx MV, Williams DM, et al. The upper arm approach for placement of peripherally inserted central catheters for protracted venous access. AJR 1992;158:427–429.
5. Selby JB, Tegtmeyer CJ, Amodeo C. Insertion of subclavian hemodialysis catheters in difficult cases: value of fluoroscopy and angiographic techniques. AJR 1989;152:641–643.
6. Andrews JC, Walker-Andrews SC, William DE. Long-term central venous access with a peripherally placed subcutaneous infusion port: initial results. Radiology 1990;176:45–47.
7. Laméris JS, Post PJM, Zonderland HM, et al. Percutaneous placement of Hickman catheters: comparison of sonographically guided and blind techniques. AJR 1990;155:1097–1099.
8. Hinke DH, Zandt-Stastny DA, Goodman LR, et al. Pinch-off syndrome: a complication of implantable subclavian venous access devices. Radiology 1990;177:353–356.
9. Rubenstein RB, Alberty RE, Michels LG, et al. Hickman catheter separation. J Parent Ent Nutr 1985;9:754–757.
10. Jaques PF, Mauro MA, Keefe B. Ultrasonographic guidance for vascular access. J Vasc Intervent Radiol 1992;3:427–430.
11. Kahn ML, Barboza RB, Kling GA, et al. Initial experience with percutaneous placement of the PAS port implantable venous access device. J Vasc Intervent Radiol 1992;3:459–461.
12. Denny DF, Greenwood LH, Morse SS, et al. Inferior vena cava: translumbar catheterization for central venous access. Radiology 1989;170:1013–1014.
13. Kaufman JA, Greenfield AJ, Fitzpatrick GF. Transhepatic cannulation of the inferior vena cava. J Vasc Intervent Radiol 1991; 2:331–334.
14. Robertson LJ, Jaques PF, Mauro MA, et al. Percutaneous inferior vena cava placement of tunneled Silastic catheters for prolonged vascular access in infants. J Pediatr Surg 1990;25:596–598.
15. Lund GB, Lieberman RP, Haire WD, et al. Translumbar inferior vena cava catheters for long-term venous access. Radiology 1990;174:31–35.
16. Mauro MA, Jaques PF. Radiologic placement of long-term central venous catheters: a review. J Vasc Intervent Radiol 1993;4:127–137.
17. Azizkhan RG, Taylor LA, Jaques PF, et al. Percutaneous translumbar and transhepatic inferior vena caval catheters for prolonged vascular access in children. J Pediatr Surg 1992;27: 165–169.
18. Hull JE, Hunter CS, Luiken GA. The Groshong catheter: initial experience and early results of imaging-guided placement. Radiology 1992;185:803–807.
19. Robertson LJ, Mauro MA, Jaques PF. Radiologic placement of Hickman catheters. Radiology 1989;170:1007–1009.
20. Morris SL, Jaques PF, Mauro MA. Radiology-assisted placement of implantable subcutaneous infusion ports for long-term venous access. Radiology 1992;184:149–151.
21. Teslo F, DeBaz H, Panarello G, et al. Double catheterization of the internal jugular vein for hemodialysis: indication, techniques and clinical results. Artif Organs 1994;18:301–304.
22. Keohane PP, Attrill H, Northover J. Effect of catheter tunnelling and a nutrition nurse on catheter sepsis during parenteral nutrition. Lancet 1983;Dec. 17:1388–1390.
23. Takasugi JK, O'Connell TX. Prevention of complications in permanent central venous catheters. Surg Gynecol Obstet 1988;167:6–11.
24. Delmore JE, Horbelt DV, Jack BL, et al. Experience with the Groshong long-term central venous catheter. Gynecol Oncol 1989;34:216–218.
25. Wechsler RJ, Spirn PW, Conant EF, et al. Thrombosis and infection caused by thoracic venous catheters: pathogenesis and imaging findings. AJR 1993;160:467–471.
26. Corona ML, Peters SG, Narr BJ, et al. Subspecialty clinics: critical-care medicine (infections related to central venous catheters). Mayo Clin Proc 1990;65:979–986.
27. Norwood S, Ruby A, Civetta J, et al. Catheter-related infections and associated septicemia. Chest 1991;99:968–975.
28. Sitges-Serra A, Linares J, Garau J. Catheter sepsis: the clue is the hub. Surgery 1985;97:355–357.
29. Liñares J, Sitges-Serra A, Garau J, et al. Pathogenesis of catheter sepsis: a prospective study with quantitative and semiquantitative cultures of catheter hub and segments. J Clin Microbiol 1985;21:357–360.
30. Brothers TE, Von Moll LK, Niederhuber JE, et al. Experience with subcutaneous infusion ports in three hundred patients. Surg Gynecol Obstet 1988;166:295–301.
31. Harvey WH, Pick TE, Reed K, et al. A prospective evaluation of the Port-a-Cath implantable venous access system in chronically ill adults and children. Surg Gynecol Obstet 1989;169: 495–500.
32. Guenier C, Ferreira J, Pector JC. Prolonged venous access in cancer patients. Eur J Surg Oncol 1989;15:553–555.
33. Greene FL, Moore W, Strickland G, et al. Comparison of a totally implantable access device for chemotherapy (Port-a-Cath) and long-term percutaneous catheterization (Broviac). South Med J 1988;81:580–583.
34. Ahmed N, Payne RF. Thrombosis after central venous cannulation. Med J Austr 1976;1:217–220.
35. Hoshal VL, Ause RG, Hoskins PA. Fibrin sleeve formation on indwelling subclavian central venous catheters. Arch Surg 1971;102:353–358.
36. Brismar B, Hardstedt C, Jacobson S. Diagnosis of thrombosis by catheter phlebography after prolonged central venous catheterization. Ann Surg 1981;194:779–783.
37. Jacobs MB, Yeager M. Thrombotic and infectious complications of Hickman-Broviac catheters. Arch Intern Med 1984; 144:1597–1599.
38. Anderson AJ, Krasnow SH, Boyer MW, et al. Thrombosis: the major Hickman catheter complication in patients with solid tumor. Chest 1989;95:71–75.
39. Haire WD, Lieberman RP, Lund GB, et al. Thrombotic complications of silicone rubber catheters during autologous marrow and peripheral stem cell transplantation: prospective comparison of Hickman and Groshong catheters. Bone Marrow Transplant 1991;7:57–59.
40. Lowell JA, Bothe A Jr. Venous access preoperative, operative and postoperative dilemmas. Surg Clinics North Am 1991;71: 1231–1246.
41. Bern MM, Lokich JJ, Wallach SR, et al. Very low doses of warfarin can prevent thrombosis in central venous catheters. Ann Intern Med 1990;112:423–428.
42. Stalter KA, Stevens GF, Sterling WA. Late stenosis of the subclavian vein after hemodialysis catheter injury. Surgery 1986; 100:924–927.

59

Vena Cava Filters

TIMOTHY P. MURPHY
GARY S. DORFMAN
ROBERT E. LAMBIASE

Background

Pulmonary and deep venous thromboembolism represent a continuum of the same disease process. Pulmonary embolism has been stated to be the third leading cause of death in this country.[1] The incidence of pulmonary embolism has been estimated at 750,000 to 900,000 cases per year, with a mortality of 120,000 to 150,000 cases per year in the United States.[2,3] Untreated, proximal deep venous thrombosis or pulmonary embolism has a 30.5 to 50.0 percent chance of recurrent pulmonary embolism, with an 18 to 26 percent mortality rate.[4–6] Eighty-five to 95 percent of pulmonary emboli arise from the iliofemoral veins,[7,8] with most of the other 10 to 15 percent arising from thrombi in the vena cava, ovarian veins, right atrium, or upper extremities.[7,9,10] Anticoagulation is the initial treatment of pulmonary deep venous thromboembolic disease in most patients. Mechanical means of interrupting the pathway of thrombi traveling to the lungs are most often reserved for patients who cannot tolerate anticoagulation, who suffer pulmonary embolism during adequate anticoagulation, or who have extensive thrombosis above the inguinal ligament that predisposes them to significant pulmonary embolism despite adequate anticoagulation.[11,12]

Virchow triad was originally postulated in 1860.[13] Just 8 years later, mechanical obstruction as a method to prevent lower extremity thrombi from traveling to the lungs was conceived.[14–16] Homans recognized in 1944 that most symptomatic pulmonary emboli arise from the lower extremity and pelvic veins, and that these proximal thrombi usually originate in the deep veins of the calf.[7,17] Homans, DeBakey, and Ochsner advocated early femoral interruption in patients who had experienced pulmonary embolism.[7,18] Such vein ligations were often performed at the common femoral level.[7] Suction of proximal thrombi from iliac veins was performed if thrombus was present in the common femoral vein on exploration, although Homans advo-

cated ligation at the common iliac level in such patients.[7] Since heparin did not become available for clinical use until 1935,[19] and warfarin was not synthesized and available for widespread clinical use until 1948,[20,21] the use of anticoagulation paralleled vein interruption in the treatment of this disease process.

Ligation of the common femoral vein fell out of favor because of the high incidence of lower extremity swelling after this treatment. Ligation of the superficial femoral vein therefore became the standard means of venous interruption in patients not eligible for or not adequately treated by anticoagulation who had thrombus limited to the calf or distal thigh.[22] However, this was less than satisfactory for patients with thrombus proximal to the junction of the superficial and deep femoral veins. Ligation of the inferior vena cava became popular in these patients.[7,22,23] By the early 1960s, comparison of inferior vena cava ligation and lower-level ligation revealed a similar operative mortality rate and a significantly lower rate of recurrent pulmonary embolism after inferior vena cava ligation.[22,23] Although mortality rates for inferior vena cava ligation as low as 2 percent were reported,[22] most series had mortality rates in the range of 12 to 15 percent.[24–26] Ligations were optimally performed directly below the renal veins because low ligation of the inferior vena cava resulted in venous stasis between the ligature and the renal veins, which could result in recurrent pulmonary embolism.[23,25,27] Immediate and severe leg swelling was a debilitating sequela, occurring in 10 to 16 percent of patients.[22,24]

To limit the undesirable venous stasis seen with inferior vena cava ligation, methods of partial interruption of the inferior vena cava were developed in the late 1960s. This was done to preserve flow through the inferior vena cava while trapping or filtering out potentially harmful emboli. These included suture plication[28] and various designs of clips designed to nar-

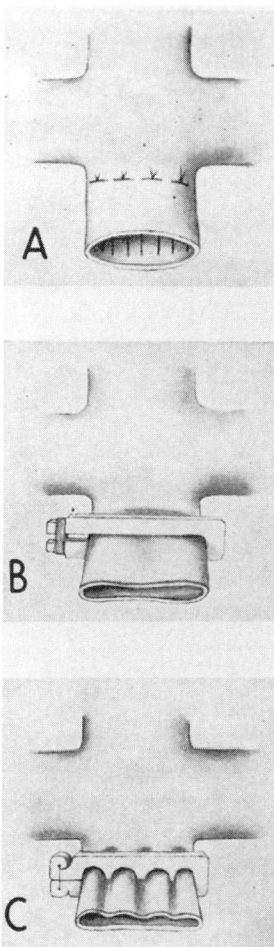

Figure 59-1. Drawing of early surgical approaches to partitioning of the vena cava. (A) "Harp-string" grid method of surgical plication popularized by Spencer. (B) Moretz clip. (C) Miles clip. (From Adams JT, Feingold BE, DeWeese JA. Comparative evaluation of ligation and partial interruption of the inferior vena cava. Arch Surg 1971;103:272–276. Copyright 1971, American Medical Association. Used with permission.)

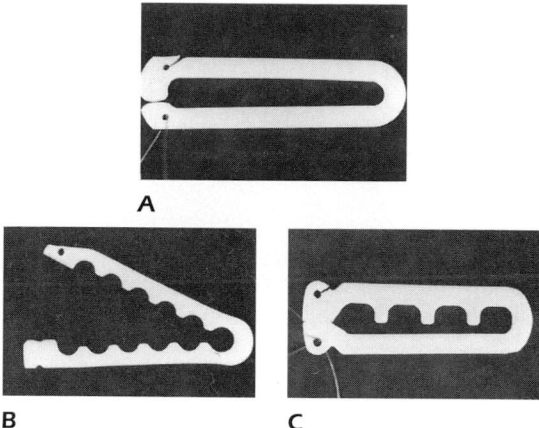

Figure 59-2. Photographs of the Moretz (A), Miles (B), and Adams-DeWeese (C) vena cava clips. The Moretz clip narrows the lumen of the vena cava to 2.5 mm; the Miles and Adams-DeWeese clips compartmentalize the lumen of the vena cava into multiple channels between 3 and 4 mm in diameter. (From Eberlein TH, Carey LC. Comparison of surgical management for pulmonary emboli. Ann Surg 1974;179(6):836–841. Used with permission.)

row the lumen of the inferior vena cava (Moretz clip) or to compartmentalize the lumen into several smaller channels (Miles and Adams-DeWeese clips) (Figs. 59-1 and 59-2).[29,30] Comparison of partial versus complete interruption of the inferior vena cava demonstrated similar procedure-related mortality and recurrent pulmonary embolism rates but a significantly lower incidence of lower extremity morbidity in the patients treated with partial caval interruption (46 versus 76 percent).[25] Clips and suture plication of the vena cava were associated with a 30 to 40 percent incidence of inferior vena cava occlusion.[16] It is interesting to note that inferior vena cava ligation was associated with immediate shock in only approximately 5 percent of patients,[25] despite causing significant transient hemodynamic alterations in experimental animals.[31]

In 1967, Mobin-Uddin et al. introduced the first transvenous device for caval interruption, the Mobin-Uddin umbrella (Edwards Laboratories) (Fig. 59-3).[32] This device was placed through the right internal jugular vein after surgical exposure through a catheter-based carrier system with an inner diameter of 9 mm (27 French), and was deployed in the inferior vena cava using fluoroscopic guidance, and therefore procedures were usually performed in the angiography department. The jugular approach was used to avoid potential iliocaval thrombus; a femoral carrier for the Mobin-Uddin umbrella did not exist.

The Mobin-Uddin umbrella was designed as an adjunct to anticoagulation in patients who experienced recurrent pulmonary embolism during adequate anticoagulation. Broad use of devices for caval interruption in patients with contraindications to anticoagulation, currently the most frequent indication for filter placement, was not common at that time. The original version of this device was intended to result in occlusion of the inferior vena cava.[32] This version consisted of six radiating stainless-steel-alloy spokes connected by a silicone membrane, which was deployed with the apex of the umbrella directed caudally (Fig. 59-4). However, it was expected that alterations in cardiac output, which had been shown experimentally to decrease by 47 percent after inferior vena cava ligation,[31] would be minimized if the time required for vena cava occlusion was prolonged enough to allow for development of collaterals. Therefore, fenestrations were

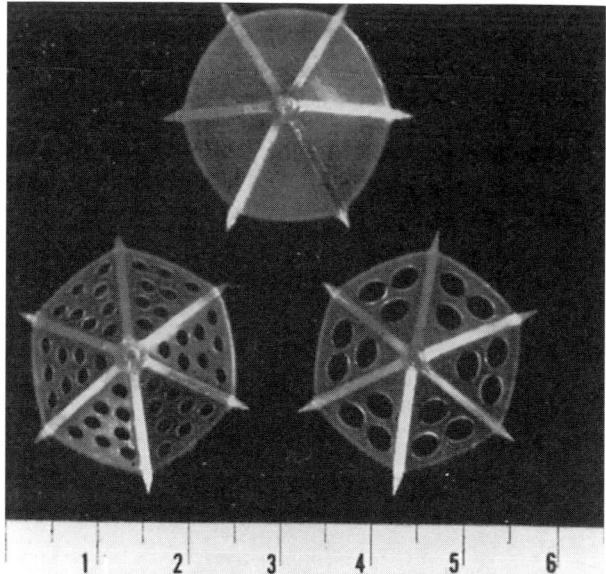

Figure 59-3. Axial view of three configurations of the Mobin-Uddin umbrella. The initial configuration consisted of six radial struts with a solid silicone membrane. The filter was later modified to contain fenestrations of 1.5 mm or 3.0 mm in the silicone membrane. (From Mobin-Uddin K, McLean R, Bolooki H, Jude JR. Caval interruption for prevention of pulmonary embolism: long-term results of a new method. Arch Surg 1969;99:711–715. Copyright 1969, American Medical Association. Used with permission.)

placed in the silicone membrane in 1.5-mm- or 3.0-mm-diameter sizes. As experience with this device accumulated, it became evident that approximately one-third of patients maintained patency of the vena cava after umbrella placement with no increase in the incidence of recurrent pulmonary embolism, which was reported as 3.6 percent in a review of 2215 patients.[33] The silicone membrane was subsequently heparin-bonded in an attempt to improve caval patency rates.

Originally, the Mobin-Uddin umbrella had an expanded diameter of 23 mm. This was increased to 28 mm in the mid-1970s because of occasional reports of proximal migration of the 23-mm-diameter umbrella. The superiority of the transvenous method of inferior vena cava interruption as opposed to surgical methods was established by marked improvement in procedure-related mortality, which was negligible for transvenous placement,[32,33,34–37] versus 8.0 to 14.2 percent for direct surgical methods of caval interruption.[38,39]

The Hunter-Sessions balloon is another transvenous device designed for inferior vena cava occlusion.[40] This device consists of a balloon mounted on the tip of a 20 French outer-diameter catheter system and has been used mainly by the jugular approach following surgical exposure of the jugular vein. After the balloon is positioned under fluoroscopic control, it is inflated,

occluding the cava. The carrier system is then detached from the balloon and removed. The only large reported series of 191 patients treated with this device demonstrated a 1.5 percent incidence of recurrent pulmonary embolism, a 0 percent mortality due to recurrent pulmonary embolism, and a relatively low incidence of lower extremity swelling following placement of the device (25 percent).[40] However, it should be noted that this rate of postphlebitic syndrome is lower than that reported with clips or umbrellas, which not infrequently maintain patency of the inferior vena cava, and is also lower than that seen in patients with lower extremity deep venous thrombosis treated with anticoagulation alone.[41–44]

The observation that patients with the Mobin-Uddin umbrellas who maintained patency of the inferior vena cava had no increased incidence of recurrent pulmonary embolism[35,45] and a lower incidence of lower extremity sequelae[35,45] led to the development of devices designed to maintain patency of the vena cava. The success of these devices led to the demise of the Mobin-Uddin umbrella, which was removed from the market in 1986. Currently, methods of caval interruption resulting in a high incidence of caval occlusion are performed infrequently, in favor of devices designed to preserve patency of the inferior vena cava while trapping clinically significant pulmonary emboli. The first such device introduced was the Kimray-Greenfield filter, now known as the Greenfield filter.

The Greenfield filter (Boston Scientific) was introduced in 1974 and is the most widely used vena cava filter to date. Despite the proliferation of many small

Figure 59-4. Radiograph of a Mobin-Uddin umbrella demonstrates the caudal orientation of the filter apex.

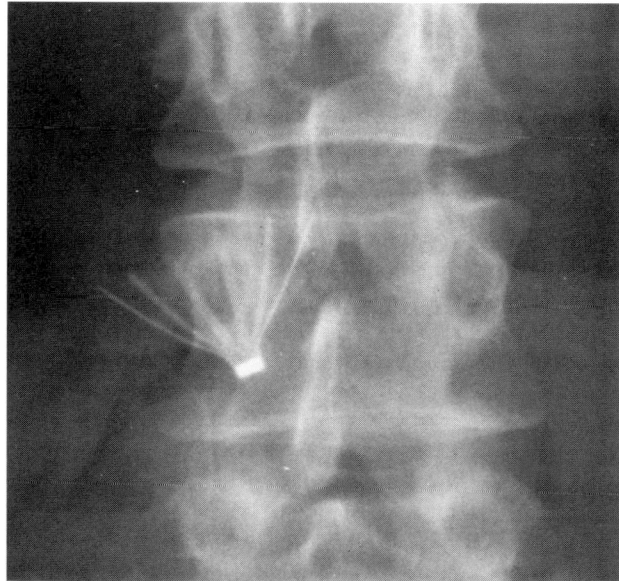

profile filter systems, the Greenfield filter remains one of the most popular vena cava filters in use today. This filter is placed transvenously through a carrier system with an outer diameter of 29.5 French. It was initially placed by surgical cutdown, usually of the right internal jugular vein but also occasionally by the right common femoral vein. Percutaneous placement was first described by Tadavarthy in 1984.[46] The filter is made of stainless steel and consists of six crimped radiating struts angled so that the resulting filter is shaped like a cone. The apex of the cone is directed cephalad. In this position, 80 percent of the volume of the cone can be occupied by thrombus, corresponding to a reduction in cross-sectional area to 64 percent.[16] This filter has demonstrated the ability to trap clinically significant emboli in vitro and in vivo,[47,48] and in clinical trials has demonstrated a rate of clinically evident recurrent pulmonary embolism of 4 percent while maintaining caval patency in 96 percent,[49] although it should be noted that reliable objective tests to assess asymptomatic pulmonary embolism and vena cava occlusion were rarely performed.

Downsizing the introducer system has become popular to facilitate percutaneous placement, to reduce procedure time and patient blood loss during the procedure, and in the hope of reducing thrombosis of the insertion site, usually the common femoral vein. Initial reports of the incidence of insertion site thrombosis with percutaneous insertion were discouragingly high, from 10 to 41 percent.[50–53] The hope of reducing rates of insertion site thrombosis also motivated development of lower-profile systems. However, modification of placement technique, including balloon dilatation of the tract and limited insertion of the large sheath into the iliac vein,[54,55] significantly reduced the incidence of insertion site thrombosis, to 10.0 to 14.3 percent.[54,55] The introduction of carrier systems as small as 9 French outer diameter has not significantly reduced these rates of insertion site thrombosis.[56]

Technique of Filter Placement

Percutaneous placement of vena cava filters is usually achieved after gaining access to a common femoral or internal jugular vein by a single-wall puncture, replacing the needle over a guidewire for serial dilators or a long angioplasty balloon of suitable size for the filter system being used (from 9 French in outer diameter for the Simon nitinol filter to 29.5 French in outer diameter for the stainless steel Greenfield filter), and finally, placing the filter introducer system through a sheath left in the vena cava and then deploying the filter. Although serial dilators were used for large-

caliber tract dilatation in the past, balloon dilatation of the tract[54] has been shown to be less traumatic to the vein[57] and to result in a lower incidence of insertion site thrombosis.[55,58] For smaller venotomies, no similar studies have been performed. The safety of percutaneous access to the vein compared with surgical exposure of the vein has been demonstrated.[59]

Vena cavograms are routinely performed before filter placement to assess the patency of the vena cava, anomalies of the vena cava, or webs or excessive narrowing of the intrahepatic portion of the vena cava.[60] Inflow of the renal veins can be determined to ensure proper positioning of the filter. Also, because approximately 3 percent of venae cavae are oversized (>28 mm in diameter)[61] and not suitable for many of the available filters, caval diameters are also routinely measured. Useful information is available in up to 27 percent of cavograms performed before filter placement, and in 15 percent of cases this information significantly affects the performance of the procedure.[60] Approximately three-fourths of percutaneous filter placements are done through the common femoral vein after the vena cava and the femoral and iliac veins are assessed. The majority of the remainder are placed by the jugular approach. Although the femoral approach potentially may induce thrombosis in the vein and rarely may cause pulmonary embolism by inadvertent manipulation through iliac or caval thrombus, the jugular approach occasionally results in death because of air embolization or trauma to the carotid or vertebral artery,[58] and therefore the femoral approach is preferred when thrombus does not prohibit it. The left femoral approach has been associated with a higher incidence of thrombosis of the insertion site than the right femoral approach when the large delivery system for the stainless steel Greenfield filter is used.[62] This is probably due to mechanical trauma to the left iliac system when one is negotiating the more acute angle encountered at the iliocaval junction to place the filter from the left side, which may be aggravated by the occasional necessity of straightening this junction to permit filter passage. The higher incidence of thrombosis of the insertion site with placement by the left common femoral vein has not been confirmed with use of the low-profile filter systems.[56] Other access sites that have been used include the left internal jugular vein and the external jugular veins.[63] Antecubital vein placement is possible with the Simon nitinol filter.

Because most inferior vena cava filters are placed for lower extremity thrombus, infrarenal placement can usually be accomplished. When thrombus in the inferior vena cava does not permit infrarenal placement, suprarenal placement is acceptable. Although occlusion of the inferior vena cava above the renal veins carries the theoretical risk of renal vein thrombosis and venous infarction of the kidneys, the collateral circulation, particularly on the left, should be sufficient to preserve renal viability despite thrombosis of the vena cava at and above the renal veins, and no increased risk of renal dysfunction with suprarenal filter placement has been reported.

Indications for Filter Placement

Deep venous thrombosis or pulmonary embolism and a contraindication to anticoagulation remain the most frequent indications for vena cava filter placement, cited in 38 to 77 percent of patients.[49,52,63-66] Absolute contraindications to anticoagulation include recent stroke or neurosurgical procedure (within 2 months), recent major surgery or trauma (within 2 weeks), active internal bleeding, intracranial neoplasm, recent ocular surgery, and heparin-induced thrombocytopenia.[67-73] Coumadin is contraindicated in pregnancy because it crosses the placenta and can cause fetal anomalies.[73] Relative contraindications include recent minor trauma (within 2 weeks), hematuria, occult blood in the stools, peptic ulcer disease, pericarditis, bacterial endocarditis, and unstable gait.[67-73] Less frequent indications for vena cava filter placement include complications of anticoagulation, which occur in 5 to 50 percent of patients and include bleeding, thrombocytopenia secondary to heparin therapy, and warfarin-induced skin necrosis.[67,71-79] Anticoagulation is associated with a 5 to 12 percent mortality rate.[67,71-79] Complications of anticoagulation are the indication for filter placement in 6 to 17 percent of patients.[49,63,65,66] In 3 to 27 percent of patients, the indication for filter placement is recurrent pulmonary embolism or proximal propagation of lower extremity thrombus while adequately anticoagulated.[49,63-66] A high risk of pulmonary embolism is seen in patients with free-floating iliofemoral or caval thrombus, which occurs in 27 to 60 percent of these patients despite adequate anticoagulation.[11,12] These situations also warrant placement of a vena cava filter, ideally as an adjunct to anticoagulation.[63]

Prophylaxis for pulmonary embolism is a term that has undergone evolution since the advent of percutaneous filter placement, and its use today may have two different meanings. *Prophylaxis* initially referred to any filter placement in a patient with deep venous thrombosis but without documented pulmonary embolism. Since percutaneous filter placement is well tolerated, with significantly less morbidity and mortality than surgical placement, *prophylaxis* now often means placement in patients without documented deep ve-

nous thrombosis or pulmonary embolism but in a high-risk clinical situation for development of the disease. Such clinical situations include surgical and trauma patients,[67,80-83] spinal cord injury patients,[82] patients in the intensive care unit,[84] patients with poor pulmonary reserve with a cardiac index less than 1.5 liters per minute,[6] patients undergoing pulmonary or lower extremity thrombolysis or thrombectomy,[6] hip fracture patients, and patients undergoing total knee arthroplasty.[85-87] These indications are controversial and not universal, and they need to be considered on an individual basis.

Evaluation and Comparison of Vena Cava Filters

The majority of filter data published to date has relied on clinical follow-up (Table 59-1). Criteria such as death, clinically apparent recurrent pulmonary embolism, and significant lower extremity swelling are the most significant adverse outcomes associated with filter placement, and traditionally clinical assessment has dominated filter literature. The problem with this approach is that such clinically significant adverse outcomes are uncommon. Reliance on clinical data will not readily demonstrate a difference between the many filter devices that are available, whereas this difference might be evident if all patients underwent rigorous follow-up with serial imaging studies. The frequent occurrence of asymptomatic pulmonary embolism has been well documented, and has been observed in 35 to 51 percent of patients with deep venous thrombosis.[88,89] Previous reports have demonstrated that thrombosis and occlusion of the inferior vena cava are usually asymptomatic,[7,22,23,33,90] and clinical follow-up will therefore underestimate this occurrence. In addition, patients with a history of lower extremity deep venous thrombosis are predisposed to the postphlebitic syndrome. Up to 79 percent of patients develop lower extremity swelling due to damage to the valves in the deep veins caused by thrombosis, and therefore clinical assessment of inferior vena cava thrombosis is dubious.[41-44] Objective evaluation of such criteria would be more fruitful, because incidences of asymptomatic outcomes, which are more common than symptomatic ones, would point to real differences in filter performance. However, the magnitude and cost of such a study have prevented analysis of currently available filters.[91]

Many filter series include follow-up data of short duration. For this disease process, in which the risk of pulmonary embolism in most patients is self-limited,

Table 59-1. Comparison of Five Vena Cava Filters*

Filter	Recurrent Pulmonary Embolism	Inferior Vena Cava Patency	Insertion Site Thrombosis	Stability	Caval Penetration
Stainless steel Greenfield	4%	95%	0–41%	Excellent; occasional migrations to heart and pulmonary arteries reported	Rare, including penetration of adjacent organs
Bird's nest	3%	97% clinical follow-up	Up to 33% (non-occlusive)	Case reports of migration to right atrium	Unknown
Titanium Greenfield	3%	100%	3.0–8.7%	11% >1 cm with new filter design	0.8% with new design
Simon nitinol	3%	79–86% imaging follow-up	10–11%	Rare; migration to heart and pulmonary arteries reported	25%, including aortic penetration in two patients
LGM (Vena Tech)	—	70–92% imaging follow-up	6–23%	14% migration >1 cm; migration rarely significant	Not significant

*Summary of available data for the five vena cava filters currently available. Comparison of published figures between filters in most cases is not reliable because of inconsistent methods of establishing outcomes. (See refs. 4, 5, 46, 49, 52–55, 63, 64, 66, 97–115.)

this approach may be justified. Because thrombus is most likely to embolize in its acute form before it becomes adherent and incorporated into the vein wall, and this process is usually complete by 3 to 6 months, the acute period following filter placement is of most interest regarding recurrent pulmonary embolism, caval thrombosis (which probably always occurs because of trapped emboli),[4,58,90] and insertion vein thrombosis. After organization of thrombus, a process that takes up to 3 to 6 months in most patients,[92] occlusion of the inferior vena cava or pulmonary embolism is probably unlikely to occur in the absence of recurrent deep venous thrombosis.[63]

There are currently five approved intracaval filters in the United States. These include the stainless steel Greenfield filter (Boston Scientific), the titanium Greenfield filter (Medi-Tech), the LGM (Vena Tech) filter (Vena Tech), the bird's nest filter (Cook, Inc.), and the Simon nitinol filter (Nitinol Medical Technologies). The Gunther filter and Amplatz filter have undergone clinical trials, most of which have been conducted in Europe. Filters differ in size, design, composition, and size of introducer. Criteria that are used to assess filters include rates of recurrent pulmonary embolism after filter placement, death rates due to pulmonary embolism after filter placement, occlusion of the filter and inferior vena cava, thrombosis of the insertion site, incidence of filter angulation and significance of filter angulation vis-à-vis filtration ability, filter migration, potential sites of insertion, and ease of placement. An ideal vena cava filter should be biocompatible and nonthrombogenic, effectively filter all clinically significant emboli, result in minimal flow dis-

turbance, be stable in the longitudinal and transverse planes within the vena cava, result in no injury to adjacent structures, be simply and safely placed, and be of low cost.[93,94] Retrievability is a debatable attribute.[94] It should be noted that most published series include data obtained mostly by clinical follow-up; very few studies have assessed filters objectively with imaging studies to document outcome according to the above criteria.

The ability of vena cava filters to trap experimental thrombi has been tested using in vitro models of the vena cava, and in animal models as well.[47,48,95,96] In Katsomouris's study, the Greenfield filter was relatively ineffective at trapping small emboli (<3 mm in diameter), whereas the Mobin-Uddin, Amplatz, Gunther, Simon nitinol, and bird's nest filters were effective in filtering most of even the smallest emboli (2 mm in diameter).[47] In tilted or eccentric position, or with prolapse or elongation of the filaments of the bird's nest filter, the Amplatz, Gunther, Simon nitinol, and bird's nest filters maintained their effectiveness in filtering emboli of all sizes.[47] The Mobin-Uddin umbrella and the Kimray Greenfield were significantly less effective in filtering even large thrombi (7 mm in diameter) when not oriented properly.[47] This finding was not confirmed, however, in an animal experiment where thrombi were injected into the vena cava of sheep.[48] In this study, the Greenfield filter removed 89 percent of emboli either 4 or 8 mm in diameter, with failures limited to emboli of the smaller sizes. No significant decrease in clot filtration was seen in four animals with the filter tilted so that the apex was against the wall of the vena cava.[48] Another animal model was used to study the LGM and titanium Greenfield filters.[86] In this study, thrombi of two sizes, 5 by 5 mm or 5 by 10 mm, were injected into eight adult sheep.[96] The LGM filter trapped 70 percent of the smaller size and 100 percent of the larger size, and the titanium Greenfield filter trapped 26 percent of the smaller size and 34 percent of the larger size.[96] In addition, the titanium Greenfield filter trapped only 37 percent of 5 × 30 mm emboli.[96] The only consistent conclusion is that the Greenfield filter appears relatively ineffective at filtering small emboli.[47,48,95,96] However, the importance of this conclusion is dubious because these small emboli may not be clinically significant and the filter may have a higher patency rate because of fewer trapped emboli.[96] Furthermore, none of these models duplicate the physiology of the inferior vena cava in humans.

Stainless Steel Greenfield Filter

The stainless steel Greenfield filter consists of six radiating struts that project downward and outward from a central point, making the shape of a cone (Fig. 59-5). The apex of the cone is directed toward the head in the vena cava. The filter is 4.4 cm in height. Each of the six legs of the filter is angled, taking a zigzag course from apex to base. At the base, each strut has a single barb or tine that anchors the filter within the vena cava. The filter is self-expanding and is deposited from the jugular or femoral vein, either by percutaneous puncture or by cutdown. A hole in the apex of the filter permits placement over a guidewire. The original introducer system has an outer diameter of 29.5 French. The filter has been modified and is now available with a 14 French introducer.

The stainless steel Greenfield filter has been used since 1973.[52] In Greenfield and Michna's review of the first 12 years of experience with this device, they reported a 4 percent clinically suspected or confirmed rate of recurrent pulmonary embolism in 469 patients.[49] By comparison, the incidence of recurrent pulmonary embolism in patients not treated with anticoagulation is approximately 30 percent,[4] and the mortality rate in patients with pulmonary embolism not treated with anticoagulation in 6 months is 25 percent,[5] demonstrating the effectiveness of this device in preventing clinically significant pulmonary embolism. A separate report by Greenfield et al. documented a 95 percent patency rate of the inferior vena cava in 59 patients using contrast and radioisotope vena cavography[97]; this has also been confirmed by other investigators.[52,53] Periprocedure mortality is rare.[49,52,53,97]

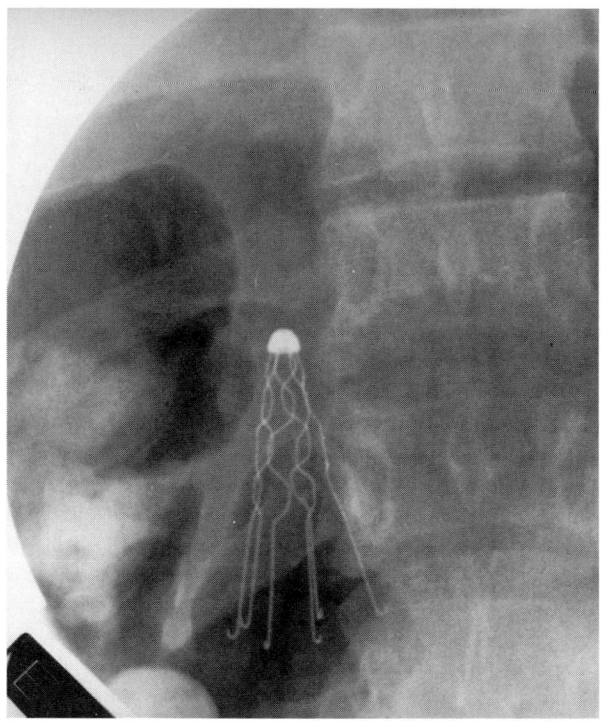

Figure 59-5. Radiograph of a suprarenal stainless steel Greenfield filter in a patient with thrombosis of the inferior vena cava extending to the renal veins.

The necessity of coordinating the vascular surgeon, operating instruments, and the radiologist with angiography equipment in the angiography suite resulted in delays and frustration for all parties involved.[98] To gain suitable access to the deep central veins, radiologists began to use dilators originally designed for the creation of large tracts for renal calculi removal, obviating the need for surgical access of deep veins. Percutaneous placement of the Greenfield filter was first reported in 1984.[46] It was achieved by puncture of either the jugular or femoral vein, placement of a guidewire in the vein through the needle, and subsequent dilatation of the tract using serial dilators up to 24 French in size, which was required to accommodate the delivery system.[98] Hemostasis after removal of the delivery system was achieved by manual compression within 15 to 30 minutes.[53,98] With the radiologist acting independently, it was found that placement of a vena cava filter lengthened the procedure time by only about 10 minutes after an inferior vena cavogram was performed.[98] Tract dilatation was later performed using an angioplasty balloon; this approach saved time and was less traumatic to the vein than multiple dilators.[54,55]

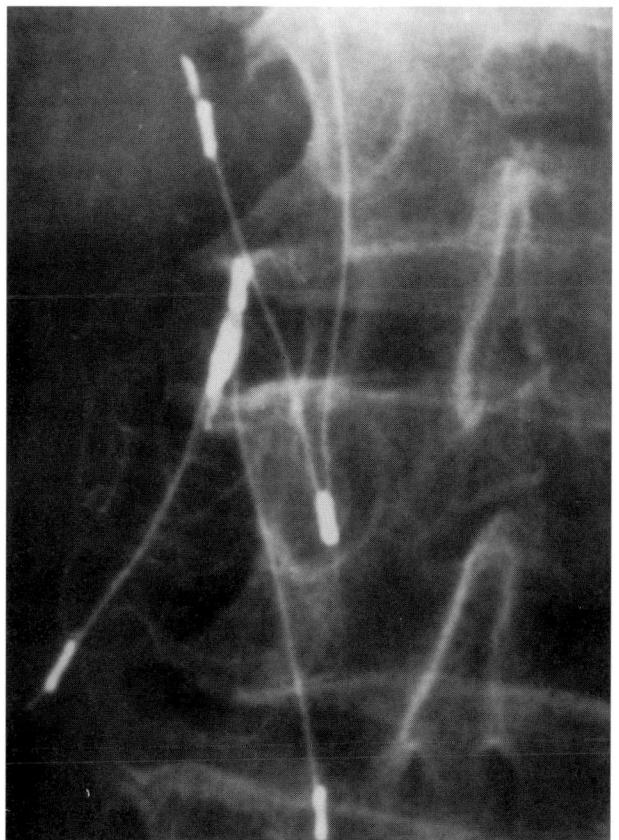
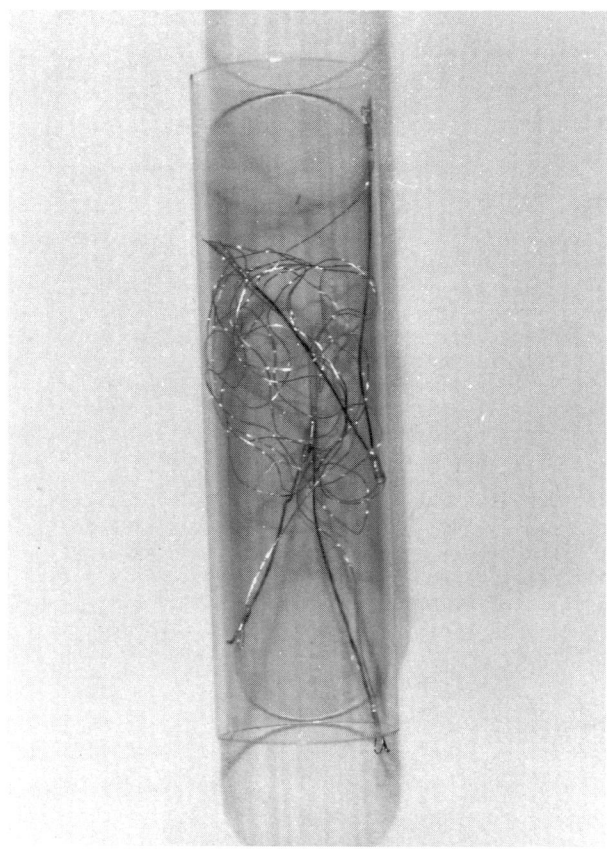

A   **B**

Figure 59-6. (A) Radiograph of the bird's nest filter showing the stabilizing struts. The filaments that constitute the nest responsible for filtration are only faintly seen. (B) Photograph of the filter in a model of the vena cava clearly shows the filaments.

Bird's Nest Filter

The bird's nest filter (Cook, Inc.) has been in use since 1982 (Fig. 59-6).[64] This filter is unique in design. Filtration is achieved by a network of four 25-cm-long filaments 0.18 mm in diameter, which during deployment are wound in such a way so that their relationship is fairly compact.[64] These filaments are anchored to the vena cava by two sets of V-shaped struts, each composed of two legs connected to each other at one end with an acute angle at their junction. The legs have barbs and loops at their ends opposite their junction point to prevent movement within the vena cava and to limit penetration of the vena cava wall. One set of struts is deposited first, with the apex directed caudally. After these are anchored firmly within the vena cava, the filaments are deployed. The filaments are not visible fluoroscopically and only occasionally are seen with plain radiography. Manipulation of the introducer sheath, which is rotated 90 degrees four times during filament deployment, minimizes prolapse of the filaments beyond the anchoring struts.[64] Finally, the second set of anchoring struts is deployed, with the apex or junction point of the legs directed cephalad, overlapping the first set of struts by at least 50 percent. The filter was initially designed for placement through an 8 French sheath, although modification of the anchoring struts necessitated increasing the size of the introducer to 12 French.[64] Since the maximum expansion diameter between the free ends of the legs of the anchoring struts is 60 mm, this filter has been particularly useful in patients with venae cavae greater than 28 mm in diameter, which is the maximum acceptable diameter for placement of the Greenfield filter and other currently available filters of similar design.[99] This filter has been placed in venae cavae up to 42 mm in diameter and has demonstrated equal clot-trapping efficiency in an in vitro oversized vena cava model with less flow disturbance than with bilateral iliac placement of other filters.[100]

Results obtained with the bird's nest filter were reported in the largest series of filter patients published

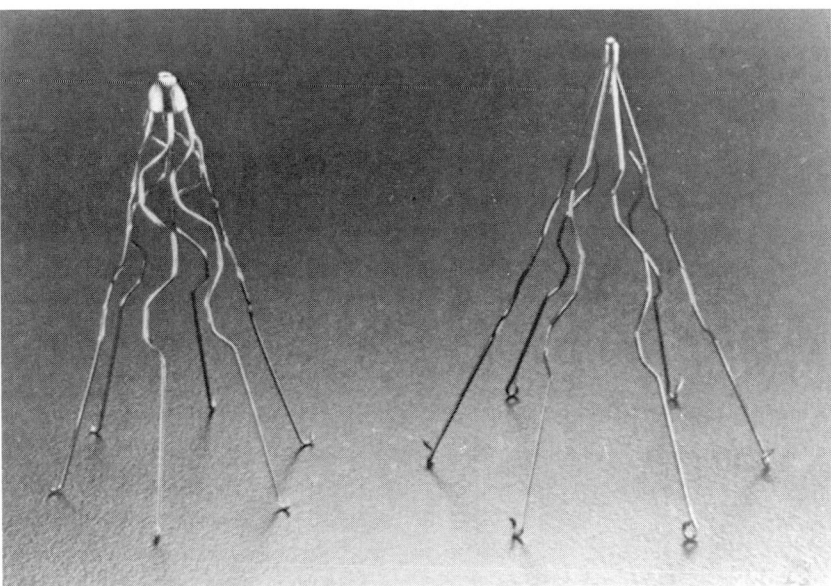

Figure 59-7. Photograph of the titanium Greenfield filter (*right*), with the stainless steel Greenfield filter (*left*) for comparison. (From Greenfield LJ, Cho KJ, Pais SO, Van Aman M. Preliminary clinical experience with the titanium Greenfield vena caval filter. Arch Surg 1989;124:657–659. Used with permission.)

to date, 568 patients.[64] Unfortunately, follow-up was almost exclusively clinical, with few imaging studies performed to document outcome.[64] In addition, duration of follow-up was short, with a minimum required follow-up of 6 months and a maximum of 5 years.[64] Twelve of 440 patients (2.7 percent) on whom 6-month follow-up information was available demonstrated clinically suspected recurrent pulmonary embolism, and 13 patients (2.9 percent) had clinical evidence of inferior vena cava thrombosis.[64] Recurrent pulmonary embolism was confirmed in only 2 patients, and thrombosis of the inferior vena cava in 7 patients. Of 27 follow-up vena cavograms performed, 6 demonstrated thrombosis; it is not stated in this report if all of these vena cavograms were obtained for symptoms.

Two configurations of the bird's nest filter have been used. The original version had flexible struts 0.25 mm in diameter. Significant migration of the filter was seen in 5 of the first 422 patients with the original filter design.[64] Migration of the filter to the right atrium occurred in 4 patients; in a fifth, the filter and a massive recurrent pulmonary embolism were found in the pulmonary artery at autopsy 10 days after filter placement.[64] Because of migration of the filter in these 5 patients, the struts were increased to 0.46 mm in diameter, and in the current model are rigid. This change required increasing the diameter of the insertion sheath from 8 French to 12 French. No migrations were reported in this series in the next 147 patients treated with the modified filter.[64] A subsequent report described 2 patients treated with the modified filter

who experienced cephalad migration of one set of anchoring struts, one to the intrahepatic inferior vena cava and the other to the right atrium.[101] The bird's nest filter has been placed uneventfully in venae cavae with diameters up to 42 mm in one report of 18 patients with vena cava diameters greater than 28 mm.[99] No filter migration was seen in the 10 patients who underwent plain radiographic follow-up in this group; the mean follow-up was 12 weeks.[99]

Titanium Greenfield Filter

The titanium Greenfield filter is similar in design to the stainless steel Greenfield filter but is slightly larger, with a length of 4.7 cm and a width at the filter base of 38 mm (Fig. 59-7).[66,102] It is approximately half the weight of the stainless steel Greenfield filter and is designed to be placed using a 12 French carrier through a 14 French sheath.[66,102] Unlike the stainless steel Greenfield filter, the filter is not placed over a guidewire. Titanium has demonstrated biocompatibility comparable to stainless steel.[102]

The original version of the titanium Greenfield filter had hooks at the base of each of the filter struts that were similar in design to those of the stainless steel Greenfield filter. However, this filter design was plagued by a high incidence of filter migration (27 percent)[66] as well as by disturbingly frequent reports of penetration of the wall of the vena cava and adjacent structures.[103,104] The titanium Greenfield filter had greater lateral force at large diameters than the stainless steel Greenfield filter, which may have predisposed it to caval penetration.[102] Therefore, the filter hooks were modified by curving them to limit penetration and angling them 80 degrees to minimize migration.[66] The modified filter design demonstrated an improved rate of migration 1 cm or greater in 11 percent in a follow-up study.[66] Caval penetration was assessed by splaying of the filter base over 5 mm in 17 of 121 patients; further evaluation with computed tomography (CT) confirmed filter penetration of the vena cava in 1 patient (0.8 percent).[66] This represented an improvement over the unacceptable 13 percent rate of caval penetration for the initial design.[66,102,103]

The titanium Greenfield filter often demonstrates crossing of one or more pairs of the filter struts after deployment; this problem was reported in a total of 7.4 percent of 181 cases.[66] The crossing results in uneven segmentation of the vena cava and in some cases may be unsatisfactory, requiring placement of an additional filter. In the authors' experience, crossing of the legs is less frequently seen with jugular placement, possibly because of the presentation of the filter struts on deployment, as opposed to the apical presentation with femoral placement.

In clinical trials the titanium Greenfield filter has demonstrated similar clot-trapping effectiveness as the stainless steel Greenfield filter.[66,102] Pulmonary embolism after filter placement was clinically suspected in 3 percent of 181 patients in one series.[66] No patients were clinically suspected of having thrombosis of the inferior vena cava, although patients were only followed for 30 days in this study.[66] Thrombosis of the insertion site has been reported in 3.0 to 8.7 percent of patients.[66,102]

Simon Nitinol Filter

The Simon nitinol filter (Nitinol Medical Technologies) is composed of a nickel-titanium alloy that has thermal memory (Fig. 59-8). This filter is molded into a predetermined shape at high temperature. When cooled, the filaments become pliable, and the filter can be straightened for introduction. The filter is cooled with iced saline as it is introduced. As it is warmed on contact with blood, it assumes its molded configuration within seconds. The filter is 3.8 cm long, and the filter dome has a diameter of 28 mm.[105] The filter is placed through a 7 French introducer (9 French outer diameter). It has six radiating legs projected from the center of the filter, each with a hook designed to minimize motion of the filter within the vena cava. In addition, the filter has a second tier of struts designed for filtration. These are located cranially to the anchoring struts and consist of seven wire loops arranged in the configuration of the petals of a flower.

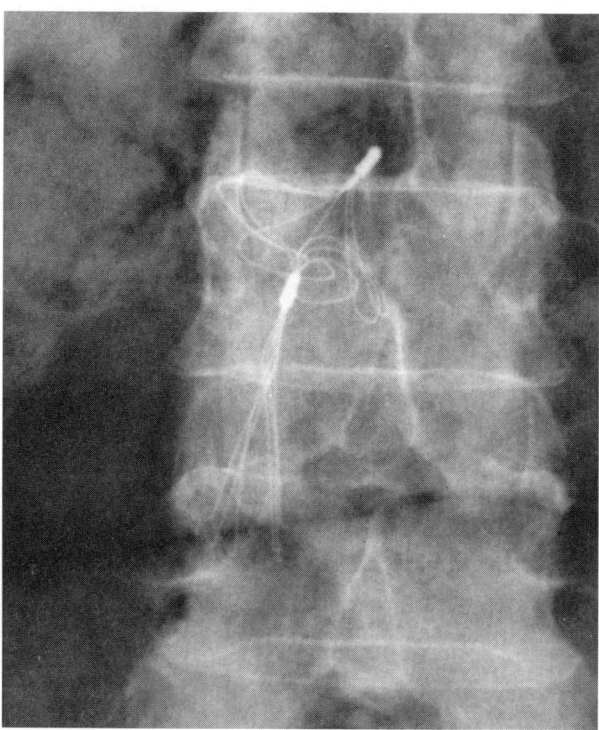

Figure 59-8. Radiograph of the Simon nitinol filter. The film demonstrates slight tilting of the filter petals compared with the longitudinal axis of the vena cava.

In preliminary data from 103 patients with Simon nitinol filters placed at 17 centers, recurrent pulmonary embolism was confirmed in 2 patients and suspected in a third, for a recurrent pulmonary embolism rate of 3 percent.[105] Subsequently, patient deaths due to pulmonary embolism or related to caval thrombosis with the use of the Simon nitinol filter have been described.[106] Occlusion of the inferior vena cava was reported in 6 of 44 patients (14 percent), and insertion site thrombosis in 5 of 44 patients (11 percent).[105] No significant filter migration was observed in this series, although 3 cases of migration to the heart or pulmonary arteries have been published.[107,108] Although tilting of the dome of the filter was observed in 55 percent of 44 patients, it has been stated that this does not affect filter effectiveness.[105] In the largest series published to date, the number of patients undergoing objective testing for each of these outcomes is not specified, and it must be presumed that all patients did not undergo such testing.

Thrombosis of the vena cava after filter placement has been the major disadvantage of the Simon nitinol filter (Fig. 59-9). In one series in which this problem was assessed, occlusion of the vena cava was seen in 21 percent of 24 patients.[109] The possibility of more frequent occurrence of vena caval occlusion in patients with malignancies has been raised, although

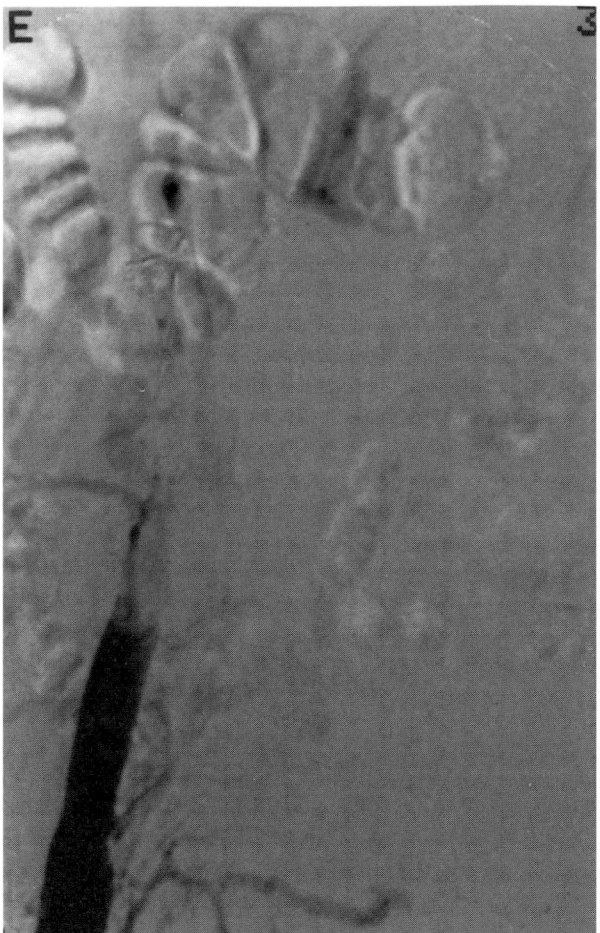

Figure 59-9. Digital subtraction vena cavogram from a patient who had a Simon nitinol filter placed 1 month previously. There is thrombosis of the vena cava at the level of the filter, with a patent lumen in the caudal inferior vena cava. The vena cava probably occluded because of trapped thrombus.

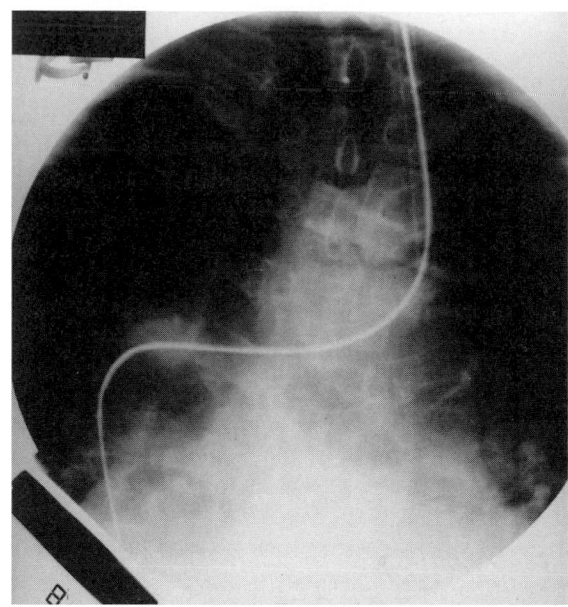

Figure 59-10. Radiograph of the extremely tortuous course through the mediastinum during filter placement from the left internal jugular vein in a patient without possible access by the right jugular system or by either femoral vein. The Simon nitinol filter was the only filter able to negotiate this course.

the number of patients on which this conclusion was based is small.[109] Filter penetration has been documented by imaging studies in 5 out of 20 patients (25 percent), including penetration of the aorta in 2 patients.[107] Tilting of the cephalad cluster of loops in undersized venae cavae has been observed, and it has been postulated that this may impart excessive torque on the filter-anchoring struts and increase the likelihood of penetration of the vena cava,[107] although this has not been proven. This series confirmed the ability of this filter to prevent pulmonary embolism; no clinically suspected postfilter emboli were seen in 20 patients with mean follow-up of 14 months.[107]

Problems such as occlusion of the vena cava and penetration of the vena cava have limited this filter's acceptance. However, the Simon nitinol vena cava filter has one clear advantage over other devices; namely, the flexibility of the filter before deployment allows

placement from virtually any access site, including the left jugular system, which may not permit placement of one of the other available filters, and the antecubital veins (Fig. 59-10). The Simon nitinol filter is used at the authors' institution most frequently in patients who do not have traditional routes of venous access and who therefore need filter placement by the left jugular or antecubital approaches, although most patients have suitable anatomy to permit placement of one of the other devices by the left jugular vein.

LGM Vena Tech Filter

The LGM Vena Tech filter (Vena Tech) is cone-shaped and has six radiating struts. It measured 4.5 cm high in its initial configuration, with a base width of 28 mm (Fig. 59-11). The filter is composed of a stainless steel alloy called Elgiloy and is stamped and point-welded. There are six longitudinal side rails attached to the struts at the base of the filter parallel to the wall of the vena cava. They are designed to contact the wall of the vena cava throughout their length, providing transverse stability.[63] The side rails were 34 mm long in the original design and therefore shorter than the diagonal struts. Hooks are punched from the metal at the cephalad ends of the side rails to provide longitudinal stability. This filter is designed for rapid deployment; indeed, slow deployment may result in incomplete opening of the filter.[63] Since incomplete opening was reported in up to 42 percent of filters placed by the jugular approach,[110] the filter was modified so that the side rails are now nearly equal in height to the filter when deployed. This was done to minimize crossing of the side rails with the diagonal struts upon filter deployment, which can result in incomplete opening of the filter.[63]

The LGM filter has been used in Europe since 1985[111]; use in the United States began in 1989.[63] This filter is the most thoroughly and objectively evaluated filter to date, with four large studies reporting mostly imaging-based follow-up.[63,111–113] The filter is effective in preventing recurrent pulmonary embolism. In five large series involving a total of 482 patients, recurrent pulmonary embolism rates of 0 to 3.5 percent were reported.[63,111–114]

Occlusion of the inferior vena cava (IVC) was studied in the first series by cavography in 90 patients 1 year after filter placement, and was present in 7 (8 percent).[111] In the second series, 60 patients underwent routine imaging studies, and the probability of vena cava patency at 8 months was 92 percent.[63] A higher

Figure 59-11. Lateral photograph of the LGM Vena Tech filter.

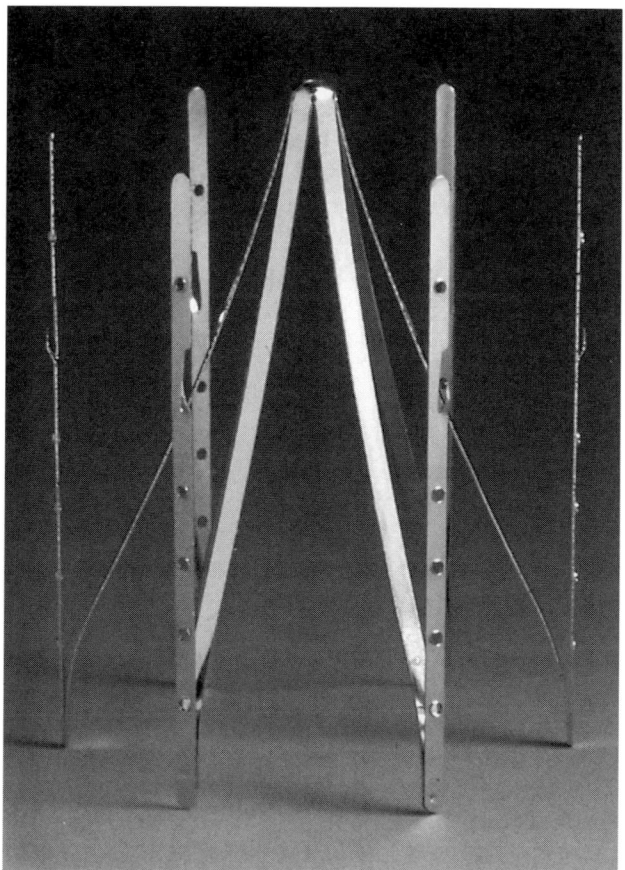

rate of thrombotic occlusion of the vena cava was reported in the third series, seen by sonography or autopsy in 14 out of 64 patients, for a rate of IVC occlusion of 22 percent.[113] This result is considerably higher than that of other reports of short follow-up[63,111] and was not confirmed in another series, in which a rate of IVC occlusion of 8 percent of 39 patients was reported.[112] In a recently published series with 2- to 6-year follow-up, the patency of the inferior vena cava as documented by transabdominal Doppler ultrasound was 92 percent after 2 years but then continued to decrease by approximately 5 percent per year thereafter, to 70 percent after 6 years.[114] This is lower than rates reported for the stainless steel Greenfield filter.[49,97] However, since imaging studies were not done to document the long-term patency of the stainless steel Greenfield filter, the difference may be attributable to closer scrutiny of the LGM filter. The observation that the patency rate of the vena cava with the LGM filter continued to decline at a consistent rate up to 6 years raises the possibility that the filter causes thrombosis of the vena cava in the absence of embolized or propagating thrombosis. Because the material is biologically stable and the normal vena cava is a very high flow structure, spontaneous thrombosis seems unlikely without constriction of the vein lumen.[107] Indeed, narrowing of the filter base was highly correlated with thrombosis of the vena cava in this series.[114] Although in previous experience this was felt to be due to retraction of thrombus, it is possible that the filter side rails incite a hyperplastic or fibrotic response in the vein wall that results in narrowing and occlusion.[114] Whether this feature is unique to the LGM filter awaits further study.

Thrombosis of the insertion site following placement of the LGM Vena Tech filter has been reported in 6 and 23 percent of patients in the two series in which this was evaluated.[63,113] Significant filter migration (1 cm or greater) was seen in 14 percent of 65 patients in one series, with a maximum migration of 3 cm,[63] and in 13 percent in another series.[112] These results were supported in one other series.[111] One centimeter is assumed to be the minimum for significant migration when assessing filter stability, because shorter migration cannot be reliably distinguished from perceived change due to parallax.

Only 1 patient of 242 (0.4 percent) demonstrated filter angulation greater than 15 degrees,[63,112,113] which is the minimum angulation required to reduce filtration ability.[47] This can be attributed to the presence of longitudinal side rails on the LGM Vena Tech filter, which provide transverse stability. One filter was noted to have spontaneously fractured on follow-up.[112,115] Caval penetration of 2 and 5 mm was reported in one series, documented by computed tomography and ultrasound.[113]

As mentioned above, incomplete opening of the LGM Vena Tech filter has been its only significant problem, and this is most frequently encountered with jugular placement. This problem was reported in between 9 and 42 percent of cases when the jugular approach was used.[63,110,112,113] However, it is interesting to note that in the two largest series reporting significant numbers of jugular filter placements in which incomplete opening of the filter was encountered (22 and 42 percent rates of incomplete filter opening),[63,110] two institutions contributed patients to both reports in the same time period, presumably the same patients. Therefore the results from both reports will be weighted toward those achieved at these institutions, because the data are not truly independent. Results obtained with the new configuration are not available.

Amplatz Filter

The Amplatz filter (William Cook, Europe; Bjaerverskov, Denmark) is designed to be retrievable. This feature may be desirable in the patient with a transient contraindication to anticoagulation, such as recent trauma or recent or impending surgery. It is also a feature with intuitive appeal, because deep venous and pulmonary thromboembolic disease is usually time-limited. Organization of thrombus is complete within 3 to 6 months.[92] If the patient can be protected from potentially fatal pulmonary emboli during this acute period with medication or filter placement, he or she usually will not require either of these treatments after that time.

The Amplatz filter is cone-shaped and has 12 radiating filaments projected outward from the apex of the cone, 6 of which contain an additional filament in a loop configuration to limit penetration of the straight leg through the wall of the vena cava.[116] To facilitate transfemoral removal of the filter, a hook is present at the apex of the cone, and the filter is deposited with the apex directed caudally.[65]

Two series of patients treated with the Amplatz filter have been published to date. In one, 52 filters were placed in 52 patients.[65] No deaths occurred during filter placement, and no patient experienced clinical symptoms of recurrent pulmonary embolism within mean follow-up of 15 months. Small (<4 mm) pulmonary emboli were discovered in 1 asymptomatic patient out of 3 who underwent autopsy.[65] Occlusion of the inferior vena cava was present in a relatively large number of patients—9 of 42 (21 percent)—who underwent follow-up examination by vena cavography, computed tomography, ultrasound, or autopsy. This rate of caval occlusion, which is higher than that reported for most other percutaneous filters, was felt to be due to the close spacing of the filter struts,[65] which probably results in increased filter efficiency for small emboli, and the inverted position of the filter cone, which causes more flow disturbance than the traditional filter position with the apex positioned cranially.[65] Only 1 of 33 patients (3 percent) who underwent objective testing for insertion site thrombosis had evidence of thrombosis of the insertion vein.[65] No filter migration greater than 1 cm was seen in 45 patients evaluated for this problem; filter angulation of 20 degrees was seen in 1 of these patients (2 percent). Because of the prong and loop design of this filter, significant penetration (>2 mm) of the wall of the inferior vena cava was not observed.[65]

Percutaneous removal of the Amplatz filter was attempted in 6 patients. Removals were complicated by incorporation of the filter struts in the intima of the vein and by occasional incorporation of the filter hook. Filter removal was fairly traumatic, resulting in intramural hemorrhage in 2 patients, which did not result in acute symptoms.[65] Three filter retrievals were described as "difficult" because of adherence of the filter to the vein wall, which takes approximately 2 to 3 weeks to occur.[65,117–119] Because 2 retrievals were performed within 24 hours, it is likely that 3 of the 4 more delayed retrievals were complicated.[65] Removability in this context therefore does not justify the little benefit that it provides.

A second series of 30 patients who underwent placement of the Amplatz filter at a different center demonstrated similar results.[116] Recurrent pulmonary embolism was documented in 2 of 30 patients (7 percent) primarily by clinical means, confirmed by ventilation/perfusion scan in 1 and by autopsy in the other.[116] Occlusion of the inferior vena cava was seen in 23 percent of patients (7 of 30). This was documented in 4 by vena cavography, in 1 by ultrasound, and clinically in 2 patients.[116] This series reported 2 of 20 filters with extension of part of the filter more than 2 mm beyond the wall of the vena cava, without symptoms or surrounding abnormality on computed tomograms.[116] Only 1 of 30 (3 percent) of patients experienced thrombosis of the insertion site after filter placement, although follow-up was solely clinical in some patients.[116] Percutaneous removal was not attempted in this series.[116] The Amplatz filter is not available in the United States.

Conclusion

Because of the high mortality of untreated pulmonary deep venous thromboembolism, mechanical interruption of the inferior vena cava is necessary in those patients with this condition who cannot be treated medically with anticoagulation, or who suffer pulmonary embolism or demonstrate proximal propagation of thrombus while adequately anticoagulated. In addition, high-risk situations exist, such as free-floating iliac or vena cava thrombus, that warrant caval interruption in addition to anticoagulation. Partial interruption of the vena cava by percutaneous placement of a vena cava filter is the method of choice for achieving this objective and is optimally performed with fluoroscopic guidance following vena cavography.

Five vena cava filters are available in the United States: the stainless steel Greenfield filter, the bird's nest filter, the titanium Greenfield filter, the Simon nitinol filter, and the LGM filter. Of these, the Greenfield filter design is slightly less effective in removing small emboli from the bloodstream than the bird's nest or Simon nitinol filter. However, it is equally effective in preventing clinically significant pulmonary embolism and has a better rate of patency of the vena cava after placement. This filter design is suitable for most patients. The bird's nest or Simon nitinol filter may be useful in patients unable to tolerate small pulmonary emboli, such as those with cor pulmonale or chronic lung disease. The bird's nest filter is ideal in patients with mega vena cava (>28 mm in diameter), and the Simon nitinol filter is useful in patients without traditional routes of access for filter placement. Since no significant differences in clinical outcome have proven superiority of one filter design over the others, it is likely that the differences are minor, and no filter is ideal for all patients. Rather, the choice of which filter to use should be made on an individual basis, until a randomized clinical trial clearly elucidates the relative benefits of each of these devices.

References

1. Evans AJ, Sostman HD, Knelson MH, et al. Detection of deep venous thrombosis: prospective comparison of MR imaging with contrast venography. AJR 1993;161:131–139.
2. Ferris EJ. Deep venous thrombosis and pulmonary embolism: correlative evaluation and therapeutic implications. AJR 1992;159:1149–1155.
3. Harmon B. Deep vein thrombosis: a perspective on anatomy and venographic analysis. J Thorac Imaging 1989;4:15–19.
4. Barker NW, Nygaard KK, Walters W, Priestley JT. Statistical study of post-operative venous thrombosis and pulmonary embolism: time of occurrence during post-operative period. Proc Staff Meet Mayo Clin 1941;16:17–23.
5. Barritt DW, Jordan SC. Anticoagulant drugs in the treatment of pulmonary embolism: a controlled trial. Lancet 1960;1:1309–1312.
6. Rohrer MJ, Scheidler MG, Wheeler HB, Cutler BS. Extended indications for placement of an inferior vena cava filter. J Vasc Surg 1989;10:44–50.
7. Homans J. Deep quiet venous thrombosis in the lower limb: preferred levels for interruption of veins; iliac sector or ligation. Surg Gynecol Obstet 1944;79:70–82.
8. Moser KM. Pulmonary embolism. Am Rev Respir Dis 1977;115:829–852.
9. Horattas MC, Wright DJ, Fenton AH, et al. Changing concepts of deep venous thrombosis of the upper extremity: report of a series and review of the literature. Surgery 1988;104(3):561–567.
10. Monreal M, Lafoz E, Ruiz J, Valls R, Alastrue A. Upper-extremity deep venous thrombosis and pulmonary embolism: a prospective study. Chest 1991;99:280–283.
11. Norris CS, Greenfield LJ, Herrmann JB. Free-floating ilio-femoral thrombus: a risk of pulmonary embolism. Arch Surg 1985;120:806–808.
12. Radomski JS, Jarrell BE, Carabasi RA, Yang S, Koolpe H. Risk of pulmonary embolus with inferior vena cava thrombosis. Am Surg 1987;53(2):97–101.
13. Virchow R, Chance F, trans. Cellular pathology. New York: Dewitt, 1860.
14. Hoagland PM. Massive pulmonary embolus. In: Goldhaber SZ, ed. Pulmonary embolism and deep venous thrombosis. Philadelphia: Saunders, 1985:179.
15. Hunter J. Observation on inflammation of internal coat of veins. Trans Soc Improvement Med Chir Knowledge (London);1793;1:18.
16. Greenfield LJ, DeLucia A. Endovascular therapy of venous thromboembolic disease. Surg Clin North Am 1992;72(4):969–989.
17. Bauer G. Venous thrombosis: early diagnosis with the aid of phlebography and abortive treatment with heparin. Arch Surg 1941;43:462.
18. DeBakey ME, Schroeder GF, Ochsner A. Significance of phlebography in phlebothrombosis. JAMA 1943;123:738–744.
19. Jaques LB. Addendum: the discovery of heparin. Semin Thromb Hemostas 1978;4:350–353.
20. Allen EV, Barker NW, Waugh JM. A preparation from spoiled sweet clover. JAMA 1942;120:1009–1015.
21. Seidman M, Robertson DN, Link KP. Studies on 4-hydroxy-coumarins: X. Acylation of 3-(alpha-phenyl-beta-acetylethyl)-4-hydroxycoumarin. J Am Chem Soc 1950;72:5193–5195.
22. Crane C. Femoral vs. caval interruption for venous thromboembolism. N Engl J Med 1964;270(16):819–821.
23. Mozes M, Adar R, Bogokowsky H, Agmon M. Vein ligation in the treatment of pulmonary embolism. Surgery 1964;55(5):621–629.
24. Nasbeth DC, Moran JM. Reassessment of the role of inferior vena cava ligation in venous thromboembolism. N Engl J Med 1965;273(23):1250–1253.
25. Adams JT, Feingold BE, DeWeese JA. Comparative evaluation of ligation and partial interruption of the inferior vena cava. Arch Surg 1971;103:272–276.
26. Amador E, Kai T, Crane C. Ligation of inferior vena cava for thromboembolism: clinical and autopsy correlations in 119 cases. JAMA 1968;206(8):1758–1760.
27. Ferris EJ, Vittimberga FJ, Byrne JJ, et al. The inferior vena cava after ligation and plication. Radiology 1967;89:1–10.
28. Spencer FC, Quattlebaum JK, Quattlebaum JK, Sharp EH, Jude JR. Plication of the IVC for pulmonary embolism: a report of 20 cases. Ann Surg 1962;155:827.
29. Miles RM, Elsea PW. Clinical evaluation of the serrated vena caval clip. Surg Gynecol Obstet 1971;132(4):581–587.
30. Eberlein TJ, Carey LC. Comparison of surgical management for pulmonary embolus. Ann Surg 1974;179(6):836–841.
31. Maraan BM, Taber RE. The effects of inferior vena caval ligation on cardiac output: an experimental study. Surgery 1968;63:966–969.
32. Mobin-Uddin K, McLean R, Bolooki H, Jude JR. Caval interruption for prevention of pulmonary embolism. Arch Surg 1969;99:711–715.
33. Mobin-Uddin K, Utley JR, Bryant LR. The inferior vena cava umbrella filter. Prog Cardiovasc Dis 1975;17(5):391–399.
34. McIntyre AB, McCready RA, Hyde GL, Mattingly W. A ten year follow-up study of the Mobin-Uddin filter for vena cava interruption. Surg Gynecol Obstet 1984;158(6):513–516.

35. Wingerd M, Bernhard VM, Maddison F, Towne JB. Comparison of caval filters in the management of venous thromboembolism. Arch Surg 1978;113:1264–1271.

36. Gomez GA, Cutler BS, Wheeler HB. Transvenous interruption of the inferior vena cava. Surgery 1983;93(5):612–619.

37. Menzoian JO, LoGerfo FW, Weitzman AF, Ezpeleta M, Sequeira JC. Clinical experience with the Mobin-Uddin vena cava umbrella filter. Arch Surg 1980;115:1179–1181.

38. McConnel D, Mulder D, Buckberg G. The placement of vena cava umbrella filters: the value of phlebography. Arch Surg 1974;108:789–791.

39. Bernstein E. The place of venous interruption in the treatment of pulmonary thromboembolism. In: Moser K, Stein M, eds. Pulmonary thromboembolism. Chicago: Year Book, 1973:312–323.

40. Hunter JA, DeLaria GA, Goldin MD, et al. Inferior vena cava interruption with the Hunter-Sessions balloon: eighteen years' experience in 191 cases. J Vasc Surg 1989;10:450–456.

41. Strandness DE, Langlois Y, Cramer M, Randlett A, Thiele BL. Long-term sequelae of acute venous thrombosis. JAMA 1983;250:1289–1292.

42. Lindner DJ, Edwards JM, Phinney ES, Taylor LM, Porter JM. Long-term hemodynamic and clinical sequelae of lower extremity deep vein thrombosis. J Vasc Surg 1986;4:436–442.

43. Browse NL, Clemenson G, Thomas ML. Is the postphlebitic leg always postphlebitic? Relation between phlebographic appearances of deep-vein thrombosis and late sequelae. Br Med J 1980;281:1167–1170.

44. Mudge M, Hughes LE. The long term sequelae of deep vein thrombosis. Br J Surg 1978;65:692–694.

45. Cimochowski GE, Evans RH, Zarins CK, Lu C, DeMeester TR. Greenfield filter versus Mobin-Uddin umbrella. J Thorac Cardiovasc Surg 1980;79:358–365.

46. Tadavarthy SM, Castaneda-Zuniga W, Salomonowitz E, et al. Kimray-Greenfield vena cava filter: percutaneous introduction. Radiology 1984;151:525–526.

47. Katsamouris AA, Waltman AC, Delichatsios MA, Athanasoulis CA. Inferior vena cava filters: in vitro comparison of clot trapping and flow dynamics. Radiology 1988;166:361–366.

48. Thompson BH, Cragg AH, Smith TP, et al. Thrombus-trapping efficiency of the Greenfield filter in vivo. Radiology 1989;172:979–981.

49. Greenfield LJ, Michna BA. Twelve-year clinical experience with the Greenfield vena caval filter. Surgery 1988;104:706–712.

50. Pais SO, Tobin KD. Percutaneous insertion of the Greenfield filter. AJR 1989;152:933–938.

51. Kantor A, Glanz S, Gordon DH, Sclafani SJA. Percutaneous insertion of the Kimray-Greenfield filter: incidence of femoral vein thrombosis. AJR 1987;149:1065–1066.

52. Pais SO, Tobin KD, Austin CB, Queral L. Percutaneous insertion of the Greenfield inferior vena cava filter: experience with ninety-six patients. J Vasc Surg 1988;8:460–464.

53. Rose BS, Simon DC, Hess ML, Van Aman ME. Percutaneous transfemoral placement of the Kimray-Greenfield vena cava filter. Radiology 1987;165:373–376.

54. Shetty PC, Bok LR, Sharma RP. Balloon dilation of the femoral vein expediting percutaneous Greenfield vena caval filter placement. Radiology 1986;161:275.

55. Dorfman GS, Cronan JJ, Paolella LP, et al. Iatrogenic changes at the venotomy site after percutaneous placement of the Greenfield filter. Radiology 1989;173:159–162.

56. Molgaard CP, Yucel EK, Geller SC, Know TA, Waltman AC. Access-site thrombosis after placement of inferior vena cava filters with 12–14F delivery sheaths. Radiology 1992;185:257–261.

57. Dorfman GS, Esparza AR, Cronan JJ. Percutaneous large bore venotomy and tract creation: comparison of sequential dilator and angioplasty balloon methods in a porcine model, preliminary report. Invest Radiol 1988;23:441–446.

58. Pais SO, Mirvis SE, De Orchis DF. Percutaneous insertion of the Kimray-Greenfield filter: technical considerations and problems. Radiology 1987;165:377–381.

59. Roberts AC, Geller SC, Waltman AC, Athanasoulis CA. Kimray-Greenfield inferior vena cava filter: safety of percutaneous insertion via the femoral vein. Radiology 1987;165(P):204.

60. Martin KD, Kempczinski RF, Fowl RJ. Are routine inferior vena cavograms necessary before Greenfield filter placement? Surgery 1989;106:647–651.

61. Prince MR, Novelline RA, Athanasoulis CA, Simon M. The diameter of the IVC and its implication for the use of vena cava filters. Radiology 1983;149:687–689.

62. Mewissen MW, Erickson SJ, Foley WD, et al. Thrombosis at venous insertion sites after inferior vena caval filter placement. Radiology 1989;173:155–157.

63. Murphy TP, Dorfman GS, Yedlicka JW, et al. LGM vena cava filter: objective evaluation of early results. J Vasc Intervent Radiol 1991;2:107–115.

64. Roehm JOF, Johnsrude IS, Barth MH, Gianturco C. The bird's nest inferior vena cava filter: progress report. Radiology 1988;168:745–749.

65. Epstein DH, Darcy MD, Hunter DW, et al. Experience with the Amplatz retrievable vena cava filter. Radiology 1989;172:105–110.

66. Greenfield LJ, Cho KJ, Proctor M, et al. Results of a multicenter study of the modified hook-titanium Greenfield filter. J Vasc Surg 1991;14:253–257.

67. Tobin KD, Pais SO, Austin CB. Reevaluation of indications for percutaneous placement of the Greenfield filter. Invest Radiol 1989;24:115–118.

68. Hirsh J. Treatment of pulmonary embolism. Annu Rev Med 1987;38:91–105.

69. Hayes SP, Bone RC. Pulmonary emboli with respiratory failure. Med Clin North Am 1983;67:1179–1191.

70. Mansour M, Chang AE, Sindelar WF. Interruption of the inferior vena cava for the prevention of recurrent pulmonary embolism. Am Surg 1985;51:375–380.

71. Carter BL, Jones ME, Waickman LA. Pathophysiology and treatment of deep-vein thrombosis and pulmonary embolism. Clin Pharmacol 1985;4:279–296.

72. Petitti DB, Strom BL, Melmon KL. Duration of warfarin anticoagulant therapy and the probabilities of recurrent thrombolism. Am J Med 1986;81:255–259.

73. Wessler S, Gitel SN. Warfarin from bedside to bench. N Engl J Med 1984;311:645–652.

74. Moore FD, Osteen RT, Karp DD, Steele G, Wilson RE. Anticoagulants, venous thromboembolism, and the cancer patient. Arch Surg 1981;161:405–407.

75. Landfeld CS, Cook EF, Flatley M, Weisberg M, Goldman L. Identification and preliminary validation of predictors of major bleeding in hospitalized patients starting anticoagulant therapy. Am J Med 1987;82:703–713.

76. Mant MJ, O'Brien BD, Thong KL, et al. Haemorrhagic complications of heparin therapy. Lancet 1977;1:1133–1135.

77. Belt RJ, Leite C, Haas CD, Stephens RL. Incidence of hemorrhagic complication in patients with cancer. JAMA 1978;239:2571–2574.

78. Doyle DJ, Turpie AGG, Hirsh J, et al. Adjusted subcutaneous heparin or continuous intravenous heparin in patients with acute deep vein thrombosis. Ann Intern Med 1987;107:441–445.

79. King DJ, Kelton JG. Heparin-associated thrombocytopenia. Ann Intern Med 1984;100:535–540.

80. Sevitt S, Gallagher N. Venous thrombosis and pulmonary embolism: a clinico-pathological study in injured and burned patients. Br J Surg 1961;48:475–489.

81. Kakkar VV, Howe CT, Flanc C, Clarke MB. Natural history of postoperative deep-vein thrombosis. Lancet 1969;2:230–233.

82. Jarrell BE, Posuniak E, Roberts J, et al. A new method of management using the Kimray-Greenfield filter for deep ve-

nous thrombosis and pulmonary embolism in spinal cord injury. Surg Gynecol Obstet 1983;157:316–320.

83. Lambie JM, Mahaffy RG, Barber DC, et al. Diagnostic accuracy in venous thrombosis. Br Med J 1970;2:142–143.

84. Habscheid W, Stratmann A, Dammrich J. Compression sonography as a screening method in thrombosis diagnosis. Dtsch Med Wochenschr 1990;115:1003–1008.

85. Cronan JJ, Froehlich JA, Dorfman GS. Image-directed Doppler ultrasound: a screening technique for patients at high risk to develop deep vein thrombosis. J Clin Ultrasound 1991;19: 133–138.

86. Woolson ST, McCrory DW, Walter JF, et al. B-mode ultrasound scanning in the detection of proximal venous thrombosis after total hip replacement. J Bone Joint Surg 1990;72: 983–987.

87. Leyvraz PF, Richard J, Bachmann F, et al. Adjusted versus fixed-dose subcutaneous heparin in the prevention of deep-vein thrombosis after total hip replacement. N Engl J Med 1983;309:954–958.

88. Dorfman GS, Cronan JJ, Tupper TB, Messersmith RN, Denny DF, Lee CH. Occult pulmonary embolism: a common occurrence in deep venous thrombosis. AJR 1987;148:263–266.

89. Huisman MV, Buller HR, ten Cate JW, et al. Unexpected high prevalence of silent pulmonary embolism in patients with deep venous thrombosis. Chest 1989;95:498–502.

90. Moran JM, Kahn PC, Callow AD. Partial versus complete caval interruption for venous thromboembolism. Am J Surg 1969;117:471–479.

91. Athanasoulis CA. Complications of vena cava filters. Radiology 1993;188:614–615.

92. Murphy TP, Cronan JJ. Evolution of deep venous thrombosis: a prospective evaluation with US. Radiology 1990;177: 543–548.

93. Yune HY. Inferior vena cava filter: search for an ideal device. Radiology 1989;172:15–16.

94. Grassi CJ. Inferior vena caval filters: analysis of five currently available devices. AJR 1991;156:813–821.

95. Palestrant AM, Prince M, Simon M. Comparative in vitro evaluation of the nitinol inferior vena cava filter. Radiology 1982;145:351–355.

96. Millward SF, Marsh JI, Pon C, Moher D. Thrombus-trapping efficiency of the LGM (Vena Tech) and titanium Greenfield filters in vivo. J Vasc Intervent Radiol 1992;3:103–106.

97. Greenfield LJ, Peyton R, Crute S, Barnes R. Greenfield vena caval filter experience: late results in 156 patients. Arch Surg 1981;116:1451–1456.

98. Denny DF, Cronan JJ, Dorfman GS, Esplin C. Percutaneous Kimray-Greenfield filter placement by femoral vein puncture. AJR 1985;145:827–829.

99. Reed RA, Teitelbaum GP, Taylor FC, Pentecost MJ, Roehm JOF. Use of the bird's nest filter in oversized inferior venae cavae. J Vasc Intervent Radiol 1991;2:447–450.

100. Korbin CD, Reed RA, Taylor FC, Pentecost MJ, Teitelbaum GP. Comparison of filters in an oversized vena caval phantom: intracaval placement of a bird's nest filter versus biliac placement of Greenfield, Vena Tech-LGM, and Simon nitinol filters. J Vasc Intervent Radiol 1992;3:559–564.

101. Rogoff PA, Hilgenberg AD, Miller SL, Stephan SM. Cephalic migration of the bird's nest inferior vena caval filter: report of two cases. Radiology 1992;184:819–822.

102. Greenfield LJ, Cho KJ, Pais SO, Van Aman M. Preliminary clinical experience with the titanium Greenfield vena caval filter. Arch Surg 1989;124:657–659.

103. Teitelbaum GP, Jones DL, van Breda A, et al. Vena caval filter splaying: potential complication of use of the titanium Greenfield filter. Radiology 1989;173:809–814.

104. Ramchandani P, Koolpe HA, Zeit RM. Splaying of titanium Greenfield inferior vena caval filter. AJR 1990;155:1103–1104.

105. Simon M, Athanasoulis CA, Kim D, et al. Simon nitinol inferior vena cava filter: initial clinical experience. Radiology 1989;172:99–103.

106. Dorfman GS. Percutaneous inferior vena caval filters. Radiology 1990;174:987–992.

107. McCowan TC, Ferris EJ, Carver DK, Molpus WM. Complications of the nitinol vena caval filter. J Vasc Intervent Radiol 1992;3:401–408.

108. LaPlante JS, Contractor FM, Kiproff PM, Khoury MB. Migration of the Simon nitinol vena cava filter to the chest. AJR 1993;160:385–386.

109. Grassi CJ, Matsumoto AH, Teitelbaum GP. Vena caval occlusion after Simon nitinol filter placement: identification with MR imaging in patients with malignancy. J Vasc Intervent Radiol 1992;3:535–539.

110. Reed RA, Teitelbaum GP, Taylor FC, et al. Incomplete opening of LGM (Vena Tech) filters inserted via the transjugular approach. J Vasc Intervent Radiol 1991;2:441–445.

111. Ricco JB, Crochet D, Sebilotte P, et al. Percutaneous transvenous caval interruption with the "LGM" filter: early results of a multicenter trial. Ann Vasc Surg 1988;2(3):242–247.

112. Taylor FC, Awh MH, Kahn CE, Lu C. Vena Tech vena cava filter: experience and early follow-up. J Vasc Intervent Radiol 1991;2:435–440.

113. Millward SF, Marsh JI, Peterson RA, et al. LGM (Vena Tech) vena cava filter: clinical experience in 64 patients. J Vasc Intervent Radiol 1991;2:429–433.

114. Crochet DP, Stora O, Ferry D, et al. Vena Tech-LGM filter: long-term results of a prospective study. Radiology 1993;188: 857–860.

115. Awh MH, Taylor FC, Lu C. Spontaneous fracture of a Vena Tech inferior vena caval filter. AJR 1991;157:177–178.

116. McCowan TC, Ferris EJ, Carver DK, Baker ML. Amplatz vena caval filter: clinical experience in 30 patients. AJR 1990; 155:177–181.

117. Lund G, Rysavy J, Hunter DW, Castaneda-Zuniga WR, Amplatz K. Retrievable vena cava filter percutaneously introduced. Radiology 1985;155:831.

118. Darcy MD, Smith TP, Hunter DW, et al. Short-term prophylaxis of pulmonary embolism by using a retrievable vena cava filter. AJR 1986;147:836–838.

119. Hunter DW, Lund G, Rysavy JA, et al. Retrieving the Amplatz retrievable vena cava filter. Cardiovasc Intervent Radiol 1987;10:32–36.

60

Abnormal Arteriovenous Communications

ROBERT J. ROSEN

Although vascular malformations have been described since antiquity, they remain one of the most commonly misdiagnosed and mismanaged conditions in clinical medicine. Because of the relative rarity of these lesions, few clinicians have gained much experience in their diagnosis and management. Unfortunately, even those with significant experience have discovered that these are often difficult and frustrating disorders to manage. This is one area where the caveat "do no harm" is particularly applicable.

The first step, and possibly the most important, is to correctly classify a lesion encountered clinically. Numerous terms have been applied to these lesions over the years, and many systems of classification have been described (Table 60-1). For practical purposes, it is helpful to divide the lesions into four major categories: hemangioma, arteriovenous fistula, arteriovenous malformation, and venous malformation. Although this categorization is not exhaustive or based on pathogenesis, it is most helpful in prognostic and therapeutic terms. Each of these lesions is distinctive enough to be discussed separately.

Hemangiomas

There is a general consensus among experts in the field of vascular malformations that the term *hemangioma* should be applied only to the benign vascular neoplasm generally encountered in infancy, which is characterized by a proliferative phase that is usually followed by spontaneous involution. The natural history and pathology of this lesion are therefore clearly different from those of true vascular malformations. The distinguishing features of the true hemangioma have been emphasized by Folkman and Mulliken and are presented in Table 60-2.[1,2]

Hemangiomas are relatively common in infancy, occurring in approximately 10 percent of children in the first year of life.[3] They may be present at birth or become manifest shortly thereafter, and may be multiple in 20 percent of cases.[4] Beginning as a small area of reddish discoloration, hemangiomas typically enter a proliferative phase in which growth can be dramatic. Pathologically, endothelial cell proliferation accounts for the rapid growth; this pattern of actual neoplastic cellular growth is not seen in true vascular malformations. Another distinguishing feature is the marked female-male predominance (5:1), as opposed to the equal distribution seen in vascular malformations.

The clinical course of the lesion during the proliferative phase depends largely on the location of the lesion. Superficial lesions may be quite disfiguring and may also show ulceration, bleeding, or infection (Fig. 60-1A). Lesions involving respiratory, visual, or digestive structures can present serious management problems. Very large lesions, particularly in the liver, can be associated with high-output congestive heart failure. Platelet trapping and subsequent thrombocytopenia (Kasabach-Merritt syndrome) is another potential complication of large lesions.

The most interesting (and fortunate) aspect of the natural history of the hemangioma is its tendency to spontaneous regression. Fully 70 percent of these lesions show substantial involution by the age of 7 years without treatment (see Fig. 60-1B), and the rest show continued resolution until the age of 12.[5] It is apparent that many treatments described in the past owed their success to this tendency toward spontaneous involution. There may be complete involution or residual discoloration or redundant skin, in some cases requiring plastic surgical intervention.

Diagnosis

Most hemangiomas can be diagnosed on physical examination, particularly when the lesion is followed over a period of time. Superficial lesions, sometimes referred to as "strawberry birthmarks," are bright red, whereas deeper lesions may show only a bluish discoloration. On palpation, these lesions are firm and spongy, reflecting the dense cellular stroma found pathologically. As stated, these lesions are usually single but can be multiple, particularly in children with hemangiomatosis of the liver. These latter children will also demonstrate hepatomegaly, bruits over the liver,

Table 60-1. Classification of Abnormal Arteriovenous Communications

Congenital
  Hemangiomas
  Predominantly venous malformations
  Multifistulous malformations
  Single fistulas
Acquired
  Tumors
    Primary vascular
      Glomus tumor
      Angiosarcoma
      Hemangiopericytoma
    Tumors with shunting
      Hypernephroma
      Hepatoma
      Others
  Fistulas
    Surgically created
      Dialysis
      Others
    Pathologic
      Traumatic
      Iatrogenic
      Infection
      Aneurysm
      Neoplasm
      Spontaneous

Adapted from Rosen RJ, Riles TS. Arteriovenous malformations. In: Strandness D, van Breda A, eds. Vascular diseases: surgical and interventional therapy. New York: Churchill-Livingstone, 1994:1226.

and, in some cases, evidence of congestive heart failure.[6] Some lesions cannot be differentiated clinically from true vascular malformations at the time of presentation, but the characteristic progression of the lesion over time will generally clarify the diagnosis.[7]

When the process of involution begins (toward the end of the first year), the color of the lesion becomes duller and the lesion becomes softer and starts to show shrinkage, generally beginning at the center and progressing toward the periphery. Ultimately, the skin over the lesion may be lighter in color than the surrounding normal skin.

Radiologic studies are generally not required for superficially located lesions but may be helpful in evaluating deep visceral lesions. Angiography demonstrates a diffusely hypervascular mass with enlarged feeding arteries, and a lobular pattern is often present. CT scanning shows a well-defined mass that shows dense enhancement after contrast is administered.[8]

Treatment

Because these lesions characteristically involute spontaneously, conservative management should be the rule. Parents may find this difficult to accept during the proliferative phase, but they should be reassured as to the natural history of the condition.

In a few situations treatment must be attempted because of bleeding, high-output failure, platelet trapping, or interference with respiratory or visual structures. Treatment is difficult at best; the primary methods described are pharmacologic therapy, radiotherapy, surgery, and embolization.

The mainstay of pharmacologic therapy is corticosteroids, which can produce marked shrinkage of the lesion. Generally a 4- to 6-week course of oral prednisone is given during the proliferative phase.[9–11] Despite a significant reported response rate, steroids used during infancy can cause significant problems, including overwhelming sepsis. This therapy has therefore generally been reserved for complicated lesions or those involving critical anatomic structures. The use of chemotherapeutic agents has also been reported in occasional cases of life-threatening hemangiomas.[12]

Like most rapidly proliferating tissues, hemangiomas are sensitive to radiation, which has been used in their treatment. However, because of concerns over long-term carcinogenesis, particularly in the head and neck region, this modality is rarely employed.[6]

Surgical resection of hemangiomas is technically difficult and rarely indicated except in lesions that interfere with breathing, feeding, or sensory development.[13] When involution is complete, plastic surgery may be considered for residual lesions or redundant skin.

Embolization therapy has been used in certain cases where specific treatment of the lesion is required. Preoperative embolization may facilitate surgical resection by significantly reducing blood loss. Selective hepatic embolization has also been used in infants with high-output congestive heart failure due to extensive hepatic hemangiomatosis.[14] This is a devastating clinical problem carrying a mortality rate of up to 80 percent

Table 60-2. Distinguishing Features of Hemangiomas and Arteriovenous Malformations

Hemangioma	Arteriovenous Malformation
Neoplasm	Congenital anomaly
30% present at birth; remainder present in first 3 months; proliferative phase: first year	90% present at birth, although many not manifest
Female-male 5:1	Female-male 1:1
Endothelial proliferation	No cellular proliferation
Growth in tissue culture	No growth tissue culture
Cellular stroma	No mast cells
Increased mast cells	No spontaneous involution; growth with individual
Spontaneous involution in 95% by age 7	May or may not require treatment
No treatment required in vast majority	

Data from Mulliken JB, Glowacki J. Hemangiomas and vascular malformations in infants and children: a classification based on endothelial characteristics. Plast Reconstr Surg 1982;69:412.

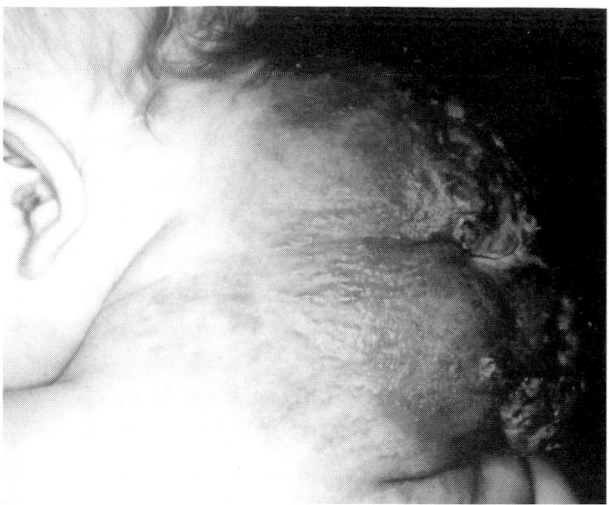

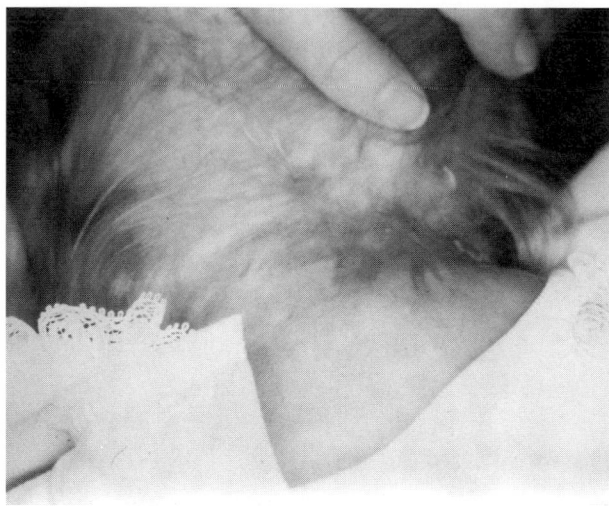

A   B

Figure 60-1. (A) Extensive hemangioma in 6-month-old girl during proliferative phase. The lesion is complicated by superficial ulceration and infection. (B) The same child at 6 years of age showing essentially complete involution with only conservative management.

because of the intractable congestive failure. These infants characteristically present with multiple cutaneous hemangiomas, hepatomegaly associated with a bruit, and severe congestive failure. In the absence of cutaneous lesions, the problem may be initially misdiagnosed as congenital heart disease. It should be noted that, like the cutaneous lesions, hepatic hemangiomas will show eventual spontaneous involution if congestive failure can be controlled during the proliferative phase.

Surgical ligation of the hepatic artery was employed in the past to reduce the degree of shunting, but this should rarely be necessary with the availability of embolization. The best results have been reported with Gelfoam pledgets, Ivalon particles, and acrylic adhesives; proximal hepatic artery embolization using coils is probably less effective. Gelfoam powder and absolute ethanol should not be used because of the risk of hepatic necrosis.[15]

Arteriovenous Fistula

An arteriovenous fistula is a direct connection between an artery and a vein. The vast majority of these lesions are acquired, usually as a result of trauma. Other causes include surgery, infection, tumor erosion, and rupture of an artery into an adjacent venous structure (e.g., carotid-cavernous fistula).

The first descriptions of arteriovenous fistulas were recorded over 200 years ago and were related to penetrating injuries or blood-letting procedures.[16] Attempts to repair these lesions constituted the earliest

efforts in vascular surgery, and the results were decidedly mixed. Initially, treatment consisted of ligating the feeding artery, which nearly always resulted in either recurrence of the fistula or gangrene of the extremity.[17,18] Subsequently, the procedure was extended to include "quadruple ligation and excision," referring to the afferent and efferent arteries and veins.[19] Although this procedure was effective for chronic fistulas with well-developed collaterals, ischemic complications developed in most acute lesions. For this reason, it became accepted practice to allow fistulas to "mature" for a period of months before excision.[20]

After Carel's description of vascular anastomosis in 1902, reconstruction of the vessels with restoration of the normal circulation became the goal, although this often proved impossible in practice even through World War II.[21] With modern reconstructive techniques, this goal can be achieved in most cases. Unfortunately, cases are still encountered on a regular basis where the same mistakes made 200 years ago are still being made, with the same clinical results.

An understanding of the architecture and physiology of the arteriovenous fistula is essential to planning proper treatment, whether by surgery or by interventional radiologic technique. The most complete description of the pathophysiology of arteriovenous connections was provided by Emile Holman, beginning in the 1920s.[22-24] Holman described the local, distal, and systemic effects of acute and chronic fistulas. Once these effects are appreciated, the difficulties in treating these lesions are much more easily understood, and certain common mistakes can be avoided. The physiol-

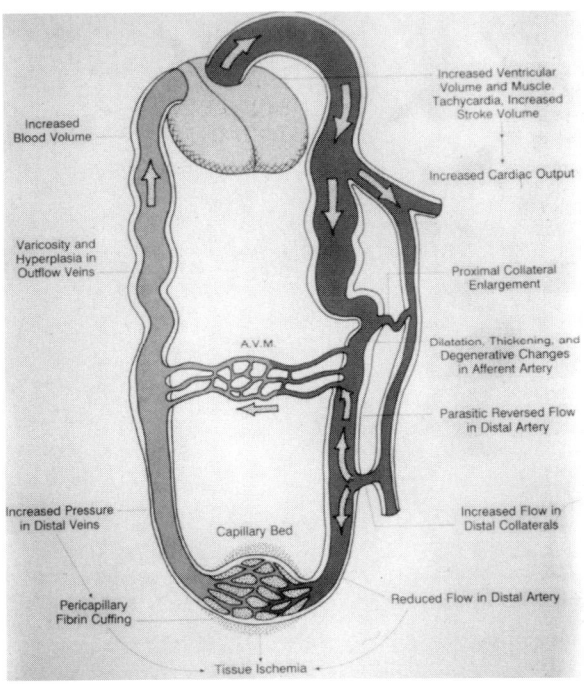

Figure 60-2. Diagram of pathophysiology of a fistulous arteriovenous communication. Most of these phenomena are also seen to a lesser degree in high-flow congenital vascular malformations. (From Holman E. The anatomic and physiologic effects of an arteriovenous fistula. Surgery 1940; 8: 362.)

ogy of an arteriovenous fistula is shown in Figure 60-2. The basic phenomenon is the creation of a low-pressure sump; various authors have made analogies to plumbing systems or electrical circuits to explain subsequent events.[25] Briefly, flow through the fistula depends on the size and length of the arteriovenous connection, with the highest flow encountered in direct side-to-side fistulas. The connection tends to enlarge over time, although small traumatic fistulas, such as those seen after renal biopsy, occasionally close spontaneously. As flow in the feeding artery increases, the feeding vessel tends to dilate and elongate. If the resistance across the fistula is lower than in the artery distal to it, a steal will develop, with eventual ischemic changes in the distal tissues. This is particularly pronounced in extremity lesions, where claudication, skin and muscle atrophy, and frank gangrene may ultimately develop. If the pressure gradient across the fistula is low enough, reversal of flow in the artery beyond the fistula will occur, further worsening the ischemia.

It is well established that an arteriovenous fistula is the most powerful stimulus known for the development of collateral arteries and veins, much more so than an atherosclerotic occlusion.[26] These collaterals can, in some cases, compensate for the steal through the fistula, although they may also show eventual re-

versal of flow. These extensive collaterals explain the predictability of recurrence of the fistula if only proximal ligation of the feeding artery is performed. Indeed, these recurrences can show such complex patterns of circulation that the original underlying fistula cannot be identified, the angiographic appearance becoming indistinguishable from that of a complex congenital vascular malformation (Fig. 60-3). It can readily be appreciated what a disservice this type of proximal ligation represents, whether performed surgically or by an embolization coil. Subsequent treatment often becomes impossible by any modality.

Other pathologic changes occur on the venous side of the fistula, including venous hypertension and enlargement of draining veins with eventual valvular incompetence and reversal of venous flow. The elevated venous pressures result in distal changes that resemble

Figure 60-3. Arteriogram of forearm of a 52-year-old patient who originally had a traumatic arteriovenous fistula in the palm of the hand from a penetrating injury. Several proximal surgical ligations resulted in resupply of the lesion by collaterals and ischemia, requiring amputation of a portion of the hand. At this time, the lesion is nearly indistinguishable from a complex congenital lesion and almost impossible to treat.

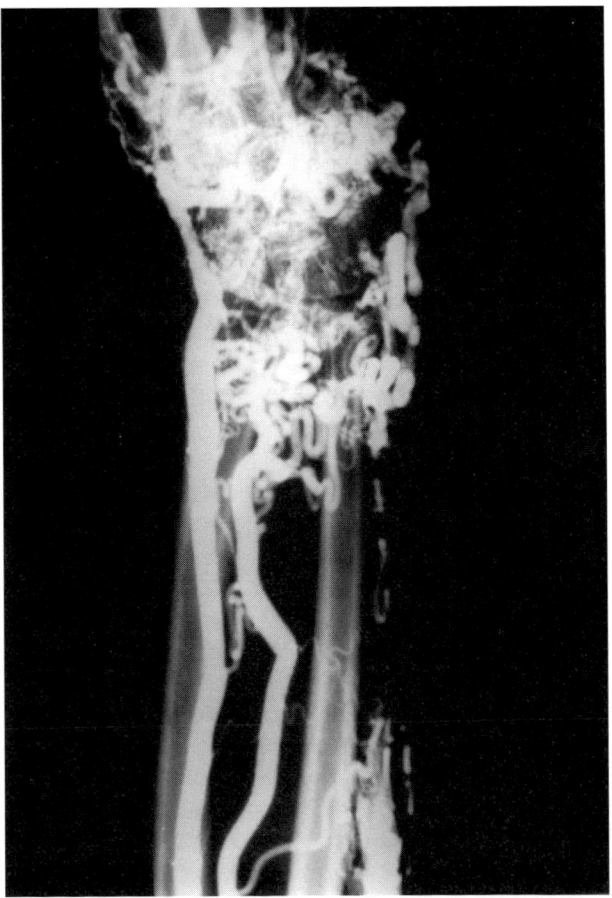

chronic venous insufficiency, with extensive varicosities, edema, thickening of tissues, and venous ulcerations. In many cases, these secondary venous abnormalities are the presenting findings. Extensive venous varicosities confined to one extremity should at least raise the question of an underlying arteriovenous fistula or malformation.

Finally, there are the systemic effects of the fistula. A detailed description of this physiology is beyond the scope of this chapter, but the changes briefly consist of the cardiovascular effects of a left-to-right shunt.[26] These effects include a decrease in peripheral vascular resistance with a secondary increase in cardiac output through an increased heart rate and stroke volume. This phenomenon can be demonstrated on physical examination by eliciting the so-called Branham-Nicoladoni sign, which consists of slowing of the heart rate when the fistula is occluded by manual compression, a reflex that is probably vagally mediated.[27,28] Blood volume is also increased in the presence of a significant fistula.

Over time, the increased circulatory work caused by the shunt leads to secondary cardiac changes, including hypertrophy and eventual dilatation. Ultimately high-output congestive failure may develop in the presence of a large fistula. It is interesting and important to note that although these generalized cardiovascular effects are commonly associated with large arteriovenous fistulas, they are rarely seen in connection with congenital vascular malformations, even large ones. The reason for this difference is not entirely understood, but appears to be related to the preservation of peripheral vascular resistance by the complex connections of the malformation as opposed to the low resistance presented by the arteriovenous fistula.[29] This difference provides a strong justification for early intervention in fistulas and a reason for conservatism in treating malformations.

From the preceding discussion, it is apparent that the treatment of arteriovenous fistulas must be directed at obliteration of the fistula, with preservation of distal flow whenever possible. In certain situations, particularly in extremity trauma, early surgical intervention will provide the best result because these fistulas are usually "side to side" or quite short, and in a large percentage of cases are associated with traumatic pseudoaneurysms (Fig. 60-4). At the present time, this type of pathologic anatomy is often difficult to treat by interventional techniques while preserving distal flow. The introduction of intravascular grafting may change this situation in the near future, however. In other types of lesions, embolization may be the initial treatment of choice, such as in carotid-cavernous fistulas

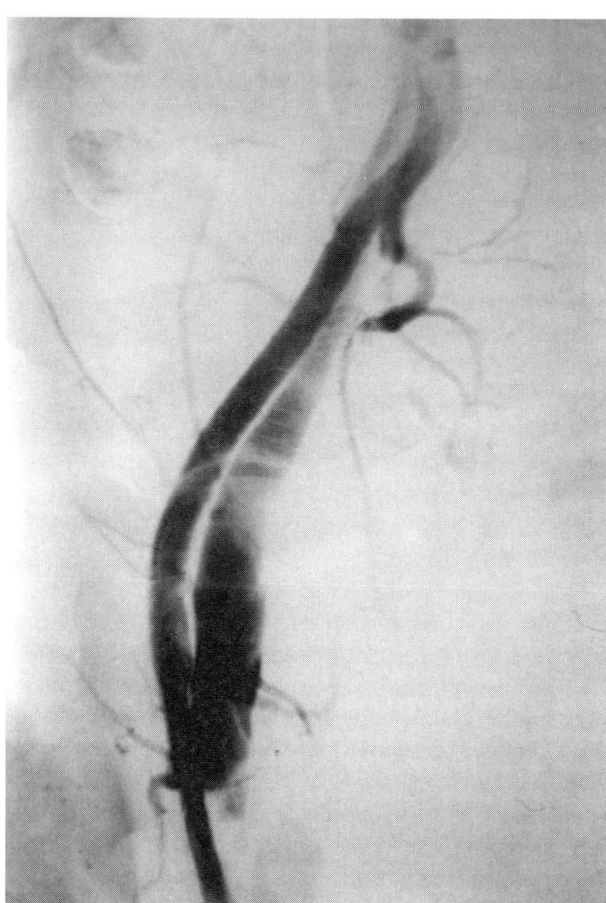

Figure 60-4. Direct femoral arteriovenous fistula several months after cardiac catheterization. These side-to-side fistulas are best treated surgically, although covered stents may be used in the near future.

(Fig. 60-5) and visceral lesions (Fig. 60-6). The embolization procedure can be directed at occluding the fistula itself (the ideal) or at isolating the segment of artery from which the fistula originates (Fig. 60-7). The choice of embolic device or material will be determined by the anatomic situation, but generally macroscopic occluding devices such as coils or detachable balloons are effective, balloons having the advantage of being flow-directed and being able to be repositioned for optimal placement.[30] The use of Gelfoam or other reabsorbable materials is probably inadvisable, and particulate materials will obviously be shunted through the arteriovenous connection. In some cases acrylic adhesive has been used to seal a small fistulous tract with preservation of the parent artery and vein (Fig. 60-8).

Once an arteriovenous fistula has been occluded, a cure can generally be anticipated and recurrences are

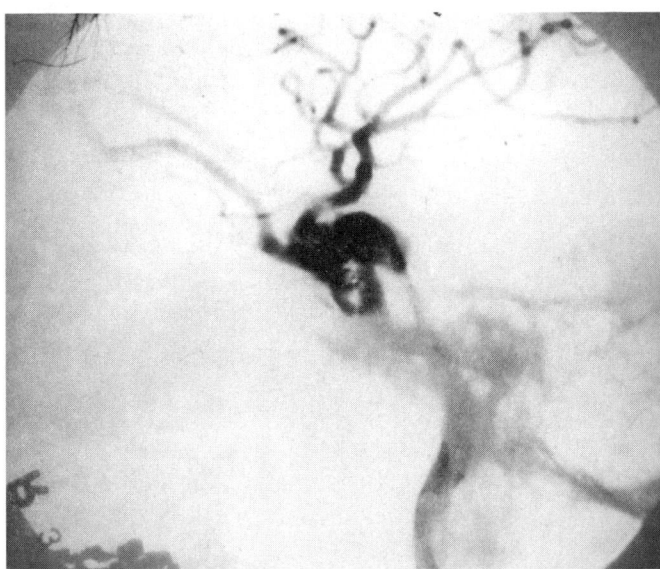

A

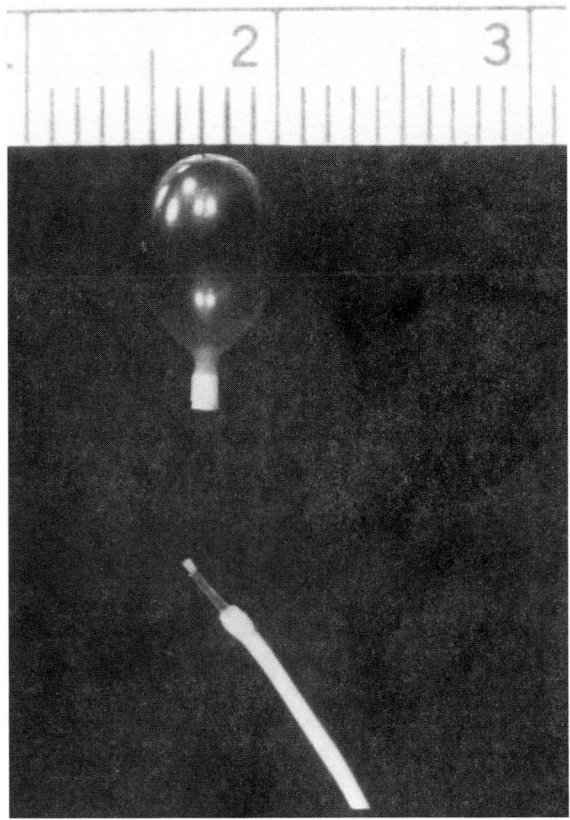

B

rare. This is unlike vascular malformations, where the patterns of supply are much more complex and recurrences common. As previously noted, however, an improperly treated fistula can become as difficult to manage as a complex congenital lesion.

Arteriovenous Malformations

Arteriovenous malformations (AVMs) are congenital anomalies that represent a focal failure of vascular differentiation in utero, generally between the 4th and 10th week of development. They are nearly always isolated lesions in otherwise healthy individuals and in most cases are not genetically transmitted. An exception is the Rendu-Osler-Weber syndrome, in which the lesions are multiple and there tends to be a strong family history.

Because these are developmental anomalies and not neoplasms, they tend to grow at the same rate as the individual, unlike the pattern of rapid growth and involution seen in hemangiomas. Depending on the size and location, AVMs can remain asymptomatic and undetected throughout life or represent a severe clinical problem. In the past, and unfortunately in the present as well, these lesions have often been misdiagnosed and mistreated, sometimes with disastrous results (Fig. 60-9). Because they tend to be stable, slow-growing lesions, conservative management is advisable in most cases. When symptoms do warrant intervention, it must be planned carefully and with the understanding that the results are not entirely predictable.

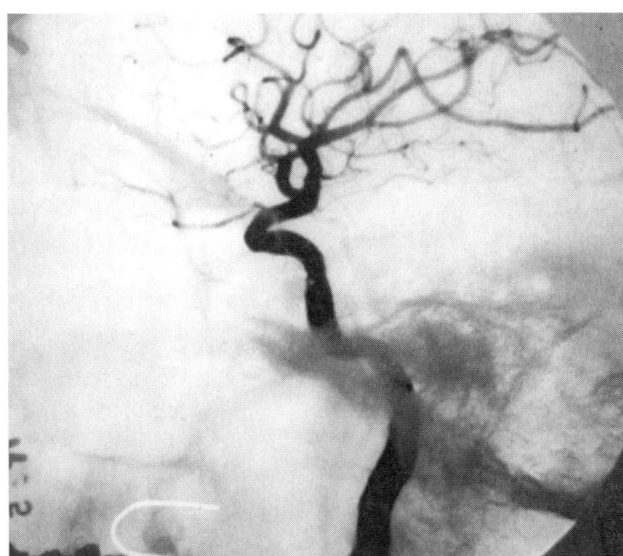

C

Figure 60-5. (A) Typical carotid-cavernous fistula following head trauma, resulting in chemosis, pulsating exophthalmos, and decreased vision. (B) Detachable balloon with self-sealing valve. Balloons offer the advantages of flow guidance, the ability to reposition, and positive occlusion. (C) After embolization of the fistula with a detachable balloon, no flow into the cavernous sinus is seen and there is preservation of the carotid-cavernous artery.

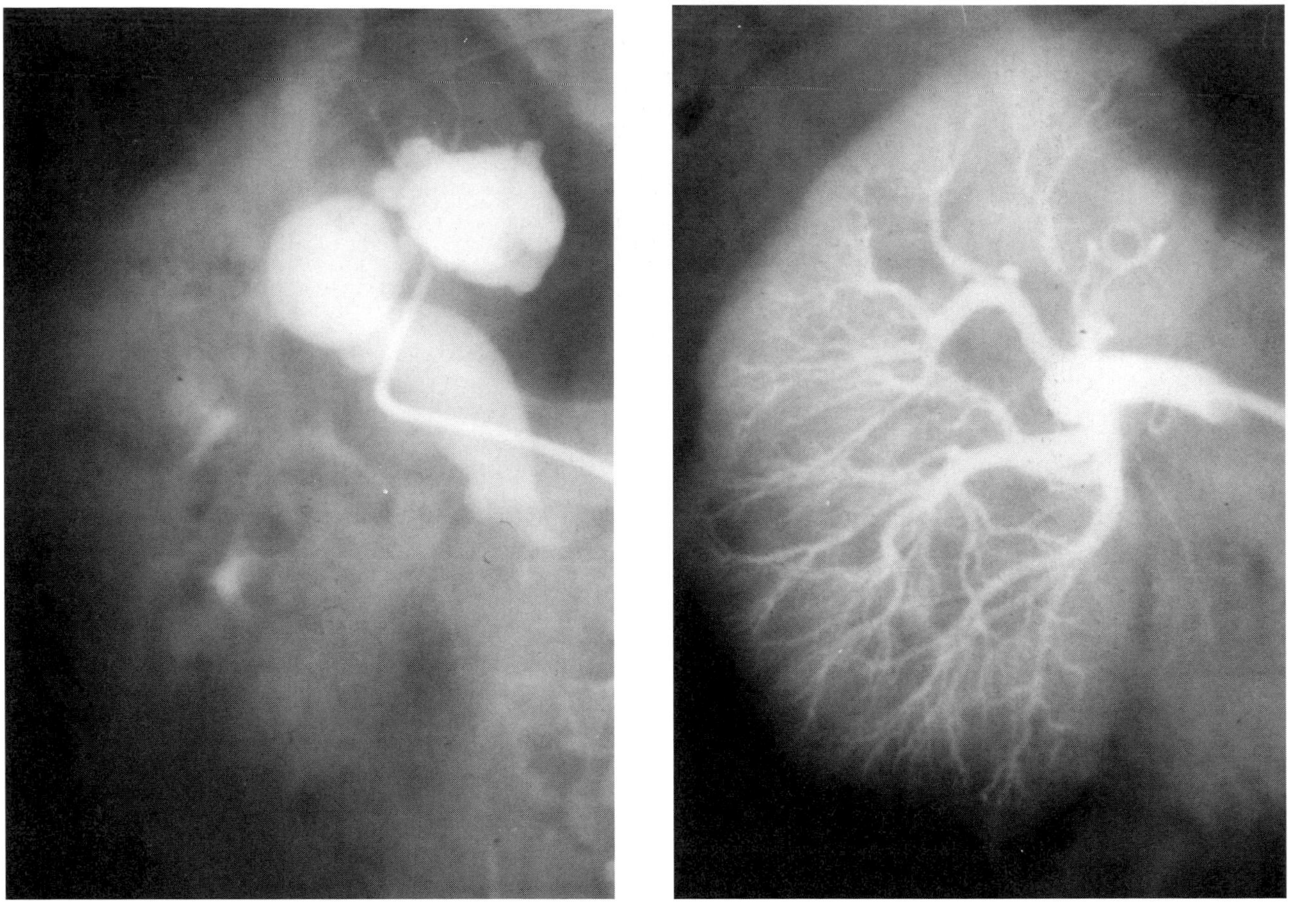

Figure 60-6. (A) Intrarenal arteriovenous fistula following stab wound to right flank. The patient presented with hematuria, hypertension, and a flank bruit. (B) After selective coil embolization of the fistula.

Figure 60-7. (A) Congenital arteriovenous fistula between axillary artery branch and right subclavian vein in a 26-year-old woman. The patient presented with complaints of pain, swelling of the arm, and distended neck veins. (B) The fistula and the distal feeding artery were occluded using platinum microcoils.

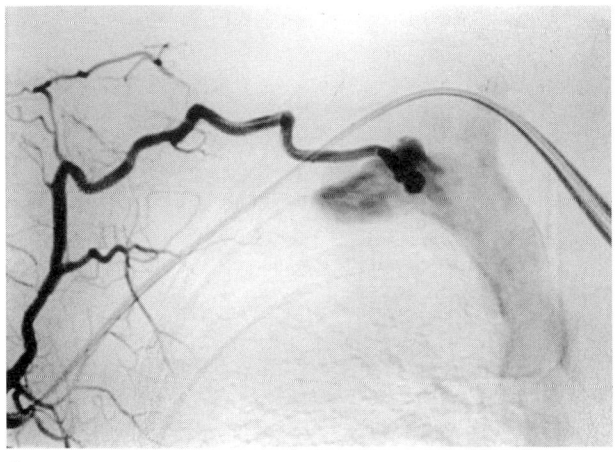

A

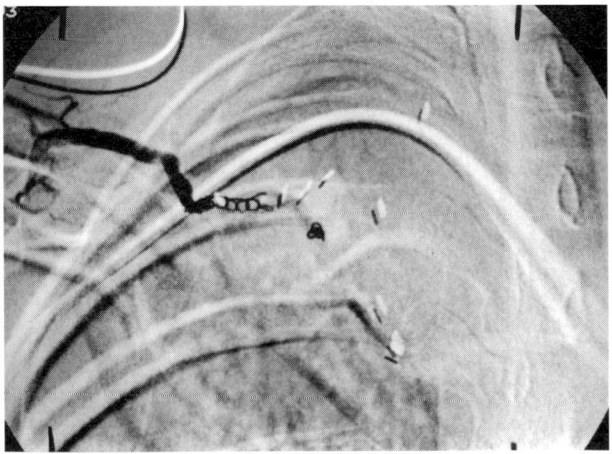

B

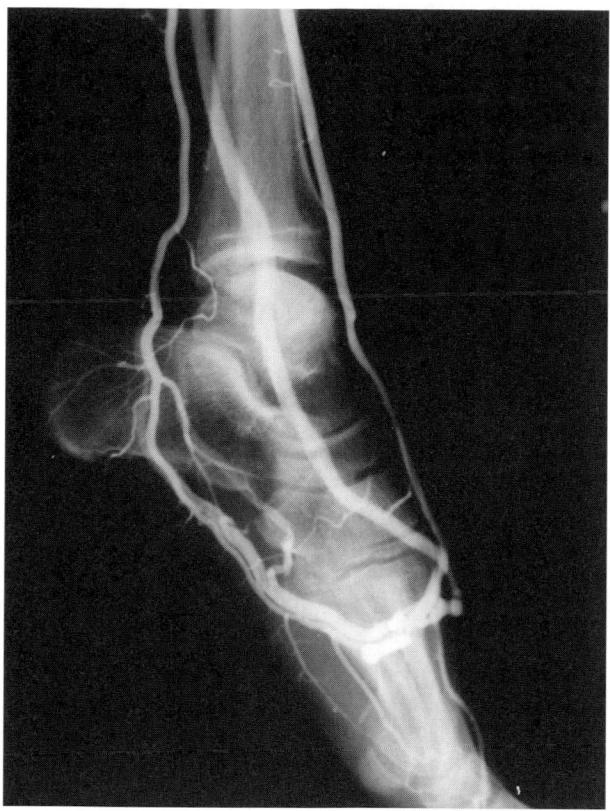

A

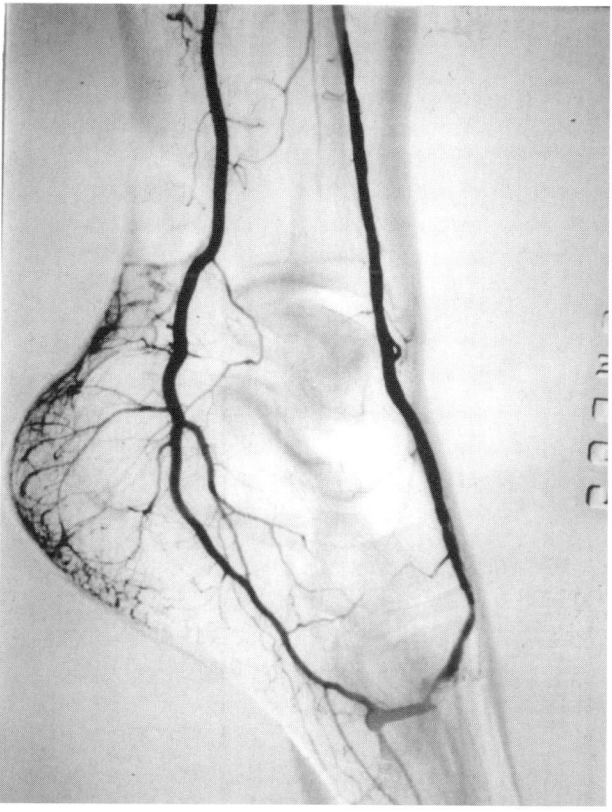

B

Figure 60-8. (A) A 33-year-old man with pain and marked swelling of the left foot several months after screw fixation of metatarsal fracture. Arteriogram shows arteriovenous fistula from the dorsalis pedis at the site of the metallic screw.

(B) The fistula was occluded using 0.2 ml of NBCA tissue adhesive through a coaxial microcatheter. Note the good preservation of normal pedal vessels.

Figure 60-9. (A) This 20-year-old woman, otherwise healthy, underwent a series of surgical ligations and amputations for what began as a localized AVM of the right foot starting at age 12. At this time, she shows breakdown of her high thigh amputation stump. (B) Arteriogram of stump

demonstrates significant residual AVM. Such catastrophic results are not uncommon after misguided attempts at treatment of high-flow vascular malformations.

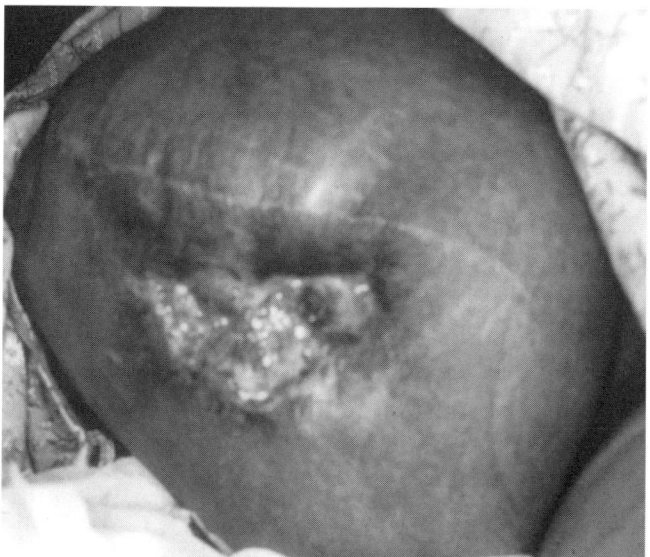

A

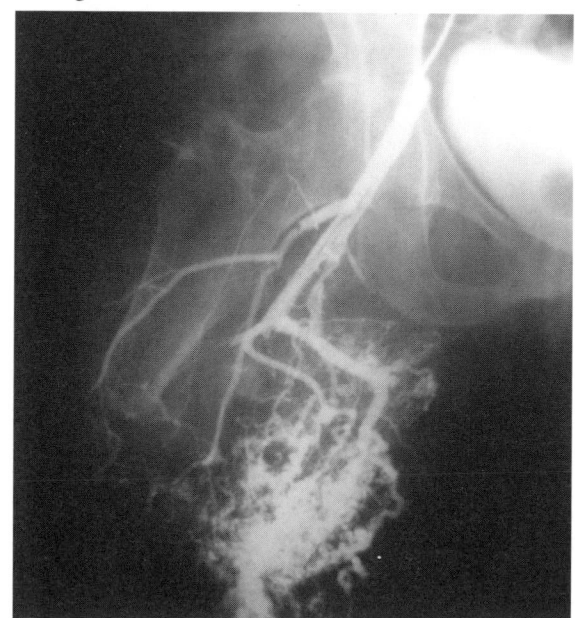

B

Clinical Features

AVMs can occur anywhere in the body, although certain anatomic sites seem more commonly affected, including the central nervous system, the pelvis, and the lower extremities. If the malformation is in a location accessible to physical examination, it generally presents as a pulsatile, nontender mass. Often the arterial pulses in the region will be bounding, and bruits or a continuous-flow murmur may be audible on auscultation. Draining veins may be prominent and may also be pulsatile. In the extremities there is often evidence of long-standing venous hypertension, including thickening of the skin, edema, and in some cases venous ulceration. Depending on the degree of steal, there may be distal ischemic changes such as atrophy or even ischemic ulceration. It is important to note that the major clinical manifestations of these lesions are often located "downstream" rather than over the lesion itself. When extremity lesions present in childhood, limb length is commonly affected, usually by overgrowth but occasionally by shortening. Focal gigantism of digits or hands and feet may also occur (Fig. 60-10).

Deep lesions of the trunk may be clinically silent, in which case they may be detected as a pulsatile mass on routine examination, or as a vascular mass found incidentally on radiologic examination. If symptoms are present, they can cover an almost unlimited spectrum, depending on the size and location of the lesion. As stated previously, generalized cardiovascular effects from an AVM are distinctly uncommon. In the au-

thor's own series of over 150 cases, only two patients with extensive pelvic malformations demonstrated high-output states (Fig. 60-11).

Although it is true that these lesions tend to grow slowly in proportion to the individual, some lesions do show periods of rapid enlargement. The two primary settings where this occurs are (1) in response to a change in the hormonal environment and (2) after unsuccessful attempts at surgical or radiologic treatment. In female patients, there is an unpredictable but definite association between menarche, pregnancy, and the clinical course of a previously stable AVM.[7] Young patients who have significant vascular malformations should be warned that pregnancy may be associated with progression of the lesion, sometimes to a marked degree. The progression does not involve any cellular proliferation but an enlargement of existing channels and recruitment of new collaterals. In the second setting, after attempted treatment, it appears that mechanically disturbing a stable lesion can result in significant worsening, again most likely because of development of new collaterals. This is most likely to occur after ligation or proximal embolization of feeding arteries or incomplete excision. It is for this reason that all treatment should be undertaken with extreme caution.

Diagnostic Studies

Lesions accessible to physical examination have characteristic findings that should permit the diagnosis to be made on clinical grounds, although the author sees at least two or three patients a year who have undergone biopsies or attempted excisions of misdiagnosed vascular malformations. Noninvasive studies will clearly demonstrate a high-flow lesion with enlarged feeding and draining vessels. Isotope studies using particles to demonstrate arteriovenous shunting have been described but are not widely used.[31] Plain radiographs are generally uninformative; venous lesions may show phleboliths, and high-flow lesions will occasionally show bone erosion or a permeative pattern that can resemble tumor involvement (Figs. 60-12 through 60-14). Disturbances in bone growth or development may also be noted in some cases.

Computed tomography (CT) and MRI are extremely valuable modalities in evaluating vascular malformations (Fig. 60-15). They demonstrate the true extent of the lesion, which is often much larger than can be appreciated on physical examination or even angiography. These techniques also clearly show the relationship of the lesion to surrounding structures; often a lesion felt to be resectable on clinical examina-

Figure 60-10. Congenital vascular malformations of the hands or feet may present as focal gigantism or overgrowth of digits.

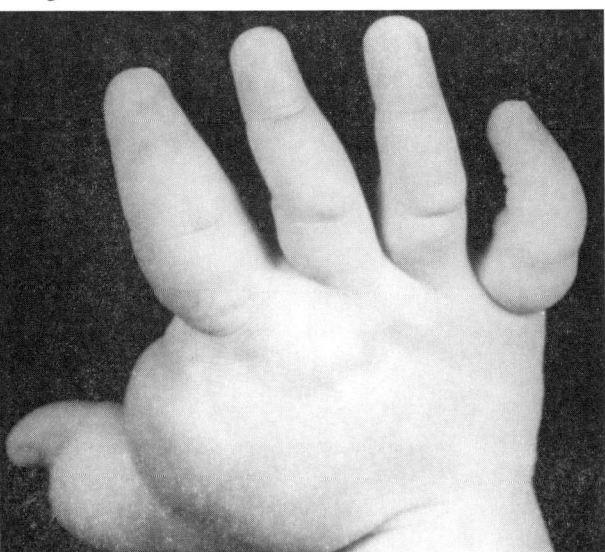

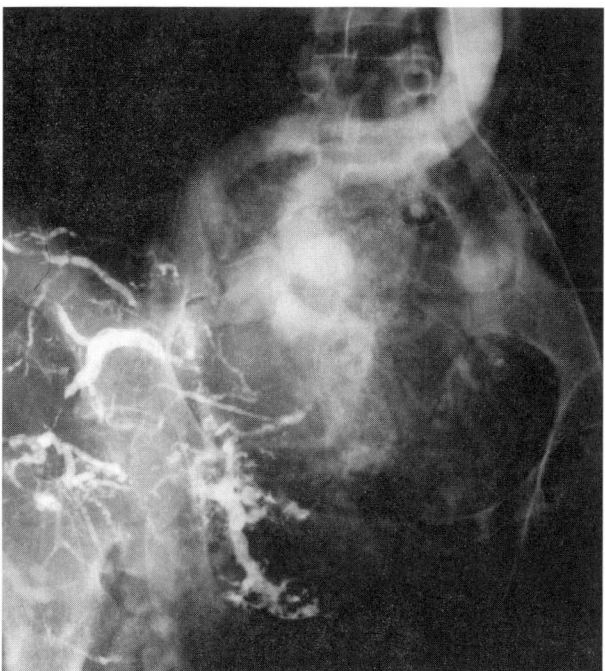

A

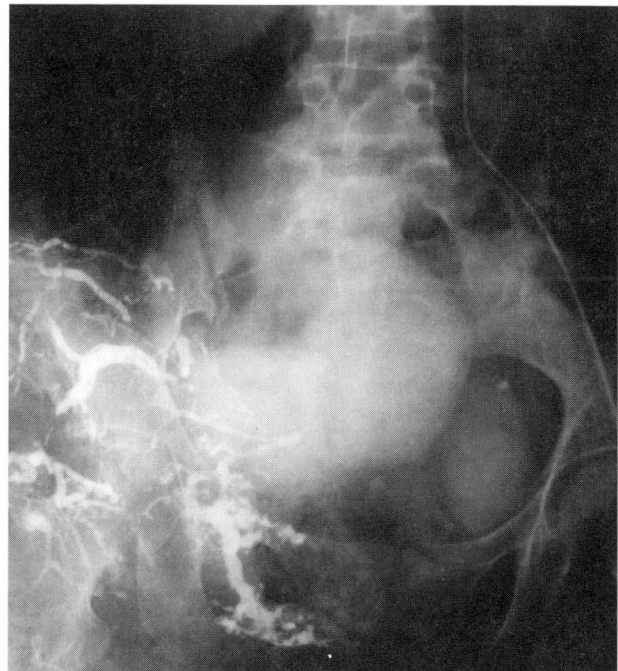

B

Figure 60-11. Unusual case of huge pelvic vascular malformation in a 23-year-old woman. The malformation was causing high-output congestive heart failure. (A) Flush pelvic aortogram shows high-flow lesion supplied primarily by an enlarged right hypogastric artery. Note the radiopaque embolic material from previous embolizations. (B) Venous phase demonstrates a hugely dilated draining hypogastric vein. (C) Chest radiograph of same patient shows marked cardiomegaly and pulmonary vascular congestion. Although the pelvic lesion was not curable, this patient's congestive heart failure has been controlled for over 10 years (and through two pregnancies) with multiple embolization procedures.

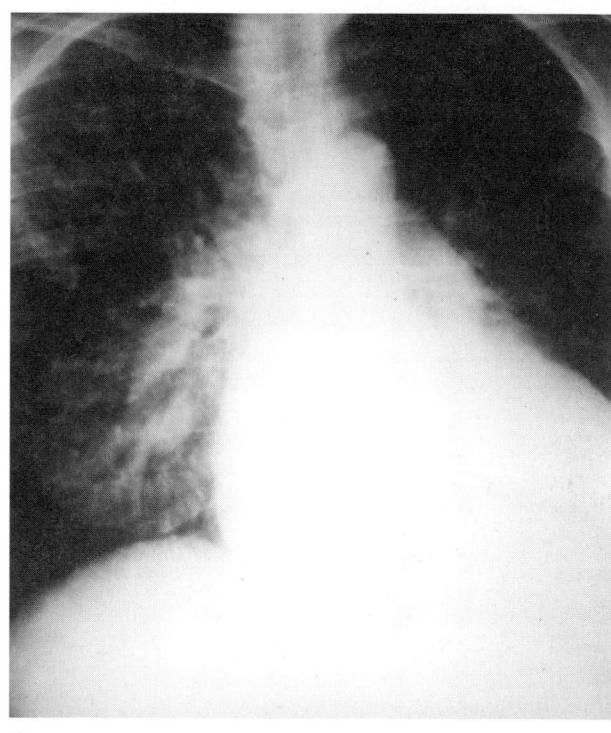

C

tion is clearly not when these studies are obtained. Such imaging modalities are also valuable as an objective baseline, which can be repeated at intervals or after intervention.

Angiography provides the most detailed depiction of vascular anatomy, although these findings can also be misleading without the additional information provided by cross-sectional studies. The author does not routinely perform diagnostic angiography unless the diagnosis is in doubt or intervention is planned, particularly in children. Nonselective studies with rapid filming will confirm the diagnosis and give an overview of the vascular supply. Detailed selective studies are not necessary until intervention is planned. The angiographic findings include enlargement and tortuosity of feeding arteries; a dense nidus of malformation, which can range from innumerable small vessels to a few large ones; and early opacification of draining veins, which may show marked dilatation. Most malformations demonstrate a primary feeding artery and multiple smaller secondary feeders. If the primary feeding artery is occluded, the secondary vessels will resupply the nidus of the lesion almost instantaneously.

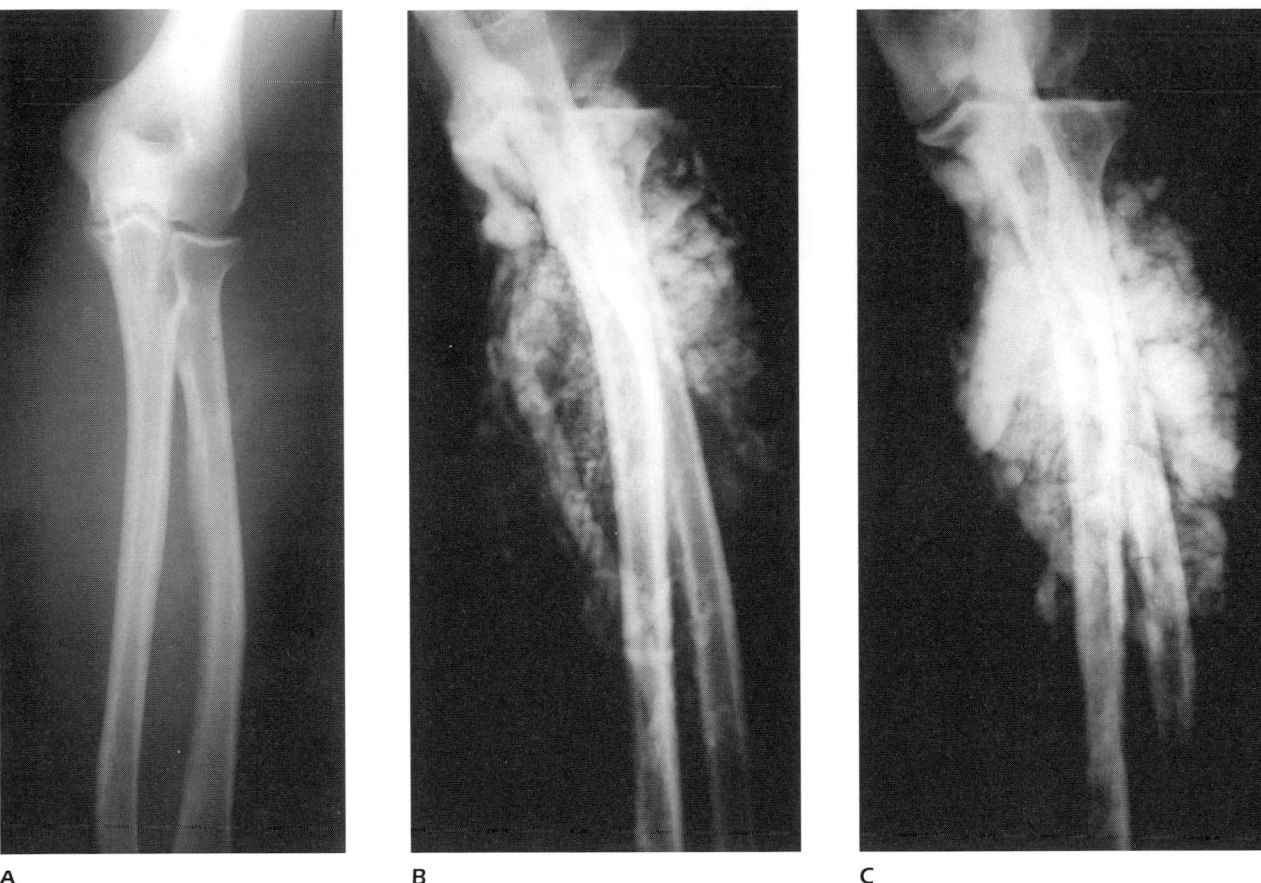

A   B   C

Figure 60-12. Plain film of forearm (A) shows completely normal bony structures, with nothing to suggest the presence of an extensive high-flow malformation (B and C). Most AVMs have little effect on regional bony structures.

Treatment

Unlike hemangiomas, which involve spontaneously, and fistulas, which can usually be permanently cured, true vascular malformations are notoriously refractory to treatment. Surgeons long ago discovered that complete resection of the lesion is rarely possible and is often associated with marked blood loss, which can be uncontrollable. The apparently more conservative approach of ligating feeding vessels almost always results in recurrence, sometimes within months. These recurrences may be more symptomatic than the original lesion and are invariably more complex anatomically because they involve numerous feeding vessels. Coping with these lesions surgically has been justifiably likened to battling a medusa. This is not to say that surgery has no role in the management of these lesions, only that it must be carefully planned with realistic goals in mind. Planning includes careful radiologic study consisting of both cross-sectional and angiographic examinations. It must also include provision for large-volume blood replacement, such as "cell saver" devices.[32-34]

Although only a minority of AVMs can be completely resected, when this can be accomplished, it probably represents the best chance of a complete cure. Partial resections and ligations, as stated, are worse than useless and should be avoided. In some cases, preoperative embolization can convert a lesion from unresectable to resectable with an acceptable blood loss.

Transcatheter embolization has now assumed a primary role in the management of congenital vascular malformations. An endovascular approach to this type of lesion makes a great deal of sense, but the apparent ease of catheterizing a feeding artery and depositing embolic devices must not tempt the angiographer into the same errors made over decades of surgical intervention. Specifically, proximal occlusion of feeding vessels, whether performed by surgical ligation or an endovascular coil, will produce the same poor clinical result with virtually guaranteed recurrence. Since these are benign lesions in relatively young patients, a long-term view of results is always necessary. A large number of these patients require only a correct diagnosis

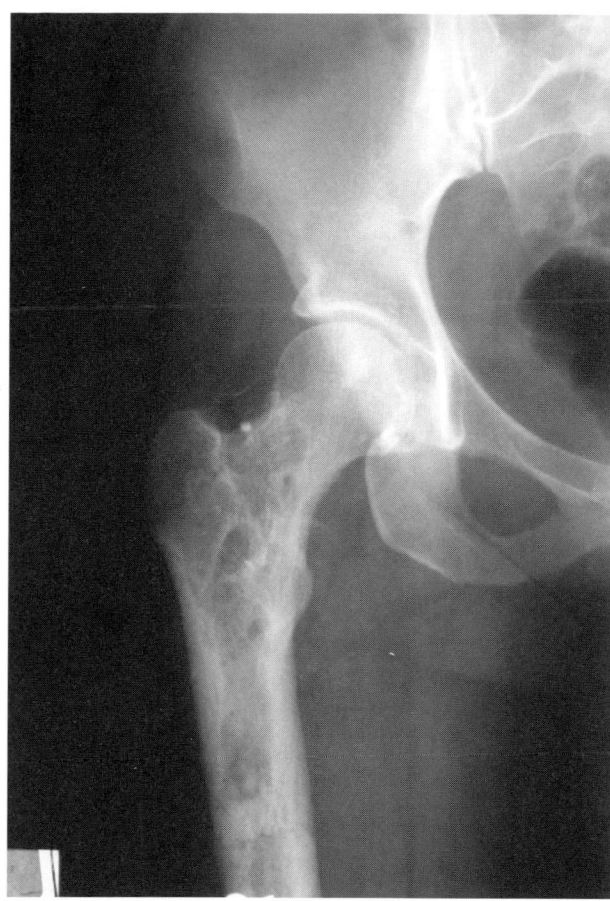

A

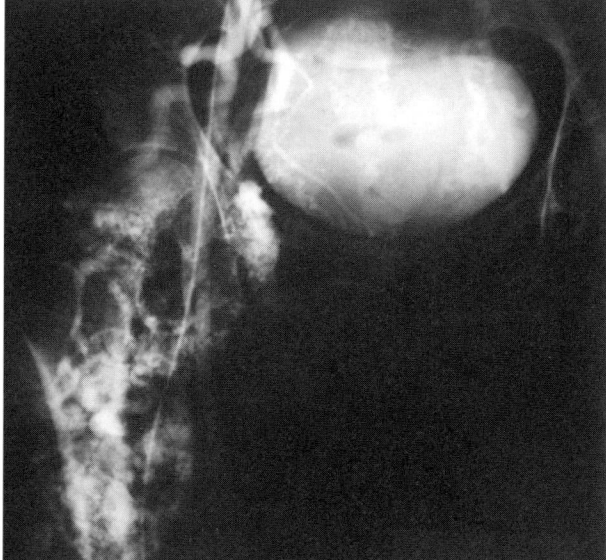

B

Figure 60-13. Some malformations do involve the bone, as in this 26-year-old woman with a high-flow malformation involving the proximal right femur. Note the plain film findings of enlarged vascular foramina and erosion of the medullary canal.

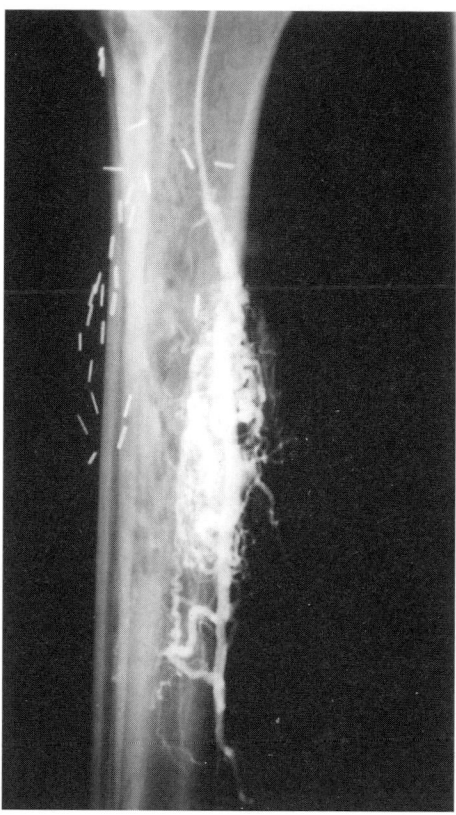

Figure 60-14. Occasionally a high-flow vascular malformation can cause extensive bone destruction, as seen in the permeative pattern of the tibia of this young woman. A pathologic fracture can have catastrophic consequences in this setting.

Figure 60-15. Cross-sectional MR image of a young man with a thigh AVM, clearly demonstrating the relationship of the lesion to surrounding muscle planes.

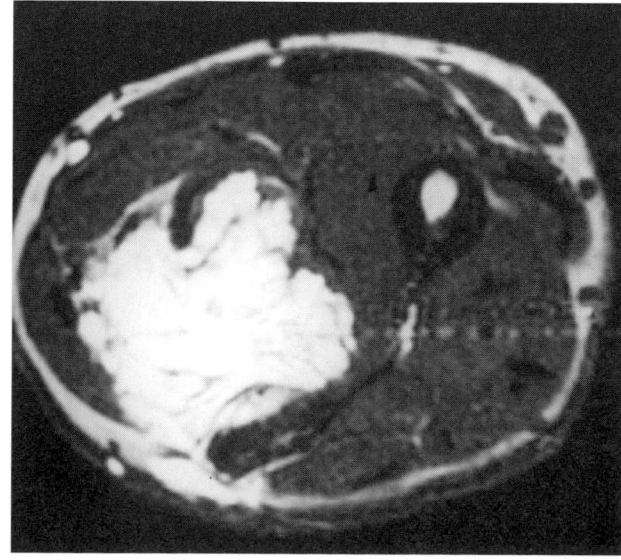

and reassurance, and the temptation to intervene must be tempered with a realistic assessment of the long-term prospects of treatment. Although complete cures can be accomplished in only a minority of cases, control of clinical symptoms can often be achieved with minimal morbidity. Both the physician and the patient should be prepared for the likelihood of repeated future procedures.

There are few conditions in which a "team approach" to treatment is more important than vascular malformations. Members of the team should include internists, vascular surgeons, interventional radiologists, plastic surgeons, orthopedists, pediatricians, and anesthesiologists. A multidisciplinary conference at which cases are presented on a regular basis can facilitate management and decision making, as well as maximize the experience of the group in dealing with these relatively unusual conditions.

The author performs virtually all embolization procedures under general anesthesia, feeling that the increased risk, time, and expense are justified by the length of these procedures and the discomfort involved in numerous superselective studies, particularly in the extremities.

A variety of embolization techniques and materials have been described over the past twenty years. Dramatic advances have also occurred in vascular imaging and catheterization. Among the most significant in the realm of treating AVMs has been the introduction and rapid refinement of digital angiography and "road-mapping" (Fig. 60-16). The ability to superimpose a live fluoroscopic image on a frozen image of the vessels, combined with the development of coaxial microcatheters and steerable guidewires, has made possible superselective catheterization of vessels that would have been nearly impossible to even image a few years ago. There is no question that the availability of better embolic materials has lagged considerably behind our ability to reach even the smallest vascular bed. There is still no embolic agent that is ideal for treating vascular malformations, meaning one that has proven long-term safety, ease of handling and delivery, permanence, and the ability to reach and occlude the nidus of the malformation.[32] Each of the devices or agents currently in use is briefly discussed.

Gelfoam

Gelfoam is an absorbable gelatin sponge and is available in several forms.[32] The most commonly used in embolization are the pledget and powdered forms. Gelfoam pledgets are generally cut into small strips or cubes and suspended in contrast for injection. Although this material is quite useful in treating acute hemorrhage and in preoperative embolization, its large size and reabsorption over a period of days or weeks make it unsuitable for treating most AVMs. This

Figure 60-16. Use of digital road-mapping in embolization of high-flow malformation in right thigh. (A) Femoral arteriogram shows large malformation supplied by the profunda femoris. (B) Digital road map image during embolization shows superimposition of microcatheter on frozen image of profunda branch about to be embolized. The medial branch has already been occluded with acrylic adhesive. (C) Final angiogram shows complete obliteration of the malformation.

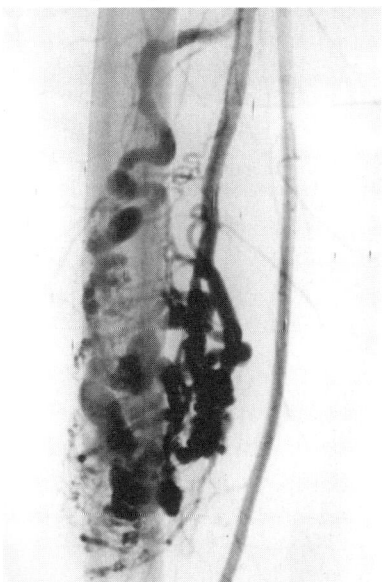

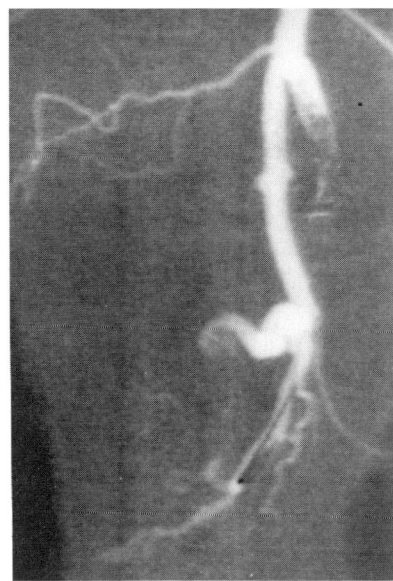

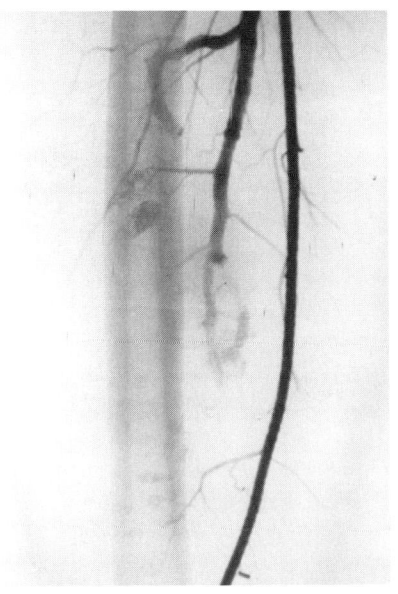

A   B   C

agent is sometimes useful for protecting normal vessels from distal embolization by occluding them proximally when other agents are used.

Gelfoam powder consists of particles as small as 40 μ in size. This material can reach the capillary level and presents a definite risk of tissue ischemia. Except when tissue infarction is intended, as in treating neoplasms, it should generally be avoided.

Coils

Stainless steel coils are among the oldest devices designed specifically for transcatheter vascular occlusion. They cause thrombosis by creating a mechanical blockade of the vessel, with thrombosis promoted by the incorporation of Dacron fibers (Fig. 60-17). Coils have the advantages of being an FDA approved device and being easy to use; they come in a wide variety of shapes and sizes and can be passed through standard selective angiographic catheters. More recently, miniaturized platinum coils ("microcoils") have become available that can be introduced through 2 and 3 French microcatheters into extremely small arteries (Fig. 60-18). They are available in unfibered and fibered types, the latter being much more effective occluding devices.

Despite their advantages, coils are unsuitable for treating most vascular malformations because of their size. The proximal occlusion caused by these devices is equivalent to surgical ligation, a technique that has long proven ineffective. Like Gelfoam, coils may be of use as proximal protective devices or to redistribute flow during embolization with other more penetrating agents.

Detachable Balloons

Detachable balloons are useful in situations where flow guidance, reversible occlusion, and repositioning are required. Examples include high-flow lesions (such as carotid-cavernous fistulas) and pulmonary AVMs. In these situations they provide unique advantages that justify their complexity and cost (Fig. 60-19). Their use is not justified as simple proximal occluding devices, and they would offer little advantage over coils in nonfistulous vascular malformations. Premade balloons of various sizes with self-sealing valves are available, replacing the tediously hand-assembled latex balloons of the past.

PVA (Ivalon)

Ivalon, or polyvinyl alcohol (PVA) sponge, was first introduced as an embolic material in 1975.[35] It is generally used in particulate form, with particle sizes ranging from 150 to 1000 μ (Fig. 60-20). Commercial preparations exist with more uniform consistency and particle size than the previous largely "homemade" types. This agent is usually injected as a suspension through standard-size catheters or microcatheter systems. The particles will follow the flow of blood until

Figure 60-17. Gianturco embolization coils consist of stainless steel coils with attached Dacron fibers to promote occlusion. They can be easily inserted through standard selective angiographic catheters and are available in a variety of sizes.

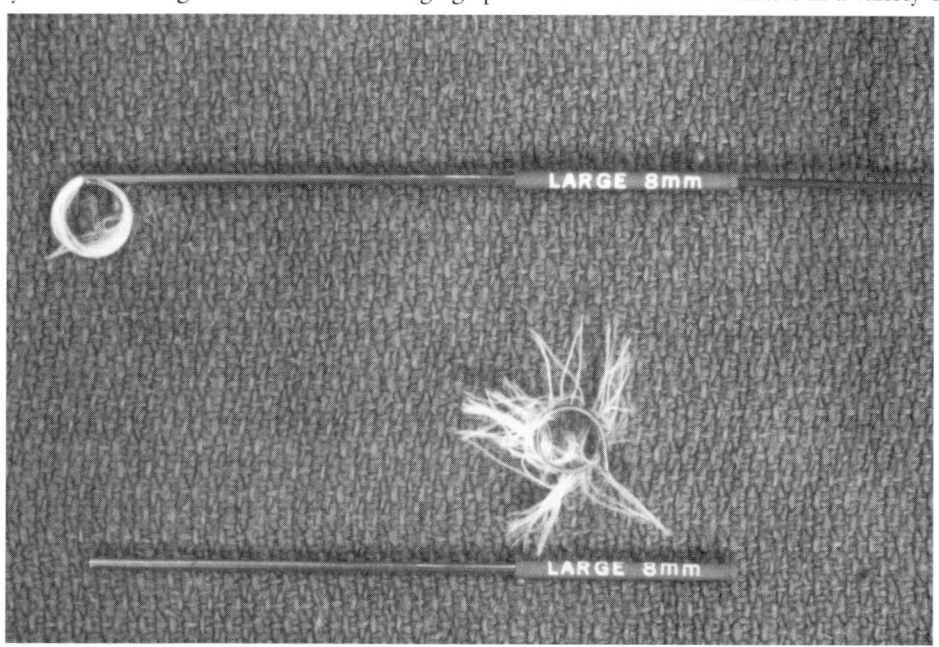

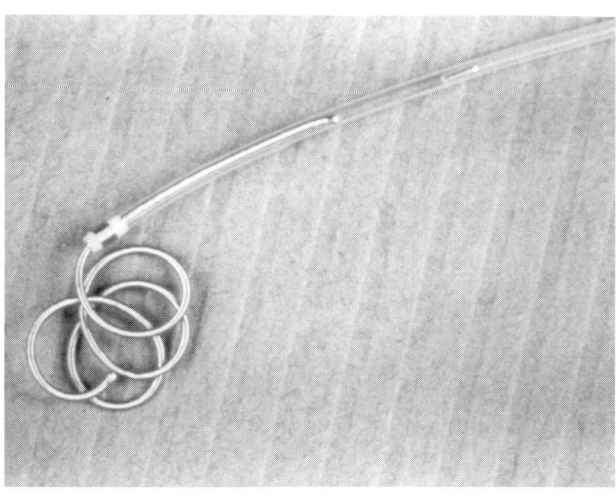

A

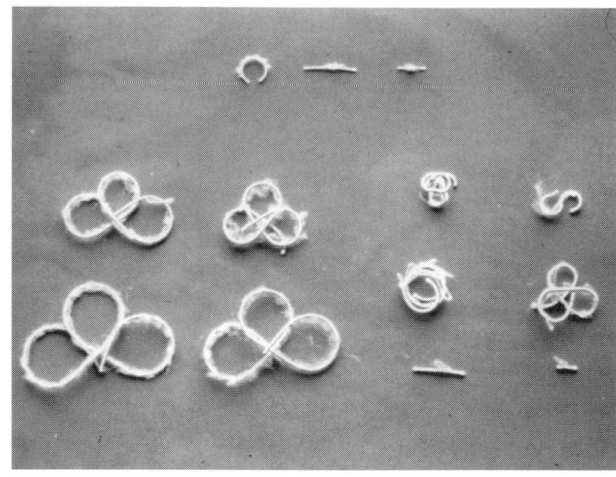

B

Figure 60-18. (A) Microcoils are available that can be passed through 2 to 3 French coaxial microcatheters. Most of these are constructed of platinum wire and so are extremely radiopaque. (B) The fibered varieties are much more effective occluding devices.

Figure 60-19. Certain high-flow lesions are best treated with detachable balloons, despite their complexity and cost. One example is the pulmonary AVM, where flow guidance and the ability to reposition optimally are critical. Loss of another type of embolic device through a pulmonary AVM will result in systemic embolization, with potentially disastrous results.

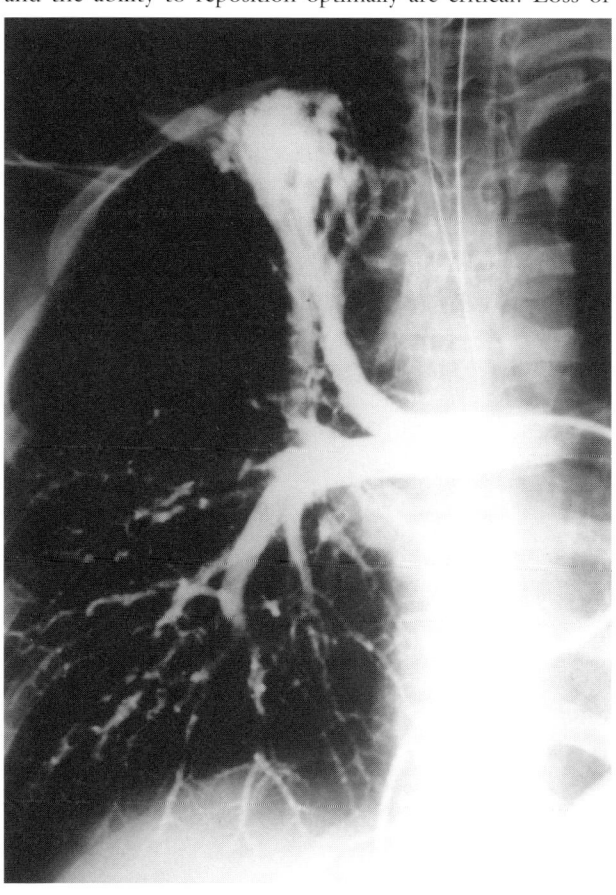

A

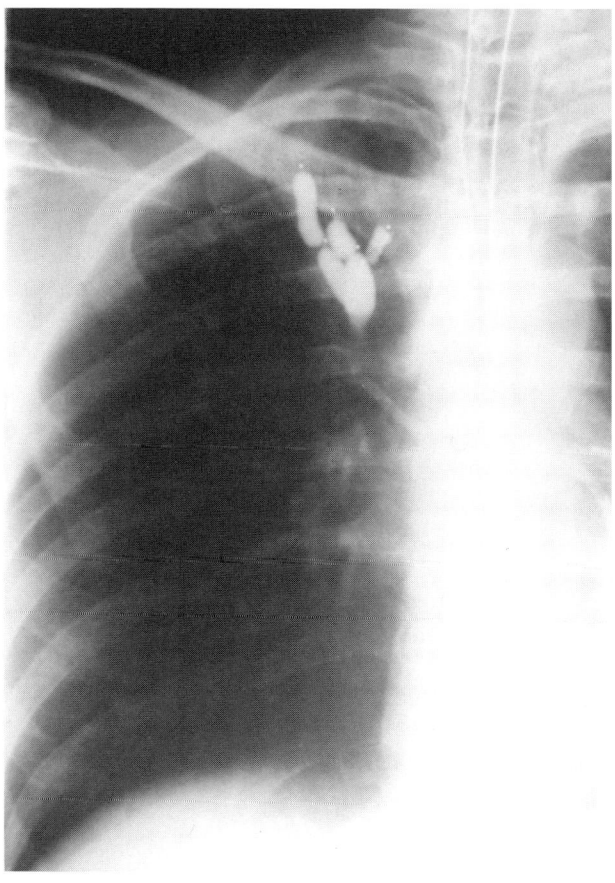

B

Figure 60-20. Ivalon, or polyvinyl alcohol foam, is generally used in particulate form, suspended in contrast. Various-size particles, from 150 to 1000 μ, are available, the choice depending on the size of the vascular matrix to be occluded.

they lodge in a vessel too small to allow further passage (Fig. 60-21). Thus different particle sizes can be selected based on the size of the vascular matrix to be occluded. It should be noted that even the smallest Ivalon particles (150 μ) are larger than those of Gelfoam powder, so there is less risk of tissue ischemia.

Because PVA is considered a permanent (nonreabsorbable) material and can be deposited deeply into vascular beds, it was hoped that this would be a suitable agent for treating AVMs. Indeed, PVA embolization can produce an impressive immediate angiographic result, with a gradual pruning of vessels and slowing of flow until stasis is reached (Fig. 60-22A to C). Unfortunately, these initial results were often followed by recurrence of the lesion, often within a period of months (see Fig. 60-22D). Further investigation demonstrated that this was due to a combination of reabsorption and recanalization.[36] Thus Ivalon has proved disappointing over the long term and may be most effective as a preoperative embolic agent. Its use may also be warranted as a "trial" agent to determine the effect of embolization on a lesion clinically; if there is significant benefit, access to feeding vessels will not have been sacrificed and more permanent agents can then be used in the event of recurrence.

Absolute Ethanol

Absolute (95 percent) ethanol is a highly potent embolic agent that causes vascular occlusion by a combi-

nation of direct toxic effect on the vessel wall and clumping of damaged erythrocytes and denatured proteins. It was initially described as an effective embolic agent in the treatment of renal tumors, where its marked tissue toxicity was desirable. This agent also has the advantages of being readily available, inexpensive, and easy to deliver through virtually any catheter system. Its use in treating AVMs was first described by Sasaki et al. in 1984[37] and was popularized by Yakes et al.[38] Although some series have reported excellent results, this agent must be used with a great deal of caution because of its toxicity. It is capable of causing considerable damage to normal tissues, particularly when used in vessels supplying mucosal surfaces, skin surfaces, and neural structures (Fig. 60-23). One must therefore be certain of all structures supplied by a feeding vessel and must also consider how distribution of the agent may change abruptly as occlusion occurs. For these reasons, the author adds metrizamide powder as an opacifying agent when using alcohol, to continuously monitor flow and distribution of the agent fluoroscopically.

The author has found alcohol to be more applicable in the treatment of venous malformations by direct injection, where the risk of tissue damage is much lower. This technique is discussed in detail in the section on venous malformations.

Figure 60-21. Particulate agents such as Ivalon will follow blood flow until they reach a vessel too small to allow further passage. Although the goal is to penetrate the nidus of the lesion, this probably seldom occurs. This fact, combined with the irregular shape of the particles, which causes incomplete occlusion, is the most likely explanation for the frequency of recurrence months after embolization with this agent.

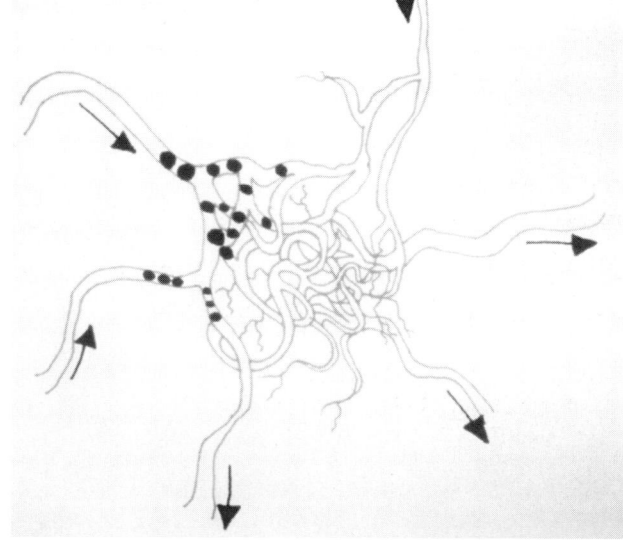

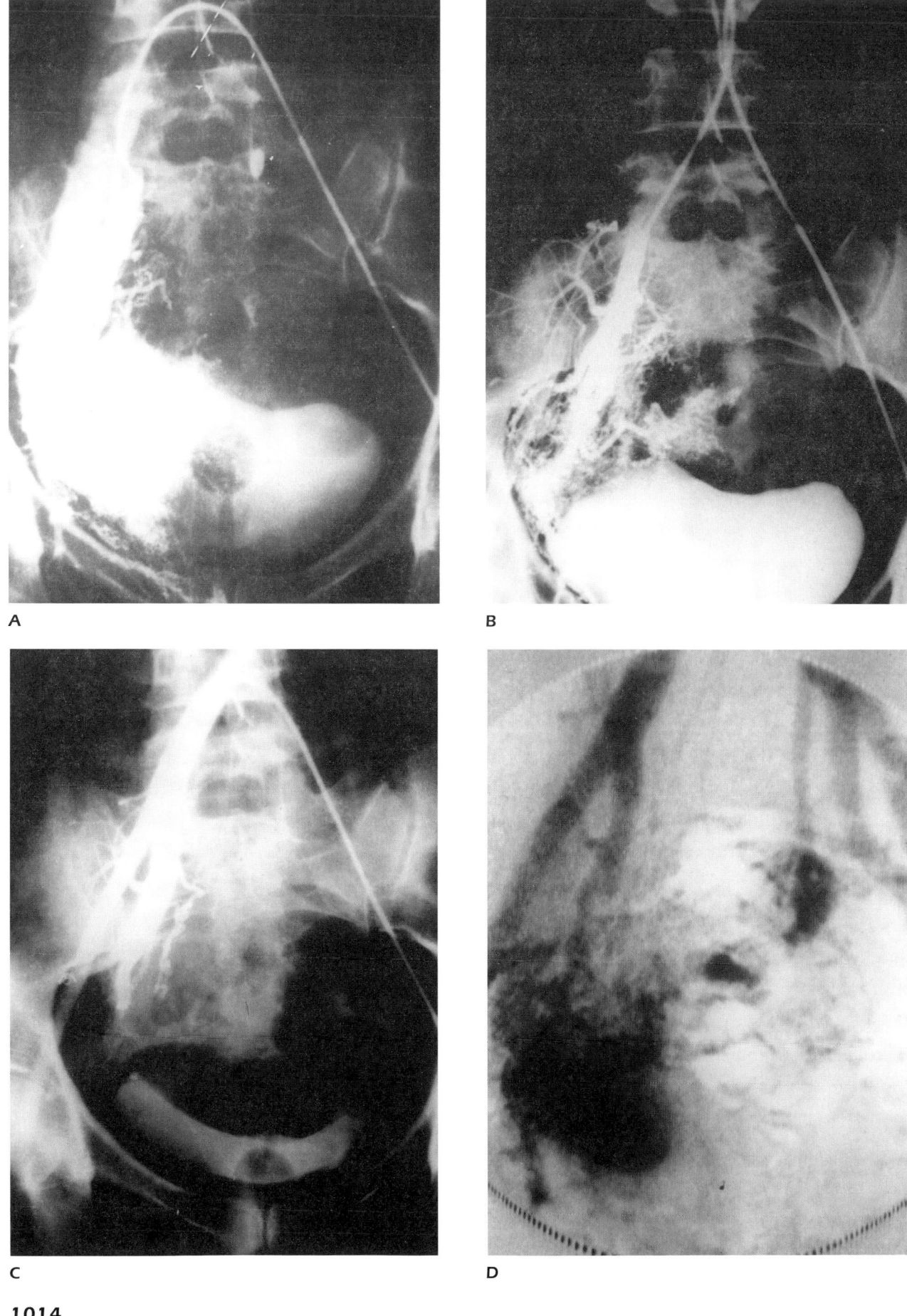

A

B

C

D

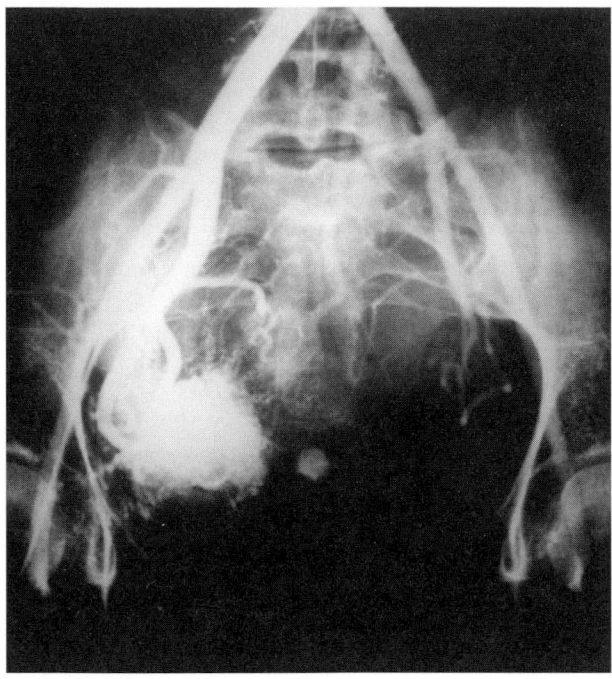

A

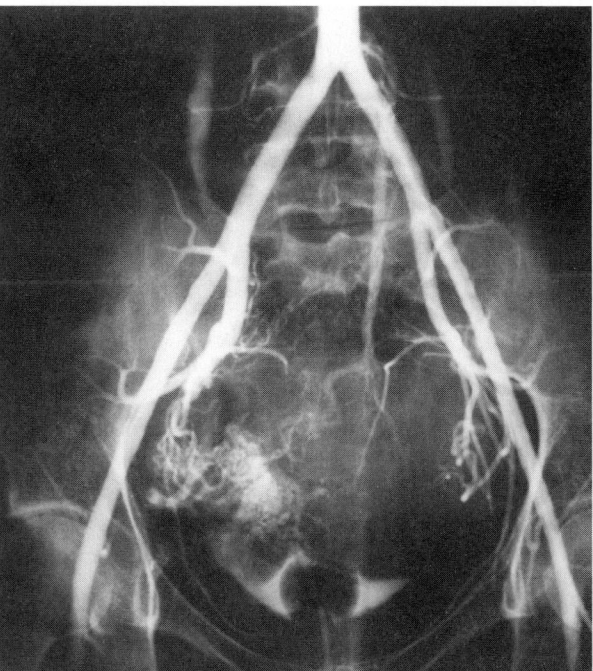

B

Figure 60-23. Intraarterial alcohol is a highly potent agent that must be used with extreme caution in treating vascular malformations. Preembolization (A) and postembolization (B) studies show a good angiographic result in this 28-year- old woman with a right pelvic AVM. Unfortunately, the alcohol caused a permanent nerve injury resulting in intractable chronic pain.

Acrylic Adhesives

Cyanoacrylates, a group of rapidly polymerizing adhesives, have been used for a variety of clinical applications over the past 30 years, and specifically for intravascular occlusion for nearly 20 years.[39] Their use has been controversial in that a wide variety of tissue reactions have been described, causing concern over long-term toxicity or even carcinogenicity. In an exhaustive review of the histotoxicity of cyanoacrylates, Vintner et al. in 1985 concluded that there was no evidence of carcinogenicity but that more work was needed in evaluating tissue reactions to these agents.[40] In most series where pathologic studies have been carried out, a chronic inflammatory reaction with foreign-body giant cells, mural inflammation, and eventual fibrosis is demonstrated. A gradual reduction in the amount of acrylic adhesive within an embolized lesion has also been documented, and correlates with radiographic observations of shrinkage or disappearance of the opaque material over time.[41] Whether this is due to phagocytosis or another mechanism is not entirely clear, but this phenomenon can be associated with recurrence of AVMs following embolization with acrylic adhesives.

Despite these problems and uncertainties, the author has seen better long-term results with acrylic adhesives in AVMs than with most of the alternative agents. This embolic material rapidly polymerizes on contact with any ionic medium, including the mildly basic bloodstream. The material is generally combined with oily contrast (Pantopaque or Ethiodol), which adds radiopacity and slows the polymerization time to allow for more controllability. Powdered tantalum metal may also be added to further increase radiopacity. This slightly viscous mixture is then delivered as close as possible to the nidus of the malformation, gen-

◄ **Figure 60-22.** Extensive pelvic AVM in a 34-year-old woman with complaint of pain. (A) Selective right hypogastric injection shows an extensive malformation with shunting into the iliac vein. (B) During embolization with PVA particles, marked "pruning" of the lesion is demonstrated. Individual branches are now visible and no shunting is seen. (C) At the end of the embolization procedure, no further filling of the lesion is seen. Note the proximal coils in the posterior division of the hypogastric artery, placed to protect this circulation from particulate emboli. (D) After an initial resolution of symptoms, the patient returned 6 months later complaining of recurrent pain. A digital intravenous study demonstrated recurrence of the lesion, a common problem after PVA embolization.

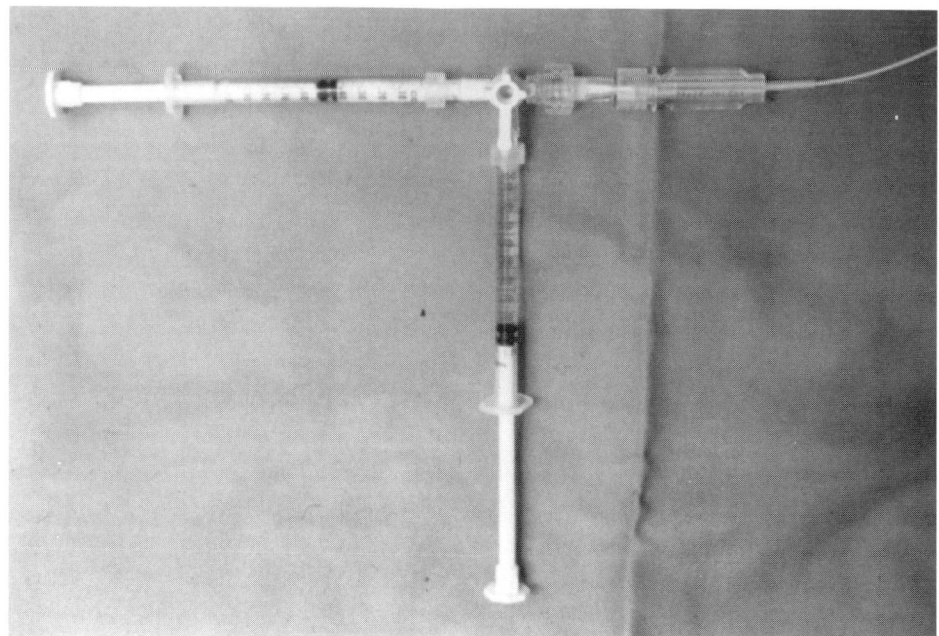

Figure 60-24. "Push" technique for delivering acrylic adhesive. A small volume of adhesive (generally 0.2–0.6 ml) is injected through the microcatheter, pushed by a bolus of nonionic flush (D_5W) to prevent polymerization inside the catheter.

erally through a coaxial microcatheter. Extremely small depositions are used, generally ranging from 0.2 to 0.6 ml, delivered as a continuous injection or with a "push" of nonionic 5 percent dextrose in water (D_5W) (Fig. 60-24). These small depositions polymerize rapidly, incorporating blood elements to produce a significantly larger cast than the volume of the agent. The goal, which cannot always be achieved, is to create a "cast" of the nidus of the lesion (Fig. 60-25). This should theoretically obliterate the low-pressure sump, which is the stimulus for the development of new collaterals and recurrences. Clinically observed tissue toxicity has been minimal in the author's experience, with no evidence of mucosal damage, tissue necrosis, or nerve damage.

Pelvic AVMs

The pelvis is one of the more common locations for AVMs to occur. The complex blood supply to this region and the numerous organs that may be involved combine to produce an extremely difficult clinical management problem.

The anatomic distribution of pelvic AVMs is quite variable, ranging from focal lesions confined to the broad ligament of the uterus to extensive lesions involving the bladder, bowel, uterus, ovaries, muscle, nerves, and even bone. The blood supply may be equally complex, the most common feeding vessels

consisting of the hypogastric, middle sacral, lumbar, inferior mesenteric, and common femoral artery branches.

Figure 60-25. Partial embolization of a right pelvic AVM using NBCA adhesive. Note the "cast" of the embolized vessels; the agent is made opaque through the addition of Pantopaque and tantalum powder.

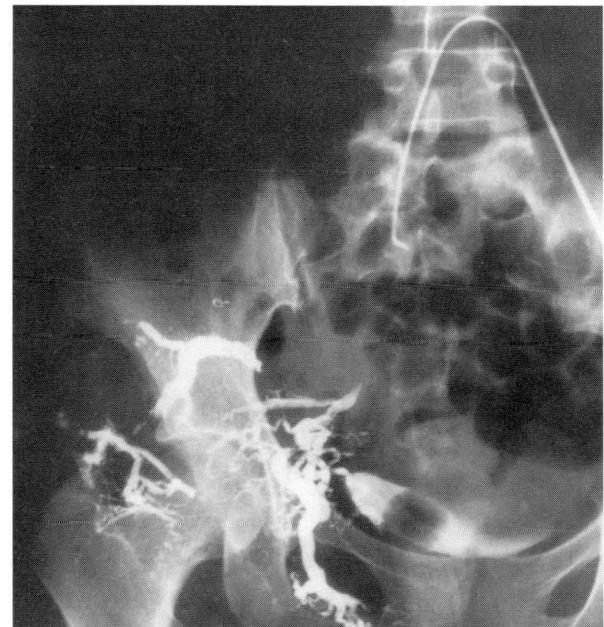

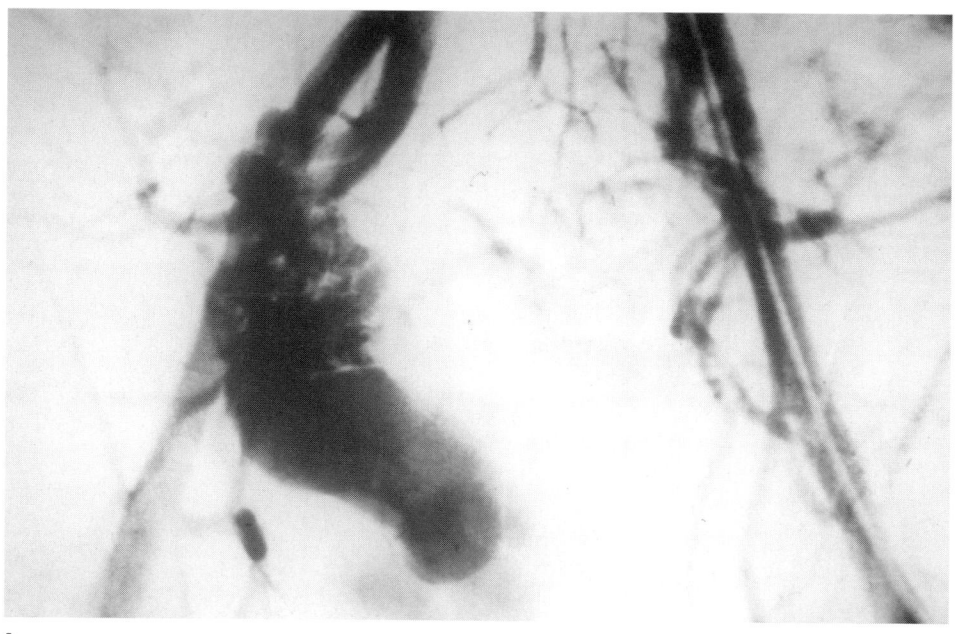

A

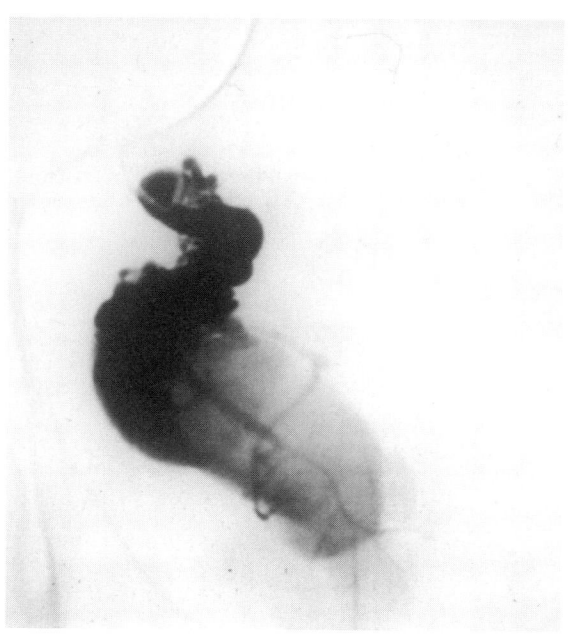

B

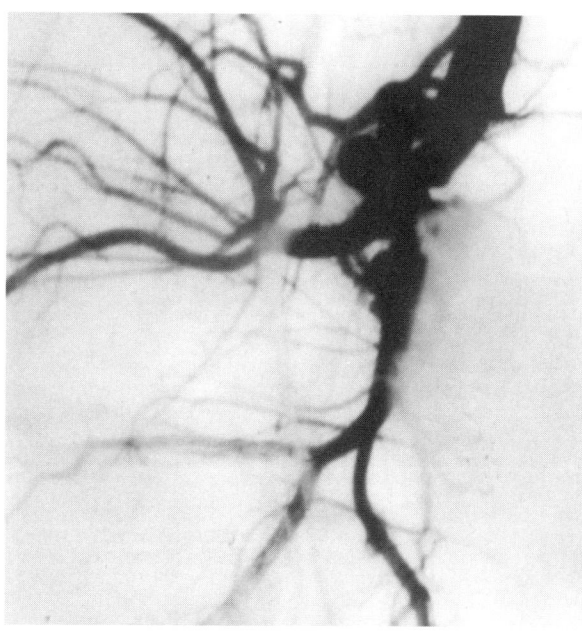

C

Figure 60-26. A 22-year-old man with complaints of pelvic pain and urinary retention. Rectal examination revealed a pulsatile mass. Pelvic arteriogram (A) demonstrates a "male" pattern AVM, with a single hypogastric artery supply wrapped around a massively dilated draining vein (B), which is responsible for the symptoms. (C) After embolization with acrylic adhesive, the lesion has been occluded with preservation of the normal hypogastric branches. This patient remained asymptomatic and without radiologic evidence of recurrence 8 years after embolization.

These lesions are most often encountered in young women. Presenting features may include local or referred pain, leg edema, abnormal menstrual bleeding or hematuria, and, rarely, high-output congestive heart failure. In male patients, the anatomic distribution tends to be simpler, often with a single hypogastric artery feeder and drainage through hugely dilated veins, which are primarily responsible for the symptoms of pain, disturbed bowel and or bladder function, and occasional bleeding (Fig. 60-26). In both male and female patients, these lesions may be asymptomatic and discovered incidentally on physical or radiologic examination.

Treatment of pelvic AVMs, particularly in female

patients, is extremely difficult. Complete cures are the exception, and recurrences are common. Thus the decision to initiate treatment must be tempered by a realistic assessment of the goals and risks involved. Surgical resection may be successful for lesions confined to the broad ligament; this is one of the few situations where radiologic studies may actually overestimate the difficulty of surgical treatment (Fig. 60-27). Although the lesion may draw feeders from multiple sources, the nidus is localized and can often be completely removed. Other lesions may be confined to the uterus, curable by hysterectomy. The author has treated one such patient with embolization who presented with severe menorrhagia (Fig. 60-28).[42] Hysterectomy was thereby avoided, and the patient later carried a full-term pregnancy uneventfully.

Unfortunately, most of these lesions are not so localized, and surgical resection is not feasible with an acceptable degree of morbidity. Palliation of symptoms, and in some cases cure, can be achieved by embolization. As always, the goal should be to obliterate the nidus rather than occlude the feeders. Most of these cases will require multiple staged procedures because of the complexity of the blood supply. Although branches of the hypogastric arteries are usually the primary feeding vessels, all of the regional arteries should be studied in order to evaluate other sources of supply or likely routes of recurrence. Ischemic complications

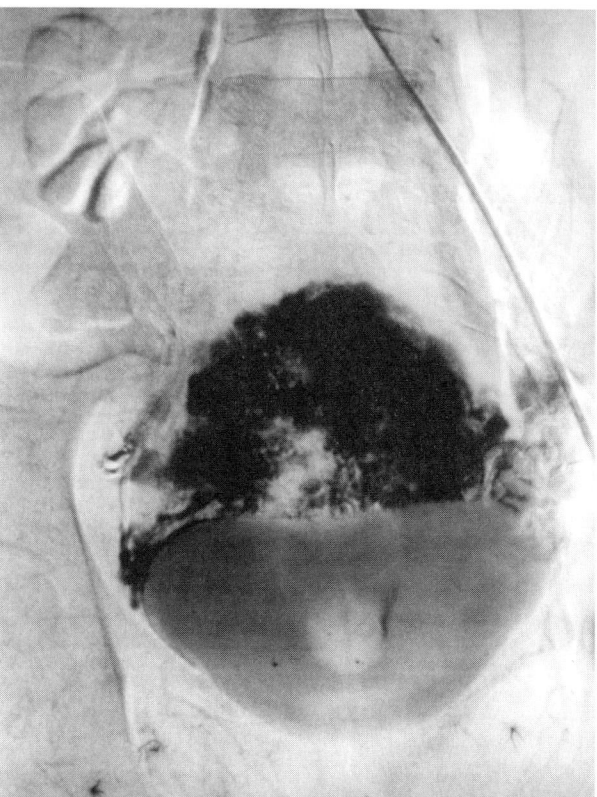

Figure 60-28. A 27-year-old woman with severe menorrhagia found to have a vascular malformation confined to the uterus. This was successfully managed with embolization.

Figure 60-27. Vascular malformation in the broad ligament of the uterus causing symptoms of pelvic pressure and pain. These lesions can often be removed surgically while preserving the uterus.

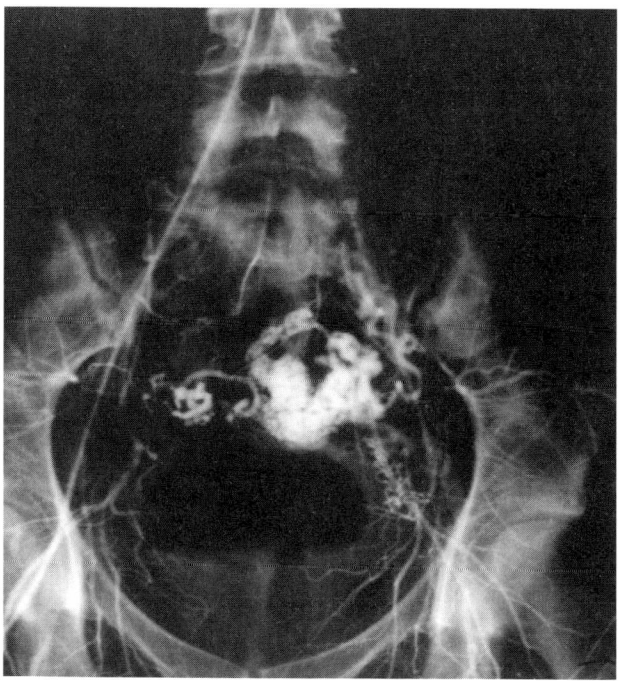

have been extremely rare, even when embolizing branches of the inferior mesenteric artery (Fig. 60-29). Caution must be used when employing agents such as Gelfoam powder or absolute alcohol, which may cause tissue necrosis through end-vessel blockade or direct toxicity.

The simpler blood supply of most male pelvic AVMs renders them much more treatable. If the nidus supplied by a single hypogastric artery can be occluded, the large draining veins will collapse or thrombose, and excellent long-term results have been achieved (Fig. 60-30).

Extremity Lesions

Extremity lesions are among the most difficult malformations to treat. They more often interfere with function than truncal or visceral lesions because of edema, muscle and nerve involvement, and distal ischemia. These lesions are also more subject to trauma during normal activity. From the standpoint of surgery or embolization it may be difficult to determine how many vessels can be sacrificed before compromising perfusion of normal tissues.

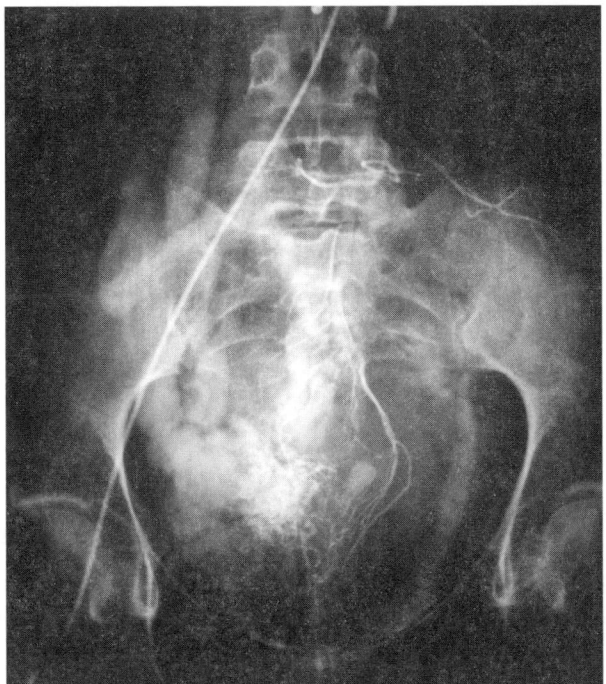

A

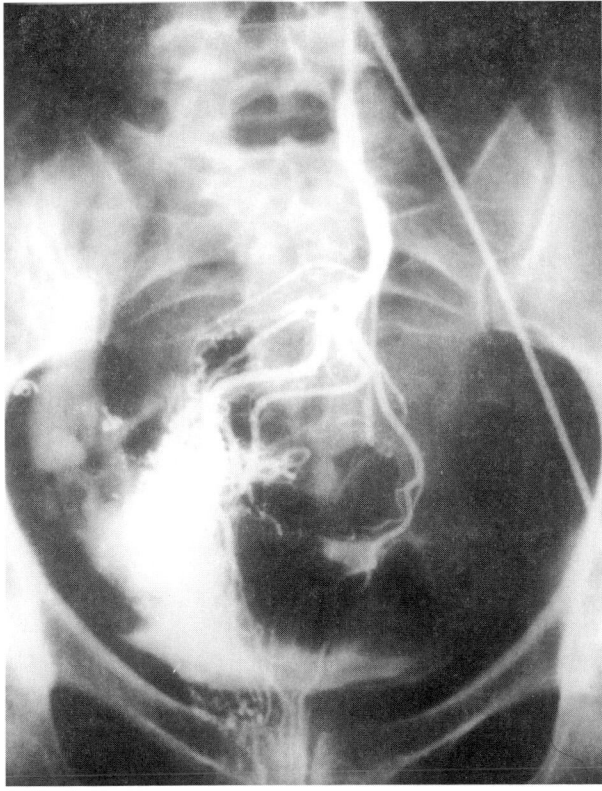

B

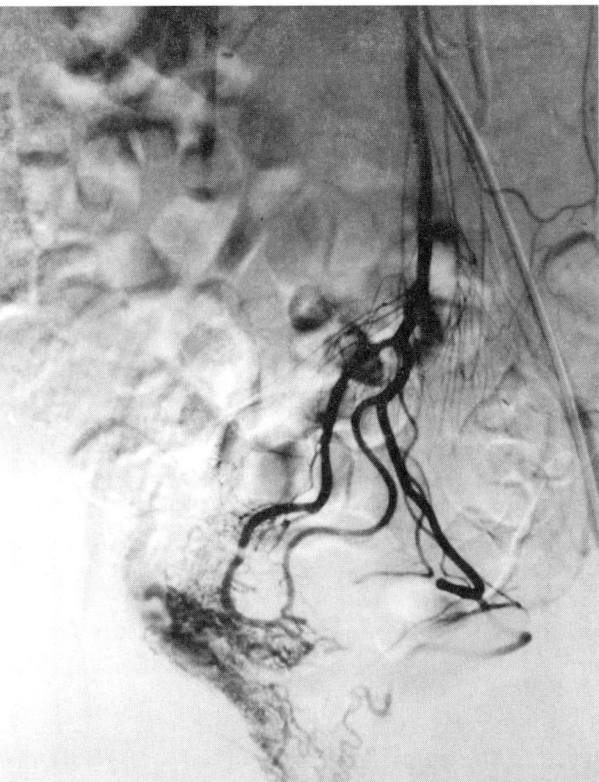

C

Figure 60-29. Three examples of women with pelvic AVMs partially supplied by branches of the inferior mesenteric artery. This type of involvement is occasionally associated with rectal pain or bleeding. Superselective embolization of the involved branches has been performed without ischemic complications.

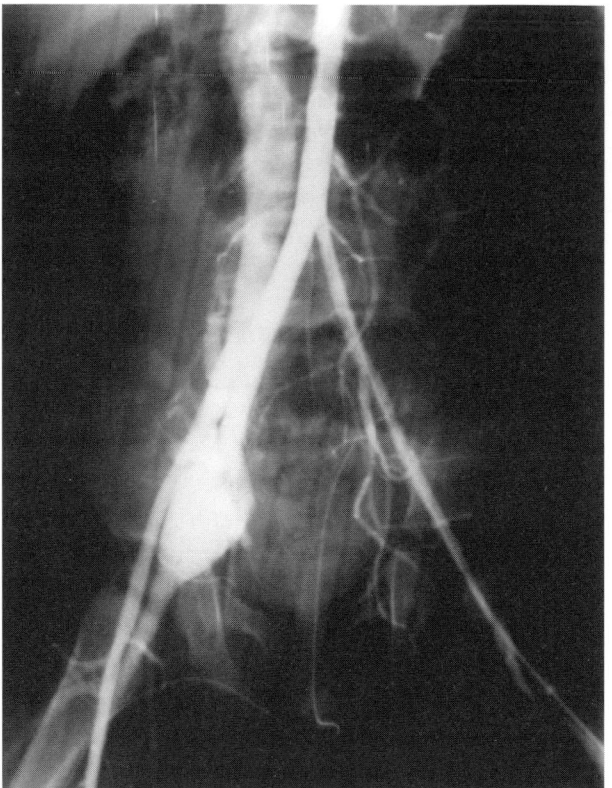

A

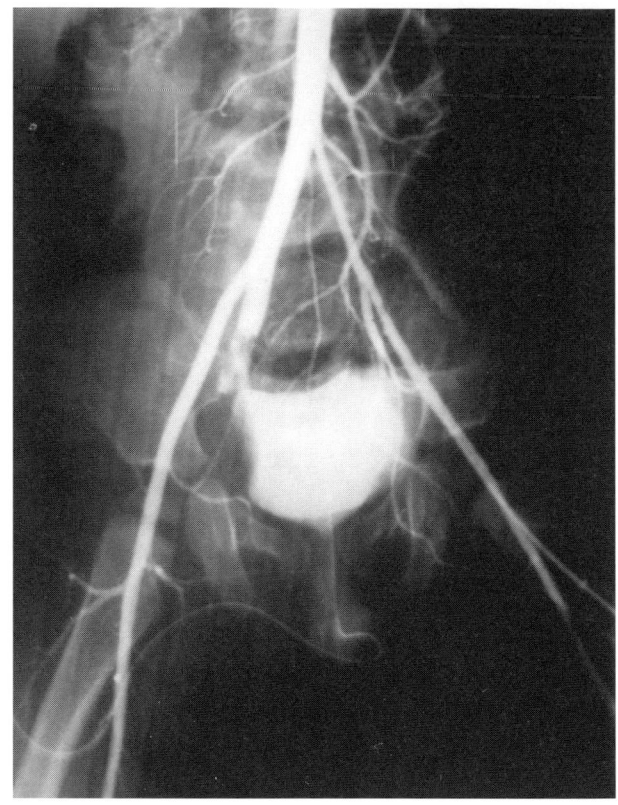

B

Figure 60-30. The youngest patient the author has treated with a "male pattern" AVM was 18 months old, presenting with overgrowth and swelling of the right leg. (A) Aortogram demonstrates marked enlargement of the right common iliac and hypogastric arteries due to the malformation, which shunts into an aneurysmally dilated vein with subsequent rapid filling of the inferior vena cava. (B) After acrylic embolization the lesion no longer fills. At 5 years of age, the child had no leg swelling and minimal leg length discrepancy.

As with other vascular malformations, proximal ligation is worse than useless, resulting in recurrence with a more complex pattern of supply. The availability of microcatheter systems and digital imaging has permitted superselective embolization of many lesions that would have been untreatable in the past (Fig. 60-31). Especially after previous ligations or embolizations, transvascular access to the lesion may be impossible or present an unacceptable risk of occluding normal vessels. Direct puncture techniques, using either adhesives or alcohol, may be technically easier and safer. The risks of intraarterial alcohol have been discussed but are particularly significant in the extremities, where the compartments containing the malformation also contain nerves and muscles, which can be damaged by this agent.

Ischemic pain, atrophy, or even tissue loss is commonly encountered with extremity AVMs. Even when the lesion cannot be eradicated completely, reducing the shunt by embolization will improve distal perfusion and can often be quite effective in relieving the most distressing clinical symptoms (Fig. 60-32). Treatment should generally be undertaken in stages, with the clinical result assessed at least 3 months after each procedure before continuing. The patient should also be aware that the lesion is unlikely to be completely eradicated and that repeated procedures may be required in the future.

Judgments as to the necessity and timing of treatment are particularly difficult in the pediatric population. Except in life- or limb-threatening situations, the author tries to avoid performing procedures on children under 5 years of age. The natural history of the lesion can be observed and there is less risk to normal

Figure 60-32. Even when extremity lesions cannot be completely eradicated, embolization to reduce the shunt can reduce or eliminate the clinical symptoms, as in this 22-year-old man before (A) and after (B) embolization of a plantar malformation. Note the surgical clips from a previous attempted resection. ▶

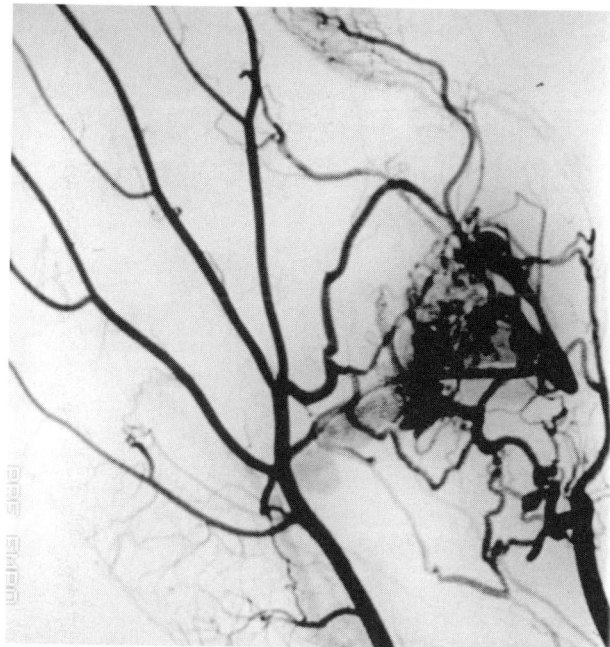

A

Figure 60-31. The availability of digital road-mapping and microcatheter systems now permits treatment of previously inaccessible lesions. This 17-year-old man had previously undergone radial artery ligation for treatment of an AVM of the palmar surface in the thenar region. He presented with pain in the hand and ischemic changes in the thumb. (A) The initial angiogram demonstrates collateralization around the ligated radial artery with multiple feeders supplying the AVM. The feeders were superselectively embolized using NBCA adhesive. (B) A repeat study 1 year after embolization demonstrates no evidence of recurrence. The patient's symptoms resolved and the ischemic changes in the thumb were reversed.

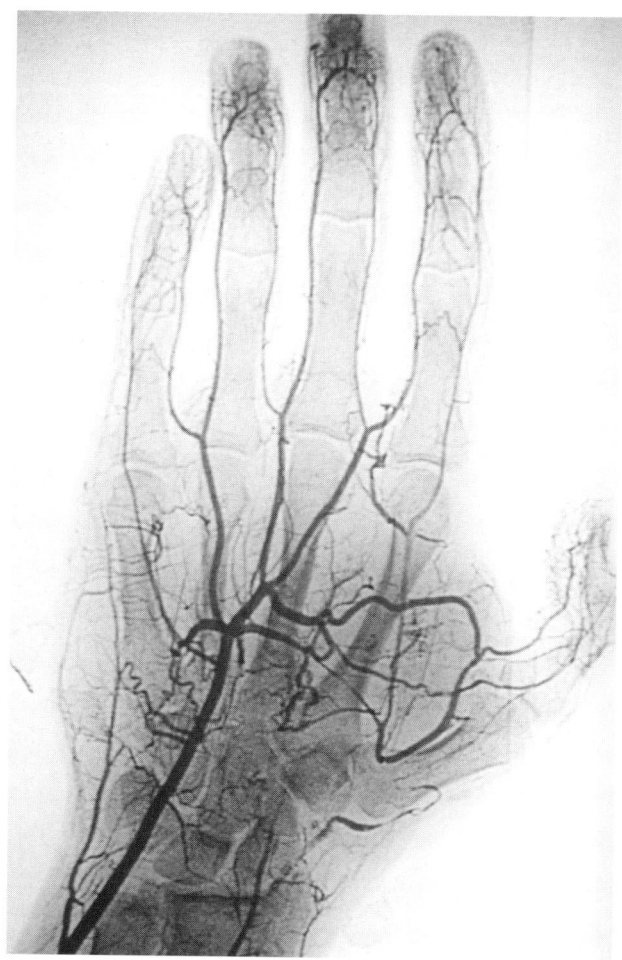

B

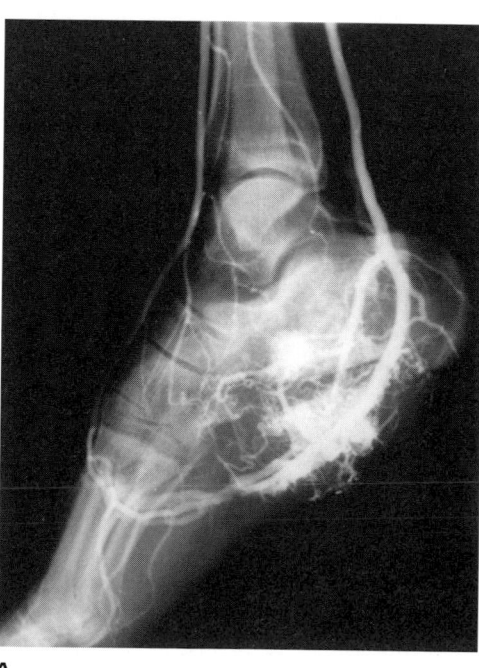

A

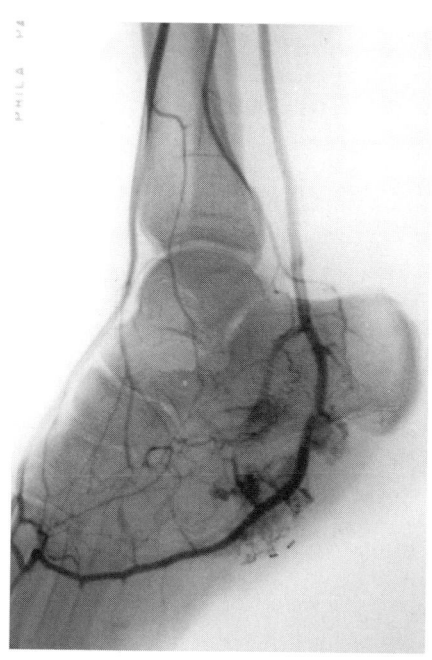

B

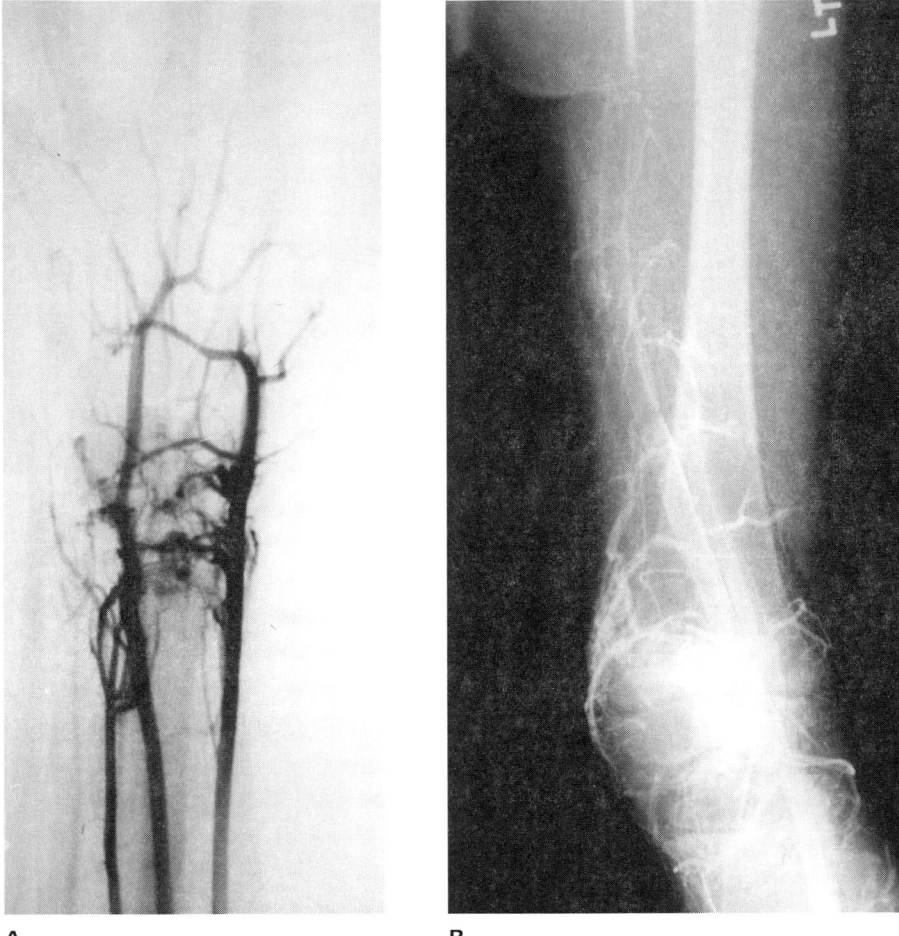

A   B

Figure 60-33. Two pediatric patients with limb overgrowth due to epiphyseal AVMs involving the wrist (A) and knee (B). The rate of growth was slowed considerably after embolization of these lesions.

vessels when the child has reached this age. The author has encountered a specific type of lesion in six pediatric patients who demonstrated overgrowth of a limb due to a vascular malformation involving the epiphyses (Fig. 60-33). After consultation with pediatric orthopedists with regard to timing of the procedure, these lesions were embolized. In three patients with an adequate length of follow-up, growth of the involved limb was slowed considerably, and it is hoped that the ultimate limb length discrepancy can be minimized using this approach.

Venous Malformations

Venous malformations are relatively common and range from anomalies of venous anatomy to focal cavernous lesions. There is also a category of "mixed" lesions, which are primarily composed of venous elements but demonstrate an arterial component when studied angiographically. As with other vascular malformations, these are not neoplastic lesions and generally show growth commensurate with growth of the individual.

Cavernous Venous Malformations

This is the prototypical venous lesion, in the past referred to as *cavernous hemangioma*. These lesions may occur anywhere in the body and are composed of irregular venous spaces with slow flow under low pressure. When they are located close to the skin surface, they have a characteristic bluish appearance and a soft, nonpulsatile compressible consistency (Fig. 60-34). They can be actively emptied by manual compression or passively by elevation of the affected part. Conversely, they can become tense and painful when engorgement occurs in the dependent position in extremity lesions and during increased intrathoracic or intraabdominal pressure in truncal lesions (e.g., Val-

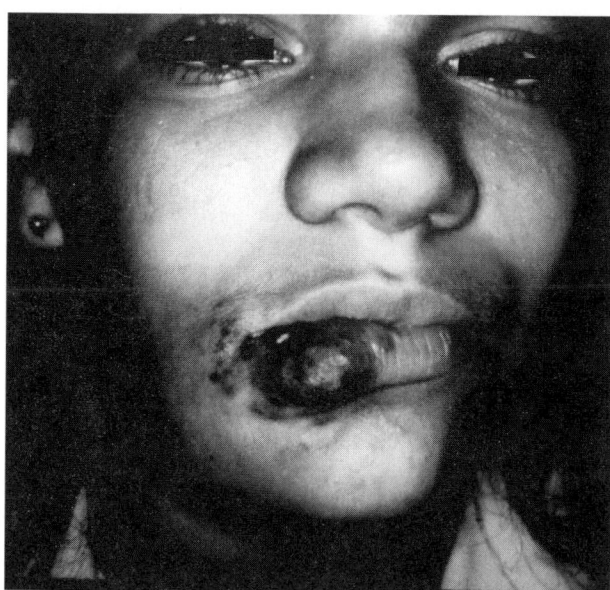

Figure 60-34. Typical cavernous venous malformation. When close to a skin surface, these lesions are soft, nonpulsatile, and compressible with a bluish discoloration. The overlying skin may be thinned to the point of spontaneous breakdown with bleeding.

salva maneuver, crying in children). These lesions are not tender unless there is superimposed acute thrombosis. Very superficial lesions may show marked thinning of the overlying skin, which may even show breakdown with spontaneous bleeding.

Noninvasive vascular studies show irregular fluid-filled spaces with slow flow. CT and MRI are extremely valuable in delineating the true extent of the lesion, which may involve a much larger territory than is evident clinically. These examinations should certainly be obtained before any surgical or interventional treatment.

Arteriography is typically unimpressive, demonstrating normal-caliber regional arteries that may show late venous staining on delayed films after high-volume contrast injections (Fig. 60-35). Occasionally a lesion that appears purely venous clinically will turn out to have an arterial component, which may alter treatment significantly.

Standard venography often fails to show any filling of the lesion from normal venous structures, although associated venous anomalies may be present. Direct puncture or "closed-space" venography is a much more effective technique for outlining these lesions; the abnormal venous structure is entered directly with a sheathed needle and then filled with contrast under fluoroscopic control (Fig. 60-36).[43] The lesion may be composed of a single irregular chamber or demonstrate multiple noncommunicating compartments.

When the capacity of the lesion is reached, opacification of small draining veins is typically observed, with eventual drainage into the normal venous system. This direct puncture technique has been extended into a therapeutic modality, as described below.

Treatment

As with any vascular malformation, cavernous venous lesions require treatment only if they are significantly symptomatic or disfiguring. Once the diagnosis is clear, patients can be reassured that these lesions generally change little over time and rarely bleed spontaneously. A more common problem is local pain due to distention of the lesion or superimposed thrombosis. The pain of distention can often be reduced by positioning or compression (e.g., support stockings or bandages). Local thrombosis is managed like any superficial phlebitis, with elevation, analgesics, and warm soaks. Anticoagulation is rarely indicated in this setting. On occasion, cavernous lesions may show the same type of progression at menarche and during pregnancy as is seen with other vascular malformations.

Figure 60-35. Diffuse cavernous venous malformation involving the hand. (A) Film from arteriogram shows normal-caliber arteries without shunting (uneven arterial filling not persistent).

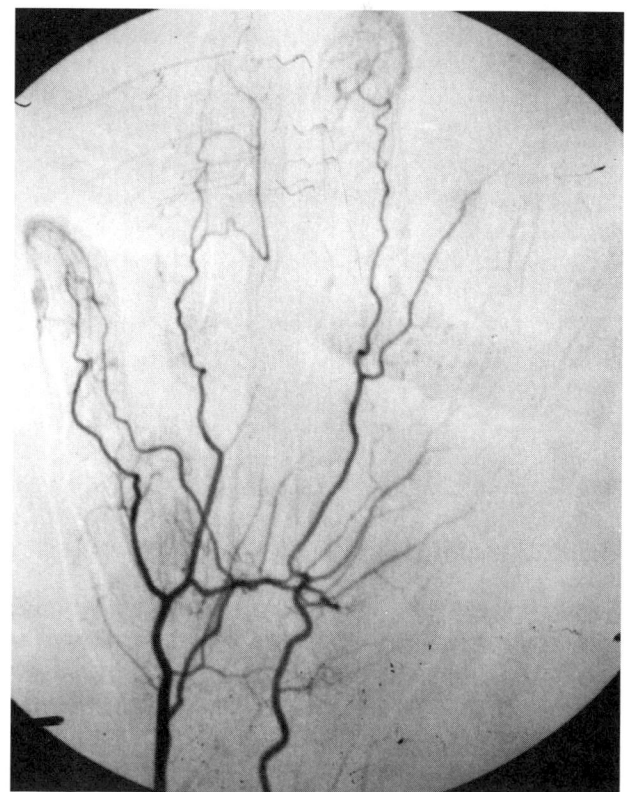

A

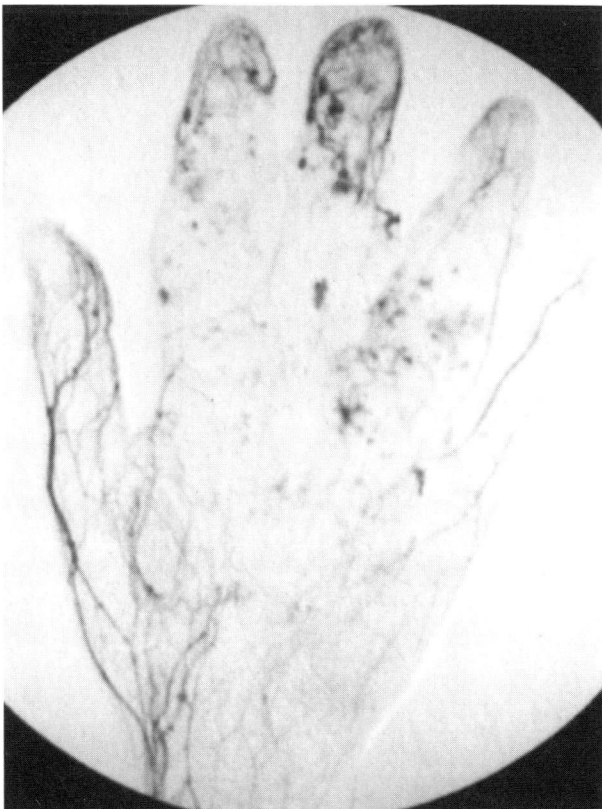

B

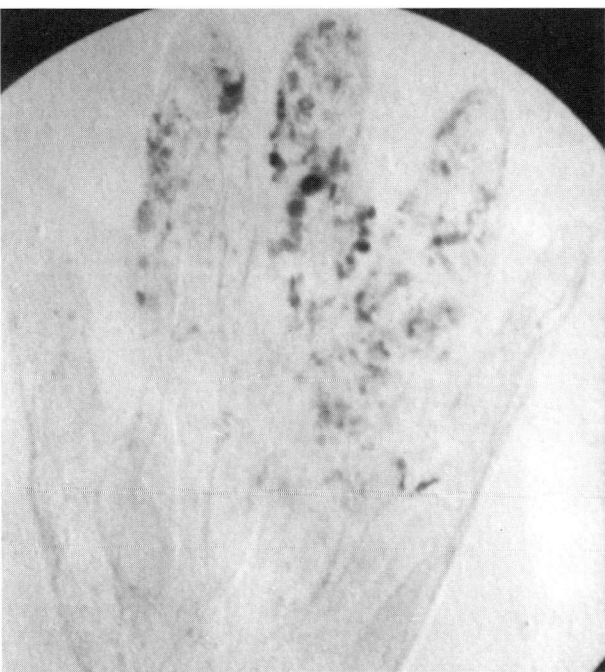

C

Figure 60-35 (continued). (B and C) Later phase films show slow filling of venous spaces, which remained filled for several minutes.

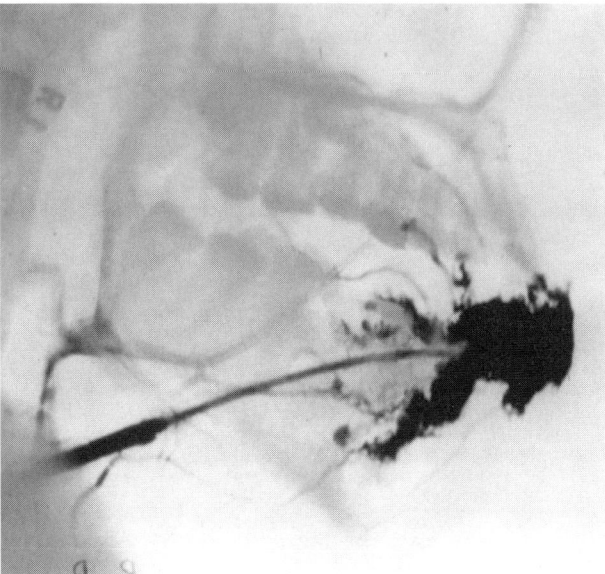

Figure 60-36. Direct puncture venography performed under anesthesia on a patient with a cavernous venous lesion of the lower lip (same patient as Fig. 60-34). Note filling of extensive irregular venous spaces with eventual filling of normal-caliber draining veins.

Complete surgical resection may be possible for localized lesions, but their true extent should first be carefully evaluated by imaging studies and direct puncture venography, since the visible component of the lesion may be only the "tip of the iceberg." Partial resections are generally associated with significant blood loss and a very high likelihood of recurrence.

Embolization of regional arterial branches in an effort to decompress these lesions was attempted in the past with little success (Fig. 60-37). The author often performs arteriograms during the initial evaluation to rule out an arterial component. This type of mixed lesion is uncommon but may benefit from combined arterial and venous embolization (Fig. 60-38).

Direct puncture embolization or sclerosis is a simple technique that has proven fairly effective in treating cavernous venous lesions. This is an extension of the closed space venography technique, involving direct puncture of the lesion using a sheathed needle inserted through the adjacent normal skin, usually under anesthesia (Fig. 60-39). Once venous blood return is observed, contrast is slowly hand-injected under fluoroscopic guidance until the capacity of the lesion is reached; this can be judged by observing small draining veins begin to fill from the periphery of the lesion toward normal regional veins. The lesion is then allowed to empty passively (active compression will often dislodge the catheter), after which the lesion is partially refilled with an opacified solution of 95 percent ethanol. Lesions with multiple noncommunicating

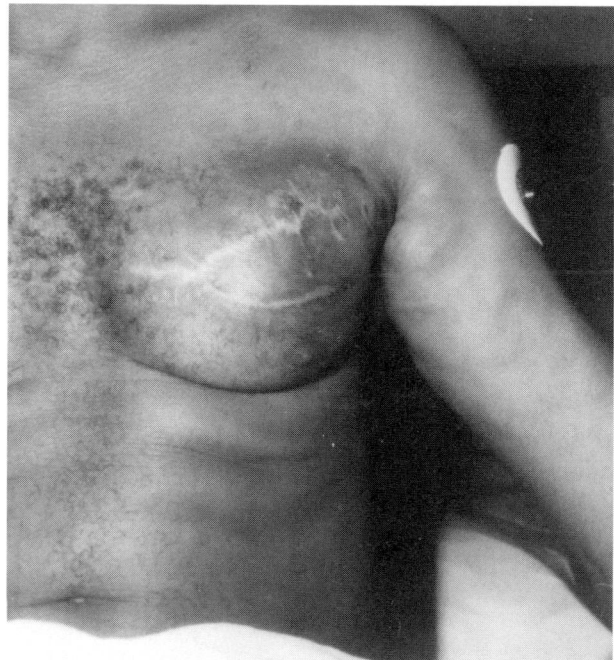

A

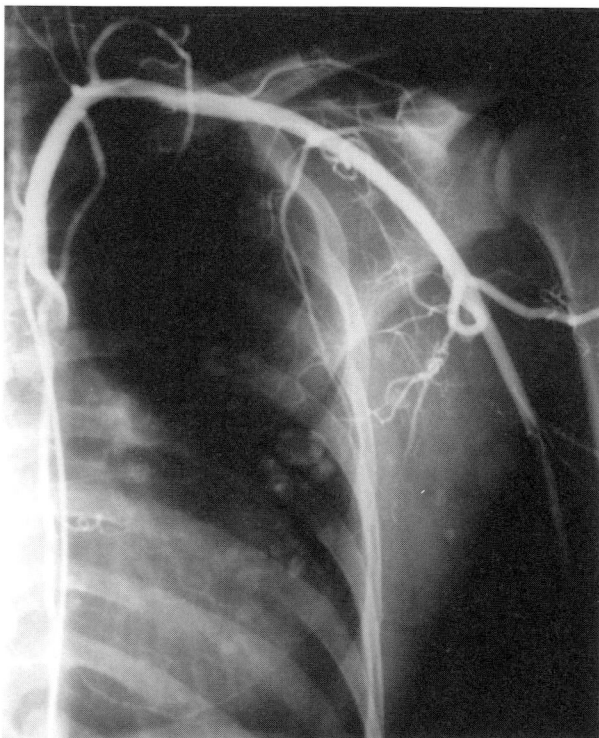

B

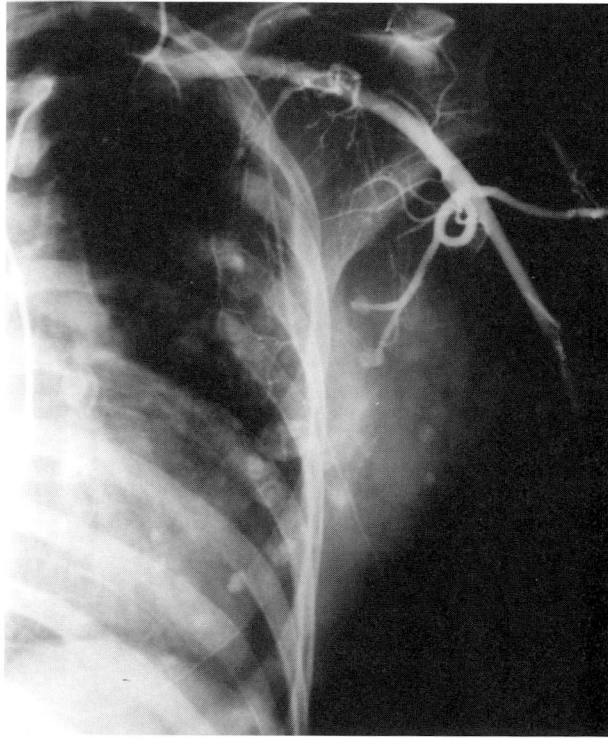

C

Figure 60-37. (A) A 25-year-old man with a large venous malformation involving the left chest wall and upper arm. Note the scars from previous unsuccessful attempts at surgical resection. (B) Left subclavian arteriogram demonstrates normal-appearing arteries in the region. Note the numerous scattered phleboliths typical of cavernous venous malformations. (C) Embolization of axillary artery branches was performed in an effort to reduce flow to the lesion, with virtually no clinical improvement. This approach has consistently proven ineffective.

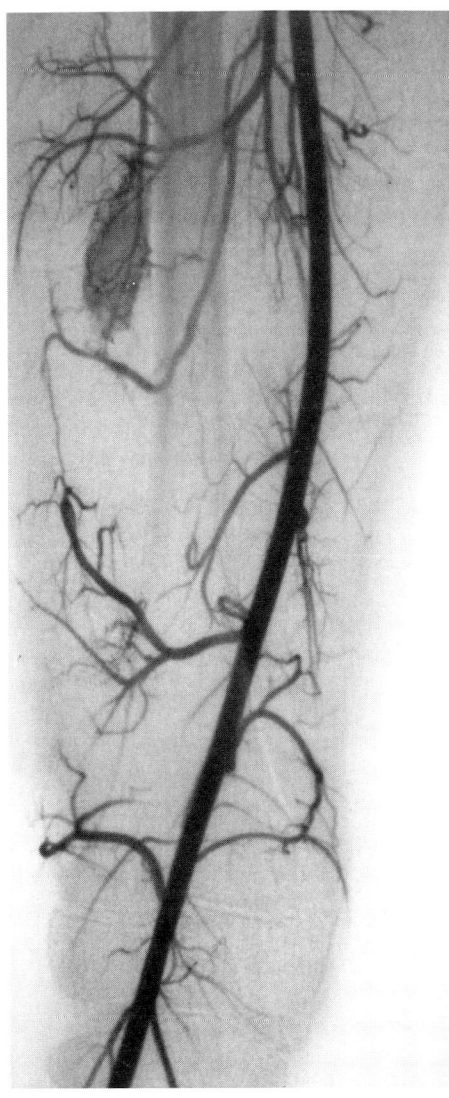

A

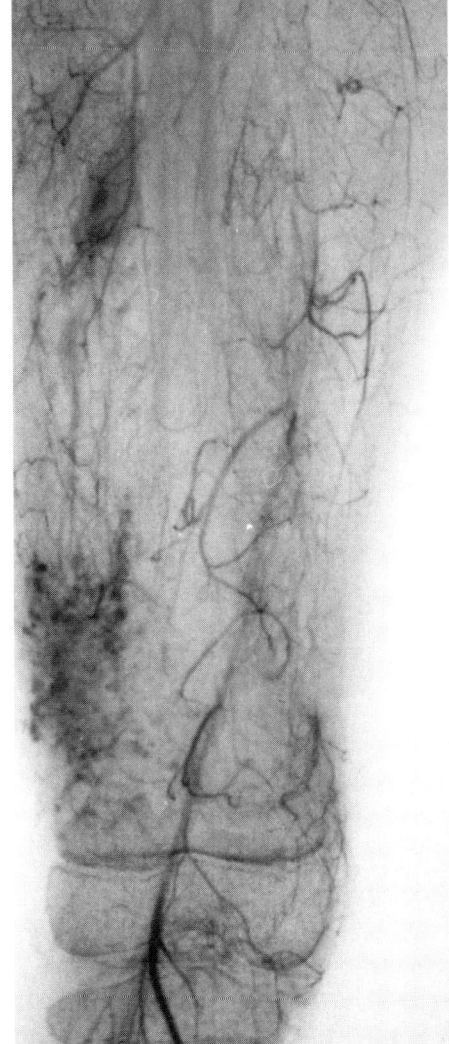

B

Figure 60-38. A 12-year-old boy with a mixed but primarily venous lesion of the right thigh. Early (A) and late phase (B) films show minimal shunting into the lesion from fairly normal caliber arterial branches. These branches were embolized, after which a direct puncture embolization of the venous spaces was performed with good results. Although these lesions are unusual, the author often performs initial angiography on apparently venous lesions to rule out an arterial component.

compartments will require multiple sites of injection. The alcohol is left in place, causing clotting of the blood and damage to the vascular endothelium lining the venous spaces. As thrombosis develops, the lesion will become enlarged and firm. A small amount of Avitene collagen suspension is injected along the tract as the catheter is withdrawn to prevent bleeding and tracking of alcohol to the skin surface, where it may cause ulceration. Signs of thrombosis (inflammation, pain, swelling) will persist for 2 to 3 weeks, and it will often require 6 to 8 weeks to observe shrinkage of the lesion. Depending on the size of the lesion, multiple treatments over time may be necessary, but the overall response has been favorable.

Klippel-Trenaunay Syndrome

Klippel-Trenaunay syndrome is probably the most frequent major venous malformation encountered clinically. The major components of the syndrome, first described in 1900, consist of (1) extensive venous varicosities usually involving a single limb, (2) hypertrophy of the entire limb, including bones and soft tissues, and (3) a large irregular birthmark over the

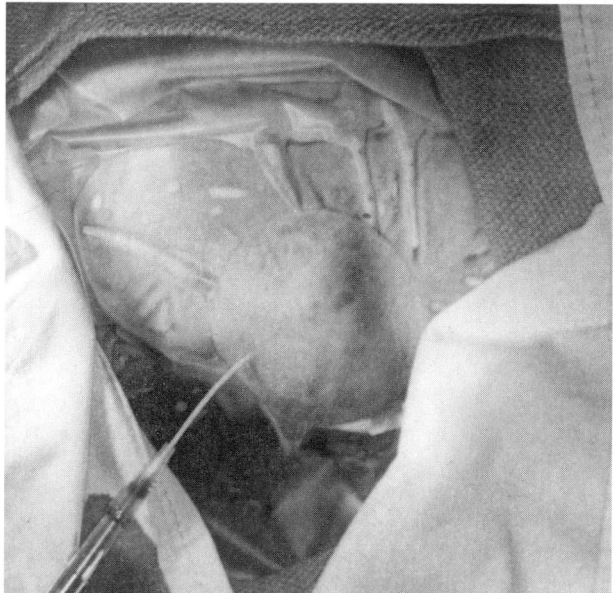

A

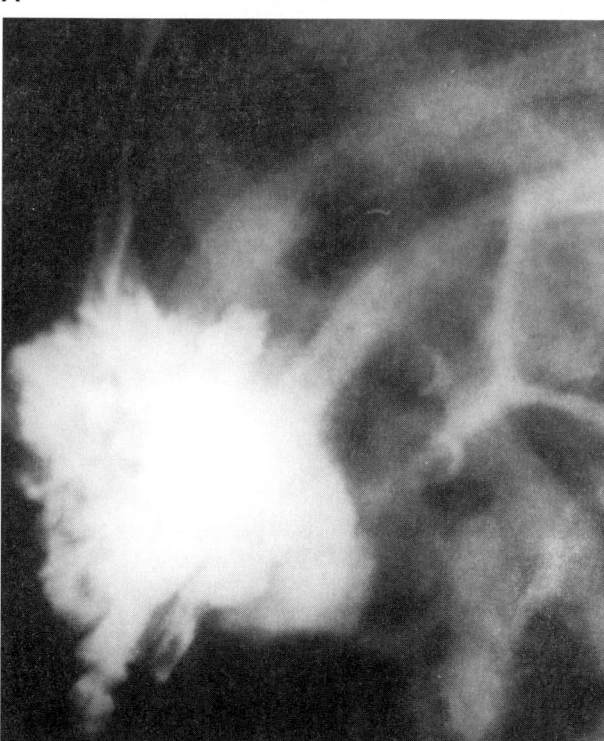

B

Figure 60-39. Direct puncture embolization of cavernous venous malformation is a fairly simple technique. (A) Under anesthesia, the lesion is entered through the adjacent normal skin using a sheathed needle. (B) Once blood return is obtained, the lesion is filled with contrast to determine its capacity. The contrast is then permitted to drain passively and the lesion is refilled with a smaller volume of opacified absolute ethanol under fluoroscopic control. The alcohol is left in place and the tract is occluded with collagen suspension as the sheath is withdrawn to prevent bleeding and tracking of alcohol to the skin surface.

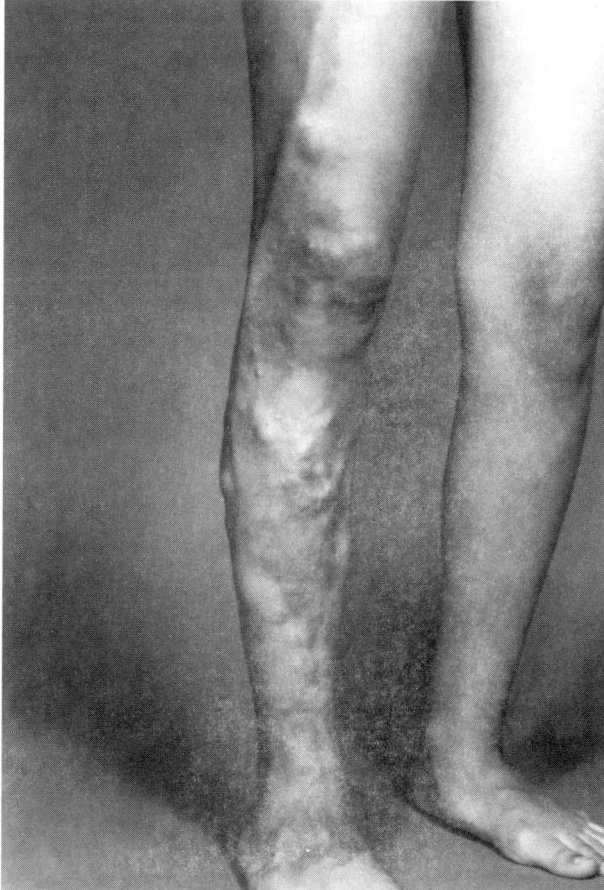

Figure 60-40. Typical findings of Klippel-Trenaunay syndrome, including unilateral leg hypertrophy, large irregular birthmark, and extensive varicosities.

affected extremity.[44] The vast majority of these cases involve the lower limb and are unilateral, a finding that suggests this diagnosis rather than simple varicose veins (Fig. 60-40). The varicosities are typically extensive and associated with changes of long-standing venous hypertension, including edema, skin thickening, ulceration, and often areas of superficial phlebitis.

Some of these patients demonstrate an anomalous or hypoplastic deep venous system on venography, often with marked hypertrophy of the varicose superficial veins, which must carry the bulk of venous return from the leg (Fig. 60-41). Most cases are confined to a single extremity, but there are severe cases that extend into the abdomen. Large cavernous spaces may occupy the entire retroperitoneum and may be associated with hematuria or gastrointestinal bleeding.[45] Plain films may show phleboliths scattered over a wide anatomic region in these patients (Fig. 60-42).

Unfortunately, there is little effective therapy for this condition other than conservative management.

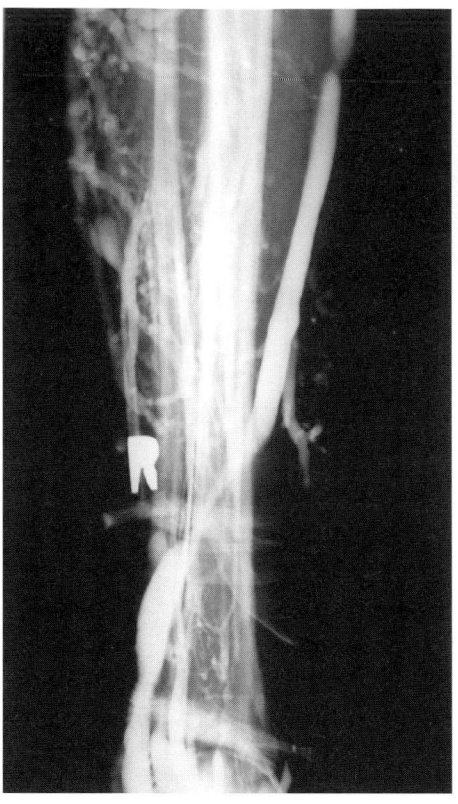

Although there have been reports of successful surgical treatment,[46,47] many patients actually get worse after these procedures. Because the primary problem may be hypoplasia of the deep venous system, removal of superficial veins may result in acute venous insufficiency with intractable leg swelling. Careful venographic evaluation should be performed before any invasive treatment, and only localized symptomatic veins should be stripped. Some of these patients also demonstrate associated cavernous venous lesions that may be amenable to direct embolization; aside from this, interventional techniques have little to offer in this syndrome.

A variant of Klippel-Trenaunay syndrome is the so-called Parkes Weber syndrome, which is clinically almost identical but on angiography demonstrates arteriovenous fistulas.[48] Some of these patients show significant improvement with embolization of these fistulous connections, often with dramatic decompression of the venous structures (Fig. 60-43). It is in or-

◄ **Figure 60-41.** Venogram of calf in patient with Klippel-Trenaunay syndrome demonstrates hypoplastic deep veins with venous return through anomalous superficial collaterals.

Figure 60-42. A 14-year-old boy with extensive Klippel-Trenaunay syndrome extending into the abdomen and retroperitoneum, associated with hematuria, rectal bleeding, and prolapsed hemorrhoidal veins. (A) Note the scattered phleboliths in the abdomen and pelvis. (B) Selective arteriograms showed no arterial abnormalities.

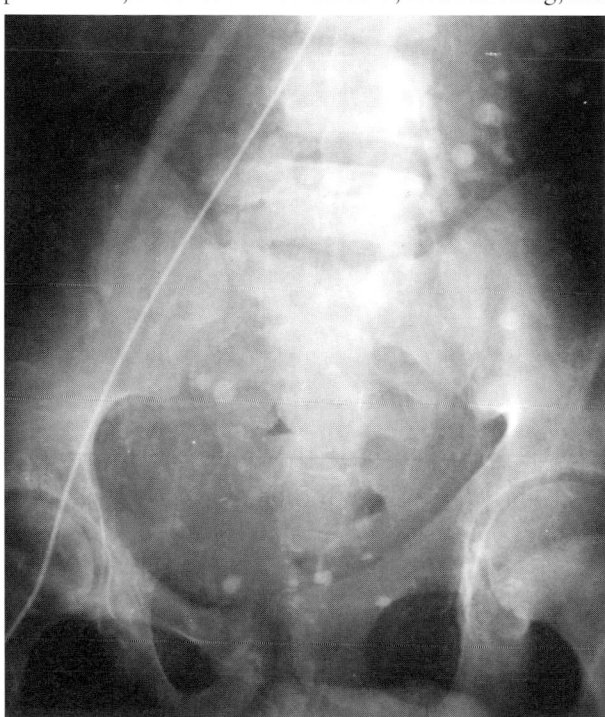

A

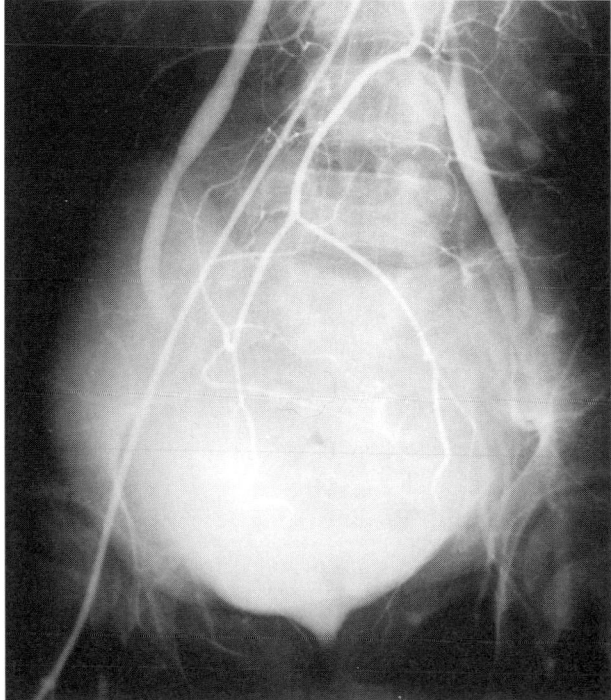

B

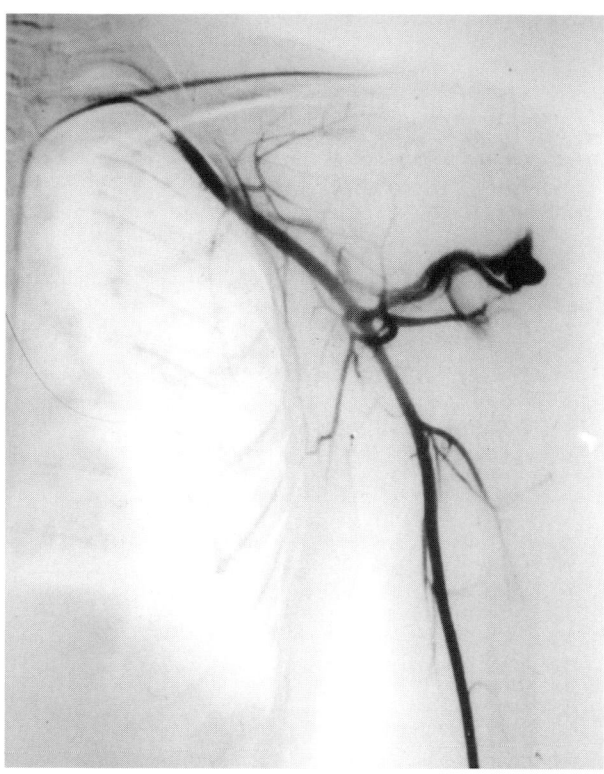

A

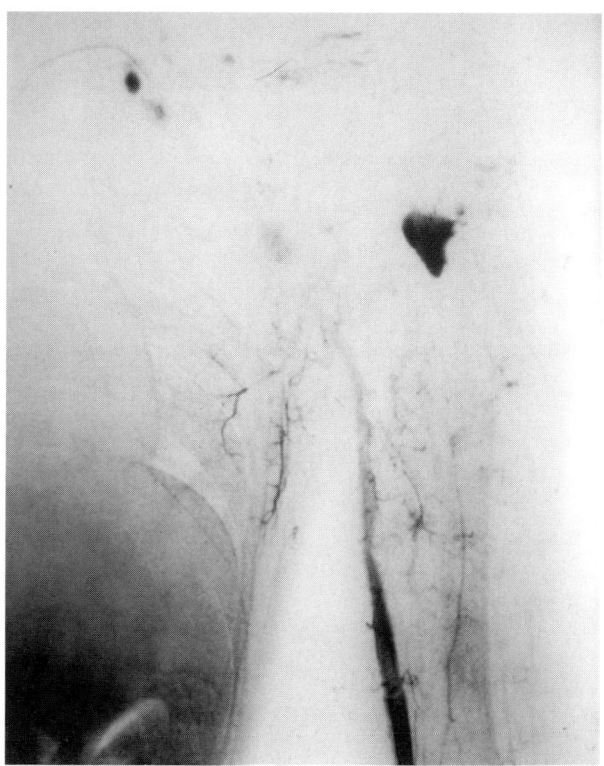

B

Figure 60-43. An 8-year-old girl with what appeared clinically to be a purely venous malformation involving the shoulder and upper arm. (A) Left subclavian arteriogram demonstrates an unexpected fistula from the axillary artery branch. (B) Later phase film demonstrates filling of cavernous venous spaces. This lesion is typical of Parkes Weber syndrome. (C) Embolization of the arterial component produced dramatic decompression and shrinkage of the lesion.

der not to miss these patients that the author performs an initial arteriogram on most patients with Klippel-Trenaunay syndrome.

References

1. Mulliken JB, Zetter BR, Folkman J. In vitro characteristics of endothelium from hemangiomas and vascular malformations. Surgery 1982;92:348.
2. Folkman J. Toward a new understanding of vascular proliferative disease in children. Pediatrics 1984;74:850.
3. Jacobs AH, Walton RG. The incidence of birthmarks in the neonate. Pediatrics 1976;58:218.
4. Margileth AM, Museles M. Cutaneous hemangiomas in children: diagnosis and conservative management. JAMA 1965; 194:523.
5. Pratt AG. Birthmarks in infants. Arch Dermatol 1967;67:302.
6. Berman B, Lim HWP. Concurrent cutaneous and hepatic hemangioma in infancy: report of a case and a review of the literature. J Dermatol Surg Oncol 1978;4:869.
7. Mulliken JB, Young AE. Vascular birthmarks in folk lore, history, art and literature. In: Mulliken JB, Young AE, eds. Vascular birthmarks, hemangiomas and malformations. Philadelphia: Saunders, 1988:114, 115.

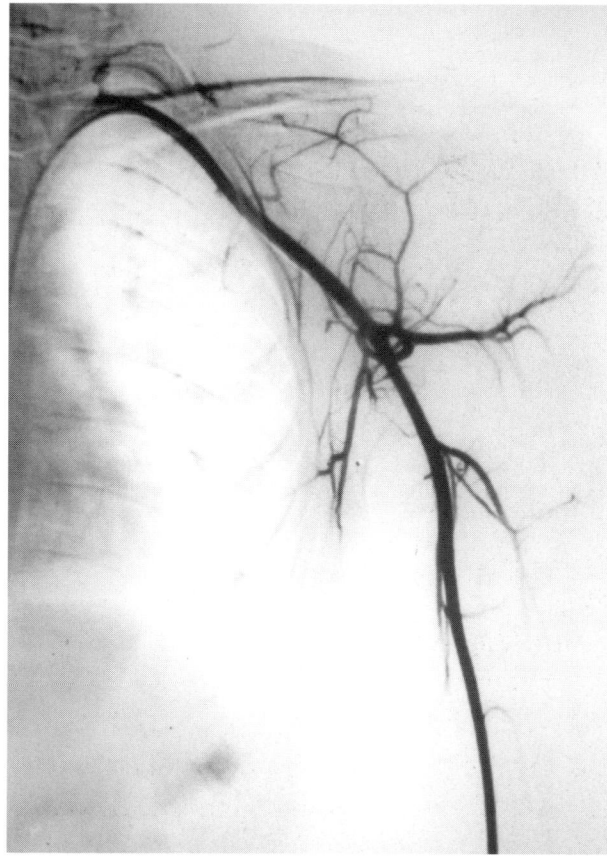

C

8. Greenspan A, et al. Imaging strategies in the evaluation of soft tissue hemangiomas of the extremities: correlation of the findings of plain radiography, angiography, CT, MRI and ultrasonography in 12 histologically proven cases. Skeletal Radiol 1992;21:8–11.

9. Zarem HA, Edgerton MT. Induced resolution of cavernous hemangiomas following prednisone therapy. Plast Reconstr Surg 1967;39:76.

10. Bartoshesky LE, Bull M, Feingold M. Corticosteroid treatment of cutaneous hemangiomas: how effective: a report on 24 children. Clin Pediatr (Phila) 1978;17:625.

11. Edgerton MT. The treatment of hemangiomas: with special reference to the role of steroid therapy. Ann Surg 1976;183:517.

12. Hurvitz CH, Alkalay AL, Sloninsky L, et al. Cyclophosphamide therapy in life-threatening vascular tumors. J Pediatr 1986;109:360.

13. Thomson HG, Ward CM, Crawford JS, Stigmar R. Hemangiomas of the eyelid: visual complications and prophylactic concepts. Plast Reconstr Surg 1979;63:641.

14. Stanley P, Grinnell VS, Stanton RE, et al. Therapeutic embolization of infantile hepatic hemangioma with polyvinyl alcohol. AJR 1983;41:1047.

15. Chuang VP, Wallace S. Hepatic artery embolization in the treatment of hepatic neoplasms. Radiology 1981;140:51.

16. Hunter W. The history of an aneurysm of the aorta, with some remarks on aneurysms in general. Med Observ Inq 1757;1:323.

17. Breschet G. Memoire sur les aneurysmes. Mem Acad R Med Paris 1833;3:101.

18. Brooks B. The treatment of traumatic arteriovenous fistula. South Med J 1930;23:100.

19. Bramann F. Arterio-venous aneurism. Arch Klin Chir 1986;33:1.

20. Blaisdell FW, Lim RC Jr, Hall AD. Revascularization of severely ischemic extremities with an arteriovenous fistula. Am J Surg 1966;122:166.

21. Shumacker HB Jr. The problem of maintaining the continuity of the artery in the surgery of aneurysms and arteriovenous fistulae: notes on the development and clinical application of methods of arterial suture. Ann Surg 1948;127:207.

22. Holman E. Arteriovenous aneurysm: clinical evidence correlating size of fistula with changes in the heart and proximal vessels. Ann Surg 1924;80:801.

23. Holman E. Arteriovenous aneurysm: abnormal communications between the arterial and venous circulations. New York: Macmillan, 1937.

24. Holman E. The anatomic and physiologic effects of an arteriovenous fistula. Surgery 1940;8:362.

25. Sumner DS: Hemodynamics and pathophysiology of arteriovenous fistulas. In: Rutherford R, ed. Vascular surgery. Philadelphia: Saunders, 1989:1007, 1015.

26. John HT, Warren R. The stimulus to collateral circulation, Surgery 1961;49:14.

27. Nicoladoni C. Phlebarteriectasie der rechten oberen Extremitat. Arch Klin Chir 1875;18:252.

28. Branham HH. Aneurismal varix of the femoral artery and vein following a gunshot wound. Int J Surg 1890;3:250.

29. Szilagyi DE, Elliot JP, DeRusso FJ, et al. Peripheral congenital arteriovenous fistulas. Surgery 1965;57:61.

30. Berenstein A, Kricheff I. Catheter and material selection for transarterial embolization: II. Materials. Radiology 1979;132:631.

31. Rutherford RB. Noninvasive testing in the diagnosis and assessment of arteriovenous fistula. In: Bernstein EF, ed. Noninvasive diagnostic techniques in vascular disease. St. Louis: Mosby, 1982:430–442.

32. Trout HH, McAllister HA, Giordano JM, et al. Vascular malformations. Surgery 1985;97:36.

33. Natali J, Jue-Denis P, Kieffer E, et al. Arteriovenous fistulae of the internal iliac vessels. J Cardiovasc Surg 1984;25:165.

34. Rosen RJ, Riles TS. Arteriovenous malformations. In: Strandness D, van Breda A, eds. Vascular diseases: surgical and interventional therapy. New York: Churchill-Livingstone, 1994:1126.

35. Tadavarthy SM, Moller JH, Amplatz K. Polyvinyl alcohol (Ivalon): a new embolic material. AJR 1975;125:609–616.

36. Lasjaunias P, Berenstein A. Technical aspects of surgical neuroangiography. In: Surgical neuroangiography. Berlin: Springer-Verlag, 1987, vol. 2.

37. Sasaki M, Tadokeoro S, Kimura S, Mori M, Kosula S, Tachibana M. Two cases of renal arteriovenous fistula treated by transcatheter embolization with absolute ethanol. Hinyokika Kiyo 1984;30:295–298.

38. Yakes WF, Haas DK, Parker SH, et al. Symptomatic vascular malformations: ethanol embolotherapy. Radiology 1989;170:1059–1066.

39. Kerber C. Intracranial cyanoacrylate: a new catheter therapy for arteriovenous malformation. Invest Radiol 1975;10:536–538.

40. Vintner V, Galil KA, Lundie MJ, Kaufmann JCE. The histotoxicity of cyanoacrylates. Neuroradiology 1985;27:279–291.

41. Rao VRK, Mandalam KR, Gupta AK, Kumar S, Joseph S. Dissolution of isobutyl 2-cyanoacrylate on long-term follow-up. Am J Neuroradiol 1989;10:135–141.

42. Markoff G, Quagliarello J, Rosen RJ, Beckman EM. Uterine arteriovenous malformation successfully embolized with a liquid polymer, isobutyl 2-cyanoacrylate. Am J Obstet Gynecol 1986;55(3):659–660.

43. Boxt LM, Levin DC, Fellows KE. Direct puncture angiography in congenital venous malformations. AJR 1983;140:135.

44. Klippel M, Trenaunay P. Du naevus variqueux osteohypertrophique. Arch Gen Med (Paris) 1900;3:611.

45. Servelle M, Bastin R, Lougue J, et al. Hematuria and rectal bleeding in the child with Klippel Trenaunay syndrome. Ann Surg 1976;183:418.

46. Servelle M. Klippel and Trenaunay's syndrome: 768 operated cases. Ann Surg 1985;201:365.

47. McCarthy R, Lytle J, Van Devanter S. The use of total circulatory arrest in the surgery of giant hemangioma and Klippel-Trenaunay syndrome in neonates. Clin Orthop Relat Res 1993;289:237–242.

48. Parkes Weber F. Haemangiectatic hypertrophy of the limbs: congenital phlebarterietasis and so-called congenital varicose veins. Br J Child Dis 1918;15:13.

61

Intraarterial Chemotherapy for Sarcomas

MICHAEL C. SOULEN

About 8000 sarcomas are detected annually in the United States, causing over 4000 deaths per year. Two thousand of these tumors arise in bone. The remainder arise mostly from mesodermal soft tissues anywhere in the body. Sixty percent of the soft tissue sarcomas are found in the extremities. Most sarcomas are sporadic, but occasionally they are associated with trauma, foreign bodies, chemical carcinogens, radiation, or genetic disorders such as neurofibromatosis, Gardner syndrome, certain gene mutations, or chromosomal abnormalities. A viral etiology exists for several animal sarcomas. Kaposi sarcoma is associated with viral infection in humans, but a specific mechanism for an oncogenic virus causing sarcomas in humans has not been elucidated.

The treatment and prognosis for these tumors depend on the grade, size, and site of the primary tumor. Sarcomas are classified histologically as low- or high-grade, with the high-grade tumors being more aggressive and therefore more likely to recur locally or distantly after resection of the primary tumor. Tumors larger than 5 cm have a worse prognosis than tumors smaller than 5 cm. Deep tumors lying close to vital neurovascular structures or organs, or violating anatomic compartments so as to prohibit wide excision, have a poorer outcome than superficially located tumors. The cell type of the sarcoma is of less prognostic importance, except for synovial sarcomas and rhabdomyosarcomas, both of which are typically very aggressive.

The initial assessment of grade, size, and location determines the type of therapy appropriate for an individual patient. Small, low-grade tumors are well treated by wide surgical resection when their location permits. Excision with a 2-cm-wide negative margin is usually curative. Large, high-grade tumors have a 50 percent recurrence rate after excision alone. For this reason, amputation was the treatment of choice for many years. However, although amputation provides excellent local control, it results in significant disability for patients, many of whom will go on to die from distant metastases anyway. Over the past 2 decades, a multimodality approach that combines surgery with adjuvant or neoadjuvant radiation therapy or chemotherapy has evolved. The goals of the multimodality approach are threefold: limb-sparing resection with preservation of function, prevention of local recurrence, and control of distant metastases.

Radiologic Staging of Sarcomas

To stage and plan multimodality therapy for sarcomas, one must assess the size and anatomic extent of the tumor relative to the affected tissue compartment, determine the involvement of adjacent neurovascular structures and regional nodes, evaluate for distant metastases, and histologically grade the tumor. Grading is determined by biopsy, and the remainder by magnetic resonance imaging (MRI) or angiography (MRA) or enhanced CT examination. CT examination of the chest and a bone scan complete the metastatic workup. Angiography is rarely required for diagnosis or staging.

Preoperative angiography is useful for large retroperitoneal or abdominal sarcomas when the organ of origin is uncertain and when one must assess for venous invasion.[1] Defining the blood supply to the tumor can help to distinguish a primary retroperitoneal mass from an adrenal or renal primary tumor. Retroperitoneal sarcomas are supplied by the lumbar arteries but can also be fed by branches of the celiac, mesenteric, and renal arteries. Retroperitoneal leiomyosarcomas can arise from the inferior vena cava (IVC) primarily (5 percent) or involve the IVC along with an extravascular mass (33 percent).

Primary and metastatic sarcomas of bone and soft tissue tend to be hypervascular, and a greater degree of hypervascularity correlates with higher histologic grade for some sarcomas. Preoperative angiography of extremity sarcomas is useful for planning intraarterial therapy and surgical resection.[2] Encasement of major vessels may require vascular bypass as part of the limb reconstruction or may preclude limb salvage surgery altogether. The patency of runoff vessels and of the palmar or pedal arches must be determined prior to resection of tibial or forearm arteries.

Limb-Sparing Resection of Extremity Sarcomas

Modern surgical techniques, including bone and neurovascular grafts, homologous and prosthetic joints, and vascularized plastic reconstructions, now permit resection with preservation of a functional limb in 85 to 95 percent of cases. Tumors that are high grade, larger than 5 cm, or lacking wide margins require adjuvant or neoadjuvant therapy to prevent local recurrence. Bulky tumors in particular may benefit from preoperative therapy, which can reduce tumor size and create better-defined planes between tumor and normal tissue.

Preoperative Radiation Therapy

Most series of soft tissue sarcomas have employed preoperative radiotherapy in the range of 40 to 50 Gy given in 200-cGy daily fractions, followed in some patients by a postoperative boost to a total of 60 Gy.[3] Local control is achieved in 70 to 100 percent of patients at 2 to 10 years, with tumor grade, size, and adequacy of margins being the major determinants of local recurrence. In most series local control is better than 90 percent, except for large tumors with poor margins.[4,5] The major problems with preoperative radiotherapy are wound complications and limb dysfunction due to fibrosis or radionecrosis. Wound complications occur in 16 to 40 percent of patients, about half of whom will require a second operation.[6,7] Secondary amputation or, rarely, death due to wound complications occurs in 1 to 7 percent of patients. Predictive factors for wound complications are preoperative radiation dose and size of excision. About 10 to 20 percent of salvaged limbs never regain function because of late effects of radiation.[8] Reducing the preoperative radiation dose decreases complications at the expense of local control.[9] In an effort to maintain local control, some centers have evaluated preoperative chemotherapy, either combined with reduced radiation doses or in place of preoperative radiation.

Preoperative Chemotherapy

Systemic chemotherapy has an established adjuvant role in the treatment of osteosarcomas, which have a strong propensity to metastasize to distant sites in spite of successful resection of the primary tumor. The benefit of adjuvant chemotherapy for soft tissue sarcomas is not as well established. Adjuvant chemotherapy may have a role in patients with more aggressive tumors. Some authors feel that patients who are intended to receive adjuvant chemotherapy may benefit from pre-operative (neoadjuvant) therapy.[9] This preoperative chemotherapy permits earlier initiation of systemic therapy without the customary delay for wound healing after surgery. In addition, blood supply to the periphery of the tumor is undisturbed, providing optimal delivery of chemotherapeutic drugs to the cells most likely to be responsible for local recurrence or dissemination during surgery. Tumor response may facilitate limb-sparing resection. The response of the primary tumor to preoperative chemotherapy predicts the sensitivity of subsequent metastases, and so helps in planning drug regimens for later treatment. Response is also strongly predictive of long-term survival. Patients with a poor pathologic response in their primary tumor to the preoperative chemotherapy have much worse long-term survival than patients with a good pathologic response, despite complete resection of the primary tumor.[10]

Unfortunately, response rates of sarcomas to systemic chemotherapy are only 15 to 30 percent, with relatively little tumor necrosis found on pathologic examination after resection. Moreover, responses tend to be slow, requiring multiple courses of chemotherapy over months with consequent delay of surgery. Preoperative administration of systemic chemotherapy has not significantly improved limb salvage rates. Experimental studies have shown that regional intraarterial delivery of chemotherapeutic drugs to the limb increases tissue concentrations by a factor of 4 to 10.[10,11] Cisplatin, doxorubicin, and 5-fluorouracil do not undergo significant first-pass extraction in the extremities, and so can be delivered regionally without sacrificing systemic levels. Transient balloon occlusion can increase local tissue levels by another order of magnitude.[11]

Intraarterial Chemotherapy for Osteosarcoma

At M.D. Anderson Cancer Center, 96 patients with osteosarcomas of the extremities were treated with intravenous (IV) doxorubicin (90 mg/m^2/96 hr) followed by intraarterial (IA) cisplatin (120–160 mg/m^2/2 hr).[12] Cycles were repeated monthly for an average of four treatments. The limb salvage rate increased from 8 to 80 percent with the use of regional therapy, and 68 percent of the tumors had 90 percent or more necrosis (Fig. 61-1). The local recurrence rate was only 6 percent, less than the local failure rate after amputation. Five-year disease-free survival was about 60 percent overall: close to 80 percent among patients with a good pathologic response (≥90 percent necrosis), but only 30 percent among patients with less than 90 percent tumor necrosis, despite the addition of high-

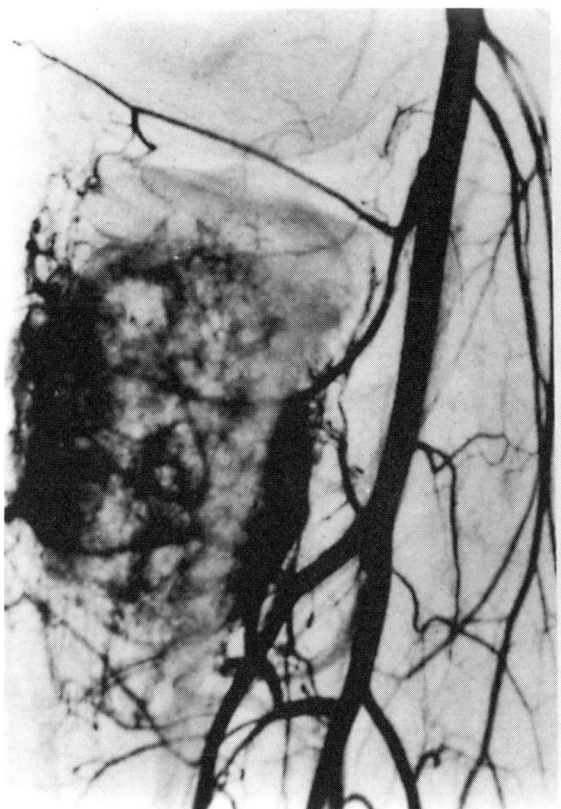
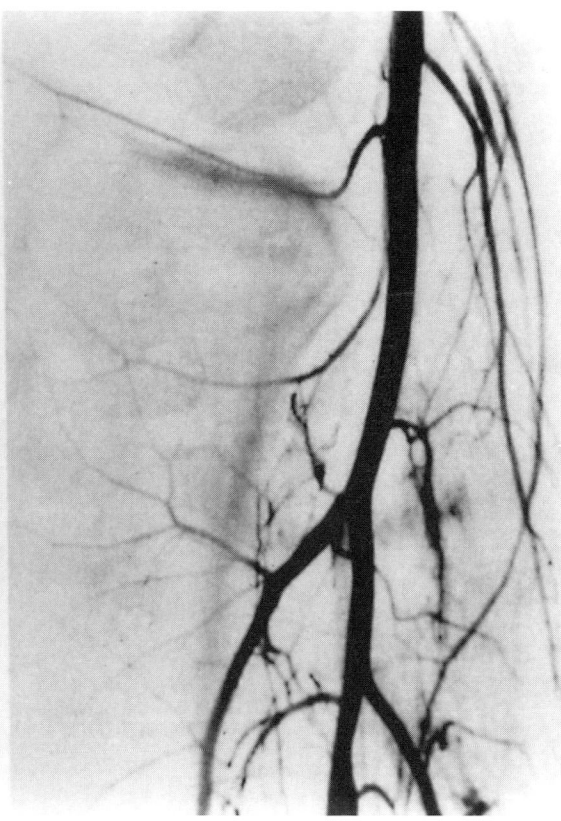

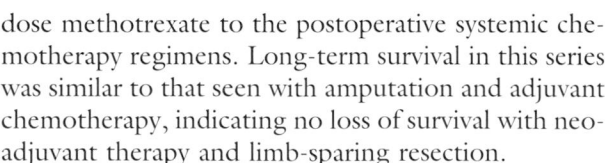

Figure 61-1. Popliteal angiogram before and after intraarterial chemoinfusion of a tibial osteosarcoma. (A) Pretreatment arteriogram shows marked tumor vascularity. (B) After two courses of chemoinfusion, the tumor stain is gone. The tumor was 99 percent necrotic at resection. (From Carrasco CH, Charnsangavej C, Raymond AK, et al. Osteosarcoma: angiographic assessment of response to preoperative chemotherapy. Radiology 1989;170:839–842. Used with permission.)

dose methotrexate to the postoperative systemic chemotherapy regimens. Long-term survival in this series was similar to that seen with amputation and adjuvant chemotherapy, indicating no loss of survival with neoadjuvant therapy and limb-sparing resection.

At the Istituto Rizzoli in Italy, 144 patients were treated with IV methotrexate (8 g/m²/6 hr), intravenous doxorubicin (60 mg/m²/8 hr), and intraarterial cisplatin (120 mg/m²/72 hr) for two cycles prior to resection.[13] All three drugs were continued systematically after surgery, with ifosfamide and VP-16 added for patients with a poor pathologic response. Limb salvage increased from 4 percent without preoperative therapy to 91 percent, with a local recurrence rate of only 1.5 percent. Seventy-eight percent of the tumors had 90 percent or more necrosis. Disease-free survival was over 80 percent at less than 3 years' median follow-up in this immature series.

At the University of California Los Angeles (UCLA),[14] 83 assorted skeletal sarcomas (57 osteosarcomas) were treated with 90 mg IA doxorubicin over 3 days followed by 3500 cGy in 10 fractions, and then resection 1 to 2 weeks later. Intravenous doxorubicin

and methotrexate were given postoperatively. Limb salvage was 100 percent, with two local recurrences (2.4 percent). Three-year survival for patients with osteosarcoma was 65 percent.

Kashdan et al.[15] delivered the entire preoperative dose of chemotherapy intraarterially (doxorubicin 80 mg/m² + floxuridine 5 mg/m² over 10 days, with two 120-mg/m² boluses of cisplatin on day 4 and day 10) for 1 to 2 cycles with resection 3 to 6 weeks later. All patients received adjuvant doxorubicin, methotrexate, vinblastine, actinomycin-D, and cyclophosphamide. Limb salvage was 89 percent, with a 4 percent local recurrence rate. Cumulative survival was 82 percent at 2 years. Improvement in resectability or tumor necrosis with the intensified and prolonged intraarterial regimen was not demonstrated in this small series.

Intraarterial Chemotherapy for Soft Tissue Sarcomas

Four series reported on the previously described UCLA protocol of 3 days of IA doxorubicin (90 mg/m²) followed by a reduced dose of preoperative radiotherapy (30–40 cGy) for large (>5 cm), high-grade soft tissue sarcomas.[14,16–18] Among 186 patients, limb salvage surgery was possible in 95 percent, with a 2 percent local recurrence rate, but wound complications remained high at 20 to 40 percent. Median survival ranged from 76 percent at 32 months to 58 percent at 56 months. At UCLA, reducing the preoperative radiation dose from 3500 to 2800 cGy in a subsequent series led to a decrease in wound complications from 35 to 20 percent and a decrease in secondary amputations from 6 percent to none.[9]

At the National Tumor Institute in Milan, Italy, 101 patients with large (mean 14 cm) soft tissue sarcomas were treated with IA doxorubicin 100 mg/m² over 8 to 9 days for two cycles and then resected.[19] Forty-five percent of these were patients with local recurrence after prior resection. Limb salvage was accomplished in 80 percent, but the local recurrence rate was 29 percent. This high rate largely reflected the high prevalence of inadequate margins in this series of very large, high-grade, and often recurrent tumors. Five-year survival was 54 percent.

Kónya and Vigváry[20] treated 51 patients with 129 short infusions (20–40 minutes) of cisplatin and doxorubicin that combined superselective infusion, chemoembolization, balloon occlusion-infusion, and tourniquet infusion. There were three complete responses. Two patients were excluded when they developed distant metastases while on the neoadjuvant protocol. Limb salvage was possible in 43 of the remaining 46 patients (93 percent). Recurrence and survival rates were not reported.

Soulen et al.[21] reported on 15 patients with very large (mean 15 cm), high-grade sarcomas treated with a prolonged multidrug IA chemotherapy regimen as outlined above for Kashdan's osteosarcoma series.[15] Limb salvage was achieved in 87 percent with no wound complications. Eleven of 15 tumors (73 percent) had 80 to 100 percent necrosis. Three-year survival was 67 percent. These limited series suggest that aggressive neoadjuvant chemotherapy can achieve limb salvage and local control rates similar to those reported with neoadjuvant radiation therapy but without the wound complications and limb dysfunction associated with radiotherapy.

Technique and Complications of Intraarterial Chemotherapy in the Extremities

The safe performance of regional chemotherapy requires attention to detail in catheter placement and careful daily examination of the patient by the interventional radiologist. Initial diagnostic angiography should be performed via an access remote from the affected limb—femoral for upper extremity tumors, contralateral leg for lower extremity tumors—to evaluate completely the arterial supply to the lesion. If no blood supply from proximal branches is detected to tumors arising distal to the knee or elbow, subsequent catheterizations can be performed ipsilaterally in an antegrade fashion to allow the patient greater mobility. An axillary or brachial approach has been used for lower extremity infusions to permit ambulation, but this technique increases the chance of catheter tip migration. Retrograde catheterization for ipsilateral infusion should not be performed because of the risk of catheter dislodgment.

Once the tumor's blood supply is mapped, a 4 to 5 French straight catheter should be placed as selectively as possible with its tip proximal to the most proximal branches feeding the tumor. Since patient motion due to drug-induced emesis is likely, the catheter must be secured as stably as possible, preferably in a location that permits a few centimeters of tip migration without jeopardizing the infusion. To avoid migration of the catheter tip into a side branch with resultant local toxicity, curved or angled catheter configurations should not be used unless absolutely necessary to achieve stable catheter positioning. Heparin-bonded catheters such as Anthron (Toray Industries, Tokyo) may help to minimize pericatheter thrombosis, though this has not been proven.

After catheter placement, patients with a femoral catheter should be placed at strict bed rest with the hips and knees straight. Systemic heparinization and daily monitoring of the activated partial thromboplastin time (PTT) are recommended by some authors to minimize arterial and venous thromboembolism. Although the benefit of heparin has not been rigorously proven, the risk of anticoagulation is low, and limb loss due to catheter-related arterial thromboembolism has been reported in the absence of adequate anticoagulation (see below). The catheterization site and the extremity being infused should be inspected daily. Some centers use periodic fluorescein injection and a Wood lamp to assess the territory infused by the catheter. Local erythema of the infused territory is normal, but focal painful myositis or dermatitis suggests migration of the catheter tip or streaming of the chemotherapy into a small branch vessel. If this occurs, the chemotherapeutic infusion should be halted immediately, since local toxicity can cause skin and tissue necrosis. Arteriography should be performed and the catheter repositioned. Catheters can be safely withdrawn and resecured but should never be advanced, since bacterial colonization of the catheter and tract can cause sepsis. If advancement or exchange of the catheter is required, a fresh puncture should be made. Use of a pulsatile infusion pump can improve mixing of the drugs with the blood and minimize streaming. The infused territory should be inspected, and the puncture site and the arterial and venous system of the catheterized and infused extremities should be examined daily for evidence of bleeding, catheter dislodgment, or thromboembolism.

Catheter-related complications increase with the duration of the infusion. In a series of 333 short (2- to 24-hour) cisplatin infusions, no catheter-related complications were reported.[22] Among series using a 3-day IA doxorubicin protocol, Eilber et al.[14] reported 2 arterial thromboses among 183 infusions. One was treated with thrombectomy, and the other led to amputation. No heparin was used in these patients. Wanebo et al.[18] reported 2 arterial thromboses among 60 infusions, both associated with inadequate anticoagulation. The outcome in these 2 patients was not reported. Kashdan and Soulen,[15,21] among a total of 73 prolonged ($\geq$10-day) multidrug infusions, reported 7 cases of arterial thrombosis requiring alteration of therapy. Five were treated with catheter removal followed by observation or prolongation of anticoagulation, 1 with thrombectomy, and 1 with thrombectomy and bypass. The bypass patient developed intractable gangrene requiring amputation. Both patients who required surgery had a subtherapeutic PTT. Twenty-four percent of 29 patients who had routine pullout arteriograms before catheter removal had small ($\leq$5 mm), nonocclusive, asymptomatic pericatheter or distal thrombi, irrespective of whether anticoagulation was therapeutic. Two additional patients developed deep venous thrombosis of the lower extremity despite therapeutic heparin infusions. Other complications included catheter dislodgment, catheter occlusion, focal skin necrosis due to local toxicity, fever requiring catheter removal, and hemorrhage remote from the catheterization site in patients who were anticoagulated and/or thrombocytopenic. Azzarelli et al.'s report of over 100 8- to 9-day IA doxorubicin infusions does not mention any complications.[19]

Intraarterial Therapy of Nonextremity Sarcomas

Sarcomas of the Axial Skeleton

Sarcomas arising in the pelvis or shoulder girdles are less amenable to resection with preservation of a functional limb, and are more likely to be unresectable than sarcomas arising in the extremities. Intraarterial chemoinfusion or chemoembolization can be performed either for palliation or to attempt to achieve sufficient tumor regression to permit resection. In small series employing IA cisplatin infusion or Gelfoam chemoembolization, often combined with systemic chemotherapy and radiotherapy, partial responses were seen in about half of patients and stabilization in most of the remaining patients.[23,24]

Gastrointestinal Sarcomas

Primary sarcomas of the gastrointestinal tract and abdomen are quite rare, and are best treated by resection. Intraarterial chemoinfusion or chemoembolization of unresectable tumors is possible if feeding vessels that are not also supplying the gut can be identified and superselectively catheterized (author's personal experience), but there is no broad experience with this technique.

Gastrointestinal and retroperitoneal sarcomas tend to metastasize to the liver. Liver metastases are treated by resection when possible. The response rates of unresectable metastases to systemic chemotherapy are relatively poor. Chemoembolization is a well-established technique for treatment of hepatoma and has been applied to a variety of liver metastases. Experience with metastatic sarcomas is limited because of the rarity of the disease. The hypervascular nature of these tumors suggests that they may be sensitive to arterially directed therapy. Two patients at M.D. Anderson Cancer Center had dramatic regression of hepatic metastases after a combination of chemoembolization and chemoinfusion.[25] The author has treated five patients using either cisplatin and Gelfoam or cisplatin/doxorubicin/mitomycin-C, iodized oil, and polyvinyl alcohol particles, with regression or stabilization in four. One became resectable for cure, with 60 percent necrosis in the resected specimen. Two patients were alive 2 years after chemoembolization. Two patients died, including the patient whose tumor did not respond and the final patient whose hepatic metastasis did respond but who died of extrahepatic metastases 6 months after chemoembolization.

Summary

Patients with sarcomas not amenable to cure by surgical resection alone because of the size, grade, or location of their tumor can benefit from preoperative therapy. In most of these patients, regional intraarterial chemotherapy permits limb-sparing resection with less morbidity than is associated with preoperative radiation therapy. Neoadjuvant chemoinfusion and limb salvage surgery enable patients to maintain a better quality of life than if they underwent amputation, with no detriment to local control or long-term survival. Regional infusion therapy requires scrupulous attention from the interventional radiologist to minimize complications.

References

1. Hartman DS, Hayes WS, Choyke PL, et al. Leiomyosarcomas of the retroperitoneum and inferior vena cava: radiologic-pathologic correlation. Radiographics 1992;12:1203–1220.
2. Mitty HA, Hermann G, Abdelwahah IF, et al. Role of angiography in limb-tumor surgery. Radiographics 1991;11:1029–1044.
3. Spiro IJ, Rosenberg AE, Springfield D, et al. Combined surgery and radiation therapy for limb preservation in soft tissue sarcoma of the extremity: the Massachusetts General Hospital experience. Cancer Invest 1995;13:86–95.
4. Wilson AN, Davis A, Bell RS, et al. Local control of soft tissue sarcoma of the extremity: the experience of a multidisciplinary sarcoma group with definitive surgery and radiotherapy. Eur J Cancer 1994;30A:746–751.
5. Pitcher ME, Fish S, Thomas JM. Management of soft tissue sarcoma. Br J Surg 1994;81:1136–1139.
6. Peat BG, Bell RS, Davis A, et al. Wound-healing complications after soft-tissue sarcoma surgery. Plast Reconstr Surg 1994;93:980–987.
7. Bujko K, Suit HD, Springfield DS, et al. Wound healing after preoperative radiation for sarcoma of soft tissues. Surg Gynecol Obstet 1993;176:124–134.
8. Keus RB, Rutgers EJT, Ho GH, et al. Limb-sparing therapy of extremity sarcomas: treatment outcome and long-term functional results. Eur J Cancer 1994;30A:1459–1463.
9. Huth JF, Eilber FR. Preoperative intraarterial chemotherapy. In: Pinedo HM, Verweij J, eds. Treatment of soft tissue sarcoma. Boston: Kluwer Academic Press, 1988:103–110.
10. Benjamin RS. Regional chemotherapy for osteosarcoma. Semin Oncol 1989;16:323–327.
11. Anderson JH, Gianturco C, Wallace S. Experimental transcath-eter intraarterial infusion-occlusion chemotherapy. Invest Radiol 1981;16:496–500.
12. Benjamin RS, Chawla SP, Carrasco CH, et al. Preoperative chemotherapy for osteosarcoma with intravenous Adriamycin and intra-arterial cisplatinum. Ann Oncol 1992;3(Suppl II):3–6.
13. Picci P, Bacci G, Ruggieri P, et al. The treatment of localized osteosarcoma of the extremities: the Italian experience. Ann Oncol 1992;3(Suppl II):13–18.
14. Eilber FR, Morton DL, Eckardt J, et al. Limb salvage for skeletal and soft tissue sarcomas. Cancer 1984;53:2579–2584.
15. Kashdan BJ, Sullivan KL, Lackman RD, et al. Extremity osteosarcoma: intraarterial chemotherapy and limb-sparing resection with 2-year follow-up. Radiology 1990;177:95–99.
16. Goodnight JE, Bargar WL, Voegeli T, et al. Limb-sparing surgery for extremity sarcomas after preoperative intraarterial doxorubicin and radiation therapy. Am J Surg 1985;150:109–113.
17. Hoekstra HJ, Koops HS, Molenaar WM, et al. A combination of intraarterial chemotherapy, preoperative and postoperative radiotherapy, and surgery as limb-saving treatment of primarily unresectable high-grade soft tissue sarcomas of the extremities. Cancer 1989;63:59–62.
18. Wanebo HJ, Temple WJ, Popp MB, et al. Combination regional therapy for extremity sarcoma: a tricenter study. Arch Surg 1990;125:355–359.
19. Azzarelli A, Quagliuolo V, Fissi S, et al. Intra-arterial induction chemotherapy for soft tissue sarcomas. Ann Oncol 1992;3(Suppl II):67–70.
20. Kónya A, Vigváry Z. Neoadjuvant intraarterial chemotherapy of soft tissue sarcomas. Ann Oncol 1992;3(Suppl II):127–129.
21. Soulen MC, Weissmann JR, Sullivan KL, et al. Intraarterial chemotherapy and limb-sparing resection of large soft-tissue sarcomas of the extremities. J Vasc Intervent Radiol 1992;3:659–663.
22. Carrasco CH, Charnsangavej C, Raymond AK, et al. Osteosarcoma: angiographic assessment of response to preoperative chemotherapy. Radiology 1989;170:839–842.
23. Marangolo M, Tienghi A, Fiorentini G, et al. Treatment of pelvic osteosarcoma. Ann Oncol 1992;3(Suppl II):19–22.
24. Fiorentini G, Dazzi C, Tienghi A. Chemofiltration and chemoembolization: new techniques in advanced pelvic bone malignancies. Ann Oncol 1992;3(Suppl II):37–38.
25. Mavligit GM, Zukiwski AA, Salem PA, et al. Regression of hepatic metastases from gastrointestinal leiomyosarcoma after hepatic arterial chemoembolization. Cancer 1991;68:321–323.

62

Percutaneous Large-Core Breast Biopsy

STEVE H. PARKER

The need for an effective, streamlined, diagnostic workup of breast problems becomes more critical as breast cancer screening becomes more commonplace and the consequent number of diagnostic breast biopsies increases. Incorporating percutaneous, automated, large-core breast biopsy into treatment allows for a complete breast lesion workup using the least financial and temporal resources.

The accuracy of stereotactic and ultrasound-guided core breast biopsy is at least equal to that of traditional localization and open surgical breast biopsy.[1-5] In addition, percutaneous core breast biopsy has significant advantages over surgical biopsy; no surgical scar will result from the biopsy, and no mammographic pseudolesion is left within the breast to confuse future interpretation. The biopsy can be set up and performed much more quickly than surgical biopsy, even the same day that the breast abnormality is detected. Because most (approximately 80 percent) breast biopsies result in a benign diagnosis, it makes little sense to perform an open surgical biopsy if a percutaneous biopsy is equally as accurate. If the patient does have breast cancer and a biopsy is performed using percutaneous core technique instead of surgery, she will frequently be spared the additional surgery of the initial diagnostic biopsy and can go directly to definitive therapeutic surgery. Furthermore, when a breast cancer is identified by percutaneous core biopsy, the surgeon performing the definitive therapeutic surgery has a much easier surgical field of operation. The surgeon does not have to operate on the distorted cavity created by a previous open surgical biopsy. Finally, when percutaneous core breast biopsy ultimately replaces open surgical breast biopsy, the potential cost savings for the United States are as large as 1 billion dollars per year.

The accuracy of the procedure depends on combining mammography, ultrasound, and interventional skills. Before an image-guided percutaneous large-core breast biopsy service is instituted, it is essential that the proper equipment and personnel are in place to ensure the appropriate workup and successful biopsy of suspicious breast lesions. High-quality mammography is essential, as is state-of-the-art breast ultrasound. Ideally, the radiologist performing the biopsies should have expertise in mammography, ultrasound, and interventional radiology. Radiologists who do not possess these fundamental skills will have difficulty successfully performing these procedures.

In addition to standard two-view mammography, spot-compression and magnification view capability are crucial for the appropriate mammographic problem solving that precedes biopsy. For mammographic biopsy guidance, the stereotactic images should be able to identify any lesion detected on a conventional mammogram. Recumbent dedicated stereotactic equipment is generally regarded as being better suited to large-core breast biopsy than adapted standard mammography or "add-on" units (Fig. 62-1). The recumbent stereotactic table can be raised, providing much more working room in and around the biopsy apparatus and x-ray tube than the "add-on" system can provide. Patient movement is rarely a problem with the recumbent unit, as opposed to the add-on unit, where patient movement can be responsible for a lesion miss. Also, with the recumbent approach, vasovagal reactions are virtually nonexistent, and the patient is not subjected to direct observation of the biopsy itself, as with the add-on. Lying on the table for long periods of time can be somewhat uncomfortable, however, and most patients find this worse than the actual biopsy. Digital, near-real-time stereotactic imaging combined with a motorized, automatic guiding device for the biopsy apparatus can reduce procedure time considerably and has partially remedied this problem.

With respect to adjunctive diagnostic measures, breast evaluation has been markedly improved with the relatively recent and significant improvements made in near-field ultrasound imaging. Older, conventional ultrasound equipment, however, cannot support the kind of decision making required for breast biopsy. It is critical to have state-of-the-art ultrasound equipment with high-frequency (7.5- to 10-MHz), electronically focused, linear array transducers

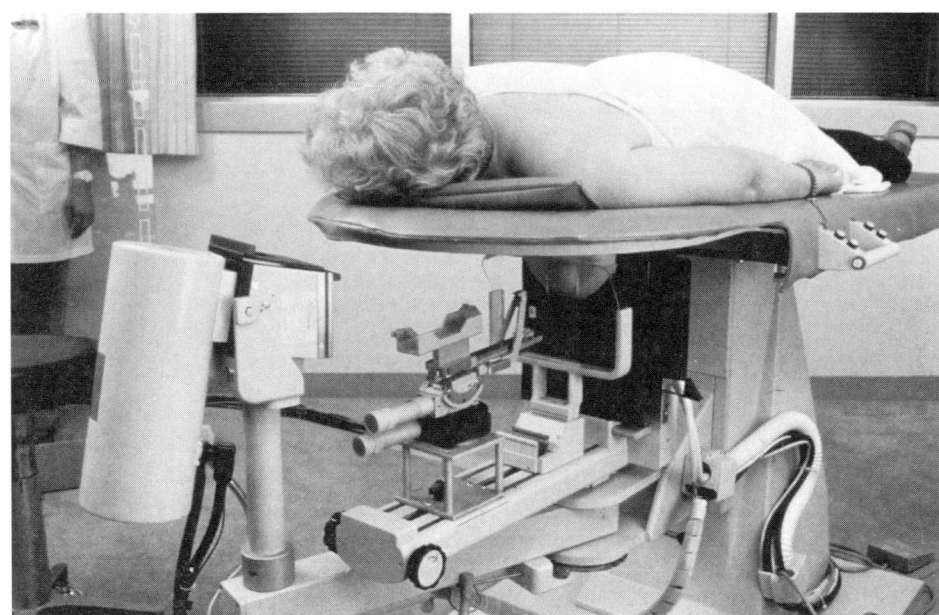

Figure 62-1. Dedicated prone stereotactic unit. These units eliminate the unwanted patient movement and vasovagal reactions common to the adapted standard stereotactic units.

configured specifically for breast imaging. The near-field resolution must be superb, with the ability to focus electronically with multiple focal zones in the first 5 to 20 mm. Older or less expensive equipment is not suitable for good breast ultrasound.

In addition to the appropriate imaging equipment for workup and biopsy guidance, large (14-gauge) needles are required to obtain surgical-quality tissue. Compared with the cytologic material obtained with fine-needle aspiration biopsy (FNAB) (Fig. 62-2), core biopsy provides histologic tissue that allows for a definitive diagnosis. For benign lesions this is especially important. Rather than the cytologic diagnosis of "no malignancy present," a definitive diagnosis such as intracanalicular fibroadenoma can be rendered (Fig. 62-3). Therefore, it is possible to differentiate between a false-negative diagnosis due to sampling error and a true-negative diagnosis such as fibroadenoma. This distinction frequently is not possible with FNAB. The possibility of a false-negative result haunts FNAB, and, as a result, surgical biopsy is frequently performed to confirm its benign nature. The patient and surgeon might understandably wonder in these instances whether the skinny needle missed the lesion or was in the lesion but failed to obtain adequate cells for diagnosis of a possible malignancy. This kind of uncertainty makes it difficult to substitute breast FNAB for surgical excisional biopsy and therefore places FNAB as another additional layer of cost and testing on top of surgical excisional biopsy. This clouded diagnostic situation is remedied with core histology.

By obtaining more definitive malignant diagnoses with the core tissue (Fig. 62-4), the patient can confidently be counseled regarding the therapeutic options, and therefore the therapeutic procedure can be rationally decided on. This is especially true for differentiating in situ from invasive carcinoma. If the cancer is found on the permanent-section core histology to be invasive, then the patient can be appropriately counseled regarding lumpectomy versus mastectomy. If the patient opts for lumpectomy, then the lymph node dissection can be done at the same time, reducing the number of surgeries from two to one. If the patient opts for mastectomy, this can confidently be performed without the need for frozen section confirmation and its attendant drawbacks. In addition, if an extensive intraductal component coexists with the infiltrating carcinoma, this can likewise be targeted and diagnosed on large-core biopsy. Armed with this refined information, the therapy team is generally more aggressive in the treatment plan.

The large-core technique not only allows for more definitive benign and malignant diagnoses but also eliminates several drawbacks of FNAB: the significant insufficient tissue rate, the need for a pathologist or cytotechnologist to attend the biopsy, and the need for a cytopathologist to interpret the sample.[5-8]

It is equally important that the core tissue be obtained with an automated, large-core biopsy device to realize the fruits of the efforts expended on pinpoint image guidance. The rapid excursion of the needle with this equipment allows for accurate sampling of

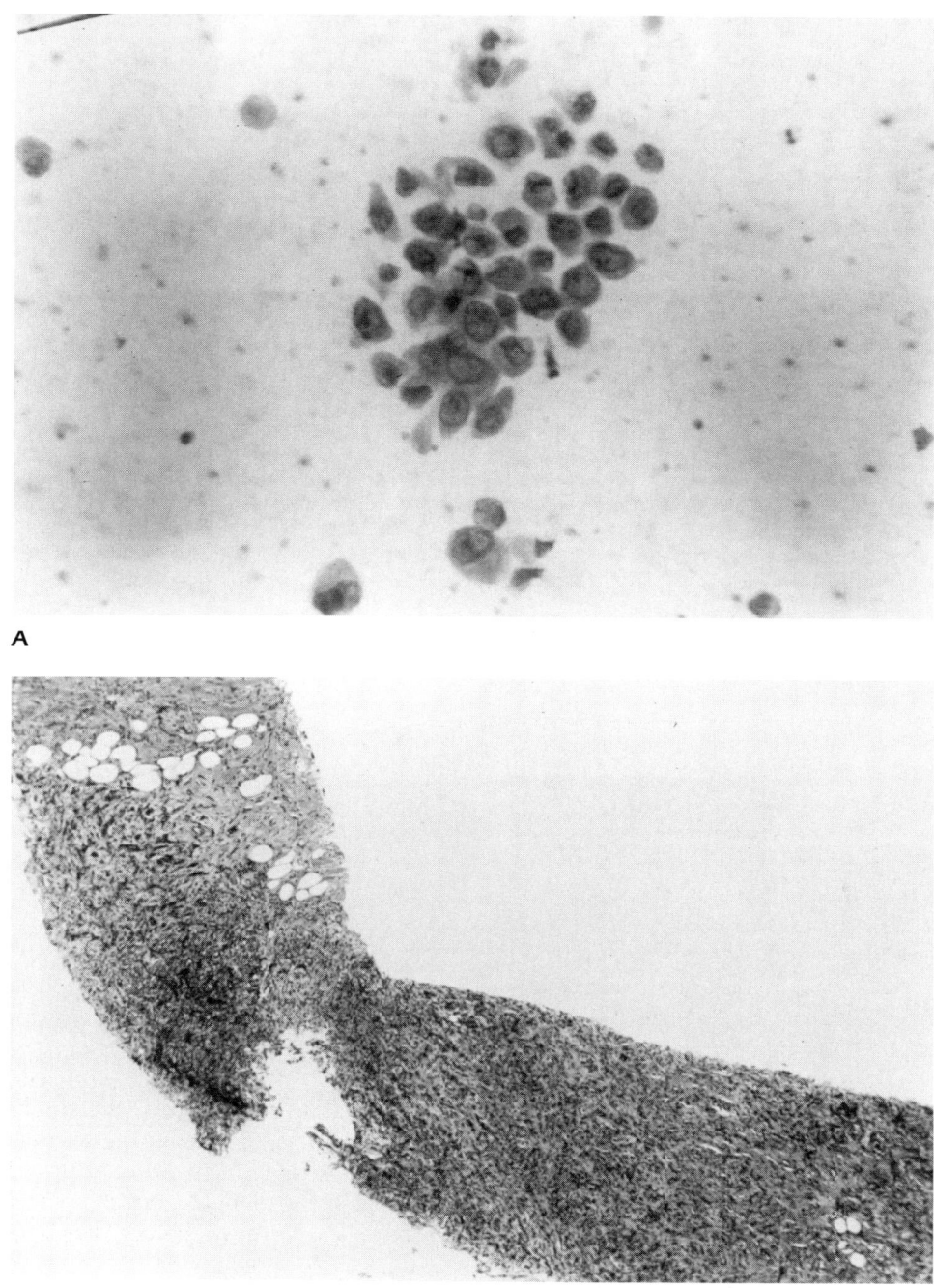

A

B

Figure 62-2. Comparison of cytology from FNAB with histology from core biopsy. (A) Cytology smear showing malignant cells, but it is impossible to determine whether the cancer is invasive or in situ. (B) Core histology demonstrates a definitive diagnosis of infiltrating ductal carcinoma.

mobile breast lesions such as fibroadenomas before they have the opportunity to slip out of the path of the needle. In addition, patient discomfort is minimized and there is little or no crush artifact compared with manual core biopsy techniques. These samples are of much higher quality than samples obtained with conventional manual "tru-cut" needles.[7]

The indications for large-core breast biopsy, with ultrasound or stereotactic guidance, are essentially the same as for surgical biopsy. In addition, because needle core biopsy is less traumatic and is as accurate as surgical biopsy, patients with less suspicious lesions are considered if physician concern or patient anxiety is high. Compared with surgical biopsy, image-guided percu-

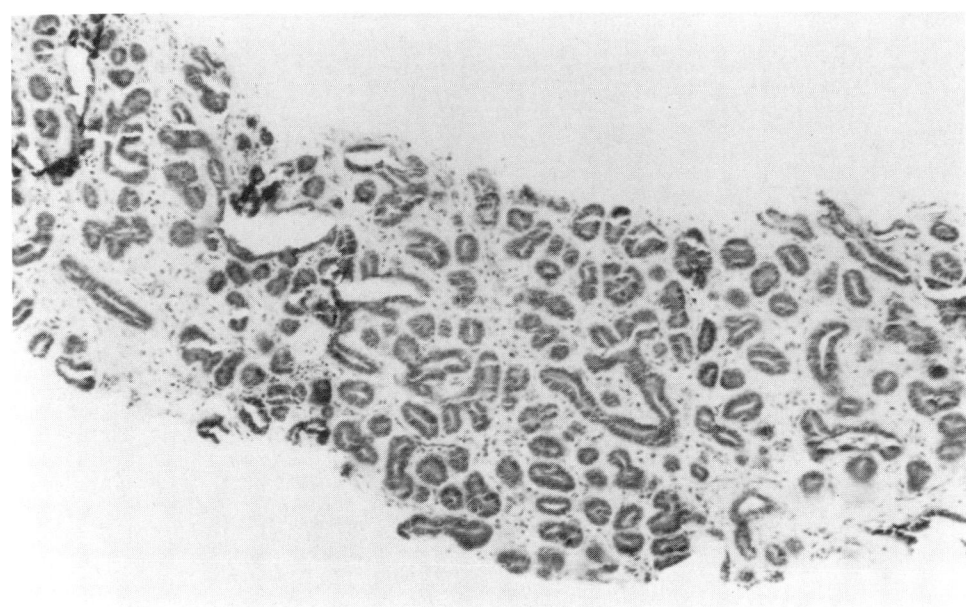

Figure 62-3. Example of benign core histology. Core biopsy specimen demonstrates an unequivocal diagnosis of a pericanalicular fibroadenoma. No surgery is required.

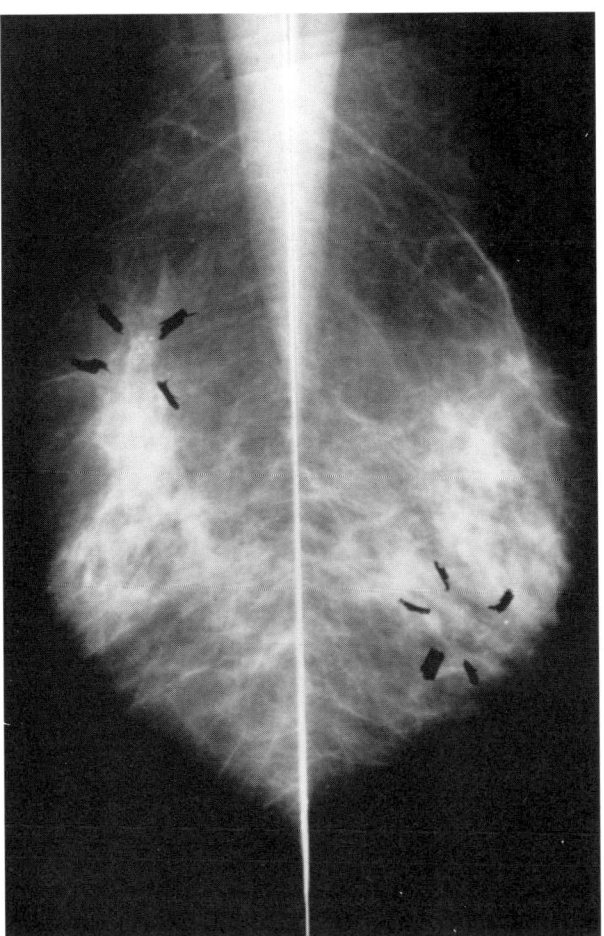

taneous biopsy is especially useful in patients with lesions seen well in only one projection, in patients with multiple lesions in one or both breasts, and in patients with questionable lesions after surgical biopsy or lumpectomy. In the sequence leading up to the decision to biopsy, any and all clinical or mammographic areas of suspicion must be thoroughly evaluated.

High-quality ultrasound is especially important in evaluating mammographically dense breasts where there is an area of clinical concern and in better characterizing mammographically detected lesions that are still unclear after appropriate mammographic workup. Ultrasound guidance is uniquely suited for lesions seen only on ultrasound and for patients who are nursing. In addition, if the lesion is seen well on both ultrasound and mammography, ultrasound guidance is preferred because it is quicker, is less uncomfortable for the patient, and produces no ionizing radiation.

If ultrasound verifies that a suspicious lesion is a

◄ **Figure 62-4.** Bilateral breast calcifications. Both areas were stereotactically core-biopsied. The histologic diagnosis of infiltrating ductal carcinoma was obtained from the lesion in the lower aspect of the right breast, and a diagnosis of degenerated fibroadenoma was made from the cores obtained from the upper left breast lesion. Thus appropriate treatment planning could be carried out for the right breast lesion and the left breast lesion could be dismissed. (From Parker SH. Percutaneous breast biopsy. New York: Raven, 1993. Used with permission.)

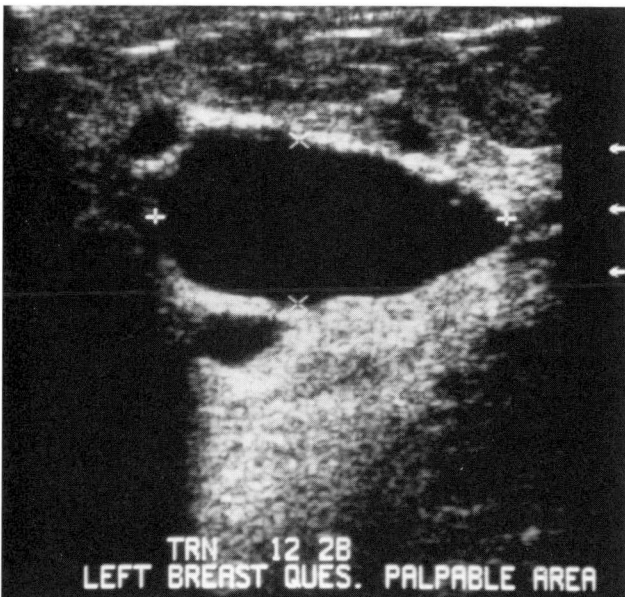

A

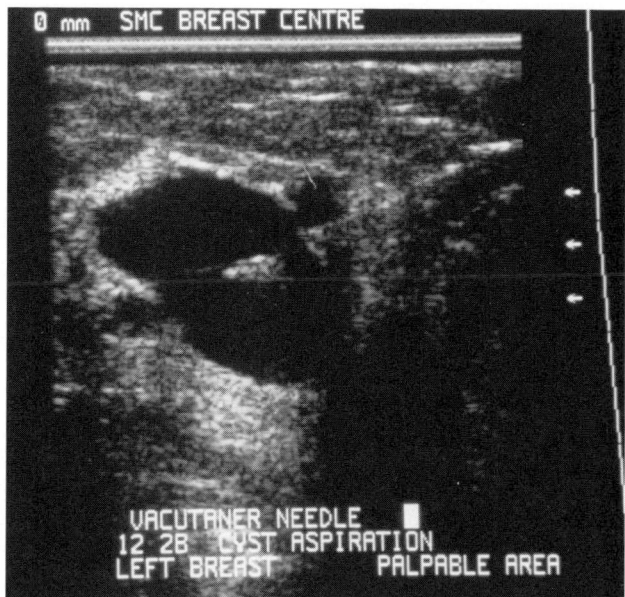

B

Figure 62-5. Cyst aspiration. (A) Symptomatic cyst as seen on ultrasound. (B) Ultrasound image showing 21-gauge vacutainer needle within cyst before vacuum of red top tube is activated. (C) Ultrasound image showing resolution of cyst subsequent to vacuum activation.

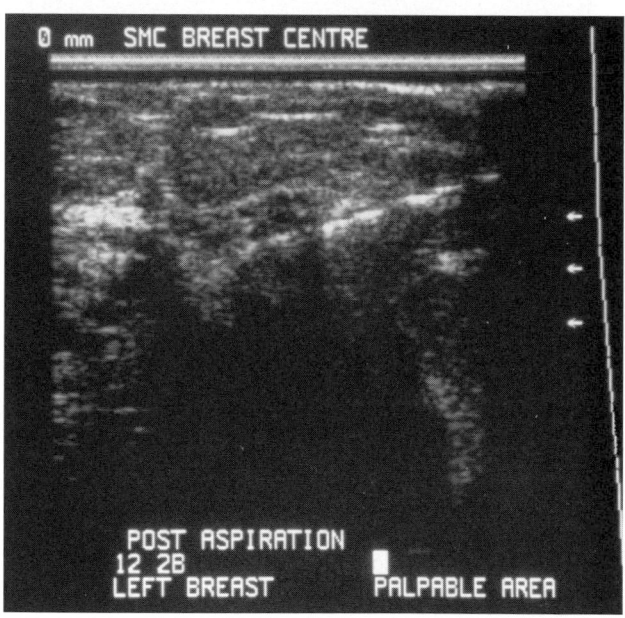

C

nonpalpable, simple cyst, it can be safely left alone. If the cyst is palpable and/or symptomatic, it can be aspirated easily using ultrasound guidance (Fig. 62-5). In cysts with questionable mammographic findings, a postaspiration mammogram can be performed to demonstrate that the mammographic lesion has resolved. There is generally no need to send the fluid from a simple cyst for analysis.

Complex cysts are aspirated for two reasons. First, there is a small but real chance that a complex cyst is associated with malignancy and that the fluid obtained may contain malignant cells. Second, solid lesions are occasionally mistaken for complex cysts. Being unable to aspirate a presumed complex cyst suggests that the lesion is solid, and the radiologist can then proceed with ultrasound-guided core biopsy.

In questionable ultrasound cases, verification that the lesion represents the suspicious mammographic lesion can be made by placing a 25-gauge hypodermic needle or retractable hook-wire needle into the lesion under ultrasound guidance. A postlocalization mammogram is then performed to prove unequivocally that the lesion seen on ultrasound is the same as that seen on mammography. The lesion can then be biopsied using ultrasound guidance.

When it comes to the actual biopsy, the interventional skills of the radiologist are especially empha-

sized. The first step in stereotactic biopsy is to take a straight craniocaudal or mediolateral scout film. Two 15-degree off-axis stereotactic views are exposed side by side on a single film (Fig. 62-6A). The biopsy gun is then locked into place in its dedicated housing. The stereo views are placed on the adjacent digitizer, and the coordinates are calculated by activating a handheld computer "mouse" at the center of the lesion and at reference crosshairs in each view. This process is performed on the computer monitor when using a stereotactic unit configured with digital imaging. Older units print out the lesion coordinates, which must be

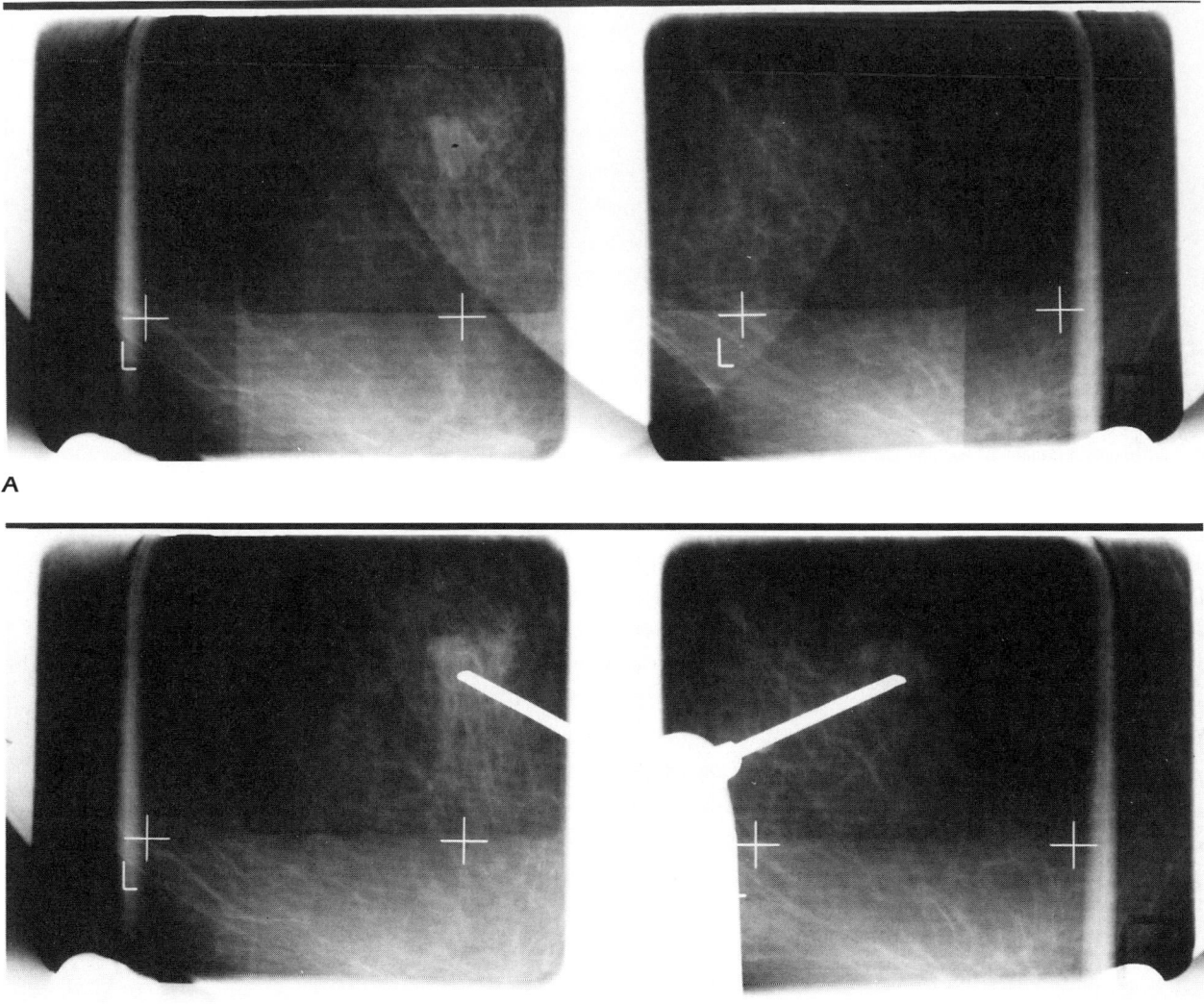

A

B

Figure 62-6. Stereotactic biopsy. (A) Stereotactic scout views of lesion with intended biopsy sites marked on the film. (B and C) Pre- and postfire views showing position of the needle to be slightly low (anterior). (D) Second postfire view after retargeting demonstrates the needle traversing the center of the lesion. The remainder of the cores could then be taken without further stereotactic images required.

manually dialed into the biopsy holder. Units with an "autoguide" place the coordinates automatically in the memory of the remote control panel attached to the main unit. The biopsy gun and needle automatically align on the proper trajectory with the push of a button.

After a small amount of local anesthetic is instilled, the gun and needle are advanced to the designated depth and stereo views are repeated to confirm the position of the needle (see Fig. 62-6B). After the gun is fired, a final set of stereo views is obtained to document that the needle has traversed the lesion (see Fig. 62-6C and D). At least five passes are made to obtain representative samples throughout the lesion. For calcification cases, a minimum of 10 cores are obtained to thoroughly canvass the region. A magnified specimen radiograph is then obtained to verify that some of the target calcifications are included in the cores. Stereotactic units equipped with digital imaging provide a faster verification of the adequacy of biopsy. A stereo pair of images can be performed after the requisite cores have been obtained to determine if some of the calcifications have been removed. Also, small pockets of air noted throughout the region of biopsy are an additional verification of the adequacy of the complete canvasing of the region. A specimen radiograph is still performed, but the patient can be released from the table before this "formality" is completed.

As a result of the need for multiple, time-consuming core acquisitions, a new device, the Biopsys Mam-

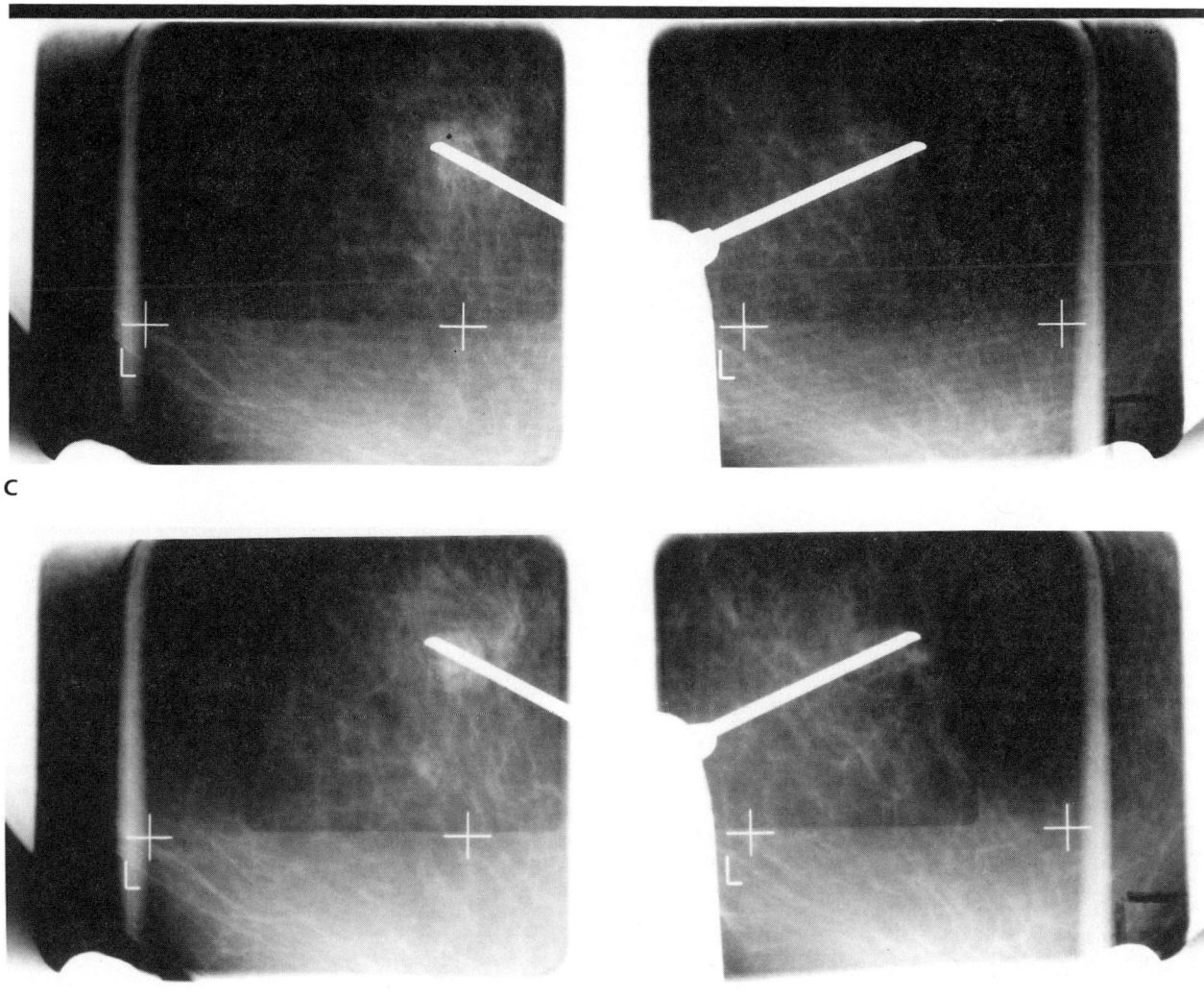

C

D   **Figure 62-6** (continued).

motome, has been introduced that allows a greater amount of breast tissue to be harvested in a much shorter amount of time. (Fig. 62-7). The mammotome probe consists of an outer hollow tube with a piercing tip. Just proximal to the piercing tip is an aperture with vacuum holes opposite the aperture. Within the outer hollow tube is positioned a hollow cutter with a sharpened end. The cutter rotates at high speed as it is advanced across tissue that has been pulled into the probe via the vacuum. The cutter is then withdrawn (while the outer portion of the probe remains within the breast) to a "specimen collection chamber," where a knock out pin pushes the specimen out the end of the cutter. This process can be repeated as many times as desired with or without rotating the probe aperture to a new "o'clock" position.

Because the conventional biopsy gun technique requires the acquisition of ten or more of the conventional cores and up to an hour or more of the radiolo-

gist's time, the mammotome's faster technique is a great help. With the mammotome, larger samples are obtained through the same size skin opening as is made by a 14-gauge core needle. Because the mammotome probe does not have to be removed from the breast after each sample acquisition, the radiologist can complete the requisite acquisition of tissue in approximately half the time as is necessary for the automated core technique. In addition, because there is contiguous tissue acquisition with the mammotome, the likelihood of sampling error should be greatly decreased.

The same protocol for biopsy described above is used for ultrasound-guided biopsy except that ultrasound is used for the image guidance portion. The free-hand technique for ultrasound-guided biopsy is preferred; that is, the radiologist holds the transducer in one hand and the biopsy needle in the other (Fig. 62-8). In this way, the transducer and needle can be more easily coordinated without the constraints of a

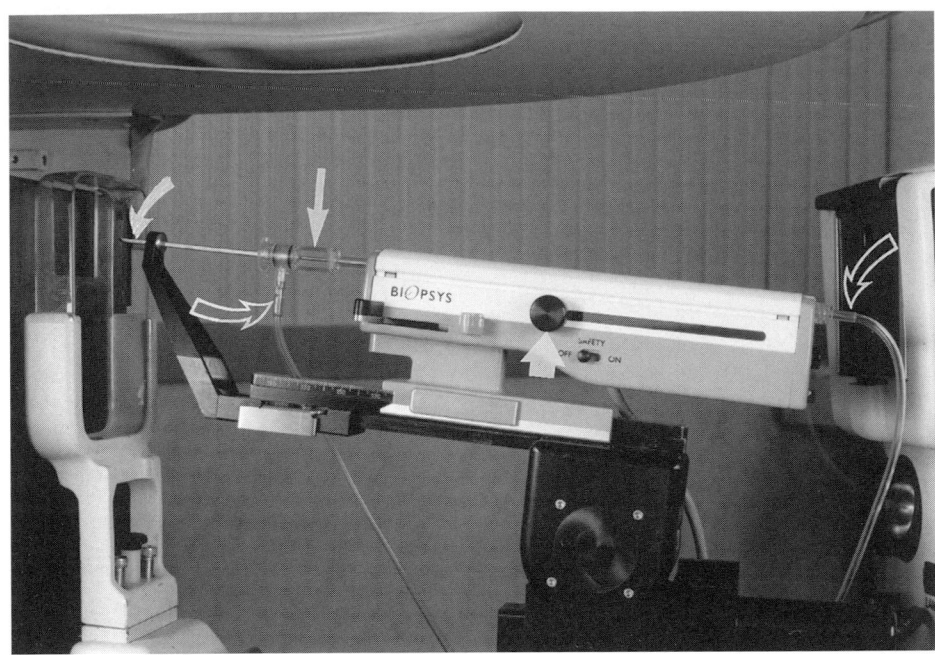

Figure 62-7. The Biopsys Mammotome. The probe is placed within or near a breast lesion and the lesion is pulled through the aperture (*curved arrow*) and into the probe using vacuum (*open arrows*). The inner rotating cutter is then advanced using the side-mounted knob (*arrowhead*). Tissue is consequently captured within the cutter and the cutter is withdrawn to the specimen chamber (*straight arrow*), while the probe itself remains stationary within the breast.

needle guide attached to the transducer. Using the free-hand technique, the needle is advanced to and fired through the lesion under real-time ultrasound observation. Continuous observation also ensures avoidance of the chest wall. Pre- and postfire images are obtained to document the needle and sample

Figure 62-8. Ultrasound biopsy. The "free-hand" technique is preferred, whereby the radiologist holds the transducer in one hand while guiding the needle with the other. (From Parker SH. Percutaneous breast biopsy. New York: Raven, 1993. Used with permission.)

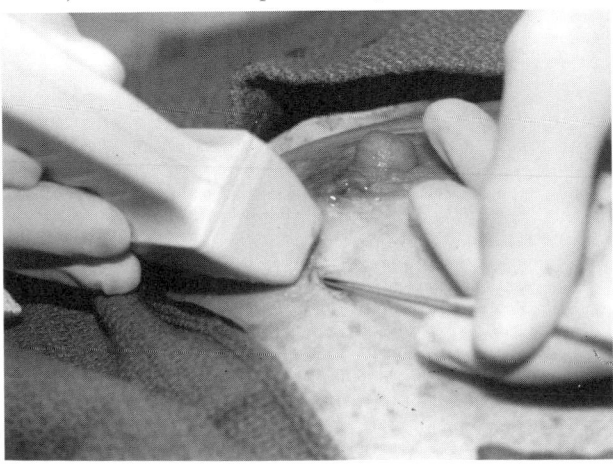

notch passing through the lesion (Fig. 62-9). In over 4000 patients biopsied with ultrasound and stereotactic percutaneous large-core technique, none experienced significant hematoma or other complication.

In conclusion, because the breast is one of the few areas of the body still subjected to open surgical biopsy and surgical biopsy has some shortcomings, it is important to try to identify an alterantive to surgical excisional biopsy. In recent years, improved needle and imaging techniques have allowed percutaneous needle biopsies to replace open surgical biopsy in most other areas of the body. Excisional biopsy, however, is still considered by many to be the current standard in the breast. Most radiologists who have attempted to extend percutaneous biopsy to breast lesions have used FNAB. Although somewhat successful in other areas of the body, FNAB has its greatest failings in the breast. On the other hand, the combination of large-core automated biopsies and pinpoint imaging provided by stereotactic mammography and ultrasound can provide reliable, definitive histologic diagnosis of both benign and malignant breast lesions, thus providing a dependable alternative to surgery. With an accuracy similar to or better than surgical biopsy but with less psychological and physical discomfort and a cost one-half to one-fourth that of surgical biopsy, large-core breast biopsy should prove a cost-effective,

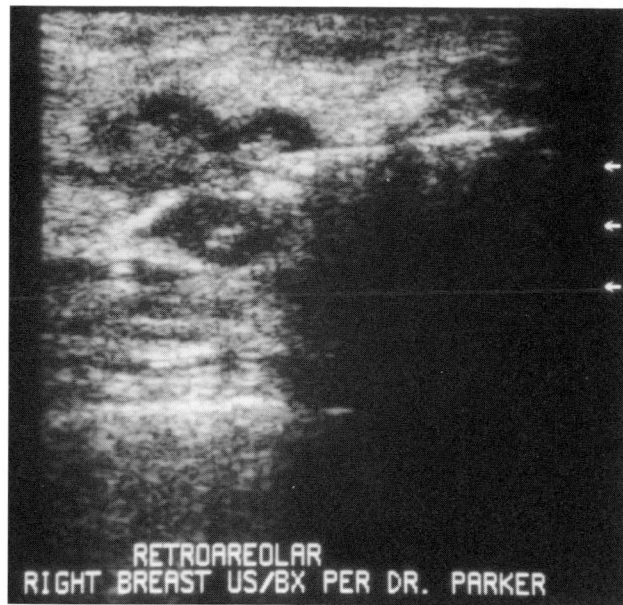
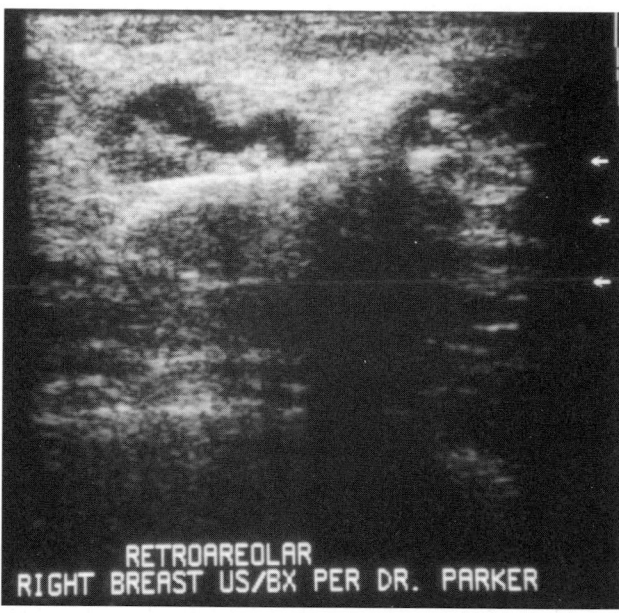

A　　　　　　　　　　　　　　　　　　　　**B**

Figure 62-9. Ultrasound biopsy. Images of the 14-gauge needle before (A) and after (B) activation of the biopsy gun. The histologic diagnosis was infiltrating ductal carcinoma.

reliable, and expedient alternative to surgical biopsy. Success with this procedure, however, requires a radiologist who is well trained and experienced in mammography, ultrasound, and especially interventional techniques.

References

1. Norton LW, Zeligman BE, Pearlman NW. Accuracy and cost of needle localization breast biopsy. Arch Surg 1988;123:947–950.
2. Parker SH, Lovin JD, Jobe WE, et al. Nonpalpable breast lesions: stereotactic automated large-core biopsies. Radiology 1991;180:403–407.
3. Parker SH, Jobe WE, Yakes WF, et al. US-guided automated large-core breast biopsy. Radiology 1993;187:507–511.
4. Elvecrog E, Lechner M, Nelson M, et al. Computer-guided stereotaxic large-core needle biopsy of the breast. Radiology 1992; 185(P):112.
5. Meyer JE. Value of large-core biopsy of occult breast lesions. AJR 1992;158:991–992.
6. Dronkers DJ. Stereotaxic core biopsy of breast lesions. Radiology 1992;183:631–634.
7. Parker SH, Hopper KD, Yakes WF, et al. Image-directed percutaneous biopsies with a biopsy gun. Radiology 1989;171:663–669.
8. Parker SH, Lovin JD, Lobe WE, et al. Stereotactic breast biopsy with a biopsy gun. Radiology 1990;176:741–747.

63

Venous Thrombolysis and Stenting

PAUL C. LAKIN

Obstruction of the superior and inferior vena cava (SVC, IVC) and their major branches may be caused by a variety of both benign and malignant pathologic conditions. Trauma, inflammatory lesions, and radiation may result in perivascular fibrosis. Neoplastic masses may either directly compress or invade major venous structures. In addition, indwelling catheters or local trauma may result in venous obstruction. Thrombosis may convert a partial obstruction into a venous occlusion. With the obstruction of major venous structures, various congestive syndromes may arise, depending upon the location of the obstruction, resulting in the IVC or SVC syndrome or severe hepatic dysfunction.

Percutaneous interventional therapy is extremely useful in treating obstructions of large veins and frequently restores the patency of the vein while reversing the congestive symptoms. Since surgical repair or bypass of obstructed venous structures, particularly in malignant obstructions, is frequently difficult or impossible, interventional therapy is crucial in these patients and frequently provides effective long-term palliation in malignant obstructions. In benign obstructions, when conventional anticoagulation therapy is not effective, surgery may also be difficult, and percutaneous interventional therapy may provide long-term patency. Three interventional modalities can be used for the treatment of venous obstruction: local thrombolytic therapy, percutaneous transluminal angioplasty, and expandable stent placement. Although these modalities may be used alone, they are most often used in combination.

In the past, the vast majority of central venous obstructions were due to malignant obstruction.[1] However, with the increased use of central venous catheters, the incidence of benign obstruction has increased. Since the appropriateness and type of intervention depend more on the underlying disease process than on the location of the stenosis, this chapter discusses the treatment of central venous obstruction on the basis of the underlying disease process rather than on the basis of anatomic location alone.

Thrombolysis

Historical Overview

Initially, thrombolytic agents were used systematically. Porter et al.[2] demonstrated the efficacy of systemic streptokinase in the treatment of patients with acute deep vein thrombosis. Systemic streptokinase and urokinase were also used for the treatment of subclavian vein thrombosis associated with transvenous pacers.[3] However, the large doses of lytic agents required and the concomitant risk of complication resulted in poor clinical acceptance. Becker et al. in 1983 described the use of local thrombolytic therapy for subclavian and axillary vein thrombosis.[4] The perfusion of lytic agents directly into the thrombus using a catheter position in or near the offending clot resulted in excellent initial results and in all cases demonstrated an underlying venous abnormality. Other reports followed with similar results.[5,6] With the increased availability of urokinase and its improved efficacy and safety,[7,8] venous lytic therapy became more accepted. In addition, the availability of angioplasty balloons and stents to treat the underlying venous abnormality propelled venous intervention to its current status.

General Principles

Like arterial thrombolysis, venous thrombolysis is best performed by the transcatheter regional infusion of thrombolytic agent directly into the area of involvement. This allows a higher concentration of the thrombolytic agent to reach the thrombus and thus results in more rapid lysis of the thrombus as well as reduced hemorrhagic complications when compared to systemic infusion. In patients with SVC and/or subclavian occlusions, one or two catheters should be placed using the femoral, transjugular, or peripheral upper extremity approach. After venography, a guidewire should be advanced through the thrombus with an appropriate multi-side-hole infusion catheter positioned with the side holes aligned within the thrombus. Because of the demonstrated increased margin of safety and efficacy, the author prefers urokinase.[7] Initially a modified pulse-spray technique is used that infuses 250,000 IU of urokinase into the thrombus over a 15-minute period. This dose may be increased to 500,000 IU depending on the thrombus bulk. If significant residual thrombus remains, the patient is returned to the hospital room and infusion thrombolysis is continued at the rate of 120,000 IU per hour through each catheter for a combined infusion rate of 240,000 IU per hour over 4 hours in a dosage regimen similar to that described by McNamara and Fischer.[9] After approximately 4 hours, the patient is restudied and the dosage is adjusted downward to a total infusion rate of 60,000 to 120,000 IU per hour. The patient is then restudied in 8 to 12 hours. All patients are treated systemically with heparin. After an initial loading dose of 5000 units of heparin, the patient is placed on a dose sufficient to maintain the partial thromboplastin time (PTT) at approximately 1.5 times normal. The PTT is reevaluated 4 and 24 hours after the start of thrombolytic therapy.

Thrombolysis is considered complete when at least 95 percent of the thrombus has been cleared, although complete clearing is optimal. If thrombolysis fails to progress at a high dosage level or if a major bleeding complication occurs, the thrombolytic treatment may have to be stopped. At this point it is necessary to make a decision regarding the treatment of the underlying lesion. Essentially all malignant stenoses should be treated with stenting. In patients with an extrinsic constrictive process, such as fibrosing mediastinitis, retroperitoneal fibrosis, or fibrosis secondary to radiation therapy, percutaneous transluminal angioplasty (PTA) alone is usually unsatisfactory and stenting is again required.

Stenting

The placement of expandable metallic stents in large veins provides the potential of long-term relief because expandable stents prevent recoil and may prevent the recurrence of stenosis. However, since intimal hyperplasia within the stent or compression of the stent may result in restenosis or occlusion, stents must be used judiciously and only when appropriate.

Historical Overview

The Maass double-helix barrel prosthesis (Medivent, Zurich, Switzerland) was one of the first stents used clinically for venous obstruction. The introductory system was rather large (7 mm in diameter) and therefore usually required a cutdown in the jugular or femoral vein for placement. It was employed successfully for the treatment of the obstruction of IVC and iliac veins in 1986.[10] However, complications, including perforation of the IVC due to the rigidity of the introductory system, were reported,[10] and the stent did not find wider clinical use.

In 1985 Wright et al. reported the placement of Z stents in the canine jugular vein and vena cava without evidence of complication.[11] Subsequently, Putnam et al. reported two patients with SVC syndrome due to malignant compression and massive thrombosis of the SVC who were treated with local thrombolytic therapy and placement of modified Gianturco Z stents with excellent results.[12] Concomitantly, Zollikofer et al. reported the use of Wallstents (Medinvent, SA, Lausanne, Switzerland) in the iliofemoral system with good short-term follow-up.[13] Palmaz stents (Johnson & Johnson Co.) have subsequently been used in subclavian and iliac veins as well as in the SVC and IVC,[14] again with good results.

Stents available in the United States include the Gianturco-Rösch Z stents (GRZ stents; Cook, Inc.), the Wallstent (Schneider USA, Inc.), and the Palmaz stent (Johnson & Johnson Co.). However, none of these stents at the time of this publication is FDA-approved in the United States for intravenous use, although Palmaz stents and Wallstents are FDA-approved for intraarterial use.

General Principles

Chapter 7 has described the various stents that are available. Although the worldwide experience with arterial stents is considerable, the experience with venous stents is limited. The records of 80 patients at the author's institution and a review of the literature, including meeting abstracts, yield fewer than 400 reported cases.[15,16] Essentially all of these cases were performed with Z stents, Wallstents, or Palmaz stents, in that order of frequency. In their application in the venous system, each of these stents has advantages and disadvantages.

Most of the cases reported in the literature were performed with either Gianturco Z stents or GRZ stents.[15] The advantage of Z stents is that they can be manufactured on site and custom-built as necessary. Thus they are a relatively inexpensive stent with a wide range of applicability. They are commercially available as a tracheobronchial stent in a double-body Z-stent design in diameters up to 35 mm in 5-mm increments. The 15-mm stent is delivered through a 14 French introducer, and the larger-diameter stents are delivered through a 16 French introducer. However, these stents are not FDA-approved for venous use. More-

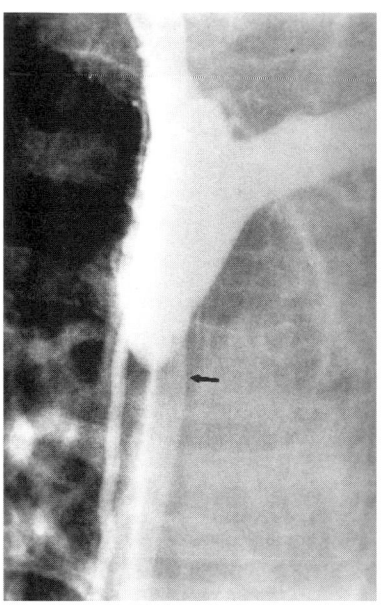
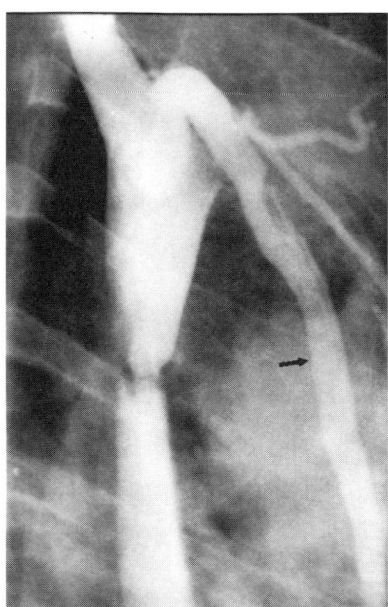
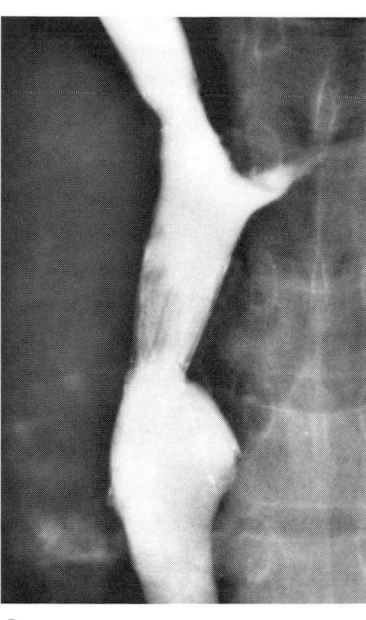

A   B   C

Figure 63-1. Benign idiopathic SVC stenosis in intravenous drug abuser. (A) Transfemoral subclavian venogram in this 42-year-old man who presented with severe SVC syndrome demonstrates severe stenosis of the SVC. Opacification of the azygos vein (*arrow*) is evident. (B) After percutaneous transluminal angioplasty (PTA) with a 12-mm balloon there is improvement in the stenosis, although azygos collateral flow (*arrow*) remains. Symptoms recurred in 4 weeks and PTA was again performed, with similar results. (C) Because of recurrence of symptoms, a double-body GRZ stent was placed, which completely resolved the symptoms. The patient remained asymptomatic until he was lost to follow-up.

over, for most short venous stenoses, a triple-body design would be more useful, and for a lengthy stenosis a single multibody Z stent is preferable. The stent chosen should have a diameter 20 percent greater than the measured diameter of the vein into which the stent is introduced to ensure stability. Since the maximum expansile strength of a Z-stent body is in its central portion and the least expansile force is at the end, the stent body should be centered on the stenosis. A single-body Z stent does not work well in a short stenosis in that it will "squirt" to a position either above or below the stenosis, and a double-body Z stent tends to center the junction of the two stents, which is the weakest portion of the stent, at the level of the tightest stenosis (Fig. 63-1). However, a double-body stent can provide the anchor for a second double-body stent to be placed that overlaps within the initial stent so that the central portion of the second body is centered in the stenosis to provide maximal expansile force.

Although Z stents have excellent expansile force, they tend to exhibit fatigue and may fracture over the long term.[17] In addition, their expansile force may result in erosion and perforation of the vein over a long period of time. Because of their minimum surface area, they can be placed across an inflowing vein with relative impunity and with little concern for occlusion of the vein.

Use of the Wallstent in the United States has been limited until recently by the maximum diameter available (12 mm), but recently the stent became available in diameters up to 24 mm. The principal advantages of the Wallstent are its ready availability in longer lengths, the relatively small size of the introducer system (11 French or less), its ease of introduction, and its flexibility. The disadvantages are the decreased expansile force in larger sizes, particularly when they are not fully expanded, and also their tendency to "squirt" from the venous stenosis to a more dilated portion of the vein if they are not carefully centered in the stenosis (Fig. 63-2). At this time Wallstents are approved for intraarterial but not intravenous use in the United States.

The balloon-expandable Palmaz stents are available in diameters up to 12 mm but can be overexpanded to larger diameters. They are approved for intraarterial use but not for venous use in the United States. The larger stents can be introduced on a 7 French balloon catheter through a 10 French sheath. Their advantages are their availability and the predictability of their location upon release (Fig. 63-3). The major disadvantage is their compressibility once they are delivered and expanded; therefore, they should not be placed in any location that is subject to compression, most notably in the subclavian or femoral regions.

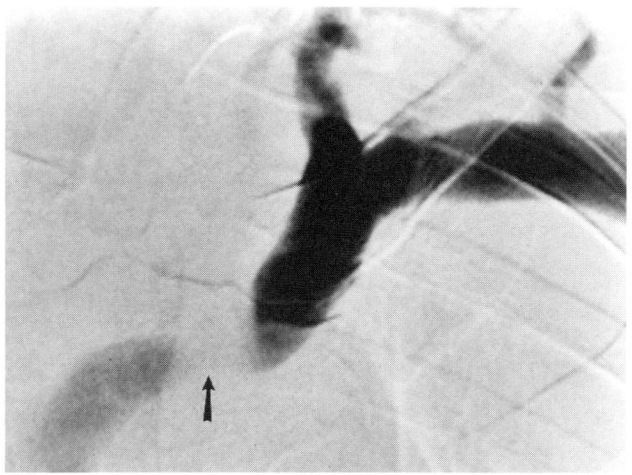

A

Figure 63-2. Brachiocephalic vein stenosis treated with a Wallstent. (A) This 46-year-old man with end-stage renal disease had recent thrombosis of his left arm dialysis fistula. After thrombolysis of the fistula, the venogram demonstrates an 80 percent stenosis (*arrow*) of the left midbrachiocephalic vein. Angioplasty with a 14-mm-diameter angioplasty balloon yielded little improvement. (B) A 16 mm × 60 mm Wallstent was deployed across the stenosis and dilated with a 14-mm balloon. It is imperative that the larger Wallstent be centered on focal stenoses to prevent migration. (C) Follow-up venography demonstrates excellent flow through the Wallstent.

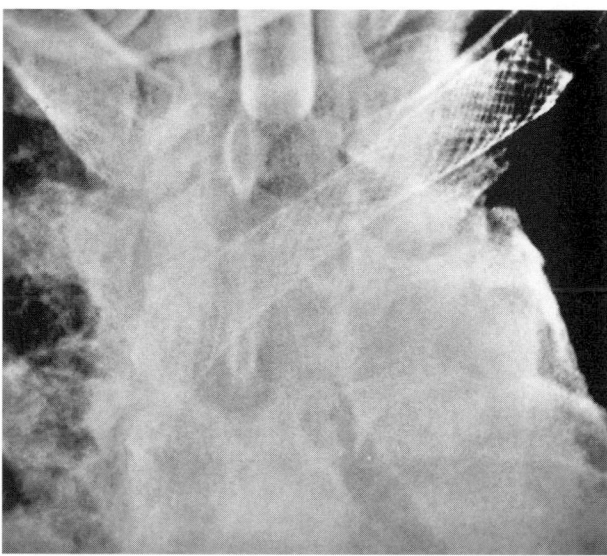

B

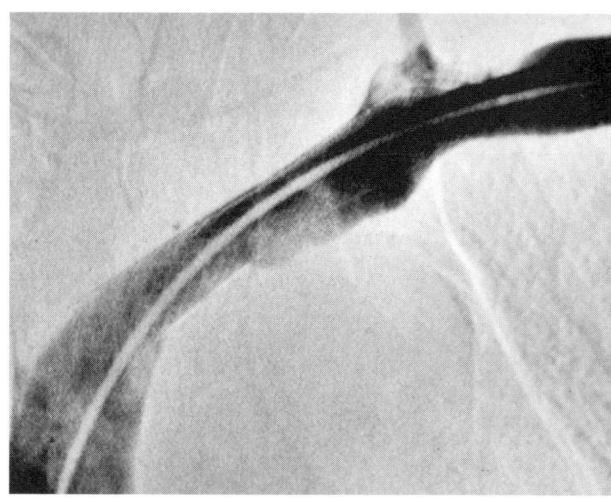

C

Before a stent is placed, venography of the involved area is performed using either serial or digital roentgenography. Vessel diameter measurements of the involved area must be available. The stent should be of adequate length to cover the stenosis and, if the anatomy allows, to extend approximately 2 cm both proximal and distal to the stenosis. This is particularly true in malignant stenoses where overgrowth or extension of the neoplasm is anticipated. If thrombus is present, thrombolytic therapy should be performed before the stent is placed. The author prefers complete thrombolysis, although occasionally stents have been placed with thrombus remaining. In these cases, additional thrombolytic therapy is usually performed. In two of the author's patients with incomplete thrombolysis originally, rethrombosis occurred within 48 hours of stent placement. Both cases responded to additional thrombolytic therapy.

Clinical Experience and Applications

Venous thrombolysis, balloon angioplasty, and stenting are effective in the management of patients with both benign and malignant stenoses or occlusions.

The ultimate choice of treatment depends both on the location of the stenosis and on the underlying pathologic process. In those patients with a shortened life expectancy, palliation of the symptoms is a much more important consideration than long-term patency.

Benign Obstructions

Subclavian and SVC stenoses related to compressive syndromes require a different approach than abnormalities related to the previous placement of central venous catheters. Lesions in patients on hemodialysis are more likely to recur after interventional therapy than lesions in patients not on hemodialysis. Therefore, hemodialysis patients are discussed separately.

Stenoses Unrelated to Hemodialysis

Stenoses of the subclavian and brachiocephalic vein and SVC have become much more prevalent with the

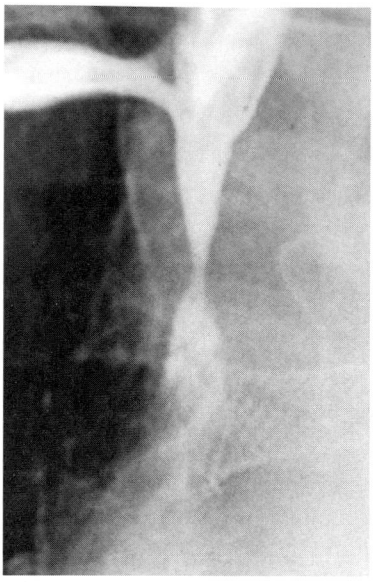
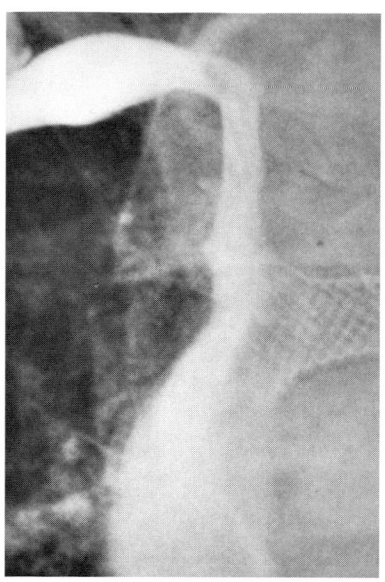
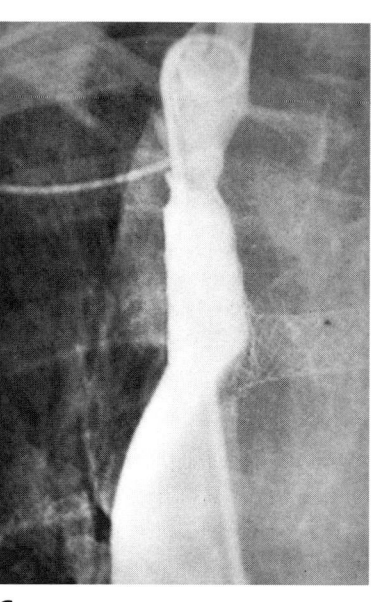

A   B   C

Figure 63-3. Right brachiocephalic vein stenosis related to a right percutaneous dialysis catheter. (A) Right subclavian venogram in a 53-year-old woman with end-stage renal disease who had multiple previous percutaneously placed right subclavian and transjugular dialysis catheters. The venogram demonstrates a tight stenosis of the right brachiocephalic vein. Previously placed Wallstents, still patent, are identified in the left brachiocephalic vein. (B) Angioplasty with a 12-mm balloon resulted in improvement. However, consider-able recoil of the vein is evident, resulting in a lumen insufficient for the right arm dialysis fistula. (C) A Palmaz stent was chosen to allow future access to the innominate vein from both the jugular and right subclavian approach and to provide minimal encroachment of the left brachiocephalic vein. After dilation of the stent to 12 mm, there is excellent flow through the right brachiocephalic vein. Washout by nonopacified blood from the left brachiocephalic vein is evident in the SVC.

increased use of central lines and indwelling catheters. Permanent cardiac pacers have also been implicated in subclavian and SVC stenosis and thrombosis.[3,18,19]

Subclavian Vein Obstruction. Benign compression of the subclavian vein may be caused by several processes and results in pain and swelling of the upper extremities. The thoracic outlet syndrome may present with venous, arterial, or brachial plexus symptoms and is caused by entrapment of these structures as they exit the thorax over the first rib and beneath the clavicle. The most common points of entrapment are (1) between the anterior and medial heads of the scalenus of the first rib (scalenus anticus syndrome),[20] (2) between the subclavius muscle, the clavicle, and the first rib, and (3) between the anomalous cervical rib and scalenus muscle. This compressive syndrome is frequently complicated by thrombosis. A previous history of intermittent symptoms can frequently be elicited.

Paget-Schroetter syndrome or effort (spontaneous) thrombosis also affects the subclavian vein and may extend into the axillary vein. It is frequently associated with transient compression of the subclavian vein between the costocoracoid ligament and the subclavius muscle during downward and backward bracing of the shoulders.[21] This syndrome most commonly occurs in young men, particularly body builders, or after intense upper body exercise.

In benign subclavian vein occlusion secondary to extrinsic compression, venous thrombolysis is only the first step in the treatment of the patient. Almost invariably, the underlying lesion will be located. Patients with idiopathic axillary and subclavian venous thrombosis without a well-defined venous lesion appear to do best with no additional treatment.[19,22] However, in those patients with an anatomic abnormality resulting in compression of the vein, a combined surgical and interventional approach frequently proves beneficial. This may either be resection of the first rib or cervical rib with subsequent angioplasty of the vein[23,24] or surgical repair of the vein. Although axillary and subclavian vein angioplasty provides excellent short-term results, long-term patency appears to be poor.[25]

In patients with venous stenosis secondary to previous catheter placements, such as central lines or dialysis catheters, who are not currently on hemodialysis, PTA alone may provide a satisfactory result. Primary stenting should be considered if significant elastic recoil is evident. In the author's experience with 16 patients treated primarily with stents, the primary patency rate was 69 percent and the secondary patency rate was 94 percent with a mean follow-up of 27 months. Patients receiving hemodialysis respond differently and are discussed separately, as already mentioned. Stenting should be considered if severe elastic recoil prevents restoration of adequate flow.

SVC Obstruction. Acute benign SVC obstruction is usually secondary to existing or previous line placement. This includes not only dialysis catheters but also catheters placed for parental nutrition, chemotherapy, and central venous pressure monitoring. SVC obstruction may also be caused by fibrosing mediastinitis, which is generally attributable to granulomatous diseases such as tuberculosis and histoplasmosis, or to radiation therapy and occasionally to mediastinal trauma. The progressive extensive compression of the SVC frequently allows time for adequate collateral flow to be established. However, with superimposed thrombosis, acute symptoms will occur.

Regardless of the etiology, if thrombosis is present, thrombolysis as described above is necessary. After the thrombolysis is completed, balloon angioplasty of the stenosis is performed. In patients with fibrosing mediastinitis, primary stenting should be performed. In stenoses secondary to a previous transvenous line or cardiac pacemaker, angioplasty alone may be adequate.[26] However, the recurrence rate of the stenoses following PTA alone is high in the SVC (see Fig. 63-1), and in the author's experience primary stenting provides an effective treatment in these patients. Rosenblum reported six patients stented for SVC obstruction, with three of these patients subsequently having a central line placed across the stent for vascular access with no recurrence or venous thrombosis.[27]

Iliofemoral and IVC Obstruction. Compression of the left iliac vein secondary to compression by the right iliac artery is thought to be the cause of the increased incidence of deep venous thrombosis in the left lower extremity.[28] In some cases, a local fibrotic stricture is identified after thrombolysis (Cockett or iliac compression syndrome). May-Thurner syndrome has a similar finding, although thrombosis of the left femoral vein is not present. Focal webs may be identified upon phlebography, and typically a 2- to 4-cm water pressure gradient is present with exercise.

Stenosis or obstruction of the iliac veins as well as the inferior vena cava may also be caused by radiation therapy, retroperitoneal fibrosis, or fibrosis secondary to trauma.

In all instances, benign stenoses of the iliac veins and IVC appear to respond best, following thrombolysis (if indicated), to primary stenting. PTA yields little

improvement because the elastic recoil in all instances is significant, since these syndromes are secondary to extrinsic compression.

In patients with iliofemoral deep vein thrombosis, Semba and Dake[29] used a transjugular approach and a regimen with either a dual-lumen multi-side-hole catheter or a coaxial system with an end-hole catheter and a thrombolytic guidewire across the thrombus. Urokinase was delivered in split doses of 75,000 to 100,000 IU per hour into each thrombolytic catheter guidewire for a total dose of 150,000 to 200,000 IU per hour. This regimen resulted in partial or complete thrombolysis in 23 of 25 limbs treated. However, only 8 required no further intervention; 2 required angioplasty alone and 13 required angioplasty with stent placement. Follow-up examination demonstrated continued patency in 11 of 12 treated iliofemoral veins at 3 months.

The author has treated two total occlusions of the IVC secondary to retroperitoneal fibrosis with thrombolysis and stenting, and these had a documented patency 5 years after stenting without intervening treatment. Iliac vein stenosis secondary to extrinsic compression responds well to stenting (Fig. 63-4). In an additional patient with postsurgical stenosis and thrombosis of the iliac vein, follow-up venography 3 years after placement demonstrated that the stent was occluded. The occlusion was not treated because the patient was asymptomatic.

Stenoses Related to Hemodialysis

Central venous stenosis in patients on hemodialysis represents a unique situation. These patients, for reasons that are yet unclear, have a much higher restenosis rate and shorter patency rate following both PTA and stenting than patients not on dialysis. Kovalik et al.[30] observed 20 patients who had hemodialysis fistula and central stenoses. In the patients with nonelastic stenoses (stenoses with greater than 50 percent improvement in the diameter of the lesion following PTA), the mean time to recurrence was 7.6 months and the recurrence rate was 81 percent. However, in those patients with elastic stenoses (less than or equal to 50 percent improvement in the diameter of the lesion following PTA), the mean time to recurrence was 2.9 months, with a 100 percent recurrence rate. The authors observed that placement of a Wallstent in individuals with nonelastic lesions resulted in no evident prolongation of the recurrence time, whereas in patients with elastic lesions there was significant prolongation of the time to recurrence. On the basis of these findings, it is appropriate in hemodialysis patients to stent those lesions that demonstrate significant elastic

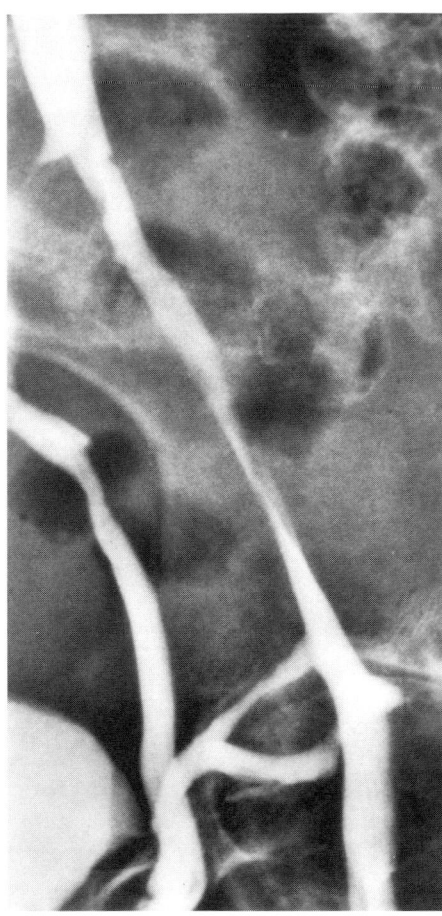

A

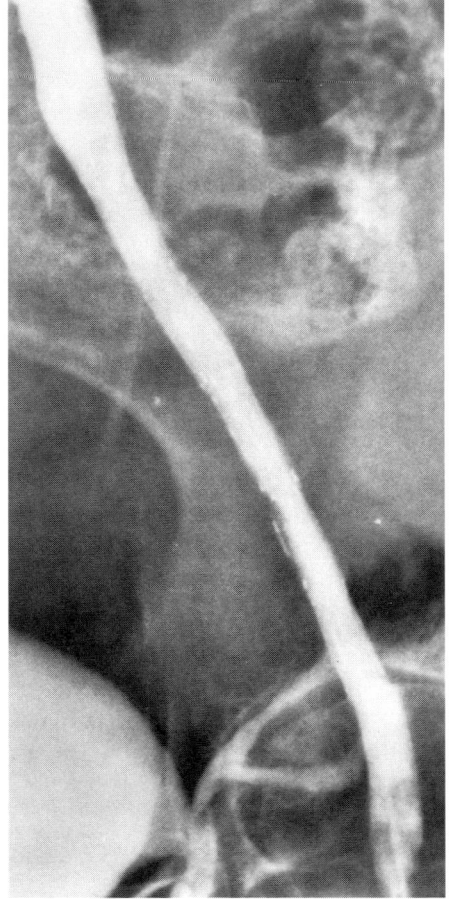

B

Figure 63-4. Iliac vein stenosis secondary to extrinsic compression. (A) After radiation therapy of the abdomen and pelvis for lymphoma, this 66-year-old woman developed persistent left leg edema. The left iliac venogram demonstrates diffuse compression of the left iliac vein. (B) After deployment of an 8 mm × 12 cm multibody GRZ stent, there is restoration of normal flow in the iliac vein. The patient became asymptomatic in 4 days and remained so.

recoil and to not stent those lesions that have minimal elastic recoil until necessary (see Figs. 63-2 and 63-3).

The author has stented 16 stenoses in 13 hemodialysis patients. The mean follow-up time was over 16 months with the longest follow-up being 65 months. The primary patency rate was 25 percent, and the secondary patency rate was 63 percent. Many of these patients have required frequent intervention to maintain patency. At the author's institution, the intervention rate in stented central stenoses in hemodialysis patients is three time the rate of intervention in benign central stenoses not related to hemodialysis. Shoenfeld et al. reported a series of 19 patients with proximal venous obstructions and primary stenting with Wallstents and/or Palmaz stents.[31] Follow-up at 17 months demonstrated a primary patency rate of 68 percent and a secondary patency rate of 93 percent.

Budd-Chiari Syndrome

Budd-Chiari syndrome is a somewhat ambiguous term applied to the classic triad of hepatomegaly, ascites, and abdominal pain. It was first described by Budd in 1845 and described further by Chiari in 1899.[32] The syndrome may be caused by an obstructive process in either the hepatic veins or the intrahepatic IVC.[33] The process may be associated with trauma; medication, especially oral contraceptives; or neoplasm, particularly leukemia. Venography demonstrates a significant stenosis of the intrahepatic portion of the IVC. Hepatic vein obstruction may be due to either focal stenosis of the hepatic vein or to extensive hepatic venous occlusion with the typical "spider web" appearance seen with hepatic venography. Surgical therapy is difficult and has an operative mortality of approximately 9 percent.[34,35] PTA alone of either the IVC obstruction or the hepatic vein focal stenosis is useful, but frequent redilation is required.[36-38] Stenting of the IVC stenosis as well as the hepatic vein stenosis provides satisfactory long-term patency.[39] The author has treated two patients with GRZ stents. At follow-ups of 3 and 6 years, respectively, there was no recurrence of symptoms and, venographically, no recurrence of the stenosis. In addition, no repeat interventions have been required. Gianturco Z stents have been most commonly used, although a case of Wallstent implantation has been reported as a bridge to subsequent liver transplantation.[40]

Portal Vein Occlusion

Portal vein thrombosis is seen in patients with cirrhosis and portal hypertension as well as after trauma and liver transplant surgery. Portal vein thrombolysis may be appropriate and is best performed using the transjugular approach to the portal system. In patients with cirrhosis or portal hypertension, a transjugular intrahepatic portosystemic shunt (TIPS) should be performed concomitantly to maintain portal vein patency after flow in the portal vein has been restored. Stenting of the portal vein is best performed with the Wallstent because of the tortuous tract presented by the transjugular approach. In patients who have portal vein stenoses and/or thrombosis after transplant surgery, the transjugular approach is again used. However, a TIPS procedure is not necessary once the portal vein stent, usually a Wallstent, has been placed.

Malignant Obstructions

The treatment of a central venous obstruction due to malignant compression is primarily for palliation because of the limited life expectancy of the patient. Most of these obstructions behave similarly, regardless of their location. However, obstructions of the intrahepatic IVC do respond well technically, although most of the patients have a very limited life expectancy. Therefore, this group will be discussed separately.

SCV and IVC Obstruction

Malignant obstruction of the SCV and IVC is invariably secondary to compression by an adjacent neoplasm, with or without frank invasion of the lumen of the venous structure. In the author's experience of 27 patients with extrahepatic central malignant venous obstruction, the majority involved the SVC and 50 percent were secondary to pulmonary malignancy. Again, in the treatment of these patients, venography of the involved area and fibrinolysis as appropriate are required (Fig. 63-5). All of these patients should be

stented primarily (at the initial interventional procedure), and the stent selected should have a diameter 20 percent greater than the expected diameter of the lumen of the involved vessel. Frequently, balloon dilation of the stent is required to obtain adequate stent expansion. In all of the author's 49 patients with central malignant venous obstruction, stents were placed primarily in the SVC or IVC. Stenting was then extended into the innominate and subclavian veins (or the iliac veins) as necessary to provide adequate inflow. Stent placement provided excellent palliation in all stented patients. Dyet et al. reported a series of 20 patients with SVC obstruction who were treated with large-diameter Wallstents. The primary patency rate was 90 percent, and the secondary patency rate was 100 percent.[41] Other series have also reported excellent palliation and patency using the Z stent[19,42-47] and the Wallstent.[48]

In patients with SVC obstruction, the congestive syndrome rapidly improved, with clearing of the symptoms in 1 to 3 days.[49] In patients with IVC obstruction, the improvement was less dramatic, with clearing in 5 to 7 days. In the author's 27 patients with extrahepatic caval obstruction, technical success was achieved in all patients. A primary patency rate of 78 percent was achieved, and the secondary patency rate was 93 percent with a mean follow-up of 5.2 months. Using a multivariate analysis, Furui et al. demonstrated that patients who have CT evidence of complete encasement of the cava by the tumor are likely to have less satisfactory short-term and long-term results.[50]

Intrahepatic IVC Obstruction

In 22 patients with intrahepatic IVC obstruction, the results are somewhat less dramatic. Two-thirds of the patients presented with both ascites and lower extremity edema, and the remainder presented with either ascites alone or peripheral edema alone. Inferior vena cavography invariably showed compression of the inferior vena cava secondary to extensive hepatic metastasis. Superimposed thrombosis was not identified in any of the patients. Pressure gradients across the cava varied from 6 to 25 mmHg, with a mean of 12 mmHg. Balloon angioplasty of these lesions is of no benefit. After placement of the multibody GRZ stent, clearing of the edema and/or ascites occurred in 4 to 8 days in essentially all patients (Fig. 63-6). Although the primary patency rate in the author's patients was 100 percent, the outlook for these patients is particularly dismal, with 50 percent of the patients expiring within 22 days. Generally, patients with ascites and peripheral edema had a considerably shorter survival than those with peripheral edema alone. Therefore, these patients

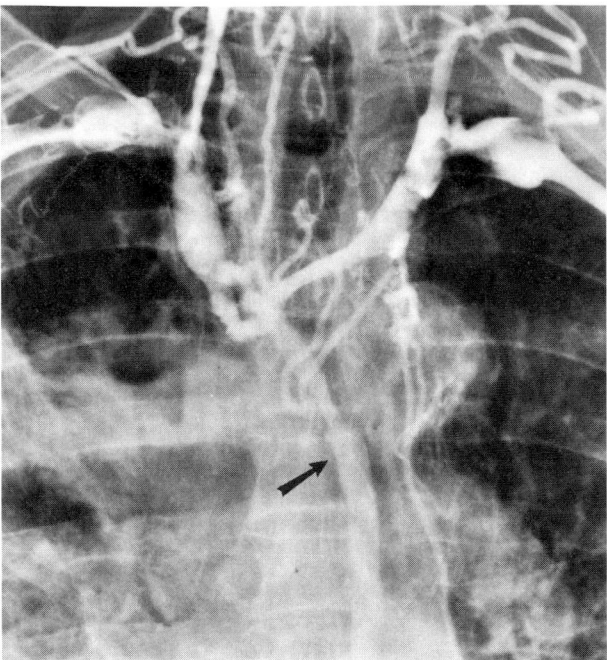

A

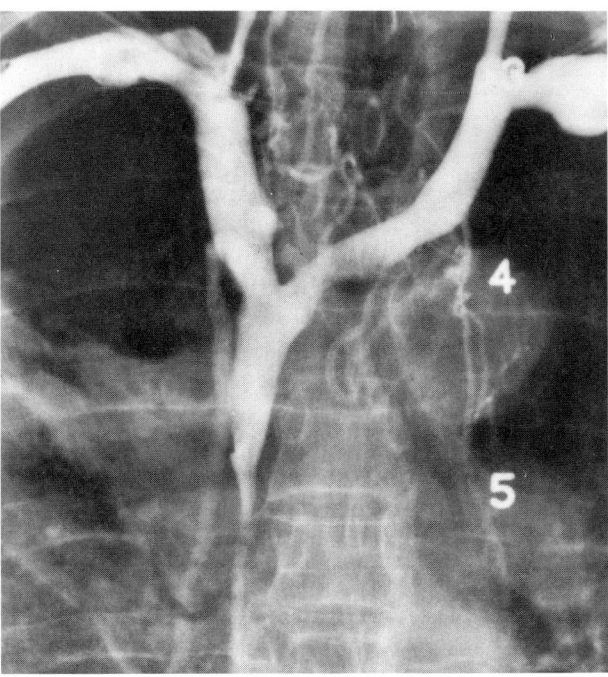

B

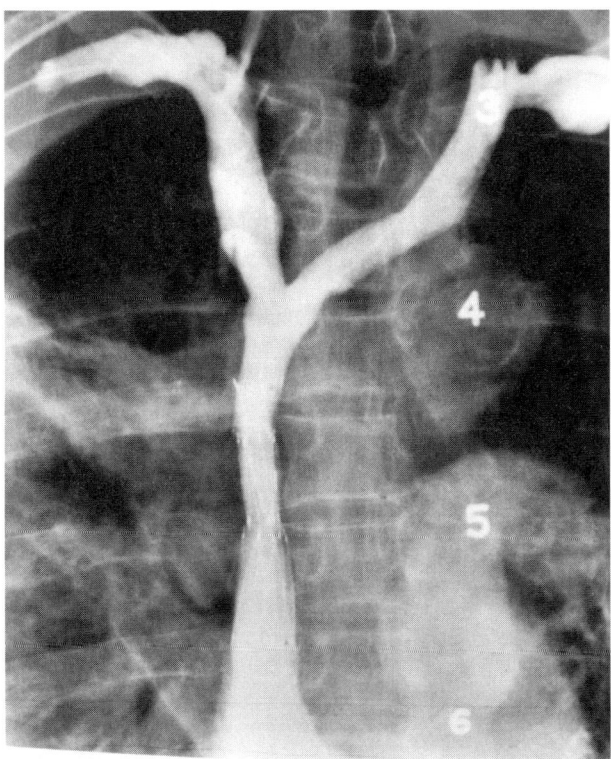

C

Figure 63-5. Thrombosed malignant SVC obstruction. (A) The initial bilateral subclavian venogram in this 68-year-old man with pulmonary adenocarcinoma demonstrates complete obstruction of the SVC with collateral flow through the azygos vein (*arrow*). Extensive thrombus is present in both the brachiocephalic veins and the SVC. (B) After thrombolytic therapy there is complete thrombolysis of the brachiocephalic veins and SVC, with the underlying SVC stenosis revealed. (C) The SVC has been stented with a triple-body GRZ stent, 18 mm in diameter and 6 cm in length. Note that the central body is centered on the stenosis (compare with Fig. 63-1). The stent was fully expanded on a chest radiograph 2 weeks later.

Complications

Complications may be secondary to thrombolysis, the actual stenting, or postprocedure anticoagulant therapy. Thrombolytic complications are reportedly lower with urokinase than with streptokinase.[7]

During stenting, vessel perforation and disruption have been reported, as well as disruption of the superior vena cava with associated cardiac tamponade.[51] Stent migration occurs[52] but is less likely with self-expanding stents. Initially, single-body Z stents were prone to be displaced to an off-center position relative to the stenosis, but this has not been a problem with multibody Z stents. Wallstents, particularly of larger diameter, may also be displaced during expansion and "squirt" from an appropriately centered position.

Palmaz stents may be kinked or crushed by external compression and therefore should not be placed in a

must be carefully evaluated to determine whether the expense of stent placement is warranted in view of the short survival time (mean 29 days in the author's 22 patients), even though the primary patency rate was 100 percent.

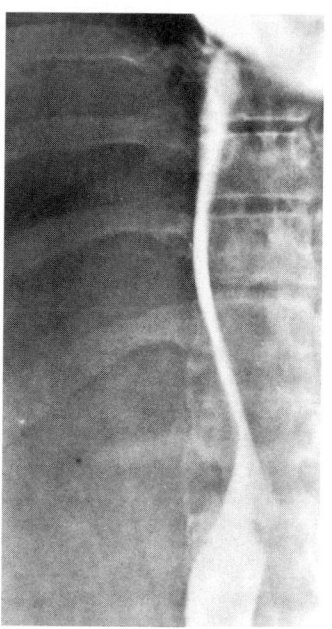 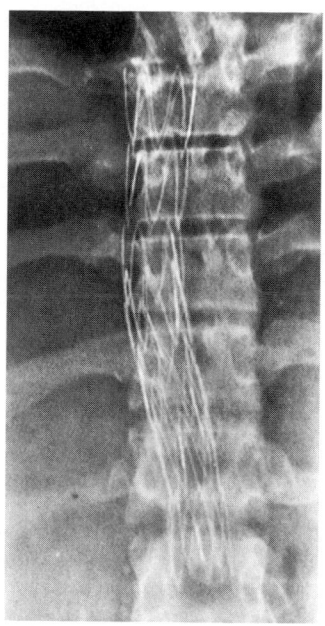 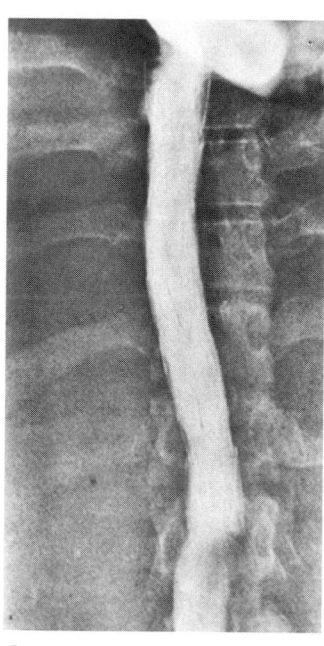

A   B   C

Figure 63-6. Intrahepatic IVC stenosis due to hepatic metastasis. (A) The inferior vena cavogram in this 44-year-old woman with occular melanoma metastatic to the liver demonstrates severe stenosis of the intrahepatic portion of the IVC. The patient had recently developed severe peripheral edema and ascites. A 19-mmHg gradient from the abdominal IVC to the right atrium was present. (B) Because of the marked hepatomegaly and the extent of the stenosis, two overlapping multibody GRZ stents were placed. The initial central stent was a 20 mm × 10 cm multibody GRZ stent, and a 20 mm × 8 cm stent was then overlapped within the central stent to provide coverage of the lesion. (C) Post stenting venogram demonstrates excellent flow through the IVC, and the gradient was reduced to 4 mmHg. The patient had complete resolution of the leg edema at 7 days with marked improvement in her ascites. There was no recurrence of symptoms before her death 2 months after stent placement.

position that is susceptible to compression or that requires flexing, such as in the subclavian or femoral regions (Fig. 63-7). However, Trerotola et al. redilated compressed Palmaz stents in lambs and found that the stents could be redilated without complication and with a 50 percent mean increase in stent diameter.[53]

Complications also result from long-term anticoagulation therapy following intervention. In the author's series of 79 patients with central venous stenoses treated by stenting, two patients with vena cava stenosis and associated abdominal metastases experienced retroperitoneal hemorrhage while anticoagulated. One of these proved fatal, and the second required no further therapy after cessation of the heparin. Postmortem examination in the fatality demonstrated the stent and cava to be intact. One additional patient succumbed to massive pulmonary hemorrhage within 24 hours of SVC stenting while being heparinized.

Postprocedure Care

Although all patients are heparinized during stent placement, anticoagulant therapy is not continued in patients receiving hemodialysis. In the author's patients who initially continue anticoagulant therapy after stent placement, anticoagulation is halted after 2 months when the stent is fully endothelialized.[11] However, in those patients who required thrombolytic therapy before stent placement or subsequent to stent placement to restore patency, anticoagulation is continued indefinitely. Because of early experience with retroperitoneal hemorrhage in two patients with advanced abdominal malignancy, the author does not routinely anticoagulate patients in whom abdominal malignancy is suspected.

Summary

The use of local fibrinolytic therapy is an excellent treatment of superimposed venous thrombosis. The treatment of the underlying lesion may be performed by PTA, although, because of significant elastic recoil, this is frequently of limited benefit. Patients with malignant extrahepatic venous obstruction should be treated by local fibrinolytic therapy and primary stenting. Patients with malignant intrahepatic IVC obstruc-

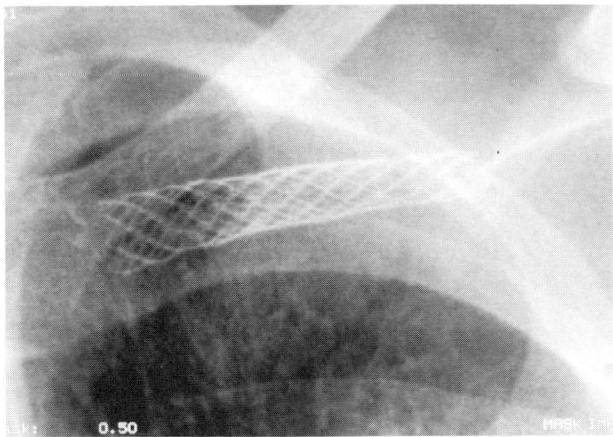

A

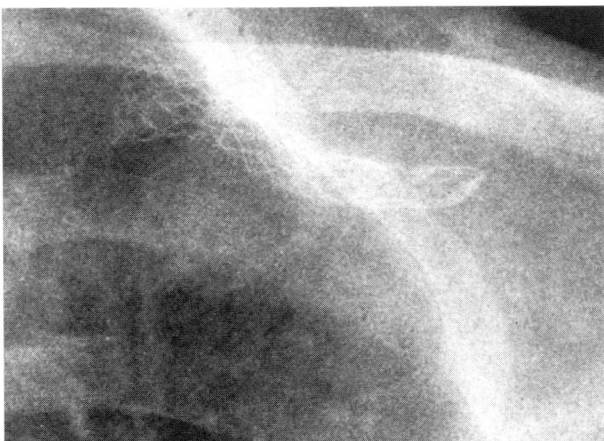

B

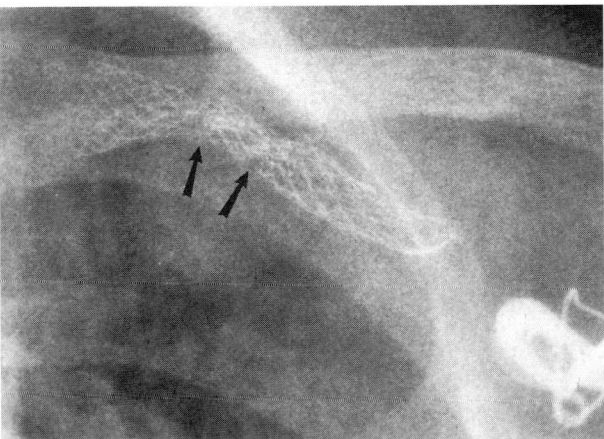

C

Figure 63-7. Compression of Palmaz stent. (A) Two overlapping Palmaz stents were placed in this 32-year-old woman with hemodialysis fistula in the left upper extremity and an 85 percent stenosis of the subclavian vein. (B) A chest radiograph 2 weeks later demonstrates compression of the stents. The fistula in the left upper extremity was not functional. (C) A chest radiograph 1 year later demonstrates further compression of the stents with fractures (*arrows*) of the stents. Complete disruption of the stent was confirmed fluoroscopically.

tion have a short life expectancy even though a high patency rate can be expected.

In those patients with subclavian stenosis associated with thoracic outlet obstruction, thrombolysis provides initial patency, but surgical intervention is frequently required. Caval and iliac venous stenoses rarely respond to PTA alone, and stenting is frequently required. In patients with dialysis-associated stenoses, elastic stenoses should probably be stented primarily but will require frequent interventions to maintain patency. Hemodialysis patients with nonelastic lesions may respond to PTA alone, but again, repeated interventions are usually required.

Acknowledgments

I want to express my appreciation to Sherri Imai for her assistance with preparing the images for this chapter, and to Linda McCall for her help with the manuscript.

References

1. Yellin A, Rosen A, Reichert N, Lieberman Y. Superior vena cava syndrome: the myth—the facts. Am Rev Respir Dis 1990;141:1114–1118.
2. Porter JM, Seaman AJ, Common HH, Rösch J, Eidemiller LR, Calhoun AD. Comparison of heparin and streptokinase in the treatment of venous thrombosis. Am Surg 1975;41:511–516.
3. Bradof J, Sands MJ Jr, Lakin P. Symptomatic venous thrombosis of the upper extremity complicating permanent transvenous pacing: reversal with streptokinase infusion. Am Heart J 1982;104:1112–1113.
4. Becker GJ, Holden RW, Rabe FE, Castaneda-Zuniga WR, Sears N, Dilley RS, Glover JL. Local thrombolytic therapy for subclavian and axillary vein thrombosis: treatment of the thoracic inlet syndrome. Radiology 1983;149:419–423.
5. Druy EM, Trout HH III, Giordano JM, Hix WR. Lytic therapy in the treatment of axillary and subclavian vein thrombosis. J Vasc Surg 1985;2:821–827.
6. Sullivan KL, Gardiner GA Jr, Shapiro MJ, Bonn J, Levin DC. Acceleration of thrombolysis with a high-dose transthrombus bolus technique. Radiology 1989;173:805–808.
7. Bell WR. Update on urokinase and streptokinase: a comparison of their efficacy and safety. Hosp Formul 1988;23:230–241.
8. Graor RA, Young JR, Risius B, Ruschhaupt WF. Comparison of cost-effectiveness of streptokinase and urokinase in the treatment of deep vein thrombosis. Ann Vasc Surg 1987;1:24–528.
9. McNamara TO, Fischer JR. Thrombolysis of peripheral arterial and graft occlusions: improved results using high-dose urokinase. AJR 1985;144:769–755.
10. Jakob H, Maass D, Schmiedt W, Schild H, Oelert H. Treatment of major venous obstruction with an expandable endoluminal spiral prothesis. J Cardiovasc Surg 1989;30:112.
11. Wright KC, Wallace S, Charnasangavej C, Carrasco CH, Gianturco C. Percutaneous endovascular stents: an experimental evaluation. Radiology 1985;156:69–72.
12. Putnam JS, Uchida BT, Antonovic R, Rosch J. Superior vena cava syndrome associated with massive thrombosis: treatment with expandable wire stents. Radiology 1988;167:727–728.
13. Zollikofer CL, Largiader I, Bruhlmann WF, Uhlschmid GK, Marty AH. Endovascular stenting of veins and grafts: preliminary clinical experience. Radiology 1988;167:707–712.
14. Elson JD, Becker GJ, Wholey MH, Ehrman KO. Vena caval

central venous stenoses: management with Palmaz balloon-expandable intraluminal stents. J Vasc Intervent Radiol 1991;2: 215–223.

15. Trerotola SO. Interventional radiology in central venous stenosis and occlusion. Semin Intervent Radiol 1994;11:291–304.

16. Lakin PC, Peterson BD, Barton RE, Uchida B, Rösch J, Saxon RR. Expandable stents in the treatment of central obstruction in the venous system. SCVIR 19th Annual Scientific Meeting (program) Abs., p 35.

17. Carrasco CH, Charnsangavej C, Wright KC, Wallace S, Gianturco C. Use of the Gianturco self-expanding stent in stenoses of the superior and inferior venae cavae. J Vasc Intervent Radiol 1992;3:409–419.

18. Ferguson R, McCaughan B, May J, Waugh R. Venous occlusion: a rare complication of transvenous cardiac pacing. Aust N Z J Surg 1992;62:977–980.

19. Becker DM, Philbrick JT, Walker FB. Axillary and subclavian venous thrombosis: prognosis and treatment. Arch Intern Med 1991;151:1934–1943.

20. McCleery RS, Kesterson JE, Kirtley JA, Love RB. Subclavius and anterior scalene muscle compression as a cause of intermittent obstruction of the subclavian vein. Ann Surg 1951;133: 588–602.

21. Falconer MA, Weddell G. Costoclavicular compression of the subclavian artery and vein. Lancet 1943;2:539–544.

22. Ameli FM, Minas T, Weiss M, Provan JL. Consequences of "conservative" conventional management of axillary vein thrombosis. Can J Surg 1987;30:167–169.

23. Perler BA, Michell SE. Percutaneous transluminal angioplasty and transaxillary first rib resection: a multidisciplinary approach to the thoracic outlet syndrome. Am Surg 1986;52:485.

24. Inazawa K, Simanuki T, Minowa T, Iijima Y, Orita H, Washio M. A case of treatment of the Paget-Schroetter syndrome with PTA and Gianturco expandable metallic stent. J Jpn Assoc Thorac Surg 1993;41:1410–1414.

25. Glanz S, Gordon DH, Lipkowitz GS, Hong J, Sclafani SJA. Axillary and subclavian vein stenosis: percutaneous angioplasty. Radiology 1988;168:371.

26. Sherry CS, Diamond NG, Meyers TP, Martin RL. Successful treatment of superior vena cava syndrome by venous angioplasty. AJR 1986;147:834–835.

27. Rosenblum J, Leef J, Messersmith R, Tomiak M, Bech F. Intravascular stents in the management of acute superior vena cava obstruction of benign etiology. J Parenter Enteral Nutr 1994; 18:362–366.

28. Taheri SA, Williams J, Powell S, Cullen J, Peer R, Nowakowski P, Boman L, Pisano S. Iliocaval compression syndrome. Am J Surg 1987;154:169–172.

29. Semba CP, Dake MD. Iliofemoral deep venous thrombosis: aggressive therapy with catheter-directed thrombolysis. Radiology 1994;191:487–494.

30. Kovalik EC, Newman GE, Suhocki P, Knelson M, Schwab SJ. Correction of central venous stenoses: use of angioplasty and vascular Wallstents. Kidney Int 1994;45:1177–1181.

31. Shoenfeld R, Hermans H, Novick A, et al. J Vasc Surg 1994; 19:532–539.

32. Murphy FB, Steinberg HV, Shires GT III, Martin LG, Bernardina ME. The Budd-Chiari syndrome: a review. AJR 1986;147: 9–15.

33. Ludwig J, Hashimoto E, McGill DB, VanHeerden JA. Classification of hepatic venous outflow obstruction: ambiguous terminology of the Budd-Chiari syndrome. Mayo Clin Proc 1990; 65:51–55.

34. Wang ZG. Recognition and management of Budd-Chiari syndrome: experience with 143 patients. Chin Med J 1989;102: 338–346.

35. Wang Z, Zhu Y, Wang S, Pu L, et al. Recognition and management of Budd-Chiari syndrome: report of one hundred cases. J Vasc Surg 1989;10:149–156.

36. Chan P, Lee CP, Lee YS. Budd-Chiari syndrome treated successfully by percutaneous transluminal balloon angioplasty. Cathet Cardiovasc Diagn 1992;27:215–219.

37. Furui S, Yamauchi T, Ohtomo K, Tsuchiya K, Makita K, Takenaka E. Hepatic inferior vena cava obstructions: clinical results of treatment with percutaneous transluminal laser-assisted angioplasty. Radiology 1988;166:673–677.

38. Martin LG, Henderson JM, Millikan WJ, Casarella WJ, Kaufman SL. Angioplasty for long-term treatment of patients with Budd-Chiari syndrome. AJR 1990;154:1007–1010.

39. Lopez RR, Benner KG, Hall L, Rösch J, Pinson CW. Expandable venous stents for treatment of the Budd-Chiari syndrome. Gastroenterology 1991;100:1435–1441.

40. Martin L, Dondelinger RF, Trotteur G. Treatment of Budd-Chiari syndrome by metallic stent as a bridge to liver transplantation. Cardiovasc Intervent Radiol 1995;18:196–199.

41. Dyet JF, Cook AM, Nicholson AA. Use of the Wallstent in the treatment of malignant superior vena caval obstruction. SCVIR 19th Annual Scientific Meeting (program) Abs., p. 35.

42. Oudkerk M, Heystraten FMJ, Stoter G. Stenting in malignant vena caval obstruction. Cancer 1993;71:142–146.

43. Furui S, Sawada S, Irie T, et al. Hepatic inferior vena cava obstruction: treatment of two types with Gianturco expandable metallic stents. Radiology 1990;176:655–670.

44. Sawada S, Fujiwara Y, Koyama T, et al. Application of expandable metallic stents to the venous system. Acta Radiol 1992; 33:156–159.

45. Irving JD, Dondelinger RF, Reidy JF, et al. Gianturco self-expanding stents: clinical experience in the vena cava and large veins. Cardiovasc Intervent Radiol 1992;15:328–333.

46. Antonucci F, Salomonowitz E, Stuckmann G, Stiefel M, Largiader J, Zollikofer CL. Placement of venous stents: clinical experience with a self-expanding prosthesis. Radiology 1992;183: 493–497.

47. Dondelinger RF, Goffette P, Kurdziel JC, Roche A. Expandable metal stents for stenoses of the venae cavae and large veins. Semin Intervent Radiol 1991;8:252–263.

48. Tacke J, Antonucci F, Stuckmann G, Mattias P, Espinosa N, Zollikofer CL. The palliative treatment of venous stenoses in tumor patients with self-expanding vascular prostheses. Rofo Fortschr Geb Rontgenstr Neuen Bildgeb Verfahr 1994;160: 433–440.

49. Rosch J, Uchida BT, Hall LD, et al. Gianturco-Rösch expandable Z-stents in the treatment of superior vena cava syndrome. Cardiovasc Intervent Radiol 1992;15:319–327.

50. Furui S, Sawada S, Kuramoto K, et al. Gianturco stent placement in malignant caval obstruction: analysis of factors for predicting the outcome. Radiology 1995;195:147–152.

51. Personal communication, Robert Feld, MD, 1994.

52. Wisselink W, Money SR, Becker MO, et al. Am J Surg 1993; 166:200–204.

53. Trerotola SO, Lund GB, Samphilipo MA, et al. Palmaz stent in the treatment of central venous stenosis: safety and efficacy of redilation. Radiology 1994;190:379–385.

Index

Index